HANDBOOK OF RESEARCH

ON SCHOOL SUPERVISION

HANDBOOK OF RESEARCH ON SCHOOL SUPERVISION

EDITED BY

Gerald R. Firth

AND

Edward F. Pajak

MACMILLAN LIBRARY REFERENCE USA

Simon & Schuster Macmillan

New York

Prentice Hall International

London   Mexico City   New Delhi   Singapore   Sydney   Toronto

Copyright © 1998 by Simon & Schuster Macmillan

Macmillan Library Reference USA
Simon & Schuster Macmillan
1633 Broadway
New York, NY 10019

Manufactured in the United States of America.

Printing number
    1 2 3 4 5 6 7 8 9 10

Library of Congress Cataloging-in-Publication Data
Handbook of research on school supervision / edited by Gerald R. Firth,
    Edward F. Pajak.
        p.   cm.
    Includes bibliographical references and index.
    ISBN 0-02-864662-2
        1. School supervision—Research—United States—Handbooks, manuals, etc.
2. School supervision—United States—Handbooks, manuals, etc. I. Firth, Gerald R.
II. Pajak, Edward, 1947-
LB2806.4.H36   1997
371.2'03—dc21   97-36964
                                                                   CIP

This paper meets the requirements of ANSI/NISO Z39.48-1992 (Permanence of Paper).

Dedicated to
Lloyd Chilton
in appreciation for
Inspiration, Consultation, and Confirmation
in shepherding this document
from wish to reality

CONTENTS

Part I

SUPERVISION AS A FIELD OF INQUIRY

Introduction   35
Isobel L. Pfeiffer, University of Akron

Part II

FOUNDATIONS OF SUPERVISION

Introduction   178
*Keith A. Acheson, University of Oregon,
and Duncan E. Waite, Appalachian State University*

Part
III
SUPERVISION AS PROFESSIONAL PRACTICE

Introduction   337
Robert J. Alfonso, East Tennessee State University

Part
IV
SPECIALIZED AREAS OF SUPERVISION

Introduction   489
Geneva Gay, University of Washington

Part
VII
SUPERVISION AS AN ORGANIZED PROFESSION

Introduction   867
Robert F. Nicely, Jr. and Iris M. Striedieck,
Pennsylvania State University

Part
VIII
THEORIES OF SUPERVISION

Introduction   1029
Allan A. Glatthorn, East Carolina University

Part
IX
FORCES AND FACTORS

Introduction 1153
Barbara Nelson Pavan, Temple University

PREFACE

"In research the horizon recedes as we advance . . . and research is always incomplete."

Mark Pattison
(1813–1884)
Chapter 10, *Isaac Casaubon, 1875*

Research is defined as the systematic investigation of a particular subject, both to develop new knowledge and to assemble pre-existing information for appropriate use.

Publication of *The Handbook of Research on School Supervision* is a milestone in the evolution of a challenging, contributing, and sometimes controversial craft in the field of American education. The handbook simultaneously serves to explore the antecedents, establish the parameters, and speculate on the destiny of supervision in educational settings. In such perspectives, the handbook connects the past through the present into the future.

One purpose was to assemble the major scholarship and research of the field in a single volume, thereby identifying its boundaries, concepts, and methods of inquiry. A second purpose was to stimulate new and future research by providing perspectives on school supervision which have not previously appeared in the literature.

This volume takes its place on a list of distinguished handbooks that have defined other aspects of American education. Originally as a project of the American Educational Research Association, the first *Handbook of Research on Teaching* was published in 1963 with Nathaniel L. Gage as editor. The second published in 1973 with Robert M. W. Travers as editor. Both volumes were published by Rand McNally and Company. A third edition of that handbook was published by Macmillan in 1986, with Merlin C. Wittrock as editor.

This current handbook is most closely related to others on teacher education edited by W. Robert Houston, Martin Haberman, and John Sikula (1990) and on curriculum edited by Phillip W. Jackson (1992) and published by Macmillan, as well as on educational administration edited by Normal J. Boyan (1988) and published by Longman.

EMERGENCE OF THE PROJECT

The idea for *The Handbook of Research on School Supervision*, as with several other volumes in the series, originally came from Lloyd Chilton in his role as education editor for Macmillan. Lloyd's inquiry on the need for a volume describing research on school supervision evoked an affirmative response. The absence of such a volume was regarded as a point of embarrassment. Despite our immediate fascination with the project when first proposed more than five years ago, other professional commitments kept the idea on the "back burner" for some time. There were also serious reservations about assuming responsibility for what would clearly be an enormous task. Lloyd's persistence and persuasiveness, however, eventually won us over. After we acknowledged the absolute need for such a handbook we were at one point admonished that it would be our fault if one did not get done.

Lloyd's challenge was accepted because we believe that a volume on school supervision as a field of study and practice deserves a place on the bookshelf alongside other publications of the genre. It also was noted that school supervision was entirely absent as a topic in previous handbooks representing related fields of education in general and of educational leadership in particular. This convinced the co-editors that a separate handbook on school supervision was needed to fill this void, while at the same time avoiding duplication of earlier works.

Consideration was also given to the fact that scholarship in the field of supervision is, to a certain extent, chronologically bimodal. One group of authors came to prominence in the 1960s and 1970s, while a second group emerged during the 1980s and 1990s. These two groups have produced distinctly different bodies of literature, although they dealt with similar recurrent themes that affect teachers and teaching. It was apparent that no unifying work existed to tie it all together. This fact led to the current handbook as serving the purpose of "passing the torch," in a sense, from one generation of scholars and researchers to another. This would amount to a codification of the literature—an attempt to link the texts, the theory, the research, and the emerging perspectives surrounding the issue of supervision in schools.

The projected, proposed, and/or posited clientele for this handbook is broad in range, long in tradition, and deep in position. Through membership in the Department of Supervisors and Directors of Instruction (DSDI) within the National Education Association instructional supervisors once represented, a large and focused category of educational leaders. Its journal, *Instructional Method*, was a distinguished publication utilized by theorists and practitioners. Many changes have occurred in both fields since the merger of DSDI with the Society for Curriculum Study in 1946 to form the Association for Supervision and Curriculum Development. While instructional supervisors as a category are far fewer in number and proportion among educational leaders, their craft is performed by many individuals bearing a wide variety of titles: instructional lead teacher, team coordinator, department head, principal, assistant principal, assistant superintendent, and superintendent, to name only a few beyond instructional supervisor and curriculum director. Once the commitment to the handbook had been made, the co-editors selected broad representation among the diversity of scholars in school supervision from within the COPIS membership and beyond. These 10 representatives comprised the Advisory Board:

Keith A. Acheson, University of Oregon (Emeritus)
Robert H. Anderson, University of South Florida
Noreen B. Garman, University of Pittsburgh
Geneva Gay, University of Washington
Allan A. Glatthorn, East Carolina University
Ben M. Harris, University of Texas - Austin
Robert F. Nicely, Jr., Pennsylvania State University
Barbara N. Pavan, Tempe University
Isobel Pfeiffer, University of Akron
Leonard A. Valverde, Arizona State University

Guidance was also obtained from staff members of three national professional leadership organizations who served as consultants to the project:

Ronald J. Areglado, National Association of Elementary School Principals
Thomas F. Koerner, National Association of Secondary School Principals
Ronald S. Brandt, Association for Supervision and Curriculum Development

Early in the process, Robert Anderson sought to obtain agreement on a definition of instructional supervision because he believed it would serve as a starting point for discussions with ASCD and AERA groups. He abandoned the quest, however, when the handbook was obviously headed toward a much broader conception than the original 24 topics had indicated.

Supervision in education has been variously defined in terms of support, prescription, assistance, training, control, dissemination, change, direction, and democracy. For purposes of the handbook the Advisory Board decided to define school supervision in the most inclusive terms possible. Casting a wide net served to ensure that the numerous manifestations of supervision, both traditional and emerging, would be represented.

STRUCTURE

The final structure of the handbook comprised 52 chapters, authored by 77 individuals, distributed among nine sections. This pattern evolved from the original list of 24 proposed chapters that were to be addressed primarily if not exclusively by members of COPIS.

During the initial meeting of the Advisory Board, the number of chapters doubled, that the suggested length of each manuscript was reduced. With recognition of the potential that the handbook could become the definitive supervision text, it was clear that other authors needed to be involved. Certain topics, including faculty development and instructional improvement in higher education, and supervision related to state departments of education, clearly required authors beyond the COPIS membership.

The lead chapter by Ben M. Harris establishes the setting and tone for the remainder of the volume by describing the perspectives and parameters of supervision in education as "not an individual but a species" (Fielding, 1742).

The five chapters of Section I examine supervision as a field of inquiry through respective lenses: historical, structural, methodological, and evaluatory, illustrating the point of Chuang-tzu (1942) that "all men seek to grasp what they do not know."

The five chapters of Section II consider the various foundations of school supervision: ideological, philosophical, psychological, sociological and anthropolical, and political, indicating the need to "love our principle, order our foundation, progress our goal" (Comte, 1851–1854).

The five chapters of Section III describe the practice of supervision, "there in the ring where name and image meet," as Auden (1937) indicated is appropriate, through functions; roles, responsibilities, and relationships, processes and techniques, teacher education, teacher involvement, and development over the teacher career span.

The six chapters of Section IV consider the concepts of supervision as manifest in academic disciplines, fine and performing arts, occupational fields, specialized education areas, service areas, and nonteaching professions, describing in the words of Maupassant (1887) that a person "who looks a part has the soul of that part."

The eight chapters of Section V observe the operation of school supervision as influenced by various levels of educational endeavor "on which all the parts are played," as suggested by Middleton (1624), including early childhood education, elementary schools, middle schools, secondary schools, district central offices, intermediate agencies, state education departments, and institutions of higher education.

The five chapters of Section VI explore the relationships of supervision to affiliated fields including educational administration, instructional development, curriculum development, staff development, and organization development, sharing Bohr's (1934) opinion that "the purpose is not to disclose the real essence of the phenomena but only to track down, as far as possible, relations between the manifold aspects of our experience."

The seven chapters of Section VII consider elements of an organized profession on the belief of Eliot (1860) that "character is destiny" through governance, preparation, teaching, legal considerations, moral precepts, and global aspects.

The six chapters of Section VIII offer theoretical dimensions of supervision with the counsel of Sherlock Holmes (Doyle, 1894) that "it is a capital mistake to theorize before one has data," including scientific, social, human, aesthetic, industrial, and international.

The four chapters of Section IX discuss the influence, impact, and/or contribution of forces and factors, including organizational, social, political, and economic; cultural and gender, and technological, like Helmholtz seeking (1862) "A perfect understanding of the action of natural and moral forces."

The closing chapter by Glickman and Kanawati regarding their examination of future directions for school supervision suggests that "fate and character are the same conception" as stated by Novalis (1798).

AUTHORS

An outline consisting of chapter titles and headings for the proposed sections was presented to the COPIS membership during the annual fall meeting at Johns Hopkins University in Baltimore in November 1992.

COPIS members were invited to submit proposals to author chapters on particular topics. With that feedback, Firth and Pajak distributed assignments considered logical in terms of capabilities, interests, and contributions of individuals. While some were obvious, others required discussion and occasionally negotiation. In choosing authors, the editors also tried to ensure gender balance and minority involvement. Direct contact with authors helped to increase the diversity, although the potential authors were already committed to other publication priorities in some instances. In some cases, organizations representing elementary and secondary school principals volunteered leadership for certain topics. In other cases, authors sought modest changes in topics and/or breadth of treatment based on knowledge of the nature and availability of existing research.

As envisioned by the Advisory Board and Project Consultants, the goals of the handbook included, but also extended, well beyond the important function of reviewing research, theories, and methods of research on supervision in education. Because of particular expertise in this field, each author nominee was invited to write a scholarly chapter on a specific topic.

Each chapter was intended to provide a thoughtful, well-organized discussion of the topic and its relation to the field of school supervision as a whole. Authors were requested to remember that the handbook was to focus on research through such questions as, What research has been done in the area? How has the research been applied to practice? What research remains to be done? It was stressed that a modest amount of data to date might enhance the importance of identifying needed research.

A guide for authors presented the procedures for completing the writing assignment. Because of the proximity of school supervision to professional practice, practitioners were invited to author chapters individually and teamed with professors as topics indicated. Many practitioners served as reviewers to critique early versions of chapter manuscripts.

REVIEWERS

The co-editors invited authors to suggest potential reviewers for their particular chapters. These suggestions were used whenever possible; however, exceptions were made when requests would have created an impossible burden for several multiply requested reviewers. As a guideline, the editors tried to use at least one reviewer whose background was close to the topic, then to reach wider as the situation required.

Authors' responses to reviews of first drafts were generally very positive. This is attributed to the fact that most negotiation about major revisions occurred during the outline stage rather than after the chapter had been drafted. In those few instances where the original outlines submitted encroached on other topics or overlooked a topic that needed to be included, suggestions were offered by the editors. Most discussion occurred at the outline stage when authors could best rethink the parameters of their chapters.

Once writing was in progress, contact with authors was delegated to the members of the Advisory Board, each of whom served as coordinator of a specific section of the handbook. Periodic progress reports were obtained from these "intermediate" advisors.

Two individuals were invited to review the manuscript of each chapter. At least one reviewer had no other relationship with the project to insure an independent and objective critique. In some cases, the member of the Advisory Board who coordinated the section in which the chapter was to appear also contributed a review. Reviewers were reminded that the handbook involved review, analysis, and projection of investigations regarding inquiry and practice in school supervision. The reviewer was requested to assist the project by providing a critique of a chapter in a topic in which he or she possessed acknowledged expertise. From the review, the author(s) received suggestions to improve the focus, quality, and/or comprehensiveness of the treatment in timely fashion to encourage incorporation of appropriate changes into the chapter prior to final submission for publication.

Members of the Advisory Board initially convened during the annual conference of the Association for Supervision and Curriculum Development at Washington, D.C., in March 1993, and again during the annual meeting of the American Educational Research Association at Atlanta, Georgia, in April. Progress reports were delivered by editors, board members, and/or authors at various meetings of ASCD, AERA, and COPIS throughout the development of the project.

The Advisory Board met during ASCD each spring, and often those members in attendance at COPIS met in the fall as well. COPIS remains the major contact point.

ACKNOWLEDGMENTS

The editors gratefully acknowledge the efforts of several key individuals without whom this volume would not have reached completion.

Dr. Dianne G. Kanawati, Research Associate, Department of Educational Leadership, University of Georgia, who more than any other single individual kept the project on track through contributions, communications, and commentary.

Dr. Ray E. Bruce, Professor Emeritus, Department of Educational Leadership, University of Georgia, whose wise counsel, deft editing, and patient encouragement improved every item entrusted to his care.

Dr. Robert J. Alfonso, Vice President for Academic Affairs, East Tennessee State University, who accepted a variety of roles in advocacy, criticism, and consultation.

Mrs. Donna Bell, Administrative Secretary, in the Department of Educational Leadership, University of Georgia, who prepared letters, contracts, documents, and manuscripts with typical charm, competence, and creativity.

Mrs. Trisha Reeves, Research Assistant, Department of Adult Education, University of Georgia, who stepped in during a critical transition period and re-established order with grace and efficiency.

Members of the Advisory Board who represented a broad array of talent, viewpoint, and careers united in common cause.

Authors who contributed 52 chapters examining various venues in which concepts of instructional supervision exist.

Reviewers who assisted in the improvement of manuscripts with careful and expert criticism.

National educational leadership organizations, including the American Association of Colleges for Teacher Education, the Association for Supervision and Curriculum Development, the Council of Professors of Instructional Supervision, the National Association of Elementary School Principals, the National Association of Secondary School Principals, the National Middle School Association, National Council for Accreditation of Teacher Education, and the National Education Association.

Dr. Russell H. Yeany, Jr., Dean of the College of Education; Dr. Richard L. Lynch, Director of the School of Leadership and Lifelong Learning; and Dr. C. Thomas Holmes, Chair of the Department of Educational Leadership, University of Georgia, who provided the encouragement, resources, and time to meet the challenge of this project.

REFERENCES

Auden, Wystan H. (1907–1973). (1937). *On This Island.* New York: Random House.

Bohr, Niels H. (1885–1962). (1934). *Atomic Theory and the Description of Nature.* New York: The Macmillan Company.

Chuang-tzu (369–286 B.C.). (1942). *The wisdom of China and India.* Lin Yutang (Ed.). New York: Random House.

Comte, Auguste (1798–1857). (1851–1854). *Systeme de Politique Positive.* Paris: L. Mathias.

Doyle, Arthur C. (1859–1930). (1894). *The Memoirs of Sherlock Holmes.* London: George Newnes, Ltd.

Eliot, George (Marian Evans Cross, 1819–1880). (1860). *The Mill on the Floss.* Edinburgh and London: W. Blackwood and Sons.

Fielding, Henry (1707–1754). (1742). *The History of the Adventures of Joseph Andrews.* London: A. Millar.

Helmholtz, Hermann von (1821–1894). (1862). *Academic Discourse.* Heidelberg: G. Mohr.

Maupassant, (Henri Rene) Guy de (1850–1893). (1887). *Mont-Oriol.* Paris: Victor-Havard.

Middleton, Thomas (1580–1627). (1624). *A game at chess.* Leyden: Ian Masse.

Novalis (Friedrich von Hardenberg, 1772–1801). (1798). *Leben des ofterdingen.* Berlin: Heilbronn.

Pattison, Mark (1813–1884). (1875). *Isaac Casaubon.* London: Longmans, Green, and Company.

CONTRIBUTORS

Keith A. Acheson is Professor Emeritus of Education at the University of Oregon and a visiting professor of education at the University of Portland. He is an active consultant with the British Columbia Teacher's Federation "Program for Quality Teaching." He joined the faculty at the University of Oregon in 1967. Active in federal programs such as Teacher Corps, regional laboratories, and research and development centers, he served as associate director of the ERIC Clearinghouse on Education Management. He is co-author of *Techniques in the Clinical Supervision of Teachers* (1997) with Meredith Gall. Dr. Acheson received his Ed.D. in Curriculum and Instruction from Stanford University.

Pamela G. Adamson is Executive Officer of Curriculum and Instruction for the Clayton County Schools in Jonesboro, Georgia. She has been a classroom teacher, instructional lead teacher, and district level curriculum specialist in the area of mathematics. She received undergraduate and graduate degrees in the areas of mathematics and mathematics education. Her doctorate from the University of Georgia is in instructional supervision with emphasis on district level leadership. She has conducted research on district innovativeness.

Judith A. Aiken is Assistant Professor of Educational Leadership at the University of Vermont. She currently teaches courses in organizational leadership, school supervision, and curriculum development. A former teacher, guidance director, principal, and curriculum director in New Jersey and Vermont, her research and writing interests have focused on curriculum, supervision, professional development, and school leadership. For the past five years, she has been involved in development and organization of university/public school collaborations and professional development school partnerships throughout Vermont. She received her doctorate in education from Rutgers University.

Robert J. Alfonso is Vice President Emeritus for Academic Affairs at East Tennessee State University. He has been dean of the College and Graduate School of Education and also associate vice president for academic affairs and dean of faculties at Kent State University. As a faculty member at the University of Alabama and the University of Georgia, he taught courses in instructional supervision. He is the author of numerous publications and papers in the field of supervision, including *Instructional Supervision: A Behavior System* (1975, 1981), co-authored with Gerald R. Firth and Richard F. Neville. He received his Ph.D. in Educational Administration from Michigan State University.

Robert H. Anderson has been a teacher, principal, superintendent, professor at Harvard University, dean of the College of Education at Texas Tech University, and more recently president of a nonprofit corporation, Pedamorphosis, Inc. At the University of Wisconsin, he studied under A.S. Barr, and at Harvard, he served briefly with W.H. Burton. In Cambridge, he worked alongside Morris Cogan, the early developer of clinical supervision, and one of his most creative students, Robert Goldhammer. Dr. Anderson has actively promoted non-gradedness and team teaching, having pioneered in both developments.

Ronald J. Areglado is Associate Executive Director of Programs at the National Association of Elementary School Principals in Alexandria, Virginia. He is responsible for planning NAESP's annual convention and professional development activities. He has been a teacher in Boston's inner city, rural school principal, superintendent, and senior manager with the Massachusetts Department of Education. He has held faculty appointments at several colleges and universities, teaching primarily in the area of educational leadership. As a consultant to both private and public sector organizations, he presents workshops and keynote addresses on leadership, personal development, and organizational change. He is co-author of *Learning for Life* (1996) on self-directed learning.

Terry A. Astuto is Professor of Educational Administration in the School of Education at New York University. Her research and writing focus on alternative organizational theories and application to schools with particular attention to creating meaning links between theory and practice. Recent publications examine school restructuring and educational reform. She received her doctorate in Educational Administration from Indiana University.

Bernard Badiali is Professor and Chair of the Department of Educational Leadership at Miami University of Ohio. He has worked closely with John Goodlad as a Leadership Associate in the National Network for Educational Renewal. His research interests have been in school renewal, and supervision and transformative leadership. He received a Ph.D. in Curriculum and Instruction from Pennsylvania State University.

Thomas E. Barone is Professor of Education at Arizona State University with a joint appointment in Curriculum and Instruction and in Educational Leadership and Policy Studies. He teaches courses in curriculum studies, teacher education, and qualitative methodology. Dr. Barone has special interests in arts-based and narrative forms of educational research. He earned his doctorate from Stanford University in Design and Evaluation of Educational Programs.

James E. Barott is Assistant Professor of Educational Administration at the University of Utah. He was acting program leader in the graduate program in Organizational Leadership and Confluent Education for the University of California at Santa Barbara. His primary areas of interest include the micropolitics of educational organizations and organizational change/persistence. Recent publications include *Changing Schools into Collaborative Organizations* and *The Confluent Approach to Organizational Change and Development.*

Michael Blakeney is Executive Assistant to the Superintendent, Community School District 19 (Brooklyn), New York City Public Schools. He has served as a high school art teacher with specializations in painting and drawing. Current research focuses on ways in which teachers make sense of comprehensive school improvement initiatives. He received his doctorate in Educational Administration from New York University.

Arthur Blumberg is Professor Emeritus of Education at Syracuse University. His books include *Supervisors and Teachers: A Private Cold War* (1974, 1980), *The Effective School Principal* (1986), *The School Superintendent* (1988), and *School Administration as a Craft* (1989). He received his doctorate from Teachers College, Columbia University.

Margaret Borrego Brainard has been an instructor in the Preservice Program in Elementary Education at Teachers College, Columbia University for three years. She has worked as a classroom teacher, special education consultant teacher, and administrator in public and private school settings for 16 years. Her research interests include alternative assessment, the theory-building strategies of beginning teachers, and supervision of programs which include special needs students in regular classrooms.

David M. Byrd is Professor in the Education Department at the University of Rhode Island. He has served as director of the Office of Teacher Education and acting head of the proposed School of Education. He was associate professor at Southern Illinois University. He has authored and co-authored over 30 articles, books and chapters including the textbook *Methods for Effective Teaching* (1994) and chapters in both the *Handbook of Research on Teacher Education* (1996) and the *Handbook of Research on School Supervision*. He presently serves as co-editor of the *Teacher Education Yearbook* series, including *Research on the Education of our Nation's Teachers, Preparing Tomorrow's Teachers: The Field Experience,* and *Research on Career Long Teacher Education*. He has a long-term professional and research interest in the preparation of teachers, preservice and in-service. He is a graduate of the doctoral program in Teacher Education at Syracuse University.

Gillian E. Cook is Associate Professor of Education at the University of Texas at San Antonio. She is responsible for the Professional Supervisor certification and graduate degree program, and also teaches in the undergraduate Interdisciplinary Studies degree program. She is the Director of the Office of Core Curriculum for the University. In addition to teaching courses in instructional supervision, she regularly conducts leadership training programs in the public schools. She is an active member of the Council of Professors of Instructional Supervision (COPIS) and the Special Interest Group on Instructional Supervision of the American Educational Research Association. She completed her Ed.D. degree at Harvard University with a focus on instructional supervision.

John C. Daresh is Professor and Chair of the Department of Educational Leadership and Foundations at the University of Texas at El Paso. He also directs the new doctoral program in Educational Leadership. He previously served on the faculties at Illinois State University, University of Cincinnati, Ohio State University (where he also directed the Danforth Foundation Principal Preparation Program), and University of Northern Colorado. He was a teacher in the public schools of Dubuque, Iowa, and Chicago. He has been a consultant for school districts, institutions, and state education departments across the United States and in numerous countries around the world. Most recently, he served as a member of the Carnegie Commission to Restructure the American High School for the National Association of Secondary School Principals (NASSP). He continues to work with the National Association of Elementary School Principals (NAESP) in a variety of professional development activities.

Mary Erina Driscoll is Associate Professor of Educational Administration in the School of Education at New York University. Her research focuses on organizational and collaborative arrangements connecting individuals to each other and to the communities in which schools and students are located. This includes the study of policies affecting schools and communities and, particularly, those bearing on the coordination of children's services at the school site. She received her doctorate in Educational Administration from the University of Chicago.

Francis M. Duffy is Professor of Administration and Supervision at Gallaudet University in Washington, D.C., as well as consultant on organization development. He has also served a classroom teacher, executive director, and instructional supervisor. His books include *Designing High Performance Schools* (1996) and *Supervising Knowledge Work* (1997). He authored a chapter in *Educational Supervision: Perspectives, Issues, and Controversies* (1997). He received his Ph.D. from the University of Pittsburgh in Curriculum and Supervision.

Gerald R. Firth is Professor of Educational Leadership at the University of Georgia where he has served for 25 years in roles including chair of the Department of Curriculum and Supervision and dean of the College of Education. He has been president of the Association for Supervision and Curriculum Development as well as ASCD affiliates in four states. As leader, scholar, and practitioner in the fields of instructional supervision and curriculum development, he has co-authored significant textbooks in both specializations: *Instructional Supervision: A Behavior System* with Robert J. Alfonso and Richard F. Neville (1975, 1981) and *The Curriculum Continuum in Perspective* with Richard D. Kimpston (1973); contributed chapters to ASCD yearbooks (1968, 1982), texts, and reference books, as well as numerous articles in professional publications, notably *Educational Leadership* and the *Journal of Curriculum and Supervision*. His experience in school systems ranges from teacher to superintendent and in higher education includes administrative and faculty roles at the University of Alabama, University of Minnesota, and State University of New York at Buffalo. He has served as director of a reform effort with small rural schools in the United States, as chief of party to the Ministry of Education in Egypt, and as consultant to bi-national schools in Central and South America and the Caribbean region. He has been major advisor for nearly 100 doctoral dissertations as well as numerous specialist projects, and master's theses. He received his doctorate from Teachers College, Columbia University.

David J. Flinders is Associate Professor in the School of Education at Indiana University, Bloomington. He was a high school and middle school English teacher. He has published widely in the areas of curriculum evaluation, teaching, instructional supervision, and qualitative research. His most recent book is *The Curriculum Studies Reader* (1997) co-edited with Stephen Thornton. Flinders is currently conducting classroom research on critical thinking as a form of reasoned inquiry. He received his doctorate from Stanford University.

Patrick Galvin is Associate Professor in the Department of Educational Administration at the University of Utah and Co-director of the Utah Education Policy Center. His research focuses on school finance, with special attention to resource utilization within school organizations. His policy studies focus primarily on issues of school finance, student achievement, and organizational structure.

Noreen B. Garman is Professor of Administrative and Policy Studies and Co-director of the Institute for International Studies in Education at the University of Pittsburgh. She teaches courses in instructional supervision, curriculum studies, qualitative research, and interpretative research. Author of numerous articles and chapters on clinical supervision, curriculum, and qualitative and interpretive research, she is presently Director of a Federation-wide teacher development project in Bosnia and Herzegovina. She received her Ph.D. from the University of Pittsburgh with specializations in curriculum and supervision.

Robert J. Garmston is Professor Emeritus of Educational Administration at California State University at Sacramento. He is a former classroom teacher and school administrator. He is a co-developer of Cognitive Coaching and Co-director of the Institute for Intelligent Behavior with Dr. Arthur Costa. Dr. Garmston is author of numerous publications on leadership, supervision, and staff development. He has made presentations and conducted workshops for educators throughout the United States and in Africa, Asia, Canada, Europe, and the Middle East.

Geneva Gay is Professor of Education at the University of Washington-Seattle. She is the recipient of the 1990 Distinguished Scholar Award, presented by the Committee on the Role and Status of Minorities in Educational Research and Development of the American Educational Research Association, and the 1994 Multicultural Educator Award, the first to be presented by the National Association of Multicultural Education. She is nationally and internationally recognized for scholarship in multicultural education, particularly as related to curriculum design, staff development, classroom instruction, and culture and learning. Her writings include more than 100 articles and book chapters, the co-editorship of *Expressively Black: The Cultural Basis of Ethnic Identity* (1987), and the author of *At the Essence of Learning: Multicultural Education* (1994).

Jeffrey Glanz is Associate Professor in the Department of Instruction, Curriculum, and Administration at Kean University of New Jersey. He teaches graduate courses in supervision, curriculum, and action research. He served on the editorial board of the *Journal of Curriculum and Supervision* and is currently an editorial board member of *Educational Studies and the Record in Educational Leadership*. He is also current editor of *Focus on Education,* the journal of the New Jersey ASCD affiliate. Dr. Glanz has authored *Bureaucracy and Professionalism: The Evolution of Public School Supervision* (1991), co-edited

Educational Supervision: Perspectives, Issues, and Controversies (1997) with Richard Neville, and is currently completing his third book, *Action Research: An Educational Leader's Guide to School Improvement.*

Allan A. Glatthorn is Distinguished Research Professor of Education at East Carolina University. He previously served as professor of education at the University of Pennsylvania. He has been a high school teacher, department head, principal, and director of two alternative schools. He is the author of 25 professional books in curriculum and supervision, including *Curriculum Renewal* (1987), *Supervisory Leadership* (1990), and *Differentiated Supervision* (1997). He has published several English textbooks, numerous professional articles, and two monographs on the English curriculum and the teaching of writing. As a consultant, Dr. Glatthorn has advised more than 100 school systems in developing versions of differentiated supervision.

Carl D. Glickman serves the University of Georgia as University Professor, Convener and Professor of the Social Foundations of Education Program, and Chair of the Program for School Improvement, which operates the nationally recognized school renewal network, the League of Professional Schools. His latest book is *Renewing America's Schools* (1993). The fourth edition of his book *Supervision of Instruction: A Developmental Approach* (1985), co-authored with Stephen Gordon and Jovita Ross-Gordon, will be published in 1998.

Lee F. Goldsberry is Associate Professor of Education at the University of Southern Maine. For the past several years, he has engaged in preparing preservice teachers, assisting experienced teachers, and contributing to local school renewal. His focus is on methods of providing classroom teachers with stimulation for and assistance with critical examination and refinement of teaching practices. Among his publications is a chapter in *Educational Supervision: Perspectives, Issues and Controversies* (1997). A former elementary school teacher, he received his Ed.D. from the University of Illinois at Urbana.

Stephen P. Gordon is Associate Professor of Educational Administration at Southwest Texas State University. He has been a teacher, supervisor, staff development consultant for a state education department, and coordinator of university outreach to schools. He is author of the book *How to Help Beginning Teachers Succeed* (1991) and co-author of the text *Supervision of Instruction: A Developmental Approach* (1985) with Carl Glickman and Jovita Ross-Gordon. His primary areas of research and writing are instructional supervision, professional development, and schools which empower.

Ruud J. Gorter is Executive Director of the Association of Educational Advisory Centers in The Hague, The Netherlands. He has served as coordinator of the National Institute for Curriculum Development (SLO) for 10 years. He

has been a special education teacher, consultant, and director of program development for an inner city school project. Dr. Gorter is a former member of the National Advisory Council for Primary Education, Secondary Education School Board, European Forum on Educational Management, European Platform on Education, Commission on Inclusion in Education, National Language Teaching Expertise Center at the University of Nijmegen, and taskforce of educational support agencies (Netherlands/Belgium). He is co-author of the Handbook on Dutch Language Teaching for Teacher Training Colleges; and editor and co-author of *Views on Core Curriculum, Core Curriculum,* and *A Comparative Analysis* (ASCD/SLO). He was the editor of the *Handbook for Counseling and Supervision in Education in The Netherlands,* published in a variety of education books and journals, including Educational Leadership. He received his doctoral degree from the Institute for Pedagogical Sciences at Utrecht University.

Gene E. Hall is Professor of Educational Leadership at the University of Northern Colorado. He spent 18 years at the national Research and Development Center for Teacher Education at the University of Texas at Austin. He also was professor of Educational Leadership at the University of Florida. He is the principal architect of the Concerns Based Adoption Model (CBAM), which has provided the conceptual framework for his career long scholarly efforts to study, assess and facilitate the change process in schools, higher education, business and government settings. He earned his Ph.D. from Syracuse University.

Ben M. Harris is M.K. Haye Centennial Professor Emeritus for the University of Texas at Austin. His professional career spans 50 years as teacher, curriculum director, instructional supervisor, personnel director, researcher, consultant, and professor. His writing, research, and teaching for the past 40 years has focused on in-service education, staff development, teacher evaluation, and instructional leadership. In addition to graduate teaching at various universities, he has conducted workshops and lectured throughout the United States; served as consultant to ministries of education in a dozen different countries; and been active in several professional organizations, particularly the Association for Supervision and Curriculum Development and Council of Professors of Instructional Supervision. His major books include *Supervisory Behavior in Education* (1963, 1975 and 1985), *In-Service Education for Staff Development* (1986), and *Personnel Administration in Education* (1992).

Richard D. Hawthorne is Professor of Curriculum and Instruction at West Virginia University. He was a member of the faculty at Case Western Reserve University for four years, and at Kent State University for 22 years. Throughout his career, Dr. Hawthorne has developed and taught courses on curriculum theory, instructional supervision, and theory and research on teaching. His most recent publications include: "Impact on Colleges of Education" in *Lessons from Restructuring Experiences* (1995), edited by N.E. Hoffman, W.M. Reed, and G.S. Rosenblugh; and

Transformative Curriculum Leadership (1995) with James G. Henderson. He completed his doctorate at the University of Wisconsin.

Helen M. Hazi is Professor of Educational Leadership at West Virginia University. Her research specialty is legal aspects affecting instructional supervision. She examines trends and critical incidents of practice associated with certification, rights, testing, development, and evaluation of professional personnel and school reform. Her work appears in books and journals such as *Educational Leadership, Phi Delta Kappan, Journal of Curriculum and Supervision, Journal of Personnel Evaluation in Education,* and the *International Journal of Educational Reform.* She is a published poet, reader of fiction, photographer, traveler, and beachcomber.

Nancy E. Hoffman is Associate Professor and Director of Field Experiences, Student Teaching, and Advising in the College of Human Resources and Education at West Virginia University. She recently edited a book on creating and sustaining professional development schools, *Lessons from Restructuring Experiences: Stories of Change in Professional Development Schools.* She completed her doctorate in Curriculum and Supervision at Pennsylvania State University.

Patricia E. Holland is Associate Professor in the Department of Educational Leadership and Cultural Studies at the University of Houston. Her research is focused on supervision as an interpretive practice through which teachers come to understand teaching and learning. She has authored or co-authored articles appearing in *Journal of Curriculum and Supervision, American Educational Research Journal, Peabody Journal of Education, Journal of Staff Development,* and *Journal of Curriculum Theorizing.* She is co-author of *Collaborative Leadership and Shared Decision Making;* and has contributed chapters to several books, including the 1992 ASCD Yearbook, *Supervision in Transition: The Principal as Instructional Leader,* and *Commissions, Reports and Reforms.*

Michael J. Hough blends competencies in educational leadership and management science as a faculty member at the University of Wollongong in New South Wales, Australia. Experience in engineering and expertise in telecommunications are combined in developing programs of distance learning in countries throughout the Pacific Basin. He has consulted with institutions, agencies, and organizations in the United States, England, Europe, and the Middle East. He returned to the University of Georgia as a visiting lecturer after earning his doctorate in Curriculum and Instruction. His dissertation research focused on preferred learning profiles for staff development to address changing needs of teachers over their professional careers.

Marie L. Howells is coordinator of Project Achieve at Martin Luther King, Jr. High School in New York City. She was a teacher of foods and nutrition, founder of a school-based

management team, and coordinator of a collaborative learning institute emphasizing cooperative interaction and interdisciplinary studies. Her professional interests and competencies involve leadership in team building. Her dissertation research focused on the role of the instructional supervisor in school restructuring from a moral perspective. She earned her doctorate from Fordham University.

Maynard J. Iverson is Associate Professor and Coordinator of the Agricultural Education Program in the Department of Occupational Studies at the University of Georgia. He also served as a faculty member in vocational/occupational education at the University of Kentucky, Auburn University, and North Carolina State University. He has taught graduate-level supervision courses in occupational education in North Carolina and Georgia for 17 years and is currently working on a major text revision. Dr. Iverson has consulted on vocational program development in Saudi Arabia and Japan, as well as in numerous states across America. He earned his Ph.D. from Ohio State University.

Edward F. Iwanicki is Professor of Educational Leadership at the University of Connecticut. He is responsible for teaching courses in the areas of instructional supervision, personnel evaluation, and program evaluation. Dr. Iwanicki has consulted with numerous school systems and state agencies in New England, Florida, Louisiana, and North Carolina on the design, implementation, and evaluation of personnel evaluation programs. Among his publications is a chapter on "Teacher Evaluation for School Improvement" in *The New Handbook of Teacher Evaluation.* He was a member of the Panel of Writers for *The Personnel Evaluation Standards* and was founding editor of the *Journal of Personnel Evaluation in Education*

Paula Jorde Bloom is Professor of Early Childhood Education at National-Louis University of Wheeling, Illinois. She has taught preschool and kindergarten, designed and directed a child care center, and served as administrator of a campus laboratory school. Her current research interests are in the areas of organizational climate and occupational stress as related to indices of job satisfaction in early childhood settings. Dr. Bloom is the author of numerous journal articles and several widely read books including: *Avoiding Burnout: Strategies for Managing Time, Space, and People; Living and Learning with Children;* and *A Great Place to Work: Improving Conditions for Staff in Young Children's Programs.* Her most recent book *Blueprint for Action: Achieving Center-Based Change Through Staff Development* provides a framework for understanding child care centers as organizations and how staff development can serve as the vehicle for improving program effectiveness. She received her Ph.D. from Stanford University.

Kim Kaiser is a faculty member at the Erickson Institute and an adjunct professor at the University of San Francisco. He teaches courses in psychology and counseling. A psychologist and licensed marriage, family, and child counselor, he has taught in classroom settings ranging from elementary school to graduate school.

Dianne G. Kanawati is a curriculum specialist serving faculty assignments at Campbell University and Durham Technical College in the Research Triangle of North Carolina. Her professional experience includes positions as teacher in public schools of Florida and as instructor in post-secondary institutions of South Carolina. As a Graduate Fellow in Educational Leadership at the University of Georgia, she contributed to programs for the Council of Professors of Instructional Supervision and the Society of Professors of Curriculum. Dr. Kanawati had a major role in the evolution of the *Handbook of Research on School Supervision.* Completing the doctorate in Curriculum and Instruction, her qualitative study generated guidelines for developing curriculum congruent with profiles of cultural, functional, or critical literacy.

Joyce Killian is Professor of Curriculum and Instruction at Southern Illinois University at Carbondale. She chairs the graduate specialty area in teacher education and supervision. Her research focuses on the professional development of teachers and the conditions that promote that growth. She has authored several chapters and numerous articles in journals including *Educational Leadership, The Journal of Staff Development,* and the *Journal of Teacher Education.* She received her Ph.D. from Pennsylvania State University in the area of Curriculum and Supervision.

James M. King is Associate Professor of Instructional Technology at the University of Georgia. A recognized instructional designer, he has worked closely with many funding agencies and corporations in the design, development, and evaluation of instructional materials including: the National Science Foundation, U.S. Department of Education, IBM, Apple Computer, Lufthansa German Airlines, Dow Chemical and Dole Foods Company. Recent design and development collaborations include CD-ROM products for Dole Foods Company, Mead Johnson Nutritionals, East Carolina School of Medicine, and the University of California-Berkeley. His current research interests focus on interface design, advanced system design, and ethics in the use of technology. His teaching areas include message design, interactive multimedia design, media utilization, telecommunications, and photographic processes. He received his doctorate in Instructional Systems Technology with an emphasis in message design from Indiana University.

Karron G. Lewis is Assistant Director and Coordinator of the Teaching Assistant Training Programs for the Center for Teaching Effectiveness at the University of Texas at Austin. She consults with university faculty members and TAs on a one-to-one basis to assist improvement of teaching, conducts departmental and university-wide workshops on a variety of topics, engages in research activities, and periodically acts as a consultant and conducts workshops for faculty members and TAs at other institutions. She is the editor of *The Journal of Graduate Teaching Assistant Development, The TA Experience: Preparing for Multiple Roles,* and *Face to Face: A Sourcebook of Individual Consultation Techniques for Faculty/Instructional Developers* and has written numerous book chapters and journal articles on both faculty and TA development.

Laura Lipton is Director of *Educational Consulting Services,* a New York-based human development firm specializing in a systems approach to change for individuals and organizations. She is a Senior Associate with the Institute for Intelligent Behavior in Berkeley, California, co-directed by Arthur Costa and Robert Garmston. Dr. Lipton pursues a writing and research agenda in the fields of organizational culture and change and cognitive science. Her recent publications include *Shifting Rules, Shifting Roles: Transforming the Work Environment to Support Learning,* with Arthur Costa and Bruce Wellman; and *Organizational Learning: The Essential Journey,* with Robert Melamede.

D. John McIntyre is Associate Dean for Teacher Education and Professor of Curriculum and Instruction at Southern Illinois University at Carbondale. He is past president of the Association of Teacher Educators, co-editor of the ATE Yearbook in Teacher Education series, and co-author of *Reflective Roles of the Classroom Teacher.* Dr. McIntyre is the recipient of the ATE Research Award and has been selected among 70 outstanding leaders in teacher education. His research focus is in the areas of teacher education and supervision, with emphasis on the field experience component.

Richard F. Neville is Professor Emeritus at the University of Maryland Baltimore County (UMBC). He has served the University of Maryland system as assistant to the dean at College Park, dean of education, dean of faculty, and dean of arts and sciences at UMBC; and completed his service as acting provost of the University of Maryland Biotechnology Institute. Dr. Neville has published in the field of supervision, including *Educational Supervision: Perspectives, Issues, and Controversies* (1997), co-edited with Jeffrey Glanz; and *Instructional Supervision: A Behavior System,* co-authored with Robert J. Alfonso and Gerald R. Firth (1975, 1981). He received his Ph.D. in Curriculum and Supervision from the University of Connecticut.

Robert F. Nicely, Jr. is Professor of Education and Associate Dean for Outreach and Faculty Development in the College of Education at Pennsylvania State University. He has served as co-editor and member of the editorial board of the *Journal of Curriculum and Supervision,* and has served as president of the Pennsylvania Association for Supervision and Curriculum Development, the Pennsylvania Educational Research Association, and the Pennsylvania Council of Teachers of Mathematics. Dr. Nicely has chaired committees and served as an editor of publications for the Association for Supervision and Curriculum Development. He has received numerous awards for his leadership, service, program development, and research.

Barbara Stock Nielsen is serving her second term as State Superintendent of Education for South Carolina. She has been a teacher, assistant principal, director of career education, and educational consultant. She has championed strategic planning for school renewal and financial accountability. In her capacity as chief state school officer, she has provided leadership to systemic reform and restructuring efforts in the state education department and school districts. Dr. Nielsen has developed initiatives in state deregulation, technical assistance, instructional improvement, and character education. She earned her doctoral degree in Educational Administration from the University of Louisville.

Dennis J. Nielsen is Professor of Educational Administration at South Carolina State University. He was a faculty member at the State University of New York at Albany and director of Program and Pupil Evaluation for the Jefferson County School District in Louisville, Kentucky. He also served as a mathematics teacher, assistant high school principal, and evaluation consultant. Dr. Nielsen is directing a federally-funded project to investigate applications of Total Quality Management strategies in restructuring rural schools throughout South Carolina. He earned his doctoral degree in Instructional Supervision at the University of Georgia. His dissertation research focused on the relationship between critical thinking and self concept of high school students.

James F. Nolan, Jr. is Associate Professor of Curriculum and Supervision at Pennsylvania State University. He is a former elementary teacher, high school teacher, and guidance counselor. He is the author of numerous articles in professional journals that focus on the topics of classroom management, reflective supervision, and peer coaching. He is co-author of *Classroom Management: A Professional Decision Making Approach*. He contributed a chapter to *Educational Supervision: Perspectives, Issues and Controversies* (1997). His major research interests are in instructional supervision, reflective practice, school and teacher change, and classroom management. He received his Ph.D. in Curriculum and Instruction from Pennsylvania State University.

Sharon Nodie Oja is Professor of Educational Psychology and Director of Field Experiences in the Department of Education at the University of New Hampshire. She has held positions as a high school mathematics teacher, a mathematics instructor in General College at the University of Minnesota, and was principal co-investigator of the National Science Foundation's Mathematics and Science Collaborative. She conducts workshops and presents papers regularly at national and international meetings, including the International Conference on Teacher Research and the Annual Portfolio Conference. She is a member of the Board of Directors for the New England Research Association. She received her Ph.D. in Developmental Education from the University of Minnesota.

James R. Okey is Professor Emeritus of Education at the University of Georgia. During his 20 years at that institution, he served programs in science education and instructional technology. He conducted research in the areas of instructional effectiveness and development of technology-delivered materials. In recent years, his work has focused on technological applications in teacher training and learner assessment.

Peter F. Oliva is retired from positions as Professor and Chair of Educational Leadership at Georgia Southern University, Florida International University, and Southern Illinois University. He has held faculty positions at the University of Mississippi, University of Florida, Indiana State University, and University of Hawaii. He taught at the high school level in New York State and Maryland. He has published numerous articles in the professional literature and is author of several textbooks in the fields of curriculum, instruction, and supervision, including *Supervision for Today's Schools* (1996) and *Developing the Curriculum* (1997).

Edward F. Pajak is Professor of Educational Leadership in the College of Education at the University of Georgia. He directs a major systemic educational restructuring initiative centered around collaboration between institutions of higher education and P-12 schools in Northeast Georgia. He has published more than 30 articles in professional journals, including the *American Educational Research Journal*, *Sociology of Education*, and the *Journal of Psychoanalytic Anthropology*. Dr. Pajak has also published two earlier books, *The Central Office Supervisor of Curriculum and Instruction: Setting the Stage for Success* (1989) and *Approaches to Clinical Supervision: Alternatives for Improving Instruction* (1993). His current research interest is the application of psychoanalytic concepts toward an understanding of social and psychological dynamics of teaching. He earned his doctorate from Syracuse University.

Barbara Nelson Pavan is Professor of Educational Administration at Temple University. She teaches courses on supervision, principalship, organizational theory, and research. She has been an elementary school teacher and principal. She has served as president of the Council of Professors of Instructional Supervision. In addition to co-authoring the book, *Nongradedness: Helping It to Happen*, she has written several chapters on instructional supervision. Her publications on supervision, nongradedness and gender differences in school administrative careers appear in *Educational Leadership*, *Elementary School Journal*, *ERIC*, *Phi Delta Kappan*, *Principal*, and *Urban Education* among others. She received her doctorate from Harvard University.

Isobel L. Pfeiffer is Emeritus Professor of Educational Leadership at the University of Akron. She held faculty positions at the University of West Georgia and the University of Georgia. Dr. Pfeiffer is co-author of *Supervision of Teachers: A Guide to Improving Instruction* and author of numerous articles in professional journals. Her educational career included teaching and leadership roles in public schools at both elementary and secondary levels, and in higher education at undergraduate and graduate levels. She is past president of the Council of Professors of Instructional Supervision and Ohio ASCD affiliate.

Donna M. Post is Associate Professor of Curriculum and Instruction and Center Coordinator of the Marion Professional Development Center for Southern Illinois University at Carbondale. She specializes in teacher education and supervision. She teaches graduate courses in instructional methods, trends in education, research design, and supervision of teaching, with special emphasis on cooperating teachers and the skills and knowledge needed to extend professional development of novice teachers. Her journal contributions include *When the Cooperating Teacher Goes on Strike: Twelve Practical Suggestions for University Supervisors, The Alien and the Alienated: The Power of Clinical Supervision in Turning the Tide with a Disgruntled Veteran Teacher, Accommodating Adult Students in Undergraduate Teacher Education Programs* (with Joyce Killian), and *Searching for Prospective Teacher Educators* (with M.M. Dupuis). She received her doctorate from Pennsylvania State University with an emphasis in teacher education and supervision.

Dwight J. Pullen is Secondary Instructional Supervisor for the Cherokee County Schools in Canton, Georgia. His responsibilities include supervision of extensive programs in vocational education. He was a teacher of agriculture at Cherokee High School and vocational supervisor at Sequoyah High School, also in Canton. He completed his doctorate in Occupational Studies at the University of Georgia. His dissertation involved the study of projected duties of the secondary vocational education supervisor in the 21st century.

Alan J. Reiman is Assistant Professor, Director of the Model Clinical Teaching Program at North Carolina State University, and Coordinator of the North Carolina Model Clinical Teaching Network, a nationally recognized consortium of universities engaged in innovative teacher education. His primary interests are in collaborative models of teacher professional development across the career span. His funded research and research publications are focused on the impact of new leadership and mentoring roles joined by guided reflection on the development of teachers. He is the co-author of *Supervision and Mentoring for Teacher Development.*

Jean M. Rhoades is Assistant Superintendent of Curriculum and Staff Development for the Polk County Schools in Cedartown, Georgia. She has been a middle school teacher and department chair, and has served on numerous curriculum committees. Dr. Rhoades conducted research on school and district responsibility for dimensions of supervisory practice in restructuring schools. She earned her doctoral degree in Instructional Supervision at the University of Georgia.

Jerrold Ross is Dean of the School of Education and Human Services at St. John's University. He was associate dean for academic affairs in the School of Education at New York University, director of the National Arts Education Research Center site at NYU, president of the New York College of Music, and director of the Town Hall in New York City. His research interests include arts education, arts education policy, and teacher education. He earned his doctorate in Music Education at New York University.

Frances O'Connell Rust is Associate Professor and Coordinator of the Undergraduate Program in Early Childhood and Elementary Education at New York University. Her research interests include teacher education, teacher beliefs, instructional supervision, and educational innovation. She designed and implemented a four-year project in staff development involving student teachers, Professional Development Laboratory, Teacher Leadership Institute, and Head Start. She is currently president of the Special Interest Group on Instructional Supervision of the American Educational Research Association. Her publications appear in the *Journal of Early Childhood Teacher Education* (1997), *Teaching and Teacher Education, Encyclopedia of Early Childhood Education* (1994), and *Journal of Teacher Education* (1988). Her most recent book, *Changing Teaching, Changing Schools* (1993), examines early childhood theory and practice and their potential for improving elementary education. She earned her doctorate in Curriculum and Teaching from Teachers College, Columbia University.

Richard D. Sawyer is an instructor in Curriculum and Teaching at Teachers College, Columbia University. He has written on school-based integrated services, school-college partnerships, teacher retention, and alternative route certification. He taught public high school in San Francisco.

Frances Schoonmaker is Associate Professor of Education and Co-director of the Preservice Program in Elementary Education in the Department of Curriculum and Teaching at Teachers College, Columbia University. She teaches courses in elementary education, in-service supervision, and curriculum studies. She authored chapters in ASCD yearbooks and articles in various professional journals. Dr. Schoonmaker has been active in the American Educational Research Association as Chair of the Special Interest Group on Instructional Supervision and Secretary of Division B. She earned her doctorate in Curriculum Studies from Teachers College, Columbia University.

Mohammed Shamsher serves as administrator on the staff of the Professional Development Division for the British Columbia Teachers Federation in Vancouver, Canada. He is the originator of "Program for Quality Teaching," a peer consultation effort to adapt the techniques of teacher supervisory practices for professional growth. His publications include *Voices of Teaching* (1990-91) and *Call to Teaching* (1992) with Ted Aoki, and *Classroom Research* (1993). He received his Ph.D. degree in Educational Policy and Management from the University of Oregon.

Arthur S. Shapiro is Professor of Educational Leadership at the University of South Florida. He has been a social worker, teacher, principal, director of secondary education, assistant superintendent, and superintendent. He was appointed professor at George Peabody College directly from the field. His writing investigates respective theories of supervision, curriculum, decision-making, and strikes. He published numerous articles and simulations in supervision, curriculum, and administration. He serves schools and other organizations as trouble-shooter and change agent. He is presently preparing manuscripts on supervising constructivist education and on diagnosing concerns in organizations.

Marilyn A. Sheerer is Professor and Chair of Elementary and Middle Grades Education at East Carolina University. She has served as a teacher, administrator, faculty member and department chair in the field of early childhood and elementary education for over 25 years. She is the author of numerous articles on curriculum, supervision, and staff development. She is a consulting editor for *Young Children* and the co-editor of the professional development column in the *Early Childhood Education Journal*.

Billie J. Sherrod is Director of Accountability at the Georgia Department of Education. Previous responsibilities during her 15 years of service with that agency include coordinator of distance learning and media programs, coordinator of test development, Quality Basic Education field administrator, and consultant for guidance and counseling programs. Her experience also includes serving as a high school counselor and a social studies teacher. She earned her doctorate in Instructional Supervision at the University of Georgia.

Wen-Haur Shieh is Associate Professor and Secretary in Chief at the National Hualien Teachers College in Taiwan. He has served as a school administrator for 13 years. As a member of the School Guidance Team at his institution, Dr. Shieh provides consulting visits to the elementary schools and is involved in the school change process. His areas of expertise are professional growth of teachers and leadership of school change. He has published articles on moral education and student teaching practices in schools. He received his doctoral degree from the University of Northern Colorado.

Neil S. Smith is a faculty member in Teacher Education at Malaspina University College in British Columbia. He has 20 years of experience in teacher education and evaluation of teachers, as consultant in organization development, and as facilitator and researcher regarding implementation of multi-district peer consultation programs. He received his Ph.D. degree from the University of Oregon.

John Smyth is Foundation Professor of Teacher Education and Associate Dean for Research at the Flinders University of South Australia. He is also Director of the Flinders Institute for the Study of Teaching. He was Senior Fulbright

Research Scholar at the University of Pittsburgh in 1990, Distinguished Scholar at the University of British Columbia in 1991, and received the Palmer O. Johnson Award from the American Educational Research Association in 1993. Dr. Smyth has authored/edited eight books, the latest of which is entitled *Critical Discourses on Teacher Development* (1995). His most recent book is entitled *Remaking Teaching: Ideology, Policy and Practice* with G. Shacklock.

Karolyn J. Snyder is Professor of Educational Leadership at the University of South Florida. In the past 20 years, over 200 publications have evolved from her work on a systems approach to change in educational institutions, which have stemmed from her major publication with Robert H. Anderson: *Managing Productive Schools: Toward an Ecology* (1986). The *School Work Culture Profile* has been translated into six languages, and is used in research projects around the world. Dr. Snyder's work on systems thinking, school change, and chaos theory has led to involvements with schools and universities throughout the United States and in Brazil, England, Finland, Germany, Holland, Hungary, Indonesia, Israel, Norway, Russia, Sweden, United Arab Emirates, and Venezuela.

Robert J. Starratt is Director of Educational Administration and Higher Education Programs in the Graduate School of Education at Boston College. He previously served as a faculty member and academic administrator at Fordham University. Besides his long affiliation with the field of supervision, his publications include *Building an Ethical School* (1994), *Transforming Educational Administration* (1996), *The Drama of Leadership* (1993), and *Leaders With Vision* (1997). He co-authored *Supervision: A Redefinition* (1993) with Thomas J. Sergiovanni. His lectures on school reform and educational leadership have taken him overseas to many communities of educators.

Iris M. Striedieck is an educational consultant with school districts in the central Pennsylvania area. She works with prospective teachers, specializing in supervision, mathematics education and multiple cultures and perspectives. She is an active reviewer, writer, and presenter for various professional organizations. She earned her doctorate at Pennsylvania State University.

William W. Swan is Associate Professor of Educational Leadership at the University of Georgia. He has served in leadership positions for special education at the local, state, and federal/national levels for over 25 years. His research interests include policy analysis for special education and general education, collaboration among general education and special education leaders, early childhood/special education, and programs for severely emotionally disturbed. He has published extensively in refereed journals, in professional texts, and has co-authored a book on interagency collaboration for comprehensive services with J.L. Morgan (1993). He has provided consultation/technical assistance to over 75 national/state/local public education and private agencies in 42 states. He received his doctorate in Research Design in Education from the University of Georgia.

Daniel Tanner is Professor in the Graduate School of Education at Rutgers University. He directs the graduate studies in curriculum theory and development. He is the author of many books including *Crusade for Democracy: Progressive Education at the Crossroads* (1991), *Secondary Curriculum: Theory and Development* (1971), *Secondary Education: Perspectives and Prospects* (1972), *Schools for Youth,* and (with Laurel Tanner) *Supervision in Education: Problems and Practices* (1987), *History of the School Curriculum* (1990), and *Curriculum Development: Theory Into Practice* (1980, 1995). He is consulting editor for the *Annual Review of Research for School Leaders.*

Conrad F. Toepfer, Jr. is Professor of Education at the State University of New York at Buffalo. He teaches courses in curriculum planning and development. A curriculum generalist with a special interest in middle level education, he has contributed widely to professional literature in general curriculum and middle level education over the past 32 years. A past president of the National Middle School Association, he chaired the Middle Level Education Council for the National Association of Secondary School Principals from 1981 through 1993.

Saundra J. Tracy is Professor and Dean of the College of Education at Butler University. Previous higher education experience includes service as a professor of educational leadership at Lehigh University and at Cleveland State University, assistant to the president of Lehigh University as an American Council of Education Fellow, Director of Education Programs for the Iacocca Institute and executive director of the Lehigh University School Study Council. Her research interests include instructional supervision and career development in education. She is co-author of *Assisting and Assessing Educational Personnel* (1993) with Robert MacNaughton. She received her Ph.D. in Educational Administration from Purdue University.

Leonard A. Valverde is Professor and Dean of the College of Education at Arizona State University. He previously served as vice president for academic affairs for the University of Texas at San Antonio. He began his career as a classroom teacher and became an instructional supervisor of mathematics teachers in the Los Angeles City School District. He taught instructional supervision concepts and leadership competencies on the graduate level at the University of Texas at Austin for 15 years. He currently is directing a Kellogg Foundation funded doctoral leadership preparation program for individuals interested in and committed to improving the educational experiences of Hispanic youth.

Duncan E. Waite is Professor and Director of the Educational Leadership Program at Appalachian State University. He has examined supervision and, especially, supervisory conferences from anthropological-linguistic and sociological points of view. His research focuses on face-to-face interactions between supervisors and teachers. His book, *Rethinking Instructional Supervision: Notes on Its Language and Culture* (1995), extended this work from an empirical base into the theoretical realm. Dr. Waite has also published in the *Journal of Curriculum and Supervision, American Educational Research Journal, Teaching & Teacher Education, Urban Education, Urban Review,* and *Theory into Practice.* He received his doctorate from the University of Oregon, where he studied qualitative research and conversation analysis.

Gene L. Wilkinson is Associate Professor of Instructional Technology at the University of Georgia. He was a faculty member at Indiana University and taught history and government in the public schools. A past president of the Georgia Association for Instructional Technology and past director of the Southeastern Regional Media Association, he is active in a number of professional organizations. He is a recognized authority on the economics, productivity, and cost-effectiveness of technology and media programs. His current research interests focus on school media services, effectiveness of media delivery systems, media selection, and cost-effectiveness analysis. His teaching areas include design and production of instructional materials, media utilization, and management of media service programs. He received his Ed.D. in Instructional Technology from Indiana University.

Carolyn J. Wood is Professor of Educational Administration at the University of New Mexico. Her research and publication interests have been focused primarily on teacher evaluation, instructional supervision, learned and taught helplessness, and participatory decision making. She has authored several multimedia presentations on topics such as learned helplessness, taught helplessness, and the ways in which instructional supervisors can teach helplessness and/or resourcefulness. She received a Ph.D. in Educational Policy and Administration from Washington University.

Karen Callison Woodward is Superintendent for Anderson School District Five in Anderson, South Carolina. As superintendent in two districts over the past 12 years, she has been recognized as the Superintendent of the Year by the South Carolina Association of School Administrators (SCASA) and the South Carolina School Boards Association (SCSBA), and was one of four finalists for National Superintendent of the Year by the American Association of School Administrators (AASA). She has served as president of SCASA and is currently President-Elect of the South Carolina Association of School Superintendents (SCASS). Active in the community, Dr. Woodward was selected the Businesswoman of the Year by the South Carolina Businesswomen's Association in 1994. During the past nine years, Dr. Woodward has led Anderson School District Five through major restructuring in organization and instruction. She received her Ed.D. degree in Curriculum and Instruction from the University of Georgia.

REVIEWERS

Robert J. Alfonso
East Tennessee State University

Robert H. Anderson
University of South Florida

Alfred A. Arth
University of Nebraska at Lincoln

Stanley B. Baker
North Carolina State University

Thomas E. Barone
Arizona State University

Roland S. Barth
Harvard University

Leslee J. Bishop
University of Georgia

Donald S. Blumenfeld-Jones
Arizona State University

Ira Bogotch
University of New Orleans

Bettye M. Bobroff
New Mexico ASCD

Ray E. Bruce
University of Georgia

Donald Bubenzer
Kent State University

Wesley E. Budke
Ohio State University

Dennis C. Buss
Rider University

Joseph J. Caruso
Framingham State College

David W. Champagne
University of Pittsburgh

George Churukian
Illinois Wesleyan University

James Cooper
University of Virginia

Arthur L. Costa
California State University at Sacramento

Arthur L. Crawley
Louisiana State University

Lori B. Crutchfield
Columbus College

John P. Dayton
University of Georgia

James G. Deegan
University of Georgia

Franny Dever
Albuquerque Public Schools

Francis M. Duffy
Gallaudet University

Donald P. Ely
Syracuse University

Ralph Fessler
Johns Hopkins University

William A. Firestone
Center for Educational Policy Analysis

Gerald R. Firth
University of Georgia

David J. Flinders
Indiana University

Lois Folsom
Mathematical Association of America

Vito A. Forlenza
Northeastern Educational Intermediate Unit

Calvin M. Frazier
Education Commission of the States

Jerome Frieberg
University of Houston

Gordon G. Fulcher
Chichester College, England

Allan A. Glatthorn
East Carolina University

Donna S. Goble
Vencor Hospital System

Donna Gollnick
National Council for Accreditation of Teacher Education

Merrie Hahn
National Association of Elementary School Principals

Ben M. Harris
University of Texas at Austin

Kenneth T. Henson
Eastern Kentucky University

Robert D. Heslep
University of Georgia

Corinne E. Hill
Governor's Office
Salt Lake City, Utah

Shirley M. Hord
Southwest Educational Development Laboratory

Karen Huffman
Braxton County School District
Sutton, West Virginia

Ronald T. Hyman
Rutgers University

Jacqueline Jordan Irvine
Emory University

William K. Jackson
University of Georgia

Joyce E. Killian
Southern Illinois University at Carbondale

Robert D. Krey
Wisconsin State University at River Falls

Linda Lambert
California State University at Hayward

John H. Lounsbury
Georgia College

John T. Macrostie
Consultant, Tasmania, Australia

John McDonald
Council of Chief State School Officers

Thomas L. McGreal
University of Illinois at Urbana-Champaign

Joseph R. McKinney
Ball State University

George E. Melton
National Association of Secondary School Principals

Edward C. Merrill, Jr.
Gallaudet University

Mary Guy Miller
Interactive Design and Development, Inc.

Petra Monro
Louisiana State University

Michael M. Morris
University of New Mexico

Richard F. Neville
University of Maryland-Baltimore County

Robert F. Nicely, Jr.
Pennsylvania State University

Susan Nicklas
Association for Supervision and Curriculum Development

James F. Nolan, Jr.
Pennsylvania State University

Sandra J. Odell
Western Michigan University

Peter F. Oliva
Georgia Southern University

Donald C. Orlich
Washington State University

Pamela O. Paisley
University of Georgia

Edward F. Pajak
University of Georgia

Jerry L. Patterson
University of Alabama at Birmingham

Charles A. Reavis
Texas Tech University

Thomas C. Reeves
University of Georgia

Judy Reinhartz
University of Texas at Arlington

Jerrold Ross
St. John's University

Kate Rousmaniere
Miami University of Ohio

Frances O. Rust
New York University

Cayce Scarborough
Auburn University

Thomas Schram
University of New Hampshire

Frances Schroonmaker
Teachers College
Columbia University

C. Paul Scott
Altamaha Technical Institute

Barbara P. Sirvis
SUNY College at Brockport

Andrew F. Smith
American Forum for Global Education

Jon Snyder
California State University at Santa Barbara

Robert J. Starratt
Boston College

Marilyn Tallerico
Syracuse University

Laurel N. Tanner
University of Houston

Stephen J. Thornton
Teachers College
Columbia University

Paul W. Thurston
University of Illinois at Urbana-Champaign

Murray H. Tillman
University of Georgia

Saundra J. Tracy
Butler University

Bruce Uhrmacher
University of Denver

Elizabeth Vallance
St. Louis Art Museum

Leonard A. Valverde
Arizona State University

Duncan E. Waite
Appalachian State University

J. Foster Watkins
Gainesville College

Karen E. Watkins
University of Georgia

Brevard S. Williams
Apple Computer, Inc.

Robert K. Wimpelberg
University of New Orleans

L. Craig Wilson
University of Delaware

Fred H. Wood
University of Oklahoma

James R. Yates
University of Texas at Austin

Joost Yff
American Association of Colleges for Teacher Education

◆ 1 ◆

PARADIGMS AND PARAMETERS
OF SUPERVISION IN EDUCATION

Ben M. Harris
UNIVERSITY OF TEXAS AT AUSTIN

INTRODUCTION

Supervision as a Field of Practice

Despite a long history of widely recognized responsibilities, an extensive literature in published sources, and legal provisions in many countries and states in the United States, the "Field" remains one that is full of controversy and uncertainty. In U.S. public schools, supervisory practice was differentiated from classroom teaching by the mid-nineteenth century as both rural county and urban city school systems emerged. Without highly centralized structures at either national or state levels, quite predictable diversity of practices, positions, and traditions emerged (Pajak, 1989b: 1–18; Krey and Burke, 1989).

As the oldest of the nonteaching positions in school operations, early supervision of schools was further differentiated from governance, finance, and general administrative practice by emphasis on inspection of student progress and enforcement of curricular prescriptions (Barr et al, 1938: 719). The advent of "free textbooks" added further emphasis to the standardization and controlling character of supervision (Westbury, 1990: 5–7). The emphasis on the individual teacher as the object of supervision as distinguished from emphasis on the student was an early reform that has only recently been challenged.

Roles, Relationships, and Functions Controversy regarding positions, roles, relationships, and functions of supervisory personnel and their practices emerged in "reform" efforts during World War I and has continued to the present time (Sergiovanni and Starratt, 1994). Controversy was fueled by the progressive education movement built on the philosophy of John Dewey (Broudy, 1981: 19) and the societal upheavals

associated with the Great Depression (Zilversmit, 1993). The expansive writings of Barr, Burton, Bruekner (1938) and Fred Ayer (1954) were among those that mapped the terrain of supervision in fine detail as instructional improvement, functional not positional, general and curricular, as well as specialized, and undergirded by the principles of democratic and humane practice. Wiles (1967) followed in this tradition with emphasis on human relationships, as did Franseth (1961), who emphasized both "leadership for improving teaching and learning" and the many positions sharing responsibility as "supervisors" (p. v). The field has witnessed almost constant changes, challenges, controversies, and fads since then (Cuban, 1990b). A major departure from the broadly defined perspectives of supervision was initiated with the dual works of Robert Goldhammer (1969) and Morris Cogen (1973) and their emphasis on clinical supervision. Despite their emphasis on clinical supervision as "special methods" (Goldhammer, 1992: 48) the "clinical approach" gradually became almost synonymous with "supervision" in its entirety.

Definitions of Supervision Much of the controversy over supervisory practice is reflected in diverse definitions. Some definitions are highly reflective of the old inspectorial emphasis on control, management, and evaluation of teaching. Other, equally narrow definitions, reflect the movement toward nearly complete autonomy for teachers and emphasize essentially service-oriented definitions of supervision (Glatthorn, 1990: 200–221). Still other definitions emphasize democratic practices (Harrison, 1968: 5–7) or systems development as central to supervisory practice (Feyereisen et al, 1970: 90–95). Bolin's (1987) historical review of definitional trends and issues focuses on "scientific," "developmental," and "Democratic," and concludes that a clear definition is "still difficult" and perplexing (pp. 370–380). Wiles and Bondi (1991: 68), stressing supervision "at the district level," identify assisting, linking, and

1

developing as the major task categories with emphasis on district, school, and classroom activities.

Even though current thought does not represent full consensus, it does have many consistencies. Some of these are contained in definitions of supervision focused on:

- Teaching and learning
- Responding to changing external realities
- Providing support, assistance, and feedback to teachers
- Recognizing teaching as the primary vehicle for facilitating school learning
- Promoting new, improved innovative practices

Defining supervision in such terms provides some sense of the scope and limits of the field of practice and generates little controversy; however, questions of roles, relationships, positions, and even skills, tasks, and functions remain without full consensus. The most conflict-prone areas of such controversy may well be those that relate to positions and relationships as well as role and function vis-à-vis evaluation of teaching (Anderson, 1989). The current trends toward increasing reliance on principals of schools and/or on teaching peers for supervisory services, however defined, raises serious questions about effectiveness, as well as about conflicting roles and functions.

Supervision as Function

Too much emphasis on diversity of practices and controversy in the field of supervision may mask the evolving character of supervision as a major function of school operations. Long-term trends in both theory and practice of supervision reflect greater emphasis on change and improvement than they do in early stages of development of the field. Other trends within this major one indicate an evolving, still emerging, and very complex picture of supervision as the improvement of instruction function in schools (Joyce, 1986). Trends that are in evidence, but which are not yet clearly integrated in either theory or practice, include emphasis on learning outcomes, teaching practices, professional development, supporting services, innovations, and restructuring, including integration of electronic technology (Kerr, 1990: 211). While much of the literature on supervisory functions stresses change and improvement in teaching and learning, it tends to do so within the context of traditional structures for curriculum, teaching, and school organization. Fullan (1993) suggests "a quantum leap" (p. vii) in which a major function of supervision could become one of management of change.

Supervisory Inquiry

Despite perennial pronouncements that supervision of instruction is passé—a thing of the past, no longer needed—or only a specific aspect of school administration, an extensive literature continues to be published. Texts in the field are numerous; new titles by major publishers are issued annually; and both general and special focus texts are fairly numerous. The periodical literature is less clearly identifiable as supervisory, but it, too, is extensive when supervision skills, tasks, and roles are cross-referenced. Research reports, like journal articles, are not easily identified by title as supervisory unless one focuses on the more specific topics related to supervisory practice (Anderson, 1989: 291).

More recently published general supervision texts reflect a fairly stable pattern of writing and publishing by both scholars and practitioners. In 1993, 40 books, mostly texts, titled specifically under "supervision" or supervisors" were listed as "in print" (Books in Print, 1993 to 1994, vol. 4). Many other texts focusing on the principalship, school administration, leadership or change process, personnel development, and curriculum planning relate to supervisory practices to some extent and greatly extend the coverage of the field.

Periodical literature focusing explicitly on supervisory practice by name is not extensive, by some standards. There are few periodicals that make supervisory research, theory, or practice the primary focus of editorial policy. On the other hand, virtually all professional journals that deal with instruction, teaching, staff development, policy, administration, or curriculum include articles directly related to supervision in schools.

Research reports relating to supervision are numerous when viewed broadly as discussed earlier with reference to journal articles. In a more narrowly defined perspective, masters theses and dissertations seem to dominate much of the research that focused specifically on supervisors, roles, functions, and relationships. Within this narrowly defined set of research reports, increasing emphasis has been directed toward the principal as "supervisor" or "instructional leader." The U.S. Office of Education (1974) enumerated theses and doctoral dissertations in supervision from 1926 to 1927, when none were listed, until 1929–1930, showing dramatic increases in such studies. The number of such studies then doubled from 1930–1931 to 1932–1933. More recent analyses of dissertations listed in the Comprehensive Dissertation Index suggest that supervision is still a topical arena for inquiry [See Exhibit 1.1]; however, staff development and other "keyword" descriptors are more commonly utilized.

Funded studies of supervision appear limited unless one examines the vast array of studies related to teaching, learning, staff development, program innovation, change process, curriculum development, and leadership. This vast body of scholarly study has been funded by foundations, state agencies, federal programs, and private business interests, as well as by universities and school districts. Much of this funding, beginning with the National Defense Education Act in the 1950s and continuing to the present, provides a substantial base of inquiry for use in guiding school supervision practice, as well as for theory-building and further research in this field.

Evaluation research, which is commonly undertaken in association with action projects and school improvement programs, provides still another knowledge base on supervision. Such inquiries rarely deal with supervisory theory or practice in specific terms even though clearly relevant. Hence, a massive, if rather chaotic, effort to improve teaching and learning has been in progress for at least 40 years. This could suggest a major challenge of this entire book—to synthesize the outcomes (and failures) of this long era of supervisory inquiry. A perplexing problem associated with stimulating, synthesiz-

EXHIBIT 1–1. Enumeration of Supervision Dissertations

		Number listed
1862–1972 [*]		
Supervision, Total		963
· Supervising	111	
· Supervision	338	
· Supervisors	281	
· Supervisory	233	
Staff Development, Total		2,200
· Training	1,800	
· Staff Development	None	
· In-service	400	
All Categories Combined		3,163

Recent Years [**]	1973–1982		1986, 1990, 1991	
	Number	Average	Number	Average
Supervision	345	34	71	24
Staff Development	1,875	187	397	132
All Categories	2,220	220	468	156

[*] Source: *Comprehensive Dissertation Index 1862–1972*, Vol. 22 and 24. Education (1973). Ann Arbor, MI: Xerox University Microfilms.

[**] Source: *Comprehensive Dissertation Index—Supplements for 1986, 1990, and 1991*, Vol. 3, Part 1: Social Science and Humanities. Ann Arbor, MI: University Microfilms.

ing, and making effective use of supervisory inquiry goes beyond the fragmentation problems suggested here. In addition, supervision as a field of inquiry suffers from the addressing of its grand complexity with simplistic paradigms, from the lack of recognition of the field as one that has architectural and engineering characteristics, and from both funding and publishing entities preoccupied with fads and quick-fixes rather than with synthesis and professional development of the field.

Paradigm Shifts and New Parameters

If we think of parameters as either constants or variables that help to determine the specific forms of a field of practice (Flexner, 1987: 1408), then new supervisory parameters of many kinds surely have emerged over the years and may well be doing so at an accelerating rate. Parameters as constants or at least not readily changing realities, however, are surely important as guides to more or less enduring features of supervisory practice. The term paradigm shifts has been widely used to emphasize changes in ways of thinking and behaving with reference to new models, patterns, ideals, or standards (McKenzie, 1975: 1298; Kipfer, 1992: 606–607). Common usage seems to suggest that paradigm shifts and new parameters are closely related in the change process and emphasize (or at least should) both departures from the past and limits and constraints. Fullan (1993: vii) emphasizes the reality of ". . . learning how to contend with forces of change—turning positive forces to our advantage while blunting negative ones."

A few shifts in the specific forms of supervisory practice which deserve critical attention as they emerge are identified here and elaborated upon later in the context of much broader changes in thinking about the very nature of schooling.

- Supervision as a broadly characterized function emphasizes improvement of teaching and learning using diverse approaches. This view of practice as more strategic, more eclectic, and less stereotyped stands in sharp contrast to views of supervision as purely instructional, purely classroom focused, purely clinical, or essentially evaluative. While hardly a new way of viewing supervision (Barr et al, 1938; Ayer, 1954; Franseth, 1961; Harris, 1963) it has received renewed emphasis in the work of Glatthorn (1984 and 1990) on "differentiated" supervision, as well as Glickman's (1990) emphasis on "developmental supervision," and is especially well exemplified in the nearly encyclopedic work of Oliva (1989).

- Supervision as a collaborative function seems to be emerging more clearly as a persistent view guiding changes in practice. The renewed emphasis on shifting toward full collaboration with stakeholders in the supervisory process is reflected in both programs and literature on peer supervision (Glatthorn, 1990: 188–199; Harris & Ovando, 1992) and site-based decision-making involving teachers and parents (Candoli, 1991; Conley & Bacharach, 1990), building on the operational principles promoted by clinical supervision advocates (Goldhammer, 1969; Cogan 1973; etc.).

- Supervision as planning for systemic change is a relatively new paradigm shift that has a shallow base in the view of both scholars and practitioners (Rivlin, 1971; Anderson, 1993). Such planning is more common in its advocacy than it is in practice because it requires the interrelating of curricular, organizational, teaching, evaluation, personnel, and policy change. Wiles and Bondi (1991: 68–70) describe 28 tasks of instructional supervision that relate to this perspective. Such complex and high-risk practices understandably emerge slowly. Current efforts to promote restructuring of school programs (Boyer, 1983; Comer 1980; Cohen 1988; Glasser, 1990; Schlechty, 1990; Sizer, 1984) give voice and sometimes vision to supervision as planning for systemic change.

These paradigm or parameter shifts are not inevitable, nor are they necessarily desirable. There are certainly others that may be equally important in considering supervision as a field of inquiry. Practices born of past changes that might also deserve thoughtful, critical scrutiny include the dramatic shift in the post–World War II era from relying on tradition-oriented instructional practices to embracing a multitude of fads with new technologies constantly in vogue (Cuban, 1985 and 1990b).

SUPERVISORY PRACTICE IN DIVERSE FORMS

Given any of the broader definitions of supervision as instructional leadership for change in schools directed toward improving teaching and learning, a variety of diverse practices is observable throughout public and private schools in both the United States and many other countries. With ample diversity, these practices are appropriately viewed from equally diverse perspectives and analytical frames of reference. Some distinctive models are utilized with sufficient fidelity that they are clearly recognizable. Still another framework for viewing and analyzing practices focuses on people, roles, and relationships involved. The organizations and structures employed to deliver supervisory services have long been a dominant frame of reference for analyzing practice. Supervisory skills and competencies are somewhat different, perhaps a most personal framework for analyzing practice.

Distinctive Models of Supervisory Practice

To be distinctive a model should have a clearly defined set of practices employed with a rationale and purposes that are supervisory in nature. Furthermore, since models often share some common practices, only those that are somewhat distinctive when compared with others are identified here. There obviously may well be others that deserve attention, and, of course, models are human inventions that one hopes will be emerging, changing, and improving over time (Tracy & McNaughton, 1993: 8–18).

Clinical Models Clinical supervision and closely related personalized models (Berman & Usery, 1966) have been among the most widely used, reported, and studied; especially since the seminal works of Goldhammer (1969) and Cogan (1973). This model receives ample attention in other chapters of this book. Nearly all variations on the clinical supervision model involve a dyadic relationship, preconferencing, focused classroom observation, and analysis, followed by postconference feedback and planning for improving teaching practice (Snyder, 1988: 262–263). Variations on this standard model have been introduced involving such practices as "establishing a base-rate of behaviors" (Boyan and Copeland, 1978), videotaping and self-analysis in lieu of an observer (Bailey, 1979; Far West Lab, 1978; Kaplan, 1980), and use of peers (Ellis et al, 1979) in a reciprocal, coaching relationship (Showers, 1985). These and other variations may have effects on the quality, effectiveness, or utility of the model, but the distinctive pattern of practices is fairly uniform (Tracy & McNaughton, 1993), even when their psychotherapeutic origins or demanding professional competencies are ignored (Seager, 1992: 2). The latest of these clinical models, "cognitive coaching" (Costa & Garmston, 1993), draws heavily on the work of prior decades, adding considerable rigor in detailing the face-to-face interactive process with emphasis on cognitive development of the teacher.

Diagnostic Models Diagnostic approaches to supervision are related to clinical models in that they are personalized and share many practices, especially conferencing, data analysis, feedback, and improvement planning. Diagnostic models are sometimes prescriptive (Glatthorn, 1984), but they have been used in nonprescriptive forms (Harris & Hill, 1982; Melnik & Sheehan, 1976; Stulac et al, 1982). Ayer discussed "diagnostic supervision" as involving self-appraisal and observations as "a common starting basis for planning instructional improvement." (1954: 175).

Distinctive features of diagnostic models include the use of formal diagnostic procedures such as tests, self-reports, structured observations, student reports, and special analytical techniques (Harris, 1984). Flanders (1970) created an obser-

vation system that became the basis for one of the earliest diagnostic models. Verbal interaction categories were designated as the focus for viewing teaching, a system of focused observing and recording was developed, and a special matrix analysis system was used as the basis for providing personalized feedback. These unique features made Flanders' Interaction Analysis one of the most widely used and studied supervisory models prior to the emergence of less-structured clinical models (Simon & Boyer, eds, 1970).

Developmental Evaluation Systems The work of Harris and Hill (1982) in designing and testing the DeTEK system (Harris, 1986) illustrates still another diagnostic model with less prescription and more collaborative involvement of the teacher. This system utilizes pretraining, teacher self-assessment, and a three-phase data-gathering, analysis, and improvement process. A survey phase involves both self-assessment and a classroom observation with analysis of data in a follow-up conference. The second, diagnostic phase uses a teacher-selected focus with self-assessment, a second observation, and student-reported data, followed by a collaborative analysis and interpretation conference. A third phase involves systematic planning, again on a collaborative basis, of a growth and improvement process. A unique diagnostic procedure called was developed for this model, simplifying data processing (Harris, 1989).

The DeKalb diagnostic supportive supervision model (1975) was designed to assist new teachers in their early years on the job. It was a rather elaborate system that involved various performance measures, teams of supervisory personnel, and external evaluation. A unique diagnostic profiling instrument was developed to guide the supervisory effort. It was also based on the assumption that teaching proficiencies must be developed in the context of real and extended field experiences rather than on college campuses. This model also represents one of the few efforts to utilize supervisory teams with individual teachers. It did not appear to "work," and therein lies another challenge to scholars and practitioners alike. Fessler and Burke (1987) describe still another diagnostic model that utilizes both assessment and self-perception data.

Training Models Staff development as training models has been widely reported by Lawrence et al (1974), Yarger et al (1980), and Grant (1981), as well as many others during the period of considerable interest in and scrutiny of such programs. Howey and Vaughan (1982) were among many observers reporting strong criticism of current practice of the time, even while new models and evaluation research were beginning to provide some clues to more effective practices. Joyce and Showers (1983) gained wide recognition for their so-called coaching model, which was, in fact, a much more sophisticated strategy for the implementation of instructional innovations. Harris, Bessent, and McIntryre (1969) had developed the "laboratory approach" early on as still another distinctive model that utilized formal training practices with high levels of involvement, insight, and motivation. Gall and Renchler (1985), Hagen (1981), Hall and Loucks (1978), and Glickman (1990) were only a few of the scholars proposing staff development models and strategies based on research and evaluation in field contexts.

Training programs and practices are too numerous and varied to be described here in any detail. They can be characterized to some degree as different from clinical and diagnostic models. Training programs tend to involve groups rather than focusing on individuals. Some utilize a workshop format addressing fairly limited outcomes, but others are more strategic in form—study groups, courses, professional development center projects (Hagen, 1981)—and lend themselves to more ambitious goals. A brief analysis of a variety of training strategies, activities, and models (Harris, 1989: 37–43) suggests an even more diverse array of known training practices, including group therapy, simulations, gaming, sensitivity training (Golembiewski & Blumberg, 1977), cooperative learning (Slavin, 1990) "synergogy" (Mouton & Blake, 1984), and computer-based programs (Wedman, 1988). The diversity of practices which is in common use with extremely different features raises many questions about process–outcome relationships, as well as cost–benefit relationships. Commonalities among many of these training practices are still evident, including a group context, a series of clearly designated "sessions" over time, one or more "trainers" or facilitators, designated anticipated learning outcomes, verbal interactions, and active involvement in job relevant activities. They also share a common feature in not being integrally a part of the actual work flow of participants, as are clinical supervision and action research. This much-neglected variable was addressed by Gant (1977) in a preliminary way as "temporary systems" and is worthy of further consideration and study.

Coaching and Mentoring Coaching and mentoring are emerging as closely related concepts. Coaching models for staff development appear to be somewhat unique in combining clinical practices and formal training, lectures, and skill training preceding the more individualized coaching activity (Joyce & Showers, 1983). This may, in part, account for its popularity in the 1980s, even though its effectiveness has yet to be established. Emphasis on peer coaching as an economical technique for providing observational feedback continues to be widely advocated and reported in use for a variety of purposes (Chrisco, 1989; Neubert & Bratton, 1987). A variation on the concept of coaching by Costa and Garmston (1993) emphasizes cognitive thought processes, but it is nonetheless essentially a clinical model using a four-phase sequence (pp. 18–22). Mentoring is often lacking in clarity as a model, yet it seems to be gaining support and taking shape, especially in work with new teachers (ASCD, 1994a).

Curriculum Development Models Curriculum development is one of the oldest of supervisory approaches to improve teaching and learning (Barr et al, 1947; Spears, 1957; Taba, 1962; Gordon, 1968). The focus of this approach is on involving teachers and supervisors in individual or group efforts to redesign and develop curricula for classroom use. The distinctive character of curriculum development models of supervisory practice is the emphasis on plans for teaching rather than on learning to apply new teaching skills, as is emphasized in most training and clinical models. Practices distinguishing such models, therefore, involve curricular goal setting and clarification via group interaction, creating lesson or unit plans, and devel-

oping instructional and assessment materials. The use of "curriculum councils" to give systematic structure and to ensure full involvement of various groups, including teachers and supervisors, is elaborately detailed by Feyereisen et al (1970: 289–299). More recently, there appears to be a renewed interest in Spears' (1957) concept of relating curriculum development and implementation to staff development (Romberg & Price, 1983; Glickman, 1990) as a response to the growing concern for systemic change in schooling that involves both curricular and organizational change (Eisner, 1990; McNeil, 1990; Tye, 1991) as well as improved teaching practice.

Organizational and Planning Models Other models of supervisory practice that have some distinction include organization development—as promoted by Schmuck and Schmuck (1990)—and action research as promoted by Stephen Corey and developed as a systematic approach in its early stages (Taba & Noel, 1957). Research in action-oriented forms appears to be gaining new momentum, as reported by Tikunoff and Mergendoller (1983), Hopkins (1993), and others using the term *teacher researcher*. This new emphasis on action research seems to be evolving from a confluence of ideas relating to Schon's (1983) "reflective practitioner," criticisms of traditional forms of formal research (Eisner, 1984), pressure for change in classroom practices, and site-based decision-making.

Strategic and systematic planning for change (Fullan & Stiegelbauer, 1991; Cunningham, 1982; Rogers, 1983; Bennis et al, 1985) are still other distinctive forms of supervisory practice that involve people working together toward improved teaching and learning (Mitchell & Cunningham, 1990). New emphasis on planning and decision-making at the local school and classroom levels (Rallis, 1990) when it focuses on instructional change becomes essentially supervisory in nature. Such planning focuses on creating both understandings and commitments to actions of a wider variety of kinds than most supervisory efforts. The participants may not be primarily teachers since parents, students, and other stakeholders may be essential to the process. In a wide-ranging review, however, Inbar (1980: 388) stresses the importance of planning that is ". . . a reflection of educational activity and the unique characteristics of educational behavior. . . ." A further distinctive feature of such planning efforts is the need to attend to changes in a wide ranging variety of system variables—rules, structures, personnel, and resources (Anderson, 1993; Cohen & Spillane, 1992; Harris, 1989: 192–194).

Teacher Evaluation Models Formal monitoring and evaluation of classroom teaching practices are among the most controversial, yet most widely utilized supervisory practices (Medley et al, 1984; Stipnieks, 1981). Whether formative or summative in nature, whether mandated or locally initiated, or whether structured or informal, "teacher evaluation" or "assessment" practices are in general use and constitute a substantial portion of what is perceived as supervision of instruction (Darling Hammond, 1992). Supervision in this mode is commonly characterized by a set of prescribed performance criteria, a formal observation, the recording of ratings, the making of judgments by the observer, and feedback in some form. These monitoring, assessing, evaluating practices are distinct from clinical and diagnostic models in that they are often more formal, lack collaboration, and are based on authoritative assumptions about relationships and misconceptions about effective teaching. These practices are also distinctively different from the clinical and diagnostic when applied uniformly, because they tend to be for all or many teachers; hence, they lack flexibility and collaborative involvement. Even when such practices are intended for purposes of improving teaching and learning, they tend to rely on coercion and rewards rather than on intrinsic motivations. Many of these practices have been formalized as systems under mandates of law or policy (Berry & Ginsberg, 1990: 156); and have been severely criticized (Harris & Monk, 1992: 169–170; Medley et al, 1984; McNeil, 1988). Crooks (1988) concludes on the basis of a review of studies that, for better or worse, ". . . classroom evaluation has powerful direct and indirect impacts."(p. 438).

People, Roles, and Relationships

Roles and role relationships have dominated ways of thinking and analyzing supervisory practices for many years. In contrast, emphasis has also been given from early periods of development of the field to the people involved broadening the focus to address people, positions, roles, relationships, and responsibilities. These are clearly not mutually exclusive ways of analyzing practices, but they are very different and influence both research and practice.

People in Positions Emphasis on people and their positions gives rise to inquiry and controversy alike. The nature of the job of the curriculum specialist has been the focus of much attention. The nature of the responsibilities of "the supervisor" as a person in a position outside the individual school organization has similarly been explored and debated over many decades (Franseth, 1961: v). Special subject supervision versus general supervision (Tracy & Haughton, 1993: 269–272) has a long history of inquiry, as has principal versus supervisor as instructional leader. Peer supervisor versus supervisor in a superordinate position and in-school supervisor versus external supervisor are a couple of the many issue-oriented ways of focusing on supervisory positions (Smyth, 1991). The supervisory character of support service personnel is undergoing increasing review (Cervera, 1990).

One serious obstacle to inquiry into supervisory practice as it relates to positions as variables is the failure of the U. S. Department of Education even to recognize supervisory personnel in their staffing reports (National Center for Educational Statistics, 1993). In the past, nonprincipal personnel were simply aggregated as "administrators" or support staff. This ignoring of complexity of staffing practices in local schools and districts unfortunately makes inquiry regarding roles and relationships more difficult. Simple survey data are currently needed regarding numbers of supervisory personnel in various positions.

Position Titles As mentioned earlier, serious barriers to understanding and focusing on more complex questions related to supervisory practices are the lack of national and state

survey data on supervisory personnel and their organizational affiliations. Position titles available in various directories are also nearly meaningless in inferring supervisory functions or roles or responsibilities beyond those of "superintendent," "administrator," and "principal" (Gorton et al, 1988: 264).

The title *principal* generally designates the person who is administrator in charge of a specific school operation. This title does not permit inferences regarding supervisory roles, of course. However, assistant principal as a title means only that some function, roles, or responsibilities are assumed at the building level; they may be mostly teaching, counseling, or custodial. The titles of director, supervisor, coordinator, consultant, head teacher, team leader, and facilitator are among hundreds of variations on supervisory titles; unfortunately, they have no clear meaning and may not be supervisory in any instructional leadership sense of the term. Many such titles are reportedly designated for purposes of salary determination, fund reimbursement, or ego satisfaction without clear functional meaning.

"What's in a name . . . a rose by any other name . . ." (Shakespeare) is undoubtedly good literature, but it is poor professional advice. Questions about terminology in supervision have often been directed at the word supervision itself for the implication of authoritativeness. The extensive use of hundreds of titles with little clear meaning, continuity, consistency, or rationale may be more critical to the problems of improving supervisory practice. Communications among practitioners and meaningful inquiry into supervisory practice is apparently hampered by this state of affairs. A worthy contribution to the field would be taxonomic studies combined with efforts at least to define, if not to standardize, titles of supervisory personnel.

Supervisory Roles Further complexity is found in dealing with people, positions, and titles related to supervision as the staffing patterns of school systems become more varied. Social workers (Cervera, 1990), librarians, school psychologists, and media specialists are only a few of the special titles or positions being utilized in supervisory roles. Their numbers are increasing, yet models of practice in supervision do not often account for or even acknowledge their work.

Roles as constructs guiding inquiry and practice are also numerous and very complex. The roles of supervisors as expert, subject specialist, curriculum developers, coach, helper, change agent, counselor, facilitator, materials provider, group process coordinator, trainer, monitor, evaluator, planner, and organizer are among those reflected in various studies and in the professional literature and dialogue of practitioners (Pajak, 1989a). These many roles, which all presumably have some relevance for supervisory practice, have rarely been studied in relationship to larger frameworks of theory, organization, or job description. Any role might be appropriately or inappropriately related to any person in any position, but it seems unlikely that all roles are appropriately embraced in practice by all supervisors.

Dimensions of Supervision in Practice Pajak's (1989a) study identifying 12 "dimensions of supervisory practice" has implications for roles as well as skills and competencies of supervisors. High levels of agreement among practitioners and scholars alike were reported for most of the 12 dimensions, even though each is a rather broadly defined area of supervisory activity, (see Exhibit 1.2 for detail). The dimensions not clearly and strongly accepted by practitioners (i.e., community relations and research and evaluation), suggest needs for further research. It is curious that scholars, too, reported lower agreement levels on the importance of these two dimensions as well as on a third. "Curriculum" as a dimension of supervisory practice of high importance appears to be somewhat at issue. Dissertation studies at the University of Georgia from 1990 to 1991 produced more detailed evidence supporting Pajak's finding in both literature reviews and practitioner surveys.

Supervisory Skills and Competencies

The functions, roles, and purposes toward which supervisory practices are directed call for technical skills and competencies as well as leadership (Leithwood & Steinbach, 1993). Whether generic leadership skills can be presumed to be adequate for high quality, professionally responsible supervision is an open issue. For instance, graduate preparation programs for supervisors are sometimes undifferentiated from those of administrators; however, the preparation of such personnel is highly differentiated in other institutions. Roles of supervisors clearly assume pre-requisite skills in many cases, but are not so clear for others. As early as 1964 Goldhammer (1992) argued for rigorous systematic classroom observation procedures as essential for effectiveness in serving teachers (p. 4); Kelley was detailing "workshop procedures" (1951); Cantor (1951) was describing discussion leading techniques; and Harris, Bessent, and McIntyre (1969) were demonstrating the "laboratory training" exercise approach.

Pajak's (1989c) study of supervisory practices focused primarily on identifying and prioritizing "dimensions" of super

EXHIBIT 1–2. Dimensions of Supervisory Practice Supported by Pajak's Study, 1989

Dimension of Practice	Percentage of Agreement on Importance	
	Practitioners (n=1,075)	Scholars (n=131)
Communications	89	83
Staff development	88	94
Instructional program	86	83
Planning and change	83	88
Motivating and organizing	80	80
Observation and conferencing	77	87
Curriculum	73	64
Problem solving and decision-making	73	80
Service to teachers	73	80
Personal development	71	83
Community relations	64	45
Research and program evaluation	57	63

Source: Pajak, E. (1989). "A Report on the Nationwide Survey of Outstanding Supervisors and University Professors." Presented at the annual meeting of the Council of Professors of Instructional Supervision, The Pennsylvania State University, November 10–12.

visory practice in central office staff positions. The highly recognized dimensions, some 12 in number, were more clearly defined in this study as clusters of skills, competencies, or behaviors.

A functional or task approach has been utilized that closely paralleled Pajak's dimensions (Harris, 1985). A rational deductive approach identified competencies and behaviors within functionally defined tasks of instructional leadership and improvement of instruction. Studies of practitioner opinions as well as scholarly studies seemed to offer support for the importance of a variety of skills or competencies such as discussion-leading (Cantor, 1951), brainstorming, role playing, and demonstrations (Neuman, 1961), as well as systematic observing. Harris (1974) identified over 200 such skills.

Supervisors' Competency Estimates In one effort to validate supervisory skills and competencies clearly within a broad spectrum of roles and responsibilities, Bailey (1985) surveyed a variety of central office supervisors in the urban Houston (Texas) area, as well as in surrounding suburban and rural school districts. Thirty-two school districts and 154 supervisors with various titles were included in this study. An inventory focusing on five of Harris' (1985: 10–12) nine task areas of supervisory practice secured self-estimates of competence on 150 statements of behavior. Forced-choice instrumentation was utilized to derive competency estimates for each of 22 tasks within the five areas of supervisory practice. Importance scores were also computed using rating of importance of the competencies for job success.

Exhibit 1.3 reports a summary of the findings from this study for all types of supervisory positions combined. The few competencies with the highest percentage of choices representing those that "best describe" supervisors' capabilities are found in the curriculum development and in-service education areas. These two areas also have some of the highest mean importance ratings. A few specific competencies were chosen with low frequencies and midrange importance ratings, especially in the areas of staffing for instruction and evaluation; however, not one of the 24 competencies had a low mean importance score, and only four of them were infrequently chosen as describing supervisors' capabilities.

This study may or may not reflect nation-wide practice with any accuracy. The variety of types of positions and kinds of school settings, however included, suggests that fairly broad-gauge roles are widely held by central office supervisors. These findings are clearly reflected in the more general findings of the Pajak study some years later.

Skills from Related Fields The scholarly literature from several fields contributed to the development and testing of skills related to supervisory practices. Group process analysis, face-to-face interaction psychiatry, training and adult learning, decision-making, planning, and problem solving are just a few fields of inquiry where scholarly thought, research, and theory building have made substantial contributions to defining and validating leadership skills directly applicable to instructional supervision.

EXHIBIT 1–3. Major Competency Scores
for Supervisory Respondents*

Competencies	Mean Choice Scores (%)	Mean Importance Ratings (0–9)
Curriculum development		
Setting goals	51.2	7.31
Designing instructional units	43.2	6.90
Developing and adapting curriculum	73.8	7.37
Materials development		
Evaluating and selecting learning materials	49.5	6.48
Producing learning materials	18.4	6.07
Evaluating use of learning resources	34.8	6.12
Staffing for instruction		
Developing a staffing plan	36.2	7.15
Recruiting and selecting personnel	12.3	6.29
Assigning personnel	28.8	6.85
Providing for In-Service Education		
Supervising in a clinical mode	48.5	6.92
Planning for individual growth	44.6	7.13
Designing training sessions	69.5	7.61
Conducting in-service	74.2	7.39
Training leadership	44.2	6.75
Assessing needs	66.0	7.31
Developing a master plan	65.6	7.18
Writing project proposal	58.4	7.26
Designing self-instructional module	14.3	5.33
Designing a training program	80.5	7.75
Evaluating Instruction		
Observing and analyzing teaching	32.0	6.87
Designing a questionnaire	15.8	5.92
Interviewing in depth	15.5	5.96
Analyzing and interpreting data	20.1	6.98

* Bailey (1985: 80 and 170–176)

Group process analysis theories and techniques were widely studied in the 1940s and 1950s. Bales' (1950) theory of group member interactions related to group effectiveness was one of the most sophisticated and useful in identifying specific skills. Flanders' (1970) focus on verbal interaction in classroom groups contributed to the refinement of observation skills and to analytical techniques. Taba (1962) devoted attention to "working with groups" (pp. 471–482) in addition to many studies that focused on observing and analyzing the culture of the classroom as supervisory efforts. Discussion leading technique as studied by Cantor (1951), Berkowitz and Bennis (1961), Maier and Hoffman (1965), and Blumberg (1968) was still another scholarly focus that identified skills and their applications to training activities in supervisory practice. More recent emphasis on group process skills has focused on leadership in groups and team building (Glickman, 1990: 111), as well as on collaborative relationships (Ovando & Harris, 1993; Smith, 1980).

Applications of concepts and techniques for working with groups of adults in more effective ways are being recognized as promising supervisory practice. Slavin (1990) and Johnson et al (1991) are notable for demonstrating the effectiveness of cooperative learning groups with children and youth. Mouton

and Blake (1984) have various models of group-centered learning with adults under the title of synergogy. The "Jigsaw Technique" for structuring group activity to optimize the use of expertise of group members has been detailed by Aronson (1978). As supervisory practice embraces teacher and parent participation in decision-making and planning for improving instruction, more concerns are raised about getting work accomplished (McGrath, 1984) and linking decision-making to the specific tasks required.

Face-to-face interaction skills and related emphasis on feedback in facilitating communications have been scholarly concerns in the fields of psychotherapy (Rogers, 1959) and communications (Feverberg, 1989), as well as in education. The use of interviewing or individual conferencing is widely reported in the literature of supervision in connection with formative evaluation (McGreal, 1982) clinical supervision (Boyan & Copeland, 1978), coaching (Costa & Gramston, 1994), and staff development (Harris, 1989: 124).

Supervisors as facilitators of both individual and group actions for improving instruction suggest still other skills often reflected in the literature. Consulting (Alpert, 1982; Gallesich, 1982; Champagne & Hogan, 1981) and coordinating are closely related areas of skill that are associated with supervisory practice as reflected in the literature, but more clearly in the titles often given supervisors, especially "consultant" and "coordinator." Supervisory skills, while not clearly defined by such titles, are inferred as being somewhat different from those of director, principal, or superintendent. The literature on educational consultation is substantial (Manolakes, 1975; Silverblank, 1979; Alpert, 1982) and consulting roles and skills are reflected therein. Coordination as a type of supervisory practice is not so clearly recognized in literature even though widely utilized as a title (Harris, 1989: 224; Washington State Department of Education, 1981; National Center for Educational Statistics, 1994).

Training skills and those related to adult learning have been the focus of scholarly concern for decades under the influence of Knowles (1984) and Mouton and Blake (1984) among others. Training skills and techniques derived from concepts of adult learning styles and preferences have influenced supervisory practices as they relate to in-service education and staff development. Presentational skills emphasizing visualization (Friant, 1983; Frielander, 1972; Lynch, 1979); use of role playing, simulations, and gaming (Sculli & Ng, 1985); more recently, the use of computers in training (Schroeder, 1983) has received substantial attention in both the scholarly and practitioner literature. Studies of the efficacy of various training techniques have been limited and skill identification is often vague. Early studies of visual media—films in particular—were numerous in the early days of "audiovisual education" but uncontrolled and highly variable utilizations of these media made conclusions about relative effectiveness difficult. More recently, studies of computer applications to training are becoming numerous but limitations of similar kinds are emerging with quality of software and rapid changes in hardware adding uncertainty to the complexity of training problems (Kerr, 1989).

Change process, visioning, and related areas of scholarly activity are full of implications for supervisory practice and inferred skill development. Everett Rogers' (1983) work in agriculture was an early effort to define the anatomy of change process, identify critical variables, and emphasize diffusion as a unique dimension, distinct from invention. Adaptation process related to implementation of innovations has also been studied by Rogers (1986), who added important insights for supervisory practice. Fullan (1982) has been instrumental in clarifying the factors associated with failures of many innovative implementation efforts in schools. Bennis et al (1985) have been synthesizers of scholarly endeavors, popularizing concepts such as change agent, risk taking, and so on. Visioning and creative thinking are still other aspects of leadership for change that have gained attention. For instance, Argyris (1982) has documented the importance of new modes of learning in directing plans for action to assure meaningful change in business and industry. His conclusions relating to promoting "double-loop" learning to avoid repeating old mistakes have implications for supervisory practice. Krug (1992) advocates five dimensions of leadership that imply diverse skills and competencies. Defining mission, managing curriculum and instruction, providing information that actively supports curriculum development, supervising teaching, monitoring student progress, and developing an instructional climate are dimensions detailed as a "constructivist perspective" (p. 433). These dimensions have much in common with those of Pajak and Harris, as well as with early pioneers in this field of school supervision.

Forms of Supervision Glatthorns's (1990) designation of "forms of supervision for teacher development" (pp. 155–199) implies differential use of supervisory practices in "clinical," "differentiated," "peer collaboration," and "self-development" forms even though it is not explicit in identifying roles and relationships. Many other reports from the field indicate roles and relationships in more fragmented ways. Van Tuider et al (1993) report on in-service education in innovative schools of the Netherlands as being "managed" by teachers with supervisors "steering" and coordinating events.

Rogers (1983), noting the extensive publishing on diffusion of innovations in the field of education, infers along with Fullan (1993) that change agent roles, which are of crucial importance in the improvement of instruction, need to be assumed by responsible personnel. Darling-Hammond (1992) is even more outspoken in asserting that ". . . we are at a point in our history where the reform movement is not going to fade away after a few years." (p. 13). She focuses on restructuring teacher education as the reform and infers formal and informal supervisory roles that apply.

Supervisory Positions

Identifying and enumerating people in supervisory positions is an important part of understanding roles, relationships, and practices, yet such identifying is not without difficulty. Studies and reports by the National Center for Educational Statistics have provided more detailed and useful data on staffing in public as well as nonpublic schools. The 1992 data provided by NCES (July 1994) is revealing of the very large enterprise that is instructional supervision in U.S. public elementary and secondary schools. The complexities of staffing practices in this field are also reflected to some extent in this same report (Exhibit 1.4).

As reported by states and "outlying areas," several categories of staff personnel include supervisors of instruction by most definitions. The largest single category is "school administrators" (approximately 122,000), followed by "school district officials and administrators" (approximately 44,000), with "instructional coordinators and supervisors" reported at approximately 30,000. Teachers, guidance counselors, librarians, and "other support staff," however, may well include supervisors in unknown numbers. The NCES report emphasizes that some "instructional coordinators are included in other staff counts and cannot be disaggregated." (1: 6–7).

Realistic estimates of instructional supervisors in public schools based on 1992 data are approximately 40,000, excluding school principals and undocumented supervisors in association with various private and public agencies that include university continuing education programs.

Based only on the estimated 40,000 instructional coordinators, supervisors, directors, and the like who are assigned to nonteaching, nonprincipal roles, there is approximately 1 supervisor for each 1,000 students, 1 for each 60 classroom teachers, or 1 per 80 instructional personnel. Variations among states, however, are substantial, as they are among districts. The 30,000 instructional coordinators and supervisors officially reported range from about 2% of the total staff in Hawaii and Puerto Rice to 0.1% in South Dakota. These officially reported supervisors typically represent 1% of the total staff.

The extensive literature focusing upon the school principal as a supervisor of instruction is a clear reflection of both the hierarchical and the numerical superiority of persons in these positions as compared with other supervisory positions. The paucity of comparable literature on approximately 40,000 other persons in supervisory positions, however, is more difficult to understand. The public expenditures for this cadre of professional instructional leadership personnel can be estimated at $200 million per year, nationwide.

EXHIBIT 1–4. Summary U.S. Public School Staff by Positions*

Pupil-Related Staff	1992–1993
Teachers	2,457,737
Instructor's Aides	427,220
Guidance Counselors	81,048
Librarians	50,136
Sub-Total Pupil Related	3,016,141
Nonpupil-Related Staff	
Instructor's Coordinators and Supervisors	30,499
School District Officials and Administrators	44,151
School Administrators	122,128
Other Support Staff (estimate only)	1,372,000
Sub Total Nonpupil Related	1,568,778
Total All Staff	4,584,919
Total Pupils	42,734,746

*Ratio of Students per Adult Staff; 9.36.
Source: National Center for Educational Statistics (1994). *Statistics in Brief: Public School Student, Staff, and Graduate Counts by State-School Year 1992–1993.* U.S. Department of Education; (July) NCES - 484.

As to numerical trends, prior estimates of local district supervisors exclusive of principals (Harris, 1985: 113) show increases from 14,000 (1960) to 27,000 (1970) and 40,000 (1992), for a total increase over those years of 286%. Teaching staffs increased approximately 200%. The massiveness of the staff resources actually or potentially contributing to improvement of the instructional programs of public school, however, is not clearly reflected in currently available data. Personnel categorized as coordinators or supervisors may be engaged in endeavors with little relationship to supervision as a function. Teachers may actually be highly involved in supervision in many instances. The school "official" and "administrator" categories inevitably include large numbers of nonsupervisory personnel, and principals may also fail to function as supervisors of instruction in many instances.

Some insights were provided by Blacklock's (1978) study of "professional staffing practices" in a single large state. The complexities reported at that time in both positions and functions of personnel are not likely to be less striking in the 1990s. In brief, Blacklock utilized a statewide professional personnel assignment data bank to analyze positions by type rather than merely by titles. Fifteen categories of personnel were identified rather than the two or three usually considered.

Exhibit 1.5 shows the names given to the professional position types and summarizes the functional scores assigned to each using Harris' two dimensions of school operations (1985: 4). An expert panel was utilized to derive estimates of pupil- and instruction-relatedness for each carefully defined position type. In this summary, the "supervisor" type is estimated to be highly instruction-related functionally (7.0 on a nine-point scale) and relatively low on the pupil-related dimension (2.4). Interpretations of these dimensional estimates were made, defining the supervision function as highly instruction-related without being highly pupil- or student-related.

EXHIBIT 1–5. Dimensional Relatedness Mean Scores for Fifteen Professional Position Types, By A Panel of Experts*

Position Types	Mean Score for Pupil Relatedness**	Mean Score for Instruction Relatedness**
Principal	4.6	6.0
Vice principal	7.0	4.8
Supervisor	2.4	7.0
Elementary teacher	8.9	8.9
Secondary teacher	8.7	8.9
Special education teacher	8.8	8.9
Librarian	6.9	6.3
Guidance	6.8	5.4
Psychologist	5.7	2.9
Audiovisual specialist	4.2	5.0
Teacher aide	7.9	7.0
Supportive service	4.2	1.8
Central administrator	1.9	2.8
Instructional administrator	2.0	5.9
Planning administrator	2.5	5.0

* The panel includes a district personnel director, an elementary principal, and alternative school principal, a professor of supervision, a professor of curriculum, a professor of educational administration, a superintendent of schools, a doctoral student in educational administration, and a director of federal programs.

** Scores computed using importance estimates scaled from 0 to 9.

This assumed that supervision involves work with teachers, curriculum, media, and other personnel, while only indirectly relating to students. Using such a rationale, these data affirm only four position types as supervisory from a functional perspective: principal, supervisor, instructional administrator, and planning administrator. These data may now be out-of-date, however, and a restudy might show changes in organizational expectations of various personnel. Furthermore, variations among communities as well as between states and regions certainly exist.

Recognizing the limitation of simplistic staffing categories suggests needs for survey and descriptive studies of more focus and depth than many now available. Such needs also gives further emphasis to the importance of research on staffing for supervision of instruction that is more systemic and function-oriented.

Organizations and Structures

Since supervisory practices in schools are inevitably linked to and a part of one or more formal organizational structures, these are important influences on and variables in supervision practice. These, too, are not as simple as might be thought. There is a tendency for research, theory, and practice to reflect implicit assumptions about the organizational structures within which supervision is practiced. For example, clinical supervision is conceptualized as a continuing or recurrent relationship between a skilled clinician and a willing, even eager, teacher with ample knowledge, skill, and time for preconferencing, focusing, observing, analyzing, interacting, planning, and re-teaching and recycling. In fact, none, some, or all of these prerequisites may be organizational realities in any given circumstance in a school. The recruitment, selection, assignment, and development of principals or other "clinicians" will be organizationally determined to some extent and influence clinical supervision as a viable reality or improbability. The size of the school, traditions, past experiences of teachers with people observing in their classrooms, expectations of principals and teachers, and, of course, union rules and constraints may all be significant variables that influence the practices supervisors employ.

From a structural perspective, the quality and variety of supervisory practice is undoubtedly influenced by budgets, organizational structures, state laws, and local policies and priorities. Several differentiated organizations for delivery of supervisory services are in existence in most communities. Central office staffs (Pajak, 1989b) generally include some professional personnel assigned supervisory responsibilities with titles ranging from superintendent of schools (Wilson & Harris, 1991) to director of instruction, or coordinator of technology services. In addition to influencing and regulating educational programs, state education agencies are often directly involved in supervisory practices that include planning, monitoring, training, materials development, and program evaluation. Other agencies that are widely influential in affecting teaching in schools are intermediate service units, professional associations, and, increasingly, private vendors, publishers, and consultants.

This array of organizations, staffed and actively engaged in promoting various changes in teaching and learning, is a part of the reality regarding supervisory practices. Little research has focused on the existence of these organizations as a multiplicity of influences. Studies of state department, central staff, and principal leadership tend to be mutually exclusive in their foci. In a few cases, when multiorganizational effects have been under study (Almanza, 1980; Sprinkles, 1993), they have been enlightening. A study of the impact of the work of the National Study of School Evaluation (1986) in the collaborative development of evaluative criteria for use in the accreditation and school improvement efforts of regional associations illustrates the promise of reward in focusing more on multiorganizational supervision influences.

Decentralization of organized supervisory services is a recurrent interest and issue (Tracy & McNaughton, 1993: 274–275). Such decentralization is often based on political rather than on effectiveness criteria; however, the site-based management trend (Hallinger et al, 1992) with the promise of more teacher autonomy requires serious attention to supervisory relationships. In practice, such organizational restructuring may produce a variety of unanticipated changes that affect supervision of instruction. For instance, Watt (1989) is highly critical of decentralization programs in the United Kingdom, arguing that equality may be sacrificed: "The emergence of freedom rather than equality . . . carries a suggestion . . . of a massive general shift to the right . . . increased educational inequality . . . is an almost inevitable outcome . . . " (p. 25).

New technologies, such as video conferencing and computer networking, are bringing disparate agencies and remote individuals into the supervisory process. For example, Dallat (1992) reports on a video-conferencing/tutoring program that links college campuses to school-based personnel. Proposals for an innovative twenty-first century school organization (Austin America 2000 Proposal, 1992) call for a variety of organizational changes, including multiage groups, team teaching, on extended school day, week, and year, home- and community-sites for specialized study, and integrated human and social services on-campus. Dryfoos (1994) describes such changes under the title of "full-service" schooling. Carroll (1989 and 1994) reports on a variety of school organizational innovations relating to scheduling, blocks of time, and so on.

Still other emerging forms of supervision involve classroom or mentor teachers as part-time supervisors. The designating of "teaching consultants" or mentor teachers to supervise novice teachers has gained recognition in both law and practice (ASCD, 1994a). Peer coaching is being utilized for staff development and program implementation purposes (Showers, 1985; Sprinkles, 1993). Diverse organizational structures are being utilized to make use of current classroom experience and to give added credibility to supervisory efforts ranging from curriculum and planning and staff development to administrative decisions and personnel evaluation (Hofsess, 1990; Reiman & Theis-Sprinthall, 1993; ASCD, 1994b; Conleg et al, 1995;)

SUPERVISION AS EVOLVING FUNCTION

Four functionally distinguishable areas of supervision in schools emerge from viewing it as a field of practice in past and present perspectives. The quality control and maintenance function, which is historically dominant, remains in high profile in some circles where national testing, graduation requirements, summative teacher evaluation, or "world class" standards are emphasized. The professional development function persists as a favorite in the literature of supervision that has a lot of emphasis on continuing adult learning, in-service training, field-based internships, and coaching. The support services function, which once focused primarily on making materials available, has expanded to embrace concerns for diverse supporting services that include media resources, clerical assistance, parental involvement, health services, and integrated technology environments. The planning for change and restructuring function is an outgrowth of early innovative efforts over the years, but it gains greater clarity and importance as the piecemeal efforts of "reform" give way to the recognized need for dramatic, even revolutionary, changes in the very character of schooling (Darling-Hammond, 1992: 13).

The Quality Assurance and Maintenance Function

Stability in instructional processes and outcomes has had a heavy emphasis in supervisory practice. Practices emphasizing expertise, overseeing, controlling, and regulating have been major targets of scholars and practitioner critics alike for many years (Barr et al, 1947; Wiles, 1967; Cogan, 1973; McNeil, 1988). These critical views have much to commend them; however, changing supervisory practices in ways that minimize limitations and assure balance among functions has not been easily accomplished. Arguments can be made for wariness in embracing changes in teaching and learning as supervisory goals, given the miserable failures and misguided efforts that have been experienced from the "platoon system" of the 1880s to the "reforms" of the 1980s (Slavin, 1989; Wayson et al., 1988; Kerr, 1989: 202.)

Quality assurance, within a context of supervision that emphasize professional development, supportive services, and thoughtfully designed changes, can hardly be ignored as an essential feature of supervisory practice. In this context, the "total quality" precepts of Deming (1993) have been rediscovered for application to supervision in schools (Holt, 1993). The focus on quality rather than on control is perhaps one useful contribution of Deming's emphasis on eliminating outmoded punitive and bureaucratic practices. Everett Rogers (1986) has emphasized the place of quality control in the implementation of innovative programs while acknowledging the importance of adaptations of designs to fit unique situations. Deming's emphasis on "constancy of purpose," however, along with training, continuous improvement, and vigorous leadership seem to favor continuity and quality control (Blankstein & Swain, 1994: 52).

Fullan (1982) is among those who have documented causes of failures of new programs even when well conceptualized and enthusiastically implemented. Top–down mandates, lack of leadership, and inadequate retraining are clearly among the errors frustrating improvement. A decade later, however, Fullan (1993: 42–49) analyzed apparent failures of new programs not erring in old ways. He cited two central problems with special significance for supervisory leadership:

1. "It is not easy to accomplish fundamental change"
2. "The hardest core to crack is the learning core—change in instructional practices and in the culture of teaching"

Sprinthall and Theis-Sprinthall (1983) provide one promising perspective on the resolution of these problems utilizing cognitive developmental theory (pp. 27–31).

Stability in organizational life is an aspect of the maintenance of quality function that may be undervalued. The U.S. public schools are unique as the primary source of custodial care for more than 42 million young persons. As such, the simple maintenance of schooling with predictability is enormously important on a daily basis in the lives of millions of people. Any change that threatens such regularity of "care" is suspect, even for purposes such as providing released time for staff development or curriculum planning.

Stability means more than predictable custodial care for 180 days each year. Curricular changes may create cognitive dissonance at home among parents and in the community among employers, and among special interest groups. Teaching practices that involve teams, aides, interns, visiting scholars, field trips, cooperative learning, new technology, or schedule flexibility may have serious repercussions among students, parents, teachers, and other citizens if they are not understood fully, implemented smoothly, and tailored adequately. Systems theory (Banathy, 1968) provides an ample basis for recognizing in advance some of the effects of any structural or process change on other parts of the larger program. The need for stability is part of the equation calling for change; hence, this emphasis as one of the supervisory functions should not be ignored. Deming and Fullan, however, have both suggested that "constancy of purpose" in the instructional improvement process calls for extended time frames of persistent effort, abandoning naive and simplistic approaches (Deming, 1993).

Respect for the wisdom of the profession has been argued on rare occasions as still another reason to make progress slowly and, hence, to give substantial emphasis to the control and maintenance function in supervision. Sarason (1990) recognized the distinction between first and second-order changes, with the former seen as those made ". . . without disturbing the basic organization features, without substantially altering the way that children and adults perform their roles" (p. 342). His distinction may mask the need for careful, selective preservation of current practice, and the restoration of selected past practices as second- and third-order changes are designed. Teaching is not a new field of human endeavor, as are robotization, laser surgery, and genetic engineering. Teaching as a formal, thoughtful, systematic practice is at least as old as Socrates and Confucius (Durant, 1939; McNeill & Sedlar, 1970). Early scientific, philosophical, methodological, and empirical studies of teaching and learning have a long and rich history (Dewey, 1916; Piaget, 1963). Scholars and practitioners need not rely on pure conjecture, political expediency, or commercial hype for guides to good practices (Eisner, 1990). Even modern scientific method has limited authority in directing supervisory practice toward change or maintenance (Hills,

1991). What works and has failed in the past, however, is much more clearly understood and informed by the wisdom of the profession and findings of research and theory (Gage, 1978) than by the diverse images of visionaries, technocrats, and politicians. This concern for cautious and reflective approaches to change was voiced by Kerr (1989: 215) with respect to technology in classrooms:

perhaps no feature of twentieth century educational practice has been more puzzling than the gap between what technology has promised and what it has delivered. . . . Teachers are dissuaded by tradition, practical constraints, lack of training, and lack of appropriate models.

One might even ask whether much of the promise of technology is not essentially commercial and not very educational.

Emphasis on outcomes-based supervision for improving teaching and learning was an early concept in supervision history when supervisors spent time with students seeing how well they could read, write, and compute rather than observing the teaching-learning process and reviewing lesson plans. This emphasis has currently gained renewed vigor and support primarily from the proliferation of tests of student achievement. The implications for judging either teaching or learning using standardized tests are numerous and often highly controversial. Even so, pressures and plans for extending this form of control via "national testing" and making use of such data to pressure, reward, and punish individual schools and teachers seem to be growing.

Countervailing influences on supervisory practices can be recognized with growing emphasis on alternative ways of measuring student achievement and outcomes. Performance assessment, alternative assessment, and authentic assessment are some of the terms being used to describe departures from standard practices. Such developments, as problematic, challenging, and promising as they are, have potential for new supervisory practices; however, the emphasis on outcomes almost to the exclusion of any emphasis on teaching, curriculum, and other factors relating to the quality of schooling, remains at the core of outcome-based policy. As such, supervisory practices may be forced into a control and maintenance mode, whether guided by narrow standardized measures, "world-class standards," or new assessment techniques.

The Professional Development Function

The emphasis on the function of promoting the growth and development of teachers as professional practitioners has a long tradition in the literature and folklore of instructional supervision. This function, however, has been much more widely embraced in theory than it has in practice (Harris, 1989). As a broad functional area of concern, professional development has at least three differing emphases:

1. Promoting effective teaching practices
2. Providing for continuous personal and professional growth
3. Changing the character of the school and teaching

These are not mutually exclusive but have distinctively different implications for supervisory practice.

Promoting Effective Teaching The emphasis on effective teaching practices is essentially one based on decades of "teacher effectiveness studies" exemplified by the work of Gage (1978), Good and Brophy (1987), Walberg and Lane (1989), Soar (1976), and many others. Although these studies are still critically reviewed by many scholars, they have provided the basis for supervisory practices that emphasize classroom observation, clinical conferencing, and lesson analysis techniques as ways of promoting improvements in teaching. The assumption that some practices are more likely to be more effective in promoting student learning provides concrete and feasible guidelines to supervisors and teachers whether clinical, formal training, coaching, or self-directed approaches are selected.

If there are clearly more and less appropriate teaching practices, then they are undoubtedly limited in number, applicability, and effect. Nearly all scholars and practitioners seem to agree on the enormous complexity of the teaching–learning process (Eisner, 1984; Shulman, 1986). Those working closely with teachers across a variety of classrooms, schools, and communities, however, often attest to the enormous chasm between known effective practices and the repertoire of most teachers (Joyce & Weil, 1986; Glickman, 1991; Harris, 1986; Dunkin, 1987). There appears to be no problem, therefore, in identifying teaching improvements worthy of supervisory attention.

The abuses of identified effective teaching practices in the hands of overzealous researchers, supervisors, and administrators have been strongly argued. Mandated punitive teacher evaluation systems such as those adopted in Texas and Georgia are clear examples of such abuse (Wayson et al, 1988; McNeil, 1988). Administrators seeking the security of specifics to use as "expectations" have similarly, attached unwarranted importance to a few teaching practices as indicators of effectiveness (Sprinkles, 1993). Private consultants and publishers have found it profitable to promote acceptance of causes such as phonics, wait-time, and programmed teaching with dubious rationale.

Personal and Professional Development The emphasis on continuing, personal, and professional development has its origins in assumptions about teaching as an art or a craft that asserts that the personal and professional behavior of teachers are inseparable and uniquely individual. This view of professional development emphasizes less formal supervisory efforts in favor of self-directed growth activities (Glatthorn, 1987) that supervisors might facilitate (Hall & Hord, 1984). Time for peer sharing, reflection, and dialogue in an environment where there is freedom to explore and reflect on one's practice (Schon, 1983) is given priority over either improving specific practices or implementing new programs. The "teacher as researcher" (Tikunoff & Mergendoller, 1983) is also closely related to this emphasis on teacher development.

Sprinthall and Thies-Sprinthall (1983) address personal and professional growth from the perspective of teachers as adult learners. They suggest the importance of recognizing the need to design programs to "promote both growth and skill acquisition." Guidelines are proposed based on a synthesis of adult learning and cognitive-developmental principles:

1. placing persons in "significant role-taking experiences"
2. providing for "careful and continuous guided reflection"

3. balancing "real experience and discussion/reflection/teaching. . . . Guided integration appears essential" (pp. 27–30).

Such programs would be continuing and involve both challenging opportunities for new experiences as well as personal, professional support.

Changing Schooling Emphasis on changing the character of the school and teaching is still somewhat different than one seeking to improve practices or to promote continuing individual growth. This emphasis derives from assumptions about the need to restructure schooling (New American Schools Development Corp., 1991). It is asserted that curricular changes are essential (Sizer, 1984; Comer, 1989; Schlechty, 1990; Tye, 1991b; Boyer, 1983; Sautter, 1994; Glasser, 1990). Structural changes that would directly affect teaching, such as team teaching, use of aides, field-based learning, home-school linkages, and technology networking, are often advocated. Even the purpose of schooling is sometimes challenged as in need of fundamental "rethinking" (Wagner, 1993).

Regardless of the specific restructuring proposals, improvement of teaching under such assumptions tends to be imbedded in a systematic planning–implementation process (Anderson, 1993). Formal training is emphasizes in such programs, and needs are dictated by the demands of the planned changes (Bennis et al, 1985) rather than by either predetermined practices or personal choices. Supervisory leadership under these circumstances is closely related to planning and implementation of a variety of changes—curricular, organizational, and instructional—all of which demand formal training (Fullan, 1991). Romberg and Price (1983) suggest even further complexities, viewing such implementation processes as involving "cultural change."

Professional development as a major function in supervision seems always to be recognized in theory and yet rarely embraced as widespread practice (Harris, 1989). That training, coaching, simulating, demonstrating, and directed practice can produce improved teaching has substantial support in research and best practice. Lack of policy commitments, money, time, and traditional misconceptions ("anybody can teach," "you learn to teach by teaching," and "a license certifies competence"), however, tend to limit the function of professional development in supervisory practice. It persists, however, as one of the emphases of supervision over time, stimulated by growing interest in major reforms. The acceptance of and emphasis on staff development for implementing structural and technological changes have fueled and renewed support among researchers and practitioners (Fullan, 1991; Glickman, 1990; Resta, 1991).

The Support Services Function

The essence of supervisory practice has been to support teaching and learning over the decades. The supervisor as a resource provider and as a communications link are only two variations on this emphasis in the field. Cogan (1973), Goldhammer et al (1980), and many other advocates of clinical supervision project an image of the "clinician" as an assistant to the teacher, providing information, offering analyses, and delivering feedback. Even when broader roles and responsibilities are emphasized, the importance of service and support are often asserted. Schon's (1983) emphasis on the "reflective practitioner" and the early influence of Carl Rogers (1959) promotion of "nondirective" approaches in a "helping" relationship are further illustrations of supervision as support services.

Developments have greatly expanded the range of these traditional services to include some consideration of service needs spawned by community involvement, integration of electronic technologies, mainstreaming of handicapped students, and elaborate testing and accountability pressures. Teaching is still a somewhat personal, private affair with a rather "loose coupling" between classroom reality and the outside world, but such insulation appears to be eroding and support service needs growth more urgently. The Education for All Handicapped Children Act passed by Congress in 1975 stimulated formal arrangements for involving school psychologists, social workers, nurses, and learning disabilities specialists in consultative and educational plan-making activities with teachers and supervisors (Gorton et al, 1988: 265–266).

A distinction can be drawn between administrative, clerical, counseling, and health services as less directly related to teaching and learning than supervisory support. Some of the newer service needs are much more directly related to teaching, instruction, curriculum, and the climate for learning. As such, they are at least potentially supervisory services. At the very least, they influence supervision as practiced in other more directly instructional ways (Harris, 1985: 6,11). Librarians and other media specialists, educational diagnosticians, social workers, psychologists, nurses, and even parole officers are increasingly sharing responsibilities for improving teaching in schools (Alpert, 1982; Blacklock, 1978; Cervera, 1990; Cohen, 1976; Decker & Associates, 1990; Dryfoos, 1994; Hodgkinson, 1991a; National Commission on Children, 1991).

Community involvement in the instructional program appears to be increasing in variety and influence. The use of advisory councils of lay persons has been amplified with growing parental involvement as classroom aides and active members of school decision-making teams. Programs for fuller utilization of the human resources of the community as visiting presenters in the classrooms or as "mentors" and tutors for individual students greatly change the curriculum and add complexity to both teaching and supervision (Barth, 1990; Cervera, 1990; Cohen, 1978; Consortium on Youth Apprenticeships, 1990; Decker & Associates, 1990; Dryfoos, 1994).

Technology integration in the instructional programs of schools calls for more than purely technological support services. Entirely new relationships between teachers and the tools of the trade are produced when electronic, computer-oriented instructional activities are employed (Davies & Shane, 1986: 15–17). Aside from the obvious need for changes in staff development and observational processes of supervisors, the need for technical assistance for teachers in deciding about new technologies—their quality, utility, and relative advantage—appears to be increasingly important. A special problem for teachers and supervisors is the extensive commercialization associated with most new electronic technology. Unlike older technologies—textbooks, recordings, workbooks, and labora-

tory equipment—electronics change rapidly, are dominated by major corporations, and tend to have methodologies of their own (Walker, 1986: 36). Technology assessment support services are clearly necessary to go beyond encouraging utilization (Squire, 1988) in order to provide the knowledge base and analytical tools for instructional decision-making by individual teachers and schools alike. If the "medium is the message" (McLuhan, 1984), then the medium must be more rigorously assessed by teachers and supervisors. (Davies, 1986; Dede, 1989).

Mainstreaming of handicapped students in the classroom has added greatly to the complexity of teaching and calls for support services not traditionally emphasized in supervisory practices. Technical support personnel such as diagnosticians, psychologists, and speech correctionists play critical roles in assisting teachers as well as parents and students in school; however, it is not realistic for each teacher to independently draw upon these service personnel. Supervision needs to be available in coordinating and facilitating the collaborative efforts of these specialists. Curricular adaptation for handicapped students is still another arena where support services are increasingly needed for assuring adaptations based on quality diagnoses, and for assisting with making materials readily available. The emotional stresses added to the life of the classroom teacher by the presence of physically and/or emotionally handicapped students in the regular classroom is a reality needing both psychological support and technical assistance even more than curricular expertise (Idstein, 1993).

Testing programs and concomitant pressures for "results" have grown in recent decades. Such programs are unfortunately not highly effective and produce serious negative side effects. Programs for better use of test data (Schalock et al, 1993), performance assessments, and more clearly diagnostic, individualized responses to student needs are being advocated. Such changes will require new assessment technologies (Quinto & McKenna, 1977) and assistance in their application to classroom settings. It seems as unlikely that teachers can be expected to undertake new assessments all alone as it seems for medical doctors to run their own laboratory tests.

SUPERVISORY INQUIRY

Scholarly inquiry directly related to the field of instructional supervision is bewildering in its diversity (Anderson, 1989). As an applied professional field of endeavor, supervision of instruction draws upon, or at least might be expected to draw upon, theory, research, and developmental efforts in many disciplines and specialties both within and outside educational systems. The sources of knowledge, therefore, are numerous, and synthesis and utilization are particularly difficult as well as promising. When supervisory practices are widely defined as diverse positions, roles, relationships, and tasks that relate to leadership for instructional improvement, then a panorama of opportunities emerge for relating research, development, and theory from many fields to professional supervisory practice.

In setting the stage for numerous in-depth reviews in other chapters in this book, this section will endeavor to sketch the general features of scholarly inquiry using selected indexes and abstracts as well as scanning articles in issues of a few scholarly journals. The focus will be on how research and other scholarly publications reflect major categories of supervisory practice. Similar analyses are utilized to focus on both scholarly and practitioner-oriented inquiry utilizing two selected journals, the ERIC Index, and a national catalog of practices.

General Features of Recent Inquiry

Robert H. Anderson (1989) observed from personal perspective and nearly a half century of professional involvement in supervision research:

I became increasingly aware of the enormous range and complexity of work being done in the related categories of general supervision, instructional improvements, instructional leadership, teacher effectiveness, teacher empowerment, and teacher improvement. . . . Soon I realized that the broad cataloguing of needed research was not appropriate. . . . The process of seeking, sorting, and sifting material from this exploding field was an "awesome' experience. . . ." (p. 291).

This perspective has guided the preparation of this overview on scholarly inquiry contributing to the field. Abstracts of masters theses and dissertations were specifically scanned with a variety of categories and keywords employed to both enumerate and identify topics of relevance to supervisory practice. A small number of scholarly journals were reviewed by scanning titles, abstracts, and the articles themselves to identify the topics of relevance that were most clearly represented. Educational Administrative Abstracts was also scanned using similar identifying and enumerating procedures.

In reporting on the general features of supervision inquiry, details will be minimized for the sake of emphasizing impression, emphases, and themes, as well as apparent omissions and limitations; however, the major categories and keywords or topics fairly consistently utilized in scanning various sources are shown in Exhibit 1.6.

Theses and Dissertations Main headings found in these abstract publications do not include supervision. They instead categorize dissertations and theses in the field of education with subheadings. Supervision-relevant studies are reported under general education administration, curriculum, adult and continuing education, and teacher training. A quick overview of master theses for 1991–1992 (Masters Abstracts International, 1993) led to the identification of at least 10 studies related to supervisory categories. Six studies focused on instructional change with keywords such as alternative schools, knowledge of educational change, middle school transition, and school culture and change. Only two theses were clearly curricular, program evaluation was the focus of only two, and personnel evaluation of only one. Three of these same theses emphasized teaching with the keywords teacher involvement, supportive relationships, and unsatisfactory teaching. By contrast, staff development topics were identified in seven titles. Six theses focused on supervision or leadership identified by keywords such as consultation, collaborative, implementation role, and supportive relationships.

EXHIBIT 1–6. Major Supervisory Categories and Keywords or Topics

Change process
- educational
- renewal
- process
- restructuring
- innovations
- leadership for

Curriculum and instruction
- development
- evaluation
- design
- improvement of
- planning
- implementing

Evaluation of personnel
- teacher assessment
- summative
- observation
- self-evaluation
- diagnostic
- ratings
- systems of
- feedback
- formative
- appraisal

Evaluation of programs
- instructional
- effectiveness
- implementation
- outcomes
- uses
- methods

Leadership for instruction
- styles
- principal
- instructional
- central staff
- school

Staff development
- training
- group process
- in-service education
- growth
- consulting
- team building
- clinical approaches
- workshops

Supervision
- instructional
- competencies
- supervisors
- tasks
- roles
- functions
- skills
- positions

Teaching and teachers
- teams
- empowerment of
- effectiveness
- problems of
- styles
- need of
- involvement of teachers

It would be unwise to try to generalize about theses topics based on such a limited review of only one year. It is nonetheless notable, that supervision as a term was not common, that staff development was strongly represented by an array of keywords—(i.e.,) facilitator, training, implementation, skill, transfer, in-service, etc., and that all major categories in Exhibit 1.6 were represented with one or more studies. Also of interest is the fact that only 10 or 12 of 276 studies listed in the area of Education appeared to be clearly supervision relevant for the year examined.

Dissertation abstracts were reviewed for 1985 and 1990, with a substantial number of studies clearly identified as supervisory relevant in both years. Studies were especially common with specific reference to "in-service education," "staff development," and "training" for staff "improvement." A keyword analysis for a limited sampling of studies reveals major emphasis on change, staff development, and leadership, as well as teaching. A substantial number of studies was focused on curriculum, supervision, and teacher evaluation. Keywords that identified these dissertation studies are listed in Exhibit 1.6. Some examples of abbreviated titles listed in the following also are indicative of the major categories of emphasis.

Abbreviated Dissertation Titles: 1985 and 1990

Change Process

- Analysis of educational reform legislation
- Contradiction and difficulty in educational change
- Directiveness vs. participation in change process
- Implementation of a middle school program

Curriculum and Instruction

- Models of school effectiveness
- Model for increasing parent and community involvement
- Time on task in middle schools
- Instructionally effective schools

Evaluation of Personnel

- Upgrading teacher performance evaluation process
- Success of beginning teachers
- Acceptance of evaluation by teachers
- Development of a teacher evaluation plan

Evaluation of Programs

- None

Leadership for Instruction

- Effects of leadership on teacher burnout
- Congruency between principal behavior and teacher effectiveness
- Effects of principal behavior on parental involvement

Staff Development

- Experiential learning for staff development
- A case study of school improvement
- Integration of instruction and staff development
- Staff development needs assessment
- Teacher perceptions of in-service education
- Training in developing the school curriculum

Supervision

- Job satisfaction of instructional services staff

Teaching and Teachers

- Characteristics of effective teaching
- Teacher motivation and effectiveness
- Interdisciplinary teaming
- Relation of teaching style to learning style

These abbreviated titles of a limited sample of dissertations cannot fully reflect the full scope of this form of research. It is interesting to note, however, the diversity of foci with recurrent attention to in-service education for school improvement, implementation of new programs, and assessment of greater effectiveness. The absence of certain topics is also worthy of note. There are few studies that focus on technical competencies and skills, innovations, or program evaluation. There are also rather few studies identified here that focus on issues of power, autonomy, role conflict, or interpersonal relationships. Sampling error could easily be responsible for this, but some of these perennial issues may be of passing interest.

Scholarly Journals The use of abstracts across a wide variety of journals was supplemented for this review by a sampling of volumes of several clearly research-oriented journals in education. Educational Administration Abstracts were used, along with selected volumes of Review of Educational Research, Educational Administration Quarterly, Social Work in Education, Journal of Educational Administration (UK), Educational Evaluation and Policy Analysis, Educational Psychological Research, Journal of Research and Development in Education, and Research in Education (Canada). These journals represent diversity more than systematic selection, but they do reveal a widespread interest in supervisory practices among diverse researchers.

A sampling of journal articles is represented in the following within eight categories that relate to supervision of instruction. These are abbreviated titles that give at least some flavor of the topics as published. A sample of some 30 articles published in the United States, Canada, and the United Kingdom are represented. These are largely scholarly journals such as those mentioned previously.

Abbreviated Titles in Selected Scholarly Journals 1986–1993

Change Process

- Restructuring schools for fundamental reform.
- Inside-outside leadership for change.
- School leadership for change.
- Radical reforms in New Zealand education.
- Principals as change agents.
- Developing a culture for change.

Curriculum and Instruction

- Research perspectives on learning and instruction.
- New forms of teaching and subject matter knowledge.

Evaluation of Personnel

- Validity of principal judgments of teacher effectiveness.
- Negative feelings toward self-evaluation among teachers.
- Developing and validating criteria of teacher effectiveness.

Evaluation of Program

- Using assessment data to improve teaching.
- Factors influencing job satisfaction in teaching.
- Innovation, school improvement, and self-renewal theory.
- Knowledge about classroom assessment possessed by teachers and administrators.
- Developing an index of school quality.

Leadership for Instruction

- A constructivist perspective on instructional leadership.
- Rethinking site-based management.

- Problems in the study of instructional leadership.
- Shared decision-making.

Staff Development

- Staff development as a function of readiness.
- Consultation and collaboration for improving teaching.
- Professional growth and support through teaching.
- Teacher concerns and complexity related to effectiveness of in-service education.
- Video-conferencing use and practice in professional development.

Supervision

- Improving the effectiveness of supervisory practice.
- Changing role of central office supervisors.
- Models of consultation for improving teaching.
- Group clinical supervision as feedback process.

Teaching and Teachers

- Motivation and incentives for outstanding teachers.
- Identification of stress factors in teaching.

This sample of abbreviated titles can hardly be regarded as fully representative of the scholarship in the field. The substantial number of articles, however, in each major category of supervision and the recurrent themes emphasizing change, restructuring, school renewal, leadership for instructional improvement, models for staff development, and supervision practices are consistent with those found in dissertations.

Reviews of Research A somewhat contrasting pattern of research publishing is suggested in the analysis of eight years of issues of the Review of Educational Research (see Exhibit 1.7). A review of all issues for 1970, 1975, 1980, 1985, 1987, 1988, 1990, and 1991 revealed that nearly half of all reviews were related to supervision of instruction. Ten reviews emphasized educational evaluation—with program and personnel combined. Five reviews were in the broad category of curriculum and instruction, with only one or two reviews in each of the categories of in-service education, supervision, and instructional leadership. In this analysis, the category of teaching and teachers was not utilized in order to focus more sharply on the other core supervisory categories.

EXHIBIT 1–7. Reviews of Educational Research Related to Supervision of Instruction: Eight Selected Years, 1970–1991

	Number
Change process	0
Curriculum and instruction	5
Evaluation of personnel	5
Evaluation of program	5
Staff development	1
Leadership for instruction	2
Supervision of instruction	2
Total Related Reviews	**20**

With only a few reviews included in each issue of this quarterly publication, it is to be expected that few would be supervisory in any one year. Eleven reviews, however, were identified as supervisory in the three years, 1970, 1975, and 1980, compared with nine such reviews in the five years, 1985, 1987, 1988, 1990, and 1991. It appears that attention to such scholarly work has diminished by reviewers publishing in this prestigious journal. The limited number of reviews in four major categories related to supervision is consistent for all years reported here. Both the decline and the omissions are similar to the declines shown in dissertations in Exhibit 1.1.

The 20 reviews published in Review of Educational Research in these years are listed as slightly abbreviated titles to give some sense of the focus of these scholarly efforts:

1970 —	Curriculum evaluation.
—	Evaluation of instruction.
—	Applied behavior in the classroom.
—	Stability of teacher effects on achievement.
1975 —	Assessing readiness for professional practice.
—	Language medium in early years for minority groups.
—	Logic of learning by discovery.
—	Studies of effects of school on learning.
1980 —	Schools in the political socialization process.
—	Organizations development in schools.
—	Educational planning.
1985 —	Moral education and moral judgments.
—	Effectiveness of bilingual education.
1987 —	Ability grouping and elementary student achievement.
—	Teacher receptivity to systemwide change.
1988 —	Controlling variables in training studies.
—	Supervision of counselors and teachers-in-training.
—	Variables influencing the acquisition of generic teaching skills.
1990 —	Effectiveness of mastery learning programs.
—	Mastery learning reconsidered.
1991 —	None.

In identifying these 20 reviews as those clearly related to supervision of instruction, others were deleted from the list even when clearly instructional in focus. Highly technical reviews of methodological issues were among those not identified. Reviews focusing on higher education were also passed over, as were others dealing with learning and student behavior with little direct focus on teaching. For instance, examples of some reviews that might have been identified in the 1990 volume include the following keywords from titles:

- community involvement
- equity and computers in schools
- studying student dropouts
- leader succession and socialization

These suggest still other scholarly works worthy of study by supervision-professionals, even if not clearly most relevant.

The Journal of Curriculum and Supervision

A special review of the issues of this journal was justified because of its unique character as the only nationwide publication devoted specifically to supervision of instruction from a scholarly perspective and sponsored by the Association for Supervision and Curriculum Development. Titles of all articles in this journal were reviewed from 1985 to 1993. Using the same eight major categories of supervision detailed in Exhibit 1.6, the titles were identified and categorized. Exhibit 1.8 summarizes the numbers of such supervision relevant articles. A sample of abbreviated titles reflecting the focus of the writing will also be reported shortly.

From a perspective of frequency of supervision articles published in this journal, it is not surprising to find both yearly volumes and individual issues well represented in one or more major categories. It is also apparent that the emphases of the journal—both curriculum and supervision—are also clearly and consistently represented by most individual articles. With some exceptions, however, major categories of evaluation, leadership, and even staff development are not well represented. Change process as a major category is also represented by a rather limited number of articles.

A sample of relevant titles is shown in the following in abbreviated form selected from those articles identified as related to one major category of supervision or another. These abbreviations are listed by year and volume number along with the name(s) of the authors. This array of 46 articles represents some 195 actually identified as supervisory and published in this journal from 1985 to 1993. These abbreviated titles appear to represent to some degree the interests and professional judgments of a group of scholars giving considerable attention to supervision and/or curriculum and instruction. These abbreviated titles also reflect a range of scholarly modes, including theorizing, researching, critiquing, program developing, and lots of dialoguing. In fact, a rather substantial numbers of articles were comments upon the articles of other writers.

Selected Abbreviated Titles Journal of Curriculum and Supervision

1985-1986

- Clinical supervision for professional development.
- Clinical supervision, technocratic mindedness.
- Critical theory and the art of teaching.
- The domain of curriculum.
- Locus of curriculum decision-making.
- Problems, methods, and solutions in curriculum.
- Psychoanalysis, teaching, and supervision.
- Teachers meet technology authoring courseware in schools.

1986-1987

- Adapting supervisory practice to teaching competence.

- The hidden curriculum.
- Systematic teacher appraisal for staff development.
- Development of theories of teaching.
- Teaching: rules, research, beauty, and creation.
- Uniformity and diversity: curricular and instructional issues.

1987-1988

- Clinical supervision, consultation, and counseling.
- A museum setting for a nonschool curriculum.
- Action research in curriculum.
- Benchmark testing and teacher and principal concerns.
- Imagination, rigor, and caring in educational reform.

1988-1989

- Describing curriculum development from inside.
- Ecology of teacher development.
- Discourse analysis of supervisory conferences.
- Artistry and teaching as a focus of research.
- Variables related to continuation of a curriculum innovation.

1989-1990

- Analyzing collaborative curriculum decision-making.
- Teacher initiated changes in curriculum and instructional practices.
- Teacher reflection in clinical supervision.
- Curriculum implementation and organization.
- Status of supervision scholarship.

1990-1991

- Middle school development and program phases.
- Supervision as a developmental art.
- A new supervisory process for improving instruction.
- Curricular insights for the beginning teacher experience.
- Curriculum leadership in facilitating deliberation.
- Implementing change through mandated testing.

1991-1992

- Principal judgments and teacher self-ratings.
- Creative curriculum for an inner city community school.
- Avoidance process and instructional supervision.
- Redefining who does supervision in school.
- Good teaching and supervision.

1992-1993

- Future curriculum possibilities.
- Curriculum definitions and reference points.
- Development of national attainment targets.
- A profile of supervisory activity at the district level.
- Reform and curriculum process in outcome-based education.
- Cooperating teacher as supervisor.

EXHIBIT 1–8. Analysis of Titles of Articles: Journal of Curriculum
and Supervision 1985 to 1993

Supervision-Related Categories	Volume and Year								Category Totals	
	#1 1985–1986	#2 1986–1987	#3 1987–1988	#4 1988–1989	#5 1989–1990	#6 1990–1991	#7 1991–1992	#8 1992–1993	No.	%
Change process	0	0	2	3	2	4	1	2	14	7
Curriculum & instruction	7	9	10	8	9	14	8	15	80	41
Evaluation of personnel	0	1	0	1	0	0	1	0	3	2
Evaluation of programs	0	0	0	1	1	1	2	3	8	4
Leadership for instruction	0	0	0	0	0	1	0	0	1	1
Staff development	0	1	1	3	1	0	2	0	8	4
Supervision	7	6	8	7	11	6	10	6	61	31
Teaching	4	3	3	3	3	2	2	0	20	10
Volume totals	18	20	24	26	27	28	26	26	195	
Percentage of articles	53	74	71	79	61	72	81	81		

The emphasis on theoretical, philosophical, and issue-oriented topics is clearly evidenced in each volume over nearly a decade. Topics associated with evaluation of either program or personnel are clearly not evident. This is consistent with long-standing efforts of supervisory specialists to distance themselves from judgmental events; however, the extensive interest in leadership and staff development reflected in both the literature and the field of practice is also largely missing in these scholarly efforts.

Of note by virtue of omission in the titles of these many scholarly writings are references to organizational life, system building, or community relationships. Even the words school, program, and district are largely absent, thereby giving the impression from the abundant use of the words teaching, curriculum, learning, and development that supervision exists in a social–organizational vacuum.

Practitioner Perspectives

A few of the many published sources addressing issues, practices, problems, and innovations in the field of school supervision are worthy of special review. The official journal of the Association for Supervision and Curriculum Development, Educational Leadership, is distributed internationally to all members of that comprehensive organization—one of the largest of all professional associations. Another renowned source—Phi Delta Kappan—is also distributed worldwide to a very large and highly diverse population of educators. These two journals are of importance in any review of scholarly thought related to supervisory practice in schools because they reflect policy, research, theory, current issues, and emerging practices in the public schools without being directed toward scholars per se. Both journals are clearly devoted instead to disseminating educational research, theory, and practice, and to keeping practitioners informed. In a sense, then, the articles accepted for publication in these journals, while not being devoted primarily to supervision of instruction, do in fact provide some perspective on the extent

and kind of interests prevailing among a wide variety of professional educators. Other selected sources of practitioner perspectives given attention here are the ERIC Index* and a catalog of the National Commission of Instructional Supervision (1986).

Educational Leadership This journal is published nine times each year and often includes 15–20 articles on a variety of topics in each issue. Research reports are not commonly published, although a regular feature includes some overviews of recent research. This journal uniquely utilizes a theme for each issue, devoting one third or more of the articles to a single theme; the other articles are an unrelated variety.

The analysis completed for reporting here on this journal involved a sample of 22 issues over a five-year period, 1990–1994. Approximately one half of all issues for this period were reviewed. The journal's themes were the focus of this analysis with individual articles given only cursory attention. Once again, the major categories of supervision previously employed in this chapter were utilized.

In brief, 19 of the 22 themes were readily identified as related to one of the supervisory categories; only three journal themes were somewhat nonsupervisory in nature. The distribution of themes by supervisory category clearly favored Teaching and Teachers. Ten of the 19 themes were identified as clearly related to other supervisory categories. Change process was the theme of three issues; similarly, curriculum and instruction, and evaluation of programs were related themes three times each. Staff development was related to a theme only once in a five-year period, and no themes were clearly related to evaluation of personnel, leadership for instruction or supervision of instruction. While 87% of all themes reviewed were supervision related, only 53% were related clearly to major categories other than teaching and teachers.

Some of these themes are shown next by date and category, providing a further sense about the specific aspects of practice included in each issue.

* ERIC refers to the Educational Resources Information Centers of the National Institute of Education.

Change Process

- Creating a Culture for Change (May 1990).
- Restructuring Schools: What's Really Happening (May 1991).
- Inventing New Systems: Systemic Change (September 1993).

Curriculum and Instruction

- Integrating the Curriculum (October 1991).
- Whose Culture? (December/January 1992).
- The Changing Curriculum (May 1993).

Evaluation and Personnel

(None)

Evaluation of Programs

- The Quest for Higher Standards (February 1991).
- Using Performance Assessment (May 1992).
- The Challenge of Higher Standards (February 1993).

Leadership of Instruction

(None)

Staff Development

- Teacher Education and Professional Development (???)

Supervision of Instruction

(None)

Teaching and Teachers

- Teaching Social Responsibility (November 1990).
- The Reflective Educator (March 1991).
- The Professional Educator (March 1993).
- Character Education (November 1993).
- Authentic Learning (April 1993).
- Improving the Odds for Students at Risk (December/January 1993).
- Teaching for Understanding (February 1994).
- Realizing the Promise of Technology (April 1994).
- Educating for Diversity (May 1994).

These themes related to supervisory categories clearly reveal a substantial focus on supervision practices. They also reveal, in the way they are worded, a strong effort to embrace the most recent fads, buzz words, and popular ideas—(i.e., cultural change, inventing systems, integrating, performance assessment, diversity, technology, authentic learning, etc.). This is consistent with the need to respond to a diverse readership, and the responsibility of a professional house organ to inform its members.

These themes also reveal little focus on past accomplishments, reinforcing standards of supervisory practice, recognizing leaders, or training in the practices of the field. The omission of themes emphasizing evaluation, leadership, and supervision combined with the limited attention to curriculum and staff development suggests rather superficial contributions to the field of instructional supervision.

A note of caution is in order. Since only 22 issues of the 45 (1990–1994) publications were reviewed and only themes were identified and categorized, the full contribution of this journal to scholarly inquiry from a practitioner-oriented perspective cannot be determined. It may be that more rigorous analysis of individually selected articles would reveal both better coverage of the concerns of supervisors and greater contribution to their practice.

Phi Delta Kappan This journal is published 10 times each year and often includes 15–20 articles on a wide variety of topics in nearly every issue. Research reports and surveys as well as public opinion polls are fairly regular features. Although the audience for this journal is very diverse, its authors tend to be reasonably scholarly in language, unhesitatingly report quantitative data, cite scholarly sources, and utilize theoretical constructs. Nonetheless, it is a practitioner's journal—the thinking-educator practitioner's journal.

This journal nearly always uses one or more clearly defined themes with two or three, or even up to 10 articles included. The analysis completed for reporting here on this journal involved a sample of 38 issues over a five year period, 1990–1994. Nearly three fourths of the issues for this time period were examined, and themes were identified and arranged by supervisory categories.

In brief, 71% of the issues were categorized with themes related to supervision of instruction. Only 11 of the 38 issues

EXHIBIT 1–9. Themes and Feature Articles in Phi Delta Kappan, 1990–1994, by Supervisory Category and Year

Date	Change Process	Curr. Develop.	Eval. of Personnel	Eval. of Program	Leadership for Instr.	Staff Develop.	Super- vision	Teaching & Teachers	Total
1989–1990	2	0	0	0	0	1	0	2	5
1990–1991	2	2	0	0	1	1	0	0	6
1991–1992	3	0	0	2	0	0	0	2	7
1992–1993	0	0	0	3	0	0	0	0	3
1993–1994	2	2	0	0	1	1	0	0	6
Total Themes (Issues)	9	4	0	5	2	3	0	4	27
Total Feature Articles	42	29	0	29	12	14	0	18	144

had themes not clearly supervisory in nature. Over 140 articles included as "Feature Articles" were directly related to one of the supervisory categories. Exhibit 1.9 provides some detail on this analysis by category.

In Exhibit 1.10, the titles of themes and "feature" sections are shown by supervisory category and year. The number of articles included in each theme or feature section is also shown. Since themes and feature sections were selected for their apparent relevance to supervision practice, it was also assumed that all articles within such sections of the issues were also supervisory in nature to some extent. Individual articles, however, were not analyzed and categorized.

The 27 list themes or "feature" sections reflect a heavy emphasis on change process, curriculum and instruction, and program evaluation, as well as teaching and staff development. A pattern of neglect in the categories of personnel evaluation and supervision of instruction is also quite clear.

ERIC Index Continuing abstracts of scholarly documents in education, the index published by the Educational Resources Information Center (ERIC) reflects an almost overwhelming amount and variety of the supervision related literature currently available. This ERIC Index includes a variety of kinds of documents, many unpublished but still available for review on microfiche. It is so broad in its coverage that the volumes almost defy detailed or comprehensive analysis. However, to ignore the scholarly work reflected in these volumes is to fail to understand adequately current thought and practice in the field of supervision of instruction.

For the purposes of highlighting the scholarly contents related to supervision of instruction, only cursory analyses of listing were undertaken and reported here. Two analyses were employed to gain some limited sense of the relationship of ERIC listings and supervisory inquiry. An array of subject headings were reviewed in the January–March 1994 volume. Within these subject headings, specific listed documents were selected by title for categorization as supervision relevant.

The subject headings that seemed to clearly contain listings of documents related to supervisory practice were:

- Change: implementation, teacher involvement, renewal, and restructuring.
- Consulting:
- Curriculum: design, development, evaluation, improvement, models, and planning.
- Evaluation: instructional, personnel, program and teacher.
- Group Process:
- Instructional: design, development, innovation, leadership, planning, and supervision.
- Leadership: development, growth, improvement, and training.
- Professional: development, growth, improvement, and training.
- Program: development, implementation, and improvement.
- School: improvement, leadership, and supervision.
- Staff: development, improvement.
- Supervision: instructional.

EXHIBIT 1–10. Themes, Features and Articles in Phi Delta Kappan: 1990–1994 by Supervisory Categories

Change Process	No. of Articles
• Reshaping Our Schools (January 1990)	2
• Learning in a Wired Nation: Bringing Schools on Line (October 1990)	5
• Networks for Educational Change (May 1992)	4
• The Politics of Educational Reform (December 1993)	4
• Redirecting Reform (March 1994)	5
• The Role of the Arts in Education (April 1992)	6
• Looking to the Future of Chapter 1 (April 1991)	6
• America 2000: A Series (November 1991)	4
• Restructuring and Education Reform (June 1990)	6
Total	42

Curriculum and Instruction	
• Youth Service (A Special Section) (June 1991)	10
• Multi-Cultural Education (September 1993)	6
• The Arts in Education (February 1994)	6
• The Rebirth of Vocational Education (February 1991)	7
Total	29

Evaluation of Personnel	
Total	0

Evaluation of Programs	
• Why Can' t They Be Like We Were? (October 1991)	4
• National Testing (November 1991)	6
• Accreditation for Schools (October 1993)	6
• Authentic Assessment: A Special Section (February 1993)	5
• Reflections on the Quality of American Education (April 1993)	8
Total	29

Leadership for Instruction	
• Leadership and Developing Leaders in Administration (March 1991)	6
• School Leadership: A Special Section (November 1993)	6
Total	12

Staff Development	
• Issues in Teacher Education (May 1991)	4
• Professional Development, Studying, Teaching, etc. (April 1994)	5
• Preliminary Findings for the Study of the Education of Educators (May 1990)	5
Total	14

Supervision of Instruction	
Total	0

Teaching and Teachers	
• Hands-on/Minds-on: Making Science Accessible (May 1990)	5
• The Middle Grades (February 1990)	6
• Learning to Read: The Never-Ending Debate (February 1992)	2
• Teaching the Children of Poverty (December 1991)	5
Total	18

With few exceptions, each of these numerous subheadings contained listings of documents with titles that indicated they contained supervision related information. A perusal of a variety of the abstracts of listed documents reveals the broad variety of literature contained in the microfiche. Some research reports, numerous unpublished papers and addresses, as well as project reports and program evaluations, are among those identified and categorized.

Exhibit 1.11 reports the frequency of listings of only a limited sample from a single volume. It cannot be estimated how representative this sample is of the mass of current documents made available by the ERIC system; however, it is clear that rather large numbers of documents are listed in supervisory categories. Once again, the key words utilized to categorize listings revealed somewhat limited documentation for personnel evaluation, leadership, and supervision by comparison with other supervisory categories.

National Commission Catalog The National Commission on Instructional Supervision published a report based on a nation-wide survey of school districts. Their Catalog of Polices Practices and Programs in Instructional Supervision (1986) represents, as of that date, the most authentic information available regarding actual supervisory practices in U.S. public schools. Each policy, practice, or program is reported separately in this document, providing brief demographic information about the district and descriptions of the focus of each. A total of 128 districts reported policies in 23 states ranging in size from 221 to 126,266 students. Practices were reported by 83 districts ranging in size from 221 to 440,000 students in 23 different states. Over 200 programs were similarly reported from 31 states in districts ranging in size from 453 to 198,000 students. For all three categories combined, a broad cross-section of U.S. school districts were represented, with notable exceptions in states such as Washington, New Mexico, Virginia, Vermont, Iowa, Delaware, and Arkansas.

Exhibit 1.12 shows the numbers of policies, practices, and programs reported in the catalog of instructional supervision by various school districts across the United States. Using key words to categorize these listings produced a pattern that indicated some attention, overall, to each of the major supervisory categories as might be expected. Heavy emphasis on personnel evaluation and supervision are departures from the emphases documented in most scholarly sources. The limited attention to program evaluation among policy, programs, and practice reports is interesting in contrast with heavy emphasis

EXHIBIT 1–11. A Limited Sample of ERIC Listings
by Supervisory Category, January–March, 1994

Supervisory Categories	No. of Listings
Change process	17
Curriculum and instruction	16
Evaluation of personnel	1
Evaluation of programs	10
Leadership for instruction	5
Staff development	27
Supervision	2
Teaching and teachers	22
Total sample	100

EXHIBIT 1–12. Polices, Practices, and Programs of Instructional Supervision Reported, 1985*

Supervisory Categories	Polices (N=128)	Practices (N=83)	Programs (N=119†)
Change process	0	0	0
	0%	0%	0%
Curriculum development	14	2	15
	11%	2%	12.5%
Evaluation of personnel	62	18	18
	48%	22%	15%
Evaluation of programs	1	2	2
	0.78%	2.4%	1.67%
Leadership for instruction	6	13	11
	5%	15%	9%
Staff development	13	13	38
	10%	15%	32%
Supervision of instruction	16	19	17
	12.5%	23%	14%
Teaching and teachers	6	14	18
	5%	17%	15%
	93%	96%	99%

* National Commission on Instructional Supervision (1985).

† Programs randomly sampled, using only one half of all listings.

‡ Some policies, practices, and programs not categorized as supervisory.

on personnel evaluation. Heavy emphasis on staff development programs makes this the dominant area reported.

Programs reported in this commission survey perhaps most clearly reflect the identifiable emphases of practitioners assembled almost a decade ago. A rather diverse array of efforts representing more than individual efforts or academic interests is seen. Some selected abbreviated titles of the 238 programs reported are:

Change Process (none)
• While not addressed specifically as programs, numerous listings refer to changes, improvements, revisions, and innovations.

Curriculum Development
• Central curriculum committee review.
• Curriculum workshops for special education.
• Individualized language arts.
• Instructional theory into practice.
• Monitoring the written, taught, tested program.
• The practice of piloting new programs.

Evaluation of Personnel
• Guidelines for teacher evaluation.
• Observation, evaluation system.
• Performance appraisal system.
• Performance-based teacher evaluation.

Evaluation of Programs
- Academic profile of school results.
- Competency-based testing program.
- Curriculum evaluation.

Leadership for Instruction
- Advanced supervision seminars.
- Future Elementary principal training.
- Improving leadership skills.
- Professional development academy.
- Secondary lead teachers.

Staff Development
- Advanced instructional methods.
- Comprehensive instructional improvement effort.
- Developing instructional skill excellence.
- Implementing comprehensive reading communications.

Supervision of Instruction
- Classroom clinical supervision.
- Clinical supervision training program.
- Consultant services in supervision.
- Improvement of instruction through supervision.
- Instructional supervision systems.

Teaching and Teachers
- Analysis of classroom instruction.
- Basic language arts skills monitoring.
- Effective teaching strategies.
- Teacher effectiveness through professional decision-making.
- Focus on questioning skills.

The emphasis on policies, practices and programs in supervisory categories in actual operation in U.S. public schools clearly suggests some departures from many scholarly and other forms of literature. This may be a consequence of time lag or perspective on what is important in this field. In either case, it raises some serious questions for scholar–practitioner consideration.

PARADIGM SHIFTS AND NEW PARAMETERS

The ways of viewing the field of supervision are shifting, as are the organizational–structural entities that shape instruction in schools. Supervisory practices are changing, and the supervisor's world of work is in flux. Research, theory, and program development must be responsive to such shifting, changing realities. It is also necessary, however, that scholarly endeavors help to guide, influence, and clarify for practitioners their alternatives and prospects for improving teaching and learning. In this section, some persistent issues, problems, and changing context that impinge on supervisory practice and research will be refocused. As a framework for this, the vision of fundamental restructuring of education will be presented,

providing the most extreme realities and far-reaching challenges for improving schooling as a basis for rethinking supervision.

The Challenge of Restructuring

More than a full half century has now passed since the excitement, fervor, promise, and controversy of the "progressive education movement" of the 1930s faded into history. This movement was a landmark and had enduring effects. As with other well-conceived, theoretically sound efforts for innovating and improving the character of schooling in America, failure of acceptance, adoption, or dissemination (Kirst & Meitser, 1985) often lead anew to even better-conceived efforts (Cuban, 1988: 86; Slavin, 1989). Each major wave of enthusiasm for educational change can offer new challenges to supervisors of instruction (Kagan, 1990).

The recurrent efforts for change in education seem to be irregular reflections of the accelerating, yet historically persistent, changes in the life of the nation. The curricular changes of the 1930s depression era were interrupted by war, but they left a legacy of kindergarten education, social studies, field trips, and much more. The spate of mathematics, science, foreign language, and related teaching innovations of the 1950s and 1960s (Shaplin & Olds, 1964) lacked durability over time, but they provided insights into the complexities of curricular change and set the stage for current efforts. The desegregation of schooling since 1954 and the restructuring of special education programs in the 1970s and 1980s are still in progress. The testing, accountability, summative teacher evaluations, and back-to-basics of the 1980s (Wayson et al, 1988) are further evidence of the persistent demands for change and improvement, even when approaches are ill advised. With few exceptions, pressures for and against changes in our schools over the past 50 years have focused on the improvement of teaching and learning, and they have not without both successes and failures (Harris & Monk, 1992: 46–49; Kliebard, 1992).

Supervisors of various kinds have presumably been intimately involved in virtually all of these change efforts in education that relate to teaching and learning (Almanza, 1980; Bailey, 1985; Berry & Ginsberg, 1990). If so, the high incidence of failure or demise of many sound instructional innovations is hardly an endorsement for continuing traditional supervision of instruction. On the other hand, many ill-conceived efforts also seem to fade away, perhaps with persistent instructional leadership always seeking a better way to help teaching and learning; however, a new and noisy chorus of criticisms, predictions of mediocrity, proposals, and visions for the future of our schools has emerged in the 1980s and 1990s. These new pressures for change suggest even more demanding roles for instructional supervisors. The social, economic, demographic, and political contexts are rapidly changing, and demands are more sweeping than ever before (Boyer, 1983; Woodring, 1983; Sizer, 1984; Lewis, 1989b; Comer, 1989; Shepard & Smith, 1989; Slavin, 1989; Cuban, 1990b; Kliebard, 1992). Darling-Hammond (1992: 13) reassures those who might be cynical that "we are at a point in our history where the reform movement is not going to fade away after a few years." It probably will "fade" and wane, and the return again. However, the challenge of instructional leadership is to take advantage of professional opportunities as they arise to promote the changes that best serve all students. In Fullan's terms, "the secret of growth and development is learning how to contend with the forces of change—turning positive forces to our advantage, while blunting negative ones" (1993: ii). Theory development and research appropriate to these demands are urgently needed.

Characterizing Restructuring

The new advocacies for change in education, and especially in teaching and learning, since the mid-1980s hardly made a harmonious chorus, but they tend to be different in character from many failed efforts of the past 50 or 60 years. The term restructuring means different things to particular advocates of technology integration (Kerr, 1990) on the one hand and those of site-base decision-making (Marburger, 1985) on the other, but both are calling for fundamental change in policy, regulation, funding, organization, curriculum, and teaching. It is, perhaps, these persistent and growing expressions of belief in radical and fundamental restructuring of education that gives excitement to the field of supervision when cynicism might be expected (Slavin, 1989). In the words of Garth Brooks, country music vocalist, "I would have missed the pain, but I'd a had to miss the dance." Supervisors of instruction will be required to go to the dance, get on the floor, and lead.

New emerging models of possibly better schools, programs, and learning outcomes all imply some break with the past or present, or both. In contrast with reforms and renewal efforts, restructuring implies that old paradigms controlling the critical features of educational programs in schools will be subject to radical and extensive alterations. Conley (1993) has provided one useful way of analyzing and projecting plans for restructuring. He identifies "dimensions" within which new structures or operational changes can take place. These include "learning outcomes," "curriculum," "time structure," "technology," and other dimensions discussed previously in this chapter in describing various models and programs.

Recurrent Themes In these most recent explorations into improving schooling, some themes seem persistent and appropriate to supervisory efforts. Leadership, visions for the future, technology applications, change process and systematic planning are widely advocated (Kaufman, 1991).

As might be expected, leadership is one of the recurring themes in the current movement toward restructuring. Teacher leadership is widely advocated (Rallis, 1990; Conley & Bacharach, 1990). Leadership for facilitation (Hall & Hord, 1987) and group consensus building are often emphasized (Patterson, 1993; Westheimer & Kahne, 1993), yet much of the emphasis on leadership is more broadly conceived as systemic change process (Wagner, 1993; Anderson, 1993; Schlechty, 1990). The concern for changes in governance is also being repeatedly emphasized (Cohen & Spillane, 1992; Raywid, 1990). Leithwood and Steinback (1993) conceptualize two dimensions of "total quality leadership" as "expertise" combined with "transformational practice," and argue that leadership for restructuring requires both. Glaser and Chi

(1988) have added to this renewed emphasis on expertise as a requirement for effective change. Yet the research literature in the field and much of the theoretical dialog give very little attention to the operational demands of either supervisory expertise or general leadership skills as applied to complex instructional transformations impinging on student, parents, vested interest and policy makers (Glickman, 1993).

Grand visions of twenty-first-century schooling are also common themes in the advocacy of restructuring. Slavin (1991) argues for a vision into "the next quarter century" that gives a strategic and developmental character to the processes of restructuring. Williams (1989) argues that our "authoritarian traditions" are in rapid decline and must be replaced by what Westheimer calls "school communities" (1993: 325). Another example of emphasis on visions unrestrained is the effort of the New American School Development Corporation (1991) in organizing a nationwide proposal writing competition for "Designs for a New Generation of American Schools." The requirements of leadership are in part visioning: "Leaders tell stories. . . . The truly innovative or visionary or transformational leader creates a new story and convinces individuals of its validity" (Siegel & Shaughnessy, 1984: 565).

Technology in education is clearly one of the major themes of restructuring in the present arena, even though the track record for audio–visual education in all of its previous forms has been poor (Kerr, 1989: 202–205; Cuban, 1985). The new emphases on electronic and computer-based technology with growing interest in hypermedia, interactivity, and networking (Dallat, 1992) are real; yet none of these show up as priority items in ASCD's (1994) survey on issues for 1994–1995.

A compelling analysis is provided of the "media revolution" and its electronic evolution as a pervasive force in society as well as in schools (Rogers, 1985; Rogers & Balle, 1986). Meanwhile, scholars and practitioners strive to sort out hype from promise in an atmosphere of intense commercial promotions. Teachers report media applications as one of their concerns (Cuban, 1985; Wedman, 1988: 51).

Change process and systematic planning are among the most extensively espoused and documented themes that relate to restructuring of schools and schooling. Cunningham (1982) and Bennis et al (1985) provide rather systematic guidelines for planning with change as the focus of attention. Fullan (1991) and Fullan and Stiegelbauer (1991), however, draw upon their analyses of decades of frustrating efforts to provide insights with direct supervisory implications. An older but somewhat provocative notion was offered by Alice Rivlin and P. M. Timpane (1975) as they reviewed Federal government efforts with some frustration. They criticize the widely held notion that progress is made if we "just try harder," tinkering with old solutions to new, more complex problem situations. Rivlin (1971) was one of the early advocates of systematic thinking, planning, and action for approaching such problems. Kaufman (1991) urges use of strategic planning in "restructuring," but thinking in curriculum planning (Glatthorn, 1994) remains quite traditional. Inbar's (1980) pleas for fuller use of systematic planning techniques is still valid and more urgent now. He argues for "analyzing and relating the mutual impact and linkages of various educational agencies on educational process, and being able to translate these into planning activities" (p. 388).

Societal Contexts for Restructuring

To advocate for dramatic changes in schooling requires a rationale of clear and urgent need. The need for extensive changes in schooling seems to derive from societal changes of the past and near-term future, as well as from the dramatic changes in the science and art of teaching that can now be utilized. The slow rate of acceptance of new practices, media, and content in schools and classrooms stands in sharp contrast to public acceptance of new drugs, appliances, cosmetics, fashions, and even community life. This slowness to change schooling has created more than a lag; indeed, it creates a wide chasm in many ways between what is needed, what is effective, and what is provided. Symptomatic of this chasm are the "National Goals" formulated by two administrations that have little to offer that will update an essentially nineteenth-century curriculum.

Changes in family structure, derived in part from women moving into the workforce, high divorce rates, and extensive acceptance of sexual freedoms with resultant escalation of demand for abortions (Hodgkinson, 1991a; Marriott, 1991; Rich, 1988), as well as child care and social services provide schools with new challenges in meeting student needs and redeveloping parent relationships (Lewis, 1994: 101).

Extensive suburbanization of housing and manufacturing in many parts of the nation have resulted in massive resegregation of neighborhoods and schools, and, also, concentrated poverty, urban decay, joblessness, and crime in central cities. Suburban American children are simultaneously insulated from cultural diversity and the world of work, while being abandoned to TV babysitting and sterile "care centers" with parents working far away. This tandem set of urban–suburban changes affects the vast majority of children and youth, creating "unteachable" situations by traditional standards in many classrooms (Hodgkinson, 1987). How does the school respond to meet the expanding needs of students in the absence of stable community life (Cunningham, 1990; Hodkinson, 1991b)?

Continuing industrialization over decades continues to have implications for change in schooling. The "motorization" of young people, the disappearance of summer work opportunities, the rising costs of both secondary and collegiate education for individuals, the long transition of years from high school to workforce acceptance, the dominance of mass media in the home via radio, television, and computer games, the pervasive influence of violence on the minds of children by exposure to war, crime, starvation, riots, and police brutality on a global scale are all continuing realities. The automation revolution that began with industrialized and mechanized farming in the 1940s and continues to the present with robotization of skilled manufacturing and clerical jobs. This has created chaos in vocational education circles and made unemployment and family bankruptcy a common experience. How do schools motivate and teach respect for work and promote career-related education under such circumstances?

Environmental questions also continue to loom large in America long after the Civilian Conservation Corps set out to restore our depleted forests, control soil erosion, and rebuild our national parks in the 1930s. Still, the "smog" problems of Los Angeles, and Houston continue, but they are joined by nuclear proliferation, destruction of the ozone layer in the atmosphere, oil spills across the oceans, and accelerating destruction of the forests and oceans on a global basis. Add the advanced decay in infrastructure and urban slum growth to our polluted globe. How does a nineteenth-century curriculum help the children of the twenty-first-century think intelligently about such staggering realities?

New capabilities for designing educational programs that serve students well are extremely promising, but they call for fundamental changes in curriculum (Apple & Beane, 1995; Boyer, 1990a and b; Slavin, 1991), school organization, health and human services, teaching, technology, community relationships, and policy. The very existence of a substantial body of unused professional knowledge and experience is a strong argument for rigorous restructuring efforts. Rich and exciting alternative curricula have been designed and tested, ranging from primary grade anthropology units to junior high school computer-based science (Texas Learning Technology Group, 1989) to simulated economics (Richmond, 1989 and 1990). Teaching practices have similarly been clearly researched for producing higher levels of learning and motivation in all students and areas of the curriculum (Gage, 1978), yet most are not in general use, while many outmoded practices persist on a large scale (Doyle, 1989). School organizational patterns (Carroll, 1994) that involve scheduling, nongradedness (Goodlad & Anderson, 1987), team teaching (English & Sharpes, 1972), interdisciplinary projects (Vasquez, 1993), work experience (Consortium on Youth Apprenticeships, 1990), and home–school relationships (Barrios, 1991; Rich, 1988) are but a few highly useful alternatives to common rigid structures. Policies that fly in the face of best-known professional practices are widespread and create persistent obstacles to quality education (Cardenas, 1995). Enlightened states and communities, however, have clearly demonstrated policies that work in reducing drop-out rates, minimizing discipline problems, and enhancing learning for all students.

Restructuring of schooling for high-quality learning requires attention to the full range of known and often neglected professional educational capabilities for change. Curriculum design and development, better teaching practices, integrated use of modern technology (Dede, 1989), and reorganizing to respond to needs and avoid bureaucratic rigidities are all essential to restructuring along with policy revisions that support and enhance the ongoing process.

New Systems and Practices

Schools as vitally important social institutions are also extremely complex in their operations, reflecting the enormity of their mission and the complexities of their changing, diverse communities (Gies & Gordon, 1991: 67–75; Swanson, 1993: 798). Improving instruction in realistic and fundamental ways calls for making dramatic changes, yet schooling must go on. This double barreled dilemma adds still more complexity to the educational change process. The school operation must change, but so must the larger society itself in expectations, support, and interactions. This complexity, however, is often utilized as an excuse for rejecting the more fundamental changes while opting for fads, simplistic "tinkering", and persisting with solution of the past (Argyris, 1982; Lewis, 1995; Rivlin, 1975).

The Realities of Change The complexities of educational change processes of restructuring proportions need to be more fully recognized and more clearly understood. It is a foregone conclusion that changes will occur in the years ahead. It is very likely that the changes will be more dramatic and involve major departures from traditions. Will these changes, however, reflect the needs of society now and for the future? Will they be well designed and implemented? Will they reflect the diversity of our nation? Will they assure the enhancement of local democratic control and still offer free, equitable, and appropriate education for children and youth? How can restructuring assure an emerging changing system of education consistent with the democratic traditions and still be more comprehensive, more responsible, more humane, and more efficient (Benne, 1990)? Misconceptions about the inevitability of "the future" and the desirability of all change can and should be rejected as supervisors give leadership, insisting upon thoughtful assessments of plausible, desirable alternative futures.

Demographic realities need to be taken into account in restructuring schooling for the twenty-first-century (Hodgkinson, 1989; Runkel, 1991: 178–179). The sheer size of the educational operation being restructured and the need to maintain an operating program while changing pose problems not to be taken lightly. Professional and lay persons alike tend to view education in the small dimensions of the local school, but in the aggregate the numbers are sometimes overwhelming. Is our society ready and able to make the sustained effort for fundamentally changing schools in 14,523 districts, in over 83,000 individual schools (NCES, 1995). Some three million teachers serve over 40 million students enrolled in our public schools at the present time (NCES, 1993: 7–8). Almost four million "newcomers" enter our kindergartens every fall. Restructuring that calls for curricular, teaching, organizational, and other changes will therefore impact directly perhaps 100 million people (e.g., students, staff, parents, and other officials) at any given time. Their values, concerns, needs, and interests must somehow be recognized and addressed. The urgent needs raise, however, serious questions about a "one school at a time" approach (Marburger, 1985). Criticism of "top down" change strategies provides clear warnings for supervisory practice, but do not give sufficient reason to continue equally failing efforts that rely on fragmented, uncoordinated approaches (Fullan, 1995). Michel's (1989–1990) review of the effects of a skilled and determined president makes clear both the power of national initiative in education as well as their limitations.

Mirvis' study (1991) of the adoption of new computer technologies on a massive scale in U.S. public and private offices warns of the importance of "a participatory change strategy coupled with extensive user training and support." The lesson to be learned is that neither top-down nor bottoms-up strategies are adequate when massive numbers of adopters, complex changes, and urgent needs characterize the situation facing leaders.

The human character of educational change reflects still other complexities, even at the school and classroom levels. In more mechanical operations and in more rigidly organized settings, undertaking restructuring has fewer complexities, but schooling is essentially a human enterprise. Everything we attempt to restructure directly affects students, teachers, and parents; in many instances bus drivers, cafeteria workers, and local businessmen are affected, too. Special features of this human reality of schooling are the long-established democratic and professional traditions of the common schools. Parents have rights, children have rights, teacher autonomy is to be respected, and the local community is rarely subservient to state or national authority. The interests of still other entities, however, are real and powerfully expressed by business leaders, governors, legislatures, and the Congress of the United States, not to mention the judiciary and churches. Restructuring in this context calls for leadership and strategic planning of the most intricate and skillful kinds (Inbar, 1980; Kaufman, 1991). Furthermore, restructuring must be viewed as a long-term continuing process, and not as response to a decision, edict, or blueprint (Carnegie Council on Adolescent Development, 1989). Mandates from the top down at any level are doomed to failure (Fullan, 1993: Barber, 1992: Cuban, 1990b; Schwartz, 1988); but local efforts and site-based decisions are not assured of easy success either. Both internal and external relationships are crucial to successful changes in school operations (Gies & Gordon, 1991: 74) that satisfy needs for quality education for all (Watt, 1989: 25).

Technical complexities abound in any innovative change effort, but school restructuring multiplies them as compared with reform and renewal. At even the simplest levels of change process, goals must be explicit; training provided; new elements of time, material, and space, arranged; trial efforts supported and monitored; feedback assured; reinforcement given; and new habit patterns established (Donahoe, 1993). When fundamental restructuring is being undertaken, these same elements of successful change are essential and necessarily tend to be amplified in both number and intensity. Goals tend to be more complex, necessarily more long-range, not as clearly defined, more difficult to communicate, and more threatening to sacred traditions as top priorities. Training requirements call for elaborate and continuous efforts ranging from basic skills development to emphasis on attitudes, values, and sophisticated departures from common practice. Evaluation, too, must be more elaborate and open-ended, with greater emphasis on involvement and feedback. All of these technical complexities for restructuring require longer time frames for implementation, often 20 or more years.

Third-Order Change Changes required for restructuring schools contrast sharply with the first- and second-order changes defined by Sarason (1990). These third-order changes are those that involve large-scale systemic, highly integrated changes. First-order changes generally refer to "reform" or "renewal" efforts. Desirable as they may be, they also run the risk of being inadequate in meeting needs—too little change and too late in effect—and they may be inefficient and costly.

Second-order changes are more fundamental, more dramatic shifts in program features or subsystem operations, but often fail in that new problem are created, leaving many closely related needs for improvements unmet.

Third-order changes focus on restructuring entire instructional systems and making either large or small change in related systems. Third-order change is necessarily cognizant of the many complexities discussed earlier, and plans to deal with them are required to enhance chances of success and assure institutionalization over time. Such restructuring changes involve staffing, decision-making, curriculum building, organizational restructuring, training and staff development, and operations research and evaluation. Such change seeks to assure relatively complete and long-term responses to the high priority needs of both students and society, drawing upon sophisticated forecasting techniques that offer more rationality and better alternatives. These kinds of changes can be more responsive to the emerging needs that are clearly recognizable or predictable. Such changes are necessarily more rigorously planned, involve many more people and institutions of various kinds and levels. Such planning and change implementation requires long time frames. They are also demanding of all kinds of supervisory expertise for their success.

Third-order changes that characterize restructuring in the most distinctive forms do not dictate the specific features of schooling for any community. On the contrary, like an educational erector set, the availability of sound theory, professional wisdom, and extensively tested innovative practices provide the "pieces" for constructing truly innovative schools for the twenty-first-century. Restructuring can provide alternatives to mandates, panaceas, back-to-basics, and pendular approaches. With vision and understanding of local needs, changes can be tailored to produce fundamental restructuring consistent with professional wisdom about the most promising shifts away from the status quo; yet, each model can be unique. Such new educational realities, however, will evolve, and not just emerge; they are fraught with difficulties calling for supervisory leadership of the most diverse, complex, and persistent kinds.

SUMMARY IMPLICATIONS

Supervision as a field of professional endeavor is here to stay, but that field is due to change substantially in the years ahead, just as will nearly all professional fields of practice. Supervision of instruction clearly comes in a diverse array of forms, with numerous models, roles, functions, and organizational structures. Efforts to simplify, narrow, restrict, or even eliminate this field are understandable, but they are hardly realistic or productive.

The unifying characteristics that make supervision a field in its own right are quite clearly reflected in a vast body of literature. Supervision is characteristically described as school related, emphasizing teaching, learning, and curriculum almost to the exclusion of larger contexts, even as change and improvements are stressed.

These traditional ways of viewing supervision in schools are still valid and useful, but they are clearly not sufficient. As the society and the schools are undergoing dramatic changes, the forms of supervisory practice must also change. As the school becomes more a part of the community (Decker, 1990), and less an isolated institution, so, too, will supervision need to become more communitywide in its focus and relationships (Dryfoos, 1994). As instructional programs and teaching be-come more experiential, multidisciplinary, and technology-supported, so, too, will supervision need to broaden its focus to embrace the entire learning environment in all its complexities. As changes are demanded, those in supervision will need to be both cautious critics resisting frivolous fads (Slavin, 1989), as well as promoters, designers, facilitators, coaches, and assessors. As the challenge of restructuring is faced squarely, supervisors will need to join teams and diversify their leadership roles.

Theory, practice, and research in the field of school supervision will need to focus more on relationships, processes, and structural outcomes and less on people, positions, and hierarchies. The current trends, which shift the focus from supervisor to principal, or from superordinate to peer, or from central staff to building staff (Watt, 1989; Glickman, 1993), almost certainly are missing the essence of necessary changes required to produce educational environments that are humane, responsive, effective, and capable of systematic renewal. A focus on relationships for effective supervision will consider whether the "right" leadership, at the "right" time, was included under the "right" circumstances. The focus on process for effective supervision will consider whether involvement is genuinely related to client needs, is directed by systematic problem solving, and adequately utilizes creative and professional expertise. The focus on structural outcomes for effective supervision will consider resultant changes in how work is carried on as well as its effects on learning. Supervision in pursuit of change must strive for institutionalization of designs for learning that are responsive to changing realities and needs. Schools that do not serve society's educational needs well are crippled and endangered. Supervisory leadership for high-quality, full-service responsiveness to the educational needs of all its children and youth is an essential function—a shared responsibility—not to be confused with business as usual.

REFERENCES

Almanza, H. K. (1980). *A study of in-service education programming associated with highly innovative programs in selected elementary schools.* Unpublished doctoral dissertation, The University of Texas at Austin, Austin.

Alpert, J. L. (1982). *Psychological consultation in educational settings.* San Francisco, CA: Jossey-Bass.

Anderson, B. L. (1993). The stages of systemic change. *Educational Leadership, 51,* 14–17.

Anderson, L. F. (1991). A rationale for global education. In K. A. Type (Ed.). *Global education: From thought to action.* Alexandria, VA: ASCD.

Anderson, R. H. (1989). A research agenda: Unanswered questions about the effect of supervision on teacher behavior. *Journal of Curriculum and Supervision, 4,* 291–297.

Argyris, C. (1982). *Reasoning, learning, and action: Individual and organizational.* San Francisco, CA: Jossey-Bass.

Aronson, E. (1978). *The jigsaw classroom.* Beverly Hills, CA: Sage Publications.

Association for Supervision and Curriculum Development. (1994a). *Mentoring: A multi-media training program.* Alexandria, VA: The Association.

Association for Supervision and Curriculum Development (1994b). *1994–1995 issues survey.* Alexandria, VA: The Association.

Austin America 2000 Proposal. (1992). *Building a comprehensive learning community: An America 2000 proposal to design a new generation of American schools.* Austin, TX: Austin Independent School District.

Ayer, F. C. (1954). *Fundamentals of instructional supervision.* New York: Harper and Brother Publishers.

Bales, R. F. (1950). *Interaction process analysis—a method for the study of small groups.* Cambridge, MA: Addison-Wesley.

Bailey, D. (1985). *Relationships among supervisor competencies, job expectations, and position types.* Unpublished doctoral dissertation, The University of Texas at Austin, Austin.

Bailey, G. D. (1979). Maximizing the potential of the videotape recorder in teacher self-assessment. *Educational Technology, 19,* 39–44.

Banathy, B. H. (1968). *Instructional systems.* Palo Alto, CA: Fearon Publishers.

Banks, J. (1991/2). Multicultural education: For freedom's sake. *Educational Leadership, 49,* 32–36.

Barber, B. R. (1992). *The aristocracy of everyone: The politics of education and the future of America.* New York: Ballantine Books.

Barr, A. S., Burton, W. H., & Brueckner, L. J. (1938). *Supervision: Principals and practices in the improvement of instruction.* New York: D. Appleton-Century.

Barr, A. S., Burton, W. H., & Brueckner, L. J. (1947). *Supervision: Democratic leadership in the improvement of learning* (2nd ed.). New York: Appleton, Century-Crofts.

Barrios, J. (1991). Family PACT: Sunnyside program educates both parents and children. *Tucson Citizen,* (November 23), Schools Section.

Barth, R. (1990). *Improving schools from within: Teachers and parents can make the difference.* San Francisco, CA: Jossey-Bass, Inc.

Benne, K. D. (1990). *The task of post-contemporary education: Essays in behalf of a human future.* New York: Teachers' College, Columbia University.

Bennis, W., et al., Eds. (1985). *The planning of change.* (4th ed.). New York: Holt, Rinehart and Winston.

Berkowitz, N. H. & Bennis, W. G. (1961). Interaction patterns in formal service-oriented organizations. *Administrative Science Quarterly, 6,* 25–50.

Berman, L. M. & Usery, M. L. (1966). *Personalized supervision: Sources and insights.* Washington, D.C.: ASCD.

Berry, B. & Ginsberg, R. (1990). Effective schools, teachers, and principals: Today's evidence, tomorrow's prospects. In B. Mitchell & L. L. Cunningham (Eds.). *Educational leadership and changing contexts of families, communities, and schools* (89th Yearbook of the National Society for the Study of Education, Part II). Chicago, IL: University of Chicago Press.

Blacklock, C. L. (1978). *Professional staffing practices related to functional practices, district characteristics, and instructional innovations.* Unpublished doctoral dissertation, The University of Texas at Austin, Austin.

Blankstein, A. M. & Swain, H. (1994). Is TQM right for schools? *The Executive Educator, 16,* 51–54.

Blumberg, A. (1968). Supervisory behavior and interpersonal relations. *Educational Administration Quarterly, 4,* 34–45.

Blumberg, A. (1984). *Report of the association for supervision and curriculum development committee on central office supervision.* VA: ASCD.

Bolin, F. (1987). Perspectives and imperatives: On defining supervision. *Journal of Curriculum and Supervision, 2,* 368–380.

Books in Print, 1993–1994. (1993). New Providence, NJ: R. R. Bowker, Reed Publishing Inc.

Boyan, N. J. & Copeland, W. D. (1978). *Instructional supervision training program.* Columbus, OH: Charles E. Merrill.

Boyer, E. (1983). *High school: A report on secondary education in America.* New York: Harper and Row.

Boyer, E. (1990a). Civic education for responsible citizens. *Educational Leadership, 48,* 4–7.

Boyer, E. L. (1990b). What to teach and how to teach it, and to whom. In S. B. Bacharach (Ed.). *Education reform: Making sense of it all.* Needham Heights, MA: Allyn and Bacon, Inc.

Browdy, H. S. (1981). Between the Yearbooks. In J. F. Soltis (Ed.). *Philosophy and education* (80th Yearbook of the National Society for the Study of Education, Part I). Chicago, IL: University of Chicago Press.

Buttery, T. J. (1988). Group clinical supervision as a feedback process. *Journal of Research and Development in Education, 2,* 5–12.

Candoli, C. I. (1991). *School system administration: A strategic plan for site-based management.* Lancaster, PA: Technomic Publishing Co.

Cantor, N. (1951). *Learning through discussion.* Buffalo, NY: Human Relations for Industry.

Cardenas, J. A. (1995). *Multi-cultural education: A generation of advocacy.* Needham Heights, MA: Simon and Schuster Custom Publishing.

Carlsen, W. S. (1991). Questioning in classrooms: A sociolinguistic perspective. *Review of Educational Research, 61(2),* 157–178.

Carnegie Council on Adolescent Development. (1989). *Turning points: Preparing American youth for the 21st century.* New York: Carnegie Corporation.

Carroll, J. (1989). *The Copernican plan: Restructuring the American high school.* Andover, MA: The Regional Laboratory for Educational Improvement of the Northeast.

Carroll, J. M. (1994). The Copernican plan evaluated: The evolution of a revolution. *Phi Delta Kappan, 76,* 105–113.

Cervera, N. J. (1990). Community agencies in schools: Interlopers or colleagues? *Social Work in Education, 12,* 118–133.

Champagne, D. W. & Hogan, R. C. (1981). *Consultant supervision: Theory and skill development.* Wheaton, IL: CH Publications.

Cogan, M. L. (1973). *Clinical supervision.* Boston, MA: Houghton Mifflin.

Chrisco, I. M. (1989). Peer assistance works. *Educational Leadership, 46,* 31–32.

Cohen, A. C. (1976). *The service society.* New York: College for Human Services.

Cohen, A. C. (1978). The citizen as integrating agent. *Rockville, MD: Department of HEW, Human Services Amongraph, Series 9,* (September).

Cohen, A. C. (1990). Giving purpose and cohesion to learning through service. *Education Week,* (November 28), 21, 22, 32.

Cohen, M. (1988). *Restructuring the education system: Agenda for the 1990's.* Washington, D.C.: National Governor's Association.

Cohen, D. K. & Spillane, J. P. (1992). Policy and practice: The relations between governance and instruction. *Review of Research in Education.* Washington, D.C.: American Educational Research Association.

Comer, J. P. (1980). *School power: Implications of an intervention project.* New York: Free Press.

Comer, J. P. (1989). *A conversation between James Comer and Ronald Edmonds: Fundamentals of effective school improvement.* Dubuqe, IA: Kendall/Hunt Publishing Co.

Conley, D. & Bacharach, S. (1990). From school-site management to participatory school-site management. *Phi Delta Kappan, 71,* 539–544.

Conley, D. T. (1993). *Roadmap to restructuring: Policies, practices, and the emerging visions of schooling.* Eugene, Oregon: ERIC Clearinghouse on Educational Management, University of Oregon.

Conley, S. et al. (1995). Teacher mentoring and peer coaching: A micro-political interpretation. *Journal of Personnel Evaluation in Education, 9,* 7–19.

Consortium on Youth Apprenticeships. (1990). *Youth apprenticeships, American style: A strategy for expanding school and career opportunities.* Washington, D.C.: The Consortium.

Costa, A. L. & Garmston, R. J. (1993). *Cognitive coaching: A foundation for renaissance schools.* Norwood, MA: Christopher-Gordon Publishers, Inc.

Crooks, T. J. (1988). The impact of classroom evaluation practices on students. *Review of Educational Research, 58,* 438–481.

Cuban, L. (1985). *Teachers and machines: The classroom use of technology since 1920.* New York: Teachers, College, Columbia University.

Cuban, L. (1990a). Four stories about national goals for American education. *Phi Delta Kappan, 72,* 265–271.

Cuban, L. (1990b). Reforming again, again, and again. *Educational Researcher, 19,* 3–13.

Cunningham, L. L. (1990). Educational leadership and administration: Retrospective and prospective views. In B. Mitchell & L. L. Cunningham (Eds.). *Educational leadership and changing contexts of families, communities, and schools* (89th Yearbook of the National Society for the Study of Education, Part II). Chicago, IL: The University of Chicago Press.

Cunningham, W. G. (1982). *Systematic planning for educational change.* Palo Alto, CA: Mayfield Publishing Co.

Dallat, J. et al. (1992). Expectations and practice in the use of video conferencing for teaching and learning: An evaluation. *Research in Education (Canada), 48,* 92–102.

Darling-Hammond. (1992). Perestroika and professionalism: The case for restructuring teacher preparation. *Excellence in Teacher Education: Helping Develop Learner-Centered Schools.* NEA School Restructuring Series. Washington, D.C.: National Education Association.

Davies, I. K. & Shane, H. G. (1986). Educational implications of microelectronic networks. In J. A. Culbertson & L. L. Cunningham (Eds.), *MicroComputers and Education* (85th Yearbook, National Society for Study of Education Part I). Chicago, IL: University of Chicago Press.

Decker, L. E. & Associates. (1990). *Community education: Building learning communities.* Alexandria, VA: National Community Education Association.

Dede, C. (1989). The evolution of information technology: Implication for curriculum. *Educational Leadership, 47,* 23–26.

DeKalb County Schools. (1975). *Performance-based certification: Supportive supervision model.* Doraville, GA: DeKalb County Schools.

DelVal, P. B. & Griffin, C. L. (1987). Implementing the clinical supervision process in special education. *Special Services in the Classroom, 4*(1/2), 17–33.

Deming, W. E. (1993). *The new economics of industry, government, and education.* Cambridge, MA: MIT Center for Advanced Engineering Study.

Dewey, J. (1916). *Democracy and education.* New York: Macmillan Co.

Donahoe, T. (1993). Finding the way: Structure, time, and culture in school improvement. *Phi Delta Kappan, 75,* 298–305.

Doyle, R. P. (1989). The resistance of conventional wisdom to research evidence: The case of retention. *Phi Delta Kappan, 71,* 215–220.

Doyle, D. (1991). America 200. *Phi Delta Kappan, 73,* 185–191.

Dryfoos, J. G. (1994). *The full-service school.* San Francisco, CA: Jossey-Bass.

Dunkin, M. J., Ed. (1987). *The international encyclopedia of teaching and teacher education.* Oxford: Pergamon Press.

Durant, W. (1939). *The life of Greece.* NY: Simon and Schuster.

Eisner, E. (1984). Can educational research inform educational practice? *Phi Delta Kappan, 68,* 447–452.

Eisner, E. (1990). Who decides what schools teach? *Phi Delta Kappan, 71,* 523–526.

Ellis, E. et al. (1979). Peer observation: A means for supervisory acceptance. *Educational Leadership, 36,* 423–426.

English, F. W. & Sharpes, K. K. (1972). *Strategies for differentiated staffing.* Berkeley, CA: McCutchan Publishing Corp.

Everett, S., Ed. (1938). *The community school.* New York: D. Appleton-Century Co.

Eylon, B. & Linn, M. C. (1988). Learning and instruction: An examination of four perspectives in science education. *Review of Educational Research, 59,* 251–301.

Far West Lab. (1978). *Institutionalization of change.* Berkeley, CA: Far West Laboratory for Educational Development.

Fessler, R. & Burke, P. J. (1987). Are you doing inquiry along these lines? Systematic appraisal of teacher performance: A conceptual supervision-staff development model. *Journal of Curriculum and Supervision, 2,* 381–389.

Feverberg, L. (1989). Communication: Key to the productivity doorway. *Journal of Organizational Communication, 10,* 3–5.

Feyereisen, K. Y. et al. (1970). *Supervision and curriculum renewal: A systems approach.* New York: Appleton-Century-Crofts.

Flanders, N. A. (1970). *Analyzing teaching behavior.* Reading, MA: Addison-Wesley.

Flexner, S. B., Ed. (1987). *The Random House dictionary of the English language.* (2nd ed. unabridged). New York: Random House Inc.

Franseth, J. (1961). *Supervision as leadership.* Evanston, IL: Row, Peterson, and Company.

Freedman, S. & Negroni, P. J. (1992). School and community working together: Community education in Springfield. In L. E. Decker & V. A. Romney (Eds.). *Educational restructuring and the community education process.* Alexandria, VA: National Community Education Association.

Friant, Ray J. Jr. (1983). *Preparing effective presentations: How to make presentations payoff.* Babylon, NY: Pilot Industries, Inc.

Friedlander, M. S. (1972). *Leading film discussions: A guide to using films for training discussion leaders, planning effective programs.* New York: Leagues of Women Voters, City of New York.

Fullan, M. (1982). *The meaning of educational change.* New York: Teachers College Press.

Fullan, M. (1991). *The new meaning of educational change.* New York: Teachers College Press.

Fullan, M. (1993). *Change forces probing the depths of educational reform.* New York: The Falmer Press.

Fullan, M. (1995). Coordinating top-down and bottom-up strategies for educational reform. In R. J. Anson (Ed.). *Systemic reform: Perspectives on personalizing education.* Washington, D.C.: Office of Educational Research and Improvement, U.S. Dept. of Education (September), 7–22.

Fullan, M. & Stiegelbauer, S. (1991). *The meaning of educational change.* (2nd ed.). Toronto: Ontario Institute for Studies in Education.

Gage, N. L. (1978). *The scientific basis of the art of teaching.* New York: Teachers College Press, Columbia University.

Gall, M. D. (1970). The use of questions in teaching. *Review of Educational Research, 40,* 707.

Gall, M. D. & Gall, J. (1976). The discussion method. In N. L. Gage (Ed.). *The psychology of teaching methods* (75th Yearbook, Part I). Chicago, IL: National Society for the Study of Education.

Gall, M. D. & Renechler, R. S. (1985). *Effective staff development for teachers: A research-based model.* Eugene, OR: Clearinghouse on Educational Management, College of Education, University of Oregon.

Gallessich, J. (1982). *The profession and practice of consultation.* San Francisco, CA: Jossey-Bass.

Galloway, C. M. (1974). Nonverbal teacher behavior: A critique. *American Educational Research Journal, 11,* 305–306.

Gant, J. et al. (1977). *Temporary systems.* Tallahassee, FL: Florida State University.

Gies, F. & Gordon, W. M. (1991). Collaborative School University Renewal Project. *National Forum of Educational Administration and Supervision Journal, 7(3),* 67–75.

Glaser, R. & Chi, M. (1988). Overview. In M. Chi et al. (Eds.). *The nature of expertise.* Hillsdale, NJ: Lawrence Erlbaum.

Glasser, W. (1990). *The quality school: Managing students without coercion.* New York: Harper and Row.

Glatthorn, A. A. (1984). *Differentiated supervision.* Alexandria, VA: ASCD.

Glatthorn, A. (1987). Cooperative professional development: Peer centered options for teacher growth. *Educational Leadership, 45,* 31–35.

Glatthorn, A. A. (1990). *Supervisory leadership: Introduction to instructional supervision.* Glenview, IL: Scott, Foresman and Company.

Glatthorn, A. A. (1994). *Developing a quality curriculum.* Alexandria, VA: ASCD.

Glickman, C. (1990). *Developmental supervision.* Boston, MA: Allyn and Bacon, Inc.

Glickman, C. (1991). Pretending not to know what we know. *Educational Leadership, 48,* 4–9.

Glickman, C. (1992). *Supervision in transition.* Alexandria, VA: ASCD.

Gliessman, D. H. et al. (1988). Variables influencing the acquisition of a generic teaching skill. *Review of Educational Research, 58,* 25–40.

Goldhammer, R. (1969). *Clinical supervision: Special methods for the supervision of teachers.* New York: Holt, Rinehart and Winston.

Goldhammer, R. et al. (1980). *Clinical supervision: Special methods for the supervision of teachers.* Boston, MA: Holt, Rinehart, and Winston.

Goldhammer, R. (1992). The Robert Goldhammer papers: Early writings of a distinguished educator. A Publication of the Council of Professors of Instructional Supervision. Tampa, FL: Pedamorphosis, Inc. (Spring).

Golembiewski, R. T. & Blumberg, A., Eds. (1977). *Sensitivity training and the laboratory approach: Readings about concepts and applications* (3rd ed.). Itasca, IL: F. E. Peacock.

Good, T. & Brophy, J. (1987). *Looking in classrooms.* (2nd ed.). New York: Harper and Row.

Goodlad, J. & Anderson, R. (1987). *The non-graded elementary school.* New York: Teachers College, Columbia University.

Gordon, I. J. (1968). A model for curriculum development decision-making. In I. J. Gordon (Ed.). *Criteria for Theories of Instruction.* Washington, D.C.: ASCD.

Gorton, Ri. A. et al, Eds. (1988). *Encyclopedia of school administration and supervision.* Phoenix, AZ: The Oryx Press.

Grant, C. A., Ed. (1981). Staff development: State of the scene and possibilities. *Journal of Research and Development in Education, 14*(Winter).

Grant, G. (1988). *The world we created at Hamilton High.* Cambridge, MA: Harvard University Press.

Hagen, N. J. (1981). A comparative analysis of selected in-service education delivery systems. Unpublished doctoral dissertation, The University of Texas at Austin, Austin.

Hall, G. & Loucks, S. (1978). Teacher concerns as a basis for facilitating and personalizing staff development. *Teachers College Record, 80,* 36–53.

Hall, G. et. al. (1987). *Taking charge of change.* Alexandria, VA: ASCD.

Hall, G. E. & Hord, S. M. (1984). *Change in schools: Facilitating the process.* Albany, NY: State University of New York Press.

Hallinger, Phillip et al. (1992). Restructuring schools: Principals' perceptions of fundamental education reform. *Educational Administration Quarterly, 28,* 330–49.

Haroutunian-Gordon, S. (1989). Socrates as teacher. In P. W. Jackson & S. Harwoutunian-Gordon (Eds.). *From Socrates to software: The teacher as text and the text as teacher* (89th Yearbook, National Society for the Study of Education, Part I). Chicago, IL: University of Chicago Press.

Harris, B. M. (1963). *Supervisory behavior in education* (1st ed.). Englewood Cliffs, NJ: Prentice Hall.

Harris, B. M. Ed. (1974). *Professional supervisory competencies.* Document #7, Special Education Supervisor Training Project. Austin, TX: The University of Texas at Austin (June).

Harris, B. M. (1984). A diagnostic model of teaching performance. *Thresholds in Education, 10,* 11–16.

Harris, B. M. (1985). *Supervisory behavior in education* (3rd ed.). Englewood Cliffs, NJ: Prentice Hall.

Harris, B. M. (1986). *Developmental teacher evaluation.* Boston, MA: Allyn and Bacon, Inc.

Harris, B. M. (1987). Resolving old dilemmas in diagnostic evaluation. *Educational Leadership, 44,* 46–49.

Harris, B. M. (1989). *In-service education for staff development.* Boston, MA: Allyn and Bacon.

Harris, B. M. & Bessent, E. W. (1969). *In-service education: A guide to better practice.* Englewood Cliffs, NJ: Prentice Hall.

Harris, B. M. & Hill, J. (1982). *Developmental teacher evaluation kit* (DeTEK). Austin, TX: Southwest Educational Development Laboratory.

Harris, B. M. & Monk, B. J. (1992). *Personnel administration in education* (3rd ed.). Needham Heights, MA: Allyn and Bacon Inc.

Harris, B. M. & Ovando, M. N. (1992). Collaborative supervision: Special application to developmental evaluation of teaching. *SANNYS Journal, 23,* 12–18.

Harrison, R. H. (1968). *Supervisory leadership in education.* New York: American Book Co.

Harrow, A. J. (1972). *A taxonomy of the psychomotor domain.* New York: McKay.

Hawkins, V. J. (1991). The social reconstruction wedge: A model for restructuring curriculum. *Journal of Curriculum and Supervision, 6,* 366–369.

Hills, J. (1991). Issues in research on instructional supervision: A contribution to the discussion. *Journal of Curriculum and Supervision, 7,* 1–12.

Hodgkinson, H. L. (1987). Changing society: Unchanging curriculum. *National Forum, 22(3),* 8-11.

Hodgkinson, H. L. (1989). *The same client: The demographics of education and service delivery systems.* Washington, D.C.: Institute for Educational Leadership.

Hodgkinson, H. L. (1991a). *Beyond the schools: How schools and communities must collaborate to solve the problems facing America's youth* (Part I). Arlington, VA: American Association of School Administrators and National School Boards Association.

Hodgkinson, H. L. (1991b). Education reform versus reality, Part I. In *Beyond the schools.* Arlington, VA: American Association of School Administrators and National School Boards Association.

Holt, M. (1993). The educational consequences of W. Edwards Deming. *Phi Delta Kappan, 75.*

Hopkins, D. (1993). *A teachers guide to classroom research* (2nd ed.). Buckingham, England: Open University Press.

Howey, K. R. & Vaughan, J. C. (1982). Current patterns of staff development. In G. Griffin (Ed.). *Staff development* (82nd Yearbook, National Society for the Study of Education. Part II). Chicago, IL: University of Chicago Press.

Idstein, P. (1993). Swimming against the mainstream. *Phi Delta Kappan, 75,* 336–340.

Inbar, D. E. (1980). Educational planning: A review and a plea. *Review of Educational Research, 50,* 377–392.

Johnson, D. W. & Johnson, R. T. (1987). *Learning together and alone: Cooperative, competitive, and individualistic learning.* Englewood Cliffs, NJ: Prentice Hall.

Johnson, D. W., Johnson, R. T. & Holubec, E. J. (1991). *Cooperation in the classroom* (rev. ed.). Edina, MN: Interaction Book Co.

Joyce, B. & Showers, B. (1983). *Power of research on training for staff development.* Alexandria, VA: ASCD.

Joyce, B. R. (1986). *Improving America's schools.* New York: Longman, Inc.

Joyce, B. R. & Weil, M. (1986). *Models of teaching* (3rd ed.). Englewood Cliffs, NJ: Prentice Hall.

Kagan, S. (1990). Readiness 2000: Rethinking rhetoric and responsibility. *Phi Delta Kappan, 72,* 272–279.

Kaplan, D. (1980). Feedback: Using video to measure teacher performance. In *Video in the classroom: A guide to creative television.* White Plains, NY: Knowledge Industry Publications, Inc.

Kaufman, R. (1991). *Strategic planning in education: Rethinking, restructuring, revitalizing.* Lancaster PA: Techonomic Publishing Company, Inc.

Kelley, E. C. (1951). *The workshop way of learning.* New York: Harper.

Keedy, J. L. (1994). Ten critical research questions in instructional supervision. *Instructional Supervision AERA/SIG, 14,* 4–5, 7.

Kerr, S. T. (1989). Pale screens: Teachers and electronic texts. In P. Jackson & S. Haroutunian-Gordonin (Eds.). *From socrates to software: Teacher as text and text as teacher* (88th Yearbook of the National Society for the Study of Education, Part I). Chicago, IL: University of Chicago Press.

Kerr, S. T. (1990). Alternative technologies as textbooks, and the social imperatives of educational change. In D. L. Elliott & A. Woodward (Eds.). *Textbooks and schooling in the U.S.* (89th Yearbook of the National Society for the Study of Education, Part I). Chicago, IL: University of Chicago Press.

Kipfer, B. A. (1992). *Roget's 21st century thesaurus in dictionary form.* New York: Dell Publishing.

Kirst, M. & Meister, G. (1985). Turbulence in America's secondary schools – what reforms last? *Curriculum Inquiry, 15,* 169–186.

Kliebard, H. M. (1992). *Forging the American curriculum essays in curriculum history and theory.* NY: Routledge, Chapman, and Hall, Inc.

Knowles, M. S. & Associates. (1984). *Angragogy in action.* Berkeley, CA: Jossey-Bass.

Krey, R. D. & Burke, P. J. (1989). *A design for instructional supervision.* Springfield, IL: Charles C. Thomas, Publisher.

Krug, S. (1992). Instructional leadership: A constructivist perspective. *Educational Administration Quarterly, 28,* 430–443.

Lawrence, G. et al. (1974). *Patterns of effective in-service education.* Gainesville, FL: College of Education, University of Florida.

Leithwood, K. & Steinbach, R. (1993). Total quality leadership: Expert thinking plus transformational practice. *Journal of Personnel Evaluation in Education, 7,* 311–317.

Lewis, A. C. (1989a). A box full of tools but no blueprint. *Phi Delta Kappan, 71(3),* 180–181.

Lewis, A. (1989b). *Restructuring America's schools.* Arlington, VA: American Association of School Administrators.

Lewis, A. C. (1994). Washington commentary: On the road to reform. *Phi Delta Kappan, 76,* 100–101.

Lynch, P. (1979). Prompt cards end those transparency fumbles. *Training/HRD, 16,* 34, 36.

McGrath, J. E. (1984). *Groups: Interaction and performance.* Englewood Cliffs, NJ: Prentice Hall.

McGreal, T. L. (1982). Effective teacher evaluation systems. *Educational Leadership, 39,* 903–905.

McGreal, T. L. (1983). *Successful teacher evaluation.* Alexandria, VA: ASCD.

McKenzie, J. L., Ed. (1975). *Webster's new twentieth century dictionary of the English language* (2nd ed. unabridged). New York: Collins-Word Publishing Co.

McLuhan, M. (1984). *Understanding media: The extensions of man.* New York: McGraw-Hill Book Co.

McNeil, L. (1988). Contradictions of control, Part I: Administrators and teachers. *Phi Delta Kappan, 70,* 334.

McNeil, L. (1990). Reclaiming a voice: American curriculum scholars and the politics of what is taught in school. *Phi Delta Kappan, 71,* 517–518.

McNeil, W. & Sedlar, J. W. (1970). *Classical China.* New York: Oxford University Press.

Maier, N. R. & Hoffman R. (1965). Acceptance and quality of solutions as related to leaders: Attitudes toward disagreements in group problem-solving. *Journal of Applied Behavioral Science, 1,* 373–386.

Manolakes, T. (1975). The advisory system and supervision. In T. J. Sergiovanni (Ed.). *Professional supervision for professional teachers.* Washington, D.C.: ASCD.

Marburger, C. (1985). *One school at a time—school based management.* Columbia, MD: National Committee for Citizens in Education.

Marriott, M. (1991). When parents and children go to school together. (August 21) *The New York Times,* National Edition, CXL.

Meckelenburger, J. A. (1992). The braking of the break-the mold express. *Phi Delta Kappan, 74,* 280–289.

Medley, D. et al. (1984). *Measurement based evaluation of teacher performance: An empirical approach.* New York: Longman.

Melnik, M. A. & Sheehan, D. S. (1976). Clinic to improve university teaching. *Journal of Teacher Education, 19,* 145–174.

Michel, G. J. (1989-1990). Educational reform by the president and the task forces of the Johnson administration. *National Forum of Applied Educational Research Journal, 3,* 60–65.

Miklos, E. (1991). Trends in doctoral research in educational administration. *The Alberta Journal of Educational Research, 37,* 297–321.

Milner, J. O. (1991). Suppositional style and teacher evaluation. *Phi Delta Kappan, 72,* 464–467.

Milroy, E. (1982). *Role-play: A practical guide.* Aberdeen: Aberdeen University Press.

Mirvis, Philip et al. (1991). The implementation and adoption of the new technology in organizations. *Human Resource Management, 30,* 113–139.

Mitchell, B. & Cunningham, L. L. (1990). *Educational leadership and changing contexts of families, communities, and schools* (89th Yearbook of the National Society for the Study of Education, Part II.) Chicago, IL: University of Chicago Press.

Mosenthal, J. H. & Ball, D. L. (1992). Constructing new forms of technology: Subject matter knowledge in in-service teacher education. *Journal of Teacher Education, 43,* 547–556.

Mouton, J. S. & Blake, R. R. (1984). *Synergogy: A new strategy for education, training, and development.* San Francisco, CA: Jossey-Bass.

Murphy, J. (1990). *The educational reform movement of the 1980's: Perspectives and cases.* Berkeley, CA: McCuthcan Publishing Corp.

National Center for Education Statistics. (1993). *Schools and staffing in the United States: Selected data for public and private schools, 1990-1991.* Washington, D.C.: U.S. Department of Education, Office of Educational Research and Improvement, NCES 93-453.

National Center for Education Statistics. (1994). *Statistics in brief: Public school student, staff, and graduate counts by state: School year 1992-1993*. Washington, D.C.: U.S. Department of Education, Office of Research and Improvement, NCES 94-104.

National Center for Education Statistics. (September 1995). *Statistics in brief. Overview of public elementary and secondary school districts: School year 1993-1994*. Washington, D.C.: Office of Educational Research and Improvement, U.S. Dept. of Education.

National Commission on Children. (1991). *Beyond rhetoric: A new American agenda for children and families*. Washington, D.C.: National Commission on Children.

National Commission on Instructional Supervision. (1986). *Catalog of policies, practices and programs in instructional supervision*. Alexandria, VA: An Unofficial Publication of the Association for Supervision and Curriculum Development.

National Study of School Evaluation, Pace, V. D. (1986). *Evaluative criteria for the evaluation of secondary schools* (6th Edition). Falls Church, VA: The National Study of School Evaluation.

Neubert, G. A. & Bratton, E. C. (1987). Team coaching: Staff development side by side. *Educational Leadership, 44*, 29–32.

Neuman, C. E. (1961). In-service education through demonstration teaching. *Journal of Secondary Education, 36*, 20–22.

New American Schools Development Corporation. (1991). *Designs for a new generation of american schools: Request for proposals*. Arlington, VA: New American Schools Development Corp.

Office of Educational Research and Improvement. (1991). *Youth indicators 1991: Trends in the well-being of American youth*. Washington, D.C.: Department of Education, U.S. Government Printing Office.

Oliva, P. F. (1989). *Supervision for today's schools* (3rd ed.). New York: Longman.

O'Neil, J. (1993). On systemic reform: A conversation with Marshall Smith. *Educational Leadership, 51*, 12–13.

Ouchi, W. G. (1981). Appendix 2: Quality circles. In *Theory Z: How American business can meet the Japanese challenge*. Reading, MA: Addison-Wesley.

Ovando, M. N. & Harris, B. M. (1993). Teacher's perceptions of the post-observation conference: Implications for formative evaluation. *Journal of Personnel Evaluation in Education, 7*, 301–310.

Pajak, E. (1989a). A report on the nationwide survey of outstanding supervisors and university professors. A Paper presented at the Annual Meeting of the Council of Professors of Instructional Supervision, Pennsylvania State University.

Pajak, E. (1989b). *The central office supervisor of curriculum and instruction: Setting the stage for success*. Boston, MA: Allyn and Bacon, Inc.

Pajak, E. (1989c). *Identification of supervisory proficiencies project*. Athens, GA: University of Georgia.

Passmore, W. A. (1992). *Sociotechnical systems design for total quality*. San Francisco, CA: Organizational Consultants, Inc.

Patterson, J. L. (1993). *Leadership for tomorrow's schools*. Alexandria, VA: ASCD.

Paiget, J. (1963). *The origins of intelligence*. New York: W.W. Norton and Co.

Policy Information Center. (1990). *From school to work*. Princeton, NJ: Educational Testing Service.

Quinto, F. & McKenna, B. (1977). *Alternatives to standardized testing*. Washington, D.C.: National Education Association.

Ragwid, M. A. (1990). Rethinking school governance. In Elmore (Ed.). *Restructuring school*. San Francisco, CA: Jossey Bass.

Rallis, S. F. (1990). Professional teachers and restructured schools: Leadership challenges. In B. Mitchell & L. L. Cunningham (Eds.). *Educational leadership and changing contexts of families, communities, and schools* (89th Yearbook of the National Society for the Study of Education, Part II). Chicago, IL: University of Chicago Press.

Rathbone, C. (1993). A multiage perspective from the writings of Lev Vygotsky. *Multiage portraits: Teaching and learning in mixed-age classrooms*. Peterborough, FL: Crystall Springs Books.

Raywid, M. A. (1994). Alternative schools: The state of the art. *Educational Leadership, 52*, 26–31.

Resta, P. (1991). The implications of distance learning for school reform. In *Innovations in distance learning*. Springfield, MA: Massachusetts Corporation for Educational Telecommunications.

Rich, D. (1988). *Mega skills: How families can help children succeed in school and beyond*. Boston, MA: Houghton Mifflin.

Richmond, G. H. (1989). The future school: Is Lowell pointing us toward a revolution in education? *Phi Delta Kappan, 70*, 232–236.

Richmond, G. H. (1990). Micro-society: Restructuring schools to restructure society. *Education Week, 13*, 28.

Rivlin, A. M. (1971). *Systematic thinking for social action*. Washington D.C.: The Brookings Institution.

Rivlin, A. M. & Timpane, P. M., Eds. (1975). *Planned variation in education: Should we give up or just try harder?* Washington, D.C.: The Brookings Institution.

Roberson, W. E. (1971). Teacher self-appraisal: A way to improve instruction. *Journal of Teacher Education, 22*, 469–473.

Rogers, C. (1959). Significant learning: In therapy and in education. *Educational Leadership, 16*, 232–242.

Rogers, E. (1983). *The diffusion of innovations* (3rd ed.). New York: Free Press.

Rogers, E. & Balle, F. (1985). *The media revolution in America and Western Europe*, Norwood, NJ: Ablex Publishing Corp.

Rogers, E. M. (1986). *Communication technology the new media in society*. New York: Free Press.

Romberg, T. A. & Price, G. G. (1983). Curriculum implementation and staff development as cultural change. In G. Griffin (Ed.). *Staff development* (82nd Yearbook, National Society for the Study of Education, Part II). Chicago, IL: University of Chicago Press.

Runkel, J. A. (1991). Schools for the 21st century. *National Forum of Educational Administration and Supervision Journal, 7*, 177–184.

Sarason, S. B. (1990). *The predictable failure of educational reform*. San Francisco, CA: Jossey-Bass.

Sautter, R. C. (1994). An arts education school reform strategy. *Phi Delta Kappan, 75*, 432–437.

Schalock, M. D. et al. (1993). Teacher productivity revisited: Definition, theory, measurement, and application. *Journal of Personnel Evaluation in Education, 7*, 179–196.

Schlechty, P. (1990). *Schools for the 21st century: Leadership imperatives for educational reform*. San Francisco, CA: Jossey-Bass Publishers.

Schmuck, P. & Schmuck, R. (1990). Democratic participation in small-town schools. *Educational Researcher, 19*, 14–19.

Schon, D. (1983). *The reflective practitioner*. San Francisco, CA: Jossey-Bass.

Schroeder, J. E. (1983). A pedagogical mode of instruction for interactive videodisc. *Journal of Educational Technology, 12*, 111–117.

Schwartz, H. (1988). Unapplied curriculum knowledge. In L. N. Tanner (Ed.). *Critical issues in curriculum* (87th Yearbook, National Society for the Study of Education). Chicago, IL: University of Chicago Press.

Sculli, D. & Ng, W. C (1985). Designing business games for the service industries. *Simulation/Games for Learning, 5*, 16–27.

Seager, G. B. (1992). Introduction: Bob Goldhammer in retrospect. In *The Robert Goldhammer papers: Early writings of a distinguished educator*. A publication of the Council of Professors of Instructional Supervision. Tampa, FL: Pedamorphosis, Inc.

Senge, P. (1990). *The fifty disciplines: The art and practice of learning*. New York: Doubleday/Currency.

Sergiovanni, T. J. & Starratt, R. J. (1994). *Supervision: A redefinition* (5th ed.). New York: McGraw-Hill.

Shaplin, J. T. & Olds, H. F. (1964). *Team teaching*. New York: Harper and Row.

Shepard, L. & Smith, M. (1989). *Flunking grades: Research and policies on retention*. New York: Falmer Press.

Showers, B. (1985). Teachers coaching teachers. *Educational Leadership, 43*, 43–48.

Shulman, L. S. (1986). Those who understand: Knowledge growth in teaching. *Educational Researcher, 5*, 4–14.

Siegel, J. & Shaughnessy, M. F. (1984). Educating for understanding. *Phi Delta Kappan, 66*, 563–565.

Silverblank, F. (1979). Analyzing the decision-making process in curriculum projects *Education, 99*, 414–418.

Sizer, T. (1984). *Horace's compromise: The dilemma of the American high school*. New York: Houghton Mifflin.

Sizer, T. R. (1988). A visit to an essential school. *The School Administrator, 45*, 18–19.

Slavin, R. E. (1989). PET and the pendulum: Faddism in education and how to stop it. *Phi Delta Kappan, 70*, 752–758.

Slavin, R. E. (1990). *Cooperative learning: Theory, research, and practice*. Englewood Cliffs, NJ: Prentice Hall.

Slavin, R. (1991). A vision for the next quarter century. *Phi Delta Kappan, 72*, 586–592.

Smith, P. B. (1980). *Group processes and personal change*. London: Harper and Row.

Smyth, J. (1991). *Teachers as collaborative learners: Challenging the dominant forms of supervision*. Philadelphia, PA: Open University Press.

Snyder, K. J. (1988). Supervision, clinical. In R. A. Gorton, et al. (Eds.). *Encyclopedia of school administration and supervision*. Phoenix, AZ: The Oryx Press.

Soar, R. (1976). An attempt to identify measures of teacher effectiveness from four studies. *Journal of Teacher Education, 27*, 261–267.

Spears, H. (1957). *Curriculum planning through in-service programs*. Englewood Cliffs, NJ: Prentice Hall.

Sprinkles, S. (1993). *Implementing a complex classroom innovation: A case study in process, problems, and potential*. Unpublished doctoral dissertation, The University of Texas at Austin.

Sprinthall, N. A. & Theis-Sprinthall, L. (1983). The teacher as an adult learner: The cognitive-developmental view. In G. Griffin (Ed.). *Staff development* (82nd Yearbook of the National Society of the Study of Education, Part II). Chicago, IL: University of Chicago Press.

Squire, J. R. (1988). Studies of textbooks: Are we asking the right questions? In P. W. Jackson (Ed.). *Contributing to educational change*. Berkeley, CA: McCutchan Publishing Corporation.

Stahl, S. A. (1990). Riding the pendulum: A rejoinder to Schickedanz and McGee and Lomax. *Review of Educational Research, 60*, 141–151.

Stearns, P. N. (1993). *Meaning over memory: Recasting the teaching of culture and history*. Chapel Hill, NC: The University of North Carolina Press.

Stipnicks, A. T. (1981). A study of teacher evaluation practices in selected school districts in the U.S. Unpublished doctoral dissertation, The University of Texas at Austin, Austin.

Stulac, J. F., et al. (1982). *Assessments of performance in teaching: Observation instrument (APT)*. Columbia, SC: South Carolina Educator Improvement Task Force.

Swanson, G. I. (1993). The hall of shame. *Phi Delta Kappan, 74*, 796.

Taba, H. (1962). *Curriculum development: Theory and practice*. New York: Harcourt, Brace and World.

Taba, H. & Noel, E. (1957). *Action research: A case study*. Washington, D.C.: ASCD.

Texas Learning Technology Group. (1989). *Touching the future: 1988-1989 field test results of the TLTG physical science*. Austin, TX: Texas Learning Technology Group, An affiliate of the Texas Association of School Boards.

The new alternative schools. (1994). A special edition of *Educational Leadership, 52*.

Tikunoff, W. J. & Mergendoller, J. R. (1983). Inquiry as a means to professional growth: The teacher as researcher. In G. A. Griffin (Ed.). *Staff development* (82nd Yearbook of the National Society for the Study of Education). Chicago, IL: University of Chicago Press.

Tracy, S. J. & MacNaughton, R. H. (1993). *Assisting and assessing educational personnel*. Noeedham Heights, MA: Allyn and Bacon, Inc.

Tye, K. A. (1991a). *Global education: From thought to action*. Alexandria, VA: ASCD.

Tye, K. A. (1991b). Conclusion: A look to the future. In K. A. Tye (Ed.). *Global education from thought to action* (1991 Yearbook). Alexandria, VA: ASCD.

U.S. Office of Education. (1974). *Bibliography of research studies in education—1926–1940, volumes 1 and 2*. Detroit MI: Gale Research Company.

Van Tulder, M. et al. (1993). In-service education in innovating schools: A multi-case study. *International Journal of Qualitative Studies in Education, 6*, 129–142.

Vasquez, O. A. (1993). A look at language as resource: Lessons from La Clase Magica. In M. B. Arias & U. Casanova (Eds.). *Bilingual Education: Politics, Practice, and Research*. (Part II, 92nd Yearbook, National Society for the Study of Education). Chicago, IL: University of Chicago Press.

Wagner, T. (1993). Systemic change: Rethinking the purpose of a school. *Educational Leadership, 51*, 24–28.

Waite, D. (1991). What would a paradigm shift in supervision look like? A paper presented to the Council of Professors of Instructional Supervision, (November).

Walberg H. J. & Lane, J. J. (1989). *Organizing for learning: Toward the 21st century*. Reston, VA: National Association of Secondary Principals.

Walker, D. F. (1986). Computers and the curriculum. In J. A. Culbertson & L. L. Cunningham (Eds.). *Microcomputers and education* (85th Yearboook, National Society for the Study of Education, Part I). Chicago, IL: University of Chicago Press.

Washington State Department of Education. (1981). *The Washington state system for coordination of staff development coordination study: A final report*. Olympia, WA: Office of the State Superintendent of Public Instruction. ERIC ED 209-240.

Watson, F. G. (1963). Research on teaching science. In N. L. Gage (Ed.). *Handbook of research on teaching* (pp. 1031–1059). Chicago, IL: Rand McNally Co.

Watts, G. D. & Castle, S. (1993). The time dilemma in school restructuring. *Phi Delta Kappan, 75*, 306–309.

Watts, J. (1989). Devolution of power: The ideological meaning. *Journal of Educational Administration (UK), 27*, 19–26.

Wayson, W. W. et al. (1988). *Up from excellence: The impact of the excellence movement on schools*. Bloomington, IN: Phi Delta Kappan Educational Foundation.

Wedman, J. F. (1988). Variations in teachers' concerns about different applications of educational computing. *Educational and Psychological Research, 8*, 51–60.

Westbury, I. (1990). Textbooks, textbook publishers, and the quality of schooling. In D. L. Elliott & A. Woodward (Eds.). *Textbooks and schooling in the U.S.* (89th Yearbook of the National Society for the Study of Education, Part I). Chicago, IL: University of Chicago Press.

Westheimer, J. & Kahne, J. (1993). Building school communities: An experience-based model. *Phi Delta Kappan, 75*, 324.

Wigginton, E. (1991-1992). Culture begins at home. *Educational Leadership, 49*, 60–64.

Wiles, J. & Bondi, J. (1991). *Supervision: A guide to practice* (3rd ed.). New York: Macmillan Publishing Co.

Wiles, K. (1967). *Supervision for better schools* (3rd ed.). Englewood Cliffs, NJ: Prentice Hall.

Wiles, K. & Lovell, J. T. (1983). *Supervision for better schools.* Englewood Cliffs, NJ: Prentice Hall.

Williams, L. (1989). The decline of the authoritarian tradition. In S. Rubenstein (Ed.). *Participative systems at work: Creating quality and employment security.* New York: Human Sciences Press.

Wilson, L. & Harris, B. M. (1991). Instructional leadership specifications for school executives: A preliminary validation study. *Journal of Personnel Evaluation in Education, 5,* 21–30.

Woodring, P. (1983). *The persistent problems of education.* Bloomington, IN: Phi Delta Kappan Educational Foundation.

Woolfolk, R. L. & Woolfolk, A. E. (1974). Effects of teacher and nonverbal behavior on student perceptions and attitudes. *American Educational Research Journal, 11,* 297–303.

Yarger, S. J. et al. (1980). *In-service teacher education.* Palo Alto, CA: Booksend Laboratory.

Zielin, C. (1986). Supervision and evaluation: The interface as administrative sub-systems. A paper presented to the National Commission on Instructional Supervision, NCIS Workshop (February). Mimeographed.

Zilversmit, A. (1993). *Changing schools: Progressive education theory and practice, 1930–1960.* Chicago, IL: University of Chicago Press.

SUPERVISION AS A FIELD OF INQUIRY

INTRODUCTION

Isobel L. Pfeiffer
UNIVERSITY OF AKRON

Although supervision has been an integral part of schools since colonial days, it has been an area of practice marked by considerable diversity and confusion. Even though some common elements can be found in the literature, controversy has often arisen regarding such factors as roles, relationships, functions, practices, and philosophy. In the preceding chapter, Harris gave an overview of supervision in education. He is optimistic in his analysis regarding emerging practices and the challenges of restructuring schools. Section I of the *Handbook* offers the reader an opportunity to view the field from four perspectives. Each chapter presents basic information, trends, philosophical implications, and predictions, all taken together. This kaleidoscopic view provides rich and interesting patterns for interpreting the changing profession.

HISTORIES, ANTECEDENTS, AND LEGACIES

In Chapter 2 Glanz chronicles major developments of school supervision over time and provides an interpretive analysis of this record. Comprehensive historical treatment of supervision has been limited, but textbooks, dissertations, yearbooks of leadership associations, and articles in professional journals contribute information about its development. Although patterns and traditions of supervision were originally brought from Western Europe, school supervision in this coun-

try has been influenced by many uniquely American factors: social and intellectual movements and activities of supervisors themselves. The conflict between bureaucracy in schools and professional autonomy has been frustrating for supervisors throughout history. They have also struggled to balance improvement of instruction and evaluation of teachers.

Seven models of supervision are presented. The first is inspection, originally performed by clergy and local committees and later by superintendents. The autocratic methods conformed to the bureaucratic organization developing in schools. Scientific management in industry influenced supervision in schools early in the twentieth century and resulted in the social efficiency model. Rating scales were introduced in an attempt to measure teacher efficiency. The democratic model emerged as supervisors tried to find new methods and themes to address the improvement of instruction. The fourth model, scientific supervision, incorporated analysis of teaching and application of scientific principles to supervision. Supervisors were striving for professional recognition through national organizations, publications, and preparation requirements. An alliance with curriculum workers was formed, and the new organization eventually became the Association for Supervision and Curriculum Development. The conception of supervision changed from status to function as it became the responsibility of numerous school personnel rather than of a single individual. Supervision as leadership was the next model to emerge with a focus on mutually acceptable goals, cooperative and democratic supervisory methods, improving instruction, research on educational problems, and professional leadership. It was followed by clinical supervision, which arose from dissatisfaction with traditional supervisory procedures. The collegiality and collaboration of this approach appealed to many educators. Since the early 1980s alternative methods of supervision, comprising the changing concepts model, have gained attention, including developmental supervision, cognitive coaching, and peer supervision.

After explaining the value of understanding a history of supervision, Glanz suggests essential topics and potential resources for further study. To eliminate "the ambiguous legacy" in the field of supervision, scholars are challenged to undertake historical investigation to understand the heritage and to focus future efforts.

MODELS AND APPROACHES

In Chapter 3, Tracy examines models and approaches used to classify research and practice in instructional supervision. Definitions of model are varied and include describing and explaining reality as well as serving as exemplars, predictors, and generators of research. Approaches refer to variations in practice within a specific model. As Tracy explains, models can be used as windows to expand horizons or as walls that limit understanding and reflection.

The structure of a model begins with goals and purpose. The continuum extends from teacher assistance/teacher development to teacher evaluation/organizational development. Although some leaders consider these two extremes to be a dysfunctional relationship, most recognize the need for supervision to link individual teacher growth and organizational improvement. Theoretical base is the second key concept for a model; however, writers in supervision have borrowed theories from fields as diverse as psychology, leadership, communication, organization, change, sociology, anthropology, and counseling. Major concepts or principles evolving from the theory must be identified. Tracy cites three examples of this: (1) control of process and content, ranging from teacher to organization/superintendent control, (2) breadth of focus extending from the teaching act to all aspects of the teacher's job description, and (3) conception of teaching with a continuum from art to science.

Because writers have selected different characteristics to develop their model schema, the author selects six classifications that represent the majority of models in the literature. Each schema is discussed in relation to the approaches of specific writers. Different treatments of clinical supervision, which is the only repeated term in the schemata, are analyzed. Criteria for model selection are recommended: values and beliefs about teaching and supervision, needs of the individual teacher, and organizational needs. Because existing models do not take many changes into account that occur in roles and responsibilities of teachers and supervisors, models in the future may require shifting emphases and developing appropriate systems, thereby creating a new window to view the field of instructional supervision.

METHODS OF INQUIRY IN SUPERVISION

The educational community, which sets parameters for legitimate inquiry and appropriate methodology, has greatly influenced research in supervision according to Schoonmaker, Sawyer, and Borrego-Brainard. A continuum of methodologies presented in Chapter 4. It begins with studies that utilize quantitative research designs and extends to qualitative research, and includes studies that use both methodologies, establishes complexities of the field and broad contextual factors.

Three critical questions were identified and developed into strands as appropriate studies were analyzed:

1. how can supervisors get the teacher to be more effective?
2. how can supervisors help teachers to become more professional in their practice?
3. how can supervisors help teachers to be more critical and self-reflective in practice?

The authors include the image of the teacher, philosophy, psychology, methodologies typically used, and goals in each strand. Clinical supervision is explored to illustrate variation in interpretation and the complexities of inquiry. Questions about the model (i.e., the design and value as a supervisory strategy), teacher–supervisor relationships, theoretical and research foundations, and problems of implementation are considered.

The authors conclude that supervisory inquiry, broadly defined, has resulted in vigorous research on many related interests including teacher effectiveness, professionalism, teacher thinking, and decision making. Multiple forms of inquiry to explore myriad issues and practices of teachers and schools are recommended for understanding supervision. To launch a new era of inquiry in supervision, it is recommended that the voices of those who have been left out of the recorded history of supervision should be considered. Supervisory information relating to race, class, gender, marginalization of women, the poor, people with special needs, and ethnic minorities can add a richer and more interesting dimension to this inquiry.

EVALUATION, ASSESSMENT, AND APPRAISAL OF SUPERVISION

In Chapter 5, Iwanicki analyzes approaches to program evaluation and personnel evaluation. Several models of evaluating curricular programs (e.g., Tyler, Stufflemean, Alkin and Popham, and Provus) are discussed, with emphasis on tailoring models to meet the evaluation needs in schools. Suggestions are made for appropriate use and interpretation of tests in program evaluation. Such evaluations provide the basis for decisions about the quality of school programs and their impact on students.

Three aspects of teacher evaluation continue in schools: a past view that rates teachers on the basis of style or trait criteria, a present view that analyzes teaching based on accepted practices, and a future view that considers students' learning. The author recommends integrating teacher evaluation with staff development and school improvement. An organizational approach to encompass these three factors is the "Teacher Evaluation and Professional Growth Cycle," which can be modified to fit the school's accountability system. Collaboration in a school environment is recommended as the most promising process for realizing student learning.

The perspectives of supervision presented in these well-documented chapters provide information about past developments and present status as well as invitations for further study. Analyses of perplexing questions and conflicts may encourage such efforts. The kaleidoscopic views represented can give the reader a greater understanding and appreciation of supervision as a field of inquiry.

·2·

HISTORIES, ANTECEDENTS, AND LEGACIES OF SCHOOL SUPERVISION

Jeffrey Glanz*

KEAN UNIVERSITY OF NEW JERSEY

> Of all the responsibilities of school operation, instructional supervision stands out as the one most discussed, yet least understood. In spite of the success that has been achieved, the administrative waterfront of American education is littered with the debris of supervisory ventures that failed to live out the storm, failed to reach the needs of classroom instruction. Some were stern and austere craft that were abandoned as unfit for the humanitarian purposes of modern supervision. Some were properly planned but neglected by their navigators. . . .
>
> Of all the responsibilities of school operation, supervision stands out as the one most in need of clarification. There is no greater challenge in the study of American education.
>
> Harold Spears (1953)

Public school supervision in the United States has been shaped and influenced by a variety of historical forces. On the one hand, there are patterns and traditions of school supervision that have been brought over from Western Europe (Button, 1961). On the other, we find that the development of school supervision took on a unique character of its own. While it is true that the importance of transplanted European values and beliefs should be understood, American education, in general, and supervision, in particular, were formed and shaped by many factors that were uniquely American (Arrington, 1972; Harris, 1890).

The history of school supervision, which is complex and distinct, is clearly a history of the interaction of the broad social and intellectual movements within American society. Although several published textbooks have traced the development of school supervision (e.g., Ayer, 1954; Beach & Reinhartz, 1989; Burton & Brueckner, 1955; Eye, Netzer, & Krey, 1971; Lucio & McNeil, 1962; Neagley & Evans, 1970; Swearingen, 1962; Wiles & Lovell, 1983), much of this history describes eras or changes in supervision as a series of disjointed and unrelated events. As a result, developments in supervision appear to be loosely connected, having little, if any, relation to one another. Moreover, supervision seems simply to reflect social movements and educational developments occurring in society. While greater attention has been paid to the historical development of supervision (Bolin &

* The author is indebted for the invaluable comments on this chapter offered by Dr. Richard F. Neville, Dr. Frances Schoonmaker Bolin, Dr. Helen M. Hazi, and Dr. Isobel Pfeiffer. Any errors or misinterpretations rest solely with the author.

Panaritis, 1992; Glanz, 1991; Karier, 1982; Pajak, 1993b; Tracy, 1995), a single, definitive, coherent historical theme that adequately explains the development of theory and practice of supervision in the United States is lacking.

The theory and practice of school supervision have certainly been influenced by a plethora of social, philosophical, economic, and political forces. For instance, economic capitalism at the turn of the century influenced school supervisors to institute production-oriented theories of school administration wherein detailed and elaborate inspectional practices dominated supervisory practice (Bolin, 1987). Furthermore, in the early twentieth century, democratic values played a key role in American education and influenced espoused theories of school administration and supervision (Pajak, 1993b). While these and many other irrefutable sociopolitical and educational connections have been advanced by historians (Bolin & Panaritis, 1992; Tanner & Tanner 1987), a coherent theory of educational history that explains why supervisory theory and practice have evolved to their present status has been elusive.

This chapter will have a fivefold purpose: (1) to review relevant historical research on the evolution of public school supervision in the United States, (2) to present a theoretical model or construct that offers a framework for understanding the historical developments of school supervision, (3) to analyze significant conceptions of supervision that may have influenced theory and practice in the field, (4) to assess the inattention to supervision history and to point out the relevance and significance of historical inquiry, and (5) to propose avenues for future research.

Although this chapter chronicles historical developments in supervision, as a professional practice and field of study, the author's particular view of supervision will necessarily focus attention to certain aspects of supervision that warrant analysis, while others might be discarded. Considering this hermeneutical and poststructuralist orientation (Denzin & Lincoln, 1994), the reader should therefore understand the author's meaning of supervision. As will be indicated, defining supervision has been a fleeting and unproductive endeavor. As attractive and seemingly crucial definition may be, perhaps, in the end, supervision as an all-inclusive and complex function cannot be captured by a single, straightforward definition (cf., Portelli, 1987). Nevertheless an understanding of supervision in this chapter was derived from the varied textbooks and articles written about it, not from the author's personal meaning of supervision. Supervision was understood chiefly as a function and role in public schools aimed at improving the quality of instruction. Particular meanings of supervision were shaped by the intent of many people throughout history as well as by events and circumstances. Consequently, unsurprising is the fact that methods varied and definitions abounded. Research garnered numerous accounts regarding the nature and conception of supervision. It from these accounts that this history emerged.

To a great extent, this chapter is meant as a chronicle and interpretive analysis of the history of school supervision. As such, the chapter is purposely reference intensive so that scholars may benefit from relevant citations. Due to the length of the chapter, transitional sentences and paragraphs between major sections will serve as reviews and setting contexts for upcoming material. So as not detract from meaning and understanding of the essential theme of this chapter, an overarching statement of purpose or advanced organizer of sorts may be in order.

This chapter will consider the evolution of thought and practice about supervision as embodying a coherent purpose, as opposed to those who might assert that supervision merely reflected developments occurring in education in general. For these historians, the history of supervision is a series of unrelated and disjointed occurrences lacking coherence and meaning. The history of supervision, albeit inauspicious at times, indicates that supervision, as a role and function, underwent significant transformations in an attempt to gain legitimacy within schools. Variously defined and often narrowly conceived, supervision, as a process aimed at in some way improving instruction, played a key role in schools. In an attempt to eschew its bureaucratic heritage, supervision evolved through several models. Each of the models since the 1930s, whether conceived as democratic, scientific, leadership, clinical, developmental, or coaching, portrayed supervision and supervisors as professional. As such, supervision became a constructive process whereby teaching could be improved. Eliminating the stigma associated with supervision and the supervisor became the field's raison d'être. Although new proposals and models of supervision were ill-fated, at times, supervision as a role and function in schools continued to find ways to improve the quality of education. The chapter will elucidate the consequences these models had for supervision as a professional practice and field of study.

More specifically this chapter will begin to detail relevant historical research on school supervision, noting significant contributions to the understanding of the function and conception of supervision. The chapter will critically analyze some of these works in terms of their contributions to the understanding of the development of supervision. Areas that can help construct a more comprehensive and coherent history of school supervision will be highlighted. This analysis will be followed by an attempt to develop a theoretical construct in order to more completely clarify the complex and extensive developments that have occurred in the history of supervision. Trends and developments occurring in school supervision will then be placed in context in relation to the theoretical construct developed in this chapter by describing seven dominant conceptions of supervision: inspection, efficiency, democratic, scientific, leadership, clinical, and "changing concepts." A more general discussion of supervision history, its relevance and significance, as well as future research efforts into the history of school supervision form the conclusion of the chapter.

REVIEW OF RESEARCH

The elements that define the history of supervision in American public education have been obscure. Most often published scholarship on the history of educational or instructional supervision has been lack-luster, minimalist in nature, repetitious, and creatively lacking historical currency. Most eminent scholars in the history of education have not probed educational supervision to any depth in the course of their work. The result has left us with an incomplete record and limited understanding of the evolution of educational supervision-one that is sparse in historical definition, interpretation, and evaluation.

According to Curriculum Leaders: Improving Their Influence (ASCD, 1976, p. 13), "a definitive history of educational supervision has not been published." Krey and Burke (1989, p. 9) posited that "there have been no exhaustive treatises published on the 'History of Supervision, . . .'." To be sure, there is ample published documentary material relating to many aspects of public school supervision in the United States, as will be noted at the end of this chapter. Unfortunately, one must concur with these statements quoted above that indicate the lack of historical inquiry into "educational supervision" (Glanz, 1977a). Perusal of any textbook on supervision and some curriculum books should give the researcher a broad overview of the history of public school supervision (e.g., Burton & Brueckner 1955; Lewis & Miel, 1972; Manis, 1985; Oliva, 1989; Wiles, 1967). Much of this history is sketchy, general, and, at times, inaccurate.

It should be noted that these texts did not primarily deal with the history of school supervision; therefore, they cannot be criticized for lack of critical analysis of the forces and movements that have shaped the field of supervision. Still, much of the field's historical understanding comes from these concise overviews that do not, to any great extent, shed light on the forces that influenced the evolution of school supervision. For greater depth, one must first look at doctoral dissertations that attempted to explore supervision historically.

Prominent Dissertations

The best general doctoral study on supervision was undertaken by Henry W. Button (1961), under the sponsorship of Raymond Callahan at Washington University titled, "A History of Supervision in the Public Schools, 1870–1950." Button began his investigation of supervision in the latter part of the nineteenth century because "the evidence suggests that there was little professional supervision before 1870" (p. 22). Button essentially explained the development of supervision in terms of a chronological narrative organized into five distinct periods: 1870–1885, 1885–1905, 1905–1920, 1920–1940, and 1940–1950.

According to Button, the origins of professional supervision occurred between 1870 and 1885. The supervisor, who was usually a county or city superintendent with little authority, was considered a "teacher of teachers." The primary function of the supervisor was to instruct poorly prepared teachers in the art of teaching. Button claimed that the methods employed by supervisors, influenced in large measure by Jeffersonian, Transcendental, romantic, and European ideals, were democratic in that concern for the individuality of the teacher was paramount (see also, Tanner & Tanner, 1987). Although Button acknowledged the authoritarian views of William Howard Payne (1875), who was the author of the first published textbook on supervision, and William Torrey Harris, who was perhaps the most prominent and influential

superintendent of the time, he concluded that theory and practice of supervision during this 15-year period were essentially democratic. He concluded his second chapter by stating that simply equating "'authoritarian' supervision with early supervision, and 'democratic' supervision with later supervision is an unacceptably crude historical generalization" (p. 46).

During the next period, stated Button, supervision was influenced by the autocrats who advocated authoritarian supervisory methods to deal with weak and ineffective teachers. Button explained that prevailing autocratic practices in supervision were influenced by the centralization of education in the latter part of the century. Button began his analysis of this period by describing "early advocates of autocratic supervision" (p. 51), such as Calkins (1882), Chancellor (1904), Edson (1893), Harris (1892), Payne (1887), and Pickard (1872). Characteristic of many supervisory strategies employed by these "autocrats" were the views and practices of William Torrey Harris. Harris maintained that "the first prerequisite of the school is order" (1871, p. 31). Nonconformity and disorganization were evils that had to be expunged, thought Harris. Freedom was not considered by Harris as a viable option for teachers. This view is best evidenced by Harris' notion of "supervisory devices," which were presumably used by the superintendent as supervisor to improve "the method of instruction or the method of discipline." Harris contended that this device also proved effective "in strengthening the power of governing a school." This device, said Harris, "is the practice of placing teachers weak in discipline on the 'substitutes' list and letting them fill vacancies here and there as they occur through the temporary absence of the regular teacher." "I have known teachers that had become chronic failures in discipline entirely reformed by a few weeks of such experience," said Harris (1892, pp. 171, 172).

Button then described a third era in which supervisory practice was patterned after "the administrator of business and industrial management views of school organization" (p. 336). Influenced especially by Taylor (1911), as well as by Cubberley (1916), Spaulding (1913), and, most closely related to supervision, by Bobbitt (1913), business and management practices dominated theory and practice in supervision between 1905 and 1920. During this time, Button explained, supervisors used rather elaborate rating scales to measure teacher efficiency. The scientific approach to supervision had emerged.

Button stated that with the advent of business, with its industrial metaphors and practices, supervision became even more autocratic and received much criticism from teachers. As a result of this mounting criticism, explained Button, supervisory theory shifted dramatically to meet the demands of a dissatisfied teaching force. The emergence of cooperative and democratic supervision occurred within this milieu.

Button concluded his study by summarizing each period that supervision seemed to have traversed. In attempting to find a pattern to explain the shifts and changes occurring in school supervision, Button stated:

An analysis of changes in supervision was an exercise in multiple causation. Supervision was molded by its social environment in society at large, by the rise of the business man, the fall of the learned scholar, the new faith in social planning. It was shaped by the schools in which it was to be practiced, by the problems of centralized control, by the innovations of Progressive education.

It was shaped by a variety of individuals, and by their beliefs. It was shaped by White, the namesake of Emerson; by Parker, Herbartian and democrat; by Harris, leading American Hegelian and defender of the status quo; by Payne, . . . by Bobbitt, . . . by Burton, . . . by Dewey, . . .

Supervision was shaped by environment, felt the imprint of individuals, and felt the influence of science; techniques and theory on analogy; and by philosophy, both explicit and formal, and implicit and informal (pp. 351–352).

Button's dissertation was the first comprehensive attempt to study the forces that shaped and influenced educational supervision in the United States. In doing so, he laid fundamental groundwork for scholars for years to come. Button's study, however, suffers from two basic flaws that will be noted briefly. The first deals with the treatment of the history of supervision in terms of periods. The writing of public school supervision cannot be undertaken by merely describing its development through periodization (i.e., specific periods tied within specific time frames). The historical trends occurring in supervision are frequently contradictory and confusing. For example, it is not possible, to state that scientific supervision began during such and such a time and was immediately followed by democratic supervision. Rather, to obtain a more realistic view, these events must be viewed as trends occurring concurrently; therefore, for instance, the notions of scientific, philosophic, cooperative, democratic, creative, authoritarian, and effective supervision expressed the trend in school supervision across the country during, at least, the 1920s and 1930s. Moreover, an underlying theme that explains why the field followed the course it did is absent from Button's overview of the historical development of supervision.

A second flaw of the Button study centers on his neglect of curriculum development occurring in cities throughout the country in the early twentieth century. An analysis of these curricular efforts provides much insight into supervisory practices in schools. Button stated that "the functions of supervision and of developing curriculum seem to have followed separate paths, so disparate as to make the consideration of both in a single study exceedingly cumbersome." "For present purposes," continued Button, "the individual in the school system is not engaged in supervision when he is considering the curriculum" (p. 3). The fact of the matter is that individuals in school systems, called supervisors, were engaged in curriculum matters. The researcher can glean important information on supervisory practice, for example, by examining cities such as Denver, where curriculum revision was occurring (Threlkeld, 1925). The fact remains that the paths taken by supervisors and curriculum workers were remarkably similar (see, e.g., Bolin, 1987; Bolin & Panaritis, 1992; Glanz, 1991, 1992a; Karier, 1982; Tanner & Tanner, 1980), and to neglect to study their interactions is to negate a valuable source into supervisory practice.

Notwithstanding these criticisms, Button is credited with initiating historical inquiry into supervision; unfortunately, not many scholars followed in Button's footsteps. The next

comprehensive attempt to study school supervision historically was a doctoral dissertation completed by Alfred Aisum Arrington (1972) titled, "An Historical Analysis of the Development of Supervision in the Public Schools of the United States from 1870 to 1970." Arrington's study, while focusing on some sources untapped by Button and extending the period of analysis by 20 years, does not provide a more in-depth analysis of school supervision. Apparently unaware of or unacknowledging Button's study, Arrington proceeded to cover the same ground, studying supervision as passing through various eras. In fact, many of Arrington's observations about supervision were repetitive and in some instances identical to the Button study.

Arrington can be credited for acknowledging the need for further historical analysis of supervision, a fairly well-written chapter on the "Era of Efficiency and Economy, 1905 to 1920," and some interesting comments and observations about the practice and theories of supervision. In sum, however, the Arrington dissertation lacks depth, critical analysis, and does not attempt to explain the evolution of supervision in an illuminating way.

The next attempt to analyze supervision historically was a doctoral dissertation completed by Glanz (1977b) titled, "Bureaucracy and Professionalism: An Historical Interpretation of Public School Supervision in the United Sates, 1875–1937." Under the sponsorship of Dr. Arno A. Bellack and Dr. Gary A. Griffin, Glanz attempted to explore the factors that influenced school supervision during a 60 year period, 1875–1937. During this time, the author contended, supervision was shaped by "two related, but sometimes opposing processes, bureaucracy and professionalism" (p. 1). The strength of Glanz's dissertation is that supervision history was not viewed simply as a chronological list of events; rather, it was analyzed through an interpretive framework.

The author noted that the study was in no way meant as a "comprehensive treatment" (p. 383) of the study of educational supervision. Glanz urged researchers to continue "the provocative venture of exploring, historically, school supervision in the United States" (p. 383). A basic flaw with the study, however, was that no theoretical explanation for the concepts of bureaucracy and professionalism were presented. Without such delineation of terms, the reader remains uncertain how these processes influenced supervision.

Published Book on Supervision History

Continuing this line of work was the first published book dealing exclusively with the history of school supervision (Glanz, 1991). *Bureaucracy and Professionalism: The Evolution of Public School Supervision* traced the rise and evolution of an occupational group in its efforts to professionalize. It offered an interpretive analysis of the factors that historically influenced public school supervision, emphasizing the unresolved dilemma between the demands of the organization (bureaucracy) and the drive for professionalism. In short, the book was about the professionalization of supervision and how it was shaped by bureaucratic organization.

The study began with an analysis of the period in which bureaucracy emerged as the chief form of school organization. The author stressed the importance that supervision played in the movement toward centralization and bureaucracy, arguing that supervision was an indispensable means by which superintendents maintained control over schools as well as inculcated certain bureaucratic values and ideas into the schools.

It was not until the turn of the century that supervision became the responsibility of a functionary other than the superintendent. Supervisors, general and special, and principals, who bore responsibility for supervising teachers, increased both in number and importance as the school system grew in size and complexity; however, the problems and tensions confronting the supervisor also grew. Due to the increasing bureaucratization of urban schools and rating procedures used by supervisors, teachers and other educators sharply criticized administrators during the early decades of the twentieth century. Torn between administrative duties and instructional responsibilities, the supervisor realized her/his precarious status in the bureaucratic hierarchy. It was in direct response to mounting criticism that supervisors, in a concerted effort to gain control over their work, sought to professionalize as a means to counteract bureaucracy.

In the 1930s, the supervisor became fully cognizant of the meaning of professional membership in a bureaucratic organization. In 1937 the members of the Department of Supervisors and the Society for Curriculum Study met to work on a yearbook on curriculum. The eventual merger of these two groups was one attempt to strengthen their efforts to professionalize (Glanz, 1995a; Van Til, 1986). Supervisors subsequently had a difficult time securing what the Association for Supervision and Curriculum Development (ASCD) during the 1950s and 1960s called "the professionalization of supervisors and curriculum workers" (Leeper, 1969). The professionalization of supervision was thwarted largely due to conflicts experienced by supervisors working in the bureaucratic school organization.

Although not exploring events after the late 1930s, Glanz contended that the same type of problems confronting supervisors in the formative period continued to frustrate efforts at professionalization. These problems, he explained, were rooted in an inherent conflict between bureaucratic and professional autonomy.

Reviewing *Bureaucracy and Professionalism* in the *History of Education Quarterly*, Robert Lowe (1992) criticized the "lumping all supervisors together" (p. 397). Furthermore, Lowe charged that most of the research undertaken focused on "what superintendents and professors of education said about supervision" (p. 397) and that research on supervisory practice in school settings was necessary. While appreciating Lowe's call for research, it would be foolish to assume that a single study could comprehensively analyze supervision by itself. This chapter on the history of supervision, while attempting to review work already done, aims to stimulate further historical investigations into the development of supervision. It is unquestionably lamentable that an important function as supervision has escaped serious and thorough historical inquiry. As Lowe recommended, continued research about supervision in many settings is necessary.

Other Historical Treatments

Other than the preceding three dissertations and one book devoted to exploring supervision, no other comprehensive attempts at exploring the origins and development of supervision have been undertaken. Selected dissertations, however, provide an overview of the history of supervision. An excellent dissertation was completed by Bolin (1983) in which she explored the writings of six influential leaders in instructional supervision: Barr, Burton, Brueckner, Miel, Cogan, and Sergiovanni. Bolin's work contains many valuable historical insights. Another dissertation that examines supervision history to some extent was completed by Fitzgerald (1991). More in depth analyses into the history of supervision, however, must be gleaned from articles that appeared as chapters in various ASCD publications.

Karier (1982), an educational historian, in an article entitled "Supervision in Historic Perspective," which was published as the lead chapter in an ASCD yearbook, attempted to weave together two periods of educational reform (i.e., what he called the common school era and the progressive liberal reform era) in terms of their influence on supervision. In a brief 13 pages, Karier did a fine job in highlighting several important issues tangentially related to school supervision.

Karier's treatment depicted supervision as being influenced by various social, political, and economic movements occurring in society at large and in education in particular. Karier noted that as the goals of American education changed, so did the ways schools were governed and the ways teachers were supervised. Early responsibility for education rested primarily with the family unit. The common school movement, championed by people like Horace Mann and Henry Barnard, was "spurred on by the passions of nationalism and the social and economic instability resulting from immigration and industrialization" (p. 3). As a result, state authority dominated educational practice. At the same time, a hotly contested political struggle dominated the educational scene. Local ward boards and administrative progressives battled over the control of urban schooling. Karier's work supports the notion that the bureaucratization of management and the professionalization of school administrators would eventually characterize American education and have consequences for school supervision.

Karier noted that by around 1921, as schools grew in population, they became more bureaucratic, and the role of the superintendency became more specialized, and a new cadre of supervisors emerged independent of the superintendent. This development was evidenced, claimed Karier, by the establishment of the Department of Supervisors and Directors of Instruction: "Thus by 1929 the trend toward professionalizing supervision as a separate field had advanced far enough to warrant a separate department in the NEA" (p. 10).

Influenced by the economic hardships of the depression, "the overall view of education was to help the younger generation adjust to the real world of pain and suffering which lay ahead" (p. 11). As social and economic conditions improved, education was influenced by advances in technology that translated into scientific management, social efficiency, and scientific measurement. By the end of the 1930s, however, a clear shift in focus occurred with emphasis on "cooperative curriculum revision, the whole child, pupil–teacher planning, democratic supervision, and life adjustment curricular goals" (p. 11). Karier concluded his brief overview of the history of supervision by noting that educators by in large did not take the lead in societal reform efforts; rather, they reacted to various movements and conditions. He attributed this reaction to the reliance on an educational bureaucracy.

Karier analyzed societal and educational forces that came to bear on supervision. One leaves Karier's chapter more fully understanding the changing nature of the supervisory process; however, one understands little about the motivations and aspirations of supervisors, nor does one get a sense of the internal forces that helped shape supervision as a professional field of study and practice.

Ten years later another yearbook, *Supervision in Transition,* edited by Carl D. Glickman, was published by ASCD (1992). Glickman commissioned Frances Schoonmaker Bolin, professor at Teachers College, Columbia University, and Philip Panaritis, a teacher in the New York City public schools, to write a chapter on educational supervision from a historical perspective. Bolin and Panaritis (1992) rose to the challenge and composed a clear, albeit brief (i.e., 12 pages), accounting of key developments in the history of supervision.

"Searching for a Common Purpose: A Perspective on the History of Supervision" acknowledged the fact that while supervision was inevitably influenced by a number of potent social and educational forces, the history of supervision is also characterized by "internal struggles over mission and a more external struggle for identity as a distinct field of practice" (p. 30). Supervision, the authors contended, "emerged as a field of practice around the turn of the century in response to increased levels of bureaucracy in schools and the public demand for more control over the curriculum" (p. 30). In discussing the further development of supervision, Bolin and Panaritis were not unlike previous historians, describing supervision as passing through various stages, beginning with "supervision as inspection," continuing with "supervision as social efficiency, and ending with "supervision as democratic leadership."

Bolin and Panaritis's historical account is valuable in two distinct ways. First, unlike Button (1961), the authors of this chapter attested to the fact that supervision and curriculum seemed to have shared common legacies. This important notion will be amplified later in this chapter. Second, they acknowledged and briefly alluded to the internal struggles supervisors faced in forging their own identity distinct from school administrators and curriculum workers.

Pajak's (1993b) article in an ASCD yearbook, although not meant as a comprehensive overview of the evolution of supervision, was interesting and noteworthy in terms of its attempt to trace 50 years of supervisory thought in four distinct categories: the supervisor as the "democratic educator," the "organizational change agent," the "corporate visionary," and the "leader as a teacher." More recently, Tracy (1995), in a brief article published in *The Clearing House,* reviewed historical developments of supervision and pointed out that "history can inform our practice and assist us in designing new adaptations of supervision better suited to the classrooms of the future" (p. 325).

Four less-recent sources that provide insight into the early evolution of supervision are: Pierce, 1935; Prince, 1901; Snow, 1939; and Suzzallo, 1906. These works reflect the importance of early methods in supervision and document actual practices of supervision in schools.

Blumberg (1985) briefly examined supervision in the mid-nineteenth century in a 10-page article published in the *Journal of Curriculum and Supervision.* Using the Annual Report of the Superintendent of Common Schools of the State of New York (1845), Blumberg highlighted various concerns of these early supervisors in areas such as teacher competency, method of teaching, staff development, and curriculum. Acknowledging that his piece was more of an "intellectually enriching experience" than a comprehensive attempt to trace the evolution of supervision, Blumberg's article represents one of only a handful attempts, as he said, to "learn about the thoughts and actions of people who years ago performed the job with which we claim to be concerned today" (p. 65).

A year later, Blumberg (1986), in a paper presented to the American Educational Research Association's (AERA) annual meeting, elaborated on his exploration into the early history of school supervision, which "if nothing else, can help practitioners (and professors, too) see themselves as part of a long chain (very loosely linked, I might add) of people who have been interested in improving the character of classroom instruction." Blumberg brought to life the writings and methods of supervision employed by early supervisors such as Payne, Greenwood, and Pickard. He also related their views to current conceptions of supervision. In concluding his paper, Blumberg prodded his colleagues to pursue the study of "what our supervisor forebears wrote about." (p. 30).

A few states have also documented the evolution of supervision. For example, see Snow's (1939) work titled, *The History of the Development of Public School Supervision in the State of Maine.*

Two significant contributions that reviewed the historical role of supervision in ASCD in its early stages (Bostwick, 1986) and in its later years (Firth, 1986) were compiled by Van Til (1986) and commissioned by the then president of ASCD, Gerald R. Firth. Both Bostwick and Firth chronicle developments, significant publications, conferences, and activities of the ASCD. Much information about the development and status of supervision can be gleaned from this source. In addition, see Davis's (1978) concise, yet historically accurate account of the formation of the ASCD as well as Nelson and Singleton's (1980) account.

There are not, unfortunately, many other historical accounts of the development of supervision other than selected general manuscripts, documents, articles, dissertations, and presentations that only tangentially relate to supervision and provide glimpses, at best, of methods and practices of supervision. Some of these include: Abelow (1934); Almack (1936); Bullough (1974); Burton (1852); Callahan (1967); Callahan and Button (1964); Cremin (1970); Cronin (1971); Cubberley (1934); Dolson (1964); Doyle (1976); Dutton and Snedden (1912); Elsbree (1939); Fuller (1989); Gear (1950); Gilland (1935); Hammock (1969); Herrick (1971); Kaestle

(1970, 1973); Katz (1968, 1987); Krug (1964, 1972); Lazerson (1971); Newlon and Threlkeld (1926); Reid (1968); Reller (1935); Rice (1893); Rousmaniere, (1992); Seguel (1966); and Zimmerman, (1994). Some other notable works, that only tangentially mention school supervision, are Callahan (1962); Campbell, Fleming, Newell, and Bennion, (1987); Cremin (1961); Cuban (1984); and Tyack and Hansot (1982).

Another source for historical information about supervision comes from textbooks that deal with the field of supervision in general. As noted earlier, much of this history relies on generalizations and cursory overviews rather than in-depth analyses. Some noteworthy historical accounts, however, are available in the following works: Gwynn, 1961; Krey and Burke, 1989; Kyte, 1930; Spears, 1953; and Tanner and Tanner, 1987. Special attention should be paid to Krey and Burke's account (1989) of supervision. The five historical time periods they outline are helpful and accurate.

In sum, then, due to lack of historical inquiry into supervision, studies that have been done tend to be general treatments rather than in-depth analyses (Krey & Burke, 1989). A number of studies are sorely needed on a wide range of topics that deal with public school supervision in the United States, as will be discussed further at the end of this chapter.

TOWARD A THEORY OF UNDERSTANDING THE HISTORY OF SUPERVISION

Reviewing research efforts into the history of supervision is at the same time uncomplicated and arduous. It is uncomplicated in the sense that little has been done to investigate supervision historically. Much work remains to be accomplished. The task is also extremely difficult in that supervision as a role and function in schools spans more than 100 years, and many loose ends need connecting. Moreover, Tanner and Tanner (1987) were correct when they stated that "the development of public education and the field of supervision are so completely intertwined that they defy separation, even for purposes of analysis" (p. 4). As Tanner and Tanner (1987) later assert, however, supervision has a distinct history that can and should be traced and explained.

In this section, a theory of history will be introduced that attempts to go beyond the assumption that supervision merely reflected movements occurring in society as a whole, and education in particular. The history of supervision is certainly a history of the interaction of broad social and intellectual movements affecting all aspects of education. The field of supervision and supervisors as educators were certainly influenced by these societal developments, as Karier (1982) and others have noted. Although further explication of these developments or forces on educational supervision warrant analysis, this chapter will primarily focus attention to more internal or organizational dynamics that influenced supervision as a professional practice and field of study. Rather than solely asking, for example, "What societal forces precipitated the emergence of democratic supervision?", a more fruitful query might be "What did supervisors do in schools to develop or support democratic practices?" In fact, supervisors were

active participants in shaping their destiny. They were, for instance, exponents of businesslike conceptions of management where supervisors acted like captains of industry in the corporate world rather than as victims of business pressures. Evidence indicates that supervisors marshalled resources to further their own professional interests.

While the historical antecedents of supervision were rooted in bureaucracy, later efforts centered on developing professional status in schools. Throughout the twentieth century, theories or models of supervision emerged in response to a need to reconcile inherent bureaucratic–professional conflicts of schooling (Glanz, 1991). Understanding this construct enables us to understand the progression of various models of supervision.

This chapter, in part, will explore how supervision moved through eras or changes by contrasting the development of seven models or conceptions of supervision: inspection, efficiency, democratic, scientific, leadership, clinical, and "changing concepts." The ways that current efforts in supervision (i.e., school-based management, peer supervision, etc.) reflect efforts to professionalize teaching, extend democratic ideals in school supervision, and circumvent bureaucratic legacies will also be discussed.

Applying the Bureaucratic–Professional Model

Bureaucracy and professionalism are important concepts for understanding the changes in the division of labor within schools (Doyle, 1976). Bureaucracy affected the underlying foundation of schooling by creating a centralized, standardized, hierarchical administrative structure (Anderson, 1968). Professionalization affected schooling by enabling some occupational groups to achieve dominant, and at times nearly monopolistic, status within the division of labor. Seen in this light, bureaucracy and professionalism are not two entirely separate and contradictory frames of reference; rather, they are complimentary processes influencing American education. The bureaucratic form of governance was indeed compatible with the efforts of professionalism; in fact, it was adopted into the internal operations of most professional groups (Abbott, 1988).

Bureaucratization and professionalization are not fixed or unitary concepts that affect occupational groups in similar ways. Indeed, the history of supervision indicates that bureaucracy and professionalism were uniquely manifested in terms of how and why supervisors struggled to achieve status within the formal organizational structure of schooling. For supervisors, bureaucracy, on the one hand, meant that they were accorded legitimate authority by virtue of their hierarchical status. As such, bureaucracy consisted of a hierarchy of authority, prescribed rules, centralized decision-making, and procedural specifications (Isherwood & Hoy, 1973). On the other hand, bureaucracy inhibited supervisors from gaining acceptance as professionals. For supervisors, prior to the 1940s, professionalism represented efforts to gain recognition for their work in schools and, at the same time, achieve a degree of dominance within the educational hierarchy. Employing more democratic supervisory methods, supervisors thought, would divert attention away from their bureaucratic heritage and enable them to achieve professional status (i.e., dominance and recognition).

The evolution of supervision as an occupation reflects the influence of bureaucracy and professionalism. Supervision emerged as a field of practice in the late nineteenth and early twentieth centuries "in response to increased levels of bureaucracy in schools and the public demand for more control over the curriculum" (Bolin & Panaritis, 1992:30; Bolin, 1987; Karier, 1982). The raison d'être of supervision and the work of supervisors in schools, especially during the first four decades of the twentieth century, was to remove the stigma of bureaucracy and to develop professional expertise as a distinct profession and occupational group. Supervisors, who desired a more professional role, were thwarted at several historical junctures.

These bureaucratic–professional conflicts precipitated a number of problems, leading to confusion in roles, status, and relationships with other school personnel. While details of this bureaucratic–professional conflict for supervisors have been elaborated in detail (Glanz, 1978b, 1979) and will be illustrated in discussing some of the models of early supervision, the essential point in this research review of the field of supervision is that efforts throughout the twentieth century have centered on refining and extending professional (often termed *democratic*) interests while simultaneously attempting to mitigate the ill-effects of bureaucracy and its autocratic heritage. Each new reform in supervision since the beginning of supervisory practice in this country has to some degree attempted to balance the aims of bureaucratic governance with professional interests.

The orientation of supervision as a status dramatically changed after World War II. Supervision, as a role performed by a specific group of school people, shifted from a specific *status* to a more general *function* performed by an array of individuals in schools (Davis, 1978). In other words, the efforts of a specific occupational group known as supervisors to achieve professional status were no longer expended. Emphasis was placed on the function of supervision and its role in terms of improving instruction. Along with this change in conception, there was a modification of the bureaucratic–professional dilemma. The problems experienced by supervisors, as an occupational group striving for professional status prior to 1940, became internalized in the function of supervision as a whole after 1940. More specifically, the bureaucratic legacy of fault-finding–inspectional supervision had become synonymous with the *evaluative* function of supervision. At the same time, the professional legacy of supervision as a helping function was tantamount to the goal of *improvement* of instruction. This *evaluation–improvement* conflict (Glanz, 1994a; Tanner & Tanner 1987) is a legacy of the bureaucratic–professional dilemma encountered by supervisors in the early part of this century.

The theory for understanding the evolution of public school supervision in the United States, especially since the late nineteenth century, is based on the bureaucratic–professional construct that affected supervision as both a role and a function in schools. This chapter will develop this theme by demonstrating how it was manifested in the theory of supervisory practice.

Research on Bureaucracy and Professionalism

In order to understand this bureaucratic–professional conceptual framework, the reader should consult a number of valuable sources. For the best and most recent overview of bureaucracy as a concept and research related to schools, see Abbott and Caracheo (1988). The foremost theoretician of bureaucracy was undoubtedly Max Weber. For an excellent overview of the work of this famous social scientist, see Gerth and Mills (1958). Several significant studies of bureaucracy include Bendix (1947), Blau (1969), Blau and Meyer (1956), Crider (1944), Crozier (1964), Eienstadt (1958), Gouldner (1954), Hall (1961), Merton (1940), Moeller (1962), Thompson (1969), and Udy, (1959). Important work on organizations include Argyris (1951), Bidwell, (1965), Blau and Scott (1962), Bolman and Deal (1991), Etzioni (1964), March and Simon (1958), Mouzeles (1969), Peabody (1964), Scott (1981), and Whyte (1955).

Although Abbott and Caracheo (1988) noted that "the amount of research on bureaucracy as it relates to schools is relatively modest" (p. 245), there are a number of worthy studies. Anderson's (1968) work is a comprehensive analysis that demonstrates the persistence of bureaucracy as the dominant form of organization in schools. Gracey's (1972) book represents an excellent study, from a sociological perspective, explaining the effects of bureaucracy on teachers and other school functionaries in a specific school system. Two important studies on educational bureaucracy from a historical perspective are Katz (1973) and Tyack (1974). In addition, see Brennan (1973), Gosine and Keith (1970), Hanot (1975), Isherwood and Hoy, (1973), Kerr (1983), Moeller (1964), Punch (1969), and Sousa and Hoy (1981).

The most useful discussions of professionalism include Cogan (1953), Corwin (1965), Doyle (1967), Dumont (1970), Foshay (1970), Freidson (1970), Lieberman (1956), Reid (1968), Stinnett (1968), and Vollmer and Mills (1966).

For insights into the professionalization of supervision and administration, see Beach (1959), Krey and Burke (1989), Leeper (1969), Mangieri and McWilliams (1981), Mosher and Purpel (1972), O'Brien (1963), and Wahle (1967).

The following studies are representative of the attempt to explore the relationship between professionalism and bureaucracy: Benson (1973), Blau and Scott, (1962), Corwin (1965), Dempsey (1969), Hall (1968), Hanson (1976), Mohr (1977), Robinson (1967), Scott (1961), Warren (1974), Wood (1971).

For insights into the relationship between bureaucracy and supervision see ASCD (1971), Eye, Netzer and Krey (1971), Firth and Eiken (1982), and Karier (1982).

The next section of the chapter will briefly describe the emergence of bureaucracy in education from its earliest days until fully entrenched by the early twentieth century. The intent in this chapter will be, in addition to highlighting relevant sources and research, to begin to construct a history of supervision that places critical developments in perspective and context. Much discussion will be afforded to early models of supervision that lay the foundation for future developments in the field. Later models will be discussed more briefly, indicating relationships to earlier models and relevance to current conceptions in supervision.

THE EMERGENCE OF BUREAUCRACY

European Antecedents and Early Developments

This cort, taking into consideration the great neglect of many parents and masters in the training of their children in learning and labor, and other implyments which may be profitable to the common wealth, do hereupon order and decree, that in every town ye chosen men appointed for managing prudential affayres of the same shall henceforth stand charged with the care of the redress of this evil, . . . and for this end, they, or the greater number of them, shall have the power to take account from time to time of all parents and masters, and of their children, concerning their calling and implyment of their children, especially of their ability to read and understand the principles of religion and the capital laws of this country . . . (Records of the Governor & Company of the Massachusetts Bay in New England, 1642, pp. 6–7).

The origins of school supervision are shrouded in obscurity. While substantial literature on the development of schooling in America exists (Cremin, 1970), discovering detailed descriptions of supervision in schools prior to the mid-nineteenth century is difficult. The earliest studies of supervision (Prince, 1901; Suzzallo 1906) give marginal treatment to the origins of both public schooling and to supervisory practice. Glimpses of supervision may be gleaned from Button, (1961), Elsbree, (1939), Kilpatrick, (1912), and Small, (1914).

The influence of European culture on colonial life and education, in particular, is unmistakable. In a cursory overview of supervision in historic perspective, Karier (1982) explained that "institutional forms of education such as the college, Latin grammar school, district school, and dame school, each in its own way institutional legacies of Medieval, Renaissance, and Reformation cultures" had a significant impact on American education. Furthermore, American schools adopted the Prussian model of graded schools. Lancasterian monitorial schools, originating in England in 1789, were prevalent in America during the early 1800s. Education in America, however, took on a unique character of its own.

American educational theory and practice reflected European patterns in some ways, but less so in many other ways. Apprenticeship, English textbooks, teaching methods, and the tutorial system were dominant educational practices in the colonies, as they were in England. More significantly, however, authority over education resided with "the parent in the family unit," not with the state (Karier, 1967, 1982).

The fundamental principles of education, as well as supervision, that we are so accustomed to today are legacies, by in large, of events occurring during Colonial times. Two landmark laws enacted in Massachusetts in 1642 and 1647, respectively, established the principles and guidelines of the American school system. With the establishment of a schooling network, albeit limited in scope and influence, colonial leaders realized the import of school supervision (Tanner & Tanner, 1987).

An examination of early records during the colonial period indicates that the term *inspector* is referred to frequently. Note the definition of *supervision* in Boston, 1709:

Be therehereby established a committee of inspectors to visit ye School from time to time, when and as oft as they shall think fit, to Enform themselves of the methods used in teaching of ye Scholars and in Inquire of their proficiency, and be present at the performance of some of their Exercises, the Master being before Notified of their Coming, And with him to consult and Advise of further Methods for ye Advancement of Learning and the Good Government of the School (Reports of the Record Commissions of the City of Boston, 1709).

Inspectors were often ministers, selectmen, schoolmasters, and other distinguished citizens. Their methods of supervision stressed strict control and close inspection of school facilities. As Spears (1953) explained: "The early period of school supervision, from the colonization of America on down through at least the first half of the nineteenth century, was based on the idea of maintaining the existing standards of instruction, rather than on the idea of improving them."

Tanner and Tanner (1987), however, in their superb yet all-too-brief historical account of early supervision, differed with the notion that early supervisory practice was merely inspectoral, devoid of the improvement of instruction. "It is fascinating, indeed, that many supervisors in early colonial America defined their role in terms of improving the quality of education rather than narrowly, as that of establishing and maintaining the schools required by the laws" (p. 9). Bolin and Panaritis (1992) implied that this view seemed accurate.

In another accounting of the early development of school supervision, Elsbree (1939) explained that the nature of supervision as inspection undertaken by selectmen, clergy, and school committees was "superficial" at best: "The hierarchy of officers common to our present city school systems was foreign to the minds of the early settlers, and professionalized supervision, with emphasis upon the improvement of instruction, was a far cry to a civilization that could scarcely provide schools and schoolmasters."

According to Spears (1953) there was a distinct group of colonists, New Englanders, that exerted the most influence in education. "The principles of American school supervision are traced directly to the settlers from New England." Although schools were established in the northeastern colonies and selectmen of towns were designated to secure teachers, little was said about the supervision of schools. It was not until the early 1700s, specifically in 1709 Boston, where committees of citizens were appointed to visit and inspect schools (Suzzallo, 1906).

Professional supervision performed by specially trained educators, as thought of today, was absent prior to the civil war. Supervision was principally carried out by local townspeople, who, for the most part, were concerned with improving education as well as with the maintenance of the schools as required by law. One might conclude that the earliest forms of lay-controlled supervision, although crude and unscientific, were democratic in nature.

The tradition of lay supervision continued after the Revolution through the middle of the nineteenth century, or, as commonly referred to, to the end of the common era. Despite the emergence of a new "American system of educational thought and practice . . . the quality of supervision would not improve appreciably" (Tanner & Tanner, 1987, p. 10). With the advent of a district system of supervision and then state-controlled supervision, the character of supervision did, in fact, change dramatically.

American schooling during the better part of the nineteenth century was rural, unbureaucratic, and in the hands of local authorities (For an example of insights into rural schools and supervisory practice, albeit to a minimal extent, see Fuller, 1982). The prototypical nineteenth-century school was a small one-room schoolhouse. According to Tyack and Hansot (1982) teachers were "young, poorly paid, and rarely educated beyond the elementary subjects." They continued: "Hired and supervised largely by local lay trustees, they were not members of a self-regulating profession" (p. 17). These ward board trustees who supervised schools were not professionally trained nor very much interested in the improvement of instruction (Button, 1961; Tyack, 1974).

America changed dramatically from an agrarian society to a highly urbanized, industrial state. As the nation changed, so, too, was there a dramatic shift in the conception of school supervision. To understand the antecedents for current practice in supervision, one must explore the development and evolution of supervision in the late nineteenth century.

Expansion and Transformation in the Late Nineteenth and Early Twentieth Centuries

In 1890, the director of the U.S. Census reported that the country "has been so broken into by isolated bodies of settlement that there can hardly be said to be a frontier line" (U.S. Bureau of the Census, 1895). The significance of this statement was not immediately recognized. For many years, westward expansion meant increased opportunity and prosperity for many Americans. The curtailment of this growth demonstrated the need for the American people to consolidate their accomplishments and formulate new goals. The events in the years to follow would reveal the gradual emergence of modern America.

In general, the second half of the nineteenth century was characterized by unprecedented growth and expansion, the disappearance of the frontier, and the emergence of a nation (Billington, 1967; Turner, 1920). This phase of American development was characterized by an unquestioning faith and confidence in the continued maturation of a country and an optimistic and spirited individualism that would pave the way for the future. In 1886, Andrew Carnegie expressed the sentiments of citizens of a growing nation only beginning to realize its potential by stating that the "United States has already reached the foremost rank among nations and is destined soon to outdistance all others in the race." He continued, "in population, in wealth, . . . in agriculture, America already leads the civilized world" (Carnegie, 1886, p. 1).

This phenomenal rate of change was accompanied by industrial expansion, economic growth, increased and concentrated wealth, higher national income, and intensified production of agricultural goods (Hays, 1957). Every aspect of American society was affected. This was especially evident in the growth of urban populations in New York, Boston, St. Louis, and Philadelphia (Schlessinger, 1933). Innovations in technology, transportation, and communication were rampant

(Cubberley, 1934). Progress was indeed the motto. The Darwinian and Spencerian doctrines were readily adopted by the Carnegies, Rockefellers, and Vanderbilts, and they provided the philosophic rationales for competitive individualism and laissez fair business practices. Although these doctrines did not go unchallenged, affluence and prosperity prevailed amid the pockets of urban poverty and overcrowded pathogenic tenements. Thus, the American paradox of progress and poverty was fully apparent well before the close of the century.

The struggle for the growth of American education, starting in the days of Horace Mann, who was characterized by Tanner and Tanner (1987) as the "first professional supervisor," continued and assumed a new dimension in the latter decades of the nineteenth century. The schoolmen, specifically superintendents, began shaping schools in large cities into organized networks. Organization was the rallying cry nationally and locally. There was a firm belief that highly organized and efficient schools would meet the demands of a newly developed industrialized age. That hierarchically organized public schools, as social institutions, would meet the crises and challenges that lay ahead was beyond doubt (Bullough, 1974; Cronin, 1973; Hammock, 1969; Kaestle, 1973; Lazerson, 1971).

During this period, faith in public education increased, transformations in the family, cities, population and economy took place, and political and social reform were pervasive. In effect, urbanization, industrialization, institutionalization, along with concomitant forms of rationality and increased efficiency, served to reorganize the socioeconomic, political order. This order would inevitably influence the character of American education, in general, and supervision, in particular. It should not be surprising, then, that the bureaucratic form of organization found justification within the upheavals of the late nineteenth and early twentieth centuries. It was not that bureaucracy was inevitable; rather, the differentiation of roles, reliance upon autonomous, rational, efficient implementation of specific goals and dependence on predictable levels of authority, control and supervision were "peculiarly suited to the fluidity and impersonality of an urban-industrial world" (Wiebe, 1967, p. 145). Bureaucratic organization, then, with its hierarchical forms of control, developed in response to a change in the socioeconomic order.

The reform movement in education in the late nineteenth century was reflective of the larger, more encompassing changes that were occurring societally. Although the nineteenth century was characterized by rapid economic growth, reformers realized that there were serious problems in the nation's schools. In the battle that ensued to reorganize the nation's schools, sources of authority and responsibility in education were permanently transformed (Tyack, 1974). By the end of the nineteenth century, reformers concerned with undermining inefficiency and corruption transformed schools into streamlined, central administrative bureaucracies with superintendents as supervisors in charge (Elsbree, 1939; Gilland, 1935; Griffiths, 1966; Reller, 1935). During this struggle, supervision became an important tool by which the superintendent would legitimize his existence in the school system (Glanz, 1978a). Within this context, theory and practice of supervision reflected the first dominant method or model, which is commonly referred to as "inspection."

Supervision as Inspection: Model # 1

Supervision was historically undertaken by the clergy and local committees through school inspections and frequent visitations (Elsbree, 1939). This inspectional function was later performed by rural and city superintendents. Gilland (1935) stated that often when the superintendent was performing the supervisory function, "a duty which ranked high in frequency of mention was that of visiting the schools" (p. 267). A prominent superintendent, James M. Greenwood (1888), stated emphatically that "very much of my time is devoted to visiting schools and inspecting the work." Three years later Greenwood (1891) again illustrated his idea of how supervision should be performed. The skilled superintendent, said Greenwood, should simply walk into the classroom and "judge from a compound sensation of the disease at work among the inmates" (p. 227). A review of the literature of the period indicates that Greenwood's supervisory methods, which relied on inspection based on intuition rather than technical or scientific knowledge, were widely practiced.

Supervisors using inspectional practices did not favorably view the competency of most teachers. For instance, Balliet (1894), a superintendent from Massachusetts, insisted that there were only two types of teachers: the efficient and the inefficient. The only way to reform the schools, thought Balliet, was to "secure a competent superintendent; second, to let him 'reform' all the teachers who are incompetent and can be 'reformed'; thirdly, to bury the dead" (pp. 437–438). Characteristic of the remedies applied to improve teaching was this suggestion: "Weak teachers should place themselves in such a position in the room that every pupil's face may be seen without turning the head" (Fitzpatrick, 1893, p. 76). Teachers, for the most part, were seen by nineteenth century supervisors as inept. As Bolin and Panaritis (1992) explained: "Teachers (mostly female and disenfranchised) were seen as a bedraggled troop—incompetent and backward in outlook" (p. 33). For further exploration of supervision to increase teacher efficiency by inspection, see Cook (1900), Cunningham (1911), Greenwood (1894), Harris (1899), and Soldan (1899).

Typifying inspectional and autocratic practices by superintendents as supervisors during this time were the practices of the most influential educator in the late nineteenth century, William Torrey Harris. Harris (1892) believed that the superintendent must be the foremost educational expert maintaining "supervisory control in the management of the schools." "The superintendent is the pilot for the whole system, and must watch the rocks and breakers, and winds and clouds, and look often from them to the eternal stars to ascertain the drift of his course." The control of a superintendent, said Harris, must be manifested both over matters concerning mechanical aspects of the schools, such as heating, ventilation, lighting, and the construction of buildings, as well as in school visitation. "School visitation," claimed Harris, "was an important responsibility of a superintendent." "Teachers," he maintained, "must accept the authority of the overseer, the expert, . . . the superintendent." According to Harris, Freedom was not a viable option for teachers. Teachers need to be told in rather definite terms, said Harris, "what is acceptable practice and what is not."

Harris' autocratic methods (1892) in school supervision were widely adopted by schoolmen of the day. Harris was known for his "supervisory devices" that were used by the superintendent to improve "the method of instruction" so that "a teacher's manner of discipline could be made milder and less tinged with petulance." One device in particular could have a "wholesome influence on the parent and the teacher" while it simultaneously corrected the "waywardness" of the pupil. "This device," explained Harris, "is the suspension of the pupil for repeated and inexcusable absence or tardiness, or for persistent and willful violation of the order of the school." A pupil's suspension or transfer would be indicative of the lack of classroom control on the part of the teacher, thought Harris. This suspension or transfer "is a gentle suggestion to the teacher to correct his or her own petulance."

Harris' methods were characteristic of supervisory practice. The nineteenth-century superintendent as supervisor believed that employing such supervisory methods would beneficially affect instruction and the quality of teaching in the schools. The mission of eliminating incompetent teachers, as the central thrust of supervision during this time, does not contradict the essential purpose of supervision that was to achieve quality schooling. In fact, supervisors maintained that the best way to achieve quality schooling was to remove "deficient" teachers. The methods employed by supervisors were inspectional and rather impressionistic, but nonetheless served to achieve the stated objective.

The practice of supervision by inspection was indeed compatible with the emerging bureaucratic school system. Supervision was perceived by many teachers as inspectional, rather than as a helping function. Because supervision as inspection through visitation gained wide application in schools, it is the first model that characterizes early methods in supervision. Other noteworthy sources that are representative of this sort of supervisory theory and practice are Calkins (1882), Chancellor (1904), Marble (1887), Maxwell (1894), Payne (1875), Pickard (1890), and White (1871).

The Bureaucratization of Supervision

The years 1890–1920, the "liberal reform era," as Karier (1982) called it, was a period in which schools, in particular, underwent enormous transformations. It was a period when schools were reorganized into an educational bureaucracy that remained the dominant form of school organization throughout the twentieth century. The origins of educational supervision as we know it today can be dated to the late nineteenth century. It was amid the upheavals of late-nineteenth-century America that supervision emerged as an important function in schools.

Supervision reflected the general tendency toward bureaucratization. As such, supervision was characterized by autocratic methods and procedures. Button (1961), in his fine descriptive history of supervision, observed ". . . that acceptance of an autocratic theory of supervision occurred because supervisors found themselves in a situation in which such a theory was highly workable" (p. 81). Supervisors did much to preserve and expand bureaucratic role relationships in schools. Bureaucracy, as Katz (1973) has pointed out, "is the crystallization of particular values" (p. 144). Supervisors and educators in general placed more value on authority, direction, and control than they did on freedom and individual initiative. Superintendents had an unwavering conviction that centralized, bureaucratic control would have an unprecedented positive influence on urban education.

The bureaucratization of public school supervision was established as a result of a number of interrelated factors. First, it was buttressed by Rice (1893), pediatrician turned educator, who suggested that supervision be the major function used by superintendents to gain jurisdiction over urban schools. Through the use of "scientific and efficient" supervision, superintendents' influence in schools would gain greater legitimacy. The autocratic methods employed by supervisors would bring order to a school system beset by confusion and incompetence. The bureaucratization of supervision took place within the larger campaign to bureaucratize schooling.

Second, the bureaucratization of supervision was furthered by the replacement of decentralized control over the schools with centralization and social efficiency. Within this context, supervision would assume much importance in order to accomplish the goals and directives of the newly established administrative organization.

Third, the idea that supervision must be performed by a central authority, possessing special training and expertise, contributed to autocratic methods of supervision. Supervisors did not favorably view the competence of most teachers. As such, they believed that the utilization of some rather drastic supervisory strategies was urgently required to reverse the ill-effects of teacher incompetence.

Fourth, the bureaucratization of supervision was supported by the ideas and philosophies of influential men, such as William Payne, William Harris, Andrew Draper, and William Maxwell. These men maintained that in order to accomplish the objectives of bureaucracy, certain dogmatic and restrictive techniques of supervision were necessary. These men fervently believed that autocratic methods would improve educational standards in the nation's school system.

Reformers in the late nineteenth century tried, in the Weberian sense, to establish a "most efficient form of administrative organization" (Blau & Scott, 1969, p. 9). Bureaucracy as conceived and instituted by the nineteenth century reformer, however, did not approach the Weberian "ideal type." In many ways the newly formed school system mirrored and perpetuated the very conditions that existed before the advent of this "new reform." "The more things change, the more they remain the same" may be aptly stated in this context (Cuban, 1994). The evidence (e.g., see Ravitch, 1974; Tyack, 1976) suggests that while many reformers were aware of this problem, more, not less, bureaucracy was applied. Supervisors wanted to perfect bureaucracy by establishing a "stringent hierarchy of higher and lower levels of authority in such a way that each lower level is subject to control and supervision of the one immediately above it" (Parsons, 1947, p. 53).

Due to the exigencies of a society rapidly changing from agrarianism to urbanism, bureaucracy was cast as the only viable option for the educational system in urban America. Supervisors at the time did not understand that bureaucracy was inimical to the goals of free inquiry and individual initiative, which are necessary ingredients for the survival and effective operation of a school. They did not imagine that bureaucracy and education, in the words of Seeley (1985), "are like oil and water—they do not mix" (p. 21). It is unfair to hurl accusations at these reformers for not seeking alternatives to bureaucracy. History, however, has shown us that bureaucracy turned out not to be the "one best system," as hoped by supervisors in the late nineteenth century, but that it was probably, in the words of Seeley (1985), the "one worst system" for education (pp. 41-49).

It was not until well into the twentieth century that supervisors realized the adverse effects of bureaucratic school organization and would decide to take affirmative steps to combat the curtailment of individual liberties. The "democratization" of supervision was in its infancy in the early years of the new century. As a result of the publication of Dewey's (1916) *Democracy and Education* and Hosic's (1920) article, "The Democratization of Supervision," which appeared in *School and Society,* "democratic supervision" would gain greater voice in schools (Hosic, 1920, pp. 331–336).

In perhaps a prophetic statement, Samuel T. Dutton (1904), a shrewd observer at the time, stated that "the efficacy of a centralized school management will be tested by the degree by which the superintendent succeeds in controlling the huge forces under his command without excessive red tape." "If centralization of power," continued Dutton, "should mean such a refinement of rules, and such curtailment of individual freedom, and such exasperating espionage as to depress the spirits and cripple the free action of teachers, there would, certainly be a reaction in favor of the earlier and more democratic methods" (p. 75).

It was in direct response to bureaucracy, supported, as will be shown, by teachers who were against the bureaucratization of supervision that supervisors in the twentieth century directed their drive toward professional autonomy and democratic methods. The chapter will now examine the beginnings of the "democratization of school supervision."

THE EMERGENCE OF PROFESSIONALISM

Importance of Schooling

It was the dawn of a new age marked by monumental transformations occurring in modern American society as a result of industrial and urban development. These transformations had promising benefits for business, industry, science, labor, agriculture, and education. The talk of progress in 1900 meant urban development, materialistic concerns, a literate populace, accentuated differences between the rich and poor, the extension of educational opportunity, and the promise of new abundance. To a large extent, nineteenth-century changes and reforms were consolidated with twentieth-century societal advancements to reach a new level of expectancy.

It was in the context of this era of optimism that progressivism arose. Progressives were hopeful that the American industrial system could be preserved from its own injustices and defects. According to the progressive thinker, the way to eliminate the maleficence of a democratic–industrial state was to be more democratic. "The remedy of the partial evils of democracy," wrote John Dewey, "is in appeal to a more thoroughgoing democracy" (Dewey, 1903, p. 196).

Progressivism, a broad social and intellectual movement, had its beginnings in the 1890s (Cremin, 1961). Lawrence A. Cremin (1959), historian of progressive education, stated that progressivism "arose during the 1890s as a many-sided protest against pedagogical narrowness and inequity." "In the universities," said Cremin, "it appeared as part of a spirited revolt against formalism in philosophy, psychology, and the social sciences. In the cities it emerged as one facet of a larger program of social alleviation and municipal reform." "Among farmers," explained Cremin, "it became the crux of a moderate, liberal alternative to radical agrarianism" (p. 160). In other words, progressivism was all-encompassing. As such, progressivism in education also took on special significance. Progressives realized that social progress was impossible without attention to reform in education. "I believe that education is the fundamental method of social progress and reform," wrote John Dewey (1959, p. 30), the leading spokesman of progressive reform.

Charles E. Merriam, professor of political science at the University of Chicago, in his comprehensive examination of civic education in the United States, stated that "[O]f all the agencies of social training, the school emerges as by far the most important in our time and country." The school's primary task, he said, was "to prepare the next generation for participation in social life. The church, the family, the group or gang, the culture system in the broadest sense of the term, all contribute to the training of the oncoming generation, but the heaviest burden is laid increasingly upon the educational institutions of the land" (Merriam, 1934, pp. 67–68). Beset by the magnitude of industrial growth, tremendous waves of immigrants, and perplexing problems of poverty in the cities, urban reformers turned to the schools for relief. Schools were seen as vital agents for eradicating inequities within society. What appeared to be irrefutable experiential and statistical evidence of the success of schools in American society buttressed the belief that reforms through schooling would reestablish justice, hope, and prosperity in America.

Thaddeus Stevens, Horace Mann, Henry Barnard, Francis W. Parker, James Carter, William McGuffey, Calvin Stowe, and other nineteenth-century school reformers laid the foundations for the conviction that the public school experience would succeed. It was people such as William Torrey Harris, William H. Payne, and Nicholas Murray Butler who helped standardize and systematize public education in the United States in the late nineteenth century. With numerous technological changes and the increased authority of the school superintendent to expertly administer the ever-growing hierarchical system of eduction, *progress* was indeed the watchword at the turn of the century.

Status of Supervision

The overall picture, however, was not a rosy one. A profound value conflict arose at the turn of the century that represented a serious source of agitation to the progressive reformer. The inheritors of the school system, shaped by nineteenth-century educators such as Harris and Maxwell, witnessed a system troubled by increased mechanization and regimentation of school practices. Many of the regimented practices that reformers in the nineteenth century sought to eradicate persisted and even, at times, grew worse in the early twentieth century. The organizational reforms of the late nineteenth century did not solve all the problems of American education, as reformers had hoped. Although not ill-intentioned, educators in the late nineteenth century formed, in essence, what could today be termed a *bureaucracy*. It would now be the task of twentieth-century educators to redefine the purposes, roles, and organizational framework of schooling within society. Reform in the nineteenth century meant uniformity. Would reform in the twentieth century take a similar stance? The problem confronting the twentieth-century reformer was whether to transform the bureaucratic school organization into a vehicle for change and democracy, or to maintain stability and authoritarian governance. The solution seemed apparent, yet strikingly elusive.

The growth of a core of supervisory officers was already occurring in the nineteenth century. For the most part, however, supervision remained the primary responsibility of the superintendent. For example, prior to 1888, "supervision" was indexed in the Annual Report of the United States Commissioner of Education (1895–1896) under the title of the "superintendent." Beginning in the 1890s, however, as schools were becoming more populated and authority was centralized, the superintendent could no longer personally supervise schools as before; therefore, responsibility of supervision was delegated to assistants. The increase of supervisory personnel was marked. In 1888–1889, the United States commissioner of education, in his annual report, stated that "the quest of supervision is an important one and is receiving increased attention." It was noted in the commissioner's annual report that "484 cities report 1,928 supervisors, or an average of four to each city-supervisory staff about 2,300." For the period, 1895–1896, the commissioner said that "it is plain that supervisory officers are becoming yearly more numerous." "The supervisory force has grown more rapidly than teachers or pupils," reported the commissioner (Annual Report of the United States Commissioner of Education, pp. 1488–1489).

Analyzing these statistics alone, however, does not provide an accurate account of public school supervision during these years. Although the school system was growing, the superintendent was not aloof from the day-to-day operations; in fact, the superintendent remained very much in charge of supervising schools. The supervisors that were appointed by the superintendent were merely involved in collecting data, reading reports, and other administrative details. The activities of these early supervisors were quite limited and closely monitored by the superintendent. Therefore, the term *supervisor,* when used prior to 1900, was really synonymous with the superintendency.

After 1900, however, as urbanization intensified and the school system was growing more complex, the superintendent lost contact with the day-to-day operations of the schools. As a result, the superintendent had to establish certain administrative and supervisory positions. In other words, supervision of schools after 1900 was the responsibility of someone other than the superintendent. There is much statistical evidence to illustrate this increase of supervisory personnel after 1900. In the period 1900–1901, the United States commissioner of education (1901) said that "the total number of supervisory officers reported is 4,733, . . . raising the number [in proportion] of teachers to supervisors from 17.6 to 18.5" (p. 1527). In 1905, it was reported that during the period 1903–1905, the increase of male and female supervisory officers was significant. The total number of supervisors during this period went from 5,119 to 5,729, an increase of 4.69 percent. In contrast, the total number of teachers went from 96,624 to 100,186, an increase of 3.69 percent (p. xxix). In 1911, the commissioner of education stated that for the year 1906, the Bureau of Education reported 6,600 supervisory officers and 106,026 teachers in cities of 8,000 population and over. For the years 1909–1910, continued the commissioner, the corresponding numbers were 11,144 and 125,246, respectively. Thus, said the commissioner, during a period of 5 years, the increase of supervisory personnel was 68.8 percent, while that of teachers was only 18.1 percent. "The ratio of teachers to supervisors in 1906 was 16.6; in 1910, it was only 11.2." These figures and statistics, said the commissioner, represented a "tendency towards a closer professional supervision of the schools" (p. 121).

Supervisors were generally former teachers who moved up the ranks. They were sometimes outside people who had influence in the community or business. There was no formal examination for becoming a supervisor; you were generally recognized by the superintendent or immediate assistants and appointed a "supervisor." Although there was no formal training for supervisors beyond the teaching degree, it was assumed that you were qualified to handle administrative and instructional functions. From the start supervisors were not well liked by teachers. Spaulding (1955) stated that supervisors "were quite generally looked upon, not as helpers, but as critics bent on the discovery and revelation of teachers weaknesses and failures, . . . they were dubbed Snoopervisors" (p. 130).

With the solidification of bureaucracy, these middle-management supervisory personnel increased in number. Supervisors, however, encountered a number of problems that in many ways inhibited their performance. As middle-management their authority was severely restricted and limited. Furthermore, job specifications, roles, and responsibilities remained nebulously defined. For example, in the early 1920s, it was admitted that "the present status of supervision is one of confusion, not to say of chaos. We have a multiplicity of names that plague us just as our unscientific alphabet does; the same function is called by different names and each name stands for a variety of functions." (Editorial, 1928).

A number of studies confirm the fact that role and function ambiguity was prevalent among supervisors during the first two decades of the twentieth century (Elliott, 1908; Fry, 1925; Melby, 1929; Moore, 1913; Neidert, 1926).

An irony was thus crystalizing. Although many agreed that supervision was important, relatively little attention was given to the supervisor after 1900. There are a number of explana-

tions for this apparent inattention to the supervisor. First, it was a time when the "superintendency" was emerging as a specialized profession and field of study. Influential men, such as Frank Spaulding, George Strayer, William Chancellor, and Ellwood Cubberley, and their ideas of business and management helped to formulate the basic theories of the emerging field. Administration, not supervision, was the prime concern. If anything, supervision, was seen as an extension of school administration, or, as one authority stated: "supervision was merely the arm of administration" (Lucio & McNeil, 1962). It was apparent that administration was the prime concern (Campbell et al. 1987).

Second, supervision did not dominate thought and discussion because there was no voice or advocate for the twentieth-century supervisor. The days of Harris' enormous influence had passed. Administering and managing a school system were of utmost concern, not the supervision and improvement of instruction in schools. It is interesting that Franklin Bobbitt, whose views will be discussed shortly, was a prominent educator who was very committed to school supervision in the early 1900s. His views regarding supervision, which were widely disseminated, could have been the rallying point by which to elevate supervision to a prominent position and field of study in its own right. As will be shown, however, his views were criticized by many, and even Bobbitt shifted emphasis to curriculum development away from school supervision after 1920 (Hobson, 1943).

Supervisors during the first two decades of the twentieth century realized the tenuous position they occupied in schools. The ill-defined nature of supervision and the indefinite and obscure status of supervisors within schools contributed to the attempt to find institutional legitimacy for their work. As a result, approximately after 1910, there was a concerted effort by these supervisors to clarify their role and function in schools.

The professionalization of supervision began as an effort to gain legitimacy in the eyes of teachers. They thought that the way to accomplish this was to devise objective, scientific methods for promoting "teacher efficiency." Supervisors were greatly influenced by Franklin Bobbitt's ideas of school management and particularly his call for "teacher efficiency." At this point in time, supervisors were not unaware of the problems they faced. They hoped that Bobbitt's ideas would revitalize interest in supervision; however, they proceeded with cautious optimism.

Supervision as Social Efficiency: Model # 2

American education after 1900 was greatly affected by numerous technological advances. During this time the "efficiency movement" gained considerably throughout American industry (Callahan, 1962). This movement also had important consequences for American education. Throughout urban cities curtailment of excessive expenditures and elimination of waste and inefficiency were priorities. As a result of the work of Frederick Winslow Taylor (1911), who published a book in 1911 titled, *The Principles of Scientific Management, efficiency* became the watchword of the day. Taylor's book stressed scientific management and efficiency in the workplace. According to Taylor, the worker was merely a cog in the business machinery and that the main purpose of management was to promote efficiency of the worker. Within a relatively short period of time, Taylorism and efficiency became household words and ultimately had a profound impact on administrative and supervisory practices in schools. Franklin Bobbitt (1913), then a professor of educational administration at the University of Chicago, tried to apply the ideas espoused by Taylor to the "problems of educational management and supervision." Bobbitt's work, particularly his discussion of supervision, is significant because his ideas shaped the character and nature of supervision for many years. On the surface these ideas appeared to advance professional supervision but in reality they were the antithesis of professionalism. What he called "scientific and professional supervisory methods" were in fact scientistic and bureaucratic methods of supervision aimed not at professionalizing but at finding a legitimate and secure niche for control-oriented supervision within the school bureaucracy.

Teacher Rating as a Function of Supervision

As a result of Taylor's rise to national prominence, *efficiency* and *scientific management* became the watchwords of the day. Taylor's work inspired Bobbitt to apply the business model to the nation's schools. Within a relatively short period of time, educational efficiency experts emerged with their own agenda for promoting better schools. Chief among the techniques that would be employed in the schools was the use of "scientific rating scales." Supervisors in the early twentieth century were very much interested in utilizing and devising "rating schemes" to measure "teacher efficiency." Their expectation was that the application of Bobbitt's scientific methods would elevate their professional status in schools. One of the early attempts to rate teachers was carried out by Joseph S. Taylor (1912), a superintendent from New York City. He explained that the measurement of teacher efficiency was essential in New York City schools. He indicated the benefits of a rating scale for teachers for which "every teacher who accomplishes the task receives a bonus, not in money, but in the form of a rating which may have money value." Teachers would later viciously attack this idea of basing salary or differentials on results of rating. Taylor also conveyed quite clearly what would result from unfavorable ratings: stating "those who are unable to do the work are eliminated." He explained that supervisors are in a unique position to improve instruction through the use of rating schemes. If the teacher is inefficient, warned Taylor, then the supervisor had every right to say, "take my way or find a better one."

Many other educators in the early twentieth century sought to apply business principles of scientific management to the problems of the school (Dalthorp, 1932; Davidson, 1913; Green, 1915; Hervey, 1921; Shiels, 1915; Skala, 1930). Several different versions of rating scales appeared in the early twentieth century (Johnston, 1917; Knight & Franzen, 1922). One of the earliest and representative methods for rating "teacher efficiency" was initiated by Edward Elliott (1910, 1915) of the University of Wisconsin. "The chief purpose of any teaching efficiency scheme," stated Elliott, "is to serve as the means of promoting development and improvement of the individual teacher." He had hoped to eliminate the rating of teachers based on personal and biased accounts. "The science of education has allowed us to devise objective methods for rating teachers." His scale included categories ranging from physical and moral efficiency to social efficiency. Points ranging from 0 to 10 would be awarded for each category based on the "observations" of the supervisor. Another significant attempt to devise a "teacher efficiency rating scale" that was widely disseminated throughout the schools was made by Arthur Clifton Boyce (1915).

The evidence indicates that these scales were used quite extensively in many schools across the nation. Supervisors, again, hoped that these "latest scientific methods" of rating teacher efficiency would give legitimacy and acceptance to their work in schools; however, criticism of these scales emerged shortly after their implementation in the schools. Writing in 1920, Harold O. Rugg (1920), then of the Lincoln School at Columbia University, stated that "the movement to rate teachers . . . needs a new impetus and a new emphasis." Rugg claimed that these "schemes" were "nearly always opposed by the teachers themselves and frequently the [supervisors] have been skeptical of their value." Rugg identified three shortcomings of rating schemes. First, the rating cards in practice "are not aimed at self-improvement," and have frequently been "an administrative scheme superimposed from above." Second, rating schemes, according to Rugg, were biased and abstract. "Rarely have such schemes been made concrete enough so that two or more rating officers rating the work of the same teacher could visualize precisely the same group of qualities." Third, concluded Rugg, the classification of traits themselves was ambiguous and ill-defined.

Rating procedures employed by supervisors were vigorouly opposed (e.g., see Elsbree, 1931; Johnson, 1922; King, 1920; *National Conference on Educational Method,* 1928). Despite these criticisms, rating schemes were widely used in schools throughout the first 25 years of the twentieth century; however, the proliferation of rating devices contributed to much confusion. No agreement was reached regarding uniform standards for measuring teacher efficiency. It was possible and often commonplace for a teacher to be rated unsatisfactorily with one scale, yet competent with another. With no agreed upon criteria for excellent teaching, college professors and supervisors began to question the efficacy of rating schemes. Criticism also mounted against rating scales because in many instances they were not used to offer any constructive advice as how to improve teaching. Rating scales were merely seen as ways of categorizing, stigmatizing, and controlling teacher behavior. Teachers argued that rating scales were not consistent with the ideals of democratic schooling and only mirrored bureaucratic and autocratic methods of the nineteenth century. For instance, Parrott (1915) commented: "They are fundamentally wrong . . . entirely unnecessary, a detriment to good pedagogy. . . . Let's rid ourselves of supervision of this sort." Many other vociferous attacks against supervisors and misuse of rating scales were prevalent (e.g., Bagley, 1918; Crabtree, 1915; Dewey, 1915; Hill, 1918; Lefkowitz; 1920; Patri, 1921). Urban (1976) discussed these criticims. Supervisors and their supporters did not succumb easily to efforts to abolish rating. Storm

(1923) responded to those who wished to eliminate rating: "We have classroom teachers who think themselves so perfect and so wonderfully professional that they need no supervision. These teachers," continued Storm, "would do away with all supervision and would sink all supervisors to the bottom of the deep blue sea. If they ever succeed," warned Storm, "our public schools will go to the bow wows." Others agreed with Storm (e.g., Judd, 1926; Newlon, 1923).

Thus, supervisors found themselves in a vulnerable position in the school hierarchy. They sought to legitimize their existence in schools by devising methods for rating teachers, hoping that this would alleviate many of their problems. Despite good intentions, however, they encountered much opposition. Teachers and other educators were dissatisfied with bureaucratic school governance that placed the teacher at the low end of the hierarchy. They were also disenchanted with emphasis placed on business ideology and "factory-type" education. Particular criticism was aimed at "rating schemes" that were used by supervisors primarily for decisions regarding promotions and salary. This was a period of time in which cautious optimism slowly turned into confirmed despair for supervisors. As a result, supervisors in the 1920s began to search for new methods and conceptions in supervision.

Democratic Methods Emerge: Model # 3

The supervisors' quest for professional autonomy to ameliorate their ill-defined status in schools, to gain legitimacy in the eyes of teachers, and to distinguish their work from administration assumed unprecedented importance after 1920. Professionalism as a process affecting supervisors represented a concerted effort to achieve some sort of internal organization, guidelines for expertise, professional training, a strong political power base, and control over their work especially during the 1920s and 1930s. The advocated theme for supervision in the post-1920 period was "the improvement of instruction," not rating efficiency. Dominant conceptions of supervision that were manifested in distinct models were now cast as means to redefine autocratic supervision as "more democratic and professional (Sergiovanni & Starratt, 1993). The attitudes, concerns, and aspirations of supervisors can best be summed up by the following anonymous (1929) poem found in *Playground and Recreation* in 1929 titled, "The Snoopervisor, The Whoopervisor, and The Supervisor."

> With keenly peering eyes and snooping nose,
> From room to room the Snoopervisor goes.
> He notes each slip, each fault with lofty frown,
> And on his rating card he writes it down;
> His duty done, when he has brought to light,
> The things the teachers do that are not right.

> With cheering words and most infectious grin,
> The peppy Whoopervisor breezes in.
> 'Let every boy and girl keep right with me!
> One, two, three, four!
> That's fine! Miss Smith I see.
> These pupils all write well. This is his plan.
> Keep everybody happy if you can.'

> The supervisor enters quietly,
> 'What do you need? How can I help today?
> John, let me show you. Mary, try this way.'
> He aims to help, encourage and suggest,
> That teachers, pupils all may do their best.

This new emphasis on "democratic supervision" gained popularity among supervisors after 1920. A review of the literature demonstrates a plethora of articles and books written about democratic supervision (e.g., Burton, 1922; Hosic, 1920; Keyes, 1921; Nutt, 1920; Sloyer, 1928; Spears, 1941). Supervisors during this period tried to alter the perception of supervision away from "snoopervision" to a more humane and democratic function.

The democratic drive in public school supervision was reflective of the general tone of American society in the 1920s and 1930s. President Woodrow Wilson, speaking before Congress in April 1917, asked for a declaration of war on Germany. Wilson incarnated the progressive idealism of the 1920s that embraced the idea that the United States' goal should be to "make the world safe for democracy." National democratic idealism influenced the urgent call for greater democracy in the nation's public schools. Speaking before the National Educational Association (NEA), Mary D. Bradford (1917), superintendent from Kenosha, Wisconsin, reaffirmed America's faith in democracy domestically and in foreign affairs. According to Bradford, "the evils of the world" were being "cured by more democracy." "That cure, more democracy," said Bradford, was being "applied to the internal affairs of the nation's schools." "The democratic trend in school administration seems to parallel this general trend in civic affairs." In her closing remarks, Bradford said that "the apparent trend of the day is moving away from autocratic and centralized management of the schools towards cooperative and democratic principles."

The most profound and comprehensive treatment of democracy in education can be found in the work of John Dewey (1903). Writing in 1903, Dewey explained that "modern life means democracy, . . . how does the school stand with reference to this matter? Does the school as an accredited representative exhibit this trait of democracy as a spiritual force?" Dewey lamented the fact that schools, "as currently constructed," do not foster democracy. James Hosic (1920), who was influenced to a great extent by Dewey, wrote an article appearing in *School and Society* entitled, "The Democratization of Supervision." Hosic cautioned the supervisor to eschew his "autocratic past." "The fact that he is invested for the time being with a good deal of delegated authority does not justify him in playing the autocrat. . . . To do so is neither humane, wise, nor expedient." Continuing to build a philosophic rationale for the supervisor's involvement in "democratic pursuits," Hosic explained that it is no longer viable to apply techniques of the past. Hosic believed, as did Dewey, that it was possible to reshape a school system originated on the idea of bureaucratic maintenance to comply with the principles of democracy.

Hosic, in his now classic article, analyzed "the factors involved in democratic supervision." They are: (1) a clear delimitation of the supervisory function, (2) genuine, constructive leadership, (3) adequate professional preparation of the supervisor, (4) scientific and impersonal standards by which to determine results, and (5) recognition of the human element. In explaining the first two factors of democratic supervision, Hosic discussed supervision as a specific function "not identical with administration," employing effective and cooperative methods best exemplified by enthusiasm, encouragement, and leadership on the part of the supervisor. In his third category, Hosic emphasized the fact that the supervisor would no longer be "chosen from the ranks merely because he was a good teacher." Professional preparation, wide experience, and "sound knowledge of educational method," said Hosic, would characterize the supervisor. Regarding the fourth point, Hosic admonished against scientific management without concern for the human element because without this element supervision becomes undemocratic, unscientific, and autocratic. Hosic insisted that the Prussian system, based on dictatorial principles, was not applicable to a country like the United States, where the democratic attitude was the "key to the future." Hosic believed, however, as did many supervisors of the time, that discipline and authority were important, but that they should "progressively be supplanted by cooperation."

Some 17 years after the publication of Hosic's article, Burton (1937) declared that democratic supervision was a reality. "Supervision is an expert technical service primarily concerned with bettering the conditions which surround learning." Burton continued, "it is sincerely hoped that the new definition [of supervision] will aid in eliminating from our thinking the implications of inspection, imposed improvement, and of the superiority–inferiority of the older relationship between supervisors and supervised." According to Burton, "democracy" had indeed suppressed "monarchical rule." The message was plain and clear: Snoopervision and whoopervision were vestiges of past supervisory practice; today's supervision is unquestionably "democratic," or so they hoped.

The Professional Orientation

Supervisors sought professional autonomy and development through the forming of a new organization and journal, the first of its kind devoted exclusively to supervision. Hosic (1924) lamented the fact that there was a dearth of literature in the field of supervision, while at the same time there was much written about administration. Hosic charged that there was a growing need for an organization dealing with the particular concerns related to supervisors and supervision. After all, continued Hosic, even the teachers had an organization in the Department of Classroom Teachers, founded in 1914; hence, the National Conference on Educational Method (NCEM) was established. *The Journal of Educational Method* proclaimed in an editorial (1922); "meanwhile, through every possible agency we shall do well to publish the fact that supervision is a distinct occupation in itself, worthy of lifelong devotion and demanding peculiar training and fitness." An examination of the publications, statements, and activities of this new supervisory organization indicates the desire by supervisors to redefine and reconceptualize supervision as a professional enterprise incorporating "democratic" methods to improve instruction in the schools.

Focusing on method, it was thought, would enable supervisors to attain professional recognition. An editorial (1922) of *The Journal of Educational Method* stated that in order for supervision to be considered a professional field of study it must provide "rigorous preparation, maintain definite standards, and give unmeasured service." The editorial continued, however, that supervision at present unfortunately lacks "methodological direction." In order to foster this direction, the editorial proclaimed that the NCEM "must publish the fact that supervision is a field of study in its own right possessing distinct method in its work in schools."

While the journal sought to promote supervision as a unique profession and supervisors as specially trained professionals, the evidence indicates that reality fell far short of expectation. Professional growth and development through special training and preparation were inadequate, to say the least. Prior to about 1930, supervisors, were selected on the basis of a minimum of undergraduate and graduate preparation, success as classroom teachers, and skill in certain administrative duties. The special supervisor was selected by the building principal or assistant superintendent on the basis of presumed expertise in a particular subject. General supervisors and principals were selected by school superintendents based on "competence in teaching, theory of supervision, and the science of measurements," said Coburn (1919), a superintendent from Michigan. In an extensive survey conducted by J. Minor Gwynn (1913) in 31 of the largest cities in the United States it was found that the conditions for eligibility, qualifications, and appointment of supervisors were less than adequate. In a majority of cities surveyed, no legal requirements or qualifications to be a supervisor existed. When stated in some cities, the legal requirements were vague and general. These requirements stated that the supervisor "'must hold a teacher's certificate,' or 'must be a practical educator.'" In most cases, "the judgment of the superintendent is depended upon to determine the eligibility of supervisors."

The subjective, nonscientific training of supervisors can be demonstrated by a reading of a book written by George C. Kyte (1931), professor of education and supervision at the University of Michigan. The book, widely used in "supervisor preparation courses," presents case studies describing problems that supervisors are likely to encounter. The student is asked to carefully read each case study and "solve the problem." The case study method was quite popular and considered effective in training supervisors. With little, if any, rigorous requirements for eligibility as a supervisor, however, supervisors quickly realized the importance of establishing more comprehensive programs for training recruits. A review of the literature after 1930 indicates more rigorous standards were established for supervisors. For example, many states established certification programs for supervisors after 1930 (Spears, 1953).

Supervisors never abandoned their dream of becoming accepted professionals within the school organization. One of the more prominent ways they hoped to accomplish their objective was to promote the idea that supervision was a "helping function," and not an obtrusive or autocratic function. "Snoopervision" and "Whoopervision" were no longer considered acceptable. Rather, the "supervisor" as a "helper" was advocated. Ethel Salisbury (1918), a special supervisor in Minnesota, claimed that in addition to being "progressive, open minded, patient, . . . and sympathetic," supervisors were professionals who cultivated democracy and cooperativeness in their relations with teachers. Indeed, the promotion of democratic ideals was an dominant theme in supervision during this time.

Supervision tried to move away from bureaucratic practices, which originated in the late nineteenth century, to a more democratic and cooperative function in order to attain a greater degree of professionalism. The principal vehicle for enhancing their goal of professionalization was the formation of the NCEM. Supervisors demonstrated their desire to improve instruction and accentuate democratic role relationships in schools principally through their journal and related publications (NCEM, 1928, 1929, 1930). It is curious to note that this newly formed organization, which attempted to promote the goals and objectives of supervisors in public schools while at the same time wanting to distinguish their work from administration, maintained a close affiliation with administrators and superintendents. In fact, the NCEM held its annual meeting under the auspices of the Department of Superintendence of the NEA.

In February 1928, the organization changed its name to the National Conference of Supervisors and Directors of Instruction. A number of prestigious educators contributed to the organization's first yearbook. Scholars like A. S. Barr of the University of Wisconsin, Orville Brim of Ohio State University, William H. Burton of the University of Chicago, and Leo J. Brueckner of the University of Minnesota added prestige and impetus to their drive toward greater professional acknowledgment. About 1.5 years later, in July 1929, the supervisory organization once again changed its name by dropping "National Conference" from its title. Becoming part of the NEA, the organization was now called the Department of Supervisors and the Directors of Instruction. Membership consisted primarily of people in local school systems throughout the country as well as in state departments of education. Perusal of the publications, statements, and activities of this association indicates a concerted effort to further the "professional orientation" of supervisors throughout the nation's schools (Van Til, 1986).

Summary and Preview

Thus far, early supervision as a role and function in schools was predominantly influenced by bureaucratic methods and practices. This was evidenced in two distinct models: inspection and social efficiency. Both models depicted the theory and practice of supervision as inspectional and impressionistic, aimed at promoting efficiency of school operations. As such, supervision as a process viewed the teacher as deficient and in need of assistance. The supervisors' use of rating schemes, which was an outgrowth of the social efficiency era, would presumably improve the quality of schooling. The similarity of the first two models was that both emerged from prevailing bureaucratic emphases in schooling. Differences

were subtle, yet significant, in that although both incorporated inspectional practices, the social efficiency model sought to refine inspection by making the process more "efficient."

Expectations fell short, however, and supervisors attempted to alter methods away from their bureaucratic legacy to more democratic practices. This third model depicted supervision as a helping and improvement function. Eliminating the incompetent teacher was no longer the central objective of supervision. Rather, improving instruction through democratic methods and practices was promulgated. The third model was a clear departure from previous methods and models. The remaining models were conceived in light of the democratic model. In other words, scientific, leadership, clinical, and other conceptions of supervision that would appear in coming years reflected the emphasis toward democratic theory and practice in supervision. Whether the efforts of supervisors was to gain professional acceptance or merely eschew bureaucratic legacies, future models would uniquely attempt to alter conceptions of supervision as a practice and field of study.

Scientific supervision as the fourth model was considered as distinct from social efficiency and entirely compatible with democratic practices (Dewey, 1929), as the discussion in the next section will indicate. Although many supervisors unfortunately conceived science in education quite narrowly and not unlike methods used during the social efficiency era, scientific supervision in theory promoted the ideals of science in education, through the application of the scientific method, and had a significant impact on school supervision. Hence, an examination of the literature of the time demonstrates that scientific supervision warrants consideration as a separate model.

The remaining models similarly uniquely established parameters and defined supervision as an autonomous and distinct function in schools. These models have a common bond in that they emerged as a reaction to bureaucracy in education and were influenced by the human relations movement beginning in the early twentieth century. Democracy in supervision implied a "deep concern for human relationships" and practices that encouraged and respected the dignity of the teacher (Spears, 1953). Each of the following models attempted to support this view of supervision, albeit in very different ways.

Scientific Supervision: Model # 4

It is clear that educators, in the 1920s and 1930s, urged for a more scientific approach applied to supervisory practice in schools and that the methods of the past were no longer viable (e.g., see Barr, 1925, 1931, 1933; Barr & Rudisill, 1931; Lancelot & Barr, 1935). The early attempts to apply science via "rating cards" was now losing favor. Burton (1930), who was a prolific writer in supervision, explained that the use of "rating schemes from our prescientific days, . . . would be wholly inadequate today." While recognizing the usefulness of rating in some instances, Burton, believed that "it is desirable and rapidly becoming possible to have more objectively determined items by means of which to evaluate the teacher's procedure." Burton mentioned the scientific and statistical work done by Barr, Gray, Brueckner, and himself as examples of "progressive development" in supervision.

One of the foremost proponents of science in education and supervision was A. S. Barr (1931). He emphatically stated that the application of scientific principles "is a part of a general movement to place supervision on a professional basis." Barr explained the importance of science in supervision and education in his *An Introduction to the Scientific Study of Classroom Supervision,* published in 1931. In his preface, Barr noted that there was much confusion in "the field of supervision." He said, correspondingly, that there was confusion regarding "supervision as a professional subject." Barr asserted that supervision could not rely solely on "existing subjects," such as philosophy, measurements, statistics, and methods of educational research as many educators believed. Rather, supervision must find its own methods in the "science of instructing teachers." Barr stated in precise terms what the supervisor needed to know:

Supervisors must have the ability to analyze teaching situations and to locate the probable causes for poor work with a certain degree of expertness; they must have the ability to use an array of data-gathering devices peculiar to the field of supervision itself; they must possess certain constructive skills for the development of new means, methods, and materials of instruction; they must know how teachers learn to teach; they must have the ability to teach teachers how to teach; and they must be able to evaluate.

"In short," concluded Barr, "they must possess training in both the science of instructing pupils and the science of instructing teachers. Both are included in the science of supervision" (pp. x, xi).

Barr objected to the use of scientific method in supervision as wholly inadequate. He described in great detail seven proposals to improve instruction. Barr said the supervisor should first formulate objectives, followed by measurement surveys to determine the instructional status of schools. Probable causes of poor work should then be explored through the use of tests, rating scales, and observational instruments. The results of supervision, continued Barr, must be measured. Most important, according to Barr, the methods of science should be applied to the study and practice of supervision. More concretely, Barr (1925) asserted that a scientific analysis of teaching is a necessary part of the training of a supervisor. "How can the scientific knowledge of the teaching process be brought to bear upon the study and improvement of teaching?" Barr contended that teaching could be broken down into its component parts, and that each part had to be studied scientifically. If good teaching procedures could be isolated, thought Barr, then specific standards could be established to guide the supervisor in judging the quality of instruction. He based his scientific approach to supervision "upon the success of the professional student of education in breaking up this complex mass into its innumerable elements and to study each objectively" (pp. 360, 363).

Another person who influenced the idea of scientific supervision was Charles H. Judd (1920). In an address before the National Association of Secondary School Principals, Judd stated that "teachers must be supervised in a fashion which is at once direct and scientific." Judd criticized the manner in which supervisors were chosen without adequate training in the science of education. In the future, he said, "they will be selected because they are equipped by mental capacities and by careful scientific study for administrative and managerial functions." Judd further urged that "both the non-supervisory attitude and the attitude of excessive supervision ought to be replaced by scientific method of determining whether classroom work is efficient or not" (pp. 30–31).

Supervisors undeniably advocated a scientific approach toward their work in schools. The establishment of a rigorous scientific base, it was thought, would elevate supervision to the lofty status it so very much desired. Barr (1931) again stated emphatically that the application of scientific principles "is a part of a general movement to place supervision on a professional basis." Burton and Brueckner (1955) argued that proper use of scientific principles could indeed elevate supervision to professional status. "Supervision . . . is moving steadily toward professional status" (p. 84). They further stated that "supervision is both scientific and democratic." They continued: "A few individuals still speak, write, and supervise as if science and democracy were antagonistic, or at least not easily combined. The truth is that each is necessary in an integrated theory and practice" (p. 82). For similar views see Snedden (1910, 1911). For a more recent overview of the scientific approach to supervision, see McNeil (1982).

The Distinction Between Supervision and Administration

Supervision, as a field, clearly tried to disavow its bureaucratic legacy by advocating democratic, professional, and scientific methods. Another major theme expressed by supervisors, principally through *The Journal of Educational Method,* was the desire to make a clear and definite distinction between supervision and administration. The major reason for this was, in large measure, due to the fact that supervisors in the 1930s wanted to isolate themselves from practices that might be perceived by teachers and others as bureaucratic. The new conception of supervision during this time was aimed at democratic relationships between teachers and supervisors. That supervisors were professional educators whose primary aim was the improvement of instruction, and not administrative inspection, was widely advocated by writers of supervision.

As previously explained, supervision was a function of the school superintendent in the late nineteenth century. Supervision was an important function used by superintendents to carry out their objectives of standardization and centralization of authority. The primary emphasis of supervision before 1900, therefore, was administrative, not instructional. The term *administrative supervision* is frequently found in the literature of the time; however, through the expansion of administrative and supervisory offices in the early twentieth century, some supervisors began to question the taken-for-granted notion that supervision must be equated with school administration. There was increasingly much discussion at local and national conventions of delineating supervisory practice from administration. As early as 1906, Prince (1906) said, ". . . when the duties of supervision become properly adjusted," then "the evolutionary lines of progress will no longer lie in methods of administration merely." Supervisors realized that if they were to become professionals, then they needed their own identity by establishing unique standards and specialized knowledge distinct from school administration. In short, they argued that supervision was primarily concerned with instruction, not administration.

In the first volume of *The Journal of Educational Method*, October 1921, Margaret Madden (1921), a supervisor in Chicago, Illinois, contended that supervision is a field of study distinct from administration. It is significant that the card index of a public library in a very large city shows one card only on the subject of school supervision. It bears the legend, 'See School Administration.'" She continued:

This does not mean that the library is ill equipped or that it is badly catalogued; it simply indicates that there is not a clear conception of the nature of supervision, . . . school supervision is not school administration; it is not school management. . . . It is a field in itself or should be directly concerned with questions of classroom instruction.

Many others advocated a distinction between supervision and administration (e.g., see Dunn, 1920; Foote, 1922; Holmes, 1927; Melby, 1932; NEA, 1930; Wagner, 1923).

The Status of Supervision: 1920–1940

Between 1920 and 1940, supervisors strove to attain recognition for their work in schools. They sought to gain control over their activities by establishing new methods and standards for performance. The primary objectives of the public school supervisor were to eschew autocracy and inspectoral supervision and accentuate cooperation and democracy. There is little evidence, however, to suggest that these "ideals" gained much popularity in the schools. The persistence of teacher criticism, the lack of specialized training in graduate schools, the problems encountered with scientific method, and the continued clamoring for professional status by writers of supervision were indicative of the difficulty supervisors had in maintaining a professional outlook (Glanz, 1991).

In their attempt to attain professional recognition, supervisors encountered problems that severely restricted their ability to accomplish their goals. First, while the organization they formed, in its early years, received notoriety (had a respectable membership of nearly 1600), by the mid-1930s the National Conference was losing members (almost a 50 percent decline) and did not attract a large audience, as it once did (Saylor, 1976). Partly for this reason the supervisory organization wished to merge with the Society for Curriculum Workers (SCW), as will be discussed in the next section. Second, supervisors experienced difficulties due to their interpretation of scientific method. Supervisors looked toward science for ready-made, immediate, utilitarian purposes. They sought to translate tentative and theoretical scientific notions into prescriptive and practical applications in schools. Their overconfidence and narrow empiricism associated with rating schemes proved to be a troubling issue in their quest for professionalism (Dewey, 1929).

A third problem that supervisors confronted concerns the nebulous distinction between supervision and administration. Supervisors had a difficult time removing the stigma associated with school administration. Administration's legacy is steeped in authoritarian school governance. Supervision after 1900 tried to disassociate itself from administrative practices of the past, but it had much difficulty in doing so. To many, supervision was a natural outgrowth of school administration. The difference between the two, it was thought, was only a matter of definition of function and that both desired to accomplish similar goals. Barr, Burton, and Bruekner (1938), echoing this sentiment, stated that the distinction between supervision and administration was a "purely academic one." "The two can be separated only arbitrarily for the sake of analysis, a separation in function is impossible" (p. 27).

Fourth, the supervisor's attempt to remove vestiges of authoritarian supervision and replace it with democratic supervision never came to fruition. In fact, some supervisors believed it was an impossible task (Newlon, 1934). Courtis (1928) realized the inherent dilemma: "Can you supervise me scientifically and respect my personality? I'm afraid not."

Moreover, teachers and other educators continued to criticize supervisors and their antidemocratic methods. The ideals of democracy were difficult to fulfill in a system of school organization which relied on authoritarian and hierarchical governance. In surveying the situation Ayer and Barr (1928) observed that the public school system maintained a rigid "line and staff type organization" flowing from the superintendent to the principal to school supervisors and then to teachers. The issue of finding a balance between bureaucracy and democracy was an intractable problem for public school supervision (Glanz, 1991).

Finally, supervisors had a formidable task in seeking professionalism because of their vulnerable status in the school hierarchy. As middle-management personnel, supervisors were often torn between their administrative obligations to the principal and superintendent and, on the other hand, to teachers. The supervisor was made responsible for handling both administrative as well as curricular matters, for supervising and evaluating teachers, and establishing school-community relations. The burden of these duties was so great that no time remained to offer assistance and guidance to teachers on a daily basis. Furthermore, the supervisor had to depend upon the superintendent and principal for authority to act, and at the same time upon the teaching staff to cooperate regarding instructional and curricular matters. As a result, the primary role of a supervisor became that of a bureaucratic functionary, overseeing the day-to-day management of the school and acting as "foreman" of teachers. Supervisors therefore found it difficult to become professionals when the demands of the school bureaucracy were so overpowering.

With the supervisory "dream" shattered (see Glanz, 1991 for a detailed explanation why supervisors had such difficulty attaining their goals), supervisors redirected their energies in the late 1930s and 1940s in another effort to attain professional recognition. An alliance with curriculum workers, they thought, would be advantageous and could elevate their status in the public schools. Professionalism assumed considerable importance in years to come.

Curriculum and Supervision

Courses of study, selection of textbooks, and other matters related to the instructional aspects of schooling were controlled in the early part of the nineteenth century by layman, school boards, and in the latter part of that century by the school superintendent. Curriculum development was minimal and episodic. The duty of the supervisor was to carry out the rigid and fixed courses of study determined by the superintendent. Curriculum was construed as that aspect of instruction controlled by the administrative members of the organization. In other words, both curriculum and supervision were under administrative control. This, of course, does not imply that school people were not concerned about curriculum. On the contrary, the evidence suggests that curricular matters were important concerns (Kliebard, 1987). Systematic attention to curriculum became a national concern in the late nineteenth century. Curriculum thinking was influenced by men such as Francis Wayland Parker and William Torrey Harris as well as by Herbartian philosophy. Curriculum issues were given voice at various important national and local meetings (Seguel, 1966). Despite some attention to curriculum, however, it remains undeniable that schoolmen were chiefly interested in structural, administrative reform to achieve their goal of standardization and uniformity of urban education, and that the superintendent took major responsibility for determining the course of study.

By the third decade of this century, however, attention to curriculum issues reached immense proportions. This was evidenced in a number of ways: (1) the widely disseminated work of Thorndike, Strayer, and Terman in scientific methods of education, (2) Bobbitt's work in Los Angeles, as well as his important book, *The Curriculum,* (3) curriculum revisions in city systems, such as Denver and Detroit, (4) the formation of curriculum bureaus, and (5) the important role played by national committees and commissions, as well as by the growing state curriculum projects (Caswell, 1966; Seguel, 1966; Tanner & Tanner, 1980; Walker, 1975). The watchword of the day was clearly *curriculum.* In place of Payne, Harris, McMurray, and Butler were men such as Kilpatrick, Cocking, Charters, Harap, Dale, and Lindquist, who were now concerned with curriculum development in schools. The administrative structure of schooling was secure; emphasis was now placed on more instructional and curricular issues.

Although interest in curriculum increased nationwide, no central "clearing house" or organization to meet the needs of curriculum workers existed. W. W. Charters (1923) stated in his significant book, entitled *Curriculum Construction,* that there was an insufficient number of studies in various curriculum areas. Charters said: "But with no central magazine existing devoted to curriculum construction, or other central agency, it is impossible to be certain that all significant studies have been secured." Charters felt that some sort of agency of curriculum was needed. Henry Harap (1928), a professor at the Cleveland School of Education, in a book entitled *The Technique of Curriculum Making,* similarly stated at the very outset that "there is a great need for continued study in the field of curriculum making." Harap emphasized that "we have not yet entirely cleared the woods," much remains to be done. Harap considered work in curriculum to be a "pioneer" venture. His own book was a "workbook," not a "theoretical treatise. "The chief aim of the volume was "to help students to make a new course of study, to revise a course of study, to evaluate a course of study and to interpret intelligently the extensive revision of curricula which is now in progress. "Harap, like Charters, inexorably tried to establish some sort of curriculum agency.

The publication of two volumes by the National Society for the Study of Education (1927), proved to be a contributing factor to the increased interest in curriculum across the country. Harold Rugg and George Counts, in a discussion of the current methods of curriculum-making, stated that "a nationwide movement is under way, . . . whatever the causes, the movement for curriculum-revision is here." Still, Rugg and Counts were highly critical of the current methods of curriculum-making. They said, "partial, superficial, and timorous 'revision' rather than general, fundamental, and courageous reconstruction characterizes curriculum-making in the public school." The authors criticized the methods used across the country as being of the "scissors and paste" type. Still, the tone and character of the yearbook was unequivocally devoted to the advocacy of a trained, competent, professional curriculum specialist.

A fundamental reason why supervisors during this period had a difficult time securing professional status commensurate to that, for example, of the school superintendency is based on the fact that curriculum, not supervision, was the primary concern among educators. Supervision had its problems in the early twentieth century. For example, supervisors, as was noted, had an arduous time finding legitimacy for their work in schools. At the same time, curriculum planning and development grew steadily and achieved wide popularity and, most importantly, was perceived as a useful function in reconstructing the courses of study. Special training in curriculum was viewed as a desirable and sought-after skill. It is important to note that curriculum specialists were not perceived, for the most part, by teachers as intrusive, but they were viewed as integral partners in the educational process. Attention in educational circles, therefore, focused on curriculum development. Supervisors realized that in order to attain their goal of professionalism they had to accommodate to curriculum issues. Before long, curriculum theory was being advanced as the new supervision. The supervisor, now equipped with new knowledge of curriculum, would be recognized as a complete professional. It was not that supervisors felt threatened (see Glanz, 1991; Krug, 1964), rather they saw an excellent opportunity to heighten their professional status by involving themselves in curriculum development. Supervisors, at this time, had no alternative. The choice was rather simple: "Get with it" or quickly sink into oblivion.

It was apparent to many by the 1930s that a unified effort on the part of supervisors and curriculum workers was necessary. Supervisors could no longer involve themselves in instructional matters without attention to and knowledge about curriculum. Curriculum workers also realized that an affiliation with supervision would be necessary to carry out curriculum revisions effectively in the schools. As a result, coordinated efforts between supervisors and curriculum experts were under way in different parts of the country. One of the early efforts at combining supervisory methods with curriculum revision was undertaken in the Detroit public schools. Stuart A. Courtis (1933), educational consultant for the Detroit school system, reported that the Detroit schools were unique in that supervisors were busily engaged in assisting curriculum specialists in various revisions of the courses of study. Courtis asserted that these efforts were "indicative of the prevalent trend at coordinating supervision and curriculum."

Perhaps the most widely publicized attempt at coordinating activities of supervision and curriculum took place in Denver under the leadership of Jesse Newlon, superintendent of schools, and A. L. Threlkeld (1926), deputy superintendent in charge of supervision. Newlon stressed that these coordinated efforts found acceptance in his school system because the schools were democratically administered. As such, efforts to combine the talents of supervisors and curriculum workers were welcomed. A conducive environment was present, said Newlon, that encouraged "curriculum experimentation, continuous curriculum revision, and teacher participation." Newlon and Threlkeld believed that supervision had a vital role to play in curriculum implementation. Newlon believed that these coordinated efforts would prove especially beneficial for supervisors. According to Newlon, curriculum involvement by supervisors gave them opportunities to work with teachers in a "joint, cooperative effort." This, Newlon felt, would enhance the perception of supervision among teachers. In an article entitled "Reorganizing City School Supervision," Newlon (1923) asked: "How can the ends of supervision best be achieved?" He maintained that the school organization must be set up to "invite the participation of the teacher in the development of courses." The ends of supervision can be realized when teacher and supervisor work in a coordinated fashion. Newlon developed the idea of setting up "supervisory councils" to offer "genuine assistance" to teachers. In this way, he continued, "the teacher will be regarded as a fellow-worker rather than a mere cog in a big machine"

The notion that supervisors should be involved in curriculum development was and is clearly recognized (Common & Grimmett, 1992; Consulting Editors, 1992; Editorial, 1929; Glanz, 1992a, 1994d; Heffernan & Burton, 1939; Society for Curriculum Study, 1932; Tanner & Tanner, 1980, 1990; Threlkeld, 1925, 1928; Wiles & Lovell, 1983).

The Joint Committee

Professional supervision reached its peak in an attempt by supervisors to align themselves, organizationally, with curriculum. Prior to the mid-1930s, the Department of Supervisors and Directors of Instruction (DSDI) and the Society for Curriculum Study (SCS) operated as two separate organizations with very little interaction between them. For a long time educators considered curriculum and supervision as two unrelated and distinct functions. Each would engage in their own activities without considering the significant interrelationships involved in the planning of curriculum and the supervision of instruction. By the mid-1930s, however, these apparently disjointed and unrelated groups formed an alliance based on a common effort "to establish a strong,

viable, dynamic organization" (Joint Committee, 1937). (For a fuller treatment of this joint effort see Glanz, 1991, 1995a).

Following this joint effort, a merger seemed inevitable. Although some opposed a merger, there is every indication that this criticism was limited and quickly overlooked. Still, Helen Heffernan of the California State Department of Education and a very active member in the DSDI voiced her opposition by stating that the supervisory organization was the stronger of the two, due to a more substantial membership, and merger would not aid their efforts toward professionalism. In addition, Heffernan stated that "curriculum development and supervision seemed to be related but not identical functions. Both required a distinctive type of expertness. . . . I have never been enthusiastic about the 'big umbrella'" (Saylor, 1976). O. L. Davis Jr. (personal communication, March 31, 1994) in a letter to the author recalled an interview with Heffernan who told him that she opposed the merger for two reasons: (1) that supervisors would have less influence in the new association than they enjoyed in the DSDI; and (2) that the men of the SCS would be more prominent than the women. According to Davis, Heffernan feared that merger with the curriculum group, which was mostly male, would eventuate in a male-dominated organization.

Regardless of these criticisms, merger was inevitable. For the most part, most supervisors and curriculum workers welcomed the merger. Many realized that the goal of professionalism that both groups hoped for could now be attained as a result of the merger. In May 1943, an editorial (1943) in the *Curriculum Journal* stated: "[T]he editor feels somewhat like the parent who is about to give away a favorite child in marriage. He approves his going, but parts with him reluctantly." Thus, the merger took place. The new organization was called the Department of Supervision and Curriculum Development. Three years later, the name was changed to the Association for Supervision and Curriculum Development (ASCD) (see Davis Jr., 1978; Glanz, 1992a, 1994c; Nelson & Singleton, 1980; Saylor, 1976; Van Til, 1986).

The End of an Era

It was during this period that supervision, faced with a deluge of demands and a dearth of creative solutions, realized, to some extent, the problem or dilemma of seeking professional status within a demanding, imposing bureaucratic organization. The supervisor's rather inauspicious birth during the early twentieth century marked the beginning of what proved to be a tide of circumstances that led supervisors to become aware of their vulnerable status and position in the school organization. The supervisor met several obstacles in the drive for professional recognition. The doctrines of science, democracy, and social efficiency were not able to elevate supervision to its ambitious goal of professional autonomy. Confronted with the possibility of obscurity and an indeterminate future, supervision renewed its striving for professional status through an alliance with the curriculum worker. These two groups of people realized that alone they would be unable to effect change or wield power to strengthen and buttress their efforts to be recognized as professionals. A merger, they thought, would enable them to establish a strong professional organization in order to effectuate the changes they desired.

Up to this time, public school supervision passed through three major periods in the United States. First, the late nineteenth century was characterized as a period in which bureaucracy flourished and supervision as inspection was prominent. Second, the period between approximately 1900 and 1920 was depicted as a time during which the supervisor realized her or his bureaucratic legacy and decided to make a conscious effort to counteract bureaucratization. During this time, supervision as social efficiency was advocated. Third, the post-1920 period was a time during which supervisors sought to professionalize. Scientific supervision and the reemergence of democracy in supervision were supported. Thus, bureaucracy and professionalism were important processes affecting the nature, conception, and direction of public school supervision.

THE EXPANSION OF DEMOCRATIC METHODS IN SUPERVISION

Changing Conceptions in Supervision

The amalgamation of supervision and curriculum, as a result of the merger, presented a host of problems for supervision and supervisors. After 1937, supervisors sought to define and clarify their role in the schools and achieve greater professional recognition. Supervision, however, was unable to break away from its heritage as an autocratic, inspectional function. With little or no conceptual foundation, deficiency of theoretical constructs, and lack of definition and direction, the supervisor's quest for professional recognition remained illusory (Glanz, 1991).

There was a dramatic shift in emphasis in the conception of supervision following the merger. After 1937, supervision was no longer considered a function to be performed by only one individual, but the responsibility of a wide array of school personnel, such as special supervisors, consultants, principals, department chairpeople, coordinators, deans, directors, and, later, even teachers. The January 1945 issue of *Educational Leadership* carried an article entitled, "Who is Supervisor?" in which the author contended that "everyone who is helping teachers do a better and more satisfying job" is called a supervisor (Rogers, 1945). The emphasis was on the functions of supervision, not on supervisor (e.g., see Doll, 1964; Lucio & McNeil, 1962; Mackenzie, 1961; Sloyer, 1945; Swearingen, 1946).

Although lacking theoretical clarity regarding what supervision actually was (e.g., Neville, 1963; Shores, 1967; Vigilante, 1964; Wiles, 1967), supervision did find some degree of focus, principally through its involvement in curriculum revision, which was widespread throughout the nation. Supervisors joined with curriculum people in a cooperative venture to make and revise curriculum. This connection to and involvement with curriculum development gained favor. During this time, supervisors were urging greater cooperative and democratic methods. Supervisors, more so than at any time in the past, advocated democratic

supervision in much stronger language and in more definite ways. "The supervision of curriculum development, . . . is fundamentally a democratic service rather than an administrative function" (Douglass, Bent, & Boardman, 1961).

As the conception of supervision changed after World War II from status to function (Davis, 1978), efforts by a specific occupational group of "supervisors" to professionalize diminished. Rather, efforts were expended into extending democratic methods in supervision, which was consistent and reflective of the prevailing democratic mood in postwar America. The literature from about 1940 through 1960 clearly reflected democratic and cooperative supervision (e.g., see Adams & Dickey, 1953; Ayer, 1954; Bartky, 1953; Boardman, Douglas, & Bent, 1953; Briggs & Justman, 1952; Burton & Brueckner, 1955; Featherstone, 1942; Moorer, 1952; Reeder, 1953; Rorer, 1943; Spears, 1953).

An influential pamphlet that called for the dismissal of traditional supervision in favor of democratic supervision was a pamphlet prepared by the Commission on Teacher Evaluation of the ASCD (1950). The pamphlet, entitled *Better Than Rating,* stated unequivocally that the improvement of instruction cannot be fostered through rating. The commission of five members appointed by the executive committee in March 1948 stated that "this bulletin opposes administrative or supervisory rating of teachers as undemocratic, as actually harmful in many instances, and as generally unproductive of wholesome change, growth and development on the part of individuals who may be affected by such practices." It is interesting that even Barr (1941), a staunch advocate of rating, stated that "teacher rating, albeit still an issue, is no longer viable." Barr realized that strong democratic leadership must replace the traditional view of "supervisor as rater."

Although supervision as a cooperative effort gained momentum, supervision became indistinguishable from curriculum development. It became difficult, if not impossible, to talk about supervision without attending to curriculum development. As one noted author put it: "Supervision is Curriculum Development" (Wiles, 1967). The inattention to supervision as a field to be studied in its own right is undeniable. Lewis and Miel (1972), in a work titled *Supervision for Improved Instruction,* lamented the lack of attention to supervision and expressed the view that "hindsight suggests that the profession went too far in its efforts to turn supervision into a helping function, a teaching function, a curricular function—anything," continued the writers, "but the function it literally names, overseeing with a view to improving the quality of an operation." An examination of supervision as a field of study and practice since 1937 reveals the lack of attention paid to school supervision apart from curriculum development. For example, a perusal of the *Education Index* evidences the lack of research dealing with school supervision. Sources on supervision were frequently listed under curriculum headings. In an issue of *Educational Leadership,* Robert J. Krajewski (1976), a professor of education at Texas Tech University, urged that if supervisory leadership was to be restored, then greater emphasis had to be placed on supervision as a field of study. The author of this article, entitled "Putting the 'S' Back in ASCD," observed that "curriculum has taken priority over supervision consistently." The tone of the article was, to say the least, doleful. The article indicated dissatisfaction with ASCD as a professional organization supposedly formed to meet the needs of both curriculum specialists and supervisors. Indeed, in October 1947, when the organization changed its name from a department to an association, the object of the association was clearly stated: "The object of the Association shall be the general improvement of instruction and supervision." The object of the association, according to Krajewski (1976), was not carried out. "There is no time to falter now," insisted Krajewski, "present indicators look promising for putting the 'S' back into ASCD" (for new insights see Krajewski, 1997).

This complaint about inattention to supervision at the expense of curriculum development is curious considering the views of many who advocated the importance of equal attention to both curriculum and supervision. "Supervision and curriculum development have always been central concerns of the Association for Supervision and Curriculum Development" (Drummond, 1975). Saylor (1966), who was president of the ASCD at the time, stated that "the national professional organization for supervisors" is ASCD. J. Harlan Shores (1967), who was president of ASCD in 1967, stated similarly that "the Board of Directors and Executive Committee are quite conscious of the 'S' in ASCD. There are times when it seems that supervision is neglected with the increased attention being given to curriculum development." He continued: "Supervision and curriculum development are as intimately related as we thought they should be." Supervisors and curriculum workers, however, never fully defined their own parameters and areas of specialization; confusion was inevitable. Supervision as a function consequently remained nebulously defined.

Supervision as Leadership: Model # 5

It is difficult and inaccurate to ascribe specific time periods to the development of supervision. Democracy in supervision cannot be described as characterizing one time frame. As was indicated earlier, democratic methods emerged early during colonial times, resurfaced in the early twentieth century as a reaction to supervision as social efficiency via rating schemes, and certainly was a dominant factor after World War II. Democratic methods in supervision were clearly expanded and clarified in the 1960s.

The political and social upheavals resulting from urban plight, concerns for justice and equality, and antiwar sentiments dramatically affected education, particularly supervision. Virulent criticisms of educational practice and school bureaucracy were pervasive (e.g., Silberman, 1970). Educators also took a serious look at supervisory practices in schools. The legacy of supervision as inspection, which found justification in the production-oriented, social efficiency era was no longer viable. Bureaucratic supervision was also not viable (Leeper, 1969). A new vision for the function of supervision was framed.

The work most representative of the 1960s was undoubtedly the anthology of articles, originally appearing in

Educational Leadership, compiled by then editor and associate director of the ASCD, Robert R. Leeper (1969). Leeper and the authors of this anthology still maintained that supervisors could achieve professional status by extending "democracy in their relationships with teachers." The way to accomplish this was to promulgate supervision as a leadership function.

The ideals of supervisory leadership were best expressed by Harris (1969):

The word leadership refers to showing the way and guiding the organization in definitive directions. New leadership is needed in this sense of the word. Two kinds are required:

1. Those in status positions must lead out with new boldness and find better ways of influencing the schools toward rationally planned, timed change.
2. New leadership positions must be created and coordinated to facilitate the enormously complex job of leading instructional change (p. 36).

Leadership issues in supervision in the 1960s were widely addressed (ASCD, 1960; Craig, Shapiro, & Schell, 1969; Curtin, 1964; Feyereisen, Fiorino, & Nowak, 1970; Franseth, 1961; Gwynn, 1961; Harrison, 1968; Hicks, 1960; Lucio & McNeil, 1962; Neagley & Evans, 1970). Although issues in leadership would gain popularity 15 years later, supervision as leadership essentially emerged in the 1960s. The principal focus of supervision during this time was a concerted effort by those engaged in supervision to provide leadership in five ways: developing mutually acceptable goals, extending cooperative and democratic methods of supervision, improving classroom instruction, promoting research into educational problems, and promoting professional leadership. Many of these foci were never clearly articulated and defined. A review of the literature of the period indicates that supervision, as a field, entered the 1970s with much ambiguity as to its role and function in schools.

Clinical Supervision: Model # 6

The field of supervision by the 1970s was plagued by many ambiguities. Markowitz (1976) stated that "the supervisor in the educational system is plagued by ambiguities. His or her position in the authority structure is ill-defined and quite often vulnerable, . . . there is a lack of clarity in the definition of his or her role and a lack of agreement on the functions associated with supervision" (p. 367). Alfonso, Firth, and Neville (1975) described this role ambiguity in terms of a "power limbo." That is, supervisors are "neither line nor staff, neither administration nor faculty, but somewhere in between" (p. 342). Wilhelms (1969) concurred that supervision had witnessed tremendous change. "Roles are changing; staff organization is swirling; titles and functions are shifting," continued Wilhelms, "But whether his title is 'principal,' 'supervisor,' 'curriculum coordinator,' or what not, the person in a position of supervisory leadership is caught in the middle" (p. x).

Lacking focus, a sound conceptual base, and purpose, supervision explored alternative notions to guide theory and practice in the field. Efforts to "reform" supervision were reflective of a broader attempt to seek alternatives to traditional educational practice. Clinical supervision grew out of this dissatisfaction with traditional educational practice and supervisory methods. Goldhammer (1969), who was one of the early proponents of clinical supervision, stated that the model for clinical supervision was "motivated, primarily, by contemporary views of weaknesses that commonly exist in educational practice" (p. 1).

The premise of clinical supervision was that teaching could be improved by a prescribed, formal process of collaboration between teacher and supervisor. The literature of clinical supervision has been replete with concepts of *collegiality, collaboration, assistance,* and *improvement of instruction.* Bolin and Panaritis (1992) explained that clinical supervision "appealed to many educators" because of its "emphasis on 'collegiality'." Ideally, theorists and practitioners maintained that clinical supervision eschewed any engagements with teachers that even remotely resembled inspectional, faultfinding supervision.

Most researchers attribute Morris Cogan (1973) as the progenitor of clinical supervision (Anderson, 1993), although Pajak (1989) credits Hill (1968) with incorporating a "lesser known version of the preconference, observation, postconference cycle" of supervision. Tanner and Tanner (1987) acknowledging Cogan's influence in developing the theory of clinical supervision, attributed the idea originating with Conant in 1936. Two of the best historical overviews of clinical supervision were done by Garman (1982) and Anderson (1993). Anderson (1993) not only highlighted the evolution of clinical supervision but comprehensively and incisively reviewed the literature on clinical supervision as well as its varied definitions. For further insights into clinical supervision see e.g., Acheson and Gall (1987); Anderson (1990); Anderson and Krajewski (1980); Daresh (1989); Goldhammer, Anderson, and Krajewski (1980); Pajak (1993a); Snyder (1988); and Tracy and MacNaughton (1993). Much information on clinical supervision can be gleaned from the many doctoral dissertations and articles published in journals such as the *Journal of Curriculum and Supervision,* too many to cite here.

Although advocated by professors and authors of textbooks, clinical supervision did not by any means gain wide acceptance in schools (e.g., see Garman, 1997). Clinical supervision received its share of criticism (e.g., Bolin & Panaritis, 1992; Tanner & Tanner, 1987). Supervision as practiced in schools remained inspectional at worst and eclectic at best. Nevertheless, throughout the 1970s educators continued to argue that democratic methods of supervision should be extended and that vestiges of bureaucratic supervision be excised. Supervision for improving instruction, promoting pupil learning, instructional leadership, and democratic practices remained as prominent goals throughout the seventies.

"Changing Concepts" Model of Supervision: Recent Developments

Since the early 1980s, public education continued to receive voluminous criticism for being bureaucratic and unresponsive to the needs of teachers, parents, and children (e.g., see Johnson, 1990). One of the prominent proposals for disenfranchising bureaucracy was the dissolution of autocratic administrative practices where overbearing supervisors rule by fiat. Favored was greater and more meaningful decision-making at the grass-roots level (Dunlap & Goldman, 1991). This translated into giving teachers more formal responsibility for setting school policies, thus enhancing democratic governance in schools (Glanz, 1992b, 1993b, 1994a; Kirby, 1991). Johnson (1990) observed that "although schools have long been under the control of administrators, local districts are increasingly granting teachers more formal responsibility for setting school policies" (p. 337).

Criticism leveled at the educational bureaucracy has had consequences for school supervision (Firth & Eiken, 1982; Karier, 1982). Educators continued, throughout this period, to consider alternative methods of supervision. In the early 1980s, developmental supervision gained attention (Glickman, 1981, 1985). By the end of the decade, transformational leadership was popular (Burns, 1978; Leithwood & Jantzi, 1990; Pajak, 1989; Sergiovanni, 1990). Other writers advanced their notions of supervision as well (e.g., see Bowers & Flinders, 1991; Champagne & Hogan, 1981; Gehrke & Parker, 1983; Glatthorn, 1984; Hoy & Forsyth, 1986; Pfeiffer & Dunlap, 1982; Schon, 1983; Wiles & Bondi, 1986). Teacher empowerment (Darling-Hammond & Goodwin, 1993) gained attention as a viable means for teachers to become active participants in decision-making processes in schools. Pajak (1993b) reviewed the literature on the "teacher as leader" during the past five years. Peer supervision (e.g., Clarke & Richardson, 1986; James, Heller, & Ellis, 1992; Leggett & Hoyle, 1987; Walen & DeRose, 1993; Willerman, McNeely, & Koffman, 1991; Zimpher & Grossman, 1992) appeared in the literature as an alternative to traditional supervision by "professionally trained supervisors," as did cognitive coaching (Costa & Garmston, 1986; 1994). Collegiality and democratic supervisory methods continued to receive notice (Alfonso & Goldsberry, 1982; Grimmett, 1990; Hargreaves, 1989; Koehler, 1990; Little, 1987; Smyth, 1991).

Although ASCD published two yearbooks on supervision during this period (1982, 1992), it was *Supervision in Transition* (1992) that marked a refinement in the changing conception of supervision as a democratic enterprise. Glickman, who was editor of the yearbook, clearly set the tone by stating emphatically that the very term *supervision* connoted a distasteful, even "disgusting" metaphor for school improvement. Instead of even using the words *supervision* or *supervisor,* educators, or what Glickman called "risk-taking practitioners," were more comfortable with terms such as *instructional leadership* and instructional leader. The transition that Glickman and the authors, of this comprehensive account of supervision, envisioned was one that valued collegiality. In the words of Sergiovanni (1992), supervision was viewed as "professional and moral."

What was *supervision,* who should be in charge of supervision, and how should supervision be performed were major questions with which educators during this period had to grapple. As in the past, consensus was elusive.

UNDERSTANDING THE HISTORY
OF SUPERVISION

The function and conception of supervision have changed historically. The earliest notions of supervision addressed the need for selectmen, committees, or clergymen to inspect the physical plant of schools and to ensure that children were receiving instruction as required by law. The legacy from the colonial period was one of lay supervision aimed at the improvement of instruction. Supervision in the late nineteenth century became little more than an inspectional function performed by local and city superintendents attempting to bureaucratize urban education. In the early 1900s supervision for social efficiency became the watchword. Influenced in part by social and economic forces, supervision in the 1920s and 1930s embraced democratic theory that would continue throughout the century, albeit in different forms.

Different historians have each reviewed the evolution of supervision by outlining various time frames and issues relevant for each period. Although some of these histories are accurately and chronologically developed, a conceptual or theoretical framework for understanding the varied shifts in emphases characterizing supervision, as a field, is absent. The research review in this chapter has attempted to place dominant conceptions or models of supervision in context by constructing a view of the evolution of the field as embedded in a bureaucratic–professional theoretical framework. What has been learned?

For some theorists and practitioners, a lesson learned is that authoritarian supervision aimed at faultfinding and suspecting the competence of teachers is anathema to modern practice of supervision. Some view the evolution of the practice of supervision as a progression from crude, unsophisticated approaches to more refined techniques and methodologies. For example, cognitive coaching (Costa & Garmston, 1994) is considered to be a refinement of more earlier clinical approaches that only emphasized behavioral changes. For others, supervision as traditionally conceived and practiced is defunct. "Instructional leadership" exists not "supervision," (Glickman, 1992). For others, current proposals and theories of supervision are merely masquerading under a miscellaneous array of names and approaches (Hazi & Glanz, 1997) in order to renounce the field's bureaucratic heritage. Fundamentally, however, supervision, regardless of what it is called, is still supervision. Its primary aim is still to assist teachers in improving instruction (e.g., see Glanz, 1997).

Regardless of one's particular stance or view of supervision, the development of supervision can best be understood in terms of a fundamental theme, as this chapter has sought to demonstrate. Supervision has always been influenced by two driving forces: bureaucracy and professionalism. Although supervision's inauspicious origins are rooted in democratic thinking, professional supervision, as widely understood, essentially emerged as a vital administrative function in schools in the late nineteenth century. Influenced by bureaucracy, as was urban education as a whole, supervisory practice was characterized as inspectional, and later redefined as an efficient, authoritative, and managerial function. Supervisors as an occupational group, beginning in the early twentieth century and continuing throughout the century, attempted to remove the stigma of the bureaucratic supervisor by employing democratic, scientific, clinical, developmental, transformative, and other similar methods of supervision. Supervision, both as a function of a specific group of people and as a field of study, has clearly endeavored to achieve professional status and recognition.

Supervision has also been influenced by another theme, not unrelated to the first. The inherent dilemma of supervision has been the attempt to seek a balance between the *improvement* and *evaluative* functions. Tanner and Tanner (1987) asserted that the conflict between the "helping" and "evaluative" functions presents almost insurmountable problems for supervisors. Supervisors have attested to this persistent, unresolved dilemma (Glanz, 1994a). Tanner and Tanner (1987) stated: "The basic conflict between these functions is probably the most serious and, up until now, unresolved problem in the field of supervision" (p. 106; see also Liftig, 1990).

The *evaluative* function of supervision is historically rooted in bureaucratic, inspectional-type supervision. Maintaining an efficient and effective school organization as well as a sound instructional program mandates that teachers are evaluated for competency. In other words, the evaluative aspect of the supervisory function emanates from organizational requirements to measure and assess teaching effectiveness. The origins of the *helping* or *improvement* function of supervision can be dated back to early democratic practices in colonial America and later in the early twentieth century. In other words, helping teachers to improve instruction and promote pupil achievement grew out of democratic theory of supervision.

Supervisors or people concerned with supervision have faced a basic role conflict; namely, the unresolved dilemma between the necessity to evaluate (a bureaucratic function) and the desire to genuinely assist teachers in the instructional process (a professional goal).

For example, role conflicts of this nature were documented by Catherine Marshall (1992) in a comprehensive study of assistant principals. Marshall stated that "an assistant principal might be required to help teachers develop coordinated curricula—a 'teacher support' function." "But this function," explained Marshall, "conflicts with the monitoring, supervising, and evaluating functions." Marshall continued, "The assistant may be working with a teacher as a colleague in one meeting and, perhaps one hour later, the same assistant may be meeting to chastise the same teacher for noncompliance with the district's new homework policy." Marshall concluded, "When they must monitor teachers' compliance, assistants have difficulty maintaining equal collegial and professional relationships with them" (pp. 6–7).

The field of supervision has attempted to resolve this basic conflict between *evaluation* and *improvement* (e.g., Blumberg, 1992; Frederich, 1984; Glanz, 1993a, 1994a, in press; Hazi, 1994; Munro, 1991; Poole, 1994; Tsui, 1995). It is clearly evident throughout the history of supervision that efforts have been made to extricate supervision from its bureaucratic heritage. In the latest ASCD yearbook (1992) which was devoted exclusively to supervision, one of the fundamental themes was the concerted effort to remove the "stigma" associated with supervision. Corrine Hill, president of ASCD at the time, corroborated the stigma of the supervisor as "snoopervisor" (p. v). Carl D. Glickman, the yearbook's editor, observed that "practitioners shun the word 'supervision'" (p. 2). Thomas J. Sergiovanni, who wrote the concluding chapter, went so far as to propose that one day "supervision will no longer be needed" (p. 203). Throughout the yearbook, it was argued that "instructional leadership" for the sole purpose of *improving* instruction was the new conception of supervision. Glickman concluded:

Supervision is in such throes of change that not only is the historical understanding of the word becoming obsolete, but I've come to believe that if 'instructional leadership' were substituted each time the word 'supervision' appears in the text, and 'instructional leader' substituted for 'supervisor,' little meaning would be lost and much might be gained. To be blunt: as a field, we may no longer need the old words and connotations. Instead, we might be seeing every talented educator (regardless of role) as an instructional leader and supervisor of instruction. If so, the old order will have crumbled.

Efforts to eliminate the stigma of the "supervisor" and of "supervision" are certainly not new. As early as the third decade of the twentieth century, Reeder (1930) affirmed that supervision as inspection was being intensely criticized by teachers and that a change in title might reduce potential conflict. Barr, Burton, and Brueckner (1947) suggested that the term *supervisor* might be replaced by "consultant" or "adviser." In the 1950s, titles such as "director" or "coordinator" were common. Less common, although prevalent were "helping teacher" "resource person" (Spears, 1953). In the 1960s and 1970s, "change agents" were in vogue. Wilhelms (1973) acknowledged the tendency for many educators to eschew the word *supervisor*.

The field of supervision has struggled with ways of defining itself (Bolin, 1987). With its bureaucratic heritage firmly entrenched, supervision has tried to reshape its image as a democratic enterprise aimed at instructional improvement. Pajak (1993b) was correct when he observed that "supervision in education has long been associated with democratic principles" (p. 176). Although democracy in supervision was first articulated comprehensively by Hosic (1920) 75 years ago, the bridge between theory and practice has been unstable. Surges and setbacks in democratic thought have characterized supervision since 1920. It is clear that supervision, realizing its inherent dilemma (viz., the evaluation and improvement issue), has tried to align itself with democratic governance. The multifarious proposals to accomplish this lofty and, perhaps, necessary objective will probably continue and that may be a good thing until, at least, supervision, as an important function in schools, finds its niche in the educational framework.

FUTURE RESEARCH

In attempting to note the histories, antecedents, and legacies of educational supervision, this chapter has reviewed relevant historical research, presented a theoretical model offering a framework for understanding the evolution of supervision, and has analyzed significant conceptions of supervision that may have influenced theory and practice in the field. An underlying purpose in writing this chapter has also been to help construct a history of the field. This final section of the chapter (based on Glanz, 1995b) will document the inattention to supervision history, explain the significance of historical inquiry, and suggest avenues for future research.

The Current Void

The proliferation of works focusing on the history and historiography of American education has been marked and comprehensive. Since the early to mid-1970s, the history of American education has expanded to include a broad range of topics and issues. History as a legitimate mode of inquiry is today unquestioned (e.g., Urban, 1982); however, supervision as a field of study and practice has regrettably escaped serious and ongoing investigation by educational historians (Glanz, 1990b, 1994b). Despite the fact that administration (e.g., Tyack & Hansot, 1982), curriculum (e.g., Schubert & Lopez-Schubert, 1980), teaching (e.g., Warren, 1989), teacher education (e.g., Houston, 1990), urban schooling (e.g., Katz, 1987) and even special education (e.g., Lazerson, 1983), for example, have received notable attention, school supervision remains unexamined and neglected (Glickman, 1985).

More than 20 years ago, ASCD (1976) itself lamented the lack of interest in supervision by stating that "a definitive history of educational supervision has not been published." In 1976, an ASCD yearbook devoted to historical analysis gave insufficient attention to supervision from a historical perspective (Davis, 1976). Others have confirmed these observations (Firth, 1986; Krajewski, 1976; Wilhelms, 1973). Glanz (1977a, 1990a) argued that "supervision as a field of study has little by way of history."

Although a formal subspecialty in historical scholarship of supervision may not be necessary, historical investigation of supervision is warranted and should receive greater attention. Before explicating why historical research in supervision has been marginalized and examining avenues for further historical inquiry, a brief description of what is meant by history, what are the benefits of historical study, and what it means to think historically about supervision should be explored.

History: Its Purpose and Benefits

The study of history is a struggle to understand the "unending dialogue between the present and the past" (Carr, 1961, p. 8). As such, the notion of temporality is relevant to understanding the flow of historical events. People and events cannot be explained only in terms of the present; they must also be understood in terms of a past and a future as well. The past, present, and future, according to Cassirer, form an "undifferentiated unity and an indiscriminate whole" (Cassirer, 1953, p. 219). Kummel explains this notion of temporality as a historical process "in which the past never assumes a final shape nor the future ever shuts its doors. Their essential interdependence also means, however, that there can be no progress without a retreat into the past in search of a deeper foundation" (Kummel, 1966, p. 50).

The experience of reflective consciousness through historical inquiry implies an awareness of the past and its interconnectedness to present conditions and future possibilities. History, then, can be understood as an attempt to study the events and ideas of the past that have shaped human experience over time in order to inform current practice as well as to make more intelligent decisions for the future (Marsak, 1970).

History is more than simply recording all past experiences and events. Historians are interested in those aspects of the past that have historical significance. Since what may be historically significant to one may be irrelevant to another, the reconstruction of the past must be undertaken from different perspectives by different people. Moreover, significance is granted only when a sufficient amount of time has lapsed in order to ensure that contemporary demands alone do not dictate what is considered historically important (e.g., see Davis, 1992). Seen in this way, history is the retelling and interpretation of significant events of the past (Stephens, 1974).

The value of history is its concreteness, its placing of events, people, and theories within context (e.g., see Goodson, 1985). History supplies the context with which to view current proposals. More fundamentally, understanding how the field has come to take the shape it has is a compelling reason to undertake historical inquiry of supervision. History can also explore antecedents of current innovations or theories. Thus, having a supervision history will deepen and strengthen identity as a field of scholarship and provide a collective consciousness (cf., Garrett, 1994).

Thinking Historically about Supervision

Theorists of supervision should not be content with developing proposals and formulating new models of supervision by systematically explaining their underlying assumptions. Similarly, practitioners should not carry out supervisory strategies merely to solve immediate problems. Instead, those concerned with supervision must continually reflect on their basis for doing what they do. Critical historical analysis will have per se a twofold effect on the field: leaders, developers, and researchers will look to the past for precedent; and those who write and theorize about supervision will view their efforts as embedded or situated in a set of historical conditions. To look for precedent, to draw upon historical responses to contemporarylike problems, and to view current proposals and models as connected to prior efforts and dilemmas is to acknowledge the field's historicity.

To be historical, then, means to be concerned with questions such as:

• How are prevailing practices and advocated theories connected to the past?

• How have significant ideas, events, and people influenced or informed current practice?

• What are the social, economic, philosophical, and political forces that have shaped the field's experience and, or theories?

• Once legacies are understood, can models of supervision that address the exigencies of the present by building on lessons of the past be formulated?

• What else can be learned from history that might help develop the field of supervision? (e.g., see Reid, 1986).

The emergence of a history of supervision demands an understanding of how the field came to be as it is, as well as how current practices and theories of supervision are outgrowths of past developments. To think historically is to break away from taken-for-granted notions that reinforce reliance on immediacy as the sole measure for theory and practice in supervision. To think historically means much more than presenting a superficial overview in the first chapter of a book or a subsection of an article. To underscore the import of history as a perspective that can provide useful information, one must continually deliberate by posing key historical questions. Tanner and Tanner's (1987) textbook on supervision, titled *Supervision in Education: Problems and Practices,* is an excellent example of the kind of historicity for which the field should strive. The authors go beyond providing an overview of the evolution of the field in the first chapter to provide a historical perspective that is reflected and taken seriously in chapters that follow.

An illustration of the lack of attention paid to supervision history is the manner in which writers in the field address the changing conceptions of the status and function of supervision. Sergiovanni and Starratt (1993), in their revised textbook on supervision, retitled *Supervision: A Redefinition,* assert that numerous changes and understandings about schooling, teaching, and leadership, among other factors, necessitate a "redefinition" of supervisory practice and theory. "This redefinition includes the disconnection of supervision from hierarchical roles and a focus on community as the primary metaphor for schooling." Through the word *community* the authors of this comprehensive, up-to-date, and widely acknowledged text on supervision denote the fact that responsibility for supervision has widened to include supervisors as well as teachers, mentors, consultants, and other school- and district-based personnel (see also Sergiovanni, 1997). Sergiovanni and Starratt, however, do maintain that "the supervisor's role remains important but is understood differently."

A tenaciously held conviction prevails that *supervisors* continue to be necessary, even essential, in an educational world that is now populated by teachers and other educators specially trained to perform supervision (e.g., see Willerman, McNeely, & Koffman, 1991). Teacher decision-making and democratic school governance is replacing bureaucratic mandates and administrative fiat (Johnson, 1990). The field of supervision over the past 50 years or so has not readily acknowledged, and has even resisted, the distinction advanced in the 1930s that supervision as a *function* is not, nor should be, necessarily located in supervision as *person*. The merger between the Department of Supervisors and Directors of Instruction (DSDI) and the Society for Curriculum Study (SCS) to eventually form the ASCD is indicative of this shift from status to function (Davis, 1978). While conceptions in the field of supervision appear to have changed, as reflected, for instance, in title changes of the various editions of Sergiovanni and Starratt's book, educators concerned with school supervision have insisted on maintaining archaic conceptions regarding its role and function. That supervision should be a democratic, cooperative function performed by those leaders engaged in improving instruction has been long recognized and advocated. Thus, without reference to past proposals and an explication of how current propositions evolved, we fall prey to reinventing the wheel again and again.

Has a history of supervision therefore been constructed? Is the field of supervision historically conscious of its traditions and legacies? To the extent that some scholars have seen the relevance of history and have, in fact, taken a historical perspective in their writings (e.g., see Anderson & Snyder, 1993; Blumberg & Greenfield, 1986; Krey & Burke, 1989), some progress has certainly been made. Notwithstanding these writings and the general acceptance of historical inquiry as a viable enterprise, only limited attention has been given to history. A perusal of textbooks, journal articles, and conference presentations clearly demonstrates this.

The Marginalization of Supervision's History

The treatment of the history of supervision as an identified area of scholarship rests on two problems. First, while some practitioners and theorists are certainly ahistorical, many others have simply given limited attention to history as a viable area of scholarship. A perusal of many textbooks on supervision, occasional dissertations, and selected journal articles demonstrates the generalized and simplistic treatment of history. As mentioned earlier in the chapter, many authors have taken a chronological approach to examining the evolution of supervision. Periodization is both arbitrary and monotonous, and it is also usually more inaccurate. Second, the attention that has been given to supervision history has been abysmally sporadic, and neither effective nor persuasive. The field characteristically remains overly pragmatic and highly prescriptive. A climate of urgency prevails in which "to do" is more valued than "to know." It is more a problem that the field's use of history lacks specificity, nuance, and power than that it is ahistorical (cf., Hazlett, 1979).

The paucity of historical research in supervision can be attributed to several fundamental reasons. Foremost is the fact that varying degrees of ahistoricism characterizes the field. Ahistoricism in supervision due to lack of knowledge of intellectual traditions and to inherited modes of behavior characterized the field for many years. While this sort of ahistoricism may be a thing of the past, practitioners and theorists continue to marginalize the importance of historical inquiry. Many assert that historical inquiry has little if any impact on day-to-day practice. Supervisors, be they assistant principals, principals, district office personnel, curriculum workers, mentors, classroom cooperating teachers, peer consultants, or educational evaluators, are burdened by demanding and challenging responsibilities of managing schools and providing instructional services to teachers (Glanz, 1994d). As such, they are very much practice oriented. Most articles in the major publications that supervisors subscribe to, such as *Educational Leadership, NASSP Bulletin, NAESP Bulletin,* and the *Journal of School Leadership,* are highly prescriptive; only a few deal with theoretical postulates, and even fewer with historical analyses.

Moreover, the nonreflective stance taken by the field of supervision is compounded by a rather different form of ahistoricism. Practitioners question the usefulness of understanding past events, and they tend to uncritically accept current ideas about supervisory practice that have their origins in the past. The persistence of bureaucratic authority in supervision reflects this tendency. Some practitioners fail to acknowledge other important sources of authority, such as "the professional and moral" (Sergiovanni, 1992). For these practitioners, the primary sources of authority for supervision will rarely change from bureaucratic to professional and moral without, at least, their understanding the origins of bureaucratic governance and how supervisors have historically been influenced by bureaucratic mandates. Ahistoricism precludes an understanding of the ways in which meanings have been sedimented in current practice. As Kliebard noted, albeit in relation to curriculum, "[U]nder these circumstances, the present almost inevitably intrudes on our understanding of the past, and the past becomes little more than a rationale for exhortations in behalf of urgent changes in the present" (Kliebard, 1992, p. 161; see also Kliebard, 1995, for insights into the value of history).

Ahistoricism is only partially responsible for lack of interest in the history of supervision. After all, the field of curriculum suffered not too long ago from historical amnesia as well. Although curriculum history has not been fully accepted, much progress has been made compared with supervision. Why, then, is the problem so pronounced in supervision? Another explanation may reside in the lack of clarity in even defining supervision (e.g., see Bolin, 1987; Holland, 1994; Smyth, 1991; Waite, 1994). Alfonso and Firth (1990) have noted that the study of supervision lacks focus largely due to the "lack of research and continuing disagreement on the definition and purposes of supervision."

To define supervision as merely "the improvement of instruction" does little to focus attention on critical dimensions of instructional supervision. Moreover, there is little if any consensus about the definitions that do abound (see Krey & Burke, 1989). A lack of clarity as to even the duties and responsibilities of supervisors has consequently been prevalent since around 1920. The fact that historical scholarship has not been taken seriously is understandable, albeit regrettable, given the absence of focus and lack of consensus as to what supervisors do. Can a field expect to attain historical maturity when difficulties prevail in both defining the field's parameters and role in schools?

Another reason why historical analysis is often ignored relates to a fundamental difficulty that, until rather recently, characterized education as a whole. The model of social research—the scientific method—and the logic that underpins it—positivism—have dominated educational and administrative theory. For supervisors, both practitioners and theorists, ontological and epistemological assumptions have shaped the kind of methodology accepted in the field. The predominance of this social science perspective has only undergone criticism in light of the emergence of qualitative analyses, including ethnographic and biographical. The traditions of positivism and the scientific method in educational research have precluded scholars of supervision, in this case, from examining the historical context out of which they operate because immediate, practical results are preferred.

Ahistoricism in supervision is compounded by a more fundamental problem. Supervision as a field of study has not received adequate attention. Harris (1964) decried the lack of research in supervision. Even *Educational Leadership,* explained Harris, "rare among nationally circulated periodicals in being devoted primarily to supervision and curriculum development . . . publishes few articles per se and few in supervision research."

More than 25 years ago, Goldhammer (1969) articulated problems in supervision in a scathing critique:

The problem is, more seriously, an internal one: that in the absence of some cogent framework of educational values and of powerful theoretical systems, operational models, extensive bodies of case material to consult, rigorous programs of professional training, and a broad literature of empirical research, supervision has neither a fundamental substantive content nor a consciously determined and universally recognized process—both its stuff and its methods tend to be random, residual, frequently archaic, and eclectic in the worst sense.

The National Society for the Study of Education (1913) has devoted only one work to supervision that was published over 80 years ago. Even ASCD presidents have noted the inattention to supervision. Muriel Crosby (1969), in an address at an ASCD annual conference in 1969, charged that supervisors "are being sold short by lack of effective leadership" [within ASCD]. Recently, Bolin and Panaritis (1992) commented on the lack of attention paid to supervision by the ASCD. "Between 1944 and 1981, ASCD had published more than 40 yearbooks; but only four of these were devoted to supervision" (p. 40). Since 1981, only two other yearbooks have been devoted to supervision. Even the yearbook dealing with improving teaching does not mention supervision (see Zumalt, 1986).

Supervision, historically, has had an identity crisis. The fields of administration and curriculum seem to have subsumed the function of supervision. Supervision as a field of study in its own right has not been recognized. Alfonso and Firth (1990) stated quite emphatically: "[S]upervision is subservient to the interests of either educational administration or curriculum." Note Goldhammer's (1969) lucid comments: "[B]y comparison to teaching, administration, and, more recently, school counseling, useful literature on supervision is disappointingly sparse. Its authors and students have constituted an energetic, but dismayingly small, minority in the educational community."

Although supervision's heritage is rooted in school administration, there have been curiously few if any textbooks on administration addressing issues specific to supervision. Authors espouse theories and processes of administration, but they rarely mention supervisory theory and practice (e.g., see Boyan, 1988). Further attesting to the subordination of supervision is the failure of many college and university departments of education to even mention supervision in their titles. The Department of Educational Studies, the Department of Curriculum and Teaching, the Department of Instruction,

Curriculum, and Administration are just a few examples of department names. Alfonso and Firth (1990) concurred: "[I]nstructional supervision has not been properly recognized in higher education. . . . With the exception of a handful of universities, supervision is not taken seriously in most graduate programs in education." Over 20 years earlier, Goldhammer (1969) proclaimed that "supervisor education has never occupied an important place in America's colleges and graduate schools of education, nor has supervision of instruction ever emerged as a systematic professional discipline" (p. viii).

The unfavorable image of supervision and supervisors has contributed to problems in the field. A vestige of the bureaucratic legacy of faultfinding, inspectional supervision remains a serious problem and still attracts much criticism (e.g., see Blumberg, 1980; Glanz, 1989; Rooney, 1993; Starratt, 1992). This negative perception of supervision continues to make it difficult for the field of supervision to gain professional legitimacy and acknowledgment.

Despite admirable and capable efforts of the Council of Professors of Instructional Supervision (COPIS), AERA's special interest group on instructional supervision, ASCD's network on supervision, the *Journal of Curriculum and Supervision* (published by ASCD), and Robert Anderson's *Wingspan* (published by Pedamorphosis), supervision has not occupied a prominent role in educational theory and practice. Although other scholars in the field have indicated reasons for the paucity of serious research about supervision in education (and certainly a more in-depth analysis of this situation is necessary), the fact remains that the field of supervision is moribund, not unlike Huebner's (1976) characterization about the curriculum field over 20 years ago.

Taken as a whole, the field of supervision is simply left with an ambiguous legacy. As Anderson (1982) posited," supervision has a rather undistinguished history, a variety of sometimes incompatible definitions, a very low level of popular acceptance, and many perplexing and challenging problems" (p. 181). According to Firth (1986), a past president of ASCD, emphasis on supervision as a field has been "at best, uneven and, at worst, disjointed" (p. 81). Without a well-defined and all-encompassing resuscitation effort that aims for consensus in purpose, definition, and vision for the future, supervision as a role and function will, at best, continue to wallow in mediocrity, remain subservient to the interests of administration, curriculum, and teaching, and, in a worst case scenario, simply become inconsequential in the educational enterprise.

Constructing a History of Supervision

To revitalize historical study of supervision, significant avenues should be considered. The following section of this chapter addresses questions regarding the research that remains to be done and the sorts of sources that might be available and useful. The recommendations offered are brief and are not meant to be comprehensive; rather, they are simply to help the field construct a more meaningful and inclusive history of supervision.

Topics for Research

The gaps in the knowledge of public school supervision are vast. First, more must be known about how supervision was conducted in various cities throughout the country. For example, were supervisors active in Portland (Oregon), Denver, and Boston? If so, who were these people and what duties did they perform? In general, how was supervision conducted in these school systems between 1900 and 1920? More data about supervisory practice from all over the nation need to be gathered. Accounts of supervisors practicing in school systems are needed, as are accounts of practicing supervisors like Gladys Potter, Prudence Bostwick, Chester Babcock, Muriel Crosby, Glenys G. Unruh, Elizabeth S. Randolph, Donald R. Frost, Benjamin P. Ebensole, Lucille G. Jordan, and Maycie Kay Southall, among others. The professional contributions of these past presidents of ASCD are little if any acknowledged through historical portrayal and analysis. Accounts of various marginalized groups such as women and African Americans also are needed. In Chapter 4, Frances Schoonmaker calls for this sort of research as well. Studies such as Cuban's (1984) extraordinary account in *How Teachers Taught,* in which he drew on a wide variety of sources including photographs, diaries, state, city, and district reports, published books, articles and addresses, unpublished monographs, and oral histories are needed.

Second, educational biographies are needed of well-known people (former school superintendents, researchers, and professors of supervision) as William H. Payne, John D. Philbrick, Andrew S. Draper, William T. Harris, Joseph M. Rice, Emerson E. White, Franklin Bobbitt, A. S. Barr, William H. Burton, Harold Spears, Charles H. Judd, Ruth Cunningham, Helen Heffernan, Hollis Caswell, James F. Hosic, Kimball Wiles, and Florence H. Stratemeyer, to mention only a few. Historical portrayals of the professional contributions of more current prominent educators, such as Alice Miel, Robert L. Leeper, William M. Alexander, J. Galen Saylor, William Van Til, Arthur Blumberg, Thomas J. Sergiovanni, and many others, would also be beneficial. Another neglected area of research has been historical treatments of the practical supervisory work of individual supervisors and those concerned with supervision in schools throughout the United States and in other countries (e.g., see Davis, 1993).

Third, the story of the merger between the DSDI and the SCS, eventually leading to the establishment of the ASCD, has not been fully told. For example, an in-depth investigation of the strong opposition to the merger by influential people as Helen Heffernan has not been undertaken. What was the nature of this opposition, what arguments were put forth, how extensive was the opposition, and why did the merger, in fact, take place? Furthermore, what were the consequences for supervision as a field of endeavor as a result of the merger (e.g., see Glanz, 1994c, 1995a)?

Fourth, various aspects of school supervision warrant further investigation. Some topics include the origins and early development of public and private school supervision, supervisory practice in Europe, in Colonial America, and during the postcolonial era, the origins and duties of special supervisors, general supervisors, principals, assistant principals (e.g., see Glanz. 1994e), and assistant superintendents, scientific supervision, teachers' reactions to supervisors, rating procedures used by supervisors, supervision in the social efficiency era, and the relationship between supervision and curriculum, and supervision and administration. In addition, more needs to be known about the persistence of the bureaucratic form of school organization. Bureaucracy, in varying degrees, has characterized the American public school system from the 1840s to the present. Firth and Eiken (1982) stated that "the delivery of supervision to schools is influenced by the type of bureaucratic structure in which such services must operate" (p. 169). The field needs to know more about how supervision was carried out in different schools that varied in degree of bureaucratization. Insight into how different generations of educators dealt with this bureaucratic phenomenon, what alternatives, if any, existed, and why certain people under different circumstances were able to circumvent the bureaucracy is also needed.

Fifth, historical analysis of supervisory practices in preservice settings would also be fruitful. Although theory and practice of supervision in schools remained fairly consistent, nuances can be discerned at various levels, such as elementary, secondary, and college (e.g., see Cramer & Domian, 1960; Douglass, Bent, & Boardman, 1961; Anderson, Major, & Mitchell, 1992). Knowledge of supervision as a function would also be greatly enhanced by examining supervision in various institutional settings, such as private, laboratory, and military post schools. Furthermore, comparing the theory and practice of supervision in noneducational fields, such as counseling and religious studies, with school supervision might yield valuable lessons (e.g., see Pohly, 1993; Williams, 1995).

Possible Sources

Sources that would provide insight into supervisory practice have not been fully tapped. Individuals concerned with historical exploration of supervision will find a number of helpful sources already available, including numerous journals, manuscripts, proceedings, and other recorded sources. Periodicals and journals that should be consulted include, for example, the *American Institute of Instruction* (1831–1908), *American School Board Journal* (1891–1949), *American Teacher* (1912–1949), *Curriculum Journal* (1931–1943), *Education* (1880–1948), *Educational Method* (1921–1943), *Journal of Education* (1875–1949), and *School Review* (1893–1949). While these periodicals are rich sources of school supervision, many other journals should be consulted as well, such as the *Atlantic Monthly, Chicago School Journal, High School Quarterly, Nation's Schools,* and *Secondary Education.*

A number of influential associations have published a variety of yearbooks, which also provide essential information. These associations include the Department of Elementary School Principals, the National Association of Secondary School Principals (Yearbooks 1–4, 1917–1920), the National Conference on Educational Method, the National Herbart Society for the Scientific Study of Teaching, the National Society for the Study of Education, and the Society for Curriculum Study.

Other useful sources include proceedings, manuals, and journals of boards of education, state education department reports annual reports of the U.S. commissioner of education, annual reports of superintendents, assistant superintendents, principals, and supervisors, U.S. Bureau of Education Circulars of Information, and other miscellaneous public school reports across the country. In addition, to explore archival and other types of correspondence pertaining to public school supervision, the following materials may serve as a worthwhile beginning: the Nicholas Murray Butler Papers in the Manuscript Room at Butler Library, Columbia University; and the Teachers College Library Archives (New York City school system). Many other documents and oral histories kept at various institutions and universities should be explored.

We need to go beyond what is readily available and find additional sources that could prove helpful. Davis (1976) argued that curriculum "needs to collect abundant sources available for study. . . . We need everything." The time has come to accord equal attention to supervision. Collection of relevant primary sources are needed. These might include diaries of school supervisors, oral histories, surveys, letters, artifacts, rating forms, records of classroom observations, logs, personal files, other kinds of personal correspondence and, of course, public documents. Photographs of supervisors at work are needed. A host of secondary sources that include published and unpublished works are required. Much of the potential data on supervision is fragmented among various sources in many different locations. Hence, a central agency or locale would facilitate further historical exploration of supervision and serve as repository of vital information about supervision. One such repository exists at the University of South Florida in the Pedamorphosis Leadership Library directed by Robert H. Anderson. Additional efforts must be made to expand the contents of this library, especially to include works involving school supervision.

Not a single dissertation solely devoted to historical examination of school supervision has been undertaken for over 20 years. Only a handful of historical accounts of supervision are available. In order to understand the field's heritage and better focus efforts for the future, significant time for historical inquiry at upcoming conventions of, for example, the ASCD, the AERA, and the History of Education Society should be allotted. A Society for the Study of Supervision History, not unlike the curriculum counterpart, might be in order.

A formal invitation to students and professors to undertake further study of the history of supervision should be made. Doctoral and even master's degree students might be encouraged to undertake historical investigations. It might be appropriate to include more historical perspectives of supervision in graduate courses. A special request to scholars like Tyack, Katz, Karier, Davis, Ravitch, Urban, Lagemann, Clifford, Warren, Anderson, Neville, Garman, Glickman, Schoonmaker, and Cuban, to cite just a few, might engage them in this provocative historical venture.

CONCLUSION

Insufficient investigation into supervision history has thwarted, in part, the efforts of the field to gain professional recognition. Instructional supervision as an ongoing and dynamic process remains an indispensable function, serving the highest ideals of schooling. Some theorists muse that supervision may no longer be necessary (e.g., Sergiovanni, 1992; Starratt, 1992, 1997); however, educational supervision that, at its best, aims to inspire and encourage teachers to excel is as much needed today as it was well over 100 years ago, when Payne (1875) published the first textbook on school supervision. While methods in supervision have changed numerous times since the days of Payne, its history remains regrettably unexplored.

The importance of the history of supervision is clear, and avenues for future research have been suggested. Now, mindful attention and careful work by individual scholars are required to yield the history that is possible.

REFERENCES

Abbott, A. (1988). *The system of professions: An essay on the division of expert labor.* Chicago, IL: The University of Chicago Press.

Abbott, M. G. & Caracheo, F. (1988). Power, authority, and bureaucracy. In N. J. Boyan (Ed.). *Handbook of research on educational administration* (pp. 239–258). New York: Longman.

Abelow, S. P. (1934). *Dr. William H. Maxwell, the first superintendent of schools of the city of New York.* Brooklyn, NY: Schebor.

Acheson, K. A. & Gall, M. D. (1987). *Techniques in the clinical supervision of teachers.* New York: Longman.

Adams, H. P. & Dickey, F. G. (1953). *Basic principles of supervision.* New York: American Book Company.

Alfonso R. J. & Firth, G. R. (1990). Supervision: Needed research. *Journal of Curriculum and Supervision, 5,* 181–188.

Alfonso R. J. Firth, G. R. & Neville, R. F. (1975). *Instructional supervision.* Boston, MA: Allyn and Bacon.

Alfonso, R. J. & Goldsberry, L. (1982). Colleagueship in supervision. In T. J. Sergiovanni (Ed.). *Supervision of teaching* (pp. 90–107). Washington, D.C.: ASCD.

Almack, J. C. (1936). Historical development of school administration. *School and Society, 43,* 625–630.

Anderson, D. J. Major, R. L. & Mitchell, R. R. (1992). *Teacher supervision that works: A guide for university supervisors.* New York: Praeger.

Anderson, J. G.. (1968). *Bureaucracy in education.* Baltimore: The John Hopkins Press.

Anderson, R. H. (1982). Creating a future for supervision. In T. J. Sergiovanni (Ed.). *Supervision of teaching* (pp. 181–190). Washington, D.C.: ASCD.

Anderson, R. H. (1993). Clinical supervision: Its history and current context. In R. H. Anderson & K. J. Snyder, (Eds.). *Clinical* supervision: Coaching for higher performance (pp. 5–18). Pennsylvania: Technomic Publishers.

Anderson, R. H. & Krajewski, R. (1980). Clinical supervision: Special methods for the supervisor of teachers. New York: Holt, Rinehart & Winston.

Anderson, R. H. & Snyder, K. J. (1993). Clinical supervision: Coaching for higher performance. Pennsylvania: Technomic Publishers.

Annual report of the superintendent of common schools of the state of New York. (1845). Albany, New York: State of New York.

Annual report of the United States commissioner of education. (1888–1889; 1895–1996). Washington, D.C.

Anonymous. (1929). The snoopervisor, the whoopervisor, and the supervisor. Playground and Recreation, XXIII, 558.

Argyris, C. (1951). The individual and organization: Some problems of mutual adjustment. Administrative Science Quarterly, 2, 1–24.

Arrington, A. (1972). An historical analysis of the development of supervision in the public schools in the United States from 1870 to 1970. Unpublished doctoral dissertation, George Washington University.

Association for Supervision and Curriculum Development. (1950). Better than rating: New approaches to appraisal of teaching services. Washington, D.C.: ASCD.

Association for Supervision and Curriculum Development. (1960). Working paper of the ASCD committee on the preparation of instructional leaders. Washington, D.C.: ASCD.

Association for Supervision and Curriculum Development. (1971). Freedom, bureaucracy, and schooling. Washington, D.C.: ASCD.

Association for Supervision and Curriculum Development. (1976). Curriculum leaders: Improving their influence. Washington, D.C.: ASCD.

Association for Supervision and Curriculum Development. (1982). Supervision of teaching. Alexandria, VA: ASCD.

Association for Supervision and Curriculum Development. (1992). Supervision in transition. Alexandria, VA: ASCD.

Ayer, F. C. (1954). Fundamentals of instructional supervision. New York: Harper and Brothers.

Ayer, F. C. & Barr, A. C. (1928). The organization of supervision: An analysis of the organization and administration of supervision in city school systems. New York: D. Appleton and Company.

Bagley, W. C. (1918). The status of the classroom teacher. National Educational Association Proceedings, 56, 55–58.

Balliet, T. M. (1894). What can be done to increase the efficiency of teachers in actual service? National Educational Association Proceedings, 32, 365–379.

Barr, A. S. (1925). Scientific analyses of teaching procedures. The Journal of Educational Method, 4, 361–366.

Barr, A. S. (1931). An introduction to the scientific study of classroom supervision. New York: D. Appleton and Company.

Barr, A. S. (1933). Science and philosophy in supervision. Education, 53, 360–366.

Barr, A. S. (1941). Teaching efficiency. Encyclopedia of Educational Research, 1280–1281.

Barr, A. S. & Burton, W. H. (1926). The supervision of instruction: A general volume. New York: D. Appleton-Century Company.

Barr, A. S. & Rudiseill, M. (1931). An annotated bibliography on the methodology of scientific research as applied to education. (Bureau of Educational Research Bulletin No. 13). Madison, WI: The University of Wisconsin.

Barr, A. S. Burton, W. H. & Brueckner, L. J. (1938). Supervision: Democratic leadership in the improvement of learning. New York: D. Appleton-Century Company.

Barr, A. S. Burton, W. H. & Brueckner, L. J. (1947). Supervision: Democratic leadership for the improvement of learning (2nd ed.). New York: Appleton-Century.

Bartky, J. A. (1953). Supervision as human relations. Boston, MA: D. C. Heath and Company.

Beach, D. M. & Reinhartz, J. (1989). Supervision: Focus on instruction. New York: Harper & Row.

Beach, F. F. (1959). Professionalization of educational administration. School Life, 42 5–8.

Bendix, R. (1947). Bureaucracy: The problem and its setting. American Sociological Review, 12, 493–503.

Benson, J. K. (1973). The analysis of bureaucratic-professional conflict: Functional versus dialectical approaches. The Sociological Quarterly, 14, 376–394.

Bidwell, C. E. (1965). The school as a formal organization. In J. G. March (Ed.). Handbook of organizations. Chicago, IL: Rand McNally and Company.

Billington, R. A. (1967). Westward expansion: A history of the American frontier. New York: Macmillan.

Blau, P. M. (1969). The dynamics of bureaucracy: A study of interpersonal relations in two government agencies. Chicago, IL: The University of Chicago Press.

Blau, P. M. & Meyer, M. W. (1956). Bureaucracy in modern society. New York: Random House.

Blau, P. M. & Scott, R. W. (1962). Formal organizations. San Francisco: Chandler Publishing Company.

Blau, P. M. & Scott, R. W. (1969). The nature and types of formal organizations. In F. D. Carver & T. J. Sergiovanni (Eds.). Organizations and human behavior (pp. 5–18). New York: McGraw-Hill.

Blumberg, A. (1980). Supervisors and teachers: A private cold war. Berkeley, CA: McCutchan.

Blumberg, A. (1985). Where we came from: Notes on supervision in the 1840s. Journal of Curriculum and Supervision, 1, 56–65.

Blumberg, A. (1986). The language of supervision: Perspectives over time. Paper presented at the annual meeting of the American Educational Research Association, San Francisco, CA.

Blumberg, A. (1992). A response to Starratt's "A modest proposal: Abolish supervision." Wingspan: A Pedamorphosis Communique, 8, 22–24.

Blumberg, A. & Greenfield, W. (1986). The effective principal: Perspectives on school leadership. Boston, MA: Allyn and Bacon.

Boardman, C. W., Douglass, H. R. & Bent, R. K. (1953). Democratic supervision in secondary schools. Boston, MA: Houghton Mifflin.

Bobbitt, F. (1913). Some general principles of management applied to the problems of city school systems (12th Yearbook of the National Society for the Study of Education, Part I, The Supervision of City Schools: pp. 7–96). Chicago, IL: The University of Chicago Press.

Bobbitt, F. (1920). Mistakes often made by principals—part I. The Elementary School Journal 20, 338–339.

Bolin, F. S. (1983). The language of instructional supervision: An historical study of the writings of six leaders in instructional supervision, 1922–1982. Unpublished doctoral dissertation, Teachers College, Columbia University.

Bolin, F. S. (1987). On defining supervision. Journal of Curriculum and Supervision, 2, 368–380.

Bolin, F. & Panaritis, P. (1992). Searching for a common purpose: A perspective on the history of supervision. In C. D. Glickman (Ed.). Supervision in transition (pp. 30–43). Alexandria, VA: ASCD.

Bostwick, P. (1986). ASCD and supervision: The early years. In W. Van Til (Ed.). ASCD in retrospect (pp. 23–32). Alexandria, VA: ASCD.

Bowers, C. A. & Flinders, D. J. (1991). Culturally responsive teaching and supervision: A handbook for staff development. New York: Teachers College Press.

Bowman, L. G. & Deal, T. E. (1991). Reframing organizations: Artistry, choice, and leadership. San Francisco: Jossey-Bass Publishers.

Boyan, N. J. (Ed.). (1988). *Handbook of research on educational administration.* New York: Longman.

Boyce, A. C. (1915). Methods for measuring teachers efficiency. Fourteenth yearbook of the National Society for the Study of Education, Part II (pp. 9–81). Chicago, IL: The University of Chicago Press.

Bradford, M. D. (1917). The democratic trend in school administration. *National Educational Association Proceedings, 55,* 234–235.

Brennan, B. (1973). Principals as bureaucrats. *The Journal of Educational Administration, 11,* 171–178.

Briggs, T. H. & Justman, J. (1952). *Improving instruction through supervision.* New York: Macmillan.

Bullough, W. A. (1974). *Cities and schools in the gilded age.* New York: Kennikat Press.

Burns, J. M. (1978). *Leadership.* New York: Harper and Row.

Burton, W. (1852). *The district school as it was.* Boston, MA: T. R. Marvin.

Burton, W. E. (1922). *Supervision and the improvement of teaching.* New York: D. Appleton.

Burton, W. H. (1930). Probable next steps in the progress of supervision. *Educational Method, 9,* 401–405.

Burton, W. H. (1937). A new definition of the function of supervision. *California Journal of Elementary Education 6,* 218–226.

Burton, W. H. & Brueckner, L. J. (1955). *Supervision: A social process.* New York: Appleton-Century-Crofts.

Button, H. W. (1961). *A history of supervision in the public schools, 1870–1950.* Unpublished doctoral dissertation, Washington University.

Calkins, N. A. (1882). School supervision. *Education, 2,* 498–499.

Callahan, R. E. (1962). *Education and the cult of efficiency.* Chicago, IL: The University of Chicago Press.

Callahan, R. E. (1967). *The superintendent of schools: An historical analysis.* Bethesda, MD: ERIC Document Reproduction Service.

Callahan, R. E. & Button, H. W. (1964). Historical change of the role of the man in the organization, 1865–1950. In D. E. Griffiths (Ed.). *Behavioral science and educational administration.* Chicago, IL: The University of Chicago Press.

Campbell, R. F. Fleming, T., Newell, L. J. & Bennion, J. W. (1987). *A history of thought and practice in educational administration.* New York: Teachers College Press.

Carnegie, A. (1886). *Triumphant democracy or fifty years' march of the republic.* New York: Charles Scribner's Sons.

Carr, E. H. (1961). *What is history?* New York: Alfred A. Knopf Publisher.

Cassirer, E. (1953). *An essay on man: An introduction to a philosophy of human culture.* New York: Doubleday & Co.

Caswell, H. L. (1966). Emergence of the curriculum as a field of professional work and study. In H. F. Robison (Ed.). *Precedents and promise in the curriculum field* (pp. 1–21). New York: Teachers College Press.

Champagne, D. & Hogan, R. (1981). *Consultant supervision.* Wheaton, IL: C. H. Publications.

Chancellor, W. E. (1904). *Our schools: Their administration and supervision.* Boston, MA: D. C. Heath and Company.

Charters, W. W. (1923). *Curriculum construction.* New York: Macmillan.

Clarke, C. & Richardson, J. (1986). *Peer clinical supervision: A collegial approach.* Paper presented at the annual meeting of the National Council of States on In-service Education, Nashville, TN.

Coburn, W. G. (1919). Preparation of supervisory and administrative officers. *National Educational Association Proceedings, 57,* 250–253.

Cogan, M. L. (1973). *Clinical supervision.* Boston, MA: Houghton Mifflin.

Cogan, M. L. (1973). Toward a definition of a profession. *Harvard Educational Review, 23,* 33–50.

Common, D. L. & Grimmett, P. P. (1992). Beyond the war of the worlds: A consideration of the estrangement between curriculum and supervision. *Journal of Curriculum and Supervision, 7,* 209–225.

Consulting Editors. (1992). Estrangement between curriculum and supervision: Personal observations on the current scene. *Journal of Curriculum and Supervision, 7,* 245–249.

Cook, J. W. (1900). How can the superintendent improve the efficiency of the teachers under his charge? *National Educational Association Proceedings, 38,* 276–287.

Corwin, R. (1965). Professional persons in public organizations. *Educational Administrative Quarterly, 1,* 1–22.

Costa, A. & Garmston, R. (1986). Cognitive coaching—supervision for intelligent teaching. In K. Tye & Costa, A. (Eds.). *Better teaching through instructional supervision: Policy and practice.* Sacramento, CA: California Schools Board Association.

Costa, A. & Garmston, R. (1994). *Cognitive coaching: Approaching renaissance schools.* Norwood, MA: Christopher Gordon Publishing.

Courtis, S. A. (1928). Ideals in supervision. *The Journal of Educational Method, 7,* 336–340.

Courtis, S. A. (1933). Curriculum construction at Detroit (*27th Yearbook of the National Society for the Study of Education, Part I:* pp. 135–162). Chicago, IL: The University of Chicago Press.

Crabtree, J. W. (1915). Rating of teachers. *National Educational Association Proceedings, 53,* 1165–1173.

Craig, W. L., Madison, B. T., Shapiro, A. S. & Schell, S. H. (1969). *Sociology of supervision: An approach to comprehensive planning in education.* Boston, MA: Allyn and Bacon.

Cramer, R. V. & Domian, O. E. (1960). *Administration and supervision in the elementary school.* New York: Harper & Row.

Cremin, L. A. (1959). John Dewey and the progressive education movement. *The School Review, 7,* 152–167.

Cremin, L. A. (1961). *The transformation of the school.* New York: Alfred A. Knopf.

Cremin, L. A. (1970). *American education: The colonial experience, 1607–1783.* New York: Harper and Row.

Crider, J. W. (1944). *The bureaucrat.* New York: J. B. Lippincott Company.

Cronin, J. M. (1971). *The centralization of the Boston schools.* Paper presented at the annual meeting of the American Educational Research Association, Minneapolis.

Cronin, J. M. (1973). *The control of urban schools.* New York: The Free Press.

Crosby, M. (1957). *Supervision as co-operative action.* New York: Appleton-Century-Crofts.

Crosby, M. (1969). The new supervisor. In R. R. Leeper (Ed.). *Changing supervision for changing times.* Washington, D.C.: ASCD.

Crozier, M. (1964). *The bureaucratic phenomenon.* Chicago, IL: The University of Chicago Press.

Cuban, L. (1984). *How teachers taught: Constancy and change in American classrooms, 1890–1980.* New York: Longman.

Cubberley, E. P. (1916). *Public school administration.* Boston, MA: Houghton Mifflin.

Cubberley, E. P. (1934). *Public education in the United States.* New York: Houghton Mifflin.

Cunningham, R. J. (1911). The relations of a city superintendent to his teachers. *American School Board Journal, 42,* 122–126.

Curtin, J. (1964). *Supervision in today's elementary schools.* New York: Macmillan.

Dalthorp, C. J. (1932). Shall we rate teachers? *Educational Method, 12,* 78–81.

Daresh, J. C. (1989). *Supervision as a proactive process.* New York: Longman.

Darling-Hammond, L. & Goodwin, A.L. (1993). Progress toward professionalsim in teaching. In G. Cawelti (Ed.). *Challenges and achievements of American education* (pp. 19–52). Alexandria, VA: ASCD.

Davidson, W. M. (1913). How to measure the efficiency of teachers. *National Educational Association Proceedings, 51,* 286–287.

Davis Jr., O. L. (1976). Epilogue: Invitation to curriculum history. In O. L. Davis Jr. (Ed.). *Perspectives on curriculum development 1776–1976* (pp. 257–259). Washington, D.C.: ASCD.

Davis Jr., O. L. (1978) Symbol of a shift from status to function: Formation of the Association for Supervision and Curriculum Development. *Educational Leadership, 35,* 609–614.

Davis Jr., O. L. (1992). Memory, our educational practice, and history. *The Educational Forum, 56,* 375–379.

Davis Jr., O. L. (1993, August). *To think and to teach with fresh insights: The inspectorial work of J. C. Hill In East London schools, 1931–1953.* Paper presented at the conference of the International Study Association for Teacher Thinking, Sweden, Gothenburg.

Davis Jr., O. L. (1994, March 31). Personal communication.

Dempsey, V. F. (1969). *An assessment of conflict between bureaucracy and professionalization in a school system.* Unpublished doctoral dissertation, New York University.

Denzin, N. K. & Lincoln, Y. S. (1994). *Handbook of qualitative research.* Thousand Oaks, CA: Sage Publications.

Dewey, J. (1903). Democracy in education. *The Elementary School Teacher, 4,* 190–197.

Dewey, J. (1915). Professional spirit among teachers. *The American Teacher, 4,* 112–117.

Dewey, J. (1916). *Democracy and education.* New York: Macmillan.

Dewey, J. (1929). *The sources of a science of education.* New York: Liveright.

Dewey, J. (1959). Introduction to the use of resources in education by E. R. Clapp. In M. S. Dworkin (Ed.). *Dewey on education* (pp. 2–18). New York: Teachers College Press.

Doll, R. C. (1964). *Curriculum improvement: Decision-making and process.* Boston, MA: Allyn and Bacon.

Dolson, L. S. (1964). *The administration of the San Francisco public schools, 1847–1947.* Unpublished doctoral dissertation, University of California at Berkeley.

Douglass, H. R., Bent, R. K. & Boardman, C. W. (1961). *Supervision in secondary schools.* Boston, MA: Houghton Mifflin.

Doyle, W. (1967). *A professional model for the authority of the teacher in the educational enterprise.* Unpublished doctoral dissertation, The University of Notre Dame.

Doyle, W. & Ponder, G. A. (1976) Sources for curriculum history. In O. L. Davis Jr. (Ed.). *Perspectives on curriculum development 1776–1976* (pp. 247–256). Washington, D.C.: ASCD.

Drummond, H. D. (1975). Foreword. In R. R. Leeper (Ed.). *Role of supervisor and curriculum director in a climate of change in role of supervisor and curriculum director in a climate of change* (pp. 5–8). Washington, D.C.: ASCD.

Dumont, M. P. (1970). The changing face of professionalism. In L. A. Netzer (Ed.). *Education, administration and change: The redeployment of resources* (pp. 21–34). New York: Harper & Row.

Dunlap, D. M. & Goldman, P. (1991). Rethinking power in schools. *Educational Administration Quarterly, 27,* 5–29.

Dunn, F. W. (1920). The distinction between administration and supervision. *Educational Administration and Supervision, 6.*

Dutton, S. T. (1904). *School management: Practical suggestions concerning the conduct and life of the school.* New York: Charles Scribner's Sons.

Dutton, S. T. & Snedden, D. (1912). *The administration of public education in the United States.* New York: Macmillan.

Editorial, (1922). Supervision as a profession. *The Journal of Educational Method, 1,* 34.

Editorial, (1928). *The Journal of Educational Method, 7,* 1–2.

Editorial, (1929). Full sail ahead. *The Journal of Educational Method, 8,* 372.

Editorial, (1943). Hail and farewell. *Curriculum Journal, 14,* 193–194.

Edson, A. W. (1893). School supervision. *Education, 13,* 391–396.

Eisenstadt, S. N. (1958). Bureaucracy and bureaucratization. *Current Sociology, 12,* 99–163.

Elliott, C. H. (1908). *Types of supervision in American cities.* Unpublished master's thesis, Columbia University.

Elliott, E. C. (1910). *Tentative scheme for the measurement of teaching efficiency.* Madison.

Elliott, E. C. (1915). How shall the efficiency of teachers be tested and recorded? *National Educational Association Proceedings, 53,* 472–473.

Elsbree, W. S. (1931). *Teachers' salaries.* New York: Bureau of Publications, Teachers College, Columbia University.

Elsbree, W. S. (1939). *American teacher: Evolution of a profession in a democracy.* New York: American Book Company.

Etzioni, A. (1964). *Modern organization.* Englewood Cliffs, NJ: Prentice-Hall.

Eye, G. G., Netzer, L. A. & Krey, R. D. (1971). *Supervision of instruction.* New York: Harper & Row.

Featherstone, W. B. (1942). Taking the super out of supervision. *Teachers College Record, 44,* 197–203.

Feyereisen, K., Fiorino, A. J. & Novak, A. T. (1960). *Supervision and curriculum renewal: A systems approach.* New York: Appleton-Century-Crofts.

Firth, G. R. (1986). ASCD and supervision: The later years. In W. Van Til (Ed.). *ASCD in retrospect* (pp. 69–82). Washington, D.C.: ASCD.

Firth, G. R. & Eiken, K. P. (1982). Impact of the schools' bureaucratic structure on supervision. In T. J. Sergiovanni (Ed.). *Supervision of teaching* (pp. 153–169). Washington, D. C.: ASCD.

Fitzgerald, J. H. (1991). *Management practices: A case study of district level supervisors and directors of curriculum and instruction in one school district.* Unpublished doctoral dissertation, University of South Florida.

Fitzpatrick, F. A. (1893). How to improve the work of inefficient teachers. *National Educational Association Proceedings, 31,* 71–78.

Foote, J. M. (1922). A state program of instructional supervision. *National Educational Association Proceedings, 60,* 1150–1154.

Foshay, A. W. *The professional as educator.* New York: Teachers College Press.

Frederich, G. H. (1984). Supervision and evaluation: Recognizing the difference can increase value effectiveness. *NASSP Bulletin, 68,* 12–13.

Freidson, E. (1970). *Profession of medicine: A study of the sociology of applied knowledge.* New York: Dodd, Mead, and Company.

Fry, M. B. (1925). *Supervision.* Unpublished master's thesis, Columbia University.

Fuller, W. E. (1982). *The ole country school: The story of rural education in the midwest.* Chicago, IL: University of Chicago Press.

Fuller, W. E. (1989). The teacher in the country school. In W. Donald (Ed.). *American teachers: Histories of a profession at work* (pp. 98–117). New York: Macmillan.

Garman N. B. (1982). The clinical approach to supervision. In T. J. Sergiovanni (Ed.). *Supervision of teaching* (pp. 35–52). Alexandria, VA: ASCD.

Garman, N. B. (1997). Is clinical supervision a viable model for use in the public schools? No. In J. Glanz & R. F. Neville (Eds.). *Educational supervision: Perspectives, issues, and controversies.* Norwood, MA: Christopher Gordon Publishers.

Garrett, A. W. (1994). Curriculum history's connections to the present: Necessary lessons for informed practice and theory. *Journal of Curriculum and Supervision, 9,* 390–395.

Gear, H. L. (1950). *The rise of city-school superintendency as an influence in educational policy.* Unpublished doctoral dissertation, Harvard University.

Gehrke, N. J. & Parker, W. C. (1983). Collaboration in staff development—variations on the concept. *NASSP Bulletin, 67,* 50–54.

Gerth, H. & Mills, W. W. (1958). *From Max Weber: Essays in sociology.* New York: Oxford, V. P. Galaxy.

Gilland, T. M. (1935). *The origin and development of the power and duties of the city school superintendent.* Chicago, IL: The University of Chicago Press.

Glanz, J. (1977a). Ahistoricism and school supervision: Notes towards a history. *Educational Leadership, 35,* 148–154.

Glanz, J. (1977b). Bureaucracy and professionalism: An historical interpretation of public school supervision in the United States, 1875–1937. Unpublished doctoral dissertation, Teachers College, Columbia University.

Glanz, J. (1978a). *Controlling the schools: An essay on the bureaucratization of school supervision in the late nineteenth century.* Paper presented at the meeting of the American Educational Research Association, Toronto, Canada.

Glanz, J. (1978b). *From bureaucracy to professionalism: An essay on the democratization of supervision in the early twentieth century.* Paper presented at the meeting of the American Educational Studies Association, Washington, D.C.

Glanz, J. (1979). *The bureaucratic–professional dilemma for supervisors and curriculum workers in schools: An historical analysis of a persistent problem.* Paper presented at the meeting of the American Educational Research Association, San Francisco, CA.

Glanz, J. (1989). The snoopervisor. *Learning 89,* 36–37.

Glanz, J. (1990a). Beyond bureaucracy: Notes on the professionalization of public school supervision in the early twentieth century. *Journal of Curriculum and Supervision, 5,* 150–170.

Glanz, J. (1990b). Supervision: A field without a past? *CSA Education Review, 2,* 55–61.

Glanz, J. (1991). *Bureaucracy and professionalism: The evolution of public school supervision.* New Jersey: Fairleigh Dickinson University Press.

Glanz, J. (1992a). Curriculum development and supervision: Antecedents for collaboration and future possibilities. *Journal of Curriculum and Supervision, 7,* 226–244.

Glanz, J. (1992b). School-based management and the advent of teacher empowerment: One administrator's view of reform. *Record in Educational Administration and Supervision, 12,* 40–45.

Glanz, J. (1993a). Review of *Teacher supervision that works: A guide for university professors and teachers helping teachers: Peer observation and assistance. Educational Studies, 24,* 325–329.

Glanz, J. (1993b). The rise and fall of school-based management: Lessons from a New York City elementary school. *CSA Leadership Journal,* 51–53.

Glanz, J. (1994a) Dilemmas of assistant principals in their supervisory role: Reflections of an assistant principal. *Journal of School Leadership, 4,* 577–593.

Glanz, J. (1994b). *History of educational supervision: Proposals and prospects.* Paper presented at the meeting of the Council of Professors of Instructional Supervision (COPIS), Chicago, Illinois.

Glanz, J. (1994c). The merger of the department of supervisors and the society for curriculum study: Effects on supervision. *Instructional Supervision Network Newsletter. 5,* 2–3.

Glanz, J. (1994d). Redefining the roles and responsibilities of assistant principals. *The Clearing House, 67,* 283–288.

Glanz, J. (1994e). Where did the assistant principalship begin? Where is it headed? *NASSP Bulletin, 78,* 35–41.

Glanz, J. (1995a). Reconsiderations: The changing curriculum. *Educational Studies, 26,* 326–334.

Glanz, J. (1995b). Exploring supervision history: An invitation and agenda. *Journal of Curriculum and Supervision, 10,* 95–113.

Glanz, J. (1997). Has the field of supervision evolved to a point that it should be called something else? No. In J. Glanz & R. F. Neville (Eds.). *Educational supervision: Perspectives, issues, and controversies.* Norwood, MA: Christopher Gordon Publishers.

Glanz, J. (in press). Improvement versus evaluation as an intractable problem in school supervision: Is a reconciliation possible? *Record in Educational Leadership.*

Glatthorn, A. (1984). *Differentiated supervision.* Alexandria, VA: ASCD.

Glickman, C. D. (1981). *Developmental supervision.* Washington, D.C.: ASCD.

Glickman, C. D. (1985). *Supervision of instruction: A developmental approach.* Boston, MA: Allyn and Bacon.

Glickman, C. D. (Ed.). (1992). *Supervision in transition.* Alexandria, VA: ASCD.

Goldhammer, R. (1969). *Clinical supervision: Special methods for the supervision of teachers.* New York: Holt, Rinehart, and Winston.

Goldhammer R., Anderson, R. H. & Krajewski, R. A. (1980). *Clinical supervision: Special methods for the supervision of teachers* (2nd ed.). New York: Holt, Rinehart & Winston.

Goodson, F. (1985). History, context, and qualitative methods in the study of the curriculum. In R. G. Burgess (Ed.). *Strategies of educational research: Qualitative methods* (pp. 121–152). Lewes: Falmer Press.

Gosine, M. & Keith, M. V. (1970). Bureaucracy, teacher personality needs and teacher satisfaction. *The Canadian Administrator, 10,* 1–5.

Gouldner, A. W. (1954). *Patterns of industrial bureaucracy: A case study of modern factory administration.* New York: The Free Press.

Gracey, H. L. (1972). *Curriculum or craftmanship: Elementary school teachers in a bureaucratic system.* Chicago, IL: The University of Chicago Press.

Green, C. C. (1915). The promotion of teachers on the basis of merit and efficiency. *National Educational Association Proceedings, 53,* 473-477.

Greenwood, J. M. (1888). Efficient school supervision. *National Educational Association Proceedings, 26,* 519–521.

Greenwood, J. M. (1891). Discussion of Gove's paper. *National Educational Association Proceedings, 19,* 227.

Greenwood, J. M. (1894). What shall be done with non-progressive and retrogressive teachers? *National Educational Association Proceedings, 32,* 383–387.

Griffiths, D. E. (1966). *The school superintendent.* New York: The Center for Applied Research in Education.

Grimmett, P. (1990). Teacher development and the culture of collegiality, part 2. *Australian Administrator, 11.*

Gwynn, J. M. (1913). The selection and tenure of office of assistant superintendents and supervisors. *National Educational Association Proceedings, 51,* 301–305.

Gwynn, J. M. (1961). *Theory and practice of supervision.* New York: Dodd, Mead, and Company.

Hall, R. H. (1961). *An empirical study of bureaucratic dimensions and their relations to other organizations characteristics.* Unpublished doctoral dissertation, Ohio State University.

Hall, R. H. (1968). Professionalization and bureaucratization. *American Sociological Review, 33,* 92–104.

Hammock, D. C. (1969). *The centralization of New York City's public school system, 1896: A social analysis of a decision.* Unpublished master's thesis, Columbia University.

Hanot, E. M. (1975). The modern educational bureaucracy and the process of change. *Educational Administration Quarterly, 11,* 21–36.

Hanson, E. M. (1976). Professional/bureaucratic interface. *Urban Education, 11,* 313–332.

Harap, H. (1928). *The technique of curriculum making.* New York: Macmillan.

Hargreaves, A. (1989). *Contrived collegiality and the culture of teaching.* Paper presented at the meeting of the American Educational Research Association, San Francisco, CA.

Harris, B. M. (1964). Need for research on instructional supervision. In R.. R.. Leeper, (Ed.). *Supervision: Emerging profession.* Washington, D.C.: ASCD.

Harris, B. M. (1969). New leadership and new responsibilities for human involvement. *Educational Leadership, 26,* 739–742.

Harris, W. T. (1890). The general government and public education throughout the country. *National Educational Association Proceedings, 28,* 481–499.

Harris, W. T. (1892). City school supervision. *Educational Review, 3,* 167–172.

Harris, W. T. (1899). How to make good teachers out of poor ones? *National Educational Association Proceedings, 37,* 310–314.

Harrison, R. H. (1968). *Supervisory leadership in education.* Litton Educational Publishing Inc.

Hays, S. P. (1957). *The response to industrialism, 1855–1914.* Chicago, IL: The University of Chicago Press.

Hazi, H. M. (1994). The teacher evaluation-supervision dilemma: A case of entanglements and irreconcilable differences. *Journal of Curriculum and Supervision, 9,* 195–216.

Hazi, H. M. & Glanz, J. (1997). *Supervision travelling incognito:* Paper presented at the meeting of the American Research Association, Chicago, IL.

Hazlett, S. (1979). Conceptions of curriculum history. *Curriculum Inquiry, 9,* 129–135.

Heffernan, H. & Burton, W. H. (1939). Adjusting theory and practice in supervision. *Educational Method, 18,* 323–328.

Herrick, M. J. (1971). *The Chicago schools: A social and political history.* Beverly Hills, CA: Sage Publications.

Hervey, H. D. (1921). The rating of teachers. *National Educational Association Proceedings, 59,* 823–826.

Hicks, H. J. (1960). *Educational supervision in principle and practice.* New York: The Ronald Press Company.

Hill, S. (1918). Defects of supervision and constructive suggestions thereon. *National Educational Association Proceedings, 56,* 347–350.

Hill, W. M. (1968). I-B-F supervision: A technique for changing teacher behavior. *The Clearing House, 43,* 180–183.

Hobson, C. S. (1943). Franklin Bobbitt: Pioneer in curriculum-making. *Curriculum Journal, 14,* 14–17.

Holland, P. E. (1994, November). *What do we talk of when we talk of supervision?* Paper presented at the meeting of the Council of Professors of Instructional Supervision, New York.

Holmes, B. E. (1927). The supervision of instruction. *Education, 47,* 556–568.

Hosic, J. F. (1920). The democratization of supervision. *School and Society, 11,* 331–336.

Hosic, J. F. (1924). The concept of the principalship—II. *The Journal of Educational Method, 3,* 282–284.

Houston, W. R. (Ed.). (1990). *Handbook of research on teacher education.* New York: Macmillan.

Hoy, W. K. & Forsyth, P. B. (1986). *Effective supervision.* New York: Random House.

Huebner, D. E. (1976). The moribund curriculum field: Its wake and our work. *Curriculum Inquiry, 6,* 153–176.

Isherwood, G. B. & Hoy, W. K. (1973). Bureaucratic structure reconsidered. *The Journal of Experimental Education, 41,* 47–50.

James, S., Heller, D., & Ellis, W. (1992). Peer assistance in a small district: Windham southeast, Vermont. In C. D. Glickman (Ed.). *Supervision in Transition* (pp. 97–112). Alexandria, VA: ASCD.

Johnson, F. W, (1922). The supervision of instruction. *The School Review, 30,* 123–129.

Johnson, S. M. (1990). *Teachers at work: Achieving success in our schools.* New York: Basic Books.

Johnston, J. H. (1917). Scientific supervision of teaching. *School and Society, 5,* 181–188.

Joint Committee on Curriculum of the Department of Supervisors and Directors of Instruction and the Society for Curriculum Study. (1937). *The changing curriculum.* New York: D. Appleton-Century Company.

Judd, C. H. (1920). The high school manager. *National Association of Secondary School Principals,* 30–31.

Judd, C. H. (1926). The principal as a supervisor of classroom teaching. *National Educational Association Proceedings, 64,* 825–831.

Kaestle, C. F. (1970). *The origins of an urban school system: New York City, 1750–1850.* Unpublished doctoral dissertation, Harvard University.

Kaestle, C. F. (1973). *The evolution of an urban school: New York City 1750–1850.* Cambridge, MA: Harvard University Press.

Karier, C. (1967). *Man, society, and education.* Glenview, IL: Scott, Foresman.

Karier, C. (1982). Supervision in historic perspective. In T. J. Sergiovanni (Ed.). *Supervision of teaching* (pp. 2–15). Alexandria, VA: ASCD.

Katz, M. B. (1968). The emergence of bureaucracy in urban education: The Boston case 1850-1884. *History of Education Quarterly, 8,* 155–188, 319–357.

Katz, M. B. (1973). *Class, bureaucracy, and schools: The illusion of educational change in America.* New York: Praeger.

Katz, M. B. (1987). *Reconstructing American education.* Cambridge, MA: Harvard University Press.

Keyes, R. K. (1921). Vision and supervision. *The Journal of Educational Method, 1,* 8–11.

Kilpatrick, W. H. (1912). *The Dutch schools of New Neatherland and colonial New York.* Washington, D.C.: U.S. Government Printing Office.

King, L. A. (1920). The present status of teacher rating. *American School Board Journal, 70,* 44–46.

Kirby, P. C. (1991). *Shared decision making: Moving from concerns about restrooms to concerns about classrooms.* Paper presented at the meeting of the American Educational Research Association, Chicago, IL.

Kliebard, H. M. (1987). *The struggle for the American curriculum: 1893–1958.* New York: Routledge & Kegan Paul.

Kliebard, H. M. (1995). Why history of education? *The Journal of Educational Research, 88,* 194–199.

Knight, F. B. & Franzen, R. H. (1922). Pitfalls in rating schemes. *The Journal of Educational Psychology, 11,* 145–155.

Koehler, M. (1990). The one world of supervision. *American Secondary Education, 18,* 26–29.

Krajewski, R. J. (1976). Putting the 'S' back in ASCD. *Educational Leadership, 33,* 376.

Krajewski, R. J. (1997). Can we put back the 'S' in ASCD? No. In J. Glanz & R. F. Neville (Eds.). *Educational supervision: perspectives, issues, and controversies.* Norwood, MA: Christopher Gordon Publishers.

Krey, R. D. & Burke, P. J. (1989). *A design for instructional supervision.* Springfield, IL: Charles C. Thomas.

Krug, E. A. (1964). *The shaping of the American high school, 1890–1920.* New York: Harper & Row.

Krug, E. A. (1972). *The shaping of the American high school, 1920–1941.* Madison, WI.: University of Wisconsin Press.

Kummel, F. (1966). Time as succession and the problem of duration. In J. T. Fraser (Ed.). *The voices of time* (pp. 31–55). New York: George Braziller.

Kyte, G. C. (1930). *How to supervise.* Boston, MA: Houghton Mifflin.

Kyte, G. C. (1931). *Problems in school supervision.* Boston, MA: Houghton Mifflin.

Lancelot, W. H. & Barr, A. S. (1935). *The measurement of teaching efficiency.* New York: Macmillan.

Lazerson, M. (1971). *Origins of the urban school: Public education in*

Massachusetts, 1870–1915. Cambridge, MA: The Harvard University Press.

Lazerson, M. (1983). The origins of special education. In J. G. Chambers & W. T. Hartman (Eds.). *Special education policies: Their history, implementation, and finance.* Philadelphia, PA: Temple University Press.

Leeper, R. R. (Ed.). (1969). *Supervision: Emerging profession.* Washington, D.C.: ASCD.

Lefkowitz, A. (1920). The product of autocracy. *The American Teacher, 9.*

Leggett, D. & Hoyle, S. (1987). Peer coaching: One district's experience in using teachers as staff developers. *Journal of Staff Development, 8,* 16–21.

Lewis, A. J. & Miel, A. (1972). *Supervision for improved instruction: New challenges, new responses.* Belmont, CA: Wadsworth Publishing Company.

Lieberman, M. (1956). *Education as a profession.* Englewood Cliffs, NJ: Prentice-Hall.

Liethwood, K. & Jantzi, D. (1990, April). *Transformational leadership: How principals can help reform school cultures.* Paper presented at the meeting of the American Educational Research Association, Boston.

Liftig, R. (1990). Our dirty little secrets: Myths about teachers and administrators. *Educational Leadership, 47,* 67–70.

Little, J. W. (1987). Teachers as colleagues. In R. Koehler (Ed.). *Educator's handbook: A research perspective* (pp. 491–518). New York: Longman.

Lowe, R. (1992). Review of the book, *Bureaucracy and professionalism: The evolution of public school supervision. History of Education Quarterly, 32,* 396–397.

Lucio, W. H. & McNeil, J. D. (1962). *Supervision: A synthesis of thought and action.* New York: McGraw-Hill.

Mackenzie, G. N. (1961). Role of the supervisor. *Educational Leadership, 19,* 86–90.

Madden, M. (1921). Some problems of method in supervision. *The Journal of Educational Method, 1,* 13–15.

Mangieri, J. N. & McWilliams, D. R. (1981). The what, how and when of professional improvement. *Educational Leadership, 37,* 535–537.

Manis, J. R., et al. (1985). *Handbook of educational supervision.* Boston, MA: Allyn and Bacon.

Marble, A. P. (1887). *The powers and duties of school officers and teachers.* New York: C. W. Bardeen.

March, J. G. & Simon, H. A. (1958). *Organizations.* New York: John Wiley.

Markowitz, S. (1976). The dilemma of authority in supervisory behavior. *Educational Leadership, 33,* 365–369.

Marsak, L. M. (1970). *The nature of historical inquiry.* New York: Holt, Rinehart, and Winston.

Marshall, C. (1992). *The assistant principal: Leadership choices and challenges.* California: Corwin Press.

Maxwell, W. H. (1894). Supervision of city schools. *National Educational Association Proceedings, 32,* 310–322.

McAndrew, W. (1922). The schoolman's loins. *Educational Review, 22,* 90–99.

McNeil, J. D. (1982). A scientific approach to supervision. In T. J. Sergiovanni (Ed.). *Supervision of teaching* (pp. 18–34). Alexandria, VA: ASCD.

Melby, E. O. (1929). *A critical study of the existing organization and administration of supervision: A study of current practice.* Bloomington, IL: Public School Publishing Company.

Melby, E. O. (1932). Can we be creative in supervision? *Educational Method, 12,* 129–133.

Merton, R. K. (1940). Bureaucratic structure and personality. *Social Forces, 18,* 560–568.

Merriam, C. E. (1934). *Civic education in the United States.* New York: Charles Scribner's Sons.

Mohr, L. B. (1977). Authority and democracy in organizations. *Human Relations, 30,* 919–947.

Moeller, G. H. (1962). *The relationship between bureaucracy in school systems' organization and teachers' sense of power.* Unpublished doctoral dissertation, Washington University.

Moeller, G. H. (1964). Bureaucracy and teachers' sense of power. *School Review, 72,* 137–157.

Moore, B. F. (1913). *Supervision of instruction in cities from 15,000 to 50,000 population.* Unpublished master's thesis, Columbia University.

Moorer, S. H. (1952). *Supervision: The keystone to educational progress.* Tallahassee: Florida State Department of Education.

Mosher, R. L. & Purpel, D. E. (1972). *Supervision: The reluctant profession.* New York: Houghton Mifflin.

Mouzeles, N. P. (1969). *Organization and bureaucracy: An analysis of modern theories.* Chicago, IL: Aldine Publishing Company.

Munro, P. M. (1991). Supervision: What's imposition got to do with it? *Journal of Curriculum and Supervision, 7,* 77–89.

National Conference on Educational Method. (1928). *Educational supervision: A report of current views, investigations, and practices—first yearbook.* New York: Teachers College, Columbia University.

National Conference on Educational Method. (1929). *Scientific method in supervision—second yearbook.* New York: Teachers College, Columbia University.

National Conference of Supervisors and Directors of Instruction. (1930). *Current problems of supervisors—third yearbook.* New York: Teachers College, Columbia University.

National Education Association. (1930). *The superintendent surveys supervision—eighth yearbook.* Washington, D.C.: NEA.

National Society for the Study of Education. (1913). *The supervision of city schools, part I.* Chicago, IL: The University of Chicago Press.

National Society for the Study of Education. (1927). *Curriculum-making: Past and present, part I.* Chicago, IL: The University of Chicago Press.

Neagley, R. L. & N. D. Evans. (1970). *Handbook for effective supervision of instruction.* Englewood Cliffs, NJ: Prentice-Hall.

Neidert, L. J. (1926). *The administrative aspects of supervisory organization in 44 American cities.* Unpublished master's thesis, University of Washington.

Nelson, R. & Singleton, H. W. (1980, April). *The merger of curriculum journal and educational method: Effects of the curriculum field.* Paper presented at the meeting of the Society for the Study of Curriculum History.

Neville, R. F. (1963). *The supervisory function of the elementary school principal as perceived by teachers.* Unpublished doctoral dissertation, University of Connecticut.

Newlon, J. H. (1923). Attitude of the teacher toward supervision. *National Educational Association Proceedings, 61,* 546–549.

Newlon, J. H. (1934). *Educational administration as social policy.* New York: Charles Scribner's Sons.

Newlon, J. H. & Threlkeld, A. L. (1926). The Denver curriculum-revision program. *Twenty-Sixth Yearbook of the National Society for the Study of Education, Part I.* Chicago, IL: The University of Chicago Press.

Nutt, H. W. (1920). *The supervision of instruction.* Boston, MA: Houghton Mifflin.

O'Brien, D. W. (1963). *Reference and deference to authority as factors affecting professional autonomy in education: A case study.* Unpublished doctoral dissertation, University of Wisconsin.

Oliva, P. F. (1989). *Supervision for today's schools.* New York: Longman.

Pajak, E. (1989). *The central office supervisor of curriculum and instruction: Setting the stage for success*. Needham, MA: Allyn and Bacon.

Pajak, E. (1993a). *Approaches to clinical supervision: Alternatives for improving instruction*. Norwood, MA: Christopher Gordon Publishers.

Pajak, E. (1993b). Change and continuity in supervision and leadership. In G. Cawelti (Ed.). *Challenges and achievements of American education* (pp. 158–186). Alexandria, VA: ASCD.

Parrott, A. L. (1915). Abolishing the rating of teachers. *National Educational Association Proceedings, 53*, 1168–1173.

Parsons, T. (1947). *Max Weber: The theory of social and economic organization*. New York: Free Press.

Patri, A. (1921). *A schoolmaster of the great city*. New York: Macmillan.

Payne, W. H. (1875). *Chapters on school supervision: A practical treatise on superintendency: Grading; arranging courses of study; the preparation and use of blanks, records and reports; examination for promotion, etc*. New York: Van Antwerp Bragg and Company.

Payne, W. H. (1887). *Contributions to the science of education*. New York: Harper.

Peabody, R. L. (1964). *Organizational authority*. New York: Atherton Press.

Pfeiffer, I. & Dunlap, J. (1982). *Supervising teachers: A guide to supervising instruction*. Phoenix, AZ.: Oryx Press.

Pickard, J. L. (1872) The extent, methods, and values of supervision in a system of schools. *National Educational Association Proceedings, 10*, 259–264.

Pickard, J. L. (1890). *School supervision*. New York: D. Appleton and Company.

Pierce, P. R. (1935). *The origin and development of the public school principalship*. Chicago, IL: The University of Chicago Press.

Pohly, K. (1993). *Transforming the rough places: The ministry of supervision*. Dayton, OH: Whaleprints.

Poole, W. (1994). Removing the "super" from supervision. *Journal of Curriculum and Supervision, 9*, 284–309.

Portelli, J. P. (1987). On defining curriculum. *Journal of Curriculum and Supervision, 2*, 354–367.

Prince, J. T. (1901). The evolution of school supervision. *Educational Review, 22*, 148–165.

Prince, J. T. (1906). *School administration*. New York: C. W. Bardeen.

Punch, K. F. (1969). Bureaucractic structure in schools: Toward redefinition and measurement.*Educational Administration Quarterly, 5*, 43–57.

Ravitch, D. (1974). *The great school wars*. New York: The Free Press.

Records of the Governor & Company of the Massachusetts Bay in New England, (1642).

Reeder, E. H. (1953). *Supervision in the elementary school*. Boston, MA: Houghton Mifflin.

Reeder, W. G. (1930). *The fundamentals of public school administration*. New York: Macmillan.

Reid, R. L. (1968). *The professionalization of public school teachers: The Chicago experience, 1895–1920*. Unpublished doctoral dissertation, North Western University.

Reid, W. (1986). Curriculum theory and curriculum change: What can we learn from history? *Journal of Curriculum Studies, 18*, 159–166.

Reller, T. L. (1935). *The development of the city superintendency of schools in the United States*. Philadelphia, PA: Author.

Reports of the Record Commissions of the City of Boston. (1709).

Rice, J. M. (1893). *The public-school system of the United States*. New York: The Century Company.

Robinson, N. (1967). *A study of the professional role orientation of teachers and principals and their relationships to bureaucratic characteristics of school organizations*. Unpublished doctoral dissertation, University of Alberta.

Rogers, V. M. (1945). Who is supervisor? *Educational Leadership, 2*, 152–154.

Rooney, J. (1993). Teacher evaluation: No more "super" vision. *Educational Leadership, 51*, 43–442.

Rousmaniere, K. (1992). *City teachers: Teaching in New York City schools in the 1920s*. Unpublished doctoral dissertation, Columbia University.

Rorer, J. A. (1943). Principles of democratic supervision. *Teachers College Record, 44*, 374–375.

Rugg, H. O. (1920). Self-improvement of teachers through self-rating: A new scale for rating teachers. *The Elementary School Journal, 20*, 674–686.

Salisbury, E. I. (1918). Supervision. *American School Board Journal, 57*, 18–23.

Saylor, G. (1966). Foreword. In L. M. Berman & M. L. Usery (Eds.). *Personalized supervision: Sources an insights*. Washington, D.C.: ASCD.

Saylor, G. (1976). *The founding of the Association for Supervision and Curriculum Development*. 10–22.

Schlessinger, A. M. (1933). *The rise of the city, 1878–1898*. New York: Macmillan.

Schon, D. (1983). *The reflective practitioner: How professionals think in action*. New York: Basic Books.

Schubert, W. H. & Lopez-Schubert, A. L. (1980). *Curriculum books: The first eighty years*. Lanham, MD: University Press of America.

Scott, W. R. (1961). *A case study of professional workers in a bureaucratic setting*. Unpublished doctoral dissertation, University of Chicago.

Scott, W. R. (1981). *Organizations: Rational, natural, and open systems*. Englewood Cliffs, NJ: Prentice-Hall.

Seeley, D. S. (1985). *Education through partnership*. Washington, D.C.: American Enterprise Institute for Public Policy Research.

Seguel, M. L. (1966). *The curriculum field: Its formative years*. New York: Teachers College Press.

Sergiovanni, T. J. (1990). *Value-added leadership: How to get extraordinary performance in schools*. San Diego, CA: Harcourt Brace Jovanovich.

Sergiovanni, T. J. (1992). Moral authority and the regeneration of supervision. In C. D. Glickman (Ed.). *Supervision in transition* (pp. 30–43). Alexandria, VA: ASCD.

Sergiovanni, T. J. (1997). How can we move toward a community theory of supervision? Wrong theory/wrong practice. In J. Glanz & R. F. Neville (Eds.). *Educational supervision: Perspectives, issues, and controversies*. Norwood, MA: Christopher Gordon Publishers.

Sergiovanni, T. J. & Starratt, R. J. (1993). *Supervision: A redefinition* (5th ed.). New York: McGraw-Hill.

Shiels, A. (1915). The rating of teachers in New York City public schools. *School and Society, 2*, 752–754.

Shores, J. H. (1967). Foreword. In R. P. Wahle (Ed.). *Toward professional maturity of supervisors and curriculum workers*. Washington, D.C.: ASCD.

Silberman, C. E. (1970). *Crisis in the classroom*. New York: Random House.

Skala, N. (1930). Superfishin' or supervision. *The Nebraska Educational Journal, 10*, 437–438.

Sloyer, G. F. (1945). Trouble-shooter and eye-opener. *Educational Leadership, 2*, 155–159.

Sloyer, M. W. (1928). Subject supervision. *Education, 48*, 475–481.

Small, W. H. (1914). *Early New England schools*. Boston, MA: Ginn and Company.

Smyth J. (1991). Instructional supervision and the redefinition of who does it in schools. *Journal of Curriculum and Supervision, 7*, 90–99.

Snedden, D. (1910). Centralized vs. localized administration of public education. *Education, 30*, 536–549.

Snedden, D. (1911). Combining efficiency and democracy in educational administration. *American School Board Journal, 42*, 2–5.

Snow, C. A. (1939). The history of the development of public school supervision in the state of Maine. *The Maine Bulletin, 41.*

Snyder, K. J. (1988). Clinical supervision. *Encyclopedia of School Administration and Supervision.* Phoenix: Oryx Press.

Society for Curriculum Study. (1932). *News Bulletin, 3.*

Soldan, F. L. (1899). The progress in public education. *National Educational Association Proceedings, 37,* 888–891.

Sousa, D. A. & Hoy, W. K. (1981). Bureaucratic structure in schools: A refinement and synthesis in measurement. *Educational Administration Quarterly, 17,* 21–39.

Spaulding, F. E. (1913). The application of the principles of scientific management. *National Educational Association Proceedings, 51,* 259–279.

Spaulding, F. E. (1955). *School superintendent in action in five cities.* Ringe, NH: Richard R. Smith Publisher.

Spears, H. (1941). *Secondary education in American life.* New York: American Book Company.

Spears, H. (1953). *Improving the supervision of instruction.* Englewood Cliffs, NJ: Prentice-Hall.

Starratt, R. J. (1992). After supervision. *Journal of Curriculum and Supervision, 8,* 77–86.

Starratt, R. J. (1997). Should supervision be abolished? Yes. In J. Glanz & R. F. Neville (Eds.). *Educational supervision: Perspectives, issues, and controversies.* Norwood, MA: Christopher Gordon Publishers.

Stephens, L. D. (1974). *Probing the past: A Guide to the study and teaching of history.* Boston, MA: Allyn and Bacon.

Stinnett, T. M. (1968). *Professional problems of teachers.* New York: Macmillan.

Storm, H. C. (1923). Three elements of effective supervision. *American School Board Journal, 66,* 113–115.

Suzzallo, H. (1906). *The rise of local school supervision in Massachusetts.* New York: Teachers College, Columbia University.

Swearingen, M. E. (1946). Looking at supervision. *Educational Leadership, 3,* 146–151.

Swearingen, M. E. (1962). *Supervision of instruction: Foundations and dimensions.* Boston, MA: Allyn and Bacon.

Tanner, D. & Tanner, L. N. (1980) *Curriculum development: Theory into practice* (2nd ed.). New York: Macmillan.

Tanner, D. & Tanner, L. N. (1987). *Supervision in education: Problems and practices.* New York: Macmillan.

Tanner, D. & Tanner, L. N. (1990). *History of the school curriculum.* New York: Macmillan.

Taylor, F. W. (1911). *The principles of scientific management.* New York: Harper and Brothers.

Taylor, J. S. (1912). Measurement of educational efficiency. *Educational Review, 44,* 350–351, 359.

Thompson, V. A. (1969). *Bureaucracy and innovation.* Alabama: The University of Alabama Press.

Threlkeld, A. L. (1925). Curriculum revision: How a particular city may attack the problem. *The Elementary School Journal, 25,* 573–582.

Threlkeld, A. L. (1928). The place of curriculum construction in the supervisory program. In *Educational Supervision—First Yearbook of the National Conference on Educational Method* (pp. 210–219). New York: Teachers College, Columbia University.

Tracy, S. J. (1995). How historical concepts of supervision relate to supervisory practices today. *The Clearing House, 68,* 320–325.

Tracy, S. J. & MacNaughton, R. (1993). *Assisting and assessing educational personnel: The impact of clinical supervision.* Boston, MA: Allyn and Bacon.

Tsui, A. B. M. (1995). Exploring collaborative supervision in in-service teacher education. *Journal of Curriculum and Supervision, 10,* 346–371.

Turner, F. J. (1920). *The frontier in American history.* New York: H. Holt and Company.

Tyack, D. B. (1974). *The one best system: A history of American education.* Cambridge, MA: Harvard University Press.

Tyack, D. B. (1976). Pilgrim's progress: Toward a social history of the school superintendency, 1860–1960. *History of Education Quarterly, 16,* 257–300.

Tyack D. B. & Hansot, E. (1982). *Managers of virtue: Public school leadership in America, 1820–1980.* New York: Basic Books.

Udy, S. H., Jr. (1959). "Bureaucracy" and "rationality" in Weber's organizational theory: An empirical study. *American Sociological Review, 24,* 791–795.

Urban, W. J. (1976). Organized teachers and educational reform during the progressive era, 1890–1920. *History of Education Quarterly, 16,* 35–52.

Urban, W. J. (1982). Historiography. In H. C. Mitzel (Ed.). *The encyclopedia of educational research.* New York: Macmillan.

U.S. Bureau of the Census. (1895). *U.S. Census of 1890.* Washington, D.C.: Government Printing Office.

Van Til, W. (Ed.). (1986). *ASCD in retrospect.* Washington, D.C.: ASCD.

Vigilante, N. J. (1964). *A role perception study of elementary principals and elementary supervisors in the state of Ohio.* Unpublished doctoral dissertation, The Ohio State University.

Vollmer, H. M. & Mills, D. L. (Eds.). (1966). *Professionalization.* Englewood Cliffs, NJ: Prentice-Hall.

Wagner, C. A. (1923). Supervision of instruction: Why? *American School Board Journal, 66,* 34–36.

Wahle R. P. (Ed.). (1967). *Toward professional maturity of supervisors and curriculum workers.* Washington, D.C: ASCD.

Waite, D. (1994). Understanding supervision: An exploration of aspiring supervisors' definitions. *Journal of Curriculum and Supervision, 10,* 60–76.

Waite, D. (1995). *Rethinking instructional supervision: Notes on its language and culture.* London: The Falmer Press.

Walen, E. & DeRose, M. (1993). The power of peer appraisals. *Educational Leadership, 51,* 45–48.

Walker, D. (1975). The curriculum field in formation: A review of the 26th Yearbook of NSSE. *Curriculum Theory Network, 4,* 3–25.

Warren, D. (Ed.). (1989). *American teachers: Histories of a profession at work.* New York: Macmillan.

Warren, S. W. (1974). *Striking teachers: Professionalism and bureaucracy.* Unpublished doctoral dissertation, Teachers College, Columbia University.

White, E. E. (1871). Ohio superintendent's association, proceedings of the annual meeting held at Sandusky City, July 4, 1871. *The National Teacher, I,* 8–12.

Whyte, W. H. (1955). *The organization man.* New York: Simon and Shuster.

Wiebe, R. H. (1967). *The search for order, 1877–1920.* New York: Hill and Wang.

Wiles, K. (1967). *Supervision for better schools.* Englewood Cliffs, NJ: Prentice-Hall.

Wiles, J. & Bondi, J. (1986). *Supervision: A guide to practice* (2nd ed.). Columbus, OH: Charles E. Merrill.

Wiles, K. & Lovell, J. T. (1983). *Supervision for better schools.* Englewood Cliffs, NJ: Prentice Hall.

Wilhelms, F. T. (1969). Leadership: The continuing quest. In R. R. Leeper (Ed.). *Supervision: Emerging profession.* Washington, D. C.: ASCD.

Wilhelms, F. T. (1973). *Supervision in a new key.* Washington, D.C.: ASCD.

Willerman, M., McNeely, S. L. & Koffman, E. C. (1991). *Teachers helping teachers: Peer observation and assistance.* New York: Praeger.

Williams, A. (1995). *Visual and active supervision: Roles, focus, technique.* New York: W.W. Norton & Company.

Wood, G. D. (1971). *The bureaucratic–professional role orientations of the public school teacher as perceived by teachers and principals.* Unpublished doctoral dissertation, North Carolina State University.

Zimmerman, J. (1994). The dilemma of Miss Jolly: Scientific temperance and teacher professionalism, 1882–1904. *History of Education Quarterly, 34,* 413–431.

Zimpher, N. L. & Grossman, J. E. (1992). Collegial support by teacher mentors and peer consultants. In C. D. Glickman (Ed.). *Supervision in transition* (pp. 141–154). Alexandria, VA: ASCD.

Zumalt, K. K. (Ed.). (1986). *Improving teaching.* Washington, D.C.: ASCD.

MODELS AND APPROACHES

Saundra J. Tracy

BUTLER UNIVERSITY

INTRODUCTION

There is little agreement as to whether we should classify the variety of research and practice in the field of instructional supervision into models and approaches. Even those that propose that models serve a useful purpose in creating our research agendas and guiding our reflection on practice cannot agree on what those models are. It is not the intent of this chapter to resolve these debates; rather, this chapter attempts to present both sides of the argument, showing how the creation of models can both enhance and hinder our understanding of supervision. The inherent bias of the chapter, however, is that models are more helpful than harmful, and that they have promoted rather than obstructed the limited research that has been conducted in the field.

The primary emphasis of the chapter is to identify those conceptual structures that have functioned as supervisory models in research and practice. While pointing out the different classification schema, the interrelationships between various authors' conceptualizations of models will be noted. The chapter also suggests a new schema that integrates the variety of existing supervisory models in new ways. The chapter concludes with a discussion of what is missing in today's models of supervision as we look at supervision in the context of a changing educational environment.

THE DEFINITION OF A MODEL

In the *Second Handbook of Research on Teaching*, Nuthall and Snook (1973) point out that the term *model* suffers from the ambiguity of constant usage. It is often used interchangeably with numerous others terms, such as approach, theory, or paradigm. When one investigates what is formally meant by the term, this constant usage continues to obscure a dominant definition. Several repeated definitions emerge, however, that can help inform our thinking about models in the field of supervision of instruction.

One common view of models is that they represent an abstraction of reality (Birnbaum, 1988), a bridge between the abstract and the practical (Knezevich, 1975). This view proclaims that models allow us to understand the elements and dynamics of a system—whether that system is a way of teaching, or supervising, or of managing an organization. Models as abstractions of reality grow out of extensive observation of practice. They distill the common elements of practice and identify the trends in a particular area. As Hoy and Forsyth note (1986), they may not exist in reality in their abstracted or pure form. Nevertheless, they are extremely practical tools for understanding a segment of the real world of supervision (Tracy & MacNaughton, 1993) and for classifying the events of that world (Van Manen, 1977).

Closely related to the idea of model as abstraction of reality is the idea of model as a conceptual lens or interpretative framework through which one views that reality (Birnbaum, 1988; Bolman & Deal, 1985; Polanyi, 1976; Sergiovanni & Starratt, 1993). As interpretative frameworks, models offer a way to interpret and organize empirical evidence (Polanyi, 1976). Bolman and Deal refer to the lens of a specific cognitive frame through which we see the world. These lenses simplify what we see, allowing certain key characteristics to stand out in bold relief while eliminating some of the remaining detail. In other words, they filter out some things while allowing others to pass through easily. Oliva (1993) notes that a model, through this distillation process, can quickly reveal the concepts held by the person who creates it. Models as frames help us to order our world. Without these screens, it is likely we would be overcome by information overload as we are bombarded by all of the details involved in the range of supervisory practice. Through this filtering process, we can explore more widely the range of practice that exists through focus on the essential characteristics. Defining models as frameworks also illustrates the danger in taking a single frame approach and the benefit of using alternative models to gain different but complementary perceptions of reality.

In addition to describing and explaining reality, Nuthall and Snook (1977) contend that models can be defined by several other purposes, such as exemplars or predictors. As exemplars, models set out a pattern or plan of assumptions and behaviors to be imitated. Education often has defined models in this way, touting a particular pattern of teaching behavior, student–teacher interaction, or supervisory behavior as preferred. Numerous workshops and in-service programs are built on the idea of models as exemplars. These workshops seldom also note that there is rarely one dominant, "correct" model in the social sciences. This is the major distinction between the use of the term *model* in the natural and social sciences (Shulman, 1986). Models merely represent one of several schools of thought in the social sciences, as opposed to "correct thought" in the natural sciences, where only a single model can be dominant at any given time.

As predictors, models give us initial insights into the potential outcomes of our practice. In their well-known *Models of Teaching,* Joyce and Weil (1980) support this view, adamantly opposing adherence to any single model. They recommend that teachers generate a repertoire of several models, adapting them, transforming them, and creating new models as they gain expertise. By this definition, a model becomes a design for learning as one uses it to guide beginning practice (Ingvarson, 1987, as cited in Sparks & Loucks-Horsley, 1990). This view is consistent with many of the strategies used in the preparation of teachers and supervisors. For example, one must begin by learning some initial supervisory skills that form a coherent pattern of behavior and are based on a consistent set of assumptions (i.e., a model); however, few would advocate that the learning ends there. As beginning supervisors try out these skills, they identify situations where they are and are not effective. The supervisory learning continues, with new skills and new patterns of behavior added to the mix. Different combinations are tried in different situations. In other words, a model serves as the starting point that helps to predict outcomes in a continuing, dynamic process of skill development. The initial model(s) learned are not intended to be the "right" way to practice supervision.

Finally, the term *model* is often defined in relation to the generation of research. Models may grow out of as well as stimulate research. Joyce and Weil (1980) suggest that models can be based on practice, empirical work, theories, hunches, and speculation about the meaning of research done by others. Maccia et al (1963) concur that models both devise and come from theory. Phenix (1986) defines a model as a pattern or structure that provides a satisfactory basis for theory construction. This structure does not serve as a criteria for judging something true or false, but rather as a guide for observation and research.

Models promote research by allowing researchers to frame questions about supervisory methods as either–or questions (Nuthall & Snook, 1973). When research is conducted within the context of a model, the researcher need not worry about the multitude of methods; a model simplifies and organizes the process of research. It also provides grounds for interpreting and generalizing the data that are obtained.

Like research on teaching, however, there is little possibility that empirical evidence can be used to prove the validity of one model over another (Nuthall & Snook, 1973),

because each model is fundamentally a claim about how supervision ought to be understood and interpreted. One rarely sees cross-model research; therefore, because models consist of a set of associated ideas organized around a particular world view, they illumine the way that researchers have organized themselves and the space in which they conduct their research. Models are the most commonly employed way to describe the research communities in supervision and their conceptions of the research problems and methods (Shulman, 1986). According to Shulman, research grows out of attention to a particular perspective that illuminates some part of the field while ignoring the rest—the filtering function of models.

This definition of a model as a generator of research should not lead us to conclude that models are the *primary* generators of research on supervision. In speaking about research on teaching, Nuthall and Snook (1973) remind us that the guiding force for much of the research on teaching has not been the discovery and systematic accumulation of empirical knowledge nor the gradual refinement of seminal models. A much more powerful impetus for research has come from debate and controversy over certain highly provocative concepts and claims about how teaching ought to be viewed. The same statement is certainly true for research on supervision.

THE STRUCTURE OF A MODEL

In describing a range of models of teaching or supervision, various authors have structured their presentations differently. The best-known treatment of models is probably found in the classic work of Joyce and Weils (1980). They identify a number of concepts that are useful in describing any given model: (1) the goals of the model, (2) the theoretical assumptions, (3) the principles and major concepts underlying the model, (4) the syntax of the model, (5) the social system, (6) principles of reaction, and (7) supporting conditions for the model. Although Joyce and Weils used these concepts to explicate their models of teaching, they are equally applicable to models of instructional supervision. Examples of each of these concepts in relation to supervision will illustrate this point.

The first three concepts used by Joyce and Weil are fairly self-explanatory. Tracy and MacNaughton (1993) identify the major *goals* of supervisory models as either assisting, assessing, or some combination of the two functions. Others, such as Iwanicki (1981) and Sparks and Loucks-Horsley (1990), speak of individual teacher growth goals and organizational development–improvement goals when describing models of supervision and professional development.

The *theory* on which a model is based is often not clearly articulated by either those describing or using the model. There are examples, however, where theory has been linked to supervisory models. Rosenshine (1986) shows how information processing theory forms the basis for the research on explicit teaching, which is the body of research used in support of Hunter's work in supervision. In referring to the same supervisory model, Tracy and MacNaughton (1989) describe its behaviorist philosophical roots.

Although closely related to the theoretical assumptions, the *underlying principles* or concepts provide more tangible details about the model and how it is practiced. Noting the strong relationship between the underlying assumptions and the shape the model takes in practice, Sparks and Loucks-Horsley (1990), treat the underlying principles and phases of model activity as one component of their models of staff development. To cite a supervisory example, Pajak's overview of the underlying principles of Mosher and Purpel's clinical model of supervision helps us to understand the phases of the model's implementation. These include the principles of (1) teaching as a patterned behavior, (2) which can be classified and studied, and (3) is subject to control and understanding (Pajak, 1993).

Joyce and Weil (1980) define the *syntax* of the model as the actual stages of implementation. If supervisors were to implement Hunter's model or Cogan's original version of clinical supervision, in what kinds of activities would they engage? Would they conduct a preconference? What kind of data on teaching would be gathered? The syntax of a model is rarely omitted. Referring back to our earlier discussion of models as exemplars, the syntax is the focus of numerous workshops on supervision, often with little additional attention given to the equally important theoretical assumptions and underlying principles.

Some scholars in the field of supervision have given a great deal of attention to the *social system* of the models. The social system refers to the roles and relationships and the kinds of norms that are encouraged by the model. Goldhammer (1969) is well-known for his detailed discussion of the preferred type of relationship between supervisor and teacher. Blumberg (1974) similarly focused primary attention on the quality of teacher–supervisor relationships in schools, proposing four supervisory styles of interaction.

Principles of reaction go a step beyond the syntax and suggest how the supervisor might respond to the supervisee in various situations. These principles provide some of the predictive capability of the model (i.e., if the teacher does *x,* then the supervisor should try *y* because *y* has been shown to be effective in previous use of this model). Goldhammer's treatment of developing a plan for the postconference gives one a prime example of this aspect of a model (Goldhammer, 1969). The supervisor is cautioned to select no more than one or two teaching behaviors for the focus of the conference. Goldhammer provides several questions to assist the supervisor in narrowing the conference focus when a number of teaching patterns have been identified.

The last component of models as described by Joyce and Weil is the *support system* referring to the supporting conditions that are necessary for the model to be effectively implemented. In their treatment of supervisory models, Tracy and MacNaughton (1993) refer to this component as the necessary skills and personnel. What specific skills are essential for effective use of the model? For example, some models require specific data collection techniques; others emphasize a very structured conference process. Who are the persons involved? While we have tended to focus on the "supervisor" and teacher, a number of supervisory models are effectively carried out among peers.

Just as models offer a means of organizing the world of practice, these components of the models help one discern the critical attributes of each model. They guide our understanding of the why and how of a model. These components also provide a means of more easily comparing and contrasting models and creating new models through eclectic combinations of their parts.

SUPERVISORY APPROACHES

As with the definition of models, there is not common agreement on the use of the term *approach* when referring to research and practice in supervision. Pajak (1993) and Tracy and MacNaughton (1993) could represent the two most common views of the term. Pajak uses the terms *model* and *approach* interchangeably. This is illustrated in his reference to *four models* of supervision in his book entitled *Approaches to Clinical Supervision.* Throughout this book, he alternates between the terms *model* and *approach.* For example, a section on the "Developmental/Reflective Models" begins with the sentence, "Advocates of the developmental/reflective approaches to supervision . . ." (Pajak, 1993, p. 10). Others similarly interchange the terms. In the 1982 Association of Supervision and Curriculum Development yearbook publication on supervision, a number of *approaches* are presented that represent most of the major *models* found in Pajak's work.

Tracy and MacNaughton distinguish between the two terms, using the term *approach* to refer to variations of practice within a particular model. These variations are all based on the same theory and underlying principles, but they may represent variations in implementation, social interactions, or required support systems. Approaches are another level of analysis of research and practice on supervision.

For the purposes of this chapter, the latter definition of terms is used; approach describes a subcategory within a model, the variations that one might observe in practice held together by the model's common conceptual base. With this discussion of the semantic differences in mind, a caution is in order. We have engaged far too often in semantic sparring. How we define *model* and *approach,* or whether we use these terms at all, is much less important than our ability to effectively communicate with each other in order to establish a solid research base and develop effective practice that ultimately improves learning and instruction. The terms are only useful as far as they assist us in this communication.

WINDOWS OR WALLS?

Supervisory models have the potential to both open up new vistas of understanding about supervisory research and practice and to severely restrict our view. Sergiovanni and Starratt (1993) use the metaphor of windows and walls to portray these benefits and dangers. They state:

Models in teaching and supervision are much like windows and walls. As windows, they help expand the view of things, resolve issues, provide answers, and give the surer footing one needs to function as a researcher and practicing professional. As walls, these same models serve to box one in, to blind one to other views of reality, other understandings, and other alternatives (p. 130).

Models as Windows

Models serve as windows when they illumine the relationship between theory and practice. A model should provide the one who views it with insights into the platform behind the practice. As Sergiovanni and Starratt (1993) note, in addition to the technical understandings that emerge from a model's conceptual schema, there is a floor of beliefs, opinions, values, and attitudes that provide a foundation for practice, the platform. According to Oliva (1993), a model quickly reveals the platform of the person(s) who designs it. This idea is consistent with Shulmans' contention that models describe the major research communities in a field of study (Shulman, 1986).

Teachers' and supervisors' platforms are rarely explicit. Their rationales for practice are more often based on broad generalizations and past experience. When models portray both the conceptual and practical sides of supervision, they therefore offer an opportunity for both practitioners and researchers to see more clearly the link between theory and practice. The practitioner's view from the window includes new detail of the "why" of practice—in applying this model, what does it say I believe about teaching and learning? The researcher sees the theory as it may be applied in the laboratory of the school through the window—what are the requirements for effectively implementing this ideal view? To make this connection between theory and practice, however, models must clearly articulate both. We have too often created supervisory models with an emphasis on the steps in practice, ignoring the equally if not more important theoretical base on which the model is built.

Models also create multiple windows by which we can view the world of practice. When the wide range of supervisory practices are taken together, they can create a confusing array of seemingly unrelated activities. In order to compare and contrast these practices, to determine their applicability in individual settings, some structure for organizing practice is necessary. Models provide such a structure. For example, as a supervisor in a school district, I look daily through the window at practice in my own setting. Even in that view, however, I may see a foggy picture of differing practices and outcomes. By applying the conceptual frame of a supervisory model to this picture, the key elements of practice that fit within that frame are highlighted. Other incongruous aspects of practice move out of view. Furthermore, if I move to another window framed by a different conceptual base, I see a different picture. As I move back and forth between these windows, I begin to be able to notice the distinct features of each and recognize the landscape on which each is painted.

According to Joyce and Weil (1980), these multiple windows allow us to expand our repertoires of effective practice in a meaningful and informed way. They do not become framed pictures, one of which is to be selected and hung on the wall. They offer us examples of others' work, from which

we extract certain elements and create our own picture. We are to transform the basic models that are put before us and create new ones. Tracy and MacNaughton (1993) are adamant that the purpose of models is to increase our awareness of research and practice in the world around us. As awareness increases, so should our repertoire of knowledge and skills. Because models represent idealized views, their fit with the practical circumstances of schools is rarely perfect. They are most appropriate, therefore, as catalysts for the eclectic selection and application of the aspects of several models—the creation of a new window. Models serve this purpose for practitioners; however, they also allow researchers to construct a new framework by demolishing hitherto accepted structures (Polanyi, 1962).

The structure created by models offers yet another benefit or window. Like a snapshot that we return to at different points in time, a model give us common structures for comparing our own beliefs and behaviors over time. In an early career stage, a particular model may best speak to our needs and abilities. A few years later, we may find aspects of other models that better address our personal and organizational needs. Returning to these same windows at a later time, we see a different picture. There is a somewhat enduring value to the models, even as some fade from favor and others are added to the list.

Thus, models can expand our horizons, adding to our understanding of the possibilities for research and practice in supervision. By itself, the concept of model is neither positive nor negative, just as no single model is good or bad. It is how we use this concept that determines whether models expand or constrict.

Models as Walls

Even if we believe that models have much to offer in enriching our understanding of the field of supervision, we must be cautious in how we use them, for models also threaten to limit understanding and stifle reflection. Three specific dangers threaten to transform the windows that models create into walls that block off our view of the outside world. These dangers are (1) creating a competitive struggle for the allegiance of the educational community among the adherents of various models, (2) conducting research and practice from the perspective of only one model, and (3) allowing models (even multiple models) to limit and define our perceptions.

The competing demands that we view the field of supervision from only one window (or none at all) is particularly dangerous in a field that suffers from a paucity of research (Alfonso & Firth, 1990) and where the dominant mindscapes do not reflect the reality of supervisory practice (Sergiovanni, 1984). Supervision is in dire need of cooperation in setting a research agenda for the field and in carefully examining practice. It can ill-afford the divisiveness that results from internal competition.

Nuthall and Snook (1973) argue that we often have used models to set up a form of competition in spite of the benefits of viewing educational theory and practice through models. Unlike the major models in the physical sciences, models in education compete as alternative views of the same body of established data. Because there is very little widely accepted established data in both supervision and teaching, models become competing ways of viewing practice. Advocates of particular models attempt to gain the allegiance of other members of the educational community to their point of view. As a consequence, there is the danger that a given model be perceived as how supervision *ought* to be interpreted and practiced. In addition, there is the danger that unreasonable claims will be made regarding a model in the attempt to increase the numbers of its proponents.

Closely related to this danger of competition is the result of it—the selection of a single model as the way in which one views the world (even though other models are available). Shulman (1986) warns against this limiting of perspective in his discussion of models or paradigms of teaching. The danger for any field of educational research, according to Shulman, is its potential corruption or trivialization by a single perspective. When a single perspective dominates, its principles quickly become the definition of "normal science" for that field.

The danger is also an individual one. Enticed by the claims of a particular model, we may be drawn to this one window, giving up our option to circulate freely from window to window. Thus, the selected window becomes a box or wall that closes us off from seeing the rest of supervision. As Van Manen (1977) notes, a particular orientation within a field has the uncanny quality of encapsulating the person who has learned to adopt it. Upon entering a specific realm of thought, one makes the rules of this realm his or her own. The evidences that flow from these rules consequently appear compelling. To move from one orientation to another feels like a transition between two worlds.

Schwab (1971) supports Van Manen's contention in his discussion of acceptance of theory. He notes that all theories in the behavioral sciences are incomplete. Nevertheless, both researchers and practitioners have the proclivity to accept a single theory as truth when it fits their own experiences. They look for what the selected theory tells them to look for, but they rarely notice those things it does not instruct them to search out. The selection of a single model, therefore, provides only one frame of reference. It often causes us to ignore or not notice those things that do not fit the picture, creating a sort of tunnel vision. Schumacher (1977) graphically illustrates this danger in his discussion of philosophical maps:

On a visit to Leningrad some years ago I consulted a map to find out where I was, but I could not make it out. From where I stood, I could see several enormous churches, yet there was no trace of them on my map. When finally an interpreter came to help me, he said, "We don't show churches on our maps." Contradicting him, I pointed to one that was very clearly marked. "That is a museum," he said, "not what we call a 'living church.' It is only the 'living churches' we don't show." It then occurred to me that this was not the first time I had been given a map which failed to show many things I could see right in front of my eyes.

The third caution related to using models to help us interpret the field of supervision is that even with the array of models available to us, we still may be limited by the multiple perspectives set before us. In other words, windows, in general, are too limiting. We need to step outside and experience the full vista, unencumbered by window frames. Schwab (1971) posits this view, suggesting that perception without the aid of organizers, categories, or theories can occur, though such perceptions may be fleeting and fragmentary. He further states that not all of our learned categories are demonstrably taught us by telling and pointing. Some come from experiences to which we were not directed.

McGill (1991) offers a slightly different twist on this same idea. He notes that the special problem of applying structures or models to teaching (and supervision) is that practitioners must apply them to fluid situations in which they often participate alone. Furthermore, as indicated earlier, the knowledge base is incomplete and the means to apply the model are not always clear. As a result, he contends that supervision historically has been other than a meaningful force for instructional improvement.

Garman (1990) echoes a similar view. Referring to clinical supervision, she admonishes us to overcome the tendency to treat mental terms as structures. By structure, she refers to our tendency to construe the actions of clinical supervision as a model or set of techniques, a representation to be carried out in its formally construed state. Her contention is that we do not learn to think and behave in certain ways through models as representations of events (Maturana, 1978, as cited in Garman). Rather, we learn through consensual interactions, thereby creating a linguistic domain.

While emphasizing the potential of models to serve as windows in the remainder of this chapter, we must keep these cautions regarding models as walls in mind lest we succumb to the temptations they represent. These arguments are perhaps somewhat moot if we consider that each of us is continually organizing the information around us, creating structures of our own, and acting based on these experiences. Although we may argue that others' structures or models are not sufficient representations of supervision, they may indeed be preferable to our own limited view. At least when we dare to explore these other models, we venture outside the realm of our own limited perceptions and experience. Therefore, the possibilities of expanding our understanding through models seem to outweigh the dangers inherent in taking this step.

THE BASES OF MODELS OF SUPERVISION

Returning to the earlier discussion of Joyce and Weils' structure of models, let us focus on the bases on which supervisory models have been built. Joyce and Weil (1980) refer to three key concepts that form this base: (1) the goals or purposes of the model; (2) the theoretical assumptions; and (3) the principles or major concepts underlying the model. These three concepts receive limited attention in the literature describing supervisory models with primary attention given to model implementation.

The Purposes of Supervisory Models

The models of supervision that have been developed over the years may be thought of as a continuum of purposes, as illustrated in Figure 3.1. Although most models can be placed toward one end or the other of the continuum, the majority are built on a combination of purposes rather than on an emphasis on a single purpose.

At the top of the continuum are the purposes ranging from assisting to assessing teacher performance. At the left end of the continuum, *supervision* is defined as helping teachers to improve instruction, which is a responsiveness to teachers' needs, reflective growth. Popham (1988, p. 270) describes assisting and assessing as the shaping of the teacher's performance so that it becomes more effective (assisting) versus the identification of weak teachers (assessing). Put more bluntly, he defines the difference as "fixing" or "firing." He contends that although we have frequently attempted to marry these two purposes in one model, it is always a dysfunctional relationship. The persons, procedures, and data utilized for these two purposes must be totally separate. Thus, he argues for supervisory models that represent one or the other end of this continuum.

Sergiovanni and Starratt (1993) differentiate between three possible purposes or points on this continuum: (1) administrative evaluation used for administrative decision-making (the left side of the continuum); (2) supervisory summative evaluation used for periodic, in-depth reflection, membership renewal, assessment of growth (a midpoint); and (3) supervisory formative evaluation for the purpose of ongoing reflective growth (the right-hand side). The addition of supervisory summative evaluation acknowledges the integral relationship between assisting and assessing as described by Hunter. In Sergiovanni and Starratt's view, this type of evaluation allows the teacher options to shape the evaluation to his/her individual circumstances and allows the supervisor the opportunity to work in a summative mode without losing the trust with the faculty.

Popham's and Sergiovanni and Starratt's thinking is not universally accepted in the field of supervision. In fact, some writers such as Hunter (1988) suggest that the term *supervision* has typically referred only to assisting. She argues, however, that the ultimate purpose of both assisting and assessing is the same: to increase teaching effectiveness. In her thinking, the continuum represents a chronological progression of events. Assessment is the logical outgrowth of assistance and achieves validity from the former; it is the assignment of a final grade after effort and instruction. To carry out either supervision or evaluation well requires the same person and process; only the purpose differs.

Hunter and others who share the view that these two purposes are inextricably intertwined, therefore, advocate models that fit somewhere along the continuum representing a blend of both purposes. For example, Hunter's version of clinical supervision emphasizes assisting, but it ultimately leads to assessment (Minton, 1979). It might, therefore, be placed slightly toward the left end of the continuum.

Hazi (1994) supports this perhaps inextricable link between assisting and assessing. She states that although

FIGURE 3.1. Continuum of model purposes

philosophically she would like to argue, as Popham does, for the separation of the supervision and evaluation processes, disentangling the knot may be an impossible and impractical task. Although many supervisors can clearly delineate these two functions, most teachers do not perceive the difference. Furthermore, evaluation law in most states only further confuses the distinctions. Hazi concludes that no amount of linguistic maneuvering is likely to reconcile the differences between supervision and evaluation for teachers, particularly if the same supervisor is charged with both functions.

The purpose of the model as defined by who is to be its primary beneficiary is closely related to the purposes of assisting and assessing teachers. For some models, the primary purpose is the professional development of the teacher based on the teacher's needs and concerns. Boyan and Copeland (1978) support this purpose in their advocacy for initiating supervision with the teacher's concern. The purpose of supervision is to respond to the teacher's concern—individual growth and development. An underlying assumption, usually unspoken, is that individual growth automatically leads to organizational health.

An emphasis on teacher development is sometimes accompanied by an overemphasis on attainment of school goals. Teaching and supervision research in the past decade have shown us that individual differences have a profound influence on the effectiveness of various supervision and staff development strategies. Furthermore, the traditional approaches to training teachers in the knowledge and skills deemed desirable by the school (i.e., staff development) have met with limited success and have often not been linked with the teacher's personal needs and perspectives (Bents & Howey, 1981). One reaction to this tradition is a renewed emphasis on teachers as adult learners, each with his or her unique learning needs. The primary beneficiary of supervision is the teacher.

On the other hand, emphasis has traditionally been given to the teacher's instructional performance as it relates to the accomplishment of overall school goals. The earliest forms of supervision certainly adhered to this purpose. Supervision was carried out in order to determine if the teacher was using appropriate teaching techniques and delivering appropriate content as defined by those who oversaw the operations of the school, usually a layboard from the community (Tanner & Tanner, 1987). This focus on the school rather than on the individual parallels the emphasis on assessment (rather than assistance). While arguably different purposes, therefore, assessment and staff development often go hand-in-hand, as do assistance and teacher development.

As with assisting and assessing, the majority of supervisory models represent a blend of both purposes. Joyce and Showers

(1988) suggest that schools must enhance teachers' individual clinical skills in conjunction with organizational initiatives to improve the instructional program. Without both purposes, innovations will not be sustained. In other words, one can not exist without the other.

Glickman has been a leading advocate in the field of supervision for combining both purposes. According to Glickman (1990), supervision can be thought of as the function that draws together the discrete elements of instructional effectiveness (i.e., individual development) into whole-school effectiveness (i.e., staff development). Supervision must create the link between individual teacher needs and school goals, which is a function that does not happen by chance.

In order to understand any model of supervision, we must therefore identify its purpose(s). This desired outcome is the ultimate destination of model implementation. Supervisors have all too often engaged in what appeared to be promising practice without fully understanding where that practice leads. A model intended to assist may be totally inappropriate for assessment. Nevertheless, there are numerous examples of just such inappropriate model implementation, sometimes because practitioners simply were not aware of the model's intended purpose.

The second key concept that forms the basis for supervisory models is the theoretical foundation. The field of supervision of instruction unfortunately suffers from the lack of its own firm base of theory and research. As Goldhammer (1969, p. viii) noted, there is an

absence of a cogent framework of educational values and of powerful theoretical systems, operational models, extensive bodies of case materials to consult, rigorous programs of professional training, and a broad literature of empirical research . . . both its study and its method tend to be random, residual, frequently archaic, and eclectic in the worst sense.

In citing this Goldhammer quote, Alfonso, Firth, and Neville (1975) add that supervision has historically relied on a descriptive approach through the identification and analysis of supervisory tasks. The result has been the dangerous conclusion that existing practices, because they are described, are appropriate practices. The study of supervision has rarely emanated from theoretical formulations. Twenty years later, unfortunately, little has changed.

In the absence of its own theoretical base, supervision has borrowed from a wide range of fields. Alfonso, Firth, and Neville (1975) determined that four fields had major implications for constructing a research-based theory of supervision. These four fields of study are: (1) leadership theory; (2) communication theory; (3) organization theory; and (4) change theory. They also initially included group dynamics theory and decision theory, later deciding that much of the information from these two fields was also included in the others. They note that numerous other fields, such as sociological theory or psychological theory, might also have been selected.

Bowers and Flinders (1991) borrow heavily from sociology and anthropology in developing a culturally responsive perspective of supervision. Their concept of supervision is built on the premise that the responsibilities of supervisors are defined, in large part, by the pervasive influence of language and culture on classroom activities. They are quite explicit as to the theoretical underpinnings of their perspective.

Madeline Hunter is probably the best-known in the field of supervision to base her work on educational psychology, gaining prominence for her work that emanates from this field. Heavily steeped in learning theory, her model of supervision references a long list of principles of learning with primary emphasis on theory and research on transfer, retention, reinforcement, and motivation. This reliance on psychological theory has been touted as perhaps both the greatest strength and greatest weakness of her work.

The list of fields that have influenced supervision is lengthy. Costa and Garmston (1994) relied heavily on counseling theory in developing cognitive coaching. The earlier key works of Goldhammer (1969) and Mosher and Purpel (1972) also illustrate the strong influence of counseling theory. Roberts (1992 a and b) and Waite (1993) base their work focusing on supervisor–teacher interactions on theories of communication and linguistics.

In other cases, the theoretical influences are less clear. The only way to determine the major theoretical influences is sometimes to examine the background of the chief proponent of the model. For example, Hunter's training in the field of educational psychology is clearly evident in her work in supervision. It is the contention of this chapter, however, that a critical aspect of model development is the description of the theoretical base. Without such background, it seems unlikely that either scholars, researchers, or practitioners can truly understand the model or its implications for practice.

In addition to the purposes and theoretical assumptions underlying the models, one must also identify their major concepts or principles. There are, of course, numerous concepts that can be instrumental in the formation of a model of supervision, with most growing out of the fields of theory just mentioned. We will consider just three examples, each illustrated by one of the three continua in Figure 3.2. Assumptions about these concepts seem to undergird most of the models of supervision proposed to date.

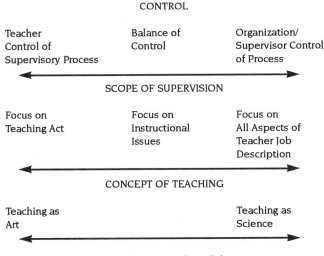

CONTROL

| Teacher Control of Supervisory Process | Balance of Control | Organization/ Supervisor Control of Process |

SCOPE OF SUPERVISION

| Focus on Teaching Act | Focus on Instructional Issues | Focus on All Aspects of Teacher Job Description |

CONCEPT OF TEACHING

| Teaching as Art | | Teaching as Science |

FIGURE 3.2. Continua of model concepts

The first is the concept of *control*. All models of supervision deal with the concept of control in some manner. In some models, such as the Teacher Concern Model of Boyan and Copeland (1978), control of the topic or focus of supervision is given to the teacher. The teacher's first responsibility in the supervisory process is to identify his or her concern. In other models, such as Hunter's, control of the "what" of the supervisory process is neither the teacher's nor the supervisor's. Research on effective teaching and learning theory predetermine the focus of supervision. In the traditional inspection model of supervision, the supervisor determined what was to be emphasized in supervision—the right-hand side of the continuum. Glickman's developmental view of supervision (1981, 1990) illustrates still another way of thinking about control. His assumptions of control are situational; control is based on the background and characteristics of the teacher and may shift back and forth on the continuum over time or in differing circumstances.

Assumptions related to control can refer to the *process* (i.e., how) of supervision as well as the *content* (i.e., what). At the left end of the continuum, the teacher selects the supervisory strategies to be utilized. These may include the types of data collected during an observation and/or conferencing strategies, areas traditionally within the control of the supervisor (the right-hand side of the continuum). Control of the process may also be held by the organization. For example, many school districts have detailed supervisory processes delineated by the contract, which allows an individual teacher (or supervisor) few choices. Although probably intended as a means of increasing teacher control over the supervisory process, one must wonder if such rigid processes do not, in fact, increase organizational control, perhaps to the detriment of both the organization and the individual teacher.

The *breadth of focus* of supervision is the second concept used here to illustrate the importance of knowing the underlying concepts of any supervisory model. Cogan (1973) discussed this concept in his development of clinical supervision. At the right-hand side of the continuum of the scope of supervision is that which focuses on the teaching act itself. Cogan's clinical supervision engaged this aspect; its principal data were to include records of classroom events based on direct observation. At the other extreme, we find supervision that can encompass all aspects of a teacher's job description—both instructional and noninstructional duties. Iwanicki's performance objectives model (1981) is an example of a model with this breadth of focus. Performance objectives need not focus solely on instructional issues; they might also deal with things such as school–community relations or extracurricular responsibilities among others. The broader the scope of the supervisory model, the more likely the model is used for assessment.

Tracy and MacNaughton (1993) also describe a midpoint on the supervision scope continuum. They refer to this midpoint as "instructional supervision," defining it as dealing with instructional issues, but extending beyond the bounds of the observable teaching act. Instructional issues might include the teacher's involvement in curriculum development, overall school improvement initiatives, and other activities that directly impact instruction. Regardless of the targeted point on the continuum, it is critical that any model of supervision note the scope of teacher activity that it covers and specifically designate those activities that are not appropriate to include.

One's conception of teaching and supervision on a continua from art to science is the final example. Although it is unusual to find an argument for perceiving teaching as pure art form or pure science, strong advocates exist for emphasizing one dominant view over the other. Eisner (1982, 1983, 1985) is one of the best known of those emphasizing teaching and supervising as art. He contends that an artistic approach to the supervision of teaching relies on the sensitivity and perceptivity of the supervisor to appreciate the significant subtleties occurring in the classroom. The supervisor utilizes the poetic and expressive potential of language to convey what has been observed. Eisner (1982) notes that the human is the instrument that makes sense of what is happening rather than relying on a scientifically derived structure of analysis. This perspective of supervision recognizes and assists to develop the individual style of the teacher.

On the other end of the continuum are models that place heavy reliance on scientifically derived principles of teaching and learning. Hunter's work is often used as an example due to her emphasis on the effective teaching research and research on learning retention, transfer, and so on. McNeil (1982), while acknowledging the limitations of much of the process–product research, suggests that some of these limitations can be overcome by newer statistical techniques such as meta analysis. Even so, he cautions against overly relying on scientific research, admonishing us to move slightly toward the middle of the continua, where knowledge is confirmed by research and also corresponds to the knowledge that grows from practice.

In each of these areas, there is no right or wrong perspective. Cogent arguments have been built to support many points along each of the continua. What we must remember is that the purpose, theory, and conceptions of a supervisory model naturally lead to implementation behaviors. Unless we can connect these behaviors with the model's bases, we have no way of comparing models, of conducting research on their effectiveness, or of reflecting on our own behaviors as practitioners of supervision.

THE CLASSIFICATION OF SUPERVISORY MODELS IN THE LITERATURE

It would be relatively easy to compare and contrast the models of supervision found in the literature if they all were constructed around some common, defining characteristic; however, they are not. In addition to the difficulty in simply identifying what models have been constructed due to the ambiguous use of the term *model,* those writers who have identified a range of models have tended to pick different characteristics upon which to develop their model schema. Almost all of the classifications are based on observation, practice, or theory; few come from actual research in supervision. Nevertheless, it is useful to consider these various classifications of supervisory models as ways to help us organize our own thinking and as a springboard for developing new schemata.

Six works that each classify supervision according to one or two dominant characteristics will be used here to illustrate. Altogether, they represent the majority of the models in the literature; however, they often interpret a given model differently. Table 3.1 presents the sources of these classifications, the chief organizing characteristics, and how those characteristics are used to define the various models. The chief organizing characteristics(s) of each will serve as the basis for our discussion. These six classification schemes share no common model with the exception of clinical supervision that is found in each. Clinical supervision is treated both as a distinct model and as the larger concept or model from which all other models are derived. This special case of clinical supervision will be explored more fully in the next section of this chapter.

Schema 1

In the Association of Supervision and Curriculum Development (ASCD) yearbook of 1982, three "faces" or approaches to supervision are presented: (1) the scientific; (2) the clinical; and (3) the artistic. These faces bear much similarity to our earlier definition of a model because they are built on a theoretical base, have underlying principles, suggest roles and relationships for both supervisor and supervisee, and establish the context in which they can succeed. The article does not, however, fully develop the phases for implementation, so it might correctly be argued that they are not presented as complete models. Due to the similarity of these "faces" with the more detailed models developed by these same authors in other works, we will examine them from the point of view of their organizing characteristics as one of the major model classifications.

The organizing characteristic for these three approaches is the *derivation of the meaning of teaching*—particularly, effective teaching. The dominant definition of effective teaching is derived from research in John McNeil's scientific approach to supervision (1982). Because the criteria for teaching effective-

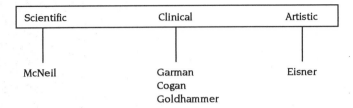

FIGURE 3.3. ASCD yearbook schema of models

ness are external to the supervisory process, both supervisor and teacher relinquish some control. Explicit strategies for implementation of this approach are not developed in this classification.

McNeil is quite candid about the limitations of research-derived criteria. He notes that the number of propositions produced through the use of scientific approaches is small in comparison to the judgments made in teaching. This research usually has merely refined existing knowledge rather than created new knowledge about teaching. Even when such refinement does occur, it is highly selective, testing only a few of the propositions about teaching that might be tested. These limited scientific findings are often divergent, raising more questions than they answer.

In spite of the problems with basing supervision on a research-derived definition of teaching, Sergiovanni (1982) admits that this scientific approach to supervision can help us to establish what is going on in teaching and what ought to be. Advocates of this approach utilize supervision to establish the level and quality of teaching actually present and hold it up against the predetermined standard—establishing the facts of what is and determining the discrepancy with what ought to be.

McNeil concludes that there are several optional directions that scientific supervision may take in the future. Researchers may abandon attempts to find practical solutions to well-

TABLE 3–1. Model organization in the literature

Source	Organizing Characteristic	Variations of the Characteristic	Models
ASCD (1982)	Derivation of the meaning of teaching	Externally derived, collaboratively derived, derived from supervisor's interpretation	Scientific, Clinical supervision, Artistic
Glatthorn (1984)	Control	Shared, self-directed, administrator-directed	Clinical supervision, Cooperative prof-development, self-directed, administrative monitoring
McGreal (1983)	Focus and purpose of supervision	Process/decision-making, specified outcome/decision-making, process/assisting, unspecified outcome/assisting	Common law, goal setting, product, clinical supervision, artistic
Pajak (1993)	Conception of professional practice	Humanistic/artistic, technical/didactic, developmental/reflective	Original clinical models, humanistic/artistic, technical/didactic, development reflective
Sergiovanni & Starratt (1993)	Professional authority	Teacher & functional authority of supervisor, teachers as colleagues, teacher alone, authority of supervisor	Clinical supervision, collegial, self-directed, informal, inquiry, advisory
Tracy & MacNaughton (1993)	Focus of supervision	Ends-oriented, means-oriented, or focus based on teachers' concerns	Instructional objective, performance objective, traditional, neo-traditional, teacher-concern

defined problems, emphasizing instead clarifying their understanding of the classroom and its problems. They might also return to the earlier practice of limiting research to highly selective questions of local import. Another option is to improve teaching through fact-finding studies, an area that has resulted in higher success than scientific generalizations. Regardless of the option chosen, it is clear that McNeil believes the scientific approach to supervision will remain one of several ways of learning about and defining teaching.

The second approach included in this overview is clinical supervision as defined by Garman (1982). The derivation of the meaning of effective teaching, according to this approach, is through the collaborative interactions of teacher and supervisor, neither of whom can fully develop or interpret the meaning of the events alone. Garman notes that there are at least two criteria that the supervisor and teacher must apply to derive the value of the operational concepts: (1) reliability and (2) utility. In attempting to understand a particular point of view, its reliability must be determined. One must ask to what degree would the same event, observed by colleagues, be recognized and described in the same way? Utility for a given purpose similarly raises the question of what is a "useful way to describe people and events so that we can understand why we perform as we do in regard to various skills?" (Garman, 1982, p. 37).

The collaborative derivation of meaning is more clearly explicated in Garman's ensuing descriptions of *collegiality, collaboration, skilled service,* and *ethical conduct. Collegiality* refers to the frame of mind one brings to the supervisory relationship. This can range from that of alienated critic to organic member where the distinction between teacher and supervisor is barely discernible. The ideal type of collaboration is characterized by a reciprocal working involvement where each member works toward achieving his or her own goals as well as those of the other person or the group. Skilled service is the result of the supervisor's prolonged and specialized training and practice made explicit to the teacher in the client–colleague relationship. Ethical conduct is the continual making of judgments based on what is fair, good, and wise.

Garman summarizes her discussion of clinical supervision by noting that a person becomes a clinical supervisor when the steps in clinical supervision become metaphor as well as method, when observation and analysis of teaching are the empirical approach inherent in skilled service as well as procedural phases—the means of deriving meaning. She concludes:

Ultimately, a person becomes a clinical supervisor when he/she can use the method, act through the metaphor, and thereby sort out the nontrivial from the trivial in order to bring meaning to educational endeavors (Garman, 1982, p. 52).

The third "face" presented in the ASCD overview is that of artisitic supervision, an approach that

relies on the sensitivity, perceptivity, and knowledge of the supervisor as a way of appreciating the significant subtleties occurring in the classroom, and exploits the expressive, poetic, and often metaphorical potential of language to convey to teachers or to others whose

decisions affect what goes on in schools, what has been observed (Eisner, 1982).

Artistic supervision focuses on the strengths in the teacher's unique style and tries to help the teacher to exploit that strength rather than emphasize aspects of style that may not be natural for the teacher. The ultimate goal of the supervisor is to assist the teacher to strengthen those values that exemplify a quality education.

Eisner differentiates between the data collected in the scientific approach versus the artistic. While the scientific is concerned with manifested behavior, the artistic approach attends to the expressive character of what students and teachers do, attempting to capture what this situation means to the people who are in it and how their actions convey such meaning. The data collected draw a rich, descriptive picture of what has transpired. Thus, the supervisor is both a "connoisseur" who appreciates what has occurred in the classroom as well as a "critic," expressing in artistic language what he or she has experienced in order to assist the teacher. The supervisor provides insights through the use of language that the teacher may be too close to see.

Precise steps for implementing the artistic approach are not discussed. Eisner does conclude, however, with a description of the eight key features of this approach. Among them are the ability to see what is significant yet subtle, to establish rapport or trust between supervisor and teacher, and to interpret events to those who experience them and to be able to appreciate their educational import. The final feature emphasizes the organizing characteristic for these three models; in the artistic approach, the individual supervisor with his or her strengths, sensitivities, and experience is the major instrument through which the educational situation is perceived and construed.

Schema 2

Glatthorn (1984) has construed supervision as a series of four options available to supervisors that should be mixed and matched as needed in Figure 3.4. Labeled "differentiated supervision," he advocates having teachers select options, thereby allowing supervisors better to focus their efforts. His range of options can be analyzed from several angles. The primary organizing theme appears to be related to issues of the purpose of supervision and control of the process. His four options are: (1) clinical supervision; (2) cooperative professional development; (3) self-directed development; and (4) administrative monitoring.

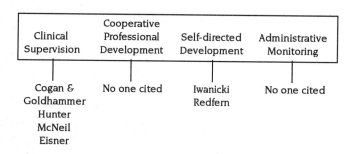

Clinical Supervision	Cooperative Professional Development	Self-directed Development	Administrative Monitoring
Cogan & Goldhammer Hunter McNeil Eisner	No one cited	Iwanicki Redfern	No one cited

FIGURE 3.4. Glatthorn's schema of models

Glatthorn's version of clinical supervision is quite different from the just-discussed Garman version. He sees scientific and artistic supervision as examples of clinical supervision, and then moves beyond these to create his own version: learning-centered supervision. The purpose of learning-centered clinical supervision is to help, not to evaluate, the teacher. Even though the purpose is to assist, the supervisor maintains significant control of the process. This point is illustrated by the target audiences for this type of supervision: (1) inexperienced teachers; (2) experienced teachers making a major shift in teaching assignment; (3) experienced teachers encountering significant problems; or (4) competent, experienced teachers who feel they can benefit from intensive supervision (Glatthorn, 1984, pp. 35–36).

As in Garman's work, the traditional steps in clinical supervision are defined. Glatthorn, however, focuses the process on the learning activities of students followed by analysis of ways in which the teacher's behavior facilitates or impedes student learning. He relies heavily on research on teaching and learning as the external criteria for this analysis, creating a combination of the Hunter and McNeil versions of clinical supervision that will be discussed later (Hunter, 1984, 1990; McNeil, 1971). His overview of this model includes detailed examples of implementation strategies, such as data collection techniques and conference agendas. As an assisting model, he strongly urges that the supervisor who assists not also be the person who ultimately must assess.

Cooperative professional development, which is Glatthorn's second option, is more often called "peer or collegial supervision." Shying away from the term *supervision,* Glatthorn defines this option as a moderately formalized process where two or more teachers work together for their own professional development. This process usually includes a minimum number of observations of each others' classes, feedback, as well as discussion of other shared professional concerns, a sequence of events analogous to those of clinical supervision. Some training in basic supervisory skills, such as data collection, data analysis, and conferencing, increases the chance of success of this option.

As in his first option, the purpose is strictly nonevaluative. He bases cooperative professional development on a small but encouraging body of research. Glatthorn acknowledges that this option is not likely to bring about major changes in instructional behavior. It does hold promise to raise the level of professional interchange in a school and to help teachers to see their colleagues and supervision in general in a new light. Quoting from a study by Nelson, Schwartz, and Schmuck (1974), he notes: "Collegial supervision can improve the attitudes and professional interdependence of . . . teachers who receive it."

The third option Glatthorn offers is self-directed development. Others (McGreal, 1983; Tracy & MacNaughton, 1993) refer to this as a goal-setting or performance-objectives model. A significant difference between their models and Glatthorn's is that each of them sees the model as useful for both assisting and assessing. Glatthorn proposes it as a self-development, nonevaluative model clearly controlled by the teacher rather than the supervisor. In spite of its nonevaluative purpose, the process is monitored by the supervisor.

The critical features of this model, according to Glatthorn, are (1) that the teacher works independently rather than being supervised by others, (2) that the teachers sets professional development goals emanating from his or her own assessment of need, (3) that a variety of resources are available to support work on those goals, and (4) that the outcomes are not used to evaluate teacher performance. This option often incorporates a number of self-appraisal techniques, such as the videotaping of one's teaching.

There are limitations to the amount of control accorded teachers in this option, according to Glatthorn. Not all teachers will want or will be able to implement this degree of self-direction. Carroll (1981) reviewed research on teacher self-appraisal and concluded that there is generally little agreement between self-ratings and the ratings of students, colleagues, and administrators. In a later edition of the same book, Barber (1990) supported Carroll's view. Hook and Rosenshine (1979) similarly concluded that teachers' reports of specific behaviors that went on in their classrooms were not particularly accurate. For those teachers who do want this level of supervisory autonomy and independence, however, this option offers a meaningful substitute for the more typical supervisory control.

Administrative monitoring is the only one of Glatthorn's models that may explicitly be used for both assisting and assessing teacher performance. Although this model should not provide the primary data for evaluation, the information gained from its brief visits realistically influence final decision-making. Glatthorn views this model as either a required option (i.e., regardless of the other options selected) or as interchangeable with clinical supervision. In other words, teacher must be involved in some supervisory process that is supervisor-directed. Glatthorn's definition of administrative monitoring is slightly different from the typical traditional evaluation model. He uses the term to refer to what others might call "drop-in" supervision. In this model, the supervisor conducts a series of brief and informal observations of teaching. In spite of the informal nature of the process, administrative monitoring should be planned by the supervisor rather than randomly conducted as time is available. The focus of these brief observations is learner-centered, which is similar to the focus of his version of clinical supervision.

Administrative monitoring is usually not an effective tool for making significant changes in a teacher's behavior. Citing research on effective schools, Glatthorn points out that effective schools are characterized by principals who are highly visible, who frequently monitor the classroom, and who stay well-informed and interested in instruction. The impact of administrative monitoring may, therefore, be felt more in the overall school climate than in visible behavioral changes of individual teachers.

Schema 3

McGreal (1983) is the third author shown on Table 3.1 who classifies supervisory models. Although his book is entitled *Successful Teacher Evaluation,* his models range from assessing to assisting. They also are classified based on the focus (i.e., process, designated, or undesignated outcomes).

Five families of models are described: (1) common law models; (2) goal-setting models; (3) product models; (4) the clinical supervision model; and (5) artistic or naturalistic models.

The common law models are those most frequently used in schools for evaluation. McGreal calls them "common law" to demonstrate that they have been in use for such a long time that they eventually gained acceptance by formalizing the procedures. The focus of this model is the process of teaching; the purpose is to make administrative decisions about performance. Control is almost exclusively held by the supervisor with the teacher a relatively passive participant in the supervisory process. Data on which a teacher's performance is judged comes primarily from classroom observation. As such, observation is synonymous with evaluation. With its major emphasis on summative evaluation, this model treats all teachers alike, using the same supervisory process regardless of experience or competence. Evaluation decisions are generally based on a simplified and standardized set of criteria, often codified in a checklist. As a result of this standardization, this model leads to comparative judgments of performance between and among teachers.

McGreal does not advocate this model; he merely acknowledges its prevalence in practice. He states that the model is not without its advantages, but each advantage can also be a disadvantage. For example, its relative ease of use with large numbers of teachers also limits teacher involvement that can result in teacher change.

McGreal next describes a goal-setting model similar to that of Glatthorn with the exception of purpose. Glatthorn offered the goal-setting model for the purpose of assisting; McGreal suggests that the individualized nature of goal setting can counteract some of the negative features of the common-law model for the purpose of evaluation. He further breaks this model into three approaches: (1) the Management by Objectives Approach (MBO); (2) the Performance Objectives Approach (POA); and (3) the Practical Goal-Setting Approach (PGSA), which is his own version. The nature of the goals and the flexibility afforded to teacher and supervisor vary among these approaches. In each, goals are prioritized based on some criteria of importance and a contract/agreement of the specified outcomes developed.

In the MBO approach, the teacher's goals are specified by and must be congruent with the goals of the broader organization. Thus, this approach has a very strong accountability orientation. The POA, which is based on the work of Redfern (1972, 1982) and Iwanicki (1981), has an added emphasis on

instructional improvement. The criteria of importance applied to goals in this approach are the responsibilities as developed in the job description. As with the MBO, it is assumed that measurable objectives will be set. The PGSA is a more flexible version of the other approaches. Goal setting is a negotiated process between supervisor and teacher, not as self-directed as in Glatthorn's version. Criteria for goal setting are based on the potential impact of the goal on student learning. As a result, goals that directly address teaching behaviors are valued more highly than are those that relate directly to the learner, to the instructional program, or to the organization. Congruent with our earlier definition of the components of a model, McGreal details a step-by-step process by which this approach can be implemented.

A third model category that also focuses on specified outcomes is that of the product model. The product model relies on measures of student performance to describe teaching effectiveness as advocated by McNeil (1971) and Popham (1973) rather than the process of instruction. Appropriate product measures include changes in students' behaviors and/or growth in skills, knowledge of subject matter, and attitudes.

In addition to the narrowed focus on student performance outcomes, McGreal differentiates this model from the goal-setting models in its purpose. He suggests that this model should be limited to formative evaluation (assisting) due to the problems associated with reliance on student outcome measures for administrative decision-making and the lack of research support. Noting growing support for the use of student data for assisting teacher development, McGreal concludes that with the cooperation of teachers, this model can be a powerful addition to assist with instructional decision-making. The detailed steps for implementation of this model are not developed.

McGreal's fourth model focuses on the instructional process rather than on its outcomes and is limited to the purpose of assisting rather than evaluating (assessing) teachers' performance. It is the only model discussed by each of the authors—clinical supervision. McGreal contends that no term has more visibility in the field of supervision than does *clinical supervision*. The data collected about this model strongly suggest that it is an effective method for improving instructional practice. By definition, however, it is not an appropriate model for assessment.

The characteristics of clinical supervision noted by McGreal are similar to those cited earlier by Garman (1982). He reinforces the collegial nature of the supervisor–teacher relationship necessary to implement clinical supervision effectively. Supervision under this model should be responsive to the teacher's needs and concerns, with the teacher deciding the course of the supervisory process. Clinical supervisors ultimately attempt to develop the teacher's own capabilities for self-supervision, making their role obsolete.

McGreal's fifth model is artistic or naturalistic, a family of supervisory approaches built from theory rather than from practice. The focus is on unspecified, open-ended outcomes used for assisting teachers to further develop their unique talents. Because the chief spokesperson for this model is Eisner (1982, 1983), McGreal's description closely parallels that described in the ASCD yearbook schema.

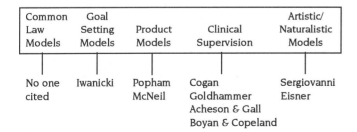

FIGURE 3.5. McGreal's Schema of Models

The artistic–naturalistic model contrasts with the goal-setting and product models because it gives attention to the unpredictable nature of teaching and to the unanticipated meanings and outcomes that can be discovered through observation and analysis. A critical assumption is that these unanticipated meanings and outcomes are legitimate and desirable, which is a view not accepted by many of the proponents of a scientific approach.

Because this model is not fully seen in practice, McGreal is less specific about the process by which it might be implemented. Like ASCD's earlier treatment of this same model, he describes the distinguishing features of data collection. This model can provide a more complete view of teaching and learning when combined with others. Its somewhat conceptually unorthodox approach to supervision enhances one's supervisory repertoire. The time and training necessary for its effective implementation practically make it an unlikely candidate for inclusion in most supervisory systems.

Schema 4

The fourth of the six authors, Pajak (1993) offers one of the most complete and detailed discussions of supervisory models in the field in Figure 3.6. His work, however, is limited to those models that can be classified as "clinical supervision." Using clinical supervision as the overarching umbrella, he describes four families of clinical models: (1) the original models of Cogan, Goldhammer, and Mosher and Purpel; (2) the humanistic/artistic models; (3) the technical/didactic models; and (4) the developmental/reflective models. Upon examination, the organizing characteristic for his classification appears to be the dominant philosophy of professional practice, particularly as it relates to a definition of teaching and learning.

The original models of clinical supervision discussed by Pajak include those of Cogan (1973), Goldhammer, (1969), and Mosher and Purpel (1972). These versions of clinical supervision share a number of common elements both historically as well as conceptually. Pajak notes that the major unifying principles of these three are collegiality and the mutual discovery of meaning in the teaching act growing out of a conceptual view drawn from modern psychological theory. These principles parallel Garman's earlier description of clinical supervision (1982) based on Cogan's work. At the same time, they represent an eclectic mix of philosophical viewpoints such as empiricism, phenomenology, behavioralism, and developmentalism. The purpose of clinical supervision for all three is to provide support to teachers (to assist) and gradually to increase teachers' abilities to be self-supervising. Central to each is a trusting relationship between supervisor and teacher that encourages open discussion and the development of shared meanings of what occurs in the classroom. Supervision is to focus on individual strengths rather than to seek out deficits.

In addition, each of these early versions of clinical supervision details the steps necessary for effective implementation. Although Cogan presents eight steps, Goldhammer five and Mosher and Purpel three, all generally begin with a collegial planning process for teaching within the context of a trusting relationship. This is followed by observation of teaching with the supervisor collecting data. Finally, the data are analyzed and discussed, and plans are made for the continuation of assistance. If one examines the nuances of the steps for each version, then additional differences come to light. For example, the preferred method of data collection varies. Goldhammer and Cogan prefer verbatim transcripts, but Cogan describes a number of other potential methods for gathering data. Mosher and Purpel assert that video or audio recordings offer a more complete and objective picture of teaching.

There are also other differences between the three versions. Mosher and Purpel see clinical supervision interwoven with the content of teaching; the supervisor should address both the what and how of teaching. Cogan would separate the two, emphasizing the teaching process over the content. Both Cogan and Goldhammer are adamant that clinical supervision be used only for improvement of performance, not for teacher evaluation.

Each version considers the teacher's needs and unique styles, but in different ways. Cogan looks strictly at teaching behaviors separate from the person of the teacher. Mosher and Purpel advocate teacher self-examination from a counseling perspective, as does Goldhammer, to a slightly lesser degree.

Pajak's second family of supervisory models is the humanistic/didactic. He references two models that fall into this category: (1) Blumberg's interpersonal intervention model (1974, 1980) and (2) Eisner's artistic approach that has been previously described. Both represent reactions to the mechanical, bureaucratic modes of supervision inherent in the 1970s, moving toward a nonprescriptive method of appreciating rather than measuring what goes on in classrooms. In spite of this common conception of the professional practice of supervision, they diverge greatly in emphasis and in exactly how that practice is to be carried out.

Blumberg's humanistic approach focuses on the quality of human relationships. As he notes in the introduction to his book describing his version of clinical supervision:

What makes this book different, then, is its exclusive focus on the human side of relationships between supervisors and teachers. It does not deal with curriculum or teaching methods, nor does it offer prescriptions for new organizational structure, or outline supervisory duties (Blumberg, 1974).

He goes on to coin a phrase to describe his aversion to the traditional supervisor–teacher relationship as "the private cold

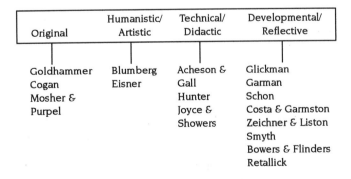

Original	Humanistic/ Artistic	Technical/ Didactic	Developmental/ Reflective
Goldhammer	Blumberg	Acheson &	Glickman
Cogan	Eisner	Gall	Garman
Mosher &		Hunter	Schon
Purpel		Joyce &	Costa & Garmston
		Showers	Zeichner & Liston
			Smyth
			Bowers & Flinders
			Retallick

FIGURE 3.6. Pajak's Schema of Clinical Supervision Models

war." According to Blumberg, rational approaches to dealing with teaching problems will be of little consequence unless one also considers the emotional dimensions of the supervisor–teacher relationship. Thus, his supervisory process relies on accommodating teachers' personal goals as well as those of the organization and assisting teachers to solve problems affecting both. His process for implementation includes a system for the supervisor's analysis of his or her own style. In keeping with the departure from a technical approach to supervision, Blumberg does not prescribe a formula-driven supervisory process. He does, however, offer a range of possibilities including the idea of a group of educators working together to explore and improve practice.

Eisner's work has already been discussed under the frameworks presented by both ASCD (1982) and McGreal (1983). Teaching is conceptually viewed as art rather than science (as discussed to some length under the ASCD classification). Pajak points out Eisner's belief that teaching is the transformation of curriculum into action; the what and how cannot be separated. Eisner notes that exquisite teaching method cannot overcome trivial or invalid content. Furthermore, Eisner takes the original clinical models' concern for teacher development to a new level by working to capture and develop the unique, creative potential of each teacher through supervision. Pajak notes that in this approach the teacher ultimately is free to accept or reject the supervisor's suggestions.

The third family or model, the technical/rational, corresponds most closely to the scientific model first described in the ASCD publication. Pajak selects three examples to illustrate this family: (1) Acheson and Gall's techniques of clinical supervision; (2) Hunter's decision-making model; and (3) Joyce and Showers' coaching model. These three share a common conception of supervision and teaching as rational practice improved through training in specific techniques. This contrasts with the *discovery* of effective methods of teaching and supervising characteristic of the humanistic/artistic family. According to Pajak, knowledge is viewed as something possessed and controlled by experts with being teachers the consumers of this knowledge. Because this knowledge of effective practice is externally derived, there is little or no need for the preobservation conference. The purpose of the postconference differs similarly from the previous models. Feedback is intended to reinforce the need for predetermined behavior patterns rather than to discover new meanings together. The emphasis on the interpersonal relationship between supervisor and teachers obviously diminishes in this family.

Acheson and Gall's version (1980, 1987, 1992) involves a detailed development of a clinical process based on three steps. These are further subdivided into 32 (1987) and 35 (1990) specific supervisory techniques. Unlike their earlier counterparts, Acheson and Gall see a natural relationship between assisting and assessing teachers, even though they prefer to have these two functions carried out by different persons. Their techniques can be used for both. They emphasize working on the content and process of teaching rather than on attempting to change teachers' personalities. Pajak contends that their criteria of good teaching come largely from the effective teaching research. The numerous

process/product studies composing this body of research have resulted in a list of effective teaching behaviors based on their correlation with student learning. Acheson and Gall particularly exemplify the technical family with their detailed and extensive range of data collection techniques.

Hunter's decision-making model, to be discussed later in Tracy and MacNaughton's classification (1993), is even more tightly wedded to the effective teaching research. She contends that the identification of the cause and effect relationship between teaching behavior and student learning increases the probability of the teacher's success. According to Hunter (1979), teaching is synonymous with decision-making. Teaching is initially predominantly science, relying on what has been learned through the scientific study of human learning. Once these behaviors are acquired, teachers use intuition to make the multitude of decisions that occur in a classroom in any given day; thus, teaching also becomes an art.

Hunter specifies a sequence of supervisory events, each guided by her templates for effective supervision. For example, six types of postconferences are described with slightly different agendas and outcomes (Hunter, 1980). She also recommends the specific technique of script taping as the preferred method of data collection (Hunter, 1983). After observation, the analysis of data is driven by the externally determined effective teaching criteria just discussed. She presents her supervisory process for the purpose of assessing teachers; however, she does not shy away from assessment, but, rather, she views it as the natural follow-up to assistance.

The final version of the technical/didactic models presented by Pajak is Joyce and Shower's coaching. Like the previous examples, coaching is based on a body of research—in this case on adult skill development. Coaching, however, does not rely on the supervisor, but is perhaps even more effectively applied by a peer (Joyce & Showers, 1980, 1982, 1988). The desired outcome of coaching is teacher professional development that ultimately affects student learning. This model, therefore, is clearly focused on assisting rather than assessing teacher performance.

Because the elements of the coaching model come from research, they must be carefully followed in the appropriate sequence. This sequence begins with reading or hearing about a particular method, seeing it demonstrated, going through several trials of practice and feedback in a simulated setting, followed by the critical element of coaching in the regular class setting. The fourth element, coaching, is the one most similar to the previous clinical supervision process. Without the other elements, however, even coaching is deemed ineffective.

Pajak concludes that Joyce and Shower's model of coaching is designed for organizational, not just individual development. They recommend that coaching teams be combined to create school and district staff development councils charged with overall school or district instructional improvement. The ultimate goal of coaching is to transform the environment of the school from one of isolation to collaboration through this carefully structured, sequential process for skill development.

The last of Pajak's categories of models is that of developmental/reflective. Included in this category is Glickman's developmental supervision (1980, 1981, 1987, 1990), Costa and Garmston's cognitive coaching model (1985, 1994), and several emerging models Pajak classifies as "reflective practice." These examples of reflective practice represent the work of Schon (1988, 1993), Zeichner and Liston (1987), Garman (1982, 1986), Smyth (1982, 1984, 1985, 1989, 1991), Retallick, as cited in Pajak, 1993), and Bowers and Flinders (1991). According to these models, the conception of professional practice is that it grows out of teachers' ability to learn from experience by critically reflecting on their own actions.

Glickman's developmental approach to supervision views supervision as the connection between individual development and overall staff development. He contends that the conception of professional practice as manifested in characteristics of teaching as a profession and the work environment in many schools is contradictory to either individual or staff development. Supervision should strive to increase teachers' decision-making ability and capacity for abstract thinking. This is only accomplished when the supervisor understands human development and can adapt his or her supervisory techniques to the developmental needs of each teacher. Glickman (1980, 1981, 1990) proposes a range of supervisory approaches based on control of the process. The nondirective approach assumes that the teacher is developmentally at a high level of abstraction and is willing to direct his or her own growth. A collaborative approach is most appropriate when supervisor and teacher have similar levels of experience and commitment to the process of improvement. On the other end of the continuum, the directive approach is used with a teacher at a low level of abstraction, who lacks the experiential base to identify alternative teaching strategies, or who is not committed to the growth process. Two versions of the directive approach are described: (1) the directive informational where the supervisor suggests a strategy but allows the teacher some choice among alternatives, and (2) the directive control where the supervisor very clearly presents the actions to be taken.

Direct assistance, which is Glickman's term for clinical supervision, is one of several useful ways of implementing developmental supervision. Following Goldhammer's five-step description of clinical supervision, he illustrates how the range of supervisory approaches (nondirective, collaborative, directive-informational, and directive-control) can be incorporated. He advocates going beyond supervisor direct assistance to include other forms of teacher development, such as peer supervision, curriculum development, in-service training, and action research, all of which he labels as methods of supervision.

Costa and Garmston's cognitive coaching model (1985, 1994) emphasizes increasing the cognitive and decision-making abilities of teachers. They build their model around the premise that teachers' intellectual capability is directly related to student learning. The three major goals of cognitive coaching are to establish and maintain trust, to facilitate mutual learning, and to enhance growth toward individual autonomy while simultaneously building interdependence with the group.

Built on the Cogan and Goldhammer foundation of clinical supervision, this version of clinical supervision is linked to teacher reflection. The three steps in the process are a planning conference, observation, and a reflecting conference, although participants may deviate from this sequence. The planning conference builds trust between supervisor and teacher, focuses attention on the teacher's goals, provides a detailed rehearsal of the lesson, and sets up the parameters of the reflecting conference. Overall, it is intended to promote self-coaching. During observation, the coach collects data on student achievement and on teaching strategies and decisions. The data collection method is determined by what is relevant and meaningful to the teacher. Finally, in the reflecting conference, the teacher is encouraged to share his or her impressions of the lesson, to draw causal relationships between teacher actions and student outcomes, and to project how future lessons might be designed to reflect what was learned from this experience of teaching. Each step is directed by the teacher with the power to coach bestowed by the teacher due to respect, leadership, and expertise to assist.

Pajak cites the thinking of several additional persons who have written about reflective practice as it relates to supervision. In Schon's version of reflective coaching, teachers and supervisors draw on their repertoires of understanding about their professional practice developed through experience. The teacher identifies unexpected student actions or outcomes, frames these events as a puzzle to be solved, and carries out experiments to reach conclusions. The supervisor's role is to encourage and provoke the teacher into such reflection. Data gathered from the observation of teaching is necessary in order to reconstruct the teaching events; however, they can lead to vulnerability and confusion on the part of the teacher, necessitating sensitive and nondirective behavior by the supervisor.

Zeichner and Liston's (1987), reflective practice targets the supervision of preservice teachers. Encouraging teachers to consider multiple aspects of an issue, to consider the outcomes of their actions on students, and to critically analyze their work with a commitment to teach all students, they delineate a number of skills necessary to accomplish these ends. Among them are skills of keen observation and reasoned inquiry. The clinical supervision process used to encourage reflection is unique in its emphasis on critical inquiry where teachers examine the moral and ethical dimensions of teaching and their relationships with broader issues and structures of schools and society as a whole. Pajak calls this philosophical emphasis one of social reconstruction. Three levels of reflectivity are possible. The first, technical reflection, concerns the effective application of educational knowledge to attain desired outcomes. The second level attempts to explain and to clarify the assumptions and beliefs underlying practice and to determine their results. The final level, critical reflection, has the teacher and supervisor consider the moral and ethical dimensions of teaching, questioning the means, ends, and contexts of teaching and learning.

Garman's conception of reflection calls for the process of clinical supervision to be carried out in a purposeful but nonritualistic way. Collegial interaction is at the heart of reflection on one's actions. A nuance of Garman's thinking not found in the others is her accompanying "reflection on recollection" (Garman, 1986). In reflection on recollection, memories of past events that are significant to the teacher can be included as part of the data. The typical method of recapturing these data is through journaling. They are interpreted in terms of their meaning in relation to current events.

Smyth and Retallick's critical consciousness, according to Pajak, is a call for changing the conditions of schooling. They propose that clinical supervision serves as a means of social control of teachers when viewed as a technical–rational process. Smyth (1991) argues against "contrived collegiality" under the guise of participation in decision-making. The three-step process for carrying out their form of reflection begins with observers helping teachers to recognize the political dimensions of their teaching and to question the ends of teacher that traditionally go unquestioned. Second, the observer creates a descriptive or narrative text of the observed classroom events. The observer plays the role of teacher-consultant willing to also have his or her professional practice critiqued by the teacher. Third, the teacher must confront his or her personal history as a teacher in order to understand present actions.

Finally, Bowers and Flinders (1991) propose that classroom events must be analyzed as growing out of the cultural ecology of the classroom rather than merely out of the actions of teachers and students. Calling their approach "culturally responsive supervision," they recommend replacing the technical view of clinical supervision with an emphasis on the social and cultural aspects of classroom life. The supervisor's role is to help the teacher be aware of the patterns of language used in interactions with and among students and to interpret these patterns in relation to social and cultural issues. The supervisors control the process, setting the agenda for supervision, assisting teachers to formulate problems of which they are unaware, providing anthropological data, reviewing these data, and providing feedback either in writing or orally. The ultimate goal of this approach is to develop culturally sensitive supervisors and teachers who can transcend the predispositions of their own dominant cultural experiences.

Schema 5

Sergiovanni and Starratt (1993) provide a fifth schema for organizing supervisory practice in Figure 3.7. They advocate that all school supervision plans be organized around a minimum of five options with teachers playing key roles in deciding which options best address their needs at a given time. These options describe various supervisory processes where teachers and supervisors play various roles. The organizing theme for their options is *professional authority*. Professional authority is defined as "informed knowledge of craft and personal expertise" (Sergiovanni & Starratt, 1993, p. 34). Using professional authority as an organizer recognizes that no one best way to supervise exists; professional knowledge is created through practice. It promotes a dialogue among teachers, provides teachers with discretion in supervision, requires that teachers hold each other accountable, and makes assistance and support available. Supervision is disconnected from the hierarchical roles of the organization.

Clinical supervision is the first option or model offered by Sergiovanni and Starratt. Reiterating the earlier work of Cogan

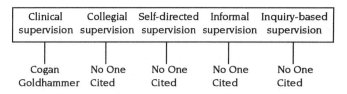

FIGURE 3.7. Sergiovanni & Starratt's Schema

and Goldhammer, they describe the cycle of working with teachers through a process that includes conferences, observations of teachers at work, and pattern analysis. A collegial relationship between supervisor and teacher characterizes the environment in which this process occurs. The assumptions underlying Sergiovanni and Starratt's view of clinical supervision are that supervisors and teachers are mutually responsible for supervision, supervision focuses on the teacher's strengths rather than weaknesses, given the right conditions, teachers are willing and able to improve instruction, teachers have many talents that often go unused; and teachers derive satisfaction from challenging work.

Relating to the organizing characteristic of Sergiovanni and Starratt's options, the authority of the supervisor in clinical supervision is functional rather than derived from the formal authority inherent in one's hierarchical position. Clinical supervision requires a partnership between the teacher and supervisor with the supervisor assuming the role of an individual with experience and insight rather than expertise. Thus, the clinical supervisor derives authority from being able to collect and provide the information desired by the teacher and from subsequently assisting the teacher to effectively use the information.

Clinical supervision, therefore, is an in-class support mechanism to provide direct assistance to an individual teacher. It is the teacher who decides the focus of the supervision and the issues to be discussed, recognizing that supervisors bring considerable influence to this selection process. Sergiovanni and Starratt are quick to note that although the steps in the process of clinical supervision look like what many supervisors do, limited examples exist of practice consistent with the assumptions on which clinical supervision is based. As teachers themselves develop skills in clinical supervision and assume responsibility for its phases, clinical supervision transitions to colleagial supervision, which is the next option proposed by Sergiovanni and Starratt.

Sergiovanni and Starratt's collegial supervision is similar to the model earlier described by Glatthorn as cooperative professional development. This model is only moderately formalized and may take a variety of forms. Teachers may group themselves in teams of two or three and carry out clinical supervision or less formal and intensive processes. Collegial supervision may extend beyond the classroom to include discussions of problems and share in lesson preparation.

Sergiovanni (1991) gives a number of guidelines for the implementation of collegial supervision that augment Glatthorn's earlier ideas. He suggests that teachers have a voice in deciding with whom they work even though the supervisor has the final responsibility for putting together collegial teams. The process should be formal enough for records to be kept on the activities involved; however, these records are nonevaluative. The supervisor's role is to provide the necessary assistance and resources for teachers to be able to carry out this collegial process. Each teacher is asked to keep a professional growth log demonstrating reflectivity and growth. The supervisor determines the effectiveness of the process by meeting at least annually with each team and its individual members.

The heart of collegial supervision, collegiality, emerges as a result of felt interdependence and professional responsibility among teachers. This option demonstrates the essence of professional authority: teachers assuming responsibility for their own and each other's professional growth.

Self-directed supervision, Sergiovanni and Starratt's third option, bears a strong resemblance to Glatthorn's self-directed model. Because teachers assume responsibility by working alone for their own professional development in this model, professional authority resides with the individual teacher. As identified by Glatthorn, performance targets are set for a year-long period, with the teacher responsible for providing evidence that the targets have been met. Sergiovanni and Starratt warn that this model runs the risk of overlooking important areas that are not initially targeted. It is most successful with teachers who prefer to work alone or who, due to schedule, are unable to collaborate with other teachers.

Informal supervision is the fourth option offered in this schema. Void of a set process, informal supervision includes the range of informal or casual encounters between supervisor and teacher. It is usually characterized by informal "drop-in" visits to classrooms, conversations with teachers about their work, and other types of informal activities. The authority base is functional; supervisors have a responsibility to be a part of all the teaching that takes place in the school. The obvious danger inherent in this option is that informal supervision may be perceived as informal surveillance. This form of supervision is best accepted in an environment where teachers routinely visit each other and share professional responsibility for teaching with supervisors. Because this option is not clearly defined by a process, it does not fully meet criteria to be described as a model. Sergiovanni and Starratt acknowledge this, describing it as a type of supervision that might become part of any option.

Inquiry-based supervision offers yet another option for supervision. This option may be carried out between teacher and supervisor or as a collaborative effort on the part of teachers. Often called "action research," this supervisory form requires the teacher to be an observer of his or her own practice. Based on the scientific method of inquiry, it probably requires the highest level of reflection and analysis of any of the options presented here.

When done individually, the teacher works closely with the supervisor in identifying a problem, developing a strategy for its solution, and in sharing findings and conclusions. Implemented as a collaborative process, problems are "co-researched," findings are shared, and teachers collectively search for implications for changing practice. Using Stratemeyer's description (1957), as cited in Sergiovanni and Starratt, action research discovers new ideas and practices, tests old ones, and explores cause and effect relationships.

Although Stratemeyer and her colleagues elaborated on the steps involved in this process, like most forms of supervision, they are neither neat nor clearly discrete phases. In general, these steps include:

1. problem identification
2. development of hunches about the problem's cause and how it might be resolved
3. testing of one or more of the hunches by collecting data, trying out the hunches in action, seeing what happens (collect more data), and evaluating or generalizing based on the evidence

Sergiovanni and Starratt do not fully develop this option as a supervisory model in their own work. Others, however, such as Glickman (1990), Sagor (1992), and Corey (1953) have provided more detailed accounts of action research as an inquiry-based approach to supervision.

A final option proposed by Sergiovanni and Starratt, but not fully developed, is the advisory system. Rather than offer a supervisory option, the advisory system is an alternative to more traditional supervision. It grew out of the movement of the 1960s and 1970s where teachers were assigned particular responsibilities in a school district to assist teachers, but where they did not view themselves as supervisors. The advisor in this process, according to Apelman (1986), (1) provides assistance at the request of the teacher, (2) has no evaluative function, (3) has no predetermined agenda, (4) addresses the teacher's needs and goals, (5) serves as a support and resource person, (6) respects teacher autonomy, and (7) develops a long-term collegial relationship with the teacher based on mutual trust. Unlike collegial supervision, the advisor is a person with functional authority to act as an advisor rather than a peer.

Schema 6

Tracy and MacNaughton (1993) provide the last schema for organizing models of supervision to be discussed in this chapter. Their schema, in Figure 3.8, includes a number of the models previously described under the other schemata organized around the focus of supervision. Three models are developed in detail: (1) the ends-oriented model; (2) the means-oriented model; and (3) the teacher concern model. Variations of the models are presented as approaches within a given model, similar to Pajak's family of models. Each model and approach is described in terms of its focus, purpose, process for implementation, skills involved, participants in the process, assumptions, and its relationship to clinical supervision. In their conceptual scheme, clinical supervision is a process that has influenced each of the models rather than presented as a distinct model.

The focus of the ends-oriented model is the attainment of predetermined objectives. These objectives may be instructional or noninstructional, depending on the approach. The strategies used to attain these objectives are left to the teacher. Approaches found within this model include the instructional objectives approach as described by McNeil and the perfor-

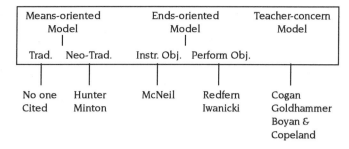

FIGURE 3.8. Tracy and MacNaughton's Schema

mance objectives approach defined by Iwanicki and Redfern. The purpose of supervision and control of the supervisory process will vary according to the individual approach.

The instructional objectives approach described by Tracy and MacNaughton is a more detailed development of the scientific model found in the ASCD yearbook (1982). While the ASCD yearbook clearly developed the theoretical basis for this variation of the ends-oriented model, Tracy and MacNaughton describe its implementation in a school setting. They note that this outcome-based approach's primary purpose is to assist teachers in helping students attain instructional objectives. An effective teacher is one who can establish appropriate instructional objectives for students and then design instruction so that students attain those objectives without undesirable side effects.

Implementation of this approach involves four key steps: (1) a preconference; (2) observation; (3) analysis and strategy; and (4) postconference. These steps parallel those of clinical supervision.

In the preconference, supervisor and teacher clarify the objectives for the lesson, the typical unit of analysis in this approach. Instructional objectives should be measurable and observable, clearly delineating the desired student outcomes. Next, the conference participants agree on what will constitute observable evidence that the objectives have been obtained and the data collection method best suited to collect that evidence. They also agree on the supervisor's role during the observation, analysis, and postconference. Finally, they discuss any aspects of the lesson unrelated to the objectives that the teacher might wish for the supervisor to observe.

In step two, the observation, the supervisor collects data as agreed upon in the preconference. McNeil (1971) prefers that the supervisor refrain from making inferences from the data during the observation. Data collected should give an objective account of exactly what occurred in the classroom. Although McNeil does not prescribe any one method of data collection, concentration on a particular aspect of the lesson suggests the use of one of the more focused observation instruments.

Step three involves analysis of the data and development of a strategy for the postconference. Lesson outcomes obtained as illustrated by the data are compared with those desired. If the outcomes were obtained, then the supervisor may analyze the teaching strategies to determine those that contributed to the desired outcomes. If not, then the super-

visor may determine what alternative strategies might have been tried.

In the last step, the postconference, supervisor and teacher collaboratively discuss the data from the lesson. They determine what teaching behaviors contributed to or detracted from objective attainment and plan for how the lesson might be taught on another occasion. New instructional objectives and related teaching strategies result from this conference.

The critical assumption of the ends-oriented model and this approach is that outcomes are more important than are the strategies to achieve them and that strategies have no value aside from their relation to an outcome. The personnel involved are typically a teacher and supervisor, although this approach could be utilized in a peer supervision mode. The primary skill is the ability to develop behavioral objectives, to collect objective data, and to conduct collaborative pre- and postconferences. Although it is rarely found in current practice, an adaptation of this approach may be the wave of the future as a response to the rising emphasis on outcome-based education.

The performance objectives approach is the second variation of the ends-oriented model presented by Tracy and MacNaughton. Their description of this approach is consistent with much of what was presented earlier as McGreal's goal-setting model or Glatthorn's self-directed development model. The focus is again on predetermined outcomes. The unit of analysis, as distinguished from the instructional objectives approach, is the broad range of responsibilities in a teacher's job description. This link with the job description gives the performance objectives approach its unique ability to relate the individual growth needs of the teacher with the needs of the organization. The purpose is for both assisting a teacher and for assessing (i.e., making administrative decisions). The time span is typically that of an entire year as opposed to an individual instructional session. Due to the evaluative nature of the approach as presented by Tracy and MacNaughton, the supervisor is almost always a superior rather than a peer.

The performance objectives approach begins operationally with the establishment of performance criteria for the teacher. These are derived from the job description of the critical areas of job performance and from an analysis of the school's needs and goals. The teacher, in collaboration with the supervisor, then sets performance objectives in a limited number of areas. Iwanicki (1984) insists that at least one of these objectives must address instructional improvement and be assisted through a cycle of clinical supervision. Performance objectives are composed of specific outcomes to be obtained, strategies for attaining these outcomes, what will serve as evidence of attainment, and a timeline for achievement.

A series of face-to-face interactions between supervisor and teacher are also part of this approach's process. Supervisor and teacher meet initially to review and revise the objectives and their related action plans. During this initial conference, it is critical that they clarify the type of support the teacher will need to accomplish the objectives. The supervisor needs to be available to assist the teacher, but the onus of responsibility for goal achievement resides with the teacher. Additional interactions should be held throughout the year to assess the teacher's progress and to adjust the objectives as necessary. At the end of the supervisory cycle, which is usually the end of the school year, the supervisor and teacher meet again to review the evidence of goal attainment, discuss the level of accomplishment, and establish new objectives for the following cycle. In both McGreal's and Tracy and MacNaughton's descriptions of this approach, this conference also serves as the final evaluation because they view this approach as useful for both teacher development and teacher evaluation. This is different from Glatthorn's presentation of a similar approach as only for assistance.

Tracy and MacNaughton caution that a weakness of this approach is the tendency in many organizations to implement it as a top-down, evaluative model with only limited regard for the needs of the individual. When a teacher's objectives are related to the principal's objectives, which are related to the superintendent's objectives, there may be unrealistic pressure placed on each lower level of the organizational hierarchy so that the top level succeeds. The long-term nature of the approach, however, which allows time for significant change coupled with its potential flexibility make it a useful addition to a supervisor's repertoire of practices.

The second model presented in Tracy and MacNaughton's schema is the means-oriented model. The focus of this model is the means or strategy used by the teacher to obtain the desired instructional outcomes. The basic premise of this model is that there is a cause and effect relationship between teaching strategy and student learning. Therefore, effective instructional practices should be the focus of supervision because their presence increases the probability that students will learn. Two approaches, which were both previously described in other schema are classified under this model: the traditional and the neotraditional.

The traditional approach is similar to that described earlier by McGreal as common-law models. This approach, which is typically used for evaluation, defines good teaching as a set of traits or characteristics. The supervisor observes to determine the presence or absence of these traits. The observed data are recorded most frequently on a checklist. One of many difficulties with this approach is the lack of weighting given to various items. As a result, appropriate dress may be of equal importance with clear delivery of lesson content. Both McGreal and Tracy and MacNaughton present this model/approach due to the fact that it is the oldest and most widely used of all the models. Neither recommend its use.

A second approach that also emphasizes the means by which teachers deliver instruction is the neotraditional. Most closely associated with the work of Madeline Hunter, this approach significantly influenced supervisory practice in the 1980s. In addition to Tracy and MacNaughton, both Glatthorn and Pajak describe this approach. For Glatthorn (1984), this approach is an example of the clinical supervision model. Pajak (1993) classifies it as a member of the technical/didactic family of models. In contrast, Tracy and MacNaughton focus on the emphasis of this approach—the delivery of instruction.

Tracy and MacNaughton note that the neotraditional, like the traditional approach, emphasizes the means of instruction or technique; however, it differs significantly in two ways. First, it stresses those teaching strategies that relate to the research on effective teaching and learning theory. Second, it focuses on instruction and does not include the broader, undifferentiated criteria typically found in the traditional approach. The underlying assumption of the neotraditional is that there is a strong correlation between certain teacher behaviors and student achievement. By focusing on those teaching behaviors, therefore, student achievement is likely to follow.

The teaching strategies of the neotraditional are externally derived from research. Even though supervisor and teacher may collaboratively analyze and discuss a lesson, what constitutes good teaching is predetermined by research, according to Hunter (1984, 1987), and to others such as Minton (1979) and Helstrom et al (1988), who subscribe to this approach. A series of critical elements of instruction is central to Hunter's approach. These elements include an anticipatory set, a lesson objective(s), input or presentation of concepts, checking for understanding, modeling, guided practice, and lesson closure. Codified by many supervisors as the necessary components of a lesson, they are perhaps the greatest source of contention surrounding this approach. Hunter was clear in cautioning that not all lessons will necessarily contain each of these elements in this sequence. Nevertheless, more than a few school district evaluation checklists contain these elements.

In addition to the elements of instruction, Hunter (1984) promoted the application of other learning principles to classroom practice. Key among these principles are those that relate to motivation, retention, transfer of learning, and reinforcement. Throughout her work, Hunter continued to add to her list of learning principles, including research on hemisphericity and other research findings to her expanding repertoire of teaching strategies. Due to the generic nature of these elements, Hunter contends that the neotraditional is an appropriate instructional approach for all subject areas and grade levels.

According to Hunter, the purpose of her supervisory approach is both to assist and to assess. There is an integral relationship between assisting and assessing teachers such that a natural outgrowth of assistance is assessment (Hunter, 1988). In practice, the neotraditional has often been viewed as an assessment tool, bypassing its intended assistance function.

Implementation of this approach is clearly defined by each of its proponents as noted by Pajak in his classification of the approach as technical/didactic. It begins with a definition of teacher competence as created by the effective teaching research and research on learning (Minton, 1979). Step two involves a diagnosis of the teacher's skills and abilities as measured against the definition of competence. This occurs through observation of the teacher in the classroom, determining areas of effective performance and areas of concern. The neotraditionalists emphasize the importance of neutral, inclusive data gathered through a technique they refer to as "scripting."

The third step is an analysis of the lesson based on the definition of effective teaching. The supervisor must consider the teacher's ability and willingness to analyze his or her own teaching and plan for the instructional conference. Carefully constructed conference questions are used to guide the teacher's analysis around the preestablished criteria. The actual format of the conference (step four) closely follows that of an effective lesson from anticipatory set through closure. While Hunter and Minton refer to the collaborative nature of the conference, critics charge that the instructional format can be manipulative. The final step, step five, is the evaluation conference that only occurs after the teacher has had sufficient time to meet the objectives of the previous instructional conferences.

Tracy and MacNaughton note that the greatest strength of the neotraditional is that it has given clarity and credibility to supervision. Many supervisors find it a way to refine the vague checklist criteria of the traditional approach into the research-based criteria that they believe will hold up under scrutiny. The supervisory process is structured and sequential, so it is readily taught. In addition, this approach deals forthrightly with the issue of assisting and assessing.

The strength of the neotraditional is also its greatest weakness. There is always the danger that its instructional components will become a rigid schedule of classroom behaviors, born out in the practices of many school districts. An additional danger is the potentially controlling position of the supervisor. Regardless of the amount of collaboration that occurs during supervision, the supervisor is ultimately placed in the position of "one who knows" in this approach.

The last model described by Tracy and MacNaughton—the teacher-concern model—focuses on the teacher's expressed need for assistance. Unlike the ends and means models, the supervisory focus is not predetermined; it is decided by the teacher rather than the supervisor or some external criteria. This model is conceptually closest to Garman's clinical model found in the ASCD yearbook (1982) and the Cogan and Goldhammer original versions of clinical supervision described by Glatthorn (1984) and Pajak (1993). It is never implemented as an evaluation/assessment model.

Tracy and MacNaughton underscore two essential elements of this model: (1) the collegial relationship between supervisor and teacher; and (2) a high degree of self-directedness on the part of the teacher. The model's primary reliance on a trusting and positive relationship between the supervisor and the teacher allows the teacher to take risks in revealing problems and concerns without fear of reprisal. Neither participant's level of openness and investment in the relationship should exceed that of the other.

Garman (1982) defines such a relationship as one where each share mutual responsibility and discover mutual potential.

Boyan and Copeland (1978), who are prime proponents of this model according to Tracy and MacNaughton, contend that recognition for needed change of teaching behavior must come from within the teacher, and not be imposed from the outside, if meaningful change is to occur. Dillon-Peterson (1986) describes this change as a self-directed process. Given the proper encouragement and support, most teachers are capable of identifying goals for change and developing strategies to attain those goals. This is also consistent with the work of Glickman (1990) and Levine (1989), who both speak of assisting teachers to increase their ability to be self-directed. They recognize that not all teachers are developmentally ready for such self-direction. Nevertheless, the goal of supervision should be to move teachers toward higher levels of self-evaluation and change.

The teacher concern model operationally closely follows the steps in the original clinical supervision process. The Boyan and Copeland version presented by Tracy and MacNaughton represents a very behavioral, technical version of this model. Pajak would undoubtedly classify it as part of his technical/didactic family of models. In this version, the supervisor and teacher begin with a clarification of the teacher's concern, behaviorally defining it in a preconference and planning for the observation. During the initial observation, the supervisor records data in order to gather a baseline determination of what is actually occurring in the classroom. These data either verify or negate the teacher's concern. Analysis of the data is led by the teacher. The role of the supervisor is to facilitate the teacher's analysis of his or her own behavior rather than to interpret for the teacher during the postconference. The key goal is teacher autonomy with the supervisor's assistance decreasing as teacher autonomy increases.

Because the teacher directs the process in the teacher-concern model, this is an appropriate model for implementing peer supervision. In considering this model for use with peers, one should also recognize that the model requires a tremendous breadth of supervisory skills. The supervisor must be able to adapt the method of data collection to meet the teacher's concern. Excellent conferencing skills are needed to ensure that communication remains nondirective.

THE SPECIAL CASE OF CLINICAL SUPERVISION

Clinical supervision is the only consistently repeated term in the six schemata just discussed. Even though it is found in the descriptions of each of the model classifications, it is treated very differently by various authors. Its treatment ranges from that of a distinct model of clinical supervision to clinical supervision as a broader concept from which numerous models are derived.

The Cogan and Goldhammer original versions of clinical supervision appear to satisfy all of the conditions required to be called a model. Even though the conditions for inclusion as a model are met, Cogan (1973) describes his version as a set of empirically developed practices rather than as a model and argues against using clinical supervision as a supervisory "cult." In reflecting on Goldhammer's original work Goldhammer et al (1980), similarly state that clinical supervision is a concept that was first articulated as a method in order to give supervisors and teachers tangible guidelines for practice. In reflecting on the origins of clinical supervision, therefore, one sees both an affinity for the practical nature of a model (window) and a concern for the potential rigidity (wall) that a model might create.

Model components found in the original versions of clinical supervision include a philosophical base, purpose, underlying principles, and steps for implementation. For example, Goldhammer et al (1993) include a philosophical framework or set of values that drives supervisory practice such as teacher initiation and analysis of practice and inquiry into practice. They describe the values embedded within clinical supervision as forming an idealized form of practice that has not yet been attained. They state, "In its present stage of development, the clinical supervision that our minds can formulate and that we seek to practice does not completely fulfill the ideal that occupies our imaginations. Day by day we know better what it is, in life and in professional life, that we are after." (Goldhammer et al, 1993, p. 42). Cogan (1973) argues that clinical supervision applies the discipline of science to transform classroom practice into artistic performance. He further draws upon social science to define the colleagial relationship that must exist between teacher and supervisor.

The second component of a model—a specified purpose—is also clearly articulated in both works. Cogan's rationale for clinical supervision is to aid the teacher to maintain and develop his or her professional competence. When the opinions of the supervisor and teacher differ, the supervisor is admonished to yield to the teacher's point of view. Such practice is clearly aimed at assisting teachers to improve rather than the summative evaluation of their performance. Goldhammer also advocates clinical supervision as a method of assistance.

Numerous assumptions underlying Cogan and Goldhammer's versions, which is the third component of a model, are defined in their works. For example, Goldhammer et al (1993, p. 52–53) give the following assumptions about clinical supervision:

1. a professional working relationship between the teacher(s) and supervisor(s)
2. mutual trust as reflected in understanding, support, and commitment for growth
3. productive tension for bridging the gap between the real and the ideal
4. supervisor knows a great deal about the analysis of instruction and learning and about productive human interaction

Cogan (1973) similarly assumes that:

1. supervision constitutes a continuation of the teacher's professional education
2. various phases of supervision are interdependent
3. supervision should break down the isolation of the classroom
4. supervision is a process of shared decision-making

Finally, the original versions of clinical supervision might be construed as a model due to the clearly defined process for implementation. Cogan presents eight steps as compared with Goldhammer's five steps; however, both include the critical elements of direct observation of classroom teaching, collection and analysis of classroom data, and face-to-face interaction between supervisor and teacher pre- and post-observation. Each author fully explicates the process.

Since these first writings about clinical supervision were published, numerous scholars and practitioners have adapted, developed, and defined clinical supervision. Some see this evolution as creating new models. Like the debate that takes place in the opening chapter of Goldhammer's second edition (1980), still others contend that clinical supervision is first and foremost a concept from which models have been derived but was never intended as a model of supervision. Let us examine each of these perspectives.

Pajak's classification of models of supervision represents the first view; clinical supervision has spawned a range of new models. As was presented in schema four, clinical supervision served as the catalyst for three new major categories of models: humanistic/artistic, technical/didactic, and developmental/reflective. Each new family of models that evolves from the original clinical supervision share at least some common assumptions and practices. They also demonstrate different philosophical underpinnings, perspectives on the processes of observation and feedback, and the nature of the supervisor–teacher relationship. Due to these differences, they are new models in their own right, distinct from their historic roots.

Three of the six schemata presented classify clinical supervision as a single and distinct model that emphasizes collegial relationships and direct assistance to the teacher in the classroom. Glatthorn creates his own version of clinical supervision by combining the works of Hunter (1984) and McNeil (1971) and maintaining the traditional steps in the process. McGreal (1983) cites clinical supervision as an assistance model adhering to the steps noted by Glatthorn. Sergiovanni and Starratt (1993) repeat a similar description. Each goes back to the earlier roots described by Cogan and Goldhammer.

On the other hand, Garman (1982, 1987) emphasizes clinical supervision as a process. In describing her ideas, Haggerson concludes that "Garman rejects the notion that clinical supervision is a model to be applied by the supervisor, but rather construes clinical supervision as a practice with concepts that can guide the practitioner's actions" (Garman et al, 1987). He continues that her view of clinical supervision is inquiry oriented because she rejects that there is any clear model of teaching to guide the supervisor's judgment. Her description of clinical supervision found in the ASCD schema suggests this same separation of process from model. It was suggested earlier that although the ASCD schema represented many of the elements of models, elements were also missing.

Tracy and MacNaughton (1993) believe that clinical supervision represents a conceptual basis for much of supervisory practice rather than serving simply as a single model. By concept, they mean that clinical supervision is a class of ideas with similar characteristics. The attitudes and methods inherent in this concept impact on and are related to all of the supervisory models in varying ways. Thus, Iwanicki's performance objectives or Hunter's neotraditional carry some of these characteristics, with each deviating in greater or lesser ways from the original concept as defined by Cogan and Goldhammer.

Glickman (Garman et al, 1987) offers a slight variation on the idea of clinical supervision as process or concept. He maintains that clinical supervision is a tool that can be used, as appropriate, to help teachers improve instruction. It is the first step available to assist the individual teacher. Its usefulness ends there for it must be augmented by other tools (i.e., strategies) to achieve broader school improvement and staff development.

Whether model, tool, process, or concept, clinical supervision is included by all of the authors mentioned here as one of the main stimuli of supervisory theory, research, and practice. Its greatest legacy, according to Anderson (1982) could be its emphasis on working directly with teachers to improve instruction. Clinical supervision has generated debate regarding the art and science of supervision and has caused researchers and practitioners to consider the need for new and integrated supervisory models and approaches. As Tracy and MacNaughton (1993, p. 323) note, "Although we may differ in our understandings of clinical supervision and in the experiential and philosophical backgrounds we bring to our debates about it, we cannot doubt how much it has contributed to our thinking about and the practice of supervision."

CRITERIA FOR MODEL SELECTION

If models are to serve as windows that illumine our research and practice of supervision, then they must expand our thinking rather than confine it to narrow patterns. Wholesale selection of any one model, regardless of its merits, is likely to be restrictive. As researchers and practitioners, we must carefully analyze the existing models in order to create new and eclectic approaches tailored to our own needs and beliefs. This analysis must encompass three major areas: (1) an analysis of values and beliefs about teaching and supervision; (2) an analysis of the needs of the individual(s); (3) an analysis of the needs of the organization.

Values and Beliefs about Teaching and Supervision

One's values and beliefs about teaching and supervision at least partially define those models or aspects of models with which one identifies. These values and beliefs, called one's "educational platform" by Sergiovanni and Starratt (1993), are the basis on which educators carry out their work and make decisions. Fenstermacher and Soltis (1986) and Tracy and MacNaughton (1993) suggest a range of views of teaching, with each based on a distinct set of values regarding the role of teacher and students, that can help guide supervisory model selection consistent with one's platform.

An *executive view* of teaching and supervising describes teachers as the managers of instruction. Recognizing the complexity of the classroom, teachers' work is seen as far more than content knowledge. Teachers must constantly react to the changing scenario of the classroom, basing their

decisions on proven effective instructional practices that increase the probability of student learning. These generic skills for managing instruction appear to be unrelated to student background, subject area, or grade level.

The value placed on research-derived criteria for teaching effectiveness places this view to the right-hand side of the art/science continuum shown in Figure 3.2. Although not diminishing the artistic element of teaching, proponents of this view believe that there is a scientific basis to the art of teaching. Tracy and MacNaughton (1993) suggest that the executive view of teaching most closely parallels the values of the traditional teacher-centered structure of teaching in the United States.

The supervisory models that most closely embody these values are those such as Hunter's, where the emphasis of supervision is on the process of teaching rather than on the product. Heavy value is placed on quantitative research to provide direction for the teacher's and supervisor's actions by clearly defining what constitutes good teaching. The supervisor believes that he or she can effectively help teachers regardless of the context or content of instruction and that certain teaching processes are essential in all instruction. The primary goal of teaching is for students to gain specific knowledge and/or skills communicated by the teacher.

A second view of teaching, the *quality management view,* is Tracy and MacNaughton's adaptation of the executive view. The primary value of this view is the creation of quality products (i.e., educated students). This view also philosophically has a scientific orientation. The focus of instruction and supervision is observable and measurable outcome behaviors as described by McNeil (1971, 1982) or in the broader context defined by Redfern (1980) and Iwanicki (1981). Instructional processes are simply the mechanisms that lead to outcomes. If one or more teaching process creates the desired outcomes, then they are encouraged but never mandated. It is assumed that there are multiple ways to achieve the same results.

Supervisors ascribing to this view hold values like:

1. all students should gain specific knowledge and skills
2. the most important student learning outcomes usually can be measured or observed
3. supervision is of most assistance to teachers when it focuses on what the teacher wants the students to achieve

Like the executive management view, teaching is still viewed as more science than art. The critical distinction is what is quantified (i.e., process or product) and the scope of the outcomes that should be considered (see Figure 3.2).

The third view of teaching and supervising is labeled the *therapist view* by Fenstermacher and Soltis (1986). This view values the individuality and self-direction of the teacher. Teachers are individuals who are concerned with helping students grow personally and reaching their highest potential. Supervision must similarly help teachers reaching their highest potential without restricting their freedom to develop. Growing out of a humanistic psychology, the primary purpose of teaching and supervision is to develop self-directed, self-actualized persons. There is no scientifically based template to describe such a person or to determine when one has achieved such status.

A key value inherent in this view is teacher's control of his or her own growth. Blumberg and Jonas (1987) acknowledge that unless teachers psychologically accept a supervisor, supervision is little more than a ritual. Even though supervisors may have legitimate access to teachers, teachers control the interpersonal access necessary for instructional improvement through supervision. Glickman similarly calls for a shift from supervisor as possessor of knowledge to supervisors and teachers as coexplorers in discovering best practice (1988). The professional power of the supervisor to assist the teacher is exercised through the professional power of the teacher (Dunlap & Goldman, 1991).

Among those models that mirror at least some of the values of the therapist view of teaching are Garman's clinical supervision, Glatthorn's cooperative and self-directed models, Pajak's developmental/reflective, and Tracy and MacNaughton's teacher concern. The supervisor and teacher in this view typically believe that (1) the assisting and assessing functions should be separated, (2) teachers' success should be measured by their individual growth rather than some uniform standard, (3) teachers grow professionally only when they have a strong personal investment in the process, (4) teachers ultimately identify those areas that are most important for student learning, and (5) the long-term potential of a teacher is more important than is the short-term performance.

These three simplified views of teaching are insufficient for describing the range of values held by both teachers and supervisors. They are used here simply to illustrate the importance of selecting practices that match one's belief system. They do not address the need to develop one's platform or to negotiate when the teacher's and supervisor's values differ. Nevertheless, the supervisor's and teacher's ability to effectively engage in supervision rests on practice congruent with personal values.

The Needs of the Individual(s)

The second area of analysis required to select an appropriate model of supervision is the needs of the individual teacher. Numerous authors note that professional development contains two components: individual and staff development (Dillon-Peterson, 1981; Fullan & Hargreaves, 1992; Levine, 1989; Sparks & Loucks-Horsley, 1990). Multiple factors influence the individual needs of the teacher. Some of the most frequently noted factors in the literature are those that relate to personal adult development issues, level of conceptual development, and career stage development.

Levine (1989) details a number of personal developmental issues that affect teacher professional growth. Referring to both phase and stage theories of adult development, she notes that all adults pass through various life crises and periods of varying focus on career issues. Family issues and personal reassessments may take precedence over professional growth issues at certain life periods. Additional personal variables such as gender also are a factor. For example, a woman may be more ready to focus on professional growth and

career advancement as her children reach young adulthood while for many males, the early to mid-thirties are the prime time for career development. These personal issues may be reflected in the level of control teachers desire in supervision, the amount of time they are willing to give to professional development, and their ability to psychologically invest in the process.

Glickman (1990) also advocates attention to teachers' developmental needs. For Glickman, a prime indicator of teachers' readiness to assume control of their own professional development is their conceptual level or ability to think abstractly. He suggests three variations of teacher–supervisor interaction based on this ability moving from teacher-directed to collaborative to directive supervision. In his mind, appropriate supervisory practice allows teachers the maximum control they are capable of assuming, with the goal to continually move teachers toward more self-direction. Research by Calhoun (1985) illustrates the need to consider both teachers' abilities to think abstractly about their own practice as well as the supervisors' level of abstraction as well.

Individual needs can also be characterized by factors related to career progression. Fessler and Christiansen (1992) detailed the characteristics common to teachers in each of eight career stages. These career stages often overlap the adult development stages or phases discussed earlier by Levine. Each has its distinct concerns, needs, and interests. For example, at the induction stage, teachers are concerned about survival (Fuller, 1969). Thus, there is an enhanced willingness to seek guidance from a supervisor and to benefit from externally defined effective practice.

In spite of the lengthy list of ways to analyze the individual needs of teachers, supervisors are cautioned at least to informally assess these needs when designing supervisory practices. Unless supervision touches the individual in a very personal way, it is unlikely to be more than a ritual that fulfills some organizational requirement but does little to actually improve instruction.

The Needs of the Organization

Because teachers and supervisors are part of educational organizations, their work must also fit into and benefit the organization as a whole. The traditional perspective of professional development has tended to emphasize organizational goals to the detriment of individual growth. We must be careful, however, that a concern for individual development does not create the reverse problem: the disregard of the needs of the organization. Glickman (1990) is a leading advocate for a blend of individual and organizational concern. He contends that supervision is the glue that holds together the discrete elements of instructional effectiveness in the school. The school can only reach its goals when teachers work together to reach common goals for students and when supervisors work with teachers in a manner consistent with the ways teachers are expected to work with students. Analyzing the needs of the organization in order to determine supervisory practice involves several elements. One must consider the historical and cultural context of the school, the structural implications, and the policy issues, among others, in identifying the organization's needs.

The cultural context of the school subtly determines what practices will succeed and what will fail. Consider a school culture that discourages collaboration and encourages individual competition or a culture that historically has been based on adversarial relationships between teachers and administrators. How successful would efforts to promote peer supervision be in this setting? Understanding the cultural context of the school requires keenly observing what events mean to those involved, not just what routinely occurs. How do persons interact with each other? What are the rituals and symbols inherent in the organization? How do teachers and supervisors define their roles in relation to others in the organization? What is the cultural perception of change? This symbolic frame for analyzing the organization gives one insights into why certain practices stimulate the organization to change and improve, while others seem to merely maintain the status quo (Bolman & Deal, 1991).

Structural aspects of the organization also greatly impact practice. They both create potential resource allocations and define power relationships within the organization. Structure can be conceptualized as the formal lines of authority within the organization or as the way the school organizes itself for instruction. If a school district's structure contains subject area supervisors for assisting teachers while building principals carry out formal evaluations, certain supervisory practices are more likely to be implemented (Tracy, 1993). A small district with "head teachers" in several elementary buildings does not overlap the principal's role when incorporating peer supervision. Each of these examples influence the lines of authority, thereby making certain supervisory relationships more or less acceptable.

Structure related to the organization for instruction include self-contained classrooms, team teaching, block scheduling, and so on. These structural configurations bring their own requirements to the supervisory process, influencing what is viewed as good teaching and supervision.

Policy considerations are yet another organizational frame that affects supervisory practice. These policies may reflect local, state, or even federal agendas. Local school boards are increasingly concerned with professional accountability. As a result, they may argue for strong policies that monitor teacher performance. In some instances, such policy pressures have resulted in negotiated agreements that spell out in detail what supervisors may and may not do, limiting the ability of teachers and supervisors to tailor supervision to individual and organizational needs.

Many states have also issued mandates relating to assisting and assessing teachers that directly influence the direction all supervisory practice takes (Tracy & Smeaton, 1993). When state policy requires supervision to focus on outcomes, such as in the state of Connecticut, district practices for assisting as well as assessing are likely to be influenced. Other state policies can have a similar effect on supervision. Districts in Pennsylvania are currently confronting major changes in their approaches to instruction based on a change in state curriculum policy. The new emphasis on outcomes-based education is likely to ultimately alter how districts supervise as well as deliver instruction.

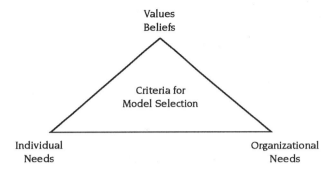

FIGURE 3.9. Criteria for Model Selection

Figure 3.9 portrays the significance of values and beliefs, individual needs, and organizational needs in selecting appropriate supervisory practice for a given setting. Because few of the models presented in this chapter were ever intended to exclusively meet all of the needs of teachers and school districts, this author argues for an eclectic approach to supervision. Such an approach draws elements from a variety of models, tailoring them to the values and needs of a specific school. Speaking practically, most schools implement bits and pieces of various models. What is missing is usually a conscious consideration of what elements best apply. Supervisory practice often evolves more from precedent and convenience than from careful analysis of needs. The authors of the Rand study on teacher evaluation (Wise et al, 1984) identified the criteria for effective evaluation practice. Although this chapter focuses more on assistance than on assessment, these same criteria seem applicable to assistance and summarize what practitioners should consider in selecting from the range of models. These criteria are:

1. the supervisory system must meet the educational goals, management style, concept of teaching, and community values of the school district
2. commitment to and resources for the system are needed
3. the school district must decide the primary purpose(s) of supervision and then match the process(es) to the purpose(s)
4. to sustain resource commitments and political credibility, the supervisory process must be seen as having utility
5. teacher involvement and responsibility improve the quality of supervision

THE NEXT GENERATION OF SUPERVISORY RESEARCH AND PRACTICE

Challenges to the Current Models

Researchers and practitioners cannot rely on the existing models of supervision presented in this chapter to address the needs of both individuals and schools in the future. These models do not take into account many of the changes currently occurring in the roles and responsibilities of teachers and supervisors, nor do they address the potential alterations in the organization of schools or the impact technology is having and will inevitably continue to have on education. It is time to begin to create the next generation of models of supervision.

The majority of the models described in this chapter are based on the assumptions that:

1. the teacher is the primary deliverer of instruction
2. teaching is an observable act
3. the teaching act occurs at a preset time and place such that the supervisor can be in attendance
4. the teacher's teaching behaviors and interactions with learners are significant events to observe in the learning environment
5. supervisor–teacher interaction is an effective way of identifying needed instructional improvement
6. supervisor–teacher interaction should occur face-to-face (Tracy, 1993b)

As the educational system on which current supervisory models are based changes, however, supervision as practiced and researched today risks obsolete. Supervision as a field of study and practice must be informed by and evolve in concert with the changing face of schooling.

Our expanding concept of the school is one of the first challenges to current models of supervision. The schoolhouse is no longer considered the only place or even the primary place where learning can and should occur. Students increasingly engage in community service, access vast amounts of information at home via computer networks, and interact with a variety of resources outside of the school in pursuit of learning. The walls of the schoolhouse do not represent the boundaries for learning.

A second challenge to the assumptions stated earlier is movement away from an emphasis on direct instruction. The individual teacher instructing a class of students who each work independently is no longer the norm in many schools. An observer in these schools will find students working cooperatively and/or teachers functioning in teams. This increased collaboration between both students and teachers is supported by a growing research base on effective teaching and learning.

Technology-rich learning environments, schools that extend into the community, and increased emphasis on collaboration all lead to radically changed roles for teachers and supervisors. Teachers become the resource providers, managers, and facilitators of students' learning more than the deliverers of instruction in these new learning environments.

Accessibility to the vast array of community resources and to technological information bases alters the teachers' role to one of resource provider, linking students with the resources necessary to attain their learning goals and helping students choose from among the variety of resources available.

Organizing the learning environment and overseeing systems for its efficient operation call for teachers to manage instruction. Although teachers have always held this managerial responsibility, it becomes more central in a high-technology environment where management may include scheduling equipment use and monitoring equipment maintenance.

The management role of the teacher frees students to learn.

Finally, the facilitator role of teachers in this new environment for learning implies a role analogous to that of supervisors today. Teachers are responsible for observing students, analyzing data on student performance, and giving feedback much as the supervisor now facilitates teachers' learning. In this role, teachers move from center stage to backstage, from director of instruction to catalyst and facilitator.

The Next Model of Supervision

It would be presumptuous to define the future model(s) of supervision. Based on the challenges to the current models, however, we can gain insights into what is missing in them and speculate about some of the elements likely to be contained in the next generation of models. In order to do so, let us return to the bases of models that were presented early in this chapter and consider what the purposes, theoretical assumptions and underlying concepts, social systems, support systems, and implementation/syntax might look like in models of the future.

The purpose or focus of supervisory models in the future is likely to shift from an emphasis on teaching to an emphasis on learning. Prior models have often assumed that the improvement of instruction naturally leads to improved student learning. Much of the current criticism of supervision and external calls for teacher accountability arise from our inability to demonstrate convincingly that supervision does, indeed, improve learning. Furthermore, these models have tended to separate teacher learning from student learning. In the learning communities of the future, all members will be expected to continually grow, regardless of the role they play. As Senge (1990) described, effective organizations will make continual learning an integral part of their cultures. As a result, supervision is likely to move away from a preoccupation with assessment to a facilitation of growth function more akin to the reflective and developmental perspectives described earlier.

The theoretical assumptions and principles underlying the model(s) will draw from a variety of fields of study. The emphasis on the differences among individuals in the organization will surely extend Glickman's and others' call for supervision grounded in developmental psychology. This research guides us to identify the stimuli that most will impact adults at varying life stages and that will promote continued growth.

As we view the entire school as a learning organization, our historical emphasis on pedagogy will not be sufficient. Supervision also must be grounded in androgogy—the theory and research on how adults learn (Cross, 1981; Kidd, 1973; Knowles, 1980; Knox, 1977). This research base acknowledges the need and ability of adults to function as life-long learners. It also suggests that most adults are capable of self-direction, of assuming responsibility for their own learning (Guglielmino et al, 1987; Tracy & Schuttenberg, 1990).

Theory and research on organizational change will also increasingly influence the field of supervision. Bolman and Deal (1991) note that although organizations are surprising, deceptive, and ambiguous entities, attempting to orchestrate organizational change reveals possibilities for creativity and effective action. Fullan (1991) points out that improving schools is far more extensive than improving the instructional performance of teachers. It is an organization/systemwide issue that must involve all those who surround teachers including those at the district, state, and federal levels. Thus, supervision cannot ignore the broader context in which teachers work if it is to have an impact on learning.

Finally, a growing body of research from the field of social psychology supports the idea that adults grow and learn best in an environment that encourages, even demands, collaboration and cooperation (Barth, 1990; Fullan, 1990; Johnson & Johnson, 1987). Conducting a meta-analysis on 133 studies of adults, Johnson and Johnson conclude that cooperation among adults "promotes achievement, positive interpersonal relationships, social support, and self-esteem" (Johnson & Johnson, p. 30). Collegial interaction should result in greater productivity and expertise and greater staff cohesion. Although peer supervision strategies are in vogue today, they often co-exist with hierarchical, one-on-one models for assisting and assessing. Effective supervision in the future must focus on group collaboration and performance while providing sufficiently detailed feedback to be useful for individual improvement within the group.

In summary, the assumptions on which this next generation of supervisory model(s) are based include:

1. the school is a community of life-long learners
2. persons are capable of taking responsibility for their own growth, of being self-directed and self-supervising, when the proper resources and support mechanisms are available
3. adult learners have their own unique needs that are distinct from those of children
4. to improve the performance of any one individual, we must consider the total organizational environment in which that person works
5. people learn best and are motivated by collaborating with others

Although no one of these assumptions by itself seems to be a radical departure from the models presented here, taken as a whole they represent a vision of supervision rarely captured in current practice.

The social system for new models of supervision will incorporate teams of professionals rather than the traditional supervisor–teacher dyad. Members of a team will have different expertise, yet they will function as equals. Roles will be defined by what one can contribute to group supervisory process rather than by formal organizational position. A collaborative relationship between team members will foster open and honest dialogue and feedback with the group assuming responsibility for the performance of its members. In such a social system, critical interpersonal interactions will involve reflective listening, giving objective, information-based feedback, and supporting and facilitating each others' work.

The support system for supervision must also change in order to establish the appropriate conditions for effective implementation of this new supervisory model. The support system includes both the people and the resources necessary. A single supervisor, which is common in the traditional models, will not have sufficient knowledge or skills to support this new paradigm. A range of people will, therefore, be needed, with each bringing his or her unique skills to the situation. The majority of these persons will probably be peers rather than individuals designated with some formal supervisory title.

Perhaps the most critical skill for those involved in improving learning will be the skill of reflection on practice. As Bolin (1987) notes, to sustain a vision, one must set aside time to reflect upon experience. Without reflection, there will be no renewal (i.e., continued growth). The significance of this skill is already well-established in the supervision literature and is advocated for several existing supervisory models (Costa & Garmston, 1994; Garman, 1986; Schon, 1983 & 1988; Smyth, 1989). It is at the heart of supervisory self-direction and assumption of responsibility for one's personal growth. Continued research is needed in how to assist people to develop reflective skills.

The implementation or syntax for the next generation of supervisory models is difficult to predict for those of us immersed in the old. Barker (1988) points out that strong adherence to a current model can result in paradigm paralysis in anticipating the new. A potential new supervisory model may be virtually invisible to those of us holding strongly to an existing model(s). In addition, those of us engaged in the research and practice of supervision today may unconsciously resist new models because we are no longer the experts when a new model is introduced. New models threaten the relevance of our scholarship and practice. Nevertheless, Sergiovanni (1991) calls us to see what we already know with new eyes. Glickman (1991) refers to capturing this vision of the possible as the opening up of suppressed knowledge. Barker (1988) suggests that the syntax of a new model should address the question, "What do we believe is now impossible to do in our field, but if it could be done would fundamentally change supervision (for the better)?"

Capturing the essence of the future supervisory model from the discussion of its purpose, theoretical assumptions, social system, and support system, it might be designated the "teacher-as-supervisor" or "self-supervision" model. Observers viewing this new model might see supervision that is personalized and diffused with teachers collaboratively assuming responsibility for analyzing and improving their own and students' performance. There will be little reliance on the expertise of a "supervisor." Teams of teachers will assist each other, collect data on student and teacher learning, and assess overall team performance. Techniques such as portfolio analysis and action research will be integral elements of this self-supervision. Technology will undoubtedly be used both to enhance teacher and student learning and to manage the learning process. Those previously designated as administrators or supervisors will be the resource providers and facilitators for supervision rather than the initiators of the process. While this may seem like an idealistic view of supervision with little basis in the current reality of teaching, we must remember that our skepticism grows out of our firm roots in the present models. In fact, this new model is already emerging. In order for it to become a reality, the field of supervision needs scholars to develop its research base and practitioners willing to risk radically new supervisory approaches. The outcome will be a new window through which we may view our field.

REFERENCES

Acheson, K. A. & Gall, M. D. (1980). *Techniques in the clinical supervision of teachers.* White Plains, NY: Longman.

Acheson, K. A. & Gall, M. D. (1987). *Techniques in the clinical supervision of teachers.* White Plains, NY: Longman.

Acheson, K. A. & Gall, M. D. (1990). *Techniques in the clinical supervision of teachers.* White Plains, NY: Longman.

Alfonso, R. J. & Firth, G. R. (1990). Supervision: Needed research. *Journal of Curriculum and Supervision,* 5, 181–188.

Alfonso, R. J., Firth, G. R., & Neville, R. F. (1975). *Instructional supervision: A behavior system.* Boston: Allyn and Bacon.

Anderson, R. H. (1982). Creating a future for supervision. In T. J. Sergiovanni (Ed.). *Supervision of teaching.* Alexandria, VA: ASCD.

Apelman, M. (1986). Working with teachers: The advisory approach. In K. K. Zumwalt (Ed.). *Improving teaching* (pp. 115–130), Alexandria, VA: ASCD.

Barber, L. W. (1990). Self-assessment. In J. Millman and L. Darling-Hammond (Eds.). *The new handbook of teacher evaluation* (pp. 216–228). Beverly Hills, CA: Sage.

Barker, J. A. (1988). *Discovering the future: The business of paradigms* (2nd ed.). St. Paul, MN: ILI Press.

Barth, R. (1990). *Improving schools from within: Teachers, parents and principals can make a difference.* San Francisco, CA: Jossey-Bass.

Bents, R. H. & Howey, K. R. (1981). Staff development—change in the individual. In Dillon-Peterson (Ed.). *Staff development/organization development* (pp. 11-36). Alexandria: ASCD.

Birnbaum, R. (1988). *How colleges work.* San Francisco, CA: Jossey-Bass.

Blumberg, A. (1974). *Supervisors and teachers: A private cold war.* Berkeley, CA: McCuthcheon.

Blumberg, A. (1980). *Supervisors and teachers: A private cold war.* (2nd ed.). Berkeley, CA: McCutcheon.

Blumberg, A. & Jonas, R. S. (1987). Permitting access: The teacher's control over supervision. *Educational Leadership,* 44, 58–62.

Bolin, F. S. (1987). Teaching as a self-renewing profession. In Bolin, F. S. & McConnell Falk, J. (Eds.), *Teacher renewal* (pp. 217–230). New York: Teachers College Press.

Bolman, L. G. & Deal, T. (1991). *Reframing organizations.* San Francisco, CA: Jossey-Bass.

Bowers, C. A. & Flinders, D. J. (1991). *Culturally responsive teaching and supervision.* New York: Teachers College Press.

Boyan, N. J. & Copeland, W. D. (1978). *Instructional supervision training program.* Columbus, OH: Charles E. Merrill.

Calhoun, E. F. (1985). *Relationship of teachers' conceptual level to the utilization of supervisory services and to a description of classroom instructional improvement.*

Paper presented to the annual meeting of the American Educational Research Association, Washington D.C., April 1985.

Carroll, J. G. (1981). Faculty self-evaluation. In J. Millman (Ed.). *Handbook of teacher evaluation* (pp. 180–200), Beverly Hills, CA: Sage.

Cogan, M. L. (1973). *Clinical supervision.* Boston, MA: Houghton Mifflin.

Corey, S. M. (1953). *Action research to improve school practices.* New York: Teachers College Press, Columbia University.

Costa, A. L. & Garmston, R. J. (1985). Supervision for intelligent teaching. *Educational Leadership,* 42, 70–80.

Costa, A. & Garmston, R. (1994). *Cognitive coaching: A foundation for renaissance schools,* Norwood, MA: Cristopher-Gordon.

Cross, K. P. (1981). *Adults as learners.* San Francisco, CA: Jossey-Bass.

Dillon-Peterson, B. (Ed.). (1981). *Staff development/organization development.* Alexandria, VA: ASCD.

Dillon-Peterson, B. (1986). Trusting teachers to know what's good for them. In K. K. Zumwalt (Ed.). *Improving teaching: 1986 ASCD yearbook* (pp. 29–35). Alexandria: ASCD.

Dunlap, D. M. & Goldman, P. (1991). Rethinking power in schools. *Educational Administration Quarterly,* 27, 5–29.

Eisner, E. W. (1982). An artistic approach to supervision. In T. J. Sergionvanni (Ed.). *Supervision of teaching* (pp. 53–66). Alexandria, VA: ASCD.

Eisner, E. W. (1983). The art and craft of teaching. *Educational Leadership,* 40, 5–13.

Eisner, E. W. (1985). *The educational imagination: On the design and evaluation of school programs* (2nd ed.). New York: MacMillan.

Fenstermacher, G. D. & Soltis, J. F. (1986). *Approaches to teaching.* New York: Teachers College Press.

Fessler, R. & Christiansen, J. C. (Eds.). (1992). *The teacher career cycle.* Boston, MA: Allyn and Bacon.

Fullan, M. (1991). *The new meaning of educational change* (2nd ed.). New York: Teachers College Press.

Fullan, M. & Hargreaves, A. (Eds.). (1992). *Teacher development and educational change.* London: Falmer Press.

Fuller, F. (1969). Concerns of teachers: A developmental conceptualization. *American Educational Research Journal,* 6, 207–226.

Garman, N. B. (1982). The clinical approach to supervision. In T. J. Sergiovanni (Ed.). *Supervision of teaching* (pp. 35–52). Alexandria, VA: ASCD.

Garman, N. B. (1986). Reflection, the heart of clinical supervision: A modern rationale for practice. *Journal of Curriculum and Supervision, 2,* 1–24.

Garman, N. B. (1990). Theories embedded in the events of clinical supervision: A hermeneutic approach. *Journal of Curriculum and Supervision, 5,* 201–213.

Garman, N. B., Glickman, C. D., Hunter, M., & Haggerson, N. L. (1987). Conflicting conceptions of clinical supervision and the enhancement of professional growth and renewal: Point and counterpoint. *Journal of Curriculum and Supervision, 2,* 152–177.

Glatthorn, A. A. (1984). *Differentiated supervision.* Alexandria, VA: ASCD.

Glickman, C. D. (1980). The developmental approach to supervision. *Educational Leadership, 38,* 178–180.

Glickman, C. D. (1981). *Developmental supervision.* Alexandria, VA: ASCD.

Glickman, C. D. (1988). Supervision and the rhetoric of empowerment: Silence or collision? *Action in Teacher Education, 10,* 11–15.

Glickman, C. D. (1990). *Supervision of instruction: A developmental approach.* (2nd ed.). Boston, MA: Allyn and Bacon.

Glickman, C. D. (1991). Pretending not to know what we know. *Educational Leadership, 48,* 4–10.

Glickman, C. D. & Gordon, S. P. (1987). Clarifying developmental supervision. *Educational Leadership, 44,* 64–68.

Goldhammer, R. (1969). *Clinical supervision.* New York: Holt, Rinehart, Winston.

Goldhammer, R., Anderson, R., & Krajewski, R. (1993). *Clinical supervision* (3rd ed.). New York: Holt, Rinehart, Winston.

Guglielmino, P., Guglielmino, L., & Long, H. (1987). Self-directed learning readiness and performance in the workplace. *Higher Education, 16,* 303–317.

Hazi, H. M. (1994). The teacher evaluation-supervision dilemma: A case of entanglements and irreconcilable differences. *Journal of Curriculum and Supervision, 9,* 1995–216.

Helstrom, C., Mass, S., Kirby, E., Krubiner, M., Helstrom, M., & Clarke, C. (1988). *Design for effective instruction.* Austrelitz, TX: Professional Growth Programs.

Hook, C. M. & Rosenshine, B. (1979). Accuracy of teacher reports of their teaching behavior. *Review of Educational Research, 49,* 1–12.

Hoy, W. K. & Forsyth, P. B. (1986). *Effective supervision: Theory into practice.* New York: Random House.

Hunter, M. (1979). Teaching is decision-making. *Educational Leadership, 37,* 62–67.

Hunter, M. (1980). Six types of supervisory conferences. *Educational Leadership, 37,* 408–412.

Hunter, M. (1983). Script taping: An essential supervisory tool. *Educational Leadership, 41,* 43.

Hunter, M. (1984). Knowing, teaching and supervising. In P. Hosford (Ed.). *Using what we know about teaching* (pp. 169–192). Alexandria, VA: ASCD.

Hunter, M. (1986). Let's eliminate the pre-observation conference. *Educational Leadership, 43*(6), 69–70.

Hunter, M. (1987). *Teach more faster.* El Segundo: TIP Publications.

Hunter, M. (1988). Effecting a reconciliation between supervision and evaluation—A reply to Popham. *Journal of Personnel Evaluation in Education, 1,* 275–279.

Ingvarson, L. (1987). *Models of in-service education and their implications for professional development policy.* Paper presented at a conference on "In-service Education: Trends of the past, themes for the future," Melbourne, Australia.

Iwanicki, E. F. (1981). A professional growth-oriented approach to evaluating teacher performance. In J. Millman (Ed), *Handbook of teacher evaluation* (pp. 203–228). Beverly Hills, CA: Sage Publications.

Johnson, D. W. & Johnson, R. T. (1987). Research shows the benefits of adult cooperation. *Educational Leadership, 44,* 27–30.

Joyce, B. & Showers, B. (1980). Improving in-service training: The messages of research. *Educational Leadership, 37*(5), 379–385.

Joyce, B. & Showers, B. (1982). The coaching of teaching. *Educational Leadership, 41,* 4–10.

Joyce, B. & Showers, B. (1988). *Student achievement through staff development.* New York: Longman.

Joyce, B. & Weil, M. (1980). *Models of teaching* (2nd ed.). Englewood Cliffs, NJ: Prentice Hall.

Kidd, J. R. (1973). *How adults learn.* New York: Association Press.

Knezevich, S. J. (1975). *Administration of public education* (3rd ed.). New York: Harper and Row.

Knowles, M. (1980). *The modern practice of adult education* Chicago, IL: Association Press/Follett.

Knox, A. B. (1977). *Adult development and learning.* San Francisco, CA: Jossey-Bass.

Levine, S. (1989). *Promoting adult growth in schools.* Boston, MA: Allyn and Bacon.

McGill, M. V. (1991). The changing face of supervision: A developmental art. *Journal of Curriculum and Supervision, 6,* 255–264.

McGreal, T. L. (1983). *Successful teacher evaluation.* Alexandria, VA: ASCD.

McNeil, J. D. (1971). *Toward accountable teachers.* New York: Holt, Rinehart, Winston.

McNeil, J. D. (1982). A scientific approach to supervision. In T. J. Sergiovanni (Ed.). *Supervision of teaching* (pp. 18–34). Alexandria, VA: ASCD.

Maccia, E. S., Maccia, G. S., & Jewett, R. E. (1963). *Construction of educational theory models* (Cooperative Research Project No. 1632). Columbus, OH: The Ohio State University Research Foundation.

Minton, E. (1979). *Clinical supervision: Developing evaluation skills for dynamic leadership.* Cassette recording. Englewood, CO: Educational Consulting Associates.

Mosher, R. L. & Purpel, D. E. (1972). *Supervision: The reluctant profession.* Boston, MA: Houghton-Mifflin.

Nelson, J., Schwartz, M., & Schmuck, R. (1974). *Collegial supervision: A sub-study of organization development in multi-unit schools.* Bethesda, MD.: ERIC Document Reproduction Service, ED 166 841.

Nuthall, G. & Snook, I. (1973). Contemporary models of teaching. In R. M. W. Travers (Ed.). *Second handbook of* research on teaching (pp. 47–76). Chicago, IL: Rand McNally & Co.

Oliva, P. F. (1993). *Supervision for todays schools* (4th ed.). New York: Longman.

Pajak, E. (1993). *Approaches to clinical supervision.* Norwood, MA: Christopher-Gordon Publishers.

Phenix, P. H. (1986). *Realms of meaning.* Ventura, CA: Ventura County Superintendent of Schools Office.

Polanyi, M. (1962). *Personal knowledge.* Chicago, IL: University of Chicago Press.

Popham, W. J. (1973). *Evaluating instruction.* Englewood Cliffs, NJ: Prentice Hall.

Popham, W. J. (1988). The dysfunctional marriage of formative and summative teacher evaluation. *Journal of Personnel Evaluation in Education, 1,* 269–273.

Redfern, G. B. (1972). *How to evaluate teaching.* Worthington, OH: School Management Institute.

Redfern, G. B. (1980). *Evaluating teachers and administrators: A performance objectives approach.* Boudler, CO: Westview Press.

Roberts, R. J. (1992a). Face-threatening acts and politeness theory: Contrasting speeches from supervisory conferences. *Journal of Curriculum and Supervision, 7,* 287–301.

Roberts, G. B. (1992b). *The relationship of power and involvement to experience in supervisory conferences: Discourse analysis of supervisor style.* Paper presented at the annual meeting of the American Educational Research Association, San Francisco, CA.

Rosenshine, B. (1986). Synthesis of research on explicit teaching. *Educational Leadership, 43,* 60–69.

Sagor, R. (1992). *How to conduct collaborative action research.* Alexandria, VA: ASCD.

Schon, D. A. (1983). *The reflective practitioner: How professionals think in action.* New York: Basic Books.

Schon, D. A. (1988). Coaching reflective teaching. In Peter P. Grimmett & Gaalen L. Erickson (Eds.). *Reflection in teacher education.* New York: Teachers College Press.

Schumacher, E. F. (1977). *A guide for the perplexed.* New York: Harper and Row.

Senge, P. M. (1990). *The fifth discipline: The art and practice of the learning organization.* New York: Doubleday Currency.

Sergiovanni, T. J. (1982). Toward a theory of supervisory practice: Integrating scientific, clinical, and artistic views. In T. J. Sergiovanni (Ed.). *Supervision of teaching* (pp. 35–52). Alexandria, VA: ASCD

Sergiovanni, T. J. (1984). *Landscapes, mindscapes, and reflective practice in supervision.* Paper presented at the annual conference of the American Educational Research Association, New Orleans, April, 1984.

Sergiovanni, T. J. (1991). The dark side of professionalism in educational administration. *Kappan, 72,* 525.

Sergiovanni, T. J. & Starratt, R. J. (1993). *Supervision: A redefinition* (5th ed.). New York: McGraw-Hill.

Shulman, L. S. (1986). Paradigms and research programs in the study of teaching: A contemporary perspective. In M. C. Whittrock (Ed.). *Handbook of research on teaching* (pp. 3–36). New York: MacMillan.

Smyth, W. J. (1982). A teacher development approach to bridging the practice-research gap. *Journal of Curriculum Studies, 14,* 331–342.

Smyth, W. J. (1984). Teachers as collaborative learners in clinical supervision: A state-of-the-art review. *Journal of Educational for Teaching, 10,* 24–36.

Smyth, W. J. (1985). Developing a critical practice of clinical supervision. *Journal of Curriculum Studies, 17,* 1–15.

Smyth, W. J. (1989). Developing and sustaining critical reflection in teacher education. *Journal of Teacher Education, 40,* 2–9.

Smyth, W. J. (1991). *Teachers as collaborative learners.* Philadelphia, PA: Open University Press.

Sparks, D. & Loucks-Horsley, S. (1990). *Five models of staff development.* Oxford, OH: National Staff Development Council.

Tanner, D. & Tanner, L. (1987). *Supervision in education.* New York: MacMillan.

Tracy, S. J. (1993a). The overlooked position of subject area supervisor. *Clearing House, 67,* 25–30.

Tracy, S. J. (1993b). Restructuring instructional supervision. *Contemporary Education, 64,* 128–131.

Tracy, S. J. & MacNaughton, R. (1989). Clinical supervision and the emerging conflict between the neo-traditionalists and the neo-progressives. *Journal of Curriculum and Supervision, 4,* 246–256.

Tracy, S. J. & MacNaughton, R. (1993). *Assisting and assessing educational personnel: The impact of clinical supervision.* Boston, MA: Allyn & Bacon.

Tracy, S. J. & Schuttenberg, E. M. (1990). Promoting self-directed learning for teacher and school improvement. *Journal of Staff Development, 11,* 52–57.

Tracy, S. J. & Smeaton, P. (1993). State mandated assisting and assessing of teachers: Levels of state control. *Journal of Personnel Evaluation in Education, 6,* 219–234.

Van Manen, M. (1977). Linking ways of knowing with ways of being practical. *Curriculum Inquiry, 6,* 207–228.

Waite, D. (1993). Teachers in conference: A qualitative study of teacher-supervisor face-to-face interactions. *American Educational Research Journal, 30,* 675–702.

Wise, A. E., Darling-Hammond, L., McLaughlin, M. W., & Berstein, H. T. (1984). *Teacher evaluation: A study of effective practices.* Santa Monica, CA: The Rand Corporation.

Zeichner, K. M. & Liston, D. P. (1987). Teaching student teachers to reflect. *Harvard Educational Review, 57,* 23–48.

⋄ 4 ⋄

METHODS OF INQUIRY IN SUPERVISION

Frances Schoonmaker, Richard Sawyer, and Margaret Borrego Brainard[1]

TEACHERS COLLEGE, COLUMBIA UNIVERSITY

Questions about the nature of supervision and how it should be studied have been raised since the early part of the century when it emerged as a profession. As new methodologies have been introduced and debated within the educational research community, scholarship in supervision has become broadly conceived and vigorous. Indeed, the shifting nature of inquiry has made drawing the boundaries of this chapter somewhat problematic.

To understand methods of inquiry within our field it is necessary to examine the antecedents of current inquiry. In doing so, however, we risk overlap with the Glanz and Harris chapters, "Histories, Antecedents, and Legacies" and "Paradigms and Parameters." We are mindful, as well, that issues of practice, particularly those related to models, processes, and techniques, are discussed in Section III because much of the inquiry we explore is related to supervisory practice. While we may draw on similar material, we do so from a different set of questions, focusing on the inquiry itself and leaving detailed study of history and practice to the designated authors.

The chapter begins with an exploration of the topical and substantive content of inquiry, taking a look at what seem to be persistent issues or questions across time. We then focus on the questions themselves, asking why they have been posed and studied in particular ways, linking the why question to contextual influences on supervision as a field of practice and images of the teacher. The clinical supervision model is explored in more depth to illustrate the complexities of inquiry. Finally, we conclude with a consideration of questions that have not been asked in the literature and thoughts about future directions for those who are interested in inquiry in instructional supervision.

SUPERVISORY QUESTIONS

The substantive issues that have been the subject of study in supervision can be roughly grouped around three organiz-

ing categories that emerge from an examination of published reports in academic journals and scholarly books from the beginning of the twentieth century:

1. the role of supervisors (including the supervisor's activities and/or the tasks of supervision)
2. the teacher's response to being supervised (including attitudes toward supervision)
3. the value of supervision or supervisory practices (including effects of supervision and of particular supervisory models and/or strategies)

The Supervisor's Role

In the early years of supervision, numerous studies were focused on the supervisor's role. Barr's often-cited descriptive study (1926) of the Detroit Public Schools examined in depth the duties and functions of supervisors. Researchers pointed to the irregularity of supervisory visits (Perrin, 1926), the wide range of supervisory activities from an organizational and administrative perspective (Ayer & Barr, 1928; Melby, 1929), and the impact of the size of school systems on supervisory strategies (Whitney, 1936). Bradfield (1953) examined 50 selected elementary schools to discover the extent to which teachers found supervisory practices to be consistent with principles of supervision. His survey concluded that the supervisor's role was seen as that of kind and understanding co-worker. These examples suggest the kind of methodologies being utilized by researchers, such as primarily surveys and comparison of quantitative data from their own survey work or from demographic material collected by school systems.

Indicative of the persistence of questions about role and function is Crosby's (1969) analysis of 60 articles on supervision that appeared in *Educational Leadership* between 1960 and 1968. Of the 60, 13 had to do with the role of the supervisor and another 15 with leadership, which could be subsumed under the discussion of roles/tasks of the supervisor. The topic remained of interest, making its way into journal articles and conference agendas, but generating little that claimed to be research. Crosby noted a scarcity of research on supervision being reported in *Educational Leadership,* implying that either research was not being conducted, or it was not being communicated to the field worker who might look to it for evidence to support the shaping of supervisory roles and functions.

Early interest in the role and function of the supervisor reflects the emergence of the field and a search for its boundaries. The scarcity of literature on this topic during the period between the late 1930s and the 1960s is reflective of the evolution of the profession and suggests a growing preoccupation with the role of supervisor in curriculum development (Glanz, 1978). Questions about role and function of supervisors persisted, however, which is perhaps reflective of a general lack of consensus over the definition of supervision (Bolin, 1987), along with the desire to promote particular forms of supervisory practice.

In recent decades, much of the research on roles and function has been organized around particular forms of supervision; examples are developmental supervision (Burden, 1982) and collegial coaching (Wilburn, 1986). Inquiry around clinical supervision has dominated the field. There are notable exceptions, among which are Blumberg's (1980) study of supervision, Grimmet's (1987) study of the role of district supervisors, and Pajak's (1989) study of supervisory proficiencies. Blumberg highlights the discrepancy between supervisors' perceptions of their role as professional and teachers' perceptions of supervisors as bureaucratic. Grimmet used semi-structured interviews to explore the role played by district supervisors in implementation of peer coaching. Pajak's survey of supervisory practice drew on a national population to explore the status of supervisory practice with a view to establishing standards. Emergent work is illustrated by Waite's examination of novice superintendents' understanding of supervision through a survey of 110 graduate students enrolled in an introductory supervisory course (1993).

The Teacher's Response to Supervision

The way teachers react to supervision has also been the topic of inquiry. This is apparent in the early years as researchers looked at teachers' reactions to general and special supervision (Nutt, 1924), attitudes toward supervision (Hart, 1930; Manning, 1954; Weber & Garfield, 1942), and supervisory preferences (Shannon, 1936). As in the study of the supervisory role, early researchers most often relied upon quantitative methodologies, primarily questionnaires and surveys, to explore guiding questions or to investigate hypotheses.

Research on teacher attitudes toward supervision has largely been focused on the value and effects of clinical supervision as a unique form of practice in recent decades. Researchers hypothesize that it will result in more positive teacher attitudes. For example, Reavis (1977), compared traditional and clinical supervision through a process–product, experimental research design that measured the verbal behavior of supervisors and teachers. Reavis concluded that clinical supervision creates a more positive level of communication between teachers and supervisors than do traditional methods.

Sullivan's (1980) review of the history and practice of clinical supervision cites research that includes, at least in part, attention to the teacher's perspective (Cook, 1976; Eaker 1972; Kerr, 1976). Of particular note is Sullivan's comment on the state of inquiry: "Research on in-class supervision as a specific area is even more inadequate. Most of the work which has been done has been conducted by doctoral students for dissertations: there appears nowhere an ongoing line of research" (p. 15).

Value and Effects of Supervisory Practice

In addition to studies that focus on the role and function of supervision and the teacher's attitudes/response to it, there are those that examine the effects of supervisory intervention with a view to proving its value. The term *effectiveness* was used interchangeably with *efficiency* during the early part of the twentieth century when supervision was influenced by scientific management. The following discussion offers a sense of the research on supervisory effectiveness.

Courtis (1919) examined the value of special or subject supervision in geography, analyzing four levels of supervision in a controlled study. Standardized test data were used as evidence of the effectiveness of particular forms of supervisory intervention (Messenger 1934; Neville, 1925; Pittman, 1921). Brueckner and Cutright (1927) documented changes in teacher behavior that they attributed to supervisory intervention, drawing upon observational data. Miel (1937) reported on the effects of cooperative planning by groups of teachers, drawing upon research being done through the Horace Mann-Lincoln Institute. In an experimental study, Kinhart (1941) examined the effect of supervision in English teaching on teachers who were considered to be equal in performance during the first semester of the year. One group was supervised for 10 hours per month using a variety of supervisory techniques such as group conference and classroom visitation, over the second semester. The other group served as a control. Kinhart concluded that the group supervised did significantly better work than did the control group. Amidon, Kies, and Palisi (1966) examined group supervision using the Flanders system of interaction analysis.

The effects of supervisory intervention are particularly interesting to current researchers. Flinders (Bowers & Flinders, 1990; Bowers & Flinders, 1991; Flinders, 1991) calls for a "culturally responsive supervision," urging supervisors to consider metaphor, nonverbal communication, and framing[2] in classroom observations and in providing teachers with feedback. Roberts (1991) (Roberts and Blase, 1993) has used discourse analysis to investigate practical problems of communication in supervisory conferences. Roberts, along with Blase (1993), explored the use of formal and informal power in interactions between prospective or practicing supervisors and teachers. Drawing on transcript analysis of over 100 supervisor and teacher postobservation conferences, Roberts and Blase concluded that personal orientation, conversational congruence, formal authority, and situational variables either constrain or facilitate conferences. Successful conferences were those in which supervisors provided a nonthreatening environment and both supervisors and teachers used personal orientation and conversational congruence strategies. Less successful conferences drew on formal authority and situational variables.

Waite (1991, 1992a, 1992b) has also been interested in analysis of conversation in supervisory conferences. He argues that supervisors' controlling behavior, as evidenced by linguistic analysis of their conversation with teachers, makes collegial relationships between teacher and supervisor problematic, but not impossible (1992b).

Several studies attempt to establish the effects of clinical supervision on teachers as well as on supervisors. Sullivan's (1980) overview of literature on clinical practice suggests a cluster of studies along these lines, many of which will be discussed when we explore the clinical model as an exemplar in inquiry.

Role, Responses, and Values: A Continuum?

Taken together, the sample studies cited suggest a variety of ways in which researchers have attempted to identify how best to improve the skills of the teacher in order to promote a more fruitful classroom experience for the student. One can imagine a continuum of methodologies, beginning at one endpoint with studies that draw upon quantitative research designs and extending through qualitative methodologies, with those studies utilizing both located somewhat in the middle. If we were to add the dimension of time, we might expect to see a clustering of more quantitative studies during the early years of supervision, when it was most influenced by scientific management, and more qualitative studies collecting along the continuum as we reach the present.

We could then see if particular questions (e.g., the role and function of supervisors) seem to lend themselves to specific methodologies. Common sense suggests that such a continuum could be enriched by tieing methodologies to underlying philosophical and psychological orientations.

While this line of exploration has an appeal, the outcome is not particularly instructive. What appear at first to be obvious relationships between methodologies used in inquiry and a philosophical continuum cannot be supported under closer scrutiny. Methods of inquiry and topics explored do not fall into clearly delineated categories. For example, it does not follow that experimental research is driven by commitments to a philosophy of positivism, whereas qualitative research relies on pragmatic and existential philosophies, although there are situations in which each of these may be true. One can certainly argue that the choice of a methodology ties one to its philosophical and psychological underpinnings, whether or not the researcher is aware of these underpinnings; however, the extent to which philosophical and psychological orientations influenced researcher choice is debatable.

There is also no easy match between goals of inquiry and methodology utilized. A classic example of the lack of congruence between method and purpose could have been Brueckner's self-assessment tool for mathematics teachers, which was devised in the 1920s and widely cited in the literature. Brueckner's purpose was to promote self-inquiry and teacher reflection. His methodology was to develop and pilot a checklist that quickly became a tool for supervisory assessment of teachers.

Both qualitative and quantitative methodologies have been used to explore the role of supervisors, teachers' responses to supervision, and its effects. Questionnaires and surveys were predominant during the early decades of the twentieth century, with some experimental designs being utilized. Forms of inquiry that are now described as qualitative research methodology were utilized, but they were not seen as "real research" until more recently.

Attempts to establish a logical continuum of supervisory inquiry by the stated purpose and topic of studies or by methodology utilized mask the complexity of the field and imposed an order on it that cannot be justified by a deeper look into the literature. *How* supervision has been studied may not be so fruitful a question as *why* it has been studied in particular ways. The focus of inquiry has clearly been on understanding the supervisor's work in the improvement of instruction; however, knowing this does not sufficiently answer the *why* question. One way to begin to do so is in becoming more aware of the contextual factors that influence the way in which supervision has been studied.

CONTEXTUAL FACTORS IN SUPERVISION

Supervision has always existed in the social "muddle" of schools and supervisory inquiry—at least the published results of inquiry that are available to us—has always existed in the ambiguous and sometimes contradictory world that bridges scholarly and practical. As a field of study, supervision has been influenced by contextual factors that confound efforts to establish clear relationships and causality in exploring methods of inquiry. Inquiry in supervision has been influenced by (1) the instrumentality of the field, (2) what constitutes acceptable scholarly work within academe, and (3) tacitly held images of the teacher.

The first two contextual "givens"—the instrumentality of supervision and the demands of the scholarly community—have formed the way in which supervision has been formally studied. While obvious, they are relatively unexplored, and they may have had more impact on the methodologies used in the study of supervision than underlying philosophical commitments or pressing problems of practice.

The Instrumentality of Instructional Supervision

Supervision is a technology, a tool used to understand and improve teaching practice, whether this is done in an authoritarian or democratic way. Until recent decades, it has been less concerned with itself than it has with the practice of teaching. Prior to the twentieth century, supervision consisted of inspection of schools by committees or by a superintendent, hired to oversee the quality of schooling. On-site supervision was later conducted by a "principal teacher," who reported to a district "area superintendent." As the profession grew from the beginning of the twentieth century, the role of supervisor came to exist in its own right, not as an add-on to the work of a superintendent, principal, or head teacher. Many researchers were preoccupied with how to move supervision from its status as an inspectorate to a role characterized by guidance in which emphasis was on facilitation of the improvement of instruction. Even so, the focus of inquiry was on supervision *in its relationship* to improvement of instruction and student outcomes, a relationship that has remained indirect. The supervisor works through teacher, curriculum, and instructional materials to influence the classroom experience of students. While it makes sense that teachers will be more effective if they have instructional support, the supervisory role has always been seen as tenuous. In 1934, Messenger wrote, "Supervision has borne the brunt of school retrenchments. Only weak, sporadic defenses have been attempted in its behalf" (p. 289).

Supervisors are vulnerable to cutbacks whenever there is an economic crisis within the schools. Supervisors are also vulnerable as various iterations of teachers as professionals—whether as democratic leaders, peer coaches, or in site-based management—seem to make the supervisor's work unnecessary or redundant because it can be performed by other school personnel including teachers themselves.

Role diffusion became a critical issue in the 1930s and 1940s, perhaps in part because of the growing emphasis on supervision as democratic leadership. The 1943 merger of supervisors and curriculum workers into a department that became the Association of Supervision and Curriculum Development (ASCD) in 1947 led to a further blurring of the role of the supervisor. There was so much enthusiasm for teacher professionalism and supervision through curriculum improvement during the 1940s and 1950s that in-class supervision seemed unnecessary to many. Articles in *Educational Leadership* pointed to role confusion experienced by supervisors (Stover, 1945; Swearingten, 1946). Mackenzie wrote an article published in 1961 that summarized thinking on this continuing trend:

"Supervisor" is used here as a generic term to include all those whose unique primary concern is instructional leadership. Supervisors may be called helping teachers, curriculum consultants, curriculum directors or assistant superintendents in charge of instruction (1961, p. 87).

The result appeared to be a lack of attention to supervision by its own professional organization and a threat to the profession (Henry, 1966; Lewis & Miel, 1972). In 1969, Eash asked if supervisors were a "vanishing breed." Eash wrote, "The supervisor's role, which has always been afflicted by vicissitudes in the halting progress toward professionalization, now conceivably faces extinction" (p. 73). In 1976, Krajewski's often-cited "Putting the 'S' Back in ASCD" appeared in *Educational Leadership*. Krajewski conducted a quantitative examination of annual conference guides for ASCD for 1971–1975, concluding, "From conference themes through special sessions, curriculum has taken priority over supervision consistently" (1976, p. 376).

The role of the supervisor continues to be questioned. More current examples are Glickman's introduction to the 1992 ASCD yearbook, which questions the conception of instructional supervision and a paper presented by Starratt at the Council of Professors of Instructional Supervision meeting in Tampa, Florida, in 1993: "A Modest Proposal: Abolish Instructional Supervision." In both of these cases, the argu-

ment has to do with whether a supervisory role is necessarily the best role to help teachers to improve their own practice, given current views about teacher authority and power.

Uncertainty over the future has prompted numerous explorations of the value of supervision. These range from "proofs of the effects" of supervision, such as those cited above in discussion of the value and effects of supervision, to collections of testimonials about its value.

The fact that supervision focuses on improvement of instruction has also meant that a great deal of the study prompted by supervisory questions is not considered inquiry in *supervision*. Scholars periodically review the literature on supervision and deplore the lack of research, as did Harris (1963), Sullivan (1980), and Blumberg (1990). While it is true that the field may suffer from lack of study of supervision, a great deal of work has been done in exploring supervisory questions. For example, much of the work on the effectiveness of teaching follows Barr's beginning line of research on teacher efficiency and effectiveness. Begun in the 1920s and extending into the 1960s, Barr's inquiry focused on teacher behavior. The idea was to better understand teacher behavior in order to improve it through supervisory intervention. The Utah Study of the Assessment of Teaching drew upon Barr's Wisconsin studies, hypothesizing that relationships between teachers, students, and others directly concerned with the education of the student could be described from classroom data focusing on interactions of teacher and student (Hughes, 1963). Medley and Mitzel (1963) studied teacher behavior by focusing on effectiveness rather than on competence, preferring to let others deal with competence "since it involves value judgments which we do not regard as part of the province of science" (p. 81). Domas and Tiedman (1950) listed more than 1000 studies of teacher competence in a review of the literature, with many patterned after Barr's interest in finding out the criteria of teacher effectiveness, which was a supervisory concern. While the teacher effectiveness research became far removed from research on supervision, it illustrates how complex and broad in scope the work of the supervisor is.

Building and strengthening a profession that is constantly threatened has been a persistent problem to supervisors and professors of supervision, and it has profoundly influenced the nature of inquiry in the field. Furthermore, the complexity of issues related to supervisory intervention has led to a siphoning of research focusing on supervision itself as researchers have become preoccupied with related matters.

Scholarly Work Within the Academic Community

Like school supervisors, professors of supervision have been affected by the vicissitudes of economics, often teaching courses in supervision as an add-on to other work. Teacher preparation, administrator preparation, staff development, and teacher professionalism are all areas that overlap with supervisory concern. Professors of supervision are also professors of preservice preparation, curriculum and instruction, school administration, educational research, or in-service teacher education—to name a few common configurations within colleges of education. Scholarly work focused on understanding supervisory history, theory, and practice has often reflected the lack of attention given to supervision within schools of education (Bolin, 1988).

The legitimacy of scholarship in the field of supervision has periodically been held in question (Blumberg, 1990; Bolin, 1988, 1990; Sergiovanni, 1990). The pressure that teacher educators face in achieving promotion and tenure within a school of education, as well as their status, has been documented by Judge (1982). Flight from those areas most closely aligned with practice has robbed field-based studies such as teacher preparation and supervision of intellectual energy and focus. Researchers interested in questions related to supervision have often had this interest channeled into other fields such as staff development, educational leadership, or research on teaching, as noted earlier.

The nature of research in supervision has also been vitally influenced by the methods of inquiry available to researchers and acceptable within the broader educational research community. While most of the research available to us through the literature has been the work of university scholars whose place in the academy required it, there are notable exceptions. These have been undertaken by large school districts interested in teacher improvement. Even these studies, however, have often been conducted by school personnel who were engaged in dissertation research and mindful of the methodologies deemed acceptable by the university or by school system directors of research, who were steeped in the traditions of university research. In any event, they have not been immune to the pressures of the scholarly community. The empirical research paradigm, so useful in the behavioral sciences, has long been regarded by many universities as *the* legitimate form of inquiry and still is, in many cases, despite the availability of other methodologies. This attitude permeates the remarks made by Banghart in introducing the *First Annual Phi Delta Kappa Symposium on Educational Research* in 1959:

Out of a matrix of verbalization [the rational–verbal approach to solution of problems] came the group of service people who felt that the primary purpose of educational research was to give service to the "people in the field." To them, research consisted of the traditional school surveys, of testing programs, of many little administrative and investigative procedures. None of these was designed to add to educational theory or to build a body of systematic knowledge in the field of education, but rather to give immediate bits of practical information . . . we now begin to see emerging a systematic body of tools available to the individual concerned with educational research. These tools are in harmony with our concept of the experimental approach, which involves control and prediction. It is through abiding by the present rules of the game that systematic knowledge can be added to the discipline of education. It is through the modern techniques of research that replications can be made and hypotheses tested. A key characteristic seems to be that any researcher can replicate and thereby test out the statements made by any other researcher. The individual who still insists upon a verbal, "thinking about" approach to the problem is no longer taken seriously. We hope, too, that most of the people concerned with educational research have outgrown the service concept. This does not mean that we need to discard "thinking"' neither do we need to discard service activities. I am only saying that these two approaches should be placed in their proper perspective (1960, p. xii).

Given the force of this viewpoint, it is not surprising to find a preponderance of work based on descriptive, correlational, and experimental research in the history of supervision.

The acceptable methodologies of the academy have unfortunately not always been most appropriate in answering the real questions faced by supervisors who are members of a profession dedicated to providing "service to 'people in the field.'" Calvert forcefully made this argument in 1938 in a critique of the history of the scientific movement in supervision. He points out that being scientific is to be commended if scientific study helps teachers to adopt better and more progressive practices. Attempts to engage in scientific research, however, often employ techniques that are not suitable to the real concerns of supervisors and divert attention from important issues.

Probably the greatest weakness in attempts to make education scientific, however, has been the choosing of the wrong problem to study—the investigator selecting some problem for which he could easily and mechanically secure statistical data that was "scientific" in appearance rather than attacking more significant, but also more difficult, problems (1938, p. 101).

Calvert's argument is not unlike that made by Findley of the Department of Research and Pupil Personnel in Atlanta, Georgia, who spoke at the Phi Delta Kappa symposium on educational research cited earlier. Findley points to the difficulty in applying findings from well- defined and well-controlled situations to the "diverse and ill-ordered" situations to be found in schools:

Spreading through the intermediary science of psychology, the controlled statistical experiment has moved into a position of high esteem in educational research. But by controlling all other factors that operate in practical settings, we have circumscribed the experiment so greatly that its scope of generalization is greatly limited and the true experiment comes in the broader applications later (1960, p. 44).

The analytical tradition does not solve the complexities of schools, but it does avoid the problem of complexity, often forcing problems analysis into two-variable relations. Furthermore, as Findley points out,

Close identification of research with the controlled experiment reduces research from its broad definition of "studious inquiry; usually critical and exhaustive investigation or experimentation having for its aim the revision of accepted conclusions in the light of newly discovered facts" (Findley, 1960, p.45).

Findley's comments, like Calvert's, echo the argument made by Dewey in *The Sources of a Science of Education*. It was Dewey's belief that those most qualified to determine what ought to be studied would be teachers themselves and that the most significant questions for research would be those that emerged from classroom practice.

Scholars in supervision, whose promotion and tenure depended upon publication, were faced with the dilemma of wanting to explore problems of real importance to teachers in ways that would be useful while meeting the demands of university scholarship. As Asbury pointed out:

A sense of optimism prompts those who do not engage in educational research to hope that what researchers do will ultimately shed some light on the treacherous footpath to improved teaching and learning. Needless to say, the very nature of the problems selected for study at times reveals that this concern is not generally shared by those persons actively engaged in the research enterprise. It has become almost axiomatic in education that the so-called "better" journals will not even consider publishing a research report unless it is so far removed from ordinary educational matters as to be totally unfathomable to in-service workers in the field. Indeed, such ordinary people as classroom teachers and principals are supposed to accept as an article of faith the notion that mysterious titles which appear in such journals might help them solve some real problems if they could only be translated into a comprehensible form of communication (p. 21).

Asbury goes on to challenge the educational research community to adopt a perspective that supports research around significant problems and needed results rather than in terms of the methods utilized to conduct the research.

Contextual factors may ultimately explain more about why supervisory inquiry has proceeded as it has than do more obvious questions that appear to drive research. One can certainly wonder how much of the scholarship on supervision, including current work, would occur without the compelling concern of scholars over promotion and tenure at the university. The opening of the research community to new forms of inquiry, however reluctantly this opening may have occurred, has contributed to a much more vigorous and healthy landscape for inquiry in the 1980s and 1990s than scholars in supervision were able to enjoy at any other time in the history of the field.

TACIT IMAGES OF THE TEACHER

In examining methods of inquiry, we bear in mind that supervision as a field of study is situated within or framed by a powerful, constraining contextual nexus that is so much taken for granted as to go unexamined. Inquiry is also influenced by the way scholars think about teachers and teaching. The roles of supervisors, teachers attitudes toward supervision, and the value of supervisory intervention—topics that have dominated the literature—have been explored through questions that emerge from powerful, tacit images of the teacher, while consciously raised by researchers. These images reflect unconscious assumptions about human beings and the social order and represent ways in which people organize and make sense of the world. Images of the teacher include views about the nature of knowledge, feeling, action, aesthetics, and ethical principals. These find their way into the framing of questions about what is important in supervision.

We identify three critical questions that seem to characterize the spirit of inquiry in supervision:

1. How can supervisors get the teacher to be more effective?
2. How can supervisors help teachers to become more professional in their practice?
3. How do supervisors help teachers to be more critical and self-reflective in practice?

The questions, and their tacit images of the teacher, do not in themselves suggest the philosophical commitments held by those who have asked them. Our purpose is to raise these commitments to consciousness through examining the questions rather than to explicate various philosophies. In doing so, we underscore the point that inquiry is seldom a tidy and straightforward process. We hope to capture some of the untidiness and complexity of inquiry in a way that is deeply respectful of both the insights and limitations as well as the commitments of those who have conducted the inquiry.

Implicitly embedded in the first question—"How can supervisors get the teacher to be more effective?"—is the image of the teacher as a *worker to be trained*. The second—"How can supervisors help teachers to become more professional in their practice?"—suggests an image of the teacher as a *professional to be enlightened*. The third—"How do supervisors help teachers to be more critical and self-reflective in practice?"—evokes an image of the teacher as a *deliberative practitioner to be supported*.

Shared questions and images of the teacher implicit in a question have spawned research by individuals with differing and sometimes contradictory philosophical commitments. For example, the main intentions of supervisory inquiry drawn from the image of *teacher as worker to be trained* is to provide directions for supervisory practice, specifically, by isolating skills that will enable supervisors to change teacher behaviors to those that produce positive pupil learning outcomes. As we shall see, many of the studies of teacher reflectiveness, which might appear to be aligned with images of the deliberative practitioner, are concerned with changing teacher thinking in order to produce particular outcomes and seem more philosophically compatible with worker images. The image of *teacher as professional* has prompted research on how supervisors can foster professional attitudes and practices in teachers. While much of this research is aimed toward sustaining job satisfactions in teachers, improving student learning and developing the teacher as a political activist are also goals of teacher professionalism. The image of teacher as *deliberative practitioner to be supported* has fostered research on how to support teachers in their efforts to be self-reflective. It assumes that the dynamic and thoughtful teacher will constantly search for the most productive ways to bridge disciplines of knowledge and interests with the skills of students. Researchers who focus on teacher reflection, however, have differing definitions of teacher thinking. Despite profound differences in ideas about means and ends of inquiry, however, scholars in supervision have shared a common commitment to improve the classroom experience of students through intervention with teachers.

How Can Supervisors Get the Teacher to Be More Effective? The Teacher as Worker to Be Trained

Research on the effectiveness of supervision was guided by the overarching question posed by Barr and that drove his research career (Bolin, 1987). It began as, "What are the criteria of efficient teaching?" This question invited the utilization of procedures for describing teaching in a "quantifiable" manner that were being developed in educational research circles, drawn from models in the natural sciences. Correlational and experimental work seeks statistically significant relationships between teacher behaviors and student outcomes, assuming that such controlled studies are the only reliable scientific bases for building teacher effectiveness. Enthusiasts continued to argue for this mode of research three decades later:

Education will begin to approach its proper level of efficiency only when we recognize that the problems of effectiveness are scientific and technical, not political. Only by inspired, sustained and systematic research in education similar to that which has graced the older sciences can education become truly effective (Fattu, 1960).

It continues to be a concern within the educational research community as researchers look for clusters of teacher behavior associated with effectiveness (Gage, 1984).

The question about efficiency evolved into one about effectiveness focusing on (1) identifying factors that facilitate or hinder teacher effectiveness and (2) measuring the relationships between supervisory interventions, teacher behaviors, and student outcomes.

Nutt's (1924) questionnaire survey of teachers of Hammond and Whiting, Indiana, and Topeka, Kansas, briefly mentioned in our discussion of teacher responses to supervision, was an early example of research on how supervisors could increase teacher effectiveness. The first part of the survey consisted of 33 items designed to elicit opinion about the helpful things supervisors do. The questionnaire divided responses into those applying to general supervision and those applying to special supervisors. In the section focusing on general supervision, "Encouragement, sympathy, and favorable comments" ranked highest in frequency of response. Of the most frequently mentioned items, Nutt classifies responses into those that focus on immediate attention to teaching problems, supervisory relationship, and indirect attack on teaching problems. The data from this section suggested that "teachers need to be made comfortable in their thinking and feeling in order to profit by the presence of the supervisor" (1924, p. 60).

There were fewer responses in the list of "Things not helpful" in supervision. Nutt surmised that "general supervisors have very largely avoided doing things really detrimental to the work of the teachers" (p. 61). In reporting "Helps desired," Nutt points out that most suggest that more be done along the lines of those things recognized as helpful.

Results for special supervision were similar to those for general supervision. Nutt points out that "special supervision has not made the same effective impression upon the teachers that general supervision has made" (p. 62). "Too much work expected" and "Too many supervisors" received the largest number of responses in the section, "Things done not helpful." Nutt notes that in comparing general with specific supervision, "one is led to conclude that special supervision has not established its case thoroughly in the minds of the teachers supervised" (p. 63). Supporting this interpretation was the fact that in general supervision, unhelpful activities were mentioned only 20 times, whereas there were 275 mentions of unhelpful things done by special supervisors. At the

same time, Nutt concludes that there was sufficient testimony in favor of special supervision to suggest "the real necessity for its development" (p. 64).

There are a number of criticisms that can be made of the report, particularly that it does not describe the methodology in sufficient detail. The merits of the study, however, may not be as important as what it represents. Nutt seems to be interested in soliciting the impressions of teachers and asks them to respond in their own words. At the same time, it focuses on quantifying responses toward the end of understanding supervisor "efficiency."

Along similar lines, Hart, a school principal, surveyed 15 school districts in Michigan in 1929; 142 teachers replied. The questionnaire survey asked teachers to respond to questions regarding number of supervisory visits and their impressions about whether the visits were helpful. Most welcomed supervision, with half responding *yes* to the question about whether supervision received made them "a better teacher." The survey provided room for teachers to list "faults" and suggestions for improvement. At least 25% of those responding listed as faults:

1. Visits are too rare to give supervisor a fair basis of judgment of the teachers' work.
2. Principals and superintendents are skilled in only a small portion of the subject that they attempt to supervise.
3. Supervisors are hesitant about offering definite and constructive help for the improvement of teaching.
4. Supervisors assume an attitude of looking for something upon which to rate the teacher rather than one of helping her to be a better teacher (1930, p. 367).

Teachers called for more frequent and lengthy classroom visitation and more helpful criticism. Among suggestions were that the supervisor stay for an entire period and make a series of consecutive visits.

Hart's study, which was one of the first published reports of research on supervision, represents the many explorations into the effectiveness of supervisory practice that have peppered the literature in supervision across time. It is also revealing in that Hart presents what continue to be common complaints about supervisory practice. It is also noteworthy that Hart called for better supervisory support for beginning teachers. Recalling his own experience as a beginning teacher—he was visited once by the county school commissioner, "the time of 'call' approximately 30 minutes" (1930, p. 365)—Hart pointed out that the situation faced by the new teacher was not changing rapidly enough. He argued that "our sympathy should extend to countless beginning teachers who take up their duties, hardly knowing 'what it is all about'" (1930, p. 365). The study again touches what is still a weak spot in supervisory practice, despite current enthusiasm for mentoring programs.

The most common methodology used in studies of the effectiveness of supervisory practice was perhaps the use of standardized tests to measure pupil gains. This was an attempt to link supervisory practices to student outcomes. Students were typically tested with achievement tests in the beginning and end of a school term. These were often accompanied by aptitude and personality tests and by adjustment inventories so that final achievement scores could be adjusted through analysis of covariance to make allowance for the influence of the student's aptitude, pervious learning, personality, or adjustment on the final scores as these were measured by tests. The mean of adjusted scores of all students in a teacher's class was compared with similar means of classes of other teachers with adjustments for effects of school and community differences if the classes were in different schools. These were usually tied to particular supervisory interventions either before testing and again after testing or by using control groups that did not receive supervisory intervention. Statements were then made about effectiveness of supervisory intervention of teacher performance. Brueckner (1933) was critical of this practice:

In the nature of things these tests to a large extent determine the curriculum. In the past this has had many unfortunate consequences, since the tests that have been used have been chiefly measures of the facts and skills that were taught and have not afforded any means of evaluating performance in respect to more intangible outcomes of learning (which, to many supervisors, are of greater value), such as character traits, appreciations, ideals, and the like. This unwise use of standard tests resulted in greater emphasis by teachers on the types of learning included in the tests, and consequently, in the neglect of other outcomes of even greater value (pp. 601–602).

The mainstream view, however, was in marked contrast to Brueckner's. Messenger (1934) of Northern Illinois State Teachers College, DeKalb, wrote an apologetic for the use of standardized tests in supervisory practice that is representative of the thinking that was well established by the early 1930s. It was so entrenched, that Whitney reported an increase in the use of standardized tests in an article in *The American School Board Journal* in 1936. More emphasis was placed on the measurement of pupil achievement in schools surveyed in 1936 than it was in an earlier survey in 1923.

Messenger, however, argued that supervision was weak as a profession and easily the victim of school retrenchments. She proposed that supervisors make their argument for supervision in facts and figures, or "definite, concrete, objective evidence to prove that their work pays":

Since in this scientific age everything that exists, it is believed, exists in some quantity, and existing in some quantity can be measured, many persons conclude that what is not measured does not exist. Figures are produced in every other line of endeavor to prove results. Since this is the common practice, the attitude of the supervisor who is indifferent to proving, when he can do so, the results of his enterprises in hard facts and cold figures is completely unintelligible to the layman (1934, p. 289).

Messenger then offers her own proofs of effectiveness of supervision as evidenced by pupil gains on The Stanford Achievement Test. Messenger points to a group of teachers who were highly trained and experienced, who believed they were not in need of supervision. A general supervisor began by testing all pupils from second to eighth grade. Tests were scored and graphs were made for each pupil. Graphs were made by half-grades and a composite graph for the whole

school. Positive and negative scores (as related to the grade norms for each subject) were reported. Teachers were "shocked" by the results.

Messenger admitted that there was no attempt made to defend the sampling of the test used, and that, in fact, the school's selection of subject matter might be better than that of the test makers. The standardized test, however, was widely used in the area, and it was believed that the district studied should perform as well as neighboring districts. Furthermore, teachers need not be limited to the material tested and could consider it a minimum. Data showed that the school was raised half a year in achievement, which seemed clear-cut evidence of the effectiveness of supervision. As far as Messenger was concerned, this more than justified use of standardized testing.

Messenger's inquiry into teacher improvement is not especially significant because of the methodology utilized or her findings, however questionable they might be. Rather, Messenger's work takes on significance in light of the contextual factors surrounding inquiry in supervision. Whatever the pressures of the college may have been to produce "research," Messenger's goal seems to be to defend supervision by means that the public would accept, "Hard facts and cold figures" (p. 289).

Not all of the inquiry that focused on the teacher as worker relied on quantifiable measures of teacher effectiveness. Among the early studies of supervisory practice was *An Analysis of the Duties and Functions of Instructional Supervisors*, by Barr, associate professor of education at the University of Wisconsin. Barr had led the study while he served as assistant director in charge of supervision for the Detroit Public Schools. Barr was concerned that supervision, as distinct from school administration, was a new field, "as yet, only vaguely defined" (1926, p. 9). His purpose was to "offer an analysis and definition of the functions of supervisors for one school system" (p. 9) in order to contribute to better relationships between teachers, school principals, and supervisors. The study was cited in the literature on supervision for the next several decades, and illustrates the development of descriptive inquiry that makes use of a variety of sources of data: (1) documents prepared by supervisors; (2) annual reports of supervisors; (3) weekly supervisory reports; and (4) daily time-cards of supervisors' work. Although we would clearly recognize it as a form of descriptive research, Barr did not consider it as such. "By research is meant the discovery and active experimental solution of current problems in subject matter, materials and methods of instruction, or in the administration of their solution in the class room" (p. 10). In Barr's thinking, the study was important background for research; real research was experimental.

Supervisors have always operated on much that is common sense, even when they felt it was not "real research." Common sense notions, however, are not always honored in the way "best practices" proven by research are honored. Brueckner (1933) offered reasons for poor work by teachers based on common sense notions, identifying those residing in the student (e.g., intelligence, attitudes, prior experience), the teacher (e.g., professional preparation, intelligence, personality), instructional materials (e.g., their supply, value), and instruction (e.g., organization of subject-matter, provision for individual differences). In doing so, he states:

It is unfortunate that at present we have so little definite information as to the exact causes of poor work in teaching. It is true that there are available several lists of "probable" causes of poor work, but they have been arrived at subjectively and in practically no case have they been experimentally validated. As a consequence, it is not possible to make as clean-cut diagnosis of teaching situations as the physician can make of physical conditions (p. 603).

At the same time, Brueckner is critical of those who attempted "to apply to educational practices the types of precise scientific techniques" that had contributed to science (p. 603). Such research paid too much attention to the impersonal and ignored a "social outlook." Borrowing techniques for science and applying them to educational problems without understanding of the purposes for which they were intended had yielded a great deal of information, but little that helped to answer the essential supervisory questions about causes of poor teaching, what is good teaching, and the like.

Brueckner recognized then what Gage (1984) has more recently argued: Factors that are characteristic of good and poor teachers "will not be specific but rather a complex of interrelated elements" (Brueckner, 1933, p. 605).

Teaching simply does not stay put. The supervisor who visits a class for the purpose of discovering the causes of poor work may see certain conditions on the day of his visit which he may infer are the underlying causes. If he is rash enough to draw any conclusions based on one single observation, he is overlooking, or else is not aware of, the well-established fact that those same conditions may not appear at all on the following day (p. 605).

Brueckner argued that the extreme variability of teaching practices needed to be considered by anyone who attempted to quantify practices that lend themselves to such treatment. Furthermore, even if data are reliable, questions of interpretation must be raised. Counting the number of questions asked in a given lesson may offer some insight into practice, but will not answer the question of appropriateness of the questions. Attempts to standardize procedures based on such studies were described as unwarranted. Brueckner was equally critical of attempts to use time analysis as the basis of allocation for subjects or teaching practices. "The fact that a supervisor may make quantitative studies of various aspects of a lesson does not mean, as is often assumed, that the procedure is scientific" (p. 606).

Brueckner's work reflects an implicit faith in development of procedures in teaching that can be experimentally validated. He laments that until such a time as this occurs, supervisors will have to rely on "compelling opinions" (p. 609).

Brueckner, along with Cutright (1927), had measured teacher "efficiency" in reading in content areas. Their study relied on observational data collected by trained observers. Brueckner and Cutright, however, did not believe that their collection and analysis of data was real research. They did believe that objective description and analysis of teaching practice could lead to correlational and experimental studies,

or "real" research. The notion that analytical, experimental, or, to use the broader term, empirical research was research was not uncommon. Scholars also routinely justified other forms of inquiry, as had Brueckner, who argued that until experimental work could be done "we must be guided by the consensus of the best available opinion" (p. 609).

Foshay (1994), speaking of the historical importance of the empirical model in educational inquiry, observed:

To conduct analytical research, one takes the educational problem apart into its irreducible elements, then seeks to discover which element, or combination of elements, best accounts for the problem. To do this, it is essential that the problem be defined in simple, quantifiable terms, such as a test score. The test score becomes the criterion by which the success of the undertaking is judged. It is also essential that the elements selected for analysis be pure—uncontaminated by other elements or variables (p. 317).

Barr envisioned a program of research to follow from the analysis of duties and functions and in general, which would include the following steps:

1. The discovery of existing instructional shortcomings and defects (possible items of improvement).
2. The search for suggestions for improved methods in the work of instructional agents in our own or other systems.
3. The formulation of a working plan for improvement.
4. The trial of the plan under experimental conditions with the selection of the successful solution on the basis of measured results, and the formulation of tentative objectives and standards of attainment.
5. The formulation of specific plans for putting the new method into operation and of standards, tests, and so on, for measuring its effects (p. 10).

The Detroit study provided a summary of supervisory activities as reported by supervisors. Attention was then devoted to an examination of the time distribution among these supervisory activities. The time distribution study tabulated the frequency of occurrence of activities reported by supervisors in regular reports, drawing on approximately 5,000 of these. In addition, two timecard studies were made. One covered a 2-year period. The second was more detailed and covered a 5 month period. Fifty supervisors noted in intervals of 10 and 15 minutes their activities and the time spent upon each. The results showed an uneven distribution of time, with the largest block (38.9%) going to *Time Spent in Research and Study*, followed by 31.9% for *Preparation of Material*. Only 10.4% of the time was spent on *Surveys, Reports, Records, Schedules*. Supervisors of today who complain that much of their time is spent in doing paper work might find this to be a surprising figure.

Barr then explored how different departments were supervised, asking how supervision varied from department to department. No uniform way of spending time was discovered and Barr pointed out that it was not possible to tell whether emphasis on one or two supervisory activities was due to the nature of work within a department, attitudes about supervision, or because of developments in particular supervisory programs.

In order to better understand the supervisor's work, Barr also did an analysis of the typewritten, mimeographed, and printed materials prepared by supervisors for use in the schools. These ranged from materials related to (1) textbooks and their selection, (2) supplies, equipment, and buildings, and (3) assistance in selection, appointment, assignment, and transfer of teachers (pp. 121–122). Review of such materials would be considered standard procedure in document analysis today.

Barr did not believe that the function of supervision was one of inspection; rather, it was to be threefold: research, training, and field work. In concluding the study, he pointed to the wide range of activities in which supervisors engage, arguing:

Supervisors have many duties other than visiting the teacher at work. The notion that the chief function of supervision is inspection finds no support in the finding of this analysis of what supervisors do. Similarly, criticisms of supervision based, as most current discussions are, upon the notion that supervision is inspection, are fallacious (p. 175).

In the Wisconsin studies Barr later went on to explore teacher effectiveness in greater detail. His work reflects a preoccupation with methods of research and a kind of wistful fantasy that if we could discover the right methodology, then we could unlock the key to teacher effectiveness.

In a critique of the teacher effectiveness literature, Nuthall (1973) pointed out that the kinds of problems addressed in the broader teacher effectiveness research and their conceptualization were limited by reliance on the experimental method that ignored the multiple domains of influence within the classroom and school, and between supervisor and teacher. Teacher behavior was seen as actions rather than intentions. When teacher behavior was of concern, the supervisor's role was to help teachers learn the probable effects of particular teaching behaviors on student outcomes so that these behaviors could be exhibited when appropriate.

A more recent line of research that attempts to influence the teacher's behavior is the research on cognitive coaching as a supervisory tool. On first examination, this work appears to be more closely aligned with images of the teacher as reflective practitioner because it addresses issues around the teacher's thinking, drawing on Schon's work. Cognitive coaching, which is a form of clinical supervision, has been described by Costa and Garmston, who note:

We define cognitive coaching as the supervisor's application of a set of strategies designed to enhance the teacher's perceptions, decisions, and intellectual functions. These inner thought processes are prerequisite to improving overt instructional behaviors which will, in turn, produce greater student learning (1986, p. 39).

Cognitive coaching seeks to understand the nature of teacher thinking and provide prompts or coaching that will enable teachers to practice more effectively. While it is concerned with teacher reflection, it is more closely aligned with the teacher effectiveness research than with emergent work on teacher deliberation.

Coaching has appeared in various iterations. Peer coaching, as described by Alfonso and Goldsberry (1980), is associated with teacher professionalism. Alfonso and Goldsberry note that the "concept recognizes the rich resources available among experienced teachers and helps create the kind of colleagueship that characterizes professionals" (p. 107). Ofek (1988) describes a peer supervision model based on a participant observation study in which peer supervision was implemented in two urban public schools in New York City, with one being an elementary and one being a high school. Ofek's model seems to be more in keeping with emergent ideas of teacher deliberation. The collegial coaching model described by Wilburn (1986) appears to be related to teacher effectiveness. Wilburn (1986) summarizes three studies of attitudes and skills of Florida teachers who participated in collegial coaching. Wilburn predicts that given changes in schools master teachers will be brought into instructional supervision, concluding that "when the critical supervisory task of conducting face to face conferences with their colleagues is examined, the collegial coaching model continues to yield effective results" (p. 50).

By asking how teachers can be made more effective, Barr and other researchers begged questions about the criteria of effectiveness. The image of teacher as worker led to a split away from what began as inquiry into supervisory practice, or how to work with the worker, and into a powerful and continuing line of inquiry on teaching, or what workers actually do. The real lesson for supervisors is that supervisory practice has many faces and dimensions, all of which continue to beg inquiry. The persistent notion that research on supervision is weak can only be supported if one sees supervision as the specific actions of supervisors. If one sees the broad and complex nature of teaching and learning encompassed by supervisory practice, then one begins to get a picture of inquiry that has moved outward in many directions.

How Do Supervisors Help Teacher to Become More Professional? The Teacher As Professional to Be Enlightened

As new approaches to research began to develop in the social sciences, interest grew in their application to educational problems. Lewin's work in studying group behavior and leadership was published in *Educational Leadership* (1944), and it intrigued scholars in supervision, notably Alice Miel and Kimball Wiles. Of particular influence on educators were Lewin's "Experiments in Social Space," published in 1939, and "Forces Behind Food Habits and Methods of Change," published in 1943 (in Wiles, 1950). Lewin's initial studies were experimental. As he began to speculate about how democratic structure and group process improve performance, facilitate group decision-making, and generally improve the satisfaction of group members, he encountered questions that did not lend themselves to experimental study.

INTERPRETIVE INQUIRY

New questions were raised by research in the social sciences, and researchers in the social sciences began to be interested in educational problems and finding new methods for studying them. Smith and Keith's (1971) study of educational innovation represents an example of how the field of inquiry was being broadened as social scientists focused on education.[3] Researchers following this new way of thinking "shared concern with intentionality and the actor's subjective interpretation (or meaning) as the basis for understanding of the social world" (Bellack, 1978, p. 21).

Bellack (1978) used the term *interpretive* to describe a common characteristic of researchers drawing on social sciences research and qualitative methodologies. The term refers to the hermeneutic tradition, or the art of interpretation to which qualitative research may be traced. The problem most concerning these researchers is how to understand a phenomenon such as supervision or teaching from the perspective of the actors within the setting. Description of the flow of events within the classroom or setting is of importance. Its underlying principles are:

1. Rejection of experimental scientific methods as the source of fact and insistence on multiple methods for understanding reality.
2. Insistence on development of methods appropriate to uniquely human characteristics and actions in society and rejection of the natural sciences as the standard for inquiry into human phenomenon.

Development of social sciences methodologies paralleled developments within supervision. Discussions of democratic supervision to be found in the literature of the 1930s and 1940s reflected interest in the opinions and intentions of teachers and called for inquiry to depart from exclusive reliance on the well-established empirical framework. While many clung to the idea that "real research" would serve education as effectively as it had served the behavioral sciences, other educators, such as Calvert (1938), who was quoted earlier, suggest a keen awareness of the need for broader forms of inquiry:

Attempts to be scientific are to be commended if they approach that goal; but unfortunately many attempts to be scientific have resulted in employing techniques not suitable to the particular problem at hand and have shifted attention away from major issues. Too often the investigator has been more interested in the "scientific appearance of his findings than in a real solution to his problem, and may have maltreated their data and generalized on insufficient evidence (p. 101).

Calvert was not alone in his call for the study of more significant problems. Brim had argued that research had led to attempts to study and to improve schools as they existed, when if researchers had understood the deeper significance of the scientific movement, they "would have challenged the entire educational structure" (1933, p. 579).

There has been a long tradition of using a broad array of approaches to inquiry in exploring supervisory problems. While they did not believe them to be research, scholars drew upon a variety of methods, including collection and analysis of observational data and document analysis (see Brueckner and Cutright, 1927, and Barr, 1926, cited earlier), often utilizing what were precursors to case study methodology and forms of action research.

The movement toward use of action research was in keeping with a growing view of the teacher as a professional who was to be enlightened in the processes and responsibilities of democracy. "Cooperative action research" focused on improving practice through systematic examination of both processes and consequences of actions. Foshay (1994) traces action research to publication of *Research for Teachers* by Buckingham in 1926. At the Horace Mann-Lincoln Institute of School Experimentation (HMLI), Caswell urged classroom experimentation. When Corey became executive officer, he began to draw upon work on "operations research" done by Collier of the U. S. Bureau of Indian Affairs, to develop what HMLI named *cooperative action research*. Teachers worked together to design classroom research and engage in both gathering and interpretation of data. Corey recognized the challenge of studying schools:

The difficulty of keeping in mind the great variety of purposes involved in such a complex activity as school teaching or supervision or administration is troublesome to everyone who seriously tries to do something about practical problems" (cited in Foshay, p. 319).

Using their own form of cooperative action research, Cooper and Miel (1948) collected material from professional diaries of teachers, principals, and supervisors. Cooper and Miel were interested in cooperation, thoughtfulness, exercise of judgment and democratic philosophy and the way educators balanced authority and freedom. This work, however, was not generally considered to be research. Classroom experimentation was descriptive and it did not lead to direct change in teacher practices.

Foshay argues that one of the lessons from cooperative action research of the 1950s was improved theory (1994, p. 320). Indeed, it may well have been the liberating influence of cooperative action research that led to broader forms of inquiry within supervision and to strengthening of conceptual and theoretical work.

Conceptual and Theoretical Work: A New Question Emerges

Theory development has not been considered research, nor should it be so. A *theory* contains a vision of how things are. *Theory building* involves looking at, viewing, contemplation, and speculation. The result is often a hypothesis or explanations about relationships. As such, theorizing is an important form of inquiry.

Those who have insisted on inquiry as *research*, and experimental work at that, have missed the boarder understanding of what it means to inquire. The Oxford Dictionary defines inquiry as "the action of seeking for truth, knowledge, or information concerning something; to search, research, investigate, examine." Theorizing and interpretive work, therefore, may be seen as inquiry in its fullest sense.

By the 1960s, scholars such as Wiles, in particular, had begun to articulate a new theoretical and conceptual base for supervision by drawing upon sociological research in human relations and organizational psychology. Wiles was among those who began to talk about teacher professionalism and held out an image of the teacher as a human resource. In supervision, Wiles' work in synthesizing relevant research from other fields of study and theorizing about supervisory practice began to open a new form of inquiry.

When Wiles wrote *Supervision for Better Schools* (1950, 1955), he believed that there was a rapidly evolving supervisory practice that lacked theoretical grounding:

The supervisors in one system may hold a philosophy and use procedures that are in direct conflict with those of supervisors in a system twenty miles away. Even within the same system teachers with several years of experience have probably encountered several types of supervision (1955, p. 5).

Wiles was concerned about practices that he believed were left over from authoritarian supervisory practice, which had the supervisor "directing and judging activity." He was no less concerned about the direction in which democratic supervision had gone, believing it to be more manipulative than democratic.

Wiles saw educational research, particularly research on supervision, as limited, and turned elsewhere to find a research base to confirm his theory of supervision. In the *Encyclopedia of Educational Research*, published in 1960, Wiles wrote, "Studies in the areas of leadership, communication, human relations, and group process all provide data which can be used to formulate hypotheses concerning the most effective procedures for supervisors to use" (p. 1442).

His own textbook had attempted to do this, as he noted in the introduction to the 1955 edition:

The entire book has been an attempt to state the implications of present research in the fields of learning, group dynamics, psychiatry, group therapy, social psychology human relations, and communications for the way in which supervisors should seek to fulfill their function (1955, p. 333).

A section entitled "Selected Significant Research" cites work that has informed his theory, including an array of studies from the natural and social sciences. A review of research on leadership for the *Encyclopedia of Educational Research*, published in 1960, led Wiles to conclude that "a supervisor who hopes to be an effective leader in the staff will be active, cooperative, and sensitive to the feelings and thoughts of others" (1960, p. 1443). Literature on group process held the following implications, "If a supervisor hopes to assist in the development of a program that has the support of the total staff, he must be concerned with improving group feeling, morale, and cohesiveness" (1960, p. 1444). Supervisors were to be skilled in communication. Reviewing literature on the effects of communication on group decision-making and productiveness, Wiles commented, "If a supervisor hopes to facilitate communication, he will work for decrease in status lines, for constant study of the process used in the group, and for desirable physical structure and competent group leadership" (1960, p. 1444). Wiles, who was aware of the role of the supervisor in curriculum leadership, reviewed literature on participatory decision-making, concluding that "the supervisor who hopes to be successful in promoting curriculum improvement will follow a procedure which involves the staff in the decision-making process" (1960, p. 1444).

According to Wiles, a supervisor should provide resources for improving the teaching-learning situation, promote creativity, and unleash the potential of teachers by establishing appropriate policies and systems of leadership, human relations, group process, personnel administration, and evaluation. Research was drawn upon to describe the necessary skills needed by supervisors in each of these areas and to refute the "trouble-causing assumptions" that must be overcome in order to provide suitable working conditions in schools. Many of the principles of supervision outlined by Wiles are shared by those who are currently interested in school restructuring and new professional roles for teachers.

Wiles cited the work of Roethlissberger and Dickinson (1939) who reported on a study done with workers for Western Electric. Productivity of workers gradually increased as working conditions were systematically improved and continued to increase even when those same benefits were removed in increments. He pointed out that concern from management toward workers can be more important to many than the conditions of their employment. Concern should be expressed by official leaders toward teachers in schools by providing a sense of fair treatment and belonging, keeping channels of communication open, and supporting teachers in capacities that reach beyond curriculum and instruction such as salary increases, staff advancement, and participation in policy formation. Wiles commented that the attention afforded to teachers in experimental schools during the 8 year study might have influenced them to put forth greater effort toward their students.

Another study by Roethlissberger and Dickinson demonstrated the need for a sense of belonging within a group. This intensive observational study concentrated on an industrial setting, where a small group produced piece work. The culture of the group regulated the amount of production. Status within the group was determined by producing enough to demonstrate interest and talent for the job, but not so much as to be regarded as an overachiever. Wiles pointed out that a new supervisor must be aware of similar norms among teachers within a school setting and work within the expectations of the group, gradually instituting change by developing organizational structures so that a faculty would begin to perceive the need to alter the status quo. He drew upon research associating productivity with authoritative rather than *laissez faire* attitudes, and proposed ways to strike a balance between the two.

The supervisor was to be aware of human relations within the school. By being aware of divisions among staff, expressing confidence in a faculty's ability to make decisions, and listening to teachers discuss their tensions and anxieties on the job, official leaders could promote harmony and decrease conflict. Wiles emphasized the need for supervisors to understand group process, drawing on studies by Lewin, Hemphill, and Jennings to show how individuals within groups influence each other in decision-making and setting the tone for work.

Wiles argued that supervision was also about removing irritating barriers and freeing the creative potential of teachers. He recommended taking inventory of the strengths and talents within a faculty, much as leading industries take inventories of the skills of workers. The supervisor could then establish means by which each person could apply their talents in dealing with problems or with innovation.

In the introduction to the second edition (1955), Wiles points out that principles outlined in the first edition were tried and tested by "graduate students and with administrative and supervisory staff groups in twenty states" (p. ix). He described events and quoted teachers and administrators extensively although, unfortunately, he rarely cited them specifically, often referring to them with descriptions such as "a teacher in a large midwestern city" or "one school in New York City." In doing so, Wiles denies the reader of the opportunity to examine the research to which he referred.

Lucio and McNeil (1969), were also interested in the basis for supervisory decisions. *Supervision: A Synthesis of Thought and Action* draws upon much of the literature that had influenced Wiles. In addition, Lucio and McNeil proposed that educators seek answers to solutions of problems and information for decision-making through site-based action research. Through action research, teachers were to build their own data base and develop problem-solving methods. A host of opportunities and considerations for research are offered, essentially drawn from empirical approaches to inquiry. Lucio and McNeil focus on the image of the teacher as professional, encouraging professional relationships between supervisor and teacher around exploration of important problems. Their concept of supervision is anchored in the scientific tradition.

With the exception of the work on teacher effectiveness, studies of supervision were few and far between. Recognizing this as a deficit within the field, Alfonso, Firth, and Neville (1979) set out to develop a textbook based on research to guide supervisory practice. They argued that "There is a reasonably clear and pertinent message for educational organizations with respect to relationships among teaching, the work system (technology), and instructional supervisory competence" (p. 11). To understand this message, the authors believed that supervisors needed to investigate research on leadership, communication, organization, and change. By presenting readers with a specific dimension of supervisory practice, such as leadership, and drawing upon a wide variety of methods of exploring the dimension, Alfonso, Firth, and Neville encouraged application of theory to practice. This work, as that of Wiles, contributed to our theoretical understanding of supervisory practice.

The need for theoretical and conceptual work in supervision had long been apparent, prompting periodic calls for building supervisory practice on stronger theory (Rorer, 1942; Shores, 1967; Wilson et al, 1969). Researchers such as Banghart (1960) might relegate theoretical and conceptual work to the heap of immature forms of inquiry used before the development of empirical techniques, perhaps classifying it among the rational-verbal approaches to problem solving. Synthesis of thought and theoretical speculation based on research from a wide array of disciplines, however, has advanced supervisory practice and has become a legitimate form of inquiry. We will explore this further in our examination of the clinical supervision model.

A new question had emerged to compete with the older teacher effectiveness question, "How do supervisors help

teachers to become more professional in their practice?" As Calvert had expressed it much earlier: "The aim of creative supervision, then, cannot be to get teachers to adopt some particular ideal pattern of teaching but rather to get them to grow and improve in 'their ways' of teaching" (1933, p. 54). Calvert believed that teachers were to be involved in experimenting with new ideas and developing their own methods from their ideas and experiences in cooperation with creative supervisory support. Creative, democratic supervision was more appropriate to a professional, who was naturally interested in self-improvement. More directive forms of supervisory practice, which had seemed appropriate when the teaching force was largely unprepared, were only appropriate in some situations where the teacher needed more support. It was Calvert's conviction that teachers who seemed unthinking and depended on authoritarian leadership had been made to be so by inappropriate supervisory leadership.

By the 1960s, supervisors were increasingly focused on themselves as professionals, and eager to extend this sense of professionalism to teachers. The strongest voice in the literature, if one can judge from the number of titles appearing in publications such as *Educational Leadership*, was about the supervisor as educational leader in curriculum development and reflected an image of the teacher as political professional. There were numerous exhortations to build democratic, cooperative group structures within schools that would prepare students for full engagement in civic responsibility, although few thought of the teacher's work as political in nature, assuming that objectivity required a political neutrality. Brueckner (1941), however, urged that professionals become involved in their communities and work toward an improved democratic social order. There were others, however, who continued to argue that the real concern of supervisors should be with classroom instruction (see Turney, 1966).

In the late 1950s, Morris Cogan, who had been interested in teacher professionalism in his early work, began to conceptualize a form of supervisory practice that he believed would honor the professional expertise of teacher and supervisor. Clinical supervision emerged in the early 1960s as a form of supervisory practice that has dominated the literature since the 1970s. We will examine the clinical model and the inquiry surrounding it to illustrate the multiple complexities of inquiry in supervision. Many of the studies of clinical supervision are focused on the teacher as professional; however, much of the critical inquiry in clinical supervision is more concerned with teacher reflection than it is with professionalism as Cogan had envisioned it, as we shall see.

How Can Supervisors Help Teachers to Be Critical and Self-Reflective in Practice? The Teacher as Deliberative Practitioner to Be Supported

The concern for teachers being brought into the supervisory process had not found full expression in inquiry around teacher professionalism. Indeed, Calvert's call for democratic supervision, written nearly five decades before Cogan, had not been exclusively a call for teacher professionalism. Calvert, who was principal of the George Washington

Elementary School in Pasadena, California, argued that "teachers' methods, to be effective, must be an outgrowth of their own ideas and experiences—a part of their own personalities and self-expression" (1933, p. 54), an argument for what sounds a great deal like the "teacher empowerment" of the 1980s. Calvert's two-part essay in the November and December issues of *Educational Method* has already been cited extensively in this chapter. The essay reads as though Calvert were already conversant with the research that Lewin was to conduct on the functioning of groups in the late 1930s and early 1940s. He observes that "Democracy is the balanced approach to a collective society toward which we are all headed—with no place for either fascistic authoritarianism or anarchistic lack of direction" (p. 54). Calvert believed that anyone whose professional responsibility included educational leadership was a supervisor. This idea of educational leadership was taken up by proponents of democratic group process in supervision during the 1930s and 1940s. Calvert's image of the teacher, however, does not appear to be contained in the image of teacher as professional. The image of teacher as deliberative practitioner assumes teacher professionalism, but it focuses on a particular kind of profession that is caring in nature and requires the caring professional to be able to make on-the-spot decisions about multiple questions related to teaching and learning. Calvert represents a long line of thinking that has seen teachers as thoughtful or deliberative practitioners when they are given the support to be so. As human beings, teachers are more than workers, more than human resources, and more than political. The conception of humans as "more than" harkens to earlier images of human beings as spiritual or transcendent in nature.

Calvert did not ask, "How do supervisors help teachers to be critical and self-reflective in practice?" This particular framing of the question is new and draws on current thinking about the nature of reflective thought. In drawing on new research from cognitive psychology, some supervisors have wondered about how to influence teacher decision-making, seeing a link between influencing thinking and teacher behavior. Costa and Gramston, whose work was discussed earlier, represent this line of inquiry, which is more akin to teacher effectiveness than it is to teacher deliberation. Teacher deliberation has not been as thoroughly studied as either teacher effectiveness or professionalism.

Other researchers have been more influenced by psychoanalytic tradition than they have by cognitive theory in their pursuit of interest in the teacher as reflective practitioner. This line of inquiry has been influenced both by humanistic philosophy and, more heavily, by pragmatic and existential thought. It implies a constructivist approach to teaching and learning that acknowledges that individuals will commit themselves to those things that draw upon their own intellectual and personal skills.

The theoretical and conceptual work of scholars such as Sergiovanni, Garman, Smyth, and Holland are closely aligned with the image of teacher as deliberative practitioner and are discussed more in depth as we review the clinical model. These theorists have as yet to articulate a rationale for deliberative practice that fully stands on its own, but they have persisted in containing their discussions within the clinical paradigm.

Nolan and Huber (1989) reviewed literature on reflective practice in supervision, observing that "although many would agree that helping teachers to become more reflective is an important goal, little is known about processes that might encourage reflective practice" (p. 126). Nolan and Huber differentiate between programs that focus on changing teacher behavior and those that seek to promote reflective practice: "Supervision from this perspective requires that the supervisor help teachers enrich the repertoire of images and exemplars that form the basis for reflective practice and help teachers use this repertoire to enhance their understanding of teaching." The following are delineated as aims of reflective supervision:

1. engaging the teacher in the process of reflective behavior
2. fostering critical inquiry into the process of teaching and learning
3. increasing the teacher's understanding of teaching practice
4. broadening and deepening the repertoire of images and metaphors the teacher can call on to deal with problems (p. 128)

In concluding their review of studies that provide empirical evidence about reflective teaching, Nolan and Huber affirm a commitment to clinical supervision.

McBride and Skau (1995) report on reflections on the supervisory process over the course of a year in which trust, empowerment, and reflection came to be seen as essentials of supervision. Their report does not offer particulars of the participant study that shaped the belief system reported, but on the system of beliefs itself. It calls for authenticity in supervision, conceptualized in much the same way as authentic assessment for students: "Similarly, authenticity in supervision within a school can be accomplished through mindful, sensitive dialogue and the provision of social support for growth and the validation of personal development" (p. 262).

For McBride and Skau, the concept of a mutually caring community is one that has implications for supervision, which "requires all parties to develop the process of trust in action and the knowledge and appreciation of one another as co-members of a single community" (p. 264).

As Nolan and Huber point out, there is a need for continued inquiry into the process of supervision for deliberative teacher action. Further theoretical and conceptual work on supervision as reflective practice in its own right, rather than as a hybrid of some other form of supervisory practice, is also needed.

The Untidy Complexity of Supervision

Now that we have looked at questions that have guided inquiry and images of the teacher implicit in each, we can begin to identify areas of confusion and overlap. An attempt to organize each of critical questions about supervision and accompanying images of teaching with exemplar studies may be found in Table 4–1. Table 4–1 further illustrates the untidy complexity of the field. While teacher effectiveness, professionalism, and reflectiveness represent images of teaching and perplexing questions that have yet to be satisfactorily answered, one cannot argue with certainty that these interests are more amenable to one form of inquiry than another. Examples can be found of both quantitative and qualitative forms of inquiry focused on each.

The emergent work on teacher deliberation is an example. Much of this work is being done in educational psychology, focusing on teacher thinking, and is experimental in nature. Supervisory inquiries into teacher thinking are sometimes closely tied to studies of the mind and reflect the desire to find out the truth of how the teacher's mind works, particularly when the supervisor is not there. The work of Costa and Gramston as well as that of Hunter has been along these lines.

Other work on teacher reflectiveness leads outward to the metaphorical, emotional, spiritual nature of human responsiveness and relies heavily on participant observation, case study, and interview data that are more qualitative in nature. Garman's work provides an example.

No form of inquiry, however, is the exclusive domain of one particular way of seeing the world. A carefully crafted participant-observation study may issue from a desire to know the truth of a thing and to examine it as it appears in "real life" rather than under controlled conditions. On the other hand, a thoughtfully constructed correlational study may issue from the desire to isolate some aspect of a problem that, in its broadest expression, is emotional or spiritual in nature.

The complexities and contradictions of inquiry are nowhere more apparent than they are in studies of the clinical supervision model.

CLINICAL SUPERVISION: CRITICAL VERSUS PRACTICAL INQUIRY

Cogan's theoretical and conceptual piece, *Clinical Supervision*, has spawned three decades of discussion and research in instructional supervision. It had generated so much excitement within the profession by the end of the 1970s that Anderson (1980) credited the concept with having brought about a "modest paradigm shift" in the field. Given the significance and volume of work generated by the clinical model, it could easily be the focus of an examination of methods of inquiry in its own right. It will be explored here, however, to illustrate the many contradictions between beliefs and actions that make categorical descriptions of inquiry in supervision such a frustrating endeavor.

It is not our intent to duplicate the numerous sources of information on the clinical model, but Cogan's theoretical and practical suggestions are explored in detail as the basis for our analysis of the nature and evolution of inquiry that the clinical model has generated. The model itself consists of what Cogan called a careful sequence of interdependent and interrelated events, the cycle of supervision:

1. Establishing the teacher–supervisor relationship
2. Planning with the teacher
3. Planning the strategy of observation
4. Observing instruction
5. Analyzing the teaching–learning process
6. Planning the strategy of the conference
7. The conference
8. Renewed planning (Cogan, 1973, p. 11)

The term *clinical* was selected both to "denote and connote the salient operational and empirical aspects of supervision in the classroom" (1973, p. 9). The model itself was to be characterized by professional collegiality, collaboration, direct observation in classrooms, analysis of observational data, and ethical conduct.

Emphasis on "collegial" relationships and support of the teacher has made clinical supervision inviting to those who favor democratic, humanistic approaches to supervision. It has also generated inquiry that is linked to the hermeneutic tradition. At the same time, Cogan's insistence on bringing about changes in teacher behavior, rooted in Thorndike's behavioristic definition of learning, has invited inquiry that is more anchored in the traditions of natural science and is often aligned with process product research. Some of the research in the hermeneutic tradition brings a critical perspective to bear on the clinical model, often challenging its assumptions, while seeming to cling to the term itself. The critical perspective has been advanced by researchers such a Sergiovanni, Garman, Smyth, and Holland. Others, such as Anderson, Glickman, Hunter, Costa, and Garmston have had a more practical orientation, focusing instead on connecting the model to broader research and developmental theory, developing aspects of the model, such as data collection and analysis, and suggesting ways to implement the model and the kinds of support supervisors need for its use.

Clinical supervision initially emerged from Cogan's work in the late 1950s and the Harvard-Newton Summer program of 1962–1963, which was developed along with Anderson and Goldhammer. Anderson recalled that it was "born out of the conscientious, sometimes agonizing search for adequate ways to plan and supervise the initial classroom efforts of the Harvard apprentices" (preservice student teachers) and to promote teacher professionalism (1986, p. 69). Cogan was concerned about the relationship between theory and practice and the way in which theory could emerge out of practice, inductively, rather than exclusively being "applied to practice as is so often the case" (Smyth, 1986b, p. 1). In 1961, Cogan started the Harvard Lexington Summer Program for in-service teachers. The first published work using the term was in 1964 (Cogan), with the first major volume on the topic in 1969, Goldhammer's book, *Clinical Supervision: Special Methods for the Supervision of Teachers*. Clinical supervision seen as differing from previous approaches to supervision in its presentation of a model and emphasis primarily on analysis rather than inspection (Sullivan, 1980).

As clinical supervision began to be practiced more widely in the early 1970s, it became the source of a growing body of literature (an interest partly promoted by considerable dissertation research at the University of Pittsburgh). Much of the early research on clinical supervision used either experimental or survey designs and frequently reflected attempts to validate the model, explore changes in teachers' behavior, and investigate teacher–supervisor relationships. Clinical supervision, however, has never developed a systematic, ongoing line of research, as Sullivan noted:

TABLE 4–1.

Teacher Effectiveness Strand	Teacher Professionalism Strand	Teacher Reflectiveness Strand
Problem: How do you get the teacher to be more efficient? Effective?	*Problem*: How do supervisors help teachers to become professional in their practice?	*Problem*: 1. How do supervisors help teachers to be critical and self-reflective in practice? 2. How do supervisors influence teacher behavior through influencing how they think about their work?
Image of the teacher: Worker to be trained.	*Image of the teacher*: A professional seeking job satisfaction	*Image of the teacher*: deliberative, capable educational leader
Philosophy: Positivism. Scientific explanation is casual in nature; inquiry is concerned with discovery of facts, modeled on natural sciences.	*Philosophy*: Humanistic. Focus on teacher needs and satisfaction.	*Philosophy*: 1. Constructivist. 2. Pragmatic.
Psychology: Behaviorist psychology, modeled on natural sciences.	*Psychology*: "Third force," drawing heavily on Maslow and human relations movement.	*Psychology*: 1. Psychoanalytic. 2. Cognitive.
Methodologies typically utilized: Patterned after natural sciences: systematic correlation and experimental control, scientific observation of phenomenon; *predominantly* the "descriptive-correlational-experimental loop," (Rosenshine & Furst, 1973) includes three phases: 1. development of procedures for describing teaching in a quantitative manner; 2. correlational studies in which descriptive variables are related to measures of student growth; 3. experimental studies in which significant variables obtained in the correlational studies are tested in a more controlled situation (pp. 122–123). Process (teaching) and product (student learning) variables are explored.	*Methodologies typically utilized*: incorporates both older methodologies and begins to apply social sciences methodologies to inquiry.	*Methodologies typically utilized*: 1. Qualitative research methodologies including case study, descriptive narrative, action research; 2. Quantitative and qualitative methodologies.
Goals: Provide direction for supervisory practice; provide directions for supervisors to change teacher behaviors to those that produce pupil learning.	*Goals*: Enable supervisors to foster teacher professional attitudes and practices that will affect their classroom performance; change the conditions of learning.	*Goals*: Influence how teachers think about their work and thus influence their teaching. 1. Equip the teacher to be self-reflective and deliberative in practice. 2. Understand the nature of teacher thinking and provide prompts/coaching that will enable the teacher to practice effectively.

Most of the cited studies which are specific to clinical supervision have very small samples and therefore have limited generalizability although they do provide suggestions for potentially fruitful research directions. Further, most of the samples, though not labeled as such, appear to be samples of convenience, often including the investigator as both subject and observer (1980, p. 23).

Although there has been little research on clinical supervision, there has been voluminous speculation about its benefits and a great deal of theoretical and conceptual work generated by the model. Common themes loop persistently throughout research reports and discourse, falling fairly loosely (but consistently) into categories that are not dissimilar

from our earlier grouping of studies around role, responses to supervision, and values of supervisory practices. Our exploration of inquiry on the clinical model is organized around these common themes:

1. Questions about the model; adequacies and inadequacies of the design of the model and its value as a supervisory strategy
2. Teacher–supervisor relationships; responses to clinical supervision
3. Theoretical and research foundations
4. The Problem of implementation

Questions About the Model

Initial research on clinical supervision was practical in orientation, considering basic questions related to the value and validation of the model. For example, Eaker (1972), considered the compatibility of its tenets and processes with the desires of teachers and administrators. His survey led to the conclusion that most teachers agreed with the assumptions of clinical supervision, but teachers were not in as strong agreement with procedures as were administrators. Turner (1976) examined how well the Goldhammer model worked with three elementary teachers. Reavis (1977), cited previously, concluded that clinical supervision creates a more positive level of communication between teachers and supervisors than do traditional methods.

A persistent question that has taken many forms over the years relates to the lack of definition of a goal of clinical instruction—or what it means to improve instruction. Cogan (1973) viewed clinical supervision as "the rationale and practice designed to improve the teacher's classroom performance." While Cogan called for supervisors to base practice on observable behavior to combat an overreliance on intuition, questions still arose about the extent to which Cogan allowed supervisors to infer needed competencies (McCleary, 1976). This concern led to a number of calls for competency frameworks (Boyan & Copeland, 1974; Harris & King, 1973; McCleary, 1976).

In contrast to a competencies approach, Sergiovanni (1976) suggested that a rigid adherence to the steps, strategies, and procedures of clinical supervision might lead to an emphasis on technocratic workflow, limiting the "conceptual capital balance" of the teacher and the supervisor. He was concerned about "the undue emphasis clinical supervision gives to teacher behavior and the corresponding apparent neglect of antecedents of this behavior" (p. 21). In arguing for a more conceptually open view of the clinical supervisory process, Sergiovanni stated:

Competency based training and performance objectives . . . are not inherently part of clinical supervision and, indeed, depending upon the enthusiasm of their advocates, may turn clinical supervision into merely another vehicle for furthering the particular ideology in question (1976, p. 21).

Garman (1982) echoed Sergiovanni's concern in questioning the "technocratic" definition of clinical supervision and argued for a more metaphorical conception of it, aligning the concepts of collegiality, collaboration, skilled service, and ethical conduct. Along with other scholars of the early 1980s, Garman called for a more teacher-empowered interpretation of the clinical model. A critical orientation to clinical supervision had emerged.

Joining Sergiovanni and Garman in the critical orientation toward clinical supervision has been Smyth (1985), who has been concerned with what might be described as inadequate views of the model, criticizing those who view clinical supervision as a delivery system through which to control teaching. In Smyth's view, it may instead promote a form of empowerment through which teachers can "problematize" taken-for-granted assumptions about teaching and institutional life. "In essence, clinical supervision stands for a view of teacher professionalism that has at its centerpiece the investment of control of pedagogical matters in the hands of teachers" (1986a, p. 33).

Holland (1988) reasoned that there are interpretive aspects in Cogan's rationale that are concerned with the understanding of the teacher for his or her actions and behavioral changes, citing Cogan (1973): "The teacher should, whenever possible and feasible, not only learn new behavior, but he should understand why he does what he does, and why it is better or worse than other things he might do." Holland examined the concept of colleagueship between supervisor and teacher, drawing on Cogan's discussion of the conference phase of the supervision cycle, in which the interpretive orientation is most apparent. Cogan had written:

Its course is unpredictable. The supervisor cannot therefore anticipate in detail how it will develop, what problems will arise, or what will force a change in direction. . . . The conference is a shared exploration: a search for the meaning of instruction (Cogan, 1973, p. 197, as cited in Holland, 1988, p. 100).

The use of data in clinical supervision is the third major interpretive component of the Cogan rationale, but one that also most strongly reflects an empirical orientation. Holland admits that Cogan did endorse the use of empirically based formal observation systems, particularly interaction analysis systems. Holland, however, saw the postobservation discussion of these instruments as "the basis for a process of hermeneutic interpretation. . . . Thus, an interpretive view of inquiry influences decisions about the empirical instruments used in clinical supervision to collect and analyze data" (1988, p. 101). Holland's interest in creating more interpretative definitions of aspects of the clinical cycle, such as focusing in on more reflective practice, has contributed to the critical tradition. Moore and Mattaliano had earlier offered an interpretive definition of clinical supervision that included helping "a teacher expand his or her perceptions of what it means to be a teacher through the discovery of strengths and weaknesses" (Moore & Mattaliano 1970, as cited in Smyth, 1986b, p. 3).

In addition to questions about the definition and the use of the model, limited inquiry has also focused on steps four and five of the clinical cycle—observing instruction and analyzing the teaching–learner process. Questions about data collection that have evolved over the decades are more in keeping with practical orientations to inquiry. Krajewski (1976) examined teachers use of Flanders Interactive Analysis and the Stanford Teacher Competence Appraisal Guide to self-appraise previously identified behavioral teaching objectives. Flanders Interactive Analysis was also used as an instrument in evaluating the model in this particular experiment. Krey et al (1977) argued that the structure of the clinical supervision model allows supervisors to create a nonpunitive determination of adequate teaching outcomes as the basis for evaluation. By the 1980s a divergence of approaches had developed to teacher observation that reflected clearly the differences between those holding practical and critical orientations to inquiry and highlighting a growing debate about the nature of the clinical model.

Garman, whose work has become more conceptual and theoretical in nature, called for the collection of "stable data," carefully getting a record of events as the basis for inductive analysis in order to empower the teacher (Garman et al, 1987). Hunter, on the other hand, used the observation to collect "script data," which the supervisor could then use as the basis for a discussion with the teacher on how to improve his or her practice (in Garman et al, 1987).

By the late 1980s, a great deal of the theoretical and speculative inquiry in supervision was focused on the question as to whether clinical supervision was as Cogan had defined it in his published work or as they believed that he intended it to be in practice. The emergent critical view was well established, dividing clinical supervision into two camps. The practical orientation to clinical supervision is closer to the teacher effectiveness strand of inquiry in its concerns and goals, even though Cogan had made teacher professionalism an objective. The critical orientation suggests several alliances: teacher professionalism as political action, seen in Smyth's work; teacher professionalism as human resources, as Sergiovanni has interpreted the clinical model; and teacher deliberation, in the work of Garman and Holland. These orientations—the practical and critical—are evidenced in reports and discussions of teacher supervisor relationships, theoretical and research foundations and the problem of implementation as well as in work focusing on adequacies and inadequacies of the design model.

Teacher–Supervisor Relationships

It is not surprising that much of the inquiry in clinical supervision has centered on the role of the supervisor in maintaining the relationship between the supervisor and teacher. The Cogan rationale gives considerable attention to the nature of "colleguality," a term coined in *Clinical Supervision*. Cogan assumes that the teacher who trusts will be willing to share his or her goals, problems, strengths, weaknesses, and, more importantly, to change his or her classroom behavior. The "collegual" relationship, however, is to be *professional* rather than personal. This is an important distinction. While the supervisor is committed to the teacher as a human being, he or she is ethically bound to remember that the clinical role is to improve the classroom experience of students through improving the teacher's classroom performance. Cogan explains that this does not mean that the "collegual" relationship is cold, distant, or neutral. It will be marked by intensity because of the close interaction between teacher and supervisor at every phase of the cycle. The interaction

Is not personal in the sense that its object is the person, as it might be in an encounter group or in psychotherapy. The target of clinical supervision is not the teacher, it is the teacher's classroom behavior. One does not have to yield one's privacy nor yet invade the privacy of others in order to participate in clinical supervision (1973, p. 71).

Maintaining the kind of professional objectivity required of the clinical supervisor requires both person and task orientation. Cogan locates the roots of person and task oriented leadership styles in industrial supervision. He points out that while there are differences in industrial and educational settings, there is much to be learned from similarities to be found between supervision in industry and in education. "At the very least," Cogan suggests, "the supervisors in both fields are trying to change human behavior." In such change, "the relationship between supervisor and supervisee certainly makes a difference" (1973, p. 50).

Many of the questions related to teacher–supervisory relationships are concerned with the issues of authority, trust, behavior change, and collaboration. We again see here practical and critical orientations to the model.

A vigorous debate has been over the question of authority. Many of the initial studies of clinical supervision were concerned with bringing about a change in the teacher's classroom behavior (Garman, 1971; Kerr, 1976; Krajewski, 1976; Skrak, 1973). As the critical orientation emerged, questions surfaced about the authority dynamic between supervisor and teacher (Frymeir, 1976; Markowitz, 1976). For example, Cogan was concerned with the possible superior–subordinate relationship between the supervisor and the teacher, stating that if a clinical supervisor is a "helper," then the teacher is someone who needs help. As a solution to this dilemma, he suggested framing the supervisor and teacher as colleagues, emphasizing mutual support and a special kind of partnership between them. In this view the supervisor would be competent in observation, the analysis of teaching, and the processes connected with the cycle of supervision. The teacher would be more competent in knowledge of curriculum, students, school, and the students' subsocieties (Cogan, 1973, 1976).

Two steps in Cogan's cycle of supervision, however, create the possibility of an unequal collegial partnership. In step three—planning the strategy of the observation—the supervisor plans the objectives, the processes, and the physical and technical arrangements for the observation and the collection of data. The teacher takes a role as determined by the supervisor's assessment of his or her development. In step six—planning the strategy of the conference—the supervisor generally develops the plan, alternatives, and strategies for conducting it in the early stages of the conference, relegating more responsibility to the teacher as he or she becomes adept at the process of identifying behavior changes and analyzing data (Cogan, 1973).

Flanders considered the question of how to guide the teacher in his or her process of self-analysis. He stated that clinical supervision's goals are not to be confused with research on teacher effectiveness; rather, they are more like action research. The supervisor takes a position toward the teacher that ranges from "high" to "low," depending on how the supervisor perceives the teacher's ability to use the instructional materials (1976). The debate over authority was still unresolved by the mid-1980s. Garman argued that "as a temporary defense as well as an early stage of identification with the role of supervisor, the use of technique should be respected" (1986a, p. 33).

Another recurring question related to authority dynamics revolved around the meaning and use of trust between supervisor and teacher. Turner (1976) supported Goldhammer's emphasis on rapport as an essential ingredient in clinical supervision. Kerr (1976) asked if clinical supervision could affect a change in teacher attitudes toward components and assumptions of clinical supervision, teacher levels of open-mindedness, and change in classroom teaching. He stated that research results indicated that the more open-minded the teacher, the greater the willingness to engage in direct two-way communication with the supervisor. Kerr suggested educating both teachers and supervisors in the clinical supervision process and making supervisors more aware of those qualities teachers find most valuable in a teacher–supervisor relationship.

The question of teacher growth and empowerment has emerged within the trust and authority debate, again reflecting practical and critical orientations as well as the split between those concerned with effectiveness and those with empowerment. Smyth has suggested that clinical supervision can act as a framework within which teachers can collaborate in constructing and interpreting their own teaching and learning theories (1984, 1985, 1986a, 1986b, 1986c, 1986d, 1988). Garman (1982) has also suggested that the image of the clinical cycle can refer to high levels of involvement and commitment that press participants toward the "connectedness" of collegiality. She has voiced concern, however, about how authentic collegiality can exist when it is the teacher's performance that is being scrutinized, and not just the supervisor's (1986a). Holland has described the importance of the joint construction of meanings within the supervisory process as a possible solution to the dilemma of authority (1988). Glickman (1988, 1985) saw teacher empowerment as related to developmental levels or stages of growth that should prompt the clinical supervisor to respond with developmentally appropriate actions. Much of this work has been theoretical and speculative in nature, with some research primarily based on interpretative methodologies (Goldsberry & Nolan, 1982; Russell & Spafford, 1986). Smyth's *Case Studies in Clinical Supervision* (1984) provides a series of windows on various aspects of the model, particularly the teacher–supervisory relationship.

Sergiovanni suggested that supervisors need to be concerned with two platforms that the teacher brings to the classroom: an espoused platform and a platform in use. The espoused theory may differ from the theory in use, which may or may not be compatible with the espoused theory. The supervisor attempts to provide "an appropriate support system and the cultivation of adaptable alternatives as the teacher seeks to modify his platform in use" (1976, p. 25). Sergiovanni's human resources view of clinical supervision places the issue of authority with the teacher. The supervisor supports, but change resides with the teacher as he or she begins to bring the two platforms into greater congruence.

Much of the inquiry centered more specifically on the supervisor been directed to exploring the inconsistency of supervisors' actions (and interactions) with teachers in the face of educational innovation. Cogan (1973) considered the inability of supervisors to offer a consistent program that includes novel educational innovation, calling for an internal logic for the professional practitioner. Gordon (1973) examined the actual behavior of supervisors in working with teachers in relation to their espoused views and beliefs. In the context of clinical supervision as improvement of teacher behavior, Gordon asked about the behaviors supervisors deem most effective in working with teachers in one-on-one conferences. He found that "advising-and-informing" was the single most reported behavior in the study (p. 462), prompting him to argue for supervisor behavior competencies. Harris (1976b), who had called for a conceptual cube model of competencies in an earlier work with King (Harris & King, 1973), considered the question of the role of the clinical supervisor in the growing accountability and competency movement of the 1970s. Harris suggested a list of 24 competencies for supervisors that related to teacher growth. This list included setting instructional goals for the teacher, designing instructional units, and providing in-service education (p. 335). Constructive teacher outcomes from such practices included a "new tolerance for critical appraisal" (p. 335).

Inquiry about the effects of clinical supervision on the teacher in the supervisory relationship has looked at improvement of teacher practice and the direction of behavioral change. It has also examined the developmental level of the teacher (Garman, 1986a; Glickman, 1985). This work has been practical in orientation. Other inquiry into the use of collaboration and discourse of clinical supervision as a framework with which to help teachers begin uncovering layers of meaning in their practice is more critical in orientation (Garman, 1986b; Holland, 1988; Smyth, 1984, 1985, 1986a). There is no one image of the teacher as skilled worker, professional (human resource or political), or reflective practitioner that emerges from a focus on the relationship between teachers and supervisors in a clinical model; rather, one glimpses multiple images, sometimes within the work of one scholar.

One of Cogan's central arguments for a clinical model had to do with the resistance of teachers to change. Citing the "failed innovations" of the 1960s, Cogan argued that the clinical supervisor could serve as change agent. He reasoned that the supervisor's role could involve functions such as developing teacher initiative and a commitment to faculty experimentation, supporting worthwhile innovations until new procedures become integrated into previous routines, and preventing intrafaculty tensions (1976, p. 12). Sullivan, however, has raised a number of questions about the relationship between clinical supervision and planned change; for example, Sullivan identifies tension at play between the emergent aspects of the change process that clinical supervision might foster and those aspects of this process that are not compatible with a clinical model. Cogan had insisted that clinical supervision focused on in-class supervision. As Sullivan commented: "If clinical supervision is to be useful in schools, the out-of-class duties traditionally associated with supervision must be dealt with in ways compatible with the design of clinical supervision" (Sullivan, 1980, p. 30).

The adequacy of support structures in schools to promote teachers as change agents, however, was questioned by Smyth (1984), who found it problematic for supervisors and administrators to supervise teachers. Smyth pointed out that the "possibility still exists for one party effectively to oppress and disenfranchise the other" (p. 27).

Theoretical and Research Foundations

While Cogan had intended to develop theory inductively from practice, the actual development of clinical theory has been problematic. Cogan had envisioned an emergent theory providing the teacher with a methodology by which to monitor improvement in practice (Smyth, 1986b). Garman, however, has questioned the consistency of Cogan's views with regard to teachers as researchers:

There was one inconsistency, however, in Cogan's writing. His earlier work on professions noted that one of the criteria for an established profession presumes a specialized body of knowledge for which practitioners, as a part of the community of scholars, are responsible for continual contributions. Yet in his 1975 article he stated, "We do not propose that school teachers should be researchers" (Garman 1986b, p. 6).

Garman went on to say that Cogan's view of teachers conducting research was understandable in the positivistic-research context of his time (1987b, p. 7).

Sergiovanni (1976) described clinical supervision as developing out of a "branch method," which is a framing that has influenced its relationship to theory:

The evolution of clinical supervision into its present form could be described as following a pattern similar to Lindblom's "branch" method. Here practices and policies evolve incrementally as decision-makers engage in "successive limited comparisons."

The branch method is in contrast to the more theory-oriented "root" method where practices and policies are derived from clear goals, the generation of alternatives, comprehensive evaluation and rational selection of the optimizing alternative. Lindblom convincingly argues that "the limitations of the second method are greater than the first" (1976, p. 20).

By the middle 1980s Garman was pointing to the paradigm shift in research from quantitative to qualitative and its effect on the nature of research on clinical supervision. Research in the hermeneutic tradition allowed teachers to be concerned with professional knowledge instead of with "scientific" knowledge (1986b). Smyth (1984) has theorized that this form of supervision can be used in an emancipatory way, allowing the teacher's own interpretations and theories to constitute the basis for his or her professional growth. Garman (1986a), however, problematized the possibility, although not the value, of teachers building theory by adapting the original techniques of Cogan. Citing Zeichner's (1980) concern that clinical supervision faces difficulty in trying to construct a systemic critical awareness in schools, Garman questions the possibly subversive role of the cooperating teacher and the press of school routines. She stresses the need, however, for teachers and supervisors to "adopt an inductive approach to inquiry and to allow for a phenomenological analysis of events as they unfold in action" (1986a, p. 29).

Sergiovanni has also questioned the problematic nature of technique to theory:

For clinical supervision to emerge as a professional field it must be based on premises underlying valid/valuable theories: Clinical supervision requires a theory which provides for normative interests and concerns; which admits to both configuration and meaning reality, which acknowledges the different existence's of espoused theories of action and theories embodied in use; which accommodates to the "clinical mind" of teachers and teaching; and which places the reconstruction of teaching at the center of its conceptual structure (1986, p. 56).

The Problem of Implementation

Although extensively discussed, clinical supervision has had only a limited impact on schools in this country, according to Sullivan: "The reality is that clinical supervision has not been widely used in schools or does it appear to completely fit into the current schemes of operation" (1980, p. 30). While one could point to the number of states and school districts that have adopted Hunter's clinical model as counterevidence, it is certainly arguable that considerable inquiry has been about various constraints to application of the clinical model in schools. A surprisingly large number of these questions about limitations to the model are subsumed by broader issues, in effect, creating a subtext to inquiry on clinical supervision. Explorations related to the problem of implementation, which has been discussed previously in relation to other studies, include:

1. Ambiguous meaning of "the improvement of practice"
2. Tension between "workflow and conceptual capital"
3. View of the model as a delivery system rather than a form of teacher empowerment
4. Supervisor–teacher role ambiguity
5. Underlying epistemology of the participants
6. Unexplored tensions between one' platform in use and espoused views
7. Conflict between behavioral aspects of the model and the goal of collaboration
8. Lack of an avenue for conflict resolution within the model
9. Conflict between school structures that limit and evaluate teachers and the goal of collaboration
10. Press of educational innovation on the model
11. Cogan method prevents teacher construction of meaning
12. Cogan method promotes teacher construction of meaning if used correctly by supervisors
13. Difference between evaluation and assessment
14. Enculturating influences of the school
15. Co-opting of supervision by the cooperating teacher

In addition to the litany of constraints to be found in research on various aspects of the model, inquiry has focused explicitly on the question of constraints. Cogan identified three sets of forces that helped shaped clinical supervision: (1) inadequacies in the preservice education of teachers; (2) the inability of teachers to relate productively to the "oscillations of educational innovation" (p. 3); and (3) the need for an "articulation of an internal logic—a rationale—for the professional practitioner" (p. 3). These forces, Cogan argued, presented the need for a rationale to provide "a psychological–sociological frame of reference for the system of procedures, attitudes, goals, relationships, and ethics that govern the practice of clinical supervision" (p. 3).

Sergiovanni (1976) who followed Cogan, theorized that the essential ingredients of clinical supervision would include "the establishment of a healthy general supervisory climate, a special supervisory mutual support system called colleagueship, and a circle of supervision comprising conferences, observation of teachers at work, and pattern analysis" (p. 20).

Harris (1976a) considered this question from the point of view of school organizational constraints and personal limitations of teachers, suggesting, "The structure of strategy which emphasizes in-classroom phenomena, analytical modes of inquiry, and verbal interaction may tend to exclude other procedures promoting change in teacher behavior" (1976a, p. 87).

It may be that implementation of clinical supervision is a problem only if one is concerned that it occur with a high degree of fidelity. Snyder, Bolin, and Zumwalt (1991) argue that in curriculum implementation, researchers have been preoccupied by fidelity of implementation and the phenomenon of mutual adaptation (which suggests that both the model and the site where it is implemented will make adjustments). An emergent view of curriculum enactment draws on a published curricula and curriculum models as one of many sources in a constructivist creation of curriculum by those participating in it. In a similar way, one might ask about the extent to which proponents of the clinical model of supervision are willing to see it adapted or to allow it to be transformed by users so that it becomes something other than clinical supervision. The concept of *fidelity*, however, has become more complex in the case of clinical supervision. It is evident in the literature that fidelity has different meanings to those who have practical and critical orientations. Those with the practical orientation have been most concerned with implementation of the model as Cogan described it in *Clinical Supervision* (1973), or following Goldhammer (1969). Scholars with a critical orientation seem to argue that Cogan's actions and intentions were not has he described them. For these scholars, fidelity seems to be to the person rather than to the practice he named.

Garman, who has been one of the most articulate defenders of clinical supervision from a critical perspective, has developed a continuing line of inquiry that seems almost completely unrelated in purpose, philosophical orientation, and practice to the model as outlined by Cogan in *Clinical Supervision*. While Garman speaks of a procedure for reflecting on action through the use of stable data and reflection through recollection that has been described as similar to Cogan's cycle (Nolan & Huber, 1989), close examination of her work suggests a very different set of assumptions about teachers and a trust of the intuitive, aesthetic, and subjective that Cogan seemed to fear. While Cogan's cycle leads to a "closed loop," to use Sergiovanni's term, Garman's procedure leads to an opening of possibilities for construal of meanings. Indeed, Garman noted that although her conception of clinical supervision had evolved she has continued to use the term *clinical supervision* out of respect for Cogan (1982). Garman (1986a) has considered how underlying philosophical orientations frame one's view of the supervision process, observing that each professional must accept the responsibility for shaping his or her own rationale through self-understanding and inquiry" a rationale that makes sense within everyday events and contributes to the professional commu-

nity one represents" (1986b, p. 2). Even so, Garman has been unwilling to let go of a name that cannot contain the process she envisions and has articulated.

Smyth, who has vigorously championed the search for meaning in teaching and supervision through clinical supervision, gives attention to the meaning of *clinical* and Cogan's construal of the term, arguing that what Cogan "clearly had in mind" was "a much less prescriptive and a more liberating view of supervision" than older forms (1985, p. 5). Smyth speaks of redeeming the process, and a "concerted and critical return to what its mentors had in mind," drawing on Sergiovanni's 1980 description of the model:

Constructing clinical supervision as a process with the capability of enabling teachers to undertake fundamental transformations of perspective goes to the very heart of the process. . . . In part, this means tearing our thoughts and actions about clinical supervision away from their marriage to purely behavioral concepts, lessening the concern with the process and procedural aspects, and deepening a commitment to tackling epistemological issues (p. 7).

Smyth has argued for the process to explore the taken for granted through a critical stance that involves "collaboration in marshalling intellectual capacity so as to focus upon analyzing, reflecting on, and engaging in discourse about the nature and effects of practical aspects of teaching and how they might be altered" (1985, p. 9).

The question remains as to whether critical advocates of clinical supervision are implicitly endorsing a way of working with teachers that is deeply embedded in Cogan's ideology by clinging to his form. A careful analysis of Smyth's work suggests that he is most interested in what might be termed a *political ecology* of practice, with teachers and supervisors working together to study the human events and processes of teaching and learning as they occur in the classroom through collection of data, analysis of patterns, questioning of meanings, and dialogue about a wide array of pertinent literature. This work seems much more at home within the context of the cooperative action research movement of the 1940s that provided the rationale and context for critical reflection on practice without the political trappings of behaviorist psychology inherent in the Cogan model. It would be interesting to see what form of supervisory practice might emerge from an energetic and thoughtful explication of cooperative action research.

The Ongoing Dialectic

Much of the inquiry in clinical supervision reflects an uneasy dialectic between aspects of clinical supervision's model and tenets (i.e., propositions) and its underlying value assumptions. Cogan's rationale hinges on one major argument: Older models of supervision do not change teacher behavior. Nolan and Hueber (1989) argue:

Changing teacher behavior is not the most important goal of the supervisor who sees teaching as reflective practice. The critical task of the supervisor from the perspective of reflective practice is to help teachers engage in reflective behavior more successfully (p. 128).

In the conclusion to their review of research on reflective practice through instructional supervision, however, Nolan and Huber claim that the basic requirements of reflective teaching "convincingly affirm the potential of clinical supervision that Cogan and Goldhammer envisioned for nurturing reflective practice" (p. 143). Much of the discussion of the emancipatory power that clinical supervision offers for the teacher to make empowered choices about professional growth is contradictory to the "bottom line" in the Cogan rationale with its focus on manifest behavior. Embedded in the rationale for *Clinical Supervision* is a value commitment that places more emphasis on teacher performance than it does on teacher thinking, intentions, and personal meaning. The clinical cycle is not designed to ask questions of personal meaning, supposing these to be outside the clinical domain. Scholars who are most concerned with questions of meaning, therefore, have reconceptualized clinical supervision and underwritten it with a new set of philosophical commitments that are not compatible with those delineated by Cogan.

In developing clinical supervision, Cogan wished to promote the professionalism of teaching. Much of the overarching inquiry in clinical supervision has been concerned with this issue. Some of these questions have examined the autonomy of teachers, the ability of teachers to connect theory to practice, and, increasingly, the teacher's search for meaning. These questions, which have surfaced repeatedly in clinical supervision, all share a persistent common denominator: the behavioral foundations of "the cycle of supervision." Born at a time when educational research was trying to become more "scientific" and following a behaviorist definition of education, clinical supervision has itself been situated in a search for meaning. The inquiry in clinical supervision shares a concern with that of traditional supervision for the improvement of practice and the relationship between the supervisor and the teacher. Unlike research in more traditional forms of supervision, however, inquiry in clinical supervision has been unusually focused on itself—especially on possibilities for teacher growth and professionalism. Much of this inquiry has been framed by the uneasy dialectic between the promise and the reality of clinical supervision.

Little inquiry in supervision has focused on the history of the profession. In calling attention to failures of traditional supervision Cogan apparently spoke outside of an historical context. Traditional images of supervision described in his rationale for clinical practice seem to draw on negative stereotypes rather than on the historical reality that includes an array of images. While arguing for enhancement of the profession of teachers, Cogan seems to have failed to see the work of teacher and supervisor together as an historic action that has a set of traditions to which both present and future are linked. There is continuity in experience in such a tradition as old practices take on new form.

Has framing the discussion of supervision around clinical supervision and fidelity to Cogan advanced the field of supervision or impeded its transformation into more powerful forms of practice? While the discussion has tried to consider the real problems of teachers, whether from practical or critical perspectives, it is arguable that these discussions have stalled progress in the field. Instead of inventing new ways of conceptualizing supervision, the critical branch of clinical inquiry has insisted on retaining the old name and many of the old processes, assuming that these can be catapulted from their behavioristic framework by bringing teachers into the process in a way that enables them to be self-critical and reflective about practice. By focusing on questions about how to make the clinical model more than it is, researchers may have precluded the opening of new questions. And, by insisting on retaining the name, proponents of clinical supervision as reflective practice have enmeshed themselves in its inherent contradictions.

Perhaps more than any other model of supervision, the clinical model illustrates the excitement as well as the frustration of attempting to come to grips with improvement of teaching and learning. There are no easy or certain ways to classify inquiry in the field. To understand it, one must become immersed in its messiness, respect is constraints, and live with its contradictions.

Summary

It is apparent that the field of supervision, while often deplored as theoretically weak and characterized by a paucity of research, has a consistent tradition of inquiry. This tradition has continued despite the fact that the existence of supervision has constantly been challenged, both at the university and within school systems. Supervisory inquiry has led to vigorous lines of research on its many related interests, such as teacher effectiveness, professionalism, and teacher thinking and decision-making.

In exploring methods of inquiry in supervision, we have heard a number of questions raised across time and around substantive issues. We have examined critical questions and images of the teacher evoked by each, images that highlight different perspectives and different underlying assumptions about the nature of knowledge and inquiry in the field. We have heard "voices" of different research traditions with differing purposes, throughout, and we have encountered a number of methodological issues.

Methodological issues vary with purposes of a given study. In those studies that apply research methodology from the behavioral sciences, researchers are concerned with the operational definition of concepts, valid and reliable measures and procedures that conform to conventional standards of practice. This empiricist, or quantitative, approach to inquiry emphasizes sense knowing and the validity of belief based on what one can see and hear under controlled conditions. It is committed to basing conclusions on facts. In its most uncritical form, empiricist inquiry equates truth and the semblance of fact that is garnered from controlled observation. Any researcher will make choices about what to observe, what to ask, and how to frame the question. An appropriately critical empiricism recognizes its own partial and limited view of facts and does not equate truth with semblance of facts.

Early supervisors were influenced by the growing field of educational research and its promise to reduce the complexities of human interaction to clearly observable and understandable facts of a situation. Facts, however, are not the only interesting product of inquiry. Facts do not assist us in understanding the meaning of a phenomenon. The empirical search for efficient and effective teachers or for the characteristics of teacher thinking does not concern itself with the teacher's intentions, meanings, and imagination. These are the concerns of most interest to researchers following the hermeneutic tradition that desires to describe the events of a situation as perceived by actors within the setting.

Research that has proceeded from social sciences methodologies and the hermeneutic tradition utilizes an array of techniques. It rejects the experimental scientific methods of the empiricist as the source of fact and insists on multiple methods for understanding reality, developing those appropriate to the uniquely human characteristics and actions of people. Some studies utilize rigorous designs that draw upon multiple methods and carefully conform to what have become acceptable canons of qualitative research. Others are more concerned with self-reporting and the perspective of participants; therefore, they do not attempt to check the validity of their data. An uncritical qualitative researcher may pose justifications, opinions, and apologetics as inquiry. An appropriately critical researcher in the interpretive tradition will be mindful of a theoretical framework that both limits and informs work.

What we would now describe as *qualitative methodology* appears in the earliest forms of inquiry in supervision. It was not considered research, however, and it took a place below empiricist approaches to inquiry in status.

Those who wish to understand supervision and its effects need multiple forms of inquiry for the exploration of myriad issues and practices of teachers and schools. Schooling is made up of both intentions and actions—persistent questions in supervision reflect this. As Bellack observed, in speaking of research on teaching; "The persistent questions are not solely in what direction and how classroom teaching might be changed, but equally important, what are the roots of classroom practices as we know them, and what are the forces in school and society that sustain them" (1978, p. 12). Bellack cites Merton (1956), who stressed that "some of the most significant problems in social inquiry emerge when there is lack of congruence between intentions and outcomes of human actions" (Bellack, 1978, p. 14).

To explore the roots of supervisory practice and the context in which they have emerged and are sustained requires an historical perspective. Research on supervision, however, has been focused on structural issues more than it has been concerned with understanding the development of these structures. One of the striking outcomes of this review of methods of inquiry has been the absence of historical inquiry.

Inquiry, broadly defined, includes more than research, extending to theoretical, conceptual, and philosophical speculation. These forms of inquiry abound in the literature on supervision. The clinical model has stimulated numerous conceptual arguments, reconceptualization of the model and theoretical and philosophical discussions.

Despite nearly a century of inquiry, there remain pressing questions about supervision that continue to invite systematic inquiry. These questions beg a larger question, "Why do the same questions keep coming up?"

We seem to have encountered a set of problems without solutions, problems that persist despite the many ways in which we have made inquiry into them. The questions around persistent problems have contradictory answers, diverting interest into methodological issues and apologetics for one form of supervision over others.

We may have reached what Langer (1957) referred to as the "tag end of an inspired era" and need new questions to guide inquiry. Questions do more than frame problems. Implications for principles of analysis and unconscious presuppositions will be within our questions. Though we admittedly live within the boundaries of our own time, context, experience, imagination, and tacit assumptions, our questions and their answers do not always reflect an understanding of these constraints. We tend to see answers as concluding or closing a search; however, if one begins to allow that there is more to be understood than can now be understood by virtue of our limits—time, context, experience, imagination—then one opens the future to movement beyond where knowledge and practice seem to have come to rest in models of practice to be defended.

NEW DIRECTIONS FOR INQUIRY

What might be questions powerful enough to launch a new era of inquiry in supervision? If, as Beane (1995) suggests, diversity in a complex world is at the center of the search for coherence, then we would do well to ask about voices of diversity in the literature on supervision. When this question is raised certain silences become apparent, representing unhonored questions or those that failed to be raised in the dominant culture. It is here that we encounter issues of race, class, and gender (including sexual identity and orientation), the marginalization of women, children, the poor, people with special needs, and racial and ethnic minorities.

It cannot be said that voices of those concerned about issues of democracy in supervisory practices within schools of a diverse society have been silent, but one has to scour the literature to find them. There were discussions of how to bring an immigrant population into the dominant culture prior to the turn of the century. Lively discussions over rural and urban supervision appear in the early literature of the 1900s. Among these is Heffernan's (1931) discussion of rural supervisors and their duties, which included placement of and adaptation of curriculum for students with special needs—handicapped children described as "deaf mutes," "amputees," and "foreign born immigrants," drawing on the language of the day. By and large, concerns for students with special needs were to be held outside of the mainstream literature. A body of literature on supervision in special areas, however, has developed and offers potential for deeper understanding of the general supervisory process.[4]

The way supervision has been organized and practiced has had profound implications for women. From the earliest history of supervision, women have assumed some positions of leadership in the field, but these women apparently entered the "conversation" being held in the mainstream literature, rather than raising issues unique to women, despite the many compelling issues faced by women teachers who constituted the largest part of the teaching force and despite the fact that these women were usually supervised by men.

Until recent decades, the literature offered few glimpses of these issues. For example, women teachers were expected to be single. Supervisors, who were expected to be aware of grounds for dismissal, were often placed in the position of enforcing policies that discriminated against women. Edwards (1925) reported on cases involving marriage as a statutory ground for dismissal of women teachers, pointing out that while laws had been upheld that authorized boards of education to dismiss teachers at pleasure, "dismissal of teachers because of marriage is regarded by the courts as unreasonable" (p. 695). Women, however, could still be dismissed by a board, however, for absence from school to give birth to a child:

Absence from school on the part of a married teacher for the purpose of giving birth to a child constitutes a neglect of duty for which she may be dismissed. The law contemplates that every teacher, married or single, be given the opportunity to fulfill the obligations of her contract. So long as such obligations are met, the law is satisfied; when they are not met, the teacher may be removed (p. 695).

The landmark publication of The Department of Superintendence, its Eighth Yearbook (1930), is silent on the subject, and the literature remained silent until recent decades. Feminist perspectives by scholars such as Garman, Hazi, Holland, and Kellan have been vigorously introduced to the field.

Policies and practices discussed in the mainstream literature on supervision were undoubtedly informed and perhaps shaped by the presence of large numbers of African Americans in segregated schools in the South and collecting in urban centers across the nation, by the immigration of Asians who were confined to ghettos in many cities, and by migrant workers and displaced farmer families who flocked to cities to find work. There is little in mainstream literature, however, to suggest that there were any issues or challenges of cultural diversity that affected supervisory practice. When mention is made at all, it is scant. For example, in a discussion of supervision practices in Fayette County, Kentucky, Baker (1923) described his aim to give each teacher at least one long-term visit during the school term, noting that "colored schools" were not slighted. Baker's account offers no clues as to the unique needs of teachers and students in segregated schools. The topic is not even mentioned in the eighth yearbook.

A special issue of *Educational Leadership*, published in March 1945, was entitled "We the Children." It was focused on intercultural understanding. The issue was organized around the words of over 1,200 young people from elementary school through college freshmen, it represented a "diversity of race, creed, and background" (Cunningham & McCue, 1945, p. 242). Seventy-nine adults representing educational institutions in cities across the country participated in collecting material for the issue. Cunningham and McCue wrote in the editor's comment:

It is with mixed feelings that we bring you these statements of children. It is with heavy heart that we record the crooked thinking and the injustice—the one no less tragic than the other. And these are our children, American children—not the youth of Hitler's Germany or the half-starved children of China or Greece. These are the children we think we are teaching to think as we lead them through the mysteries of reading, writing, and arithmetic. These are the children we cheat of their democratic birthright unless we teach them to think as clearly in the realm of man's relationship to man as in the area of the relationship of two to two.

It is with joy we bring you the statements of young people who have learned to reason with vigor and act with courage and conviction. There is high hope for our world in the words of some youngsters who recognize our problems with remarkable clarity and express an eagerness to help rid our country of intercultural strife.

While *Educational Leadership* was one of the primary journals read by supervisors, there did not appear to be any follow-up regarding what school supervisors as a unique group might do to further the goals advanced in this forward looking issue.

The Journal of Negro Education was a source for airing questions related to supervisory practice in segregated schools. For example, following school desegregation laws of 1950s questions about the future of principals and teachers in segregated schools took on a new urgency (Coutnen, 1975; Groff, 1961; Spruill, 1960; Thompson, 1953). Anticipating changes in the future, Thompson questioned the future status of "Negro principals and supervisors" (p. 100), anticipating that desegregation would bring competition for jobs. In a study of African American teachers, Spruill (1960) drew upon a review of the literature on desegregation and integration, a survey questionnaire to 280 teachers in desegregated schools, and case studies of 28 teachers in nine of the schools surveyed. He concluded that Negro teachers have a high degree of preparation, and that they have been accepted by other teachers and parents in the states surveyed. Groff (1961) surveyed heads of education departments of selected Negro colleges in the South, calling for continued optimism and "vigorous efforts to protect the civil rights of teachers" (p. 11). Meanwhile, the mainstream literature on supervision was virtually silent in response to these compelling supervisory issues of desegregation.

Clifton M. Claye (1962) examined leadership behavior of principals by using a leader behavior questionnaire with 73 teachers and 31 principals who were students of staff members at Texas Southern University. Claye asserted:

Just why the Negro principal sets for himself a higher standard of leadership behavior than he actually does indicates that his efforts to meet the expectations of a particular reference group (and certainly it is not teachers) controls, to an extent, his leadership behavior . . . there is some validity in our assumption that the dual role of the Negro principal in carrying out his responsibilities to two different ethnic groups creates for him a kind of dilemma (p. 526).

Coutnen (1975) also focused on the role of the administrator, including supervisory personnel, and concluded that women and minorities both suffer from role stereotypes and are often pitted against each other for promotion. Stereotypes are different for women and blacks in that jobs for blacks do not include supervising white teachers. Women are out of the loop because of perceptions about their role in society. Coutnen observed that current discussion of minorities was limited to blacks, particularly the black principal:

More than quality education disappeared with the black principal. In the Old South, educational administration was one of the few vocations in which a black could achieve affluence, power, and middle-class respectability, and this opportunity vanished. In addition, a black principal was often the most prominent black citizen, a community leader. . . . Finally, for black children, the black educator was often the only available role model that suggested it was possible for a black to exercise authority or leadership, and this, too, was lost (p. 12).

Following desegregation, African American principals were often transferred to central office desk jobs or relegated to roles below the rank of principal, usually working with dissident blacks in a school with biracial enrollment and primarily white staff. "The belief seems to be that blacks are only capable of supervising blacks" (Coutnen, p. 14).

Townsel and Banks (1975) wrote about the challenges of urban school administration:

We must insure that the democratic dream is not killed by a lack of competent Black people striving to keep it alive. . . . One hangup in the democratic process is that educators generally accept intellectually and verbally democratic ideals but lack the emotional participation (p. 421).

Education in segregated schools presented a unique case. Education of Native Americans had been taken out of the hands of public schools and placed with the Bureau of Indian Affairs. Work on supervision in Native American contexts has only recently begun to be aired in mainstream arenas. The 1984 Mokakit Conference, "Establishing Pathways to Excellence in Indian Education" (McCue, 1986), included a paper on "Native Indian Education and Clinical Supervision," by Este. Warner (1991, 1992) has begun a line of research looking at American Indian women. A study reported in 1991 used Festinger's dissonance avoidance theory along with Bruner and Tagirui's implicit personality theory to explore the relationship between variables of ethnicity and sex-role stereotype and job satisfaction among 114 American Indian female supervisors, some of whom were supervisors in education. Findings suggest that Native American female supervisors feel that to be seen in their role has had a negative influence. They were particularly uncomfortable with sex–role stereotypes. Warner observed that

"While historic study has revealed that stereotypes of American Indian women were founded in misinterpretations of observations from a dominant culture, many have remained primary in modern descriptions of Native American women" (p. 4).

In reporting on needs of Native American education, Latham (1984) drew on data derived from observations conducted on 16 reservations in the United States. Number 15 in the list of 15 needs is "adequately supervise teachers." The paper calls for more supervision.

While issues of cultural diversity are beginning to surface in the mainstream literature, it is apparent that a great deal of restoration needs to be done to bring into supervision discourse voices that have been marginalized. Inquiry should continue into current issues and problems of supervision in culturally diverse contexts, as well as in areas that serve students with special needs, and historical inquiry is needed to help us piece together a more balanced picture of the past. The kind of information necessary for restoration will be found in mainstream academic journals or research reports of years past as well as in the diaries of school teachers, students, and supervisors who worked in segregated schools, schools with large immigrant populations, ghetto schools, and schools on reservations. It will be found in letters and unpublished autobiographies, school records and newspaper accounts, folklore and tradition, but until we pull together many fragments of information, we will not have a coherent and inclusive center to the field of supervision. Doing so, however, will mean a much broader, richer and more interesting definition of inquiry around new questions that we have yet to imagine.

If we were to think about this review of methods of inquiry in supervision, with its projection of issues and questions, as a series of voices inviting us forward, then it is critical for us to consider those who have been left out of our recorded history. It is also critical that we constantly ask ourselves who is not being heard in the present because we have neither the vision nor the experience to know how to listen to their questions. In its fullest, richest sense, education must always extend an open invitation to the unheard of, the unspeakable, and the unthinkable—an invitation to break into and challenge our assumptions and our thinking with new questions, new issues, and new possibilities. Surely, inquiry in supervision demands no less.

REFERENCES

Alexander, W. (Ed.). (1968). *The high school of the future: A memorial to Kimball Wiles*. Columbus, OH: Merrill.

Alfonso, R., Firth, G. R., & Neville, R. F. (1979). What is supervision? *Supervision for today's schools*. New York: Longman.

Alfonso, R., & Goldsberry, L. (1980). Colleagueship in supervision. In T. J. Sergiovanni (Ed.). *Supervision of teaching* (pp. 90–107). Alexandria, VA: ASCD.

Amidon, E. J., Kies, K. M., & Palisi, A. T. (1966). Group supervision. *The National Elementary Principal, 55*(5), 54–58.

Anderson, R. H. (1982). Creating a future for supervision. In T. J. Sergiovanni (Ed.). *Supervision of teaching* (pp. 181–190). Alexandria, VA: ASCD.

Anderson, R. H. (1986). The genesis of clinical supervision. In W. J. Smyth (Ed.). *Learning about teaching through clinical supervision* (pp. 8–18). Dover, NH: Croom Helm.

Asbury, C. A. (1976). Why educational research is of limited use to the community. *The Journal of Negro Education*, 21–26.

Ayer, F. C. & Barr, A. S. (1928). *The organization of supervision*. New York: D. Appleton & Co.

Baker, G. M. (1923). Supervision in Fayette County, Kentucky. *American School Board Journal 67*.

Banghart, F. W. (Ed.). (1960). *First annual Phi Delta Kappa symposium on educational research*. Bloomington, IN: Phi Delta Kappa.

Barr, A. S. (1926). An Analysis of the duties and functions of instructional supervisors: A Study of the Detroit supervisory organization. *Bureau of Educational Research, Bulletin No. 7.* Madison, University of Wisconsin.

Barr, A. S. & Reppen, N. O. (1935). The attitudes of teachers towards supervision. *Journal of Experimental Education, 3,* 237–301.

Beane, J. A. (Ed.). (1995). Conclusion: Toward a coherent curriculum. In *Toward a coherent curriculum.* Alexandria, VA: ASCD.

Bellack, A. A. (1978). *Competing ideologies in research on teaching.* Uppsala Reports on Education 1. Uppsala, Sweden: Department of Education, University of Uppsala.

Blumberg, A. (1980). *Supervisors and teachers: A private cold war.* Berkeley, CA: McCutchan Publishing Co.

Blumberg, A. (1990). Toward a scholarship of practice. *Journal of Curriculum and Supervision. 5,* 236–243.

Bolin, F. S. (1987). On defining supervision. *Journal of Curriculum and Supervision, 2,* 368–380.

Bolin, F. S. (1988). Does a community of scholars in supervision exist? *Journal of Curriculum and Supervision, 3,* 296–307.

Bolin, F. S. (1990). The status of supervision scholarship. *Journal of Curriculum and Supervision, 5,* 244–246.

Bowers, C. A. & Flinders, D. J. (1991). *Culturally responsive supervision: A handbook.* New York: Teachers College Press.

Bowers, C. A. & Flinders, D. J. (1990). *Responsive teaching: An ecological approach to classroom patterns of language, culture and thought.* New York: Teachers College Press.

Boyan, N. & Copeland, W. D. (1974). A training program for supervisors: Anatomy of an educational development. *Journal of Education Research 68,* 100–116.

Bradfield, L. E. (1953). The extent to which supervisory practices in selected elementary schools of Arkansas are consistent with generally accepted principles of supervision. Cited in Wiles, K. (1960). Supervision. In C. Harris (Ed.). *Encyclopedia of educational research* (pp. 1142–1148). New York: Macmillan.

Brim, O. G. (1933). Reconstructing our concept of scientific supervision. *Education, 53,* 577–587.

Brueckner, L. J. (1925). The value of a time analysis of classroom activity as a supervisory technique. *Elementary School Journal, 25,* 518–521.

Brueckner, L. J. (1933). The supervisory analysis of teaching. *Education,* 601–619.

Brueckner, L. J. (1941). Family life and the curriculum. *Curriculum Journal, 12,* 58–61.

Brueckner, L. J. & Cutright, P. (1927). A technique for measuring the efficiency of supervision. *Journal of Educational Research, 16,* 323–331.

Burden, P. R. (1982). *Developmental supervision: Reducing teacher stress at different career stages.* Paper presented the Annual Meeting of the Association of Teacher Educators.

Calvert, E. T. (1938). Democratic and creative supervision in principle and practice, part I and part II. *Educational Method, 18,* 54–60, 100–104.

Claye, C. M. (1962). Leadership behavior among Negro principals. *The Journal of Negro Education, 31,* 521–526.

Cogan, M. L. (1973). *Clinical supervision.* Boston, MA: Houghton Mifflin.

Cogan, M. L. (1976). Rationale for clinical supervision. *Journal of Research and Development in Education, 9,* 3–19.

Conley, D. T. (1988). District performance standards: Missing link for effective teacher evaluation. *NASSP Bulletin, 5,* 78–83.

Cook, G. E. (1976). Supervisors for the classroom: A study of the professional growth of educational supervisors in a program of clinical training. *Dissertation Abstracts International 38,* 735A.

Cooper, J. & Miel, A. (Eds.). (1948). *Personal experiences with supervision: excerpts from professional diaries.* Unpublished paper.

Cornbach, L. (1975). Beyond the two disciplines of scientific psychology. *American Psychologist, 30,* 116–127.

Costa, A. & Garmston, R. (1986). Cognitive coaching: Supervision for intelligent teaching. *Wingspan, 3,* 38–43.

Courtis, S. A. (1919). Measuring the effects of supervision in geography. *School and Society, 10,* 61–70.

Coutnen, D. (1975). *Women and minorities in administration.* National Association of Elementary School Principals. Washington, D.C., Oregon University, Eugene. ERIC Clearinghouse on Educational Management.

Crosby, M. (1969). The new supervisor: Caring, coping, becoming. In R. Leeper (Ed.). *Changing supervision for changing times.* Washington, D.C.: ASCD.

Cunningham, R. & McCue, L. C. (1945). We the children: Boys and girls discuss intercultural understanding. *Educational Leadership, 2,* 242.

Domas, S. J. & Tiedeman, D. V. (1950). Teacher competence: An annotated bibliography. *Journal of Experimental Education.*

Eaker, R. E. (1972). *An analysis of the clinical supervisory process as perceived by selected teachers and administrators.* Unpublished doctoral dissertation, The University of Tennessee.

Eash, M. J. (1969). Is systems analysis for supervisors? *Educational Leadership,* 482–489.

Edwards, I. N. (1925). Marriage as a legal cause for dismissal of women teachers. *Elementary School Journal, 25,* 692–695.

Fattu, N. A. (1960). A survey of educational research at selected universities. In F. W. Banghart (Ed.). *First annual Phi Delta Kappa symposium on educational research* (pp.1–21). Bloomington, IN: Phi Delta Kappa.

Findley, W. G. (1960). The impact of applied problems on educational research. In F. W. Banghart (Ed.). *First annual Phi Delta Kappa symposium on educational research* (pp. 43–54). Bloomington, IN: Phi Delta Kappa.

Flanders, N. A. (1976). Interaction analysis and clinical supervision. *Journal of Research and Development in Education, 9,* 47–57.

Flinders, D. J. (1991). Supervision as cultural inquiry. *Journal of Curriculum and Supervision, 6,* 87–106.

Foshay, A. W. (1994). Action research: An early history in the United States. *Journal of Curriculum and Supervision, 9,* 317–325.

Frymier, J. R. (1976). Supervision and the motivational dilemma. *Journal of Research and Development in Education, 9*(2), 36–46.

Gage, N. L. (1984). *The scientific basis of the art of teaching.* New York: Teachers College Press.

Garman, N. B. (1971). *A study of clinical supervision as a resource for college teachers of English.* Doctoral dissertation, University of Pittsburgh.

Garman, N. B. (1982). A clinical approach to supervision. In T. J. Sergiovanni (Ed.). *Supervision of Teaching* (pp. 35–52). Virginia: ASCD.

Garman, N. B. (1986a). Getting to the essence of practice in clinical supervision. In W. J. Smyth (Ed.). *Learning about teaching through clinical supervision* (pp. 19–38). Dover, NH: Croom Helm.

Garman, N. B. (1986b). Reflection, the heart of clinical supervision: A modern rationale for professional practice. *Journal of Curriculum and Supervision, 2,* 1–24.

Garman, N. B., Glickman, C. D., Hunter, M., & Haggerson, N. L. (1987). Conflicting conceptions of clinical supervision and the enhancement of professional growth and renewal: Point and counterpoint. *Journal of Curriculum and Supervision, 2,* 152–177.

Glanz, (1977). *Bureaucracy and professionalism: An historical interpretation of public school supervision in the United States, 1875–1937.* Doctoral dissertation, Teachers College, Columbia University.

Glickman, C. (1985). *Supervision of instruction: A developmental approach.* Boston, MA: Allyn and Bacon.

Glickman, C. (1988). *Supervision and Instruction: A developmental approach.* Boston, MA: Allyn and Bacon, 1985.

Glickman, C. (1992). *Supervision in transition.* Alexandria, VA: ASCD.

Goldhammer, R. (1969). *Clinical supervision special methods for the supervision of teachers.* New York: Holt, Rinehart, and Winston.

Goldsberry, L. & Nolan, J. F. (1982). *Reflective supervisory conference.* Unpublished manuscript. Pennsylvania State University.

Gordon, B. (1973). One–to–one conferences: Teacher and supervisor. *Educational Leadership, 30*(5), 459–463.

Grimmet, P. P. (1987). The role of district supervision in the implementation of peer coaching. *Journal of Curriculum and Supervision, 3,* 3–28.

Groff, P. J. (1961). School desegregation and the education of Negro teachers in the South. *Journal of Teacher Education, 12,* 8–11.

Harris, B. (1976a). Limits and supplements to formal clinical procedures. *Journal of Research and Development in Education, 9,* 85–89.

Harris, B. (1976b). Supervisor competence and strategies for improving instruction. *Educational Leadership,* 332–335.

Harris, B. M. & King, J. D. (1973). *Instructional leadership competencies for supervisors of special education.* Document #2. Austin, TX: University of Texas.

Hart, M. C. (1930). Supervision from the standpoint of the supervised. *Education, 50,* 364–368.

Henry, J. (1966). Vulnerability in education. *Teachers College Record, 64,* 144.

Holland, P. E. (1988). Keeping faith with Cogan: Current theorizing on a maturing practice of clinical supervision. *Journal of Curriculum and Supervision, 3,* 97–108.

Hughes, M. M. (1963). Utah study of the assessment of teaching. In Bellack, A. A. (Ed.). *Theory and research in teaching* (pp. 25–36). New York: Bureau of Publications, Teachers College, Columbia University.

Jackson, P. W. (Ed.). *Handbook of Research on Curriculum* (pp. 402–435). New York: Macmillan.

Judge, H. G. (1982). *American graduate schools of education: A view from abroad.* New York: Ford Foundation.

Kerr, T. G. (1976). *An investigation of the process of using feedback data within the clinical supervision cycle to facilitate teachers' individualization of instruction.* Doctoral dissertation, University of Pittsburgh. *Dissertation Abstracts International 37:* 1374A.

Kinhart, H. A. (1941). *The Effect of Supervision on High School English.* Cited in Wiles, K. (1960). Supervision. In C. Harris (Ed.). *Encyclopedia of Educational Research* (pp. 1142–1148). New York: Macmillan.

Krajewski, R. J. (1976). Putting the 's' back in ASCD. *Educational Leadership, 33,* 376.

Krey, R. D. et al. (1977). Assumptions supporting structure in clinical supervision. *Contemporary Education, 49,* 16–23.

Langer, S. (1957). *Philosophy in a new key.* Cambridge: Harvard University Press.

Latham, G. I. (1984). *Fifteen most common needs of Indian education.* Paper presented at the National Indian Child Conference. Albuquerque, NM.

Lewin, K. (1944). The dynamics of group action. *Educational Leadership,* 195–200.

Lewis, A. J. & Miel, A. (1972). *Supervision for improved instruction: New challenges, new responses.* Belmont, CA: Wadsworth Publishing Co.

Lucio, W. H, & McNeil, J. D. (1969). *Supervision in thought and action.* New York: McGraw-Hill.

Mackenzie, G. N. (1961). Role of the supervisor. *Educational Leadership, 29,* 87.

Markowitz, S. (1976). The dilemma of authority in supervisory behavior. *Educational Leadership, 33,* 367–372.

McCleary, L. E. (1976). Competencies in clinical supervision. *Journal of Research and Development in Education, 9,* 30–35.

McBride, M. & Skau, K. G. (1995). Trust, empowerment, and reflection: Essentials of supervision. *Journal of Curriculum and Supervision, 10,* 262–277.

McCue, H. A. (Ed.). (1986). Selected papers from the Mokakit Conference "Establishing Pathways to Excellence in Indian Eduction" (1st, Ontario, Canada, July 25–27, 1984). Vancouver, B.C.: Mokakit Education Research Association, Faculty of Education, the University of British Columbia.

Medley, D. M. & Mitzel, H. E. (1963). The scientific study of teacher behavior. In A. A. Bellack (Ed.). *Theory and research in teaching* (pp. 79–90). New York: Bureau of Publications, Teachers College, Columbia University.

Melby, E. O. (1929). *A critical study of the existing organization and administration of supervision: A study of current practice.* Northwestern University Contributions to Eduction School Education Series. Bloomington, IL: Public School Publishing.

Merton, R. (1956). *Social theory and social structure.* Toronto, Canada: Collier-Macmillan. In A. A. Bellack (Ed.). (1978). *Competing ideologies in research on teaching.* Uppsala Reports on Education 1. Uppsala, Sweden: Department of Education, University of Uppsala, p. 17.

Messenger, H. R. (1934). Supervision does pay! *Educational Method, 13,* 289–294.

Miel, A. (1937). Barriers to improved instruction. *Teachers College Record,* 434–440.

Miel, A. (1937). Learning to plan together. *Teachers College Record, 48,* 391–403.

Moore, J. & Mattaliano, A. (1970). *Clinical supervision: A short description.* West Hartford, CT: West Harford Public Schools.

Neville, C. E. (1925). Supervision through simplified testing. *Elementary School Journal, 25,* 696–699.

Nolan, J. F. & Huber, T. (1989). Nurturing the reflective practitioner through instructional supervision: A review of the literature. *Journal of Curriculum and Supervision, 4,* 126–145.

Nuthall, G. (1974). Contemporary models of teaching. In R. Travers (Ed.). *Second handbook of research on teaching* (47–76). Chicago, IL: Rand McNally.

Nutt, H. W. (1924). The attitude of teachers toward supervision. *Educational Research Bulletin, 3,* 59–64.

Ofek, A. (1988). *Peer supervision: A promise for the future.* Unpublished paper.

Pajak, E. (1989). *Identification of supervisory proficiencies project.* Alexandria, VA: ASCD.

Perrin, H. A. (1926). The local status and activities of general supervisors in city schools. *Elementary School Journal, 26,* 345–356.

Pittman, M. S. (1921). *The value of school supervision demonstrated with the zone plan in rural schools.* Baltimore, MD: Warwick & York.

Reavis, C. (1978). Clinical supervision: A review of the research. *Educational Leadership, 35,* 360–363.

Reavis, C. A. (1977). A test of the clinical supervision model. *Journal of Educational Research, 70,* 311–315.

Reavis, C. A. (1978). Research in review/clinical supervision: A review of the research. *Educational Leadership, 70,* 580–584.

Roberts, J. (1991). *Face-threatening acts and politeness theory: Contrasting speeches from supervisory conferences.* Paper presented at the Annual Meeting of the American Educational Research Association. Chicago, Il.

Roberts, J. (1992). *The relationship of power and involvement to experience in supervisory conference: Discourse analysis of supervisor style.* Paper presented at the Annual Meeting of the American Educational Research Association. San Francisco, CA.

Roberts, J. & Blase, J. (1993). *The micropolitics of successful supervisor-teacher interaction in instructional conferences.* Paper presented at the Annual Meeting of the American Educational Research Association. Atlanta, GA.

Rorer, J. A. (1942). *Principles of democratic supervision.* Contributions to Education No 858. New York: Teachers College, Columbia University.

Roethlissberger, P. J. & Dickinson, J. D. (1939). *Management and the worker.* Cambridge, MA: Harvard University Press.

Rosenshine, B. & Furst, N. (1973). The use of direct observation to study teaching. In R. Travers (Ed.). *Second handbook of research on teaching* (pp. 122–183). Chicago, IL: Rand McNally.

Russell, T. & Spafford, C. (1986, April). *Teachers as reflective practitioners in peer clinical supervision.* Paper presented at the annual meeting of the American Educational Research Association. San Francisco, CA.

Sergiovanni, T. J. (Ed.). (1975). *Professional supervision for professional teachers.* Alexandria, VA: ASCD.

Sergiovanni, T. J. (1976). Toward a theory of clinical supervision. *Journal of Research and Development in Education, 9,* 20–29.

Sergiovanni, T. J. (Ed.). (1982). The context for supervision. In *Supervision of teaching* (pp. 108–118). Alexandria, VA: ASCD.

Sergiovanni, T. J. (Ed.). (1982). Toward a theory of supervisory practice: Integrating scientific, clinical, and artistic views. In *Supervision of teaching* (pp. 67–78). Alexandria, VA: ASCD.

Sergiovanni, T. J. (1985). Landscapes, mindscapes, and reflective practice in supervision. *Journal of Curriculum and Supervision, 1,* 5–17.

Sergiovanni, T. J. An emerging scholarship of practice. *Journal of Curriculum and Supervision, 5,* 247–252.

Shane, H. G. & Weaver, R. A. (1976). Educational developments anticipating the 21st century and the future of clinical supervision. *Journal of Research and Development in Education, 9,* 90–98.

Shannon, J. R. (1936). Teachers' attitudes toward supervision. *Educational Method, 16,* 9–14.

Shores, J. H. (1967). Foreword. In W. H. Lucio (Ed.). *Supervision: Perspectives and propositions.* Washington: ASCD.

Skrak, N. D. (1973). *The application of immediate secondary reinforcement to classroom teaching observations in clinical supervision.* Doctoral dissertation, University of Pittsburgh. *Dissertation Abstracts International, 34,* 1140A.

Smith, B. O. (1963). Toward a theory of teaching. In A. A. Bellack (Ed.). *Theory and research in teaching* (pp. 1–10). New York: Bureau of Publications, Teachers College, Columbia University.

Smith, L. M. & Kieth, P. M. (1971). *Anatomy of educational innovation: An organizational analysis of an elementary school.* New York: John Wiley and Sons.

Smyth, J. W. (1984). Teachers as collaborative learners in clinical supervision: A state-of-the-art review. *Journal of Education for Teaching, 10,* 24–38.

Smyth, J. W. (1985). Developing a critical practice of clinical supervision. *Journal of Curriculum Studies, 17,* 1–15.

Smyth, J. W. (1986). *Peer clinical supervision as "empowerment" versus "delivery of service."* Paper presented at the annual meeting of the American Educational Research Association, San Francisco, CA.

Smyth, J. W. (1986a). Perspectives and imperative. Clinical supervision: Technocratic mindedness, or emancipatory learning. *Journal of Curriculum and Supervision, 1,* 331–340.

Smyth, J. W. (Ed.). (1986b). *Learning about teaching through clinical supervision.* Dover, NH: Croom Helm.

Smyth, J. W. (1986c). Cinderella syndrome: A philosophical view of supervision as a filed of study. *Teachers College Record, 88,* 367–388.

Smyth, J. W. (1986d). Towards a collaborative, reflective and critical mode of clinical supervision. In J. W. Smyth (Ed.). *Learning about teaching through clinical supervision* (pp.59–84). Dover, NH: Croom Helm.

Smyth, J. W. (1988). A "critical" perspective for clinical supervision. *Journal or Curriculum and Supervision, 3,* 136–156.

Snyder, J., Bolin, F., & Zumwalt, K. (1991). Curriculum implementation. In P. W. Jackson (Ed.). *Handbook of Research on Curriculum* (pp. 402–435). New York: Macmillan.

Spruill, A. W. (1960). The negro teacher in the process of desegregation of schools. *Journal of Negro Education, 29,* 80–84.

Stover, G. F. (1945). Trouble-shooter and eye-opener. *Educational Leadership, 2,* 158.

Sullivan, D. G. (1980). *Clinical supervision: A state of the art review.* Alexandria, VA: ASCD.

Swearingten, M. E. (1946). Looking at supervision. *Educational Leadership, 3,* 150.

Thompson, C. H. (1953). Editorial comment. *The Journal of Negro Education, 22,* 99–101.

Townsel, C. W. & Banks, L. A. (1975). The urban school administrator—a black perspective. *The Journal of Negro Education. 44,* 421–429.

Travers (Ed.). *Second handbook of research on teaching,* pp. 122–183. Chicago: Rand McNally.

Turner, H. M. (1976). *The implementation and critical documentation of a model of clinical supervision: A case study.* Doctoral dissertation, University of California. *Dissertation Abstracts International* 37:4772A.

Turner-Mueke, L., Russel, T., & Bowyer, J. (1986). Reflection-in-action: Case study of a clinical supervisor, 40–49.

Turney, D. (1966). Beyond the status quo: A reappraisal of instructional supervision. *Educational Leadership, 24,* 665.

Waite, D. (1991). *Supervisors' talk: Conversation analysis and ethnography of supervisory conferences.* Paper presented at the Annual Meeting of the American Educational Research Association. Chicago, IL.

Waite, D. (1992a). Instructional supervision from a situational perspective. *Teaching and Teacher Education, 8,* 319–332.

Waite, D. (1992b). The instructional supervisor as a cultural guide. *Urban Education, 26,* 423–440.

Waite, D. (1993). *Novice supervisors' understanding of supervision.* Paper presented at the Annual Meeting of the American Educational Research Association. Atlanta, GA.

Warner, L. S. (1991). *American indian women: The double bind.* Paper presented at the Annual Conference of the American Association of School Administrators. New Orleans.

Warner, L. S. (1992). *Matriarchal decision-making.* Paper presented at the "Colors of the Heart" Conference of the National Association for Women in Education. San Francisco, CA.

Weber, C. A. & Garfield, S. L. (1942). Teachers' reactions to certain aspects in-service education. *Educational Administration and Supervision, 28,* 463–468.

Whitney, F. L. (1936) Trends in methods of teacher improvement. *The American School Board Journal, 93,* 18–19.

Wilburn, K. T. (1986). Collegial coaching: A new challenge for instructional supervision. *Wingspan, 3,* 47–51.

Wiles, K. (1955). *Supervision for better schools* (2nd ed.). New York: Prentice Hall.

Wiles, K. (1960). Supervision. In C. Harris (Ed.). *Encyclopedia of Educational Research* (pp. 1142–1148). New York: Macmillan.

Wiles, K. & Lovell, J. T. (1975). *Supervision for better schools.* Englewood Cliffs, NJ: Prentice Hall.

Wilson, C., et al. (1969). *Sociology of supervision: An approach to comprehensive planning in education.* Boston, MA: Allyn and Bacon.

Zeichner, K. (1980). Myths and realities: Field-based experiences in preservice teacher education. *Journal of Teacher Education, 31.*

NOTES

1. Also contributing to the chapter were Stephen Ellwood and Bil Johnson, who worked with us during the spring and summer of 1994, and doctoral students in the seminar, "Supervision and Curriculum Improvement," at Teachers College, Columbia University, spring 1994 and spring 1995.

2. Flinders suggests that "our words and behavior frame social interactions such as work, play, humor, or teaching," and that communication frames "function as boundaries separating various types of reality" and tell us what we are to expect (1991, p. 99).

3. For a more detailed discussion of the Smith and Keith study and the effect of applying social sciences methodologies to educational situations, see Snyder, Bolin, and Zumwalt, "Curriculum Implementation," in Philip W. Jackson (Ed.). *Handbook of Research on Curriculum* (pp. 402–435). New York: Macmillan.

4. An example is the supervisory literature that has emerged in TESOL. Fanselow (1987, 1988) has developed a nondirective method of supervising in TESOL that has been widely used. Gebhard (1984) offers a summary of models of supervision in TESOL.

5. An example is the supervisory literature that has emerged in Teaching English as a Second Language (TESOL). John F. Fanselow (1987, 1988) has developed a non-directive method of supervising in TESOL that has been widely used. J. G. Gebhard (1984) offers a summary of models of supervision in TESOL.

· 5 ·

EVALUATION
IN SUPERVISION

Edward F. Iwanicki

UNIVERSITY OF CONNECTICUT

INTRODUCTION

The focus of this chapter is on the role of evaluation in supervision as a process of inquiry. This chapter is based on the views of Sergiovanni and Starratt (1983) that supervision is the process of working with and through people to better achieve the goals of the school organization. In adopting this position the assumption is made that schools exist for two purposes: (1) to foster student learning and (2) to promote meaningful professional growth among staff. Staff are the human fabric of the school organization. Students' learning potential is realized to the extent that the school system invests continually in the development of its human fabric.

Given this position on supervision, it is clear that the two major functions of evaluation are to determine how successful the school has been in (1) achieving its students' learning potential (i.e., program evaluation) and (2) developing the capabilities of its staff (i.e., personnel evaluation). These two functions were viewed historically as distinct. Doctoral programs developed to train evaluators for the social action programs of the 1960s did not address personnel evaluation issues. Personnel evaluation was something administrators or supervisors did. We have begun to view these two functions as complementary only recently. More will be said about this later in the chapter.

The intent of this chapter is to focus analytically on the critical developments in the fields of program and personnel evaluation in an attempt to provide the reader with an understanding of what has been accomplished as well as what

needs to be addressed to make evaluation more responsive to the decision-making needs of school leaders. It is not to provide a comprehensive review of the literature in these fields. Evaluation is a critical tool for school-site decision-making.

PROGRAM EVALUATION

Evaluation Defined

What is program evaluation? Simply stated, *evaluation* is the process of obtaining accurate information for educational decision-making. This definition is important because it conveys clearly the notion that evaluation is not simply testing, as some may still believe. We can collect a range of information appropriate to the outcomes being evaluated through the evaluation process. Some information may be quantitative (i.e., numerical), whereas other information may be descriptive (i.e., qualitative). The important criterion is whether or not the information collected is accurate, not the type of information collected. Evaluations are too often based on test scores that are assumed to be accurate because they are numerical data. We sometimes find out later that our evaluation findings are flawed because the test was not a valid measure of the students' performance. Numbers can lie.

The second aspect of this definition that is important is the focus on educational decision-making. Data collected through the evaluation process need to be analyzed carefully and transformed into information about the program being exam-

Author's Note: The author expresses his thanks and appreciation to the following colleagues for the support and feedback they provided during the preparation of this chapter: Gerald R. Firth, University of Georgia; Thomas L. McGreal, University of Illinois; Philip A. Streifer, Avon (CT) Public Schools. It is also important to acknowledge the contributions that numerous other colleagues and students have made to the development of the views presented in this chapter.

ined. Decisions then need to be made on the basis of this information. These decisions may range from continuing the program as is to making minor modifications to restructuring the program, to terminating the program. A decision, however, needs to be made. Some, such as House (1973), have found that evaluations tend to be used to make decisions only when the findings either support what the decision-maker really wants to do or what the decision-maker needs to do politically.

A critical extension of this definition is the distinction Scriven (1967) makes between formative and summative evaluation. The goal of summative evaluation is to make a judgment about the value or worth of a program. The role of formative evaluation is to provide feedback for improvement while a program is in progress. Formative and summative evaluation have a role–goal relationship. If quality feedback for improvement is provided while the program is in progress, then we can make adjustments where necessary and improve our chances of ending up with a worthwhile program. In defining worth, Scriven goes beyond whether the program has achieved its objectives. Worth is determined by taking all relevant factors into consideration and then deciding whether the program has made the desired difference for participants.

Scriven's work is particularly important for two reasons. First, it supports the need for quality evaluation while a program is in progress, as well as at the conclusion of the program. Second, it takes us beyond the notion of goal-attainment and forces us to address the issue of program worth. In a more recent piece, Scriven (1991) addresses a number of questions that he been raised about formative and summative evaluation since he introduced these terms in 1967. In this work, he cautions that formative evaluation should not be taken lightly. If we do not invest adequate resources in formative evaluation, we will do a sloppy job and will not provide the feedback necessary to support the development of a worthwhile program. Furthermore, he notes that formative evaluation can lead to summative decisions. For example, we may decide to implement a drastically different approach to teaching writing. After three months of formative feedback, it might be seen that this program is still not catching on. The teachers dislike it; the parents are complaining; and the children are saying "Do I have to?" more often. This may be sufficient evidence to discontinue the program and to move to a more productive alternative. Without such formative monitoring, we could have lost a full year of appropriate instruction in writing. Even worse, however, we could have ingrained in the students a distaste for writing.

Who Makes the Decision?

Viewing evaluation as decision-making raises the issue of who makes the decisions about the program being evaluated. Let us examine the scenario of a school system that contracted with an external evaluator to assess the effectiveness of its new writing program. The evaluation will be conducted according to the procedures agreed upon with the oversight of the assistant superintendent for curriculum and instruction. The external evaluator will submit quarterly progress reports to the assistant superintendent as well as a final evaluation report with recommendations. When the assistant superintendent is satisfied with the evaluator's final report, it will be submitted to the superintendent's cabinet, and subsequently to the board of education. Who, then, makes the decision about the effectiveness of the writing program?

In addressing this question, it is helpful to refer to the discussion of the four generations of evaluation provided by Guba and Lincoln (1985). They labeled the first generation that began at the turn of the century the *technical generation*. Evaluation then was synonymous with measurement and testing. Students were administered standardized tests and program effectiveness was determined by comparing their standing to others in the appropriate reference group. The second generation that emerged in the mid-1940s was called the *descriptive generation*. This was Tylerian objective-oriented evaluation. Standardized tests could be used, but the focus in determining program effectiveness was on whether students demonstrated the behaviors specified in the program objectives. They called the third generation, which became more prevalent in the mid-1960s, the *judgmental generation*. While program effectiveness was still determined by comparing student performance with the expectations set forth in the program objectives, standards were developed to guide the decision-making process. A program was effective to the extent that students met these standards. Guba and Lincoln have noted that these first three generations of evaluation all followed the scientific paradigm in which the focus on objectivity was paramount.

When following the scientific paradigm, it is fairly clear that the evaluator would make decisions about the effectiveness of a program based on an analysis of the information collected. In returning to the scenario described earlier, the external evaluator would make some decisions about the effectiveness of the writing program when crafting the recommendations included in the final report. The role of the assistant superintendent, the superintendent's cabinet, and the school board is twofold: (1) to review and validate the recommendations, and (2) to take appropriate action on the recommendations once they are validated. Validating the recommendations of the evaluator is a critical step. It requires reading the evaluation report carefully and then stepping back and asking some critical questions:

1. Are the recommendations consistent with the findings?
2. Are the findings based on an appropriate analysis of the information collected?
3. Could the findings be biased by factors external to the program?

The issue of whether the findings of an evaluation are biased by factors external to the program is what is referred to in the research design literature as "validity threats" (Campbell & Stanley, 1963; Cook & Campbell, 1979). For example, let us assume that the writing program that is being evaluated included a technology component. All students at grades 5 to 8 are required to go to the writing lab at least twice a week for 30 minutes in addition to their usual instruction in language arts. Furthermore, let us assume that the evaluation of this new program showed that students' writing performance did not improve substantially, even though students perceived their writing lab experience as beneficial. As a member of the board of education, I am perplexed by this finding, so I discuss it with my son, who happens to be in the seventh grade. What I find through this conversation is that the need to schedule two writing lab sessions per week made it difficult for my son's teacher to schedule students for special educational services. Thus, she used classroom time in language arts for this purpose. A decision like this would bias the outcomes of the evaluation because students were not receiving all the language arts instruction they were supposed to receive. Such validity threats need to monitored closely when conducting school-based evaluations.

Guba and Lincoln (1985) would argue that such validity threats could be reduced by moving away from the scientific to a more naturalistic, responsive paradigm for evaluation. They call this fourth-generation evaluation the *negotiated generation*. The fourth-generation evaluator is more a facilitator and less an expert. One of the initial responsibilities of the fourth-generation evaluator would be to meet with the various stakeholders associated with a program to identify the questions they would like to see answered through the evaluation. An initial list would be compiled and consensus would be reached through discussion. The methods for conducting the evaluation would be determined in a similar manner. While the evaluator would share technical expertise, it would not be imposed on the constituents. Although the evaluator would collect and analyze information, that evaluator would not draft conclusions or recommendations; Instead, the evaluator would facilitate discussions by which the constituents would arrive at their own conclusions. As a participant observer, the evaluator would become familiar with the operation of the program and use this information as a teacher to help the constituents to understand what is really happening and to identify areas where program change may be necessary. Thus, fourth-generation evaluation tends to become collaborative action research (Sagor, 1993) facilitated

by a person or persons with a good repertoire of both qualitative and quantitative research skills.

While there are many positive features to the practice of fourth-generation evaluation in schools, Scriven (1992) puts this discussion into appropriate perspective when he states that an evaluator who does not make a judgment about the worth of a program is simply not doing the job. He supports this position with reference to the decline of the automobile industry in the 1970s. Evaluations were certainly going on during this period, but people were simply telling each other what they wanted to hear. The automobile industry did not begin to recover until it began to respond to the criticism of external groups such as the Consumer Union. A parallel in education was the experience with the new math programs of the 1960s and early 1970s. While those involved in developing many of the new math programs heralded their success, little attention was given to teachers' concerns about the impact of such programs on students' computation skills. For the evaluation process to be effective, we need to include many of the positive features of fourth-generation evaluation. While involvement and collaboration are important as teachers and administrators make decisions about the quality of the programs in their schools, the periodic review of such decisions by an external evaluator or evaluation group is critical.

Evaluation and Accountability

Discussions of evaluation and decision-making usually lead to questions of accountability. Who is accountable to whom for what? Alkin (1972) has identified three types of accountability in schools: goal, program, and outcome accountability. Each of these types is described in Table 5.1 in terms of who is accountable, to whom they are accountable, and for what they are accountable. It is clear from Table 5.1 that accountability for the outcomes of schooling is not the sole responsibility of the teachers, as the public often likes to believe. This responsibility is shared by school board mem-

TABLE 5–1. Accountability Types

Type	Who is Accountable	To Whom (Primary Responsibility)	For What
Goal Accountability	School Board	Public	Selecting measurable goals and objectives for the school district and allocating the resources necessary to support quality programs to achieve these objectives.
Program Accountability	Superintendent and central office staff	School Board	Develop and/or select quality programs of instruction to achieve the objectives of the school district.
Outcome Accountability	Principals and their building	Superintendent and central office staff	Achieving the outcomes stated in the objectives of the school district at a performance standard appropriate to the grade or instructional level of the students being taught.

Adapted from Alkin, M.C. (1972, p. 4).

bers, the superintendent and central office staff, and principals and teachers. Because each group has primary responsibility for specific aspects of the school program does not mean that accountability is a hierarchical process. The board does not set goals and objectives independently of the central office staff, who develop the instructional programs and then simply pass them onto the principals and their staffs. Instead, the three groups must work collaboratively in setting the goals and objectives for the school district, developing programs of instruction, and setting performance standards for students. Teachers and principals are more receptive to being held accountable for student outcomes when they have been involved in setting the performance standards and in determining what programs of instruction will be used in the classroom.

A new perspective on who is accountable to whom has been added as we begin to look at total quality schools (Bonstingl, 1992; English & Hill, 1994), school-site decision-making, and the movement toward schools as learning organizations (Fullan, 1993). Individual accountability in this case is being replaced by organizational accountability, especially as it pertains to teachers. Rather than holding individual teachers accountable for student outcomes, performance standards are developed for schools. Improvement plans are then developed collaboratively by teachers and administrators for areas where students are not meeting the expectations set forth in these standards. If we view schools as learning organizations, then these improvement plans are well thought out approaches for strengthening the teaching–learning process in particular areas. In viewing schools as learning organizations, these approaches are more hypotheses than solutions. We "get smarter" about the teaching and learning needs we are addressing through the process of implementing these plans, and we continually adjust our plans based on these new insights until the desired student outcomes are achieved. As we adopt this evolving, organizational learning approach to school improvement, we sometimes find that even our valued standards might need to be rethought. In adopting this approach, the methods of collaborative action research guide the process of school improvement more than the more linear, traditional approaches to research. The spirit of this organizational learning approach to school improvement is captured by this comment voiced by professional staff in the Dade County (Florida) Schools: *We have many successes because we are allowed to fail.*

It is interesting to see that organizational accountability is being considered as the basis for pay for performance programs in states such as Kentucky (Gong & Reidy, 1996), Tennessee (Sanders & Horn, 1994), and Texas (Webster & Mendro, 1995). Teachers and administrators in schools that achieve their school improvement standards are rewarded monetarily, while others are not. The impact of such pay for performance programs needs to be monitored closely in coming years. At first glance, some have dismissed these programs because they are based on complex statistical models that attempt to create a level playing field on which all schools can be compared. It is certain that no statistical model could do this! Others, however, claim that high-speed, rela-

tively inexpensive computers have led to developments that make this possible. While it is appropriate to validate the models used to make decisions in such approaches to school-based accountability, the rewards and sanctions aspects of these approaches merit even more careful scrutiny. If particular schools continue to be rewarded consistently over time and others are not, then what differential impact will this have on teacher motivation and student learning? The works of Frase (1992), as well as of Hatry and Greiner (1985), raise a number issues that need to be addressed when accountability for school improvement is linked to teacher compensation.

The sociopolitical agenda that underlies some state accountability programs is particularly interesting. Oescher, Black, Gunning, and Brooks (1996) note that school effectiveness may be determined on an absolute or relative basis. When determining school effectiveness on an absolute basis, common performance standards are set for all schools. When determining school effectiveness on a relative basis, performance standards are set for each school using complex statistical models that take into consideration factors such as students' prior achievement, race, English language proficiency, and socioeconomic status. Some argue that such relative approaches are more equitable because they create an "even playing field" where all schools are in a position to be rewarded. Others question whether such approaches are ethical because they result in lower performance standards for schools that have higher concentrations of students from economically disadvantaged home backgrounds.

The current attention to rewards and sanctions is somewhat surprising, because there is no evidence to support the theory that accountability models aimed at sanctioning programs or personnel have had a positive effect on the quality of education. During the 1960s and 1970s, much rhetoric was espoused to claims that only those ESEA Title I and Title III programs that were shown to be effective would continue to be funded. During the 1970s and 1980s, considerable attention was given to developing teacher evaluation models that would "weed out" the less effective teachers. Such movements created a distaste for the evaluation process. As evaluation became a "four letter word," it was more difficult to collect the types of data necessary to support meaningful school improvement and staff development efforts. It is interesting, however, that the school systems with the reputations for high-quality programs and teaching were those that relied heavily on evaluation evidence when making decisions about programs and personnel. Evaluation was not viewed negatively in such school systems because it was used to set directions for improvement rather than to reward or sanction. In many respects these school systems were ahead of their time. These school systems were at the forefront of the total quality movement (Walton, 1986) because evaluation was being used less to prove and more to improve. They were functioning as learning organizations where evaluation was used to help teachers and administrators to get smart about their school improvement and staff development needs. It is clear from such experiences that schools are truly accountable when the primary purpose of evaluation is to improve teaching and learning in all classrooms.

Program Versus Instructional Evaluation

Reading Recovery is an example of a program that has been adopted by a number of school systems. A number of Reading Recovery teachers are hired within each system. If one is evaluating the effect of Reading Recovery on students assigned to a particular teacher, this is instructional evaluation (e.g., What progress did Ed's students make?). If one is evaluating the effect of Reading Recovery on all participants in the school district, then this is program evaluation. Such evaluations are usually conducted by summarizing program effects on teachers.

Both types of evaluation should be conducted. As teachers become involved in the instructional evaluation process, it is important to make sure that they understand the evaluation procedures that they will implement in their classrooms; particularly, what information will be collected, when and how this information needs to be collected; and how it will be used to make decisions about their students' learning. Through their involvement in instructional evaluation, teachers become informed participants in the program evaluation process. Their becoming informed participants increases the probability that they will collect timely and accurate information about the impact of the program at the classroom level. This in turn lends credibility to the program evaluation process.

When teachers are not intellectually invested in the instructional evaluation process, they tend to be more haphazard about collecting the evaluation information needed for program evaluation purposes. For example, if teachers were required to administer a reading test which they knew little about, then they would view this task as an infringement on their instructional time and would deal with it as expediently as possible. They would not follow directions for administration as closely and their students' reactions would not be monitored as carefully as if the teachers were informed participants in the evaluation process. This lack of investment would tend to erode the credibility of the program evaluation findings.

Can involving teachers in the evaluation process also erode its credibility? When teachers realize they have a crucial stake in the outcomes of the evaluation, won't they bias the results in their favor? Although this could happen, the chances are slim when the purpose of the evaluation is to improve teaching and learning in the classroom. If the purpose of the evaluation is to reward or sanction performance, then the collection of evaluation data needs to be monitored carefully to insure that such bias is not introduced.

Evaluation Models

The 1960s was a very fertile period for the development of program evaluation thought. Numerous grants were made available for developing new methods for the evaluation of social action programs. Doctoral and postdoctoral fellowships were available for training evaluators in these emerging methodologies. These research and training grants included ample funds for travel to conferences and meetings where extensive and sometimes heated discourse on the strengths and weaknesses of these methodologies emerged. As Popham (1975) noted, this period produced a varied menu of evaluation models to meddle with and/or muddle through.

While the models movement was interesting in that it resulted in varied conceptions of evaluation, it fell short in providing direction to the evaluation process in schools. Successful applications of some of the more promising models to the evaluations of social action programs during the 1960s and 1970s were sparse. Although many states passed legislation that required school districts to systematically evaluate their curricular programs on an ongoing basis, few school systems turned to the available models for guidance in this regard. What became apparent at that time was that evaluation is as much a belief as it is a methodology. When program evaluation was an emerging field, some school personnel believed that the time and effort devoted to this activity would benefit the educational process. Other school personnel were undecided about the utility of the program evaluation process. Too many school personnel believed that evaluation was a waste of time and money and that these resources would be better used to support instruction. Little progress was made in implementing new evaluation methodologies in those school systems where evaluation was not perceived to be worthwhile.

The problem school system personnel encountered in applying these models to the evaluation of curricular programs was their generic nature. For example, the CIPP model (Stufflebeam 1967, 1969, 1983) is a well thought out conception of program evaluation that has had a broad impact on evaluation thought and practice. The logic followed by Stufflebeam in developing this model is:

- The goal of evaluation is to improve program quality
- To improve program quality, accurate decisions must be made
- To make accurate decisions, one must be aware of the decision alternatives and be able to make sound judgments regarding these alternatives
- Sound judgments require quality information about the alternatives
- To obtain quality information, a systematic process of data gathering must be established that yields data which are valid, reliable, timely, pervasive, and credible
- Thus, evaluation is a systematic process of gathering data to facilitate decisions directed toward the improvement of program quality

Furthermore, Stufflebeam identified four types of decisions that can be made regarding an educational program. Planning decisions define the program *context*. Programming decisions identify program *inputs*, which include available human and material resources as well as the program design and implementation strategies. Implementation decisions while the program is in *process* assess its impact on an ongoing basis and identify any defects in the program design or the manner in which the program is being implemented. Recycling decisions at the conclusion of the program focus on the quality of the program *products* and the need to make any adjustments in the program context, inputs, or processes.

The title "CIPP" was derived from four types of decision-making: context, input, process, and product. The objective, method, and relation to decision-making of these four types of evaluation are summarized in Figure 5.1.

Tailoring Evaluation Models to School Needs While school personnel had no difficulty following the logic of the CIPP model, problems were encountered when it became time to apply the four types of decisions to particular programs, particularly in the areas of context and input evaluation as they apply to curricular programs. It was difficult for teachers and administrators to take the generic descriptions of these aspects of the CIPP model and apply them, for example, to the evaluation of a reading program. It became evident that if evaluation was to have an impact on school practice, then it would be necessary to tailor the models being developed to the specific needs of school personnel. Figure 5.2 includes an overview of how the CIPP model was tailored to the evaluation of curricular programs in schools. This approach was developed over a number of years with graduate students in evaluation courses at both Boston College and the University of Connecticut. In addition to completing various readings in evaluation and about the CIPP model, these students reviewed thoroughly Tyler's (1950) *Basic Principles of Curriculum and Instructions.* Figure 5.2 includes an overview of the four phases of the curriculum development process based on Tyler's work as well as the key evaluation questions

that need to be addressed at each phase. Figure 5.2 was derived over time from a rather lengthy and comprehensive set of considerations for evaluating curricular programs. While these considerations were appropriate for professional curriculum developers, school personnel did not view them as manageable for use by teachers and administrators. The key questions presented in Figure 5.2 are those that practitioners believe capture the essence of the curriculum evaluation process.

Figure 5.2 is being presented as an appropriate point of departure for school personnel who wish to approach the evaluation of their curricular programs systematically. Some school systems have reworded the seven questions so they are more appropriate to the curriculum development process in a particular school context or discipline. While some school systems have expanded the list of questions, this should be done with caution. It is best to pilot the curriculum evaluation process with a manageable set of questions and then, as a result of this experience, to decide which questions need to be addressed as the evaluation process is continued.

In addition, the approach to evaluation shared in Figure 5.2 does not have to be applied in its entirety. For example, a school system may have no concerns about the needs being addressed by its social studies curriculum at the primary grades or about the quality of the instructional and evaluation materials that have been developed, while it is concerned

	Context Evaluation	Input Evaluation	Process Evaluation	Product Evaluation
Objective	To define the *operation context,* to identify and assess *needs* in the context, and to identify and delineate *problems* underlying the needs.	To identify and assess *system capabilities,* available input *strategies,* and *designs* for implementing the strategies.	To identify or predict, in process, defects in the procedural design or its implementation, and to maintain a record of *procedural events* and *activities*	To relate *outcome information* to objectives and to context, input, and process information.
Method	By describing individually and in relevant perspectives, the major subsystems of the context; by comparing actual and intended inputs and outputs of the subsystems; and by analyzing possible causes of discrepancies between actualities and intentions.	By describing and analyzing available human and material resources, solution strategies, and procedural designs for relevance, feasibility, and economy in the course of action to be taken.	By monitoring the activity's potential procedural barriers and remaining alert to unanticipated ones.	By defining operationally and measuring criteria associated with the objectives, by comparing these measurements with predetermined standards or comparative bases, and by interpreting the outcome in terms of recorded input and process information.
Relation to Decision-Making in the Change Process	For deciding upon the *setting* to be served, the *goals* associated with meeting needs and the objectives associated with solving problems (i.e., for planning needed changes).	For selecting *sources of support,* solution *strategies,* and procedural *designs* (i.e., for programming change activities).	For *implementing and refining the program design and procedure* (i.e., for effecting process control).	For deciding to *continue, terminate, modify or refocus* a change activity, and for linking the activity to other major phases of the change process (i.e, for evolving change activities).

FIGURE 5.1. The CIPP Evaluation Model—A Classification Scheme of Strategies for Evaluating Educational Change.*

*From Stufflebeam, D. L. (1967, p. 128).

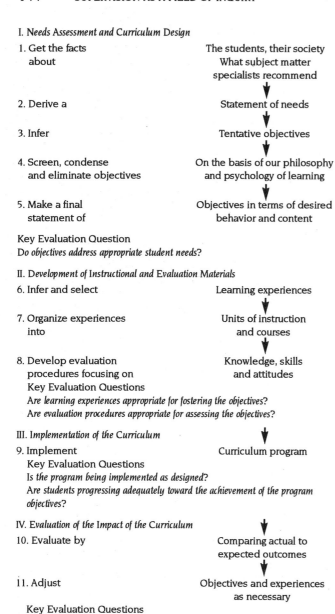

I. *Needs Assessment and Curriculum Design*

1. Get the facts
about   The students, their society
                         What subject matter
                         specialists recommend

2. Derive a   Statement of needs

3. Infer   Tentative objectives

4. Screen, condense   On the basis of our philosophy
and eliminate objectives and psychology of learning

5. Make a final   Objectives in terms of desired
statement of   behavior and content

Key Evaluation Question
Do objectives address appropriate student needs?

II. *Development of Instructional and Evaluation Materials*

6. Infer and select   Learning experiences

7. Organize experiences Units of instruction
into   and courses

8. Develop evaluation   Knowledge, skills
procedures focusing on   and attitudes
Key Evaluation Questions
Are learning experiences appropriate for fostering the objectives?
Are evaluation procedures appropriate for assessing the objectives?

III. *Implementation of the Curriculum*

9. Implement   Curriculum program
Key Evaluation Questions
Is the program being implemented as designed?
Are students progressing adequately toward the achievement of the program objectives?

IV. *Evaluation of the Impact of the Curriculum*

10. Evaluate by   Comparing actual to
                         expected outcomes

11. Adjust   Objectives and experiences
                         as necessary

Key Evaluation Questions
Have the students achieved the program objectives?
Where is it necessary to modify the objectives or aspects of the program?

FIGURE 5.2. Overview of the Curriculum
Development Process
Based on Tyler, R. W. (1950)

with the students' inability to master the outcomes desired. Thus, this school system would focus its evaluation activities on questions dealing with Phases III and IV of the curriculum development process. It is also important to note that the process presented in Figure 5.2 is cyclic. Once adjustments in the social studies curriculum are made at Step 11, this school system should cycle back through the more relevant evaluation questions during the next school year to be sure that students are now achieving the desired outcomes.

As noted in Figure 5.2, the first question addressed through the curriculum evaluation process is whether appropriate stu-

dent needs are being met. Needs assessment merits particular attention because two problems tend to arise when dealing with this process. First, some school personnel believe it is not necessary to conduct needs assessments. Their arguments go something like this:

We adopted this program because it has been considered to be the best in this field by prominent school systems across the nation. No program would achieve such notoriety if it were not appropriate to the needs of students.

or

This program has been recommended highly by the National Council of Teachers of Xxxxxx. Certainly, it must be meeting appropriate student needs.

Second, some school personnel view needs assessment as a process of discrepancy analysis:

Yes, we do a needs assessment at the beginning of each year. All students are pretested and then we review the results to determine what needs to be taught.

In both cases, school personnel are avoiding the most critical question in the needs assessment process: What do students need to know and be able to do in this particular discipline? This question is often avoided because there is no absolutely correct answer. The answer is a function of the beliefs of the members of the school community and arrived at through value analysis (Guba & Lincoln, 1982; Scriven & Roth, 1977). It is critical because what we claim to value is our definition of quality in a particular discipline. Achieving program outcomes does not mean that we are providing our students with a quality education, unless we have evidence confirming that these outcomes are most appropriate to these students' needs.

Once a value analysis has been conducted to determine what students need to know and be able to do in a particular discipline, then it is appropriate to conduct a discrepancy analysis to identify what needs to be taught. The needs assessment process, however, should not end here. Once we know what needs to be taught, a resource analysis needs to be conducted to determine whether we have the human and material resources necessary to achieve these outcomes with our students. If sufficient resources are not available, then program expectations would need to be adjusted appropriately. It is very important to note that our definition of a quality education in a particular discipline and our ability to be successful in providing such a quality education are determined largely through the value and resource analysis aspects of the needs assessment process. It is critical for school system personnel to keep this point in mind as they revise their curricula in light of the new national standards being published in various disciplines.

The product of Phase I—Needs Assessment and Curriculum Design—is a listing of objectives. Stake (1970) made the critical observation that these objectives are data that reflect our values and priorities in a particular discipline as well as in the process of schooling. Some, such as Thurow (1992), claim that the problem of school quality in the United States is a function of our inability to set curriculum objectives that meet challenging, world-class standards. In order to address such claims, it is important to adopt a global perspective on education and to be able to justify why we have made particular choices for our students.

The evaluation questions addressed in Phase II of the curriculum development process in Figure 5.2 deal with the appropriateness of both the learning experiences and the evaluation procedures. The question dealing with the appropriateness of the learning experiences is particularly important as we adopt more constructivist, cross-disciplinary approaches to instruction. Likewise, the question dealing with evaluation materials is critical as schools implement more authentic performance assessments. This question dealing with evaluation procedures is also important from the perspective of whether procedures have been developed for monitoring *all* students' progress on a continuous basis.

Some time has been taken to discuss the evaluation questions addressed in the first two phases of the curriculum development process to show that these questions are critical to the design of a quality curriculum and cannot be taken for granted. When teachers say these issues have been addressed adequately, it is important to ask for evidence to support their claims. Curriculum quality is a function of the extent to which student outcomes and learning experiences have been thought out well and integrated appropriately with both formative and summative evaluation procedures. Koberg and Bagnall (1972, p. 32) put the value of such careful curriculum planning into appropriate perspective with their statement: "Design is the process of making dreams come true."

Approaches to curriculum development as outlined in Figure 5.2 are sometimes criticized for being too linear. This does not have to be the case. As we analyze student needs and begin to identify the outcomes of a program, we see that some can be prespecified through the development of meaningful goals and objectives. In other cases, we need to follow Eisner's (1969, 1994) paradigm of expressive objectives. With expressive objectives an experience is described in relation to how students will benefit from that experience; for example, *by participating in a summer educational enrichment program in a multicultural, urban setting, suburban students will develop an appreciation of the city and its many cultures.* Student performance regarding this objective would be monitored using a pool of criteria created to assess the effect of that experience. Some of these criteria could be identified while the experience is being planned. Others could be added while observing the students as they participate in the experience. Still others could be added from conversations with students during and after the experience. Potential criteria of success for this objective might include students:

- feeling comfortable walking around the city
- talking to people from other cultures
- sampling food from other cultures
- participating in the celebrations of other cultures
- knowing how their culture is both similar to and different from that of others
- sharing their culture with others
- introducing their families to the city and its many cultures

Not all students would be expected to benefit from the experience in the same way, but each student would be expected to benefit in some meaningful way. Thus, a three-step process could be used to evaluate the success of the summer enrichment program. First, program staff would review the criteria and decide which are most important to the success of the program, which are important, and which, if any, are of little importance. Criteria of little importance would not be considered further. Next, the percentage of students who met each criterion would be calculated and this percentage would be used to rank the criteria from high to low. This step would provide a perspective on how successful the program was in helping students to meet the more important criteria for the objective. Finally, individual students' profiles of performance across the criteria would be examined to decide who benefited from the summer enrichment program. Standards could be set to make this decision. For example, it could be determined that a student must have met at least five of the eight most important criteria to be successful.

Influence of Other Evaluation Models on Evaluation Practice
The focus in this section has been on a discussion of evaluation models and how they can be tailored to program evaluation needs in schools. An approach to the evaluation of curricular programs based on the works of Tyler (1950) and Stufflebeam (1967, 1969, 1983) was shared. The question might arise as to whether this approach would change dramatically if an evaluation model other than the CIPP model were used. There probably would be little difference if another evaluation model were used because most models address the same basic categories of decision-making (i.e., planning, programming, implementing, and recycling), even though they address them somewhat differently. The four basic phases of the curriculum development process are listed in Table 5.2, followed by the key components included in some of the evaluation models that have been used extensively in schools. In reviewing Table 5.2, it is evident that the Center for the Study of Evaluation Model (Alkin, 1969) is quite similar to the CIPP model, except that process evaluation is broken into implementation and progress evaluation. Implementation evaluation focuses on whether the program is being implemented as designed, whereas progress evaluation deals with the interim effect of the program on student outcomes and whether adjustments need to be made in the program design. Because both of these issues are addressed by Stufflebeam in process evaluation, the differences between these two models have more to do with configuration than with substance. In the Discrepancy Evaluation Model (Provus, 1971), planning and programming issues are dealt with at the program design stage. Implementation issues are addressed in a manner similar to the other evaluation models. Program cost is broken down as a critical issue in making recycling decisions. With respect to substance, the Provus model is similar in many ways to the models advanced by Stufflebeam and Alkin.

While Table 5.2 provides a comparison of only some of the more popular evaluation models, Gallegos et al (1992) completed a comprehensive review and analysis of the school evaluation models being used across the nation. Through

TABLE 5–2. A Comparison of Evaluation Models

The Curriculum Development Process (Tyler, 1950)	CIPP Model (Stufflebeam, 1967)	Center for the Study of Evaluation Model (Alkin, 1969; Popham, 1975)	Discrepancy Evaluation Model (Provus, 1971)
I. Needs Assessment and Curriculum Design (*Planning*)	Context	Needs Assessment	⌐
II. Development of Instructional and Evaluation Materials (*Programming*)	Input	Program Planning	Program Design
III. Implementation of the Curriculum (*Implementing*)	Process	Implementation Evaluation	Program Operation
		Progress Evaluation	Program Interim Products
IV. Evaluation of the Impact of the Curriculum (*Recycling*)	Product	Outcome Evaluation	Program Terminal Products
			Program Cost

their work they rated the models and provided a series of recommendations for enhancing the effectiveness of a school evaluation model (Gallegos et al, 1992, pp. 33–35). An abridged version of these recommendations is as follows:

• The evaluation model should be developed and implemented with broad participation from those who will be affected by its design and impact (i.e., principals, teachers, support staff, students, parents, and community representatives). Such involvement will provide different but important perspectives, and will encourage others to assume ownership for school evaluation and improvement.

• The focus of evaluation needs to be on issues of quality, equity, and fairness. While some attention needs to be paid to compliance needs that result from federal and state laws, as well as from local school district policies, this should be minimized.

• The evaluation process must identify the broad range of needs appropriate to the students being served. It is not enough to focus the needs assessment process on minimum compliance standards established by state and federal laws.

• The evaluation model should contain a school improvement component that focuses on outcome in all domains (i.e., cognitive, affective, psychomotor). A comprehensive set of performance measures needs to be used to systematically assess the effect of the school's programs on students' academic and social growth.

• Outcome measures other than achievement test scores need to be included in the evaluation model. It should contain measures of quality that relate to the broad range of student and professional staff performance and growth.

• A total systems approach must be used when developing the evaluation model. Databases should be established and should include demographic information, disaggregated test results, attendance data, school dropout information, assessed needs of students, and results of school climate surveys.

• The context of the school and its surrounding community must be taken into consideration as evaluation decisions are made.

• The evaluation model, including the school improvement component, should be reviewed periodically by a properly trained review team to be sure it is doing what it is supposed to be doing in an effective and efficient manner.

• Realistic figures for evaluation need to be included in the school budget.

The Role of Testing in the Evaluation Process

While testing is not the same as evaluation, testing is commonly used to gather data in the program evaluation process. The purpose of this section is to address some testing issues which are critical to the program evaluation process. The practice of testing dates back to almost 2000 BC (Dubois, 1966) when the Chinese organized a very involved civil service examination system. The definition of a *test* used in developing this system is provided in Figure 5.3. A test is a sample of some population of skills. We look at students' performance on that sample and make inferences back to the original population. In Figure 5.3, the focus is on computation skills. When we administer a computation test, students complete some sample exercises. We then look at the test results and make inferences about their performance on the original population of computation skills. The key issue in testing is whether we can make *accurate* inferences about students' performance on the population of skills only if the test sampled that population accurately. This is test validity. A valid test samples the population of skills accurately and thus allows us to make accurate decisions about what students have learned.

Validity Issues in Testing When developing a test, a table of specifications needs to be constructed to ensure that the outcomes fostered in the unit or course of instruction are sampled accurately. There are many good texts on achievement-test construction that provide guidance on the development of such a table (Airasian, 1994; Popham, 1995; Stiggins, 1997). The *Handbook on Formative and Summative Evaluation of Student Learning* (Bloom, Hastings, & Madaus, 1971) is a classic reference for the construction of classroom achievement tests. Teachers too often construct tests by flipping through the book at the end of a unit or course and identifying the topics to be tested. Because this approach does not result in a test that accurately samples instruction, the test is not a valid measure of what students were supposed to learn in that unit or course.

When selecting a test, its validity can be evaluated by addressing the following questions:

1. Does the test look like it measures what was taught in the course?
2. Does this test measure the objectives of the course?
3. Does this test measure the objectives of instruction?
4. Does the test measure the objectives in the way they were taught?

The first question addresses what has been referred to as traditionally as *face validity*. Does the test appears to be valid? If so, then a more in-depth examination is made by addressing the next question of whether the test measures the objectives of the course. Higher-quality, commercially developed tests have tables of specifications that list the outcomes that are measured by the instrument. Thus, the validity of an instrument can be determined by comparing the objectives of the course to the outcomes measured by the test. Let us assume that this approach has yielded three tests that have potential for evaluating the outcomes of a particular course. Each test has about an 80% overlap with the course objectives.

As we proceed to examine the validity of these instruments, we focus on what actually happened during instruction by asking the teachers of this course to check off those course objectives that were actually taught. For a variety of reasons, teachers may not cover all of the course objectives. Thus, there could be a substantial difference between the objectives of a course and those actually fostered in the classroom. Let us say that comparing the objectives of instruction to the outcomes measured by the tests showed that two of the tests were clearly superior. The final step in assessing the validity of these instruments would be to examine the actual test exercises to determine which test does the best job of measuring the objectives of instruction in the manner in

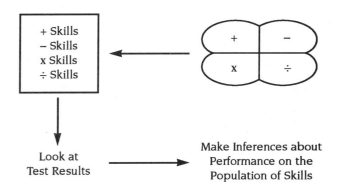

FIGURE 5.3. Definition of a Test

which they were taught. At this stage, there are numerous reasons for selecting one test over another. For example, the context in which the problems are presented in one of the tests may make it better for use in an urban school environment. One test may be more desirable than the other because metric rather than conventional units of measure are used.

It is important to note that the approach used to assess the validity of a test is very closely related to the process of curriculum mapping. We address the issue of validity to ensure that there is congruence among (1) the objectives of the school curriculum, (2) the skills actually fostered in the classroom, and (3) the outcomes measured by the unit or course test. If a test measures outcomes that are different from those included in the curriculum and fostered in the classroom, then it does not provide an accurate assessment of schooling.

The issue of validity needs to addressed very carefully when comparing curricula (Walker & Schaffarzick, 1972). For example, consider a school system that cannot decide which of two elementary school science programs it should adopt at grades K–6. Thus, it opts to pilot both programs for 3 years, compare student performance among programs, and then make a final selection. Although this may sound like a reasonable approach, it is very difficult to select a test that is a valid measure of both programs, because their outcomes are different. We saw this in the 1960s and 1970s when we attempted to evaluate the new science curricula. If we used the Harvard Project Physics test, students in this program outperformed those in PSSC Physics. The reverse happened when we used the PSSC Physics test. If we compromise by testing the outcomes common to both programs, then we end up ignoring how students performed with respect to the distinguishing features of each of these curricula.

When comparing curricula, it is often best to use two tests. Use a valid test to measure the outcomes of elementary science program A and another such test for elementary science program B. At the end of the 3 years, compile the test results in terms of what students in program A learned and what students in program B learned. The decision as to which program to adopt then becomes a value decision. Which set of outcomes do we value more?

Validity is the most important consideration when developing or selecting a test, and it should not be confused with reliability. While the focus of validity is on how accurately a test measures some population of skills, reliability focuses on how consistently a test measures that population. Ebel (1972) used the Anne Oakley analogy to illustrate the concepts of validity and reliability. Think of Anne involved in a shooting contest with an amateur as part of a charity benefit. The amateur steps to the firing line first and fires her six shots. They all hit in approximately the same spot, but at the fringe of the target. This amateur is consistent (reliable), but not accurate (valid). Anne then steps up and buries all her shots into the core of the bull's eye. Anne is consistent (reliable), as well as accurate (valid). In target shooting as well as in testing, accuracy (validity) is prized over consistency (reliability). As illustrated in this target-shooting example, if a test is accurate, it tends to be consistent. If a test is consistent, then we cannot conclude that it is valid without comparing what that test measures to the outcomes actually fostered during instruction.

Types of Tests and the Purposes of Testing The definition of a test presented in Figure 5.3 is also useful for clarifying the types of tests that are used to measure student achievement. Three types of achievement tests tend to be used in schools: norm-referenced, domain-referenced, and criterion-referenced tests. The type of test used is a function of the type of inference we wish to make regarding the population of skills. If we wish to know how students rank in comparison to other students with respect to the overall population of computation skills, then we use a norm-referenced test. *Norm-referenced tests* are the commercially developed, standardized achievement tests commonly used in schools. The strengths of such instruments lie in how students rank with respect to others at the national, regional, or state levels, rather than in telling us what students know and are able to do with respect to computation.

If we want to know what students know and are able to do with respect to computation, we need to use a domain- or criterion-referenced test. *A domain-referenced test* would be constructed if we want to make inferences about whether students have mastered the desired outcomes in each of the four domains of computation: addition, subtraction, multiplication, and division. If we want to make inferences about which objectives students have mastered in each of the four domains, then we would use a *criterion-referenced test*. To make such mastery decisions, standards are established at the domain or objective level. These standards or cut scores are the number of items a student would need to answer correctly to demonstrate mastery of a domain or an objective.

It is important to note that as we move from a norm- to a domain- to a criterion-referenced test we are obtaining finer, more in-depth information about student performance. In order to make these more-specific inferences, we need to take a larger sample of the population by increasing the number of items on the test. Thus, test length increases proportionally as we move from a norm- to a domain- to a criterion-referenced test. It is important not to confuse a criterion-referenced test with what some have called "objective-referenced tests." These tend to be commercially developed norm- or domain-referenced tests that provide an objective mastery report. While this mastery report may be useful, it only deals with the specific objectives sampled by that test. In the case of a norm-referenced test, objectives are sampled that are both critical to

the population of skills and which also maximize variation among students. Thus, the objective mastery report for such a norm-referenced test would provide only a fraction of the information available from a criterion-referenced test.

The decision as to what type of test to use should be a function of the purpose of testing. The four basic purposes of testing are as follows:

1. to assess educational needs so students are placed appropriately in instruction
2. to monitor student progress to provide both the teacher and the student with ongoing feedback to guide the instructional process
3. to assess student achievement to grade or certify mastery
4. to provide parents and the public with accountability information

For example, it is common for school systems to use loosely constructed criterion-referenced tests to place students in instruction and to monitor their progress. As higher stakes mastery decisions are made, it is necessary to develop good quality, domain-referenced tests. While such domain-referenced tests are appropriate for sharing accountability information with parents and the public, they are often supplemented with norm-referenced tests, so the achievement of students in the school district can be compared with that of students at the state, regional, or national level.

Some may wonder whether it is acceptable to make placement decisions and to monitor student progress with loosely constructed criterion-referenced tests. It is important to note that loosely constructed does *not* mean poorly constructed. Loosely constructed criterion-referenced tests are constructed by teachers with considerable thought and integrated into the instructional process. It is important to integrate such testing with the instructional process so testing does not detract from instruction. During the 1970s, some school systems implemented formal criterion-referenced systems for monitoring student progress on a weekly or biweekly basis. These approaches were abandoned because too much time was spent on testing and the record keeping was too cumbersome. As is widely recognized today, testing should serve instruction rather than detract from it. The more we integrate testing with instructional decision-making on a day-to-day basis, the better.

Some may be skeptical of using teacher-built tests to guide instructional decision-making because of the problems associated with such tests, particularly their validity. Validity is not a problem here because teachers use these tests only as guides in the decision-making process. They then reassess the appropriateness of their decisions as they work with the students. For example, Sue, who is a new student at a school, was assigned to a particular level of algebra based on a teacher-built placement test. After the first week, it was evident that Sue knew the material and was not being challenged appropriately. At that time the teacher met with Sue to reassess what she knew and was able to perform in algebra and assigned her to a more appropriate class. As another example, a middle-school teacher quizzed her class on the components of a novel before moving into literary analysis. Although it was clear that some reteaching was necessary, she

TABLE 5–3. Comparison of Various Types of Assessment

	Objective test	Essay test	Performance assessment
Purpose	Sample knowledge with maximum efficiency and reliability	Assess thinking skills and/or mastery of a structure of knowledge	Assess ability to translate knowledge and understanding into action
Typical exercise	Test items: Multiple-choice True/false Fill-in Matching	Writing task	Written prompt or natural event framing the kind of performance required
Student's response	Read, evaluate, select	Organize, compose	Plan, construct, and deliver original response
Scoring	Count correct answers	Judge understanding	Check attributes present, rate proficiency demonstrated, or describe performance via anecdote
Major advantage	Efficiency—can administer many items per unit of testing time	Can measure complex cognitive outcomes	Provides rich evidence of performance skills
Potential sources of inaccurate assessment	Poorly written items, overemphasis on recall of facts, poor test-taking skills, failure to sample content representatively	Poorly written exercises, writing skill confounded with knowledge of content, poor scoring procedures	Poor exercises, too few samples of performance, vague criteria, poor rating procedures, poor test conditions
Influence on learning	Overemphasis on recall encourages memorization; can encourage thinking skills if properly constructed	Encourages thinking and development of writing skills	Emphasizes use of available skill and knowledge in relevant problem contexts
Keys to success	Clear test blueprint or specifications that match instruction, skill in item writing, time to write items	Carefully prepared writing exercises, preparation of model answers, time to read and score	Carefully prepared performance exercises; clear performance expectations; careful, thoughtful rating; time to rate performance

Adapted from Stiggins, R. A. (1987, p. 38).

was surprised that two students who seemed to understand the concepts in class scored poorly. Thus, she reviewed their quiz results with them and found that they really did need additional instruction on the components of a novel. In summary, using loosely constructed criterion-referenced tests for placement and monitoring purposes supports good instructional decision-making as long as teachers validate these decisions as they continue with the instructional process.

The area in which the most attention needs to be devoted to improve testing practices in schools is the development or selection of domain-referenced tests to grade students or to certify mastery. Such summative decisions are high-stakes decisions that need to made on the basis of high-quality tests with evidence to support their validity. Table 5.3 (Stiggins, 1987) includes a comparison of the types of assessment techniques that can be used when constructing such instruments. Although much attention is being devoted in schools to the development of performance assessments that can include portfolios and that require students to apply what they have learned to authentic, "real"-world problems (Wiggins, 1993), objective and essay test exercises still have a place in the valid assessment of student outcomes. It is important to review the considerations in Table 5.3 and then construct or select tests that include exercises appropriate to the student outcomes being assessed. It is not unusual to include a variety of exercises in a mastery test. For example, objective exercises could be used to assess students' comprehension of critical concepts; an essay component could be used to assess students' ability to analyze important issues, and a performance task could be used to assess whether students can apply what they have learned in solving authentic problems. The National Council on Measurement in Education (NCME) has published some good instructional modules on developing performance assessments (Stiggins, 1987) and on using portfolios of student work in instruction and assessment (Arter & Spandel, 1992). These are excellent resources to consult when delving into the process of performance assessment.

Developing a Policy Statement on Testing The road to havoc is paved with good intentions often applies to testing practices in schools. Discussions of the role of testing in schools such as this one are read and accepted by well-meaning teachers and administrators who want to change what is happening in their schools, but they experience difficulty moving ahead. One strategy that has helped to improve testing practices in some schools is to develop district policies on testing. An outline of some of the issues that should be addressed in developing such a policy is presented in Figure 5.4. Although developing such a policy statement can be challenging in larger school districts, it can be especially rewarding in many ways. For example, one large school district saved several thousand dollars in developing such a statement because it found that it was able to consolidate a number of its testing programs. Another school district started to see its standardized test results being used in a more productive way. In the past, principals and teachers received reams of computer-generated reports each year without any guidance as to how these data should be used. In developing the testing policy, central office personnel clarified how these results should be used in making decisions about students and programs and also reduced the amount of data coming back to principals and teachers to only what they needed to make these decisions. Less tends to be more when sharing test data with schools. In some settings, the district policy statement on testing has been used as a planning document. In addition to those testing practices in place, it has included provisions for tests being developed. For example, one school system decided to develop mastery tests in science, social science, writing, and literature at the end of grades 2–6. Its policy statement included a description of what these instruments would look like, a timeline for their development, and a plan for reporting and using the results.

When dealing with the procedures for testing, it is important to make sure that test administrations are spread out appropriately through the year. Too much testing at a particular time of the year can lead to test fatigue and can disturb the continuity of instruction. It is also important for tests to be administered properly. With all other factors being equal, students tend to do better on standardized achievement tests when (1) parents are informed of the testing, (2) students are encouraged to get a good night's rest beforehand and to have

I. Purposes of Testing

II. Test Instruments
   A. Basic Skills areas to be tested as well as the rationale for focusing on these areas.
   B. Types of instruments to be used (i.e., norm, criterion, or domain referenced).
   C. Description of the actual test instruments selected.
   D. Grade levels at which these instruments will be used.

III. Procedures of Administering the Test Instruments
   A. Time of the year at which instruments will be administered.
   B. Specific approach to be employed in administering these instruments.

IV. Information Provided by the Test Instruments
   A. Specific types of reports and/or feedback to be received.
   B. Specific description of how this 8information will be used to evaluate curricular programs and student progress.
   C. Specific procedures for using evaluation feedback to improve the educational process.

FIGURE 5.4. Proposed Outline for a School District Policy Statement on Testing

a good breakfast on the day of the test, (3) teachers approach the testing experience positively and encourage students to do their best, (4) testing takes place in the students' regular classroom without distraction, (5) administration procedures are followed carefully, and (6) teachers check the background information that students record on their answer sheets. Teachers need to make sure that this background information is accurate, because some norms take into consideration a student's age, sex, and/or grade placement. Although it makes good sense to attend to such factors when administering a standardized achievement test, it is disturbing to see how often some of them are ignored.

The Role of Standardized Testing in the Program Evaluation Process

Standardized tests are often used to evaluate school programs because parents and the public are interested in how their students perform compared with other students in the state, region, or nation. Problems result when attempts to make such comparisons are made using grade equivalent scores. Some people think they understand grade equivalent scores when they really do not. Let us take the example of a school system that tests all of its sixth grade students using a standardized basic skills achievement test in early October. By definition, the average student would score 6.1 on this test. Six (6) stands for the sixth grade and one (1) for the first month of school. The results reported back to this school system are as follows:

Area Tested	Mean Grade Equivalent Score
Reading	6.2
Language	6.5
Mathematics	7.1

Let us assume three conclusions were drawn from these results as follows:

1. Students scored above the national average in all three basic skill areas.
2. Students did better in mathematics than in language, and better in language than in reading.
3. In mathematics our sixth grade students are one year ahead of the other students in the nation.

Only the first conclusion is correct. The second conclusion is not correct because we cannot compare grade equivalent scores across tests because they are normed independently of each other. Because 7.1 corresponds to the average score of a seventh grader in the first month of school, it was concluded that students were a year ahead in mathematics. The problem is that all a score of 7.1 tells us is that our students got the same score on this test as the average seventh grader who took the same test in the first month of school. The third conclusion would be correct only if there was evidence that this test did in fact measure what students need to know and need to be able to do in mathematics at the beginning of the seventh grade. When we examine the test specification in this manner, we tend to find that our students have done well, but not well enough to conclude that they are one year ahead in the actual mathematics curriculum.

The problem of grade equivalents is more than a problem of score interpretation. Assessing the growth of students over time is also a problem. First, there is the problem of how to calculate mean grade equivalent scores. Three methods of calculating grade equivalent score means are as follows:

1. Calculate the mean of the grade equivalent scores,
2. Calculate the mean of the raw scores and then convert this mean into grade equivalent units,
3. Calculate the mean of the standard scores and then convert this mean into grade equivalent units.

A comparison of the effect of these methods on the outcomes of the evaluation of a compensatory reading program is illustrated in Table 5.4. The goal of this program was to show six months' mean growth in reading comprehension. Depending on the method used to calculate the means, the program either met or surpassed its goal. Iwanicki and St. Pierre (1974) analyzed a large data file of students' standardized test score records. Successive random samples were drawn from this file and grade equivalent score means were calculated for each sample using the three methods. The trend that emerged through this process was that Method 1, averaging the grade equivalents directly, tended to produce a lower estimate of the mean than did either of the other two methods.

It is interesting to apply this finding to Figure 5.5. In Figure 5.5, the mean reading growth of middle-school students is compared over two years. Think of the pair of columns as a comparison of the performance of last year's fifth graders to this year's fifth graders. Although we are comparing two different groups, students in this school system tend to be fairly homogenous over time. The central office staff was somewhat

TABLE 5–4. Mean Grade-Equivalent Test Score Growth Calculated Using Alternative Methods for the Gates-MacGintie Reading Test Reading Comprehension Grade 2 (N=80)

Methods Used to Calculate Means	Pretest Results	Post test Results	Growth
Mean of the G.E. Scores	1.49	2.08	.59 (6 months)
Mean of the raw scores converted to G.E. units	1.36	2.05	.69 (7 months)
Mean of the standard scores convert to G.E. units	1.40	2.19	.79 (8 months)

perplexed by the decrease in scores at grades 5–8, because a major initiative was launched during Year 1 to improve reading performance at the middle school. Upon examining the scoring order form, we found that the grade equivalent means were calculated by Method 2 in the first year (higher estimate) and Method 1 in the second year (lower estimate). Thus, we hypothesized that the trend downward could have been a function of how the means were calculated. We were correct. When the publisher forwarded means calculated by Method 2 for year two, it became evident that there was a slight upward trend in reading performance at grades 5–8 in Year 2. What we can conclude from this discussion is that if we must use grade equivalent scores to report basic skill growth over time, then we should be consistent in the method used to calculate these scores, and preferably use Methods 2 or 3.

The meaning of good mean growth is another issue that needs to be addressed when reporting grade equivalent score growth over time. Is a year's growth for every year in school good growth? The answer is sometimes *yes,* and sometimes *no.* Figure 5.6 includes grade equivalent score growth curves for students at the tenth, fiftieth, and ninetieth percentiles. Note that the average expected growth for students at the tenth percentile is four months per year, at the

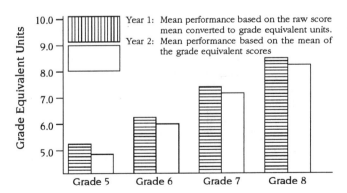

FIGURE 5.1. Comparison of Mean Reading Growth for Two Subsequent Middle School Classes*

* Note that both classes were quite similar in ability

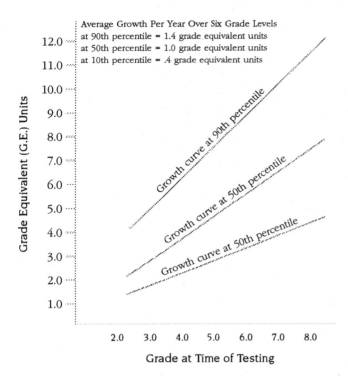

FIGURE 5.6. Illustration of the Differential Rates
of Growth in Grade Equivalent Units for
Different Percentile Ranks Based on CTBS
Total Reading Performance, Form Q.
Graphic format adopted from Wrightstone et al (no date)

50th percentile it is ten months or one year, and at the 90th percentile it is one year and four months. Thus, one year's mean growth is outstanding for students at the tenth percentile, good for students at the fiftieth percentile, but below expectations for the more capable students at the ninetieth percentile. During the late 1960s and early 1970s, some concern was raised that students in compensatory educational programs were not exhibiting one year's growth for every year in the program. Since the students participating in such programs tended to be below the twenty-fifth percentile, one year's growth was not a realistic expectation. To estimate what grade equivalent score growth should be expected over time, we need to begin with the mean grade equivalent and percentile scores which the group received on the pretest. We should then turn to the posttest norms and convert the pretest mean percentile into a grade equivalent score. The estimate of expected grade equivalent growth is the difference between the actual pretest and the derived posttest means.

It should be clear from this discussion that there are a number of serious problems that can be encountered when using grade equivalent scores for program evaluation purposes. If grade equivalent scores must be used, then it is important to proceed with caution. Although there are a number of good alternatives to grade equivalents that could be used for research purposes, parents and policy makers have difficulty understanding these approaches. The most reasonable and understandable alternative to grade equivalent scores is to use percentile scores. If the mean percentile rank

in reading for students at the beginning of grade 3 is 63, then we can tell parents and policy makers that the average student in this school system scored better than 63% of the students who took this test nationally. If we want to monitor reading achievement for a group of students over time using a particular test or test battery, then we can examine what happens to the percentile ranks over time. If the percentile rank stays the same, then this indicates that students are making progress consistent with their initial performance. If the percentile rank increases, then this indicates that student performance has been enhanced. A decrease in percentile rank indicates that students have fallen behind their reference group in reading. A sample longitudinal array of basic skill achievement test data is provided in the box:

| | Mean Percentile Rank | | |
Grade	Reading	Language	Mathematics
3	56	58	65
4	54	60	66
5	58	57	68

In examining this array in reading, we see a slight drop from grade 3 to grade 4 and an increase from grade 4 to 5 that results in an overall trend of improved performance for this cohort. An advantage of using percentiles is that mean scores can also be compared qualitatively across the areas tested. On this battery of tests, students tended to score consistently higher in mathematics than they did in either language or reading.

Some caution needs to be taken when using percentiles. Because they are not equal interval scores, the differences between percentile scores near the mean are less that the differences toward the extremes. Thus, we can make qualitative comparisons within or across test score means, but we cannot make quantitative comparisons. For example, at grade 4 we can say students did better in language than they did in reading, and better in mathematics than in language, but we cannot say the difference between math and reading is twice that between language and reading. Dealing with unequal interval scores tends to be more of a problem when comparing means that fall into the top or bottom deciles. In such situations, percentiles can be standardized by converting them into normal curve equivalents. Such conversions can be made easily using a simple table provided by the test publisher.

Using Domain-Referenced Tests in the Program Evaluation Process

When using domain-referenced tests in the program evaluation process, the focus is on what students have learned, rather than on how students rank. If objective domain-referenced tests are used to evaluate programs, standards or cut scores need to be set to determine at what level(s) students have mastered the outcomes of a unit or program. With essay tests or performance assessments, rubrics are usually developed to determine the students' level(s) of mastery. Current texts in classroom and performance assessment, as well as general references in educational measurement, provide a range of perspectives on the development of cut scores and rubrics. Once such standards are developed, the evaluation process consists of simply displaying the test data with respect to the standards and then making a judgment about the value or worth of the results. For example, one school system decided to test all of its students in the basic skills at the end of grades 2, 4, and 6 using a domain-referenced test. Performance on this test was evaluated using the same standards as those employed in Kentucky (Guskey, 1994, p. 26) as follows:

Distinguished: The student has a deep level of understanding of the concept or process and can complete all important parts of the task. The student can communicate well and offer insightful interpretations or extensions (generalizations, applications, and analogies).

Proficient: The student understands the major concepts, can do almost all of the task, and can communicate concepts clearly.

Apprentice: The student has gained more understanding and can complete some important parts of the task.

Novice: The student is beginning to show an understanding of new information or skills.

The data in reading for the first year are presented below for one school:

Percentage of Students at Each Performance Level in Reading			
Performance Level	Grade 2	Grade 4	Grade 6
Distinguished	10	15	20
Proficient	50	60	65
Apprentice	30	15	10
Novice	10	10	5

The results presented are encouraging because the combined percentage of proficient and distinguished readers increases with grade level from 60% at grade 2 to 85% at grade 6, but is this really good? Can we accept that 15% of the students are not at least proficient by the end of grade 6? Is it appropriate that only 25% of our students have reached the distinguished level? These are the types of decisions we need to make as we reflect on what we value most for our students in reading.

The use of such standards for evaluation purposes also has implications for grading. While the literature on grading indicates that grades should reflect what students have learned, this is often not the case in schools (Stiggins, Frisbie, & Griswold, 1989). In going back to the data just shared, we could equate the four performance levels with grades of A, B, C, and D. F would be reserved for those students who exhibit novice level performance and little effort to improve (i.e., poor class participation, erratic homework, refusal to stay after school for help, frequent absences). Although such grades would reflect what students have learned, would parents be willing to accept such a grade distribution where a quarter or less of the students receive an A in reading? Such considerations need to be addressed during the next few years as schools better align their grading practices with the outcomes of classroom assessments. Guskey (1996) provides some interesting perspectives on how schools can better communicate with parents what students are learning.

School-Based Evaluation in Perspective

A summary perspective on the issues discussed so far in this chapter is presented in Figure 5.7. There are two sections to this figure. The first part includes a basic approach to educational programming in schools based on the work of Stiggins (1997) and supported by the earlier work of Tyler (1950). This basic approach should be viewed as a planned process with considerable flexibility, not as overly linear.

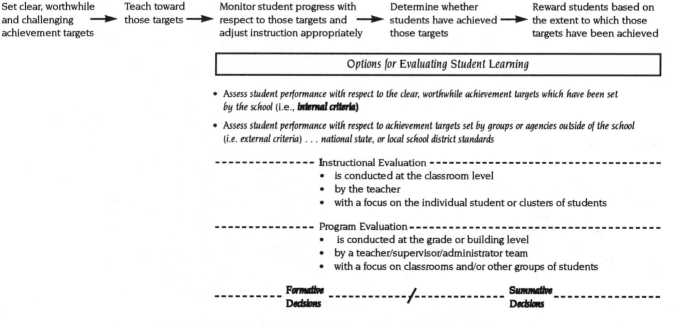

FIGURE 5.7. An Evolving Perspective on School-Based Evaluation
A Basic Approach to Educational Programming in Schools

Although we plan curricula using the literature in combination with our best professional judgment, we need to be sufficiently flexible to modify such programs if they are not meeting appropriate student needs.

The second part of Figure 5.7 includes the options for evaluating student learning as we implement the basic approach to educational programming. In practice, the school evaluation process begins with a focus on internal criteria, the worthwhile achievement targets set by school staff. As instruction commences, individual teachers monitor their students' progress on a formative basis as part of the instructional evaluation process. These teachers periodically get together with supervisory and/or administrative staff to discuss the progress that their students are making and to address ways in which they might deal with any difficulties that their students are encountering. This is the formative aspect of program evaluation, and it may result in adjustments in how a program is being implemented.

At key times during the school year (it is hoped at least quarterly), teachers administer summative assessments to their students as part of the instructional evaluation process. They review the results and make decisions about what their students have learned and about the effectiveness of their instruction. Teachers then meet and share these decisions with their colleagues, including supervisory and/or administrative staff, as part of the program evaluation process. The accomplishments of students are documented and directions are set for how instruction will continue through this process. Through this debriefing, decisions are also made about how this segment of the curriculum will be taught subsequently.

The final option in Figure 5.7 deals with using external criteria (i.e., achievement targets set by groups or agencies outside the school) to evaluate student learning. The purpose of the evaluation process is primarily summative: How well did our students perform compared with others on some external examination? It is best to address this question by first sharing the results of external examinations with teachers for their review and analysis. Teachers would identify areas in which their students did well, areas in which their students' performance needs to be strengthened, and potential strategies for strengthening students' performance in these areas. Once teachers have completed their reviews and analyses, they would be brought together with supervisory and/or administrative staff to share and discuss their findings. Through such discussions, consensus would be reached as to how students in the school compared with others who took the test and what needs to be done to improve students' performance in the future.

The approach just described for the school-based evaluation of student learning is not new. Rogers (1974, p. 9) shared Sarason's (1971) description of how John Dewey used evaluation to guide the decision-making process when he was principal of the laboratory school at the University of Chicago.

1. Dewey met weekly with the teacher "in which the work of the prior week was gone over in light of the general plan, and in which teachers reported the difficulties met in carrying it out. Modifications and adaptations followed. Discussion in these meetings was a large

means in translating generalities about aims and subject matter into definite form." These meetings were not about "administrative matters" but about ideas, their implementation, success, and failure

2. Cooperative social organization applied to the teaching body of the school as well as to the pupils. . . . It was the principal's task to create those conditions which would be the antithesis of "teaching as a lonely profession." What comes through in the description, casually and almost incidentally, is the degree of hourly and daily interaction among teachers.

3. Dewey was an investigator who, when the school was enlarged and put on a departmental basis, he chose directors who were also investigators. Each director weekly furnished reports containing "data of the problems for study and discussion in the weekly informal conference of teachers, as well as in the more formal seminar groups and larger pedagogical club meetings."

4. Dewey considered informal interchange among teachers to be an essential characteristic of the culture of the school. Teachers had free periods in order to visit and advise with other groups and teachers. The function of the free period was not a respite from a weary task but a stimulus to intellectual exchange.

5. A parent association was formed and it was expected that the parents would be concerned about educational issues. The association had an educational committee to which parents came with their criticisms and suggestions and "in quiet consultation with the teachers were often able to correct a bad habit formed in a teacher or, by revealing a teacher's plan to the parent, the teacher was able to remove his objections and reconcile him to the particular method in question."

The approach to school evaluation that Dewey used is similar in many respects to what principals of more effective public and nonpublic schools are doing today. Why, then, is this approach not being used more broadly in schools? Although for years we have attributed the lack of interest in evaluation to the need for better methods, better training, and more resources, a better answer may be that a culture of inquiry is lacking in too many schools. As Campbell (1969) has noted, we are not an experimenting society, thus, this orientation is reflected in how we approach the process of schooling. When we adopt new curricula, the expectation is that we will adopt the right one. If major flaws happen to be detected when this new program is implemented, then somebody must have made a mistake. School boards apparently have not read that change needs to be experimental. When we change our approach to schooling with the expectation that learning will be strengthened or enhanced, we need to validate that expectation and be ready to pursue other alternatives if necessary (Calhoun, 1994). The challenge of school leadership is to create a culture of inquiry and renewal in which evaluation can be used in this manner to strengthen or enhance teaching and learning in the classroom.

Evaluation as Decision-making about Teaching and Learning

The previous discussion of program evaluation issues focused heavily on making decisions about the quality of school programs and their effect on students. Not much was said about making decisions about the quality of teaching until Figure 5.7 was introduced. The primary reason for this is that the program evaluation literature did not focus on the quality of teaching until the early to mid-1990s. It was almost as if programs were teacherproof. The assumption tended to be made that if a program was designed well and implemented properly, then students would learn regardless of who the teacher was. When reference was made to teachers in evaluation reports, the discussion tended to focus on whether they implemented the program properly in the classroom with little reference to the quality of instruction.

Attention began to be devoted to the quality of teaching in the mid-1970s. Better schools were built in the 1950s. Major strides were made in improving the quality of curriculum and instruction in the 1960s and early 1970s. As parents and the public became more accountability minded and concerned about the outcomes of schooling in the 1970s, their attention turned to the teachers. If better facilities, programs, and instructional resources were not producing the desired results, then the problem must be the teachers. It was at this time that the foundation began to be set for the reforms in teacher education and certification that were initiated when we were declared *A Nation at Risk* (1983). New policies and initiatives in teacher evaluation tended to parallel states' reforms in teacher preparation and certification. The rationale in many cases tended to be that we should not expect more from beginning teachers than we did from more experienced educators.

A common approach to the evaluation of teaching that became prevalent in the 1980s was to develop a classroom observation system based on the process–product research and to apply that system to both the certification assessment and local teacher evaluation processes. The strength of such systems was that they helped to develop a common language of instruction among teachers and administrators that was lacking at that time. The problem with these systems was that they tended to focus on teaching without making direct linkages to learning. Evaluation decisions tended to be made on the basis of whether teachers demonstrated the desired teaching behaviors, with little reference to the learning that was actually taking place in the classroom.

Thus in the early 1990s, two types of evaluation processes were being implemented in schools. Program evaluations were being conducted to make decisions about the quality of school programs and their impact on student learning. Teachers were being evaluated to determine whether their performance was consistent with the teaching standards in their school systems; however the linkage between teaching and learning was not being made. As we look to the future, it is critical that the evaluation of teaching be linked to student learning. As Scriven (1994) has noted, the issues of merit and worth in the evaluation of teaching cannot be addressed until we make this linkage. As we move into the section of this chapter dealing with teacher evaluation, the need to continually make this linkage is an overriding theme. Teaching has little value or worth unless it is tied directly to student learning. This notion is not new, as evidenced by the following passage taken from the records of Massachusetts Bay Colony (Kyte, 1930 p. 4).

This Court, taking into consideration the great neglect of many parents and masters in the training up of their children in learning. . . , do hereupon order and decree, that in every town ye chosen men appointed for managing the prudential affairs. . . , shall have the power to take account from time to time, of all parents and masters, and of their children. . . , especially of their ability to read and understand the principles of religion and capital laws of this country.

TEACHER EVALUATION

The success of a teacher evaluation program is affected by three critical factors as follows:

- How we think about teacher evaluation
- How we organize for teacher evaluation
- How we conduct the teacher evaluation process

Most attention is devoted to the third factor, which deals with the methodology of teacher evaluation. This is unfortunate, because the success of a teacher evaluation program is more a function of philosophy and organization than it is of the methods we employ. If we believe that the goal of teacher evaluation is to strengthen or enhance the quality of teaching and learning in schools and to organize our schools in a manner consistent with this belief, then whatever methods we select or devise to evaluate teaching will help us to achieve our goal. The problem with teacher evaluation is that school systems often implement methods that are neither consistent with their beliefs nor with the manner in which their schools have been organized. Each of these critical factors will be discussed further in this chapter.

How We Think About the Teacher Evaluation Process

Three views of teacher evaluation have and continue to prevail in schools:
Past: evaluation focuses on rating teachers on the basis of style or trait criteria
Present: evaluation focuses on analyzing teaching on the basis of accepted practices
Future: evaluation focuses on analyzing teaching on the basis of what students learn.

The first view of rating teachers on the basis of style or trait is illustrated in Figure 5.8. It was not uncommon to find this approach being applied through the mid-1970s. Although Figure 5.8 illustrates the application of the traits approach, it is also interesting to note its date. Spears labeled this approach *Yesterday's Supervisory Formula* in 1941, yet it was still in common use almost 40 years later. It was interesting to ask practicing school administrators in the mid-1970s why they employed this approach. The most common rationale was tradition. At that time administrators rose up through the ranks in their school systems. This often included some apprenticeship to prior principals. Teacher evaluation practices tended to be handed down as a legacy from one administrator to the next, without much thought as to whether better and more effective practices might be employed.

FIGURE 5.8. Yesterday's Supervisory Formula, Parts I and II. From Spears, H. (1941, p. 382)

During the 1980s, many school systems moved away from the more traditional evaluation practice of rating teachers on the basis of style or trait criteria to analyzing teaching on the basis of accepted practices. This was due largely to the substantial investment that many states made in beginning teacher assessment. Much of what LEAs learned from the certification assessment of beginning teachers affected how they evaluated their novice and veteran teachers. It made good sense during the 1980s to focus evaluation on the analysis of teaching. The assumption was that if the evaluation process focused on the analysis of teaching, then feedback would be used to strengthen, enhance, or reinforce particular teaching skills, and thus, enhance student learning. Although this approach may have improved the quality of classroom teaching, there is little evidence (i.e., other than general perceptions) of its effect on student learning. If the goal of teacher evaluation is to improve the quality of teaching and learning in schools, then we have been only partially successful. As we look to the future, we need to focus our attention more on using teacher evaluation to improve the quality of student learning.

In order to adopt a student-learning focus in the teacher-evaluation process, we need to place a different emphasis on the analysis of teaching and adopt a more constructivist orientation to teaching and the teacher evaluation process. In doing so, we need to adopt the perspective that teaching is thinking about:

- what students need to know and be able to do
- what the teacher can do to foster such learning
- how successful the teacher has been in achieving the desired outcomes
- how the teacher should teach a particular lesson or unit of instruction the next time.

Given that teaching is thinking, it follows that teacher evaluation becomes a conversation between a teacher and another professional (i.e., administrator, supervisor, peer) about teaching. It focuses on what students know and are able to do, and on what the teacher can do to strengthen or enhance that level of learning in the classroom. Once student learning is analyzed, this information is used to make recommendations to strengthen or enhance teaching by reflecting back on the criteria or indicators of effective teaching. The major difference between this approach and what is happening now in many schools is that the analysis of student learning is the point of departure for the conversation instead of some construct of effective teaching. The basic promise of this approach is that by using student learning as the point of departure in the teacher evaluation process, we enhance the probability of arriving at recommendations that will have a direct effect on student learning.

In adopting this more learning-focused approach to the evaluation of teaching, it is important to emphasize that conversation is an opportunity for the teacher and evaluator to engage in deep, meaningful dialogue about the teaching-learning process, rather than casually exchanging ideas. In order for such dialogue to take place, it may be necessary for subject area supervisors, department heads, and peers to become more involved in the evaluation process. Dialogue is meaningful when makes sense to the teacher. Such dialogue is productive in that it leads to recommendations for improving or enhancing the quality of teaching and learning in the classroom. A school system knows whether it is taking a learning-focused approach to the evaluation of teaching by reviewing a sample of its teacher evaluation reports. If clear recommendations are made for strengthening teaching AND learning in the classroom, then the school system is taking a learning-focused approach to the evaluation of teaching.

Supervision or Evaluation?

A question often raised concerning this orientation to the teacher evaluation process is whether this is really teacher supervision rather than evaluation; or stated differently, is this really formative rather than summative teacher evaluation? From an academic perspective, the approach being advocated is supervisory or formative because it provides feedback concerning teacher performance for purposes of improvement. It is also summative or evaluative in that the information collected is used to judge the value or worth of a teacher's performance. From a practical perspective, it is difficult to specify beforehand whether teacher performance is being evaluated for formative or summative purposes. Let us consider a school system in which the teacher evaluation process consists of (1) a fall conference where directions for teacher improvement are mutually determined, (2) three classroom observations during the school year to assess the teacher's progress in the improvement areas identified, and (3) a final evaluation conference in the spring. For the vast majority of teachers in this school system, feedback provided through the fall conference and following each classroom observation would be formative or supervisory; it is feedback for the purposes of improvement. At the spring conference, a summative judgment would be made regarding the extent to which the teacher improved in those areas identified in the fall conference. For most teachers, formative and summative evaluation would assume a role–goal relationship in the classic sense as advocated by Scriven (1967). The role of formative evaluation would be to provide ongoing constructive feedback to teachers as they engage in their programs and professional development efforts for the purpose of maximizing their value or worth when summative decisions are made regarding their performance.

Let us now apply this process to a specific teacher. In mid-October, an elementary school principal observes Teacher X and finds this teacher's performance to be marginal. Through discussions with other staff, the principal finds that this teacher's performance has been affected by a recent personal crisis. In the observation conference, the principal begins wisely with the focus on the teacher: "How have things been going for you?" The teacher confides that a recent personal crisis has been doubly frustrating because it has been affecting the teacher's classroom performance. After considerable discussion of the matter, the principal and teacher agree that it would be best for all concerned to arrange for an immediate personal leave for the teacher.

In analyzing this case, it is difficult to determine whether the classroom observation was conducted for formative or summative purposes. The original intent was formative, but the information collected resulted in a summative decision to remove the teacher from the classroom. This case illustrates the point that although the intent of an effective teacher evaluation process is strongly formative or supervisory in nature, the orientation of the process can and must change dramatically when feedback indicates that a teacher is not performing adequately in the classroom.

Teachers recognize that there is not a clear distinction in practice between supervision and evaluation as it pertains to their performance in the classroom. It makes little difference to them whether the espoused purpose of a conference is supervisory or evaluative. They view all conferences as evaluative in that some decision is made regarding their performance, either for the purposes of providing feedback for improvement or for judging their effectiveness. When a written conference report is prepared and included in their personnel files, this is legally summative feedback. As one teacher noted, "Drop the weasel words. It's all evaluation. Areas we need to strengthen are identified, but we know what will happen on our final evaluation if we don't improve in those areas." In summary, teachers view the distinction often made in the literature between supervision and evaluation or between formative and summative evaluation as academic and not relevant to the actual practice of teacher evaluation. Rather than attempting to make such distinctions when working with teachers, it is more productive to introduce teacher evaluation as a process that is primarily improvement–oriented, while recognizing that the process can lead to teacher dismissal in those rare cases where efforts to facilitate improvement have not been successful.

HOW WE ORGANIZE FOR TEACHER EVALUATION

Few writings have had as dramatic an impact on the practice of teacher evaluation as *Teacher Evaluation in the Organizational Context* (Darling-Hammond, Wise, & Pease, 1983). As illustrated in Figure 5.9, these authors indicate that there is a relationship between the organizational structure of schools, the prevailing theory of education and concept of teaching in the school, the role of the school administrator, and the approaches to teacher evaluation employed. In schools organized along more rationalistic or bureaucratic lines, the teacher is viewed as a laborer or craftsman who has little or no input into the formulation of expected student outcomes, and the instructional procedures for fostering those outcomes may be externally prescribed. Within such school settings, the administrator operates more as an inspector who monitors the extent to which prescribed procedures are followed and expected student outcomes are achieved. The school organizational structure in such settings would be more characteristic of McGregor's (1960) Theory X, Argyris' (1964) infancy orientation, Likert's (1961) Systems I and II, and Sergiovanni and Starratt's (1983) human relations approach. Teacher evaluation tends to be focused on whether teachers are doing what they were told and achieving those student outcomes expected by the school administration.

In schools organized along more humanistic or naturalistic lines, the teacher is viewed as a professional or artist who participates in the identification of desired student outcomes and who exercises professional discretion in selecting appropriate instructional strategies to foster these outcomes. Within such school settings, the administrator operates more as a leader who coordinates and facilitates the efforts of the teaching staff to maximize the achievement of school outcomes. The school organizational structure in such settings would be

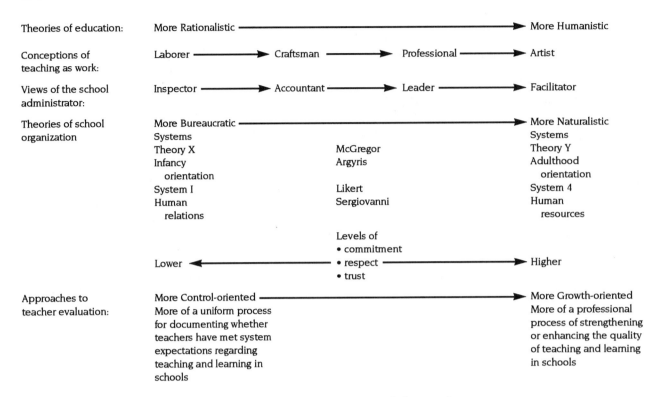

FIGURE 5.9. Some Assumptions and Their Implications
for the Role of Teacher Evaluation in Schools
Based on Darling-Hammond, Wise, & Pease (1983)

more characteristic of McGregor's Theory Y, Argyris' adult-hood orientation, Likert's Systems III and IV, and Sergiovanni and Starratt's human resources approach. The focus of teacher evaluation tends to be on cooperation and collaboration in determining school improvement needs and addressing these needs through continuous program improvement and professional development activities. A humanistic or naturalistic approach to school organization is necessary, if the goal of teacher evaluation is to improve the quality of teaching and learning. With this approach, we build the higher levels of commitment, respect, and trust necessary professional staff to implement more growth-oriented approaches to the teacher-evaluation process.

Figure 5.9 can be used to predict whether a more professional, growth-oriented approach, to the teacher-evaluation process can be implemented in school systems. For example, take the Taylortown Board of Education. It believes that teachers are being paid "darn" well, they should be responsible and pay for their own professional development. The board ensures that the 180 school days are focused on the teachers doing what they are paid to do—teach kids. Those mandatory in-service days that are required are organized around programs that meet what the board and central office administrators perceive to be the critical staff development needs of teachers, in order for the school system to comply with new state mandates. This is clearly a bureaucratic school organization. Thus, it is difficult if not impossible, to imple-

ment a more professional approach to teacher evaluation in this setting. By contrast, the Demingville Board of Education has always believed in the need to support teachers' professional development. Resources are provided to support teachers taking courses and attending conferences, provided such activities benefit the school system. Numerous teacher-initiated staff and professional-development programs have been planned at the team/department, building, and school system levels. Although all such activities are not conducted during released time, the equivalent of 14 half days have been allocated for staff and professional development activities. A professional, growth-oriented approach to teacher evaluation is most consistent with the organizational structure of the Demingville Public Schools.

In summary, the organizational context of a school determines the type of teacher-evaluation process that can be implemented effectively. This has important implications for state level teacher-evaluation reform efforts. Although a state may be encouraging its school systems to implement more professional, growth-oriented approaches to teacher evaluation, these approaches will tend to "catch on" best only in those school settings organized along more naturalistic lines. School organization along more naturalistic lines is not always a function of how the school system is organized. Weick's (1976) research on school organizations as loosely coupled systems indicated that staff in individual school buildings have considerable control over their destinies. For this reason we can find schools both "beacons of success" and "pockets of pestilence" that are anomalies given the other characteristics of the school systems in which they reside. More successful schools are healthy school organizations (Miles, 1965) in which teachers function as professionals in a climate of respect and trust. Healthy school organizations are those in which (1) goals are clear and accepted by staff, (2) good communication exists, (3) staff are empowered to make decisions, and (4) staff derive a sense of fulfillment from their work. The probability of implementing productive teacher evaluation practices in healthy school contexts in which teachers function as professionals is excellent, especially compared with those schools organized along more traditional, bureaucratic lines of authority, where teachers are viewed more as workers than as professionals.

It is important to note that in many schools, bureaucracy is a culture to which adminstrators and teachers have become accustomed, not something that is imposed on them. In more bureaucratic, hierarchical schools, principals and teachers are told what to do, and are not encouraged to think as professionals. This can become a comfortable arrangement in settings where the problems are serious, the resources are limited, and learning distractions are plentiful. Principals and teachers in such school settings do not have to be accountable. They can just blame the system.

Integrating Teacher Evaluation with Staff Development and School Improvement

Even in successful schools, where principals and teachers function as professionals, effective teacher evaluation practices may not be having an appreciable effect on student learning. The reason for this is largely due to the fact that teacher evaluation is implemented in isolation rather than in combination with other school improvement initiatives. Teachers may all be growing professionally in these settings, but they are doing so in so many different ways that the effect of such growth on the quality of learning in the school is difficult to determine. In addition, effective teacher evaluation programs that are implemented in isolation are eventually placed on the "back burner" when the next school initiative comes along. As one teacher commented, "We gave teacher evaluation a lot of attention a few years ago when the new process came in, but now we are into math manipulatives." Thus, as indicated in Figure 5.10, schools must approach the processes of teacher evaluation, staff development, and school improvement in an integrated, rather than in a disjointed, manner. The primary focus in this integrated approach is on school improvement. In schools where a continuous or total quality improvement process is in place, teacher evaluation and staff development can be used productively to support that improvement so that it has an appreciable impact on student learning. As Murphy (1987, p. 160) has noted, "One of the conclusions of the recent school improvement research is that schools work better when the parts fit together, when plans and activities are coordinated in a common effort to reach important school goals." By fitting the parts together through the more integrated approach, teacher evaluation has a more discernible impact on what happens in classrooms.

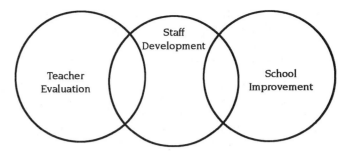

A More Disjointed Approach

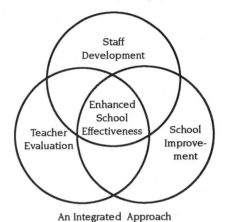

An Integrated Approach

FIGURE 5.10. Approaches to Organizing the Teacher Evaluation, Staff Development, and School Improvement Processes
From Iwanicki (1990, p. 167)

For example, one school set the following improvement goal: *Students will meet world class standards in mathematics in three years.* Given this goal, some implications were drawn for teaching and learning as noted:

- More problem-solving activities will be included in the teaching of mathematics
- Students will be involved more actively in the instructional process through the use of manipulatives and group projects
- Students will exhibit an increase in problem-solving ability on district and state performance measures.

This goal and its associated implications set a focus for staff development and teacher evaluation. As classroom observations were conducted, aspects of teaching problem solving were a focus (albeit not the sole focus) of the conversations that transpired in both the pre- and post-observation conferences. This goal and its associated implications also created a broad range of possibilities that teachers pursued in developing objectives that served as the basis of their professional growth plans. Some professional growth plans were even developed collaboratively by teams of teachers. As the superintendent commented, "When the process is done this way there is less threat and teachers understand how it will make a difference for kids." The commitment to and active involvement of the superintendent in this integrated approach to teacher evaluation is critical to its effective implementation (McLaughlin & Pfeifer, 1988).

Role of Teacher Evaluation in Systemic School Reform

It is particularly important to integrate teacher evaluation with school improvement as school systems become involved in systemic school reform initiatives. Much of the focus of systemic reform in schools is on content standards and performance standards. The work on content standards consists of developing curriculum frameworks that specify what all students should know and be able to do. These frameworks include content that is both challenging to students and critical to the discipline being studied. They are constructed to enable students to develop higher-level understandings and complex problem-solving abilities. The specific outcomes that students are expected to demonstrate in a discipline are conveyed through performance standards. O'Day and Smith (1993) caution that the focus on only content and performance standards is the same as adopting an input–output orientation to curriculum reform, which is an approach that was unsuccessful in the 1960s. They contend that the chances of achieving challenging performance standards through the development of curriculum frameworks may not be good unless school inputs and classroom processes are aligned with the intents of these frameworks. To achieve such alignment, O'Day and Smith propose that the concept of school standards be expanded to include both resource standards and practice standards:

In our current conception, school standards would have three parts. They would spell out criteria for determining whether a school (1) has the essential human and other materials to offer all of its students the opportunity to learn the content of the curriculum frameworks to a high level of performance (resource standards), (2) actually implements a program of study likely to provide its students such an opportunity (practice standards), and (3) meets challenging goals, as measured by the percentage of students who successfully achieve a high performance level (outcome or performance standards). (p. 275)

Upon further examination of the work of O'Day and Smith, it becomes evident that resource and practice standards focus on (1) resource issues and (2) aspects of curriculum and instruction related to the quality of teaching and learning in the classroom. With respect to the quality of teaching and learning in the classroom, the school standards (i.e., resource, practice, and performance) address the following questions:

1. To what extent do teachers possess the knowledge and skills necessary to implement the new curriculum frameworks effectively?
2. To what extent are teachers properly implementing the new curriculum frameworks in the classroom?
3. To what extent are students successful in achieving the desired outcomes of the new curriculum frameworks?
4. Where is staff development needed to support teachers' efforts to implement the new curriculum frameworks more effectively?

These questions are essentially the same as those addressed through the teacher evaluation process, especially when this process is being implemented in a professional, growth-oriented manner.

Teacher Evaluation in Organizational Context Today

Before leaving this section, it is important to return to Figure 5.9. While the work of Darling-Hammond et al has helped us to better understand the impact of the organizational context on teacher-evaluation practices in schools, the literature has evolved considerably since 1983. Rather than organizing more effective schools along human resources lines, the literature would now support structuring schools as learning organizations (Fullan, 1993; Senge, 1990). The focus of the principals' and teachers' efforts in a learning organization is on continually getting smarter about how the school is operating so that adjustments can be made where necessary to improve the quality of teaching and learning. Thus, change tends to be the only constant in a learning organization. Within this context, the principal would lead and facilitate in a transformational sense. As transformational leader, the principal would be responsible for working with staff to set a school vision and to develop and implement programs consistent with that vision (Leithwood & Duke, 1994). The role of the teacher would be expanded beyond professional and artistic, to include leadership and responsibility for the implementation and continuous improvement of school programs. In schools designed as learning organizations, teacher leaders would share responsibility with their principals, for the continuous improvement of school programs. Although the focus of teacher evaluation in such schools would continue to be on enhancing the quality of teaching and learning through professional growth and school improvement, the responsibility for evaluation would be shared more broadly with teacher leaders and peers.

It is interesting to monitor reactions to the directions that have been set for teacher evaluation in this section of the chapter. Educators tend to agree that teacher evaluation should focus on improving the quality of teaching and learning through professional growth and school improvement. The need to analyze teaching on the basis of what students learn makes sense to most educators. Members of the school community are also quite receptive to the notion of integrating teacher evaluation with staff development and school improvement. The need to begin with school improvement as the anchor in implementing this approach is well understood. Finally, the idea of sharing responsibility for this type of evaluation with teachers has not been met with much resistance. Why, therefore, are people not moving in this direction more quickly? It is a paradigm problem (Barker, 1992). Stated simply, a *paradigm* is a set of rules that establish boundaries. If we play by these rules, then we are assured a modicum of success, or at least safety. Because the directions being advocated in this section of the chapter are not consistent with the conventional paradigm of teacher evaluation, many school systems are uneasy about moving in this direction—but why should they do so? As Barker notes, they should do so because the old paradigm is not working. While conventional approaches to teacher evaluation produce a lot of paper, evidence of their impact on improving teaching and learning in schools is too scant to justify their continuation—but what evidence is there that the approach being advocated here will be any better? There is some, but it too is scant. When we change to a new paradigm, we tend to do so on faith that new paradigm makes better sense.

As schools move to a new paradigm, whether it be in teacher evaluation or in other areas, the way in which we communicate the new paradigm to members of the school community is critically important. When changing the process of teacher evaluation, this paradigm shift is usually made by developing a new handbook and implementing a professional development program to orient members of the school community to the procedures described in this handbook. At the conclusion of a very-well-planned professional-development program, some confusion often exists as to how this new approach differs from what has been done in the past. Thus, it is important to continually monitor this change and to clarify perceptions as necessary.

In analyzing such change, using the work of Bowman and Deal (1991), we address the structural, human resource and political frames when adopting new approaches to teacher evaluation, but we do not give sufficient attention to the symbolic frame. We are careful in drafting our new policies and making sure that we have the appropriate staff resources to implement them. We also make a concerted effort to gain the support of our professional organizations for the new teacher evaluation process, but we often do not do much to change the culture of teacher evaluation. This is an important issue to address, because we have a negative, or less than positive tradition of teacher evaluation in many school settings. It is easier to change a less than positive culture with symbols than it is with words. Figure 5.11 includes two examples of how symbolism has been used to change the culture of teacher evaluation. In 1991, the Enfield (Connecticut) Public Schools revised its teacher evaluation

handbook. The basket weave on the cover of the handbook was used to emphasize the need to integrate teacher evaluation with professional growth. In 1993, the Louisiana Department of Education implemented a new Professional Accountability Program that included teacher assessment for state certification as well as local teacher evaluation. The logo presented in Figure 5.11 was included on all program materials to emphasize the focus on teaching, learning, and professional growth. As in such examples, symbolism goes farther than words in changing the culture of and attitude toward teacher evaluation in schools.

This section on how we organize for teacher evaluation is important for two reasons. First, this issue is not addressed in most discussions of effective teacher evaluation practices. Second, this is the most critical aspect of effective teacher evaluation. Teacher evaluation will not be productive (i.e., will not have an appreciable impact on student learning) unless it is implemented in a professional school setting and integrated as an ongoing process of continuous school improvement. Effective teacher evaluation is more an issue of appropriate organization than it is of appropriate instrumentation.

HOW WE CONDUCT THE TEACHER EVALUATION PROCESS

There are four basic aspects to the teacher evaluation process:

- Philosophy regarding the goals of teacher evaluation
- Purposes for which we evaluate teachers
- Criteria we use to evaluate teachers
- Procedures we employ when evaluating teachers

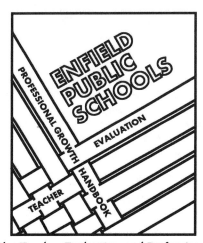

Cover of the Teacher Evaluation and Professional Growth Handbook in the Enfield (CT) Public Schools

Logo of the Louisiana Department of Education Professional Accountability System

FIGURE 5.11.
Two Examples of Using Symbolism to Change the Culture of Teacher Evaluation

Each of these aspects will be discussed in the following sections.

Philosophy and Purposes for Teacher Evaluation

The philosophy and purposes are the foundation of the teacher evaluation process. The philosophy includes the goal(s) of teacher evaluation (i.e., to improve the quality of teaching and learning in schools) as well as the basic beliefs about schools, teaching, learning, and evaluation that guide the process. The purposes state how teacher evaluation will be used in schools. The purposes that appear most often in teacher evaluation programs are:

1. Accountability, to assure the public that only effective teachers continue in the classroom.
2. School Improvement, to promote continuous school improvement and the enhancement of student learning.
3. Professional Growth, to foster the professional growth of new and continuing teachers.
4. Selection, to ensure that the best qualified teachers are hired.

School districts too often develop a statement of philosophy and purposes and then focus their efforts on developing a teacher evaluation process without looking back at this statement. These school districts get caught up in the procedures rather than in the substance of teacher evaluation. The substance of the evaluation process lies in its philosophy and purposes. A teacher evaluation process is effective to the extent that it is successful in achieving its goal(s) and purposes. If the goal of teacher evaluation is to improve the student learning experience, then the process is effective to the extent that it is making this happen.

The effectiveness of a teacher evaluation program should be assessed by reviewing teacher evaluation reports rather than procedures. If the evaluation reports provide evidence that the program is successful in achieving its goal(s) and purposes, then it is a good program. To the extent that a purpose is not being achieved, then the evaluation procedures need to be strengthened in that area.

Evaluation Criteria

It is important to state clearly in writing the criteria that will be used to evaluate teachers. The Indicators of Effective Teaching (Iwanicki, 1993) presented in Figure 5.12 have been adapted by a number of school systems for the evaluation of their teachers. As noted in Figure 5.13, each of these indicators is elaborated upon further by providing:

• a rationale (i.e., first paragraph) that describes why that indicator is important to teaching effectiveness
• a description of the defining attributes that will be used to evaluate the teacher
• a listing of the key aspects of each defining attribute

The indicators dealing with instruction (II–XI) were taken from the Connecticut Competency Instrument and the others

---

Planning

I. The teacher effectively plans instruction.

Management of the Classroom Environment

II. The teacher promotes a positive learning environment.
III. The teacher maintains appropriate standards of behavior.
IV. The teacher engages the students in meeting the objectives of the lesson.
V. The teacher effectively manages routines and transitions.

Instruction

VI. The teacher creates a structure for learning.
VII. The teacher develops the lesson effectively, using appropriate instructional techniques.
VIII. The teacher presents appropriate content.
IX. The teacher uses appropriate questioning techniques.
X. The teacher communicates clearly, using precise language and acceptable oral expressions.

Assessment

XI. The teacher monitors student learning and adjusts teaching when appropriate.

Professional Responsibilities

XII. The teacher performs noninstructional duties.
XIII. The teacher assumes responsibility for meaningful professional growth.
XIV. The teacher assumes leadership for school improvement and professional growth.

FIGURE 5.12. The Indicators of Effective Teaching
From Iwanicki (1993, p. 3)

---

were adapted from the North Carolina Teacher Performance Appraisal Instrument. Once an initial draft of the indicators was compiled, it was refined through a three-step process. First, a number of teachers and administrators reviewed the indicators and provided their feedback. Because the indicators were derived from instruments used to evaluate beginning teachers, it was important to modify them appropriately so they would apply to the evaluation of more experienced, veteran teachers. Practicing educators in graduate classes at the University of Connecticut then reviewed the indicators and provided their feedback. These students reviewed the indicators within the context of Berliner's (1988) continuum of teacher development (i.e., novice, advanced beginner, competent, proficient, expert). Finally, the indicators were reviewed in light of the literature on teaching effectiveness for experienced teachers. Covino (1991), who validated a set of proficiencies for experienced teachers in Connecticut, reviewed the indicators and provided feedback on how they could be revised to better reflect the literature on effective experienced teachers. The feedback obtained from these three sources was used to develop the final version of the indicators of Effective Teaching. Given the manner in which the indicators were developed, they are clearly what Scriven (1987) would call duty-based descriptors of effective teaching. Teachers have been very receptive to the clarity with which

The Teacher Promotes a Positive Learning Environment

1. Rapport
   - Teacher establishes rapport by demonstrating patience acceptance, empathy, and interest in students
   - Teacher avoids sarcasm, disparaging remarks, and sexist or racial comments
   - Teacher maintains a positive social and emotional tone

2. Communication of Expectations
   - Teacher encourages all students to do their best

3. Motivation of Students to Learn
   - Teacher motivates students by exhibiting his or her own enthusiasm for what is being taught
   - Teacher selects learning tasks that are meaningful and relevant to students
   - Teacher helps students to focus their energies on the learning task by instilling a "you can do it" attitude
   - Teacher rewards students for their accomplishments

4. Physical Environment
   - Teacher establishes a classroom environment that is safe and orderly
   - Teacher establishes a classroom environment that is conducive to learning

The teacher is responsible for the nature and quality of teacher–student interactions in his or her classroom. The teacher's perception of students and their abilities directly affects students' responses and achievement, and the teacher's interactions with students should be positive and designed to enhance the learning environment. It is critical that the teacher understands, respects, and accepts cultural diversity and promotes such understanding and respect among students. The teacher, therefore, establishes and maintains a positive social and emotional tone by creating a physical environment con-

ducive to learning and maintaining both positive teacher–student and student–student interactions.

Defining Attributes

There are four defining attributes of promoting a positive learning environment. They reflect the use of a variety of techniques for promoting positive teacher–student interactions and a physical environment that is conducive to learning.

1. Rapport: The teacher establishes rapport with all students through positive verbal and non-verbal exchanges and by demonstrating patience, acceptance, empathy, and interest in all students. Sarcasm and disparaging remarks are not appropriate. Every effort should be made by the teacher to maintain a learning environment that is free from anger and hostility.
2. Communication of expectations: The teacher creates a climate where students are empowered to function as independent, responsible learners and encouraged to achieve at the highest level consistent with their abilities. Expectations for success may be explicitly verbalized or communicated through the teacher's approach to assigning tasks, rewarding student efforts, and providing help and encouragement to students.
3. Motivation of students to learn: The teacher motivates students for the learning process by exhibiting his or her own enthusiasm or passion for the content and for learning. The teacher selects learning tasks that are meaningful and relevant to students and helps students to see the worth of these tasks. The teacher creates task interest, helps students to focus their energies on the learning task by instilling a "you can do it" attitude, and rewards them for their accomplishments.
4. Physical environment: The teacher establishes a physical environment that is safe and orderly and creates an atmosphere, through classroom arrangements and displays, that is conducive to learning.

Some Key Aspects of Indicator II

FIGURE 5.13. An Example of How Each Indicator is Elaborated Upon
From Iwanicki (1993, pp. 9–10, Reference 3)

the indicators have been spelled out and with their potential for challenging teachers to develop higher levels of proficiency.

The Indicators and Defining Attributes of Effective Teaching were developed as a point of departure for school systems as they worked to refine their criteria for the evaluation of classroom teachers. In practice they were adopted by some without much modification because they were perceived as a good frame of reference for guiding teachers and evaluators in their conversations about how teaching and learning could be enhanced in the classroom. The intent was not to develop performance standards to assess the quality of teaching. As noted in Table 5.5, teacher assessment is different from teacher evaluation. When making certification decisions we need well-defined standards and criteria to determine whether or not an individual should be granted a license as a result of the assessment that has been conducted. When making decisions about teaching quality, we need a well-thought-out conception of effective teaching that serves as a guide for the teacher's development through the evaluation process. Because evaluation is more contextual than assessment is, it is difficult, if not impossible, to develop

meaningful criteria and standards for rating teaching for evaluation purposes. This problem of valid and reliable measurement in the evaluation of teaching (as compared with licensure assessment) is acknowledged in *The Personnel Evaluation Standards* (Joint Committee on Standards for Educational Evaluation, 1988). In addition, the current literature on teacher evaluation (Good & Mulryan, 1990; McGreal, 1990; Schwab & Iwanicki, 1992) does not advocate using teacher ratings in the evaluation process except for self-evaluation. When teacher ratings are used in the evaluation process, evaluation conferences focus less on teaching and more on the ratings. The evaluation conference becomes more of a forum for negotiating ratings than for discussing how teaching can be strengthened or enhanced.

Training Toward the Indicators

From Figure 5.13, it is evident that each indicator is elaborated upon extensively. Thus, it is no small task for an evaluator to develop a good understanding of the defining attributes for all the indicators and to be able to apply them appropriately in the teacher evaluation process. The indicators and

TABLE 5–5. Distinction Between Teacher
Assessment and Teacher Evaluation

Question	Assessment	Evaluation
What is the purpose?	To determine whether a teacher can teach effectively	To determine whether a teacher teaches effectively
Who is assessed?	Beginning teachers	Beginning and experienced teachers
What approach is used?	State certification assessment procedures and standards	Local teacher evaluation program
Who is responsible for assessment?	State department of education	Local school districts
What is the end product?	Certificate that signifies that the person has the ability to implement those practices deemed necessary for a person entering the teaching profession	Evidence that effective teaching is taking place in the classroom and that teacher evaluation is being used to strengthen or enhance the quality of teaching and learning in schools

defining attributes are the language of instruction that is used in the teacher-evaluation process. If an evaluator does not know this language well, then the quality of evaluation suffers. Even when systems deal with this issue by providing extensive training for their evaluators, there is some drift over time in their understanding of the defining attributes. One approach for reducing this drift is to develop an "Essence of the Indicators" sheet. This piece is developed by the evaluators at the end of their training. They review the defining attributes for a particular indicator in small groups and then list those behaviors that they believe capture the essence of what a teacher must do with respect to that indicator to optimize learning. The small groups then compare their lists and reach consensus. A sample list for the indicator (in Figure 5.13), *II. The Teacher Promotes a Positive Learning Environment*, is as follows:

• Students are treated with dignity and respect (no sarcasm, diversity is valued)
• All students are encouraged to learn
• Teacher is enthusiastic about what is being taught
• Teacher maintains a safe and orderly classroom environment (physically and psychologically)

The "Essence of the Indicators" sheet that results from this process should be no longer than one page, double sided. As evaluators refer back to this sheet during the evaluation process, it keeps them on target with respect to the essence of each indicator.

Identifying the Critical Indicators of Effective Teaching One reaction to the indicators in Figure 5.12 is that these are all

well and good for beginning teachers, but are they all appropriate for the evaluation of veteran teachers. Veteran teachers must be proficient in all areas, but once they become proficient in some of these areas, they should no longer be a focus of the evaluation process. For example, Bachrach, Conley, and Shedd (1987) looked at proficiency as a two-step process: (1) Can the teacher do it? (2) Can the teacher do it with variety? Consider classroom management as an example. The competent teacher can maintain order. The proficient teacher maintains order, and does it with variety. Some students are reminded of the rules. A warning look is sufficient for others. A few students are given more attention than others. There is no need to deal with classroom management when helping this proficient teacher to grow as a professional.

What, then, do we focus on with our cadre of proficient, veteran staff? To obtain some insights into this issue, the indicators were cross-referenced with the Core Propositions of the National Board for Professional Teaching Standards (NBPTS, 1989, p. 4) as listed below:

1. Teachers are committed to students and their learning
2. Teachers know the subjects they teach and how to teach those subjects to students
3. Teachers are responsible for managing and monitoring student learning
4. Teachers think systematically about their practice and learn from their experience
5. Teachers are members of learning communities

These core propositions have been developed to guide the assessment of experienced teachers to determine whether they meet rigorous standards for the teaching profession. Thus, if there is overlap between an indicator and a core proposition, there is a good probability that the indicator addresses a critical aspect of what successful experienced teachers need to know and be able to do to facilitate meaningful student learning. The NBPTS Core Propositions are cross-referenced with the indicators in Table 5.6. From Table 5.6, it is evident that there is considerable commonality between the core propositions and the general categories used to group the indicators in Figure 5.12:

• Core Propositions 1 and 4 have much in common with Planning
• Core Proposition 3 has much in common with Management of the Classroom Environment and Assessment
• Proposition 2 has much in common with Instruction
• Proposition 5 has much in common with Professional Responsibilities

Furthermore, the following indicators overlap considerably with the core propositions. Thus, if an argument were to be made for a subset of "critical indicators" that address what successful, experienced teachers needed to know and be able to do to facilitate meaningful student learning, then these five indicators would certainly be included.

TABLE 5.6. Relationship Between the Indicators
of Effective Teaching and The National Board for
Professional Teaching Standards Core Propositions

Indicators	NBPTS Core Propositions				
	1	2	3	4	5
Planning					
I	✓			✓	
Classroom Management					
II	✓		✓		
III			✓		
IV			✓		
V			✓		
Instruction					
VI					
VII	✓	✓			
VIII		✓			
IX		✓			
X					
Assessment					
XI			✓		
Professional Responsibilities					
XII					✓
XIII				✓	✓
XIV					✓

From: Iwanicki & Rindone (1995, p. 87).

  I. The teacher effectively plans instruction
 II. The teacher promotes a positive environment for learning
VII. The teacher develops the lesson effectively using appropriate instructional techniques
 XI. The teacher monitors student learning and adjusts teaching when appropriate
XIII. The teacher assumes responsibility and leadership for meaningful school improvement and professional growth

Moving Beyond the Indicators of Effective Teaching It has become evident that all of the Indicators of Effective Teaching are important for teachers at the early stages of their careers. As just discussed, some of these indicators remain critical even at the later stages of a teacher's development. The problem with the Indicators of Effective Teaching is that they are generic indicators. As shown in Figure 5.14, the generic indicators are necessary, but they are not sufficient descriptors of effective teaching. They need to be complemented by grade/content-specific teaching standards, especially at the later stages of a teacher's development. When good, experienced teachers are asked what they are doing to strengthen their teaching, they usually describe something that is central to the subject or grade level they are teaching: "I'm integrating a unit on bioethics into my biology course" or "I'm trying to develop better ways of helping second graders to understand part–whole relationships." As we look to develop better approaches to teacher evaluation in the future, grade/content-specific teaching standards need to be crafted to address this complementary dimension of teaching. The grade-specific standards should be based on the developmental needs of students. The content–specific standards should be based on the discipline being taught. For example, the National Council of Teachers of Mathematics Standards for teaching mathematics would be an excellent point of departure for developing grade/content-specific standards for the teaching of mathematics.

Evaluation Procedures

A good way to structure the process of teacher evaluation is to begin with the goal of teacher evaluation, to decide what needs to be done from a personnel standpoint to reach that goal, and then to develop a teacher evaluation process that supports such personnel decisions/practices. If the goal of teacher evaluation is to enhance the quality of teaching and learning in schools, then we need to (1) hire the best and brightest teachers, (2) induct these new teachers into the profession properly, (3) foster the professional growth and school improvement initiatives of newer and more experienced teachers, and (4) take appropriate action in those situations in which effective teaching is not taking place in the classroom.

Role of Evaluation in Teacher Selection One of the more important evaluation decisions a school system makes is the decision to hire a particular teacher. Because very few teachers are denied tenure and only a scant number are dismissed for performance reasons, being hired almost ensures a teacher a job for as long as he or she wishes to teach in that school system. Thus, it is essential for the school system to hire the best qualified candidates. Many school systems have well-

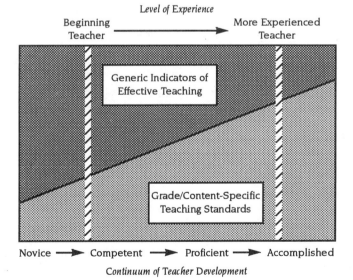

FIGURE 5.14. Relative Emphasis on Generic Indicators
of Effective Teaching and Grade/Content–Specific
Teaching Standards at Various Stages of Experience
and Teacher Development
From Iwanicki & Rindone (1995, p. 88)

developed selection procedures that ensure that the best qualified candidates are hired. In such systems, teachers are hired on the basis of demonstrated teaching ability, and not only on paper credentials. Hiring teachers based on paper screening is still common in many school systems. It is important for LEAs to employ coherent teacher selection procedures that ensure this first and most important evaluation decision is made properly.

Role of Evaluation in Teacher Induction Hiring the best and brightest teachers enhances the quality of education in a school system to the extent that such teachers are inducted into that system properly. We can set high expectations for these new teachers and provide them with the necessary support to meet these expectations or we can virtually leave them alone to be assimilated by the normative culture of the professional peer group they form. The literature advocates that it is best to structure the process to achieve the outcomes desired and not to leave induction up to the professional peer group the teacher forms by chance. Schools that have problems with the induction of new teachers should consider implementing Peer Assistance and Review (PAR) programs.

In PAR programs, the induction and evaluation of beginning teachers is handled by trained specialists (i.e., PAR consultants). These are usually classroom teachers who have been selected to participate in the program on a full-time basis for up to 3 years. At the end of this period these teachers return to their classrooms. PAR consultants are responsible for seeing that PAR guidelines are followed in the induction and evaluation of new teachers. Throughout the PAR program, support for beginning teachers and those new to the school system is provided by peers. The decision as to whether a teacher meets system expectations and should be granted a subsequent one-year or continuing contract is made by a PAR committee that reviews the report and recommendations of the PAR consultant. The PAR committee is usually comprised of an equal number of teachers and administrators.

A problem with PAR programs is the cost, because full-time staff are assigned to the program and outside assistance is needed periodically to train PAR consultants. The advantages based on the experiences of districts using such programs (e.g., Des Moines, Iowa; Columbus, Ohio) is that new teachers are inducted into the profession properly and only qualified teachers are rehired and granted tenure. School boards that have implemented PAR programs are convinced that they are worth the investment for two reasons. First, and foremost, PAR provides the appropriate support system to strengthen and enhance the performance of beginning teachers. This is particularly important in urban areas where for a time, good beginning teachers were leaving for other positions, not because they did not want to teach there, but because the system was not helping them to learn how to deal with the difficult problems they were encountering in their classrooms. Second, PAR is effective in identifying those beginning teachers who are not qualified to continue to teach in the system (about 6%).

Role of Evaluation When There Is Concern about a Teacher's Effectiveness A second advantage of PAR programs is that they can also be used when there is concern about an experienced teacher's effectiveness. If there is reason to believe that an experienced teacher is not effective, then that teacher can be referred to PAR. That teacher's performance is reviewed and the PAR Committee decides whether such performance justifies placing the teacher in the PAR program. If a teacher is placed in PAR, then the PAR Committee would decide in time whether remediation efforts were sufficiently successful for the teacher to exit the PAR program or it would recommend dismissal. In school systems where PAR programs have been implemented, they have been sufficiently successful in removing ineffective teachers.

One of the criticisms of teacher evaluation is that because almost everyone is granted tenure and almost nobody is fired, the process "has no teeth." This is due largely to the fact that building administrators often do not have the time and the training to make difficult evaluation decisions, such as those that affect a teacher's employment status. This time and expertise is available to the school system through PAR programs.

The intent here is by no means to create the impression that PAR programs need to be implemented to facilitate the dismissal of ineffective teachers. Documentation and due process are critical to dismissing an ineffective teacher, and such considerations can be addressed without implementing a PAR program. Although dismissing an incompetent teacher is costly and time-consuming, because of legal fees and the need to document the problem and what has been done to ameliorate the situation, it is not difficult. Determination and stamina are the keys to the success of the termination process. An alternative to termination is to negotiate a resignation with incentives for the teacher: "You know, Ed, winter break is coming up and I know each year you look forward to going off to your retreat in the mountains. It probably won't be as enjoyable for you and your family this year knowing that you will be coming back to a series of hearings, etc. We could make it easier for all of us. I am in a position to put you on leave with full pay and benefits through August, provided you submit your resignation at this time." Although this approach tends to be more common in business, those in the public sector often find it distasteful. Although we may be giving the teacher a bonus for being incompetent, this approach has some advantages. The biggest advantages are (1) it is usually less expensive than going through a termination hearing and (2) the teacher will be gone.

Role of Evaluation for Professional Growth and School Improvement The primary focus of teacher evaluation in most schools has been on professional growth and school improvement. The Teacher Evaluation and Professional Growth Cycle (Iwanicki, 1990; 1993) focuses primarily on these two aspects of teacher evaluation. The key features of this three-year cycle are described in Figure 5.15. In applying this cycle, three factors are considered when evaluating experienced teaches: (1) performance in the classroom based on observations, (2) professional growth, based on mutually determined objectives, and (3) self-evaluation. Efforts were made in the 1970s and early 1980s to evaluate teachers with respect to these three factors on a yearly basis. The results were not gratifying. Teachers tended to develop shorter-term, bland objectives, tied to the recommendations that resulted

YEAR 1—APPRAISAL

Focus: To conduct a thorough appraisal of teacher performance in light of the indicators of effective teaching

Events: a) Fall conference to discuss and initiate the appraisal process
    b) Minimum of three classroom observations, each with follow-up conferences resulting in a written *Classroom Observation Report*
    c) Spring evaluation conference to discuss the teacher's *Appraisal Report* and to develop a *Professional Growth Plan* for the next two years. This plan is based on objectives that can focus on
        1) Strengthening performance with respect to the indicators of effective teaching
        2) Professional growth initiatives
        3) School improvement targets

Orientation: This is a collegial but accountability-oriented process where the evaluator assumes leadership for evaluating teaching. The teacher and the evaluator use this information as they work collaboratively to develop a two-year *Professional Growth Plan* to strengthen or enhance the teacher's performance.

YEAR 2—SUPPORT

Focus: To support the teacher, as work begins, on the objectives that serve as the basis of his or her Professional Growth Plan and to monitor progress in this regard

Events: a) Fall conference with supervisor to review objectives and to decide how the teacher's progress will be supported and monitored
    b) At least two conferences to support and to monitor the teacher's progress toward objectives
    c) Formal classroom observations and informal class visits as necessary
    d) Spring conference to complete the teacher's *Spring Progress Report on Objectives*

Orientation: This is a collegial partnership, where the supervisor supports and guides the teacher's efforts to achieve the objectives which serve as the basis of his or her Professional Growth Plan.

YEAR 3—CONTINUED PROFESSIONAL GROWTH

Focus: To provide the teacher with the opportunity to
    a) pursue what needs to be done to achieve the objectives that serve as the basis of his or her Professional Growth Plan
    b) conduct a self-evaluation and to reflect on where he or she is going professionally

Events: a) Fall conference with supervisor to review what the teacher needs to do to achieve his or her objectives, to discuss what strategies the teacher might use to conduct a self-evaluation, and to reflect upon his or her performance
    b) Interim evaluation conferences as necessary
    c) Formal classroom observations and informal class visits as necessary
    d) In spring the teacher completes the *Final Evaluation Report*, which is forwarded to the evaluator. This report includes a self-assessment of
        1) the extent to which the teacher's objectives have been achieved, and
        2) those indicators of effective teaching which will provide the focus for his or her future professional development

Orientation: This is a reflective process in which the teacher assumes a more direct role in evaluating his or her performance and in setting a direction for future professional development.

FIGURE 5.15. An Overview of the Teacher Evaluation
and Professional Growth Cycle.

From Iwanicki (1993, p. 28)

from classroom observations. Self-evaluations were conducted in a cursory manner. When teachers were confronted with such concerns, they commented, "If you want us to address these aspects of evaluation in a meaningful manner, then give us the time to do so." Thus, the Teacher Evaluation and Professional Growth Cycle was developed to spread out these three critical aspects of teacher evaluation so they could be addressed thoughtfully.

Administrators also experienced difficulty in managing a teacher evaluation program that focused on these three critical aspects of teaching each year. Time constraints prevented them

from observing all classrooms and developing meaningful professional growth plans for all teachers. The Teacher Evaluation and Professional Growth Cycle was developed so administrators could work closely with roughly one-third of their staffs, each year in the analysis of their classroom performance, as well as in the development of their professional growth plans. Thus, an administrator responsible for the evaluation of 30 professional staff would work closely with about ten teachers. This 1:10 evaluator-to-teacher ratio is realistic because experience has shown that an administrator can effectively evaluate between ten and fifteen staff members each year.

The Teacher Evaluation and Professional Growth Cycle is a good point of departure for strengthening teacher-evaluation practices. For example, in the Appraisal phase, a series of classroom observations are conducted to analyze teaching and learning in the classroom. Rather than spreading out these observations over the school year, it might be better to conduct this analysis of teaching and learning in reference to a two to three week unit of instruction selected by the teacher, preferably a unit that the teacher has difficulty teaching. The teacher and evaluator would meet before the unit commenced to:

• review and discuss the teacher's instructional plan, including the objectives of the unit
• make suggestions for strengthening that plan
• consider others who might participate in the evaluation process (i.e., peers, supervisors, curriculum consultants)
• identify the performance measures that will be used to monitor student progress
• schedule classroom observations for those key lessons where feedback to the teacher would be most helpful

Throughout the evaluation of this unit, the analysis of teaching would be based largely on what students have accomplished.

The cognitive perspective that teaching is thinking is essential as we focus teacher evaluation on student learning. As noted earlier in this chapter, teaching is thinking and teacher evaluation is a conversation about that thinking. The three basic questions that guide that conversation are the following:

• Did the teacher focus on worthwhile objectives?
• Did the teacher treat the students with dignity and respect?
• How successful were students in achieving these objectives?

If a teacher is successful in fostering worthwhile objectives with all students and maintains an atmosphere of dignity and respect, then that teacher is doing a good job. The focus of the evaluation conversation would be on reinforcing those aspects of teaching that contributed to the success of that lesson. To the extent that the answers to any of the preceding questions are anything other than *yes,* then the dialogue focuses on aspects of teaching that need to be strengthened. The key feature of this approach is the idea that the recommendations for strengthening, enhancing, or reinforcing teaching are based on an analysis of what students are learning. The evaluation process too often deals with an analysis of teaching in light of best practices. While the recommendations that result have direct implications for enhancing teaching practice, they may have little impact on what students are actually learning in the classroom. As one teacher noted, "They have taught me to dance like Madeline [Hunter], but my kids are not learning better."

A traditional hierarchy of formal authority has been built into the Teacher Evaluation and Professional Growth Cycle: the evaluator, supervisor, and teacher. It is time for this formal authority structure to become more functional. Those with the most expertise need to take leadership in the teacher

evaluation process at the appropriate times. This means that evaluation needs to be a more collaborative process in which teachers assume a more active role in their evaluations and in the evaluation of their peers. Although administrators and supervisors have traditionally assumed the leadership in conducting observation conferences, teachers now need to assume more responsibility for this role. If teaching is thinking, then who is in a better position to analyze teaching than the teacher him- or herself, with input from an informed peer, administrator, or supervisor who is skilled in facilitating reflection?

In summary, the purpose of this first year of the cycle is to conduct a thorough appraisal of a teacher's performance. This appraisal should be related directly to student learning in the teacher's classroom, and every effort should be made to involve peers appropriately in the conversations that contribute to this appraisal. At the conclusion of this phase, teachers develop professional growth plans to strengthen or enhance their performances. This professional growth plan provides a focus for the teacher evaluation process in the support and continued professional growth years of the cycle. Toward the end of the continued professional growth year, teachers are expected to complete a Final Evaluation Report that (1) documents what they have accomplished with respect to their professional growth plan and (2) identifies potential directions for professional development during the next round of the cycle.

While the Teacher Evaluation and Professional Growth Cycle is being implemented effectively in a large number of school systems, very few systems adhere strictly to the procedures in Figure 5.15. As a school system begins to implement the cycle, needs often arise that make it necessary to modify the process. In most cases, such modifications are made in the number of observations conducted during the appraisal year and in the length of the cycle. Many school systems have experienced difficulty in conducting a minimum of three formal classroom observations with each teacher involved in appraisal. In some cases, the minimum number of required observations has been reduced to two. In other cases, informal classroom visits are being substituted for formal observations to reduce the amount of paperwork associated with formal observations. With respect to the length of the cycle, some school systems have allowed their teachers to extend the objectives included in their professional growth plans for a year or two. Thus, the length of the cycle would vary from three to five years. Another option that some school systems are considering is to abandon the cycle and to implement a process of continuous school improvement and professional growth with the understanding that all teachers will be appraised at least once every five years.

Whether uniformity or flexibility is applied in the implementation of the Teacher Evaluation and Professional Growth Cycle is a matter of style. The more important issue is one of productivity. How effectively is the school staff strengthening or enhancing teaching and learning through the integration of school improvement with the staff development and teacher evaluation processes? In discussing this issue with administrators, they often comment that productivity in teacher evaluation is sacrificed because of the inordinate amount of time that is spent on reports that document the obvious and do little more than fulfill a bureaucratic need.

An interesting alternative for reporting the accomplishments of a school is to use vignettes. A vignette is a short, rich story of the progress a school is making in strengthening or enhancing teaching and learning. Such a story would begin with a description of and rationale for the school improvement needs being addressed. An overview would then be provided about how the school is addressing these needs. This overview would include a description of how staff development and teacher evaluation are being integrated with the school improvement process. The progress the school is making in meeting its improvement needs would be documented in the final section of the vignette. Such a vignette would be shared and celebrated with the school community each spring and then forwarded to the board of education. The reaction of some central office personnel and school board members to this alternative has been, "My board would never accept this!" Those who reject this alternative summarily should take the pile of teacher evaluation reports received from a typical school at the end of the year and try to identify how the evaluation process has enhanced teaching and learning in that school. The use of vignettes may become a bit more attractive to them after this experience.

The term *vignette* was chosen for a school's report on its improvement efforts because it tended to be a neutral concept. Most school staff would not have any preconceived notions of what might be contained in a vignette. Thus, they would tend to be more open to the concept and give careful thought to how such a report should be crafted. As the vignette concept has been shared, some school systems have decided that *portfolio* is a better term. Because portfolios were being used in these settings to monitor student achievement as well as the professional growth of teachers and administrators, a school-level improvement portfolio fit better with the system's overall approach to accountability. What the document is called is not as important as the need to develop a report that conveys what staff have accomplished through their efforts to integrate their teacher evaluations and professional development activities with the school improvement process.

MINDSCAPES AND LANDSCAPES, THEORY AND PRACTICE, AND THE NEW PRINCIPAL STANDARDS

This chapter commenced with the perspective that supervision is the process of working with and through people to better achieve the goals of the school organization. Evaluation is critical to this process because program evaluation is used to monitor progress toward school goals as well as to judge the value or worth of what has been accomplished. In addition, teacher evaluation is used to develop the human fabric of the school organization by continually promoting the meaningful professional growth of staff. The focus of the prior two sections of this chapter has been on how these processes of program and personnel evaluation can be imple-

mented in a complementary manner to enhance teaching and learning in schools. It is important to reflect on the direction that is being advocated in this chapter using Sergiovanni's (1985) metaphor of "mindscapes" and "landscapes." Some may believe that using evaluation as a process of inquiry to enhance teaching and learning is merely a mindscape or theory that has little relevance to the landscape of school practice. This is not to say evaluation should not be used in this way; the point is that these methods of evaluation are just not consistent with the reality of what happens in schools. This reality, however, is changing rapidly because of the new standards for principals that are being developed at the state and national levels.

During the 1980s, considerable emphasis was placed on the principal as an instructional leader. During this period numerous studies produced long lists of the competencies or proficiencies of the effective principal. In a sense, these efforts were culminated in the publication of *Principals for Our Changing Schools: Knowledge and Skill Base,* by the National Policy Board for Educational Administration (Thomson, 1993). This work included a compilation of what principals need to know and be able to do with respect to the 21 domains that comprised the principalship. As we moved into the 1990s, it became evident that the notion of the principal as instructional leader was problematic in that it focused the accountability for school improvement on the principal without the sufficient involvement and leadership of other members of the school community. Thus, the principal began to be viewed more as a transformational leader. Although the principal was still accountable for school improvement, responsibility and leadership for change was shared appropriately with other members of the school community. What did this mean, however, for the knowledge and skill base for preparing, certifying, and evaluating principals?

The New Principal Standards

As states addressed this issue, the National Policy Board for Educational Administration made clear that its *Knowledge and Skill Base* was not developed to define the principalship; rather, it was to serve as a resource for state and other agencies to consult as they defined the principalship within their contexts. Some states used this resource to refine their listings of competencies or proficiencies. Others states, such as Connecticut and North Carolina, broke with tradition and developed standards for the preparation of their principals. Stated simply, standards are the big ideas that define the principalship. In Connecticut, these were the big ideas that defined the principal as a learning-focused leader. The standards that have been drafted to guide the preparation and certification of principals in Connecticut are presented in Figure 5.16. Figure 5.17 includes an elaboration of Standard VII.—Student Standards and Assessment.

These standards have been shared to show that the role of the principal has changed and the landscape is clearly evaluation-oriented, especially with respect to Standards VII–X. The directions advocated earlier in this chapter are critical to what a principal needs to know and be able to do with respect to these standards. Performance assessments in

I. *The Educated Person*

The principal possesses an understanding of the educated person; and engages staff, parents, and the community in developing a common vision of the educated person and in identifying the implications of that vision for students and the school's programs.

II. *The Learning Process*

The principal possesses a contemporary, research-based understanding of learning theory and human motivation, communicates that understanding to teachers and parents, and uses that understanding to promote the continuous improvement of student learning.

III. *The Teaching Process*

The principal possesses a knowledge of teaching that is grounded in research and experience, and uses that knowledge to foster teachers' reflection on the impact of their professional beliefs, values, and practices on student learning.

IV. *Diverse Perspectives*

The principal understands the role of education in a pluralistic society, and works with staff, parents and community to develop programs and instructional strategies that incorporate diverse perspectives.

V. *School Goals*

The principal actively engages members of the school community to establish goals that encompass the school's vision of the educated person and in developing procedures to monitor the achievement of those goals.

VI. *School Culture*

The principal utilizes multiple strategies to shape the school culture in a way that fosters collaboration among the staff and the involvement of parents, students, and the community in efforts to improve student learning.

VII. *Student Standards and Assessment*

The principal works with the school community to establish rigorous academic standards for all students and promotes the use of multiple assessment strategies to monitor student progress.

VIII. *.School Improvement*

The principal works with staff to improve the quality of school programs by reviewing the impact of current practices on student learning, considering promising alternatives, and implementing program changes that are designed to improve learning for all students.

IX. *Professional Development*

The principal works with staff to plan and implement activities that promote the achievement of school goals, while encouraging and supporting staff as they assume responsibility for their professional development.

X. *Integration of Staff Evaluation, Professional Development, and School Improvement*

The principal works with staff to develop and implement an integrated set of school-based policies for staff selection, evaluation, professional development, and school improvement that results in improved teaching and learning for all students.

XI. *Organization, Resources, and School Policies*

The principal works with staff to review organization and resources, and develops and implements policies and procedures to improve program effectiveness, staff productivity, and learning for all students.

XII. *School–Community Relations*

The principal collaborates with staff to create and sustain a variety of opportunities for parent and community participation in the life of the school.

FIGURE 5.16. Connecticut State Department of Education Draft Standards for School Principals.
From: Connecticut State Department of Education (Draft: May 28, 1996)
Do not cite or quote without CSDE permission.

teacher evaluation, data-based decision-making, and school improvement are currently being developed to assure the public that prospective principals in Connecticut are proficient in such areas. Connecticut is not unique in this regard. The Interstate School Leaders Licensure Consortium (ISLLC) has been formed through the Council of Chief State School Officers. More than 20 states are participating in this consortium, which has been formed to facilitate collaboration in the development of standards and assessments for the certification of school leaders.

Some may question whether this focus on evaluation really makes a difference. This issue was addressed by validating the Connecticut Standards for School Principals through the Successful Principals Study (Iwanicki et al, 1994). This was a two-phase study. In Phase I, principals were asked to identify up to five colleagues who were highly successful at enhancing teaching and learning in their schools. All principals who were nominated were asked to complete the Successful Principal Survey. This survey included a list of the performances for each of the 12 standards. For each standard, principals were asked to (1) rate the importance of

each performance to their success in their current role and (2) check up to three performances that were absolutely essential to their success. While all performances (68) were rated as important, an analysis of the absolutely essential performances was particularly interesting. Iwanicki, Gable, and Smith (1994) factor–analyzed the 30 performances that principals deemed to be absolutely essential. Six factors were confirmed through this process, two of which are presented shortly. These factors clearly provide evidence that evaluation is perceived as an absolutely essential aspect of a successful principal's performance.

IV. Facilitates the Development and Implementation of Programs that Meet High Standards

The principal . . .

1. Works with staff to ensure that all groups of students achieve at high levels.
2. Develops with the school community rigorous academic standards for student performance.

VII. Student Standards and Assessment

The principal works with the school community to establish rigorous academic standards for all students and promotes the use of multiple assessment strategies to monitor student progress.

Knowledge and Skills

The principal is familiar with contemporary curriculum frameworks and current national and state discussions about standards for student learning.

The principal understands curriculum design models, including how to plan and implement a framework for instruction and how to align curriculum with anticipated outcomes.

The principal understands the implications of the school's vision of the educated person for the identification of academic standards for students.

The principal knows how to involve staff and community in the identification and development of standards for student learning.

The principal understands that ongoing assessment is essential to the instructional process.

The principal understands the attributes and applications of sound student assessment and possesses multiple strategies to monitor student progress.

Dispositions

The principal believes that all children can learn an intellectually demanding curriculum.

The principal is committed to using assessment to identify student strengths and promote student growth rather than to deny students access to learning opportunities.

The principal believes that setting intellectually demanding standards is critical to improving the learning of all students.

The principal is committed to using student learning as the basis for evaluating school success.

Performances

With the school community, the principal develops rigorous academic standards for student performance.

The principal works with teachers to assess individual student and group performance.

The principal works with staff to implement multiple assessment strategies to monitor individual and group progress.

The principal promotes practices and programs that contribute to the achievement of academic standards by all students.

The principal ensures that all students make continuous progress toward academic standards.

FIGURE 5.17. Connecticut State Department of Education Draft Standards for School Principals.

From Connecticut State Department of Education (Draft: May 28, 1996) [Do not cite or quote without CSDE permission]

---

3. Promotes practices and programs that contribute to the achievement of academic standards by all students.
4. Ensures that all students make continuous progress toward academic standards.

V. Maintains a Coherent Program of School Improvement, Professional Development, and Staff Evaluation

The principal . . .

1. Incorporates school goals into teacher appraisal objectives.
2. Incorporates school goals in the planning of professional development activities.
3. Works with staff to develop programs and incorporate practices that help all children reach high achievement standards.
4. Works with staff to create a plan for professional development activities that promotes staff growth and the achievement of school goals.
5. Works with staff to improve teaching and learning for all students by linking staff selection, teacher evaluation, professional development, and school improvement to student standards and school goals.
6. Promotes and reinforces a culture of staff collaboration and collegiality by sharing decision-making authority and delegating responsibility as staff pursue improved teaching and learning for all students.

Some skeptics may question the credibility of such evidence. Do successful principals really do these things or did they just say they do? Phase II of the Successful Principals Study addressed this question through five qualitative follow-up studies with different groups of principals as follows:

- Elementary school—suburban (Nocera, 1995)
- Elementary school—urban (Fusco, 1995)
- Middle/junior high school—suburban (Wolters, 1995)
- Middle/junior high school—urban (Russo, 1996)
- High school—suburban (Carmelich, 1995)

The successful principals in each group were ranked from high to low based on the number of times they were listed as successful by their colleagues. The top three principals in each group comprised the sample for the qualitative study. Each principal was shadowed for a number of days, documents and artifacts were reviewed, and interviews were conducted. Analyses of the qualitative data confirmed further that successful principals do use evaluation effectively to enhance teaching and learning in their schools.

In the words of the futurist, Joel Barker (1992), there is no question that the paradigm of school leadership has changed. While good principals still need to manage schools well, the evaluation of their effectiveness is becoming more a function of how well they can facilitate school improvement; however, is school improvement not the process of working with and through people to better achieve the goals of the school organization? If so, then supervision is clearly at the core of learning-focused leadership. Critical to such leadership is accurate information about programs and personnel to facilitate decision-making. Thus, the role of evaluation in supervision as a process of inquiry is to provide school leaders with accurate information for making decisions about the quality of teaching and learning.

CONCLUSION

The focus of this chapter has been on evaluation as a process of making decisions about the value or worth of an educational program. It is important to note that there is a difference between making a decision about value versus worth (Scriven, 1992). The decision as to whether an outcome has value is dichotomous. Either an outcome has value or it does not. For example, most measurement experts would agree that understanding the concept of *reliability* is of value to school leaders. On the other hand, they would agree that knowing the formulas for calculating the reliability of a test would not be of value to school leaders. While value is dichotomous, worth is continuous and cumulative. For example, in addition to reliability, it is of value for school leaders to understand the concept of validity. A professional development program that helps school leaders to develop an understanding of both the concepts of reliability and validity would have greater worth than one that focuses only on reliability.

It is important to understand this distinction between value and worth when evaluating school curricula. Most would agree that it is worthwhile to teach reading up through the primary grade levels. Is it worthwhile, however, to continue to teach reading to the majority of students at grades 5 and beyond? When do we make the break between learning to read and reading to learn? A logical time would be when teaching reading no longer adds to the worth of the language arts program. Streifer (1996) would argue that this notion of worth should be approached through the process of bench marking. The school curricula should include benchmark expectations for student performance in each discipline by grade level such that the worth of the school learning experience would be enhanced as students moved from benchmark to benchmark. Assessments would be developed to monitor students' progress with respect to these benchmarks. The transition from learning to read to reading to learn would be made when students have demonstrated mastery of the skills required to satisfy the benchmark for being a proficient reader.

Streifer argues further that the commonly used standardized achievement tests are inappropriate for use in the benchmarking process in higher-performing school systems. He contends that students in such school systems perform well when applying conventional norms, but such performance is not consistent with what the school system could achieve if higher, more worthwhile benchmarks were set for students. If standardized tests are to be used in the benchmarking process, Streifer advo-

cates that more challenging norms be developed for higher-performing schools, such as the ones Educational Records Bureau has set for independent schools. Thus, the goal of evaluation is to facilitate decision-making that enables a school system to maximize the potential worth of the educational program it can provide for its students. As we use benchmark assessments in the evaluation process to make decisions about the worth of school programs, it is important to keep in mind that people make decisions. Test scores do not speak for themselves. As Madaus (1988) cautions:

Those concerned with curriculum, teaching, and learning must make the case that test information be one piece of information used alongside other indicators, when a person(s), rather than a test score, authorizes a critical decision about pupils, teachers, programs, schools, or school systems (p. 115).

Who is accountable for the development and implementation of worthwhile school programs? We all are—school board members, superintendent and other central office staff, building administrators, classroom teachers, parents, and community members. We are all members of the system and school learning organizations who need to respond to the challenge of providing a high-quality education for students. We can be successful in meeting this challenge only if we learn to get smarter together about what we hope to accomplish. Getting smarter together about what we hope to accomplish requires reflection, conversation, collaboration, and commitment. It is important to reflect on the progress we are making in implementing school programs and to share these reflections in conversations with colleagues to develop a better understanding of what has been accomplished and what needs to be done. As we set directions for strengthening or enhancing our school programs, we need to pursue these directions with the support and collaboration of colleagues who share the common commitment of providing a high quality education for all students. As Fullan and Stiegelbauer (1991, p. 349) have noted,

All successful change processes are characterized by collaboration and close interaction among those central to carrying out the changes. If we are to accomplish change in education, we have to, in Bruce Joyce's coruscating phrase, "crack the walls of privatism." Privatism and professional development are closely and inversely linked. Alliances provide greater power, both of ideas and the ability to act on them.

Such collaboration in a school environment where evaluation provides quality information for decision-making is essential to the success of supervision as a process of inquiry and improvement. This approach clearly has the most promise for developing the human fabric of the school organization so students' learning potential is realized.

REFERENCES

Airasian, P. W. (1994). *Classroom assessment* (2nd ed.). New York: McGraw-Hill.

Alkin, M. C. (1969). Evaluation theory development. *Evaluation Comment, 2*(1), 2–7.

Alkin, M. C. (1972). Accountability defined. *Evaluation Comment, 3*(3), 1–4.

Argyris, C. (1964). *Integrating the individual and the organization.* New York: Wiley.

Arter, J. & Spandel, V. (1992). Using portfolios of student work in instruction and assessment. *Educational Measurement: Issues and Practices, 11*(1), 3644.

Bacharach, S. B, Conley, S. C., & Shedd, J. B. (1987). A career development framework for evaluating teachers as decision-makers. *Journal of Personnel Evaluation in Education, 1*(2), 181—194.

Barker, J. A. (1992). *Paradigms: The business of discovering the future.* New York: HarperBusiness.

Berliner, D. C. (1988). Implications of studies of expertise in pedagogy for teacher education and evaluation. In the Proceedings of the 1988 ETS Invitational Conference - *New directions for teacher assessment* (pp. 39–65). Princeton, NJ: Educational Testing Service.

Bloom, B. S., Hastings, J. T., & Madaus, G. F. (1971). *Handbook on formative and summative assessment of student learning.* New York: McGraw-Hill.

Bowman, L. G. & Deal, T. E. (1991). *Reframing organizations: Artistry, choice, and leadership.* San Francisco: Jossey-Bass.

Bonstingl, J. J. (1992). *Schools of quality: An introduction to total quality management in education.* Alexandria, VA: ASCD.

Calhoun, E. F. (1994). *How to use action research in the self-renewing school.* Alexandria, VA: ASCD.

Campbell, D. T. (1969). Reforms as experiments. *American Psychologist, 24,* 409–429.

Campbell, D. T. & Stanley, J. C. (1963). *Experimental and quasi-experimental designs for research.* Chicago, IL: Rand McNally.

Carmelich, R. E. (1995). *A study of what successful Connecticut suburban high school principals do to enhance teaching and learning in schools.* Unpublished doctoral dissertation, University of Connecticut, Storrs (UMI# 9533116).

Cook, T. D. & Campbell, D. T. (1979). *Quasi-experimentation: Design and analysis issues for field settings.* Chicago, IL: Rand McNally.

Connecticut State Department of Education. (1996, May 28). *Draft standards for school principals.* Hartford, CT: Bureau of Research and Teacher Assessment, Author.

Covino, E. A. (1991). *Effective teaching behaviors of experienced Connecticut teachers: A validation.* Unpublished doctoral dissertation, University of Connecticut, Storrs (UMI# 9129921).

Darling-Hammond, L, Wise, A. E., & Pease, S. R. (1983). Teacher evaluation in the organizational context: A review of the literature. *Review of Educational Research, 53*(3), 285–328.

DuBois, P. H. (1966). A test-dominated society: China, 1115 B.C.-1905 A.D. In A. Anastasi (Ed.). *Testing problems in perspective* (pp. 29–36). Washington, D.C.:American Council on Education.

Ebel, R. L. (1972). *Essentials of educational measurement.* Englewood Cliffs, NJ: Prentice-Hall.

Eisner, E. W. (1969). Instructional and expressive objectives: Their formulation and use in curriculum. In W. J. Popham (Ed.). *AERA monograph on curriculum evaluation: Instructional objectives.* Chicago, IL: Rand McNally.

Eisner, E. W. (1994). *The educational imagination: On the design and evaluation of school programs* (3rd ed.). New York: Macmillan.

English, F. W. & Hill, J. C. (1994). *Total quality education: Transforming schools into learning places.* Thousand Oaks, CA: Corwin Press.

Frase, L. E. (Ed.). (1992). *Teacher compensation and motivation.* Lancaster, PA: Technomic Publishing.

Fullan, M. (1993). *Change forces: Probing the depths of educational reform.* New York: The Falmer Press.

Fullan, M. G. & Stiegelbauer, S. (1991). *The new meaning of educational change.* New York: Teachers College Press.

Fusco, P. T. (1995). *A study of what successful Connecticut urban elementary school principals do to enhance teaching and learning in schools.* Unpublished doctoral dissertation, University of Connecticut, Storrs (UMI# 9541593).

Gallegos, A. M., Benjamin, R, Candoli, C., & Wegenke, G. (1992).

Consumer report on school evaluation models. (Work funded by OERI, U.S. Department of Education - Grant No. R117Q00047). Kalamazoo, MI: The Evaluation Center at Western Michigan University.

Good, T. L. & Mulryan, C. (1990). Teacher ratings: A call for teacher control and self-evaluation. In J. Millman & L. Darling-Hammond (Eds.), *The new handbook of teacher evaluation: Assessing elementary and secondary school teachers* (pp. 191–215). Newbury Park, CA: Sage.

Gong, B. & Reidy, E. F. (1996). Assessment and accountability in Kentucky's school reform. In J. B. Baron & D. P. Wolf (Eds.). *Performance-based student assessment: Challenges and possibilities* (pp. 215–233). Ninety-fifth Yearbook of the National Society for the Study of Education (Part I). Chicago, IL: The University of Chicago Press.

Guba, E. G. & Lincoln, Y. S. (1982). The place of values in needs assessment. *Educational Evaluation and Policy Analysis, 4*(3), 311–320.

Guba, E. G. & Lincoln, Y. S. (1985). Fourth generation evaluation as an alternative. *Educational Horizons, 63*(4), 139–141.

Guskey, T. R. (Ed.). (1994). *High stakes performance assessment.* Thousand Oaks, CA: Corwin Press.

Guskey, T. R. (Ed.). (1996). *Communicating student learning.* Alexandria, VA: ASCD.

Hatry, H. P. & Greiner, J. M. (1985). *Issues and cases in teacher incentive plans.* Washington, D.C.: The Urban Institute Press.

House, E. R. (Ed.). (1973). *School evaluation: The politics and process.* Berkeley, CA: McCutchan.

Iwanicki, E. F. (1990). Teacher evaluation for school improvement. In J. Millman & L. Darling-Hammond (Eds.). *The new handbook of teacher evaluation: Assessing elementary and secondary school teachers* (pp. 158–170). Newbury Park, CA: Sage.

Iwanicki, E. F. (1993). *A handbook for teacher evaluation and professional growth in more productive schools.* Storrs, CT: Connecticut Institute for Personnel Evaluation, Department of Educational Leadership, University of Connecticut.

Iwanicki, E. F., Carmelich, R. E., Fusco, P. T., Nocera, L. L., Russo, T. F., & Wolters, L. C. (1994). *The successful principals study* (a technical report). Storrs, CT: Connecticut School Administrator Performance Appraisal Project, Department of Educational Leadership, University of Connecticut.

Iwanicki, E. F., Gable, R. K., & Smith, E. V. (1994). *Factor analysis of the successful principals survey* (A technical report). Storrs, CT: Connecticut School Administrator Performance Appraisal Project, Department of Educational Leadership, University of Connecticut.

Iwanicki, E. F. & Rindone, D. A. (1995). Integrating professional development, teacher evaluation, and student learning: The evolution of teacher evaluation policy in Connecticut. In D.L. Duke (Ed.). *From accountability to professional development: The evolution of teacher evaluation policy* (pp. 67–98). Albany, NY: SUNY Press.

Iwanicki, E. F. & St. Pierre, R. G. (1974). *A comparison of three methods of calculating grade equivalent score means* (A technical report). Chestnut Hill, MA; Center for Field Research and School Services at Boston College.

Joint Committee on Standards for Educational Evaluation (1988). *The personnel evaluation standards.* Newbury Park, CA: Sage.

Koberg, D. & Bagnall, J. (1972). *The universal traveler.* Los Angeles, CA: William Kaufman.

Kyte, G. C. (1930). *How to supervise: A guide to educational principles and progressive practices of educational supervision.* Boston, MA: Houghton Mifflin.

Leithwood, K. & Duke, D. (1994, October). *Defining effective leadership for Connecticut's schools.* Storrs, CT: Connecticut School Administrator Performance Appraisal Project, Department of Educational Leadership, University of Connecticut.

Likert, R. (1961). *New patterns of management.* New York: McGraw-Hill.

Madaus, G. F. (1988). The influence of testing on the curriculum. In L.N. Tanner (Ed.). *Critical issues in curriculum* (pp. 83–121). Eighty-seventh Yearbook of the National Society for the Study of Education (Part I). Chicago, IL: The University of Chicago Press.

McGreal, T. L. (1990). The use of rating scales in teacher evaluation: Concerns and recommendations. *Journal of Personnel Evaluation in Education, 4*(1), 41–58.

McGregor, D. (1960). *The human side of enterprise.* New York: McGraw-Hill.

McLaughlin, M. W. & Pfeifer, R. S. (1988). *Teacher evaluation: Improvement, accountability, and effective learning.* New York: Teachers College Press.

Miles, M. B. (1965). Planned change and organizational health: Figure and ground. In *Change processes in the public schools* (pp. 11–34). Eugene, OR: Center for the Advanced Study of Educational Administration, University of Oregon.

Murphy, J. (1987). Teacher evaluation: A conceptual framework for supervisors. *Journal of Personnel Evaluation in Education, 1*(2), 157–180.

National Board for Professional Teaching Standards. (1989). Toward high and rigorous standards for the teaching profession: Initial policies and perspectives of the National Board for Professional Teaching Standards. Washington, D.C.: Author.

National Commission on Excellence in Education. (1983). *A nation at risk: The imperative for educational reform.* Washington, D.C.: U.S. Department of Education.

Nocera, L. L. (1995). *A study of what successful Connecticut suburban elementary school principals do to enhance teaching and learning in schools.* Unpublished doctoral dissertation, University of Connecticut, Storrs.

O'Day, J. A. & Smith, M. S. (1993). Systemic reform and educational opportunity. In S. H. Fuhrman (Ed.). *Designing coherent education policy: Improving the system* (pp. 250–312). San Francisco: Jossey-Bass.

Oescher, J., Black, W., Gunning, S., & Brooks, C. R. (1996). *Estimating school effectiveness with the school performance model* (A technical report). Baton Rouge, LA: Louisiana Department of Education.

Popham, W. J. (1975). *Educational evaluation.* Englewood Cliffs, NJ: Prentice-Hall.

Pophan, W. J. (1995). *Classroom assessment: What teachers need to know.* Needham Heights, MA: Allyn and Bacon.

Provus, M. M. (1971). *Discrepancy evaluation.* Berkley, CA: McCutchan.

Rogers, V. A. (1974). A sense of purpose. *The National Elementary Principal, 53* (4), 4–10.

Russo, T. F. (1996). *A study of what successful Connecticut urban middle school principals do to enhance teaching and learning in schools.* Unpublished doctoral dissertation, University of Connecticut, Storrs.

Sagor, R. (1993). *How to conduct collaborative action research.* Alexandria, VA: ASCD.

Sanders, W. L. & Horn, S. P. (1994). The Tennessee Value-Added Assessment System (TVAAS): Mixed-model methodology in educational assessment. *Journal of Personnel Evaluation in Education, 8* (3), 299–311.

Sarason, S. B. (1971). *The culture of the school and the problem of change.* Boston: Allyn and Bacon.

Schwab, R. L. & Iwanicki, E. F. (1992). Can performance based salary programs motivate teachers? Insights from a case study. In L. Frase (Ed.). *Teacher compensation and motivation* (pp. 151–183). Lancaster, PA: Technomic Publishing.

Scriven, M. (1967). The methodology of evaluation. In R.W. Tyler (Ed.). *Perspectives of curriculum evaluation* (pp. 39–83). Chicago, IL: Rand McNally.

Scriven, M. (1987). Validity in personnel evaluation. *Journal of Personnel Evaluation in Education, 1*(1), 9–23.

Scriven, M. (1991). Beyond formative and summative evaluation. In M. W. McLaughlin & D. C. Phillips (Eds.). *Evaluation and education: At quarter century* (pp. 19–64). Ninetieth Yearbook of the National Society for the Study of Education (Part II). Chicago, IL: The University of Chicago Press.

Scriven, M. (1992, July). *A perspective on the evolution of evaluation thought.* Center for Research on Educational Accountability and Teacher Evaluation (CREATE) National Evaluation Institute, Snowmass, CO.

Scriven, M. (1994). A unified theory approach to teacher evaluation. In A. McConney (Ed.). *Toward a unified model: The foundations of educational evaluation* (pp. 1–12). Kalamazoo, MI: Center for Research on Educational Accountability and Teacher Evaluation (CREATE), Western Michigan University.

Scriven, M. & Roth, J. (1977). Needs assessment. Reprinted in *Evaluation Practice, 11*(2), 135–144.

Senge, P. M. (1990) *The fifth discipline: The art and practice of the learning organization.* New York: Doubleday.

Sergiovanni, T. J. (1985). Landscapes, mindscapes, and reflective practice in supervision. *Journal of Curriculum and Supervision, 1*(1), 5–17.

Sergiovanni, T. J. & Starratt, R. J. (1983). *Supervision: Human perspectives.* New York: McGraw-Hill.

Spears, H. (1941). *Secondary education in American life.* New York: American Book Company.

Stake, R. E. (1970). Objectives, priorities, and other judgmental data. *Review of Educational Research, 40*(2), 181–212.

Stiggins, R. J. (1987). Design and development of performance assessments. *Educational Measurement: Issues and Practices, 6*(3), 33–42.

Stiggins, R. J. (1997). *Student-centered classroom assessment* (3rd ed.). Saddle River, NJ: Merrill.

Stiggins, R. J., Frisbie, D. A., & Griswold, P. A. (1989). Inside high school grading practices: Building a research agenda. *Educational Measurement: Issues and Practices, 8*(2), 5–14.

Streifer, P. A. (1996, February 29). *Standardized tests and teacher evaluation: Problems and solutions.* Paper presented at the Connecticut Leadership Academy Workshop Series for School Superintendents on Issues in Personnel Evaluation, Meriden, CT.

Stufflebeam, D. L. (1967). The use and abuse of evaluation in Title III. *Theory Into Practice, 6*(3), 126–133.

Stufflebeam, D. L. (1969). Evaluation as enlightenment for decision-making. In W. H. Beatty (Ed.). *Improving educational assessment & an inventory of measures of affective behavior* (pp. 41–73). Washington, D.C.: ASCD, NEA.

Stufflebeam, D. L. (1983). The CIPP model for program evaluation. In G. F. Madaus, M. Scriven, & D. L. Stufflebeam (Eds.). *Evaluation models: Viewpoints on educational and human services evaluation* (pp. 117–141). Boston: Kluwer Academic Publishers.

Thomson, S. D. (Ed.). (1993). *Principals for our changing schools: The knowledge and skill base.* Fairfax, VA: National Policy Board for Educational Administration.

Thurow, L. C. (1992). *Head to head.* New York: William Morrow and Company.

Tyler, R. W. (1950). *Basic principles of curriculum and instruction.* Chicago, IL: University of Chicago Press.

Walker, D. & Schaffarzick, J. (1972). Comparing curricula. *Review of Educational Research, 44*(4), 83–112.

Walton, M. (1986). *The Deming management method.* New York: Perigee Books.

Webster, W. J. & Mendro, R. L. (1995, January). *Evaluation for improved school level decision-making and productivity.*

An invited presentation at the Hawaii Institute on Assessment and Accountability. Honolulu: Hawaii Department of Education.

Weick, C. (1976). Educational organizations as loosely coupled systems. *Administrative Sciences Quarterly, 21*(2), 1–19.

Wiggins, G. (1993). Assessment: Authenticity, context, and validity. *Kappan, 75*(3), 201–214.

Wolters, L. T. (1995). *A study of what successful Connecticut suburban middle school principals do to enhance teaching and learning in schools.* Unpublished doctoral dissertation, University of Connecticut, Storrs (UMI# 9529200).

Wrightstone, J. W., Hogan, T. P., & Abbott, M. M. (no date). *Accountability in education and associated measurement problems* (Test Service Notebook 33). New York: Test Department, Harcourt Brace Jovanovich.

Part

· II ·

FOUNDATIONS
OF SUPERVISION

INTRODUCTION

Keith A. Acheson
UNIVERSITY OF OREGON

Duncan E. Waite
APPALACHIAN STATE UNIVERSITY

In Section II, several academic disciplines that inform and undergird supervision are examined. In turn, each of these disciplines, which are the foundations of supervision, offers diverse perspectives on the field. An understanding of these distinct fields and their contributions to supervision provides insight into the field as a whole, and, for the reflective practitioner, provides a measure of insight into the individual's beliefs, knowledge, attitudes, and behavior. In short, these disciplines inform the practice of supervision for the collective and for the individual.

IDEOLOGY OF SUPERVISION

A broad sphere that bears upon the political and psychological concerns of supervision is the ideological one. In Chapter 6, Dully traces the historical development of certain ideologies (which he terms *paradigms*) that have dominated educational thought in America. Borrowing from the work of Argyris and Schön, Duffy contends that there has always been a marked difference between the espoused theories in the

field of supervision and the theories in use by supervisors. Duffy traces the development of supervisory thought through the historical epochs of American education; however, he makes the case that the supervision "paradigm-in-use" has remained remarkably consistent throughout almost 300 years of American education; that being supervision as inspection.

In his discussion of the "reform era" of American education, Duffy makes clear his belief that very little has changed. Traditional forms of supervision, including clinical supervision, are indicted in the perpetuation of the status quo. He believes there will be little change without systemic reorganization. To accomplish major, basic change in schools and school systems, Duffy advocates knowledge–work supervision, a spin-off of Total Quality Management (a spin-off that, as he envisions it, suffers few, if any, of the shortcomings of TQM). This new paradigm "uses instructional supervision as *the* management process for designing high-performance schools that will subsequently assure quality improvement in schooling."

Duffy's argument stems from his contention that schools are knowledge organizations that perform knowledge work.

Like Garmston, Lipton, and Kaiser, Duffy envisions new roles for supervisors engaging in his knowledge–work supervision. Knowledge–work supervisors would scan the school's system and sub–system boundaries, monitoring communication and taking corrective action to enhance the processes. Such supervisors would also supervise teachers' deliberations, or efforts at problem solving. As a new and different approach, Duffy anticipates serious resistance to knowledge–work supervision by what he views as the supervision establishment. He contends however, that only such radical systemic change as he proposes has any hope of improving American education.

PHILOSOPHY OF SUPERVISION

A discipline that is traditionally far broader than any of the others in this section is that of philosophy. From it psychology has been spawned, ideologies have emerged, politics have been waged, battles fought, and nations wrought. In Chapter 7, Neville and Garman address some of the implications that arise when supervision is viewed from this lofty perspective.

The discipline of philosophy, like that of psychology, anthropology, and sociology, is concerned with meaning according to these authors. They state that "the philosophy of educational supervision may be viewed as a search for meaning as regards the purposes and processes of supervision in educational organizations." This entails "the investigation of the ideas, principles, and values which provide the intellectual footing on which educational supervision is based." This philosophy of educational supervision derives from educational philosophy, historical traditions, and sociocultural circumstances.

In stating their case for the explicit examination of philosophy of supervision, Neville and Garman contend that

"the philosophy of supervision may be construed as a belief system, as the aggregate of the convictions, values, and dispositions that serve to guide the process of school supervision. Absent a belief system said process is ill prepared to contend with the uniqueness, uncertainties, and opportunities that accompany decision-making that goes beyond an instrumental definition of curriculum, teaching, and supervision."

These authors proceed to provide a historical overview of the development of American educational thought (i.e., philosophy), with special attention given to the historical development of the philosophy of school supervision. They discuss the various branches of philosophy—ontology, epistemology, axiology, and metaphysics—as to relevance for American education, teaching, and supervision. As a result of their examination, the authors claim that a "philosophy of supervision is not a procedure, a list of steps, or a paradigm. It is not a model or an inventory of practices. Rather, a philosophy of school supervision is a belief system derived from the 'intersection' of thought, reality, knowledge, and human values in the search for understanding about education and the process of supervision."

Neville and Garman explicate the relations between supervision and leadership from a philosophical perspective. They clearly state that "the equation of educational supervision with leadership combines ideas and traditions that have accompanied the transformation of supervision from scholastic–authoritarian inspection, through the dreams and conflicts of the Enlightenment, to democratic vistas. This evolution is the struggle to secure socio–political forms that affirm the individual in the quest for knowledge and human actualization." Like several of the other authors of this section, Neville and Garman posit several provocative questions such as "Is there such a thing as supervisory leadership and, if so, what beliefs guide its development?"

Examining the "narrative turn" in philosophy, Neville and Garman metaphorically equate a supervisor's philosophy with her story:

"The supervisor's story is her narrative of events and experiences that combine with knowledge and a moral/ethical frame to support an ideal of service. The supervisor's story is the public declaration of a belief system—which comprises the coda of a professional role. . . . Where a supervisor's story is authentic and meaningful—where knowledge construction, experience, and risk-taking co-exist, the covenant, the social contact among colleagues in their search for meaning, will characterize the philosophy of supervisory leadership."

They conclude by stating the supervision is philosophy in action.

PSYCHOLOGY OF SUPERVISION

Perhaps the discipline most closely related to supervision is psychology. Whether one adheres to humanist psychology, cognitivist psychology, constructivist psychology, behavioral psychology, family systems theory, or some other school of thought affects what supervision is viewed to be by researcher and by practitioner.

In Chapter 8, Garmston, Lipton, and Kaiser consider the evolution of psychology as a discipline. *Psychology* is defined by the authors as "the science dealing with the mind and mental processes related to the sum of a person's feelings, thoughts, theories, values, motivations, traits, decisions, behavior, physiology and learning." Theories abound within the broad scope of this field that are immediately applicable to pedagogy <u>and</u> andragogy—that is, to learning for both children and adults.

Garmston et al relate the development of psychological thought to the historical development of school supervision. They characterize clinical supervision as an "eclectic blend of diverse and dichotomous viewpoints—phenomenology and empiricism, behaviorism and developmentalism." They refer to Cogan and Goldhammer's clinical supervision as "a compote of psychological orientations." Supervision and supervisors begged, borrowed, and stole from diverse psychological theories to patch together the various models or approaches of school supervision, some of which are still in use today.

Garmston et al go a long way in simplifying and untangling the various knots, webs, and strands of psychological thought woven through most theories of school supervision. The authors forcefully make the case that the thinking behind supervision, whether clear and consistent or vague and contradictory, holds serious ramifications for the work we do:

"When these varied approaches are considered from a psychological perspective, distinct, dichotomous and far reaching consequences emerge. In practice, these deeply held psychological orientations create unstated agreements about the nature of the supervisory relationship, its purposes, assumptions about both adult and student learning, and the intrinsic worth of the persons being supervised."

The authors concentrate on psychological theories that deal with adult development. After reviewing each of the five schools of psychological thought—the behaviorist, psychodynamic, cognitive, existential/humanistic and family systems—the authors settle upon and advocate an approach they term "constructivist-developmental." This approach is grounded in systems theory. The definition of *supervision* their treatment yields is "a process that creates qualitative shifts in the construction of meaning by bringing heightened awareness within each part and of the whole-simultaneously." Supervision becomes a form of mediation: "supervision is a mediational activity rather than a parenting process." The authors conclude by advocating an approach to supervision that is a mediation of professional and organizational development. Such an approach, the authors believe, requires that supervisors become "social ecologists," concerned with the environments and systems surrounding teachers' work as much as with the individuals themselves.

ANTHROPOLOGY AND SOCIOLOGY OF SUPERVISION

As scholarly disciplines, anthropology and sociology would claim even broader spheres such as the study of humans and the study of society. Older disciplines, of course, tend to see them as "Johnny-come-latelies." In Chapter 9, Waite examines anthropology and sociology from the perspective of one who is primarily interested in the supervision of teachers, but also as one who recognizes the insights that can come from consideration of these disciplines. He cites a practicing supervisor and her conviction that training as an anthropologist should be an essential part of every administrator's preparation. Waite traces the genesis and development of anthropology and sociology in broad strokes. He then delimits the subfield within each of these disciplines that deal specifically with education. Along the way, Waite examines the development of the major constructs of both fields, their issues and controversies. In the final section of this chapter, Waite surveys the supervision literature that is informed by either an anthropological or sociological perspective.

Waite finds a continuing methodological and theoretical sophistication represented in the literature of supervision; though he points to a few authors' seemingly carefree application of certain sociological and anthropological terms. "School culture" remains a loosely defined and understood term in some of the writing of the supervision and leadership

fields, Waite contends. He sees a danger in such loose application of terms.

Reiterating his opening admonition for more widespread training in anthropology and sociology, Waite finds ready application for the research methodologies of these fields to the work of supervisors and administrators. He believes that questions concerning school and schooling can generate rich insights when framed from either an anthropological or sociological perspective:

What are the political, economic, structural, and historical sociological influences, patterns, and forces impinging upon supervision and its domain?
Can these be connected and, if so, how?
What is the nature of knowledge that supervisors possess or exhibit?
What is the view of knowledge, the epistemology, supervisors, or a particular supervisor, hold(s)?
What is the impact of a particular supervisory epistemology upon the relationship (i.e., the process) between supervisor and teacher?
How is the supervisory epistemology influenced by the structures within which the supervisor works and what is the influence of that epistemology upon the work setting?

All of these questions are framed from a sociological perspective.

Some questions Waite poses from an anthropological perspective include: "Is there a definite culture of supervision?" and, "What is the deep personal meaning attached to being a supervisor?" Waite poses still more questions meant to prompt the thinking and the inquiry of supervisors and supervision.

POLITICS OF SUPERVISION

Other influences on school supervision can be discerned through an analysis from a political point of view. In Chapter 10, Barott and Galvin investigate the political dimensions of supervision. Barott and Galvin take this perspective in giving thought to costs, stakes, democratic and autocratic influences, along with other pressures that come from the political sphere. They begin with the seemingly simple premise that "the purpose of supervision in educational organizations is to create an environment in which teachers are able to teach and students are able to learn." By defining supervision as an organizational phenomenon, however, the authors demonstrate that issues of conflict and scarcity inevitably complicate the reality of supervisory practice. The potential for both conflict and collaboration simultaneously exists among constituencies within schools, they note, and limitations of time and energy inevitably result in scarcity. These facts, Barott and Galvin point out, are not adequately addressed by the most prominent scholars in our fields. Politics and economics are important because they explain the reason behind the much lamented observation that school leaders usually devote little time and energy to instructional leadership generally, and to supervision specifically.

Barott and Galvin argue convincingly that "supervision is an inherently political act," by which they mean that supervision includes activities related to resource allocation, conflict negotiation, and agreement of purpose. Second, they posit that "supervision is inherently an economic activity" that involves choices of cost and benefit among individuals. In this chapter, the authors focus their discussion on the micropolitics and microeconomics of the circumstances and environment in which school leaders operate—the school building.

In a discussion of the micropolitics of educational organizations, a distinction is made between two functions of government: service and politics. Most supervision literature addresses only the first of these, assuming that "stakes" such as purpose, role, and process are given, while overlooking the inevitably conflictual, contradictory, paradoxical, negotiated reality of organizational life. Barott and Galvin's elaboration on the economics of organizational contexts illustrates how tangible resources, as well as intangibles like time, expertise, attention, and even affection, are strategically distributed. This currency of costs and benefits, as well as more conventional measures (e.g., personnel, materials, facilities, and equipment) interact with the political dimension to determine the success or failure of supervisory aims such as innovation and collaboration.

The authors elaborate on the theme of micropolitics by examining the "domestic affairs" of the school site, as well as the "foreign affairs" faced within the organization's environment. Issues to be resolved in both instances include: "What are the stakes?" "Who governs?" and "How do they govern?" The political ideology of schools and several political myths concerning education are also addressed.

In the end, Barott and Galvin return to their original premise and note that "(g)ood teaching and successful learning don't just happen because of good intentions." They call for a perspective of supervision that recognizes that the learning environment of schools is constantly negotiated through the interplay of numerous exchanges among teachers, students, parents, and community members, and that conflict and costs fundamentally constrain, influence, and shape the nature of supervision within the school context. Such a view entails a recognition of "both the costs of collaboration and the benefits of conflict," as well as that "individuals, given a choice, will choose the less costly alternative." The authors

conclude with the observation that the preparation of future supervisors should go beyond normative and moral issues that are most commonly dealt with, and focus on "how schools really work and why," as well as the limits of influence, to make schools both more democratic and productive.

The points of view and insights that can be derived from these chapters are illuminating and provocative. Taken individually, each chapter offers a fresh and provocative perspective on our field. Taken collectively, these chapters provide an essential education in supervision. There is much to be learned from the disciplines represented here that can help those of us who focus narrowly on the day-to-day supervision of pre–service teachers, in–service teachers, and beyond–service teachers.

Some time ago at a section meeting of the American Educational Research Association devoted to teacher supervision, a question was asked: How should a supervisor respond to a teacher who typically has a very small portion of class members on task, and explains this observed phenomenon as "God's will." Members of the panel did not have immediate answers. It is interesting, in retrospect, to consider after reading these chapters what responses might be made from a philosophical point of view, a psychological perspective, an anthropological or sociological slant, an ideological or political position, or from an eclectic, ecumenical thos. One might say, "Take data as if you were B. F Skinner, but give feedback as if you were Carl Rogers." Another could claim, "Using an Hegelian dialectic, here is an antithesis for your thesis. What shall we posit as a synthesis?" Still another could say, "Given the evidence from evolutionary psychology, what shall we assume God had in mind for these children?" Finally, there is, "As Aristotle (or Socrates, via Plato) would have said. . ." From the viewpoint of "corporate America" we might ask, "Will these young people be able to push the buttons that have pictures of hamburgers, or assets and liabilities, to draw conclusions?"

Answers to the most perplexing questions concerning supervision and schooling may be lodged in the ensuing chapters. If they are not, some important questions certainly are. For researchers, asking the best question is often preferred to having ill-conceived answers.

· 6 ·

THE IDEOLOGY OF SUPERVISION

Francis M. Duffy

GALLAUDET UNIVERSITY

INTRODUCTION

An *ideology* is a body of ideas supporting an economic, political, or social theory. Instructional supervision is a process for working with teachers to improve instruction and to promote their professional growth. An ideology of supervision, therefore, is a body of ideas supporting a general theory of instructional supervision.

An ideology can also be thought of as a paradigm. The word *paradigm* comes from the Greek *paradeigma,* which means "model, pattern, example." Kuhn (1962), a scientific historian, introduced the concept of paradigm to the world of science. Kuhn described a paradigm as "accepted examples of actual scientific practice, examples which include law, theory, application, and instrumentation together—[that] provide models from which spring particular coherent traditions of scientific research." He continued: "Men whose research is based on shared paradigms are committed to the same rules and standards for scientific practice" (p. 10).

Smith (1975) said a paradigm is based on a shared set of assumptions about the world. A paradigm, he said, explains the world to us and helps us to predict its behavior. Paradigms help to create a set of expectations about what will probably occur in our world based on a shared set of assumptions. Finally, Smith said, "When we are in the middle of the paradigm . . . it is hard to imagine any other paradigm" (p. 19).

Barker (1992) defines a paradigm as a " set of rules and regulations (written or unwritten) that does two things: (1) it establishes or defines boundaries; and (2) it tells you how to behave inside the boundaries in order to be successful." This definition could just as easily be used to define an ideology.

In the world of education, persistent historical ideologies (or paradigms) are found in the problems that educators encounter. These problems include figuring out how to govern schools, how to teach, what to include in curricula, managing the relationship between schools and their environments, and how to supervise. As time passed, educators' per-

ceptions of these problems changed as well. The changing perceptions are reflected in the dominant ideology of a particular time period. The dominant ideology, adapting Barker's (1992) definition of a paradigm to education, does two things: (1) it establishes or defines boundaries for practice, and (2) it informs practitioners about how to behave inside those boundaries in order to be successful. This chapter guides readers through a brief history of four dominant ideologies of supervision and concludes with a description of what the author believes is an evolving ideology that is currently influencing the practice of supervision.

THE IDEOLOGIES OF SUPERVISION IN RETROSPECT

The four periods of American instructional supervision identified by Eye, Netzer and Krey (1971) are used to organize a historical view of the ideology of supervision. The four periods identified by these authors are: the Period of Administrative Inspection, the Period of Efficiency Orientation, the Period of Cooperative Group Effort, and the Period of Research Orientation. The author believes these four periods represent the dominant ideologies of supervision—the four "big" ideas: inspection, efficiency, cooperative group effort, and research orientation.

The Period of Administrative Inspection (1642–1875)

During the seventeenth and eighteenth centuries, supervision was primarily inspectoral in nature and process (Alfonso, Firth, & Neville, 1981). The ideology of supervision-as-inspection put supervision in the hands of committees of ministers and lay people who focused on inspecting schools to ensure that teachers conformed to religious and moral standards prescribed by the communities. The Period of Administrative Inspection can be subdivided into the three eras: the colonial era, the post-Revolution era, and the Common School era.

The Colonial Era The history of the American educational experience began with English colonists recreating the school system of their home country. The New England colonies were primarily settled by Puritans following the religious doctrines of John Calvin. In New England, there was a clear relationship between church, state, and school. Education was viewed as a way to become literate in sacred scripture, Calvinist doctrine, and the general laws of the commonwealth. The Puritans believed uneducated people could easily be corrupted by Satan.

To ensure children's literacy, the Massachusetts General Court passed the Law of 1642 (Gutek, 1970), which required parents to attend to their child's ability to read and understand the principles of religion and the laws of the Commonwealth. In 1647, the General Court of Massachusetts enacted the "Old Deluder Satan Law" (Gutek, 1970), which required towns of 50 or more families to appoint a teacher of reading and writing. Towns of 100 or more families were also expected to appoint as Latin teachers to prepare students for entry to college.

These early school laws created several legal precedents that influenced the ideology of supervision of that time. First, the state now could *require* education. Second, state authorities could supervise and control schools. Third, public funds could be used to support education.

The curriculum of early New England town schools consisted of reading, writing, and religion. One of the most popular colonial school books was the "New England Primer" that first appeared in 1690. This book illustrates the close relationship between religion and reading in early New England. It consisted primarily of 24 rhymes (one for each letter of the alphabet) to assist children in learning to read. Many of these rhymes had religious themes.

The Middle Atlantic colonies were comprised of colonists from many different religious backgrounds and different European countries and traditions. Because of the diversity of language, culture, and religion, there was no common ground upon which to build an educational system. Government consequently neglected education in this region, resulting in the establishment of many private schools that were supported by churches and other organizations.

The colonial South was built around the agricultural plantation society. Little communication existed between large plantations, so there was no sense of community as existed in New England. The plantation also promoted rigid social class distinctions that divided the population into three groups: (1) landowners, (2) lower socioeconomic group; (i.e., "poor whites"), and (3) Negro slaves (Gutek, 1970).

The isolation of Southern plantations resulted in the use of tutors to teach children of the landed gentry. The education of the Southern gentleman had two major emphases: a code of ethics based on the concept of chivalry; second, practical instruction in the management of the basic agricultural unit. As a leisure class of people, Southern gentlemen also developed an interest in oratory. The Southern colonial society produced such orator-statesmen as Washington, Jefferson, Madison, and Monroe.

The "poor white" population was usually confined to small farms on infertile land. Education of "poor white" children was informal, usually provided by parents and focusing on hunting and farming techniques. This kind of schooling focused on survival, and resulted in a large class of illiterate people—a condition that later inhibited the progress of the South in later years.

After being uprooted from Africa, Negro slaves were forced to give up their lives in a hunter–herdsman–farmer society to take up the lives of enslaved plantation laborers. Education of slaves was direct and informal. The slave learned the tasks of his or her new position (i.e., field hand, mechanic, blacksmith, or domestic servant). Plantation owners generally made no attempt to teach slaves reading or writing (although there were a few exceptions).

The Postrevolution Era After the American Revolution, the diverse colonies blended together to form a national consciousness, but colonial forms of education did persist. Even so, there was increased debate over curricular content for introducing students to the new federal government and the developing national culture. For Constitutional reasons, the early federal government was reluctant to become involved in financing education, which resulted in individual states taking on this responsibility. Massachusetts was the first state to pass laws to finance education. Other New England states followed. The Middle Atlantic states continued to experiment with various kinds of private education. The South continued to lag behind in its organization and control of education.

In the New England schools of the late eighteenth century, it was common to hire one teacher for the winter term and another for the summer term. This meant that many winter-term teachers were farmers who sought to supplement their farming income with winter teaching (Lemlech & Marks, 1976). To qualify as a schoolmaster, the person had to study English grammar, arithmetic, algebra, geography, surveying, and rhetoric. After 2 years at an academy, the teacher was considered ready to teach. A typical contract for a winter term teacher stipulated:

- Must teach 25 students for 80 days
- The school term will begin the first week after Thanksgiving.
- Must be honest and of high moral character.
- Each child must be taught as much as he is capable of learning.
- At the end of the term a report identifying student progress in each subject must be submitted to the trustee.

(Lemlech & Marks, 1976, p. 8)

Several features of this contract influenced the ideology of supervision during that period. It specifically stipulated that children be taught as much as they were capable of learning, the teacher must document student progress in each subject, and a teacher's moral character was a qualification for teaching.

These requirements for teaching stood in sharp contrast with the fact that teaching was not considered a good career choice.

Ministers, servants, and misfits were typical teachers. Teaching was extremely nonselective during the nationalistic phase, and newspapers of the period suggest that teachers were noted for their incapacity for other types of employment. Many teachers were indentured servants who occupied their spare hours performing chores such as grave digging, leading the church choir, planting crops, or conducting wedding and funeral services (Lemlech & Marks, 1976, pp. 12–13).

A typical teacher of this era was given four new American textbooks for the entire school term. These books were Noah Webster's *American Spelling Book* (1783), Nicholas Pike's *Arithmetic* (1788), Lindley Murray's *English Grammar* (1795), and Jedediah Morse's *Elements of Geography* (1795). Teaching methods were mainly recitation, copying lessons, listening to lessons, and questioning individual students.

During this era, several plans for a national educational system were proposed. Benjamin Rush proposed that the federal government set up a new form of educational structure that would promote education to reinforce the principle of patriotism. Benjamin Franklin proposed a change from the traditional Latin Grammar School to a new curriculum that focused on practical skills, utilitarian crafts, and English grammar. Thomas Jefferson's plan emphasized that education should be a political rather than a religious function. He encouraged states to control education. Although none of these plans was accepted when first proposed, each of them contained principles that influenced later education reformers.

After 1800, various societies were formed to provide education to poor children not served by the church. The Free School Society, which was formed in New York City in 1805, was a major proponent of the Lancaster Method of teaching (Rippa, 1988). This method was developed by Joseph Lancaster, a schoolmaster in England who needed more teachers and adopted the practice of using monitors. The Lancaster Method became especially popular in industrial towns and cities with expanding populations of low-income residents.

The Common School Era Another important element of the Period of Administrative Inspection was the establishment of the Common School. The Common School preceded the contemporary public school. It was developed to promote literacy and citizenship in all people. The United States was changing from a young, agricultural republic into an industrial nation. For the children of new immigrants, schools facilitated the learning of a new language and a new way of life. As the Western frontier expanded, class distinctions were replaced by the democratic fellowship of the frontier. All of these societal changes promoted a change from the sectarian, religious foundation of schools to the patriotic, utilitarian bases of the common schools.

James G. Carter of Massachusetts was one of the leaders of the movement toward common schools. He criticized the prevalent system that used untrained teachers, tolerated irregular attendance of students, and used short school terms. He stressed the importance of the inductive teaching methods of Bacon and supported the views of Pestalozzi. Pestalozzi and Fellenberg had reformed the Prussian system of education by developing a uniform curriculum, designing standardized teacher certification requirements, and arguing for general taxation to support schools (Gutek, 1970).

Carter's most severe criticism was aimed at the district system for organizing and controlling schools. Since the beginning of educational organizations in the United States, the states passed on the responsibility for maintaining public schools to the communities, who, in turn, passed the responsibility onto school districts. According to Rippa (1988), the district control of schools "degenerated into local political feuds leading to chaotic school conditions." In 1837, as chairman of the Massachusetts' House Committee on Education, Carter persuaded the Massachusetts' Legislature to enact the Law of 1837, which created the first truly effective state board of education in the United States (Rippa, 1988). The board appointed Horace Mann to serve as the first chief state school official.

Horace Mann's life was devoted to the development of the Common School. He imagined a school that would be state-supported, publicly controlled, and of such excellent quality that all parents would want to send their children to that school. Mann also envisioned the public school as a unifying force in society that would assemble the diverse segments of America into one nation. Mann served as secretary of the Massachusetts State Board of Education from 1837 to 1848. "More than anyone else, Horace Mann stirred the American conscience with his pleas for a tax-supported system of common schools" (Rippa, 1988, p. 106).

As common schools were established it became necessary to train enough competent teachers to staff these schools. Secondary schools were initially presumed to be sufficient education for the common school teacher. Horace Mann and other educators, however, were convinced that secondary schools could not provide the kind of education needed for a new generation of teachers. In 1839, Mann was instrumental in establishing the first public normal school (a teacher training institution) in Massachusetts (Lemlech & Marks, 1976). Mann also advocated an increase in teachers' salaries to attract more competent individuals to teaching (Gutek, 1970). State teaching institutes were also arranged once or twice a year to demonstrate teaching problems and skills. Henry Barnard introduced the first institute in Connecticut in 1839 (Lemlech & Marks, 1976). By 1845, state professional associations for teachers existed, and in 1857 the National Teachers Association, which later to become the National Education Association, was established in Philadelphia.

The Ideology of Supervision-as-Inspection Despite the wide variety of schools and the diversity of their organizational structures and teaching practices, the predominant form of educational supervision during this period was administrative inspection.

The policies, purposes, standards, and curriculum of colonial schools were not determined by the teacher; rather, they were determined by a governing board that exercised some kind of supervision and approval. As mentioned earlier, a teacher's contract typically stipulated that each child be taught as much as he or she was capable of learning and that reports on student progress must be submitted to the trustees of the school. In reality, the inspector or supervisor often made judgments about the teacher rather than about the teaching or the students' learning (Eye, Netzer, & Krey, 1971). Teachers were expected to meet specific requirements. The most common requirements were "religious orthodoxy, loyalty to the civil government, and moral acceptability" (Butts & Cremin, 1953).

In addition to moral judgments, inspection often focused on the teacher's ability to manage the school and meet the requirements of the prescribed curriculum. The inspector made decisions on the basis of what he thought he saw. Improvement of instruction was not an issue. There was a stern, disciplinary relationship between the inspector and the teacher. When problems surfaced, the solutions often resulted in the dismissal of the "defective" teacher.

The power to inspect schools was originally in the hands of selectmen (i.e., town representatives) or of church ministers. As the administration of schools was delegated to school districts, inspection was performed by the school committee, which was like a school board. Finally, the authority to inspect schools was delegated from the school committee to the school superintendent.

As towns grew in size, their schools grew. With larger schools, several teachers might be employed in one building. One teacher was often given administrative duties, thus becoming the principal teacher (later being called the "building principal"). Supervision, however, remained primarily in the hands of the school committee and superintendent. The principal teacher was not expected to supervise "except as the wishes of the citizenry were made known through the lay committee" (Alfonso, Firth, & Neville, 1981, p. 22). Instruction was improved by enforcing prescribed teaching exercises and techniques.

Dickey (1948) describes this period of educational supervision when he says, "The first attempts at supervision were characterized by three fundamental approaches: (1) authority and autocratic rule; (2) emphasis upon the inspection and weeding out of weak teachers; and, (3) conformity to standards prescribed by the committee of laymen."

The common school movement and the growth of American cities led to the transfer of local supervision from the superintendent to the principal teacher. By 1830, cities were growing so quickly and school enrollment was escalating so rapidly that school superintendents were unable to give personal attention to the supervision of schools. The logical next step was to delegate the management of schools to the principal teachers (Pierce, 1935).

Supervision provided by principals during this period was an extension of the school superintendent's office. The principal performed the kinds of inspections that had previously been conducted by lay committees during the eighteenth century when they made supervisory visits to schools. Principals were expected to train teachers about "approved" teaching materials and techniques. Teachers were judged by their compliance with the rigidly prescribed courses of study. Classroom visitation was the accepted method to determine if a teacher was conforming to these prescribed materials and techniques.

The key operational verb for supervision during this period was "inspect." Inspection in the early days of colonial education was conducted by church or town leaders. Later, it was done by school committees or superintendents. In this period, inspectoral responsibilities were delegated to principal-teachers. However, the basic rationale for inspection never changed: observe teachers to determine if they measure up to a prescribed set of standards and methods.

The Period of Efficiency Orientation (1876–1936)

This period began in the aftermath of the Civil War. For the Southern states, the devastation of the Civil War made the development of schooling difficult. The major battles of the war obliterated many Southern towns. Railroads were destroyed, the banking system was in ruins, there was no currency or credit, and half the white men between the ages of 18 and 35 had been killed or seriously maimed (Rippa, 1988). The colleges and private academies of the South closed, and for the next generation the policies of "Radical Reconstruction" destroyed attempts at educational reform. The Southern people were hopelessly in debt because of the economic policies of Reconstructionist governments, and public education suffered because of this.

In contrast to the devastation and poverty of the South, the North was more prosperous than ever during the postwar years. Northern cities, factories, and railroads expanded. Economic policies developed during and after the war benefited northern industrialists. John D. Rockefeller was making headway on building his oil empire that would eventually comprise 90% of the nation's oil output. Andrew Carnegie was climbing from the ranks of impoverished immigrants toward becoming a multimillion dollar steel magnate. This was the beginning of industrial America.

In industrial America, by the early 1900s, more than 1.7 million boys and girls under the age of 16 were working long hours in the fields and factories (Rippa, 1988). The era was characterized by 16-hour work days, unsafe working conditions, and frequent industrial accidents. It is ironic that the business leaders who created and supported the deplorable working conditions in their factories criticized the "narrow vision of the school room" and the inefficiency of public schools (Rippa, 1988). According to Rippa, the National Association of Manufacturers (NAM) even proposed changes in school curricula that would meet the needs of industrial society. Most of these proposals suggested more vocational training in the public schools.

The NAM berated public schooling for what it called "gross inefficiency." In one of its official statements, the NAM suggested that the juvenile delinquent sent to a reformatory had a better chance of becoming a skilled worker and earning better wages than the average boy who attends public school. "The factory is where the school should be. . . . In that way we will get results and get something that will be a benefit to industrial America" (Rippa, 1988, p. 141). American businesses were demanding efficiency in schooling. They believed that too much money was being spent on "ornamental" branches of learning, while "forty percent of high school graduates haven't a command of simple arithmetic, cannot multiply, subtract and divide correctly in simple numbers and in fractions. Over forty percent of them cannot accurately express themselves in the English language" (Rippa, 1988, pp. 142–143).

American educators bowed to the pressure of American business leaders. Schools slowly adopted the business ideology that stressed the need for efficient workers and citizens. School administrators applied the techniques of industrial society to the operation of schools. Educators devised tests and measurements in an attempt to decrease "waste" and increase efficiency. The function of public schooling was narrowed to "teaching specific skills and attitudes that mirrored the business world and molded the individual to fit into an industrial society." (Rippa, 1988, pp. 144–145).

As American education moved toward an orientation of efficiency in schooling, a number of European educational reformers began to exert influence on American schools that was in conflict with the ideology of industrial efficiency. Jean Piaget expounded on his theory of developmental stages in human cognition. Johann Pestalozzi offered his views on education based on children's sense perceptions. Friedrich Froebel offered the concept of kindergarten. Maria Montessorri developed her approaches to sensory education. Alfred Binet's work on measuring intelligence began to have its impact on American schooling.

In addition to the influence that these European educational reformers were having on American schooling during this era, there was also an American educator-philosopher that was having an impact. His name was John Dewey. Dewey arrived at the University of Chicago in 1894. Along with his wife, Alice Chipman Dewey, he established the Laboratory School at the university. The Laboratory School gave Dewey the opportunity to experiment with some of the educational ideas that he and his wife had.

Dewey's Laboratory School differed from other schools of the industrial ilk in that it was child-centered. Pupil interests determined the curriculum. Students were encouraged to "learn by doing." Dewey's school believed in "a spirit of freedom and mutual respect," "self-discipline among the children," and "the growth of self-directive power and judgment" (Rippa, 1988, p. 185). Dewey's emphasis on problem solving to develop mental abilities was really a return to the inductive reasoning advocated by Francis Bacon in the seventeenth century. Dewey's ideas caught the imagination of American educators, and he became the chief spokesperson for the "new education" movement that began to evolve during this period.

Another important development during this era was the Normal School Movement. Schools were undergoing significant changes, and teacher training was also being radically changed. Prior to the Civil War, several normal schools were established to train teachers. These schools were usually 2-year programs and were thought to be adequate for educating elementary teachers. As secondary education became more prevalent, a need emerged for more highly trained teachers for the secondary schools.

After the Civil War, several normal schools changed from 2-year programs to 4-year teacher colleges. In addition, a small number of colleges and universities established chairs of pedagogy (i.e., most often within departments of philosophy or psychology) to train secondary school teachers. These 4-year programs enriched the traditional teacher training curricula by adding liberal arts subjects and the study of educational theory.

Dewey's influence and the Normal School Movement changed the characteristics of the American teacher. Changes in the teachers resulted in changes in teaching. Teachers became more skillful at asking questions. Teachers needed a more extensive knowledge of their subject matter. There was more of a focus on learning through experience, or, as it was also known, "object learning": "Teachers tried to use real objects in the classroom and began to consider motivation to keep children interested. To develop motivation, it became necessary to plan lessons in advance, and the teacher was emancipated from the textbook" (Lemlech & Marks, 1976, p. 26).

In 1877, John Philbrick, who was superintendent of Boston Public Schools, stated that "merely looking on and seeing teachers is not the supervision of instruction which is to be expected of principals" (Alfonso, Firth, & Neville, 1981, p. 27). This is one of the first statements of this period that suggests the emergence of a multidimensional role for supervisors that would have them doing more than inspecting teachers.

Prior to this era, administrative inspectors audited teachers, textbooks, and pupils. When a teacher was judged ineffective, he or she was dismissed. By the end of the nineteenth century, which was the early stage of the Efficiency Orientation to schooling, supervisors were beginning to act more like managers of their educational organizations. The supervisor was compared with a factory foreman. Students were the "raw material," teachers were the workers who processed the material, and the schools' administration was organized to promote efficiency and effectiveness. Students were marched through hallways from room to room under a rigid system of order and discipline. Teachers were expected to obey procedural codes. Teachers were supervised using the inspectoral paradigm, but the principles of scientific management (Taylor, 1911) were incorporated into supervisory practice to achieve industrial efficiency. Supervisors now aspired to a "science of teaching" and tried to control teacher behavior and its effect on student performance (Alfonso, Firth, & Neville, 1981).

"The impact of business practices and ethics upon education was strong. The visibility of rapid industrial development and the underlying management identifications made precision and efficiency the guiding stars of most public enterprises" (Eye, Netzer, & Krey, 1971, p. 24). The functions of administration and supervision in schools began to separate and expand. The administration of schools began to be handled by a business manager. With a business manager in place, the superintendent became primarily responsible for instruction. Supervisors, then, became responsible to the superintendents of instruction. Having a full-time supervisory position meant that supervisors spent more time with teachers trying to improve instruction.

Supervisory roles changed, and supervisory attitudes toward teachers changed. Journal articles of this period described helpful relationships between supervisors and teachers, using such words as *conferencing, improving, constructive,* and *growth.* This change in attitude was in sharp contrast to the attitudes of the administrative inspection era.

In 1911, the National Education Association (NEA) established a Committee on the Economy of Time. This committee published four major reports between 1915 and 1919. The committee advocated the use of scientific methodology to study educational problems. They constructed tests to determine instructional efficiency, reviewed textbooks to determine what was being taught, studied adult activities to identify socially worthwhile knowledge, and examined the problems of the nation to determine social needs (Alfonso, Firth, & Neville, 1981). By compiling this scientific evidence, the committee developed a basis for advocating their selection of subject matter and teaching methods.

Although a lot of educational research was conducted during the 1920s and 1930s, supervisors simply informed teachers of the findings and their implications. Directives and guidelines for teachers were developed based on the research findings. Teachers were expected to comply. Scientific efficiency was added to the inspectoral paradigm and supervision was still not a democratic process, although there were indications of movement in this direction.

The Period of Cooperative Group Effort (1937–1959)

There were several events in American society that had an important impact on education during this era: the Great Depression, increased educational opportunities for women, and the beginning of the Civil Rights Movement.

The Great Depression In October 1929, the collapse of the stock market led to the Great Depression. The economic effects of this depression were devastating—prices dropped, factories closed, real estate values declined, new construction stopped, and banks failed. Sharp reductions in school revenues also caused the closing of many schools. For example, 770 schools closed in 1 month (Rippa, 1988). Some communities even began to charge tuition to attend school. Those students who could not pay were excluded from public schooling.

The general uncertainty of this era was evident in the writing of social science educators of the time. For example, some textbook authors during the 1930s began to criticize American industrial practices instead of glorifying them, as they had in the past (Rippa, 1988). The business community reacted bitterly to the criticism of America's free enterprise economy. In fact, by the end of the 1930s several textbooks critical of American business practices were condemned by the American Legion, the Advertising Federation of America, and the New York State Economic Council. The authors of these critical books were depicted as promoters of "creeping collectivism" (Rippa, 1988). Several communities even conducted book burnings.

Improved Educational Opportunities for Women During this time period, educational opportunities for women also increased. Discrimination against women was deeply rooted in American culture. For generations, customs and laws restricted a woman's social position in a man's world. In the early years of American society, girls were excluded from the New England town schools. Girls learned to read and write from their mothers or in dame schools. A few communities began to allow girls to attend the Latin grammar schools toward the end of the eighteenth century, but only in the early mornings or late afternoons when the boys had already been taught. A secondary education was rarely available to colonial girls, and a collegiate education was unthinkable. In

1783, one young girl who had passed the entrance examination to Yale was declared "fully qualified, except in regard to sex" and was denied admission (Rippa, 1988, p. 234).

The nineteenth century saw women demanding equality in greater numbers. They rallied for the right to vote long before the conclusion of the Civil War. For many leaders of the women's movement of that era, the right to education became a rallying cry for the movement as a whole. Education could open doors and pave the way toward political equality. Despite their political efforts, however, women continued to receive their education in female seminaries and other gender-segregated schools. Some of these schools prepared women as teachers long before the opening of normal schools.

Teaching became one of the few socially acceptable occupations for women. The newly established normal schools of this era catered almost exclusively to women. Men increasingly worked in factories or lived on the Western frontier, while women were encouraged to go into teaching because they could be paid less than men. This trend continued throughout the nineteenth century.

In 1920, women won the right to vote with a Constitutional Amendment. They then began to demand many of the same privileges that men enjoyed. They increasingly entered the work force, demanded equal pay for equal work, earned advanced college degrees, and generally began to move toward intellectual and social equality with men. This movement gained momentum throughout this period in American education.

The Civil Rights Movement For almost a century after the Civil War, separate schools for black children was the accepted norm in American education. In 1896, the U.S. Supreme Court supported the "separate but equal" doctrine of *Plessy v. Ferguson.* "Separate" facilities and services for blacks were ruled constitutional as long as they were "equal" to those enjoyed by whites.

Until World War II, the black community offered little resistance to the "separate but equal" doctrine of education. As the war began to bring integration to the armed forces, however, returning black soldiers moved their families north in search of a better life. With this mobility, and attending increases in political power, blacks also began to demand equality of educational opportunities—opportunities that were not provided under the "separate but equal" policy.

The increasing expectations and demands of the black community for more educational opportunities resulted in a historically significant Supreme Court decision: *Brown v. Board of Education of Topeka.* This decision reversed the 1896 "separate but equal" doctrine. The Court ruled that segregation in public schools on the basis of race or color deprived the individual of equal protection of the law as guaranteed by the Fourteenth Amendment. This judicial decision, however, did not bring a sudden end to segregated schools because the Court's ruling could not change decades of public attitudes. It took years of boycotts, mass demonstrations, court-ordered school busing, and, finally, the passage of the Civil Rights Act of 1964 to bring about changes in schools and other public agencies.

The Ideology of Supervision-as-Cooperative Group Effort
Within the milieu characterized earlier, cooperative-democratic approaches to supervising teachers began to emerge. The social transformations of the Great Depression and the increased involvement of women and minorities in American society saw movement toward wide participation in the formulation of social and educational policy. There was an emerging emphasis on allowing teachers to participate in the decision-making processes and to share the responsibility for improving instruction at the level of the school district. This attitude was expressed by Kyte (1930) when he said that democratic supervision was supposed to provide for the "maximum development of the teacher into the most professionally efficient person she is capable of becoming."

Research in group dynamics during this time period promoted the concepts of social psychology (e.g., Roethlisberger, Dickson, & Wright, 1939). Supervision was seen as a dynamic process that encouraged the interchange of ideas among professionals. All people working in the schools were expected to be sensitive to each other as professionals. Perceptual accuracy was stressed based on the rationale that the more accurate people's perceptions are, the greater the opportunity to solve difficult problems. Improved one-on-one and group communication, sensitivity to others, professionalism, and interpersonal cooperation were all important elements of supervisory ideology of this time period.

"The democratic supervision of the 1930s (characterized by kind treatment of the individual) evolved into cooperative enterprise (group decision-making) in the 1940s and 1950s and ushered in the concept of the supervisor as an agent for change" (Wiles, 1955). The change-agent concept viewed teachers as the key individuals for identifying and analyzing instructional problems and as the key player for implementing needed changes. The cooperative actions of a supervisor and a group of teachers were thought to make both parties aware of the strengths and needs within the group. The teachers' self-direction was a primary goal of the supervisory process. "A pupil learns more when he assumes responsibility for his learning. A teacher is more effective when he is responsible for making the final decision on what constitutes an appropriate teaching procedure" (Wiles, 1955).

Within this ideology, the sharing of responsibility with teachers was not intended to displace the supervisor's leadership. The supervisor was not supposed to wait passively for teachers to identify and act on problems. Supervisors were expected to provide teachers with an ordered conceptual framework for the consideration of teaching problems. Working within this framework, teachers were encouraged to clarify and act upon instructional problems.

The Period of Research Orientation (1960–present)

This period began with Russia's launching of Sputnik that suddenly made Americans doubt the effectiveness of their schooling. This fear was the basis of what now has become known as the Educational Reform Movement, which is in fact a series of movements that continues today. A short history of the reform movement is provided as an overview of this period.

The history of American education is a history of reform movements; for example, the reformers during the period 1900–1950 were known as *administrative progressives.* These reformers had common training, interests, and values. They were the first generation of professional leaders, mostly men, who would serve lifelong careers as city superintendents, education professors, state education officers, or foundation officials. They had a fundamental and common faith in the science of education.

The administrative progressives supported changes they thought would produce efficiency, equity (as *they* defined it), accountability, and expertise. They called their program of reform "reorganization." The reorganization movement, which is the opposite of what we mean today by restructuring, was remarkably successful. Many of the reforms made by this movement persist today. A summary of some of the accomplishments of this movement shows how successful the administrative progressives were in institutionalizing their changes:

- The control of urban school districts was centralized in small, elite boards and decision-making was delegated to experts (i.e., to school superintendents)
- Small, rural districts were consolidated and one-room schools were abolished
- "Largeness" was celebrated, as opposed to "smallness"
- Curricula were designed to match assumed differences of ability and economic destiny of students—as opposed to giving all students a solid grounding in academic subjects
- Hierarchies of curriculum experts and supervisors were created to tell teachers what and how to teach—as opposed to giving them greater autonomy in the classroom
- Efforts were made to replace the vagaries of local lay politics with the authority (or science) of educational practice

In the 1950s, and even more intensely in the 1960s, critics hacked at the reforms of the administrative progressives. A new politics of education emerged with groups demanding a role in the decision-making process. These new politics were significantly empowered by the *Brown v. the Board of Education* desegregation case and the civil rights movement. The message that resulted from these two events was not lost on groups such as Hispanics, feminists, and parents of handicapped children. These new, socially motivated politics undermined the status quo and modified old structures of power and school programs.

Changes made in schools during the 1960s included:

- mandated racial desegregation (primarily through busing)
- an attack on institutional sexism (e.g., by improving hiring practices)
- new bilingual education programs
- an introduction of ethnic curricula (e.g., black studies curricula)
- new, focused attention to the needs of students with disabilities
- the equalization of school finance

- state and federal government mandates for greater parental involvement through school-community councils
- African-Americans demanding greater community control of schools in urban ghettos
- school curricula saw an expansion of course electives that resulted in greater student choice
- alternative schools were created, as well as schools within schools and schools without walls
- IQ testing and academic tracking were attacked
- teachers demanded greater power over their professional lives, especially through such means as unionization and the establishment of teacher centers

In sum, reformers of the 1960s demanded dispersion and decentralization of educational decision-making, as well as an increased role for federal and state governments.

As the changes of this period were incorporated into the school system, however, no new coherent model of school governance emerged—the same old model from previous eras prevailed. The educational system instead responded by grafting these newly mandated changes onto the old structure of the system; the result being larger, more complex, and fragmented bureaucracies to deal with the mandated changes.

The primary result of the 1960's reform movement was not decentralization like it existed in the 1800s, nor was it modest centralization like the administrative progressives sought; instead, it was, as Meyer (1980) calls it, "fragmented centralization." As noted by Meyer, fragmented centralization meant that *everybody and nobody* was in charge of public education with the result that educational leaders—the insiders— lost their sense of control over schooling.

After 20 or so years of turmoil in education, 1980 saw the emergence of a new reform movement—the *Back to Basics* movement. The popular diagnosis of the 1980s was that the existing crisis in education was the result of the educational ferment during the 1960s and 1970s. This ferment, it was believed, disrupted learning, thereby resulting in a decline in educational achievement that, in turn, endangered the nation's competitiveness.

The early 1980s saw a spate of reports, books, and articles on the condition of the American education system. Let me give you a few examples of these. In April 1983, *A Nation At Risk: The Imperative for Educational Reform* was released by the National Commission on Excellence in Education. This report criticized the performance of American schools by suggesting several major causes of their poor performance; that is, the curriculum was too diluted with elective courses and academic standards were too low, students spent less time studying and they used their inschool time inefficiently, and few highly qualified students were entering the teaching profession, thereby suggesting the need to overhaul teacher preparation programs.

In September 1983, the Carnegie Foundation for the Advancement of Teaching released a report called *High School: A Report on Secondary Education in America*. The report, which was a bit more optimistic about our nation's schools than many of the other reports of that era, proposed a 12-point "Agenda for Action" to remedy some of the problems facing the schools. Examples of these recommendations are:

- Develop a core curriculum focused on literacy and language with additional requirements in art, health, work, and community service
- Expand guidance services to help students with career planning beyond high school
- Encourage diverse teaching techniques with flexibility in scheduling and an emphasis on student participation
- Establish school–business partnerships

In addition to these four specific recommendations, there were several suggestions for improvement related to teachers' level of preparation, salaries, workloads, and incentives for professional development.

A book on reform published in 1983 was *A Place Called School: Prospects for the Future,* by John Goodlad. This book resulted from an 8-year study of public schools, entitled "A Study of Schooling," that was conducted by Goodlad. The bulk of Goodlad's book describes and analyzes what he thinks schools and schooling are all about. The final two chapters in his book propose an agenda for school improvement. Several of Goodlad's recommendations are:

- increase local school site control
- provide teachers with more planning time
- develop a core curriculum
- design ungraded classes that maximize the interaction between older and younger children
- use peer teaching and cooperative learning
- develop teams of teachers with leadership being provided from within the teams
- create a fourth phase of schooling for students 16–20 years of age that is organized around experimental education and community agencies and which focuses on independent work, study, and volunteer service as a transition to adult life

In 1984, *Horace's Compromise: The Dilemma of the American High School* was published. This was the first major publication resulting from *A Study of High Schools* cosponsored by the National Association of Secondary School Principals and the Commission on Educational Issues of the National Association of Independent Schools. *Horace's Compromise*, written by Ted Sizer, is based on direct observations of public and private high schools in the United States and abroad. The title alludes to a fictional high school teacher whose characteristics are a composite of many of the teachers observed in the study. Through the eyes of this fictional character, Sizer describes the practical problems of education and the compromises that are often forced by the system. Among his many suggestions for improving high schools, Sizer suggests:

- The high school should be devoted to the development of mind and character

- The high school curriculum should be simplified by reducing it to four areas
  - inquiry and expression
  - mathematics and science
  - literature and the arts
  - philosophy and history
- New student evaluation systems should be developed that are based on multiple indices of student performance, instead of course credits
- Teachers should be given more time to respond to students' work through a personalized form of coaching that would require reductions in student–teacher ratios
- Bureaucratic structures should be altered to give local school staffs an opportunity to develop high expectations for students that are built upon trust, rather than on formal regulations

Two other significant reports of the mid-1980s were *Tomorrow's Teachers*, published in 1986 by The Holmes Group, and *A Nation Prepared: Teachers for the 21st Century*, published in 1986 by the Carnegie Task Force On Teaching As A Profession. Both of these reports focus on reforming teacher preparation programs. Both reports suggest that initial teacher preparation should occur at the graduate level of education. Both also stress the need for teachers to have command of their subject matter, primarily by majoring in the field that they wish to teach during their undergraduate years. The Holmes Group Report suggests that professional preparation courses should be improved by teaching specific subjects that are based on recent research. The Carnegie Report also suggested the establishment of a National Standards Board to develop and administer licensing examinations.

In addition, the Holmes Group Report recommends a career ladder that has three levels—instructor, professional teacher, and career professional—whereas the Carnegie Report proposes to restructure the teaching force into four categories—licensed teachers, certified teachers, advanced certificate holders, and lead teachers.

These, and other reform-minded books and reports, immediately preceded the current interest in restructuring schools—an interest that emerged around 1986.

Today, many critics believe that effective educational reform must result in the restructuring of schools. Advocates of restructuring often call for such changes as an increase in the decentralization of authority, more autonomy for teachers with opportunities for collegial decision-making, getting students to think and to demonstrate their competence, more parental involvement, and smaller schools.

Raywid (1990) has written about restructuring in such a way as to shed some light on the meaning of the term. She describes three distinct kinds of school reform efforts: pseudo-reform, incremental reform, and reform by restructuring.

Pseudo-reform Pseudo reform provides changes that are really quite superficial. These include building repairs, expanding exceptions to school policies, lengthening the school day, and increasing minimum achievement scores for school athletes.

Sheer rhetoric, or "symbolic politics," Raywid said, is the most common kind of pseudo reform. Raywid suggests that another frequent example of pseudo-reform is the establishment of a task force; for example, a School Improvement Task Force. She noted that sometimes the convening of the task force *is* the reform. Some cynics of the task force structure claim that the effectiveness of the task force can be restricted to symbolic reforms right from the beginning, depending on how the task force is constituted. Regarding this observation, Raywid wrote: "To include on a task force all interest groups with a stake in the issues virtually insures the continuation of the status quo."

Incremental Reform Incremental reform is more ambitious than pseudo-reform. These reforms aim to improve educational practice. Most reform proposals are of this type. They typically focus on new arrangements or on the implementation of a new practice.

One of the difficulties associated with incremental reform is that schools are notoriously difficult to change. One major reason for this difficulty is the interconnectedness among various parts of the school organization. Several reformers (e.g., H. Dean Evans and Ted Sizer) have noted that in order to change almost anything of significance in schools, a great deal must be changed simultaneously. This condition is reflected in the title of an article by Evans (1983) in the *Phi Delta Kappan*: "We must begin educational reform every place at once." Like a successfully completed jigsaw puzzle, every piece is connected to everything else. You cannot change one piece without altering those pieces that are connected to it. Incremental reforms tend to focus on one piece of the organization without considering required changes in other connected pieces.

Restructuring Restructuring focuses on the fundamental arrangements of the school organization that either support or constrain effective educational practice. Raywid said that because of the interconnectedness of various components of the school organization, any change in the school organization, no matter how minor it may initially appear, will require major changes. Thus, when reasonable and desirable changes appear too complex or too unworkable, it might be time to examine the underlying organizational structures that make them too complex or unworkable. This is what restructuring is all about.

Many critics are convinced that schools are put together in the wrong way and that it is now time to reconsider such fundamental structures as:

- how children are grouped for instruction
- how educational material is divided and packaged for instructional presentations
- how student learning is evaluated

These critics point out that even after a dozen years of serious educational reform efforts to improve the quality of schools, the same pejorative stories that drew the educational community to the excellence movement in the first place are still being heard (e.g., falling test scores, rising dropout rates, and the continuing discovery of yet another set of schools deteriorating rapidly).

For these and other reasons, in 1986 the excellence movement took a noticeable turn away from "reform" and toward "restructuring." Raywid pointed out that proponents of restructuring propose one or both of two significant changes:

• a fundamental and pervasive alteration in the way education is organized and institutionalized
• alterations in the way in which public schools are governed and held accountable

Furthermore, supporters of restructuring hardly agree on what aspects of the school organization should be changed. Despite this lack of agreement about specific changes, two broad restructuring strategies have emerged:

• site-based management
• schools of choice

Both of these strategies, although obviously different in their goals, have common features. Both represent some kind of decentralization of decision-making; both seek to broaden the current base of educational decision-making; and, both talk of changed accountability structures. The goals of each strategy will now be briefly described.

Site-Based Management Site-based management seeks to improve schools by altering the ways in which the schools are governed. There are two key moves to accomplish this goal. First, decision-making power for budget, staff, and instruction is shifted from central office to individual schools. Second, decision-making in an individual school is shared among administrators, teachers, parents, and the community. The underlying logic is that each school decides for itself which kinds of changes and improvements it will undertake.

The practice of site-based management has not been around for a long time; therefore, there is not a lot of evidence to support its effectiveness. There is evidence, however, to suggest some major difficulties in instituting this kind of restructuring. The evidence includes observations that:

• central office staff are highly resistant to shifting authority to individual schools
• often shared decision-making in individual schools is set-up as a process of giving teachers a voice in an advisory body, but not giving them a vote in a decision-making body
• at its worst, a site-based management group becomes just another committee that is not identified and elected by the faculty but appointed by the building principal
• research indicates little correlation between site-based management and increased student achievement

Schools of Choice The schools of choice strategy is based on the premise that parents ought to be able to choose the schools that their children attend. Mary Ann Raywid, who is an advocate of the choice strategy, said that "the record of the last two decades makes choice a more promising strategy." The relative success of the choice strategy seems to lie in school officials freeing and supporting teachers to design and implement distinctive programs from among which families can choose. Teachers are invited (not assigned) to become program designers and innovators by working together with other teachers with similar interests.

More than 20 states have adopted some form of parental choice, according to the U.S. Department of Education. These plans range from those that allow students to transfer to any public school they desire to initiatives that permit students to take some classes at local colleges. Former President George Bush cited choice among public among public schools as a cornerstone of school improvement. Policy analysts Chubb and Moe (1990) of the Brookings Institution gave the movement a lift with their book, *Politics, Markets, and the Nation's Schools*. The book, based on longitudinal data, calls for restructuring education by allowing parents to choose among both public and private schools.

Some critics of choice, such as Albert Shanker (1990), president of the AFT, argue that choice does not necessarily translate into students flocking to better schools because parents might rank such factors as convenience above academic quality. He has said, "The assumption that the choices people would make would be based on academic quality is wrong." Another critic of choice, Diane Berreth (1991), deputy director of the Association for Supervision and Curriculum Development (ASCD), cites concerns that choice might stratify schools along racial or socioeconomic lines. She also says that choice "is being significantly oversold" given the available research evidence. Moreover, she claims that educators may neglect more promising initiatives, such as school-based management, if hard-sell campaigns for choice go unchecked. She says that "good schools are good because of the commitment, the talent, and the knowledge of the educators who work in them, and the engagement and motivation of the parents and students. Those conditions exist in schools with choice and in schools without choice."

In addition to the suggestions for school-based management and schools of choice, the National Governors Association (NGA) has developed a framework for school restructuring similar to that expressed by other experts. NGA says that restructuring should focus on:

1. The *modification of curriculum and instruction* to support higher-order thinking skills by all students. In addition, the use of instructional time must be more flexible, learning activities must be made more challenging and engaging, and student grouping practices should promote student interaction and cooperative learning.

2. *Authority and decision-making* should be decentralized so that the most educationally important decisions are made at the school site. Teachers, administrators, and parents should set the basic direction of the school and determine strategies and organizational and instructional arrangements needed to achieve them.

3. *New staff roles* must be developed so that teachers may work together more readily to improve instruction. Experienced and skilled teachers should provide support to beginning teachers, plan and develop new curricula, or

design and implement staff development. An increased use of paraprofessionals should be considered. Principals need to provide the vision to help shape new school structures, lead talented teachers, and take risks in an environment that rewards performance rather than compliance.

4. *Accountability systems* must be designed to link clearly rewards and incentives to student performance at the building level. Schools must have more discretion and authority to achieve results, and then be held accountable for results. States must develop measures to assess valued outcomes of performance of individual schools and link rewards and sanctions to results.

The past 100 years have provided several significant educational reform movements. Each of these movements made its mark on the educational system. The current reform movement had its origins in the early 1980s. The first wave of this reform movement started with the 1983 report, "A Nation At Risk"; the second wave of this movement followed with the 1986 Carnegie Report, entitled "A Nation Prepared . . ."; and the third, and current, wave of reform, now known as restructuring, emerged almost concurrently with the second wave in 1986.

Although there is little agreement about specific changes that should be made in the organization of schools, two broad restructuring strategies have evolved. These are site-based management and schools of choice. Each has its proponents and critics. There are also many field-based examples of restructuring projects; however, none of these projects seems to be systemic in method or design (i.e., the restructuring only focuses on a few pieces of the school system and not on the *entire* system). If these projects are not systemic, then it is likely that the improvements that are made will not persist or will be canceled out by problems in other parts of the school system.

The Ideology of Supervision with a Research Orientation The dominant paradigm of supervision during this ideological period is Clinical Supervision (Cogan, 1973; Goldhammer, 1969; Goldhammer, Anderson, & Krajewski, 1980) and myriad variations of it (e.g., Differentiated Supervision [Glatthorn, 1984], Developmental Supervision [Glickman, 1985], Diagnostic Supervision [Seager, 1978], and Cognitive Coaching [Costa & Garmston, 1993; Costa, Garmston, & Lambert, 1988]. Other variations on this theme include teachers supervising teachers (e.g., Alfonso & Goldsberry, 1982), with the core supervisory process remaining focused on the classroom behavior of teachers. Because of the popularity and pervasiveness of this ideology of supervision in the professional literature, a concise history of it is provided.

The roots of Clinical Supervision are in the late 1940s and early 1950s (Powell, 1980) when Dr. James Conant, then president of Harvard University, recommended that the education of future teachers, particularly their introduction to the classroom environment, be conducted under the auspices of a truly talented university professor who was also an experienced school teacher (Conant, 1963). Influenced by Conant's recommendation, which may have been perceived more as a mandate, the teacher education program at Harvard in the 1960s transformed itself into a program that emphasized the use of clinical experiences in the preparation of teachers.

The clinical paradigm for supervising teachers emerged from work done at the Harvard School of Education in the 1960s. Two professors in the School of Education (Morris Cogan and Robert Anderson) actively pursued the development of intimate and intellectually challenging relationships with their students (e.g., Robert Goldhammer, Barbara Nelson Pavan and G. Bradley Seager, Jr.). The paradigm of supervision they developed came to be known as *Clinical Supervision.*

The initial development of Clinical Supervision, as a formal model described in the literature, is attributed to Morris Cogan (Acheson & Gall, 1992; Glatthorn, 1990; Goldhammer, Anderson, & Krajewski, 1980). Cogan was director of secondary student teaching at Harvard. He, and those working with him, used Clinical Supervision in summer workshops with graduate students who were preparing for teaching careers. Robert Anderson, a professor-colleague of Cogan's, had a major role in directing the summer workshops, and he significantly contributed to the development of the principles of Clinical Supervision. Robert Goldhammer, a doctoral student of Robert Anderson's and a junior faculty member in the summer workshop program, also contributed to the early development of the paradigm of Clinical Supervision. In fact, Goldhammer refined Cogan's early conceptualization of Clinical Supervision, and, with Robert Anderson serving on his dissertation committee, completed a dissertation on Clinical Supervision. Subsequent to completing the dissertation, Goldhammer wrote the manuscript for the first text on Clinical Supervision, with the last chapter completed by Robert Anderson after Goldhammer's untimely death in 1969, called *Clinical Supervision: Special Methods for the Supervision of Teachers.* In 1973, Cogan published his text on Clinical Supervision, which was called *Clinical Supervision.* The current model of Clinical Supervision is anchored securely to both of these seminal works.

Cogan borrowed the adjective *clinical* from other fields of science to indicate that a key element of the supervisory process is the collection of data in the actual classroom where the teacher is working with students and where the supervisor is present as part of the ongoing activity (Goldhammer, Anderson, & Krajewski, 1980). The importance of inclass observations is repeatedly emphasized as the key element that distinguishes Clinical Supervision from other forms of general supervision (Acheson & Gall, 1992; Glatthorn, 1990; Goldhammer, et al, 1980; Hopkins & Moore, 1993). Smyth (1985) notes that the original philosophy of Clinical Supervision was to learn in the setting where the craft was being practiced. In addition, Acheson and Gall (1992, p. 9) reiterate that the use of the word *clinical* suggests a "face-to-face" relationship between teacher and supervisor and a focus on the teacher's actual behavior in the classroom.

Goldhammer (1969) thought of Clinical Supervision as a series of five sequenced events he called *stages.* Cogan (1973) presented the cycle of Clinical Supervision using eight *phases.* In the revised edition of Goldhammer's original book, Anderson and Krajewski (1980) retained Goldhammer's original five stages while noting Cogan's important contributions, even commenting that "it seems reasonable to claim that there are no major differences in the structure of the cycle of supervision as described by the two authors" (p. 32). Acheson and Gall (1992) presented another variation of Clinical Supervision by condensing the cycle to three phases. The common elements found in these variations of the cycle of Clinical Supervision are (1) a preobservation or planning conference between the supervisor and teacher, (2) an inclass observation of teaching, (3) an analysis of observational data coupled with strategic planning for instructional improvement, (4) a feedback conference for joint data analysis and discussion of the analysis by the supervisor and teacher, and (5) a final analysis of the Clinical Supervision process to determine its effectiveness and to plan for future supervisory activities.

Although the three basic models of Clinical Supervision previously described (i.e., Acheson and Gall's, Cogan's, and Goldhammer's) are most often described in the literature, other variations of Clinical Supervision have emerged over the years. Glatthorn (1990) criticized the traditional models, suggesting that they lack a theoretical perspective, provide no opportunity for conceptual development, and offer little flexibility to practitioners in determining how the model should be implemented. He then offers a set of ten professional development modules to use in varying combinations in a manner that he labels as *differentiated supervision*. Hopkins and Moore (1993) hold to Goldhammer's traditional five-stage model, but they heavily emphasize the teacher as a change agent in the classroom, which harkens back to Wiles' (1955) views on teachers-as-change-agents, which were in turn linked to the ideology of supervision-as-cooperative group effort. Hopkins and Moore also suggest that the primary goal of Clinical Supervision is the professional growth of the teacher.

While these models differ slightly from each other in terms of specific emphasis, all are variations of the original paradigm developed by Cogan and Goldhammer. Another model that evolved from Clinical Supervision that is strikingly different because of its popularity and because of the robust criticism it garnered is the variation developed by Madeline Hunter (1984), which she also called *Clinical Supervision*.

Hunter's model was developed based on research findings that were claimed to support the relationship of specific teaching strategies to instructional effectiveness (Tracy & MacNaughton, 1989). In Hunter's model, the emphasis of supervision is on how the teacher teaches with the supervisor functioning in an authoritative role rather than in a collaborative one. Tracy and McNaughton describe Hunter's model as a highly prescriptive one that involves (1) developing a job description of what a good teacher does, (2) collecting and analyzing data from the classroom based on a description of good teaching, (3) holding a conference where the supervisor helps the teacher analyze his or her teaching, and (4) providing a period of assistance before holding an evaluative conference.

Hunter's model, which became known as *I-TIP* (Instructional Theory Into Practice) model, became especially popular in the 1980s and fit well with the ideology of supervision based on a research orientation. Administrators and supervisors were attracted to the model because it had specific criteria for analyzing teaching, it was applicable to all subject areas, and it had the ability to introduce accountability into educational practice (Tracy & MacNaughton, 1989).

Hunter's model is criticized in the literature for its use of external criteria as a measurement of teaching effectiveness and its hierarchial nature that creates a power relationship between a supervisor and teacher, rather than being the collegial relationship suggested by Cogan and Goldhammer's models (Blake & DeMont, 1990; Garman, 1990; Jerich, 1990; Pavan, 1986; Smyth, 1985, 1988; Tracy & MacNaughton, 1989).

Another refinement of the basic Clinical Supervision paradigm is the introduction of the concept of "reflective thinking." Several authors (e.g., Coe, 1990; Nolan, 1989; Nolan & Huber, 1989; Pavan, 1991; Sergiovanni & Starratt, 1993; Smyth, 1985, 1988) suggest the importance of allowing the opportunity for reflective thinking on the part of the teacher and supervisor as a way of exploring the qualitative nature of teaching. These writers point to Goldhammer's (1969, p. 51) vision of Clinical Supervision as a vehicle for "transforming schools from places where teachers go through unthinking rituals to places where teachers understand what they are doing and why."

The principle of reflective thinking is derived from Schön (1983). He promulgates a highly collaborative process between the supervisor and teacher that is centered on substantive issues of concern to the teacher. Schön uses the term *coach* rather than *supervisor,* and he suggests that the coach must think *with* the teacher, in a nonthreatening manner, about the substantive issues at hand. The coach and the teacher work together toward finding solutions to problems identified by the teacher. The principles of reflective thinking and coaching are reminiscent of the principles of democratic supervision espoused during the era of supervision-as-cooperative group effort.

Because of its cyclical nature, Clinical Supervision was coopted by the practice of teacher evaluation (e.g., Manatt, 1988). Although most practitioners and professors of supervision recognize that teacher evaluation is necessary in some form, especially for compensation and promotion systems, it is also acknowledged that the roles of supervisor and evaluator do not easily exist side-by-side. Garman (1990) acknowledges that Clinical Supervision has become synonymous with evaluation despite scholarly arguments to the contrary, but he agrees with others in the field of supervision (e.g., Acheson & Gall, 1992; Glatthorn, 1990; Goldhammer, et al, 1980; Hazi, 1994; Nolan, 1989; Smyth, 1985, 1988) that the roles are not compatible and should be separated.

Clinical Supervision has also evolved toward models of peer supervision (e.g., Alfonso & Goldsberry, 1982; Galvez-Hjornevik, 1986). In the 1990s, Clinical Supervision is being cast as a peer inquiry process conducted by mentor teachers, lead teachers, or instructional coaches rather than by principals or other administrators (Pavan, 1991). This trend supports the observation that Clinical Supervision may be evolving as a tool for promoting the professional growth of teachers rather than as an evaluation process. This trend is further supported by evidence that the cycle is being used more often in response to higher public expectations for education and by a desire to provide broader avenues of professional growth for teachers and administrators (Anderson, 1993; Blake & DeMont, 1990). The results of Clinical Supervision field projects also suggest that professional growth may be occurring as evidenced in increased collaboration among school-based professionals, a lowering of institutional barriers to collaboration, and enhanced self-understanding for teachers as a result of the collaborative relationships (Anderson, 1993; Coe, 1990). Once again, the influence of the ideology of democratic supervision is seen.

A major criticism of Clinical Supervision is that it takes time to do it correctly. To make the process effective in bringing about significant and meaningful change adequate time must be allotted for its successful implementation (Anderson, 1993; Coe, 1990; Garman, 1990; Herbert & Tankersley, 1993; Nolan, 1989; Nolan & Huber, 1989). The allotment of adequate time for Clinical Supervision suggests that the school district must make a long-term commitment to the process of Clinical Supervision.

Although a school district must make a commitment of resources to make Clinical Supervision work effectively, an epistemological analysis of the literature suggests that there. is no convincing data to support the effectiveness of Clinical Supervision as a method for improving instruction or promoting professional growth on a consistent, whole-system basis. Even though there are case studies describing how Clinical Supervision significantly assists individual teachers, there is no evidence to suggest that the process helps teachers across an entire school district to improve teaching or to grow professionally. School superintendents are consequently reluctant to commit money and human resources to a process that may not produce desired results in an era of shrinking budgets and community dissatisfaction with the quality of schooling.

Argyris and Schön (1974) provide a useful way of distinguishing between what people say they believe in and what they actually do. For example, if supervisors are asked what their theory of supervision is, then their oral response are what Argyris and Schön call their *espoused theory of action.* If their *true* theory of supervision is to be known (i.e., the one they are actually practicing), however, their supervisory behavior needs to be observed and described. Argyris and Schön call these observed behaviors the supervisors' *theory in use.* Borrowing and modifying these concepts, then, it is possible to point out another problem with Clinical Supervision (i.e., Clinical Supervision is the dominant *espoused paradigm* of supervision); however, it is *not* the dominant *paradigm in use* in schools. The dominant paradigm in use is derived from the ideology of *supervision as inspection* that has stayed in school organizations for more than 300 years. This dominant paradigm in use can be described as observe to evaluate, evaluate, punish, reward, or ignore. This observation is supported by teachers' perceptions of supervision as being an inspection process (Acheson & Gall, 1992; Hazi, 1994; Smyth, 1985). Thus, although the ideologies of supervision espoused by academics and "enlightened" practitioners have changed over time (as described earlier in this chapter), the dominant ideology in use in public schools has not.

One possible explanation of why the dominant ideology in use has remained essentially unchanged throughout more than 300 years of schooling in America is that the espoused ideologies that were developed really did not improve instruction or promote professional growth of teachers *throughout* a school district, although they may have helped individual teachers to improve and grow. Because these various espoused ideologies required so many resources to use them, the guardians of the status quo (i.e., school administrators and school boards) were reluctant to throw scarce resources at processes that were not proven to be effective (e.g., in an address to the Council of Professors of Instructional Supervision in the early 1980s in Austin, Texas, Nolan Estes, a former superintendent of the Dallas, Texas, school district, said, "The reason more superintendents don't support instructional supervision is that there is no evidence that it makes any difference in schools.")

If the dominant paradigm in use (i.e., administrative inspection) is to be supplanted, then the contending paradigm must offer the guardians of the status quo a process that can produce results (i.e., that can improve instruction throughout an *entire* school district). The paradigm proposed for the future is derived from the evolving Ideology of Quality Improvement movement in America.

The Ideology of Quality Improvement

The Quality Improvement movement has made significant inroads to the world of business and industry, and it is beginning to influence administrative and supervisory practice in education (e.g., Rinehart, 1993; Sevick, 1993). The Quality improvement movement ideology is reminiscent of the Period of Efficiency Orientation described earlier in this chapter, but it goes far beyond the principles of efficiency. It also incorporates principles of democracy in the work place as reflected in the Period of Cooperative Group Effort. It is additionally reminiscent of the research orientation to supervision.

Because the current Quality Improvement movement resembles these earlier periods in the history of supervision, and because the movement is associated with the business world, some educational elite are opposed to the ideas of this movement. This opposition is often heard in the stinging criticism of people who suggest using business practices in schools. The argument is that schooling is not a business and, therefore, business practices have no place in schools. Schooling, however, is a business. It is a business in the not-for-profit sector of America's organizations. School districts have business purposes, they have missions and objectives, and they have financial goals. The similarities between school organizations and other organizations are striking, as any professional who crosses back-and-forth from the worlds of schooling and business can confirm.

A short history of the Quality Improvement movement is provided to help readers catch a glimpse of the "big" ideas associated with this movement. A concise description of the most popular paradigm of quality improvement (i.e., total quality management, or TQM) is provided. A critique of TQM is offered followed by a description of a new supervision paradigm, designed especially for schools, that may be able to overcome these criticisms.

A Short History of the Quality Improvement Movement
TQM is a management philosophy that attempts to rethink the way organizations operate. TQM holds at its core the belief that quality is the goal of an effective organization and that the customer is the judge of that quality. In the best companies, TQM embodies four key principles:

- Focus on adding value to the customer while developing positive working relationships with customers and suppliers
- Continuous improvement of work processes that are based on continuous learning of employees
- Involving the right people at the right time in the continuous improvement process
- Establishing needed and productive linkages between and among organizational units

W. Edwards Deming, a physicist and statistician, is considered the father of TQM. He was a professor at New York University and wrote more than 170 papers and books on TQM. In addition, he consulted with organizations throughout the world since the years immediately after World War II. After the war, Deming lectured in Japan at the request of the Japanese Union of Scientists and Engineers. Japanese leaders in business and industry credit Deming for motivating them to achieve their astonishing growth over the past 50 years.

Deming stresses the importance of assuring quality *during* the production cycle. He does not believe that quality is achieved *after* the product leaves the assembly line. In his mind, measuring the quality of the final product and repairing or scraping inferior goods is an expensive and inefficient method for ensuring quality. In his mind, quality, is built into the production cycle—from start to finish (Aguayo, 1990).

Between 1950 and 1990, Deming crystallized his ideas about quality by developing his "Fourteen Points." Deming also referred to these 14 points as *principles* or *obligations* of management. Sashkin and Kiser (1993, pp. 29–33) review the 14 points:

1. Create constancy of purpose for improvement of product and service
2. Adopt the new [TQM] philosophy
3. Cease dependence on mass inspection
4. End the practice of awarding business on price tag alone
5. Improve constantly and forever the system of production and service
6. Institute training
7. Institute leadership
8. Drive out fear
9. Break down barriers between staff areas
10. Eliminate slogans, exhortations, and targets for the work force
11. Eliminate numerical quotas
12. Remove barriers to pride of workmanship
13. Institute a vigorous program of education and improvement
14. Take action to accomplish the transformation

A Critique of TQM Juran (1989), Ishikawa (1985), Taguchi and Clausing (1990), and Crosby (1979, 1986) joined Deming as leading thinkers and innovators in quality improvement. All of these people have said that quality shortcomings rest with management and management systems. There is no disagreement with this conclusion; however, the reason most managers do not use TQM principles effectively is that they lack an understanding of *how to change* traditional, bureaucratic organizations (Sherwood & Hoylman, 1992). Beer, Eisenstat, and Spector (1990) also explain why most change programs do not result in anticipated changes. They say expected changes are not realized because the change programs are:

guided by a theory of change that is fundamentally flawed. The common belief is that the place to begin is with the knowledge and attitudes of individuals. Changes in attitudes . . . lead to change in individual behavior . . . and changes in individual behavior, repeated by many people will result in organizational change. . . . This theory gets the change process exactly backward. In fact, individual behavior is powerfully shaped by the organizational roles that people play. The most effective way to change behavior, therefore, is to put people into a new organizational context, which imposes new roles, responsibilities, and relationships on them" (p. 159).

Fundamental and enduring improvements in quality come *only* with fundamental changes in the way an organization is structured, together with changes in the way people are viewed and managed, and, therefore, with changes in the way work is thought of and performed. With TQM, however, these fundamental changes are *not* happening.

Sherwood and Hoylman (1992, pp. 4–8) describe seven major reasons why many TQM efforts have not realized their potential. These are:

1. The methods produce small successes soon and seduce us into believing we are making significant improvements
2. Project–orientation leads to piecemeal changes rather than systemic change
3. Training is often believed to be synonymous with implementation
4. The focus is management control rather than self-control
5. A technique approach [to quality improvement] cannot work
6. Staff cannot be the leaders
7. The role of leadership is often misunderstood

To create quality improvement programs that work effectively, Sherwood and Hoylman (1992, pp. 14–22) recommend seven guiding principles. These are:

1. The way an enterprise is organized determines how well customers are served
2. Substantial improvements come from systemic change
3. The change process is collaborative in design and implementation
4. If you want people to do a good job, give them a voice in how their work is done
5. The building block of organizational change is the unit of work—the team
6. The change process itself is competently managed
7. The vision stretches expectations of what is possible: Dream big!

The application of TQM in schools is in its early stages (e.g., Blankstein & Swain, 1994; Bradley, 1993; Sallis, 1993; Teeter & Lozier, 1993). It is meeting with resistance because of its close association with business and industry, and because many school practitioners are aware that TQM is not being implemented effectively in the business world. To overcome some of the problems associated with TQM such as those described earlier by Sherwood and Hoylman, the author of this chapter proposes a new paradigm for supervision that uses instructional supervision as *the* management process for transforming school districts into high-performing learning organizations that will subsequently assure quality improvement in schooling. The proposed paradigm (1) establishes or defines boundaries for instructional supervision for transforming school districts, and (2) informs practitioners about how to behave inside those boundaries so they can be effective. An in-depth description of the model is found in Duffy (1996a, 1996b).

KNOWLEDGE WORK SUPERVISION®*

The paradigm of *Knowledge Work Supervision* is derived from the literature on quality improvement (e.g., Deming, 1982; Crosby, 1986, Ishikawa, 1985; Juran, 1989; Taguchi & Clausing, 1990), knowledge work (e.g., Drucker, 1993; Knights, Murray, & Willmott, 1993; Pava, 1983), sociotechnical systems design (e.g., Hanna, 1988; Lytle, 1991; Pasmore, 1992, 1988; Pasmore, Francis, & Haldeman, 1982; Trist, 1969; Trist, Higgin, Murray, & Pollack, 1965), and organization development (e.g., Argyris & Schön, 1978; Burke, 1982). As a proposed paradigm that may be perceived to be in competition with the dominant espoused and "in-use" models of supervision, it is sure to meet with resistance. The potential for this resistance is noted by Nagatomo (1993):

When the rise of a new theory suggests a change of direction in scholarship, history attests to a common pattern of reaction among the established intellectual community. There is often flat dismissal or at best vehement attack in order to kill and bury the theory, especially if it signals an imminent as well as immanent possibility of shaking the secure and comfortable foundation upon which the existing paradigm of thinking rests (pp. ix–x).

The Dominant Paradigms of Instructional Supervision

A *paradigm* is a pattern, example, or model that guides thought or behavior. Barker (1992) defines a paradigm as "a set of rules and regulations (written and unwritten) that does two things: (1) it establishes or defines boundaries; and (2) it tells you how to behave inside the boundaries in order to be successful."

There are currently two dominant paradigms of supervision in the field of education. One is primarily espoused in the literature (Clinical Supervision and variations of it) and the other is primarily practiced in schools (i.e., supervision-as-performance evaluation).

Clinical Supervision focuses on helping individual teachers to improve teaching and to grow professionally. Clinical Supervision's approach to these goals is the process of one supervisor working with one teacher at a time, collecting observational data about that teacher's classroom teaching, analyzing the observational data, reporting the analyses back to the teacher, making plans for that teacher's improvement of teaching and professional growth, and then moving on to work with another teacher. There are myriad variations of Clinical Supervision; for example, Differentiated Supervision (Glatthorn, 1984), Developmental Supervision (Glickman, 1985), Cognitive Coaching (Costa & Garmston, 1993; Costa, Garmston, & Lambert, 1988) and Diagnostic Supervision (Seager, 1978). Variations on this theme include teachers supervising teachers (Alfonso & Goldsberry, 1982), with the core supervisory process remaining focused on the classroom behavior of teachers.

Even though the research on the effectiveness of the Clinical Supervision paradigm is primarily anecdotal, many professionals have strong beliefs about the value of using this approach with individual teachers. On the other hand, an epistemological analysis of what is known about the effectiveness of Clinical Supervision indicates: (1) it is not commonly practiced in schools (supervision-as-performance evaluation is the dominant paradigm-in-use) and (2) when it is used, there is no evidence that it is effective for improving teaching throughout an *entire* school system, although there is some anecdotal evidence that it helps a few, select teachers.

There is also no research evidence that the supervision-as-performance evaluation helps improve instruction. This paradigm probably prevails because it pretends to be scientific and objective, yet it is very subjective in terms of how evaluation criteria are set, interpreted, and applied. Its subjectivity is increased because it relies on classroom observations as the primary source of data on a teacher's effectiveness (like its counterpart, Clinical Supervision). Its focus on individual behavior, as with Clinical Supervision, contributes to its inability to help improve instruction throughout an entire school district. This conclusion is supported by a quote by Beer, Eisenstat, and Spector cited earlier in this chapter when they noted that change (e.g., improving instruction) does not happen by changing individual behavior.

Despite the apparent ineffectiveness of Clinical Supervision and supervision-as-performance evaluation, professional educators are faced with the challenging task of trying to improve instruction throughout an entire school system. If the espoused and in-use paradigms of supervision cannot help educators to improve instruction *throughout* an entire school system, then there is a need for one that can help them accomplish this goal.

Knowledge Work Supervision

Knowledge Work Supervision is a new way of supervising instruction. Using this model, practitioners examine and simultaneously improve three sets of key organizational variables: the school district's knowledge work processes, its social architecture, and its environmental relationships.

---

* *Knowledge Work Supervision* is a registered mark of The F.M. Duffy Group.

Although the model is new, many practitioners are using components of the model; for example, school districts are assessing environmental expectations and developing powerful vision statements to guide their movement into the future. This new model was developed by bundling tested organizational improvement methods with innovative ideas for improving knowledge work.

Knowledge Work Supervision assumes that the work of school districts is knowledge work. Knowledge work uses information to produce new knowledge, design products, or deliver services. High-quality knowledge work has five components: quality information, key people who participate in an exchange of this information, varied forums for exchanging this information, effective technological devices to support the work, and high-quality work procedures and organizational functions (adapted from Pava, 1983). Knowledge organizations also have an intricate social architecture, composed of Motivators, Satisfiers, Quality of Work Life, Skills, and Working Conditions, that interacts symbiotically with the knowledge work processes. Finally, knowledge organizations exist within a broader environment. Practitioners must make simultaneous improvements in all three areas to transform their districts into high-performing learning organizations.

Knowledge work uses information to produce knowledge, design products, or deliver services. Drucker (1993) noted that in 1880, about 9 out of 10 workers made and moved things. Today that ratio is down to one out of five. The other four out of five workers, he said, are knowledge workers. These workers converse on the phone, write reports, solve problems, create innovative designs, educate others, and attend meetings. Drucker (1985) posits that the central social problem of our new, knowledge society is to make knowledge work productive and knowledge workers achieving. Because teachers' knowledge is the "tool" they use to do their jobs, they are knowledge workers.

Knowledge work in schools happens inside teacher's heads. It is the thinking that occurs so teachers can do their jobs effectively and with a high degree of quality. Drucker (1995) alluded to the nature of knowledge work when he said: "knowledge workers own the tools of production. . . . Increasingly, the true investment in the knowledge society is not in machines and tools. It is in the knowledge of knowledge workers" (p. 246).

Knowledge work in school districts is manifested primarily as teaching behavior. Knowledge work is not done in a step-by-step manner because of human capability to think along several lines simultaneously, relate apparently unrelated information, and draw conclusions on the basis of intuition. Knowledge work consists of activities that can be done in parallel, separated from each other, or in a variety of sequences. Knowledge workers often cannot decide future work until some results of the current work activities are completed. Knowledge work is often consequently experienced as chaotic, even though it is not. An example of knowledge work in schools is the pattern of decisions made by a teachers while teaching. When they are on their feet, their minds are racing. They have learning objectives in mind. While teaching, new examples of the points they are trying to make pop into their heads. Students ask questions that take them off the course

temporarily. They return to their original direction when a story reinforcing their objectives comes to mind. They look at the clock and realizes they must bring their lessons to a close. Before closing they make one last point triggered by a student's question during the first minute of class—a full 45 minutes earlier. Knowledge work cannot be improved by supervising the behavior of individual teachers.

Work processes that are linear and sequential support knowledge work. A linear work process is a sequence of steps that must be followed so that step one is completed before beginning step two, and so on. This process is "the total collection of processes, procedures, instructions, techniques, tools, equipment, machines, and physical space used to transform the organization's inputs into the desired outputs (products or services). X is transformed into Y by doing Z" (Lytle, 1991).

In a school district, the supportive linear work process is the instructional program, kindergarten through 12 grade, within which students must complete first grade before moving into second grade, and so on. Resources (inputs) are poured into the instructional program with the intention of providing students with a high-quality education (desired outputs).

Improving Knowledge Work Practitioners improve the linear instructional program by examining that work process to identify where mistakes are made, or where potential for mistakes exists. Then, they take actions to correct the mistakes or to eliminate the possibility of making them.

Improving nonlinear knowledge work in schools, on the other hand, requires different actions. Remember that knowledge work in school districts occurs primarily inside the heads of teachers and it is manifested in their classroom teaching. Remember, too, Drucker's (1995) just-cited characterization of knowledge work. The broad actions needed to improve knowledge work are:

- Improve the quality and timeliness of key information teachers need to teach effectively
- Assure that teachers interact with the key people with whom they should be exchanging critical information
- Provide teachers and key people with a variety of structured, semi-structured, and informal forums for exchanging information (e.g., in structured workshops, informal "brown bag" lunches, or national conferences)
- Examine and improve any devices (e.g., computers), work procedures (e.g., lesson planning), and organizational functions (e.g., administration and supervision) that support teaching.

Knowledge Work Supervision provides a systemic and systematic model for achieving these improvements. The structure of the *Knowledge Work Supervision* paradigm is shown in Figure 6.1.

Knowledge Work Supervision is a brand new model. Its newness leads skeptics to say, "Give us some examples of school districts using this model." The response is, "There are none—yet." Many districts, however, are using components of this new model. Because proven organizational improvement

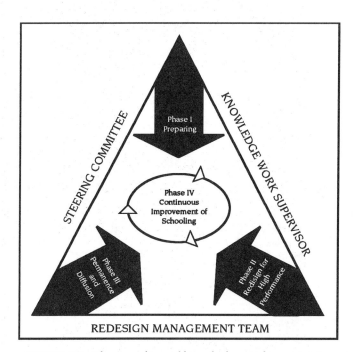

FIGURE 6.1. The paradigm of knowledge work supervision

methods are combined with innovative methods for improving knowledge work, it is believed that *Knowledge Work Supervision* can achieve its purposes.

Knowledge Work Supervision is complex because school districts are complex systems. The paradigm offers a methodical model to examine and simultaneously improve three sets of critical organizational variables affecting the overall performance of a school district. The paradigm also views a school district as a system and provides methods to improve all pieces of the system, not just the instructional program or the curriculum.

Knowledge Work Supervision takes time. It is designed to be used continuously for the life of your organization. There are no "quick fixes" for increasing the performance levels of knowledge organizations. If practitioners go for a quick fix, then they go for failure.

When *Knowledge Work Supervision* replaces the dominant supervision paradigms, there will be a better fit between supervisory processes and the purpose, goals, and outcomes of a school district that wants to become a high-performing learning organization. When supervision becomes a function that transforms school districts into high-performing learning organizations, it will finally make a difference for an entire school district instead of for select teachers. It is also believed that this new kind of supervision will respond effectively and simultaneously to both human and organizational needs and, therefore, move individuals, groups, *and* the whole organization toward higher levels of performance.

If applied consistently and with patience, *Knowledge Work Supervision* will move school districts toward higher levels of performance through organizational learning. Furthermore, although a district uses *Knowledge Work Supervision*, it will

never perfectly achieve its new vision because that vision is a moving target. Through Phase IV of the paradigm (the Continuous Improvement of Schooling), however, and because the *Knowledge Work Supervision* cycle is repeated for the life of the organization, school districts will move *continuously* toward that vision. It is a school district's life-long journey of organizational learning and continuous renewal that will raise its level of organizational performance. Nothing less will do it!

CONCLUSION

This chapter presented a historical overview of the ideologies of supervision that dominated the literature on supervision (i.e., the Period of Administrative Inspection, the Period of Efficiency Orientation, the Period of Cooperative Group Effort, and the Period of Research Orientation). It was posited that although educational literature suggests these ideologies resulted in changes in supervisory practice, the dominant paradigm for supervisory behavior has in fact remained relatively constant over 300 years of American education (i.e., supervision-as-inspection, which is most often experienced as performance evaluation).

Clinical Supervision was described as the dominant paradigm of supervision described in the literature. It was suggested that Clinical Supervision was linked to the ideologies of cooperative group effort and the research orientation to supervision. Although Clinical Supervision is espoused as the model-of-choice for supervising teachers, the dominant model-in-use, is in fact once again supervision-as-inspection or performance evaluation.

It is proposed that an evolving ideology of supervision is the Ideology of Quality Improvement. The quality improvement movement is making inroads education; however, the dominant espoused model of quality improvement, TQM, is not viewed as significantly effective primarily because it overlooks important principles for changing organizations.

Using the literature and real-world experiences of theorists and practitioners from several interrelated fields (i.e., knowledge work, sociotechnical systems design, business process re-engineering, and organization development), and drawing from his own experience as a teacher, supervisor, professor of administration and supervision, and organization development consultant, the author conceptualized a new paradigm for supervision that can be used to transform entire school districts into high-performing learning organizations. This paradigm is called *Knowledge Work Supervision*. This process was generally described.

It is predicted that the paradigm of *Knowledge Work Supervision* will be met with resistance because it offers a different view of how to supervise instruction. The paradigm requires supervisors to shift their attention from supervising individual teachers to supervising three sets of key organizational variables: the district's knowledge work processes, its social architecture, and its relationship with its external environment. Improvements must be made in all three areas simultaneously and continuously. This different view of the supervision world view challenges the traditional theories and models of supervision that all focus on individual teachers and, therefore, is sure to meet with resistance. From what is known about organizational improvement, however, *Knowledge Work Supervision* offers a more effective process for transforming schools into high-performing learning organizations. There is absolutely no evidence that traditional supervision can do this.

References

Aguayo, R. (1990). *Dr. Deming: The American who taught the Japanese about quality*. New York: Carol Publishing Group.

Acheson, K. A. & Gall, M. D. (1992). *Techniques in the clinical supervision of teachers: Preservice and in-service applications* (3rd ed.). White Plains, NY: Longman.

Alfonso, R. Firth, G., & Neville, R. (1981). *Instructional supervision: A behavior system*. Boston: Allyn & Bacon.

Alfonso, R. & Goldsberry, L. (1982). Colleagueship in supervision. In T. Sergiovanni (Ed.). *Supervision of teaching*. Alexandria, VA: ASCD.

Anderson, C. R. (Ed.). (1993). *Voices of change: A report on the clinical schools project*. Washington, D.C.: American Association of Colleges for Teacher Education Publications (ERIC Document Reproduction Service No. ED 353 252).

Argyris, C. & Schön, D. (1974). *Theory in practice: Increasing professional effectiveness*. San Francisco: Jossey-Bass.

Argyris, C. & Schön, D. (1978). *Organizational learning*. Reading, MA: Addison-Wesley.

Barker, J. A. (1992). *Future edge: Discovering the new paradigms of success*. New York: William Morrow and Co.

Beer, M., Eisenstat, R. A., & Spector, B. (1990). Why change programs don't produce change. *Harvard Business Review, 68*(6), 158–166.

Berreth, D. (1991). Personal correspondence with the author.

Blake, N. & DeMont, R. (1990). From checklist evaluation to clinical supervision. *Executive Educator, 12*(3), 14–15.

Blankstein, A. M. & Swain, H. (1994). Is TQM right for schools? *Executive Educator, 16*(2), 51–54.

Bradley, L. H. (1993). *Total quality management for schools*. Lancaster, PA.: Technomic.

Burke, W. W. (1982). *Organization development: Principles and practices*. Boston: Little, Brown.

Butts, R. F. & Cremin, L. A. (1953). *A history of education in American culture*. New York: Holt, Rinehart, and Winston.

Chubb, J. & Moe, T. (1990). *Politics, markets and America's schools*. Washington, D.C.: Brookings Institute.

Coe, D. (1990). *Toward collegial inquiry: Is there more to clinical supervision than the improvement of practice?* Paper presented at the annual meeting of the American Educational Research Association, Boston, MA.

Cogan, M. L. (1973). *Clinical supervision*. Boston: Houghton-Mifflin.

Conant, J. (1963). *The education of American teachers*. New York: McGraw-Hill.

Costa, A. L. & Garmston, R. J. (1993). Cognitive coaching: A strategy for reflective teaching. *Wingspan, 9*(1), 4–7.

Costa, A. L., Garmston, R. J., & Lambert, L. (1988). Evaluation of teaching: The cognitive development view. In S. J. Stanley & W. J. Popham (Eds.). *Teacher evaluation: Six prescriptions for success* (pp. 145–173). Alexandria, VA: ASCD.

Crosby, P. B. (1979). *Quality is free: The art of making quality certain*. New York: New American Library.

Crosby, P. B. (1986). *Running things*. New York: McGraw-Hill.

Deming, W. E. (1982). *Out of crisis*. Cambridge, MA: MIT Press.

Dickey, F. G. (1948). Developing supervision in Kentucky. *Bulletin of the Bureau of School Services, 20*(3).

Drucker, P. F. (1993). Professionals' productivity. *Across the Board, 30*(9), 50.

Duffy, F. M. (1996a). *Designing high performance schools: A practical guide to organizational reengineering*. Delray Beach, FL: St. Lucie Press.

Duffy, F. M. (1996b). *Supervising knowledge work: Transforming school districts into high performing learning organizations*. Unpublished book manuscript submitted for publication.

Evans, H. D. (1983). We must begin educational reform every place at once. *Phi Delta Kappan, 65*(3), 173–177.

Eye, G., Netzer, L., & Krey, R. (1971). *Supervision of instruction*. New York: Harper & Row.

Galvez-Hjornevik, C. (1986). Mentoring among teachers: A review of the literature. *Journal of Teacher Education, 37*(1), 6–11.

Garman, N. B. (1990). Theories embedded in the events of clinical supervision: A hermeneutic approach. *Journal of Curriculum and Supervision, 5*(3), 201–213.

Glatthorn, A. A. (1984). *Differentiated Supervision*. Alexandria, VA: ASCD.

Glatthorn, A. A. (1990). *Supervisory leadership: Introduction to instructional supervision*. Glenview, IL: Scott, Foresman/Little, Brown.

Glickman, C. D. (1985). *Supervision of instruction: A developmental approach*. Boston, MA: Allyn and Bacon.

Goldhammer, R. (1969). *Clinical supervision: Special methods for the supervision of teachers*. New York: Holt, Rinehart and Winston, Inc.

Goldhammer, R., Anderson, R. H., & Krajewski, R. (1980). *Clinical supervision* (2nd Ed.). New York: Holt, Rinehart, and Winston.

Gutek, G. (1970). *An historical introduction to American education*. New York: Thomas Y. Crowell Co.

Hanna, D. P. (1988). *Designing organizations for high performance*. Reading, MA: Addison-Wesley.

Hazi, H. M. (1994). The teacher evaluation-supervision dilemma: A case of entanglements and irreconcilable differences. *Journal of Curriculum and Instruction, 9*(2), 195–216.

Herbert, J. M. & Tankersly, M. (1993). More and less effective ways to intervene with classroom teachers. *Journal of Curriculum and Instruction, 9*(1), 24–40.

Hopkins, W. S. & Moore, K. D. (1993). *Clinical supervision: A practical guide to student teacher supervision*. Dubuque, IA: Wm. C. Brown Communications.

Hunter, M. (1984). Knowing, teaching and supervising. In P. L. Hosford (Ed.). *Using what we know about teaching*. Alexandria, VA: ASCD.

Ishikawa, K. (1985). *What is total quality control? "The Japanese way."* Englewood Cliffs, NJ: Prentice Hall.

Jerich, K. (1990). *An analysis of a staff development program in clinical supervision and the realities of the K-12 instructional setting: Evaluating its impact for special groups and the usefulness in the supervisory process*. Paper presented at the annual conference of the National Council of States of In-service Education, Orlando, FL (ERIC Document Reproduction Service No. ED 329 516.)

Juran, J. M. (1989). *Juran on leadership for quality*. New York: The Free Press.

Knights, D., Murray, F., & Willmott, H. (1993). Networking as knowledge work: A study of strategic interorganizational development in the financial services industry. *Journal of Management Studies,* *30*(6), 975–995.

Kuhn, T. S. (1970). *The structure of scientific revolution.* Chicago, IL: University of Chicago Press.

Kyte, G. (1930). *How to supervise.* Boston, MA: Houghton Mifflin Co. Lemlech, J. & Marks, M. (1976). *The American teacher (1776–1976).* Bloomington, IN: Phi Delta Kappa Educational Foundation.

Lytle, W. O. (1991). *Socio-technical systems analysis and design guide for linear work.* Plainfield, NJ: Block-Petrella-Weisbord.

Manatt, R. P. (1988). Teacher performance evaluation: A total systems approach. In S. J. Stanley & W. J. Popham (Eds.) *Teacher Evaluation: Six prescriptions for success.* (pp. 79–108). Alexandria, VA: ASCD.

Meyer, J. W. (1980). *The impact of the centralization of educational funding and control of state and local educational governance.* Stanford University, Institute for Research on Educational Finance and Governance.

Nagatomo, S. (1993). Translator's Introduction. In Y. Yuasa (Ed.). *The body, self-cultivation, and ki-energy.* Albany, NY: State University of New York.

Nolan, J. F. (1989). Can supervisory practice embrace Schön's view of reflective supervision? *Journal of Curriculum and Supervision, 5*(1), 35–40.

Nolan, J. F. & Huber, T. (1989). Nurturing the reflective practitioner through instructional supervision. *Journal of Curriculum and Supervision 4*(2), 126–145.

Pasmore, W. A . (1988). *Designing effective organizations: The sociotechnical systems perspective.* New York: Wiley & Sons.

Pasmore, W. A. (1992). *Sociotechnical systems design for total quality.* San Francisco, CA: Organizational Consultants, Inc.

Pasmore, W. A., Francis, C., Haldeman, J., & Shani, A. (1982). Sociotechnical systems: A North American reflection on empirical studies of the seventies. *Human Relations, 35*(12), 1179–1204.

Pava, C. H. P. (1983). *Managing new office technology: An organizational strategy.* New York: The New Press.

Pavan, B. (1986). A thank you and some questions for Madeline Hunter. *Educational Leadership, 43*(6), 67–8.

Pavan, B. (1991). *Determining the usages of clinical supervision.* Paper presented at the annual meeting of the American Educational Research Association, Chicago (ERIC Document Reproduction Service No. ED 336 374).

Pierce, P. R. (1935). *The origin and development of the public school principalship.* Chicago, IL: University of Chicago Press.

Powell, A. (1980). *The uncertain profession: Harvard and the search for educational authority.* Cambridge, MA: Harvard University Press.

Raywid, M. A. (1990). The evolving effort to improve schools: Pseudo-reform, incremental reform, and restructuring. *Phi Delta Kappan, 72*(2) 139–143.

Rinehart, G. (1993). Building a vision for quality education. *Journal of School Leadership, 3*(3), 260–268.

Rippa, S. A. (1988). *Education in a free society* (6th ed.). New York: Longman.

Roethlisberger, F. J., Dickson, W. J., & Wright, H. A. (1939). *Management and the worker: An account of a research program conducted by the Western Electric Company, Hawthorne Works, Chicago.* Cambridge, MA: Harvard University Press.

Sallis, E. (1993). *Total quality management in education.* London: Kogan Page.

Sashkin, M. & Kiser, K. J. (1993). *Putting total quality management to work: What TQM means, how to use it, and how to sustain it in the long run.* San Francisco: Berrett-Koehler.

Schön, D. (1983). *The reflective practitioner: How professionals think in action.* New York: Basic Books.

Seager, G. B., Jr. (1978). *An introduction to diagnostic supervision.* Unpublished manuscript, University of Pittsburgh.

Sergiovanni, T. J.& Starratt, R. J. (1993). *Supervision: A redefinition* (5th ed.). New York: McGraw-Hill.

Sevick, C. (1993). *Can Deming's concept of total quality management be applied to education?* Paper presented at the Annual Conference on Creating Quality Schools (ERIC Document Reproduction Service No. ED 3629971).

Shanker, A. (1990). The end of the traditional model of schooling and a proposal for using incentives to restructure schools. *Phi Delta Kappan, 71*(5), 345–357.

Sherwood, J. J. & Hoylman, F. M. (1992). *The total quality paradox: Why isn't TQ working?—How we can make it work!* Unpublished manuscript.

Smith, A. (1975). *Power of the mind.* New York: Ballantine Books.

Smyth, W. J. (1985). Developing a critical practice of clinical supervision. *Journal of Curriculum Studies, 17*(1), 1–15.

Smyth. W. J. (1988). A "critical" perspective for clinical supervision. *Journal of Curriculum and Supervision, 3*(2), 136–156.

Taguchi, G. & Clausing, D. (1990). Robust quality. *Harvard Business Review, 68*(1), 65–72.

Taylor, F. (1911). *The principles of scientific management.* New York: Harper and Row.

Teeter, D. J. & Lozier, G. G. (Eds.) (1993). *Pursuit of quality in higher education: Case studies in total quality management.* San Francisco, CA: Jossey-Bass.

Tracy, S. J. & MacNaughton, R. H. (1989). Clinical supervision and the emerging conflict between the neo-traditionalists and the neo-progressives. *Journal of Curriculum and Supervision, 4*(3), 246–256.

Trist, E. L. (1969). On socio-technical systems. In W. Bennis, K. Benne, & R. Chinn (Eds.). *The planning of change* (2nd ed.). New York: Holt, Rinehart, and Winston.

Trist, E. L., Higgin, G. W., Murray, H., & Pollack, A. B. (1965). *Organizational choice.* London: Tavistock Publications.

Wiles, K. (1955). *Supervision for better schools.* Englewood Cliffs, NJ: Prentice Hall.

7

THE PHILOSOPHICAL PERSPECTIVE
ON SUPERVISION

Richard F. Neville
UNIVERSITY OF MARYLAND BALTIMORE COUNTY

Noreen B. Garman
UNIVERSITY OF PITTSBURGH

INTRODUCTION

This chapter[1] addresses the nature and origins of educational supervision from a philosophical perspective. It is an attempt to examine aspects of our intellectual and educational traditions that gave rise to patterns of schooling and the supervisory arrangements set in place to guide their maintenance and development. An effort is made to conjoin various themes from the treasure trove of our philosophical and educational history as a way of examining the lineage, and the contemporary forms, that comprise the foundations of educational supervision.

A *foundation* implies a support system, a base, and, in a more poetic sense, it refers to the fundamental principles—the ideas that advance creative thought, action, and the purpose of social institutions. For example, the surge of thought during the Enlightenment of the eighteenth century engendered ideals regarding the nature of humanity and authority. Its themes of reason, natural goodness, and the plausibility of attaining the "good life" in the here and now were pronounced by Kant, Rousseau, Voltaire, Newton, Locke, and "in the colonies" by Franklin, Jefferson, and Paine, among others. The generations who read and advanced their works, from the laws of gravity to the nature of human relations, set the foundation for an age of reason, romanti-

cism, and revolution (Brinton, 1963). The spirit of the Enlightenment sought to release individuals from dogmatic authority toward individualism, empiricism, and scientific reasoning. It may be referenced as the "era when modernity began," and it got its name, "as Kant explained later in the eighteenth century, from the enterprise of spreading light into the dark corners of the human mind" (Appleby et al, 1994, p. 36). Learning was wrested from the clergy, "science led the way", and all areas of inquiry and knowledge could be systematized (Appleby, p. 36).

Our nation was born, in the wake of the Enlightenment, and an educational system emerged. State and local governments worked to shape their constitutionally reserved educational authority and responsibility. In keeping with the nation's growth and educational needs, as educational activity advanced supervisory arrangements were close at hand. Early on, educational supervision was as varied in form as the hamlets, villages, towns, and districts that were developing across the landscape of America. As to the purpose of supervision, however, there was great clarity and agreement. These were formative years; hence, supervision was "oversight," with duties specified to sustain the task of keeping school in accordance with local values and the democratic predilections of a new nation.

By contrast, educational supervision in contemporary America is something of a conundrum. There is considerable dissonance in terms of the concepts, structures, and organizing principles that combine to form supervisory theory and practice. Out of this dissonance, however, critical energy has emerged that confronts the long-prescribed notion, expressed in many guises, of educational supervision as "oversight"—as inspection—as logical positivism—as reductionism—with theory and practice that affirms the primacy of "the supervised" as a core substance of education. This view, ably presented and documented in this handbook, holds that supervisors are teacher advocates, agents of moral and ethical discourse, sharers of power, activists in the transformation of authoritarian hierarchical structures, and colleagues in knowledge generation and pedagogy.

The philosophy of educational supervision may be viewed as a search for meaning as regards the purpose and process of supervision in educational organizations; it goes beyond inventories of practice and task analysis to the investigation of the ideas, principles, and values that give shape and definition to supervision in its antecedent and contemporary forms. Such inquiry is in large measure guided by aspects of our educational history and philosophy from whence the story of educational supervision is derived; they are the traditions that have nurtured the roots and the forms of educational supervision. It is not that simple, however, because the story shifts as ideas and circumstances are subject to reason, knowledge (i.e., interpretation), and cultural mood. These factors form a dynamic reality and ultimately define "the place called school," which, given the pluralism that is America, expresses a diversity of beliefs about curriculum, instruction, and supervisory practice.

FRAMES OF REFERENCE

An exploration of the philosophical features of educational supervision (i.e., the systems of belief that prompted its evolution) is bounded by certain general ideas or propositions about the nature and status of educational supervision as a field of study, the likes of which include the following issues.

• Research activities directed at the history, philosophy, and evolution of educational supervision both in theory and practice have been limited in scope (Bolin 1992; Glanz 1995; Smyth 1986a).

The major problem with the study of supervision is that while there has been a plethora of research and much hortative literature on the practicalities of doing supervision, there has been virtually no attempt to stand back and look at the area of study itself, what it purports to be, where it has come from, what it aspires to, where it is headed, and how it relates to discussion and debate in the broader area of philosophy of science. As Toulmin (1972, p. 84) argued any field that hopes to make any conceptual advances must remain continually open to criticism and change if it is to move beyond being a mere pretender. It is, above all, this ability to develop an inquiring inner eye on itself, that represents the hallmark of a field of study (Smyth, 1986a, p. 3).

• The nature and understanding of the philosophy of educational supervision is resolutely linked with the history and the themes of American education.

"Indeed some would argue that all philosophers deal with the history of philosophy from the moment they reflect on some past thought or idea. And, since once a thought has been proposed or even entertained its recollection implies that it is part of the past, it turns out that philosophical reflection is inextricably tied to the reflection on the history of philosophy. Accordingly, no philosopher can escape the history of philosophy" (Garcia, 1992).

In one sense, the history of philosophy investigates the doctrinal influences of past thinkers, including the "rational reconstruction of their positions," (Campbell, 1992, p. 8) while doing philosophy historically seeks to "enrich" self-understanding and insight into the present; the historical philosopher is "operating with a strong sense of his or her situatedness in history where truth is not 'correctness' but 'revelatory and transforming' fully sensitive to the 'inherited past yet going beyond it" (p. 10). The philosophy of educational supervision confronts the inherited past as a pathway to refined understanding of the supervisory process and its possibilities rather than as a confirmed truth.

• The need for energized and imaginative approaches to educational supervision will increase as the organization and process of education confronts changes in the conceptualization of knowledge, communication technologies, including the reconfiguration of learning contexts.

In the near future, students will have access, they will be able to "download" vast store houses of information related to all aspects of our intellectual traditions. The race to build the information superhighway is ongoing. There is talk of "empowering individuals and launching a new age of digital democracy" (Gormery, 1994, p. 9). Indeed, some business and government officials appear to desire access for all where the American public school is the "consummate broad organization" that has "loose coordination in autonomous districts," provides the ultimate laboratory for the artful and personal uses for the riches of the information age. Is it inevitable? The virtual aspects of community seems to be assured while informed analysts have registered vigorous concerns: Postman (1992) sees "the Technology story" without a moral center, which puts efficiency, interest, and economic advance in its place. Roszak (1994) writes, "The irony behind (information) technology is the tendency it encourages in some of its most talented and enthusiastic developers to cheapen—or even to try to replace—the mind that created the technology in the first place."

"Numerous forms of technology—rich learning environments—illustrate a dramatic shift in the traditional paradigm of education. . . . The boundaries of time and space inherent in our old paradigms of schooling are being called into question in these technology-rich learning environments. . . . The disparities . . . between the existing supervision paradigms and potential new ways of delivering instruction does not mean that the practice of supervision is necessarily obsolete. They do, however, challenge supervisors to seek new paradigms of supervision that alter current instructional supervision practices in response to technology's impact on education" (Tracy, 1993).

• Exploring the philosophy of educational supervision and its links with history, literature, and the social sciences is essential to the construction of ideas and concepts—the stuff of philosophy and its attendant quest for knowledge (meaning) about educational process and instructional leadership.

"Supervision as a field of study is still a mere pretender because it has never had the moral courage to separate itself from its origins in the mainstream of educational management. Instead of further refining or proliferating the forms of supervision—developmental, scientific, artistic, clinical or whatever—we need to totally rethink our perspective including the social, cultural, and pedagogical relationships we believe are important and whatever we believe is indispensable about the nature of teaching and learning" (Smyth, 1989, p. 169).

Without attention to these dimensions our grasp of the philosophy of supervision will be wanting—like a theater production without a first or second act—or a mosaic with gaping holes—an image less than satisfying to the eye, touch, and mind.

- Supervision in educational contexts appeared very early in the history of American education and the theories behind it, past and present, more contemporaneously referred to as "models"—are demonstrated in practice and reflect publicly affirmed or tacitly understood principles about the nature of educational supervision and its place within the process of education.

Glanz (1995, pp. 102–105) affirms that the marginalization of supervision's history results from inadequate knowledge of intellectual traditions, a nonreflecting stance taken by scholars of educational supervision, the strengths of social research—the scientific method and the logic of positivism that has dominated educational and administrative theory.

- The evolution of democratic institutions and their organizational manifestations declare the struggle to fulfill the essential principles and the truths of American society; educational leaders, including supervisors, have been part and parcel of the struggle to construct knowledge to inform the educational process amid the clash of values and cultural change.

The active society and the "advent of the postmodern period has been marked by the rapid rise of a new technology of knowledge which serves data collection and analysis, simulation, and systems analysis." This propelled the emergence of organizations "specializing in the production and processing of knowledge. . . . As a result, society has much more information about itself, a development which generates a whole new set of options for societal control, new decisions to be made and a range of processes to be guided" (Etzioni, 1968, pp. 9–10).

- The philosophy of educational supervision is a belief system used to construct the configuration of supervisory activities that support the cohesiveness of the school as a community and, through the understanding of shared and diverse values, to guide the design and the authenticity of the school as a learning environment.

"For school renewal to endure, every school and district in our land needs principles that transcend the interests of any individual and that are derived from constituents. These principles must be congruent with a definition of the core values of democracy: freedom, justice, and equality as well as life, liberty, and the pursuit of happiness for all. These principles will not be swayed by politics, fools, or special interests" (Glickman, 1993, pp. 23–24).

In support of these principles: "We need communities—and school organizations that balance diversity and unity—and provide an open climate for dissent and an opportunity for subcommunities to retain their identity to provide the social bonds that sustain the moral voice, while avoiding tight networks that suppress pluralism and dissent." Such school communities would be neither oppressive nor hierarchical, but would be places where diversity is respected and common bonds nurtured (Etzioni, 1993, pp. 120–123).

- Supervision is made of language, whether text or talk, discourse is central to practice . . . what we say really matters . . . and how it is that we persuade one another in the situation at hand. We are challenged to pay attention to how language influences the thought and conduct of those we work with, and more important, what our language tells us about our own dispositions and motives (Garman, 1994).

"The decade of the 1980s has seen a revolution in thinking about the basis of educational inquiry and practice." As Clifford Geertz (1980) announced at the beginning of the decade, "Something is happening to the way we think about the way we think." This movement, often referred to as the "rhetorical turn" (Eisner, 1982; Rorty, 1967; Sills & Jensen, 1992), emphasizes that the central goal of social inquiry is the interpretation of meaningful human practices. As scholars have turned away from the traditional rational/technical explanations of knowledge claims and toward heuristic understandings reflected in debate and discussion, there is a revival of interest in rhetoric and discourse."

In these matters, Flinders (1991b) provides an ecological perspective as regards language, thought and the influence of metaphor:

"Sensitivity to the metaphorical nature of language is important on two counts. First, it allows supervisors to assess the conceptual boundaries of the key metaphors used in both the classroom and supervisory feedback. These boundaries constitute what our language brings into focus as well as what it hides. Second, metaphor highlights the connections between language, culture, and thought—connections that need to be recognized if supervisors are to understand the significant cultural differences in how various educational situations are experienced by different participants in the process."

- Supervision, particularly educational supervision, is intended to illuminate, through reason and interpersonal respect, the course and the opportunities of education as reflected in the primacy of the teaching act and the conditions of learning.

This statement connotes the moral dimension of supervision and the compact among supervisor, teacher, students, and community in the creation of the good society:

"That is to say, teaching of its very nature assumes a caring for the one taught and a respect for the integrity of what is being taught and its connection to the past, present, and future life of the community. Not to care for the person being taught, or to distort the meaning of what is being taught, violates the very idea of teaching. Supervision is an activity that involves another in supporting and furthering that caring for the learner and respect for the significance of what is taught. The moral authority of the supervisor is joined with the moral authority of the teacher" (Sergiovanni & Starratt, 1993, XVIII).

• Philosophy is a close companion of history. The record of human existence and travails goes beyond a chronology of events and social circumstance. As important as the record is, in form and meaning, its interpretation is a matter of continued reconstruction. If the historical record is to be more than a story, chronicle, or annal, it needs to account for past events in the recognition that history is not "constructs created by the historian" to be slavishly affirmed in thought and action.

History might be better understood as Carr (1961) viewed it: "Provisional selection of facts and a provisional interpretation . . . which undergo subtle and perhaps partly unconscious change through the reciprocal action of one over the other. And this reciprocal action also involves reciprocity between present and past. The historian and the facts are necessary to one another. . . . What is history? . . . it is a continuous process of interaction between the historian and his facts, an unending dialogue between the present and the past." Finkelstein (1992) wrote that history, in the contemporary context, has acquired many meanings, "utterly irrelevant on the one hand, and as totally powerful on the other"; an apparent contradiction "discovered in the last two decades, that historians function like other mythmakers in society. Through their analyses of the past, they reveal meaning and, when they do it well, make sense of reality" (Finkelstein, p. 255). Finkelstein interprets educational history "as an evolving series of narrative visions, that have, over time, revealed ever more nuanced and complete aspects of the U.S. educational past and the limits and possibilities of education" (Finkelstein, p. 257).

In his trenchant review of research in the history of curriculum, Kliebard (1992) explains that the history of education was characterized for a long time by a kind of "missionary goal and evangelism" that led to a "fatal parochialism," where the recurring theme was "an unrelenting line of progress," where the "victory of democratic forces over the rule of entrenched aristocracy and elitism" was pronounced. He references Bailyn's (1960) work as a turning point away from "celebratory" history toward a more expansive, interdisciplinary, and critical approach to the history of education/curriculum. Supervision as one aspect of our educational institution has suffered the same limitations. It remains to be seen whether the meaning and values that define educational supervision will attract a level of study and research commensurate with its role and potential for instructional leadership.

What sets philosophy apart from history? (1) It does not contain propositions merely descriptive of events or ideas for which there can be direct empirical evidence, (2) it contains propositions whose function is to describe logical relations among ideas, (3) its propositions may lack reference to time and provenance, and (4) its propositions deal primarily with universals rather than with individuals (Garcia, 1992 p. 60). Taken together history and philosophy seek meaning in human experience—because the synthesis of fact, information, description, and values is as much a product of human art as the ideas and concepts that flow from them (Garcia, 1992).

To our end consideration of the philosophy of supervision should be sensitive to the integrative nature of its relationship with history in formulating description and interpretation of the belief system(s) that form the boundaries of educational supervision—from whence purpose, organization, technique, and procedure are ultimately derived.

• Models of supervision are not discrete patterns of function but are most often forms of practice derived from the integration of tradition (historical and philosophical perspectives) and evolving professional knowledge. There is an ever present tension between the long held views of the past and more recently developed ideas about schooling, curriculum, teaching, and authority in educational organizations.

Dewey (1920, pp. 101–102) called for a philosophical reconstruction "which should relieve men of having to choose between an impoverished and truncated experience on one hand and an artificial and important reason on the other. . . . It would destroy the division of men of goodwill into two hostile groups. It would permit the cooperation of those who respect the past and institutionally established with those who are interested in establishing a freer and happier future. For it would determine the conditions under which the funded experience of the past and the continuing intelligence which looks to the future can effectively interact with each other."

Tyack and Cuban (1995) examine the character and dimensions of school reform through the use of "historical evidence and case studies." They probe the continuity, the persistence over time of the "grammar of schooling" that is "the organizational form that govern instruction" while contrary forms are set aside (p. 5). They see change as a "more gradual and piecemeal" process for such efforts require "political and organizational savvy—and collective action" (p. 109); and they offer a reminder that "in a democracy, fundamental reforms that seek to alter the cultural construction of a [real school] cannot succeed without lengthy and searching public dialogue about the ends and means of schooling" (p. 109). This dialogue is essential to the philosophy of supervision because without it forms of supervisory practice will likely demonstrate a stubborn and comfortable continuity with a "division of labor and hierarchical supervision," such as those espoused by the efficiency models of industry (p. 109).

• Supervision has had a long-standing and continuing presence in the evolution of American public education; it has been characterized by an incessant struggle to go beyond the conceptualization of supervision as inspection—as oversight, beyond supervision as a rational technical system of control—toward an understanding of supervision based on collegial discourse and the sharing of responsibility and authority with teachers who are essential agents in instructional leadership.

"The major problem with traditional forms of supervision (and clinical supervision is by no means completely immune from this criticism) is that they are conceptualized as a delivery of a service to those deemed to be in need of it. No matter how benevolently 'it is done' (emphasis in the original) . . . efforts of this kind are ultimately self defeating because they are premised on managerial and undemocratic ways of working; such forms of supervision create 'dependence' rather than independence. It is not the teachers' agendas, issues and concerns that are being addressed, but rather those of someone within the administrative or bureaucratic hierarchy" (Smyth,

1991a, pp. 2–3). "Until fairly recently, there was an exclusive preoccupation with the bureaucratic use of instructional supervision as a form of social control over teachers and teaching, albeit in the guise of enhancing efficiency" (Smyth, p. 7).

- "Traditional" forms of educational supervision, conceptually at least, abound with change. Whatever the terms used to describe these changes the examination of the ideas and beliefs that sustain them is the province of the philosophy of supervision.

In the 1992 Association for Supervision and Curriculum Development (ASCD) yearbook, Supervision in Transition, editor Carl D. Glickman captured the dynamic quality of supervision in his challenge to the contributing authors:

"Over the past decade, school supervision has been in the midst of swirling, transitional views. One view of supervision—as a district-based, inspector-type function carried out by line supervisors who understand generic processes of effective teaching—has gained ascendancy. A shifting view of supervision as a school-based collegial process, based on reflection, uncertainty, and problem solving, has been finding acceptance in schools that are recasting the roles and responsibilities of teachers. A further area of shifting views has been from an emphasis on pedagogy to focus on the interaction of content (subject knowledge) and instruction. These transitions in supervision have created volatile issues, tugging at the security of peoples' professional lives, and changing previous organizational structures" (Glickman, 1992, pp. 2–3).

- The philosophy of supervision may be construed as a constantly evolving belief system, which reflects the aggregate of the convictions, values, and dispositions that serve to guide the process of educational supervision. Absent a belief system said process is ill prepared to contend with the uniqueness, uncertainties, and opportunities that accompany decision-making that goes beyond an instrumental definition of curriculum, teaching, and supervision.

Sergiovanni and Carver (1980, p. 20) refer to these ambiguities as the "web of tension," where disagreement, dialogue, and controversy that centers on tasks and problems can be a stimulus to individual and organizational creativity—when sustained by a belief system or value framework.

Tanner and Tanner (1987, pp. 339—344) caution that philosophy is not an "esoteric and self-serving exercise but as an outlook that serves as a compass or regulator to guide and test concrete practices." This outlook is intended to support teachers and supervisors in their efforts to create "an effective environment for learning" in accordance with societal ideals, the maturity levels of the learners, and learning experience consonant with the needs and interest of the learner and organized knowledge structures.

Another caution is in order: Supervisory decisions and the actions that accompany them are not a philosophy in their own right. They reflect a vision, however tentative, of what should be in the "public square" of supervisory practice. It is when vision and decisions correspond to a belief system that is grounded in experience, knowledge, and personal values that we have the makings of a philosophy. In these terms, a belief system is more than a supervisory platform, for as crucial as it is for the supervisor to have an agenda that is confirmed by agreed upon goals and procedures, it is even more important that the said platform be supported and sustained by a foundation of beliefs and values that, although not permanent, are essential to thinking, conversation, and action.

- In the final analysis, educational supervision is a leadership process that evolved in tandem with the development of formal educational arrangements. It has frequently served as a management support system absorbed with the particulars of organizational efficiency to the exclusion of instructional leadership that ventures to engage with teachers and community in the pursuit of educational excellence.

We hasten to add that the obverse of this statement is often true: Where educational supervisors moderate management tasks and engage with teachers and community to promote the conditions of learning, they exercise instructional leadership based on ideas, not regulations, on shared visions, not worn traditions, on the advance of mutual responsibility, not legal authority.

"In establishing idea-based leadership, principals have a special responsibility to share their visions of what school can become, but they must do this in an invitational mode, not in the command or sell modes usually advocated by business writers. Why is an invitational mode right for schools and why are the command and sell modes wrong for schools? Because school leadership should be directed to connecting parents, teachers, and students morally to each other, and to their responsibilities as defined by shared purposes. In schools, moral connections cannot be commanded by hierarchy or sold by personalities, but must be compelled by helping people to accept their responsibilities" (Sergiovanni, 1996a).

Sergiovanni's admonition to principals is patently applicable to supervisors in their "stewardship" of instruction and the learning opportunities of students.

These general ideas and commentaries serve as background to the further discussion of the ideas and beliefs that attended the development of our systems and patterns of educational supervision. They are not all-inclusive, but they may be sufficient to frame the discussion. Please be advised: This chapter is not a philosophy of supervision; there is no one philosophy of supervision—there are no immutable truths nor one set of strategies or skills that define the process: This chapter is intended to prod a more personal examination of the traditions and beliefs that set the purposes, decisions, and activities of educational supervision.

KEY CONCEPTS: A MEASURE OF MEANING AND INTERPRETATION

Philosophy

It is generally understood that philosophy is one of the oldest forms of intellectual inquiry. From its ancient roots to its present contentious forms, it seeks to direct thought, observation, and conversation in the examination of ideas, concepts, and the work of social institutions. Recall that philosophy comes from its Greek language roots—philos— which means love of, fondness, and sophia, which means wisdom (Ferm, 1969; Brennan, 1967). Given that wisdom is difficult to define, the meaning of philosophy as the love of wisdom is not all that helpful. People talk about the philosophy of art, music, politics, education, and religion—the full range of life experience. In this sense, they probably mean "general theory of" or "point of view." When someone affirms, "this is my philosophy," it implies that this stated position is his or her perspective. It is the theory or the stance that this said person holds when looking at a particular topic or subject. It is very much a personal perspective—a general point of view in a given area (Ferm, 1967, p. 15).

In a traditional or foundational sense, philosophy joins three areas of investigation: metaphysics, which is concerned with reality and the nature of existence; epistemology, where the concern is the nature of knowledge and how we acquire knowledge; and axiology, which is the study of values and ethics. These dimensions of fundamental philosophy are seen by many observers as relics of the history of philosophy because they reflect the search for universal truths and principles that hold good everywhere, irrespective of any difference in place or object (Riley, 1959, p. 289). This approach seems to disparage considerations of utility and may cut short the deliberative process or the personal exploration of ideas and their potential consequences. It casts a shadow that continues to bear on the way we think about existence and cultural forms, including the organization of educational systems.

Metaphysics

In metaphysics, philosophers seek to distinguish between reality and what appears to be real. They examine what the world is about to better grasp the order and nature of things. They contemplate issues of existence and reality. Metaphysics is the most fundamental and comprehensive of inquiries because questions about reality and the ultimate nature of things underline all particular inquiries (Glymour, 1992, Chapter 1). Individuals struggle with the problem of reality as they seek meaning amid the clamor of existence. "What's it all about?" is the inevitable query. The search may follow different paths, such as mental or spiritual reflection (i.e., idealism), material or physical properties (i.e., realism), the combination of the spiritual and the physical, the concept of the twofold truth of faith and reason, or a view of reality that is relative to circumstance, a reality that is constructed and tentatively held, where the limits of convention are set aside in favor of new forms of discourse from which no one is excluded (i.e., pragmatism). (Bayles, 1966, Rorty, 1979; Ulich, 1961). In his discussion of pragmatism qua philosophy Rorty (1987) offers the following critique of metaphysics and traditional philosophy:

So pragmatists see the Platonic traditions as having outlived its usefulness. This does not mean that they have a new non-Platonic set of answers to Platonic questions to offer, but rather that they do not think we should ask these questions any more. When they suggest that we not ask questions about the nature of Truth or Goodness, they do not invoke a theory about the nature of reality or knowledge or man which says that there is no such thing as Truth or Goodness. Nor do they have a "relativistic" or "subjectivist" theory of Truth or Goodness. They would simply like to change the subject (Rorty, p. 27)

In his seeming rejection of traditional metaphysics, Rorty proposes the consideration of new approaches; such as pragmatism, hermeneutics, and edifying discourse, in the search for new forms of self description (Baynes, Bohman, & McCarty, 1987, p. 22). Reality so conceived is more an ongoing effort to advance personal knowledge, growth, and meaning about the order of things, and not a search for absolutes or certainty (Dewey, 1916; Polanyi, 1958; Rorty, 1994). This view of a dynamic reality and the constancy of change need not deny the traditions and values of the past; indeed, it may help to refine traditional perspectives, their cultural relevance, and expression in the community (Dewey, 1916). In this sense, the educational supervisor is a reality builder and interpreter. She contributes to the understanding of the ideas, forms, and structures that represent the organization of the school and the process of education. She struggles with the diversity of students, teachers, and public concerns, and works to bring together the range of properties, strengths, and needs that characterize the reality and richness of the school community. She engages with colleagues in order to find meaning in the teaching act that goes beyond prescribed arrangements. She seeks to set the conditions that transform the school into a laboratory of ideas and individual development, which is a fundamental concern for the continued emergence of democratic values in a society marked by alternative values and more than a small measure of tumult (Pritzkau, 1959). The supervisor struggles with the pressures of modernity trying to sort the noise and tensions of existence in support of education that is authentic and personal for all involved: the effort to better grasp, "What it's all about."

Epistemology

Another area of philosophy—epistemology—concerns the nature and scope of knowledge, such as what is known and how it is acquired (Hamlyn, 1972). "The epistemologist, however, is concerned not with whether or how we can be said to know some particular truth but with whether we are justified in claiming knowledge of some whole class of truths or, indeed, whether knowledge is possible at all" (Hamlyn, p. 9). The process of "knowing" has inspired diverse interpretations across the history of philosophy from the ancients to post modern philosophers: The recollection or discovery of universal truths; as a product of reason and empiricism; the result of analytical thought; a concern with truth and whether or not knowledge constructs (i.e., fact, information, or personal speculations) meet the conditions of truth, belief, and evidence (Scheffler, 1965); an individual quest for personal knowledge (Polyani, 1958); and challenges to general assertions about the objectivity of knowledge and the stability of language (Appleby, et al, 1994). All societies distinguish between knowledge on the one hand and belief on the other. "Knowledge is that which is entitled to general acceptance and trust; belief is that which one or more individuals, rightly or wrongly, happen to cleave to." What counts as knowledge in one society may count as belief in another (Barnes, 1990, p. 60). Extending this concern to supervision, one might reasonably question the extent of our knowledge about supervision and the balance of knowledge as against belief. In addition, if philosophy is in large part configured by beliefs, then it is the belief system enriched and more valid as operating principles when knowledge, however tentative in nature, is the ground of theory and practice?

Schrag (1992) cautions that efforts to derive "educational implications from traditional epistemological 'isms' (e.g., realism, idealism) are, regrettably, neither philosophically current or educationally illuminating"; today, epistemology is most often discussed as "foundationalism" and "coherentism" (p. 269); he proposes that curriculum designers (i.e., leaders) and research confront issues "concerning knowledge that are at root philosophical," but does not believe that "standard philosophical approaches will be that helpful" (p. 268). Schag prefers to account for the link between educational ideas and knowledge by identifying and interpreting "major educational traditions" and their connection to views about "*what knowledge is most worthy of transmission* and more important, *where it is to be found,* and *how it is to be transmitted*" (emphasis in the original, p. 269).

Greene's (1994) essay on epistemology and educational research explores the traditions of "knowledge construction" and the emerging importance of "perspective and point of view in educational inquiry" to include "the recent contributions of feminist epistemologies and new modes of uncovering and presenting ideas, such as narrative and story" (Darling-Hammond, 1994, p. XV). Greene's thinking on the status and meaning of epistemological pursuits is, in part, expressed thusly:

Epistemology, viewed as a normative activity focused on evaluating discourse in terms of its relation to a trans-historical truth, is generally understood to have reached its end. But this does not eradicate the questions involving what constitutes knowledge, what validates knowledge claims, how truth is defined, how social and cultural traditions affect scientific investigations, how "understanding" differs from "knowledge", what "meaning" signifies, and what belief systems and locations, in the world have to do with the determination of what is to be taken to be real and true (Greene, 1994, p. 425).

In the same volume, Fenstermacher (1994, pp. 3–56) addresses "The Knower and the Known: the Nature of Knowledge in Research on Teaching." He examines varied aspects of knowledge, with regard to teaching: What is known about effective teaching; what teachers know about teaching, the generation of knowledge about teaching, and the epistemological consideration of two types of knowledge about teaching: *formal* knowledge (i.e., propositional or informational knowledge that is "science oriented"), and *practical* knowledge (i.e., that which is concerned with practice, knowing how, competence or performance).

On these matters, Grimmet and MacKinnon (1992) offer a comprehensive analysis of "craft knowledge" (i.e., "the accumulated wisdom derived from teachers'- and practice-oriented researchers' understanding of the meaning ascribed to the many dilemmas inherent in teaching") (Grimmet & MacKinnon, p. 428). They link craft knowledge with judgment of an aesthetic variety, which in turn "relies heavily on intention, care, and empathy for pupils"; it is a form of knowledge that is "steeped in morality and ever critical in its search for meaningful schooling and benefit for pupils" (pp. 428–429). They reference Shulman's (1987) categories of knowledge that are basic for teaching (i.e., context knowledge, general pedagogical knowledge, curriculum knowledge, pedagogical content

knowledge, knowledge of learners, knowledge of education contexts, and knowledge of educational ends, purposes, and values, as well as their philosophical and historical grounds), and they "argue" that Shulman's pedagogical content knowledge "is epistemologically different" from his other categories (Grimmet & MacKinnon, pp. 386–387) because it is derived from "a considered response to experience in the practice setting, and though related to knowledge that can be taught in the lecture hall, it is formed over time in the minds of teachers through reflection" (Shulman, p. 387).

Grimmet and MacKinnon identify "crafty teachers" as individuals who, in the "dexterous, ingenious sense," want to "transform classrooms—and ultimately schools—into places in which all students become celebrated learners controlling their own inquiries" (Grimmet & MacKinnon, p. 429).

Fenstermacher (1994) points to "a growing body of literature that gives attention to the differences between men and women with respect to knowing." He references the work of Code (1991) and Gilligan (1982), while both he and Greene (1994) reference the work of Belanky, McVicker, Clinchy, Goldberger, and Tarule (1986) as scholarship that advances the consideration of knowledge types and women's ways of knowing (Greene, 1994, pp. 20, 450). In Greene's words: "The writers discuss the suppression of self as *separated* knowers given to positing an objectively existent world," which women "experience social obligations" that affect their ways of knowing and "conclude with reminders of the importance of the relatedness, collaboration, and the kind of knowing that is grounded in actually lived experiences" (Greene, p. 451).

The reviews of research and knowledge on teaching by Greene, Fenstermacher, Grimmet, and MacKinnon speak indirectly to the construction of knowledge about supervision. They confront the field in terms of the knowledge base that guides thought, speculation, research, and the activities that constitute supervisory performance. What do supervisors know? Is there substantive formal, theoretical, and practical knowledge about the concept and process of supervision? Is our knowledge of the field an extension of the teachers' knowledge base, or is administrative theory, or some combination of the two, the source of knowledge about supervision? Does Pajak's (1989) supervisory proficiencies project offer a beginning knowledge base as constructed from the literature and the perceptions of instructional leaders? Because knowledge, however defined, is vital to thinking about any area of human concern, what are the messages of formal propositional knowledge, practical knowledge, and craft knowledge to the philosophy and practice of educational supervision? One message is clear: Consideration of the philosophy or practice of supervision presumes general and specific knowledge, and not necessarily "certain" knowledge, about the process of supervision and the organizational culture (i.e., the reality) in which it is expressed because as a field of study supervision depends on the discovery or construction of knowledge pertinent to the process of educational supervision.

Axiology

Another dimension of philosophy—axiology—concerns values, which are those relatively permanent dispositions of thought and belief that configure our sense of goodness, evil, and beauty. As a separate area of philosophy the study of value is often broken down into *aesthetics,* which is the question of beauty, and *ethics,* which concerns issues of right and wrong. In many ways, the study of values is the most interesting and the most perplexing aspect of philosophical inquiry (Frankena, 1972), given that consensus about what we value in society and in organizations is subject to varying degrees of personal or group modification. It is of no small consequence what supervisors of whatever disposition believe and value. The view we hold about reality or knowledge will help determine the value judgments we make, but value judgments, however made, will in large measure determine our actions and behavior. Our values are an intimate and vital part of our humanity that give order to the pattern of our existence. Supervisors engage with and assess the process of education and instructional activities as an extension of value orientations derived from experience, knowledge, and cultural imprint. The supervisors' reality (i.e., the school and its community) is fraught with diverse perspectives that require a blending of those values to be admitted as a basis for discourse and those values to be accepted (Pritzkau, 1959). The value dimension is an essential condition, if not the source, of a philosophy of supervision because it shapes our moral stance and personal integrity.

If philosophy turns on critical reflection as to the justification of human beliefs, then the analysis of language the concepts in which beliefs are expressed, is important. More vigorously stated, philosophy is the discipline that involves creating concepts: "The object of philosophy is to create concepts that are always new" (Deleuze & Guattari, 1991, p. 5).

The question—What is philosophy? can perhaps be posed only late in life, with the arrival of old age and the time for speaking correctly. In fact, the bibliography on the nature of philosophy is very limited. It is a question posed in a moment of quiet restlessness, at midnight, when there is no longer anything to ask. It was asked before; it was always being asked, but too indirectly or obliquely; the question was too artificial, too abstract. Instead of being seized by it, those who asked the question set it out and controlled it in passing. They were not sober enough. There was too much desire to do philosophy to wonder what it was, except as in stylistic exercise (Delueze & Guattari, 1991, p. l).

In a more irreverent tone, Midgley (1992) asks the question: Is philosophy like plumbing? They are both activities that arise because elaborate cultures have, a fairly complex unnoticed system beneath the surface:

Each system supports vital functions while each is hard to repair when something goes wrong. Neither system has had a single designer— instead, they have given overtime and are constantly being altered piecemeal to fit changing demands as the ways of life above them have concepts we are living by malfunction, they do not drip through the ceiling or swamp the kitchen floor. They just quietly distort and obstruct our thinking. Yet, when things go wrong, we somehow readjust, shift, or restate the assumptions we have inherited. This is the stuff of philosophy. And, suggestions for change may come from among the spectrum of those who ponder the nature of things including poetry and the other arts. Shelly is noted to have said that the poets are among the unacknowledged legislators of mankind (Midgley, 1992, pp. 139–140).

At another level, where philosophical inquiry offers guidance in practical affairs, it prompts the development of principles or general ideas as a guide to decision-making while helping to establish a "philosophical spirit" with due recognition of the work and the intellectual turmoil required to advance knowledge and meaning. As conceptualized by Carruthers (1993), philosophy is the struggle to interpret the unknown:

[I]t is the front trench in the siege of meaning and truth. Science is the captured territory; and behind it are those secure regions in which knowledge and art build our imperfect and marvelous world. Philosophy seems to stand still, perplexed; but only because she leaves the fruits of victory to her daughters the sciences, and herself passes on, divinely discontent, to the uncertain and unexplored. Science is analytical descriptions, philosophy is synthetic interpretation.

As the systematic examination of knowledge and belief, philosophy may be at a turning point. "It simply cannot go on as it has" because traditional Platonic traditions have for many observers "outlived its usefulness" (Baynes, Bohman, & McCarthy, 1987, p. 2). The call is for the transformation of foundational philosophy whereby the concepts of transcendent and universal truths, and metaphysical first principles, are set aside. Efforts to transform Platonic traditions are directed to the reconstruction of these notions in accordance with the frailty of human condition because knowledge and truth, tentative in nature, are "bound up" with fundamental human interests (Baynes, Bohman, & McCarthy, pp. 11–12). The center of philosophy lies in certain questions that the reflective mind finds naturally puzzling. It is done just by asking questions, arguing, trying out ideas, and wondering how our concepts really work (Nagel, 1987, p. 4).

Given the complexity of defining philosophy, it is appropriate to recall that the philosophy of educational supervision is rooted in the historical and cultural formulations of our nation. As American education unfolded from the tensions and strivings of a developing nation to one of unrivaled world power, the issues of personal rights, privileges, and responsibilities have been confronted through an unparalleled interplay of the past and the genius of this relatively new democratic experiment. American society and its educational system have therefore developed structures, forms, and processes to sustain and refine the core of the culture and belief. As the society contends with its reality with its beliefs, knowledge, and purpose, including the source and definition of these constructs, there is an inevitable conversion of these thoughts to the work and leadership of the school of which educational supervision is a part. Smyth (1986b) refers to these tensions as a "crisis in the professions," as an epistemological struggle between the "technical–rationality" of the positivist, "where theory is separate from practice" and the emergent paradigm of reflective action which emphasizes forms of knowing that disavow the separation of theory from practice" (Smyth, pp. 12–13).

In these terms, a philosophy of educational supervision is not a procedure (i.e., a list of steps or a paradigm). It is not a model or an inventory of practices. Rather, a philosophy of educational supervision is the continuous process of constructing a belief system derived from the intersection of thought, reality, knowledge, and human values in the search for understanding about education and the process of supervision. You do not straight out adopt a philosophy of supervision as some "verbal chain," although we often adopt procedures or models exclusive of the philosophical concepts that inhere in them. The challenge is to engage in thought and conceptual analysis that relates to the meaning of the "intersection" of ideas that constitute the belief system and, hence, the foundation of a philosophy and consequent supervisory decisions and behavior. This is not a proforma exercise or a building of an outline of descriptors. It is meant to be an earnest, "dialectical" process (Smyth, 1986b) that explores: (1) the nature—the reality of school supervision; (2) the knowledge structures, however tentative, that give shape to this reality; and (3) the values that help make the belief system a guide to action and supervisory decisions.

Supervision

As hazardous (i.e., as challenging and potentially confining) as definitions can be, they give focus to the essence or meaning of things. They serve to guide discussion, and they help to give structure to knowledge and ideas in their various forms. Definitions are also corrigible in the light of new information or changes in the social context from whence they came. We are quite matter-of-fact about the meaning of educational supervision. In the past, there had not been much thought and analysis given to its defining properties save for the long-standing adage to serve teachers and improve instructional programs. If we are to understand supervision as a concept and a process, and if the many public exchanges about purpose, policy, and activities are to be understood, then its definition is important dialectically and for informed practice Glanz (1996, Chap. 2) comments that defining supervision

"has been a fleeting and unproductive endeavor. As attractive and seemingly crucial definition may be, perhaps, in the end, supervision as an all-inclusive and complex function, cannot be captured by a single, straight forward definition" (cf. Portelli, 1987).

In his history of educational supervision, however, he derived a definition based on various writings that supervision is a "function and a role in public schools aimed at improving the quality of instruction." That is a concept that reflects the intent of people over time as well as events and circumstances that provide the context within which meaning is formed (Glanz, Chap. 2). His historical reconstruction examines the record, promotes discourse, and avoids an ideological stance that may resonate with something other than history. One might classify his efforts as "hermeneutical studies" (i.e., dealing with and clarifying the meaning of texts) as well as nontext in the search for meaning and "hidden messages" (Diesing, 1991, pp. 105–107).

Bolin and Panaritis (1992) report two areas of common agreement about the identity and definition of supervision: (1) the function is important irrespective of whom is responsible for the process, and (2) the primary concern is the improvement of classroom practice for the benefit of students, regard-

less of the particular form of supervisory practice (p. 31).

Aside from these consensual areas, the equation of supervision as "expertise" accompanies the development of the school as a formal organization and as a unity within a larger bureaucratic system that is often obsessed with the specialization required by its twin goals of efficiency and effectiveness. Barr, Burton, and Bruerckner (1947), who were seminal thinkers in educational supervision since the 1920s, conflate the ideas of supervision as cooperative activity and expert technical service. Bolin's (1983) scholarship suggests a dualistic aspect to their view of supervision:

Burton (1922) first conceived of supervision as a carefully organized, cooperative activity designed to improve teaching through inspiring, encouraging, and if necessary, redirecting or terminating teachers' work. . . . improving the teaching act across a range of activities including the rating of teachers (Bolin, p. 373).

Bolin reminds us that Burton came to believe that supervisors while urging teachers to apply "principles of learning based on child growth and development must look at the implications of these perspectives for supervisors" (Bolin, p. 373). She also noted the definition of Barr, Burton, and Brueckner (1947): "Supervision is in general what it has been in modern times, an expert technical service primarily concerned with studying and improving the conditions that surround learning and pupil growth." These themes continue to be evident in the discussion of the definition (i.e., the nature and intent of educational supervision). A measure of these discussions is expressed in the following commentaries.

As early as 1943, Miel et al envisaged supervision as a service and support to teachers. She proposed that the concept of "consultant service" supplant supervision, given its heavy overtones of inspection and conformity to bureaucrative rules and regulations (Bolin, 1983, pp. 168–169). Supervision as a planned program for the improvement of instruction was the theme advanced by Wiles (1955), who emphasized that supervision was "assistance in the development of the teaching learning situation." It was the contention of Burton and Brueckner (1955) that the primary function of all supervision is leadership and the encouragement of the leadership function among teachers, staff, and community participants, while they also asserted that the chief function of supervisors "is the evaluation and improvement of instruction." Franseth (1951) affirmed a social orientation that supervision should contribute to the educational program so "the quality of living should be improved because of it." In the 1950s and 1960s, the encyclopedists defined supervision as the efforts of "designated school officials" toward providing leadership to all educational personnel in terms of the (1) improvement of instruction and professional growth of teachers, (2) selection and vision of educational objectives, (3) material of instruction, and (4) the methods of teaching and evaluation. During this period, professional associations registered concern about the conditions of learning and the supervisor's role in creating an environment that helps teachers reach the maximum of their professional potential by working to create a "climate" that promoted "involvement," group process, and shared responsibility for the development of curriculum. These definitions project an image of supervision as service to others without relinquishing the manager's role, including the line responsibilities the role of supervisor implies. The struggle to cast off the yoke of evaluation is marked by a certain caution or hesitation. It likely reflects the tension between the commitment to democratic precepts and the clarion call of efficiency and effectiveness.

Glickman (1985) reaffirmed that "supervision refers to the school function that improves instruction through direct assistance to teachers, curriculum development, in-service training, group development, and action research." He also described supervision as the "glue" of a successful school (i.e., as the function that draws together discrete elements of instruction for "whole-school action") as basis for illuminating common goals and shared responsibility (Glickman, p. 4).

Krey and Burke (1989) inventoried the definition of supervision from the historical record from the early colonial period. They provide succinct statements of definition as advanced in early legislation, in community mandates, and by formal leaders of an ever-developing educational system. Krey and Burke organized their litany of definitions according to periods: administration inspection (1645–1975) through the period that they identify as unification (1976–present). The "unification" period appears to stress supervision as a service to teachers as a form of educational leadership intended to invigorate the teaching–learning process. Their review may serve as a starting point for the conceptual analysis of supervisory thought and its change over time.

More recently, educational supervision has been explained by Sergiovanni and Starratt (1993) as a process that has a moral essence drawn from its involvement with the intrinsic moral qualities of teaching and learning. Such a process goes beyond "human relations," technical skills, and the "effectiveness" syndrome:

As a process supervision involves a "standing over" a "standing above" in order to achieve a larger or deeper view of the educational moment, to gain a vision of the whole as it is reflected and embodied in its parts. In short supervision is not so much a view of a teacher by a superior viewer; it is vision, a view of what education might mean at this moment, within this context, for these particular people. Perhaps more accurately, the process of supervision is the attempt by a segment of the community of learners to gain this super-vision of the educational moment within their reflective practice, so that their insight into the possibilities of that moment can lead to the transformation of that moment into something more satisfying and productive for them (p. 182).

Pajak (1993) reviewed the development or, as he expressed it, the "deconstruction" of clinical supervision. Recognizing the seminal work of Goldhammer (1969), Mosher and Purpel (1972), and Cogan (1973), Pajak presented "four categories or families of models" of clinical supervision: original clinical, humanistic/artistic, technical/didactic, developmental/reflective. These models offer a view of supervision based on the principles of collegiality, interpersonal relations, teaching strategies, and teacher cognitive development as essential tenets in the process of supervision from a clinical perspective.

Holland (1994) examined the meaning of supervision, more specifically the way we "talk about it," by reviewing "nearly three dozen popular and representative textbooks on the nature and practice of supervision published in the past sixty years" (Holland, p. 1). She reports that interpretations of supervision presented in these texts reflect the influence of "practical expediency" from which the functional requirements of supervisors are derived: curriculum, staff development, and teacher evaluation. She noted the commonality of these functional requirements and signals the "differences in the way these functions and the process and the techniques for carrying them out are discussed" (Holland, p. 2). Why are there variations in the way supervision texts present and discuss the purportedly common functions of supervision? Holland answers by pointing to the variability of the various "grand narratives" (Lyotard, 1989), which are the structures of the "language game" that authors use to frame their interpretations. Holland (1994) portrays four academic grand narratives: philosophical democracy, positivist solid science, instrumentalist management, and phenomenology as derived from her "qualitative content analysis of the representative texts in her study" (Holland, p. 3). She emphasizes that two or more of the narratives may "coexist" within a text, and that each of the narratives "wends its way through the sixty-year time-span" that was the focus of her review.

The significance of Holland's study, in part, relates to the construction of the "grand narratives" as derived from the language and the concepts employed by scholars of educational supervision. She has provided a framework for studying and translating the language of supervision as a preface to understanding its nature and intentions. She has not set aside the issue of definition; rather, she guides the quest for the meaning and challenges of supervision beyond conventional wisdom toward an enlightened understanding of the process and its responsibilities. In this sense one may conjecture that the definition of supervision is a mark and a force in our formal systems of education whose nature and properties will reflect the surgence and the shifts of knowledge, diversity of thought, and civility in the larger society.

In the mode of Holland's supervision as "grand narratives," Sergiovanni and Starratt's (1993) concept of supervision as a process reflects her narrative category of "philosophical democracy," which is an approach that seeks to promote the achievement and advancement of the individual as a core requirement for "society's collective progress" (Holland, p. 4). She would also place Glickman's developmental supervision, a process characterized by directive, collaborative, and nondirective supervision geared to the teachers' stage of professional development, as an example of her grand narrative category, "positivist social science," which emphasizes knowledge of the individual and the social structures generated from social science research.

Grumet (1978) provides a vivid "backward glance" on the meaning of supervision "to peruse or to scan a text." She offers a poetic and idealized portrait:

Imagine the monk performing this task, inspecting the text for errors, for minute deviations from an original manuscript that has been copied, perhaps even illuminated. What does this supervision look for? Smudges? Omissions? Does he bend to the work, eyeing each word and disregarding the meaning of the aggregate as the skilled copy reader who trains himself to examine surface content only? Are his standards for the work shared by the one who executed it, both participating in a practice so saturated with their common faith that the criteria for scrutiny needs scarcely be uttered?

In our view that the answer to all these questions is *yes* because the monk's task and the supervisor's responsibility were preordained by a particular philosophical construct, a dualistic reality, where transcendent revelation sets the profile of knowledge and the "good life." It may be that the issues of "style and design" were matters of some limited negotiation, but consideration of the intent and interpretation of the text was to await another time when knowledge would go beyond revelation and scholasticism to the discovery and construction of knowledge to a time of new nation states, political systems, and institutions. In this sense the concept of supervision, and the role of the supervisor (e.g., Abbot, magistrate, selectman, principal teacher, whomever) emerged and continues to emerge as a part of the larger process of cultural and institutional development. As we are better informed about the human condition, the nature of individuals and the "overall form of a civilization—the principle—material or spiritual—of a society, the significance common to all the phenomena of a period . . . the face of a period" (Foucault, 1972, p. 9), we are more capable of understanding the origins and nature of supervision: "The problem is no longer one of tradition, of tracing a line, but one of division, of limits; it is no longer one of lasting foundations, but one of transformations that serve as new foundations, the rebuilding of the foundations" (Foucault, p. 5). The task is to grasp the historical and the cultural "face" of supervision, for in recognizing the particulars surrounding its evolution there is an awareness, a respect for its traditions, that partakes in the process of transforming the concept in an environment of competing belief systems.

Flinders (1991) examines the ubiquitous and the "tacit characteristics" of culture through the use of metaphysical images as a "framework for culturally responsive supervision." He views the term *supervision* as a

metaphor that generates an image of professional practices . . . and as derived from "business and industry the term signifies the responsibility of one person to oversee the work of others. When we apply the concept to the business of running a school, its cultural baggage is not lost in the transition from one field to another. The vocabulary supervisors use to describe their work and the work of teachers makes a difference in shaping the most basic lessons of our professional development." . . . The message concerns the cultural parameters, the language and the conceptual tools which "inform what supervisors look for in the classroom, as well as how they provide feedback to teachers" in an artful "blend of both routine and reflection" (Flinders, 1991, pp. 103–104, 105–106).

Glickman (1985) registers concern about the limitations, if not the distortions, of the term *supervision,* given its traditional connotations of hierarchy, status, and evaluation. He prefers the more dynamic or professional form of the concept—coaching, collegiality, professional development or critical inquiry—which McBride and Skau (1995, pp. 275–276) find to be in keeping with a supervisory belief system based on trust, empowerment, and reflection; one that fosters "an enlivened community of educational practitioners," one that provides the

"glue . . . the force . . . that draws the discrete elements of instructional effectiveness into whole school action" (Glickman, 1989, p. 5).

Smyth (1986b) petitions that our study of supervision go beyond the technicalities of the process, that our thinking focus, on the "ground" of supervision that is the "values and ideals purportedly implicit in the notion of supervision," and not on the "figure." As Smyth contends, a preoccupation with the "technical and the instrumental," features of supervision will serve to set aside "important moral, ethical, political, and philosophical questions" (Smyth, p. 10).

Ornstein (1992) considers the way in which philosophy connects to the provenance of education and curriculum. It may be seen as "theories in education" as "interpreted clusters, bundles, or sets of interpretation, analysis, and understandings about educational phenomenon" (p. 4) that have a "reciprocal relationship" to the action we take. So conceived theories and action "inform each other" in the quest for wisdom about the substance and structure of education. They provide a direction in the "what and how" of educational goals, and a framework for curriculum decision-making (pp. 10–11). Ornstein's overview of "educational philosophies" affirms Dewey's (1916) proposals that "philosophy may be defined as the general theory of education . . . the laboratory in which philosophical distinctions become concrete and tested." This suggests philosophy as the prime mover, as a source of educational values and beliefs from whence codes of belief, theory and practice, curriculum, administration, and supervision are derived. The philosophy of supervision in this context—or reality—represents the array of principles derived from the metaprinciples of philosophy and education. These principles are essential elements of the supervisor's belief system and bear directly on the needs and aspirations of people, the process of education, the teaching compact, and the school as a communitarian enterprise. The strands and forms of supervisory activity are part of the fabric of the school organization and, as some have suggested, the "glue" of the instructional program.

These definitions, however diverse, reject supervision as inspection. They deny an authoritative hierarchical concept of professional relationships. In varying degrees, they propose an approach to supervision that is humanistic, collegial, and participatory. This approach values individuals, their strengths, capacities, and needs. It has the potential to energize the process of education and to become a source of strength and enrichment for the educational process. The matter of definition is not pedantry; rather, it is a continuing professional responsibility that is vital to the outline and refinement of educational supervision. The matter of definition includes ideas, knowledge (such as it is), values, and social context. It is a primer in the search for an illusive "truth" and belief about a role and process that is a presence in the reality of educational systems. Definition is not superfluous; it is an imperative and very much a part of the philosophy of supervision. If educational supervision is to qualify as a field of study with a structure, syntax, and beliefs, however tentative, then

those of us in the area of supervision need to work in ways that enable us to challenge taken-for-granted, even cherished assumptions about the area. Above all we need to develop reflexive capabilities

THE PHILOSOPHICAL PERSPECTIVE OF SUPERVISION • 211

so as to transcend what we think we know about supervision, and develop alternatives, even oppositional possibilities of what it might mean to be involved in the theory and practice of supervision (Smyth, 1986a).

SUPERVISORY MODELS AS BELIEF SYSTEMS

In this volume, Glanz presents an exhaustive history of educational supervision. His chapter (see Chap. 2), and his other scholarly works (Glanz, 1977, 1991) provide a historical framework long lacking in the scholarship of educational supervision. His work is "synergistic" (Boyer, 1992) in that he integrates the historical record with developments in supervisory theory and practice. He registers his intent to

introduce a theory of history that attempts to go beyond the assumption that supervision merely reflects movements occurring in society as a whole, and in education, in particular, the history of supervision is the history of the interaction of broad social and intellectual movements affecting all aspects of education (Glanz).

Glanz's history of supervision is "processed" beyond a "fetishism of facts" in order to conduct a conversation about the story of educational supervision. He posits the integration of fact, interpretation, and imagination as "models" or "dominant conceptions" including supervision as inspection, supervision as social efficiency, democratic supervision, scientific supervision, clinical supervision, supervision as leadership, and changing concepts of supervision. These "models" might best be thought of as operational definitions. They clarify the development of supervisory theory and practice as related to prevailing historic or cultural themes and conditions. Our discussion of the philosophy of supervision is framed by Glanz's history and the perspectives of Bolin and Panaritis (1992) on the history and "common purpose" of supervision. This decision assumes that these models and perspectives provide a structure for the examination of ideas and beliefs that helped to shape educational supervision. The intent is to extend the conversation about supervision to the ideas and the beliefs that are reflected in the record of supervisory theory and practice.

Supervision as Inspection

Inspection, the dictionary tells us, is an act or process of looking into things. It is very much a "careful critical investigation or scrutiny of objects or events." Inspections are completed by persons who are officially appointed to oversee matters of public interest in order to ascertain the quality or the "state of things." It might be reasonably assumed that the inspection process is guided by clearly defined notions of "what should be" conducted by an agent who has knowledge of that which is being scrutinized. The inspector would ideally secure first-hand, valid information as a base for evaluation and modification, as may be required of the matter being inspected. These terms of definition obviously express an ideal type that implies consummate precision, order, and rationality. We know, however, that the variance between def-

inition and reality, in most things, is substantial, especially in matters that attend to social organizations and the human condition.

As the story is often told, supervision began early in the history of American education. As educational activities evolved the inspectional nature of supervision continued through the colonial and the early national period of the "common school," through the course of the progressive transformation to the present. This suggests that "supervision as inspection" has persisted in a variety of forms across the history of American education, even other "models" have emerged. It is often defined in terms that belie its inspectional nature and intent for the ideas—the belief systems that sustain the practice of supervision as inspection have changed in accordance with prevailing images of curriculum, instruction, and organizational structure, if not the goals of education. Even though efforts have been made to change the image of supervision as control and evaluation, "it is not," in Smyth's (1991) words,

altogether clear that we have severed the connection between instructional supervision and the industrial model . . . which evokes feelings . . . of an impersonal hierarchical process of inspection and quality control . . . it is not just a matter of changing the lexicon; the real issues go far deeper, frequently to the very basis of the intent and purpose of the supervisory process.

Supervision as inspection had its start in the belief system of the early colonial clergy and lay leaders. Through a "priesthood of all believers," shared convictions as to the purpose of life and the import of education were pronounced. Recall that those who settled America were generally common people seeking to advance themselves and to provide for their well being economically and for political and religious reasons (Cremin, 1980).

The concern of American colonists for education was born of necessity, lest their children grow up "barbarous in the wilderness" (Spiller et al, 1963, p. 16). This concern was especially great in New England and Virginia, although the response to the wilderness condition was different. In New England, villages quickly set up schools for their children. Indeed, the Puritan fathers established Harvard College (1636) to

insure a learned ministry and provide a nursery of learning for their sons. In Virginia the wealthier planters hired tutors and the less well-to-do organized plantation schools and shared the expense of the teacher; those who were able sent their sons and sometimes daughters to England for advanced education.

In 1693 Virginia established the college of William and Mary for the same motives that had prompted the founders of Harvard in Massachusetts (Spiller et al, 1963, pp. 16–18).[2]

The Puritans of New England "have left an indelible mark on the American character," including our educational institutions. We remember the Puritans as a religious reform movement in sixteenth and seventeenth century England that was committed to "purifying" the Church of England from the orthodoxy of Rome (Flower & Murphey, 1977, p. 4). The Puritans saw the world as being in God's control, as defined in the precepts of Calvin's theory: God's hand held the world together; He is the creator, Lord and master of the universe; His sovereignty is unconditional, His power is infinite and His will arbitrary and unconstrained; He determines all events, is omniscient and transcendent hence human knowledge can never adequately depict Him.

The Puritan God is mysterious, inscrutable, and absolutely sovereign; the covenant between God and the brethren, "the elect," was direct and unyielding. Moral relativism was not to be found. (Kurtz, 1972, p. 84; Flower & Murphey, 1977). Discipline was needed: Individuals capable of controlling themselves and taking responsibility for their lives in a stable social order based on a contract between people and the Deity. This is

an order of those who rule themselves in their personal lives . . . But the initial thrust is not toward democracy but rather to a kind of elite rule. The godly, the disciplined, ought to rule over themselves through agreement, but over the unregenerate through force if necessary. . . . The saints control themselves, they admonish each other, but they rule the ungodly coercively (Taylor, Chapter 1).

The Puritans rejected the authority of a distant and hierarchical church and stressed the privacy of their covenant with God. An essential factor in this relationship was the ability to read. It was the precondition for a first-hand personal association with God's word, particularly as pronounced in the Bible (Wolterstorff, 1972, Vol. 2, p. 9). The urgency of providing schools and teachers was immediately addressed, as was the oversight of teachers and students.

As the poet has said: "Adversity is the quickest and most unerring of tutors." During the first century and a half of settlement in America the colonists spent most of their time and energies in practical pursuits, as required in a

raw and unexploited continent. By 1760, however, some cities, particularly Boston and Philadelphia, had excellent grammar schools, and throughout the colonies public spirited citizens were laboring to increase educational opportunities. Stern Calvinists were convinced that education was necessary to combat the devil, and the more easy going deists were equally certain that education was needed to bring about man's perfection to virtue. The doctrine of universal educational opportunities, which Thomas Jefferson advocated near the turn of the eighteenth century, was already incipient, and movements were on going which would change the ideal of education into something akin to a religious conversion (Spiller et al, 1963, p. 17).

As these developments unfolded, the primacy of the Puritan traditions waned. Conversions were down. The ministers lamented "New England's declension" and called for revival. Jonathan Edwards came forward as the apologist for the Puritan faith and tradition. As he sought to advance a spirit of renewal other ideas engaged the attention of those who were inclined to go beyond revelation and to pursue the continuities of faith, reason, and practical intelligence. Such were the inclinations of Benjamin Franklin, Thomas Paine, and Thomas Jefferson. Franklin converted to deism and championed the cause of reason, rejecting the authority of scriptural revelation, prophecies, and miracles (Schneider, 1963, pp. 33–35). The deists rejected the Calvinist notion of the sinfulness of humanity; they supported religious freedom and the

separation of church and state (Flower & Murphey, 1977, pp. 99–101). They conceived of God as the first cause (i.e., the designer of the order of the universe), where all events are determined by material law; therefore, nature is a manifestation of the goodness of God (Kurtz, 1972). Deism affirms the "oneness of humanity" and marks the rise of secularism and toleration of the thoughts of others, which may be its major legacy. Their moral philosophy was humanistic and reflected the principles of the Enlightenment that expressed an optimistic faith and the use of science, reason, and education as instruments of human progress (Kurtz, 1972, Vol. 1, p. 84).

The early statesmen of the new republic (i.e., Jefferson, Madison, John Adams, and Hamilton) had a vision of government that went beyond practical affairs to consider both "the buried sources power [and] the moral aspects of good government." The principles espoused by these philosopher statesmen combined to define a national ideology: our objectives, our character as a people, our economic and social patterns, and our Americanism (Spiller, et al, p. 146). It is written that Jefferson was the "greatest of them all"; he examined his own beliefs carefully, as well as the design and practice of good government because citizens are to be led by "reason and persuasion and not by force" in a republic (Spiller, pp. 147–158). He was eager to find every device and policy that would prove humanity capable of governing itself in freedom and virtue (Ketcham, 1972).

Although Jefferson's achievements in the development of education in his beloved Virginia were limited, the import that he assigned to education was ever strong (Cremin, 1980, pp. 107–114). He championed the development of the University of Virginia and the course of popular schooling as essential to political life, freedom, and an educated citizenry—the source of leadership in the republic. "The entire scheme Jefferson maintained was founded upon the view that human nature was not fixed, that man was essentially improveable, and that education was the chief means of affecting that improvement" (Cremin, pp. 111–112). Whatever the limits of his practical achievements in education, and the limitations of his proposals and actions with regard to slavery and the education of women, the "influence of Jefferson's educational thought, during the nineteenth century and into the twentieth, was powerful and pervasive" (Cremin, 1980, pp. 113–114).[3]

The revolutionary spirit expressed a theory of knowledge based on reason as the source of "self-evident principles," where the truths deduced from them were "certified" by national law, intuition, and the use of the senses (White, 1978). Reason becomes the servant of revelation by preparing the ground for intuitive thought and understanding (Cassirer, 1932, p. 46). In the Jeffersonian sense essential truths about the nature of humanity and governments were not innate, imprinted on the soul; rather, they were intuitions derived from reason and logic, abetted by education and a government obliged to aid, or at least protect, the individual right to pursue happiness (White, 1978). The revolutionary leaders intuitively knew it was right to rebel against Britain and to "dissolve the political bonds that connect them" because independence was more than morally possible, it was morally necessary (White, 1978, pp. 13–19). Jefferson was optimistic about the ability of the majority to be educated and to consciously ascribe to the "self-evident truths" of the revolution and the moral capacity to sustain them (White, p. 268). At another time, Dewey would consider the appeal to self-evidence and intuition as conservative, undemocratic, and authoritarian because it implied a faculty of mind employed only by the few who might seek to impose their views on the many (White, 1978, pp. 13–14)

As significant as the early American political philosophers were to the birth of the republic, it was the family and the local community that had the responsibility for education (i.e., the transmission of the social, religion, and cultural heritage) (Karier, 1982, pp. 2–3). This was not an easy task because it was a time when long-revered traditions and virtues were being confronted by Enlightenment perspectives, the realities of war, the politics of independence, and Yankee ingenuity (Schneider, 1963, pp. 36–37). The family and the community were joined "in a relation of profound reciprocity." To put it another way, "individual families are the building blocks out of which the larger units of social organization are fashioned." As expressed by the "Puritan" preacher (Demos, 1986, pp. 27–29):

A family is a little church and a little commonwealth, at least a lively representation thereof, whereby trail may be made of such as are fit for any place of authority, or of subjection, in church or commonwealth. Or rather, it is a school where in the first principles and grounds of government are learned: whereby men are fitted to greater matters in church and commonwealth (Gouge, London, 1622).

Under these circumstances, proposals about the education of youth were expressed in strict moral codes and a distrust of human nature. In this time, educational supervision as inspection resonates with the traditions of foundational philosophy: reality is dualistic (i.e., the here and now, which is but a moment in the overall scheme of things), and it is transcendent (i.e., reality that is beyond human calculation and apprehension, which is in the keeping of Divine providence). Knowledge in this sense of reality is derived from the acceptance of a revealed good that shapes the values, aspirations, and behavior of the individual and the community, not from our senses.

Given this code of belief supervision as inspection was required. The curriculum was ordained and mastery of "the word" grounded in catechetical learning. Although feverish ministerial pronouncements provoked the heart and mind, reading and writing were required intellectual skills in order to gain direct access to the revealed word. The selectmen, town fathers, or committeemen who supervised gave careful scrutiny to "objects and events" in the work of the schoolmaster in the school and beyond. The task was straightforward and was defined by the tenets of the church and legislated proficiency in reading and writing: They were doing supervision, they were talking supervision, and they were legislating supervision. They were "enlightened" agents because they were ministers and selectmen; they knew what to look for, and it was not creative pedagogy or empathetic interaction between the teachers and the taught. This was not a democratic exercise inclined toward the unfoldment of

human capacities; rather, it was "oversight" as mandated by the covenant. This was supervision as inspection driven by a core of universal beliefs with the intent to exact conformity under the conditions of a prescribed course of study and the performance of students. In this age, supervision as inspection sought to confirm, a pervading moral theme regarding personal relationships and the life of the community rather than a checklist of performance. While supervision as inspection would continue, the belief system supporting it would modify, as the beat of history, the discovery of a personal concept of God, "manifest destiny," the process of science, and the mix of faith and reason stirred the passions of a new nation.

Inspection: Change and Promise

In the early 1800s, the harsh, rigid Puritan faith was in decline (Curti, 1959, p. 96). Many Calvinist clergy were attracted to the vigor of reason, rejecting teachings that seemed to be contrary to a more deliberative understanding of the nature of things. A major controversy, raised by the Unitarians, centered around the issue of the Trinity, but this controversy was more than a question of doctrine because it involved fundamental differences in world view (Flowers & Murphey, 1977, Chapter 1). Like Franklin and Jefferson, the Unitarians were children of the Enlightenment. They espoused the cause of reason and benevolence in the humanistic sense of these terms. In the advances of science, many saw clear proof of the power and the scope of human reason: They were not afraid to follow where it led, even in questions of theology, and they rejected the notion of humanity's innate depravity and affirmed their faith in the moral capacity of rational men (Flower & Murphy, Chapter 1). For others, social morality substituted for the older, weakened religiosity:

Humanitarian agitators from the ministerial, farming, and commercial classes, joined the crusade against slavery, war, intemperance, imprisonment for debt, and harsh penal conditions; they battled heroically for the rights of women, the insane, and the underprivileged in a context marked by depression, unemployment, and child labor (Curti, 1959, pp. 95–96).

As Demos (1986, p. 31) described these times:

The brave new world of nineteenth-century America was, in some respects, a dangerous world—or so many people felt. The new egalitarian spirit, the sense of openness, the opportunities for material gain, the cult of the "self-made man": all this was new, invigorating, and liberating at one level—but it also conveyed a deep threat to traditional values and precepts. In order to seize the main change and get ahead in the ongoing struggle for "success," a man had to summon energies and take initiatives that would at the very least exhaust him and might involve him in terrible compromises. At the same time he would need to retain some place of rest and refreshment—some emblem of the personal and moral regime that he was otherwise leaving behind.

Between 1820 and 1850, educational leaders struggled to secure public support and supervision of the common elementary school (Curti, 1959, p. 194). They confronted stubborn opposition to taxation for school support and concern about limitations on local control. Despite opposition, systems of state-supervised schools were developed—even in the West, where problems of settlement held back cultural developments (Curti, 1959, pp. 194–196). Before the Civil War, except in the south, the battle for state support and state supervision of public education had been won. At the start of the nineteenth century, no state had a system of public elementary, secondary, or higher education. By 1860, every state had the first two, and several had public colleges and universities (Nye, 1974, p. 376). The concept of the "common school" (i.e., one free and open to all, of excellent quality, and common in the sense that children of all backgrounds would be served) was closer to realization.

The function of supervision was legislated in Massachusetts in 1826, providing that town committees would "have the general charge and superintendents of all public schools." This included "the power to direct and supervise the teachers activity in the classroom" as a function that is largely dependent upon visitation and inspections . . . a function that has been associated with the committee idea from the beginning" (Suzzallo, 1969, pp. 146–147). Where inefficient or weak performance was discovered, school authorities could "(1) discharge or decline to hire such a teacher or (2) so direct and supervise his work so that it would become more effective" (Suzzallo, p. 145).

In these times, educational supervision was but a bit player. It continued to be expressed in the heavy tones of the Calvinist tradition that stressed education for conformity and the ordered life. On the one hand it was a general theory of education and instruction, whereas it was a definition of how to keep school on the other hand. It prescribed what was good for teachers and students, and the program of instruction was bounded by Christian themes and the exegesis of enlightened ministers and lay leaders. It was not unlike the approach of supervision as inspection during the colonial period, which emphasized knowledge gained from drill and practice, and the frailty of human understanding. It was different in the sense that creed and the particulars of religious belief were moderated by a trust in providence, themselves, and the institutions they were building to help realize personal freedoms—the promise of the new republic. Tyack and Hansott (1982, p. 3) inform us that:

many of the public school promoters of the mid-nineteenth century were convinced that America was literally God's country, the land He had chosen to bring about redemption of mankind. . . . This process of redemption was not passive or deterministic, however; the common school crusaders regarded themselves as God's chosen agents. This sense of being part of a large providential plan infused even ordinary tasks with large meaning . . . school leaders retained much of this earlier moral earnestness and sense of mission, but they lost much of the specific content of millenialism—they drew on a newer aspiration to control the course of human evolution scientifically through improving education.

Stimulated by faith in the idea of progress, leaders such as Horace Mann, Henry Barnard, and Catherine Beecher (Cremin, 1980) looked to public education as the instrument for achieving a society in which morality and religion could be respected, where citizens would be law abiding and industrious, where crime and pauperism were no more, and where property and life were secure (Cremin, 1980; Tyack & Hansott, 1982). By 1840, the United States possessed a clear understanding of its identity which for some observers was based on three things:

(1) An equality of expectation—each American could legitimately hope for personal and material security, (2) religious sentiment—the churches were a powerful cohesion factor in American civilization, (3) on the conviction that the nation had a moral commitment to lead the world to a better future (Nye, 1974, p. 5).

As Barlow wrote in his epic poem, The Columbiad (as quoted in Schneider, 1963, p. 64):

> Instruction clear a speedier course shall find,
> And open earlier on the infant mind.
> No foreign terms shall crowd with barbarous rules
> The dull unmeaning pageantry of schools;
> Nor dark authorities nor names unknown
> Fill the learn'd head with ignorance not its own;
> But wisdom's eye with beams unclouded shine,
> And simplest rules her native charms define;
> One living language, one unborrow'd dress
> Her boldest fights with fullest force express;
> Triumphant virtue, in the garb of truth,
> Win a pure passage to the heart of youth,
> Pervade all climes where suns or oceans roll
> And warm the world with one great moral soul.

Tocqueville (1838) observed that Americans pay little attention to philosophy because they have no philosophical school of their own (which would change with the advent of pragmatism later in the nineteenth century); however, because "the inhabitants use their minds in the same manner, and direct them ascending to the same rules; that is to say, without ever having taken the trouble to define the rules, they have a philosophical method common to the whole people" (Reeves, Bowen, & Bradley, editors, 1838, p. 3). Tocqueville defines the philosophical method of America as the tendency to:

Evade the bondage of the system and habit", the limitations of "family maxims, class opinions, and in some degree of national prejudices", where tradition is a "means of information and existing facts only as a lesson to be used in doing otherwise and doing better; to seek the reason of things for oneself, and in oneself alone; to tend to results without being bound to means, and to strike through the form to the substance—such are the principal characteristics" (Reeves et al, p. 3).[4]

The growth of cities became marked about 1830 and continued thereafter at a rapid pace: The national population had grown from 4 to 31 million between 1790 and 1860, and the country quadrupled in size–to include new areas of diverse climate, topography, resources and population (Nye, 1974). This created problems in the management and supervision of the local schools. The Quincy Grammar School in Boston

(1847) is usually cited as the first graded school, and early school board records indicate that Cincinnati placed all departments of school under a single head prior to 1838 (Pierce, 1935, p. 9). St. Louis and Chicago soon afterward achieved similar arrangements where all programs and grades were under the direction of one principal in each building, all the other teachers being assistants (Pierce, p. 9). In Boston, the single principal–teacher arrangement was set in 1855, whereas New York, as late as 1889, still had "23 schools—each having male, female, and primary departments." As late as 1903, many of the elementary buildings in the boroughs of Manhattan and the Bronx, it was found that two, in some cases three independent principals existed under the same roof (Pierce, p. 9).[5]

In 1837, the Massachusetts Board of Education was organized, and a secretary, Horace Mann, was appointed. As identified in the Act, the duties for this position were to "collect information on the actual condition and efficiency of the Common Schools and other means of popular education" and to diffuse information on effective practice, "to the end, that all children of the Commonwealth who depend upon Common Schools for instruction, may have the best education which these schools can be made to impart" (Mann, 1855, p. VII). He held county conventions throughout the state, where, over time, he lectured on the Common School, the preparation of teachers, education in a republic, God, man and educational responsibility, and a historical view of the importance of education. His "sermon" on the Common School (1837), his first as secretary, was testimony to his abiding concern for education that nurtures the mind and the soul to "inspire the love of truth as the supremest goal and to clarify the vision of the intellect to discuss it." His admonition combined Enlightenment philosophy and an evangelical petition to recognize the merits of the "great cause" of education:

We want a generation of men above deciding great and eternal principles upon narrow and selfish grounds . . . men capable of taking up their complex questions, and of turning all sides of them toward the sun, and examining them by the white light of reason, and not under the false colors which sophistry may throw upon them. We want no men who will change, like the vanes of our steeples, with the course of the popular wind; but we want men who, like mountains, will change the course of the wind. We want no more of these patriots who exhaust their patriotism, in landing the post; but we want patriots who will do for the future what the past has done for us. We want men capable of deciding, not merely what is right, in principle,—that is often the smallest part of the case;—but we want men capable of deciding what is right in means, to accomplish what is right in principle. We want men who will speak to the great people in counsel and not in flattery. We want god-like men who can tame the madness of the times, and, speaking divine words in a divine spirit can say to the raging of passion, "Peace, be still," and usher in the calm of enlightenment, reason and conscience (Mann, 1855, pp. 52–53).[6]

In these times, the position of the "principal teacher" (i.e., the controlling head of the school) was a matter of concern to assistant teachers. In 1839, the Common School Teacher's Association of Cincinnati asked the Board of Education to define the "relative duties" of "principals and assistant teachers" (Pierce, p. 11). The Board offered detailed description of the responsibilities of the teacher and the assistants: The principal teacher was to (1) function as the head of the school, (2) regulate the classes and course of instruction of all students, (3) give necessary instructions to his assistants, (4) instruct assistants, (5) refrain from impairing the standing of the assistants, especially in the eyes of their pupils, and (6) require the cooperation of his assistants (Pierce, p. 12). The Board emphasized that "principal teachers" were selected based on "their knowledge of teaching methods, the characteristics of children, and common problems of schools." A lack of firmness was not tolerated and mutual cooperation between principal teacher and the assistant teacher was deemed essential, "because without it, good order and teaching efforts would suffer" (Pierce, p. 12). These Board actions offer clear evidence of supervision as inspection, which were to be conducted by a duly appointed official whose professional experience and knowledge were to address "the regulation" of the school in terms of management, including oversight of the "teacher assistants." In this sense, the inspection model has matured, for responsibility goes beyond an inventory of student deportment and recitation to the idea of a formal relationship between "principal teacher" and "teacher assistants," based on the continuing opportunity to scrutinize the work of teachers and the performance of students, a clear understanding of what should be taught and the virtues to espouse; and a clear line of authority purportedly based on "professional knowledge" as well as tradition. This was supervision as inspection, whose definition was drawn from a nation's faith in progressive change, human rights, and responsive independence, which is a faith in the "natural power of freedom" (Schneider, 1963) as so passionately expressed in Mann's *Lectures on Education* (1855).

Blumberg's (1985) commentary on supervision in the 1840s recounts the exhortations of the superintendent of the common schools of New York as to the significance of public schools: "On the flourishing condition of our schools, repose the hopes of the present and the destinies of the future" (Blumberg, p. 19). And even more dramatically, "the only salvation for the republic is to be sought for in our schools" (Blumberg, p. 19). Blumberg also notes the superintendent's efforts to classify teachers: those that were "first class"—an honor to the profession—spark the interest of their students, adapt instruction to the capacities of their pupils and teach students to think for themselves, "second class teachers"—a very respectable class of teachers who teach more words than ideas, the "third class"–very ordinary—and the "fourth class," "decidedly bad teachers . . . actually cramming the mind with error" (Blumberg, p. 60).

There were hints, however, of change. Some of these early superintendents were concerned about the quality of teaching and methodology. In Blumberg's words,

[T]heirs was not merely a mission to spread schooling, but to spread what they conceived to be an educational experience for youngsters. Perhaps they realized that to perpetuate a system of instruction that involved little more than memorizing and reciting would mean the end of their grandiose dream, a society in which the schools would lead the way to civility and understanding" (Blumberg, pp. 56–65).

This vision was simultaneously a concern for the individual, the promise of American democracy, and a marked sensitivity to refining the process of education within the structure of a traditional, "essentialist" approach to the curriculum: promotion of intellectual growth; education of the competent person; mastery of subject matter; and teaching of traditional values (Ornstein, 1992, p. 13). Supervision in this context walked a path between the traditions of generations past and the practical struggles of diverse communities building a nation. Supervision was not a professional role, save for the early state superintendents, whose energy and vision affirmed long-standing precepts while hinting at the proposition that values and knowledge are not separate from the stream of human experience. Hear Mann (1855) again: "We want men capable of developing what is right in principle. . . . but we want men capable of deciding what is right in means, to accomplish what is right in principle." Schoolmen, as educational leaders and supervisors, faced a contest of Puritan values, the philosophy of a disciplined life with Franklin's practical benevolence and secular humanism (Schneider, 1963, p. 36) that rejects by inference supervision as defined by a "prominent jurist" in 1834: "[Teachers] in the number and the qualifications [necessary] we can never have, unless they are properly *trained*, and properly *examined*, and *watched*, and *controlled*" (Burton, 1961, p. 21).

Before the Civil War, the gains of the revolution were being consolidated and transcendentalism, which is a distinctive American intellectual tradition, became an influential literary movement from about 1836 to 1860 (Moran, 1972, Vol. 5, p. 479). It has been defined as a form of "idealism" as a "class of ideas or imperative forms, which did not come by experience, but through which experience was acquired—by the intuitions of the mind" (Moran, p. 479). Transcendentalism contained the "final liberation of America's liberal consciousness from the Calvinism that the Unitarians had already done much to ameliorate" (Moran, p. 480). Its advocates included, among others, Ralph Waldo Emerson and Henry David Thoreau. While some of a transcendentalist persuasion were willing to accept the validity of revelation, they wanted to extend the vision of the Enlightenment to go beyond ordinary experience to achieve direct union with God because they saw "the universe as far richer and deeper than empirical philosophy would allow" (Kurtz, 1972, Vol. 1, p. 86). They challenged a blind adherence to convention and custom and strived for social progress, they affirmed natural rights and equality, and they labored for the abolition of slavery. In addition, they engaged in social reform, and struggled with philosophical problems such as the human relationship with God, nature, and spirituality (Flower & Murphey, pp. 401–403). Scholars reference transcendentalism's "vitalizing effect upon American art and literature and indeed upon the development of American democracy as a whole" (Spiller, et al, p. 346).[7]

As transcendentalism nudged the complacency of America's intellectual traditions, an evolving public school structure required a cadre of teachers who were qualified in terms of basic knowledge as well as a standard, model, or pattern of teaching. Developments in American culture and thought, and the ideas of the European "sense teachers," sparked the development of the normal school. The normal school pronounced a teaching methodology that went beyond the litany of memorization and recall, and beyond the subject disciplines of the curriculum as separate forms of knowledge. Drawing upon the philosophic "social contract" of Rousseau (1712–1778) and educational visionaries of the nineteenth century, such as Frederick Froebel, Johann Pestalozzi, and Johann Herbart, it offered a kind of natural pedagogy that emphasized the integration of mental, moral, and manual education. Their efforts reflect Rousseau's theories of natural goodness, the importance of sense data, the natural environment, and a notion of interest and "child centeredness" (Butts & Cremin, 1964, pp. 380–381).[8]

As the normal school contributed to the professional development of teaching, it also supported the emergence of the "principal teacher" and what might be called "proto-supervision," which is the earliest phase of in-school supervision such as it appears in the early definition of the principal-teacher's role. In addition to "keeping school," these definitions begin to prescribe that "oversight" should include the review of teaching performance and some measure of "staff-development" of working with teachers on matters related to classroom organization, management, curriculum, and teaching method. The development of the normal school was a signal event in the development of supervision. If there was a "norm" for teaching practice, then it could be taught, observed, and supervised.[9]

Another dimension of teacher education in the nineteenth century was the "teacher institute," which is akin to what we call staff development in the form of workshops or short courses. Tanner and Tanner (1987, pp. 20–21) indicate that the term *institute* was first used in connection with a 2-week convention for teachers in Ithaca, New York, in 1843. These activities helped to spread the normal school presence widely among teachers and school districts (Harper, 1939). They were to provide information about successful methods of "arranging the studies and conducting the disciplines of instruction of public schools" (Tanner & Tanner, 1987, pp. 20–21), which was an idea as expressed by early superintendents gained:

ground among those entrusted with the supervision of our schools, that all who will shall have the opportunity of improving; and that those who will not, shall no longer desecrate the educational temples of our land, nor disgrace a profession which ought to be as sacred as the priesthood (Blumberg, 1985, p. 63).[10]

Following the Civil War, William Torey Harris was the most commanding figure in American education (Curti, 1957, pp. 310–347). He was a teacher for 8 years, he served as superintendent of the St. Louis public schools (1868–1880), and was subsequently as the U.S. commissioner of education (1889–1906). His career combined the study of idealistic philosophy and educational leadership. He studied Hegel and worked to professionalize school administration. He was the "great consolidator of the pre–Civil War victories" in American education (Cremin, 1961, p. 15).[11]

After 1870, school administration advanced and directed attention to the organization of schools and school systems. Leaders such as E. E. White, Francis W. Parker, and W. N.

Hailman agreed that the purpose of the school was "to develop the innate abilities of each individual. Education was a process of *unfolding*, a developmentof the unique qualities of each individual . . . the teacher was to be an artist," said White, whose methods "must bear the impress of the teacher's image and pulsate with the life which he breathes into it" (Callahan & Button, 1964, pp. 73–74). White (1871) petitioned for supervision that would cultivate the artistry of teaching and avoid the dangers of "mechanical supervision" while recognizing that "supervision must secure conformity. . . . produce certain results and awaken and encourage a spirit of professional inquiry and experiment." He asks:

How can a corps of teachers be subjected to efficient supervision without reducing them to operative? The difficulty lies in the fact that success involves the adjustment of two apparently antagonistic principles. That there be necessary system, there must be a good degree of uniformity in instruction and management, and, in order that the teacher may do true work, he must have freedom. All operative work fails in the school room. Men and women are not educated by machinery. The teacher must be an artist, working by his own methods and embodying his own ideas. It is only when he rises to this standard that he uses his best powers.

Like his counterparts in New York, Boston, Philadelphia, and Chicago, Harris was faced with thousands of children and too few teachers and classrooms. He started grading schools, with students moving through on the basis of regular and frequent examinations. Harris adhered to supervisory practices that were successfully used in Boston, Chicago, and Cincinnati, where the primary schools, which were "tributary" to the grammar schools, were under the supervision of the grammar school principal. Harris wrote (1871) that:

Our principals as beginning supervisors as well as instructors and the schools under their charge are becoming uniform in their degree of excellence. Close daily supervision is the only method of securing the desired result and one can scarcely believe how great a degree of efficiency may be regarded in a corps of teachers of average ability, until he actually sees it exists . . . under the management of a principal who knows how to perform his duty (Pierce, 1935, p. 61).

Like Franklin, Harris believed in rugged individualism, yet he supported industrial development and urbanization as benefiting the spread of a better life—less mindful of the severe problems to accompany these developments (Curti, 1959, p. 319). He "constructed" an educational philosophy that he hoped would create a truly democratic community in the emerging urban, industrial America of his day (Cremin, 1988, p. 164).

How different was Harris' idealism from the evolutionary perspectives of Darwinism (*The Origin of Species*, 1859) that stimulated scientific explanation beyond the physical sciences to the concerns of psychology and the social sciences (Hofstadter, 1959)? As Darwin recorded in his notebook: "[T]he line of argument often pursued throughout my theory is to establish a point as a probability by induction and to apply it as a hypothesis to other points and see if it will solve them" (Herbert, 1987, p. 9). The spirit of science would converge with compelling social, economic, and political forces:

the reconstruction of a nation; the human problems attendant to a tide of immigrants of varied cultured backgrounds; the challenges and miseries of industrialization, and the incessant growth of cities and the slums, with their myriad social problems; and the emergence of organizations, agencies, and bureaucratic systems intended to regulate all manner of things in a rational and efficient manner (Cremin, 1961).

America faced another considerable change in the nineteenth century: the end of "economic man," where most individuals engaged with nature and one another in shaping an existence; where personal properties and resilience, together with social and cultural conditions, shaped an individual's options and degrees of freedom (Drucker, 1939). Something important was ending. The frontier experience was about over (Brands, 1995). In its stead, "industrial man" predominated, where individuals are bent to the machine, technical energy, and an impersonal authority. As the frontier disappeared, a new American frontier—cultural and cognitive pluralism—confronted the reality of the nation's ethos (Levine, 1996; Schrag, 1992). Universal forms will need to be reworked, transformed from fixed and finished ideas into active forces to extend the Enlightenment search for a "deeper order of things" (Cassirer, 1951). In this process the transformation of the school was dulled by rigid structures where teaching practices sought "obedience, uniformity, productivity, and other traits required for minimum participation in bureaucratic and industrial organizations" (Cuban, 1984, p. 240). Although there were many instances where educators and social activists provided services according to the needs and interests of children and families, there was, in the schools, a "stubborn continuity" of teacher-centered instruction (Cuban, 1984). This was explained in part by the structure of schools as a reflection of "prevailing social norms, values, and behavior," where pedagogical practices "mirror the norms of the larger class and economic system (as a) primary mechanism for social control" and "deeply embedded" individual and shared beliefs about the purpose of schooling, the role of subject matter, the organization of the classroom; and the exercise of authority (Cuban, 1984, pp. 240–245).

Cuban (1984) summarized the features of public schools in late-nineteenth century America as graded, rows of bolted down desks; where teachers often had limited formal training, and with a rigidly defined curriculum—a stolid picture—"a terrain familiar to teachers and students today" (Cuban, p. 18). Finkelstein's (1989) analysis of teaching practice (i.e., "patterns of teaching") during the same period included an infrequent pattern—the "Interpretor of Culture"—a teacher who, despite an authoritarian tendency to "bring children under the command of rules and regulations," develops a personal and special connection with students:

"No matter what era or culture, material or political setting, there are persistent qualities in the relationship between students and teachers in schools. Nineteenth-century primary school teachers, like generations of teachers before and after them, acted as agents of communication mediating between the symbolic worlds of informal conversation and the more structured ones of books. When they taught students in school, they initiated them into a chain of "interlocking conversations", and introduced new elements into it. The schools over which they presided were specialized universes linking students to the written word, and ways of thinking, seeing, knowing, feeling, believing that might have been otherwise unimaginable" (Finkelstein, 1989, pp. 8–9).

Because instruction is the oft-referenced focus of educational supervision, Cuban's analysis of the persistence of traditional patterns of teaching (1890–1980) is a matter of genuine importance for supervisors. The degree of congruence, the tensions and discontinuities between the belief systems of teachers and supervisors, about the purpose and nature of instruction, is surely at the heart of the matter in developing and expressing a philosophy of supervision. The practice of teaching and the supervision of teaching are deeply rooted in the beliefs from whence theory, decisions, and practice are derived. In this contemporary, postmodernist, post-structionalist age culture is made up of many meanings that individuals use to guide their lives, and their professional activities. For Geertz (1995) "those meanings are inside a culture, not outside it," and they must be "entered and understood, like a novel." In these terms the job of the supervisor is in part to facilitate the discourse needed to make belief systems more public and intelligible among people and organizational groups. Pritzkau (1959) advanced this theme as "total value admissions," as distinct from "total value acceptance" where the curriculum leader/supervisor advances the conditions for discourse. An essential aspect of building an environment that respects individuals and builds the sense of community. This does not mean an absence of values and beliefs on the part of the supervisor; rather, it suggests that diversity of beliefs, "when ingeniously juxtaposed," can shed light on one another to abate the seemingly irreconcilable gap between "me and you"/"Us and Them" (Geertz, 1995). These values set aside the tenets of inspection for public engagement about the goals, knowledge, and values of education/instruction that aspires to advance citizenship, virtue, and the common good. This is more the promise of educational supervision, however, because the evolution of complex organizations and bureaucracies in nineteenth-century America offered a conceptual system for the continuation of educational supervision as inspection. This is a philosophy virtually mandated by the growth of population centers, the power of business and industry, the grading of schools, an expanding curriculum, increasing cultural diversity, and a burgeoning school system urgently attending to matters of organization, management, and control. As Glanz (1991) recounts:

Superintendents sought to legitimize their control over schools . . . and in their zeal to gain control and increase efficiency . . . supervision became little more than an institutional, perfunctory mechanism by which the superintendent would manage and maintain control over schools. A school system based on bureaucratic organization, with supervision as the primary means to oversee school operations, they thought, would serve the best interests of American education. The fallacy of such an agreement would soon be clearly evident; however, relief would fall short of expectation.

In this period of development supervision as inspection runs its course, reflecting a view of humanity that is bounded by history and the precepts of "old world" traditions that were eventually moderated by Enlightenment ideals of human nature and social institutions. It reflects traditional (Essentialism) philosophy (Ornstein, 1992, pp. 13–16). Beliefs and values were fixed and universal (i.e., in the manner of knowledge that was revealed), as part of a defined religious and cultural heritage. The curriculum and the role of the teacher conformed to this heritage. Knowledge was fixed, subjects were codified, and instruction in the oral tradition was the rule. In its best sense school was to preserve this heritage and supervision was to insure its transmission, but there were stirrings. Emerson views "mankind" as essentially good, engaged in a "struggle for personal integration" through the "creative achievements of human culture" where concern for traditional ideals and absolutes are humanized and challenged, for life's purpose is to acquaint each man with himself (Moran, 1972, Vol. 2, p. 477). Darwinism was to "undermine the established authority of idealism" and change the idea of nature from a "fixed system into one of dynamic change" where "substance and essence were replaced by process and event" (Kurtz, 1972, Vol. 1, p. 87). In sum:

When the Protestant dissenters from Europe tended to become the conformists of America, the spirit of the frontier and new waves of immigration forced them either to retreat or to develop. The mind of this country could not allow itself to slacken for long on a single line of thought. Cotton Mather was offset by the Enlightenment and the transcendentalism of Emerson and Josiah Royce by the pragmatism of William James and John Dewey (Ulich, 1961, pp. 273–274).

From the period of the colonial "transplantation" to the cultural diversity of contemporary America, the need for educational supervision that engages and respects people, and sets conditions for the construction of personal knowledge, is clear. Supervision as inspection, however, will persist in different forms as the champion of a tired and frequently debilitating idea.

Supervision and Social Efficiency[12]

Early twentieth-century America experienced continued immigration, urbanization, and industrialization. There were 19 cities with a population of 100,000 or more in 1880. By 1900 the number had increased to 36, and to 50 by 1910. There were two streams of immigrants to the cities: from rural America and from foreign lands (Morrison & Comminger, 1962, p. 449). The attendant problems were complex: The dissonance between the individualistic moral code of an agrarian society with that of an industrial and integrated social order; the reach of big business and its control of material resources and labor; the unequal distribution of wealth; and the denial of constitutional and political rights to blacks and other minorities (Comminger, pp. 443–444).

This tremendous growth in urban America put great pressure on all forms of social service. City governments, often plagued by corruption and graft, struggled with the assistance of private agencies to respond to the need of the diverse population of city dwellers. The municipal leaders were the frequent target of "muckrakers" who sought to uncover corruption in American officialdom.

Karier (1982, p. 7) views this industrial development as pivotal to the nation's systems of "mass production, distribution, and consumption," and with it the emergence of the "regulatory state" spawned by political progressives of the era as they sought to "rationalize and regulate the political, social economy." A productivity revolution took hold as the ideas of scientific management (i.e., planning, analysis, organization, and production) were "trumpeted" across industrial America (Drucker, 1993). Under these circumstances, the building and organization of schools was a major undertaking. They became a ready target for social engineering and the precepts of industrial technology and management. Campbell et al (1987) described this period:

In the wake of the massive social and economic upheaval . . . scientific management seemed to offer a way of bringing logic and organization to production processes while, at the same time, it tilted the pendulum of authority from industrial decisions to management—where they would more directly control what was perceived to be a recalcitrant work force (Campbell et al, 1987, p. 25).

In 1881, Frederick W. Taylor was a foreman in a steel plant. He began to apply knowledge to the analysis and engineering of work. Taylor, who had problems with eyesight, set aside a university education and took a job as an apprentice machinist, where his metal work inventions eventually made him wealthy. Although he is often viewed as a champion of the management class, Drucker indicates that Taylor was concerned about the antipathy between management and labor, and that Taylor's main concern "was for the creation of a society in which capitalists and workers had a common interest in productivity . . . and to improve efficiency" (Drucker, (1994)[13, 14]

One of Taylor's goals was to promote a relationship where the worker could benefit from productivity because "the knowledge which every journeyman has of his trade is his most valuable possession. It is his great life capital" (Gross, 1964). Taylor's first innovation was to gather knowledge about the work process, tabulate it, improve it through analysis and further tabulation, and finally reduce it to "laws, rules, and even mathematical formula" (Gross, p. 123). Through careful observation of a worker's performance he wanted to discern the best array of work procedures to the benefit of efficiency and the goals of the organization. This process enabled Taylor to standardize work in terms of method and tools. Workers ostensibly could be assigned a job for which they were best fitted, through selection and training. Taylor challenged tradition and applied research to the world of work, avowing that such analysis permitted the "exploration" of the worker's development, "allowing him to advance to the highest level that his natural abilities would allow"; "that it was cooperation between labor and capital that brought success." For Taylor this "was the most important message" (Perrow, 1979, pp. 63–64). There was considerable resistance to Taylor's methods of analysis for he proposed a division of tasks among supervisors with the consequence that the line production worker was receiving directions from different managers and technical experts (Gross, 1964, p. 124). Managers failed, he suggested, because they had not devel-

oped the structures necessary to bring order and discipline to the workplace. Taylor (1911) attacked the "old world" system of management where each worker had the final responsibility for a job, was isolated in the workplace, and had little advice from the management (p. 25). He proposed that management gather all the "traditional knowledge" possessed by the "workmen" as the initial step in building a "science" of work, followed by training and "hearty cooperation," with an "equal division of the work" between the workmen and management (pp. 36–37), where management takes on the responsibility of organizing and planning. This science of work consists of task analysis (p. 39), time and motion studies, training, and close cooperation between management and the workmen—"the essence of modern scientific or task management" (p. 26).

Taylor (pp. 120–121) related his task analysis concept to the school as:

No efficient teacher would think of giving a class of students an indefinite lesson to learn. Each day a definite, clear-cut task is set by the teacher before each scholar; stating that he must learn just so much of the subject; and it is only by this means that proper systematic progress can be made by the students. The average boy would go very slowly if, instead of being given a task, he was told to do as much as he could. All of us are grown-up children, and it is equally true that the average workman will work with the greatest satisfaction, both to himself, and to his employer, when he is given each day a definite task which he is to perform in a given time, and which constitutes a proper day's work for a good workman. This furnishes the workman with a clear cut standard, by which he can, throughout the day measure his own progress, and the accomplishment of which affords him the greatest satisfaction.

Another Taylor, J. S. (1912), proposed the fundamentals of scientific management to the organization of a school system: (1) where the industrial task analysis system is applied, and "experts" supervise the teacher and "suggest the processes that are most efficacious and economical"; and (2) where teachers who accomplish the prescribed tasks are given a bonus, and "those who are unable to do the work are eliminated, either thru the device of a temporary license or of a temporary employment" (p. 351).

Pajak (1993) registers a strong caution as to the effect of Taylor's theories on educational supervision. He agrees that there was some link, "but its impact is often vastly overestimated." He references Callahan and Button (1964) and their view that scientific management had but moderate influence on educational supervision because "the problems of supervision and of teaching method were not readily amenable to investigation in the management frame of reference nor with the techniques available" (Callahan & Button, 1964, p. 90). Many reform-minded American educators, however, were drawn to Taylor's ideas, caught-up in the storm of social criticism and the political reform of progressivism. They found a degree of congruence between Taylor's principles of supervisory management and the developing science of education: Thorndike's (1911) Law of Effect and Law of Exercise, and Woodworth's (1901) work on the transfer of training, and the themes of "Progressivism" in education," the use of the schools to improve the lives of individuals," and the application "in the classroom of pedagogical principles derived from new scientific research in psychology and the social sciences" (Cremin, 1961). The tremendous growth in school population, bureaucratization, the diversity of cultural backgrounds of the students, and the escalating costs of education were accompanied by calls for reduced expenditures and overall efficiency (Campbell, 1991, p. 22) as a palliative to these conditions.

Given this "efficiency movement" educational supervisors directed their attention to the needs and the perceived "deficits" of teachers with on-the-job training and the determination of "objective standards and specifications for the educational product" (Bolin & Panaritis, 1992, p. 34). Indeed,

Franklin Bobbitt (1913) called for standardization in the curriculum, based on the real life needs of adult citizens. . . . Charters developed a framework for thinking about teaching . . . and supervisors began devising rating scales for measuring teacher efficiency and effectiveness in ways that they believed to be more objective than had previously been possible" (Bolin & Panaritis, p. 34).

Scientific management and bureaucratic supervisory methods would "legitimate and secure a niche for control-oriented supervision with the school bureaucracy" (Glanz, 1996).

Sergiovanni and Starratt (1993, p. 12) describe scientific management as a "classic autocratic philosophy of supervision" where workers are "appendages of management and, as such, are hired to carry out prespecified duties in accordance with the wishes of management." Their translation of scientific management to educational supervision is addressed in the following:

[T]eachers are viewed as implementors of prescribed curriculum systems; close supervision is practiced to ensure that they are teaching in accordance with approved guidelines and teaching protocols; control, accountability, and efficiency are emphasized within an atmosphere of clear-cut, manager-subordinate relationships. Though vestiges of this brand of supervision can still be found in schools, by and large traditional scientific management is not currently in favor. Its basic premises and precepts, however, are still thought to be attractive by many policymakers, administrators, and supervisors. The ideas have not changed, but strategies for implementing them have.

The ideas included in this summary statement correspond to Smyth's (1991a) position that it takes more than "changing the lexicon" to rid educational supervision from the vestiges of scientific management because "the real issues go far deeper, frequently to the very basis of the intent and purpose of the supervisory process" (Smyth, 1991a, p. 5).

Raymond E. Callahan's book, *Education and the Cult of Efficiency* (1962), offers historical analysis and insight on the efficiency movement in education. Karier (1982, p. 8), however, questions Callahan's portrayal of educators as being vulnerable to business pressures. Karier refers to the scholarship of Joseph Cronin, *Control of Urban Schools,* and David Tyack's *One Best System* (1974) as showing "that school leaders were not as much victims of business influence and pressure as they were exponents of it" (Karier, p. 8). In this

regard, Tyack (1974, pp. 126–147) recounts the centralization movement and the acceptance of the corporate model in urban education, where "the new school managers" supported the vesting of "power in a small committee of successful men" in order "to emulate the process of decision-making used by men on the board of directors of a modern business corporation." They would help to reorganize schools to fit the new economic and social conditions of an urban–industrial society and ridiculed the "exceedingly democratic idea that all are equal," urging that "schooling be adapted to social stratification" (Tyack, p. 126). This description links to Pajak's (1993, p. 163) discussion of Edward C. Elliott's writing on the distinction between "administrative efficiency" and "supervisory efficiency," where the former demands "centralization of administrative power" and the latter "required decentralized, cooperative, expert supervision." Bureaucratization, with its centralized professional authority, aimed to keep the schools separate from inept and politically corrupt control, and to advance the use of "systematic and efficient" supervisory activities as a necessary condition for the support and improvement of teaching (Glanz, 1991, pp. 42–43).

The pursuit of efficiency was a struggle to produce goods and services, and in the private industrial sector to produce wealth. For most individuals the struggle was to survive during a period of rapid change, where energy and skills were necessary to secure a livelihood, given the dependence upon the fortunes of an unpredictable and impersonal industrial system. The realities of mechanized work (i.e., conformity, hostile work environments, and attendant social problems) were almost Dickensian.

The culture of the production system requires the constant refinements of science, technology, and engineering. It requires particular skills, prescribed performance, from management and the work force. Training and retraining are constant features of industrial efficiency. A "Web of Rules" governs the relationship of supervisor and worker. Rights, duties, and responsibilities are explicitly defined: "The industrial system creates an elaborate 'government' at the work place or community" (Kerr et al, 1960, p. 41). In this context, the moral code of the individualistic agrarian society is set aside. "There is no place for the extended family"; its function is restricted, and "it engages in very little production; it provides little, if any, formal education and occupational training; the family is substantially displaced by professional management" (Kerr et al, pp. 35–36). Industrial living was a clash of cultures, of language, and of values. A vision of what was possible was reserved for the few, while the many were bound to work in situations that constrained thought and denied individuality. This was the time of "industrial man," when resources, including those human, were used to maximize profit with a minimum of expenditure and human support services. Reality was the condition of the balance sheet, not an awareness of the difficulties of the human condition. Knowledge and the evidence needed to confirm it were discovered through the code of observation and sense-data, as preface to task analysis, and the measurement of the industrial credo: efficiency and effectiveness.

To the extent that educational leaders and supervisors acquiesced to the formulas and mandates of industrial efficiency, they were remaking the belief system, either knowingly or by default, around which supervisory programs and activities had heretofore developed. In keeping with supervision in decades past the inspectional character of the supervisor's work remained constant, but there was a departure in that the system of beliefs shifted to accommodate changing concepts of reality and knowledge. *Reality* was the struggle of survival, of being, in the here and now. The educational supervisor espoused the particulars of the teaching method, the use of time: the standardization of the curriculum and the "educational product," and the use of rating scales for measuring teacher effectiveness (Bolin & Panaritis, 1992, p. 34). The individual teacher as a source of ideas was not a consideration because conformity and bureaucratic structures ruled the day. Under these circumstances the tones of idealism and universal truths, where knowledge and the good life are found in tradition, faith, and reason, were muted. Discovery, science, technology, and objectivity forged systems of knowledge production that challenged traditions and announced the concept of the supervisor as an authority based on status in the school hierarchy. The advancement of supervision as a professional collegial function was to await another day.

Efficiency endures as a driving force in many schools. Whether it reflects a political accountability mentality or an earnest professional commitment that goes beyond the bounds of organizational concepts (e.g., mission, goals, objectives, instructional strategies, "systems analysis," and "total quality management") remains to be seen. Where efficiency is an authentic commitment, it seeks to arrange the conditions of learning to support the intellectual, emotional, and moral development of each student. It reflects a belief system that assumes that human intelligence can be developed, and that everyone has the ability to learn. Finally, it tries to affirm the primacy of teaching and human potential.

In this sense, educational efficiency is a state of mind, a blending of the particulars of reality, resources, and collegial decision-making in support of learning. It is distant from an idea of "industrial man," where individuals are pressed to conform so as to maximize predetermined results. Educational supervision drawn in the image of efficiency may be rational and predictable in its commitment to the primacy of the instructional program. It may be energized in the pursuit of objectives in the face of obstacles and imperfect information, it may be dynamic and participatory in its expression, or it may be ritualized, characterized by "mindless doing," impersonal action, and regulated by rules and procedures that sap instruction of its vitality, while fermenting self-interest and competition.

This efficiency business appears beholden to science, pragmatism, and the pressures of modernity. The "genteel tradition" of American philosophy, Calvinism, and transcendentalism is eroded, if not supplanted, by the pragmatism of Pierce and James, a "theory of thought and truth . . . where ideas are not mirrors, they are weapons; their function is to prepare us to meet events, as future experience may unroll them" (Santayana, 1913). In something of a lament, Santayana cautions about the limitations of such systems of thought:

Everywhere is beauty and nowhere is permanence, everywhere an incipient harmony, nowhere an intention, nor a responsibility, nor a plan. It is the irresistible suasion of this daily spectacle, it is the daily contact with things so different from the verbal discipline of the schools, that will, I trust, inspire the philosophy of your children.

Smyth (1984) would not offer much solace regarding Santayana's petition because he finds the features of supervision as inspection/social efficiency persisting:

Despite a half century of cooperative supervision, human relations supervision, supervision as curricular development, and various other forms of supervision in schools, it is not clear that even today we have severed the connection between supervision and the industrial–managerial model with which it has been so closely affiliated.

Democratic Supervision

The efficiency movement of early twentieth-century America came under strong criticism from workers, trade unions, and federal agencies. As society registered concern about the plight of workers and families, corporate reform began to take stock of the nature of work and the psychology of human behavior (Campbell, et al, 1987, p. 4). Those who petitioned for greater democratic control of affairs were countered by the theme of individualism and competition as the true reflection of the American ethos (Butts Cremin, p. 351). In the face of these tensions, John Dewey's, *Democracy in Education* (1916) illuminated an educational theory and pedagogy that seemed consistent with the needs and stated ideals of an increasingly diverse, democratically inclined society.

In the early 1880s, while teaching high school, Dewey struggled with the conflicting authorities of religion and science. He eventually worked out a theory of truth that described the human mind interacting with the "contingencies of an unstable, ever-evolving nature," and that the contradictions of reality are best seen as "fruitful collisions yielding, in the Hegelian sense to a higher synthesis of thought" (Diggins, 1989, p. 79). He concluded that thought seeks to change reality, that it is brought into existence, that it is made, it is utility, "and its meaning lies in its consequences and its value is its usefulness" (Diggins, 1989, p. 79). As Dewey reworked pragmatic theory, he brought together the logic of Charles Pierce and the humanism of William James, and reformulated pragmatism into a "theory of the general forms of conception and reasoning," and instrumentalism, which sought to bridge the dualism in modern thought—"the separation of science and values, knowledge and morals" (Thayer, 1972, Vol. 6, p. 434).

To some observers, *pragmatism* describes an "expedient approach to things, ungoverned by moral principle." For Dewey, however, it was a challenge to the traditional methods of finding truth. His pragmatism rejected the assumption that the test for truth

is the correspondence between our thoughts about the world and the world as it really is. At the heart of pragmatism was the notion that the truth of a statement or belief depends on its usefulness in making sense and guiding action (Sandel, 1996, p. 35).

Dewey's philosophy helped Americans to make their peace with the modern world (i.e., to address the alternatives) between science and faith, individualism and community, and democracy and expertise (Sandel, 1996). In his philosophical pursuits, Dewey explores education as a necessity of life, as a social function, and as a process of growth:

A society which makes provision for participation in its good of all its members on equal terms and which secures flexible, readjustment of its institutions through interaction of the different forms of associated life is insofar democratic. Such a society must have a type of education which gives individuals a personal interest in social relationships and control, and the habits of mind which secure social changes without the introduction of disorder (Democracy and Education, 1916, p. 99).

In this view of things, intelligence is not a function of faculty psychology to be trained through exercise, nor is it a pursuit "of truth for its own sake; it is a process of making over one's environment into something more satisfactory to one's needs and desires." In its very essence, it involves action (Spiller, et al, 1963, p. 1280).

A fundamental idea of Dewey's educational philosophy is the unity of the "intimate and necessary relation between the process of actual experience and education"; he was aware that the general principles of his progressive ideas do not solve the problems of the practical management of schools; rather, they set new problems that have to be worked out on the basis of a new philosophy of experience (Dewey, 1929). He cautioned that an educational philosophy, based on freedom and experience, may become as dogmatic as the tradition it challenges if its theory and practices "are not based upon critical examination of its own underlying principles" (Dewey, 1929). Education was central to Dewey's pragmatism and democratic yearnings. It was a process that would cultivate the habits of mind and character, intellectual and moral patterns that would enable citizens to take up the "mutual responsibilities of a shared public life." This kind of education combined schooling with the work of other social and political institutions. Schools for Dewey "would be small communities that would prepare children to engage in a democratic public life . . . to advance the common good" (Sandel, p. 36).

In the Deweyean school rote learning is banished; rather, students explore problems whose solutions make a difference in practice. Their interest would be maintained by dealing with problems that arose in the course of their own growth. Prescription from the outside world would be reduced and experimentation encouraged, and subject matter would be adjusted to the child, rather than the child to the subject matter. The old distinction between cultural and vocational training would be abolished, for that part of the environment is most important part. Much of the child's education would consist of active involvement with things, ideas, and cooperative activities (Spiller, et al, pp. 1281–1282).

In the Child and Curriculum (1902), Dewey petitioned against the traditional, scholastic notion of the curriculum. Subject matter, he affirmed, was not "something fixed and ready-made in itself, outside of the child's experience as something hard and fast." He conjectured on the nature of the world in which the child lived and offered the child as the "starting point, the center, and the end." The development and the growth of the child is the ideal. "It alone furnished the standard; to the growth of the child, all studies are subservient; they are instruments valued as they serve the needs of growth" (p. 9). In the School and Society, first published in 1899, Dewey dealt with the school's social aspects: the school in relation to the growth of children, and the school as an institution. In this latter regard, he was concerned with the waste of human potential when organization is wanting and hurtful to the process of education. He wrote:

[S]o when we speak of organization, we are not to think simply of the externals; of that which goes by the name "School System"—the School Board, the Superintendent, and the building, the gauging and promotion of teachers, etc. These things enter in but the fundamental organization is that of the school itself as a community of individuals in its relations to other forms of social life. All waste is due to isolation. Organization is nothing, but getting things into connection with one another, so that they work easily, flexibly, and fully. I desire to call your attention to the isolation of the various parts of the school system, to the lack of unity in the aims of education, to the lack of coherence in its studies and methods (School and Society, pp. 63–64).

Not all informed observers supported Dewey's "break with tradition." Robert Maynard Hutchins, then the young president of the University of Chicago, responded to Dewey's instrumental concept of education with a series of forceful books, including The Higher Learning in America (1936) and Education for Freedom (1943). Hutchins discounted Dewey's instrumental concept of thinking and education, while affirming "that truth is everywhere the same . . . at any time, in any place, under any political, social, or economic conditions" (1936, p. 66), and adding, that the schools should, "leave experience to life, and set about our job of intellectual training" (1936, p. 70).

The meaning and the importance of Dewey's perspectives have remained controversial, often on the basis of personal taste rather than on careful appraisal and critical judgment, which is problematic but not unusual in the assessment of ideas and social action. If the organization and process of education is to be expressed in the spirit and practice of democracy, in accordance with the principles of individual growth and development, then matters of school organization and leadership must be similarly ordered. Because the philosophy, curriculum, and instructional program of the school are most specifically manifest in the actions and decision-making of teachers, the congruence of their efforts with the notion of education as experience, problem-solving, and personal development will be advanced by supervision that values individuals and collegiality in the exploration and development of plans of action. This recognition of supervision as a necessary adjunct to the support of teaching in a democratic mode asks that matters of efficiency and inspection be recognized for what they are—predetermined casts that mold or shape a product or result with a consequence of limited meaning, use, and potential. It is surely much more difficult to open matters of collegial interaction and authority, yet they are most likely the conditions that will sustain inspired and vitalized teaching. Tocqueville's comment on the intellectual character of democracy in America is that "democracy pushed to its furthest limits is . . . prejudical to the art of government." We sense, by observation and experience, that our social institutions, including education, have scarcely approached our limits. There is no evidence that democratic principles and processes have been overused; indeed, we have not had a glimpse of such limits.

Democracy is not a "rampant pursuit of self-interest but the unfolding of a person's distinctive capacities." It is a "way of life that educates citizens to be capable of intelligent action" (Sandel, 1996, p. 35). Glanz (Chap. 2) and Campbell et al. (1987) detail some of the factors contributing to the rise of democratic supervision in the 1920s, such as the quest for professional stature, various dimensions of organizational development, and required expertise. The dominant theme, however, was the improvement of instruction. Glanz reviews what he describes as a "classic article" by James Hosic: "Democratization of Supervision" (1920). This article resolutely declares the important mission of supervision as equated with educational statesmanship. In Hosic's terms, the supervisor must build a relationship with teachers that reflects mutual trust and confidence. This relationship is sustained by consultation, mutual engagement in matters of instruction, and empathetic leadership because the supervisor's role is "many sided," being "first in enterprise, first in effort, first in appreciation, first in the hearts of his colleagues" (Hosic, 1920, p. 334). These conditions are supported by professional preparation, scientific standards, and concern for the human side of the enterprise, all of which converge as a testimony of will and shared commitments. Supervision, Hosic affirms, succeeds as it nurtures a learning environment, problem-solving, construction of knowledge and an ethical disposition which reflects the primacy of people. It is distant from the precepts of "scientific management"; it expresses an approach to supervision that avoids bureaucratic entanglements and leadership based on traditional authority.

This idea of democratic supervision is in stark contrast to the corporate view of educational organization where the emphasis is on jurisdictional areas, regulations, official duties, authority, and technical superiority (Roth & Wittich, 1978, p. 973). The corporate/bureaucratic system has a badge of precision about it; individuals have relatively unambiguous roles and responsibility; there appears to be the mark of knowledge, continuity, unity, and, ostensibly, a reduction of friction. The office holder in such an organization has typically completed a course of study, has a working capacity related to a role with prescribed functions, has a distinctly elevated status, especially where the demand for expert capacity is required and is evidence (Roth & Wittich, pp. 958–959). In the Weberian sense bureaucracies "will develop more perfectly the more it is dehumanized, the more completely it succeeds in eliminating . . . all purely irrational and emotional elements." Bureaucracy, however, inevitably accompanies mass democracy as a mechanism to insure equal treatment and opportunity in organizational life or before the court (Roth & Wittich, p. 983). The democratization of society is favorable for bureaucratization, although democracy riles against a distant and privileged class of leaders whose rule often stifles the spontaneity, freedom, and self-realization of their employees, which are the hallmark conditions of a democratic system.

The democratic view of school leadership evolved as a result of change in school organization and as a reaction away from autocratic and authoritarian supervisory practices. It drew its strength from the ideas of educational reformers and was founded on beliefs about democratic rights, cooperation, and the nature of social organizations (Campbell, 1987, pp. 49–50). We well know that democracy means shared governance—it provides for personal participation in policy deliberations and decisions. All members of the organization ideally have an opportunity to contribute and to influence decisions where each person's voice carries a weight related to the merit of the idea presented. An indispensable part of democratic process is a lively and educationally concerned professional cohort. Apathy is detrimental to the deliberative process because the strength and the validity of ideas, proposals, and decisions will be determined by the range of ideas, experience, and insight that is directed to the matter under consideration. Because situations are continuously in a state of flux the supervisor, as an agent of instructional development, has a responsibility to engage with individuals and groups in a manner that sets the conditions for mutual consideration, for a professional "dialectical" approach to supervision, that "not only regards teaching problematically, but which mobilizes teachers into dialogue among themselves toward pedagogical consciousness about teaching and the broader social context of their work" (Smyth, 1991, p. 32). A democratic setting or culture can nurture such discourse because it ascribes to a deliberate process where "what's right" is a search, not a product. It is a process for formulating a plan(s) of action and gathering resources. The focus of the process is the construction of knowledge, however tentative, being subject to use and modifiable depending upon results, new ideas, or change in the context. It is not the "engineering of consent" (Apple & Beane, 1995, p. 5); rather, it is an authentic expression of a belief system that expresses:

1. The open flow of ideas, regardless of their popularity
2. Faith in the individual and collective capacity of people to create possibilities for resolving problems
3. The use of critical reflection and analysis to evaluate ideas, problems, and policies
4. Concern for the welfare of others and "the common good"
5. Concern for the dignity and rights of individuals and minorities
6. An understanding that democracy is more than idealized set of values that guide, must guide, our life as a people than an "ideal" to be pursued
7. The organization of social institutions to promote and extend the democratic way of life (Apple & Beane, pp. 6–7)

A significant issue concerns the "reconciliation of democracy and expertise" (Mohr, 1994). Supervisors are assigned roles, functions, and responsibilities that equate to power. The assumption of these assignments is knowledge and expertise. Does this conflict with a democratic and transforming approach to supervision? Is "democratic supervision" an academic notion separate from the reality of the school as a complex organization? Does equalizing legitimate power do away with the "coordinating benefits" of hierarchical structure? Our reading of Mohr suggests that the "conflict" may be reconciled where the goals of the organization are grasped as shared purposes; where the "workers" and the experts are "one and the same people"; where a "voluntaristic" model of democracy pervades the organization; and where the right to exercise authority is up to the individual to decide when and where to assert that right. Mohr's "voluntarist" pattern of participation is one that requires official authority to be decentralized, but *not* the actual exercise of authority." He emphasizes the importance of agreement about goals/purpose and "quality norms" as the basis for reconciling the dilemma of democracy and expertise, which is generally seen in unit organizations such as schools as a precondition to the growth and development of people, the construction of knowledge, and the advance of the school as a learning community.

Dewey's pragmatic philosophy was one of action, rather than contemplation, as well as the authentic voice of an American democratic philosophy (Spiller, et al, 1963, p. 77). His democratic principles have challenged succeeding generations to promote the participation of its members in the quest for the "good life," and "such a society must have a type of education which gives individuals a personal interest in social relationships . . . and the habits of mind which secure social changes without introducing disorder" (*Democracy and Education*, p. 99).

Ravitch (1983) explored the contributions of Dewey's philosophy to the progressive movement in education and faults the leadership of that movement for being more political than intellectual. She recognizes that the political instinct of the movement has been the basis for much of Dewey's influence, "for the American public has expected education to solve complex social problems" (Diggins, 1989, p. 80). On the other hand, Ravitch reports that the "radical faith" of the early progressives that "culture could be democratized without being vulgarized" (Cremin, 1961) was forgotten and that the progressive inclinations of the professional establishment "had strayed far from the humane, pragmatic, open minded approach advocated by John Dewey; it had deteriorated into a cult whose principles were taught as dogma and whose critics were treated as dangerous heretics" (Ravitch, 1983, p. 79).

Democratic supervision is a dramatic departure from the traditions of inspection and the rigid protocols of the efficiency movement. It values the uniqueness of individuals, the human experience, and the belief in practical intelligence that does not deny, but is also not confined by the traditions of the past. Democratic supervision affirms the process of constructing knowledge, not receiving (i.e., idealism) or discovering (i.e., realism) it. Democratic supervision conceives of knowledge and ideas, as plans of action, to be tested in the design of educational environments as instruments of development, change, and social reconstruction. Such a process is accepted as an idea to be tested, not as an article of faith or discovered truth. Democratic supervision exalts in the energy of a learning community that sparks imagination and the involvement of different constituents. Democratic supervision is enriched by knowledge and experience as a point of departure for the release of creative thinking and practical judgments, not as a pattern of truth. Democratic supervision has

a different perspective on reality, the notion or idea of knowledge, and the values that guide the decisions by which we live. It remains to be seen whether or not a democratic philosophy of educational supervision can contend with the ambiguities and tensions of knowledge construction and alternative values that it affirms to cherish.

Scientific Supervision

Supervision in the modern age was bound to affirm the spirit and methods of science. This age of discovery, relative values, and tentative truths was reflected in patterns of scholarship, economic productivity, the organization of work, and social organization. Given such cultural dynamics, supervision stepped away from the thinking of the past to a posture where knowledge and its uses were to be discovered. There would be less deference to the traditions of revelation and an antecedent reality. In his examination of "Conceptions of Knowledge" and the school curriculum, Schrag (1992) speaks of the scientific tradition as a "hybrid"—a combination "of the philosophical and apprenticeship traditions" where knowledge and understanding are discovered—a tradition that is "forward-rather than backward-looking." This tradition prepared the advent of "educational science," including supervision. It served to promote the professionalization of educational supervision as a legitimate actor in the administrative structure. Scientific supervision required that authority and status would be conferred on the basis of training, experience, knowledge, and expertise. Educational supervisors were to grasp the methods of science (i.e., structured observation, experimentation, and measurement) as a device for concept formation, theory building, and the definition of supervisory activities consonant with educational principles derived from democratic dispositions.

Science has been described as an "institutionalized art of inquiry" (Nagel, 1961). It often promotes the achievement of "reliable knowledge concerning fundamental determining conditions" as to various events and places. For Nagel science contributes to "the emancipation of the mind" from ancient fears and superstitions. It serves to shake the "intellectual foundations" of traditional dogmas and to weaken "unreasoned customs" that provide the "protective cover for the continuation of social injustices." It challenges the merits of alternative assumptions "concerning matters of fact and social policy" (Nagel, p. VII). Dewey's reconstruction in philosophy portrayed science as a process of pursuit, not a coming into possession of immutable truths, but a process that, "eschews the domination of custom" where the great innovators in science "are the first to fear and doubt their discoveries."

Pragmatism, which is the philosophical stance of Pierce, Dewey, and James, allied with science to challenge traditional discourse in favor of examining the consequences of thinking, actions, and experience. The idea of ultimate certainty was rejected as a mythology of times past. In its place pragmatism, given its action-oriented nature, attached itself to all aspects of the American culture (Kurtz, 1967). The connection between science, modernity, and supervision was made real in Frederick Taylor's "Scientific Management" (1911). Recall that Taylor and his colleagues applied knowledge, derived from observation, analysis, and technical definitions, to the study of work and its supervision (Campbell et al, 1987; Drucker, 1993; Gross, 1964). They were quite determined, even passionate, about the use of systematic observation to construct the definition of tasks and required worker performance. In these terms education was increasingly viewed as an applied science wherein theoretical and practical questions about education and learning could be investigated. Educational systems and many university scholars shared a strong "faith" in scientific study that became a hallmark of reform. Educational researchers "embraced the scientific movement" and probed human learning using quantitative scientific procedures to assay virtually everything: physical, mental, and moral qualities, as well as students' abilities, performance, and rates of progress (Campbell et al, 1987).

Scientific supervision was viewed as an answer to the lack of clearly defined standards (McNeil, 1982, p. 18). Under these circumstances, determining efficient teaching methods and effective teaching was difficult at best. Franklin Bobbit (1913) saw scientific supervisors as addressing two initial tasks: "guiding teachers in the selection of methods and preparing and renewing teachers" (McNeil, p. 18). Nutt (1920), who was an early analyst of educational supervision reported that supervisors came to the public schools "in response to a pressing demand for the improvement of teachers." He asserted that supervision entered the educational field

on broad general ideas and theories" gradually becoming more specific in role and function until it became recognized "as a definite educational science distinctly set off from the job of teaching on the one hand and the job of administration on the other hand." And he presaged its future: "the growth and development of this relatively new science will be determined by the worthiness of the contributions that it makes to the training of teachers and the improvement of the work of the public schools" (Nutt, p. 231).

In Barr's work, Bolin discerns an "unwavering" commitment to the "methods of science" that "evolved from . . . an amalgamation of the principles of scientific management and behavioristic psychology to a point of view that recognized science as a tool for thinking about and seeking to understand phenomena" (Bolin, p. 50). He sought to advance the spirit of "scientific inquiry" so teachers could approach the process of teaching and attendant problems more systematically. His "insistence" on a scientific approach to supervision "was based on the conviction that the school experience of students could best be enhanced through intensive cultivation of a scientific point of view by those who worked with both the teachers and supervisors" as agents of educational development. So conceived, Barr's scientific supervision sought the professional growth of teachers through the study of instructional issues—a kind of "scientific problem solving"—not "some sort of scientific autocracy modeled upon scientific management of big business" (Bolin, pp. 49–50).

Barr defined core dimensions of supervisory knowledge and ability in a manner consistent with the spirit of science: analyze teaching situations, use of data-gathering devices, develop means, methods, and materials of instruction, and teach teachers, and evaluate; in short, supervisors must possess training in the science of instructing pupils and teachers—

for both are aspects of the science of supervision (Glanz). It appears that Barr and other theorists of scientific supervision were influenced by Dewey's ideas, which connect thought and action—where in a "theory of scientific method . . . united in the conduct of scientific inquiry," where "unintelligibility disappears, and the nature and course of modern science becomes clear" (Ratner, 1939, p. 114). In McNeil's view Barr's most important conclusion is "that the constituents of effectiveness are not found in teacher, pupil or in situation, but in the relationships that exist among the three at any time and place" (1982, p. 23).

Bolin (1983) conveys Burton's view of the import of supervisory leadership where teachers are "assisted" and "encouraged" in the ordered study and experimentation of their work. This approach abhors "coercion" and regards "all educational workers as coworkers in the improvement of education" (Burton, et al, 1947). Improvement required a balance between the "scientific" and "philosophical" methods, where the scientific method is concerned with facts, reliability, and validity, whereas the "philosophical method was concerned with what ought to be, and how to deal with the known facts, with discovering the best policies in light of the known facts with aim, value, and meaning. . . . Those things valued by a society were the ends of its programs of education." Burton registered the importance of understanding the relationship between science and philosophy (Bolin, 1983, pp. 110–112).[15]

The curriculum must surely include those skills and knowledge which are clearly useful in life. These the scientific method will discover in place. But the curriculum must also contain material leading to insights, attitudes, and understandings which seem at first glance to be not immediately useful. These values are, however, more useful than the limited practical knowledge just mentioned. Both the scientific and the philosophic method will attempt to discover and describe these. Finally, the philosophic method will attempt to determine the kind of life from which scientific method extracts skills and knowledge for the curriculum (Burton, 1934, p. 429).

Brueckner "shared a common definition of supervision with Barr and Burton." Even though he "relied upon" Thorndike's principles of learning he held that:

the products of learning could not be limited to the observable, outward behavior of an individual. The language that Brueckner offered to teachers was often couched in the medical metaphor. He spoke of diagnosis, description, analysis, and prescription, yet he urged that "teachers engage in self-diagnosis and analysis and that the tools so designed be applied with insight" (Bolin, p. 144).

McNeil (1982) introduced his summary of scientific supervision by affirming that supervision so ordered "began the optimistic promise to deliver both a more just authority for teacher improvement and great gains in student achievement." Although the promise was never realized McNeil opined that research activity would continue to support the development of supervisory practice through "theoretical research to explain what occurs in classrooms" and "through practical research whereby practitioners and researchers together try to resolve limited problems in particular school situations"(McNeil, p. 18).

In his review, McNeil describes the 1930s as a shift in supervision away from the search for final conclusions to the use of research results for "sharpening observation and further thinking" (McNeil, p. 19). In the 1940s scientific supervision turned toward principles associated with democratic ideals: participation, shared decision-making, and the import of group processes in defining activities and goals-particularly as these principles relate to facts and principles "established by the process of science." By the 1960s the democratic action research orientation of supervisors was criticized for shortcomings in quantitative methods and conceptualization of the problems under investigation (McNeil, p. 21). Research on teaching, which was the primary emphasis of supervisory leaders, was consequently taken over by professional researchers who were technically competent to define and structure the research activity as illustrated by Nathan Gage's, *Handbook of Research on Teaching* (1963) (McNeil, p. 22).

McNeil projected, quite correctly, that scientific supervision would take "the direction of social research" and would become" only one among several analytical methods," including the "ordinary knowledge of supervisors and teachers." It would be derived from "common sense, empiricism, and thoughtful speculation" (McNeil, p. 31). He also observed that the case for scientific supervision had not been won: "There is an erosion in America's faith in science, so there is a lack of confidence that research in teacher effectiveness will ever fulfill its promise" (McNeil, p. 31).

Sergiovanni (1989, pp. 93–105) defines science as "systematized knowledge derived from observation and experiments to determine the nature of principles of what is being studied." He recognizes the limitations of science and cautions against "scientism" (i.e., instances that "extend the authority of science beyond its accepted bounds"). To avoid the "breakdown" of scientific investigations into scientism, Sergiovanni argues that

we should avoid an allegiance to a single line of research; . . . we need to view research findings, however discovered, less as truths and more as insights and understandings. The purpose of research in our field is not to discover the right answer but to help better understand the conditions of our practice" (Sergiovanni, p. 101).

Such understanding may very well reflect "the poetry" of professional practice that "provides insights and frames" that enable us to go beyond "the boundaries of our models and algorithms" (Sergiovanni, p. 93). In a related view, Smyth (1986b) sees supervision as suffering from an "affiliation with an outmoded interpretation of science" that is "value-free objectivist propelled by notions of technical rationality," which is a concept of science that begets "social engineering in the guise of neutral science" (Smyth, 1986b, p. 3). In this view, the character of science should not be defined as the mechanical application of one or another analytic method. It is a much larger narrative wherein methods of investigation and analysis are chosen because of their relevance to the perceived problem:

In a word there is no single scientific method. There is however a systematic relationship between the identification of a problem—and

the subsequent choice from among available methods of observation and measurement," and any effort sharply to separate the two is doomed (Robinson, 1995, pp. 331–332).

Goldsberry (1986) distinguishes between clinical and scientific rationality by construing clinical rationality as a "tool for sorting the interconnections or perceived and hypothesized facts," not as a "tool for the exploration or discovery of general principles, as in the scientific method." Having made this distinction, he urges that supervision helps teachers to identify their "systematic biases and temper them with additional information."

The counterpoint to scientific supervision is one that is inspired by an artistic view of communication and the discovery of meaning. As McNeil summarized the emergence of scientific supervision Eisner (1982) sketched an artistic approach to supervision that

relies on sensitivity, perceptivity, and knowledge of the supervisor as a way of appreciating the significant subtleties occurring in the classroom, and that exploits the expressive, poetic, and often metaphorical potential of language to convey to teachers and to others whose decisions affect what goes on in schools, what has been observed.

An artistic approach to supervision, aims to inspire the quality of life in school. This concept of supervision cannot be a "stop and shop" procedure. An artistic form of supervision goes beyond codified observation and seeks to understand and to interpret the teaching act "by applying educational not simply statistical criteria" (Eisner, p. 66). Eisner summarized the demands of an artistic approach to supervision:

That attention be paid to the process of classroom life and that this process be observed over extended periods of time; that rapport be established between supervisor and those supervised so that dialogue and a sense of trust can be established; that the individual supervisor with his or her strengths, sensitivities, and experience is the major instrument through which the educational situation is perceived and its meaning constructed (Eisner, 1982, pp. 65–66).

Interjecting an artistic approach in the discussion of scientific supervision is intended as a reminder that the knowledge base and the values that obtain to educational supervision are not divulged through one disciplinary culture or one definition of the process of knowing. It is ill-advised to impute the infallible guarantees to the discovery of truth and knowledge to science. Although scientific study is an important dimension of supervisory programs it is an incomplete formula for the study of teaching and instructional programs. Given the personal and value-laden nature of the teaching act other forms of inquiry and knowledge generation are required if supervisory efforts are to go beyond measurement to an expanded understanding of the conditions of learning.

In this spirit Sergiovanni (1982), advanced an *integrated view* of supervision (i.e., scientific, artistic, clinical). He proposed a framework for analyzing "domains of inquiry" as opposed to the meaning of "what is? and what ought to be?" In this view theories of practice derived from this analysis would illuminate different problems in supervision because facts and value are not separated, as is often the case with traditional science; rather, fact and value are essential to inquiry and meaning. An integrated view of knowing and supervisory practice focuses on the meaning of events in the development of a theory of supervision and evaluation of teaching (Sergiovanni, 1982, pp. 67–78).

Kuhn's well-known work, *The Structure of the Scientific Revolution* (1962), ignited a challenge to the long-standing belief as to the objectivity of science. He argued in part that each science has an "overarching paradigm and the community of scientists reinforce the dominant paradigm," and "only when forced by mounting evidence" will they confront the "anomalies that their research turns up—and this is the stuff of scientific revolutions" (Appleby, et al, 1994, p. 164). Under these circumstances:

[S]cientists most of the time are sequestered, not only from rival theories, but also from larger social economic, and political interests. In that situation and under the guiding influence of their paradigm, they routinely do normal science. Only a dramatic, theoretical innovation, the now famous paradigm shift, will shake them loose from their theoretical moorings and permit the emergence of new revolutionary science. Kuhn did *not* say that these shifts occur in opposition to the methods of science or without regard for empirical work (Emphasis added, Appleby et al, 1994, pp. 164–165).

Kuhn's account of science offers a foundation for examining a sociological view of scientific knowledge: Such knowledge is inherited; its transmission relies on the authority of the teacher and the text, as well as the "artful use of various pedagogic devices; with an emphasis on the association of belief and practice—theory and practical accomplishment," and on the identification of the scientific paradigm as the "fundamental unit in the transmission of scientific knowledge" (Barnes, 1990, pp. 64–65). Kuhn "shows that neither an initial choice of scientific paradigm nor a choice between competing paradigms is fully intelligible in terms of logic and experience alone." A paradigm should not be thought of as embodying a set of rules that determine research practice . . . but likened to a "judicial decision in the common law, it is an object for further articulation" (Barnes, p. 65). Although Kuhn had no interest in opening the door to relativism he was "blamed almost immediately for the rising skepticism about science." He was accused of modifying the notion of an "objective, empirical science into the hopelessly subjective" (Appleby et al, p. 165). His work seemed to be a "retreat from the heroic model of scientists with their special purchase on truth," yet for many informed observers heroic science was "philosophically correct and morally necessary" (Appleby, p. 165). Its rational methods can address complex human problems, and it was the foundation for "progress and rationality in the West . . . a generation of historians and scientists were not about to sacrifice it on the altar of social explanations" (Conant, 1947, pp. xii–xiii).

The debate over the objectivity of history and science is often identified with postmodernism "an outlook that stresses the constricted and arbitrary character of any explanatory framework" (Burbules & Rice, 1991, p. 395). The question then became, How so? Beliefs and values for those of a postmodern persuasion are "infinitely variable and highly contin-

gent." Hence, efforts to advance one system over others are denied because such claims discourage further investigation or allow investigation only on one's terms. Postmodernism challenges these restrictions and rejects absolutes (e.g., the idea of a single rationality, morality, or "ruling theoretical framework for the analysis of social and political events"). It attributes "power or dominance" to all social and political discourse, and because there is no "sustainable norms of rationality and value, then all educational discourse is political." Absolutes therefore serve to enfranchise certain groups over others (Burbules & Rice, 1991, p. 395), which is to say that those who champion a prevailing ideology secure power. They define the limits of discourse and set the boundaries for creative thought and action. One might conjecture that an approach to educational supervision that limits or denies articulation of "nonruling theoretical frameworks," in a postmodern sense, denies constituent energy and risk taking in favor of a prescribed rationality (Burbules & Rice, pp. 393–396).

Appleby et al (1994) want to parse the debate about history's relationship to scientific truth, objectivity, postmodernism, and the politics of identity in a more positive, less cynical framework. While they express a belief in skepticism "as an approach to learning as well as a philosophical stance" for such a system of thought excites learning by challenging traditions, they caution that complete skepticism can be debilitating. "It casts doubt on the ability to make judgments or draw conclusions . . . truths about the past are possible, even if they are not absolute, and hence are worth struggling for" (Appleby, et al, pp. 6–7).

Postmodernists appear to reject modernism with its pronouncements of certainty, knowledge, and truth. They recall twentieth-century horrors of war, genocide, and famine, and they question the claims of progress and the promise of the Enlightenment. Revered intellectual traditions and cultural forms once thought to be sacred are suspect. Appleby et al, (1994, p. 17) express their interpretation to this perspective as follows:

Contemporary disillusionment frames our examination of heroic science. Compromised by two world wars and a long cold war in which science and technology played critically important roles, heroic science looks flawed, today no longer workable as the foundation of all truth-seeking in this or any other culture. Science has lost its innocence. Rather than being perceived as value free, it is seen as encoded with values, a transmitter of culture as well as physical laws. Even the truth still found in science seems different in character-more provincial, less absolute-than it did to the enlightened eighteenth century forbearers who first glorified in it. True to their age late twentieth century historians of western science have been skeptical in ways that the true believers of the eighteenth century Enlightenment and beyond would have found unimaginable, as well as irreverent. In this skeptical and iconoclastic vein they examine the history of western science in order to discover how culture acquired its distinctively absolutist image of science" (Appleby et al, p. 16).

Horgan (1996) challenges the view that science will continue to progress as a knowledge-generating, truth-seeking process because scientists uneasily confront the limits of knowledge, the fallibility of theories past, and the challenge of questions that seem to go beyond human capacities to where there are no answers, only more questions.

It is not surprising that the science community has made a strong response to postmodern perspectives. Gross and Levitt (1994) declare that postmodernists thought does not have a "well-defined theoretical position with respect to science." There is, however, a "uniformity of tone, and that tone is ambiguously hostile." These authors recognize the legitimate concern that many people have on some of the uses of science, but they register surprise at the open hostility toward the content of scientific knowledge and the assumption that "scientific knowledge is reasonably reliable and rests on sound methodology." They are distressed that postmodernists want ideas "long favored and championed by western culture over the centuries . . . stripped of their claims to universality and timelessness, and uncontextual validity." This is because these ideas are viewed as local truths or structures that make sense only within a certain context of social experience and political system (Gross & Levitt, 1994, p. 38). Those of a traditional persuasion have little patience with the imputation that science is a restrictive and arbitrary framework, and they are dismayed that the power, potential, and contributions of modern science are suspect particularly as this suspicion is voiced by some colleagues in the academy.

Under these conditions, objectivity must deal as much with the voices of the critics as with champions of science. We can not "ignore the subjectivity of the author." Standards of objectivity must be constructed that recognize that all histories start with a particular individual and reflect "her or his personal and cultural attributes." A new standard of objectivity is proposed:

[O]ne that, concedes the impossibility of any research being neutral (that goes for scientists as well) and accepts that knowledge seeking involves a lively, continuous struggle among diverse groups of truth seekers. Neither admission undermines the viability of stable bodies of knowledge that can be communicated, built upon, and subjected to testing (Appleby et al, p. 254).

Waite (1995) provides strong cautionary comments about the process of science and supervision in a postmodern age. The supervisor, he writes, is challenged by "the malaise of modernity" that has provided a deep and pervading questioning of, among other things, science and scientific certainty. Waite is concerned that supervisors who practice conventional techniques, unaware of the trends of modernity, "may inadvertently contribute to power differentials and an incoherent sense of community, in short, to the alienation, atomization, and disenfranchisement of teachers" (Waite, p. 117). He prefers "dialogic supervision" as a corrective approach to mediate the "reductionist" character of most supervisory interactions, "which reduces what gets talked about" and serves "particular aims" while ignoring or excluding others where the teacher usually gets "short shrift in the conventional clinical supervision cycles" (Waite, pp. 118–119). Waite comments, therefore, that teachers are "disempowered," whereas a dialogic approach recognizes the "constant interaction between meanings" and helps to exclude one-dimensional monologic talk where the supervi-

sor delegates the search for meaning to a protocol (i.e., a template) of interaction.

These severe tensions of belief that in part are associated with modern and postmodern views of science, history, and knowledge need to be addressed. Separation and distrust among individuals, particularly educational leaders, interrupts the dialog needed to advance the search of the individual and community for knowledge, meaning, and fraternity. If we intend to "celebrate differences," then we "must broaden an understanding of others and through this our understanding of ourselves." In some strong measure maintaining discussion and dialog "across differences" is essential to the aims of "personal development and moral conduct," which is very much the cause of education and its surrogate, supervision (Burbules & Rice, 1991, p. 413).

We are further cautioned that experimental knowledge, which is phenomena developed in the laboratory setting, may appear as local knowledge, "that which is strongly dependent upon the practices employed in its making" (Golinski, 1990, pp. 492–505). The problem here is the "transition of knowledge from private to public spaces" (Golinski, p. 496). The relationship between science and its "audiences" requires greater awareness of the practice by which knowledge is developed so as to better understand the strategies and varied resource required to move local knowledge to the "public square."

Scientific knowledge in supervisory contexts often seeks the companionship of a democratic social system, so the definitions, limitations, procedures, and experimental findings gain a more public authority as an expression of a culture where discourse, ideas, and plans of action related to knowledge constructions and belief are a community value distinct from "truth" delivered from "foreign parts." Supervision has an ally in science as the course of events raises doubts, questions, hypotheses, speculations, and the like, which can be served by authentic conversation about professional concerns, not a limited notion of "technical rationality."

When McNeil (1982) concluded his analysis of "scientific supervision," he pondered its future in the light of America's essential optimism and "sense of efficiency." He recognized that supervisors "want a knowledge base to free them from charges of personal arbitrariness in their supervisory practice." He speculated that the future of scientific research will take the direction of "social research in general" and that scientific research will be but one analytic method for the development of instruction, as evidenced by the import of "ordinary knowledge" won by "common sense, empiricism, and thoughtful speculation." McNeil expressed "little hope" for an authoritativeness to supervision because research, he noted, does not cover the whole terrain of classroom problems. It is also highly unlikely that "teachers and supervisors will agree that any finding is sufficiently established to serve as the final word of authority (McNeil, pp. 31–32). He foresaw a return to action research on questions of importance to the local community, as well as objective experiments to "improve the science of pedagogy; and improvement of teaching through fact-finding" (1982, pp. 33–34). Other testimony about the perceived limits of scientific supervision appear to echo Nagel's caution that not all existing sciences present the highly integrated form of systematic explanation. In many domains of social inquiry the idea of a rigorous logical system remains as "an ideal" (Nagel, 1961, p. 4). To the extent that the scientific investigations indicate patterns of relations across a wide range of "fact" and information one might find some explanatory principles and propositions about these facts. The combination of these facts, principles, and propositions may be construed as a "logically unified body of knowledge," a tentative statement of knowledge subject to continued examination, analysis, and applications (Nagel, 1961, p. 4).

The quest for knowledge as a guide to supervisory behavior and leadership has continued in the full recognition that scientific approaches constitute one part of the process of developing knowledge about supervision. As one calling of philosophy is to challenge the authority of science, so should the philosophy of supervision challenge the forms, ideas, and practices of supervision beyond "wishful thinking" and a "scientific theology." The principles and propositions that result from these efforts, given the artistic and human essence of teaching, are likely to be temporary guidelines, as knowledge, fact, and circumstance modify and rearrange themselves under the press of an evolving reality. Along with other ways of knowing, the power and precision of science as an approach to the discovery and construction of knowledge should contribute to the belief system or philosophy of educational supervision. In addition, given the accelerating development of communication technology and instructional alternatives supervision will likely be expressed as both an applied science and as an artistic enterprise. Curriculum and instruction will take many forms and these forms will shape the learning environment. Teacher decisions on the congruence between instructional options and individual needs and interests, long the theme of "progressive education," may be more readily attainable. These conditions raise a host of issues, philosophical and practical, but "science and engineering," the electronic-virtual world view, has/will become a major aspect of the teachers professional responsibilities and, therefore, by definition a major concern of the educational supervisor. In this realm of speculation, Alvin and Heid Toffler (1995). forsake the postmodern perspective for the "prefuture." They chart a "new civilization" beyond the first wave (i.e., agricultural revolution) and their second wave (i.e., industrial revolution and mass society) to the "third wave," which they see as "globally integrated, cybernetic, an information driven society . . . which will have consequences for all aspects of living from family life to political institutions." They envision this globally integrated civilization as "vibrantly democratic" where decision-making is decentralized as required by the diversity of information sources, culture, production, and politics. No one will be set aside because "the energies of whole peoples will be required and the collective imagination unleashed." How will we define and prepare for the supervision of a steadily increasing technological school and classroom? Tracy (1993, 1996) has considered the question in terms of a shift in the long-standing paradigm or model of American education with a consequent shift in the paradigm of supervision: From classrooms with prescribed curriculum, traditional teaching modalities charac-

terized by substantial levels of "teacher talk," to a paradigm that "personalizes the learning process for all children, removes the "limitations of time and space," and "changes the role of the teacher" in the direction of "resource provider." With regard to supervision Tracy hazards the notion that in an age of science and its bedfellow technology it will "become personalized and diffused"; indeed, she projects, "the new instructional supervision paradigm may be *Teacher As Supervisor* (Tracy, 1993, pp. 128–131).

Clinical Supervision

The attempts to bring together scientific approaches and democratic ideals were evident in the collaborative efforts by Barr, Burton, and Brueckner. Their supervision textbook had spanned four decades in its various editions and titles (Bolin, 1987). By the mid-1950s it was no longer the primary college textbook in supervision. Their work, however, signaled a focus on in-class supervision and the importance of portraying a practical approach to supervising teachers face-to-face, yet with concerns for human agency. In the writing and research at this time, it was becoming apparent that there were typically two contexts (i.e., perspectives) from which authors located supervisory practice. One perspective assumed that supervision is located primarily at the school level and includes a wide range of techniques reflected in various events associated with the improvement of instruction (i.e., in-class supervision/evaluation, curriculum development, staff development, etc.). Another perspective suggested that the major context for supervision is the classroom where actual teaching takes place. Techniques of observation and conference began to emerge as parts of a defining practice. From 1955 to 1965 at Harvard University, colleagues Morris Cogan, Robert Anderson, David Purpel, and others were working in classrooms with supervisors and teachers. Robert Goldhammer, as a graduate student, was swept up in the challenge of articulating in-class supervision. Cogan coined the term *clinical supervision*. He later wrote his seminal book, *Clinical Supervision* (1973), using his earlier experiences at the Harvard-Newton and Harvard Lexington Summer programs to fashion an eight-phase approach to supervising teachers in their classrooms. Goldhammer's dissertation was also a version of clinical supervision, and his sudden and tragic death in 1968 prompted his mentor, Robert Anderson, to edit his work for publication in 1969. These two texts launched a vital field known as clinical supervision. In 1980, Anderson and Krajewski published a second edition of the Goldhammer text. By this time, the practice had become a prominent subfield of supervision with a growing scholarship.

Although Cogan (1973) and Goldhammer (1969) are the acknowledged seminal authors in the tradition, their notions of "clinical" experience" and "clinical professorship" were echoing through the educational environment at Harvard in the 1940s and 1950s (Powell, 1980). James Conant (1963), then president of Harvard, proposed that there be "intermediaries between the basic social sciences and the future practitioner," particularly, that the induction of the teacher into a classroom through practice teaching should be under the supervision of an experienced school teacher who holds high rank as a university professor and . . . should also be in close touch with the new developments in the educational sciences.

It is noteworthy that Robert Anderson, a well-known author in the field, became a tenured clinical professor under the Conant initiative. In their activities at Harvard in the mid-1950s and 1960s, Cogan and Goldhammer worked in clinical programs and fashioned their portrayals of in-class supervision from the daily events of practice. Cogan called his depiction a "rationale," while Goldhammer referred to his version as "methods." In their writing, however, both remained close to the events of in-class supervision for their descriptions. Most educators accept the following as the basic sequence of events: establishing a relationship with the teacher, observing classroom teaching, analyzing classroom scenarios, and holding a conference with the teacher. To articulate the events in methodological form, both authors compartmentalized them. Cogan called them "phases"; Goldhammer labeled them "stages." Both authors emphasized the cyclical nature of the events, indicating that the series of phases could not be construed as a single *event,* but rather must be repeated several times in order to establish a comprehensive working relationship with the teacher. This repetitive set became known as "the cycle of clinical supervision." Their texts therefore, established the basis for subsequent interpretations of the nascent practice. It is interesting to note that the cycle of supervision combined elements of scientific method (i.e., observation, data gathering, analysis, inference-making) with democratic ideals (i.e., establishing a collegial relationship with the teacher). This mix of ideals invited subsequent philosophic orientations to emerge in the following years.

Instrumental versions of clinical supervision began to appear from the early texts. Mosher and Purpel (1972) plucked a piece out of the larger portrayal of clinical supervision that they claimed is a general objective: "planning for, observation, analysis, and treatment of the teacher's classroom performance." The piece they described in one chapter defines clinical supervision as the "actual (i.e. observable) teaching performance and the results of teaching." At this point we begin to see clinical supervision viewed functionally as an instrument, or tool, in their interpretation of in-class supervision. They stress counseling theory and, in particular, ego counseling for the basis of supervisory practice.

Acheson and Gall (1980) expanded their instrumental version to include functional applications for planning, observing, and holding conferences with teachers. Glickman (1985) situated his version of supervision in developmental theories grounded in psychology. He used clinical supervision instrumentally as in-class supervision as he portrayed schoolwide supervision in general. McGreal (1983) is representative of the evaluation enterprise that has adopted clinical supervision for the practice of in-class personnel evaluation of teaching. These instrumental perspectives had their roots in the philosophic orientation of scientific realism. The assumption was that research on teaching would eventually give educators the necessary findings to be able to posit how effective teaching could be generalized. Meanwhile, supervision took the improvement of the teacher's instruction as its goal. In this period dilemmas regarding the results of clinical supervision were evident because there were no clear standards of practice for teachers. "Improvement of instruction" was a nebulous goal, compounded by the assumptions of scientific realism (i.e, that generalizations regarding effective teaching were possible for the supervisor to make). In the 1970s through to 1985 scholars in supervision looked to the enormous amount of research being conducted in the nationally funded Research and Development Centers focused on determining the characteristics of effective teaching, which seemed to hold promise for supervisory practice.

By the middle of the 1980s, several philosophic forces were converging in educational thought. First, it was clear that the promises made by those who espoused scientific realism were exaggerated. The research on effective teaching had too many anomalies to help supervisory scholars and practitioners shape their work (Sergiovanni, 1989). Second, Donald Schon (1983) had published his book, *The Reflective Practitioner,* which became a defining text for professionals in many fields. Schon's ideas came at a time when supervisors needed a new perspective on what "improvement of instruction" meant. Clinical supervisors could now guide educators (including themselves) toward becoming reflective practitioners. Schon's work was derived from the earlier philosophic writings of John Dewey (1933). (It is interesting to note that Schon's dissertation focused on Dewey's philosophic influences.) Third, the intellectual scholarship in all fields was beginning to reflect the challenges of postmodernism.

One aspect of the postmodern influence, often referred to as the "rhetorical turn" (Garman, 1994), emphasizes the interpretation of meaningful human practices as the central goal of social inquiry. In the educational discourses, scholars were beginning to debate the notion of multiple perspectives for research paradigms. Soltis (1984) published his important article, "On the Nature of Educational Research," in *Educational Researcher,* which articulated at least three different paradigms, or world views, that could serve as the ground for research: empirical (i.e., scientific realism), interpretive (i.e., hermeneutic), and critical (i.e., critical theory). By 1989, the *Encyclopedia of Education, Vol. 1,* had listed three approaches under "Supervision and Curriculum" that assumed different philosophic positions: the applied science approach, the interpretive-practical approach, and the critical emancipatory approach. Thus, in the 1980s, major philosophic shifts were beginning to influence supervisory research and practice in general and clinical supervision in particular. The interpretive perspective in clinical supervision was being articulated by Holland (1988, 1989, 1990) as well as by Garman, (1982, 1986, 1990, 1993). John Smyth (1986, 1988) began to represent the critical perspective in clinical supervision in the early 1980s.

As the 1990s reaches its last years, clinical supervision continues to occupy a place in supervision scholarship, in part due to the postmodern orientations of Smyth, Holland, Garman, Waite, and others who have been willing to change the philosophic discourses in the field of school supervision in general. The clinical supervision tradition has continued for five decades. The discussions periodically reflect the possibility of an impending demise. In 1991, at the American Educational Research Association's Annual Meeting, there was a session titled, "Isn't it High Time to Bury Clinical Supervision." In a chapter that debates the efficacy of clinical supervision for use in public schools, Garman (1996) describes the 1990s version as follows:

[F]irst of all, it is about people—acting with their hearts and minds toward understanding each other; it is directed toward the personal rather than the institutional (to personal practice rather than institutional programs). The practice is discursive, with emphasis on the nature of discourses among the participants and their authentic educative relationships. Clinical supervision has a moral/ethical dimension which serves to guide the encounters (Garman & Haggerson, 1993) and a critical dimension which continues to challenge the pretense of certitude. Most important, the meaning of clinical supervision is embodied in the individual stories that are fashioned from genuine dialogue, honest introspection, and the willingness to struggle toward wisdom in practice.

Supervision as Leadership

In our discussion of clinical supervision, we mentioned that two perspectives on supervision have emerged as related to the context, or place, where supervision is situated. One perspective takes the classroom as the context where face-to-face interactions with teachers and students happen. This is the context associated with clinical supervision. The other perspective focuses on supervision at the institutional level and includes a wide range of functions such as curriculum development, staff development, and in-class supervision/evaluation as these activities serve to support classroom instruction. One of the newer concepts that serves to frame the perspective of school-wide supervision is leadership. The equation of educational supervision with leadership combines ideas and traditions that have accompanied the transformation of supervision from scholastic–authoritarian inspection through the dreams and conflicts of the Enlightenment to democratic vistas.

What is a leader? Under what conditions or circumstances is leadership expressed? What is the purpose of leadership? Does it take varied forms? Is it assigned by position or apportioned by circumstance among constituent members of the organization? What is known about leadership? Comprehensive responses to these questions have been provided elsewhere. Our task is to consider another question: Is there such a thing as supervisory leadership and, if so, what beliefs guide its development?

A leader may be defined as one who, by force of character, ideas, genius, or strength of will, is able to arouse and direct others in conduct and achievement (i.e., dictionary). These descriptors may be valid, but they only hint at the features of leadership in a world of continuing human interactions. The "traits theory," which is the "great man" interpretation of leadership, provides a limited message about leadership in a culture marked by diversity of thought and conditions. In our "organizational society" (Etzoni, 1968, 1993; Presthus, 1978) the meaning of leader and the process of leadership will depend upon the context or setting in which they are found (Spitzburg, 1985). In this regard, "kind of insti-

tution" refers to the goals, the history, and the culture of the group or organization. It also refers to the internal structure, the nature of the organization, the work undertaken, and the pattern of working relationships. Leaders and leadership, therefore, can be manifest in different forms and at different levels of social responsibility. They are vital signs as to the stability and effectiveness of group activity. Suffice it to say that leadership continues to be both powerful and puzzling:

"Powerful because it contains the implication of direction or redirection of peoples lives, actions, and aspiration, yet puzzling because the determinants of effective leadership remain so poorly understood. It is impossible for any social structure to endure if there is continued absences of leadership" (Alfonso, et al, 1981, p. 94).

Beyond general definition and theoretical constructs, Stogdill (1974) summarized the research that focused on the "traits" and characteristics of leaders for the period 1904–1970 (Stogdill, pp. 35–91). After completing this Herculean task, he constructed a comparative analysis of factorial studies of leadership published in the period 1945–1970. The studies were surveys of leadership in military and industrial contexts (Stogdill, p. 92), where "the most frequently occurring factors are descriptive of various skills of the leader . . . these factors describe the leader as making effective use of interpersonal, administrative, technical, and intellectual skills." These factors also related to the leader's "relationship with his group," where the factor profile included maintaining: cohesiveness; coordination-teamwork; standards of performance; informal group control (freedom); and nurturing behavior. The other factors configured personal characteristics of the leader such as: emotional balance, assuming responsibility, ethical conduct, communication, energy, courage, and maturation (Stogdill, p. 96). In summarizing the order of the frequency of the factors, Stogdill wrote, "certain skills and capabilities-interpersonal, technical, administrative, and intellectual"-enable the leader to be of value to the organization-especially as related to group cohesiveness, drive, and productivity." This is particularly the case when the leader possesses "a high degree of task motivation, personal integrity, communication ability, and the like" (Stogdill, p. 96).

Stogdill's (1974) work introduced a breadth of systematic thinking about the theory and practice of leadership. Given the complexity of the subject, he commented that "it is not surprising that many individuals who attempt leadership find themselves bewildered by their lack of success. Nor is it surprising that those who attain this status find the path difficult indeed" (Stogdill, p. 415). Bass and Stogdill (1990) referenced later Machiavelli's warning: "There is nothing more difficult to take in hand, more perilous to conduct, or more uncertain in its success than to take the lead in the introduction of a new order of things" (Bass & Stogdill, p. 4).

More recently, the dominant paradigm for the study of leadership goes beyond research on traits, situation, organizational climate, and contingency models to something more dynamic. Leadership begins to be seen as a transaction—an exchange between leaders and constituency: "Leaders exchange rewards and benefits to subordinates for the fulfillment of agreements with the leader" (Bass & Stogdill, 1990,

p. 53). Sergiovanni and Starratt (1993) describe transactional leadership as a "favor for a vote—a granted request here for a future request there." These transactions are governed by instrumental values (i.e., fairness, honesty, loyalty) where the leader monitors the procedures and the arguments. Beyond "transaction" is a form of leadership that affirms the importance of "collective motivation" where constituents, who were formally designated leaders, and others identify with the "goals and values" of the organization (Bass & Stogdill, 1990, p. 903); this is transformational leadership, which Sergiovanni and Starratt (1993, p. 186) have defined thusly:

[A]n exchange among people seeking common aims, uniting them to go beyond their separate interest in the pursuit of higher goals . . . concerned with end values such as freedom, community, equity, justice, brotherhood. It is that leadership which calls people's attention to the basic purpose of the organization, to the relationship between the organization and the society. Transformational leadership changes people's attitudes, values, and beliefs, from being self-centered to being higher and more altruistic.

Where democratic-transformational leadership is an actuality, the commitment of the membership is to one another and to organizational goals in which individual growth in part depends. Such organizations evidence collaboration and consensus building regarding goals, as well as a level of communication that provides feedback of results as a guide to individual and group performance (Bass & Stogdill, 1990, p. 1129).

Burns (1978) noted that the transformational leadership recognizes the need to engage the full person in the saga of the organization. It seeks to develop individual capacities, and it is a belief system, a value system whereby constituents are turned into leaders (Bass & Stogdill, 1990), where leadership may pass from one individual to another.

In the educational context, we suggest a distinction between administrative and supervisory leadership. The higher administrative levels of the organization tends to be management bound. Given the increasing complexity of educational organizations such leadership is important. It helps to guide the course of organizational development and may set the conditions for the emergence of leadership across the system by providing resources, motivating, clarifying mission, and provoking the intellectual vitality of individuals in a manner consistent with democratic principles. Whereas supervisory leadership tends to be proximate to the instructional program, to the dynamic of teaching, supporting a culture that makes instructional leadership and decisions the agenda of the local school community, where planning and actions are not separated from those responsible for doing it (Alfonso, et al, 1981, Chap. 1). In the spirit of transformational leadership, Sergiovanni (1996) wrote:

For schools to work well, we need theories of leadership that recognize the capacity of parents, teachers, administrators and students to sacrifice their own needs for causes they believe in. We need theories of leadership that acknowledge that parents, teachers, administrators and students are more norm-referenced decision makers than individual decision makers. Instead of making individual calculation based on self-interest, we should acknowledge that people are

response to norms, values, and beliefs that define the standard of living together as a group and that provide them with meaning and significance (p. 14).

Supervisory leadership at the school or program level is a shared responsibility that confronts the reality of the school: the aggregate of the needs, skills, knowledge, and values of all those who comprise the school community. Instructional supervisory leadership shares responsibility for activating the "covenant." It works to analyze the conditions of learning (i.e., the local school environment and the particulars that attend to the instructional program). It works to nurture intellectual skills and the moral sense that sustains democracy and the sense of self in a community (Etzoni, 1993, pp. 89–115). Such general propositions about supervisory leadership mirror Arygris' early work (1957–1960) and his concern that organizations that emphasize tight controls and authoritarian leadership places employees in an environment that is incongruent with mature, healthy personalities where, among other things, they are expected to be passive, dependent, and subordinate.

Harris (1975) defined *leadership* as an "active, purposeful, skilled influencing of people to facilitate change" where "consideration and initiation of structure" frame instructional leadership that balances friendly concern with supervisory expertise. Harris' philosophic perspective aspires to a form of supervisory leadership that Blumberg identifies with openness and accessibility (1980, p. 37), "an egalitarian, nonbureaucratic, atmosphere where all resources have equal input—where the ideas of teachers are respected and judged on their merit," wherein the supervisor serves as a consultant who is available, competent, and empathetic in collegial interactions. This approach to supervision reflects a humanistic/artistic view of the role and practice of supervision. It is "tension-laden" because personalized supervision asks for "reciprocal mutual confrontation" in a professional relationship that is marked by trust, concern, and responsiveness (Berman, 1971). Given the complexity of organizational life and the demands of the "public interest" this is no small task. The jury is still out on the extent to which Blumberg's "private cold war" has abated in the cause of supervisory practice informed by more recent developments in leadership, organizational theory, and clinical models.

Sergiovanni has devoted much of his scholarship to the study of educational leadership. He has synthesized concepts and principles from the humanities, and from social and behavioral sciences, and has generated ideas, and creative formulations, as a guide to further study of leadership behavior.

Although Sergiovanni (1971) defined *supervision* as a human dimension of school leadership, he balked at endorsing the human relations motif when used as a method "to help people feel good about themselves while it failed to incorporate them as actual shareholders in the educational enterprise" (Sergiovanni, 1971, p. 57). It was too often applied, "Sergiovanni declared . . . without any alteration in the belief system of those who had applied it control, authority, and management were still the framework upon which decision rested" (Bolin, 1983, p. 235). Sergiovanni speculated about various models (i.e., scientific management, bureaucratic, collegial, and political theories) of educational leadership-as "lenses through which school leaders may look at the schools and better understand their own work" (Bolin, p. 239). He urged that these models be seen as "complementary rather than competing lenses through which school leaders may look at the schools and better understand their own work" (Bolin, p. 239). He contends (1979) that leadership models are too often conceptually flawed and are neglectful of "substantive leadership," which focuses on "how things are to be accomplished to the serious neglect of questions of value, mission, and worth": "What the leader stands for and communicates to others is more important than how he or she behaves in any particular set of circumstances" for "supervision requires both head and heart" (Sergiovanni, 1979, pp. 241–244).

Alfonso and Goldsberry (1982) projected the advantages of a collegial approach to supervision: (1) human resources are mobilized in a collective effort to improve instruction; (2) the ability of teachers to contribute to instructional development is recognized; and (3) the implementation of instructional innovations are more likely to occur "in schools having active colleagueship." To advance the conditions of colleagueship, "school leadership" needs to espouse and model this perspective by providing "structured opportunities for meaningful collaboration and interaction" (Alfonso & Goldsberry, p. 97).

Sergiovanni (1990) proposed a "value-added" approach to leadership that "emerges from a synthesis of traditional management theory and recent studies of successful school and corporate cultures" (p. 3). This work challenges customary forms of "value leadership" that emphasize direction, control, and designated rewards (p. 4). Value-added leadership requires, among other things, a shared sense of purpose that invigorates the school by "building a covenant comprising purposes and beliefs that bonds people together . . . that provides them with a sense of what is important, a signal of what is of value" (p. 20) that is based on (1) empowerment (i.e., authority and obligation are shared), (2) enablement (i.e., means and opportunities are provided and obstacles are removed), and (3) enhancement (i.e., a function of empowerment and enablement that leads to more enhancement, commitment and extraordinary performance) (p. 96). In the spirit of democracy value added leadership combines "freedom with obligation," which "is the secret of genuine accountability" (1990, p. 143).

Sergiovanni and Starratt (1993) offer a dynamic interpretation of supervisory leadership that reflects essential human and organizational conditions consisting of "five basic elements":

1. It is grounded in essential meanings about human persons, society, knowledge, growth, learning, and schooling.
2. It is energized by a vision of what education might and should be.
3. It involves the articulation of a vision of schooling that all can embrace.
4. It seeks to embody the vision in institutional structures, frameworks, and policies.
5. It celebrates the vision and seeks its continuous renewal (p. 188).

This vision advances the understanding of the school as a learning community sustained by beliefs in human potential, "their sacred value, the moral quality of human striving, the necessity as well as the difficulty of self-governance." It is energized by a vision of what education might and should be, and it "seeks to embody the vision in its institutional structures, frameworks, and policies" (Sergiovanni & Starratt, 1993, p. 188). Sergiovanni (1996) calls for a Community Theory of leadership that goes beyond bureaucratic control and personal authority, beyond a "Follow me because of my position" or "Follow me because I make it worth your while . . . " toward a theory of leadership that emphasizes "building a shared followership," "not on *who* to follow but on *what* to follow" (p. 83):

Community members are not asked to comply in response to clever leadership processes or in response to aspects of the leaders personality. They are asked to respond to substance. Leadership in communities is idea based; the goal is to develop a broad commitment to shared values and conceptions that become a compelling source of authority and what people must do. . . . [For the] quest for virtue involves selflessly serving and building a community (Sergiovanni, pp. 83, 96).

Maxcy (1984) cautions that debates about schooling need

critically imaginative vision that sees leadership as a community effort to redesign schools for the maximization of the interests of that community for the school is not simply an organizational complex, with function and structure, peopled by workers exercising some status or role.

He anticipates the view of education as "living texts," a process of reconstituting human freedom through a new linguistic community, and a "new pragmatism, in the face of technology and totalitarianism" that promotes a "nonfoundational continuous conversation" where leadership will confront new ways of knowing (Maxcy, p. 19).

One is tempted to say that the research and scholarship in leadership has left us with the clear view that things are far more complicated than initially believed. In fact, they are so complicated and contingent that it may not be worthwhile to spin out more and more qualifications (Perrow, 1986). In this regard, for those concerned with educational supervision as leadership, Pajak's (1993b) work offers some relief and considerable information. He has presented an informed and vivid picture of varied concepts of educational leadership. He has fashioned a schema that summarizes changes "shifting conceptions" in theory and action from the decade of the 1940s through the 1990s. He illuminates the progression of the educational leader as "democratic" (1940s–1950s) to the 1990s view of the "teacher" as the educational leader. This latter view captures the sense of the school as a human system and a learning organization. It suggests, at least in part, that the school may be conceived of as the aggregate of the properties (i.e., knowledge, beliefs, values) of the teachers, students, and other constituents that make up the school community. Pajak outlined the challenge of educational leadership as a "recommitment to the value of democracy as a moral imperative . . . that our profession and society desperately need" (Pajak, p. 180). This theme was also expressed in his earlier work (1989) on the dimensions of professional practice: knowledge, skill, and values that characterize effective supervision. In addition to a substantial knowledge base and consistent with Schon's (1983, 1987) "reflection-in-action," Pajak identifies optimism and a high regard for people as "the heart of this belief system." This study is significant on a number of counts. It codifies conventional wisdom on the range of knowledge and skill areas that define the practice of educational supervision. It affirms the unity of knowledge, skill, and values as important components of a supervisory belief system. It also outlines a direction for continued discourse and further research.

In the midst of many claims about the nature and purpose of leadership, Starratt's *The Drama of Leadership* (1993) provides a challenging yet approachable interpretation of the structures and dynamics of leadership. Referencing the contributions of other scholars, Starratt outlines progress:

1. Leadership "can not be treated in isolation from historical social context, nor in isolation from the qualities of followers"
2. Leadership as a moral activity
3. Leadership includes substantive as well as instrumental rationality; it "is involved with management by meaning and by values as well as short term objectives"
4. Leadership prompts "extraordinary talent and effort of the members of an organization"
5. "Leadership is essential for modern democratic institutions and societies" (Starratt, 1993, pp. 13–14).

This is leadership "broadly based throughout society, rather than a leadership exercised by a select few" for the burden of leadership must be shared if societies are to be renewed in postmodern societies (Starratt, p. 136) so conceived leaders, "will understand that their power does not come from the force of their personalities, but from the power of values that ground human life as meaningful and worthwhile" (Starratt, pp. 137–138).

There is no escaping power but supervision as leadership may secure its distribution so it will be negotiated and exchanged. This requires "trust," which is a relationship marked by honesty, integrity, and an authentic sense of respect among the members of the school community (McBride & Skau, 1995). Fukuyama (1995) adds his voice to the importance of "trust" in successful organizations where members act in the group's interest rather than being propelled by selfish or opportunistic considerations. He sees "trust" arising from what he calls "spontaneous sociability," which has its roots in "intermediate institutions," family ties, religious communities, and other cultural agencies. Given the sorry state of many institutional forms leaders need to nurture a "culture of trust" as a correlate of Starratt's "postmodern sensibility."

To Gardner (1995), leadership is best understood as a story with the assumption that the leader has a story to tell and has the ability to tell it, unless the message becomes static in the noise of organizational life. What may appear to be a romantic concept of leadership is better understood as an issue of group and personal identity where the contract among the participants is nurtured by a capacity to share stories, authentic messages that link people to the work in the community. In this sense, a leader's story (i.e., the essential theme or message about fact and circumstances) is not overwhelmed by rational structures and the press of ever-increasing technical expertise. The supervisor's story is a narrative of events and experiences that combine with knowledge and a moral/ethical frame to support an ideal of service. The supervisor's story is the public declaration of a belief system that comprises the coda of a professional role. Where the story is of doubtful authorship (i.e., where it lacks authenticity), its message is transitory and short on meaning. On the other hand, where a supervisor's story is authentic and meaningful (i.e, where knowledge construction, experience, and risk-taking co-exist), the covenant (i.e., the social contract among colleagues in their search for meaning) will characterize the philosophy of supervisory leadership.

Smyth (1996) asked "What would it mean if we were to redraw the educational boundaries of educational/instructional supervision," if we stripped away "the crustaceans of nearly a century of research, scholarship and practice," and developed an "alternative agenda" where supervision was understood as a process of "working with students, teachers, parents and community groups"—an agenda that would go beyond accountability and the trappings of hierarchy to an emphasis on

an agenda from within schools; artistic and narrative forms of portrayal of locally created experiences and visions of what people in schools are trying to do [that focus] on the structure, context, and location within which teaching and learning are occurring [as a basis for analyzing teaching and learning to help the school community to identify] "disabling or debilitating circumstances and what might be done about them politically (bracketed text added) (pp. 290–291).

Smyth advanced the concept of supervision as a "process of self-study" where schools are committed "to recreate themselves as discursive, critical, and collaborative communities" (p. 292).

This evolution in our understanding of supervisory leadership conveys the struggle to secure sociopolitical forms that affirm the individual in the quest for knowledge and human actualization. Supervision conceived as leadership, therefore, is essential in establishing the conditions that will stimulate creative energies and reflective judgments. It engages the mind and experience of many, such as designated administrative officers, teachers and staff, and students and community. Such beliefs are consonant with the values and concerns of a democratic and multicultural society, and they are indispensable to supervision's primary function: improving the education of students in the public schools, which is a precondition to the promise of America—the freedom of heart and mind to shape and power one's course of life as an individual and a citizen. We have often thought and talked in this manner. We have less often, and frequently with cause, acted to provide supervisory leadership to the full advantage of the educational process. Glickman (1993) declares that the answer, for all engaged in the institution and process of education, "is simple," and his answer speaks clearly to supervisory leaders:

1. We must realize that the basic goal of our schools is to prepare students to engage productively in a democracy
2. We must organize and operate our own schools in accord with the democratic principles of our society
3. Teaching and learning between students and teachers must demonstrate, in actions, the relationship between education and democracy—the power of learning for engagement in real issues (Glickman, p. xii).

Levine (1996) maintains that "a people's culture is safe only insofar as it continues to ceaselessly examine and understand itself" (p. 169). He references Whitehead's observation that a society "must prevent its codes, its rules, its cannons—its entire symbolic system—from becoming fixed and hard . . . they require revision in the light of reason or they will ultimately decay either from anarchy, or from the slow atrophy of a life stifled by useless shadows" (p. 169). Such ideas continue as cogent principles for the unfoldment of transformational supervision.

These perspectives on leadership are related to what Sergiovanni (1996b) identifies as a "Community Theory of Supervision" (p. 275), where educational purposes are shared and understood and persuasion rests on "example" and the "tapping of inner moral forces." Such an approach is a "reciprocal" relationship among colleagues, where leaders/supervisors are part of the order of things, "even as they attempt to change it," as they are obliged to fulfill the moral dimensions of their responsibilities as instructional leaders (p. 275).

These ideas and concepts confront tired and worn notions of supervisory leadership in education. The challenge requires a search for meaning beyond organizational structures and hollow activity. A philosophy of educational supervision is therefore distant from any claims or pretense of certitude. It is beyond the tenets of inspection from decrees about what is right and the sovereignty of tradition. These themes do not deny the stories, traditions, and institutional forms of the past. They are attributions of supervisory leadership that seek to go beyond ritualized adoption of bureaucratic standards of procedure and to express efficiency as one class of actions crafted to support the conditions of learning, not as an abstract concept or as an end. They recognize the order, power, and potentialities of science as one way of knowing, while also recognizing its frailties and fallibility. They reflect the importance of knowledge and skill, and they affirm the reconciliation of expertise and democracy. They ascribe to supervisory leadership, which nurtures leadership as a shared capacity rather than as a role or position. They affirm the "valuing of human beings" and promote the development of the school as a laboratory of ideas charged by the authority of democratic principles and a moral code consonant with the principles of mutual respect and trust in service to each other, and likewise to students and community. Education and supervision thus conceived partner in the continuing search for a civil and moral society.

As Hodgkinson (1983) voiced the cannon of his statement on leadership, we would similarly affirm that supervision is

philosophy in action. It is the public expression of a belief system (i.e., of decision-making) dedicated to the service of individuals and the school as a community. It is the enduring pursuit of knowledge, meaning, and shared values. It is an energy system (i.e., a leadership process) uniquely capable of contributing to the development of educational programs, which serve the diverse multicultural society that is America.

SUMMARY

This chapter explored the development of supervision in terms of the belief systems and values that comprise the story of educational supervision in American culture. This path links the discussion of supervision to particular historical themes and philosophical sentiments framed by general "models," or, as we called them, "operational definitions" of supervision. So ordered, this plan provides a focus for defining and interpreting concepts and propositions about educational supervision.

Because interpretation requires a level of definition, our discussion began by examining the concepts of philosophy and supervision. In the first instance, philosophy was referenced in its disciplinary, foundational form as a search for understanding by considering the reality, knowledge structures, and values that form individual or institutional perspectives. While this foundational tradition continues to spark critical discussion on matters of universal human concern, including its own meaning and relevance, we assumed a more applied posture: The consideration of the philosophy of educational supervision would best be grounded in an examination of ideas, values, and changes in thinking that inspire the evolution of supervisory thought and practice.

The discussion of supervisory models and attendant belief systems begins with *inspection,* which is a pattern of authority based on an orthodoxy of revealed truth where supervision underscores a commitment to a fixed system as it contends with the perplexities of an emerging culture and alternative values. The *efficiency* movement in supervision reflects the impact of accelerated social change, the authority of science and technology, and a progressive temperament that engendered supervisory arrangements consistent with the meta themes of science and social science. *Democratic* supervision and Deweyean pragmatism emphasize the process of education as individual growth and self-realization as essential to the fulfillment of the American ethic, where supervision is conceived of as shared governance, involvement, and the development of individual capacities: It is action oriented in the pursuit of meaning and knowledge. *Scientific* supervision espouses the methods of science as a means of discovering general principles of supervisory behavior as derived from hypothesis building, observable facts, quantitative measurement, and freedom from emotional bias. Supervision that is so conceived enables teachers to engages in the systematic analysis of their programs and teaching behavior in advance of student learning. *Clinical* supervision is located in the classroom, which is where teaching unfolds, techniques of observation and conference are expressed in a manner that combines scientific method and democratic ideas, and collaborative interaction and interpersonal respect demonstrate a moral endeavor through "reflection-in-action," which is to say "that philosophy derives its mission from the context in which we live and work." Supervision as *leadership* eschews one paradigm or design (i.e., one set of traits, tasks, or set of skills); rather, it is a dynamic enterprise that subverts conformity, transforming things (i.e., concepts, values, knowledge, and practice) in the quest for a learning community (i.e., a laboratory of ideas) and a harbor for "cognitive pluralism" and "pedagogical leadership."

By examining these models or "narratives" of educational supervision, we have attempted to complement historical fact and circumstance, examine supervision from a cultural–value-oriented perspective, and give moment to the values and belief systems that are the source of supervisory philosophy and practice. This is, to be sure, only a beginning at interpreting events and ideas related to the story of educational supervision.

CONCLUSION

There is no one philosophy of supervision. The models or dominant patterns of supervision represent different systems of belief and value. They remain in process in varied and combined forms in different contexts. This may suggest limited knowledge about supervision or it may speak to the difficulty of reconciling the process with organizational mandates and the human, artistic side of teaching and educational leadership. As in so many aspects of our personal and professional lives, a philosophy of supervision is an amalgam of ideas, knowledge, and belief. It is not an equation drawn from one model or "predominant pattern" of supervision. It is more a constant reconstruction or refinement of the principles that reconcile the promise of "pedagogical leadership" with the reality of the school as a culturally derived formal organization. The philosophy of supervision is a call for a personal and continuing examination of the purpose, knowledge, and values that configure the process and potential of educational supervision. This is the stuff of wisdom and responsible supervision.

REFERENCES

Acheson, K. & Gall, M. (1980). *Techniques in the clinical supervision of teachers: Preservice and in-service applications.* New York: Longman.

Aldridge, A. O. (1959). *Man of reason: The life of Thomas Paine.* New York:

Alfonso, R. J., Firth, G. R., & Neville, R. F. (1981). *Instructional supervision: A behavior system.* Boston, MA: Allyn and Bacon.

Appleby, J., Hunt, L., & Jacob, M. (1994). *Telling the truth about history.* New York: W.W. Norton.

Argyris, C. & Schön, A. (1974). *Theory in practice: Increasing professional effectiveness.* San Francisco: Jossey-Bass Publishers.

Bailyn, B. (1960). *Education in the forming of American society: Needs and opportunities for study.* The Institute of Early American History and Culture, Williamsburg, VA: The University of North Carolina Press-Chapel Hill.

Barnes, B. (1990). Sociological theories of scientific knowledge. In R. C. Obly et al (Eds.). *Companion to the history of modern science.* London, England: Routledge.

Barr, A. S. (1931). *An introduction to the scientific study of classroom supervision.* New York: D. Appleton.

Barr, A. S. & Burton, W. H. (1926). *The supervision of instruction: A general volume.* New York: D. Appleton.

Barr, A. S., Burton, W. H., & Brueckner, L. J. (1938). *Supervision: Democratic leadership in the improvement of learning.* New York: D. Appleton-Century Company.

Barr, A. S., Burton, W. H., & Brueckner, L. J. (1947). *Supervision: Democratic leadership in the improvement of learning* (2nd ed.). New York: D. Appleton-Century Company.

Bayles, E. E. (1966). *Pragmatism in education.* New York: Harper and Row.

Baynes, K., Bohman, J. & McCarthy, T. (Eds.). (1987). *After philosophy: End or transformation?* Cambridge, MA: The MIT Press.

Bass, B. M. (1990) *Bass and Stogdill's handbook of leadership.* New York: The Free Press.

Belenky, M., Clinchy, B., Goldberger, N., & Tarule, J. (1986). *Woman's ways of knowing: The development of self, voice and mind.* New York: Basic Books

Berman, L. M. & Usery, M. L. (Eds.). (1966). *Personalized supervision: Sources and insights.* Alexandria, VA: ASCD.

Blumberg, A. (1980). *Supervision and teachers: A private cold war.* Berkeley, CA: McCutchan.

Blumberg, A. (1985). Where we came from: Notes on supervision in the 1840s. *Journal of Curriculum and Supervision, 1,* 56–65.

Bobbit, F. (1913). Some general principles of management applied to the problems of city school systems (*12th Yearbook in the National Society of the Study of Education, Part 1, The Supervision of City Schools;* pp. 7–96). Chicago, IL: The University of Chicago Press.

Bolin, F. (1983). *The language of instructional supervision, 1922–1982.* Unpublished doctoral dissertation, Teachers College, Columbia University.

Bolin, F. S. (1987). On defining supervision. *Journal of Curriculum and Supervision, 2,* 368–380.

Bolin, F. & Panaritis, P. (1992). Searching for a common purpose: A perspective on the history of supervision. In C. D. Glickman (Ed.). *Supervision in Transition* (pp. 30–43). Alexandria, VA: ASCD.

Bowers, C. A. & Flinders, D. J. (1991). *Culturally responsive teaching and supervision: A handbook for staff development.* New York: Teachers College Press.

Boyer, E. L. (1990). *Scholarship reconsidered.* Princeton, NJ: The Carnegie Foundation for the Advancement of Teaching.

Brennan, J. G. (1967). *The meaning of philosophy.* New York: Harper & Row.

Brinton, C. (1950). *Ideas and men: The story of Western thought.* Englewood Cliff, NJ: Prentice Hall.

Burbules, N. C. & Rice, S. (1991). Dialogues across difference: Continuing the conversation. *Harvard Educational Review, 61*(4), 393–413.

Burns, J. M. (1978). *Leadership.* New York: Harper Torchbooks.

Burton, W. H. (1922). Supervision and the improvement of teaching. New York: D. Appleton.

Butts, R. & Cremin, L. A. (1964). *A history of education in American culture.* New York: Holt, Reinhart and Winston.

Button, H. W. (1961). *A history of supervision in the public schools,*

1870–1950. Unpublished doctoral dissertation, Washington University, St. Louis.

Callahan, R. E. (1962). *Education and the cult of efficiency: A study of the social forces that have shaped the administration of the public schools.* Chicago, IL: University of Chicago Press.

Callahan, R. E. & Button, H. W. (1964). Historical change of the role of the man in the organization. In D. E. Griffiths (Ed.). *Behavioral Science and Administration*, pp. 73–92. National Society for Study of Education. Chicago, IL: Distributed by University of Chicago.

Campbell, R. (1992). *Truth and historicity.* New York: Oxford University Press.

Campbell, R. F., Fleming, T., Newell, L. J., & Bennion, J. W. (1987). *A history of thought and practice in educational administration.* New York: Teachers College Press.

Carr, E. H. (1961). *What is history?* New York: Alfred A. Knopf.

Cassirer, E. (1955). *The philosophy of the enlightenment* (translated by Fritz C.A. Koelln and James P. Pettegrove). Boston, MA: Beacon Press.

Code, L. (1991). *What can she know? Feminist theory and the construction of knowledge.* Ithaca, NY: Cornell University Press

Cogan, M. (1973). *Clinical supervision.* Boston, MA: Houghton-Mifflin.

Conant, J. B. (1947). *On understanding science: An historical approach.* New Haven: As cited in Appelby et al, 1994: 16.

Conant, J. (1963). *The education of American teachers.* New York: McGraw Hill.

Cremin, L. A. (1961). *The transformation of the schools.* New York: Alfred A. Knopf.

Cremin, L. A. (1970). *American education: The colonial experience, 1607–1783.* New York: Harper and Row.

Cremin, L. A. (1980). *American education: The national experience, 1783-1876.* New York: Harper and Row.

Cremin, L. A. (1988). *American education: The metropolitan experience, 1876–1980.* New York: Harper and Row.

Cuban, L. (1984). *How teachers taught: Constancy and change in American classrooms, 1890–1980.* New York: Longman.

Curti, M. (1959). *The social ideas of American educators.* Paterson, NJ: Littlefied, Adams.

Davies, B. (1989). Education for sexism: A theoretical analysis of the sex/gender bias in education. *Educational Philosophy and Theory, 21, No.1.* As quoted in Barbules and Rice. 1991: 393.

Deleuze, G. & Guattari, F. (1991). *What is philsophy.* As translated by H. Tomlinson & G. Burchell (1994). New York: Columbia University Press.

Demos, J. (1986). *Past, present and personal.* New York: Oxford University Press.

Dewey, J. (1910). *How we think.* Boston, MA: D.C. Heath.

Dewey, J. (1916). *Democracy and education.* New York: Macmillan.

Dewey, J. (1933). *How we think: A restatement of the relation of reflective thinking to the educative process.* Boston, MA: D.C. Heath.

Diesing, P. (1991). *How does social science work.* Pittsburgh, PA: University of Pittsburgh Press.

Diggins, J. P. (1989, Autumn). The philosopher in the schoolroom. *Wilson Quarterly,* 76–82.

Drucker, P. F. (Spring 1993). Of the knowledge society. *Wilson Quarterly,* 52–71.

Drucker, P. F. (Nov. 1994). The age of social transformation. *The Atlantic Monthly,* 53–80.

Edwards, P. & Pap, A. (1973). *An introduction to philosophy: Readings from classical and contemporary sources.* New York: The Free Press.

Eisner, E. (1988, June-July). *The primary of experience and the politics of method.* Educational Researcher.

Eisner, E. W. (1982). An artistic approach to supervision. In T. J. Sergiovanni (Ed.). *Supervision of Teaching* (pp. 53–66). Washington, D.C.: ASCD.

Etzioni, A. (1993). *The spirit of community: Rights, responsibilities and the communitarian agenda.* New York: Crown Publishers, Inc.

Fenstermacher, G. D. (1994) The knower and the known: The nature of knowledge in research on teaching. *Review of Research in Education, 20,* 3–56.

Fiedler, F. E. (1967). *A theory of leadership effectiveness.* New York: McGraw-Hill.

Fiedler, F. E. (1971). *Leadership.* New York: General Learning Press.

Finkelstein, B. (1989) *Governing the young: Teacher behavior in popular primary schools in nineteenth-century United States.* New York: Falmer Press.

Finkelstein, B. (1992). Educational historians as mythmakers. *Review of Research in Education, 18,* 255–297.

Flinders, D. J. (1991a). Supervision as critical inquiry. *Journal of Curriculum and Supervision, 6*(2), 87–106.

Flinders, D. J. (1991b). *Supervision reconsidered: An ecological perspective.* Unpublished paper presented at the meeting of the Council of Professors of Instructional Supervision, Houston.

Flower, E. & Murphey, M. (1977). *A history of philosophy in America.* New York: Capricorn Books.

Foucault, M. (1972). *The archeaology of knowledge.* As translated by A. M. Sheridan Smith. New York: Pantheon Books, Random House.

Foucault, M. (1980). Power/knowledge: Selected interviews and other meetings (1972–1977), translated by Colin Gordon, (Ed.), Leo Marshall, John Mepham, & Kate Soper. New York: As referenced in Appelby et al, 1994.

Franfort, J. (1951). *Before philosophy: The intellectual adventure of ancient man.* Middlesex, England: Penguin Books.

Garcia, J. J. E. (1992). *Philsophy and its history: Issues in philsophical historiography.* New York: State University of New York Press.

Gardner, J. (1995). *Leading minds: An anatomy of leadership.* New York: Basic Books.

Garman, N. (1980). Theories embedded in the events of clincial supervision: A hermeneutic approach. *Journal of Curriculum and Supervsion, 5*(3), 201–213.

Garman, N. (1982). The clinical approach to supervision. In T. Sergiovanni (Ed.). *The supervision of teaching.* Alexandria, VA: ASCD.

Garman, N. (1986). Reflection, the heart of clincial supervision: A modern rationale for professional practice. *Journal of Curriculum and Supervision, 2*(1), 1–24.

Garman, N. & Haggerson, N. (1993). Philosophic consideration in the practice of clincial supervision. In R. Anderson and K. Snyder (Eds.). *Clinical supervision: Coaching for higher performance.* Lancaster, PA: Technomic Press.

Garman, N. (1994). Beyond the reflective practitioner and toward discursive practice. *Teaching and Teachers' Work, 2*(4), 1–7.

Garman, N. (1997). Is clinical supervision a viable model for use in public schools? A no position. In J. Glanz & R. F. Neville, *Educational supervision: Perspectives, issues, and controversies.* Boston, MA: Christopher-Gordon Publishers, Inc.

Geertz, C. (1980, Spring). *Blurred genres: The refiguration of social thought.* American Scholar 49.

Geertz, C. (1988). *Works and lives: The anthropologist as author.* Stanford, CA: Stanford University Press.

George, W. (1622). Of domestical duties. As referenced in Demos, J. (1986) *Past, present, and personal* (p. 27), New York: Oxford University Press.

Gerth, H. H. & Mills, C. W., translators, (1946). *From Max Weber: Essays in sociology.* New York: Oxford University Press.

Giddens, A. (1990). *The consequences of modernity.* United Kingdom: Polity Press, in association with Basil Blackwell.

Giddens, A. (1984). *The constitution of society.* Berkely, CA: University of California Press.

Gilligan, C. (1982). *In a different voice: Psychological theory and women's development.* Cambridge, MA: Harvard University Press

Giroux, H. A. (1983). *Theory and resistance in education: A pedagogy for the opposition.* New York: Bergin and Garvey Publishers, Inc.

Glanz, J. (1990). Beyond bureaucracy: Notes on the professionalization of public school supervision in the early twentieth century. *Journal of Curriculum and Supervision, 5*(2), 150–170.

Glanz, J. (1991). *Bureaucracy and professionalism: The evolution of public school supervision.* Rutherford, NJ: Fairleigh Dickinson University Press.

Glanz, J. (1995). Exploring supervisory history: An invitation and agenda. *Journal of Curriculum and Supervision, 10,* 95–113.

Glickman, C. (1985). *Supervision of instruction: A developmental approach.* Boston, MA: Allyn and Bacon.

Glickman, C. (Ed.). (1992). *Supervision in transition.* Alexandria, VA: ASCD.

Glickman, C. (1993). *Renewing America's schools: A guide for school based action.* San Francisco, CA: Jossey-Bass Publishers.

Glymour, C. (1992). *Thinking things through: An introduction to philsophical issues and achievments.* Cambridge, MA: The MIT Press.

Goldhammer, R. (1969). *Clinical supervision: Special methods for the supervision of teachers.* New York: Holt, Rhinehart, Winston.

Goldhammer, R., Anderson, R. H., & Krajewski, R. J. (1980). *Clinical supervision: Special methods for the supervision of teachers.* New York: Holt, Rhinehart, Winston.

Goldsberry, L. F. (1986). The reflective mindscape. *Journal of Curriculum and Supervision, 1*(4), 348.

Golinski, J. The theory of practice and the practice of theory: Sciological approaches to the history of science. *ISIS, 81,* 492–505.

Gomery, D. (1994, Summer). In search of the cybermarket. *Wilson Quarterly, 18*(3), 9–17.

Grass, B. M. (1964). *The managing of organizations: Volume 1.* New York: The Free Press of Glencoe, the Crowell-Collier Publishing Company.

Greene, M. (1965). *The public schools and private vision.* New York: Random House.

Greene, M. (1989). Educational philsophy and teacher empowerment. In proceedings of the national forum of the Association of Independent Liberal Arts College for Teacher Education, Indianpolis, IN, June 1989.

Greene, M. (1994). Epistomology and educational research: The influence of recent approaches to knowledge. In L. Darling-Hammond (Ed.). *Review of Research in Education, 20,* Washington, D.C.: American Educational Research Association, pp. 423–464.

Griffiths, P. A. (Ed.). (1967). *Knowledge and belief.* London, England: Ely House, Oxford University Press.

Grimmet, P. P. & MacKinnon, A. M. (1992). Craft knowledge and the education of teachers. *Review of Research in Education, 18,* 385–456.

Grumet, M. R. (1978). *Supervision and situation: A methodology of self report for teacher education.* A paper presented at the AERA annual meeting.

Hamlyn, D. W. (1972). History of epistemology. In P. Edwards, (Ed.). *The Encyclopedia of Philosophy* (Vol. 3) pp. 8–38. New York: Collier Macmillan Publishers.

Hare, P. H. (Ed.) (1988). *Doing philosophy historically.* Buffalo, NY: Prometheus Books.

Hargreaves, A. (1994). *Changing teachers, changing times: Teachers' work and culture in the postmodern age.* London, England: Cassell Publishers.

Harper, C. (1939). *A century of public teacher education: The story of the state teachers colleges as the evolved from the normal schools.* Washington, D.C.: American Association of Teachers Colleges, a Department of the National Education Association.

Harris, B. M. (1975). *Supervisory behavior in education (2nd ed.).* Englewood Cliffs, NJ: Prentice Hall.

Hodgkinson, C. (1983). *The Philosophy of Leadership.* New York: St. Martin's Press.

Holland, P. (1988). Keeping faith with Cogan: Current theorizing in a maturing practice of clincial supervision. *Journal of Curriculum and Supervision, 3*(2), 97–108.

Holland, P. (1989). Reading between the lines: Exploring the supervisory conference through discourse analysis. *Journal of Curriculum and Supervision. 4*(4), 380–382.

Holland, P. (1990). A hermeneutic perspective on supervision scholarship. *Journal of Curriculum and Supervision. 5*(3), 252–255.

Holland, P. (1994). *What do we talk of when we talk of supervision?* Paper presented at the meeting of the Council of Professors of Instructional Supervision, Instruction Supervision. Fordham University, New York.

Hosic, J. F. (1920). The democratization of supervision. *School and Society, 11,* 331–336.

Huebner, D. (1966). Curriculum language and classroom meanings. In J. B. MacDonald & R. H. Leeper (Eds.). *Language and Meaning,* Washington D.C.: ASCD.

Hutchins, R. M. (1936). *Higher learning in America.* New Haven: Yale University Press.

Johnson, W. R. (1994). "Chanting Choristers": Simultaneous recitation in Baltimore's nineteenth-century primary schools. *History of Education Quarterly, 34*(1), 1–23.

Kanigel, R. (Summer 1996). "Frederick Taylor's Apprenticeship." *Wilson Quarterly,* 44–51.

Karier, C. (1982). Supervision in historic perspective. In T. J. Sergiovanni (Ed.). *Supervision of Teaching* (pp. 2–15). Alexandria, VA: ASCD.

Kerr, C., Dunlop, J. T., Harbison, F., & Myers, C. A. (1960). *Industrialism and industrial man: The problems of labor and management in economic growth.* Boston, MA: Harvard University Press.

Ketcham, R. (1965). *Benjamin Franklin.* New York: Macmillan.

Ketcham, R. (1972). *Thomas Jefferson.* In P. Edwards, (Ed). *The Encyclopedia of Philosophy,* 4, 259–260. New York: Collier Macmillan Publishers.

Kliebard, H. M. (1992). Constructing a history of the American curriculum. In P. W. Jackson (Ed.). *Handbook of research on curriculum: A project of the American Educational Research Association.* New York: Macmillan.

Koapman, G. R., Miel, A., & Misner, P. (1943). *Democratic school administration.* New York and London, England: D. Appleton-Century Co.

Krey, R. D. & Burke, P. J. (1989). *A design for instructional supervision.* Springfield, IL: Charles C. Thomas.

Kurtz, P. (1972). American philosophy. In P. Edwards, (Ed.). *The encyclopedia of philosophy,* vol. 1, 83–93. New York: Collier Macmillan Publishers.

Levine, L. W. (1996). *The opening of the American mind: Cannons, culture, and history.* Boston, MA: Beacon Press.

Lewis, R. W. B. (1958). *The American Adam: Innocence, tragedy and tradition in the nineteenth century.* Chicago, IL: University of Chicago Press.

Lucio, W. H. & McNeil, J. D. (1962). *Supervision: A synthesis of thought and action.* New York: McGraw-Hill.

Lyotard, J. F. (1989). *The postmodern condition: A report on knowledge.* Minneapolis, MN: University of Minnesota Press. As referenced in P.E. Holland (1994).

Mann, H. (1855). *Lectures on education.* Boston, MA: Ide and Dutton. As reprinted by the Arno Press & The New York Times, New York, 1969.

Maxcy, S. J. (1991). *Educational leadership: A critical pragmatic perspective.* New York: Bergin and Garvey.

McBride, M. & Skau, K. G. (1995). Trust, empowerment and reflection:

Essentials of supervision. *Journal of Curriculum and Supervision,* 10(3), 262–277.

McNeil, J. D. (1982). A scientific approach to supervision. In T. J. Sergiovanni (Ed.). *Supervision of Teaching,* (pp. 18–34). Alexandria, VA: ASCD.

Midgley, M. (1992). Philosophical plumbing. A. P. Griffiths (Ed.). *The impulse to philosophise.* Royal Institute of Philosophy Supplement: 33, Cambridge University Press.

Miel, A. (1946). *Changing the curriculum: A social process.* New York: Appleton-Century Crafts.

Mohr, L. B. (1994). Authority in organization: On the reconciliation of democracy and expertise. *Journal of Public Administration Research and Theory, Part 4, 1,* 49–65.

Moran, M. (1967). New England transcendentalism. In Paul Edwards (Ed.). *The Encyclopedia of Philosophy, Vol. 5.* New York: Collier Macmillan Publishers.

Moran, M. (1972). Henry David Thoreau. In Paul Edwards (Ed.). *The Encyclopedia of Philosophy, Vol. 8.* New York: Collier Macmillan Publishers.

Morrison, S. E. & Commanger, H. S. (1962). *The Growth of the American Republic, Vol. 2.* New York: Oxford University Press.

Mosher, R. & Purpel, D. (1972). *Supervision: The reluctant profession.* Boston, MA: Houghton-Mifflin.

Nagel, E. (1961). *The structure of science: Problems in the logic of scientific explanation.* New York: Harcourt, Brace and World, Inc.

Nagel, T. (1987). *What does it all mean?* New York: Oxford University Press.

Nutt, H. W. (1920). *The supervision of instruction.* Boston, MA: Houghton-Mifflin.

Nye, R. B. (1974). *Society and culture in America.* New York: Harper and Row, Publishers.

O'Brien, C. C. (1996). *The long affair: Thomas Jefferson and the French Revolution, 1785–1800.* Chicago, IL: University of Chicago Press.

Ornstein, A. C. (1992). Philosophy as a basis for curriculum decision. In A. C. Ornstein & L. S. Behar (Eds.). *Contemporary issues in curriculum.* Boston, MA: Allyn and Bacon.

Pajak, E. (1989). *Identification of supervisory proficiencies project.* A report based on research conducted at the University of Georgia under contract with the ASCD.

Pajak, E. (1993a). *Approaches to clinical supervision: Alternatives for improving instruction.* Norwood, MA: Christopher Gordon Publishers.

Pajak, E. (1993b). Change and continuity in supervision and leadership. In G. Cawelti (Ed.). *Challenges and achievements of American education* (pp. 158–186). Alexandria, VA: ASCD.

Perrow, C. (1979). *Complex organization: A critical essay,* (2nd ed.). Glenview, IL: Scott, Foresman and Company.

Pierce, P. R. (1935). *The origin and development of the public school principalship.* Chicago, IL: The University of Chicago Press.

Polanyi, M. (1958). *Personal knowledge: Towards a post-critical philosophy.* New York: Harper and Row.

Portelli, J. P. (1987). On defining curriculum. *Journal of Curriculum and Supervision, vol. 2,* 354–367.

Postman, N. (1992). *Technology: The surrender of culture to technology.* New York: Alfred A. Knopf.

Powell, A. (1980). *The uncertain profession: Harvard and the search for educational authority.* Cambridge: Harvard University Press.

Pritzkau, P. T. (1959). *The dynamics of curriculum development.* Englewood Cliffs, NJ: Prentice Hall.

Ratner, J. (Ed.). (1939). *Intelligence in the modern world: John Dewey'a Philosophy.* New York: Random House.

Ravitch, D. (1983). *The troubled crusade: American education 1945–1980.* New York: Basic Books, Inc.

Riley, W. (1959). *American thought: From puritanism to pragmatism and beyond.* Gloucester, MA: Peter Smith Publishers.

Robinson, D. (1995). *An intellectual history of psychology* (3rd ed.). Madison, WI: The University of Wisconsin Press.

Rorty, R. (1967). *The linguistic turn: Recent essays in philosophical method.* Chicago, IL: University of Chicago Press.

Roszak, T. (1994). The cult of information: *A neo-buddite treatise on high techs artificial intelligence and the art of thinking.* Berkley, CA: University of California Press.

Sandel, M.J. (1996, May 9). "Dewey Rides Again." A review of Alan Ryan's *John Dewey and the High Tide of American Liberalism. The New York Review of Books, 43,(8),* 35–38.

Sandburg, C. (1936). *The people, yes.* Orlando, FL: A Harvest Book, Harcourt Brace & Company (1990), originally published by Harcourt Brace and Company in 1936.

Santayana, G. (1913). *Winds of doctrine.* London, England: J. M. Dent & Co. As reprinted in: *The American intellectual tradition,* (2nd ed.), Vol. 11. D. Hollinger & C. Copper (Eds.). 1993. New York: Oxford University Press.

Schrag, F. (1992). Conceptions of knowledge. In P. W. Jackson (Ed.). *Handbook of Research on Curriculum. A project of the American Educational Research Association* (pp. 268–301). New York: Macmillan.

Scheffler, I. (1965). *Conditions of knowledge: An introduction to epistemology and education.* Chicago, IL: Scott, Foresman and Company.

Schneider, H. W. (1963). *A history of American philosophy.* New York: Columbia University Press.

Schon, D. (1983). *The reflective practitioner: How professionals think in action.* New York: Basic Books, Inc.

Sergiovanni, T. J. (1982). Toward a theory of supervisory practice: integrating scientific, clinical, and artistic views. In T. J. Sergiovanni (Ed.). Supervision of Teaching. Alexandria, VA: ASCD.

Sergiovanni, T. J. (1989). Science and scientism in supervision and teaching. *Journal of Curriculum and Supervision, 4*(2), 93–105.

Sergiovanni, T. J. (1990). *Value-added leadership: How to get extraordinary performance in schools.* San Diego, CA: Harcourt, Brace, Jovanovich.

Sergiovanni, T. J. & Starratt, R. J. (1993). *Supervision: A redefinition* (5th ed.). New York: McGraw-Hill.

Sergiovanni, T. J. (1996). *Leadership for the schoolhouse.* San Francisco: Jossey-Bass Publishers.

Sergiovanni, T. J. (1997). How can we move toward a community theory of supervision? Wrong theory/wrong practice. In J. Glanz & R. F. Neville (Eds.). *Educational Supervision: Perspectives, issues, and controversies,* Norwood, MA: Christopher-Gordon Publishers, Inc.

Sergiovanni, T. J. & Carver, F. D. (1980). *The new school executive: A theory of administration.* New York: Harper and Row Publishers.

Sergiovanni, T. J. & Corbally, J. E. (1984). *Leadership and Organizational Culture.* Urbana, IL: University of Illinois Press.

Sills, C. & Jensen, G. H. (Eds.). (1992). The *philosophy of discourse: The rhetorical turn in 20th centrury thought.* Portsmouth, NH: Boynton/Cook Publishers.

Simon, H. A. (1947). *Administrative behavior.* New York: Macmillan.

Smyth, J. (1984). Toward a critical consciousness in the instructional supervision of experienced teachers. *Curriculum Inquiry,* Ontario Institute for Studies in Education. New York: John Wiley & Sons.

Smyth, J. (1986a). Cinderella syndrome: A philosophical view of supervision as a field of study. A paper presented at the annual meeting of the American Educational Research Association, San Francisco, CA.

Smyth, J. (Ed.). (1986b). *Learning about teaching through clinical supervision.* London, England: Croom Helm.

Smyth, J. (1988). A critical perspective for clinical supervision. *Journal of Curriculum and Supervision, 3*(2), 136–156.

Smyth, J. (1989). An alternative and an educative agenda for supervision as a field of study. *Journal of Curriculum and Supervision, 4*(2), 162–177.

Smyth, J. (1991a). Instructional supervision and the redefinition of it in the schools. *Journal of Curriculum and Supervision, 7*, 90–99.

Smyth, J. (1991b). *Teachers as collaborative learners: Challenging dominant forms of supervision.* Philadelphia, PA: Open University Press.

Smyth, J. (1992). Teachers' work and the politics of reflection. *American Educational Research Journal, 29*(2), 267–300.

Smyth, J. (1997). Is supervision more than surveillance of instruction. In J. Glanz & R. F. Neville (Ed.). *Educational supervision: Perspective, issues, and controversies.* Norwood, MA: Christopher-Gordon Publishers.

Soltis, J. (1984). On the nature of educational research. *Educational Research, 13*(10), 5–10.

Spears, H. (1953). Improving the supervision of instruction. Englewood Cliffs, NJ: Prentice Hall.

Spiller, R. E., Throp, W., Johnson, T. H., Canby, H. S., & Ludwig, R. M. (1963). *Literary history of the United States* (3rd ed.). New York: Macmillan.

Starratt, R. J. (1992). After supervision. *Journal of Curriculum and Supervision, 8*, 77–86.

Starratt, R. J. (1993). *The drama of leadership.* Washington, D.C.: The Falmer Press.

Stogdill, R. M. (1974). *Handbook of leadership.* New York: Free Press.

Suzzallo, T. H. (1969). *The rise of local school supervision in Massachusetts.* New York: Arno Press.

Tanner, D. & Tanner, L. (1987). *Supervision in education: Problems and practices.* New York: Macmillan.

Taylor, C. (1987). Overcoming epistomology. In K. Baynes, J. Bohman, & T. McCarthy (Eds.). *After philosophy: End or transformation?* Cambridge, MA: The MIT Press.

Taylor, F. W. (1911). *The principles of scientific management.* New York: Harpers.

Thorndike, E. L. & Woodworth, R. S. (1901). The importance of improvement in one mental function upon the efficiency of other functions. *Psychological Review, 8.*

Thorndike, E.L. (1911). *Animal intelligence: Experimental studies.* New York: Macmillan.

Tocqueville, A. D. (1838). *Democracy in America.* As translated by Harry Reeve, Esq., with notes and bibliography by Phillips Bradley. New York: Vintage Books, Random House, 1945.

Tracy, S. (1993). Restructuring instructional supervision. *Contemporary Education, 64*(2).

Tracy, S. (1997). Will technology replaced the role of the supervisor? In J. Glanz & R. F. Neville (Eds.). *Educational supervision: Perspective, issues, and controversies.* Norwood, MA: Christopher-Gordon Publishers.

Turner, B. S. (1992). *Max Weber: From history to modernity.* New York: Routledge.

Tyack, D. & Cuban, L. (1995). *Tinkering toward utopia: A century of public school reform.* Cambridge, MA: Harvard University Press.

Tyack, D. B. (1974). *The one best system: A history of American education.* Cambridge, MA: Harvard University Press.

Tyack, D. B. (Fall 1976). Pilgrim's progress: Toward a social history of the school superintendency, 1860–1960. *History of Education Quarterly*, 257–300.

Tyack, D. B. & Hansot, E. (1982). *Managers of virtue: Public school leadership in America, 1820–1980.* New York: Basic Books.

Ulich, R. (1950). *History of educational thought.* New York: American Book Company.

Van Doren, C. (1991). History of knowledge: Past, present and future. Secaucus, NJ: Birch Lane Press.

Veatch, H. B. (1990). *Swimming against the current in contemporary philosophy.* Washington D.C.: The Catholic University of America Press.

Whitehead, A. N. (1927). *Symbolism: Its meaning and effect.* New York: Fordham University Press, 1985: 87–88.

Wiles, R. (1967). *Supervision for better schools.* Englewood Cliffs, NJ: Prentice-Hall.

Weber, M. (1978). *Economy and society: An outline of interpretive sociology.* G. Roth & C. Wittich (Eds.). Translators, Ephraim Fischoff, et al. Berkeley, CA: University of California Press.

NOTES

1. This chapter is admittedly incomplete and more a beginning to our examination of this compelling topic than a straightforward report of research findings. We have drawn extensively from the work of many colleagues and other scholars and ask their pardon for errors of fact and interpretation. We are particularly indebted to the work of: Jeffrey Glanz, Patricia Holland, Edward Pajak, Frances Schoonmaker (formerly Bolin), Thomas J. Sergiovanni, John Smyth, and Robert J. Starratt.

2. In the pattern of colonial development, the English eventually dominated. By 1689, English settlements stretched in a continuous line down the North American coast from what is now Maine to the Carolinas. The decisive influence of their culture, however, was more than numbers of people or technical know how. It was in large measure education because the English conceived of the colonies as "permanent, self sustaining communities where education, among other intellectual pursuits, were to flourish," not as temporary arrangements (Cremin, 1980).

3. Conor Curise O'Brien's (1996) highly critical book on Jefferson, *The Long Affair: Thomas Jefferson and the French Revolution, 1785–1800*, announces that traditional historians have made Jefferson a sacred icon—a prophet of America's civil religion. O'Brien challenges this tradition and connects certain ills of contemporary America to Jefferson (e.g., racism and the antifederal inclinations of various militia rebel groups who make distorted claims about Jefferson's "holy cause of freedom"). Gordon S. Wood concludes his review of O'Brien's book (The New York Review of Books, Vol. XLIX, No. 3, February 2, 1997) with the following reminder: "Jefferson belongs in the eighteenth century, but he did make many ringing statements in celebration of liberty and equality that have resounded throughout our culture, indeed the world's culture, for the past two hundred years. It is these transcendent statements that we need to honor, not the eighteenth-century slave holder who remains inextricably enmeshed in a lost and distant past.

4. Tocqueville traveled in America in 1831 with his friend and colleague Gustave de Beaumont. They were young French noblemen (i.e., magistrates) sent by the minister of the interior, to examine the prison system and to report back their findings. Their unofficial purpose was to write about democracy, to "examine the nature and working of democracy as it might be applicable in Europe . . . as a working principle of society and government." *Democracy in America* continues to offer insights on the nature of democracy and patterns of belief in American life during the early national period.

5. As urban school population and costs rose the monitorial system developed by English educators, "most notably" Joseph Lancaster, took hold for a time in America. It was based on two "pedagogical innovations" that were attractive to school managers and supervisors,

(i.e., principal/teachers): subject matter carefully sequenced accompanied by an "elaborate system of directives for teaching it"; the use of older students as monitors–to teach the younger children (Cremin, 1980, p. 396). Its use was greatest in the 1820s ("there were about 150 Lancasterian schools in the country"), but the system fell out of favor in the 1830s (Cremin, p. 396). In theory, the Lancasterian system would make it possible to maintain the practice of individual recitation (Johnson, 1994, p. 4), which had been a feature of pedagogy in the one-room district school. In 1839, Baltimore set aside the monitorial method of instruction, over time being replaced which by "simultaneous recitation," where "students of varying degrees of preparation recited the same material together as a group . . . remained a widespread pedagogical technique in Baltimore and other cities, even into the 1890s" (p. 3). Johnson indicates that the evidence from Baltimore "suggests that neither the monitorial method nor incipient bureaucracy created dull, monotonous, and indifferent routines in nineteenth-century urban schools. Instead, these features can be attributed at least in part to simultaneous recitation, a pedagogic method that quickly supplanted monitorial instruction in Baltimore, and which, for the remainder of the century, blunted some of those characteristics, such as competition and hierarchy, that we associate with school bureaucracy. Simultaneous recitation, then, provides a different lens through which to view the history of nineteenth-century urban schools" (p. 4).

6. After his election to Congress (1848) Mann lashed out against the evils of slavery–"how it polluted our free institutions and endangered our American experiment" (Curti, 1959, p. 136); how it contaminated private and public morals—and was an institution that was, "barbarous in nature, with which no compromise could be made." His vision for American education remained strong throughout his life, that the schoolroom shared the interests of society and personal life; each citizen, "should be imbued with a feeling for the wants, and a sense of the rights of others, as participants in the work of government" (Curti, 1959, pp. 132–136).

7. Emerson (1803–1882), son of a Unitarian clergyman, attended Boston Latin School, then Harvard, after which he "became a schoolmaster while he continued to study extramurally at Harvard Divinity School" (Moran, 1972, Vol. 2, pp. 477–479). He was appointed a pastor of a church in Boston (1829), after which (1833) he went to Europe to study and shape his philosophical outlook. He had difficulty reconciling himself with society's values that were "essentially one of the property of fences, of exclusiveness." His writings became a part of the "general intellectual consciousness of America" (Moran, p. 479). Thoreau (1817–1861) has been described as an anarchist and a revolutionary (Moran, 1972). He had a brief "skirmish with school teaching but soon after devoted himself to literature and the study of nature." He worked with Emerson for a time when his intellectual development was guided by the ideas of transcendentalism. Thoreau's concern for natural history reflected his interest in "concrete communion with nature." Recall his essay, "Civil Disobedience," where he espoused the principle of action on the dictates of one's own conscience (Moran, 1972, Vol. 8, pp. 121–122).

8. Harper (1939) documented the story of teacher education for the period 1839–1939. His book, *A Century of Public Teacher Education,* was subtitled, "the story of the state teachers colleges as they evolved from the normal schools." Harper recounts the events of 1825 when Governor De Witt Clinton recommended to the New York state legislature that it "concerns itself with the problem of securing a supply of competent teachers"—or "suffer the failure of democratic representative government" (Harper, 1939, p. 14).

9. Tanner and Tanner (1987) point to the importance of the normal school to the "common school idea and the very survival of a free republic". They emphasize the contribution of the normal school to the professionalization of teaching and reference the awareness of the early leaders of American education (Mann, Carter, Barnard) as to the distinction between *teaching school* and *keeping school* (Tanner & Tanner, 1987, p. 17).

10. Tyack and Hansot (1982, pp. 48-49) describe the teacher institutes as "short-term conventions" that "often followed the format of religious revivals." Like the "dignified denominationally sponsored revivals of the 1830s and 1840s," the meetings focused on pedagogy and expressed a distinctly spiritual and moral dimension.

11. Harris wrote voluminously in philosophy, literary criticism, the arts, and on questions of politics and economics. In Hegal, he found a philosophy which was optimistic and idealistic–a perspective which in his judgment, "infused the world with divine purpose" and which, "like Christianity, endowed the individual with a noble and immortal destiny" (Spiller et al, p. 972). Hegalianism appeared to justify the "existing order and authorities" as an "unfolding of objective reason that "lifted the individual to a higher plane of self realization" while regarding the "individual and the solidarity of the society as one and the same." According to Harris, the individual could only be realized "through the family, school, church, and state" (Spiller et al, 1963, p. 972).

12. As reviewed by Kliebard (1992, pp. 162–167) *social efficiency* was a term popular "in the early part of the 20th century." It described "the social and educational doctrine that lay behind reforms such as certain recommendations of the Cardinal Principles Report," completed by the NEA in 1918. Krug (1964) "reintroduced the term," which he "defines as a blending of two forces for change in American education, education for social control and education for social service" (Kliebard, p. 163).

13. In Drucker's view few thinkers in history have had "a greater impact than Taylor; and few have been so willfully misunderstood and so assiduously misquoted . . . Taylor has suffered because history has proven him right and the intellectuals wrong; . . . Taylor is ignored because contempt for work still lingers, above all among the intellectuals; . . . His reputation has suffered precisely because he applied knowledge to the study of work" (Drucker, 1993).

14. In 1878, Taylor finished an apprenticeship in a pump manufacturing firm in Philadelphia. He moved on to a steel mill, where he became chief engineer, developing "time and motion study, pay incentive schemes, work standards, and other innovations, which together made for what he saw as a new *science*, one promising even cheaper, more efficient production." In 1910, then-attorney Louis Brandeis argued before the Interstate Commerce Commission that the railroads did not need a "rate hike," "they need a dose of scientific management. . . . Taylor's system of science-bred industrial efficiency." In Taylor's scheme, management and labor would have their quarrels resolved by "science, the impartial arbiter would decide." One observer reports that "Taylor's thinking had become part of our moral inheritance" (Robert Kanigel, Frederick Taylor's apprenticeship. *The Wilson Quarterly*, Summer 1996, pp. 44–51).

15. Bolin's (1983) comprehensive analysis of the writings of leaders in the area of instructional supervision for the period 1922–1982 included the work of: Arvid S. Barr; William H. Burton; Leo J. Brueckner; Alice Miel; Morris Cogan; and Thomas J. Sergiovanni. Her study provides a thorough and poignant examination of their work particularly as related to: meanings and definitions; supervision and the educational practices of teachers; and the stability of their proposals over time (Bolin, p. 22). She has clarified the evolution of supervisory thought including "scientific" perspectives.

8

THE PSYCHOLOGY OF SUPERVISION

Robert J. Garmston

INSTITUTE FOR INTELLIGENT BEHAVIOR

Laura E. Lipton   **Kim Kaiser**

EDUCATIONAL CONSULTING SERVICES   ERICKSON INSTITUTE

INTRODUCTION

As schools enter the twenty-first century, the most significant change in the view of supervision is that the one-on-one work of a supervisor is only a partial, limited, and limiting aspect of the work. As schools become self-renewing institutions, workplaces in which learning is valued, understood, and practiced by all, supervisory interactions will be built on reciprocal relationships in groups and learning partnerships. Outcomes of mutual growth and professional development will drive the supervisory interaction. Three reasons exist for this. First, the knowledge base about teaching and learning is vast, intricate, and growing, and the most efficient way for educators to gain and maintain proficiency in its application is through group oriented professional development activities. The second reason is the growing realization that the culture of the workplace influences professional practice more than acquisition of a pedagogical knowledge base. The contemporary supervisor, therefore, must be a social ecologist with the skills to maintain and nurture a healthy school system. The third reason is that a counterpoint of divergent voices is our evolutionary promise. Valuing and celebrating diversity is the well-spring of creative unity. Supervision has the potential to create a world view that in the differentiation lies our strength to evolve and that growth is fostered by dialogue.

We will examine several dominant schools of psychological thought in this chapter and relate their contributions to supervision practices in the past, present, and future. We believe it useful for the student of educational supervision, supervisors of supervisors, and supervisors themselves to have an understanding of the supervision models that exist and might exist, along with their prevailing psychological principles and assumptions. In addition, based on an examination of the research on levels of adults development, we will present supervisory approaches that are most likely to promote professional growth. With this knowledge, educators can:

1. Analyze the supervisory model(s) being used to determine psychological foundations. If only a single psychological orientation is being represented, the model may be inadequate.
2. Compare the psychological principles of the supervision model in use with the adopted pedagogical views on learning. Without congruence, teachers will receive two messages, creating a shortcut to professional schizophrenia, teacher burnout, and cynicism.
3. Develop self-renewing work environments that draw on the psychological principles found in systems theory and which bear a potent relationship to adult learning and development.

Finally, we confess that this treatment of psychological foundations of supervision is influenced by our own interpretation of the aims of schooling in a democratic society. We desire students who are life-long learners, who employ moral reasoning, who have the capacity to examine their own systems of reasoning, who have skills of independence and interdependence, and who are informed, thoughtful, caring, and participating citizens in a local, state, national and world community.

We ultimately, envision schools in which the function of supervision evolves into a collaborative, systems orientation in which learning about instruction is everyone's responsibility. In such schools, both the role and term of supervision as it is presently practiced become anachronistic.

We will define psychology in this chapter as the study of the mind and all its mental activities. We will suggest that the psychology of supervision involves the interplay of the physiological phenomena, personal experiences, and constructed meaning making of all parties involved in an interaction, and we will review the antecedents to present practice through the lenses of their psychological orientations. Based on a constructivist-developmental approach to human development, defined in this chapter, we will suggest a reconceptualization of supervision. We invite the reader to rethink the role of supervision, and to consider the relationship between supervision and individual growth, student learning, and school change as we describe nine principles of supervisory mediation. Finally, through an examination of nine psychological principles of organizational interactions, we will ask the reader to consider new goals and purposes for supervisory practice related to reshaping the culture of schools.

We will conclude with our vision of the promises and potential of supervisory practice in creating self-renewing organizations, and raise considerations for further study regarding reciprocal patterns of influence among schools and communities, preparation programs, supervisors, and school staffs, and the students they serve.

CONTEXT

Six Premises Regarding the Role of Psychology in Supervision

There are six premises that illuminate the role psychology plays in educational supervision and drive the thinking in this chapter.

1. *Psychological Principles Form an Invisible Foundation of Supervision*
   Ever since supervision emerged as a special area of study and practice in the late 1800s, conceptions of supervisory purposes have evolved that have roughly paralleled pedagogical ideas about the purposes of schooling. Psychological principles, often unstated, are an important part of the foundation for each pedagogical approach and, indeed, for each model of supervision. Making these principles explicit, understanding their relationship to supervisory goals, and understanding their relationship to dominant views of student learning and curriculum construction are prerequisite to making informed choices from among current and emerging supervisory models.

2. *Congruence in Psychological Orientation Will Improve Instruction*
   For supervisory practices to improve instruction, congruence in the psychological interactions across three contexts

must be met. First, the knowledge base upon which pedagogical and supervision practices are based must be broad and inclusive, utilizing research on cognition, child development, adult development, motivation and behavior, discipline specific pedagogy, and general pedagogy (Darling-Hammond with Sclan, 1992), with clearly articulated psychological orientations evident in the each arena. Second, there must be a clear and consistent delineation between evaluation and other major components of a professional growth program, such as administrative coaching, peer coaching, staff development, and action research (Costa, Garmston, & Lambert, 1988). In prevailing practice, the purpose of evaluation, and thus its underlying psychology, is discrepant from the psychological foundations espoused for supervision, which is intended to foster professional growth. Research on evaluation reveals no evidence that it improves instruction. In some cases this research actually produces negative correlations with teachers' effectiveness, as measured by student achievement gains (Ellett, Capie, & Johnson, 1981). Finally, and perhaps most importantly, it is our premise that the psychological values and assumptions of the supervisory model must be congruent with the values and assumptions of the instructional model.

3. *Personal Decisions are Based on Individual Psychology*
   All decisions are based on psychological phenomena. In other words, perceptions, emotions, and cognitive maps shape the construction of meaning that directs behavior. The majority of reform literature recognizes that while teachers must function as knowledgeable professionals collaborating for the benefit of students (Glickman, 1993; Sergiovanni, 1994; Fullan, 1993), they are, simultaneously, independent artisans needing the capacity to make a myriad of contextually based decisions (Darling-Hammond, Wise, & Pease, 1983). Effective teachers make decisions that represent the best match-in-the-moment from their knowledge base, skills, and experiences to the daily interactions with curriculum design and student interactions (Saphir, 1987). These processes of decision-making are grounded in a person's psychology. Thus, it is important and necessary for supervisory practice to be guided by understandings of the psychological principles that guide adult development and teacher decision-making (Clark & Peterson, 1986; Costa & Garmston, 1994).

4. *Communication Occurs on a Verbal and Nonverbal Level*
   People display both verbal and nonverbal behavioral manifestations of their psychological states. Supervisors must be aware of these cues in others, as well as their own verbal and nonverbal messages in order to promote interactions of enhanced communication, trust, and learning (Grinder, 1993; Lankton & Lankton, 1983).

5. *Psychological Stress Inhibits Cognitive Functioning*
   At certain thresholds, psychological stress limits cognition and decision-making capacities. Supervisors therefore need understandings and skills that enable them to design and conduct supervisory interactions in ways that minimize distress; however, they must also maximize positive levels of stress, or eustress, related to developing the skills, habits, and norms of professional rigor (Caine & Caine, 1991; MacLean, 1978).

6. *An Individual's Psychology Is Influenced by the Larger System in Which He or She Is a Part*

An individual's cognition, decisions, and subsequent behaviors are influenced more by the culture of the workplace than they are by personal biography (Frymier, 1987; Olds, 1992; Rosenholtz, 1989). A key function of supervision, then, is to shape an environment that fosters growth. The supervisory process attends both to interactions between individuals and groups, and interactions between individuals and the work environment. It concerns itself as much with the environment in which individual educators operate as it does with the individuals themselves.

Psychology

Psychology developed in the late nineteenth century as the offspring of philosophy and experimental physiology. Since its emergence as a special science, it has continued to embody the philosophical spirit of inquiry in its endeavor to examine human nature and behavior. Psychology has attempted to answer philosophical questions about the relationship between subject and object, the distinction between part and whole, the nature of meaning, and the distinction between individual and society and world. In exploring these questions, psychology has drawn both from the experience of clinical practice and the data of academic research.

A more complete review of psychology than is offered here would examine the lenses of specializations like experimental psychology, neurobiology, learning theory, drug therapy, and psychometrics. Even such an array of different lenses, however, produces a selective orientation because they are primarily the product of Eurocentric culture. As such, they represent only one set of the "psychologies" that people in many times and places have articulated. For example, they exclude the psychologies of indigenous people and those stemming from Eastern traditions, which offers one of the most extensive sources of well-formulated psychologies. Though there are multiple schools of psychological thought in Eastern traditions, all share some common features. These include phenomenological methods, which seek to describe the nature of a person's immediate experience. Each is concerned with human movement toward an ideal mode of being that anyone can attain who diligently seeks to do so. The path to this transformation encourages far-reaching changes in personality, usually through some form of meditation.

For the purposes of this chapter, we shall focus our attention primarily on the period in European history starting with the late nineteenth century and several Western models of psychological thought that evolved from that era. On that basis, psychology today is defined as the science dealing with the mind and mental processes related to the sum of a person's feelings, thoughts, theories, values, motivations, traits, decisions, behaviors, physiology, and learning. Psychology encompasses the mental activity that influences cognition that results in behavior. The sum of a person's mental activity is influenced by personal history, developmental factors, cognitive style, cultural dispositions, educational theories and beliefs, modality preferences, states of mind, adult developmental stages, and metaphors of personal identity (Costa & Garmston, 1994). Each of these, and their relationships to supervision, will be explored in the sections that follow.

It should be noted that our review of psychological literature revealed that categorizing psychological orientations is a fluid affair. Major contributors to the study of psychology are treated differently by different scholars in the field. Based on our survey of dominant thinking in the field and for the purposes of this chapter, we have clustered major contributors into five schools of psychological thought: (1) behaviorist, (2) psychoanalytic, (3) humanistic/existentialist, (4) cognitive, and (5) family systems therapy. The first three schools—behavioral, psychoanalytic, and cognitive—represent a commonly agreed upon division of psychological approaches that have influenced American psychology (Friman et al, 1993). The latter two schools—humanistic/existential and family systems therapy—are both well established and have introduced unique viewpoints, existential philosophy, and systems theory into the discipline. We also reference Neurolinguistic Programming as a psychological influence on current thinking and practice. Each of these psychological perspectives incorporates formulated assumptions about the nature of human beings, views on learning, sources of motivation, and considerations regarding adult development that have relevance to our study on the psychology of supervision.

Supervision

Glickman (1985) defines supervision as "the school function that improves instruction through direct assistance to teachers, curriculum development, in-service training, group development, and action research" (p. xv). Bolin and Panaritis (1992) support this definition and report that only two areas existed by the early 1990s in which a loose consensus had been built regarding supervision. First, that supervision is primarily concerned with the improvement of classroom practice for the benefit of students, regardless of what else may be entailed. Second, that the function of supervision is an important one, regardless of who carries it out (i.e., a superintendent, principal, supervisor, curriculum worker or peer).

In this chapter, we will introduce the potential of a third purpose for supervision, to influence the growth and development of all members of the school organization, increasing their capacity for learning and their potential for effectiveness on individual tasks and collaborative endeavors. We suggest, therefore, supervision has three special functions. These are to (1) improve instructional practice, (2) develop an individual educator's potential for learning, and (3) improve the organization's capacity for creating self-renewing work environments. Supervision has classically included a fourth purpose: the service of organizational needs such as informing personnel decisions, tenure, promotion, dismissal and assignment. In this chapter, we are excluding supervisory function related to personnel decisions and focusing on the three supervisory functions identified.

The Improvement of Practice The methods with which supervisors work toward instructional change and improvement in practice largely determine the degree of receptivity and response to the challenges for rigor they will receive from teachers (Grimmett, Rostad, & Ford, 1992). An informed application of psychological principles is likely to increase teachers' motivation for change and result in the improvement of practice in three areas: (1) a teacher's practice within their personal style of teaching, (2) the general practice of an individual teacher, and (3) the practice of teaching in general. The first—improvement of a teacher's practice within their personal style—would concern continual growth within an individual's preferred modes, including cognitive style, representational systems, and educational belief system. The second—improvement in the general practice of an individual teacher—would include an increase in effectiveness with students, which is a continually expanding repertoire of instructional strategies that may extend beyond unconscious style preferences, contextual decisions regarding classroom management, outcomes for their classes and individual students, and classroom-based assessment and instructional planning.

The third aspect of improvement of practice regards extending collective knowledge in the field of pedagogy. Sergiovanni (1992) suggests that "there is a difference between concern with one's teaching practice and concern with the practice of teaching" (p. 210). One critical dimension of supervision is its capacity to strengthen, to enhance, and to improve teaching practice itself. Concern for teaching practice includes the broad knowledge base regarding instructional repertoire, deep content understandings, knowledge of the structure of the disciplines, developmental knowledge about learning, and valued outcomes for students and schools, as well as the practical concerns and issues addressed by teachers on a daily basis.

Developing Individual Potential for Learning The second dimension of supervision is to develop an individual's potential for learning.

For some teachers, the press for change in instructional practice represents a high-pressure disturbance generating much anxiety, internal seething, and agitation, together with a sense that an overwhelming muddle is busily at work dismantling the stability of their world. For others, the press for change rekindles waning enthusiasm; stimulates a sense of wonder, excitement, and mystery about learning; and absorbs their interest in a manner that inspires a quiet confidence and serenity (Grimmett, Rostad, & Ford, 1992, p. 185).

Supervision that focuses on an individual's learning potential will incorporate strategies to produce productive, or syntonic, tension, and to reduce dystonic tension that inhibits cognitive capacity. It will promote professional inquiry and reflection in all phases of teaching: during planning, while teaching, and after instruction. Furthermore, it will facilitate the construction of meaning through the analysis of instructional events.

An inquiry-oriented supervisory process will result in self-directed practitioners who engage in a problem-posing, problem-solving stance toward their practices. Supervision of this type requires an understanding and application of psychological dynamics that is developmentally appropriate and challenges individuals toward a greater ability to think abstractly,

work strategically, and operate with a clear, conscious intention. It will require supervisors to become continually more conscious regarding their own thinking and meaning making, to engage in reflection regarding their own practice, and to model self-directed, problem-solving behaviors. This type of supervisory environment has the potential to support Sergiovanni's (1992) vision "of a day when supervision [as it is presently practiced] will no longer be needed" (p. 203).

Improving the Organization's Capacity for Self-Renewal The third dimension of supervision is to develop the organization toward continual self-renewal. Organizational factors often serve to depress ingenuity, creativity, and imagination, thereby deflating the potential for self-actualization and internal motivation. For some time, Gestalt family therapy has asserted that there is no such thing as an "individual," in the dynamic sense, that we exist only as part of a relatedness, without which we do not survive (Kempler, 1991, p. 267). In *Personality and Organization,* Argyris (1957) concluded that organizational work environments that are controlling, bureaucratic, and hierarchial reduce adults to childlike behavior such as passivity, dependence, subordination, and lack of self-control and self-awareness (Clark & Astuto, 1994). More recently, and in regard to schools, Frymier (1987) and Rosenholtz (1989) report that the work culture is more important than are personal biographies, prior knowledge, previous training, and skills in determining the cognitions, attitudes, and behaviors of teachers. In addition, advances in the new sciences have offered further understandings of how natural systems work (Wheatley, 1992). Several of these systems principles are especially important to schools. First, schools are dynamical systems that are being constantly affected by many variables, each of which is influencing another, which is influencing another, and so on. Second, tiny events in dynamical systems can produce major consequences. Third, natural systems are self-organizing, iteratively playing out simple designs in repetitive patterns that grow to comprise complex wholes. In nature, relationships, energy, and information are the essential stuff of life and growth. This also appears to be true in schools.

The contemporary supervisor, then, recognizes that the school environment itself influences adult learning just as certainly, if not as observably, as sunlight, moisture, and plant life creates rich and fertile jungles. As a social ecologist, this supervisor seeks to establish an inquiry-oriented, reflective work culture that fosters independence, interdependence, and promotes the development of self-authoring responsible practitioners engaged in collaborative self-renewal for the benefit of all students.

AN EVOLUTION OF SUPERVISORY PRACTICES AND THEIR PSYCHOLOGICAL ROOTS

Background

Educational goals, conceptions of learning, instructional and curricular priorities, and supervisory practices adjust to the social, political, and psychological climate of their era.

During the twentieth century, changing expectations and public demands for greater control over what was taught in school resulted in the concurrent emergence and development of the fields of supervision and curriculum. These same broad social and psychological trends influenced the character of supervision. During the latter part of the twentieth century, there are alternating logs and parallels, congruencies and incongruencies between the development of psychological principles in academic practice and clinical practice and their application in school practice. For example, in the 1940s education, led by John Dewey and others, followed a strong trend toward greater socialization; however, academic psychology during this same period was almost exclusively behavioral, while clinical practice was predominantly psychoanalytical. During the 1950s, dramatic events in science moved schools toward modernizing the curriculum, while at the same time the gestalt orientation of the mind as organizer of raw perceptual data reintroduced a cognitive approach to clinical practice.

In the 1960s, however, reflecting current social trends, education renewed its orientation toward humanistic values. This orientation had striking parallels to practice in psychotherapy. Both fields were focused on a person-centered approach, with the major tenet being that individual choice is a prerequisite to growth. In the 1970s, while schools emphasized a process–product, research-based orientation, psychological practice continued to develop in the humanistic traditions. During the 1980s, an emphasis on teaching effectiveness based on a set of predominantly behavioristic learning principles emerged out of the research-driven, process-product paradigm of the 1970s (Rubin, 1982). In contrast, in the field of psychology during this period, social factors were causing a redefinition of the learning unit from a focus on the individual to working with the family as a system.

The 1990s finds supervision in transition. As in the 1960s, there appears to be a confluence emerging between school supervision and energy in academic and clinical practice in psychology. Research into perception is informing our understanding of how the mind organizes data physiologically, biochemically and cognitively (e.g., see Csikszentmihalyi, 1993; Edelman, 1992; Ornstein, 1991; Sternberg, 1983). Developments in quantum physics and evolutionary biology (e.g., see Briggs, 1992; Chopra, 1989; Wheatley, 1992) are offering new perspectives on personal and organizational development. These dual influences are setting new directions for supervisory practice. While a behaviorally oriented clinical supervision is therefore still a dominant mode of prac-

tice, reflective, teacher-centered supervisory interactions are being reported with increasing frequency (Glickman, 1992; Grimmett, Rostad, & Ford, 1992).

It is not surprising that the definition of supervision has fluctuated with the changing times. The role of the supervisor has historically been steeped in the controversy that mirrors the divergent views of educational outcomes and the psychological basis of classroom practice. Supervisory models have most frequently followed the contemporary view of learning and development. The role of supervisors has been described variously as one of administrator, analyst, change agent, counselor, critic, and monitor/evaluator based on orientations that include managerial, clinical, technological, aesthetic, humanistic, and performance-based (Pohland & Cross, 1982).

The section that follows overviews five schools of psychological thought, as well as the additional influence of Neurolinguistic Programming as a foundation for exploring the psychological neuristics of modern supervisory practice.

Five Schools of Psychological Thought

As can be seen in Figure 8.1, our literature review suggests five established schools of psychological thought that we offer as a framework for our discussion: (1) behaviorist, (2) psychoanalytic, (3) humanistic/existentialist, (4) cognitive, and (5) systems theory. As a foundation for an exploration of the psychological antecedents of supervisory practice, we begin with a brief description of each of these five schools of psychological thought, focusing on their views of motivation, learning, and development. We will also briefly describe the influence of Neurolinguistic Programming.

1. The Behaviorists Behaviorism classically focuses on the relationship between a stimulus and an organism's response. The mechanism of stimulus and response is the main model used to understand human behavior. All behavior is seen as a response to stimulus (Watson, 1913). The influence of past events or of mental processes is seen either as nonexistent or as secondary to what is occurring in the present. Individual behavior can be shaped and controlled by the individual's response to observable stimuli (Skinner, 1972). This view emphasizes the study of observable behavior and learning as the acquisition of a set of functional responses to stimuli (Hull, 1937). It holds a neutral, cause and effect view of human nature that like Newton's mechanical view of the universe implies that if you control the stimuli, then you will be able to predict and shape future behavior.

Behaviorst	Psychodynamic	Cognitive	Existential/ Humanistic	Family Systems
Mechanical stimulus-response to external environment	Internal drives seeking balance between conflicting forces	Reasoning which is produced by and which produces internal schema	Self discovery leading to realization of full potential	Development of the self is interdependent with development of the other

FIGURE 8.1. The primary organizing principles for the construction of meaning viewed from five schools of psychological thought

This school holds that pursuit of pleasure and avoidance of discomfort are the primary motivations underlying behavior. Rewards produce a pleasurable experience or lessen discomfort. Punishments produce discomfort or lessen rewards. In the strictest sense for this school of thought, "learning is a kind of habit which links together chains of individual stimulus-response behaviors" (Lowry, 1971, p. 193). By selecting the desired behaviors and reinforcing them, behavior is said to be shaped. "From learning how to talk to doing brain surgery, differentiation and shaping of responses to obtain less variability is the end goal" (Lundin, 1977, p. 187). Development is the result of learning and is observable in behavior. Thus, the course of development is quantitative and linear (Miller, 1993).

We do not need to try to discover what personalities, states of mind, feelings, traits of character, plans, purposes, intentions or other prerequisites of autonomous man really are in order to get on with a scientific analysis of behavior. . . . Thinking is behaving. The mistake is in allocating the behavior to the mind. (Skinner, 1972 p. 47)

As behaviorist theory evolved, researchers began to discover behaviors that appeared to call for an explanation involving more than simple connection between stimulus and response. Some behaviorists adopted the formula S–O–R in which an organism stands between stimulus and response. Succeeding generations of behaviorists have put behaviors into this O that are not observable, such as thought and problem-solving processes. Behavioral approaches to therapy began to move beyond the strict behaviorist theorists, such as B. F. Skinner, to acknowledge that the organism, or the individual, is in some way involved with the ways in which the self operates to influence or to mediate the relationship between the environmental stimuli and individual response. These contemporary behavioral orientations, such as *social learning theory* and *cognitive behavior therapy,* are most relevant to our discussion of supervisory practice. From a behavioral perspective, the focus of supervision is on changing observable behavior in the present.

The Social Learning approach is found in the work of Bandura (1977), which adds cognitive mediational processes to the stimuli and reinforcement of external events. Wolpe (1958) also acknowledged the influence of intervening internal variables while adhering to the classical conditioning concepts of Pavlov and Thornedike. The addition of cognitive psychology to the behavioral focus on observable behavior has led to the cognitive behavioral work of Meichenbaum (1977) and to the highly effective work with emotional disorders of Beck (1976) and Burns (1988).

2. Psychoanalytical Theorists Contrary to the behaviorist's insistence that psychological events must be observable by a third party, Freud, the founder of modern psychological thinking, developed a psychology that focused on mediating internal drives seeking balance between conflicting forces. Freud's formulations are important to any examination of Western psychology because they shaped the conceptual bowl from which all other theorists dipped. Freud's work used individual introspection to observe the inner workings of the psyche. He described an inner world that is divided into three competing parts: the *id,* the *ego,* and the *superego.* Observable behavior is driven by the demands of internally generated instinctual forces or *drives,* which are sexual in nature, that dwell in the *unconscious,* hidden from awareness. In his view, the organism must deal with two sources of stimuli: internal instinctual "psychosexual" drives whose intensity is reduced through gratification, and the demands of the environment. The organism mediates or balances the demands of these two stimuli through the activity of the "ego," which derives its power from reason, delay, conscious awareness, and insight. Behavior is thus seen as the result of reconciling competing forces within the personality. The psychoanalytic view of human nature thus emphasizes perpetual internal conflict and defense. The psychoanalytic view is called *psychodynamic* because it refers to the working together of several parts of the psyche.

Contrary to the behavioral conception of learning as the accumulation of effective stimulus–response pairings, learning in the psychoanalytic approach is the process of developing an ego that is capable of mediating between the instinctual urges of the id, the critical demands of the superego, and the survival requirements of reality. Learning, then, is the development of an ego that uses conscious awareness and rationality to appraise the real world accurately and to respond to it. The development of an effective ego enables the organism to bring unconscious forces to consciousness. This activity is the therapeutic goal of psychoanalysis: "To strengthen the ego, to make it more independent of the superego, to widen its field of perception and enlarge its organization, so that it can appropriate fresh portions of the id. Where Id was, there Ego shall be. It is a work of culture—not unlike the draining of the Zuider Zee" (Freud, 1933, p. 544). Thus, learning is directed toward the reduction of unconscious motivation and the development of conscious awareness.

The psychoanalytical approach to human consciousness has given rise to several contemporary schools of psychotherapy. Among Freud's many successors, Jung and Adler were two of the most influential. Each gave rise to many schools of thought and practice. Jung's (1934) *analytical psychotherapy* traces the expressions of the collective unconscious that all people share. Adler (1963) included social and political factors in his analysis.

The *self psychology* of Kohut (1971) emphasizes the importance of empathic mirroring in the individual's development. Mahler's (1975) studies on separation and individuation processes has also been a major influence on contemporary psychotherapy. One of the most popular of the psychoanalytic approaches is perhaps *transactional analysis* (Berne, 1964).

3. Cognitive Theorists Cognitive theory's main ideas come from the Stoic philosophers "who considered man's conceptions (or misconceptions) of events rather than the events themselves as the key to his emotional upsets" (Beck, 1976, p. 3). Cognitive theorists hold that human behavior is determined by "cognitive structures" composed of internally generated sets of mental *representations* of reality. These internal structures are essential for perception and can be manipulated or examined through the process of reasoning. The nature of these cognitive structures is described in metaphors ranging from mental maps to computers. In all of these theories, however, human behavior and motivation are understood to be determined by thinking, and not by feeling. It explains behavior in terms of mental processes and information processing, and it holds a neutral view of human nature.

Learning for cognitive theorists involves the acquisition of cognitive structures or schemas that inform healthy behavior. The two most influential schools of developmental thought that have arisen from the cognitive approach are those of Piaget (1948, 1952, 1967) and the information-processing theorists. Information-processing theorists use the computer as a model for human behavior and study the changing relationship between input and output as learning and development occur. Flow diagrams, computer programs, and tree diagrams are used to describe the mental processing that would have to occur to produce the outputs observed (Siegler, 1991). Information-processing theorists look at the specific rules that a learner uses to perform a task, carefully analyze the learner's actions, and then attempt to write a flow diagram or a computer program that can generate the sequence of actions (Klahr, 1992). Development is seen to occur as "children acquire new strategies, rules, scripts, representations, deeper levels of processing, or a broader knowledge base, depending on the particular approach" (Miller, 1993, p. 278).

In contrast, Piaget held that at specific points in their development, children dramatically change their ways of thinking (Piaget, 1967). Whereas information-processing theorists look for rules to guide behavior, Piaget looked for the underlying logic. He described cognitive development as a series of overlapping periods ranging from infancy through adolescence that involve major changes in the way an individual processes information and uses logic. Piaget's work provided the foundation for an examination of stage theory in adult development. His work was later extended by Kegan (1992, 1994), who elaborated the stages of cognitive development through adulthood. In addition, cognitive psychology, spurred on by research in computing and neurophysiology, was developing clinical approaches to emotional disorders based on new understandings of thought processes.

4. Humanistic/Existentialist Theorists In the humanistic/existential approach, the inherent wisdom of the organism is relied upon and is accessed through turning attention to the individual's present, here and now, experience. For these theorists, behavior is understood as being engaged in the process of constructing a durable self-image by the subjective nature of our perception of the world, by the meanings that one experiences, and by the organism's need for personal growth, or self-actualization, which is the full expression of one's potentials. These theories emphasize the movement toward self-actualization and the construction of a functional self-image to explain behavior. Self-actualization, as defined by Rogers, is based on the organism's inherent tendency to develop all its capacities in ways that serve to maintain or enhance the organism. The difference between maintenance and enhancement is seen in the work of Maslow (1968).

Maslow, a prominent humanist, offered a theory of motivation in which individuals move through a hierarchy of levels of human needs from fundamental physiological needs (e.g., food, water, sleep) and psychological needs (e.g., security, affection, affiliation, esteem) toward the satisfaction of meta-needs (e.g., higher-level, growth needs, such as justice, order, beauty, and unity, culminating in "self-actualization" or "self-transcendence").

As compared with the cognitive theorists, the humanistic/existential school holds a positive, philosophic view of human nature. The individual is seen as engaged in a continuing process of self-discovery that allows one to accurately observe and appropriately interpret one's inner and outer worlds. There is no end or goal of coming to a complete understanding of one's self or the world. Learning how to engage in this process is the focus of therapy.

For this school, the influence of environmental, psychodynamic, and historical causes of behavior are minimized. To understand the causes that give rise to an individual's behavior and experience, we must attempt to look at the world from that person's point of view (i.e., to see it as they see it). This is called the *phenomenological approach*. Phenomenology is a theory of perception described by existential philosophy that studies the individual's experience of the world from that individual's point of view. "[P]henomenology emphasizes direct experience, what it means to the one who experiences, and what he communicates of this experience to others" (Lana, 1976, p. 49).

5. Systems Theory Systems theory emphasizes the importance of communication, the dynamics of the construction of a shared reality, and the maintenance of the hierarchy of relationships that compose the system. Systems theory in psychology emerged from work with families in which the cause of behavior is no longer seen to come from one source or from one individual; behavior is mutually co-created by the dynamics of the larger system of relationships (i.e., family) of which the individual is a member (Haley, 1976). Human behavior is not determined by the interactions of individual conscious and unconscious processes alone; rather, they must be understood holistically (i.e., seen within the context of a part operating within a larger whole). Systems theory is the study of "wholes," which are self-organizing systems that maintain their integrity while embedded in and composed of other systems. Olds (1992) describes the implications of systems theory thusly: "We are wholes relative to our smaller parts (organs, molecules, atoms) but parts relative to the larger wholes in which we are embedded" (p. 89).

Systems theory is both holistic and synergistic, meaning that looking at the action of each of the parts individually does not allow one to see the action of the whole (e.g., much as looking at all the parts of an automobile spread out on your front lawn will not necessarily give you an idea of what they can do when put together). Looking at the part alone without looking at the whole will conversely not allow you to see the function of the part. Systems have their own requirements for survival (e.g., a car cannot function without tires), and individuals within systems will feel pressure to act in accordance with the needs of the system (e.g., to roll over in

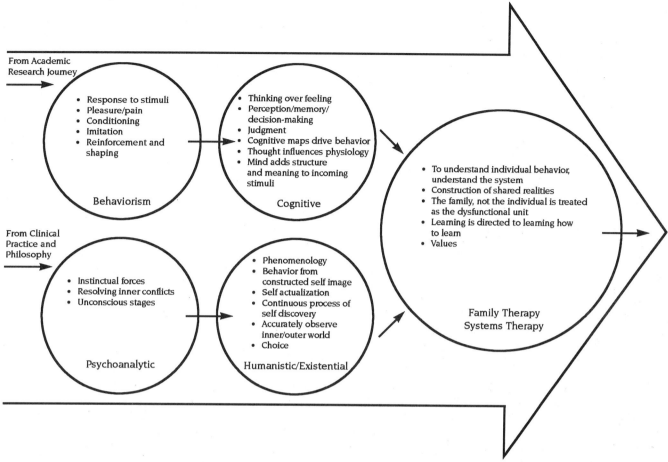

FIGURE 8.2. Development of psychological thought
influencing supervision practices

order to get to where you want to go). Motivation is thus seen as a mutual dynamic, operating from both the top down and the bottom up, determined by the needs of the individual and the needs of the system.

Learning is directed toward learning to learn (Bateson, 1972, p. 277). The first level of learning requires the ability to learn the rules that govern the interactions of the system and to be able to produce those behaviors. These rules include values, goals, shared meanings, and acceptable modes of conduct. On occasion, however, the system itself will require new behaviors in order to adapt to the changing demands of its environment (e.g., moving to a new house, children leaving home) and will require individuals to generate new behaviors not previously included in the system repertoire to meet the system's need to adapt. This is learning how to learn, creating and enacting new behaviors in the present using information from and familiarity with the system's past (Fig. 8.2).

Other Influences In the early 1970s, an eclectic approach to human psychology began to make itself felt in the fields of clinical psychology, management, leadership, teaching, and supervision. This work, initiated by Bandler and Grinder

(1976), examined the neurological and linguistic foundations of excellence in human behavior. "It was agentic, goal-oriented, pragmatic and as with most forms of science—utilitarian and useful, interested in prediction, control, and potential change" (Olds, 1992, p. 57). Initial modeling was done with such luminary figures in therapy as Perls, Satir, and Erickson. From these studies, a body of information began to be assembled that was theory free. Stemming primarily from cognitive-behavioral and psycholinguistic roots, it sought to observe, understand, and be able to teach others the specific building blocks of high performance in any field—therapy, athletics, leadership, and so on. Neurolinguistic Programming (NLP), as it came to be called, built upon the foundations of existing psychological schools of thought to provide an eclectic approach to human growth and development. "The cognitive-behaviorally compatible school of Neurolinguistic Programming . . . shows its allegiances to an active, goal-oriented, agentic stress on excellence, person power, clean crisp action, decisiveness, and a whole technology of tools for change" (Olds, 1992, p. 161).

The premise that thoughts, feelings, behaviors, and intentions are comprised of sets of sequenced mental representations in forms of pictures, sounds, feelings, smells, and tastes is fundamental to NLP. By understanding the structure of human experience (i.e., the nature and sequencing of these representations) one can understand high performance and teach for it, just as one can identify the subjective structure of maladaptive behaviors, and eliminate them. NLP practitioners draw on an extensive repertoire of behaviorally oriented principles to evoke human learning in a client-centered, humanistic/existentialist context. Their basic assumptions include a sense that humans possess a wise and benevolent unconscious that will consistently make the best choices for the person available to them in the moment, as well as a belief that language represents internal reality and that it can be used as a mediational tool to support persons in modifying their internal models and, consequently, their behaviors and performance.

These five psychological theories—behaviorist, psychoanalytical, cognitive, humanistic/existential and systems theory—and the perspectives gleaned from NLP, form the basis for our description and analysis of the psychological orientations of recent, present, and potential future supervisory practice.

To establish a context for considering the role of supervision in the twenty-first century, and the psychological heuristics upon which it will be based, we begin with the evolution of supervisory practice parented by Anderson, Cogan, and Goldhammer's initial conception of clinical supervision. While each of the subsequent (i.e., second-generation) models is born of a common genealogy, each has matured, embodying significantly different applications to practice stemming from different psychological orientations.

Using the Classroom As Clinic: Four Models of School Supervision and Their Psychological Roots

As originally conceived, clinical supervision was an eclectic blend of diverse and dichotomous viewpoints: phenomenology and empiricism, behaviorism and developmentalism (Garman, 1982; Pajak, 1993). Early research on the original model of clinical supervision suggested that it existed as a support for intellectual development designed to give a teacher useful insights into instructional practice (Flanders, 1976; Shane & Weaver, 1976, Krajewski, 1982).

Cogan and Goldhammer's clinical supervision was a composite of psychological orientations. According to Krajewski (1982), clinical supervision was an objective technology for improving instruction. As such, it required supervisory skills in interpersonal communication (humanistic/existentialist), reducing subjectivity (cognitive theorist), and data collection around a specific instructional focus (behaviorist).

Researchers and writers in the field of educational supervision have attempted to organize and categorize the divergent approaches. Two distinct categories have been described by Tracy and MacNaughton (1989) as neotraditionalists and neoprogressives. The neotraditionalists, such as Hunter, Joyce, and Showers, as well as Popham, focus on the more behavioral aspects of clinical supervision: the scrupulous collection of observation data to discern whether and to what degree teachers are displaying specific instructional behaviors. Drawing from the humanistic/existential and cognitive theorists, the neoprogressives, such as Garman, Costa, and

Garmston, as well as Glickman, place a high value on the relationship and interrelational aspects of clinical supervision.

Another categorization of supervision models is provided by Glanz (1994). He describes seven approaches to supervision that come about as the result of the interaction of broad social and intellectual movements affecting all aspects of education. He places these seven models of supervision into three major categories. Supervision as *inspection* emerged as a response to the bureaucratic needs of urban education in the late nineteenth century. During an emergence of professionalism period, *efficient, democratic, and scientific* supervision then developed as attempts to remove the stigma associated with inspectional supervision. Finally, *supervision as leadership, clinical supervision,* and a *changing conceptions model* came into being in a category Glanz labels the expansion of democratic methods in supervision.

While many categorical descriptions of supervision could offer a potential framework for an examination of the psychology of supervision, we have chosen Pajak's (1993) descriptions of the original clinical supervision model, and three orientations that stem from it to organize our analysis of the psychological foundations of school supervision. These four categories are the original clinical models and three of its derivations: the technical/didactic models, the artistic/humanistic models, and the developmental/reflective models.

Clinical Supervision: The Original Model Initiated in the late 1950s at Harvard by Anderson, Cogan, and Goldhammer, clinical supervision was a response to the traditional, industrial model of supervision that was based on close inspection and control. Clinical supervision offered a move away from this bureaucratic, behavioral mode toward a cyclical process of planning, observation, diagnosis, changed, and renewed planning. This first generation of clinical supervision was originally designed as part of the teacher education program to support the learning of their teaching interns. It was envisioned by its developers as both a process in which supervisor and teacher would engage in a series of sequential steps that would repeat as a cycle of supervision, and a concept that held that clinical supervision involved at least two people, one of whom is a teacher. Classroom-based data would be collected and analyzed to improve instructional performance (Krajewski, 1982).

According to Morris Cogan (1973):

Clinical supervision is focused upon the improvement of the teacher's classroom instruction. The clinical domain is the interaction between a specific teacher or team of teachers and specific students, both as a group and as individuals. Clinical supervision may therefore be defined as the rationale and practice designed to improve the teacher's classroom performance. It takes its principal data from the events of the classroom. The analysis of these data and the relationship between teacher and supervisor form the basis of the program, procedures, and strategies designed to improve the students' learning by improving the teacher's classroom behavior (p. 120).

Clinical supervision conceptually involves an "up-close" interaction between two people who are concerned with improvement of classroom instructional practice, and with the study of individual performance (Cogan, 1973; Goldhammer,

1969). This interaction provides an opportunity for "analysis of behavioral data [leading to] the develop[ment] of categories of analysis *after* teaching has been observed, rather than beforehand" (Goldhammer, 1969). As clinical supervision evolved, sequential processes, or "cycles of supervision," with a specified number of steps were delineated (Cogan, 1973; Goldhammer, 1969).

Clinical supervision was goal-oriented and systematic, yet flexible. The clinical supervisory process worked to develop clarity about the outcome of a lesson being observed, the purpose of the data, and the professional goals of the teacher. While this process was systematic, it also flexed to the teaching styles and the preferences of individual teachers. Furthermore, clinical supervision required mutual trust and rapport nurturance. Mutual trust is the binding element in clinical supervision. While trust is established over time, rapport is the glue that adheres the individuals in the moment-to-moment-interaction.

When it is viewed holistically, the original clinical supervision model had an eclectic blend of several schools of thought at its psychological roots. The notion that learning can be achieved by the reinforcement of positive behaviors and the extinction of negative behaviors is fundamental to the behaviorist view. Aspects of the clinical supervision model are oriented toward this view in that the methods are grounded in the collection of behavioral data and rely more on teacher's observable actions than they do on their thinking processes. The data is then used as a basis to reinforce behaviors identified as effective and to eliminate those that were not.

In its original conception, however, the sequential process and gathering of empirical data was intended to support an inquiry-based method through which new teachers would begin to develop understandings about their craft. Through this process, individuals would be freed from preconceived notions regarding practice and be able to create contextually based procedures and strategies toward increased effectiveness. Garman (1982) described this concept:

The processes implicit in the cycle of supervision can become inquiry methodology for one to generate theory. The empirical qualities of observation and analysis, two of the phases of the "cycle", help the novice to quantify events in order to be free from judgmental preconceptions. Personal empowerment releases one's senses to savor the aesthetics of teaching and learning. Freedom is won through patience and devotion, through careful documentation of accumulated experiential knowledge. . . . Somewhere, in the rigor of inquiry, the clinical spirit is born (p. 37).

Viewed from this perspective, the original model of clinical supervision is steeped in both cognitive theory and humanistic/existential psychology. According to cognitive theory, judgment and decision-making play an important role in directing behavior. Human behavior is determined by cognitive structures that are composed of internally generated sets of mental representations of reality. Cognitive approaches hold that humans are designed to organize their observations and experiences into a coherent set of meanings and to adapt to new observations and experiences. Precedence is given to reasoning, which is a thought-based approach to the diagnosis and resolution of problems. This view concerns itself with thinking, knowing, perception, understanding, memory, decision-making, and judgment. The first generation of clinical supervision worked to bring a rich data base to teachers to enable analysis of their practice, thereby producing better informed decisions regarding it.

The humanistic/existential orientation suggests that the individual is engaged in a constant process of self-discovery. By our choices, we create ourselves; by choosing to commit ourselves to our choices we give the world meaning. We are continually in the process of becoming aware of the rippling effects of what our choices are creating (i.e., of the evolving consequences of our actions). An illuminating example of the marriage of these two psychological perspectives is Kelly's (1965) notion that we construct theory from the processing of our interactions in the world. Bridging the two psychological orientations of cognitive development and humanistic/existential thinking, his work suggests that through continual experiences, and the processing of those experiences, practitioners form their own theories regarding practice and personal definitions of their professional identities.

Thus, based on its original conception, and the psychological understandings of the time, the first generation of clinical supervision represented a blend of psychological perspectives: behaviorist, cognitive theorist, and humanistic/existential. The interpretation and application of the original process varied across settings, based on an organization's psychological and philosophical orientations to practice, as well as the purposes and perspectives of the supervisor.

These divergent philosophical and psychological roots led to various interpretations and applications of the clinical model during the latter part of the twentieth century. The first generation of clinical supervision bore the fruit of three specific offspring. These second generation schools of supervisory thought were the technical/didactic models, the artistic/humanistic models, and the developmental/reflective models (Pajak, 1993).

TECHNICAL/DIDACTIC MODELS. During the 1980s, a technical/ didactic model of supervision that was strongly rooted in behavioral psychology was prevalent. In fact, of all the models studied, the technical/didactic process comes closest to having a single orientation to one school of psychological thought. The behavioral school views learning as an increasing ability to consistently produce desired responses. Learning is fostered through the application of conditioned positive reinforcement, such as money or social approval. Rather than focusing on an individual practitioner's discovery of best practice, the technical/didactic models attempt to foster conformity of practice based on the acquisition and application of specific skills. The instructional skills identified were those indicated by the current research to be most effective in achieving predetermined student outcomes.

Technical/didactic models of supervision rely heavily on the sequential, linear procedure outlined in the original clinical models. They are based on an assumption that the skills of effective teaching are context-free, existing independently from the specifics of a particular classroom or school setting.

They employ classroom observation as a primary feedback source for reinforcing a specific and predetermined model of teaching that has been identified as desirable. The function of supervisory interactions is to teach the proper enactment of certain behaviors that comprise preselected teaching strategies that have been documented as "effective" by researchers in education. Thus, supervisors encourage teachers to pay attention to, and to monitor, specific behaviors, including allocation and use of time, establishing and verifying instruction at the appropriate level of difficulty, demonstration and modeling, and checking for learner understanding through active participation.

This approach to supervision stems from and aligns with process–product paradigms that drove research in effective instruction during the 1970s and early 1980s. The prevailing technology of instruction was dependent upon a prescribed set of effective teaching behaviors, preset learning objectives, criterion-referenced assessment measures, and skill and drill practice. According to the technical/didactic perspective, supervision is a "tool for implementing behaviors, skills, and strategies that are discovered or invented outside the classroom being observed" (Pajak, 1993, p. 150). There is little opportunity for the individual teacher's search for understanding or for personal expression of meaning. Pajak offers three primary examples of the technical/didactic approach to supervision: Hunter's decision-making, Joyce and Showers' Peer-Coaching, and Acheson and Gall's Technical Model (see Table 8.1).

TABLE 8–1. Technical/Diadactic Models

	Fundamental Premises	Psychological Foundation	Data Sources/ Collection Methods	Supervisory Structure	Unique Features
Hunter's Decision-Making Model	• Supervision in an analytical process of diagnosis and prescription based on specific principles of learning	Dominant Orientation: • Behaviorist Ancillary Orientation: • Humanistic/existential • Cognitive theorist (in Stage 5 conferences)	Script taping detailing teacher actions and subsequent student behaviors	• Five-phase cycle: (1) extensive in-service, to teach a cause–effect relationship between specific teacher behaviors and student outcomes; (2) classroom observation and script taping; (3) analysis of the data by the supervisor; (4) the supervision conference during which a collaborative, trust-building interaction occurs between the supervisor and the teacher; and (5) follow-up through repetition of the clinical cycle and additional feedback and guided practice as deemed necessary to support and accelerate teacher growth.	• No preobservation conference • Data analyzed by supervisor to determine and label patterns of teacher behavior
Joyce and Shower's Peer-Coaching Model	• The informed application of theory into practice promotes growth and learning for students and teachers	Dominant Orientation: • Behaviorist Ancillary Orientation: • Humanistic/existential	• Use of a clinical assessment form to determine presence/absence and frequency/ consistency of pre-determined set of instructional behaviors	• Four phases: (1) study, individually or in small groups, of the theoretical basis or rationale of a particular instructional method or model of teaching; (2) live or videotaped demonstration of the instructional strategy or technique being studied; (3) several cycles of practice with the new method in mini-lessons conducted first with their peers as students and then in the classroom, with feedback provided by a colleague/partner; and (4) coaching by a trusted partner for companionship, support, ideas and on-going feedback.	• Supervisory exchange occurs between peers • Observations done by colleagues • Promotes coaching as a powerful process for establishing a community of adult learners
Acheson and Gail's Technical Model	• Teachers will have a positive reaction to supervision steeped in their own specific concerns/issues	Dominant Orientation: • Behaviorist/social learning theory Ancillary Orientation: • Humanistic/existential	• Use of a large variety of data collection methods	Three stage cycle: (1) Planning conference (2) A classroom observation (3) Feedback conference	• Allows for the nurturing of a personal style of teaching and supervision • Interactive, democratic, teacher-centered

Hunter's Decision-Making Model. Hunter's Decision-Making Model is the most purely behaviorally oriented of the three Technical/Didactic models of supervision described by Pajak. The supervisor analyzes detailed data collected during a classroom observation to identify patterns of teacher behavior that adhere to a specific set of teaching and learning principles. The supervisor's data analysis is used to develop a plan for the postconference, which can take one of six distinct forms. These conference forms differ in their intended objectives and are designed to be matched to teachers' varying levels of ability and readiness.

The supervisor begin might to enter the realm of the cognitive theorists (i.e., the self-actualizing aspects of the humanistic perspective only at the most advanced stages of the Hunter conference forms. In fact, Hunter assumes that supervisors should begin with teachers at the first level, which is a conference designed to reinforce effective teaching behaviors. Hunter makes a clear distinction between supervision and evaluation, and recommends that the same individual serve both roles. She perceives supervision as a complex monitoring task that includes diagnosis of teaching deficits and prescription of specific knowledge and skills acquisition toward improvement. In contrast, evaluation is the decree of a bottom-line judgment and the placement of each teacher in a predetermined category.

Joyce and Showers' Peer-Coaching Model. Like Hunter's Decision-Making Model, Joyce and Showers Peer Coaching Model relies on a prescribed set of instructional behaviors to determine teacher effectiveness. Four major areas—(1) models of teaching, (2) curriculum and curriculum implementation, (3) school effectiveness and (4) teacher effectiveness—provide the essential skill set for the Peer-Coaching Model.

In contrast with Hunter's approach, however, the coaching model relies on peer observation and data collection, using a clinical assessment form to assess the presence, absence, and frequency and consistency of a specific, predetermined set of instructional behaviors. There is no summative judgment involved, simply the collection of data for subsequent analysis by the coaching partners. There is clearly formative judgment, however, regarding the presence or absence, frequency, and adequacy of specific behaviors. This model promotes coaching as a powerful process for establishing a community of adult learners who are engaged in a continual study of their craft knowledge and who share common understandings and language regarding teaching. Furthermore, coaching cultivates a climate of professionalism and a supportive structure to ensure transfer of newly acquired skills into consistent classroom practice. According to Joyce and Showers, coaching provides the necessary forum for the incremental learning, application, and practice of potent, research-based strategies necessary for inclusion in a teacher's instructional repertoire.

A dominant behavioristic orientation is evidenced in Joyce and Showers strong belief that a specific set of technical skills for effective teaching can be taught and learned. Their emphasis in this model, however, on the development of collegial relationships built on trust stems from a humanistic/existential perspective. They suggest that learning is most likely when colleagues work collaboratively without a hierarchical struc-

ture and are free of evaluation. In fact, they strongly recommend that evaluation be completely excluded from the coaching experience and conducted by someone not involved in that process. This separation allows coaching to provide a safe environment within which teachers will take risks and experiment with new strategies.

Acheson and Gall's Technical Model. Acheson and Gall's supervisory model focuses on improving instruction by focusing on a teacher's classroom behaviors. In contrast with the two preceding applications, however, this version of the technical/didactic models leans heavily on the social learning theory school of behavioral psychology. Social learning theory views psychological functioning as being caused by the reciprocal interaction of three sets of influences: behavior, cognitive processes, and environmental factors. "In the social learning approach, the influence of environmental events on behavior is largely determined by cognitive processes, which govern what environmental influences are attended to, how they are perceived, and how the individual interprets them" (Wilson, 1980, p. 240).

This supervisory model suggests that a supervisor is responsible for supporting a teacher's acquisition and development of specific behavioral and intellectual skills through the systematic collection and mutual analysis of objective data. This model exemplifies the behaviorist school of social learning theory, which suggests that:

[P]ersonal and environmental factors do not function as independent determinants; rather they determine each other. Nor can "persons" be considered causes independent of their behavior. It is largely through actions that people produce the environmental conditions that affect their behavior in a reciprocal fashion. The experiences generated by behavior also partly determine what individuals think, expect, and can do, which in turn, affect their subsequent behavior (Bandura, 1977, p. 345).

ARTISTIC/HUMANISTIC MODELS. The Artistic/Humanistic models present a shift in practice from the behavioral aspects present in the original model of clinical supervision. As the name suggests, these models embrace the humanistic/existential aspects of that first generation clinical model, and evolved as a response to the technical, bureaucratic, prescriptive interpretations that were prevalent during the 1970s. This contrast is described by Grimmett, Rostad, and Ford (1992):

The dominant model of instructional supervision is marked by a disputable assumption: instructional supervisors have access to a scientific knowledge base and set of analytical skills that are beyond the orbit of the regular classroom teacher. Supervisors sometimes talk about "instructional improvement" as if it were something they do to teachers rather than the outcome of carefully nurtured teacher development (p. 187).

Pajak offers two examples that illustrate different dimensions of the artistic/humanistic orientation to supervision. While both of these models are rooted in a humanistic psychological orientation, they offer two distinct interpretations. The humanistic approach, which is illustrated by Blumberg's Interpersonal Intervention Model (1974), has the nature and quality of the relationship between the teacher and supervisor as its focus. The artistic perspective is described in Eisner's Artistic Approach, which suggests that educators must use their individual sensibilities and be both private connoisseurs and public critics of excellent practice. This orientation holds the supervisory role as one of consultant, or informational resource, to the practitioner.

Blumberg's Interpersonal Intervention Model. Because the technology of teaching is uncertain and complex, Blumberg presents schools as centers of inquiry where supervisors and teachers collaborate as problem solvers. He suggests that this orientation would require an alteration of the ways in which practitioners view the function of supervision and the nature of schools. According to Blumberg, this shift could be accomplished through open, honest, collegial interactions between supervisors and teachers where supervisors focus on establishing and maintaining trusting relationships. He believes that supervisors must demonstrate an active concern regarding classroom practice, as well as formalize the support networks between teachers. Furthermore, they must offer themselves as models of adult learning, displaying reflective behaviors, being willing to make mistakes, and requesting feedback on their own behaviors.

Blumberg's interpersonal intervention model incorporates the humanistic/existential views of Kelly (1965) and Rogers (1980). For Kelly, an individual, like a scientist, creates a set of conscious and unconscious hypotheses about the nature of the world. This personal construct allows one to predict, and, it is hoped, to control the course of events. Kelly focused on individuals' potential to reconstruct their lives by changing the negative beliefs that might be part of their personal constructs. Like Kelly, Rogers stressed the human potential to choose their view of themselves and others. Feeling or information that does not fit with the self-image is considered incongruent. According to Rogers, you are best able to actualize your potential if your self-image is congruent with your actions, thoughts, and feelings. Development is a process of maximizing the potential by accepting information about oneself in as realistic and honest a manner as possible. Thus, people with a close match between their self-image and their ideal self tend to be the most secure and confident.

The concept of mutual growth reflected in Blumberg's model echoes the Rogerian contention that both the clinician and the client are developed in successful counseling. This growth orientation extends beyond instructional issues to interpersonal dynamics of the entire school setting. There is a presumption, in Rogerian thought, that there is a basic unity to personality that is best understood as a process rather than as an entity. According to this belief, fully functional people are self-aware and open to new experiences. They are not hostile or defensive, and they maintain harmonious relations with others in which there is unconditional positive self-regard. Rogers describes three "core conditions" that would enable individuals to move on their own towards this level of functioning if embodied by someone else in the social environment. These conditions are (1) accurate empathy, (2) unconditional positive regard, and (3) congruence. In accurate empathy an individual attempts to understand another's world and feel what it would feel like to live in that world as

if he or she were that client. Accurate empathy involves four steps: (1) immersing the self in the other's feeling world, (2) experiencing that world as if you were in it yourself, (3) having an active experience of your own and the other's feelings, and (4) becoming aware of surrounding implicit feelings that are on the edge of the other's awareness. The practice of accurate empathy also requires that one checks in with the other and ask for feedback about the accuracy of what you are experiencing. In this way, meanings and feelings are shared and explicated. Unconditional positive regard for the other is based on confidence in the other's self-actualizing tendency, and it is communicated through nonjudgmental understanding and genuine response. Genuine response is a function of congruence that is the ability to know one's own inner experiencing and to feel free to express that in one's outward behavior. When these core conditions are met, by being present in another, then the individuals will move toward healthy, harmonious functioning because of their own self-actualizing tendency.

Blumberg's supervisory model is based on authentic relationships of this type. The model is steeped in the humanistic/existential school of psychology in that it relies on the premise that we are continually becoming, and that the focus of our choices and concerns give meaning and authenticity to our lives. Inherent in Blumberg's model is his recognition that individuals seek to satisfy psychological needs in their work environment. For Blumberg, relationships and responsibility are the keys to satisfying adults' needs. He believes that supervision and evaluation can be conducted by the same individual, provided that the functions remain distinct and that evaluation does not enter into the interpersonal intervention. Any conflicts between the two distinct functions must be confronted directly and honestly. He bases his orientation to supervision on Levinson's (1968) three categories; (1) *ministration*, which involves the need for supportive relationships and close connections to and guidance from others, (2) *maturation*, which recognizes the necessity of growth and development opportunities, and (3) *mastery*, which involves the need to control one's environment (see Table 8.2).

Eisner's Artistic Approach. According to Eisner (1982), an artistic approach to supervision

relies on the sensitivity, perceptivity, and knowledge of the supervisor as a way of appreciating the significant subtleties occurring in the classroom, and that exploits the expressive, poetic, and often metaphorical potential of language to convey to teachers or to others whose decisions affect what goes on in schools, what has been observed (p. 59).

This orientation is closely connected to one perspective of the humanistic/existential school of psychology known as *phenomenology*. Phenomenology is the belief that what we "know" exists as a construction of reality. What we are aware of at any given moment is our phenomenological field, which is the composite of our personal, subjective experience of reality. The phenomenological field includes all that we are aware of at any given moment. The phenomenological paradigm suggests that which can be known exists only

TABLE 8–2. Artistic/Humanistic Models

	Fundamental Premises	Psychological Foundation	Data Sources/ Collection Methods	Supervisory Structure	Unique Features
Blumberg's Intervention Model	• Teaching is uncertain and complex, therefore supervisors and teachers should be collaborative problem-solvers	Dominant Orientation: • Humanistic/ existentialist	Data gathered collaboratively; includes inter-personal, or noninstructional aspects of the classroom	• Data analysis and application are the responsibility of the teacher, with support from the supervisor during authentic, growth-producing interactions.	• Highly teacher-centered • School is a center of inquiry • Supervisor is a model of adult learning
Eisner's Artistic Approach	• Teaching is an artistic process in which the curriculum is transformed to fit the context (i.e., based on the teacher's style, values, pedagogical outlook) • Curriculum content (i.e., what is taught) is as vitally important as instructional repertoire (i.e., how it is taught)	Dominant Orientation: • Humanistic/ existentialist	• Classroom events are captured and shared in vivid, metaphorical language • Interpreted as art critic	• Supervisor shares rich descriptions of classroom activities and serves as both connoisseur, appreciating what has occurred, and critic, publicly voicing reactions	• Emphasis on the self-actualization of the teacher • Use of metaphor to promote teacher's insights • Search for aesthetic relationship

in people's minds in the form of constructed realities, and that the relationship of the knower to the knowable is characterized by the interactions through which the knower comes to know (Guba & Lincoln, 1985, p. 140).

Eisner's model has as its heart an investment in the sense-making "human instrument" that is the teacher. As teachers are differentiated by their personal styles and strengths, this model is focused on an appreciation of the characteristics of individual teachers. It is designed to nurture and develop their particular talents.

In contrast with Blumberg's model, which focuses on the noninstructional nature of interpersonal relationships, Eisner's Artistic Approach to supervision is strongly rooted in instructional and curricular issues. In fact, Eisner believes that teachers must have a clear understanding of curriculum and an extensive instructional repertoire in order to personalize their teaching to meet the diverse needs of individual students. Teaching is viewed as an artistic process that is guided by the teacher's values, beliefs, and personal outlooks. It is a transformation of the curriculum to fit the context. In other words, how true is the artist to their medium? Supervisors must therefore attend to what is being taught, as well as to how it is being taught.

Eisner identifies two key roles for supervisors: that of connoisseur and that of critic. The connoisseur of teaching appreciates both the particular nuances and traits of the performer, or teacher, as well as the overall quality of the performance, or teaching. That is, "both the general level of teaching competence and the unique characteristics of the performance would be perceived and appraised" (Eisner,

1982, p. 61). Supervisors as critics must express their reactions to the performance "publicly" in order that they be useful and significant to others. Eisner suggests that the supervisor as critic functions to help others appreciate what has occurred. Educational connoiseurship is the process that provides the content for the educational critic. The critique should be expressed through the artistic use of language, which sets an aesthetic context for the observed event.

This model has its dominant roots in humanistic/existential psychology. From a phenomenological perspective, various and continued interactions produce a construction of shared interpretations of events. Through interaction, as well as through interpretation of the behaviors, gestures, and actions directed toward them by others, individuals attempt to see themselves as others see them. In this way, they acquire definitions of themselves, as well as learn to change themselves. Eisner sees the role of the supervisor as enabling individuals to appreciate and to recognize aspects of a situation to which they may be too close. Interpretation of these events, through use of metaphor and vividly descriptive language, explicates patterns, relationships, and significant concepts. There is a search for congruence between the teachers' actions and their intentions. The emphasis here is on the self-actualization of the teacher via the development of general qualities such as flexibility, creativity, ingenuity, and novelty, as well as each teacher's unique talents.

THE DEVELOPMENTAL/REFLECTIVE MODELS. In the late 1980s, another branch of supervisory thought emerged that arose from the cognitive theory orientations of the first generation of clinical supervision. The developmental/reflective models presume that teaching and learning are influenced by the personal, social, organizational, historical, political, and cultural contexts within which they operate. They embrace the principles of cognitive theory, promulgating that a teacher's cognitive operations regarding instruction are just as important, if not more important, than are their specific instructional behaviors. Teachers are decision-makers involved in context-specific practice. In these models, the supervisory interaction is aimed at mediating the teachers' thinking, perceptions, beliefs, and assumptions as they work toward self-improvement and increasing complexity of cognitive processing: They seek to reinforce and to expand the relationships between teachers' thought and intentions and their performance.

This philosophy and practice of supervision brings with it an emerging focus on a teacher's cognitive development that is based on the belief that growth is achieved through the development of intellectual functioning. Supervision is directly related to changes in teacher thinking. Each of these models combines, to differing degrees, the cognitive theorist perspective with aspects of the humanistic/existential and family systems orientations; however, the Piagetian view that the individual is the active agent of learning is central to the developmental models.

This perspective presents a vivid contrast to the prescriptive, systematic forms of professional development and instructional improvement inherent in behaviorally oriented technical/didactic models. Hilgard and Atkinson (1967) contrast the views of the behaviorists and cognitive learning theorists in this way:

Does the rat learn a chain of movements in running from the start of an alley to the food box at the end, or does it learn the location of the food. . . . If the rat learns a maplike representation of the environment, so that it can take new paths and short cuts, then it has acquired a cognitive structure (p. 306).

Pajak offers a variety of examples of this orientation to supervision: Glickman's Developmental Supervision, Costa and Garmston's Cognitive Coaching, and the Reflective Practice models of Schön, Zeichner and Liston, Garman, Smyth, and Retallick, and Bowers and Flinders.

Glickman's Developmental Supervision. Glickman offers an eclectic approach in that his work offers a continuum of supervisory actions that range from directive to collaborative to nondirective. This model combines the psychological orientations of the behaviorists, the humanists, and the cognitive theorists. It is a bridge between the technical/didactic models and the emergence of reflective models.

Glickman's model is highly contextual and attentive to both the complexity of the teaching practice and the differing needs of individual teachers. It encompasses the work of the developmental theorists, such as Loevinger (1976), Kohlberg (1971), Hunt (1971), and Piaget (1948, 1952), and it is rooted in the premise that adults progress through a continuum of stages. Glickman believes that a supervisor can facilitate development through these stages toward high lev-

els of commitment to schoolwide concerns and the ability to think abstractly about instructional practice through strategic and conscious interaction. A five-step clinical sequence is suggested toward this end (see Table 8.3).

Developmental supervision relies on one-to-one interactions between the supervisor and teacher, although it suggests that collaborative interaction and dialogue between all of the adults in the school is highly desirable. Toward this end, Glickman encourages action research and group problem-solving sessions where teachers work to explore school-based problems, identifying issues, gathering information, and generating potential plans for improvement. The supervisor's role here shifts to developing problem-solving and group process skills, again along a continuum based on the developmental needs of the group.

Costa and Garmston's Cognitive Coaching. Cognitive coaching offers a model, or framework, that both promotes and serves as a guide for reflection. This model derives from a rich marriage between the cognitive theorists and the humanistic/existentialists. It has evolved to include neurolinguistic principles and systems theory in its goals and approaches. These schools of thought are applied consistently throughout the process. Cognitive coaching facilitates practitioners' abilities to reframe their experiences given their "existing repertoire of examples, images, understandings, and actions" (Schon, 1988, p. 25), and to transform those experiences so that the particular experience is seen as only one of many possible versions. Cognitive coaching widens the professional possibilities for exploration and experimentation by enhancing the ability to reframe and to reexamine familiar patterns of practice, and to reconsider the underlying assumptions that direct action. Thus, the ultimate purpose of supervision in this model is to enhance the teacher's capacity for self-modification.

The three fundamental goals of cognitive coaching are (1) establishing and maintaining trust (i.e., trust in self, trust in a coaching relationship, trust in the coaching process and trust in the organizational environment to provide continued support while evolving towards a collaborative, self-renewing culture, (2) facilitating learning, which is the restructuring or alteration of mental processes, and (3) enhancing growth toward holonomy (Costa & Garmston, 1994). Holonomy is expressed as an individual's achievement of a balance between being autonomous and self-authoring, and functioning collaboratively and interdependently. Holonomy is expressed as a high level of resourcefulness in five states of mind: efficacy, flexibility, craftsmanship, consciousness, and interdependence. Skillful cognitive coaches can recognize temporary "stuckness" and facilitate resourcefulness. To do so, they must themselves function holonomously. The capacity for learning and self-modification increases as development in these states of mind occurs.

To achieve these goals, cognitive coaches employ a specific set of strategies designed to enhance an individual's thought processes, thereby affecting their overt behaviors toward improved professional practice, and ultimately increasing their capacity for critically self-reflective practice. As in Blumberg's model, Rogerian principles of accurate

TABLE 8–3. Developmental/Reflective Models

Model	Fundamental Premises	Psychological Foundation	Data Sources/ Collection Methods	Supervisory Structure	Unique Features
Glickman's Developmental Supervision Model	• Through strategic and conscious interaction, a supervisor facilitates teacher cognitive developmental growth	Dominant Orientation: • Cognitive theorist; Ancillary Orientations: • Behaviorist; • Humanistic/ existentialist	• Objective data (agreed upon in the pre-conference and collected by supervisor during classroom observation)	• Five phase cycle: 1) a preconference; 2) a classroom observation during which the data is collected by the supervisor; 3) supervisor analyzes and interprets the data, and then chooses a postconference strategy from the three options (directive, collaborative or non-directive); 4) a postconference; and 5) a critique (either done at the postconference, or on a separate occasion) in which the clinical cycle is examined for refinements or improvements.	• Relies on developmental continuum based on teacher's level of abstraction and commitment; • Three supervisory options: directive, collaborative, non-directive, depending on supervisor's analysis of teacher's level of development; • Three supervisory options: directive, collaborative, non-directive, depending on supervisor's analysis of teacher's level of development
Costa and Garmston's Cognitive Coaching Model	• Based upon four assumptions: (1) the non-routine and complex nature of teaching requires constant contextual decision-making; 2) all behavior is directed by our individual and subjective perceptions; 3) to skillfully change behavior requires a change in perception; and 4) effective coaching mediates the perceptual changes and capacities for reasoning and decision-making that promote behavioral changes towards more effective practice. • The purpose of supervision is to increase the capacity for self-modification	Dominant Orientation: • Cognitive Theorist; Ancillary Orientations: • Humanistic/ existentialist; • Systems theory	• Objective data (agreed upon in the planning conference and collected by supervisor and/or teacher during classroom observation and/or events)	• Three-phase cycle: (1) Planning conference; (2) Classroom observation; (3) Reflecting/applying conference; • Three phase cycle: 1) pre-observation, 2) collection of data, and 3) post-observation	• Three fundamental goals: 1) trust; 2) learning; and 3) holonomy; • Emphasis on supervisory use of linguistic and relationship tools to mediate cognitive development; • Coaching relationship can be developed with anyone in the school community; • The principles and skills are not limited to formal interactions
Reflective Models: Schon's Reflective Action, Zeichner & Liston's Reflective Coaching, Garman's Reflective Heart, Smyth & Retallick Critical Consciousness, Bowers & Flinders' Cultural Responsible Supervision	• Practitioners build a knowledge base derived from reflection on their own practice; • Reflection promotes an examination of implicit assumptions and values that drive teaching decisions, holding them open to potential revision	Dominant Orientation: • Cognitive Theorist; Ancillary Orientation: • Systems Theory (Smyth & Retallick; Bowers & Flinders); Behaviorist: • Bowers & Flinders	• Schon: Three levels of interaction; a) students w/learning phenomena; b) teacher w/students; and c) supervisor with teacher; • Zeichner & Liston: Specific instructional event; as well as teacher's reflections on professional goals; • Garman: Specific instructional events; as well as reflections on recent instructional events; • Smyth & Retallick: A descriptive narrative of instructional events; • Bowers & Flinders: Focus of observational data based on specific guides		• Zeichner & Liston: Teacher's cultivate skills in inquiry, engage in seminars, and maintain reflective journals; • Garman: Teachers reflect on action and on recollection; • Smyth & Retallick: Supervision liberates teachers from prevailing assumptions through critical analysis of their school setting; Supervision process is reciprocal; • Bowers & Flinders: Supervisor illuminates unconscious patterns which drive teaching decisions; analysis within the cultural context of the classroom

empathy, unconditional positive regard, and personal congruence guide the relationship-building work of the coach. Certain neurolinguistic principles are also applied to achieve rapport in the moment, which is believed necessary for the mediation of cognitive processes. The cognitive coaching model is then predicated upon a set of maps and tools that invites the shaping and reshaping of thinking and problem-solving capacities, for both the coach and those being coached, when combined with these nonjudgmental ways of being and working with others. The coach's function varies across four phases of instruction: planning, teaching, analyzing/reflecting, and applying.

The ability to work effectively with one's self and others across style differences and philosophical preferences is integral to this model. Fundamental to the effectiveness of the supervisory interaction is the capacity to work within the teacher's world view. As a result, the viewpoints of both participants are widened, enabling an exploration of new ideas and new behaviors that offer expanded perspectives, yet are consistent with the teacher's existing beliefs and values.

Cognitive coaching marries the psychological orientations of the cognitive theorists and the humanists by incorporating the basic principles of knowledge construction suggested by Bruner (1959), Feuerstein et al (1980), Piaget (1948, 1952), and Taba (1962); human developmental sequences based upon the work of Piaget, Kohlberg (1971), and Erickson (1950); human dynamics theories of Rogers (1980), Perls (1969, 1973) and Satir (1972); and psycholinguistics theories of Chomsky (1957, 1965), Bandler and Grinder (1976). Based on the work of these theorists, coaches develop a set of linguistic tools, including questioning skills that incorporate the use of syntax and positive presuppositions to promote thinking and response behaviors that use wait time, paraphrasing, clarifying, and probing for specificity. This model attends to the linkages between physiology and cognition. Cognitive coaches become skillful with the elements of rapport (i.e., posture, gesture, language, tonality, and breathing), which become important tools for building and maintaining trust in the moment, particularly in the event of tension, miscommunication or anticipated difficulty.

Reflective Practice: Five Perspectives. Pajak offers five distinct perspectives that put forth reflective practice as the process that has the greatest potential for developing the moral, ethical, and social sensitivity necessary for excellence in education. These are Schon's Reflective Coaching, Zeichner and Liston's Reflective Action, Garman's Reflective Heart of Clinical Supervision, Smyth and Retallick's Critical Consciousness, and Bowers and Flinder's Culturally Responsive Supervision. The basis of each of these models of reflective practice lies in challenging taken-for-granted assumptions and beliefs and holding them open to examination and potential revision. In this way, they are steeped in a cognitive theorist orientation. The notion of exploratory experimentation requires a cycle of inquiry and reflection in which the practitioner is defined as a builder of repertoire rather than as a collector of procedures and methods (Schon, 1988). Schon (1987) described this cycle:

It is initiated by the perception of something troubling, or promising, and it is determined by the production of changes one finds on the whole satisfactory or by the discovery of new features which give the situation new meaning and change the nature of the questions to be explored (p. 151).

Most of the models described by Pajak employ the sequential process of the clinical supervisory model developed by Goldhammer: a preobservation conference, collection of observational data, a postconference, data analysis, and some form of feedback. It is through this cyclical process that educators recognize doubt or uncertainty, draw inferences based on previous experiences, choose a course of action, and finally test their inferences and choices through further reflection (Grimmett & Erickson, 1988; Schon, 1983).

This reconstruction of experience is subjective, and is based on the individual's perceptions and self-view. Rooted in cognitive theory, reflective practice is highly contextual. It is based on the institutional culture and the variables involved with the specific event.

[T]he primary source of validity in the propositions produced as results, must lie not in their validity as statistical generalizations . . . but in the extent to which practitioners who reflect-in-action in the light of them are able to use them to design effective interventions, confirm action-oriented hypothesis, or gain new insights into the phenomena of practice (Schon, 1988, p. 28).

Schon's Reflective Coaching. Schon suggests that practitioners use the perspective of their own experiences to frame problems and to select professional goals. In order to develop the teacher's capacity to do so, Schon suggests that the supervisor function as a coach who attends to three levels of interaction. The first level is the student's interaction with a learning phenomena (i.e., printed information or a particular concept); the second level is the teacher's interaction with the student (i.e., the teacher's inferences, interpretations, and choices regarding subsequent action); the third level is the supervisor's interaction with the teacher (i.e., their own inferences, inquiries, and responses to the teacher). In each interaction, there are relevant questions designed to cut to the core of the experience and provide fuel for reflection.

Schon is mindful that the organizational constraints imposed upon practitioners may deter from this process. He purports, however, that working within these constraints with continued experimentation and the development of a theory-in-use through conscious examination of practice will work to help eliminate the very impositions that may be constraining (see Table 8.3).

Zeichner and Liston's Reflective Action. Zeichner and Liston contrast routine action, which is habituated, traditional, and potentially impulsive with reflective action, which is grounded in careful and persistent examination of practices and beliefs. According to Zeichner and Liston, reflective teachers are clear about their position within the political and social contexts of their work environment; they are highly conscious about the type of practitioner they would like to be; and they are aware of the knowledge and skills they need to develop to actualize their beliefs. This model is rooted in Dewey's predispositions toward learning, open-mindedness, responsibility, and wholeheartedness, as well as the psychological school of cognitive theory.

In this model, reflective teaching is the central goal, and teachers must cultivate skills in inquiry, engage in seminars designed to broaden their perspectives, and maintain reflective journals. The supervisory process is based on the clinical model of formal observations, conferences that focus on the specific instructional event that was observed, and the teacher's ongoing professional growth. During the teacher–supervisor interaction, attention is given to the teacher's own analysis of the connections between intentions, beliefs, and related behaviors, the institutional and social context of their teaching techniques, the appropriateness of the content as well as process, and any unanticipated effects or outcomes related to curriculum, instruction, or social interaction in the classroom. Supervision is designed to invite consideration of changes based on the teacher's reflection, not directly to change teacher behavior.

Garman's Reflective Heart of Clinical Supervision. Garman's model of supervision is highly consistent with the traditions of the original model of clinical supervision. Like Cogan and Goldhammer, she asserts that reflection lies at the heart of practice. She believes it is the responsibility of every practitioner to develop a professional identity that includes a personal rationale for teaching. The supervisor's primary function is to support teachers in their own generation of knowledge. This, she suggests, is done through two kinds of reflection: reflection on action, in which a practitioner studies immediate events, and reflection on recollection, in which a review of recent events is used as data. The reflection on action mode follows the traditional preconference, observation, and analysis/interpretation sequence. It is the teacher who interprets the data, with the support of the supervisor and potentially with relevant literature in the field. Garman also adds two steps to reflection-on-recollection: construal and confirmation. During construal, the supervisor supports the teacher's construction of insights, principles, and practical understandings that will inform future practice. During confirmation, the teacher and supervisor confirm the results of the process and seek outside expertise to broaden their new learnings.

Smyth and Retallick's Critical Consciousness. Smyth and Retallick view supervision as a liberating, collaborative action that can free teachers from any constraining assumptions about practice. They believe that the supervisory process should involve teachers in reflectively analyzing their own practices and in developing theories appropriate to their needs and situations. They foresee this process as one in which teachers critically examine their own school settings, becoming politically involved in challenging prevailing assumptions and forging new dimensions for schools. The supervisor–teacher relationship is reciprocal in that either party can call to question embedded assumptions and beliefs regarding practice.

Though they write separately, both Smyth and Retallick agree on four procedures that would foster examination and questioning of the moral, ethical, social, and political practices prevalent in schools: (1) problematizing teaching through a dialogue wherein supervisors help teachers to explore the traditionally unexamined social and political purposes of their practices; (2) observing and creating text about teaching wherein the observer offers data as a descriptive narrative of the classroom events and consults with the teacher in the interpretation of the teaching episode presented; (3) confronting personal biography and professional history, which includes questioning authoritarian assumptions that have led to teacher dependency and docility, as well as a self-examination of the origins of a teacher's personal values, definitions, practices, and beliefs, which is a step used to explore consciously and potentially redirect relationships and interactions in all aspects of the school; (4) refocusing and acting, where attention is paid to developing shared frameworks of meaning regarding the clinical supervisory practice.

Bowers and Flinder's Culturally Responsive Supervision. As distinct from the other reflective models, Bower and Flinder's Culturally Responsive Supervision presents a strong foray into systems theory with its emphasis on the influence of external systems on the students' lives and the teacher's decisions. Its minor roots extend from cognitive psychology, based on a faith in the capacity of individuals to integrate multiple forces into complex meaning systems.

Bowers and Flinder's take an ecological perspective and argue that the role of supervision is to inform and sensitize teachers to the broad social, political, and cultural issues prevalent in schools. They believe that social and cultural issues, such as single parenting, drug abuse, and gender discrimination influence classroom functioning. They suggest that culturally determined assumptions direct students', as well as teachers', perceptions and behaviors, and must be examined within the classroom ecology. Thus, knowledge is open to negotiation and interpretation based on past patterns, present usefulness, and future concerns.

The role of supervision is to spotlight unconscious patterns of language and response behaviors that teachers are using and to analyze these patterns in light of the social and cultural climate of the classroom. In this way, teachers will develop sensitivity to the differing strengths, and needs of their students. The supervisor serves as a consultant who can assist teachers in increasing their consciousness regarding their instructional choices and actions, adapting their practices to align with the differing social and cultural learning patterns of their students.

Bowers and Flinders believe that the supervisor should control the focus of the observation based on the information in 11 detailed guides that they have developed. Through a clinical supervisory process, the supervisor serves "as a connoisseur of culture, rather than a neutral observer, who focuses the teacher's attention on issues of race, gender, culture, and environmental concerns" (Pajak, 1993, p. 306).

Distinctions in Practice From a Psychological Perspective: A Summary When these varied approaches to supervisory practice are considered from a psychological perspective, distinct, dichotomous, and far-reaching consequences emerge. In practice, these deeply held psychological orientations create unstated agreements about the nature of the supervisory relationship, its purposes, its assumptions about both adult and student learning, and the intrinsic worth of the persons being supervised. These agreements are acted out by both parties in the relationship, with differing degrees of effectiveness depending upon their match with deeply held psychological assumptions regarding contexts, such as instruction, that are outside the supervisory transaction. For example, supervision can be seen as teaching specific skills and solving specific problems. The supervisor is an educator who provides information, analyzes data, and develops strategies for interacting with the teacher based on a preconceived learning agenda. Supervision can also be seen as a life-expanding endeavor of human development. The supervisor is alternately a mediator, a consultant, a co-learner, or a coach.

The development of supervisory models has many characteristics in common with the evolution of psychological theories. All schools of psychology have dipped into the well of psychoanalytic theory that had its source in early clinical practice and philosophy, and have later models of school supervision (see Figure 8.2). General influences from this orientation persist today in popularized characterizations of the Freudian constructs of id, ego, and superego that have become sort of a mythological truth in North American consciousness. In supervision, subject-object theory and practices based on assumptions about developmental stages (Kegan, 1994) reflected in such models as Developmental Supervision (Glickman, 1985), Cognitive Coaching (Costa & Garmston, 1994), and five models of Reflective Practice (Pajak, 1993) can trace portions of their origins to psychodynamic theory. From academic research, which is more visible in its supervisory manifestations, surges behaviorism predicated on assumptions of cumulative learnings that occur as the environment acts on the individual. The technical/didactic models express this view in their emphasis on the installation of specific teaching behaviors through supervisory feedback. In these models, supervision is organized around the detailed collection of data regarding the absence or existence, frequency, adequacy, and consistency of these predetermined behaviors, which will be reinforced or extinguished as deemed appropriate by the supervisor.

For all of the other psychological perspectives, learning is about the individual acting on and with the environment. To varying degrees, it occurs inside the individual. In these models, classroom data sets a context for learning, and is used to provide rich description, as in Eisner's artistic approach, to illuminate alternative possibilities, to support teacher-centered analysis and problem-solving, and to focus on broad-based issues that affect learning and various aspects of practice.

For example, the cognitive theorists hold that humans are driven to process their experiences by organizing and adapting. Thus, meaning is made and learning occurs through the continual interaction of the individual with the environment. Developmental supervision offers an example of supervision based on this psychological school, which is in turn based on its premise that supervision is part of a life-long process of evolution toward more complex differentiation.

The heart of Roger's existentialist view is the belief that personality is a process, not an entity. This process involves a continual move toward actualization that goes beyond Maslow's deficiency needs to more sophisticated differentiation of functions and gives rise to the meaning making system identified as the self. Learner-centered models, such as the developmental/reflective approaches to supervision, are derived from this perspective. These models call on the process of supervision to "encourage teacher introspection in order to discover context-specific principles of practice." (Pajak, 1993, p. 10). From a humanistic/existential perspective, the source of motivation is the continual construction of the self toward increased capacities for maintenance and enhancement. Thus, humanistically based models rely on the professional identity of the teacher as one that seeks to learn and strives for continual improvement.

How does one choose a supervisory model? Sergiovanni and Starratt (1988) contend that choosing, interpreting, and applying one is largely dependent on several variables: initiating, mediating, and effectiveness. Initiating variables will include the supervisor's own meaning making system and inherent assumptions, beliefs, and values about professional identity, the role of supervision, the motivation level of the staff, the expectations of the institution, and so on. Mediating variables include the meaning making systems of the staff, their attitudes regarding their work, the institution, the role of supervision, their level of commitment, and so on. Effectiveness variables involve qualitative and quantitative data about the organization, such as student performance levels, the quality of school–community relationships, and levels of job satisfaction for the staff.

The following is an argument for a developmental perspective to school supervision. We find merit with Sergiovanni and Starratt's contention that the mediating variables holds the most promise for school improvement. Furthermore, many studies support the notion that the most profound and enduring effect of school supervision will be its attention to the growth of the individuals that comprise the organization (Glassberg, 1979; Harvey, 1967; Hunt & Joyce, 1967; Sprinthall & Thies-Sprinthall, 1982; Thies-Sprinthall, 1980; and Witherall & Erickson, 1978) toward the ultimate and self-renewing growth of the organization itself (Frymier, 1987; Rosenholtz, 1989). From this standpoint, it is critical to understand the patterns and stages of human development:

[B]ecause the way in which the person is settling the issue of what is "self" and what is "other" essentially defines the underlying logic (or psychologic) of the person's meaning. Since what is most important for us to know in understanding another is not the other's experience, but what the experience means to him or her, our first goal is to grasp the essence of how the other composes his or her private reality (Kegan and Lahey, 1984, p. 113).

AN EMERGING PSYCHOLOGY OF SUPERVISION

The dominant practice of supervision in the 1990s is based on a clinical model. Emerging efforts toward instructional improvement and school renewal, however, produced varied models and configurations that included aspects of, yet differed from, the clinical model. One of these major new developments is the entrance of teacher choice. In consultation with a supervisor, a teacher can decide what type of supervisory model to employ. Labeled by many districts as "professional growth plans" or "supervision for growth," teachers can select from such options as traditional clinical supervision, peer coaching, cognitive coaching, action research, portfolio-driven data collection, or contextually defined personalized growth plans.

Dominating these newly emerging models is a focus on teacher development. The emphasis on the developmental nature of human values and behaviors is in accord with the work of Adler, Maslow, Piaget, Erikson, Kohlberg, Kegan, and others, who see the powerful role of growth and change in humankind. The central process that moves individuals into dynamic, ever-evolving lives is one of conflict and choice.

As people move through developmental stages, they are caught between "natural" wants and needs and the necessity of obeying rules in order to avoid punishments; between idiosyncratic impulses and desires and the incentive to conform in order to receive rewards, the return of favors, and the approval of others; between the desire to explore deviant kinds of behavior and the avoidance of unacceptable behavior because of guilt instigated by censure from legitimate authorities; between conflicting sets of personal values; and ultimately between condemnation by others and self-condemnation. Such conflicts are the main "moto" or condition for "upward" movement. . . . [M]ovement is spurred not simply by reasoning about higher modes of thinking but by day-to-day exposure to concrete choices that reflect moral conditions (Burns, 1978, p. 428).

While it is an expectation that teachers develop professionally throughout their careers and it is clear that adults have the capacity to continue to develop throughout their lives, there are alternate views regarding the ways in which they do so. Development typically refers to a change in form over time, usually on a continuum from relatively simple to complex. Driving these changes for adults are both maturational factors within the individual and interactional factors between the personal characteristics of the individual, their experiences, and the environment. Two schools of thought have arisen from work in adult development. Age-related task development theorists, such as Sheehy (1976) and Levinson (1965), believe that there are specific roles, tasks, and coping skills necessary at different times of life, and that generalizations can be made regarding behaviors during one's 20s, 30s, 40s, and so on. On the other hand, life-cycle theorists believe that there are a series of stages, with transitions between each, through which humans progress. They emphasize that progression through these stages is determined more by experience than it is by chronology.

As we consider adult development, we follow the thinking of the life-cycle theorists, who include Piaget (1948), Kohlberg (1971), Loevinger (1976), Hunt (1971), and Kegan (1992, 1984). These psychologists view adult development as a progression from "concrete, undifferentiating, simple, unstructured patterns, of thought to more abstract, differentiating, and complex patterns of thought" Burden (1990, p. 312). The domains of individual growth differ for each: Piaget's work explores cognitive growth and the understanding of physical phenomena, such as space, time, and causality; Kohlberg's work describes changes in orientation toward authority, self, and others in making morally based decisions; Loevinger explores ego development as individuals move from conformity through emotional independence toward self-understanding and personal identity; Hunt's work indicates increasing degrees of cognitive flexibility, creativity, and tolerance for stress as individuals advance in their conceptual systems development; Kegan's work examines developmental growth in how persons make meaning of their experiences. Knowledge of such developmental changes informs decisions about the needs, concerns, interests and abilities of teachers at various points in their development, and contributes to establishing professional goals and professional development programs.

Relating Teacher Performance to Factors of Adult Development

Like all adults, teachers exhibit various characteristics as they move through developmental phases. As they develop professionally, however, teachers also express different skills, behaviors, attitudes, and concerns in relation to their teaching careers. Burden (1990) identifies three specific arenas of development: (1) specific job skills (such as teaching methods, classroom management, and curriculum implementation), (2) attitudes and concerns (such as professional identity and job satisfaction), and (3) job-related circumstances (such as changes in assignment, involvement in additional responsibilities, and participation in professional development). Furthermore, a comprehensive set of research indicates that teachers' developmental levels have a direct correlation to their performance in the classroom, as well as their interactions with other adults in the school environment. This research indicates that teachers who function at higher conceptual levels are capable of greater degrees of complexity in the classroom and are more effective with students. For example, teachers with more advanced conceptual levels are more flexible, stress tolerant, and adaptive in their teaching style (Harvey, 1970; Hunt, 1971; Hunt & Joyce, 1967). Thus, they are able to assume multiple perspectives, employ a variety of coping strategies, and apply a wide repertoire of teaching models. Furthermore, they are responsive to a wider range of learning styles and culturally diverse classes (Harvey, Prather, White & Hoffmeister, 1968; Hunt, 1975; Hunt & Joyce, 1967). Teachers at higher levels of conceptual development can take an allocentric perspective, employing the learner's frame of reference in instructional planning, teaching, and evaluation (Hunt & Joyce, 1967). They are more supportive to students in regard to formulating hypotheses and analyzing and evaluating information (Joyce, Weil, & Wald, 1973). Understanding and being sensitive to this information can inform supervision practices with teachers toward developmental growth and offer fertile arenas for facilitating learning.

The Psychology of a Constructivist– Developmental Orientation

People maintain a capacity for learning over most of their adult lives, and, under certain circumstances, increase their capacity for learning as they age. The desirability of teachers' continuing mental growth is widely accepted. For example, the National Board for Professional Teaching Standards (NBPTS), expects teachers to steadily extend their knowledge, perfect their teaching, and refine their evolving philosophy of education. To achieve this goal, the Board expects highly accomplished teachers to consider reflection on their practice as central to their responsibilities. In another standard, the NBPTS calls for teacher collaboration with colleagues to improve schools and to advance knowledge and practice in their field (NBPTS, 1993). If supervision is to contribute to teachers' ability to achieve these standards, and indeed to increase their capacity for learning and self-modification throughout their professional lives, then a constructivist–developmental approach is a logical direction.

A constructivist–developmental view of supervision combines two fields of inquiry: constructivism and a more recent body of information regarding developmental stages in adult life. *Constructivism* is closely connected to a Kantian model of knowledge, and combines the cognitive theorist, humanistic/existentialist and, to a lesser degree, systems theory schools of psychology. Based on a Piagetian orientation to human development, a constructivist approach attends to developments in the way in which an individual constructs reality (i.e., how he or she makes meaning). In this case, it is the way in which a teacher or a supervisor makes meaning of their role (i.e., how they construct their professional identity). According to this theory, people respond to events and experiences based on their system of meaning. *Development* is described as a qualitative change in a person's meaning system.

The constructivist–developmental approach to adult development is rooted in the work of cognitive theorists including Dewey (1938), Mead (1934), Bruner (1959), and Piaget (1952), the developmental theoritsis such as Kohlberg (1971), and Kegan (1984), and the humanistic/existentialist perspective of such practitioners as Rogers (1980) and Kelly (1965). Concepts inherent in this theory include:

1. For human beings, development is founded on their constructions of reality, or how they make meaning. Our meanings are more something we are, and not so much something we have.
2. Our experience is shaped by our meaning system. "We do not understand another's experience simply by knowing the events and particulars of the other but only knowing how these events and particulars are privately composed." (Huxley, in Kegan & Lahey, 1984, p. 202)
3. To a large extent these meaning systems give rise to our behavior. Even those behaviors that appear to be irrational, or inconsistent, may be coherent and understandable when viewed through the perspective of the individual taking the action.
4. Our thoughts, feelings, and behaviors are organized by our system of meaning, except during periods of transition and evolution between one system and another.
5. Albeit that individuals are each unique, there are striking generalizations that can be made regarding the underlying structures of meaning making systems, and to the sequence of growth changes (Kegan & Lahey, 1984).

Two fundamental understandings are also inherent in this perspective: (1) Growth is not automatic, but occurs only with mediation, or appropriate interaction and experience between the individual and the environment, and (2) behavior can be understood by an individual's particular developmental stage (Sprinthall & Sprinthall, 1980).

Supervisory models founded on these psychological principles attend to adult life span development and the personal construction of knowledge. In that they subscribe to the development of relational understandings and the assimilation of new schema, or ways of understanding the world, they are based in cognitive theory. There is a phenomenological underpinning to constructivism, however, in that individuals are the composite of their experiences, that meaning is derived through the mediation of experience, and that they ultimately expand their world view by processing new experiences based on previous ones. Kelly is considered by many to be the first person to formally bring a constructivist perspective to the humanistic/existential orientation in the fields of personality theory and mental health. Rogers (1959) held that the basic unity of personality is a process not an entity. This process is understood in the context of the self's efforts to maintain, and the experience of transforming, the self-system. "A developmental perspective naturally equips one to see the present in the context both of its antecedents and potential future, so that every phenomenon gets looked at not only in terms of its limits, but its strengths." (Kegan, 1982, p. 30). Thus, we recognize that human growth occurs as a series of qualitative changes in an individual's construction of meaning.

We suggest that these qualitative changes in meaning can also be described from a systems-theory perspective. Qualitative changes encompass the recognition of our possibilities or ways of being. From a systems perspective, qualitative change is the emergence of new abilities and possibilities that come into being as you view yourself within the context of the whole within which you are participating. At each point you have capabilities and possibilities that are only available when you see the whole system (Olds, 1992; Zohar & Marshall, 1994). Supervision is potentially a process that creates qualitative shifts in the construction of meaning by bringing heightened awareness within each part and of the whole—simultaneously. This process is participatory, dynamic, and system oriented because the process itself is part of the whole.

Evolving Stages of Adult Meaning Making

Because of the complexity of teachers' work, the nature of their discretionary decisions, and the modeling teachers provide for student emulation, supervision's attention to adult development in the areas of ego maturity, principles of moral and ethical reasoning, and increased conceptual complexity is important. An individual's system of meaning making addresses the central influences on an individual's decision-making capacity. Kegan and Laskow Lahey (1984) argue that development in adult meaning making has more to do with qualitative changes in a person's meaning system than it does with aging. Based on Kegan's (1982) original work on evolutionary phases in adult development, they describe three systems of meaning in adulthood; Interpersonal, Institutional, and Postinstitutional.

The first system is the Interpersonal, so called because of a continuing dependency on relationships with external authorities that guide meaning making . This stage is entered and developed somewhere between the teens to the early 20s. The second system is the Institutional, when individuals achieve their own psychological "institution" with its own rules, standards, and authority. The third system on this evolutionary continuum is the Postinstitutional. At this stage the adult has an institution, but can mentally step outside it to question its assumptions and logic. While in the Institutional stage the adult tends to be threatened by data that challenge the assumptions and logic of its "psychic institution," the adult can question these systems of logic at the Postinstitutional stage.

In each phase of development, the preceding stage is subsumed into the next, where it is still accessible and still functional, but is no longer dominant. Kegan (1994) elaborated on the psychological structure within each system in his detailed work, "In Over Our Heads: The Mental Demands of Modern Life." He reports that as few as one third of adults may fully attain the institutional stage and that very few adults, and none before age 40, attain Postinstitutional reasoning. An overview of these three systems follows, with a discussion of their relationship to supervision.

1. Interpersonal As individuals mature, they learn to regulate their impulses and make plans, fulfill goals, and meet needs. During childhood, the self tends to make others captive of its needs and is almost exclusively egocentric in its views and habits. Somewhere around adolescence this world view begins to change and give way to the first adult system of meaning, the Interpersonal Self. The Interpersonal meaning system begins to regulate what now becomes a subsystem of individual needs, goals, and single point of view. The person can move back and forth between his or her own and others' needs and viewpoints.

At the Interpersonal stage, thinking becomes abstract, and self-knowledge includes awareness of patterns of dispositions, needs and preferences. Analysis of interaction between categories is possible. Cause–effect thinking, goal setting, loyalty to ideals or a community, and commitment to and capacity for self-improvement are manifested in the Interpersonal Self. Personal identity, however, is dependent on relationships. The Interpersonal Self derives identity by being in a dependent relationship to persons or ideas.

The key to understanding the structure of the Interpersonal Self is to focus on the nature of what it means to be in "relationship." For some people, the dependency is on a relationship to another, or other, important individuals; for others, it may be to a set of ideas or values that guide, or potentially dictate, their choices. "The essence of the structure of the Interpersonal world view is that the self has internalized, uncritically accepted and identified with the values, beliefs, and expectations of 'others' in the social surrounding" (Lahey, 1995). These others can include any group or organization that explicitly communicate a set of values, beliefs, norms, and expectations, or specific schools of thought (e.g.,

democracy, constructivism, cooperative learning). "The Interpersonal Self's identity is founded on whatever the values, beliefs, norms and expectations are of the particular important other people, institutions or schools of thought. These are uncritically accepted by the self" (Lahey, 1995).

A dilemma is created for this individual when confronted with conflicting principles or ideas within the relationship. For example, the choices of a teacher who has an Interpersonally constructed relationship with the whole language movement will be informed by his or her understanding of this movement. If he or she was facing a problem with a particular child, then this teacher might go back to specific references (e.g., a professor, the person who ran the seminar he or she attended, a resource book, etc.) to find ideas for addressing the problem. This process would be straightforward if a case example in a text that matched the specific situation could be accessed, or a specific authority (i.e., the professor) would prescribe what to do. If the need arose this teacher could generalize from the reference. A problem would arise if this teacher surfaced contrary recommendations from two expert sources. "Without a self that has the structural ability to make up one's mind, the Interpersonal Self is left to 'decide' on bases like, which person is the 'real' expert? Which idea is closer to the one s/he thinks more experts would agree with? etc." (Lahey, 1995).

2. Institutional When the self moves on to the next system of logic, it does not abandon the old system, the Interpersonal, but now holds this as a subsystem of a larger one, the Institutional. At this stage of development the self no longer *is* the interpersonal point of view, it now *has* the interpersonal as an option with which to operate. The person at this new stage becomes self-authoring:

Rather than having the pieces of oneself co-owned and co-determined in various shared psychological contexts, the person brings the power of determination into the self and establishes the self as a kind of psychic "institution," an organization which the self is now responsible for running and regulating. In common language, the person evolves an identity" (Kegan and Lahey, 1984, p. 204).

The Institutional Self can reflect upon thoughts, feelings, intentions, behaviors, relationships, and their effects: They can monitor and modify their decisions and behaviors as long as they are consistent with the "rules" of their self-developed system. The limit of the Institutional system, however, is that it is *too* self-referencing. It lacks a capacity for correction of itself and "risks the excesses of control that may pertain to any government not subject to a wider context in which to root and justify its laws. Personal well being is linked to the smooth running of one's own system" (Kegan & Lahey, 1984, p. 204).

Persons functioning at this stage of reasoning can create relationships of caring and congeniality, but they are not dependent upon them for feelings of personal worth. Teachers at the Institutional stage are autonomous. They are self-authoring, self-owning, self-initiating, and self-dependent. They set their own standards, perform self-evaluation, and rate personal assessment as more reliable and important than external evaluation. A limitation for these persons, however, can be that they get locked into perpetuating their own systems as a goal and miss the opportunity to engage in critical reflection and modification of their own systems. These persons can be closed to information or ideologies that challenge their systems of meaning (see Figure 8.3).

3. Postinstitutional In the Postinstitutional system, the self no longer *is* the organization, it *has* organizations. The self is more than its temporary organization. The prevailing principle of organization is not ultimate and a predetermined orientation to conflict and information is transcended. No ideology is considered ultimate.

Teachers at this level of meaning system reflect on and modify their own organization of self. They view the principal and other adults as individuals who are neither loyalists nor foes in regard to their own or the school's programs or positions. They recognize that those meanings are constructed knowledge, amenable to reinterpretation, examination, and modification. Furthermore, they possess the ego strength and cognitive capacity for flexibility of thought, and they can value and consider new data and other person's points of view.

The Postinstitutional Self has a great respect for individual differences, is open to questions, possibilities, conflict and reconstruction, and value ambiguity. Persons at this stage of development have style flexibility and value collaborative decision-making. They regard conflict as opportunity for learning and personal change. They are more committed to processes of continual inquiry and exploration than they are to preserving a product. They refer to values in addition to behaviors in analyzing and learning from their own work. They have a capacity for self-modification and question system norms, objectives, and practices in a quest for continual improvement (see Figure 8.3).

Kegan (1994) describes this continuum of developing capacities as emanating from the evolving inner logic of the "subject–object" relationship around which it is organized.

Subject (We are)	Object (We have)
Those elements of our knowing or organizing that we are identified with, tied to, fused with, or embedded in. We cannot be responsible for, in control of, or reflect upon that which is subject. Subject is ultimate.	Those elements of our knowing or organizing that we can reflect on, handle, look at, be responsible for, relate to each other, take control of, internalize, assimilate, or otherwise operate upon. It is not the whole of us, it is distinct enough from us that we can do something with it. Object is relative.

This logic is applied by Kegan (1994) to describe increasingly complex "orders of consciousness" that are believed to evolve in sequence with each successive epistemology containing the last. According to this hierarchy, the Interpersonal Self assigns point of view and enduring dispositions, needs, preferences to "object." At this level, the principle of cross-categorical knowledge (i.e., the capacity to subordinate durable categories to the interaction between them) makes their thinking abstract. Their feelings can be attributed to their own inner processing of events, not assigned to the events themselves. Their self-reflective emotions such as guilt or self-

Interpersonal	Institutional	Post-Institutional
• Identity is defined by relationships with person(s) or ideas	• Self-authoring, self-initiating	• Reflects on and modifies own organization of self
• Seeks validation from external criteria	• Validated by internal criteria	• Open to questions
• Self has internalized, uncritically, the values and beliefs of others	• Sets own standards; self-evaluation	• Committed to continual inquiry
• Occupies a dependent stance	• Occupies an independent state	• Occupies an interdependent state
I am my relationship	I have relationships	There are relationships and I am part of them

FIGURE 8.3. Three systems of adult meaning
(Adapted from Robert Kegan and Lisa Laskow Lahey.)

confidence can be assigned to their own dispositions and treatment of life events, not life itself. They are capable of loyalty and devotion to a community of people or ideas larger than the self.

The Institutional Self assigns abstractions, mutuality, interpersonalism, inner states, subjectivity, and self-consciousness to "object." This person operates from the principle of system/complex (i.e., the capacity to gather cross-categorical constructions into a complex or integrated system permits the creation of a mental structure that subtends, subordinates, acts upon, directs, and actually generates the meaning of one's relationships). The Postinstitutional Self applies the principle of transsystem and transcomplex (i.e., the capacity for recognition of our multiple selves) for the capacity to see conflict as a signal of our overidentification with a single system, for the sense of our relationships and connections as prior to and constitutive of the individual self, and for an identification with the transformative process of our being rather than the formative products of our becoming. At this level "object" is assigned to institution, relationship-regulating forms, self-authorship, self-regulation, and self-formation.

As persons grow in cognitive complexity they progress through stages of adult meaning making, increasingly assigning a greater portion of their experience to "object" and less to "subject."

Implications for Growth According to Kegan (1982, 1994), growth is continual movement. Mediation of developmental growth through stages of meaning making is facilitated by an understanding of the developmental level from which an individual is presently constructing meaning. Each of these levels is comprised of two facets that need to be differentiated in a discussion of supervisory practice: the *structure* through which the self is constructed (i.e., the way in which the individual is making sense) and the *content* that defines the world view (i.e., the information or belief system that informs, or in some cases dictates, choices). For example, the structure of meaning making for the Interpersonal Self is an uncritical acceptance of an important "others" set of values. The content for meaning making will be contained in the specific value set (e.g., cooperative learning, teaching for thinking, academic rationalism). Thus, supervisory behaviors that validate a persons' source of meaning making or conclusions will be perceived as supportive when support is defined as confirming the content of the present level of meaning making . While support of this type may be comforting, it may not be growth promoting. Growth requires productive tension or discomfort. A distinction must also be made between nonproductive and productive (i.e., growth-promoting) tension. "The forms of conflict, tensions and discomfort are critical to being able to judge which will be syntonic, and which dystonic for the individual" (Lahey, 1995).

An understanding of Kegan's theory allows supervisors to differentiate interactions, establish appropriate expectations, and make predictions regarding behaviorial responses in an effort to maximize growth opportunities and engage in productive supervisory exchanges with diverse school faculties. This knowledge is fundamental to achieving the second function of supervision stated at the beginning of this chapter: developing teachers' capacity for learning. Levine (1989) wrote:

If developmental stage affects the degree to which we can hear ourselves and colleagues and the level of irritation that can be evoked by discrepant world views, [we] will have to listen hard to [our] own voices, talk with and listen to colleagues, and monitor the range of responses that individuals manifest. When an individual displays signs of discomfort or irritation, thinking about the source of the disruption in developmental terms may add a new layer of insight to one's understanding (p. 114).

In summary, Kegan's work describes adult development as an evolving journey toward greater mental complexity and away from perceiving the self as separate from others and center of the universe. The descriptions detailing growth in mental complexity are consistent with cognitive and developmental theorists, whereas the movement from an ego-centered existence to experiences of self as a complete, integrated, self-expressive, autonomous person stems from the humanistic/existential school of psychology. Csikszentmihalyi (1990) observed:

In the past few thousand years—a mere split second in evolutionary time—humanity has achieved incredible advances in the differentiation of consciousness. We have developed a realization that mankind is separate from other forms of life. We have conceived of individual human beings as separate from one another. We have invented abstraction and analysis—the ability to separate dimensions of objects and processes from each other, such as the velocity of a falling object from its weight and its mass. It is this differentiation that has produced science, technology, and the unprecedented power of mankind to build up and to destroy its environment.

But complexity consists of integration as well as differentiation. The task of the next decades and centuries is to realize this underdeveloped component of the mind. Just as we have learned to separate ourselves from each other and from the environment, we now need to learn how to reunite ourselves with other entities around us without losing our hard-won individuality (pp. 239–240).

This capacity to reunite ourselves (i.e., to be an interdependent member of an evolving community) is to be holonomous (Costa & Garmston, 1994). In the next section we will describe five states of mind of a holonomous person and the implications for supervision as mediation of adult development.

States of Mind Supporting Movement Through Adult Stages of Development

Person's reasoning at Kegan's Institutional level of meaning making are self-authoring, self-initiating, and autonomous. These are the very qualities required to achieve self-growth in professional skills and knowledge, which is one of the aims of the NBPTS. It is unlikely, however, that teachers operating at this level of meaning are fully capable of the interdependence necessary to achieve the NBPTS standard for collaboration. The very self-sealing logic and psychic need to protect inner logic that characterizes this stage of development interferes with the capacity to function interdependently.

We describe the qualities needed to operate interdependently, yet maintain a clear sense of personal integrity, as holonomy. An assumption of unity and oneness as opposed to fragmentation, isolation, and separateness is basic to holonomy (Costa & Garmston, 1994; Koestler, 1972; Samples, 1981). Interdependence in reasoning, and the corresponding capacity to function holonomously requires a complex mental organization in which the self (i.e., that which one is identified with, fused with, inseparable from) has evolved to allow for one's experience to be something one has rather than something one is. Holonomous persons would reason at the Postinstitutional stage in Kegan's model. They would be autonomous *and* capable of questioning their own assumptions and organization of meaning.

The term *holonomy* comes from the Greek in which *holos* means whole and *on* means part. Koestler (in Olds, 1992) offers this description: "The dynamic system, or 'holon,' a two-sided Janus-like concept reflecting that each level system is a whole relative to its constituent parts and a part relative to the next larger level whole" (p. 76).

This notion of relational, or holistic, thinking is fundamental to the psychological orientation of systems theory. Costa and Garmston (1994) wrote:

Autonomous individuals set personal goals and are self-directing, self-monitoring, and self-modifying. Because they are constantly experimenting and experiencing, they fail frequently, but they fail forward, learning from the situation. But autonomous persons are not isolated or mechanical in their work; rather, they also participate significantly in their organization. They operate in the best interests of the whole while simultaneously attending to their own goals and needs. In other words they are at once independent and interdependent—they are holonomous" (p. 129).

In studies of peak performers (Garfield, 1986), in descriptions of effective leaders (Covey, 1990), in examinations of self-actualizing persons (Maslow, 1968), and profiles of highly evolved educators (Costa & Garmston, 1994), descriptions and manifestations of certain qualities of mind appear repeatedly. Costa and Garmston (1994) have identified five specific qualities, or states of mind: efficacy, flexibility, craftsmanship, consciousness, and interdependence. These five states are valued by personnel directors at organizations identified by Peter Senge to be "learning organizations" (Liebmann, 1993). Taken together, these five states of mind are held to be the deepest resources of holonomous persons—autonomous yet community-minded, cognitively complex, and high achieving.

These states of mind function as a set of perceptual filters that affect the construction of meaning. Certain filters, such as cognitive style and representational systems, represent differences in physiological preferences about the way one knows. Others, such as culturally influenced dispositions and educational beliefs, influence what one knows, or one's values. The states of mind, however, influence the capacity for knowing and the capacity for learning. In other words, the states of mind are filters contributing to epistemological capacity, not epistemological style.

States of mind are developmental in nature. Empirical data, developed by associates of the Institute for Intelligent Behavior working with cognitive coaching (Costa & Garmston, 1994; Edwards, 1993; Lipton, 1993) indicate that they are mediatable through environmental influences and supervisory intervention. While research studies relating the two are not yet available, it appears that sturdy parallels exist along the progression of Kegan's five "orders of consciousness" (1994) and developing capacities within Costa and Garmston's five states of mind (1994).

As individuals develop higher systems of reasoning, these states of mind mature, they become more complex, more accessible by the self, and they become habits of mind ultimately contributing to the ability to function at Kegan's Postinstitutional stage of making meaning. At any stage of development, however, states of mind are always transitory, and their presence and potency may be influenced by stressful moments, environments, and performance anxiety. At higher stages of development, the states of mind are more complex and are more quickly recoverable through mediation by self or colleague.

Efficacy To be efficacious requires cross-categorical meaning making, which is a cognitive capacity that emerges during the Interpersonal stage of adult development. Efficacy is a psychological condition experienced as a state. Feeling powerless is a psychological condition experienced as a state. To experience the condition, "I *want* to feel in charge," *and* the condition, "I *am* feeling powerless," involves holding these two categories together. "The self's experiencing derives not from either of these categories but from their relationship" (Kegan, 1994, p. 361). When an individual believes that one's own actions can influence events, the individual has formed a relationship between locus of control, self, and a new class called, "I can make a difference." This is the foundation for the state of mind of efficacy.

Efficacy is more than believing one can make a difference, it is also being willing and able to do so. Garfield (1986) found that the primary locus of control for peak performers was internal not external. One element that stands out clearly among peak performers is their virtually unassailable belief

in the likelihood of their own success, and their track records reinforce their beliefs.

Efficacy is a catalytic state of mind because it is a determining factor in the resolution of complex problems. If a person feels little efficacy, then blame, withdrawal, and rigidity are likely to follow. Persons with robust efficacy, however, are likely to expend more energy in their work, persevere longer, set more challenging goals, and continue in the face of barriers or failure. Efficacious people regard events as opportunities for learning, believe that personal action produces outcomes, control performance anxiety by accessing personal resources, and recognize what is not known by the self and seek to learn. They are self-modifying.

A number of advantages have been identified for helping teachers develop high degrees of efficacy. Low-efficacy teachers spend more time in small group instruction (e.g., 50% as compared with 28% for high efficacy teachers), are more likely to provide a student with the answer, ask another student or permit other students to call out the answer than high efficacy teachers. They also use more criticism and less persistence in failure situations (Gibson & Dembo, 1985). Higher efficacy teachers exhibit less stress, (Edwards & Newton, 1994; Greenwood, Olejnik, & Parkay, 1990) miss fewer days of school (Gibson & Dembo, 1985), and use more solution-oriented conflict message strategies (Grafton, 1987) than lower-efficacy teachers. High teacher efficacy has been correlated with reading achievement, whole class instruction (Tracz & Gibson, 1986) and higher locus of control (Greenwood, Olejnik, & Parkay, 1990).

One study that looked at the relationship between efficacy and curriculum implementation showed that two states of mind—teachers' efficacy and interdependence—significantly predicted the successful implementation of the new curriculum guides (Poole & Okeafor, 1989). Neither efficacy nor teacher interactions alone produced a significant difference in use of the curriculum, but together they brought about change. Rosenholtz (1989) found that teachers' efficacy influenced students' basic skills and mastery, and Fullan (1982) regards teacher efficacy as a vital factor for successful implementation of change.

In the Rand Corporation's seminal research on school effectiveness, Berman and McLaughlin (1977) found that teacher efficacy was the single most consistent variable related to school success. The efficacy identified by the Rand Corporation study is what Fuller, Wood, Rapoport, and Dornbusch (1982) label "organizational efficacy," or the link between what a group sees as valued goals and their expectation that those goals can be achieved by participating in the organization.

Flexibility As persons achieve Kegan's level of Postinstitutional logic, they value and more consistently view situations from multiple perspectives. Piaget called this the "overcoming of egocentrism." Flexibility is prerequisite to the state of mind of interdependence. It allows one to see others from a broader perspective in which self and others are both players in a larger drama in which they are simultaneously the central cast and only playing walk-on parts, not as representatives of a role or in regard to the degree of agreement with one's own views. We argue that flexibility, too, is developmental in nature. It requires, at least momentarily, a setting aside of self and relegating what one perceives to the status of "object" in order to view it other than from an egocentric perspective.

Flexibility includes being able to shift perceptual positions at will. There are many possible perceptual viewpoints: temporal (i.e., past, present, future), centricity (i.e., egocentric, allocentric, macrocentric), representational system (i.e., auditory, kinesthetic, visual). The state of mind of flexibility capacitates this shift. For example, peak performers studied by Garfield (1986) displayed an ability for flexible attention. These individuals could shift from microattention in which they focused on detail and precision, to macroattention, which enabled the discernment of patterns, themes, and holistic concepts.

The developmental ladder of flexibility parallels the ability to operate with cross-categorical constructions to form complex or integrated structures. This is the essential state of mind for working with social diversity. At this level, the individual can recognize the wholeness and distinctness of other people's ways of experiencing and making meaning.

Flexibility is a prerequisite to valuing diverse perspectives. Flexible teachers listen empathically with their ears, eyes, heart, and mind from the student's perspective, and from the parents, and from the curriculum's, and from their interpretation of the overarching aims of schooling. They are cognitively empathic with students, which enables them to predict misunderstandings and anticipate the most useful learning experiences.

Like efficacy, flexibility is also related to risk taking. Perkins (1983) describes creative persons as living on the edge, always pushing the frontier, generating new knowledge, experimenting with new ways, and constantly growing into new abilities. Persons experiencing the state of mind of flexibility can set aside their own opinions to understand others', and they can situationally adjust their own cognitive style, culturally influenced dispositions, and modality preferences.

Craftsmanship Craftsmanship is about striving for mastery, grace, and economy of energy to produce exceptional results. It is about learning as a continuing journey. Studies from the League of Professional Schools (Glickman, 1993) find that in schools where faculties are the most successful, teachers have the highest dissatisfaction with the results of their work. Success, for craftsmanlike people, produces self-imposed higher standards in an ongoing cycle of improvement. In a study using cognitive coaching with university professors, Garmston and Hyerle (1988) found that as craftsmanship increased, professors grew in their ability to be critically self-reflective and effective in producing self-analysis and evaluation.

Craftsmanship means knowing that one can continually perfect one's craft and be willing to pursue ongoing learning. To appreciate this state of mind, consider the mindset of expert performers (e.g., musicians, artists, teachers, craftspersons, and athletes). They take pride in their work and consistently strive to improve their current performance.

Craftsmanship (i.e., the drive for elaboration, clarity, refinement, and precision) is the energy source from which persons ceaselessly learn and deepen their knowledge, skills, and effectiveness. People engaged in the state of mind of craftsmanship persevere to resolve disequilibrium between present and desired states, and to create, hold, calibrate, and refine standards of excellence, as well as to monitor and manage refinements in their own thought and language.

Consciousness To be conscious is to be aware of one's thoughts, feelings, behaviors, intentions and their effects. At the Postinstitutional stage, individuals can mentally stand outside themselves and the immediate system in which they are operating, and beyond that to the systems in which the present system is just a part of a greater whole. We propose that consciousness develops along stages paralleling that of movement through Kegan's (1982, 1994) stages of meaning making Institutional stage persons, engaged in self-reflective consciousness, can be aware of their own intentions and outcomes, selectively attend to their own and others' styles, values, and behaviors, and generate, hold, and apply criteria for making decisions. As we develop toward the Postinstitutional stages of reasoning, our consciousness of self or "subject" has grown more flexible, and we can assign to "object" our own ways of making meaning, ideologies, and dominant egocentric locus of perspective. In addition, as more of one's experience is assigned to "object," more is directable by the individual, offering greater choices and, correspondingly, greater efficacy.

Consciousness is another of the states of mind with particular catalytic properties for the other states of mind, meaning making, and choices in behaviors. It is *the* state of mind prerequisite to self-control and self-direction. "Although every human brain is able to generate self-reflective consciousness, not everyone seems to use it equally." (Csikszentmihayli, 1993, p. 23). Consciousness means that we are aware that certain events are occurring, and we are able to direct their course. As adults, everything we feel, smell, hear, think, see, or remember, and what we can assign to "object" is potentially a candidate for entering consciousness, yet the nervous system has definite limits on how much information it can process at any given time.

Interdependence While one may work interdependently, live in community, vote, or take place in family or workplace dialogues, actual reasoning from within the state of mind of interdependence is quite different from just being a member of a group. In order for one to be interdependent, certain psychological prerequisites must exist regarding subject–object relations.

As with the other four states of mind, we contend that interdependence is developmental. The manifestation of a state of mind of interdependence for an Institutional Self will be qualitatively different from that of a Postinstitutional Self. At more complex levels of development, more of a person's experience has been assigned to "object," thus, the person operating at this level exercises some very advanced reasoning. For example, they can consider protracted conflict as meaning that each has become identified with the places of the conflict: They can also consider the conflicting relationship in which one finds oneself to be an expression of one's own incompleteness taken as completeness, or regard protracted conflict as a likely sign of one's own identification with false assumptions of wholeness, distinctness, completeness, or priority. Individuals at this stage can view conflict as an opportunity to transform themselves. Few people, notes Kegan (1994), ever reach this stage of complexity, and never before middle age.

As persons transition from Institutional to Postinstitutional thought, the state of mind of interdependence can include a sense of kinship that comes from a unity of being, a sense of sharing a common habitat (e.g., class, school, neighborhood), and a mutual bonding to common goals, shared values and shared conceptions of being. German sociologist Ferdinand Tonnies calls this way of being *Gemeinschaft.* Interdependent people's sense of self is enlarged from a conception of *me* to a sense of *us* (Sergiovanni, 1994). They understand that transcending the self and becoming part of the whole does not require the loss of individuality. It invites the loss of egocentricity instead.

As interdependence develops, it is characterized by altruism, collegiality, and giving self to group goals and needs. Interdependent persons both contribute to a common good, and they draw on the resources of others. They value dialogue and are able to hold their own beliefs and actions in abeyance in order to lend their energies to the achievement of group goals. People experiencing highly developed states of interdependence believe that conflict is an opportunity for growth, envision the expanding capacities of the group and its members, and value and draw upon the resources of others.

Implications for Supervisory Practice

Attempts to strengthen the individual's capacity to create an orderly inner life that conserves psychic energy, enables reasoned choice, and produces growth are common to all schools of psychology. In this respect all modern schools of psychology recognize that an individual's experience of reality is separate from the external world. Thus, psychological theorists and practitioners have sought to understand human behavior and, where appropriate, modify it through strategies devoted to improving the inner life, rather than the environment in which the individual functions.

The practical application of this understanding in the field of supervision is that an individual's decisions and their subsequent behaviors are based on the markings on the mental maps, not the actual territory. If adults construct meaning from their experiences, a central question for educators becomes: Can supervision practices be designed to facilitate these constructions and to focus them toward increasing cognitive complexities? We believe that an understanding of the processes of meaning construction and a knowledge of mediational techniques can foster supervision designed to promote such growth. Five concepts that are fundamental to an understanding of how supervision, working through the medium of verbal exchange, can mediate development: (1) the stored experiences of a person's history constitute a structure of reference experiences from which all meaning

emanates, (2) these reference experiences and their meanings can be represented in logically well-formed verbal expressions at a level of Deep Structure, (3) both Deep and Reference Structures find expression in what we say and how we behave (Surface Structures of language and behavioral manifestations), (4) the behavioral structures transmit affective and cognitive messages often outside the awareness of the sender, and (5) the language portion of the Surface Structure can be used to mediate changes in Reference Structures as a result of supervisory exchanges. These concepts are elaborated in the discussion that follows.

SUPERVISION AS MEDIATION

As supervision practices work to support the development of ever-increasing complexity in mental constructs, a knowledge of the role these mental maps play in professional judgments is important. The role that language plays in revealing and mediating refinements in the mental models from which teachers make their decisions and generate their behaviors is of equal value.

The theoretical image presented in Figure 8.4 derives from transformational grammar, psycholinguistics, and studies of

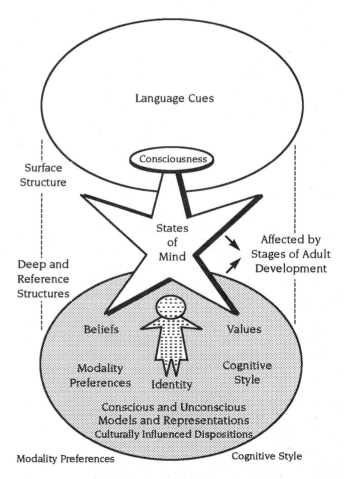

FIGURE 8.4. Moving from deep to surface structure

the verbal transactions of unusually effective therapists with their clients (Bandler & Grinder, 1976). Three theorems guide its application in supervisory work (Garmston & Wellman, 1995). First, that the sum of an educator's constructed meanings reside internally at conscious and unconscious levels and serve as the criteria for perceptions, decisions, and behavior. Second, that when these meanings are given form through language, they become accessible to both parties in a verbal transaction. Third, that through the medium of language, these meanings and the perceptions, decisions, and behaviors that result from them can be refined, enriched, and modified.

The Structure of Subjective Experience

Reference Structures Housed in the Reference Structure are personal models of reality derived from stored experiences transmitted through sensations (e.g., kinesthetic, auditory, visual, olfactory, and gustatory), filtered by cultural and neurological mechanisms. Human neurological filters allow perception of some data, but not others. Individuals perceive and store data according to personal predispositions for assimilating information from different modalities and with different cognitive styles. This storage and interpretive process begins before speech. Once begun, it interacts with meanings created from earlier stored experiences representing a point of view from which new experiences are assimilated and accommodated. This Reference Structure is illustrated in Figures 8.4–8.6.

UNIVERSAL PROCESSES OF HUMAN MODELING. The knowledge that all information making up this structure has been influenced by generalizations, deletions, and distortions is important to understanding the Reference Structure. The processes of generalization, deletion, and distortion are both neurological and psychological, and they contribute to efficiency in human learning, and to understanding the self as "a point of view that unifies the flow of experience into a coherent narrative" (Brunner, in Kofman & Senge, 1993). Bandler and Grinder (1976) refer to generalizations, deletions, and distortions as "the universal processes of human modeling, the rules of representations themselves." (p. 57) All information gathered throughout one's life is affected by these three factors, which in turn is now additionally influenced by the individual's developing point of view.

Generalization. Generalization is the process of experiencing by which components or pieces of a person's model of the world become detached. These experiences, then, come to represent the entire category of which the experience really is only an example. Each person makes many generalizations that are useful and appropriate in some situations, but not in others.

It is not uncommon for people to form generalizations from very little data. For example, a negative experience with an individual supervisor might lead to the generalization that all supervision is bad. Whether or not a generalization is useful must be evaluated with regard to a particular context. For example, "active engagement in learning is beneficial" might

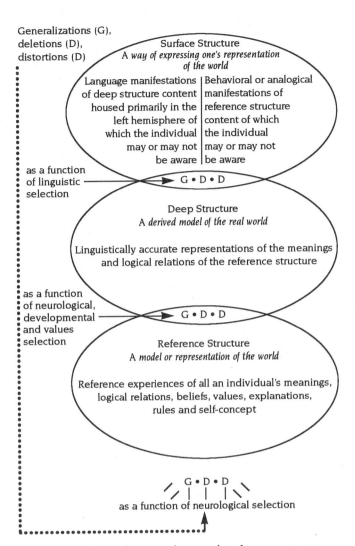

FIGURE 8.5. Reference, deep and surface structures

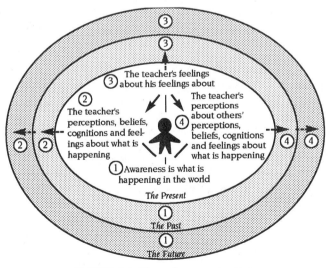

FIGURE 8.6. The reference structure and 12 reflective positions

be a useful generalization, whereas "girls have a low capacity for math" would be limiting.

Deletion. Deletion is a second coping method that can be potentially limiting. Deletion is the process by which one selectively pays attention to certain aspects of experience and excludes others. This process allows one not to be overwhelmed by external stimuli; however, the same process can be limiting if one deletes portions of experience necessary for a full and rich model of the world. For example, to delete awareness of a ticking clock might be useful during a test period, but teachers who delete evidence of student boredom from their experiences would be limiting their own experience as well as that of their students.

Distortion. Distortion is the process that allows one to make shifts in how sensory data is experienced. Without this process one could not plan or create (e.g., design a lesson or develop a curriculum); however, one can also limit oneself with distortion in many ways. For example, "all behavior is positively motivated" might be a useful distortion, whereas a teacher who distorts all student failures by blaming the students limits the performance of both the teacher and the students.

Figure 8.4 displays five other propositions regarding the Reference Structure: (1) its constructions are influenced by developmental growth through Kegan's stages of adult meaning making and the five states of mind, (2) consciousness is the access port for mediating Deep and Surface Structures, (3) the filters of modality preferences and cognitive style influence the Reference Structure in three ways (i.e., at the initial level of screening sensory input, in the styles of attending to internal experiences, and in the manner in which both external and internal data are processed and stored), (4) culturally influenced dispositions have a central role in interacting with all the filters and all the meanings being constructed by the individual, and (5) that portion of the Reference Structure available to verbal articulation will be expressible in the Deep Structure.

Figure 8.6 adds a final elaboration on our presentation of Reference Structure. Satir, and Bandler and Grinder (1976) initially observed that humans perceive events from multiple positions. For example, during a lesson teachers can reflect upon what is occurring in at least four ways: (1) with a direct sensory experience of what is occurring, (2) through their thoughts or feelings about what is happening, (3) through their students' perceptions about what is happening, or (4) through their own metacognition. Furthermore, these reflections on experience can occur before an event, during an event, or afterward. Any of these 12 presentations of reality can become useful arenas for supervisory dialogue.

The similarities of these human multiple realities to quantum systems has been noted by Zohar and Marshall (1994):

Then, too, both indeterminate quantum systems and our human imagination involve "superpositions." They contain several possible realities all juxtaposed, one on top of the other, that they explore simultaneously by throwing out "feelers" toward the future. Quantum systems do this to test out the most stable future energy state; our imagination does it to test out the best possible future life scenarios.

Deep Structure The Deep Structure is a well-formed linguistic expression of the meanings and logic of the Reference Structure. Were it articulated, it would be a full linguistic expression of all the representations and meanings a person has made of one's experience. It will carry the exact same deletions, distortions, and generalizations of experience that originally formed the Reference Structure.

Surface Structure The Surface Structure is the verbal expression of the Deep Structure. It is literally "what people say." It utilizes the grammatical rules needed to convey meaning. The Surface Structure reflects the generalizations, deletions, and distortions held in the Deep Structure. In addition, further generalizations, deletions, and distortions may be added. For example, "high school teachers teach content, not students," is a generalization that may be held in Deep Structure. As expressed in the Surface Structure, this same generalization will appear, but perhaps with additional linguistic deletions, or distortions: "High school teachers don't care about students."

These changes have derived from transformations that have occurred on the journey from Deep to Surface Structure and offer cues to understanding an individual's Reference Structure. Because the Surface Structure represents the Deep Structure, supervisory interactions that modify Surface Structure can also serve to mediate Deep and Reference Structures, to recover experiences, and to expand choice to assist persons in modifying their own Deep Structures.

This level of meaning structure is accessible through verbal interaction and physical cues. In addition to linguistic representations, analogic or nonverbal representations of the Deep and Reference Structure will also be present. Some of these behavioral manifestations include bilateral gesturing, which indicates access to both right and left brain hemispheres, eye shifts as manifestation of visual, auditory, or kinesthetic processing, and breathing shifts in which the brain has more or less access to oxygen with resulting changes in levels of stress. In some cases both digital and analogic representations meld into one form as occurs with voice pitch, rhythm, pace, volume, and intonation (see Figure 8.5).

Mediation of Experience is Achieved through Verbal Transactions

To mediate is to intervene between a learner and the learner's environment, illuminating potentially relevant data from which the learner constructs new meanings. As we shall describe later in more detail, viewing supervision as a mediational activity rather than as a parenting process is a key to emerging forms of supervision. Verbal language is the primary tool of supervision as mediation because the goal of mediation is to bring information from Reference and Deep Structures to a place of interaction and influence in the Surface Structure. For supervision to be mediative, a vision of the ideal must be held. We submit that this ideal would include development through Kegan's states of adult development and Costa and Garmston's five states of mind. While various scholars will hold differing views of what constitutes the ideal educator, the important point is that whatever the vision, mediation must take into account the many filters of perception that influence the construction of the Reference Structure.

Supervisory practices that mediate for developmental growth reach into the Reference Structures through linguistic and analogic transactions. Spoken language is the most accessible arena wherein one can interact with an individual's assumptions and experiences that inform points of view, pedagogical content knowledge, application of teaching repertoire, cause–effect reasoning, states of mind, decision-making strategies, knowledge of students, beliefs, and values. Supervisors can employ a set of linguistic tools to reconnect persons with Reference Structures and, in so doing, enrich models of reality and bring choices to the conscious level that were not perceived before. Thus, over time, mediative exchanges facilitate increased awareness and a reconstruction of meaning in increasing accord with more complex stages of adult development.

Linguistic Tools The three universal modeling processes (i.e., generalizations, deletions, and distortions) are expressed at the Surface Structure in language patterns. Thus, supervisors can use a set of linguistic tools that recover deletions, challenge generalizations and distortions, and invite greater precision and accuracy in language. These verbal transactions have the effect of reconnecting the speaker with experiences and mental models. They make possible corresponding adjustments to Deep and Reference Structures to expand a teacher's perception and to increase his or her capacity for meaning making and resulting behavioral choices. This use of language for mediative purposes falls into three categories: gathering information, identifying and challenging limits in the speaker's mental maps, and challenging semantic ill-formedness.

GATHERING INFORMATION. Mediational supervisory practices recognize when a deletion has occurred and aim to assist the person in recovering the deleted information to aid in restoring a fuller representation of the experience.

"I don't understand." "You don't understand what?"
"I want students to learn." "In what ways do you want them to learn?"
"Half my class is struggling" "What is happening for the other half?""
They did it poorly." "What do you mean by poorly?"

Mediative supervisory transactions will also challenge nominalizations. These are experiences that have been transformed from process words (i.e., verbs) to events or nouns. Reversing nominalizations helps one to see that what they had assigned to an event, and therefore could not control, can now be considered a process in which they have an active role.

"I don't get any *recognition*." "In what ways would you like to be *recognized*?""
They need more *help* than I can give." "What *kinds of help* do they need?"

IDENTIFYING AND CHALLENGING LIMITS IN THE SPEAKER'S MENTAL MAPS. Generalizations often appear in speech with words such as *all, every, always, never,* and *nobody.* Challenging

these universal quantifiers assists speakers in finding the exceptions to their generalizations and affords them more choice. Rule words, or modal operators of limitation or necessity, such as *I can't, I have to, I must, It's necessary that,* also convey the speaker's perception of limited choice.

CHALLENGING SEMANTIC ILL-FORMEDNESS. The third grouping of language distinctions is concerned with recognizing and challenging statements that are semantically ill-formed. To do so allows the speaker to examine portions of their mental map that may contain distortions. Three classes of semantic ill-formedness are cause and effect, mind reading, and lost performative.

Cause and effect involves the belief that some action on the part of one person can cause another person to act in a certain way or experience a certain emotion.

"They make me mad." "How do they make you mad?"
"Parents have prevented me from teaching about things that are important to me." "How have they made you do that?"

Mind reading refers to the belief on the part of the speaker that one person can know what another person is thinking or feeling without a direct communication from the second person.

"Everybody thinks I'm talking too much in meetings." "What data do you have that gives you that impression?"

In statements that convey a lost performative, the performance criteria for a judgment has been lost from the Surface Structure of the communication.

"This is the right way to do this?" "The right way for whom?"
"This was a poor seminar." "How would you define poor?"

The Construction of the Reference Structure

Perceptual Veils "Whatever we call reality, it is revealed to us only through an active construction in which we participate" (Prigogine, in Csikszentmihalyi, 1993, p. 61). This phenomenolgical perspective is a recurring theme in many cultures. Before speech appeared in humans, the processing of information was entirely introsomatic (i.e., it took place within the body through the sense organs of nose, mouth ears, eyes, and tactile senses. When speech appeared, however, information processing became extrasomatic as well. Information could now be passed from generation to generation through myth and legend, orally at first, and then later in writing.

Both religion and science have universally been the most important organs of extrasomatic knowledge created by humans (Csikszentmihalyi, 1993). Religions, which have existed for thousands of years on different continents under differing conditions, carrying different customs, and worshipping in different languages, have all transmitted one agreed upon truth: The senses lie. Veils of perception obscure reality. Twentieth-century findings in quantum physics have now added a scientific voice to this view (Wheatley, 1992).

Idiosyncratic experiences influence the development of the brain. In addition, they contribute to the mind's construction of meaning (Edelman, 1992). These experiences include the circumstances of gestation, birth, gender, country of origin and residence, race, childhood events, historical period of adolescence, socioeconomic conditions, family structure, significant personal memories (i.e., conscious and unconscious), and work history. Interpretations of all these experiences are further influenced by interactions with developmental factors, stages of adult meaning making , and states of mind, which are themselves the product of constructed meaning, and the perceptual filters that will be listed shortly. Meaning is thus constructed as a result of experiences that are physiological, emotional, and cognitive. These meanings constitute one's psychology (i.e., the organization of one's thinking, feeling, and acting over a wide range of human functioning). We will examine how certain of these filters interact to shape individual realities.

Knowledge of perceptual filters and their contribution to someone's ways of knowing are important to the field of supervision for three reasons. First, they offer cues about the influences on an individual's construction of reality. Second, because certain filters are related to stages of cognitive, moral, and ego stage development (Kegan, 1994), we can maintain a developmental view in working with individuals, and be alerted to more or less "normal" patterns and potentially appropriate mediational activities. The third reason is related to rapport. Whether in dyadic or group settings, rapport is prerequisite to the occurrence of complex mental activity (Lankton & Lankton, 1983; O'Connor & Seymour, 1990; Schmuck & Runkel, 1985). Because rapport is manifested by matching the verbal and nonverbal communication style of others, knowledge of and attention to the perceptual filters of others enhances communication, thinking, and development.

We earlier described two filters of capacity: *stages in adult systems of meaning making* (Kegan, 1982, 1994) and *five states of mind*, (Costa & Garmston, 1994). We will now describe two filters of style: *cognitive style* and *modality preferences*. These perceptual filters represent differences in preferences about the way one knows, not about one's competencies or capacities in knowing. They are differences in epistemological style, they are not epistemological. They remain relatively unchanged over a person's lifetime. We will then examine two filters modifiable by experience and affected by developmental factors: *culturally influenced dispositions* and *educational beliefs*. Finally, we will describe a perceptual filter, (i.e., *metaphors of identity)* that is a manifestation of the confluence and influence of all the preceding perceptual filters and, yet, is modifiable itself.

COGNITIVE STYLE. Cognitive style describes the brain's preference for organizing information, not its capacity for learning. As delineated in numerous models and theories (for example, see Myers-Briggs Type Indicator, 1957. preference in cognitive style tends to range along a continuum from highly organized, detail-oriented, and linear-sequential, to divergent, spatially oriented, and global. Cognitive style is evidenced by behaviors, characteristics, and mannerisms that indicate underlying psychological frames of reference. It can be determined through a number of valid, reliable instruments, including the Myers-Briggs Type Indicator and Herman Witkin's Field Dependence–Independence Theory

(Witkin, et al, 1973) of cognitive style indicates that most adults lean toward one of two poles: (1) field independent, which is evidenced by exacting attention to detail where perception is not influenced by the background, or (2) field independent, in which the organization of information is strongly influenced by the background, or context. While an individual's preference for cognitive style appears to be relatively fixed over one's lifetime, each person can become more "bicognitive" (i.e., situationally adept at more than one style).

Knowledge of cognitive style is important in supervision because it is a primary filter for what is perceived: parts or wholes, relationships or things. Cognitive style preferences offer information regarding ways in which teachers' perceptions, intellectual processing, and instructional behaviors differ (Guild & Garger, 1985). Over time, Witkin and his associates became convinced that field dependence–independence influences both perceptual and intellectual functioning as well as personality traits such as social behavior, career choice, body concept, and defense (Witkin, Goodenough, & Cox, 1975).

The mediational supervisor will adjust interactions with teachers depending on the teacher's prevailing style. In one account of this style flexibility, teachers reported that the supervisor "shone the flashlight of attention on the part of their brains that they typically did not use" (Garmston with Linder & Whitaker, 1993).

REPRESENTATIONAL SYSTEMS. Mediative supervisors are sensitive to the unique ways each person processes information. Human thought occurs in pictures, sounds, feelings, tastes, and smells. These same neurological pathways are used to represent experience internally. In western culture, the primary systems in which persons think are the visual, auditory, and kinesthetic. Most individuals will favor one or two, even though this modality dominance may not be part of their conscious awareness.

To understand how experiences are organized within one's Reference Structure, two types of cues are useful: language and eye movement. Surface Structure language offers a view of thinking processes. As supervisors listen to teachers talk, they may discover that the majority of words are from one of the sensory-based representational systems. This is an indicator of how the person is representing this experience at this time in their Reference Structure. It is also a cue that the most effective interactions will be those that use language that matches the dominant representational system. Costa and Garmston (1994) wrote:

"Regrettably, the research and literature on language congruence has been rife with misunderstandings and methodological errors. But several solid studies (see for example, Einspruch and Forman, 1985) and our own experience, have affirmed the relationship between language and representational systems" (p. 63).

A second cue is eye movement. With the advent of research in brain specialization, scientists have investigated the relationship between particular types of eye-movement patterns and variations in brain functioning. Several researchers agree that eye movements indicate differences in cognitive involvement and hemispheric dominance. Costa and Garmston (1994) pointed out that eye-movement patterns provide a kind of external graph of internal sensory activity. For example, in most eye movements to the upper left of the person's face indicates that past visual memories are being accessed, while eye movements in a lower-left direction indicate accessing of an internal auditory process.

While cognitive style and modality preferences prescribe the form in which meanings are processed in the Reference Structure, the next two filters (i.e., culturally influenced dispositions and belief systems) are about the content of the Reference Structure. While all perceptual filters convey deletions, generalizations, and distortions, these next two especially contribute to distortions in the making of meaning and the exercise of day-to-day logic.

CULTURALLY INFLUENCED DISPOSITIONS. America is a nation of immigrants. Where once only indigenous people lived, successive waves of people arrived, bringing with them culturally influenced habits of making meaning, being, and communicating. People come from different countries and continents and belong to different races and genders, which also represent a culture, causing the metaphor for the American people to move from the "melting pot" to the "salad bowl" to the "hyphenated-American." As the field of supervision matures in this country, it is gradually coming to understand that different cultures have their own ways of being, and it is critical to develop an understanding and respect for these differences.

By culture, we are referring to the "cumulative deposit of knowledge, experience, meanings, beliefs, values, attitudes, religions, concepts of self, the universe, and self-universe relationships, hierarchies of status, role expectations, spatial relations and time concepts acquired by a large group of people in the course of generations" (Samovar & Porter, 1972, p. 3). We include the special ways one's gender, race and national heritage contribute to making meaning and communicating in this definition. Gilligan (1982), who conducted extensive research in female moral development, finds that a woman's "perception of self is so much more tenaciously embedded in relationships with others [than a man's] and whose moral dilemmas hold them in a mode of judgment that is insistently contextual." (p. 102) To be both female and a person of color in America, wrote Featherstone (1994), is to "live [the] 'theater of the absurd,' understand at least two languages, speak in a variety of voices and view the world always from at least two perspectives" (p. 5).

Culture influences the content of the Reference Structure. Communicating across cultures complicates understanding one another. As Tannen (1990) observed, "[W]hen speakers from different parts of the country, or of different ethnic or class backgrounds [or gender] talk to each other, it is likely that their words will not be understood exactly as they were meant" (p. 13). Tannen describes male–female conversations as a form of cross-cultural communication: "While men speak and hear a language of status and independence, women are more likely to speak and hear a language of connection and intimacy . . . they speak different 'genderlects.'" (Tannen, 1990, p. 42) Furthermore, the American workplace culture tends to reward a decontexualized, objective style, and to

suppress a more personalized narrative style of communicating. In the workplace and in classrooms, males speak more frequently and for longer periods of time. In contrast, women tend to "dart in and out around the edges of the conversation, interjecting brief remarks that have the effect of 'asides' between masculine perorations" (Kegan, 1994, p. 213). In such contexts as psychotherapy, however, where the personalized narrative style has been institutionalized, women speak most frequently and the longest, and it is the men who make brief comments on the side.

Race also exerts influence, permeating all the other perceptual filters. Featherstone (1994, p. 2) said:

Skin is the great significator. It is the first thing people see and is used to define who one is and to what one can "rightfully" aspire. The privileges, or lack thereof, attached to different shades of skin, texture of hair, shape of eye or gender are encoded into the social fabric. More than we care to admit, our socialization often makes us complicit in living out myths devised by others. Our Authentic Selves are lost; we behave as though our realities are only skin deep.

Caucasians probably cannot comprehend the intensity of and permanent effect on the perceptual filters that the deeply scarring experiences of racism and colorism exert, nor how common these experiences seem to be. One African American woman writes, "I maintained two stances in the world. The outward one conquered obstacles, projected an 'in charge' IMAGE. The inward one, a battered dark-skinned child who believed she could do nothing to be acceptable, whose identity was her victimization." (Featherstone, 1994, p. 15.)

She is describing what we term her *personal identity*. It is the last perceptual filter we will treat. As we will describe, it is at once a manifestation of all the other filters, the culminating lens through which we make meaning, and the lens, if and when altered, creates the most behavioral changes (Dilts, 1990, 1994).

It is clearly beyond the scope of this chapter to detail differences in how the construction of meaning, developmental growth, and subsequent communications are influenced by gender, race, workplace cultures, and the scores of varying subgroups, cultures, and regional orientations within the United States. Modern supervision, however, demands knowledge and sensitivity to these cultural influences, particularly in New York, Texas, Florida, California, and other areas within the United States that experience high rates of immigration, where supervision must concern itself with further complexities regarding the influence of national culture on relations with relatively recent immigrants.

Each national environment shapes a kind of national mental programming. These common orientations have their roots in a shared set of beliefs about the country's history, and are reinforced because the nation, as a unit, shares many culture-shaping institutions (i.e., a government, an army, laws, an education system and a media network. Hofstede (1991) reports findings from a study of workers in multinational companies employing workers from 41 different nations. Four dimensions of national culture were examined for their influence on supervisory relations: (1) degrees of certainty, or the degree to which a society feels threatened by uncertain and ambiguous situations; (2) power distance, or the extent to which a society accepts that power in organizations is distributed unequally; (3) relationship or task orientation, or the extent to which the dominant values in a society are either "masculine" (i.e., task, assertiveness, money) or "feminine" (i.e., quality of life, caring for others and people) and (4) individual or group style preferences.

Hofstede's study revealed a wide variety of differences across these dimensions based on nationality. His work dramatically demonstrates the influence of clear national profiles and suggests that they exert a strong influence on individual personality.

EDUCATIONAL THEORIES AND BELIEF SYSTEMS. Whether they verbalize them or not, educators hold deep beliefs about their work, their students, the role of schools in society, the curriculum, and teaching and learning. These beliefs are powerful predictors of behaviors, and they drive the perceptions, decisions, and actions of all players on the education scene. Beliefs are formed early and tend to self-perpetuate. Changing beliefs during adulthood is a relatively rare phenomenon, and beliefs about teaching are well-established by the time a student gets to college (Pajares, 1992).

In their seminal work on educational beliefs, Eisner and Vallance describe five belief orientations that guide teachers' instructional decision-making: (1) Cognitive Processor, (2) Self-Actualizer, (3) Technologist, (4) Academic Rationalist, and (5) Social Reconstructivist. The following is taken from Costa and Garmston's (1994) treatment of their work.

Cognitive processors. Cognitive processors are drawn to psychologist and educational theorists, including Bloom, Bruner, Taba, Sternberg, Piaget, Feuerstein, Montessori, Suchman, and DeBono. They have an orientation to cognitive psychology, and they tend to believe that the central role of schools is to develop rational thought processes, problem solving, and decision-making. Persons with this orientation would most likely select instructional strategies that involve problem solving and inquiry methods, use terms like *intellectual development, cognitive processes, metacognition,* and *thinking skills,* organize teaching around the resolution of problems, employ the Socratic Method, and present discrepant events for students to explore and analyze.

Self-actualizers. Self-actualizers share an orientation with humanistic/existential psychology, and believe teaching should be child-centered. They view the teacher as a facilitator of learning, and believe the purpose of teaching is to bring out the unique qualities, potentials, and capacities in each child, a gardener of children's potential. These teachers value multisensory instruction, student choice, self-directed learning, and individualized instruction.

These teachers often value student autonomy and look for increases in autonomy as a central measure of teaching effectiveness. They are drawn to such psychologists and educational theorists as Maslow, Ashton Warner, Combs, Rogers, Simon, and Leonard.

Technologist. A third educational belief system is that of the technologist. These teachers may be influenced by the behavioral psychology of Skinner, Pavlov, and Thorndike, and may be attracted to such education authors as Mager,

Popham, and Hunter. They place strong emphasis on accountability and measurable learning. Their metaphor for education may be similar to that of a computer with an input, throughput, output system. These teachers are often skilled at task analysis and they are interested in learning systems with opportunities to diagnose entry levels and to prescribe according to what is known and what is yet to be learned.

Academic rationalist. A fourth belief system is that of the academic rationalist. Some of the philosophic company of this group includes Ravitch, Hirsch, Bestor, Bennett, and Finn. These teachers are drawn to teacher-centered instruction, believing that knowledgeable adults have the wisdom and the experience to know what is best for students. Their metaphor for education is the transmission of the major concepts, values, and truths of society, and they may consider students as clay to be molded or vessels to be filled. They value and are highly oriented toward increasing the amount and rigor of student learning. These teachers are often drawn to essential truths, classics, the great books, and traditional values. They appreciate basic texts and the teaching strategies of lecture, memorization, demonstration, and drill. They evaluate students through summative examinations, achievement testing, and content mastery.

Social reconstructivist. The fifth category of educational beliefs draws from the orientation of the system theorists. These educators are often concerned with the problems of society, the shrinking world, the future of the planet, and major crises such as destruction of the food chain, the hole in the ozone, protection of wildlife, and the threat of overpopulation. They view the learner as a social being (i.e., a member of a group, a responsible citizen, one who identifies with and is proactive regarding the environmental ills and social injustices of the day).

These teachers believe that this is a world where we must care for our neighbors and take action at the grassroots level. Their metaphor of education is as an instrument of change, and they believe that schools are the primary institution in our society charged with the responsibility of bringing about a better future and a better world. They are drawn to authors like Ferguson, Harmon, Toffler, Samples, Naisbitt, Houston, and Freire.

Metaphors of Identity

An individual's metaphors of identity dominate the Reference Structure. The perceptual filters described earlier and one's personal history interact to create a sense of personal identity: a perspective from which all ongoing meaning is constructed and whose view is dominant in the Reference Structure. To support a person in expanding his or her sense of personal identity may be one of the most potent interventions of supervision. The metaphors educators use to describe their work may disclose much about their implicit beliefs about learning and teaching, their conceptions of the content disciplines, and their perceptions of their professional role. For example, teachers might see themselves as "conduits," which may represent teaching as a mechanical process of transferring knowledge from one mind to another. Other teachers may view their role as "travel agents" who tour students through a survey of the content exploring various domains. Still others may describe their functions as, in a popularized cliché, "A guide on the side, rather than a sage on the stage." We offer a story to illustrate the particular psychological influence metaphors of identity have on one's behavior.

In 1994, a New York garment executive was kidnapped and held in a deep pit in Central Park while the kidnappers negotiated for ransom. This 60-year-old man, when lowered into the pit, said to himself, "I am a marine," and in so evoking the memories of what it meant to be a tough, survive-at-all-costs marine nearly 40 years earlier, weathered this ordeal in remarkably good shape. Our everyday metaphoric expressions of identity (e.g., I am a marine, teacher, administrator, supervisor, French teacher, or foreign language teacher) form unconscious patterns that create and organize meaning in our lives. These metaphors become filters out of which we make sense of events (e.g., of course, he's a union member; or, what did you expect, she's a board member), symbolize our identity, and shape our beliefs and actions. Dilts (1990, 1994) theorizes that to intervene with a person's sense of identity is the most far-reaching influence one can bring to another's perceptions, thoughts, and behaviors short of intervening with one's spiritual life. Dilts' hierarchy of interventions begins at the lowest level of impact with changes in the environment, and continues in nested fashion focusing on behaviors, skills, capabilities, values/beliefs, identity and spirit. Garmston (1990) describes how identity shifts occurred for teachers engaged in peer-coaching programs and how the resulting shifts dramatically changed their sense of what it meant to be a professional, as well as their feelings of responsibility and services to the school.

Metaphors carry invisible filters in the form of unconscious goals, values, beliefs, and presuppositions (Faulkner, 1991). For example, in the metaphor "teacher as gardener," the unconscious goals are probably growth and bearing fruit, the values may embrace nurturance and individual progress, the beliefs may stipulate that gardening is loving work, that the soil must be tilled, watered, and fertilized, and the presuppositions probably include self-actualization (i.e., seeds have within them the unique patterns of their own maturity). With every metaphor, some experiences will become more important and embellished, while others will be diminished or deleted. A gardener probably pulls and discards weeds, yet the teacher who sees herself as a gardener of learning probably deletes that notion from her self-concept. The supervisor who recognizes the meaning, thereby giving power of identity metaphors, understands a great deal of the psychology of the individual teachers and will communicate differently with the teachers who see themselves as artists, or performers, or generals, or parents, or mechanics, and so on.

To summarize, we are building a case for supervision as a mediating factor in adult development. In Figure 8.4 we described a Reference Structure for housing all of an individual's meanings, logical relations, beliefs, values, rules, and identity. This Reference Structure continually reconstructs itself based on a variety of perceptual filters. Two of these—states of mind and stages of adult development—carry epis-

temological capacity and, we argue, are developmental. Two are about preferences in the way one knows: cognitive style and modality systems. Two are mediatable through experience, cultural dispositions, and belief systems. Finally, metaphors of identity are both a summarization of all the teacher's systems of meaning and an organizer for future experiences. Supervisory transactions that consciously interact with Deep Structure meanings through the Surface Structure language will be most efficient in mediating instructional decision-making and in accelerating the development of adult capacities. Language skills, however, are not enough alone for mediational transactions. Trust and rapport are prerequisite to a willing partnership in exploring meanings and teaching decisions. Supervision, then, becomes a mediational activity that requires pedagogical knowledge, language skills, and human relations sensitivity.

NEW GOALS: SUPERVISION AS MEDIATION OF PROFESSIONAL AND ORGANIZATIONAL DEVELOPMENT

The emerging focus on human development places teachers and their development at the center of educational change (Fullan & Hargreaves, 1991). Supervision becomes the mediation of adult learning and development. The range of necessary supervisory skills extends beyond observing instructional behaviors and relating those behaviors to students' learning and the broad research base on effective practice. Supervision from a constructivist–developmental perspective also includes mediative strategies designed to facilitate the construction and expansion of the teacher's reflective capacities, understanding, and interpretive process. From this orientation the most effective supervisors will have a wide repertoire of interactive strategies and will be able to vary their approach in a variety of one-to-one interactions based on individual developmental differences (Glickman, 1985). As described by Costa and Garmston (1994), the supervisor as a mediator of teacher growth is one

who diagnoses and envisions desired states for others; constructs and uses clear and precise language in the facilitation of other's cognitive development; devises an overall strategy through which individuals will move themselves toward desired states; maintains faith in the potential for continued movement toward more holonomous states of mind and behavior; and possesses a belief in his or her own capacity to serve as an empowering catalyst of others' growth (p. 132).

When a supervisor can interact with teachers in ways that the teachers themselves experience as support, supervision will be more effective and growth more likely (Kegan & Lahey, 1984). This ability incorporates, and largely depends upon, the supervisor's knowledge of adult developmental needs, stages, and intervention strategies that are appropriate to each stage, and the supervisor's fluency with these knowledge bases in guiding interactions with teachers.

Up to this point, we have examined four supervision

models practiced as sets of one-to-one interactions. We have explored their roots in four schools of psychology: behaviorist, psychodynamic, humanist/existentialist, and cognitive. A fifth school of psychology, pioneered in family systems therapy, has now emerged in a constructivist–developmental approach to supervision. This more recent orientation to supervision blends systems theory with humanist/existential and cognitive approaches and offers fresh ways of viewing the supervisor and teacher relationship. Whereas in all previously described models the supervisor applied skillful interventions within the relationship to promote growth in others, the supervisor in a systems theory perspective is an integral part of the relationship. The supervisor is reciprocally affected within the relationship, and both are influenced by the larger system, or work culture in which they are a part. In the next two sections we will explore, first, supervision as a developmental mediation for individuals, and, second, supervision as a systems mediation, modifying the work culture itself.

Blending a Constructivist–Developmental and Systems Approach

Throughout the history of psychological thought, the relationships and relative importance between part and whole have been a focus for debate. Gestalt theorists have treated the mind as an organizer of the whole, while the behaviorists emphasized part to whole and stimulus–response patterns as a foundation for learning. Psychoanalytical theorists and personality theorists have treated the psyche as if it was composed of opposing parts in continual conflict, while the existential/humanistic approach has assumed a kind and wise unconscious naturally striving for self-actualization. Systems theory adds a new dimension by investigating the unique properties that arise when parts interact to form a new functional whole. From a systems viewpoint, causation is no longer attributable to one part of the system, such as the human being or the environment. Causation is said to arise from circularity. In other words,

systems are constantly modified by recursive circular feedback from multiple sources from within and from outside the system. When one describes the causal components of systemic change, it is not acceptable to espouse a linear view of causality that identifies only one factor as determining the subsequent behavior of a system. (Guttman, 1992, p. 42).

Systems theory as a therapeutic model introduced an important shift in psychological thought: Family therapists no longer view themselves as external agents who manipulate the family system from a position safely outside it (Hoffman, 1981). Therapists as part of the family system requires that they see themselves as part of what is being observed. In this way, the distinction between observer and observed becomes much less clear. Therapists learn to join the system and to intervene as a part of the dynamic system, not as a manipulator of it.

Attributes of Mediational Interactions

When we apply this psychological orientation to supervision, it places the supervisor as a part of the dynamic system, creating a view of interactions that mediates the making of meaning for both learners, supervisor and teacher. This view of supervision requires that the supervisor is no longer separate from the learning, but that it is an integral part of the relationship or system. A mediator is one who enters a relationship between a person and their experience by directing conscious awareness to that data in the experience that has the potential of being growth producing. Both persons are affected in this process. Feuerenstein (1988) reported that three attributes are most important in distinguishing a mediated learning experience from other forms of interaction: (1) intentionality and reciprocity, (2) transcendence, and (3) mediation of meaning.

Intentionality and Reciprocity Feuerstein describes intentionality and reciprocity as:

A mediated interaction . . . is marked by an intention animating the mediator . . . as he interposes himself between the [individual] and the sources of the stimuli. The intention of the mediator affects the three partners involved in the interaction; the stimuli to be perceived, the [individual] and the mediator. All of them are changed by the intention to mediate. Intentionality transforms the triangular relationship . . . creating within the [individual] the prerequisites for cognitive modifiability (p. 62).

As a result, the intention of the mediator is to provide a mediational learning experience, change is brought to the stimuli. The stimuli is no longer the teacher's simple need to identify a learning objective for a group of students. With the mediator's questions, the stimuli has become something more, as well as a description of how the teacher will know when the learning is achieved. The teacher is also changed by the mediational interaction, becoming more alert, more conscious, and more deliberate in consideration of his or her learning objectives and evidence procedures. Change is also occurring simultaneously, and with reciprocity, for the mediator in this experience. Because the mediator's role requires responses from the teacher in order to know if the mediation is successful, the mediator attends to the teacher's verbal and nonverbal behaviors, using these as signals in a feedback spiral in which the mediator monitors and makes adjustments in his or her own behaviors. Furthermore, the mediator ceases to be a separate agent, becoming instead a part of a system with the teacher that carries and continues to influence both of them. Finally, over time, the mediator is also changed because he or she has constructed new meaning from these interchanges (e.g., meaning about the other person, learnings about the relationship, about instruction, and about him- or herself).

Transcendence Transcendence in a mediative experience is related to both what is to be mediated and how. Content is selected for its potential to transcend the needs of the moment. Talking with a teacher about the design of lessons in general is more powerful than talking about a particular lesson. We can, however, talk about one lesson in ways that are generalizeable to lesson design. Furthermore, in a mediative exchange, there are ways of engaging in dialogue about this lesson in which the primary goal is one that transcends this conversation toward developing the capacity to think about lesson design with increased consciousness, craftsmanship, and flexibility. The ultimate goal of transcendence is the promotion of adaptability and self-mediation.

Mediation of Meaning Finally, to be a mediative learning experience, meanings and values are the consistent subtext of the interchange. Mediational transactions express a presupposing of human modifiability, a valuing of reciprocity in relationship, of individuation, of constructivist learning, of interdependence and self-confidence, competence, flexibility, consciousness, and a continuous reaching for high standards in the execution of learning experiences for students.

NINE PRINCIPLES OF MEDIATING PROFESSIONAL DEVELOPMENT. The following nine principles presuppose a reciprocal, constructivist–developmental approach to the one-on-one supervisory exchange. They are an extension of Feuerstein's (1988) work in mediated learning, Lankton and Lankton's (1983) principles of therapeutic intervention, and some of the Developmental/Reflective Models of Supervision, including Costa and Garmston's (1994) Cognitive Coaching.

We propose them as criteria for selecting or designing supervisory practices intended to mediate adult development. Like the constructionist–developmental approach, they draw from multiple psychological foundations: subject–object theory, cognitive, humanistic/existentialist, psychodynamics, systems theory, and the cognitive–behavioral orientations of neurolinguistics.

People act on their internal maps of reality and not on sensory experience. Each person perceives the world from his or her own unique Reference Structure, seeing it through filters of immediate (and always limited) sensory perception, personal history, belief systems, sociocultural experiences, pedagogical biases, representational systems, and cognitive styles. Each will base decisions on these constructed models of reality (Bandler & Grinder, 1976). This cognitive principle encourages participants to learn how the world appears to each other by nonjudgmentally gathering data to understand the other person's Reference Structures and its construction.

The more dimensional, detailed, and accessible the reference structure, the more effective a person's decisions. This psycholinguistic and cognitive principle reminds the mediator that both planned and spontaneous interactions are most potent when they have a goal of transcendence (Feuerstein, 1988). Capacity building for teacher learning, perception, and decision-making through the continuous articulation of increasingly complex maps about all the systems in which the teacher is both a part and a whole is a continuing aim of mediative supervision. Whatever the short-term supervision goal, the overarching aim is the continuous development and integration of new knowledge. This is true of declarative, procedural, and conditional knowledge, pedagogical knowledge, content-specific pedagogical knowledge, knowledge of one's discipline, knowledge of self, knowledge of students, and the decision-making processes in which these are applied.

Meet the other person in their own reference structure. The meanings each person has constructed is the only starting place for continued learning. According to this phenomenologist perspective drawn from humanistic/existential psychology, mediation must occur within the other person's models of teaching learning and self. Rapport enables one to connect with another person psychologically. In turn, rapport makes more potent the skillful use of linguistic tools to understand the Reference and Deep Structure from which another person operates. This is merely a starting point for a mediative interaction, however, not a destination. It is not necessary, nor is it always desirable, for the mediator to stay in the other person's model.

People make the best choice for themselves at any given moment. This humanistic/existential principle presupposes a positive unconscious and positive intentions. It does not suggest that people make the best choice possible, only the best choice they perceive to be available to them at the moment. Individuals will make their best choice according to their model of the world. Certain stages of meaning making will predispose one to have certain choices more apparent than others. Because cognitive psychology reveals that high levels of stress will limit access to thinking, personal models, internal resources, and choice, this principle suggests that supervision function free from judgments and evaluations that would limit the system's ability to work constructively with teachers. Mediators who act on this principle discover that teacher resistance disappears. Resistance persists only in a system of resistance.

Provide choice; never take choice away. Individuals as choosers is a cornerstore of existentialist psychology. When an attempt is made to limit people's choices, they are often drawn stubbornly to the choice that has been removed. Effective mediators exercise and offer options. They also operate on the notion that by expanding a teacher's consciousness (i.e., awareness of behaviors, thoughts, feelings, and theories), they expand choice.

Respect all messages. Empathy, respect, and responses calibrated to the communications of the other person are critical resources that the mediator brings to learning interactions. In the tradition of humanist psychology and psychodynamics, skilled mediators are aware that communication is occurring at many different levels at once. They attend to and respect both verbal and nonverbal messages. This capacity is enhanced by being attuned to subtle elements of communication-voice tone, gestures, breathing, facial expressions, eye shifts, and metaphors of identity.

The resources each person needs lie within his or her own neurology and personal history. The roots of this principle emerge from many psychological schools of thought: subject–object theory, psychodynamics, behaviorist, cognitive, and humanistic/existential. Personal resources draw from the reservoir of the Reference Structure and include the sum total of learnings from accumulated experiences, problem-solving skills, and access to the five states of mind. This access increases one's capacity to be (1) conscious (i.e., aware of and therefore able to direct thoughts, feelings, intentions, and behaviors), (2) flexible (i.e., able to examine events from varied temporal positions and multiple perspectives), (3) craftsmanlike (i.e., setting high personal standards and tirelessly working to learn and refine one's work), (4) efficacious (i.e., knowing one can persevere past barriers, seeing problems as learning opportunities), and (5) interdependent (i.e., drawing on and contributing to others in order to produce greater work). Supervision can facilitate access to these inner resources in the moment and mediate the developmental growth of these resources over time.

The greater the adaptability, the more effective a person is at achieving outcomes. Bateson (1972) called this the law of requisite variety. This systems theory and neurolinguistic orientation observes that the more repertoire teachers have, the greater flexibility and choice they have in terms of instructional strategies and classroom management, and the more effective they are in service of a range of different types of learning needs. The same is true of mediators or any person in a growth-producing relationship. When mediations fail, it is frequently due to the mediator's inability to exercise the needed flexibility (Erickson, in Zeig, 1980; Feuerstein, 1988).

Outcomes of mediative supervision are achieved at the psychological level. Professional decisions and behaviors are the manifestation of meaning an individual makes from the intersection of complex psychological dynamics, both intrapersonal and interpersonal. This neurolinguistic principle states that several levels of communication about these processes operate simultaneously (Lankton, 1980). One of these is the social level message, which is usually verbal. Another is the psychological level that is usually reflected in the voice tone, eye accessing cues, breathing, gesture, and inflection or emphasis. When these two levels of communication are incongruent, the psychological message will determine the outcome of the communication. This principle reminds mediators to be conscious of and clearly intentional about their own levels of communication, as well as to be aware of the communications of the other person. Garman (1982) observes,

Early in supervisory practice, the supervisor develops a keen ear for precise vocabulary and, in a sense, becomes bilingual. He/she acquires one language which speaks about the inner world of personal feelings and attitudes and another for describing, interpreting and judging the outer world of professional acts and consequences. (pp. 45–46).

These nine principles offer a psychological foundation for one-on-one supervisory practice that is reciprocal, mediative, and developmental. At the level of one-to-one interaction this orientation provides the greatest movement along a continuum of complexity in meaning making. While we place great importance on mediative strategies to support teacher development, we believe that the traditional view of one-to-one

interaction is highly limited. We are seeing evidence in the literature and in our work with schools that a move from the individual construction of knowledge to the social construction of knowledge constitutes new goals for leadership. In this era of developing learning organizations (Senge, 1990), empowered employees (Block, 1987), schools as communities (Sergiovanni, 1994; Barth, 1990), and renaissance schools (Costa & Garmston, 1994) we predict that supervision will evolve beyond the concept of classroom as the primary clinical setting for teacher development and embrace the whole school as an arena for adult learning. Because the culture of the workplace is the most important determinant in shaping the behaviors of its members (Frymier, 1987; Garmston & Wellman, 1994; Rosenholtz, 1991) the school environment and the conditions of work become a focus for and a target of development (Grimmett, Rostad, & Ford, 1992). As we conclude this chapter, we extend the theme of reciprocal influence and a systems theory approach to school supervision and explore the development of the organization as another major function of supervision.

New Roles for Supervisors: The Supervisor as Social Ecologist

The psychological foundation for supervisory practice intended to cultivate a growth-oriented work culture will be informed by a rich array of psychological schools of thought. For example, the behaviorists recognize that the environment is a critical factor that influences individual learning and behavior. Humanistic/existential principles would frame the context of relationships and guide the moment-to-moment transactions. Intellectual rigor and reflective practice toward continuous improvement would derive from the cognitive–developmental theorists. Finally, any effort at influencing the organization must place a strong emphasis on the relationships throughout the organization. Systems theory, which is predicated on the notion that any system is comprised of levels of relationship, or systems within systems, each of which influences and is influenced by the other, becomes a primary psychological heuristic for supervision as organizational development.

Systems theory offers a psychological orientation for organizational growth. Supervision as systems intervention contrasts with models in which professional growth along a developmental continuum is facilitated through one-to-one interactions between supervisor and teacher. The application of systems theory to organizational development shifts the arena for mediative interactions from dyadic exchanges to whole school involvement.

Viewing schools as dynamical systems and supervision from a systems theory orientation opens new ways of operating for individuals in supervisory positions. The supervisor becomes a social ecologist who focuses the resources of the organization in order to increase the system's capacity for adaptation and ongoing learning. The evolution from promoting individual pursuit of knowledge and achievement of goals toward emergent, creative learning communities in which the organization itself gets smarter requires no less than a transformation of a personal attitude.

It requires that each one of us . . . let go of our fixed perceptions, our habits . . . our single-minded pursuit of personal gain and . . . devotion to our own corner. It requires, instead, that we stand poised and alert, poised to let our inner freedom give rise to the unfolding, common reality of self and community (Zohar and Marshall, 1994, p. 135).

Thus, the contemporary supervisor will be conversant with pedagogy and skilled in the psychological nuances of mediative interventions, and will also have an understanding of schools as systems that influence and are influenced by the choices and actions of the individuals comprising them. This systems theory approach views human beings as

unique, complex, whole individuals who grow up and live the majority of their lives in various human and organizational systems. Parts (people) are always seen in relation to and interacting with other parts to create a dynamically changing whole (Horne and Passmore, 1991, p. 313).

In other words, within an organization, or any system, the development of the self is interdependent with the development of the other. By being sensitive to the needs and nuances of the system, and their own part within it, systems-oriented supervisors broaden the base and distribute the functions of supervision. They work to dissolve fragmentation, competition and reactiveness (Kofman & Senge, 1993), and they nurture collaboration, experimentation, and professional reflection. Supervision as social ecology becomes system gardening through a set of energies devoted to developing learning organizations.

Organizational learning (i.e., the development of new capabilities, practices and policies) occurs over time in a continuous cycle of theoretical reflection, practical conceptualization, action, assessment, and reflection on action. Such work requires systems thinking in addition to successful cognitively oriented approaches because schools' most important challenges are functions of their systems, not their parts. Organizational development requires vision, values, and goal focus, skills at generating, interpreting, and using data, ability to initiate and manage adaptation; gathering and focusing resources, and developing and nurturing interdependence (Garmston & Wellman, 1994). In these efforts, collaboration becomes as important as competitiveness has been in the past. Looking good becomes less important than being good. In communities of learning, teachers and supervisors admit to not knowing, seek help from others, and seek to be taught. Proactiveness instead of reactivess and creation rather than problem solving become the dominant practices.

Costa and Garmston (1994) claim that such schools, holonomous schools that honor independence and interdependence simultaneously, are necessary for high performance and continuous refinement. As part of a learning organization, the ecologically minded supervisor moves the school toward holonomy by directing resources toward developing community, fostering reflective practice, and increasing the capacity of the system toward adaptation and growth.

Developing Community A community is a complex network of interdependent relationships. The community draws from a shared repository of resources (i.e., their collective potential). It is not held together by "a complex calculus of self-interest nor by any set of bureaucratic rules. It draws, rather, on its common culture and on the autonomous authority of that culture—on its 'collective patterns of thinking, feeling and action' and on their common expression" (Zohar & Marshall, 1994, p. 99).

Supervisory attention to community building is central to any school improvement effort because workplace culture (i.e., the shared values, quality of relationships, and collaborative norms of the workplace) have greater influence on what professionals do than do the knowledge, skills or the personal histories of either workers or supervisors (Rosenholtz, 1991; Sergiovanni, 1994). Providing opportunities for individuals to interact in a public forum, developing norms of collaboration, inquiry and experimentation, and fostering the establishment of a common, or shared culture becomes the focus of supervision. Action research groups and other forums for probing deeply into instructional practice pry at the very core of professional values and identities. These latter forms of collaboration are most compatible with the research claims regarding teacher professionalism, reflection, and efficacy. They are, however, also the least common forms found in practice (Little, 1984). Collaboration must be linked to norms of continuous improvement (Fullan, 1990) that are connected directly to deepening understandings about the instructional process and improving student learning. Collaborative cultures respect individuality, value diversity, establish expectations for continuous growth and improvement, develop problem-coping and conflict-resolution strategies, and embrace life-long learning that involves reflective practice, inquiry, and skill development (Fullan & Hargreaves, 1991). Dialogue is essential to this process. Activities such as coteaching, peer coaching, and curriculum development affect individual choices and require dialogue between practitioners.

In learning communities, conflict and disagreement about change, scarcity, diversity, and power are fundamental communities to successful change. Conflict of this nature is constructive and inquiry-oriented when it is addressed in forums in which colleagues question underlying assumptions, probe for specificity regarding the alignment of actions with values, and examine practice for intentionality of purpose and effectiveness of outcomes. These forums are driven by a combination of humanistic/existential principles of human relationships and cognitive theorist strategies for theory building. "Inquiry is the engine of vitality and self-renewal" (Pascal, 1990, p.14). Shared norms develop from the opportunity for individuals to try on their new understandings within a group. Norms of collaboration include behaviors that increase dialogue among educators in order to solve problems, learn more about teaching and learning, and increase organizational effectiveness in-service of student learning. Seven such norms have been elaborated by Baker and Shalit (1992): pause, paraphrase, probe, put ideas on the table, presume positive intentions, pay attention to self and others, and balance advocacy and inquiry.

Collaborative cultures also support risk taking when practitioners engage in rigorous reflection on their practice with a mutual willingness to question underlying assumptions (Little, 1982; Hargreaves, 1990). Reflective practice increases comfort with professional uncertainty and supports the notion of conscious experimentation and continued professional growth. In these collaborative communities, the five states of mind (i.e., efficacy, flexibility, craftsmanship, consciousness and interdependence) prevail as values, goals, standards, and self-organizing principles (Costa & Garmston, 1994).

It is critical in this effort to remember that organizations are dynamical systems. If schools and school districts were comprised of only their physical elements (e.g., buildings, classrooms, playgrounds, parking lots) redesigning schools could be accomplished through the precise construction of a blueprint for change. Innovative and new designs could be initiated at the drawing board and communicated via these clear, concise, rational schematics. Schools are comprised of people, however, not constructed of neatly laid-out right angles. The school is the community, teachers, students, administrators, custodians, and support staff all interacting with each other. It is the rich diversity of those who inhabit our schools that enables them to be vital and stimulating places. It is precise because schools are the composite of their human condition, however, that they are nonrational arenas. As stated earlier, schools have their own organizational cultures in which tacit knowledge and commonly held understandings direct behaviors and inform actions to a much greater extent than do decontextualized programs and policies. Supervision efforts must therefore take into account individual needs and concerns about innovation, celebrate their rich cultural and ethnic diversity, and recognize the need to develop positive, enduring, and shared norms about the purpose of schooling and the process of change.

Developing community and supporting change efforts in organizations requires individuals to manage personal psychological transition during periods of change. Individuals accommodate change with metaphoric thinking (e.g., the language of ceremony, ritual, and myth), and not with the language of linear, logical functions that are often attributed to left-brain operations. Organizational heroes and heroines, stories and anecdotes, celebrations, and opportunities to grieve connect with meaning making on a deep, intuitive level.

The power to improve or rebuild comes from within. Reweaving the strands of individual talents and energy into a rich cultural tapestry, humans create the art form of culture through imagination and social interaction. Thereafter, it shapes and gives meaning to their experiences. . . . Building from within on a . . . foundation of experience, values, and beliefs . . . will revitalize and transform the public schools. . . . The secret lies in the soul of every school and the hearts of those who give it life, zest and magic (Deal, 1984, p.66).

The nonrational aspects of organizational culture (e.g., the myths, symbols, rituals, and metaphors) are therefore levers for systemic change.

Promoting Work Cultures of Reflective Practice Reflective practice offers a potent process for enhancing the power of the supervisory interaction toward professional growth and school renewal. Rosenholtz (1991) suggests that teachers develop new conceptions of their work through communica-

tions with their supervisors or colleagues in which "new aspects of experience are pointed out with fresh interpretations" (p. 3). Reflection keeps practitioners continually fresh through opportunities to consider their experiences in previously unthought of dimensions. Costa and Garmston (1994) describe a renaissance school in which humans are makers of meaning, both consciously and unconsciously, from experience. "All members of the school community are continual and active leaders . . . and . . . [l]eadership is the mediation of both the individual's and the organization's capacity for self-renewal" (p. 10).

The nonroutine nature of teacher's work (Rosenholtz, 1991), requires complex, contextual decision-making and an inquiry-oriented approach to practice. Reflection facilitates development of problem-solving skills by fostering an ability to reframe experience, generate alternatives, make inferences based on prior knowledge, and evaluate actions to construct new learnings. Reflection involves recasting a situation as a result of clarifying questions, reconsidering assumptions, and generating a wider range of alternative responses or actions.

Sergiovanni (1992) suggests that teachers need to "create knowledge in use as they practice becoming skilled surfers who ride the wave of the pattern of teaching as it unfolds" (p. 210). This level of professional ability requires contextually based, systematic experimentation and reflection. Without reflection, progress is uninformed, and change in practice is haphazard. When teachers are viewed as generators of knowledge about teaching, however, rather than simply as consumers, supervisors can become collaborators in analysis and synthesis of new understandings that are steeped in the context of their own settings. A primary purpose of supervision becomes the improvement of practice through the acquisition of deeper understandings and broader views of the possibilities inherent in the teaching–learning process. Supervision becomes a "function, not a role" (Nolan & Francis, 1992, p. 56) that can be performed by many and various people in the school, in one-to-one or group interactions. As Sergiovanni (1992) asserts, the authority for supervision "can come from the inside as easily as the outside" (p. 204). Based on this belief, anyone in the school community can offer supervision (e.g., supervision of self, of colleagues, or a group), and everyone should be encouraged to do so.

When teachers engage in the process of generating knowledge about their own teaching, "their teaching is transformed in important ways: [T]hey become theorists articulating their intentions, testing their assumptions, and finding connections with practice" (Cochran-Smith & Lytle, 1990, p. 8). Supervisory actions should be designed to provide resources, offer information, and otherwise support and motivate practitioners to engage in this type of systematic experimentation and reflection, encouraging educators to coalesce theory out of their own practice.

Collaborative supervisory approaches that promote reflection would cause practitioners to develop new patterns of thinking and alternative perspectives from which they can take a fresh look at the challenges of their work and from which they can generate personal theories of practice. Furthermore, based on a systems theory approach, influencing professional practice would involve shaping the work environment to support these behaviors as organizational norms.

Increasing the Capacity of the System The pace and complexity of change assure of us of no more calm waters and no final destination in our continual journey toward excellence. By their very nature, dynamical systems cannot be guided with linear planning, nor can long-term outcomes be predicted with precision. In such mileu, the intention of organizations to follow predetermined plans toward the achievement of predetermined outcomes shifts to an intention of continual discovery and evolutionary planning (Fullan, 1994). In order to navigate the years ahead, each member of the organization must be able to manage personal change, support others (e.g., students, parents, and faculty) in their change process, and contribute to the continued learning of the group.

The capacity of the organization is maximized through the simultaneous development of the system and of its individual members. "As individuals, we are not only what we *are* or *do*, but also what we *might* be or *might do*. If we share our wishes, fears, dreams, and images . . . we become bound together into a group that transcends any one definition of itself in actual behavioral roles" (Zohar & Marshall, 1994, pp. 194–195). To fully capacitate the organization, neither collectivism (i.e., the tendency of the group to think as one unit), nor individualism (i.e., the maintenance of rigid attitudes or fixed positions) will work. In a collectivist organization, each member defines him- or herself in terms of the group. Sacrificing personal identity for social identity limits the creative contributions made possible by the voices of individuals. On the other hand, when group members adopt an individualistic attitude, they can be cut-off from the richness and resourcefulness of the group, closed to the ideas of others, and less likely to evolve as a continually learning group. "Neither attitude is conducive to the emergence of a community spirit in the group" (Zohar & Marshall, 1994, p. 132)

Systemic change, however, can only be realized when consciously articulated values are used as operational benchmarks for gathering feedback and reflecting on practice for individuals and groups. Quality is controlled by an intrinsic, shared understanding of what quality means and the desire to achieve it, not by programs, policies, rules, and structures.

Value-driven reflection of this nature, or double-loop learning, allows an organization to grow and learn from its experience, gathering feedback from events within the organization. Agryris (1994) offers the following metaphor to illustrate the contrast between single-loop, or behavior-driven and double-loop, or value-driven learning:

Single-loop learning . . . is incremental and adaptive, something like a thermostat that is set to turn on the heat if the room temperature drops below 68 degrees . . . double loop learn[ers] correct errors by examining the underlying values and policies of the organization . . . [like] an "intelligent" thermostat that can evaluate whether or not 68 degrees is the right temperature for optimum efficiency (p. 27).

Double-loop learning is especially useful when problems are complex or difficult. Based on their experience in organizational change, leaders in Dade County, Florida, offer the following mandate:

Supervisory practices must promote a climate in which it is both safe and encouraged for areas that were formerly private and off limits to discussion to become public and subject to discussion. In such a climate, change and improvement become more highly prized than constancy and predictability; and single-loop learning gives way to double-loop learning (Dreyfuss, Cistone, & Divita, Jr., 1992, p. 85).

CONCLUSIONS

The findings from developmental psychology and adult life-span theorists raise anew questions about the ultimate goals of schooling in American society, or, for that matter, any society dedicated to democratic forms of governance and/or participation in postbureacratic organizational structures. For example, in this chapter, we drew upon Kegan's (1982, 1994) Postinstitutional System, a state of reasoning in which thinking is characterized by a fluid and macrocentric logic in which the self is not the center of the universe, nor are the self-devised prevailing principles of self-governance ultimate and fixed. Instead, in Postinstitutional reasoning, predetermined orientations to conflict and information are transcended and the self is freed to think and act in interdependent ways.

During the late 1980s and well into the 1990s, movement was noted in schools and businesses toward organizations that would require this level of operation in order to function. For example, in *The Fifth Discipline,* Senge (1990) noted:

[L]earning organizations are organizations where people continually expend their capacities to create the results they truly desire, where new and expansive patterns of thinking are nurtured, where collective aspiration is set free, and where people are continually learning how to learn together (pp. 3–4).

Kegan and Lehay (1984) offer Torbert's vivid contrast between bureaucratic structures that develop individuals beyond the institutional level, and those that hold or restrict people to it. He suggests that stifling organizations have the following characteristics: (1) they maintain focus on doing the predefined task, (2) the viability of the product becomes the overriding criterion of success, (3) standards and structures are taken for granted, (4) they focus on quantitative results based on defined standards, (5) reality is conceived of as dichotomous and competitive (e.g., success–failure, in-group–out-group, leader–follower, legitimate–illegitimate, work–play, reasonable-emotional, etc). In these organizations, there is allegiance to tradition, precedent, and tried and true methods. Predetermined structures exist to produce predefined outcomes that are evaluated by preset standards of quality. The organization is invested in the system as is.

In contrast, developmental, evolving organizations engage in shared reflection about larger (i.e., wider, deeper, more abstract) purposes of the organization. They focus on development of an open interpersonal process, with disclosure, support, and confrontation on value–stylistic–emotional issues. Evaluation centers on the effects of one's own behavior on others in the organization and on formative research on the effects of the organization on the environment (i.e., social accounting). There is direct facing and resolution of paradoxes (e.g., freedom-control, expert vs. participatory decision-making, etc.). There is an appreciation of the particular historical moment of this particular organization as an important variable in decision-making.

These organizations have the following characteristics: (1) they develop creative, transconventional solutions to conflicts; (2) they display commitment, over time, to a deliberately chosen structure that is often unique in the experience of the participants or among similar organizations; (3) they place a primary emphasis on horizontal rather than vertical work–role differentiation; and (4) they foster the development of symmetrical rather than subordinate relation with "parent" organizations. There is a vested interest in their own development in these growth-promoting organizations. There is a commitment to self-reflection, open-system information seeking, and feedback loops with the possibility of redefining goals, procedures, and criteria. These attributes amount to an "institutional capacity for intimacy" (p. 221).

Costa and Garmston (1994) label organizations with these qualities Renaissance Schools, with their essence representing

rebirth and awakening, a reenergizing of values, a reconnecting with natural forces found in the universe, a recognition of the innate capacities for human development, both individually and in groups. . . . [An amalgamation of psychological perspectives, these schools are] at once a celebration of the limitless potential and creativity of the human spirit and a means of continuous improvement towards ideals (p. 187).

We believe that educational organizations that embody these characteristics are vitally important to our continued evolution as a nation.

It is our contention that a psychology of supervision is simultaneously influencing and being influenced by the psychology of the workplace. Schools are socially constructed realities. The work site exerts a strong influence on the teachers' interpretation of roles, preferences for work structures, and receptivity to work redesign. Understandings are contextually based, affected by the interactions and social-information processing at specific work sites (Hart, 1990). This chapter suggests that a constructive–developmental approach to the growth of the individuals within the organization, combined with a systems theory understanding regarding psychosocial dynamics, is a necessary approach to a psychology of supervision in order to achieve the educational environments and the educational outcomes that foster the ideals of the postinstitutionalist ethic.

As compared to approaches that emphasize norms of health and humanistic normlessness, the constructive–developmental perspective provides a basis for norms of growth. Among Kohlberg's most important, long-argued, and carefully exposed points is the instruction that goals for intervention cannot derive their justification from science or social science alone. Psychology can study and demon-

strate the changes of personality, but the determination that a change is preferable . . . is intrinsically a philosophical question (Kegan, 1982, p. 293).

Considerations For Further Study

In this chapter, we have presented a view of the psychological heuristics that would be operant in such an organization. This view raises provocative questions regarding the functions and contexts of supervisory practice in supporting adults toward increasingly complex systems of meaning. For example, there can be no serious treatment of supervision or the psychology of supervision without examining the supervisors themselves, including their orientations to practice, their philosophies regarding education, and their own meaning making systems. What are the implications for preservice and in-service programs in preparing educators with the skills, knowledge, and attitudes mandated by a constructivist–development view? What designs are necessitated for a workplace that supports them? How will the rich diversity of perspectives, cultures, personal experiences, along with presently held meaning systems inform and influence the growth of educational organizations, their individual members, and the communities they serve? What levels of dialogue need to be initiated and sustained, nationally and locally, to explore the possibilities? Finally, as we consider a psychology of supervision, how can we be informed by the multiple perspectives of our practice?

Much like the idealized relationship between supervision and pedagogy, we seek a congruency of perspective between supervisory practices and organizational values. Supervision becomes a fractal representation of similar values, assumptions, and beliefs that permeate the organization, recognizing the reciprocal and adaptive nature of evolution. Thus, we suggest some learning from open-systems evolutionary biology, which locates the force of change, of life, in the interactions between the individual and the environment, and not simply within them.

We conclude this chapter with a final question: "What is the relevant system to which supervision should be attending; is it the teacher, the interactions between teacher and students, supervisor and teacher, teachers, supervisors, and the greater school community, or all of the above and others interacting with one another?" This view of a psychology of supervision would

not place an energy system within us so much as it places us in a single energy system of all living things. Its primary attention, then, is not to shifts and changes in an internal equilibrium, but to an equilibrium in the world, between the progressively individuated self and the bigger life field, an interaction coupled by both and constitutive of reality itself (Kegan, 1982, p. 43).

REFERENCES

Adler, A. (1963). *The practice and theory of individual psychology.* Paterson, NJ: Littlefield, Adams.

Argyris, C. (1994). Education for leading-learning. *The learning organization in action.* New York: American Management Association.

Baker, B. & Shalit, S. (1992). *Seven norms of collaboration.* Berkeley, CA: Group Dynamics Associates.

Bandler, R. & Grinder, J. (1976). *The structure of magic II.* Palo Alto, CA: Science and Behavior Books, Inc.

Bandura, A. (1977). *Social learning theory.* Englewood Cliffs, NJ: Prentice Hall.

Barth, R. (1990). *Improving schools from within.* San Francisco: Jossey-Bass.

Bateson, G. (1972). *Steps to an ecology of mind.* New York: Ballantine Books.

Beck, A. T. (1976). *Cognitive therapy and the emotional disorders.* New York: International Universities Press.

Beck, A. T. (1985). Cognitive therapy, behavior therapy, psychoanalysis and pharmacotherapy: A cognitive continuum. In M. Mahoney & A. Freeman (Eds.). *Cognition and psychotherapy.* New York: Plenum.

Berger, P. & Luckmann, T. (1967). *The construction of social reality.* Garden City, NY: Anchor Press.

Berman, P. & McLaughlin, M. W. (1977). *Federal program supporting educational change: Factors affecting implementation and continuation.* Santa Monica, CA: Rand Corporation.

Berne, E. (1964). *Games people play.* New York: Grove Press.

Block, P. (1987). *The empowered manager.* San Francisco, CA: Jossey-Bass.

Blumberg, A. (1974). *Supervisors & teachers: A private cold war.* Berkeley, CA: McCutcheon.

Bolin, F. & Panaritis, P. (1992). Searching for a common perspective: A perspective on the history of supervision. In C. Glickman (Ed.). *Supervision in transition: ASCD yearbook* (pp. 30–43). Alexandria, VA: ASCD.

Briggs, J. (1992). *Fractals, the patterns of chaos.* New York: Simon & Schuster.

Brunner, J. (1959). *The process of education.* Cambridge, MA: Harvard University Press.

Burden, P. (1990). Teacher development. In R. W. Houston (Ed.). *Handbook of research on teacher education* (pp. 311–328). New York: MacMillan.

Burns, D. (1980). *Feeling good: The new mood therapy.* New York: New American Library.

Burns, M. (1978). *Leadership.* New York: Harper & Row.

Caine, R. & Caine, G. (1991). *Teaching and the human brain: Making connections.* Alexandria, VA: ASCD.

Chomsky, N. (1957). *Syntactic structures.* The Hague: Mouton.

Chomsky, N. (1965). *Aspects of the theory of syntax.* Cambridge, MA: MIT Press.

Chopra, D. (1989). *Quantum healing: Exploring the frontiers of mind/body medicine.* New York: Bantam Books.

Clark, C. & Peterson, P. (1986). Teachers' thought processes. In M. Whittrock (Ed.). *Handbook of research on teaching* (3rd ed.) pp. 255-296. New York: Macmillan.

Clark, T. & Astuto, T. (1994). Redirecting reform: Challenges to popular assumptions about teachers and students. *Phi Delta Kappan,* 75(7), 512–520.

Cochran-Smith, M. & Lytle, S. (1990). Research on teaching and teacher research: Issues that divide. *Educational Researcher, 19*(2), 2–11.

Cogan, M. (1973). *Clinical supervision.* Boston: Houghton-Mifflin.

Costa, A. & Garmston, R. (1994). *Cognitive coaching: A foundation for renaissance schools* (p. 59). Norwood, MA: Christopher-Gordon Publishers, Inc.

Costa, A., Garmston, R., & Lambert, L. (1988). Evaluation of teaching: A cognitive development view. In Popham, W. J. & Stanley, S. J. *Teacher evaluation: Six prescriptions for success* (pp. 145–172). Alexandria, VA: ASCD.

Covey, S. (1990). *The 7 habits of highly effective people: Powerful lesssons in personal change.* New York: Simon and Schuster, Fireside Edition.

Csikszentmihalyi, M. (1993). *The evolving self: A psychology for the third millennium.* New York: Harper Collins Publishers, Inc.

Csikszentmihalyi, M. (1990). *Flow: The psychology of optimal experience.* New York: Harper & Row.

Darling-Hammond, L. & Sclan, E. (1992). Policy and supervision: Supervision in transistion. In C. Glickman (Ed.). *1992 ASCD Yearbook* (pp. 7–29). Alexandria VA: ASCD.

Darling-Hammond, L., Wise, A. E., & Pease, S. R. (1983). Teacher evaluation in the organizational context: A review of the literature. *Review of Educational Research, 53*(3), 285–328.

Deal, T. (1984). Searching for the wizard: The quest for excellence in education. *Issues in education, 2*(1), 56–67.

Dewey, J. (1938). *Experience and education.* New York: Macmillan.

Dilts, R. (1990). *Changing belief systems with NLP.* Cupertino, CA: Meta Publications.

Dilts, R. (1994). *Effective presentation skills.* Capitola, CA: Meta Publications.

Dreyfuss, G., Cistone, P., & Divita, C. Jr. (1992). Restructuring in a large district: Dade County, Florida. In C. Glickman (Ed.). *Supervision in transition: ASCD yearbook* (pp. 77–96). Alexandria, VA: ASCD.

Edelman, G. (1992). *Bright air, brilliant fire: On the matter of the mind.* New York: Basic Books.

Edwards, J. L. & Newton, R. R. (1994). *The effects of cognitive coaching on teacher efficacy and empowerment.* Paper presented at the Annual Meeting of the American Educational Research Association, San Francisco, CA.

Edwards, J. L. (1993). The effect of cognitive coaching on the conceptual development and reflective thinking of first year teachers (doctoral dissertation, The Fielding Institute, Santa Barbara, CA). *Dissertation Abstracts International, 54/03-A,* AAD93-20751.

Einspruch, E. & Forman, B. (1985). Observations concerning research literature on neuro-linguistic programming. *Journal of Counseling Psychology, 32*(4), 569–589.

Eisner, E. (1982). An artistic approach to supervision. In T. Sergiovanni, (Ed.). *Supervision of teaching: ASCD yearbook* (pp. 53–66). Alexandria, VA: ASCD.

Ellett, C. D, Capie, W., & Johnson, C. E. (1981). *Teacher performance and elementary pupil achievement on the Georgia Criterion Referenced Tests.* Athens, GA: Teacher Assessment Project, University of Georgia.

Erickson, E. H. (1950). *Childhood and society.* New York: W. W. Norton.

Faulkner, C. (1991). *Metaphors of identity: Operating metaphors and iconic change* (cassette recording). City Unknown: Genesis II.

Featherstone, E. (1994). *Skin deep: Women writing on color, culture and identity.* Freedom, CA: The Crossing Press.

Feuerstein, R., Rand, Y., Hoffman, M. B., & Miller, R. (1980). *Instrumental enrichment: An intervention program for cognitive modifiability.* Baltimore, MD: University Park Press.

Feuerstein, R., Rand, Y., & Rynders, J. (1988). *Don't accept me as I am: Helping "retarded" people to excell.* New York: Plenum Press.

Flanders, N. (1976). Interaction analysis and clinical supervision. *Journal of Research and Development in Education, 9*(2), 47–48.

Freud, S. (1933). *The complete introductory lectures on psychoanalysis* (p. 544). Trans. J. Strachey. New York: W. W. Norton.

Friman, P. C., Allen, K. D., Kerwin, M. L. E., & Larzelere, R. (1993). Changes in modern psychology: A citation analysis of the Kuhnian thesis. *American Psychologist,* 48, 658–664.

Frymier, J. (1987). Bureaucracy and the neutering of teachers. *Phi Delta Kappan, 69*(1), pp. 9–14.

Fullan, M. & Hargreaves, A. (1991). *What's worth fighting for? Working together for your school.* Andover, MA: Regional Labs.

Fullan, M. (1982). *The meaning of educational change.* New York: Teachers College Press.

Fullan, M. (1990). Staff development, innovation and institutional development. In B. Joyce (Ed.). *Changing school culture through staff development: ASCD yearbook.* Alexandria, VA: ASCD.

Fullan, M. (1993). *Change forces: Probing the depths of educational reform*. New York: The Falmer Press.

Fuller, B., Wood, K., Rapoport, T., & Dornbusch, S. (1982). The organizational context of individual efficacy. *Review of Educational Research, 52*(1), 7–30.

Garfield, C. (1986). *Peak performers: The new heroes of American business*. New York: William Morrow and Company, Inc.

Garman, N. (1982). The clinical approach to supervision. In T. Sergiovanni (Ed.). *Supervision of teaching: ASCD yearbook* (pp. 35–54). Alexandria, VA: ASCD.

Garmston, R. (1990). Is peer coaching changing supervisory relationships? Some reflections. *California Journal of Curriculum and Supervision, 3*(2), 21–27.

Garmston, R. & Hyerle, D. (1988). Professors' peer coaching program: Report on a 1987–1988 pilot project to develop and test a staff development program for improving instruction at California State University, Sacramento, CA: California State University, Sacramento.

Garmston, R. & Wellman, B. (1994). *Developing the adaptive organization*. Paper presented for the National Education Association, Washington DC.

Garmston, R. & Wellman, B. (1995). Adaptive schools in a quantum universe. Alexandria, VA: ASCD. *Educational Leadership, 52*(7), 6–12.

Garmston, R., Linder, C., & Whitaker, J. (1993). Reflections on cognitive coaching. *Educational Leadership*. Alexandria, VA: ASCD, *51*(2), 57–61.

Gibson, S. & Dembo, M. H. (1985). Teachers' sense of efficacy: An important factor in school improvement. *The Elementary School Journal, 86*(2), 173–184.

Gilligan, C. (1982). *In a different voice: Psychological theory of women's development*. Cambridge: Harvard University Press.

Glanz, J. (1994). *History of educational supervision: Proposals and prospects*. Paper presented to the Council of Professors of Instructional Supervision at the ASCD Annual Conference, Chicago, IL.

Glassberg, S. (1979). *Developing models of teacher development*. (ERIC Document Reproduction Service No. ED 171 685), March.

Glickman, C. (1985). *Supervision of instruction: A developmental approach*. Boston: Allyn & Bacon, Inc.

Glickman, C. (1992). *Supervision in transition: ASCD yearbook*. Alexandria, VA: ASCD.

Glickman, C. (1993). *Renewing America's schools: A guide for school based action*. San Francisco: Jossey Bass.

Goldhammer, R. (1969). *Clinical supervision: Special methods for the supervision of teachers*. New York: Holt, Rinhart and Winston, Inc.

Grafton, L. G. (1987). *The mediating influence of efficacy on conflict strategies used in educational organizations*. Paper presented at the Annual Meeting of the Speech Communication Associates, Boston, MA.

Greenwood, G. E., Olejnik, S. F., & Parkay, F. W. (1990). Relationships between four teacher efficacy belief patterns and selected teacher characteristics. *Journal of Research and Development in Education, 23*(2), 102–106.

Grimmett, P. & Erickson, G. (1988). *Reflection in teacher education*. New York: Teachers College Press.

Grimmett, P., Rostad, O., & Ford, B. (1992). The transformation of supervision. In C. Glickman (Ed.). *Supervision in transition: ASCD yearbook* (185–202). Alexandria, VA: ASCD.

Grinder, M. (1993). *Envoy: Your personal guide to classroom management*. Battle Ground, WA: Michael Grinder and Associates.

Guba, E. & Lincoln, Y. (1985). *Effective evaluation* (p. 140). San Francisco, CA: Jossey-Bass.

Guild, P. & Garger, S. (1985). *Marching to different drummers*. Alexandria, VA: ASCD.

Guttman, H. (1992). Systems theory, cybernetics, and epistemology. In A. Gurman & D. Kniskern (Eds.). *Handbook of family therapy, (Vol. 2, p. 42)*. New York: Brunner/Mazel.

Haley, J. (1976). Development of a theory: A history of a research project. In C. E. Sluzki & D. C. Ransom (Eds.). *Double bind: The foundational of the communicational approach to the family*. New York: Grove & Stratton.

Hargreaves, A. (1990). Contrived collegiality: The micropolitics of teacher collaboration. In J. Blase (Ed.). *The politics of life in schools*. Berkeley, CA: Sage Press.

Hart, A. W. (1990). Impact of the school social unit on teacher authority during work redesign. *American Educational Research Journal, 47*(3), 503–532.

Harvey, O. J. (1967). Conceptual systems and attitude change. In C. Sherif & M. Sheif (Eds.). *Attitude, ego involvement and change*. New York: Wiley.

Harvey, O. J. (1970). Beliefs and behavior: Some implications for education. *The Science Teacher, 37*, 10–14.

Harvey, O., Prather, M., White, B., & Hoffmeister, J. (1968). Teacher's beliefs, classroom atmosphere, and student behavior. *American Educational Research Journal, 5*, 151–166.

Hilgard, E. R. & Atkinson, R. G. (1967). *Introduction to psychology* (p. 306). New York: Harcourt Brace.

Hoffman, L. (1981). *Foundations of family therapy*. New York: Basic Books.

Hofstede, G. (1991). Cultures and organizations: Software of the mind. London: McGraw-Hall.

Horne, A. M. & Passmore, J. L. (1991). *Family counseling and therapy* (2nd ed.). Itasca, IL: Peacock Publishers.

Hull, C. L. (1937). Mind, mechanism and behavior. *Psychological Review, 44*, 1–32.

Hunt, D. (1971). *Matching models in education*. Toronto: Ontario Institute for Educational Studies.

Hunt, D. (1975). Person-environment interaction: A challenge found wanting before it was tried. *Review of Educational Research, 45*, 209–230.

Hunt, D. & Joyce, B. (1967). Teacher trainee personality and initial teaching style. *American Educational Research Journal, 4*, 253–259.

Hunt, D. E. & Joyce, B. R. (1967). Teacher trainee personality and initial teaching style. *American Educational Research Journal, 4*(3), 253–255.

Joyce, B., Weil, M., & Wald, R. (1973). The teacher-innovator: Models of teaching as the core of teacher education. *Interchange, 4*, 47–59.

Jung, C. (1934). *The archetypes and the collective unconscious*. Collected works. Vol. 9, Part 1, Bollingen Series XX. Princeton, NJ: Princeton University Press, 1968.

Kegan, R. (1982). *The evolving self*. Cambridge, MA: Harvard University Press.

Kegan, R. (1994). *In over our heads: The mental demands of modern life*. Cambridge, MA: Harvard University Press.

Kegan, R. & Lahey, L. (1984). Adult leadership and adult development: A constructivist view. In B. Kellerman (Ed.). *Handbook on socialization theory and research* (pp. 199–229). Chicago: Rand McNally.

Kelly, G. (1965). *A theory of personality*. New York: W. W. Norton.

Kelly, G. (1954). *The psychology of personal constructs*. New York: W. W. Norton.

Kempler, W. (1991). Gestalt family therapy. In A. M. Horne & J. L. Passmore (Eds.). *Family counseling and therapy* (2nd ed.). Itasca, IL: Peacock Publishers.

Klahr, D. (1992). Information processing approaches to cognitive development. In M. H. Bornstein & M. E. Lamb (Eds.). *Developmental psychology: An advanced textbook* (2nd ed.). Hillsdale, NJ: Erlbaum.

Koestler, A. (1972). *The roots of coincidence*. London: Hutchinson.

Kofman, F. & Senge, P. (1993). Communities of commitment: The heart of learning organizations. *Organizational Dynamics, 33*(2), 5–23.

Kohlberg, L. (1971). From is to ought. In T. Mishel (Ed.). *Cognitive development and epistemology*. New York: Academic Press.

Kohut, H. (1971). *The analysis of the self*. New York: International Universities Press.

Krajewski, R. (1982). Clinical supervision: A conceptual framework. *Journal of Research and Development in Education, 15*(2), 38–43.

Lahey, L. (1995). Personal communication with the authors.

Lana, R. (1976). *Foundations of psychological theory*. New York: Halsted Press.

Lankton, S. (1980). *Practical magic: Applications of neuro-linguistic programming in clinical psychotherapy*. Cupertino, CA: Meta Publications.

Lankton, S. & Lankton, C. (1983). *The answer within: A clinical framework of Ericksonian hypnotherapy*. New York: Brunner/Mazel.

Levine, S. L. (1989). *Promoting adult growth in schools: The promise of professional development*. Boston: Allyn and Bacon.

Levinson, D. (1965). *Seasons of a man's life*. New York: Alfred A. Knopf.

Liebmann, R. (1993). *Perceptions of human resource developers as to the initial and desired states of holonomy and managerial and manual employees*. Unpublished doctoral dissertation, Seton Hall University, South Orange, NJ.

Lipton, L. (1993). Schools as learning communities: Cultural conditions to support school renewal. *NYC challenge: Building a community of learners*. Journal of the NYC ASCD: 20–25.

Little, J. (1982). Norms of collegiality and experimentation: Workplace conditions of school success. *American Education Research Journal, 19*, 325–340.

Little, J. W. (1984). Seductive images and organizational realities in professional development. *Teachers College Record, 86*, 84–102.

Loevinger, J. (1976). *Ego development*. San Francisco, CA: Jossey-Bass.

Lowry, R. (1971). *The evolution of psychological theory* (p. 193). Chicago: Aldine.

Lundin, R. W. (1977). Behaviorism: Operant reinforcement. In R. Corsini (Ed.). *Current personality theories* (p. 187). Itasca, IL: F. E. Peacock.

Mahler, M., Pine, F., & Bergman, A. (1975). *The psychological birth of the human infant*. New York: Basic Books.

Maslow, A. H. (1968). *Toward a psychology of being* (2nd ed.). Princeton, NJ: Van Nostrand.

MacLean, P. (1978). *A mind of three minds: Educating the triune brain*. The 77th Yearbook of the National Society for the Study of Education (308–342). Chicago: Chicago University Press.

Mead, M. (1934). Kinship in the Admiralty Islands. *Anthropological Papers of the American Museum of Natural History*, New York, Vol. 34, Part II, pp. 181–358.

Meichenbaum, D. (1977). *Cognitive-behavior modification: An integrative approach*. New York: Plenum.

Myers-Briggs Type Indicator. (1957). Princeton, NJ: Educational Testing Services.

Miller, P. (1993). *Theories of developmental psychology* (p. 278). New York: W.H. Freeman.

National Board for Professional Teaching Standards. (1993). *Five core propositions: What accomplished teachers should know and be able to do*. Washington, DC.

Nolan, J. & Francis, P. (1992). Changing perspectives in curriculum and instruction. In C. Glickman (Ed.). *Supervision in transition* (pp. 30–43). Alexandria, VA: ASCD.

O'Connor, J. & Seymour, J. (1990). *Introducing neuro-linguistic programming: The new psychology of personal excellence*. Hammersmith, London: Harper Collins Publishers.

Olds, L. (1992). *Metaphors of interrelatedness: Toward a systems theory of psychology*. Albany, NY: SUNY Press.

Ornstein, R. (1991). *The evolution of consciousness*. New York: Simon and Schuster.

Pajak, E. (1993). *Approaches to clinical supervision*. Norwood, MA: Christopher-Gordon Publishers, Inc..

Pajares, M. F. (1992). Teachers' beliefs and educational research: Cleaning up a messy construct. *Review of Educational Research, 62*(3), 57–64.

Pascale, P. (1990). *Managing on the edge*. New York: Touchstone.

Perkins, D. (1983). *The mind's best work: A new psychology of creative thinking*. Cambridge, MA: Harvard University Press.

Perls, F. S. (1969). *Gestalt therapy verbatim*. Lafayette, CA: Real People Press.

Perls, F. S. (1973). *The gestalt approach: Eyewitness to therapy*. Palo Alto, CA: Science and Behavior Books.

Piaget, J. (1948). *The moral judgment of the child*. Glencoe: Free Press.

Piaget, J. (1952). *The origins of intelligence in children*. New York: International Universities Press. Originally published in 1936.

Piaget, J. (1967). *Six psychological studies*. New York: Random House.

Pohland, P. & Cross, J. (1982). Impact of the curriculum on supervision. In T. Sergiovanni (Ed.). *Supervision of teaching* (pp. 133–152). Alexandria, VA: ASCD.

Poole, M. G. & Okeafor, K. R. (1989). The effects of teacher efficacy and interactions among educators on curriculum implementation. *Journal of Curriculum and Supervision, 4*(2), 146–161.

Rogers, C. (1957). The necessary and sufficient conditions of therapeutic personality change. *Journal of Consulting Psychology, 21*, 95–103.

Rogers, C. (1959). A theory of therapy, personality, and interpersonal relationships, as developed in the client-centered framework. In S. Koch (Ed.). *Psychology: A study of a science* (Vol. 3) pp. 184–256. New York: McGraw-Hill.

Rogers, C. (1980) *A way of being*. Boston: Houghton-Mifflin.

Rosenholtz, S. (1989). *Teachers' workplace: The social organization of schools*. New York: Longman, Inc.

Rosenholtz, S. (1991). *Teachers' workplace: The social organization of schools*. New York: Teachers College Press.

Rubin, L. (1982). External influences on supervision: Seasonal winds and prevailing climate. In T. Sergiovanni (Ed.). *Supervision of teaching* (pp. 170–179). Alexandria, VA: ASCD.

Samovar, L. A. & Porter, R. E. (1972). *Intercultural communication: A reader*. Belmont, CA: Wadsworth Publishing Company, Inc..

Samples, R. (1981). *Mind of our mother*. Reading, MA: Addison-Wesley.

Saphir, J. & Gower, R. (1987). *The skillfull teacher: Building your teaching skills*. Carlisle, MA: Research for Better Teaching.

Satir, V. (1972). *Peoplemaking*. Palo Alto, CA: Science and Behavior Books.

Schmuck, R. & Runkel, P. (1985). *The handbook of organizational development in schools* (3rd ed.). Prospect Heights, IL: Waveland Press, Inc.

Schön, D. (1983). *The reflective practitioner: How professionals think in action*. USA: Basic Books USA, A Division of Harper Collins.

Schön, D. (1987). *Educating the reflective practitioner*. San Francisco: Jossey-Bass.

Schön, D. (1988). Coaching reflective teaching. In P. Grimmett & G. Erickson (Eds.). *Reflection in teacher education*. New York: Teachers College Press.

Senge, P. (1990). *The fifth discipline: The art and practice of the learning organization*. New York: Doubleday.

Sergiovanni, T. (1985). Landscapes, mindscapes, and reflective practice in supervision. *Journal of Curriculum and Supervision, 1*(1), 5–17.

Sergiovanni, T. (1992). Moral authority and the regeneration of supervision. In C. Glickman (Ed.). *Supervision in transition: ASCD yearbook* (pp. 203–214). Alexandria, VA: ASCD.

Sergiovanni, T. J. (1994). *Building community in schools.* San Francisco: Jossey-Bass.

Sergiovanni, T. & Starratt, R. (1988). *Supervision: Human perspectives* (4th ed.). New York: McGraw-Hill.

Shane, H. & Weaver, R. (1976). Educational developments anticipating the 21st century and the future of clinical supervision. *Journal of Research and Development in Education, 9*(2), 90–98.

Sheehy, G. (1974). *Passages: Predictable crises of adult life.* New York: E. P. Dutton.

Siegler, R. S. (1991). *Children's thinking* (2nd ed.). Englewood Cliffs, NJ: Prentice Hall.

Skinner, B. F. (1972). *Beyond freedom & dignity.* New York: Bantam Books.

Sprinthall, N. A. & Theis-Sprinthall, L. (1980). Educating for teacher growth: A cognitive-developmental perspective. *Theory Into Practice, 19,* 278–286.

Sprinthall, N. A. & Theis-Sprinthall, L. (1982). Career development of teachers: A cognitive developmental perspective. In H. Mitzel, *Encyclopedia of educational research* (5th ed.). New York: Free Press.

Sprinthall, N. A. & Theis-Sprinthall, L. (1983). The teacher as adult learner: A cognitive-developmental view. In G. Griffen (Ed.). *Staff Development, 82nd Yearbook of the National Society for the Study of Education.* Chicago, IL: University of Chicago Press.

Sternberg, R. (1983). Components of human intelligence. *Cognition, 15,* 1–48.

Taba, H. (1962). *Curriculum development.* New York: Harcourt, Brace & World.

Tannen, D. (1990). *You just don't understand.* New York: Ballantine Books.

Theis-Sprinthall, L. (1980). *Promoting the conceptual and principled thinking level of the supervising teacher.* Unpublished research report, St. Cloud State University, Minnesota.

Tracy, S. & MacNaughton, R. (1989). Clinical supervision and the emerging conflict between the neo-traditionalists and the neo-progressives. *Journal of Curriculum and Supervision, 4*(3), 246–256.

Tracz, S. M. & Gibson, S. (1986, November). *Effects of efficacy on academic achievement.* Paper presented at the Annual Meeting of the California Educational Research Association, Marina del Rey, CA.

Watson, J. B. (1913). Psychology as the behaviorist views it. *Psychological Review, 20,* 158–177.

Wheatley, M. (1992). *Leadership and the new science.* San Francisco: Berrett-Koehler.

Wilson, E. O. (1980). *Sociobiology: The abridged edition.* Cambridge, MA: The Belknap Press of Harvard University Press.

Witherell, C. S. & Erickson, V. L. (1978). Teacher education as adult development. *Theory into Practice, 17,* 229–238.

Witkin, H. A., Oldman, P. K., Cox, W., Erlichman, E., Hamm, R. M., & Ringler, R. (1973). *Field-dependence-independence and psychological differentiation: A bibliography.* Princeton, NJ: Educational Testing Service.

Witkin, H. M., Goodenough, D., & Cox, P. (1975). *Field dependent and field independent cognitive styles and their implications.* Princeton, NJ: Educational Testing Service.

Wolpe, J. (1958). *Psychotherapy by reciprocal inhibition.* Stanford, CA: Stanford University Press.

Zeig, J. (1980). *Ericksonian approaches to hypnosis and psychotherapy.* New York: Brunner/Mazel.

Zohar, D. & Marshall, I. (1994). *The quantum society.* New York: William Morrow and Company, Inc.

·9·

ANTHROPOLOGY, SOCIOLOGY, AND SUPERVISION

Duncan E. Waite

APPALACHIAN STATE UNIVERSITY

Jeanne Fulginiti (1986) credits her being an educational anthropologist for the successes she has experienced as a department head, a vice-prinicpal, and a program director.[1] The skills she learned and applied as an anthropologist have allowed her, as an administrator, to:

determine how teachers, students, and parents perceive school settings . . . [to] gain easy entry into existing social groups and . . . to assess current issues, discover shared meanings in group perceptions, understand and prioritize situations that require immediate attention, and quickly identify key people in school and community (p. 20).

Fulginiti went ever further in suggesting that training as an anthropologist should be part of every administrator's preparation. For, as she argues adeptly:

As large scale federally-funded efforts have given way to state mandates in public education, one thing has remained constant. American children still attend local schools. Teachers and administrators spend most of their careers in a single school system. Therefore, it is essential that each school deal with its own cultural diversity (or lack of it) and provide experiences which fit students to live in a multicultural world. The most cost-efficient means of securing a good public education for each child rests with well-educated staff in each local district. Anthropology and ethnographic research skills should be a vital part of each district's staff development program (p. 21).

Staff development, as we know (Oliva, 1993), is part of the supervisor's domain.

Anthropologist Paul Bohannan (1968) wrote of three primary areas in which anthropology was relevant for educators. First, he wrote, anthropology was important as a content area. Second, "anthropology, better than any of the other social sciences, provides a method of investigation that is suitable for the study and evaluation of classroom procedures and cultures" (p. 161). His third area consisted of the benefits that could be derived through application of anthropological field work techniques that offer "great insight into some of the problems of teachers, both during their training and in their classrooms" (p. 161). This is the short list, and it is easily expandable. Adding supervisors to the list of beneficiaries broadens the relevance of anthropology and sociology for education and foreshadows what will be at the heart of this chapter.

In this chapter I will discuss the contributions the fields of anthropology and sociology have made, or have the potential to make, to supervision. The influences of these fields on the theory of supervision will be examined, as will the influence anthropology and sociology have had and will have on research in the field.

In order to accomplish such a task with any semblance of coherence, it will be necessary first to delimit what is meant by the terms *anthropology* and *sociology,* and to sketch their theoretical and methodological developments.[2] A discussion of the past theoretical applications made to supervision from these two disciplines will follow. That, in turn, will be followed by a discussion of the research into supervision that has been informed by anthropological and sociological perspectives. The chapter concludes with a call for further research. Research opportunities available in the field of supervision will be extrapolated from a combination of what has been neglected to date and what areas show promise in the near future.

The assignment of reviewing the confluence of anthropology, sociology, and supervision is a rewarding task in that all of these fields have converged in the study of and the improvement of schools. That is not to say, however, that the whole of the field of sociology, for instance, is concerned with schools. It is not. There is, however, a respected, well-established subfield of sociology that deals specifically with the sociology of education, just as there is a discrete branch of anthropology that deals with the same.

287

Coming at this topic from the other direction, though, the task is somewhat more difficult. Sifting through the literature of supervision for studies sociological and anthropological is a daunting one. Moreover, many of the studies of supervision in either a sociological or anthropological vein are doctoral dissertations, and these sources prove elusive and increasingly inaccessible, with many institutions of higher education now charging for the privilege of borrowing dissertations done there. The task is also made more difficult by the fact that much of the current literature and field methods used in studies of supervision are now of the third or fourth generation. That is, the genesis of the research methods and literature informing studies of supervision have often become part of our taken-for-granted belief system, our worldview, so that acknowledgment is seldom paid to the founding fathers (and mothers) of those esteemed traditions. This problem is but one aspect of the phenomenon identified in the literature of sociology as the "double hermeneutic" (Giddens, 1990, p. 15). Giddens, a sociologist, wrote:

[T]he development of sociological knowledge is parasitical upon the lay agents' concepts; on the other hand, notions coined in the meta-languages of the social sciences routinely reenter the universe of actions they were initially formulated to describe. . . . Sociological knowledge spirals in and out of the universe of social life, reconstructing both itself and that universe as an integral part of that process (pp. 15–16).

The phenomenon of the double hermeneutic makes the task of chronicling sociological and anthropological concepts and methods in supervision an unusually tricky one. The difficulty stems from the fact that terms and concepts from these fields have entered our language at a fundamental, yet still nebulous, level. Terms like *culture* and its derivative, *school culture* (e.g., Joyce, 1990), permeate our talk about schools and school leadership/supervision (e.g., Sergiovanni, 1984). Educational anthropologist Harry Wolcott (class notes, April 1989) used to say that culture was not there until the anthropologist put it there, which may have been true during the early days of his pioneering work. As examples, however, talk of culture today (from anthropology) or role (from sociology), although perhaps technically imprecise, is on the tongue of nearly every neophyte educator. My task, therefore, as I have come to view it, is in part to separate out the research and theory that is well-grounded in anthropology and sociology from the pretenders, the charlatans, and the faddists.[3]

The task of delimiting anthropological and sociological contributions made to the field of supervision is also fraught with problems of another sort that stem from the phenomenon that the anthropologist Geertz (1983, p. 19) referred to as "blurred genres." It was Geertz's observation that the social sciences were continuing a trend of leakage, one into the other, leading to what he termed the "refiguration of social thought." To underscore his point, Geertz asks, "What *is* Foucault—historian, philosopher, political theorist? What Thomas Kuhn—historian, philosopher, sociologist of knowledge?" (p. 20).

Though one may still point with some certainty at a core repository of knowledge, theory, and method for each of the social sciences, there are overlapping areas between almost all of them. An example of this is interest in sociology in the study of the sociology of culture. Is this the same as or different from social anthropology? Issues such as these will be explored in the pages to follow.

ANTHROPOLOGY AND ITS DEVELOPMENT

Of the two social sciences—anthropology and sociology—covered in this chapter, anthropology is by far of the more recent vintage.[4] By all accounts, it has its roots in American academia, especially that of American pragmatism. Early anthropologists blended their skills as linguists and observers of traditional (i.e., indigenous) peoples and their ways of life. Franz Boas (1858–1942) is indisputably the father of American anthropology (Stocking, 1982).[5] Boas' contribution to anthropology on a global scale cannot be overestimated because he, almost singlehandedly, lead anthropologists into the field.[6] Erickson (1984) credits the Polish anthropologist, Bronislav Malinowski, with initiating what he refers to as "scientific ethnography" (p. 53). He then contrasts scientific ethnography with what had gone before. Jacob (1987) notes that "holistic ethnography developed primarily from the work of Franz Boas in the U.S. and Bronislaw Malinowski in England." She continues:

Contemporary holistic ethnographers do not explicitly focus on the theoretical formulations of these early anthropologists, but in varying ways draw on the work of Boas and Malinowski as a legacy for their own assumptions and methods (p. 10).[7]

Prior to the work of Boas and Malinowski, most cultural studies had basically been written either by travelers or by "arm-chair" anthropologists.[8]

Unlike the traveler, the trained anthropologist brought to the field an explicit—more often implicit—ethnological perspective, within which his [/her] description was conducted, as well as an ethnographic concern for the local meanings of behavior (Erickson, 1984, p. 53).

Erickson distinguishes ethnology from its sister, ethnography:

[E]thnography portrays events, at least in part, from the points of view of the actors involved in the events. . . . Ethnology contrasts with ethnography, and the two are interdependent in the researcher's conduct of inquiry. "Ethnology" literally means the study of the meaning, or significance, of a human group's organization and customs. The "meaning" to be elucidated by ethnology is not the meaning of a behavior complex within the context of the particular culture in which it is found, as in ethnographic analysis. The project of ethnology is to identify the principles of order in the social behavior of mankind as a whole. Its method is comparative (p. 52).

This, then, becomes a useful jumping-off point in the discussion of anthropology. A gross distinction between anthropology and sociology, offered to orient the reader, is that sociology was traditionally concerned with the study of modern, developed (or developing, i.e., industrializing) societies, just as traditional anthropology was concerned with studying "primitive" cultures, although this state of affairs has changed for both disciplines, as will be shown. Anthropology undertakes the study of a group of people, not always exotic, their modes of behavior and beliefs, and the interrelationship of them. Anthropology has a distinct, although often misunderstood, disciplinary identity with unique potential for the study of American society and its schools. Spindler and Spindler (1983a) held that:

Anthropologists attend to symbols, ceremonies, rituals, communities, language and thought, beliefs, dialects, sex roles and sexuality, subsistence and ecology, kinship, and a multitude of other topics in ways that historians, sociologists, political scientists, and psychologists will not, because of the heritage of experience with "other" cultures from primitive to peasant to urban away from home (p. 73).

Anthropology, technically speaking, includes four branches: physical anthropology, archaeology, cultural anthropology, and linguistic anthropology. There are some (e.g., Zaharlick, 1992), however, who include applied anthropology as another of its subdisciplines. These four fields can be subdivided still further. However beneficial this "four field" distinction may be for anthropologists to locate themselves within the field, a cursory reading reveals the relevance of especially two of these fields (i.e., cultural anthropology and linguistic anthropology) for supervision specifically and studies of schooling generally (Zaharlick, 1992).[9]

As noted earlier, the field of linguistics is a prime example of a blurred genre. As a field, it has struggled for a distinct and separate identify. Linguistics has also benefited from its unique status, bridging the fields of anthropology, sociology, English and English literature, philosophy of knowledge, and cultural studies. For instance, sociology and anthropology influence linguistics in particular ways. In the study of language, especially the interplay between language and culture, anthropology has developed an area of study termed *the ethnography of speaking* and, later, *the ethnography of communication* (Gumperz & Hymes, 1964). For its part, sociology has developed the fields of sociolinguistics and conversation analysis. In the struggle to find its own identity, linguistics developed a similar, yet distinct, field of discourse analysis (Fairclough, 1989). Each of these methods of studying language takes a particular slant, informed by the discipline that spawned it. "The achievements of linguistics," wrote Fairclough,

have been bought at the price of a narrow conception of language study. It is a paradoxical fact that linguistics has given relatively little attention to actual speech or writing; it has characterized language as a potential, a system, an abstract competence, rather than attempting to describe actual language practice (pp. 6–7).

Much of the criticism of linguistics proper, such as that cited earlier (Fairclough, 1989), has actually been in response to what may have been greatest and most controversial contribution of linguistics to the human sciences to date: the development of the idea of structuralism and its widespread acceptance and application in other fields. The Swiss linguist, Ferdinand de Saussure (1916), is credited with starting the

structuralist revolution, which was a remarkable breakaway from the conventional thinking of his day, historical linguistics (Agar, 1994). de Saussure made a distinction between the spoken language, *parole*, and the language of the collective, whole and systematic, *langue*. Linguists, argued de Saussure, study language, *langue*, not speech, *parole*. Of particular interest to de Saussure and the generations of linguists since was the structure of a language and the relation of its parts. He advocated the synchronic, as opposed to diachronic, study of language as a system. These notions romanced anthropologists as well (e.g., see Lévi-Strauss' [1963] *Structural Anthropology*), who looked for the overall structure of a culture and the relations of its parts (see Note 27).

The area of most concern to us, that of cultural anthropology, has benefited from de Saussure and the adaptation of his ideas (Agar, 1994). Even such notables as Boas, Edward Sapir (Boas' student), and Benjamin Lee Whorf (Sapir's student) were taken with de Saussure's ideas, especially as they concerned the interplay of language and culture. Many cultural anthropologists, and a subgroup interested in cognitive anthropology, were set on determining how language could illuminate culture. As Agar points out, however, most, though not all, early anthropologists were interested in defining culture through its internally consistent dynamics, structures, and relations. Whorf was an exception, in more ways than one. Whorf tied language and culture together and examined the effects each had on the other. His work resulted in the well-known Sapir–Whorf hypothesis. Briefly stated, the Sapir–Whorf hypothesis holds that the language a person speaks influences how he or she perceives the world.[10]

Agar's (1994) critique of the early anthropologists, as well as Fairclough's (1989) critique of linguists, is basically that they separate the two systems, language and culture. For anthropologists, language was a research tool, a means to an end, with that end being culture. Linguists study language apart from its meaning (the Sausserian emphasis on *langue*). Agar, following the lead of Friedrich (1989), insists on marrying the two concepts in the study of what Friedrich terms *linguaculture* (p. 307). Linguaculture, for Friedrich, sidesteps the difficulties wrought by

the decades-long balancing act between "language and culture" ("how much of each?"), "language in culture" ("culture in language?"), and . . . recognize[s] that the real world and much of our ongoing research involve a common ground that is shared by both phenomema in question, and that the common ground is usually more important than what is not shared.

The linguacultural order, like language itself, is constituted by the interaction between and the integration along many variables, which should usually be seen as continuous. The linguacultural order has ethical, political, and other implications that variously jell, organize, and even motivate individuals and groups of individuals. . . .

Linguacultural ideology . . . is not about how our ideas of language are determined or at least defined by cultural values, but rather how the complementary processes by which values implicit in a language determine, define, and affect the culture, particularly its political economic dimensions (p. 307).

Still, and all their methodological differences aside, the focus of the study of sociolinguistics, discourse analysis, conversation analysis, and the ethnography of communication constitutes their commonality. Linguistics, anthropology, and sociology again share common boundaries that sometimes overlap, but are sometimes discreet. It is not always easy to separate their interrelated concepts into disciplines neatly.

Returning to anthropology per se and its development, I shall concern myself in this discussion with the fields of cultural anthropology and anthropological linguistics, although there may be some bleeding into closely related fields and subfields. Anthropology as a field and anthropologists as its practitioners and theorists have remained misunderstood and subject to romantization, especially by the American public. The educational anthropologist, Harry Wolcott (1992), noted how, in the popular mind, anyone conducting qualtiative research in general and ethnography in particular was conducting research "just like Margaret Mead" (p. 26). Romantic and popular notions of anthropology have proved to be both a boon and a bane to the modern anthropologist. The field as a whole and individuals within it have not gone clearly out of their way to dispel such popular myths. Wolcott and those who follow him, however, are clearly not "like Margaret Mead," to the degree and in the sense that modern astronomers are not like Galileo Galilei, nor are modern medical researchers like Louis Pasteur.[11]

Anthropology has both suffered and benefited from its checkered past. Early anthropological/ethnographic accounts were written by travelers (e.g., missionaries, priests, career military men, and colonial governors) (Pratt, 1992).[12] In this way, anthropologists, to their dismay, often become associated with the conquest and subjugation of other peoples and cultures (Said, 1979, 1989; Vidich & Lyman, 1994). Boas (Stocking, 1982) himself claimed to have "incontrovertible proof" that the United States during World War I employed spies in the guise of anthropologists. This, he wrote, will cause "every nation . . . [to] look with distrust upon the visiting foreign investigator who wants to do honest work, suspecting sinister designs" (pp. 336–337).

Anthropology as a field and anthropologists as individuals, however, have been endowed with the capacity, even encouraged, to be reflexive (i.e., to examine themselves, their aims, and their methods).[13] Thus, and not without a certain amount of angst, anthropology has been able to regenerate itself; indeed, the current era is fraught with such soul-searching regeneration and rehabilitation (Marcus, 1994). As noted this rehabilitation of anthropology has been occasioned by the reflexive nature of those within the field combined with the postcolonial assertiveness of previously subjugated peoples (see Ferguson et al, 1990) and the relatively recent effort in cultural interpretation to represent "the native's point of view" (Geertz, 1983).[14] Taken to its logical extreme, and aided by intellectual movements in other social sciences (Giddens, 1984),[15] this effort to represent the other's point of view, the so-called emic perspective, has produced what Marcus (1994) refers to as "messy texts" and what Clifford (1983) lauds as the polyvocality of some recent ethnographies.

To come to this point, however, anthropology has passed through many stages. Anthropology is generally considered to be concerned with culture (Zaharlick, 1992), although there are those who claim that anthropology is known equally well by the methods employed by its practitioners (Agar, 1994). Even the seemingly benign term culture, however, has evolved, sometimes peacefully, sometimes more violently. The foci of study of anthropologists, the methods by which these foci were studied, and the associated theories and concepts of anthropology have exhibited change and refinement. For example, Spindler and Spindler (1983a) commented on the historical movement within anthropology away from grand or comphrehensive treatments of culture (i.e., "studies of the whole" [p. 52]), to a "new" anthropology that is more concerned with "specific institutions, cultural settings, and contexts rather than American culture as a whole or a community as a window to a larger cultural whole" (p. 55).

Early ethnography was intent upon determining a developmental, comparative explanation of peoples and their evolution (Vidich & Lyman, 1994). This agenda grew from an interest in the origins of cultures and civilizations, and was influenced by social Darwinism. As primarily a "first world" project, this effort served to rationalize the first world's "natural" superiority, as other people were consigned to the category of "primitive." The "discovery" and study of diverse peoples around the globe caused serious problems for early fifteenth- and sixteenth-century theologists and cosmologists: "Such a profusion of values, cultures, and ways of life challenged the monopolistic claim on legitimacy and truth of the doctrines of Christianity" (Vidich & Lyman, 1994, p. 26). These issues emerged in the debates between Bartolome de Las Casas and Juan Gines de Sepulveda at the Council of Valladolid over how to consider the original inhabitants of the Americas. Gines de Sepulveda argued a position derived from Aristotle's doctrine of natural slavery, whereas de Las Casas argued for the native's human rights.

These issues, even though removed in time from our own, still echo in the schism between relativistic and universalistic values.[16] These same issues infuse epistemic claims in all the social sciences, especially in anthropology, and these issues emerge in discussions about "the insider's" and "the outsider's" points of view (i.e., the emic and etic perspectives, respectively, as mentioned earlier). The methodological question becomes, "How is it possible to understand the other when the other's values are not one's own?" (Vidich & Lyman, 1994, p. 26).

As already sketched briefly, the colonial period was characterized by travel writings and by the writings of missionaries, soldiers, colonial administrators, and traders. Even during this time and among this group there was disagreement as to the role the writers thought they should play, and the sides they thought they should take. Some clearly felt that colonization was in the best interests of the "natives" in that it facilitated their "advancement." Others believed indigenous peoples were best left alone. Many of this later group were Marxists (Vidich & Lyman, 1994, p. 27), who believed "that precapitalist natives would practice some form of primitive communism." Still others were uninterested in either of these two issues and turned their attention to questions of acculturation. They were interested in the processes by which some groups became acculturated rapidly and others retained aspects of their traditional culture or resisted acculturation completely.[17]

Informing the anthropological discussion of acculturation was the application of social Darwinism. To a great degree, acceptance of the idea of social Darwinism allowed anthropologists to set aside concerns about moral relativism and, instead, "permitted the assertion that there existed a spatiotemporal hierarchy of values" (Vidich & Lyman, 1994, p. 27). Vidich and Lyman assert that "these values were represented synchronically in the varieties of cultures to be found in the world, but might be classified diachronically according to the theory of developmental advance" (p. 27). This notion of a comparison of cultures along an evolutionary continuum is credited to Comte and his comparative method (Vidich & Lyman, pp. 27–28). Comte proposed that there were three stages of moral development: savagery, barbarism, and civilization: "The peoples assigned to these stages corresponded to a color-culture hierarchical diachrony and fitted the ethnocentric bias of the Occident" (p. 28).

According to Vidich and Lyman (1994), ethnologists' acceptance of this Comtean schema "vitiated the need to grant respect to these cultures on their own terms—that is, from the perspective of those who are its participants" (p. 28). This acceptance also made the work of the Eurocentric ethnographer much easier; all that was required was to classify cultures according to this existing scheme. Vast projects were undertaken to catalogue the world's cultures in this way, of which the most notable, if only for its size and scope, was the Human Relations Area Files, housed at Yale University (p. 28).

In the United States, early and continuous work of an anthropological nature was done with Native Americans. The newly arrived Europeans' attitude toward the inhabitants of the Americas was a curious mixture of religious co-optation (i.e., conversion through missionary work) and armed subjugation. Due to the inherent and continuous culture contact/culture clash between these peoples, there was ample opportunity to gain and disseminate information and misinformation about the Native Americans. Again, as in other parts of the world, initial contact was established by European-American missionaries, soldiers, and traders.

The missionaries, especially the early Calvinists and Puritans, experienced little success in converting the native population, due, primarily, to "having misjudged both the Indians' pliability and their resistance to an alien worldview" (Vidich & Lyman, 1994, p. 29). Still, these efforts continued. These contradictory attitudes, those of conversion and subjugation, influenced both U.S. policy toward native peoples and popular and academic dispositions toward them: "As one consequence, the several tribes of North American aborigines would remain outside the ethnographic, moral, and cultural pale of both European immigrant enclaves and settled white American communities" (p. 30).

The establishment of the Bureau of Indian affairs and, a short while later, the ethnology section of the Smithsonian Institution contributed, in their own ways, to the study of these indigenous others and to the advancement of anthropology as a field. An important development in this area was the organization of the U.S. Bureau of Ethnology and the Committee on the North-Western Tribes of Canada (Clifford, 1983). "The Committee's first agent in the field was the nineteen-year veteran missionary among the Ojibwa, E. F. Wilson" (p. 122). Before long, he was replaced by Franz Boas. Boas was trained as a physicist, but he identified himself as an anthropologist. His unique admixture of scientific training and dedication ushered in the era of scientific ethnography. Clifford quotes George Stocking on this point specifically. Wilson's replacement with Boas, wrote Stocking,

marks the beginning of an important phase in the development of British ethnographic method: the collection of data by academically trained natural scientists defining themselves as anthropologists, and involved also in the formulation and evaluation of anthropological theory (Stocking, 1992, p. 20).

Boas was soon joined by others who Stocking (p. 20) referred to as the "intermediate generation," including A. C. Haddon and Baldwin Spencer. This group was characterized by the development and intermingling of "the empirical and theoretical components of anthropological inquiry" (Clifford, 1983, p. 122).

The establishment of intensive participant-observation, however, is credited to Malinowski and his followers (Clifford, 1983; Stocking, 1992).[18] Participant-observation had an intense field experience as its hallmark that was characterized by the anthropologist's mastery of the vernacular, a year-long field study at a minimum, and an "undergoing [of] a personal learning experience comparable to an initiation" (Clifford, 1983, p. 122). The anthropological intent was to be able to speak as/for cultural insiders.

This anthropological intent, that of speaking as/for insiders, carried with it certain dangers, dilemmas, and demons. There was always the danger the anthropologist would "go native" (i.e., become *totally* enculturated in the other culture) and choose not to return to his or her primary culture. As an academician, the anthropologist's purpose is understood to be cultural translation, "making the strange familiar" (Erickson, 1984). That is, anthropologists were "professional strangers" (Agar, 1980), crossing borders and boundaries in an attempt to understand others, and then returning to the anthropologist's home culture to communicate (i.e, translate) what was learned. This hard-earned knowledge would be lost if the anthropologist was not to return. The failure to return is seen as a kind of betrayal to one's home culture, one's professional community, and one's professional duty.[19] In addition, one cannot overestimate the psychic costs incurred by anthropologists who freely suspend their own cultural norms, give up the security of their support networks, and immerse themselves in unfamiliar lifeways (Crapanzano, 1977; Estroff, 1981; Malinowski, 1967; Stoller, 1989). These were the risks to which Malinowski, Boas, and others exposed the field, even though they were willingly incurred by their followers, imbued with a certain amount of romanticism, and eventually assumed mythic proportions.

Malinowski's brand of fieldwork (i.e., a marriage of empirical and theoretical research) persists today; however, responding to changing world conditions (i.e., the collapse of the empires and of colonialism, coupled with the postmodern condition alluded to earlier), anthropology has evolved to include anthropological study of one's home culture as well as other, more "exotic" ones. This process has had tremendous benefit for the field of education (as well as for anthropologists), as will be shown.

Our knowledge of life in schools (e.g., Spindler, 1982) has benefited from the movement toward more focused anthropological study, the so-called new anthropology already mentioned; however, such knowledge has had its cost. Although some have heralded the movement in anthropology toward studies of practice (Ortner, 1984; Pelissier, 1991), there are those who remind us that it is often the case that studies of this type obfuscate the historical antecedents to current conditions and practices (Sahlins, 1981; Spindler & Spindler, 1983a; Zaharlick, 1992). To put it another way, it could be argued that synchronic studies of schooling (or whatever) may neglect the diachronic. Anthropology, especially, gains its power from comparative analysis (Spindler & Spindler, 1983a; Zaharlick, 1992); but that power is weakened if history, and with it historical change, is left out of the mix.

Doing the Anthropology of Schools

As a field, anthropology and education, or, as it is sometimes known, educational anthropology, is concerned with several areas: bilingual/bicultural education—including multicultural education—the culture of the classroom and school, cultural congruence and incongruence between home and school, modes of education and thought, research methods for the study of educational phenomena, and the teaching of anthropology (Pelissier, 1991).[20]

Roberts (1976, p. 3) adeptly drew the relevance of anthropology and education, one for the other, when she wrote:

The concept of culture when applied to education insists, then, on perceiving the learner as a complicated person living in a complex human environment who acquires through enculturation over the entire life span the total shared way of life of a given people. This is accomplished through a variety of socialization techniques that express relative solutions to universal needs of the human species within the constraints of the physical world.

The relevance of anthropology for education is particularly pronounced when speaking of the subfield of applied anthropology. Bohannan (1968) enumerated three areas in which anthropology could be of benefit to education, and these were listed at the opening of this chapter. In developing his last point (i.e., that of the application of anthropological field techniques by teachers) Bohannan draws several analogies between the ethnographer and the teacher. One of the most strikingly similar attributes anthropologists in the field share with teachers (and supervisors) is that each "must learn to work within an ascribed status, perhaps trying to change it a little, but more importantly, understanding the constrictions that it puts on your activities and your opportunity to learn" (p. 163). There have been numerous other adaptations and applications of ethnographic field methods and techniques for educators (i.e., teachers, supervisors, and administrators) (Fulginiti, 1986; Gearing & Hughes, 1975; Sitton, 1980; Sitton, Mehaffy, & Davis, 1983; Strahan, 1983; Wagner, 1990).

Early anthropologically informed studies of education include Henry's (1966) On Education,[21] Wax, Diamond, and Gearing's (1971) Anthropological Perspectives on Education, the early work of George and Louise Spindler at Stanford University (Spindler, 1955a, 1955b; Spindler & Spindler, 1983b), and that of Solon Kimball at Teachers College, Columbia University (Wolcott, 1988).

Even before there was interest in educational anthropology specifically, dyed-in-the-wool anthropologists attended to child-rearing practices in the U.S. and elsewhere. Studies such as Mead's (1928) Coming of Age in Samoa promoted a comparative perspective, comparing American civilization with other, "simpler," societies as one method of understanding U.S. educational practices (Eddy, 1987). Even Malinowski was concerned with the role education played in the lives of children in the United Kingdom, Africa, and elsewhere (Eddy, 1987; Roberts, 1976).

Building upon the work of its pioneers, "as a recognizable intellectual pursuit, anthropology and education made its real gains in the next generation" (Wolcott, 1988, p. 12). The educational anthropologists who made headway in the United States included Bohannan, Gearing, Kimball, the Spindlers, Tax, and the Waxes, as well as their intellectual progeny.[22]

Eddy (1987) posited two distinct epochs in the formation of the field of educational anthropology, although, others may no doubt be delimited. She distinguished the "formative years," 1925–1954, from the years of "institutionalization and specialization," 1955 to the (then) present. For Eddy, the formative years of educational anthropology were characterized by an increased interest in anthropology, both among the general U.S. population and government and private funding agencies. During this time, anthropology took root in U.S. universities, with an expansion of the number of departments of anthropology and "the growth of an interdisciplinary movement in the social sciences" (p. 7). In its early years, anthropology was often incorporated with sociology in the creation of new departments. As Eddy notes, "at this time, anthropology was a young science, and those who entered it typically came by a roundabout way of professional training and experience in other fields" (p. 8); for example, note the careers of Malinowski, Boas, Bateson, and many other early anthropologists. In summing up the formative years, Eddy noted that they "occurred within the context of disciplinary developments in theory and research methodology that advanced anthropological studies of contemporary peoples in a rapidly changing world" (p. 9).

The demarcation between the formative years and the years of the "institutionalization and specialization" of educational anthropology is marked for Eddy (1987) by the Stanford Conference of 1954. Spindler, who was the host, assembled "twenty-two anthropologists and educationists" (Spindler, 1984, p. 3), including Kroeber, Mead, and Henry, for a 4-day conference "centering on how anthropology and education might be beneficial to each other" (p. 3). Spindler himself remarked how "many seem to regard this conference as the beginning of educational anthropology" (p. 3). The papers presented and much of the ensuing dialogue are reported in Education and Anthropology (Spindler, 1955a).

Spindler remarks on four of the conference themes he found relevant: "the search for a philosophical . . . [and] theoretical articulation of education and anthropology"; "the necessity for sociocultural contextualization of the educative process"; "the relation of education to 'culturally phrased' phases of the life cycle"; and "the nature of intercultural understanding and learning" (1984, p. 4). He measured the contributions in each of these areas made by conference participants against the contributions which have been made since. For each of these areas, Spindler generally recommended that more attention be paid by researchers and theorists. The nostalgic tenor of his musings are apparent: "I miss discussions such as [Jules] Henry's in the current educational anthropology literature" (p. 7).

Eddy (1987) characterizes the ensuing years (i.e., "1955 to the [then] present") as years in which anthropology and its subdiscipline, educational anthropology, became institutionalized: "Dozens of departments [of anthropology] were founded where none had existed before or an anthropology severed joint departmental relationships with sociology" (p. 15). The expansion and refinement of "the areal and theoretical interests of anthropologists" was also characteristic of this period:

No longer dominated by the models of structural-functionalism introduced by Malinowski and Radcliffe-Brown and the culture–personality paradigms of Mead and others, contemporary sociocultural anthropology is noteworthy for theoretical diversity, eclecticism, and debate (p. 16).

Eddy (1987) also chronicled the development of anthropologically informed curricula and curriculum materials. Some of these projects included National Science Foundation support for the Anthropology Curriculum Study Project (ACSP), the Education Development Center's *Man: A Course of Study*, the University of Minnesota's Project Social Studies, the Teacher Resources in Urban Education Project (Project TRUE), and the Culture of Schools program, transferred after a year-and-a-half to the American Anthropological Association, put under the direction of Fred Gearing, and renamed the Program in Anthropology and Education (pp. 18–19).

Interest in anthropology and education sustains a professional academic journal, *Anthropology and Education Quarterly* (established in 1977), which is the organ of a professional organization of educational anthropologists, the Council on Anthropology and Education (CAE), a section of the American Anthropological Association established in 1968. Eddy (1987) cites the parallels between the CAE, its tenets, and those of earlier generations of anthropologists. First, she states, is a concern with cross-cultural and comparative studies of contemporary peoples. Second, is the consideration of the United States as a multicultural society. Third, is "reaffirmation . . . that anthropology should be concerned with child development and learning in all the various ways and environments in which they occur" (p. 20). Fourth, is the insistence that anthropologically informed research has implications for educational policy. Finally, the recognition that education occurs within contexts of "sweeping cultural, social, political, economic, and technological change" (p. 20).

This list sums up the mission of educational anthropologists, and their accomplishments to date are also catalogued in Eddy's (1987) essay. They include strides made in understanding the complex cognitive and sociolinguistic processes in classrooms and schools, the gradual addition of ethnographic methods among the canons of educational research, attention to education in developing countries, and an increase of educational anthropologists employed in nonacademic positions (p. 21). Another rich area of anthropological research, and one that will not be covered in any depth here, even though it is highly pertinent to supervisors, is the area of teacher culture (Feiman-Nemser & Floden, 1986).[23]

The degree of agreement to be found in the writings of Eddy (1987) and Pelissier (1991) is remarkable. The noticeable differences are remarkable also. Pelissier takes a more conceptual, as opposed to chronological, survey of the field and its developments. Pelissier focuses upon modes of thought, cross-cultural and everyday cognition, socialization, communication style, and modes of education (p. 76).[24] Embedded within Pelissier's discussion is the theme of change. Cultural processes are no longer viewed as one-way phenomena, with the child or novice as a passive recipient. Anthropology and educational anthropology have provided us with an interactional understanding of cultural processes (e.g., Dorr-Bremme, 1990; McDermott, 1977; McDermott & Roth, 1978; Mehan, 1979, 1980; Mehan & Griffin, 1980; Schieffelin & Ochs, 1986). Interactional perspectives permit a view of culture that runs counter to previous structural, deterministic views. The actor is no longer viewed as hapless victim to the tyranny of a static, dark, oppressive culture. In the interactional view, actors and system interact in dynamic fashion, with one influencing the other.

The interactional view in anthropology has several important consequences for our thinking about culture, cognition, change, individuality, and agency (Ortner, 1984).[25] Interactional approaches, together with research approaches in language socialization (e.g., Schieffelin & Ochs, 1986) that focus on the active participation of the child, novice, or other in the processes studied, "emphasize a dialectic between agency and structure" (Pelissier, 1991, p. 84). Although the interactional approach may have been open to criticism due to its excesses (e.g., privileging the individual agent over the larger society, culture, or structure), developments in anthropology and sociology (as will be discussed shortly) have reconciled the extreme positions.[26] These reconciliations are discussed by Ortner under the terms of practice, practice theory, action, and praxis (p. 127).

The essential questions addressed by an action approach, for Ortner (1984), include those of understanding where "'the system' comes from—how it is produced and reproduced, and how it may have changed in the past or be changed in the future" (p. 146). Other foci of the action orientation in anthropology, and two that have particular relevance for education, are how the system shapes practice and how practice shapes the system (Ortner, 1984). Illumination of these two essential questions regarding schools has profound implications for teachers, supervisors, administrators, and educational policy makers. I shall return to a more detailed discussion of the specific applications and relevancies of anthropology to supervision after a brief sketch of the history of sociology and the sociology of education.

SOCIOLOGY AND ITS DEVELOPMENT

Whereas anthropology had as its early mission the explication of the Other, the "primitive," the exotic, via theoretical treatments concerned with culture, sociology, which was founded in industrialized and industrializing European nations, concerned itself with the effects of industry on society and the individuals constitutive of those societies. "Culture concerns the *way of life* of the members of a given society, *society* refers to the *system of interrelationships* that connects together the individuals who share a common culture" (Giddens, 1991, p. 35).[27] Vidich and Lyman (1994, p. 23) state the mission of sociology:

[T]he analysis and understanding of the patterned conduct and social processes of society, and of the bases in values and attitudes on which individual and collective participation in social life rests.

Fine (1992, p. 88), however, noted:

[T]he core questions of sociological discourse involve how social order is possible, how change occurs, how conflict is mediated, the nature of organized human activity, and the melding of agency and structure.

Sociology covers such broad topics as demography, community, organization, and change. Sociology has its roots in Comtean empiricism (Giddens, 1991; Vidich & Lyman, 1994), and was heavily influenced by social Darwinsim, attributed to the sociologist Herbert Spencer (1820–1903), who coined the phrase "survival of the fittest" (Giddens, p. 38). It was Aguste Comte (1789–1857) who coined the term *sociology* (Giddens, p. 847). Sociology's later-day adherents included Emile Durkheim (1858–1917), Georg Simmel (1858–1918), Max Weber (1864–1920), and Karl Marx (1818–1883), each of whom has left his mark on the field.[28] Early sociological treatises were theoretical in nature. Many of the sociologists mentioned were concerned with the changes taking place in nineteenth-century industrializing societies (e.g., primarily Europe and the United States). Durkheim, Weber, and Marx especially were concerned with the effects of industrialization; they wrote of such changes in terms of class, labor, bureaucratization, and capital.

In the United States, sociology was advanced by two theorists especially, George Herbert Mead (1863–1931) and Talcott Parsons (1902–1979), although it was heavily influenced by the American pragmatist movement, itself lead by William James. It is interesting that these two American sociologists spawned quite distinct branches of American sociology. Parsons is credited with reviving the social evolution argument, which had been neglected since the heyday of the social Darwinists (Vidich & Lyman, 1994, p. 29). Parsons argued for four evolutionary universals found in even the simplest action systems: religion, communication through language, kinship, and technology. Evolution toward more complexity was seen as a functional adaptation. Parsons' writings, especially those written during the apex of the Cold War between the United States and Soviet Russia, contributed to the sense that the United States had "arrived at the highest stage of societal development" and fostered the idea that

economic progress was inherent in industrialization and that nation building coincided with capitalism, the gradual extension of democratization, and the orderly provision of individual rights. . . . Despite the pointed criticisms of the comparative method that would continue to be offered by . . . [at least one] school of sociohistorical thought . . . a Comtean outlook survived within sociology in the work of Talcott Parsons and his macrosociological epigoni (p. 29).

This movement in sociology really only ended with the fall of the Soviet Union and the end of the Cold War, although there were those who feared the end of history itself (Fukuyama, 1992). Since that time, there has been increased interest in "post" movements (e.g., postmodernism, postcapitalism, postindustrialism, poststructuralism).

Because it was involved with macrosociological phenomena, Parsons' type of sociology benefited from quantitative and theoretical analyses. Parsons' name is associated with the school of thought referred to a functionalism, a mantle he inherited from Comte and Durkheim (Giddens, 1991, p. 851).[29] Mead, on the other hand, contributed to a branch of American sociology concerned more with microsociological and qualitative analyses. Along with Herbert Blumer (1937, 1969, 1972), Mead prepared the way for the introduction and development of the concept of symbolic interactionism, which, in turn, produced several theoretical/methodological branches of its own, most notably those of ethnomethodology and conversation analysis.[30]

Denzin (1992, p. xiv) allows that symbolic interactionism:

is that unique American sociological and social psychological perspective that traces its roots to the early American pragmatists James, Dewey, Peirce, and Mead. It has been called the loyal opposition in American sociology . . . the most sociological of social psychologies. . . . In its most canonical form . . . it rests on three assumptions: first, that "human beings act toward things on the basis of the meanings that the things have for them" [Blumer, 1969, p. 2] . . . second, that the meanings of things arise out of the process of social interaction; and third, that meanings are modified through an interpretative process which involves self-reflective individuals symbolically interacting with one another.

Certain sociological methods were developed contemporaneously alongside this new theoretical perspective. Denzin (1992, p. xv) lists a few that have been influenced by, and in turn influenced, symbolic interactionism: The "new" ethnography, postmodern ethnography, "structural, articulative, semiotic, and practical" ethnography, grounded theory, the biographical, life history method, the performance science, feminist ethnography, creative interviewing, conversational analysis, and "the more traditional interviewing, fieldwork, and participant observation practices" are some sociological methods associated with symbolic interactionism, specifically, and with more qualitatively-based sociology generally.

A clear break with traditional sociological methods is usually traced to the so-called Chicago School of fieldwork (Adler & Adler, 1987, pp. 8–20). Adler and Adler attribute this revolution in sociological research technique to Robert Park and Ernest Burgess, operating out of the University of Chicago's Department of Sociology in the 1920s.[31] These initiators stressed to their students "the importance of using the city of Chicago as a laboratory to study human nature and society" (p. 9), and the importance of seeking the subjective point of view of those whom they studied "by striving for empathy and an imaginative participation in the lives of others."

While it was not the vogue at the time to write explicitly about the methods used in conducting a particular study, enough information can now be gleaned to ascertain that Anderson's *The Hobo* (1923), Cressey's *The Taxi Dance Hall* (1932), Thrasher's *The Gang* (1927), and Landesco's *Organized Crime in Chicago* (1929), among others, involved the use of those naturalistic field methods that would later be defined more formally as participant observation. These include prior membership, participation in the group's activities, using covert roles, consciously attempting to penetrate fronts, cross-checking accounts, and generally hanging out (Adler & Adler, 1987, p. 9).

The University of Chicago Department of Sociology's national preeminence in fieldwork has since ebbed and flowed. Park retired from Chicago in the early 1930s and Burgess became somewhat inactive (Adler & Adler, 1987). Other universities, most notably Columbia and Harvard, set the standard of sociological research. Talcott Parsons was at Harvard. The field turned to public opinion polling and survey research, more deeply rooted in the quantitative research paradigm.

During the postwar period, however, a second generation of Chicago fieldworkers emerged. This second generation is linked to such people as Herbert Blumer, Everett Hughes, William Lloyd Warner, Anselm Strauss, David Reisman, Howard Becker, and Erving Goffman. The second generation of Chicago fieldworkers is credited with developing and codifying the methods of participant observation (Adler & Adler, 1987).[32] Adler and Adler believe that

the participant observation fieldwork conducted and codified by this second generation of Chicagoans has persisted in influence to the present day. Most of the current fieldwork texts present the practice and philosophy advocated by these individuals, and it has come to stand as the "classical," or "Chicago School" tradition in field research (p. 11).

Other permutations of this approach have since appeared. Adler and Adler (p. 20) cite what they refer to as the "California Sociologies of Everyday Life" strand of fieldwork: a more existential approach, built upon the work of the early Greek Sophist, Thrasymachus, and the more recent existential philosophies of Martin Heidegger, Jean-Paul Sartre, Maurice Merleau-Ponty, the phenomenology of Edmund Husserl, and the hermeneutics of Wilhem Dilthey.

Another variation of sociology is that which has come to be known as the "Iowa School" of symbolic interactionism and, later, the New Iowa School. These movements, based on the work of Manford Kuhn, have come to reconceptualize sociological (and Meadean) terms such as *self, other, role-taking,* and so on, which are then

fitted to a processual theory of sociation (Simmel), which stresses temporality (shared pasts, projected futures), emotionality, and power. Simmel, Mead, Blumer, Goffman, Stone, and Strauss are reworked to fit an interactionist social psychology (Denzin, 1992, p. 15).

Doing the Sociology of Education

In the introduction to their book, *How Schools Work: A Sociological Analysis of Education*, Bennett and LeCompte (1990) point to the major sociological theories of education, subsumed under two umbrella categories. These larger categories are comprised of the social transmission theories and the social transformation theories. For Bennett and LeCompte, the social transmission theories include those of functionalism, structural functionalism, conflict theory, and reproduction theory. The social transformation theory category includes those of interpretive theory and critical social theory.

Functionalism and structuralism have been sketched earlier in the treatment of their development and influence in anthropology and I shall not deal with them here. Bennett and LeCompte's (1990) treatment of structural functionalism, however, warrants some discussion. According to these authors, structural functionalists, "believe that social structures must function effectively and in cooperation with others in order for societal health to be maintained" (p. 5). This type of sociologist also holds that any structure found in a society must have some function that probably serves the system as a whole: "Functionalists view educational systems as one of the *structures* which carry out the *function* of transmission of attitudes, values, skills and norms from one generation to the next" (p. 6). Structural functionalists believe that a naturally healthy system is in equilibrium or stasis. According to this view, then, healthy systems avoid conflict, and gradual change is preferred.

The proponents of conflict theory include Marx and Simmel, among others (Bennett & LeCompte, 1990). These theorists held that the organization of society depended upon its economic system and patterns of ownership of property. These patterns introduce conflict when there is a differential distribution of resources. As social institutions, schools are then seen as sites where this conflict and contestation get played out.

Related to, yet distinct from, conflict theory is the other major transmission theory: reproduction theory (Bennett & LeCompte, 1990). If one accepts that resources are indeed differentially distributed, then how do they come to be so? Are there systems and processes in place to guarantee that they remain so? In American education, especially, these questions speak to the heart of the Horatio Alger myth. Is an individual solely responsible for his or her destiny, or are there social forces that determine one's life chances? Social reproduction theorists and researchers believe that society's structures, inequalities and all, reproduce themselves intergenerationally. These theories and the sociological issues involved fuel and inform the current debate concerning agency and structure (discussed more at length shortly).

Much of the work on educational inequality and the relation of those inequalities to one's life chances was conducted by sociologists. In the United States, the Coleman study

(Coleman, 1966; Coleman, Hoffer, & Kilgore, 1982) illuminated the inequalities fostered by American education. Other theoreticians, particularly Marxists and neo-Marxists, further developed the ideas of inequitable social reproduction (Bourdieu & Passeron, 1977; Bowles & Gintis, 1976; Giroux, 1981, 1983; Willis, 1981b).[34]

It was Pierre Bourdieu (1986, 1988) who developed and popularized the concept of cultural capital. Like other forms of capital wealth, cultural capital, can be transmitted from generation to generation. This represents one of the (many) processes through which inequalities are perpetuated.[34] Giddens (1991, pp. 526–528) takes Paul Willis' (1981b) book, *Learning to Labor: How Working Class Kids Get Working Class Jobs,* as representative of empirical work in social reproduction theory, although Willis (1981a) himself situates it in the area of cultural production.[35] Willis (1981a, 1981b) contributes to our understanding of how schools contribute to the social reproduction of the relationships among social classes, often subtly so. "Education mystifies itself," Willis (1981a, p. 54) reminds us. This is to say that it often works in insidious ways. Schools and education and industry policy makers do not necessarily set out to produce so many blue collar workers, so many middle managers, so many technocrats, and so many owners. Still, argue the reproduction theorists, that is the result. Schools stratify and sort as much as they educate and liberate. This process is complex, however, and schools are only one factor in the equation. Other social institutions and processes contribute to social inequalities. Interactional researchers, however, have often been unable or unwilling to examine other than local phenomena, which is a point to which I shall return in the conclusion. Herein lie indications of a major point of contention among sociologists: What is to be the level of analysis?

Hargreaves (1985) discussed this very issue in terms of the macro/micro debate, although there has been an increasing interest in "mesodomain analysis" (Hall, 1991). The issue under discussion also influences the theoretical debates within sociology. For example, many sociologists (and anthropologists, too) believe part of their mission should be to elaborate or build some grand theory (/theories) to explain social phenomena. Others question such "totalizing attempts of sociology" (Craib, 1992, p. 7).

Interpretive and critical theory, the last of Bennett and LeCompte's (1991) theoretical approaches to the sociology of education, together comprise the social transformation theories. These authors distinguish the interpretive theories as being derived from phenomenology, ethnomethodology, and symbolic interaction, and they cite the work of Cicourel (1964), Garfinkel (1967), and Blumer (1969) as having contributed to its development. In this regard, interpretive theory is strikingly similar to that cast by Pelissier (1991) as the interactional branch of anthropology. The distinction, aside from the obvious one that the first is situated in sociology and the second in anthropology, is that the interpretivists' focus on the social construction of meaning in social interactions. Another strikingly similar field to that of interactional anthropology is the micropolitical strand within sociology (e.g., Ball, 1987; Blase, 1991; Schempp, Sparkes, & Templin, 1994).

The micropolitical perspective is informed by symbolic interactionism and concerns itself with such sociological constructs as power and control. Although filling a long-neglected void in sociology, the micropolitical and other interactionist perspectives have themselves been the target of criticism (Reynolds, 1987). Even those who write in the field have recognized and attempted to address the perceived limitations of the interactionist and micropolitical approaches. Schempp, Sparkes, and Templin (1994) note how the micropolitical perspective ignores "larger structural issues" (p. 449). Reynolds, citing other critics, notes how interactionist approaches tend to be ahistorical, noneconomic, embued with "certain philosophical and ideological biases" (p. 135), "culturally and temporally limited" (p. 136) to modern societies and their personality types, lacking in "a proper appreciation of the role of social power in human affairs" (p. 136), "far too quaint and/or exotic" in their "portrait[s] of social reality" (p. 136), and that they either ignore or have "an improper understanding of both social organization and social structure" (p. 136). Other authors in the field have moved to rectify these shortcomings of the interactionist approach (Fine, 1992; Hall, 1991). These efforts have lead Fine to speak of newer interactionist approaches as "synthetic," a term with positive connotations for him in this regard.

A milestone in the development of the interpretivist school of sociology of education was the advent of the "new sociology of education" (Young, 1971). The focus of the new sociology of education was on classroom interactions, the analytic categories and concepts used by educators, and sociological studies of curriculum, including questions of the sociology of knowledge. Interpretive sociology of education can be distinguished from critical theory in that interpretivists focus more on microaspects while critical theorists attempt to link micro- and macro-levels of analysis. Another distinction is that critical theorists place an emphasis on the agency of the individual, the power of individuals to transform oppressive social structures and processes (Bennett & LeCompte, p. 21). Once more, we see the differential weighting put on either micro- or macro-levels of analysis by these various schools and their proponents; and the issue of structure and agency is again raised.

Notable critical theorists working in U.S. education today include Michael Apple, Henry Giroux, Joe Kincheloe, Peter McLaren, and Ira Shor, although this list is not exhaustive. Critical theory, a term coined by Max Horkheimer, has benefited from the work of the Frankfurt School, especially Horkheimer, Theodor Adorno, and Herbert Marcuse, Antonio Gramsci, and Paulo Freire (Bennett & LeCompte, 1991, pp. 24–26). Critical theorists are concerned with social inequities and their production/reproduction. They concentrate on issues of class, gender, and race, and, in education, how schools contribute to the disempowerment and marginalization of certain groups and individuals. Although critical theory was originally grounded in a Marxist analysis of society, its influence and its explanatory power have gained it adherents who would not refer to themselves as Marxist, or even neo-Marxist.

Power is a fundamental theme of critical theory, especially the asymmetries of power, whether interactional or systemic. For example, Apple (1986) has contributed to thinking on the deskilling of teachers, a process whereby teachers are distanced from the conceptualization of curriculum. So-called teacher-proof curricula and materials are a result of this essentially disempowering process, although there are also other, more insidious results, such as alienation and resistance. Critical theorists stress the active role teachers must take as transformative intellectuals in addressing the injustices of society and in the empowerment of students.

Interpretivists methodologically rely heavily upon the research methods of anthropology and qualitative research in general, grounding their work in phenomenology and symbolic interactionism. Critical theorists do likewise, although out of concern for empowerment they are more likely to engage in collaborative or participatory action research (Carr & Kemmis, 1986; Habermas, 1973; Hall, 1984; Kincheloe, 1991; Latapí, 1988, e.g.). Not all collaborative action research, however, has social justice as an agenda (e.g., see Glickman, 1990; Sagor, 1992).

Newer forms of ethnography have begun to emerge (Marcus, 1994; Robinson, 1995; Thomas, 1993). One of these, critical ethnography (Thomas, 1993), weds the critical theorist's political and emancipatory agenda with a strong grounding in qualitative sociology. Anthropology also has its brand of critical ethnography (Herzfeld, 1987). These methodological developments (e.g., Marcus' "messy texts," Robinson's "ethnography of empowerment," and Thomas' "critical ethnography") reinforce the break qualitative sociologists have made with their positivist predecessors. These methods of doing social science research reiterate the need for the subject's (/subjective) point of view. At the same time, and adding fuel to the flame, such canons of positivistic and experimental research as objectivity (Lather, 1986b), generalizability (Firestone, 1993), and validity (Lather, 1986a; Wolcott, 1990) have come under fire from various quarters.

Both social transmission and transformation theories have, theoretically, given way to new or more refined theories. Poststructuralism has succeeded structural-functionalism (e.g., Cherryholmes, 1988). A new dialogue on the politics of position has offered a critique of critical theory (Burbules & Rice, 1991; Ellsworth, 1989; Minh-ha, 1986-1987; Shilling, 1991), and even questioned the traditional sociological categories of race, class, and gender as being essentialist and normalizing. For example, Shilling's work on *embodiment*, which extends Bourdieu's (1986, 1988) notions of *habitus* and cultural capital, relocates the physical body as a site for many of the social processes discussed by other social theorists. Processes such as accumulation and conversion of (embodied) capital, the forces of social production and reproduction, and the processes of oppression and resistance, for Shilling, are centered on and concerned with the body. Shilling's conceptualization of the body allows for much more complex analyses than the traditional sociological categories of race, class, and gender permit.

Evolution of the theoretical precepts of sociology are often prompted by critique. For example, critical theory itself has been criticized, as I have shown earlier, for an oversimplistic representation of asymmetrical power relationships (Bennett & LeCompte, 1990). Bennett and LeCompte have suggested that

the emancipation advocated by critical theorists is predicated upon Western and European notions of power and group relations. Imposing this view on people who are not part of that tradition is no less authoritarian, say the critics, than other kinds of oppression (p. 30).

Others also have begun to question both critical and feminist discourse (Gore, 1993).

It is usual, and in response to criticism, for another candidate theory with greater or truer explanatory power to be advanced. One candidate with potential to resolve the theoretical dilemmas currently operant in sociology is Giddens' (1984) formulation of structuration (i.e., "the structuring of social relations across time and space" [p. 376], although Giddens himself, and his theories, are also subject to critique (Cohen, 1989, 1991; Craib, 1992).[36]

Attention to structuration reconciles the interactional and structural perspectives while it resolves the micro/macro dichotomization of research foci and units of analysis. The concept of structuration is not overly deterministic, and it allows for agency in the processes whereby patterned historical human interactions structure those selfsame interactions and future ones. The applicability of this theory to education, educational institutions, and the sociology of education has already been demonstrated (Shilling, 1992).

Sociology has benefited from both evolution brought on by critique as well as from the rethinking and renewed application of more traditional sociological concepts and their application within the (post)modern context. A case in point is Deegan's reworking (1989) of Goffman's (1959) and Turner's (1974) dramaturgical analyses of everyday life. Another case in point is Platt's sociology of sociology (1976). Each of these bodies of work is reflexive. In the first instance, they combine sociological and anthropological concepts, and adjust them to suit the times, extending them in novel ways. In the second instance, they illuminate the practices of sociology itself.

With the development of anthropology, anthropology of education, sociology, and the sociology of education, now outlined, I will turn to discussion of the application of these fields in supervision.

ANTHROPOLOGY AND SOCIOLOGY IN SUPERVISION

The Role of Anthropology and Sociology in the Development of Supervision Theory

Education benefits from all the human sciences. To paraphrase Giddens, one might say that education is parasitical upon the human sciences. Supervision is as well. Several chapters in this handbook attest to the fact that areas such as psychology (see Chap. 7), philosophy (see Chap. 8), political science (see Chap. 9) and ethics (see Chap. 40) inform the field of supervision. Each area, however, fills a particular niche. The same can be said of anthropology and sociology. As disciplines concerned with human interaction, however, human communion and communities, along with human meaning making, in all their multifaceted and wonderously complex instantiations across the globe, indeed as disciplines concerned with the human condition writ large, anthropology and sociology have the potential to make profound impacts upon both the theory and practice of supervision and, by implication, upon the practice of schooling and the future life-worlds of students.

Supervision authors have glimpsed the potential of anthropology and sociology and have worked to incorporate concepts from these fields into their work. Oliva (1993, p. 22) lists sociology and communication theory among the foundations of supervision. Lucio and McNeil (1969, p. xi) suggest that supervision is informed by phenomenological views of individual behavior, although they conceive of this as a psychological construct, along with theories of knowledge, group dynamics, and social anthropology, as well as such theories of change, role, oganizations, and communications.

Writing around the edge of supervision (i.e., in the area of educational/instructional leadership), authors like Sergiovanni (1984) and Deal (1987) delve into the elusive concept of "school culture" and how a supervisor or other administrator might change it.[37] Deal defines culture as "the way we do things around here" (p. 5). Sergiovanni also considers one of the functions of the cultural leader to be to explain "the way things operate around here" (p. 9).

At an elementary level, these theoretical treatments serve to alert the reader to the existence and gross effects of culture. Such treatments of culture, however, run the risk of being ill-conceived and perhaps even erroneous.[38] For instance, "the way we do things around here" privileges the behavioral aspects of human existence and may get confused with distinct and sociologically-derived concepts such as role. "The way we do things around here" may scratch the surface of such cultural enactments as ritual, although there is much more to even that phenomenon than the observable behaviors. "The way we do things around here," however, ignores other important anthropological concepts and constructs. It ignores the ideational (i.e., the meaning) behind the act. For instance, an early and oft-cited definition of culture is Goodenough's (1957, p. 167):

A society's culture consists of whatever it is one has to know or believe in order to operate in a manner acceptable to its members, and do so in any role that they accept for any one of themselves.

Less often cited, however, Goodenough continues:

By this definition, we should note that culture is not a material phenomenon; it does not consist of things, people, behavior, or emotions. It is rather an organization of these things. It is the forms of things that people have in mind, their models for perceiving, relating, and otherwise interpreting them.

There is another, hidden danger in facile applications of culture and other anthropological concepts (see Note 36). One problem with the undertheorization of the concept of culture, for example, is that it reinforces naive and stereotypical understandings and applications. Readers come to believe they understand culture and its effects in schools, for

example, and delve no further, whether into the extensive anthropologically-informed literature or in further contemplation of doing their own research. If they do, then the utility of such research becomes suspect when based on such flimsy foundations.

Ethnography, anthropology, and sociology stand to better inform us of educational processes and their impacts, but we must guard against simply reinforcing commonsense, taken-for-granted, and often mistaken notions if we are to realize the potential of those endeavors. Zaharlick (1992) argues the point similarly. In referring to a study by Ogbu (1974), she reasons how:

There are a number of other ways in which the understandings resulting from ethnographic research can contribute to the improvement of educational and school practice. . . . Ogbu's study pointed out how people who live and work in close proximity often understand very little about even the most basic conditions of each other's lives. Lacking this information, they often rely on stereotypes and "common sense" assessments of the other's basic living conditions. These stereotypes in turn make it all the more difficult for people to accept information that might contribute to better understanding. Ethnography, in this case, was able to reveal how inadequate and erroneous most of these "common sense" views were and provide a basis for the development of better informed educational policies (p. 123).

Other supervision authors have contributed more to our understanding of culture and the role culture plays in schools and in supervision. For example, Glatthorn (1990) employs culture in his discussion of organizational leadership and change. Even though his definition of culture (p. 58) tends toward the ambiguous, he does recognize the problematic nature of the term and attempts a clarification. Leaning on the work of Firestone and Wilson (1983), Glatthorn recounts three key aspects of the content of culture (i.e., the belief system, the norms, and the traditions) and four major ways content is made manifest: through the language of members, the rituals and ceremonies, the myths and folklore, and the icons and symbols used. He even touches upon, if only briefly, the issue of cultural transmission in his discussion. There is finally a glimmer here of a more complex understanding and application of anthropologically-derived terms and concepts to supervision/instructional leadership.

Sergiovanni and Starratt (1993) have refined the concept of culture and its applicability for supervision even further. For instance, they make an important distinction between school climate and school culture:

[T]he climate metaphor leads one to think more about the interpersonal life in schools. Culture leads one deeper into the life of the school, into the tacit world of beliefs and norms, into the realm of meaning and significance (p. 97).

They also distinguish levels of culture. For them, the levels of culture include: (1) the artificats of culture, what people say, how people behave, and how things look; (2) the perspectives of members, the shared rules and norms, definitions of situations, and what constitutes acceptable behavior;

(3) the level of values; and (4) assumptions.[39] An important contribution Sergiovanni and Starratt have made in the discussion of school culture is in the consideration of the historical aspects of culture. They encourage us to consider, "How does a school's past live in the present?" (p. 94).

Other authors have contributed to the evolution of our understanding of the interplay between anthropology and supervision (Bowers & Flinders, 1990, 1991; Flinders, 1991; Gearing & Hughes, 1975; Kilbourn, 1984; Waite, 1992b, 1995). Although I eschew a formal definition of culture other than that of "a unified system of meaning that people ascribe to their lives, both personal and professional" (Waite, 1992b, p. 437, fn. 2), I have sketched the outline of a supervisor culture through examination of the extant literature *and* practitioners' voices. I posited then that supervisor culture includes belief in individualization, professional autonomy, which resulted in a norm of noninterruption of the lesson observed, and avoidance of a direct style of communication with teachers when in conference, although each of these norms may be violated if the warrant to do so is strong enough. I went on to list the possible warrants that may cause supervisors to violate the norms mentioned. These include concern for the (student) teacher, concern for the students (i.e., for their physical and psychological well-being), the supervisor's philosophical orientation, and perceived time pressures.

Gearing and Hughes (1975) are concerned primarily with observation, and how teachers, principals, and supervisors may get at the routines that occur in classrooms and staff rooms: "If you are a principal or supervisor, some . . . array of routines will become evident [through doing ethnography] in your staff meetings and workshops" (pp. 21–22). As to the necessity of doing ethnography for the educator, Gearings and Hughes wrote:

[I]f you do ethnography, an important fact about the behaviors in your place [of work] will be revealed: namely, that virtually all of those seemingly diverse behaviors are bits and pieces of certain well-established routines which regularly unfold in your place (p. 19).

This is an excellent example of the "new anthropology" (Spindler & Spindler, 1983), which is no longer quite so new, that takes interactional or microcultural processes as its focus. I have similarly suggested (Waite, 1995) a situationally contexted approach to supervision in which the supervisor and the teacher analyze the numerous contexts and processes in which they and the students take part. This is done, first, in order to understand them, and, second, to affect them.

Likewise, Kilbourn (1984) perceives numerous and viable similarities between clincial supervision and ethnographic research. These similarities include the fact that "clinical supervision and ethnographic research . . . focus . . . on particular classroom events and the process of clincial supervision capitalizes on the kind of knowledge obtained in ethnographic studies" (p. 173).

Bowers and Flinders (1990, 1991; Flinders, 1991) examine the ideational aspects of school culture and supervisor culture much more deeply. They are especially concerned with "metaphor, nonverbal communication, the teacher's gatekeeping role, framing, gender-specific uses of humor, and the privileging of written over spoken language" as aspects of "the hidden cultural patterns of classroom teaching" (Bowers & Flinders, 1990, p. 192). In their treatise, they expose some of the assumptions of supervision, such as the assumption that "supervision is based on forms of rationality divorced from tradition and culture" (p. 195). In their discussion of "supervision as technology" they comment on the taken-for-granted assumption that "supervision . . . is only a tool or method for engineering social change" (p. 195), claiming that such beliefs exhibit a "technicist orientation."

These authors express a concern with the supervisor's awareness or lack of awareness of how supervision "techniques 'use' them [the supervisors] at the same time as they use the techniques" (Bowers & Flinders, 1990, p. 196). The assumption of supervisors and certain models of supervision is that "actual teaching behavior is assumed to exist independent of the supervisor, out there waiting to be discovered" (p. 197). They question the objectivity of supervisors' observations (see also Waite, 1995), although their major concern is how assumptions "hide the sociocultural and political nature of professionalism by limiting the supervisor's role to that of a technician" (p. 198). "If we accept an image of supervisors that denies their cultural embeddedness," they suggest, "then observation techniques operate foremost as a set of blinders; that is, they restrict rather than enhance perception" (p. 198). Bowers and Flinders are concerned with the assumptions that make of the supervisor a technician and put out of focus her or his cultural embeddedness, and not with observation per se. They recommend that supervision become a process of inquiry, qualtitative inquiry to be specific, which is a topic to which I shall return in the conclusion of this chapter, and culturally responsive, especially in bringing the implicit curriculum to the level of awareness.

Flinders (1991) wrote of supervision as cultural inquiry in much the same vein. His rationale is that supervisors ought to penetrate beyond the superficial, observable traces of teacher behavior in their analyses and evaluations (i.e., in their observations). His argument is that in order to understand the teacher's experience, inference must be based upon "judgments informed by 'thick' description and interpretation, the primary tools of cultural analysis" (p. 87). Flinders' project involves "extending the epistemology of culture into the practical realms that guide a supervisor's observations, discussions, and evaluations of classroom teaching" (p. 87). He asks that supervisors become knowledgable in and considerate of the uses of metaphor, nonverbal communication, kinesics, prosody, and the cultural frames of interactions, as employed by teachers and students in the classroom and by supervisors themselves.

Other anthropologically-informed treatments of supervision include those of Alfonso (1986), Head (1992), and Migra (1976). Alfonso's paper examined the *in-service* supervisor through a theoretical treatment of the role school culture plays as a restraint to teachers (i.e., as an "unseen supervisor"). Head and Migra both dealt with *preservice* supervision. Of these two studies, Migra focused on student–teacher supervision and university supervisors in great detail. Head's treatment of student teaching as initiation dealt with supervision only tangentially, concentrating instead on the student teacher's experiences with the cooperating teacher. Head notes how student–teacher supervision is viewed as an undesirable task, yet she remarks how both cooperating teachers and university supervisors expect that student teachers will be radically affected by the experience. Migra (1976) found that cooperating teachers, student teachers, and building principals oriented to the university supervisor as a mediator and messenger. For their part university supervisors were often the first, if not the only, people to view the student teachers as professionals.

The sociologically-informed theoretical aspects of supervision are more numerous (i.e., more well established). For example, Gerald Firth (personal communication, May 24, 1994) recalled how sociological concepts were employed by the curriculum and supervision faculty at Teachers College, Columbia University, during his tenure as a student there. There has been at least one complete book devoted to a sociological treatment of supervision (i.e., Wilson, Byar, Shapiro, and Schell's (1969) *Sociology of Supervision*) in addition to numerous articles and dissertations.

Wilson et al (1969) contributed a model of what they termed "tripartite power" in schools, which combined consideration of person, plan, and position to explain organizational change. They also added to our understanding of the influences of the nonlocal community on schools. Throughout their discussion, these authors invoked not only sociologists and sociological theory, but anthropologists (e.g., George Kneller [1965]) and anthropological theory as well. For example, Wilson et al wrote of the enculturation processes that are a part of education (p. 94) of the "cultures of poverty" (p. 128), as well as of "culture distortion" and "culture lag" (pp. 152, 153, respectively). A substantial portion of their book is devoted to a discussion of three case studies, which are primarily employed to illustrate their theory of supervision and organizational change, although there is no explicit mention of the methodology or methodologies by which the data for these case studies were either gather or analyzed.

Likewise, another case study of supervision that describes a supervision conference (Kyte, 1971) reports no specific theory, sociological or anthropological, informing the analysis and interpretation. Although the author is explicit regarding the procedures used, the reader is left without a theory on which to hang the study's findings, or a relevant body of literature with which to relate or compare them. Research in supervision, [e.g., in the area of the supervisory conference (Hamann, 1989; Roberts, 1992; Waite, 1992a, 1993, 1995; Zeichner & Liston, 1985)] pays much more explicit attention to both theory and method, although none of the studies cited could reasonably be classified as sociological in nature.[40]

Other book chapters and articles borrow sociological concepts in the development of their arguments (e.g., Geddis, 1988; Lovell, 1967; Lucio, 1969). In his foreword to *The Supervisor: New Demands, New Dimensions*, Lucio makes explicit the beliefs informing the symposium that his book reported. He wrote that, undergirding the symposium, were the beliefs that:

[A] responsible profession should . . . take account of social forces and self-knowledge . . . [and] should recognize an obligation to be responsive to the needs of the social order which houses it, but should seek at the same time to keep such responsiveness under some systematically planned order and control (p. xii).

A systems paradigm dominated much of supervisory thought throughout the 1950s and 1960s (e.g., Lovell, 1967). Lovell wrote of the areas from which "supervisory behavior derives its distinctive features" as:

(1) The characteristics of human beings in schools; (2) The nature of the "social systems" in which instructional supervisory behavior occurs; (3) The nature of teaching and learning; [and] (4) The organizational structure of schools (p. 16).

Three of these areas are clearly sociological in nature.

Ham's (1986) study of the cognitive development and supervisory effectiveness of school administrators employed the case study method as an essential component, although the whole study was described by the author as a "microethnography" (p. 69).[41] The case studies of five principals' were analyzed according to five themes: the school context, supervisory style, appreciation of individual teacher needs, the principal's personal philosophy of supervision, and the principal's degree of self-reflection (p. 112). Among her findings were those that indicated that administrators functioning at the higher cognitive stages saw problems more globally, possessed a wider repertoire of problem-solving skills, functioned more effectively in complex situations, and were more empathic. As a result of her study, Ham holds that most programs in educational leadership do not distinguish between the espoused theories and theories in use of pre-sent or future leaders" (p. 169). Involvement with the author/researcher in collaborative action research increased the principals' confidence in their ability "to identify, confront, and deal effectively with school or district problems" (p. 174).

Furthermore, Ham's (1986) study seemed to validate the assumptions underlying both Glickman's (1985) Developmental Supervision and Glatthorn's (1984) Differentiated Supervision. Ham expressed her beliefs, based on the study reported, that "one 'best' supervisory model does not exist" (p. 182). "The most effective principals or supervisors," she found, "were those able to match appropriate models or strategies to the specific needs and developmental levels of their teachers" (p. 182). Finally, Ham underscored others' previous findings in stating her belief that:

[S]upervision can enhance a teacher's belief in a cause beyond oneself . . . [that] supervision can facilitate goal congruence between teachers, administrators, students, and parents . . . [that] supervision involves creating workplaces which provide autonomy as well as involvement in mutual decision-making . . . [that] supervision can stimulate teachers to share common purposes and activities . . . [and that] supervision can challenge teachers by encouraging them to assume new roles and promoting their growth to higher levels of abstract thinking (pp. 182–183).

Another sociologically-based study was that done by Keaster (1989). This study is unique in that it applied Goffman's (1955, 1967) concept of facework in an examination of how principals supervise, and why. Findings from this qualitative study indicated that principals deemphasized supervision even though they considered supervision to be their most important job. Supervision was distinguished from monitoring: Monitoring "meant checking up on the teachers to make sure they were doing their job" (p. 225), whereas supervision had a "less threatening identity aimed at offering suggestions concerning instruction." It is ironic that the principals Keaster studied supported the strict curricular controls imposed by the district and would monitor more if they could (i.e., if they had more time). Keaster argued however, that such monitoring would not be for the sole purpose of control. Citing other reasons given for principals' monitoring of teachers (e.g., "getting a 'reading' of the school,'" "improving personal knowledge of activities," "the growth and development of teachers," "providing a 'relief' from the office," and "simply enjoying being in the classroom") Keaster implied that principals do quite a bit of it. The principals studied gave no stated support for extending autonomy to teachers.

Grounded in Goffman's (1955, 1967) concept of facework, Keaster (1989) examined the phenomena of avoidance, overlooking, and discretion on principals' parts as explanations as to how and why they attempt to "save face" when supervising teachers.[42] He found no support for the contention that principals either avoid or overlook problems. Discretion, however, was displayed by the principals studied, and teachers' interviews corroborated this. Facework was essentially discounted as a reason for principals' deemphasis of supervision.

Keaster (1989) examined six possible reasons why supervision may be deemphasized by principals: acceptable teacher competence; psycho/social motivations, which concerned the facework mentioned previously; structural factors; a flawed technology of supervision; a view of teaching as an art; and, the principal's coping with inconsistent external, and possibly conflicting, regulations (p. 234). By far, the strongest support in his study pointed to structural factors as constraints on principals, preventing them from supervising as they felt they should. The study's theme that found the most support had to do with time and time constraints (i.e., with principals having a "wide span of control with insufficient resources") (p. 275) to meet the demands. This was considered to be a structural constraint.

This brief discussion has hinted at how language, culture, the wider society, and the structures of schools have an impact on supervision, and vice versa. The studies cited, however, whether empirical or theoretical, have only *begun* to realize the potential anthropology and sociology hold for supervision. In concluding, I will suggest some other questions, applications, and areas of promise.

SUMMARY AND DISCUSSION

It was with a deep sense of deja vu that I read George Spindler's article, "Education in a Transforming American Culture," from a 1955 issue of the *Harvard Educational Review*. He wrote:

"The American public school system," and the professional educators who operate it, have been subjected to increasingly strident attacks from both the lay (noneducationist) public, and from within the ranks. . . . [T]hese attacks can best be understood as symptoms of an American culture that is undergoing transformation—a transformation that produces serious conflict. . . . [T]his transformation . . . [is] a problem in culture change that directly affects all of education, and everyone identified with it (p. 145).

Though now more than 40 years old, Spindler's message retains its force and relevance, which is that of "the functional utility of understanding, and of insight into the all-encompassing transformation of American culture and its educational–social resultants" (p. 156). One of the major differences between then and now is that now there is a second and third generation of educational anthropologists and sociologists about the business of studying American schools and educational processes. To what can/should they turn their attention? What studies would be of the most interest to those of us in supervision? What areas of study hold promise to fulfill Spindler's "functional utility of understanding"?

The trend within sociology seems to be toward a synthesis of agency and structure (Fine, 1992; Giddens, 1984). Studies of this sort, with a focus on supervisors and supervision, are sorely needed. That is, how are the parts connected to the whole? What are the parts? What are the units of analysis? Is it the individual supervisor, the supervisor–teacher dyad, the student, the teacher, the classroom, the school, or community? What is the nature of the relationships that ensue? What are the political, economic, structural, and historical sociological influences, patterns, and forces impinging upon supervision and its domain? Can these be connected and, if so, how?

What is the nature of knowledge that supervisors possess or exhibit? What is the view of knowledge, the epistemology, supervisors, or a particular supervisor, hold(s)? What is the impact of a particular supervisory epistemology upon the relationship (i.e., the process) between supervisor and teacher? How is the supervisory epistemology influenced by the structures within which the supervisor works and what is the influence of that epistemology upon the work setting?

There have been initial contributions in some of these areas. Smyth (1992) wrote of the "teachers' work and the politics of reflection," tying current trends in teacher professional development with global political and economic phenomena (see also Smyth's chapter this volume, Chap. 49.) What does this mean for supervision and supervisors? Are they likewise constrained by national and global economic trends and philosophies? What are the ramifications at the local level? What are the ties? These questions ask that research into supervision follow anthropology and sociology in seeking to link local, micro-phenomena to, first, the meso-level, and, later, the global or macro-level phenomena. They also speak to the efficacy of agency and may inform the agency/structure discussion. On the other hand, are there areas of supervisory practice untouched by more global phenomena? If so, what are they and how is supervision enacted in these arenas?

Giroux (1992) has also challenged educational leaders and leadership preparation programs to educate for democracy. Even though it is ostensibly a political agenda, what would the ramifications be of such an agenda for supervision and supervision preparation programs? Indeed, a concern with democracy and democratic education has surfaced in Glickman's writing (Glickman, Gordon, & Ross-Gordon, 1995) and that of others (Waite, 1995). What do democratic *processes* look like in action? What are their essential characteristics? The answers to these questions might be forthcoming from an application of the action and interactional theories and methodologies practiced in anthropology and sociology.

What will be the results of current reforms upon supervision, its theory and practice? If teachers further professionalize, to become reflective practitioners and empowered decision makers, will supervision as now conceived become superfluous? Will it simply take another form? What of the new roles being considered for teachers and administrators (Schlechty, 1990)? If these concepts take hold, what will be the implications for supervision? Even though I have not dealt at length with the sociology of organizations, it seems that this area is ripe with research possibilities.

Is there a definite culture of supervision? If so, what are its characteristics? What aspects are part of a national identity, and what are purely local and/or idiosyncratic? There is opportunity here for research into all levels of culture. Shilling (1991) emphasized the theoretical leverage offered by consideration of embodiment, and others have discussed it as well (Sparkes, 1994). What is the deep personal meaning attached to being a supervisor? What about supervisors of other races, classes, and genders? Although I have not dealt explicitly with demographics (another sociological construct), who are supervisors? Are they primarily Euro-American males? Are females represented in supervisory positions, and in what percentage and in what roles? Are more women aspiring to supervisory positions? If this is indeed a trend, what are

its causes and what are its effects? Again, what is the meaning they ascribe to being a supervisor? Is it influenced by their identity? How? Does their identity influence their supervision as well?

The linkage between supervision and research has been well established in the literature of supervision (e.g., Flinders, 1991; Wilson et al, 1969), with authors imploring supervisors to do more research themselves. Little seems to have come of such supplications. What kind of research do supervisors need to engage in? What kinds are they engaged in at present? It is an exciting age in educational research. Alternate methodologies, most having roots in anthropology and sociology, are coming to the fore. Qualitative methods such as ethnography, conversation analysis, phenomenology, narrative inquiry, and participatory action research have established themselves in academe. Will it be long before they become part of teachers' and supervisors' repertoires? How should they be taught (i.e., preservice or in-service)? How should they be reinforced? Will studies done with these alternative methods carry any weight with decision makers? With boards of education? What might need to be done so that they will carry such force?

What would be the supervisors' role if teachers were to become researchers? How does participation in, for example, action research, meet the staff development and curriculum development needs of teachers? Close to the ground, what does such participation look like? What are its effects?

More questions have unfortunately been raised than answered in this chapter. That is as it should be. I certainly do not mean to imply that the preceding questions represent the horizon of possibilities. No one can suggest such a thing, and certainly not in advance, and for all time. I have succeeded in my efforts if what I have written here is taken as a springboard, a jumping-off place, for further inquiry into supervision—further inquiry of an anthropological and/or sociological kind.

REFERENCES

Adler, P. A. & Adler, P. (1987). *Membership roles in field research.* Newbury Park, CA: Sage.

Agar, M. (1980). *The professional stranger: An informal introduction to ethnography.* New York: Academic Press.

Agar, M. (1994). *Language shock: Understanding the culture of conversation.* New York: William Morrow and Company, Inc.

Alfonso, R. J. (1986). *The unseen supervisor: Organization and culture as determinants of teacher behavior.* Paper presented to the annual meeting of the American Educational Research Association, San Francisco.

Althusser, L. (1972). Ideology and ideological state apparatuses. In B. Cosin (Ed.). *Education: Structure and society* (pp. 242–280). Harmondsworth, UK: Penguin.

Apple, M. W. (1986). *Teachers and texts: A political economy of class and gender relations in education.* New York: Metheun.

Anderson, N. (1923). *The hobo.* Chicago: The University of Chicago Press.

Ball, S. J. (1987). *The micropolitics of the school: Towards a theory of school organization.* London: Methuen/Routledge.

Bennett, K. P. & LeCompte, M. D. (1990). *The way schools work: A sociological analysis of education.* New York: Longman.

Bernstein, B. (1977). *Class, codes and control (Vol. 3). Toward a theory of educational transmission* (2nd. ed.). New York: Routledge & Kegan Paul.

Blase, J. (Ed.). (1991). *The politics of life in schools: Power, conflict, and cooperation.* Newbury Park, CA: Sage.

Blumer, H. (1937). Social psychology. In E. P. Schmidt (Ed.). *Man and society* (pp. 144–198). Englewood Cliffs, NJ: Prentice-Hall.

Blumer, H. (1969). *Symbolic interactionism.* Englewood Cliffs, NJ: Prentice Hall.

Blumer, H. (1972). Symbolic interaction. J. P. Spradley (Ed.). *Culture and cognition: rules, maps, and plans* (pp. 65–83). San Francisco: Chandler.

Bohannan, P. J. (1968). Field anthropologists and classroom teachers. *Social Education, 32,* 161–166.

Bourdieu, P. (1986). The forms of capital. In J. G. Richardson (Ed.). *Handbook of theory and research for the sociology of education* (pp. 241–258). New York: Greenwood Press.

Bourdieu, P. (1988). *Language and symbolic power.* Cambridge: Polity Press.

Bourdieu, P. & Passeron, J. (1977). *Reproduction in education, society, and culture.* Beverly Hills, CA: Sage.

Bowers, C. A. & Flinders, D. J. (1990). Culturally responsive supervision. In C. A. Bowers & D. J. Flinders, *Responsive teaching: An ecological approach to classroom patterns of language, culture, and thought*. New York: Teachers College Press.

Bowers, C. A. & Flinders, D. J. (1991). *Culturally responsive teaching and supervision: A handbook for staff development*. New York: Teachers College Press.

Bowles, S. & Gintis, H. (1976). *Schooling in capitalist America*. New York: Basic Books.

Brown, R. H. (1977). The emergence of existential thought: Philosophical perspectives on positivist and humanist forms of social theory. In J. D. Douglas & J. M. Johnson (Eds.). *Existential sociology* (pp. 77–100). Cambridge: Cambridge University Press.

Britzman, D. P. (1986). Cultural myths in the making of a teacher: Biography and social structure in teacher education. *Harvard Educational Review, 56*, 442–456.

Burbules, N. C. & Rice, S. (1991). Dialogue across differences: Continuing the conversation. *Harvard Educational Review, 61*, 393–416.

Carr, W. & Kemmis, S. (1987). *Becoming critical: Education, knowledge, and action research*. London: Falmer Press.

Cherryholmes, C. H. (1988). *Power and criticism: Poststructural investigations in education*. New York: Teachers College Press.

Cicourel, A. V. (1964). *Method and measurement in sociology*. New York: The Free Press.

Clifford, J. (1983). On ethnographic authority. *Representations, 1*(2), 118–146.

Cohen, I. J. (1989). *Structuration theory: Anthony Giddens and the constitution of social life*. London: MacMillan Education.

Cohen, I. J. (1991). Social theory of modern societies: Anthony Giddens and his critics; The consequences of modernity. *The British Journal of Sociology, 42*(4), 638-641.

Coleman, J. S. (1966). *Equality of educational opportunity*. Washington, D.C.: U.S. Government Printing Office.

Coleman, J. S., Hoffer, T., & Kilgore, S. (1982). *High school achievement: Public, Catholic and private schools compared*. New York: Basic Books.

Craib, I. (1992). *Anthony Giddens*. London: Routledge.

Crapanzano, V. (1977). On the writing of ethnography. *Dialectical Anthropology, 2*, 69–73.

Cressey, P. G. (1932). *The taxi dance hall*. Chicago: The University of Chicago Press.

Deal, T. E. (1987). The culture of schools. In L. T. Sheive & M B. Schoenheit (Eds.). *Leadership: Examining the elusive* (pp. 3–15). Alexandria, VA: ASCD.

Deegan, M. J. (1989). *American ritual dramas: Social rules and cultural meanings*. New York: Greenwood Press.

Denzin, N. K. (1992). *Symbolic interactionism and cultural studies*. Oxford, UK: Blackwell.

de Saussure, F. (1916). *Cours de linguistique générale*. Paris: Payot. [1958. *Course in general linguistics* (W. Baskin, Trans.). New York: Philosophical Library.]

Dorr-Bremme, D. W. (1990). Contextualization cues in the classroom: Discourse regulation and social control functions. *Language in Society, 19*(3), 379–402.

Eddy, E. M. (1987). Theory, research, and application in educational anthropology. In G. D. Spindler (Ed.). *Education and cultural process: Anthropological approaches* (2nd ed.). pp. 5–25. Prospect Heights, IL: Waveland Press.

Eisenhart, M., Shrum, J., Harding, J., & Cuthbert, A. (1988). Teacher beliefs: Definitions, findings, and directions. *Educational Policy, 2*(1), 51–70.

Ellsworth, E. (1989). Why doesn't this feel empowering? Working through the repressive myths of critical pedagogy. *Harvard Educational Review, 59*, 297–324.

Erickson, F. (1984). What makes school ethnography 'ethnographic'? *Anthropology and Education Quarterly, 15*, 51–66.

Erickson, F. (1986). Qualitative methods in research on teaching. In M. C. Wittrock (Ed.). *Handbook of research on teaching* (3rd ed.) pp. 119–161. New York: Macmillan.

Erickson, F. (1987). Conceptions of school culture: An overview. *Educational Administrtion Quarterly, 23*(4), 11–24.

Estroff, S. E. (1981). *Making it crazy: An ethonography of psychiatric clients in an American community*. Berkeley, CA: University of California Press.

Fairclough, N. (1989). *Language and power*. London: Longman.

Fay, B. (1977). How people change themselves: The relationship between critical theory and its audience. In T. Ball (Ed.). *Political theory and praxis* (pp. 200–269). Minneapolis, MN: University of Minnesota Press.

Fay, B. (1987). *Critical social science: Liberation and its limits*. Ithaca, NY: Cornell University Press.

Feiman-Nemser, S. & Floden, R. E. (1986). The cultures of teaching. In M. C. Wittrock (Ed.). *Handbook of research on teaching* (3rd. ed.) pp. 505–526. New York: Macmillan.

Ferguson, R., Gever, M., Minh-ha, T. T., & West, C. (Eds.). (1990). *Out there: Marginalization and contemporary cultures*. New York: The New Museum of Contemporary Art.

Fine, G. A. (1992). Agency, structure, and comparative contexts: Toward a synthetic interactionism. *Symbolic Interaction, 15*, 87–107.

Firestone, W. A. (1993). Alternative arguments for generalizing from data as applied to qualitative research. *Educational Researcher, 22*(4), 16–23.

Firestone, W. A. & Wilson, B. L. (1983). *Using bureaucratic and cultural linkages to improve instruction: The high school principal's contribution*. Eugene, OR: Center for Educational Policy and Management, University of Oregon.

Flinders, D. J. (1991). Supervision as cultural inquiry. *Journal of Curriculum and Supervision, 6*, 87–106.

Friedrich, P. (1989). Language, ideology, and political economy. *American Anthropologist, 91*(2), 295–312.

Fukuyama, F. (1992). *The end of history and the last man*. New York: Free Press.

Fulginiti, J. M. (1986). Ethnography in school administration. *Practicing Anthropologist, 8*(3/4), 20–21.

Garkinkel, H. (1967). *Studies in ethnomethodology*. Englewood Cliffs, NJ: Prentice Hall.

Gearing, F. O. & Hughes, W. (1975). *On observing well: Self-instruction in ethnographic observation for teachers, principals, and supervisors*. Amherst, NY: The Center for Studies in Cultural Transmission.

Geddis, A. N. (1988). Using concepts from epistemology and sociology in teacher supervision. *Science Education, 72*, 1–18.

Geertz, C. (1975). On the nature of anthropological understanding. *American Scientist, 63*(1), 47–53.

Geertz, C. (1983). *Local knowledge*. New York: Basic Books.

Giddens, A. (1984). *The constitution of society*. Berkeley, CA: University of California Press.

Giddens, A. (1990). *The consequences of modernity*. Stanford, CA: Stanford University Press.

Giddens, A. (1991). *Introduction to sociology*. New York: W. W. Norton & Company.

Giroux, H. A. (1981). *Ideology, culture and the process of schooling*. Philadelphia: Temple University Press.

Giroux, H. A. (1983). Theories of reproduction and resistance in the new sociology of education: A critical analysis. *Harvard Educational Review, 53*, 257–293.

Glatthorn, A. A. (1984). *Differentiated supervision*. Alexandria, VA: ASCD.

Glatthorn, A. A. (1990). *Supervisory leadership: Introduction to instructional supervision*. Glenview, IL: Scott, Foresman and Company.

Glickman, C. D. (1985). *Supervision of instruction: A developmental approach*. Boston: Allyn and Bacon.

Glickman, C. D. (1990). *Supervision of instruction: A developmental approach* (2nd ed.). Boston: Allyn and Bacon.

Glickman, C. D., Gordon, S., & Ross-Gordon, J. (1995). *Supervision of instruction: A developmental approach* (3rd ed.). Boston: Allyn and Bacon.

Goffman, E. (1955). On face-work. *Psychiatry, 18*, 213–231.

Goffman, E. (1959). *The presentation of self in everyday life*. Garden City, NY: Doubleday.

Goffman, E. (1961). *Asylums: Essays on the social situation of mental patients and other inmates*. Chicago: Aldine.

Goffman, E. (1967). *Interaction ritual: Essays in face-to-face behavior*. Chicago: Aldine.

Goffman, E. (1974). *Frame analysis: An essay on the organization of experience*. Cambridge, MA: Harvard University Press.

Goodenough, W. H. (1957). Cultural anthropology and linguistics. In P. L. Garvin (Ed.). *Report of the seventh annual round table meeting on linguistics and language study* (pp. 167–173). Washington, D.C.: Georgetown University Press.

Goodson, I. F. (Ed.). (1992). *Studying teachers' lives*. New York: Teachers College Press.

Gore, J. M. (1993). *The struggle for pedagogies: Critical and feminist discourses as regimes of truth*. New York: Routledge.

Gumperz, J. J. & Hymes, D. H. (Eds.). (1964). The ethnography of communication. *American Anthropologist, 66*(1).

Habermas, J. (1973). *Theory and praxis* (Trans. J. Viertel). Boston: Beacon Press.

Hall, B. (1984). Research, commitment and action: The role of participatory research. *International Review of Education, 30*, 289–299.

Hall, P. (1991). In search of the meso domain: Commentary on the contributions of Pestello and Voydanoff. *Symbolic Interaction, 14*, 129–134.

Ham, M. C. (1986). The impact of collaborative action research in promoting the cognitive development and enhancing the supervisory effectiveness of five school administrators (doctoral dissertation, Vanderbilt University). *Dissertation Abstracts International, 47*, 3259A.

Hamann, J. M. (1989). Conversational analysis of successful and unsuccessful supervision conferences between supervision and student teachers. *Dissertation Abstracts International, 50*, 1631A (University Microfilms Inter-national no. 8919910).

Hargreaves, A. (1985). The micro-macro problem in the sociology of education. In R. G. Burgess (Ed.). *Issues in educational research: qualitative methods* (pp. 21–47). London: Falmer Press.

Hargreaves, A. (1990). Teachers' work and the politics of time and space. *Qualitative Studies in Education, 3*(4), 303–320.

Hassan, I. (1993). Local education, global concerns: The United States and Japan. *The Georgia Review, 47*(2), 285–00.

Head, F. A. (1992). Student teaching as initiation into the teaching profession. *Anthropology and Education Quarterly, 23*, 89–107.

Henry, J. (1966). *On education*. New York: Random House.

Herzfeld, M. (1987). *Anthropology through the looking-glass: Critical ethnography in the margins of Europe*. Cambridge, MA: Cambridge University Press.

Jacob, E. (1987). Qualitative research traditions: A review. *Review of Educational Research, 57*(1), 1–50.

Joyce, B. (Ed.). (1990). *Changing school culture through staff development*. Alexandria, VA: ASCD.

Keaster, R. D. (1989). The logic of confidence and the supervision of instruction: Perceptions and practices of elemen-

tary school principals (doctoral dissertation, University of New Orleans). *Dissertation Abstracts International, 51*, 362A.

Kilbourn, B. (1984). Ethnographic research and the improvement of teaching. In H. Munby, G. Orpwood, & T. Russell (Eds.). *Seeing curriculum in a new light: Essays from science education* (pp. 162–181). Lanham, NY: University Press of America.

Kincheloe, J. L. (1991). *Teachers as researchers: Qualitative inquiry as a path to empowerment*. London: Falmer Press.

Kneller, G. (1985). *Educational anthropology*. New York: John Wiley and Sons.

Kyte, G. C. (1971). The supervisor–teacher conference—a case study. *Education, 92*(2), 17–25.

Lacey, C. (1977). *The socialization of teachers*. London: Methuen.

Landesco, J. (1929). *Organized crime in Chicago*. Chicago: Illinois Association for Criminal Justice.

Latapí, P. (1988). Participatory research: A new research paradigm? *The Alberta Journal of Educational Research, 34*, 310–319.

Lather, P. (1986a). Issues of validity in openly ideological research: Between a rock and a soft place. *Interchange, 17*, 63–84.

Lather, P. (1986b). Research as praxis. *Harvard Educational Review, 56*, 257–277.

Leis, P. E. (1972). *Enculturation and socialization in an Ijaw village*. New York: Holt, Rinehart and Winston.

Lévi-Strauss, C. (1963). *Structural anthropology*, Vol. 1 (C. Jacobson & F. G. Schoepf, Trans.). New York: Basic Books.

Lévi-Strauss, C. (1966). *The savage mind* (2nd ed.). Chicago: The University of Chicago Press.

Lortie, D. C. (1975). *Schoolteacher: A sociological study*. Chicago: University of Chicago Press.

Lovell, J. T. (1967). A perspective for viewing instructional supervisory behavior. In W. H. Lucio (Ed.). *Supervision: Perspectives and propositions* (pp. 12–28). Washington, D.C.: ASCD.

Lucio, W. H. (Ed.). (1969). *The supervisor: New demands, new dimensions*. Washington, D.C.: ASCD.

Lucio, W. H. & McNeil, J. D. (1969). *Supervision: A synthesis of thought and action* (2nd ed.). New York: McGraw-Hill.

Malinowski, B. (1967). *A diary in the strict sense of the term* (N. Guterman, Trans.). New York: Harcourt, Brace & World.

Malinowski, B. (1976). Native education and culture contact. In J. I. Roberts & S. K. Akinsanya (Eds.). *Educational patterns and cultural configurations: The anthropology of education* (pp. 42–61). New York: David McKay.

Marcus, G. E. (1994). What comes (just) after "post"? The case of ethnography. In N. K. Denzin & Y. S. Lincoln (Eds.). *Handbook of qualitative research* (pp. 563–574). Thousand Oaks, CA: Sage.

McDermott, R. P. (1977). Social relations as contexts for learning in school. *Harvard Educational Review, 47*, 198–213.

McDermott, R. P. & Roth, D. R. (1978). The social organization of behavior: Interactional approaches. In B. J. Siegel (Ed.). *Annual Review of Anthropology* (Vol. 7) pp. 321–345. Palo Alto, CA: Annual Reviews Inc.

Mead, M. (1928). *Coming of age in Samoa*. New York: William Morrow and Company, Inc.

Mehan, H. (1978). Structuring school structure. *Harvard Educational Review, 48*, 32–64.

Mehan, H. (1979). *Learning lessons: Social organization in the classroom*. Cambridge, MA: Harvard University Press.

Mehan, H. & Griffin, P. (1980). Socialization: The view from classroom interactions. *Sociological Inquiry, 50*(3/4), 357–398.

Metz, M. H. (1986). *Different by design: The context and character of three magnet schools*. New York: Routledge & Kegan Paul.

Metz, M. H. (1987). Teachers' pride in craft, school subcultures, and societal pressures. *Educational Policy, 1*(1), 115–134.

Migra, E.D. (1976). The transition from theory into practice: A microethnography of student teaching as a cultural practice (doctoral dissertation, Kent State University). *Dissertation Abstracts International*, *37*, 6247-A.

Minh-ha, T. T. (1986/87). Introduction. *Discourse, 8*, 3–9.

Ogbu, J. U. (1974). *The next generation: An ethnography of education in an urban neighborhood.* New York: Academic Press.

Oliva, P. F. (1993). *Supervision for today's schools* (4th ed.). New York: Longman.

Ortner, S. B. (1984). Theory in anthropology since the sixties. *Comparative Studies in Society and History, 26*(1), 126–166.

Ost, D. H. (1991). The culture of teaching: Stability and change. In N. B. Wyner (Ed.). *Current perspectives on the culture of schools* (pp. 79–93). Cambridge, MA: Brookline Books.

Peirce, C. S. (1960). *Collected papers.* In C. Hartshorne & P. Weiss (Eds.). Cambridge, MA: Harvard University Press.

Pelissier, C. (1991). The anthropology of teaching and learning. In B. J. Siegel (Ed.). *Annual review of anthropology*, Vol. 20 (pp. 75–95). Palo Alto, CA: Annual Reviews Inc.

Platt, J. (1976). *Realities of social research.* New York: Halsted Press.

Pratt, M. L. (1992). *Imperial eyes: Travel writing and transculturation.* London: Routledge.

Reynolds, L. T. (1987). *Interactionism: Exposition and critique.* Dix Hills, NY: General Hall.

Ritzer, G. (1994). *Sociological beginnings: On the origins of key ideas in sociology.* New York: McGraw-Hill.

Roberts, J. (1992). Face-threatening acts and politeness theory: Contrasting speeches from supervisory conferences. *Journal of Curriculum and Supervision, 7*, 287–301.

Roberts, J. I. (1976). Introduction. In J. I. Roberts & S. K. Akinsanya (Eds.). *Educational patterns and cultural configurations: The anthropology of education* (pp. 1–20). New York: David McKay.

Robinson, J. (1995). *The ethnography of empowerment.* London: Falmer Press.

Sagor, R. (1992). *How to conduct collaborative action research.* Alexandria, VA: ASCD.

Sahlins, M. (1981). *Historical metaphors and mythical realities: Structure in the early history of the Sandwich Islands kingdom.* Ann Arbor, MI: University of Michigan Press.

Said, E. W. (1979). *Orientalism.* New York: Vintage.

Said, E. W. (1989). Representing the colonized: Anthropology's interlocutors. *Critical Inquiry, 15*(2), 205–225.

Schempp, P. G., Sparkes, A. C., & Templin, T. J. (1993). The micropolitics of teacher induction. *American Educational Research Journal, 30*, 447–472.

Schieffelin, B. B. & Ochs, E. (1986). Language socialization. In B. J. Siegel (Ed.). *Annual review of anthropology* (Vol. 15) pp. 163–191. Palo Alto, CA: Annual Reviews Inc.

Schlechty, P. C. (1990). *Schools for the 21st century: Leadership imperatives for educational reform.* San Francisco: Jossey-Bass.

Sergiovanni, T. J. (1984). Leadership and excellence in schooling. *Educational Leadership, 41*(5), 4–13.

Shilling, C. (1991). Educating the body: Physical capital and the production of social inequalities. *Sociology, 25*, 653–672.

Shilling, C. (1992). Reconceptualizing structure and agency in the sociology of education: Structuration theory and schooling. *British Journal of Sociology of Education, 13*(1), 69–87.

Sitton, T. (1980). The child as informant: The teacher as ethnographer. *Language Arts, 57*, 540–545.

Sitton, T., Mehaffy, G. L., & Davis, O. L., Jr. (1983). *Oral history: A guide for teachers (and others).* Austin, TX: University of Texas Press.

Smyth, J. (1992). Teachers' work and the politics of reflection. *American Educational Research Journal, 29*(2), 267–300.

Sparkes, A. (1994). Self, silence and invisibility as a beginning teacher: A life history of lesbian experience. *British Journal of Sociology of Education, 15*(1), 93–118.

Spindler, G. D. (Ed.). (1955a). *Education and anthropology.* Stanford, CA: Stanford University Press.

Spindler, G. D. (1955b). Education in a transforming American culture. *Harvard Educational Review, 25*(3), 145–156.

Spindler, G. D. (Ed.). (1982). *Doing the ethnography of schooling: Educational anthropology in action.* New York: Holt, Rinehart & Winston.

Spindler, G. D. (1984). Roots revisited: Three decades of perspective. *Anthropology and Education Quarterly, 15*(1), 3–10.

Spindler, G. D. & Spindler, L. (1983a). Anthropologists view American culture. In B. J. Siegel (Ed.). *Annual review of anthropology* (Vol. 12) pp. 49–78. Palo Alto, CA: Annual Reviews Inc.

Spindler, G. D. & Spindler, L. (1983b). Review essay: The case studies in education and culture from cradle to grave. *Anthropology and Education Quarterly, 14*(1), 73–80.

Stocking, G. W., Jr. (Ed.). (1982). *A Franz Boas reader: The shaping of American anthropolgy.* Chicago: University of Chicago Press.

Stocking, G. W., Jr. (1992). *The ethnographer's magic and other essays: In the history of anthropology.* Madsion, WI: University of Wisconsin Press.

Stoller, P. (1989). *The taste of ethnographic things.* Philadelphia: The University of Pennsylvannia Press.

Strahan, D. B. (1983). The teacher and ethnography: Observational sources of information for educators. *Elementary School Journal, 83*(3), 195–203.

Thomas, J. (1993). *Doing critical ethnography.* Newbury Park, CA: Sage.

Thrasher, F. M. (1927). *The gang.* Chicago: The University of Chicago Press.

Turner, V. (1974). *Dramas, fields, and metaphors: Symbolic action in human society.* Ithaca, NY: Cornell University Press.

Vidich, A. J. & Lyman, S. M. (1994). Qualitative methods: Their history in sociology and anthropology. In N. K. Denzin & Y. S. Lincoln (Eds.). *Handbook of qualitative research* (pp. 23–59). Thousand Oaks, CA: Sage.

Wagner, J. (1990). Administrators as ethnographers: School as a context for inquiry and action. *Anthroplogy and Education Quarterly, 21*, 195–221.

Waite, D. (1990/1991). Behind the other set of eyes: An ethnographic study of instructional supervision (doctoral dissertation, University of Oregon, 1990). *Dissertation Abstracts International, 51*, 3708A.

Waite, D. (1992a). Supervisors' talk: Making sense of conferences from an anthropological linguistic perspective. *Journal of Curriculum and Supervision, 7*, 349–371.

Waite, D. (1992b). The instructional supervisor as a cultural guide. *Urban Education, 26*(4), 423–440.

Waite, D. (1993). Teachers in conference: A qualitative study of teacher-supervisor face-to-face interaction. *American Educational Research Journal, 30*, 675–702.

Waite, D. (1995). *Rethinking instructional supervision: Notes on its language and culture.* London: Falmer Press.

Walker, J. C. (1985). Rebels with our applause? A critique of resistance theory in Paul Willis's ethnography of schooling. *Journal of Education, 167*(2), 63–83.

Wax, M. L., Diamond, S., & Gearing, F. O. (Eds.). (1971). *Anthropological perspectives on education.* New York: Basic Books.

Willis, P. (1981a). Cultural production is different from cultural reproduction is different from social reproduction is different from reproduction. *Interchange, 12*(2/3), 48–67.

Willis, P. (1981b). *Learning to labor: How working class kids get working class jobs.* New York: Columbia University Press.

Wilson, L. C., Byar, T. M., Shapiro, A. S., & Schell, S. H. (1969). *Sociology of supervision*. Boston: Allyn and Bacon.

Wolcott, H. F. (1988). "Problem finding" in qualitative research. In H. T. Trueba & C. Delgado-Gaitan (Eds.). *School & society: Learning content through culture* (pp. 11–35). New York: Praeger.

Wolcott, H. F. (1989). Class notes.

Wolcott, H. F. (1990). On seeking—and rejecting—validity in qualitative research. In E. Eisner & A. Peshkin (Eds.). *Qualitative inquiry in education: The continuing debate* (pp. 121–152). New York: Teachers College Press.

Wolcott, H. F. (1992). Posturing in qualitative research. In M. D. LeCompte, W. L. Milroy, & J. Preissle (Eds.). *The handbook of qualitative research in education* (pp. 3–52). San Diego: Academic Press.

Young, M. F. D. (1971). *Knowledge and control: New directions for the sociology of education*. London: Collier-Macmillan.

Zaharlick, A. (1992). Ethnography in anthropology and its value for education. *Theory into Practice, 31*(2), 116–125.

Zeichner, K. M. & Liston, D. (1985). Varieties of discourse in supervisory conferences. *Teaching and Teacher Education, 1,* 155–174.

NOTES

1. Author's Note: I wish to thank Art Crawley, Jim Deegan, Catherine Emihovich, Mary Hauser, Tom Schram, George Spindler and Harry Wolcott for their contributions to this chapter.

2. I have fortunately not been asked to define supervision. I shall leave that to more able and ambitious colleagues and scholars.

3. If I err along the way, through sins of commission and omission, I must beg the reader's forgiveness in advance.

4. Some of the social sciences not covered in this treatment include those of economics, political science, psychology, human geography, philosophy, and literature and literary criticism (including journalism). Several of these fields are covered in other chapters in this volume (see Chaps. 5, 6, 8, 38, and 47).

5. Of Boas' contribution to American anthropology, Roberts (1976, p. 4) writes of him as "probably the most influential American anthropologist of this century, [and who] was probably the first to write on anthropology and education when in 1898 he discussed the teaching of anthropology at the university level."
   The distinctions between American and continental anthropology, on the one hand, and between American sociology and, especially, British sociology, on the other will become more critical in the discussion to follow concerning research methods.

6. It is interesting to note, as do Eddy (1987) and Roberts (1976), that as Margaret Mead's professor, Franz Boas, influenced her choice of sites and topical research interests.

7. That Boas and Malinowski shared the stage, so to speak, was due, in part to their contemporaneity, and, in part, to the romanticism associated with fieldwork, a romanticism not demythed by the anthropologists. On the contrary, anthropologists themselves greatly contributed to the mythic character fieldwork came to possess in the public's eye (Stocking, 1992, pp. 57–58). Stocking wrote: "Even in America, which had its own Boasian variant of the mythic field work character, Malinowski's influence was asserted, both from a distance and in person on periodic visits."

8. Vidich and Lyman (1994, p. 44, fn. 15) credit Margaret Mead with being "the earliest of the nonmissionaries to ethnograph a Pacific Island."

9. The other two fields (i.e., archeology and physical anthropology) shall be treated here only as ancillary fields and of limited relevance.

10. This is the admittedly weak version of the Sapir–Whorf hypothesis, the one with which I am more comfortable. The strong version of the hypothesis holds that the language a person speaks *determines* how the world is perceived. This is termed *linguistic determinism* (Agar, 1994, p. 67). The weak version, as I stated, simply holds that language influences perception of the world. This is *linguistic relativity,* the precursor of cultural relativsim.

11. Of course, there *are* similarities *and* differences, which are remarkable in both cases.

12. These, of course, were the accounts written "in the field," so to speak. As was mentioned earlier, there have been those accounts (e.g., Fraser, 1940) that were written by people who never did such traveling.

13. Clifford (1983, p. 119) refers to ethnographic fieldwork as "an unusually sensitive method."

14. Ortner (1984) makes note of the fact that, for anthropology specifically, and perhaps for the humanities more generally, "The other major contribution of the Geertzian framework [the first being the argument that 'culture was not something locked inside people's heads, but rather is embodied in public symbols, symbols through which members of a society communicate their worldview, value-orientations, ethos . . . to one another, to future generations—and to anthropologists' (p. 129)] was the insistence on studying culture 'from the actor's point of view' (e.g., 1975). Again, this does not imply that we must 'get into peoples' heads.' What it means, very simply, is that culture is a product of acting social beings trying to make sense of the world in which they find themselves, and if *we* are to make sense of a culture, we must situate ourselves in the position from which it was constructed" (p. 130).

15. This theme will be revisited in the discussion of sociology.

16. See Hassan (1993), for example, especially as to how these issues influence current thinking about education.

17. Acculturation and its twin process, enculturation, have often been the primary focus of educational anthropologists, especially when studying other cultures, or have been the foci that have lead anthropologists into questions of schooling. Malinowski (1976, p. 42) reminds us, however, that "education is bigger than schooling."

18. Stocking (1992, p. 57) notes how Malinowski's *Agronauts of the Western Pacific* set the standard and established the discourse of

anthropological fieldwork: "[N]o other early published work of the prewar [WWI] cohort paid such explicit and extended attention to ethnographic (as opposed to interpretative) method." "A man of great ambition," wrote Stocking (p. 58), "and no mean entrepreneurial talent, he [Malinowski] was able to make of himself the spokesman of a methodological revolution, both within anthropology, and in some ways more important, to the nonanthropological academic and intellectual community."

19. This same problem presents itself to sociologists as a distinct possibility. Adler and Adler (1987, p. 24) cite the fear among some sociologists that overinvolvement will cause "researchers to go native, they may fail to return from the field. Existential sociologists feel strongly that throughout their research, fieldworkers must maintain a commitment to the academic world to write their descriptions, observations, and analyses of their settings. The danger of overinvolvement thus lies in the seduction of the setting, enticing sociologists to transfer their allegiances elsewhere."

20. Of the intersection of anthropology and education in the area of multicultural education, Spindler (1984, p. 9) comments how "multicultural education programs abound, but anthropology is only weakly represented, if at all."

21. Of Jules Henry's work, Roberts commented that it represents "the most fully developed outline of education to be produced by an anthropologist" (Roberts, 1976, p. 9).

22. These "intellectual progeny" include Harry Wolcott, Henry Trueba, Bob Tabachnick, Ray McDermott, and, still within the same academic genealogy even though a generation or two removed, Ray Barnhardt, Heewon Chang, Mary Hauser, Geoff Mills, Tom Schram, and myself, among numerous others. Another branch of the "family tree" includes those who studied under Fred Gearing, himself a student of Sol Tax: Catherine Emihovich (former editor of *Anthropology & Education Quarterly*), Paul Epstein, Elmor Dougherty, and Alan Tindall. Fred Erickson studied with Paul Bohannan. George Spindler (personal communication, July 30, 1994) describes Fred Gearing and Murray Wax as "independent starters," essentially products of other disciplines and/or mentors.
Rather than simply an exercise in name dropping, such discussions of academic lineage reveal important influences in the field of anthropology and anthropology in education. Such a project in sociology and the sociology of education would be equally edifying, although somewhat more difficult. One such geneology is Ritzer's (1994, pp. 182–187) discussion of the sources of influence upon one noted sociologist, Gary Alan Fine.

23. The obvious argument is that supervisors should be cognizant of teacher culture in their day-to-day professional lives. Less obvious, though nonetheless important, is the theoretical leverage gained by supervision theorists and educational anthropologists alike when examining supervisor culture. After all, anthropology is concerned with comparative cultural analysis. Interested readers might wish to consult Britzman (1986), Eisenhart et al (1988), Erickson (1986), Feiman-Nemser and Floden (1986), Goodson (1992), Hargreaves (1990), Lacey (1977), Lortie (1975), and Metz (1986, 1987) to begin.

24. Use of the term *socialization* in an anthropologically based discussion may trouble some readers. It is generally understood that socialization speaks to a sociological concept, that of recruiting new members to socially accepted and defined roles (another sociological term). The parallel in anthropology is expressed in the term *enculturation,* or, variously, *acculturation.* See Leis (1972, pp. 4–6) for a resolution of the apparent confusion of terms. Leis distinguishes socialization as the manner in which one learns to behave in a particular society and encul-

turation as involving development of a world view. Both are processes of humanization. For now, let us accept the "slippage" as an example of blurred genres.

25. Educationists are more interested in application than they are in understanding for understanding's sake (Zaharlick, 1992). Notions of culture change have been appropriated by such authors, especially in the areas of organizational change, in the form of (school) cultural change (e.g., Firestone & Wilson, 1989; Ost, 1991). Ost lists seven strategies educational leaders/supervisors might implement to change the culture of their schools: (1) "hybrid introduction" (p. 86) (i.e., filling positions with persons who are familiar with the culture yet sufficiently different as to incite and support change); (2) "technologic seduction" (p. 86) (i.e., technology itself, according to the assumptions behind this strategy, causes change); (3) alternative credentialing efforts (i.e., alternative paths to teaching open the doors to those who have not been socialized or enculturated to the extent that those who follow the traditional path have); (4) early recruitment (i.e., identifying and targeting diverse groups and populations provides a wider pool of potential teacher candidates, thus altering the culture of teaching); (5) counteracting the influence of existing teaching culture (i.e., "In addition to the four processes described above, counteractive strategies . . . help first- and second-year teachers . . . ward off the conservative self-perpetuating qualities of existing teaching culture") (p. 87); (6) exposing myths and misrepresentations to the public (i.e., this is a form of "'whistle blowing,' in the sense of exposing inconsistencies internal to [the] organization and perpetuating serious consequences") (p. 88); and (7) "managed change through structural changes" (i.e., used, writes the author, "to challenge embedded assumptions and establish a new pattern of operation") (p. 88). These and other strategies of cultural change suffer to the extent that they are ill-informed (i.e., not informed by studies "on the ground") or lapse into either oversimplified or overly ambitious social engineering projects. An example of this type of project, of particular interest to supervisors and supervision theorists, is the transplantation of the Jeanes supervision model to Africa in 1925 (Eddy, 1987, p. 11; Malinowski, 1976, pp. 48, 51, 54). Eddy notes "that in 1925 the Carnegie Foundation made the first of many grants to African education and provided funds to the Kenya Education Department for the development of a Jeanes school to train supervisors for village schools. . . . [Such efforts] represented what was then considered to be the best thought on educating the 'backward races'. . . . Even at that time, the philosophy was controversial within American education, and later historical events demonstrated clearly that it appraised inadequately the educational needs and aspirations of both African and American blacks" (p. 11).

26. Giddens (1984), a sociologist, notes what he refers to as a phenomenological turn in the social sciences, and laments that most of the contemporary humanities have fallen under its sway. As a remedy, he proposes structuration; briefly, an investigation of the interplay between agency and structure.
Pierre Bourdieu (1978) suggests that a theory of practice must take into account the agent and the structure, the agent's understanding, and the social scientist's understanding, his or her embeddedness, as well. For Bourdieu the goal is to "make . . . a science of the dialectical relations between the objective structures to which the objectivist mode of knowledge gives access and the structured dispositions within which those structures are actualized and which tend to reproduce them" (p. 3).

27. Denzin (1992, p. 22), however, makes the claim that symbolic interactionists, practitioners of one branch of sociology, believe that "'society' is an abstract term which refers to something that sociologists have invented in order to have a subject matter."

28. It is interesting to note that in their *A Critical Dictionary of Sociology*, Boudon and Bourricaud (1989) list Comte, Durkheim, Machiavelli, Marx, Rousseau, Schumpeter, Spencer, Tocqueville, and Weber as those who have made major contributions, "the main founders of sociology" (p. 5), to the field and each merits separate treatment in their dictionary.

29. Functionalism, although developed by Comte and Durkheim, was actually given impetus by anthropologists (Giddens, 1991, p. 851). Functionalism basically looks to the functions of parts of a society or culture in relation to the whole and its continuity. For anthropologists, especially, this theory represented a radical departure from the previous work done by travel writers, missionaries, colonial administrators, and arm-chair ethnographers. Functionalism, however, has its detractors and critics (see Giddens, 1984, pp. 263–274). There are many processes and states that the theory of functionalism, especially Parsons' evolutionary variety, cannot adequately explain, most notably the temporal coexistence of the cultures in various of Parsons' stages. Functionalism is usually contrasted with another major social theory—structuralism. Structuralism comes from linguistics and is usually attributed to Ferdinand de Saussure (1857–1913). de Saussure initiated a movement in linguistics that has come to be known as "abstract objectivism" (Todorov, 1984, p. 33). In de Saussure's formulation, linguists were to study abstract systems of language (*langue*) rather than systems of *use* or speaking (*parole*). de Saussure's contribution lay in his argument that the meaning of words derive from the structure of language, not from the objects to which they refer. He further suggested that meaning derives from the differences between related concepts which the rules of language recognize and codify. de Saussure's conception of language and meaning undergirded the establishment of semiotics, a study of nonlinguistic meanings. Structuralism was adopted by anthropologists; in fact Claude Lévi-Strauss (1966) popularized the term. Giddens (1991) notes that structural analyses have been done of kinship, myth, religion, and so on, but, he claims, that even though "many writers on sociological theory have been influenced by notions drawn from structuralism . . . [s]tructuralist thought has weaknesses that limit its appeal as a general theoretical framework in sociology" (p. 856).

30. The contributions of Charles Sanders Peirce (1960) to symbolic interactionism, especially, cannot be overlooked. Straddling the genres, to borrow from Geertz, of sociology and the philosophy of mind, Pierce articulated "the relationship of action to meaning, the properties and functioning that experience must assume in order to acquire the status of knowledge" (Brown, 1977, p. 89). His groundbreaking work resulted in a "theory of symbols—a semiotics of knowledge, conduct, and reality" (p. 89). Also notable in this regard is the work of Erving Goffman and his substantial contribution to our understanding of face work, ritual, and nonverbal messages (Goffman, 1955, 1959, 1963, 1967, 1974), along with more macrosociological treatment of totalizing institutions (1961).

31. George Herbert Mead was a professor in the philosophy department at The University of Chicago at the time.

32. Denzin (1992) makes finer distinctions than do the Adlers. Concerned primarily with symbolic interactionism, he posits no less than four generations, within seven phases of its development that he refers to as: "the canon" (1890–1932), "empirical/theoretical" (1933–1950), "transition/new texts" (1951–1962), "criticism/ferment" (1963–1970), "ethnography" (1971–1980), and "diversity/new theory" (1981–1990). Goffman, Strauss, Stone, and Becker fall in Denzin's third generation of interactionists, while Adler and Adler identify them with the second generation of the Chicago school.

33. It may seem inappropriate to situate Giroux with the neo-Marxists; a label he might contest. Giroux is often more closely associated with the critical theorists. This distinction, however, represents an example of Geertz' (1983) blurred genres. The line between conflict theorists (Marxists and neo-Marxists) and critical theorists remains fuzzy.
Pierre Bourdieu could likewise be claimed by sociologists and anthropologists alike. Note even his blurring of the distinctions between sociology and anthropology in the simple phrase "cultural capital." His *Outline of a Theory of Practice* (Bourdieu, 1977) is a decidedly anthropological text.

34. I would like to direct the interested reader to Paul Willis' (1981a) informative essay on the phenomena of cultural production, in which he critiques Althusser's (1972), Bernstein's (1977), Bourdieu and Passeron's (1977), and Bowles and Gintis' (1976) formulations of cultural (re)production. To summarize his project, he notes in that essay the contribution each of the above theorists has made and critiques and extends their work in adapting it to his ethnographic study of "the lads" (Willis, 1981b).

35. A critique of Willis' (1981b) work can be found in Walker (1985), although Willis' work was generally seen as a breakthrough in its use of empirical data to verify and contribute to the theory of cultural (re)production. Reproduction theories in general are critiqued in Bennett and LeCompte (1990, p. 20). Critiques of reproduction theories generally question their structuralist assumptions, arguing they ignore or slight issues of agency. See Fay (1977, 1987) for a more detailed and well-reasoned argument concerning agency.

36. Cohen's (1991) critique of Giddens' work centers on what he perceives as the ontological weakness of that work. Giddens deals explicitly in many of his volumes with questions of ontology and "ontological security" (Giddens, 1990) (i.e., "the confidence that most people have in the continuity of their self-identity and in the constancy of the surrounding social and material environments of action" (p. 92). "The reason ontological security has loomed large in Giddens' account of subjectivity is that it ties subjectivity to agency and praxis, rather than letting it float free" (Cohen, 1991, p. 640). Cohen suggests that subjective intentionality has been overlooked by Giddens and that "a full range of responses in terms of human being rather than doing have been set aside" (p. 640). He also claims that Giddens lacks "an ontological conception of human socialization which would connect structuration theory to human biology on the one hand, and feminist theory on the other" (p. 641).

37. Erickson (1987) questions the utility and accuracy of such uses of the term *culture*: "A problem with such usage is that it leaves the term without distinct content and leaves the phenomenon of culture in the school invisible and tacit—it's somehow in the air and all around us but we can't see it or talk about it" (p. 12). Such usages as those by Deal (1987), Sergiovanni (1984), and others exemplify the point made in the introduction of this chapter about the double hermeneutic, where social science concepts filter into and alter everyday life, and vice versa.

38. Allan Glatthorn (1990, p. 58) notes how "predictably, a complex anthropological concept like *culture*, in common use by business leaders and educators without a background in anthropology, is used in various and, at times, inaccurate ways."

39. In an apparent effort to facilitate examination of one's school culture, these authors have provided a checksheet inventory which might actually reveal more of a school's climate than its culture, according to the authors' own distinctions between the two concepts.

40. Of these, however, only Waite's (1992a, 1995) work is explicitly anthropological.

41. See Mehan's (1978) "Structuring School Structure," for example, for discussion of microethnography.
42. I have examined Face Threatening Acts (FTAs) in supervisory conferences in some detail (Waite 1990/1991, 1992a). I found that supervisors generally mitigate suggestions and criticisms in conferences, with a likely explanation being that they sought to save face for the teacher, and not threaten his or her professional autonomy.

·10·

THE POLITICS OF SUPERVISION

James E. Barott

UNIVERSITY OF UTAH

Patrick F. Galvin

UNIVERSITY OF UTAH

INTRODUCTION: A CONCEPTUAL ORIENTATION

The purpose of supervision in educational organizations is to create an environment in which teachers are able to teach and students are able to learn. This simple definition belies a subject of enormous complexity. Rather than define supervision as a set of specific tasks or ideologies, we have framed the concept as an organizational phenomena. Supervision is strongly influenced and shaped by how people within an organizational environment govern their activities (e.g., how teachers help teachers, how parents work with administrators, and how students claim the right to make decisions within the school). Within this context, we view supervision as including the process by which meaning and values are negotiated and enacted. In this chapter, we will focus on issues of conflict and costs in an effort to more fully describe the nature and character of supervision. To do this, we will draw on the disciplines of politics and economics. These fields of study are particularly well suited for our task and, we believe, are especially well suited for examining the micropolitical and economic issues underlying supervision.

Supervision means many things to different people. Meanings range from close monitoring of another's "productivity" to embodying an attitude that engenders creativity and collaboration on the job. The question of which of these two stereotypes of product and process is the "true" form of supervision is not something we wish to touch. Rather, we prefer to define supervision as an organizational phenomena. We first note that schools are, above all else, systems of interdependent activities. This interdependency among constituent groups within schools (i.e., teachers, parents, administrators, students, and community members) means that the

potential for collaboration and conflict simultaneously exist (Pfeffer, 1981). The potential for collaboration exists because the work of educating students requires the combined effort of all its organizational members. No one individual or single group of educators can adequately provide the education necessary for students to succeed in the complex environment in which they live. At the same time, these interdependencies create the potential for conflict because intentions, goals, means, and ideologies vary. We may all intend to help children to learn to the best of our abilities, but the means by which we pursue such goals will certainly differ. The potential for very real and legitimate disagreements exists with these differences. Thus, we argue that conflict and collaboration are simply two sides of the same coin and that current conceptualizations of supervision do not adequately recognize the extent to which conflict shapes supervision.

The nature of supervision is also influenced by a second organizational characteristic of schools: scarcity. Dollars and cents are not the only resource we have in mind here. While educational agencies may not have all the money they want to provide services, time may be the dearest resource available to educators. Intentions and goodwill may be limitless, but time and expertise are not. The commitment of one's expertise to one program necessarily reduces the time and expertise available for other needs within a school. Thus, when individuals seek to promote the commitment of resources to a set of activities, the interests and values of other activities are at least partially denied. Like interdependency, scarcity strongly influences the shape and action of supervision within school organizations. The presence of scarcity raises a political side of supervision that is frequently downplayed or ignored. We explicitly incorporate the politics of supervision into our discussion.

A third element of school organizations that shapes the nature and character of supervision within schools is the distribution of costs and benefits among organizational members. Schools operate with limited resources. Given choices about how to organize and produce educational services, educators, like members of virtually any organization, will be attentive to the relative costs of alternative ways of organizing. Supervision, either in a collaborative or conflictual form, takes time. The argument we make is that the cost of alternative ways of supervision influences the final choice of which approach is adopted and adapted to a school environment.

These organizational factors strongly influence how we perceive the business of supervision at the micro (i.e., school or classroom) level. Supervision is more than one individual or a set of individuals observing and helping teachers teach so students can learn. Rather, it includes the complex interactions of all the members of school as they negotiate how services are produced and delivered, who carries the cost of such activities, and who garners the benefits. Teachers working with other teachers is one form of supervision. Students interacting with teachers to influence how teachers teach and students learn is another form. Supervision in our perspective is better thought of as an organizational phenomena that is bound by organizational constraints and opportunities. The literature about supervision is thick with description about the contribution of collaboration to successful supervision. The influence of conflict and costs as these affect efforts to promote environments where teachers can teach and students learn is less recognized.

BACKGROUND

During the last decade, the idea that principals should act as curriculum or instructional leaders has gained considerable momentum and legitimacy. These ideas stem in part from a growing sense of concern about the productivity of our public schools. A series of national and state reports contributed to the sense that more curricular accountability and content was required to right past wrongs. These initiatives were fueled in part by the effective school's literature, which generally found that principals were instrumental in the success of schools producing proficient students. Thus, according to Sergiovanni and Starratt (1993), as well as Goldring and Rallis (1993), the role and responsibility of the principal has expanded to include leadership in curricular areas. The idea is not an unpopular one with school leaders in the field. When school administrators are asked to rank how they wish to spend their time, the idea of curriculum leader is consistently first (Hoy & Forsyth, 1986). The problem, however, is that when asked how they actually spend their time, curriculum leadership is always near the last item. Normative claims about what educational leaders ought to do are not consistent with what, in general, they actually do.

The literature about supervision, and more specifically about the supervision of instruction, is grand in its scope. This is to say that the literature is ideological in character. Thus, for example, Sergiovanni and Starratt (1993) argue that the authority for supervision is vested in moral acts of caring and community rather than in hierarchy and bureaucracy. Goldring and Rallis (1993), in what is perhaps the most grounded treatment, describe supervision relative to the need to control change and reform. Glickman, Gordon, and Ross-Gordon (1995) adopt a human development school of thought, while Neagley and Evans (1980), as well as Oliva (1989), purport a human relations perspective. Hoy and Forsyth (1986) draw heavily on the literature about effective schools and school organization. Each perspective in its own right contributes to an understanding of the business of supervision. Although each approach has its own logic and purpose, none explicitly accounts for why school leaders do not spend more of their time acting as instructional leaders.

To understand the conflicts and dilemmas that constrain and shape the behavior of supervisors, we believe it is necessary to move from the theory described earlier to a more grounded theory that illuminates the microcosm of schools. The purpose of this chapter is to discuss two perspectives that are especially appropriate to this purpose. Reference to these perspectives identifies two fundamental realities that we believe underlie the business of supervision within educational organizations. First, supervision is an inherently political act. This does not mean that we think supervision is amoral or inhumane, but rather that supervision includes the processes by which resources are allocated, conflicts negotiated, and agreements about the purposes of education are ultimately reached. Such a process is the embodiment of politics in our perspective. Second, supervision is inherently an economic activity. One of the strongest themes underlying the literature about supervision, regardless of one's perspective, is that of the productive school. The purpose of supervision, as noted earlier, is to create an environment and climate in which teachers are able to teach effectively and students are able to learn efficiently. The reforms that have pushed supervision into the limelight are largely about enhancing the productivity of schools. In this light, supervision is an economic activity.

In this chapter, we will frame our perspective in terms of the micropolitics of supervision and the microeconomics of supervision. If politics is about the conflictual allocation of resources and economics is about the influence of cost on choices, then these perspectives have much in common. These perspectives specifically recognize the dynamic social and personal processes that exist within organizations. Recognition of scarcity, conflict, self-interest, cost, and bounded rationality all contribute to a more realistic picture of supervision within the school setting. If, as Sergiovanni and others argue, our theories of supervision profoundly influence the way in which we enact practice, then theories that incorporate these dynamic processes of school organization seem of particular importance. A microperspective, which focuses on the immediate circumstances and environment in which school leaders operate, provides the means by which to examine those dynamic processes. The application of micropolitical and microeconomic concepts to that perspective provides one method to enrich our sense of those dynamic processes. Such an understanding is essential for appreciating the potential opportunities, as well as limitations, of supervision within the environment of public education.

ORGANIZATIONS AS POLITICAL ENTITIES

Unit of Analysis

We have selected the school building as the organizational level on which to focus our attention in this chapter. The building or site level is the immediate organizational unit within which the principal and classroom teacher work, children are instructed, and direct supervision occurs. At the same time, it is important to recognize that the school is nested in multilevel governmental structures. The organizational politics of the building site is the micropolitics of a subunit of a larger complex organization: the school district. In turn, the school district is a local government unit, variously connected to other local governments, as well as to the state and national governments.

Although national and state educational policies have some direct implications for the building, most of these are primarily translated into the micropolitics of the building through the local school district. As Iannaccone has noted, "rather than follow a pure democracy model, the local school is better seen as an administrative unit whose decisions are made for it at the central office and board level" (1975, p. 57). In practice, the channels of authority and structured interactions between the school building and the school district's central office can be treated as the major links between the macro- and micropolitics of education. In the past, these linkages, and the structure of interaction around these linkages, reflected the legal, bureaucratic chain-of-command that flows from the state through the local school district board and central office initially impacting on the principalship and the building administration. The more recent development of collective bargaining has created an additional line of interaction between the building and the teacher's organizations that represents the faculty in negotiations. It also maintains supervision of the implementation of the labor contract, most frequently through grievance mechanisms and procedures.

The larger politics of education is the relevant political environment for the micropolitics of education as "macropolitical processes and especially changes in these have a significant effect upon the internal and external politics of the school building" (Iannaccone, 1975, p. 43). The politics of a school building involve many aspects of the intraorganizational affairs of the complex system of American public schools. Its politics are shaped to a significant degree by the impact of the larger system of which it is a component. Focusing on the site level without acknowledging its relation to the larger educational political system would therefore ignore much of what shapes the internal politics of the building. At the same time, the macropolitics of education is not the focus of our discussion. We will, therefore, give as little attention to the macropolitics of education as possible, but as much as seems necessary.

The Micropolitics of Educational Organizations[1]

Scholars in the politics of education subfield have long recognized that schools are political systems (Campbell et al,

1985; Campbell et al, 1987; Iannaccone, 1975, 1977; Stroufe, 1977; Wirt & Kirst, 1975). Research on the micropolitics of schools has conceptualized schools as political entities that are dependent on diverse constituencies and variously serve as vehicles for political socialization, objects of political contest, and arenas of political negotiation (Ball, 1987; Blase, 1991b; Malen, 1995; Marshall & Scribner, 1991).

The referents for the micropolitics of education as used here are as follows. The *micropolitics of education* is

concerned with the interaction and political ideologies of social systems of teachers, administrators and pupils within school buildings. These may be labeled as internal organizational subsystems. It is also concerned with the issues of interaction between professional and lay subsystems. They may be called external systems (Iannaccone, 1975, p. 43).

The preceding definition, as well as the discussion that follows borrows heavily from the seminal work of Laurence Iannaccone (1975, 1977, 1991) and Betty Malen's more recent work (1993, 1994a, 1994b, 1994c, 1995).

Definition of Politics

"Politics is the process by which a society's persistent social values are translated in policy . . . and thence into a multitude of rules, regulations, and administrative decisions" (Iannaccone, 1991, p. 467). It is that set of interactions that influence and shape the authoritative allocation of values (Easton, 1965a, 1965b; Wirt & Kirst, 1992). As Wirt and Kirst (1975, p. 4) have pointed out, "the essence of the political act is the struggle of men and groups to secure the authoritative support of government for their values." It follows that the political function of educational government is to manage conflict.

A basic principle underlying this definition is that of scarcity: Every social system has more potential demands for resources of value than it can establish and distribute. The establishment of value priorities and the distribution of valued resources scarce enough to be the source of conflicts require that social systems develop mechanisms to avert chaotic conflicts and self-defeating wars. Any ongoing social system with stability has mechanisms to make decisions (i.e., allocations) that its members will support, tolerate, or find acceptable (i.e., are more or less authoritative). Such allocations, the mechanisms by which they are made, and especially the attempts by individuals and groups to influence these, are what is meant by politics. Although this is similar to decision-making, "a politics perspective's unique focus is on processes for producing policy from conflict" (Iannaccone, 1991, p. 467). As Schattschneider (1975) has stated, "all politics deals with the displacement of conflict or efforts to resist the displacement of conflicts" (p. 68). The political process is illustrated graphically in Figure 10.1.

The process of translating conflicting social values into policy requires a set of arrangements by which a particular society governs itself. Banfield and Wilson (1963) have distinguished two functions of government: the service func-

FIGURE 10.1.

tion and the political function. The *service function of government* is those processes or activities that meet perceived social needs such as the need for education. This is the function on which most of the supervision literature is focused. From this perspective supervision is viewed as facilitating and monitoring the service delivery. An organization becomes a vehicle designed to enhance efficiency.

The *political function of government* is those processes and activities that exist to manage conflict and settle disputes between contesting coalitions. The emphasis here is on the potential conflicts avoided or exploited within school buildings, as well as between the building and lay subsystems. Supervision in this context is framed as governing or monitoring the political function of educational governments.

The research on the service function and the research on the political function of educational governments are usually based on fundamentally different assumptions. The research literature on the supervision of the service function tends to assume stasis, order, regulation, consensus, and solidarity. Munificence is also assumed. For example, classroom teachers are assumed to have enough time and attention to go around. Cost, including time, expertise, and monetary resources, is also rarely considered.

It is more important for our discussion that this literature generally assumes the service function as given. It assumes that the stakes are settled and that the service function of schools is to teach or socialize children in a caring manner. In addition, who the supervisor is and who is supervised is a given, and not open to question. How the supervisor supervises (i.e., the processes, strategies and tactics of supervision) tend to be normative and at times utopian. In other words, "best practice" or how we "should" supervise is given a lot of attention. Underlying ideologies, myths, and assumptions are also taken for granted, and unexamined. Finally, organizational structure is framed as functional and rational.

The research literature on the politics of supervision rests on an entirely different set of assumptions. This literature generally assumes continual conflict, negotiation, contradiction, paradox, coercion, and domination. Scarcity is also assumed. There is never enough to go around. Cost is also an issue. In contrast to the research on the service function, research on the political function assumes that the service or task functions of the organization are undecided, continually negotiated, and in conflict. It assumes that stakes are a matter of continual contest. In addition, who the supervisor is and who is supervised is a matter of negotiation, contest, and conflict. How the supervisor supervises (i.e., the processes, strategies, and tactics of supervision) is assumed

to be driven by political considerations as well as by monitoring and transaction costs. Underlying ideologies, myths and assumptions are questioned and examined. Finally, organizational structure is framed as a function of previous conflicts and costs.

In this chapter we will be operating from the second set of assumptions as we address what the literature tells us about the politics of supervising educational organization at the site level.

DEFINITION OF ECONOMICS AND THE ORGANIZATIONAL CONTEXT

Economic inquiry examines the influence of cost on the processes by which productive activity is coordinated within the market, which includes organizations (see Barney & Ouchi, 1986; Demsetz, 1995; Hoenack, 1983; Leibenstein, 1987; Williamson, 1976). Economic thought has much to say about how individuals collaborate around common production processes. We believe that such thought is particularly relevant to the study of supervision in education because, whatever else one may say, it is fundamentally about how educators coordinate their interests, values, resources, skills, and time to produce effective services. Such a process can certainly be thought of in economic terms.

Many educators are justifiably wary of the application of economic ideas to education. To these critics Callahan's work in his book *Education and the Cult of Efficiency*, stands as documented evidence of the danger principles of scientific management[2] pose to schooling. Indeed, the reactions by virtually every author about supervision to the notions of scientific management are vehement and definitive: Scientific management is both conceptually bankrupt and, perhaps, morally bankrupt as well (Alfonso, Firth, & Neville, 1981; Glickman, Gordon, & Ross-Gordon, 1995; Sergiovanni & Starratt, 1993).

It is interesting that Callahan (1962) is not so vehement about his critique of scientific management. After detailing the excruciating story of what the indiscriminate implementation of scientific management meant for education, with its emphasis on procedures for cost cutting and outcome surveys, Callahan suggests that there existed a tragedy in its failure to improve schools:

[T]he essence of the tragedy was in adopting values and practices indiscriminately and applying them with little or no consideration of educational values or purposes. It is not that some of the ideas from the business world might not have been used to advantage in educational administration, but that the wholesale adoption of the basic values as well as the techniques of the business/industrial world, was a serious mistake in an institution whose primary purpose was the education of children . . . if educators had sought "the finest product at the lowest cost"—a dictum which is sometimes claimed to be a basic premise in American manufacturing—the results would not have been unfortunate. But the record shows that the emphasis was not at all upon "producing the finest product" but on "the lowest cost" (p. 244).

We will argue in this chapter that costs strongly influence choices and organizational behavior, particularly in such a labor-intensive task as education. The consideration of how costs affect choices within an organization does not require one to abandon his or her values, sense of community, or morals. Rather, recognition of the complexity of costs and their influence on behavior within an organization helps one understand why the task of implementing good ideas, like those proposed about supervision, are not always easy realized.

Economic thought begins with a simple and intuitively obvious proposition: individuals make choices, whether in their private lives or in their capacity as members of organizations (Monk, 1990; Thomas, 1971). An assumption most economists work with is that individuals make decisions with complete and accurate information and thus do so consciously and rationally. Organizational theorists are less willing to accept such an assumption. March and Simon (1958), for example, are well noted for arguing that individuals are bounded in their rationality, which is to say that even in an environment with perfect information, no one individual has the capacity for processing, evaluating, and acting on all the information necessary to ensure perfect rationality. When we refer to economic thinking, we work from a model that recognizes the autonomy of individuals as well as their bounded rationality (see Barney & Ouchi, 1986; Demsetz, 1995; Hoenack, 1983; Leibenstein, 1987; Williamson, 1976 for good introductions to this line of inquiry, which is variously described as the new institutional economics or, as we prefer, organizational economics). Thus, within an organization individuals may act with their own best self-interest,³ but they do so without complete or accurate information. Work agreements within an organization are necessarily incomplete and open to interpretation. It is not surprising, in such a view of individuals and organization, that we think conflict and collaboration are fundamental components of even the best of systems. Indeed, conflict and collaboration are essential to the vitality of all good organizations.

Supervision, according to many key scholars (Glickman, Gordon, & Ross-Gordon, 1995; Goldring & Rallis, 1993; Neagley & Evans, 1980; Oliva, 1989), is, among other things, about ensuring that the resources and skills available to schools can be used effectively and efficiently.⁴ This literature is certainly much more sensitive to the goals, values, and circumstances of education than was the literature based on industrial models of supervision; however, recognizing the legitimacy of values, community, and caring does not forego a concern about production. For example, Goldring and Rallis (1993), while explicitly recognizing the organizational and social reforms that affect schools, argue that principals have an explicit responsibility to "take charge" and supervise school improvement. Successful principals, these authors argue, "must be acutely aware of their political and organizational environments. Ultimately, these environments have enormous impact on the extent to which principals can be in charge" (p. 142). The notion of control identified by Goldring and Rallis is not meant to represent power over teachers and parents and students. Rather, the concept of "take charge" is meant to reflect the idea of authority, as discussed by Sergiovanni and Starratt (1993), with all its incumbent rights and responsibilities. The notion of take charge, however, also means making tough choices about what is produced and how it is produced within the school. In this perspective, the issue is an economic one where the comparative framework that balances costs and benefits is important.

The following discussion accepts arguments about the potential benefits of supervision (Goldring & Rallis, 1993; Sergiovanni & Starratt, 1993). Indeed, most public school administrators, as mentioned earlier, see supervision as one of their primary responsibilities, even though they report it frequently occupies the least amount of their time. One might argue that administrators dedicate a small but sufficient amount of time, but that is not how these administrators see it (Hoy & Forsyth, 1986). They want to dedicate more time to supervision, especially curricular supervision. Why, therefore, do they not follow through on the desire? Why do authors of texts about supervision, after so many years of discrediting "scientific management," still need to argue for collaborative supervision that is sensitive to the values and goals of school organizations? An analysis of costs as they affect choice and behavior within organizations provides some insight to the question. In the next section, the discussion turns to delineating and defining the nature of costs as economists think about them. These ideas are then applied to the analysis of an illustrative case that details the influence of costs as they affected the operation of a collaborative enterprise. The illustrative case highlights the role of costs as they affected this collaborative effort and frames the political problems inherent in supervision.

Definition of Costs

According to Thomas (1971) in his book, *The Productive School: A Systems Analysis Approach to Educational Administration*, one of the most important contributions of economics to educational administration is the notion of costs. It is not unusual for most educators to equate costs with expenditures. Costs as expenditures are defined as the monetary outlay associated with the purchase of educational inputs: teachers, desks, books, facilities, buses, and so on.

Economists describe costs more broadly to include consideration of nonmonetary factors associated with production. These include consideration of one's time, expertise, attention, interest, and perhaps affection. Consideration of nonmonetary costs is particularly important for understanding efforts to implement new ideas in education. The salaries and overhead costs are often fixed, but the indirect and nonmonetary costs associated with how teachers distribute and use their time are not. Thus, if one is to understand the influence of costs on choices about adopting innovations, then a consideration of the nonmonetary costs as well as direct monetary costs is essential. To illustrate the point, imagine a teacher considering whether to adopt fully an administrative innovation, such as a new computerized grade book. The teacher knows that learning how the system works will take time and mean that he or she will not have that time available for developing a desired science project on solar power. Thus, adopting new innovations has important implications for the distribution of the teachers' time as well as for the potential learning of students within the environment. These circumstances represent what economists describe as opportunity costs. If the teacher takes the time to adopt the innovation, then students may lose the opportunity to learn about solar power. The ideas of "foregone learning" and "foregone productivity" are central to an understanding of how opportunity costs influence our choices within an organizational context.

In the most general sense, economists describe all costs as opportunity costs (i.e., that which is given up rather than what is put into the system). When principals or other innovators seek to implement changes in educational systems, they generally talk about the direct costs and potential benefits of such efforts. They rarely elaborate or consider the full range of costs, and more specifically the opportunity costs. These costs, however, and their impact on potential benefits, are what we believe are crucial to understanding whether an innovation is adopted or abandoned.

Although all costs can be understood in a broad sense as opportunity costs, economists generally divide costs into three categories of polarities: (1) direct and indirect; (2) public and private; (3) monetary and nonmonetary. These have been introduced earlier, they will now be more formally defined. Furthermore, two additional cost categories will be discussed: (4) transaction costs; and (5) agency costs. These additional categories are particularly relevant for understanding the practice of supervision.

Direct costs involve hiring personnel and purchasing materials. These costs or expenditures are generally accounted for by a school's budget report. These are the costs most frequently cited by educators and the lay public, and they are largely funded by legislative grants. These sources of revenues and the related costs are obviously important because they frame the obligations and responsibilities of individuals within the organization. At a microlevel, however, individuals still have considerable latitude or discretion about how they implement their job descriptions. We will argue shortly that nonmonetary costs also strongly influence choices and behavior.

Indirect costs include such factors as depreciation of buildings and equipment. Other indirect costs may include property and sales tax exemptions provided to businesses within a school district. Indirect costs are not directly related to program expenditures, but they are costs indirectly associated with the program.

Public and private costs refer to the degree to which the cost of any particular action falls upon the individual versus society at large. An innovation that requires a teacher to participate in a workshop at the expense of leisure time is an example in which the costs are private in nature. By contrast, if a school system hires additional staff to relieve teachers during their normal work hours so they can participate in the workshop, then the costs are distributed across society at large (i.e., because tax dollars are used to pay for the substitute teachers) and illustrate an example of public costs. Private costs represent foregone opportunities for individuals and their families. Private costs are reduced when public contributions increase. Social costs are the sum of private and public costs (Thomas, 1971).

Monetary costs may be either direct or indirect, and they may be paid by either society or by the individual. Tuition and taxes represent direct monetary costs to parents with students in school. Foregoing leisure activities to support student learning is an illustration of nonmonetary costs. According to Thomas (1971), nonmonetary costs within a school include those costs associated with the allocation of time. For example, when a student is assigned to a teacher's classroom, there are associated costs for the teacher as well as for the other students within the classroom. The creation of a new curriculum necessarily foregoes time available for other instructional opportunities.

Although the preceding categories help one to recognize the range of costs that influence organizational behavior, they fail to capture the complexity of decision-making within an organization. It is useful to think of the procedure by which individuals seek collaboration as an exchange. Individuals within organizations do not act with total autonomy. What they do with their time and resources often affects the capacity of others within the organization to complete their work. This is a familiar point in education wherein the second grade teacher depends upon the work of the teacher in first grade and the third grade teacher is dependent upon the work of the second grade teacher. An interdependency exists. In the best of all worlds, one would simply let others know about their instructional plans and goals so that they could align their instructions, in a complementary way. Such an alignment, however, requires a lot of information, which is neither inexpensive, nor always available. Thus, efforts to coordinate activities within an organization are dependent upon resources and conditions over which one may not have control.

Transaction costs refer to those costs associated with keeping the system running, but they do not contribute directly to the productivity of the system. Arrow (1971) and Williamson (1986) describe these costs as transaction costs or coordination costs. They suggest that these costs can be visualized as the points of friction that tend to drag or slow a system down. For example, they represent the cost of communicating about a program, writing up formal agreements about what all the parties will do, supervising or monitoring behavior within the organization, and reacting legally if individuals fail to live up to their agreements. We argue that these issues are ubiquitous to all organizations, including schools.

Red tape stands as an illustration of the issue. In its worst form, red tape is simply an exercise in accountability that has little to do with the actual service being offered. In a world of perfect information, there would be no need for such accountability procedures because in such a world one would simply know whether teachers, for example, were using resources in ways consistent with the intention of the funding agent. Such information, unfortunately is not readily available, and the expense of acquiring it detracts from the overall efficiency of any plan being implemented. Transaction costs are an often overlooked but significant source of costs that can profoundly alter the cost–benefit ratio of program efforts within organizations. The implications are familiar. Who has not heard teachers say, I love this program but it requires too much effort and time to maintain? The failure of many programs is not their ineffectiveness; rather, it is that the costs of maintaining these programs are simply greater than individuals are willing to bear.

The problem is not limited to funding agencies. In any team effort, there are times when it is necessary to discuss whether every one is pulling his or her weight. The threat of shirking (i.e., taking advantage of the fact that others can not easily assess your effort) raises the need for monitoring and possibly writing agreements that then need enforcement. All these efforts are costly and require resources that cannot then be applied to the tasks at hand. Organizations seek ways of structuring their work to reduce transaction costs and enhance organizational efficiency. Strategies to reduce these costs, however, are not easily achieved. One problem is that plans for reducing transaction costs can carry with them different burdens and benefits for different individuals and groups within an organization. Plans that are not perceived as equitable can actually exacerbate transaction costs, making a program so inefficient that it is abandoned despite its rich potential for offering teachers opportunities to teach and students opportunities to learn. Recognizing the presence and influence of transaction costs on individual choice within an organization is important for understanding supervision.

Agency theory draws attention to another category of costs: those associated with issues of ownership and control. Public education is owned by taxpayers. These owners are sometimes referred to as the "De Jure" owners (Michaelsen, 1981). Be this as it may, school administrators actually hold the reins and are called the "De Facto" owners. Thus, the problem for owners of agencies like schools is one of figuring out how to monitor the decisions of the mangers (i.e., de facto owners) hired to conduct the agency's business. On the other hand, if managers were able to know exactly what and how to conduct the business of the owners, then the problem of monitoring would be minimized. Schools have unfortunately been castigated for the last few decades for failing to provide graduates ready for the labor market, or well prepared for the university. The current rush of parental involvement and business involvement in public education might be interpreted as a mechanism by which these vested groups of taxpayers (i.e., de jure owners) are becoming more closely involved in decisions about how schools operate. Such involvement is costly. Agency theory examines the means by which de jure owners seek efficient ways of monitoring the behavior of de facto owners. Agency costs describe the direct and indirect, private and public, monetary and nonmonetary costs associated with such a problem. These costs are fundamentally about supervision, but they are rarely addressed or considered in the debate about supervision in educational environments. Such a failure overlooks important sources of influence affecting the structure and behavior of organizational members seeking ways for resolving the need for supervision and their desire to minimize the cost. This is an important analytic perspective, particularly about the problem of promoting effective and fair supervision practices that involve parents and community members within the governance of schools.

If collaboration and community involvement are a means of producing more effective results (i.e., enhanced student learning of desired knowledge and skills), then one must recognize the similarity of such propositions to those of scientific management. The goal and purpose of scientific management was not necessarily to establish power relations by which management could dominate workers. Rather, as Callahan noted, the purpose was to find low-cost strategies by which to produce desired results. These early efforts unfortunately failed to keep in mind the quality of the services provided, thus pursuing low cost without regard to the quality. These early efforts also failed to promote efficiency, or to recognize, the legitimacy of the values, norms, and culture of schools and schooling, or the complexity of the tasks of education. The current stream of literature about supervision and schools certainly recognizes the values, norms, and culture of school and schooling, but it appears to ignore completely the influence of costs as they affect both the production choices of constituent members of schools and the quality of services offered. Using the previous definitions we will argue that more attention to costs, without losing sight of the values and norms of schools, will enhance the chances of achieving both effective schools and constructive school reform.

Supervision: Cooperation, Conflict, and Efficiency

In the previous sections, we defined basic concepts and terms relative to the disciplines of politics and economics. These disciplines help to frame our understanding of supervision within educational organizations. Indeed, referencing these disciplines helps to clarify a fundamental goal for the organization, (i.e., finding efficient ways of managing collaboration and conflict).

Collaboration, particularly in terms of a learning community, has emerged as the cornerstone for discussions about supervision in education. We believe that the call for collaboration is more than ideological. Learning requires a collaborative effort between student and teacher. In this respect, collaboration can be thought of as the dominant value driving the organization of schooling. Recalling Callahan's admonitions of scientific management for its failure to recognize the value and norms that characterize schooling, collaboration may be more than a good idea: It may be essential for effective and efficient education.

Mobilizing support for collaboration[5] does not eliminate conflict. Even in an environment where everyone is supportive of the purposes of an educational initiative, there is bound to be conflict about how the associated tasks should be divided and coordinated among constituent members of the organization. This is inevitable because decisions about how to divide and coordinate tasks within a school impact the individual interests and efforts of teachers and students. If an initiative or policy conflicts with the specific instructional goals and methods of a teacher, then an administrator should not be surprised to meet resistance. At this moment, supervision changes from an effort to mobilize collaborative support for an initiative to the management of conflict. Conflict emerges from a legitimate debate about how the burdens and benefits of a program initiative should be distributed among organizational membership, not from some psychology about the resistance to change or mean spiritedness.

A case example illustrates the point. In a small rural school district, high school math students were unable to receive advanced math classes (i.e., calculus) because of limited enrollments. Because community members were unwilling to consolidate their district with their larger neighboring district, the superintendent of the smaller district proposed a collaborative set of math classes for the two districts. This meant that the more able students of the smaller district could travel to a school in the larger district that was less than ten miles away and take calculus. The problem for the math teacher in the smaller district was that he was left with an even smaller number of students of less ability. Whereas his previous instruction relied on the more able students to generate classroom discussion and mentor the less able students, the class was now largely remedial in character, with unmotivated students. Furthermore, because the math teacher in the smaller district had a limited number students and resources, his curriculum focused on basic skills rather than on precalculus. Thus, when students from this small district tried to fit into the calculus curriculum of the math teacher in the larger district, there was trouble because these new students were not well prepared for the coursework. This collaborative program, which initially seemed so perfectly suited to the problem identified by administrators, failed to serve anyone's needs in the end; however, it did generate considerable conflict, and any potential benefits from the plan were soon lost as teachers, parents, and students spent their time arguing about perceived injustices rather than learning in the classroom.

Collaboration is a good word, but it does not mean much until one considers the details of an arrangement. In the preceding example, the conflict that ensued, which was significant for teachers, administrators, parents, and students, stemmed largely from a concern about how the costs and benefits of the plan to produce more learning would be distributed. In this respect, the problem can be understood as both economic and political. Indeed, the reason for the plan was the belief that collaboration between a small and larger school district would enable economics of scale that would in turn lower production costs while enhancing learning outcomes.

The effect, however, was to create burdens, which can be thought of as costs, that teachers, parents, and students were unwilling to accept. There were direct costs that both schools had to absorb in terms of transportation, accounting of texts, and attendance. These were minor, but they were noted by administrators in both schools. There were many indirect, nonmonetary costs. For example, although the students were interested in gaining advanced math classes, they noted that it meant that they had to forego other opportunities in their home school. Some of these opportunities were social, whereas others were academic. Both sources of cost were reluctantly borne by students. The teachers of both schools complained that the changes in student enrollments posed barriers to their teaching and to their student's learning. In the larger school district, the visiting students from the smaller school district required additional support from the teacher, which slowed down the progress of other students. Transaction costs were particularly high for teachers, administrators, and students. First, teachers were trying to coordinate their activities so as to better fit the collaborative plan,

which is a process that takes considerable time that might have been better used for other purposes. Students found the administrative time checking in and out of each district as they traveled between schools to be a frustrating use of their time. Administrators at the district level and school level found more and more of their time absorbed in the mechanics, negotiations, and renegotiations associated with this seemingly simple proposal.

Although none of these costs was huge in and of itself, the costs cumulatively began to wear on all the participants. Administrators found that they were spending lots of time in meetings coordinating such items as schedules, vacations, snow day policies, and disciplinary policies. In addition, the conflict these collaborative programs created required a lot of monitoring and long discussions with upset teachers and students. Finally, parents became unhappy because they felt that educators were spending too much time trying to maintain a very small part of the services offered by the schools.

The preceding example was not extraordinarily contentious or complex in nature. Other observers might choose to describe the events differently, but we observe here the role of costs and conflict affecting the administration of a collaborative program. Any potential efficiencies gained by the schools or, more specifically, to the few students from the smaller district were certainly canceled out by the costs administrators, teachers, parents, and even the students were required to bear.

Our purpose is not to challenge the utility of collaboration. It is certainly possible that this situation and others like it could be worked out successfully. Rather, the example illustrates the presence and influence of costs on strategies to produce educational services. Even if consensus about the utility of a given strategy exists, there is always the potential for conflict about how such a strategy should be implemented. Where supervision is about the assignment of tasks and the achievement of coordinated action, these issues of cost and conflict are essential for thinking about the nature of supervision. It is in this way that we view the subject of supervision, a point graphically illustrated in Figure 10.2.

The overlap of the circles identifying different domains is meant to be illustrative, not proportional (i.e., we have no specific idea about how much of supervision overlaps with economics and politics). Nonetheless, we argue that one must recognize both the political and economic aspects of supervision if one is to understand clearly and substantively the nature of the supervision. Other aspects of supervision, such

FIGURE 10.2.

as curriculum and personnel management, as well as communication and social relations, could be included in the preceding circles or be identified in separate circles. If one tried to capture all the relevant domains that affected the realm of supervision, then the number of circles in the figure would be impossible to track. The practice of supervision is complex.

The preceding model simplifies the complexity, but it is not intended to ignore the debate about the nature and character of supervision. For example, in their textbook about educational administration and leadership, Razik and Swanson (1995) dedicate several chapters to the evolving and conflicting theories of leadership and supervision in education. The discussion is framed as a paradigmatic contest (à la Kuhn, 1962) between positivism and postmodern theories of social organization. The argument, generally speaking, is to say that mechanical metaphors of supervision generated from the social sciences of the 1930s are inappropriate to schools. In the opinion of these authors, postmodern theories of social science, which are constructive, critical, interpretative, holistic, and developmental, are more appropriate and useful.

This dichotomy between positivism and postpositivism is a frequent format for discussing literature about supervision and educational leadership. For example, Hoy and Forsyth (1986) clearly present the task of supervision in technical terms, which breaks the concept of supervision into discrete components: philosophy; social system; formal and informal organization; organizational climate; the teacher; the student; classroom climate; classroom arrangements; and evaluating performance. This model exemplifies the tradition of positivism that seeks to quantify and define the components of production to enhance effectiveness. By contrast, Sergiovanni and Starratt (1993) explicitly challenge the premise of supervision as a management science and argue instead for a more humanistic and holistic perspective. These authors argue that supervision is a moral, not a technical, act. The authority for such action rests upon "the obligations and duties that teachers feel as a result of their connection to widely shared community values, ideas, and ideals" (Sergiovanni & Starratt, 1993, p. 31). This notion of moral authority is not unrelated to what Hodgkinson (1983, p. 43) describes as metavalues, which are concepts that are so desirable and widely entrenched that they seem to be beyond dispute. Sergiovanni and Starratt argue that "when moral authority is in place, teachers respond to shared commitments and felt interdependence by becoming self-managing" (p. 31).

This last point seems vaguely wishful to us. Oliva (1989) states: "Theoretically, we could dispense with the services of supervisors if—a very improbable if—all teachers were dynamic, knowledgeable, and skillful" (p. 34). Such views about the nature and character of supervision go too far in reacting to models of what Hoy and Forsyth (1986) describe as "close" supervision: the bureaucratic models of control and dominance. The literature about supervision appears to have long held on to this foil for its evolving arguments about self-management. Power, these authors argue, is bad. Moral authority, however, is good.

By contrast, we contend that all organizations are confronted with the need to coordinate their resources to some productive end. Cyert and March (1963) and Pfeffer (1978) propose that these ends or organizational goals are set through a process of negotiation between members of dominant coalitions. However they are derived, the choice about what to produce and how to produce it will at times conflict with the specific interests and goals of individual members within the organization. Thus, a critical responsibility for any successful organization is to limit the discretionary behavior of individuals operating with organizational resources and authority. This is not to say that employees cannot have any authority; rather, the organization has an interest in ensuring the efficient production of its goals before it allows individual members to pursue their individual agendas. Etzioni (1961) describes the issue of compliance as one of a few universal laws governing organizations. The nature and practice of supervision is about this universal law.

If one rejects the proposition of self-management and accepts the necessity of compliance to organizational goals and strategies, then it is inevitable that conflict must be managed. In the following sections, we will draw specific attention to the political content of supervision. Our focus in these sections is on the micropolitics of supervision, where most of the interaction takes place. The discussion would ideally integrate political and economic factors. In fact, although these factors are inextricably linked in practice, they are extremely difficult to discuss in an integrated fashion. Thus, for reasons of clarity, we will simplify the discussion by separating our presentation so that economic issues are discussed first, and then micropolitical issues. The reader is encouraged to link points made in this first section with those made in the following sections.

THE MICROPOLITICS OF SUPERVISION

The following discussion of the politics of the school is organized into two broad areas: Domestic Affairs, in which we focus on the internal politics of the school building, and Foreign Affairs, in which we focus on the political interaction of the building and its local environment.

Domestic Affairs

The research on the micropolitics of the school's domestic affairs focuses on the interaction and political ideologies of administrators, teachers, and students within the school building. From a micropolitical perspective, the focus is on the conflictual interactions of a school site's internal constituent groups. The research in this area indicates that administrator, teacher, and student political interactions center on three fundamental areas of contest. The first contest is over the allocation of valued resources or stakes. In the case of the domestic affairs of the school, this is primarily conflict over the distribution of valued resources and what services the school provides. The second conflict concerns who controls or governs (i.e., who has the legitimate right to decide as well as monitor domestic policy and in what domain). The third area of contest is over the system's political ideology and its underlying assumptions. In this section, we will also address how supervisors supervise (i.e., what are the strategies and tactics employed by the supervisors and the supervised?).

What Are the Stakes? The issue of the distribution of stakes, or, "Who Gets What?" (Lasswell, 1936) is concerned with the allocation of resources and services. This emphasis is on the stakes allocated and mechanisms of allocation. Stroufe (1977) offered the following definition:

> Politics has to do with the distribution of stakes within a society or group. "Stakes" means jobs, money, prestige, influence, status, or even acceptance of ideas. People care enough about such stakes to try actively to influence their distribution. To this end they develop and husband their influence, and seek to use it wisely to affect the distribution of stakes (p. 190).

In the domestic politics of the school, the principal, teachers, and students have multiple stakes which are contested. Contests occur over budget, discipline, personnel, curriculum, instruction, evaluation, and so on (Malen, 1995; McLeese, 1992). The focus is again on the authoritative allocation of valued resources as well as mechanisms of allocation (Easton, 1965a; Easton, 1965b; Wirt & Kirst, 1989). Whether the school is providing appropriate educational services as defined by the various constituent groups is sometimes at issue. At other times, contests revolve around whether individuals or groups are getting their perceived fair share of valued resources (e.g., time, supplies, supportive parents, and fluent learners).

Who Governs? The second area of contest is concerned with who governs. This area of contest between the school's building level constituent groups is both territorial and topical. It is fought over who has the legitimate right both to make decisions and to monitor their implementation on what topics and in what territorial domains. The principally contested territories are over control of the building and control of the classroom. In addition to territorial contests, who supervises what topical areas is also a matter of contest. Contested topics include curriculum, budget, personnel, and instruction (Malen, 1995; McLeese, 1992).

The research findings on who governs in which territorial and topical domains are quite clear. The dominant territorial pattern is that principals control building-level policy and teachers control classroom instruction. In topical areas, administrators are acknowledged by teachers to have preeminence in matters that involve decisions about security in the school, school boundary issues (e.g., representing the school to the attendance area), school–community communications, budget, and personnel (Conley, 1991; Weiss, 1993). Administrators are also seen as having special responsibility for the evaluation and certification of instructional programs and teaching. In this last area, however, administrator behaviors are carefully circumscribed to meet legal requirements of accountability rather than to interfere in the classroom. Teachers see topics such as curriculum and instruction as their prerogatives.

Both parties are interested in maintaining their authority over their particular domains while they acquire influence in the other's domain (Bacharach, Bauer, & Shedd, 1986; Rowan, 1990). Some overlapping jurisdiction occurs in this area when administrators seek to mandate new curricula or major changes in instructional processes. This sort of action can push such issues into matters of contest. In general, however, teachers are acknowledged by most administrators to have the right to organize the learning process in their area, usually by grade levels in the lower schools and subject areas in the upper schools.

The stakes for all constituent groups are two things. The first is influence. The second is discretionary latitude, which is sometimes mislabeled autonomy. From a political frame of reference, the demands for influence and discretionary latitude are political ideologies. In effect, they are a "demand to be allowed to use one's expertise with a minimum hindrance from others" (Iannaccone, 1975, p. 45). Between administrators and teachers, the conflict is between administrator control and teacher discretion. Between teachers and students, the conflict is between teacher control and student discretion. The prize in each case is the right to decide. The political process around who governs between the principal and teachers is illustrated graphically in Figure 10.3.

From a micropolitical perspective, the argument over who governs is a contest over the relative citizenship rights of the various constituent groups in these territorial and topical domains. This leads us to an examination of the nature of the school as a polity.

As we stated earlier, the process of translating conflicting social values into policy requires a set of arrangements by which a particular society governs itself. This set of arrangements includes its constitution and the institutionally defined members of a body politic. From a micropolitical frame of reference, organizational membership groups or strata are viewed as the constitutionally related constituent groups of the polity. One obvious feature of school organization is the stratified nature of its major constituent groups: administrators, teachers, and students (Blase, 1991a; Marshall & Mitchell, 1991; Opotow, 1991).

The political significance of the stratified structure of the school is revealed in how constituent group membership becomes a basis for the governance roles of organizational members. The presentation of types of persons in governance statuses is the basic reality of representation. All organization is the mobilization of bias toward political action, whether that fact led to the organization or not. This fundamental bias of the social structure of educational organizations may be seen in the strength of the separations among its major status categories. These categories define the school's major constituent groups and produce a sense of identity within each. In addition, they establish boundaries between each and provide different bases of definition for representation.

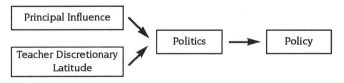

FIGURE 10.3.

A central concern from a micropolitical perspective is the part played by each constituent group in the governance of the polity. In fact, the specific nature of a polity is revealed by the relationship of its constituent groups to its politics. This relationship is defined by the rights and obligations of each constituent group in the polity's governance. The specific nature of a polity is defined more precisely by the institutionally defined role of each constituent group in translating conflicting social values into building policy, rules, regulations, and administrative decisions.

The school's organizational status definitions serve to define the nature of each constituent group's access to policy making. They also carry major implications for participation in organizational supervision and governance. First, the strength of the status boundaries limits the interaction across statuses, restricting these interactions to a narrow pattern of formal relationships most of the time. On the other hand, the same boundaries and strengthened sense of identity within statuses tend to increase the potential development of systematic interaction within each status. The influence of this stratified structure therefore tends to increase access to peer networks for the mobilization of influence. At the same time, it tends to decrease interaction across statuses.

The significant threat of major conflict erupting between the different status groups is also implicit in this arrangement. The potential for conflict between the building's three major constituent groups, administrators versus teachers versus pupils, is always present. As Schattschneider's (1975) model indicates, however, the nature of politics itself results in certain conflicts becoming dominant at the expense of other potential conflicts. In fact, the pupils as a mass become actively engaged in the micropolitics of the building only rarely in extreme periods of political conflict.

A political perspective uses the categories of citizen, subject, and alien to describe the nature of a constituent group's rights and obligations in the polity's governance. Subjects, as the term indicates, are subject to the rule of the polity (i.e., they are required to obey the laws and regulations of the polity). Citizens are subjects who have the right to participate in the polity's law-making processes; however, there may be considerable variation in the relative citizenship rights of different constituent groups within a polity. Within schools, "administrators and teachers are both subjects and citizens of the polity, with differences in their citizen rights, displaying tension along the line of cleavage separating them" (Iannaccone, 1991, p. 468). In fact, these two constituent groups are continually engaged in struggles over their relative citizenship rights and obligations. For example, Blase (1991) described this tension between teachers and administrators over degrees of teacher participation in site-level governance. Other studies have illustrated how teachers seek to readjust the existing balance under the banner of professionalism (Noblit, Berry, & Dempsey, 1991). Using a different tactic, teacher organizations have attempted to readjust this balance through the labor contract.

There are also constituent groups who are subject to the laws of the polity they dwell in. Although they are not considered aliens, they still do not participate in its rule-making and civic dialogue. Students are such a group. Students, who are the largest constituent group in the school, are subjects who are not citizens and who cannot become citizens (i.e., there is no route to citizenship status for them). When the largest category of a polity's members is a class of persons who neither share in its governance by right, nor are able to acquire that right through their efforts, then the polity involved is a caste society. A caste, unlike a social class, is a status from which one cannot move through social mobility into another class within the same social system. "The school viewed in micropolitical terms has as its defining polity feature, its essential governance attribute, the character of a caste society" (Iannaccone, 1991, p. 469).

Caste polities display predictable features. First, there is always tension between castes, and the threat of disruption of the system is always present. Second, each caste has a tendency to conceal its inner workings, internal differences, and intrastratum conflicts from the other castes. Hence, strategies to conceal their activities from members of other castes are a normal way of doing business. The different classes of citizens, in this case teachers and administrators, avoid revealing the tensions that exist between them to other subject castes, especially the student caste. This is done to prevent potential threats to their citizenship status. As a result, the citizens do not engage in open debate, critical self-examination, and dialogue over significant policy issues. For this reason, the governance of caste societies displays many more petty value conflicts that do most other polities. This is so precisely because they avoid confronting their more significant tensions. The pursuit of these more significant tensions threatens to destroy the fragile authority structure of the polity.

The tendency toward the prevention of major conflicts is built into the school's micropolitical structure, its ideology, and its decision-making processes. The political outcomes of the school's micropolitics usually reinforce this same tendency toward the prevention of conflict. This paradoxically helps to explain why there are so many petty political clashes in schools. One way to avoid a big conflict is to create conditions that siphon off conflicts into many petty fights. This is why in schools, as in small rural towns, the etiquette of gossip characterizes teacher talk, and petty political crises are so prominent. These serve to fill the vacuum created by the absence of open political debate with a loyal opposition (Iannaccone, 1967; Willower, 1970).

How Do They Govern? We will now turn our attention to the strategies and tactics of the supervisors and the supervised in the governance process. Research on policy making and its monitoring at the building level suggests that the school is usefully viewed as a negotiated order (Hanson, 1979). A negotiated order is one in which organizational members and constituent groups are involved in a pervasive and complex web of decision-making processes. These decision-making processes involve the use of informal negotiations and bargaining processes and result in give-and-take agreements. A negotiated order stands in contrast to a social order based solely on formal hierarchical top-down governance processes. The existence of a negotiated order depends upon conflicting legitimated sources of authority. In the case of the school, the dominant conflicting sources of authority are the legal bureaucratic chain-of-command versus the authority of professional expertise.

A structural view of the internal politics of the school building displays two different ways of arranging its components. The one most frequently noted in connection with the school's governance is the hierarchical arrangement of the school. In its simplest conceptualization, this arrangement is viewed as the legal chain-of-command running from the school's administration to its teaching staff to the students. The primary function of this hierarchical structure is presumed to be the governance of school building affairs, including the activities of the task structure. Much of the bureaucratic chain-of-command of this authority structure reflects external governance conditions imposed from the macrolevel rather than the microlevel internal task accomplishment needs of the school. As a result, this hierarchical authority structure contains many elements that have been superimposed upon the school.

The second structural arrangement is based upon the school's educational task accomplishment. This second structure partly rationalizes and coordinates the educational services of the school. The primary features of this task structure are derived from the school's client-serving nature as an educational delivery organization. The authority of this zone is based upon professional expertise around this task accomplishment. This zone of authority is shaped by the professional discretion of the classroom teacher.

Each of these zones of authority reflects quite different, but related, school features. The competing territorial and topical domains discussed earlier arise from these two different zones of authority that are structurally built into the school. Principals' authority stems from their position in the legal bureaucratic chain-of-command whereas teachers' authority is based upon professional expertise around task accomplishment.

These two structures may be described using a loosely drawn analogy from larger political systems. The task structure of the organization may be viewed as what is governed. Its components may thus be seen as the categories of persons whose behavior is governed in the school as a political entity. The hierarchical authority structure may be seen in this analogy as its government. Together these form the major micropolitical structure of the school's domestic affairs.

Continuous informal negotiation substitutes for all-out political war between these two zones. Hanson's (1979) research on schools displays these two basically different spheres of authority, which he labels the "administrators' zone" and the "teachers' zone." As these zones interact and overlap, they produce a third decisional sphere. This third sphere, which he labels the "contested zone," is where most of the day-in, day-out negotiations take place.

The contested zone may expand or contract depending upon several factors. Some of this area's nature results from the interdependence of factors in the other two. Hanson offers the following examples:

The personnel in the Silverwood schools were continually observed in the process of informal negotiation. Students negotiated with teachers for less homework; teachers negotiated with janitors for repairing the light fixture now instead of later in the day; teachers negotiated with administrators for more instructional materials, dif-ferent room assignments, or new committee assignments; administrators negotiated with teachers for increased vigilance in the halls; administrators negotiated with parents for increased participation in school affairs or more patience and understanding with the school reading program. The end product of the ongoing negotiation process is to bring order and stability to the potentially disruptive contested zone (Hanson, 1979, p. 125).

Why this process instead of the simple issuing of commands or making formal demands? The answer lies in the complex and subtle realities of the nature of the work involved as well as the nature of the social system. Every group in the organization, whether administrators, teachers, nonteaching staff, or students, has significant pocket veto power. Simply working to the rule and doing exactly what the directive specifies and not more would effectively wreck the operation. This is so because rules, by their very nature, explicate minimum standards. Hence, there is the built-in need for day-in, day-out negotiations.

Because topics and terrains of interest to all parties fall in contested zones, principals, teachers, and students negotiate who will have influence on what topics in what territories. They constantly broker the boundaries of their respective spheres of influence. In doing so, they negotiate what if any changes will be permitted in school policies and practices, whose conception of the school will prevail, and who will monitor it (Ball, 1987; Malen, 1995).

Principals and teachers maintain control of their respective zones by employing a number of tactics. Principals maintain control of the governance of the schoolwide policy making system in a number of ways. In formal arenas, such as faculty and committee meetings, they control decision-making processes by setting the agenda, as well as controlling the meeting format and information flow (Ball, 1987; Corcoran, 1987; Gronn, 1984; Malen & Ogawa, 1988; Mann, 1974). The capacity to set the agenda and control the meeting format allows principals to confine agendas to issues of their choosing. This tactic is used by principals to keep the focus on safe issues while avoiding or containing conflict (Marshall & Mitchell, 1991). In some schools, teachers recognize that the agenda items set by the principal are trivial and tangential (Mauriel & Lindquist, 1989) and depict options for input as token gestures or pseudoparticipation that rubber stamp decisions that have already been made (Ball, 1987; Johnson, 1989, 1990). Finally, principals can overturn troubling decisions by simply not implementing them.

The principal uses the existing formal governance structures of the school to serve a number of important political functions. First, they are used as vehicles to air complaints (Ball, 1987; Mann, 1974; McLeese, 1992). The principal can also use them as forums to rally support for preexisting policies (Hanson, 1991; Malen, 1993, 1994a). These structures also serve symbolic functions and can be used as symbols of teachers' and students' right to have a voice in decisions. Principals can also stigmatize and silence teachers through rhetorical devices that define discussion as subversive action (Anderson, 1991; Ball, 1987). This capacity to control and manipulate information allows principals to manage the meanings ascribed to actions (Anderson, 1991) as well as to shape decision-making premises. Pettigrew (1973) found that administrators who control information and choose to filter it can have as much influence over decisions as if they were to make the decisions themselves. Teachers are reluctant to challenge the principal's meanings and decision-making premises for a number of reasons, not the least of which is fear of social and professional sanctions (Ball, 1987; Corcoran, 1987; Duke, Shower, & Imber, 1981; Weiss, Cambone, & Wyeth, 1992). Professional norms also serve to mute dissent, minimize conflict, and maintain stability (Malen and Ogawa, 1988).

In some instances, principals recruit supportive teachers as school council members as a means to form coalitions of like minded teachers (Bryk et al, 1993; Hanson, 1981; McLeese, 1992; Weiss & Cambone, 1993). Principals can less formally selectively consult with teachers. These tactics allow them to preempt or coopt resistance (Ball, 1987; Blase, 1988). On the other hand, principals can limit opponents' access to the formal governance system, thereby working to divide faculties into fragmented factions (Ball, 1987).

As a function of their formal position in the governance system, principals can control and allocate discretionary resources as a managerial prerogative. This is further compounded by the limited authority and the modest supports provided to school-based governance structures (David & Peterson, 1984; Fish, 1994; Stevenson & Pellicer, 1992). This is true even in schools that are actively following a site-based management model. Researchers in this area have found that teachers become worn down by the demands of site-based management and skeptical of the prospects for meaningful influence at the organizational level (Johnson, 1990; Malen, Ogawa, & Krantz, 1990). While endorsing the ideal of participatory democracy, some principals also become frustrated by the demands of participatory processes and struggle to retain control over issues perceived to fall within their topical and territorial domains (Bennettet al, 1992; McLeese, 1992).).

Teachers know that principals have the authority to allocate a number of valued resources. In addition to discretionary funds, principals can adjust assignments, influence evaluations and promotions, and otherwise affect teachers' well being (Malen, 1995). The principal can use these resources and sanctions to broker agreements or grant favors. These agreements and favors are used to silence opposition, produce indebtedness, and induce loyalty (Ball, 1987; Blase, 1988).

Principals also employ strategies to influence teachers in informal arenas. They use moral persuasion (Greenfield, 1991), recognition, and praise as means to influence the domestic politics of the building (Blase & Kirby, 1992; Greenfield, 1991). Conflictual interactions between principals and teachers are a major source of stress for both parties (Bridges, 1970; Marshall & Mitchell, 1991). They "tend to manage these tensions through polite exchanges that maintain and mirror the traditional pattern of power" (Malen, 1995, p. 155). As in any polity, informal exchanges between principals and teachers "bring an acceptable degree of order and stability" to the school (Hanson, 1981, p. 266). They also tend to make change an incremental if not an incidental outcome (Ball, 1987; Malen 1991).

All of the preceding tactics are means whereby the principal governs. They use these tactics to maintain their zones of influence, impact the decisional sphere, and effectively "block, stifle, dissuade, or ignore groups in school" (Ball, 1987, p. 79; Berman & McLaughlin, 1978; McLaughlin, 1987). For these reasons, teachers generally employ a set of protective and promotional strategies (Blase, 1988, 1989) with principals. Blase (1988) has formulated these responses into a typology of teacher learned responses: Acquiesce; Conform; Circumvent; Sabotage; and Passive Resistance. Teachers are also vulnerable to the criticisms of peers and students (Blase, 1988). Thus, they tend to "insulate themselves from interactions that can damage their reputations, diminish the quality of their work life and disrupt their ability to carry out their responsibilities in ways congruent with their views and values" (Malen, 1995, p. 157).

The prominent pattern in studies that address the domestic affairs of the school is a set of governance tactics that sustain conventional roles and zones of influence. Formal committees and everyday interactions between principals and teachers both work to maintain these conventional arrangements (Little, 1990; Malen, 1993). Both principals and teachers seek to defend and preserve their respective spheres of influence and maintain a climate of harmony in the school (Ball, 1987; Blase, 1991a). In these ways, the likelihood that traditional patterns of influence will be challenged is reduced and the likelihood that established patterns will be sustained is increased. In effect, "teachers purchase discretion within classrooms by relinquishing their opportunity to influence school policy" (Corwin, 1981, p. 276). School administrators, who have been socialized as teachers and tend to share the ideology of teacher discretion in the classroom, usually support this division. Because of these dynamics, incremental changes may occur, but major changes in the basic governance structure of the school rarely happen (Berman, Weiler Associates, 1984; Bryk et al, 1993; Malen, 1993; McLeese, 1992; Weiss & Cambone, 1993). As a result, principals retain control over school-level policy and teachers retain discretion over classroom-level practice.

We will now turn our attention to the interactions and ideologies of teachers and students. Teachers engage in two sorts of activities in the governance of the teaching and learning process in the classroom. First are those activities that are necessary to teach expertly. Second are those activities that are needed to invoke the students' cooperation in their own learning. The need to involve students in their own learning produces a dilemma for teachers. They may use their legal authority and expert power to govern student behavior, or, alternately, they may rely upon eliciting the students' cooperation via shared decision-making processes. This dilemma is rooted in the fact that students must be psychologically engaged in their own growth. Moreover, much of what students must do to use the expert guidance of the teacher must be done by students when the teacher is not present and therefore unable to provide close supervision.

In some professions, this dilemma is partly resolved by the fact that practitioners and their clients engage in a pattern of self-selection in which each chooses the other. In public education, compulsory education laws mitigate against this option. Students do not choose their teachers and teachers do not choose their students (Carlson, 1964). Compulsory education laws mandate that students accept the service, at least at the level of being in the school, and that teachers accept their students, at least at the level of allowing them in their classrooms.

Students cannot legally reject being in school, and as such they have no choice of whether to belong to the polity. Some mitigation of this extreme picture does exist. For example, some students drop out, wealthy students may select private schools, home schooling is an option for some, and informal interaction with teachers and the principal by parents can produce changes in classroom assignments. On the whole, however, students have little choice about whether or where they will be placed in the organization. Thus, they are compelled by law to be a member of the school organization and of a particular classroom most of the time. Their conditions of membership are not theirs to determine, and they have no organizationally legitimated discretion at all. The law, however, cannot and does not determine how students respond to that reality. In fact, the students' response to this situation is the only freedom they have. As a result, some degree of alienation usually characterizes the nature of the student's response. This dynamic is one source of the demand for teacher discretion.

In addition, students do not directly pay teachers for educational services. Teachers are paid by the larger society through its macropolitical governance structures. For this reason, client choice has little direct relationship to the economic base of education. There are two major consequences that flow from this fact. First, the teacher–student relationship is weakened by the absence of an economic bond. Second, this mode of payment produces an economic bond between the teacher and the larger society that sometimes mitigates against student representation (Iannaccone, 1975).

In public schools, both the range of choices for mutual selection and the economic bond is absent. These factors attenuate the teachers' dilemma. Teachers need the discretion that will allow them to use their judgment and shuttle between the use of legal authority and the use of shared decision-making processes. Without a significant degree of discretion, the teacher lacks the capacity to make that choice in the governance of the classroom. Most teachers realistically combine some of each of these strategies. Teacher tactics are easier to develop if the turf is well bounded and the belief in teacher discretion is well established. The stronger this boundary, the greater the teacher's discretion. For these reasons, teachers work to maintain control of the governance of the classroom. Principals, who were socialized as teachers, tend to support this as long as control in the classroom is maintained. One role of the principal's office, school board regulations, and the central office is to help protect the teacher's influence and discretion in the classroom. In the process, teachers trade control of organizational-level policy for control of the governance of the classroom.

This demand for professional discretion and the belief in it as a primary value is common to all professions. Stated most simply, it arises because of the need of professionals to make judgments about what to do with specific clients and

their needs. A professional needs discretionary latitude. As previously explained, discretionary latitude is a demand to be allowed to use one's expertise with minimal hindrance from others. Discretionary latitude is required even in a tutorial arrangement. It is needed more in a classroom, where a range of pupils are found; consequently, the most generally shared work-related political norm of the building is for teacher-discretionary latitude in their control of their classes.

As we stated earlier, the teacher must alternate between the use of bureaucratic authority inherent in the teacher role and the building of warm affective bonds needed to produce the motivation for learning. A requirement of considerable latitude in teacher discretion is implicit. That latitude in effect allows the teacher to operate sometimes in conflict with the hierarchical and bureaucratic structure of the school in order to meet the responsibilities for effective learning. The classroom viewed as a micropolitical entity is therefore fraught with potential conflicts. Restricting the scope of these is an essential aspect of the classroom social structure. The outcome of this condition is an uneasy balance within the classroom. It produces another uneasy balance between teachers, administrators, and the pupil social system within the building.

The norm of professional discretion in the classroom is the predominant ideological demand the work flow structure places upon the chain of command. This norm may be seen in several of its correlates. These include the assumption of a single teacher as the classroom teacher. It is seen in the norm that those criticisms are confined to the etiquette of peer gossip, however critical other teachers may be about one's teaching. Sharing such criticism with parents, administrators, and especially pupils is a major norm violation. It is also seen in teacher demands that administrators stay out of classrooms except under carefully prescribed procedures required for principals to carry out their legal responsibilities. At the building level, the same norm underpins the faculty's claim for preeminence in instructional decisions. Here, more than in the classroom, that claim confronts the legal and administrative demands that limit it. A balance between these potentially conflicting values is maintained through the development of a negotiated social order. That social order is the central synthesis of structure, process, and ideology that gives the school as a political entity its basic character.

The dominant conflict of the building between the hierarchical authority structure and the task–accomplishment structure sharply defines who may participate in the school's political conflicts. This cleavage defines teachers and administrators as the major contestants. At the same time, it defines the largest proportion of the members of the building organization, (i.e., students and noncertified employees, as well as its attendance area public) as spectators (Schattschneider, 1975). These groups are not represented as active participants in the political conflict.

This dominance of the structural relationship between teachers and administrators as the central political cleavage has a second consequence. It avoids the issues most significant to groups in the audience by neglecting or subordinating these to the ones of most interest to the customary contestants. The kinds of conflicts most significant to pupils and parents are suppressed by the teacher-versus-administrator cleavage around which the dominant political conflicts occur. The most obvious of these are the conflicts between teachers and pupils. The prevention of these potential classroom conflicts from expanding to become part of the battles of the building is a major function of the dominant cleavage. The socialization of vice principals teaches them to look for this potentially disruptive conflict and head it off before it starts (Marshall & Greenfield, 1985). The suppression of the conflict of the classroom indirectly but powerfully shapes the battle lines of the building. It is most important to note that the politics needed to maintain such a system results above all in inertia and a static polity.

At the same time, a significant source of potential conflicts is created by the existence of this structural arrangement. It is akin to the normal tension found in any political system between those who govern and the governed. As in the case of larger political systems, the governance structure also appears to be more obviously political than do the structures of groups governed. Nevertheless, the structural organization of the governed is more fundamentally significant in the politics of any polity. Following Schattschneider's (1975) model, the governed are the audience of political activity. It is to be expected that the interplay between the authority and the task accomplishment structure will be fertile territory for political conflicts. It is as if a no-man's land of at least potential warfare were implicitly structured into the school as a political entity.

The most politically significant features of the building's structures are those found at the points of intersection between the formal authority structure and the task structure. The political function of the chain-of-command may be better understood when it is seen as a conflict defining, conflict-limiting, and conflict-resolving structure. These functions are most observable at those points where this governmental structure intersects with the work flow or service structure. The salient sets of interactions at those intersection points primarily involve teachers and administrators. The formal interaction between components of the task structure and the legal governance structure are the axes around which most of the micropolitics of the building is observed. The more visible allocation of stakes involving bargaining, negotiations, and decision-making adjustments take place around this axis. It is politically naïve to view these as only interpretive decisions about the specific meanings of board policies and central office directives. This is also true of the legal interaction around union contract management and grievances. Informal interactions and day-to-day implementation of understandings going beyond the formal contract are similarly found around the same axes.

The pressure transmitted through chain-of-command from the external macropolitics of the district are also lodged on this axis. Pressures from the micropolitical environment of the parents and the neighborhoods of the building's attendance area also come to rest on the same axis as that for decision-making. This is so whether those pressures are transmitted through the administrative structure or through the felt pressures expressed by teachers.

Much of this is taken for granted. It is ironic that it is the unasked questions or the assumptions that lead to questions not being asked that often display greater policy influence than the ones raised. The assumption that things are done as they are because that is the way we do it here, or it has always been done that way, is an indicator of enormous power. The most powerful areas of potential conflict are often the ones neglected by the unasked questions. Such questions include whether children should be educated by public authority, as well as how they should be educated.

The meaning and significance of such assumptions for the micropolitics of the school cannot be adequately understood using the concepts of structure and process alone. The concept of political ideology must be added to understand the impact of the school's assumptive foundations on its politics.

The Political Ideology of the School Ideologies are the underlying assumptions or political myths on which the governance of educational organizations is based. An ideological approach pays particular attention to the assumptions, beliefs, and norms of the constituent groups of the school. Its point of departure is the consistent finding that in all social systems, some beliefs become normative. In the formation of even primary groups, certain customary ways of behaving become accepted as expected of group members. Shared expectations about behavior become group norms. These are the standards by which member behaviors are judged and rewarded or sanctioned. Political ideology refers to shared beliefs and assumptions about standards for behavior with respect to governance. This includes beliefs about the behavior of both those who govern and those who are governed.

Ideological assumptions guide the politics of the building in both its definition of conflicts and in its incremental decision-making processes. Incremental quiescent political processes of day-to-day allocation of stakes are largely routine consequences of decisions made by persons in their organizational roles. These may be teachers, administrators, custodians, or secretaries. They may be leaders of informal groups of the adults and the students of the building. The norms, regulations, policies, and other criteria guiding these routines are reflections of established political ideologies. These routines and the values allocated by them depend upon ideological underpinnings. Beliefs about authority are, therefore, an essential factor in supporting and shaping the routine, seemingly apolitical distributions of stakes in the school.

Political ideology also guides the choice of political conflicts. As we stated earlier, the choice of conflicts through the definition of most salient issues for political action is the central strategy of politics (Schattschneider, 1975). That choice, however, is not a simple exercise of will. In addition to political ideology, it reflects the realities of organizational structures and the perception of threat from other policies and interests. It is most important that the choice is shaped by conceptualizations of the social situation and the categories for classifying information. These are often not thought of as politically relevant.

Obvious normative beliefs appear as prescriptive statements about what should or should not be done. The most concretely stated beliefs of a governance system appear in the forms of constitutions, laws, regulations, and policy statements. Among the less obvious, seemingly purely cognitive categories for classifying facts, events, and persons carry evaluative connotations. Thus, even apparently purely descriptive conceptualizations of the structures for allocating values carry some evaluative connotations. Status categories identifying groups of persons in terms of the school's work flow similarly carry connotations of appropriate political participation in the decision-making of the chain-of-command.

We often take for granted our conceptualizations of categories of persons within an organization. As a result, we seldom think about the normative implications for political participation implicit in those categories we use for organizational members. The concepts of status and role categories we each use also carry with them a sense of group identification. Verbal indicators of that sense may especially be seen in the distinction between we and they or pronouns of ownership (e.g., ours and theirs). Such identification points to two related social aspects. It points to the direction of social solidarity that may be expanded or contracted in political action. It also points to the opposite side of the same coin (i.e., the cleavages that exist and may be distended into conflicts). Thus, conceptualization of status and role categories simultaneously tends to unite some people for collective action and separate them from others as either potential opponents or as not politically relevant for specific political action.

The political ideology of the school is shaped by the potential conflicts between the school's competing sources of authority. The typical expression of the building's myth of authority seeks to balance off the legal demand for influence and accountability against the claims of professional discretion. The competing claims of these values combined with the looseness of linkages at the intersections of the legal authority and work-flow structures produce two effects. Political conflicts at these points are usually defined ideologically as issues of influence and accountability versus discretion. This core ideology also justifies a negotiated order rather than justifying administrative commands as the rational organizational implementation of hierarchical policy.

The negotiated order of the school is what it is largely to avoid the more explosive and disruptive political conflicts that could threaten the professional discretionary latitude of administrators and teachers. The danger that extended expansion of any of these conflicts could turn into a war around teacher discretion and building administrator influence tends to severely limit these conflicts. As a result, the basic ideology tends to suppress rather than open up conflicts. In the process, many small conflicts come and go, leaving a residue of unfinished and incomplete business, with its frustration and lowering of morale rather than conflict resolution. Dramatic changes in policies and programs do not take place without accepting the risks of political conflict. The school's political ideology is bent toward incrementalism in policy changes instead. Most of the time, the dominant ideology of the building micropolitics moves toward stasis rather than change.

This political ideology carries two major implications for the politics of the building. Discretion in any political system must be traded off against influence. Discretion for the teacher within the classroom may increase the teacher's

potential influence over the pupils in the room. It at least creates the conditions of discretionary latitude for such influence. The same commitment to classroom teacher discretion, however, sharply reduces the influence possible to teachers on one another's classroom behavior. For example, attempts by some teachers to change the teaching behavior of others through formal offices or faculty meeting decisions usually fail. On the other hand, proposals for buildingwide action that can be linked to expanding teacher discretion are likely to elicit the support of other teachers.

In addition, the ideology of discretion for classroom teachers places demands upon the building administration to protect the classroom from both central office and local parent influence. Thus, the major functional problem in the foreign relations of the school is to maintain professional latitude without sacrificing public support. The predominant ideology consequently shapes the building's foreign policy toward building discretion through strengthening barriers against its environment. The short-run gains in professional discretion are won at a cost. The long-run results increase the isolation of schools and decrease their public support.

Foreign Affairs

We now turn our attention to the external politics of the site level through an examination of the school's foreign affairs. The politics of the school's foreign affairs are concerned with managing or channeling the conflict that occurs between the building and its local environment. This leads to a focus on the political interactions and ideologies of the building, its immediate neighborhoods, and the school district. Our focus is specifically on the conflictual interactions of professionals and lay subsystems at the building level. A building's external politics (i.e., its foreign relations) may be seen both in its relationships with its immediate neighborhoods as well as with its interaction with the flow of authority from the super system of which it is a legal component. As we stated earlier, larger political and institutional forces as championed by the state, church, professional organizations, and community interest groups will be largely, but not entirely, mediated by the district. We will attend to the implication of this for the micropolitics of the building in greater detail in the following pages.

In this section of our discussion, we will first focus on the interaction between the administrative policy making system of the building and parents. In broad terms, the research in this area indicates that the political interactions between the principal and parents center on two fundamental areas of contest. The first is conflict over the allocation of valued resources or stakes. This is primarily conflict over the distribution of valued resources and whether the school has provided appropriate educational services. The second area of contest concerns who governs (i.e., who has the legitimate right to decide and monitor policy). In addition to these two areas of contest, we will also address how school conflict is governed or supervised (i.e., what are the processes and strategies that are employed in the supervision of building level conflict by the various constituent groups and coalitions, by the governors and the governed).

What Are the Stakes? In the micropolitics of the school, the administrative policy making system of the school and the building-level public have multiple stakes that may be contested. Areas of contest include, but are not limited to, discipline, curriculum, programs, finance, personnel selection, and evaluation (For a review, see McLeese, 1992). In addition, the amount of resources allocated, the disbursement of rewards or sanctions, and the meaning of propriety and fairness are also matters of concern and contest (Blase, 1989, 1991a). The focus here is on the authoritative allocation of valued resources (Easton, 1965a; Easton, 1965b; Wirt & Kirst, 1989) (i.e., whether the school is providing appropriate educational services).

The principal, teachers, parents, lay public, various interest groups, the district, and institutional agents (e.g., church, state, and professional organizations) are all potential players in conflicts over stakes. Who will and who will not become involved in these conflicts is dependent upon a number of issues. These include the definition of the conflict, the strength of individual and group interests, the discrepancy between "what is" and "what should be," who has access to the existing governance mechanisms of the building, and so on.

Who Governs? The second area of contest concerns who governs and who is governed. It is specifically concerned with who has the right to participate in the governance of the polity as well as the relative citizenship rights of the various constituent groups. Citizenship rights include the capacity to define the conflict, set the agenda, make policy and rules, decide issues, and construct organizational meanings. It is also important to note who controls and has access to information.

The research indicates that much of the professional and public tension centers on who has the legitimate right to influence or decide policy (Malen, 1995). This conflict plays out in a contest over parental influence versus the latitude of discretion of the administrative policy making system of the building. The ability of the administrative policy making system of the building to manage conflicts that arise as parents try to influence school policy is a central issue in the micropolitics of the building (Summerfield, 1971). Influence versus discretionary latitude is again at stake in this political contest. The political process around who governs is illustrated graphically in Figure 10.4.

The research findings on the relative citizenship rights of parents and school professionals at the building level are quite clear. The traditional pattern is that principals control organizational level policy, teachers control classroom instruction, and parents provide support (Davies et al, 1977; Jennings, 1980; Malen et al, 1990). Principals and teachers consistently maintain that it is their right to make school policy, whereas the role of parents is perceived as endorsers of the professional's decisions (Davies, 1980, 1987; Mann, 1974; Moles, 1987). Although parents often express concern with this position (McLeese, 1992), they usually accept it (Davies, 1981; Malen & Ogawa, 1988).

This theme of the limited role of parental influence is evident in a number of studies. It has been found in studies of program specific advisory committees (Davies, 1980, Fisher, 1979, Shields & McLaughlin, 1986) as well as in site-based decision-making bodies (Berman, Weiler Associates, 1984; Bryk et al, 1993; Malen & Ogawa, 1988). Parent councils have been characterized as pro forma units and public relations vehicles, not as democratic decision-making bodies or policy making entities (Davies, 1987; Mann, 1974, 1977; Popkewitz, 1979). In addition, parent councils rarely function as forums for meaningful discussion of significant issues or for professional–parent problem solving. (Davies, 1980; Davies et al, 1977; Malen et al, 1990). For example, in studies of parent councils, the issues of budget, personnel, and program are rarely addressed (Davies, 1980; Fisher, 1979; Jennings, 1980). In other studies, parents have typically depicted council agendas as trivial and identify issues they would prefer to discuss, but which they are not able to raise (Davies, 1987; Malen & Ogawa, 1988; Mann, 1974). At the building level, the councils tend to be "artificial bodies" in which opportunities to influence policies are "more significant on paper than in practice" (Berman, Weiler Associates, 1984, p. 166). The research evidence indicates that parent council interactions have not substantially affected the distribution of educational services (Berman, Weiler Associates, 1984, p. ii; Malen et al, 1990).

To compound the issue, council membership itself rarely reflects the economic, social, racial, or ethnic composition of the school community it purports to represent (Conway, 1984; Malen et al, 1990; Mann, 1975, 1977). Parent influence is especially restricted for low-income and minority populations (DeLacy, 1992; Fine, 1993). This propensity for participation to be socially stratified suggests that matters of race, ethnicity, and economics affect parent access to, hence prospects for, influence in these areas (Fine, 1993; Malen & Ogawa, 1988; Mann, 1977).

All of this research speaks to the limited citizenship rights of the building-level public. Parents are alien to the building-level politics, procedurally as well as structurally. Although they and their children may be subject to the policies of the schools, they have almost no citizenship rights in the policy making system beyond that of supporting policies as set by the principal and teachers. At the microlevel, the answer to the question "Who governs?" is clearly the administrative policy making system of the building.

How Do They Govern? The third issue we will address concerns the strategies and tactics of managing conflict that are employed by the supervisor. Conflicts arise when parents assert their right to influence school policy, place demands for change on the school, or otherwise challenge the discretionary latitude of professional educators. Administrative pro-

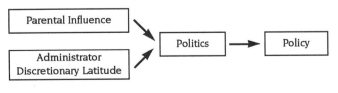

FIGURE 10.4.

fessionals are aware that parental criticisms can threaten the stability and legitimacy of the school. This potential threat of parents becoming involved in policy making has been framed by administrators as fears of "intrusion" by "outsiders" (Hempel, 1986, p. 136). The administrator's "anxieties about the school's ability to withstand scrutiny and conflicts . . . are ever present" (Malen, 1995, p. 149).

Iannaccone and Lutz (1995, 1970) have shown that parents move to political action when there is a mismatch between community expectations and school operations. Events such as desegregation plans, curricular changes, school closures, and so on signal parents that mismatches exist. When these mismatches exceed the parents' "zone of tolerance" (Iannaccone & Lutz, 1970), they act. Despite the ever-present and contagious nature of parent–school conflict, the traditional pattern of the principal controlling organizational-level policy, teachers controlling classroom instruction, and parents providing support is usually maintained. This occurs for a number of related reasons and in a number of mutually reenforcing ways.

Principals employ a number of strategies in an attempt to manage the conflict that occurs as a result of the intrusion of the parents into the policy making process. Summerfield (1971) found that the principals he studied used four situationally derived strategies to contain conflict and procure deference. First, principals may act as leaders of neighborhood interest groups. From this position, the principal works to define the conflict as between the neighborhood interest groups and the district. In the process, the principal deflects the conflict away from the building. With community support, the principal is able to secure symbolic and material resources from the district. In turn, this leads to increased community support and public deference to school administrators in exchange for their hard work and success in securing resources. Second, principals may act as agents of central school authorities. A lack of organized community interest leads the principal to behave as a representative of district authority, not of the interests of the neighborhood. This strategy serves to avoid conflict and to secure deference through the limited knowledge parents have about the school and its educational processes. Third, principals may become the target of parental discontent. In this role, the principal "seeks to reduce the endless conflict by either absorbing or reflecting it within the neighborhood" (Summerfield, 1971, p. 93). This was the least successful strategy for reducing conflict at the building level. Deference in this case is secured through problem denial. This strategy works to deflect the conflict away from the district. Finally, principals act as nice neutrals (i.e., they occasionally call on the community to petition the central district, but they typically operate so that discontent is not aroused). Deference is secured by sustaining the perception that the school is doing well. All of these strategies seek to deflect and minimize conflict between parents and the school building. All are context dependent, and some are obviously more successful than others.

As illustrated earlier, there is considerable variation among school buildings regarding the extent to which collaboration or conflict exists between the building and its attendance area. In some cases, the micropolitics of the building and its attendance area combine into effective collaborative influence on the central office. In other cases, the micropolitics of the building, which lacks an organized attendance area political support system, is less effective in its impact on central office. In yet other cases, conflicts between the building and its attendance area weakens its impact on central office, sometimes leading to hostility from the central office.

How well-knit the external structures of the building are to both its macrolinkages and its micro–local-attendance-area linkages is an important political question. It makes a significant difference to the building's capacity to conduct its external relationships. "Since principals who act as spokespersons for neighborhoods are better positioned to secure allocations, patterns of neighborhood politics may have consequential effects on the distribution of resources to schools" (Malen, 1995, p. 154). The strength of the building's foreign policy toward either or both of its external fields is interdependent. When its attendance area linkages are well established and friendly, its capacity to mobilize support from its area for help from the central office on dealing with problems, including the acquisition of special resources, is greater than when its linkages are weak or its relationship is hostile. In addition, the stronger and more friendly its relationships around the chain-of-command, the more it can call upon the help of the macrosystem in dealing with its attendance area problems. The most significant consequences on the micropolitics of education made by its external relations of both sorts is likely to be seen in the discretionary latitude the building has. The prize for each of these worlds running in each direction is the same. The language used may be different. Up and down the chain-of-command run the terms *control* and *autonomy,* respectively. In and out of the building and its attendance area are the labels, parent influence or community control versus professional autonomy. The prize, however, is the degree and character of discretionary latitude within the building.

Principals also use their positions to preempt or to curb parent voices. In effect, they act as gatekeepers or buffering agents (Thompson, 1967, Scott, 1992) to filter parental demands. For example, sources of stress are typically managed through cordial, ceremonial exchanges (Malen, 1995). In addition, parents get stonewalled or sanctioned when they provoke critical conversation (Fine, 1993; Malen & Ogawa, 1988). Norms surrounding professional prerogatives and harmonious interactions also work to mute discussion, muzzle conflict, and maintain traditional patterns of power (Huguenin, Zerchkov, & Davies, 1979; Malen & Ogawa, 1988). In addition, studies have shown that principals actively work to socialize parents into both supportive and submissive roles (Goldring, 1993; Malen et al, 1990). All of these tactics act to impact the politics of the building in potent ways. In effect, they work to buffer the building-level policy making system from lay influence and to maintain principal discretion over the school's domestic policies.

Another tactic principals use to curb dissenting parent voices is to leverage the composition of formal school councils. Their formal position in the governance system enables them to invite and to appoint supporters to formal committees as well as to coopt vocal critics. In this way, principals can mobilize factions and forge coalitions (Blase, 1991a; Hanson, 1981) as well as limit the authority delegated to critical parents. This enables principals to create an aura of smooth sailing and mutual admiration (Mann, 1974). They may also direct contentious topics to private arenas, such as a subcommittee of principals and teachers (Malen & Ogawa, 1988). In these ways and others, principals attempt to "maintain smooth operations by deflecting fundamental challenges to those operations" (Bryk et al, 1993, p. 7) and, thereby, reinforce existing patterns of power and privilege (Rollow & Bryk, 1993a).

The administrative policy making system of the school uses formal parent groups to fulfill a number of functions. In addition to the buffering function mentioned previously, these groups perform an important symbolic function. They create the impression of parent involvement (Huguenin et al, 1979), serve as symbols of parents' right to a voice in decisions, and act as signs that the organization recognizes that right. Each of the preceding symbolic functions serves to provide the school with legitimacy. Parent councils also provide a means for contentious issues to be brought "into a supportive structure under the control of the district and school administrators" (Shields & McLaughlin, 1986, p. 8). They serve as vehicles to air complaints and assuage concerns (Mann, 1974; McLeese, 1992). They also function as forums to rally support for and reduce resistance to policies made elsewhere. The formal arenas can regulate conflict, reduce the likelihood that familiar influence relationships will be challenged, and increase the chances that established relationships will be sustained (Malen et al, 1990; Popkewitz, 1979).

Principals can also control resources, information, and decision-making processes. This enables them to employ a number of additional tactics. First, by controlling resources, they can limit the resources and supports they provide to formal parent organizations (Berman, Weiler Associates, 1984; Fager, 1993). The control of resources also allows principals to withhold rewards (e.g., not letting parents have a favored teacher). Principals can also manage conflict by controlling information. For example, they can limit the information they provide on actual school operations.

As a function of their formal position, principals can also control decision-making processes. One vehicle that principals use to control the decision-making process is through controlling the agenda of formal and informal meetings. Controlling the agenda allows the principal to choose which conflicts he or she wants to address or avoid. The choice of conflicts through the definition of the most salient issues for political action is the central strategy of politics (Schattschneider, 1975). This strategy dates back to at least the English Revolution of the seventeenth century. Harrington, writing in *Oceana*, saw the definition of alternatives and the choice of conflicts as the supreme instrument of power.

Any complex social system is replete with potential conflicts. Every social system is similarly replete with opportunities for social collaboration. Only a few of the many issues within a political entity can be given attention at any time. Hence, the choice of which potential conflicts are exploited for expanded conflict is a central strategy in politics.

The selection of certain issues as legitimate for political activity automatically defines some others as illegitimate. Furthermore, other issues become subsumed under the most salient ones through their redefinition. Some issues must be suppressed in order to produce the collaboration needed to exploit the most salient conflicts. Thus, the choice of issues for political conflict automatically defines other issues and positions on issues as supportive, opposing, and irrelevant. Issues are only meaningful in political conflicts because people hold them with enough commitment to clash over them. Because given issues are significant in different ways to various groups of people, the choice of issues implies a choice of potential allies, probable opponents, and defines the probable audience. This is why the ultimate political acts are the struggles over defining which conflicts are fought.

Parents are reluctant to challenge these dynamics for a number of reasons. Foremost is that they lack the resources, information, and decision-making authority accorded to the principal by the bureaucratic chain-of-command. In addition, parents tend to exhibit a deference to the expertise of professionals. Parents who become involved in school governance also tend to have served and to support orientations, and they have an appreciation for being invited to join the council (Berman, Weiler Associates, 1984; Chapman & Boyd, 1986; Salisbury, 1980). In addition, the principal's ability to maintain control of the conflict is further augmented by the teachers' willingness to align with the principal to keep major issues under the purview of professionals (Berman, Weiler Associates, 1984; Mann, 1974). All of these factors serve to reinforce principal discretion at the expense of lay influence.

We do not mean to imply that the building level public exerts no influence on the school. As Summerfield (1971) illustrated, organized interest groups of neighborhood parents have an influence on the nature of the school and the strategies and tactics employed by the principal. Parents certainly exert influence on important aspects of the school and principals do placate the demands of select parents. For example, as a means of managing conflict with parents or community groups, principals may selectively enforce discipline policies. This allows them to "avoid direct confrontation with outsiders," notably parents who might expand the scope of conflict by involving the board, the courts, or others (Corbett, 1991, p. 94). Under pressure from high-status parents, principals also learn to finesse requirements, to "wink" at improprieties, and to develop "live and let live" agreements (Hempel, 1986, p. 27). Principals have also been known to press teachers to alter grades, modify class content, adjust homework, or grant favored status to students in particular programs (Blase, 1988). These actions demonstrate that parents do have some influence on school policy and that principals are not simply buffers that insulate the school from outside forces. Principals serve a bridging function as "arbiters of disputes, negotiators of private compacts, and conduits for parent influence on programs and practices" (Malen, 1995, p. 153).

On the other hand, the preferential treatment accorded some groups of parents often occurs at the expense of less vocal or powerful parents (Malen, 1995). Corbett (1991) has suggested that microsized deals have "more than microsized" effects (p. 87). For example, the preferential treatment of some parental demands has been shown to undermine teachers' efficacy, lower morale, intensify stress, and erode commitment. This happens particularly when the deals violate building and teacher norms. In addition, special treatment to some may impact student attitudes and student access to programs (Blase, 1988; Corbett, 1991).

The strategies and tactics employed by the principal are primarily designed to avert or contain conflict (Hempel, 1986; Wiles, 1974). In all cases, principals surface as key actors whose primary political responsibility is to "minimize conflict between the community and the neighborhood school" and the district (Summerfield, 1971, p. 93). The political strategies and tactics of the administrative policy making systems in its foreign affairs is essentially the politics of privatization (Schattschneider, 1975). This is "a politics that confines the scope of conflict to safe issues, restricts the game to insider exchanges, and puts the emphasis on the acquisition of acquiescence" (Malen, 1995, p. 159). In Schattschneider's (1975) political model, conflict is the root of all politics. The contagiousness of conflict (i.e., the tendency to expand its scope) is its pivotal fact. The dynamics of politics that dictate its strategies and tactics are found in the perennial tension between conditions for restricting the scope of political conflicts or privatizing conflict, and those for expanding their scope or socializing conflict.

Schattschneider's model contains two basic components: (1) the two significantly smaller groups actively in conflict, and (2) the vastly larger passive crowd of spectators who could enter it as contestants rather than remain in the audience. These may range from spectators fascinated by the conflict to the inattentive and bored. Because they vastly outnumber the active contestants in political struggles, even a small proportion of the audience switching from passive observers to active participants in the conflict will change its nature and its outcome. The audience is never truly neutral, but its bias toward action is unknown until it acts. Hence, the spectators are the most difficult part to predict of the calculus of all political conflicts. Destroying the customary barriers between the usual contestants and their traditional audience is, therefore, the most dangerous of all political acts. In nation-states, it results in revolution.

Even a relatively small transformation of audience participation into political action has significant impact. An astute political analyst, therefore, watches the audience to see whether a change in the scope of conflict is underway. This is often more useful than watching the traditional contestants. More precisely, changes in the highly permeable boundary mechanisms that separate the audience from the combatants will indicate changes in at least two aspects of the political conflict. The first are realignments within the organization of the competing coalitions, including their leadership and the status and role characteristics of their members. The second aspect is related to the first. All organization is the mobilization of bias for action, and changes in organization will change the values at issue. Changes in the organization of either coalition leads to changes in the issues that are most salient in the conflict. Every different combination of contestants and issues will involve the dominance of some issues

and the subordination of others. This is why control of the scope of conflict is the prime instrument of political strategy. When conflicts become socialized, the leading coalitions on both sides of an issue have more to lose than the stakes at issue in the immediate conflict. If the normally passive members of the organization get into the fight, the leading coalitions could lose their leadership as well as their definition of the issues.

The contagious nature of political conflicts is what gives meaning to the set of interactions that influence and shape the authoritative allocation of values. Social conflicts are fundamentally contagious. The mechanisms that authoritatively allocate values exist to avert chaotic conflicts and self-defeating wars. In the school, these mechanisms result in the privatization of conflict, incrementalism in decisions, and routinization of decision-making processes. Privatization and socialization are two poles of that set of interactions that influence and shape the authoritative allocation of values. Privatization describes the prevailing conditions of stasis in the micropolitics of the school. Socialization is more useful for describing the rare conditions of major political change. Schattschneider's model, more importantly, helps us to understand the implicit threat that the spread of conflict holds for the school's common value assumptions.

Privatization submerges basic value questions, whereas socialization raises them. It is especially true in privatized political systems that "established power is so tenacious of its prerogatives that rather than part with any of them it will often by blind resistance invite the loss of all of them" (MacIver, 1965, p. 287). The tendency toward privatization helps the advantaged, but it also detaches them from the rest of the polity. This eventually leads to increases in conflict when the larger polity undergoes major social change (Iannaccone, 1977).

The supervision of educational politics is a perennial struggle between privatizing conflict, which restricts its scope, and socializing conflict, which expands its scope. As stated earlier, the control of the scope of conflict is the primary instrument of political strategy. One way to restrict the scope of conflict is to localize it. One way to expand the scope of conflict is to democratize it. "Privatization of conflict is exactly what the structures of educational government and the political ideology resulting from the reform at the turn of the century produced" (Iannaccone, 1977, p. 260). We will now address the ideology of the municipal reform movement, which continues to extend a profound effect on educational institutions (Tyack & Tobin, 1994; Tyack & Hansot, 1982; Tyack, 1974) in the following section. The section on political ideology, which follows, draws heavily on the work of Iannaccone (1977) in *Three Views of Change in Educational Politics*.

Political Ideology and Myths Political theorists concerned with ideology emphasize the fact that all governance is a complex of norms. In his *Web of Government*, MacIver (1965) views the system of beliefs held by a society about the nature and proper function of government as the web that holds it together. He places special emphasis on those beliefs that have long been held by a political entity. These often-taken-for-granted beliefs are powerful elements in that web. These beliefs are usually the product of previous but forgotten political conflicts.

The central political beliefs of any political entity are those about who should govern what. MacIver terms these beliefs the "myth of authority," emphasizing their historical development rather than challenging their validity. People's conceptualizations and normative beliefs about authority are central to any political entity because these guide their responses to four related questions: (1) What should be decided? (2) Who should decide? (3) What types of procedures and processes should be employed? and (4) What criteria should guide? An ideological approach to the school as a political entity centers attention on the beliefs about authority that are most salient for describing the school's politics (i.e., that set of interactions that influence and shape the authoritative allocations of values). These beliefs operate as the ideological assumptions that guide day-in, day-out decisions through routine processes. As discussed earlier, they result in incremental policy change. Every policy system rests upon such beliefs or political myths.

The general policy process of the distribution of stakes and incremental change in educational organizations rests upon general agreement about basic ideological principles.

Any even loosely organized set of interlocking generalizations or principles about social organization . . . is of enormous help to policy analysis. . . . All policy analysis rests to a degree on ideology so defined. . . . In effect an ideology takes certain beliefs out of the gunfire of criticism. . . . These beliefs . . . can thereafter be introduced into policy analysis as though they were settled fact. . . . Even mistaken beliefs can serve . . . because we chose a common set of assumptions (Lindblom, 1968. p. 23).

Such assumptions are characteristically answers to basic questions that are no longer seen as questions. They are never seriously raised for deliberation within the incremental decision-making process, which allocates valued resources in a day-in, day-out process (Sarason, 1983). For example, these questions include whether children are to be educated by public authorities. Other assumptions include the appropriate balance of parental, general public, and professional influence over education. These issues run so deep and are so pervasive in their implications that the systematic pursuit ultimately to resolve these would result in struggles that none of the contesting parties would survive. Such questions may in fact be unresolvable. They do, however, become "periodically . . . compromised and redefined within the assumptions of the dominant political doctrine of an era" (Iannaccone, 1977, p. 262).

We subordinate such basic controversies in essentially two ways. We break the underlying basic conflicts into many smaller conflicts at each level of government. These are then dealt with in thousands of microsocial units including the school site. The processing of each of these smaller conflicts is guided by policy assumptions into routinization of conflicts through incremental decisions based to a large extent on implicit value assumptions. These guiding policy values and assumptions run so deep that they are taken for granted. A description of the day-to-day politics of the school is consequently sterile if it ignores the more dangerous political conflicts subordinated by the very day-in, day-out politics.

The school building is subject to and embodies political ideologies that are imposed on it from the larger political system. The roots of the larger politics of education are to be found in the ideology of the municipal reform movement. The substitution of conflicts (i.e., replacing the most fundamental issues such as whether children should be educated by public authorities with less basic ones) is one of the most remarkable achievements of the municipal reform. That replacement produced a set of political myths that appeared to resolve the recurrent issues in education. They were operationally removed for an era, which is the best one can ask of a political formula that removed essentially unresolvable issues from public debate. Municipal reform doctrines have become the ideology that underlies fundamental policy assumptions in education. These tenets have been the basis of educational policy analysis for much of the twentieth century. They have only recently begun to come under attack.

There are three major doctrinal tenets of the municipal reform movement. The first is the separation of politics and education or the apolitical political myth. The second is the myth of the unitary community. Finally, the third is the political myth of administrative neutral competency.

THE SEPARATION OF POLITICS AND EDUCATION The first myth is the separation of politics and education or the apolitical political myth. This myth was justified as necessary for enhancing the efficiency and effectiveness of educational service delivery and governance. A number of political mechanisms were developed to operationalize this ideology. First, the size of school boards was reduced and school district elections were separated in time from other local elections. In addition, school district boundary lines were drawn in a manner not coterminous with other local governments. School board membership selection was framed as a nonpartisan process. The impact of this myth and its associated mechanisms was to disadvantage the neighborhood political base and to privilege a managerial elite. The invisible agenda was the transfer of power from one class to another and, some argue, to take advantage of the social inequality in neighborhoods as a political device to disenfranchise the poor. As a result, the "wrong" people were kept out of educational politics and the conflicts were privatized. Schattschneider (1975) pointed out that privatized political systems open up politics to interest groups. Schools now became more vulnerable to organized economic and social elites within the district as those who led the reform movement sat on the boards.

The fundamental character of educational politics was changed in another way as well. The weakening of the neighborhood had implications for the influence of parents on educational service delivery and supervision. More important for our discussion, microlevel and building-level political issues also tended to get lost in the centralized at-large board structure.

THE UNITARY COMMUNITY The second myth of the municipal reform movement was that of the unitary community or the melting pot philosophy. It argued that a single unitary community existed and that the United States manifested no social or economic cleavages. All special interest became subordinated to this single-community interest. This myth is a necessary element in the apologia for the power of the few. The reformer's demand was to implement an elite educational system for all. In the process, the needs and values of ethnic or class neighborhoods were ignored as they were considered to be hostile to good education.

This myth is a distinctly macrodistrict political orientation. It encourages boards to focus on educational issues and delivery at the general level rather than concerning themselves with educational ends as they relate to the individual pupil. The municipal reform developed a system that shifted the political center of gravity from the neighborhood and the school building to the central office. Neighborhood participation was reduced, making it difficult for parents and local community members to influence decisions about educational outputs. The micropolitics of the site became a kind of political wasteland, eventually occupied by managed PTAs and noneducational groups that appeared during episodic upheavals. The separation of politics from education, combined with the unitary community view as exposed by the prevailing ideology, destroyed the micropolitics of the neighborhood as it took power from the working classes and poor in order to empower the native, white, upper middle-class, and professional elites. Little attention was paid to the loss of power by the clients of education.

Administrative Neutral Competency The third myth is the political myth of administrative neutral competency. Institutions of American administration have generally been organized and operated to pursue successive value orientations (Kaufman 1956). Jacksonian democracy dominated most of the nineteenth century. The municipal reform doctrine that followed was based on the apolitical myth that administrators should operate as professional experts in their public service area and make decisions that are value free and apolitical. This myth led to the myth of administrative neutral competency as well as to the rise of professional managers. The predominant belief was that educational government should be directed by nonpartisan managers who meet high standards of professional expertise. These high standards of professional expertise were to be assured through credentialling requirements.

This myth also led to a "scientific" or linear and decontextualized approach to problem solving that assumed the validity of the results as long as the methodology was sound and experts interpreted the data. In effect, this approach to management evolved as a buffer ideology against a variety of competing value systems. Those who commanded technical knowledge under these circumstances controlled the system. The political myth of the neutral competency of school professionals became interdependent with the techniques of governance, knowledge construction, and information flow. A technique is a way of knowing applied to the world of people that also serves as a means of control. This is the sense in which knowledge is power. Technique, however, although interdependent with political myths, is never a substitute *for* the myth. The tendency toward privatization in educational government is a ten-

dency toward that impossible substitution as it cuts the power more and more in favor of those who have the technique (Harrington, 1747). As Brogan (1949) warned:

It is a dangerous and idle dream to think that the state can be ruled by philosophers turned kings or scientists turned commissars. For if philosophers become kings or scientists commissars, they become politicians and the powers given to the state are powers given to men who are rulers of states, men subject to all the limitations and temptations of their dangerous craft (p. xvi).

This myth removed education from an arena of conflicting value systems. In doing so, it changed the nature of the questions being asked. It also changed the nature of what "should" be: A good school was the same for all and an expert was best able to determine the nature of a good school. It became widely accepted that schools should and could be run independently of competing value systems, ethnic, or racial backgrounds. Issues discussed became technical, while questions of values, purpose, and effects were ignored.

This ideological commitment to professionalism in the governance and operation of educational services became a vehicle for the supremacy of the superintendent over lay boards and the principal over the neighborhood. With its professional credentialism requirements and belief in professional expertise, this ideology served to close the boundaries between the school and its neighborhood as parents were granted very little opportunity to see what was going on inside the system.

In summary, the municipal reform substituted a nonparty, elite interest group politics for that which had existed. It resolved the issue of the many versus the few in the wielding of political influence in educational government. Power was placed in the hands of the upper-middle-class few. These ideologies also determined that the politics of the local educational authority would be about general district macroissues of finance rather than about building-site microissues such as teaching and learning. These myths are obviously not apolitical. "The reform doctrine is a thoroughgoing apologia for power of the strong administrative state" (Iannaccone, 1977, p. 283). The impact of the political myths of the municipal reform movement was an increase in professional influence at the expense of lay control.

CONCLUSION

The current literature about supervision in education calls for a fundamental reform of social and work relations within public schools. Where school and home were once divided by professional and private interests, they are now seen as necessary partners, with each contributing to the production of learning. The call for collaboration between schools, homes, and businesses is more than an ideological proposal. It is seen as an essential strategy for effective and excellent schools, where teachers can teach and students can learn. Authors such as Glickman, Gordon, and Ross-Gordon (1995) and Oliva (1989) have defined supervision in terms of skills and tasks that promote collaboration among all the organizational members of schools. Although the specifics of our analysis of supervision differ in content from those of these authors, our intent is not in conflict with theirs. For example, Glickman, Gordon, and Ross-Gordon (1995) argue that supervision is not a matter of an individual monitoring the work of other "employees." Rather, these authors argue that supervision is the product of many individuals working to make sense and meaning out of the tasks related to education. Our model of supervision similarly highlights the significance of supervision as the product of numerous exchanges among teachers, parents, students, and community members, which cumulatively define the environment in which teachers teach and students learn.

Good teaching and successful learning do not just happen because of good intentions. Schooling is a very complex process that requires the coordinated efforts of everyone concerned. We have described these circumstances as a negotiated order, whereby teachers, parents, students, and community members are all part of a learning community. Because the goals, means, and ideologies of each group vary, the politics of supervising educational organizations at the building level occurs in the context of this negotiated order. This negotiated order allows the groups to collaborate while it works to prevent all out war between them. Such an effort is costly and often carries with it political costs that are not fully recognized in the literature about supervision.

In this chapter, we introduced conflict and costs as fundamental constraints influencing the shape and character of supervision within schools. Indeed, we argued that supervision was better understood as an organizational phenomena involving all members rather than an individual phenomena (cooperative or otherwise). School organizations are above all else systems of interdependent activity. In addition, school organizations function in environments of scarcity, in which there is never enough to go around. This interdependence between the school's constituent groups under conditions of scarcity means that the potential for both collaboration and conflict exist simultaneously. The potential for collaboration exists because organizational citizens and subjects must work with and through others in order to get things done. At the same time, this interdependence creates conflict because goals, means, and ideologies vary.

Conflict and collaboration arise when individuals and groups come into contact. Without contact, there can be neither conflict nor collaboration. For example, it is extremely unlikely that either conflict or collaborative agreements will occur between a middle school in Louisiana and a high school in California. Both collaborative agreements and conflict are far more likely to occur between a middle school and a high school within the same school district. Successful supervision requires that organizational members are aware of this dialectic and have the ability to work with both collaboration and conflict.

In school organizations, the major points of conflict and collaboration that shape the politics of the school building and constrain supervision occur at the boundary between the organization's primary constituent groups: administrators, teachers, students, and parents. The first conflict we reviewed in this chapter is the perennial tension between administrator influence and teacher discretion in the domestic affairs of the

buildings. The second is the tension between teacher influence and student discretion. Finally, the third is the tension between parental influence and professional discretion in the foreign affairs of the building. There is no ultimate resolution to any of these points of tension, nor is it likely that thinking people would want all the influence to be in any one of these camps. Conflicts, therefore, usually range around the degree of influence sought by each group, as well as a contest between the conflicts for dominance.

We view the activities of organizational members and groups as constrained by both economic and political factors. For this reason, we have attempted to expand the way we think about supervision in educational organizations by focusing on both the costs of collaboration and the benefits of conflict. We believe both are essential to a good theory about supervision and that they must be taken into account if we want to explain supervisory behavior in schools. By contrast, the current literature highlights collaboration as the central figure around which a vision of supervision is developed and tends to neglect both the costs and conflict. Sergiovanni and Starratt (1993) carry this argument to its logical conclusion by arguing that good supervisors are guided by a moral leadership. By moral leadership, they argue that the authority for supervision ought to be housed in social values common to all educators, parents, and students. From this perspectives, collaboration is a win–win situation in which, by consensus around common values, the supervision of education becomes self-managing.

A clear sense that costs exist among alternative means of action, and, more, that the distribution of benefits and burdens associated with these alternative means varies is missing from this argument. One of the assumptions operating in our model is that individuals, when given a choice, will choose the less costly alternative, especially if they believe the quality of service is comparable. Comparing total program costs of alternative means of production, however, is not enough because the distribution of benefits and burdens will vary with different programs. Thus, holding total costs constant, one program for supervising a math program may rely more on parental and community involvement than another, which may rely more on teachers as the means for supervision. The choice between programs obviously has important political and economic implications for who bears the cost of such an activity as well as who maintains control over decisions. Recognition of these constraints on choice does not provide answers for what to do in a specific circumstance, but such an awareness does provide current and future educators with clarity about "what is" rather than simply "what ought to be."

In training future educators, we do them a disservice by focusing only on the normative and moral aspects. We must work to educate both the public and future school personnel about how schools really work and why, and about the limits of their potential influence. To do this properly requires that we devise systems of explanation, or theory if you will, that gives these people some leverage with this social reality. Only in this way can we begin the long and arduous task of changing our schools into the democratic institutions and productive environments that students deserve and our communities require.

REFERENCES

Alfonso, R., Firth, G., & Neville, R. (1981). *Instructional supervision: A behavior system* (2nd ed.). Boston, MA: Allyn and Bacon.

Anderson, G. (1991). Cognitive politics of principals and teachers: Ideological control in an elementary school. In J. Blase (Ed.). *The politics of life in schools: Power, conflict and cooperation* (pp. 120–138). Newbury Park, CA: Sage.

Arrow, K. J. (1971). *Control in larger organizations: Essays in the theory of risk-bearing.* Chicago, IL: Markham.

Bacharach, S. B., Bauer, S., & Shedd, J. B. (1986). The work environment and school reform. *Teachers College Record, 88,* 241–256.

Ball, S. J. (1987). *The micropolitics of the school: Towards a theory of school organization.* London: Methuen.

Banfield, E. C. & Wilson, J. Q. (1963). *City politics.* Cambridge, MA: Harvard University Press.

Barney, J. & Ouchi W. G. (Eds.). (1986). *Organizational economics.* San Francisco, CA: Jossey-Bass Inc.

Bennett, A. L., Bryk, A. S., Easton, J. Q., Kerbow, D., Luppescu, S. & Sebring, P. A. (1992). *Charting reform: The principals' perspective.* Report on a survey of Chicago Public School principals. Chicago, IL: Consortium on Chicago School Research.

Berman, P. & McLaughlin, M. (1978). *Federal programs supporting educational change, VIII.* Santa Monica, CA: Rand.

Berman, Weiler Associates (1984). *Improving school improvement: A policy evaluation of the California school improvement program.* Berkeley, CA: Berman, Weiler Associates.

Blase, J. (1988). The politics of favoritism: A qualitative analysis of the teachers' perspective. *Educational Administration Quarterly, 24,* 152–177.

Blase, J. (1989). Teachers' political orientation vis-à-vis the principal: The micropolitics of the school. In J. Hannaway & R. Crowson (Eds.). *The politics of reforming school administration* (pp. 113–126). New York: Falmer Press.

Blase, J. (1991a). The micropolitical orientation of teachers toward closed school principles. *Education and Urban Society, 27*(4), 356–378.

Blase, J. (1991b). The micropolitical perspective. In J. Blase (Ed.). *The politics of life in schools: Power, conflict and cooperation* (pp. 1–18). Newbury Park, CA: Sage.

Blase, J. & Kirby, P. C. (1992). *Bringing out the best in teachers: What effective principals do.* Newbury Park, CA: Corwin Press.

Bridges, E. M. (1970). Administrative man: Origin or pawn in decisionmaking?. *Educational Administration Quarterly, 6,* 7–24.

Brogan, D. W. (1949). Preface. In Bertrand de Jouvenel, *Power: The natural history of its growth,* J. F. Huntington (Trans.) p. xvi. New York: Viking Press.

Bryk, A. S., Easton, J. Q., Kerbow, D., Rollow, S. G., & Sebring, P. A. (1993). *A view from the elementary schools: The state of reform in Chicago.* Chicago, IL: Consortium on Chicago School Research.

Callahan, R. E. (1962). *Education and the cult of efficiency.* Chicago, IL: The University of Chicago Press.

Campbell, R. F., Cunningham, L. L., Nystrand, R. O., & Usdan, M. D. (1985). *The organization and control of American schools* (5th ed.). Columbus, OH: Charles E. Merrill.

Campbell, R. F., Fleming, T., Newell, L. J., & Bennion, J. W. (1987). *A history of thought and practice in educational administration.* New York: Teachers College Press.

Carlson, R. O. (1964). Environmental constraints and organizational consequences: The public school and its clients. In D. E. Griffiths (Ed.). *The sixty-third yearbook of the National Society for the Study of Education* (pp. 262–276). Chicago, IL: University of Chicago Press.

Chapman, J. & Boyd, W. L. (1986). Decentralization, devolution, and the school principal: Australian lessons on statewide educational reform. *Educational Administration Quarterly, 22,* 28–58.

Conley, S. (1991). Review of research on teacher participation in school decision-making. In G. Grant (Ed.). *Review of research in education* (pp. 225–265). Washington, D.C.: American Educational Research Association.

Conway, J. (1984). The myth, mystery and mastery of participative decision-making in education. *Educational Administration Quarterly, 20,* 11–40.

Corbett, H. D. (1991). Community influence and school micropolitics: A case example. In J. Blase (Ed.). *The politics of life in schools: Power, conflict and cooperation* (pp. 73-95). Newbury Park, CA: Sage.

Corcoran, T. B. (1987). *Teacher participation in public school decision-making: A discussion paper.* Paper prepared for the Work in America Institute.

Corwin, R. (1981). Patterns of organizational control and teacher militancy: Theoretical continuities in the idea of "loose coupling." In A. C. Kerckhoff (Ed.). *Research in the sociology of education and socialization* (Vol. II) pp. 261–291. Greenwich, CT: JAI Press.

Cyert, R. M. & March, J. G. (1963). *A behavioral theory of the firm.* Englewood Cliffs, NJ: Prentice Hall.

David, J. L. & Peterson, S. M. (1984). *Can schools improve themselves?* San Francisco, CA: Bay Area Research Group.

Davies, D. (1980). School administrators and advisory councils: Partnership or shotgun marriage. *NASSP Bulletin, 62*–66.

Davies, D. (1981). Citizen participation in decision-making in the schools. In D. Davies (Ed.). *Communities and their schools* (pp. 84–119). New York: McGraw-Hill.

Davies, D. (1987). Parent involvement in the public schools. *Education and Urban Studies, 19*(2), 147–163.

Davies, D., Stanton, J., Clasby, M., Zerchkov, R. & Powers, B. (1977). *Sharing the power: A report on the status of school councils in the 1970s.* Boston, MA: Institute for Responsive Education.

DeLacy, J. (1992). *The Bellevue evaluation study* (second report). Seattle: University of Washington Institue for the Study of Educational Policy.

Demsetz, H. (1995). *The economics of the business firm.* Cambridge, MA: Cambridge University Press.

Duke, D. L., Shower, B. K., & Imber, M. (1981). *Teachers as school decisionmakers.* Stanford, CA: Stanford University Institute for Research on Educational Finance and Governance.

Easton, D. (1965a). *A systems analysis of political life.* NewYork: Wiley.

Easton, D. (1965b). *A framework for political analysis.* Englewood Cliffs, NJ: Prentice Hall.

Etzioni, A. (1961). *A comparative analysis of complex organizations.* New York: The Free Press.

Fager, J. (1993). *The "rules" still rule: The failure of school-based management/shared decision-making in the New York city public school system.* New York: Parents Coalition for Education in NYC.

Fine, M. (1993). [Ap]parent involvement: Reflections on parents, power and urban public schools. *Teachers College Record, 94,* 682–709.

Fish, J. (1994). *Institutionalizing the fiction of site based management.* A paper presented at the annual conference of the American Educational Research Association, New Orleans, LA.

Fisher, A. (1979). Advisory commitees—Does anybody want their advice? *Educational Leadership, 7,* 254–255.

Glickman, C. D., Gordon, S. P., & Ross-Gordon, J.M. (1995). *Supervision of instruction: A developmental approach.* Boston, MA: Allyn and Bacon.

Goldring, E. B. (1993). Principals, parents and administrative superiors. *Educational Administration Quarterly, 29,* 93–117.

Goldring, E. B., & Rallis, S. F. (1993). *Principals of dynamic schools: Taking charge of change.* Newbury Park, CA: Corwin Press.

Greenfield, W. L. (1991). The micropolitics of leadership in an urban elementary school. In J. Blase (Ed.). *The politics of life in schools: Power, conflict and cooperation* (pp. 161–184). Newbury Park, CA: Sage.

Gronn, P. C. (1984). "I have a solution. . . ." Administrative power in a school meeting. *Educational Administration Quarterly, 20*(2), 65–92.

Hanson, E. M. (1979). *Educational administration and organizational behavior.* Boston, MA: Allyn and Bacon.

Hanson, E. M. (1981). Organizational control in educational systems: A case study of governance in schools. In S. B. Bacharach (Ed.). *Organizational behavior in schools and school districts* (pp. 245–276). New York: Praeger.

Hanson, M. (1991). Alteration of influence relations in school-based management innovations. Paper presented to the American Educational Research Association, Chicago, IL.

Harrington, J. (1947). *The oceana* (3rd ed.). London: A. Miller.

Hempel, R. L. (1986). *The last little citadel.* Boston, MA: Houghton Mifflin.

Hodgkinson, C. (1983). *The philosophy of leadership.* Oxford, England: Basil Blackwell.

Hoenack, S. A. (1983). *Economic behavior within organizations.* New York: Cambridge University Press.

Hoy, W. K. & Forsyth, P. B. (1986). *Effective supervision: Theory into practice.* New York: McGraw-Hill.

Huguenin, K., Zerchykov, R., & Davies, D. (1979). *Narrowing the gap between intent and practice: A report to policymakers on community organizations and school decision-making.* Boston, MA: Institute for Responsive Education.

Iannaccone, L. (1967). *Politics in education.* New York: Center for Applied Research in Education.

Iannaccone, L. (1975). *Education policy systems: A study guide for educational administrators.* Fort Lauderdale, FL: Nova University.

Iannaccone, L. (1977). Three views of change in educational politics. *(76th Yearbook of the National Society for the Study of Education;* pp. 255–286). Chicago, IL: The National Society for the Study of Education.

Iannaccone, L. (1991). Micropolitics of education: What and why. *Education and Urban Society, 23,* 465–471.

Iannaccone, L. & Lutz, F. (1970). *Politics, power and policy: The governance of local school districts.* Columbus, OH: Charles E. Merrill.

Iannaccone, L. & Lutz, F. (1995). The crucible of democracy: The local arena. In Scribner & Layton (Eds.). *The study of educational politics* (pp. 39–52). London: Falmer Press.

Jennings, R. E. (1980). School advisory councils in America: Frustration and failure. In G. Baron (Ed.). *The politics of school government* (pp. 23–51). New York: Pergamon Press.

Johnson, S. M. (1989). School work and its reform. In J. Hannaway & R. Crowson (Eds.). *The politics of reforming school administration* (pp. 95–112). New York: Falmer Press.

Johnson, S. M. (1990). *Teachers at work: Achieving success in our schools.* New York: Basic Books.

Kaufman, H. (1956). Emerging conflicts in the doctrine of public administration. *American Political Science Review, 50,* 1057–1073.

Kuhn, T. S. (1962). *The structure of scientific revolutions.* Chicago, IL: University of Chicago Press.

Lasswell, H. D. (1936). *Politics: Who gets what, when, how?* New York: McGraw-Hill.

Leibenstein H. (1987). *Inside the firm: The inefficiencies of hierarchy.* Cambridge, MA: Harvard University Press.

Lindblom, C. E. (1968). *The policy making process.* Englewood Cliffs, NJ: Prentice Hall.

Little, J. W. (1990). The mentor phenomenon and the social organization of teaching. In C. Cazden (Ed.). *Review of research in education* (pp. 297–351). Washington, D.C.: American Educational Research Association.

Lortie, D. (1969). The balance of control and autonomy in elementary school teaching. In A. Etzioni (Ed.). *The semi-professions and their organizations.* New York: Free Press.

MacIver, R. M. (1965). *The web of government.* New York: Free Press.

Malen, B. (1993). "Professionalizing" teaching by expanding teachers' roles. In S. L. Jacobson & R. Berne (Eds.). *Reforming education: The emerging systemic approach* (pp. 43–65). Thousand Oaks, CA: Corwin Press.

Malen, B. (1994a). Enacting site based management: A political utilities approach. *Educational Evaluation and Policy Analysis, 16,* 249–267.

Malen, B. (1994b). *Enhancing the information base on Chicago school reform: A commentary on the Consortia's governance stream of research.* Paper presented at the request of the Consortia on Chicago School Research. Chicago, IL: University of Chicago Center for School Improvement.

Malen, B. (1995). The micropolitics of education: Mapping the multiple dimensions of power relations in school politics. In Scribner & Layton (Eds.). *The study of educational politics* (pp.147–167). London: Falmer Press.

Malen, B. & Ogawa, R. T. (1988). Professional-patron influence on site-based governance councils: A confounding case study. *Educational Evaluation and Policy Analysis, 10,* 251–279.

Malen, B. Ogawa, R. T., & Kranz, J. (1990). What do we know about school-based management? A case study of the literature—A call for research. In W. H. Clune & J. F. Witte (Eds.), *Choice and control in American education* (Vol. II) pp. 289–432. London: Falmer Press.

Mann, D. (1974). Political representation and urban school advisory councils. *Teachers College Record, 75,* 270–307.

Mann, D. (1975). Democratic theory and public participation in educational policy decisionmaking. In F. M. Wirt (Ed.). *The polity of the schools* (pp. 5–21). Lexington, MA: D. C. Heath.

Mann, D. (1977). Participation, representation and control. In J. Scribner (Ed.). *The politics of education.* Yearbook for the National Society for the Study of Education (pp. 67–93). Chicago, IL: University of Chicago.

March, J. G. & Simon, H. A. (1958). *Organizations.* New York: John Wiley.

Marshall, C. & Greenfield, W. D. (1985). The socialization of the assistant principal: Implications for school leadership. *Education and Urban Society, 18*(1), 3–6.

Marshall, C. & Mitchell, B. A. (1991). The assumptive worlds of fledgling administrators. *Education and Urban Society, 23,* 396–415.

Marshall, C. & Scribner, J. D. (1991). It's all political. *Education and Urban Society, 23,* 347–355.

Mauriel, J. J. & Lindquist, K. M. (1989). *School-based management doomed to failure?* Paper presented at the annual conference of the American Educational Research Association, San Francisco, CA.

McLaughlin, M. W. (1987). Lessons from experience: Lessons from policy implementation. *Educational Evaluation and Policy Analysis, 9,* 171–178.

McLeese, P. (1992). *The process of decentralizing conflict and maintaining stability: Site council enactment, implementation, operation and impacts in the Salt Lake City School District, 1970–1985.* Doctoral disseration, Department of Educational Administration, University of Utah, Salt Lake City, UT.

Michaelsen, J. B. (1981). A theory of decision-making in the public schools: A public choice approach. In S. Bacharach (Ed.). *Organizational Behavior in Schools and School Districts* (pp. 208–241). New York: Praeger Publishing.

Moles, O. C. (1987). Who wants parent involvement? *Education and Urban Society, 19,* 137–145.

Monk, D. H. (1990). *Educational finance: An economic approach.* New York: McGraw-Hill Publishing Company.

Neagley, R. L. & Evans, N. D. (1980). *Handbook for effective supervision of instruction.* Englewood Cliffs, NJ: Prentice Hall.

Noblit, G., Berry, B., & Dempsey, V. (1991). Political response to reform: A comparative case study. *Education and Urban Society, 23*(4), 379–395.

Oliva, P. F. (1989). *Supervision for today's schools* (3rd ed.). New York: Longman.

Opotow, S. (1991). Adolescent peer-conflicts: Implications for students and for schools. *Education and Urban Society, 23,* 416–441.

Pettigrew, A. M. (1973). *The politics of organizational decision-making.* London: Tavistock.

Pfeffer, J. (1978). The micropolitics of organizations. In M. W. Meyer (Ed.). *Environments and organizations* (pp. 29–50). San Francisco, CA: Jossey-Bass.

Pfeffer, J. (1981). *Power in organizations.* Marshfield: Pitman.

Popkewitz, T. S. (1979). Schools and the symbolic uses of community participation. In C. A. Grant (Ed.). *Community participation in education* (pp. 202–223). Boston, MA: Allyn and Bacon.

Razik, T. A. & Swanson, A. D. (1995). *Fundamental concepts of educational leadership and management.* Englewood Cliffs, NJ: Prentice Hall.

Rollow, S. G. & Bryk, A. S. (1993a). Democratic politics and school improvement: The potential of Chicago school reform. In C. Marshall (Ed.). *The new politics of race and gender* (pp. 97–106). New York: Falmer Press.

Rowan, B. (1990). Commitment and control: Alternative strategies for the organizational design of schools. In C. Cazden (Ed.). *Review of Research in Education* (pp. 353–389). Washington, D.C.: American Educational Research Association.

Salisbury, R. H. (1980). *Citizen participation in the public schools.* Lexington, MA: D. C. Heath.

Sarason, S. B. (1983). *Schooling in American: Scapegoat and salvation.* New York: Free Press.

Schattschneider, E. E. (1975). *The semi-sovereign people* (2nd ed.). New York: Holt, Rinehart, and Winston.

Scott, W. R. (1992). *Organizations rational, natural and open systems.* Englewood Cliffs, NJ: Prentice Hall.

Sergiovanni, T. J. & Starratt, R. J. (1993). *Supervision: A redefinition* (5th ed.). New York: McGraw-Hill Inc.

Shields, P. & McLaughlin, M. (1986). *Parent involvement in compensatory education programs.* Stanford, CA: Center for Educational Research at Stanford.

Stevenson, K. R. & Pellicer, L. (1992). School-based management in South Carolina: Balancing state-directed reform with local decision-making. In J. J. Lane & E. G. Epps (Eds.). *Restructuring the schools: Problems and prospects* (pp. 123–139). National Society for the Study of Education. Berkeley, CA: McCutchan.

Stroufe, G. E. (1977). Politics and evaluation. In J. D. Scribner (Ed.). *The politics of education* (76th Yearbook of the National Society for the Study of Education; pp. 287–318). Chicago, IL: University of Chicago Press.

Summerfield, H. L. (1971). *The Neighborhood bases politics of education.* Columbus OH: Charles E. Merrill.

Thomas, J. A. (1971). *The productive school: A systems analysis approach to educational administration.* New York: Wiley.

Thompson, J. D. (1967). *Organizations in action.* New York: McGraw-Hill.

Townsend, R. G. (1990). Toward a broader micropolitics of schools. *Curriculum Inquiry, 20,* 205–224.

Tyack, D. (1974). *The one best system: A history of American urban education.* Cambridge, MA: Harvard University Press.

Tyack, D. & Hansot, E. (1982). *Managers of virtue: Public school leadership in America, 1820–1980.* Basic Books.

Tyack, D. & Tobin, W. (1994). The "grammar" of schooling: Why has it been so hard to change. *American Educational Research Journal, 31*(3), 453–479.

Waller, W. (1932). *The sociology of teaching.* New York: Wiley.

Weiss, C. H. (1993). Shared decisionmaking about what? A comparison of schools with and without teacher participation. *Teachers College Record, 95*(1), 68–92.

Weiss, C. H. & Cambone, J. (1993). Principals' roles in shared decisionmaking. Revised version of paper presented at the American Educational Rsearch Association, Atlanta, GA.

Weiss, C. H., Cambone, J., & Wyeth, A. (1992). Trouble in paradise: Teacher conflicts in shared decisionmaking. *Educational Administration Quarterly, 28,* 350–367.

Wiles, D. K. (1974). Community participation demands and local school response in the urban environment. *Education and Urban Society, 6*(4), 451–468.

Williamson, O. E. (1976). Transaction-cost economics: The governance of contractual relations. *Journal of Law and Economics, 22,* 233–261.

Williamson, O. E. (1986). The economics of governance: Framework and implications. In Langlois (Ed.) *Economics as a process, essays in the new institutionalist economics* (pp. 171–202). Cambridge: Cambridge University Press.

Willower, D. J. (1970). Educational change and functional equivalents. *Education and Urban Society, 2,* 385–402.

Wirt, F. M. & Kirst, M. W. (1975). *The political web of American schools.* Boston, MA: Little, Brown.

Wirt, F. M. & Kirst, M. W. (1992). *Schools in conflict: The politics of education.* Berkeley, CA: McCutchan.

NOTES

1. We would like to thank the following individuals for their time and effort in reviewing our chapter: Jon Snyder, Teacher Education Program, Graduate School of Education, University of California, Santa Barbara; Gary Crow, Department of Educational Administration, Graduate School of Education, University of Utah; and Rebecca Raybould, Department of Educational Administration, Graduate School of Education, University of Utah.

2. Recall that the ideas of Fredrick Taylor and scientific management were introduced in the 1930s and Callahan wrote his book about the "cult of efficiency" in 1962, so the references (if not the practice) are hardly fresh.

3. It should be noted that self-interest is not always, if ever, rationally defined, nor is it a single or clearly defined variable. Nonetheless, the idea of self-interest exists within the collective interests of a group.

4. For the sake of clarity, it is worthwhile distinguishing between these two words: *effectiveness* refers solely to measures of outcomes, whereas *efficiency* is a ratio of outcomes to costs. Thus, one could have a very effective program, but one that cost a fortune. An efficient program may be less effective, but one with which even the most frugal tax payer would be pleased.

5. Speaking parenthetically, this is how we describe the purpose of many of the current textbooks on supervision in education. In this respect, these textbooks serve a distinctly political function.

◆ III ◆

SUPERVISION AS PROFESSIONAL PRACTICE

INTRODUCTION

Robert J. Alfonso
EAST TENNESSEE STATE UNIVERSITY

The six chapters in Section III present a broad perspective on past, current, and future professional practice of supervision. Each chapter can stand alone. However, read or studied as a package, the chapter provide the scholar or practitioner of school supervision with a comprehensive analysis of the practice of supervision and the way that these professional roles have been manifested in organizational arrangements, behaviors, and processes. These chapters make clear the complex nature of school supervision, its varied and changing patterns, and the differing perceptions among scholars of school supervision about what should constitute appropriate and effective professional practice. Both persistent and emerging issues concerning the focus of school supervision are addressed: the individual teacher; a larger group; the school as the unit of change; the role of teachers themselves in supervision; and the practice of supervision from the point of introduction to the profession to its responsibility for teacher development during a career.

FUNCTIONS OF SCHOOL SUPERVISION

This section begins with a comprehensive analysis and description by Anderson and Snyder of the functions of school supervision. In Chapter 11, they trace the evolution of school supervision, noting how changes in supervisory func-

tions during the past century have been directly related to the emerging challenges that schools have faced and the resulting professional issues that have also needed to be addressed. Supervisory functions, in their view, have always been a product of the contemporary school culture in existence at a given time. As the context in which schooling takes place has changed, the authors demonstrate, through analysis of research and practice, that the function of supervision has been on a steady, although not unbroken, evolutionary track. The authors refer to these various functional shifts as stages, each clearly identifiable and each having not only some traceable cultural or organizational causes, but also having its own strong advocates. They identify these stages, progressively, as authoritarian control and evaluation of teachers, followed later by a focus on team development and interpersonal collaboration, and in the most recent past an orientation to systems analysis and the development of the whole school as a learning community.

In the second part of the chapter, the authors examine current approaches to supervision functions through a discussion of the school as a unit of change (as contrasted with historical emphasis on the teacher as the focus of supervisory change efforts). They include "lessons" from corporate America, and include an analysis of culture development and culture change as essential components of this approach. They also provide evidence for the critical role of the principal as cultural architect.

Lastly, in the third part of Chapter 11, Anderson and Snyder present their more visionary concept of the kind of supervision that will be needed as schools undergo dramatic changes in the 21st Century. This discussion deals with new anticipated demands on school leadership; it shares perspectives from the quality management literature; and suggests a change model designed to guide leaders in the process of school development. A report on a school district partnership and the results of a research study that highlights the emerging role of the school principal/supervisor are presented not as prescriptions but as useful data and guidance for those who recognize the need for schools and leadership to respond to the changing needs of students. The authors emphasize strongly the need for visionary leadership for the transformation of schools.

ROLES, RESPONSIBILITIES, AND RELATIONSHIPS

Glatthorn examines the great variety of roles, responsibilities, and relationships that are characterized under the general rubric of school supervision. He demonstrates in Chapter 12 how supervisory services that exist at different levels relate to each other and how services are affected at one level by activities at another. He identifies what he refers to as three spheres of influence: roles external to the school district, roles within school districts, and roles within the individual school. Glatthorn gives the term *supervision* a broad interpretation, in which he includes all those who are formally assigned responsibility for improving instruction and curriculum. This includes persons who do not carry the title of supervision, but whose duties so define them.

He recognizes what is almost an historical obsession with trying to identify and list the tasks performed by supervisors at these three levels. Indeed, the literature, as Glatthorn notes, is replete with such lists—although it is frequently not clear how the lists were generated or what validity they might have.

In developing a conceptual framework for the analysis of roles, the author uses two bodies of literature: research on learning (to keep the focus on student learning) and studies and theoretical analyses of the roles of supervisors. He identifies five foci for school supervision: quality of instruction, quality of curriculum, quality and quantity of instructional resources, school and classroom climate, and the quality of the school's relationship with parents and community. In his analysis of roles, Glatthorn concludes that a supervisor could adopt one of three major orientations: evaluation, improvement, or maintenance. On-going processes are the result of day-to-day activities selected to carry out responsibilities. These three dimensions form the conceptual framework that he uses to examine supervisory roles across the three spheres of influence.

Glatthorn's thorough analysis provides a clear portrayal of the complex web of effort and responsibilities called "supervision." It is both seen and unseen, close at hand and at a distance. He also highlights for us the connections and relationships among supervisory efforts in schools, district offices, state departments, and higher education.

PROCESSES AND TECHNIQUES OF SUPERVISION

In Chapter 13, Holland points out the difficulty in identifying or clarifying essential techniques and processes in any profession in the absence of accepted standards of practice. It is from standards of practice that a determination can be made of legitimate actions that can be provided in response to client need. She recognizes that the lack of professional standards is a general problem in education and has led to easy acceptance of a wide array of techniques—some stemming directly from local school conditions and others coming from the writing of scholars. Schools have been subject to continuous change efforts and prescriptions—many from well-meaning persons and groups. But without professional standards of practice, they are all too subject to the latest fad or the persuasion of an influential spokesperson. She further argues that this condition is "exemplified" in the field of instructional supervision, noting that its processes and techniques are characterized by practical expediency and even intellectual anarchy.

Holland comments on the debate between those who argue that in-class supervision is the "real thing" and those who argue for supervision in a broader context—school level supervision. Obviously, there are those who argue that it is not a choice, but that both are needed. Which approach one advocates, however, has a major bearing on the processes and techniques that are considered important. An orientation to school level supervision leads, for example, to processes and techniques related to evaluation, staff development, and curriculum development. There is an extensive body of research on classroom observation, and Holland provides examples of how a process leads to techniques; the two processes resulting from an in-class supervision orientation are observation of teaching and the supervisory conference. Holland concludes that the absence of standards of practice allows for processes and techniques which represent quite divergent perspectives on the theory and practice of supervision. Her discussion of process orientation is an effective corollary to the preceding chapters by Anderson and Snyder and by Glatthorn.

SUPERVISION IN TEACHER EDUCATION

Supervision as an essential component of teacher education is analyzed by McIntyre and Byrd in Chapter 14. They include in their discussion early field experience and student teaching, professional development schools, and other emerging patterns of supervision related to the preparation of teachers. Supervision of student teachers requires the use of a number of the same skills that would be used with in-class supervision as described by Holland in the preceding chapter; however, the relationship between the supervisor and a teacher and that of the university supervisor and the student teacher are quite different. The university supervisor and the student teacher are still in a teacher-student relationship and evaluation and a final grade (and licensure) are the final outcome. In a school district, the supervisor and the teacher are both professionals in the same organization, with all the influence of the larger organization, such as its culture, its goals, its hierarchy, and its history. The question has been raised before as to whether supervision of student teachers is truly supervision or whether it is teaching—an off campus extension of a professor's responsibility.

Regardless, McIntyre and Byrd describe the problems of the field experience and student teaching inherent in trying to clarify the purpose and goals. They echo the theme of Holland in blaming this situation on the absence of theoretical underpinnings for field experience and for teacher education as a whole. The importance of student teaching has long been recognized, but it often received little but lip service in university programs. In more recent years, however, more research has addressed this activity, and new forms of induction, most notably professional schools, have emerged.

One of the frequently difficult aspects of field experience is treated at length by the authors. They refer to the "supervisory triad of the student teacher, university supervisor, and cooperating teacher. It is fraught with difficulty for all, but especially for the student teacher. Not only are there differences in understanding about the purpose and goals of student teaching, but there are disagreements about the student teacher's role, one which shifts during the experience. In addition, McIntyre and Byrd point out that the three members of the triad may have very different philosophical positions about schools and teaching. This situation is only exacerbated when roles in the triad are not clearly delineated.

TEACHER INVOLVEMENT IN SUPERVISION

Goldsberry focuses his attention in Chapter 15 on in-class supervision, but more specifically on the involvement of teachers in this process. One way to view supervision is as what supervisors do, their skills, and their behavior. Goldsberry, however, is interested in supervision as the *interaction* that occurs between a supervisor and a teacher, asserting that "teacher involvement is a requisite for educational supervision." Goldsberry's chapter is an example of those scholars who place a particular value on "in-class" supervision. It is interesting to consider it alongside Holland's chapter on "Processes and Techniques." While acknowledging existing perspectives on clinical supervision, he states that only two conditions are necessary for studying teacher involvement in supervision: that a teacher is receiving assistance from at least one other person in refining teaching behavior, and that it is based at least in part on direct observation of teaching practice.

Critics have long complained that supervision is something done to teachers and too seldom for them. Goldsberry goes further in suggesting that it should be something done *with* them, arguing that if teachers are not consciously involved in the examination and refinement of teaching, they are not engaged in (part of) supervision.

The extremely complex question is raised as to what outcomes are desired from supervisory interventions, what interventions may bring about certain results, knowing when desired results have actually occurred, and to what extent inter-

ventions are affected by personality, by attitudes toward teaching and learning, by the nature of the teacher's involvement, and by the characteristics of the intervention itself. Goldsberry also discusses the particularly difficult question of knowing when improved teaching has resulted. Often improved teaching is described (or assumed to result) even in the absence of good information about preceding performances.

He concludes that meaningful and documented changes in teaching practice can occur as a result of supervisory intervention when teachers are actively involved and when they are given opportunities to reflect on their practices and to share their perceptions of altered practice. Goldsberry's careful analysis of practice and research dealing with teacher involvement leads to the conclusion that it is essential if we are serious about improving practice. Yet, except in certain progressive school districts, in "light house" projects, or in university research studies, much supervision is still what Goldsberry calls "nominal," rare observation followed by little meaningful discussion. In describing possible relationships for teacher involvements he analyzes roles of mentors, coaches, and consultants, and associated strategies and desired consequences.

TEACHER DEVELOPMENT ACROSS THE CAREER SPAN

Prior chapters in this section deal with issues such as functions, roles, student teaching, processes and teacher involvement. Throughout these there runs the underlying issue of the proper foci for school supervision. Should it be for school wide improvement, attempting to change a culture? Should it emphasize more refined techniques of observation or conferencing, focusing on the individual teacher and the classroom? In Chapter 16, Oja and Reiman draw on theory and research in adult development; they conclude that research directed at school restructuring (and ultimately improved practice) must be connected to research on teachers' professional concerns and life cycle transitions.

There was a time when a teacher education graduate was considered a finished product, or approximately so. Some years ago, that assumption was widely discredited and a variety of staff development programs and supervisory interventions have sought to contribute to teacher growth, skill acquisition, and, in a general sense, the professional development of teachers. Many efforts were without theoretical or research foundation, and much of the effort was built on an insufficient knowledge base. Oja and Reiman assert that on one end of a continuum, supervision for teacher development was based on a psychoanalytic conception of teacher growth. In this view, supervision should help teachers face themselves and understand how early experiences have shaped present deliberations. At the other end of the continuum has been the process-product model, drawing on behavioral psychology. The authors also suggest that some theories for teacher development are extremely broad and consequently too abstract to be sufficiently useful; other theories tend to be so concerned with specifics as to become too narrow to provide adequate explanations.

In creating their conceptualization of supervision for teacher development across the career span, the authors utilize the extensive body of knowledge already available concerning stages of adult cognitive development, age theories (adult age-related transitions), career phases, and moral development, for example, and indicate the implications for supervision of the Teacher Career Cycle Model.

The model presents a comprehensive research based approach to modifying supervisory practice. It is likely that much of the disenchantment that has characterized teachers' perceptions of supervision is a result of practices that operated without regard to the changes in adults in their life/career cycles. Without such awareness and without sensitivity to them, supervision can be unproductive at best and a negative experience at worst. Research and knowledge of adult development and life cycle issues have increased dramatically in recent years. As this knowledge base begins to be adapted by educational researchers and practitioners, it can only improve the practice of supervision. Oja and Reiman conclude that "If we knew what adult maturity and development is, then we should also know what supervision ought to be."

The views presented in these six chapters provide significant perspectives on the professional practice of supervision. Although the authors take different approaches to the practice of supervision, the mosaic created by their analyses is a useful one for any person interested in the study and practice of supervision.

•11•

FUNCTIONS OF SCHOOL SUPERVISION

Robert H. Anderson
UNIVERSITY OF SOUTH FLORIDA

Karolyn J. Snyder
UNIVERSITY OF SOUTH FLORIDA

INTRODUCTION

In the last several decades the functions of school supervision have been undergoing remarkable change. The rapid increase in numbers and varieties of at-risk students along with the virtual transformation of the work place are calling the nature of school supervision into question. Schools are no longer predictable social institutions with predictable student needs. Teachers now find themselves inventing new teaching processes and programs more often, which causes supervisors to question the utility of their practice.

In this chapter the supervisory functions that have evolved over the century are explored in relation to the changing schooling challenges and resulting professional issues. What we see is that historically the literature of supervision focused almost exclusively upon the work that needs to be done to help individual teachers improve their instructional services to children. The first part of this chapter examines this literature. The literatures of education including supervision have been increasingly focused upon the total school as the entity within which change occurs, and the nature of the principal's role as leader (and provider of supervision in the change process for instructional improvement) has received much attention. The second part of this chapter explores how the shift in supervisory functions has occurred as a result of this new focus on the school. Even more recently, with the so-called Quality revolution underway, functions related to the change process are coming to be understood at least partly in terms of influencing the school work culture and empowering work groups so that they can perform at higher levels. Part III of the chapter examines the implications of this "revolution," in

terms of the functions now identified with the role of supervisor. It is therefore intended that the reader will understand the shift that has been made from attention focused on individual teachers to the school as a unit and then to ways through which the needs of the client (student) become central to the total school-development efforts.

SCHOOL SUPERVISION FUNCTIONS: DEFINITIONS AND PERCEPTIONS

Introduction

Glanz's chapter in this volume (see Chap. 3) examines the historical dimension of supervision in the schools. Some of that material will be revisited in this chapter, but our effort here will be devoted to the functional dimension: Over the years, what have been seen as the normal or characteristic activities in which persons with the label, *supervisor,* are expected or obliged to engage in as part of their work activity? What specific duties or responsibilities have been, or are being, attached to the role? These questions guide our inquiry as we seek to understand how supervisors have been viewed over the years within the larger educational establishment(s) they serve.

Dearth of Research Data At the outset it may be appropriate to note that although there has always been, and continues to be, an extensive literature base regarding supervisory functions, almost none of that literature includes research concerning these functions. Earnest, even intense, opinions are regularly offered with respect to the "legitimate" activities in which supervisors should, or should not, participate. Often these opinions relate to the "helping versus judging" dilemma, and the bulk of these opinions rests on the argument that supervisors should not be involved in (administrative) evaluation activities. Another body of opinion(s) concentrates on the extent to which supervisors should, or should not, focus on clinical supervision with individual teachers. Of course, there are other debates.

To our knowledge the advocates of one or another position on such issues have not buttressed their statements with quantitative or other data. Some investigations have sought to assess the benefits to the school situation (i.e., especially with regard to children's learning) of the work done by supervisors, but none of these efforts has succeeded in illuminating whether various supervisory functions have the sort of impact upon learning that justifies the costs of providing such services. In the material that follows, therefore, supervisory functions are being reviewed largely through the lenses of scholarly opinion.

Functional Definitions In seeking to define the functions of supervision, drawing upon the opinion-dominated literature, Bolin and Panaritis (1992) concluded that there are essentially only two areas around which a loose consensus has been built over the years:

1. The function of supervision is an important one, whether it is carried out by a superintendent (as in the early history of the field), a supervisor, a curriculum worker, or a peer.
2. Supervision is primarily concerned with the improvement of classroom practice for the benefit of students, regardless of what else may be entailed (e.g., curriculum development or staff development) (p. 31).

In what follows, these two areas of agreement will frequently be illustrated or confirmed.

Historical Transitions from Early-Stage Inspection and Control Functions to Assisting and Enabling Functions

Conceptual Framework There appear to have been three types of evolutions over time with respect to conceptual frameworks in supervision: (1) With respect to the supervision of individuals, there has been a century-long switch from teacher control and evaluation, to teacher development, and to various clinical formats for coaching (i.e., both top-down, and among peers); (2) with respect to the supervision of teachers in groups, the movement has been toward promotion of peer coaching, of mutual assistance within teams, and of other forms of collaboration; and (3) with respect to promotion of total-school development, the movement has been toward systems-thinking approaches.

With respect to trends over time in the supervision of individuals, and within the literature, both earlier in this century and in the past 20 or 30 years, most scholars have referred to the fact that as cities grew after about 1840 and as schools became more complex institutions, it was necessary or at least

convenient to rely upon a very ill-trained and ill-educated teaching workforce. In turn, it was convenient to provide that workforce with very detailed instructions and very close "inspection."

In large part because of the influence of Horace Mann, who advocated the adoption of age-graded schools as per the Prussian model, one solution to the insufficient preparation of elementary teachers was to divide the curriculum into tightly-segmented portions, each defining a year's work for the child, so that each teacher need only become an expert in that 1-year segment of the total program. Various historians suggest that this resulted in such a narrow range of expertise that some teachers, capable enough of managing, for example, the third grade program, would have floundered at least initially if told on short notice to teach one of the two lower grades.

There simultaneously emerged graded textbook materials, in each case very specific to the supposed capabilities of the children in its age-grade range. There is not much information in historical accounts to suggest that the suppositions about grade-level difficulty were consciously adapted or geared to research-derived postulates about child/youth development. Over time there also emerged very specific teachers' guides to insure systematic and on-time coverage of the text material.

The function of the inspector, or supervisor, was therefore largely related to enforcement of expectations, including faithful teacher use of the guidelines and maintaining a brisk enough pace so that the content for that grade would indeed be completely covered by the end of the year.

As a wistful commentary on the situation a century or more later, there remain many elementary and secondary schools in which faithful adherence to prescribed curriculum, guidelines, and schedules continues to be a major concern of supervisors. It is also dismaying that the practice of aggregating pupils within a strict 1-year age range had no scientific or philosophic justification, but originated simply as a way of standardizing practice among very amateur teachers. Such an arrangement remains popular even among the much more professional teacher workforce in modern schools.

Reflecting upon nineteenth-century practice, most historians tend to acknowledge that the simplistic graded system combined with tight controls upon teachers' daily behavior and decisions made a contribution to the development of a workable public school system. These historians also observe that the rather severe environment that the system nurtured, during this period in American social history, was somewhat harmonious with the social/religious environment surrounding the schools. Within that environment obedience (e.g., to established authority and employers) was very highly valued and respect for positive elements in human nature (i.e., particularly as they may relate to motivation for learning or motivation for work) was minimal.

It is also useful to note that, apart from the "moral imperatives" that prevailed in mid–nineteenth-century society, there was only the most primitive understanding even among scholars concerning human growth and development, human motivation, and the facilitation of learning. There was also only a primitive understanding of adult work behavior and organizational productivity. It remained for the full impact of the Industrial Revolution and subsequent "scientific management" to cause business/industrial leaders and others, such as school supervisors/superintendents, to revise their thinking about how to stimulate appropriate work behavior.

In an early work, Spears (1953) postulated that there were four distinct periods in the history of supervision: (1) the Colonial Period down to the Civil War, with an emphasis on inspection, done by lay people; (2) the later nineteenth century, which had the same emphasis, but with professional officials doing the supervision; (3) the period between roughly 1910 and 1935, responsibility was divided between principals and special supervisors; and (4) the period after 1935, which features cooperative educational leadership, with involvement also by coordinators, curriculum directors, and consultants. These time divisions up to the mid-1950s are similar to those identified by Beach and Reinhartz (1989), who traced the shift to an emphasis up to 1970 upon curriculum development and "change" broadly defined, and then to a period they label the Clinical and Accountable Period (1970–1980). Since 1980, they note, the field has been in a managerial and entrepreneurial stage.

Fitzgerald (1991), who focused in particular upon the evolution of district-level supervision, propounds that there have been seven time periods during which supervision has evolved. The first, from about 1850 to 1876, is associated with the development of cities and the appearance of "graded" schools calling for the standardization of services. He labels the second period, 1876–1910, "Growth by Need," and links it with maturing industrialism and the beginnings of professionalism in such fields as psychology, medicine, engineering, government, and education. Beginning about 1910, Fitzgerald continues, the impact of F. W. Taylor's scientific management caused a new emphasis upon efficiency which was later criticized in Callahan's landmark 1962 volume, *Education and The Cult of Efficiency*. This was followed by a period, marked by pronouncements around 1930 that supervision was being given over to middle management (i.e., the school principal), during which time supervisors were defined as staff officers and resource persons.

Following Sputnik in 1957, a period began during which time the focus was primarily upon the improvement of curriculum, especially mathematics and science, and during which the numbers of district-based supervisory specialists also grew markedly. This focus gradually shifted toward the improvement of instruction (1978-1986) and featured attempts to implement the growing body of research concerning effective teaching, effective staff development, and generic teaching skills.

Fitzgerald labels the current period (1986 ff.) as "Redefinition: The Supervisor as Manager." The supervisor is seen as manager of support systems rather than actually being the support system, occupying a role and carrying out functions that are in many ways a radical departure from the roles and functions of previous periods.

Lieberman and Miller (1992), in commenting upon the emphasis in research at different historical points, suggest that it was group process in the 1950s; it was subject-matter mastery in the 1960s; it was process–product and generic teaching behaviors and traditions in the 1970s and 1980s; and it was teaching within the context of the classroom in the late 1980s, with particular interest in notions of teacher inquiry, reflective practice, craft knowledge, and collaborative research. Lieberman and Miller also noted two competing views: deficit training versus growth and practice, which defines teachers as professionals and "seeks to develop structures to enable them to collaborate with colleagues and participate in their own renewal and the renewal of their schools" (p. 1051).

The Wiles Contribution The focal changes over time, as noted by Lieberman and Miller, are reflected in writings over a 33-year period associated with the work of Wiles. Wiles was one of the most prominent writers in the field of supervision. His influential book appeared in its first edition in 1950. Subsequent editions while Wiles was still alive appeared in 1955 and 1967, after which two editions were produced by Lovell in 1975 and 1983. It is possible to examine these five editions to obtain a sense of the changes, or evolutions, that took place in supervisory emphasis and functions.

In the first edition of Wiles (1950), an opening chapter entitled "What is the Function of the Supervisor?" sets the stage by pointing to five necessary skills: leadership, human relations, group process, personnel administration, and evaluation. The second edition (1975) includes virtually the same ideas, although it provides a different opening chapter that seeks to define supervision. Within the third edition (1967), there is more elaborate treatment of supervision as curriculum development. "Supervision has the responsibility for effecting continuous improvement in the curriculum," (1967, p. 93), and of supervision as improving instruction (i.e., there are "three facets of the process of improving instruction: the person-to-person interaction, the in-service education program, and the provision of materials of instruction," p. 117).

This emphasis is continued in the fourth edition (1975), in which Lovell observed that since 1957 (Sputnik) the responsibility for the initiation of change had been shifting from the supervisor as "change agent" to

assisting in the decision as to desirable changes, assisting in innovation, supplying the many types of resource help necessary in innovation, coordinating the incorporation of innovations into the program in such a way that student programs would have continuity, assisting in the evaluation of innovation, helping the staff become aware of the variety of alternatives being proposed, assisting in the choice of the alternative that seemed most appropriate in the system, and developing a plan and design that would determine the types of innovations to be supported financially (1975, p. 127).

In Lovell's continuing commentary, a strategy of directed change, often from persons outside of public education, was seen as diverting responsibility for curriculum development from the local school system to outside forces (e.g., university specialists in the disciplines). "Second thoughts," however, led to suspicion that these outside forces were not necessarily prompting needed improvements, although working with community leadership in the planning of changes was coming to be seen as a major supervisory function.

In the chapter defining supervision as "improving instruction," Lovell includes a lengthy section on Direct Interaction with Teaching Behavior, which notes the conflict between provisions of a support system, on the one hand, and assisting with evaluation activities on the other. Preferring the provision of a technical and psychological support system, Lovell proceeds to examine the planning process and the instructional process as observed and analyzed by the supporting supervisor. In the material that follows, about what he calls the "evaluation behavior system," Lovell refers to the emerging importance of collegial supervision within various interaction systems that are available.

The fifth edition (1983) of the Lovell–Wiles work may be viewed as a fairly current representation of the functions of supervision. It has a strong section on "Collaborative Supervision," which puts it in reasonable synchrony with other discussions of personal support functions and culture-building as key ingredients of supervisory work. Defined as "necessary tasks" of supervision are:

1. provision for psychological and technological support
2. helping people to communicate
3. helping people to help and be helped by each other
4. helping people to accept each other
5. coordination of the contributions of highly specialized people toward the needs of human beings in the learning environment
6. utilization of the total staff in the system of instructional supervisory behavior
7. leadership behavior to promote and facilitate change
8. release of human potential
9. curriculum development, coordination, and evaluation
10. continuous development and evaluation of educational goals (p. 129)

The Lovell–Wiles 1983 edition also has a great deal more to say about clinical supervision than was included in prior editions, but perhaps more significant is that the volume includes material, under the chapter heading "Supervision is Facilitating Human Development," that underscores the importance of at least half of the preceding listed tasks.

Other Reflections: Ayer A 1954 volume by Ayer reflects the extent to which the definition of supervisory functions has departed from top–down, inspection-oriented definitions. Ayer identifies supervision as "the most noble and dynamic of educational endeavor" (p. 2) and traces the work of the major writers in the field (e.g., Burton, Barr, Brueckner, Wiles, Melchior, Briggs, & Justman), all of whom pointed to the improvement of instruction as the guiding general concept. Ayer observed that the improvement of human relations, and the quality of living within the school, became a central concept as reflected in the writings of K. Wiles and also J. A. Bartky (1953), stating that "it is the function of supervision to maintain existing programs of instruction as well as that of improving them" (p. 7).

Ayer (1954) then drew upon a 1952 administration textbook by Miller and Spalding in which four groups of employees were identified: the doers (e.g., teachers or custodians), the recorders of what is done (e.g., bookkeepers, social workers, and again teachers), those who seek to improve the ways in which others do things (e.g., supervisors and consultants), and the administrators. He then noted that the major developments in professional supervision include teacher training supervision, special supervision, special service supervision, and administrative supervision.

Relating Past Practices to More Recent Developments Before leaving this discussion, which has looked at supervisory functions largely vis-à-vis individuals, it seems appropriate to look at several developments in the final third of the twentieth century that had significant implications for supervisory functions. The first and perhaps most important such development has been the (re)emergence of flexible patterns for organizing schools and for aggregating pupil groups. Whereas until the mid-1960s the prevailing and presumably effective arrangement in elementary schools was the self-contained classroom with a single-age pupil cohort, the literature in the mid-1990s is very close to unanimous in support of multiaged pupil cohorts and at least some significant form of teacher teaming or collaboration. This is not to say that the traditional arrangement has given significant ground; rather, it seems to be true that most schools are at least discussing the taking of steps in the direction of possible alternative arrangements. Many middle schools have similarly been moving in the direction of multiage pupil cohorts within a multidisciplinary, thematic, team-taught program, and the same changes are occurring in a fair number of secondary schools.

While it is not the province of this handbook to discuss teacher teaming and heterogeneous pupil grouping in detail, it is important here to note that pupils with different backgrounds and experiences need to learn together, and teachers need to work within collegial arrangements. Meeting these needs creates a very different environment within which the supervisor functions. A different constellation of class/team management problems, and different opportunities, arises for teachers. The supervisor's work with both individual teachers and groups of teachers takes on new dimensions. In both cases, expertise becomes essential in how to help individuals and groups (i.e., pupils and/or teachers) to function comfortably and efficiently.

In this connection, it may be useful to point out that when the concept of team teaching was first explored in the late 1950s, it derived from two basic assumptions: first, that working alone provides insufficient opportunity for professional career growth and satisfaction; second, that curricular and pedagogical advances would more likely occur within a lively and interactive setting. Shaplin and Olds (1964) and their colleagues at Harvard University have provided a thorough and balanced account of team teaching's early history. As a postscript to that volume, it might now be observed that both of the major books that subsequently appeared on the topic of clinical supervision (Cogan 1973; Goldhammer 1969) were nurtured and shaped during the years when team teaching, which provided for them a context, was first being developed. The understandings that underlie practices of collegial interchange (peer supervision) were also sharpened during the summer programs (1960–1965) that were sponsored by Harvard for the training of team personnel.

When clinical supervision emerged in the early 1960s, it had a significant influence upon the work and functions of the supervisor, and, coinciding as it did with teaming, it also created a new dynamic for peer-level "supervisory" interactions. Many of the procedures and attitudes associated with clinical supervision influenced the ways that teachers began to observe and react to each others' work. Such terms as *peer supervision, mentoring,* and *collegial assistance* acquired stronger valence within the partnership frameworks that became more prevalent. A corollary to these developments was that supervisors, whose essential mission has always been to influence teacher thought and action, assumed a somewhat new function, the role of advisor and consultant to teachers seeking to help each other. Pajak (1993) has provided a particularly comprehensive report on the many varieties of clinical supervision that can be found in today's schools.

Program Development Functions

As reflected in the very name of the professional association that speaks most directly to the work of supervisors (i.e., The Association for Supervision and Curriculum Development, ASCD), supervision is inextricably connected with program development, and virtually all persons whose title includes a variant of "supervision" carry heavy responsibility for both maintaining and improving the programs that are offered to students. This section will examine the four major dimensions of this responsibility.

Curriculum Development In the current context, within virtually all supervision textbooks now in use, the broad rubric of curriculum development subsumes at least the following tasks:

1. identification and provision of resources and research information
2. providing connections with regional, state and national curriculum efforts
3. coordination of work groups and task forces
4. representing or identifying technological tools
5. coordination of action research

In the following discussion each of these categories will briefly be examined. The comments represent what the majority of authors of supervision textbooks appear to perceive; hence, individual citations are limited.

INFORMATION AND RESEARCH. In the first category, the supervisor is generally expected to keep in touch with the curriculum literature and to make public note of important books, booklets, journals, monographs, and other sources that may be useful to curriculum committees or task forces, to groups of teachers working on particular problems, and to individual teachers. The supervisor is similarly expected to be alert to new instructional materials as they become available and to make suggestions to groups or individuals for whom such materials may be useful. Participation in regional, state, or national meetings in which curriculum matters are discussed and where instructional materials may be on display is common in the work schedules of supervisors.

Relating to the information function is the provision function. It is the supervisor in many schools or districts who is responsible for procurement, and even for the distribution, of such materials. The observation that the effective supervisor needs to own a station wagon or its equivalent because of the delivery services involved is not unusual.

CONNECTIONS. The second category includes those activities, often growing out of the aforementioned information functions, related to maintaining active connections with curriculum workers and experts across the land. Much of this occurs within the context of professional meetings, workshops, and institutes, some of which are sponsored by professional associations, others that are sponsored by state agencies or networks, entrepreneurial organizations, or universities. In larger districts, the supervisor(s) may also perform this function by bringing projects or persons from such organizations into the district for consultation or other services.

COORDINATION OF GROUPS. The third category includes the work that supervisors do in stimulating, guiding, and coordinating curriculum work groups and task forces, both within the district as a whole and within individual schools. The supervisor actually sometimes functions as the convenor or chair of such groups, although his or her role is more often that of a consultant, resource person, or ex-officio member of the working unit.

Emerging within the leadership literature is a strand of thought that links the growing knowledge base for adult learning (e.g., as reflected in the writings of Knowles [1984], Brookfield [1986], and Houle [1980] with the almost-overwhelming inflow of writings about how worker output and morale can be raised to higher levels. After reviewing these sources Anderson (1989) noted that there are three common threads: (1) most adults prefer to learn and work in a social context; (2) helping work groups function well is a cost-effective, productive activity for managers and supervisors; and (3) work cultures are healthy when members value group and organizational goals and when day-to-day decisions related to the goals are made at the operations level (p. 296).

It would seem to follow that with these conclusions before them, supervisors will seek to "coordinate" work groups within the district and to play an active role in increasing the numbers and the effectiveness of cooperative work groups. Functioning as a "culture builder" within the district could well be one of the most worthwhile functions for the supervisor to play.

TECHNOLOGY. The fourth category is a relative newcomer to the list of supervisor's functions within the framework of curriculum development. It refers to the growing need for teachers to be knowledgeable about, and skillful in the use of, the abundance of electronic resources now coming into common use in classrooms or in schools.

ACTION RESEARCH. "Action research" may not be the most appropriate label for this category, because the term frequently describes data-collection and investigative activities in connection with which there is little if any effort to link results with hypotheses or to seek truly definitive answers to perceived problems. All the same, from the literature, including the journals of professional organizations, one learns that a great many teachers and other school workers are busily involved in carrying out a variety of studies and working together in order to solve problems. Whether they constitute "low level" research or not, these activities often invigorate those involved and generate discussion and experimentation that benefit the program in some way. It is very appropriate to the function of the supervisor to be involved in encouraging and coordinating such efforts.

Foshay (1994) has examined the history of action research, and urged those in consultant roles to take a respectful approach and seek to learn about how teachers, who are generally disinterested in theory, think about their instructional problems and ways to solve them.

Instructional Improvement Within this major area of functional responsibility, the supervisor is expected to have considerable influence upon the instructional program, particularly the instructional decisions and behavior of classroom teachers. Some of this influence is exerted at the district level, some at the local school level, and some in individual or team classrooms. Providing leadership toward instructional improvement, which is an all-inclusive function in some senses, calls for playing a number of roles.

One important function is to be centrally involved in the district's/school's efforts to identify what good instruction is by asking such questions as: What are the knowledges, skills, and attitudes that are related to higher instructional performance? What standards or goals should be adopted and respected within the district? How can we tell when the best possible learning environment is in existence? What are the elements of pedagogical craftsmanship?

Mandated instructional approaches sometimes provide the approved answers to these questions. During the 1980s, a number of states adopted systems for identifying instructional competences. One example was Florida, where a great deal of effort went into developing a research-based teacher evaluation system in what became known as the Florida Performance Measurement System (FPMS). Derived from empirical studies on teaching, and organized into domains with definitions, examples, and principles of effective teaching, FPMS defined such concepts of teacher performance as rule explication, group alert, review of subject matter, academic feedback, concept development, emphasis, and task attraction and challenge. A good review of the FPMS system is found in a chapter by Bullerman, Borg and Peterson (1993). In FPMS, the supervisor's function is to make certain that these teaching behaviors are being regularly utilized.

Somewhat similar functions are/were carried out in schools or school systems in which the so-called Madeline Hunter Model of teaching has been officially adopted or mandated. In what was identified by Hunter as a clinical supervision model, it was the responsibility of the supervisor to determine the extent to which this definition of good instruction was being followed. Critics of the Hunter system noted that such an approach became a form of teacher evaluation rather than of supervision (Hunter, 1988; Pavan 1987).

Beach and Reinhartz (1989) observed that it is the function, rather than the title, that defines an instructional supervisor. They declare that anyone (e.g., superintendent, central office staff member, principal or assistant principal, department head, or consultant) who has the responsibility for working with teachers to increase the quality of student learning through improved instruction falls within that category. Such persons have these duties or functions:

1. formulating, implementing, and evaluating goals for the school and/or the teacher.
2. developing, implementing, and evaluating curriculum.
3. supervising and evaluating personnel and providing staff development opportunities.
4. developing and managing resources for the teaching-learning process.
5. evaluating instructional materials and programs for classroom use.

The roles associated with these functions include planner, organizer, leader, helper, evaluator or appraiser, motivator, communicator, and decision maker (pp. 8–11).

Mentoring and *coaching* are terms now prominent in the literature of supervision. A publication on coaching (Anderson & Snyder, 1993) included chapters by Hosack-Curlin on examining peer coaching among teachers, Giella and Stanfill on the institutionalization of peer coaching in an entire district, Pajak and Carr on mentor teachers and peer coaches, and by Nielsen on technical coaching. These authors provide excellent summaries of the literature on these topics.

Again with respect to the function of promoting instructional improvement, supervisors work with task forces, committees, and other groups that seek to define effective instructional practices and influence progress toward this goal. Related to this function is that of assisting specialists, broadly defined to include both central-office "directors" of curriculum areas and those teachers within the schools with acknowledged expertise, who in turn provide assistance and services to school staffs.

Staff Development (Human Resource Development) The extent to which teachers and others in the schools have been shedding their long-standing hostility to staff "in-service" programs and embracing opportunities for growth under the rubric of "staff development" is of interest. Although not all districts have come to the point where their teachers place high value upon human resource development as a major force in their professional growth and success, it appears that in a great many districts teachers are being offered a rich menu of workshops, training sessions, institutes, and other services. Teacher response to these opportunities has been reported to be generally positive.

Supervisors frequently play important roles in such human resource development offerings, although in many districts there is now a full-time staff, headed by a ranking central office person, that is responsible for managing the programs. Those direct-supervision functions that involve the supervisor either as an actual visitor to teachers' classrooms or as the coordinator of supervisory classroom visits being carried out by peers/colleagues are now often included under the heading of "Staff Development."

Supervisors increasingly function as either advisors to, or resource persons for, those involved in clinical supervision or other direct, hands-on work with teachers (Anderson & Snyder, 1993). Among the challenges faced by those who would supervise classroom teachers is understanding the relative professional maturity of each teacher and knowing how to adapt supervisory behavior accordingly. Within the notion of "contingency supervision," as associated with the work of Hersey and Blanchard (1977), is awareness that for some workers it is necessary and appropriate to be very directive as, probably, was the nineteenth-century inspector, whereas for others it is appropriate to adopt a stance between directive and consultatory, and for others the best approach is to give ample authority/leeway to the skillful professional whose performance will surely be exemplary.

Snyder and Anderson (1986) have developed a management training program within which "clinical supervision," including contingency approaches, is 1 of 10 supervisory approaches. In their schema, "staff development" in all of its many dimensions is the key to moving schools successfully in productive directions.

Within the latest (1992) edition of the *Encyclopedia of Educational Research,* in which there is no essay on supervision per se, Lieberman and Miller provide an essay on "Professional Development of Teachers." Within this essay there is a subsection on staff development and school improvement. These authors note that the two functions, developing staff and improving schools, are "reciprocal and inextricably connected" (p. 1049). A subsection follows on staff development as culture building, with the culture-building metaphor drawn from their earlier work (Lieberman & Miller, 1979). Respectful mention is made of the landmark work by Sarason (1971), who pointed out that unless changes are being made in the basic way that people go about their work, technical changes in textbooks, procedures, instructional methods, and organizational arrangements are doomed to be merely "illusory."

Sarason's early work and the contributions of Lieberman and Miller, as noted earlier, are congruent with a substantial literature in which the building of a dynamic and goal-oriented "work culture" (Deal & Kennedy, 1982; Snyder & Anderson, 1986) is identified as one of the major activities or functions with which school leaders need to be associated. Although school leaders, in this context, also include persons with line authority, there is a strong indication within the literature, especially that which concentrates upon supervision, that culture building is a domain within which people in supervisory assignments have a particular, even central, part to play.

Lieberman and Miller also take note of an AERA paper by Little (1981), noting that successful staff development ensured collegial work conditions by promoting open discussion of issues, shared understandings, and a common vocabulary. Showers, Joyce, and Bennett (1987) embellish this thinking by observing that "all teachers need social support as they labor" (p. 86) and that staff development that generates cognitions about practice is the most effective.

Further to the topic of staff development are links between the work of Costa and Garmston (1994), Fullan (1993), Glickman (1990), Senge (1990a), Sergiovanni and Starratt (1993), and others. In his foreword to a new volume on cognitive coaching by Costa and Garmston (1994), Glickman observed that his research time in the late 1970s was spent largely on the interactions between supervisors and teachers. Within the literature at that time, Glickman noted, there was a void in the personal, cognitive, and developmental nature of human interactions. Through his emerging work on developmental supervision he sought to address this void by putting humans, with all their magnificent complexities, into the supervision equation. As he became acquainted with the idea of cognitive coaching as developed by Costa and Garmston, he saw it as a harbinger of new educational demands, expectations, and reforms in the 1990s, with schools working together for democratic renewal. The goal, as he came to see it, was to make teaching a more dignified and thoughtful profession.

Costa and Garmston (1994), in the volume admired by Glickman, sought to define the three goals of what they have labeled cognitive coaching as (1) establishing mutual trust, defined as an assured reliance on the character, ability, or strength of someone or something, (2) facilitating mutual learning (i.e., the engagement and transformation of mental processes and perceptions), and (3) enhancing growth toward holonomy. The latter term, borrowed from Koestler, represents the twin goals of individual autonomy, on the one hand, and collaboration, working interdependently with others on the other. A key concept, in the authors' minds, is that the ultimate purpose of coaching is to modify teachers' capabilities to modify themselves. The role of the coach is therefore to help individuals to thrive simultaneously in the two behaviors, both on their own terms and as members of the professional community.

In a journal description of the cognitive coaching process as used with two teachers, Garmston (Garmston, Linder, & Whitaker 1993) notes that the process "seemed to facilitate access to the lesser used sides of their brains" (p. 57) and to help teachers to expand their repertoire of teaching styles, exploring untapped resources within themselves.

DEVELOPMENTAL SUPERVISION. Returning to Glickman, who is one of the most influential shapers of current thought about supervision, we note his selection of the term *developmental supervision* to signal the approach that is most appropriate when working within a professional context.

Glickman identified five major "tasks" of supervision in his 1985 textbook. These tasks, all related to the improvement of instruction, were direct assistance, providing one-to-one feedback to teachers, in-service education (i.e., providing learning opportunities to teachers), curriculum development, providing for changes in teaching content and instructional materials, group development, providing for instructional problem-solving meetings among teachers; and action research, providing teachers with ways to evaluate their own teaching, Glickman devotes much of his text to detailing how these five "tasks can be performed so that teachers take individual and collective responsibility for instructional improvement" (p. 257).

PEER ASSISTANCE: COGNITIVE COACHING. A very strong trend, in practice and as reflected in the literature, is for the helping function long associated with the formal role of supervisor to be extended to persons in other roles, especially "peers" or others with essentially equal status. It is quite likely the growing dissatisfaction with the literally self-contained work model combined with growing acceptance of team-teaching arrangements, in numerous forms, that has stimulated professional conversation within schools and created greater willingness to be involved in mechanisms within a framework of partnership, such as collegial assistance, collegial coaching, and some versions of mentoring. Within this context, the person occupying the more formal supervisory role is sometimes accepted as a partner and behaves in much the same manner as would a literal peer.

Costa and Kallick (1993) have added a useful phrase, "the critical friend," to the literature describing the helping functions carried on in healthy school situations. Identified as a "trusted person who will ask provocative questions and offer helpful critiques" (p. 49), the critical friend plays an important role both in the expansion of one's professional repertoire/insights, as well as in stimulating self-evaluation and promoting higher levels of thinking about one's work. Costa and Kallick note that the idea of critical friend applies to all role levels (e.g., teacher, administrator) and can in fact be a valuable tool in staff development (p. 51).

The metaphor of "coaching," as fully developed in the work of Joyce, Showers, and others, has become a synonym for certain of those helping functions for which supervisors are often responsible, but also, and perhaps especially, for the collegial-assistance functions in which peers engage. Reference is therefore emerging in the literature, to the function that supervisors can play (e.g., with teaching teams or partnership/coaching teams, in training, and in counseling peers in their efforts to work together).

Evaluation and Assessment As indicated at the outset of this chapter, the extent to which persons with the label *supervisor* should be involved in the administrative functions that result in personnel decisions (e.g., tenuring, promoting, rewarding) is much discussed in the supervision literature, with the overwhelming weight of argument running against such involvement. In one review of this problem, Anderson (1990–1991) identified those functions for which the term *administrative supervision* seems appropriate. This should not involve the supervisor whose role responsibilities relate to growth-inducement, which falls within the term *supportive supervision.* These administrative functions include career stage reviews, pretenure, and periodic affirmation or reconfirmation, recognition-associated reviews, merit-related applications or reviews, and criterion-related assessments, problem-associated supervision, informal, intensive, or due-process supervision, and organizational goal attainment (p. 109). Anderson's position was that there should be a "presumption of competence" with respect to educational workers, in keeping with the legal concept of "presumption of innocence," and that the day-to-day relationships of supervisors should be predicated upon positive predictions of motivation and performance.

Subsumed under the category of organizational goal attainment in the Anderson model would be quality control, to ensure compliance with legal and statutory requirements, and other functions that protect the society's investment in the education of its children. Such supervisory behaviors also explicitly serve to protect and enhance the standards and ideals that characterize the education profession's noblest purposes.

By contrast with these observations/conclusions concerning supervisor involvement in data gathering and analysis, most commentators on the evaluation responsibility within school districts seem agreed that it is proper, even central, within the supervisory role. Such a role facilitates the development of standards/criteria of excellent performance, in working out policies and procedures for teacher evaluation, and in providing counsel/assistance/services to teachers with respect to the improvement of skills and the elimination of deficiencies. In an Olympics analogy, the figure skater is ultimately dependent upon the judge's view, but he or she has a close and positive relationship with the coach who provides guidance and assistance. The instructional supervisor does not belong in the role of judge, or at least so claim virtually all of those who write about supervision. In practice, however, it is sometimes difficult to keep the coaching and the judging functions clearly separated from each other.

Organizational Maintenance and Development Functions

A great many of the functions for which supervisors are held responsible have to do with the general day-to-day maintenance and survival of the school or district (e.g., in the acquisition and distribution of resources). Other functions have to do with planning and preparing for the future (e.g., in developing new curricula), or in preparing for the anticipated revolution in uses of technology. In general, it seems that supervisors, more than administrators, are also expected to be active and proficient in discovering and sharing new knowledge, both practical and theoretical.

Among current textbooks on supervision, one by Wiles and Bondi (1986) makes note of several functions that are not as explicit in other textbooks. One has to do with the search for, and the management of, funding from various internal and outside sources (pp. 11, 13). In this connection, they comment on the role of "following the flow of monies to ensure their application to intended programs." Another reference is to the supervisor's role in "enforcing statutory requirements" (p. 16). A third, and somewhat more complex, function is described as management of change. As the manager of change, according to these authors, the supervisor becomes responsible for complying with many of the legislative mandates coming down upon the schools along with expectations growing out of the general trend toward a "systems mentality" that links the cycle of accountability with the cycle of curriculum improvement.

While the previously mentioned functions tend to be largely administrative in the minds of most writers, it is probably true that many supervisors do indeed find these responsibilities to be part of their workloads.

Redefining the Leadership Role A growing number of writers ascribe responsibility for leadership functions to nonadministrative roles within the schools, including that of supervisor. There is a built-in difficulty in separating official (i.e., line-officer) responsibility from the obligations that belong to such other roles as teachers, counselors, team/department chairs, and "supervisors," although as members of these other roles become more expert and responsible "professionals" it becomes natural for them to be accepted as other-than-followers. This tendency is one of the root ideas in worker-level decision-making, and in the related notion of giving individual school staffs more responsibility and more opportunity for shaping both ends and means.

As teachers and others evolve from the traditional subordinate orientation toward one in which superordination is shared at "grass-roots" levels, the functions of both line and staff officers in the schools change to at least some extent from command to coordination, from directing to orchestrating, from persuasion to enablement, and from controlling knowledge/information to assisting in its generation and circulation. The extent to which this requires or suggests redefinition of (among other roles) the supervisor's functions is only now being explored in the literature.

Among the writers whose views on these matters are currently of special interest is Sergiovanni. With Starratt he has produced a 1993 (Fifth Edition) volume the very title of which is *Supervision: A Redefinition*. These authors stress the importance of developing an Educational Platform, within which are identified the supervisor's convictions and sometimes unspoken assumptions, beliefs, attitudes and values about the nature of supervisory work. They also seek to redefine schools as communities, rather than as organizations, and to consider supervision as "an essential process within the complex and continuous dynamic of reinventing schools" (p. xix).

Function-Related Dilemmas Although the preceding material has already revealed some of the uncertainties associated with supervision, it may be helpful here to identify four categories within which these uncertainties become troublesome. These are: (1) imprecise definitions of roles and functions; (2) line versus staff responsibilities (notably, evaluation and assessment versus service and assistance), (3) administrative cooptation; and (4) changing contexts and requirements.

First, we might re-examine what has been said (e.g., by Bolin & Panaritis, 1992) as cited earlier, about the function of supervision: It is important no matter who carries it out, and its primary concern should be the improvement of practice in order to benefit students. That there is considerable confusion anyway about the functions of supervision is due to the fact that for many writers there is almost no limit to the activities in which a supervisor might legitimately engage. Harris (1963) has long been one of the strongest and most persistent advocates of the view that supervision involves almost "anything that school personnel do with adults or things for the purpose of maintaining or changing the operation of the school in order to directly influence the attainment of the major instructional goals of the school" (p. 11).

Related to the supervision function, Harris also argued in 1963, are five processes, planning, organizing, leading, con-trolling, and assessing, ten tasks (i.e., arranging for in-service education, curriculum development, organizing for instruction, staffing, orientation of new staff members, providing facilities, providing materials, relating special services, developing public relations, and evaluation), and eight skills, writing, listening, observing, empathizing, diagnosing, synthesizing, visualizing, and analyzing (pp. 12–14).

Although "functions" are not necessarily synonymous with "dimensions," it may be useful to note that in an ASCD-sponsored research project, Pajak (1989) sought to define the knowledge, attitudes and skills most closely associated with outstanding supervisory practice. The 12 dimensions associated with outstanding supervisory practitioners were: communication, instructional program, motivating and organizing, curriculum, service to teachers, community relations, staff development, planning and change, observation and conferences, problem solving and decision-making, personal development, and research and program evaluation (Pajak, 1989, p. 128).

In a treatment of supervisory functions written during the expansion period that followed World War II, Gwynn (1961) indicated that the main responsibilities of the supervisor may be identified as of three kinds: (1) to give individual help to the teacher, (2) to coordinate and make the instructional services of the school more available to all personnel, and (3) to act as a resource person for the superintendent and other administrative personnel, as a special agent in training teachers in service, and as an interpreter of the school and its program both to school personnel and to the public (p. 27).

In order that these responsibilities may be competently discharged, continued Gwynn, the supervisor must be capable of performing these major tasks:

1. To aid the teacher and the principal in understanding children better.
2. To help the teacher to develop and to improve individually and as a cooperating member of the school staff.
3. To assist school personnel in making more interesting and effective use of materials of instruction.
4. To help the teacher to improve his (sic) methods of teaching.
5. To make the specialized personnel in the school system of maximum assistance to the teacher.
6. To assist the teacher in making the best possible appraisal of the student.
7. To stimulate the teacher to evaluate his (sic) own planning, work, and progress.
8. To help the teacher to achieve poise and a sense of security in his (sic) work and in the community.
9. To stimulate faculty groups to plan curriculum improvements and carry them out cooperatively, and to assume a major responsibility in coordinating this work and improving teacher education in service.
10. To acquaint the school administration, the teachers, the students, and the public with the work and progress of the school (pp. 27–31).

Gwynn, it seems worth noting, was one of the first writers on supervision to recognize that the advent of team approaches to instruction is likely to modify the supervisor's relationship with individual classroom teachers. Providing leadership for the organization and functioning of teaching teams, and helping to develop the professional competencies required by this cooperative approach, was seen as a new responsibility for the supervisor (Gwynn, p. 32). Gwynn further observed that teaming provides built-in supervision at least for interns and beginning teachers who are included; graduated professional experiences can be arranged within the more flexible organization for inexperienced and less able members. It was noted as a benefit that the team leaders and master teachers are capable of providing professional help to team members, which could "free supervisors to devote more time and energy to top-level leadership for curriculum development and the organization and evaluation of instruction" (Gwynn, p. 32). This latter work would, he predicted, become more important as higher-quality learning is promoted through differentiated staffing and as greater demands are thereby stimulated for curriculum modifications. As a final note in this remarkably insightful early analysis, Gwynn observed that such curriculum developments "will open doors to supervisors that permit them to exercise greater leadership for research—a much neglected responsibility of educational leadership" (pp. 32–33).

Returning to more recent work, Oliva (1993) voices his views concerning the confusion about role definition among current textbook writers/authors in supervision. Within a chapter examining historical and current descriptions of the tasks of supervision, Oliva observes that there has not been, and there continues not to be, much agreement among supervision writers and specialists concerning role definition or the appropriate functions of supervision. The orientations of these writers range from persons who link administrative and supervisory tasks together to those who seek a total separation of such functions, from persons highly committed to affective forms of support to those who have a strong academic-discipline focus. He notes that the lack of agreement becomes even more troubling when one reads the job descriptions published by school districts and realizes the enormous range of expectations with which "supervisors" are faced, some of which scarcely differ from the job requirements of other roles.

Oliva then proceeds to define a model based on roles within three domains: instructional development, curriculum development, and staff development. Four roles that are prominent within the model are coordinator, consultant, group leader, and evaluator, with the latter relating to assisting teachers rather than to administrative decision-makers, in examining their work.

The Four Dilemmas As noted, there are four major dilemmas that confront workers in supervision roles.

IMPRECISE DEFINITIONS OF ROLES AND FUNCTIONS. As long as there is uncertainty about the specific parameters within which the supervisor is expected to engage, he or she is free to invent or adopt a definition that feels comfortable and within the range of perceived interests and talents. He or she is also at the mercy of superordinates who are equally free to invent new or different definitions. Thus, there is no assurance that

supervisory time and energy will in fact be devoted to "the improvement of classroom practice for the benefit of students" (to requote Bolin & Panaritis, 1992). There is also no assurance for supervisors concerning the legitimacy of their efforts, and the psychological and other rewards for success in these efforts.

LINE VERSUS STAFF RESPONSIBILITIES: EVALUATION AND ASSESSMENT OF PERSONNEL VERSUS SERVICE AND ASSISTANCE PERSONNEL. Whether or not supervisors should be involved, even in indirect ways, in the processes of teacher evaluation, remains a delicate question, even though the preponderance of opinion in the literature proscribes such involvement.

Even at its best, the relationship between classroom teachers, and other operations-level personnel, and their supervisors is somewhat tainted by the risk that is at least imagined by teachers whenever they expose their actions and thoughts to the scrutiny of a supervisor. Because of the historically negative views held by teachers of supervisors, often with good reason, it might be acknowledged, supervisors have sought for many decades to project the image of friend, counselor, helper, and nonthreatening ally. This becomes difficult when district job descriptions for supervisors include evaluative responsibilities. The image of a friend and counselor can be shattered whenever or if ever a supervisor's knowledge of one's strengths and weaknesses or opinions about adequacy are brought into the administrative evaluation equation.

Future-oriented views of education generally dismiss the traditional view of supervision as an evaluative function and propose or endorse a variety of collegial arrangements within which the promotion of professional growth and success has high priority, and judgmental assessment is seen as a wasteful activity except where either reclamation or dismissal, each as an action that protects the well-being of children, seem to be the only alternatives. From this viewpoint, the extensive involvement of administrative or supervisory officers in routine evaluation functions is unproductive and wasteful. By contrast, enabling such officers to devote more of their energies to the positive support of individual and organizational growth is a much more defensible policy.

Des Dixon (1994) asserted that "responsibility for the formative evaluation of teachers (and hence the routine supervision that is implicit in formative evaluation) must be taken away from principals and given to counselors, who would be employed by every school board to help teachers plan their professional growth" (p. 365). While it might be suggested that principals and supervisors do in fact function as counselors in many situations, Des Dixon's emphasis upon that term is a useful reminder of the functions involved.

This view of supervisor-as-helper is consistent with that propounded by Anderson (1990–1991), with the aforementioned essay arguing for a "presumption of competency" in supervisory approaches to teachers. His term, "supportive supervision," which focuses upon growth inducement, was seen as a label for the far-more-important "helping" aspect of supervisory work. Its subsets include the stimulation of professional growth, improvement of the quality of teaching, invigoration of the organization, contributing to the accomplishment of district and individual "stretch goals," facilitation of the development and implementation of new programs, assisting groups to accomplish their missions, fostering self-evaluation on the part of both individuals and groups, and nurturing a healthy work culture.

ADMINISTRATIVE COOPTATION: SUPERVISOR INVOLVEMENT IN NON-PER-SONNEL-RELATED ADMINISTRATIVE DECISIONS, AND IN DISTRICT RESPONSES TO PRESSURES AND OVERLOADS. Anderson (1988) has noted that many school districts seem to be constantly over-loaded with paperwork, and tasks related to the production thereof, and that they are constantly under pressure from either state, federal, or other agencies. This pressure also comes from what are euphemistically called "interest groups," such as book censors, conservative rightist groups, special-cause advocates, and other groups with axes to grind. The beleaguered school board or superintendent often diverts the energy of supervisors from their appointed tasks in order to help fight or fend off these pressures (e.g., in the collection of defense information or even in representing the district in public gatherings).

CHANGING CONTEXTS AND REQUIREMENTS. In the world of "restructuring," under new pressures for "accountability," at a time when bureaucracies are making at least some efforts to downsize or to "flatten" themselves and to transfer decision-making power to operational levels, and during moments of major transition as school boards are infiltrated by pressure-group members, the context within which all school person-nel, including supervisors, pursue their functions may be changing in ways that generate confusion or frustration.

A fifth group of dilemmas, or at least changing circum-stances to which supervisory personnel must adjust, would include new definitions of optimal instructional approaches, new ways of managing and of making decisions, new rela-tionships between schools and their environment, and new emphases upon providing a learning environment for adults and children alike.

As different ways of perceiving the optimum teaching-learning environment emerge, as technology becomes a more active force in that environment, as site-based decision-mak-ing becomes more prevalent in both authentic and superficial forms, as school districts become more integrally involved with universities through Professional Development Schools, and as other changes occur for which the all-purpose word *restructuring* is frequently used, new challenges and new requirements attach to the role of supervisor. Inspectorial and other administration-related functions, although still promi-nent in some places in supervisors' lives, become secondary as people-helping, program-developing, network building, and culture-creating assume greater importance.

Within the literature of site-based management, not much has been said about the impact upon supervisory roles of the shift of at least some responsibility from the central office to the local school site. Burke and Fessler (1994) have addressed this question, drawing data from their experiences in Wisconsin, where shared decision-making and related restructuring efforts are being actively pursued. They point to the effects upon the supervisor's role of assessing the impact of schooling, identifying a new vision for the school, and

designing/implementing school improvement plans related to that vision. In these activities, the supervisor is a key source of resource data for decision-making.

The supervisor also becomes a supportive member of, and a model for, teams as they work toward viable management systems. They are then responsible for provision of the staff development program promoting teacher growth and renew-al; such responsibility requires expertise in planning, organiz-ing, and implementing staff-development programs plus knowledge of outside sources of help and consultation. Supervisors must also have skills in site-based research and action-research methodology, which will become more prevalent as the staff seeks data and direction. They must also function as prompters of self-analysis and reflection within the staff. In the words of Burke and Fessler, this calls for mov-ing "from one 'doing' supervision to one who is engaged in 'making supervision happen'" (p. 47).

In a final comment, these authors state that more than any-one else in the organization, the supervisor(s) must play a central role in accountability. Among the ways this is accom-plished is through supporting collaboration and consensus building among teachers and administrators (p. 48).

Section Summary

The previous section attempted to trace the evolution of supervisory functions over the years, and to provide a com-prehensive overview of those functions as reflected in scholar-ly opinion, the research literatures, and current practices in the school culture/organization. A portrait of supervision going through several stages of metamorphosis emerges, beginning with the authoritarian control and evaluation of individual teachers, progressing toward team development and interper-sonal collaboration, and coming to a focus upon systems think-ing and the development of the entire school, concluding with a focus upon systems thinking and the development of the school as a learning community. We now turn, then, to a sec-tion examining the development of schools as units of change and how this influences supervisory functions.

DEVELOPING THE SCHOOL AS A UNIT OF CHANGE: THE SUPERVISORY CHALLENGE OF THE 1970S AND 1980S

During the 1970s and 1980s, a shift in supervisory empha-sis emerged, moving from improving teaching exclusively. Workshops on teaching strategies flourished, and follow-up clinical supervision began to play an increasingly important supervisory function. Educators began to consider emerging problems that spanned the classroom, yet influenced instruc-tion and learning. Hence, these decades were filled with the dual supervisory functions of training and coaching individual teachers, and also engaging the help of teachers to improve schoolwide programs and services.

What were the problems in schools that required a new supervisory function? In 1984, Goodlad reported themes and patterns from a study of 1,000 classrooms across America that painted a dismal portrait of schooling that failed to capture the human spirit. The overarching characteristics that Goodlad found were blandness of learning and teaching activity, flatness of the emotional climate, and a lack of intellectual and emotional vigor for learning; no one seemed to care about this lifeless condition. Teachers and students tended to work in isolation and were engaged in endless, often meaningless, tasks. The conditions of teaching and learning themselves perhaps influenced student success rates. Unless this pattern is changed, urged Goodlad, schools will ultimately fail in their mission as a social institution.

At this same time, *A Nation At Risk* (1983) was published from the U.S. Department of Education. It called for a major overhaul of schooling as we now know it. This document created a furor that spawned reform efforts in teacher evaluation and curriculum in most states. Concern for the survival of the school as a social enterprise began to raise new questions about the purpose and function of supervision. The bureaucratic supervisory functions of teacher control and compliance were clearly in doubt, and they seemed no longer to serve the purpose they once served. Questions during this decade centered around the quality of leadership and supervision that was needed to revitalize the school as a social institution.

During the 1970s and 1980s, educators at all levels began to shift their attention from the teacher as the unit of development to the school (Goldhammer, 1969; Heathers, 1972; Weber, 1971; Williams et al, 1974). The effective schools research movement, which sought to identify school effects patterns that correlated with student success, produced evidence over time that the quality of school life, as well as of teaching and learning practices, were directly correlated with the quality of the principal. It was claimed that essentially the principal makes the difference in the success of students, schoolwide (Austin, 1979; Brookover & Lezotte, 1979; Edmonds, 1979; Vanezky & Winfield, 1979). A wave of reforms followed, primarily at the state level, to direct schools to integrate what was being learned through research activity about school effects. The principal emerged as the instructional leader, one who became directly involved in the supervision of teachers in the classroom, and who directed the instructional improvement process schoolwide. The central office supervisor, largely a curriculum expert by the 1970s, was virtually replaced by the principal as the primary supervisor of teachers and of teaching. This second part of this chapter will focus on the changing functions of school supervision during the 1970s and 1980s, and the roles that emerged for the principal as the instructional leader and primary supervisor.

The reform efforts and the innovations that were developed to advance school improvement will be discussed. In the first section the nature of reform efforts is examined, and the influence of public policy on schools, which provides a context for developing schools as units. In the second section the multiple forces on the school as a unit are explored, as educators ask how the school work culture can be developed to alter the dismal patterns of complacency. In the third section the emphasis on teacher development will be examined as it relates to school improvement issues. Finally, in the last section implications for the changing functions of supervision are examined that grow out of the school improvement movement.

Educational Reform and Restructuring

Educational Reform While there was a growing interest in the school as a unit of change, initiatives were launched in most states during the first wave of reform in the 1980s that continued an idiosyncratic approach to change, and which failed to build upon the effective schools research findings. In the aggregate, these reform efforts tended to further fragment and isolate schooling programs and services rather than to strengthen schools as units of change, and their effects produced few positive results (Fuhrman, Elmore, & Massell, 1993).

Murphy (1991) observed that this phase of reform emphasized centralized control and higher standards for teacher and student performance. Two assumptions prevailed: (1) the poor quality of teachers accounts for the poor performance of students, and (2) teacher quality can be improved through top–down mandates. State reform initiatives for students centered on higher graduation requirements, new curriculum controls, and state testing programs. Reform initiatives for teachers included teacher certification and evaluation systems, and master/mentor teacher programs. More than 1,000 new pieces of legislation emerged during this era, which, Conley et al (1988) noted, served to reinforce the bureaucratic structure of school organization. Reform efforts were formulated without teacher involvement, and, in fact, many proposals implicitly blamed teachers for the deficiencies of schools.

According to Fuhrman et al (1993), a second wave of reform shifted attention from isolated programs and teachers to the school as a unit. State agencies, still playing a major role in reform, launched new pilot programs to enhance the school as a unit of influence on students. One strategy was school-based management, which shifted decision-making about curriculum, budget, and staffing from the district to the school level. School planning systems were issued through state directives to ensure a school improvement focus. Expectations mounted for improving instruction, and with this came a wide array of staff development programs as a resource to teachers. Parental involvement and student choice also emerged as initiatives that enhanced local school decision-making.

Along with a focus on school improvement, there also was an expectation for high levels of academic learning, often with conflicting policies for the work required. In addition, drop-out-prevention and retention programs grew in numbers as educators sought to control for high student success rates, as well as for graduation requirements, curriculum testing, and entry requirements for teachers. The research studies on the second wave of reform initiatives, however, report little positive effects from the policies that emerged (Fuhrman et al, 1993).

Restructuring Schools The restructuring movement in education paralleled that in business and industry, and was embraced in education in response to the shallow effects of the earlier reform movements. Lally (1991) observes that discussions of reorganization in the latter part of the 1980s focused not only on the school, but also on state departments of education. The school now was seen as needing support, rather than inspection, for it to succeed with accountability and restructuring mandates. The National Alliance for Restructuring Education (NARE) is but one example of new structures that emerged to assist its members in addressing restructuring challenges (Taylor & Levine, 1991). The NARE focus centered on (1) assessment tools, (2) accountability results, and (3) managing change. Emphasis was given to training teachers, changing the school's culture, improving student outcomes, and launching site-based management. The effective schools, research findings and patterns were also used by educators in restructuring efforts, as schools also sought to improve their instructional programs and effects upon students.

Patterns began to emerge from "restructuring" innovations throughout the country. According to Murphy (1991) these included:

- changes in organizational structure
- changes in governance
- redesign of teachers' work
- reallocation of resources
- improvements in the process of teaching and learning.

Accomplishing these changes centered around strategies for curriculum and instruction practices, governance and finance, equity, partnerships, choice, and empowerment (Hansen, 1989). Technology became a tool to advance restructuring at both the instructional and management levels (Collins, 1991; David, 1991; Sheingold, 1991).

The role of supervision within a climate of "school improvement" faced new questions because of the changing role of teachers, as well as because of the changing school populations. With increasing demands from at-risk and special student populations, many wondered what the function of the school principal was. The expanding special populations, and the legislative and supervisory challenges they presented, also raised new issues about their influence on reform agendas and new policy initiatives (Sage & Burrello, 1986). New knowledge bases began to surface for principals that reflected the needs of at-risk populations (Valesky & Hirth, 1992), and new school management competencies eventually centered around the needs of all school populations (Missouri Department of Education, 1989). Sailor (1991), who is a specialist in "Inclusion," argued for special education to be focused at the school rather than at the district level, where the entire staff has responsibility for all students. He further observed that a new window of opportunity had finally evolved for integrating special students into the mainstream of school life. The new *inclusion movement* was launched at the end of the 1980s to advance the integration of programs at the school level, and to alter the influences of schooling on all student populations.

Another approach to restructuring that emerged in many states, such as Kentucky, was nongradedness and continuous progress (Anderson, 1992). A movement that began more than 30 years ago is now viewed by many in the 1990s as a set of concepts and arrangements that will permit greater flexibility and variation in the learning environment, thereby enhancing student success patterns for all populations. Anderson and Pavan (1993) report that research studies published between 1968 and 1990 tended to favor nongradedness on standardized measures of student achievement.

What will supervision become within nontraditional learning environments? At the dawn of the last decade in the twentieth century, the Governors' Association published a monograph called *Time for Results* (1991). In it they ask the question, Who will manage the school? They described the leaders as those with a vision of what they want their schools to be, who are able to translate the vision into school goals and teacher expectations, who create a climate of support, and who share decision-making with the faculty. This document influenced the writing of President George Bush's reform document, *America 2000* (1991), which argued for the school as the site of reform, where teachers, principals, and parents together provide leadership for the school. Bush went on to argue that reinventing schooling meant breaking the mold in order to build schools for the next century, and that it required making a commitment to create places that foster learning. This was a call for a schooling revolution. What were the functions of school supervision to become within a national climate of restructuring and reinventing schools?

Making Schools Work Through Culture Development By the mid-1980s, the negative impact upon teacher morale that resulted from the first wave of reform became troublesome to school officials and to legislators alike (Conley et al, 1988). The national morale problem seemed to relate to the lack of teacher participation in shaping reform policies and programs at any level of the education enterprise. The Carnegie Foundation (Boyer, 1988) conducted a study of 20,000 teachers nationwide to determine the dimensions and the extent of teacher involvement in decision-making. They found that teachers helped to shape curriculum and to select textbooks, but that they were not involved in making other critical decisions, such as selecting teachers and principals, participating in teacher evaluation, deciding on staff development activity, building budgets, determining student placement, writing promotion and retention policies, and setting standards of student conduct. Boyer charged that public schools cannot be fixed without the help from teachers (i.e., those who manage classrooms). He called for a "school report card" to be prepared each year that would identify school improvements made, as well as problems to be pursued. Teachers, he urged, must become full partners for improving the nation's schools.

In another document, Conley et al (1988) concluded that teachers were already assuming greater responsibility for interdependent managerial functions through such mechanisms as quality circles, peer assistance programs, and career ladders. Teachers are already line managers, they argue, having direct and ongoing contact with the school system's primary workers or clients (i.e., its students), and that as such they should have an equal voice in decisions made about the central management issues of running a school and a district. At issue was the bureaucratic practice of separating the functions of supervisors and workers. Their posture demanded a closer integration between the management decision-making functions at district, school, and classroom levels, which was an example of systems thinking rather than bureaucratic activity. They also argue that involvement in decision-making needs to be more than a concession to teachers; it must also be viewed as a necessity for shaping new forms of schooling.

Dialogue about school-based management (SBM) flourished as teachers became involved in mostly administrative matters. In time, those who were involved in SBM began to center on more philosophical issues, other than budget and staffing, that had broad implications for the demise of traditional bureaucratic systems and the rise of more organic approaches to organizational development. Questions like these arose: "Is the function of school improvement to enhance bureaucratic systems in schools?" "Are we developing new and more flexible kinds of working learning and management systems?" (Conley et al, 1990). David (1991) analyzed research reports on school-based management and drew the following conclusions:

1. SBM differs from school improvement in that it represents a realignment of power and responsibility of schools in relation to the school district.
2. Autonomy and shared decision-making represent the two major areas of development in SBM.
3. Decisions made at the school level should include distribution of resources, personnel decisions, and curriculum decisions.
4. School-based teams or committees are universally used to facilitate school-based decision-making. Membership on these teams includes teachers, community leaders, parents, and administrators.
5. Preliminary research results support an improvement in morale and in professionalism among participants.

In a national study on the implementation of SBM throughout the United States, Herman and Herman (1993) found that 44 states reported initiatives that were either permitted or mandated (Kentucky and Texas). The patterns among the states encompassed decentralized budget-making authority, personnel decision-making, curricular decision-making, and school-based councils. Extensive training in collaboration and group decision-making was found as well, along with time for professional interaction and multiple measures of accountability.

With teacher involvement as an emerging pattern in school improvement initiatives, new relationships evolved among and within role groups, and supervision shifted in many places from a telling to a leadership function for teacher development. While instructional innovations flourished during the 1980s, the focus for school renewal was clearly no longer on the individual teacher and the classroom. The school was coming to be viewed as a unit of interdependent functions rather than as a collection of isolated and independent programs and services.

Work Culture Development: A Systems Perspective As school leaders experimented with new forms of decision-making at the school site, and made alterations in instructional programs

and delivery systems, issues surfaced about what it would take to make schools work for all student populations. The powerful effects of cultural forces were observed in a study by McFaul and Cooper (1983), where the school's traditional work culture virtually prevented the successful implementation of clinical supervision practice. Mistrust, role isolation, and defensive work patterns existed and actually prevented honest exchange, feedback, and peer support from evolving. "The School" was in need of a new definition. Within the reform literatures over the past decade, new images of the school as an organization evolved. Sergiovanni (1994) promoted the concept of the school as a community. He pointed to the difference between schools as organizations that are based on contracts and rewards, and schools as social communities that are bound by moral commitment, trust, and a sense of purpose.

A composite of the school's work culture evolved from the work of Snyder and Anderson (1986), and drew support from more than 400 research summaries from the business and education literatures. The *Managing Productive Schools* model provides a construct for reporting this research base, and is built on systems thinking. The four interdependent dimensions of the work culture include school planning, staff development, program development and school assessment. Summaries of the 400 studies are reported shortly (Snyder & Giella, 1987).

SCHOOL PLANNING Productive schools are driven by a few stretch goals that are identified through a shared decision-making process. Goals are then subdivided into tasks and assigned to both permanent and temporary work groups and teams. The groups cooperatively develop action plans to accomplish their tasks. Within a group context, individuals establish performance goals that specify their intended contributions to the school's/team's success. The resulting organizational plan becomes the focus for professional work, development, and assessment.

STAFF DEVELOPMENT In productive schools, plans are made for knowledge and skill acquisition that is important for achieving school and team goals. Staff members make workshop plans as they anticipate their collective needs and seek the best available resources. An important finding is that teachers' development processes are creatively stimulated when some form of coaching follows a workshop. Furthermore, when work groups (i.e., the building blocks of successful organizations) are provided with skill-building opportunities, the capacity for shared inquiry and problem solving is enhanced. Collaborative forms of quality control are viewed as developmental and provide adjustment opportunities for the organization.

PROGRAM DEVELOPMENT When educators examine the student learning challenges they face in their school, better solutions evolve when the growing knowledge base is utilized. Students master knowledge and skills to the extent that the following conditions exist: (1) instruction is matched with readiness levels, (2) instruction is guided by clear expectations and procedures, (3) active and interactive task engagement is managed, and (4) positive reinforcement and correctives are provided to ensure certain levels of mastery. Solutions to learning problems occur when leaders facilitate problem-solving and development activity, and then generate the necessary resources.

SCHOOL ASSESSMENT Productive organizations have complex assessment systems that measure the extent to which goals are achieved. Work groups assess the results of their work, individuals are assessed for their contributions to the school's outcomes, and student assessment data serve as a feedback measure for improving the instructional program. Assessment data provide a feedback loop for short-range planning and for long-range growth targets.

Advancing Systems Thinking With the introduction of systems thinking into the organizational literature, and with the dramatic shift in the roles of supervisors (i.e., from controllers to coordinators and culture-builders), new insights emerged that concerned both the changed role of line officers as well as the changed role of staff personnel.

It was becoming commonplace by the late 1980s, for workshops to include training in planning, collaboration, coaching, instructional improvement, and assessment. In her study of "A+ schools" in Arizona, Fuentes (1992) found that collaborative forms of school planning, staff and program development, and assessment were evident in each school, yet there was no interdependence among the four work culture dimensions. This meant that school goals, staff development activity, program development efforts, and school assessment in all schools were not aligned; hence, they were unrelated functions. In addition, she learned that the culture of collaboration that existed among the adult professionals in each school had not permeated the classroom to any extent.

Senge (1990a) argued that it is an illusion to consider the world as separate and unrelated forces. He presented core disciplines for building the learning organization. The discipline of personal mastery goes beyond competence and spirituality, and refers to approaching one's life work as a creative endeavor, as living life from a creative, as opposed to a reactive, viewpoint. Mental models are deeply ingrained assumptions, generalizations, or even images that influence how we understand the world and how we take action. Changes in mental models occur as teams learn together and build a shared vision. Later, Senge and Lannon-Kim (1991) observed that the key to transforming schools into learning organizations lies in understanding the individual and collective capabilities needed to build such institutions. The power of the learning organization resides in its ability to engage in that basic human drive, to learn. They argue that the challenge for leaders is to turn collective energy into a shared vision that is compelling for all members of the organization.

The old model of leadership, where the top thinks and workers carry out the plans, must give way to integrated thinking and acting at all levels (Senge, 1990b). The traditional view of leaders as special persons who set direction, make key decisions, and energize the troops, is deeply rooted in an individualistic and nonsystemic worldview. In learning organizations, Senge further argues, the leader's role dif-

fers dramatically and requires the ability to build a shared vision, to challenge prevailing mental models, and to foster more systemic patterns of thinking. The new supervisory roles include that of designer, teacher, steward, and systems thinker. To develop a learning organization, the work team becomes the learning laboratory for professional work. The supervisor's focus for development therefore shifts from the individual teacher to the work team, and to the team's function within the school's development process. The supervisor's function is to stimulate continuous learning on the work team about the craft of teaching, especially as it relates to specific student populations being served.

Restructuring efforts that are designed to transform the workplace of schools require both new job-specific knowledge for supervisors and professional workers, and also new conceptual frames and tools for productive partnerships (Snyder, 1993). Professional development programs will necessarily move from isolation to integration, from policy and compliance orientations to problem solving and invention, and from deficiency reduction to capacity building. A shift in the purpose of professional development activity is likely, progressing from the segmentation of functions to the integration of overall orientations, beliefs, values, and practices. New supervisory functions evolved to develop instructional teams and departments as vibrant work units, focusing on professional capacities to address challenges. The professional development of team members will require the interdependence of school/team goals, training opportunities, and follow-up coaching. It will provide for dimensions of adult learning that include readiness, concepts, demonstrations, practice, feedback, and transfer. Developing new professional capacities through training and follow-up coaching activities is the foundation for transforming schooling outcomes.

It now can be argued that systems thinking is dynamic and will lead naturally to the demise of independent and isolated functions within schools, and replace the fragmented work patterns found in bureaucratic organizations. A central concept in systems thinking in the 1990s is interdependence, which is defined as the integration, and eventual fusion, of resources, information, and systems across units for the pursuit of new outcomes. Representing a profound reshaping of the internal world of thought for supervisors, systems thinking will become operative when coupled with skills in surfacing assumptions and in balancing inquiry and advocacy (Senge, 1993). The models that matter, Senge predicts, are the systemic understandings that can lead to significant change. These will eventually become new shared mental models that evolve through continuous dialogue about challenges, assumptions, and visions of the future.

Challenges in Teacher Development

During the 1980s, along with new interests in school improvement everywhere, teachers and principals became skilled in various models of clinical supervision. The seminal publications on this topic were prepared by Cogan (1973) and Goldhammer (1969, with later editions prepared by Anderson & Krajewski, 1980, 1993). Almost simultaneous movements for improving schools and improving the quality of teaching existed by the end of the 1980s. It was perceived by many that clinical supervision would provide teachers with feedback on their classroom work patterns, and it grew in importance as a strategy for helping teachers to acquire more effective teaching behaviors.

The Goldhammer model of clinical supervision emphasized five stages: preobservation conference, observation and data collection, data analysis, feedback, and cycle analysis. Cogan's model reflected similar stages in the observation cycle, although there were eight in number. The relationship between training and coaching was promoted by Joyce and Showers (1980) by introducing an adult learning model to guide training and feedback; its purpose was for teachers to develop executive control over new instructional processes. Little (1985) developed a coaching model to foster "skilled pairs," with four stages of development that include focus, hard evidence, interaction, and predictability and reciprocity. The concepts of cognitive coaching (Costa & Garmston, 1986) built upon the values of professional learning and autonomy. The supervisor's task was to enhance the teacher's perceptions, decisions, and intellectual functions in order to produce greater autonomy and effect on student learning.

After tracing its evolution, Pajak (1993) examined four "families" of "classifications" of clinical supervision that have appeared over 30 years that include the original models, humanistic and artistic models, technical and didactic models, and developmental and reflective models. It is significant that Pajak concludes his study with a strong appeal for "democratic supervision," which respects democratic values (i.e., equality, participation, social justice, and personal responsibility) and seeks to create action-oriented, learning-focused communities in schools.

In addition to the varieties of clinical supervision models that evolved in the 1980s, questions surfaced about the relationship between its practices and other schooling functions. A systems model was introduced by Snyder (1981) that linked clinical supervision practice interdependently with overall school improvement plans, instructional improvement initiatives, and school evaluation activity. She further argued for a clinical supervision function that was developmental rather than inspectional (i.e., many educators began to adopt the clinical supervision method for a new approach to teacher evaluation), and which linked interdependently with other school improvement functions, such as to a school's goals, to staff development programs, to instructional program development, and to school assessment. Given the findings of the Fuentes (1992) study mentioned earlier, the absence of systems thinking for school development had not yet been established by even some of the best schools. Supervision of instruction must function interdependently with other work culture dimensions for schools to grow well as units of influence on students.

How have these separate interests (i.e., improving both schools and teaching) influenced the functions of supervision? With the advent of the 1980s' educational reform movements, the functions of supervisors have changed dramatically. In 1990 Richardson published a report on the new profile of the Kentucky supervisor. He noted that supervision is a long-term, continuous process designed to assist teachers in enhancing learning opportunities for students. Richardson documents that teachers' primary help comes from one another, and that they are highly critical of the quality of assistance they receive from instructional leaders, who are called supervisors and principals.

By now some experts urged for supervision to move beyond teaching competence as a focus for their work, and instead to help teachers to build professional partnerships within and across schools and institutions. The primary supervisory task for the decade ahead (at least) was to encourage teachers to solve the problems they face together. Opportunity, information, and resources that are too often denied to teachers are what teachers need to build productive partnerships. Snyder and Anderson (1988) identified two conditions for empowerment. The first of these is an organizational culture that includes stretch goals, reward and recognition systems, opportunities for development, and group sharing and networking opportunities. The second condition focuses on synergogical learning environments for teachers. A *pedagogical approach* to supervision centers around telling teachers what they need to learn and to do. An *andragogical approach* addresses individual teacher learning that is related to job problems. *Synergogical learning* embraces cooperative learning among teachers as they address new job challenges together.

Teachers have begun to work together through various forms of peer-coaching arrangements, perhaps because changes in the job of supervisor trail behind alterations in teaching work patterns. Garmston (1987) uses the term *technical coaching* to refer to the improvement of teaching. His premise is that teachers will improve their instruction if they are presented with objective data that have been gathered in their classroom. Technical coaching guidelines were prepared for teachers to use as follow-up to a training program on innovative reading strategies (Nielsen, 1993). Nielsen observed from her research that teachers tended to use the new skills in their regular instruction along with technical coaching follow-up; that all strategies were used appropriately; concern evolved from the teachers about how the new skills were affecting them personally; teachers rated coaching very effective in helping them to acquire the new skills; and coaches felt that they refined their own skills for helping teachers develop new skills.

Hosack-Curlin (1993) observed in her study that peer coaching empowers teachers to transcend the isolation that is typical in schools, and provides a support structure for teachers to acquire new skills that will be integrated into classroom work. From her experience in managing the research project, she argued that the school leader must demonstrate the value of coaching by providing resources and opportunities for peer coaching to be effective. In addition, teachers need actually to be involved in designing and managing the peer coaching program, which encourages continuous professional growth within the school.

What is the impact of peer coaching? Garmston (1989) found several patterns from a large-scale study. Some teachers report that peer coaching stimulates transformations in self-perception and their relations with supervisors. For other teachers, not much seems to have changed. Teachers report that their principals respond in a variety of ways to coaching, either as neglecters, resisters, or supporters. The quest in the later part of the 1980s, Garmston noted, was to advance the practice of supervision in ways that were proportionate to the interests and needs of teachers, who by then were learning a variety of new teaching techniques.

The Role of the Principal as Supervisor and Cultural Architect

By the end of the 1980s the principal had emerged as the primary supervisor of teachers, with central office supervisors focusing more on helping and assisting teachers with new curriculum. In addition, "instructional leadership" and "school culture builder" had been added to the list of major new job expectations. Lewis (1988) observed that schools must work harder at sharing the authority for making important decisions. School leaders, he noted, will think longer term, look beyond their own schools place emphasis on vision and values, become outstanding managers, and develop changing organizations.

While the literature reports examples of new supervisor, instructional leadership, and culture-builder roles, other research studies document that, for the most part, principals do not perform these new roles to any extent, still playing a traditional administrative function for the school. Pitner (1988) drew themes from descriptive studies, which include several of the following work patterns of principals: (1) low degree of self-initiated activities; (2) discontinuity; (3) emergencies; (4) unpredictable work flow; (5) events near the office; (6) time spent with student discipline; (7) maintenance and control issues; (8) not involved in classroom activities; (9) instructional leadership not a central focus; and (10) not involved in core issues of the school.

Principals spend little time observing teachers and value keeping peace in the school environment, observes Greenfield (1988), while teachers are responsible for all instructional matters. Hultman (1989) draws similar conclusions from an analysis of many studies conducted on the work of principals in recent decades. He concluded that administrators continue to focus on administrative work only, while teachers are responsible for instruction. When principals interact with teachers, it typically concerns administrative matters rather than instruction. The work of administrators, Hultman contends, is only marginally related to instruction. A different picture is beginning to emerge that shows evidence of the fusion of instruction and administration. Luehe (1989) found that principals as supervisors are no longer inspectors; rather, they are colleagues who work with teachers to identify instructional problems and serve as resource persons. Although instructional supervision has become the major focus of the job, in theory, principals spend less than 20 percent of their time on this function. There clearly appears to be a gap between what scholars perceive principals ought to do as instructional leaders, and the operative demands of the principalship.

McAfee (1990) identified 12 instructional leadership competencies from a large national sample of principals that verifies the enlargement of supervision functions beyond improving teaching. There is a blend between administrative and instructional dimensions to their changing job in the following list of principal competencies. The list appears in the order of importance to principals: communication, observing and conferencing, instructional programs, motivation and organizing, planning change, staff development, community relations, problem solving and decision-making, personal development, service to teachers, curriculum, and research and program evaluation.

As a result of the administration/instructional leadership job dilemma, and in anticipation of the principal's changing work for the twenty-first century, the National Association for Elementary Principals (1990) developed a few projections about the changing role of principals within which an instructional supervisory function exists:

- principals will be the leader of leaders
- expectations for high-performing schools will rise
- the role of instructional leader will grow
- school-based accountability will increase
- the need for continuous professional development will increase
- requirements of the adult learner must be addressed

The challenges for school leaders have changed in recent decades as the principalship has been transformed from a maintenance job to one of managing change, which requires the involvement of the entire education community in research, training, practice, and dialogue. A systems approach to developing schools provides a conceptual framework or mental model for the development of a new age of schooling. Attention to the school's culture and its development is critical to the school's ability to serve all student populations.

The next part of this chapter presents a glimpse of twenty-first century schooling challenges, and identifies ways in which the Quality revolution holds promise for transforming schooling. Within emerging views of schooling, and the changing role of the teacher, the function of supervision remains largely an unanswered question. Emerging trends are examined in the next section, many of which hold promise for reinventing schools.

EMPOWERING SCHOOL WORK TEAMS: THE 21ST CENTURY SUPERVISORY CHALLENGE

Along with all other social institutions, schools are shedding bureaucratic characteristics in order to become more responsive to changing demographics, and to the knowledge and skills that are now required in the workplace. The schools of tomorrow are likely to be invented in places where leaders have a vision of a different kind of schooling, and possess the knowledge and skills to empower others to respond to emerging challenges through networks and partnerships. The supervision and leadership task for a new age of schooling is to stimulate continuous innovation, which alters the outcomes of schooling for all student populations, rather than to manage for teacher compliance with outdated standards of work. The functions of supervision that were once characterized by *control of programmed performance* later centered on the *development of teachers and schools as units*. These two functions are now being reshaped by *visionary leadership and facilitators* at each school site, while *developing and empowering professionals to respond* to the changing needs and requirements for all students to succeed.

In the first part of this section the changing social context of schools will be examined, which places new demands on school leadership and supervision. In the second part the emerging literatures of quality management and systems thinking provide perspectives on the changing functions of supervision. A model of change that grows out of an examination of emerging literatures is presented in the third part to guide leaders in the school development process. New supervisory functions for transforming schools are reported in the fourth section. These four sections together provide a portrait of a school's new visionary leader, the newest in the evolutionary functions of the school supervisor.

A Changing Social Reality

Schooling Demographics As we enter the information age, schools are faced with an almost unmanageable challenge of preparing a growing at-risk youth population for work in the twenty-first century. The changing demographics of communities and their schools are presenting educators with mounting challenges for addressing the needs of the ever-more-numerous at-risk populations (Hodgkinson, 1991). In his 1993 publication, Hodgkinson provides convincing information: "The lowest 40 percent of students are in very bad educational shape, a situation caused mostly by problems they brought with them to kindergarten, particularly poverty, physical and emotional handicaps, lack of health care, difficult family conditions, and violent neighborhoods (pp. 619–623)." The middle 40 percent of students, he continued, are able to complete college, while the top 20 percent are found in the top percentages of performance on international measures. Even though the bottom 40 percent are at-risk primarily for social rather than educational reasons, an argument might be made that the schooling enterprise has also failed to respond adequately to changing social conditions, and therefore is an at-risk social institution. The social demands placed on every school are now raising questions about the feasibility of standard programs and services that have evolved over the last century within bureaucratic traditions.

Any major school reform effort must consequently address the needs of at-risk groups. To do so requires a transformation of school work cultures, and of the programs and services that are provided. Hodgkinson (1993) goes on to recommend that a "seamless web" of services, combining education, health care, housing, transportation, and social welfare, be provided within communities, and that the major focus for educational reform be on those American children who are at greatest risk. The effects of neglect can no longer be tolerated, he argued, because unless these populations possess capacities for full-community participation, the negative effects on communities will continue to mount and may in time virtually cripple our society. The implications of those conclusions for the functions of supervisors are far-reaching.

The time-worn supervisory function of helping teachers to learn specific predefined sets of instructional behaviors is no longer sufficient to meet the growing needs of students. The current schooling challenges of at-risk populations will require routine invention and experimentation by teachers, with supervisors as partners in the quest.

New Definitions of Work While the American at-risk populations are expanding, as are many consequent at-risk schools, so also are the requirements of the workplace. The SCANS Report (1992) provided every school in America with a radically different image of current job demands from those that typically guide instruction and learning within the K–12 schools. The SCANS snapshot of "workplace know-how" calls for reinventing schooling work structures, programs, and services, including supervision. A central message from the report is that the outcomes of schooling for the information age must go far beyond minimal basic skills in traditional isolated subject areas; they must prepare students with more fundamental capacities for productive participation in community life.

To equip students with competence in the SCANS workplace know-how will require fundamentally new forms of schooling that build capacities for students over time. These include the following dimensions: the productive use of resources, interpersonal skills, information search, systems functioning, and technology; the foundation skills that include the traditional "basics" of reading, writing, and computation; and the creative and critical thinking and personal qualities that add value to the workplace. When considering the revolution of the workplace that students will face after their schooling years, along with the challenges of growing at-risk populations, a virtual rethinking of adult and student work and its outcomes is a fundamental issue for restructuring schooling. Anything short of radical change will be inadequate for schools to remain viable as a social institution. Both teaching and supervision will take on new characteristics.

The Work Culture Revolution In order that schools may respond to new challenges, many of the deep-rooted traditions of schooling face extinction. In their place, dynamic and energetic work cultures will evolve. What seems to be happening both in the United States and throughout the world is a virtual transformation of governments, agencies, institutions, industry, and businesses, all of which are responding to rapid changes in the environment and to technological pressures (Snyder, Anderson, & Johnson, 1992).

The renovation of American education, from preschool to graduate school education, has become a national priority in the 1990s. A century ago, the transformation from an agrarian to an industrial society caused the one-room schoolhouse to become obsolete. Transformation into an information age will require as fundamental a restructuring of schooling. To keep pace with social and economic changes, every schooling dimension will be altered (i.e., standards and assessment, instruction, technology, school management, supervision, and work cultures).

The fundamental traditions of work are at issue for all social agencies. Bureaucratic systems that have been honed over the past century, and which had perhaps served well the needs of an age gone by, are rapidly being replaced with more fluid and responsive forms of work. Chubb and Moe (1990), who are policy analysts from the Brookings Institution, observed that the school organization's objective in the past was to deliver programs and services that were well designed by experts, and for schools to improve those over time. This bureaucratic approach to program development is now recognized by many as obsolete.

In rethinking the function of leadership that drives restructuring efforts, Fullan, in his book on change (1993), provides a definition. He suggested that "change agentry" requires four capacities: *personal* vision-building, inquiry, mastery, and collaboration. For each of these four capacities, the institution has a counterpart: *shared* vision-building, organizational structures, norms and practices of inquiry that focus on organizational development and know-how, and on collaborative cultures of work. These two interrelated forces (i.e., personal and organizational), he observed, are dealt with simultaneously. The change agent must have the requisite personal capacities before change can be managed within an organization.

Visionary leaders are needed for the revolution in schooling, those who understand the scope of transforming work cultures, and the challenges of designing responsive systems. To engineer the change process successfully, leaders are driven by a moral obligation to respond to the needs of students, their families, and the community (Sergiovanni, 1992). In other words, the real challenge of the supervisor is to develop learning organizations within schools that have the capacity to adjust constantly to changing conditions. A learning organization is skilled at modifying its own behavior to reflect new knowledge and insights about meeting customer requirements.

Changing Schools Is not Easy Schooling traditions have tenacious roots, and revising them to any extent will require an altogether new understanding of the dynamics of change. To illustrate the enduring strength of habits and traditions, and the challenges faced in uprooting bureaucracies, there is a discouraging conclusion from an experiment funded by the Annie Casey Foundation. In the early 1990s, $40 million was spent on a social experiment to alter the life chances of disadvantaged youth in four cities (Welhage, Smith, & Lipham, 1992). A 3-year study of the project concluded that fundamental changes in programs, policies, and structures had not occurred, that most interventions were only supplemental to traditional educational programs, and that few workers were prepared to use evaluation data to assess the impact of innovations.

Three major causes were identified for the lack of impact in the Casey experiment: (1) the maintenance of traditional cultures of all agencies involved supported inertia that prevented change; (2) the lack of visionary leadership from any agency, which led to action without direction and focus; and (3) people who did not have the skills to work together as decision-making bodies. Reversing the years of powerlessness, the researchers determined, will require more than cluster teams and committees. Leadership must make a moral

commitment to youth, they argued, which stimulates a shared vision among all partners for the success of the youth. Students need to become engaged in authentic work, which provides the context for professional dialogue and reflection. The staffs of the varying supporting agencies need to become empowered to respond to needs, with the resource base being strengthened to support innovation and success.

School Work Culture Profiles What does it take to transform a work culture of habit, fear, and isolation? Snyder, Acker-Hocevar, and Wolf (1994) reported findings from a multisite case study of change over time within 28 schools, that supervisors have a vision of success for all student populations, and that they also possess the skills for changing traditional work cultures over time, and stimulating fundamental change. The perceptions of teachers from these schools is shared here to illustrate the complexity of the supervisor's work by presenting the multiple voices of teachers.

PERCEPTIONS OF SCHOOL CHANGE. The first question asked whether teachers believed schools have changed, and to what extent. They were then asked to explain their responses. Teachers who felt that *schools had changed for the better* offered the following explanations. In the more mature work cultures (as measured on the School Work Culture Profile-SWCP, Snyder, 1988), the responses given most often for contributing to school improvement were: team teaching, interdisciplinary curriculum, cooperative learning, collaborative decision-making, better-defined goals, teacher opinions solicited, and a supportive administration. These characteristics were common in all the schools studied, and suggest the positive influence that a structure for collaboration generates. The administrations in these schools support teaching teams, and teachers feel valued for their input at all levels.

There were a number of teachers who believed *schools have changed for the worse*. The reasons for schools worsening might be categorized into three large areas: (1) social forces and lack of student discipline; (2) multiple teacher roles that are distracting to "teaching"; and (3) administrative policies that detract from meeting the needs of all students. Teachers indicated the negative impact that social ills are having on their students and classrooms. Students are coming to school without a sense of respect for teachers or learning, and teachers do not feel that parents are helping to combat this problem. Some teachers consequently feel that they are working in isolation to be a disciplinarian for these "disrespectful" students—a job for which they never applied. One might argue that these teachers need more training in strategies for different populations. Nevertheless, the perceptions of these teachers provide information for the supervisor's next challenge.

In addition to the isolation that many teachers feel, there is an overwhelming sense of being overworked by the multiple roles that they are asked to play, from teacher to disciplinarian, and from paper pusher to learner. (It is interesting to note that for teachers in the less-mature cultures, a strong support system that is built around team teaching and group work does not yet exist.) Finally, the administration, according to these teachers, does not help to alleviate teachers' problems. Some teachers indicated a lack of administrative support, suggesting that teachers do not have the right to make decisions in their classrooms; rather, decisions are guided more by the desires of the parents and community. Other teachers indicated inconsistent support from the administration, suggesting that the administration sometimes values teacher input and decisions, and sometimes it does not. This inconsistency has developed a sense of apathy on the part of some teachers.

There is a small cluster of teachers who feel that *schools have not changed much at all*. According to them schools are engaged in the motions of change with no real substantive moves taking place. According to these teachers, change occurs about every 10 years, but it never results in anything new. They recognize the talk of change, but they do not see any movement. This is an important finding, as change processes are slow. It is possible that the current restructuring efforts will transpire new systems of operating, if the shift is derived from a philosophically and fundamentally new base. In order for this to happen, however, the change process has to be nurtured and reinforced over time. Teacher perception is a major resource and source of energy for principals to employ in developing the school's capacity to address challenges.

JOB SATISFACTION. Teachers were asked if they were very satisfied with their jobs, moderately satisfied, or less than satisfied. They were then asked to explain their answers. It is interesting that teachers were more satisfied with their jobs in the more mature schools, yet they were not necessarily unsatisfied with their jobs in the less-mature school work cultures. This finding could suggest that teachers come to schools with a built-in intrinsic motivation that centers around a love for teaching and helping students to grow.

Of the reasons given by teachers for job satisfaction, several factors were the strongest: "I make a difference" was offered by more teachers than any other response, coupled with "team teaching," "a positive, supportive administration," "freedom to take risks," and "the empowerment of teachers to be proactive" in their schools and classes.

"Low pay," "overcrowded classes," and "too much paperwork" were the three most stated reasons why teachers were dissatisfied with their jobs. In light of these factors, however, they remained in teaching because they make a difference in the lives of their students. Other factors that contributed to a negative work culture were the lack of administrative support and freedom to take risks in their classrooms, and a lack of respect from students and parents, along with appreciation from the administration. These teachers felt burdened from the amount of work without adequate compensation in the form of recognition, respect, and professional treatment.

DEFINING SCHOOL GOALS. A clear distinction was found about goal setting between more- and less-mature work cultures. The denser the patterns of collaboration in the work culture, the more mature is the work culture overall. In the more-mature cultures goals are set by the entire faculty, and by representatives of the parents and community. These are maintained by leadership teams and weekly or biweekly faculty meetings. The goals permeate the school and are embraced

by all. In the less-mature cultures, goals are set collaboratively, but not by the entire staff; consequently, not all voices are represented. Some also feel that goals are mandated by the principal in relation to the state and district mandates, and that "collaboration" exists just to appease the staff. Finally, goals in some schools are not communicated clearly to the entire school; consequently, a confusion about the school goals exits.

PROFESSIONAL ENHANCEMENT. All schools reported the same avenues for professional enhancement: workshops, in-service, and outside readings. Schools that scored higher on the SWCP, however, added the factor of principal support and encouragement, a principal who keeps current with schooling trends, and working in groups and on teams. In the lower-scoring schools, where the work culture was not as advanced, opportunities were provided but not necessarily perceived to be supported by the administration. Teachers were not encouraged to advance themselves, and they were often discouraged by the lack of release time made available. Schools that were higher scoring on the SWCP had principals that encouraged and supported teacher advancement, providing them with release time and opportunities to identify their training needs. In addition, the higher-scoring schools employed more team teaching, which teachers indicated was the strongest growth experience because they were able to share and learn from one another daily.

What has been learned about change is that developing a strong culture of collaboration is developmental, and the speed with which this occurs relates to the professional readiness of the staff rather than to the number of years engaged in change. Two of the most mature work cultures in the study were found in schools that had existed for little more than 1 year in which the principals were able to select the faculty. The challenge, it seems, is for principals to view time as a nonlinear variable, and to transform the conditions of isolation and fragmentation into those that are cohesive, and which support a common focus and a common way of working and learning together, over time. The amount of time varies in different contexts and professional environments and traditions. Building staff readiness and capacity to innovate within collaborative structures is the real work of supervisors.

The Work Culture Revolution

As supervisors seek to develop collaborative work cultures, the question arises: What are the standards or patterns of work found in high performing organizations? The most significant evolution in organizations thus far is perhaps the worldwide interest in Quality Management, and its impact on the work culture and effects. In 1994, an entire issue of *Wingspan* (Snyder, 1994a) was devoted to an analysis of major publications about the Quality Revolution. A research team from the University of South Florida reviewed more than 50 major works on Quality: those from the original scholars, new standards for the Quality workplace, schemas for work team empowerment within Quality organizations, and works that are closely related to the Quality literatures. The philosophical foundations of the Quality literatures provide educational leaders with powerful concepts for guiding the overhaul of schooling. A revolution in the work culture is required for schooling to perform useful educational functions for a rapidly changing society and workplace. Selections from the *Wingspan* essays by Snyder, Rigsby, Acker-Hocevar, and Perkins will be reported in the sections that follow.

About the Revolution In the last decade, Total Quality Management (TQM) has merged internationally as a guide for the work culture revolution in business, industry, and social institutions of all kinds. In the early years of this century, the focus of quality was on the supervisory control of individual workers, who were trained to "do things right" (Garvin, 1988). By midcentury, the focus had shifted from individual workers to the organization as a unit for improvement and development, under the new label of "quality control." Now, at the end of the twentieth century, the object of organizational improvement has moved from the worker and organization to the customer, who determines quality by placing value on programs, products, or services. Successful organizations today respond to customer needs through continuous organizational development, and this happens in work teams that are empowered to make things work for the customer.

The early "quality" leaders (Deming, 1986; Ishikawa, 1985; Juran, 1988; 1992) demonstrated the power of information and statistical analyses for refining products, services, and programs to meet quality standards, and to enhance marketplace value. The statistical tools and systems thinking that have evolved over the last century of quality are now used by high-performing organizations to continuously improve the quality of products and services to meet customer needs.

Work culture principles have evolved into standards for American industry in its quest for superiority in the marketplace. The national award for "quality" is known as the Baldrige Award, and it is given to those companies who demonstrate high performance in all the Quality standards (Steeples, 1992). Quality has been defined by some Baldrige winners as meeting, and exceeding, customer requirements in relation to delivery, communication, and service dimensions. To stimulate "quality" in the workplace, many states now have a similar award, such as the new Florida Sterling Award, and the Minnesota, Kansas, and New York Quality awards.

Transforming schools so that rigid policies are abandoned is likely to occur with TQM practices. The client-success focus for improvement represents "upside-down" thinking. When it is used as the basis for shared decision-making it can transform the quality of services and programs, and their delivery. Thinking in terms of "systems" for delivering quality will lead naturally to the demise of independent and isolated functions within schools, and will replace the basic fragmented work patterns found in bureaucratic organizations.

Strategic planning, according to Juran (1992), determines the quality of products and services that are produced. Goals are moving targets, he observed, that change in response to new challenges that come over the horizon: new technologies, new competition, social upheaval, threats, and opportunities. Strategic thinking and planning, driven by client needs

and systems thinking, can offset traditional reliance on static laws, programs, structures, and practices, and they can alter the outcomes of schooling for all populations.

Dynamic work environments center around implementing strategic plans cooperatively, gathering information regularly through both quantitative and qualitative measures, and constantly improving services to meet customer requirements. Work teams, rather than managers, in new work environments are empowered with skills and knowledge to use information for continuous improvement (Jablonski, 1991). The work context focuses on using client information to constantly (and forever) improve programs, products, and services to meet their needs. Continuous improvement, noted Bowles and Hammond (1992), is the work of everyone at all levels of the organization. The products/programs/services are improved, and all employees receive training routinely, and adjustments are constantly made to the strategic plan.

The Quality literatures provide perspectives on transforming the school's work culture, which will become the major new function of the supervisor. The leadership challenges for facilitating development efforts, and for empowering professionals will become the new supervisory focus.

A Philosophy for the Transformation of Work Cultures Total Quality Management is not a new program. It is not a package of prescribed behaviors for administrators and workers, nor is it a "quick-fix" for ailing organizations and dysfunctional work cultures. It does not bring about immediate results. It is not a project to be undertaken by "management" alone. It is not boss–management. It cannot be encultured through slogans, exhortations to workers, or "go team" posters and buttons. It is not crisis management, nor does it propose that problems be viewed as a reflection of workers or students who could do better if they tried harder. It is not a method for managers to gain better control of the workforce or teachers to regain control of the classroom.

Total Quality Management is a transformational philosophy and way of work within a culture that is characterized by continuous improvement of processes and the elimination of waste. It is a cycle of planning, doing, studying, and acting on data for the improvement of processes. It is breakthrough thinking that focuses on the possibilities and opportunities for improvement. It is many small steps toward a better way of work. It is a team-driven, cooperative, and collaborative approach to a focus on customer requirements and customer satisfaction. It is noncoercive lead-management, along with long-term, permanent change in thinking. It is employee involvement at every level as well as student involvement in the planning of learning experiences. It is training and education for employees aimed at improving professional practices as well as self-improvement. It demands organizational constancy of purpose that is established and guarded by top-level management.

The management philosophy of Deming (1986), and of other leaders in the Quality field, including Crosby (1984), Feigenbaum (1983), and Juran (1988, 1989, 1992) was initially popularized as manufacturing industries began to practicing "quality control." This new way of thinking and working grew to include design engineering and management. These principles, applied to management, have come to be known as the principles of TQM. Over time, the application of Quality principles has spread to many service industries as well as to manufacturing industries.

Deming (1986, 1993) is credited with contributing to a cultural revolution in the Japanese workplace through his teachings in quality management principles. He is often regarded as the father of TQM, although he does not care for the label. In 1960, he was awarded the *Japanese Second Order Medal of the Sacred Treasure* for his contributions to the quality transformation in Japanese industry and the resulting economic growth. In his honor, the annual Deming Prize for improvement of quality and productivity was established in 1980 by the American Statistical Association. The same management principles that revolutionized Japanese industry, according to Deming, may be used to improve the processes utilized in American organizations no matter how big or how small, whether producing services or products.

Deming's work suggests that a major new function for supervisory work is a focus on the customer (i.e., students, parents, community), rather than on the teacher or the school. When client needs become clear, then school goals and strategic plans follow, as does the assistance to teams of teachers. The relatively new measurement emphasis will assist supervisors to base school improvement decisions on data, basing improvement on the plan/do/study/act cycle.

A Guide To Organizational Transformation According to Steeples (1992), some of the reported outcomes of a quality culture in business include increased employee satisfaction, higher attendance, less turnover, increased safety, and the increased health of employees. She relates that lower-scoring companies on the national Baldrige criteria tend to have more passive leadership. The leadership in these companies tends to react to customer systems, and has limited methods of measuring the systems in place to guide decision-making. Because some systems lack ongoing process evaluation, little change or improvement is noted. In contrast, high performing companies have aggressive quality goals, benchmarks that are time-driven, and systems in place that are responsive to customers. These companies gather data, and make decisions that are based upon data. High-performing companies, most importantly, make a major investment in human resources (Naisbitt & Auburdene, 1985).

The Baldrige Award criteria, from the U.S. Department of Commerce, is built around key concepts that Steeples (1992) included in her book about the Baldrige criteria.

1. Quality is defined by the customer.
2. Senior leadership needs to create clear quality values, and build the values into the day-to-day operation procedures of the company.
3. Quality is the result of well-designed and executed systems.
4. Continuous improvement must be part of the management of all systems and processes.
5. Companies need to develop goals as well as strategic plans to achieve quality leadership.
6. Cycle time reduction needs to be institutionalized.
7. Data-based decision-making guides the decision-making process.
8. Employees must be trained in the notions of quality.
9. A major part of the system design should be to prevent defects.
10. Companies need to communicate quality requirements to suppliers.

The new standards define quality and provide an overall direction for organizations to begin building their internal capacities for change. By defining standards and indicators that benefit customers, organizations are provided with a road map for change that produces results to benefit constituents. Developing the capacities for change requires a movement toward systemwide thinking about solutions to problems, while simultaneously embracing the concepts inherent in learning organizations, the end result of which could be a learning society. This end can be achieved if all community groups work closely together for the attainment of a learning community.

Quality principles are equally appropriate for transforming the classroom work culture, and a supervisory function of the teacher who manages the work of students. Byrnes, Cornesky, and Byrnes (1992) argue that if teachers believe they manage 85 to 90 percent of the teaching and learning processes and systems, then they change their role from the inspector of students' work to the supervisor of the processes of work. Teachers as supervisors can affect the quality of learning in their classrooms. The principal's challenge is to work with teams of teachers and others to transform the work cultures of both the school and classrooms into responsive and adaptive systems of work.

Work Teams: The Basic Units of Transformation The work of teams is the organizational wave of the future for schools because collaboration and a "sense of community" within and between all departments and levels of the school organization have replaced work isolation. Teams are interdependent units of work charged with continually improving processes, products, and services.

Levering (1988) characterizes good workplaces as fun places to work where there is sense of family, and risk-taking is encouraged. In a good workplace, trust is a function of the partnership that exists between the levels of employees, where team-playing, not rivalry, is the norm. Productive workplaces foster fair treatment, respect, and trust throughout the work environment. The productive workplace provides the impetus for creative problem solving and quality initiatives to evolve.

Wellins, Byham, and Wilson (1991) discuss self-directed work teams, small groups who are empowered to manage their own work on a daily basis in formal permanent organized structures. This exciting concept goes further than most team configurations because these workers both handle their job responsibilities and also plan and schedule their own work, make production-related decisions, take action to solve problems, and share leadership responsibilities. This level of worker involvement is highly rewarding, these authors noted, and empowered teams can be a vital part of overall business strategy. Workers involved in self-directed work teams are empowered to improve their jobs and make meaningful contributions to the effectiveness of their organizations.

Shilliff and Motiska (1992) discussed continuous quality improvement through teamwork, up and down and across organizational lines. The leader plays an important role in providing support, guidance, and direction to the quality effort. Cooperative-team interaction that fosters cooperation and communication among all levels of management and workers is advocated over the adversarial model that pits management's forces of influence against workers' forces of resistance.

Miller and Krumm (1992) examine self-managed teams from the workers' perspective, showing how problems can be solved efficiently and cooperatively. Being empowered to make decisions, teams are charged with maintaining an attitude that promotes cooperation and commitment. A team must be cohesive and understand its mission, its reason for existence, and its responsibility and level of authority in order to accomplish its work.

Ryan (1992) presents a team approach to total quality control/just-in-time. Here, management is accountable for developing and maintaining teamwork within and across departmental barriers, with top-level management's commitment required. Ryan discusses three main types of teams, but the success of continuous improvement efforts is directly related to the ability (and willingness) of top-level executives to cope with change in the organizational power structure.

A common theme among these authors is the necessity of acceptance and support from top-level leadership, the supervisor, in order for teams to carry out their work effectively. Another important theme is that those closest to the work have the greatest opportunity to know the work and to know what needs to be done to improve the processes. Work is not done in isolation in quality environments; it takes the concerted efforts of specialized teams to define it and to improve it continually.

Shilliff and Motiska (1992) offer a suitable summary when they observe that a totally integrated quality culture incorporates teamwork across organizational lines. This way of work necessitates a change in individual attitudes, beliefs, ideas,

work objectives, and relationships. Teams at every level of the organization are working together to define and refine the nature of the work that takes place. Top management must create and improve the quality culture in order to drive out fear throughout the organization, from worker through top management. The result will be a total quality culture, an integration of the socio/technical/quality systems, and the wave for the future.

The individual teacher is no longer the unit for development; rather, it is the work team of teachers and other staff members. Hence, to develop the school and classroom work cultures, the supervisor devotes energy and resources at the team level, functioning as a visionary leader, facilitator, developer of talent, and as one who empowers the team to produce results for students.

Moving Schools Toward a Quality Culture

Shedding bureaucratic patterns of work and replacing them with more responsive systems will require both visionary leaders as well as those who understand the nature of changing work cultures over time, and their supervision. The primary operational value in a *bureaucratic system* is control, which is accomplished in educational agencies through enduring program and employee policies, restrictive time parameters, and predetermined levels of acceptable performance for leaders, teachers and students. Furthermore, traditional management practices ensure that workers are dependent upon established policies and practices. Hammer and Champy (1993) found from their research in business that many tasks performed by employees have nothing at all to do with meeting customer needs. The tasks are done simply to satisfy the internal demands of the company's own organization. Transforming schoolwork cultures from a control to a responsiveness orientation requires both knowledge about new outcomes of schooling and an understanding of the function of change over

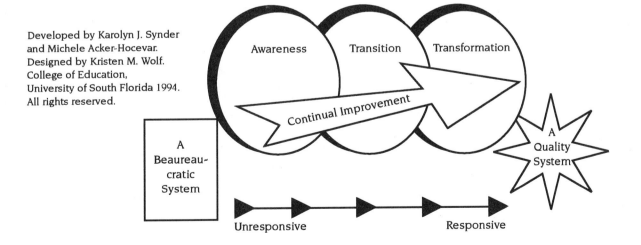

FIGURE 11.1. Quality change process model
toward customer success and satisfaction

time within the work culture (see Figure 11.1).

Bureaucratic structures in schools typically tend to be unresponsive to deviations from the norm, except for such practices as transferring students into "special education" programs. The special populations have expanded over the years, and with them many new, and often independent, programs, services, and funding patterns have also emerged. A call for reversing the practice of isolating "nonnormal" students is picking up speed. Inclusion of all types of students into regular education programs signals that the time has come to view all student populations as special, and to abandon the outdated view of "normal populations" (Rude & Rubadeau, 1992). The conditioned response of professionals over this century has been to abrogate responsibility for those who cannot succeed within conventional programs. This is a bureaucratic response that needs to be abandoned.

The *quality system* found at the other end of the responsiveness continuum is fundamentally different in its purpose and delivery of services. Its goal is to identify specific student population needs rather than to fit students into "canned" programs. Given a "responsiveness" orientation, professionals are free continually to innovate in order to enhance customer success and satisfaction. Rather than requiring dependence upon established practice, workers in high-performing organizations are encouraged to function independently as professionals, and to work interdependently to achieve new purposes. Systems thinking encourages professionals at many levels of the hierarchy to assume responsibility for the overall success of services, products, or programs, with customers determining the levels of satisfaction. For example, nongradedness and continuous-progress forms of schooling are escalating as educators seek to break out of traditional graded and lock-step programs and organizational patterns (Anderson & Pavan, 1993).

Transforming structures, policies, and programs from the control emphasis of the bureaucratic system to responsive patterns found in customer-driven systems requires attention to the development of the work culture over time. A "quality" system stimulates the development of work teams, networks, and partnerships as routine structures for inventing better futures.

Three developmental levels of organizational performance are conceptualized to provide general direction for school growth over time. In *The Awareness Phase,* professionals become acquainted with quality concepts, standards, and values, as well as their implications, while improvement efforts focus on professional development and on the improving isolated programs. The work culture at this stage might best be characterized by "tinkering with the system" as professionals explore a new way of life. In *The Transition Phase,* the staff begins to understand that systems thinking is required for everything in the school, and new linkages are formed between and among program and services. Flexible work structures are consequently evolving as professionals begin to explore "responsiveness" aspirations. The third level, *The Transformation Phase,* is characterized by a new belief system about work that is shared by the entire staff. Emphasis has shifted from the organization and its systems to the needs of customer groups, both internal and external to the organiza-

tion. Responding to client needs and interests, through continuous innovations, is becoming a way of life in the last phase, where partnership structures flourish that span organizations to provide resources and energy for work. Emphasis has shifted from student performance within isolated programs, to performance in community life as an adult worker and family member (see Table 11.1).

New Supervisory Functions for Transforming Schools

Based on the broad interest in Quality management among educators in the 1990s, Acker-Hocevar (1994a) and Snyder (1994 a & b) worked with school districts in Florida to develop a Quality system that would address the major themes found in Quality criteria for work culture excellence, which would also address issues that are being addressed within the education enterprise. The purpose of the Education Quality System (EQS) is to enable school leaders to plan their change initiatives over time within a context that is

---

TABLE 11-1. Organizational Development Phases

BUREAUCRATIC Phase

Focus:	Institutional policies, programs, and regulations
Beneficiary:	State and district policymakers
Decision-Makers:	Policymakers
Outcomes:	Compliance with policy, program guidelines, and regulations
Data:	Gathered to meet policy requirements

AWARENESS Phase

Focus:	Program improvement and professional development
Beneficiary:	Professional educators and programs/services
Decision-Markers:	Principal and school improvement team, task forces
Outcomes:	To meet school improvement requirements
Data:	Are collected to meet state requirements

TRANSITION Phase

Focus:	Organizational growth and improvement
Beneficiary:	The organization
Decision-Markers:	Principal, many staff, advisory council, parents, district linkages, schools, teams, and some students
Outcomes:	Beginning systems interdependence and capacity building for organizational change
Data:	Base line used for compliance, problem solving, and decision-making

TRANSFORMATION Phase

Focus:	Continuous systemic improvement
Beneficiary:	The internal/external customers
Decision-Makers:	Customers, suppliers, schools, districts, and communities
Outcomes:	Student preparation for twenty-first century work, family community. Self-renewing organization: to enhance responsiveness
Data:	Synthesis of data is the driving force in decision-making models

QUALITY Phase

	Institutionalization of the continuous improvement cycle

defensible, and for the purpose of enhancing professional empowerment and the success rates of students. The question guiding the development was, What world-class standards of high-performing organizations will be helpful for guiding the transformation of schools and districts? The new socially constructed system responds to collective perceptions of both existing and emerging challenges. It also reflects the extensive research found in the schooling reform and Quality Management literatures.

Overview There are nine dimensions of the Education Quality Benchmark System, six Performance Areas, and three Results Areas (see Figure 11.2). The six interdependent Performance Areas provide the energy for work within educational institutions. They also create the synergy for three inner dimensions of the model that produce Results in the Quality system. The six interdependent Performance Areas include *Visionary Leadership, Strategic Planning, Systems Thinking and Action, Information Systems, Continual Improvement,* and *Human Resource Development.* These Performance Areas are together expected to produce the Results found in work cultures that foster improved performance to affect customer success and satisfaction. Customer requirements, which are internal as well as external to the institution, drive organizational development over time and create a high synergy for institutional responsiveness to customer needs.

PERFORMANCE AREA 1: VISIONARY LEADERSHIP. A vision for the organization's future guides work throughout the system, and has positive effects upon the direction of the change for different customer groups.

Leaders initiate intervention in the system to unfreeze the organization and begin the change process. Top leadership defines and supports the change process through clear communication, and by providing initial resources, translating systems thinking, and trusting people to begin the journey of ongoing continual improvement. Leadership translates the vision into how the organization will look (i.e., structures), and what behaviors (i.e., results) one should begin to see. Leaders also communicate and reinforce a customer focus and quality values within the context of a learning organization, where the customer is an integral part of feedback in the learning process. decision-making about processes and strategies that will improve the system are left to teams that are held accountable for their results at all levels of the institution, whether at the district, school, university, college, or classroom levels.

PERFORMANCE AREA 2: STRATEGIC PLANNING. A comprehensive plan for achieving the vision of the organization is shaped by all stakeholders, and includes the vision, overall mission, the mission of different subunits and/or departments, and their corresponding goals and action plans. A quality management and control system guides quality improvement systems to benefit customer groups.

Strategic planning differs from action planning, and includes a comprehensive projection of fundamentally new approaches to work. A strategic plan incorporates (1) a vision

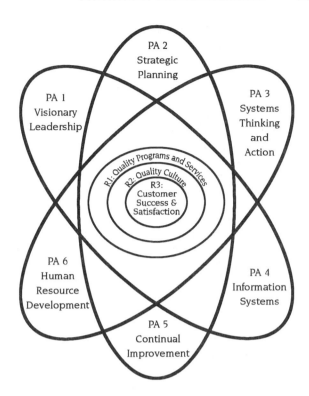

FIGURE 11.2. Quality performance system
(PA = Performance Area; R = Results)

of future conditions for customer groups, (2) quality performance areas to align performance patterns, (3) organizational mission, goals, and outcomes, (4) intervention systems, programs for removing barriers, and innovations, (5) work structures that expand beyond traditional boundaries, (6) multiple action plans, both simultaneous and over time, (7) a quality management system, (8) quality improvement processes, and (9) a description of how quality requirements are deployed, understood, and achieved by all units.

PERFORMANCE AREA 3: SYSTEMS THINKING AND ACTION. An interdependency of units within the organization provides energy for work to influence the organization's performance. The system ensures full participation, empowerment, and cooperation among role groups.

Systems thinking and action reflects knowledge about and application of interdependent processes and functions within the organization's boundaries. It also recognizes that as one part of the system changes, the entire system is affected. Forces outside the educational system will exert pressure on institutions to change. Systems thinking views the people, materials, and time as resources to meet customer needs. In operation, all work units function interdependently with others to achieve outcomes. The isolated and independent performance of roles and units impedes growth in the system as a whole. The decisions that guide the system are related to the system's constancy of purpose or basic aims. Systems are continually aligned with the overall purposes of the organization. Blaming people for problems is not consistent with systems thinking, nor is the isolation of professional workers and units. Organizational processes are instead examined, and barriers to growth are routinely identified and eliminated.

PERFORMANCE AREA 4: INFORMATION SYSTEMS. A complex information system communicates changing conditions, customer needs, and the effects of programs and services. Information influences the continual improvement process. Benchmark, and comparison data are readily available to those who need it for improvement purposes.

Data systems enable workers to store and retrieve information, and to analyze the effects of programs and services over time on different customer groups. Information guides organizational decisions about where to allocate resources for customer groups, and is a basis for improving programs, services, and the training and utilization of human resources. Prevention of problems is built into the system's problem-solving and identification mechanism through information systems. Workers have a clear understanding of statistical process control (SPS), where the concepts of variance, and common and special causes are delineated, understood, and applied. There is continuous and ongoing communication among the various groups of stakeholders within and outside the system to identify future problems.

PERFORMANCE AREA 5: CONTINUAL IMPROVEMENT. Continual improvement is a way of life as the organization responds to changing customer needs, both internally and externally.

Continual organizational/institutional improvement examines the manner in which workers interpret and institutionalize the concept of improvement. Established ongoing assessment of processes leads to improved results and innovation continually throughout the system. Problem-solving mechanisms are used on a routine basis. Multiple information systems and technology assist workers in gathering data from multiple customer groups to make better decisions about programs, services, and functions. Interdependence among all systems enables the institution to improve at meeting customer needs.

Performance Area 6: Human Resource Development. A comprehensive developmental system enhances the professional capacities of professional workers and leaders to respond to emerging demands in the workplace.

Human resource development underscores the importance of commitment in cultivating new skills and knowledge as it relates to changing customer requirements. Professionals are encouraged to view their work as continually developing within a learning community. Growth in a Quality work environment emphasizes systems and the skills needed for collaborative decision-making and action. Multiple resources for knowledge acquisition are accessible to all employee groups in the organization through diverse and experimental delivery systems. A wide range of development opportunities includes: training, observations, conferences and seminars, becoming a trainer, networking, and coaching and mentoring. Employees are recognized routinely for their individual and group performance; their successes become the organiza-

tion's lore. Stories are told again and again to reinforce the values and beliefs that underpin the organizational purpose and philosophy.

EQS Results Areas (RA)

RA 1: QUALITY PROGRAMS AND SERVICES. Programs and services represent the processes and interventions that are designed to achieve the desired results of the system.

Quality programs and services are the result of improvements and innovations to meet customer requirements, which are both immediate and long-term. Program and service data demonstrate that programs and services meet or exceed different customer group's needs and expectations. Services and programs are benchmarked against standards, and are assessed for their effects on customer groups. Objective measures are gathered routinely to confirm improvement. Trends and current levels of Quality and operational Performance are measured on a routine basis. Customer and supplier relationships operate interdependently across programs and services to satisfy customer needs.

RA 2: QUALITY CULTURE. A work culture evolves within the organization that builds upon the interdependence of systems, work units, and resources, and keeps work focused on customer needs.

A Quality culture is the result of a common, ever-evolving vision that guides organizational change and innovation within the system, and among partnerships and networks with other educational institutions, social agencies, and businesses. A common language emerges, with shared values and norms to guide the process of continual improvement. The success of the organization drives the development of the culture to make further improvements through pilots and other innovations that impact results on customers. Networks and partnerships across and within organizational boundaries utilize resources in new ways to benefit customer groups. The organization is optimistic about meeting the needs of customer groups based on their ability to implement innovations through pilots, networks, partnerships, and customer responsiveness.

RA 3: CUSTOMER SUCCESS AND SATISFACTION. Data are gathered regularly to assess how well customer needs are being met by programs and services, as well as to align improvements and innovations with the new information.

Data trends in customer success and satisfaction, both internally and externally, document continual improvement in the area of customer success and satisfaction. The system empowers workers who are closest to the processes to make ongoing and continual improvements. Customers may be described as either primary or secondary, and either internal or external to the system. The primary and secondary *internal* customers are workers within the organization at all levels. The primary customer of a particular work unit is the immediate beneficiary of its work. The secondary internal customer is any customer group within the organization who is indirectly affected by the work unit's work and results.

The primary *external* customers of the education system

are students and their parents and/or guardians. The secondary external customers of the educational organization are community agencies, businesses, and, ultimately, society. External customer groups benefit by the responsiveness and commitment of the internal customers to the changing requirements in the environment reflected in the way the organization does business. The EQS holds promise for guiding supervisory work, and for benchmarking the change process over time in developing schools.

The Principal's Voice: Supervising School Change How does the Quality framework relate to the real work of supervisors? In the 28-school study of change (Snyder, Acker-Hocevar, & Wolf, 1994) the principals were interviewed about their experiences in managing change over time as they shifted teacher focus to a student-success orientation. The themes and patterns that emerged from the data closely matched the Quality model in the previous section. The principals' voice provides important clues about the real work of supervisors toward the end of the 1990s.

Visionary Leadership The focus of the principal's vision centers around success for all student populations. The clarity of this image seems to drive their strategic thinking and planning as principals manage the change process. Almost equally important is the vision for the school's work culture, which is described in many different ways around the central theme of staff collaboration. A vision of student success seems to have a corollary of staff success in working together toward common ends that influence students. The mission of the school focuses on preparing students for life success, which is a departure from mission statements of past schooling decades. There is a sense of urgency for all populations, especially the at-risk populations, to be prepared for a changing work world and to be able to make a contribution to the community.

Principals seem to be driven by their belief that all students want to and can succeed with what is required of them in school, and that the staff working together makes a difference as they function as a force for change in the lives of students. They see their challenge as one of encouraging the staff to invent constantly more powerful programs and services, and to do so in teams. Quality is everyone's job, they reported consistently, where the focus is on the success of students. According to principals, not all teachers are ready to participate in transforming schools; consequently, their strategy for realizing the vision is to develop the talents of all professionals at the school.

Strategic Planning A vision of student success for all populations does not belong only to the principal; rather, it is shared by the staff as well. This vision guides strategic-planning processes. School improvement goals are established through consensus building, with many principals reporting the use of the Delphi-Dialogue Technique (Snyder & Anderson, 1986) every year as a structure for total staff involvement in school improvement planning. Goal-setting activities include teachers, parents, students, and community leaders.

Action planning directs the work that is implicit in the school improvement goals because task forces and teams develop a blueprint for their own work. A wide assortment of temporary and permanent structures are designed for goal-related work. Goals tend to become the responsibilities of many task forces and/or teaching teams because the work is divided. Principals report that the simple action planning of the past decade is evolving into more in-depth study groups before decisions are made. Simple solutions are being replaced more often by comprehensive plans and long-lasting changes. Teachers are receiving training in collaborative planning and accountability for results, and they are learning skills for facilitating collaborative ventures. As plans are made, many innovative staff arrangements are being tried to enhance the use of human resources. Grant writing by teachers seems to flourish in the more mature work cultures.

Systems Thinking and Action Any discussion of people working alone is gone, as is being responsible for tasks in isolation. Structures that foster both articulation across curriculum and grade levels seem to flourish, while cross-functional teams focus on the integration of curriculum and services to meet student needs. Principals report that the practice and concept of isolation is shed gradually, unless they select their own staff, and this requires training and coaching, and taking on new challenges. Multiaged and nongraded teams were found both as pilots in elementary schools and in every middle and high school in our study. Many secondary principals reported that departments are a thing of the past because teachers explore integrated programs to enable students to explore real social challenges. These pilots are viewed as places to test new structures and processes for learning while still maintaining traditional programs.

Several examples of systems thinking were consistent across schools. For example, inclusion programs seem to flourish as teachers work together to integrate special education students and their programs into the regular classroom. Interdisciplinary learning programs seem to focus on a major theme while integrating separate curriculum areas. Multi-aged teams integrate students of many ages while they work together on common projects. Networks and partnerships seem to be thriving in the more developed cultures, and these span the teaching team to make use of additional resources and opportunities. Advisory councils and leadership teams now seem to address challenges that are common to the school as a whole, and solve problems that affect all units. The traditional boss-principal has been replaced with a leadership team that represents the various units, and this team fosters interdependence among work groups.

Information Systems This area represents the greatest change. The question, How are we doing? seems to prompt a search for new ways to gather information. While schools have excelled in gathering information for district and state offices, the traditional kinds of data are not particularly useful for planning and improvement purposes. Most principals shared that the staff is seeking to gather new kinds of information that will inform their planning. Thus, the question looms large: What kind of information will help? Parent and community survey data are being used more often now for improvement planning. Analyzing accomplishments, in relation to goals, points out areas for improvement.

The biggest area of change perhaps relates to student performance data. Principals continue to pay attention to the following data as they ask new questions: attendance, test performance, honor roll, annual comparisons, bus referrals, percentages going to college, and grade distributions. New curriculum rubrics offer new kinds of information on student progress, and teachers are learning new skills to analyze the information. Many schools have measurement task forces to explore new ways to gather information that is useful in decision-making. Most principals report pilots that are testing and developing the concept of student portfolios. This somewhat new approach to data collection and reporting of student progress raises altogether new questions about useful and reliable information. Additional issues of information are raised within the context of continuous progress structures. Most principals seem excited about the potential that new forms of information will have for guiding the planning and daily decision-making processes.

Continual Improvement School improvement in past decades was based on many kinds of influences and information. Principals reported a shift in their thinking about the function of reliable information for making decisions about improvement. Most shared that they are beginning to explore the meaning of data-based kinds of improvement. For example, continuous progress structures seem to lend themselves well to team accountability for improvement. Teachers are shifting from "improving to meet guidelines" to "improving to help students succeed."

Empowerment is an issue in continual improvement, with not all teachers being ready or willing to assume new kinds of improvement responsibility. About one-third of the teachers from these schools seem pleased about empowerment opportunities, whereas the other two-thirds are still in transition. It is interesting that not many principals perceived that large groups of negative or disinterested teachers exist; the discrepancy between teachers was the degree of willingness to be responsible for improvements.

Many school improvement goals focus on pilots for whole language, continuous progress, integrated curriculum, and authentic forms of assessment. Principals spoke about pilots as a strategy to test new ideas, and they seemed less inclined to launch new innovations schoolwide until their success could be predicted. Piloting with eager teachers seems to work in adapting innovations to local conditions.

The leadership team is viewed by principals as a major force for innovation. In the past leadership teams may have been more concerned with monitoring compliance patterns; they are now often the sparks for innovation. The leadership team also seems to be the training ground for new school leaders because they develop new systems and strategies schoolwide to enhance the interdependence of programs and services.

Human Resource Development No principal in any school mentioned teacher evaluation during any of the interviews. The practice still continues, but when principals think about developing their schools they focus on the professional development of the staff. In fact, many spoke about development of others as an investment in the future of the school; professional growth was the chief strategy that principals used for advancing the school's work culture. The goal of human resource development today is empowerment (i.e., developing knowledgeable and skillful professionals who can meet new challenges). Although important, discussion of compliance with regulations seems to be a backdrop for development.

Professional development systems in these schools are extensive, and they include workshops, teachers as trainers, conferences, seminars, book clubs, visitations, graduate work, and leadership development. There seems to be a strong linkage between the school improvement goals and the focus of the staff development programs within a given year because new knowledge and skills are viewed as enabling strategies. Little mention was made of curriculum-focused training; rather, talk centered on development centers around new innovations and pilot systems, as well as on tools for working collaboratively. Training for teams focuses on facilitation in goal setting, planning, action and results, group problem solving, and personality inventories that enhance group work. Peer coaching and problem solving now seems to be a natural way of working within teams because professionals learn with and from each other to advance the school's capacity to enhance success.

All principals reported recognition programs for teachers and teams. When teachers understand the power of recognition they develop programs to salute students, as well as parent volunteers and community agencies and businesses. In fact, the negative climate of the school has been replaced in most schools with the celebration of successes and optimism for the future. Principals report that one of their major strategies has been to "keep the staff pumped up" during the change years. Teachers are now making use of those same strategies for recognizing the success and contributions of others.

Quality Programs and Services The effects of visions, strategic plans, systems thinking and action, information systems, continual improvement, and human resource development have stimulated new kinds of programs and services. Many principals reported that they have stopped using textbooks, and tracking and retention practices. All seemed to be exploring alternative ways to enhance student success.

For instruction, information bases are guiding decisions more often for student placement rather than for age and grade level. Pilots of integrated curriculum are changing the role of teacher to facilitator, and student to worker and producer. Forms of cooperative learning are replacing competition and isolation as a structure for work, and the biggest change can be seen in high schools. Nongraded structures K–12 have replaced tracking patterns, and are helping more students to succeed. Tutorials that span age levels function to help students at all ages. Technology has begun to cause a revolution in learning, replacing the teacher function of dissemination and drill. This has encouraged new facilitative roles to evolve for the teacher.

The most prevalent form of program development is an

integrated curriculum within teams and continuous progress structures. New programs tend to center around real-life community challenges. They are guided by rubrics that specify levels of performance for students in many subject areas. Most principals feel that integrated and continuous progress programs will become institutionalized, and sense that they and their staffs are only beginning to understand the potential for students. Authentic assessment pilots tend to be limited to reading and writing, with the expectations that the concept will be expanded when there is a greater understanding of how the concepts can be operationalized. Additional pilot program include inclusion, career and business programs, and college articulation. The greatest observation, perhaps, is the changing role of the student in the learning process from individual recipient of information to team producer of products.

Quality Culture Principals report a shift over time from a "me" to a "we" culture of work. Parents and community agencies and business seem more integrated into the school's life now and are partners in the development of youth. A climate of success has replaced a crisis orientation from past years as school cultures move from chaos to clarity of focus for invention. The new interdependent work structures have stimulated those who were eager to grow, and many of the "old timers" have been revitalized to become a force for change. A sense of family is evolving that focuses on "community," where a continuity of caring is evolving for all students and staff. The big story centers around the extent of parent and community involvement in the daily life of the school. The walls of school isolation are disintegrating and being replaced with open doors to participate in the life of the community.

Within most of the schools, perhaps, a "learning community" is forming that asks new questions and has the confidence to explore and examine options continuously. What keeps the change process moving? Principals report a growing sense of moral responsibility among the staff to do whatever it takes to help all students succeed, especially with the at-risk populations. A focus on students seems to provide the energy that stimulates continuous development from the staff. The picture of collaboration certainly exists within teams, but it also now extends to other teams, task forces, networks, and partnerships.

Customer Success and Satisfaction What effect is the changing work culture having on student populations? Rather than sharing numbers of new student performance patterns, principals shared new collections and concentrations of adult energy to help more students succeed. Most principals reported noticeable growth patterns for at-risk populations. Programs for parents included volunteers, councils and task forces, mentors, tutors, dinners, events featuring students, training, and transportation. Considerable effort has been made by principals to engage local businesses and agencies in the school's challenges; consequently, the list of participating organizations is extensive. Schools now seem to be more integrated into the community structure, and any sense of school isolation from the community is gone. Many programs also exist for students to work (e.g., in nursing homes) and to shadow professionals

to learn about career options. While test scores do not seem to be the most useful measure of student success today, many new approaches are enabling students to become participants within their communities, while still in school, and to interact with the community in its daily life.

When principals are trained in the knowledge and skill bases for managing change, their school work cultures tend to reflect patterns found in productive workplaces. Change occurs over time, and is a different phenomenon in each community. Change is not time bound; rather, it is determined by the readiness of the faculty to address the challenges they face. Some of the most mature cultures were found in schools that will be a little more than 1 year old. Developing an interdependence among planning, staff development, program development, and assessment work culture systems requires a common focus and a shared vision of success for all students, all of which evolves over time.

Teacher perceptions of the change process is seen as developmental and contingent upon the degree of common focus for school improvement, as well as the extent of involvement in decision-making processes. Teachers in the more mature cultures tend to see priorities and challenges in similar ways, and to be involved in shaping the new programs and services. Pilots are strategies for developing workable ideas that may eventually influence the entire school, whereas teachers view themselves as learners who are empowered to make contributions to school improvement.

Principals who understand the change process tend to be successful in engineering school development. A strong vision of success for the school permeates the culture and drives continuous program and professional development. Collaboration takes many forms as cultures mature, beginning within teams, and moving out to task forces, networks and partnerships. The leadership team is a major source of school energy that stimulates innovation and nurtures exploration. The more highly developed the culture, the more ready and capable the staff is to try new ideas and to study their effects.

This story of change in 28 schools provides a snapshot of supervision in schools in transition. The themes and patterns reported here provide useful indicators of maturing work cultures, and suggest strategies that work in their development. Mastering the change process appears to be a major challenge for supervisors as leaders today in the redesign of work in schools, and in the programs and the services that affect students.

CONCLUSIONS

During the twentieth century school supervision was launched as a control function to ensure the compliance of teachers with predetermined performance patterns for the prevailing view of "teacher." In the last half of the twentieth century, the idea of teacher development emerged as a need, which led to the new field of staff development, within which adaptations of clinical supervision and peer-coaching arrangements evolved. In the latter part of this century, teachers and principals began to work in collaborative arrangements to address pressure challenges schoolwide.

Supervisors began to shift from an authoritarian to a facilitation function in school development for the enhancement of professional performance.

More is perhaps required of principals than new competencies. Snyder et al (1992) argue that no new budget, curriculum, law, instructional strategy, calendar or schedule, union contract, planning system, or organizational structure has the power within it to transform schooling so that every student succeeds routinely. Only leaders who have a vision of new schooling futures for all students will succeed in turning the schooling business upside down because out of their dreams comes the energy to overhaul outdated education structures, decision-making processes, programs, and traditions. The major task in restructuring is to nurture cooperative problem solving that centers around the question, "What do our students need next?" Reinventing schooling requires that educators be willing to shed outdated traditions and together create new, more vibrant forms of schooling. The future of school restructuring and accountability may rest upon four conditions:

- a vision of success for all students
- plans shaped by school partners
- a work culture that nurtures and expects development and success
- staff empowerment and commitment to provide the energy system for success.

As schools prepare for the next century, there is growing concern for the increasing at-risk populations and their well-being in school, as well as for the information that now exists about marketplace competencies and for the capacity of the education enterprise to transform the culture of work in schools so that more students succeed. Success needs to be measured, both in relation to traditional school requirements, and also in relation to twenty-first century job requirements.

At the dawn of the twenty-first century, many schools have moved beyond a compliance orientation to work. Principals, teachers, and other partners are more often engaged in new work arrangements because they use existing knowledge and together invent more responsive services. The Quality movement in industry, together with the change era in education, has led to a new view of the functions of school supervision.

The compliance expectations from supervisors as bosses are gone. In their place now are more visionary leaders who empower knowledgeable professionals to invent continuously responsive services. The Education Quality Benchmark System, the 28-school study on school change, provides examples of school leaders who are preparing schooling for a new age. The next century of schooling belongs to the inventors, risk takers, and those who have a dream of a better schooling future for all students. Out of the continuous interdependence of all role groups and institutions in the education enterprise, new forms of schooling will be born to meet the challenges ahead. The new schooling future will depend in large measure on the transformation of the supervisory function to a visionary leader who empowers high-performing professionals to continuously respond to education challenges.

Promising new supervisory functions have been identified in this chapter that hold promise for the transformation of schooling and its effects upon the changing student populations and the emerging job requirements of the marketplace. The challenge for a supervisor is to function as a visionary leader and a change agent for engineering staff participation in creating more responsive cultures of work in schools. A new set of supervisory functions includes:

1. visionary leadership for anticipating the direction of school change
2. strategic planning, which includes teachers and customers, and that provides a comprehensive blueprint for change
3. systems thinking that will stimulate interdependence among work groups, and foster networks and partnerships for development endeavors
4. information systems that generate useful information to guide improvement decisions
5. continual improvement as a cultural norm
6. human resource development programs that stimulate continuous learning for work teams and for the school community

The future of supervision as a field of practice and inquiry may well rest upon the collective capacity of educational leaders to respond to the new demands of the workplace called school. New functions of school supervision will evolve from a response to the new demands of twenty-first century schooling, or else supervision as a function will cease

REFERENCES

to play a role in the schooling process.

Acker-Hocevar, M. (1994a). *The content validation of standards, outcomes and indicators for organizational development in region IV of Florida.* Unpublished doctoral dissertation proposal, University of South Florida, Tampa.

Acker-Hocevar, M. (1994b). Quality standards: A guide to organizational transformation, and book reviews. *Wingspan, 10*(1), 6–11.

Anderson, R. H. (1988). Political pressures on supervisors. In L. Tanner (Ed.). *Critical issues in curriculum* (pp. 60–82). Chicago, IL: University of Chicago Press.

Anderson, R. H. (1989). Unanswered questions about the effect of supervision on teacher behavior. *Journal of Curriculum and*

Supervision, 4, 291–297.

Anderson, R. H. (1990–1991). Presumption of competence. *National Forum of Educational Administration and Supervision Journal, 7*(3), 101–110.

Anderson, R. H. (1992, April). *The nongraded elementary school: Lessons from history.* Paper presented at the annual meeting of the American Educational Research Association, San Francisco.

Anderson, R. H. & Pavan, B. N. (1993). *Nongradedness: Helping it to happen.* Lancaster, PA: Technomic.

Anderson, R. H. & Snyder. K. J. (1993). *Clinical supervision: Coaching for enhanced performance.* Lancaster, PA: Technomic.

Austin, G. R. (1979). Exemplary schools and the search for effectiveness.

Educational Leadership, 37, 10–14.

Ayer, F. C. (1954). *Fundamentals of instructional supervision.* New York: Harper and Brothers.

Bartky, J. A. (1953). *Supervision as human relations.* Boston: D. C. Heath & Company.

Beach, D. M. & Reinhartz, J. (1989). *Supervision: Focus on instruction.* New York: Harper & Row.

Bolin, F. S. & Panaritis, P. (1992). Searching for a common purpose: A perspective on the history of supervision. In C. D. Glickman (Ed.). *Supervision in transition* (pp. 30–43). Alexandria, VA: ASCD.

Bowles, J. & Hammond, J. (1992). *Beyond quality: new standards of total performance that can change the future of corporate America.* New York: Berkley Publications Group.

Boyer, E. L. (1988). *Report card on school reform: The teachers speak out.* Princeton, NJ: Carnegie Foundation for the Advancement of Education.

Brookfield, S. D. (1986). *Understanding and facilitating adult learning.* San Francisco: Jossey-Bass.

Brookover, W. B. & Lezotte, L. W. (1979). *Changes in school characteristics coincident with changes in student achievement.* East Lansing, MI: Institute for Research on Teaching. College of Education, Michigan State University (ERIC Document Reproduction Service No. ED 181005).

Bullerman, M., Borg, J., & Peterson, D. (1993). Research bases for enhancing teaching and learning: Essential skills. In R. H. Anderson & K. J. Snyder (Eds.). *Clinical supervision: Coaching for higher performance* (pp. 325–345). Lancaster, PA: Technomic.

Burke, P. J. & Fessler, R. (1994). The changing role of supervision in site-based management. In R. J. Krajewski (Ed.). *Supervision: new roles and all: Fast forward 2* (pp. 41–48). Madison, WI: Wisconsin Association for Supervision and Curriculum Development.

Bush, G. (1991). *America 2000.* Washington, D.C.: U.S. Department of Education.

Byrnes, M. A., Cornesky, R. A., & Byrnes, L. W. (1992). *The quality teacher: Implementing total quality management in the classroom.* Port Orange, FL: Cornesky & Associates Press.

Callahan, R. E. (1962). *Education and the cult of efficiency.* Chicago: University of Chicago Press.

Chubb, J. & Moe, T. (1990). *Politics, markets and America's schools.* Washington D.C.: Brookings Institute.

Cogan, M. L. (1973). *Clinical supervision.* Boston: Houghton Mifflin.

Collins, A. (1991). The role of computer technology in restucturing schools. *Phi Delta Kappan, 73,* 28–36.

Conley, S. & Bacharach, S. B. (1990). From school-site management to participatory school-site management. *Phi Delta Kappan, 71,* 539–544.

Conley, S. C., Schmidle, T., & Shedd, J. B. (1988). Teacher participation in the management of school systems. *Teachers College Record, 90,* 259–280.

Costa, A. L. & Garmston, R. (1986). The art of cognitive coaching: Supervision for intelligent teaching. *Wingspan, 3,* 38–43.

Costa, A. L. & Garmston, R. J. (1994). *Cognitive coaching: A foundation for renaissance schools.* Norwood, MA: Christopher-Gordon Publishers, Inc.

Costa, A. L. & Kallick, B. (1993). Through the lens of a critical friend. *Educational Leadership, 51*(2), 49–51.

Crosby, P. B. (1984). *Quality without tears: The art of hassle-free management.* New York: McGraw-Hill.

David, J. L. (1991). Restructuring and technology: Partners in change. *Phi Delta Kappan, 73,* 37–40, 78–82.

Deal, T. E. & Kennedy, A. A. (1982). *Corporate cultures: The rites and rituals of corporate life.* Reading, MA: Addison-Wesley.

Deming, W. E. (1986). *Out of the crisis.* Cambridge, MA: Massachusetts Institute of Technology Center for Advanced Engineering Study.

Deming, W. E. (1993). *The new economics for industry, government, and education.* Cambridge, MA: Massachusetts Institute of Technology Center for Advanced Engineering Technology.

Des Dixon, R. G. (1994). Future schools and how to get there from here. *Phi Delta Kappan, 75,* 360–365.

Edmonds, R. R. (1979). Effective schools for the urban poor. *Educational Leadership, 37,* 15–18, 20–24.

Feigenbaum, A. V. (1983). *Total quality control* (3rd ed.). New York: McGraw-Hill.

Fitzgerald, J. H. (1991). *Management practices: A case study of district level supervisors and directors of curriculum and instruction in one school district.* Unpulished doctoral dissertation, University of South Florida, Tampa, FL.

Foshay, A. W. (1994). Action research: An early history in the United States. *Journal of Curriculum and Supervision, 9,* 317–325.

Fuentes, E. (1992). *Work cultures of evolving schools: Observational analysis of practice.* Unpublished doctoral dissertation, Harvard University, Cambridge, MA.

Fuhrman, S. H., Elmore, R. F., & Massell, D. (1993). School reform in the United States: Putting it into context. In S. L. Jacobson & R. Beene (Eds.). *Reforming education: The emerging systemic approach* (pp. 3–27). Thousand Oaks, CA: Corwin Prss.

Fullan, M. (1993). *Change forces: Probing the depths of educational reform.* London: Falmer Press.

Garmston, R. (1989). *Is peer coaching changing supervisory relationships?* (ERIC Document Reproduction Service No. ED 315854).

Garmston, R. (1987). How administrators support peer coaching. *Educational Leadership, 44*(5), 18–26.

Garmston, R., Linder, C., & Whitaker, J. (1993). Reflections on cognitive coaching. *Educational Leadership, 51*(2), 57–61.

Garvin, D. A. (1988). *Managing quality: The strategic and competitive edge.* New York: The Free Press.

Glickman, C. D. (1985). *Supervision of instruction: A developmental approach.* Boston: Allyn and Bacon.

Glickman, C. D. (1990). *Supervision of instruction: A developmental approach* (2nd ed.). Boston: Allyn and Bacon.

Goldhammer, R. (1969). *Clinical supervision: Special methods for the supervision of teachers.* New York: Holt, Rinehart and Winston.

Goldhammer, R., Anderson, R. H., & Krajewski, R. J. (1980). *Clinical supervision: Special methods for the supervision of teachers* (2nd ed.). New York: Holt, Rinehart and Winston.

Goldhammer, R., Anderson, R. H., & Krajewski, R. J. (1993). *Clinical supervision: Special methods for the supervision of teachers* (3rd ed.). Fort Worth, TX: Harcourt Brace Jovanovich.

Goodlad, J. I. (1984). *A place called school: Prospects for the future.* New York: McGraw-Hill.

Governors' Report on Education. (1991). *Time for results.* Washington, D.C.: Department of Education.

Greenfield, W. D. (1988). Moral imagination, interpersonal competence and the work of school administrators. In D. E. Griffiths, R. T. Stout, & P. B. Forsyth (Eds.). *Leaders for America's schools: The report and papers of the national commission on excellence in educational administration* (pp. 207–232). Berkeley, CA: McCutchan.

Gwynn, J. M. (1961). *Theory and practice of supervision.* New York: Dodd, Mead & Company.

Hammer, M. & Champy, J. (1993). *Reengineering the corporation: A manifesto for business revolution.* New York: HarperCollins.

Hansen, K. (June 1989). *The anatomy of restructuring: Strategies for reforming American education* (ERIC Document Reproduction Service No. ED 310504).

Harris, B. M. (1963). *Supervisory behavior in education.* Englewood Cliffs, NJ: Prentice Hall.

Heathers, G. (1972). Overview of innovations in organizations of learning. *Interchange, 3*(2–3), 47–68.

Herman, J. L. & Herman, J. J. (1993). A state to state snapshot of school-based management practices. *International Journal of Educational Reform, 2,* 256–262.

Hersey, P. & Blanchard, K. H. (1977). *Management of organizational behavior: Utilizing human resources* (3rd ed.). Englewood Cliffs, NJ: Prentice Hall.

Hodgkinson, H. (1991). Reform versus reality. *Phi Delta Kappan, 73,* 9–16.

Hodgkinson, H. (1993). American education: The good, the bad, and the task. *Phi Delta Kappan, 74,* 619–623.

Hosack-Curlin, K. (1993). Peer coaching among teachers. In R. H. Anderson & K. J. Snyder (Eds.). *Clinical supervision: Coaching for higher performance* (pp. 231–249). Lancaster, PA: Technomic.

Houle, C. O. (1980). *Continuing learning in the professions.* San Francisco: Jossey-Bass.

Hultman, G. (1989). The state of the art of school administration: A review of facts and theory. *Scandinavian Journal of Educational Research, 33*(2), 123–162.

Hunter, M. (1988). Effecting a reconciliation between supervision and evaluation: A reply to Popham. *Journal of Personnel Evaluation in Education, 1,* 275–279.

Ishikawa, K. (1985). (D. J. Lee, Trans.). *What is total quality control? The Japanese way.* Englewood Cliffs, NJ: Prentice Hall.

Jablonski, J. R. (1991). *Implementing total quality management: An overview.* San Diego: Pfeiffer.

Johnson, W., Snyder, K. J., Anderson, R. H., & Johnson, A. (1993). *The school work culture profile: A statistical analysis and strategy* (ERIC Document Reproduction Service No. ED 355282).

Johnson, W., Snyder, K. J., Anderson, R. H., & Johnson, A. (1994, April). *Assessing school work culture: An analysis and strategy.* Paper presented at the annual meeting of the American Education Research Association, New Orleans.

Joyce, B. & Showers, B. (1980). Improving in-service training: The messages of research. *Educational Leadership, 37,* 379–382, 384–385.

Juran, J. M. (1988). *Juran on planning for quality.* New York: The Free Press.

Juran, J. M. (1989). *Juran on leadership for quality: An executive handbook.* New York: Free Press.

Juran, J. M. (1992). *Juran on quality by design.* New York: The Free Press.

Knowles, M. (1984). *The adult learner: A neglected species* (3rd ed.). Houston: Gulf Publishing Co.

Lally, K. (1991). Changing of the old guard: States turn towards helping rather than regulating. *The School Administrator, 48*(3), 8–12.

Levering, R. (1988). *A great place to work: What makes some employers so good (and most so bad).* New York: Random House.

Lewis, A. (1988). *Challenges for school leaders.* Arlington, VA: American Association for School Administrators.

Lieberman, A. & Miller, L. (1992). Professional development of teachers. In M.C. Alkin (Ed.). *Encyclopedia of educational research* (6th ed.) pp. 1045–1052. New York: Macmillan.

Lieberman, A. & Miller, L. (1979). *Staff development: New demands, new realities, new perspectives.* New York: Teachers College Press.

Little, J. W. (1985). Teachers as teacher advisors: The delicacy of collegial leadership. *Educational Leadership, 43*(3), 34–46.

Lovell, J. T. & Wiles, K. (1983). *Supervision for better schools* (5th ed.). Englewood Cliffs, NJ: Prentice Hall.

Luehe, B. (1989). The principal and supervision. Elementary Principal Series No. 4. ERIC ED3115914.

McAfee, A. L. (1990). *The importance of twelve dimensions of effective supervisory practice derived from educational literature as perceived by selected principals.* Unpublished doctoral dissertation, University of Georgia, Athens, GA.

McFaul, S. A. & Cooper, J. M. (1983). Peer clinical supervision in an urban elementary school. *Journal of Teacher Education, 34*(5), 34–38.

Miller, G. L. & Krumm, L. L. (1992). *The whats, whys & hows of quality improvement: A guidebook for continuous improvement.* Milwaukee: ASQC Press.

Miller V. & Spalding, W. B. (1952). *The public administration of American schools.* Yonkers, NY: World Book Company.

Missouri Department of Elementary and Secondary Education. (1989). *Missouri special education administrator's manual.* Jefferson City, MO: Missouri Department of Elementary and Secondary Education.

Murphy, J. (1991). Helping teachers prepare to work in a restructured school. *Journal of Teacher Education, 41*(4), 50–56.

Naisbitt, J. & Auburdene, P. (1985). *Re-inventing the corporation: Transforming your job and your company for the new information society.* New York: Warner Books.

National Association of Elementary School Principals. (1990). *Principals for 21st century schools.* Alexandria, VA: National Association of Elementary School Principals.

Nielsen, L. A. (1993). Technical coaching: Equipping professionals with basic and emerging tools for enhancing performance. In R. H. Anderson & K. J. Snyder (Eds.). *Clinical supervision: Coaching for higher performance* (pp. 251–265). Lancaster, PA: Technomic.

Oliva, P. F. (1993). *Supervision for today's schools* (4th ed.). New York: Longman.

Pajak, E. (1989). *Identification of supervisory proficiencies project: Final report.* Athens, GA: Dept. of Curriculum and Supervision, Division of Educational Leadership, College of Education, University of Georgia.

Pajak, E. (1993). *Approaches to clinical supervision: Alternatives for improving instruction.* Norwood, MA: Christopher Gordan Publishers.

Parkinson, A. (1990). *An examination of the reliability and factor structure of the school work culture profile instrument.* Unpublished doctoral dissertation, University of South Florida, Tampa, FL.

Pavan, B. N. (1987). *Hunter's clinical supervision and instructional models: Research in schools utilizing comparative measures* (ERIC Document Reproduction Service No. ED 273 606).

Perkins, G. C. (1994). Work teams: The basic units of transformation, and book reviews. *Wingspan, 10,* 11–12.

Pitner, N. J. (1988). School administrator preparation: The state of the art. *Leaders for America's schools: The reports and papers of the national commission on excellence in educational administration* (pp. 367–402). Berkeley, CA: McCutchan.

Reavis, C. A. & Griffith, H. (1991). *Restructuring schools: Theory and practice.* Lancaster, PA: Technomic.

Richardson, M. D. (1990). *The Kentucky supervisor: A research profile* (ERIC Document Reproduction Service No. ED 331156).

Rigsby, K. L. (1994). Total quality management: A philosophy for the transformation of work cultures, and book reviews. *Wingspan, 10*(1), 4–5.

Rude, H. & Rubadeau, R. J. (1992). Practices for principals as special education leaders. *The Special Education Leadership Review, 1*(1), 55–62.

Ryan, J. M. (1992). *The quality team concept in total quality control.* Milwaukee: ASQC Quality Press.

Sage, D. D. & Burrello, L. C. (1986). *Policy and management in special education.* Englewood Ciffs, NJ: Prentice Hall.

Sailor, W. (1991). Special education in the restructured school. *Remedial and Special Education, 12,* 8–22.

Sarason, S. B. (1971). *The culture of the school and the problem of change.* Boston: Allyn and Bacon.

Senge, P. M. (1993). Transforming the Practice of Management.

Human Resource Development Quarterly, 4, 5–32.

Senge, P. (1990a). *The fifth discipline: The art and practice of the learning organization.* New York: Doubleday.

Senge, P. (1990b). The leader's new work: Building learning organizations. *Sloan Management Review, 32*(1), 7–23.

Senge, P. & Lannon-Kim, C. (1991). Recapturing the spirit of learning through a systems approach. *The School Administrator, 48*(9), 8–12.

Sergiovanni, T. J. (1992). *Moral leadership: Getting to the heart of school improvement.* San Francisco: Jossey-Bass.

Sergiovanni, T. J. (1994). *Building community in schools.* San Francisco: Jossey-Bass.

Sergiovanni, T. J. & Starratt, R. J. (1993). *Supervision: A redefinition* (5th ed.). New York: McGraw-Hill.

Shaplin, J. T. & Olds, H. F., Jr. (Eds.). (1964). *Team teaching.* New York: Harper & Row.

Sheingold, K. (1991). Restructuring for learning with technology: The potential for synergy. *Phi Delta Kappan, 73,* 17–27.

Shilliff, K. A. & Motiska, P. J. (1992). *The team approach to quality.* Milwaukee: ASQC Quality Press.

Showers, B. Joyce, B., & Bennett, B. (1987). Synthesis of research on staff development: A framework for future study and a state-of-the-art analysis. *Educational Leadership, 45*(3), 77–87.

Snyder, K. J. (1981). Clinical supervision in the 1980s. *Educational Leadership, 38,* 521–524.

Snyder, K, J. (1988). *The school work culture profile: A diagnostic instrument.* Tampa, FL: Managing Productive Schools.

Snyder, K. J. (1993). Competency development: Linking restructure goals to training and coaching. In R. H. Anderson & K. J. Snyder (Eds.). *Clinical supervision: Coaching for higher performance.* Lancaster, PA: Technomic.

Snyder, K. J. (1994a). (Ed.). Welcome to the quality revolution; quality education standards in Florida: An emerging construct [special issue] and book reviews. *Wingspan, 10*(1).

Snyder, K. J. (1994b). The quality revolution in schools: A Florida partnership venture. *International Journal of Educational Reform, 3*(3), 279–289.

Snyder, K. J., Acker-Hocevar, M., & Snyder. K. M. (1994, April). *Organization development in transition: The schooling perspective.* Paper presented at the annual meeting, American Educational Research Association, New Orleans.

Snyder, K. J. & Anderson, R. H. (1986). *Managing productive schools: Toward an ecology.* Orlando: Academic Press.

Snyder, K. J. & Anderson, R. H. (1988). Empowering groups of teachers to solve school problems. *Record, 8,* 19–21.

Snyder, K. J., Anderson, R. H., & Johnson, W. L. (1992). Transforming work cultures and learning patterns: The school-based management

challenge. *International Journal of Educational Reform, 1,* 291–297.

Snyder, K. J. & Giella, M. (1987). Developing principals' problem solving capacities. *Educational Leadership, 45*(1), 38–41.

Spears, H. (1953). *Improving the supervision of instruction.* New York: Prentice Hall.

Steeples, M. M. (1992). *The corporate guide to the Malcolm Baldrige National Quality Award: Proven strategies for building quality into your organization.* Milwaukee: ASQC Quality Press.

Taylor, B. O. & Levine, D. U. (1991). Effective school projects and school-based management. *Phi Delta Kappan, 75,* 394–397.

U.S. Department of Labor, The Secretary's Commission on Achieving Necessary Skills. (1992). *Learning a living: A blueprint for high performance. Part I.* Washington, D.C.: Dept. of Labor, Secretary's Commission on Achieving Necessary Skills.

U.S. National Commission on Excellence in Education. (1983). *A nation at risk: The imperative for educational reform: A report to the nation and the Secretary of Education, U. S. Department of Education.* Washington D.C.: The Commission.

Valesdy, T. C. & Hirth, M. A. (1992). Survey of the states: Special education knowledge requirements for school administrators. *Exceptional Children, 58,* 399–406.

Vanezky, R. L. & Winfield, L. F. (1979). Schools that succeed beyond expectations in reading. *Studies in Education.* Newark, DE: University of Delaware (ERIC Document Reproduction Services No. ED 1977484).

Weber, G. (1971). *Inner-city children can be taught to read: Four successful schools.* Washington, D.C.: Council for Basic Education.

Welhage, G., Smith, G., & Lipham, P. (1992). Restructuring urban schools: The new futures experience. *American Educational Research Journal, 29,* 51–93.

Wellins, R. S., Byham, W. C., & Wilson, J. M. (1991). *Empowered teams: Creating self-directed work groups that improve quality, productivity, and participation.* San Francisco: Jossey-Bass.

Wiles, J. & Bondi, J. (1986). *Supervision: A guide to practice* (2nd ed.). Columbus, OH: Charles E. Merrill Publishing Company.

Wiles, K. (1950). *Supervision for better schools.* New York: Prentice Hall.

Wiles, K. (1955). *Supervision for better schools* (2nd ed.). New York: Prentice Hall.

Wiles, K. (1967). *Supervision for better schools* (3rd ed.). New York: Prentice Hall.

Wiles, K. & Lovell, J. (1975). *Supervision for better schools* (4th ed.). New York: Prentice Hall.

Williams, R. C., Wall, C. C., Martin, M., & Berchin, A. (1974). *Effecting organizational renewal in schools: A social systems*

·12·

ROLES, RESPONSIBILITIES, AND RELATIONSHIPS

Allan A. Glatthorn

EAST CAROLINA UNIVERSITY

This chapter will examine the various roles subsumed under the generic term, *supervisor*, placing special emphasis on the relationships between those roles as executed at the several levels of governance and organization. In this sense the chapter examines how the supervisory services provided at specific levels (as described in Chapters 23–30) relate to and affect each other. In order to capture the wide range of services thus provided, the term *supervisor* is used in its broadest sense to identify any individual formally charged with the responsibility of improving curriculum and instruction. Thus, there are individuals employed by state departments of education, who are identified by some title other than "supervisor," who do not observe or confer with teachers, but who spend much of their time developing materials designed to improve curriculum and instruction at the classroom level. In this sense, therefore, they are "supervisors" for the purposes of this chapter.

The chapter is organized by first presenting a conceptual framework designed to provide an organizing structure for what follows. That conceptual framework is then used in examining in turn three spheres of influence: roles external to the school district (e.g., as supervisors in state education departments, educational service agencies, and institutions of higher education); roles within school districts (e.g., chiefly central office supervisors); and roles within the individual school (e.g., administrators and team leaders).

A CONCEPTUAL FRAMEWORK FOR ROLE ANALYSIS

The literature seems replete with reports that list the tasks performed by supervisors at all three levels. Some of these (e.g., Pajak, 1989) analyze the responsibilities of supervisors in general; others (e.g., Madrazo and Hounshell, 1987) focus on supervisors in special subject areas. In most instances both types of studies simply provide a list of activities in which supervisors reported being engaged. For example, the

Madrazo and Hounshell study surveyed science teachers with respect to the following activities, under the rubric of "the coordinator as a supervisor of science": make regular visitations to schools; follow-up school visitations with meetings or conferences; follow-up school visitations with written reports; participate in administrative planning with supervisors; visit and observe science teachers with supervisors; participate in disseminating the science programs in the community. Such lists of specific tasks do not seem very useful either in understanding the special nature of the role or in making the role more productive and meaningful.

The conceptual framework presented here was derived from two bodies of literature. First, in order to structure the framework so that it emphasized student learning, the research on learning was reviewed. Four research syntheses were most helpful (Cotton, 1990; Fraser et al, 1987; Wang, Haertel, & Walberg, 1990; Wang, Haertel, and Walberg, 1993). Each synthesis was analyzed to determine the general factors that affected student achievement. Each factor was listed, and the source was identified. Similar factors were grouped together, in order to eliminate redundancy. The results were then reviewed to identify the groups of factors that met two criteria: (1) they were under the direct influence of the school; (2) they were significantly associated with better student achievement.

This analysis resulted in the identification of five groups of factors considered salient, conceptualized here as the *foci* of supervision.

1. The quality of instruction, especially as such instruction fostered the development of students' cognitive and metacognitive skills and involved positive teacher–student social interactions.
2. The quality of curriculum, including the use of specific objectives, the implementation of a well-coordinated curriculum, and the linkage of assessment to curriculum.
3. The quality and quantity of instructional resources, including the time allocated to a subject, the use of classroom

time for learning, and the textbooks and other materials used to support learning.

4. The school and classroom climate, especially as that climate was orderly, learning-focused, and motivating.
5. The quality of the school's relationship with parents and the community, especially as that relationship fostered a home environment supportive of schooling.

These five factors are considered the foci of supervision: They are the elements with which the supervisor can be centrally concerned.

The second body of literature included those studies and theoretical analyses of the roles of supervisors. A comprehensive review of the ERIC data base and of current texts in supervision was undertaken to identify sources that gave explicit attention to the tasks or functions of supervision, regardless of role. Several sources were most useful here (Harris, 1985; Miller, Smey-Richman, & Woods-Houston, 1987; Oliva, 1984; Pajak, 1989; Pajak, 1990; Parramore, 1990; Tanner & Tanner, 1987). The intent was to discover major patterns, not to identify specific practices. A comprehensive list of the tasks was developed. The list was then reviewed to identify major patterns and groupings, rather than to focus on specific tasks. This analysis of the literature indicated that the ascribed roles of supervisors could be analyzed into two major categories: *orientations* and *on-going processes*.

First, it was determined that supervisors could adopt one or more of three orientations.

Evaluation

Assess existing components in order to identify strengths and weaknesses, and to undertake research into existing practices. A supervisor concerned with assessing the quality of a new curriculum guide would be manifesting an evaluation orientation.

Improvement

Undertake systematic action to strengthen and improve existing components. A supervisor involved in developing a new curriculum guide would be demonstrating an improvement function.

Maintenance

Carry out those activities designed to support existing structures, programs, and personnel. Thus, a supervisor chiefly concerned with ensuring that teachers are implementing an existing curriculum would be viewed on that occasion as having a maintenance orientation.

It should be noted that these three orientations might be seen as a recurring cycle of change: evaluate the existing component; take steps to improve, based upon that evaluation; maintain the new form of the component.

In much of the literature prescribing tasks and functions, the *maintain* orientation is identified with an "administrator/coordinator" role; the *evaluate* and *improve* is matched with a "supervisor/consultant" role (e.g., see Parramore, 1990). In reality, however, supervisors typically function as

both administrators and consultants, as Erb (1988) determined.

The on-going processes were those day-to-day activities used by the supervisor in order to carry out the assigned responsibilities. The following processes were identified in this manner: assigning and allocating; planning and organizing; communicating and conferring; coaching and modeling; motivating; observing; problem solving; and fostering the supervisor's own professional growth.

The resulting conceptual framework includes the three dimensions: foci, orientations, and on-going processes. It is hoped that the conceptual framework could be used both as a research tool that guides the design of studies of supervisory roles and as a resource for practice, enabling superintendents and supervisors to delineate the role expectations clearly. For illuminating issues of practice, the conceptual framework could be used either by generalists, who are expected to supervise teachers in several subject areas, and specialists, who are typically expected to work with teachers in a special subject area.

ROLES EXTERNAL TO THE SCHOOL DISTRICT

Three agencies external to the school district impact upon curriculum and instruction at the classroom level: state departments of education, educational service agencies, and institutions of higher education. State departments and their service agencies affect indirectly all classroom teachers, whereas institutions of higher education tend to impact chiefly upon student teachers and their cooperating teachers.

Before examining the roles and responsibilities of supervisors in state educational agencies, it would be useful to provide a context for those roles because professional assignments are determined primarily by agency functions and agendas.

The research on educational policy making at the state level indicates that states are generally becoming much more active and controlling, with the activity focusing on three functions: curriculum policy, assessment, and teaching (see Massell & Fuhrman, 1994, for a detailed review of initiatives in these three areas). As James (1991) notes, this increase in the exercise of state authority is one of the major changes in American education over the past decade, ironically coming about at a time when the rhetoric of reform emphasizes local control, school-based management, and teacher decision-making. The increased activity also comes at a time when many agencies are reporting reductions in staff size (Fuhrman, 1994).

Much of this increased activity at the state level involves the development of "curriculum frameworks," a term that is currently being used to describe a variety of curriculum documents. Curry and Temple (1992) identified two types of frameworks: "traditional frameworks," which in their terms are often rigid and prescriptive taxonomies of subject matter objectives, unrelated to other components of the educational system; and "progressive frameworks," which are less prescriptive, are more likely to emphasize themes and concepts, and underscore the linkages between curriculum, instruction, and assessment.

Whether traditional or progressive, the number of such state frameworks is increasing. A study by Blank and Dalkilic (1992) of state curriculum activity in science and mathematics concluded that 42 states at the time of the survey had mathematics frameworks, 30 had science frameworks, and another 14 were developing science frameworks. In 22 of the states with mathematics frameworks, the respondents indicated that the frameworks had a direct relationship to the state testing program, whereas 10 noted an indirect relationship. Massell and Fuhrman note that 15 states, as of late 1993, had already implemented curriculum frameworks, whereas 30 others were embarked on the development of such materials.

The impact of such frameworks on local districts seems to vary considerably. In their study of this issue in Florida, Michigan, and California, Cantlan, Rushcamp, and Freeman (1990) identified two distinct patterns of local district response to state mandates. Those districts whose response pattern was identified as "district autonomy/compromise" had sufficient resources and commitment to design their own curricula that focused on local needs and priorities. Supervisors in such districts maintained the integrity of the curricula that they had developed while making the minimal changes needed to conform with state guidelines. On the other hand, those districts whose pattern was identified as "district compliance/augmentation" implemented state curriculum policies, while at the same time augmenting those policies with locally developed curriculum initiatives.

Is increased state control of the curriculum desirable? The review by Cohen and Spillane (1992) concludes that such control results in greater consistency in the curriculum, which in turn seems associated with higher student achievement. The authors, however, point out several cautions in interpreting the evidence: most studies reveal only modest effects; most rely upon standardized achievement tests as the measure of student learning; and there are too many causal ambiguities. These cautions lead them to conclude that the research does not offer much support for efforts in the United States to increase curricular consistency.

These state frameworks are likely to be given serious attention by teachers when such guides are accompanied by state-mandated tests. A review of the factors influencing teacher planning indicated that state and districts tests were a significant determiner of teachers' planning decisions (Glatthorn, 1993). A six-state study by Porter, Smithson, and Osthoff (1994) of testing policies and practices in mathematics and science led to three conclusions: (1) testing is more commonly used as a policy instrument at the elementary than at the high-school level; (2) testing is more prevalent in mathematics than it is in science; and (3) states with a curriculum reform agenda had testing programs that were not congruent with that agenda. Although the conventional wisdom holds that most teachers resent the imposition of state testing policies, Porter and colleagues found that teachers in South Carolina, which had one of the most prescriptive policies with respect to testing, saw the state tests as a "necessary evil" (p. 154).

A similar increase in state activity has been noted in the area of teaching. Massell and Fuhrman note five domains of state activity: salaries and incentives, preservice education, inservice training, certification, and evaluation. Levels of activity in these five domains varied considerably, as their review concluded. Thirty states had set minimum salaries by 1986. Thirty-nine states had expanded certification requirements by 1990 to include assessment of basic skills and professional knowledge; however, only eight states reported funding staff development activities at the local district in 1990.

State activity in the assessment of teachers perhaps deserves a closer look. A study by Sclan and Darling-Hammond (1992) determined that 45 states and the District of Columbia have instituted systematic programs to evaluate beginning teachers. The authors note that most of those programs base the assessment of performance on the teacher's ability to perform certain prescribed "generic" skills, supposedly derived from the research on teacher effectiveness. They point out several limitations to such lists: they ignore the classroom context; they minimize the significance of the subject; they exclude others bodies of research (e.g., child development and student motivation); they result in a passive style of teaching; and they minimize teacher reflection and problem solving. In light of these limitations, four states—Georgia, Louisiana, Virginia, and Florida—have either dropped such programs or modified them substantially.

ROLES AND RESPONSIBILITIES OF STATE SUPERVISORS

Identifying the specific roles and responsibilities of state supervisors is difficult. As Lusi (1994) noted, there are no recent studies of activities of state departments of education; therefore, her description relies heavily on a dated 1967 study by Campbell, Sroufe, and Layton. A tentative delineation of those roles, however, can be accomplished by analyzing that context and reviewing the small body of literature that is available. It should be kept in mind that in understanding the results of such analyses, the specific duties of state staff would vary considerably, depending upon both the extent of state regulation and the particular office to which a staff member was assigned.

Given those caveats, those processes suggest that several responsibilities would be important for staffs of state departments of education now and in the near future.

Two of those responsibilities might be considered "conventional" because they seem to have been important in the past.

First, many state supervisors continue to assist local schools by providing supervisory services as requested. In doing so, their focus is on instruction, primarily, and their orientation is to improve (i.e., to use the concepts in the framework proposed here). Dowling and Yager's (1983) survey of state science supervisors determined that providing such local consultation was the primary activity of these subject specialists; however, they noted that their survey indicated that state science supervisors believed their roles were becoming more regulatory in nature and less supportive. In addition, Davis (personal communication, April 18, 1994) reported that the professional staff of the North Carolina Department of Public Instruction often works with individual schools in subject areas where local expertise is not available or serves the needs of special student populations.

Second, state supervisors continue to make on-site visits to coordinate the accreditation process and to monitor compliance with state regulations, thereby embodying a maintenance function that focuses primarily on curriculum. As Lusi (1994) notes, however, such functions seem to be less important now than they were in previous years: There are a small number of state staff personnel and a large number of teachers.

Four of those roles might be seen as "emerging" because the evidence suggests that they are becoming increasingly important during a period of reform and restructuring.

First, state supervisors are very involved in developing new testing programs and in assisting districts in administering such tests and interpreting the results. The focus is on curriculum, and the orientation is to evaluate. This function, obviously, would be primarily performed by staff assigned to the state testing office. Such staff typically have special expertise in test development. A 1992 survey by Blank and Dalkilic concluded that state activity in the area of science and mathematics testing was increasing markedly. Twenty-seven states required a science achievement test; 46 required a math achievement test; 5 needed a science competency test; 21 asked for a math competency test. Twenty states were developing alternative types of assessments in mathematics, and 16 were doing so in science.

Second, state staff seem more occupied in assisting groups who are developing curriculum frameworks. Once again the focus stayed on the curriculum, with an improvement orientation. As Curry and Temple (1992) pointed out, the development of such frameworks typically requires at least 2 years of work by a comprehensive committee of experts from across the state. It is assumed that state department staff would play an active role in nominating members of such committees, developing the knowledge base, organizing meetings, building consensus, and reporting and disseminating the results of the process. An example of the comprehensive involvement of several groups of educators is provided in the *South Carolina Visual and Performing Arts Framework* (South Carolina Department of Education, 1993). The writing team included 15 educators from universities and school systems who were assisted by an editor and a technical assistant. Seven of the state staff served as facilitators, and five university and school-based specialists served on the review panel.

There is also some evidence that, at a time when accountability is considered essential, states are assuming a more active role in providing targeted assistance to low-performing school systems. Such special assistance may take several forms: recommending consultants; providing training to district and school leaders; reviewing school improvement plans; assisting school administrators in interpreting and using test results. Fuhrman and Fry (1989) term such assistance "differential" aid because it is not provided equally to all schools across the state. When such assistance is provided, the foci probably include both curriculum and instruction, with an improvement orientation.

Finally, state supervisors are engaged to a greater extent than they were previously in monitoring the application of teacher appraisal systems and in developing alternative systems. As noted earlier, almost all states now have a mandatory teacher evaluation system in place. Such systems typically specify that districts submit detailed reports with respect to their use. In addition, several states are in the process of developing alternative systems that are less anchored in a particular model of teaching, give more attention to the use of measures other than classroom observation, and place more emphasis on teacher growth and less on accountability (e.g., see Stiggins & Duke's 1988 recommendation of a three-track evaluation system). This continuing interest in teacher appraisal is most often expressed by state supervisors assigned to personnel offices. Such staff would typically provide a regulatory function by reviewing reports from local districts and a supportive one by conducting training workshops on the development of alternative systems. The focus here is on instruction, with an evaluation orientation.

THE IMPACT OF STATE REFORM ON DISTRICTS, SCHOOLS, AND TEACHERS

The evidence suggests that these state initiatives, however delivered, have had a moderate impact at the local level. Porter, Smithson, and Osthoff (1994) concluded their study of 18 high schools in six states by noting that state activity in curriculum development and testing had increased the number of students taking mathematics and science courses, enrollments in remedial courses focused on state tests, and the number of students taking college preparatory science and mathematics. Schools had responded by counseling students into taking an academic curriculum and in developing magnet schools.

How have teachers responded to state control of curriculum and testing? Earlier studies concluded that state mandates in the areas of curriculum and testing undermine the professional autonomy of teachers and lower teacher morale (e.g., see McNeil, 1986.) Later studies, however, indicated that the teachers surveyed did not report that state initiatives reduced their autonomy. Porter, Smithson, and Osthoff (1994) concluded that the science and mathematics teachers in their study found state regulations appropriate and with positive effects. Archbald and Porter's study (1994) of high school mathematics and social studies teachers indicated that the teachers reported high degrees of personal control over content and pedagogy, even in states and districts characterized as having high levels of control in curriculum and testing. They also reported finding little evidence that teachers feel less efficacious because of the constraints of state and district policies in curriculum and testing.

Educational Service Agencies

The second external organization impacting on teacher development is the Educational Service Agency (ESA), a unit that functions organizationally between the state and the local school district. These agencies are given several different names; a study by Stephens and Turner (1991) identified such designations as education service cooperative, boards of cooperative services, regional educational service center, educational improvement center, intermediate school district, county office of education, intermediate unit, and cooperative education service agency. The term used by Stephens and Turner, *educational service agency*, is the one used in the following discussion.

These educational service agencies can be classified into three types, using a typology developed by Stephens and Turner. The special district ESA is a legally constituted unit of school government between the state and the local district. The special district ESA tends to be highly structured by legislation or state education agency regulations and have lay control. It also tends to have its programs determined by member districts and the state, and it receives fiscal support from local, regional, state, and federal sources. The regionalized ESA is a regional branch of the state education agency. It tends to be structured by state regulations only, have a professional advisory board, offer services determined almost exclusively by the state, and be funded chiefly by state and federal funds. The final type, cooperative ESA, is a loose consortium of local districts. It is structured by intergovernmental regulations or statutes and is composed of representative member local districts. It is focused on an agenda that is determined almost exclusively by member districts, and it is funded by local and state funds, supplemented by some federal funds. As of 1990, the time of the Stephens–Turner study, 23 states had some type of ESA.

Functions, Services, and Delivery Modes of ESAs The role of the professional staff of such agencies is affected by the functions those agencies perform. Stephens and Turner identify five current functions: improve the educational opportunities of schools in the state, with a special concern for rural schools; improve equality of education in regions of the state, with services to the handicapped given special attention; improve the quality of education in the schools of the state; promote cooperation among schools of the state; and provide services desired by the local schools. It might be inferred from such a list that the foci include curriculum and instruction, and that the orientation is to improve.

To accomplish these purposes the ESAs typically provide five kinds of programmatic services: direct instructional services to students; instructional support services to staff of Local Education Agencies (LEAs); management services to LEAs; services to state agencies; and services to nonpublic schools. Stephens and Turner predict that there will be an expansion of ESA activity in each type of service in the coming years.

These services are typically provided in one or more delivery modes, according to an earlier study by Firestone, Rossman, and Wilson (1983a): long-term project assistance; training workshops; brief interactions over the telephone or face-to-face; and visits to resource centers. The Firestone, Rossman, and Wilson study concluded that one of the factors promoting the use of such services was the extent of congruence between the way that LEA administrators wanted ESA field agents to act and the way these agents actually carried out their roles. Administrators surveyed in this study expressed a preference for field agents who possessed the following characteristics: a high level of professional expertise; effective interpersonal skills; responsiveness to the district's unique needs; accessibility; and timeliness of nondirective assistance. As Firth and Eiken (1982) noted, these agents include generalists, subject specialists, grade level specialists, coordinators of special programs, and consultants for innovative projects.

Relationship of ESAs with State and Local Systems Although there is great variation from state to state with respect to the operations of these agencies, some understanding of how they serve to connect the state agency with local school systems can be gained through a closer examination of how they were operating in North Carolina at the time this chapter was written. (This noting of the time factor is important because these North Carolina centers were undergoing a comprehensive review with respect to their functions.) The North Carolina designation for these agencies is technical assistance centers (or TACs, which they are usually called).

In the view of the state superintendent of education, the primary function of such centers in North Carolina is to work directly with local school districts to improve student achievement, noting that staff development is not an essential component of such direct assistance (Nelson, 1993). The individual at the state level who is directly responsible for coordinating the activities of the TACs is Nancy Davis, executive director for staff development and technical assistance centers. Davis also sees the chief function of the TACs as working directly with school systems to improve student achievement, chiefly through providing staff development and technical assistance (personal communication, April 18, 1994). In her view the TACs are concerned primarily with providing service, not checking on compliance.

Davis meets twice monthly with the directors of the state's five centers to keep them informed about current developments at the state level (especially the development of legislation affecting education), help them identify concerns, and facilitate the sharing of ideas. In addition to these group sessions, Davis confers frequently with individual directors.

Because the staff at the local centers are now considered generalists, Davis noted that state department subject specialists often render direct service to individual schools.

What happens at the regional centers in North Carolina? While there is variation across the state, the operations of the Northeast Technical Assistance Center (NETAC) can provide some general insight, although this center seems to be one of the most active in the state. The director of NETAC is Jeanne Meiggs, whose center serves 20 school systems and 194 schools within those county systems. Meiggs has 16 professionals on her staff who are considered generalists. She meets monthly with the 20 superintendents to communicate information from the state, inform them of center activities, discuss common problems, and receive their input with respect to services needed (personal communication, March 21, 1994). She also elicits their concerns, which are then passed on to Davis in Raleigh. From Meiggs' perspective, the primary mission of the center is to provide service to all the districts in the region, although the state department has directed her to pay special attention to low-performing systems. In addition to this central service function, Meiggs identified three other major responsibilities for the center: to provide current information to districts and schools on research and exemplary practice; to facilitate communication between the state office and district offices; and to provide some regulatory monitoring with respect to such programs as Chapter 1 and vocational education.

One of the 16 professionals on her staff is Billy Revels, whose title is "instructional specialist." Revels, who has worked at the center for 20 years, is specifically assigned to work with two school systems, although any of the systems served by the center may call upon his services (personal communication, March 14, 1994). Although his primary contacts are with central office professionals (e.g., assistant superintendent for instruction, director of instruction, and supervisor) and with school principals, he occasionally provides workshops for classroom teachers. His performance appraisal report lists his primary responsibilities as: to assist the local district in developing and implementing its school improvement plans; to evaluate such plans; to serve as liaison with the local district and the TAC; to coordinate programmatic support services; to assist in identifying and analyzing district problems; to collaborate with other consultants; and to plan and organize activities.

Effectiveness of ESAs How effective are such centers? Few seem to have been subjected to a rigorous evaluation. Two studies, however, do shed some light on this question. An earlier survey of school systems in New Jersey and Pennsylvania by Firestone, Rossman, and Wilson (1983b) reached several conclusions with respect to how administrators viewed these agencies. They appreciated receiving services in three broad areas: curriculum and instruction, school management, and coping with the external environment (e.g., state and federal agencies). They believed that such assistance is constructively provided when the relationship of the ESA with their systems is characterized by mutual knowledge and trust, working intimacy, ease of access, and on-target assistance. They also noted that the characteristics of ESA staff made a difference in relation to the use of agency services. The following staff characteristics made an important difference: content expertise, "school savvy," interpersonal skill, and a responsive attitude.

A more recent study evaluating the staff development programs of a North Carolina agency, reported in Nelson's (1993) doctoral dissertation, reached several conclusions. First, several groups of stakeholders (including classroom teachers) perceived the staff development activities as effective; however, stakeholders were uneven in their understanding of the mission of the center, and the communication between the center and the local education agencies was not perceived as completely coherent and reciprocal. In addition, teachers and administrators reported that they did not have appropriate involvement in the staff development planning process. Nelson's study also determined that the talent and enthusiasm of the center's consultants were perceived as allowing them

to overcome resource and structural constraints. Nelson concluded that the ESA can be an effective means of conceptualizing and implementing planned change across school districts.

Some understanding of the factors that interfere with the effectiveness of these agencies is provided by Firth and Eiken's (1982) analysis of their limitations: Relationships among supervisory personnel at the several levels are not clearly specified; state supervisors often bypass service agency personnel and work directly with classroom teachers; service agency staff often bypass district supervisors in the same manner; and it is more difficult for service agency personnel to establish the critical personal relationships with classroom teachers from many school systems.

Impact of ESAs on Classroom Teachers As implied in the preceding discussion, the ESA serves as the primarily linch-pin between the state agency and the local school district. As such its major clients seem to be district and school administrators, impacting on classroom teachers primarily through staff development workshops. There is some evidence, however, that the impact of ESAs on classroom teachers is minimal at best. The study by Firestone, Rossman, and Wilson (1983a) determined that classroom teachers had little direct contact with ESA staff. For 1 year, the median number of contacts was: through long-term projects, 0; through workshops, 1; by telephone, 1; in face-to-face interactions, 3; through the use of the ESA resource center, 0.

As school systems make increasing use of school-based management models, it is quite likely that classroom teachers will experience more direct contact with service agency staff in the near future. Young (1989) predicts that such increased contact with local schools on the part of the service agency will be primarily in the areas of instructional services, data processing, consultation, and staff development.

Institutions of Higher Education

For decades the standard model of university faculty/classroom teacher relationships was what Goodlad (1994) called a "one-way street," in which teachers and administrators flocked to universities for advanced degrees. The only exception to that one-way flow was made by a university supervisor making occasional visits to supervise student teachers. As a consequence, the standard image of institutions of higher education held by many practitioners was that of an aloof, remote, and irrelevant organization that welcomed educators only as a source of income and schools only as a convenient site for student teaching.

The model and the image seem to be changing. As Goodlad noted, the large number of teachers already holding a master's degree and the increase in school-based staff development both presage a continuing decline in the number of teachers and administrators undertaking graduate work and those involved in university-sponsored staff development.

It is more important to note that the significant interest in new forms of collaboration between universities and schools is gradually changing that negative image of the university.

While that collaboration takes many forms, most seem to create new relationships between university faculty and classroom teachers that are based upon a mutual respect for the viewpoints and contributions of both scholars and practitioners. The governance of the new collaboratives, such as the numerous "professional practice schools," reflect that mutuality: University faculty and school representatives have an equal voice in determining policy and making key decisions. (See Levine, 1992 for a useful review of the forms and functions of such collaboratives.) In some collaboratives, university faculty provide both remedial and advanced instruction to secondary students. In many collaboratives, university faculty and classroom teachers function as equal partners in joint efforts to improve the organization, both the school and the university. Cooperating teachers and university faculty function as equal members of instructional teams of both methods courses and student teaching seminars. Cooperating teachers in many instances have assumed primary responsibility for supervising the student teachers assigned to them (e.g., see University of North Carolina Model Clinical Teaching Network, 1992.)

Despite those major changes, the chief avenue by which university faculty and classroom teachers interact is the student teaching experience, and it is that aspect that will be examined in the rest of this section.

Overview of Roles and Relationships

Although most experts in the field of student teaching tend to speak only of the "triad" (i.e., the university supervisor, the cooperating teacher, and the student teacher), a careful analysis of the student teaching experience suggests a much more complex picture. The following description draws primarily from four sources (Diamonti & Diamonti, 1975; Feiman-Nemser & Buchmann, 1987; Guyton & McIntyre, 1990; Zahorik, 1988).

First, the university supervisor is influenced by those holding two other roles (i.e., university administrators and other faculty members). As Glatthorn and Coble (1995) note, the dean of the school of education can play an effective leadership role in improving the status of university supervisors, providing them with the resources they need, and ensuring that the hidden curriculum of the school of education supports the goals and purposes of student teaching. The duties of the administrator of field experiences, as enumerated by Guyton and McIntyre (1990), suggest several ways in which this administrator influences the university supervisor, as well as the cooperating teacher and the student teacher. These are: prepare the student teaching budget; select, orient, and provide in-service for the supervisors and the cooperating teachers; determine eligibility of and place student teachers; maintain records and prepare reports; handle public relations; set up seminars; make final decisions regarding student teachers. As Diamonti and Diamonti (1975) concluded, instructors of methods courses expect the supervisor to provide a link between theory and practice.

The cooperating teacher is similarly a member of a complex role set. The cooperating teacher is influenced in three ways by his or her peers: They influence what the teacher

decides to teach; they have an indirect influence on the methods the teacher uses; and they establish and reinforce norms about peer interactions and professional development (see Glatthorn's 1990 review of the research here). The school principal often has both a direct and an indirect influence on the cooperating teacher and the student teacher. The direct influence comes about when the principal plays a key role in the placement of the student teacher, supervises and evaluates the cooperating teacher, assists in the orientation of the student teacher, and provides evaluative feedback on the performance of the university supervisor. The principal exerts a powerful indirect influence as he or she exercises a leadership role in establishing and maintaining a supportive environment for teaching and learning.

If student teaching is to become a valid component of teacher education, then the cooperating teacher must go beyond these predictable roles, as Feiman-Nemser and Buchmann (1987) argue. They challenge the cooperating teacher to carry out the following functions: Talk aloud about what they do in making decisions about their own teaching, demonstrate how to extend the thinking of elementary or secondary students, alert student teachers to interpret signs of understanding or confusion in their students, and stimulate student teachers to talk about their teaching-related decisions and questions.

Finally, the student teacher similarly has certain predictable and nonstandard roles. The predictable ones include becoming oriented to the school, becoming informed about the students, learning the norms and expectations of the cooperating teacher, observing the cooperating teacher and other teachers, planning units and lessons in conjunction with the cooperating teacher, conducting minilessons and full lessons, and participating in student teaching seminars.

The student teacher, however, is much more than a submissive apprentice, imitating the cooperating teacher. First, there are clearly demarcated stages for the student teacher as he or she moves from an observer to an autonomous teacher. While several researchers have formulated these stages quite differently, the conceptualization offered by Sacks and Harrington (1982) seems most useful. They identify these six stages: anticipation, entry, orientation, trial and error, integration/consolidation, and mastery. As the student teacher moves through these stages (however delineated), there seems to be a clearly discernible movement from the student's perception of the professional self as an unsure apprentice to that of a confident teacher. Calderhead (1987) characterizes the final phase of student teacher development as an opportunity to experiment, when the student teacher discovers his or her own style of teaching.

Also, several teacher education programs are attempting to broaden the role to include that of teacher-researcher. Several reports note success in carrying out projects that involve the student teacher as a collaborator in action research (e.g., see, Cochran-Smith & Lytle, 1993; Kull, Oja, & Ellis, 1991).

In understanding the problems inherent in these complex relationships, it seems most useful to examine the root causes and the negative consequences, rather than simply to tick off a random list of difficulties. The root causes of the numerous problems cited in the literature can be categorized into five groups: organizational, structural, interpersonal, professional, and practical.

The organizational cause inheres in the obvious fact that neither the university nor the school system perceives the development of student teachers as one of its high-priority responsibilities. Thus, administrators of both institutions provide few resources and weak leadership, with a range of problems resulting. Diamonti and Diamonti (1975) argued from an organizational perspective that the problems themselves serve three organizational purposes. First, they serve as a form of conflict management, because the supervisor can use them as excuses for not being able to do a better job. Second, they serve the university because they keep the supervisors so busy that they are unable to critically analyze the situation and raise embarrassing questions. Finally, they serve the schools by keeping them from having to deal with pressures from the outside to change and reform.

There are two structural causes: the instability of the triad and role ambiguity. As Yee (1968) noted in an early analysis, groups of three are inherently unstable. Experts in group relationships observe that almost every three-person group breaks down into a "two against one" situation. In the case of the student teaching triad, the cooperating teacher and the student teacher typically see themselves as allied against the supervisor, with the student teacher perceiving the cooperating teacher as the more influential source of expertise (American Association of Colleges for Teacher Education, 1991).

Role ambiguity is a major factor complicating the triad's relationships. As noted earlier, the three roles are often undefined; and each incumbent brings to his or her role a unique conceptualization. The result is general confusion, especially as the issue focuses on the responsibilities of the university supervisor and the cooperating teacher. In a survey of close to 400 university supervisors, cooperating teachers, and student teachers, Bain (1991) concluded that there were significant differences in perceptions of primary responsibility for implementing supervisory functions. In five areas the university supervisors and cooperating teachers were in agreement, whereas student teachers reported a different perspective: observing the student teacher routinely and reacting to teaching; tying theory to practice; encouraging the student teacher to attempt various styles and strategies; helping the student teacher to understand how students learn; helping the student teacher to think about effective instruction. In each of these five, the student teachers were inclined to give the cooperating teacher the dominant role. (For further evidence of role ambiguity, see Grimmett & Ratzlaff, 1986; Richardson-Koehler, 1988.)

The interpersonal causes are the personal elements built into any complex set of relationships. Two issues need special note here. To begin, the supervisor, cooperating teacher, and student teacher often differ in their belief systems, especially with respect to their conceptualizations of teacher effectiveness, their understanding of their own and each other's roles, and their expectations for the student teaching experience. Those conflicting belief systems exacerbate the power struggle, the other interpersonal factor at work here. The university supervisor and the cooperating teacher often become involved in a subtle power struggle over who knows more about teaching, who will be the final authority about issues of teaching and learning, and who will be the chief determiner of the student teacher's professional fate. In Barrow's (1976) view, the relationship is an unbalanced one, with the cooperating teacher exercising inordinate control.

The professional causes at work involve the selection and training of both cooperating teachers and supervisors. Cooperating teachers are typically selected by the school principal from among the teachers who are willing to accept the responsibility. Many of these volunteers, Grossman (1992) observes, see the assignment of a student teacher as an "on-site sabbatical" that will free them from the demands of the classroom for a few weeks. University supervisors are often selected from the ranks of doctoral students, whose primary concern is the completion of their doctoral program, not the supervision of student teachers. Despite the obvious need for developing the special skills of supervising student teachers, neither the cooperating teachers nor the university supervisors are provided with systematic training. The teacher education program may provide one orientation session for cooperating teachers and one brief workshop for its supervisors, but only a few exemplary programs seem to take the training task seriously (see Boydell, 1986; Richardson-Koehler, 1988).

Finally, the practical cause of lack of time often makes the experience a frustrating one for all three members. The university supervisor is usually a doctoral student faced with the consuming demands of course work and dissertation, the student teacher spends a full day at the school and then returns to campus for courses and seminars, and the cooperating teacher still has classes to prepare and teach. Many of the teachers whom Johnson (1990) studied indicated that the inordinate time demands of supervising student teachers was the main reason they were reluctant to volunteer.

All those causes give rise to an array of negative consequences that prevent student teaching from fully achieving its potential as a growth experience. One useful means of examining those consequences is to analyze them in relation to the standard components of clinical supervision: pre-observation conference, observation, analysis, and debriefing.

While some experts in the field debate the value of the preobservation conference for supervising experienced teachers, there is general agreement that this conference has value for the student teacher, primarily to develop planning skills and ensure that the lesson to be taught is well organized (e.g., see Acheson & Gall, 1987). Two major problems develop here. First, the supervisor and the cooperating teacher hold differing views about the nature and value of such plans. They also often communicate these varied perspectives in separate conferences with the student teacher, who then feels conflicted about the plans that should be made. While most supervisors believe in the importance of detailed daily lesson plans that focus on learning objectives, experienced teachers give greater importance to unit plans and tend not to use a rational process that focuses on objectives. Many teachers make only brief notes to themselves for their daily planning, relying instead on mental scripts for the lesson to be taught. (For a review of the research on teacher planning, see Glatthorn, 1993.)

To be effective, observations should be systematic, regular, and frequent. In another work (Glatthorn, 1990), this author recommends that the supervisor implement several cycles of observation in which diagnostic observations, which scan the classroom broadly, alternate with focused observations, which use a narrow lens to examine specific aspects of teaching. The research on the observation practices of both supervisors and cooperating teachers indicate that they often observe without a systematic plan. Lemma (1993) determined that the cooperating teachers' observations declined after the first 3 weeks of the student teaching experience.

The analytic process may be the most important because it is here that the supervisor attempts to assess the learning that occurred, identifies the factors that both facilitated and inhibited that learning, assesses the student teacher's proximal zone of professional development, and makes tentative plans for a debriefing conference that will foster reflection. The evidence suggests that neither the university supervisor nor the cooperating teacher brings to bear such a sophisticated analysis, focusing instead on a small number of "effective teaching skills" to identify several "good points" and perhaps one or two "areas for improvement." In this sense they embrace an orientation that Zeichner and Tabachnick (1982) identify as "technical-instrumental," a point of view that focuses on the techniques of teaching.

The conference that results from such a superficial analysis is predictable. The supervisor dominates the talk, giving advice, praising, and sharing personal anecdotes. Seven of the 10 supervisors studied by Zahorik (1988) used such an approach in the conference, a style that he identifies as an active style emphasizing prescribing and interpreting. The active style results in a conference dominated by the university supervisor or the cooperating teacher. O'Neal and Edwards (1983) found in their study of cooperating teacher–student teacher conferences that the cooperating teacher did 72 percent of the talking—talk that focused on the methods and materials of instruction.

Despite the difficulties that beset the student teaching experience and the consequent reservations of some critics about the overall value of student teaching, evidence provides support for its continuation. Seventy-seven percent of university supervisors and 70 percent of the cooperating teachers surveyed agreed that student teaching prepares students more than adequately for their first full-time assignment (American Association of Colleges of Teacher Education, 1991).

Whether student teaching will persist in its present form is another issue. The growth of professional practice schools (or professional development schools) will undoubtedly increase the influence of the field-based faculty. Grossman (1992) reports that the "site supervisor," as they are called in schools cooperating with the University of Washington/Seattle, meets weekly with all student teachers, orients them to the program, and observes and evaluates them. No use is made of university supervisors.

Roles Within School Districts

Within the school district, a network of significant actors exercises both an indirect and a direct influence on classroom teachers. The superintendent and the assistant superintendent (or associate superintendent) exert a powerful indirect influence on classroom teachers as they function in positions of line authority with respect to the school board, whom they serve, and the principals, whom they supervise. In addition, administrators of special programs or areas, such as the director of finance and the director of personnel, have a direct impact on the professionals and programs whom they supervise. Finally, an array of instructional supervisors (designated with various titles) have both a direct and an indirect influence on classroom teachers. Because of the complexity and importance of the roles of this last group of central office staff, the following discussion focuses on their functions and effects.

Before turning to the research on the roles and effectiveness of these individuals, it should be noted that the literature review is complicated by the fact that many of the research reports speak of "supervisory services" without specifying whether such services were provided by a central office supervisor, a principal, or a department chair. For example, the Cawelti and Reavis (1980) study of administrators and teachers from sixteen school systems determined that only 25 percent of the teachers rated "supervisory services" as high, without specifying the source of such services. In resolving such ambiguity, each source was read carefully to determine if it included any terms (e.g., *district, school,* or *principal*) that would suggest the primary location of the supervisor. It was assumed that the term *supervisor* (and its derivatives) denoted "central office supervisors," but only if the article implied a district basis and if some other role, such as principal or department chair, was not specifically identified.

Titles and Definitions

These individuals hold a variety of titles, such as central office staff, curriculum coordinator, secondary supervisor, elementary instructional coordinator, and supervisor of reading and language arts. Parramore (1990) offers a generic term: Central Office Curriculum and Instruction Professionals. As she uses the term, it includes all the staff members in the superintendent's office who have responsibilities in the areas of curriculum and supervision of instruction. The definition thus emphasizes both location (i.e., in the superintendent's office) and areas of responsibility (i.e., curriculum and supervision of instruction). The following discussion accepts the Parramore definition, but it simplifies the term by identifying such individuals as *central office supervisors.*

The District Context

In order to understand the roles and functions of these supervisors, it would be helpful to examine the district context in which they serve. Although the district context was ignored for many years as researchers and practitioners emphasized the school as the locus of improvement, scholars have begun analyzing the nature of effective school districts. One of the most useful of such analyses is that offered by

Wimpelberg (1987), whose first "proposition" of central office leadership states the case rather forcefully:

Instruction in most schools is not likely to improve unless a leadership consciousness at the district level develops in such a way as to forge linkages between schools and central office, among schools, and among teachers within schools (p. 106).

Such a consciousness, he notes, is forged through an exchange process in which central office and school administrators both challenge and support each other.

The means by which district administrators and supervisors accomplish this role of instructional leadership are several, as the following summary indicates.

1. District leaders provide a foundation for excellence: They work to establish a culture and climate of excellence and communicate values, norms, expectations, and goals supporting excellence.
2. District leaders support the development of principal leadership through high-quality programs of selection, evaluation, and professional development.
3. District leaders develop coherent, clear, and systematic plans for school-based management that reflect the schools' need for autonomy and encourage school-based problem solving, while respecting the district's need for coordination and standardization.
4. District leaders provide effective programs for the selection, assignment, evaluation, development, and reward of effective teachers.
5. District leaders create and maintain positive relationships with the communities they serve, developing a supportive environment, encouraging collaborative relationships, and buffering the schools from undue turbulence.
6. District leaders develop and implement systems of program and student evaluation that provide for authentic assessment of learning; they use the results of such assessments in identifying emerging problems and planning for school improvement.
7. District leaders establish, maintain, and use effectively open channels of communication—with the community, the school board, school administrators, and teachers.
8. District leaders enable the development of high quality curricula that ensure effective coordination and articulation throughout the district, while respecting the schools' need for a measure of curricular autonomy.
9. District leaders work with the school board to provide adequate resources and allocate those resources in an equitable manner and in response to demonstrated need. (Cuban, 1984; McLaughlin, 1992; Miller, Smey-Richman, & Woods-Houston, 1987; Purkey & Smith, 1985; Schlechty, 1985; Wimpelberg, 1987.)

In exercising these functions, McLaughlin (1992) notes that district leaders work to establish a district-level professional community that is fragile and difficult to achieve, but instrumental in developing an overarching sense of inclusion, influence, and pride. The central office supervisors can obviously play a vital role in the performance of all these functions.

Roles and Responsibilities

In his seminal work, Pajak (1989) uses such terms as *puzzling, fragmented,* and *defying interpretation* to characterize the roles and responsibilities of central office supervisors. He also warns that an unduly restrictive definition of the role may limit the effectiveness of supervisors in interpreting and giving meaning to the complex reality of schools.

Neither textbook authors nor researchers in the field have heeded that warning. First, several authors of texts in supervision have stipulated their lists of tasks and responsibilities, often without providing a rationale for their conceptualization. The earliest such attempt may have been the formulation presented by Burton in 1922, which identified five general roles: the improvement of the teaching act; the improvement of teachers in service; the selection and organization of subject matter; testing and measuring; and the rating of teachers.

More recently, one of the most influential analyses to appear in supervisory texts was that presented by Harris in the 1975 edition of his text, whose model, as Sullivan (1982) indicated, was at the time a "widely accepted . . . model of supervisory work" (p. 450). Harris identified these 10 tasks of supervision: developing curriculum, organizing for instruction, providing staff, providing facilities, providing materials, arranging for in-service education, orienting staff members, relating special pupil services, developing public relations, and evaluating instruction. The list seems to be a useful collection of needed tasks, but Harris did not indicate how it was derived and cited specific references for only 3 of the 10 tasks.

In the current period five major studies have gone beyond simply prescribing supervisory tasks. Sullivan (1982) used Mintzberg's (1973) classic analysis of managerial tasks to analyze supervisory activities. In the Mintzberg formulation, three categories of managerial work subsumed 10 roles:

INTERPERSONAL: Figurehead; Leader; Liaison
INFORMATIONAL: Monitor; Disseminator; Spokesperson
DECISIONAL: Entrepreneur; Disturbance Handler; Resource Allocator; Negotiator

Sullivan determined that there were high concentrations of supervisory activities in three categories: resource allocator, monitor, and disseminator.

Hall, Putman, and Hord (1985) used interviews and observations of central office supervisors in nine states, focusing on their role in the change process. They concluded that central office personnel held both line (i.e., responsible for evaluating subordinates) and staff (i.e., responsible for evaluating programs, not people) positions, noting that this distinction affected how teachers perceived them: Line persons were rarely seen in the schools, whereas many teachers noted that staff supervisors were there in the schools when needed. They also determined that those with line positions had substantially more power than did those in staff roles. The district personnel whom they studied had only vague notions of their specific responsibilities, unless the superintendent expressly stipulated their functions; similarly, teachers were unclear about the responsibilities of central office personnel. The study also determined that those holding staff positions in the central office performed a variety of functions, such as providing materials and ideas, providing staff development, visiting classrooms, meeting with department heads, meeting with other staff personnel, scoring tests, developing curriculum, monitoring and evaluating curricula, adopting textbooks, and planning.

Pajak's (1990) 12 "dimensions of supervisory practice" is perhaps the most extensive study of the roles of central office supervisors. He and his doctoral students reviewed 300 research documents and 18 supervision textbooks, listing knowledge, attitudes, and skills cited in at least two of the references. The results of this analysis were then collapsed into 12 categories: community relations, staff development, planning and change, communication, curriculum development and implementation, improving the instructional program, service to teachers, observing and conferencing, problem solving and decision-making, research and program evaluation, motivating and organizing, and personal development.

In her study of supervisors in the southeastern states, Parramore (1990) used a list of nine "functions or activities" that she indicated were derived from a review of the literature. The functions/activities she identified for purposes of her survey included coordinate curriculum development, lead staff development/in-service activities, develop/select textbooks and instructional materials, coordinate daily operations of instructional programs, visit/observe in classroom and confer with teacher, evaluate school program(s), manage routine administrative tasks, work directly with inexperienced teachers, and evaluate teachers for personnel decisions.

Finally, Snyder, Fitzgerald, and Giella (1992) have developed and validated a model that reconceptualizes the primary role of the supervisor as a manager of resources, rather than as a resource or helper. Their model identifies four major functions, each with specific job dimensions:

PLANNING (district and department goal setting; work organization; performance planning)
STAFF DEVELOPMENT (staff development design and training; clinical supervision design and training; work group and leader development)
PROGRAM DEVELOPMENT (designing and managing an instructional program; resource development and management)
ASSESSMENT (quality control; assessing achievement)

Both the lists proposed by textbook authors, based upon their conceptualizations of the role, and those by researchers, derived from an analysis of the literature, seem to have some major limitations. They do not focus on the critical elements important in learning. They do not distinguish between orientations that are substantially different, and they tend to mix ongoing processes (e.g., communicating) with the essential foci. It is hoped that the conceptual framework proposed at the beginning of this chapter overcomes these difficulties.

Despite these limitations the lists of tasks have been useful in guiding research studies on how supervisors spend their time. The results are strongly influenced by the researcher's conceptualization of the tasks. For that reason, the research yields mixed conclusions.

As noted earlier, in an observational study of central office supervisors Sullivan (1982) determined that there were high concentrations of activities in three of the Mintzberg managerial task areas: resource allocator (30 percent), monitor (19 percent), and disseminator (16 percent). Ninety-eight percent of the activities reported fell into one or more of the managerial areas. In analyzing the means by which these tasks were accomplished, the same study concluded that the major portion of the supervisor's time (61 percent) was spent in verbal communication. On the base of these data Sullivan concluded that the supervisor's major purpose is maintenance of the day-to-day operation of the school district.

The importance of the maintenance function was underscored in Richardson's (1987) study of Virginia instructional supervisors, who reported spending most of their time on routine maintenance functions, even though they wanted to spend more time on curriculum development and instructional leadership. Female supervisors reported spending more time on evaluation and improvement activities than did the males. A study by Erb (1988) of 46 central office supervisors in Pennsylvania suggested a greater emphasis on the improvement of instruction. More than half (i.e., 51.8 percent) of the work week was devoted to such improvement activities as observing and conferring with teachers, developing curriculum, conducting in-service programs, and conducting research.

The study of supervisors in 24 Maryland districts by Roberts and Newcombe (1984) revealed that these professionals had relatively large supervisory loads, and were responsible for supervising 94 teachers in seven schools. They reported spending 30.7 percent of their time in observing and assisting teachers, the most time-consuming of all their duties. In general the purpose of those observations was to make summative evaluations of the teacher's performance. Attending meetings was second in terms of time devoted, with 10.3 percent of their time devoted to this activity. Those studied also reported that administrative issues took time away from supervision.

The 95 supervisors from southeastern states whom Parramore (1990) studied reported that the following activities were most time-consuming (with rankings noted): (1) manage routine administrative tasks; (2) coordinate curriculum development; (3) coordinate daily operations of instructional programs; (4) lead staff development; (5) develop/select texts and other instructional materials. When asked to rate the same activities in relation to their importance, however, those surveyed reported a different ranking: (1) coordinate curriculum development; (2) lead staff development; (3) develop/select texts and other materials; (4) visit/observe in classroom and confer with teachers.

Using his "12 dimensions," Pajak (1990) surveyed 987 educational leaders in the United States and Canada who were reputed to be outstanding leaders. More than half of those surveyed strongly agreed that all the dimensions were important to supervisory practice. From the perspective of these leaders, the six most important dimensions, with the percentage strongly agreeing as to its importance noted in parentheses, were: communication (89 percent); staff development (88 percent); instructional program (86 percent); planning and change (83 percent); motivating and organizing (80 percent); and observation and conferencing (77 percent).

A case study by Fitzgerald that was reported in Snyder, Fitzgerald, and Gielia (1992) used categories derived from their conceptualization of supervision as management to determine that supervisors in a Florida district allocated their time as follows: resource management, 23 percent; work group development, 22 percent; staff development, 16 percent; program management, 15 percent; work organization, 13 percent; monitoring and evaluation, 3.3 percent; goal setting, 2.2 percent. "Performance planning" and "coaching/clinical supervision" were not observed.

While it is difficult to make precise comparisons across studies in which the conceptualization of the role varies so widely, the data from the studies cited would suggest that the chief foci are curriculum and instruction, the major orientation is a maintenance one, and the communication process is most frequently used.

Effectiveness of Central Office Supervisors

How effective are central office supervisors in their evaluation, maintenance, and improvement efforts? The available research on this issue presents a somewhat mixed picture: some studies underscore the value of central office supervisors, but others suggest that teachers do not generally hold a high regard for the services provided by central office supervisors.

Hall, Putman, and Hord (1985) determined that the district office personnel whom they studied were both the source and impetus of many of the innovations implemented in the district, even though they did not seem to be aware of the apparent differences in how they approached elementary schools as compared with secondary schools. The credibility accorded by classroom teachers to central office supervisors in this study was affected chiefly by three elements: their teaching assignment prior to joining the district office (i.e., high school teachers seemed to distrust supervisors with an elementary background), the length of time the supervisors had been away from the classroom, and teachers' perceptions of supervisor usefulness.

Some of the studies that emphasized the value of central office supervisors were intentionally biased by focusing on supervisors reputed to be successful. The most important of these, perhaps, is Pajak's (1989) in-depth study of 10 central office supervisors reputed to be successful practitioners. His study led him to conclude that effective central office supervisors reduced uncertainty with respect to the instructional program, provided stability and predictability, supported a district culture that valued continuing improvement, added to the store of knowledge, and facilitated "sense-making" on the part of administrators and teachers.

Floyd's (1987) study of four central office supervisors who had received rewards for outstanding service concluded that for these effective supervisors the fragmentation and ambiguity of the role were actually positive factors. Instead of being constrained by an overly prescriptive role definition or feeling handicapped by role ambiguity, these effective leaders capitalized upon the role ambiguity by interpreting their func-

tions broadly and flexibly. The flexibility required for effective performance, she concluded, stemmed from three factors: fragmented focus, paradoxical visibility, and authority ambiguity. Her study also concluded that cognitive complexity was a key factor in the effectiveness of central office supervisors.

Although the 81 teachers in Martin's (1990) study reported that they were more satisfied with their principal's supervision than they were with their supervisors', they did report increased pedagogical confidence when their supervisors took time to work with them and demonstrated a collegial relationship.

On the other hand there have been numerous studies over the past few decades that concluded that teachers hold a generally negative view of the supervision they receive. Several early studies underscored the negative feelings that teachers held about supervisors and supervision. Blumberg and Amidon (1965) found that most of the teachers in the Philadelphia area whom they surveyed found supervision to be a waste of time. Seventy percent of the teachers in Heishberger and Young's (1975) study perceived their supervisors as potentially dangerous. In his (1980) work Blumberg concluded that what occurs in the name of supervision is a waste of time, as teachers see it, and that the character of the relationships between supervisors and teachers can best be described as a "cold war" (p. 5).

More recent studies confirm these earlier negative findings. In a national survey that asked teachers to evaluate the effectiveness of varied sources of teaching knowledge and skill, only 31.5 percent rated "consultation with grade-level or subject-level specialists" as "definitely effective" and only 12.9 percent gave the same rating to "in-service training provided by your school district" (National Education Association, 1988). Only two sources were rated as "definitely effective" by more than half the respondents: 91.5 percent credited their own experience, and 52.2 percent pointed to consultation with other teachers.

From the standpoint of district supervisors, even more discouraging results were presented in a study comparing teacher attitudes in 1984 with those in 1964 (Kottkamp, Provenzo, & Cohn, 1986). Using the data collected in 1964 from Dade County (Florida) teachers for Lortie's (1975) study as a basis for comparison the researchers surveyed teachers from the same county in 1984, asking (among other questions) which indicators a good teacher is most likely to use in judging personal effectiveness. In 1964, 58.9 percent reported that "general observations of students" was the most influential; in 1984, this indicator was again rated highest, with 37.3 percent so indicating. On the other hand, only 2.9 percent of the 1964 group and 6.0 percent of the 1984 group indicated that they would rely on principal assessments; and 1.2 percent (1964) and 2.8 percent (1984) would rely upon assessments made by supervisors.

One of the few studies examining the influence of central office supervisors in the implementation of a new program was Grimmett's (1987) study of the role of district supervisors in the implementation of peer coaching in a school district in British Columbia. While the participants identified two supervisors and the director of instruction as the primary initiators and supporters of the project, almost all the participants held the district responsible for the lack of successful implementation in seven of the eight schools. Teachers in the one school where the project seemed to be implemented successfully credited the school principal's leadership and energy. Specific criticisms of district supervisors were offered by 24 of the 29 participants were lack of communication, lack of refresher and follow-up courses for teachers, nonavailability of resources and help from the resource person, and inadequate monitoring and field-based work by supervisors during the implementation stage.

Four groups of factors seem to make a difference in the functioning of central office supervisors: the district, the school, the supervisor, and the teacher.

Several district factors seem influential. First, as Alfonso (1986) points out, the culture of the district influences teacher behavior and can either facilitate or hinder supervisor effectiveness. If there is a district culture that values continuing improvement and collegiality, there is a greater likelihood that supervisors will perform accordingly. In addition, the leadership of the district makes a difference. As Hall and Guzman (1984) concluded, if the district leaders are active initiators and supporters of school improvement, then central office supervisors respond with the same proactive stance. The nature and clarity of the role also exercise a strong influence on performance. Although Floyd's study suggested that role ambiguity could be construed as a liberating force, Hall and Guzman note that central office supervisors emphasize the maintenance function because they are spread so thin. Grimmett (1987) concluded that one factor in the failure to implement the peer coaching program was the lack of clarity with respect to the responsibilities of the central office supervisor and those of the school principal.

The organizational status of the role is also a determiner. Supervisors are generally positioned in a "staff" relationship in the organizational structure, lacking the formal power of line authority. In the typical district, principals report to, and are accountable to, the superintendent, not to central office supervisors. As Hall, Putman, and Hord (1985) determined, the line/staff distinction very much influences how other professionals perceive central office supervisors. The physical location of the district office also makes a difference. Several studies indicate that teachers prefer to seek assistance from those near at hand, immediately accessible, who share their world (e.g., see Bird & Little, 1986). If the elementary teacher needs help with a scientific concept, he or she is more likely to turn to a colleague rather than to call a science supervisor sitting in a remote office.

Finally, the "loose coupling" of the district with the schools makes it difficult for district supervisors to affect change at the school level. As Weick (1976) first noted, school systems are not tightly linked bureaucracies in which orders from the top are carried out through all subordinate levels. The research instead presents a picture of individual classrooms that are loosely connected into a school network, and individual schools that operate with a high degree of autonomy. Weick's theory was confirmed in Deal and Celotti's (1980) study of the influence of district and school policies and practices on the individual classroom. In examining this issue with respect to whether teachers used indi-

vidualized instruction and team teaching, they concluded that open space architecture and a specially funded state reform effort were the influential factors, not district or school policies and procedures.

School factors are also influential. The core values of the school administrators and teachers can once again facilitate or constrain the work of central office supervisors. Principals who value openness, who recognize the worth of external sources of expertise, and who publicly affirm their positive views of district supervisors are obviously more likely to create an environment where central office supervisors are welcomed and used effectively. As Owens (1987) notes, the "clans" or cliques to which teachers belong can also exercise a very strong socializing force on members, establishing and enforcing norms of behavior. If clan leaders openly mock central office "snoopervisors," then it is highly unlikely that members will call upon the services of such individuals. Blumberg (1983) argues that schools are "weakly normed" systems where teachers are reluctant to put pressure upon each other to improve performance, tolerating a wide range of behavior among their colleagues.

In addition, the resources available at the school level would affect attitudes toward central office supervision. The faculty of a small elementary school staffed only by a principal and classroom teachers would clearly place more value on central office supervisors than would a faculty in a large high school with a capable cadre of department chairs.

The third group of influencing factors are those that involve the supervisor. The characteristics and skills of the supervisor are obviously critical factors in determining the way in which supervisory services are received. Two reviews of the research on the characteristics of effective supervisors suggest that the following attributes characterize effective supervisors (Glatthorn, 1990; Glickman & Bey, 1990).

1. The supervisor's power derives from his or her competence, not from the authority of the role.
2. The supervisor projects a sense of calmness and emotional detachment during times of stress.
3. The supervisor is perceived as a powerful advocate for the teacher, not as a subservient tool of administration.
4. The supervisor focuses on important issues involving the quality of instruction, not on the trivial and inconsequential.
5. The supervisor is authentic in providing a supportive relationship, demonstrates strong interpersonal skills, and projects a sense of caring and consideration.
6. The supervisor and the teacher share a common perception of the functions of supervision and use a common language in talking about teaching.
7. The supervisor uses a style of supervision that seems congruent with the teacher's needs and level of development.

The supervisor's work is also complicated by an inherent role conflict, as Blumberg (1980) noted. Many supervisors are expected to perform both a helping and an evaluating role, which are roles that resonate with built-in tensions. As he points out, teachers are concerned that expressing a need for help will be interpreted as a sign of weakness.

The final group of factors are the teacher-related factors. Blumberg (1980) noted several factors that complicate the work of supervisors. First, most teachers are protected by tenure laws, which assume competence; thus, there are few negative sanctions for failing to improve. Second, teachers enjoy autonomy in their classrooms. Even principals have difficulty in monitoring their performance or in requiring specific teaching behaviors. Another complicating factor is the isolated nature of the teacher's work. This isolation reduces the ability of supervisors to intervene even when such intervention seems necessary. The complexity of teaching also means that there is no one right way to teach; thus, advice from supervisors about how to teach is often suspect, especially if it is couched in absolute terms. Finally, Blumberg noted, defensiveness seems to occur in many helping relationships. Teachers assume that supervisors' suggestions imply a deficiency in their present way of teaching.

All of these factors taken together would suggest that the "cold war" is endemic to the nature of educational organizations and the special conditions of the supervisor–teacher relationship, and is not a result of personality flaws or skill deficits.

WITHIN THE SCHOOL

We will now review the research on supervision within the school, beginning by examining the school context as it influences supervision. We will then review the research on the supervisory services and functions as carried out by: the principal, the assistant principal, and teachers with special supervisory roles.

The School as a Special Context for Supervision

The difficulties of generalizing about supervisory services and relationships are made clear by understanding the complexity of the school as a setting for supervision. This section analyzes that context and the proximal factors that influence it, ignoring the distal influences of the state and the educational service agency for the purposes of this section.

Several groups of factors seem to make a difference in how supervisory services are delivered and used at the school level: external factors, the school culture, the structural elements, the instructional technology in use, and the staffing.

External Factors Three external elements seem to influence school-based supervision. First, as Peterson (1989) indicated, the configuration of the district has an impact: In districts with few schools and small central office staff, schools would be expected to play a more active role. In addition, the superintendent's leadership plays a role here. As McLaughlin (1992) emphasizes, strong district leadership can foster learning communities where teachers are committed to their professional development.

The collective bargaining agreements negotiated by teachers' unions are also perceived as external elements that have a constraining effect on supervision. In her review of the impact of collective bargaining on teacher evaluation,

Johnson (1987) noted that many contracts specify who will conduct the evaluation, how frequently they will be completed, and how many classroom observations are required. This is not to suggest, however, that unions necessarily play an adversarial role. Kerchner (1986) noted that union activism often results in a new social relationship between teachers and principals that is based upon reciprocity of influence more than on obedience to authority. He points out that most teachers, even the most militant union members, do not see any conflict between being a good teacher and an active union member.

School Culture The culture of the school will obviously play a key role in determining how teachers use school-based supervisory services. The following values would seem to support extensive and effective use of school-based services:

1. Better learning for all students is the central mission of the school, and better teaching is the central means by which that mission is accomplished.
2. Teaching is a complex science and art that is never fully mastered.
3. Improved teaching performance requires objective feedback from multiple sources.
4. Other professionals in the district and in the school can be trusted as sources of encouragement and feedback.

As Firestone and Wilson (1985) point out, principals can counter the negative effects of loose coupling by systematically modifying the culture so that it supports the use of supervisory services.

Structural elements As the term is used here, structural elements refer to the level of schooling, the size of the school, and the extent of school-based decision-making. While early researchers identified an image of instructional leadership that they believed applied uniformly to all schools, most experts in the field are now convinced that no single model will apply uniformly to elementary, middle, and high schools. Glatthorn and Newberg (1984) identify three factors that make leader-influence patterns in secondary schools different from elementary schools: There is less consensus among principals and teachers on school goals, the departmental structure of secondary schools reinforces the autonomy of the secondary subject teacher, and the secondary principal working with teachers who perceive themselves as subject matter specialists has less "expert power" than does the elementary counterpart, who guides the work of teachers who see themselves as child-centered generalists. As Peterson (1989) suggested, the size of the school is also an obvious influence: The principal who heads a faculty of 20 teachers can clearly have more direct influence than one who leads a faculty of 100.

One of the elements often cited in the literature is the degree of decision-making extended to the schools, supported by principals, and exercised by teachers. Although the principles of school-based management would suggest that schools involved in such projects would have a greater degree of autonomy with respect to how supervisory services

are utilized, research suggests otherwise. Weiss' (1992) longitudinal study of six high schools that had some form of
school-based decision-making and six that did not seems
typical here. Only three teachers out of 191 indicated that
teaching was a focus of school decisions, with no difference
between the two groups of schools. Weiss concluded that
adoption of school-based decision-making does not appear
to be related to a concentration on schoolwide issues of
teaching and learning. Firestone (1991) reached a similar
conclusion in his study of 11 urban high schools. Although
the teachers in his study were highly committed to jobs that
gave them autonomy and influence, they were not interested in issues of curriculum and instruction, choosing instead
to focus on student discipline and teaching schedules.
Bimber's (1993) review of the literature on school decentralization concluded that most school-based decision-making
programs gave authority to schools over only such marginal
items as safety, career education, and parent involvement.
Some support for giving teachers greater control over school-
based decisions is provided by Osterman's (1989) study,
which concluded that such distribution of control does not
necessarily decrease principal authority and that supervision
does not decrease teacher authority.

Instructional technology As the term is used here, instructional technology refers to the means by which the school
accomplishes its mission of student learning; in simpler
terms, it refers to the curriculum and instructional processes
in use. Scholars who study organizations contend that the
clarity and complexity of that technology influence how
administrators behave (e.g., see Hallinger & Murphy, 1987).
A higher degree of clarity is present when the school supports a specific approach to instruction, such as direct
instruction, and clearly delineates the curriculum objectives
that are to be mastered. Hallinger and Murphy argue that
closer supervision is possible in situations characterized by
high clarity and that it is more likely to have positive results;
on the other hand, they assert, when the technology is more
nebulous, highly directive supervisory behavior may be
counterproductive.

Staffing Finally, the composition of the teaching staff will
play a role in determining which supervisory style is most
likely to be well received by teachers. Hallinger and Murphy
noted several factors relating to staff composition that are
influential: age, years of experience, educational level, intelligence and conceptual level, and attitudes toward the organization. They hypothesize that as teaching staffs mature and
stabilize, principals will shift from more formal directive
supervisory approaches to more informal, indirect styles. In
addition, the leadership structure would be an obvious influence. As Peterson (1989) indicated, if team leaders and
department chairs are given released time to observe and
confer with teams and departments, then school-based
supervision is more likely to occur.

In a sense, then, when the question is asked, "What is
supervision like at the school level?" the only reasonable
response is, "Which school?"

An Overview of Supervisory Services at the School Level

Even though it is extremely difficult to predict the type of
services that will be provided in a particular school, a general
picture can be developed from the research. Before examining
individual roles, it would therefore seem useful to understand
this more global view. The references supporting this general
picture are cited in the individual sections that follow.

Most of the research would suggest the following general
set of relationships. First, in almost every school, there is a
principal who aspires or claims to be an instructional leader,
but who seems uncertain about how such a role is operationalized and is overwhelmed by the tasks of administering
the school. In larger schools, the principal is aided by an
assistant principal, who is typically assigned teacher-evaluation tasks, as well as "bad boys, books, and buses" (to use the
terminology of seasoned assistant principals). These assistant
administrators also have aspirations of leadership. In elementary and middle schools, teachers are typically organized into
grade level teams, whereas the subject department reigns
supreme in high schools. Both team leaders and department
chairs are expected to assist with supervision, but they are
saddled with too many additional tasks and not enough time.
Novice teachers may be assigned a mentor teacher to guide
them over the difficulties of the first 2 or 3 years. The experienced classroom teacher, surrounded by all this supervisory
help, turns to competent peers for advice and support.

As Hall and Guzman (1984) and Duffy (1985) both pointed out, these separate roles interact in very complex ways.
Understanding those interactions is crucial to gaining insight
into the change process in schools. In Hall and Guzman's
field studies of high school leadership patterns, they found
several different combinations of principals, assistant principals, department chairs, and central office supervisors providing effective instructional leadership. In their study of
Maryland school systems, Roberts and Newcombe (1984)
determined that the individuals holding these interlocking
roles differed markedly in their perceptions of the purpose,
philosophy, and process of supervision.

The Principal

In presenting a description of the principal as supervisor,
this section will review the research on the importance of the
principal's supervisory role, the foci for principal supervision
and the methods the principal uses to supervise, and teacher
attitudes toward the principal's supervisory efforts.

The Importance of the Supervisory Role In determining how
significant the supervisory role is perceived for principals, it
would first be useful to determine what priority principals
should give this function. Three sources can provide an
answer: the recommendations of experts; the beliefs of principals, and the perceptions of teachers. Experts in the field of
instructional leadership are uniform in suggesting that principals should play an active role as "instructional leaders." In
most of the literature, that role gives primary emphasis to the
supervision of the instructional staff (e.g., see Peterson, 1989;

Smith and Andrews, 1989; Weber, 1987). When principals are asked about how much time they should devote to instructional supervision, they typically respond that they should spend more time than they are actually spending. For example, the 203 principals surveyed in Osborne and Wiggins' (1989) study reported that they believed they should give "personnel" a second priority (out of nine task areas), while they actually give it fourth priority, behind program development, student behavior, and student activities. In their 2-year study of secondary schools, Little and Bird (1987) found that, in schools where classroom observation is valued, teachers expected administrators to make an observation at the beginning of a unit and then observe how the unit unfolds over several days. They note that teachers would consider it rude for the administrator to observe only once and then not observe for several months.

How important is supervision in the principal's actual performance of the role? The general answer derived from several studies is that such a function has a relatively low priority; principals seem to spend most of their time on management issues, generally observing each teacher twice a year.

Research studies that rely upon principal surveys underscore this general finding. The study of 716 high school principals by Pellicer et al (1988) concluded that these principals spent relatively more time on school management than they did any other task, devoting on the average about an hour a day on informal classroom observations. Similar findings were reported by Osborne and Wiggins (1989) in their study of secondary principals from Oklahoma. As had been determined in a similar 1977 study, school management was their highest priority in terms of tasks actually performed, with the broad field of "personnel" ranking fourth of nine functions. In reporting the number of formal observations each year, Anderson (1990) concluded that two-thirds of the K–12 principals in the Detroit metropolitan area spent the equivalent of two class periods supervising each teacher. The principals observed in the study by Roney et al (1990) spent about 34 percent of their total time on office management, 12 percent on school-system interaction, but only 4 percent on instructional management.

The findings of these studies, which relied chiefly upon surveys of principals, are confirmed in those assessing teacher perceptions. In the survey by the National Education Association (1988) of close to 1,800 members, slightly more than half (i.e., 54 percent) of these teachers reported that they speak to a building administrator only a few times a week. The same low level of contact was reported by Indiana vocational agriculture teachers: 38 percent reported that their principals observed them twice a year; 10 percent reported no observations (Martin, 1985). The researcher concludes that an "alarming number" of these teachers had limited formal contact time with school administrators regarding the supervision of instruction (p. 3). Most of the 115 teachers studied by Johnson (1990) reported that classroom observations by the principal were infrequent and largely symbolic. Harvey and Levin's (1984) survey of the perceptions of 644 Pennsylvania teachers with respect to supervision found that 48 percent reported being observed only once or twice during the year, and that these observations lasted from 11 to 30 minutes.

The picture is not uniformly bleak, however. Hallinger and Murphy's (1985) study of 10 elementary principals from a single school district found that these principals supervised and evaluated instruction more closely than previous studies had indicated. Teachers, supervisors, and the principals themselves reported that of 11 instructional management tasks, "supervising and evaluating instruction" was the function receiving the highest rating. The researchers note that this surprising finding may have resulted from the fact that the superintendent in this district had implemented a 4-year school improvement program that emphasized, among other elements, the active role of the principal as a supervisor.

The quality of leadership is also a factor in considering how important teachers view principal leadership. Smith and Andrews (1989) asked the teachers in their survey to rate their principals as either a strong, an average, or a weak leader; they then asked several questions about the principal's effectiveness as a communicator. When these teachers were asked if their principal provided frequent feedback to them regarding classroom performance, the results varied considerably, depending upon how strong the teachers perceived the principal to be: 68 percent of those with a strong leader indicated that their principals did provide such feedback; 29 percent of those who considered their leader as average so reported; and only 18 percent of those with a weak leader noted that they received frequent feedback about their teaching.

It seems reasonable to conclude that most principals do not give supervision a high priority, unless there is district pressure to do so or unless the principal seems to be an active leader of instruction. The research by Hurley (1990) is illuminating: He concluded from his interviews with 28 principals that both the superintendent and the teachers influenced the principal to devote more time to student discipline, whereas very few of the messages principals received from superintendents and teachers dealt with curriculum and personnel functions.

Methods and Foci of Principals' Supervision It would probably be assumed that principals performed most of their supervision by focusing on instructional strategies and using direct observation of teaching; however, the research suggests a more complex picture. First, as noted earlier, they do make classroom visits to observe teachers' instructional skills, typically observing teachers about twice a year. In most cases those observations are followed by a debriefing conference. Such observations and conferences often have a monitoring function: 59 percent of the principals in Anderson's 1990 study indicated that the purpose of their supervision was administrative, monitoring and accountability; only 22 percent reported that they used clinical supervision to improve instruction.

Experts in the field, however, have challenged principals to go beyond this somewhat narrow concern and to use other methods.

Several have suggested that principals would make a more lasting impact by changing the culture of the school. As Fullan (1992) argued, principals can make a more pervasive impact on their schools by developing collaborative cultures rather than by instituting several unrelated innovations. He encouraged principals to emphasize the following in working with teachers: vision building, norms of collegiality and continuous improvement, problem solving and conflict resolution strategies, and life-long teacher development. Sergiovanni (1992) made essentially the same point, but underscored the importance of grounding collegiality in a school that sees itself as a community, not as an organization. Firestone and Wilson (1985) believe that the principal can offset the disadvantages of loose coupling by strengthening the cultural linkages at the school level.

Several studies of the principalship also concluded that more attention needs to be given to the routine behaviors of principals as subtle but strong influences on the quality of instruction. The most useful formulation of the concept of *routine behaviors* is probably that provided by Bossert et al (1982). They identified goal setting and planning, monitoring, evaluating, communicating, scheduling, allocating resources, and organizing, staffing, modeling, governing, and filling in as the routine behaviors having an impact on the quality of instruction. Peterson (1989) identified the systematic use of such behaviors as *indirect leadership*, which facilitates leadership in others by providing supportive conditions for teaching and setting challenging standards. Lee's (1987) in-depth study of one principal over the course of a year reached a similar conclusion: This effective principal achieved her goal of better learning for all chiefly through her routine actions. As Lee puts it, "she used those /routine/ activities as opportunities to assess progress with respect to her goals and to further movement toward achieving her vision" (p. 91). Pfeifer's (1986) study of 85 elementary and secondary teachers concluded that, from their perspective, principals provided instructional leadership when they attend to the everyday realities of life in schools, protecting them from uncertainty and creating a supportive environment.

In general, the research cited earlier suggests that the principal's chief orientation is maintenance, the major focus is instruction, and the primary process is observing.

Teacher Attitudes toward Principal Supervision In general, teachers report negative attitudes toward their principals' supervision; however, several factors seem to affect how teachers view their principals as supervisors.

Several studies suggest that teachers do not generally place a high value on the supervision provided by their principals. In a study that compared the responses of Dade County teachers in 1964 with those responding to a similar survey in 1984, only 9.4 percent of the 1977 group and 3.6 percent of the 1984 cohort indicated that the school principal was the source from whom they received the most help with curriculum and methods (Kottkamp, Provenzo, & Cohn, 1986). The largest percentage of both groups reported that "other teachers in the school" were the chief source—36.6 percent of the 1964 group and 36.0 percent of the 1984 group. Only one third of the teachers in the NEA survey noted earlier reported that their principals gave them helpful suggestions. These teachers rated consultation with building administrators as among the least effective source of 14 possible sources of knowledge and skills. When the teachers in Poole's (1994) study were asked about whom they sought out for advice on

instructional matters, they always mentioned the teachers whom they respected first; only a few indicated that they turned to the principal, and it was usually in relation to noninstructional matters on those occasions.

The "very good" teachers involved in Johnson's (1990) research reported several sources of dissatisfaction with their principals as supervisors: The formal supervision they provided was useful for dismissal purposes, but not for improvement; administrators rarely offered useful advice; the supervisory process rarely provided an opportunity for teacher growth.

This general picture of teacher dissatisfaction, however, requires a closer examination. Three principal factors seem to affect how teachers feel about their principal as supervisor. First, the leadership ability and supervisory skills and attitudes of the principal seem to make a difference. As noted above in the report of the Smith and Anderson, teachers who saw their principals as "strong leaders" differed along several dimensions from those who perceived their principal as "average" or "weak" as a leader. One item is especially illuminating here. When teachers were asked if they believed that improved instructional practice resulted from interactions with their principal, their responses differed significantly as follows: 80 percent of those with a strong principal agreed, 49 percent, those with an average principal, and 25 percent, those with a weak principal.

Lyman's (1987) study of 150 Kansas teachers concluded that principals were able to build trust in the supervisory process when they manifested the following behaviors: conveyed a positive tone, demonstrated a genuine interest in the teacher, made frequent and on-going observations of teaching, gave prompt and specific feedback, exhibited good listening skills, and provided support to the teacher.

Several studies also suggest that the principal's "style" affects teachers' perceptions of the value of principal supervision. The term *style* is used variously in these studies to identify certain pattern aspects of behavior. Blumberg and Greenfield (1980) concluded that an individualistic and idiosyncratic ideology toward the job made a positive difference.

Huff, Lake, and Schaalman (1982) determined that principals were more effective with teachers when they used a participatory style and persuaded, rather than dictated. As the Glickman and Bey (1990) review concluded, several studies indicate that teachers generally prefer a communication style that they perceive as *collaborative*, rather than directive or nondirective. One interesting exception to this general finding is the Richardson and Sistrunk (1989) study, which surveyed 192 high school teachers and concluded that greater emotional exhaustion and depersonalization were associated with the principal's use of collaborative supervision.

The final influential factor receiving close examination is the conceptual level of the principal and the teacher. Glickman (1985) argued that the principal should adapt supervisory style to the conceptual level of the teacher; however, the review by Glickman and Bey (1990) concluded that the exactness of Glickman's "developmental" model based on conceptual theory is "suspect" (p. 557). Several studies support this conclusion. Grimmett and Crehan (1987) concluded that conceptual matching was not a determining factor in whether supervision improved the teacher's classroom management skills; such improvement took place only when they shared a common language and were both at a moderate or high conceptual level. Calhoun's (1985) review of the research and the results of her own study led her to conclude that there were no significant relationships between teachers' conceptual levels and the frequency of requests for direct assistance, the variety of services sought, the location of resources sought, the use of resources, or the perceived availability of supervisors.

The Assistant Principal

The principal is usually aided by an assistant principal in larger schools. If two assistant principals are assigned, then one is usually identified as *assistant principal for curriculum and instruction.*

In addition to the number of assistant principals, other factors influence the extent to which the assistant plays an active role in supervision. The most important of these is the principal's perception of the assistant's role. Several of the subjects of Marshall's (1993) study of "career" assistant principals indicated that the principal was the primary determiner of the assistant's scope of work. Hall and Guzman (1984) reached the same conclusion in examining the role of the assistant principal as a change agent. The career aspirations and role preferences of the assistant also influenced how the role is carried out. Smith's (1987) survey of the recommendations of close to 800 principals and district administrators concluded that "visiting classrooms to observe teachers" would be an essential experience for assistant principals who aspire to the principalship.

The role of the assistant principalship as actually implemented is a fragmented one. The 263 secondary assistant principals surveyed by Norton and Kriekard (1987) validated 59 competencies that they considered essential for carrying out their roles. More than half of the assistant principals in the 1988 study by Pellicer and others identified 30 duties as important in understanding the assistant's role. These 30 duties included eight under school management, six under staff/personnel, six under curriculum and instruction, four marked as community relations, three in student activities, and three in student services. When asked to rate these duties with respect to the degree of responsibility, these assistants ranked "evaluation of teachers" third, after "student discipline" and "school policies." "Instructional methods" was ranked fifteenth according to the same criterion. The researchers note that these data suggest that the duties of assistant principals have changed very little since 1965, when a similar study was completed. They will change in the future if school systems heed the recommendations of the National Association of Secondary School Principals (NASSP) Council on the Assistant Principalship (1991). The council strongly recommended that the role be reconceptualized to emphasize involvement in teacher evaluation and supervision and active participation in instructional leadership.

There is a paucity of studies that focus on the effectiveness of assistant principals as supervisors; many studies, such as the 1988 NEA research, ask teachers about their attitudes toward "school administrators," without distinguishing between the principal and the assistant. The Dade County (Florida) teachers in the 1986 study by Kottkamp, Provenzo, and Cohn ranked "assistant principal for curriculum" second (after "other teachers") as the source from which they received the greatest help with respect to curriculum and methods; 22 percent of those surveyed so indicated, while only 3.6 percent identified the principal as the greatest source of help.

Teachers with Special Supervisory Roles

Three groups of teachers are sometimes assigned special supervisory roles. Department chairs and team leaders are often expected to provide minimal supervision to the teachers in their work groups. In some schools, a "teacher consultant" is assigned specific supervisory duties. A mentor teacher is frequently formally assigned the task of supervising novice teachers. The following discussion reviews the limited research with respect to these teachers with a special supervisory assignment.

Department chairs are for the most part found only in high schools, where the departmentalization of the curriculum results in a subject-focused organizational structure. Many elementary principals appoint an experienced teacher as a grade-level team leader. Staffing at the middle school level is more varied. Some middle schools are organized by subject, with one teacher expected to provide leadership, whereas other middle schools that emphasize interdisciplinary curricula use a grade-level organization similar to that of the elementary school; and some use both structures.

Of these two leadership roles (i.e., department chair and team leader), the former role has been studied more often. Several studies illuminate the functions served by departments. For most secondary teachers, the department is their primary reference group: The department is the place where they learn norms of behavior, develop professional affiliations, and find their professional identity. The 39 "very good" teachers in Johnson's (1990) study reported that the department served several functions: it provided socialization and training for new members; it was a source of encouragement and recognition; it helped them to maintain standards; it gave them an opportunity to be creative and influential; and it helped them to improve their teaching through joint planning, peer observation, team teaching, and staff development. Several of these functions obviously have a direct impact on teacher performance. Although Johnson (1990) noted much variation in the way departments function, she pointed out that they influence teacher performance in several indirect ways as well. Some departments develop their own curriculum guides, many select textbooks for the students, and many assign teachers to courses. In high schools that use school-based management approaches, the department also serves as the primary vehicle for involving teachers in decision-making. While the structure for such involvement is in place, however, there is no assurance that the departmental organization fosters teachers' participation in the process. Pink's (1983) research concluded that, while the high school administrators believed that instruction was the concern of department chairs, departments did not in reality meet; thus, there was no forum in which instructional issues could be conducted.

The degree of influence of the department seems to depend upon both the chair and the subject matter. First, the way department chairs conceptualize their roles influences the way they perform their duties. Johnson noted that those who see themselves primarily as teachers work with teachers as peers, but those who view themselves as administrators spend more time in overseeing teachers' work and in monitoring their implementation of school and district policies.

Johnson concluded from her own and others' research that the subject matter affiliation of teachers also affects their views about the department: Mathematics teachers seem to achieve departmental consensus rather readily, whereas social studies teachers insist on charting their individual paths.

How effective is the department chair or the team leader? Slightly more than 12 percent of the teachers in the Kottkamp, Provenzo, and Cohn (1986) study indicated that either a department chair, grade-level chair, or resource teacher was the source from whom they received the most help with curricular and instructional issues; in contrast, only 3.6 percent saw the principal as the most helpful.

The resource teacher is typically found in the elementary school, helping teachers deal with the burdens of implementing curricula in five or six different subjects. In this author's experience, most seem to be assigned special responsibilities in either mathematics or reading. The study of the consulting teacher's role in school improvement by Gersten et al (1986) concluded that while these teacher specialists were helpful in assisting teachers new to the project, they were very reluctant to give feedback to other teachers. Some consulting teachers explained this failure by citing district policy, which made clear that they could help, but that they could not evaluate teachers, without specifying the difference.

A larger body of research is available on the mentors, generally indicating that they perform valuable services to the novice teachers assigned to them. Huling-Austin (1990) points out that they have various titles, such as mentor, support teacher, helping teacher, peer teacher, and buddy teacher.

In analyzing the role of the mentor, this author (Glatthorn, 1990) concluded from a review of the literature that five mentor roles and functions seemed to make a difference in relation to the success of the relationship: counselor, listening empathically to the novice's concerns; orienter and resource guide, helping the novice know about and gain access to community and school resources; model, providing a model of effective teaching and committed professionalism; source of feedback, giving supportive and constructive feedback to the novice about his or her performance; and advice-giver, offering professional advice about the curriculum, discipline, testing, and lesson planning. Huling-Austin and Murphy (1987) determined from their study of first-year teachers that the mentors helped them in 14 different areas, with the area of "someone to talk to/listen to" mentioned most frequently. Even though the conceptualization of the role may differ somewhat, experts in the field agree that a clear delineation

of the role is essential for the success of the mentoring program (e.g., see Newcombe, 1988; Willis & Auer, 1988).

The research strongly underscores the importance of the mentor in the professional development of novice teachers, as Huling-Austin's (1990) review concludes. Several factors seem to be crucial in the success of the mentor–novice relationship. First, as Huling-Austin indicates, certain personal characteristics of the mentor seem to matter: prior experience in assisting student teachers and novices; years of experience as a classroom teacher; willingness to commit time to the relationship; high status within the school and the profession; awareness of the novice's developmental needs.

In addition, certain matching of characteristics matters. In an early study of mentoring outside the field of education, Levinson (1978) recommended that the mentor should be half a generation (8–15 years) older than the protege. His research convinced him that if there is a full generation's difference, then the relationship is more likely to become a parent/child one. From her review of the research, Galvez-Hjornevik (1986) concluded that the mentor and the novice should not be of different genders: Male/female pairs must deal with the potential of sexual tensions and public scrutiny. Some research also indicates the desirability of the mentor and novice holding similar educational belief systems and having a similar teaching assignment (see Huling-Austin, 1988).

In addition to these personal characteristics, certain features of the program seem influential. Huling-Austin (1990) cites four from her review of the research: the program addresses the felt needs of novices; the program is flexible, changing as the novice gains greater skill and confidence; the program is the result of collaborative efforts of state departments, teacher-training institutions, school districts, and schools; the program supports the placement of novices in teaching assignments likely to lead to success.

Not all mentoring programs are successful. Kennedy's (1991) studies of novice teachers persuaded her that those teachers who had a mentor were not necessarily more successful than were those who did not. She noted that novices are strongly influenced by the traditional models of teaching that they have observed as elementary, secondary, and college students. She has also determined that many mentors do not have sufficient content knowledge to help novices. Finally, she argued, mentors may be effective teachers of children, but they are not necessarily effective teachers of teachers. Caruso's (1990) study noted the absence of genuine collaboration among principals, mentors, and novices. He attributed this failing to two factors: Principals and mentors were unclear about their respective roles, and a state policy requiring confidentiality between mentor and novice clearly inhibited discussions between the principal and the mentor.

SUMMARY

The general picture of supervisory roles and relationships can obviously be understood from several perspectives. One of the most useful could be that of the classroom teacher.

From the viewpoint of the teacher in the classroom, how do all these roles relate to the teacher's daily life with students?

To begin with, the state department of education, acting at the behest of state legislators, sets broad and permeable limits, focusing chiefly on teacher evaluation, curriculum, and student assessment. Those departments then act through their educational service agencies to assure compliance with policies and to provide the support needed for effective implementation of state and programs. In an era of educational reform, when most states are playing a very active role, the stance of state departments and their service agencies might best be characterized as a combination of improvement and maintenance. While the classroom teacher has little direct contact with supervisors from state offices or their service agencies, the teacher is aware and generally accepting of the boundaries drawn by the state, knowing that the protection afforded by the closed classroom door shields the teacher from any unwarranted intrusion by state officers or their agents.

The classroom teacher has relatively little contact with district supervisors, who seem chiefly engaged with maintaining the system as it is, giving most of their attention to the administrative requirements of the role. The teacher tends to perceive the district supervisor as a somewhat remote and relatively unhelpful professional, except in those cases where the supervisor has chosen to play a highly active role as resource provider and consultant.

At the school level, the teacher finds that colleagues are the most helpful resource, although the unstated norm of projecting self-sufficiency often gets in the way of genuine collaboration. At the high school, the department plays a central role for its members. At the middle and elementary levels, the grade-level team performs some of the same functions, albeit in a less forceful manner. The teacher's chief contacts with school administrators come through very brief informal exchanges that take place during the day and from two formal observations, whose main purpose is system maintenance through evaluation.

REFERENCES

Acheson, K. A. & Gall, M. D. (1987). *Techniques in the clinical supervision of teachers: Preservice and in-service applications* (2d ed.). New York: Longman.

Alfonso, R. J. (1986). *The unseen supervisor: Organization and culture as determinants of teacher behavior.* Paper presented at annual meeting of the American Educational Research Association, San Francisco (ERIC Document Reproduction Service No. ED 277 141).

American Association of Colleges for Teacher Education. (1991). *RATE IV: Teaching teachers: Facts & figures.* Washington, D.C.: Author.

Anderson, S. A. (1990). *Current supervisory and evaluation practices: Paradoxes and deficiencies* (ERIC Document Reproduction Service No. ED 332 279).

Archbald, D. A. & Porter, A. C. (1994). Curriculum control and teachers' perceptions of autonomy and satisfaction. *Educational Evaluation and Policy Analysis, 16,* 21–39.

Bain, C. (1991). *Student teaching triads: Perceptions of participant roles.* Paper presented at annual meeting of the Northern Rocky Mountain Educational Association (ERIC Document Reproduction Service No. ED 338 620).

Barrow, L. K. (1976). *Power relationships in student teaching.* Paper presented at annual meeting of the American Educational Research Association, San Francisco.

Bimber, B. (1993). *School decentralization: lessons from the study of bureaucracy.* Santa Monica, CA: Rand.

Bird, T & Little, J. W. (1986). How schools organize the teaching occupation. *Elementary School Journal, 86,* 493–511.

Blank, R. K. & Dalkilic, M. (1992). *State policies on science and mathematics education 1992.* Washington, D.C.: Council of Chief State School Officers.

Blumberg, A. (1980). *Supervisors and teachers: A private cold war* (2nd ed.). Berkeley, CA: McCutchan.

Blumberg, A. (1983). *Supervision in weakly normed systems: The case of the schools.* Paper presented at annual meeting of the American Educational Research Association, Montreal (ERIC Document Reproduction Service No. ED 239 381).

Blumberg, A. & Amidon, E, (1965). Teacher perceptions of supervisor-teacher interaction. *Administrator's Notebook, 14*(1), 1–4.

Blumberg, A. & Greenfield, W. (1980). *The effective principal: Perspectives on school leadership.* Boston: Allyn & Bacon.

Bossert, S., Dwyer, D., Rowan, B., & Lee, G. (1982). The instructional management role of the principal. *Educational Administration Quarterly, 19*(3), 34–64.

Boydell, D. (1986). Issues in teaching practice supervision research. *Teaching and Teacher Education, 2,* 115–125.

Burton, W. H. (1922). *Supervision and the improvement of teaching.* New York: Appleton-Century.

Calderhead, J. (1987). *Cognition and metacognition in teachers' professional development.* Paper presented at annual meeting of the American Educational Research Association, Washington, D.C.

Calhoun, E. F. (1985). *Relationship of teacher's conceptual level to the utilization of supervisory services.* Paper presented at annual meeting of the American Educational Research Association, Chicago (ERIC Document Reproduction Service No. ED 269 841).

Campbell, R. F., Sroufe, G. E., & Layton, D. H. (Eds.). (1967). *Strengthening state departments of education.* Chicago: Midwestern Administrative Center, University of Chicago.

Cantlan, D., Rushcamp, S., & Freeman, D. (1990). *The interplay between state and district guidelines for curriculum reform in elementary schools.* East Lansing, MI: Center for the Learning and Teaching of Elementary Subjects, Michigan State University.

Caruso, J. J. (1990). *Supervisory roles and responsibilities of principals to teacher leaders and novice teachers in four Connecticut schools: A close-up look.* Paper presented at annual meeting of the American Educational Research Association, Boston (ERIC Document Reproduction Service No. ED 321 389).

Cawelti, G. & Reavis, C. (1980). How well are we providing instructional improvement services? *Educational Leadership, 38,* 236–240.

Cochran-Smith, M. & Lytle, S. L. (1993). *Inside/outside: Teacher research and knowledge.* New York: Teachers College Press.

Cohen, D. K. & Spillane, J. P. (1992). Policy and practice: The relations between governance and instruction. In G. Grant (Ed.). *Review of research in education, 18* (pp. 3–50). Washington, D.C.: American Educational Research Association.

Cotton, K. (1990). *Effective schooling practices: A research synthesis, 1990 Update.* Portland, OR: Northwest Regional Educational Laboratory.

Cuban, L. (1984). Transforming the frog into a prince: Effective schools research, policy, and practice at the district level. *Harvard Educational Review, 54,* 129–151.

Curry, B. & Temple, T. (1992). *Using curriculum frameworks for systemic reform*. Alexandria, VA: ASCD.

Deal, T. E. & Celotti, L. D. (1980). How much influence do (and can) educational administrators have on classrooms? *Phi Delta Kappan, 71*, 471–473.

Diamonti, M. & Diamonti, N. (1975). An organizational analysis of student teacher supervision. *Interchange, 6*(4), 27–33.

Dowling, K. W. & Yager, R. E. (1983). Status of science education in state departments of education: An initial report. *Journal of Research in Science Teaching, 20*, 771–780.

Duffy, F. M. (1985, March). *Analyzing and evaluating supervisory practice*. Paper presented at annual meeting of the Association for Supervision and Curriculum Development, Chicago (ERIC Document Reproduction Service No. ED 254 896).

Erb, R., Jr. (1988). *The nature and scope of instructional supervision functions of district-wide supervisors and their relationship to student performance on the Pennsylvania Educational Quality Assessment Inventory*. (Doctoral dissertation, Lehigh University, 1988). *Dissertation Abstracts International, 49*, 1636–A.

Feiman-Nemser, S. & Buchmann, M. (1987). When is student teaching teacher education? *Teaching and Teacher Education, 3*, 255–273.

Firestone, W. A. (1991). Increasing teacher commitment in urban high schools: Incremental and restructuring options. In S. C. Conley & B. S. Cooper (Eds.). *The school as a work environment: Implications for reform* (pp. 141–168). Boston: Allyn & Bacon.

Firestone, W. A., Rossman, G. B., & Wilson, B. L. (1983a). *Only a phone call away: local educators' views of regional educational service agencies*. Philadelphia: Research for Better Schools.

Firestone, W. A., Rossman, G. B., & Wilson, B. L. (1983b). *The study of regional educational service agencies: Summary of findings*. Philadelphia: Research for Better Schools.

Firestone, W. A. & Wilson, B. L. (1985). Using bureaucratic and cultural linkages to improve instruction: The principal's contribution. *Educational Administration Quarterly, 21*, 7–30.

Firth, G. R. & Eiken, K. P. (1982). Impact of the school's bureaucratic structure on supervision. In T. J. Sergiovanni (Ed.). *Supervision of teaching* (pp. 153–169). Alexandria, VA: ASCD.

Floyd, M. K. (1987). Flexibility and central office supervisors: The instrumental function of fragmentation, invisibility, and ambiguity. Paper presented at annual meeting of the American Educational Research Association, Washington, D.C. (ERIC Document Reproduction Service No. ED 282 311).

Fraser, B. J., Walberg, H. J., Welch, W. W., & Hattie, J. A. (1987). Syntheses of educational productivity research. *International Journal of Education, 11*, 145–252.

Fuhrman, S. H. (1994). Legislatures and education policy. In R. F. Elmore & S. H. Fuhrman (Eds.). *The governance of curriculum* (pp. 30–55). Alexandria, VA: ASCD.

Fuhrman, S. H. & Fry, P. (1989). *Diversity amidst standardization: State differential treatment of districts*. New Brunswick, NJ: Center for Policy Research in Education, Rutgers University.

Fullan, M. G. (1992). Visions that blind. *Educational Leadership, 49*(5), 19–20.

Galvez-Hjornevik, C. (1986). Mentoring among teachers: A review of the literature. *Journal of Teacher Education, 37*(1), 121–126.

Gersten, R., Davis, G., Miller, B., & Green, W. (1986). *The role of the instructional supervisor in school improvement*. Paper presented at annual meeting of the American Educational Research Association, San Francisco.

Glatthorn, A. A. (1990). *Supervisory leadership*. New York: HarperCollins.

Glatthorn, A. A. (1993). *Learning twice: An introduction to the methods of teaching*. New York: HarperCollins.

Glatthorn, A. A. & Coble, C. R. (1995). Leadership for effective student teaching. In G. A. Slick (Ed.). *The Field Experience*. Thousand Oaks, CA: Corwin.

Glatthorn, A. A. & Newberg, N. A. (1984). A team approach to instructional leadership. *Educational Leadership, 41*(5), 60–63.

Glickman, C. D. (1985). *Supervision of instruction: A developmental perspective*. Boston: Allyn & Bacon.

Glickman, C. D. & Bey, T. M. (1990). Supervision. In W. R. Houston (Ed.). *Handbook of research on teacher education* (pp. 549–568). New York: Macmillan.

Goodlad, J. I. (1994). *Educational renewal: Better teachers, better schools*. San Francisco: Jossey-Bass.

Grimmett, P. P. (1987). The role of district supervisors in the implementation of peer coaching. *Journal of Curriculum and Instruction, 3*, 3–28.

Grimmett, P. P. & Crehan, E. P. (1987, May). *A study of the effects of supervisory intervention on teachers' classroom management performance*. Paper presented at annual meeting of the Canadian Association for Teacher Education, Hamilton, Ontario (ERIC Document Reproduction Service No. ED 282 326).

Grimmett, P. P. & Ratzlaff, H. C. (1986). Expectations for the cooperating teacher role. *Journal of Teacher Education, 37*(6), 41–50.

Grossman, P. (1992). Teaching to learn. In A. Lieberman (Ed.). *The changing contexts of teaching* (91st Yearbook of the National Society for the Study of Education: pp. 179–196). Chicago: University of Chicago Press.

Guyton, E. & McIntyre, D. J. (1990). Student teaching and school experiences. In W. R. Houston (Ed.). *Handbook of research on teacher education* (pp. 514–534). New York: Macmillan.

Hall, G. E. & Gutman, F. M. (1984). *Sources for leadership for change in high schools*. Paper presented at annual meeting of the American Educational Research Association, New Orleans (ERIC Document Reproduction Service No. ED 250 815).

Hall, G. E., Putman, S., & Hord, S. M. (1985). *District office personnel: Their roles and influences on school and classroom change: What we don't know*. Paper presented at annual meeting of the American Educational Research Association, Chicago (ERIC Document Reproduction Service No. ED 271 808).

Hallinger, P. & Murphy, J. (1985). Assessing the instructional management behavior of principals. *Elementary School Journal, 86*, 217–247.

Hallinger, P. & Murphy, J. (1987). Instructional leadership in the school context. In W. Greenfield (Ed.). *Instructional leadership* (pp. 179–203). Newton, MA: Allyn & Bacon.

Harris, B. M. (1975). *Supervisory behavior in education* (2nd ed.). Englewood Cliffs, NJ: Prentice Hall.

Harris, B. M. (1985). *Supervisory behavior in education* (3rd ed.). Englewood Cliffs, NJ: Prentice Hall.

Harvey, P. L. & Levin, J. (1984). *Teachers' perceptions of supervision*. Paper presented at annual meeting of the American Educational Research Association, New Orleans (ERIC Document Reproduction Service No. ED 259 456).

Heishberger, R. & Young, J. (1975). Teacher perceptions of supervision and evaluation. *Phi Delta Kappan, 57*, 210–213.

Huff, S., Lake, D., & Schaalman, M. L. (1982). *Principal difference: Excellence in school leadership and management*. Report submitted to the Council of Educational Management. Tallahassee, FL: Florida Department of Education.

Huling-Austin, L. (1988). *A synthesis of research on teacher induction programs and practices*. Paper presented at annual meeting of the American Educational Research Association, New Orleans.

Huling-Austin, L. (1990). Teacher induction programs and internships. In W. R. Houston (Ed.). *Handbook of research on teacher education* (pp. 535–548). New York: Macmillan.

Huling-Austin, L. & Murphy, S. C. (1987). *Assessing the impact of teacher induction programs: Implications for program development.* Paper presented at annual meeting of the American Educational Research Association, Washington, D.C. (ERIC Document Reproduction Service No. ED 283 779).

Hurley, J. C. (1990). *The organizational socialization of high school principals: A description and analysis.* Paper presented at annual meeting of the American Educational Research Association, Boston (ERIC Document Reproduction Service No. ED 320 281).

James, T. (1991). State authority and the politics of educational change. In G. Grant (Ed.). *Review of research in education, 17* (pp. 169–224). Washington, D.C.: American Educational Research Association.

Johnson, S. M. (1987). Collective bargaining. In V. Richardson-Koehler (Ed.). *Educators' handbook: A research perspective* (pp. 553–574). New York: Longman.

Johnson, S. M. (1990). *Teachers at work: Achieving success in our schools.* New York: Basic Books.

Kennedy, M. M. (1991). Some surprising findings on how teachers learn to teach. *Educational Leadership, 49*(3), 14–17.

Kerchner, C. T. (1986). Union-made teaching: The effects of labor relations on teacher work. In E. Z. Rothkopf (Ed.). *Review of research in education, Volume 13* (pp. 317–352). Washington, D.C.: American Educational Research Association.

Kottkamp, R. B., Provenzo, E. F., Jr., & Cohn, M. M. (1986). Stability and change in a profession: Two decades of teacher attitudes, 1964–1984. *Phi Delta Kappan, 67,* 559–567.

Kull, J. A., Oja, S. N., & Ellis, N. E. (1991). *Models of collaborative supervision involving teacher educators and school personnel in new roles and activities via collaborative teams.* Paper presented at annual meeting of the American Educational Research Association, Chicago (Education Document Reproduction Service No. ED 352 350).

Lee, G. V. (1987). Instructional leadership in a junior high school: Managing realities and creating opportunities. In W. Greenfield (Ed.). *Instructional leadership: Concepts, issues, and controversies* (pp. 77–99). Newton, MA: Allyn & Bacon.

Lemma, P. (1993). The cooperating teacher as supervisor. *Journal of Curriculum and Supervision, 8,* 329–342.

Levine, M. (1992). A conceptual framework for professional practice schools. In M. Levine (Ed.). *Professional practice schools: linking teacher education and school reform* (pp. 8–24). New York: Teachers College Press.

Levinson, D. J. (1978). *Seasons of a man's life.* New York: Knopf.

Little, J. W. & Bird, T. (1987). Instructional leadership: "close to the classroom" in secondary schools. In W. Greenfield (Ed.). *Instructional leadership: Concepts, issues, and controversies* (pp. 118–138). Boston: Allyn & Bacon.

Lortie, D. C. (1975). *Schoolteacher.* Chicago: University of Chicago Press.

Lusi, S. F. (1994). Systemic school reform: The challenges faced by state departments of education. In R. F. Elmore & S. H. Fuhrman (Eds.). *The governance of curriculum,* pp. 109–130. Alexandria, VA: ASCD.

Lyman, L. (1987, March). *Principals and teachers: Collaboration to improve instructional supervision.* Paper presented at annual meeting of the Association for Supervision and Curriculum Development, Orlando (ERIC Document Reproduction Service No. ED 280 186).

Madrazo, J. M., Jr. & Hounshell, P. B. (1987). The role expectancy of the science supervisor: Results of research in supervision. *Science Education, 71*(1), 9–14.

Marshall, C. (1993). *The unsung role of the career assistant principal.* Reston, VA: National Association of Secondary School Principals.

Martin, O. L. (1990). *Instructional leadership behaviors that empower teacher effectiveness.* Paper presented at annual meeting of the Mid-South Educational Research Association, New Orleans.

Martin, R. A. (1985). *Supervisory communications and support linkages between high school principals and teachers.* Paper presented at annual meeting of the American Educational Research Association, Chicago (ERIC Document Reproduction Service Number ED 263 669).

Massell, D. & Fuhrman, S. (1994). *Ten years of state education reform, 1983–1993.* New Brunswick, NJ: Consortium for Policy Research in Education, Rutgers University.

McLaughlin, M. W. (1992). How district communities do and do not foster teacher pride. *Educational Leadership, 50*(1), 33–35.

McNeill, L. M. (1986). *Contradictions of control: School structure and school knowledge.* New York: Routledge and Kegan Paul.

Miller, R., Smey-Richman, B., & Woods-Houston, M. (1987). *Secondary schools and the central office: Partners for improvement.* Philadelphia: Research for Better Schools.

Mintzberg, H. (1973). *The nature of managerial work.* New York: Harper & Row.

NASSP Council on the Assistant Principalship. (1991). *Restructuring the role of the assistant principal.* Reston, VA: National Association of Secondary School Principals.

National Education Association. (1988). *The conditions and resources of teaching.* Washington, D.C.: NEA Research Division.

Nelson, J. A. (1993). *An evaluation of staff development activities of the Northeast Technical Assistance Center (North Carolina).* (Doctoral dissertation, East Carolina University, 1993). *Dissertation Abstracts International, 54,* 2043A.

Newcombe, E. (1988). *Mentoring programs for new teachers.* Philadelphia: Research for Better Schools.

Norton, M. S. & Kriekard, J. A. (1987). Real and ideal competencies for the assistant principal. *NASSP Bulletin, 71*(501), 23–31.

O'Neal, S. & Edwards, S. (1983). *The supervision of student teaching.* Paper presented at annual meeting of the American Educational Research Association, Montreal.

Oliva, P. F. (1984). *Supervision for today's schools* (2nd ed.). New York: Longman.

Osborne, W. D., Jr. & Wiggins, T. (1989). Perceptions of tasks in the school principalship. *Journal of Personnel Evaluation in Education, 2,* 367–375.

Osterman, K. F. (1989). *Supervision and shared authority: A study of principal and teacher control in six urban middle schools.* Paper presented at annual meeting of the American Educational Research Association, San Francisco (ERIC Document Reproduction Service No. ED 307 678).

Owens, R. G. (1987). The leadership of educational clans. In L. T. Sheive & M. B. Schoenheit (Eds.). *Leadership: Examining the elusive* (pp. 16–29). Alexandria, VA: ASCD.

Pajak, E. (1989). *The central office supervisor of curriculum and instruction: Setting the stage for success.* Boston: Allyn & Bacon.

Pajak, E. (1990). *Identification of dimensions of supervisory practice in education: Reviewing the literature.* Paper presented at annual meeting of the American Educational Research Association, Boston.

Pajak, E. F. (1992). A view from the central office. In C. D. Glickman (Ed.). *Supervision in transition* (pp. 126–140). Alexandria, VA: ASCD.

Parramore, B. M. (1990). *Changing roles and realities of central office curriculum and instruction professionals.* Research Triangle Park, NC: Southeastern Educational Improvement Laboratory.

Pellicer, L. O., Anderson, L. W., Keefe, J. W., Kelley, E. A., & McCleary, L. E. (1988). *High school leaders and their schools: Volume 1, a national profile.* Reston, VA: National Association of Secondary School Principals.

Peterson, K. D. (1989). *Secondary principals and instructional leadership: Complexities in a diverse role.* Madison, WI: National Center on Effective Secondary Schools, University of Wisconsin-Madison.

Pfeifer, R. S. (1986). *Enabling teacher effectiveness: Teachers' perspective on instructional management.* Paper presented at annual meeting of the American Educational Research Association, San Francisco (ERIC Document Reproduction Service No. 270 868).

Pink, W. T. (1983). *Instructional leadership: The role of the administrative team and student achievement.* Paper presented at annual meeting of the American Educational Research Association, Montreal (ERIC Document Reproduction Service No. ED 238 194).

Poole, W. L. (1994). Removing the "super" from supervision. *Journal of Curriculum and Supervision, 9,* 284–309.

Porter, A. C., Smithson, J., & Osthoff, E. (1994). Standard setting as a strategy for upgrading high school mathematics and science. In R. F. Elmore & S. H. Fuhrman (Eds.). *The governance of the curriculum* (pp. 138–166). Alexandria, VA: ASCD.

Purkey, S. C. & Smith, M. S. (1985). School reform: The district policy implications of the effective schools literature. *Elementary School Journal, 85,* 353–389.

Richardson, G. D. & Sistrunk, W. E. (1989). *The relationship between secondary teachers' perceived levels of burnout and their perceptions of their principals' supervisory behaviors.* Paper presented at annual meeting of the Mid-South Educational Research Association, Little Rock, AR (ERIC Document Reproduction Service No. 312 763).

Richardson, S. C. (1987). *Actual and ideal role perceptions of instructional supervisors in the public schools of Virginia.* Paper presented at annual meeting of the Southern Regional Council on Educational Administration, Gatlinburg, TN.

Richardson-Koehler, V. (1988). Barriers to the effective supervision of teaching: A field study. *Journal of Teacher Education, 39*(2), 28–34.

Roberts, J. M. E. & Newcombe, E. I. (1984). *Supervision: Practice and preference in the state of Maryland.* Philadelphia: Research for Better Schools (ERIC Document Reproduction Service No. ED 252 914).

Roney, R., DeLong, M., Bloomer, D., & Lindsey, C. (1990). *Time use by teachers and school administrators.* Paper presented at annual meeting of the American Educational Research Association, Boston (ERIC Document Reproduction Service No. ED 321 353).

Sacks, S. R. & Harrington, G. N. (1982). *Student to teacher: The process of role transition.* Paper presented at annual meeting of the American Educational Research Association, New York.

Schlechty, P. C. (1985). District level policies and practices: Supporting effective school management and classroom instruction. In R. M. J. Kyle (Ed.). *Reaching for excellence: An effective schools sourcebook* (pp. 117–129). Washington, D.C.: U.S. Government Printing Office.

Sclan, E. & Darling-Hammond, L. (1992). *Beginning teacher performance evaluation: An overview of state policies. Trends, and issues paper No. 7.* Washington, D.C.: ERIC Clearinghouse on Teacher Education.

Sergiovanni, T. J. (1992). Why we should seek substitutes for leadership. *Educational Leadership, 49*(5), 41–45.

Smith, J. A. (1987). Assistant principals: new demands, new realities, and new perspectives. *NASSP Bulletin, 71*(501), 9–12.

Smith, W. F. & Andrews, R. L. (1989). *Instructional leadership: How principals make a difference.* Alexandria, VA: ASCD.

Snyder, K. J., Fitzgerald, J. H., & Giella, M. (1992). *An empirical validation of a management construct for district level supervisors.* Paper presented at annual meeting of the American Educational Research Association, San Francisco (ERIC Document Reproduction Service No. ED 348 745).

South Carolina Department of Education. (1993). *South Carolina visual and performing arts curriculum framework.* Columbia, SC: Author.

Stephens, E. R. & Turner, W. G. (1991). *Approaching the next millennium: Educational service agencies in the 1990s.* Arlington, VA: American Association of Educational Service Agencies.

Stiggins, R. J. & Duke, D. (1988). *The case for commitment to teacher growth: Research on teacher evaluation.* Albany, NY: State University of New York Press.

Sullivan, C. G. (1982). Supervisory expectations and work realities: The great gulf. *Educational Leadership, 39,* 448–451.

Tanner, D. & Tanner, L. (1987). *Supervision in education: Problems and practices.* New York: Macmillan.

University of North Carolina Model Clinical Teaching Network. (1992). *Learning to teach in North Carolina.* Chapel Hill, NC: Author.

Wang, M. C., Haertel, G. D., & Walberg, H. J. (1990). What influences learning? A content analysis of review literature. *Journal of Educational Research, 84,* 30–43.

Wang, M. C., Haertel, G. D., & Walberg, H. J. (1993). Toward a knowledge base for school learning. *Review of Educational Research, 63,* 249–294.

Weber, J. R. (1987). *Instructional leadership: A composite working model.* Eugene, OR: ERIC Clearinghouse on Educational Management, University of Oregon.

Weick, K. E. (1976). Educational organizations as loosely coupled systems. *Administrative Science Quarterly, 21,* 1–19.

Weiss, C. H. (1992). *Shared decision-making about what? A comparison of schools with and without teacher participation.* Cambridge, MA: National Center for Educational Leadership, Harvard University.

Willis, C. L. & Auer, B. R. (1988). *Beginning teachers and professional development.* Elmhurst, IL: North Central Regional Educational Laboratory.

Wimpelberg, R. K. (1987). The dilemma of instructional leadership and a central role for central office. In W. Greenfield (Ed.). *Instructional leadership: Concepts, issues, and controversies* (pp. 100–117). Boston: Allyn & Bacon.

Yee, A. H. (1968). Interpersonal relationships in the student teaching triad. *Journal of Teacher Education, 19,* 95–112.

Young, J. (1989). *Site based management: Implications for educational service agencies.* Paper presented at annual meeting of the Association of School Business Officials, Orlando, Florida (ERIC Document Reproduction Service No. ED 313 814).

Zahorik, J. A. (1988). The observing-conferencing role of university supervisors. *Journal of Teacher Education, 39*(2), 9–16.

Zeichner, K. M. & Tabachnick, B. R. (1982). The belief systems of university supervisors in an elementary student-teaching program. *Journal of Education for Teaching, 8,* 34–53.

·13·

PROCESSES AND TECHNIQUES IN SUPERVISION

Patricia E. Holland

UNIVERSITY OF HOUSTON

This chapter explores the processes and techniques employed in the practice of instructional supervision. At first glance, such a task would seem to be a straightforward operation of description and classification of processes and techniques that are readily identifiable in both theoretical and practical literature in the field of supervision. Upon looking more closely at that literature, however, one discovers that *process* and *technique* are rather slippery terms, quite glibly used and indicating an ill-defined corpus of supervisory practice.

In order to begin to probe beneath the surface of glib reference and nonspecific usage of the terms *process* and *technique,* consider the point that in other professions, such as medicine, law, or engineering, there is an acceptance of "standards of practice." These standards provide an articulation by the professions themselves of those processes and techniques considered to be within a range of legitimate actions toward clients.

Education, however, has not been delimited by such standards. Rather, a tendency toward acceptance of any and all processes and techniques has prevailed. At best, this lack of generally accepted standards of educational practice has allowed the creation of a wide range of techniques out of local school conditions and scholarly deliberations. At worst, it permits us to indulge in delusion and pretense. While the desirability of establishing more precise educational standards is a topic for debate in venues other than this chapter, it is important here to note that without standards of practice, a critical stance by the professional community toward processes and techniques—most particularly toward those that are questionable—is difficult, if not impossible.

The lack of professional standards to clarify processes and techniques of professional practice in education is well exemplified in the field of instructional supervision. As will become clear in this chapter, the research reveals that as a practice with no statement of standards, supervision is characterized by processes and techniques that reflect both practical expediency and intellectual anarchy. Furthermore, the research reveals that supervision is paradoxically multitheoretical and atheoretical at one and the same time.

Before scrutinizing the research on processes and techniques of instructional supervision, however, the words *process* and *technique* need to be specifically defined as they will be used in the context of this chapter. The casual frequency with which these words are used by scholars and practitioners of supervision suggests something of the nature of supervision as both a field of study and practice. What the casual and familiar use of these words tells us is that supervision, along with other educational specializations, has adopted a language of technical-rationality that suggests a consistent and ordered theory and practice. The words also imply something about the expectations that steer the practice of supervision. It can be expected that the practice of supervision is somehow both constant and knowable. Because one purpose of this chapter is to challenge the sufficiency of these implicit assumptions, definitions will be used that make it possible to construe supervision more precisely in terms of its "processes" and "techniques."

It is worth noting that the very lack of professional standards of practice makes varying definitions of processes and techniques of supervision possible, and even inevitable. Furthermore, as will become readily apparent to any reader familiar with the field of supervision, this chapter represents only one possible way of classifying, clarifying, and understanding supervisory processes and techniques. Such arbitrariness remains inescapable in the absence of standards to delimit the nature and range of supervisory practice.

Following definition of the terms *process* and *technique,* actual research in supervision—both theoretical and empirical—will be examined to see what processes and techniques have been identified. Finally, questions will be raised about the current state of research on the processes and techniques of supervision. To what extent does this research reflect prevailing and emerging views of schooling? What epistemological perspectives underlie the research on supervisory processes and techniques? Do these perspectives offer useful ways to construe the practice of supervision?

PROCESS DEFINED

Thirteen definitions are found in the Oxford English Dictionary (1971) for the noun *process*. While some of these definitions are obsolete or have specialized meanings in law, logic, or biology, there are several definitions that address the most common understanding of process as the carrying out of action in a regular and serial fashion. The most useful of these definitions for the context of supervision is: "A continuous or regular action or succession of actions, taking place or carried out in a definite manner, and leading to the accomplishment of some result" (OED, 1971).

This definition of *process* indicates that acts of supervision are governed by a rationale and assumptions about their intended outcome. For instance, classroom observation is a process by which the supervisor can collect a record of events in a classroom. For example, the intent of the observation might include the necessity for a school district to evaluate the quality of teaching in the district. The assumptions for the observation might relate to the cooperative, compliant, or resistant nature the teacher brings to the observation. In any case, the process has a complex set of intents and assumptions as a part of its meaning.

Agreement among scholars and practitioners about the intent and assumptions of supervision, however, is only reached on the broadest of bases (i.e., the improvement of instruction). The vagueness of this statement of intent should caution those who would describe supervision as process. Furthermore, as the definition of *process* suggests, acts of supervision should be found to be regular, definite, and continuous. In other words, the practice of supervision should be recognizable in particular, specified, and readily identifiable actions. As the research in supervision reveals, there is agreement only in a very general sense about what these actions are or ought to be.

These disclaimers about supervision as a process, or even as an assortment of processes, is not meant to negate the notion of supervision as a process. Rather, they are intended to alert the reader that the process of supervision is not well defined either in terms of its intents and assumptions, nor in terms of standard practices for its conduct. These disclaimers are also intended to raise questions about the kind of process that supervision is, whether it is one best characterized within the familiar discourse of technical-rationality, or whether other epistemological frames better explain its intents and assumptions.

TECHNIQUE DEFINED

The use of the term *technique* in conjunction with *process* in the context of supervision insinuates that the two are related, in that *techniques* are specific behaviors for carrying out a process. For example, the process of classroom observation may involve the supervisor using the particular technique of recording observation data by writing down the direct dialogue of teacher and students on the left half of a sheet of paper, leaving the right half of the page for the supervisor's analysis of the verbatim data.

The Oxford English Dictionary adds an interesting dimension to that implied relationship between process and technique. The primary definition of *technique* is:

The manner of artistic execution or performance in relation to formal or practical details (as distinct from general effect, expression, sentiment, etc.); the mechanical or formal part of an art, especially of the fine arts; also skill or ability in this deportment of one's art; mechanical skill in artistic work (OED, 1971).

Its emphasis on the artistic, albeit on the practical and mechanical aspects, is most interesting about this definition.

In the context of techniques of supervision, this definition suggests that techniques require more than just technical knowledge or skill. They are discriminating choices that draw on knowledge and skill, and combine them in uniquely appropriate ways to suit particular supervisory contexts. Thus, the supervisor's choice of the split-page recording technique for classroom dialogue reflects an exercise of informed judgment in selecting that particular technique from among various other possibilities because it promises to provide the teacher and supervisor with the most valuable form of information about the observed classroom.

As such, techniques can be seen as what distinguish supervision as a professional practice, making it something that not just anyone can automatically do well. The linking of techniques with the process of supervision (i.e., that familiar combined reference to processes and techniques) raises the practice of supervision beyond ordinary activity to a level of "connoisseurship," or knowledgeable perception, that Eisner (1982) has described as important in the practice of supervision to see what is significant yet subtle.

THEORETIC SOURCES FOR LANGUAGE OF PROCESSES AND TECHNIQUES

The preceding definitions suggest that the language of processes and techniques in supervision should reflect both the precise and specialized nature of supervisory practice (i.e., process) as well as the element of artistic choice and skill in its performance (i.e., technique). In fact, processes and techniques of supervision tend to be discussed in ways that reduce processes to formulas and techniques to generic prescriptions for practice. How and why does such reductionism occur?

Klinchoe (1991) offers one explanation. In an impassioned plea to recognize and include teachers as researchers—a notion some scholars see as a component of supervision (e.g., Glickman, 1985)—Klinchoe argues that teaching "promotes an obsessive concern with means (techniques of instruction) over ends (critical examination of educational purpose)" (Klinchoe, 1991, p. 6). He leaves no doubt about the limitations imposed when means/techniques are a primary focus. He quotes Tolstoy in the guise of an artist character from *Anna Karenina*, who responds to Vronsky's intended compliment of his technique with an angry scowl: "He had often heard this word technique, and was utterly unable to understand . . . a mechanical facility for painting or drawing, entirely apart from its subject" (Tolstoy, 1981, p. 62). Like Tolstoy's artist, Klinchoe argued that making technique the sole basis for judging good teaching is reductionist because by failing to take concerns about the ends of educational endeavors into consideration, teaching becomes an act isolated from its intended goal (i.e., student learning).

Another explanation for the reduction of processes of supervision to formulas, and techniques to prescriptions for practice can be found in the very language most commonly used to discuss educational practice. As Schon (1983) has pointed out, the language of professional practice has long been expressed in what he calls "technical rationality." This dominant view of professional knowledge is characterized as the application of scientific theory and technique to the instrumental problems of practice. In education, this applied science approach has perpetuated the notion that educational practices are grounded in sciencelike theories and that the competent practitioner "applies" these theories to the daily events of her or his work. The application (or action) is articulated through various processes and techniques considered to be the "practical" part of practice.

Foster (1986) offers further insight into reductionism as reflected in the language of supervisory processes and techniques by describing the orthodox or mainstream theory in educational administration (of which school supervision may be considered a part) as "functionalism." Foster claims that "the majority of the theoretical and research-based work done in educational administration reflects a functionalist frame of mind" (p. 59), which he goes on to describe as follows:

Taking its legacy from Taylorism, human relations, and systems theory, the research within this frame tends to be positivistic, objectivistic, and supposedly neutral . . . In general, mainstream theorists in educational administration espouse quantitative research that explores categories of behaviour derived from structural-functional analyses of school organizations. The literature is rife with studies of communication patterns, role structures, school climate, motivational patterns, and so on. All of these studies assume that organizations are concrete entities populated by role players and that systematic study of these entities will yield reliable and predictable knowledge. Science, not philosophy, governs in the hope that a critical mass of empirical studies will eventually result in the accumulation of a verified, or at least not falsified, body of knowledge that will rationalize practice (pp. 59—60).

Foster's description of the functionalist approach leaves no room for a practice of supervision that contains elements of subjective artistry in its performance. Functionalism, as it governs the study of supervision, produces a language of research that delimits the practice of supervision by seeking to demonstrate the effectiveness of certain processes and techniques. In that such research tends to ignore, or at best, broadly classify supervisory contexts, it employs a discourse and a view of the nature of knowledge that is dominant both in education and in the overall culture.

Such narrow views further contribute to reductionist notions that divorce process and techniques from a larger context of intent and meaning. According to Van Manen (1977), we live in a culture where the knowledge industry is dominated by an attitude of accountability and human engi-

neering. Marcuse (1966) presents a similar argument about the way instrumental thinking has permeated our imagination. This attitude is reflected in educational practice in a preoccupation with prescribed procedures, control, and means–ends criteria of efficiency and effectiveness. This technical–instrumental attitude is reflected in an emphasis on practical relevancy in the language of educational programs. Such practical relevancy is expressed in terms of how best to increase teacher "competency" and supervisory "effectiveness." For the supervisor, this means that he or she must learn to apply a variety of techniques to bring about instructional "improvement."

This relationship between knowledge and practical action is made up of an accumulation of practical insights in the form of principle-governed techniques derived from research and propositional theory. As Van Manen (1977) pointed out, "it is very difficult for educators not to invest knowledge and theory with technical significance" (p. 210). In other words, it is taken for granted that practitioners will express their actions in the form of processes and techniques.

"The dominant position of empirical-analytical science in education," says Van Manen, "assures that the practical question is converted almost automatically into an instrumental one" (p. 210). Instrumental questions are posed as: How can the teacher become more effective? How can the supervisor be more productive? Van Manen suggested that such questions are not inherently bad, but that there are other, perhaps more important questions to be asked, that find little expression in the dominant language of educational research and practice.

According to Schon (1983), instrumental questions reflect the penchant for professionals to draw on applied science as the basis for practice, which is a custom he traces through the last 300 years of the history of Western ideas and institutions. "Technical rationality," says Schon, "is the heritage of positivism, the powerful philosophical doctrine that grew up in the nineteenth century as an account of the rise of science and technology to the well-being of mankind" (p. 31). Scholars often refer to another movement which grew out of positivist thought. As Anderson (1990) pointed out, for some decades, notably from the late 1920s to the late 1960s, research in psychology (and also in education) was dominated by the behaviorists. Researchers in the two fields espoused an approach that limited study to that which could be observed, rather than giving attention to human thought, and dealt only with measurable physical behaviors. Thus, the educational processes and techniques were expressed in behavioral terms and instrumental language gained legitimacy in the research community.

The important point made by Schon and other scholars who wrote about this proclivity for articulating processes and techniques within such interrelated rubrics as technical-rationality, instrumentalism, functionalism, and empirical-analytical science is that these epistemological stances are accepted as part of our culture; they form a collective frame of mind. The influence of this frame of mind on supervision had been recognized by Sergiovanni and Starratt (1971). In the first edition of their supervision text, they described conditions in the schools as representative of the larger society's "cult of efficiency and its underlying 'technical rationality'" (p. 215). They cite Ellul (1964) and his thorough analysis of the saturation of Western society by technological rationality.

The foregoing critique of the language of technical-rationality and its influence on supervision certainly suggests that such language imposes limits on both theory and practice by casting supervision too narrowly and overemphasizing processes and techniques. Such a critique, however, is not to be read as implying that there is no appropriate place for the articulation of processes and techniques as a part of supervision. Garman, (1982, 1990), who is generally critical of instrumentalist approaches to supervision, makes just this point using clinical supervision as an example of supervisory practice. She (1986a) pointed out that the seminal authors, Cogan (1973) and Goldhammer (1969), described clinical supervision through their own experiences with the processes and techniques. In the 1960s and 1970s, clinical supervision came to be thoroughly identified with its process and techniques. Garman suggested, however, that the "technique" aspect signifies a "nascent practice" that may, at the outset of training, provide the novice with

a sense of knowledgeableness and helps the novice fend off the anxiety stirred by new tasks. As a temporary defense as well as an early stage of identification with the role of supervisor, the use of technique should be respected. It serves the would-be practitioner's progress, being used with increasing sophistication by those who are growing professionally, and remaining a sterile defense to be used by those who are not (1986a, p. 320).

Garman's statement provides an appropriate caution to hold in mind as consideration is given to research that has been conducted in the field of supervision.

WHAT IS MEANT BY RESEARCH?

The influence of technical-rationality is found both in the language of supervision and in the way that research in the field is commonly viewed. Empirical research tends to come to mind when research is mentioned. Such research focuses on studies of the actual practice of supervision and seeks to determine the relative effectiveness of specific processes and techniques. Thus, a self-perpetuating system of inquiry is created. An emphasis on processes and techniques in supervision is reinforced by the designs of research studies and vice versa.

While empirical studies are certainly valuable to both scholars and practitioners of supervision, they leave out important considerations of such things as the intellectual frameworks, values, beliefs, and purposes that underlie particular forms of supervisory practice. By concentrating exclusively on processes and techniques, research neglects other equally important issues in delineating supervision as a professional practice.

These neglected issues are the ones that concern the intangible aspects of practice (i.e., those frameworks, values, beliefs, and purposes), how they relate to each other, and how they inform the selection of particular processes and

techniques that are the focus of theoretical or conceptual research in supervision. Such work is unfortunately not often recognized as a form of research in a practice that, as has been discussed, is dominated by rational-technical, instrumentalist perspectives. They are relegated to a lesser status as interesting essays, rather being regarded as solid, valuable, and usable research in their own right.

In the following sections of this chapter devoted to exploring existing research on processes and techniques in supervision, such theoretical or conceptual research will be considered along with the more familiar empirical research. This inclusive approach to research allows a better understanding of what various processes and techniques represent as choices for the professional practice of supervision.

CONTEXTS FOR RESEARCH IN SUPERVISION

In the research on supervision, both empirical and conceptual, there are typically two contexts within which authors locate supervisory processes and techniques. One context assumes that supervision occurs primarily at the school level and includes a wide range of techniques that are reflected in various events associated with improvement of instruction. Such events include evaluation of teachers, curriculum development and implementation, and staff development.

A second context for supervision presumes that the classroom is the major setting for supervision because it is where actual teaching takes place. Within the context of in-class supervision, techniques of observation and conference become the focus.

Although the two contexts of school supervision and in-class supervision are both represented in the research, there is an underlying and unresolved tension within the field among scholars who align with one context or the other (e.g., witness the Ben Harris–Morris Cogan discussions that occurred during early sessions of the Council of Professors of Instructional Supervision). School supervision advocates argue that in-class supervision is too narrow a focus for supervisory practice. Proponents of in-class supervision argue that the classroom is where the action is. In reality, the tension is over the *primacy* of techniques associated with the two contexts (i.e., which techniques have more validity) because ultimately the techniques begin to define which context of supervision has more legitimacy (i.e., what supervision is really about).

School-Level Supervision

Much of the material about school-level supervision is found in textbooks. This discussion of school level supervision will, therefore, concentrate primarily on the ways in which these texts construe supervision. It is important to point out that because textbooks are a primary source of information for students in university courses about the conceptual bases of supervision, they exert considerable influence, especially on practitioners' views of what constitutes supervision. A review undertaken for this chapter of nearly three dozen popular and representative textbooks reveals that roughly two thirds of these books describe *supervision* as a school-level function, despite the fact that Eye et al (1971) noted that the "common image of supervision is that of classroom visitation" (p. 289). This is not to say that in-class supervision is ignored; rather, it is subsumed and often accorded relatively minor importance within the larger role of school supervision.[1]

How is it that these texts construe school supervision, and, more specifically, the processes, and techniques associated with its practice? In large part, an answer to this question derives from the influence of practical expediency on school supervision. Practical expediency emphasizes the "functional" in that word's definitional sense of "the kind of action or activity proper to a person, thing or institution" (OED, 1971). Such practical expediency is reflected in three functions that broadly characterize school-level supervision: the need to evaluate teachers, the need to conduct and oversee professional development, and the need to develop of curriculum. These functions tend to be discussed in quite general terms and describe similar methods or processes by which they are carried out by supervisors.

These three functions, and the processes associated with their execution, are readily mentioned in the table of contents of supervision texts published across the past six decades. As has been pointed out elsewhere (Holland, 1995), however, it is not the similarity of reference to common processes that is most significant; rather, it is instead different underlying theoretical and philosophical perspectives. It is also important to note that techniques as well as processes representing various perspectives can be found to coexist within a single text. It is interesting that such generalization and commingling convey an implicit assumption that knowledge within the field of supervision is somehow homogenous. It is an assumption that may get in the way of developing the professional standards of practice currently lacking in supervision.

Evaluation of Teaching Turning now to the processes and techniques associated with each of the three functions of school level supervision,[2] let us begin with evaluation of teaching, the function out of which supervision historically evolved (Lucio & McNeil, 1969). Evaluation of teaching is essentially treated as a management function intended to insure "quality control" over teachers' performance. As such, evaluation is construed as a measurement process and is based in classroom observation. Difficulties with such processes, however, have long been recognized. In 1938, Barr, Burton, and Breukner pointed out the "problem involved in the evaluating of teaching through the use of observational techniques, as it is usually done" (p. 382). They introduced observation instruments as techniques offering greater objectivity and specificity to what aspects of teaching were in fact being measured. They also called for multiple data collection points. Despite their optimism about such instruments, these authors also cite a study by Barr of the validity of activity analyses of teaching that yielded no statistically significant difference between good and poor teachers (Barr et al, 1938).

Nonetheless, interest in the development of instrumentation that would base evaluation of teaching in specified performance measures continued. For example, Lucio and McNeil (1969), discussed "a proposal for teacher evaluation, based on principles related to the teacher's tasks" that included techniques for specifying instructional objectives, pre-assessing instructional objectives and pupil entry behavior, and evaluating instructional objectives (p. 248). What had been added to the process and techniques of evaluation of teaching in 30 intervening years between Barr, Burton, and Breuckner's 1938 text and supervision texts of the late 1960s is typified in Lucio and McNeil's 1969 text. It is an emphasis on a process wherein "supervisor and teacher jointly define the objectives of instruction, specify the pertinent and necessary procedures required to accomplish these purposes, and determine in advance the evaluation methods to be applied" (Lucio & McNeil, 1969, p. 249). This process of collaborative negotiation marks the addition of a different perspective in supervisory evaluation. The process of evaluation, therefore, becomes more democratic and it acknowledges the lived experience (i.e., phenomenology, of the teacher, and the classroom).

As the process of evaluation became more sensitive to differences in teachers and in the contexts of their teaching, supervision came to be seen more as a helping function. This trend was lamented by Lewis and Meil (1972), who claimed that it had gone too far, that supervision had lost its claim to "the function it literally names, overseeing with a view to improving the quality of an operation. . . . We believe supervision is such a monitoring function and that its root concern is enhancing the quality of an operation" (p. 43). Lewis and Meil, however, did not propose a process based on the use of traditional observational rating systems, dismissing these as "interfering with the cooperative planning and mutual learning function" of supervision. Rather, they argued for evaluation grounded in data documenting the teaching–learning process that could then be analyzed and used to improve teaching. Lewis and Meil exemplify a subtle pattern found in the textbooks of the 1970s to integrate the measurement and helping processes of supervisory evaluation. The existence of recognizable standards that determine the quality of teaching behaviors remains only implicit in the process Lewis and Meil describe.

Attempts to make these standards explicit came in the next decade with the advent of the Hunter model. Most educators are certainly familiar with the model of teaching and supervision that Hunter developed and marketed so successfully in the 1980s. Hunter tied supervision and the evaluation of teaching to a generic seven-step teaching process assumed to apply universally to any teaching context (Hunter, 1984), although she claimed that her model is not focused on the presence or absence of those steps, but rather that it looks for "temporal sequencing" and "the flow of a lesson" (Haggerson et al, 1987). During the 1980s, classroom observation and the collection of data recording teacher's behaviors within the model's categories became the norm for evaluation of teaching throughout the United States, and as far afield as Australia (Smyth, 1991). Despite Hunter's claim that her teaching model was not intended to serve as a checklist for the presence or absence of specified practices within each and every lesson, it was—to the dismay of supervision scholars (Hazi &

Garman, 1988; Gibboney, 1987)—implemented in that way by many states and districts (e.g., see Hazi, 1989, for a discussion of the Florida FPMS evaluation system; Crawford, 1989, for a discussion of the Texas TTAS system). For example, Texas had a statewide evaluation process that gathered data about teachers' performance, or lack thereof, for 65 indicators of effective practice. These indicators were primarily derived from Hunter's model, giving greater specificity to behaviors expected as evidence of the seven-step teaching process (Crawford, 1989).

Widespread implementation of instruments based on the Hunter model brought evaluation of teaching full circle back to a traditional measurement practice of rating a teacher based on externally defined and universally prescribed behaviors assumed to be associated with good teaching, which Sergiovanni decried as "scientism" (1989). The 1990s have begun to see the pendulum swing away from such limited views of teaching practice. Discussions of supervisors' evaluative practices recognize multiple and varied processes for evaluating teachers as well as the existence of a wide range of competent teaching styles and different contexts within which teaching and learning occur. For example, Gitlin's (1989) "horizontal evaluation" describes a collaborative model for evaluation of teaching. Sergiovanni and Starratt's 1995 edition of their supervision text describes such evaluation processes as clinical supervision, portfolios, Eisner's (1972) educational connoisseurship and criticism, Scriven's duties-based evaluation (1988), and evaluation based on assessment of authentic student learning such as that described by Murphy and Hallinger (1989). These more individualized techniques suggest that supervisory evaluation is reclaiming its phenomenological orientation.

Staff Development Professional or staff development is closely linked to evaluation of teaching as a function of supervision (McQuarrie & Wood, 1991). In the supervision texts, staff development is often accomplished through in-service programs for teachers that were designed "for the purpose of improving, expanding and renewing the skills, knowledge, and abilities of staff personnel" (Dull, 1981). Such training is seen as both preparing teachers for evaluation, and as remediation for those whose evaluations show them to need additional help. The processes and techniques of staff development tend to reflect the same distinction between rational-technical approaches, which commodify knowledge needed for good teaching, and the phenomenological approaches attending to teachers' individual needs and teaching contexts.

Evidence of the phenomenological perspective is found in research that shows that in-service programs are most successful when they are part of a larger program that includes processes of peer support and classroom follow-up (Joyce & Showers, 1980; McLaughlin & Marsh, 1978). In addition, Hall and his associates (Hall et al, 1975) have shown that in-service programs also need to consider teachers' levels of concern about a particular program or innovation.

Glickman's model of developmental supervision (Glickman, 1985; Gordon, 1990) offers a good example of these findings applied to specific techniques for in-service activities that are appropriate for teachers with low, moderate,

and high abilities of abstract thinking. Glickman (1985) describes abstract thinking as "the ability to determine relationships, to make comparisons and contrasts between information and experience to be used to generate multiple possibilities in formulating a decision" (p. 57). Techniques of explanation and demonstration are recommended for low-abstraction teachers; of classroom practice, peer supervision, and observation for teachers of moderate abstract thinking ability; and modification of classroom practice through teams, brainstorming, and group problem solving for teachers capable of high abstraction (Glickman, 1985, pp. 285–287).

The techniques suggested by Glickman illustrate how the processes and techniques of staff development programs are construed more broadly than are the traditional, rational-technical process of imposed, in-service presentations to large groups of teachers who perceive them as irrelevant to their needs. Despite recurring criticism in the literature on staff development (Wood & Thompson, 1980, who describe them as "the slum of American education"), such in-service presentations continue to be recognized as a common process for addressing teachers' professional development needs. Their persistence, both in the textbooks and in practice, offers a good example of how supervision, lags behind such research and continues to promote ineffective practices of staff development by failing to articulate standards of practice based in available research. Harris (1975) offered a distinction between in-service and advanced professional development that suggests that such functions are significantly different. He maintained that in-service programs are intended to provide learning opportunities for teachers, while advanced preparation offers training and knowledge needed to move to different or higher level positions.

It is interesting, given his clear separation of these two purposes of staff development, that Harris provides a list of 23 widely accepted activities or techniques of supervision that make no distinctions among techniques appropriate for either purpose. These techniques include large group activities, such as lecturing, panel presentations, and demonstrations, small group activities, such as buzz sessions and discussion, and individual activities, such as interviewing and classroom observation. His list implies that such techniques are generic to all purposes for staff development, which is a rational-technical notion implicit in supervision texts prior to Glickman's differentiation of techniques based on teachers' developmental level discussed earlier.

Despite its shortcoming in accounting for teacher needs, Harris's list does offer evidence of another important distinction to be made in a discussion of processes of staff development in supervision. This distinction is that even in the textbooks where the emphasis is primarily on supervision as a school-level function, staff development is seen as a process best conducted on both a school- or departmentwide basis and on an individual level. As Oliva (1989) has pointed out, directors of staff development and principals, who are responsible for creating master plans for their districts or schools, need to employ processes for planning, implementation, and evaluation of staff development programs at both group and individual levels. As such, the process of staff development implicitly includes both the rational-technical and the phenomenological perspective.

Curriculum Development The third function of school-level supervision is curriculum development. As Tanner and Tanner (1987) have pointed out in their review of the history of supervision, "supervision and curriculum development operate hand in hand." Despite assertions of an estrangement between curriculum and supervision (*Journal of Curriculum and Supervision*, 1992), this connection between supervision and curriculum has been an important characteristic of supervision in this century, and the involvement of supervisors in processes of curriculum development has transformed supervision from its origins as a monitoring function to its present status as a practice requiring specialized, professional knowledge and skill. It has also led to descriptions of the process of curriculum development in supervision that reflect the same tensions between the universal and particular, the rational-technical and the phenomenological, that have been described in the other functions of supervision (i.e., evaluation of teaching and staff development).

Oliva (1989) attempts to resolve this tension by noting that supervisors employ a variety of processes in their work with curriculum.

When supervisors help teachers either individually or in groups to make decisions about programs as opposed to methods, they are working in the domain of curriculum development. As curriculum leaders, supervisors direct teachers in the study of scope and sequence, of balance, and of articulation. They are in the curriculum arena when they help faculties try out innovative programs like learning centers, remedial laboratories, open education and nongrading (Oliva, 1989, p. 50).

By placing the focus of curriculum development as a supervisory process on "programs as opposed to methods," Oliva attempts to combine techniques for rational-technical prescription and techniques addressing individualized experience with curriculum.

Three fundamental processes appear in textbook discussions of supervisors' work in curriculum development. Oliva (1989) has categorized these processes as planning, implementation, and evaluation (p. 268). The first of these, planning, is frequently discussed in terms of specific techniques for developing statements for learning goals and behavioral objectives to guide content and instructional activities. For example, Firth and Newfield (1984) distinguish between curriculum goals that are phrased in terms of "input statements" that offer general direction but which allow teachers and students freedom to determine specific subject matter content, and "output goals" that more narrowly specify the material expected to be learned and even the behaviors students will evince to demonstrate their learning.

The second process in curriculum development is that of implementation. Wiles and Bondi (1986) have referred to this process in rational-technical terms as essentially a "management system that takes the basic plan for changing or improving the curriculum and 'drives' it toward completion" (p. 108). A less mechanistic view of this process is provided by Sergiovanni and Starratt (1988), who describe the unique vantage point of the supervisor who is able to identify necessary modifications and provide feedback by being in a position to observe the curriculum in use.

The third process of curriculum development is evaluation. As an observer of enacted curriculum, the supervisor is again in a position to evaluate its effectiveness. The textbooks, however, tend to neglect the advantage supervisors have to gather rich qualitative data about curriculum, and they describe the process of curriculum evaluation as one that is measurement based (Harris, 1975; Lucio & McNeil, 1969; Oliva, 1989).

In-Class Supervision

Turning now to the classroom as the second major context for supervision, a marked difference between the research in school-level and in-class supervision becomes apparent. There is a greater volume of empirical research about in-class supervision as well as a greater representation of in-class supervision in journals and dissertations than is the case for school-level supervision. For example, 195 ERIC citations and 25 dissertation abstracts exist for processes of instructional supervision. One hundred nineteen ERIC citations and 9 dissertation abstracts were found for techniques of instructional supervision. This more extensive body of literature creates a greater complexity in terms of the perspectives that underlie the processes and techniques described.

In-class supervision is broadly characterized by two processes: observing teaching and conferring with teachers. These are the two processes that are assumed within clinical supervision[3] which, in its various permutations, is the most widespread practice for in-class supervision. While there is general agreement about the processes of observation and conference, there is considerable diversity of opinion when it comes to their intended purposes and in the techniques recommended for their execution. In fact, it is at the level of technique that varying perspectives on in-class supervision become most evident. The differences among these perspectives, however, is often masked by general reference to clinical supervision's processes of observation and conference. In order to understand the differences among the theoretical perspectives underlying in-class supervision, it becomes important to look at the techniques used in its processes.

Observation of Teaching The first of these processes for in-class supervision (i.e., observation of teaching) has been discussed in terms of a wide variety of techniques (Learn, 1991). The purpose of the following discussion of observation techniques is not intended to provide an exhaustive list of such techniques as they have been explicated in the research on supervision; rather, it is to selectively describe particular techniques in order to illustrate broad categories within which they can be grouped. An excellent overview of observation techniques for the practice of in-class supervision has been compiled by Acheson and Gall (1992).

One category of observation techniques is already familiar from the previous discussion of school level supervision (i.e., rational-technical instrumentation). Observation techniques within this category rely on the use of predetermined and specifically designated criteria for teacher and student behaviors. Implicit in these techniques is an evaluative intent. Observed teaching and learning are assessed according to the presence or absence of specified criteria, or the extent to which the criteria are present. These criteria indicate standards with which to compare actual teaching and learning.

The type of observation instruments most commonly associated with in-class supervision are checklists. In their simplest form, such checklists provide a list of teacher behaviors, although student behaviors are sometimes also included. These behaviors are assumed to correspond to some general or specific model of good teaching. Official state- and district-level evaluation of teaching forms (e.g., Texas' TTAS and Florida's FPMS) are an obvious example of such instruments. However, these documents are rarely used for improving instruction, only for summative evaluation. A better example of a checklist intended for use in instructional supervision is the Stallings' Observation System (Stallings, 1986). This observation instrument is designed in two separate parts to capture teacher and student behaviors identified in research on effective teaching. It is the first part that offers a good exemplar of an observation checklist. It compares the time spent by teachers and students on 64 variables of student and teacher behavior with criteria time measures in each variable. It is this ability to compare the amount of time spent on the behavioral variables identified on Stallings' checklist in an actual classroom against the specified criterion standards that allows the supervisor and teacher to use the observation data to analyze teaching and identify a teacher's particular strengths and weaknesses.

The second part of the Stallings Observation System provides an example of another significant observation technique: the interaction analysis instrument. Stallings' instrument—the Five-Minute Interaction Profile (FMI)—employs timeline coding to tabulate verbal interactions in an observed classroom. It again correlates these data with criterion standards for their occurrence. The Stallings FMI offers a more complex version of what is perhaps the best known and most researched observation technique—the Flanders Interaction Analysis System (Flanders, 1970)—which identified 10 categories within which to classify all classroom communication. Flanders' system was so popular in the 1960s and 1970s that an entire chapter was devoted to its use in Cogan's 1973 text on clinical supervision.

While observation instruments such as those that have been discussed specify what is to be sought in observation, other techniques rely on contextually determined qualitative data and are more phenomenological in their orientation. One category of such techniques can be classified as "constructionist" in nature. The term *constructionist* is used here in the sense described by Schon (1987) to describe techniques for generating observation data that are "determined by kinds of reality individuals create for themselves, the ways they frame and shape their worlds" (Schon, 1987, p. 322). The most familiar of such techniques, what Acheson and Gall (1992) have descriptively named the "selective verbatim," is traditionally associated with the practice of clinical supervision (Goldhammer, 1969, 1992; Cogan, 1973). Using this observation technique, the supervisor gathers as complete a written record as possible of exactly what is said. This record is "selective" in that it only captures a particular feature, or a few closely related features, of the teaching/learning context. An important characteristic, of the selective verbatim technique is that

the supervisor and teacher identify and agree on what types of verbal behaviors or interactions will be recorded prior to the observation. Thus, selective verbatim as a constructionist technique requires that decisions about what is important to observe become the responsibility of participants in the supervisory process.

Other constructionist techniques draw more directly from ethnographic research methods. For example, Bowers and Flinders (Bowers & Flinders, 1991; Flinders, 1991) document the use of field notes similar to those generated by anthropologists "in which the supervisor records ongoing events as well as observational themes" (p. 25). These field notes are then used to identify "patterns of tacit, cultural knowledge" (p. 26) that can be examined by the supervisor and teacher for their implications about teaching and learning as they occur—and as they might better occur—in the cultural context of the classroom.

Observation as it is conducted within the supervisory process of peer coaching (Joyce & Showers, 1982), or cognitive coaching as Costa and Garmston (1994) have called it, also employs observation techniques for constructionist purposes. Peer coaching, however, does not specify particular observation techniques. Rather, a teacher selects techniques that look like they will provide the kind of information he or she wants about his or her teaching. Thus, peer coaching assumes that teachers have knowledge of a variety of observation techniques and the skill to choose those that appear to be relevant to their particular professional development needs and goals. The observation techniques used in peer coaching are therefore highly contextualized and personal, and, as such, constructionist.

Another category of phenomenologically oriented observation techniques is distinguished from constructionist techniques by a relatively greater degree of interpretation of the events of teaching and learning. Whereas constructionist techniques are primarily focused on what qualitative researchers refer to as "thick description" (Stake, 1978), interpretive techniques shift the emphasis from empirical description to explication of the meaning events have for the observer. One such interpretive technique is described by Eisner (1979) as "educational criticism." While studies of this technique have virtually been limited to Eisner's doctoral students at Stanford, it has attracted attention in the educational literature because of Eisner's status as a leader in the "paradigm wars" of educational research during the late 1970s and 1980s. Eisner is widely recognized as a champion of qualitative, and particularly interpretive, approaches to educational inquiry. His technique of educational criticism rests in his claim that a paradigmatic model for inquiry is found in the arts, both in producing art and in inquiry into the work of artists (i.e., criticism). Important features of the product of educational criticism that locate it within the interpretive perspective are that it is both subjective and representational in nature. As a technique, educational criticism offers a vicarious *experience* of the critic's view of life in a particular classroom. Educational criticism produces accounts that provide rich ethnographic detail and compelling narrative text.

Another technique of interpretive observation is teacher journaling (Bolin, 1988; Zeichner & Liston, 1987), the most subjective of all observation techniques. Journal writing is used by teachers to record their own observations and impressions about their teaching experiences. Such records form a stable text that serves as a basis for the teacher's reflection and questioning of her practice. For example, Bolin's (1988) study of student teachers' use of journals showed that values and beliefs about teaching as well as actual teaching experiences surface in journals. Supervisors can use the issues raised in teachers' journals to help define a program of supervisory assistance that is highly responsive to teachers' own expressed needs and ideas.

The Supervisory Conference The second supervisory process that characterizes in-class supervision is the supervisory conference. Conferencing as a supervisory process occurs in various forms: preconferences prior to observation of instruction, postconferences in which observation data are examined and analyzed, conferences that involve a supervisor and one or more teachers, and conferences of two or more teachers. It is not the form of supervisory conferences, however, that is most distinguishing. Rather, techniques of the supervisory conference merit consideration because of the distinctions various techniques make apparent between rational-technical and phenomenological approaches to supervision.

A distinction within the literature on supervisory conferences is made between conferences whose style and purpose is directive and those whose style and purpose is nondirective (Blumberg & Amidon, 1965; Glickman, 1985). According to Glickman, there are also collaborative conferences that combine directive and nondirective styles and purposes. The techniques employed in directive conferences are consistent with a rational-technical orientation, while collaborative and nondirective conferences are more phenomenologically aligned (Holland, 1989).

Examples of techniques used in directive, rational-technical-oriented conferences include those with evaluative and didactic purposes. Hunter's (1980) description of the evaluative conference, as one among six types of conference, offers an excellent example. During postobservation conferences used for summative evaluation, according to Hunter, "a teacher's placement on a continuum from 'unsatisfactory' to 'outstanding' will be established and the teacher will have the opportunity to examine the evidence used" (Hunter, 1980).

Such an evaluative thrust of postobservation conferences has long been an aspect of clinical supervision and is historically well documented by Weller's Multidimensional Observation System for the Analysis of Interactions in Clinical Supervision (Weller, 1971), which is used to study patterns of verbal communication in supervisory interactions. If one presumes that evaluation exists against some normative view of effective teaching, then the instrument rates the teacher's performance on the standards against which she is being judged. More recently, Waite's (1995) ethnolinguistic studies of supervisory conferences have revealed similar patterns of judgment and criticism of teaching behaviors according to implied or explicit performance standards.

While evaluative techniques are found only in postobservation conferences, didactic techniques are also evident in preobservation conferences. As Mosher and Purpel (1972) described, the intention of such techniques is "teaching" the teacher alternative and assumedly more effective pedagogical strategies. Over the years, a number of studies have supported the use of directive, didactic behavior in the conference (Holland, 1989). These studies suggest that novice teachers may actually prefer such techniques, seeing them as providing needed help and information. In contrast to purely evaluative techniques, didactic techniques leave identification of appropriate and effective teaching practices to the supervisor rather than imposing them through generic observation instruments and specified models of teaching.

As Glickman (1985) has noted, "the belief behind directive behaviors is that the supervisor knows better than the teacher what needs to be done to improve instruction." Such a belief is consistent with the tendency of rational technical thinking to commodify knowledge and create hierarchies based on the possession of greater or lesser amounts of required knowledge. On the other hand, nondirective and collaborative conference techniques reflect phenomenological assumptions that are more democratic. Knowledge is created by those who use it, and is generated out of contexts of lived experience, which in the case of supervision mean teaching, learning, and supervision itself.

Collaborative and nondirective techniques seek the creation of knowledge as better understanding by both teacher and supervisor of how pedagogical decisions affect the nature and quality of instruction and learning. Studies examining actual conferencing behavior, such as Kindsvatter and Wilen's (1981) analysis of conferencing skills, emphasize the technique of supervisors posing questions that engage teachers in high-level thinking skills as they analyze their teaching and develop strategies to improve classroom performance. This pattern supports Blumberg and Amidon's (1965) landmark study of teachers' perceptions that a supervisor's indirect behaviors of asking and listening best enabled them to gain insight into themselves.

Collaborative and nondirective conferencing techniques are most often discussed in terms of developing the teacher's own personal understanding. Cogan (1973) described the process as the supervisor anticipating the teacher's needs and, in the actual interaction of the conference, encouraging teachers to assume their own share of responsibility for analyzing their teaching behavior and for planning its improvement. In addition to personal understanding, however, collaborative and nondirective conferencing techniques also help teachers gain critical awareness of cultural dimensions of schooling and of the interaction between school and society (Gitlin & Smyth, 1989). An important technique for such purposes is that teachers confer with each other as colleagues in a peer supervision relationship. Smyth (1987) envisions such encounters as opportunities for teachers to discuss their teaching with each other in ways that move beyond casual conversation or attempts at quick fixes for problems. He proposes that teachers employ techniques of rigorously questioning or "problematizing" their practice, and describes encounters in which "teachers can actively intervene in their own teaching so as to challenge the conventional wisdom of established practices" (Gitlin & Smyth, 1989).

CONCLUSION: SUPERVISION AT THE CROSSROADS

This chapter began with an expression of concern about the lack of articulated standards of practice in the field of supervision. It was assumed that such standards would allow a critical stance that would clarify processes and techniques appropriate to the professional practice of supervision. As the preceding review has shown, however, the absence of standards of practice allows for processes and techniques that appear to represent widely divergent perspectives on the theory and practice of supervision.

While these different perspectives are in themselves enough to bring supervision to a crossroads, additional factors are also affecting how supervision is defined and practiced. For example, the trend to site-based management raises questions about both the place and function of supervision, and emerging challenges from the religious right suggest that processes and techniques of mediation may become an important part of a supervisor's practice. These examples illustrate changes that are occurring in the ways schools are thought about and, by extension, the way supervision needs to be envisioned.

How might research on processes and techniques of supervision deal with these challenges of widely diverging theories of practice and changes in the organization of schooling? In part, the answer depends on what schools will look like in the future. Strike (1990) has described three normative models of schooling, each of which would lead to different kinds of supervisory processes and techniques. The first of these models, "bureaucratic democracy," would place supervisors in traditional hierarchical management positions in which they would be responsible for generating rules and procedures for implementing policy, and for monitoring compliance with policy. It is a role that makes supervision a school-level function requiring rational-technical, instrumentalist processes and techniques for evaluation, staff development, and curriculum development. Such processes and techniques would be for purposes of establishing and maintaining effective management systems.

The second model is "professionalism." Strike quotes Darling-Hammond's (1985) explanation of the nature of professionalism in education: "At the core of the definition of a profession is the notion that its members must define and enforce their own standards of practice" (p. 212). This statement suggests that schools organized according to principles of professionalism would involve a conceptualization of in-class supervision, based in service, and attentive to the teacher's perceptions of their needs and experiences—in other words, a phenomenological perspective.

The third normative model of schooling is that of "communitarian democracy." As Strike explains this model, it is an organizational structure

where those who must implement or undergo group decisions are full participants in the discussions that produce them . . . it allows for high levels of participation in decision-making by those most directly affected, it makes decisions dialogically, and its tends not to create hierarchical structures (Strike, 1990, p. 369).

This model has considerable potential for resolving what appear in the research on supervisory processes and techniques as conflicting interests between school-level supervision and in-class supervision, and between rational-technical and phenomenological perspectives. In a communitarian democracy, rational-technical processes and techniques of supervision would be used at the decision of teachers, administrators, parents, and even students to create school-level supervisory practices that serve their needs. Phenomenological perspectives would be represented in dialogic processes of questioning and examining teaching and practices.

Processes and techniques of supervision do not exist in a vacuum. They are utilized by real supervisors and teachers within the contexts of real schools. As such, the relationship between organizational models of schooling and particular processes and techniques of supervision is an important consideration for future research. In fact, it may help to establish standards of practice at least within particular school contexts.

REFERENCES

Acheson, K. & Gall, M. (1992). *Techniques in the clinical supervision of teachers* (3rd ed.). New York: Longman.

Anderson, W. (1990). *Reality isn't what it used to be.* San Francisco: Harper and Row.

Barr, A., Burton, W., & Breuckner, L. (1938). *Supervision: Democratic leadership in the improvement of learning.* New York: Appleton-Century-Crofts.

Berman, P. & McLaughlin, M. (1978). *Federal programs supporting educational change Vol. 8: Implementing and sustaining innovations.* ED 159 289. Santa Monica, CA: Rand Corporation.

Blumberg, A. & Amidon, E. (1965). Teacher perceptions of supervisor-teacher interactions. *Administrator's Notebook, 14,* 1–4.

Bolin, F. (1988). Helping student teachers think about teaching. *Journal of Teacher Education, 39,* 48-54.

Bowers, C. & Flinders, D. (1991). *Responsive teaching: an ecological approach to classroom patterns of language, culture and thought.* New York: Teachers College Press.

Cogan, M. (1973). *Clinical supervision.* Boston: Houghton Mifflin Company.

Consulting Editors, Journal of Curriculum and Supervision (1992). Estrangement between curriculum and supervision: Personal observations on the current scene. *Journal of Curriculum and Supervision, 7*(3), 245–249.

Costa, A. & Garmston, R. (1994). *Cognitive coaching: A foundation for renaissance schools.* Norwood, MA: Christopher-Gordon Publishers, Inc.

Crawford, J. (1989). *Reliability and validity analysis of the Texas teacher appraisal system.* Unpublished dissertation, University of Houston.

Darling-Hammond, L. (1985). Valuing teachers: The making of a profession. *Teachers College Record, 87*(2), 205–218.

Dull, L. (1981). *Supervision: School leadership handbook.* Columbus, OH: Charles E. Merrill Publishing Company.

Eisner, E. (1979). *The educational imagination: On the design and evaluation of school programs.* New York: Macmillan Publishers.

Eisner, E. (1982). An artistic approach to supervision. In T. Sergiovanni (Ed.). *Supervision of teaching.* Alexandria, VA: ASCD.

Ellul, J. (1964). *The technological society,* trans. by J. Wilkerson. New York: Alfred A. Knopf.

Eye, G., Netzer, L., & Krey, R. (1971). *Supervision of instruction.* New York: Harper & Row Publishers.

Firth, J. & Newfield, J. (1984). Curriculum development and selection. In J. Cooper (Ed.). *Developing skills for instructional supervision.* New York: Longman.

Flanders, N. (1970). *Analyzing teaching behavior.* Reading, MA: Addison-Wesley.

Flinders, D. (1991). Supervision as cultural inquiry. *Journal of Curriculum and Supervision, 6*(2), 87–106.

Foster, W. (1986). *Paradigms and promises: New approaches to educational administration.* Buffalo, NY: Prometheus Books.

Garman, N. (1986a). Getting to the essence of practice in clinical supervision. In J. Smyth (Ed.). *Learning about teaching through clinical supervision.* London: Croom Helm.

Garman, N. (1986b). Clinical supervision: Quackery or remedy for professional development. *Journal of Curriculum and Supervision, 1*(2), 148–157.

Garman, N. (1990). Theories embedded in the events of clinical supervision: A hermeneutic approach. *Journal of Curriculum and Supervision, 5*(3), 201–213.

Garman, N. & Hazi, H. (1988). Teachers ask: Is there life after Madeline Hunter? *Phi Delta Kappan, 69*(9), 669–672.

Gibboney, R. (1987). A critique of Madeline Hunter's teaching model from Dewey's perspective. *Educational Leadership, 44,* 46–50.

Gitlin, A. (1989). Educative school change: Lived experiences in horizontal evaluation. *Journal of Curriculum and Supervision, 4*(4), 322–339.

Gitlin, A. & Smyth, J. (1989). *Teacher evaluation: Educative alternatives.* New York: The Falmer Press.

Glickman, C. (1985). *Supervision of instruction: A developmental approach.* Boston: Allyn and Bacon, Inc.

Goldhammer, R. (1969). *Clinical supervision: Special methods for the supervision of teachers.* New York: Holt, Rinehart and Winston, Inc.

Goldhammer, R. (1992). *The Robert Goldhammer papers: Early writings of a distinguished educator.* Tampa, FL: Pedamorphosis, Inc.

Gordon, S. (1990). Developmental supervision: An exploratory study of a promising model. *Journal of Curriculum and Supervision, 5*(4), 293–307.

Haggerson, N., Garman, N., Glickman, C., & Hunter, M. (1987). Conflicting conceptions of clinical supervision and the enhancement of professional growth and renewal: Point and counterpoint. *Journal of Curriculum and Supervision, 2*(2), 152–177.

Hall, G., Loucks, S., Rutherford, W., & Newlove, B. (1975). Levels of use of the innovation: A framework for analyzing innovation adoption. *Journal of Teacher Education, 26*(1), 52–56.

Harris, B. (1975). *Supervisory behavior in action* (2nd ed.). Englewood Cliffs, NJ: Prentice Hall.

Hazi, H. (1989). Measurement versus supervisory judgment: The case of Sweeney v. Turlington. *Journal of Curriculum and Supervision, 4*(2), 211–229.

Holland, P. (1989). Implicit assumptions about the supervisory conference. *Journal of Curriculum and Supervision, 4*(4), 362–379.

Holland, P. (1995). What do we talk of when we talk of supervision? Paper presented to the Conference of Professors of Instructional Supervision, New York.

Hunter, M. (1980). Six types of educational conferences. *Educational Leadership, 37,* 409.

Hunter, M. (1984). Knowing, teaching and supervising. In P. Hosford (Ed.). *Using what we know about teaching.* Alexandria, VA: ASCD.

Joyce, B. & Showers, B. (1982). Improving in-service training: The message of research. *Educational Leadership, 39,* 379–385.

Joyce, B. & Showers, B. (1982). The coaching of teaching. *Educational Leadership, 40,* 4–10.

Kincheloe, J. (1991). *Teachers as researchers: Qualitative inquiry as a path to empowerment.* London: The Falmer Press.

Kindsvatter, R. & Wilen, W. (1981). A systematic approach to improving conference skills. *Educational Leadership, 38,* 525–529.

Learn, R. (1991). Perspectives in the literature on the centrality of observation in instructional supervision. Unpublished dissertation, University of Pittsburgh.

Lewis, A. & Meil, A. (1972). *Supervision for improved instruction: New challenges, new responses.* Belmont, CA: Wadsworth.

Lucio, W. & McNeil, J. (1969). *Supervision: A synthesis of thought and action.* New York: McGraw-Hill Book Company.

Marcuse, H. (1966). *One dimensional man.* Boston: Beacon Press.

McQuarrie, F. & Wood, F. (1991). Supervision, staff development, and evaluation connections. *Theory Into Practice, 30*(2), 91–96.

Mosher, R. & Purpel, D. (1972). *Supervision: The reluctant profession.* Boston: Houghton Mifflin Company.

Murphy, J. & Hallinger, P. (1989). Equity as access to learning: Curricular and instructional treatment differences. *Journal of Curriculum Studies, 21*(3), 132.

Oliva, P. (1989). *Supervision for today's schools* (3rd ed). New York: Longman.

The compact edition of the Oxford English dictionary (1971). Glasgow: Oxford University Press.

Schon, D. (1983). *The reflective practitioner.* New York: Basic Books.

Schon, D. (1987). *Educating the reflective practitioner.* San Francisco: Jossey-Bass Publishers.

Scriven, M. (1988). Evaluating teachers as professionals: The duties-based approach. In J. Popham (Ed.). *Teacher evaluation: Six prescriptions for success.* Alexandria, VA: ASCD.

Sergiovanni, T. (1989). Science and scientism in supervision and teaching. *Journal of Curriculum and Supervision, 4*(2), 93–105.

Sergiovanni, T. & Starratt, R. (1971). *Emerging patterns of supervision: Human perspectives.* New York: McGraw-Hill.

Sergiovanni, T. & Starratt, R. (1988). *Supervision: Human perspectives,* New York: McGraw-Hill.

Sergiovanni, T. & Starratt, R. (1995), *Supervision: A redefinition* (5th ed). New York: McGraw-Hill, Inc.

Smyth, J. (1986). Developing a critical practice of clinical supervision. *Journal of Curriculum Studies, 17*(1), 1–15.

Smyth, J. (1988). A critical perspective for clinical supervision. *Journal of Curriculum and Supervision, 3*(2), 136–156.

Smyth, J. (1991). Instructional supervision and the redefinition of who does it in schools. *Journal of Curriculum and Supervision, 7*(1), 90-99.

Stake, R. (1978). The case study method in social inquiry. *Educational Researcher, 7,* 5–8.

Stallings, J. (1986). Using time effectively: A self-analytic approach. In K. Zumwalt (Ed.). *Improving Teaching.* Alexandria, VA: ASCD.

Strike, K. (1990). The ethics of educational evaluation. In J. Millman & L. Darling-Hammond (Eds.). *The new handbook of teacher evaluation: Assessing elementary and secondary school teachers.* Newbury Park, CA: Sage Publications.

Tanner, D. & Tanner, L. (1987). *Supervision in education: Problems and practices.* New York: Macmillan Publishing Company.

Tolstoy, L. (1981). *Anna Karenina.* Cited in C. Bly, *Letters from the country.* New York: Penguin Books.

Van Manen (1977). Linking ways of knowing with ways of being practical. *Curriculum Inquiry, 6,* 205–228.

Waite, D. (1995). *Rethinking instructional supervision: Notes on its language and culture.* London: The Falmer Press.

Weller, R. (1971). *Verbal communication in instructional supervision.* New York: Teachers College Press.

Wiles, J. & Bondi, J. (1986). *Supervision: A guide to practice* (3rd ed.). Columbus, OH: Charles E. Merrill Publishing Company.

Wood, F. & Thompson, S. (1980). Guidelines for better staff development. *Educational Leadership, 37*(5), 374–378.

Zeichner, K. & Liston, D. (1987). Teaching student teachers to reflect. *Harvard Educational Review, 57,* 23–48.

NOTES

1. Notable exceptions to the emphasis on schoolwide supervision are found in those few texts that focus on clinical supervision. Examples of such texts are: Goldhammer, 1969; Cogan, 1973; Acheson and Gall, 1987. These works will be discussed in greater detail in the section of this chapter on in-class supervision.

2. The discussion of the functions of supervision in this chapter are not intended to be an exhaustive inventory of processes and techniques described in the literature. Rather, the objective is to provide an overview of the nature of the discourse about processes and techniques for school-level and in-class supervision.

3. Classic texts on clinical supervision are Goldhammer (1969) and Cogan (1973). Acheson and Gall (1992) provide practical information about the process and techniques of clinical supervision and a review of related research. The Garman's (1983, 1986a, 1986b, 1990) and Smyth's (1985, 1986, 1988) writings offer notable current perspectives on clinical supervision.

·14·

SUPERVISION IN TEACHER EDUCATION

D. John McIntyre
SOUTHERN ILLINOIS UNIVERSITY

David M. Byrd
UNIVERSITY OF RHODE ISLAND

The purpose of this chapter is to examine research in the area of supervision as conducted throughout teacher education. In that regard, attention will focus on the early field experience and student teaching phases of undergraduate and/or graduate teacher preparation, supervision through professional development schools, and other innovative or emerging patterns of supervision related to teacher education. We will not address issues related to the supervision of practicing teachers in schools because that topic will be more than adequately addressed throughout the handbook.

Glickman and Bey (1990) stated that substantially less research literature is available on supervision in preservice teacher education than on in-service education. They state that supervision in preservice teacher education has been sporadic, with many areas not covered. This chapter will provide a vehicle for other teacher educators to examine the current state of supervision in teacher education and to help focus questions that will formulate a research agenda in this area for the future.

THEORETICAL FRAMEWORK FOR TEACHER EDUCATION AND SUPERVISION

In order to examine the status of preservice teacher education supervision, one must first understand the theoretical underpinnings of field experiences, in general, and teacher education, as a whole. The lack of a theoretical framework or a clear set of goals for the development and implementation of field experiences has long been lamented by teacher educators. It has been argued that no agreed-upon definition of the purpose and goals for the field component of teacher education exists (McIntyre, 1983; Watts, 1987; Zeichner, 1987; Guyton & McIntyre, 1990). This lack of focus and purpose for

field experiences both emanated from a similar problem existing in teacher education programs as a whole and affected the direction, or lack thereof, of supervision conducted throughout the teacher education program. Without a direction or vision for the teacher education program, supervision would most likely also be conducted without clearly stated goals and would serve to further exasperate the link between field experiences and campus-based courses, between theory and practice. As Cromwell and Browne (1993) stated, the need for clearly stated goals for a teacher education program is critical for supervision because "if we do not know where we are going, it will be very hard to get there and difficult to educate others about their choices along the way" (p. 41).

Goodlad, Soder, and Sirotnik (1990) discovered that the typical teacher education program was comprised of a collection of courses, various field experiences, and student teaching. Each of these components appeared to be separate from the others and was taught by a variety of faculty who had little or no communication with each other. They stated that it was not uncommon for cooperating teachers not to have the slightest notion of the program's goals, or for them to have any idea whether any existed.

Emerging Unifying Theoretical Frameworks

McIntyre, Byrd, and Foxx (1996) stated that evidence has emerged to indicate that theory and practice are becoming integrated in teacher education programs, and that a set of goals and objectives are creating a common theme or model throughout these programs, including the supervision of field experiences. A major force in this evolution is the standards adopted by the National Council for Accreditation of Teacher Education (NCATE) in 1987. These standards require participating institutions to explicate a conceptual framework and knowledge base that undergirds the purpose, processes, and outcomes of their teacher education program. The model and knowledge base adopted by the institutions must unify all components of a program, including campus courses and field and laboratory experiences. One of the major means for unifying these particular components is through supervision.

Although the NCATE standards do not specify a common model to be adopted by all institutions, there does appear to be a trend emerging toward program goals and models that develop teachers who are reflective decision makers, and not mere technicians. For example, Liston and Zeichner (1991) propose that the aims of teacher education programs should focus on developing teachers who are able to identify and articulate their purposes, who can choose the appropriate instructional strategies, who understand the social experiences and cognitive orientations of their students, and who can articulate their actions. Effective teachers must have an understanding of the activity of teaching and have a greater understanding of the political and social context of schooling. Farber, Wilson, and Holm (1989) supported this framework for teacher education by asserting that teachers must be sensitized to the full range of sociopolitical and personal consequences of student practice; they must examine the moral and professional ambiguities in the process of schooling; and they must critically examine the consequences of standard practice.

Constructivism, Reflective Teachers, and Supervision

The trend toward developing a theoretical framework in teacher education is resulting in a movement away from a positivist orientation to a more constructivist approach to teacher preparation (Alkove & McCarty, 1992). A positivist teacher education program assumes that outside forces determine standards and that people conform to established practices and follow mandates handed down by those in authority. These programs tend to create teachers who are followers, who do as they are told, and who communicate this to their students.

The constructivist framework emphasizes the growth of the prospective teacher through experiences, reflection, and self-examination. Constructivist programs recognize that teachers are primarily persons who enter the program processing values and beliefs that form the foundation from which they make professional choices. Student teachers within this framework view teaching as ongoing decision-making rather than as a product or recipe. These student teachers learn that significant education must present learners with relevant problematic situations in which the learner can manipulate objects to see what happens, to question what is already known, to compare their findings and assumptions with those of others, and to search for their own answers. As a result, constructivist teacher education must provide prospective teachers with the same orientation and experiences in both coursework and field experiences. The link between the two components is the supervision provided throughout field experiences.

This emergence of constructivist teacher education programs has resulted in the movement toward developing

reflective teachers (i.e., Eby, 1992; Roth, 1989; Valli, 1992; Zeichner & Liston, 1987). Cohn and Gellman (1988) said that reflective inquiry involves raising questions as to the appropriateness of teacher action in any given situation. The emphasis on reflectivity or inquiry in teacher education is predicated on the assumption that teaching is a complex and normative activity that requires continual decision-making and problem solving. Teachers must learn to be inquirers who can make connections between the theory and methods that are available to them and the practical situations they encounter in differing contexts.

Preservice students must practice reflectivity and observe it being practiced by experienced teachers. Bullough (1989) asserted that teacher education programs should restructure all field experiences so students can engage in reflective decision-making and can act on their decisions in the spirit of praxis. He believed that reflective field experiences should begin during the first semester or quarter of the preservice teacher's program, and should emphasize the study and critique of the school and cultural context within which they will be working. Changing the conditions of student teaching and supervision is of primary importance if reflectivity is to become a true objective of teacher education programs.

The notion of modifying the conditions of student teaching is a common theme among teacher educators who advocate the development of reflective teachers. For example, Britzman (1991) stated that student teachers possess a personal biography that shapes their expectations of "real school life." The courses that these students take throughout their teacher education program are viewed as impractical and too theoretical. Student teaching is the opportunity to link theory and practice; however, it too often serves to widen the gulf between the two. The role of student teaching in the process of merging theory and practice emphasizes the importance of the supervision process. As teacher education students spend more time in field experiences, the importance of those who supervise these experiences also increases (Metcalf, 1991). As Guyton and McIntyre (1990) stated, "supervision processes are what make up the event called student teaching" (p. 527).

The movement toward defining the purpose of field experiences and toward clarifying the goals of teacher education is encouraging. This action is assisting our profession in determining the kinds of teachers we desire to prepare for future classrooms and aids in guiding the entire thrust of the teacher education program, including the supervision process. Quantifiable and qualitative data, are missing, however, that will enable teacher educators to determine if these programs are, indeed, preparing more thoughtful, reflective teachers that are more effective in the classroom than are those prepared in more traditional, apprentice-type programs.

RELATIONS WITHIN THE SUPERVISORY TRIAD

The activities and processes of supervision of preservice teacher education is linked to a triad that consists of a student teacher, university supervisor, and cooperating teacher (Glickman & Bey, 1990). Many of the problems that arise during the supervisory process arise out of the conflicting philosophies of conservative cooperating teachers and liberal university supervisors that place stressful demands on the student teacher (Vickery & Brown, 1967). It is interesting that Peterson (1977) found that students, prior to student teaching, anticipate philosophical disagreement between cooperating teachers and university supervisors, and are thus not surprised that conflict occurs.

Numerous studies have found differences in understanding among cooperating teachers, college supervisors, and student teachers about each other's roles, expectations, decision-making, and the process for policy formation (Castillo, 1971; Copas, 1984; Grimmett & Ratzlaff, 1986; Kapel & Sadler, 1978). There are even disagreements as to the student teacher's role (Gettone, 1980). These disagreements are partly based on the developmental nature of field experiences in which students' roles often change over time. This phenomenon is evidenced by the fact that Calderhead (1987) found that even student teachers' perceptions of their own roles shifted over the course of student teaching. There are also differences in opinion, however, that go beyond each group having similar perspectives, yet these different expectations are relative to the speed with which student teachers develop a full range of abilities and dispositions. For example, cooperating teachers and student teachers perceived that the most important factor during student teaching was the development of self-confidence.

Student teachers and cooperating teachers occasionally have such severe philosophical differences that the student teacher reconsiders his or her career choice and the cooperating teacher questions her or his continued role as a teacher educator (Wiggins & Clift, 1995). On the other hand, college supervisors and school administrators considered application of theory into practice as the most important issue during student teaching (Tittle, 1974). It is interesting that student teachers rated experimentation during student teaching of much higher value than cooperating teachers, supervisors, or administrators. Therefore, although triads of student teachers, cooperating teachers, and college supervisors work together in productive ways every day, their interactions are not without tension and some angst. A good portion of this tension seems to be caused by a lack of communication and agreement as to the responsibilities of each member of the triad.

It is perhaps not surprising that Wiggins and Clift (1995) found that student teachers often have opposing beliefs "with no apparent awareness of the inconsistency" between these beliefs (p. 10). Examples of opposing beliefs included the "obligation of the teacher to be an external motivator as opposed to the obligation of the students to have an innate motivation to learn," "the importance of individualizing instruction as opposed to concerns for equality and avoiding favoritism" and "the desire to be a friend to . . . students as opposed to [the] need to be an evaluator" (p. 11). That student teachers possess opposing beliefs is not in and of itself necessarily a concern, unless the conflicting views appear to be keeping student teachers from functioning adequately. Data clearly show that this was the case, at least for the student teachers in this study. From a supervisory standpoint, it is an important finding that the student teachers under study both had opposing beliefs that created conflict during student

teaching and that these conflicts were not recognized or resolved by supervisory interactions between the student teachers, cooperating teachers, and university supervisors.

Kagan (1990) provided additional insight into the phenomenon by suggesting that teacher and teacher educator attitudes and behaviors are a direct result of the norms of their workplace. She said that schools can be low-consensus (i.e., isolated and pluralistic) or high-consensus (i.e., with agreement as to goals and desirable teaching methods), and that sharing a professional culture or sense of what its members hope to accomplish is an important characteristic of successful, or what Rosenholtz (1989) calls "consensus," schools. University faculty, on the other hand, are described as a highly fragmented, pluralistic group, similar to teachers in low-consensus schools. Although academic freedom is central to being a professor, teacher educators and teacher education programs appear to define the term *low-consensus* (Howey & Zimpher, 1989; Wisniewski & Ducharme, 1989). As stated previously, however, NCATE standards require that "the unit has high quality professional education programs that are derived from a conceptual framework(s) that is knowledge-based, articulated, shared, coherent, consistent, with the unit and/or institutional mission and continuously evaluated" (NCATE, 1995, p. 15).

Even with this accreditation requirement, many teacher education programs continue to struggle with the development and integration of a unifying focus/purpose. This issue of shared vision for teacher education is an essential attribute of successful teacher education programs that is further elevated by Howey and Zimpher (1989) in *Profiles of Preservice Teacher Education*. Their analysis of teacher education programs at six distinct types of higher education institutions supported the importance of having "conceptually coherent programs [which] enable needed and *shared* faculty leadership to engage in more generative and continuing renewal by underscoring collective roles as well as individual course responsibilities" (1989, p. 242). If a lack of consensus on campuses exists in relation to direction and goals for teacher education programs, then one cannot be surprised to find a lack of agreement between the campus and the field regarding goals, roles, and responsibilities expected of student teachers, cooperating teachers, and university faculty.

Howey and Zimpher's interviews with cooperating teachers provide some evidence of the range of perceptions held by cooperating teachers. Cooperating teachers were asked "whether they believed the students today appear to be better prepared to teach than they were formerly" (p. 142). Most responded in a positive manner. For example, one teacher responded, "Of course, it depends upon the student teacher you work with in terms of how you see the program, but I've had excellent student teachers to work with. I'm amazed at how much know-how they have when they come into the classroom and how willing they are to try things" (p. 142). Cooperating teachers, however, also had concerns. The following response is illustrative of these concerns:

I think the whole approach to training teachers is wrong. I think all people going into education should spend at least the first two years—or maybe more—in liberal arts. . . . My students don't always know some of the basics in American history. They don't know . . . they haven't read basic works of literature. And it's not because they don't want to, they haven't had the opportunity (p. 144).

These exchanges provide some indication of the range and strength of opinions held by teachers on the issue of teacher preparation. Discussion of the content preparation of student teachers is a good example of the type of issue about which university professors, supervisors, and cooperating teachers may have differing opinions.

Communication during student teaching and the need for understanding as to the purposes, roles, and responsibilities during supervision is generally accepted in principle, yet it is hard to achieve. Whether or not college or university faculty agree with the perception of a cooperating teacher that a student teacher's content preparation is incomplete, without discussion and analysis, this issue is likely to cause concern for the student teacher and potentially all future student teachers in a building or district. There is ample information available from professional specialty organizations on recommended levels of content preparation and valid data on the importance of adequate content preparation (see the content preparation in this chapter) for this issue to be resolved; however, issues less rich in data must also be open for review to support clear recommendations.

In addition to the call for a common knowledge base for teacher education programs, there has also been discussion of the need for the delineation of the roles and responsibilities of each triad member. These roles and responsibilities have been outlined in college/university student teaching handbooks and in state teacher education program approval standards, such as those developed by the National Association of State Directors of Teacher Education and Certification (NASDTEC), and the national accreditation standards of NCATE. Delineating roles and responsibilities, however, is only the first step toward ensuring that each member of the triad commits to fulfilling them. Without commitment to implementation, handbooks and approval programs will not improve student teaching or the supervision of teacher education students. Many programs, however, are beginning to address the issues regarding the roles and responsibilities of cooperating teachers and university supervisors effectively (Bennett, Ishler, & O'Loughlin, 1992; Cochran-Smith, 1991; Guyton, 1989; Heathington, Cagle, & Blank, 1988; University of Arizona Cooperating Teacher Project, 1988; Wolfe, Schewel, & Bickman, 1989). Exemplary programs and practices are the necessary building blocks for establishing and maintaining collaborative relationships.

Cooperating Teachers

Teachers perceive that their cooperating teachers had the most significant influence on them during student teaching (Evertson, 1990; Glickman & Bey, 1990; Karmos & Jacko, 1977; Manning, 1977; Metcalf, 1991). Blocker and Swetnam (1995) stated that cooperating teachers are the professionals most available to the student teacher for advice, direction, and support. Student teachers observe and interact with cooperating teachers for more time than they observe any other

professional in their training. Because these observations and interactions take place with the contextual knowledge, background information, and immediate factors that influence the cooperating teachers' behavior, they overtly and subtly influence the student teacher's attitude and behaviors. In addition, it is the cooperating teacher who provides the majority of assessment regarding the student teacher's teaching, planning, and student behavior.

In 1991, the American Association of Colleges of Teacher Education released a report of a survey of 228 cooperating teachers. They reported the following statistics regarding the "typical" cooperating teacher:

- White (96%)
- Female (75%)
- 43 years old
- Has taught for approximately 16 years
- Has been in the same school for approximately 12 years
- Holds a masters degree (50%) or a certificate of advanced study or doctorate (10%)
- Represents all grade levels with about 60% in elementary classrooms and 40% in secondary classrooms

The attitudes of student teachers is perhaps the variable most strongly shaped by cooperating teachers as the semester progresses (Dunham, 1958; Johnson, 1969; Price, 1961). Mahan and Lacefield (1976) found this specifically true of students' attitudes toward schooling. When discrepancies existed between the attitudes of student teachers and cooperating teachers, the movement of the student was in the direction of the teacher. Student teacher attitudes seem to become more custodial and negative with a focus on classroom management, control, and lesson completion, without concern for student progress (Dispoto, 1980; Iannacone, 1963).

Whereas studies have supported the general trend of movement of students' attitudes toward that of their cooperating teachers, there is a growing perception that the cooperating teacher alone is not responsible for this shift (Bryant, 1982). For example, Horowitz (1968) discovered that there were no statistically significant shifts in student teachers' views of teaching from pre- to post-student teaching at the conclusion of student teaching. Boschee, Prescott, and Hein (1978) found that there was no significant relation between student teachers' educational philosophy after student teaching and that of cooperating teachers. Zeichner (1979) points out that some student teachers do not adopt the attitudes of their cooperating teacher and that researchers should determine why some student teachers resist socialization while others do not.

The merging of the classroom behaviors of student teachers and their cooperating teachers has, to this point, been conflicting. Studies by Price (1961), Seperson and Joyce (1973), and Zevin (1974) have indicated adoption and movement of student teachers toward their cooperating teachers' classroom style. Flint (1965) discovered that although there was no relationship between student and cooperating teacher behavior before student teaching, the student teachers' classroom verbal behavior correlated significantly with that of their cooperating teachers at the end of a three-week assignment.

Seperson and Joyce, however, found this influence pervasive only during the first few weeks of student teaching. McIntyre, Buell, and Casey (1979) reported that student teachers do not model the verbal behaviors of their cooperating teachers.

Whereas the majority of the research on field placements has focused on attitudinal changes, there is a growing body of research concerned with other characteristics of the cooperating teacher. In a study to determine if characteristics of field placements had a relationship to students' final evaluations, Becher and Ade (1982) placed students in three settings: (1) teacher models good teaching; (2) teacher gives feedback to the student teacher; (3) teacher allows the opportunity for innovation. They found that there was a lack of a strong relationship between the modeling of good practice by cooperating teachers and the final performance ratings of field experienced students. This finding is of major interest because the selection of cooperating teachers who are perceived as good role models is a pervasive criterion for placement of student teachers. It would seem that being a good role model, in and of itself, is not sufficient to bring about positive behaviors in students. Possible reasons for this finding might be that students could not recognize an effective model, cooperating teachers had little knowledge of the benefits of modeling (Joyce, Showers, & Rolheiser-Bennett, 1987; Joyce and Weil, 1986), or the cooperating teachers lacked expertise in guiding student practice. The results of feedback given to field experienced students were mixed (i.e., highly positive for the last two semesters and negative for the first); whereas the results for innovation were highly positive in the first and last, but not during the second. These results are more difficult to explain. Perhaps they were due to the perception by students and their cooperating teachers that students were to develop and practice, but not imitate, their teachers. In addition, one would expect that high-feedback teachers would provide additional feedback on the criterion used for the final evaluation and that this would aid student performance on the final evaluation.

Because the pervasive perception regarding the selection of cooperating teachers is that of a good role model, it is interesting to note a study by Blocker and Swetnam (1995). The results of their survey indicated that the most important criteria for selecting cooperating teachers is the recommendation of the building principal, evaluations of previous student teacher supervision, and at least three years of classroom experience. It was also important that the teacher volunteered and had held her or his position a minimum number of years. The criterion used by the building principal to recommend cooperating teachers was not investigated and is still an interesting variable to be studied by future research.

Conferencing is often considered the most critical component of teacher education supervision. Through conference, university supervisors and cooperating teachers develop a productive and cooperative relationship with teacher education candidates. Foremost attention must be given to establishing a positive working relationship with an emphasis on interpersonal communications skills. All members of the supervision triad need to exhibit a respect for others, communicate in clear, concrete, and nonjudgmental terms, and encourage the active participation of one another in decision-making and goal setting (O'Shea, Hoover, & Carroll, 1988).

Wilkins-Canter (1996) investigated the frequency, conditions, content, and methods of feedback provided by the cooperating teacher to the student teacher. She discovered that most feedback is provided on a daily basis and lasted between 5 and 15 minutes, depending on the topic being discussed or the magnitude of the problem. Although the time most preferred to provide feedback was during the school day or after school, most feedback occurred at the end of the school day. Feedback occurring immediately after an observed lesson was less frequent. The feedback tended to focus on discipline, instruction, and student concerns. Feedback on discipline focused on classroom and behavior management. Discussions regarding instruction centered on lesson plans, long-term planning, time management, and learning styles. The topic of student concerns dealt mainly with student attitudes, attendance, motivation, and personal problems.

Richardson-Koehler (1988) reported that cooperating teachers are typically unwilling to share negative criticism with their student teachers. She pointed out that in three-way meetings between the cooperating teacher, student teacher, and university supervisior, cooperating teachers tended to defend the student teachers regarding issues about which they had privately expressed concern to the university supervisor beforehand. In addition, Zimpher, deVoss, and Nott (1980) found that cooperating teachers tend not to provide students with feedback and critical analyses of their teaching.

Wright, Silvern, and Burkhater (1982) investigated whether cooperating teachers demonstrate or give direction on how to carry out activities that were perceived by university faculty and the cooperating teachers as instructionally important (i.e., first, reading to class; second, conducting oral reading lesson with an audience situation; and third, guiding pupils to more extensive reading). They found that more than half the students did not recall receiving instruction to perform any of the listed tasks. Furthermore, teachers were much more likely to demonstrate an activity than they were to give directions. These studies on modeling point out that students need to observe and to model the behaviors of cooperating teachers if they are to gain the maximum benefits from their cooperating teachers' experience and knowledge. Until cooperating teachers are trained to give directions and to demonstrate activities, their influence on the development of the student teachers' skills should be questioned. This situation is perhaps best interpreted by Copeland (1977), who suggested that the ecology of schooling is the major variable in the development of student teacher skills, rather than the influence of the cooperating teacher.

Many teacher educators have called for the formalized training of cooperating teachers as supervisors (Brennan, 1995; Copas, 1984; Cornbleth & Ellsworth, 1994; Randolph, Slick, & Collins, 1995). Killian and McIntyre (1986) found that teacher education students appear to have brief, impersonal interactions with their students and that they avoid conflict and substantive discussion with cooperating teachers. In a study designed to overcome this phenomenon, McIntyre and Killian (1986) developed a course on instructional supervision for cooperating teachers and preservice students. A control group did not receive information on instructional supervision. In examining the differences in interactions of teacher education students and cooperating teachers, they found that teacher education students paired with trained cooperating teachers received significantly more feedback. In addition, the student teachers spent more time preparing and planning, and interacting with their own students. They concluded that cooperating teachers need training in communication skills and that training should promote reflective thinking if teacher education students are to master this skill. The assumption that representatives from the university must also promote an atmosphere of communication, feedback, and reflection if these factors are to be present during student teaching is implied in this study. In a related study, Hauwiller et al (1988–1989) found that a series of short-term in-service workshops provided by university supervisors for cooperating teachers appears to be an effective method for improving communication. Cochran-Smith (1991a) suggested that student teachers can learn to be reformers if they are placed with experienced teachers who are attempting to reform their classrooms. This process of reform is maximized when there is a supportive linkage between the university and the schools.

Thorlacius (1980) reported that, when cooperating teachers were trained in Cogan's model, their conference behavior changed and they moved toward the collegial approach and away from the directive approach, and supportive behavior increased in both cooperating teachers and student teachers. Chandler (1971) found that, if cooperating teachers received no training in supervision, then they dominated more than 60 percent of the talk in the conferences. In additon, their level of discourse tended to be more convergent and nonevaluative than if they had received training.

Training for cooperating teachers is delivered in a variety of formats. Pullman (1995) describes a series of workshops for cooperating teachers and university supervisors that emphasizes the writing of the summative evaluation of the student teachers. She stresses the importance of developing skills in the writing of a statement that will be read by prospective employers. Colton and Sparks-Langer (1992) described a 4-day workshop that began with a series of readings and discussions regarding the characteristics of thoughtful, self-directed teachers and theoretical underpinnings of student teaching supervision. Further sessions centered on interpersonal skills, to bolster self-esteem and problem solving. Weiser (1995) suggested a variety of approaches to train cooperating teachers, including biweekly seminars located in several convenient locations, correspondence courses with appropriate technology, on-campus course work that will be accepted as part of a degree program, building-level training done by university supervisors, and use of interactive technology that would allow direct communication between the university and schools that are hosting student teachers.

University Supervisor

The university supervisor often has been criticized for not fulfilling the role of instructional leader (Diamonti, 1977). A number of studies have reported that the university supervi-

sor has little measurable effect on student teachers' attitudes or behavior (Sandgren & Schmidt, 1956; Schueler, Gold, & Mitzel, 1962). Morris (1974) placed 96 student teachers in one of two groups (i.e., those with a university supervisor and a cooperating teacher and those with a cooperating teacher alone). She found no significant differences, as measured by the final evaluations of the student teachers, in classroom performance or adjustment, between the group that had a university supervisor and the group that did not.

Additional data on university supervision does point to a level of influence by clinical faculty on student teachers. Bennie (1964) discovered that experienced teachers perceived that university supervisors improve student teachers' performance. In addition, Friebus (1977) found that university supervisors play a role as "coaches," providing suggestions and support about specific teaching problems. The most important role played by university supervisors, however, results from the uncritical relationship between cooperating teachers and their student teachers. Zimpher, deVoss, and Nott (1980) found that cooperating teachers do not provide students with feedback and critical analyses of their teaching, and that without the input of university supervisors, student teachers would be left to analyze their own teaching performance. In addition, this study reported that university supervisors provide needed support in defining and communicating program goals and in phasing the student into classroom activities. Corrigan and Griswold (1963) found those student teachers with certain university supervisors became more positive in their attitudes toward teaching, schools, and children. These students perceived their university supervisors as influencing their perceptions on these variables. One of the most comprehensive descriptive studies of student teaching was conducted by Griffin et al (1983). A major finding was that the most significant characteristic of student teaching was the central role played by supervision, and that while the university supervisor plays a role in supervision, the cooperating teacher plays the most prominent role. The university supervisor is viewed as the more tolerant, secure, and independent member of the triad, being more progressive and possessing a higher level of self-esteem than the cooperating teacher. An additional finding is that university supervisors and cooperating teachers do not apply a shared knowledge base during discussions or conferences. This in turn perhaps leads to the perception by student teachers that although university supervisors could have been more helpful, they were perceived as people they could talk to about both professional and personal issues (i.e., as opposed to cooperating teachers with whom they carried on only professional dialog). Whereas openness describes one major positive characteristic of university supervisors, however, research also points out the lack of an atmosphere for rigorous inquiry, which may limit the potential for increasing student analysis or what is often referred to in the literature as reflection. Future studies may do well to investigate the appropriate balance between openness and reflection.

Koehler (1984) reported that university supervisors perceived that their primary duties centered on providing support for student teachers, while facilitating growth and moderating conflict resolution between cooperating teachers and student teachers. Additional roles, in ascending order, included serving as a liaison between the university and the schools, providing a set of common expectations for cooperating teachers and student teachers, providing support for student teachers both professionally and personally, securing favorable placements, orienting student teachers to schools, evaluating student teachers primarily relative to growth rather than to specific skills or knowledge, providing feedback from observations, and conducting seminars. Most supervisors reported major problems, such as the breakdown of communication or working to ensure that the members of the triad worked together as a team.

University supervisors perceived effective supervisors in much the same way cooperating teachers and student teachers did (i.e., as cooperative, flexible, hardworking, having a sense of humor, and able to work with others). Moreover, the university supervisors reported that they believed themselves pressed for time and overtaxed with a range of responsibilities.

Enz, Freeman, and Wallin (1995) reported on a study aimed at discovering the most important roles and responsibilities as perceived by cooperating teachers, university supervisors, and student teachers. The roles and responsibilities ranked as the most important (in rank order) were: observe student teachers' lessons and provide feedback, provide moral support and encouragement to the student teacher, facilitate feedback conferences between student teacher, cooperating teacher, and university supervisor; review student teacher responsibilities and timelines, and evaluate the quality of student teachers' lesson plans. There was remarkable congruence among the three groups of the triad regarding these perceptions.

Zahorik (1988) reported on the perceptions of the observing–conferencing role of the university supervisor. To be specific, he examined the types of supervision that existed and the techniques that were used to conduct the observation and conferencing phases of supervision. Three main types of supervision were employed, including behavior prescription, idea interpretation, and person support. Behavior prescription supervisors told student teachers to use certain instructional and management acts and to avoid others. This type could be delineated even further. For example, the scholar supervisor presented research evidence to the student teachers about effective teaching practices and urged the student teacher to use the behaviors. The master supervisor prescribed instructional and management practices from the perspective of an experienced expert teacher. The mentor supervisor presented wise advice to the student teacher. The mentor did not recite research findings or claim to be an expert teacher. Finally, the critic supervisor carefully collected evidence regarding the student teacher's teaching, provided analysis and interpretation of the behaviors used, and suggested and supported actions to be taken by the student teacher.

Supervisors who used idea interpretation presented beliefs to the student teacher that the supervisor had about what classrooms and schools ought to be like. Supervisors using this approach were typically either humanist supervisors or reformer supervisors. The humanist supervisor raised the consciousness of the student teacher about questionable classroom and school practices, and suggested ways to bring about change. The reformer supervisor was more emphatic about the actions the student teacher ought to take.

The third type (i.e., person support) focused on facilitating student teacher decision-making by creating a climate that permitted and encouraged student teachers to think for themselves. The therapist supervisor listened intently to the student teacher, picked up on his or her reactions, reflected the student teacher's analysis and helped the student teacher devise a plan of action. The advocate supervisor eliminated or reduced those forces in the classroom or school that prevented the student teacher from being a responsible decision maker. The inquirer supervisor served as a questioner of the student teacher with the intent of having the student teacher examine her or his teaching, evaluate the effectiveness of various practices, and decide on further action.

A difference has been reported among supervisors regarding the time spent visiting and observing student teachers. Spivey (1978) and Herbster (1976) reported that supervisors who were generalists reassigned more student teachers than did those who were subject specialists. They also spent more time working with the student teachers than did the specialists. Kersh (1995) recommends that university professors serve as university supervisors because they are in the unique position to evaluate the teacher education program as it relates to student teaching and, thus, would be able to modify weak program elements. In addition, the university professor would be in a position to recruit graduate students. It is interesting that Kersh does not mention anything about the university professor's knowledge of supervision or ability to supervise student teachers.

Cole and Knowles (1995) have suggested that the role of the university supervisor be reconceptualized. They suggest that the role of the university supervisor be modified to supervising the *process* of student teaching. This shift would reorient the university supervisor's role from supervising actual practice to preparing the context for and continuing the facilitation of professional development. It involves paying closer attention to the links between field experiences and the formal aspects of the preparation program, contexts for developing emerging practice, mutual coherence of perspectives, and ways of facilitating and supporting preservice teacher development. Cole and Knowles would view the university supervisor of the future as placing less emphasis on evaluation and more emphasis on preparation of both the narrow and broad contexts associated with preservice teachers' learning from field experiences.

Additional research has been conducted on the concept of "clustering" student interns in schools and setting up what Oja (1988) calls Teacher Supervision Groups (TSGs), which are made up of cooperating teachers, the building principal, and the university supervisor. The groups met biweekly during the school day while the university interns were working independently in classrooms. TSGs focused on alternative models of supervision and the role that adult development plays in supervision. Action research projects appeared to assist the cooperating teachers in their investigation and understanding of supervision. Supervisors continued to meet with each intern and her or his cooperating teacher on a biweekly basis, and to hold weekly seminars with cluster interns to get their impressions and to discuss a range of issues regarding their internships. Major outcomes centered on the benefits teacher educators and teachers gained by finding a professional way to talk with others about teaching and supervision.

Training for university supervisors is rarely addressed in the student teaching literature (Metcalf, 1991). Glatthorn and Coble (1995) stated that university supervisors should be selected with the same care as cooperating teachers are chosen, and that they should be provided with similar training in supervision. French and Plack (1982) described a system of preparation of graduate students who served as university supervisors at the University of Minnesota. Training consisted of a series of orientation meetings focusing on supervisory duties, responsibility, and expectations. Once they started to observe student teachers, the graduate assistants were accompanied by the student teaching coordinator, who provided feedback and guidance. The graduate assistants were monitored throughout the semester and attended weekly seminars. In support of this training, Lamb and Montague (1982) also discovered that graduate assistants could become effective supervisors if provided with training.

Student Teachers' Reflection and Analysis

The third member of the supervisory team is the student teacher. As the concept of reflective practice has taken hold, increasing amounts of research have begun to center on the student teacher and his or her experiences, reflections, and analyses.

A central theme in the Alexander et al (1992) study of preservice students' written reflections on lessons they had taught found that students had an orientation toward practicality. Their concerns were pragmatic, such as promotion of classroom discussion, questioning, and the intricacies of lesson planning. Schleuter (1991) found that music student teachers were initially most concerned with student enjoyment, but as they gained experience, student achievement became their primary goal. The importance of being able to relate to others was also shown to be an important variable in a study of student teachers in an English-as-a-foreign language program in Israel (Kalekin-Fishman & Kornfeld, 1991). Results suggest that human relationships were the most important variable in determining the degree of success during student teaching. In a study of knowledge student teachers gain about students, Kagan and Tippins (1991) found that elementary teachers were intimately involved with students and were able to provide rich descriptions of students. Secondary student teachers, on the other hand, were judged to be more aloof and less attuned to students. Kagan and Tippins (1992) found that when elementary and secondary student teachers were given various linear lesson plan formats, they differed as to which aspects were most helpful. Secondary student teachers used planning to help them remember materials or facts. Their plans became more detailed and fact oriented as the semester progressed. Elementary student teachers used plans to organize thoughts and material, but they never referred to the written plans while teaching. As the semester progressed, their plans became less detailed and served more as a supplement to teacher guides.

A study by Ellwein, Graue, and Comfort (1990) brought some additional clarity to the study of student teacher reflection by focusing broadly on student teachers' reflections of success and failure. They found seven elements that formed a multidimensional concept of student teachers' evaluation of their teaching, based on interviews of student teachers regarding successful lessons and in those described as failures: student characteristics, implementation, planning, lesson uniqueness, management, student teacher characteristics, and lesson content. The reactions of students to lessons, lesson implementation, and the uniqueness of the lesson were all prominent in interns' descriptions. Student teachers appeared to judge successful lessons based on the level of "student interest, participation, and, to a lesser extent, learning" (p. 5). Whereas all elements were generally discussed by both elementary and secondary student teachers, there was some difference in frequency with respect to which elements were discussed. For example, elementary teachers were more likely to mention planning as the cause of unsuccessful lessons, whereas secondary teachers often characterized problems related to their lesson implementation as reasons for failure. Elementary teachers were also more likely to mention lesson implementation and uniqueness of the lesson as elements of success.

Sparks-Langer et al (1990) also studied the ability of teacher education students to reflect upon their performance. This study took place during a prestudent teaching "block" that promoted reflection on issues of curriculum and methodology through linked campus classes and a field experience. Review of students' reflections indicated that students were able to think about successful and less successful lessons, and to describe what they thought contributed to the success or lack of success of lessons. In general, "students with lower course achievement . . . [had] more difficulty applying the course concepts and principles than . . . higher-achieving students" (p. 28). Higher achieving students (90 percent of all students) were able to analyze events that took place in their classrooms using pedagogical principles and contextual factors, such as student characteristics, subject matter, or community factors. For example, students functioning at this level might relate a technique such as cooperative learning to the fact it provides for "repeated positive experiences with children from different backgrounds" (p. 27).

In a related study, Rodriguez (1993) found that "student teachers entered teacher education programs with a revealing awareness of their beliefs, not only about teaching and learning, but also about the possible barriers that may interfere in their professional growth" (p. 217). Students appreciated the usefulness of their university coursework, but they still wished that there were more attempts made to introduce content and procedures of a practical nature (i.e., discussion of videotaped school scenarios in which a teacher is working through a problem such as classroom management or using various instructional techniques to teach complex concepts to both receptive and unreceptive students).

In a study of two student teachers' well-remembered events, Carter and Gonzalez (1993) found a need for student teachers to have opportunities to relate theory to practice. The successful student teacher recalled events that point to orientation being focused on curriculum and the "process of enacting the curriculum with students." In particular, this student teacher appeared to recognize that enacting a curriculum in a classroom situation depended largely on students' interests and cooperation, and that one's own actions were connected to how students reacted to content. The unsuccessful teacher, on the other hand, remembered her mistakes and feelings of being inadequate. Rather than focusing on the curricular or instructional implications of teaching, this student teacher focused on eliciting sympathy by mentioning inexperience and by using humor in relation to errors or problems perceived and made. In addition, this student teacher did not reflect on teaching, but focused instead on gaining more experience and attempting to copy the behaviors of the cooperating teacher. Furthermore, the student teacher did not understand how to merge what was observed into functional instructional activities. Carter and Gonzalez suggested that when using cases or videotapes, university professors need to ensure that students have descriptions of teaching/learning and teachers' reflections about the same events. Moreover, cooperating teachers need to share their thoughts about lessons with students as a way for them to gain understanding of the decision-making process teachers use.

Discussions of success and failure, as perceived by the student teacher, appear to be a fertile area for supervisors to begin activities to strengthen reflectivity. It is clear that student teachers need to begin to clarify their beliefs and to put their beliefs into practice throughout their programs.

In summary, a lack of clearly agreed to and delineated goals, roles, and responsibilities both hampers teacher education programs in general, and also more specifically hinders the effectiveness of the triad as a supportive alliance to advance the growth and development of the student teacher. During student teaching, a primary focus is on supervision; however, the potential for supervision to assist student teacher growth is not met fully due to problems of communication and delineation of roles and responsibilities of all participants. For example, if the student teaching experience is perceived as "not going well," then members of the triad can either begin to communicate or they can retreat into silence. If the choice becomes one of silence, then the student teacher can lose sight of the need for reflection and growth and simply focus on survival and graduate. The cooperating teachers may recognize that a problem exists, but they may not have a quick solution, and concern for the welfare of their own students often causes them to distance themselves from the student teacher's failure. The university supervisor, who by definition is not present on a daily or even weekly basis, may be viewed as a disconnected observer/evaluator, or, worse yet, as an uninformed guest in the classroom. As such, the university supervisor may be considered an inappropriate choice to involve in assessing and facilitating solutions or interventions. Cooperating teachers and university supervisors can only hope to promote an atmosphere of reflection in which problems can be solved by understanding each others' roles and through common understandings and open communication.

Even if open communication exists, however, we have limited understandings of how supervisors can best support teacher growth and development. This is perhaps due to the subtle nature of the behaviors they hope to influence: an atmosphere in which student teachers can reflect on complex issues and gain assistance in thinking about how to best promote student learning. For example, student teachers need a supportive atmosphere in which to reflect on difficult issues, such as when to give feedback to students versus when to reteach a concept or skill to students, or how to use long-term positive reinforcement to improve the ecology of the classroom. Although these are interesting questions during on-campus discussions, they take on added urgency and form the bases for success or failure in the context of student teaching, both for the student teacher and for the students they are teaching now and those they will teach in the future.

The next section of this chapter will deal with evaluation and assessment of teaching. Both have direct application to the improvement of supervision in teacher education.

EVALUATION

How teaching experience is evaluated, judged, or supported is an important topic for all teacher education programs. Despite the level of deliberation teacher education faculty give to the issue of investigating the central essence of teaching and developing a conceptual framework for teacher education programs, the evaluation of students often rests largely on a behavioral psychology and individual skill-based orientation (Howey & Zimpher, 1989). Teacher education programs have made great strides toward helping teacher education students gain insight through reflection and development of portfolios. Ongoing observation, supervision, and the resulting evaluation, however, still often come primarily through what Howey and Zimpher have called "periodic evaluative snapshots framed by debatable criteria of 'teaching effectiveness.' The conception of teaching as primarily cognitive and problem oriented in a highly complex environment could receive more attention" (p. 217).

Analysis of the processes for evaluation during field experiences evaluation has shown a lack of critical review and often a confusing lack of common regard as to the distinction between outstanding and ineffective teaching (Diamonti, 1977; Vittetoe, 1972). There is also considerable debate regarding the role of university supervisors and cooperating teachers and whose authority and opinion is judged most relevant. One of the main premises for placing student teachers in a room with a cooperating teacher is the capacity for an experienced teacher to give feedback and support. Numerous studies, however, have found that cooperating teachers are not especially critical nor evaluative (Killian & McIntyre, 1986; McIntyre & Killian, 1986; Zimpher et al, 1980). Although cooperating teachers are often called upon to provide written evaluations of student teachers, they may not provide evaluation as an ongoing part of the student teaching experience, but rather only in isolated instances such as an orchestrated call for midterm and final evaluation form completion.

A related concept to reflection is the view that professional preparation should be established around the concept of professional competence based on practical reasoning (Koff, 1988). The assumption that teachers think about teaching before, during, and after teaching is consistent with this premise. The conduct of teachers, therefore, results from their beliefs about what is good teaching, their experience, and their empirical beliefs about what will happen if they implement an action along with their belief that a situation calls for a particular action at a given time. Competence is consequently premised on a teacher being able to articulate the practical arguments on which a course of action is grounded.

As stated earlier in the chapter, the goal of preparing reflective teachers has been called for widely and adopted by many teacher education programs during the past decade. In a review of 42 self-study reports of institutions seeking NCATE approval, Christensen (1996) found that 31 programs had identified a theme to describe its program. Nine of those programs listed reflective practice as their central theme. This is not surprising in that the outcry for greater emphasis of teacher reflection has been a consistent one. The central aim of reflection is to improve the education of children by assisting teachers in the improvement of the teaching/learning environment through contemplation on what has been and what should be.

Teacher reflection is presently not firmly established in the culture of teacher education in respect to the evaluation of student teachers; however, reflective activities, journal writing, and portfolio development, which support the concept of the college/university student as a reflective professional, are becoming a universally accepted part of teacher education. The transition from simply requiring these activities of student teachers to embedding them as the focus of the evaluation and supervision of student teachers is still a work in progress. This task is made more difficult by the seeming incompatibility of the promotion of self-analysis and reflection and the mandate to teacher education programs adequately to ensure that only the competent enter and continue in the teaching force.

Zimpher and Ashburn (1985) refer to the existence of two distinct conceptual frameworks for arriving at truth, each of which has potential ramifications for the improvement of supervision of the student teachers. These conceptual frameworks or paradigms each have separate principles, standards, and approaches for conducting research (Guba, 1981).

These conceptual frameworks (i.e., the empirical and the naturalistic perspective) have been used primarily by researchers to gain understanding of the practice of teaching and learning. These same conceptual frameworks, however, also have applicability to the supervision and evaluation of teachers. Those supervisors whose preference tends toward the empirical are disposed to base their review of teaching on concepts that have a strong empirical foundation, such as academic engagement, wait time, structuring behavior, or cooperative learning. Those with a more phenomenological orientation are more likely to take a holistic approach and open themselves to what appears important to themselves and the student teacher. Central to this orientation is the tenet that supervision requires an inquiry-oriented approach, which Zeichner and Tabachnick (1982) felt "fosters a critical orientation on the part of student teachers toward both their teaching and the contexts that surround it" (p. 41).

Some see a controversy taking place around the question of what type of research (i.e., quantitative or qualitative) is best suited to provide information to improve teacher education. From

their reading of journal articles and papers, however, Ducharme and Ducharme (1996) noted that "most teacher educators appear to have embraced a fusion" (p. 1033). A fusion of both of these approaches during supervision would have supervisors, cooperating teachers, and student teachers using both approaches to aid their understanding of teaching.

Patton (1980) refers to borrowing and combining parts from pure research methodologies to create mixed methodological strategies. In bringing this technique to teacher education, a university supervisor, a cooperating teacher, and a student teacher might choose a topic for review and analysis. For example, they might review the literature on academic engagement or cooperative learning. After a review of the findings, techniques, or attributes from this often quantitative research base, the triad members could begin to investigate the implementation of the concept in the classroom. It is important that the collection of information on the topic under study be from a number of sources. The student teacher, cooperating teacher, and supervisor would not depend exclusively on their own perception of an effect of cooperative learning in the classroom; rather, they would confer with all participants, including the students working in cooperative learning groups. In this example, empiricism serves as a source of direction for selection of an appropriate teaching strategy. Cooperative learning, and a qualitative approach to encouraging reflection about teaching, helps to ensure successful analysis and implementation.

This process need not take place in one direction, from empirical to naturalistic. An issue might just as easily originate from the student teacher's reflection or from observations by the cooperating teacher or university supervisor that leads to a perception that an issue should be investigated in a more empirical manner or that the empirical literature might bring insight into effective procedures.

The move toward a blending of conceptual frameworks will not allay all the doubt associated with effectiveness of current practices for the evaluation of field experiences. The reliability of evaluations provided by clinical faculty and cooperating teachers will still be of concern to those worried that if something can not be quantified and agreed upon by trained observers, then it has little value. It is generally accepted, however, that the types of information collected on low-inference evaluation forms often do not give a true measure of the success of student teachers in the complex classroom environment in which they worked.

For the vast majority of student teachers, the issue is not whether they have mastered individual teaching skills or should even gain a license to teach, but rather whether we have given them the support they need to be reflective and to grow as teachers in the future.

PREPARATION AND INDUCTION

First-year teachers have increasing opportunities to work with veteran teachers in mentoring programs that help to socialize them into teaching. The number of beginning teachers participating in mentoring programs has doubled in the last decade, and tripled since the early 1970s. Approximately half of all teachers working in public schools have participated in an induction program for new teachers (Choy et al, 1993).

Many early induction programs have tended to focus on evaluation rather than on mentoring, with California and Connecticut being notable exceptions. These first programs were apt to require beginning teachers who participated to be observed and evaluated on a generic set of teacher behaviors with little emphasis on the context in which the teacher worked (Darling-Hammond with Sclan, 1992; Little, 1987; Rosenholtz, 1985). Induction programs that support new teachers and help them gain skills and solve real problems, however, can make a significant difference in the retention rate of beginning teachers (Darling-Hammond & Sclan, 1996; Pontecell & Zepeda, 1996).

Qualifications of New Teachers

A distressing trend seems to be emerging relative to beginning teachers. The pool of teachers is generally now stronger, both academically and professionally, than it was in the 1980s. Even during the 1980s, however, studies (Book, Freeman, & Brousseau, 1985; Fisher & Feldmann 1985) have shown that teacher education majors' ACTs/ SATs and GPAs (i.e., overall and in courses taken outside education) were equal to nonteacher education majors. In 1990, 50 percent of all qualified teachers had a GPA of 3.25 or better, compared with 40 percent of all college graduates. There is a subset of beginning teachers, however, whose academic preparation does not support their qualification to teach (Gray et al, 1993). In 1987–1988, approximately 80 percent of those teaching in the public schools had a college major or minor in the major area of certification. In 1990–1991, only 66 percent of new public school teachers had either a major or a minor in their area of licensure. Beginning teachers who do not enter teacher education programs during the typical undergraduate years, sometimes referred to as delayed entrants into teacher education, were even less likely to have a license and a major or minor in the subject field they taught: Less than 50 percent met both these criteria. In addition, 15 percent of newly hired teachers held no license in 1990–1991, and 12.5 percent held a substandard license of a temporary or emergency nature. The majority of these teachers were hired to work in private schools where licensure is not state mandated; however, 10 percent of the first year teachers in public schools did not hold a license in the major field in which they taught, while 17 percent held a substandard license.

This data raises two important questions. First, does this duality of qualification lead to diminished learning for children? A number of studies have investigated the relationship between pedagogical training and teacher classroom performance. These studies have shown that uncertified and novice teachers without pedagogical training do not have the pedagogical knowledge, or knowledge of diverse students needed to translate their knowledge of subject matter into effective instruction (Clarridge, 1990; Hawk, Coble, & Swanson, 1985). In other words, they could not get students on task, plan or develop appropriate goals, motivate students, manage the classroom, deal with discipline problems, give feedback, or use a variety of teaching techniques. They did not ask questions, involve students, or provide guidance for students, but they did tend to provide too much content without regard to whether students were learning.

The second question is perhaps of even greater importance: How do teachers with lesser qualifications enter the profession? The literature on alternative teacher preparation provides additional insight into both of these questions.

Alternate Routes

There appear to be three distinct types of alternate certification programs. The first are programs developed for individuals looking for a midcareer change to teaching, usually involving teacher preparation at the graduate level. A confusing aspect of the alternate certification movement is that, whereas some states classify programs of this type as alternate routes, others classify them with other state-approved traditional routes to licensure. The second type of alternate certification programs are those that shorten the time required for certification by states reducing the requirements for certification. These programs offered by states or by school districts often provide little formal preparation prior to hiring, and they rely on supervision during the first year as the central training focus. Darling-Hammond (1992) has documented that supervision is unfortunately often lacking or inadequate in these programs. The third type of alternate certification program is really not a program at all; rather, it is defined by the policies states employ to hire teachers under emergency hiring practices. Emergency hiring typically requires assurances that no licensed personnel are available.

The success of alternate certification programs was evaluated in a RAND Corporation study (Darling-Hammond, Hudson, & Kirby, 1989). Teachers in the midcareer graduate preparation programs were compared with those prepared in short-term, often as little as two-week, programs. Teachers who participated in the graduate programs were more satisfied with the amount and quality of their preparation. They reported fewer problems as they began their first careers and perceived they would remain in teacher education to a greater extent than would their colleagues trained in short-term programs.

In addition, the short-term alternate certification students in many ways had similar backgrounds to unlicensed teachers employed on emergency or other substandard certificates. It is surprising, perhaps, that data on these recruits show them to be younger than the average teacher education student and likely to be right out of college. The average age of teacher education students has increased over time, and the students often have varying lengths of employment in other fields. A series of studies has shown that both noncertified and short-term certification teachers had lower grade point averages than did other teacher education students, especially in shortage areas such as mathematics and science (Darling-Hammond, 1992; Gray et al, 1993; Natriello et al, 1990; Stoddart, 1992).

Issues for Policy Makers and Teacher Educators

Although there may be disagreement over whether holding a license to teach is fully equated with excellence, the majority of evidence to date supports the position that fully prepared and licensed teachers are more effective than those who lack one or more typical licensure requirements, such as, major or minor in the field taught, knowledge of teaching and learning, and supervised field experiences (Darling-Hammond, 1992). Second, this duality in which we have both improving and decreasing qualifications for two distinct subsets of teachers does not help our efforts to eliminate growing inequalities between wealthy and poor schools in this country (Darling-Hammond, 1995). Urban schools and schools with the highest proportion of minority students were most likely to hire unlicensed teachers and teachers recruited through alternative certification programs that often offered only minimum preparation and occasionally little supervision or induction (Choy et al, 1993; Darling-Hammond, 1990).

Both traditional undergraduate and nontraditional students, therefore, are best served by a developmental approach that provides multiple field experiences directly tied to coursework. In this type of program, students have the opportunity to try out what they are learning and to observe outstanding instruction. In this way, students develop a repertoire of strategies based on research, observation, and their own success with children before they take on the sole responsibility for education of a group of students. Learning to teach is developmental, and children suffer when a teacher fails.

Professional Development Schools

Professional development schools hold some promise for changing the culture of schools and teacher education programs; however, collaboration and partnerships are not new to teacher education. The need for beginning teachers to have experiences during their early preparation has historically led to partnerships between college/university teacher education programs and school districts. Professional development activities for in-service teachers have also provided the opportunity for collaborative efforts between higher education institutions and school districts. Collaboration, however, does not occur without problems. These inherent challenges are perhaps all too often unacknowledged.

The professional development school movement attempts to improve education of preservice and in-service teachers through school-based collaborative partnerships. Variously referred to as professional development schools (Holmes Group, 1986, 1990), clinical schools (Carnegie Corp., 1986), or professional-practice schools (Levine, 1988), the goal is to improve the education of teachers by serving as models for inquiry, best practices, and the power of collaborative relationships between higher education and the public schools. In function, professional development schools (PDSs) are sometimes compared with the use of teaching hospitals in medical education. The promise of professional development schools, therefore, is to begin the process of moving from a situation in which colleges and universities make requests for placements for preservice students in schools to one in which true partnerships are formed with schools and efforts made to improve jointly the education environment for children, prospective teachers, practicing teachers, and college/university faculty.

In a review of professional development schools, Stallings and Kowalski (1990) found that a number of professional development schools have been formed since 1988. They were able to find only three, however, that had made attempts to evaluate the effects of partnership. They suggested that without needed research on the effects of this concept, "teacher-preparation and certification policies are being made by state legislatures on the basis of passionately held philosophical beliefs and guesses" (p. 262). Research on professional development schools has increased since 1990.

Frankes, Valli, and Cooper (1997) assessed the state of research on the four primary goals for professional development schools and compared the extent to which these goals have been achieved. The four goals reviewed were teacher as researcher, teacher as decision maker, teacher as teacher educator, and teacher as political activist (Holmes Group, 1990).

The professional development school model has encouraged research to take place within partner schools. There are numerous examples of teachers making decisions to involve themselves in research-related activities (e.g., action research projects, research sharing, and study to improve school practice) (Berry & Catoe, 1994; Jett-Simpson, Pagach, & Whipp, 1992; Lemlech, Hertzog-Foliar, & Hack, 1994; Snyder, 1994). Studies tend to be small scale and not involve the entire school. In a survey of all the skills viewed as important for teachers within professional development schools, however, research was viewed as the least important (Moore & Hopkins, 1993).

Regarding teacher as decision maker, the primary change that has taken place involves teacher empowerment and the development of new roles and democratic structures (Francis, 1992; Witford, 1994). Teachers have typically taken leadership in a number of activities: leading meetings, interviewing student teachers, PDS budget review, delivering of college courses, and motivation of other teachers (Miller & Silvernail, 1994; Romerdahl, 1991).

A primary goal for professional development schools is premised on the belief that classroom teachers would help to bring campus instruction and the problems of schools into greater agreement. Collaboration in planning, teaching, and supervision would bring about greater articulation and lead to improved schools and teacher preparation. The majority of studies in this area report on the enhancement of mentoring for student teachers and the increased frequency of college/university faculty teaching in the schools, and teachers teaching college courses (Berry & Catoe, 1994; Boles & Troen, 1994; Grossman, 1994; Gehrke, Young, & Sagmiller, 1991).

The greatest gap between calls for improvement in practice through professional development schools exists in the area of equity. Professional development schools, as proposed by the Holmes Group, would strive to bring greater social justice and equality to schools. There is little published evidence of the achievement of this goal beyond the creation of a number of professional development schools in urban areas. It should be noted that these professional development schools were often created with the expressed purpose of urban teacher preparation, school improvement, and equity enhancement.

Although there is not a large research base on professional development schools, Fankes, Valli, and Cooper (in press) concluded that professional development schools show great promise, yet they face many challenges. If they are to succeed, then they must overcome the demands of increased workload, difficulties in attempting to empower teachers in traditionally hierarchical schools, and the challenges of productively involving university faculty in the life of schools.

The Role of Supervision

What does this have to do with teacher education and supervision? First, we need to continue to recruit highly qualified individuals to teaching. Second, we need to continue to support the improvement of teacher education by ensuring that students have adequate content preparation, knowledge of teaching and learning, and supervised field experiences linked to campus coursework with support for reflection. Third, we can improve teacher effectiveness by improving support during the first crucial teaching years through formal mentoring and coaching programs, whether in professional development schools or other organized partnership efforts.

MULTICULTURALISM/DIVERSITY

We may need look no further for reasons why we need to invest in multicultural education than to know that teachers express concern relative to their preparation to work in multicultural classrooms (Banks, 1994, 1991; Gollnick & Chinn, 1986). After all, teachers will have to teach an increasingly varied student population that is "diverse in race, class, language, and sex-role socialization patterns" (Grant & Secada, 1990, p. 404).

Surprisingly limited amounts of research have been completed on the important topic of preparing teachers to work with diverse populations. Some important findings, however, do emerge.

- Significant numbers of student teachers lack knowledge and empathy about the effects of institutional racism; they do not perceive that education has the power to change peoples' thoughts and actions, and they view diversity as a problem, not as a resource (Lauderdale & Deaton, 1993; Moultry, 1988; Paine, 1989).
- Student teachers lack empathy in regard to the effects of institutional racism, and they show a lack of confidence in the ability of education to change the ways people think and act (Moultry, 1988).
- Preservice programs in multiculturalism teach students to have greater awareness and understanding of multicultural concepts; however, there tends to be little implementation of these concepts during field experiences (Grant & Koskela, 1986).
- Teacher education students and experienced teachers often have low expectations for poor students of color, and teacher education students are often reticent about working in diverse settings and interacting with students and parents from these settings (Zeichner, 1993).
- Preservice teachers need encouragement and the opportunity to use a rich range of teacher strategies, experience the

maintaining of high expectations, and reflect on the outcomes of their efforts (Bennett, 1988; Contreras, 1988; Wayson, 1988).
- Community field experiences for preservice teachers can help them to develop cultural sensitivity and intercultural teaching competence (Zeichner & Melnick, 1996).
- Student teachers are likely to be apprehensive and have misconceptions about working in diverse settings. Apprehension about classroom management and relating to students is common. Student teachers who have successful experiences make attempts to relate personally to students as individuals by risking personal revelations, reacting to and accepting student voice, handling racial confrontations, and bringing multicultural concepts to the curriculum. Building trusting relations tends to be both more important and difficult than the literature has acknowledged (Valli, 1996).

In summary, teacher education students do not enter preparation education programs with the skills, knowledge, and attitudes essential for success in teaching diverse populations of students. Second, although teacher education students can be taught to have greater awareness and understanding of issues regarding multicultural education, they do not necessarily implement what they have learned without support and direction. Third, preservice students need to be placed in schools where they have the opportunity to experience a diverse student population if they are to later work competently in such settings. Fourth, teacher education students need to be encouraged to create an environment of mutual respect and break down barriers (often of their own making) between themselves and their students. Fifth, teacher education students need to be encouraged and supported in analyses of practice and the effects of practice on students.

CONTENT PREPARATION

Concern about the competence of teacher candidates has resulted in increasing dissatisfaction with the state of teacher education. Suggested reforms have centered on three types: (1) increase the preparation in subject matter content knowledge; (2) increase field-based experiences; (3) decrease hours in teaching methods and other pedagogical courses (Berliner, 1985). During the mid-1980s, the debate over the importance of subject matter courses as opposed to education coursework was a central issue in the literature. There was an outcry for adoption of accreditation standards and certification mandates that required additional content preparation, in some cases at the expense of educational coursework. The authors of *A Nation at Risk* (National Commission on Excellence in Education, 1983) stated that teacher education programs included too many courses in the area of educational methods, and not enough in content areas of subjects taught in public schools. This claim, which was never substantiated on empirical grounds, was continually reiterated by various groups and reports, including The Holmes Group (1986), the Carnegie Forum on Education and the Economy

(Carnegie Corporation, 1986), and other groups both within and external to education (Sikula, 1990).

While the literature on this issue continues to advance, too often "the debate continues on ideological rather that empirical grounds" (Ferguson & Womack, 1993). Study relative to the importance and relationship of subject-matter and education coursework on teacher preparation, therefore, needs to continue. Reviews have found that teacher education courses have a positive effect on future performance (Ashton & Crocker, 1987; Darling-Hammond, 1991; Evertson, Hawley, & Zlotnik, 1985). Ball and McDiarmid's (1990) review supports the notion that knowledge of subject matter is important to teaching. Additional support for the importance of content knowledge comes from the research on teachers assigned outside their areas of expertise. Hawk, Coble, and Swanson (1985) specify that mathematics teachers teaching outside their area of expertise are less successful. Druva and Anderson's (1983) meta-analysis discovered that education and science coursework was positively associated with successful science teachers. In a review of teacher education programs, Veenman (1984) found that programs that emphasized subject matter training over education coursework were less effective. Studies comparing liberal arts majors with education graduates (Copley, 1974; Denton & Lacina, 1984; Grossman, 1990) indicated education majors had greater skills in the areas of classroom management, lesson introduction and summary, communication skills, pedagogical knowledge, and ability to meet the needs of students and to relate information in an interesting manner. The finding from a series of studies that increasing the subject-area requirements for teachers beyond those commonly required for certification does not improve teacher effectiveness is of interest (Ashton & Crocker, 1987; Evertson, Hawley, & Zlotnik, 1985).

Further assessment related to this issue by Ferguson and Womack (1993) measured the extent to which education coursework, subject-matter coursework, and NTE Specialty Area Tests (as a test of subject knowledge) predicted teaching performance of students. Grades from courses in education proved to be the most powerful predictors of teaching effectiveness, followed by grade point averages in a liberal arts major, and NTE specialty test scores. Furthermore, perhaps due to a required 2.5 grade point average for admission to teacher education programs over the last decade (due to increased state program approval requirements and NCATE), no difference in the quality of instruction was indicated between students with lower and higher overall GPAs.

Subject matter knowledge of teachers is typically thought to be especially relevant to the secondary education majors, whose certification is directly related to a content field (e.g., English, mathematics, history, biology, etc.); however, there is a growing interest in the issue of content preparation for elementary teachers, especially in mathematics. A noteworthy study by Ball (1990) helps to bring to this issue lucidity and move this debate forward. She investigated the subject matter knowledge of preservice elementary and secondary mathematics teachers. Her data challenge many commonly held assumptions about the adequacy of content preparation for both elementary and secondary teachers. The first assumption her research challenges is that the traditional mathematics

curriculum taught in elementary schools is not difficult. She found that college students had difficulty with the explanation of mathematical concepts beyond the simple use of rules and procedures. Students who were generally able to "invert and multiply" when dividing fractions could not explain why this was being done. In addition, her research challenges whether traditional mathematics classes provide teachers with all they need to know to teach mathematics effectively to students. Ball found that although elementary education majors study very little mathematics and secondary students study significantly more (often majoring in mathematics or its equivalent), neither had "meaningful [mathematical conceptual] understanding nor knowledge with which to figure out such understandings on the spot" (p.463). Ball stated,

[I]n mathematics . . . we find less difference in substantive understanding between elementary and secondary teacher education candidates than one might expect (or hope). Although the latter, because they are mathematics majors, had taken more mathematics, this did not seem to afford them substantial advantage in articulating and connecting underlying concepts, principles, and meanings (p. 463).

Ball went on to explain that this was true for "good" mathematics students (majors) and for the mathematics students (majors) not planning to teach.

A related study by Floden, McDiarmid, and Jennings (1996) was undertaken to investigate where in the elementary education curriculum reforms advocated for elementary school mathematics conceivably could be housed. It was found that methods instructors could take responsibility for teaching knowledge of content, but prefer to concentrate on attitudes toward mathematics and on teaching methods. If methods instructors do not accept responsibility for providing an environment that supports elementary education students' mathematical understanding, the question for teacher education faculty and supervisors is: Who will assist student teachers and beginning teachers in gaining this knowledge? Simply leaving beginning teachers to seek information on their own as they contend with the complex task of setting up a new classroom seems to be a recipe for failure. Without formal support, we can anticipate teachers shying away from implementing the mathematics reform content and, perhaps, the teaching of mathematics in general.

In summary, the preparation of elementary mathematics teachers appears to be inadequate—simply requiring a major in mathematics is not going to prepare teachers who can explain the complexity of division of fractions beyond simply stating the rules, or bring understanding of mathematics to students that enables them to relate mathematics to problems they encounter in life.

Research supports subject matter preparation as an important, although perhaps poorly understood, prerequisite for effective teaching. McDiarmid, Ball, and Anderson (1989) believe teachers need a flexible understanding of the students, learning, and content they teach in order to make instructional decisions relative to appropriate selection of subject matter and instructional strategy. Feiman-Nemser and Buchmann (1989) state the problem for teacher education: "Teachers must know things worth teaching" (p. 366). As supervisors, we must, therefore, ensure that our teacher education students struggle with their own understanding of the concepts they teach and that children are not left with knowledge of rules without understanding. If we wait until student teaching to address this issue, our impact is likely to be minimal. This research has major implications for the subject matter preparation of teachers, the content and methodology utilized in methods' courses, and the ways students are supported and supervised during field experiences.

CONCLUSION

The goal of this chapter was to analyze the research on supervision in teacher education and to use this analysis to suggest areas for improvement. Research on supervision in teacher education has not been conducted in a systematic fashion. Much of this problem is the result of a lack of a well-conceived theoretical base for field experience.

An examination of research on supervision during both preservice and in-service field experience brings forth certain factors that may help in this analysis. The first factor is the realization that the practice of teaching without analysis and reflection does not lead to professional growth. Research on

the role of cooperating teachers and supervisors has reported some influence on student teachers' attitudes, but the larger question of how to shape their behavior is largely unknown. Even universally accepted notions, such as placing students with "good" role models, have not been shown to be reflected in improved student evaluations. A more open contextual approach is perhaps needed in research and evaluation. The supervision of field experiences is of critical importance. We must begin to utilize methodologies that allow us to understand the complex world of teaching and to present this world to students and teachers during field experience so that they might learn to better analyze the teaching–learning process.

Finally, when teaching at the preservice or in-service level is not going well, the situation occurs minute by minute, hour by hour, and day by day. A discussion among the triad members once every 2 or 3 weeks during student teaching can boarder on farce. Observation and discussion between a practicing teacher and supervisor on an inconsistent and almost perfunctory basis is no better. Prevention of failure needs to be a tenet of teacher education for both novice and experienced teachers. The supervision of these experiences—along with content and methodology—must be considered a foundation of teacher education.

REFERENCES

Alexander, D., Muir, D., & Chant, D. (1992). Interrogating stories: how teachers think they learn to teach. *Teaching and Teacher Education, 81*(1), 59–68.

Alkove, L. & McCarty, B. (1992). Plain talk: Recognizing positivism and constructivism in practice. *Action in Teacher Education, 14*(2), 16–22.

American Association of Colleges of Teacher Education (1991). *Rate IV, teaching teachers: Facts and figures.* Washington, D.C.: Author.

Ashton, P. & Crocker, L. (1987). Systematc study of planned variations: The essential focus of teacher education reform. *Journal of Teacher Education, 38*(3), 12–18.

Ball, D. L. (1990). The mathematical understandings that prospective teachers bring to teacher education. *Elementary School Journal, 90*(4), 449–466.

Ball, D. L. & McDiarmond, G. L. (1990). The subject matter preparation of teachers. In W. R. Houston (Ed.). *Handbook of research on teacher education* (pp. 437–449). New York: Macmillan.

Banks, J. (1991). *Teaching strategies for ethnic studies.* Boston: Allyn & Bacon.

Banks, J. (1994). *Multiethnic education: Theory and practice.* Boston: Allyn & Bacon.

Becher, R. & Ade, W. (l982). The relationship of field placement characteristics and students potential field performance abilities to clinical experience performance rating. *Journal of Teacher Education, 33*(2), 24–30.

Bennett, C., with Okinaka, A. & Xiao-yang, W. (1988). *The effects of a multicultural education course on preservice teachers' attitudes, knowledge and behavior.* Paper presented at the annual meeting of the American Educational Research Association, New Orleans.

Bennett, R., Ishler, M., & O'Loughlin, M. (1992). Effective collaboration in teacher education. *Action in Teacher Education, 14*(1), 52–56.

Berliner, D. (1985). Laboratory settings and the study of teacher education. *Journal of Teacher Education, 36*(6), 2–8.

Berry, B. & Catoe, S. (1994). Creating professional development schools: Policy and practice in South Carolina's PDS initiative. In L. Darling-Hammond (Ed.). *Professional development schools: Schools for developing a profession* (pp. 176–202). New York:

Blocker, L. S. & Swetnam, L. A. (1995). The selection and evaluation of cooperating teachers: A status report. *The Teacher Educator, 30*(3), 19–30.

Book, C., Freeman, D., & Brousseau, B. (1985). Comparing academic backgrounds and career aspiration of education and non-education majors. *Journal of Teacher Education, 36*(3), 27–30.

Boles, K. & Troen, V. (1994). *Teacher leadership in a professional development school.* Paper prepared for the 1994 AERA Conference in New Orleans.

Brennan, S. (1995). Making a difference for student teachers through the careful preparation of supervisors. In G.A. Slick (Ed.). *Making the difference for teachers: The field experience in actual practice* (pp. 93–102). Thousand Oaks, CA: Corwin Press.

Britzman, D. (1991). *Practice makes practice.* Albany, NY: State University of New York Press.

Bryant, B. (1982). *Shaping teacher expectations for minority girls: A teacher training module.* Paper presented to Women's Educational Equity Act Program, Washington, D.C.

Bullough, R. (1989). Teacher education and teacher reflectivity. *Journal of Teacher Education, 40*(2), 15–21.

Calderhead, L. (1987). *Cognition and metacognition in teachers' professional development.* Paper presented at the annual meeting of the American Educational Research Association, Washington, D.C.

Carnegie Corporation of America. (1986). *A nation prepared: Teachers for the 21st Century.* New York: Carnegie Corporation of New York (ERIC Document Reproduction Service No. ED 268 120).

Carter, K. & Gonzalez, L. (1993). Beginning teachers' knowledge of classroom events. *Journal of Teacher Education, 44*(3), 223–232.

Castillo, J. B. (1971*). The role expectations of cooperating teachers as viewed by student teachers, college supervisors, and cooperating teachers.* Unpublished doctoral dissertation, University of Rochester.

Chandler, B. (1971). *Levels of thinking in supervisory conferences.* Paper presented at the annual meeting of the American Educational Research Association, New York.

Christensen, D. (1996). The professional knowledge-research base for teacher education. In J. Sikula (Ed.). *Handbook of research on teacher education* (2nd ed.) pp. 38–52. New York: Macmillan.

Choy, S. P., Henke, R. R., Alt, M. N., Medrich, E. A., & Bobbitt, S. A. (1993). *Schools and staffing in the United States: A statistical profile, 1990–1991.* Washington, D.C.: NCES, U.S. Department of Education.

Clarridge, P. B. (1990). Multiple perspective on the classroom performance of certified and uncertified teachers. *Journal of Teacher Education, 41*(4), 15–25.

Cochran-Smith, M. (1991). Reinventing student teaching. *Journal of Teacher Education, 42*(2), 104–118.

Cohn M. M. & Gellman, V. C. (1988). Supervision: A developmental approach for fostering inquiry in preservice teacher education. *Journal of Teacher Education, 34*(2), 2–8.

Cole, A. L. & Knowles, J. G. (1995). University supervisors and preservice teachers: Clarifying roles and negotiating relationships. *Teacher Educator, 30*(3), 44–56.

Colton, A. B. & Sparks-Langer, G. (1992). Restructuring student teaching experiences. In C. D. Glickman (Ed). *Supervision in Transition. The 1992 ASCD Yearbook.* Alexandria, VA: ASCD.

Contretas, A.R. (1988). *Multicultural attitudes and knowledge of education students at Indiana University.* Paper presented at the annual meeting of the American Educational Research Association, New Orleans.

Copas, E. (1984). Critical requirements for cooperating teachers. *Journal of Teacher Education, 35*(3), 26–30.

Copeland, W. (1977). *The nature of the relationship between cooperating teacher behavior and student teacher classroom performance.* Paper presented at the annual meeting of the American Educational Research Association, New York.

Copley, P. O. (1974). A study of the effect of professional education courses on beginning teachers. Springfield: Southeast Missouri State University (ERIC Document Reproduction Service ED 098 147).

Cornbleth, C. & Ellsworth, J. (1994). Teachers in teacher education: Clinical faculty roles and relationships. *American Educational Research Journal, 31*(1), 49–70.

Corrigan, D. & Griswold, K. (1963). Attitude changes of student teachers. *Journal of Educational Research, 57*(2), 93–95.

Cromwell, R. R. & Browne, C. S. (1993). A clinical supervision program prepares teachers to become change agents. *The Teacher Educator, 28*(2), 37–46.

Darling-Hammond, L. (1990). Teachers and teaching: Signs of a changing profession. In W. R. Houston (Ed.). *Handbook of research on teacher education* (pp. 267–290). New York: Macmillan.

Darling-Hammond, L. (1991). Are our teachers ready to teach? *Newsletter of the National Council for the Accreditation of Teacher Educators, 1,* 6–7, 10.

Darling-Hammond, L. (1992). Teaching and knowledge: Policy issues posed by alternate certification for teachers. *Peabody Journal of Education, 67*(3), 123–154.

Darling Hammond, L. (1995). Inequality and access to knowledge. In J. Banks (Ed.). *Handbook of research on multicultural education* (pp. 465–483). New York: Macmillan.

Darling-Hammond, L., Hudson, L., & Kirby, S. N. (1989). *Redesigning teacher education: Opening the door for new recruits to science and mathematics teaching.* Santa Monica, CA: RAND Corporation.

Darling-Hammond, L., with Sclan, E. (1992). Policy and supervision. In C. Glickman (Ed.). *Supervision in transition* (pp. 7–29). Alexandria, VA: ASCD.

Darling-Hammond, L. & Sclan, E. (1996). Who teaches and why: Dilemmas of building a profession for twenty-first century schools. In J. Sikula (Ed.). *Handbook of research on teacher education* (2nd ed.) pp. 67–101. New York: Macmillan.

Denton, J. J. & Lacina, L. J. (1984). Quantity of professional education coursework linked with process measures of education. *Teacher Education and Practice, 1*(1), 39–46.

Diamonti, M. (1977). Student teacher supervision. *Educational Forum, 41*(4), 477–486.

Dispoto, R. (1980). Affective changes associated with student teaching. *College Student Journal, 14*(2), 190–194.

Druva, C. & Anderson, R. D. (1983). Science teacher characteristics by teacher behavior and student outcome: A meta-analysis of research. *Journal of Research in Science Teaching, 20*(5), 467–479.

Ducharme, E. & Ducharme, M. (1996). Needed research in teacher education. In J. Sikula, (Ed.). *Handbook of research on teacher education* (2nd ed.) pp. 1030–1046. New York: Macmillan.

Dunham, D. (1958). *Field attitudes of student teachers, college supervisors, and student teachers toward youth.* Unpublished doctoral dissertation, Indiana University.

Eby, J. (1992). *Reflective planning, teaching, and evaluation for the elementary school.* New York: Merrill.

Ellwein, M. C., Graue, M. E., & Comfort, R. E. (1990). Talking about instruction: Student teachers' reflections on success and failure in the classroom. *Journal of Teacher Education, 41*(4), 3–14.

Enz, B. J., Freeman, D. J., & Wallin, M. B. (1995). Roles and responsibilities of the student teacher supervisor: Matches and mismatches in perception. In D. J. McIntyre & D. M. Byrd (Eds.). *Preparing tomorrow's teachers: The field experience. Teacher Education Yearbook IV* (pp. 131–150). Thousand Oaks, CA: Corwin Press.

Evertson, C. (1990). Bridging knowledge and action through clinical experiences. In D. D. Dill (Ed.). *What teachers need to know* (pp. 94–109). San Francisco: Jossey-Bass.

Evertson, C. M., Hawley, W. D., & Zlotnik, N. (1985). Making a difference in educational quality through teacher education. *Journal of Teacher Education, 36*(3), 2–10.

Farber, P., Wilson, P., & Holm, G. (1989). From innocence to inquiry: A social reproduction framework. *Journal of Teacher Education, 40*(1), 45–50.

Feiman-Nemser, S. & Buchmann, M. (1989). Describing teacher education: A framework and illustrative findings from a longitudinal study of six students. *The Elementary School Journal, 89*(3), 365–377.

Ferguson, P. & Womack, S.T. (1993). The impact of subject matter and education coursework on teaching performance. *Journal of Teacher Education, 44*(1), 55–63.

Fisher, R. L. & Feldmann, M. E. (1985). Some answers about the quality of teacher education students. *Journal of Teacher Education, 36*(3), 37–40.

Flint, S. (1965). *The relationship between the classroom verbal behavior of student teachers and the classroom verbal behavior of their cooperating teachers.* Unpublished doctoral dissertation, Columbia University.

Floden, R., McDiarmid, G. W., & Jennings, N. (1996). Learning about mathematics in elementary methods courses. In D. J. McIntyre & D. M. Byrd (Eds.). *Preparing tomorrow's teachers: The field experience* (pp. 225–241). Thousand Oaks, CA: Corwin Press.

Francis, R. W. (1992a). *Issues in establishing rural professional development schools.* Paper presented at the Annual Rural and Small Schools Conference.

Francis, R. W. (1992b). Issues Carnegie Corporation of New York. (1986) *A nation prepared: Teachers for the 21st century.* New York: Carnegie Corporation of New York. ED 268 120

Frankes, L., Valli, L., & Cooper, D. (1997). Continuous learning for all adults in the PDS: A review of the research. In D. M. Byrd & D. J. McIntyre (Eds.). *Research on the lifelong education of teachers.* Thousand Oaks, CA: Corwin Press.

French, C. & Plack, J. (1982). Effective supervision: A system that works. *Journal of Physical Education, Recreation and Dance, 53*(3), 43–46.

Friebus, R. J. (1977). Agents of socialization involved in student teaching. *Journal of Educational Research, 70*(5), 263–268.

Gehrke, N., Yung, D., & Sagmiller, K. (1991). *Critical analysis of the creation of a new culture: A professional development center for teachers.* Paper presented at the annual meeting of the American Educational Research Association, Chicago, IL.

Gettone, V. G. (1980). Role conflict of student teachers. *College Student Journal, 14*(1), 92–100.

Glatthorn, A. A. & Cobble, C. R. (1995). Leadership for effective student teaching. In G. A. Slick (Ed.). *The field experience: Creating successful programs for new teachers* (pp. 20–34). Thousand Oaks, CA: Corwin Press.

Glickman, C. D. & Bey, T. M. (1990). Supervision. In W.R. Houston (Ed.). *Handbook of research on teacher education* (pp. 549–566). New York, NY: Macmillan.

Gollnick, D. & Chinn, P. (1986). *Multicultural education in a pluralistic society.* Columbus, OH: Charles Merrill.

Goodlad, J., Soder, R., & Sirotnik, K. (1990). *Places where teachers teach.* San Francisco: Jossey-Bass.

Grant, C. A. & Koskela, R. (1986). Education that is multicultural and the relationship between preservice and campus learning and field experiences. *Journal of Educational Research, 79*(4), 197–203.

Grant, C. A. & Secada, W. G. (1990). Preparing teachers for diversity. In W. R. Houston (Ed.). *Handbook of research on teacher education* (pp. 403–422). New York: Macmillan.

Gray, L., Cahalan, M., Hein, S., Litman, C., Severynse, J., Warren, S., Wisan, S., & Stowe, P. (1993). *New teachers in the job market, 1991 update.* Washington, D.C.: U.S. Department of Education, OERI.

Griffin, G., Barnes, S., Hughes, R., O'Neal, S., Defino, M., Edwards, S., & Hukill, H. (1983). *Clinical preservice teacher education: Final report of a descriptive study.* Austin: Research in Teacher Education Program, Research and Development Center for Teacher Education, University of Texas at Austin (ERIC Document Reproduction Service No. ED 240 101).

Grimmett, P. P. & Ratzlaff, H. C. (1986). Expectations for the cooperating teacher role. *Journal of Teacher Education, 37*(6), 41–50.

Grossman, P. L. (1990). *The making of a teacher: Teacher knowledge and teacher education.* New York: Teachers College Press.

Grossman, P. L. (1994). In pursuit of a dual agenda: Creating a middle level professional development school. In Darling-Hammond (Ed.). *Professional development schools: Schools for developing a profession* (pp. 50–73). New York: Teachers College Press.

Guba, E. G. (1981). Criteria for assessing the trustworthiness of naturalistic inquiries. *Educational Communication and Technology Journal, 29*(2), 75–91.

Guyton, E. M. (1989). Guidelines for developing educational programs for cooperating teachers. *Action in Teacher Education, 11*(3), 54–58.

Guyton, E. M. & McIntyre, D. J. (1990). Student teaching and school experiences. In W. R. Houston (Ed.). *Handbook of research on teacher education* (pp. 514–534). New York: Macmillan.

Hauwiller, J., Abel, F., Ausel, D., & Sparapani, E. (1988–1989). Enhancing the effectiveness of cooperating teachers. *Action in Teacher Education, 10*(4), 42–46.

Hawk, P. P., Coble, C. R., & Swanson, M. (1985). Certification: It does matter. *Journal of Teacher Education, 36*(3), 13–15.

Heathington, B., Cagle, L., & Blank, M. (1988). Seeking excellence in teacher education: A shared responsibility. *Teacher Educator, 23*(4), 19–29.

Herbster, D. L. (1976). Generalists versus specialists in the supervision of student teachers. *Teacher Educator, 11*(3), 32–34.

Holmes Group, Inc. (1986) *Tomorrow's teachers: A report of the holmes group.* East Lansing, MI: The Holmes Group. Inc.

Holmes Group, Inc. (1990). *Tomorrow's schools.* East Lansing, MI: The Holmes Group, Inc.

Horowitz, M. (1968). Student teaching experiences and attitudes of student teachers. *Journal of Teacher Education, 19*(4), 317–324

Howey, K. & Zimpher, N. (1989). *Profiles of preservice teacher education.* Albany, NY: State University of New York Press.

Iannacone, L. (1963). Student teaching: A transitional stage in the making of a teacher. *Theory into Practice, 12*(2), 73–80.

Jett-Simpson, M. Pugach, M. C., & Whipp, J. (1992). Portrait of an urban professional development school. A paper presented at the annual meeting of the American Educational Research Association, San Francisco.

Johnson, J. (1969). Change in student teacher dogmatism. *Journal of Educational Research, 62*(5), 226–241.

Joyce, B., Showers, B., & Rolheiser-Bennett, C. (1987). Staff development and student learning: A synthesis of research on models of teaching. *Educational Leadership, 45*(2), 11–23.

Joyce, B. & Weil, M. (1986). *Models of teaching* (3rd ed.). Englewood Cliffs, NJ: Prentice-Hall.

Kagan, D. M. (1990). Teachers' workplace meets the professors of teaching: A chance encounter at 30,000 feet. *Journal of Teacher Education, 41*(4), 46–53.

Kagan, D. M. & Tippins, D. J. (1991). The evolution of functional lesson plans among twelve elementary and secondary student teachers. *Elementary School Journal, 92*(4), 477–489.

Kalekin-Fishman, D. & Kornfeld, G. (1991). Constructing roles: Cooperating teachers and student teachers in TEFL: An Israeli study. *Journal of Education for Teaching, 17*(2), 151–163.

Kapel, D. E. & Sadler, E. J. (1978). *How much involvement in student teaching: A study of cooperating teachers.* Paper presented at the annual meeting of the Association of Teacher Educators, Las Vegas.

Karmos, A. & Jacko, C. (1977). The role of significant others during the student teaching experience. *Journal of Teacher Education, 28*(5), 51–55.

Kersh, M. (1995). Coordinating theory with practice: A department chair's perspective. In G.A. Slick (Ed.). *The field experience: Creating successful programs for new teachers* (pp. 99–110). Thousand Oaks, CA: Corwin Press.

Killian, J. E. & McIntyre, D. J. (1986). Quality in early field experiences: A product of grade level and cooperating teachers' training. *Teaching and Teacher Education, 2*(4), 367–376.

Koehler, V. (1984). *University supervision of student teaching.* Paper presented at the annual meeting of the American Educational Research Association, New Orleans.

Koerner, M. (1992). The cooperating teacher: An ambivalent participant in student teaching. *Journal of Teacher Education, 39*(2), 28–34.

Koff, R. (1986). The socialization of a teacher: On metaphors and teaching. In *Tension and Dynamism: The Education of a Teacher* (Conference proceedings). Ann Arbor: University of Michigan.

Lamb, C. E. & Montague, E. J. (1982). *Variables pertaining to the perceived effectiveness of university student teaching supervisors.*

Paper presented at the annual meeting of the Southwest Educational Research Association, Austin, TX.

Lauderdale, W. B. & Deaton, W. L. (1993). Future teachers react to past racism. *Educational Forum, 57*(3), 266–276.

Lemlech, J.K., Hertzg-Foliart, H., & Hackl, A. (1994). The Los Angeles professional practice school: A study of mutual impact. In L. Darling-Hammond (Ed.). *Professional development schools: Schools for developing a profession* (pp. 156–175). New York: Teachers College Press.

Levine, M. (1988) *Professional practice schools: Building a model.* Washington, D.C.: Center for Restructuring, American Federation of Teachers. SP031702

Liston, D. & Zeichner, K. (1991). Critical pedagogy and teacher education. *Journal of Teacher Education, 169*(3), 117–137.

Little, J. W. (1987). Teacher as colleagues. In V. Richardson-Koehler (Ed.). *Educator's handbook. A research perspective* (pp. 491–518). New York: Longman.

Mahan, J. & Lacefield, M. (1976). *Changes in preservice teachers' value orientations toward education during year-long, cluster, student teaching placements.* Paper presented at the annual meeting of the American Educational Research Association, San Francisco, ED 124 534.

Manning, D. (1977). The influence of key individuals on student teachers in urban and suburban settings. *Teacher Educator, 13*(2), 2–8.

McDiarmid, G. W., Ball, D. L., & Anderson, C. W. (1989). Why staying one chapter ahead doesn't really work: Subject-specific pedagogy. In M. C. Reynolds (Ed.). *Knowledge base for the beginning teacher* (pp. 193–205). Oxford: Pergamon.

McIntyre, D. J. (1983). *Field experience in teacher education: From student to teacher.* Washington, D.C.: Foundation for Excellence in Teacher Education and ERIC Clearinghouse on Teacher Education.

McIntyre, D. J., Buell, M., & Casey, J. P. (1979). Verbal behavior of student teachers and cooperating teachers. *College Student Journal, 13*(3), 24–244.·

McIntyre, D. J., Byrd, D. M., & Foxx, S. M. (1996). Field and laboratory experiences. In J. Sikula (Ed.). *Handbook of research on teacher education* (pp. 171–193). New York: Macmillan.

McIntyre, D. J. & Killian, J. E. (1986). Student teachers' interactions with pupils and cooperating teachers in early field experiences. *Teacher Educator, 22*(3), 2–9.

Metcalf, K. K. (1991) The supervision of student teaching: A review of research. *The Teacher Educator, 26*(4), 27–42.

Miller, L. & Silvernail, D. (1994). Wells junior high school: Evolution of a professional development school. In L. Darling-Hammond (Ed.). *Professional development schools: Schools for developing a profession* (pp. 28–49). New York: Teachers College Press.

Moore, K. & Hopkins, S. (1993). Professional development schools: Partnerships in teacher preparation. *Contemporary Education, 64*(4), 219–222.

Morris, J. E. (1974). The effects of the university supervisor on the performance and adjustment of student teachers. *Journal of Educational Research, 67*(8), 358–362.

Moultry, M. (1988). *Multicultural education among seniors in the College of Education at Ohio State University.* Paper presented at the annual meeting of the American Educational Research Association, New Orleans.

National Commission on Excellence in Education. (1983). *A nation at risk.* Author.

National Council for Accreditation of Teacher Education (1987). *NCATE Standards, procedures, and policies for the professional education units for the preparation of professional school personnel at basic and advanced levels.* Washington, D.C.: Author.

National Council for Accreditation of Teacher Education (1995). *Standards, procedures & policies for the accreditation of professional education.* Washington, D.C.: Author.

Natriello, G., Zumwalt, K., Hansen, A., & Frish, A. (1990). *Characteristics of entering teachers in New Jersey.* Paper presented at the 1988 annual meeting of the American Educational Research Association, Boston.

Oja, S. N. (1988). *A collaborative approach to leadership in supervision* (Final Report OERI 400-85-1056). Durham: University of New Hampshire, Department of Education.

O'Shea, L. J., Hoover, N. L., & Carroll, R. G. (1988). Effective intern conferencing. *The Journal of Teacher Education, 39*(2), 17–21.

Paine, L. (1989). *Orientation towards diversity: What do prospective teachers bring?* (Research report 89-9). East Lansing: Michigan State University, National Center for Research on Teaching and Learning.

Patton, M. Q. (1980). *Qualitative evaluation methods.* Beverly Hills: Sage Publications.

Peterson, G. (1977). *Belief and judgment policies in student teaching: Institutional differences and distribution of knowledge.* Paper presented at the annual meeting of Midwestern Psychological Association, Chicago.

Ponticell, J. & Zepeda, S. (1996). Making sense of teaching and learning: A case study of mentor and beginning teacher problem solving. In D. J. McIntyre & D. M. Byrd (Eds.). *Preparing tomorrow's teachers: The field experience* (pp. 115–130). Thousand Oaks, CA: Corwin Press.

Price, R. (1961). The influence of supervising teachers. *Journal of Teacher Education, 12*(1), 471–475.

Pullman, S. E. (1995). Evaluating student teachers: The formative and summative process, In G. E. Slick (Ed.). *The field experience: Creating successful programs for new teachers* (pp. 55–73). Thousand Oaks, CA: Corwin Press.

Randolph, D. L., Slick, G. A., & Collins, L. (1995). Development and supervision during practicum placement: A comparative study. *The Teacher Educator, 30*(4), 16–24.

Richardson-Koehler, V. (1988). Barriers to the effective supervision of student teaching: A field study. *Journal of Teacher Education, 34*(2), 28–34.

Rodriquez, A. J. (1993). A dose of reality: Understanding the origin of the theory/practice dichotomy in teacher education from the students' point of view. *Journal of Teacher Education, 44*(3), 213–222.

Romerdahl, L. (1991). *Shared leadership in a professional development center.* Paper presented at the annual meeting of the American Educational Research Association, Chicago.

Rosenholtz, S. J. (1985). Effective schools: Interpreting the evidence. *American Journal of Education, 93*(3), 352–388.

Rosenholtz, S. J. (1989). *Teachers' workplace: The social organization of schools.* New York: Longman.

Roth, R. (1989). Preparing the reflective practitioner: Transforming the apprenticeship through the dialectic. *Journal of Teacher Education, 40*(2), 31–35.

Sandgren, D. L. & Schmidt. (1956). Does practice teaching change attitudes toward teaching? *Journal of Educational Research, 50*(8), 673–680.

Schleuter, L. (1991). Student teachers' preactive and postactive curriculum thinking. *Journal of Research in Music Education, 39*(1), 46–63.

Schueler, R., Gold, B., & Mitzel, H. (1962). *Improvement of student teaching.* New York: City University of New York, Hunter College.

Seperson, M. & Joyce, B. (1973). Teaching style of student teachers as related to those of their cooperating teachers. *Educational Leadership, 31*(1), 146–151.

Sikula, J. P. (1990). National commission reports of the 1980s. In W. R. Houston (Ed.). *Handbook of Research on Teacher Education* (pp. 72–82). New York: Macmillan.

Snyder, J. (1994). Perils and potentials: A tale of professional development schools. In L. Darling-Hammond (Ed.). *Professional development schools: Schools for development of a profession* (pp. 98–125). New York: Teachers College Press.

Sparks-Langer, G. M., Simmons, J. M., Pasch, M., Colton, A., & Starko, A. (1990). Reflective pedagogical thinking: How can we promote it and measure it? *Journal of Teacher Education, 41*(4), 23–32.

Spivey, D. A. (1978). *The subject area specialist approach versus the generalist approach in the supervision of student teaching.* Unpublished doctoral dissertation, University of Tennessee.

Stallings, J. & Kowalski, T. (1990). Research of professional development schools. In W. R. Houston, (Ed.). *Handbook of research on teacher education* (pp. 251–266). New York: Macmillan.

Stoddart, T. (1992). Los Angeles Unified School District intern program: Recruiting and preparing teachers for an urban context. *Peabody Journal of Education, 67*(3), 84–122.

Tittle, C. (1974). *Student teaching: Attitude and research bases for change in school and university.* Meutchen, NJ: Scarecrow Press.

Thorlacius, J. (1980). *Changes in supervisory behavior resulting from training in clinical supervision.* Paper presented at the annual meeting of the American Education Research Association, Boston, MA.

University of Arizona Cooperating Teacher Project (1988). *Final report: Project portrayal; program assessment report; practice profile.* Tucson, AZ: College of Education.

Valli, L. (Ed). (1992). *Reflective teacher education: Cases and critiques.* Albany: State University of New York Press.

Valli, L. (1996). Trusting relations, preservice teachers, and multicultural schools. In D. J. McIntyre & D. M. Byrd (Eds.). *Preparing tomorrow's teachers: The field experience* (pp. 26–40). Thousand Oaks, CA: Corwin Press.

Veenman, S. (1984). The perceived problems of beginning teachers. *Review of Educational Research, 54*(2), 143–178.

Vickery, T. R. & Brown, B. (1967). *Descriptive profiles of beliefs of teachers.* Paper presented at the annual meeting of the American Educational Research Association, New York.

Watts, D. (1987). Student teaching. In M. Haberman & J. M. Backus (Eds.). *Advances in Teacher Education* (Vol. 3) pp. 151–167. Norwood, NJ: Ablex.

Wayson, W. (1988). *Multicultural education among seniors at Ohio State University.* Paper presented at the annual meeting of the American Educational Research Association, New Orleans.

Weiser, S. (1995). Rewarding the practicing professional. In G. E. Slick (Ed.). *Making the difference for teachers: The field experience in actual practice.* Thousand Oaks, CA: Corwin Press.

Whitford, B. L. (1994). Permission, persistence, and resistance: Linking high school restructuring with teacher education reform. In Darling-Hammond (Ed.). *Professional development schools: Schools for developing a profession* (pp. 74–97). New York: Teachers College Press.

Wiggins, R. A. & Clift, R. T. (1995). Opposition pairs: Unresolved conflicts in student teaching. *Action in Teacher Education, 17*(1), 9–19.

Wilkins-Canter, E. A. (1996). Providing effective cooperating teacher feedback. In D. J. McIntyre & D. M. Byrd (Eds.). *Preparing tomorrow's teachers: The field experience. Teacher Education Yearbook IV.* Thousand Oaks, CA: Corwin Press.

Wisniewski, R. & Ducharme, E. (1989). Why study the education professorate? An introduction. In R. Wisniewski & E. Ducharme (Eds.). *The professors of teaching: Inquiry* (pp. 1–10). Albany: State University of New York Press.

Wolfe, D., Schewel, R., & Bickman, E. (1989). A gateway to collaboration: Clinical faculty programs. *Action in Teacher Education, 11*(2), 66–69.

Wright, P. J., Silvern, S. B., & Burkhater, B. B. (1982). An evaluation of teacher input in field-based instruction. *Journal of Research and Development in Education, 15*(2), 34–37.

Zahorik, J. A. (1988) The observing-conferencing role of the university supervisors. *Journal of Teacher Education, 34*(2), 9–14.

Zeichner, K. M. (1979). *The dialectics of socialization.* Paper presented at the annual meeting of the Association of Teacher Educators, Orlando.

Zeichner, K. M. (1987). Toward an understanding of the role of field experiences in teacher development. In M. Haberman & J. M. Backus (Eds.). *Advances in Teacher Education* (Vol. 3, 99. 94–117). Norwood, NJ: Ablex.

Zeichner, K. M. (1993). *Educating teachers for cultural diversity.* East Lansing: Michigan State University, National Center for Research on Teacher Learning.

Zeichner, K. M. & Liston, D. (1987). Teaching student teachers to reflect. *Harvard Educational Review, 57*(1), 23–48.

Zeichner, K. M. & Melnick, S. (1993). Community field experiences and teacher preparation for diversity: A case study. In D. J. McIntyre & D. M. Byrd (Eds.). *Preparing tomorrow's teachers: The field experience* (pp. 41–61). Thousand Oaks, CA: Corwin Press.

Zeichner, K. M. & Tabachnick, B. R. (1982). The belief systems of university supervisors in an elementary student teaching program. *Journal of Education for Teaching, 8*(1), 35–54.

Zevin, J. (1974). In the cooperating teachers' image: *Convergence of student teachers' behavior p atterns with cooperating teachers' behavior patterns.* Paper presented at the annual meeting of the American Educational Research Association, Chicago (ED 087 781).

Zimpher, N. L. & Ashburn, E. (1985). Studying the professional development of teachers: How conceptions of the world inform the research agenda. *Journal of Teacher Education, 36*(6), 16–26.

Zimpher, N. L., deVoss, G. G., & Nott, D. L. (1980). A closer look at university student teacher supervision. *Journal of Teacher Education, 31*(4), 11–15.

·15·

TEACHER INVOLVEMENT IN SUPERVISION[1]

Lee F. Goldsberry

UNIVERSITY OF SOUTHERN MAINE

INTRODUCTION

The purpose of this chapter is to explore teacher involvement in supervision so that the reader can consider how research has been and might be used to better inform our practice. Although several studies are examined to ground our considerations, this chapter does not attempt to review all the research germane to this expansive topic. As seen in this chapter, "teacher involvement" is a requisite for educational supervision and a necessary focus for research in the field. The reader may well ask: "How is 'teacher involvement in supervision' a meaningful topic?" "What sets the focus of 'teacher involvement' apart from the other chapters in this book?" Those are two excellent questions. Please continue to interact with this chapter by raising such questions. To begin, it seems important to discuss precise meanings of the terms that provide our focus.

Teacher involvement in supervision

To begin at the most general level, schools exist to influence the learners who attend them. Teaching (i.e., curriculum and instruction, to some) exists as the primary mechanism for directing that intended influence. Supervision is an organizational effort to examine and improve teaching. As viewed in this chapter, then, supervision is a function of the school organization, not a role. This function specifically consists of working with teachers to improve teaching, regardless of the job title (i.e., role) of the person who does it. You might ask, How is that different from staff development? That is another good question. Staff development is also a function of the school organization usually intended to improve teaching. When properly done, supervision and staff development should clearly be interconnected. Supervision (i.e., as discussed in this chapter) is separated from other forms of staff development by both its particular focus on an individual's teaching practice and its "close in and personal" form. This chapter focuses upon direct supervision, or what some (e.g., Acheson & Gall, 1990; Cogan, 1973;

Goldhammer, 1969) have called "clinical supervision." Some (e.g., Goldsberry, 1984) have suggested that certain conditions, such as preobservation conferences or a reflective approach, need to exist for an approach to be called "clinical supervision" correctly. Russell and Spafford (1986) stated: "Clinical supervision seeks to foster the autonomy and independence of the teacher, with a view to enabling the teacher to become more analytical of his or her own teaching behavior" (p. 3). As sound as such perspectives might be, the only two conditions that are deemed necessary for inclusion in this chapter are (1) that at least one other person is assisting a classroom teacher refine teaching practices, and (2) that it is based at least in part on direct observation of teaching practice. Some form of communication, whether face-to-face conference or written exchange, is necessary for such assistance. Given this perspective, the importance of teacher involvement in the process is apparent. Teachers who are not involved in the deliberate examination and refinement of teaching are not engaged in supervision.

The reader might also ask how supervision is different from teacher evaluation. In practice, there is often no difference. Many teachers associate supervision with the annual ritual of being observed by an administrator for the sole purpose of rating their teaching. Others would say that their supervisor does not evaluate them, only their principal does. Teacher evaluation is a process for assuring competent performance from teachers in all areas of duty and, sometimes, for assisting with the improvement of teaching. In these latter cases, the functions of teacher evaluation and supervision are combined. As is discussed later in this chapter, some believe that combining official organizational judgments about teaching competence with efforts to refine teaching practice is doomed to fail. It should simply be noted that supervision is sometimes combined with formal teacher evaluation, and that sometimes it is separated from it. Questioning whether such a combination inhibits or promotes teacher involvement in the ongoing improvement of practice is surely germane to our focus. Little teaching reform seems likely when a teacher is participating in a ritual of being observed and of receiving another's opinion of her or his teaching successes and failures, but without genuine involvement. Just as teaching depends upon learner involvement to succeed, supervision requires teacher involvement to do its job. Teacher evaluation is, therefore, a process for determining and reporting the "goodness" or "effectiveness" of a teacher's overall performance, whereas supervision is an organizational process involving direct observation and conferral designed to help a teacher enhance personal performance. While supervision may also be related to other job requirements, the focus in this chapter is on supervision of teaching performance.

Chapter Overview

The skeletal questions section which follows explores the questions that we might expect or want research on supervision to examine before we review some of the enormous body of work that has been done. This skeletal structure will both offer us an opportunity to wonder, which is a necessary disposition for those who interact with research, and serve as an organizer for the exploration of the topic. The next section addresses forms of involvement in supervision. In this part of the chapter, the labels applied to different roles charged with forms of educational supervision are discussed and a conceptual ordering of these terms is suggested. The labels identified in this section (e.g., supervisor, mentor, coach, and consultant).[2] become the subsection headings for subsequent sections in which some of the literature and research pertaining to each of them are examined. The third section of the chapter addresses research methods used to explore teacher involvement in supervision and attempts to respond to the skeletal questions that frame this exploration. The conclusion section addresses challenges for those who wish to continue the study of teacher involvement in supervision.

Skeletal Questions

If you read the preceding section and chose to interact with the chapter, then you have already identified a set of interests in the topic. These may be in the form of questions. The overarching question that frames this chapter is, What do we know and what do we want to know about teacher involvement in supervision? Practitioners very often "cut to the chase" and simply ask, "What works?" Cutting to the chase can be very efficient if we know what beast we are chasing. When it turns out to be our own tail, however, efficiency seems rather unimportant. What *are* we chasing here? To be general to the extent of being vague, the purpose is to explore the ways in which teachers are involved in supervision to determine what insights we might garner that will help us study and practice supervision well. To move beyond vague, we will have to be explicit about "well." The first question we need to consider, therefore, is "What are the desired consequences of supervisory interventions?"

Desired Consequences In the introduction, it was suggested that improved teaching seems to be the only supervisory consequence that has so far gained consensus approval. As with most seemingly clear and direct answers, this one prompts several new questions, such as:

What (or who) determines what good (or improved) teaching is?

What evidence do we need about the learning that results to determine the value of the teaching?

Is learning that produces higher scores on standardized tests always desirable?

Must we consider the attitudinal consequences for the learners as part of the assessment of teaching?

As you readily can see, agreeing that supervision must improve teaching to be successful does not bring us to the promised land, but it does bring us closer. Although our own values and hopes for education may lead us to challenge or reject learning goals that others embrace, a fundamental question that should guide our exploration of teacher involvement in supervision remains. What evidence is sought or used to indicate whether or not teaching is improved? This question suggests a parallel to using evidence of learner accomplishment as an indicator of teaching success (i.e., evidence of improved teaching is seen as a necessary, but not necessarily sufficient, indicator of the success of supervision).

Dewey (1938) suggested that educative experiences necessarily promote rather than inhibit the learner's continued involvement in active learning. It could similarly be suggested that a second indicator of supervisory success is the teacher's increased (or at least maintained) enthusiasm for examining and refining personal practice. What evidence is sought or used to indicate teachers' continued or heightened enthusiasm for teaching and for involvement in supervision?

There is an old saw about the difference between a teacher with 20 years of experience and a teacher with 1 year of experience repeated 20 times. As the distinction suggests, the exemplary teacher has experience, and learns from it. While the complexity of teaching in our society and dealing with numerous learners in many very different local contexts makes "having all the answers" about teaching practice impossible, some teachers manage to refine their questions over the years, getting some answers, and ever-more sophisticated questions. Another consequence of supervision might be that teachers are better able to grasp the complexities and idiosyncrasies involved in interacting with multiple learners: They are better able to adapt teaching tactics to meet changing learners and times. It is clear that part of this increased savvy might be the ability to articulate connections between teaching purposes and teaching tactics, between intended and actual consequences, and between general purposes and the adaptations made for unusual learners or circumstances. Some writers (e.g., Colton & Sparks-Langer, 1992; Glickman, 1984; Oja & Reimen chapter in this book; Thies-Sprinthall & Sprinthall, 1987) suggest that the thought process involved in examining and refining teaching practice is developmental; therefore, supervision must minimally adapt to the ways teachers see and understand classroom events and teaching itself to be successful. That supervision should help teachers discover and use questions that will help them better understand and monitor their own teaching is often also suggested or implied. Newton et al (1994) suggested that "if teachers at higher stages of development have greater empathy, more flexibility, additional coping strategies, and a better understanding of contextual and cultural differences, then schools should provide the means to encourage adults to attain those levels of development" (p. 1.10). As we consider research on teacher involvement in supervision, then, what evidence is sought or used to indicate teachers' conceptions of teaching, and their ability or tendency to reflect on personal teaching practices?

It is ironic that for a job that has one interacting with learners most of the time, teaching has been characterized as "lonely" or isolated work (Jackson, 1968; Lortie, 1975). Creating teams or partnerships that provide "sounding boards" or collaborative problem identification and solution is one approach to counteracting the isolation of the job and, simultaneously, building commonalities among different subjects or grades that may benefit learners. What evidence is sought or used to indicate teachers' disposition to work with fellow educators to enhance teaching practices?

We thus began with improved teaching as a goal and then added enthusiasm for using supervision as a way to enhance teaching, refine or enrich thinking about teaching, and enhance disposition for collaborative work as desired consequences of supervision. Each of the three subsequent goals is worthy because of its likelihood to contribute to improved teaching. As we explore the consequences of teachers' involvement in supervision, we will, therefore, first look to see if there is any direct evidence of improved teaching, then see if there is evidence of any of our three subgoals. Starting with this set of desired consequences allows us to question our own conception of supervisory goals. For instance, the reader may feel that the most important subgoal are been overlooked. If so, another should be added to determine if it would change how to review or design research in exploring teacher involvement in supervision. The awareness that this conception could well be limited raises another question to be pursued: What evidence is sought or used to indicate other consequences that help us determine supervisory success? These questions and others that will guide our analysis appear in Figure 15.1.

Supervisory Interventions Now that we have established questions that will guide our exploration by specifying examined consequences of teacher involvement in supervision, we next examine questions of cause. It is clear that any form of supervisory intervention is intended to contribute positively to some desired consequence. What aspects of supervisory practice or other conditions are suggested as contributing to observed consequences? A specific subquestion related to our present focus is, What attributes of teacher involvement in supervision are suggested as influencing observed consequences? These questions will help us to identify practices and structural attributes of supervision that seem to contribute to its success. The answers to these questions regarding approaches and techniques offer hope to modify future supervision efforts to maximize success, as long as the advocated practices are well-grounded. How might it be determined that suggestions or conclusions are truly well-grounded?

These two sets of questions—those regarding intended consequences and intervention strategies—form the core of the second section of this chapter. As varying forms of supervisory programs are discussed, a focus on desired consequences and on intervention strategies will be deliberate. Most exploration of research method will be left for the third section.

Questions of Research Method The grounding of the findings and conclusions reported by researchers regarding supervisory approaches and techniques depends upon the rigor and relevance of the design of the investigations themselves. What research approaches and techniques are suggested as useful for examining teacher involvement in supervision? Given the several possible consequences that might warrant our inquiry, what data collection tools are used to ascertain and document relevant aspects of supervisory intervention and their consequences? Because supervisory interventions typically involve at least three role groups (i.e, supervisor, teacher, and learners served by the teacher), it might help us to identify what role groups inform us as to characteristics of teacher involvement in supervision and their intended and observed consequences. Because supervision is an intervention, and because interventions take time, we might wonder what the duration of the intervention and related data collection is. Because supervision of teachers is a skilled service (Garman, 1982), we might be curious as to what information is reported regarding supervisory preparation or expertise for those

What consequences are desired from supervisory interventions?

Who are the intended beneficiaries of supervisory interventions?

How are desired consequences of supervisory interventions documented and assessed?

How do variations of teacher involvement contribute to achieving these desired consequences?

How is the intervention strategy determined?

What features characterize supervisory interventions?

What rationale supports the structure of the supervisory intervention?

How are the relative contributions of different segments of the supervisory intervention documented and assessed?

How do variations of intervention strategy relate to variations of teacher involvement?

What characteristics describe the research method?

How are desired consequences of supervisory interventions documented and assessed?

Whose perceptions of supervisory interventions and their consequences are solicited?

How are data regarding supervisory interventions collected?

How do the methods of collecting data regarding supervisory interventions influence the data that are collected?

How are variations of teacher involvement documented and judged as contributing to supervisory success?

FIGURE 15.1. Skeletal Questions

who deliver the service. Because we understand that any learning situation is influenced by the expectations and attitudes of the learners, we might want to know what procedures are used to determine relevant conditions prior to the supervisory intervention. Because we also know that local conditions can have powerful influences on both the design and consequences of any intervention, we might ask how local contextual variables are determined and reported. Anyone who has taken (or been taken by) a basic research methods course would have learned to ask to what extent is generalizability of the findings or conclusions suggested and supported by study elements (e.g., sample size and procedure, comparison or control samples). There are probably several other questions that occur to the reader about the research design and implementation when teacher involvement in supervision is concerned. A moment's reflection is appropriate about the circumstances that you believe would have telling influences on how we explore teacher involvement in supervision. If you wanted to explore the questions you have raised earlier about teacher involvement in supervision, what study procedures might be considered in order to provide as rigorous and conceptually solid investigation as possible? If you compare your ideas with the designs of studies that you review, you may be surprised by what you find.

FORMS OF INVOLVEMENT

How can teachers be involved in supervision? How should they be involved? Stop for a minute and record your initial thoughts on desired teacher involvement in the function of supervision. Consider the roles that teachers might play, as well as characteristics of their intellectual and emotional involvement that you deem desirable and undesirable. Next, consider whether these roles and characteristics are indeed appropriate for all teachers or if they may vary with teacher differences. For example, should a brash, overconfident beginning teacher participate in the same roles with the same characteristics as the talented experienced teacher who lacks confidence? Do you believe it is important for role and characteristics of teacher involvement to shift in adaptation to each teacher's wants, abilities and needs? If so, how and why? And, how would you expect research on supervision to acknowledge and accommodate such idiosyncratic adaptations? Please consider your own beliefs now.

If you concluded that the function called *supervision* should indeed vary in consideration of the differing traits and desires of individual teachers, then you are certainly not alone. Such scholars as Glickman (1985) and Glatthorn (1984) have written at length about the nonsense they perceive in delivering the same treatment regardless of symptoms or history of the client. Indeed, the analogy to the physician's charge to prescribe individualized procedures or medications after skillfully diagnosing the individual patient's problems and related conditions has often been offered. Many have observed that the medical analogy places sole responsibility for determining the treatment on the supervisor and regards the teacher as playing little part in the decision-making other than to provide requested information

tion and to follow the prescribed treatment plan. While our medical colleagues may cringe at the simplistic characterization of the doctor–patient relationship, we have ample grist in our stereotypical view of the educational supervisor to warrant suspicions about prescriptive approaches. Elsewhere the differences among nominal, prescriptive, and reflective approaches to supervision have been discussed (Goldsberry, 1988). The question of teacher's autonomy seems pertinent as one of the considerations in examination of teacher involvement in supervision for our purposes here.

Autonomy is certainly a relative feature in teaching. Few would argue that classroom teachers should be permitted to discuss any topic that occupies their own interests with the children they teach. Even fewer would insist that a teacher be permitted to punish children in any fashion he or she found "effective." Indeed, there is a tension between "micromanaging," where the supervisor intrudes on the discretion of the teacher to the point of inhibiting the ability to teach creatively or adaptively, and "laissez-faire" operations, where the teacher can do anything that is legal in the classroom. Sergiovanni and Starratt (1983) call this tension the "autonomy-coordination dilemma." Those who have tried to work with teaching teams or with integrated curriculum across high school departments can fully appreciate the need for coordination in schools. We do not need to look at such extreme examples either. Any school faculty that has tried to develop curricular consistency across grade level or between academic subjects has first-hand experience with the need for coordination. In a utopian society, all teachers would perhaps exercise their autonomy in ways that required no outside assistance to assure coordination and common purpose. Until we inhabit such a wonderful place, organizational coordination is needed to develop and articulate common purpose and to plan and implement curricula to achieve it. Supervision is one organizational function, with staff development and curriculum development being two others, that most schools employ in an attempt to reach necessary coordination. Different approaches to supervision address different balance points between the organizational purpose to coordinate and the ideal state of orchestrated autonomy.

The literature on supervision has distinguished several different supervisory roles with differing balance points. As outlined in Figure 15.2. These roles include supervisor, mentor, coach, and consultant. Although it is difficult to distinguish among these roles discretely, and it is true that different writers and practitioners use the terms interchangeably, an attempt will be made to clarify conceptual differences among them so that we might consider the aims and effects of each in terms of teacher involvement in supervision.

The supervisor is generally not a classroom teacher. Most often, the teacher's supervisor is a building administrator, usually the principal. Some large school districts employ central office supervisors or districtwide specialists in curriculum and instruction whose work includes working with teachers to improve both the content and manner of teaching. The supervisor is usually, but not always, also charged with formally evaluating the teacher's performance for employment decisions. In any case, the teacher's involvement in this form of supervision is in the role of recipient of supervision.

Supervisor generally sets boundaries for teacher autonomy. If teacher crosses spoken (or even unspoken) boundaries, supervisor has authority to "remediate." Supervisor has organizational blessing to direct teaching behavior using own expertise and preferences as a guide.

Mentor advises teacher of established (by policy or norm) boundaries. If teacher crosses spoken (or unspoken) boundaries, mentor's expectation is to advise as to established standards. If actions outside of boundaries continue, mentor is expected to inform supervisor.

Coach advises teacher boundaries inherent in skill or approach being coached. Coach's understandings of the proper application of the method serve as standards. Coach determines "rightness" of method. May report proficiency with method to supervisor or to mentor.

Consultant serves at pleasure of teacher. Advises regarding perceived "goodness" of practice. Teacher is at liberty to act upon or to ignore advice. Standards are determined by teacher and communicated to consultant. Consultant may challenge teacher's reasoning, but (barring malpractice) teacher's reasoning prevails.

FIGURE 15.2. Autonomy as a function
of supervisory role

Teacher as Recipient

What does research tell us about teacher involvement in supervision when the teacher is the recipient? First, it is advisable to distinguish student teaching supervision or any form of preservice supervision from the supervision of regularly employed teachers. The design, delivery, and, arguably, even the purposes of supervision differ considerably between preservice and in-service recipients. The special case of preservice supervision is discussed later. The focus here is on the in-service teacher as a recipient of supervision. What questions would be raised to explore teacher involvement in supervision when the teacher is the recipient (and hopefully beneficiary) of the services of a person employed at least in part to provide such supervision? You might start with questions of definition and logistics, such as:

What is the job title of the supervisor?
How often does the supervisor observe the teaching of each teacher?
How does the supervisor communicate the results of these observations to the involved teacher or to others?
What are the procedures of the supervisory act?

You might then consider questions of intent and success, such as:

What type of participation is expected from the teacher?
How do teachers perceive the usefulness of this supervision for improving their teaching or for any other intent?
What evidence is collected to support assertions of either teaching or supervisory effectiveness?
How are the specifics of the process documented and assessed?

Finally, you might consider questions of research method, such as:

What techniques are used to gather and interpret data?
How might the procedures used in the study have influenced the findings?
Are the author's conclusions supported by the collected data?

These questions should remind the reader of the skeletal questions raised earlier in this chapter, and of the questions you personally wish to explore. The implication is that research is, or at least should be, a disciplined attempt to answer our serious questions and not simply a rite of passage.

One question that is often raised regarding supervisory interventions (or other interventions, for that matter) is: What characteristics of the intervention produce the desired results? This is clearly an important question to answer if the goal is to apply successful intervention strategies to subsequent efforts; however, there a powerful assumption is embedded in the question (i.e., that characteristics that produce a desired result in one setting will also do so in another). Pajak and Glickman (1989) cite Ripley (1983) as indicating that attitude change can be influenced by the personality of the recipient as well as by the nature of the intervention. They refer to the work of Brown and Newman (1982) and Newman, Brown, and Braskamp (1980) as indicating that supervisory behaviors, like making specific recommendations for change, may be preferred by teachers with an external locus of control, but not by others. Some teachers might, therefore, respond to a supervisor's suggestions differently from others. The effects of supervisory interventions are perhaps greatly influenced by the attitudes toward teaching and learners that the individual teachers bring to the supervisory experience, by the nature of the teacher's involvement in the experience, *and* by the general characteristics of the supervisory intervention. Several other contextual variables (e.g., participants' mood or energy level, the physical setting of the supervision, or the norms of the school) also influence the effects of supervisory interventions. If such factors seem likely to influence the consequences of supervision, then the attempt to generalize cause–effect relationships with the nature of supervisory interventions as the sole "cause" may be doomed as oversimplistic. This observation does *not* imply that disciplined inquiry into supervisory interventions and into teachers' involvement in such interventions is futile. It does suggest, however, that good supervision and good research into supervision, like good teaching, need to be sensitive to the multiple influences that may contribute to observed consequences. The search for better understanding of what can be done to achieve desired consequences can be abetted by deliberate and careful inquiry into present practices if the temptation to overgeneralize findings and conclusions is assisted.

Desired Consequences for the Recipient of Supervision

What evidence is used to consider the success of supervision? For our exploration of dependent measures used to examine the effects of clinical supervision, Pavan's (1985) review of research is very instructive. Among the supervisory outcomes mentioned in this review are:

- measures of student achievement (Congdon, 1979; Huskey, 1977; Mayfield, 1983; Spaulding, 1984)
- observed changes in supervisory behavior (Johnson, 1983)
- observed changes in teaching behavior (Clapper, 1981; Fishbaugh, 1983; Johnson, 1983; Kerr 1976; Krajewski, 1976)
- student ratings of teaching behavior (Krajewski, 1976; Lafferty, 1980)
- student reports of changes in teaching behavior (Shuma, 1973)
- supervisor attitudes toward supervision (Sears, 1984; Snider, 1978)
- supervisor consistency in evaluation (Faast, 1982)
- supervisor perceptions of student achievement (Congdon, 1979)
- supervisor's post-observation conference behavior (Reavis, 1977)
- teacher assessments of supervisory communication (Reavis, 1977)
- teacher attitude changes on global measures such as Minnesota Attitude Inventory (Clapper, 1981; Krajewski, 1976; Spaulding, 1984)
- teacher attitudes toward in-service teacher education (Wiley, 1980)
- teacher attitudes toward learners (Wiley, 1980)
- teacher attitudes toward supervision (Arbucci, 1976; Bisbee, 1983; Fishbaugh, 1983; Johnson, 1983; Lafferty, 1980; Lindstrom, 1983; Mattes, 1983; Myers, 1975; Sears, 1984; Shuma, 1973; Snider, 1978)
- teacher attitudes toward teaching (Fishbaugh, 1983; Shuma, 1973; Wiley 1980)
- teacher attitudes toward themselves (Shuma, 1973)
- teacher level of use measures (Bisbee, 1983; Joyce, 1982)
- teacher level on stages of concern measures (Bisbee, 1983; Joyce 1982)
- teacher perceptions of student achievement (Congdon, 1979)
- teacher perceptions of supervisory behavior (Clapper, 1981; Faast, 1982; Witt, 1977)
- teacher reflective or self-analytic behavior (Lafferty, 1980; Shuma, 1973)
- teacher reports of changes in teaching behavior (Lindstrom, 1983)
- time spent in supervision (Arbucci, 1976)

Researchers are apparently considering several variables as indicative of supervisory success. Some of these involve direct teacher involvement through reported teacher perceptions, attitudes, or reflections. Some forms of teacher involvement (e.g., reporting perceptions of supervisory helpfulness, positive attitudes toward supervision and improving teaching, or focused reflection) are, therefore, seen as evidence, per se, of supervisory success. Although there may indeed be justification for considering active and positive teacher engagement as a desired result of supervision, it may be secondary to improved teaching and improved student learning. The use of

indicators that focus on areas other than improved performance by either teacher or learners is discussed further in the third section. The focus for now will be on the desired consequences for the teacher as recipient of supervision.

Improved Teaching as a Consequence What constitutes "improved teaching"? The most straightforward answer to this question is that some aspect of teaching gets better over time. In order to document that an aspect of teaching has improved, one needs, therefore to compare subsequent performance with preceding performance and identify at least one aspect that is better with no corresponding loss in another aspect. This discussion seems so elementary that one may wonder why it is even mentioned. The reason is that such comparison is seldom done. The way many researchers would advise us to proceed (i.e., collecting ample baseline data on teaching performance, and then intervening and collecting similar data after the intervention to compare to the baseline) involves systematic assessment or evaluation of teaching performance. Anyone who has spent any time within the culture of schools knows that such systematic assessment of teaching performance is time consuming, costly, and disruptive to the daily routines and, often, to faculty morale.

Some researchers argue that the concepts or actions associated with "effective and ineffective teaching . . . must be identified, defined, classified, exemplified, and documented" (Bullerman, Borg, & Peterson, 1993, p. 328). Following this reasoning, the State of Florida invested in the development of the Florida Performance Measurement System (FPMS), which is based on "teacher performance indicators shown by research to affect student learning. . . . The screening/summative instrument combined all of the indicators in thirty-nine abbreviated statements, convenient for making observations" (Bullerman, Borg, & Peterson, 1993, p. 329). Using this approach, "good teaching" is operationally defined and teaching is judged by the presence or absence of target behaviors. For example, if the presence of higher-level cognitive questioning is associated with good teaching, then one might chart the frequency of higher-level questions and compare the actual frequency with some standard for the desired frequency. If the frequency corresponds to the desired frequency, then the assessment of the teaching is favorably influenced. In complex systems, the greater the discrepancy between the observed frequency and the desired frequency, the greater the reduction in the score for the teaching episode. Such algorithmic approaches to teacher evaluation generally do not consider contextual variables, or even the qualities of the target behavior. For example, there are seldom ways to differentiate well-worded or well-timed higher-level questions from poorly worded or ill-timed ones. If one considers "good teaching" to be a highly adaptive set of behaviors that will vary with the interest levels, prior knowledge, and emotional states of the learners, as well as with the nature of the learning objectives and peculiarities of the subject and topic at hand, then attempts to standardize a set of teacher behaviors that will constitute good teaching, irrespective of these varying conditions, seems impossible. On the other hand, if one accepts that some teaching behaviors (e.g., stating clear learning objectives, or providing positive reinforcement for learners who meet or exceed learning goals) are generally reliable indicators of good teaching, then identifying these indicators and using them wisely as we plan and assess teaching seems reasonable. Once again, the nature of teacher involvement in the process is pivotal for success. If teachers discuss any criterion and accept it as important for their teaching success, then it would be reasonable that they may profit from an observer's descriptive accounting of that behavior during a teaching episode. Furthermore, if a teacher has time and assistance for considering the criterion behavior in light of the particular lesson within its context, then the importance of that criterion may be enhanced or diminished for that particular episode. If the process requires active teacher consideration of the positive and negative consequences experienced by the learners from any particular teaching behavior or set of behaviors, then that teacher is likely to use the fruits of her or his considerations in future teaching. If, however, the teacher is not engaged in such considerations, but rather feels coerced into behaviors he or she doubts have meaningful influence on learning, then resistance is predictable. This reasoning suggests that researchers should document teachers' perceptions of altered teaching tactics, as well as their frequency *while being formally observed*. The ability to use a particular teaching behavior will interact with the way teachers think about good teaching to determine what behaviors will be used when no one else is watching.

In a study that examined the comparative benefits of a "traditional supervisory process, consisting of an observation and postobservation conference . . . (with an) experimental supervisory process, which was the same as the traditional model except that after observing the teacher's lesson the supervisor taught the same lesson to the teacher's next class" (pp. 118–119), Elgarten (1991) found that teachers "tended to carry out more suggestions when they saw the suggestions modeled (demonstrated) by their supervisors" (p. 123). It may have been important that the supervisors in this study were subject-specialists (e.g., mathematics). Elgarten compared the demonstration results with the results of traditional supervision delivered by the same supervisors and found significantly greater adoption of suggested changes in the experimental group. This finding again tends to support the notion that extra energy in the supervisory process is likely to produce more change on the part of the teaching techniques used by the teachers. The extra attention perhaps engages teachers in a less cursory way than does the typical brief and sporadic visit. What do we know about teachers' involvement in thought as part of supervisory interventions?

Teacher Thinking as a Consequence Nolan, Hawkes, and Francis (1993) reviewed six case studies of clinical supervision and concluded that "clinical supervision under certain conditions can lead to powerful changes in teachers' thinking about instruction and instructional behavior" (p. 54). Nolan et al also concluded that five process characteristics "appear to have a cumulative, positive impact on teacher thinking and behavior" (p. 56). These process characteristics are:

1. Whatever the formal roles of the participants are, the successful cases emphasized that a collegial relationship

between supervisor and teacher was established. "In developing collegiality, the qualities of the relationship appeared to be more important than the organizational roles of the participants" (p. 55).
2. Teachers determined the changes to be made. Nolan et al called this "controlling the products of supervision"—the central idea of which was the teacher tended to employ tactics that he or she felt worth trying, and tended to ignore or halfheartedly try tactics that seemed imposed.
3. Supervision is marked by frequent teacher–supervisor interactions over extended periods of time. . . . (I)n some of these cases, it took several cycles of clinical supervision or coaching before . . . conferences became productive and teachers were willing to examine those aspects of their teaching in which they felt most vulnerable (Kilbourn, 1982; Nolan & Hillkirk, 1991; Robinson, 1984).
4. The provision of descriptive observational data for the teacher's consideration. Nolan et al emphasize the importance of sharing the observational data with the teacher prior to the postobservation conference so that each participant can be prepared to discuss personal interpretations.
5. Facilitated reflection on teaching, wherein the supervisor encouraged and focused teacher thinking about their own teaching. Nolan et al observed that "the cognitive dissonance that arose when teachers did not see a match between their thinking and actual events seemed to be the most powerful impetus to reflection and change" (p. 56). They also emphasized that such supervisors reflected on their own performance and adapted when they found their own dissonance.

The six cases analyzed by Nolan et al seem to suggest that teacher involvement as a recipient of supervision can be elicited in a positive and useful manner, even though only four of the six cases involved the direct form of supervision by an organizational superordinate addressed in this section. It should be noted that these four were all principals. The fifth case involved a fellow teacher serving as a peer consultant and the sixth looked at a university instructor serving as consultant.

Russell and Spafford (1986) offer a first-person account of a beginning teacher's experiences with clinical supervision. The teacher reports developing "a better concept of myself as teacher . . . (one who) felt less like a child and more like the professional adult I was supposed to be" (p. 7) during the first year of teaching. "When I volunteered for clinical supervision in my second year, it was considered 'breaking of the ranks' (by fellow teachers) because it meant working more closely with the administration of the school, something teachers were not eager to do" (p. 7). Russell and Spafford conclude that advantages could be realized by involving teachers in peer clinical supervision, a practice considered below in the mentor, coach, and consultant sections.

It is noteworthy that each of these cases clearly involved much more than the cursory inspection model found to be the norm by Lovell and Phelps (1977) and by Goldsberry, et al. (1984).[3] For supervision to achieve the depth of teacher involvement that is associated with improved teaching, the talent, time, and energy devoted to the process must perhaps far exceed the ritualistic annual inspection. The evidence collected to date supports this conclusion, but it is clearly insufficient to establish the point firmly. The expanded, more intense efforts at clinical supervision *are* more costly than the cursory ritual. Does the increased effort translate to better learning for the students?

Improved Learning as Consequence Whatever other consequences may be desired, supervision is clearly intended to contribute to improved teaching. Does teacher involvement in supervision translate to improved learning for students? In her thorough and scholarly review of clinical supervision studies employing pre- and postintervention measures, Pavan (1985) deliberately sought effects on learner achievement from clinical supervision. Though Pavan observed that "the relationship between clinical supervision and student achievement is probably the most difficult, if not impossible, to determine" (p. 19), she still reviewed four completed and two "in-progress" studies of this relationship. Of the four completed studies, only one (Mayfield, 1983) reported significantly higher achievement from students whose teachers participated in clinical supervision. Pavan's thorough scrutiny of the Mayfield study led her to conclude "that teacher and principal effects and gross differences in supervisory time have more influence on student achievement than clinical supervision" (p. 28).

Pavan's study is important for the illustration of two separate points. First, although the improvement of teaching is the central purpose for supervision, the achievement of students is seldom reported in the research on supervision. Second, when student achievement is considered, it is usually in the form of a mean score on some multiple-choice examination. Both of these observations have implications that will be discussed later. Suffice it to say for now that there is insufficient data available to support that supervision of teachers has any causal relationship to documented student achievement.

Informed Personnel Decisions as a Consequence

Most school systems, rightly or not, charge those who supervise teachers with the dual responsibility of helping all teachers develop professionally and of evaluating those same teachers for personnel action. This combination of accountability and professional development as part of the supervisory mission has drawn starkly differing appraisals from highly regarded scholars. McLaughlin and Pfeifer (1988) state:

[A]ccountability and improvement not only are compatible objectives; they are necessary partners. Just as a combination of pressure and support is necessary to focus attention on teacher evaluation throughout the district and foster the conditions that enable, so too do teachers need both pressure and support to grow professionally. . . . A strategic combination of pressure and support are as important at the individual level, we see, as they are at the institutional level. They support reflective practice (p. 85).

The notion that summative evaluation of teaching supports reflective practice among teachers is sharply challenged by Hargreaves and Dawe (1990) who suggested that "within these initiatives, under the aegis of professional collaboration and personal development, lurks an administrative apparatus of surveillance and control" (p. 239).

At the core of each perspective lies a different assumption about teacher involvement in such relationships. McLaughlin and Pfeifer (1988) envision "control based in professional values and motivation" (p. 83) and a collaborative culture in which active teacher involvement provides a combination of individual accountability and institutional accountability. In contrast, Hargreaves and Dawe (1990) asserted that "supervision is incompatible with healthy coaching relations. The presence of evaluation prejudices the necessary willingness to show weakness and vulnerability in order to gain support" (p. 238). It is possible that both views are correct. Both agree that "technical" systems that impose solutions upon teachers are antithetical to reflective practice, and unlikely to produce either a collaborative culture or meaningful reform of teaching practice. Indeed, both might agree with Byrne's (1994) assertion that:

[T]he nonparticipation of teachers in decisions that bear directly on their daily work environment leads both to a decline in self-esteem and to strong feelings of external control by others. Over time, these effects take their toll, manifesting themselves first in terms of job stress and ultimately in perceptions of diminished personal accomplishment (p. 665).

Can formal teacher evaluation be done in a manner that promotes a collaborative culture and contributes to meaningful improvement of the teaching/learning environment? These scholars seem to hold differing opinions on this question as well. McLaughlin and Pfeifer support their assertions with anecdotal data from four case studies of school districts that have heavily invested in implementing meaningful teacher evaluation programs. Sharing cases where formal teacher evaluation is documented as contributing to, rather than detracting from, active teacher involvement in the collaborative challenge of improving the learning environment seems persuasive that teacher evaluation can be done in a manner that supports rather than undermines teacher development. Deeper examination may still be needed. The long-term consequences of combining efforts toward regular and systematic teacher evaluation ultimately might undermine efforts to establish a collaborative spirit of inquiry and acceptance of varied perspectives.

How can research into teacher involvement help us address this controversial issue? Can we deliberately design supervisory interventions to contribute both to accurate assessment of present teaching performance and to active teacher involvement in the refinement of subsequent teaching? These questions foreshadow the discussion of "consequential validity" (Shulman, 1994) found in the final section of this chapter. Such questioning will surely bring us to attend to aspects of the supervisory intervention itself.

Intervention Strategy

The stereotypical image of teacher supervision has a silent and stern observer watching a stereotypical classroom with its rows of student desks filled with polite, clean, smiling children facing a smiling, lecturing teacher pointing to a math problem on a chalkboard. One imagines a Norman Rockwell painting done in the 1950s. The supervisor is always male, whereas the teacher is always female. How or when they confer is left undisclosed. Teacher lore, however, has its own stereotypes about supervisory feedback. It could come, if it comes at all, in a written summary or in the briefest of meetings where the supervisor provides the same kind of one-way judgment-giving proclamations he could in writing. In either case, it begins with a general compliment (e.g., "I really enjoyed visiting your class. I always enjoy watching good teachers at work."), moves on to the obligatory "suggestion for improvement" (e.g., "You might consider writing your objective for the lesson on the board at the beginning of the lesson."), and concludes with the customary blessing (e.g., "I'm really glad to have a teacher like you on my faculty."). The stereotype has supervision as ritualistic, often condescending, and harmless—like a visit to the dentist when he or she says: "Everything looks great. See you in six months." According to the stereotype, however, if there is ever an effort to hold a serious discussion after the examination, then the teacher is in trouble—the equivalent of hearing about a pending root canal. According to the stereotype, therefore, educational supervision is either innocuous or threatening. Stereotypes can be dangerous. What systematic information do we have that describes the procedures of supervision in schools?

It is sad to say, but not much. Although there are many descriptions of how supervision is conducted in specialized programs (i.e., often related to preservice teacher education), few attempts have been made to collect descriptive information as to "typical" classroom teachers' experiences with supervision. Guthrie and Willower (1973) examined 350 observation reports from a single school district written by 26 principals or assistant principals using content analysis. They distinguished between "ritualistic" and "goal oriented" ("those that referred to a specific instructional situation and conveyed the writer's attempt to report and . . . improve educational practice" p. 285) statements. They also distinguished among comments that judged existing practice as positive, negative, or neutral. Of 1,433 coded statements, they found 1,237 (86 percent) to be ritualistic compared to 196 (14 percent) goal oriented; 990 (70 percent) to be positive judgments, 403 (28 percent) to be negative, and 40 (3 percent) to be neutral; and only two (00.1 percent) that were negative and goal-oriented, or that described and attempted to help address current practice that was not seen as effective. The analysis of observation reports depicts a ritual that is anything but threatening. Guthrie and Willower called this complimentary ritual a "ceremonial congratulation" and concluded that "the observation report is unlikely to be a vehicle for the promotion of serious dialogue on instruction" (p. 289). Such a portrayal sadly supports the teacher-lore stereotype of supervision as a superficial process with no teacher involvement (i.e., not even apprehension) and with no discernible benefit for teaching and learning in the school. Is this truly the norm? What do we know about supervisory practices on a larger scale? This study perhaps misrepresents common supervisory practice.

Lovell and Phelps (1977) sought to collect and share descriptive information about the supervision teachers received in

Tennessee. Seventy-three percent of responding teachers reported that the building principal observed them teaching at least once during the school year, while 82 percent reported conferring with the principal at least once regarding the instructional program. "Interestingly, more than 80 percent of the teachers reported no observations by or conferences with a general or special supervisor" (pp. 226–227). Both principals and teachers reported brief conferences, with many lasting less than 10 minutes. These Tennessee teachers reported that, usually, observations were not

scheduled in advance, not requested, not preceded by a conference, and not followed by a conference or written report. Most teachers felt confident while being observed and reported that observations were not disruptive to the class. However, only 44% of the teachers found that observations were usually helpful. Conversely, the majority of principals and supervisors reported that observations were usually scheduled in advance, preceded by a conference, and followed by a conference and written report (p. 227).

This fascinating phenomenon of different respondent groups reporting contradictory findings is not unique.

Inspired by Lovell's efforts, Goldsberry and colleagues (Goldsberry et al, 1984) developed and administered the Survey of Supervisory Practices (SSP) to more than 4,000 Pennsylvania teachers and their supervisors. The SSP has also been used to examine teachers' perceptions of supervisory practices in Canada (Mandrusiak, 1988), in Alaska (Fenton et al, 1989), and in New Jersey (Corn, 1986). According to Goldsberry et al supervisors are usually principals and assistant principals who observe and confer with teachers twice annually. Conferences usually occur after, but not before, classroom observations. Although most supervisors report the primary purpose of such observations and conferences is to assist teachers to improve their teaching, nearly three quarters of teachers report the primary purpose as either "to comply with legal requirements" mandating such observations or to rate their teaching (Goldsberry et al, 1984). As in the Lovell and Phelps study, supervisors in the SSP studies often reported higher frequencies of supervisory services and more positive perceptions of both intent and effects of supervision than did the teachers. Unlike the Lovell and Philip study, Goldsberry et al matched teachers and supervisors so that the teacher respondents were supervised by the supervisor respondents.

Although Blumberg (1980) characterizes the relationship between supervisors and teachers as a "private cold war," nearly three quarters of teachers responding to the SSP across different settings chose "supportive" as a descriptor of the supervision they received. As with the Lovell and Phelps (1977) study, teacher respondents seemed to portray supervision as a nonthreatening, harmless process. Both of the large-scale surveys of teacher perceptions (Goldsberry et al, 1984; Lovell & Phelps, 1977) reported that teachers generally found supervision *not* helpful for improving teaching. Goldsberry et al also reported a significant interaction between the identification of potential teaching improvements and the helpfulness of the supervisory process for improving instruction. It is not surprising that teachers who reported that possible improvements were identified as part of the supervisory process were much more likely to find supervision helpful for improving their teaching than were those who reported that no potential improvements were identified. Still, 42 percent of teachers reported that *no* potential improvements were identified.

In short, the Lovell and Phelps and the SSP studies provide a snapshot of central tendencies of supervision provided in those places where principals are the primary supervisors. This picture of sporadic service, which was intended to improve teaching but was perceived as a "supportive" act of ritualized rating, verifies many teachers' perceptions of supervision as nominal service (i.e., neither doing much good nor much harm, neither threatening nor stimulating, but supportive). Goldsberry et al (1984) do identify six components of the supervisory process that correlated significantly with teachers' perceptions of helpfulness for improving teaching: (1) the occurrence of postobservation conferences; (2) the awareness of the supervisor of the teacher's lesson plan for the observed lesson; (3) the teacher's perception that the purpose of the observation was to improve teaching; (4) the identification of potential teaching improvements; (5) the teacher's perception that the supervisor stimulated thought about teaching; and (6) the teacher's perception that the supervisor emphasized student achievement. These six features were not representative of most teachers' perceptions about the supervision they received, but when they were present, teachers were highly likely to report that supervision was helpful for improving teaching. Although further study is needed, the initial impression from these survey results is that teacher involvement in supervision is usually minimal, and that it is more of casual participation in an innocuous ritual than it is either a helpful engagement or a distasteful intimidation. Goldsberry et al (1984) advise considerable caution in generalizing beyond the study population. However, if the findings are generalizable, teacher involvement in the six factors mentioned may contribute to supervisory success.

Remarkably little is known about the nature or the even frequency of teachers' involvement as recipients of supervision. The supervisory inspection (i.e., the sporadic observation of teaching for the purpose of rating general competence) seems to be the most common practice, but until more descriptive data are collected even that conclusion relies on generalizing from localized and aging studies. Although many believe that such inspections produce defensive reactions from teachers (e.g., Blumberg, 1980; Hargreaves & Dawe, 1990), available data support the conclusion that the ritual is perceived as a harmless and often useless exercise that was aptly labeled by Guthrie and Willower (1973) as the "ceremonial congratulation."

Are there studies that illuminate alternative views of teacher involvement in supervision as the recipient, even if these views may be localized? The answer is, *Yes.* For example, Pavan (1985) systematically looked for studies examining clinical supervision and its consequences for in-service K–12 teachers and their learners. Given this focus and her emphasis on studies employing "pre-post test measures or an experimental control group research design" (p. 4), she identified and reviewed 29 studies exploring clinical supervision. While it may be reasonably argued that her focus and delimitations led Pavan to situations more intense than those typically found in supervi-

sory practice, her careful scholarship helps us to examine supervision in those settings, however rare, where "clinical supervision" is deliberately attempted and where one type of disciplined investigation is undertaken. Pavan emphasizes methodological concerns more than noteworthy findings regarding supervisory practice. She concluded that "most of the studies reported more positive, though not necessarily statistically significant, attitudes after clinical supervision implementation" (p. 26). It is noteworthy for our examination that at least two of the studies reported by Pavan (Clapper, 1981; Fishbaugh, 1983) involved peer supervision, where one would suppose that different types of teacher involvement would occur. Pavan observed that in at least one of these cases, "peer supervision rather than clinical supervision seemed the more important factor" (p. 9). Based on Pavan's scholarly review, studies specifically exploring clinical supervision seem to find teachers engaged more actively in the examination and adaptation of teaching practices than those (e.g., Goldsberry et al, 1984; Lovell & Phelps, 1977) that surveyed schools, irrespective of their espoused use of clinical supervision. Pavan's findings further support the notion that when unusual steps are taken to bolster the rigor of instructional supervision, teachers are generally more involved, have more positive attitudes, and possibly improve teaching practices. If supervision is an innocuous ritual in most settings, and a genuine attempt is occasionally made to involve teachers and to improve the teaching/learning environment through meaningful supervision that proves useful, then both portrayals of supervision (i.e., innocuous ritual and helpful intervention) may be accurate in varied settings.

Fenton et al (1989) compared three approaches (i.e., "cooperative, supervisor controlled, and minimal") to supervision. Teachers who participated in the cooperative approach (i.e., defined as an approach involving a series of conferences and observations in which the supervisor provides encouragement and monitors progress as the teacher works on self-selected instructional improvement goals) found supervision to be more helpful than did teachers in the other groups. Most of these teachers specifically reported that: (1) the purpose of supervision was to improve instruction, while most teachers in other groups saw the purpose as simple compliance with a mandated policy; (2) the supervisor was aware of the plan for the lesson to be observed, while other groups did not perceive this; and (3) the innovations tried as a result of supervision (i.e., all groups reported trying new practices) were worthwhile, while most teachers in other groups did not. The nature of the supervisory intervention again seems to vary considerably and to have an influential effect on both teacher involvement and on teachers' perceptions of supervision's usefulness. Fenton and colleagues reported that teachers in each group generally perceived supervision positively. The cooperative group, however, were more positive than were the other two groups to a statistically significant degree. While 92 percent of all teachers reported that the teacher evaluation associated with the supervision was fair, the cooperative model was most often identified as organized, productive, systematic, and collaborative. The cooperative group was also most likely to report that trust was needed and present.

Whether called clinical supervision or not, the logical

assumption that the manner in which the supervisory program is delivered makes an important difference in the effects of supervision has been supported in the research literature. Based on their thorough analysis of a single case of clinical supervision, Grimmett and Crehan (1990) concluded that even when a productive supervisory relationship has been established the teacher's reflective behavior is inhibited when the supervisor imposes personal frames of reference that are different from the teacher's frames. Herbert and Tankersley (1993) observed that even when two different supervisors use similar questions during postconferences the consequences can be quite different in terms of teacher reflection. Like Grimmett and Crehan, they concluded that using the teacher's perspective as a focus and encouraging connections between the teacher's perceptions of different aspects of the situation will elicit the desired reflection. The supervisor drawing comparisons between the teacher's actions and those of others was found to limit the frames of reflection of their supervisers. In short, the degree and nature of teacher involvement in the supervisory process seems crucial to supervisory success.

In summary, the nature of the supervisory intervention varies considerably in the research reviewed. The norm seems to be a minimal approach characterized by rare observation and little meaningful discussion of teaching. This portrayal corresponds to what Goldsberry (1988) has called "nominal supervision." Teacher involvement in this common approach is almost nonexistent, as are its consequences for instructional improvement. Other approaches seem more time-consuming, more costly, and more effective. Reviewed research supports the hypothesis that as teacher involvement increases, so does the perceived usefulness for improving teaching. Moreover, it could be argued that whenever a serious attempt is made to provide supervision focused on improving the teaching–learning environment, teachers perceive it as helpful. More study is clearly needed to test these hypotheses. The very form of the research method will perhaps influence the findings.

Consider the research reviewed so far. Are any patterns discernable between the methods used to collect data and the reported findings? This question will be discussed in more depth in the third section.

If the "top–down" relationship of an organizational superordinate interacting with a subordinate might inhibit open collaboration, as has been suggested by some, as noted earlier, how might an organization create a less inhibiting structure for generating support to refine teaching practice? Establishing mentor–protégé relationships between effective, experienced teachers and beginning teachers will perhaps help.

Mentors and Beginners

What is a "mentor," and how does he or she differ from a supervisor? A mentor is generally an experienced practitioner who guides the development of an inexperienced one. As this notion pertains to educational supervision, a mentor would be an experienced, and sometimes expert, teacher who guides the induction process of a new teacher. Many of us have profited from "mentors" who were not recognized by any organization for their helpful function. When an experienced teacher takes a novice "under wing," an informal mentorship may begin. These self-selected, naturally evolving relationships may be very valuable for both mentor and protégé, but they are difficult to institutionalize. Mentor programs in schools are generally hybrids of naturally arising mentorships and supervision. A mentor is specifically "an experienced teacher who is 'a master of the craft of teaching and personable in dealing with other teachers; an empathic individual who understands the need of a mentorship role'" (Zimpher & Reiger, 1988, cited in Zimpher & Grossman, 1992, p. 145). Because mentors are generally classroom teachers with limited or no "line authority," the role is less bosslike than supervisor. Because teacher-mentors are generally assigned and their functions defined organizationally, the role is generally more formal and externally determined than the naturally evolving mentorships.

Such school-defined roles raise special questions regarding teacher involvement in supervision. Two teachers are now involved. Do both profit? In similar ways? How does the role discrepancy in the relationship influence benefits? What qualifies a teacher to become a mentor? In this section, research exploring mentorship programs is discussed with special emphases on role definition, process characteristics, and evidence of consequences.

Although the roles called "coach" and "consultant" in this chapter often are labeled interchangeably in the literature, the "mentor" function is consistently seen as an experienced teacher helping a beginner. The nature of the interaction, however, how mentors are selected, how beginners are matched with mentors, the extent to which (if at all) either participant is prepared for the role, and the intended frequency and duration of the interaction, are the variables. As might be imagined, these variations cause considerable differences in the role and effect of mentors among various mentor programs. In a scholarly review of the mentor phenomenon, Little (1990) observed: "Mentor roles are markedly ambiguous. Throughout the implementation literature observers record the uncertainties of mentors, administrators, and teachers regarding the central purposes of mentorship and the specific behavior in which mentors should or might engage" (p. 313). Following the structure established earlier, this section begins with an examination of the intended consequences of mentor programs, and then examines the nature of the intervention.

Desired Consequences of Mentor Programs

The special needs of beginning teachers are often cited as justification for mentor programs. Beginners are generally willing and often eager for helpful advice from more experienced colleagues. In fact, one study (Tellez, 1992) found that 98 percent of beginning teachers reported seeking help from other teachers. One focus for a mentor is clearly to assist a beginning teacher adjust to the demands of a complex job. Veenman (1984) documented that the transition from teacher preparation into the first teaching job is often traumatic for teachers in different countries. Whether called "transition shock" or "Praxisshock, . . . the concept is used to indicate the collapse of the missionary ideals formed during teacher training by the harsh and rude reality of everyday classroom life" (p. 143). By reviewing previous studies, he reported that beginning teachers often abandon democratic or student-centered practices in favor of authoritarian ones. Veenman concludes that much further study is needed, including

comprehensive developmental studies of the beginning teacher . . . systematic study of variations in forms of training and assistance, and the relationships of these different training experiences with the personality characteristics of the beginning teachers and with the social settings in which they work (p. 168).

It seems, therefore, that one purpose for a mentor program is to provide a supportive orientation to the school and the complex job of teaching, possibly with the idea of preserving some entry ideals.

As with all forms of supervision, improved teaching practice by the beginning teacher is another desired consequence of mentor programs. The emphasis on supporting a beginner going through a difficult transition sometimes collides with the emphasis on improving teaching practice. The extent to which a mentor should directly work to improve teaching practices is at issue. For example, Anctil (1991) focused on such direct assistance that she called "instructional coaching" as a crucial function for the mentor, while Yosha (1991) focused on emotional support for the beginner as the principal function of a mentor, asserting: "It is important to remember that the role of mentors is to assist and not evaluate" (Yosha, 1991, p. 6). (The issue of involving mentors in formal evaluation and a more elaborate comparison between the Anctil and Yosha studies are discussed further shortly.) It seems as if the term *evaluate* may hold some ambiguity. As discussed earlier, teachers often associate "evaluation" with their experiences with formal teacher ratings that are typically superficial and unhelpful. Even when mentors are not reporting to anyone other than the beginner being observed, however, there is a form of judging the efficacy of teaching strategies and tactics that requires the mentor to evaluate observed teaching if her or his expert judgment is to be made available to the teacher in the form of advice or suggestions. Could it be that practicing mentors feel a tension between "being supportive" and confronting the beginner with the bad news that the teaching is not seen as "good"? In some cases, perhaps, mentors are placed in a position where their actions will differ if they see their primary client being the beginning teacher rather than the learners served by the beginner. In such cases, the two most obvious goals of most mentor programs (i.e., to help the beginner "fit in" and to help the beginner improve teaching practice) may clash. When the unspoken norm is to honor differing teaching styles regardless of one's beliefs about their effectiveness, this clash seems most likely.

In general, mentors reported allowing beginners to make their own decisions and being careful to avoid prescribing solutions. . . . Their reticence to engage in direct forms of teaching or coaching might be attributed to the strong norms of privacy among teachers (Feiman-Nemser & Floden, 1986) or to uncertainty about their own knowledge. Our repeated exposure to these teachers suggests, however, that most were genuinely concerned with advancing their beginners'

interest in and ability to think through their own problems (which often requires an indirect approach), and they were willing to share their own expertise. . . . With few exceptions, the mentors reported building relationships where advice could be given in a comfortable, collegial manner" (Wildman et al, 1992, p. 207).

One wonders if many mentors develop the relationship with the beginning teacher to discuss the full range of their insights candidly. The development of candor may be different from comfort with giving tactfully chosen advice.

A third goal for some mentor programs is to assist the beginner to develop skills of self-evaluation and adaptation.

In guided participation, an experienced mentor assesses the level of the beginner and gradually moves him to higher levels of cognitive functioning. This process requires active collaboration, interpersonal skills, the ability to assess another's developmental level, and interactive dialog (Colton & Sparks-Langer, 1992, p. 158).

Where this is an explicit aim of the mentor program, a priority is implicitly placed on the mentor's candidness regarding her or his perceptions of teaching adequacy. The presumption is that mentors will help beginning teachers *accurately* evaluate their personal teaching practices. The yardstick most commonly available to the mentor to gauge accuracy of the beginner's evaluation is naturally the mentor's evaluation. One wonders if mentors who judge teaching performance differently from the beginners they serve are seen as helpful by those beginners. One also wonders what happens when the mentor observes teaching practices she or he deems unacceptable but is unable to persuade the beginner of their unworthiness. *Another controversial goal for some mentor programs is to provide information for personnel decisions.*

Informed Personnel Decisions as a Consequence

Does a mentor evaluate a beginner's teaching? If so, to whom is the evaluation communicated? Perhaps more than in formal supervision, the question of teacher evaluation frames a difficult issue around the intended consequences of mentor programs. While it is easy to espouse a "helpful and supportive" mentor program that is "nonthreatening," advocating a specific function for the mentor of a beginning teacher who is not successfully working with students seems very difficult. Noting the "distinction made between assistance and assessment," Zimpher and Grossman (1992) compare two models of mentor programs, one in which assistance is provided while assessment is strictly avoided and one (called "peer assistance and review" or PAR) in which the mentor "offers the same kinds of assistance . . . while also providing periodic assessments that ultimately factor into a review panel's decision to retain the beginning teacher on a regular contract" (p. 143).[4]

Citing Schmidt, Zimpher and Grossman report the Ohio Education Association's (OEA) position on the issue:

"Our position is that teachers who evaluate other teachers should do so for the purpose of improving the performance of the teacher being evaluated." . . . [The OEA] assert[ed] that teachers who know that their evaluators could eventually recommend their discharge will be less likely to discuss the difficulties they are encountering (Schmidt, 1990, p. 22) (Zimpher & Grossman, 1992, p. 144).

For these reasons one mentor program studied by Zimpher and Grossman deliberately separated the mentor service from personnel evaluation.

The only irony worth reporting is repeatedly, at the culmination of a year's work in a role that was to be strictly assistance oriented, mentors complained about their lack of involvement in the principal's decisions on contract renewal for the beginning teachers in the program (Zimpher & Grossman, 1992, p 149).

In some cases, mentor programs serve to ascertain that beginning teachers have acquired teaching skills to some degree of proficiency. Schaffer, Stringfield, and Wolf (1992) report a mentor program in which beginning teachers

were required to demonstrate competence in (a) managing instructional time, (b) managing student behavior, (c) instructional presentation, (d) monitoring student performance, (e) providing instructional feedback, (f) collegiality, (g) analyzing teaching, and (h) using a variety of teaching models (p. 182).

This particular study employed trained observers using the Stallings Observation System (SOS) to collect descriptive information of the beginners' teaching. The authors report:

Each SOS profile contains three types of information on 51 specific teaching behaviors that research has shown to be related to student achievement gain. Teachers are provided with normative data, a criterion performance level for effective teaching, and their performance on that dimension. A typical profile indicates that a teacher is performing at or above criterion on several dimensions, below criterion on others. The SOS profile is not used prescriptively. The information is presented as data for teachers to use in considering in-class behavior they may want to modify or build upon" (p. 183).

Mentor programs are seldom reported to have such a sharp focus on specific teaching behaviors. As one might expect from a program with such precision in its expectations, beginning teachers demonstrated considerable progress on the identified teaching behaviors, regardless of the explicit avoidance of prescriptive behavior from mentors. (Two other factors that may have contributed to the growth experienced by these beginning teachers are the combination of a university-based teacher induction program with experienced teachers serving as mentors and deliberate follow-through over a 2-year induction period. These likely influences will be discussed further shortly.)

Professional Development for Mentors

A final consequence often associated with mentor programs is professional payoff for the experienced teachers who serve as mentors. Reported programs often claim experienced teachers both refine their own teaching practices and report renewed enthusiasm for their own work. Given the norm of autonomy that works powerfully in some school settings, however, teachers who serve as mentors may find themselves caught in a professional bind. As Little (1990) explained:

Ironically, teachers may move from classroom teacher, with substantial discretion over the manner of their work, to a mentorship that finds them exercising less discretion and accommodating more constraints. . . . Teachers who have served as mentors or teacher leaders decline to do so again; the intended career incentive is diluted both for them and for the colleagues who have witnessed their defeat (Hart, 1989). Faced with mounting dissent, the institution makes moves to render the role harmless—and thus useless (Bird, 1986). The prospect of increased organizational capacity is weakened. The standard of mutual benefit is compromised (p. 315).

Given this possibility for mentor programs to work against the mutual benefits desired for both mentor and beginner, careful monitoring of actual effects seems clearly warranted.

Who are Mentors?

If mentors themselves are expected to gain from their work with beginners, then is it logical to make someone whose teaching has stagnated a mentor? Because the mentor is intended to influence the beginner's teaching practices, should the mentor not be one who models and understands exemplary teaching practices? Does a teacher need skills other than those required for successful teaching to be a successful mentor? Ackley and Gall (1992) think so. Among the skills important for mentors they identified are listening, problem solving, interpersonal ease, cheerfulness, friendliness, knowledge of subject, technical proficiency, demonstration, confidence-building, resource-building, support, and collaboration. Wildman et al (1992) agree. From their investigation, they listed 12 characteristics for mentors that

were reported consistently across all data sources by both mentors and beginners: (1) willing to be a mentor; (2) sensitive—that is, they know when to back off; (3) helpful, but not authoritarian; (4) emotionally committed to their beginners; (5) astute—that is, they know the right thing to say at the right time; (6) diplomatic—for example, they know how to counteract bad advice given to their beginners by others; (7) able to anticipate problems; (8) nurturant and encouraging; (9) timely in keeping the beginners appraised of their successes; (10) careful to keep the beginners' problems confidential; (11) enthusiastic about teaching; (12) good role model at all times (p. 211).

These characteristics certainly seem desirable. One wonders how they might be assessed, and how many potential mentors may possess all these skills or characteristics. Are they all equally important? If a mentor is "diplomatic—for example, knows how to counteract bad advice given to their beginners by others," but is not exactly "a good role model at all times," then might that teacher still be a successful mentor? If a teacher has marvelous problem-solving skills, but is less than cheerful most of the time, then will the beginner not profit? Might serving as mentor help a teacher develop or strengthen some of these skills? If so, is this done at the expense of the beginner? Careful examination of the relative benefits of each of these skills or characteristics has not been done (and, perhaps, cannot be done, as is discussed later in the conclusions section). Moreover, it seems likely that however skilled and committed the mentor may be, the extent to which the beginner (or mentor) benefits seems inextricably related to the nature and duration of the intervention.

Intervention Strategy

Because initiating a mentor program for beginning teachers where none existed involves money, time, and meaningful operational change, such efforts are usually impelled by forces external to the local school district, and very often at the state level. Like many large-scale political solutions to problems that are ill-defined and often idiosyncratic, the fervor that led to many states adopting teacher induction programs involving mentors in the mid-1980s has declined noticeably in the fiscal and political climate of the mid-1990s. Two consequences seem worthy of note. First, as fiscal resources and short-lived hype diminish, local commitment and intervention procedures might atrophy or die out completely. Could mentor programs, with their heavy demand on teacher time and energy, become the same kind of nominal ritual that instructional supervision has in many places? Because the impetus for change often came from afar, might local leadership quickly abandon the priority on teacher induction, resorting to the much easier "sink-or-swim" approach? When external resources and emphases are reduced, it seems logical to forecast a corresponding diminishing effect in many localities. Only longitudinal studies can explore whether mentor programs will be other than another "flash-in-the-pan" educational reform that has no lasting effect on either children or schools. In the review for this chapter, no study covering more than 3 years after the initiation of a mentor program was discovered.

A second and obvious consequence of school reform emanating from state-level policy is that the target population for the designed intervention is larger. This often has implications for research design (discussed in the third section), as well as for program implementation. Basic implementation features, such as who becomes a mentor, how mentors are selected and prepared, the actual expectations for observing teaching, and the time for meeting with the beginner, are highly varied. For our focus on teacher involvement in the supervision of instruction, the variance is no less. Some mentors (e.g., see Lemberger, 1992) and some researchers (e.g., Anctil, 1992) emphasize direct consideration of the beginner's teaching practices and direct communication as to how they might be improved as a necessary feature of the mentor service. Others (e.g., see Lemberger, 1992; Yosha, 1991) view the mentor's function as providing more of a supportive, and less of an intrusive, orientation to school life. To illustrate how these differing perspectives can influence research findings, consider the following case study:

A Tale of Two Studies

It was the best of programs; it was the worst of programs. Well, neither really. Really it was two different perspectives on one program, Connecticut's Beginning Educator Support and Training (BEST) program. Both studies were presented at the Annual Meeting of the American Educational Research Association (AERA) in Chicago in 1991. Together, they provide what I find to be an intriguing stereoscopic view of a single program.

Mentors in the BEST program have "articulated responsibilities which include:

a) meeting regularly (average once a week for a minimum of 30 minutes per week) with beginning teacher over the course of the year;

b) meeting and observing at least eight times per year with the beginning teacher in each other's classroom. (Some of these sessions should be demonstrations of effective teaching practices by the mentor while others should be focused on the beginning teacher's teaching. The observations of beginning teachers should be accompanied by focused formative feedback.);

c) providing support for the development of the beginning teacher's skills focused on the Connecticut Teaching Competencies (i.e., planning of instruction, classroom management, instruction and assessment of student learning);

d) assisting the beginning teacher in preparing for the BEST assessment process;

e) recording meetings and activities with the beginning teacher (a–d) in the mentor log; and

f) completing the appropriate follow-up training program" (Anctil 1991, p. 2).

Questions of Intervention Strategy

Anctil (1991) used "telephone surveys of mentors and beginning teachers, and mentor logs completed by mentors and signed by both the mentor and beginning teacher" (p. 2) as data sources, while Yosha (1991) used "telephone surveys; . . . focus group discussions; . . . site visit interviews; and . . . letters from practicing mentors to teachers contemplating becoming mentors" (p. 2). Sampling procedures are not explicit in either study. I assume that these two researchers are independently analyzing the same data set from telephone surveys. [This possibility is supported by correspondence of frequencies in the rare cases when data from the same questions are reported. e.g., both researchers report 49 percent of beginners rated the quality of mentoring 'very high' (Anctil 1991, p. 7; Yosha 1991, Figure 15.2).] Another possibility, however, is that the two studies are reporting on two different samples drawn from the same population of mentors and beginning teachers in the BEST program.

Data from Telephone Surveys

Yosha reports: "Being observed frequently, as well as observing veteran teachers frequently enabled novices to learn techniques for interacting with students, organizing lessons, and obtaining and developing new materials" (1991, p. 4, emphasis in original). Anctil provides more information as to the meaning of being observed frequently (as reported by beginning teachers): "Beginners reported the frequency of mentor observation as follows: 15 percent—weekly; 33 percent—monthly; 36 percent—less than monthly; 11 percent—one time; 5 percent—never. Report of beginning teacher observation of mentors was somewhat less: 7 percent—weekly; 18 percent—monthly; 27 percent—less than monthly; 14 percent—one time; 34 percent—never. . . . (A) large percentage (85 percent) of beginning teachers reported that their mentors provided them with clear, constructive feedback that helped them improve their teaching. [Yosha (1991, pp. 2–3) reports the identical finding.] The frequency of mentors providing feedback on beginning teachers' teaching was reported as follows: 27 percent—weekly; 40 percent—monthly; 23 percent—less than monthly; 6 percent—one time; 5 percent—never" (pp. 4–5).

Another display of Anctil's data highlights a curious finding:

frequency of observation by mentor		feedback on beginners' teaching
15 percent -	weekly	- 27 percent
33 percent -	monthly	- 40 percent
36 percent -	less than monthly	- 23 percent
11 percent -	one time	- 6 percent
5 percent -	never	- 5 percent

Apparently, mentors are providing feedback (on a weekly and monthly basis) on beginning teachers' teaching without observing the teaching. If the respondents in Anctil's study are representative of those in Yosha's study, then slightly more than half of the beginners who reported the benefits of frequent observation were observed less than once a month.

Anctil also reports novices' responses regarding frequency of observation of the mentor while teaching: "7 percent—weekly; 18 percent—monthly; 27 percent—less than monthly; 14 percent—one time; 34 percent—never" (1991, p. 5). Apparently, beginning teachers in the BEST program have very different experiences in terms of observing their mentors teach: One in four report such observations at least monthly, while one in three do not observe the mentor's teaching at all.

Meetings between mentor and beginner occurred much more often than observations. Anctil (1991) reports that 8 percent of beginners surveyed reported meeting daily with their mentors; 67 percent, weekly; 18 percent, monthly; and 7 percent less than monthly. Apparently, the aim of the BEST program for beginners to meet regularly with their mentors was being met.

Data from Mentors' Logs
Anctil's analysis of mentor logs provides another perspective on the frequency of observations: "In approximately one out of ten (mentor logs) in the study, a pattern of frequent observation (at least once per month) was identified, with specific observation focus noted. . . . In approximately half of those logs identified as 'frequent observation,' notation was made of follow-up conferences. However, within these notions, feedback was rarely mentioned specifically" (pp. 10–11). Approximately 70 percent of the mentors' logs documented 2–3 observations over the course of the year. Twenty percent had no evidence of observation.

We begin with a relatively low inference level question: How often do mentors in the BEST program observe beginning teachers teaching? At one level, we are informed that both the intent and actual practice is "frequent" observation. According to novices' responses to Anctil's telephone surveys, actual observations varied considerably with 15 percent of respondents being observed weekly while 16 percent of respondents were observed once or never. These same responses indicated that nearly half of the novices were observed at least monthly, but the analysis of the mentors' logs revealed documentation of only 10 percent being observed monthly.

How can this be? Is someone not being truthful. Perhaps, though, mentors were not reliable about entering observations into their logs. Perhaps, beginning teachers responded with impressions rather than with precise frequencies when confronted with the telephone survey, and perhaps, when they weren't exactly sure which of two responses was accurate, they systematically chose the one most favorable. Whatever combination of factors contributed to it, the discrepancy leaves us unable to say with any confidence how often these beginning teachers were observed. Even if we accept the telephone survey data as completely accurate, we are left with the information that as many teachers (15 percent) are observed once or never during the school year as are observed weekly. This huge variation in the nature of the service provided by the mentor leaves us with a very poor foundation from which to assess the contributions of the service.

The point of this discussion of frequency of mentor observation is not that these are poor studies. Quite the contrary, with the benefit of Anctil's findings we have information that stimulates our curiosity and begs further inquiry. Rather, the present point is that when we set out to explore teacher involvement in supervision, we must discipline ourselves to gather and report data (as Anctil so admirably models) that enable the reader to ascertain the extent to which the nature and amount of teacher involvement is similar among the collection of teachers studied. Obviously, if different mentors and beginning teachers are participating in highly varied experiences, then it is not practi-

cal to try to generalize as to the nature of or benefits from the mentor experience from their aggregate responses. For example, if the vast majority of responding beginners report "frequent observation" by mentor as a helpful characteristic of the BEST but the data show these same respondents experience a range of observation from "weekly" to "never," it is difficult to support an assertion that "frequent observation contributed to beginners' developing better teaching practices." Anctil provides us with actual findings (i.e., the responses of the mentors and novices as opposed to her interpretations of them) that enable us to see how discrepant frequency of observation is across her sample. From her study, we have learned that the "frequent" observation that is intended as a defining characteristic of mentorship in the BEST program is not routinely practiced. This information strongly implies that the experiences of the participants (both mentors and novices), and thus the benefits, are idiosyncratic not common.

The mentors' logs also provided Anctil with information regarding the nature of mentor-beginner interaction. "At least 15 percent of the logs revealed the following pattern: rather than recording activities and focus of the meetings, mentors wrote glowing descriptions of the skill and energy levels of beginners, with lengthy, subjective, global comments as to the quality of the teaching observed. These logs were evaluative in nature, and extremely positive in tone. . . . In approximately one quarter of the logs, a pattern of noninstructionally based conversations were documented around such topics as: school district budgets, school policies, evaluations by building administrators, the injustice of the assessment process, biographical notes about the beginner, meeting set-up and arrangements, school calendars, faculty meetings, reduction-in-force policies, and recreational activities" (Anctil 1991, p. 10).

In short, the analysis of mentor logs conveys a very different impression than did the results from the telephone survey. In Anctil's words: "Discrepancies exist between survey data (perceptual data recalled over extended period of time) and log data (data recalled and written down from week to week). It appears that information from both mentors and beginning teachers is both quantitatively and qualitatively different on surveys than was actually reported in logs. It seems that log information may be more accurate given that reports are written while activities are more current" (p. 13). Another possible influence is that respondents may have tended to respond positively to items on the telephone survey out of a sense of loyalty or affection for their colleague. Such a "halo effect" may have had both mentors and beginners selecting ways of responding that would not offend their partner nor shed a negative light on their own performance. Again, another possibility for the discrepancy between the data sources is that mentors' logs inaccurately captured characteristics of the experience, perhaps due to haste with or lack of commitment to log entries. Though confounding, a clear virtue of the Anctil report is the deliberate presentation of these discrepancies so that subsequent studies might help illuminate the confusion.

Other Data Sources
Recall that Yosha interpreted data drawn from focus group discussions, site visit interviews, and letters from practicing mentors to teachers contemplating becoming mentors, as well as telephone surveys. Did these data sources yield the same puzzling contradictions? No. In Yosha's words: "What we found were patterns in experience and feeling. Trends. The data echo each other regarding benefits. That is, what respondents told telephone interviewers, they also told their colleagues and facilitators in focus groups and field staff workers at site visits" (Yosha 1991, p. 2). Apparently, only the mentors' logs produced discrepant findings.

Questions of Consequences
Where does this leave us with the more ambitious accountability questions that drive both of these studies? In Yosha's words: "What,

then, are the outcomes (of the BEST program) for teachers? What benefits has this induction program reaped? What are the payoffs?" (p. 1). Anctil's question was different: "The overarching purpose of this study was to investigate the accountability of mentors in Connecticut. In other words, are they doing what they are paid to do?" (p. 2). Both researchers report perceptions as to the consequences of the mentorship.

How do beginning teachers perceive the mentor service? Well, "93 percent of beginning teachers rated the amount of time spent with mentor 'adequate' or 'more than adequate'" (Anctil 1991, p. 3). Given the vast differences in classroom observation time reported earlier, it appears that time spent with mentor is deemed adequate or better whether one is observed weekly or very rarely.

"One question asked novices in the spring of their first year of teaching was, 'Has the mentor made a real difference in your becoming a more competent teacher?' Eighty-five percent (85 percent) agreed strongly or somewhat that the mentor had made a real difference. A subsequent question was, 'Has the mentor made a real difference in your adjustment to teaching?' Seventy-nine percent (79 percent) agreed that the mentor had made a real difference" (Yosha 1991, p. 2). Two responses were combined to yield the "agree" category reported. Forty-four percent of the respondents said "strongly agree" to the "becoming a more competent teacher" question, while another 41 percent responded "agree somewhat." Forty-one percent of the respondents said "strongly agree" to the "adjustment to teaching" question, while another 38 percent responded "agree somewhat." One wonders if "agree somewhat" translates to "not much," and if the rest of the respondents (15 percent and 21 percent) said "disagree" or "not at all."

Yosha reports roughly half (49 percent) of respondents strongly agreed that the "first year would be more difficult without (a) mentor" and that the "quality of support was 'high' or 'very high'" with 25 percent to 30 percent of respondents selecting "agree somewhat" to each item. This leaves at least 20 percent of respondents who did not even "agree somewhat" to these assertions. "Despite positive beginning teacher responses regarding specific assistance provided by mentors before, during, and after assessment (49 percent of beginners rated the quality of mentoring 'very high'), 46 percent stated that they could do without the mentor, and that the mentor was not needed" (Anctil, 1991, p. 7). If these two researchers are indeed using the same data set, then this final observation that nearly half of the beginning teacher respondents felt the mentor unnecessary helps us interpret the "somewhat agree" response. If almost half of beginning teachers tell us that the first year would be more difficult without the mentor, and that the quality of the service is "very high," and at the same time almost half tell us that the mentor is not needed, many of those who call the service unnecessary must also be selecting the "agree somewhat" response for its helpfulness. This suggests that grouping the "strongly agree" and the "agree somewhat" responses into an "agree" category (as Yosha sometimes does) may be misleading.

Improving Teaching or Moral Support?
Yosha concludes that the BEST program is highly successful, and asks: "How can we doubt that the teaching profession itself can profit from a systematic, structured induction program that brings these results?" (p. 9). Anctil, however, offers a different perspective: "For the most part, mentors appear to be energetically engaged in many support activities with beginning teachers. They spend much time in discussions about teaching. In addition, much time is spent discussing topics of interest to themselves and to beginning teachers. It appears that many of these topics, however, are not directly related to instruction. Both surveys and logs indicate what seems to be an *inordinate amount of time providing moral support and emotional support*" (p. 13, emphasis added).

"First, the major benefit perceived by novices is that an assigned mentor is someone to talk to and provide support" (Yosha, 1991, p. 4). The characterization of moral support seems to differ sharply between these two researchers. Anctil (1991) is clear in her appraisal that the lack of clear focus on refining the beginner's teaching practices is a disappointment: "It is apparent that a small percentage of mentors take their roles as instructional coaches more seriously than others" (p. 14). She goes on to recommend: "Provide mentors, during follow-up training, with explicit verbal review of the expectations for their role, including meeting, observation, assistance in developing teaching competencies, and preparing for assessment" (p. 15).

So What?
Given these two studies, it seems that we have some basis for the following assertions regarding the experiences of beginning teachers participating in these studies:

1. The nature of the experience is highly varied from one beginner to the next. One might be observed by the mentor weekly; another might only be observed once over the course of the year.
2. Both mentors and beginning teachers report "adequate" meeting time and general satisfaction with the program.
3. Apparently mentor logs provided data that are inconsistent with data collected through telephone surveys, focus group interviews, and other self-report means, with logs indicating less frequent classroom observation and an inconsistent focus on teaching practices.

The most intriguing aspect of this comparison, however, is the tone of the conclusions drawn from what appears to be the same data set, or at the very least, a different sample from the same population. Yosha is clear in her appraisal that the induction program is highly successful. Although she does suggest questions for future study, she interprets the data set as strongly positive. "The pattern is clear. There are mutual benefits for participants" (Yosha 1991, p. 9). Anctil, however, is obviously disappointed at what she sees as the rarity of mentors assuming an instructional coach role. Her recommendations clearly suggest steps that should be taken "with the goal of improving mentor accountability" (Anctil, 1991, p. 15).

How can we explain how two researchers see the same program so differently? First, Anctil's disappointing data came from an analysis of mentor logs, a data source mentioned but apparently not analyzed by Yosha. One clear possibility is that the data are influenced or distorted by the way they are collected. Anctil suggests this is the case, and gives more credence to the log data because they are collected during the process and not in recall. The logical possibility of respondents giving overly positive responses as a form of personal or collegial loyalty would support this explanation. A rival, and equally credible, possibility is that in the press of providing time-intensive service, the mentors simply did not thoroughly report events in their logs. This possibility would have us view log data more, not less, skeptically. As with much good research, these studies raise some questions that should be addressed by future research. Data are needed to inform us as to how valid data collected both by surveyed self-report and by logged self-report are. Such studies are relatively easy to design, and labor intensive to conduct because they would require some form of direct observation of actual practices to be compared to varied forms of self-report.

Apart from the obvious difference in the data source, another possibility is equally intriguing as influencing the tone of these two studies: focal bias, as in the old adage that one is more likely to find something which is look for. Anctil seemed to be seeking evidence that beginning teachers were getting real help with acquiring and refining teaching techniques. She is disappointed at the dearth of such evidence and notes, "Both surveys and logs indicate what seems to be an inordinate amount of time providing moral support and emotional support" (Anctil, 1991, p. 13). Yosha does not seem to be looking for evidence of instructional coaching, rather: "Our purposes at the time were *to provide moral support* for the new practitioners and to be available for problem solving if teachers requested it" (Yosha, 1991, p. 3, emphasis added). Unsurprisingly, this candid advocacy position from the interviewer parallels the responses of the interviewees regarding the benefits received from a mentor: "First, the major benefit perceived by novices is that an assigned mentor is someone to talk to and provide support" (Yosha, 1991, p. 4). What constitutes "support"? Apparently, Yosha might suggest that encouraging words and availability for problem solving would. Anctil might argue that deliberate observation of teaching techniques and constructive coaching, whether requested or not, should be present. These two studies, when compared, support the need for careful articulation of the dependent variables or target indicators that we select as representatives of "success." They also illuminate the need for researchers to examine their data sources critically, questioning the assumption of validity. The triangulation of discrepant data sources that Anctil presents permits the reader to discover legitimate confusion. To be sure, confusion is not always desired as a result of our inquiries. Still, as Anctil's study admirably illustrates, it enables us to raise needed questions that may result in richer, if delayed, gratification of our need for accurate information.

For the focus at hand, though, some results are clear. First, the nature of teacher involvement in this one statewide mentor program is highly varied both for mentor and for beginner. As was the case in our exploration of more traditional supervision, it seems that both the nature of involvement and the benefits received are more idiosyncratic than generalizable among participants. Again, this suggests a need for much more examination of *how* a particular supervisory form is implemented.

The Varied Nature of Teacher Involvement as Mentor

The ways in which mentor teachers are involved with beginning teachers varies in states other than Connecticut. Tellez (1992) reported that while 75 percent of the beginning teachers she studied reported seeking help from other teachers, only 7 percent reported seeking help from the mentor. In fact, more of her respondents said they would seek help from university advisors (i.e., the program she studied had a deliberate university follow-up component), another teacher, or even a family member or friend, rather than from their mentor. Several researchers (e.g., Ackley & Gall, 1992; Anctil,

1991; Feiman-Nemser & Floden, 1986; Tellez, 1992) reported that beginners rarely sought or received help with the technical skills of teaching. This indicates that at least in some mentor programs the intended relationship denoted by the term *mentor* is not being realized.

Lemberger (1992) identified "three levels of assertiveness" demonstrated among 17 mentor teachers in a single California school district. She based her assertiveness continuum on three elements: "the mentor's willingness and ability to *exert expertise and authority* over colleagues; . . . the mentor's willingness to interact with colleagues *inside the classroom*; and . . . the mentor's interactions with colleagues of appropriate *intensity and duration* " (p. 96). Frequent classroom observations were apparently not characteristic of the intended mentor program in California, as in Connecticut. Given the demonstrated disparity in frequency of classroom visitation in Connecticut, where frequent visits were intended, one might suspect that without a clear expectation for such direct, in-classroom support, mentors might avoid it completely. The mentors that Lemberger called "strongly assertive" did not.

Only a few mentors had the courage to engage in frequent classroom observations, demonstrations, and one-to-one peer coaching with colleagues. It was this very rare willingness to cross another teachers' threshold and interact intensively *in the classroom* that was the distinguishing feature of the effective strongly assertive mentors (p. 198, emphasis in original).

Lemberger (1992) is clear as to her assessment of the "strongly assertive" mentor:

It is those few, those six (of 17 studied) strongly assertive mentors who are the promise of what teacher leaders can accomplish. Despite the structural problems of the cellular schools, and the ambiguities of the mentor legislation and its local implementation, those six showed that mentors with courage can begin to fill that vacuum of instructional leadership in schools, can effectively help new teachers and others to improve their curricular understandings and enlarge their teaching repertoires. But much more needs to be done so that a higher percentage of teacher leaders can be successful in helping teachers (p. 198).

It is certain that not all studies of state-developed mentor programs reach the conclusion that the service as delivered is only rarely close to the intent. Wildman et al (1992) drew information from 150 mentor–beginner dyads "as part of a midyear day-log training session for mentors" (p. 206). Relating to the reluctance to engage beginners assertively discussed earlier, Wildman et al noted:

In general, mentors reported allowing beginners to make their own decision and being careful to avoid prescribing solutions. . . . Their reticence to engage in direct forms of teaching or coaching might be attributed to the strong norms of privacy among teachers (Feiman-Nemser & Floden, 1986) or to uncertainty about their own knowledge (p. 207).

Although they do note this reluctance to appear assertive or prescriptive as well as the oft-mentioned obstacle of too little time for mentor-beginner interaction, Wildman et al concluded:

Mentors did not take the expedient route to solving problems and smoothing over difficulties for their beginners. Indeed, the range of helping strategies used, many involving time-consuming reflection, modeling, and collaborative problem solving, suggests that mentors have a serious desire to help develop real competence, not just to offer emotional support. On the basis of these findings, we believe that teachers can achieve many of the expectations evoked by the broader cultural images of mentoring. In this regard, our conclusions contrast with those of Little (1990) who concluded that mentoring programs, especially those arising from state reform mandates, often result in a narrow, utilitarian focus (p. 212).

A Question of Preparation

The importance of preparing classroom teachers to serve as mentors has often been emphasized in the literature (e.g., Colbert & Wolff, 1992; Kent, 1985; Thies-Sprinthall, 1986) How *are* mentors prepared to serve the needs of beginning teachers? Could deliberate preparation help overcome the norms of privacy and egalitarian status that might inhibit teachers from taking "the mantle of mentorship" (as Lemberger, 1992, calls it)? If mentors assume the responsibilities to assist beginning teacher development, how are they provided with the skills and time to fulfill this charge?

For induction programs to work, systematic intensive supervision is requisite for beginning teachers. A mentor role is complex, requiring "higher order" ability to demonstrate, to observe, and to coach. It is not reasonable to assume that minimally trained classroom teachers can achieve a level of competence to provide differentiated intensive supervision. In fact, there should be a real worry that well-meaning but poorly trained "buddies" may pass on the "wrong set" of the secrets of the trade" (Thies-Sprinthall, 1986, pp. 18-19).

Little (1990) reported that nearly 40 percent of districts in the California Mentor Teacher Program allocated no resources after mentor selection to help these teachers acquire understanding or skills related to the mentor function (citing Bird & Alspaugh, 1986). Little also reports that

there are virtually no studies that trace the contributions made by postselection training to the subsequent performance of mentors, or to the success in relationships with teachers or administrators. No studies compare mentors who receive training with those who are left to their own resources (p. 309).

Although the importance of thorough preparation for mentors has been cogently argued, its provision is rare and its benefits largely undocumented. In one study (Ganser 1993) involving 24 mentors, five widely different types of experience were cited as preparation: participation in a year-long, university-based program as a mentor; participation in a year-long; university-based program as a beginning teacher; brief workshops sponsored by a local school district; brief workshops sponsored by a regional educational service agency; and participation in a college course focusing on student teacher supervision were listed. One of the 24 mentors reported having no preparation.

Some researchers (e.g., Anctil, 1992; Schaffer, Stringfield, & Wolf, 1992; Thies-Sprinthall, 1986; Yosha, 1992) do report more than cursory preparation, but no studies indicating the

long-term consequences of such preparation on mentor or beginner performance was found. There is support for the assertion that preparation is necessary for effective work as a mentor. For example, consider the comments of Joy (a beginner) regarding the contributions of her mentor (Marsha):

I think there needs to be more training for mentors in classroom observation and analysis. I think it was real difficult for her (Marsha) to observe me. I don't think teachers have the training that principals do. Their training allows principals to come and observe and give the correct feedback. I think I needed a more structured program like a clinical supervisor at the beginning. It's just such a trial and error process sometimes. I know that's a part of getting into the profession; but in this situation, there was no one around and I felt real isolated. There were many days I felt at a loss because I had no feedback from anyone around me. It's just not the same when you wait to go tell somebody about your (instructional) day until after it's over (Ackley, 1991, p. 95).

Ackley reports that Marsha also characterized her preparation to serve as mentor as insufficient.

A Question of Time

Those who control mentor programs, whether teachers or administrators, signal the importance they attribute to mentor roles by the amount of time they allocate for mentors' work, by policies that govern when the work . . . can be done, and by the formal and informal expectations that define what work counts as mentoring (Little, 1990, pp. 309–310).

The norms of schools allow precious little time for classroom teachers to observe one another, much less time during the school day to discuss such observations. The need for frequent observations for beginning teachers has often been mentioned. Frequent observations "enabled novices to learn techniques for interacting with students, organizing lessons, and obtaining and developing new materials" (Yosha, 1991, p. 6). The meaning of *frequent* in settings where experienced teachers are rarely observed, however, is in doubt. As discussed earlier, the range of observations can be from daily to never. Is observing a beginning teacher one time a month "frequent" or, more germane, helpful for improving teaching practice?

Benefits to Mentors

The effects of serving as a mentor on an experienced teacher's own teaching efforts can be negative as well as positive. Noting that mentor teachers will often use less release time than allocated to observe and confer with a beginning teacher, Little (1990) comments:

Release time that draws teachers away from the primary classroom responsibilities underscores, perhaps ironically, the marginal status of mentoring activity by placing teachers' work with fellow teachers in competition with the fundamental work of the classroom. To fulfill the obligation of mentoring, mentors risk compromising other valued institutional goals and increasing the strain on themselves as individuals (p. 311).

Tellez (1992) observed that beginning teachers see themselves as a burden when the mentor assigned to them is busy with personal teaching and with other administrative chores.

Do mentors benefit from working with beginners? If so, how? The evidence is not conclusive. There is some suggestion that the school climate may actually improve as a result of beginning a mentor program. Ackley and Gall (1992) report that in three of five schools studied, the teachers not directly involved in the mentor program had formed discussion groups focused on school improvement with those who were involved. Lasting effects on experienced teachers may result from establishing a successful mentor program, but the evidence still needs to be collected.

As in the case with regular supervision, mentor programs seem to vary considerably from one another. In fact, based on a comparison of mentor programs in Los Angeles and Albuquerque, Feiman-Nemser and Parker identify "three perspectives on mentoring in relation to teacher induction. The first casts mentors as local guides; the second casts mentors as educational companions; and the third sees them as agents of cultural change" (1992, p.16) They suggest the nature of the mentor program varies with the context. If this plausible conclusion is accurate, then studies of teacher involvement in mentor programs will need to consider carefully the contextual factors that may enhance or inhibit desired results.

Finally, although it may be somewhat cynical to suggest, one wonders if mentor programs were a passing fancy, started and studied only when fashionable and when resources were available. In times when many schools are facing reduced budgets and faculty, expensive programs for beginning teachers often seem expendable. Indeed, establishing and maintaining a costly mentor program may only be justifiable when a district has several new teachers. How might experienced teachers be involved in the delivery of supervision when few or no new teachers are being hired?

Coaches and Established Teachers

Working with experienced teachers, who have successfully endured the first years of teaching and who have earned the status of tenure or "continuing contract," is different from working with beginners. Some (e.g., Fuller & Bowe, 1975) have observed that once teachers have passed the "survival" stage, when they focus on their own abilities to adjust to the working life of schools, they can then focus on the technical and learner-centered concerns that stimulate ongoing refinement of teaching strategies and practices. Harsh stereotypes sometimes paint experienced teachers as old dogs who have no interest in new tricks, whose practices have not changed in many years, and who have "retired-on-the-job." Either image, sadly, can be accurate, and the feebleness of most staff development for practicing teachers does little to promote one or to thwart the other.

Two different views of "coaching" have emerged in educational literature. The first of these, which is often associated with the scholarly work of Showers and Joyce (e.g., Joyce & Showers, 1987; Showers & Joyce, 1987; Showers, Joyce, & Bennett, 1987), is intended to work in conjunction with established staff development programs to increase the likelihood

that advocated practices will actually be implemented in the classroom (i.e., "transfer of training"). In this approach, teachers are systematically introduced to some teaching method (e.g., a model of teaching, aspects of direct instruction, or a writing process) that they are encouraged to use in their own teaching. The coach then follows the teachers into their own classrooms and helps them apply the method or technique successfully. In this instance, the coach draws on her or his advanced expertise or experience with the method, offering informed appraisals of the teacher's initial efforts, supporting the change process during often clumsy first efforts, and guiding the teacher to a practiced mastery of the method. This role (i.e., the more expert educator guiding the initial efforts of an experienced teacher to master a new teaching method) is the one called *coach* in this chapter.

The second approach that is also commonly referred to as coaching (e.g., Costa & Garmston, 1994; Nolan & Hillkirk, 1991) differs in that the focus of classroom observation is idiosyncratic to the teacher, rather than an attempt to apply a focus already determined as a district or school goal. Drawing from the writings on clinical supervision (especially Goldhammer, 1969; Cogan, 1973), this second approach emphasizes skilled observation of teaching and related conferral as a vehicle for helping experienced teachers achieve whatever performance improvement they may choose. Rather than the coach using personal expertise with the specific teaching approach to determine the criteria for successful performance, "(t)he teacher determines what the coach shall look for as criteria for excellence in terms of student behavior and teacher behavior" (Costa & Garmston, 1994, p. 14). To emphasize the powerful functional difference suggested by the client (here, the teacher) that determines the criteria for success, the role in which the classroom observer serves to assist the teacher refine teaching practice *without reference to criteria for success other than the teacher's own* is called a *consultant* in this chapter, and is further explored in the next section.

The process of employing a *coach* in this review consists of one with expertise in some aspect of teaching, but without line authority observing and conferring with an experienced teacher. Coaching, therefore, differs from supervision in that the coach lacks line authority, and from consultation in that the coach possesses and uses superior expertise in a specified aspect of teaching. A "coach," as used in this chapter, differs from a mentor in that mentors work exclusively with beginning teachers, whereas coaches work with experienced teachers as well as with beginners. This function has also been called "technical coaching" (Garmston 1987), and "advisor" (Caruso, 1987).

"Coaching occurs at the point where the trainee attempts to implement the new teaching strategy in the classroom" (Showers, 1987, p. 66). The coach is typically an experienced teacher who has received special preparation to work with her or his colleagues (e.g., Gilman & Miller, 1988; Phelps & Wright, 1986), although Showers points out that a coach might be an administrator or a college professor. The general purpose for such coaching is to improve the learning of students by refining the teaching practices of teachers. The coach is presumed to have expertise in the specific aspect of teaching serving as the focus for the staff development and coaching. Peer coaching models often provide preparation for teacher/coaches in some aspect of teaching who then work to help their colleagues apply the studied technique with their students. It is important to draw the distinction between preparation "in some specific aspect of teaching" and preparation in the coaching process. Areas of coaches' expertise include general teaching effectiveness (Avila, 1990; Gilman & Miller, 1988; Phelps & Wright, 1986; Sparks & Bruder, 1987), the writing process (Caruso, 1987) and mathematics (Gersten & Kelly, 1992; Madsen & Lanier, 1992). Coaching may include actual modeling of desired teaching strategies or techniques (Gersten & Kelly, 1992). The area of the coach's expertise becomes a focus for the observation and for the improvement of teaching. A "writing process coach" will address improvements in the design and delivery of the literacy curriculum (even as a part of teaching math or social studies if the "writing-across-the-curriculum" approach is in place) with some expertise, but probably will not address direct instruction or role-playing activities in a similar fashion. The presumed expertise of the coach (i.e., the shared idea that she or he has greater capability in the focus area than the teacher using the service) is a defining characteristic of this role.

Desired Consequences of Coaching Programs

The first intended benefit of coaching is generally enhanced teaching in some specific way. As Glatthorn (1987) indicated, the focus of coaching is the mastery of teaching skills. Whether the intended refinement focuses on better use of advance organizers, of the writing process, or of higher-level questions, the focus is on teacher performance. "One of the purposes of coaching . . . (is) to keep teachers practicing new strategies in their classrooms and provide support through the period when the new strategy was awkward, and students were unsure what was expected of them" (Showers, 1987, p. 63). This does not include judging the teacher's performance as part of formal personnel evaluation. There is an implicit assumption in coaching programs that when teachers gain proficiency with the focus of the coaching, students will benefit. Whether the focus addressed is direct instruction, a classroom management approach, or an established method for teaching inquiry, the presumption of a coaching approach is that if the teacher learns to apply the approach well, then students will benefit. This focus on the skill involved in the specific teaching act, rather than on the context of the setting or the students' performances, has led some (e.g., Hargreaves & Dawe, 1990) to criticize it. "Technical coaching fits excellently into an educational system which is becoming ever more inclined to bureaucratic forms of control over its employees in order to secure the implementation of centrally-determined standard forms of 'effective' instruction" (Darling-Hammond, 1985; McNeil, 1986)" (Hargreaves & Dawe, 1990, p. 234).

Improved Student Achievement Scant evidence of learners' performance or attitude improvement resulting from coaching programs exists. Coaching episodes are most often deemed "successful" based on their reported consequences for teachers. Evidence too often consists solely of teacher self-reports

that the coaching was beneficial without suggesting how the learners being served or teaching practices have benefited. When asked directly about student benefits from the teacher's involvement in a peer coaching project, teachers often respond positively, but vaguely (Sparks & Bruder, 1987). "Nine (of 36 participating) teachers reported greater student success, and some backed up their claims with specific examples" (Sparks & Bruder, 1987, p. 55). In this same study, between 70 percent and 75 percent of respondents indicated that the students were "very likely" benefiting, and were more involved and attentive during lessons. Both these general, positive impressions of the classroom teachers and general, positive impressions given by students when asked for "perceptions of teachers" (Gilman & Miller, 1988) demonstrate that something good can be associated with such coaching programs, but much more specific examination of actual benefits received by coaches, teachers with whom they work, and the students who are the ultimate beneficiaries is needed.

When student achievement measures are used, the connection between the achievement and the contribution of coaching is necessarily tenuous. For example, Ross (1992) reported a significant relationship between student achievement in history and a self-reported "use of coach" score; however, there was no classroom observation involved in the coaching Ross studied, just voluntary consultation (i.e., highly varied in frequency and nature) between teachers and the "coaches" assigned to them. Moreover, the study left Ross wondering about the value of student achievement as a dependent variable. "Despite the importance of student achievement as the ultimate criterion of school success . . . a case could be made that teacher practice is a more immediate measure of coaching effects and that classroom observation is the best evaluation tool" (Ross, 1992, p. 63).

One reviewed study was exceptional in that it attended to and reported information about both teacher performance and student achievement. Gersten and Kelly (1992) studied a coaching project involving four secondary special education teachers working with an innovative videodisc program entitled, "Mastering Fractions." Kelly, who was identified as a research associate at the University of Oregon, served as coach for the intervention that included the introduction of the videodisc curriculum, as well as in-class coaching of the four teachers. Regarding student achievement, Gersten and Kelly reported:

On the criterion-referenced tests administered to students, the average pretest score for the four groups was 31 percent and the average posttest score was 83 percent. This represented a growth of 52 percent, indicating that the teachers' implementation of the videodisc program was reasonably effective in teaching the relevant concepts and algorithms to students who had repeatedly failed to learn the same content (p. 45).

Although the authors make no attempt to separate the effects of the videodisc curriculum (i.e., apart from referring to an earlier study of the same videodisc program, but with no coaching, which has less consistently positive results), and the localized nature of the study makes generalizations to other settings inappropriate, the study does present a plausible and well-documented case of a new teaching approach combined with coaching contributing to learner achievement.

[This study is discussed both in the intervention segment and in the research method section, and it serves as a model for suggestions made in the conclusions of this chapter.]

Improved Teaching Practices Given the technical focus of the coaching program (i.e., to assist teachers in translating methods or techniques advocated and introduced in staff development sessions), it seems remarkable that so few studies actually attempt to document the teachers' implementation of advocated techniques in the classroom. Some researchers, however, do take pains to examine classroom practices after coaching (e.g., Gersten & Kelly, 1992; Miller, Harris, & Watanabe, 1991).

Miller, Harris, and Watanabe (1991) explored the effects of a "5-week summer practicum to provide learning strategies instruction to upper elementary through high school students" (p. 183) with six experienced teachers. Frequencies of both effective and ineffective teaching behaviors as categorized by the FPMS were collected through direct observation of teaching behaviors during 15-minute FPMS observations at four different intervals (i.e., a baseline prior to coaching, two during the active coaching segment of the study while the teachers taught learning strategies to groups of upper elementary through high school students, and one at least three months after the coaching intervention while the teachers were working in their regular settings). Despite "inconsistent performance from one day to the next" on the frequencies of effective and ineffective behaviors of the FPMS, the findings "clearly demonstrate consistent improvement over time" (p. 186). Each teacher demonstrated a marked increase in effective teaching behaviors from baseline to follow-up. If one accepts the FPMS as an accurate measure of effective teaching practices, then it is clear that this combination of practicum and coaching increased effective teaching practices in the university setting and that effective teaching practices occurred more frequently during subsequent teaching in the teacher's work setting than they did during the baseline observation in the university setting.

The desire to improve teaching practices suggests the need to identify specific aspects of the desired approach that are deemed necessary for the faithful application of the approach and to assess the extent to which these vital practices are actually employed in the teacher's classroom. Gersten and Kelly (1992) identified and observed six specific teaching behaviors. They then employed coaching with both written and verbal feedback focused on these behaviors. They concluded that "the coaching was found to affect a variety of teacher techniques, consistently resulting in an observable increase in positive approaches and a decrease in inappropriate behaviors" (p. 45). Although there are problems associated with using frequency of teaching behaviors as a sole measure of coaching success, which Gersten and Kelly do *not* do, it does seem reasonable to expect research of the effects of coaching to document changes in teaching behavior as one indication of the consequences of such coaching. It is surprising to note that few researchers have used direct observation of teaching to collect such documentation.

In short, although very few studies conscientiously examine and document how teaching practices are changed during and after coaching, those that do, report favorable changes. These findings support the assertion that coaching can indeed influence classroom teaching practices. If such coaching also serves to develop communication among classroom teachers regarding the relationship between teaching strategies and consequences for learners, then the benefits could extend beyond the specific focus of the coaching.

Enhanced Collegiality When "peer coaching" is employed, two concurrent purposes are often mentioned. One, of course, is to help with the technical improvement of teaching practice. The second, nearly as obvious, aims to provide a sense of community or collegiality in the work setting. The insightful observations raised by Little (1990) and discussed in the previous section of this chapter regarding the mixed benefits of release time to observe another teach may also apply to coaching programs. It is probable that most teachers value time to talk to one another and to observe other teachers, although not necessarily to have their own teaching observed, as long as it does not detract from their own teaching responsibilities. Building school communities and the common language often associated with them takes time away from students. What evidence exists to support the notion that coaching programs truly have a positive influence on a sense of professional community? Is there support for the suggestion that time away from one's own teaching may be seen as counterproductive?

Gilman and Miller (1988) report significant differences on "teachers' perceptions of other persons ($p < .01$), attitude toward administrators ($p < .05$) and attitude toward differentiated staffing ($p < .01$)" (p. i), as well as on student perceptions of teacher effectiveness after a seven month coaching experience. To their credit, Gilman and Miller conscientiously reported that teachers "attitude toward other teachers" declined, although not statistically significantly ($p = 0.14$), at the same time "perceptions of others" increased significantly. Given the general, but not uniform, tendency of posttest scores to exceed pretest scores, the authors concluded that "the effectiveness of Teachers Teaching Teachers in enhancing positive educator attitudes and beliefs is demonstrated by the results of this study" (p. 12). Such a conclusion may be warranted, but the finding that attitudes toward other teachers were actually diminished is puzzling and deserves further study.

Teachers who participate in a coaching program commonly report favorably about the experience (e.g., Avila, 1990; Phelps & Wright, 1986). "'The thing I liked most about peer coaching is being able to watch someone else teach. I have picked up some good ideas. I have also realized that I'm not the only one with certain problems'" (unnamed teacher, cited by Avila, 1990). While such positive sentiments seem to be a regular benefit of such programs, one wonders if the real appreciation is for the opportunity to watch another teacher work (i.e., the old notion once called intervisitation) and not for the systematic attention to particulars of performance that "coaching" implies. Such peer support without a technical focus is perhaps worthwhile, per se. Byrne (1994) suggested "that self-esteem is a critical and controlling factor in the predisposition of teachers to burnout" (p. 667), and that peer coaching provides such support in ways that supervisors cannot.

The extent to which teachers take active involvement in, or self-esteem from, coaching programs is not well documented. The vague "we-liked-it" sentiment often offered by teachers who participated in coaching tells us too little about the nature of their involvement or the specific benefits realized. Deeper study will likely reveal that different teachers benefit in different ways, and that coaching programs themselves are highly varied. Along with the individual needs and interests of teachers who participate, the actual benefits realized seem highly dependent upon how these interventions are conceived and implemented.

Intervention Strategy

As coaching has been defined in this section (following Joyce & Showers), it is a deliberate classroom observational approach to follow-up staff development efforts. There are, therefore, two separate segments of the coaching process (i.e., the initial instruction on the targeted teaching strategy and the provision of in-class observation and guidance on the application of the strategy) that can contribute to the success of the coaching program. Coaching interventions vary considerably in the relative emphasis given to instructional and classroom observational components. For instance, Gersten and Kelly provided two 1-hour training sessions prior to an elaborate in-class segment in which each participant was observed a minimum of 10 times over 30 days. In contrast, Miller, Harris, and Watanabe (1991) provided a 5-week summer practicum that included coaching teachers' work with upper elementary through high school–aged students as part of the practicum, and then observed one 15-minute teaching episode in the teachers' work settings to determine the continued use of practicum teaching strategies in the teacher's own classrooms. Ross (1992) reports a coaching program where the six coaches visited the classrooms of the 18 teachers with whom they worked only when invited. The total number of classroom visitations reported in this study was two, and these were invitations to demonstrate, rather than to observe, teaching. Although this approach falls outside the definition of supervision used in this chapter because no classroom observation was involved, it is mentioned to illustrate the variations of interventions that are called "coaching" in the literature.

As varied as the coaching programs are, so, too, are the descriptions of the frequency and procedures of the coaching process. For instance, Caruso (1987) gave brief, but helpful, details about the classroom observations done by coaches (whom he calls "advisors") in his study:

Advisors offer intensive support during initial phases of their work with a teacher. This means three classroom visits per week. At the beginning advisors assume primary responsibility for teaching (writing) but, over time, roles gradually shift. By the third or fourth month, advisors gradually withdraw and eventually drop in on classrooms once a week for support visits. On the average, they work with seven teachers during a given time period (Caruso, 1987, p. 70).

In contrast, Gilman and Miller (1988) noted that "teachers exposed to the techniques were given feedback through peer observation" (p. 8). They did not report frequency or duration of observations or related conferences, nor did they discuss the nature of the coaching process at all. Although they concluded that "follow up is important. The program had a

means of follow-up which proved to be effective" (p. 12), these authors reported no description of the follow up.

Given that many published studies of coaching efforts provide very little information regarding the frequency of classroom observation and related discussion, it is probably not surprising that the nature of the coach's or the teacher's involvement in coaching conferences is often undisclosed. Gersten and Kelly, however, provided a very helpful description of their coaching process.

After the observation, the coach shared her observations, which typically included some specific quantifiable data (e.g., number of students who actively participated, number of times teacher provided informational feedback to students experiencing difficulty, student engagement rate). These meetings pinpointed aspects of the lesson deemed to be effective and productive, as well as one or two areas that seemed to require improvement. The coach then developed one or two specific suggestions, explaining to the teacher why she thought the new techniques would help ameliorate the problem. When appropriate, she offered to model the new strategy the next day. She also provided reasons why she felt the suggested strategy would enhance the students' learning or motivation. The coach asked whether the teacher had any issues he or she wished to discuss, or was experiencing any problems above and beyond what was observed that particular day. The coach also noted the extent to which the teacher implemented suggestions made in the previous sessions, and the observed impact on students (Gersten & Kelly, 1992, p. 42).

Such accounts of the coaching process inform the reader's consideration of the involvement of both coach and teacher. Given present research on coaching in schools, we are again confronted with the great variation among coaching interventions and must conclude that teachers' involvement in coaching is equally varied.

Consultants and Teachers

In this chapter, *consultants* are those educators, usually fellow teachers, who observe teaching and confer regarding the quality of the teaching, but without a specific focus other than that selected by the teacher being observed. Consultants in this context do not claim expertise in a specific aspect of teaching as coaches do, but they may have special preparation that provides them with expertise in the process of consulting. The central distinction lies in the observer's responsibility for a predetermined focus, and her or his presumed expertise for this focus. Because coaching programs are designed to transfer advocated approaches or practices into the classroom, the coach is responsible for understanding central aspects of desired approach or practice and for helping the teacher successfully apply the approach or practice in the classroom. "Is this being done the way it is supposed to be done?," is a question that implies performance standards and fidelity to the techniques or model being applied, and the coach's responsibility to the teacher for guidance toward these standards as reflected in the coach's subjective appraisal. In contrast, the focus of the consultant's observation is idiosyncratic to the concerns and context of the teacher being observed. Rather than the coach's charge to help the teacher faithfully apply key aspects of the targeted innovation, the consultant's mission is to help the teacher identify a focus relevant to that teacher and the setting in which she or he works, and then to help the teacher assess and improve teaching related to that focus.

Two types of consultation seem worthy of distinction. Some consultants (e.g., Garmston, Linder, & Whitaker, 1993; Hillkirk & Nolan, 1990; Kent, 1985; Little, 1985; Ross & Regan, 1995) are people who are not engaged in the daily demands of classroom teaching and who avail themselves and their consulting services to regular classroom teachers. Those who practice this *one-way* consultation need to acquaint prospective teacher-clients with the intents and procedures of the service and then, commonly, wait for requests. Other programs (e.g., Anastos & Ancowitz, 1987; Holt. 1992; Raney & Robbins, 1989; Sparks & Bruder, 1987) prepare classroom teachers to observe and to confer with one another and then, typically, to arrange for alternating observations where teachers both observe and are observed by their partners. This *reciprocal* consultation generally involves both teachers in the preparation phase and arranges for reciprocal observation cycles either as part of or subsequent to the preparation. The clear intent in both one-way and reciprocal consultation is to assist the teacher being observed in both the collection of relevant observational data and the interpretation of these data so that new understandings might lead to adaptations in teaching performance.

Garmston (1987) referred to this consultation process as "collegial coaching." "*Collegial coaching* is directed . . . to the context of teaching and to the processes of self-reflection and professional dialogue among teachers needed to improve practice and to alter the organizational context in such a way as to assist that improvement" (Hargreaves & Dawe, 1990, p. 231). Teacher involvement in examining the whole of classroom practice in the specific context of a single classroom and then determining a personal focus distinguishes this consultation process from coaching wherein the general focus for improvement (e.g., the writing process or predefined elements of effective teaching) is again determined externally and prior to the first preobservation conference.

Nolan and Hillkirk (1990) perhaps draw the distinction best. They suggest that coaching, which they refer to as "a technical model of peer coaching," involves workshops on instructional effectiveness "followed by peer coaching visits in which the peer coaches judged the effectiveness of the teacher's use of the techniques presented in the workshop" (p. 4). In contrast, a consultant, who uses what they call "a reflective model of peer coaching," would take

on the role of colleague whose primary interest (is) to help the teacher reflect on the efficacy and appropriateness of his/her behavior, goals, beliefs, and values. The teacher assume(s) the role of primary decision maker concerning the desirability of his/her teaching behavior (Nolan & Hillkirk 1990, p. 4).

The consultant, therefore, is one who assists the teacher with the assessment and refinement of teaching practice. This emphasis on the teacher who receives the service being the judge of good practice, as opposed to the supervisor's or coach's conception or conformity to standard practice, separates the consultant function from the rest.

According to Costa and Garmston (1994), who call their approach to consulting "cognitive coaching,"

the assessment of teacher growth will focus on the degree to which teachers develop the capacity to analyze, evaluate, and self-prescribe their own growth. . . . Ultimately, teachers will assume the responsibility for evaluating themselves. The role of the coach [consultant, as used in this chapter] becomes one who facilitates teachers' capacities to evaluate themselves (p. 166).

This conceptual distinction between coaching and consulting is not always clear in practice. Many coaches serve as consultants because they broaden their discussions to areas beyond the preselected focus. Many consultants do have expertise in aspects of teaching performance and function as coaches, using this expert power to guide suggestions. Although the conceptual lines may blur in practice, the distinction between teachers trying to apply a predetermined innovation faithfully and trying to examine and evaluate personal teaching performance to select and modify idiosyncratic features seems powerful enough to warrant separate labels for the service.

Desired Consequences of Consulting Programs

Although improved student achievement, improved teaching practices, and enhanced collegiality are clearly desired consequences of consulting, as they are of coaching—or of any form of supervision of teachers, for that matter—the consultant has a clear and mediating goal in mind. The consultant "helps, provokes, and encourages a teacher to reflect on her own practice . . . that is, her effort to make explicit to herself what she is seeing, how she interprets it, and how she might test and act on her interpretation" (Schön, 1988, p. 22).[5]

Self-evaluation as a goal produces a tension between accountability and autonomy. To put it simply, what do consultants do when they witness what they consider to be inept teaching from teachers who judge the same teaching as excellent? In many schools, an egalitarian norm defines differences in teaching as different "styles" and presupposes that no one style is superior to another. Such a presupposition makes confronting poor teaching unacceptable because "it's just a different style." This norm often manifests itself as one teacher who is involved as a consultant to another utters, "Who am I to judge his teaching?" The tension between accountability and autonomy may be addressed by establishing a set of standards that the consultant helps the teacher apply in the self-evaluation process. For example, Costa and Garmston (1994) suggested that their cognitive "coaches will be alert to indications that teachers are moving toward (1) valuing process goals of thinking, creativity, and collaboration; (2) valuing conceptual development more than content coverage; (3) becoming more empathic toward students, and (4) striving for more lofty and global society goals" (p. 170). Assuming that the teachers being consulted also endorse these aims and seek to refine their own practices to better achieve them, then the consultant can indeed become a facilitator who helps teachers refine teaching based on guided self-evaluation. If the goal is to elicit conformity to these tenets, however, *irrespective of the individual teacher's agreement with them,* then the process is fairly called coaching because in consultation the defining characteristics of teaching success are discretionary with the teacher.

This marriage of improved teaching with guided self-evaluation logically leads to drawing evaluative judgments from the teacher rather than relying upon the observer's critical appraisal of teaching performance. The assumption that the teacher's expertise is at least equal to that of the consultant is implicit in this arrangement. The consultant's function, therefore, is to inform the teacher of observations, of the consultant's interpretations (perhaps), and possibly of any implications the consultant believes such interpretations may have for learner consequences and for subsequent teaching practice. The teacher who is observed, therefore, considers information provided by the consultant and decides what, if anything, to do differently. The teacher's perceptions that the consultation process is helpful, therefore, often serves as an indication of consulting success. As was the case with services provided by mentors discussed earlier, it seems important to distinguish between the teacher's appreciation of interaction that is friendly and personally supportive from the teacher's ability to identify specific improvements in the teaching/learning process. The former may produce a sense of affiliation that benefits the teacher, whereas the latter addresses benefits received by the learners served by the teacher. Intended consequences for consultation programs, therefore, generally include improved teaching, enhanced teacher self-evaluation, and heightened collegiality.

Improved Teaching Sparks and Bruder (1987) thoughtfully discussed a reciprocal consultation project in two Ann Arbor, Michigan, elementary schools. Using both questionnaires and interviews to inform them, the authors concluded that the consultation process was "useful in improving collegiality, experimentation, and student learning" (p. 57). It is noteworthy for our focus that, even though a clear majority of the 36 teachers reported the general helpfulness of the program (e.g., after the intervention 89 percent reported receiving feedback on their instruction; 75 percent reported that the advice they had received about instruction was "very helpful"; 70 percent reported they tried new things in the classroom frequently; 67 percent reported they were much more confident when trying new things; 59 percent reported they were very likely to keep trying a new approach even if it didn't go well at first; and 70 percent reported that their students were "very likely" learning more), only 25 percent reported "greater student success, and some backed up their claims with specific examples" (p. 56). Teachers apparently find it easier to report general satisfaction and their own tendency to innovate than they do to identify indicators of increased learner success. More studies building upon the work of Sparks and Bruder might help us to distinguish the benefits such involvement has for the teachers who participate from the benefits realized by the learners.

Similar findings are reported by Clarke and Richardson (1986), who noted that, although teachers often find corroboration for what they are already doing, few attempt meaningful changes in teaching practices as a result of consultation. Three of 11 teachers in their study made major adaptations in teaching practices, whereas two others made slight changes and six reported no changes at all.

Enhanced Self-Evaluation Given the explicit aim in many consultation programs of promoting and enhancing self-evalua-

tion by teachers, the paucity of documentation of such deliberation is surprising. Some (e.g., Cook, 1985) collect observations and notes regarding participant behavior during the preparation stage. Many use written comments by the participants as a data source illuminating teachers' thoughts about the process. Some interview participants to determine the quality and extent of self-evaluative behavior. There is still scant evidence supporting the claim that either preparation for or participation in consulting programs enhance teachers' self-evaluation skills or practices.

The best indication that self-evaluative practices and dispositions are enhanced perhaps comes from those studies that examine individual cases (e.g., Gitlin & Price, 1992; Grimmett & Crehan, 1990; Holt, 1992; Nolan, Hawkes, & Francis, 1993). Consider the following excerpts from Holt (1992):

The purpose of consultation is to *stimulate self-evaluation and critical thinking.* Therefore, consultant behaviors in all conferences ought to include questions that provoke genuine evaluation and critical thinking (p. 1, emphasis in original).

I asked if she'd like me to observe groups working entirely on their own. She responded with a "no" saying they were not ready to be on their own. I then asked her, "How do you envision (your students) becoming ready?" This question required her to clarify her notion of when her students might be "ready" to function independently and visualize what that would look like. . . . It also prompted a discussion of modeling, another part of (the teacher's) platform (p. 2).

The information gathered (during the observation) seemed to provide a perspective that (the teacher) had not seen herself, as she was more engaged in the book topic questions than in the group process. A conflict became evident a little farther on when she discussed being torn between focusing the group on the questions they had been assigned or allowing the students' "side-tracking" to set their agenda. This conflict between doing what the Reading Curriculum says vs. letting their interests guide the discussion seemed problematic to her (e.g.,"I don't know. It's hard. The Reading Curriculum says . . . got off topic. . . . If there's a certain amount of time. . . .") considering her belief that ". . . life-long learning in children involves teaching process skills and not just assessing final products." An element of this issue, to stay or not to stay on the predetermined topic, continued to pop up throughout our discussion and was never resolved. Looking at my observer's notes, I notice one or two opportunities I missed to pursue it more completely. For instance, I asked, "So, is it okay for kids to get off on a tangent—or is that their way of dealing with questions?" Unfortunately, this was one of those yes or no questions! Better phrased this might have led (the teacher) into clarifying some of her sense of values (i.e., the value of student-directed tangents vs. the top-down directive of a mandated curriculum) (pp. 3-4).

Did Holt document heightened self-evaluation from the teacher? That is possible. She does present evidence that the process contributed to the self-evaluative process. It is perhaps more important that Holt demonstrated a well-developed and focused pattern of self-evaluation as a consultant. Because Holt was involved in a program of reciprocal consultation, it seems plausible to conclude that such thinking would extend to evaluating her interactions with her own learners. Testing this speculation about the habits of mind demonstrated in supervisory conferences transferring to disciplined inquiry outside the conference setting seems a fruitful line for further study.

Enhanced Collegiality Heightened Enhanced collegiality is the most commonly reported effect of consultation programs (e.g., Clarke & Richardson, 1986; Cook, 1986; Goldsberry, 1980; Raney & Robbins, 1989). Conferences based on classroom observations can be very rewarding to experienced teachers (Little, 1985). Whether the rewards are derived from affirmation of present teaching practices, as Clarke and Richardson (1986) suggested, or satisfaction stems from improving one's teaching practices is difficult to say. One wonders again if the data collection procedures are sensitive enough to distinguish productive collegiality from the contrived collegiality that Hargreaves and Dawe (1990) discussed, to separate teacher satisfaction with collaborative and fruitful partnerships from teacher gratitude for the opportunity to shed some of the job's isolation.

Grimmett, Rostad, and Ford (1992) revealed two teachers' appraisals of the interactions during consultant conferences:

I remember . . . thinking, my goodness, I'm not (faking it) at all, I really am being open and honest, and I was amazed because this represents a change even from the first preconference where I had a feeling of awkwardness about opening up, and now (three observations later) I'm opening up without any degree of discomfort (p. 199).

I could have told her how to do all this stuff . . . but I don't think that's the point. The point is that she feels comfortable with what she decides to do . . . I'm not playing dumb, I'm just shifting the expertise (p. 200).

Is the "expertise" shifted to the teacher who is observed, or to a collaborative one? The distinction seems important for distinguishing between the "neutral observer" role (Goldsberry, 1992), in which the judgments and suggestions of the observer are never revealed, and the "full partner" (Goldsberry, 1992) or "organic member" (Garman, 1982) role, in which each party shares the responsibility for evaluating teaching practices and offering ideas. Which is more collegial? Are consultants who keep their judgments private and avoid conflicting perspectives less threatening, and, thus, more collegial than those who reveal judgments and confront differing perceptions and perspectives? When teachers report feeling "safe and supported," do they mean protected from the judgments of others or encouraged to confront them? Much goes on in the names of collegiality and collaboration. Hólt (1992, quoted earlier) makes it clear that confronting her partner teacher with potential conflicts and challenging her partner to resolve the conflict is part of her own function as consultant. The disequilibrium or cognitive dissonance associated with such challenging behavior is generally associated with discomfort, rather than comfort. When teachers report that consultation is comfortable and nonthreatening, should we interpret this perception as consulting success?

Intervention Strategy

Because the consultation service is based on the assumption that "peers" (i.e., educators with equal expertise) can be very helpful to each other in the refinement of teaching strategies, preparation focuses on the process using observation and conferral (unlike in most coaching programs where the focus of the coaching effort is also a preparation focus). The prepara-

tion often (e.g., Cook, 1985; Goldsberry, 1980) includes observation cycles in which the participants practice advocated procedures and skills with the explicit understanding that questions, concerns, or observations regarding the process were to be raised as part of the preparation process. Goldsberry (1980) included "process observers" during conferences in this preparation phase to assist in documenting the consultant's technique and to focus self-evaluative discussion around consultation, just as the consultant focused self-evaluative discussion around observed teaching.

A common strategy for observations by consultants is to collect data pertaining to a focus selected by the teacher being observed. Teachers new to the process will often focus the observer's attention on student behavior. Many teachers move to focusing observations on their own teaching tactics over time. Clarke and Richardson found that by the third observation more than half of the teachers studied "asked their observer to give them feedback on specific teaching skills" (1986, p. 10). While these researchers found that all 11 consultants discussed observation focus and data collection tools with teachers during the preobservation conference (with the teacher having the right of approval of both focus and tool), collected ample observational data, and shared these data with the observed teacher during postobservation conferences, "only three observers gave specific suggestions for improvement, . . . and only one team engaged in active and productive problem solving. . . . The common approach was to provide requested data along with many positive comments but seldom solving the identified problem" (pp. 12–13).

Cook (1985) observed that frustration with the process occurred during the second observation cycle, and concluded that at least part of this was due to a predictable "slump" that occurs "when learners are becoming sophisticated enough to understand the complexity of the process, but are not yet skilled enough to handle this complexity" (p. 5). If this phenomenon is indeed common, then providing practice cycles with structured debriefing meetings may be a helpful part of consultant preparation.

How many cycles of observation and conferral are necessary to reap the intended consequences from consultation? The answer probably varies considerably, depending on the history of teacher cooperation in the setting, with the disposition of individual teachers for collaborative learning or for disciplined inquiry, with other demands on participants' time and energies, and a score of other factors. As with formal supervision, the notion that something more is necessary than a one-shot, quick fix intervention is well supported. The ability of the classroom observer to detect nuances of classroom interaction that can have dramatic implications for learners, the development of interpersonal trust between consultant and teacher, and the progressive benefits of examining and experimenting with different teaching tactics all demand more time and energy than is routinely available among colleagues in schools. The depth of and benefits from teacher involvement in consultation, as with the other forms of supervision, require multiple observation cycles. If we examine such interventions closely focusing on the qualities and depth of teacher involvement, then perhaps we can identify factors that greatly enhance the likelihood that teachers and the learners they serve will profit.

RESEARCH METHOD

Early in the chapter, several skeletal questions were raised to guide our exploration of research into teacher involvement in supervision. Having reviewed literature on several different forms of such involvement, it seems fitting to review these questions and to offer responses.

What Consequences Are Desired from Supervisory Interventions?

Who Are the Intended Beneficiaries of Supervisory Interventions? It is rational to expect the ultimate beneficiaries of all school services to be the learners served by the school. It is reasonable, then, that studies examining supervisory interventions intended to improve student achievement or attitudes might be expected to document changes in learner performance or demeanor. This is rarely done. Supervisory interventions are most often assessed by teacher, not student, responses to them. It can certainly be fairly argued that teachers are also intended beneficiaries of supervisory services. Unlike fringe benefits of employment, however, that are intended to compensate the employee for work, supervision is intended to heighten job performance. It is neither intended as, nor often perceived as, a "fringe" benefit. It is logical that it is supposed that if teaching improves, then learner benefits increase. This would be true by definition if we documented teaching improvement only by observed learner benefits. We sometimes simply ask teachers, however, if they found supervisory services "helpful" as a way of documenting supervisory success. Can you imagine a teacher who has been deprived of meaningful discussion about personal teaching practices reporting that a program is "helpful" simply because it offers an opportunity to discuss one's work, without seriously attempting to refine it? Can you also imagine a teacher who has present practices acknowledged as "good," or "professional," or even "impressive," by a knowledgeable colleague finding such rare recognition "helpful"? While the psychic benefits of such "helpfulness" may indeed lead to untold benefits for that teacher's students, would it not be preferable that the benefits be told?

Suggesting that supervisory services that have positive effects on a teacher's morale or self-confidence are highly likely to enhance learning by that teacher and by the teacher's students is surely plausible. Documenting both enhanced teacher attitudes *and* related gains by students still seems preferable. Future studies should directly explore the connections between a teacher's involvement in supervision and related student benefits.

How Are Desired Consequences of Supervisory Interventions Documented and Assessed? As suggested earlier, teacher responses to survey items and interview questions are too commonly the sole source of data regarding supervisory consequences. Such devices could be helpful if they were specifically designed to elicit teacher reports as to attempted changes in teaching practices and their observed effects for students. In fact, a disciplined attempt to draw an explicit account from teachers of the tactics they have used for specific purposes with specific learners as well as a disciplined assessment of the consequences of those tactics might well serve both supervisory and research purposes. Such questions are too seldom even asked.

Given the emphasis on teaching performance and standards of performance in contemporary literature, it seems incongruous that so little documentation of teaching performance appears in the literature on educational supervision. Skilled performers generally study their own work by reviewing their own performances. Dance moves, golf swings, actors' gestures, and even courtroom performances by lawyers are analyzed by reviewing them on video tape. Unexamined performance deprives the performer from recognizing and relishing successful aspects of performance as well as from discovering and refining unsuccessful aspects. Disciplined documentation of teaching tactics and their effects for learners seems essential both for sound inquiry into teaching practice and for successful supervision. Documentation of such efforts would be a fruitful addition to the professional literature.

How do variations of teacher involvement contribute to achieving these desired consequences? Although empirical evidence is scant, a fair hypothesis based upon present studies is that when supervision actively engages teachers in systematic inquiry and adaptation of teaching actions, participants judge the process fruitful regardless of whether a supervisor, mentor, coach, or consultant is providing the skilled service. Engaging a colleague in focused discussion based upon observed teaching practice seems to be helpful to the teacher involved in supervision.

The chief advantage of peer-delivered approaches to supervision seems to be the mutual benefit to the teacher who observes a colleague at work. This advantage may be counteracted if the nature of the discussion is focused on interpersonal support rather than disciplined support with inquiry into practice. "Feel good" assessments of supervisory interventions should be replaced with documentation of changes in teaching tactics and strategies accompanied by careful appraisal of resulting learner benefits. Involving the teacher in reasoned adaptation of performance again seems to be the key to successful supervision. Documenting learner benefits of such adaptation seems to focus "success" on the most reasonable dependent variable.

How Is the Intervention Strategy Determined?

What Features Characterize Supervisory Interventions? Apart from observed performance followed by some form of feedback (i.e., usually a face-to-face conference), the features of supervisory interventions vary greatly. Some are delivered by organizational superiors, some by peers, and some by people from a university. Some involve cycles of observations and conferences, some use workshops followed by observations, and some make use of observations only when requested. Unless the nature of the process is scrupulously documented and reported, it is impossible to determine the nature of teacher involvement. Research reports often leave the nature and quantity of observational data and the interactive process used in conferences undisclosed. Until these features are better documented, the basis for and kinds of teacher involvement in inquiry on teaching practices will remain invisible.

What rationale supports the structure of the supervisory intervention? The only commonality here seems to be the belief that teachers will profit from structured observation and feedback. Although the literature on clinical supervision espouses that cycles of observations and conferences are necessary for meaningful supervision, many studies of supervisory practice are based on one or two iterations. While many authors discuss the importance of promoting and supporting teachers' reflection on personal practice, few document how reflective behavior is elicited by the intervention design.

How Do Variations of Intervention Strategy Relate to Variations of Teacher Involvement? When there is a presumption of expertise on the part of the supervisor, mentor, or coach, interventions are more likely to be prescriptive. When the supervisor, mentor, coach, or consultant seeks to reinforce the egalitarian norm, all decisions are often left to the teacher being observed.

Although beginning teachers often demonstrate an apparent eagerness for assistance in examining their performance, interventions with more experienced teachers may resist being observed while teaching and take steps to make it nonthreatening. Interventions with both beginners and veteran teachers sometimes make observations invitational (i.e., waiting for a teacher request to be observed). One wonders if these interventions undermine or reinforce the notion that teaching is a private act. Might some teachers see inviting an observer to witness teaching as an admission of inadequacy, or as cause to put on a show? Might teachers involve themselves differently when observations are routine than when they are rare, or when they are spontaneous or regular rather than when they require an invitation?

An unstated assumption of many studies seems to be that the nature of the supervisory process is constant irrespective of contextual or interpersonal variations. Do you believe that a person supervises essentially the same when confronting a model lesson as when dealing with an unsuccessful one? What about when working with an outspoken and confident friend as opposed to a timid stranger? If the practices of teaching should be varied with the dispositions of the individual learners and the nature of the teaching goals, should not the practices of supervision be equally adaptive? The rationale for and documentation of key variations of strategies in supervisory practice are often overlooked, even as we seek to develop teachers as "reflective practitioners."

What Characteristics Describe the Research Method?

How Are Desired Consequences of Supervisory Interventions Documented and Assessed? Learner benefits are occasionally documented with standardized or criterion-referenced test results. Learner benefits and other desired consequences are more often identified through reports of teachers being supervised. Surveys and interviews of teachers and their supervisors, mentors, coaches, or consultants are the most common forms of data collection. Relying on such self-report requires caution in interpreting results. (This notion is elaborated in the next section.)

Whose perceptions of supervisory interventions and their consequences are solicited? As just mentioned, the immediate participants are the usual informants.

How Are Data Regarding Supervisory Interventions Collected? Responses to surveys and interviews of participants again provide the most used data source regarding the nature of supervisory interventions. Authors of papers and articles will often describe general characteristics of the supervisory process based upon their own involvement with it. Systematic observational data are rarely collected regarding the nature of supervisory interventions. When it is done, these studies generally focus on the supervisory conference and categorize verbal interaction. Participants are seldom asked to report specific attributes or the *qualities* of supervisory intervention.

How Do The Methods of Collecting Data Regarding Supervisory Interventions Influence The Data That Are Collected? This is, of course, a matter for conjecture. Given the general reliance on perceptions of participants, any tendency for these informants to emphasize either a positive or negative portrayal could lead, even unintentionally, to a systematic distortion of data or a *halo effect*. As mentioned earlier, the few studies that have compared reports from supervisors with those of teachers being supervised, indicate that supervisors tend to view supervision more favorably than do recipients. Recipients who like their supervisors perhaps respond favorably as well. One might reasonably expect that recipients who dislike either the supervisor or the supervisory process may report overly negatively. When questions regarding the utility of supervisory interventions are raised, asking questions that elicit information regarding specific aspects and their consequences (e.g., Are preobservation conferences helpful for refining planning skills? Does the supervisor ask useful questions?), seems preferable to simply asking for a respondent's general impressions.

In some studies, those who supervise also collect data on the supervisory process and consequences. In these cases special steps should be taken into assure that respondents are candid.

How Are Variations of Teacher Involvement Documented and Judged As Contributing to Supervisory Success? In general, except in studies focusing on interactions in a single supervisory dyad, they are not. A worthy exception to this tendency to neglect individual variations is found in the Gersten and Kelly (1992) investigation of coaching in which adaptations for each of four participating teachers are discussed in brief case reports. Although each of the four teachers reported that the coaching program was helpful, these researchers concisely documented variations in the process and varied results for each of the coaching recipients. As must be apparent to the reader by now, more research like the Gersten and Kelly study and case studies that examine interventions carefully enough to document qualities of teacher involvement in supervision are needed.

WHAT DO WE KNOW

Having considered all of the preceding information what have we learned about teacher involvement in supervision? It is clear that honest and able efforts have been made to explore how teachers and learners might benefit from different forms of supervision. Nevertheless, we know too little about teacher involvement in supervisory programs, and how such involvement serves the ultimate purpose of improving the learning experiences of the students served by our schools. Based on the good work that has been done, however, we do know more about the inquiry that remains to be done, and why it is so difficult to do. This closing section describes five serious obstacles to both the development of meaningful teacher involvement in supervision and to the disciplined study of such involvement. These obstacles are: (1) the blurring of the concept of supervision; (2) the lack of consensus on the proper dependent variable; (3) the imprecise notions of desired teacher involvement; (4) the pretense that supervisory interventions can have predictable and reproducible consequences across contexts and teachers; and (5) the persistent reliance on "quick fixes" in educational reform. After examining each obstacle, future research is suggested that can help us better understand teacher involvement in supervision and how such involvement can contribute to improving educational vitality in our schools.

Blurring of the Concept of Supervision

When one examines the multiple forms of supervisory interventions examined in this chapter carefully, the distinguishing characteristics of "supervision" seem illusive. Recall that the studies reviewed were initially delimited by the conditions that (1) at least one other person was engaged in helping a classroom teacher improve teaching performance (2) based on the actual observation of that performance. As an organizer, this loose view of supervision allowed us to consider a wide array of actual practices from instances when a supervisor worked with a single teacher intensely (e.g., Bureau, 1992) to studies using mentor teachers (e.g., Anctil, 1991), coaches (e.g., Gersten & Kelly, 1992), and consultants (e.g., Nolan & Hillkirk, 1990). Although observations of classroom teaching were almost always included, the nature of these observations was seldom vividly described. What, if anything, do observers record during these sessions? How long do the observations last and how representative are they of the teacher's work? Does the teacher ever voice his or her appraisal of teaching strategies or otherwise discuss teaching during conferences? Apart from the case studies and their "thick descriptions," questions such as these are rarely addressed in the reported research.

Such details are perhaps overlooked because the writers expect the readers to understand that the norms for observations of experienced teachers include annual or semi-annual observations of from 20 to 45 minutes in which the observer records any impressions that capture her or his fancy, and thereafter communicates minimally with the observed teacher. If so, this is troubling because observations thus conducted can be expected to evoke much less teacher involvement than more regular classroom visits during which the observer records descriptive information regarding a focus that the teacher has previously voiced as important to the success of the lesson, and then makes times for a thorough and mutual exploration of the information collected in the observation.

Imagine how our understandings of both the supervisory and the research processes might change if supervision of teaching were commonly understood to include such characteristics as:

- a preobservation conference in which the teacher acquaints the supervisor with relevant contextual information for the lesson to be observed and agrees on a focus for observation that has specific relevance to that lesson's success

- an observation (or set of observations) specifically designed to allow the supervisor to record descriptive data that would inform specific questions regarding the lesson's success

- an understanding that both supervisor and teacher would have access to recorded information and time to interpret it

- a postobservation conference in which both teacher and supervisor engage in a genuine sharing of ideas and interpretations culminating in the teacher's decision of appropriate follow-up actions and related data collection

- a time in which the helpfulness of the supervisory process is carefully and honestly appraised, and, if necessary, adapted.

These skeletal characteristics begin to develop an expectation of teacher involvement in the supervisory process as well as a set of structures to elicit that involvement. These probably are recognized as characteristics of the clinical supervision process advocated by Cogan (1973), Goldhammer (1969), Acheson and Gall (1980), and others. Given the information available in the few studies of supervisory practice in schools (e.g., Lovell & Phelps, 1977), few teachers would recognize these as characteristic of any form of supervision they have experienced. The sad fact seems to be that supervisory practice in schools bears little resemblance to that described in professional literature. Teachers might logically think of supervision as what their supervisors do. This may help us to understand why teachers seem so leery of supervision at the same time that they seem so enthusiastic about mentoring or coaching programs that follow a clinical supervision process. Future research will perhaps help demonstrate that, when teachers are meaningfully involved in a thoughtful and collaborative examination of the practices they use in their own teaching, they will respond appreciatively, whether the helper is called supervisor, principal, mentor, coach, or consultant.

Does it matter whether we call the function of skilled observing and conferring with teachers supervision or something else? If the term *supervision* is commonly associated with inept, bureaucratic, intrusive behavior, then perhaps it should simply be called something else? For example, consider the project in which

supervisors and project directors used the terms reflective supervision, clinical supervision, and peer coaching interchangeably to refer to the supervisory process. The formal name given to the supervisory process for teachers was peer coaching. *This was done to help them distinguish this project from the typical supervision which they had experienced throughout their careers* (Nolan & Hillkirk, 1990, p. 2 - emphasis added).

A common response to the observation that teachers associate "supervision" with inept past practices has been to argue that we should change terms. This may be a pragmatic option, but when people misunderstand concepts (whether "supervision" or "liberty"), then another option is to educate them.

The blurring of concept is not limited to programs that are called supervision either. For example, consider the following: "Because mentoring involves highly personal interactions, conducted under different circumstances in different schools, the roles of mentoring cannot be rigidly specified. . . . Mentoring, like good teaching, should be defined by those who will carry it out" (Wildman et al, 1992, p. 212). The wisdom in this stance recognizes that nuances and subtleties of practice must be responsive to the context and people with whom one works. Nevertheless, one suspects that Wildman and colleagues would agree that some broad definition of the functions of a mentor must be commonly understood for the role of mentor to have any meaning at all.

We see, therefore, that different individuals have differing meanings for the term *supervision;* where can this blurred concept lead us? Until we have some common understanding of supervision and related terms like coaching, we cannot reasonably explore teacher involvement in it. Those who study and advocate "teaching" do not seem deterred when they encounter others who oversimplify the term to mean standing in front of rows of desks and lecturing to bored students. We exemplify good teaching by studying and discussing the best of its practices, not the worst. We need to do the same for supervision in any of its forms. Those who write of supervisory practices and their consequences must be careful to distinguish between good practice and malpractice. Both by describing the general elements of the supervisory intervention in detail to allow the reader to visualize key practices and by documenting adaptations to context and individual scrupulously, researchers and writers on supervisory interventions can provide enough of a window for readers to begin to understand the nature of teacher involvement in the process.

Lack of Consensus on the Proper Dependent Variable

When we are studying teaching effects, we must ultimately try to assess the consequences, whether anticipated or not, for learners. As we try to determine the effects of supervision, we are naturally concerned with effects for both teachers and learners. The supervision of *teaching,* as opposed to supervision of teachers, addresses planning, delivery, and evaluation of teaching performances or other activities. Attention must be focused, therefore, on how the teacher's actions influence the learners. To do this appropriately, one must observe elements of each.

Do not ask, then, whether data regarding supervisory interventions should focus on teacher actions or on learner consequences. Who would ask if medical research should focus on elements of the treatment or on the responses of the patients? One obviously cannot fairly assess medical interventions without considering specific aspects of the treatment in direct relation to specific responses of the patient. Too much supervisory research, however, seems to neglect collecting data addressing both *specific* teaching adaptations made by teachers and some sensible appraisal of how students are influenced.

From the perspective of exploring teacher involvement in supervision, one final focus is necessary. Might the nature of the process and the idiosyncratic nature of each teacher's involvement with such supervision have dramatic influence on who benefits and how? It seems likely. If the supervisory process is most beneficial when adapted to the setting and even to the individuals who participate, then it may be futile to search for precise and generalizable answers to questions like, "How does formal teacher evaluation affect professional development?" If we reason that the answer to that question is likely, "it depends," then our research might be better focused "on what" does it depend? Examining and documenting elements of human interaction and engagement within supervisory relationships, therefore, is crucial to assess teacher (or supervisor) involvement in the process.

These observations lead to three specific suggestions for future research that will contribute to our understanding of teacher involvement in supervision: (1) to document differences in teaching practice by clearly describing what teaching behavior is changed and how; (2) to explore how the judgments of "good" and "poor" (or successful vs. unsuccessful) teaching practices, as well as supervisory practices, are grounded in meaningful consequences for students; and (3) to attend to (and report) the interaction between the human relationship enjoyed by supervisor and teacher and the productiveness of supervisory interventions.

The reliance on subjective self-report that seems to dominate research into supervisory practices might be called the "happy camper" syndrome (i.e., "I really enjoyed this, so it must be good"). How these campers would answer, "good for what?" is often unclear in the research reports. Certainly, teachers may enjoy it, but how does teaching and learning improve? It will be impossible to determine the success of a supervisory program or of teacher involvement in it until this question is addressed.

Cooperate and Graduate

William D. Johnson, one of my finest teachers, called the game two preservice teachers would play when asked to observe and evaluate each other's teaching "cooperate and graduate." He regretted that rather than engage one another in a collaborative inquiry of teaching purposes, practices, and effects, students would often say nice things so that the partner would also say nice things. The implication was that it is better to avoid confronting one another with the difficult inquiry into teaching excellence in favor of the easier and more comfortable courteous praise of each other. In addition, it is easier . . . and more comfortable. In these days when teacher comfort poses as a purpose for supervision, cooperate and graduate becomes a seldom spoken norm of tolerating, even praising, mediocre teaching. If we want more from teacher involvement in supervision, then what exactly do we expect?

One mediating aim for supervisory programs is often disciplined and assisted self-evaluation of teaching performance. The emphasis on teacher self-evaluation often translates into an explicit role-reversal from most traditional "top–down" images. Supervision is often construed as a situation in which a more powerful and presumably, more expert worker observes the practice of another and offers judgments and suggestions. The supervisor's judgment clearly prevails in such relationships. Two options to this supervisory dominance are available in a one-to-one setting. First, the two participants can try to achieve some parity of power and reason through each judgment or suggestion as partners. When disagreements occur that lead to differing courses of action, these partners would negotiate and search for a decision that both could support. The second option turns the stereotypical power arrangement upside-down and assigns all decision-making power to the teacher who is observed. Although this second option is generally the route taken in cases of impasse (i.e., because there is little recourse other than coercive power when someone takes an adamant stand), the first option *suggests a more rigorous interaction before impasse is concluded.* In short, the consultant, coach, or supervisor using the second option may actually permanently withhold her or his own opinions and suggestions in deference to the teacher's ideas and interpretations. While it may well be desirable in many cases to elicit and focus evaluative judgments from the teacher who is observed prior to sharing the observer's judgments, total withholding of such judgments is the antithesis of collaboration. Indeed, it seems reasonable to suggest that one effect of continually deferring to the judgments of another is minimizing reflective interaction needed for joint problem solving.

Perhaps the best documentation of this phenomenon is the Clarke and Richardson (1986) study of a consultation project in an elementary school. They report:

Most partners felt they were able to be open and honest but qualified that idea with such statements as

- "He was such a good teacher, I only had to give positive comments and that was easy."
- "No problems if I dealt strictly with the requested data and gave no judgmental feedback."
- "At first, I structured the data collection procedure for my observer so no judgments of my teaching skills would be discussed. I couldn't handle that."
- "When observing the students, (it was) very easy to be open, but when asked to observe her teaching, I found it difficult."
- "I would have real difficulty being absolutely honest with a peer. Some teachers would get mad. But, I suppose, for this program to be successful, you must be able to be very honest."

The only team (dyad) that engaged in constructive criticism and active problem solving was a team that normally met as a grade level every week, participating in these processes on a regular basis prior to the onset of the project (pp. 14–15).

Little's (1990) observation of mentors may well apply to any form of teacher observation: "The emphasis on comfort and harmonious relations between . . . (teachers) may preclude productive confrontation with important but difficult matters of practice (Hollingsworth, 1989)" (p. 329). That teachers who observe other teachers might emphasize harmony at the expense of candor is more than conjecture. Eight of 11 teachers in the Clarke and Richardson study reported enjoying "the comfortable, supportive atmosphere created by peer supervision, but felt a need for the objective and honest feedback that a supervisor could provide" (1986, p. 17).

As we better collect information regarding the relationships between supervisory processes and teaching adaptations, and between teaching adaptations and student benefits (as discussed in the previous section), we will be better able to understand the nature of teacher involvement that leads to successful supervisory practice. This will call for less superficial assessments of teacher involvement and probably for more intense and uncomfortable forms of that involvement. Such research will require investigators to articulate and assess specific expectations for teacher involvement in supervision.

Imprecise Notions of Desired Teacher Involvement

Exactly what kinds of teacher involvement do we want in supervisory interventions? It is beyond the scope of this chapter to reveal the "holy grail" regarding ideal teacher involvement. Rather, four specific factors that may have substantial influence on supervisory success will be suggested in the hope that these will stimulate the reader to generate others. These are: (1) establishing foundational assumptions regarding good teaching and supervision; (2) drawing initial judgments; (3) grounding judgments in learner consequences; and (4) viewing altered teaching practices as hypotheses to be tested.

What is good teaching? When I was a beginning teacher, the answer was clearer than it is to me now. To be flip, I could say that good teaching was simply teaching that my supervisor liked. If she liked the overhead projector, then good teaching involved using it. To be more serious, good teaching meant that the kids in my class had fun. As I have aged, I have come to believe that some very important lessons are not fun—but they are still crucial. At one point, I believed that kids having fun irritated my supervisor, who seemed to think that the way they expressed themselves at such times was "out-of-control." The point here is not to ask which one of us was right—we both were. Rather, the point is that we too often act as if everyone understands and agrees to a vision of "good teaching." In the supervisory interventions I would like to see, participants (e.g., observer and observed) will discuss characteristics and intended effects of desired teaching practice as well as desired supervisory practice as a foundation for working together. The process could thereby be assessed and adapted formatively as the participants worked collaboratively to tinker with the form of the work to better serve its intended function.

Drawing initial judgments of performance can be done by either performer or critic. When the performer does it, the intended, although not always realized, focus is on self-evaluation and improvement. When the critic does it, the focus is always on adapting one's performance to meet the expectations of another. There are perhaps times when such external guidance is helpful. In any case, it makes sense to examine whose evaluations are spoken when one examines teacher involvement in supervision. The process of eliciting critical self-evaluation is quite different from the process of delivering external judgment in ways that elicit compliance or even open consideration. Whether the supervisory intervention involves an expert serving as coach or mentor to an inexperienced colleague or a peer working as a consultant, the process for discussing observations and reaching judgments should be explicit.

Grounding judgments in learner consequences means that practitioners and researchers will not debate what makes good teaching without connecting the teaching practice to intended learner outcomes. My teaching may well have been improved by my using the overhead projector to placate my supervisor, but how would I know without observing the way in which the visuals helped the learners understand?

This emphasis on discovering and using observed learner consequences as one judges teaching strategies and tactics leads directly to viewing altered teaching practices as hypotheses to be tested. Visually depicting or reinforcing key concepts using an overhead projector may indeed be sound teaching practice in theory, but how will I know that my own efforts are having the desired effect? This is a question to be raised and addressed as part of supervisory conferences. The answers will be as varied as there are educational practices and settings. When teachers and those who supervise them engage in collaborative inquiry into teaching practices, formally stating reasons for adapting teaching performance as hypotheses for how the learners will benefit from proposed changes serves to connect both teacher and supervisor to the learner, who is the intended beneficiary of our services. Testing these hypotheses then becomes the best measure both of teacher involvement in supervision and of supervisory success.

The Pretense that Supervisory Interventions Can Have Predictable and Reproducible Consequences Across Contexts and Teachers Is Puzzling

The effects associated with clinical supervision or with peer coaching or with supervision by any other name will depend upon human and setting idiosyncrasies. The person who supervises, the person who is supervised, the press of other events and conditions, the frequency of classroom observations by others, and the reputations and histories of the participants all influence the consequences of a supervisory intervention. When we ask how a supervisory approach influences teaching and learning in a setting while pretending that interpersonal and contextual variables are inconsequential, it is tantamount to asking what effects wearing a skimpy bathing suit has without attending to audience or setting. Supervision is a form of human, interpersonal interaction. As such, it is as variable as friendship, parenthood, sales, or any

other form of people engaging other people. As we explore teacher involvement in supervision, we must be sensitive that differences in people, in places, and in circumstances will surely make differences in successful supervisory practice. Rather than pretending otherwise, investigations should help readers appreciate the special circumstances that characterize the intervention, people, and setting being studied.

Persistent Reliance on "Quick Fixes" in Educational Reform

Persistent reliance on "quick fixes" in educational reform is a colossal problem. How long do you believe it would take to develop productive teacher involvement in a new supervision program? Very many of the studies of supervision have occurred in the very first year of a program. Many of the mentor studies occurred between 1986 and 1992, when several states were investing heavily in teacher induction programs. Much of what we do in the name of school renewal supports the jaded attitude often heard from teachers that "we will outlast this, too." Although supervision in some fashion has been a customary presence in schools for a long period, studies of teacher involvement in supervision are seldom designed to surface effects that take time to emerge.

The few studies that do take a disciplined look at a supervisory intervention over time are very helpful. For instance, Greene (1992) collected data over a 3-year period (1985–1988) that addressed teacher involvement in a clinical supervision program. She carefully noted how some aspects of the supervisory interaction evolved during that time. For example:

Over the project's three years, the ratio of supervisor providing information to teacher analyzing information changed from 2:1 to 1:1. The increases in supervisors accepting or using teachers' ideas and in teachers accepting or using supervisors' ideas were statistically significant (p. 138).

Such shifts could clearly not have been observed in a study lasting only a few months, as most do.

Even more telling than Greene's (1992) documentation of the successful evolution of the supervisory process is her portrayal of the developing level of discourse:

Even after three years, however, the content of most conferences and teacher discussions focused primarily on relatively low-level and non-threatening behaviors—questioning skills and student on-task behaviors. Only toward the end of the third year did teachers begin to reflect on, analyze, and try to address more complex teaching behaviors and student outcomes (p. 139).

Generating thoughtful and interactive teacher involvement in supervision takes time. The press for quick results and the impatience reflected in fads in school reform work against providing the time needed both to genuinely engage teachers in meaningful supervision and to conduct useful studies of such programs.

Finally, teacher supervision does lead to professional development, but not without considerable resources (both personal and financial), effort, goodwill, commitment, and an unshakable vision of teachers as competent professionals able and willing to take control of their own professional lives (Greene, 1992, p. 148).

The same might be said about research that examines teacher involvement in supervision. Shulman (1994) has urged researchers to consider *consequential validity* as they plan, deliver, and assess intervention research. In essence, when the consequences of one's intervention on the people or organizations being studied are consistent with the values endorsed by the investigators, the study has consequential validity. Thus, if the manner in which we investigate teacher involvement in supervision contributes to the involvement we endorse, then the study would have consequential validity. Given the brevity

of many interventions and the superficiality with which teacher involvement is determined, we must wonder about the consequential validity of such studies.

If you have engaged in this chapter as actively as hoped, then you have identified several unanswered questions that address your concerns about teacher involvement in supervision. Please pursue those questions, then share your work with the rest of us who seek to better understand and promote teacher involvement in supervision for the benefit of the learners they serve.

REFERENCES

Ackley, B. & Gall, M.D. (1992). *Skills, strategies, and outcomes of successful mentor teachers.* Paper presented at Annual Meeting of American Educational Research Association, San Francisco, CA.

Ackley, B. C. (1991). *The role of mentor teachers in Oregon's beginning teacher support program. Dissertation Abstracts International, 52,* 3247A. (University Microfilms No. 92-05,786)

Anastos, J. & Ancowitz, R. (1987). A teacher-directed peer coaching project. *Educational Leadership, 45* (November), 40–42.

Anctil, M. (1991). *Mentor accountability: Acting in accordance with established standards.* Paper presented at American Educational Research Association, Chicago, IL.

Archer, V. T. (1990). A blueprint for teacher empowerment: Peer clinical supervision. *Dissertation Abstracts International, 51,* 822A. (University Microfilms No. 90-02, 262)

Ariza-Menendez, M. (1992). *Interns' assessment of teachers: Perceived usefulness of developmental feedback.* Paper presented at American Educational Research Association, San Francisco.

Avila, L. (1990). *Peer coaching to enhance the effectiveness of bilingual education teachers.* Paper presented at the Annual Conference of the National Council of States on In-service Education, Orlando, FL.

Barbour, C. (1971). Levels of thinking in supervisory conferences. Paper presented at American Educational Research Association, New York.

Bauer, L. K. (1986). Teacher attitudes toward supervisory practices of elementary school principals. *Dissertation Abstracts International, 47,* 1540A .

Bird, T. & Little, J. W. (1983). *Finding and founding peer coaching: An interim report of the application of research on faculty relations to the implementation of two school improvement experiments.* Paper presented at American Educational Research Association, Montreal.

Blackbourn, R. L. (1983). The relationship between teachers' perceptions of supervisory behaviors and their attitudes toward a post-evaluative conference. *Dissertation Abstracts International, 45,* 694A.

Blumberg, A. (1980) *Supervisors and teachers: A private cold war* (2nd ed.). Berkeley, CA: McCutchan.

Borg, W. R., Kallenbach, W., Morris, M., & Friebel, A. (1969). Videotape feedback and microteaching in a teacher training model. *Journal of Experimental Education, 37*(4).

Brande, R. T. (1980). Supervisory behaviors which contribute to the improvement of instruction: An analysis of teacher and supervisor perceptions. *Dissertation Abstracts International, 41,* 4897A.

Bullerman, M., Borg, J., & Peterson, D. (1993). Research bases for enhancing teaching and learning: Essential skills. In R. H. Anderson & K. J. Snyder (Eds.). *Clinical supervision: Coaching for higher performance.* (pp. 325–345). Lancaster, PA: Technomic Publishing Co.

Bureau, W. E. (1992). Seeing supervision differently: The processes of facilitating change in a veteran teacher's beliefs. *Dissertation Abstracts International, 53/05,* 1331A (University Microfilms No. 92-07, 628).

Byrne, B. M. (1994) Burnout: Testing for the validity, replication, and invariance of causal structure across elementary, intermediate, and secondary teachers. *American Educational Research Journal, 31*(Fall), 645–673.

Carr, J. & Dunne, K. (1991). *The New Hampshire mentor project: Bridging the gap between concept and application.* Paper presented at the Annual Conference of the National Council of States on In-service Education, Houston, TX.

Caruso, J. (1987). The role of teacher advisors in improving writing instruction. *Journal of Staff Development, 8*(1), 67–73.

Chunn, G. F. (1985). Perceptions of teachers and principals concerning behaviors and attitudes that contribute to an effective supervisory cycle. *Dissertation Abstracts International, 6,* 2494A.

Clark, E. D., Smith, R. D., Thurman, R. A., & Baird, J. E. (1984). *Supervisors' feedback to student teachers* (ERIC Document Reproduction Service No. ED 257 794).

Clarke, C. & Richardson, J. A. (1986). *Peer clinical supervision: A collegial approach.* Paper presented at National Council of States on In-service Education. Nashville, TN.

Colbert, J. A. & Wolff, D. E. (1992) Surviving in urban schools: A collaborative model for a beginning teacher support system. *Journal of Teacher Education, 43* (3, May-June), 193–199.

Colton, A. B. & Sparks-Langer, G. (1992). Restructuring student teaching experiences. In Carl D. Glickman (Ed.). *Supervision in transition: The 1992 ASCD yearbook* (pp. 155–168). Alexandria, VA: ASCD.

Cook, G. E. (1985). *Teachers helping teachers: A training program in peer supervision.* Paper presented at Annual Conference of Association of Teacher Educators. Las Vegas, NV.

Copas, E. M. (1984). Critical requirements for cooperating teachers. *Journal of Teacher Education, 35* (6, Nov.–Dec.).

Costa, A. L. & R. J. Garmston. (1994) *Cognitive coaching: A foundation for renaissance schools.* Norwood, MA: Christopher-Gordon Publishers, Inc.

Cryan, J. R. (1972). *Supervisor verbal style as related to the quality of interpersonal relations.* Paper presented at American Educational Research Association, Chicago.

Cuff, W. A. (1978). Indirect versus direct influence in supervisory conferences and student teachers' levels of needs. *Dissertation Abstracts International, 39,* 4877A.

Dalton, G. W., Thompson, P. H., & Price, R. L. (1977). The four stages of professional careers—A new look at performance by professionals. *Organizational Dynamics, 6,* 19–42.

Darling-Hammond, L. & McLaughlin, M. W. (1995) Policies that support professional development in an era of reform. *Phi Delta Kappan, 76*(8, April), 597–604.

Davie, G. S. (1986). Teachers' and principals' perceptions of the performance and importance of instructional supervisory behaviors of the principal in schools using or not using clinical supervision (elementary). *Dissertation Abstracts International, 47,* 1944A.

Dawson, J. L. (1982). Clinical and nonclinical supervision of student teachers. *Dissertation Abstracts International, 43,* 2638A.

Dean, K. (1982). *Supervision of student teachers: How adequate?* (ERIC Document Reproduction Service No. ED 079 256).

Dewey, J. (1938) *Experience and Education.* New York: Collier.

Diaz, J. Z. (1991). Teacher perception of the instructional evaluation process: An exploratory study. *Dissertation Abstracts International, 52,* 3136A.

Elgarten, G. H. (1991). Testing a new supervisory process for improving instruction. *Journal of Curriculum and Supervision, 6*(2),118–129.

Erickson, F. (1993) Foreword. In M. Cochran-Smith & S. L. Lytle (Eds). *Inside/outside: Teacher research and knowledge* (pp. vii–ix). New York: Teachers College Press.

Feimen-Nemser, S. & Parker, M. B. (1992) *Mentoring in context: A comparison of two U.S. programs for beginning teachers. NCRTL special report.* East Lansing, MI: National Center for Research on Teacher Learning, Michigan State University.

Fenton, R., Stofflet, F., Straugh, T., & DuRant, M. (1989). *The effects of three models of teacher supervision: Cooperative, supervisor controlled and minimal.* Paper prepared for Division A of American Educational Research Association, San Francisco.

Finley, D. A. (1990). Teachers' perceptions of evaluation: Process versus person, with implications for instruction improvement. *Dissertation Abstracts International, 52,* 32A (University Microfilms No. 91-16, 735).

Flinders, D. J. (1991). Supervision as cultural inquiry. *Journal of Curriculum and Supervision, 6*(2), 87–106.

Fuller, F. & Bowe, O. (1975) Becoming a teacher. In K. Ryan (Ed.). *Teacher education. Seventy-fourth yearbook of the National Society for the Study of Education* (pp. 25–52). Chicago, IL: University of Chicago Press .

Funk, F. F., Hoffman, J. L., Keithley, A. M., & Long, B. E. (1978). *The influence of feedback from supervising teachers on a student teaching program* (ERIC Document Reproduction Service No. ED 211 492).

Ganser, T. (1993). *How mentors describe and categorize their ideas about mentor roles, benefits of mentoring, and obstacles to mentoring.* Paper presented at Annual Meeting of the Association of Teacher Educators Los Angeles.

Garman, N. (1995) Mentoring as discursive practice. In M. Zeldin & S. S. Lee (Eds.). *Touching the future: Mentoring and the Jewish professional* (pp. 28–35). Los Angeles, CA: Hebrew Union College—Jewish Institute of Religion.

Garmston, R., Linder, C., & Whitaker, J. (1993). Reflections on cognitive coaching. *Educational Leadership, 51*(2), 57–61.

Gehrke, N. & Kay, R. (1984). The socialization of beginning teachers through mentor-protege relationships. *Journal of Teacher Education, 35*(3), 21–28.

Gersten, R. & Kelly, B. (1992). Coaching secondary special education teachers in implementation of an innovative videodisc mathematics curriculum. *Remedial and Special Education, 13*(4), 40–51.

Gibson, R. J. (1985). The effectiveness of clinical supervision in modifying teacher instructional behavior. *Dissertation Abstracts International, 46* 2499A.

Gilliss, G. (1988) Schön's reflective practitioner: A model for teachers? In P. P. Grimmett & G. L Erickson (Eds.). *Reflection in Teacher Education* (pp. 47–53). New York: Teachers College Press, and Vancouver, B.C: Pacific Educational Press.

Gilman, D. A. & Miller, M. (1988). *An examination of teachers teaching teachers.* Research Report, Indiana State University, Terre Haute, Professional School Services (ERIC Document Reproduction Service No. ED 302 878).

Gitlin, A. & Price, K. (1992) Teacher empowerment and the development of voice. In C. D. Glickman (Ed.). *Supervision in transition.*

The 1992 Yearbook of the ASCD (pp. 61–74). Alexandria, VA: ASCD.

Glatthorn, A. A. (1987). Cooperative professional development: Peer-centered options for teacher growth. *Educational Leadership, 45*(3, November), 31–35.

Goldsberry, L. Three functional methods of supervision. *Action in Teacher Education, 10*(3), 1–10.

Goldsberry, L. (1980). *Colleague consultation: Teacher collaboration using a clinical supervision model.* Unpublished doctoral dissertation, University of Illinois, Urbana-Champaign.

Goldsberry, L., Harvey, P., Hoffman, N., Levin, J., Badiali, B., & Vadella, R. (1984) *The survey of supervisory practices.* Cornish, ME: Schoolworks.

Gray, W. A. & Gray, M. M. (1985). Synthesis of research on mentoring beginning teachers. *Educational Leadership, 43*(3), 37–43.

Greene, M. L. (1992). Teacher supervision as professional development: Does it work? *Journal of Curriculum and Supervision, 7*(2), 131–148.

Grimmett, P. G., Rostad, O. P., & Ford, B. (1992) The transformation of supervision. In C. D. Glickman (Ed.). *Supervision in Transition: The 1992 yearbook of the ASCD* (pp. 185–202). Alexandria, VA: ASCD.

Grimmett, P. P. & Crehan, E. P. (1990). Barry: A case study of teacher reflection in clinical supervision. *Journal of Curriculum and Supervision, 5*(3), 214–235.

Hanson, M. (1992). *Peer evaluation among teachers: Acceptance of alternative roles.* Paper prepared for American Educational Research Association Annual Meeting, San Francisco.

Hargreaves, A. & Dawe, R. (1990). Paths of professional development: Contrived collegiality, collaborative culture, and the case of peer coaching. *Teaching and Teacher Education, 6*(3), 227–241.

Harris, J. G. C. (1990). What factors make a difference in terms of teachers' acceptance of peer coaching? *Dissertation Abstracts International, 51,* 2712A (University Microfilms No. 91-01, 464).

Herbert, J. M. & Tankersley, M. (1993). More and less effective ways to intervene with classroom teachers. *Journal of Curriculum and Supervision, 9*(1), 24–40.

Holt, A. (1992) *Colleague consultation, a self-evaluation: Putting down on paper thoughts that range through my head on a daily basis.* Unpublished manuscript.

Huling-Austin, L. L. (1990). Squishy business. In T. M. Bey & C. T. Holmes (Eds.). *Mentoring: Developing Successful New Teachers.* Reston, VA: Association of Teacher Educators.

Jackson, P. (1968) *Life in Classrooms.* New York: Holt, Rinehart, & Winston.

Joyce, B. & Showers, B. (1987). Low-cost arrangements for peer-coaching. *Journal of Staff Development, 8*(1), 22–24.

Kennedy, M. M. (1991, November) Some surprising findings on how teachers learn to teach. *Educational Leadership, 49,* 14–17.

Kent, K. M. (1985, November) A successful program of teachers assisting teachers. *Educational Leadership, 43,* 30–33.

Koballa, T. R. Jr., Eidson, S., Finco-Kent, D., Grimes, S., Kight, C. R., & Sambs, H. (1992). Peer coaching: Capitalizing on constructive criticism. *Science Teacher, 59*(6), 42–45.

Lamb, C. & Montague, E. (1982). *Variables pertaining to the perceived effectiveness of university student teaching supervisors.* Paper presented at the Annual Meeting of the Southwest Educational Research Association, Austin, TX.

Leggett, D. and Hoyle, S. (1987). Peer coaching: One district's experience in using teachers as staff developers. *Journal of Staff Development, 8*(1), 16–20.

Lemberger, D. J. (1992). The Mantle of a Mentor. *Dissertation Abstracts International, 52,* 2892A (University Microfilms Order No. 9203618).

Lemma, P. (1993). The cooperating teacher as supervisor: A case study. *Journal of Curriculum and Supervision, 8*(4), 329–342.

Lieberman, A. (1995) Practices that support teacher development. *Phi Delta Kappan, 76*(8, April), 591–596.

Little, J. W. (1985) Teachers as teacher advisors: The delicacy of collegial leadership. *Educational Leadership, 43*(3, November 1985), 34–36.

Little, J. W. (1990a). The mentor phenomenon and the social organization of teaching. In C. B. Cazden (Ed.). *Review of Research in Education, 16,* 297–351.

Little, J. W. (1990b). Teachers as teacher advisors: The delicacy of collegial leadership. *Educational Leadership, 43*(3), 34–36.

Lortie, Daniel. (1975) *Schoolteacher: A sociological study.* Chicago: University of Chicago Press.

Lovell, J. T. & Phelps, M. S. (1977) Supervision in Tennessee as perceived by teachers, principals, and supervisors. *Educational Leadership, 35*(3), 226–228.

Madsen, A. L. & Lanier, P. (1992). *Improving mathematics instruction through the role of the support teacher.* Institute for Research on Teaching, Michigan State U., East Lansing, Michigan.

Mandrusiak, B. J. N. (1988). *A study of supervision and evaluation practices in Strathcona County: The development of a teacher supervision and evaluation program plan.* Unpublished Master's Thesis. Edmonton, Alberta: The University of Alberta.

Mattes, R.G. (1983). A comparative study of teachers' perceptions of teacher development and supervisory practices under clinical and traditional supervision practices in selected Colorado schools. *Dissertation Abstracts International, 44,* 940A.

Mayer, R. & Goldsberry, L. (1993). Searching for reflection in the student teaching experience: Two case studies. *Teacher Education Quarterly, 20*(1), 13–27.

Mayfield, J. E. (1983). The effects of clinical supervision on pupil achievement in reading. *Dissertation Abstracts International, 44,* 940A.

McIntyre, D. J. & Killian, J. E. Students' interactions with pupils and cooperating teachers in early field experiences. *Teacher Educator, 22*(2), 2–9.

McLaughlin, M. W. & Pfeifer, R. S. (1988). *Teacher evaluation: Improvement, accountability, and effective learning.* New York: Teachers College Press.

Miller, S. P., Haris, C., & Watanabe, A. (1991). Professional coaching: A method for increasing effective and decreasing ineffective teacher behaviors. *Teacher Education and Special Education, 14*(3), 183–191.

.Newton, A., Bergstrom, K., Brennan, N., Dunne, K., Gilbert, C., Ibarguen, N., Perez-Selles, M., & Thomas, E. (1994). *Mentoring: A resource guide for educators.* Andover, MA: The Regional Laboratory for Educational Improvement of the Northeast and Islands.

Nolan, J. F. & Huber, T. (1989). Nurturing the reflective practitioner through instructional supervision: A review of the literature. *Journal of Curriculum and Supervision, 4*(2), 126–145.

Nolan, J., Hawkes, B., & Francis, P. (1993). Case studies: Windows onto clinical supervision. *Educational Leadership, 51*(2), 52–56.

Nolan, J. F. & Hillkirk, K. (1990). *The impact of skilled reflective supervision on veteran teachers.* Paper presented at annual meeting of American Educational Research Association, Boston.

Nolan, J. F. & Hillkirk, K. (1991). The effects of a reflective coaching project for veteran teachers. *Journal of Curriculum and Supervision, 7*(1), 62–76.

O'Neal, S. R. (1983). *An analysis of student teaching cooperating teacher conferences as related to the self-concept, flexibility, and teaching concerns of each participant.* Paper presented at American Educational Research Association, Montreal.

Odell, S. J. & Ferraro, D. P. (1992). Teacher mentoring and teacher retention. *Journal of Teacher Education, 43*(3), 200–204.

Olsen, D. G. & Heyse, K. L. (1990). *Development and concerns of first-year and reentry teachers with and without mentors.* Paper presented at annual meeting of American Educational Research Association, Boston.

Osterman, K. F. (1984). Supervision in public schools: An examination of the relationship between supervisory practices of principals and organizational behavior of teachers. *Dissertation Abstracts International, 46,* 572A.

Pajak, E. & Glickman, C. (1989). Informational and controlling language in simulated supervisory conferences. *American Educational Research Journal, 26*(1), 93–106.

Pavan, B. N. (1985). *Clinical supervision: Research in schools utilizing comparative measures.* Paper presented at American Educational Research Association, Chicago.

Pavelich, B. (1992). *Peer Coaching Within the Internship, Monograph No. 10.* Saskatchewan University, Saskatoon College of Education.

Phelps, M. S. & Wright, J. D. (1986). *Peer coaching—A staff development strategy for rural teachers.* A paper presented at the 11th National Conference of the National Council of States on In-service Education, Nashville, TN.

Phillips, M. D. & Glickman, C. D. (1991). Peer coaching: Developmental approach to enhancing teacher thinking. *Journal of Staff Development, 12*(2), 20–25.

Powell, N. C. (1982). The relationship existing between clinical supervision and certain teacher attitudes. *Dissertation Abstracts International, 43,* 3177A.

Raney, P. & Robbins, P. (1989). Professional growth and support through peer coaching. *Educational Leadership, 46*(8, May), 35–38.

Reiman, A. J. & Edelfelt, R. A. (1991). *The opinions of mentors and beginning teachers: What do they say about induction?* Dept. of Curriculum and Instruction, North Carolina State University, Raleigh (Eric Document Reproduction Service No. ED 329 519).

Reiman, A. J. & Thies-Sprinthall, L. (1993). Promoting the development of mentor teachers: Theory and research programs using guided reflection. *Journal of Research and Development in Education, 26*(3), 179–185.

Rogers, M.G. (1986). Teacher satisfaction with direct supervisory services. *Dissertation Abstracts International, 47,* 4260A.

Ross, J. A. (1992). Teacher efficacy and the effects of coaching on student achievement. *Canadian Journal of Education, 17*(1), 51–65.

Ross, J. A. & Regan, E. M. (1995) "When I was successful, they made it seem like luck": District consultants' responses to feedback from principals and others. *Journal of Curriculum and Supervision, 10*(2, Winter), 114–135.

Rothman, L. S. (1981). Effective and ineffective supervisory behaviors of college supervisors as perceived by secondary school cooperating teachers. *Dissertation Abstracts International, 42,* 2086A.

Russell, T. L. & Spafford, C. (1986). *Teachers as reflective practitioners in peer clinical supervision.* Paper presented at meeting of American Educational Research Association, San Francisco.

Sands, R., Parson, L. A., & Duane, J. (1991). Faculty mentoring faculty in a public university. *Journal of Higher Education, 62*(2).

Schweitzer, S. M. (1990). Performance-based teacher evaluation in the state of Missouri: Teachers' perspectives. *Dissertation Abstracts International, 53,* 2359A.

Sergiovanni, T. J. & Starratt, R. J. (1983). *Supervision: Human perspectives* (3rd ed.). New York: McGraw-Hill.

Schaffer, E., Stringfield, S., & Wolf, D. (1992) An innovative beginning teacher induction program: A two-year analysis of classroom interactions. *Journal of Teacher Education, 43*(3), (M/J), 181–192.

Schön, D. A. (1988) Coaching reflective teaching. In P. P. Grimmett & G. L. Erickson (Eds.). *Reflection in Teacher Education* (pp. 19–29). New York: Teachers College Press, and Vancouver, B.C: Pacific Educational Press.

Shahzade, J. B. (1983). The match of style and conceptual level of university supervisors with student teachers in relationship to supervisor effectiveness. *Dissertation Abstracts International, 44,* 2449A.

Showers, B. (1987). The role of coaching in the implementation of innovations. *Teacher Education Quarterly, 14*(3), 59–70.

Showers, B. (1988) *Skills teachers need as learners to master and implement new skills and strategies.* Eugene, OR: Booksend Laboratories

Showers, B., Joyce, B., & Bennett, B. (1987). Synthesis of research on staff development: A framework for future study and a state of the art analysis. *Educational Leadership, 45*(3, November), 77–87.

Shulman, L. (1988) The dangers of dichotomous thinking in education. In P. P. Grimmett & G. L Erickson (Eds.). *Reflection in Teacher Education* (pp. 31–38). New York: Teachers College Press, and Vancouver, B.C: Pacific Educational Press.

Shulman, L. (1994) *Discussion of portfolios and consequential validity.* Presentation at the Portfolio Conference, Cambridge, MA.

Smith, S. C. (1985). The effects of clinical supervision on teachers' autonomy and perceptions of productive relationships. *Dissertation Abstracts International, 46,* 3003A.

Smith, D. J. (1992). *Intern perspectives on the quality of cooperating teacher supervision. Monograph No. 9.* Saskatchewan University of Saskatoon, College of Education.

Smylie, M. A. (1992, September) Teachers' reports of their interactions with teacher leaders concerning classroom instruction. *Elementary School Journal, 93,* 85–98.

Sparks, G. M. & Bruder, S. (1987, November). Before and after peer coaching. *Educational Leadership, 45,* 54–57.

Spaulding, J. W. (1984). A study of the implementation of a clinical supervision model in the Santee, California, School District. *Dissertation Abstracts International, 44,* 2948A.

Sriza-Menendez, Maria (1992). *Interns' assessment of teachers: Perceived usefulness of developmental feedback.* Paper presented at the American Educational Research Association annual meeting, San Francisco.

Starratt, R. J. (1992). After supervision. *Journal of Curriculum and Supervision, 8*(1), 77–86.

Stein, R. D. (1985). The relationship between principal supervisory behavior and teacher burnout. *Dissertation Abstracts International, 46,* 577A.

Tabachnick, B. R., Popkewitz, T. S., & Zeichner, K. M. (1979–1980). Teacher education and the professional perspectives of student teachers. *Interchange, 10*(4), 12–29.

Taylor, S. M. (1984). Teachers' perceptions of intensive supervisor/teacher relationships (phenomenology). *Dissertation Abstracts International, 46,* 953A.

Tellez, K. (1992). Mentors by choice, not design: Help-seeking by beginning teachers. *Journal of Teacher Education, 43*(3), 214–221.

Thies-Sprinthall, L. (1986). A collaborative approach for mentor training: A working model. *Journal of Teacher Education, 37*(6), 13–19.

Thies-Sprinthall, L. & Sprinthall, N. A. (1987). Experienced teachers: Agents for revitalization and renewal as mentors and teacher educators. *Journal of Education, 169*(1), 65–79.

Veenman, S. (1984). Perceived problems of beginning teachers. *Review of Educational Research, 54*(2), 143–178.

Vukovich, D. (1976). *The effects of four specific supervision procedures on the development of self-evaluation skills in pre-service teachers.* Paper presented at American Educational Research Association, San Francisco.

Wildman, T. M., Magliaro, S. G., Niles, R. A., & Niles, J. A. (1992). Teacher mentoring: An analysis of roles, activities, and conditions. *Journal of Teacher Education, 43*(3), 205–213.

Williams, R. E. H. (1986). The relationship between secondary teachers' perceptions of supervisory behaviors and their attitudes toward a post observation supervisory conference. *Dissertation Abstracts International, 47,* 1976A.

Yosha, P. (1991). *The benefits of an induction program: What do mentors and novices say?* Paper presented at American Educational Research Association, Chicago.

Zimpher, N. L., deVoss, G. G., & Nott, D. L. (1980). A closer look at university student teacher supervision. *Journal of Teacher Education, 31*(4), 11–15.

Zimpher, N. L. & Grossman, J. E. (1992). Collegial support by teacher mentors and peer consultants. In Carl D. Glickman (Ed.). *Supervision in transition: The 1992 ASCD yearbook* (pp. 141–154). Alexandria, VA: ASCD.

NOTES

1. The author acknowledges the invaluable assistance of Marianna Estabrooke in all stages of the development of this chapter, especially for the thorough and insightful review of relevant literature. Thanks go to Jim Nolan for his careful review and thoughtful suggestions on the draft of this chapter.
2. Supervisory relationships in preservice teaching, often called "student teaching," are excluded from consideration in this chapter, largely due to the expansiveness of the topic.
3. The Lovell & Phelps and the Goldsberry et al studies are discussed shortly.
4. The authors mention without elaborating that PAR "consultants" also intervene with experienced teachers who are experiencing

problems in the classroom. Such interventions would be considered a specific form of supervision in this chapter because the consultant is assigned an evaluative function that contributes to decisions regarding subsequent employment of experienced teachers.

5. Schön refers to this process as "reflective supervision" and to the deliverer as "coach." While the process may indeed be part of supervision, mentoring, or coaching as used in this chapter, it is seen as a *defining characteristic* of consulting, reflecting the reliance on teacher's reasoning, rather than supervisory authority or fidelity to *externally* determined performance standards in consultation.

·16·

SUPERVISION FOR TEACHER DEVELOPMENT ACROSS THE CAREER SPAN

Sharon Nodie Oja
UNIVERSITY OF NEW HAMPSHIRE

Alan J. Reiman
NORTH CAROLINA STATE UNIVERSITY

INTRODUCTION

Instructional supervision for teacher development is emerging as an increasingly important focus for school reform and educational excellence. Efforts at "restructuring" have reminded us that, as more schools become decentralized and engage in shared decision-making, there is a concomitant need for personal and professional development for teachers. In this chapter, the authors review a broad array of research on instructional supervision for teacher development across the career span. Two general questions guide the review of literature: To what degree do teacher characteristics, attitudes, career phases, conceptions of self, and intellectual, interpersonal, and moral dispositions determine the explicit and implicit interactions between the teacher and students or colleagues? To what degree can such psychological development be deliberately promoted?

The literature of teacher development is relevant to instructional supervision in that new forms of supervision are emerging in the form of mentors, peer coaches, school-based teacher educators, clinical teachers, collaborative action researchers, and instructional study teams. These new supervisory and assistance roles for teachers support professional growth and development experiences for preservice teachers, beginning teachers, and experienced teachers. Thus, another purpose for this chapter is to draw implications and common

themes from the theory and research on supervision for teacher development and point to practical applications in teacher education and ongoing staff development. The review is organized into three parts: theory and research literature on adult psychological growth and development; theory and research on design and implementation of deliberate programs to promote preservice, induction, and in-service teacher development; and common themes and implications for supervision and teacher education across the career span.

MAJOR TRADITIONS OF TEACHER DEVELOPMENT

Typically, teachers begin their careers in a teacher-preparation program at a college or university, are inducted into their careers during an initial 2- to 3-year period, and, with support, become experienced educators. Teachers learn and develop over the course of their careers, and there are many models that describe this developmental and career progression (Burden, 1990; Lanier & Little, 1986).

In this review, the developmental progression is described through analysis of four major traditions of teacher development (Pintrich, 1990). These models include the stage and structure literature, the information processing literature, the beliefs and affect literature, and the cognitive style literature. As one might expect, each developmental tradition has a dif-

The authors are grateful for the comments of chapter reviewers Saundra Odell (University of Nevada, Las Vegas) and Pam Paisley (University of Georgia).

ferent set of assumptions about the adult learner and how the process of development unfolds. Furthermore, each tradition places differing degrees of emphasis on "what" develops. After an analysis of the four models, the authors will turn to the question of how the field of supervision can design and implement programs that promote learning and development. Before introducing the four models, however, prior models of supervision for teacher development are described.

Prior Models of Supervision for Teacher Development

The importance of supervision as a process for promoting teacher development across the career span had not, previously, received adequate theoretical and research attention. At least part of the problem was related to definition. Supervision was most often practiced as a kind of hierarchical control of the supervisee by a principal or central office administrator. A larger problem, however, was the application of models that were insufficient to explain and guide program development. For example, one conception of supervision was based on the global psychoanalytic conception of teacher growth in the tradition of Jersild (1955). Such a view was based on the assumption that present behaviors are largely a function of very early childhood experiences. Supervision must help teachers to face themselves and to understand how early experiences have shaped present behaviors. Such a model clearly was limited as a directing construct for supervision and for teacher growth.

At the other end of the continuum has been the process–product model. Deriving its intellectual heritage from behavioral psychologists such as E. L. Thorndike, specific teacher behaviors were identified as supervisory objectives. The model relied heavily on correlational research rather than the concerns, attitudes, and dispositions of teachers in different learning contexts (Darling-Hammond & Sclan, 1992). The skills were shaped through behavior modification, and the teachers were expected to integrate such discrete behaviors (a process) to promote student learning (a product). A number of state departments of education employed this model as they mandated evaluation of beginning and experienced teachers. As Shulman (1986) has pointed out, however, the teaching/learning process is not a linear one-way street; instead, it looks more like a busy intersection at rush hour.

The inadequacies of the prior paradigms have been all too apparent as they have been implemented. In their place, a series of new initiatives has been appeared over the last decade. The goal is broad: to create a firm basis in theory and research for the practice of professional teacher development through supervision. This emergent paradigm envisions supervision as a variety of deliberate and planned individual and group activities/interventions that promote learning about instruction and development. Many questions still remain unanswered, however, and it is probably appropriate only to suggest the possibility of an emerging consensus.

Part of the difficulty relates to the study of supervision for teacher development. Can an emergent developmental paradigm accommodate quantitative and qualitative research models? Can, for example, the classic stage and structure conceptions of growth and development, with reliance on nomothetic data, be extended to explain idiographic and individual dif-

ferences? The dilemma of broadly focused versus narrowly focused theory certainly presents additional difficulties. Katz and Raths (1985) have addressed this dilemma most provocatively with their "Goldilocks principle." Some theories for teacher development are extremely broad and abstract. The theoretical "bed" is too big for the actual process of teacher growth. Some of the psychoanalytic and humanistic theories are certainly exemplars of such broad propositions. However, as Katz and Raths also note, there is another side to the problem. Theory and research can be so focused on specifics that they are excessively narrow as an explanatory framework. The process–product behavioristic approach to supervision represents a case in point. Teacher complexity is whittled down to a few correlational propositions: "If this teacher behavior is present, then you can anticipate these learner outcomes." This is an example of a theoretical "bed" that is too small. Goldilocks is a metaphor for supervisory models that shift from place to place hoping to find a better fit. In the absence of careful integration of theory, research, and best practices, the discipline of supervision will wander from fad to fad, without the means to more effectively promote teacher development. There are no simple explanations for how developmental theory informs supervisory practice or how practice affects theory. Both are clearly essential to supervision for teacher development.

Stage and Structure Models in Teacher Development

There have been significant gains in both theory and research within the classical stage and structural framework of human development, with implications for the adult learner in general and the teacher in particular. There are, however, two different strands to the model: the organismic and the contextual (or lifespan) (Lerner, 1986).

Organismic Perspective In the stage and structure models, the organismic perspective assumes that the person is the focus of development and that the individual is actively constructing meaning from experience. Further major theoretical assumptions are that all persons process experience through cognitive structures, that this construction of meaning progresses through distinct phases or stages, that each new stage/structure represents a qualitatively different and more complex cognition and personality, and that the sequence is both hierarchical and invariant. More complex levels are conceptualized as more adequate in the use of problem-solving strategies, more flexible in modes of thought and action, and more comprehensive in understanding and applying democratic principles for conflict resolution. For example, according to this view of teacher development, expert teachers at more complex developmental levels do not just have more knowledge and experience, but their knowledge, values, feelings, and problem solutions are organized in qualitatively different and more complex ways that are necessary for resolving complex "human-helping" problems.

Furthermore, stages and structures as the focus of development represent cognitions and behaviors in a variety of domains of growth. Each domain is a unique part of human growth and development. For example, conceptual development represents the domain of rational process and problem-solving researched by Piaget (1972), King and Kitchener (1994), Arlin (1993), Case (1992) and Hunt (1974). Ego development is a related domain that can be conceptualized as self-knowledge. Loevinger's research (1976) has been a major source of knowledge of the stage/structural conception of personality in this area. Moral and ethical judgment is a third domain and is related to how persons in a democratic society view questions of social justice and fairness. Kohlberg's original research (1969) as well as the work of Rest and Narváez (1994) have framed inquiry in this area.

Other domains may be added to our understanding of the process of adult interpersonal and intrapersonal growth. For instance, Gardner (1993) has looked at stages of aesthetic development, and Selman (1980) has researched stages of interpersonal relations. Sternberg (1986) has acknowledged the need to better understand a domain for creativity. These theorists, however, have concentrated their inquiry on children and adolescents. Much work needs to be done before implications can be drawn for adult growth.

In the domain of conceptual development, there were suggestions by Piaget (1972) that adults might continue to develop in formal operations. The hallmarks of formal operational thinking (Flavell, 1985) are:

1. abstract thinking and the ability to consider a variety of possibilities;
2. combinatorial thinking, which involves considering all possible combinations of ideas;
3. hypothetical thinking;
4. projective thinking, which requires thinking ahead;
5. metacognitive thinking; and
6. the ability to be self-reflective.

However, there has been an ongoing assessment problem because of horizontal decalage. DeLisi and Staudt (1980) found that physics, political science, and English majors were more likely to display formal operations on problems related to their major.

Arlin (1986, 1990) presents a theoretical construct for continued adult growth, conceptualizing a fifth stage in the Piagetian sequence called postformal operational thinking. Specific cognitive elements representing the postformal stage (problem finding) include:

1. complementarity (connecting unrelated or even contradictory ideas in a new way);
2. detecting asymmetry;
3. openness to change (remaining flexible);
4. redefinition of limits, intuition and taste for levels of significance; and
5. preference for creativity and originality.

However, there have been no cross-sectional or longitudinal studies to validate Arlin's assumptions. Likewise, Basseches's (1984, 1986) empirical research on dialectical thinking and Richards and Commons's (1984) research on systems thinking have described the possibility of adults going beyond the formal operations thinking stage to a level where reasoning is not just about a set of variables but about systems of thought.

Hunt's (1974) cross-sectional research, on the other hand, confirmed adult differences in the ability to conceptualize between concrete and abstract thinking. His research established the predictive validity of conceptual level stages (CL) and the parallel behaviors. Miller's (1981) meta-analysis of over 60 studies of conceptual level supported the construct of conceptual level. Miller concluded that persons functioning at higher stages of conceptual level exhibited behaviors such as:

1. a reduction in prejudice;
2. greater empathic communication;
3. greater focus on internal control;
4. longer decision latencies;
5. more flexible teaching methods; and/or
6. more autonomy and more interdependence.

Hunt (1976, 1981) integrated the preceding list denoting higher-stage teachers as able to "read and flex" in the classroom, which meant the ability to change the learning environment in accord with pupil needs. Longitudinal research, however, to examine the stage and sequence pathway is still needed.

Perry's (1970, 1981) research on "positions" of conceptual and epistemological thinking has also been extremely helpful to our understanding of college student growth. This developmental theory and research has enjoyed great popularity in the field of higher education. Perry's focus was with the content and "deep" structure of college students' reasoning about intellectual relativism that is confronted in college classrooms. Interviewing 140 students from Harvard and Radcliffe about their college experiences, Perry described the students moving through nine stages during their four years of college. The stages fall into three broad categories. The initial category describes students who are absolutists and believe that every intellectual problem has a right or wrong answer. At the middle level in Perry's scheme, students relate to intellectual inquiry from a more relativistic perspective. The final stages in Perry's model describe students who examine intellectual problems from multiple perspectives and who make commitments to a perspective based on their values. There has been no study of adult samples to examine whether, in Perry's scheme, adults continue to mature in conceptual and epistemological development.

Perhaps the most significant research on cognitive and conceptual development with adults is the work of King and Kitchener (1994). Their work was begun in the 1970s, when they revisited Perry's work. They extended his work on conceptual dualism, relativism, and committed relativism into a framework denoted by stages of reflective judgment. Using an elaborate interview schedule with ill-structured problem-solving scenarios, their method involved rating interviews according to levels of the Reflective Judgment Index (RJI). Correlation coefficients were in the +.90 level for interrater and test–retest reliability. Their longitudinal sample was composed of 80 subjects retested over a ten-year period. Additionally, they have collected cross-sectional data on almost 1,700 subjects. Results indicate that adults move through a stage and sequence in reflective judgment from authority-based concrete thought, to quasi-reflective abstract thought, and then to "true" reflective judgment. This highest stage is similar to Schon's (1987) description of reflection in action, van Manen's (1977), critical reflection, and Dewey's (1933) original conception of scientific problem solving. It is also closely related to Hunt's highest conceptual stage.

King and Kitchener found that adult growth is slow, yet there were no regressions, no one skipped a stage, and the problems posed were context resistant. Furthermore, they found that age by itself does not predict growth in reflective judgment. More important predictors were informal education and professional development. Their research provides support for the contention that a developmental stage framework can be applied to the process of conceptual growth of teachers.

Another developmental domain that has been investigated is self-knowledge or ego (personal) (Erikson, 1963; Loevinger, 1976) development. In contrast with King and Kitchener's emphasis on how adults come to know something, Erikson's and Loevinger's focus has been with how the person comes to understand him- or herself and others. Loevinger submitted that the development of ego has five major characteristics. First, stages are defined as plateaus that define children and adults. Second, the current ego stage of a person is structural. There is inner logic to each stage, and the stages have a progression. Third, there are research methods for identifying ego stages. Fourth, self-knowledge or ego development progresses along a continuum of differentiation and complexity. Each ego stage is more complex than the last, and none can be skipped in the course of development. Fifth, the conception of an ego domain applies to all ages.

Loevinger's elaborate model of the stages (milestones) and transitions in the growth of self-knowledge (ego) is not related to chronological age. Different individuals may stabilize at certain plateaus and, consequently, not develop beyond that stage. An individual is only designated as operating at a particular stage if the whole pattern of characteristics of that stage are demonstrable (Oja, 1991). A brief summary of the stages identified by Loevinger follows.

At the *impulsive stage,* the person uses bodily impulses to maintain the formation of a separate identity. Persons at this stage are strongly dependent and demanding; value others for what they can "give to" the individual; prefer absolute judgments; and categorize people as good or bad.

At the *self-protective stage,* persons control their impulsiveness in anticipation of rewards or punishments. Rules are acknowledged at this stage and are used to one's advantage. Blame is placed on others when goals are not reached. Thus, persons at this stage tend to be exploitive, deceptive, manipulative, and preoccupied with control and personal advantage.

At the *conformist stage,* persons place strong trust for their welfare and self-knowledge in the family, peer group, and/or socially approved norms. Rules are obeyed because the group accepts them. Belonging is most important and persons are afraid of appearing to be different. Beliefs and values are molded by the expectations of others, and behavior is viewed in terms of external actions and concrete events rather than inner motives.

At the *self-aware transition* between the prior conformist stage and the subsequent conscientious stage, there is an increase in self-awareness and a nascent understanding of multiple possibilities in problem solving. There is an increased capacity for self-reflection, although feelings are often expressed in vague and global terms. Loevinger found this stage to be the predominant level for adults in the United States.

At the *conscientious stage,* a person is able to combine short and long-term goals, to self-criticize and self-evaluate, and to feel responsibility for developing an adult conscience. Rules are internalized and guilt is the consequence of breaking inner rules. Behavior is interpreted in terms of feelings, motives, beliefs, and patterns rather than simple actions. Achievement is driven by self-chosen standards, and persons at this self-knowledge (ego) stage are preoccupied with obligations, rights, and ideals that are defined more by inner personal standards and less by the need for external recognition and acknowledgment.

At the more complex *individualistic level,* a person has a heightened sense of individuality joined with an increased awareness of emotional dependence on others. Self-reflection is characterized by a greater tolerance of ambiguity as well as an increased valuing of interpersonal relationships. Persons at this stage, however, have difficulty reconciling the inner conflict that arises from conflicting needs and responsibilities.

At the *autonomous level,* the person now is able to reconcile conflicting needs, ideals, and perceptions. Ambiguous and seemingly incompatible ideas, beliefs, and options can be united at this stage. In particular, the person accepts other persons' needs to make personal choices and to learn from mistakes. Most important, the person at this stage realizes the limitations of autonomy. Mutual interdependence is highly valued in interpersonal relationships as a result.

Finally, at the *integrated stage,* which is admittedly more difficult to describe because cases are rare (Cook-Greuter, 1990), there is further reconciliation of conflicting needs and issues and the embracing of both individuality and interdependence.

Related case studies of the development of self-knowledge have been undertaken by Kegan (1982). He describes a similar progression of stages in self-perception and understanding. However, he names the stages differently to focus more on the balance achieved at each new stage.

The early plateaus of self-knowledge (i.e., impulsive and self-protective) are characterized by conceptual confusion, externalization of blame, and manipulation. Progression to the conformist stage represents a qualitative shift where belonging and social acceptability are preeminent. The conscientious stage is characterized by another qualitative shift through the self-awareness transition. At this stage, the person exhibits conceptual complexity, long-term goals, and differentiated feelings. Finally, at the autonomous and integrated stages, there is a high tolerance for ambiguity as well as a realization that conflict is a part of the human condition.

In the organismic perspective, another strand of reasoning that builds upon the basic Piagetian framework is the moral domain. Kohlberg's theory and research of moral reasoning (1976) is based on interviews and in-depth analysis of peoples' reactions to moral dilemmas. Kohlberg's work uncovered six stages of moral justice reasoning that were clustered into preconventional, conventional, and postconventional reasoning.

At the preconventional level, the individual resolves dilemmas based on obedience to or fear of authority and punishment (i.e., stage 1, punishment and obedience), or is concerned primarily with satisfying his or her own needs, thus making relationships one-way only (i.e., stage 2, instrumental purpose).

At the conventional level, the individual is concerned about conforming to group norms (i.e., stage 3, conformity) or maintaining and preserving societal order (i.e., stage 4, social systems maintenance). Two-way relationships are realized at the conventional level.

At the postconventional level, the person agrees that what is just is based on the social contract and on principles such as the greatest good for the greatest number (i.e., stage 5, social contract). At the final stage (i.e., stage 6, universal ethical principles), ethical principles such as justice, equality, and dignity are the basis of decision-making.

Kohlberg (1984) reported that his subjects always progressed slowly through the moral reasoning sequence in an invariant order, without regressions in stages or skipping. The subjects were retested every four years over a 20-year span and their pattern of a gradual increase in moral reasoning can be viewed as strong research validation of the stage/structure model. The method of assessment, the moral judgment interview (MJI), reported reliability coefficients in excess of +.95 for interrater and test–retest situations.

Another longitudinal study (Rest, 1986) of high school, college, and graduate students also clearly shows the same trends from less complex to more complex judgment in the domain of moral reasoning. Rest's research, in addition, indicates highly similar stages of moral justice reasoning through 40 cross-cultural comparisons, including Western, non-Western, industrialized, and nonindustrialized countries. These findings are congruent with Kohlberg's cross-cultural studies (Snarey, 1985) in some 50 countries, as well as more recent work by Gielen (1991).

Questions have been raised about whether there is any relationship between one's ability to reason at more complex moral reasoning levels and one's behavior. The most up-to-date research on this relationship comes from a large group of studies across a variety of professions (Rest & Narvaez, 1994). There is a consistent trend in these studies for more ethical behavior at the more complex moral reasoning stages. For example, a meta-analysis of nine studies by Chang (1994) revealed consistently positive relationships between higher levels of moral judgment and democratic classroom discipline. In a review of studies of the accounting and auditing professions, Ponemon and Gabhart (1993) reviewed a number of empirical studies and reported three major findings: studies indicated that members of the public accounting profession were not reaching their potential for higher levels of ethical reasoning; findings showed that ethical reasoning as described by Rest (1986) may be an important determinant of professional judgment such as disclosure of sensitive information; and unethical and dysfunctional audit behavior, such as underreporting of time on an audit time budget, may be systematically related to the auditor's level of ethical reasoning.

As a final case in point, Self and Baldwin (1994) summarize the results of 30 years of research with ethical reasoning in medicine. Studies in this area have primarily used Rest's Defining Issues Test (1986), Kohlberg's Moral Judgement Interview (1984), and the Gibbs and Widaman (1982) Social/Moral Reflection Measure. A number of studies examined the relationship between the moral reasoning stage and behavior. Among the findings discussed was the statistically significant ($p < .07$) relationship between higher moral reasoning scores and physicians' orientation toward patients and professional colleagues. Physicians at higher moral reasoning levels were more allocentric with patients, had fewer malpractice claims, and were more open to peer review.

Longitudinal work with ego and moral development has required major revisions in our understanding of human growth. Perhaps the most significant work is that of Lee and Snarey (1988). Their longitudinal study with a sample of over 600 adults examined stage growth in the domains of ego or self-development based on Loevinger's work (1976) and moral judgment based on the work of Kohlberg (1969). Adults demonstrated a pattern of slow growth in both domains. However, the rate of growth varied. During early adulthood (ages 19 to 29), ego development with its emphasis on self-knowledge and interpersonal relations was found to be in advance of moral development. During middle adulthood (ages 30 to 49), the scores were equal for ego and moral stages. For the older group (ages 50 to 80), there was another shift with moral judgment in advance of the ego stage.

These findings outline important, needed changes for adult development. Lee and Snarey concluded that cognitive stages should be conceptualized as a series of interrelated domains, such as ego, moral, and conceptual domains. Furthermore, adults do have the potential for stage growth. Such growth, however, varies by age and phase, with ego or self-development as primary growth during early adulthood and moral judgment as primary growth during late adulthood. The process of stage growth clearly may continue throughout the life span. It is interesting to note that these findings offer empirical support for the theoretical positions of Erikson. Ego development, with its focus on identity and relationship, mirrors Erikson's emphasis in early adulthood. Lee and Snarey's midpoint also parallels Erikson's view of generativity and care. The final phase, with its focus on social justice, connects to Erikson's view of wisdom and integrity. What may be emerging is concurrent validity for connecting cognitive developmental stage theory to Erikson's psychosocial framework.

Life-Span Perspectives In stage and structure models of teacher development, the life-span perspectives contrast and complement the organismic perspectives. In contrast with the organismic approach, which focuses on stage, structure, and the construction of meaning, the life-span and life-cycle theorists describe problems, personal issues, and career tasks persons face during their lives. Assumptions of this approach are that developmental change is a lifelong process which is multidirectional (there can be different patterns and trajectories for growth). Patterns in adults' age-related transitions have been reported by a number of theorists (e.g., Erikson, 1963; Levinson, 1986; Neugarten, 1968; and Veroff & Veroff, 1980).

Age theories suggest a pattern of adult tasks beginning with the transition from adolescence to adulthood during the late teens and early twenties; moving into the twenties for a period of provisional adulthood and initial commitments. In the late twenties or early thirties, a transition period of examination and questioning of the initial life structure may result in reaffirmation of initial commitments or trigger a change in career and in personal relationships. The thirties are often a period of settling down, reaffirming commitments, setting long-term goals both for work-related and family-related activities, and often choosing a career as the most highly valued investment of one's time and energy. Career-related goals become even more important in the late thirties and early forties, when the adult is concerned with becoming his or her own person. While work relationships are important, the adult seeks to break away from advisors and mentors in order to become more independent in work. A midlife transition involving another round of questioning one's priorities and values occurs in the early forties, with the realization that time is finite and success and achievement have limitations. A restabilization period follows with further investment in personal relationships. Transitions in the fifties are followed in the sixties by restabilization often marked by pleasingly mild and gentle reactions to life's experiences or a vigorous sense of flourishing.

At each of these different ages, the adult is trying to create a better fit between the life structure he or she has defined and the reality of life's challenges. Age-related phases do not fit completely for all adults. Age alone is not totally predictive of the dilemmas adults face. Life-ages, however, can be helpful to supervisors who want to recognize and understand the nature of their colleagues' dilemmas.

There are a number of extensive reviews of life-age and life-cycle theories. For instance, see Chickering and Havinghurst (1981) for a review of major theories and Hagestad and Neugarten (1985) for a discussion of sociological changes (political, technological, economic, and demographic), age norms, the social clock, and on-time and off-time crises that can result in life-cycle changes. Levinson's (1986) discussion of structure building and structure changing is particularly important to a developmental conception of life periods in adulthood.

Developmental life-cycle researchers often rely on interviews for their data on how adults at specific ages deal with the tasks of adulthood. They gather systematic and repeated self-reports in addition to other types of questionnaire data to create a phenomenological perspective. Limitations to the generalization of this work revolve around issues of socioeconomic status, gender, race, history, and marital status of participants of the studies from which the theories were developed.

Age-related life-cycle theorists hypothesize that the negotiation of certain life tasks may indeed have a significant impact upon the functioning of the individual. Supervisors need to recognize the legitimacy of these age-related tasks and issues and investigate how supervisory programs can respond to and provide for teachers' continuing needs to confront off-time events; rework life-cycle issues of identity, intimacy, generativity, and integrity; negotiate life-structure transitions; and balance continual periods of transition and stability.

A variety of researchers in teacher education have used age-related life-cycle literature to better understand phases of a teacher's career. Krupp (1987) summarizes the general characteristics, key concerns, and implications for staff development planning for seven phases of teachers' lives from the early twenties to retirement. Her scheme most closely relates to Levinson's age-related phases of adult development. Krupp concentrates on helping supervisors to understand and motivate teachers in the second half of life.

Huberman's (1993) life-cycle research with Swiss teachers with 5 to 40 years of teaching experience uses the methodology of collaborative autobiography to analyze teachers' career paths, attitudes and perceptual changes. The data are treated qualitatively and statistically. His work raises issues about the empirically disjointed nature of teachers' development, which can result in either rigid or flexible endpoints.

Vonk and Schras (1987) focus on professional development during the first four years of teaching in the Netherlands and Burden (1990) summarizes a number of life-cycle studies of beginning teachers and experienced teachers, mostly from the United States. Recent research on beginning teachers has yielded a wealth of recommendations on effective ways to supervise and mentor beginning teachers and train experienced teachers as mentors. See, for example, an outstanding summary of research and mentor in-service training strategies and materials in Newton et al (1994); this training guide bridges the life-span perspectives on teacher development with the organismic cognitive–developmental perspectives of ego/self, moral/ethical, and cognitive/intellectual development of teachers.

While cognitive–developmental theory (the organismic perspective) has charted the relationship between selected aspects of development and behavior, the life-span career development model has focused on ages and phases of occupational progression. In general, the theory and limited research on teacher career development reports some changes in career experiences and knowledge, as well as changes in a teacher's attitudes toward teaching, commitment to teaching, and career satisfaction. Career events such as preparation, entry into, and retirement from teaching are central aspects of the theories on career cycles (Fessler & Christensen, 1992; Huberman, 1993). Although the preservice and induction levels of a teacher's career have received more careful investigation during the 1980s (Houston, 1990), in general, research on teacher career cycles is absent. Most of the theory is based on two studies, one by Fessler and Christensen (1992) and the other by Huberman (1993). Both studies, with samples of 160 teachers, found general support for their theories. As more is learned about phases within the career cycle, one may be able to better predict the kinds of supervision that are needed. The growing understanding of the induction phase for teachers has certainly bolstered public policy and hastened the development of better support programs for beginning teachers. Still needed in the stage and structure models of teacher development, however, is greater synthesis of the career cycle literature with the cognitive-developmental research.

Information Processing and Expertise Models in Teacher Development

In the information processing and expertise model of development, either child or adult cognitions are conceptualized as representing a linear continuum from the less complex to greater amounts of cognitive complexity and fluency. Such a model does not connote a stage and structure framework where development moves through an invariant sequence of cognitive transformations as the person is constructing meaning from experience. Instead, the model focuses more attention on specific cognitive processes, such as how an individual inputs, stores, and retrieves information. In a manner similar to computer modeling and artificial intelligence, cognitions are charted along a series of dimensions such as short-term and long-term memory according to "chunking", cue association, and mnemonics (Anderson, 1990). For example, the research on teacher expertise has focused on comparing experts and novices at a specific moment in time. How does the expert or novice teacher "chunk" pedagogical skills during a particular lesson? The research has not, however, addressed the developmental process by which the experts have constructed their complex knowledge base (Pintrich, 1990).

In addition to showing how persons input, store, and retrieve information, the information-processing model proposes some type of metacognitive or self-regulatory function. Although metacognition has come to have a variety of meanings, it most often refers to two aspects of cognition: the awareness of and knowledge about cognition, and the control and regulation of cognition (Flavell, 1979; Peterson, 1988). Self-regulation, monitoring, and volition are essential to metacognition (Bandura, 1986; Weinstein & Mayer, 1986). Self-regulation activities involve changing behavior to better match a particular task, based on practice with feedback. Monitoring activities include tracking during performance of a task, and volition entails initiating and controlling emotions and environmental distractions. Thus, metacognition requires attention, volition, and online changes of cognition as learning tasks are undertaken. For example, a teacher mentor might demonstrate metacognition when preparing supervision and assistance plans for a beginning teacher, monitoring or "reading" colleague behavior, and self regulating (or "flexing") supervisory assistance as a function of feedback from the novice teacher.

The metacognitive view also suggests that structure (e.g., lesson plans, supervisory and coaching plans, and demonstration lessons) can serve as external and vital supports or scaffolds to guide learning. Clark and Peterson (1986) have shown how lesson plans serve as a needed support for novice teachers, while experienced teachers do not need this external support. It is interesting to note that David Hunt's work (Miller, 1981), which is reviewed earlier in the stage and structure model of teacher development, also discussed the importance of differentiated structure according to the developmental needs of the adult learner. He also described the need for teacher educators and supervisors to "read and flex" support and assistance based on the needs of the adult learner.

Although, by far, most of the work in the information-processing and expertise model has focused on the process of student learning (Pintrich, Marx, & Boyle, 1993), it can be applied to adults in general and specifically to the development of cognitions in adult teachers. The goal of the model is to outline a system of cognitive learning which will lead to conceptual mastery. Prior research has shown quite clearly that teachers, like adults in general, either distort or ignore information which is in conflict with their current preferred cognitions. The classic research by Nisbett and Ross (1980) provided multiple examples of such failures in syllogistic reasoning and inadequacy of adult judgment in general. The need for improving cognitive processing is clearly compelling.

Thus far, the major effort in this area has focused on cognitive information processing and teacher planning (Clark & Yinger, 1987). The approach, which derives from the teacher as decision maker, has charted the actual planning systems employed by teachers with different amounts of experience. Additionally, there are recorded differences between the novice teacher planner and expert teacher planner in metacognition (Royer, Cisero, & Carlo, 1993). Also, an earlier review did show some specific differences in domain knowledge, organization of information, and tacit knowledge (Carter, 1990).

The current state-of-the-art efforts with this model are both promising and problematic. The promise is that the framework will decipher how teachers learn and reach higher levels of complexity as decision makers. On the other hand, the assessment problems in this area are substantial. In a massive review, Royer, Cisero, and Carlo (1993) focused only on the instructional question: How reliable and valid are the measures employed to assess the acquisition of cognitive change? In supervision for teacher development terms, can the measurement of improved cognitve planning and other aspects of metacognitions be considered adequate basis for intervention and assistance programs? The answer appears to be a strong negative. Royer, Cisero, and Carlo (1993) wrote, "In all of the research that we read, there was not a single report of a reliability index for an assessment procedure, and indices of validity were available only as inferences of the form" (p. 235). As a result, their conclusion was that significant research on so-called authentic assessment is a necessary prior step to any procedures designed to promote the acquisition of metacognitive skills in either students or adults. The theory certainly has many potential benefits as a causal explanation of the critical link between teacher cognition and effective classroom performance, but this framework remains to be validated before supervisory and assistance programs can emerge.

Affect and Beliefs in Teacher Development

Affect and beliefs are important aspects of teacher development because they address individuals' feelings, goals, and concerns as maturing adults; however, the cognitive models of development tend to ignore affect. An exception is Loevinger's stage and structure framework for self-development, reviewed earlier, which is perhaps one of the most extensively researched theories of the developing self. The thoughts (beliefs) and feelings about self, others, and environment are assumed to guide what persons choose to do and how persistent they are once they have made their choice.

Although the number of motivational models is literally bursting at the seams, the authors will review two conceptions of motivation that have direct bearing on development. One conception of motivation relates to a person's expectation to be successful. In a classic body of research by White (1959), research uncovered empirical support for the concept of intrinsic motivation, called competence motivation. White found that all persons have an intrinsic need to be competent and that competence grows through stages when there is positive interaction in a positive environment. deCharms (1968) and more recently, Deci (1975, 1980), and Deci and Ryan (1985) began to explore how persons form beliefs about self-determination. deCharms used the terms *origins* and *pawns* to describe students who believed they were able to control their actions versus students who believed others controlled their behavior. The overriding message of their research is that persons who have a belief that they can self-determine positive outcomes (internal locus of control) experience higher achievement and higher self-esteem. Conversely, those persons that do not believe they self-determine positive outcomes (external locus of control) experience less achievement and lower self-esteem. This is sometimes referred to as *learned helplessness* (Kuhl, 1987). It should be pointed out that this relationship is not linear. Pintrich (1990) finds a curvilinear relationship between age, locus of control, and achievement. The strongest relationship exists for adolescents.

A related field of study examines the relationship between expectancy beliefs and performance (Weiner, 1979, 1985). Attributional theory submits that persons' attributions of success or failure mediate future expectations. Weiner's studies show that individuals who attribute success to internal causes like personal skill tend to expect to succeed in the future. When the person encounters failure, he or she attributes the failure to external and unstable events.

Affective components include persons' emotional and cognitive reactions to the task or innovation. A number of researchers have examined affect, self-worth, and self-actualization (e.g., Covington, 1984; Kleibur & Maehr, 1985; Maslow, 1970; McKeachie, 1984; Weiner, 1986; Wlodkowski, 1988). In general, these scientists have addressed the basic question: How does the task make you feel?

Related research on teacher concerns was inaugurated by Frances Fuller in the late sixties. Working with undergraduate teacher education majors, Fuller initiated a series of clinical studies to examine student teachers' motivations and affective concerns toward teaching.

Emerging from the field trials was Fuller's seminal article "Concerns of Teachers: A Developmental Conceptualization" (1969). Fuller proposed that student teacher "concerns" could be categorized and the categories represented a relationship between the amount of teaching and the category of concerns expressed (preteaching phase: no concerns; early-teaching phase: concern with self; midteaching phase: concern with task; and late-teaching phase: concern with students/impact). Fuller proposed a model of "personalized" teacher education. In this model, education curriculum and field experiences would be structured so that they match the current phase of the preservice student.

Fuller's colleagues applied concerns theory to teachers across the career span. In particular, this new line of research explored the concerns of teachers who were engaged in educational innovations. Called the Concerns Based Adoption Model (CBAM), a paper and pencil questionnaire was designed to assess concerns of educators. Early work addressed reliability and validity issues, and only later was the questionnaire applied in cross-sectional and longitudinal studies (Burden, 1990).

More recently, Hall and Rutherford (1990) conducted a review of concerns studies over a twenty-year period. They found the model to be a reliable means of assessing teachers and teacher educators involved in the change process. Nonetheless, a number of methodological problems have not been resolved. As Hall and Rutherford acknowledge, "Most data collections have been one-time occurrences. In only one study is there a control group, and when multiple data assessments of Stages of Concern have been made, the time interval has not been very long" (1990, p. 11). An additional concern about the CBAM is that it may "fake high." The instrument requires respondents to recognize concerns, thus potentially prompting respondents to acknowledge concerns they might not have.

Cognitive Styles in Teacher Development

The cognitive styles tradition in teacher development, encompassing many different learning-style models, has been investigated primarily to improve the immediate and long-term results of instruction. Claxton and Murrell (1987), in their extensive review of the research on fifteen major learning-style models, use a four-part framework to divide the learning-style research into four levels: personality (the core characteristics of one's personality), information-processing (how one takes in and processes information), social interaction (how students tend to interact and behave in a classroom), and instructional preference (learning and classroom environments). They suggest that at the basic personality level, learning-style traits are the most stable and least subject to change. At the other end, the cognitive styles grouped into the classroom environment level are less stable and more amenable to change through intervention.

Among the most widely known learning-style measures in education are the Kolb (1985), Myers-Briggs (Myers & MacCaulley, 1985), and Witkin (1962). The Witkin and Myers-Briggs learning styles are personality-type inventories and purport to describe a person's core personality traits. The Kolb Learning Style Inventory represents an information-processing model, describing how persons tend to take in and process information. Internal and test/retest reliability as well as construct and predictive validity for these three learning-style measures are outlined in Curry's (1990) taxonomy. Curry evaluates the field of learning styles and recommends thirteen learning style measurement systems as the strongest existing learning style conceptualizations, all with underlying constructs that have been supported by correlations with other measures and by acceptable indices of reliability and validity. Curry points out that areas for continuing concern about the operationalization of the wider array of learning-style literature include: 1. confusion in definitions; 2. weakness in reliability and validity of the measurements; and 3. identification of relevant characteristics in learners and instructional settings.

Witkin (1962) proposed a field dependence–independence theory of cognitive style based on the concept of differentiation. Human development progresses in terms of an increasing polarity between the inner self and outer reality. Human infants exist in an undifferentiated state in which no boundaries are experienced between the self and others. However, in the process of differentiation, the individual begins to perceive him- or herself as separate from others and to experience a clear definition of what is identified as belonging to the self. The process of differentiation is developmental; the goal is to develop a completely autonomous self. Over 2,000 research studies have been conducted between 1962 and 1981 using Witkin's Field Dependence/Independence model (Cantwell, 1986). The research studies compare field dependence/independence to attributes such as occupational choice, intelligence, personality characteristics, and learning.

Learners who show greater field dependence tend to process information more globally. They are more sensitive to contextual and social information in the learning situation and tend to possess greater interpersonal skills and social skills. Field-dependent learners are particularly responsive to external reinforcement, both social and material (Rollack, 1992). Field dependents have an interpersonal orientation, seek closeness to others, pay selective attention to social cues, are social and interested in people, and are effective in interpersonal situations (Cantwell, 1986).

The field-independent learner is less affected by external influences. This learner has an ability to develop strategies for organizing and restructuring information and tends to take a more analytic approach to learning. Results of studies that have considered the relationship between academic achievement and field dependence/independence indicate that field-independent students consistently perform better than field-dependent students in virtually every curriculum area studied (Davis, 1991).

The above characteristics distinguish the style attributes of field dependence/independence. They may be visualized as dimensions on a continuum rather than discreet categories. Cantwell (1986) reports that the Group Embedded Figures Test (GEFT) is a powerful tool for assessing cognitive style, and the results of studies of the psychometric aspects of the GEFT support the quality of the instrument. The test has been used in a broad spectrum of studies and is inexpensive, quick to administer, and a valid and reliable instrument (Panek, Funk, & Nelson, 1980). The GEFT consists of 18 various geometric figures, each of which contains an embedded figure that the subject must locate. Raw scores are assigned to quartiles. A higher quartile signifies a greater level of field independence. The quartile norms are: primary field dependent, secondary field dependent, secondary field independent, and primary field independent. Field dependence/independence concepts represent not a state of being, but a way of perceiving. Further, Witkin (1962) states that these attributes are pervasive across the personal domains of body concept, psychological defenses, and perceptual and cognitive functioning. Finally, style shows a constancy over time.

Witkin, Goodenough, and Kamp (1967) reported a trend toward increasing field independence up to adulthood. However, there tends to be a tendency toward a return to more field dependent preferences after age 17 especially among females. Hammer, Hoffer, and Williams's (1995) research lends support to the proposal that girls are less field-dependent when young, and at a certain point females make a shift to more field dependence. When researchers examine sex differences in field dependence/independence, they find that females, college-aged and beyond, exhibit more field dependence than males (Forns-Santacana, 1992; Fritz, 1992; Hammer, Hoffer, & Williams, 1995; Rollack, 1992). Feminists find difficulty with the perceived greater value placed on field independence as the top end of the continuum. Haaken (1988) argues that a different way to look at this cognitive style difference would be to shift the value dimension and state that field dependence (women's ways) is really more valuable. She states that field dependence suggests a pattern that connects the inner world with outer reality and gives value to the context of the experience.

The Myers-Briggs Type Indicator (MBTI) (Myers & McCaulley, 1985) is a cognitive-style instrument that is based on Jungian theory. According to Jung (1923), people perceive the world in two distinct ways (i.e., sensing or intuition), and people use two distinct ways to reach decisions (i.e., thinking or feeling). In addition to the mental functions are people's preference for extroversion or introversion and people's attitude toward life, which is either judging or perceptive. Thus, in a work situation, for example, people can be categorized as sensing types or intuitive types, thinking types or feeling types, extroverts or introverts, and judging types or perceptive types. The MBTI uses these categories to develop four different scales or dimensions: sensing versus intuition (S–N), thinking versus feeling (T–F), extroversion versus introversion (E–I), and judging versus perception (J–P).

Extensive research has provided only indirect evidence of differences in learning style by MBTI type (e.g., see Gordon, 1984; Lawrence, 1984; among a wealth of others). For example, sensing-feeling type learners may be characterized as sympathetic, friendly, interpersonal, and prefer learning activities like group projects, show and tell, team games, directed art activities, and personal sharing. Sensing-thinking type learners are realistic, practical, and pragmatic, and their preferred learning activities include workbooks, drill and repetition, demonstrations, dioramas, and competitions. Intuitive-thinking type learners are logical, intellectual, and knowledge oriented, and they prefer independent study, essays, logic problems, and debates. Intuitive-feeling type learners are curious, insightful, and imaginative; they prefer creative art activities, imagining, boundary-breaking, dramatics, and open-ended discussion.

Studies of types of students compared to types of teachers have found striking mismatches. For example, data from the Center for Application of Psychological Types at the University of Florida at Gainesville indicate that many school districts in California show a rather consistent distribution of teacher and administrator types as follows: 56% sensing–judging types; 36% intuitive–feeling types; 6% intuitive–thinking types; and only 2% sensing–perception types. And the profile for the corresponding California school children is quite different: 38% of the students are sensing–judging types; 12% intuitive–feeling types; 12% intuitive-thinking types; and a significant 38% of the children are sensing–perceptive types. Belonging to so massive a majority, however, the SJ educators unconsciously assume their views to be the norm and are continuously surprised when colleagues take issue with them. The goal of understanding the types is to promote dialogue among teachers about the effect of such mismatches and the implications for curriculum design.

Research using the MBTI has been useful when the focus is on the teacher (Claxton & Murrell, 1987). These kinds of questions and the ways in which they are asked usually reflect the teacher's own preference for sensing or intuition. Sensing types ask questions that seek facts and details; they want responses that are predictable. Intuitive types ask questions that call for synthesis and evaluation and usually invite imagining and hypothesizing. The MBTI has a high face validity. Upon taking the MBTI, people say that it describes their personality well. Teachers who understand the types can generally develop ways to orient their courses more toward their students. Using the MBTI can foster dialogues between supervior and supervisee about how they teach or learn. Also, teachers can become more sensitive to consequences of match and mismatch with their students.

Much research on the construct, validity indices, and relationship to other measures continues to be generated using the MBTI. One interesting study by Redford, McPherson, Frankiewicz, and Gaa (1995) reported that of the four personality dimensions of the MBTI, the sensing–intuition dimension was the only one to have a positive relation to subjects' level of moral reasoning as measured by the Defining Issues Test. In a study of intentions in handling conflict, Percival, Smitheram, and Kelly (1992) report that extrovert–thinking–judging types preferred competing; extrovert–feeling–judging types preferred collaborating; extrovert–thinking–perceiving types preferred accommodating; and all introverted types preferred avoiding, except the introvert–thinking–perceiving types who preferred compromising. In a study of burnout in occupational health nurses, emotional demands and a lack of caring for others were associated with the measure of burnout only for MBTI feeling types, whereas mental demands and lower ambitiousness were associated with the measure of burnout only for MBTI thinking types (Garden, 1989). In a study of reading teachers using both the MBTI and the Kolb learning style measurements, Stice, Bertrand, Leuder, and Dunn (1989) found that whole language and skills teachers tended to be MBTI feeling types rather than thinking types. Phonics teachers tended to be judging types, while whole language teachers tended to be perceiving types. Skills teachers tended to be concrete-experience learners, while whole language teachers tended to be active-experimentation learners.

Kolb's (1984) Learning Style Inventory deals with style as well as concepts of learning and individual development. It is a well–established model that has been used as a basis for selecting and sequencing learning activities. This cognitive style model is based in Dewey's focus on experience-based learning, Lewin's focus on active learning, and Piaget's focus on intelligence as the result of the interaction of the person and the environment. The model describes how people generate concepts, rules, and principles to guide their behavior in new situations based on experience, and how they modi-

fy these concepts in order to improve their effectiveness. Thus, the process of learning as defined by Kolb is both active and passsive, concrete and abstract.

The Kolb model is a four-mode repeating cycle in which *concrete experience* stimulates *reflection and observation,* leading to the *formation of abstract concepts* and generalizations, which leads to the testing of these concepts by *active experimentation* in new situations. Ultimately, this leads one to modify one's concepts, to create new experiences, and to begin the cycle again. The Learning Style Inventory (Kolb, 1985) measures one's strengths and weaknesses as a learner in the four modes of the learning process. No individual mode of the four is better or worse than another. Even a totally balanced profile is not necessarily best. The key to effective learning, says Kolb, is being skillful in each mode when it is appropriate to the learning activity. A high score on one mode may mean a tendency to overemphasize that aspect of the learning process at the expense of others. A low score on a mode may indicate a tendency to avoid that aspect of the learning process. The four modes are described next. (See Kolb (1981) and Royatzis and Kolb (1991) for further discussion).

A high score on concrete experience (CE) represents a receptive, experience-based approach to learning that relies heavily on feeling-based judgments. High-CE individuals tend to be empathetic and "people-oriented." They generally find theoretical approaches to be unhelpful and prefer to treat each situation as a unique case. They learn best from specific examples in which they can become involved. A high score on abstract conceptualization (AC) indicates an analytical, conceptual approach to learning that relies heavily on logical thinking and rational evaluation. High-AC individuals tend to be oriented more toward things and symbols and less toward other people. They learn best in authority-directed, impersonal learning situations that emphasize theory and systematic analysis. They are often frustrated and benefit little from unstructured discovery learning approaches, such as exercises or simulations. A high score on active experimentation (AE) indicates an active, doing orientation to learning that relies heavily on experimentation. High-AE individuals learn best when they can engage in such things as projects, homework, or small group discussions. They dislike passive learning situations such as lectures. These individuals tend to be extroverts. A high score on reflective observation (RO) indicates a tentative, impartial, and reflective approach to learning. High-RO individuals rely heavily on careful observation in making judgments and prefer learning situations such as lectures that allow them to take the role of impartial objective observers. These individuals tend to be introverts.

A recent examination of the construct validity of the Kolb learning-style instrument scored normatively (on a Likert scale) produced strong support for the four separate learning abilities theorized by Kolb (Geiger, Boyle, & Pinto, 1993).

In most of the learning style models, the implication is that a person has a major cognitive style that can be measured and that the style does not change. The learning for teachers is to recognize their own style and learn how to work with others who have different styles. There is little or no research about how one's preferred style incorporates aspects of other learning styles. Kolb (1985), however, does note that an indication of maturity in one's learning style is the ability to use all four of one's learning modes equally well depending on the needs of the situation.

A related issue in the cognitive-style research is whether optimal results are achieved when persons are systematically matched to curriculum instructional methods according to their learning style or whether, for some purposes, they ought to be carefully mismatched (e.g., exposed to alternative learning styles). When the goal is to provide individuals with the opportunity to become sensitive to and proficient in multiple learning strategies (Shipman & Shipman, 1985), then Snow and Lohman's review (1984) suggests matching one's individual style to instructional format for the initial stages of learning and then moving to systematic mismatches as the student becomes more proficient with the material. We note that this discussion of match and constructive mismatch was previously delineated by Hunt (1974).

APPLICATIONS TO SUPERVISION FOR TEACHER DEVELOPMENT

The previous section analyzed recent research and theory of the four major traditions of teacher development (stage and structure, information processing, beliefs and affect, and cognitive style). There is a possibility of an emerging consensus. For example, the stage and structure paradigm accommodates both quantitative and qualitative research models and links the more common nomothetic data with idiographic data that addresses individual differences. Likewise, recent research on information processing and metacognition has charted teacher planning systems and highlighted the need for differentiated structure and scaffolds for the adult learner. The cognitive-style literature focuses attention on the concept of matching learning strategies to one's cognitive-style for initial support in new learning, and the research on beliefs and affect help explain the affective dissonance experienced during new learning. Further, there have been major new contributions at both the theoretical and empirical levels in the constructivist framework, with implications for teacher supervision and teachers as adult learners.

As was noted, there is a growing body of evidence supporting positive relationships between more complex stages and more adequate use of problem solving strategies, more flexibility in modes of thought and action, and greater understanding and application of democratic principles in resolution of conflict. The theory and research outlined in the previous section are evidence of an increasing focus on practice that derives directly from the basic research. That research demonstrates that: (1) adult learners have the potential to develop to more complex levels and stages, and (2) greater complexity or psychological maturity implies a more adequate performance in complex human interactions. Before discussing selected applications of the developmental traditions to supervision across the career span (e.g., preservice, induction, and in-service teacher education), conditions for effective supervision programs are reviewed. We define supervision holistically as a deliberate set of actions/interventions between educators (e.g., teachers, counselors, students, and administrators) in pairs or groups that promote learning about instruction as well as mutual growth and development.

Conditions for Promoting Growth and Learning: Role-Taking (Action), Social Interaction, and Reflection

The translation of developmental theory to supervisory practice originates in the work of three practical theorists: George Herbert Mead (1934), Lev Vygotsky (1978), and John Dewey (1933, 1963). Mead described the importance of role-taking as a catalyst for growth. Specifically, he maintained that active participation in a complex "real world" activity, as opposed to role playing or simulated experience, offered tremendous potential for development.

Social interaction has its roots in the work of Vygotsky. He stressed the importance of discourse to development. As an example, he might encourage prospective teacher supervisors to meet periodically to discuss their new roles. Such discussion or social networking presents the adult learner with a variety of perspectives and problems to resolve, thus encouraging individuals to develop a number of domains or frameworks for thinking and problem solving. The key to Vygotsky's account of development is his postulation of the zone of proximal development (1978), which is typically described as any person's range of potential for learning and development, where the development is framed by the social environment in which it takes place (Smagorinsky, 1995). Development is heterogeneous (Tulviste, 1991) in that the social construction of meaning in Vygotsky's zone of proximal development (ZPD) occurs simultaneously in several domains. In a Vygotskyan sense, the teacher can perform at a developmentally more advanced level when assistance and coaching are provided than when acting alone. This difference in level of performance or development implies that the adult learner has a range of potential rather than some fixed state of ability, as is purported by some in the cognitive styles developmental tradition.

A final contributor is Dewey (1933, 1963) who, for most of his scholarly life, strove to integrate theory and practice. He was fond of saying that there was nothing quite as theoretical as good practice. Like Mead and Vygotsky, Dewey elaborated on the important interplay between action and reflection or *praxis*. He recognized that there are major differences inherent in the content of experience: working as an attendant at the car wash is not equivalent to tutoring a 6-year-old to read. Education (and supervision) therefore must address the fundamental tasks, predicaments, and performances in teaching, as well as the many forms of dialogue (oral and written) between the participants in supervision. The coach must also know when to "stretch" the colleague's functioning slightly beyond his or her current preferred style of problem solving.

All developmental theorists agree on the final component (stretching), that new cognitive-structural learning begins with a "perturbation" or knowledge disturbance. The idea was perhaps most central to Piaget's final reformulation of equilibration theory (Piaget, 1985). In particular, Piaget tried to describe more specifically how equilibration can lead to essentially new and more complex forms of thought, a process of *reflective abstraction.* Development from one level to the next is motivated by a need to reconcile "perturbations" that may include contradictions to a person's current preferred ways of understanding and solving problems, and *lacunae,* or gaps in knowledge. Many developmentalists have shared with Piaget, Kohlberg, and Loevinger a sustained curiosity in the generativity of intelligence and the progressive increase in rigor observed in intellectual and affective development (Chapman, 1992, p. 46). Knowledge disturbance and its role in equilibration has been a major focus of developmental inquiry. The learner is confronted with problems which the current cognitive structures cannot solve adequately.

Early studies prompted the identification of elements that were necessary for cognitive-structural growth (Sprinthall & Thies-Sprinthall, 1983). A number of studies were conducted over the next 15 years to test the effectiveness of these elements for educational programming. The elements are outlined below.

Role Taking (Not Role Playing) This condition involves selecting a helping experience in a real world context, such as supervision, mentoring, action research, tutoring, peer coaching, or working in a community internship. The role taking (action) precedes and shapes the reflection that grows out of the new experience. The duration of the experience did not need to be substantial. Two to three hours of role taking per week are as potent as 12 hours (Exum, 1980).

Reflection Sequenced readings, journals, and discussions of the role-taking experiences are crucial. Experience by itself is not enough. In fact, experiential learning standing alone can be just as ineffective as listening to lectures. A series of field studies have underscored the important role reflection plays in cognitive-developmental growth (Reiman, 1988; Reiman & Parramore, 1993; Sprinthall, Hall, & Gerler, 1992; Sprinthall & Scott, 1989).

Furthermore, one cannot assume a sophisticated capacity for reflection in the supervisee and supervisor. It has become obvious, first in secondary school programs and later with supervising teachers in training, that reflection requires educating. There is a need for *guided reflection* rather than a spontaneous outpouring of ideas or concrete description of events.

Balance Experience and reflection must be in balance or praxis. Experience by itself is insufficient. Excessive reflection without experience also misses the point. Instead, what are needed are provisions for guided reflection to follow the role-taking activity each week. Too great a time lag between the experience and the reflection halts the growth process.

Continuity There is an old learning truism that spaced learning is superior to massed learning. This truism applies to the complex goal of affecting the cognitive structures in the conceptual, ego, and moral domains. Such a goal requires a continuous interplay between the experience and reflection. A one- or two-week workshop followed by a helping experi-

ence does not promote growth. Instead, at least one semester and preferably two are required for significant structural growth (Mosher & Sullivan, 1976).

Support and Challenge In the instructional phases of the role-taking programs, Thies-Sprinthall (1984) essentially rediscovered Vygotsky's zone of proximal growth (1978). Piaget (1964) had documented the problems of assimilation/accommodation and disequilibration. Since the intervention required the participants to engage in a more complex role with greater responsibility, persons often found themselves in the middle of a "knowledge perturbation."

The response of the instructor/supervisor then becomes crucial. One cannot simply follow the "values clarification" format, i.e., "If the experience is uncomfortable, you can pass." Rather, there is a need to support the participants but not to eliminate the challenge. This may be the most complex and demanding pedagogical requirement of the intervention. Vygotsky's zone, or what Hunt calls the arena for a constructive mismatch, does require substantial "reading" and "flexing" (Hunt, 1976) on the part of the instructor or supervisor. Structural growth does not come cheaply. In fact, significant "personal loss" can be involved in moving to more complex levels of development.

These five elements were originally employed with adolescents. However, a number of studies with preservice and in-service teachers investigated whether the five elements were both necessary and sufficient for cognitive-structural growth as well as professional development. As this shift in research has occurred, a number of refinements were made to the elements. Specifically, the initial role-taking experiences as designed—for example, applying counseling skills— were too diffuse for teachers to apply in their own classrooms. A more focused approach to role-taking and more interplay between the action and reflection were needed (Sprinthall, Reiman, & Thies-Sprinthall, 1993).

Much has been written about the change process (Fullan, 1991; Joyce & Showers, 1995). Research and experience illustrate that institutional and individual change are multidimensional, interacting with the institution as well as a person's varying career levels, developmental stages (or growth states), and affective concerns. Change works or doesn't work on the basis of individual and collective responses to that change (Fullan, 1991, p. 46). Encouraging shared meaning through sustained interactive discourse drives change.

Fuller's work (1969), noted earlier, is a case in point. Her research has helped explain the affective dissonance that accompanies a learner's recognition that one's own current system of problem solving is inadequate. Her phases of personal concern—self–task–impact—represent different levels of affective awareness of the need to improve on one's ability to adopt new and more complex problem-solving strategies. The successful resolution of each phase propels the person forward in the change process.

During each phase, because of the affective dissonance, there is a need for support and what Hans Furth (1981) calls an atmosphere of relaxed reflection. This view of relaxed reflection can be observed in the practice of support groups or mentoring relationships. Those persons who coordinate the support groups must be aware of Fuller's phases of concern, realizing that persons will be at various levels of affective dissonance.

Thus, the current theory for developmental supervision and instruction includes an equal emphasis on the affective and the cognitive. One criticism that is often voiced by philosophers such as Peters (1978) and psychologists such as Lapsley (1991) is that the cognitive developmental framework is devoid of feelings. In fact, affect plays an important role in teacher developmental supervision programs. The dissonance created by new role-taking activities must be addressed for cognitive-structural change to occur.

Applications to Preservice Education

The cognitive-structural model of teacher development and the information processing and metacognitive model have supervisory applications in the preservice teacher education arena. Early work reported by Glassberg and Oja (1981), Glassberg and Sprinthall (1980), and Oja and Sprinthall (1978) produced some promising trends in promoting cognitive-structural growth of teachers and student teachers. The intervention studies showed that cognitive structural growth could be promoted but that more potent formats as well as a greater amount of time were needed.

A crucial new direction was uncovered by Thies-Sprinthall (1980). The study found a clear example of the negative effects of ignoring cognitive-structural stages in the process of student-teaching supervision. In a version of attribute treatment interaction, Thies-Sprinthall found that cooperating teachers functioning at very modest levels of development based on Rest's measure of moral-judgment reasoning (Rest, 1986) and Hunt's measure of conceptual complexity (Hunt, 1971) did, in fact, negatively and inaccurately evaluate their student teachers who functioned at high levels on both measures. The study raised two major issues for supervision: (1) What happens when there is a negative mismatch in a learning experience such as supervision, and (2) could the training of school-based supervisors constitute a role-taking experience that might promote both conceptual and moral development?

Newmann (1993) examined student teachers' ability to represent real life teaching problems. Using Case's (1992) neo-Piagetian cognitive-structural framework, Newman investigated a nonrandom sample of 39 intermediate student teachers. Faculty supervisors also completed rating forms and observations of the student teachers. Results indicated that student teachers grew in complexity of problem representation during the student teaching practicum, an example of complex role taking with reflection. Newman also found that student teachers at more complex levels would coordinate more pupil differences.

Reiman and Parramore (1993) examined the growth potential of additional role-taking experiences with guided reflection. In a nonrandomized study, the experimental group participated in an additional role-taking experience (tutoring) along with intensive guided reflection. Dependent variables included conceptual complexity and moral judgment reasoning. There were no significant differences in conceptual complexity, but students

in the experimental group did show significant gains in moral judgment reasoning. Similarly, Watson (1995) studied the effects of a role-taking curriculum with guided reflection for students participating in their first education foundations and field experience course. The study found significant gains in both conceptual complexity and moral judgment reasoning. These studies, although not definitive, do outline a growing body of research on cognitive-structural interventions in the preservice teacher education arena.

An emerging area of work is being conducted on the use of portfolios and portfolio assessment for student learning and student–teacher reflection. A number of researchers and practitioners (Kieffer & Morrison, 1994; Paulsen, Paulsen, & Meyer, 1991; and Wolf, 1991) have argued that portfolios, as portrayed by multiple sources of evidence collected over time in relevant settings, can promote both learning and development. Wagner and Brock (1996) have linked portfolio assessment to Vygotsky's zone of proximal development. They argue that the social dialogue (Resnick, 1991) between student teachers as they develop portfolios encourages greater learning about the teaching/learning process. In this framework, the supervisor may provide more structure and demonstration as the student teachers begin their new role, but as the student teachers begin to process and learn the strategies needed to manage instruction, supervisor support gradually fades. Thus, the supervision is constantly anticipating and planning supervision and coaching that is slightly ahead of the supervisees' current levels of learning and development.

Another application of portfolios in student teaching is text interpretation. Drawing from the information processing model, this perspective (Wertsch & Bivens, 1992) considers text (e.g. portfolios, journals, and clinical supervision audio and videotapes) as "thinking devices" that the student teacher can engage in dialogue, and, thereby, construct new meanings. For example, the student teacher might predict the outcome of a particular lesson and then debate/discuss the outcome with other student teachers. These practical approaches borrow from the cognitive-structuralist tradition as well as the metacognition literature. To date, however, there is little empirical research on the relationship between student teacher portfolio assessment and performance, cognitive-structural growth, and metacognition.

Applications to Teacher Induction

Teacher induction, according to Huling-Austin (1990), "is best understood in the larger context of teacher education, which is often described as a continuum represented as follows: preservice-induction-in-service. Viewed in this context, it becomes clear that programs to address the induction period need to function both as logical extensions of the preservice program and as entry pieces in a larger career-long professional development program" (p. 535). Induction programs acknowledge that beginning teachers need unique kinds of support and assistance in order to both learn and develop as teachers and to adjust to the difficult challenges faced in the initial years as a classroom teacher.

In a comprehensive review of teacher induction programs and internships, Little (1990) and Huling-Austin (1990) summarized the goals of induction efforts: to improve teaching performance, to increase retention, to promote professional self-efficacy, and to transmit the culture of the school to beginning teachers. Huling-Austin also attempted to summarize the research base supporting the goals just reviewed. Her analysis found evidence that quality induction programs do improve teaching performance, increase retention, promote self-efficacy and professional well being, and transmit the culture. In most cases, however, these conclusions are based on a small number of evaluation studies of state-mandated induction programs that relied on self-report as the primary source of data. An exception is the Teacher Induction Study (Hoffman et al, 1985; Hoffman et al, 1986; Huling-Austin & Murphy, 1987) that traced through qualitative and quantitative measures the implementation of state legislative mandates in induction programs in 26 national sites. Among the most significant findings was the importance of the support teacher. A cluster of studies found the support teacher/mentor to be the most powerful and cost-effective intervention in the induction program. For example, in a study by Huling-Austin, Putman, and Galvez-Hjornevik (1986), beginning teachers reported that having a support teacher was the single most helpful aspect of their induction program. Odell (1987) provides a list of important mentor characteristics, including successful teaching experience, close proximity to the beginning teacher, empathy, openness to learning, and receptiveness to the ideas of the novice colleague.

There is no disagreement that beginning teachers need support, mentors, and teaching assignments that are reasonable. But perhaps the most helpful aspect of Huling-Austin's review of teacher induction literature (1990) is the identification of unresolved issues. For example, it is unclear what is meant by a successful beginning teacher. How should the support teacher and/or supervisor be prepared for the role, and how much release time is necessary for support staff to successfully fulfill their role? To what degree can deliberate induction programs promote new learning, growth and development, and professional attitudes? Are some contexts more facilitative of new teachers' professional growth?

In the information processing and expertise model of the young adult learner, the work of Clark and Peterson (1986) examined how novice teachers need to develop detailed lesson plans because many teaching knowledge structures and skills are inaccessible to them. There is a need for external direction (scaffolds) by the support teacher. Accordingly, the concept of metacognitive control and self-regulation of cognition becomes a psychological rationale for particular kinds of assistance to the novice teacher.

The research of Veenman (1984) and Reiman and Parramore (1994) has dramatized the difficulties experienced by novice teachers. Beginning teachers often have few planning periods and some of the most difficult teaching assignments. The affect and beliefs model of teacher development offers important theoretical support for attention to beginning teachers' emotions. Beginning teachers may learn more readily when they have opportunities to meet with their peers in a setting free of evaluation. Deliberate support group programs might ameliorate beginning teachers' concerns.

Thies-Sprinthall and Gerler (1990), in their theoretical and program review of support groups for beginning teachers,

state, "It can be argued that novices in any high-stress, unfamiliar yet demanding new role may need more than individual supervision by a master teacher. Group support can be an important complement to individualized help" (p. 19). Developmental theorists such as Furth (1981) and Vygotsky (1978) recommended that a supportive atmosphere is necessary if adult learners are to master new and complex thought and action.

Fuller's work (1969) is a specific application of the ideas outlined by Furth and Vygotsky. She demonstrated the positive effects of support groups for student teachers. Studies by Herring (1989) and Paisley (1990) have found positive trends in beginning teachers' movement through Fuller's phases of concern. Also, a study of a large school system's implementation of support groups for over 200 beginning teachers (Reiman et al, 1995) found positive trends in the amelioration of self-concerns and a gradual movement toward task and impact concerns.

Applications to In-service Education

Preparing Teachers as Supervisors A program by Thies-Sprinthall in 1984 framed a crucial new direction for the interventions. She created a method of using a training model from Weil and Joyce (1978) in concert with the development conditions described earlier (e.g., role taking, guide reflection, balance, continuity, and support and challenge). Specific and focused skills of supervision were taught to teachers in a sequence of rationale, demonstration, peer practice, and generalization for each component. The role taking was to become a teacher supervisor (i.e., mentor or clinical teacher). Journals and readings were added for guided reflection. The program was equivalent to a two-semester course in order to assure continuity.

One of the major goals of the curriculum was to prepare the teachers to apply different models of supervision based on the developmental needs of their colleagues (e.g., student teachers, beginning teachers, or experienced colleagues). This was organized around the work of David Hunt, who identified the need to systematically vary the amount of structure depending on needs of the learner. Examples of differentiated needs were concrete or abstract, immediate reinforcement or spread out, numerous advance organizers or few and assignments were focused or extended (see Table 16–1.).

The overall atmosphere in the class meetings encouraged the discussion of *ideas and feelings* in a relaxed mode, using the Vygotsky, Furth, and Freire instructional principles. The results of the researched program firmly established two points. It was almost impossible to provide the necessary structure, reflection, and support for experienced teachers who were at very modest levels of development. Teachers at the less complex levels on the Defining Issues Test of moral judgment and low conceptual level on Hunt's Paragraph Completion Test never could make meaning from the coursework. On the other hand, for the majority of teachers, the results were quite positive. Their gains on both developmental instruments were significant. Instructor observation, audiotapes of instruction, narrative accounts, and interviews cross-validated the empirical results (Thies-Sprinthall, 1986).

TABLE 16–1. Differentiation of structure.

Factors	High Structure	Low Structure
Concepts	Concrete	Abstract
Time span	Short	Long
Time on task	Multiple practice	Single practice
Advance organizers	Multiple use of organizers	Few (if any) organizers
Complexity of learning task	Divided into small steps and recycled	Learning tasks clustered "into wholes"
Theory	Concretely matched with experiential examples	Generalized including action research
Instructor support	Consistent and frequent	Occasional

From the Thies-Sprinthall studies, it was concluded that role taking in the form of supervision skills was a highly appropriate means of promoting the intellectual and moral growth of in-service professionals. Further examination of the reflection component of the experience, however, raised questions about whether a rather generic method of responding each week to journals was as effective as it might be. It was certainly not sufficiently developed to the point where other teacher educators could employ it. Ever since John Dewey (1933), at least, educators have grappled with the problem of how to learn from experience. The current vogue in teacher education and supervision is to focus on developing reflective practitioners (Costa & Garmston, 1986; Korthagen, 1993; Nolan & Huber, 1989; Reiman & Parramore, 1993; Russell & Spafford, 1986; Schon, 1987; Sergiovanni, 1985; Zeichner & Liston, 1987). The difficulty, of course, is the sophisticated and subtle problem of how to extract complex meaning from experience.

Earlier interventions had shown that cognitive-structural complexity determines how deeply the person can both perceive and analyze. This discovery was confirmed by Cummings and Murray (1989) in a study of the relationship between teacher beliefs and developmental stage. Perry's opening chapter (1970), where he describes three college students at three levels of complexity with widely different interpretations of test questions, is yet another case in point. The questions were obviously identical, but the interpretations of meaning depended upon the stage of the college student.

The process of refining journal feedback became the process of starting where the learner is and then gradually mismatching. Mismatching, as it turns out, is not as easy in practice as in theory. If no connection was made with the proximal zone, in the Vygotsky sense, no growth would occur; yet such a zone varies in accordance with variations in the complexity levels of the teacher. A flexible framework was needed to guide reflection that itself could be differentiated. Reiman (1988) created a systematic method of dialoguing in journal responses which allowed the instructor to match and mismatch the writing samples. The method, following Friere, included equal attention to the thoughts and emotional themes presented in journal form. The format is included in Table 16.2. It was first employed with teachers

TABLE 16–2. Summary of categories guiding written reflections.

Interaction	Journal Pattern	Instructor Response
1. Accept feelings	1a. Teacher has difficulty discerning feelings in both self and others	Share own feelings
	1b. Teacher discerns feelings in both self and students	Accept feelings
2. Praises or encouragement	2a. Teacher doubts self when trying new teaching strategies	Offer frequent encouragement
	2b. Teacher has confidence when attempting new instructional strategies	Offer occasional support
3. Acknowledges and clarifies ideas	3a. Teacher perceives knowledge as fixed and employs a single "tried and true" model of teaching	Relate ideas to observed events and clarify how ideas affect students' lives
	3b. Teacher perceives knowledge as a process of successive approximations and employs a diversity of models of teaching	Accept ideas and encourage examination of hidden assumptions of pedagogy
4. Prompts inquiry	4a. Teacher rarely reflects on the teaching/learning process	Ask questions about observed events in teaching/learning
	4b. Teacher consistently reflects on diverse aspects of the teaching/learning process	Ask questions that encourage analysis, evaluation, divergent thinking and synthesis of theory/practice and broader societal issues.
5. Provides information	5a. Teacher disdains theory, prefers concrete thinking, and has difficulty recalling personal teaching events	Offer information in smaller amounts, relate to observed practice, and review regularly
	5b. Teacher employs abstract thinking, shows evidence of originality in adapting innovations to the class and is articulate in analysis of his or her own teaching	Relate information to relevant theory and contrast with competing theories
6. Gives directions	6a. Teacher needs detailed instructions and high structure, is low on self-direction, and follows curriculum as if it were "carved in stone"	Offer detailed instructions but encourage greater self-direction
	6b. Teacher is self-directed and enjoys low structure	Offer few directions
7. When problems exist	7a. Teacher has difficulty accepting responsibility for problems and blames students	Accept feelings and thoughts, use "I" messages and arrange a conference
	7b. Teacher accepts responsibility for actions	Accept feelings and thoughts

preparing to become mentors. The quasi-experimental study showed that without the systematic responses, journal entries remained at the initial levels. Furthermore, the group of teachers who participated in the guided-reflection dialogues showed significantly greater gains in both moral and conceptual complexity. The system, though labor intensive, does show how the learner's level of reflective complexity can be promoted through journal dialoguing. An elaboration of the study is included in Sprinthall, Reiman, and Thies-Sprinthall (1993).

Recent studies by DeAngelis-Peace (1992) and Mann (1992) have applied the same model to a group of in-service school counselors being educated as counselor–mentors and to a group of college students being trained to tutor high school students. The DeAngelis-Peace study found results similar to those of Reiman and Thies-Sprinthall. The counselors developed higher-order cognitions as measured by the Hunt (CL) index and exhibited higher-order supervisory skills in practice (e.g., both structural and behavioral change). Mann similarly found college tutors developing higher-order cognitions as measured by the Perry scale. Within-group analysis of the journals also revealed qualitative differences in how the tutors reflected on their experience. Tutors identified as on the "high road" to development wrote journal entries that included more perspective taking, more personal disclosure of feelings, and more effective diagnosis of pupil learning difficulties and needs. These results are consistent with the work of Anson (1989) who analyzed college student writing for evidence of cognitive-developmental level.

Teacher as Collaborative Inquirer Educators have argued that action research and collaborative inquiry bolster professional development. Action research has been integrated into teacher preparation and teacher supervision activities at some universities (Zeichner & Liston, 1987). Oja and Smulyan (1989) studied collaborative inquiry as a complex new role assumed by teachers. Using a cognitive-developmental framework, they were interested in how sustained participation in an action research project changed teachers' conceptual complexity, empathy, and perspective taking. They employed a multicase study design that analyzed key elements of effective collaborative action research. They used theory in group dynamics and adult development to explain how individual teacher researchers and groups develop.

Their findings suggest that "the type and quality of collaborative action research is dependent upon the developmental stages of the teachers involved" (p. 136). Once again, the overall format included regular opportunities for the participants to meet and discuss *ideas and feelings* in a relaxed mode using the Vygotsky, Furth, and Freire instructional principles. Transcripts of these meetings over the two years of the ARCS project permitted careful observation and analysis of five teachers over the duration of the project. The investigators found that a teacher's cognitive-developmental stage perspective defines a meaning system through which the teacher interprets and acts on issues related to teaching and action research. In particular, at the conformist stage of ego/self development (Loevinger, 1976), they documented a teacher's tendency to conform to external rather than self-evaluated

standards with little appreciation of multiple possibilities in problem-solving situations. At the conscientious ego/self stage, the teacher researcher shifted toward more self-evaluated standards and demonstrated a fuller recognition of individual differences in attitudes. Finally, at the transition between individualistic and autonomous stages of ego development, the teacher– researcher assumed multiple perspectives, utilized a wider variety of coping behaviors in response to school and research team pressures, employed a larger repertoire of group process and change strategies, and was very self-reflective and highly effective in collaborative action research.

Teacher as Instructional Peer Coach Glickman (1990) and Gordon (1990) have encouraged a developmental view of supervision, maintaining that knowledge of how teachers grow and develop must serve as a guiding framework for supervisors. An understanding of how teachers can become more cognitively complex, more empathic, and more flexible in instruction is a necessary prerequisite for supervisory work. Their work broadened understanding of the role of cognitive development in teachers' change process. They have begun to explore, along with associates, possible interventions to assist teachers to move to more complex stages of moral and conceptual development.

Phillips and Glickman (1991) studied the potential of new role taking as well as the other four elements with a group of teachers interested in peer coaching. Over a seven-month period, the teachers were introduced to supervisory strategies which they learned to employ with their colleagues. Once again, there were opportunities for demonstration, practice, and feedback. Additionally, frequent opportunities were provided for reflection on the experience. The goal of the program was to develop supervisory/peer coaching skills and higher-order cognitive complexity. While the sample size was small (22), Phillips and Glickman found their program did raise the teachers' conceptual levels and helped reduce teacher isolation.

Preparing Teachers to Employ the Discourse Method Sergiovanni (1992) has recently emphasized the need to combine the "managerial imperative" with the "moral imperative" in creating a "covenantal relationship" of all participants in a school (p. 104). A comparable idea can be found in Kohlberg's "just community" concept (Kohlberg, 1985; Mosher, 1980; Oser & Althof, 1992; Power, Higgins, & Kohlberg, 1989) and in work with the discourse approach (Oser, 1992, 1994).

A study by Oser (1991) complements some of the findings on role taking that were just reviewed. Working in German schools with 84 (K–12) teachers, Oser implemented two interrelated methods for in-service teacher education. One method involved 30 hours of training in what he termed the Discourse II method. The content and process included dilemma discussions focused on issues of justice, care, and teaching effectiveness. The overall objectives of the training were to promote higher-order moral reasoning and higher-order teaching skills. In order to evaluate these objectives, Oser employed a broad set of outcome measures, questionnaires, interviews, video lessons, student evaluations, and moral judgment indices. Based on these assessments, he found the training to produce a reduced security orientation, less single-handed conflict management, and more interactive teaching methods.

The second method employed the Just Community model. Based on Kohlberg's work in the United States, Oser created a school community of teachers and pupils involving all the elements of the Just Community. Town meetings led by students allowed the communicty to discuss and vote on discipline methods as well as school policy methods. The use of Discourse II strategies. (e.g., teacher–learner dialogues) was incorporated. After two years of study, Oser commented, "The most astonishing effect is not on the side of the students. The teachers developed in a most dramatic way (1991, p. 225). They behaved as Discourse II teachers. As a result, Oser concluded that teachers reached an equilibrium across the three domains of justice, care, and truthfulness.

Rulon (1992) has reported similar outcomes in her staff development work with a Just Community high school. Rulon found that teachers first needed to become comfortable with a version of Oser's Discourse II method. Rulon found that participation in the Just Community town meetings did promote developmental growth among the teachers over the two-year period. A comparison group of teachers showed no change on either qualitative or quantitative assessments.

Role Taking for School-Based Teacher Educators The research base for the elements is continuing to expand and indicates that role taking without reflection does not promote growth. The research results also indicate that experienced school teachers can perform the functions of a new role as supervisor with a high degree of competence, if the preparation program follows the Joyce model and is of sufficient length. Gordon (1990) acknowledges this outcome in his study of 47 teachers. Without a more sustained long-term approach, outcomes are short-changed.

Even more important may be the findings that indicate that experienced teachers can also become school-based teacher educators (i.e., a cadre of "clinical" faculty, Reiman & Thies-Sprinthall, 1977). For example, in a select group of North Carolina public schools, there is now a network of some 40 two-person teams of school-based teacher educators in 12 school systems, who instruct their colleagues in year-long courses in developmental supervision and coaching. The overall network now consists of 1,500 teachers educated in the new role of mentor and school-based teacher educator, with full instructional responsibility. The network was started about 10 years ago with one university faculty member (NC State University) and 12 experienced teachers from one school system. The program can be conceptualized as an operational example of the "triple T" framework, with university faculty as the third T, experienced school-based teacher educators as the second T, and mentor teachers as the first T. The mentors then serve to induct both preservice and beginning teachers in their initial assignments. Such a model of staff development involves a series of interacting components. The new teachers gain from careful mentoring. The mentors improve their own teaching skills, and the school-based teacher educators develop a new set of skills as teacher educators and become models for their colleagues.

The numerous interventions just described employed the five elements and suggest an emerging framework for supervisors, teacher educators, and school-based teacher educators wanting to employ more vigorous and sustained educational interventions.

The elements of the intervention—role taking, guided reflection, balance, continuity, and support and challenge—imply that there is no quick road to teacher growth and development. There needs to be a careful interplay between the new experience and reflection. Although the conditions have been applied most directly to teacher supervision, there are a growing number of studies with counselors, tutors, and health professionals that have supported the claims of the original basic research.

CONCLUSIONS AND DIRECTIONS FOR RESEARCH IN SUPERVISION FOR TEACHER DEVELOPMENT

The question of needed goals for educational supervision usually raises a heated debate. Educators and teacher educators almost never have spoken as a unified voice, and it is to be expected that a diversity of views abound. On the question of overall purpose, the divergence is quite visible.

Policymakers have generally favored supervisory roles that are more evaluative. For example, the teacher performance-based assessment movement utilized supervision as a screening strategy. Its goal was to promote teacher demonstration of fundamental (some would say basic) teaching strategies. At the other extreme is supervision as a humanistic approach: to be fully human and to reach full potential as a teacher requires process, spontaneity, authenticity, and genuineness. Supervision under the first approach is highly structured and based on scoring the effectiveness of the supervisee. It is rare that a feeling of collegiality prevails. At the opposite end, supervision as a humanistic process often is characterized by little structure and an anything-goes philosophy, another possible case of supervision as rampant relativism.

In the last decade, a series of research studies has raised the possibility of a new synthesis for supervision. Instead of an either–or approach to supervision, the goal could be the promotion of both views in the form of psychological maturity. Is teacher leadership not the ability to use the mind and the heart in unison?

The elements of psychological maturity have been explored by educational researchers. On the intellectual side, the elements would include the ability to relate ideas in a flexible and adaptive fashion, to symbolize experience, to think in a field-independent manner, and to reflect critically on experience; however, these intellectual skills are necessary but not sufficient.

Douglas Heath (1977, 1991) has been conducting a longitudinal study of the factors that predict success and happiness in adult life. His work has uncovered a second set of elements that are present in psychologically mature persons. The ability to act allocentrically, to be autonomous, to be humorous, and to have a disciplined commitment to humane democratic values comprises the second set. The challenge, then, for supervision is to promote both intellectual and personal development. Both sides of the human condition require development if persons are to live significant and successful lives.

The work of Sternberg (1986) supports Heath. He notes that professionals have equated cognition and cognitive development almost exclusively with abstract reasoning (e.g., cognitive-structural model), speed of learning (e.g., information-processing model), and problem solving (e.g., stage and structure, information processing, and cognitive style). He posits that wisdom and creativity are additional domains of personal growth. His definition of wisdom includes concepts such as judgment, fairness, interpersonal sensitivity, perceptiveness, and information seeking. Arlin's recent work on wisdom and teaching (1990, 1993) cites a number of cross-sectional and longitudinal studies that have inquired into wisdom as an important domain of personal development.

Regarding creativity, Sternberg identifies imagination, unconventionality, aesthetics, flexibility, and the novel integration of information. A study by Sternberg and Davidson (1985) summarized the apparent lack of creativity in adults. And a careful and systematic study of superior academic achievers at Johns Hopkins University (Janos & Robinson, 1985), classified the Phi Beta Kappa graduates as "stable, stodgy, and unoriginal." The students were very intelligent in conventional terms but lacked creativity.

Supervision for the development of educational leaders for school and community requires that educators attend to the theory and research on psychological maturity, wisdom, and creativity. Intelligence is not enough. Instead, educational leaders need to develop wisdom and creativity. This clearly is a broadening of the goals for supervision.

The recent efforts to explore interprofessional development (Corrigan & Volas, in press) have argued that professional development must begin to span a number of helping professions, including teaching, social services, counseling, and health services. Supervision can play a central role in helping teachers to bridge across these disciplines. Perhaps the intervention approaches described earlier can point the way toward a framework of educational programming that can promote teacher development across a number of partially independent domains, like conceptual complexity, empathy, perspective taking, and creativity, while building the necessary skills to work in complex professional systems. What domains hold promise for future research and program design?

Directions for Research in Supervision for Teacher Development

There is an African proverb that wisely proclaims, "It takes the whole village to teach a child." It may also be a truth that *it takes the whole community to prepare a teacher.* In this final section, the authors explore the future potential of the previous statement by identifying domains of psychological maturity for teacher development across the career span that could guide future research and program initiatives. In particular, an exhaustive longitudinal study by Heath (1991) has shown a number of dimensions that predict success in adult life and that could become a kind of rosetta stone for what we want teachers to become.

Greater Teacher Autonomy and Interdependence A number of supervision studies have looked at teacher autonomy and interdependence. A five-year case study of a single teacher (Kilbourn, 1982) indicated that direct supervision helped the teacher develop greater autonomy and confidence. Likewise, a study by Osterman (1984) compared six middle schools where supervision was actively practiced and schools where supervision was neglected. The self-report study indicated that teachers in schools with little supervision saw themselves as having little influence on school practice. In schools where supervision was practiced regularly, teachers showed greater satisfaction and interdependence (e.g., commitment to working with colleagues and to improving the school).

Thies-Sprinthall (1986) reported findings from a qualitative study of school-based teacher educators that had participated in a rigorous preparation program (two courses, six graduate hours) for their roles as supervisors. The findings, based on interviews, reviews of supervisory audiotapes, participant observation, and journals indicated that the participants in the intervention showed greater autonomy in supervisory skills and more frequently acknowledged the collegial nature of supervision. McIntyre and Killian (1987) similarly reported an investigation of the influence of supervisory training (one course, three graduate hours) on the cooperating teachers and early field-experience students. Questionnaires and interviews were used for data collection. Education for the role of supervisor was found to have a significant effect particularly in the areas of planning, preparation, and the preservice students' performance. Cooperating teachers who participated in the preparation program, were, in most cases, able to autonomously employ the skills introduced to them in the course. Post hoc analysis did indicate, however, that the skills were not adapted by all cooperating teachers. Thus, teacher autonomy and interdependence is a promising domain of development that warrants further study.

Improved Teacher Integration Integration is characterized as relational and organizational skills and developed logical reasoning skills. Studies of supervisors' thoughts, judgments, and behaviors have related closely to the area of teacher integration. Studies include Glickman (1985), Gordon (1989), Grimmett and Housego (1983), Hunt (1987), Pajak and Glickman (1989), Reiman (1988), and Thies-Sprinthall (1980), reviews of supervision studies by Glickman and Bey (1990) and Kagan (1988), and a meta-analysis by Holloway and Wampold (1986). The research has attempted to understand teachers' decision-making processes, supervisors' planning for conferences, how supervisors self-analyze the teaching/learning process, and conceptual complexity. From this collection of studies, the researchers have implied that "supervisors' thought could be a more critical factor in determining success than a particular set of supervisory behaviors or approaches" (Glickman & Bey, 1990, p. 554).

Therefore, future efforts to improve integration and conceptual complexity represent a hopeful direction for supervision. The ability of the supervisor to "read and flex" according to the needs of the colleague, to be sensitive to the colleague's background and interests, and to chart a supervisory course that accommodates to the complex needs of both the supervisor and the colleague shows promise in explaining successful supervision (Glickman & Bey, 1990).

Increased Teacher Stability Stability can be defined as having enduring professional relations, having confidence in oneself, and having persistence in professional goals. A number of supervision studies are instructive. Richardson's participant observation study (1988) highlighted the importance of providing stability for the student teacher. Her study identified the importance of routines. Although cooperating teachers had well-established routines for classroom practice, little or no attempt was made to explain the structure to the student teachers. As a result, the student teachers expressed confusion and frustration, and little stability was reached during the student teaching experience.

Stein (1985) examined the relationship between elementary school teachers' burnout and the discrepancy of teacher and supervisor views of supervisory behavior. Burnout was related to teachers who received few supervisory visits. Parker (1986) studied two groups of 12 first-year teachers. The experimental group received a formal program of supervision and the comparison group received no support. Outcomes of the study were: (1) greater attrition occurred in the comparison group, and (2) a majority of the teachers in the experimental group planned to remain in teaching after five years. Huling-Austin (1990) reviewed a number of studies that compare groups of beginning teachers who received support and supervision with groups that received no assistance. From the evidence available, it appears that some of the programs with more formalized support and supervision programs are retaining more first-year teachers.

Increased Teacher Reflection and Higher-Order Thinking (Symbolizing Experience) Reviews of supervision by Glickman and Bey (1990), Holloway and Wampold (1986), and Kagan (1988) have identified the effects of supervision on increased teacher reflection and higher-order thinking. Holloway and Wampold reviewed and classified 24 studies into two areas: (1) investigations of conceptual-level effect on counseling performance, and (2) the effect of structure in the supervisory or training environment on demonstrated counseling abilities. The findings for the second area showed that high conceptual-level counselors functioned better than low conceptual-level counselors under low structure. Furthermore, as high structure was introduced, there was little improvement in high conceptual-level performance, but low conceptual-level counselors made substantial gains. Findings support matching supervisory style to counselors' cognitive level. Kagan's review of four studies of conceptual level confirmed its importance to supervisory practice. However, greater empirical validation is needed. In particular, she calls for greater examination of how context interacts with conceptual level. Glickman and Bey identify five studies that show how supervision can increase higher-order thinking. An example is the research of Phillips (1989), who studied conceptual thought and levels of higher-order thinking as dependent measures of teachers who participated in peer supervision. Phillips found that supervision can stimulate teachers to higher stages of thinking.

Russell and Spafford (1986) employed a case study approach of one beginning teacher. Their findings showed how a supervisory process can influence teachers' reflection and understanding of the teaching/learning process. Zeichner and Liston (1985) found that high conceptual-level supervisors generated the greatest amount of reflective discourse during supervisory conferences with their student teachers. Reiman and Parramore (1993) found that carefully guided reflection by the supervisor encouraged higher moral judgment reasoning.

Improved Collegiality and Perspective Taking The majority of the studies in this area rely on anecdotal information. There are a few notable exceptions, and these are now reviewed. A study by Thies-Sprinthall (1984) employed an overlapping research design to identify whether teachers being prepared for the role of supervisor grew in empathy and higher-order thinking. Pretest–posttest measures of conceptual level and moral judgment reasoning, interviews of participants, written artifacts, questionnaires, and audiotapes were used. Findings indicated that all participants employed greater levels of empathy in posttests of listening. A study by Oja (1978) studied the effects of weekly supervision. The quasi-experimental study showed significant gains for the experimental group in moral reasoning, conceptual complexity, and empathy levels, all indicators of increased allocentrism. In addition, a growing number of studies have examined the role of indirect supervision through support groups to new professionals. A study by Paisley (1990) and a review by Thies-Sprinthall and Gerler (1990) show that beginning teachers' concerns (Fuller, 1969) can shift more swiftly to students when provisions are made for support groups. More studies are needed, but this is a promising type of new teacher assistance that warrants attention. Finally, Oja, Diller, Corcoran, and Andrew (1992) describe how on-site collaborative supervisory teams in schools are successful ways to supervise beginning teachers toward greater autonomy and greater perspective taking. Oja (1990-1991) describes how school-based collaborative supervisory teams of cooperating teachers working with a university supervisor lead to improved collegiality within the school, between the university and the school, and greater understanding and perspective taking on the part of both school and university teacher educators.

An Emerging Paradigm

The proposed domains for future research raise the possibility of a new synthesis of goals for supervision. Rather than choosing a clinical, humanistic, or diagnostic approach to supervision, the goal would be the promotion of a form of general psychological maturity. On the intellectual side, the elements would include the ability to integrate ideas in logical fashion and to think in a field-independent way. Teachers and supervisors also would be capable of symbolization (i.e., being reflective, imaginative, and able to represent ideas in a variety of forms). These intellectual and creative competencies are necessary but not sufficient. Heath (1991), who has been conducting a longitudinal study for over 30 years, has studied the factors that predict success in adult life. Both integration and symbolization are important. But he has found three other dimensions of psychological maturity that are required. One dimension is other-centeredness. This means that the person can take multiple perspectives and is able to empathically feel and care for others. A second dimension is autonomy. This means that the person possesses the ability to judge independently, to be self-reliant, to form interdependent relationships, and to have the courage to act on democratic principles. A final dimension is stability. This means that knowledge is readily accessible and this person recovers resiliently from the pebbles in the shoe of life. McClelland (1973) similarly suggested that maturity and competence, rather than scholastic aptitude, ought to guide educational programs.

It would be a mistake to assume that the dimensions described by Heath imply an ideal endpoint or final destination, where, in Heath's words, "we can breath a deep sigh,

relax forever, and become blissfully comatose" (Heath, 1991, p.68). Mature persons (and supervisors) realize that life can never be taken for granted and that one is continuously adapting to new events. In many challenging situations, we need to adapt afresh. Naturally, these new experiences spur the possibilities of renewed maturing.

Perhaps the most important point is that maturity can be encouraged. Contrary to the views of Rousseau, supervision could be framed around encouraging the growth in the five dimensions of maturity: autonomy and interdependence, integration, stability, reflection and higher-order thinking, collegiality and perspective taking. The work in teacher development and adult development has supported much of Heath's research regarding these five domains of growth. If we know what adult maturity and development are, then we also should know what supervision ought to be.

REFERENCES

Anderson, J. R. (1990). *The adaptive character of thought.* Hillsdale, NJ: Lawrence Erlbaum Associates.

Anson, C. (1989). Response styles and ways of knowing. In C. Anson (Ed.). *Writing and response* (pp. 332–366). Washington, D.C.: National Council of Teachers of English.

Arlin, P. K. (1986). Problem finding and young adult cognition. In R. Mines & K. Kitchener (Eds.). *Adult cognitive development* (pp. 22–23). New York: Praeger.

Arlin, P. (1990). Wisdom: The art of problem finding. In R. J. Sternberg (Ed.). *Wisdom: Its nature, origins, and development* (pp. 230–243). New York: Cambridge University Press.

Arlin, P. (1993). Wisdom and expertise in teaching: An integration of perspectives. *Learning and Individual Differences, 5*(4), 341–349.

Bandura, A. (1986). *Social foundations of thought and action: A social cognitive theory.* Englewood Cliffs, NJ: Prentice-Hall.

Basseches, M. (1984). *Dialectical thinking and adult development.* Norwood, NJ: Ablex.

Basseches, M. (1986). Dialectical thinking and young adult cognitive development. In R. A. Mines & K. S. Kitchener (Eds.). *Adult cognitive development: Methods and models* (pp. 33–56). New York: Praeger.

Belenky, M. F., Clinchy, B. M., Goldberger, N., & Tarule, J. (1986). *Women's ways of knowing: The development of the self, voice, and mind.* New York: Basic Books.

Burden, P. (1990). Teacher development. In R. Houston (Ed.). *Handbook of research on teacher education* (pp. 311–328). New York: Macmillan.

Cantwell, Z. M. (1986). The group embedded figures test. In D. J. S. Keyser & C. Richard (Ed.). *Test critiques (Vol. 5).* Kansas City, MO: Test Corporation of America.

Carter, K. (1990). Teachers' knowledge and learning to teach. In R. Houston (Ed.). *Handbook of research on teacher education* (pp. 291–310). New York: Macmillan.

Case, R. (1992). *The mind's staircase.* New York: Lawrence Erlbaum Associates.

Chang, F. Y. (1994). School teachers' moral reasoning. In J. Rest & D. Narvaez (Eds.). *Moral development in the professions: Psychology and applied ethics* (Chapter 4). Hillsdale, NJ: Lawrence Earlbaum Associates.

Chapman, M. (1992). Equilibration and the dialectics of organization. In H. Beilin & P. Pufall (Eds.). *Piaget's theory: Prospects and possibilities* (pp. 39–59). Hillsdale, NJ: Lawrence Erlbaum Associates.

Chickering, A. W. & Havighurst, R. J. (1981). The life cycle. In A. W. Chickering and Associates (Eds.). *The modern American college* (pp. 16–50). San Francisco: Jossey-Bass.

Clark, C. M. & Peterson, P. L. (1986). Teachers' thought processes. In M. C. Wittrock (Ed.). *Handbook of research on teaching* (3rd ed.) pp. 255–296. New York: Macmillan.

Clark, C. M. & Yinger, R. K. (1987). Teacher planning. In C. D. Berliner & B. V. Rosenshine (Eds.). *Talks to teachers* (pp. 342–365). New York: Random House.

Claxton, C. S. & Murrell, P. H. (1987). *Learning styles: Implications for improving educational practices* (ASHE-ERIC Higher Education Report No. 4). Washington, D.C.: Association for the Study of Higher Education.

Cook-Greuter, S. (1990). Maps for living: Ego-development theory from symbiosis to conscious universal embeddedness. In M. M. Commons, C. Armon, L. Kohlberg, F. A. Richards, T. A. Grotzer, & J. D. Sinnott (Eds.). *Adult Development* (pp. 79–104). New York: Praeger.

Corrigan, D. & Udas, K. (1996). Creating, collaborative, child- and family-centered education, health, and human services systems. In J. Sikula (Ed.). *The second handbook of research on teacher education* (pp. 893–921). New York: Macmillan.

Costa, A. & Garmston, R. (1986). Student teaching: developing images of a profession. *Action in Teacher Education, 9*(3), 5–11.

Covington, M. (1984). The motive for self worth. In R. Ames & C. Ames (Eds.). *Research on motivation in education: Student motivation* (pp. 77–113). Orlando, FL: Academic Press.

Cummings, A. & Murray, H. (1989). Ego development and its relation to teacher education. *Teaching and Teacher Education, 5*(1), 21–32.

Curry, L. (1990). *Learning styles in secondary schools: A review of instruments and implications for their use.* Madison, WI: National Center on Effective Secondary Schools, School of Education, University of Wisconsin-Madison.

Darling-Hammond, L. & Sclan, E. (1992). Policy and supervision. In C. Glickman (Ed.). *Supervision in transition: Yearbook of the Association for Supervision and Curriculum Development* (pp. 7–29). Alexandria, VA: ASCD.

Davis, J. K. (1991). Educational implications of field dependence–independence. In S. Wapner & J. Demick (Eds.). *Field dependence–independence.* Hillsdale, NJ: Lawrence Erlbaum Associates.

DeAngelis-Peace, S. (1992). A study of school counselor induction: A cognitive developmental mentor supervisor training program. Unpublished doctoral dissertation, North Carolina State University, Raleigh, NC.

deCharms, R. (1968). *Personal causation.* New York: Academic Press.

Deci, E. L. (1975). *Intrinsic motivation.* New York: Plenum.

Deci, E. L. (1980). *The psychology of self-determination.* Lexington, MA: D. C. Heath.

Deci, E. L. & Ryan, R. (1985). *Intrinsic motivation and self-determination in human behavior.* New York: Plenum.

DeLisi, R. & Staudt, J. (1980). Individual differences in college students' performance on formal operations tasks. *Journal of Applied Developmental Psychology, 1,* 108–208.

Dewey, J. (1933). *How we think: A restatement of the relation of reflective thinking to the educative process.* Chicago: Henry Regnery.

Dewey J. (1963). *Experience and education.* New York: Collier.

Erikson, E. H. (1963). *Childhood and society* (2nd ed.). New York: W. W. Norton.

Exum, H. (1980). Ego development: Using curriculum to facilitate growth. *Character Potential, 9,* 121–128.

Fessler, R. & Christensen, J. (1992). *The teacher career cycle: Understanding and guiding the professional development of teachers.* Boston: Allyn and Bacon.

Flavell, J. H. (1979). Metacognitive and cognitive monitoring: A new area of cognitive-developmental inquiry. *American Psychologist, 34,* 906–911.

Flavell, J. H. (1985). *Cognitive development.* Englewood Cliffs, NJ: Prentice-Hall.

Forns-Santacana, M. (1993). Differences in field dependence–independence in cognitive style. *Psychology in the Schools, 30*(2), 76–80.

Fritz, R. L. (1992). *A study of gender differences in cognitive style and cognative volition.* Paper presented at the American Vocational Association Convention, St. Louis, MO (ERIC Document Reproduction Service ED 354379).

Fullan, M. G. (1991). *The new meaning of educational change* (2nd ed.). New York: Teachers College Press.

Fuller, F. (1969). Concerns of teachers: A developmental conceptualization. *American Educational Research Journal, 6*(2), 207–226.

Furth, H. (1981). *Piaget and knowledge.* Chicago: University of Chicago Press.

Garden, A. M. (1989). Burnout: The effect of psychological type on research findings. *Journal of Occupational Psychology, 62*(3), 223–234.

Gardner, H. (1993). *Multiple intelligences: The theory in practice.* New York: Basic Books.

Geiger, M. A., Boyle, E. J., & Pinto, J. K. (1993). An examination of ipsative and normative versions of Kolb's revised Learning Style Inventory. *Educational and Psychological Measurement, 53*(3), 717–726.

Gibbs, J. C. & Widaman, K. F. (1982). *Social intelligence: Measuring the development of sociomoral reflection.* Englewood Cliffs, NJ: Prentice-Hall.

Gielen, V. (1991). Research on moral reasoning. In L. Kuhmerker (Ed.). *The Kohlberg legacy* (pp. 18–38). Birmingham, AL: REP.

Glassberg, S. & Oja, S. N. (1981). A developmental model for enhancing teachers' personal and professional growth. *Journal of Research and Development in Education, 14*(2), 59–70.

Glassberg, S. & Sprinthall, N. (1980). Student teaching: A developmental approach. *Journal of Teacher Education, 31*(2), 31–35.

Glickman, C. (1985). *Supervision of instruction: A developmental approach.* Needham Heights, MA: Allyn and Bacon.

Glickman, C. (1990). *Supervision of instruction: A developmental approach.* Boston: Allyn and Bacon.

Glickman, C. & Bey, T. (1990). Supervision. In R. Houston (Ed.). *Handbook of research on teacher education* (pp. 549–568). New York: Macmillan.

Gordon, L. (1984). *Learning styles as a facet of personality: A review of research involving the MBTI.* Presentation at the annual meeting of the American Educational Research Association, New Orleans.

Gordon, S. (1989). Developmental supervision, supervisor flexibility, and the post-observation conference. Unpublished doctoral dissertation, University of Georgia, Athens, GA.

Gordon, S. (1990). Developmental supervision: An exploratory study of a promising model. *Journal of Curriculum and Supervision, 5*(4), 293–301.

Grimmett, P. P. & Housego, I. E. (1983, May). Interpersonal relationships in the clinical supervision conference. *Canadian Administrator, 22,* 8.

Haaken, J. (1988). Field dependence research: A historical analysis of a psychological construct. *Signs, 13*(2), 311–339.

Hagestad G. O. & Neugarten, B. L. (1985). Age and the life course. In R. H. Binstock & E. Shanas (Eds.). *Handbook of aging and the social sciences* (2nd ed.). pp. 35–61. New York: Van Nostrand Reinhold.

Hall, G. & Rutherford, G. (1990, April). *A preliminary review of research related to stages of concern.* Paper presented at the annual meeting of the American Educational Research Association, Boston, MA.

Hammer, R. E., Hoffer, N., & Williams, K. (1995). Relationships among gender, cognitive style, academic major and performance on the Piaget water level task. *Perceptual and Motor Skills, 80,* 771–778.

Heath, D. (1977). *Maturity and competence.* New York: Gardner.

Heath, D. (1991). *Fulfilling lives: Paths to maturity and success.* San Francisco: Jossey-Bass.

Herring, R. (1989). Psychological maturity and teacher education: A comparison of intervention models for preservice teachers. Unpublished doctoral dissertation. North Carolina State University, Raleigh, NC.

Hirsh, S. & Kummerow, J. (1989). *Life types.* New York: Warner.

Hoffman, J., Edwards, S., O'Neal, S., Barnes, S., & Paulissen, M. (1986). A study of state-mandated beginning teacher programs. *Journal of Teacher Education, 37*(1), 16–21.

Hoffman, J., Griffin, G., Edwards, S., Paulissen, M., O'Neal, S., & Barnes, S. (1985). *Teacher induction study: Final report of a descriptive study* (Report No. 9063). Austin, TX: University of Texas at Austin, R & D Center for Teacher Education.

Holloway, E. L. & Wampold, B. E. (1986). Relation between conceptual level and counseling-related tasks: A meta-analysis. *Journal of Counseling Psychology, 33,* 310–319.

Houston, R. (Ed.). (1990). *Handbook of research on teacher education.* New York: Macmillan.

Houtz, J. C., LeBlanc, E., Butera, T., & Arons, M. F. (1994). Personality type, creativity, and classroom teaching style in student teachers. *Journal of Classroom Interaction, 29*(2), 21–26.

Huberman, M. (1993). *The lives of teachers.* New York: Teachers College Press.

Huling-Austin, L. (1990). Teacher induction programs and internships. In R. Houston (Ed.). *Handbook of research on teacher education* (pp. 535–548). New York: Macmillan.

Huling-Austin, L. & Murphy, S. C. (1987). *Assessing the impact of teacher induction programs: Implications for program development.* Paper presented at the annual meeting of the American Educational Research Association, Washington, D.C. (ERIC Document Reproduction Service No. ED 283 779).

Huling-Austin, L., Putman, S., & Galvez-Hjornevik, C. (1986). *Model teacher induction project study findings* (Report No. 7212). Austin, TX: University of Texas at Austin, R & D Center for Teacher Education.

Hunt, D. (1971). *Matching models in education: The coordination of teaching methods with student characteristics.* Toronto: Ontario Institute for Studies in Education.

Hunt, D. E. (1974). *Matching models in education.* Toronto, Canada: Ontario Institute for Studies in Education.

Hunt, D. E. (1976). Teachers' adaptation: Reading and flexing to students. *Journal of Teacher Education, 27,* 268–275.

Hunt, D. E. (1981). Teachers' adaptation: Reading and flexing to students. In B. Joyce, C. Brown, & L. Peck (Eds.). *Flexibility in teaching* (pp. 59–71). New York: Longman.

Hunt, D. E. (1987). *Beginning with ourselves: In practice, theory, and human affairs.* Cambridge, MA: Brookline Books.

Janos, P. & Robinson, N. (1985). Psychosocial development of intellectually gifted children. In F. D. Horowitz & M. D. O'Briend (Eds.). *The gifted and talented: Developmental perspectives* (pp. 149–196). Washington, D.C.: American Psychological Association.

Jersild, A. (1955). *When teachers face themselves.* New York: Teachers College Press.

Joyce, B. & Showers, B. (1995). *Student achievement through staff development.* New York: Longman.

Jung, C. G. (1923). *Psychological types.* London: Rutledge & Paul Kegan.

Kagan, D. (1988). Research on the supervision of counselors and teachers-in-training: Linking two bodies of literature. *Review of Educational Research, 58*(1), 1–24.

Katz, L. & Raths, J. (1985). A framework for research on teacher education programs. *Journal of Teacher Education, 36,* 9–15.

Kegan, R. (1982). *The evolving self.* Cambridge, MA: Harvard University Press.

Kieffer, R. & Morrison, L. (1994). Changing portfolio process: One journey toward authentic assessment. *Language Arts, 71*(6), 411–418.

Kilbourn, B. (1982). Linda: A case study in clinical supervision. *Canadian Journal of Education, 7*(3), 1–24.

King, P. & Kitchener, K. (1994). *Developing reflective judgment: Understanding and promoting intellectual growth and critical thinking in adolescents and adults.* San Francisco: Jossey-Bass.

Kleibur, D. A. & Maehr, M. (Eds.). (1985). *Advances in motivation and achievement: Motivation and adulthood.* Greenwich, CT: JAI Press.

Kohlberg, L. (1969). Stage and sequence: The cognitive–developmental approach to socialization. In D. Geslin (Ed.). *Handbook of socialization theory and research* (pp. 347–480). New York: Rand McNally.

Kohlberg, L. (1976). Moral states and moralization. In T. Lickona (Ed.). *Moral development and behavior: Theory, research, and social issues* (pp. 2–15). New York: Holt, Rinehart, & Winston.

Kohlberg, L. (1984). Essays on moral development (Vol. 2). *The psychology of moral development: The nature and validity of moral stages.* San Francisco: Harper & Row.

Kohlberg, L. (1985). The just community approach to moral education in theory and practice. In M. W. Berkowitz & F. Oser (Eds.). *Moral education: Theory and application* (pp. 27–87). Hillsdale, NJ: Lawrence Erlbaum Associates.

Kolb, D. A. (1981). Experimental learning theory and the learning style inventory: A reply to Friedman and Stumpf. *Academy of Managment Review, 6*(2), 289–296.

Kolb, D. A. (1984). *Experiential learning: Experience as the source of learning and development.* Englewood Cliffs, NJ: Prentice-Hall.

Kolb, D. A. (1985). *Learning style inventory and technical manual.* Boston: McBer and Company.

Korthagen, F. (1993). Two modes of reflection. *Teaching and Teacher Education, 9*(3), 317–326.

Krupp, J. A. (1987). Understanding and motivating personnel in the second half of life. *Journal of Education 169*(1), 20–46.

Kuhl, J. (1987). Feeling versus being helpless: Metacognitive mediation of failure-induced performance deficits. In F. E. Weinert & R. H. Kluwe (Eds.). *Metacognition, motivation, and understanding* (pp. 217–235). Hillsdale, NJ: Lawrence Erlbaum Associates.

Lanier, J. E. & Little, J. W. (1986). Research on teacher education. In M. Wittrock (Ed.). *Handbook of research on teaching* (3rd ed.) pp. 527–569. New York: Macmillan.

Lapsley, D. (1991, November). *Moral psychology in the post-Kohlbergian era.* Paper presented at the Annual Meeting of the Association for Moral Education, Athens, GA.

Lawrence, G. (1984). *Learning style as a facet of personality: A review of research involving the MBTI.* Presentation made at the annual meeting of the American Educational Research Association, New Orleans, LA.

Lee, L. & Snarey, J. (1988). The relationship between ego and moral development. In D. Lapsley & C. Power (Eds.). *Self, ego, and identity* (pp. 151–178). New York: Springer-Verlag.

Lerner, R. (1986). *Concepts and theories of human development.* New York: Random House.

Levinson, D. (1986). A conception of adult development. *American Psychologist, 41*(1), 3–13.

Little, J. (1990). The mentor phenomenon and the social organization of teaching. In B. Cazden (Ed.). *Review of research in education* (Vol. 16, 297–351). Washington, D.C.: American Educational Research Association.

Loevinger, J. (1976). *Ego development.* San Francisco: Jossey-Bass.

Maccallum, J. (1993). Teacher reasoning and moral judgment in the context of student discipline situations. *Journal of Moral Education, 22*(1), 3–18.

Mann, A. (1992). A quantitative and qualitative evaluation of a peer tutor training course: A cognitive-developmental model. Unpublished doctoral dissertation. North Carolina State University, Raleigh, NC.

Maslow, A. (1970). *Motivation and personality.* New York: Harper & Row.

McClelland, D. C. (1973). Testing for competence rather than for "intelligence." *American Psychologist, 28,* 1–14.

McIntyre, J. & Killian, J. (1987). The influence of supervisory training for cooperating teachers on preservice teachers' development during early field experiences. *Journal of Educational Research, 80*(5), 277–282.

McKeachie, W. J. (1984). Does anxiety disrupt information processing or does poor information processing lead to anxiety? *International Review of Applied Psychology, 33,* 187–203.

Mead, G. H. (1934). *Mind, self, and society.* Chicago: University of Chicago Press.

Miller, A. (1981). Conceptual matching models and interactional research in education. *Review of Educational Research, 51*(1), 33–84.

Mosher, R. L. (Ed.). (1980). *Moral education: A first generation of research and development.* New York: Praeger.

Mosher, R. L. & Sullivan, P. (1976). A curriculum in moral education for adolescents. *American Psychologist, 25,* 911–924.

Myers, I. B. & McCaulley, M. H. (1985). *Manual: A guide to the development and use of the Myers-Briggs Type Indicator.* Palo Alto, CA: Consulting Psychologists Press, Inc.

Neugarten, B. L. (1968). *Middle age and aging.* Chicago: University of Chicago Press.

Newmann, L. (1993). The beginnings of expertise: A neo-Piagetian perspective on student teachers' representation of the problem of adapting differences among learners. *Learning and Individual Differences, 5*(4), 351–371.

Newton, A., Bergstrom, K., Brennan, N., Dunne, K., Gilbert, C., Ibarguen, N., Perez-Selles, M., & Thomas, E. (1994). Mentoring: A resource and training guide for educators. Andover, MA: Regional Laboratory for Educational Improvement of the Northeast and Islands.

Nisbett, R. & Ross, L. (1980). *Human inference: Strategies and short-comings of human judgment.* Englewood Cliffs, NJ: Prentice-Hall.

Nolan, J. & Huber, T. (1989). Nurturing the reflective practitioner through instructional supervision: A review of the literature. *Journal of Curriculum and Supervision, 4*(2), 126–145.

Odell, S. (1987). Teacher induction: Rationale and issues. In D. Brooks (Ed.). *Teacher induction: A new beginning* (pp. 69–80). Reston, VA: Association of Teacher Educators.

Oja, S. N. (1978). A cognitive-structural approach to adult conceptual, moral, and ego development through in-service teacher education. Unpublished doctoral dissertation, University of Minnesota, Minneapolis, MN.

Oja, S. N. (1990–1991, Winter). The dynamics of collaboration: A collaborative approach to supervision in a five-year teacher education program. *Action in Teacher Education, 12*(4), 11–20.

Oja, S. N. (1991). Adult development: Insights on staff development. In A. Lieberman & L. Miller (Eds.). *Staff development for education in the 90s* (pp. 37–60). New York: Teachers College Press.

Oja, S. N., Diller, A., Corcoran, E., & Andrew, M. D. (1992). Communities of inquiry, communities of support: The five-year teacher education program of the University of New Hampshire (pp.3–23). In L. Valli (Ed.). *Reflective teacher education: cases and critiques.* New York: SUNY.

Oja, S. N. & Smulyan, L. (1989). *Collaborative action research: A developmental approach.* London: Falmer.

Oja, S. N. & Sprinthall, N. A. (1978). Psychological and moral development of teachers (pp. 117–134). In N. A. Sprinthall & R. L. Mosher (Eds.). *Value development as the aim of education.* Schenectady, NY: Character Research Press.

Oser, F. (1991). Professional morality: A discourse approach. In W. Kurtines & J. Gewirtz (Eds.). *Handbook of moral behavior and development* (Vol. 2) pp. 191–228. Hillsdale, NJ: Lawrence Erlbaum Associates.

Oser, F. (1992). Morality and professional action: A discourse approach for teaching. In F. K. Oser, A. Dick, & J. L. Patry (Eds.). *Effective and responsible teaching: The new synthesis* (pp. 109–125). San Francisco: Jossey-Bass.

Oser, F. (1994). Moral perspectives on teaching. In L. Darling-Hammond (Ed.). *Review of research in education* (pp. 57–128). Washington, D.C.: American Educational Research Association.

Oser, F. & Althof, W. (1992). *Moralische Selbstbestimmung: Modelle der Entwicklung und Erzieklung in Wertebereich: Ein Lehrbuch* (Moral autonomy: Developmental and educational models). Stuttgart: Klett.

Osterman, K. F. (1984). Supervision in public schools: An examination of the relationship between supervisory practices of principals and organizational behavior of teachers (doctoral dissertation, Washington University, 1984). *Dissertation Abstracts International, 46,* 572A.

Paisley, P. (1990). Counselor involvement in promoting the developmental growth of beginning teachers. *Journal of Humanistic Education and Development, 29,* 20–31.

Pajak, E. & Glickman, C. (1989). Informational and controlling language in simulated supervisory conferences. *American Educational Research Journal, 26*(1), 93–106.

Panek, P. E., Funk, L., & Nelson, P. E. (1980). Reliability and validity of the Group Embedded Figures Test across the life span. *Perceptual and Motor Skills, 50,* 171–174.

Parker, L. S. (1986). The efficacy of a teacher induction program in providing assistance and support to first-year teachers. (Doctoral dissertation, University of Wisconsin, 1986). *Dissertation Abstracts International, 47,* 872A.

Paulsen, F. L., Paulsen, P. R., & Meyer, C. A. (1991). What makes a portfolio a portfolio? *Educational Leadership, 48*(5), 60–63.

Percival, T. Q., Smitheram, V., & Kelly, M. (1992). Myers-Briggs type indicator and conflict-handling intention: An interactive approach. *Journal of Psychological Type, 23,* 10–16.

Perry, W. G. (1970). *Forms of intellectual and ethical development.* New York: Holt, Rinehart, & Winston.

Perry, W. G. (1981). Cognitive and ethical growth: The making of meaning. In A. W. Chickering (Ed.). *The modern American college* (pp. 76–116). San Francisco: Jossey-Bass.

Peters, R. (1978). The place of Kohlberg's theory in moral education. *Journal of Moral Education, 7,* 147–157.

Peterson, P. (1988). Teachers' and students' cognitional knowledge for classroom teaching and learning. *Educational Researcher, 17,* 5–14.

Phillips, J. (1989). A case study evaluation of the impact on teachers of the implementation of a peer coaching training program in an elementary school. Unpublished doctoral dissertation, University of Georgia, Athens, GA.

Phillips, M. & Glickman, C. (1991). Peer coaching: Developmental approaches to enhancing teacher thinking. *Journal of Staff Development, 12*(2), 20–25.

Piaget, J. (1964). *Psychology of intelligence.* Totowa, NJ: Littlefield, Adams.

Piaget, J. (1972). Intellectual evolution from adolescence to adulthood. *Human Development, 15,* 1–12.

Piaget, J. (1985). *The equilibration of cognitive structures.* Chicago: University of Chicago Press.

Pintrich, P. R. (1990). Implications of psychological research on student learning and college teaching for teacher education. In R. Houston (Ed.). *Handbook of research on teacher education* (pp. 826–857). New York: Macmillan.

Pintrich, P., Marx, R., & Boyle, R. (1993). Beyond cold conceptual change: The role of motivational beliefs and classroom contextual factors in the process of conceptual change. *Review of Educational Research, 63*(2), 167–199.

Ponemon, L. & Gabhart, D. (1993). *Ethical reasoning in accounting and auditing.* Vancouver, Canada: Canadian General Accountants' Research Foundation.

Power, C., Higgins, A., & Kohlberg, L. (1989). *Lawrence Kohlberg's approach to moral education.* New York: Columbia University Press.

Redford, J., McPherson, R. H., Frankiewicz, R. G., & Gaa, J. (1995). Intuition and moral development. *Journal of Psychology, 129*(1), 91–101.

Reiman, A. J. (1988). An intervention study of long-term mentor training: Relationships between cognitive-developmental theory and reflection. Unpublished doctoral dissertation, North Carolina State University, Raleigh, NC.

Reiman, A. J., Bostick, D., Lassiter, J., & Cooper, J. (1995). Counselor- and teacher-led support groups for beginning teacher: A cognitive-developmental perspective. *Elementary School Guidance and Counseling, 30*(2), 105–117.

Reiman, A. J. & Parramore, B. (1993). Promoting preservice teacher development through extended field experience. In M. O'Hair & S. Odell (Eds.). *Teacher education yearbook I: Diversity and teaching* (pp. 111–121). Fort Worth, TX: Harcourt Brace Jovanovich.

Reiman, A. J. & Parramore, B. (1994). A collaborative investigation of beginning teachers' assignment, expectations, and development. In M. O'Hair & S. Odell (Eds.). *Teacher education yearbook II: Partnerships in teacher education.* Orlando, FL: Harcourt Brace Jovanovich.

Reimen, A. J. & Thies-Sprinthall, L. (1997). *Mentoring and supervision for teacher development.* New York: Addision-Wesley Longman.

Resnick, L. (1991). Shared cognition: Thinking as social practice. In L. B. Resnick, J. M. Levine, & S. D. Teasley (Eds.). *Perspectives on socially shared cognition* (pp. 1–20). Washington, D.C.: American Psychological Association.

Rest, J. (1986). *Moral development: Advances in research and theory.* New York: Praeger.

Rest, J. & Narvaez, D. (1994). *Moral development in the professions: Psychology and applied ethics.* Hillsdale, NJ: Lawrence Erlbaum Associates.

Richards, F. A. & Commons, M. L. (1984). Systematic, metasyrematic, and cross-paradigmatic reasoning: A case for stages of reasoning beyond formal operations. In M. L. Commons, F. A. Richards, & C. Armon (Eds.). *Beyond formal operations: Late adolescent and cognitive development* (pp. 92–140). New York: Praeger.

Richardson, V. (1988). Barriers to the effective supervision of student teaching: A field study. *Journal of Teacher Education, 39*(2), 28–34.

Rollack, D. (1992). Field dependence/independence and learning condition: An exploratory study of style vs. ability. *Perceptual and Motor Skills, 74*(3), 807–819.

Royatzis, R. F. & Kolb, D. A. (1991). Assessing individuality in learning: The Learning Skills Profile. *Educational Psychology, 11*(3–4), 279–295.

Royer, J., Cisero, C., & Carlo, M. (1993). Techniques and procedures for assessing cognitive skills. *Review of Educational Research, 63*(2) 201–243.

Rulon, D. (1992). The just community: A method for staff development. *Journal of Moral Education, 21*(3), 217–224.

Russell, T. L. & Spafford, C. (1986, April). *Teachers as reflective practitioners in peer clinical supervision.* Paper presented at the annual meeting of the American Educational Research Association, San Francisco, CA.

Schon, D. (1987). *Educating the reflective practitioner.* San Francisco: Jossey-Bass.

Self, D. J. & Baldwin, D. C. (1994). Moral reasoning in medicine. In J. Rest & D. Narvaez (Eds.). *Moral development in the professions* (Chapter 8). Hillsdale, NJ: Lawrence Erlbaum Associates.

Selman, R. (1980). *The growth of interpersonal understanding.* New York: Academic Press.

Sergiovanni, T. (1985). Landscapes, mindscapes, and reflective practice in supervision. *Journal of Curriculum and Supervision, 1*(1), 5–17.

Sergiovanni, T. (1992). *Moral leadership.* San Francisco: Jossey-Bass.

Shipman, S. & Shipman, V. C. (1985). Cognitive styles: Some conceptual, methodological, and applied issues. In E. W. Gordon (Ed.). *Review of research in education* (pp. 229–291) Washington, D.C.: American Educational Research Association.

Shulman, L. (1986). Paradigms and research programs in the study of teaching: A contemporary perspective. In M. Wittrock (Ed.). *Handbook of research on teaching* (pp. 3–36). New York: Macmillan.

Smagorinsky, P. (1995). The social construction of data: Methodological problems of investigating learning in the zone of proximal development. *Review of Educational Research, 65*(3), 191–212.

Snarey, J. (1985). Cross-cultural universality of socio-moral development. *Psychological Bulletin, 97*(2), 202–232.

Snow, R. E. & Lohman, D. F. (1984). Towards a theory of cognitive aptitude for learning from instruction. *Journal of Educational Psychology, 76,* 347–376.

Sprinthall, N. A., Hall, J., & Gerler, E. (1992). Peer helping: Counselors and teachers as facilitators. *The Peer Facilitator Quarterly, 9*(4), 11–15.

Sprinthall, N. A., Reiman, A. J., & Thies-Sprinthall, L. (1993). Role taking and reflection: Promoting the conceptual and moral development of teachers. *Learning and Individual Differences, 5*(4), 283–299.

Sprinthall, N. A. & Scott, J. (1989). Promoting psychological development, math achievement, and success attribution of female students through deliberate psychological education. *Journal of Counseling Psychology, 36*(4), 440–446.

Sprinthall, N. A. & Thies-Sprinthall, N. A. (1983). The teacher as an adult learner: A cognitive developmental view. In G. Griffin (Ed.). *Eighty-second yearbook of the National Society for the Study of Education* (pp. 24–31). Chicago: University of Chicago Press.

Stein, R. D. (1985). The relationship between principal supervisory behavior and teacher burnout (doctoral dissertation, University of Illinois, 1985). *Dissertation Abstracts International, 46,* 577A.

Sternberg, R. J. (1986). Intelligence, wisdom, and creativity: Three is better than one. *Educational Psychologist, 21*(3), 175–190.

Sternberg, R. J. & Davidson, J. E. (1985). Cognitive development in the gifted and talented. In F. D. Horowitz & M. D. O'Brien (Eds.). *The gifted and talented: Developmental perspectives* (pp. 37–74). Washington, DC: American Psychological Association.

Stice, C. F., Bertrand, N. P., Leuder, D. C., & Dunn, M. B. (1989). Personality types and theoretical orientation in reading: An exploratory study. *Reading Research and Instruction, 29*(1), 39–51.

Thies-Sprinthall, L. (1980). Supervision: An educative or miseducative process? *Journal of Teacher Education, 31*(4), 17–30.

Thies-Sprinthall, L. (1984). Promoting the developmental growth of supervising teachers: Theory, research programs, and implications. *Journal of Teacher Education, 35*(3), 53–60.

Thies-Sprinthall, L. (1986). A collaborative approach to mentor training: A working model. *Journal of Teacher Education, 37*(6), 13–20.

Thies-Sprinthall, L. & Gerler, E. (1990). Support groups for novice teachers. *Journal of Staff Development, 11*(4), 18–23.

Tulviste, P. (1991). *The cultural-historical development of verbal thinking.* Commack, NY: Nova Science Publishers.

van Manen, M. (1977). Linking ways of knowing with ways of being practical. *Curriculum Inquiry, 6,* 205–228.

Veenman, S. (1984). Perceived problems of beginning teachers. *Review of Educational Research, 54*(2), 143–178.

Veroff, J. & Veroff, J. B. (1980). *Social incentives: A life-span developmental approach.* New York: Academic Press.

Vonk, J. H. C. & Schras, G. A. (1987). From beginning to experienced teacher: A study of the professional development of teachers during their first four years of service. *European Journal of Teacher Education, 10*(1), 95–110.

Vygotsky, L. (1978). *Mind in society.* Cambridge, MA: Harvard University Press.

Wagner, R. L. & Brock, D. (1996). Using portfolios to mediate literacy instruction and assessment. In L. Dixon-Kraus (Ed.). *Vygotsky in the classroom* (pp. 161–174). White Plains, NY: Longman.

Watson, B. (1995). Early field experiences in teacher education: A developmental model. Unpublished dissertation, North Carolina State University, Raleigh, NC.

Weil, M. & Joyce, B. (1978). *Social models of teaching: Expanding your teaching repertoire.* New Jersey: Prentice-Hall.

Weiner, B. (1979). A theory of motivation for some classroom experiences. *Journal of Educational Psychology, 71,* 3–25.

Weiner, B. (1985). An attributional theory of achievement motivation and emotion. *Psychological Review, 92*(4), 548–573.

Weiner, B. (1986). *An attributional theory of motivation and emotion.* New York: Springer-Verlag.

Weinstein, C. & Mayer, R. (1986). The teaching of learning strategies. In M. C. Wittrock (Ed.). *Handbook of research on teaching* (3rd ed.) pp. 315–327. New York: Macmillan.

Wertsch, J. & Bivens, J. (1992). The social origins of individual mental functioning: Alternatives and perspectives. *The Quarterly Newsletter of the Laboratory of Comparative Human Cognition, 14*(2), 35–44.

White, R. W. (1959). Motivation reconsidered: The concept of competence. *Psychological Review, 66*(5), 297–332.

Witkin, H. A. (1962). *Psychological differentiation.* New York: John Wiley, Inc.

Witkin, H. A., Goodenough, D. R., & Kamp, S. A. (1967). Stability of cognitive style from childhood to young adulthood. *Journal of Personality and Social Psychology, 7*(3), 291–300.

Wlodkowski, R. J. (1988). *Enhancing adult motivation to learn.* San Francisco: Jossey-Bass.

Wolf, K. (1991). The school teacher's portfolio: Issues in design, implementation, and evaluation. *Phi Delta Kappan, 73*(2), 129–136.

Zeichner, K. & Liston, D. (1985). Varieties of discourse in supervisory conferences. *Teaching and Teacher Education, 1*(2), 155–174.

Zeichner, K. & Liston, D. (1987). Teaching student teachers to reflect. *Harvard Educational Review, 57*(1), 23–48.

Part

·IV·

SPECIALIZED AREAS OF SUPERVISION

INTRODUCTION

Geneva Gay

UNIVERSITY OF WASHINGTON

The six chapters in Section IV cover a wide range of topics and reveal a number of common traits about supervision among them. These commonalties are evidenced both within and among the categorical areas of research reviewed. The topical areas examined by Cook in Chapter 17 include supervision in the academic subjects offered in schools, such as mathematics, science, social studies, reading, and English language arts. In Chapter 18, Rust, Astuto, Ross, Driscoll, and Blakeney examine supervision in and for arts education, including the fine arts, music, and drama. Supervision in occupational education fields or "education for work" is considered by Iverson and Pullen in Chapter 19. These are commonly referred to as technical-vocational education or the "practical arts," and include the areas of exploratory, traditional, school-to-work, and coop apprenticeship programs in both secondary and postsecondary educational settings. In Chapter 20, Swan focuses on supervision of instructional programs and personnel for children within the 12 areas of disability that constitute special education: intellectual disabilities, specific learning disabilities, visual impairments, emotional and behavioral disorders, hearing impairments, orthopedic impairments, autism, traumatic brain injuries, and developmental delays. The issue of concern to Nolan in Chapter 21 is supervision of specialists who provide student support services outside of regular classrooms. The analyses are limited to only school counselors and psychologists. In Chapter 22, research on supervision of clinical practice in

nonteaching professions is reviewed by Hawthorne and Hoffman. The specific professions included are social work, counseling practices, nursing, and medicine.

Despite the diversity of topics covered by these chapters, they share certain commonalties which provide an important element of cohesion to the section. Two factors account for this. The first is that the authors used a similar paradigm to organize the research review and analysis of their respective topics. It includes six major parts: (1) a historical sketch of the development of the field of interest and supervision functions within it; (2) theoretical models of supervision employed in the fields of study; (3) effective methods of and alternative approaches to supervision; (4) influences within the field of specializations that affect how supervision is performed; (5) roles and responsibilities of supervisors; and (6) research interests, issues, and needs related to supervision. The second factor contributing to the cohesion among these chapters is a set of common themes which emerge from the separate analyses.

The reviews and analyses presented in these chapters reveal a scarcity of well-defined research on supervision in the various fields of specialization. The research that does exist tends to concentrate on defining the personal characteristics, roles and functions, and perceived satisfactions with the practices of supervisors. It relies heavily upon data from survey questionnaires and self-report measures. Systematic evidence generated from empirical and observational studies on the effects of actual supervisory practices is virtually nonexistent. In their chapter, "Supervision in Nonteaching Professions," Hawthorne and Hoffman speak eloquently about this state of affairs. They observe: "When the developmentally oriented models of supervision [in the counseling professions] are examined in terms of their effects on counseling practices, little firm knowledge has been generated that informs supervisory practice. Surveys of supervisors and supervisees are equally interesting but lack the types of evidence that give direction or add to the conduct of supervision." As a result, much of the "research" reported in the chapters in this section are, in fact, summaries of "theoretical literature" which provide explanations of various theories, methods, models, challenges, and needs for discipline-based supervision. Its emphases are substantively more conceptually definitional and prescriptive than empirical, descriptive, and effectual. On this point, Hawthorne and Hoffman explain that "the dominance of positivist and practical . . . perspectives . . . appears to keep the research questions descriptive and utilitarian rather than interpretative and critical." While they are speaking specifically about research on supervision in the counseling professions, similar emphases are revealed in the other professions discussed in this section as well.

Four important findings resulted from research on the roles and responsibilities of supervisors across the various professions. First, supervisors are expected to perform similar leadership and management functions. These include the development of content knowledge and task competence; program planning, administration and development; program and personnel evaluation; research, inquiry, and data analysis; and interpersonal and human relations. Second, regardless of the profession, more supervisory time and effort are devoted in practice to knowledge transmission, planning, and administrative tasks than to any of the other responsibilities. Hawthorne and Hoffman found that in nursing, medicine, and social work, supervision is commonly conceptualized as "administrative oversight, education and information update, development from novice to expert, emotional support, professional induction, clinical teaching, and oversight of treatment of the client/patient." Nolan concludes from his analysis of the counseling professions that "much of what passes for supervision is really administrivia." A third finding across the chapters is the existence of a persistent discrepancy between what supervisors should do and what they actually do in practice. This discrepancy is acknowledged by both supervisors and those whom they supervise, and in most instances there is strong agreement between them about the nature of the divide between theory and practice. Despite a wide variety of functions proposed by theory, in practice supervision tends to be limited to transmitting knowledge about effective approaches and techniques. The underlying assumption is that the acquisition of this knowledge is sufficient to guarantee its application. Fourth, across the various professions examined, little definite knowledge has been generated from research which informs supervisory practice in any systematic and significant way. The most prevailing influences continue to be theoretical and conceptual.

Another important issue for the authors of the chapters in this section, individually and collectively, is the challenge imposed upon supervisory conceptions and practices by the complexity and diversity of efforts in the various fields of specialization. These fields require multitasked and multititled supervisors. One manifestation of these challenges is the question of whether administrators trained in general supervisory principles and techniques are sufficiently prepared to supervise special programs or whether supervisors should be specialists in the fields in which they are expected to provide leadership. For example, are school principals competent to supervise special education, school counseling programs, personnel, and pedagogy? Is one supervisor adequately prepared to supervise art, music, and drama? Is there anything "generic" or "universal" about quality supervision across social work, clinical counseling, medicine, and nursing? Another factor in the supervision specialist versus generalist debate is whether composite or "integrated" fields of study and professional practice, such as special education, the fine arts, the health services, and occupational education are best served by "composite" supervisory approaches, or whether each of the components in these fields should be treated separately.

None of the research reviewed by the authors fully supports the generalist or "composite task performance" supervision point of view. The closest is the position taken by Cook in her chapter, "Supervision in Academic Disciplines," Swan's chapter, "Supervision in Special Education," and Nolan's chapter, "Supervision in Service Areas." They endorse both specialized and generalized training and functions for supervisors. Cook's research reviews led her to conclude:

In subject area supervision, content and skills may vary from discipline to discipline, but supervisory situations, conditions, characteristics, and problems seem to cross all areas of the curriculum. . . . On the one hand, supervisors in one area can learn from those in other areas, and new knowledge in one area can easily be adapted or applied to another. On the other hand . . . [a] mathematician looks at the world in different ways than a poet, and the historian, the artist, and the scientist view the past, present and future in different ways . . . [T]o ignore the uniqueness of each field is to miss its richness and vitality.

Swan's review of research and practices related to supervision in special education indicates that it is increasingly characterized by collaboration among specialists and generalists. This is becoming even more routine as practices of including students with disabilities in general education programs expand. Consequently, Swan suggests that "effective supervision of special education instruction can be provided by a building level leader in collaboration with a special education leader using a general education supervision model . . . within the context of the unique dimensions of special education. " Nolan concludes that it is "preferable to have supervisors of school counselors who possess expertise in both counseling and supervision."

The authors of the other chapters endorse specialized supervision for their professional fields, while simultaneously recognizing that in actual practice it encompasses both universal and particularistic functions. Comments made by Rust and associates in their chapter, "Supervision in the Fine and Performing Arts," are illustrative of this endorsement. They conclude, "In arts education, the assessment of instruction must, of necessity, address the ways of knowing and skilled activity that are central to a given area, hence, a need for arts supervisors who are themselves experienced arts educators." Despite this preference, these authors devote a lot of time to describing the complexity of the work art educators and supervisors do as both generalists and specialists. The standards for counseling supervisors adopted by the American Association of Counseling and Development and discussed by Jackson include a combination of specialized and general competencies and tasks.

Several other salient "messages" emerge from the issues examined, research reviewed, and findings reported in these chapters about the present conditions and future needs of supervision in different professions. One is that supervision, as a visible and definitive task earmarked for performance by professionally educated personnel, is very susceptible to historical developments, changing conceptual orientations of professions, and financial expediency. The first two types of influences are natural expectations as professions grow and develop, and can produce positive results, relative to further clarifying the purposes, roles, and effects of supervisory functions. However, the latter influence is highly constraining, and can have detrimental effects. Recent reductions in the availability of funds and allocation patterns across different educational programs and priorities have either blurred lines of distinction between supervisors and other educational leaders or eliminated supervisory positions entirely. Cases in point are arts education, special education, and occupational education. In their respective chapters, the authors in this section explain these processes in detail. The analyses by Rust and associates demonstrate that, when school funding is low, arts education programs are among the first to be streamlined or totally eliminated. According to Iverson and Pullen and to Swan, the emergence of pedagogical emphases on mainstreaming and "integrated curriculum" and reductions in state funding are causing some school districts to question the need for supervisors in occupational and special education and reassign supervisory tasks to school administrators. Thus, multipurpose, multidisciplined supervisors are becoming a common reality. These individuals are expected to perform so many different tasks that the depth of their discipline-based knowledge and technical skills in any of them is minimal.

Many professional fields do not have any systematic endeavors called supervision per se. This appears to be more apparent the further the field is away from education as a professional endeavor, and especially in K-12 schools. In fact, as the performance sites of where supervisory functions occur become more distant from teaching and the education profession, they assume the character of administration and management rather than supervision in the truest sense. The chapters in this section that deal with academic disciplines, special education, and occupational education report more research on supervision as a wide range of tasks to be performed than those dealing with medicine, nursing, counseling, social work, and the performing arts. Even within the conventional educational arenas, supervision is more evident in areas of specialization which place strong emphasis on the mastery of specific performance skills instead of more generalized competencies. Supervision as a specifically defined function is consequently more identifiable in occupational and special education than the academic disciplines and the arts.

In the nonconventional teaching fields (e.g., medicine, nursing, social work, the counseling professions), supervision is more visible and definitive in some than others. Hawthorne and Hoffman suggest that this pattern is gender-related. They found that "male-dominated professions [such as medicine] do not have what we even broadly construe to be the supervision of professional practice." However, "female-dominated professions [nursing, social work] always have direct supervision of practice." This observation can be extended to various roles in the conventional education profession as well, although none of the authors in this section makes this assertion. The actions of classroom teachers, who are predominately female, are more likely to be subjected to close and systematic supervisory scrutiny than the functions of school administrators, who are predominantly male.

It also appears that supervision is less evident and less significant in professions considered to be more "scientific" or otherwise ascribed "high status." Supervision is more prominent and routinized in public precollegiate educational programs but far less so in private professional endeavors and higher education. It is less prominent in science-related professions like medicine than in applied fields such as teaching and nursing. Hawthorne and Hoffman attribute these patterns to "assumptions of certainty about the knowledge base and procedures developed and refined under the scrutiny of scientific examination." The exceptions to these patterns in the areas of specialization analyzed in this section are special and occupational education in K–12 schools. Supervision in them is more clearly demarcated than in the academic disciplines. This may be a function of federal and state funding of special education and occupational programs, which allows for the employment of supervisory personnel. The regular local funding of math, science, social studies, and language arts programs do not make these kind of provisions.

The analyses presented in these chapters indicate that supervision is inversely related to the professional maturation of members of different professions. It tends to be more overt, prominent, and systematic for younger professionals, and drops off significantly, to the point of being nonexistent, as individuals matriculate from the status of novice to expert. For instance, more actual research is available on supervision of preservice students and new teachers than for in service, experienced teachers. This is also true for the supervision of counselors, social workers, doctors, and nurses-in-training. They receive most of their supervision prior to their full-fledged induction into the profession. This practice seems to suggest that, once professionals have mastered the knowledge and skills of their specializations, they will engage in self-regulatory behaviors by acting ethically and competently in practice; monitoring, assessing, and, when necessary, correcting their own performance; and directing their own self-renewal and future professional development. "Masters" and "experts," it is assumed, do not need any external supervision; they can supervise themselves.

All of the authors in this section agree that more research is needed and should be qualitatively different from what currently exists. Most of the existing data reported come from self-reports, surveys, and anecdotal records, which emphasize personal characteristics that effective supervisors should possess and the roles and responsibilities they are expected to perform. Future studies should include more well-crafted empirical studies, observations of actual supervisory practices, analyses of the outcome effects of different supervisory techniques on the performance of the supervised, and examinations of the full spectrum of supervisory functions in regard to diverse situations, contexts, and clientele. Supervision in all the professions is in dire need of more thorough investigations of and a greater union among research, theory, and practice. Cook offers some challenging and enticing advice, which is a fitting summary of current affairs and a mandate for future directions in supervision across the professions. She contends that for too long supervision research has attempted to reduce complex issues to simplistic dictates to make them more manageable and computable. This is not a fruitful direction to pursue in the future. Instead, researchers should resist the temptation of easy answers, stop avoiding the complexities inherent in the profession, deepen their analyses to achieve results of greater substantive significance, and broaden the parameters of their investigations. These changes in research emphases and methodologies will lead to the development of a comprehensive profile of what constitutes the dynamic essence of supervision as practiced, as opposed to what is only theorized.

·17·

SUPERVISION IN ACADEMIC DISCIPLINES

Gillian E. Cook

UNIVERSITY OF TEXAS AT SAN ANTONIO

INTRODUCTION

Supervision takes place within particular settings and contexts. There is a generally accepted common set of responsibilities and proficiencies that are characteristic of supervision across the academic disciplines (e.g., Pajak, 1989). Textbooks in supervision consistently treat supervision as equally applicable to all subject areas and all grade levels. However, supervisors work with teachers whose focus is upon the content, concepts, knowledge, and skills in and across specific disciplines such as English language arts, mathematics, social studies, and science.

In recent years, there has been a steady movement in the supervision literature toward situation-specific supervision. In 1981, Glickman described three approaches to supervision which are dependent upon the level of abstraction and level of commitment of the teacher. Zimpher and Howey (1987) presented four types of teaching competence and related these to different supervisory approaches. Garman (1986), Sergiovanni (1984), and Smyth (1987) emphasized the importance of teachers' reflective practice and the specialized role of the supervisor in facilitating this teacher-centered and idiosyncratic type of supervision.

There has, however, been virtually no attention paid in recent years to supervision that is designed to address the specific characteristics of separate academic areas. John-Steiner (1985) and Gardner (1983) have identified different ways of thinking or "intelligences" that are found among scientists, musicians, mathematicians, artists, and poets. While there are "habits of mind" (Martinello & Cook, 1994) that cross all disciplines, there are also concepts, "languages," and approaches to inquiry that are specific to each discipline (Gardner & Boix-Mansilla, 1994). In supervision texts and other literature related to supervision, these differences are seldom, if ever, addressed.

Some research in supervision has a discipline orientation, but this is usually restricted to specific content and skills. For example, Columbro (1964) described the components of literature, communication, and linguistics in the English language arts curriculum and suggested that a major role of English supervisors is to help teachers to know these components. Vogt (1991) focussed on characteristics of effective reading instruction in her observation guide for reading supervisors. Shrigley (1980) identified 25 characteristics of science supervisors. Most of the other research related to supervision in the academic areas addresses questions that cross discipline lines. These inquiries are valuable contributions to the field of instructional supervision, but they do not reflect specific ways of thinking in any particular discipline.

This chapter will therefore examine various aspects of research which appear to cross academic boundaries, even though the research itself was conducted within specific disciplines.

METHODOLOGY

To locate research on supervision in the academic areas, searches were conducted in the ERIC files (1966–1994), *Education Index* (1983–1994), and *Dissertation Abstracts International* (1929–1993), focusing on supervision in the areas of English language arts, mathematics, reading, science, and social studies. Current journals in supervision, such as *Educational Leadership* and the *Journal of Curriculum and Supervision,* were also examined for recent research studies in the academic areas. Several studies covered more than one academic area, particularly those which addressed student teaching supervision. While relevant studies on student teaching supervision were included, this area was not a focus of the searches.

The emphasis in this search was upon formal qualitative or quantitative research, including descriptive and empirical studies. Simple descriptions of practice were treated with caution and were selected only if the data were subjected to some form of analysis. Articles that were primarily prescriptive without a supporting research base were not included.

The concept of "supervision" was defined broadly but with a clear focus upon the educational supervisor who is in schools working directly with individuals or groups of teachers to improve teaching and learning. Typical roles included central office supervisors specializing in one or more subject areas, principals (particularly in elementary schools), department chairs in middle or high schools, and subject area specialists within the schools (particularly reading specialists).

The searches yielded 51 relevant research studies in the following areas:

10 general (across several disciplines)
8 English language arts
3 English as a second language (not a primary area of search; these emerged from other searches)
5 mathematics
9 reading
14 science
2 social studies

Approximately 30 additional studies were initially identified, but proved either not to be relevant to the focus of this chapter, or to be prescriptive rather than descriptive. The selected studies were found in dissertations (19), journal articles (20), and ERIC ED documents (12).

Analyses of these studies yielded three major categories, with several subcategories, that form the framework for this chapter:

Supervisory Roles and Responsibilities
    Characteristics of supervisors
    Supervisory responsibilities
    Role expectations and actual responsibilities
Supervisory Methods
    Programs in action
    Aspects of supervision
    Interaction and politics
The Effectiveness of Supervision
    Instructional improvement
    Teacher attitudes
    Supervisory effectiveness

The final sections of the chapter present a summary of findings and recommendations for future directions in research.

SUPERVISORY ROLES AND RESPONSIBILITIES

One of the continuing questions in instructional supervision is: What does the supervisor do? Job descriptions or supervision texts give partial answers, but the reality of the supervisor's world is both complex and changeable. Roles are affected by a broad spectrum of situational factors, including the expectations of administrators, teachers, and the supervisors themselves.

In this section, therefore, there is no definitive answer to the question, but rather an overview of research efforts to explore the complex world of supervisors in terms of what they are like, what they are expected to do, and how this compares with what they actually do.

Characteristics of Supervisors

Surveys reported by Al-Habeeb (1981), Caruso (1991) Cook, Duke, Owen, and Schiff (1983, 1985), Ellis (1977), Hutchinson (1973), Lee (1958), Suhor (1985), and Urquia (1975) examine the personal characteristics and professional backgrounds of supervisors in a variety of fields. Caruso found that most early-childhood supervisors are women, while Al-Habeeb's population of secondary English supervisors in Saudi Arabia were all men.

Caruso's research shows that, while the supervisors in his surveys were predominantly young, their years of experience as supervisors were very similar to the English language arts supervisors surveyed by Cook and her colleagues. Thirty-nine percent of Caruso's sample had less than 4 years of experience; 30% had 4–9 years; and 31% had over 9 years. Cook and her colleagues found an average experience of 6.33 years; 48% had less than 6 years and 81% had less than 10 years. Hutchinson's survey of science supervisors in Florida showed similar results, with a majority having less than 10 years of experience.

Most supervisors have both experience in teaching and training in supervision. Al-Habeeb found that the supervisors in his survey had extensive experience in teaching, as did the principals in Urquia's study of reading supervision and the science supervisors in Lee's survey. Certification is required in many states. Both Caruso and Cook et al found that most of their samples had the appropriate certification, though as many as one-third of the respondents had gained certification after taking a supervisory position. Academic preparation varied across the studies. In science, both Lee and Ellis reported that all their respondents had at least a master's degree, as did 53 of the 54 supervisors in Hutchinson's study. Caruso, however, reviewed a number of studies in early childhood education and found that up to 25% of early-childhood supervisors did not have a bachelor's degree.

Ongoing training reported by supervisors in Cook and her colleagues' sample included graduate studies, workshops and in-service meetings, conference attendance, on-the-job training, and reading professional literature. Caruso recommended that early childhood supervisors pursue graduate studies, or, in some cases, obtain undergraduate degrees, and receive on-the-job training. Urquia bewailed the lack of subject-specific in-service or graduate work in reading among the principals she surveyed, a concern that Hutchinson also raised since he found that only 22% of the science supervisors had undergraduate work in science.

Supervisors do have differing backgrounds, and they also have a wide variety of titles: director, specialist, consultant, coordinator, supervisor, or demonstration teacher (Caruso, 1991; Cook et al, 1983, 1985; Madrazo & Hounshell, 1987). Jackson (1966) discovered that much science supervision in Oklahoma was being carried out by "quasi-supervisors": teachers who performed supervisory duties on a part-time basis. Ellis (1977) reported that approximately half of his respondents had "science" in their title. There was no evidence in the literature as to whether these varied titles affected the supervisor's job expectations. However, the research did indicate a wide variety of responsibilities.

Supervisory Responsibilities

Madrazo and Hounshell (1987) reported that, in a national survey conducted through the National Science Teachers Association's Division of Supervision, the roles of the science supervisor, in order of preference, were:

1. instruction
2. curriculum
3. staff development
4. implementation
5. management
6. assessment
7. assignment, transfer, and load.

Surveys conducted by Beisenberg and Yager (1991, 1992), Hutchinson (1973), Perrine (1984), and Shrigley (1980) in science; Mack (1991) in reading; and Florez-Tighe (1984) in English as a second language support these major categories, though some of the specific descriptors vary from study to study.

"Instruction" may include the determination of district and school goals and objectives, helping teachers to select specific instructional strategies, and the provision of materials and resources. "Curriculum" can be exemplified as the development or selection of curriculum at the district, school, or grade level, and may include making decisions on controversial topics. "Staff development" implies the provision of formal and informal in-service opportunities for teachers, and may involve the development of in-service models as well as the more traditional provision of workshops.

Clinical supervision may be perceived as a form of staff development, or it may be more closely related to "implementation," since it usually involves the supervisor and teacher working on immediate, classroom-based issues. Other types of "implementation" include helping teachers to implement specific programs through advice, demonstration lessons, collaborative problem-solving, support for teacher innovations and ideas, and the direct improvement of student learning.

"Management" is a necessary part of the supervisor's role, and may include professional meetings for teachers, the coordination of federal and other special programs, fundraising, budgets, and gaining visibility and public recognition for the district or school and its programs.

"Assessment" incorporates a wide spectrum of responsibilities from large-scale program evaluation to teacher assessment, recognition, and rewards, and the evaluation and reporting of student progress. A related area of responsibility, which is mentioned less frequently, is that of "assignment, transfer, and load," whether at the district or school level.

These general areas appear in nearly all surveys and descriptions of supervisory responsibilities, though the specific descriptors or tasks may vary; however, although these roles are generally expected of all supervisors, the daily life of the supervisor may not reflect the expectations of the role, particularly in terms of relative importance and the amounts of time given to each responsibility.

Role Expectations and Actual Responsibilities

Six studies addressed the topics of role expectations and actual responsibilities in supervision in academic areas. Lee (1958) and Madrazo and Hounshell (1987) examined different perceptions of the role of the science supervisor among different groups of professionals. Perrine (1984), also focusing on science supervisors, compared perceptions of teachers and supervisors concerning ideal and actual characteristics of the role. Ritz, Cashell, and Felsen (1981; Ritz & Cashell, 1980) looked at science teachers' and supervisors' perceptions of supervisors' effectiveness. Mack (1991), in her study of reading supervisors, examined the perceptions of reading supervisors in Pennsylvania about desired and actual roles. Dillingham (1966) compared the values placed upon supervisory practices by supervisors and by schools. What all six researchers found was that the differences were remarkably small.

Madrazo and Hounshell (1987) asked groups of superintendents, supervisors, principals, secondary teachers, elementary teachers, and college teacher-education professors to rate various aspects of the role of science supervisor as a resource for science teaching, in implementing the science program, in in-service programs, as a leader in science teaching, and as a supervisor. The only significant differences among the groups related to the categories of "in-service," where secondary teachers were more favorable toward the role than were superintendents, and "supervision," where there seemed to be a difference in expectations about the role of the supervisor as evaluative or as supportive.

A similar study was conducted by Lee (1958) to compare values that science supervisors, general supervisors, and a jury of science educators placed upon a range of supervisory practices. He found that the values espoused by the jury were consistently higher than the actual performance reported by the supervisors, due to lack of support and an area too large to serve properly, a problem also identified by Al-Habeeb (1981). Supervisors ranked "methods" highest, as did the jury, but they ranked "research" lowest, while the jury ranked it third in a list of eight areas of responsibility.

Ritz, Cashell, and Felsen (1981; Ritz & Cashell, 1980) used the Science Supervisor Rating Scale (SSRS) to compare the perceptions of science teachers and science supervisors concerning the effectiveness of supervision. They found that the supervisors rated themselves as more effective than the teachers did in the categories of instructional intervention (such as staff development) and in interpersonal and supporting activities. The researchers suggested that these differences in perception contributed to the "cold war" described by Blumberg (1980).

Perrine's (1984) study compared the perceptions of teachers and supervisors concerning ideal and actual components of supervision, including communication (i.e., one-way or two-way), working relationship assisting or directing), leadership style (democratic or autocratic), creativity/confidence (positive or negative), personnel position staff or line), initiating structure (positive or negative), consideration (positive or negative), and decision-making (group or autonomous). Results showed that teachers had higher expectations from supervision than the supervisors did. However, there was little difference in the two groups' perceptions of the actual role, which indicated the need for a clearer communication of realistic expectations to teachers.

Mack's (1991) study of reading supervisors in Pennsylvania indicated little difference between desired and actual roles. Supervisors were actually performing 9 of the 11 most desired roles, and were performing least often most of those roles that they least wished to perform. However, supervisors reported that they would like to give more attention to all the roles, a finding similar to that of Al-Habeeb (1981), who expressed concern that English supervisors in Saudi Arabia were unable to interact frequently with teachers because they were responsible for large numbers of teachers scattered across extensive urban and rural areas.

Dillingham (1966) compared the value placed upon supervisory practices in English language arts by a group of selected Texas secondary schools and a second group of selected schools across the nation with the values identified by a selected group of English and general supervisors. She found that the supervisors' group placed a higher value upon supervisory practices than the schools in either Texas or the nation did. Another finding was that while the supervisors placed the greatest emphasis upon experimentation, the Texas and national schools gave the greatest emphasis to curriculum development. Both schools and supervisors, however, emphasized curriculum analysis, communication skills, orientation meetings, professional meetings, and slow and gifted students, areas that are echoed in virtually all the research on supervisory roles.

In looking across this research, several common characteristics emerge:

1. The range of supervisory responsibilities is broad but reasonably consistent across all the studies, including curriculum, instruction, implementation, assessment, and management of programs.
2. Supervisory roles within this broad range are often poorly defined or not clearly communicated to teachers, which can create dissonance between the supervisors and those they work with.
3. There is sometimes a gap between what responsibilities are desirable and what can actually be done. This gap may be seen between the perceptions of "experts" and those of practitioners, between the expectations of supervisors and of teachers, and between supervisors' desired roles and their actual responsibilities.
4. Supervisory roles appear to differ very little across the various academic areas except in terms of curriculum content and subject matter.

Who is a supervisor, and what are the responsibilities of the role? This overview of research in several academic areas suggests that this is probably not the right question to ask. General guidelines are consistently agreed upon; details

depend upon the particular situation and the expectations or administrators, fellow supervisors, and teachers. In addition, this situation changes constantly over time. Perhaps a more fruitful line of inquiry would be the exploration of what variables are commonly influential in the determination of a specific role and what strategies supervisors use to delineate and refine their individual roles over time.

SUPERVISORY METHODS

In this section, the realities of the supervisor's world are examined in a variety of ways: descriptions of programs in action; research-based examination of specific aspects of supervision; and consideration of the politics and interactions within supervisory relationships.

Programs in Action

Most of the descriptions of programs in the literature are anecdotal rather than research-based. However, four studies included a research component to determine the qualities of the program. Berg (1986) described a preservice clinical supervision program at San Diego State University, where students were asked to respond to a questionnaire about the program. The National Clearinghouse for Bilingual Education (NCBE) used a broad perspective to look at supervision in bilingual education and special language programs (1987/1988). Bush, Moss, and Seiler (1991) examined an alternative to traditional student teaching in mathematics. Abbott (1992) explored the use of peer supervision to implement recommendations of the National Council of Teachers of Mathematics (NCTM).

In these studies, several common characteristics of effective supervision programs were identified. Successful programs involved long-term relationships between supervisors and teachers. For example, in Berg's study, supervisors using a clinical supervision model spent considerably more time with the student teachers than did those in the control group. The programs described by the NCBE staff extended over one to three years. The alternative to student teaching for secondary mathematics teachers described by Bush, Moss, and Seiler involved teams of high school teachers in extensive professional activities, such as working closely with student teachers, teaching in university courses, regular meetings, and attending professional conferences.

A second common characteristic was the participatory nature of the supervisory experiences. Supervisors and teachers were engaged in joint planning and program development, and played an active and valued part in the implementation of the program. Supervisory models used in these programs included clinical supervision (Berg et al, 1986), peer supervision (Abbott, 1992), team supervision (Bush, Moss, & Seiler, 1991), and site-based training (NCBE, 1987/1988). All these models are collaborative and democratic rather than autocratic or authoritarian.

Collaboration is closely allied to participation, but also implies that all partners, including administrators, supervisors, and teachers or student teachers, work together toward a common end: the improvement of instruction. For example, Abbott's study examined a district-wide effort to implement the NCTM standards in high schools. The NCBE staff identified three exemplary collaborative programs designed to improve bilingual education in specific sites across the country. The program described by Bush, Moss, and Seiler used team supervision to provide richer experiences in mathematics for teachers, supervisors, and student teachers alike, and ultimately to improve mathematics teaching and learning in the classroom.

A fourth common characteristic of these programs was that they all involved training for the supervisor in addition to professional development for the teachers or student teachers. Training of master teachers was seen as an integral part of the programs described by Berg et al and Bush, Moss, and Seiler. The NCBE staff presented three programs which provided extensive and ongoing training for leadership teams and local teacher trainers. The peer supervision model described by Abbott provided mutual training and support in a situation where teachers learned both to supervise and to improve their own teaching.

What were the results of these participatory, collaborative, long-term training programs? Bush, Moss, and Seiler (1991) identified four benefits that were also apparent in the other programs:

- the quality and depth of supervision and advice from teachers were greatly enhanced
- teachers were more willing and comfortable to take responsibility for supervision
- new teaching ideas and strategies were learned
- theory and practice blended better

In addition, Berg et al reported that student teachers learned to evaluate themselves in a clinical supervision program, and Bush, Moss, and Seiler found that teacher participation enhanced the credibility of the methods courses. The NCBE staff and Abbott also found an improvement in the quality of instruction.

These four studies took a broad perspective as they examined these supervision programs. Five other studies employed a narrower focus in their examination of supervision in practice.

Aspects of Supervision

Supervision is a multifaceted phenomenon, and the researchers discussed in this section each examined specific aspects or features of supervision. Garman (1971) looked at the effects of clinical supervision on teaching assistants in college English compared to teaching assistants who had no supervision, while Fraenkel (1992) examined the results of joint supervision versus single supervision for student teachers in mathematics and English. The effectiveness of specific tools and techniques in supervision was explored by Harder (1968), who looked at the use of videotaping in training secondary school social studies teachers, Heimler (1959), who conducted a survey to determine the content of a proposed guide for the supervision of high school science programs, and Goode (1968), who used research findings to develop

case studies in science supervision. These studies incorporate, to some degree, the principles of collaboration, participation, and training that were exemplified in the broader studies described earlier.

Garman's study (1971) compared two groups of teaching assistants. One group was provided a teaching seminar, while the other group was provided additional support in terms of clinical supervision, planning sessions, and a demonstration class. She found that the group with additional clinical supervision was much more likely to make changes in teaching than the control group.

Fraenkel (1992) described a program in which student teachers in English and mathematics were supervised jointly by supervisors from the English and mathematics departments and supervisors from the Education department. He found no significant differences between these student teachers and the control group who were supervised only by education professors, though the student teachers who were jointly supervised valued the additional time and advice that they received and found the experience a positive one. However, the joint supervision could be more accurately described as parallel supervision, since the subject-area supervisors and general supervisors did not work together in any way.

Harder (1968) found that videotaping of student teachers was somewhat effective in changing behavior and that student teachers tended to become more indirect in their teaching as a result of the experience. However, he pointed out that videotaping had several disadvantages: technically, it could not give an accurate or complete picture of classroom interaction; and it resulted in very high anxiety for the student teacher.

Heimler (1959) used questionnaires on science status and science teaching problems and a review of literature on instructional supervision to develop a guide for high school science supervision in New York central schools. This guide was designed to provide schools with suggestions and information about the identification and analysis of science teaching problems, a discussion of the supervisor's role and supervisory methods and techniques, and recommendations for science programs in a small school.

In a somewhat similar study, Goode (1968) used the information gained from a literature search to develop case studies related to the role of the science supervisor. These case studies were responded to by a jury of science educators and science supervisors, and the results were compiled into an instrument for evaluating supervisory behavior.

It is disappointing that among the many descriptive and prescriptive articles about supervisory approaches, tools, and techniques, so little research has been conducted to ascertain their effectiveness. The few articles discussed here begin to give some verification to the generally accepted precepts of collaboration, participation, long-term involvement, and training, but the studies are too diverse to lead to more specific generalizations.

Supervision is both interpersonal and political in nature, and, therefore, it is more likely to be examined in idiosyncratic and subjective ways. Some researchers have undertaken the examination of those political and interpersonal characteristics of the supervisory process.

Interaction and Politics

The perception of supervision as a political activity, in the broadest sense of the term, has been gaining emphasis. Perhaps in reaction to the positivist stance apparent in much of the effective teaching research of the 1970s and 1980s, theorists began to identify and clarify other philosophical bases in supervision. Clinical supervision, which had its genesis in the late 1950s, began to take on new and varied interpretations. Haggerson (1987) chronicled a symposium in which Hunter, Garman, and Glickman presented conflicting conceptions of clinical supervision. Meanwhile, Sergiovanni and Starratt (1979, 1983) had been espousing "human resources" supervision, which had a very different conceptual and theoretical base from the older authoritarian and "human relations" approaches. Schön's (1983) definition of the reflective practitioner added to new concepts of supervisory interaction. Smyth (1986) incorporated reflection into his model of "emancipatory learning" within historical, social, and cultural contexts. In 1987, Smyth offered "dialectical supervision" as an empowering approach for teachers. Flinders (1991) developed a framework for "culturally responsive supervision."

As supervision moved into this complex political arena of philosophies and situations, some researchers looked at politics and interaction and explored implications and applications within their own academic areas. For example, Rex (1989) examined the micropolitics of supervision of secondary school English student teachers, while Waite (1993) studied the interactive processes that occur between teacher and supervisors. Thompson and Williams (1985) proposed the use of dissonance to cause change, while Vogt (1991) provided guidelines to deal with change.

Certain commonalities emerge from these studies. Both Rex and Waite defined supervision as a political situation where there are agendas, contexts, and "cultures." In order to deal with this situation, Rex suggested negotiation rather than relying upon communication; Waite identified three models of communication: adversarial, passive, and—the one he espoused—collaborative.

What are some of the effective techniques within this negotiation or collaborative communication? They include careful observation, active listening, support together with suggestion, and the provision of needed resources.

The issue of change underlies these political situations. As human beings, we both welcome and fear change. Change is necessary but seldom easy. To promote change, Thompson and Williams suggested that the creation of confusion is necessary for teachers who are no longer learners, and that "until dissonance is created, any attempt to change them . . . is likely to fail" (1985, p. 14). Confusion, or cognitive dissonance, is a powerful impetus for change, but it can also cause distress. As Vogt suggested, therefore, the supervisor must also provide time for change to occur, knowledge and understanding, support, and resources. She also pointed out that effective supervisors must also be open to new ideas and approaches.

Effectiveness is to some degree a relative term. Does effectiveness mean that the supervisor fulfills expected roles and responsibilities? Does it refer to teacher comfort in a supervisory role? Does it imply that teachers change for the better?

Effectiveness in supervision research appears to be as poorly defined as supervision itself. In the next section of this chapter, we will focus on the effects of supervision on pupils, teachers, and supervisors.

THE EFFECTIVENESS OF SUPERVISION

There are a limited number of studies that directly address the effects of supervision on pupil achievement, teacher attitudes, and supervisory behavior in specific academic areas: reading, mathematics, and science.

Instructional Improvement

Seven studies were identified that explored the effects of supervision upon instruction. Four of these looked at student performance; the other three examined teachers' instructional behavior.

The findings related to student achievement were equivocal. Rosser (1980) compared six county districts in Alabama that had reading supervisors with a matched set without reading supervisors to see if there were significant differences in reading scores at the second, fourth, and sixth grade level. She found no significant differences in total reading achievement between the two groups of students.

Morrill (1966) compared two types of supervision for reading teachers. The control group of teachers was provided with consultant help on a one-to-one basis at the request of the teacher or building principal, while teachers in the experimental group were given a half-day release twice a month to meet with other grade-level teachers and the consultant, to share ideas and discuss problems. The apparent effects on children's learning were questionable because of the differences between the classes in earlier years. However, teacher attitudes in the experimental group were markedly more positive, with the teachers expressing feelings of confidence, capability, and colleagueship.

Mayfield (1983), on the other hand, in her study of third grade students in Detroit, found significant differences in reading levels between students whose teachers received clinical supervision and those whose teachers did not. The clinical supervision group scored significantly higher on the reading comprehension section of the California Achievement Test.

Snippe (1992) examined the effects of instructional supervision and staff development upon the learning of a new method of teaching multiplication in fifth grade mathematics classes. No significant differences were found in terms of the time teachers spent on the new strategy, but students in the experimental groups were able to solve mathematical problems at a higher level of abstraction and outperformed the control group on tests based directly on the content of the curriculum. It appeared that these results came from a combination of instructional supervision and in-service meetings, rather than from instructional supervision alone.

Trosky (1971) looked at the relationship between teacher questioning and a series of three supervisory conferences designed to modify those questions from recall to higher cognitive levels. She found that four of the five teachers in the study did make changes in questioning, while the fifth teacher understood how to do so, and felt that more conferences would be helpful.

The methodology, subject area, research questions, and populations in these four studies were so varied that no definite conclusions can be drawn. The major implication is that more studies need to be carried out to investigate the effects of supervision upon student learning.

Fitzpatrick and Charter (1986) conducted a large-scale study to investigate how instructional leadership functions and school policy factors affected the extent to which secondary school mathematics teachers implemented instructional strategies presented in a staff development program. One section of this study focused particularly on instructional supervision and evaluation procedures. The results are difficult to decipher because there is no clear demarcation between instructional supervision and a fairly traditional evaluation program. However, some of the general findings are similar to those reported in other parts of this chapter. For example, the researchers reported that there was a positive relationship between the total amount of support teachers received and the extent to which they applied the instructional strategies. Some of the elements of this support system were that: (1) teachers' professional opinions were valued right from the beginning of the program; (2) teachers had the opportunity to work collaboratively with their peers; (3) administrative support for the program was provided; and (4) the new instructional strategies were modeled and discussed.

A study by Elgarten (1991) examined the effects of modeling in more detail. Using Bandura's observational learning theory as a theoretical base for the study, Elgarten hypothesized that the 48 New York City mathematics teachers in his sample who were supervised with the use of modeling by the supervisor would implement the supervisor's suggested changes with more frequency than those who did not have any modeling; that teachers who were given a list of suggested changes would implement more changes than those who received no list; and that teachers who received modeling by the supervisor and a list of suggested changes would implement more changes than those who received only modeling, only a list, or neither. His findings showed that the teachers carried out a significantly greater number of suggestions when they saw them modeled, but that the list had no significant effect upon the number of suggestions that were carried out. While this study is clearly predicated upon a highly directive model of instructional supervision, the findings do show the value of modeling in supervision. Meanwhile, direct suggestions seem to have little effect upon teacher behavior, perhaps because this approach does not provide for participation or collaboration and does not give teachers control over their own teaching or professional growth.

These last two studies, together with others reported earlier, suggest that teacher perceptions and attitudes affect both the supervisory relationship and the outcomes of that relationship. There are several studies that address teacher attitudes more directly.

Teacher Attitudes

Six studies, two of which included Sistrunk as a coauthor (Kennebrew & Sistrunk, 1989; Richardson & Sistrunk, 1988),

looked as teacher attitudes as a variable in considering the effectiveness of supervision. Stronck (1987), for example, conducted a survey of 1,614 elementary school and 529 secondary school science teachers in British Columbia to ascertain what type of district-level science coordination was perceived to be most satisfactory. Elementary teachers clearly preferred having a designated science coordinator, though they also indicated that a working group of teachers—or, to a lesser degree, an administrator or teacher working informally—could provide satisfactory supervision. Secondary school teachers were most satisfied with a coordinator who had responsibilities for only the secondary school grades, and slightly less satisfied with a K–12 science coordinator. A lower preference was given to a general-subjects supervisor. Both elementary and secondary teachers clearly valued having a designated science coordinator.

Foley (1986) took a more detailed look at elements of supervision as he examined the relationship between teacher/supervisor attitude toward the clinical supervision model and effective teaching in elementary reading classes. He found that teachers felt more positive about the principles of clinical supervision than about the details of the clinical supervision model, but that all teachers demonstrated a relationship between attitude toward clinical supervision and their ability to provide instruction. This has implications for supervisors who use clinical supervision and college professors who teach clinical supervision. As Goldhammer (1969), one of the pioneers of the clinical supervision model, suggests, supervision must be "inherently humane, conceptually tough, grounded in intellectual humility, and based upon a determination to discover more about reality and to construct behaviors that are rationally related to such discoveries" (p. 55).

Trosky (1975) described a training program in clinical supervision for reading supervisors and the effects of this program upon teachers in two schools; a small rural school and a large urban elementary school. Her findings indicated that teachers found supervision effective when the supervisor, in a series of conferences, helped them identify and attain goals; when observation and analysis of teaching focused on the teacher's expressed interests and needs, and when time was allocated for supervisory conferences.

Several approaches to supervision have been categorized, described, compared, and often prescribed over the years. Glickman (1981) identified three categories of supervisory behavior, which he termed directive, nondirective, and collaborative. Three studies used the Supervisory Behavior Description Questionnaire developed by Sistrunk (1982), this questionnaire used these three categories of supervisory behavior. The researchers looked for correlations between principals' supervisory behavior as perceived by teachers and other variables related to teacher attitudes. Their results varied considerably. Richardson and Sistrunk (1988) looked at the relationship between teachers' burnout and their perceptions of principals' directive, nondirective, or collaborative behavior. Their findings indicated that teachers felt high levels of emotional exhaustion when their principals used collaborative supervision; that teachers preferred nondirective principal behavior when they were engaged in curriculum development and staff development, and that directive supervisory behavior was preferred in evaluation.

In Kennebrew and Sistrunk's (1989) study, the variables were principals' supervisory behavior (directive, collaborative, and nondirective) and school climate as measured on the NASSP School Climate Survey. Their findings were different from Richardson and Sistrunk's in that they found that the administrative aspects of school climate, which included curriculum development, staff development, organization for instruction, and program evaluation, correlated negatively with directive and nondirective supervisory behavior, but positively with perceived collaborative behavior of school principals.

Williams (1986) conducted a study of 120 secondary school teachers in English, mathematics, science, and social studies in Mississippi to explore the relationship between teachers' perceptions of supervisory behavior in an evaluation conference (directive, nondirective, or collaborative) and their attitudes toward the postobservation supervisory conference. She found that there was no correlation. Teachers' attitudes did not seem to be influenced by their perceptions of the principals' behavior as directive, nondirective, or collaborative.

These contradictory results may arise, in part, from the particular variables in each study. As Richardson and Sistrunk concluded, there are tasks in which teachers preferred to be told what to do, and other tasks in which they preferred to be left alone. A generally collaborative style of leadership on the part of the principal and a supportive school climate should be sensitive and responsive to these specific needs and preferences. In addition, the studies were limited to the supervisory behavior of principals, and supervision appears to have been related closely to evaluation. While principals do serve important supervisory roles, the hierarchical nature of the relationship between principal and teacher and the role of principal as evaluator tend to affect this relationship and make it difficult to develop a true democratic collaboration.

These studies examined the effects of supervisory behavior on teachers. Other studies focus more directly on the supervisor and supervisory effectiveness.

Supervisory Effectiveness

How is effectiveness defined? These studies relied upon teacher perceptions of effectiveness, but did not clearly define what the concept meant. Negley (1962) designed a study to determine the nature of the relationship which existed between the practices of authoritarian, "midauthoritarian," and nonauthoritarian supervisors and their effectiveness as perceived by social studies teachers. Criteria for "effectiveness" included common understandings of the curriculum among teachers and supervisors, confidence in the supervisor, and the teachers' feeling that they were working effectively with their supervisor toward improved instruction. Findings showed that authoritarian behavior did not correlate with perceived effectiveness in any area.

Wolfer (1978) examined the relationship between supervisory effectiveness and supervisory responsibility by asking science supervisors and the teachers they worked with to complete rating scales. In addition, twelve situational factors were studied as they related to the effectiveness/responsibility correlations. Analysis of the data indicated that there was a positive relationship between effectiveness and responsibility, though the correlations varied from task to task. There was agreement between supervisors and teachers as to the strength of the correlations from task to task. The situational factors did not generally affect the strength or direction of the correlations, though the amount of time the supervisor was able to devote to supervisory responsibilities and the clarity of role expectations were positively related to ratings of both responsibility and effectiveness.

It is difficult to draw conclusions from the studies in this section. Since supervision appears to be very complex and highly situational in nature (see, for example, Waite, 1992), there is a real danger in trying to isolate specific variables related to effectiveness. Future research could include broad and rigorous ethnographic studies of supervision in action and its effects upon schools, teachers, and, ultimately, children's learning.

Summary of Findings and Conclusions

In 1988, Murphy compiled an annotated bibliography of journal articles specifically related to the study of supervision. The articles she identified are more general in nature than those on supervision in academic areas reviewed in this chapter, but her selections provide a useful overview of writings on supervision in the 1980s. In this bibliography, certain trends are apparent, which include:

- Multiple models of supervision
- An awareness of the significance of underlying philosophical theories
- A humanistic and people-centered approach
- Continued confusion as to whether supervision is designed for improvement, evaluation, or both and
- An understanding of the need for training for supervisors.

These trends are also apparent in the research reviewed in this chapter and will therefore form a broad framework for the discussion of findings in this section.

Multiple Models of Supervision

Murphy identified a number of articles that discussed a variety of models or approaches in instructional supervision (Gebhart, 1984; Haggerson, 1987; Hunter, 1980; Zimpher & Howey, 1987). These differing models may lead to contradictory expectations by teachers and role confusion by supervisors (McDaniel, 1981). Articles reviewed in the first section of this chapter (Caruso, 1991; Cook et al, 1983, 1985; Madrazo & Hounshell, 1987); show a wide number of job titles, roles, responsibilities, and expectations which also lead to role confusion. In addition, there is often a discrepancy between ideal and actual components of supervision (Mack, 1991; Perrine, 1984).

These varied models, perceptions, and discrepancies may be due in part to the situational nature of supervision. Supervision is affected by a large number of factors, including the content of the field. For example, reading supervisors and science supervisors have to deal with content, skills, and problems endemic to the actual discipline and approaches to teaching within that discipline (Goode, 1968; Heimler, 1959; Vogt, 1991). This broad and complex range of responsibilities means that the supervisor must develop an extensive variety of approaches to meet these demands effectively.

Another aspect of situational supervision is that situations are not simple or static. For example, the demands and expectations placed upon the supervisor may vary depending upon the nature of the task. Richardson and Sistrunk (1988) found that teachers prefer different types of supervision related to different tasks, such as teacher evaluation or curriculum development. A collaborative, participatory approach in which the supervisor and teacher share responsibility seems most effective for ongoing professional growth and change over time. As Etzioni (1961) suggests, however, supervisory behavior should vary according to the desired goal, the complexity of the task, and the extent to which participant involvement and commitment is required. Richardson and Sistrunk (1988) reported that, in evaluation, teachers preferred a direct approach so that they knew what was expected of them, while in curriculum development, they preferred a nondirective style that allowed them to get on with their work.

Underlying Philosophical Theories

In looking at the articles identified by Murphy (1988), one is struck by the evidence of a variety of philosophical beliefs related to instructional supervision. For example, Pajak (1986) looked at theoretical advances in psychoanalysis and their implications for supervision; Sergiovanni (1984), Smyth (1987), and Tracy and MacNaughton (1986) and examined the characteristics of the traditional "technical" approaches to supervision and offered philosophically based alternatives; Garman (1986) and Turner-Muecke (1986) emphasized the role of reflection-in-action in facilitating professional development; and Copeland (1980), May and Zimpher (1986), and Tracy (1984) offered alternative approaches to supervision based upon varying philosophical bases.

There was little overt discussion of theoretical bases in the research reviewed in this chapter, but hypotheses were based upon a variety of assumptions and beliefs. Perhaps the most obvious example is Elgarten's (1991) study of the effects of modeling, based explicitly upon Bandura's observational learning theory. Concepts of direct, nondirect, and collaborative approaches in supervision appeared in a number of studies and formed the basis for Sistrunk's (1982) Supervisory Behavior Description Questionnaire, which was used in studies by Kennebrew and Sistrunk (1989), Richardson and Sistrunk (1988), and Williams (1986). Beliefs about teacher burnout (Richardson & Sistrunk, 1988) and school climate (Kennebrew & Sistrunk, 1989) were used as variables in research studies. The influence of human relations theories in business was apparent in the emphasis upon teacher collaboration, participation and empowerment (Abbott, 1992; Berg et al,1986; Bush, Moss, & Seiler, 1991; and NCBE, 1987/1988).

Another way for philosophical orientation to be incorporated in research is through standards and statements developed by professional associations. For example, Wolfer (1978) used a list of supervisory tasks developed by a National Science Supervisor's Association commission in his study of secondary school science supervisors. Abbott (1992) used NCTM standards as a criterion in her study of mathematics teachers engaged in peer supervision. As new standards are developed for teaching and learning in the various academic disciplines, there is opportunity for further research in supervision related to these standards.

The clarification of the philosophical bases of supervision is essential if the effectiveness of supervision is to be considered. Contradictory findings about the efficacy of a particular supervisory approach may be due not only to situational factors but also to the philosophical assumptions of the participants and researchers.

Humanistic Approach

In her bibliography, Murphy included Diamond (1980), who presented a humanistic and clinical model of supervision, and Johnston and Holt (1983), who prescribed a process of supervision designed to be anxiety-reducing. Is humane supervision necessarily anxiety-reducing? Teachers who are in a state of high anxiety are unlikely to be particularly effective either in teaching or supervisory situations. For example, Richardson and Sistrunk (1988) found that collaborative supervision was associated with high levels of emotional exhaustion and burnout. However, it is not clear whether humaneness can or should be equated with a lessening of anxiety. As Sergiovanni and Starratt (1983) suggested, "human relations" supervision, where the emphasis is on creating a feeling of comfort, is not necessarily effective. Productivity is not achieved merely by assuring the happiness of teachers. Some of the research examined in this chapter supports this view. Thompson and Williams (1985) proposed that some level of confusion is necessary to encourage change. In most of the literature under review, there was an assumption that active collaboration and participation will lead to long-term effectiveness and satisfaction.

The nature of change is complex and often poorly understood, in spite of the extensive work conducted in this field by scholars such as Argyris (1982), Fullan (1991), and Rogers and Shoemaker (1971). It is a human paradox that we both fear and welcome change. Supervisors tend to criticize their teachers for refusing to change, yet teachers deal constantly with their own change and their student's change. Research on supervision deals constantly with change. Although the concept of change is not the explicit subject of most of the research reviewed here, implicit assumptions and beliefs about change underlie much of the methodology and findings. Some of these assumptions include the following, identified by Martinello and Cook (1994):

1. There must be motivation for the change. Thompson and Williams (1985) suggested that this motivation comes from a feeling of dissonance. Suggestions, particularly when accompanied with support and respect, can also bring about change (e.g., Garman, 1971; Rex, 1989; Vogt, 1991; Waite, 1993).
2. Successful change involves shared meanings and beliefs. The importance of sharing and understanding basic philosophical stances has been addressed above. It is possible

that some of the lack of shared role definition and expectations described by researchers such as Madrazo and Hounshell (1987) arises from a lack of shared goals and visions about education in general and supervision in particular.

3. All participants must have ownership of the change. The collaborative, participatory programs and models described by Abbott (1992), Berg et al (1986), and the NCBE (1987/1988) provide evidence for the significance of this characteristic. Empowerment is a word that is used frequently, but is not always implemented with true understanding of the relationships between participation and power.

4. Change takes time. As Fullan (1991) suggests, change is not an event but a process that takes a great deal of interaction, negotiation, and energy. Successful programs described by researchers such as Berg et al (1986), Garman (1971), and the NCBE (1987/1988) emphasize the need for long-term programs if change is to occur. Teachers lead busy and complicated lives. If supervision is to be successful, it is essential that appropriate and sufficient time be allowed for teachers to learn, grow, and change.

Improvement and Evaluation

There has been an ongoing discussion about the responsibility of the supervisor related to instructional improvement and teacher evaluation. In Murphy's bibliography, an article by McCarty (1986) suggested that supervision and evaluation may be two irreconcilable processes. However, supervision cannot be totally devoid of evaluation. Perhaps one of the major issues is that of teacher perceptions. If the teacher perceives the process as evaluative and, therefore, threatening, it is this perception that will color the relationship and its effects, no matter how well-intentioned and supportive the supervisor may be (Kennebrew & Sistrunk, 1989; Richardson & Sistrunk, 1988; Williams, 1986).

Teacher perceptions are a significant factor in supervisory effectiveness and teacher change. Many of the studies reviewed in this chapter recognize this fact and examine perceptions as major variables or findings (Foley, 1986; Stronck, 1987).

A Need for Training

Successful supervision, like any other complex process, needs training. Warner (1980) emphasized the importance of developing a cadre of trained professionals in clinical supervision, and Killion and Harrison (1985) described a successful training program for the implementation of clinical supervision. The necessity for training in supervision is supported by the certification requirements for supervisors in most states in the United States, the number of courses and programs offered at colleges and universities, and the many textbooks in the field. Training was taken for granted in much of the research reviewed in this chapter, but some programs emphasized a strong training component (NCBE, 1987/1988), and other articles called for more supervisory training (Caruso, 1991; Urquia, 1975).

The research reviewed in this chapter is conducted within specific subject areas, but the findings are applicable across the disciplines. In subject-area supervision, content and skills may vary from discipline to discipline, but supervisory situations, conditions, characteristics, and problems seem to cross all areas of the curriculum. This is both comforting and dismaying. On the one hand, supervisors in one area can learn from those in other areas, and new knowledge in one area can easily be adapted or applied to another. On the other hand, however, some of the important characteristics of thinking and inquiring in the separate disciplines are ignored. A mathematician looks at the world in different ways than a poet does. The historian, the artist, and the scientist view the past, present, and future in different ways. Supervisors in different fields should be able to use the unique characteristics and modes of thinking generic to that field to strengthen supervisory relationships and promote more effective learning and teaching. This is one of the areas that seems ripe for research.

DIRECTIONS FOR RESEARCH

Ellis (1991) examined integrative reviews of supervision literature that indicated that research in supervision has been "largely haphazard, atheoretical, and rife with a host of methodological flaws"; that "the vast majority of supervision models have not been tested or verified empirically"; and that "the cumulative knowledge in supervision is disparate and poorly organized and thus offers little to theory, research, or practice" (p. 238).

This is also true of supervision research in the academic areas. It is difficult, and sometimes impossible, to make sound generalizations, draw comparisons among studies, or verify findings because of the wide differences among the studies.

In addition, there is a surprising paucity of research pertinent to the use of generalist versus specialist supervisors. Questions that were rarely if ever addressed in the research examined here and that could form a basis for new studies include the following:

1. Is there an increase in the use of generalist supervisors or in the use of specialist supervisors in the academic disciplines?

2. Do teachers prefer help from a specialist or a generalist? Is there any evidence that a specialist supervisor is more effective than a generalist, or vice versa ? (See Stronck [1987], who found that teachers at all grade levels in schools in British Columbia were most satisfied when there was a designated district-level science supervisor as opposed to a working group of teachers or informal supervision by an administrator.)

3. Does grade level make a difference in preference for a generalist or a specialist?

4. Is there more demand for specialists in certain subject areas, such as science or reading?

A major recommendation in this chapter is for much more research. In addition to new directions for research, there is a need for replication of studies so that there may be verification or new comparable findings.

This is particularly urgent in the area of effectiveness. The research in this area is scant and spotty. There is seldom a clear definition of effectiveness in any study, and much of the research examines limited variables rather than addressing the broader question of what supervision is ultimately designed for: the enhancement of student learning.

This may be understandable in an era where we have difficulties in understanding student learning and how to assess it. However, this is all the more reason why research in supervision should examine student learning in a broad perspective. This perspective can encompass the environment, the teacher, the learner, and those variables, including supervision, that support or interfere with learning.

Such research may have to take new directions. Performance assessment has implications for research in supervision, as elsewhere. As we learn how to assess complex learning processes in students, we can also learn to look more accurately and thoroughly at the complex processes of teaching. Teacher portfolios, for example, have the potential to open up new areas of research related to supervision.

Ethnographic research is no longer in its infancy in education. However, there is little evidence of ethnographic research in supervision in the academic areas. Rich, textured descriptions of supervision within specific subject areas can enable to reader to gain deeper understanding of how teachers and learners conduct inquiry in science, mathematics, literature, art, music, or gymnastics, and how supervision can enhance such thinking and learning.

There is a vast difference between simple elegance and simplistic solutions. For too long, we have been content to seek the latter, to reduce complexity in order to make it manageable and computable. Research in supervision now needs to accept the whole messy complexity of teaching, learning, and supervision; to persevere; to resist the easy answers; and to strive for elegant solutions. As in all fields of study, those elegant solutions emerge from risk taking, from patience and persistence, from intensive and extensive experience and observation, and from intuition developed through rigorous exploration and shared ideas and knowledge.

Researchers in supervision need both to broaden and narrow their explorations. They need to explore the many rich related fields—psychology, neurology, management, communications, counseling, and leadership—to gain understanding of how people learn, develop, and change. They also need to focus upon specialized areas within the curriculum to see how the content of the different fields of study—their languages, "grammar," paradigms, and assumptions—affect the ways that people think within those fields. Scientific inquiry is different from historical research; explorations in art differ from investigations in mathematics. To be sure, there are commonalities in thinking across the disciplines, but to ignore the uniqueness of each field is to miss its richness and vitality. As Gardner and Boix-Mansilla (1994) write, "Whereas subject matters are seen as collections of contents that students need to learn, disciplines entail particular modes of thinking or interpreting the world that students need to develop" (p. 202).

As we discover more about how people think, inquire, dream, create, and communicate, supervision itself takes on new dimensions and moves from the traditional linear model to a complexity full of life, wonder, and unexpected beauty. Research must accept and incorporate that complexity so that we begin to understand it more fully, and through understanding, to honor and respect the role of supervision in education.

REFERENCES

Abbott, L. Y. (1992). Using a peer supervision model to implement recommendations of the NCTM standards in algebra classes in an urban school system. *Dissertation Abstracts International, 53,*10A, 3465.

Al-Habeeb, M. M. S. (1981). Evaluation of instructional supervision of English programs at the intermediate and secondary schools in Saudi Arabia. *Dissertation Abstracts International, 43,* 01A, 60.

Argyris, (1992). *Reasoning, learning, and action: Individual and Organizational.* San Francisco: Jossey-Base.

Beisenberg, P. & Yager, R. (1991). The school science supervisor: A necessity for a quality program. *School Science and Mathematics, 91,* 152–156.

Beisenberg, P. & Yager, R. (1992). Wanted: Science supervisors. *The American School Board Journal, 179,* 45–46.

Berg, M. et al. (1986, February). *Partners in supervision: A clinical supervision model program, San Diego State University.* Paper presented at the Annual Meeting of the Association of Teacher Educators, Atlanta, GA.

Blumberg, A. (1980). *Supervisors and teachers: A private cold war* (2nd. ed.). Berkeley, CA: McCutchan.

Bush, W., Moss, M., & Seiler, M. 1991). An alternative to traditional student teaching. *Mathematics Education, 84,* 533–537.

Caruso, J. (1991). Supervisors in early childhood programs. *Young Children, 46* (6), 20–26.

Columbro, M. N. (1964). A conceptual framework for the teaching and supervision of high school English. *Dissertation Abstracts International, 25,* 11, 6587.

Cook, G. E., Duke, C., Owen, F., & Schiff, P. (1983). *Summary of questionnaire results: Subcommittee on the Status of Supervision of the CEE Commission on Supervision and Curriculum Development* (ERIC Reproduction Service No. ED 255 930).

Cook, G. E., Duke, C., Owen, F., & Schiff, P. (1985). ERIC/RCS report: Roles and responsibilities of today's English language arts supervisors. *English Education, 17*(3), 170–173.

Diamond, S. (1980). Micro-supervisory experience, humanistic and clinical format. *NASSP Bulletin, 64*(434), 25–29.

Dillingham, F. E. (1966). A study of emphasis placed on supervisory practices in the supervision of English. *Dissertation Abstracts International, 27,* 01A, 50.

Elgarten, G. H. (1991). Testing a new supervisory process for improving instruction. *Journal of Curriculum and Supervision, 6*(2),118–129.

Ellis, M. (1991). Research in clinical supervision. *Counselor Education and Supervision, 30,* 238–251.

Ellis, R. F. (1977). The status of science supervision in Florida school districts. *Dissertation Abstracts International, 38,* 04A, 1748.

Etzioni, A. (1961). *A comparative analysis of complex organizations.* New York: Free Press.

Fitzpatrick, K. & Charter, W. W. (1986). *A study of staff development practices and organizational conditions related to instructional improvement in secondary schools: Final report* (ERIC Reproduction Service No. ED 266 558).

Flinders, D. J. (1991, Winter). Supervision as cultural inquiry. *Journal of Curriculum and Supervision, 6*(2), 87–106.

Florez-Tighe, V. (1984). Instructional leadership and supervision in special language programs. In J. Denton, W. Peters, & T. Savage (Eds.). *New directions in teacher education: Foundations, curriculum, policy* (ERIC Reproduction Service No. ED 253 509).

Foley, R. P. (1986). A study of the relationships between attitudes toward clinical supervision and effective teaching behaviors in elementary reading classes. *Dissertation Abstracts International, 47*, 08A, 2821.

Fraenkel, J. R. (1992, April). *Joint vs. single supervision.* Paper presented at the Annual Meeting of the American Educational Research Association, San Francisco, CA.

Fullan, M. (1991). *The new meaning of educational change.* New York: Teachers College Press.

Gardner, H. (1983). *Frames of mind: The theory of multiple intelligences.* New York: Basic Books.

Gardner, H. & Boix-Mansilla, V. (1994). Teaching for understanding in the disciplines and beyond. *Teachers College Record, 96*, 198–217.

Garman, N. B. (1971). A study of clinical supervision as a resource for college teachers of English. *Dissertation Abstracts International, 32*, 12A, 6835.

Garman, N. B. (1986). Reflection, the heart of clinical supervision. *Journal of Curriculum and Supervision, 2*(1),1–24.

Gebhart, J. G. (1984). Models of supervision: Choices. *TESOL Quarterly, 18*, 501–514.

Glickman, C. D. (1981). *Developmental supervision: Alternative practices for helping teachers improve instruction.* Alexandria, VA: ASCD.

Goldhammer, R. (1969). *Clinical supervision: Special methods for the supervision of teachers.* New York: Holt, Rinehart, and Winston.

Goode, J. M. (1968). The development of an instrument to evaluate certain practices in science supervision. *Dissertation Abstracts International, 29*, 03A, 759.

Haggerson, N. L. (1987). Conflicting conceptions of clinical supervision, and the enhancement of professional growth and renewal. *Journal of Curriculum and Supervision, 2*, 152– 157.

Harder, R. J. (1968). A study in the supervision of social studies: Student teachers utilizing video-tape techniques. *Dissertation Abstracts International, 29*, 12A, 4183.

Heimler, C. H. (1959). A guide for science supervision in the New York State Central School. *Dissertation Abstracts International, 20*, 10, 3999.

Hunter, M. (1980). Six types of supervisory conference. *Educational Leadership, 37*, 408–412.

Hutchinson, J. M., Jr. (1973). A study of science supervision in the public high schools of Louisiana. *Dissertation Abstracts International, 34*, 08A, 4911.

Jackson, T. V. (1966). The scope and nature of quasi-supervision in the state of Oklahoma with focus upon the status and role of quasi-supervisors of secondary science and mathematics. *Dissertation Abstracts International, 26*, 07, 3720.

John-Steiner, V. (1985). *Notebooks of the mind: Explorations of thinking.* Albuquerque, NM: University of New Mexico Press.

Johnston, J. H. & Holt, L. C. (1983). Data-based instructional supervision and self-analysis. *NASSP Bulletin, 67*(463), 22–23.

Kennebrew, J. L. & Sistrunk, W. E. (1989, November). *Principals' supervisory behavior and school climate.* Paper presented at Annual Meeting of the Mid-South Educational Research Association, Little Rock, AR.

Killion, J. P. & Harrison, C. R. (1985). Clinical supervision: Comprehensive training for success. *Journal of Staff Development, 6*, 96–101.

Lee, V. W. (1958). The evaluation of supervision of secondary-school science instruction. *Dissertation Abstracts International, 19*, 09, 2289.

Mack, K. (1991). Actual and desired roles of reading supervisors. *Journal of Reading, 34*, 568–570.

Madrazo, G. M. & Hounshell, P. B. (1987, January). The role expectancy of the science supervisor: Results of research in science supervision. *Science Education, 71*(1), 9–14.

Martinello, M. L. & Cook, G. E. (1994). *Interdisciplinary inquiry in teaching and learning.* New York: Merrill.

May, W. T. & Zimpher, N. L. (1986). An examination of three theoretical perspectives on preservice field supervision. *Journal of Curriculum and Supervision, 1*, 83–99.

Mayfield, J. E. (1983). The effects of clinical supervision on pupil achievement in reading. *Dissertation Abstracts International, 44*, 04A, 940.

McCarty, D. J. (1986). Supervision and evaluation: Two irreconcilable processes? *Clearing House, 59*, 351–353.

Morrill, K. A. (1966). A comparison of two methods of reading supervision. *Reading Teacher, 19*(8), 617–621.

Murphy, D. (1988). Selected annotated bibliography. *Action in Teacher Education, 10*(1), 83–87.

National Clearinghouse for Bilingual Education (1987/1988). *Innovative staff development approaches: New focus, NCBE Occasional Papers, No. 4* (ERIC Reproduction Service No. ED 296 584).

Negley, H. H. (1962). Effectiveness in the supervision of social studies in relationship to the extent of authoritarianism in the practices of supervisors. *Dissertation Abstracts International, 23*, 10, 3694.

Pajak, E.F. (1989). Identification of supervisory proficiencies project: Final report. Unpublished manuscript, University of Georgia, Athens, GA.

Perrine, W. G. (1984). Teacher and supervisory perceptions of elementary science supervision. *Science Education, 68*(1), 3–9.

Rex, L. (1989). The micropolitics of supervision. *English Education, 21*(3), 170–181.

Richardson, G. D. & Sistrunk, W. E. (1988, November). *The relationship between secondary teachers' perceived levels of burnout and their perceptions of their principals' supervisory beliefs.* Paper presented at the Annual Meeting of the Mid-South Educational Research Association, Louisville, KY.

Ritz, W. C. & Cashell, J. G. (1980). "Cold war" between supervisors and teachers. *Educational Leadership, 38*(2), 77–78.

Ritz, W. C., Cashell, J.G., & Felsen, M. F. (1981). The effectiveness of science supervisors and their membership status within a faculty. *Journal of Research in Science Teaching, 18*, 229–240.

Rogers, E. M. & Shoemaker, F. F. (1971). *Communication of innovations: A cross-cultural approach.* New York: Free Press.

Rosser, J. D. (1980). Relationship of reading supervision and children's reading achievement. *Dissertation Abstracts International, 41*, 08A, 3510.

Schön, D. A. (1983). *The reflective practitioner: How professionals think in action.* New York: Basic Books.

Sergiovanni, T. J. (1984). Expanding conceptions of inquiry and practice in supervision and evaluation. *Educational Evaluation and Policy Analysis, 6*, 355–365.

Sergiovanni, T. J. & Starratt, R. J. (1979). *Supervision: Human perspectives.* New York: McGraw-Hill.

Sergiovanni, T. J. & Starratt, R. J. (1983). *Supervision: Human perspectives* (2nd. ed.). New York: McGraw-Hill.

Shrigley, R. L. (1980). Science supervisor characteristics that influence their credibility with elementary school teachers. *Journal of Research in Science Teaching, 17*, 161–166.

Sistrunk, W. E. (1982, April). *The Supervisory Behavior Description Questionnaire, Forms 1 and 2, as research instruments.* Paper presented at the Mississippi Inter-University Conference on Educational Administration.

Smyth, W. J. (1986). Clinical supervision: Technocratic mindedness, or emancipatory learning? *Journal of Curriculum and Supervision, 1,* 331–340.

Smyth, W. J. (1987). Cinderella Syndrome: A philosophical view of supervision as a field of study. *Teachers College Record, 88,* 567–588.

Snippe, J. (1992, April). *Effects of instructional supervision on pupils' achievement.* Paper presented at the Annual Meeting of the American Educational Research Association, San Francisco, CA.

Stronck, D. (1987). Teachers' attitudes toward science coordination in British Columbia's school districts. *Science Education, 71*(1), 21–27.

Suhor, C. (1985). Survey of language arts supervisors reveals more work, fewer resources—and optimism. *Educational Leadership, 43*(3), 85–86.

Thompson, E. & Williams, L. (1985). Creating confusion to encourage change. *English Education, 17*(1), 14–17.

Tracy, S. J. (1984). Expanding the view of instructional supervision: Shared and borrowed concepts from supervision of counseling. *Clearing House, 57,* 281–283.

Tracy, S. J. & MacNaughton, R. H. (1986). The neo-traditional approach to instructional supervision: Problems, promises, and options. *Contemporary Education, 57,* 130–134.

Trosky, O. S. (1971, April). *Modifications in teachers' questioning behavior in the development of reading comprehension and a series of supervisory conferences.* Paper presented at the meeting of the International Reading Association, Atlantic City, NJ.

Trosky, O. S. (1975). A training program for reading supervisors. Unpublished manuscript, The University of Manitoba.

Turner-Muecke, L. A. (1986). Reflection-in-action: Case study of a clinical supervisor. *Journal of Curriculum and Supervision, 2*(1), 40–49.

Urquia, S. T. (1975). Professional growth activities and in-service needs of northern Virginia public school elementary principals in the supervision of reading. *Dissertation Abstracts International, 36,* 05A, 2563.

Vogt, M. E. (1991, November). An observation guide for supervisors and administrators moving toward integrated reading/language arts instruction. *Reading Teacher, 45,* 206–211.

Waite, D. (1992). Instructional supervision from a situational perspective. *Teaching and Teacher Education, 8,* 319–332.

Waite, D. (1993). Teachers in conference: A qualitative study of teacher-supervisor face-to-face interviews. *American Educational Research Journal, 30,* 675–702.

Warner, A. R. (1980). Quick fixes don't work. *Educational Leadership, 37,* 424, 443.

Williams, R. E. (1986, November). *The relationship between secondary teachers' perceptions of supervisory behaviors and their attitudes toward a post observation supervisory conference.* Paper presented at the Annual Meeting of the Mid-South Educational Research Association, Memphis, TN.

Wolfer, H. A. (1978). Effectiveness of supervision vs. supervisory responsibility: A study of this relationship among secondary science supervisors in the state of Massachusetts. *Dissertation Abstracts International, 39,* 02A, 604.

Zimpher, N. L. & Howey, K. R. (1987). Adapting supervisory practices to different orientations of teaching competence. *Journal of Curriculum and Supervision, 2,* 101–127.

·18·

SUPERVISION IN THE FINE AND PERFORMING ARTS

Frances O. Rust, Terry A. Astuto, Mary Erina Driscoll, Michael W. Blakeney
NEW YORK UNIVERSITY

Jerrold Ross
ST. JOHN'S UNIVERSITY

Imagine a moment in a secondary school day: An art teacher is teaching painting to an introductory class of ninth graders. Some students have special artistic talents; many enjoy what they are doing, but do not consider art to be a major part of their high school curriculum. Some have had inadequate early experiences and don't want to be there; others are having little success in other aspects of their school days, and this is one place in which they feel engaged and comfortable. Some are students with disabilities for whom this is one of their few "regular" classes. This scene is repeated in music, in drama, in dance. Throughout the arts education program, the diversity of students in arts classes and the variety of reasons for their being there are significant factors in understanding the role and place of the arts in education.

Now imagine other moments. The "art cart" goes by. A high school principal is worried about the spring concert, or the annual play, or the winter art exhibit. A music teacher is traveling between the three elementary schools where she works. A fifth grade teacher asks the art teacher for help with her bulletin boards. Dance and drama teachers are negotiating with administrators and custodians for time to use the auditorium or the gym. A music teacher is contacting community members and businesses for donations of sheet music and instruments. A middle school team of teachers asks for help in integrating the arts into their interdisciplinary curriculum. A school board member is concerned about the choice of music for the holiday concert. A community group questions the propriety of work included in the school's art exhibit. Moments like these are commonplace in arts education.

Arts education is simultaneously central and marginal to the curriculum of schools. It reaches throughout the school—far beyond art, music, and drama classrooms—and into the community. It is rooted in culture, and the debates of the broader society become part of the foreground here perhaps more strongly than in any other aspect of education. Generation X, the diversity of a multicultural society, wealth and poverty, access and discrimination, politics, economics, fears, hopes, dreams, failures, promises—all dimensions of students' experiences are entwined in the arts, but the arts occupy a marginal position in the curriculum of both elementary and secondary education, largely because of a general conception of the arts as enrichment rather than an essential and basic part of education (Geahigan, 1992). "The arts," Williams (1987) writes,

have been assigned a marginal position in today's curriculum, and arts education is valued almost exclusively as a means of enhancing self-expression and creativity, rather than as an organized body of knowledge requiring the same kind of substance and intellectual rigor we expect in the sciences and humanities. No wonder, then, that in an era of belt-tightening of our school systems, art programs are often among the first to be cut, or that large numbers of our students never develop an appreciation or understanding of the arts. (pp. 12–13)

In the wake of California's Proposition 13, school districts throughout that state and in other parts of the country have followed California's lead toward lower expenditures for schools. Arts programs have either been cut back severely or abandoned. Where these programs do exist, they are, for the most part, treated in one of the following ways:

• As "special" classes: This is often the case in elementary schools where art and music classes might be given once a week for each grade in a school.

506

- As "electives": This is frequently the model in middle schools and high schools where students have the option to add arts-related courses to their basic, required courses in order to fill out their class schedules. Students who have special needs, such as the learning disabled or speakers of English as a second language, and disruptive students often find themselves unable to participate in elective arts classes because of the necessity of using such "extra" time for support classes.
- As "after school" activities: In both elementary and secondary schools, art, drama, and music clubs and lessons, and band, orchestra, and chorus rehearsals are part of the after-school/after-classes life of schools. These are often provided on school grounds by school faculty for a growing number of students who have nowhere to go until their parents return home from work.

The status of the arts in education reflects what Geahigan (1992) describes as a

deep-seated ambivalence about the significance of the arts and their value in American education, an ambivalence that persists to this day. Ever inclined toward the practical, American educators have tended to regard the arts as more enjoyable than necessary, as something to be attended to after the serious business of school had been finished. (p. 2)

An emphasis on the arts in education has been conspicuously absent from recent national and statewide reform efforts, such as Education 2000 or New York's Compact for Learning. Despite a strong movement toward developing integrated curricular and instructional approaches—a movement powered by the research of cognitive psychologists (Bruner, Gardner, Perkins), curriculum theorists (Eisner, Jackson, Noddings), and educators (Atwell, Graves, Heath, Holt) that demonstrates the importance of multisensory engagement in learning and, conversely, the estrangement from their studies felt by many students who experience only rote learning—there has been relatively little support given to bringing the arts into the general curriculum of both elementary and secondary education. Hence, arts educators—art, dance, drama, and music teachers—in the vast majority of schools around the country find themselves on the periphery of schooling, short on funding, few in number, often teaching their specialization alone without the support of colleagues, and rarely engaged in the mainstream of curriculum and instruction.

Given the tenuous position of the arts in schools, the issue of how to support the work of arts educators in their multifaceted and often ill-defined roles in schools and classrooms becomes very complex. How important is it, for example, that arts educators be supervised by educators with expertise in the fields of art education, music education, or drama education? Are there supervisory issues in arts education that are common across the elementary and secondary curriculum, or should there be a different set of standards used for guiding and evaluating the work of arts educators? Can an art educator supervise the work of a drama teacher and vice versa? What should be the focus and content of supervision in arts education? What strategies and approaches work best to support the work of arts educators in schools?

The purpose of this chapter is to explore these and other questions as they relate to supporting arts educators and arts education in schools and facilitating their professional development and success. In addressing these questions, we have considered:

1. a framework for understanding the place of the arts in the overall curriculum;
2. the professional, classroom, and school contexts in which arts educators work; and
3. ways of promoting the professional development of arts educators.

THE PLACE OF THE ARTS IN THE CURRICULUM

Arts education can help elementary and secondary school students to reach out

"beyond prime time" and understand the unchanging elements in the human condition. It can teach them to see and hear as well as read and write. It can help them understand what civilization is so that as adults they can contribute to it. In a culturally diverse society, it can generate understanding of both the core and multiplicity of America's culture. In an age of television, it can teach our children how the arts can be, and have been used. In a world made smaller by modern communication and travel, it can teach them how the cultures and civilizations of other countries affect attitudes, beliefs and behavior. It can help our children develop the skills for creativity and problem-solving and acquire the tools of communication. It can help them develop the capacity for making wise choices among the products of the arts which so affect our environment and daily lives (National Endowment for the Arts, 1988, p. v).

While this statement by the National Endowment for the Arts paints a clear picture of the potential of arts education, in many parts of the country, educators, policy makers, and members of the arts communities are actively engaged in a debate about the importance of the arts in elementary and secondary schools, about the appropriate content of an arts education curriculum, and about appropriate pedagogy. This conversation has a long history. Wolf (1992) identified several distinct stages leading to the present state of the arts curriculum. This evolution yields a framework that is helpful for understanding ways in which arts educators think about the content of their curricula and ways in which the arts are perceived in education.

The arts, Wolf writes, are now viewed by many as "a distinct form of knowledge, requiring sustained and demanding work and yielding kinds of empathy, understanding, and skill both equal to and distinctive from those available in chemistry, civics, or shop" (p. 945). However, this journey towards envisioning the arts as a way of knowing has not been easy and is far from complete. Such a vision departs radically from the earliest forms of American arts education.

Wolf argues that the inclusion of the arts in the curriculum of the nineteenth-century common school was a mixed blessing. The arts were assured their place in the curriculum, albeit as marginal subtext, and, like other subjects, were used as tools of Americanization. Music and art became "a *common* curriculum—a conveyor of values rather than a form of knowledge, to be sure—but necessary, not just nice" (p. 948). This nineteenth-century focus on a particularized set of values and the emergence of the "cult of efficiency" (Callahan, 1962) converged in a way that had a marked effect on the arts curriculum. Wolf observes:

It was a strange kind of Faustian bargain. The arts were admitted to the common curriculum—so long as they served virtue, religion, citizenship, and industry and so long as they assumed the look, the practices, and the diction of industrial or clerical work (p. 948).

With the advent of Dewey's (1934) work and the Progressive movement, the arts acquired a new status. The school became a place to nurture and free a child's creativity rather than a factory in which those natural impulses and talents were constrained. The arts presented unparalleled opportunities for the kind of free expression urged by Progressive educators. Children were seen as full-fledged artists in their own right (Wolf, 1992, p. 950).

Child development theory and, in particular, an emphasis on children's thinking and cognitive development, played an important role in the 1960s and 1970s in reshaping arts educators' views of children's abilities in music and art. The developmental abilities of children were fostered, Wolf (1992) writes, by appropriate experiences that enabled them to grow in their understanding of the arts:

A number of researchers and educators became involved in an effort to describe the stages of development *in order to provide a reasoned basis for arts instruction*. . . . But what was new was the emphasis on how children *worked* their way from stage to stage, rather than "just" discovering new possibilities for reference and expression in their paintings and drawings (p. 951).

In concert with the new research on cognitive development, the arts began to lay claim to the power to develop skills germane to many academic subjects, such as reasoning and close observation, and asserted their importance in developing abilities unique to artistic expressions. This new perspective on the arts had implications for arts educators. As Wolf (1992) points out,

Finally, the place of teaching and the role of instruction were acknowledged. More than designing generous environments or productive methods, educators were clearly responsible for sustaining and informing their students' work (p. 953).

Spurred on by the recent research on intelligence conducted by cognitive scientists such as Bruner et al (1966), Gardner (1983 and 1990), Perkins and Leondar (1977), others with Harvard's Project Zero, and supported by both public and private funding sources, arts education today has begun to emerge in some circles as an important means of achieving curricular integration and addressing the needs of increasingly diverse groups of learners. This current stage of the evolution of the arts curriculum derives from the belief that "artistic or aesthetic knowledge is different from other kinds of knowing in fundamental ways: in intention, in modes of making meaning, in its method and view of truth or excellence" (Wolf, 1992, p. 955).

The emergence of this new way of understanding and the recognition that aesthetic knowledge must be built on a thoughtful and engaged mix of doing, observing, and guided learning has enormous implications for the role and place of the arts in the curriculum of general education.

Burton (1994) moves us toward a vision of curricular integration in which the arts are on an even footing with other areas of the curriculum. Such a vision, Burton notes, requires radical change in the ways teachers teach and learners learn, for it implies "a willingness to abandon the confines of traditional subject matter altogether" (1994, p. 488). It also implies a rethinking of the ways in which we work in schools, not a simple reorganization of the curriculum to accomplish integration of subject areas:

First, artistry and skill do not simply emerge out of curriculum organization however thoughtfully designed and implemented; rather there is mounting evidence that the degree to which interdisciplinary infusion will actually enhance artistic knowledge and skills is dependent on the level of competence acquired within the discipline itself—learning in art. The second point is that whatever the curriculum format, the shaping of visual images through the transformation of materials plays a powerful, unifying, and integrating role. For it is in the process of shaping visual images that children explore, inquire, discover, reflect, imagine, develop new skill and synthesis [sic] responses in expressive form. Thus, the real question for curriculum planners is how to avoid sacrificing learning in art to learning through art and vice versa. Just as the fragmented curriculum of the kind that we now have in many schools can destroy continuity and concentration, so an integrated or interdisciplinary curriculum can forfeit depth and richness for cursory variety (p. 489).

While Burton is speaking directly to the issue of the visual arts in education, the same issues apply to the dramatic and musical arts (Miller & Coen, 1987; Surace, 1992). In each area, as Gilmore (1994) writes,

What we need is art teaching that emphasizes the process of thinking in symbols, that makes us use "texts" that help students at all levels learn how to begin to question, to think independently of received everyday meanings, and to begin to be ready to challenge inherited cultural meanings (p. 518).

To accomplish this, teachers must, as Jackson (1994) points out, "have integrated at least some of art's lessons into our own ways of responding to the world, including what we do as teachers. Only then will we be in a position to invite our students to do the same" (p. 547).

The evolution of the arts curriculum described by Wolf (1992) and the implications for teaching addressed by Burton (1992, 1994) and Jackson (1994) point to the tensions inherent in arts education and, thus, in the roles of arts educators. These include

- art for all and art for the talented;
- art as an outlet for creativity and art as authentic, disciplined, thoughtful practice;
- art as part of the common curriculum and art as a distinctive area of knowledge; and
- art to enable technical proficiency and art to introduce students to cultural traditions that can inform performance.

These philosophical and professional tensions are intriguing and healthy. As Lagemann (1994) observed: "If debating the value of the arts and their place in schools can enlarge our deliberations from the narrowly utilitarian to the more humane and enduringly significant, then surely such debates are essential to the well-being of this society" (pp. 437–438). There is a temptation, however, to engage in these conversations apart from the realities of the arts in schools. This is unfortunate. The improvement of arts education and the professional development of arts educators should be grounded in school and classroom contexts.

THE CONTEXT OF ARTS EDUCATION

The work of arts educators is nested in the broader societal domain in which debates about the purposes of school and the need for reform occurs. For the past decade, the emphases in school reform and improvement have been driven by goal setting and the specification of increased (or at least different) standards to guide student achievement. *Education 2000* of the Bush administration and the *Goals 2000: Educate America Act* of the Clinton administration reflect beliefs about the purpose of schools as the instrumental servants of the economy and capitalism. That translates into a curriculum intended to prepare today's children for tomorrow's workforce. The content of the curriculum targets literacy, math, and science. Renyi (1994) traces this focus to "the definition of the public schools as institutions designed to effect social rather than intellectual development" (p. 443). This perspective on the purposes of schools has meant trouble for arts education. Goodlad (1992) observed:

There has been a downside to the centrality of universal schooling defined instrumentally that arguments for schools committed to education for its own sake have not been able to counter—a downside not favorable to the arts. We have only to look at the standardized tests used to determine the health of our schools to realize that the arts simply do not count; what is not measured is not important. The impact of this instrumental paradigm on the place of the arts in schools is exacerbated by other popular perceptions. For example, the arts are "soft" and better suited to the nursery school and kindergarten years where women teachers dominate. They are to be left behind for the "tough" subjects—mathematics and sciences—in the more masculine world of schooling that tends to follow. Also, the arts are to a considerable extent tactile—more of the hand than the head—and so, goes the thinking, are not within the core of truly intellectual subjects. And as for talent and giftedness, the classic sorting machine is the intelligence test and its dependence on linguistic and quantitative abilities as the determinants of IQ (p. 195).

Now, as in the past, interest in and support for the arts in education has waxed and waned with the cycles of change in education and the political and economic forces at work in the country as a whole. As McLaughlin (1987) notes,

All of this arts education momentum at the national and state level should indicate that the conditions for educating children in the arts are improving. This improvement comes after a series of severe cutbacks in arts education during the late 1970s, the result of fiscal crises in school systems (especially in large urban centers and rural districts) and of the emphasis on "back to basics education."

Still, the status of arts education in local schools remains grim. States such as California and Massachusetts, through referendum tax reform, have eliminated arts education in their elementary schools. . . . New York City has mandated visual arts and music curricula in the elementary schools, yet has not mandated specialists to teach these areas. Chicago reports that there are only 28 specialists combined in visual art, music and dance who serve all of the elementary schools in that city.

Advocates for arts education at the local level often times do not exist. The advocates who are there do not have adequate information to convince superintendents of education or school boards of the need for arts education for students that includes cultural literacy as a main goal. Even school systems which have established arts education as an important goal lack the resources needed to design truly effective arts curriculum; therefore, principals, arts specialists and classroom teachers still are a long way from making the arts central to a student's school program (p. x).

A utilitarian perspective on the purposes of schools names the arts as irrelevant and squeezes the arts education curriculum into spaces in the school day left over by curricular focuses that matter more. In his pioneering study of schools, Goodlad (1984) notes that the inclusion of the arts in the curriculum of elementary schools correlates significantly with the length of the school week and the use of instructional time: In schools where the instructional week is over 23 hours (slightly more than the average for his sample), time is given to the arts; when it is under 23 hours, the arts are virtually absent.

In recent times, there have been a number of arts education programs implemented in schools, the progress of which has made them interesting case studies and valuable models for educational reformers. According to Fowler (1980), successful programs have certain common characteristics. They:

- relate the arts to each other and to other school subjects of study;
- strengthen existing art and music programs while expanding to others like theater, dance, environmental design, photography, film making, and the literary arts;
- draw more fully on community resources—artists as well as arts and cultural organizations;
- meet the special needs of special children—both the gifted and the handicapped; and
- help reduce personal and racial isolation (p. 17).

Brooks (1991) reviewed 13 programs across the country—including programs such as Harvard's Project Zero, New York City's Cultural Advisory Concil (CAC), and Minnesota's Comprehensive Arts Planning Program (CAPP). Her findings are similar to those of Fowler (1980). In the successful programs that Brooks described:

1. administration and teachers are deeply involved in the development of a plan and of curriculum for the arts programs, and they stayed involved;
2. there was a strong commitment of funds and necessary resources;
3. there was commitment to ongoing staff development; and
4. these programs benefited from good coordination.

Brooks' summary echoes the findings of Medeja (1973) whose intensive study of a large Midwestern school system was one of the first comprehensive studies of an arts in education program.

Like other researchers looking into the change process (Berman & McLaughlin, 1978; Fullan, 1993), York (1989), who was studying corporate involvement in three arts education programs in schools, found that the educational initiatives he was studying were discontinued once the money supporting them had run out. In each case, he found the support of teachers' efforts to use the new programs, the visibility and status given these initiatives, and communication between teachers and administrators to be critical to the longevity of the programs in the schools.

Vallance's (1991) study of an arts education program in the seventh grade at Harding Junior High School, in Cedar Rapids, Iowa, demonstrates how schools "create extraordinary programs from relatively ordinary resources, often in mysterious or at least unpredictable ways" (p. 381). Harding's seventh grade curriculum includes a full year of arts education, a requirement that exceeds the district's minimum. A high ratio of arts educators (9 of 53 full-time teachers for 950 students) provide more arts electives than any other junior high school in Iowa. The principal and teachers tap into a wide array of community resources in ways that energize the artistic life of the school, and simultaneously, connect the students and the school to the artistic life of the community. And, Vallance shows, the students participate:

In addition to the required general art and music, Harding offers in the course of a year five fine arts classes, six crafts classes, orchestra, two periods of band, five dramatics classes, and choir at three levels. There is a full-time teacher associate assisting the music teacher. Students elect these classes in droves. The 950 or so students at Harding produce (with some overlap) over 700 enrollments in the visual arts courses during the year, the highest of any junior high in Iowa, and over 600 enrollments in music courses; most of these, needless to say, are students opting to exceed the seventh grade requirements (p. 385).

Harding's teachers and administrators created a school context in which the arts are central, accessible and fully integrated into students' lives both in and out of school. Underlying the arts curriculum at Harding Junior High is a seriousness of purpose that is focused on learning, experiencing, and developing intelligent consumers of the arts. In his study, Vallance (1991) "uncovered" the commitments of teachers, administrators, parents, and the community that were critical in creating this environment:

Being intelligent consumers requires early and serious exposure to numerous art forms, and this exposure is guided by commitment (1) to the role of the community in nurturing artistic appreciation and expression; (2) to a belief that the arts should be accessible to all; (3) to the importance of personal initiative and involvement in the arts and (4) to a belief that the arts should be taken seriously (p. 388).

These commitments support and are supported by a school context in which

1. school-wide policies recognize the legitimacy of arts education;
2. a collaborative professional community enacts curricular linkages;
3. the principal is an enthusiastic spokesperson for arts education, providing resources and connections to the areas of the artistic community; and
4. synergistic relationships with the school maintain community support.

In the case of Harding, Vallance (1991) observes:

The legitimacy of art is proclaimed in the low teacher-pupil ration, in the number of electives, in the daily class meetings, and in the full-year requirement for art. All of these provide the time for the teachers to treat art in an appropriately serious way but all require financial resources and sanctions from the administration (p. 394).

School policies often marginalize the arts. This is most evident in decisions about assignments of students and teachers, class schedules, and allocation of resources. Both Goodlad (1984) and Eisner (1992) note that, in most American schools, the arts receive about two hours of instructional time per week at the elementary school level and are generally not a required subject of study at the secondary school level. This communicates the limited importance accorded the arts, but, as Eisner observes, it has other implications as well:

Thus, time represents both value and opportunity: value, because it indicates what is considered significant; opportunity, because the school can be thoughts of as a culture of opportunity. A culture in the biological sense is a place for growing things. Schools, too, are cultures. They are cultures for growing minds, and the directions this growth takes is influenced by the opportunities the school provides. These opportunities are defined by the school's program—its curriculum—and by the artistry with which teachers mediate that program. A school in which the arts are absent or poorly taught is unlikely to provide the genuine opportunities children need to use the arts in the service of their own development (p. 592).

As Goodlad (1992) observed, many believe that the arts are "soft," that is, that they do not fit within a framework that stresses the disciplined thinking required for mathematics and science. The one exception here, writes Geahigan (1992), "is the study of literature, in large part because of its ties to the language arts, the very core of the public school curriculum" (p. 2). Along with beliefs about the content of the curriculum go assumptions about learning and student achievement, which further reduce room for the arts. It is common practice in schools, write Goodlad (1992) and Renyi (1994), to make access to the arts available only *after* basic requirements have been fulfilled and then generally to academically gifted and talented students. Goodlad's (1984, 1992) data show how "slow learners" and children of poverty are often denied access to the arts:

Slow students find themselves not only in the low-track classes featuring lower status and more immediately utilitarian subject matter, but also in additional remedial courses in the basic subjects. Since entry into college is viewed by counselors and, ultimately, by these students, as unlikely, the need to think about future employment opens up the vocational education alternative. The combination of taking the courses required for graduation and a sequence of vocationally oriented courses pushes the arts to the margins for most. These are students predominantly from economically marginal backgrounds and many are also members of minority groups. Artistic talent among these young people is as widespread as it is among those students who enjoy the luxury of greater choice. Most of these curricularly disadvantaged students not only are deprived of the opportunity to prepare for lifetime enjoyment of the arts but also are cut off from initial access to the long road that could lead to development of this talent (pp. 198–199).

Such beliefs about curriculum, learning, and achievement constrain professional practice in education and especially in arts education for they close off to teachers and to learners what Maxine Greene (1992) describes as "situated knowing" (p. 505), the ability of "people (old or young) [to] be personally present to what they are doing or what they are attending to. . . . Only conscious, active moves toward the work at hand," she notes, "can lead to the opening of new perspectives or the breaking through of crusts of conformity" (p. 495).

Stake, Bresler, and Mabry (1991) observed that the conversations by leaders in the field of arts education do not map onto the classroom realities of arts educators where, as Oddliefson (1994) notes, "arts educators are laboring under intolerable conditions, not the least of which is the general attitude that what they teach is irrelevant" (p. 448). Stokrocki (1990) observed that, especially at the secondary school level, arts educators teach large classes in short time blocks with inferior and inadequate supplies, in poor facilities. Student class schedules are built around requirements and "academic" subjects; in this framework, the arts serve as "fillers." Teachers' schedules are often built in blocks and their lunch and/or preparation periods and other responsibilities occur while their students are in arts classes. At the elementary and middle school levels, the same patterns are in evidence. In addition, there are generally too few arts educators to teach too many students. Hershfeld (1993), for example, found: "In New York City, two thirds of public elementary schools have no art teachers, and only two of the city's 32 school districts have an art and music teacher in every school. This means it is impossible to meet state requirements that students take at last one arts course before they graduate" (p. 40).

Where strong arts education programs exist, as Remer (1980) points out, they are generally found in school systems that developed effective general education programs. These school systems, Remer notes, have the following characteristics:

1. *A commitment to quality education for all children.* Along with this goes the establishment of a mechanism for systemic change and innovation.
2. *A commitment to quality education through the arts.* A significant number of chief school officials, administrators, teachers, and parents subscribe to the belief that teaching and learning through the arts improves the quality of education for all children. . . . They have found that, by incorporating the arts into all aspects of schooling, children develop positive attitudes towards learning, a stronger sense of themselves, and a keener awareness of the world around them.
3. *The creative use of existing human, financial, and physical resources.*
4. *A coherent, collaborative approach to program planning and development.* Programs are planned, developed. operated, and assessed by those who participate in them. Consequently, these programs related to the actual strengths and needs of individual schools and make use of the appropriate resources in the schools and community. Professional consultants in the arts and education are involved in the planning and development process.
5. *An organic program design.* Though they will vary from school to school, effective arts in general education programs have at least three related points of emphasis in common:
   a) Strong programs in all the arts for all children;
   b) Interdisciplinary teaching and learning; and
   c) Effective and regular use of community cultural resources, including services provided by artists and arts institutions.
6. *A continuing curriculum and staff development effort.* Program planning and development occur simultaneously with curriculum and staff development workshops, seminars, and meetings.
7. *On-going internal and external documentation and evaluation.* Evaluation of the school's efforts in program planning and development are continuous, largely internal, and address questions of effectiveness in terms of the goals and objectives the school has set for itself. Judgments about quality and achievement are made by those best in the position to render and make use of them, and modifications are made as soon as they are needed.
8. *An effective communication network.* A conscious and systematic effort is made to share information about the school's new arts programs, and problems and prospects are discussed within the school, with other schools and cultural institutions, and with community advisory groups.
9. *A broadened and humanistic concept of schooling.*
10. *An increased commitment to and understanding of the change process in education.* School systems that have developed effective arts in general education programs have not only improved the quality of teaching and learning in their schools but also developed a greater understanding of the change process. This process is generally most effective when the individual school is viewed as a social unit and the most powerful agent for progressive change in education (pp. 237–239).

The studies of Brooks (1991), Medeja (1973), Vallance (1991), and York (1989) bear out Remer's (1980) observation that "when an entire school system embarks on an arts in general education project, certain kinds of changes take place in the schools and community" (p. 237). These studies provide a useful way to frame a discussion of the school context in which arts education can be effectively and successfully situated, and they help to define the parameters of the work of those who guide and support the work of arts educators in schools.

PROMOTING THE PROFESSIONAL DEVELOPMENT OF ARTS EDUCATORS

In its study *Toward Civilization: A Report on Arts Education*, the National Endowment for the Arts (1988) makes the following observation about arts education in the schools:

We have found a gap between commitment and resources for arts education and the actual practice of arts education in classrooms. Resources are being provided, but they are not being used to give opportunities for all, or even most, students to become culturally literate. The arts are in general not being taught sequentially. Students of the arts are not being evaluated. Many arts teachers are not prepared to teach history and critical analysis of the arts (p. v).

"This condition," the authors of the report conclude, "is *not* worse now than it has been" (p. v).

Arts education is, for the most part, on the periphery of schooling. To move it to center place and to move school administrators and arts educators towards the expansive, constructivist vision articulated by Burton (1992, 1994), Greene (1994), Jackson (1994), Wolf (1992), and others requires a radical rethinking not only of the curriculum but also of the conduct of and conditions for art education in schools. "For art education to truly mature," writes Wright (1994), "we need to unshackle our traditional notions of creativity and invent a new art education dedicated to substance and meaning" (p. 57).

Houser (1991) draws on the work of Vygotsky to construct a structure for teaching the arts that blends creating, knowing, collaborating, and critiquing:

If, as Vygotsky has suggested, all cognitive construction is socially mediated, then it is clearly counterproductive to insist that students engage in cognitive exercises which have not been designed with respect to relative social and personal context(s). Although art education remains at the forefront of experientially based pedagogy, there is little evidence to indicate that social mediation as a component in the construction of meaning in art has received specific attention (p. 33).

Houser (1991) proposes a "collaborative processing cycle of art education" based on Harste, Short, and Burke's (1988) "authoring cycle," which was derived from Bruner (1960). He describes this cycle as a "participation structure which engages students in dynamic analysis and evaluation of each other's art work—both process and product" (p. 35). The cycle consists of eight steps:

1. Creation of a safe, intellectually stimulating environment
2. Exposing student artists to a variety of media, styles, and techniques
3. Experiential periods of "play" with an emphasis on process
4. Beginning planning for the creation of a piece that has personal significance to the student, drawing on personal experience
5. Small group or partner exchange to share thoughts and reactions with ample time for reflection and feedback
6. Revisions in view of active reflections on peer feedback
7. Repeat small group or partner exchange or provide for whole class display and critique
8. Invention to further artistic engagement (p. 37).

An important part of the cycle that Houser (1991) has defined is, obviously, critique. Teachers guide these sessions by establishing topics for self and group evaluation: original intentions, audience, media selection, special challenges, and descriptions of ways in which collaboration influences individual decision-making:

The emphasis of the critique, as always, is the search for meaning through the construction of knowledge. . . . Teachers are instrumental in establishing the desired learning environment. In addition to modeling the kinds of questions which lead to greater understanding, they may also render insightful evaluative judgments. However, the teacher's opinions and observations must remain entirely open for challenge or rebuttal. This opportunity for reciprocity is an underlying principle of fair play, and subsequently, of environmental safety (p. 36).

Godfrey (1992) describes other skills and abilities that are also required of arts educators, including familiarity with new media technologies such as the computer and the video recorder.

The most critical dimensions of classroom context relate specifically to curriculum and instruction. Burton (1992) distinguishes between two ways of teaching art: "art with a capital *A*" and "art with a small *a*." Those who teach art with a capital *A* "teach conventional techniques and formulas—the trick of the art trade" to their students. They do this, Burton holds, "in the name of having children behave 'as artists' in order to be initiated into the vernacular of artistry" (p. 15). According to Burton, this approach, while typical of the teaching of many arts educators, runs counter to the constructivist notion of learner-centered pedagogy in which the skills and techniques associated with an arts form are learned in a context and at a time and level of complexity that are appropriate for the learner.

Art with a small *a* calls for teachers to select out of their "own repertoire(s) of understanding just those insights that will best serve children at different times in the growth and development" (p. 15). This requires that we

rethink our ideas of artistry with a big A, recast them in the context of ideas about representation and symbolic capacities . . . embark on the difficult task of rethinking our own conventional conceptions, tracking them back, so to speak, to their origins in human experience so that we can come to know the many and different levels, nuances, and interweaving out of which our own insights have grown to artistic maturity (p. 16).

This activity of rethinking and reconceptualizing is a prerequisite to teachers making wiser decisions about how and what to teach their students.

Stake, Bresler, and Mabry (1991) propose thinking about arts education as deep discussions between teachers and students about those things that they have come to cherish—ranging from the artistic to the seemingly mundane. "Our children," they write, "need to be encouraged to explore, to see, and hear with other eyes and ears, to sense the power of understanding that can be gained from another's point of view, to translate their own thoughts and feelings into a socially communicable and engaging form" (p. 345). These "shared cherishings," argues Jackson (1994), increase awareness of what someone else has found worthwhile. Of course, as Jackson points out, such an approach raises questions: How do teachers engage in these conversations with students in an environment of "intimacy and warmth"? How will teachers realistically find a place for these reflections in a crowded curriculum within a demanding day? And, most important, how will these conversations move from the "simply diversionary" to the educative? Answers to these questions have to do with the ways that the work of arts educators is understood and supported in schools.

Clearly, these are calls for substantive change in the teaching of the arts, and the changes envisioned are such that, if they are successfully implemented will have an impact that will be felt far beyond the arts education environment. As Shapiro, Place, and Schneidenhelm (1973) note, "one of the important results of an artist's involvement in the school is a new, improved level of energy in the whole school population" (p.14). The issue, then, becomes one of determining the optimal environment for arts education.

Research on administration, supervision, and evaluation of arts education programs in the schools has two major foci: 1. arts teaching and teachers, and 2. the implementation of arts programs.

SUPERVISING AND EVALUATING ARTS TEACHING AND TEACHERS

The central dilemma of supervision and evaluation of arts educators is whether to consider their work as generally the same as or radically different from the work of other teachers. Fowler (1988) holds that "the artist who teaches cannot escape the need to master teaching techniques" (p. 75), and he is not alone in this judgment. Still, there is the issue of the specialized knowledge and techniques that are central to the artistic experience and how these are recognized, nurtured, and assessed. Who should assess the work of arts educators? Should arts education supervisors be specialists in their areas or should they be generalists? What skills, attitudes, and knowledge do arts educators value most in those who provide leadership in schools? What do they need to support their work?

Mills (1991b) found little uniformity in the ways in which the position of arts supervisor is construed in schools. He writes that "each arts supervisory position and its circumstances (title, job description, staff, school district) seem to be unique" (p. 13). In large districts, the position is often a full-time one in which the arts supervisor and his or her staff work through the district office of curriculum and instruction. In small districts, "the person providing district wide leadership (in the arts) may spend a portion of the school day teaching and will probably share a secretary. In other school districts, an administrator such as a principal or curriculum director may be assigned responsibility for coordinating the arts; in still others, a supervisors of *one of the arts* may be assigned as supervisor of *all of the arts*" (p. 13).

In her study of the perceptions of music supervisors, Porter (1994) notes that the demands on music supervisors' time from other areas of the school are so great that they hinder their ability to work effectively to support the work of music educators. "Supervisors," she writes, "need to have the freedom to be the *music* supervisor and not have constraints from other responsibilities such as discipline hearings or visual art supervision. The effectiveness of the music supervisor as it relates to the music instructional program will continue to be limited as long as the music supervisor has multiple responsibilities" (p. 110).

Topping (1991) found that there were some interesting and intriguing differences in the ways in which arts supervisors are perceived by school administrators and arts teachers:

Educators tend to perceive multi-arts coordinators differently than single focused art coordinators. Principals and other administrators typically value the views of generalists more than specialists because of their perceived ability to understand the "big picture" while coordinating arts programs. The generalist tends to be closer to the power structure and thus can have more influence in helping teachers with budget and scheduling matters. On the other hand, art teachers have greater respect for the art coordinator's in-depth knowledge of the art field and often feel that the specialist can give them more assistance and understanding (p. 79).

Topping concludes his discussion with what he describes as "a clear bias" towards

having specialists as art coordinators whenever feasible. The specialist's technical mastery and conceptual awareness far outweigh the comprehensive vision and political acceptance of the generalist. The specialist provides the optimal art curriculum, instructional, and staff development because of time, availability, greater content knowledge, and more staff acceptance (p. 82).

Topping (1991), however, like Eisner (1994), Mills (1991b), and others, recognized that the economics of education do not always permit this optimal arrangement. He suggested the use of outside consultants with expert knowledge in art education as well as engaging arts coordinators in staff recruitment/ selection, peer coaching, and curriculum/staff development. "Although I am partial toward the specialist," Topping writes, "the key challenge is for selected art leaders in each school system to draw upon available resources to provide an optimal art program. This is especially critical in this conservative era where the existence of creative self-expressions is threatened by an overemphasis on the cognitive aspects of art" (p. 82).

It is a fine line that arts education supervisors walk these days, a veritable tightrope strung between opinion poles. How do we know whether a teacher is teaching well? Who defines the standard of good teaching? These are among the perennial questions in schooling, and they take on a special significance in the area of arts education in which the judgment of quality can be so subjective on the part of teachers, supervisors, students, and communities.

Glass (1993) recommends an integration of formative and summative evaluation methods and of working with supervisors who are both generalists and specialists. "Most successful evaluation programs," he writes,

contain four critical elements which contribute to their success. First, the school system is committed to providing all the necessary resources to operate the evaluation program. There is a strong sense of support to the process and product and a belief that the results are well worth the effort. Second, there is an understanding that all administrative participants must be well trained in the philosophy and mechanics of the adopted program of evaluation. As new administrators are added, they must be trained in the program. Teacher participants must also be trained in the process and informed of the district's expectations. Third, there needs to be a sense of collaboration between the teacher and the evaluator. The evaluation process is viewed as a joint effort with all aspects of the process being conducted in a humane and collegial manner. A feeling of give and take is evident and the concerns of all participants are heard and discussed. Finally, the process involves an integration of the district's goals and the teacher's unique and specific instructional strategies (p. 41).

In his research on evaluation and support of marginal art teachers, Glass (1993) found that most school systems subscribe to what McGreal (1983) describes as "common law approaches" to evaluation. According to Glass,

A common law process occurs when a school district has used an evaluation program for so long that it appears to be "married" to the program. These systems give lip service to teacher improvement as their prime purpose, but really only provide for termination or tenure evaluations. Although formative on the surface, they are really summative in operation (p. 41).

Glass (1993) rejects models that focus on student achievement as a gauge of teacher competence. He found the most effective approaches to supervision and evaluation to be those that engage teachers as partners in the process. Among those that he cites is an *objective setting model* described by Redfern (1980), which begins with the teachers conducting a self-assessment of their strengths and weaknesses. "The model," writes Glass,

addresses problems with validity by involving the teacher in the process of determining the criteria of evaluation. After the objectives have been established, the teacher and evaluator work on the process of identifying strategies to address them. The evaluation team, comprised of the teacher and the evaluator, also review the process of conducting the evaluation experience. This process usually involves establishing a series of scheduled and unannounced site visits to observe the teacher. A visit is usually preceded by a pre-conference and followed by a post observation conference. The observation process allows the evaluator to monitor the teacher's performance in comparison to district expectations and provide constructive feedback. At the close of the agreed upon evaluation period, the team reviews the overall results of the teacher's efforts and plans for future improvement (p. 47).

Redfern's (1980) is similar in many ways to Goldhammer, Anderson, and Krajewski's (1980) expansion on the *clinical supervision* model developed by Cogan (1973). As Glass (1993) notes,

Most forms of evaluation tend to oversimplify the nature of teaching by starting with predetermined criteria. Clinical supervision, by contrast, derives issues from the teaching situation and takes seriously the teacher's analysis. Supervision is a partnership in inquiry with the supervisor as a more experienced practitioner instead of an aloof expert (p. 53).

In these models, there is a collegial relationship between teachers and supervisors. Each begins with an understanding of teachers as skilled practitioners. Thus, they are particularly appropriate in the field of art education, where the individual artistry and expertise of the teacher is a critical element of instruction. In the right environment and given a collaborative interaction between the supervisor and teacher, these approaches can move supervisory interaction close to what Eisner (1982) describes as an *"artistic approach"* to supervision:

By artistic I mean using an approach to supervision that relies on the sensitivity, perceptivity, and knowledge of the supervisor as a way of appreciating the significant subtleties occurring in the classroom, and that exploits the expressive, poetic, and often metaphorical potential of language to convey to teachers or to others whose decisions affect what goes on in schools, what has been observed. In such an approach to supervision, the human is the instrument that makes sense of what has gone on. The major aim is to improve the quality of educational life in schools (pp. 59–60).

In this context, the issue of evaluating teachers' work goes beyond checklists. It incorporates all those elements that are intrinsic to good teaching in any field: knowledge of content, classroom management, instructional planning, skilled interaction with students, and assessment of student progress. It speaks both to and from teachers' lived experience in the classroom and in the school. In arts education, the assessment of instruction must, out of necessity, address the ways of knowing and skilled activity that are central to a given area; hence, there is a need for arts supervisors who are themselves experienced arts educators. And this in turn leads to consideration of the issue of how specialized the arts supervisor should be.

Porter (1994) found that music supervisors and coordinators in Georgia thought it was essential that music education programs be guided and supported by music educators:

The uniqueness of music as a subject did, however, imply that the music supervisor could function in a unique way. Because many educators are not trained musicians or music educators, they would not be as suited to the supervision of a music program as a music supervisor. There were needs of teachers present that were best met by someone who understood the subject matter (p. 111).

Others, like Glass (1993), suggest that *peer coaching* can provide an effective means of supporting teachers. However, he notes, "districts must be ready to give extensive, sophisticated training of such coaches" (p. 297). "An effective coach," writes Glass,

needs to be a skilled observer of teacher and student behavior. Also, the coach needs to be able to capture information related to the various behaviors demonstrated by the teacher and the teacher's students. Therefore, the coach needs to possess excellent data collection skills. The coach should be able to analyze the collected data, determine which aspects of the observed teacher's performance facilitated student learning and which elements detracted from learning, and be able to provide appropriate feedback . . . (p. 295).

O'Donnell and Crow (1991) point out that this is a role for which many arts educators are not prepared. Most of the arts educators whom O'Donnell and Crow interviewed had an understanding of the role of supervisor/administrator that included "familiarity with three . . . forms of leadership . . . charismatic, bureaucratic, and human relations. The one unfamiliar form of leadership was collegial" (p. 92). O'Donnell and Crow found that "[arts] teachers with 4–12 years of teaching experience were more likely [than teachers with less experience] to justify a collegial staff development plan for its interpersonal benefits" (p. 97). They attribute this openness to stages of teacher development:

If these individuals with 4–12 years of experience perceive that they have achieved basic mastery of teaching practice, they may be more interested in professional relationships with colleagues. This is the stage that Katz (1977) refers to as the renewal stage of teacher development when the teacher is rewarded by meeting peers, formally and informally, rather than developing skills in the mechanics of teaching, as was done in the earlier career stage (p. 97).

Arts educators, O'Donnell and Crow (1991) point out, may be different from other teachers in that, for them, "art teaching is a primary professional choice rather than a default for those who cannot make it as an artist" (p. 99). Therefore, arts educators who are prepared to work collegially with other arts educators bring to their work a commitment to the field as well as a deep understanding of the discipline itself. "The profession at large," write O'Donnell and Crow,

should also realize the unique assets that the art teacher brings to administration. The nature of the art teacher's work includes broad contact with other teachers, school building administrators, and district administrators, thereby providing opportunities to grasp the 'big picture.' The tendency to have had experience working directly with adults provides the art teacher with more opportunities to develop interpersonal skill necessary for effective administration. Art teachers are more likely to have had broad community contacts through such activities as sponsoring art exhibits, judging juried shows, and contributing to community art projects. This community contact broadens and enriches the skill that art teachers bring to administration. Acknowledging these unique and critical skills permits us to move beyond the proverbial coach-to-principal tracks and encourage art teacher-to-principal career tracks (pp. 99–100).

While the work of O'Donnell and Crow (1991) focused exclusively on art teachers moving into supervision and administration in schools, their findings are echoed in Porter's (1994) study of the perceptions of music supervisors and coordinators and seem both relevant and appropriate to understanding the work and the ethos of other arts educators, whether they are musicians, dancers, actors, or writers. Often, opportunities to work with and move arts educators into supervisory positions in schools become possible when districts are implementing new programs that require ongoing, onsite work to support teachers' use of innovation.

IMPLEMENTING NEW ARTS PROGRAMS IN THE SCHOOLS

According to Hord, Rutherford, Hauling-Austin, and Hall (1987), both "bottom-up" and "top-down" change initiatives can work in schools:

We have seen both approaches result in effective change and in improved practices in the classroom, school, and school district. The important factor in all cases, whether at the single teacher level or at the level of all teachers across a district, is the support and assistance provided to make the change. If properly facilitated, both strategies can work (pp. 7–8).

York's (1989) study of various arts-in-education initiatives bears out the observation of Hord et al. (1987), but Brooks (1991), Fowler (1980), and York (1989) also make clear that the success of such initiatives is dependent on a clear understanding of the initiative and on commitment from the central office. As Berman and McLaughlin (1978) pointed out almost 20 years ago, "'who originated a project did not matter. . . . What did matter was 'how' project planning was carried out, regardless of the source of the idea" (pp. 74–75). Innovations proposed by teachers or by the community that do not gain support from the district office and the principal of the school appear to fail at the outset.

The critical issue here is leadership. Successful innovations, according to Berman and McLaughlin (1978), are those in which the new program is institutionalized and the process of making the innovation a part of the life of a school and ensuring its continuation, long after initial seed monies have been curtailed and early supporters have moved on to other things, inevitably falls to the school principal or to instructional supervisors.

In arts education, both principals and supervisors are critical of the outcome of new programs. Brooks (1991) found that an "arts manager" was an extremely useful "buffer between teachers and an authoritative principal" (p. 228). She also found that "implementation of a creative program is better served with an open leadership style that encourages problem solving" (p. 229). Porter's (1994) finding that human relations skills were critical to the effectiveness of music supervisors in their interactions with administrators and teachers underlines the often delicate negotiation that is required to maintain strong arts programs in the framework of general education.

As noted above, O'Donnell and Crow (1991) found that among the art educators whom they studied, collegial forms of leadership were the least well understood. They observed that "the move from art teacher to art administrator involves a career change from one professional role to another" (p. 87), and they surmise that such a move occasions a radical reassessment of one's work:

First, balancing the three orientations of artist, teacher, and future administrator is more difficult than balancing the roles of teacher and future administrator. Second, the balance of artist and teacher permits both collegiality and solitude in work. But the move to administration disrupts that balance by running the risk of decreasing collegiality.

Administration has been characterized as a "lonely job for the person at the top" (Jackson, 1977) (p. 88).

The difficulty for arts educators moving into supervisory and administrative positions has to do with the image or understanding of the role and work of supervisors and administrators and recognizing that the move to arts administrator/supervisor does not need to signal a break with prior experience. It can, in fact, be seen as synchronous with earlier work.

Brooks (1991) recommends that in complex program innovations similar to the one that she studied,

key people need to be involved in the planning process. The notion here is that the planning of the project is almost as important as implementation, particularly because the planning phase sets the context for implementation. Therefore, when unpredictable occurrences arise, the people involved from the ground floor up have a greater understanding of the dynamics of the change effort and they can explain the sequence of events and give reasons for why something did or did not happen rather than exhibiting victimization of circumstances (p. 228).

Such engagement calls for leadership from supervisors and administrators that values community and creates a norm of collegiality.

The arts supervisor's reach, like that of arts teachers, extends far beyond the classroom and the school building. It is the parents and the community who inevitably affect the outcome of innovations in arts education, for they are the ones who have the last word in what their children learn. The supervisor's willingness and ability to create community around arts education is critical. As Brooks (1991), Fowler (1980), and York (1989) discovered, principals and superintendents can articulate the need for an arts program and demonstrate their support, but it is the arts supervisor who bridges the divide between teachers and administrators, who sets a climate for collegial interaction among teachers—not just among arts teachers—who supports and guides teachers in the translation of theory to practice, and who acts as "town crier" to the community, bringing news of what is happening in the school and voicing the rationale for those activities—translating practice into theory.

SOME FINAL THOUGHTS

In this chapter, we have attempted to explore ways in which administrators and supervisors can support arts educators and arts education. There is no question that arts education has been in a tenuous position in schools for some time—at once both essential and a frill, central to the work of general education and on the margins of schooling. Because their work both requires and allows for creativity and nontraditional approaches, arts educators, like early childhood educators, often find themselves alone at the cutting edge of innovation. We have made an effort here to show the tremendous potential inherent in the work of arts educators for integration and a broad-based, meaningful revisioning of the curriculum of elementary and secondary education. We have tried to substantively describe the complexity of the work of arts educators and particularly arts supervisors, who must operate both as generalists and specialists combining their artistry and love of their area of the arts with a commitment to education for all through their work of supporting and guiding arts educators in the schools. The power of the arts to transform the lives of children, and thus, of the nation, is so great that there is no question that the important work of arts education must be recognized and supported not just in affluent areas but across the country in urban and rural schools and in elementary and secondary school settings.

REFERENCES

Berman, P. & McLaughlin, M. W. (1978). *Federal programs supporting educational change: Vol. VIII. Implementing and sustaining innovations.* Santa Monica, CA: Rand Corporation.

Brooks, K. (1991). Implementation of an art in education program in an elementary setting: A case study of a curricular innovation. Unpublished doctoral dissertation, Teachers College, Columbia University, New York.

Bruner, J. S. (1960). *The process of education.* New York: Vintage Books.

Bruner, J. S., Oliver, R. R., & Greenfield, P. (1966). *Studies in cognitive growth.* New York: John Wiley & Sons.

Burton, J. M. (1992). Art education and the plight of the culture: A status report. *Art Education,* 7–18.

Burton, J. M. (1994). The arts in school reform: Other conversations. *Teachers College Record, 95*(4), 477–493.

Callahan, R. E. (1962). *Education and the cult of efficiency: A study of the social forces that have shaped the administration of public schools.* Chicago, IL: University of Chicago Press.

Cogan, M. L. (1973). *Clinical supervision.* Boston, MA: Houghton Mifflin.

Dewey, J. (1934). *Art as experience.* New York: G. P. Putnam's Sons.

Eisner, E. W. (1982). An artistic approach to supervision. In T. J. Sergiovanni (Ed.). *Supervision of teaching* (pp. 53–66).

Eisner, E. W. (1992). The misunderstood role of the arts in human development. *Phi Delta Kappan, 73*(8), 591–595.

Eisner, E. W. (1994). *The educational imagination: On the design and evaluation of school programs* (3rd ed.). New York: Macmillan. Alexandria, VA: ASCD.

Fowler, C., (Ed.). (1980). *An arts in education source book—A view from the JDR 3rd Fund.* New York: The JDR 3rd Fund.

Fowler, C. (1988). *Can we rescue the arts for America's children? Coming to our senses—10 years later.* New York: American Council for the Arts Books.

Fullan, M. G. (1991). *The new meaning of educational change.* New York: Teachers College Press.

Gardner, H. (1983). *Frames of mind: The theory of multiple intelligences.* New York: Basic Books.

Gardner, H. (1990). *Art education and human development.* Los Angeles, CA: Getty Center for Education in the Arts.

Geahigan, G. (1992). The arts in education: A historical perspective. In B. Reimer & R. A. Smith (Eds.). *The arts, education, and aesthetic* knowing. *Ninety-first yearbook of the National Society for the Study of Education, Part II* (pp.1–19). Chicago, IL: University of Chicago Press.

Gilmore, J. C. (1994). Educating imaginative thinkers. *Teachers College Record, 95*(4), 508–519.

Glass, W. R. (1993). A framework for the evaluation and support of marginal teachers with specific reference to art teachers. Unpublished doctoral dissertation, Teachers College, Columbia University, New York.

Godfrey, R. (1992). Civilization, education, and the visual arts: A personal manifesto. *Phi Delta Kappan, 73*(8), 596–600.

Goldhammer, R., Anderson, R. H. & Krajewski, R. J. (1980). *Clincal supervision: Special methods for the supervision of teachers.* New York: Holt, Rhinehart & Winston.

Goodlad, J. I. (1984). *A place called school.* New York: McGraw-Hill.

Goodlad, J. I. (1992). Toward a place in the curriculum for the arts. In B. Reimer & R. A. Smith, (Eds.). *The arts, education, and aesthetic knowing.* (91st yearbook of the National Society for the Study of Education, Part II: pp.192–212). Chicago, IL: University of Chicago Press.

Greene, M. (1994). Carpe diem: The arts and school restructuring. *Teachers College Record, 95*(4), 494–507.

Harste, J. C., Short, K. G., with Burke, C. (1988). *Creating classrooms for authors: The reading-writing connection.* Portsmouth, NH: Heinemann.

Hershfeld, A. (1993, September 22). The strategic good sense of arts education. *Education Week, 13*(3), 40.

Hord, S. M., Rutherford, W. L., Hauling-Austin, L. & Hall, G. E. (1987). *Taking charge of change.* Alexandria, VA: ASCD.

Houser, N. O. (1991). A collaborative processing model for art education. *Art Education, 44*(2), 33–37.

Jackson, P. W. (1977). Lonely at the top: Observations on the genesis of administrative isolation. *School Review, 85*, 425–432.

Jackson, P. W. (1994). Thinking about the arts in education: A reformed perspective. *Teachers College Record, 95*(4), 542–554.

Katz, L. (1977). *Talks with teachers.* Washington, D.C.: National Association for the Education of Young Children.

Lagemann, E. (1994). For the record: The arts and educational debate. *Teachers College Record, 95*(4), 435–441.

McGreal, T. L. (1983). *Successful teacher evaluation.* Alexandria, VA: ASCD.

McLaughlin, J. T. (1987). *A guide to national and state arts education services.* New York: American Council on the Arts.

Medeja, S. S. (1973) *All the arts for every child: Final report on the Arts in General Education Project in the School District of University City, Missouri.* New York: JDR 3rd Fund.

Miller, A. & Coen, D. (1994). The case for music in the schools. *Phi Delta Kappan, 75*(6), 459–461.

Mills, E. A., (Ed.). (1991a). *Supervision and administration: Programs, positions, perspectives.* Reston, VA: National Arts Education Association.

Mills, E. A. (1991). The need for a supervisor. In E. A. Mills, (Ed.). *Supervision and administration: Programs, positions, perspectives* (pp. 11–18). Reston, VA: National Arts Education Association.

National Endowment for the Arts. (1988). *Toward civilization: A report on arts education.* Washington, D.C.: Author.

Oddliefson, E. (1994). What do we want our schools to do? *Phi Delta Kappan, 75*(6), 446–451.

O'Donnell, K. & Crow, G. M. (1991). From art teacher to art supervisor: Views of teacher collegiality. In E. A. Mills, (Ed.). *Supervision and administration: Programs, positions, perspectives* (pp. 83–97). Reston, VA: National Arts Education Association.

Perkins, D. & Leondar, B. (Eds.). (1977). *The arts and cognition.* Baltimore, MD: Johns Hopkins University Press.

Porter, B. E. E. (1994). The role of the music supervisor in Georgia: Perceptions of practicing music supervisors/coordinators. Unpublished doctoral dissertation, University of Georgia, Athens, GA.

Redfern, G. B. (1980). *Evaluating teachers and administrators: A performance object approach.* Boulder, CO: Westview.

Remer, J. (1980). Ten characteristics of school systems that have developed effective arts in general education programs. *An arts in education source book—a view from the JDR 3rd Fund* (pp. 237–239). New York: The JDR 3rd Fund.

Renyi, J. (1994). The arts and humanities in American education. *Phi Delta Kappan, 75*(6), 438–445.

Shapiro, S. R, Place, R. & Schneidenhelm, R. (1973) *Artists in the classroom.* Hartford, CT: Connecticut Commission on the Arts.

Stake, R., Bresler, L. & Mabry, L. (1991). *Custom and cherishing: The arts in elementary schools.* Urbana, IL: Council for Research in Music Education.

Stokrocki, M. (1990). A cross-site analysis: Problems in teaching art to preadolescents. *Studies in Art Education, 31*(2), 106–117.

Surace, E. (1992). Everyone wants to join the chorus. *Phi Delta Kappan, 73*(8), 608–612.

Topping, R. J. (1991). Art specialist vs. art generalist: Timely considerations. In E. A. Mills (Ed.). *Supervision and administration: Programs, positions, perspectives* (pp. 77–82). Reston, VA: National Arts Education Association.

Vallance, E. (1991). Alchemy in Iowa: Arts education at Harding Junior High School. *Teachers College Record, 92*(3), 381–395.

Williams, H. M. (1987, March/April). Philanthropy and art education: The role of the private foundation. *Design for Arts in Education, 88*, 12–13.

Wolf, D. P. (1992). Becoming knowledge: The evolution of art education curriculum. In P. W. Jackson (Ed.). *Handbook of research on curriculum* (pp. 945–963). New York: Macmillan.

Wright, J. (1994). The artist, the art teacher, and misplaced faith: Creativity and art education. *Art Education, 43*(6), 50–57.

York, G. T. (1989). Arts education in the public schools: Three case studies of corporate involvement. Unpublished doctoral dissertation, Teachers College, Columbia University, New York.

·19·

SUPERVISION IN OCCUPATIONAL
EDUCATION FIELDS

Maynard J. Iverson
UNIVERSITY OF GEORGIA

Dwight J. Pullen
CHEROKEE COUNTY (GEORGIA) SCHOOLS

INTRODUCTION

The purpose of this chapter is to review the research on supervision related to the vocational-technical, or "practical arts" educational programs in the United States. Although there are many facets of skill training at work across the nation, the lion's share of what little research is available comes from the level that has been in existence longest, the secondary school vocational program. We have chosen to concentrate on this level for several reasons: (1) the relative availability of research in these traditional, long-established programs; (2) the extensive experience that we have had in the secondary school arena; and (3) the shared conviction that, for many youngsters, high school vocational programs are the last, best chance for job preparation—the dropout from secondary school is unlikely to go on to postsecondary technical preparation or higher education.

The danger in this approach, however, is that the reader may come to the conclusion that the *only* occupational education occurring in America is in its public high schools. That would be a huge error, for much of America's working-age population is currently engaged in work-related educational programs. Indeed, education for work in the United States can be described as widespread, provided in both public and private settings, involving myriad agencies and organizations, and encompassing traditional as well as "high-tech" areas of

employment. For this reason, we chose the more inclusive term, *occupational education,* as both the title of the chapter and in frequent references throughout.

The advent of the vocational supervisor in secondary schools is a parallel development with federal legislation that proliferated in the 1970s and 1980s when as much as one-third of a school's budget could be from state and federal "vocational" funds. Thus, it is important for the reader to see the flow of legislation over the years, which we have included in some detail. At the time of this writing, a significant restructuring of vocational-technical education is taking place under various and often restrictive legislation. Acting in concert with the reduction in federal funding, many states have enacted laws which are changing the appearance and emphasis of secondary school vocational education—mostly toward integration with academic subjects. If the pending school-to-work legislation is successful, many skill-centered vocational programs—particularly trade and industry programs—will largely disappear from the public schools. To fill the void, many states are upgrading and expanding one- and two-year postsecondary technical educational systems, in both technical institutes and occupational divisions of community colleges. Proprietary vocational schools are also expanding.

A likely result of this restructuring is the demise of high school vocational supervisors as we have known them. In the new structure, the supervisor of occupational programs—exploratory, traditional, school-to-work and coop/apprentice-

ACKNOWLEDGMENTS We would like to express our appreciation to the following reviewers of the preliminary draft of this chapter; we invite their participation in the future revision of the chapter: Dr. Wesley E. Budke, Dr. C. Cayce Scarborough, Dr. Curtis Finch, Dr. C. Paul Scott, and Dr. J. Foster Watkins.

518

ship education—will undoubtedly wear several hats such as assistant principal, assistant superintendent, or curriculum coordinator. In Georgia, we are already seeing this occur as a common reality.

Much of the literature has focused on the role of the occupational supervisor. Thus, we have attempted to trace development from the federally mandated and funded state supervision in the Vocational Education Act of 1917, to the local supervisor of the 1980s to the multitasked and multititled supervisor of the 1990s. A somewhat unexpected finding in the Pullen (1996) study of future roles of the supervisor of occupational programs is that visionary leaders in vocational-technical education foresee a continuation of many current functions, such as curriculum management and instructional improvement. Where the supervisor of the future will function and what the extent of his or her powers to influence the system of education for work will be are subjects for study, discussion, and perhaps a peek through a crystal ball. We invite the reader to join us in this quest. The following sections may provide fodder for the effort.

DESCRIPTION OF OCCUPATIONAL EDUCATION

Occupational fields of education are viewed by the professional educator as generic terminology reflecting formalized experiences involved in the exploration and preparation for work (Finch & McGough, 1982). Contemporary occupational education occurs in a wide range of settings, among greatly varied clientele. Public secondary schools and postsecondary institutions comprise a large number of programs, which are usually referred to as vocational and technical education, respectively, and are under the auspices of the United States Department of Education for some funding and reporting purposes. The current total enrollment in these schools is difficult to determine, but several agencies gave an indication of the size of the programs as follows:

Secondary schools: The United States Department of Education (USDE) reported that, in 1992, 24% of public secondary students qualified as "vocational students" by having enrolled in three or more occupational courses (USDE, 1994). Multiply this figure by the approximately 12 million public secondary students in 1995, and you come up with 2.8 million students enrolled in vocational programs.

Postsecondary schools: The Digest of Educational Statistics (USDE, 1995) listed the postsecondary technical enrollment in the United States for the 1992–1993 school year as 1,027,713 students. Since the 2-year, postsecondary school is a rapidly growing sector of the field, it can be assumed that there were approximately 1.5 million students enrolled in public postsecondary/technical education by 1995. Thus, by extrapolation, it can be estimated that nearly 4.5 million students were enrolled in American public secondary and postsecondary vocational and technical education programs during the 1995–1996 school year.

Another agency that oversees public occupational education in the form of employment and training is the United

States Department of Labor. Public training programs that have operated under the Manpower Development and Training Act (MDTA), the Comprehensive Employment and Training Act (CETA), and the more recent Job Training Partnership Act (JTPA), have involved hundreds of thousands of nontraditional, handicapped, or socioeconomically disadvantaged, at-risk individuals.

Occupational education and training are also provided extensively by corporations, unions, the military, government agencies, private schools, and for-profit businesses. According to the *Statistical Abstract of the United States* (U.S. Department of Commerce, 1995) 69% of the more than 50 million Americans who were engaged in adult education programs in 1990 and 1991 were taking job-related education or training.

Because of the diversity of efforts which can be described as occupational education and the inherent difficulty in examining these disparate and often emerging fields, the authors chose to limit the discussion of supervision to that which is found in public secondary and postsecondary educational institutions. Many of the findings and recommendations of research within this sector of the field will, of course, have some application to the other programs across the spectrum. To understand supervision in the context of occupational education, however, one must first look at the origins and trace the development of the field.

DEVELOPMENT OF OCCUPATIONAL EDUCATION

The first form of occupational or vocational education was apprenticeship. The traditional apprenticeship lasted from two to seven years, during which the apprentice was taught the skills of the trade by a master. According to Finch and McGough (1982):

the master was to provide the apprentice with the same religious, moral, and civic instruction that he gave his own sons. In this context, the master served as a teacher-leader-worker. He had responsibility for developing the total individual, one who was competent in a craft and would be a contributing member of society (p. 4).

Apprenticeships have continued to be used today in many industries and educational institutions. However, modern apprenticeships sadly seem to have lost the concepts of the whole person and of helping each individual become a contributing member of society. Today, apprenticeships are much more skill-specific and focused on development of a competent, specialized worker.

The federal government had no initial interest in education. However, the country was still very young when support for public education began. The 1785 Land Ordinance set aside one section (640 acres) in each western township for education. The 1787 Northwest Ordinance noted congressional concern and support for public education (Finch & McGough, 1982).

The first federal legislation to support vocational education was the Morrill Land-Grant Act of 1862. The grant provided 30,000 acres (or more, depending on the number of senators and representatives) to each state to establish agricultural and mechanical colleges. The second Morrill Act of 1890 provided additional annual funding for the land grant colleges and established funds for traditionally black institutions (Finch & McGough, 1982).

In 1914, Congress established the Commission on National Aid to Vocational Education. The Commission's purpose was to determine if vocational education was needed and to what extent federal funding was necessary. The Commission's report was largely responsible for the passage of the Smith-Hughes Act of 1917. The Smith-Hughes Act is considered to be the Magna Carta of vocational education. It created the Federal Board for Vocational Education and required each state to develop a similar board. The Act provided each state with a yearly appropriation for vocational education of $5,000 through 1923 and $10,000 per year thereafter. The law required each federal dollar to be matched by state and local dollars in the areas of trades and industry, agriculture, and home economics. A key aspect of the law was the provision of state supervisors of agriculture, home economics, and trade and industry education (Oravet, 1989).

Since the Smith-Hughes Act, many federal acts have affected vocational education. A brief description of the major acts through 1977 was developed by Finch and McGough (1982):

1918 Smith-Sears Act (Public Law 64–347): The first vocational-rehabilitation legislation. This legislation helped disabled veterans discharged from the armed forces to return to civil employment.

1920 Smith-Fess Act (Public Law 65–178): Made it possible for civilians to receive vocational rehabilitation if they were disabled in industrial accidents during civil employment.

1929 George-Reed Act (Public Law 66–236): Increased appropriations for vocational agriculture and home economics.

1934 George-Ellzey Act (Public Law 70–702): Refunded the expired George-Reed Act and provided funding for trade and industry programs.

1937 George-Dean Act (Public Law 73–245): Replaced the expired George-Ellzey Act, with the added inclusion of funding for distributive education.

1943 Barden-LaFollette Act (Public Law 74–673): Provided vocational rehabilitation for men disabled and classified as unfit to serve in the armed forces.

1946 George-Barden Act (Public Law 79–586): Increased funding for existing programs and expanded the role of the federal government.

1946 Employment Act of 1946 (Public Law 79–304): Established the President's Council of Economic Advisors and was designed to provide for the elimination of unwanted unemployment.

1954 Vocational Rehabilitation Act (Public Law 83–565): Provided for relieving existing shortages in rehabilitation personnel and facilities.

1958 National Defense Education Act (Public Law 85–864): Provided for technician training and guidance services.

1962 Manpower Development and Training Act (Public Law 87–415): Provided for occupational training and placement for disadvantaged persons.

1963 Vocational Education Act (Public Law 88–452): Provided for equal opportunity for all citizens to receive occupational education and employment, especially the disadvantaged and unskilled populations of America included the first allocation of funds for vocational supervisors at the local level (Public Law 89-329).

1965 Education Professions Development Act: Provided support for potential and current occupational education leaders to develop and update their administration and supervision skills.

1968 Vocational Education Amendments of 1968 (Public Law 90–576): Provided for the cancellation of all previous vocational education legislation except the Smith-Hughes Act. It served to extend and solidify the federal commitment to vocational education and earmarked funds for the disadvantaged.

1972 Education Amendments of 1972 (Public Law 92–318): Created the Bureau of Occupational and Adult Education, which is a part of the United Stated Office of Education. It also expanded the role of vocational education for special-needs students.

1973 Comprehensive Employment and Training Act (Public Law 93–203): Provided for a consolidation of numerous special-needs programs into a revenue-sharing concept that is managed by local prime sponsors (local communities); assumed much of the responsibility of MDTA and was aimed at hard-core unemployed youth and adults having no occupational skills.

1975 Education for All Handicapped Children Act (Public Law 94–142): Required all state plans to provide high-quality educational programs for the handicapped within a "least restrictive environment."

1976 Vocational Education Amendments of 1976 (Public Law 94–482): Provided for extension of services funded by the 1963 and 1968 acts.

1977 Youth Employment and Demonstration Projects Act (Public Law 95–93): Provided for the creation of a youth-adult conservation corps and the preparation of teenagers and young adults for work. It was aimed at school dropouts and potential dropouts (pp. 25–26).

Iverson (1995) provided the summary from 1978 through 1994:

1978 Comprehensive Employment and Training Act (Public Law 95-524): A continuation of 1962 and 1973 Act; ensured coordination and cooperation among all federal, state, and local private and public agencies involved in the vocational education and training of workers.

1982 The Job Training Partnership Act (Public Law 97–300): Established programs to prepare youth and unskilled adults for entry into the labor force.

1984 Carl D. Perkins Vocational Education Act (Public Law 98–524): Established funding authorization for a five-year period focused on improving vocational programs and serving special populations.

1988 Family Support Act (Public Law 100–485): Established the Jobs Opportunity and Basic Skills Training (JOBS) program, which was to ensure that needy families with children obtain the education, training, and employment that will help them avoid long-term welfare dependency.

1990 Americans with Disabilities Act (Public Law 100–336): Mandated elimination of discrimination, established standards for assessing discrimination, and assured congressional authority to enforce the fourteenth Amendment.

1990 Individuals with Disabilities Education Act (IDEA) (Public Law 101–476): Required that every student with a disability receive transition services from school to adult life.

1990 Carl D. Perkins Vocational and Applied Technology Education Act (Public Law 101-392): Brought the largest ever federal funding authorization for vocational education—up to $1.6 billion a year through 1995, with a major portion of funds earmarked for "tech prep" programs and greater opportunities for disadvantaged people.

1994 School-to-Work Opportunities Act (STWOA, Public Law 103-239): Addressed the need for well-defined transition from secondary to postsecondary institutions or training programs. Three core components of learning were identified: (1) school-based learning that emphasized high academic and occupational instruction; (2) work-based learning that provides for ongoing training and mentoring; and (3) connecting activities that bridge academic and workplace learning.

1994 Goals 2000: Educate America Act (Public Law 103-227): Provides a framework for meeting the National Education Goals; state participation is voluntary. The National Education Goals are as follows:

1. All children will start school ready to learn.
2. At least 90 percent of students will finish high school.
3. Students will leave grades 4, 8 and 12 with demonstrated competence in English, math, science, foreign languages, civics and government, economics, arts, history, and geography.
4. Teachers will have access to programs for the continuous improvement of their skills.
5. The United States will be first in the world in math and science achievement.
6. Every adult will be literate and possess the skills to compete in a global economy.
7. Every school will be free of drugs and violence.
8. Every school will promote involvement of parents in their children's education.

1994 National Skills Standards Act (Public Law 103-227): Established a National Skills Standards Board to serve as a catalyst in stimulating the development and adoption of a voluntary national system of skill standards and of assessment and certification of attainment of skill standards.

While federal legislation has had a major impact on the development of occupational education and its supervision, the emergence of state and local institutions has also greatly influenced the field. State supervision, supervision in local systems, and local institution supervision have resulted because of the strengthening of state and local agencies involved in occupational education.

CURRENT STATUS OF OCCUPATIONAL SUPERVISION

At a time of increased national emphasis on preparation for work, vocational-technical educators face perhaps the greatest challenge to the survival of their programs. The success of vocational-technical education in the past has been a direct result of strong state supervisory leadership. Today, in many if not most states, reductions in vocational leadership at the state level have placed even greater responsibility on the local vocational supervisor. Yet, only a few states have well-articulated programs for development of this local leadership. A compounding factor is the practice of local systems to have the vocational supervisor jointly assigned to wear two or more hats—such as assistant principal and vocational supervisor. This practice, along with the use of noncertified personnel, has weakened the influence of the vocational supervisor in local school systems.

A paucity of research specific to supervision in vocational-technical education led the authors to conduct a survey of major institutions involved in the University Council for Vocational Education. Nearly all respondents at the 20 institutions surveyed reported some form of certification for vocational supervisors in secondary schools in their respective states, but only five indicated that their states had certification for postsecondary supervisors. Even then, the respondents were concerned about the change in state policies toward more generic certification. Fourteen institutions had academic programs for the certification of secondary school vocational (and, in a few cases, postsecondary/technical) supervisors. Programs varied substantially in length and course requirements. However, a pattern of "core" courses appeared to center around pragmatic courses, such as curriculum, philosophy, foundations, and administration/supervision. Other courses often included in approved programs were: special needs, school law, leadership, policy, and program-specific areas.

Faculty qualifications for teaching the supervisor certification programs were most often experience as local or state supervisors and some—but often limited—course work in their respective doctoral programs. Research reported by the active institutions as being specific to vocational-technical supervision was often limited to student theses and occasional professional articles and developmental projects. The survey indicated a general need for policies and programs to address the emerging field of vocational-technical supervision.

RESEARCH IN OCCUPATIONAL SUPERVISION

Supervisory positions are relatively new in the total scheme of occupational (vocational/technical) education. Federal/state funding for occupational supervisory positions was first provided by the Vocational Educational Act of 1963, as was mentioned previously. Since 1963, studies have been conducted to identify leadership attributes, tasks and competencies, and the general role of the occupational supervisor.

An early study (Stephens, 1967) found that in Utah the vocational administrator was primarily involved with planning, training, and evaluating personnel. Loudermilk and Webb (1973) studied vocational administrators in Texas. They concluded that the primary area of concern was in planning and program development.

A Missouri researcher (Sireno, 1973) could not obtain agreement on the actual role of the local vocational school director. He found a lack of uniformity concerning the minimum requirements of the local vocational leader.

Harrington (1973) studied competencies judged essential for vocational administrator effectiveness. Harrington found that knowledge-based competencies were more often considered essential than competencies of attitudes and skills.

Holt (1973) noted no significant differences between the actual and ideal roles of Tennessee directors of vocational education. Professional activities and administration and supervision had a high priority rating, while community interaction and research activities were considered low priority.

A study of perceived leader behavior and teacher morale was conducted by Laird (1974). Laird used the LBDQ-Form XII and found a significant positive relationship between perceived leadership behavior and teacher morale.

Klein (1974) identified the basic management and leadership skills needed for mid-management vocational personnel. He labeled them as:

1. human relations;
2. local, state, and federal relations;
3. business/industry-education relations;
4. planning and budgeting;
5. research and inquiry;
6. administrative operations; and
7. evaluation and accountability.

Ericksen (1975) attempted to identify the "ideal" leadership role of local Minnesota vocational education administrators. He noted that the "ideal" leader should hold a master's degree, have three to four years of work experience, place emphasis on vocational education and administration, and be responsible for programs for educating students from kindergarten through adulthood.

Desirable qualifications for the area vocational center director in South Carolina were defined by Bell (1975). He identified them as: a master's degree, 4–6 years of teaching experience, and secondary principal or supervision certification with one or more vocational endorsements.

Aiken (1976) studied the actual and ideal dimensions of leadership behavior of vocational education directors in Tennessee. The directors were more effective in accomplishing tasks than in interpersonal skills.

A Michigan study (Rosenthal, 1976) compared job satisfaction of vocational teachers to the perceived leadership role of vocational education administrators. Rosenthal found a higher level of job satisfaction among teachers who perceived that the administrator possessed high interpersonal skills than among teachers who perceived that the administrator possessed high task-oriented skills.

The Vocational Research Coordinating Unit of the Alabama State Department of Education (1976) noted, "The ideal applicant for the positions of local vocational director and area vocational center administrator possesses a master's degree, at least 6 years of vocational teaching experience, at least three years non-teaching experience, a secondary certificate endorsed in one or more vocational areas, and preferably endorsement as a principal or supervisor" (p. 12).

Howard (1981) studied the relationship between tasks performed by vocational supervisors, their importance, and school size. He noted that vocational supervisors considered business and financial management-related tasks to be the most important and staff development activities to be the least important functions performed.

Bryant (1983) used the Leader Effectiveness and Adaptability Description Instrument developed by Hersey and Blanchard (1977) to compare the demographic characteristics and leadership behaviors of female vocational teachers with those of female vocational administrators. She noted that both groups used high task/high relationship as their predominant leadership style and that administrators used all four styles more often than the teachers.

In Oklahoma, Sharpton (1985) studied the leadership styles of 24 area vocational administrators. Sharpton utilized the Management Style Diagnosis Test developed by Reddin (1970) and found the high task/high relationship leadership style to be the most prominent. In a similar study, Cimperman (1985) wanted to determine if differences existed in the perceived leadership styles of male and female administrators in the Wisconsin Vocational, Technical, and Adult Education System. The high task/high relationship leadership style was perceived to be dominant in all administrators.

A study of Midwestern vocational administrators by Baugher and Schlichting (1986) identified general administration, instruction, and supervision as the primary role functions.

In Ohio, Barrick (1989) conducted a study of burnout and job satisfaction of vocational supervisors. He concluded that a large number of vocational supervisors were experiencing high levels of burnout and noted that the Ohio vocational education program and local schools must address this issue.

Oravet (1989) utilized the Management Style Diagnosis Test developed by Reddin (1974) to study the dominant leadership styles of Alabama's high school principals and area vocational center directors. The results showed no statistically significant differences between the perceived leadership styles of the two groups.

In an effort to define vocational leader attributes, Moss and Liang (1990) reviewed a large number of publications. From the available information they developed the following list of attributes:

I. CHARACTERISTICS
  A. Physical
    1. Energetic with stamina
  B. Intellectual
    2. Intelligent with practical judgment
    3. Insightful
    4. Adaptable, open, flexible

5. Creative, original, visionary
6. Tolerant of ambiguity and complexity
C. Personal
7. Achievement-oriented
8. Willing to accept responsibility
9. Assertive, takes initiative
10. Confident, accepting of self
11. Courageous, resolute, persistent
12. Enthusiastic, optimistic
13. Tolerant of stress and frustration
14. Trustworthy, dependable, reliable
15. Venturesome, risk taker
16. Emotionally balanced
D. Ethical
17. Commitment to the common good
18. Personal integrity
19. Evidences highest values and moral standards

II. KNOWLEDGE AND SKILLS
A. Human Relations
20. Communication with others
21. Tactful, sensitive, respectful
22. Motivation of others
23. Networking
B. Management
24. Planning
25. Organizing
26. Team building
27. Coaching
28. Managing conflict
29. Managing time and organizing personal affairs
30. Managing stress
31. Using leadership styles appropriately
32. Holding ideological beliefs appropriate to the group
C. Cognitive
33. decision-making
34. Problem solving
35. Gathering and managing information (p. 13)

In an effort to utilize the identified attributes, Moss, Johansen, and Barry-Craig (1991) developed and tested the Leader Attributes Inventory (LAI) instrument. "As envisioned throughout its development, two of the potential uses of the LAI by vocational educators are 1) as a tool for program evaluation and 2) as a self-assessment" (p. 27).

Finch, Gregson, and Faulkner (1991) examined the leadership behaviors exhibited by successful secondary and postsecondary vocational education administrators. They discussed leadership behaviors related to the seven identified areas: physical, intellectual, personal, ethical, human relations, management, and cognitive. They also noted: "Future vocational education administrator preparation programs should target key leader attributes and ensure that these attributes are accounted for in the preparation experience" (p. 31).

In a study for the National Center for Research in Vocational Education, Finch, Gregson, and Reneau (1992) focused on things that supervisors do: comprehensive leadership development, resource selection and use, and leadership development resources and resource selection. They empha-

sized the need to build leadership programs around the individual, giving thought to where the person is, where he or she is going, and where he or she will end up. They also noted: "It is clear that many types of potentially useful leadership development resources are available. Most of these resources are not specifically designed for use in vocational education leadership development; however, it appears that many may be easily adapted to vocational education settings and clientele" (p. 29).

Moore, Crudup, and Vander Wall (1992) surveyed school superintendents, principals, vocational teachers, and local vocational directors and found the directors had four primary activities: administration, instruction, program promotion, and personnel. They noted that the vocational directors needed to be more substantially involved in program promotion and more moderately involved in personnel. The authors quoted *The Report of the Panel of Consultants on Vocational Education* (cited in Moore et al, 1972): "The leadership of vocational education will determine both its quality and effectiveness. In a rapidly changing world this leadership must be dynamic and forward looking, able to adapt its thinking to the constantly changing situation which it faces" (p. 63). The authors affirmed that this 1963 report still holds significance for today's leaders.

THE IDEAL VOCATIONAL SUPERVISOR

Minimum requirements or entry level qualifications of the vocational supervisor vary somewhat in the literature. A general summary from the literature provides these essential basic requirements: the vocational supervisor should hold a master's degree, have three to four years of nonteaching work experience, have four to six years of teaching experience, hold administration or supervision certification with one or more vocational endorsements, and should ideally exhibit the 35 attributes identified by Moss and Liang (1990).

The vocational supervisor is primarily concerned with planning, program development, and evaluating personnel. It is generally noted that knowledge-based competencies are more important than skill-based competencies. Likewise, administration and supervision activities are considered more important than research activities. Basic management and leadership skills can be labeled as follows: human relations; local, state, and federal relations; business/industry education relations; planning and budgeting; research and inquiry; administrative operations; and evaluation and accountability. The effectiveness of the vocational supervisor and teacher morale are directly related to the perceived abilities of the supervisor.

In order to be more effective, the vocational supervisor must utilize self improvement. The ideal leader should know his or her own strengths and weaknesses. Many instruments have been developed to assist in this self-assessment process. The Management Style Diagnosis Test (Reddin, 1970), the Leader Effectiveness and Adaptability Description Instrument (Hersey & Blanchard, 1977), the Myers-Briggs Type Indicator (Myers & Myers, 1987), the Leader Behavior Analysis II (Blanchard, Hambleton, Zigarmi, & Forsyth, 1991), and the

Leader Attributes Inventory (Moss & Johansen, 1991) have been used often in vocational supervisory studies. The professionally oriented supervisor can develop an individualized leadership plan to capitalize on strengths and improve weaknesses through utilization of one or more of these instruments.

FUTURE VOCATIONAL SUPERVISORS' DUTIES

As the new century approaches, vocational supervisors must perform duties necessary to conduct programs which prepare students for both further education and entry into the world of work. The worker of the future will engage in life-long learning. All educators should ask themselves, "Are we preparing the graduates of the year 2000 and beyond for life after high school?" To this end, one can make the argument that the vocational supervisor must understand the duties which need to be performed in the next century.

Vocational supervisors and instructors in secondary schools are especially challenged to meet these demands. They should try to prepare students to enter postsecondary educational institutions or the world of work. Toffler (1974) stated, "All education springs from some image of the future. If the image of the future held by society is grossly inaccurate, its educational system will betray its youth" (p. 3).

Changes in vocational education may best be implemented through the vocational supervisor. According to Ryan and Norton (1991), "As a leader you must expect change, welcome change and encourage change—change not just for the sake of change, but for the sake of building schools and programs that put quality first" (p. 39). Their research indicates that supervisors can either take the easy way and react to events and changes proposed by others or take charge and lead their faculties and communities in positive directions. The time has come for occupational educators to look to the future and find those possible directions for improving the quality of educational programs. More specifically, it is time for the vocational director to admit that improvements are needed and then accept the leadership responsibilities for that change.

Much current supervisory research focuses on leadership for vocational education. The need for vocational leadership is defined, dimensions of leadership are defined, and attributes of the leaders are defined; however, the desired behaviors and performance expectations of that leader are *not* defined. Valentine (cited by Moore, Crudup, & Vander Wall, 1992) called "for a clear definition of the role and responsibilities of the local vocational director, since the local director plays such an important role in the delivery of vocational education, and since the implementation of that role can create conflicts" (p. 64). Many conflicts can be avoided if the role of the supervisor is clearly defined. Bjorkquist (1982) noted the need to identify the functions of vocational supervision as follows:

In one sense, it seems unimportant to identify which functions are supervisory and who does the supervising. It can be argued that it doesn't matter what we call supervision or who does it, as long as it gets done. Analogously, we can say that it doesn't make any difference what an automobile is called as long as it provides transporta-

tion. However, we expect that those who buy, sell, repair, and have contact with automobiles on a frequent basis will know make, model, and year. This identification information is useful to those concerned about the functioning of an automobile. Similarly, the identification of supervision is important to those who do it. If the quality of supervisory practice in vocational education is going to be improved, the improvement effort needs to be focused. This requires that the tasks of supervision in vocational education be identified (pp. 27–28).

Wenrich (1990) believed that the principal/supervisor is the key figure for quality and equity in education. Defined duties act as a road map to assist the supervisor in implementing quality educational programs. Before attempting to define the duties of the vocational supervisor, one should understand the purpose of the vocational supervisor.

The *Dictionary of Occupational Titles* (U.S. Department of Labor, 1991) has the following performance-oriented definition of the director of vocational training:

Directs and coordinates vocational training programs for public school system, according to board of education policies and state education code. Confers with members of industrial and business communities to determine human resource training needs for apprenticeable and nonapprenticeable occupations. Reviews and interprets federal and state vocational educations codes to ensure that program conforms to legislation. Prepares budget and funding allocations. Plans and develops joint programs in conjunction with other members of education staff. Organizes committees to provide technical and advisory assistance to programs. Coordinates on-the-job training programs with employers, and evaluates progress of enrollees in conjunction with program contract goals (p. 77).

The definition given for vocational supervision in the *Dictionary of Occupational Titles* generally describes the function of the supervisor. Bjorkquist (1982) presented the functions in the following specific categories:

1. To develop and evaluate the accomplishment of program goals.
2. To develop and provide for the implementation of curriculum.
3. To maintain facilities and equipment and procure supplies and materials.
4. To maintain records, and gather data about operations.
5. To relate to public groups about the program.
6. To communicate by writing, speaking, and listening
7. To promote the development of the abilities of the work group members.
8. To build and maintain faculty morale, and professional outlook toward responsibilities.
9. To help select and induct new staff members, assign responsibilities, and make recommendations for personnel decisions (p. 35).

Iverson (1983) also developed a list of the major tasks of supervisors and extrapolated their application to occupational education, based on teachers' experience, as follows:

1. Developing curriculum
2. Organizing for instruction
3. Providing staff

4. Providing facilities
5. Providing materials
6. Arranging for in-service education
7. Orienting staff members
8. Relating special student services
9. Developing public relations
10. Evaluating instruction

A national research project conducted by Pajak (1990) developed what he identified as the 12 dimensions of supervisory practice, but not necessarily in occupational education:

1. Communication: ensuring open and clear communication among individuals and groups throughout the organization;
2. Staff Development: developing and facilitating meaningful opportunities for professional growth;
3. Instructional Program: supporting and coordinating efforts to improve the instructional program;
4. Planning and Change: initiating and implementing collaboratively developed strategies for continuous improvement;
5. Motivation and Organizing: helping people to develop a shared vision and achieve collective aims;
6. Observation and Conferencing: providing feedback to teachers based on classroom observation;
7. Curriculum: coordinating and integrating the process of curriculum development and implementation;
8. Problem Solving and decision-making: using a variety of strategies to clarify and analyze problems and to make decisions;
9. Service to Teachers: providing materials, resources, and assistance to support teaching and learning;
10. Personal Development: recognizing and reflecting upon one's personal and professional beliefs, abilities, and actions;
11. Community Relations: establishing and maintaining open and productive relations between the school and its community;
12. Research and Program Evaluation: encouraging experimentation and assessing outcomes (p. 78).

The *Dictionary of Occupational Titles* (1991), Bjorkquist (1982), Iverson (1983), and Pajak (1990) all defined or identified useful and vital duties of the supervisor. Collectively, they may be summarized into the following list of vocational supervisors' duties:

1. Provide communication: Work with staff and community leaders to provide open communication for the improvement of the vocational department.
2. Develop and evaluate program goals: Work with all stakeholders in the development and evaluation of program goals.
3. Develop instructional program: Support and coordinate efforts to develop curriculum, improve instructional programs, and provide for the needs of all students.
4. Coordinate personnel management: Assist in the selection and induction of new staff members, provide staff devel-

opment activities, evaluate the effectiveness of staff members, and build and maintain faculty morale.
5. Provide services to teachers: Maintain facilities and equipment and provide supplies, materials, resources, and assistance to support teaching and learning.
6. Coordinate community relations: Establish and maintain open and productive relationships between the vocational department and the community.
7. Provide business management: Develop budgets, maintain records, research and gather information for program improvement, and ensure that the department is in compliance with all federal, state, and local rules and regulations.
8. Solve problems: Identify and analyze problems and make the necessary decisions for solutions.
9. Develop personally: Reflect on one's beliefs and abilities and participate in actives for professional improvement.

A national Delphi study (Pullen, 1996) attempted to identify the duties of the secondary vocational supervisor for the twenty-first century. A national panel of experts, nominated by the department chairs of the member institutions of the University Council on Vocational Education, provided lists of duties which they felt were necessary for the twenty-first century. The Delphi technique was used to seek consensus from the members of the panel of experts as to the importance of the identified duties. A list of 134 specific tasks were generated in the open-ended first round; panelists reached consensus on all but 15 items in the second round; 10 more items were approved in subsequent rounds. However, five items failed to achieve consensus. The panel generally thought that occupational supervisors would likely continue many traditional functions, but with new emphasis on electronic communication, school-to-work initiatives, and state-of-the-art supervision methods, such as Total Quality Management (TQM).

FUTURE DIRECTION OF OCCUPATIONAL EDUCATION

Recent federal legislation provides today's vocational student with better services. The Carl D. Perkins Vocational and Applied Technology Education Act, the School-to-Work Opportunities Act, and the Goals 2000: Educate America Act have focused national attention on vocational education and its future direction. Much attention has been given to the integration of academic and vocational education, which has the potential of ensuring that secondary school students who were previously viewed as noncollege bound will have the option of going to work, entering postsecondary occupational education, or going on to college. This assumes that every secondary school student must be prepared for vocational training beyond high school, entry into the world of work, or higher education. With this in mind, the vocational supervisor must insure that occupational programs meet the needs of current and future vocational students. Therefore, the vocational supervisor must understand the duties required and be prepared to perform them in order to meet these needs.

"Seamless" education, "life-long learning," "tech-prep," and "school-to-work" are buzzwords of the 1990s used to describe continuous education. If they are successfully implemented, these movements have the potential for preparing students to move successfully from school, to careers to a full life. The term *continuous education* indicates that the educational process can no longer stop with formal education. Apple (1983) noted, "The next two decades will be a time of increasing conflict in the curriculum. Solutions to many of the problems that are now taking shape will require coordinated efforts between educators and the larger society" (p. 321). Educators are now forced to deliver programs based on societal demands, but society must be ready to proceed where formal education stops.

In a review of six national reports, including the Council of Chief State School Officers (1991), the National Assessment of Vocational Education (1989), the National Center on Education and the Economy (1990), the Secretary's Commission on Achieving Necessary Skills (1992), the Southern Regional Education Board (1992), and the William T. Grant Foundation (1988), Lynch, Smith, and Rojewski (1994) identified eight common reform themes:

1. Guaranteed Access to Education, Training, and Employment—Students must have access to jointly planned educational endeavors. Alliances between educational agencies must be planned and the business/industry community must be involved in the educational process.
2. Meaningful Participation of All Students—High quality education must be provided for all students. Flexible and alternative service delivery systems will be used for students with special needs. Support services will be developed to address the whole student rather than school-only needs.
3. Early Orientation to Work—Work orientated activities should be provided for all students. Career guidance and workplace understanding would be taught to younger students.
4. Integrated Theoretical and Practical Knowledge (Academic and Vocational)—The integration of academic theory and vocational education practice is imperative. New or revised programs must be rigorous, challenging, have high standards, and be technologically up-to-date.
5. Employers, Employee Organizations, and Community and Social Services Must Assume Responsibility for the Development of Youth Employment Skills—Schools, businesses, and communities should work together to plan, organize, and develop systems of employment preparation.
6. Student Assessment—To meet the challenges of a changing workplace students will complete a structured, highly focused, and challenging program of study. Traditional and non-traditional (performance testing, assessment of student projects, on the job assessment, portfolios, etc.) student assessments will determine achievement.
7. Policy Directive and Guidance—Policy-related reforms are needed within public education. These initiatives should include redesigning curriculum, establishing performance standards, coordinating services, improving employment readiness, and evaluating program effectiveness.
8. Improved Teacher Training and Staff Development—Improvement in teacher education departments and strengthened and expanded staff development will insure that teachers are ready to meet the new demands (pp. 104–111).

These reform themes transcend secondary vocational education and provide implications not only for the entire scope of occupational education but for education in general. Additional research is needed, however, to validate and evaluate the reform themes. Other aspects of occupational supervision also merit further study.

SUGGESTIONS FOR FURTHER RESEARCH

One can argue that occupational education programs are only as good as the supervisors of those programs, which may explain the extensive research conducted in the past on roles, attributes, duties, and effectiveness of supervisors. Studies related to roles and duties should be repeated periodically to ensure that current needs are being met. National studies often overlook specific needs of certain geographical areas; thus, it is recommended that state or local studies be conducted on the supervisor's role. Successful supervisors should be examined not only for their attributes and qualities but also for their efforts to improve themselves.

In many schools, vocational supervisors are assigned nonvocational duties; research is needed to determine what effect this has on the quality of the supervision given to vocational programs.

Preparatory programs for supervisors should also be studied in order to identify their strengths and weaknesses. Research to determine the needs of recent graduates of occupational supervision preparation programs should be done at regular intervals in order to assure program effectiveness.

Research should be conducted to determine what effects other agencies play in the supervision of occupational education. In the era of apprenticeships and school-to-work programs, studies which focus on the private sector's involvement would be valuable. The roles played by training and development agencies and local, state, and federal departments of labor need to be defined and evaluated.

Additional research is also needed to validate the nine duties outlined in the previous section. The following questions need to be addressed: Are the duties and their components valid for the twenty-first century? Are duties defined that will *not* be required in the twenty-first century? What duties will be required in the twenty-first century that have not been identified?

Because of the keen interest seen nationally in the integration of academic and vocational education, research is needed to determine what effects the Carl Perkins Vocational and Applied Technology Education Act, the School-to-Work Opportunities Act, and the Goals 2000: Educate America Act have had on occupational education and its supervision.

Most occupational education programs in America depend on the financial largess of the political system. The advent of the block grant and the shift from Federal to state and local control have potential for significant impact on how the programs are conducted and supervised. Research is needed to guide the inquiry into the effects this major change has in the funding patterns and to give scientific credibility to the findings.

IMPLICATIONS FOR THE PROFESSION

Occupational education will undoubtedly continue in some form at nearly all levels in American society, especially in light of the recent economically and technologically spurred impetus for lifelong learning. Vocational/technical/occupational educators have the major task of providing applied knowledge to *all* students, regardless of their circumstances or handicaps.

Occupational educators must continue to update their own skills and receive input from business, industry, and the community in the development of educational policy. These educators must also prepare students for the changes that will take place in the workplace in the foreseeable future.

Because of their advanced training and experience, supervisors will likely play a major part in managing change within programs of occupational education. The preparation of supervisors, including provision of the experience and training needed for them to conduct high quality programs as funds become scarce, is a major challenge for universities across the nation. Researchers will continue to provide the keys to unlock means for accomplishing change in occupational education.

REFERENCES

Aiken, W. C. (1976). The leadership behavior of selected local administrators of vocational education in Tennessee (doctoral dissertation, University of Tennessee, 1976). *Dissertation Abstracts International, 37*(8), 5074-A.

Alabama State Department of Education. (1976). *Role perceptions of the position of local vocational administrator in Alabama.* Montgomery, AL: Research Coordination Unit, Division of Vocational Education.

Apple, M. W. (1983). Curriculum in the year 2000: Tensions and possibilities. *Phi Delta Kappan, 64*(5) 321–326.

Barrick, R. K. (1989). Burnout and job satisfaction of vocational supervisors. *Journal of Agricultural Education, 30*(4), 33–39.

Baugher, S. L. & Schlichting, H. O. (1986). A profile of Midwestern vocational education administrators. *Educational Horizons, 65,* 12–15.

Bell, W. L., Jr. (1975). The role of the secondary area vocational center director in the State of South Carolina (doctoral dissertation, University of Tennessee, 1975). *Dissertations Abstracts International, 36*(5–6), 3611-A.

Bjorkquist, D. C. (1982). *Supervision in vocational education: Management of human resources.* Boston, MA: Allyn and Bacon.

Blanchard, K. H., Hambleton, R. K., Zigarmi, D., & Forsyth, D. (1991). *Leader behavior analysis II.* Escondido, CA: Blanchard Training and Development, Inc.

Bryant, D. D. (1983). A comparison of the leadership style range and leadership effectiveness of female administrators and teachers in vocational education (doctoral dissertation, Rutgers University, 1983). *Dissertation Abstracts International, 43*(5), 1518-A.

Cimperman, R. M. (1985). A comparison of perceived primary leadership style, style range, and leadership style adaptability of female and male administrators in the Wisconsin vocational, technical and adult education system (doctoral dissertation, University of Wisconsin-Milwaukee, 1985). *Dissertation Abstracts International, 46*(8), 24461-A.

Ericksen, D. O. (1975). An analysis of the role of the local vocational program director in Minnesota (doctoral dissertation, University of Tennessee, 1975). *Dissertation Abstracts International, 36*(5–6), 3614-A.

Finch, C. R., Gregson, J. A., & Faulkner, S. L. (1991). Leadership behaviors of successful vocational education administrators. *The Journal of Vocational Education Research, 16*(1), 1–33.

Finch, C. R., Gregson, J. A., & Reneau, C. E. (1992). *Vocational education leadership development resources: Selection and application* (Report No. CE-062-054). Berkeley, CA: National Center for Research in Vocational Education (ERIC Document Reproduction Service No. ED 349 471).

Finch, C. R. & McGough, R. L. (1982). *Administering and supervising occupational education.* Prospect Heights, IL: Waveland.

Harrington, C. T. (1973). Essential competencies of vocational education administrators in the State of Illinois (doctoral dissertation, Northern Illinois University, 1973). *Dissertation Abstracts International, 34*(9–10), 5818-A.

Hersey, P. & Blanchard, K. H. (1977). *Management of organizational behavior* (3rd ed.). Englewood Cliffs, NJ: Prentice Hall.

Holt, R. A. (1973). The role of the director of vocational education at the public school district level in the State of Tennessee (doctoral dissertation, The Univeristy of Tennessee, 1973). *Dissertation Abstracts International, 34*(5–6), 2472-2473-A.

Howard, W. R. (1981). The identification of tasks performed by vocational supervisors of comprehensive high schools in Georgia and their importance in relationship to school system size (doctoral dissertation, Georgia State University, 1981). *Dissertation Abstracts International, 42*(3), 1117-A.

Iverson, M. J. (Ed.). (1983). *Selected papers on major tasks of the occupational education supervisor.* Unpublished class project in ED 608, Raleigh, NC: North Carolina State University, Department of Occupational Education.

Iverson, M. J. (1995). *Federal legislation for occupational education.* Unpublished handout for EOS 806 class, Athens, GA: The University of Georgia, Department of Occupational Studies.

Klein, G. A. (1974). A study of basic management skills for mid-management vocational leadership personnel (doctoral dissertation, Georgia State University, 1974). *Dissertation Abstracts International, 35*(9–10), 6585-6586-A.

Laird, R. E. (1974). The relationship of leader behavior of principals and teacher morale in the vocational centers of Maryland (doctoral dissertation, University of Maryland, 1974). *Dissertation Abstracts International, 35*(5–6), 3589-A.

Loudermilk, W. B. & Webb, E. S. (1973). *Perceptions of vocational administrators and high school principals regarding the role of the vocational administrator.* College Station, TX: Texas A & M University.

Lynch, R., Smith, C., & Rojewski, J. (1994). Redirecting secondary vocational education toward the 21st century. *Journal of Vocational Education Research, 19*(2), 95–116.

Moore, G. E., Crudup, S., & Vander Wall, W. J. (1992) The actual and desired roles of local vocational directors: A comparison of perceptions. *Journal of Vocational Education Research, 17*(3), 63–88.

Moss, J., Jr. & Johansen, B. P. (1991). *Conceptualizing leadership and assessing leader attributes* (Report No. CE-058-194). Berkeley, CA: National Center for Research in Vocational Education (ERIC Document Reproduction Service No. ED 333 178).

Moss, J., Jr. & Liang, T. (1990). *Leadership, leadership development, and the National Center for Research in Vocational Education* (Report No. CE-056-172). Berkeley, CA: National Center for Research in Vocational Education (ERIC Document Reproduction Service No. ED 325 645).

Myers, P. B. & Myers, K. D. (1987). *Myers-Briggs type indicator* (9th ed.). Palo Alto, CA: Consulting Psychologists Press, Inc.

Oravet, K. V. (1989). A comparison of the perceived leadership styles of directors of area vocational centers and high school principals within the state of Alabama (doctoral dissertation, University of Alabama).

Pajak, E. (1990). Dimensions of Supervision. *Educational Leadership, 48,* 78–81.

Pullen, D. J. (1996). Secondary vocational supervisors' duties: A futures study utilizing the Delphi technique (doctoral dissertation, University of Georgia).

Reddin, W. J. (1970). *Management effectiveness.* New York: McGraw-Hill.

Reddin, W. J. (1974). *Management style diagnosis test* (3rd ed.). Fredericton, New Brunswick, Canada: Organizational Tests, Ltd.

Rosenthal, J. S. (1976). Leadership role perceptions of vocational education administrators as related to job satisfaction of teacher coordinators in Michigan (doctoral dissertation, Arizona State University). *Dissertation Abstracts International, 37*(6), 3323-3324-A.

Ryan, R. D. & Norton, R. E. (1991) Leadership and planning for future. *The Vocational Education Journal, 66,* 39–40.

Sharpton, L. F. H. (1985). Leadership styles of administrative personnel in the area vocational schools in the State of Oklahoma (doctoral dissertation, Oklahoma State University, 1985). *Dissertation Abstracts International, 46*(12), 3699-A.

Sireno, P. J. (1973). The role of the local vocational education director in the area vocational schools in Missouri (doctoral dissertation, University of Missouri, 1973). *Dissertation Abstracts International, 35*(9–10), 6441-A.

Stephens, J. F. (1967). *Analysis of questionnaires completed by Utah vocational directors.* Salt Lake City, UT: Research Coordinating Unit, Utah State Department of Education.

Toffler, A. (1974). *Learning for tomorrow: The role of the future in education.* New York: Random House.

U.S. Department of Commerce. (1995). *Statistical abstract of the United States.* Washington, D.C.: U.S. Government Printing Office.

U.S. Department of Education. (1994). *National assessment of vocational education: Final report to Congress.* Washington, D.C.: U.S. Government Printing Office.

U.S. Department of Education. (1995). *Digest of educational statistics.* Washington, D.C.: U.S. Government Printing Office.

U.S. Department of Labor. (1991). *Dictionary of occupational titles* (4th ed.). Washington, D.C.: U.S. Government Printing Office.

Valentine, I. E., et al. (1979). Role clarification and determination of the responsibilities for administrative in Colorado. Final report. Colorado State University, Ft. Collins. Department of Vocational Education.

Wenrich, R. C. (1990). The comprehensive high school—Is it still viable?. *NASSP Bulletin, 74,* 26–32.

·20·

SUPERVISION IN SPECIAL EDUCATION

William W. Swan
UNIVERSITY OF GEORGIA

OVERVIEW*

Supervision is one of five major functions of school operations—general administration, supervision, teaching, management, and special services (Harris, 1975, pp. 4–7). Building level leaders (principals, assistant principals, supervisors, designees) supervise instruction by working to maintain or change the school operation in ways that directly influence the teaching processes to promote student learning (Harris, 1975, p. 10). Supervision directly impacts on three of Wang, Haertel, and Walberg's (1993) six metaanalytically formulated theoretical constructs of school learning—design and delivery of curriculum and instruction, classroom practices, and student characteristics.

Tasks associated with building level supervision include: developing the curriculum; organizing for instruction; providing staff, facilities, and materials; arranging for in-service education; orienting staff members; relating special pupil services; developing public relations; and evaluating instruction (Harris, 1975, pp. 11–12). These tasks are accomplished by educational leaders through assessing, prioritizing, designing, allocating resources, coordinating, and directing (Harris, 1975, pp. 14–15).

Supervision is a critical role for special education administrators, directors, coordinators, and supervisor (Billingsley & Jones, 1993; Osborne, DiMattia, & Curran, 1993; Zadnik, 1985). Supervision of special education instruction often includes specific tasks associated with special education in addition to those for building level leaders. Such additional tasks include monitoring for compliance issues (budgeting, implementing rules and regulations, certification requirements, suspension/expulsion actions); recruitment/retention of special education and related services staff; facilitating collaboration among general and special education professionals, with emphasis on instructional/curricular adaptations in inclusive settings; and directly supervising other special education leaders, special education staff, support staff, and related services staff to enhance student learning (Osborne et al, 1993; Podemski, Marsh, Smith, & Price, 1995).

Supervision of special education personnel in a school is the responsibility of a building level leader. Most often, a building level leader and a special education leader collaborate to effectively supervise special education instruction. Collaboration is a complex interpersonal and professional relationship between two or more parties (e.g., building level leader and special education leader) who share common goals, mutual commitments, resources, decision-making, and evaluation responsibilities (Bartel, 1977; Swan & Morgan, 1993). Specific collaboration between a building level leader and a special education leader must be individually negotiated between each leader, based on the unique knowledge and skills of each and the needs of the community of learners and the school. While some supervisory approaches combine the generalist (e.g., building level leader) and the specialist (e.g., special education leader) roles, collaboration emphasizes meshing the knowledge, skills, and experiences of two specialists—both the building level leader and the special education leader—to create an environment that maximizes the effectiveness of supervision of instruction for *all* students. For example, in some school systems, the assistant principal, in collaboration with a special education leader, is responsible for special education in a particular building, for example, Henry County Schools (Jordan, personal communication,

ACKNOWLEDGMENTS I would like to express appreciation to five special education leaders—Drs. Richard Downey, Joan A. Jordan, Ann Glendinning, Barbara Sirvis, and James R. Yates—and four graduate students—Frank Carbo, Odis Johnson, Sherry LaBoon, and Susan Walker—for reviewing an earlier draft of this manuscript and providing suggestions for improvement in content and structure.

* This chapter assumes that the reader has basic knowledge concerning Public Laws 94–142 (The Education for All Handicapped Children Act of 1975) and 101–119 (The Individuals with Disabilities Education Act, Amendments of 1991) and relevant state legislation. This chapter was written prime to the enactment of Public Law 105-117, the Individuals with Disabilities Act Amendments of 1997. For those readers who do not have this knowledge, a supplemental reading list is provided before the References section.

1996) and Lowndes County Schools, both in Georgia (Lanier, personal communication, 1996).

Collaboration among leaders has become more important with the increased emphasis on including students with disabilities in general education classes (inclusion); general and special education leaders collaborate to demonstrate effective supervision of instruction for teams of general and special education teachers. Specific approaches to the collaboration between building level leaders and special education leaders have been operationalized in formal training programs such as the Principal Training Simulator in Special Education/Collaborative Leadership Development programs (Burrello & DeClue, 1990; Burrello, Schrup, & Barnett, 1990; Swan, 1993), which can be used for both preservice and in-service preparation.

Effective supervision of special education instruction can be provided by a building level leader in collaboration with a special education leader using a general education supervision model (e.g., Harris' [1975] actions to accomplish tasks necessary to accomplish supervision of instruction) within the context of the unique dimensions of special education. Figure 20.1 provides a representative description of these components for supervision, beginning at the bottom with collaboration between the building level and special education leaders who use a filter of dimensions unique to special education supervision to determine their actions to accomplish supervision tasks to supervise instruction in an array of special education instructional alternatives (at the top). One example of such alternatives may include the following: inclusion classes (both general education and special education teachers collaborating in classes with students); a general education teacher in a class with a special education teacher consulting or collaborating with the general education teacher periodically; a special education teacher in a resource special education class with some students with disabilities mainstreamed in some general education classes; and a special education teacher in a self-contained class with a special education teacher and students who are minimally mainstreamed in a few general education classes.

CONTEXT

Supervising special education instruction is challenging because it occurs in a unique multidimensional arena (see Figure 20.1, shaded area); several of these dimensions were specified by Brown and Swan (1985) and have been adapted for use in this context. This section examines dimensions that have an impact on supervision. It then specifies commonalities and uniquenesses of supervision for building level leaders and special education leaders.

Legal Foundations

Federal law and corresponding state law require provision of providing special education and related services to students with disabilities. The Individuals with Disabilities Education Act (IDEA, 1992), formerly the Education for All Handicapped Children Act of 1975 (as amended), and complimentary state legislation guarantee each student with a disability a free appropriate public education in the least restrictive environment through the implementation of an individualized education program (IEP). The supervision of general education personnel and special education personnel (e.g., teachers certified in the areas of disability, special education administrators and lead teachers, other specialized teachers, teacher aides, and therapy aides) and other related personnel (e.g., occupational therapists, physical therapists, nurses, social workers, psychologists, bus drivers and monitors, custodians, and food service personnel) is a challenging undertaking for both building level leaders and special education leaders. Building level leaders and special education leaders work with both individual educators and related services personnel and groups or teams of these individuals to provide each student with a high quality education individualized to meet each student's needs.

The implication for the legal foundations dimension is twofold. The rules, regulations, and policies to implement the IDEA at the federal, state, and local levels require significant knowledge and expertise on the parts of building level leaders and special education leaders. Furthermore, the continuing annual changes in the implementation of IDEA, based on legislative changes, court orders, and evolving best practices, provide a challenging environment in which educational leaders must be knowledgeable to provide effective supervision.

Areas of Disability

There are 12 distinct areas of disability: intellectual disabilities (mild, moderate, severe, and profound), specific learning disabilities, severe emotional/behavioral disorders, speech/language impairments, visual impairments/blindness, hearing impairments/deafness, deafness/blindness, other health impairments, orthopedic impairments, autism, traumatic brain injuries, and significant developmental delay (for children ages 3 to 5 years only). The proportion of students with disabilities is approximately 10% of the total student population. Instruction in each of these areas requires adaptations of curriculum and instruction, which are facilitated by building level leaders and special education leaders who possess the requisite knowledge and skills in each area.

Figure 20.2 displays the array and number of specialized knowledge items (K) and skills items (S) judged essential for the instruction of students with disabilities in eight of the 12 areas (Council for Exceptional Children [CEC], 1995; Swan & Sirvis, 1992). These knowledge and skills items are contained in a Common Core (rectangular/lower block), which is essential for all areas of disability. It is organized into eight components:

I. Philosophical, Historical, and Legal Foundations of Special Education
II. Characteristics of Learners
III. Assessment, Diagnosis, and Evaluation
IV. Instructional Content and Practice
V. Planning and Managing the Teaching and Learning Environment
VI. Managing Student Behavior and Social Interaction Skills
VII. Communication and Collaborative Partnerships
VIII. Professionalism and Ethical Practices

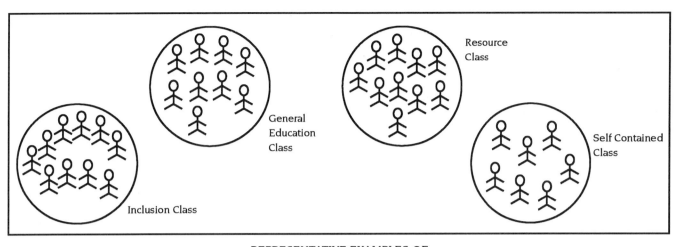

REPRESENTATIVE EXAMPLES OF
INSTRUCTIONAL ALTERNATIVES

Developing Curriculum	Arranging for Inservice Education
Organizing for Instruction	Orienting Staff Members
Providing Staff	Relating Special Pupil Services
Providing Facilities	Developing Public Relations
Providing Materials	Evaluating Instruction

TASKS ASSOCIATED WITH SUPERVISION

Assessing	Allocating Resources
Prioritizing	Coordinating
Designing	Directing

ACTIONS TO ACCOMPLISH SUPERVISION TASKS

Legal Requirements	Itinerancy of Staff
Areas of Disability	Reform Movements
Age Groups	Evolving Best Practices
Personnel Recruitment/Retention	Special Education Leadership
Location of Services	Preservice/Inservice Training Leaders

CONTEXT: DIMENSIONS UNIQUE TO SPECIAL EDUCATION SUPERVISION

LEADERS

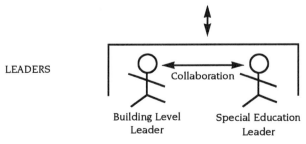

FIGURE 20.1. Supervision of special education instruction:
an overview.

Harris, 1975, pp. 11–12

Harris, 1975, pp. 14–15;

Burrello and Declue, 1990;
Burrello et al, 1990;
Swan, 1993;
Swan and Morgan, 1993).

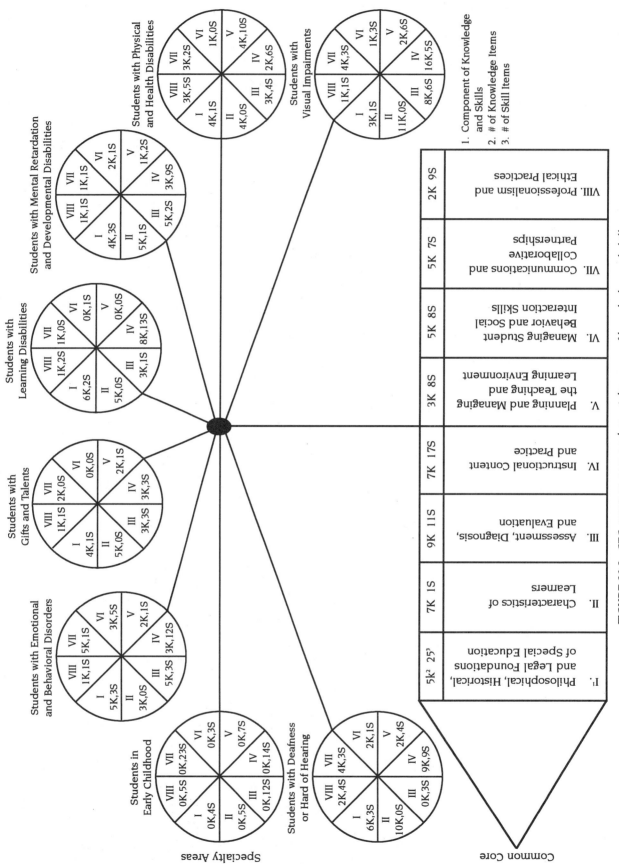

FIGURE 20.2. CEC common core and specialty areas of knowledge and skills for beginning special educators (CEC, 1995; Swan & Sirvis, 1992).

The figures above each of these components indicate the number of knowledge items (K) and the number of skill items (S) in each component. For example, Component IV—Instructional Content and Practice (7K 17S) has 7 knowledge items and 17 skills items (CEC, 1995, pp. 15–16). A sample knowledge item from this component is: Techniques for modifying instructional methods and materials. A sample skill item from this component is: Choose and use appropriate technologies to accomplish instructional objectives and to integrate them appropriately into the instructional process.

Eight Specialty Areas (e.g., Students with Deafness or Hard of Hearing) are depicted in circles in Figure 20.2 above the Common Core. Each of the Specialty Areas provides knowledge items and skills items *in addition* to the Common Core knowledge items and skills items. For example, in the specialty area Students with Deafness or Hard of Hearing, Component IV—Instructional Content and Practice (9K, 9S) has 9 knowledge items and 9 skill items. A sample knowledge item is: Information related to American Sign Language (ASL) and existing communication modes used by students who are deaf or hard of hearing. A sample skills item is: Modify the instructional process and classroom environment to meet the physical, cognitive, cultural, and communication needs of the child who is deaf or hard of hearing (e.g., teacher's style, acoustic environment, availability of support services, availability of appropriate technologies) (CEC, 1995, pp. 22–23). Additional specialized knowledge and skills are required for related services personnel (e.g., occupational therapists, physical therapists, and speech/language pathologists) and other content, such as vocational education.

The implication for supervision for areas of disability is that building level leaders and special education leaders need to possess both knowledge and skills in these multiple, distinct areas to effectively supervise both general education and special education teachers and to assist them in improving their instructional efforts to improve student learning. Based on formal preservice/in-service training and/or real-world experiences in a classroom with students with disabilities, a building level leader often possesses some of the requisite knowledge and skills for supervising effectively in some areas of disability because of the relatively large number of students served, such as students with learning disabilities, mental retardation/developmental disabilities, or emotional/behavioral disorders. In this situation, the building level leader can provide effective day-to-day supervision and collaborate with the special education leader on specific problem situations. Furthermore, in those general education classes which include students with disabilities, the building level leader and special education leader must work collaboratively with the general education and special education teachers to model the desired collaborative behavior in providing quality services.

However, in other areas, such as physical and health disabilities and visual impairments, the building level leader may need to collaborate more directly with the special education leader for specific knowledge and skills. It may also be necessary for the special education leader to obtain consultative assistance from other professionals in areas in which neither leader has the necessary knowledge and/or skills to meet specific student, teacher, and classroom needs.

Age Groups

Special education spans the age range from birth through 21 years of age—infants/toddlers, preschool, elementary, middle/junior high, and high school, including transition into the community and postsecondary education and training. The supervisory, curricular, and instructional issues for each of these age groups reflect a scope that has significant and distinctive depth as well as breadth in providing comprehensive services to these students.

The implication for supervision for age groups dimension focuses on the expertise and time of a special education leader in collaborating with multiple building level leaders. While a building level leader usually focuses expertise (in breadth and depth) on one of the age groups listed above and in one building, the special education leader must possess or access expertise in all the age groups for all the buildings in a system. The emphasis on collaboration between multiple building level leaders and a special education leader provides instructional continuity and effective transition across age ranges/groups for students. While each building level leader and a special education leader can negotiate the collaboration effectively, the special education leader does have multiple yet individual collaborative efforts with each building level leader. The result is a significant work load for a special education leader. This dimension as well as the areas of disability combine to require that the special education leader work with building level leaders to increase their expertise in selected areas through continuous improvement efforts and to collaborate for problem solving in a variety of situations.

Personnel Recruitment/Retention

There are significant shortages of qualified special education teachers, related services personnel, and local and state leaders in special education (Billingsley, 1993; U.S. Department of Education, 1992; *U.S. News and World Report*, 1995). Attrition of special education personnel is also significant. The severity of shortages and attrition varies across local districts, specialty areas, and states depending on an array of variables (Smith-Davis & Billingsley, 1993).

One of the more significant problems related to retention and recruitment is certification/licensure. While the particulars vary in the states, a teacher must be certified/licensed in the appropriate disability area in order to teach students. The disability areas are often used as a means to guide and accredit college and university personnel preparation programs and certification/licensure in the states. For example, the CEC Common Core and Specialty Areas of Knowledge and Skills for Beginning Special Educators (CEC, 1995; see Figure 20.2) are now being used by the National Council of Accreditation of Teacher Education (NCATE) to accredit college and university preparation programs in special education. This action will probably expand to influence the requirements for state certification/licensure and may enhance reciprocity among the states. Also, the requirements for speech-language pathologists are specified by the American Association of Speech, Language, and Hearing. The requirements for occupational and physical therapists are specified by their professional organizations as well.

In addition to individual areas of certification/licensure, some states use generic or global areas of special education certification (e.g. "interrelated" in Georgia and "varying exceptionalities" in Florida), which often incorporate programs for students with emotional/behavioral disorders, specific learning disabilities, and intellectual disabilities. Some states use generic areas of certification only. While reciprocal certification across state lines does exist for some states, it is not universal. The shortage of personnel and the need for varied and distinct expertise create a problem in identifying personnel who meet minimal requirements and also providing them with adequate supervision to enhance their instructional knowledge and skills to provide high quality educational and related services.

There are several implications for supervision for recruitment and retention. First, there is a need to conduct year-long recruiting efforts for qualified personnel in all areas, which takes time from the special education leader's supervision. Second, it is necessary for both the building level leader and the special education leader to develop and implement effective induction programs for new staff along with continuing staff development and support programs for existing staff in order to maintain and improve the expertise of current teachers and related services personnel. It is generally much more cost effective to support existing staff than it is to hire new staff. Collaboration among building level leaders and special education leaders provide a means to meet recruiting and retention needs not only in individual schools but across the system as well.

Location of Services

Special education must be provided to a student in the student's least restrictive environment—a setting which maximizes a student's interaction with nondisabled age peers—unless partial or full removal is required for the welfare of the student or other students. Considering the "inclusion" initiative (i.e., educating the student in a general education environment to the maximum extent possible), an increasing number of students are being educated in general classes in their home schools. Thus, there is less clustering of students with disabilities and more dispersion of teachers of special education and related services personnel to general classes. In addition, many students spend significant portions of their middle and high school years at community sites. The variety of locations and alternatives presents a geographical and management challenge to a special education leader in collaborating effectively with building level leaders and general and special education teachers in a variety of settings.

The implications for supervision for location of services is twofold—a focus on effective scheduling and placement of teachers and students on an annual basis depending on student needs and an increased amount of time to visit a variety of teachers in more classrooms. For a building level leader, this may mean that more teachers can be observed in a shorter period of time; for example, a building level leader can supervise a general education teacher and a special education teacher collaboratively in one classroom rather than two. A special education leader may collaborate to supervise a special education teacher in a variety of classrooms rather than one. Scheduling may produce more or fewer classes and teachers to be supervised on an annual basis. As a result, building level leaders and special education leaders must increase collaborative efforts to provide the supervision that is needed and target the special education leader's time on problematic situations.

Itinerancy of Staff

Many special education teachers teach students in more than one school based on the location of services, the number of students to be served, and the needs of those students. In many cases, it is the norm for special education personnel (e.g., interrelated or varying exceptionality teachers, speech-language pathologists) to teach in two schools and for related services personnel (e.g., occupational therapists, physical therapists) to provide therapy in several locations. Thus, many related services personnel may have multiple supervisors in multiple buildings. The special education leader may provide instructional supervision through collaboration with multiple supervisors for one related services person in a timely and effective manner.

The implication for supervision for itinerancy is a special education leader's need to collaborate with multiple building level leaders to provide effective supervision assistance to selected personnel in multiple locations. In many situations, building level leaders need to collaborate with each other to ensure that critical services are provided and that personnel are adequately supervised.

Reform Movements

While many general education reform movements have excluded students with disabilities from their plans, the major reform movements in special education focus on improving the teaching and learning for *all* students (Berreth, 1992). The specific reforms of "inclusion" for students with special needs in general classrooms, of merging special education with general education to form a unitary system (e.g., CASE Future Agenda for Special Education: Creating a Unified Education System, 1993; National Association of State Boards of Education, 1992), of meeting the needs of *all* students through site-based management (McNulty, 1992), of restructuring, and of revised funding mechanisms reveal continuing dynamic and fundamental changes in the delivery of special education services. These, in turn, require continuing adaptation with changes in legislation, rules, regulations, policies, personnel preparation, and leadership and supervision approaches. There is no area in which there are more court actions which influence how services will be provided to students than in special education.

The implication for supervision of special education is the need to continually update knowledge and skills on the part of building level leaders and special education leaders. The increased emphasis of reform movements to include *all* students requires increased knowledge and skills for both sets of leaders and an increasing need for collaboration to stay current with constantly changing expectations for all.

Evolving Best Practices

Best practices are continually evolving based on changes through research, legislation, or court orders. For example, recent legislative changes have placed priorities on services on infants and toddlers (birth to two years of age) who have disabilities and their families, on providing transition services for infants and toddlers to preschool programs (three to five years of age), on transition services for students 16 years of age (or 14 years of age as appropriate) who are making the transition from school to work or postsecondary education, and creating new disability categories for autism and traumatic brain injury that suggest additional adaptations for knowledge and skills in curriculum and instruction. The current emphasis on inclusion has resulted in the development of a variety of additional models, such as collaborative teaching, partial participation, or the redirection of all pullout programs, to create a generalist who is a support teacher for all students in a class. These models are related in some ways to past efforts, such as the Regular Education Initiative and mainstreaming. The evolving best practices in all 12 areas of disability and additional priorities create a constant, forced learning situation for building level leaders and special education leaders in order to be on the required cutting edge of instructional efforts.

The implication for both sets of leaders for evolving best practices is the time required to be aware of, learn, implement, and supervise the continuing changes of evolving best practices. The need to participate in a variety of learning opportunities regarding continuing developments on the part of both sets of leaders and the sharing of information requires both opportunity and time.

Special Education Leadership Pool

The number of special education leaders is limited. In small systems, the position of special education leader is often part time and coupled with either a concurrent teaching assignment or with other specialized programs, such as Title I (Billingsley & Jones, 1993). In larger systems, there may be additional personnel assigned to special education leadership and supervision; however, the number of schools to which they are assigned tends to be large. In many states, there are limited or no certification requirements for special education leaders and there are few institutions of higher education which provide graduate education opportunities in special education leadership (Jones, Robinett, & Wells, 1994). A special education leader is almost always appointed to a staff or technical position in the central office rather than a line position; the primary tools which this leader uses to directly supervise or provide technical assistance and collaboration are information and expertise. Consistent with site-based management emphases, the building principal is often the special education leader in the school (Rude & Rubadeau,

1992). The special education leader, recognizing these parameters, constantly works at being proactive to provide technical assistance collaboratively to other educational leaders but is often placed in the situation of resolving complex programmatic and legal problems rather than enhancing the quality of instruction.

The implication for supervision in this dimension is that there is limited time for special education leaders and that their time is usually focused on collaborative problem solving with building level leaders rather than direct supervision. This suggests that building level leaders and special education leaders need to acknowledge each other's expertise as well as their time constraints to maximize the effective supervision of instruction in special education.

Preservice and In-service Training of Leaders

Building level leaders need knowledge and skills in educating students with disabilities; special education leaders need knowledge and skills in general education leadership. While existing preservice training programs for general education leaders do not generally include specific knowledge and skills in the area of special education, the existing preservice training programs for special education leaders generally include some specific knowledge and skills in general education leadership. In-service training and collaboration are the most common means for both groups to obtain the knowledge and skills they need to work effectively in educating *all* students.

The implication for supervision for this dimension is the need for both sets of leaders to participate collaboratively in obtaining additional knowledge and skills through continuous improvement opportunities and sharing of cutting-edge information. Examples of such opportunities include weekend-long seminars, leadership institutes, and preconference specialty sessions at professional meetings.

Summary

The special education leader works collaboratively with building level leaders, other personnel, and groups at *all* professional levels in *all* schools and *all* departments at one time or another to collaborate in supervising instruction in special education and other areas as requested. The multiple dimensions of the context of special education instruction provide an opportunity to maximize leadership knowledge and skills to improve the quality of instruction for *all* students. The most effective manner to provide supervision is through a collaborative effort between building level leaders and special education leaders.

Commonalities and Uniquenesses of Supervision for Building Level Leaders and Special Education Leaders

While collaboration between leaders provides for the most effective supervision of instruction, there are several characteristic commonalities and uniquenesses in supervision between most building level leaders and most special education leaders. In terms of perspective, building level leaders tend to focus first on depth and breadth in their buildings and then on systemwide efforts; special education leaders tend to focus first on depth and breadth in special education and then on general education. Building level leaders hold administrative line positions and use powers of position, expertise, reward, information, influence, and charisma; special education leaders hold staff positions and focus on powers of expertise, information, influence, and charisma. Building level leaders have primary expertise and experience in general education instruction and leadership and gain expertise in special education instruction; special education leaders have primary expertise and experience in special education instruction and leadership and gain expertise in general education instruction and leadership. Building level leaders focus on day-to-day supervision and problem solving in their buildings while special education leaders focus on some day-to-day supervision and emphasize problem solving in buildings system-wide. Individual leaders are blurring the stereotypes through their efforts at continuous improvement in critical areas, which enables them to be more effective leaders in a variety of situations.

CURRENT PRACTICE AND RESEARCH

The research literature in the supervision of special education is sparse for several reasons. First, research in supervision has tended to focus on general education. Second, few research journals focus on special education leadership. Third, the context for special education supervision provides significant challenges for conducting research studies. Descriptions of available research in special education supervision are grouped in the following areas: roles, alternative approaches, professional organization parameters, special education leader concerns/teacher perceptions, and personnel preparation.

Roles

Two significant research studies have examined the roles of special education leaders concerning supervision. Harris and King (1975), in collaboration with the Texas Education Agency and the Bureau of Education for the Handicapped (U.S. Office of Education), led the Special Education Supervisor Training Project to develop both a specific competency-guided program for the preparation of special education instructional supervisors and a generic competency-guided program for the preparation of educational leaders of all kinds. They focused on supervisors whose primary assignment was to work as change agents with teachers and others to improve instruction. Using multiple sources (e.g., education, communications, psychology, political science, sociology, and law) and a variety of techniques (e.g., review and analysis of the literature, Delphi Technique using experts from the field as well as higher education, and pilot testing in the field with supervisors), they developed a generic model of competency specification for instructional supervisory personnel. This generic model was

developed by identifying knowledge, skills, and values which were placed in three competency domains: problem solving, supervisory leadership job tasks, and human relations. These competencies were then grouped into seven critical competency areas—curriculum, materials, staffing, organization, special services, public relations, and in-service education—all focused on improving instruction (see Figure 20.3). Critical competencies for both generic and special education supervision (Harris & King, 1975, Appendices A and B) were provided, including rationale statements and illustrative performance examples. A preparation program for the array of competencies (including the array of subcompetencies for each critical competency) with specifically designed assessment instruments is referenced. The preparation program was individualized for each supervisor.

Ten years later, using a combination of Rockert's (1982) work on critical success factors and the critical incident approach, Zadnik (1985) studied the roles of local special education leaders by identifying the factors which are critical to successful performance. Using a reference group of boundary

Task Area	Critical Competencies
Curriculum	• Setting instructional goals • Designing instructional units • Developing/adapting curricula
Materials	• Evaluating and selecting learning materials • Producing learning materials • Evaluating the utilization of learning materials
Staffing	• Developing a staffing plan • Recruiting and selecting personnel • Assigning personnel
Organization	• Revising existing structures • Assimilating programs • Monitoring new arrangements
Special Services	• Analyzing and securing services • Orienting and utilizing specialized personnel • Scheduling services • Evaluating the utilization of services
In-service Education	• Supervising in a clinical mode • Planning for individual growth • Designing in-service training sessions • Conducting in-service training sessions • Training for leadership roles
Public Relations	• Informing the public • Involving the public • Utilizing public opinions

FIGURE 20.3. Critical competencies for supervision, Special Education Supervisor Training Project (Harris & King, 1975, Appendices A & B).

spanners—including local directors of special education, state directors of special education, the Council of Administrators of Special Education (CASE) state presidents, and professors of special education administration—Zadnik identified 53 critical success factors for local special education directors. Employing Sergiovanni's (1984) framework, Zadnik grouped the 53 critical success factors into five areas—technical, human, educational, symbolic, and cultural—and two dimensions—personal and organizational. An examination of the 53 items reveals that eight critical success factors are related to the supervision (see Figure 20.4).

Zadnik (1985) and Burrello and Zadnik (1986) then asked a group of 236 effective administrators (nominated by the reference group) to rank the critical success factors in terms of criticalness and difficulty. Of the eight factors listed in Figure 20.4, one item was ranked in the top five in both criticalness

Human—Personal

• The special education administrator must take a personal interest in subordinates and provide them with positive reinforcement on their performance.

Human—Organizational

• The special education program must establish rapport and a close working relationship with regular education and be responsive to building level personnel, problems, and concerns.

Education—Personal

• The special education administrator must develop and maintain a knowledge base of regular education assessment, curriculum, and instruction and anticipate their potential impact on special education.

Education—Organizational

• The special education program must improve the competencies of teachers and support personnel by establishing exemplary supervision and evaluation procedures.

• The special education program must foster the personal and professional growth of each staff member through planned staff development activities.

Cultural—Personal

• The special education administrator must establish and communicate a sense and direction which allows staff to develop a sense of worth and pride in their work.

Cultural—Organizational

• The special education program must proactively recruit potential employees by promoting and marketing the program's strengths and qualities.
• The special education program must stimulate and foster the creativity of staff by actively promoting and marketing their skills and talents.

FIGURE 20.4. Critical success factors related to supervision (Zadnik, 1985).

and difficulty: "The special education program must establish rapport and a close working relationship with general education and be responsive to building level personnel, problems, and concerns." This item was ranked first in criticalness and second in difficulty.

Consistent with Zadnik's (1985) findings, CASE (1993) projects that the special education leader's roles will continue to change with increased emphasis on facilitation, advising, and occasionally advocacy or monitoring. Principals in individual buildings will oversee *all* aspects of the curriculum and instruction, including the plans for children with disabilities. The roles of the special education leaders will continue to be based on educational information and expertise. The legal requirements of federal and state legislation place special education leaders in unique supervisory positions. The supervision role will become more and more collaborative as the special education leader provides increased technical expertise in critical situations.

Billingsley and Jones (1993), in their studies of special education supervision in rural areas, suggested an array of roles for special education instructional supervisors including establishing program descriptions, establishing comprehensive staff development programs, providing individualized assistance to teachers, developing and modifying curricula, facilitating IEP development and implementation, the coordination of services and programs, providing and coordinating instructional resources, facilitating the induction of staff members, and evaluating instructional programs. They suggest that individual systems in rural areas may each identify one person or may work together to form cooperatives—either formal or informal—to provide the needed supervision. They also emphasize the importance of a focus on the building level in terms of responding to needs, in addition to a focus on the system level needs. As they examine the assignment of these roles to personnel, Billingsley and Jones emphasize that expertise is the key criterion for the assignment of critical responsibilities and that alternative assignments could be made to principals, teachers, and special education leaders based on their areas of expertise.

Guerra, Jackson, and Madsen (1994) suggest that the current emphases on site-based management and inclusion of students with disabilities in settings with their nondisabled peers will create significant shifts in leadership behavior. They developed three policy statements which suggested the need for such change: the promotion of students with disabilities through site-based management; the integration of general and special education, thereby eliminating the dual systems that currently serve children; and, the need for improved quality of programming and services to students with special needs. A collaborative supervision approach incorporating both general education administrators at the building level and special education leaders will probably be necessary to implement policies such as these.

Other Professional Organization Parameters

In addition to supervising special education teachers, principals, with assistance from special education leaders, may supervise a variety of related services personnel (such as physical therapists, occupational therapists, speech-language pathologists, psychologists, and social workers. Many of these related services personnel belong to professional organizations which have their own supervision requirements based on their own research, best practices, and standards. For example, physical therapists are members of the American Physical Therapy Association (APTA, 1992) which requires an organizational plan, policies, and procedures which define supervisory functions and relationships. The APTA provides a structure for supervision which includes observation, an appropriate and written staff development plan for education and training, and periodic review of physical therapy support personnel (aides). Building level leaders (and, where appropriate, special education leaders) must supervise physical therapists consistently with these guidelines.

The American Occupational Therapy Association (1994) has developed an approved *Guide for Supervision of Occupational Therapy Personnel*. The organization recognizes that occupational therapy practitioners may be administratively supervised by others such as principals, facility administrators, or physicians and recommends procedures for doing so along a continuum from close (daily) through minimal (as needed but less than monthly). Further, the amount, degree, and pattern of supervision may vary depending on the employment setting, the method of service provision, the practitioner's competence, and the demands of service. Specifics are provided for registered occupational therapists, certified occupational therapy assistants, occupational therapy aides, technicians, and students with differential expectations for entry level through advanced areas for each level of professional.

The American Speech-Language-Hearing Association (ASHA, 1985, 1989) has specified guidelines for supervising speech-language pathologists through a position paper and in a tutorial guide based on its research, best practices, and standards. These comprehensive requirements focus on specific knowledge, skills, and supervisory practices working with principals, special education leaders, and speech-language pathologists who hold the Certificate of Clinical Competence. The rules and procedures for conducting supervision are specified in detail. As with many accrediting programs, the American Speech-Language-Hearing Association is reconsidering its structure, the nature of its standards, and its methods of operation as conditions change in higher education and society (O'Toole, 1996).

These additional sets of guidelines and requirements and their continuing refinement and change impact the supervision of these personnel by adding another set of parameters to a fairly small number of people for supervision in collaboration with other potential leaders. Inadequate consideration of these supervision guidelines and requirements may create significant problems in retaining staff and meeting minimal performance standards.

Alternative Approaches

Most special education leaders who obtain formal leadership instruction receive their supervision training in general educational administration (Jones et al, 1994). The array of alternative supervision approaches used in general education is used in special education as well. The research on alternative approaches tends to focus on teacher preparation programs, continuing education programs, and supervision of related services personnel.

DelVal and Griffin (1987) studied the clinical supervision process in special education in the public schools of Quincy, Massachusetts. Their six-phase approach focused on supervising and evaluating "with" teachers, not "to" teachers. Their results indicated that there was a need for valid criteria for measuring teacher performance before such activities. They also found improved collaboration in many activities both among special education teachers and between general and special education teachers. DelVal and Griffin encouraged clinical supervision efforts as an integral part of their interactive leadership program.

Peer coaching is another supervision approach which has been used and studied in special education. In one study, peer coaching with videotape feedback was found to increase effective direct instructional behaviors by low performing preservice teachers (Morgan, Menlove, Saltzberg, & Hudson, 1994). In another study, Lignugaris-Kraft and Marchand-Martella (1993) studied peer coaching using students in the latter part of their programs as supervisors. They found that this increased teachers' interactive teaching skills in a direct instructional practicum. A format for supervision was developed in response to a series of recommendations for a task force in this study. Anderson and Ritter (1988) studied the effectiveness of peer consultation and in-service leadership by using special education personnel to work with general education personnel. Through participation in a three-course university graduate credit sequence, 61 special education personnel achieved competencies in providing in-service courses with follow-up peer consultation. The second component of the training was to conduct awareness activities and workshops in local schools. Approximately 45 percent of the trainees implemented the in-service training, and about one-half of them were successful according to project criteria. Barriers to implementation included lack of local school district support, preference for informal consultation rather than formal in-service programs on the part of local district personnel, lack of follow-up to in-service programs, and participant perception that they were better trained for consultation than for in-service delivery. Peer consultation was clearly preferred over in-service programs. In a study of continuing professional development of urban educators, Elliott Jackson, and Alvarez (1993) found that a peer mentor support approach emphasizing the concerns of the individual being supervised, the school, and the school system was the most effective.

Indicators of reflective practice were observed in a study of high school special education resource teachers' instructional decision-making (Bartleheim & Evans, 1993). The results indicated that managing instructional problems required a significant degree of personal responsibility based on teachers' behaviors.

A collaborative approach—using a team of university supervisor, school supervisor, and student—in educating speech-language pathology students was found to be effective if it included frequent and effective communication (Baldes et al, 1977). Shapiro (1994) studied the effectiveness of four systems of interaction analysis in analyzing supervision conferences for speech-language pathology students; all four had strengths depending on the situation and the personnel involved.

Collaborative supervision is the approach which is most consistent with the current reform effort aimed at developing a unified system of education in which the principal is the instructional leader for *all* education in a building (CASE, 1993; McLaughlin & Warren, 1994; NASBE, 1992; Sage & Burrello, 1994). Collaborative supervision focuses on the principal as the building leader for instruction for *all* children (Rude & Rubadeau, 1992; Van Horn, Burrello, & DeClue, 1992). The principals in these studies were considered to be effective and relied on the central office special education staff for direct support and consultation rather than direct involvement with building level programs. This approach assumes that principals and teachers in a building are effective in providing quality instruction and that principals are basically autonomous in the day-to-day management of their programs.

One means of facilitating collaborative efforts between general education leaders—such as principals—and special education leaders is participation in joint training opportunities such as The Principal Training Simulator in Special Education (PTSSE), Collaborative Leadership Development (Burrello & DeClue, 1990; Burrello et al, 1990), an adaptation of the paradigm developed by Dwyer et al (1985). These simulation-based educational experiences focus on a common paradigm for leadership, including supervision, for both general education and special education leaders as reform takes place.

In one study of the impact of such collaborative training efforts, Hostetter, Jordan, Swan, and Draper (1994) provided information on the training of 367 educational leaders from 81 local and state education agencies in Collaborative Leadership Development (Swan, 1993), an adaptation of the PTSSE (Burrello et al, 1990). Thirty-nine principals and special education directors from 24 agencies trained other general education and special education leaders. Participants included superintendents, associate and assistant superintendents, principals, assistant principals, special education directors, counselors, and university faculty. Results indicated that 97.1 percent of the participants believed that the training would benefit them as educational leaders and that 91.5 percent anticipated changes in their leadership behavior based on the training.

In a more in-depth study, Lehner (1993) followed up 12 teams of principals and special education leaders in Georgia three months after they had participated in Collaborative Leadership Development (Swan, 1993). He found that the principals and special education leaders reported using the collaborative leadership skills they learned as a result of the training, that principals and special education leaders took similar actions and used similar strategies when resolving conflict involving general and special education, that special education leaders interacted more often with central office personnel in critical incidents than principals, and that the reported major benefits of the training were increased skills in collaboration, staff empowerment, and meeting individual student needs.

Special Education Leader Concerns and Teacher Perceptions

Johnson and Burrello (1987) studied special education leaders in both single districts and cooperative or intermediate units in Indiana (n = 15) and Massachusetts (n = 20). They conducted interviews and obtained ratings of particular factors of leadership. The results indicated that special education administrators needed to perceive themselves as supportive persons to teachers. They also found that special education leaders were concerned with maintaining and enhancing program quality and collaboration with general education leaders. Arick and Krug (1993) found a significant need to increase the collaboration between regular and special education leaders, based on the perceptions of special education administrators. There is a need to increase the number of administrators trained with knowledge and skills in special education. It appears that the emphasis for special education leaders is to model desirable behavior with principals/designees to ensure that adequate supervision is provided to special education and related services personnel. However, special education teachers and related services personnel may need individualized supervision from principals/designees, with assistance from special education leaders.

Teachers and supervisors' perceptions of the need for and provision of supervision appear to differ, sometimes significantly. Breton, Donaldson, and Gordon (1991), in a study of resource room teachers in Maine, found that the majority of teachers received minimal supervision, and many indicated they received none at all. Thirty-nine percent identified the building principal as the primary supervisor and 53 percent identified the special education director as the supervisor, suggesting that a variety of options were used in providing supervision to teachers. An alternative explanation is that special education teachers may wish to receive more supervision from both the principal and the special education leader in concert.

Higgins, Brown, and Swan (1987) surveyed 454 secondary school teachers—382 in general education and 72 in special education—in an urban school system which emphasized site-based management. Organizational identification and perceived intraschool conflict were examined. They found that both groups identified with the school and the district level department at a greater than neutral level. General education teachers identified more strongly with their individual school than district level, but not much more strongly, and special education teachers identified equally with both their individual school and the district level. As identification with either the individual school or the district level office increased, conflict decreased. Suggested rationale for these results include high levels of collaboration among teachers and leaders and site-based management efforts which include teacher emphases.

Billingsley (1993) found that special education teachers cited a lack of support from central office administrators, more often than lack of support from the principal, as a reason for attrition. Furthermore, both special and general education teachers who experienced higher levels of principal support were likely to be less stressed, more committed to their school division, and more satisfied with their jobs, than those receiving lower levels of support. A definition of "administrative support" is complex, but it includes supervisory functions. Interpretations, however, remain difficult and additional research is needed. In a study of students with specific learning disabilities, Houck and Rogers (1994) found significantly differing perceptions on the focus of a variety of areas regarding integration, which suggests that more supervision is needed to facilitate the integration of students with disabilities. Bordieri (1988), using Herzberg's motivators and hygiene factors to study occupational therapists and leaders, found that both occupational therapists and supervisors provided similar positive perceptions of job satisfaction when the supervisor was seen as a person who was knowledgeable and demonstrated skills on the job.

Educational leaders and teachers have varied perceptions on the necessary or desirable quantity and quality of supervision provided by leaders. Special education teachers appear to want supervision from the building principal/designee along with supervision from the special education leader who has particular knowledge and skills concerning the instruction and curricular issues which are presented by student with disabilities. Clarification of expectations and responses to individual needs by both general education and special education leaders are necessary to provide effective supervision to these people.

Personnel Preparation

Jones et al (1994) surveyed personnel preparation programs in special education administration/supervision across the country. Their survey results revealed a total of 94 programs which provided coursework—certification only, degree programs, or a combination thereof. Supervision of special education was one of the most frequently required courses and was most often taught in a department of educational administration. There was a consistent effort to include special education administration/supervision/leadership in regular education administration/supervision/leadership program units or to provide for collaboration between departments of special education and departments of general educational administration/ leadership.

Paolucci-Whitcomb, Bright, and Carlson (1987) studied general education and special education leadership personnel from 1981 to 1987 using the Interactive Leadership Program (ILP) at the University of Vermont. ILP was a process of treating people with equality and parity so that each person's perception and expertise is utilized to help increase the productivity and quality of their work lives. Competency areas included communication, leadership, team planning, and school improvement. The major purpose of the ILP was to facilitate improved educational services for all children and youth, especially those with disabilities, through a new training approach for regular and special educators. The faculty modeled the interactive process with significant success. Specific results included the following: 91 percent of participants completed the ILP concentration within expected time limits; team members rated the ILP 9 on a 10-point scale, indicating a high level of satisfaction with the program; primary changes included

integration of training for special and general education administrators and use of this approach; and special education leadership training was improved. They concluded that interaction among educators builds commitment to quality programming.

The CASE Future Agenda (1993) recommends that personnel preparation programs for principals include specific courses and experiences in educating students with disabilities. Considering the reform movements and the emphasis on site-based management, the need for principals to have significant knowledge and skills in educating these students is critical. The Principal Training Simulator in Special Education (Burrello et al, 1990) is one approach to providing such experiences.

RESEARCH AGENDA

There are several priority areas in which research should be conducted to explore the effectiveness of supervision of special education instruction. First, we need to examine the impact of excluding special education from reform agendas (e.g., America 2000, 1991) to determine if such exclusion significantly affects the quantity or quality of supervision of special education teachers and related services personnel. How would the inclusion of special education as an integral part of all educational reform efforts affect supervision? What are effective vehicles to provide supervision of special education and related services personnel in inclusive ways in each school? How should leaders collaborate to provide the most effective supervision for *all* personnel using all available resources? Under what conditions does the provision of effective supervision positively impact student achievement?

Second, we should consider the continuing and increasing educational reform movements in both breadth and depth. There is a need to determine the most effective roles for principals/designees and special education leaders to ensure that effective supervision is provided to special education personnel and to combinations of general education and special education personnel in inclusive service delivery alternatives. These new service delivery alternatives will require all those associated with them to increase their knowledge and skills in multiple dimensions, including supervision.

Third, we must recognize the role of the building principal/designee in supervising *all* personnel in the building. Research needs to determine the most effective ways to increase the knowledge and skills of principals and other designated supervisors of special education personnel. Vehicles include preservice courses, in-service courses, institutes, mentorships, peer consultation, shadowing, and other creative alternatives. An effective and efficient means to educate all educational leaders is necessary for continuous improvement. The results of effective use of these knowledge and skills would be the reduction of unnecessary problem situations and an increased amount of time to focus on instructional and curricular improvement for *all* students.

Fourth, research should determine which supervision approaches are most effective under which series of resources and constraints. Time and resources are always limited. What are the most effective means to meet the supervision needs of teachers and related services personnel?

Fifth, how can *all* educational leaders—both administrators and teachers—work collaboratively to provide necessary supervision to *all* personnel in schools rather than drawing arbitrary limits on who can do what with whom and when? Dynamic ways of collaboration among *all* leaders for the benefit of *all* students must be explored. Research can identify those practices which work most effectively under specific situations with given resources and constraints.

CONCLUSION

It is a time for each of us as leaders to build collaborative bridges over the divisive walls which allow one group of educators, and one group of students, to be isolated from one another. Supervision may be one of the most effective and essential vehicles to maximize the knowledge and skills of *all* teachers for the benefit of *all* students.

REFERENCES

America 2000: An education strategy (1991). Washington, D.C.: U.S. Government Printing Office.

American Occupational Therapy Association. (1994). *Guide for supervision of occupational therapy personnel.* Alexandria, VA: Author.

American Physical Therapy Association. (1992). *Standards of practice for physical therapy.* Alexandria, VA: Author.

American Speech-Language-Hearing Association Committee on Supervision in Speech-Language Pathology and Audiology. (1985, June). *Clinical supervision in speech-language pathology and audiology (position statement)* pp. 57–60. Rockville, MD: American Speech-Language-Hearing Association.

American Speech-Language-Hearing Association Committee on Supervision in Speech-Language Pathology and Audiology. (1989, March). *Preparation models for the supervisory process in speech-language pathology and audiology (tutorial)* pp. 97–106. Rockville, MD: American Speech-Language-Hearing Association.

Anderson, D. M. & Ritter, S. A. (1988). Training district personnel as peer consultants and in-service leaders: Implementation and evaluation of a training program. *Special Services in the Schools, 4*(1/2). Reprinted in L. C. Burrello & D. E. Greenburg (Eds.). *Leadership and supervision in special services: Promising ideas and practices* (pp. 77–95). New York: The Haworth Press.

Arick, J. R. & Krug, D. A. (1993). Special education administrators in the United States: Perceptions on policy and personnel issues. *The Journal of Special Education, 27*(3), 348–364.

Baldes, R. A., Goings, R., Herbold, D. D., Jeffrey, R., Wheeler, G., & Freilinger, R. (1977). Supervision of student speech clinicians. *Language, Speech, and Hearing Services in the Schools, 8*(2), 76–84.

Bartel, J. M. (1977). The collaborative process for service integration. In (Eds.). *The service integration project: Final report.* Durham, NC: Lloyd Shore.

Bartleheim, F. J. & Evans, S. (1993). The presence of reflective-practice indicators in special education resource teachers' instructional decision-making. *The Journal of Special Education, 27*(3), 338–347.

Berreth, D. G. (1992). Restructuring: Where we've been and where we're going. *The Special Education Leadership Review, 1*(1), 5–10.

Billingsley, B. S. (1993). Teacher retention and attrition in special and general education: A critical review of the literature. *The Journal of Special Education, 27*(2), 131–174.

Billingsley, B. S. & Jones, P. R. (1993). Instructional supervision in special education: Strategies for rural programs. *Rural Special Education Quarterly, 12*(2), 3–9.

Bordieri, J. E. (1988). Job satisfaction of occupational therapists: Supervisors and managers versus direct service staff. *The Occupational Therapy Journal of Research, 8*(3), 155–163.

Breton, W. A., Donaldson, G. A., & Gordon, A., Jr., (1991). Too little, too late? The supervision of maine resource room teachers. *Journal of Special Education, 25*(1), 114–125.

Brown, C. L. & Swan, W. W. (1985). *Budget planning and preparation for special education under the Quality Basic Education Act.* Atlanta: South Atlantic Regional Resource Center (Ft. Lauderdale, FL) in collaboration with Georgia Council of Administrators of Special Education and Georgia Department of Education/Program for Exceptional Children.

Burrello, L. C. & DeClue, L. (1990). *Instructors manual: Training materials for the principal's training simulator in special education.* Bloomington, IN: Indiana University.

Burrello, L. C., Schrup, M. C., & Barnett, B. G. (1990). *The principal as the special education instructional leader: Training materials for the principal training simulator in special education.* Bloomington, IN: Indiana University.

Burrello, L. C. & Zadnik, D. J. (1986). Critical success factors of special education administration. *The Journal of Special Education, 20*(23), 20–26.

Council for Exceptional Children. (1995). *What every special educator must know: The international standards for the preparation and certification of special education teachers.* Reston, VA: Author.

Council of Administrators of Special Education. (1993). *CASE future agenda for special education: Creating a unified education system.* Albuquerque, NM: Author.

DelVal, P. B. & Griffin, C. L. (1987). Implementing the clinical supervision process in special education. In L. C. Burrello & D. E. Greenburg (Eds.). *Leadership and supervision in special services: Promising ideas and practices* (pp. 17-34). New York: The Haworth Press,

Dwyer, D. C., Lee, G. V., Barnett, B. G., Filby, N. N., Towan, B., & Kojimoto, C. (1985). *Understanding the principal's contribution to instruction: Seven principals, seven stories.* San Francisco: Far West Laboratory for Educational Research and Development.

Elliott, M. A., Jackson, Y., & Alvarez, C. (1993). Continuing professional development for urban special educators. *Teacher Education and Special Education, 16*(1), 73–82.

Guerra, P., Jackson, J. S., & Madsen, C. (1994). Site-based management and special education: Policies, implications, and recommendations. *The Special Education Leadership Review, 2*(1), 59–71.

Harris, B. M. (1975). *Supervisory behavior in education* (2nd ed.). Englewood Cliffs, NJ: Prentice Hall.

Harris, B. M. & King, J. D. (1975). *Competency specifications `for instructional leadership personnel,* document #7 (rev.). Austin, TX: Special Education Supervisor Training Project, The University of Texas at Austin.

Higgins, D. R., Brown, C. L., & Swan, W. W. (1987). Organizational identification and perceived intra-school conflict among secondary special education and regular education teachers. *Special Services in the Schools, 4*(1 & 2), 95–102.

Hostetter, C., Jordan, J. A., Swan, W. W., & Draper, I. (1994, November). *Collaboration—Promising practices and partnerships.*

Annual meeting of the National Association of Directors of Special Education, Grand Rapids, MI.

Houck, C. K. & Rogers, C. J. (1994). The special/general education integration initiative for students with specific learning disabilities: A "snapshot" of program change. *Journal of Learning Disabilities, 27*(7), 435–453.

Johnson, V. L., Jr. & Burrello, L. C. (1987). Critical success factors in rural and urban special education administration. *Special Services in the Schools, 4*(1/2). Reprinted in L. C. Burrello & D. E. Greenburg (Eds.). *Leadership and supervision in special services: Promising ideas and practices* (pp. 1–16). New York: The Haworth Press.

Jones, P. R., Robinett, M. K., & Wells, D. L. (1994). Administration and supervision of special education: Where is training available? *CASE in Point, 8*(1), 37–52.

Lehner, G. P. (1993). *Collaborative leadership development: Impact on leadership behaviors of principals and special education directors.* Unpublished doctoral dissertation, University of Georgia, Athens.

Lignugaris-Kraft, B. & Marchand-Martella, N. (1993). Evaluation of preservice teachers' interactive teaching skills in a direct instruction practicum using student teachers as supervisors. *Teacher Education and Special Education, 16*(4), 309–318.

McLaughlin, M. J. & Warren, S. H. (1994). Restructuring special education programs in local school districts: The tensions and the challenges. *The Special Education Leadership Review, 2*(1), 2–21.

McNulty, B. A. (1992). Restructuring and special education: A state administrator's perspective. *The Special Education Leadership Review, 1*(1), 13–17.

Morgan, R. L., Menlove, R., Saltzberg, C. L., & Hudson, P. (1994). Effects of peer coaching on the acquisition of instructional skills by low performing preserving teachers. *The Journal of Special Education, 28*(1), 59–76.

National Association of State Boards of Education. (1992). *Winners all: A call for inclusive schools.* Alexandria, VA: NASBE Study Group on Special Education.

Osborne, A. G., Jr., DiMattia, P., & Curran, F. X. (1993). *Effective management of special education programs: A handbook for school administrators.* New York: Teachers College, Columbia University.

O'Toole, T. J. (1996). *Current initiatives for standards in certifying and accreditation of speech-language pathologists.* South Atlantic Regional Resource Center Reports—Emerging Issues and Trends in Education. Stillwater, OK: National Clearinghouse of Rehabilitative Training Materials.

Paolucci-Whitcomb, P., Bright, W. E., II, & Carlson, R. V. (1987). Interactive evaluations: Processes for improving special education leadership training. *Remedial and Special Education, 8*(3), 52–61.

Podemski, R. S., Marsh, G. E., II, Smith, T. E. C., & Price, B. J. (1995). *Comprehensive administration of special education.* Englewood Cliffs, NJ: Merrill Publishing.

Public Law 94-142. *Education for All Handicapped Children Act of 1975,* 20 U.S.C., 1400, 89 Stat. 793 (1975).

Public Law 102-119. *Individuals with Disabilities Education Act, Amendments of 1991,* 20 U.S.C. S 1400 *et seq.* (1992).

Rockert, J. F. (1982). The changing role of the information system executive: A critical success factor perspective. *Sloan Management Review, 24,* 3–13.

Rude, H. A. & Rubadeau, R. J. (1992). Priorities for principals as special education leaders. *The Special Education Leadership Review, 1*(1), 55–62.

Sage, D. D. & Burrello, L. C. (1994). *Leadership in educational reform—an administrator's guide to changes in special education.* Baltimore, MD: Paul H. Brookes Publishing Co.

Sergiovanni, T. (1984). Leadership and excellence in schooling. *Educational Leadership, 41*(5), 4–14.

Shapiro, D. A. (1994). Interaction analysis and self study: A single-case comparison of four methods of analyzing supervisory conferences. *Language, Speech, and Hearing Services in the Schools, 25,* 67–75.

Smith-Davis, J. & Billingsley, B. (1993). The supply-demand puzzle. *Teacher Education and Special Education, 16*(3), 215–220.

Swan, W. W. (1993). *Collaborative leadership development: An adaptation of the principal training simulator in special education.* Atlanta, GA: Division for Exceptional Students, Georgia Department of Education.

Swan, W. W. & Morgan, J. L. (1993). *Collaborating for comprehensive services for young children and their families.* Baltimore, MD: Paul H. Brookes Publishing Co.

Swan, W. W. & Sirvis, B. (1992). CEC knowledge and skills for beginning special education teachers. *Teaching Exceptional Children, 25*(1), 16–20.

U.S. Department of Education. (1992). *Fourteenth annual report to Congress on the implementation of the Individuals with Disabilities Education Act.* Washington, D.C.: U.S. Government Printing Office.

U.S. News and World Report (1995, December 30). The graduate guide, p. 22.

Van Horn, G. P., Burrello, L. C., & DeClue, L. (1992). An instructional leadership framework: The principal's leadership role in special education. *The Special Education Leadership Review, 2*(1), 41–54.

Wang, M. C., Haertel, G. D., & Walberg, H. J. (1993). Toward a knowledge base for school learning. *Review of Educational Research, 63*(3), 249–294.

Zadnik, D. J. (1985). Critical success factors of special education administrators. Unpublished doctoral dissertation. Bloomington, IN: Indiana University.

SUPPLEMENTARY READINGS FOR SPECIAL EDUCATION

Hallahan, D. & Kauffman, J. (1994). *Exceptional children: Introduction to special education* (6th ed.). New York: Allyn and Bacon.

Lewis, R. B. & Doorlag, D. H. (1995). *Teaching special students in the mainstream* (4th ed.). Englewood Cliffs, NJ: Prentice Hall.

·21·

SUPERVISION IN SERVICE AREAS

James F. Nolan, Jr.

PENNSYLVANIA STATE UNIVERSITY

INTRODUCTION

The purpose of this chapter is to review the research on supervision of pupil personnel specialists, those professionals who serve students in professional support roles which are usually carried on outside the confines of the classroom. Although there are other professionals, such as school nurses, who function in pupil personnel roles, this review will focus on the supervision of two groups of pupil personnel specialists: school counselors and school psychologists. Both school counselors and psychologists provide a variety of services to children from preschool through high school. School counselors provide comprehensive developmental guidance and counseling programs for students from kindergarten through twelfth grade. They provide support for both students and teachers by focusing their attention on a wide variety of issues, including school adjustment, academic problems, family problems, behavioral counseling and management, student self-esteem, career education, and substance abuse prevention. They accomplish their work through a variety of mechanisms, including one-to-one counseling sessions with students, group counseling sessions for students, delivering instruction to large groups of students within the classroom, providing consultation with teachers and parents, and consulting with and arranging for appropriate services from social service agencies and other providers within the local and state communities.

The role of the school psychologist varies somewhat from school district to school district. In some schools, school psychologists are almost exclusively engaged in leading multidisciplinary teams, which are charged with responsibility for evaluating students who may be eligible to receive special education services. In other districts, school psychologists engage in many of the same activities as school counselors, but with a more restricted population of students. These students need assistance that requires different expertise from that of the school counselor. The role of the school psychol-

ogist has changed rapidly in recent years because of the "regular education initiative" or "inclusion" movement. As a result of inclusion, the task of assessing students for placement in special education settings is diminishing in favor of providing support to the regular classroom teacher to enable all students to be successful there. In most situations, school counselors and psychologists work closely together to provide the services that students need, and they are structurally aligned within the school as an organization.

The remainder of the chapter will be divided into three parts. The first section will provide an overview of the research on the supervision of counseling in general. This research provides an important backdrop for understanding the research that deals specifically with the supervision of both school counselors and psychologists, since school counselors and school psychologists can really be considered a subset of the entire population of counselors and counseling psychologists. This general overview of the research on the supervision of counselors will focus on four major subtopics: models of counseling supervision, methods of counseling supervision, variables which affect the supervisor-counselor relationship, and research strategies and issues in the supervision of counselors.

The second section of the chapter will focus specifically on the research concerning the supervision of school counselors and will provide some directions and questions for future research. The final section of the chapter will focus on the research concerning the supervision of school psychologists and provide suggestions for future research in this area.

SUPERVISION OF COUNSELING

Supervision has been recognized as a specialty area within the counseling profession since the early 1980s (Dye & Borders, 1990). Since the early 1980s, the amount of research in the area of supervision of counseling has grown tremendously, and doctoral coursework in supervision has been added at many institutions across the country. In fact, specialized coursework in supervision is required for doctoral programs that seek accreditation from the Council for the Accreditation of Counseling and Related Programs. (Dye & Borders, 1990). The impetus for the development of supervision as a specialty area within the counseling profession reached a milestone in 1989, when the American Association for Counseling and Development (AACD) (Now the American Counseling Association) adopted standards for counseling supervisors. These standards, which were developed over several years, require that counseling supervisors must:

1. be effective counselors;
2. possess effective personal and professional traits;
3. be knowledgeable about the ethical and regulatory aspects of the profession;
4. possess a conceptual understanding of the nature of the supervisory relationship;
5. possess a conceptual knowledge of supervision methods and techniques;
6. possess a conceptual knowledge of the counselor development process;
7. be competent in case conceptualization and management;
8. be competent in client assessment and evaluation;
9. be competent in oral and written case reporting and recording;
10. be competent in evaluating counselor performance; and
11. be knowledgeable about counseling and counselor supervision (AACD, 1990).

The development of these standards and the impetus over the last decade toward the professionalization of the role of counselor supervisor have led to considerable research in the area of counseling supervision. This research can be used as the foundation for the supervision of school counselors and school psychologists. Despite the fact that much of the research in the area of counselor supervision has focused on the supervision of counselors in training, the body of knowledge which has been accumulated does provide important insights for the supervision of practicing counselors and psychologists as well. We have divided that body of knowledge into four key areas: models of supervision, methods of supervision, key variables in the supervision process, and research strategies and issues.

Models of Supervision.

Therapy Based Supervision Bernard (1992) grouped counseling supervision models into five categories: psychotherapy-based, developmental, alternative conceptual models, parallel process, and personal growth. Though it is certainly legitimate to consider these models as five separate entities, for purposes of this discussion it is sufficient to discuss two distinct approaches to the supervision of counselors: therapy-based supervision and developmental supervision.

All of those specific models (psychodynamic, person-centered, behavioral, parallel process, personal growth) which we have classified as therapy-based share the common assumption that the process of supervision is an extension of, or a parallel process to, the process of therapy. Therefore, the supervisor's thinking and behavior as a supervisor should match or closely parallel his or her behavior and thinking as a therapist, and the relationship between the supervisor and counselor should parallel the relationship between counselor and client (Freeman, 1992). This notion is quite similar to Goldhammer's (1969), who believed that the process of teacher supervision should be a model for the process of teaching and learning. Therapy-based models assume that learning is the primary outcome of both therapy and supervision, that the theory which underlies one's model of therapy can be applied equally to both supervisee and client, and that the supervision and therapeutic contexts are equal or parallel (Bernard & Goodyear, 1992). The goals that are espoused by these approaches include not only the growth of the counselor as a professional but also the growth of the counselor as a person. They also include a resolution of personal issues and concerns that would be addressed in a therapeutic context.

Although empirical evidence concerning the efficacy of therapy-based approaches is very limited, therapy-based supervisory approaches do offer the advantages of: (1) allowing supervisors to behave in ways which are congruent with their behaviors as counselors; (2) providing models of therapeutic behavior for the counselor during the supervisory process; and (3) helping the counselor to develop empathy for his or her clients. On the other hand, therapy-based approaches have limitations as well. Supervisors are likely to have a very difficult time supervising counselors who do not share the same orientation toward counseling, and the supervisor may be inclined to ignore client issues during the supervisory process, focusing instead on the counselors' personal issues.

Developmental Supervision Though therapy-based approaches to supervision dominated the field during the early history of counseling supervision, developmental approaches to supervision have dominated the literature during the last 20 years. Developmental models of supervision (Loganbill, Hardy, & Delworth, 1982; Stoltenberg, 1981; Wiley & Ray, 1986) assert that becoming a counselor is a developmental process during which the prospective counselor passes through a series of stages. In each stage, the counselor faces a predictable series of personal and professional issues and tasks that must be resolved successfully if development to the next stage is to continue. Developmentalists believe that effective supervisors help trainees resolve the stage-related issues by employing stage-relevant supervisory interventions (Galassi & Trent, 1987). Most developmental models propose a three- or four-stage model of development. In Stage 1, the preservice counselor is dependent and insecure, lacks insight, and tends to engage in categorical rather than flexible and adaptive thinking. The theory is that counselors in this stage require a supportive, structured supervisory relationship, with direct instruction in counseling. In Stage 2, trainees begin to define themselves more clearly as individual counselors and begin the journey from dependence to autonomy. Counselors at this stage naturally experience some confusion, internal conflict, and conflict with their supervisors as they strive to gain independence and a more fully developed sense of who they are (Borders & Leddick, 1987). Supervisors at this stage should begin to provide less direct instruction and greater modeling and make more use of demonstrations. During the third stage of development, preservice counselors become more flexible in their thinking, more insightful about client issues, more tolerant of diverse points of view in counseling, and more self-confident. They also become more aware of their own personal motivations as counselors. Supervisors are urged to engage in more collaborative supervision during this stage of development, sharing their thoughts as colleagues and challenging their supervisees' notions as they would those of a respected colleague (Galassi & Trent, 1987). In the final stage, counselors reach the stage of independent practitioner. They develop the ability to really work with others in colleague consultation. Developmental supervision in short holds that counselors progress from dependence to conditional dependence to autonomy and from categorical thinking to flexible and adaptive thinking. The theory asserts that development to these higher levels of functioning is optimized when counselors are supported with congruent supervisory behavior as they make their way through a series of conflicts that surround eight counseling issues: personal competence, emotional awareness, autonomy, identity, respect for individual differences, counseling purpose and direction, personal motivation, and ethical responsibility (Loganbill, Hardy, & Delworth, 1982).

Research is somewhat supportive of developmental models of counseling supervision. Perceptions of both supervisors and supervisees are generally consistent with developmental models. Their perceptions seem somewhat more consistent with counselor development than with how supervisory behavior matches to counselor developmental level. It does appear, however, that the supervisory relationship becomes more collegial over time and that the substance of supervision seems to change from an early emphasis on counseling skills to a later emphasis on personal and relationship issues (Worthington, 1987). Holloway (1987) asserted that there is consistent support for counselor development between the initial graduate practicum and the final internship but very little empirical evidence of changes within the time period from the end of the first practicum to the beginning of the final internship. Bernard and Goodyear (1992) claim that while developmental models are widely applicable and helpful in focusing on progress over time, they may be too rigid, and they fail to account for divergent developmental paths and cases of no growth or developmental relapses. Developmental models of counseling supervision nevertheless present a cogent theory of counselor development and supervisor behavior, and they do enjoy some empirical support.

Methods of Supervision

Individual Supervision There is a variety of interventions that have been advocated for the process of counselor supervision, although research concerning the effectiveness of the various methods is scarce. We can generally identify two distinct approaches to supervisory interventions: methods of individual supervision and group supervision. *Individual supervision* refers to a supervisor who works one to one with a counselor to examine and improve the counselor's performance and professional development. Strong advocates of psychotherapy-based models of counseling are limited in terms of supervisory interventions to those methods which are congruent with the underlying therapeutic model. Advocates of alternative models are free to chose from a variety of intervention techniques. It is possible to classify all of these variations under four general methods of individual supervision: (1) self-report; (2) use of audio- and videotapes; (3) skill acquisition training; and (4) live observation.

Self-report refers to an intervention in which the counselor provides a report of the counseling session to the supervisor soon after the counseling session and the supervisor and counselor attempt to process the session through the counselor's recollections. This method is often augmented by the use of the counselor's process notes. Hart (1982) acknowledges the difficulties which counselors face as they attempt to make objective self-observations, as well as the potential for enhanced self-evaluation. Hart nevertheless, asserts that self-report is a useful supervisory strategy when combined with other interventions.

A second popular method of individual supervision is the use of audio- and videotape recordings to provide a record of the counseling session. This record is then used as the basis for analysis by both supervisor and counselor. The analysis may be accomplished in a variety of ways. One model is simply viewing the tape together and talking about key incidents and behaviors. A second strategy involves separate viewing or listening to the tapes, followed by written critiques of the tapes by each partner, and, finally, a conference in which the two partners come together and compare their written critiques. A third model is labeled as interpersonal process recall (Kagan, 1988). In interpersonal process recall, the supervisor and counselor watch a videotape or listen to an audiotape together, and the supervisor asks confrontational but nonjudgmental questions, such as: "What were you thinking at that point?" or "Given the client's nonverbal behavior, what do you think she made of that comment?"

Skill acquisition training refers to a variety of approaches in which the supervisor teaches new skills to the counselor. Popular approaches to skill acquisition have included microtraining, in which counselors attempt to learn a variety of new skills through a step-by-step format, including theory, demonstration, practice, and feedback (Forsyth & Ivey, 1980). This approach is quite similar to the model of staff development training advocated by Joyce and Showers (1995). A second approach to skill acquisition involves role playing on the part of counselors in training, with appropriate feedback provided by the supervisor. A final approach to skill acquisition involves modeling and demonstration of counseling sessions by the supervisor. Akamatsu (1980) claimed that the use of live or video models was quite effective in skill development when accompanied by practice and feedback by the supervisor. Hart (1982) also claimed that observing the behavior of a supervisor who was acting as cotherapist was an effective method for skill development.

Research on this method of supervision indicates that practice and feedback are key elements in the acquisition of new skills by beginning counselors.

The fourth method of supervision involves live observation of the counselor by the supervisor. This method has been used less frequently than the other three because of its potential intrusiveness and resulting discomfort on the part of the client. However, Worthington (1984) reported that counselor performance improved when live observation was used, and Bernard and Goodyear (1992) assert that live observation may create discomfort but does not have any negative effect on the therapy outcome. The research on the use and efficacy of various methods of individual counselor supervision is very limited (Bernard & Goodyear, 1992).

Group Supervision The method of supervision which has been most widely used in counseling and counselor education during the last decade is group supervision. Group supervision typically is a problem-oriented approach, in which a supervisor works with a small group of three to six supervisees and helps the supervisees become more adept at analyzing and resolving difficult issues and concerns that arise during their work with clients. Case notes or audio- and videotapes are used as the basis for analysis by the supervisor and group.

Borders (1991a) provides a description of one systematic approach to peer group supervision. Using this approach, one of the counselors in the group identifies questions that he or she has concerning a particular client and requests feedback from the group. Group members watch a videotape of the counseling session, with each group member focusing on a different aspect of the counselor-client interaction. For example, one member might observe the counselor's nonverbal behavior; another might observe the client's nonverbal behavior; a third member might focus on the use of some particular counseling technique or skill; and a fourth member might focus on viewing the tape from a particular therapeutic perspective. The counselor presents the case to the group during the group supervision session, the group views the tape, and the supervisor then facilitates a discussion of the tape. The discussion concludes with a summary by the supervisor or one of the group members. The supervisor acts as a process observer and provides feedback on the group processes and interactions that have occurred during the discussion. In addition, Borders advocates that the supervisor vary his or her behavior in accordance with the developmental level of the group, becoming more directive with neophytes and more collaborative with advance counselors.

Bernard and Goodyear (1992) assert that group supervision provides several distinct advantages, including the following:

1. enhanced reflection on the part of counselors;
2. enhanced perspective taking beyond oneself;
3. providing reassurance, validation, and a sense of belonging;
4. establishing a peer review process; and
5. minimizing the dependence-authoritarian role conflicts which can be present in one-to-one supervisory relationships.

Holloway and Johnston (1985) claim that the field of counselor training is at a very rudimentary level in its attempt to explain and understand group supervision, because there has been little empirical research concerning its efficacy. They believe that group supervision makes intuitive sense, but that there are neither adequate models nor convincing empirical approaches. They also identified the following research questions which should be pursued in studies concerning group supervision:

1. What should be the goals of group supervision?
2. What role should the supervisor adopt?
3. What balance among didactic material, case conceptualization, and interpersonal process is most productive?
4. What is the role of evaluation in group supervision?
5. What unique contribution to counselor development does group supervision make?

Variables Affecting the Supervisory Process

Gender This section of the chapter focuses on two factors which can have a positive or negative impact on the supervisor-counselor relationship: gender and culture. Both issues have received growing attention in the counselor supervision literature.

Although many writers hypothesize that gender differences can have a significant impact on the relationship between supervisor and supervisee, empirical studies concerning the impact of gender are mixed. Behling, Curtis, and Foster (1988) asserted that same-sex pairings generally work out best, but they also cautioned that this finding is not universal. In their study, female-female dyads tended to be the most positive while female trainee-male supervisor dyads tended to be most problematic, due to sexist behavior on the part of the supervisor. Thyer, Sowers-Hoag, and Love (1988) reported relatively the same trends but reported that gender accounted for only about 5 percent of the variance in determining satisfaction with the supervisor-supervisee relationship. Worthington and Stern (1985) reported that same-gender dyads resulted in self-reported closer relationships and greater supervisor influence for supervisees, but they reported no significant differences for supervisors. They also reported that male supervisors and supervisees reported better relationships than females did. It seems that gender differences between supervisor and supervisee can exert some influence on relationship satisfaction, especially for supervisees, but the magnitude of that impact is in question.

One aspect of gender differences which has been explored in greater depth is the impact of gender on the dimension of power within the supervisory relationship. Stoltenberg and Delworth (1987) reported significant differences in the types of power employed by supervisors (using French and Raven's typology of social power bases). According to their findings, male supervisors were more likely to make use of referent power, while female supervisors were more likely to employ expert power bases. Nelson and Holloway (1990) studied 20 matched-gender and 20 mixed-gender supervisory dyads, finding subtle but important differences in the power relationship. They reported that regardless of gender the supervisor tended to play a more directive, didactic role than the supervisee. They also suggested that both male and female supervisors were more encouraging of male supervisees who assumed power roles within the relationship than they were of female supervisees who assumed power roles. This finding is compounded by the fact that female supervisees tended to relinquish the power roles to individuals they perceived as experts more readily than their male counterparts did. It is, therefore, less likely that female supervisee's will enjoy an equal power relationship, regardless of the gender of the supervisor.

Culture In the last 20 years, the literature on cross-cultural counseling has increased exponentially, but the scarcity of empirical information on which to base our understanding of cross-cultural counseling is striking (Leong & Wagner, 1994). Leong and Wagner define cross-cultural counseling as a supervisor-supervisee relationship in which the supervisor and supervisee come from different cultures. However, the examples which they provide are confined to differences in racial and ethnic identity (e.g., white, African American, Latin American, Native American). Other cultural variables, such as socioeconomic status, gender, educational level, geographic location, and religious affiliation are apparently not included in this definition. Bernard (1994), in response to Leong and Wagner, prefers the label *multicultural counseling* because it "keeps us more vigilant of a variety of cultural variables whereas cross-cultural tends to imply a more singular cultural focus" (p. 168). Whatever label one uses, the burgeoning literature in this area of inquiry is far more theoretical than empirical.

In terms of theoretical conceptions of multicultural issues in counselor supervision, Bernard and Goodyear (1992) present a cogent overview of some of the issues involved, They begin with Pedersen's (1987) conceptualization of several common assumptions that reflect a Western bias in the traditional helping professions. These assumptions are:

1. an emphasis on the individual as opposed to the family or community;
2. fragmentation of learning into the traditional disciplines;
3. an over dependence on the value of decontextualized abstraction;
4. an overemphasis on independence as opposed to interdependence;
5. neglect of the client's natural support system;
6. dependence on logical, linear thinking as opposed to systemic or cyclical thinking;
7. a focus on the part of the helper on changing the individual rather than changing the system; and
8. an overemphasis on the present with a resultant neglect of the client's history.

These assumptions are compounded by our inherent ethnocentrism, which tends to lead us to assume that our view of the world is normal and right rather than culturally and politically contextualized.

These often implicit assumptions on the part of client, counselor, and supervisor can lead to the development of conflicts within the supervisory relationship. Ryan and Hendricks (1989) identified five such sources of conflict within cross-cultural supervisory relationships:

1. differences in cognitive orientation, such as verbal vs. nonverbal or field dependence vs. field independence;
2. differences in motivational orientation, such as external vs. internal locus of control;
3. differences in communication style, such as talkative vs. not talkative;
4. differences in value orientation, such as self-reliance vs. interdependence or humility vs. self-expression; and
5. differences in sensory orientation, such as auditory vs. visual.

Bernard and Goodyear (1992), in an attempt to help prospective counselor supervisors deal with the potential conflicts which are inherent in cross-cultural supervisory relationships, advocate five foci for supervisor preparation: development of a pluralistic philosophy, development of knowledge about particular cultures, consciousness-raising activities, experiential training, and contact with minorities. They have also developed a five-stage model of cross-cultural awareness which includes the following stages:

1. *unawareness:* The individual has not given serious thought to cultural, racial or ethnic differences or their meaning and influence;
2. *beginning awareness:* The individual begins to develop some cognitive dissonance and sense of discomfort concerning such differences;
3. *conscious awareness:* The individual shows a full awareness of racial, ethnic, and cultural differences but is unable to integrate such differences into any useful way of acting;
4. *consolidated awareness:* The individual takes positive actions to promote intergroup understanding and social change; and
5. *transcendent awareness:* The individual's life is characterized by appropriate responsiveness in a variety of cultural environments.

Priest (1994) has also developed a conceptualization of the stages which supervisors go through as they develop multicultural awareness. He identified six specific developmental stages:

1. a denial stage in which the supervisor denies that there are appreciable cultural differences that can impact the supervisory relationship;
2. a dissonance stage in which the supervisor begins to recognize cultural differences but does not know what to do about them;
3. a discovery stage in which the supervisor attempts to identify cultural differences and similarities that impact the supervisory relationship;
4. a self-analysis stage in which the supervisor attempts to identify where he or she fits into the overall scheme;
5. a skilled stage in which the supervisor identifies thought processes and communication patterns that facilitate supervision; and

6. an integrated stage in which the supervisor formulates multiple supervisory methodologies that are respectful of the supervisee's culture and interactive style.

Leong and Wagner (1994) identified three empirical studies of cross-cultural supervision in their comprehensive review of the literature. A study by Vander Kolk (1974) found that race had a significant impact on supervisee expectations for their supervisors in terms of variables such as respect, empathy, and congruence. Black trainees expected supervisors to be less congruent and empathetic. Cook and Helms (1988) surveyed 225 minority trainees about their perceptions of cross-cultural counseling supervision. They found that one factor, perceived supervisor liking, accounted for 70 percent of the variance in determining satisfaction with supervision. If supervisees felt liked and cared about by the supervisor, they were generally satisfied with supervision. Hilton, Russell, and Salami (in Leong and Wagner, 1994) studied the impact of supervisor racial background and level of support on the perceptions of female trainees concerning supervisory effectiveness. High levels of supervisor support were significantly related to perceptions of effectiveness, but there was no main effect for race and no interaction effect. Leong and Wagner drew the following conclusion concerning empirical research.

Thus, the answer to our first question, "what do we know?" is very little. There are a number of theoretical hypotheses from different authors and many of these converge, but even these remain untested. Empi-rically it seems safe to conclude that (a) race can have a profound influence on the supervisory process, particularly in terms of trainees' expectations for supervisor characteristics like empathy, respect, and congruence; (b) race can influence a supervisee's perception of supervisor liking; and (c) there are some circumstances under which race does not seem to influence supervision (p. 128).

Leong and Wagner (1994) identify several questions which should be pursued in future studies of the effects of culture on counseling supervision. These questions include:

1. Is cross-cultural counseling a developmental process?
2. Do the various models of cross-cultural counseling apply to all interracial triads, or do we need specific models for specific racial combinations?
3. How does the supervisor's ethnicity influence his or her role?
4. What techniques can help supervisors promote awareness, increase knowledge, and develop cross-cultural counseling skills in their trainees?
5. How would our knowledge be enhanced if race and ethnicity were treated as complex psychological variables rather than as nominal categories?

Bernard (1994) recommends the following parameters for supervision in her attempt to summarize the implications of the empirical and theoretical literature on multicultural counseling supervision:

1. Supervisees must be at least as multiculturally sensitive as their clients, and supervisors must be as least as multiculturally sensitive as their supervisees.

2. Training programs must determine at what level of multicultural development a trainee is ready for clinical practice and for entry into the profession.
3. Supervisors must rely on both multicultural and developmental models of supervision to understand the readiness of supervisees to be challenged multiculturally, and choose fertile moments to do so.
4. Supervisors must be offered supervision to enhance their own multicultural development.

Research Strategies and Issues

The focus of much of the research on the counselor supervision process has been on structural variables, such as gender, experience level, and culture or on the use of particular conceptual models such as developmental supervision. Most of the research has also employed cross-sectional designs and self-report measures and rating scales to assess supervisee satisfaction with the supervisory process (Kagan, 1988). Ellis's (1991) summary of research on counselor supervision provides a very dismal picture of the progress thus far. "The proliferation of research in supervision has been largely haphazard, atheoretical, and rife with a host of methodological flaws, and the vast majority of supervision models have not been tested or verified empirically" (p. 238). Although Ellis's evaluation seems overly critical, Borders (1989) does provide some support for the critical nature of these comments: "Little progress has been made toward answering the critical question posed six years ago, 'What supervision interventions by which supervisors will lead to what outcomes for which supervisees?'" (p. 16). It is clear that the field would be well served by a greater focus on the supervisory process itself and on the outcomes of the supervisory process for both supervisor and supervisee. In fact, the literature is completely silent on the outcomes of the supervisory process for the supervisor. We need studies that would enable researchers to link direct supervisory events with outcomes for supervisors, supervisees, and clients (Borders, 1989).

Bernard and Goodyear (1992) write that the current state of counselor supervision is in the first stage of scientific development—the discovery stage, in which important variables are identified through descriptive studies. Although cross-sectional survey research has been helpful in identifying important variables such as gender and culture, there is a great need for other research strategies. These strategies have the potential to identify important variables that are not amenable to discovery through surveys. Among the variety of research designs that could prove fruitful, Bernard and Goodyear put particular emphasis on the use of qualitative research (e.g., phenomenology), case studies, interaction analysis-type studies, and what they label as the "events paradigm" approach. Events paradigm research seems quite similar to what others have labeled "action research." Bernard and Goodyear assert that increased use of these other approaches should result in the identification of other important variables, which can then be manipulated during stage two of the development process: aptitude-treatment interactions. Holahan and Galassi (1986) have described an additional research strategy that would seem to be quite appropriate for studying the counselor supervision process: the single case design. Using this multiple baseline design, data concerning effectiveness are collected prior to any intervention, at multiple points during the intervention process, and at some follow up point in time to assess residual impact.

It is important to try to avoid some of the methodological issues which have hindered counselor supervision research in the past when designing studies that are intended to examine the events of counselor supervision, the relationship between these events, and the outcomes for supervisee, supervisor, and client. Bernard and Goodyear (1992) suggest that researchers pay attention to the following methodological issues:

1. the need to attempt to increase sample size in studies which are intended to lead to generalizations. Although increasing sample size is admittedly difficult, many survey studies to date have used very small samples. If appropriate sample sizes cannot be obtained, it might be preferable to conduct more detailed multiple case studies;
2. the need to use longitudinal and sequential designs in addition to cross-sectional designs;
3. the need to provide more detailed information about raters when raters and rating scales are employed;
4. the need to provide more detailed information about participants as well as contexts;
5. the need to avoid using participants in multiple roles within the same study, for example, as supervisor in one dyad and supervisee in another. If such "double dipping" is unavoidable or even desirable for some reason, its effects, advantages, and disadvantages should be fully explored;
6. the need to develop well-accepted and clear operational definitions of terms and constructs that are important to the study;
7. the need to develop rigorous instruments developed specifically for research on counselor supervision; and
8. the need to limit the overreliance on self-reported satisfaction as a measure of supervisory effectiveness. When self-reported satisfaction is used as a measure, greater attempts should be made to identify other outcomes which are associated with satisfaction.

With this overview of the research on the supervision of counseling in general as a backdrop, we can now turn our attention to the research on the supervision of school counselors and school psychologists.

SUPERVISION OF SCHOOL COUNSELORS

Research to Date

The research on the supervision of school counselors is extremely limited. Despite the scarcity of research in the field, however, it is possible to draw one reasonably strong conclusion: school counselors receive very little supervision. As is the case with teachers, it appears that school counselors receive much more intense, high quality supervision during their preservice education period than they do at any other point in

their professional careers. What Boyd and Walter said in 1975 remains essentially unchanged. School counselors are like cacti—they survive without many nutrients from the environment, and much of what passes for supervision is really administrivia.

Several studies which have been conducted on the status of school counselor supervision have used a conceptualization of supervision developed by Barret and Schmidt (1986). Barret and Schmidt reported that in 1986 most supervision of school counselors was carried out by principals and other school administrators who had little or no educational preparation in counseling. They also wrote that there appeared to be very little agreement about what constitutes effective school counselor supervision in the literature. These authors went on to develop a model of school counselor supervision which consisted of three phases:

1. an administrative phase carried out by administrators, which focuses on meeting contractual obligations such as attendance, punctuality, relating to staff, completing paperwork, etc. This aspect of supervision is closely related to personnel evaluation;
2. a program development phase, which focuses on the counselor's contribution to the overall guidance and counseling program; and
3. clinical supervision, which refers to developmental supervision carried out by a supervisor specifically prepared in counseling, which is intended to improve the counselor's skills.

Roberts and Borders (1994) used this three-category model of supervision as the basis for a survey which they conducted with school counselors in North Carolina. One hundred and 68 counselors (a 37 percent return rate) responded to their survey concerning their postdegree supervisory experiences. Eighty-five percent of the respondents replied that they did experience some administrative monitoring by the principal. Monitoring activities ranged from monthly meetings to yearly personnel reviews. Seventy percent reported receiving some program supervision, typically delivered by the principal or by the director of the counseling program within the school district. Supervisory activities in this category also ranged from once a month to once a year. Only 37 percent of the counselors responded that they received any clinical supervision, despite the fact that the vast majority of their time at work was spent in counseling activities. As Roberts and Borders wrote: "most supervision consists of a mandated discussion between a school counselor and a school principal (or director of counseling) during an annual review conference" (p. 155). The study also revealed that the majority of counselors wanted additional program and clinical supervision. They desired at least a monthly clinical supervision process with a supervisor who had a counseling background. Unfortunately, supervisors who fit this description were not in abundance.

These findings are quite similar to the findings from earlier studies by Usher and Borders (1992) with a national sample. Survey results in this earlier study, from a stratified random sample of 106 school counselors (a 51 percent return rate), indicated that the school counselors desired a task-oriented style of supervision and wanted to focus the supervisory process on developing specific skills and techniques.

Sutton and Page (1994) conducted a survey concerning the supervision of school counselors in Maine. These researchers surveyed 533 school counselors and received responses from 493, an amazing response rate of 92 percent. The researchers defined clinical supervision as "an intensive, interpersonal, focused relationship, usually one to one or small group in which the supervisor assists the counselor as he or she learns to apply a wider variety of assessment and counseling methods to increasingly complex counseling cases" (p. 34). They also limited the definition of *clinical supervisor* to a trained professional (counselor, social worker, mental health professional, or psychologist) who has at least five years of experience in the field. Using these definitions, 20 percent of the respondents said that they were receiving clinical supervision. Thirty seven percent responded that they saw no need for clinical supervision while 48 percent responded that they perceived a need for clinical supervision. Respondents viewed the most important goals for clinical supervision as: taking appropriate actions with clients, developing counseling skills and techniques, and formulating treatment plans.

Counselors appear to want clinical supervision; however, the establishment of a productive process of clinical supervision for counselors is not always easy. One study which also used Barret and Schmidt's three-category model attempted to move the process of school counselor supervision away from administrative monitoring by the principal toward clinical supervision by the director of counseling (Henderson & Lampe, 1992). These researchers used Goldhammer's five stages of clinical supervision to implement a clinical supervision model which used observational data from live observations and videotapes to improve counselor performance. The researchers encountered two major difficulties in attempting to implement the model. First, the counselors, prior to the move toward clinical supervision, had received very little substantive feedback from the principal during administrative monitoring. When the director of counseling attempted to provide substantive feedback, some counselors became quite resentful. Second, some of the directors of counseling lacked supervisory skills; no doubt this explains some of the counselor resistance described above. This lack of supervisory preparation results from the fact that most of the directors are master's-level counselors who received little or no supervision as practitioners. Most counselor preparation programs reserve training and coursework in supervision for doctoral students.

What should we conclude from the literature on counselor supervision? First, it appears that counselor supervision is a rare phenomenon. In most cases, counselors receive administrative monitoring or evaluation. Second, it appears that school counselors desire more clinical supervision. Third, it is difficult to implement productive clinical supervision of school counselors—even when counselors desire supervision—because many directors of school counseling programs have little training in supervision and school principals have little background in counseling. We can finally conclude that the one activity which does occur less frequently than supervision of school counselors is research concerning the supervision of school counselors.

Future Needs

There are several pressing needs for research on the supervision of school counselors. First, there is a need for commonly understood definitions of counselor supervision, as distinct from counselor evaluation. Borders (1991b) has provided definitions which should prove very useful. She defines counselor supervision as a set of ongoing activities that enhance professional development of counselors using teaching, counseling, and consulting skills to work toward mutually agreed upon goals. She defines counselor evaluation as judging and determining the worth or value of the counselor's performance. Additional guidance concerning this distinction could be provided by the literature on instructional supervision (see Pajak, 1993).

A second useful step would be to develop some comprehensive conceptualization of the multidimensional role of the school counselor, which could be used as the basis for thinking about the appropriate targets for supervisory interventions. Schmidt (1990) has provided a conceptualization which divides the school counselor's work into six major areas:

1. program planning, including time management, program development and management, and general organization;
2. counseling, including individual and group techniques and processes as well as diagnostic and follow-up processes;
3. consulting, including advising students, teachers, and parents;
4. coordinating, including management of referral processes, communication with others, and student advocacy;
5. student appraisal, including both standardized and nonstandardized testing and assessment; and
6. professional practices and development, including continuing education and ethical issues such as confidentiality.

Schmidt also offers a variety of ways in which data concerning counselor performance can be collected. He suggests using:

1. live observation of classroom teaching and other large group presentations;
2. video- and audiotapes of counseling sessions;
3. interviews with counselors concerning particular cases;
4. simulations;
5. collection of artifacts, such as case reports, referrals, handbooks, and policy manuals;
6. collection of time schedules;
7. case records; and
8. surveys to gather feedback from teachers, parents, and students.

The combination of these data collection strategies and the conceptualization of the counselor's role would provide the basis for developing a comprehensive plan for counselor supervision and evaluation.

The literature on counseling supervision places a great deal of emphasis on group supervision of counselors; however, the literature on the supervision of school counselors has little to say about group supervision. One exception is a doctoral dissertation by Bigley (1985), which suggested that group supervision resulted in increased empathy, respect, and genuineness for an experimental group of school counselors, as opposed to a control group that did not receive group supervision.

All of those who are engaged in the process of school counseling, school counselor supervision, and school counselor education must invest energy in establishing a base of research and knowledge that can be used to enhance the quality of school counselor supervision as well as school counseling services. At this point in time, given the scarcity of research in the field, almost any study would make a contribution, but there are particular questions which need to be pursued as an agenda for research on the supervision of school counselors.

Directions for Future Research

Research on the supervision of school counselors is clearly needed. The lack of research in this subspecialty area is quite astounding when one considers the considerable attention which the supervision of counselors has received in the general counseling literature. A variety of research designs, including qualitative studies, case studies, survey and interview studies, correlational studies, and experimental designs, need to address questions in at least four different areas: supervisory personnel, supervisor preparation, supervision models and methods, and supervision outcomes.

Personnel The literature in school counseling supervision indicates that principals are responsible for much of the supervision and also asserts that trained counselors should be delivering clinical supervision rather than principals. Although this assertion makes intuitive sense, there is no real empirical evidence on the effectiveness of counselor supervision provided by principals as opposed to counselor supervision provided by trained counselors. Henderson and Lampe (1992) found that the directors of counseling with whom they worked had difficulty providing effective supervision due to a lack of preparation in supervision. This study leads the reader to question whether the outcomes of supervision might have been better with a principal who was, despite a lack of counseling expertise, a skilled supervisor. A similar question has been raised in the literature on teacher supervision; should principals supervise teachers in instructional areas where the principal does not have content expertise. It would clearly be preferable to have supervisors of school counselors who possess expertise in both counseling and supervision. Until such experts are present in school systems, it would be beneficial to have empirical studies which examine the necessity for content expertise on the part of the supervisor. There is also a need for studies that examine questions concerning the types of preparation programs that can be developed to equip master's-level counselors with supervisory skills, as well as that types of programs that can be developed to help principals acquire essential knowledge about counseling. We also need studies which examine the plausibility and effectiveness of using peer counselor supervision. Peer coaching and peer consultation seem to be very useful strategies for improving instruction (see the Chapter by Goldsberry in this volume). Could these strategies also be effective for improving counseling? We need studies which examine this question.

Preparation One explanation for the difficulty in finding qualified supervisors for school counseling, as noted earlier, is the fact that most school counselors have master's-level training, while supervisory preparation is typically limited to doctoral students. While it may not be possible to provide master's-level students with all of the useful supervisory preparation, it would still be possible to provide some training in supervision. The question seems to be: What training and in what knowledge, skills, and attitudes? This raises an excellent question for research. What knowledge, skills, and disposition are critical for the supervisor to produce positive outcomes in the supervision of school counselors? The 11 standards for counseling supervisors developed by the American Association for Counseling and Development (now the American Counseling Association) could be used as the basis for designing reputational studies of supervisors of school counselors who have been recognized as outstanding by their knowledgeable peers. Case study, survey, and interview designs focusing on these exemplary practitioners should be helpful in sorting out which of the 11 AACD (now ACA) competencies are most critical for supervision of school counselors. These critical elements could then be incorporated into preparation programs at the master's level.

An additional question is: What preparation is necessary for counselors to benefit from counselor supervision? Little attention is paid to the knowledge, skills, and attitudes of the supervisee. Supervision is clearly a two-way street. Is the supervisor the only one who requires preparation, or are the outcomes of school counselor supervision enhanced when both partners have preparation in supervision? This is an important question which might contribute helpful information to those individuals who are engaged in the preservice preparation of school counselors.

Models and Methods of Supervision The current literature does not help enlighten us about the models of supervision and the supervisory methods which are employed in the supervision of school counselors. Among the research questions which need to be investigated are the following:

1. What models of counselor supervision are currently being used in the supervision of school counselors?
2. How should models of supervision for counselors in general be adapted to meet the specific needs of school counselors?
3. What is the proper balance among the three types of supervision advocated by Barret and Schmidt (1986): administrative monitoring, program supervision, and clinical supervision?
4. Are there schools and or school districts that currently employ models of school counselor supervision that could be used as exemplars for other schools and school districts?
5. Which of the various counselor supervision methods have been used and advocated in the general literature on counseling (live observation, audio- and videotapes, self-report, skill acquisition, and group supervision), and which methods are currently being used with school counselors?
6. What are the advantages and disadvantages of each of these methods of general counselor supervision when they are applied to the supervision of school counselors?

7. Are there certain methods of general counselor supervision that are more effective (effectiveness would need to be defined operationally) for school counselor supervision?
8. Are there other methods of supervision which might be useful for and effective for school counselor supervision?

Outcomes Border's (1989) question concerning general counselor supervision—"What supervision interventions by which supervisors will lead to what outcomes for which supervisees?" (p. 16)—is also very appropriate for research on the supervision of school counselors. Very little has been written concerning the expected outcomes for supervision of school counselors, and even less has been written concerning the resulting outcomes. Many research questions can be pursued in this area, including:

1. What are the intended outcomes for supervisors, counselors, and clients of the counselor supervision programs that are currently in place in schools?
2. Are these intended outcomes actually realized through the process of counselor supervision, and, if so, under what conditions?
3. Which supervisory models and methods lead to which supervisory outcomes for supervisors, counselors, and clients?
4. What unintended outcomes for supervisors, counselors, and clients result from the process of school counselor supervision?
5. What role does gender play in producing the intended and unintended outcomes that result from school counselor supervision?
6. What role does culture play in producing the intended and unintended outcomes that result from school counselor supervision?

Although there are additional research questions which need to be addressed, focusing on research studies in these four key areas (personnel, preparation, models, and outcomes) would be a major step towards establishing a solid knowledge base concerning high-quality supervision of school counselors.

SUPERVISION OF SCHOOL PSYCHOLOGISTS

Research to Date

Supervision of school psychologists has been mandated by the National Association of School Psychologists (NASP) since 1977 (Knoff, 1986). According to Knoff, the NASP guidelines call for supervision of one hour per week during practica and internships for preservice school psychologists. They also require one hour per week of supervision for credentialed school psychologists during the first three years of professional practice. Knoff reported that the American Psychological Association (APA) also requires that nondoctoral, credentialed school psychologists receive one hour per week of supervision by a doctoral-level school psychologist.

Very little, unfortunately, is known about the supervision that school psychologists actually receive (Zins, Murphy, &

Wess, 1989). These researchers surveyed a national random sample of 490 school psychologists drawn from a NASP membership list. Eighty two percent of those contacted responded to the questionnaire, which asked whether they were currently receiving clinical supervision. Clinical supervision was defined as direct one-to-one efforts to help the school psychologist improve his or her professional skills. The researchers made a clear effort to separate clinical supervision from administrative monitoring or evaluation. Twenty three percent of the respondents reported that they received individual or group clinical supervision by a trained psychologist. Thirty to 40 percent of those receiving clinical supervision, however, reported that they received it less than once a week. The most commonly reported supervision method was a weekly meeting to review psychoeducational reports and case reviews and to receive feedback from the supervisor concerning these reports and case reviews. The majority of those receiving such supervision reported some modest benefit from it. Almost half of those who responded to the survey said that no supervision by a trained school psychologist was available to them.

Other than the two studies noted above, there is really no literature to speak of concerning research on the supervision of school psychologists. As Knoff (1986) put it, "our research is virtually non-existent in the supervision area" (p. 545).

Future Research

Knoff (1986) identified five major research thrusts that were needed in the area of supervision of school psychologists:

1. the development of empirically determined models of qualitative professional development and supervision specific to school psychology;
2. the identification, examination, and validation of supervisory issues, behaviors, and characteristics and their relationship to supervisory effectiveness;
3. the development of training standards for supervisor knowledge, skills, and dispositions;
4. the development of valid, reliable systems for evaluating supervisory service delivery; and
5. the development of studies which relate supervision causally to effective services.

Despite the fact that more than 10 years have passed since Knoff laid out this research agenda, it still seems very appropriate for guiding research in this field.

In addition to Knoff's useful general conceptualization, some of the specific questions which were posed above to form a research agenda in the supervision of school counselors would be excellent questions for inquiry in the supervision of school psychologists. There are questions concerning the personnel involved in supervision and their preparation, such as:

1. Can nonlicensed professionals who are trained as supervisors provide effective supervision for school psychologists?
2. What preparation is essential for equipping school psychologists with the knowledge, skills, and dispositions that are needed to be an effective supervisor of school psychologists?

3. What role, if any, can peer coaching and peer consultation play in the supervision of school psychologists?
4. What preparation do peer coaches and counselors require?

There are also questions concerning models and methods of supervision such as:

1. Are there exemplary programs for the supervision of school psychologists which are currently being used in schools and school districts which can serve as a models for others?
2. What general models of counselor supervision are currently being employed in the supervision of school psychologists?
3. What are the advantages and disadvantages of these general models of counselor supervision when they are applied to the supervision of school psychologists?
4. Are there effective models of supervision which are unique to the supervision of school psychologists?
5. Which methods of counselor supervision that have been used and advocated in the general literature on counseling (live observation, audio and video tapes, self-report, skill acquisition, and group supervision) are currently being used with school psychologists?
6. What are the advantages and disadvantages of each of these methods of general counselor supervision when they are applied to the supervision of school psychologists?
7. Are there methods of general counselor supervision that are more effective for the supervision of school psychologists?
8. Are there other methods of supervision which might be useful and effective for the supervision of school psychologists?

There are also questions concerning the outcomes of the supervision of school psychologists:

1. What are the intended outcomes for supervisors, psychologists, and clients of the psychologist supervision programs of that are currently in place in schools?
2. Are these intended outcomes actually realized through the process of psychologist supervision, and, if so, under what conditions?
3. Which supervisory models and methods lead to which supervisory outcomes for supervisors, psychologists, and clients?

4. What unintended outcomes for supervisors, psychologists, and clients result from the process of school psychologist supervision?
5. What role does gender play in producing the intended and unintended outcomes that result from school psychologist supervision?
6. What role does culture play in producing the intended and unintended outcomes that result from school psychologist supervision?

SUMMARY

A very rich literature base has developed during the last fifteen years concerning the supervision of counseling in general. The theoretical work in this domain has been excellent, resulting in well conceptualized models and methods of supervision and well thought out guidelines concerning the competencies which counselor supervisors should possess. There is also rich theoretical literature concerning the potential impact of structural variables such as gender and culture on the counselor supervision process.

The empirical literature in the field of counselor supervision still lags far behind the theoretical literature. Much of the empirical work that has been done has relied on self-report measures, survey designs, and cross-sectional research. There is a need to expand the types of research strategies that have been employed as well as a need to focus future activity on outcome-oriented research and research designs that link outcomes to antecedent and process variables.

Much of the empirical research that has been done has focused on preservice counselors, especially on the supervision of preservice practica experiences. There has been extremely limited research on the supervision of credentialed, practicing counselors. The field of counselor supervision, nevertheless, has a great deal to offer to scholars who are interested in pursuing research in the supervision of school counselors and psychologists. These two areas have been sorely neglected to date. This chapter hopefully provides generative ideas that will give rise to focused and sustained inquiry. This inquiry will be useful in the improvement of school counseling and psychological services and will ultimately prove beneficial to students.

REFERENCES

American Association for Counseling and Development. (1990). Standards for counseling supervision. *Journal of counseling and development, 69,* 30–32.

Akamatsu, T. (1980). The use of role play and simulation techniques in the training of psychotherapists. In A. K. Hess (Ed.). *Psychotherapy supervision: Theory, research, and practice* (pp. 209–225). New York: John Wiley.

Barret, R. J. & Schmidt, J. J. (1986). School counselor certification and supervision: Overlooked professional issues. *Counselor Education and Supervision, 26,* 50–55.

Behling, J., Curtis, C., & Foster, S. A. (1988). Impact of sex-role combination on student performance in field instruction. *The Clinical Supervisor 6,* 161–168.

Bernard, J. M. (1992). The challenge of psychotherapy-based supervision: Making the pieces fit. *Counselor Education and Supervision, 31,* 232–237.

Bernard, J. M. (1994). Multicultural supervision: A reaction to Leong and Wagner, Cook, Priest, and Fukuyama. *Counselor Education and Supervision, 34,* 159–171.

Bernard, J. M. & Goodyear, R. K. (1992). *Fundamentals of clinical supervision.* Boston, MA: Allyn and Bacon.

Bigley, M. (1985). Peer group supervision with school counselors: An examination of two models. Unpublished doctoral dissertation, Temple University, Philadelphia, PA.

Borders, L. D. (1989). A pragmatic agenda for developmental supervision research. *Counselor Education and Supervision, 29,* 16–25.

Borders, L. D. (1991a) A systematic approach to peer group supervision. *Journal of Counseling and Development, 69,* 248–251.

Borders, L. D. (1991b) Supervision doesn't equal evaluation. *The School Counselor, 38,* 253–255.

Borders, L. D. & Leddick, G. R. (1987). *Handbook of counseling supervision.* Alexandria, VA: ASCD.

Boyd, J. D. & Walter, P. B. (1975). The school counselor, the cactus, and the supervisor. *The School Counselor, 23,* 103–107.

Cook, D. A. & Helms, J. E. (1988). Visible racial/ethnic group supervisee's satisfaction with cross cultural supervision as predicted by relationship characteristics. *Journal of Counseling Psychology, 35,* 268–274.

Dye, H. A. & Borders. L. D. (1990). Counseling supervision: Standards for preparation and practice. *Journal of Counseling and Development, 69,* 27–29.

Ellis, M. V. (1991). Research in clinical supervision: Revitalizing a scientific agenda. *Counselor Education and Supervision, 30,* 238–249.

Forsyth, D. R. & Ivey, A. E. (1980). Micro-training: An approach to differential supervision. In *Psychotherapy supervision: Theory, research, and practice* (pp. 242–261). New York: John Wiley.

Freeman, S. C. (1992). C. H. Patterson: On client centered supervision: An interview. *Counselor Education and Supervision, 31,* 219–226.

Galassi, J. P. & Trent, P. J. (1987). A conceptual framework for evaluating supervisor effectiveness. *Counselor Education and Supervision, 27,* 261–269.

Goldhammer, R. (1969). *Clinical supervision: Special methods for the supervision of teachers.* New York: Holt, Rinehart, & Winston.

Hart, G. M. (1982). *The process of clinical supervision.* Baltimore, MD: University Park Press.

Henderson, P. & Lampe, R. E. (1992). Clinical supervision of school counselors. *The School Counselor, 39,* 151–157.

Holloway, E. L. (1987). Developmental models of supervision: Is it developmental? *Professional psychology: Practice and research, 18,* 209–216.

Holloway, E. L. & Johnston, R. (1985). Group supervision: Widely practiced but poorly understood. *Counselor Education and Supervision, 25,* 335–345.

Holohan, W. & Galassi, J. P. (1986). Toward accountability in supervision: A single case illustration. *Counselor Education and Supervision, 26,* 166–174.

Joyce, B. & Showers, B. (1995) *Improving student achievement through staff development* (2nd ed.). New York: Longman.

Kagan. D. M. (1988). Research on the supervision of counselors and teachers in training: Linking two bodies of literature. *Review of Educational Research, 58,* 1–24.

Knoff, H. M. (1986). Supervision in school psychology: The forgotten or future path to effective services. *School Psychology Review, 15,* 529–545.

Leong, F. T. & Wagner, N. S. (1994). Cross-cultural counseling supervision: What do we know? What do we need to know? *Counselor Education and Supervision, 34,* 117–131.

Loganbill, C., Hardy, E., & Delworth, V. (1982). Supervision: A conceptual model. *The Counseling Psychologist, 10,* 3–42.

Nelson, M. L. & Holloway, E. L. (1990). Relation of gender to power and involvement in supervision. *Journal of Counseling Psychology, 37,* 473–481.

Pajak, E. (1993). *Approaches to clinical supervision: Alternatives for improving instruction.* Norwood, MA: Christopher Gordon Publishers.

Pedersen, P. C. (1987). Ten frequent assumptions of cultural bias in counseling. *Journal of Multicultural Counseling and Develop-ment, 9,* 16–24.

Priest, R. (1994). Minority supervisor and majority supervisee: Another perspective of clinical reality. *Counselor Education and Supervision, 34,* 152–158.

Roberts, E. B. & Borders. L. D. (1994). Supervision of school counselors: Administrative, program and counseling. *The School Counselor, 38,* 86–93.

Ryan, A. S. & Hendricks, C. O. (1989). Culture and communication: Supervising the Asian and Hispanic social worker. *The Clinical Supervisor, 7,* 27–40.

Schmidt, J. J. (1990). Critical issues for school counselor performance appraisal and supervision. *The School Counselor, 38,* 86–93.

Stoltenberg, C. D. (1981). Approaching supervision from a developmental perspective: The counselor complexity model. *Journal of Counseling Psychology, 28,* 59–65.

Stoltenberg, C. D. & Delworth, V. (1987). *Supervising counselors and therapists: A developmental approach.* San Francisco, CA: Jossey Bass.

Sutton, J. M. Jr. & Page, B. J. (1994). Post-degree clinical supervision of school counselors. *The School Counselor, 42,* 32–39.

Thyer, B. A., Sowers-Hoag, K., & Love, J. P. (1988). The influence of field instructor-student gender combination on student perception of field instructor quality. *The Clinical Supervisor, 63,* 169–179.

Usher, C. H. & Borders, L. D. (1992). Practicing counselors' preferences for supervisory style and supervisory emphasis. *Counselor Education and Supervision, 33,* 66–79.

Vander Kolk, C. (1974). The relationship of personality, values, and race to anticipation of the supervisory relationship. *Rehabilitation Counseling Bulletin, 18,* 41–46.

Wiley, M. & Ray, P. (1986). Counseling supervision by developmental level. *Journal of Counseling Psychology, 33,* 439–445.

Worthington, E. L. (1984). An empirical investigation of supervision of counselors as they gain experience. *Journal of Counseling Psychology, 31,* 63–75.

Worthington, E. L. (1987). Changes in supervision as counselors and supervisors gain experience: A review. *Professional psychology: Research and practice, 18,* 189–208.

Worthington, E. L. & Stern, A. (1985). Effects of supervisor and supervisee degree level and gender on the supervisory relationship. *Journal of Counseling Psychology, 32,* 252–262.

Zins, J. E., Murphy, J. J., & Wess, B. P. (1989). Supervision in school psychology: Current practices and congruence with professional standards. *School Psychology Review, 18,* 56–63.

·22·

SUPERVISION IN NONTEACHING PROFESSIONS

Richard D. Hawthorne and Nancy E. Hoffman

This chapter presents a review of research on supervision of clinical practice in several nonteaching professions: social work, counseling specialities, medicine, and nursing. Research on supervision in the professional fields of engineering, architecture, and accountancy were also considered but are not pursued. Following unsuccessful attempts to locate published research reports in these areas, we sought advice from several colleagues in the respective fields. We find that there appear to be no reported studies of supervision in those areas because there is no supervision in a developmental, educational, or evaluative sense. The dominant perspective is that once licensure is obtained, there is no further need for "supervision." There has been no focus of inquiry into how new professionals are socialized into those professions following formal preparation and internship experiences.

The reviews of the research literature related to supervisory practices and impact in social work, counseling, medicine, and nursing were guided by the following questions:

1. What is meant by "the supervision of clinical practice" in each of the professional practice fields, and how and why did it emerge and evolve?
2. What theoretical perspectives and language are used to interpret and render meaningful the research questions posed, to select the forms of inquiry engaged, and to guide the critical analyses and discussions of findings?
3. What are the dominant tools of inquiry and forms of analysis used in the research conducted in each of these fields of practice?
4. What are the major findings and insights gleaned about supervisory policies and practices in these four nonteaching professions?
5. What implications for the study of instructional supervision can be derived from the theoretical perspectives, the questions asked, the modes of inquiry engaged, and the key understandings and insights evolving from the research efforts focusing on supervision in nonteaching professions?

We limited most of our review to studies reported in the literature during the past twenty years. If a piece of work or a theoretical framework was reported at an earlier time and cited by researchers in their rationales, it is reported here, too. We have examined several synoptic texts on supervision in the professions, as well as pertinent journals, ERIC, and other abstract services. We intended to restrict the review to research on supervision of practicing professionals, not to attend to the research on the supervision of students in practica or internships. This proved to be far too restrictive in several of these professions, for reasons that will become evident. The vast majority of research on supervision in these professions has indeed been in relation to the clinical practice development of novices seeking initial licensure or certification.

SUPERVISION OF CLINICAL SOCIAL WORK

The Context and History of Research on Supervision in Clinical Social Work

Social work started with volunteers providing assistance to families in need, due to such circumstances as the lack of support by an alcoholic parent, death of a spouse or divorce and related lack of work skills or places of employment for women, and various financial and health-related problems affecting a parent and, thus, a family. Supervision of social workers and their activities initially entailed recruiting volunteers, providing minimal training of people to serve as "friendly visitors" to the homes of the destitute, organizing the activities and deployment of the volunteers, and supporting and retaining the volunteers—who more often than not were overwhelmed by the poverty and the subhuman living conditions they so frequently encountered. With the development of the social and behavioral sciences, as well as the development of a shared wisdom born of experience, a field of study and professional practice emerged. Social work became less a matter of charity and volunteerism and more a professional practice (Kadushin, 1992a; Munson, 1983).

Some of the professionalized work focused on individual cases and involved therapeutic and training interventions. Another dimension involved group therapy and training, and a third was defined by community and organizational assistance, ranging from legal and financial information to assertiveness and empowering training. As the needs became more diverse, the social and psychological problems of individuals and families became more complex; the number of people in need became increasingly large; and the responsibilities of governmental, hospital, and social service agencies became more defined and demanding. With the decline of other psychiatric workers over a 30-year period, social workers emerged as the largest single group delivering psychotherapeutic services to individuals with relatively mild psychological problems, such as communication, stress, neuroses, and other nonpsychotic conditions (Munson, 1983).

Tension increased between the professional autonomy and authority of the social worker, whose historical roots were grounded in casework, and the bureaucratized organizations, which were defined by control through regulations and procedures. Charged with the responsibility of providing efficient therapeutic and problem-solving services to families and children, while staying within the ever-growing rules and regulations governing social services, the practice of social work supervision became more administrative than educational or supportive. The reaction against oppressive forms of interpersonal relations and the greater concern for social and political action that characterized the field in the late 1960s and early 1970s influenced the supervision of social workers (Kadushin, 1992a). That period was followed by another period that emphasized accountability and efficiency, traits which are evident in social work policies and practices today. As teachers search for professional empowerment, social workers are struggling to reassert their professional autonomy within the constraints of governmental and private for-profit agencies. We turn to the array of inquiry on supervision practices related to social workers and their professional conduct, with this brief contextual account in mind.

Harkness and Poertner (1989) made the case that supervisory practice and research on supervision of social work paralleled the contextual changes described above. They argue that the focus of supervision shifted from the case and client to the qualities of social workers and their training. Research on supervision in social work became circular, as a consequence, losing sight of the client. Harkness and Poertner have proposed a three-part research agenda to redirect concern back to the client. They proposed that inquiry about supervision attend to the analysis of supervisory behaviors that are connected to improved caseload outcomes. Only when supervisory practice is connected with improved client outcomes, they argue, will theory become substantive and useful (Harkness & Poertner, 1989). One could also argue that such inquiry requires a robust body of descriptive studies that identify context, intervening and outcome variables, and the relationships obtained between them, before explanatory theories can be formulated. Others will argue in contrast that looking for the causal relations of supervisory behaviors, con-

text, supervisee attributes, and client attributes will necessarily miss the ambiguous and uncertain connections between professional practices and client outcomes.

Barretta-Herman (1993) contends that the focus of theoretical development and research on the supervision of independent social work practitioners has been in relation to the neophyte, in-training, or newly trained social workers, not on measured improvements in the client. Supervision has served as the primary mechanism for professional development, the reduction of isolation for the independent worker, and providing support, given the emotional demands of the practice. Barretta-Herman believes the supervisor's role is "to reflect, critique, challenge, and support the practitioner in maintaining the highest level of competence possible through continual extension and refinement of his or her skills and knowledge" (p. 61). The unstated assumption is that when practitioners are given support and are engaged in reflection, their repertoire of understanding and actions is extended and refined, thus serving the client more fully and effectively.

The changing contextual dimensions of social work and supervision of social work have in turn influenced research on supervision of social work practices. In the following sections, we attempt to capture the conceptual, theoretical, and analytical aspects of research on supervision in social work that have evolved in the changing contexts over the past several decades.

Supervision in Clinical Social Work Defined

Supervision in clinical social work practice has evolved through several stages and today includes several dimensions. Munson (1979) offers the following pragmatic conception of supervision in the context of social workers' practice: "Supervision is viewed by most workers as the main channel of accountability, a means of protecting clients, and the chief source of professional development and support for the worker" (p. 240). Supervisory practices in clinical social work have been defined by Kadushin (1992a) in terms of three functions: (1) educational (learning how to practice social work with the assistance of an experienced social worker and to maintain an up-to-date understanding of policies and practices); (2) administrative, "the correct, effective, and appropriate implementation of agency policies and procedures . . . to assure adherence to policy and procedure"; and (3) the "expressive-supportive leadership function," which provides moral support, a sense of belonging, and a feeling of security and hope (Kadushin, 1992a, pp. 19–20). Munson (1983) offers another perspective by referring to such activity as the supervision of clinical social work: "an interactional process in which a supervisor has been assigned or designated to assist in and direct the practice of a supervisee in the areas of teaching, administration, and helping" (p. 3).

The contemporary conceptions of supervisory practice seem to coalesce around a developmental/educational element, an administrative element, and a helping/supportive element. The roots of these elements are readily recognizable in the history of social work practice itself. They also become apparent in the theoretical perspectives of research on supervisory practices and their impact on social work practices.

Theoretical Perspectives of the Research Inquiry about the clinical aspects of social work has been heavily influenced by psychotherapeutic, social psychological, and educational paradigms. Because social workers, and thus the supervisor social worker, are extensively engaged in psychotherapeutic counseling and have ongoing preparation related to marriage and family assistance, alcohol and drug therapy, HIV support counseling, and a host of similar areas, it is quite natural that the inquiry about supervisory relation would reflect similar perspectives. Educational perspectives are appropriate, because much of the relationship between supervisor and supervisee is viewed as training, information giving, and fostering personal-professional development. There is no evident theoretical perspective that might be recognized distinctly as supervision of social work research. The perspective taken in relation to conducting research about the supervisory dimension in many professions stems from the foundational disciplines or fields that frame the practices of that profession—thus, it makes sense that social psychology and counseling have a strong influence on the conceptualization of research interests in the supervision of social work.

The predominate research design used in the study of supervision of social work is descriptive in nature, with a few experimental studies and even fewer qualitatively oriented designs evident. Munson (1979) made an observation that still appears to be accurate: "Little experimental research on field instruction has been attempted; what research has been carried out is generally of the participant-observer variety and has been generalized to agency supervision, even though the demands and goals of field instruction and professional supervision are separate and distinct" (p. 240).

The lack of critically oriented (feminist, emancipatory, political, social class) inquiry is surprising given the history and nature of social work itself. There are only hints at raising questions about the ideological meanings or emancipatory/ oppressive impacts of supervisory practices.

The areas of social work supervision that have been of interest to researchers (who have been primarily doctoral students) include: supervisory roles and functions, characteristics of supervisors, supervisor and social worker relations, stress, and the forms and effects of supervisory practices. A brief presentation of works reported and representative of these areas follows.

Supervisory Roles and Functions Supervision as identified earlier by Kadushin (1992a) was grounded in his analysis of several studies of supervisors' self-reports about their work. Descriptive studies by Kadushin (1992b), Melichercik (1984), Patti (1983), and Poertner and Rapp (1983) are representative of the inquiries conducted in this area. Each of the studies added specific examples but did not alter the basic practical definitions of the three functions. All, with the exception of the Melichercik study, used survey instruments.

Melichercik (1984) collected data via logs kept by 85 supervisors who worked in social welfare agencies. The subjects used a precoded log to record the percentage of time spent on four categories of activity. The findings were consistent with those obtained across the other studies: administrative tasks dominated the role of the supervisors.

Melichercik recommended that, because the educational and supportive functions of supervision have been displaced by administrative functions, the conceptualization of supervision ought to reflect the management functions more fully. Melichercik's claim is reflected in a study conducted by the Wisconsin Department of Health and Social Service in 1978 (well before Melichercik's analysis), which focused on identifying the tasks supervisors performed. While a good deal of variation was reported, over 60 percent of the tasks were administrative in nature (e.g., assigning, coordinating, and evaluating work; hiring, promoting, and terminating personnel; program and budget management; and handling complaints) (cited in Kadushin, 1992a, p. 23). Supervision in group work and in community organizations has less well-defined parameters or activities due, in Kadushin's judgment, to the amount of relative autonomy in an ill-defined role (1992).

One of the most extensive studies of supervisory practices was conducted by Kadushin (1974), who surveyed 750 supervisors and 750 supervisees. He found that two-thirds of each of the groups were female, and the supervisors were slightly older than the supervisees. Supervisors were "responsible" for an average of four to five workers. Individual conference is the principal context for supervision. The conferences average three to four times per month and last from one hour to one and a-half hours each. Fourteen percent reported that group supervision was the primary supervision context.

Kadushin asked the supervisors and supervisees to identify which form of power they felt was most salient to the supervisee, using the French and Raven construct of five different bases of social power (expert, positional, coercive, reward, and relational). The intent was to discover the particular source of power that supervisees accepted as the basis for "supervisors' authority." He found that supervisors overwhelmingly perceived (95.3 percent of responses) that the expert power base would be most salient to the supervisees. Of the supervisees, 65.5 percent also perceived expert power to be most salient while 21.1 percent perceived positional power to be the most salient.

Another section of the survey asked supervisors to review a list of supervisory functions and to rank them (1) in terms of those which occupied the most time and (2) in terms of greatest preference. The supervisees were asked to rank the functions from most important to least important. Both identified "teaching the casework aspects of the job"—the knowledge, skills and attitudes the supervisee needs for effective job performance—as most important and occupying most of the conference time (Kadushin, 1974).

A final section of the survey elicited supervisors' reactions to 39 supervisory behaviors. Behaviors identified as those desired of an ideal supervisor included: competence in social work practice and supervision, understanding and acceptance of the supervisee, openness to criticism, freedom to acknowledge shortcomings, and willingness to grant the supervisee autonomy and encourage him or her to be independent (Kadushin, 1974).

Scott's (1965) study of supervisors working in a public welfare agency underscores how central the issue of professional autonomy has been for social workers and supervisors over the past several decades. He identified two types of professional functioning: *autonomous,* where the individual has several degrees of freedom to make decisions and act independently of the organization that functions as a base of operation, and *heteronomous,* where the professional is subordinate to the organization's administrative framework. He found that in the mid-1960s, most social workers functioned in a heteronomous model.

Munson (1980) administered a questionnaire to 64 supervisors and 65 supervisees across 19 agencies to examine the relationship between structure and authority. The two groups' perceptions of actual and preferred structure, authority, frequency, and initiation of conferences were incongruent. The structure of the supervisory relation, according to Munson, did not have impact on the outcomes of the supervision.

Characteristics of Supervisors

A related focus of inquiry is the demographic characteristics of social work supervisors and the social-psychological attributes of social workers. A 1986 analysis of the membership of the National Association of Social Workers showed that of the 125,000 members, 5,605 were identified as supervisors. The vast majority held a master are social work degree (MSWs), 68 percent were female, and over 60 percent were in their thirties and forties (cited in Kadushin, 1992a). These were similar to Munson's findings in his 1975 analysis of social work supervisors (Munson, 1983). Vinokur-Kaplan and Hartman's (1986) demographic analysis of child welfare supervisors found that approximately 15 percent were African Americans.

Kolb (1981) examined the cognitive frameworks and learning approaches of social workers and found that most used what he termed a "concrete-active" orientation. Kolb described the perspective most social workers bring to their daily practice: "The dominant philosophy is pragmatism and truth as defined by workability. Inquiry centers around the question of how actions shape events. The case study is the common method of inquiry and analysis" (p. 244). It would seem reasonable to extrapolate that if social workers approach sense making this way, and since supervisors are social workers, then supervisors are likely to be equally pragmatic and experientially grounded. Scott (1990) acknowledged the influence of experiential knowledge on social work practice and argued that practice wisdom or clinical judgment has been ignored in the study of how social workers (and supervisors) think and solve problems during the conduct of practice. Kolb (1981) suggested that cognitive schema and clinical supervision may be fruitful perspectives to use in the qualitative study of why social workers practice as they do. Attention to how professionals think, make decisions, and make judgments is emerging as a promising focus of inquiry for the role of supervision of professionals.

Race and Gender More recent studies examine issues related to the factors of race and gender. For example, Jayaratne et al (1992) conducted a study in which African-American social workers' perceptions of African-American and white supervisors were compared. The survey of 201 private and public agency social workers randomly selected from the membership of the National Association of Social Workers showed no significant differences in the responses related to the factors of emotional support, evaluation, and social undermining. African-American social workers did report more criticism from African-American supervisors than from white supervisors. In the public agency context, the African-American female supervisors were viewed as less supportive and most critical, while in the private agencies, white male supervisors were reported as holding those same characteristics.

Munson (1979) found that male social workers who were supervised by females reported they were quite satisfied; in fact, they reported higher satisfaction than males supervised by males. This is similar to Mathews's (1983) findings and Dailey's (1983) observation that male social workers' attitudes seem to be more androgynous than men in general and have little concern about receiving supervision from women. In contrast, several studies examined the reactions of supervisees to assertiveness, harassment, and helping behaviors (see Kadushin, 1992a).

Supervisor and Supervisee Relationship The supervisor-supervisee relationship has been the center of interest for several researchers. Goldstein, Heller, and Sechrest (1966) observed that the nature of the supervisor-supervisee relationship was a very powerful variable in determining the supervisee's openness and receptivity to the supervisor's efforts to educate toward change (Kadushin, 1992a). Through analyses of tape-recorded conferences, Nelson (1973, 1974) reported what she characterized as a high-frequency use of supportive statements by the supervisor. She felt such statements were essential in the reduction of tension between the supervisor and supervisee.

This domain of inquiry is reviewed in some depth by Kadushin (1992a), who employs psychotherapeutic constructs in discussing the transference of sibling or parent-child conflicts to the supervisor-supervisee relation. Others suggest transference of problems the supervisee was having with his or her client to the supervisor-supervisee relationship (Kadushin, 1992a, p. 240). Here again is evidence of the psychotherapeutic orientation of social work, which in turn becomes an interpretive framework of the supervisor and researcher of social work supervision.

The developmental model of supervision is another key framework in the conduct of supervision. Hogan (1964) set forth four stages of supervisee development and offered recommendations for supervisory practices deemed congruent with each of the stages. Fisher (1989) took on the formidable task of empirically examining Hogan's development hypothesis of supervision. "While the assumption that supervision should vary according to the trainee's developmental level appears to be axiomatic to the field, few empirical studies have challenged or confirmed this hypothesis" (p. 58) .

The Fisher study examined the foci of supervisory conferences in relation to the developmental levels of the participating marriage and family therapists. The conferences of six supervisors with 16 supervisees who had been identified as beginning or advanced therapists were audiotaped and interviews were conducted with the supervisees to identify the supervisory behaviors deemed most helpful. The communication styles and the type of supervisor-supervisee relation perceived to be most helpful were also identified. The tapes were analyzed using the Supervision Focus Coding System developed by Fisher to rate the foci. The options or categories in the coding system included: case observations, case conceptualizations, intervention strategies and goals, personal thoughts and feelings, request for information from others, feedback, supervision relationship, general therapy, comments, and other (Fisher, 1989). The results of the study showed no significant differences between beginning and advanced supervisees and the focus of the conference or the style of communication used. While the study is not robust enough to refute the Hogan developmental axiom, it raises interesting questions and provides useful tools for examining the extent to which supervisory behavior is differentiated across supervisees.

Live Supervision One of the basic supervisory approaches that has been studied in some depth is called live supervision. Live supervision involves using a one-way mirror or closed-circuit television and a telephone so that the supervisor is able to intervene if the supervisee is having difficulty, if the client is in potential harm, or if the supervisor wants to assist the supervisee by making suggestions during the session. While this approach is used a great deal in the supervision of family therapists, little was known about its effects or the thinking of the supervisors as they used it. Lewis and Rohrbaugh (1989) distributed a questionnaire to 278 marriage and family therapists in Virginia to obtain greater understanding of what the therapists viewed as important about the use of live supervisory practices. Almost one-third of the respondents indicated that they used live supervision. They also reported that the supervisors viewed the clarity, timing, and parsimony of the phoned-in suggestions as the most important factors of live supervision.

A different twist on the live supervision approach reflects newer technology, with the supervisee wearing a wireless receiver in the ear (bug-in-the-ear or BITE) that is capable of "picking up" the short-wave signal and messages from the supervisor. Gallant, Thayer, and Bailey (1991), using clinical judges in a prepost design, found that BITE-feedback can contribute to improving therapists' clinical behaviors. A more extensive review of BITE-related studies is presented in the counseling supervision section of this chapter.

Effects of Supervisory Strategies Several researchers have explored the effects of different approaches to supervision on the supervisee and the client. Harkness (1987) investigated the effects of asking mental health workers about successful client outcomes and compared the results with normal supervisory practices. The two treatments involved the supervisor asking or referring infrequently to client outcomes over an eight-week period during supervisory sessions with the worker. The other treatment involved frequent references by the supervisor to client outcomes. The findings showed increased client satisfaction under the client outcome-focused supervision.

In another study, Harkness and Hensley (1991) used an experimental design in which two forms of supervisory practice were used with two female and two male staff members over a 16-week period. One treatment used a mixed supervi-

sory function (administrative, training, and clinical consultation) approach, followed by the second treatment which focused on the client. The findings suggested that the type of supervision did make a difference in relation to client outcomes, with significantly greater satisfaction by the clients.

Spira (1986) examined the satisfaction of experienced MSW subjects with private and agency-based supervision provided by other social workers and psychologists. Ninety-five percent of the subjects indicated that they were well satisfied with private supervision while only 25 percent were well satisfied with agency supervision, 38 percent were dissatisfied, and nearly the same number indicated ambivalence. Spira reported that the subjects who received private supervision viewed increases in self-awareness, theoretical knowledge, and technique more than subjects who received agency supervision did. An apparent key difference in the two forms of supervision was that in private supervision, the supervisor modeled and talked through interventions with clients, where the agency supervisors didactically provided suggestions without experiential demonstrations or mentoring.

Stress and Burnout

The role of supervisors in relation to social workers' stress and burnout behaviors has also been a major focus of inquiry. Some (Ewalt, 1980; Patti, 1979; Woodcock, 1967) have investigated the stress related to the transition from social worker to supervisor while others (see Kadushin, 1992a, pp. 233–277) examined stress and burnout experienced by social workers, contributing factors, and forms of supervisory assistance that help social workers and administrators address those factors. It is quite clear that the problem of burnout in social work practice is a matter of central concern and that supervision is viewed as a source of support in helping social workers cope with the enormous stress that defines social work—regardless of its source and manifestations.

Summary of Research on Social Work Supervision

The topography of research on the supervision of social work practice shows a disjointed and ahistorical aggregate of studies. The most extensive studies are of a survey nature, with demographic characteristics and role functions as the focal points. A few studies have turned to the analysis of supervisor-supervisee conferences in order to obtain descriptions of the behaviors actually engaged in and the perceived and assessed effects they have. Clearly, the supportive function that Kadushin set forth as one of the three supervisory functions has received little examination by researchers, yet it is viewed as critical to maintaining balance in an intensely emotionally packed profession such as social work.

RESEARCH ON SUPERVISION IN COUNSELING PROFESSIONS

The research activity related to the supervision of counseling practices is broadly cast and represents a large volume of studies—also conducted primarily by doctoral students

(Bernard & Goodyear, 1992). The reviewers relied heavily on a recent synoptic text by Bernard and Goodyear (1992), which has a comprehensive chapter on research issues and methods for establishing the parameters of the pertinent research activity related to several counseling professions. *The Clinical Supervisor, Counselor Education and Supervision, The Journal of Counseling Psychology*, and the *Counseling Psychologist* were the primary referents for recent studies. This review includes research on supervision related to several specific counseling professions, such as school counseling, community counseling, counseling psychology, career counseling, and marriage and family counseling. There are historical and foundational as well as clinical roots that are shared by counseling and social work, thus providing a broad base of shareable research.

Supervision of Counseling Practice: An Operational Definition

Bernard and Goodyear (1992) define supervision as:

An intervention that is provided by a senior member of a profession to a junior member or members of that same profession. This relationship is evaluative, extends over time, and has the simultaneous purposes of enhancing the professional functioning of the junior member(s), monitoring the quality of professional services offered to the clients she, he, or they see(s), and serving as a gatekeeper for those who are to enter the particular profession (p. 4).

The supervisee in this definition is most frequently a trainee developing counseling or psychotherapy competence, though Bernard and Goodyear (1992) acknowledge "the increasing frequency of postgraduate supervision" (p. 4). The roots of counseling supervision are the same as those of social work, which began to assure that the client was receiving quality care. With the growth of caseloads, the public's demand for greater accountability, and the professionalization of social work in the 1930s, supervision shifted focus from the client to the social worker therapist (Harkness & Poertner, 1989). In spite of the shared heritage and clinical skills, supervision serves a socialization function in the specific professions where senior counseling psychologists, counselors, or school counselors mentor junior members of the same specialty areas. The evaluative aspect is a clear and pervasive role of supervision of the various counseling trainees. Whether or not evaluation would play such a clear role with experienced counselors is not clear.

The theoretical perspectives which ground supervision and the research on supervision of counseling have been strongly influenced by three ideological forces: psychotherapy, human development theories, and positivist empirical assumptions and research methods. The constructivist perspective of cognitive psychology has found expression in the study of supervision. Bernard and Goodyear (1992) make the observation: "Supervision models often have developed as extensions of therapy theories" (p. 224). They add that "it is natural for supervisors to use therapy as the lens through which they view supervision. The tendency to do so, however, likely will weaken as supervision research grows in both volume and sophistication" (p. 225).

The relatively recent impact of development theories on supervisory practices and research agendas on supervision stems from the works of several scholars with particular recognition given to the work of Stoltenberg (1981). The developmental perspective "describes a sequential learning process that all supervisees undergo in developing from novice to expert counselors" (Borders, 1989a, p. 16). Borders observes that "despite a predominant focus on developmental models in the recent supervision literature, there is still little empirical information about the actual conduct of effective supervision" (p. 16).

The desire for more focus on the effects of supervisory practices supported by appropriate and mature supervision research is reflective of the views set forth by Holloway and Hosford (1983) and echoed by Ellis (1991). Both have pointed out the limitations of the research on supervision in counseling and argue for the development of "a science of supervision." Holloway and Hosford (1983) stated:

Our theories need to predict what types of supervision techniques will result in what types of trainee outcomes for which type of trainee. When such a prescriptive model is developed and tested, we will have a science of supervision (p. 75).

Bernard and Goodyear (1992) build from the Holloway and Hosford (1983) three stages for creating a science of supervision:

(1) one of descriptive observation in which a phenomenon is observed in its natural environment; (2) one in which important, specific variables are identified and relationships between and among them are clarified; and (3) one in which a theory is developed, based on the empirically derived evidence about variables and their interrelationships (p. 225).

They then set out four basic approaches for doing descriptive inquiry, including qualitative research, case study research, interactional research, and "An Events Paradigm" (p. 228). Several studies using the interactional and case study approaches are reviewed later in this section. Bernard and Goodyear (1992) cite Kiesler (1966) as they argue against the assumption that all clients with a particular disorder constitute a homogeneous group and thus will respond in predictable and common ways to a particular intervention treatment (p. 228). It is inappropriate to assume that trainees constitute a common group for whom a particular teaching approach or supervisory intervention will be equally effective. They suggest that the aptitude-treatment interaction model (Cronbach & Snow, 1977) is the most appropriate perspective to take if substantive insights about practice are to be obtained. This is the model used by researchers investigating conceptual systems theory, such as Harvey, Hunt, and Schroeder (1961).

The history of research on supervision of counseling practice has been driven by the positivist perspective and has moved from a focus on "proving the effectiveness" of alternative models of counseling the counselor, to using rather broadly defined developmental features, to multifaceted descriptive analyses of supervisor-supervisee transactions and more refined studies of supervisee developmental stages, contextual variables, specific interventions, and supervisee learnings. The research perspective continues to be positivist in character and in search of models and their effects in specific conditions with supervisees with specific developmental traits. Borders (1989a) sets forth a proposed pragmatic research agenda which would set aside further research on "new and improved" descriptive models and would devote energy to

creating prescriptive instructional approaches. 'Technical manuals' would (a) specify target skills and supervision outcomes, (b) outline the steps of a particular supervision approach designed to promote those outcomes, and (c) provide methods for evaluating the premises of the models (p. 17).

A second prohibition that Borders (1989a) suggested was to stop using self-reports as dependent measures. Borders cited concerns about the lack of correspondence between reported perceptions and degrees of satisfaction with the observed behaviors and measured changes deemed major limitations by several critics of past supervision research; she suggested that self-reports be discontinued as valuable. She argues instead for in-depth analyses of actual supervisory contexts and transactions: "These designs allow researchers to directly measure the behaviors of supervisor, supervisees, and clients, and to explore the relationships of these behaviors." (p. 20) Borders also recommends a moratorium on research in academic settings, with a reciprocal shift to more research in field settings or more natural supervisor-supervisee interactional contexts.

Many of the concerns of Borders and others may have been heard. Many of the more recent studies have been case studies, content analyses of field-based conferences, and analyses of supervisors and supervisees' thought processes and problem-solving activities. It is to these and other studies that we now turn in order to obtain a sense of the research problems deemed worthy of pursuit and the findings and insights that those studies yielded. The general topics of the following sections are: (1) models of supervision and the developmental levels of supervisees, (2) forms of supervision, (3) supervisor-supervisee conference interactions, (4) supervisor-supervisee relationships, and (5) cognitive structures and problem-solving strategies.

Developmental Levels and Models of Supervision Studies have described and assessed several different developmental models of supervision. As indicated earlier, the premise of the developmental approach is that counselors in training each bring their own developmental level to the process of learning and are best served through the use of interventions that take into account the developmental stage of the supervisee. Stoltenberg's (1981) four-level developmental model has been the most prominent and the focus of many empirical studies. Kagan (1988) reviewed these studies and reported: "All of these studies employed *self-report questionnaires* completed either by supervisors and/or trainees at specific points in the counseling curriculum. . . . Longitudinal data were never obtained, nor were behaviors actually observed. Results from virtually all of these studies supported a developmental model" (p. 5). Almost all participants felt that there was move-

ment from one level of development—and thus perspective and understanding—to a more independent and complex level.

The Heppner and Roehlke (1984) studies represent the analysis of self-reported reactions and judgments obtained from supervisees across three training levels (beginning practicum, advanced practicum, and doctoral interns) in relation to (1) influence processes between supervisors and supervisees, (2) supervisees' perceptions of supervisor behaviors that were effective, and (3) supervisees' perceptions of events that occurred during the semester they felt were most important. The findings were congruent with a developmental perspective, showing differential behaviors, judgments, and events clustered according to the three training levels. McNeill, Stoltenberg, and Pierce (1985), Rabinowitz, Heppner, and Roehlke (1986), and Reising and Daniels (1983) used a similar design and report similar findings.

Forms of Supervision The clinical literature is rich with recommendations for the conduct of supervision, including forms of direct supervision of supervisees in clinical contexts. It is not surprising that there is a paucity of empirical research that describes, from an observational perspective, what the various forms of supervision look like in actual practice and what the effects appear to be when each is used in a systematic fashion.

Live supervision is one form of supervision used heavily in training programs and far less in the field for logistical reasons. Bernard and Goodyear (1992) distinguish between live observation and live supervision: "the former being a method of observing the supervisee but not interacting with supervisee during the session (except in cases of emergency) and the latter being a combination of observation and active supervision during the session" (p. 62). A few researchers have examined the use of live supervision in general and the use of specific techniques and their effects. Bubenzer, West, and Gold (1991) sent a questionnaire to 432 institutions to ascertain the respondents judgments about the importance of live supervision and the supervisory methods and frequency of sessions that they used. Of the 307 returns, 51 percent used live supervision. Of that group, 85.3 percent used live supervision weekly and 12.5 percent used it biweekly.

One technique that is used quite frequently in counselor practica training sessions is the phone-in procedure. In this procedure, the supervisor observes the trainee in a counseling session with a client using a one-way mirror. When the supervisor believes the supervisee or client needs assistance, or a strategy needs further extention or refinement, the supervisor uses a telephone to talk with the supervisee and give suggestions during the session, rather than taking notes and discussing options after the session. In their study of the phone-in procedure, West, Bubenzer, Cantrell, and Arnold (1992) surveyed supervisors of marriage and family therapy counselor trainees, who were instructed to read a supervision case and select the most appropriate phone-in response from five options. Those supervisors who gave the "correct" response had themselves received supervision via the phone-in procedure.

Studies on the bug-in-the-ear (BITE) technique—where the supervisee wears a wireless earplug and the supervisor has a microphone and is thus able to talk directly to the supervisee without being heard by the client or otherwise disturbing the relationship between the supervisee and the client—have been reviewed by Gallant and Thyer (1989). Experimental studies by McClure and Vriend (1976) and Tentoni and Robb (1977) found very positive effects. McClure and Vriend found extended or short cues to supervisees and other procedures to be most effective. Tentoni and Robb (1977) compared 10 client outcomes with counselors using BITE and ten using conventional postsession feedback techniques. The BITE group scored significantly higher on the Counselor Evaluative Rating Scale.

The use of videotapes, postsession conference reviews, and other forms of supervision were not found to be the topics of research.

Supervisor-Supervisee Conference Interactions The discourse used in supervisory conferences has been of interest to Holloway and her colleagues (Holloway, 1982; Holloway & Wampold, 1983; Holloway & Wolleat, 1981). For the most part, they described the typical frequencies and patterns of verbal behaviors using a modified Blumberg Interaction Analysis (BIA; 1980). Holloway and Wolleat (1981) used the BIA to examine the stability of supervisory behaviors between supervisors working with the same supervisees and the stability of a supervisor's behavior between sessions with the same supervisee. They reported significant differences between the frequencies and patterns of verbal behaviors of supervisors across supervisees and between sessions of the same supervisor and supervisee. Holloway (1982) identified predictable patterns of supervisory behaviors during samples of five supervisors' audiotapes of the third, sixth, and ninth sessions with their supervisees. The Blumberg coding system has been effectively used to examine actual supervisory verbal behaviors and identify patterns and relationships that had not been examined.

Supervisor-Supervisee Relationships A large number of studies have been conducted in which a variety of factors in the supervisor-supervisee relationship have been the focus. Some have addressed the gender, race, specialty, or level of experience of the supervisor and supervisee and the effects, if any, on the satisfaction of the supervisee. Usher and Borders (Borders & Usher, 1992; Usher & Borders, 1993) administered a two-part national survey to practicing counselors regarding their supervisory preferences. In their 1992 study, they found that school counselors preferred less frequent supervision than nonschool counselors did and the school counselors preferred a counselor rather than another helping professional to serve as their supervisor. They also found that 45 percent of the school counselors had received no post-degree supervision. The second stage of the study focused on counselors' preferences for supervisory style and found that the experienced counselors preferred the consultative style over the teaching or didactic style. They also preferred supervision that emphasized the conceptual, personalized, and process

skills over professional behaviors. This is consistent with more mature and independent professionals who want support and ideas that enhance their practice.

Supervisory experience does not result in significant differences between experienced and novice supervisors' preplanning, verbal behaviors, or other related supervisory functions (Marikis, Russell, & Dell, 1985; Stone, 1980; Worthington, 1984). Handley (1982) looked at the relation between supervisors' and supervisees' ratings of the supervisory relationship and their respective satisfaction with it. The Myers-Briggs Type Indicator (MBTI) was used to identify cognitive styles, and other rating scales were used to measure independent variables. The results showed relationships between some MBTI scales and perceptions of the interpersonal relationships. The possibility of a relationship between cognitive styles and the supervision process was raised, but it needs more investigation. These studies used self-reported data rather than observational data. Gender is generally not a significant factor in the supervisor-supervisee relationship (Worthington & Stern, 1985).

Cognitive Structures and Problem-Solving Strategies The final area of research on supervision of counseling practices is one set forward by Bernard and Goodyear (1992) and Borders (1991, 1992) as a most promising area for research on counseling supervision. Central to this line of inquiry is the belief that the supervisor in various ways influences the schemata counselors develop to make sense of and guide their counseling practices. Cognitive development models (see Harvey, Hunt, & Schroeder, 1961) set forth hierarchical levels of conceptual functioning from concrete to abstract forms. There is little research that examines in some sophistication the relationship between supervisors' conceptual frameworks and reflective or constructivist learning behaviors in conference settings and this relationship's effects on how supervisees think and act during the conference or in practice.

Summary of Research on Supervision in Counseling Professions

With full allegiance to the positivist history of psychologically grounded inquiry, the effort to develop a science of supervision in counseling is strong in its conviction and admittedly weak in its movement. Although the developmentally oriented models of supervision are examined in terms of their effects on counseling practices, little firm knowledge has been generated that in turn informs supervisory practice. Surveys of supervisors and supervisees are equally interesting but lack the types of evidence that give direction or add to the conduct of supervision.

The three most promising aspects of research on supervision appear to be the use of technology (e.g., BITE), the systematic analysis of actual supervisor-supervisee sessions (e.g., Blumberg analytic system), and the investigation of the cognitive and moral development of practitioners, with particular attention to the novice-expert evolution in making decisions, framing problems, and making judgments.

SUPERVISION OF CLINICAL MEDICINE

The Context of Research on Supervision in Clinical Medicine

While medicine is now an established profession with relatively standardized and controlled education for and admission to the profession, that has not always been the case. Although the first American medical school was established in 1765, there was no standard pattern of entry into medical practice in America. In the 1700s, most physicians entered practice after a brief and informal apprenticeship, although a few completed academic training and an extended apprenticeship. During the 1800s, the number of medical schools grew from four to 160, and many of these were proprietary schools of questionable quality. There were no common standards for medical school curricula, faculty, length of training, or entry into practice. It is estimated that as many as three fourths of those who entered medical schools prior to the Civil War entered practice without completing their medical education. By the early 1900s, the quality of medical education had become a public concern (Hughes, Thorne, DeBaggis, Gurin, & Williams, 1973).

In 1910, the Carnegie Foundation commissioned Abraham Flexner to study medical education in North America. Flexner's highly critical report, which emphasized the need for a strong academic base in science, followed by extended clinical experience in a teaching hospital, was the impetus for a dramatic upgrading and standardization of medical preparation. By 1920, the number of American medical schools had declined from 160 to 87 and standards for medical education based on Flexner's report meant greater control over recruitment, training, and medical practice (Hughes et al, 1973).

One result of the development of a lengthy and quite standard training for physicians has been strong internal control of the medical profession and entry into the profession. A number of professional organizations and licensing boards govern the medical profession, including federal and state licensing and accrediting agencies, the American Medical Association (AMA), and the Association of American Medical Colleges (AAMC). These organizations play a major role in setting the agenda for medical education and, thus, strongly affect the direction of the research literature on medical education and induction into the profession. The AMA has published *Future Directions for Medical Education* (1982) and the AAMC has issued a number of reports that establish new directions for medical education, including *Physicians for the Twenty-First Century* (1984) and *Clinical Education of Medical Students* (1986). These reports emphasize the need for medical education to promote professional expertise, clinical thinking, and problem solving skills. Although these reports establish new directions and goals for medical education and induction, Flexner's report and other writings continue to set the standard by which current innovations in medical education are measured (see, for example, Ebert, 1992).

Definition of Supervision in Clinical Medicine

Supervisory practice in medicine is influenced by the profession's extended and standardized period of induction into clinical practice, which typically begins with a series of clerkships during the third and fourth years of medical school, and progresses through internship and three or more years of residency. This gradual induction into clinical practice reflects the ongoing influence of Flexner's "learning by doing" approach to medical education (Ebert, 1992) and creates a learning environment oriented toward the development and assessment of clinical practice. The induction into clinical practice and the process of supervising this experience are referred to in the medical literature as *clinical teaching*. In medicine, the term *supervision* typically refers to the oversight of a patient's course of treatment. Clinical teaching may be defined as individual or small-group educational interactions which involve a patient, a teacher or preceptor who is typically an experienced physician or resident, and an inductee who may be at any stage of the induction process, including residency.

Physicians who have completed the extended induction and licensure process may choose to continue their education by seeking certification in a speciality. Whether they specialize or not, they are required to enhance their performance by choosing a certain number of continuing medical education (CME) credits. CME typically focuses on information transfer rather than interaction with another professional centering on the physician's own clinical practice (Mazzuca et al, 1990). The best comparison for CME in education would be the traditional in-service education model, in which groups of teachers are given information by experts. Although a number of articles have been written on the importance of lifelong learning, and CME standards have been set for continuing licensure, research on the effectiveness of CME has been inconclusive. Hayes, Davis, McKibbon, and Tugwell (1984) reviewed 248 studies of CME and concluded that CME had potential to "improve physician behaviors" (p. 61), but they also noted that CME was not held accountable for improved physician performance or improved patient care. In a review of the literature on CME, Lanzilotti, Finestone, Sobel, and Marks (1986) concluded that it was important to design CME programs which facilitate the development of self-directed learning and self-evaluation. Jennett and Pearson (1992) describe a number of innovative approaches to CME that depart from the traditional didactic approach: technological networks that encourage dialogue with peers, problem-based learning based on clinical problems or examination of patient health records, and individual learning contracts. These new approaches do not seem to be the norm at this point, but they indicate the directions where CME may move in coming years, directions which may be more effective in improving practice.

The profession also utilizes other approaches to quality control: formal peer review boards that adjudicate complaints about the practice of licensed physicians, quality assurance boards that consider the costs of medical care, and informal discussion of clinical problems through informal consultations among physicians and in-house morbidity conferences.

Research on patient outcomes has traditionally focused on the impact of particular treatments: only recently have researchers begun to examine the role of the individual physician in patient outcomes (Norcini & Shea, 1993). Although questions of professional competence or conduct have long been relegated to state licensure boards, some medical speciality areas have established recertification programs that include demanding evaluations of competence (Norcini & Shea, 1993). There seems to be no supervision, as we envision it in education, of the practice of experienced physicians and, therefore, no research on it. The medical profession concentrates its supervisory efforts on the extended induction into professional practice. The remainder of this review will therefore examine the existing research on supervision of the extended induction process.

Theoretical Perspectives of the Research

Inquiry about clinical teaching in medicine is strongly influenced by positivist and experimental research perspectives, with more interpretive approaches only beginning to appear in the literature (Dinham & Stritter, 1988). The research on clinical teaching typically uses a behavioral perspective and focuses on the role of context in clinical education, reactions of supervisees to particular strategies, accurate assessment of clinical competence, the characteristics and preparation of effective preceptors, or the relationship of scientific knowledge to practice.

Context

One of the changes in medical education that has affected clinical teaching is the increased use of nonacademic and ambulatory care settings as clinical sites. As inductees have been placed in sites away from the medical school and its full-time faculty, the use of part-time faculty as preceptors has increased enormously. An important strand of the research on clinical education has examined the impact of these changes by studying interactions with preceptors, reliability of part-time preceptors' evaluations of competence, types of inductee activity, and inductees' and preceptors' time allocations in various clinical education settings.

A number of studies have used questionnaires to compare inductees' perceptions of the learning environment in a variety of clinical settings (Biddle & Smith, 1984; Patel & Dauphinee, 1985). Other researchers have examined the variance in sites less holistically, often by having inductees record the time spent in specific clinical activities, interacting with preceptors, and waiting (Bornsztein & Julian, 1991; Bradford & Schonfield, 1986; Friedman, Stritter, & Talbert, 1978; Schamroth & Haines, 1992; Talbert, Stritter, & Riddle, 1981). Friedman, Stritter, and Talbert's findings were confirmed in 1981 when Talbert, Stritter, and Riddle again found that clerkships done in community and teaching hospitals were not systematically different. Differences existed by site, rather than by the academic hospital or community hospital categorization. The researchers concluded that community hospitals can be effective clerkship sites.

In 1991, Walter, Zweig, and Hosokawa used direct observation to examine both inductees' and preceptors' use of time in different clinical settings. They found that inductees spent about 44 percent of their time with patients, 21 percent interacting with preceptors, and 13 percent waiting without interaction. The second phase of this research moved beyond time allocation, analyzing verbal interactions to produce descriptions of the ways preceptors interacted with inductees. Eighty percent of the interaction between preceptors and inductees was spent in case presentations, questioning, and making recommendations for case management.

Other studies have examined preceptors' use of time in their clinical education role, an especially complex issue since the preceptor's role as a clinical educator is only part of his or her daily work. These studies include observation of preceptors' clinical education activities during rounds (Wilkerson, Lesky, & Medio, 1986), a comparison of the time preceptors spent on specific educational activities in inpatient and ambulatory settings (Taylor, Dunn, & Lipsky, 1991), and a comparison of inductee and preceptor perceptions of the time preceptors spent on various educational activities (Calkins, Arnold, Willoughby, & Hamburger, 1986). The findings of Wilkerson, Lesky, and Medio (1986) seem to be representative. They found that the strategies most likely to be used by residents serving as preceptors were lecturing or modeling at the bedside. Preceptors rarely referred to literature, gave feedback, asked thought-provoking questions, or demonstrated specific techniques. In short, preceptors rarely made effective use of the unique learning opportunities inherent in the clinical setting.

Strategies

A second strand of the clinical education research has focused on the impact of specific strategies on the performance of inductees. Many of these strategies are related to methods of communicating expectations, providing feedback, or fostering clinical reasoning. Since most preceptors have had little or no formal training in teaching or supervision, many of the strategies being studied are quite basic. Powers and Draeger (1992), for instance, examined the impact of direct instruction and supervised practice on inductees' confidence in their own performance of procedures traditionally learned through a "see one, do one, teach one" approach. They found that the majority of inductees were more confident after direct instruction and supervised practice.

Using questionnaires, a number of researchers have examined inductee and/or preceptor perceptions of feedback practices (Gil, Heins, & Jones, 1984; Harth, Bavanandan, Thomas, Lai, & Thong, 1992; Irby, 1986). Other researchers have examined the effect of particular feedback strategies on inductee performance. These strategies have included use of computer simulations (Lincoln et al, 1991), criterion referenced evaluation forms (DaRosa, Mazur, & Folse, 1984), videotaping and critiques (Scheidt et al, 1986), the use of real and simulated patients as the stimulus for performance (Simek-Downing, Quirk, & Letendre, 1986), and the use of specific learning objectives to guide inductees' practice (Locksmith, Mundy, & Passmore, 1992). The results of these studies do not establish any particular strategy as superior, but they do reinforce the value of feedback and interaction in improving inductee performance.

Since the development of clinical reasoning or reflective practice is a particular goal of clinical education, researchers have also studied the effect of various strategies on its development. Schwartz, Donnelly, Nash, and Young (1992) compared the relative effects of traditional Socratic questioning and problem based learning (PBL) in the clinical setting. They found that PBL was equivalent to traditional instruction in increasing students' factual knowledge and superior in improving clinical problem solving skills. Rogers, Swee, and Ullian's (1991) examination of the transfer of decision-making training to clinical practice revealed that 15 hours of decision-making training prior to a clerkship was not associated with higher ratings on clinical problem solving. Foster (1981) studied the effect of preceptor questioning patterns on clinical performance. Many of these studies utilized self-report questionnaires to document practice and its impact. In an unusual departure from the behavioral model which characterizes most research on clinical education, Simpson, Dalgaard, and O'Brien (1986) examined inductee and preceptor perceptions of the nature of knowledge. Studying students, residents, and instructors, they concluded that with increasing experience comes an increasing acceptance of the role of uncertainty in medicine. They recommend that preceptors emphasize the uncertainty of medical knowledge as they guide the development of novices' clinical reasoning.

Assessment of Competence

A third focus for research on clinical education is the accurate assessment of clinical competence. This has long been an issue in the profession, but recent additions to the standards for the profession emphasize interpersonal skills, reflection, and other important but less quantifiable aspects of performance, and have led to considerable research in this area. The addition of more and more varied clinical faculty and clinical education settings has also prompted this research.

Studies of the reliability of preceptor ratings of clinical competence are common. Davis, Inamadan, and Stone (1986) found that individual faculty ratings of students' medical knowledge and relations with coworkers were most reliable and ratings of interpersonal skills were least reliable. While some researchers have studied the reliability of preceptor performance ratings in particular settings (Littlefield et al, 1991), others have examined the impact of various ways of arriving at ratings, such as faculty forums (DaRosa et al, 1984), small group discussions (Rosenblum, Platt, Wetzel, & Rosenthal, 1992), and the use of printed evaluation forms (Dean & Johnson, 1977) or structured outlines (Elks & Sawyer, 1992) to increase the reliability of ratings of clinical competence.

Other researchers have explored the number of direct observations of the inductee's practice that are required for reliable evaluation of clinical practice. In a study of the number of observations of performance required for a preceptor to reliably assess clinical competence, Carline, Paauw, Thiede, and Ramsey (1992) found that, regardless of a preceptor's experience or setting, seven observations of performance were needed for a reliable rating of overall performance in a 12-week clerkship. As many as 27 observations were required to reliably rate particu-

lar interpersonal aspects of clinical performance. In another study of performance evaluations in a 12-week clerkship, O'Donohue and Wergin (1978) found that average ratings of clinical performance were more reliable than individual ratings.

Another area of growing emphasis is the use of peer and self assessments (Gordon, 1992; Wooliscroft, TenHaken, Smith, & Calhoun, 1993). Forsythe, McGaghie, & Friedman (1986) found that two factors seemed to relate to overall assessments of clinical competence, cognitive abilities, and interpersonal skills. Both supervisors and peers accurately assessed the cognitive abilities, but supervisors were more discriminating than peers in their assessments of interpersonal skills. In a 1992 review of the literature on self assessment, Gordon concluded that medical training does not do a good job of developing self-assessment skills and that research is needed on the development of these skills and their transfer to the workplace.

With the introduction of the standardized patients (lay people trained to exhibit certain syndromes), many studies have examined the use of nonphysicians in evaluating clinical performance and compared these ratings with traditional preceptor performance ratings (Colliver & Williams, 1993; Mumford, Schlesinger, Cuerdon, & Scully, 1987; Schnabl, Hassard, & Kopelow, 1991; Templeton, Kerr, Tripp, Smith, & Couch, 1988). In Colliver and Williams' 1993 review of research on the use of standardized patients, they reported that more than 50 studies have documented the validity and the reliability of standardized patients' evaluations of clinical performance.

Preceptors

The characteristics and preparation of effective preceptors is a fourth strand in the research on clinical education. A number of questionnaire studies that asked inductees or preceptors to describe best clinical teaching practice are evident in the literature (Anderson, Hess, Rody, & Smith, 1991; Bland, Schmitz, Stritter, Aluise, & Henry, 1988; Calkins, Arnold, Willoughby, & Hamburger, 1986; Gjerde & Coble, 1982; Irby, Ramsey, Gillmore, & Schaad, 1991; Jolly & Macdonald, 1987; MacDonald & Bass, 1983; Miller, 1982; Shellenberger & Mahan, 1982; Skeff, Campbell, & Stratos, 1985; Wolverton & Bosworth, 1985). These studies support the notion that preceptors who are personally accessible, interact more, focus more clearly, and use questions to promote higher level thinking are perceived as more effective.

Other researchers have explored the relationship between specific characteristics or behaviors and inductee perceptions of preceptors effectiveness. Irvy (1987), for example, explored the relationship of faculty rank, involvement, and nature of relationship and inductees' perceptions of a preceptor effectiveness. Preceptors who had specific goals for their clinical teaching asked more questions and used more high level questions were rated as more effective by inductees (Edelstein, 1981). Crandall (1993) and Irby (1992) had similar findings. Irby found that preceptors who were considered experts planned their interactions with inductees in advance, later reflected on these interactions, and were quick to diagnose the problems of both patients and inductees in the clinical setting. In interviews, Crandall found that expert preceptors exemplified Schon's model of reflection in action, knowing in action, and reflection on action. In a study of beliefs about their clinical teaching, Valerio (1992) found that preceptors' clinical practices were congruent with their beliefs and that their own clinical education was the source for those beliefs about effective preceptoring. In a study which casts doubt on the outcomes of many studies of preceptor practices, the validity of data gathered using self report was questioned (Hartman & Nelson, 1992). This study found that the behaviors reported by preceptors and the behaviors observed by the researchers were not strongly correlated.

The relationship between preceptors' level of content expertise and their interactions with inductees has also been studied by a number of researchers (Davis, Nairn, Paine, Anderson, & Oh, 1992; Eagle, Harosym, & Mandin, 1992; Schmidt, Van Der Arend, Moust, Kokx, & Boon, 1993). The increasing emphasis on PBL and case methods led Davis, Nairn, Paine, Anderson, and Oh (1992) to investigate the impact of faculty members' expertise in content on interaction and learning. This study found no significant differences in interaction, but students working with faculty members who had more content expertise were more satisfied and scored higher on relevant exams. Eagle, Harosym, and Mandin (1992) had similar findings. PBL groups led by content experts generated more learning issues per case and the issues were more congruent with the case.

The impact of training preceptors has also been studied by a number of researchers. These studies have examined the improvement of clinical teaching through the use of various faculty development programs which present information on effective clinical teaching strategies (Anderson, Hess, Rody, & Smith, 1991; Bland, Hitchcock, Anderson, & Stritter, 1987; Brennan, McWhinney, Stewart, & Weston, 1985; Edwards, Kissling, Plauche, & Marier, 1986; Edwards, Marier, & Kissling, 1985; Hitchcock, Stritter, & Bland, 1992; Jewett, Greenberg, & Goldberg, 1982). Stuart, Orzano, and Eidus (1980) studied a program in which expert preceptors directly observed the practice of less experienced preceptors and offered feedback. The videotaping of the novice preceptors' interactions with inductees prior to and after this feedback indicated significant increases in preceptor skill.

Summary of Research on Supervision in Clinical Medicine

It seems that the goal of the research on clinical teaching is to identify specific, standardized strategies that develop and assess the clinical competence of inductees most efficiently. A behavioral perspective guides the research on supervision of clinical practice in medicine in almost all cases. Even though the research on inductees clearly indicates that classroom knowledge does not necessarily predict clinical performance, the research on clinical teaching seems to assume that giving preceptors information about effective and efficient ways to supervise clinical practice will result in the use of those approaches. The research also has assumed, until recently at least, that self report on practice is accurate and that inductee and preceptor perceptions of events are similar. The observational apprenticeship Lortie (1975) describes as so influential on the classroom practice of teachers is also evident in preceptor practices, which are clearly dominated by the Socratic

questioning and "learning by doing" approaches advocated by Flexner. The research on clinical teaching in medicine seems to focus on technical and implementation issues, not the basic assumptions on which practice is founded. Few studies in the research literature address less observable issues like beliefs or certainty of knowledge, although there seems to be a growing recognition of the need for new approaches to research. This literature is currently intended to fine tune practice, not revolutionize practice, although the growing recognition of the value of new approaches to research has the potential to dramatically change research in the field.

SUPERVISION OF PRACTICE IN NURSING

Context of Research on Supervision in Nursing

In 1992, Aydelotte described three programs which currently lead to a first professional degree in nursing: diploma programs operated by hospitals; associate and baccalaureate degree programs operated by universities, colleges, or community colleges; and graduate degree programs at the masters' and doctoral levels operated by universities. Despite obvious differences in admission requirements, program, faculty, and graduation standards, all these programs lead to eligibility for the same licensing examination and the same title: professional nurse. Although standards are set by the national accrediting organization for nursing, the National League for Nursing (NLN), and state agencies, there is no one set of standards that all nursing programs must meet. It is still, as Christman noted in 1979, "almost impossible to generalize about a nurse's abilities, codify colleagueships with other types of care providers, or set meaningful standards for nursing practice" (p. 21). Unlike medicine, nursing has not standardized the education and induction of novices into the profession. Calls for restructuring nursing education date back to the 1923 Goldmark report (cited in Aydelotte, 1992), which urged that nursing education move away from apprenticeship-style hospital training toward more professional education. Unlike the Flexner report, the Goldmark report inspired very little reform, perhaps because reform of nursing education was perceived as reform of women's education, perhaps because of nursing shortages (Grace, 1983), or perhaps because of the dominant status physicians have maintained in the field of healthcare. In fact, the debate over the appropriate form of preparation for nurses continues, fed by debate within the profession and external forces such as health care reform, and complicated by the variety of contexts in which nurses practice, nursing's status as a female occupation, and the more interrupted career paths traditional for women (Aiken, 1992; Grace, 1983).

Definition of Supervision in Nursing

In nursing, as in medicine, the term *supervision* most often refers to the oversight of a patient's course of treatment. The induction into clinical practice and the process of supervising this experience are generally referred to as *clinical teaching*.

Clinical teaching may be defined as individual or small group educational interactions that involve a patient, a teacher or preceptor who is typically a nurse educator or an experienced nurse, and a prospective or novice nurse completing a nurse education program or beginning a first nursing assignment. Experienced nurses who mentor novice nurses are generally referred to as *preceptors*.

Theoretical Perspectives of the Research

Because the nursing literature has focused considerable attention on the development of professional expertise in both nursing education and nursing practice, this review will include research on clinical teaching in nursing education, research on induction, and research on the development of practicing nurses. Research in clinical teaching and induction has focused on the impact of context, specific strategies or characteristics, and the preceptor role. Research on the development of practicing nurses has focused on involvement in continuing education and the development of practical knowledge. Perhaps because there is such disparity in the preparation of novice nurses, nursing literature has traditionally addressed clinical teaching, induction, and professional growth. Daggett, Cassie, and Collins (1979) noted that "nursing clearly has the largest literature on clinical teaching," although little of it was based on research (p. 153). As nursing programs have become baccalaureate, master's, and doctoral programs at institutions of higher education, research has become a more integral part of the nursing culture and literature. Although much of the research on nursing has been quantitative, the profession has adopted qualitative research strategies in recent years. Methodological diversity is seen as a strength in nursing research, and combinations of quantitative and qualitative methodologies are frequently found in current nursing research (Hinshaw, 1992).

Context

Nurses practice and complete clinical practica in an increasing variety of contexts, and the impact of context on the development of clinical expertise has been a frequent focus for research. Reilly and Oermann's (1992) review of the literature on context reported many studies which examined the scope of settings for clinical practice, the perceived value of varied settings, and the selection of clinical practice sites. Few studies examining the effect of various settings on the development of clinical expertise were reported. The methodology of research on contexts ranges widely. At one end of the spectrum are massive questionnaire studies like McEwen's (1992) national survey of the contexts in which nurses complete clinical experiences. At the other end are small interview studies which intensively examine particular contexts. Baillie's (1993) phenomenological interview study of eight students, who completed eight-week practica placements in community placements, is an example of the smaller qualitative study in this area of research. Baillie examined the impact of context on perceptions of the nurse role by interviewing students and preceptors and carefully documenting the placement context. In a study employing both quantitative and qualitative methodologies to examine the impact of context on outcomes, Anderson (1991a) explored the impact of preceptors on the development of nurses' moral reasoning in hospital versus community placement contexts.

Strategies

Research on clinical teaching in nursing has often focused on role modeling and interpersonal skills (Marriott, 1991). Many of these studies have used questionnaires to gather student nurse perceptions of their clinical instructors and clinical experiences (Anderson, 1991b; Brown, 1981; Kleehammer, Hart, & Keck, 1990; Knox & Mogan, 1985; Pugh, 1988). In a typical study, Anderson (1991b) found that students perceived role modeling as one of the most effective strategies a preceptor could use to teach the roles and functions of a staff nurse; preceptors saw role modeling as one of the least effective strategies. A number of these studies have found that clinical instructors' interpersonal skills are very important to students, although clinical instructors tend to be more concerned about professional competence (Marriott, 1991). The literature suggests that being a good role model and offering feedback are valued by both students and clinical instructors, although they do not always agree on their relative importance (Brown, 1981; Flagler, Loper-Powers, & Spitzer, 1988; Knox & Mogan, 1985; Mogan & Knox, 1987; Pugh, 1988; Windsor, 1987).

Other studies have explored student responses to specific strategies employed in clinical teaching. For example, Hawks and Hromek (1992) found that students felt that learning contracts in clinical settings empowered them. Lyte and Thompson (1990) examined the use of diaries to promote reflection and communication among preceptors, faculty, and students. Other researchers have studied the question of flexible schedules (Wolfe & Sands, 1981) and learning style-related strategies (Ismuert, Ismuert, & Miller, 1992). Studies in this area have addressed a wide variety of strategies, with a growing emphasis on the development of reflection and clinical reasoning.

Another group of studies has examined clinical instructors' use and perceptions of various strategies. A number of self-report and survey studies have been done in this area (see reviews by Mariott, 1992; Reilly & Oermann, 1992; Van Hoozer et al, 1987). These studies have found that generic teaching skills, personal traits, relationships with students, and nursing competence are perceived by clinical instructors as important to effective teaching (Reilly & Oermann, 1992). In a more open-ended and outcome-oriented study of the strategies instructors and students associated with higher clinical performance scores, Brasler (1993) found that participation in formal support groups was not correlated with better clinical performance scores. In this study, support from nurse friends, emotional support from a preceptor, and preceptor skills were associated with better clinical performance scores. A review of the literature on clinical instructors' evaluations of student performance (Orchard, 1991) suggested that there are disparities in expectations, difficulties in documenting assessments of clinical decision-making, and a need for both training and multiple inputs in clinical evaluation. There is, once again, a increasing focus on the development of clinical decision-making.

Preceptors

In recent years, the use of preceptors in nursing has grown and studies of the role, selection, preparation, and practice of preceptors have become an important part of the research on nurse development. Studies have examined the use of preceptors in nursing education and induction (Peirce, 1991; Rosenlieb, 1991), the selection of preceptors (Hartline, 1993; Westra & Graziano, 1992), and the impact of preceptored experience on novice nurses' professional orientation, confidence, and clinical performance (Anderson, 1990; Bellinger & McCloskey, 1992; Jairath, Costello, Wallace, & Rudy, 1991; McGrath & Princeton, 1987; Oermann & Navin, 1991; Peirce, 1991; Welborn, 1991, Yonge, & Trojan; 1992). Preceptors' values (Ferguson & Calder, 1993), the training that preceptors receive (Bizek & Oermann, 1990; Rittman, 1992), and the impact of preceptor training on practice and outcomes have also been topics for a number of studies (Hagopian, Ferszt, Jacobs, & McCorkle, 1992; Westra & Graziano, 1992).

A number of researchers have studied the transition into nursing and preceptors' impact on the transition, recognizing the different subcultures of nursing education and nursing practice. In 1990, Hamel used participant observation to study the experience of neophyte nurses making the transition from the nursing education subculture to the nursing work subculture. She found that neophytes were afraid of making errors, found the transition unpleasant, felt that efficiency and task were valued over nursing's psychosocial aspects, and had difficulty organizing the tasks they faced. Preceptors had trouble articulating the work subculture, provided minimal support to the new nurses, and seemed to lack understanding of the preceptor role. However, another study of the transition to work (Jairath, Costello, Wallace, & Rudy, 1991) found that preceptors facilitated the transition to nursing practice and improved neophytes' performance.

A number of studies have focused directly on preceptors' practice. Davis, Sawin, and Dunn (1993) used qualitative research strategies to study the strategies of expert preceptors, finding that they approached the task of precepting with two distinct styles: "incremental structure" and "sink or swim." The sets of strategies articulated by these expert preceptors included orientation strategies, strategies used with all students, and strategies used differentially according to the needs of the student. Krichbaum's (1991) study of critical care preceptors found many similarities in the practice of effective preceptors and the practice of effective clinical teachers, including organizing, timely feedback, appropriate questioning, and demonstration of a positive approach toward teaching and learning. Taylor (1989) surveyed clinical nursing faculty to determine how they allocated their time in supervising clinical work. These faculties indicated that they preconferenced with the supervisee, observed, and held a postconference. They reported spending 51 percent of their time in observations, 38 percent in role modeling, 25 percent in various types of data preparation and analysis, and 16 percent in conferences. Hsieh and Knowles (1990) examined the development of relationships among preceptors, instructors, and novice nurses, concluding that effective relationships addressed seven issues: trust, expectations, support, honest

communication, mutual respect, encouragement, and mutual sharing. Although the research is not conclusive, preceptors seem to have the potential to make a positive contribution to nurses' professional development, especially if they have some training in the role and have good interpersonal and analysis skills.

Continuing Education

The continuing education of nurses has long been a concern in the profession, perhaps because women tend to follow more interrupted career paths than men. Many nurses participate in continuing education that is required in their workplace, creating a setting for study of the impact of continuing education on professional practice. Recent studies have examined this issue in a variety of ways. Many studies have asked nurses what they feel they should learn more about (see, for example, Duffy & Fairchild, 1989). Some researchers have looked at the impact of managerial behavior on nurses' sense of freedom to practice (Paunonen, 1991) and levels of stress (Revicki & May, 1989). Blais, Duquette, and Painchard (1989) explored nurses' participation in continuing education, finding that cost and conflicting role demands were the most frequently cited reasons for nonparticipation in continuing education outside the workplace. Other studies have explored the value of specific approaches to professional development, such as portfolios. Hart (1990) reviewed the literature and suggested that peer review and peer consultation be linked to facilitate the continuing professional development of nurses.

Although some individual studies have found that continuing education programs were effective in improving nursing practice (see, for example, Cox & Baker, 1981), Gosnell's (1984) review of the literature concluded that research on the effectiveness of continuing education in improving nursing practice was not conclusive. Cervero, Rottet, and Dimmock (1986), who have done a series of studies of continuing professional education (CPE) and nurses, have sought to determine why CPE is sometimes effective and sometimes not. They suggest that research on CPE needs to ask much more complex questions to get good answers, offering the following question as a starting point: "Under what conditions and for which types of individuals are which characteristics of a CPE program most likely to improve professionals' performance?" (p. 83).

Clinical Practice

Benner's (1984) book, *From Novice to Expert: Excellence and Power in Clinical Nursing Practice*, provides a research-based model of clinical skill acquisition based on data gathered from more than 1,200 nurses, using questionnaires and interviews. Benner documents the development of the clinical expertise which allows expert nurses to behave in an orderly way without rigid rule following, acting on the subtle hunches and feelings that lead skilled nurses to attend to particular aspects of the clinical situation.

Applying the Dreyfus model of skill acquisition to nursing, Benner (1984) identified areas of practical knowledge and stages in the development of clinical knowledge. Benner identified six areas of practical or clinical knowledge, "the knowledge that accrues over time in the practice of an applied discipline" (p. 1), and five stages in the development of expertise: novice, advanced beginner, competent, proficient, and expert. Benner notes that these areas and stages are context-based and that practitioners are often unaware of their own growth in and use of practical knowledge.

The six areas of clinical knowledge identified by Benner are: "(1) graded qualitative distinctions, (2) common meanings, (3) assumptions, expectations, and sets, (4) paradigm cases and personal knowledge, (5) maxims, and (6) unplanned practices" (p. 4). The area of graded qualitative distinctions refers to the expert nurse's ability to detect subtle changes in a patient's condition, changes that are often significant only in light of the patient's history. Common meanings are the set of responses and options shared by expert nurses working in a particular context. Benner defines assumptions, expectations, and sets as elements, often outside formally recognized knowledge, which occur in narrative accounts of practical situations and help define the possibilities a nurse sees in a clinical situation. Paradigm cases and personal knowledge are the clusters of events and experiences which guide a nurse's approach to a particular clinical issue. Maxims are the "cryptic instructions" (p. 10) given by expert practitioners that are fully understood only by other expert practitioners. Maxims can alert researchers and novices to areas where clinical judgment is important. Unplanned practices are the areas of practice that are informally delegated to nurses, often as new procedures or technology are introduced. Nurses develop considerable expertise in these rarely defined or studied areas. Benner suggests that these areas of clinical knowledge, which she further defines, are the foundation for clinical reasoning in nursing. Definition and discussion of these areas make it easier for nurses to extend and refine their clinical reasoning.

Benner's model offers a structure for career ladders, professional development programs, and research on the development of expertise in nursing and in other applied disciplines. The model's attention to the subtleties of context, experience, implicit knowledge, and judgment are congruent with nursing researchers' growing awareness of the nonbehavioral aspects of excellent practice. The model and the research on which it is based may stimulate researchers in other fields to examine the clinical knowledge and reasoning that are the heart of practice in applied disciplines.

Summary of Research on Nursing Supervision

Nursing is an applied discipline in which knowledge accumulates over time as nurses engage in clinical practice. Traditional didactic CPE and clinical teaching that focus on explicit knowledge and specific behaviors have little to do with development of the informal, practical knowledge that expert nurses exhibit. Cervero, Rottet, and Dimmock (1986) have suggested that a good starting point for future research on CPE would be, "Under what conditions and for which types of individuals are which characteristics of a CPE program most likely to improve professionals' performance?" (p.

83). Benner's (1984) study of clinical nursing practice provides a model for examining the clinical reasoning CPE seeks to improve. Nursing research has recognized and begun to examine the subtle nonbehavioral aspects of clinical practice that are so important in any applied field. This research on clinical reasoning in nursing may also provide a valuable starting point for the study of clinical reasoning in other applied disciplines.

CHAPTER SUMMARY AND IMPLICATIONS FOR RESEARCH ON INSTRUCTIONAL SUPERVISION

This review of research on supervision of professional practice in social work, the several counseling fields, medicine, and nursing was organized around five questions. We return to the first four of those questions, summarize the research reported across the fields, and frame implications for future research on instructional supervision.

1. *In each of the professional practice fields, what is meant by "the supervision of clinical practice" and how and why did it emerge and evolve?*

The conceptualizations of supervision across the clinical practice fields include such functions as administrative oversight, education and information update, development from novice to expert, emotional support, professional induction, clinical teaching, and oversight of treatment for the client or patient. Perhaps the most significant difference is that between the preservice meaning of supervision functions in the counseling professions and in nursing and medical preservice education and the preservice and in-service meanings of supervision in social work and education practices. There are in-service seminars, correspondence courses, and other forms of training and information updating in all of these professions. In the health and counseling professions, there is no supervision in the sense of systematic review of or reflection on one's practice by or with another person. The assumption is that the professional practitioner has mastered the knowledge and skills that define the essence of the practice, will conduct him- or herself ethically, will actively seek and use new insights and skills, and will use standardized procedures and judgments to guide their practice. The assumptions of certainty about the knowledge base and procedures developed and refined under the scrutiny of scientific examination may also contribute to the belief that ongoing supervision of practice is unnecessary once it has been certified that the individual has mastered that stable body of practice knowledge.

It is noteworthy that these professions are historically male-dominated fields of practice. Supervision beyond initial preparation and licensure varies extensively between historically male-dominated and historically female-dominated professions. Male-dominated professions do not have what we even broadly construe to be the supervision of professional practice; female-dominated historically professions have always had direct supervision of practice.

2. *What theoretical perspectives and language were used to frame the research questions, to select the forms of inquiry engaged, and to guide the discussions and derivation of implications?*

While there are assumptions and perspectives represented in all research efforts, much of the research reviewed here can be characterized as virtually atheoretical. The questions asked across the fields have been largely generic in nature: Who are supervisors? What do they do? What do supervisors and supervisees talk about during conferences? How do supervisors think and make clinical judgments? We have seen research reflecting developmental, psychotherapeutic, and cognitive constructivist learning theories in counseling, and social construction of knowledge theoretical orientations in nursing. In a few cases, grounded theory is the assumed perspective, and the questions, analyses, and interpretations have emerged more from the context than from *a priori* theoretical perspectives.

It is also clear that while some behavioral and social science theories are used in the research on supervision, there is little evidence that critical theory has become an active frame of reference. We found only a single reference in the social work area that suggested the importance of inquiry about gender, race, ethnicity, education, and other social and political identifiers in relation to power, influence, approach, enactments, and impact. The dominance of positivist and practical perspectives about research and understanding appears once again to keep the research questions descriptive and utilitarian, rather than interpretive and critical.

Research problems and questions center around the personal characteristics of supervisors; what supervisors do and what the perceived satisfactions and effects of those practices are from the vantage points of the supervisees; and what the actual professional practices are and how they relate to supervisees' beliefs, reasoning, and professional practices.

3. *What are the dominant tools of inquiry and forms of analysis used in the research on supervision in each of the nonteaching professional practices?*

The dominant tools of inquiry include the survey questionnaire, interview protocols, and systematic observation protocols that enable the recording of supervisor-supervisee talk and the tone of their interactions. The tools of qualitative inquiry are beginning to emerge in the conduct of inquiry about supervision. Interview questions, journals, logs, stories, and shadowing of supervisors and practitioners (e.g., Benner, 1984) are some of these researchers' tools.

The forms of analysis used in quantitative studies tend to be directed toward describing patterns of supervisors' beliefs, perceptions, and behaviors and their relationships with demographic variables, supervisees' beliefs, perceptions, and behaviors. Some strongly believe that the effects of certain supervisory practices on the beliefs, thoughts, and enactments of practitioners can be and should be the focus of contemporary research. A different perspective is that the forms of analysis should lead toward greater understanding of the complexities and meanings of supervisory practices. Perhaps

more important is the need to bring all forms of inquiry to the search for understanding of the multiple aspects of supervisory practice and to assess the impact—intended and unintended—on the quality of professional practice and client status.

4. *What are the major findings and insights gleaned about supervisory policies and practices in these nonteaching professions?*

There are no major findings or insights to report, beyond the acknowledgment that there are multiple and very diverse images of supervision of professional practice used to locate and frame research problems and that there is little sustained or focused inquiry taking place (counseling being the notable exception). This is more a function of the preparadigm status of research on supervision than of the studies reviewed. The overwhelming statement from the review is that research along the lines pursued has not for the most part been fruitful.

Borders's (1992) call for a shift toward the study of the clinical reasoning of supervisors and supervisees is reflective of the search for more promising research problems. Clinical reasoning and enactment has been the emphasis of clerkships in medical education for years. What has not been evident in the medical research has been the role of the mentor on the development of clinical reasoning by novices. Benner's (1984) work is pivotal in this regard because it provides both an approach to and insights about how to describe and interpret clinical reasoning.

5. *What implications for the study of instructional supervision can be derived from this review of research on nonteaching supervision?*

a. View teaching and continuously learning about how to teach as complex cognitive, affective, social, and political phenomena—not as a simplistic "show it, do it, and integrate it" undertaking.

b. Direct research about instructional supervision toward understanding the clinical reasoning and judgments of teachers and supervisors.

c. Provide the necessary time and support for conducting research on instructional supervision as if it was a serious matter.

d. Establish lines of sustained inquiry by faculty and graduate students to replace the apparently disjointed and ahistorical inquiry done largely by doctoral students.

e. Use multiple forms of inquiry to inquire about the complex human activities encompassed by instructional supervision.

The lack of imagination in the inquiry on nonteaching supervision and the lack of a moral centering on matters of consequence in relation to understanding the phenomena and enhancing those aspects most likely to have high impact on the quality of life and learning for all in schools are also matters to be taken seriously in the conduct of inquiry about instructional supervision.

REFERENCES

Aiken, L. H. (1992). Charting nursing's future. In L. H. Aiken & C. M. Fagin (Eds.). *Charting nursing's future: Agenda for the 1990s* (pp. 3–12). Philadelphia: J. B. Lippincott.

Anderson, D. C., Harris, I. B., Allen, S., Satran, L., Bland, C. J., Davis-Feickert, J. A., Poland, G. A., & Miller, W. J. (1991). Comparing students' feedback about clinical instruction with their performances. *Academic Medicine, 66*(1), 29–34.

Anderson, J., Hess, G., Rody, N., & Smith, W. (1991). Improving a community preceptorship through a clinical faculty development program. *Family Medicine, 23*(5), 387–288.

Anderson, S. L. (1990). Senior preceptorship: Faculty-preceptor collaboration. *Nursing Connections, 3*(4), 21–30.

Anderson, S. L. (1991a). Do student preceptorships affect moral reasoning? *Nursing Education, 16*(3), 14–17.

Anderson, S. L. (1991b). Preceptor teaching strategies: Behaviors that facilitate role transition in senior nursing students. *Journal of Nursing and Staff Development, 7*(4), 171–175.

Aydelotte, M. K. (1992). Nursing education: Shaping the future. In L. H. Aiken & C. M. Fagin (Eds.). *Charting nursing's future: Agenda for the 1990s* (pp. 462–484). Philadelphia, PA: J.B. Lippincott.

Baillie, L. (1993). Factors affecting student nurses' learning in community placements: A phenomenological study. *Journal of Advanced Nursing, 18*(7), 1043–1053.

Barretta-Herman, A. (1993). On the development of a model of supervision for licensed social work practitioners. *The Clinical Supervisor, 11*(2), 55–64.

Bellinger, S. R. & McClosky, J. C. (1992). Are preceptors for orientation of new nurses effective? *Journal of Professional Nursing, 8*(6), 231–237.

Benner, P. (1984). *From novice to expert: Excellence and power in clinical nursing practice.* Menlo Park, CA: Addison-Wesley.

Bernard, J. M. & Goodyear, R. K. (1992). *Fundamentals of clinical supervision.* Boston, MA: Allyn & Bacon.

Biddle, W. B. & Smith, D. V. (1984, April). *Evaluation of clinical electives: Factors differentiating between clinical training sites.* Paper presented at the annual meeting of the American Educational Research Association, New Orleans, LA.

Bizek, K. S. & Oermann, M. H. (1990). Study of educational experiences, support, and job satisfaction among critical care nurse preceptors. *Heart and Lung, 19*(5), 439–444.

Blais, J. G., Duquette, A., & Painchard, G. (1989). Deterrents to women's participation in work-related educational activities. *Adult Education Quarterly, 39*(4), 224–234.

Bland, C. J., Hitchcock, M. A., Anderson, W. A., & Stritter, F. T. (1987). Faculty development fellowship programs in family medicine. *Journal of Medical Education, 62*(8), 632–641.

Bland, C. J., Schmitz, C. C., Stritter, F. T., Aluise, J. A., & Henry, R. C. (1988). Project to identify essential faculty skills and develop model curriculum for faculty development programs. *Journal of Medical Education, 63*(6), 467–469.

Borders, L. D. (1989a). Review of supervising counselors and therapists: A developmental approach. *The Clinical Supervisor, 7,* 161–166.

Borders, L. D. (1989b). A pragmatic agenda for developmental supervision research. *Counselor Education and Supervision, 29,* 16–24.

Borders, L. D. (1991). Supervisors' in-session behaviors and cognition. *Counselor Education and Supervision, 31,* 32–47.

Borders, L. D. (1992). Learning to think like a supervisor. *The Clinical Supervisor, 10*(2), 135–148.

Borders, L. D. & Usher, C. H. (1992). Post-degree supervision: Existing and preferred practices. *Journal of Counseling and Development, 70,* 594–599.

Bornsztein, B. & Julian, T. M. (1991). Quantifying clinical activity in a multi-site clerkship in obstetrics and gynecology. *Obstetrics and Gynecology, 78,* 869–872.

Bradford, W. D. & Schonfield, J. R. (1986). Study of required clerkships in internal medicine in U. S. and Canadian medical schools. *Journal of Medical Education, 61*(3), 157–162.

Brasler, M. E. (1993). Predictors of clinical performance of new graduate nurses participating in preceptor orientation programs. *Journal of Continuing Education in Nursing, 24*(4), 158–165.

Brennan, M., McWhinney, I. R., Stewart, M., & Weston, W. (1985). A graduate program for academic family physicians. *Family Practice, 2*(3), 165–172.

Brown, S. T. (1981). Faculty and student perception of effective clinical teachers. *Journal of Nursing, 20*(9), 4–15.

Bubenzer, D. L., West, S. D., & Gold, J. M. (1991). Use of live supervision in counselor preparation. *Counselor Education and Supervision, 30,* 301–308.

Calkins, E. V., Arnold, L. M., Willoughby, T. L., & Hamburger, S. C. (1986). Docents' and students' perceptions of the ideal and actual role of the docent. *Journal of Medical Education, 61*(9, Pt. 1), 743–748.

Carline, J. D., Paauw, D. S., Thiede, K. W., & Ramsey, P. G. (1992). Factors affecting the reliability of ratings of students' clinical skills in a medicine clerkship. *Journal of General Internal Medicine, 7*(5), 506–510.

Cervero, R. M., Rottet, S., & Dimmock, K. H. (1986). Analyzing the effectiveness of continuing professional education at the workplace. *Adult Education Quarterly, 36*(2), 78–85.

Christman, L. (1979). Professional nurse responsibility and accountability. In *Nursing's influence on health policy for the eighties* (pp. 21–23). Kansas City, MO: American Academy of Nursing.

Colliver, J. A. & Williams, R. G. (1993). Technical issues: Test application. *Academic Medicine, 68*(6), 454–460.

Cox, C. L. & Baker, M. G. (1981). Evaluation: The key to accountability in continuing education. *The Journal of Continuing Education in Nursing, 12,* 11–19.

Crandall, S. (1993). How expert clinical educators teach what they know. *Journal of Continuing Education in the Health Professions, 13*(1), 85–98.

Cronbach, L. J. & Snow, R. E. (1977). *Aptitudes and instructional methods.* New York: Irvington.

Daggett, C. J., Cassie, J. M., & Collins, G. F. (1979). Research on clinical teaching. *Review of Educational Research, 49*(1), 151–169.

Dailey, D. M. (1983). Androgyny, sex role stereotypes, and clinical judgement. *Social Work Research and Abstracts, 19*(1), 20–24.

DaRosa, D. A., Mazur, J., & Folse, R. (1984). The effects of standardized feedback on orthopedic patient evaluation skills. *Journal of Medical Education, 59*(12), 969–970.

Davis, J. K., Inamadan, S., & Stone, R. K. (1986). Interrater agreement and predictive validity of faculty ratings of pediatric residents. *Journal of Medical Education, 61*(11), 901–905.

Davis, M. S., Sawin, K. J., & Dunn, M. (1993). Teaching strategies used by expert nurse practitioner preceptors: A qualitative study. *Journal of American Academic Nurse Practitioners, 5*(1), 27–33.

Davis, W. K., Nairn, R., Paine, M. E., Anderson, R. M., & Oh, M. S. (1992). Effects of expert and non-expert facilitators on the small-group process and on student performance. *Academic Medicine, 67*(7), 470–474.

Dean, R. E. & Johnson, T. M. (1977). The surgical clerkship in the community hospital. *Journal of Medical Education, 52*(1), 59–65.

Dinham, S. M. & Stritter, F. T. (1986). Research on professional education. In M. C. Wittrock (Ed.). *Handbook of research on teaching* (3rd ed.) pp. 952–970. New York: Macmillan.

Duffy, S. A. & Fairchild, N. (1989). Educational needs of community health nursing supervisors. *Public Health and Nursing, 6*(1), 16–22.

Eagle, C. J., Harasym, P. H., & Mandin, H. (1992). Effects of tutors with case expertise on problem-based learning issues. *Academic Medicine, 67*(7), 465–469.

Ebert, R. H. (1992). Flexner's model and the future of medical education. *Academic Medicine, 67*(11), 737–742.

Edelstein, R. A. (1981, April). *A model for analyzing precepting in the clinical setting.* Paper presented at the annual meeting of the American Educational Research Association, Los Angeles, CA.

Edwards, J. C., Kissling, G. E., Plauche, W. C., & Marier, R. L. (1986). Long-term evaluation of training residents in clinical teaching skills. *Journal of Medical Education, 61*(12), 967–970.

Edwards, J. C., Marier, R. L., & Kissling, G. E. (1985, April). *Improving clinical teaching: Focus on residents.* Paper presented at the annual meeting of the American Educational Research Association, Chicago, IL.

Elks, M. L. & Sawyer, J. W. (1992). Scripted oral examinations of internal medicine students' clinical skills with simulated patients. *Academic Medicine, 67*(7), 484.

Ellis, M. V. (1991). Research in clinical supervision: Revitalizing a scientific agenda. *Counselor, 30,* 238–251.

Ewalt, P. L. (1980). From clinician to manager. In S. White (Ed.). *New directions for mental health services: Middle management in mental health* (pp. 1–10). San Francisco, CA: Jossey-Bass.

Ferguson, L. M. & Calder, B. L. (1993). A comparison of preceptor and educator valuing of nursing student clinical performance criteria. *Journal of Nursing Education, 32*(1), 30–36.

Fisher, B. L. (1989). Differences between supervision of beginning and advanced therapists: Hogan's hypothesis empirically revisited. *The Clinical Supervisor, 7*(1), 57–74.

Flagler, S., Loper-Powers, S., & Spitzer, A. (1988). Clinical teaching is more than evaluation alone. *Journal of Nursing Education, 27*(8), 342–348.

Flexner, A. (1910). *Medical education in the United States and Canada: A report to the carnegie foundation for the advancement of teaching* (Bulletin No. 4). Boston, MA: Updyke.

Forsythe, G. B., McGaghie, W. C., & Friedman, C. P. (1986). Construct validity of medical clinical competence measures: A multitrait-multimethod matrix study using confirmatory factor analysis. *American Educational Research Journal, 23*(2), 315–336.

Foster, P. J. (1981). Clinical discussion groups: Verbal participation and outcomes. *Journal of Medical Education, 56*(10), 831–838.

Friedman, C. P., Stritter, F. T., & Talbert, L. M. (1978). A systematic comparison of teaching hospital and remote-site clinical education. *Journal of Medical Education, 53*(7), 565–573.

Gallant, P. J. & Thyer, B. A. (1989). The "bug-in-the-ear" in clinical supervision: A review. *The Clinical Supervisor, 7*(2/3), 43–58.

Gallant, P. J., Thyer, B. A., & Bailey, J. S. (1991). Using bug-in-the-ear feedback in clinical supervision: Preliminary evaluations. *Research on Social Work Practice, 1*(2), 175–187.

Gastel, B. & Rogers, D. E. (Eds.). (1989). *Clinical education and the doctor of tomorrow.* New York: New York Academy of Medicine.

Gil, D. H., Heins, M., & Jones, P. (1984). Perceptions of medical school faculty members and students on clinical clerkship feedback. *Journal of Medical Education, 59*(11, Pt. 1), 856–864.

Gjerde, C. L. & Coble, R. J. (1982). Resident and faculty perceptions of effective clinical teaching in family practice. *Journal of Family Practice, 14*(2), 323–327.

Goldstein, A. P., Heller, K., & Sechrest, L. B. (1966). *Psychotherapy and the psychology of behavior change.* New York: Wiley.

Goodyear, R. K., Abadie, P. D., & Efros, F. (1984). Supervisory theory into practice: Differential perceptions of supervision by Edstein, Ellis, Polster, and Rogers. *Journal of Counseling Psychology, 31*(2), 228–237.

Gordon, M. J. (1992). Self-assessment programs and their implications for health professions training. *Academic Medicine, 67*(10), 672–679.

Gosnell, D. J. (1984). Evaluating continuing nursing education. *The Journal of Continuing Education in Nursing, 15,* 9–11.

Grace, H. K. (1983). Nursing. In C. H. McGuire, R. P. Foley, A. Gorr, & R. W. Richards (Eds.). *Handbook of health professions education.* San Francisco, CA: Jossey-Bass.

Hagopian, G. A., Ferszt, G. G., Jacobs, L. A., & McCorkle, R. (1992). Preparing clinical preceptors to teach master's-level students in oncology nursing. *Journal of Professional Nursing, 8*(5), 295–300.

Hamel, E. J. (1990). *An interpretive study of the professional socialization of neophyte nurses into the nursing subculture.* Unpublished doctoral dissertation, University of San Diego.

Handley, P. (1982). Relationship between supervisors' and trainees' cognitive styles and the supervision process. *Journal of Counseling Psychology, 29*(5), 508–515.

Harkness, D. R. (1987). *Social work supervision in community mental health: Effects of normal and client-focused supervision on client satisfaction and generalized contentment.* Unpublished doctoral dissertation, University of Kansas.

Harkness, D. & Hensley, D. (1991). Changing the focus of social work supervision: Effects on clients. *Social Work, 36*(6), 506–512.

Harkness, D. & Poertner, J. (1989, March). Research and social work supervision: A conceptual review. *Social Work, 34*(2), 115–119.

Hart, G. (1990). Peer consultation and review. *Australian Journal of Advanced Nursing, 7*(2), 40–46.

Harth, S. C., Bavanandan, S., Thomas, K. E., Lai, M. Y., & Thong, Y. H. (1992). The quality of student-tutor interactions in the clinical learning environment. *Medical Education, 26*(4), 321–326.

Hartline, C. (1993). Preceptor selection and evaluation: A tool for educators and managers. *Journal of Nursing and Staff Development, 9*(4), 188–192.

Hartman, S. L. & Nelson, M. S. (1992). What we say and what we do: Self-reported teaching behavior versus performances in written simulations among medical school faculty. *Academic Medicine, 67*(8), 522–527.

Harvey, O. J., Hunt, D. E., & Schroeder, H. M. (1961). *Conceptual systems and personality organization.* New York: Holt, Rinehart, and Winston.

Hawks, J. H. & Hromek, C. (1992). Nursing practicum: Empowering strategies. *Nursing Outlook, 40*(5), 231–234.

Hayes, R. B., Davis, D. A., McKibbon, A., & Tugwell, P. (1984). A critical appraisal of the efficacy of continuing education. *Journal of the American Medical Association, 251,* 61–64.

Hekelman, F. P., Vanek, E., Kelly, K., & Alemagno, S. (1993). Characteristics of family physicians' clinical teaching behaviors in the ambulatory setting: A descriptive study. *Teaching and Learning in Medicine, 5*(1), 18–23.

Heppner, P. P. & Handley, P. G. (1981). A study of the interpersonal influence process in supervision. *Journal of Counseling Psychology, 28*(5), 437–444.

Heppner, P. P. & Roehlke, H. J. (1984). Differences among supervisees at different levels of training: Implications for a developmental model of supervision. *Journal of Counseling Psychology, 31*(1), 76–90.

Hewson, M. G. (1991). Reflection in clinical teaching: An analysis of reflection-on-action and its implications for staffing residents. *Medical Teacher, 13*(3), 227–231.

Hinshaw, A. S. (1992). Nursing research: Weaving the past and the future. In L. H. Aiken & C. M. Fagin (Eds.). *Charting nursing's future: Agenda for the 1990s* (pp. 485–503). Philadelphia, PA: J. B. Lippincott.

Hitchcock, M. A., Stritter, F. T., & Bland, C. J. (1992). Faculty development in the health professions: Conclusions and recommendations. *Medical Teacher, 14*(4), 295–309.

Hogan, R. A. (1964). Issues and approaches to supervision. *Psychotherapy: Theory, Research, and Practice, 2,* 139–141.

Holloway, E. L. (1982). Interactional structure of the supervision interview. *Journal of Counseling Psychology, 29*(3), 309–317.

Holloway, E. L. & Hosford, R. E. (1983). Towards developing a prescriptive technology of counselor supervision. *The Counseling Psychologist, 11*(1), 73–77.

Holloway, E. L. & Wampold, B. E. (1983). Patterns of verbal behavior and judgements of satisfaction in a supervision interview. *Journal of Counseling Psychology, 30,* 227–234.

Holloway, E. L. & Wolleat, P. L. (1981). Style differences of beginning supervisors: An interactional analysis. *Journal of Counseling Psychology, 28*(4), 373–376.

Hsieh, N. L. & Knowles, D. W. (1990). Instructor facilitation of the preceptorship relationship in nursing education. *Journal of Nursing Education, 29*(6), 262–268.

Hughes, E. C., Thorne, B., DeBaggis, A. M., Gurin, A., & Williams, D. (1973). *Education for the professions of medicine, law, theology, and social welfare.* New York: McGraw-Hill.

Irby, D. M. (1986). Clinical teaching and the clinical teacher. *Journal of Medical Education, 61*(9), 35–45.

Irby, D. M. (1992). How attending physicians make instructional decisions when conducting teaching rounds. *Academic Medicine, 67*(10), 630–638.

Irby, D. M., Ramsey, P., Gillmore, G., & Schaad, D. (1991). Characteristics of effective clinical teachers of ambulatory care medicine. *Academic Medicine, 66*(1), 54–55.

Irvy, D. M. (1987). Factors affecting ratings of clinical teachers by medical students and residents. *Journal of Medical Education, 62*(1), 1–7.

Ismeurt, J., Ismeurt, R., & Miller, B. K. (1992). Field dependence and independence: Considerations in staff development. *Journal of Continuing Education in Nursing, 23*(1), 38–41.

Jairath, N., Costello, J., Wallace, P., & Rudy, L. (1991). The effect of preceptorship upon diploma program nursing students' transition to the professional nursing role. *Journal of Nursing Education, 30*(6), 251–255.

Jayaratne, S., Brabson, H. V., Gant, L. M., Nagda, B. A., Singh, A. K., & Chess, W. A. (1992). African-American practitioners' perceptions of their supervisors: Emotional support, social undermining, and criticism. *Administration in Social Work, 16*(2), 27–43.

Jennett, P. A. & Pearson, T. G. (1992). Educational responses to practice-based learning: Recent innovations in medicine. *New Directions for Adult and Continuing Education, 55,* 29–40.

Jewett, L. S., Greenberg, L. W., & Goldberg, R. M. (1982). Teaching residents how to teach: A one-year study. *Journal of Medical Education 57*(5), 361–366.

Jolly, B. & Ho Ping Kong, H. (1991). Independent learning: An exploration of student grand rounds. *Medical Education, 25*(4), 334–342.

Jolly, B. & Macdonald, M. M. (1987). More effective evaluation of clinical teaching. *Assessment and Evaluation in Higher Education, 12*(3), 175–190.

Jones, J. A. (1985). A study of nurse tutors' conceptualization of their ward teaching role. *Journal of Advanced Nursing, 10*(4), 349–360.

Jones, J. G., Cason, G. J., & Cason, C. (1986). The acquisition of cognitive knowledge through clinic experiences. *Medical Education, 20*(1), 10–12.

Kadushin, A. (1974, May). Supervisor-supervisee: A survey. *Social Work, 19,* 285–297.

Kadushin, A. (1992a). *Supervision in social work* (3rd ed.). New York: Columbia University Press.

Kadushin, A. (1992b). Social work supervision: An updated survey. *The Clinical Supervisor, 10*(2), 9–27.

Kagan, D. M. (1988). Research on the supervision of counselors and teachers-in-training: Linking two bodies of literature. *Review of Educational Research, 58*(1), 1–24.

Kleehammer, K., Hart, A. L., & Keck, J. F. (1990). Nursing students' perceptions of anxiety-producing situations in the clinical setting. *Journal of Nursing Education, 29*(4), 183–187.

Knox, J. E. & Mogan, J. (1985). Important clinical teacher behaviors as perceived by university nursing faculty students and graduates. *Journal of Advanced Nursing, 10,* 25–30.

Kolb, D. A. (1981). Learning styles and disciplinary differences. In A. A. Chickering & Associates (Eds.). *The Modern American College* (pp. 232–255). San Francisco, CA: Jossey-Bass.

Krichbaum, K. E. (1991). *The relationship between specific teaching behaviors and achievement of clinical learning outcomes by baccalaureate nursing students.* Unpublished doctoral dissertation, University of Minnesota.

Lanzilotti, S. S., Finestone, A. J., Sobel, E., & Marks, A. D. (1986). The practice integrated learning sequence: Linking education with the practice of medicine. *Adult Education Quarterly, 37*(1), 38–47.

Lewis, W. & Rohrbaugh, M. (1989). Live supervision by family therapists: A Virginia survey. *Journal of Marital and Family Therapy, 15*(3), 323–326.

Lincoln, M. J., Turner, C. W., Haug, P. J., Warner, H. R., Williamson, J. W., & Bouhaddou, D. (1991). Iliad training enhances medical students' diagnostic skills. *Journal of Medical Systems, 15*(1), 93–110.

Littlefield, J. H., DaRosa, D. A., Anderson, K. D., Bell, R. M., Nicholas, G. G., & Wolfson, P. J. (1991). Accuracy of surgery clerkship performance raters. *Academic Medicine, 66*(9, Supp.), S16–S18.

Locksmith, J. P., Mundy, W. M., & Passmore, G. G. (1992). Student and faculty perceptions of interactive learning in the radiology clerkship. *Investigative Radiology, 27*(10), 875–879.

Lortie, D. C. (1975). *School teacher: A sociological study.* Chicago: University of Chicago Press.

Lyte, V. J. & Thompson, I. G. (1990). The diary as a formative teaching and learning aid incorporating means of evaluation and renegotiation of clinical learning objectives. *Nursing Education Today, 10*(3), 228–232.

MacDonald, P. J. & Bass, M. J. (1983). Characteristics of highly rated family practice preceptors. *Journal of Medical Education, 58*(11), 882–893.

Mahan, J. M. & Shellenberger, S. (1983). Changes in students' perceptions of clinical teaching as a result of general practice clerkships. *Medical Education, 17*(3), 155–158.

Marikis, D. A., Russell, R. K., & Dell, D. M. (1985). Effects of supervisor experience level on planning and in-session verbal behavior. *Journal of Counseling Psychology, 32*, 410–416.

Marks, J. L. & Hixon, D. F. (1986). Training agency staff through peer group supervision. *Social Casework: The Journal of Contemporary Social Work, 87*(7), 418–423.

Marriott, A. (1991). The support, supervision and instruction of nurse learners in clinical areas: A literature review. *Nurse Education Today, 11*(4), 261–269.

Mathews, G. (1983). *Supervision in human sevices in Kent and Muskegon counties, Michigan.* Kalamazoo, MI: Western Michigan University.

Mazzuca, S. A., Vinicor, F., Einterz, R. M., Tierney, W. M., Norton, J. A., & Kalasinski, L. A. (1990). Effects of the clinical environment on physicians' response to postgraduate medical education. *American Education Research Journal, 27*(3), 473–488.

McClure, W. J. & Vriend, J. (1976). Training counselors using absentee-calling systems. *Canadian Counselor, 10*, 120–126.

McEwen, M. (1992). Community health nursing clinicals: An examination of the present and ideas for the future. *Journal of Nursing Education, 31*(5), 210–214.

McGaghie, W. C., Frey, J. J., Stritter, F. T., & Shahady, E. (1981). A multi-component program to increase family physicians' faculty skills. *Journal of Medical Education, 56*(10), 803–811.

McGrath, B. J. & Princeton, J. C. (1987). Evaluation of a clinical preceptor program for new graduates: Eight years later. *Journal of Continuing Education in Nursing, 18*(4), 133–136.

McNeill, B. W., Stoltenberg, C. D., & Pierce, R. A. (1985). Supervisees' perceptions of their development: A test of the counselor complexity model. *Journal of Counseling Psychology, 32*, 630–633.

Meleca, C. B., Schimpfhauser, F. T., Witteman, J. K., & Sachs, L. A. (1983). Clinical instruction in medicine: A national survey. *Journal of Medical Education, 58*(5), 395–403.

Melichercik, J. (1984). Social work supervision in transition: An exploration of current supervisory practice. *Social Worker Travailleur Social, 52*(3), 108–112.

Miller, M. D. (1982). Factorial validity of a clinical teaching scale. *Educational and Psychological Measurement, 42*(4), 1141–1147.

Mogan, J. & Knox, J. E. (1987). Characteristics of "best" and "worst" clinical teachers as perceived by university nursing faculty and students. *Journal of Advanced Nursing, 12*, 331–337.

Mumford, E., Schlesinger, H., Cuerdon, T., & Scully, J. (1987). Ratings of videotaped simulated patient interviews and four other methods of evaluating a psychiatry clerkship. *American Journal of Psychiatry, 144*(3), 316–322.

Munson, C. E. (1979a). Evaluation of male and female supervisors. *Social Work, 24*(2), 104–110.

Munson, C. E. (1979b). *Social work supervision: Classic statements and critical issues.* New York: Free Press.

Munson, C. E. (1980). Differential impact of structure and authority in supervision, *Arete. 6*(1), 3–15.

Munson, C. E. (1981). Style and structure in supervision. *Journal of Education for Social Work, 17*(1), 65–72.

Munson, C. E. (1983). *An introduction to clinical social work supervision.* New York: Haworth Press.

Nelson, J. C. (1973). *Early communication between field instructors and casework student.* Unpublished D.S.W. dissertation, School of Social Work, Columbia University.

Nelson, J. C. (1974). Relationship communication in early fieldwork conferences. *Social Casework, 55*, 237–243.

O'Donohue, W. J. & Wergin, J. F. (1978). Evalution of medical students during a clinical clerkship in internal medicine. *Journal of Medical Education, 53*(1), 55–58.

Oermann, M. H. & Navin, M. A. (1991). Effect of extern experiences on clinical competence of graduate nurses. *Nursing Connections, 4*(4), 31–38.

Orchard, C. (1991). Factors that interfere with clinical judgments of students' performance. *Journal of Nursing Education, 31*(7), 309–313.

Parenti, C. M. & Harris, I. (1991). Faculty members' ratings of the importance and the discriminating powers of nine aspects of students' clerkship performances. *Academic Medicine, 66*(9), 561.

Patel, V. L. & Dauphinee, W. D. (1985). The clinical learning environments in medicine, pediatrics, and surgery clerkships. *Medical Education, 19*(1), 54–60.

Patel, V. & Cranton, P. A. (1982, March). *An alternative study of transfer of learning in clinical evaluation.* Paper presented at the annual meeting of the American Educational Research Association, New York.

Patti, R. J. (1979). From direct service to administration: A study of social workers' transitions from clinical to management roles. *Administration in Social Work, 3*, 131–151.

Patti, R. J. (1983). *Social welfare administration: Managing social programs in a developmental context.* Englewood Cliffs, NJ: Prentice-Hall.

Paunonen, M. (1991). Changes initiated by a nursing supervision programme: An analysis based on log-linear models. *Journal of Advanced Nursing, 16*(8), 982–986.

Peirce, A. G. (1991). Preceptorial students' view of their clinical experience. *Journal of Nursing Education, 30*(6), 244–250.

Panel on the General Professional Education of the Physician. (1984). Physicians for the twenty-first century. *Journal of Medical Education, 59*(11, Pt. 2), 1–208.

Poertner, J. & Rapp, C. A. (1983). What is social work supervision? *Journal of Clinical Supervision, 1*, 53–67.

Powers, L. R. & Draeger, S. K. (1992). Using workshops to teach residents primary care procedures. *Academic Medicine, 67*(11), 743–745.

Pugh, E. J. (1988). Soliciting student nurse input to improve clinical teaching. *Nurse Educator, 13*(5), 28–33.

Rabinowitz, F. E., Heppner, P. P., & Roehlke, H. J. (1986). Descriptive study of process and outcome variables in supervision over time. *Journal of Counseling Psychology, 33*, 292–300.

Regan, S. & Martha, G. (1987). Teaching clinical reasoning in a clinical clerkship by use of case assessments. *Journal of Medical Education, 62*(1), 60–63.

Reising, G. & Daniels, M. H. (1983). A study of Hogan's model of counselor development and supervision. *Journal of Counseling Psychology, 30*, 235–244.

Revicki, D. A. & May, H. J. (1989). Organizational characteristics, occupational stress, and mental health in nurses. *Behavioral Medicine, 15*(1), 30–36.

Rittman, M. R. (1992). Preceptor development programs: An interpretive approach. *Journal of Nursing Education, 31*(8), 367–370.

Rogers, J. C., Swee, D. E., & Ullian, J. A. (1991). Teaching medical decision-making and students' clinical problem solving skills. *Medical Teaching, 13*(2), 157–164.

Rosenblum, N. D., Platt, O., Wetzel, M., & Rosenthal, R. (1992). Effect of context on the rating of students by faculty and house staff in a clinical clerkship. *Academic Medicine, 67*(7), 485.

Rosenlieb, C. O. (1991). *Preceptorships in baccalaureate nursing programs for registered nurses.* Unpublished doctoral dissertation, University of Pittsburgh.

Schamroth, A. J. & Haines, A. P. (1992). Student assessment of clinical experience in general surgery. *Medical Teacher, 14*(4), 355–362.

Scheidt, P. C., Lazoritz, S., Ebbeling, W. L, Figelman, A. R., Moessner, H. F., & Singer, J. E. (1986). Evaluation of a system providing feedback to students on videotaped patient encounters. *Journal of Medical Education, 61*(6), 585–590.

Schmidt, H. G., Van Der Arend, A., Moust, J. H., Kokx, I., & Boon, L. (1993). Influence of tutors' subject-matter expertise on student effort and achievement in problem-based learning. *Academic Medicine, 68*(10), 784–791.

Schnabl, G. K., Hassard, R. H., & Kopelow, M. L. (1991). The assessment of interpersonal skills using standardized patients. *Academic Medicine, 66*(9, Supp.), S34–S36.

Schwartz, R. W., Donnelly, M. B., Nash, P. P., & Young, B. (1992). Developing students' cognitive skills in a problem-based surgery clerkship. *Academic Medicine, 67*(10), 694–696.

Schwenk, T. L. & Whitman, N. A. *Residents as teachers: A guide to educational practice.* Salt Lake City, UT: University of Utah School of Medicine, Department of Family and Community Medicine.

Scott, D. (1990). Practice wisdom: The neglected source of practice research. *Social Work, 35*(6), 564–568.

Scott, W. (1965). Reactions to supervision in a heteronomous organization. *Administrative Science Quarterly, 10,* 65–68.

Shellenberger, S. & Mahan, J. M. (1982). A factor analytic study of teaching in off-campus general practice clerkships. *Medical Education, 16*(3), 151–155.

Simek-Downing, D. L., Quirk, M. E., & Letendre, A. J. (1986). Simulated versus actual patients in teaching medical interviewing. *Family Medicine, 18*(6), 358–360.

Simpson, D. E., Dalgaard, K. A., & O'Brien, D. K. (1986). Student and faculty assumptions about the nature of uncertainty in medicine and medical education. *Journal of Family Practice, 23*(5), 468–472.

Skeff, K. M., Campbell, M., & Stratos, G. (1985). Process and product in clinical teaching: A correlational study. *Proceedings of the Annual Conference on Research in Medical Education, 24,* 25–30.

Spira, L. (1986). M.S.W.'s speak: Experiences in agency and private supervision. *Clinical Social Work Journal, 14*(1), 79–91.

Stoltenberg, C. (1981). Approaching supervision from a developmental perspective: The counselor complexity model. *Journal of Counseling Psychology, 28*(1), 59–65.

Stone, G. L. (1980). Effects of experience on supervisor planning. *Journal of Counseling Psychology, 27*(1), 84–88.

Stritter, F. T. & Hain, J. H. (1977). A workshop in clinical teaching. *Journal of Medical Education, 52*(2), 155–157.

Stritter, F. T., Baker, R. M., & McGaghie, W. C. (1983). Congruence between residents' and clinical instructors' perceptions of teaching in outpatient care centres. *Medical Education, 17*(6), 385–389.

Stritter, F. T., Kappelman, M. M., Irby, D. M., & Skeff, K. M. (1983). Symposium: The study and improvement of clinical instruction. *Proceedings of the Annual Conference on Research in Medical Education, 22,* 262–269.

Stuart, M. R., Orzano, A. J., & Eidus, R. (1980). Preceptor development in residency training through a faculty facilitator. *Journal of Family Practice, 11*(4), 591–595.

Talbert, L. M., Stritter, F. T., & Riddle, M. H. (1981). A clinical clerkship in a multicenter setting: An appraisal. *Journal of Reproductive Medicine, 26*(8), 421–424.

Taylor, C. A., Dunn, T. G., & Lipsky, M. S. (1991). Time spent by preceptors on specific educational activities in inpatient and ambulatory-care settings. *Academic Medicine, 66*(2), 121.

Taylor, D. E. (1989). *Preparing nurses to practice in contemporary health care systems: An analysis of the instructional and supervisory practices as perceived by nursing faculty teaching in clinical settings.* Unpublished doctoral dissertation, University of Maryland at College Park.

Templeton, B. B., Kerr, R. M., Tripp, J. N., Smith, M. U., & Couch, K. W. (1988). The training and use of nonmedical observers to evaluate the clinical skills of medical students. *Journal of Medical Education, 63*(8), 652–654.

Tentoni, S. C. & Robb, G. P. (1977). Improving the counseling practicum through immediate radio feedback. *College Student Journal, 12,* 279–283.

Usher, C. H. & Borders, L. D. (1993). Practicing counselors' preferences for supervisory style: Supervision emphasis. *Counselor Education and Supervision, 33*(2), 66–79.

Valerio, N. M. (1992, April). *Medical residents' beliefs and actions: Implications for clinical teaching during work rounds.* Paper presented at the annual meeting of the American Educational Research Association. San Francisco, CA.

Van Hoozer, R. S., Albanese, M. A., Bratton, B. D., Croft, M. J., Gjerde, C. L., Ostmoe, P. M., & Weinholtz, D. (1987). *The teaching process: Theory and practice in nursing.* Norwalk, CT: Appleton-Century Crofts.

Van Rosendaal, G. M. & Jennett, P. A. (1992). Resistance to peer evaluation in an internal medicine residency. *Academic Medicine, 67*(1), 63.

Vinokur-Kaplan, D. & Hartman, A. (1986). A national profile of child welfare workers and supervisors. *Child Welfare, 65*(4), 323–335.

Walter, L. L., Zweig, S. C., & Hosokawa, M. C. (1991). A process evaluation of a required primary care clerkship. *Family Medicine, 23*(7), 547–548.

Welborn, B. P. (1991). *Influence of precepted experience on professional role orientation of nursing students.* Unpublished doctoral dissertation, University of North Carolina at Chapel Hill.

West, S. D., Bubenzer, D. L., Cantrell, R. P., & Arnold, M. S. (1992). Using the phone-in procedure: Supervision of supervisees. *The Clinical Supervisor, 10*(2), 185–193.

Westra, R. J. & Graziano, M. J. (1992). Preceptors: A comparison of their perceived needs before and after the preceptor experience. *Journal of Continuing Education in Nursing, 23*(5), 212–215.

Wilkerson, L., Lesky, L., & Medio, F. J. (1986). The resident as teacher during work rounds. *Journal of Medical Education, 61*(10), 823–829.

Windsor, A. (1987). Nursing students' perceptions of clinical experience. *Journal of Nursing Education, 26*(4), 150–154.

Wolfe, M. L. & Sands, R. F. (1981, October). *A comparison of the performance of registered nurse students in flexible and traditional clinical courses.* Paper presented at the annual conference of the Evaluation Network, Austin, Texas.

Woodcock, G. D. (1967). A study of beginning supervision. *British Journal of Psychiatric Social Work, 9,* 66–74.

Wolverton, S. E. & Bosworth, M. F. (1985). A survey of resident perceptions of effective teaching behaviors. *Family Medicine, 17*(3), 106–108.

Woolliscroft, J. O., TenHaken, J., Smith, J., & Calhoun, J. G. (1993). Medical students' clinical self-assessments: Comparisons with external measures of performance and the students' self-assessments of overall performance and effort. *Academic Medicine, 68*(4), 285–294.

Worthington, E. L. (1984). Empirical investigation of supervision counselors as they gain experience. *Journal of Counseling Psychology, 3*(1), 63–75.

Worthington, E. L. & Stern, A. (1985). Effects of supervision and supervisee degree level and gender on the superviso-ry relationship. *Journal of Counseling Psychology, 26,* 64–73.

Yonge, O. & Trojan, L. (1992). The nursing performance of preceptored and non-preceptored baccalaureate nursing students. *Canadian Journal of Nursing Research, 24*(4), 61–74.

Part

• V •

LEVELS OF SUPERVISION

INTRODUCTION

Robert H. Anderson

UNIVERSITY OF SOUTH FLORIDA

In all occupations, there is a recognized need for two types of "supervisory" activity. One function, which is increasingly identified as more important, is to provide assistance to workers for the purpose of strengthening and expanding the quality of their work. The other has the additional intention of providing evaluative information while also seeking to enhance the well-being of the organization as well as the worker. Labels such as "helping" for the first function and "judging" for the second help to define the contribution that supervisors make. The authors of this volume place a far greater value on the helping function; it is almost an article of faith that under supportive conditions, nearly all reasonably qualified workers can achieve in an acceptable if not admirable way.

In this section, the authors examine several of the various settings or levels in which educational workers carry out their responsibilities. At each level, it becomes evident that the opportunities, challenges, and work cultures are unique. Therefore, different atmospheres of supervision exist within these levels. In this section, these atmospheres are examined in detail.

In the early chapters of this section, the authors examine the functions played by supervision within instructional environments—places where pupils or students are served directly by teachers and other professional personnel. Some educational workers—many of whom have had prior experience working directly with children and youth in the schools—are employed at central district offices, intermediates agencies, or state education departments. Three later

chapters examine the supervisory roles played in these noninstructional agencies.

EARLY CHILDHOOD EDUCATION

Sheerer and Bloom start the reader at the beginning of the learning spectrum: supervision in early childhood education. They point to the great diversity that can be found and mention that there is great variation in the standards for staff employment at this level, as well as in the types of preparation programs that exist.

Much of the chapter discusses the varied contexts of early childhood supervision as found in child care programs, family day care, nursery school and preschool, Head Start, prekindergarten, kindergarten, and the primary grades.

The authors describe their model for viewing supervision from a social systems perspective, noting that the titles and functions of supervisors are varied and that several different roles (executive director, program director, educational coordinator, and head teacher) are involved. They discuss the typical characteristics of supervisors and the education and training that they bring to their roles.

Another major section of the chapter looks at models of supervision and staff development and includes discussion of common threads within the models. A brief section follows on supervision in Denmark and Guyana. Afterwords, the authors offer some interesting suggestions for increasing research on supervision in early childhood education.

ELEMENTARY SCHOOLS

Areglado discusses supervision in elementary schools. He uses a recently completed national study of 90 principals as a lens to consider whether practice reflects established research and theory. This chapter acknowledges the importance of both supervision and school improvement and the relationship between them, but it also calls attention to numerous constraints to classroom supervision that elementary school principals face. These include inadequate knowledge, limited availability of time, the large size of schools, responsibility for professional and noncertified staff, and district-wide negotiated contracts that impose uniformity of process. Such constraints and competing job demands create a dilemma for principals who are dedicated to improving student, teacher, and school performance.

Almost all the principals studied use a simplified three-stage version of clinical supervision—preconference, classroom observation, and postobservation conference. While some might be heartened by of the prevalence of even this limited application of clinical supervision, Areglado points out that the complex richness of the original models proposed by Goldhammer and Cogan has been lost. Most elementary principals rely on data-gathering systems that are used district-wide and involve "some form of numerical or letter-coded scale." Also, very few principals use audio or videotape or other technology to aid in recording data. A preponderance of elementary principals consistently employ a collaborative approach when conferencing with teachers, without regard for teachers' developmental needs, even though these principals express an appreciation for instruction that allows for student differences. Areglado reports that most principals fail to differentiate between formative and summative evaluation processes. The result is that, despite good intentions of principals, many teachers continue to view supervision as unimportant and irrelevant to their professional growth.

Areglado also notes that principals themselves receive little supervisory support from superintendents and few ask for assistance from mentors or networks of colleagues. He concludes that the problems of supervision in schools are systemic in nature and proposes a series of recommendations for improving the preparation of principals and policies that can make successful and meaningful supervision a more common reality.

MIDDLE SCHOOLS

Toepfer examines the role played by supervision in middle schools, where supervisory practices differ from the traditional supervisory approaches used in elementary and secondary schools. Noting that the concept of the middle school and the implementation of collective negotiations coincided historically, he suggests that this became a positive factor as there emerged a supportive and interactive relationship between supervisory and instructional personnel.

Toepfer discusses the contribution that middle schools can make to vertical program continuity and presents in historical perspective the gradual shift away from "junior editions" of senior high schools toward more developmentally responsive schools for the young people whom Eichhorn described as transescents. These schools tended to value collaborative instructional and staffing approaches along with interdisciplinary teaching strategies, and somewhat differentiated modes of supervisory support were needed. He traces the need for team teaching and supervisory support, and notes that supervision in teaming arrangements had to depart from traditional line/staff direct observations procedures.

Toepfer's comments about the problem of establishing trust and the desirability of colleagueship and peer coaching arrangements are of great interest, as is the section describing how instructional improvement needs have changed in the direction of coordinated, cooperative effort.

Toepfer takes a critical view of "restructuring", which he sees as a form of cutting and pasting, and urges that revisioning or reconceptualizing are more appropriate, along with developing new supervisory approaches to meet new program goals. These approaches must reject many old assumptions and practices and be more flexibly suited to the many uniquenesses in middle school situations. The three illustrative situations that he presents in detail are of particular interest and value.

Collaborative learning arrangements call for supervisory services of a different nature from those geared to the isolated-teacher pattern. Toepfer pays detailed attention to the challenges involved. He notes that supervisory practices specific to the needs of teamed teachers have largely failed to emerge and reports some of the examples and commentaries that are now available, including those about peer coaching. He then presents two situations that feature innovative and effective instructional improvement: one from a middle school in Naples, Florida and one from Dallastown, Pennsylvania. This is followed by a particularly insightful analysis that concludes with the hope that new paradigms will be developed that will respond effectively to the new demands for improved supervisory support.

SECONDARY SCHOOLS

Aiken and Tanner offer an in-depth look at supervision in the secondary school through an extensive and comprehensive historical review of the literature. They begin with a brief critique of general research in the supervision field and define a duality in theory and practice between a "production efficiency" model and a "professional growth" model of supervision. They trace the roots of the former, with its view of the school as factory and the supervisor as manager, to the late nineteenth century, when educational administration and supervision first emerged. The latter appeared after World War I and has offered a counterpoint to the production efficiency model for many decades. Aiken and Tanner favor the professional growth model of supervision, which they consider to be closely linked to curriculum development.

The authors associate the origins of scientific management and its fixation on efficiency and economy with the rise of state authority and industrialization in the United States during the late nineteenth century. Scientific management was challenged by progressive reformers and the result was an alternative view of supervision as "democratic instructional leadership" that emphasized support of teachers and an experimental attitude toward instruction. This democratic impetus served to focus on the professionalization of supervision in the 1930s and 1940s. The evolution of this idea is documented by the authors in writings that span most of the twentieth century, continue through the increased federal involvement and civil rights movement of the 1950s and 1960s, and culminate in recent discussions about what appears to be an estrangement between supervision and curriculum as fields of study.

Curriculum leadership is the essence of supervision for Aiken and Tanner, and democratic problem solving grounded in the philosophy of progressive education is the process undergirding school success. In the final third of their chapter, contemporary issues affecting secondary schools—and all of education—are addressed in detail, including the implications of initiatives to nationalize education in the United States, the restructuring movement, changing teacher roles, competency-based education, differentiated staffing, clinical supervision, the supervisor as change agent, and collaborative problem solving. They conclude with a call for an integrated or interrelated approach to curriculum that requires collaboration among teachers from various academic areas to improve student learning in secondary schools. Their recommendation also unifies supervision and curriculum leadership and makes both more relevant to current debates about educational renewal at the secondary level.

DISTRICT CENTRAL OFFICES

Pajak, Adamson, and Rhoades open their chapter with historical information which, although focused on the central office, is in fact a broad and illuminating overview of the school district and how its organization, its services, and its ability to pursue new goals and purposes have evolved over time.

A portion follows that discusses applications of Mintzberg's ten categories of managerial behavior to supervisory work. In the next section, they report various research activities and analyses that bolster the view that successful supervisors function as transformational leaders who exercise moral influence by personally representing and advocating, as a core value, the benefit of instruction to students.

One section depicts supervisors as "backstage" or "behind the scenes" influencers of the official "onstage" work enacted by teachers, school administrators, and the school board. This is followed by a section that examines questions about supervisors as either generalists or content specialists. These authors would support the conclusions that these workers have different perspectives on their roles and that both types of supervisor make significant contributions.

The authors then tackle the question of how school restructuring might alter the roles and functions of central office supervisors as well as others. The stories they relate will doubtless stimulate much thought and discussion.

The most provocative section of the chapter, labeled "A Question of Balance," credits Fullan with proposing a systematic, symbiotic relationship between restructuring schools and school districts and examines the emerging body of literature that is illuminating that relationship. The chapter concludes with a well-crafted and informative summary and makes several excellent suggestions for further research.

INTERMEDIATE AGENCIES

Sherrod traces some of the early history of education that led to the creation of educational service agencies (ESAs), which, as she notes, exist as a structural layer between local school systems and the state agency. ESAs provide services that support instructional improvement, such as staff development and curriculum development, as well as individual consultative assistance to teachers. She notes, however, that there has been very limited research on ESAs, particularly vis-a-vis supervision. She, therefore, has chosen to expand her assignment in this handbook in order to explore the origins of ESAs, the purposes served by them, the three types of ESAs that have emerged, the legislative mandates behind ESAs, their mission, their governance, funding sources, characteristics, the services they provide, and evaluations that have been carried out.

A concluding portion examines the great need for additional research. It will be useful to doctoral students and others who are seeking important questions to investigate. A pervading theme of the chapter is that instructional supervision has been an integral component of ESAs since their inception, and this continues to be so, particularly in smaller school systems.

STATE EDUCATION DEPARTMENTS

In Chapter 29, on Supervision from State Education Departments, the Nielsens provide an inside look into effects by state departments of education to initiate, implement, and sustain systemic change. Beginning with a brief historical review of traditional organizational practices, which once dominated state education departments, the authors describe research as the new basis for systemic change in education. A background of general trends across the nation is established from the 1996 Status Report of State Systematic Education Improvements by the Council of Chief State School Officers. Against this background, the authors describe two decades of educational reform in South Carolina. Using South Carolina as a prototype, 22 separate initiatives involving leadership by the State Department of Education in conjunction with school districts and other agencies are described and their contributions in support of achievement of high academic standards are critiqued.

The Nielsens discuss the difficulties faced by staff members representing state education departments accustomed to a hierarchial structure with responsibilities to direct, regulate, and evaluate in shifting toward an organizational paradigm with expectations to lead, guide, and support reform initiated by local schools and districts. Supervision from state departments of education is examined in light of practices emerging to enhance these new leadership functions. The Nielsens contend that research needs in education call for the federal government to support program innovations by states and school districts, for state education departments to take an active role in research, and for the private sector to be involved in research efforts in various states.

HIGHER EDUCATION

Lewis addresses the topic of improving instruction in higher education. The chapter opens with the assertion that "staff development" is a better term than "supervision" when discussing the improvement of teaching and learning in higher education. The term "supervision" embraces instructional improvement, organizational development, and personal development.

The chapter looks first at the history of faculty development in higher education, then presents a overview of the structures and functions of several models, and, finally, examines the research on teaching and learning in higher education. Faculty development, once limited to the sabbatical leave (a Harvard invention in 1810), has been stimulated since about 1970 by changes in society that are symbolized by student protests and manifested in the economy by budgetary and related shortages. There has been only slow implementation of suggestions for supporting the personal and professional growth of faculty, although government and foundation support have played an important role.

Lewis notes the absence of required preparation in pedagogical theory and practice for college teachers, who are dubbed "pedagogical amateurs." As academic burnout and reduced budgetary support began to take their toll in the 1980s, a faculty development movement emerged. In the 1990s, cries for "accountability" added to the pressure for instituting faculty development programs, and these have been increasing steadily. The vitality of colleges and universities is enhanced by faculty development. As is exemplified in this chapter.

Lewis then looks at how faculty development programs are staffed, the characteristics of such programs (which differ quite widely), the stages through which each organization usually must pass, the factors that are involved in the process of improving teaching, and the various program models that can be found.

The chapter then presents charts and descriptions of four major structural variations. These include: (1) the campus-wide center; (2) the multi-campus cooperative program; (3) special purpose centers; and (4) development components of other academic programs.

Lewis discusses staff development in junior and community colleges, reviews research that has been done on teaching in higher education, and describes interventions being used to improve college teaching. The report of 24 strategies identified by Lucas for improving teaching effectiveness in a department will be of special interest to the reader.

Lewis urges more objective research into the effectiveness and attractiveness of various approaches to faculty development, and observes that recent and enormous advances in teaching, learning, and technology call for energetic effort on the part of faculty developers to help "bring each faculty up to speed."

SUPERVISION IN EARLY CHILDHOOD EDUCATION

Marilyn A. Sheerer

EAST CAROLINA UNIVERSITY

Paula Jorde Bloom

NATIONAL-LOUIS UNIVERSITY

INTRODUCTION

The diversity of the field of early childhood education is perhaps its most defining feature. Programs of different design, philosophy, and quality abound; indeed, there is no one prototype indicative of the norm. According to Spodek (1993), although there is a coherence to the field of early childhood education, programs vary by age (e.g., infant/toddler, school aged), by the characteristics of their clients (e.g., low and high income, special needs, ESL children), by purpose (e.g., half-day enrichment, full-day child care), by philosophy (e.g., Montessori, Head Start, High Scope), and by institutional sponsorship. States provide monies for public kindergarten; the federal government supports child care centers and Head Start; churches sponsor nursery school programs; private corporations provide on-site day care centers; parents support preschool cooperatives; public schools incorporate programs for 4-year-olds; and various agencies operate family day care homes. The variety and complexity are pronounced.

Prerequisite qualifications for professionals working in the varied settings are also quite diverse. Phillips (1994) explains this diversity by noting that " . . . two sets of standards for staff qualifications exist: regulatory standards and voluntary professional standards. And the regulatory requirements governing child care programs are inconsistent" (p. 215). Early childhood education professionals employed in the public school setting must meet state teacher licensure requirements, but, outside the public school arena, there is significant variation. Whitebook, Howes, and Phillips (1989) compiled the following data on personnel from 227 child care centers: 12 percent held bachelor's degrees or graduate degrees in a field related to early childhood education, 24 percent had at least one high school course in early child-

hood education, 7 percent had vocational training related to early childhood education, 19 percent had some related college education, and 38 percent had no education related to the field. Willer and her colleagues (1991) documented that, in 1990, 41 percent of teachers in centers had 16 or more years of education, although not necessarily in early childhood education.

An alternative route to increasing competency in early childhood education has been the Child Development Associate (CDA) System and Competency Standards (1992), which allows on-the-job access to professional training. This credential considers the context in which the child care worker is employed and uses a portfolio format to demonstrate competencies.

The largest professional organization, the National Association for the Education of Young Children (NAEYC), has worked to promote high-quality early childhood programs for young children from birth through age 8 by defining developmentally appropriate practices and standards for early childhood education professional preparation programs (NAEYC, 1994). The reality, however, is that programs that provide preparation and training for those working with young children are as disparate as the services themselves (Willer, 1994). Some emphasize educational and developmental theory and research, whereas others focus on practice and application. Programs in community colleges often stress working with younger children; and four-year degree programs tend to highlight the kindergarten through age 8 group. To add to the complexity, child care and early education services are often funded and regulated by separate agencies, a differentiation that creates a false dichotomy between care and education for young children.

An arm of NAEYC, the National Institute for Early Childhood Professional Development, has been working to articulate an agreement between 2- and 4-year colleges relative to the current differentiation between associate and bachelor's degrees. The Institute also continues to work on standards for the preparation of early childhood administrators and supervisors and standards for trainers.

A discussion of supervision in the early childhood field must take into consideration this remarkable diversity and complexity. Although staff needs are rather similar from program to program, staff supervision is affected by the sponsorship of the entity, the educational philosophy and goals, the available funding, and staff qualifications (Caruso & Fawcett, 1986). The following descriptions of program types and implications for supervision provide a framework for discussing the training of supervisors and for reviewing the relevant research.

THE VARIED CONTEXTS OF EARLY CHILDHOOD SUPERVISION

Child Care Programs

Although child care programs originated in the United States as a government-sponsored service for poor families, they have expanded over the past two decades to include families from all socioeconomic levels, due to the increased participation of women in the labor force. The term "child care" (also known as "day care") generally refers to programs that operate for extended hours, usually on a year-round basis, and offer services to children from infants to toddlers through school age, including special needs and bilingual children (Decker & Decker, 1992). Child care programs involve the education and care of children who are separated from their parents for all or part of the day. A key characteristic of these programs is the length of time children and staff spend together on a daily basis.

Within this context, staff are challenged to design flexible, developmentally appropriate activities for children which address their needs. Specific routines such as using the toilet and napping are important, as well as socialization and language development. Supervisors in these settings are presented with the challenge of guiding staff to meet the total needs of the child—cognitive, physical, social, and emotional. Because the prerequisite requirements for staff who work in these settings are often minimal, supervisors may find this challenge somewhat overwhelming. The entry-level early childhood education professional may have no background in developmental theory but may have extensive hands-on experience with very young children. Consequently, the supervisor has to provide on-the-job training to assist the caregiver in internalizing and implementing developmentally appropriate practices. Often it means helping the teacher or caregiver move away from the idea of "school" and structured teacher-oriented activities as an appropriate model for instruction. Moreover, because of funding inadequacies, staff turnover remains a significant problem (Bloom, 1992), and supervisors receive the full impact of this reality. They may invest time and energy into the training of a teacher or aide, only to have the individual leave the program after a short time.

A second challenge for the supervisor is finding time to meet with staff within the child care context. Because teachers work on staggered shifts due to the length of the day, it is difficult to find common down times (e.g., during nap) when the entire staff is on site. In addition, limited financial resources in child care do not usually allow for the provision of substitutes during meeting times. The supervisor in this setting is forced to be very creative in promoting staff cohesiveness and group decision-making.

Variations in the above patterns exist in particular child care programs, depending on their sponsorship. For example, corporate-sponsored child care generally enjoys expanded resources, particularly with respect to working conditions, staffing, and fringe benefits related to personnel. But in privately owned, government-funded, and franchised child care, financial restrictions can impact the ability of supervisors to carry out thoughtful, consistent practices. When funding is more adequate, for example, substitutes can be employed to cover while the entire teaching staff participates in a staff development activity.

Although infant/toddler programs often fall within the general category of child care, they can also be designed from different perspectives. For example, there are part-time programs for infants and their teen mothers to address parenting concerns, and there are infant/toddler stimulation programs for special needs children. Each setting requires a supervisor to perform a somewhat different role. Within the child care context, the supervisor assists the direct caregiver in integrating care and stimulation in a developmentally appropriate manner. In programs where parents are regularly involved, the supervisor may serve as a direct parent educator. Close, effective communication with parents is a must in all settings involving infants and toddlers, and the supervisor is often responsible for guiding staff in this programmatic area.

School-age care is a relatively new facet of the child care arena. Here again, the prerequisite qualifications for staff are minimal. Because the programs are usually quite small, supervisors often work alongside teachers for whom they are responsible (Caruso & Fawcett, 1986). Within a given school district, there may be a number of school buildings in which before- and after-school care is provided. The supervisor is faced with the challenge of finding ways to pull together these part-time employees for planning and staff development programs.

Family Day Care

Family day care usually refers to care given in the home of a nonrelative for up to twelve hours a day (Caruso, 1986). Infants and toddlers are more likely to be served in this setting, but preschool and elementary-school-aged children are also participants. Not all of the homes falling under this classification are licensed, because families frequently seek such care through private arrangements in immediate neighborhoods. In most states, the regulation of family day care programs falls under the auspices of the state social service agency (Decker & Decker, 1992).

Prerequisite qualifications for day care home providers are extremely low; overall, the providers tend to be less educated than their center-based counterparts (Eheart & Leavitt, 1986). The supervision/training system available to providers does not appear to be consistent or widespread. According to Young and Zigler (1986), family day care is the least regulated form of child care. Corsini, Wisensale, and Caruso (1988) view the United States as having a loosely supervised system of family day care.

In a more recent report, Galinsky et al (1994) confirm the variable quality of child care provided in home-based settings. Only 9 percent of the homes studied were rated as being of good quality, whereas 56 percent were adequate, and 35 percent were inadequate.

Supervision within the context of day care homes, therefore, can be challenging. Supervisors work with providers of varying ability and experience in physical environments that reflect a range of comfort and opportunity. There appears to be a need for individually designed training in these settings (Caruso & Fawcett, 1986).

Nursery School/Preschool

Nursery school is the term usually applied to half-day programs for 3- and 4-year-olds that focus on social and academic skills. They are often characterized by their alternate-day attendance options, with different teachers for the respective sessions, and they predominantly serve middle- and upper-class families (Decker & Decker, 1992). Nursery schools are privately owned for the most part or sponsored by churches and nonprofit social service agencies. The director usually teaches in addition to supervising, and parents often volunteer in the programs. Some of these preschool programs are very specialized in terms of their curriculum (e.g., Montessori); and the expectations of parents are sometimes very high with respect to academic preparation.

Supervision in these settings is highly informal. Directors usually work alongside their colleagues. Quite often, the teachers have degrees in a variety of disciplines, but not necessarily in early childhood education. Because of the part-time nature of the teachers' work, it is difficult for a supervisor to get the staff together for program planning. In addition, money is rarely allocated in these settings for in-service training or staff development.

The nursery school model has been adopted by many teacher-training colleges and universities that have established laboratory facilities. Many of these were initiated as part of the child-study movement of the early 1900s (Decker & Decker, 1992). Within these settings, the supervisor has the added challenge of assisting staff in meeting the training needs of student teachers as well as the developmental needs of young children.

Head Start

Head Start was initiated in 1965 by the federal government to address the needs of disadvantaged preschool children (Decker & Decker, 1992). It is administered by the Agency for Children and Youth of the Department of Health and Human Services, which awards grants to public agencies, private non-profit organizations, and some school systems.

The most common format for Head Start programs is the half-day preschool model, although in recent years the model has begun to expand to include full-day services. Essential components of the program are parent involvement; health, nutrition, and social services; and education, including curriculum, home-based, multicultural, special needs, child abuse, and infants and toddlers.

The Head Start Performance Standards define minimum performance expectations for all Head Start programs (v.s. Department of Health, Education, and Welfare, Office of Human Development, 1975). There is also a self-assessment system which identifies training needs, as well as a pool of consultants in each region of the United States to provide technical assistance to the individual programs.

Supervisors working within this system have the benefit of clearly defined guidelines for supervision and training. At the same time, their supervisory role may be more challenging because they are also expected to work with less educated parents as key players in the program's operation (Caruso & Fawcett, 1986). The low-income variable in Head Start programs also impacts the perspective and experiences of the staff and, consequently, has implications for supervision.

Prekindergarten, Kindergarten, and Primary Grades

Early childhood programs within the public school domain have expanded widely over the past 20 years. These programs include special at-risk programs for prekindergarten-aged children; half-day or full-day kindergartens for 5-year-olds; and the first through third grades of the regular elementary school. Although private entities such as a nursery school or parochial school may operate all of the above noted options, these program types are most prolific within the public school arena. Therefore, they abide by teacher certification requirements and are usually more formal and academically oriented.

Supervisors of prekindergarten, kindergarten, and primary school teachers in public schools are required to have certification as a principal or supervisor, and they are likely to have more narrowly defined roles than supervisors of preschool teachers in other settings (Caruso & Fawcett, 1986). Although public school supervisors have to meet very specific criteria in order to function in their roles, they often have no background in early childhood education. They may find it difficult, therefore, to implement some of the practices advocated by NAEYC in its *Developmentally Appropriate Practices for Primary Age Children* (Bredekamp, 1989). The Report of the ASCD Early Childhood Consortium (Day, 1992) summarizes survey data in which early childhood teachers state that principals frequently make administrative decisions that are counter to what early childhood educators believe is developmentally appropriate for young children. Other researchers have proposed that this situation may be caused in part by the different focus of the elementary school principal and superintendent. Caruso (1989) believes that these administrators are often more involved in evaluation outlined by collective bargaining agreements than in on-site supervisory practices which keep them in touch with the programmatic aspects of the early childhood classrooms.

In her study of young children with disabilities in five different school contexts, Capper (1990) found the same situation. In all the schools studied, principals were almost totally uninvolved in the early childhood program. Supervision of early childhood services at the building level is often delegated to other persons in the district.

SUPERVISION FROM A SOCIAL SYSTEMS PERSPECTIVE

Bloom, Sheerer, and Britz (1991) present a model for looking at the child care organization from a social systems perspective (Figure 23.1). This model underscores the importance of looking at supervision, one of the processes operating within a center, in light of other systemic variables.

Early childhood programs are generally classified according to their legal form of organization or by their source of funding (Decker & Decker, 1984). The legal governing structure relates to whether a program is for profit, nonprofit, public, or private. In various ways, the formal structure of a program determines its philosophy, physical structure, and policies and procedures. It becomes important, therefore, to look at supervision in early childhood education from a systemic perspective. A program whose mission statement does not address the professional development of staff as a priority will have very different supervisory goals and responsibilities than a program like Head Start, which has a defined set of training standards. For example, a supervisor in a Head Start program operated by a nonprofit social service agency has to abide by both the performance standards set by the government agency (external environment) and the more informal guidelines of the agency (culture and structure). On the other hand, the owner/director of a private, for-profit child care center has to adhere to only the minimum standards (structure) set by the licensing agency in that state. The type, frequency, and quality of the supervision experienced by the staff in these two different settings, as well as the supervisors' level of job satisfaction, are two specific outcomes which can be contrasted with respect to systemic variables.

Roles and Characteristics of Supervisors

The titles and functions of individuals who have supervisory responsibilities in early childhood are varied. Some of the more common designators are: director, educational coordinator, supervisor, head teacher, and mentor. Because they perform a variety of duties, supervisors often find it difficult to balance their varied assignments. For example, in a small center, the director may be the person responsible for supervision; in a larger program, a head teacher may supervise other teachers or aides. In either case, supervision is seldom the sole component of the work of these individuals (Caruso & Fawcett, 1986).

Many supervisors in early childhood programs enter their positions directly from classroom teaching. Caruso (1982) found that teachers have often been promoted to supervisory roles because of their excellent work with children. Other supervisors have come from special education backgrounds

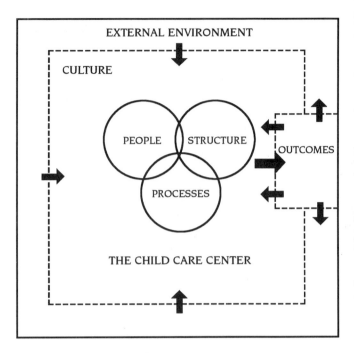

FIGURE 23.1. Child care centers as organizations: a social systems perspective

or the social studies field; while still others may hold only high school diplomas. Consequently, few of them have had specific training in supervision; rather, they tend to know and understand children and families. Although such knowledge is helpful, it does not provide the prerequisite knowledge and skills for guiding other adults in carrying out their responsibilities.

Supervisory Roles

Caruso (1991) provides descriptions of the primary responsibilities of the most common positions related to supervision:

Executive Director. The executive director is the chief administrator of a large child care agency that may comprise several social service programs, including health, nutrition, and education. Reporting to the board of directors, the executive director supervises program heads and, indirectly, other employees within the organization. Administrative and fiscal responsibilities are a major part of the executive director's role.

Program Director. A program director runs the day-to-day operation of a program. Some, such as Head Start directors, manage programs that are part of larger organizations or day care agencies that have an overall director. Other directors, such as those who manage small, private, or nonprofit independent child care centers, have more autonomy. Some program directors administrate more than one program; others also teach. Because program directors are on-site and work directly with staff, supervision is a major part of their job.

Educational Coordinator. Educational coordinators are responsible for the educational component of an agency or program. Working in the areas of supervision, staff development and training, and curriculum development, they strive toward the goal of ensuring that classrooms and staff function according to the program guidelines and for the greatest benefit to children in the program.

Head Teacher. Although head teachers primarily work with children, they usually oversee the functioning of one or more classrooms. Because of their qualifications, they supervise other teachers. Head teachers, in turn, may be supervised by the educational coordinator or the program director (pp. 20–21).

Other early childhood supervisors include: teachers who supervise assistants and aides; college faculty who supervise preservice teachers; child development associate trainers who may supervise classroom staff preparing to be assessed for the Child Development Associate (CDA) credential and outside consultants from resource centers or state agencies who sometimes work on-site with a program or with individual teachers.

Characteristics of Supervisors

Research on the background characteristics of early childhood supervisors is limited. Overall, findings show that supervisors are generally young, predominantly white, and female (Caruso, 1991). In his New England study, Caruso (1989) found that more than one-half of the supervisors were under age 40. In her study of 990 Illinois directors, Jorde-Bloom (1989) found a mean age of 40. Whitebook et al (1989) report that 21 percent of directors in their sample were under age 30.

With respect to the education and training of persons in supervisory roles, there is considerable diversity. Jorde-Bloom (1989) reported that 72 percent of the Illinois directors held bachelor's degrees, and 22 percent had obtained master's degrees. In their national sample, Whitebook et al (1989) found that 42 percent of directors in their sample had earned a bachelor's degree. Caruso's study of 10 states (1982) indicated that 62 percent of the 184 supervisors had earned bachelor's degrees. He also reports that 75 percent of the supervisors in his New England study (Caruso, 1989) held bachelor's degrees, most of which were in the field of education. In all the research cited, it has been found that there are supervisors with degrees outside of education, such as psychology, history, and social work. Caruso (1991) concludes that many individuals in supervisory positions come to their jobs with limited knowledge of group care for young children.

Child care directors are typically promoted to their positions from the ranks of teachers (Bloom, 1992). In Caruso's study (1989), the majority of those assuming supervisory roles from outside the early childhood education field began teaching in public schools. In a survey of New York directors, Norton and Abramowitz (1981) found that 78 percent of the directors in their sample had previously been head teachers or assistant directors. In an Illinois sample (Jorde-Bloom, 1989), 86 percent of the directors had classroom experience.

Experience as a supervisor is another important variable. Caruso (1982) found that 39 percent of the supervisors had four years or less of experience and 31 percent had nine years of experience or more. In his New England sample, Caruso (1989) found that 23 percent had four years or less of supervisory experience, 24 percent had four to nine years of experience, and 44 percent had been supervising for nine years or more. Several studies have shown that directors remain in their positions an average of five years. (Jorde-Bloom, 1989; Whitebook et al, 1989).

Most directors or supervisors seem to have put together a patchwork system of coursework, in-service professional development, and on-the-job training (Bloom, 1992). Directors with concentrated course work in child care management and supervision are rare. Fifty-six percent of the child care administrators in the Norton and Abramowitz (1981) study indicated that they had no courses or workshops in early childhood administration. In Jorde-Bloom's Illinois study (1989), 38 percent of the directors reported that they had not had a single course relating to the administration of educational programs prior to assuming their administrative roles.

Caruso and Fawcett (1986) summarize the picture related to the characteristics of early childhood supervisors as follows:

The multiplicity of supervisory roles; the variability of background, experience, education, and training among supervisors; and the necessity of fulfilling duties outside of supervision are in a very real sense indicators of the evolving nature of early childhood education. As early childhood professionals upgrade their skills and strive to make the field more professional, job qualifications, titles, and responsibilities are likely to become more uniform (p. 27).

TRAINING AND SUPERVISION: THE CONNECTION TO QUALITY

There is a clear paucity of research on the background characteristics of supervisors, their supervisory practices, and their level of training as these variables relate to program effectiveness in early childhood programs. Little systematic inquiry has been conducted on the role supervisors play in influencing the contextual factors that support or inhibit quality experiences for young children (Bloom, 1992).

In a study of 103 programs (Jorde-Bloom, 1989), directors' levels of formal education proved to be the strongest predictor of overall program quality as measured by compliance with accreditation criteria of the National Association for the Education of Young Children. The second most significant predictor was specialized training in early childhood education and program administration. Years of experience teaching or directing a child care center were not a significant predictor of overall program quality.

According to Jorde-Bloom's data, the majority of respondent directors indicated that skill in supervising staff should be required before an individual assumes the role of center director. Descriptive data from this sample indicated that directors averaged only six semester hours of coursework in early childhood administration, which may or may not have focused on supervision. Their strong feelings about the necessity of demonstrating competence in supervision prior to assuming a supervisory role in early childhood programs appears to be the result of their own experience in dealing with important supervisory issues.

In a more recent study, Bloom and Sheerer (1991) investigated the impact of training in the area of organizational theory, leadership, and program administration on program quality and organizational climate. Thirty-four Head Start directors, program coordinators, and teachers participated in a 16-month master's program. Effectiveness of the training model was assessed through feedback from the participants themselves regarding changes in their knowledge and skills; feedback from supervisors and colleagues attesting to changes in behavior or attitudes; and independent observations by an outside party looking at changes in actual on-the-job behavior. With respect to the participants' perceptions, the data indicated that the training program significantly impacted their perceived level of competence in the supervision knowledge and skill areas assessed.

Pre- and post-tests of organizational climate in 10 centers where participant directors held supervisory positions showed significant change in a positive direction. It appears that those areas that achieved the greatest degree of positive change were those in which the director (the participant in the training) had a great deal of control, including clarity in program procedures, opportunities for teachers' professional growth, and degree of decision-making influence given to teachers. One might conclude from these results that, as the directors became more sure and confident of their own supervisory ability, they were able to institute organizational practices that improved the quality of work life for their employees (Bloom & Sheerer, 1991).

MODELS OF SUPERVISION AND STAFF DEVELOPMENT IN EARLY CHILDHOOD

Research has shown that high-quality child care depends on well-oriented, trained, and supervised staff members (Whitebook, Howes & Phillips, 1989). Given the aforementioned level of educational preparation of many child care teachers and aides, the director or supervisor is called upon to provide on-site training and education as part of his or her supervisory responsibilities. Such training and education are, in essence, synonymous with the professional development of child care staff. As stated by Rodd (1994), "leaders of early childhood centers will assume greater responsibility for on-the-job training, development, and supervision of their staff" (p. 104). The literature reflects a variety of models which define the nature of supervision and staff development in the early childhood field.

Some writers have promoted the idea of the uniqueness of early childhood programs with respect to supervision and leadership. Phillips (1994), for example, discusses the idea of the lack of clear distinction among the roles of the adults in child care settings. She suggests that cooperative leadership and effective teaming are the essential skills for promoting quality. Rodd (1994) also speaks of a team model of supervision where the leader shares supervisory responsibility.

In their book, *Guide for On-Site Supervision*, Koralek, Colker, and Dodge (1993) present what they call a practical tool for trainers and supervisors in early childhood education. They provide a prescriptive framework to guide supervisory intervention and to insure high quality early childhood programming within each of five component areas. They detail the items, interactions, or approaches that should be present and offer concrete suggestions for what the supervisor should do to implement corrective actions. Their guide addresses the multiplicity of supervisory roles by covering center-based programs as well as family day care. The overall intent of the authors is stated in their introduction:

Trainers and supervisors need to work hand-in-hand with caregivers, teachers, and providers over time to make certain that plans, practices, and approaches are being implemented in ways that serve children well.

A somewhat different perspective is promoted in *Growing Teachers: Partnerships in Staff Development* (Jones, 1993). In this publication, Jones and other contributors present a supervisory model that stresses facilitation, not training, and underscores the importance of the supervisor in helping staff to become reflective practitioners. Taking a constructivist viewpoint, these writers describe staff development activities that are more open in design. Philosophy and practices are defined, but the outcomes are not. The facilitators, as supervisors, are independent of the system that employs the teachers, and thus are free to encourage teachers' thinking rather than evaluate their performance. Teachers' stories are used as the vehicles for empowerment and continual growth.

Newman, VanderVen, and Ward (1992) discuss supervision as a key element of employing older adults in child care. They emphasize that ongoing, supportive supervision by knowledgeable supervisors is especially important for older adults. Their model outlines individual, private, scheduled sessions between older adults and supervisors; group and peer supervision and coaching; mentoring programs; and informal supervisory contacts.

Caruso and Fawcett (1986) propose a developmental model of supervision, taking into account the supervisors' cognitive abilities, their level of professional development, and their stage in life. The supervisors' knowledge of self and their own developmental paths are also important in this model. Integrating the work of Fuller and Brown (1975), Glickman (1981), and Katz (1972), Caruso and Fawcett view supervision as a reciprocal process in which the supervisor and the teacher influence each other's behavior. Given the varied backgrounds of professionals in early childhood, their model allows supervisors to work closely with staff members and foster their development as adult learners.

A comprehensive model of developmental supervision is presented by Bloom, Sheerer, and Britz (1991), along with concrete strategies and approaches for implementing the model. These authors promote an individualized model of staff development, in which the supervisor works to facilitate the movement of the child care employee to the next stage of professional competence. Table 23–1 presents a framework for differentiating supervision and professional development by accommodating individuals at different stages in their careers. For each career development stage, a supervisory style, corresponding staff development goals, strategies, and content areas are suggested. The emphasis is on the "match" between developmental level and the selected supervisory behavior.

Rodd (1994) also views supervision as a form of continuing staff development in which staff competence is the overriding objective. She states that "supervision is no longer con-

Table 23–1. A Model of Staff Development

Career Development Stage	Supervisory Style	Goals of Staff Development	Staff Development Strategies	Content Areas of Staff Development
Survival	Directive	Help develop specific competencies in the classroom and realistic expectations for measuring success and progress. Increase perceived level of competence and effectiveness.	• modeling/guidance • direct coaching • on-site workshops • college classes • support and encouragement • articles and books to read selected by director, mentor • hands-on activities	• instruction methods in art, music, science, math, language arts, drama, etc. • child development • nutritional practices • health and safety • arrangement of physical environment
Consolidation	Directive	Help individuals apply what they have learned about children to new situations. Help them begin to analyze belief system and effectiveness of different instructional strategies.	• released time to visit other centers • conferences and workshops • college classes • feedback from videotaped segments of instruction • self-selected books, articles • peer observation, coaching	• multiculturalism • parent relations • child observation and assessment techniques • children with special needs • children's learning styles • childhood stress
Renewal	Directive, collaborative	Help individuals sustain enthusiasm about work. Help them explore their many interests and find ways to generate more challenging responsibilities.	• in-depth institutes • collegial support groups • sharing ideas with new staff • involvement in development of new curricular materials • visit other centers • expanded role in local professional organizations	• time management • stress management • child advocacy • cross cultural child rearing • adult learning styles • conflict management • curriculum innovations (e.g., computers)
Maturity	Nondirective	Provide opportunities for them to expand their expertise in related areas. Help individuals broaden their sphere of responsibility for the training and supervision of others.	• classroom research • presentation at conferences • leadership role in professional organizations • in-depth institutes, seminars • involvement in development of new curriculum policies • mentoring others	• program administration • budget/finance • grantsmanship • program evaluation • group dynamics • supervision techniques • public speaking and presentation skills • legal issues, social policy

sidered to be the sole responsibility of one individual, that is, the leader, but more appropriately is regarded as a two-way process between leader and staff member" (p. 105). Rodd advocates a team model of supervision, with peer observation and emphasis on adult learning styles. She also provides a developmental focus by noting, "Effective supervisors will match the model of supervision to the needs and the stage of professional development of the team members" (p. 106).

Wilmshurst (1984) described a training model specifically designed for Head Start which establishes the following goals for child development supervisors employed by the Los Angeles County Head Start Program: increased ability and desire to train staff, increased knowledge of workshop subject matter, and increased commitment to the supervisor role. The focus of the model is to provide training on the use of a variety of supervisory techniques, which can enhance the supervisor's skill in providing day-to-day support and feedback to teachers. Other areas covered are communication and conflict management. As a model, this approach embodies many of the same elements as clinical supervision.

Borrowing a concept from the Reggio Emilia program of early childhood education, in which the "pedagogista" functions as a resource person for the teachers, Carter and Curtis (1994) propose the "supervisor as coach model." Under this framework, "real professional development occurs as a result of teachers setting goals for themselves and getting the support they need to translate theory into practice" (p. 161). Supervisors then help teachers to select their own goals and push teachers to observe, reflect, and practice new skills. There is also an emphasis on individual development and uniqueness. Overall, this model is constructivist in its philosophical orientation and design.

Further delineation of the role of the Head Start education coordinator as a supervisor is provided in *A Guide for Education Coordinators* (1986). The supervisory functions outlined in this model emphasize observations of teachers, home visitations, adherence to performance standards for teachers and classrooms, and motivation as a supervisory variable. This document serves as the established framework for providing supervision in most Head Start programs.

COMMON THREADS WITHIN EARLY CHILDHOOD SUPERVISORY MODELS

Although there are numerous supervisory philosophies and approaches proposed for early childhood programs, there are also some threads of commonality among them. First, there is an emphasis on the individual employee and his or her developmental level. This emphasis may be the direct outgrowth of the developmental model advocated for children in child care programs.

A second common theme seems to be the idea of the supervisor as a close participant in the supervisory process. Rather than a hierarchical model, the proposed models are more collaborative and designed to empower the teacher. *Teamwork* is the term frequently used in supervisory discussions; and there is a frequent reference made to open communication. Supervision in most early childhood programs is a more informal process, largely because of the close proximity of director or supervisor and staff.

The supervisor's modeling of effective teaching and caregiving behavior is another common element because of the great variability of the experience and education levels of caregivers (Caruso, 1989). The incorporation of both supervision and evaluation into the director's or supervisor's role is another reality in early childhood programs, particularly those outside the public school arena. Ideally, the functions of supervision and evaluation are best implemented when kept separate. The fact remains, however, that most early childhood supervisors have to do both at least some of the time (Champagne & Hogan, 1981). This situation tends to compound the challenge for early childhood supervisors, due to the aforementioned informality of the relationships in most programs.

CROSS-CULTURAL RESEARCH ON SUPERVISION

Several studies have been conducted on the topic of supervision in early childhood programs in other countries, with the intention of contrasting them with models in the United States. Corsini (1988), for example, looked at family day care in Denmark and focused on the importance of a supervisory framework for insuring quality day care practices. He underscores the importance of a clearly defined training program for family day care supervisors. In addition to a three-year course of study that focuses on theoretical and practical issues associated with young children and their care, supervisors received ongoing in-service training. The supervisors then delivered training to the day care providers and were available to them for two hours each morning by phone. The caseloads did not exceed 50 children; the supervisors were available to parents for meetings and discussions; and the supervisors visited the day care homes twice a month. Corsini concludes that, in contrast to the Denmark model, the United States does not have a supervised system of family day care. He cited the lack of support from the government and regulatory agencies as the primary reason.

O'Toole (1990) reviewed a program for disabled young children in Guyana which emphasized the training of local supervisors from the community. This supervisory model included a physiotherapist and educational psychologist as intermediate supervisors, a 15-month training course through adult education, ongoing in-service programs, and local control and involvement. According to O'Toole, the goal of the program was to promote confidence in the local, community-based supervisor and to develop the family's respect for the local supervisor. The intermediate supervisor deliberately avoids taking over the responsibility for the child from the local supervisor and the family. In contrast, the United States models of early intervention have more typically employed specialists and "experts" to work with special needs children.

IMPLICATIONS FOR FUTURE RESEARCH

Research on supervision within the context of early childhood is scarce. Due to the identified diversity of programs and models, we do not have a clear idea what level of training, experience, and education are necessary to administer and/or supervise a program effectively. According to Caruso (1991), the field needs more research reflecting comprehensive descriptions of supervisors. Most of the existing research is regional and uses small sample populations. Such descriptions need to focus on a variety of variables, including personality, administrative or supervisory style, developmental level, cognitive abilities, and dispositions. The field would benefit from "supervisor stories," presented in much the same vein as the teacher stories that have been generated over the past decade, as well as particular descriptive data. Such interpretive cases might illuminate particular approaches and strategies and their connection to supervisory effectiveness.

Second, there is a need for research on the relationship between background characteristics of supervisors and supervisory practices and how this relationship affects program quality. As the profession expands its Center Accreditation to encompass more early childhood programs, it would be beneficial if data were collected on supervisors in these programs for further analyses. If we postulate that the director or supervisor is really the "gatekeeper to quality" (Jorde-Bloom, 1992), we need the research data to substantiate the importance of this position more clearly.

Because the early childhood field is dominated by women, supervisory relationships most often entail women supervising women. As Caruso (1989a) points out, little is known about the implications of the female world of supervision because there is little research on this topic. Although increased attention is given to the supervisory and management role of women in business and industry, little is known about these same issues in early childhood education. Perhaps the emphasis women place on relationships, nurturing, and feelings comes into play within the supervisory context. Research in this area would most likely generate very interesting data.

Researchers of supervisory practices may also be interested in promoting the idea of the administrator or director as researcher, paralleling the action research role of teachers. Such research would generate more in-depth insight into the thinking and approaches used by early childhood supervisors in varied contexts. Just as Ayers's *To Teach: The Journey of a Teacher*

(1993) focuses on the somewhat mysterious processes involved in teaching and learning, the journey of a supervisor might unveil some of the processes inherent in the role of a supervisor.

The challenge in the early childhood field is to look with greater scrutiny at the role and effectiveness of individuals with supervisory responsibilities. Goodlad (1984), in his study of schooling across the United States, investigated the rela-

tionship of the principal to high-quality schools. We need to continue research of this same question as it pertains to the early childhood director or supervisor. Identification of those variables that impact quality in early childhood programs must be an integral part of this research. This research, in turn, must be part of the broader agenda for further professionalizing the early childhood field.

REFERENCES

Ayers, W. (1993). *To teach: The journey of a teacher*. New York: Teachers College Press.

Bloom, P. J. (1992a). Staffing issues in child care. In B. Spodek & O. Saracho (Ed.). *Issues in child care*. New York: Teachers College Press.

Bloom, P. J. (1992b, Spring). The child care center director. *Educational Horizons*, 138–145.

Bloom, P. J., Sheerer, M., & Britz, J. (1991). *Blueprint for action: Achieving center-based change through staff development*. Illinois: New Horizons.

Bloom, P. J., Sheerer, M., Richard, N., & Britz, J. (1991). *The Head Start leadership training program*. Final report to the Department of Health and Human Services. Illinois: National-Louis University.

Bredekamp, S. (1989). *Developmentally appropriate practices for primary age children*. Washington, D.C.: National Association for the Education of Young Children.

Capper, C. (1990). Exploring community influences on leadership and reform: A micro-level and macro-level analysis of poverty and culture. ED 320379.

Carter, M. & Curtis, D. (1994). *Training teachers: A harvest of theory and practice*. MN: Redleaf Press.

Caruso, J. (1982, April). Characteristics of 184 early childhood supervisors and their settings. Paper presented at the Rhode Island Early Childhood Conference, Providence, RI.

Caruso, J. (1989a). *Early childhood, elementary, and secondary supervisors and supervision: A description and comparison*. Paper presented at the fall meeting of the Council of Professors of Instructional Supervision, University Park, PA.

Caruso, J. (1989b). *New England day care supervisors*. Unpublished manuscript.

Caruso, J. (1991, September). Supervisors in early childhood programs: An emerging profile. *Young Children, 46*(6), 20–26.

Caruso, J. & Fawcett, M. T. (1986). *Supervision in early childhood education*. New York: Teachers College Press.

Champagne, D. & Hogan, R. (1981). *Consultant supervision: Theory and skill development*. IL: CH Publications.

Child development associate assessment system and competency standards: Preschool caregivers (1992). Washington, D.C.: Council for Early Childhood Professional Recognition.

Corsini, D. (1988). Family day care in Denmark: A model to be emulated. ED 331620.

Corsini, D., Wisensale, S., & Caruso, G. (1988). Family day care: System issues and regulatory models. *Young Children, 43*, 17–23.

Creative Associates (1986). A guide for education coordinators in Head Start: Resource papers. Washington, D.C: Author.

Day, B. (1992). The education and care of young children. Report of the ASCD Early Childhood Consortium. ED 348148.

Decker, C. & Decker, J. (1992). *Planning and administering early childhood programs*. Columbus, OH: Merrill.

Eheart, B. K. & Leavitt, R. L. (1986). Training day care home providers: Implications for policy and research. *Early Childhood Research Quarterly, 1*, 119–132.

Fuller, F. & Brown, O. (1975). Becoming a teacher. In K. Ryan (Ed.). *Teacher education: The 74th yearbook of the National Society for the Study of Education* (part 2, pp. 25–52). Chicago: University of Chicago Press.

Galinsky, E., Howes, C., Kontos, S., & Shinn, M. (1994). *The study of children in family child care and relative care: Highlights of findings*. New York: Families and Work Institute.

Glickman, C. (1981). *Developmental supervision: Alternative practices for helping teachers*. Alexandria, VA: ASCD.

Goodlad, J. (1984). *A place called school*. New York: McGraw-Hill.

Jorde-Bloom, P. (1989). *The Illinois directors study*. Evanston: Illinois Dept. of Children and Family Services.

Katz, L. (1972, October). Developmental stages of preschool teachers. *Elementary School Journal, 73*, 50–54.

Koralek, D., Colker, L., & Dodge, D. (1993). *The what, why, and how of high-quality early childhood education: A guide for on-site supervision*. Washington, D.C.: National Association for the Education of Young Children.

National Association for the Education of Young Children. (1994). NAEYC position statement: A conceptual framework for early childhood professional development. *Young Children, 49*(3), 68–77.

Newman, S., VanderVen, K., & Ward, C. (1992). *Guidelines for the productive employment of older adults in child care*. Pittsburgh, PA: Generations Together.

Norton, M. & Abramowitz, S. (1981). Assessing the needs and problems of early childhood administrators/directors (ERIC Document Reproduction Service No. EB 2008963).

O'Toole, B. (1990). A community based rehabilitation project with disabled children in Guyana. ED 331244.

Phillips, C. B. (1994, November). The challenge of training and credentialing early childhood educators. *Phi Delta Kappen, 76*(3), 214–217.

Rodd, J. (1994). *Leadership in early childhood: The pathway to professionalism*. New York: Teachers College Press.

Spodek, B. (1993). *Handbook of research on the education of young children*. New York: Macmillan.

U.S. Department of Health, Education, and Welfare, Office of Human Development (1975). *Head Start performance standards*.

Whitebook, M., Howes, C., & Phillips, D. A. (1989). *Who cares? Child care teaches and the quality of care in America*. Final report of the National Child Care Staffing Study. Oakland, CA: Child Care Employee Project.

Willer, B. (1994). A conceptual framework for early childhood professional development. In J. Johnson & J. McCracken (Eds.). *The early childhood career lattice: Perspectives on professional devel-*

opment (pp. 4–23). Washington, D.C.: National Association for the Education of Young Children.

Willer, B., Hofferth, S., Kisker, E., Divine-Hawkins, P., Farguhar, E., & Glantz, F. (1991). *The demand and supply of child care in 1990.* Washington, D.C.: National Association for the Education of Young Children.

Wilmshurst, A. (1984). A program to improve teacher performance in head start classrooms based on a trainer of trainers approach. ED 257588.

Young, K. T. & Zigler, E. (1986). Infant and toddler day care: Regulations and policy implications. *American Journal of Orthopsychiatry, 53,* 43–55.

·24·

SUPERVISION IN ELEMENTARY SCHOOLS

Ronald J. Areglado

NATIONAL ASSOCIATION OF ELEMENTARY SCHOOL PRINCIPALS

INTRODUCTION

The relationship between supervision and school improvement has become an intense focus for both researchers and practitioners. The result is an appreciation of the importance of translating theory into practice in both higher education and the schools. Those of us who have witnessed and contributed to this evolution of supervision as a scholarly and serious endeavor should feel a sense of pride that supervision has become an essential element in both teacher and instructional improvement. But the rejoicing may be premature.

How is the vast and rich knowledge base of effective supervision finding its way into schools and into the ways that principals carry out this aspect of their work with teachers? How well are principals doing the job of supervision? Has the burgeoning interest in the topic transformed their thinking and reshaped their approaches to supervision? These questions are best answered by principals themselves.

In this chapter, 90 principals discuss their views on supervision and offer lessons that are sobering as well as inspirational. Their stories cast light on what theorists and practitioners must do to enhance supervisory practices in our schools.

Brian walked into his office at 3:35 P.M., closed the door behind him, and sank into his chair. I had been waiting 30 minutes to talk with him about the supervisory strategies he uses with his teachers. He explained that he had been detained, and he apologized for being late. I assured him that I more than understood. As a former elementary school principal, I know firsthand the frenetic schedule a principal deals with in the course of the day. When Brian had collected his thoughts, we began our discussion.

The conversation lasted about an hour. I thanked Brian for his time and left him to continue with his day. As I reflected on our visit, I was reminded of Arthur Blumberg's superb book, *Supervisors and Teachers: A Private Cold War* (1974), in which he explores the dynamics of supervisory practice.

His comments in one particular chapter, "The Problem Is in the System, Not the People," summarize what I was finding in schools across the country: "Supervision in the schools tends to be a ritualized, sterile process that bears little relationship to the learning of youngsters" (p. 5). Today, principals continue in large measure to engage in supervisory practices that contribute very little to more effective instruction and student achievement.

It is important to note at the outset that the problem rests primarily with the process of supervision, not the intentions of principals or teachers. It can be argued, however, that people define the system and that opportunities exist for people to redesign the system and make supervision a more meaningful process. There is no better time than the present to capitalize on a growing movement to have teachers assume more responsibility for school change and improved instruction (Lieberman, 1992).

From late 1994 through 1995, I interviewed 90 elementary school principals across the United States (see Tables 24–1 and 24–2).

The purpose of my investigation was confined to how supervisory practices are generally carried out in schools. I therefore chose not to gather or disaggregate the data I collected beyond what is found in Tables 24–1 and 24–2. (See the National Association of Elementary School Principals Ten Year Study [Doud, 1988] for a more comprehensive profile of principals in America's schools.)

Brian is representative of the principals in this study in terms of age, years as a principal, his school size, and the number of teachers he supervises. He is principal of a suburban school on the outskirts of a medium-sized Midwestern city. His school, Mark Twain Elementary, draws students from both rural and metropolitan areas. As was the case in all of my interviews with principals, the conversation with Brian focused on eight questions:

1. How often do you formally observe teachers each year?
2. What information-gathering instruments do you use?

TABLE 24–1. (School Size N=90)

School Location	Number of Schools	Average Student Population (Low/High)	Average Number of Teachers (FTE) (Low/High)
Urban/Metropolitan	23	576 (486/873)	49 (32/68)
Suburban	38	430 (370/639)	33 (24/37)
Rural	29	287 (143/375)	21 (18/34)
Composite		431	34.3

TABLE 24–2. (Personal Data N=90)

Principals by Gender	Average Age (Low/High)	Years as Principal (Low/High)
Male - 47	54 (33/64)	14 (3/27)
Female - 43	45 (31/66)	11 (3/28)
Composite	49.5	12.5

3. Is there a specific process that you use?
4. How do you differentiate between supervision and evaluation; do you use completely different techniques for each process?
5. Are you free to use alternative supervisory processes?
6. To what extent are you satisfied with your school's existing practice of supervision? Why?

   Scale: 1 = Very dissatisfied;
   2 = Dissatisfied;
   3 = Satisfied;
   4 = Very satisfied

7. What do you do to enhance your supervisory skills? How often?
8. Who supervises you? How often?

THE NUMBERS GAME: FREQUENCY OF FORMAL OBSERVATIONS

Brian quickly pointed out that he is the sole administrator in his school and that he is also responsible for the supervision and evaluation of 12 noncertified staff, such as cafeteria workers, maintenance staff, clerical workers, and both instructional and noninstructional aides. His duties are consistent with those of all but 14 principals I interviewed. For those 14, the task of total supervision is shared by individuals such as central office coordinators and administrative directors, who monitor subject specialists and special education staff. Eleven of the 90 principals have assistant principals and student populations in excess of 550 children. (Note: one school principal has over 720 students, a faculty of 55 teachers, and no assistant principal.)

Brian explained that the master contract negotiated by administration and faculty obligates him to formally supervise nontenured teachers five times a year. For tenured teachers, he is required to formally observe lessons no more than five times every three years. For all formal observations, he is required to complete a written summary, which is shared with the teacher, signed, copied, and placed in the teacher's personnel file. Eighty-three of the principals interviewed have similar administrative requirements delineated within their teachers' contracts.

Brian's observations last approximately one hour, exclusive of any pre- or postobservation conferences he might have with a teacher. He estimates that the entire cycle is completed in approximately three hours. We calculated that he devotes about 60 hours annually to formal supervision of Mark Twain's four nontenured staff members. He conducts formal observations of tenured faculty on an average of twice a year, with each cycle also lasting approximately three hours, for a total of 180 hours yearly.

In comparison with the other 76 principals, who have total responsibility for staff supervision, Brian spends more time with nontenured teachers than his colleagues and about the same time with experienced or tenured faculty. Interestingly, those with administrative assistance do not spend appreciably more time in formal observations of their teachers. It is important to note that out of approximately 1,080 hours in a school year, Brian is spending 240 hours (nearly 22 percent) of his time in formal supervision. The average time spent with each teacher ranges from a high of 15 hours (1.4 percent) to a low of 6 hours (.56 percent) annually.

Brian does a lot of informal observations of his staff, and it is evident that he knows a considerable amount about instructional practices in his school. We speculated that he is in every classroom several times a week, which adds another 30 minutes each day to the supervision process.

When similar analyses were done with Brian's colleagues, there was a range of responses. Carol, a veteran principal of a rural school, was surprised to learn that she doesn't spend more time in supervision. Sandy, a five-year principal of a suburban school, was relieved to learn that she devotes as much time to supervision as the data indicates. Michael, however, said that he wished he had more time to spend with his teachers; many principals echoed his statement. He added that he would like to spend more time with experienced teachers to provide them with more feedback on their teaching and to affirm their skills as competent teachers. Three principals stated frankly that the size of their schools prevented them from working intensively with their marginal teachers—those who are experienced, but in need of help with new instructional techniques and redress of mediocre teaching. The vast majority concurred that inordinate demands on their time, such as meetings, paperwork, and crisis management, are all factors that reduce the time for more ongoing and routine formal supervision.

Most principals feel that the supervisory requirements of their work are extremely beneficial and gratifying. They rate the importance as extremely high in terms of responsibility. However, 17 (nearly 19 percent) did not agree. Instead, they maintain that their teachers, as a result of experience or expertise, do not need regular supervision. As a result, they feel justified in spending their time on other aspects of the job, such as public relations, budgeting, trouble shooting, and administrative tasks.

IMPORTANT FACTORS IN HIGH ACHIEVING SCHOOLS

Smith and Andrews (1989) examined essential aspects of high performing schools and found that they are led by principals whose teachers see them as strong instructional leaders. Their study, conducted with elementary school principals in the Lake Washington School District in Kirkland, Washington, reveals that principals consider improvement of instruction to be their most important responsibility. Principals were first asked to indicate how much time they should spend on tasks such as instructional improvement and then to keep a log of the actual time they spent on these tasks over a two-week period. The ideal percentage of time to be spent on improvement of instruction was stated by the group as a whole to be 35 percent. The actual time logged was 24 percent. Brian's spends about 22 percent of his time in supervision and, when his informal time is combined with his formal time, he calculates the total to be approximately 31 percent. He is, therefore, closer than his colleagues in Washington to the "ideal" they cited. In fact, in comparison with his peers in this survey, he was on the high end of a range that extends from 17 percent to his own 31 percent.

Impressions

Time devoted to formal supervision is affected by the size of a principal's school, job requirements, and personal beliefs about the significance of supervision. In schools with administrative support for the principal, there appears to be no significant increase in formal supervision of staff. Principals who make supervision a priority tend to extend their work weeks beyond 50 hours and spend time on weekends catching up on "administrivia." All principals report increasing job demands and constraints such as teacher contracts and the adoption of shared decision-making processes have created additional areas for accountability and a corresponding decrease in time for staff supervision.

About 81 percent of the principals interviewed believe supervision is among the most important aspects of their work. It should be noted that the 19 percent who regard supervision as less important contradict the findings of research on instructional improvement. In either case, the stark reality is that traditional supervisory models place exclusive responsibility for supervision on the principal and thus limit opportunities to effectively monitor and assist staff. This raises serious questions about the feasibility of improving teacher performance and student achievement. Equally compelling are teachers' perceptions of their principals as instructional leaders. They view principals as strong leaders by the frequency of classroom observations and how visibly present they are throughout the school (Wing, 1987).

INFORMATION-GATHERING INSTRUMENTS

I asked Brian to show me the forms or data-gathering instruments he uses in formal observations of teachers. He explained that the forms were developed by a group of teachers and administrators who focused on rather perfunctory aspects of teaching methodology, such as lesson planning, goals and objectives, classroom management, and use of supplemental materials. For each section, there is a five-point rating scale with space for overall comments in each of six sections. Brian indicated he uses the forms primarily as talking points to promote dialogue. He acknowledged the procedures were developed by the district to create uniformity throughout the system, from kindergarten to twelfth grade. Although they serve that purpose well, he feels the process is too rigid and forces conformity. The district's previous, more varied process had been legally challenged when a teacher was recommended for dismissal. The hearing officer ruled in favor of the teacher, based on inconsistencies in the process. Following this event, the superintendent convened a task force to develop a uniform approach to data gathering.

In my interviews with other principals in the study, I learned that some have no formal instruments or forms for supervision, whereas others must follow systematic procedures similar to those used in Brian's district. A pattern seemed to emerge. In smaller schools or districts, there are more opportunities to use a variety of procedures. Of the 90 principals interviewed, 32 (36 percent) have the latitude to devise their own models. Anne, a rural principal with eight years of administrative experience, was specifically trained in observation techniques early in her career. She was previously a teacher for nine years. Anne believes her tenure in the classroom gives her keen insight into what to look for in supervising teachers. She has the freedom to create her own data gathering process, and it is apparent from the areas of emphasis on her forms that she and her staff understand both sophisticated pedagogy and methodology. It is the most comprehensive form that I reviewed.

Most principals who have the freedom to develop their own models were vague when asked how a comprehensive system might look, or they felt that limited time mitigated against creating such a system. In fact, in all but seven instances, the instruments that are being used were acquired from other school districts and modified to accommodate local circumstances. The seven principals who have created their own systems did so in collaboration with staff, using models from other districts and reviewing research on supervisory techniques and instructional practices. Those principals who felt bound by bureaucratic constraints considered the question moot.

Impressions

Approximately 82 (92 percent) of the principals interviewed use data-gathering systems that were either developed by their respective school districts or borrowed from other districts and modified to meet their needs. Only seven (8 percent) of the group have created their own systems. Sixty-six (73 percent) of the instruments have some form of numerical or letter-coded scale. Teachers ironically appear to be "graded" in the same manner as their students.

An examination of the forms revealed they focus on general categories of teacher behavior and do not appear to provide substantial insight into sound developmental practice. Those systems that were developed by teachers and principals seem more sophisticated, with an approach to instruction that includes current research on child development and methodology.

Only five principals use any form of technology such as audio- and videotape recorders or laptop computers when recording data. The other 85 principals use various forms of scripting on paper. Only six principals have had training in data collection using technologies such as Flanders Interactional Analysis or mapping. It appears the use of technology in the supervisory process is limited for most principals and should be considered a topic for future professional development.

TYPES OF SUPERVISORY PROCESSES USED WITH STAFF

Virtually all principals (88) use a modified clinical supervision model (Cogan, 1973; Golhammer, 1969), with preobservation conferences, observations, and postobservation conferences. Principals generally first meet with teachers to discuss the objectives of the lesson and teaching strategies that will be used. This conference is followed by the observation. The principal and teacher then meet to review the lesson, share comments, reconcile ratings where applicable, and perform administrative details, such as obtaining signatures and passing out forms to designated persons.

It is clearly evident that the clinical model has been seriously compromised. Not one principal in the study uses the eight phases in Cogan's model of clinical supervision. Not one, in fact, could recall each of the steps, and nearly all were surprised to learn that there were eight phases. When the 66 principals who use rating systems were told that such scales are antithetical to true clinical supervision, their comments echoed this statement from Brian: "Between what the system dictates and the limited time I have, I'm doing the best I can." It was hard to determine whether they were apologizing or lamenting their inability to undertake more comprehensive approaches to supervision.

Brian's comments underscore the tension that occurs between most teachers and principals in the supervisory process. Many teachers view supervision as something that must be done to satisfy the system's needs rather than the personal and/or professional needs of the teacher (Blumberg, 1980). I found Brian and his colleague's desire to help teachers improve their skills to be sincere, however. I concluded that they are doing the best they can, given the parameters of their situation.

The few principals like Anne who have developed a more comprehensive process of supervision also depart from Cogan's theoretical model of clinical supervision, citing limited time available to effectively complete all aspects of the cycle. I found in these instances that more discussion takes place about the lesson (phases 2 and 7), but in no instance did I find both principals and teachers engaged in actually planning the lesson collaboratively.

Although 98 percent of the principals use a preconference/observation/postconference model, they have varying approaches to the postconference segment in which findings are shared with teachers. Approximately 39 (43 percent) of the principals use elements of Developmental Supervision

(Glickman, 1985). Brian explained that he is more directive with his four nontenured staff. He points out the strengths and weaknesses in their lessons, and is more likely to direct them to other teachers or resources for help in improving their effectiveness. He is more collaborative with the rest of his staff, encouraging give and take in analysis of the lesson. He indicated that he is essentially nondirective with only two teachers. Both of them are truly gifted teachers, in his opinion, and need little or no direction from him.

Brian and I discussed his use of a collaborative style with the most of his teachers. I wanted to understand if they really are at a stage in their development that necessitates such an approach or if this is, in reality, a function of Brian's personal style. As a result of our conversation, Brian came to realize that he enjoys interactions with teachers on a variety of levels and that this work is the most meaningful to him. He remarked that helping staff and, ultimately, students succeed is "the essence of my work." Brian's comments speak for 78 (about 87 percent) of his colleagues, who find that they remember why they became educators when they can talk with staff about curriculum and instruction.

Most of the 51 principals (56 percent) who don't use a differentiated style are collaborative in nature and don't appear to make distinctions between the development and competence levels of their teachers. It appeared to be primarily a matter of leadership style. Only two principals appeared directive in their approach to analyzing lessons with their teachers. Tom, an experienced urban principal, says his staff wants to hear about his observations and interpretations of their lessons. As principal of the same school for nearly 18 years, he feels he knows his teachers extremely well and maintains that his approach to supervision meets the needs of his staff. He tended to resist taking a more introspective look at his style and its implications for other areas of dealing with staff.

Impressions

The overwhelming majority of principals interviewed were candid in their remarks about how they adjust various supervisory models to accommodate their needs. This supports research findings that teachers and supervisors don't always practice according to theory, but rather in response to realities they face and experiences they acquire (Sergiovanni & Starratt, 1993).

In addition, nearly all of the principals appear to reconnect with their personal motivations for becoming educators when they talk with faculty about teaching. It is apparent that they truly enjoy this part of their work, despite the procedural and time constraints. A statement from Maurice best expresses what I heard in extensive conversations with his colleagues: "I can justify just about any part of this demanding work when I am able to sit in on classes, interact with teachers and kids, and then talk about the craft of our profession with staff members. It's the most important and rewarding aspect of what I do."

Given the preponderance of principals who use a collaborative style with teachers, there appears to be a need for principals to develop a broader view of supervision. Such a view should include the premise that teachers represent diverse levels of development, knowledge, and skill, and that matching supervisory options to these differences is essential. Several developmental theorists such as Costa (1982) and Glickman (1985) have articulated how such matching can be achieved to meet individual needs and enhance the supervisory process.

SUPERVISION AND EVALUATION

Sergiovanni (1991) writes: "Evaluation is, and will remain, an integral part of the process of supervision, and the results cannot be ignored by principals and teachers" (p. 282). One of the most nettlesome aspects of the supervisory process is the tension caused by ambiguity when principals perform both supervision and evaluation and attempt to differentiate between the two. Supervision is often described as a formative process that helps teachers improve instruction (Cogan, 1973). The emphasis is on *helping*, not *judging* the performance of teachers. Information gathered about a teacher, however, may be used by administrators for rewarding, retaining, or terminating them (Barber, 1985). There is ample evidence in the literature to highlight the resulting contempt with which teachers regard evaluation (Blumberg, 1980).

I asked Brian how he addresses this problem with his staff. He shrugged and reminded me that the district's model is largely the result of teachers' union grievances adjudicated several years ago. He explained that his system makes no true distinction between supervision and evaluation. Although he uses a different form for summative evaluations, Brian admits he is influenced by, and has included in annual staff evaluations, incidents he has observed during his formal classroom visits.

He showed me both systems used in his school. The evaluation form was organized in the same overall manner as the form used for supervisory sessions. Data such as attendance, cooperation with parents, attention to administrator requests, and evidence of professional development were included to differentiate it from the supervisory form—and the form was even printed on a different color of paper. Brian conceded that he is uncomfortable with the duality of his role. He enjoys observing and working with teachers to improve their knowledge and skills, but he knows that the specter of evaluating performance complicates his efforts.

Earlier in my visit, Brian encouraged me to ask four members of his staff to share their overall perceptions of the supervisory practices at Mark Twain School. Their comments mirrored Brian's own discomfort with the process. They were quick to point out, however, that they trust Brian and value and respect his feedback. Evidently their professional relationship allows both parties to engage in meaningful conversation about improvement of instruction.

The collegial atmosphere in Brian's school is representative of most schools I visited. The 75 other principals with sole responsibility for supervision and evaluation all use different instruments, but only 11 (15 percent) have established different processes. Anne, mentioned earlier in this chapter, has the most thoughtful approach. She is principal of a rural school of 278 students in the Northeast and is responsible for overall supervision of 25 teachers and 13 noncertified staff.

Reflecting on her years as a teacher, Anne remembers how she watched her principal struggle with the paradox of supervisory (formative) and evaluative (summative) responsibilities. She says she decided to address this issue early in her tenure as a principal. She and her staff agreed they would always evaluate what they were doing in terms of program improvement and student achievement. The distinction would be in *how* one or the other was carried out and *what* was evaluated. The formative aspects of their work together emphasize ongoing ways to utilize insight from the teachers and the principal on how to improve instruction. No judgments or ratings are used. The summative component of their improvement model is established at the beginning of the school year and delineates *what* is to be evaluated at the conclusion of the year. Criteria, goals, and obstacles are identified, monitored regularly, and then evaluated in terms of attainment. Both models are in place and operating concurrently.

I asked Anne how information on a teacher's unsatisfactory performance would find its way into a summative evaluation and if such information would compromise the process or her relationship with staff. She described a situation where it had been necessary to recommend nonrenewal of a teacher to her superintendent. There had been serious deficiencies that surfaced in classroom observations. In the process of coaching the teacher, she recognized the need to develop a corrective plan for improvement. She explained to the teacher that issues warranted moving the mutually accepted plan into a summative mode. At the point she determined the teacher had not satisfied conditions of the plan, Anne had accumulated clear evidence to support nonrenewal. She says she realized at the time that formative and summative processes could not be separated. She and the staff consequently discussed the philosophical and ethical foundations of their improvement models. During my conversations with Anne and her staff, I was impressed to find that they have come to a deep understanding of what they believe about their work and their responsibilities for professional growth. Anne and her staff have created a remarkable supervision and evaluation system founded on qualities of mutual respect, integrity, and trust that are unrivaled in the other schools I visited.

Impressions

One could not help but be inspired by the thoughtfulness, sensitivity, and effectiveness of the work being done in Anne's school. I found none of her counterparts in this study to be as skillful or knowledgeable as she is in differentiating between supervision and evaluation. Approximately 83 of the principals (92 percent) are dealing with this issue in ways similar to Brian. Even those schools with curriculum supervisors or directors do not differ significantly in their approaches. Within this group, only 18 principals have really struggled with the dual roles of supervision and evaluation. The remaining 65 principals are moderately concerned with the matter. Three of the six principals not mentioned have developed reasonably satisfactory options, while the other three have not addressed the question. It is, therefore, not surprising that the "cold war" between teachers and principals continues, albeit with degrees of intensity. My findings in this area underscore an urgent need for further examination and extensive principal training.

ALTERNATIVE SUPERVISORY PROCESSES

Each of the principals interviewed in this study readily agreed on expectations for differentiated instruction to meet diverse needs and learning styles. Many spoke with conviction and eloquence about appropriate developmental approaches and conveyed strong philosophical and research bases for their beliefs. My classroom visits in a number of their schools provided evidence that their perceptions of how teachers structure lessons and deal with student differences are reasonably consistent.

In discussions of alternative approaches to supervision, however, 79 principals (about 88 percent) did not apply the same philosophy to their teachers. As indicated earlier, 39 (43 percent) use a developmental supervision approach with staff (Glickman, 1985), but mostly in terms of their "talk style." All of the principals understand the rationale for a differentiated system of supervision and realize that teachers are different and respond differently to various supervisory approaches (Glatthorn, 1984; Glickman, 1985). Yet only 11 (about 12 percent) actually use such a system.

Why is there such a striking dichotomy between their understanding of teacher differences and the reality of their practice? I found several reasons:

1. *Organizational constraints.* In many cases, issues such as negotiated contracts and policies limit a principal's supervisory options.
2. *Time.* Given the inordinate demands on both their teachers and themselves, many principals are unwilling to ask teachers to become more involved in alternative supervisory approaches.
3. *Knowledge.* Fourteen (almost 16 percent) of the principals admitted they are not knowledgeable about the range of possibilities for creating different strategies. They haven't been exposed to demonstration or model approaches, nor have they explored the literature.
4. *Cultural Norms.* I was not able to interview teachers extensively; however, I did talk with teachers in at least 20 schools. I learned that, in 17 of the schools, attitudes toward supervision range from enthusiastic to indifferent. Teachers feel their principals are sincere in their attempts to supervise, but contend they don't learn much from the supervision. The majority view the process as a chance for their principals to praise them for their teaching and to encourage them to keep up the good work. Others who have received minimal supervision have been told they don't need it because they are good teachers. A few teachers in two of the schools resent supervision. One of these teachers said that "the process trivializes what I do and demeans me as a professional when my hard work is reduced to some asinine checklist."

Teachers in three schools expressed high levels of approval for the supervisory process. They feel that their principals understand instruction, emphasize improved student performance as the purpose of supervision, actively involve them in the process, and treat them with professional and personal respect. Their needs for recognition and validation are being met. Despite differences in the demographic makeup of their schools (one is an urban school in the Northwest with a majority of ESL students; one is a suburban school in the Southwest; and one is a predominantly white rural school in the Northeast), they share common characteristics, such as clear and high expectations about learning for children and adults. Each principal, according to staff, is visibly present and in and out of classrooms regularly. A spirit of collegial support is evident. Teachers take responsibility for all children. Time, energy, and resources are dedicated to building a strong learning community. Teachers find supervision to be a positive experience characterized by lively and diverse approaches that are accepted as a natural part of the school's way of life (Sergiovanni, 1991). In Juan's school, a sign stating "Inquiry is encouraged in our school at all times," is permanently displayed. Anne's teachers reflect her regard for the import of teaching. One teacher described it as "a moral commitment to children and our future." He added, "we are constantly challenged to examine the how, what, and why of our teaching." An enthusiastic new teacher in Kathy's school remarked that every teacher is a resource, openly offering to help him. "They're dedicated to making sure I succeed," he said with a sense of pride and sincerity.

Juan, the passionate and dynamic principal of Willard School, explains a central quality of successful supervisory practice: "I encourage and expect teachers to appreciate and honor student differences. I have to model my beliefs with them if they are to believe the depth of my sincerity." Willard is an inner-city elementary school located in the Pacific Northwest. The student population of 560 represents 30 foreign languages. By my measure, however, student performance is impressive.

"Our approach to supervision is really simple," says Juan. "We do lots, and I mean *lots*, of informal supervision. Our purpose is very clear. We work hard to improve teaching and learning and everyone is held accountable for doing that!" Juan emphasized that teachers are accountable to each other and to him. In turn, he is accountable, not just to his superiors, but to the students, parents, and teachers.

I asked Juan about his supervisory approaches with his staff. His response was quite succinct: "What works." As he elaborated on the meaning of this phrase, it was evident that he has vast knowledge of the varied teaching styles of his teachers, their maturity as professionals, and their personality differences. He describes two fundamental approaches to working with staff. One is to ask questions and the second is to listen carefully. Based on what he learns, Juan and his teachers determine which models will help teachers improve their skills.

His staff relies heavily on alternative supervision models. For example, Juan has created a collegial supervisory model in which pairs or teams of teachers "contract" to assist one another for the school year. "I'm aware of what they're focusing on, but I don't get involved with the process," he says.

In another informal supervision arrangement, Juan makes brief and informal visits to a teacher's class. A script of his observation notes is given to the teacher, or he and the teacher may have a quick meeting. "We discuss their interactions in more detail if either the teacher or I feel the need to do so," he says. Juan estimates that less than 10 percent of his informal observations result in prolonged "feedback sessions," as he calls them. In those instances, either he wants more information, or the teacher wants to discuss his comments in detail.

Juan's system is quite large and there are bureaucratic and organizational obligations regarding supervision and evaluation. He says that he fulfills these responsibilities, but he has also worked effectively to convince his staff (and union officials) that the ongoing challenge for staff and for him is to go beyond policies or contracts if they are to build an excellent school. As a result, the Williard school's culture embraces teachers who are committed to its mission and discourages the uncommitted from either remaining at Willard or applying there in the first place.

I inquired about other alternative models of supervision at Willard. Juan explained that several teachers are working on self-directed supervision in which teachers set goals, maintain logs and/or portfolios throughout the year, and meet with him at the end of the year to review progress and create a professional development plan. This is an option reserved only for nontenured staff.

Juan is also working to create a partnership with a neighboring school to encourage the creation of clinical supervision teams at each school. Teams would assist one another by observing lessons, planning joint professional development projects, and encouraging short-term teacher exchanges.

Alternative approaches at Willard are the most expansive and eclectic of the 90 schools in this study. However, there are other schools in which a high regard for supervision addresses issues of teachers' differences and approaches to meet their needs. Anne uses a blend of models strengthened by her ability to closely match styles and by her interactions with staff. Kathy also has a sound knowledge of adult development and has created options similar to those in both Juan's and Anne's schools.

Impressions

One can easily understand why teachers might look askance at supervision. When an overwhelming number of principals (79) do not adjust for teachers' abilities, styles, and willingness to explore alternative forms of supervision, the consequences cannot be good. Sergiovanni (1991) best summarizes what seems more the rule than the exception:

The word supervision is too much a part of our history for it to be wished away. Its negative overtones would be lessened considerably, however, if principals were clearer as to its intent, more specific as to its definition, less dogmatic about how it is to be implemented, more appreciative of its complexities, and more accepting of teachers as partners in its implementation (p. 281).

Good principals focus their efforts on the aforementioned issues. In the best schools to emerge in this study, principals inspire, encourage, and support alternative supervisory practices. They join their teachers in training to provide sound observation and supervisory techniques. They take time to engage in the actual process, often at the expense of their own time to finish other work. They also work within the system to overcome obstacles to achieving their desired ends. They are unafraid to challenge conventional thinking, and they create a school climate that makes learning for students *and* adults a priority. They have proven that an atmosphere where excellence, risk taking, and collegiality are rewarded can be created in virtually any school in which courageous, visionary leadership exists.

LEVEL OF SATISFACTION: INSIDE THE NUMBERS

Each of the 90 principals was asked to rate his or her level of satisfaction with the supervisory processes used in their school. The distribution of their responses is summarized in Table 24–3.

The group is almost equally divided between overall dissatisfaction (43 percent) and satisfaction (57 percent) with the supervisory practices in their respective schools. Those who are either very dissatisfied or dissatisfied are frustrated by time constraints or bureaucratic limitations. Those who indicated they are satisfied had a greater variety of reasons for their satisfaction. Of the 11 principals (15 percent) who use multiple processes, only three (3 percent) are very satisfied. The other six are using extremely conventional models that are perceived by their teachers as having little or no value to them. Roger, an urban school principal, and Gwen, principal of a large suburban school, seem to epitomize the hierarchical and authoritarian styles of their four colleagues.

Almost half of the principals in the study (42, or 47 percent) are reasonably comfortable with their approach to supervision. Their range of sophistication, however, is the most diverse. For example, although Juan's supervisory options are the most expansive, he feels that he can do more, despite the high degree of satisfaction his teachers have. Brian is satisfied with his efforts, even with the limitations he encounters, although he is careful to distinguish between his commitment to the process and the procedures within the process. Other principals, like Carol and Sandy, are largely satisfied with both their efforts and their district's procedures. Their teachers are also reasonably positive, if not totally satisfied. The teachers do contend, however, that their feelings are more indicative of respect for their principals. They still believe that the process of supervision has made little difference in their work.

The 43 percent of principals who are dissatisfied also have faculty who are unhappy with the process. In this instance,

TABLE 24–3. Range of Respondents (N = 90)

Rating Scale	Number of Respondents	Percentage of Respondents
1. Very dissatisfied	14	15 percent
2. Dissatisfied	25	28 percent
3. Satisfied	42	47 percent
4. Very satisfied	9	10 percent

the tensions are most reflective of Blumberg's findings (1980). Both sides are resigned to the inherent status quo, and neither side appears ready or willing to address the question of improvement. Despite these findings, almost 87 percent of the schools (78) reflect a climate in which students' needs are being met and where teaching is considered important. The 12 remaining schools in this group reflect corresponding dissatisfaction with supervision and the belief that they are not strong learning communities.

Impressions

Although 51 (57 percent) of the 90 principals surveyed express overall satisfaction with supervisory procedures in their schools, it is disconcerting that only nine (10 percent) feel very satisfied, particularly when six demonstrate no keen insight into effective practice. Thus, only three schools (3 percent) have congruence between comprehensive supervision models and high teacher satisfaction.

Forty-two principals (47 percent) expressed satisfaction with their models. Some, like Juan, have every reason to be very satisfied, but their high expectations for staff, students, and themselves compel them to continue researching and creating even better systems. Leaders of this caliber, however, comprise no more than 4 percent of this category.

In this area of analysis, only seven principals (8 percent) appear to be doing an exemplary job in supervising staff. The implications for additional study and improvement are clear.

TURNING THE TABLES: THE SUPERVISION OF PRINCIPALS

It appeared potentially instructive to learn how the principals in this study are supervised by their superiors and if alternative forms of supervision, such as peer-assisted leadership models or "critical friend" arrangements, were utilized. Only three (about 3 percent) have any semblance of supervision from superiors, and the focus appears to be primarily on evaluation of performance. Five (about 6 percent) have established informal networks with other principals that resemble peer-assisted models. They meet approximately four to six times a year to discuss problems, to exchange information, or to plan a project that might be carried out at their individual schools. Two principals (about 2 percent) have established mentor relationships with other educators, one with a university professor and the other with a retired superintendent who is a former employer.

When asked to characterize the assistance their superintendents offer them, 81 principals (90 percent) indicated that they have support to improve their skills by attending workshops or conferences, albeit with financial and time limitations, ranging from three days (in state) to unspecified amounts of time that can be negotiated. Financial support ranges from no money in the school budget to a high of $1,200.

None of the principals indicated that they have a formal cycle of supervision with their superintendents. Most principals maintained that their superintendents are readily available and accessible to assist them if they seek help. All principals have regularly scheduled meetings, but these gatherings are designed to take care of management issues and rarely focus on professional development.

Mark, a veteran rural principal, captured the feelings of most principals when he spoke about the loneliness of the position. He said, "The only time I get attention is when something goes wrong. My boss expects me not to burden him, teachers and parents expect me to solve all their problems yesterday! Thank goodness I'm very self-directed and able to handle most of the issues that surface daily; but I wish I had someone to help me with my development. I've been doing this job for nine years, and I'm not sure what I really need to improve."

In the 11 schools in this study that have assistant principals, four of the principals work in a truly collaborative way with their assistants. One of the best arrangements is in a suburban school in the Northeast. Beth and her assistant, have worked out an arrangement in which they offer each other regular feedback on performance. They almost appear to be coprincipals of their school, which serves 638 pupils. While talking with them, I learned that they meet nearly every morning to plan their schedule of activities, and that they try to meet at the end of each day to discuss what has taken place that day. This assistant principal has worked with Beth for six years, declining one principal position, because "it wasn't a good match." He finds Beth very willing to share responsibility, but he also knows that she is the boss. When I asked if they felt their conversations were a form of collegial supervision, they seemed to think they were to some degree.

According to Beth, however, their primary goal is to "keep each other abreast of all the things going on at our school." She added, "we do critique one another a lot, but quite frankly it's not as extensive as it could be. Thomas is really able—he's ready to be a principal. I see my role as helping him get that first job."

Thomas explained, "I respect Beth a great deal and support her. I do tell her things I observe about her dealings with staff and I usually ask her why she did something a certain way. It helps me to ask myself how I might handle the same issue." Beth agreed it is a relationship that is built on years of trust and respect, but neither party feels they have spent time building a comprehensive supervisory model focusing on mutual professional development.

Impressions

Most principals in the study have no extensive internal supervisory processes in place. Discussions with their superintendents about performance seem to focus more on specific tasks to be accomplished, rather than any meaningful dialogue about ongoing professional development. As a whole, the group feels any plans to enhance their abilities are a product of their own initiative. As Brian stated, "the majority of principals I know usually attend workshops that give us information about new trends in education. I know these conferences provide only enough knowledge to make me dangerous, but I'm smart enough to read or talk to other principals familiar with the ideas presented before I go ahead and try them out in my school."

The vast majority of the principals are on their own. Only ten (about 11 percent) actively seek to network with colleagues or mentors in reflecting on their work. For whatever reasons, supervision of the 90 principals is a serious shortfall. Although all are evaluated on a yearly basis, even that process lacks a comprehensive and systematic approach according to 83 (93 percent) of the principals. Three principals (3.3 percent) invite teachers to evaluate their performances. One principal has parents' perceptions included in his yearly evaluation. Despite the value such information may have, it must be noted that this feedback is part of summative evaluation, *not* formative supervision.

CONCLUSIONS

These are some concerns raised by the findings of this study:

1. Despite the emphasis on school restructuring and the love affair with site-based management, not much has changed since Blumberg's penetrating and critical look at the ineffective practice of supervision (1974). Organizational and bureaucratic constraints, in part, limit principals and teachers from creating alternative forms of supervision to improve practice. In short, the more things change, the more they stay the same.
2. There is an expansive body of knowledge about effective teaching and the competencies of skillful teachers (Saphier & Gower, 1987). There is equally impressive research on a range of perspectives about supervision, including the moral and ethical dimensions of supervision, the psychosocial dynamics of practice, and the foundation and practice of supervision (Sergiovanni & Starratt, 1993). Theorists have developed a wide array of techniques that principals can use to observe and record teacher behavior (Acheson & Gall, 1987). A number of schools have developed effective models of supervision that can be replicated and that place teachers at the heart of improving supervisory practice (Livingstone, 1992).

   This rich and abundant body of knowledge sadly has not found its way into a majority of the schools in this study. Only 11 (15 percent) principals use different supervisory processes; 83 (92 percent) of them made no distinction between supervision and evaluation; and, although we intellectually know more about adult learning theory, practice suggests otherwise. Only 39 (43 percent) use a developmental supervision style with teachers who have a range of experience and expertise.
3. Principals feel a sense of isolation. Most have no sustained network to help them address complex issues that arise in staff supervision, nor do they have individuals they can turn to for assistance in improving their own skills. Little time is spent on professional development or reflective practice (Schon, 1987). With sharply reduced budgets, few funds are available to support in-service training to help principals and staff upgrade their knowledge and skills.

4. By their own admission, only 9 principals (10 percent) surveyed are very satisfied with the methods of supervision in their schools, and only three (3 percent) are practicing what could be considered appropriate supervision. Most of the principals who expressed satisfaction with what they were doing are using conventional approaches. Teacher comments reinforce the perception that supervision is not meaningful in most schools. There is, therefore, general consensus among teachers and their principals that the effectiveness of supervision is marginal, and there is considerable room for improvement.

WHAT SHOULD BE DONE?

In a follow-up to this study, six of the principals were asked to share their impressions of what should be done to improve the nature of supervision in elementary schools. The following is a summary of their comments:

1. Universities that prepare individuals for the principalship must spend more time in the areas of instructional improvement and performance assessment (supervision and evaluation of staff). Aspiring principals should receive more intensive theoretical training in assessment and should work with professors and principals in practicing techniques of supervision and evaluation. Their preparation should expose them to effective teaching, observational methods, and developmental and differentiated supervision models.
2. Because improved student achievement is related to sound instructional practice, school systems must support efforts to strengthen supervision. Union leaders must work with administrators to broaden contractual language to promote flexibility within the process and permit others to supervise teachers. School districts must similarly encourage and support principals' efforts to develop alternative models, such as instructional improvement teams comprised of master teachers and administrators. Supervision must become a shared responsibility with emphasis on the formative nature of the process. Differentiated models must also be used to reduce the limitations imposed on principals, who must supervise as many as 50 school personnel.
3. Time and money must be set aside to train leadership teams and to develop their knowledge and skills. Universities can play an important role by forming partnerships with schools to bring theory and practice together and to create, test, and disseminate the best approaches to supervision.
4. Technology is not used effectively. Ways to record data, share information, and enhance training can be of great value to educators. Communication via the Internet, establishing national networks for supervision, and the use of interactive video for training purposes can provide current information about best practices in a cost-efficient manner. Teachers can use taped video recordings of their own teaching for self-analysis of their work in relation to district-developed criteria. Schools must elevate the status of professionals who are capable of becoming self-directed learners.

Students can also play a role in support of supervision. Commensurate with students' ages and abilities, feedback mechanisms can be developed to help teachers and principals understand how students view teaching performance.

5. Policies governing summative evaluation, formative evaluation, and supervision must be made clearer. All stakeholders involved in efforts to improve educational outcomes must understand the philosophy and intent of each of these approaches to school improvement. As a result, existing ambiguities about their differences and their intentions will be coherent and understood.

6. Principals need support to improve their skills. The "critical friend" and peer-assisted leadership models should be expanded. National and state principals' associations, in cooperation with school districts, can create resource banks to match principals with colleagues for a specified time. Shadowing techniques, as well as portfolios and other artifacts of principals' work in supervision can help strengthen their abilities. Principals must also become more reflective and proactive in terms of expanding their competencies.

A FINAL THOUGHT

Supervision is a powerful tool for school improvement. Both teachers and principals extol the benefits they receive when it is done well. Unfortunately, the findings of this study, as well as studies done by other investigators, suggest that often it is not done well. The consequences are teacher and principal skepticism, cynicism, and indifference about the value and purpose of supervision. Moreover, poor and ambiguous supervisory practices create a climate of suspicion and mistrust of principals who publicly speak about instructional leadership and excellence in schools.

All educators have a vested interest in the improvement of supervision. In fact, they have a moral and ethical obligation to do so. The needs of young learners must not be ignored as we continue to engage in processes we know are not working. Ours is an honorable profession rooted in the commitment to help children reach their potential. Let us do no less for each other.

REFERENCES

Acheson, K. D. & Gall, M. D. (1987). *Techniques in the clinical supervision of teachers: Preservice and in-service applications* (2nd ed.). White Plains, NY: Longman.

Barber, L. W. (1985). *Improving teacher performance: Formative evaluation.* Bloomington, IN: Phi Delta Kappa.

Blumberg, A. (1980). *Supervisors and teachers: A private cold war* (2nd ed.). Berkeley, CA: McCuthan.

Cogan, M. (1973). *Clinical supervision.* Boston, MA: Houghton Mifflin.

Costa, A. L. (1982). *Supervision for intelligent teaching: A course syllabus.* Orangevale, CA: Search Models Unlimited.

Doud, J. L. (1989). *A ten-year study: The K-8 principal in 1988.* Alexandria, VA: National Association of Elementary School Principals.

Glickman, C. (1985). *Supervision and instruction: A developmental approach.* Boston, MA: Allyn and Bacon.

Goldhammer, R. (1969). *Clinical supervision: Special methods for the supervision of teachers.* New York: Holt.

Lieberman, A. (1992). Teacher leadership: What are we learning? In C. Livingston (Ed.). *Teachers as leaders: Evolving roles* (pp. 159–165). Washington, D.C.: National Education Association.

Livingston, C. (Ed.). (1992). *Teachers as leaders: Evolving roles.* Washington, D.C.: National Education Association.

Saphier, J. & Gower, R. (1987). *The skillful teacher: Building your teaching skills.* Carlisle, MA: Research for Better Teaching.

Schon, D. A. (1987). *Educating the reflective practitioner: Toward a new design for teaching and learning in the professions.* San Francisco: Jossey-Bass.

Sergiovanni, T. J. (1991). *The principalship: A reflective practice perspective* (2nd ed.). Needham Heights, MA: Allyn and Bacon.

Sergiovanni, T. J. & Starratt, R. J. (1993). *Supervision: A redefinition* (5th ed.). New York: McGraw-Hill.

Smith, W. & Andrews, R. (1989). *Instructional leadership: How principals make a difference.* Alexandria, VA: ASCD.

Wing, D. J. (1987). *The examination of staff perceptions of the importance of characteristics associated with strong instructional leadership at the elementary, middle, and high school levels.* Doctoral dissertation, University of Washington.

25

SUPERVISION IN
MIDDLE LEVEL SCHOOLS

Conrad F. Toepfer, Jr.
STATE UNIVERSITY OF NEW YORK AT BUFFALO

INTRODUCTION

This chapter uses the term *middle level schools* to consider the evolution of supervisory practices at that school level. Clark and Clark (1994) noted that the term *middle level school* has been increasingly used as a collective descriptor for all schools and programs between elementary and high schools. The middle level of the nation's school's system was the last to emerge. In a similar manner, emerging middle level supervisory practice has differed from traditional supervisory approaches in elementary and high schools.

This writer's first experience as a school supervisor predated the emergence of collective negotiations in public education. The supervision literature has long recommended staff empowerment and involvement in cooperatively planning instructional improvement. Barr (1937) suggested that supervision take better advantage of teacher understandings of instructional needs and issues and urged supervisors to extend teacher involvement in identifying their concerns for improving teaching and learning.

In the mainstream of educational practice, however, vertical line and staff relationships have not empowered staff. By the power of their personality and clarity of intent, individual supervisors have increased staff involvement in defining instructional improvement goals. Too often, however, illusions of "democratic" supervision have not extended beyond enlightened despotism. The reality is that supervision has remained an administrative function in which there are those who supervise and those who are supervised. In the worst circumstances, the division of authority and responsibility between line and staff approaches a "plantation mentality."

After World War II, the supervision literature espoused the need to move to democratic supervision (Adams & Dickey, 1953; Boardman, Douglas, & Bent, 1953; Briggs & Justman,

1952; Burton & Brueckner, 1955; Crosby, 1957; Hammock & Owens, 1955; Wiles, 1952). Burton and Brueckner (1955) viewed supervision as a social process and felt that supervision had to democratize its practice to meet changing needs to improve teaching and instruction.

Democracy, supported by scientific findings, clearly recognizes that leadership and creativity appear on all levels and in all types of persons. Problem-solving by means of group attack is fundamental to progress within democracy. All this makes the older relationships between leader and led wholly untenable, and the traditional processes of imposition and direction impossible. All persons ideally become co-workers and participants in the co-operative formulation, execution and evaluation of everything from general aims and policies to the minutiae of everyday procedure (p. 9).

Burton and Brueckner recommended the following as targets for involving staff in defining supervisory and curriculum planning agendas:

a) Common agreement on values, attitudes, and meanings within the group or openly expressed desire to critically evaluate certain of these factors.
b) Full and free opportunity for co-operative participation in all activities which affect the life of the group.
c) Easy and effective communication without which interaction cannot take place.
d) A process, channels, and controls through which interaction and communication are carried on, and through which common values, attitudes, and meanings may be disseminated or changed (p. 31).

Acheson and Gall (1980) contended that supervision needed to help educators develop ownership in establishing their goals for professional improvement as well as in developing specific means to accomplish those goals. However, the mainstream of supervisory practice has largely continued to remain "inspectorial," evaluating teacher performance in venues defined at line levels. Much more than in supervision, curriculum planning has extended staff involvement in the way Burton and Brueckner hoped would occur in the entire supervision-curriculum planning continuum. Beane, Toepfer, and Alessi (1986) noted: "Thus curriculum planning articulation activities will increasingly require redefinition of supervision as a means to support professional growth in both line and staff positions" (p. 337).

While staff gained greater involvement and decision-making through curriculum planning activities, the need to redefine supervisory functions persisted. In many situations, this status quo resulted in supervision being more "benevolently despotic" than democratic. It was not until the 1960s that teachers moved to gain power in their relationships with line administrators and supervisors.

A SHIFT OF CONTROL

The failure of supervision to interface line and staff functions during the next decade probably contributed to the emergence of collective negotiations in schools. Teachers sought not only to improve salary and benefits, but to gain empowerment to make professional decisions outside of the domination of line functions. Roles for educators at all levels strained even the best of supervisory-staff relations that some situations had achieved. Bovee (1967) identified the potential dangers that this shift had to overcome.

If we invert, shorten, and paraphrase the famous comments of Clemenceau (World War I French Commander-in-Chief), "War is too serious a business to leave to the generals," we express the question at the heart of the American system of education today. Across the country, teachers are asking this question, "Is education too serious a business to be left to the administrators and supervisors?"

This teacher demand for involvement in decision-making, in a much broader context than heretofore, has challenged current practices in school organization, curriculum, textbook selection, in-service education, pupil-teacher relations, and working relationships with supervisors and administrators.

The attitude of administrative and supervisory personnel toward the new "teacher militancy" has tended to fall into three categories: awareness, awareness with regret, and awareness with concern for channeling the new teacher involvement into a better educational system. Since greater teacher involvement in the total operation is obviously here to stay, the time is overdue for administrators to reassess their roles and to help leadership in a new cooperative effort which has the potential for the greatest improvement American education has ever seen (p. 5).

Although Burton and Brueckner had focused on the need to involve teachers in supervision and curriculum planning, it was the emergence of collective negotiations in schools which pushed that agenda forward. As collective negotiations were established in schools, Harnack (1967) commented:

What about the role of the administrator, supervisor, and curriculum worker? Obviously their functions will change. The basic differences will be that educational workers in administration, supervision, and curriculum (as well as other areas) will provide services designed to support the teacher who makes decisions. The key word is "support."

This idea emphasizes that, in terms of priority, the teacher's classroom decisions will come first. Then, if the teacher needs the support of other persons to carry out his task, these persons will act to aid the teacher. Basically, the teacher will determine if a supportive service is necessary, when the service is needed, and how much it is needed (p. 34).

Those circumstances provided exciting opportunities for administrators and supervisors to extend invitations for staff involvement in instructional improvement activities. However, continued resistance of line personnel to move in that direction only frustrated attempts to improve line-staff interaction. Then ASCD Executive Secretary Neil Atkins (1983) pointed to the need to reconceptualize supervision as a supportive service and to finally interrelate and involve line and staff personnel in improving educational practice.

We need to look at what all this means for the supervisory function. The greatest contribution that the present occupants of these positions could make would be to seize the leadership in newly defining the purpose and function of supervision in the support system (p. 10).

The middle level school concept was being established at the time collective negotiations were implemented in schools. That innovation began refining and extending functions and purposes that the junior high school education had defined 50 years before. Middle school changes and developments initiated in middle schools depended upon professional investment and ownership by middle school staff. It was absolutely essential that staff be willing to consider and implement the instructional dimensions of the middle school concept.

This writer's involvement with middle level education over the past 40 years has led to the following conclusion: Supportive posture, service, and interaction among supervisory and instructional personnel in middle level schools has been a key factor in the remarkable educational progress made at that level over the past 35 years.

A MIDDLE EDUCATIONAL FOCUS

Lucio and McNeil (1972) maintained that "supervision must recognize and encourage leadership throughout the instructional spectrum" (p. 61). Middle level education's intervening position between elementary and high school has created some unique supervisory tasks. It is important that those differences be understood in their interfaced context with elementary and high school supervisory concerns. The educational developments unique to the middle level also suggest possibilities for rethinking supervisory procedures and practices at other levels.

School districts serve three different developmental levels: young children, young adolescents, and maturing adolescents/young adults. Too often, school district-wide programs become casually interfaced sequences of largely free-standing programs within each school level. District-wide educational effectiveness resides in: (1) how well programs at each school level attend to the developmental needs of students at that level; and (2) how well elementary, middle level, and high school programs articulate and blend together. Lack of vertical program continuity continues to create problems requiring district-wide attention.

District-wide curriculum and program articulation establishes some overarching supervisory tasks. For example, the middle level school's position in the district-wide structure creates both "transition-in" tasks from elementary school practice and "transition-out" tasks to high school programs. Elementary-middle level and middle level-high school transition panels facilitate program interface needs (Johnston et al, 1985). Elementary-middle level panels consist of a representative group of teachers from both the last elementary and first middle level program grades. Middle level-high school panels consist of a representative group of teachers from both the last middle level and first high school program grades.

Each panel works on program/curriculum/learning articulation issues with the principals and representative parent groups. The goal is to strengthen vertical program continuity and make certain that curriculum changes made at one school level do not create gaps or overlaps in articulation of programs from one school level to the next. Transition panels can help base curricula and school programs on what students can do at each level. They also increase the awareness of those needs among all three levels in the local district. The objective of district-wide program articulation can be successfully achieved through such linkages (Toepfer, 1986).

Roderick (1991) identified a significant concern that requires supervisory attention at both district-wide and specific school levels. She found that students experiencing serious difficulty in their transition from one school level to the next are at greater risk of dropping out of school than those students who perform poorly in elementary school.

The results of this study challenge the conventional belief that dropouts are youth who can be distinguished early on in their school careers by their poor grades and lack of attendance. Late-grade dropouts, on average, did recover from losses incurred during the first year of middle school or high school (p. 18).

The Roman God, Janus, had two faces, each pointing in the opposite direction. Truly caught in the middle, middle level school programs must articulate with those at both district elementary and high schools. Collective wisdom about the nature of middle level education does not equal that of elementary and high school education. Both lay and educator audiences are much less aware of the purposes and characteristics of, and reasons for, a separate program unit between elementary and high school. Particular developmental and instructional needs of young adolescents differ from, while others blend with, needs that students manifest before and after their middle level school years.

Young children begin elementary school at relatively close developmental positions. Their individual growth and development differentiates over the next few years. Developmental ranges widen during their middle school years as that diversity becomes the hallmark of young adolescence. Those ranges narrow during the high school years as individuals approach and sometimes achieve the fullfillment of much of their potential.

Ranges of physical, social, emotional, and intellectual development that characterize human development during this period are wider than those of elementary or high school students (Kramer, 1985). Tasks faced and pressures experienced during early adolescence are extremely stressful. Episodic growth during this epoch may be extremely rapid at some points and minimal at others.

We call them "early," "emerging," or "young" adolescents. However, lack of a clear and separate descriptor for this stage of development has probably contributed to the lesser conventional wisdom about middle level education. Eichhorn (1966) defined this stage as *transescence* (based on the words *transition* and *pubescence*). Although his descriptor has never gained wide acceptance, it has clarified the nature of the tasks youth face in their metamorphosis during those years. He defined transescence as:

the stage of development which begins prior to the onset of puberty and extends through the early stages of adolescence. Since puberty does not occur for all precisely at the same chronological age in human development, the "transescent" designation is based upon the many physical, social, emotional, and intellectual changes that appear prior to the puberty cycle to the time when the body gains a practical degree of stabilization over these complex, pubescent changes (p. 3).

"One size fits all" expectations are particularly ineffective in middle level schools. Adopting elementary and high school supervisory practices as bases for middle level supervisory practice has also been ineffective. Supervisory procedures and activities should be developed in response to instructional and program needs unique to that particular educational level. As that is done at the middle level, appropriate elementary and high school procedures can be adapted to develop a supervisory program that responds to the range of those needs in the middle level school.

A HISTORICAL PERSPECTIVE

We are approaching the centenary of events that made the United States the first Western nation with an intervening educational focus between elementary and high school. The establishment of the junior high school initiated what has become a three-level educational system focused respectively on children, young adolescents, and maturing adolescents/young adults.

Initial events leading to the establishment of the junior high school were not based on curricular needs. Harvard University President Charles Eliot (1898) led the reorganization of the American elementary and secondary structure from an 8–4 to a 6–6 balance. Maintaining that seventh and eighth grade students were ready to study secondary school content, his goal was to shorten elementary school in order to better prepare entering college students. Soon afterward, the Committee on the Equal Division of the Twelve Years in the Public Schools between the District and the High School (1907) recommended subdividing the six-year high school into two equal school units.

The six-year scheme is for those who might be able to pursue their general education beyond the primary school. It ought to be subdivided into two administrative sections: (1) a junior high school of three years extending from the twelfth to the fifteenth year; and, (2) a senior high school also of three years, covering the period from the fifteenth year to the eighteenth year (p. 27).

Such thinking fostered the notion that junior high schools should be "junior editions" of senior high schools. The committee also felt the junior high school would "bridge the gap" that some felt existed between elementary and high school.

The junior high school was not initially developed to meet the educational needs of young adolescents. That awareness evolved as attention was drawn to differences in young adolescent educational needs from those of older students. Psychologist G. Stanley Hall (1905) described failings of existing middle grade curricula for young adolescents. He pointed to the need for schools to focus on student needs during that period.

The pupil is in the age of spontaneous variation which at no period of life is so great. He does not want a standardized, overpeptonized mental diet. It palls on his appetite. He suffers from mental ennui and dyspepsia, and this is why so many and an increasing number refuse some of the best prepared courses (p. 509).

In large measure, the promulgation of junior high programs such as those in Berkeley, California (Bunker, 1909) and Columbus, Ohio (Shawan, 1910) established the need for something other than miniature high schools. Over the years, that recognition led to what later became a distinct middle level educational identity. In the past decade, this has become known as *developmentally responsive education*. The recently published new edition of *This We Believe* (National Middle School Association, 1995), makes the following statement.

The importance of achieving developmentally responsive middle level schools cannot be overemphasized. The nature of the educational programs young adolescents experience during this formative period of life will, in large measure, determine the future for all of us (p. 33).

Circumstances in American education at the beginning of the twentieth century, however, were focused on a dual system of elementary and secondary schools. Educational purposes were framed in the realities of the demands of life and opportunities for students when they left the school system. In 1900, only 20 percent of students completed high school.

Students who lacked intellectual ability or initiative entered the work force upon reaching the required age for leaving school. Many students who possessed the abilities for higher education but lacked the financial resources also left school early. A goal of those early junior high schools was to keep more students in school through ninth grade. The junior high school gained acceptance and spread rapidly (Briggs, 1920):

The junior school is accepted in theory, and its possibilities have proven so alluring that the movement for reorganization is well under way in both urban and rural districts. The physical redistribution of the grades seems assured; but if, having accomplished that, educators rest content, they will have missed the one great educational opportunity of their generation for real educational reform. There is a

demand for purposes so clear and cogent that they will result in new curricula, new courses of study, new methods of teaching, and new social relationships—in short, a new spirit which will make the intermediate years not only worthwhile in themselves, but also an intelligent inspiration for every child to continue, as long as possible, the education for which he is by inheritance best fitted. In its essence then, that will assure the best results possible for each individual early adolescent as well as for society at-large (p. 367).

Such a middle level curricular identity began to emerge in 1920. That largely occurred because, unlike the initial impetus directed by college and university educators, most of those interested in studying and working with the junior high school during that interval were curriculum/instruction specialists rather than administration/organization specialists. Junior high school curriculum innovations over the next 40 years led to the evolution of the middle school, which subsequently evolved into the concept of "middle level education." The emergence of integration, exploration, articulation, and differentiation as junior high school curriculum functions (Gruhn & Douglas, 1947) specified the uniqueness of the junior high school curricular changes.

Around 1960, this rubric was supported by medical data that documented the increasingly earlier onset of puberty and the extent of differences between individuals of the same age. Eichhorn (1966) used that data to develop a curriculum model which became central in defining what became known as the middle school concept. During the 1970s and 1980s, middle level instruction continued to shift attention from *what* should be taught to *how* should it be taught.

The emergence of the middle school concept created a nagging but meaningless "turf" confrontation between some junior high and middle school advocates. Persisting through the 1970s, it distracted particular efforts to refine middle level educational initiatives. In 1981, Melton coined the term "middle level education" as a descriptor for all school programs between fourth and ninth grades focused on educating young adolescents (Melton, 1995). Diffusing the "junior high versus middle school" argument, that term has become the common descriptor for the middle grades. Clark and Clark (1994) noted:

The terms "middle level school" and "middle level education" were first used extensively by the research team of the Dodge Foundation/NASSP National Study of Schools in the Middle (Valentine et al, 1981). . . . These terms, however, gained general acceptance among junior high and middle school educators largely through the energetic efforts of George Melton, who popularized the terms through his work throughout the nation and his numerous presentations at state, regional, and national conferences and conventions (p. 6).

Development of collaborative instructional approaches and teaching strategies in middle level schools created needs for supervisory support that varied from elementary and high school practices. Teaming practices and interdisciplinary teaching are now evolving into curriculum and learning integration approaches (Beane, 1993, 1995). Middle level educational curriculum and program practices continue to create needs for differentiated modes of supervisory support. Against this background, let us consider those needs in middle level schools.

COLLABORATIVE SUPERVISION

The next two sections consider middle level instructional improvement practices that responded to changing instructional practice at that level. Unruh's and Turner's (1970) concern also reflected middle level school supervision's need to more effectively monitor, support, and evaluate those developments: "As new forces influence instruction, supervision will need to establish evaluative techniques more sophisticated and better designed than ever before" (p. 278).

Evolving middle level school needs for supervisory support focused on instructional practices rather than on the total performance of individual teachers. This requires the supervisory environment Burton and Brueckner (1955) recommended: "Competent supervision does not merely aid persons to solve their problems; it provides the conditions under which all may participate as free agents in the solutions of common problems" (p. 5).

Collaborative instruction, particularly through interdisciplinary team teaching, is a growing middle level instructional hallmark. Collaborative instructional practice requires supervisory approaches that accommodate instructional needs beyond the demands of working with individual teachers. Line and staff issues that required line-staff collaboration to improve instruction emerged during the early years of the middle school movement. Although collaborative supervisory practice has been slow to develop, it was recommended long before the emergence of middle level educational practice.

Harold Shafer, chairperson of the ASCD Commission on Problems of Supervisors and Curriculum Workers (1967), identified general supervisory concerns that were also emerging in middle level instructional practice. He stated that educational change in American schools will be possible

only when the classroom teacher becomes the nucleus of a group of professionals and paraprofessionals who work with him in educating children, only when he is looked upon as the key professional person in the education of children utilizing and coordinating the talents and contributions of a supportive staff—only then will the schools be able to provide all children with the education they must have to be contributing members of society (p. 6).

Shafer noted that many principals and supervisors had an aversion to becoming a part of a team in which the classroom teacher was the coordinator, and they did not see themselves as the supportive staff of the classroom teacher. He saw further complications because few classroom teachers were prepared to be team leaders and to use a supportive staff. Another problem in the rise of collective negotiations in education centered around identifying who would speak for supervisors and represent them in negotiations.

Team teaching developed from and extended earlier junior high school core curriculum approaches. This has created the need for collaborative instructional leadership that differs from traditional elementary and high school program supervisory approaches. Anderson (1966) captured what evolving instructional shifts in middle level school programs would create, thus requiring different supervisory support.

Three words that are used with increasing frequency in discussions of educational improvement are excellence, flexibility, and efficiency. Excellence is what we want each child, no matter how different he is from all the others, to reach—that state of physical health and intellectual-psychological maturity of which he is potentially capable. Flexibility means having and exploiting a number of alternatives in the use of personnel, facilities, and resources in responding to the needs and interests of children. Efficiency is the performance of carefully defined tasks at the lowest possible cost in time, money, and energy (p. 8).

The need for more collaborative approaches to improve instruction in middle level schools was probably never better stated. Evolving differences of both kind and degree in middle level instructional approaches have not been broadly recognized beyond the middle level school units in local districts. There is a persistent need to develop a conventional wisdom based on the uniqueness of middle level educational needs similar to what exists at early childhood/elementary and high school levels.

For the most part, site-based management and shared decision-making models have not interfaced supervisory support with team teaching and other collaborative instructional approaches. That will require examination of system-wide instructional needs, which could be facilitated by establishing a linkage of school unit transition panels.

That linkage would also broaden understanding of the unique instructional needs within each school level in the district. Anderson's concern to move toward "excellence, flexibility, and efficiency" required such an interface. The development of instructional improvement efforts based upon unique middle school level needs required establishment of that context. As will be discussed later, Anderson's notions about team teaching (1966) identified what became the basis for effective middle level school teaming arrangements. However, the delegation of responsibilities to teams required departures from traditional line/staff direct observational procedures.

As the 1970s dawned, clinical supervisory models developed from Cogan's (1973) seminal work. Clinical supervision sought to build staff trust in supervising the total performance of individual teachers. Its emergence during the spread of collective negotiations in schools probably limited the success of collective negotiations in building teacher trust in evaluation by line supervisory personnel at that time. Collective negotiations undoubtedly fueled staff concerns about Unruh and Turner's (1970) question,"who evaluates the instructional program?" (p. 179).

Staff mistrust of line authority persists. Evolving middle level educational practice has attempted to deal with a concern Sizer (1992) later observed in high schools.

If there is a quality that best characterizes the American school system, it is mistrust. The mistrust is so pervasive that we barely notice it. It is staggeringly costly—soaks up endless hours and saps morale. Trust cannot be mandated. Yet, it is the cheapest, most sensible, and for us, most radical means for reform (p. 7).

Supervisory behaviors that build staff trust have been important in improving middle level educational practice. Glickman, Gordon, and Ross-Gordon (1995) discussed criteria for selecting supervisory approaches appropriate to specific situational needs. Their range from directive control behaviors and directive informational behaviors to collaborative behaviors responds to needs for differentiated middle school supervisory approaches. The "variability" they identified is important for improving team teaching and other collaborative middle level educational practices.

1. Individual or group levels of development, expertise, and commitment may vary. . . . When working with an individual or group with widely fluctuating characteristics, a collaborative approach would probably be most effective (p. 186).
2. Characteristics of teachers and groups might change in certain situations . . . The developmental supervisor sometimes must change supervisory behaviors in order to adapt to a change in the teacher or the group's situation (p. 187).

This specified Alfonso's and Goldsberry's (1982) earlier notion of "colleagueship":

Does "colleagueship in supervision" refer to teams of supervisors working together to improve the effectiveness of schools and simultaneously to refine their own professional skills? Does it suggest that supervisors and teachers should pursue these ends in partnership? Or does it suggest that teachers should collaborate with one another for the same reasons? To all three questions, the answer is yes (p. 95).

The supervisory literature has not focused on middle level instructional practices based on collaborative relationships developed over the past 25 years. That is another indication of the lack of conventional wisdom about instructional practices specific to middle level educational needs.

Earlier, Galloway and Mulhern (1973) spoke of the need for developing collegial relationships in supervisory practice.

The collegial relationships between and among teachers has been minimized and undersold as a means of growth. Given time and opportunity, teachers can not only learn from each other, but also serve as confidants for feedback on teaching approaches and as respondents to treating philosophy and style. . . . Without this opportunity, it is easy to retreat into a shell of secrecy and become defensive about teaching (p. 34).

While speaking of the characteristics of highly successful supervisors, Sergiovanni (1987) later noted:

Highly successful leaders practice the principle of power investment. . . . They understand that teachers need to be empowered to act—to be given the necessary responsibility that releases their potential and makes their actions and decisions count (p. 187).

While statements of such general needs continue to appear, supervisory practice developed at the middle level has largely remained a "closet phenomenon." Instructional improvement in middle level schools has been facilitated by collaboration among teachers and between teachers and line leadership. The transformation of supervision discussed by Grimmett, Rostad, and Ford (1992) defined what was needed to deal with middle level educational supervisory needs.

Teacher development takes place within a culture of interdependent collegiality when teachers reflectively transform their classroom experience. In this transformational perspective, supervision becomes a process in which teachers develop profound and fresh appreciations of the learners' perspective, the classroom context, and their own role as an active enabler of student learning (p. 186).

However, clinical efforts need to focus on instructional improvement concerns that are unique to middle level schools. Goldhammer, Anderson, and Krajewski (1993) suggested that peer interactions were needed to facilitate such concerns. The subsequent development of peer coaching addressed those needs at staff and classroom levels (Costa & Garmston, 1994; Garmston, 1990; Garmston, Linder, and Whitaker, 1993; Shon, 1988) and provided that collegial means for middle level schools.

Such practices certainly are not unique to middle level schools. They have, however, been developed and are used there much more than at either elementary or high school levels. There is, however, a lag in supervisory practices developed as specific responses to those practices.

CHANGING INSTRUCTIONAL IMPROVEMENT NEEDS

Myers, Kifer, Merry and Foley (1924) spoke of the need to substitute coordination and leadership for supervision and direction. They saw a critical need to develop

cooperative procedures through which the members of the staff may effectively participate in the improvement of the educational establishment. Formerly the teacher was a nonentity with reference to these matters. Today and tomorrow, administration and supervision must learn how to share these responsibilities with the teaching staff (p. 128).

Burton and Brueckner (1955) stated: "The primary function of supervision of all types is leadership, plus the encouragement and recognition of leadership in any other persons" (p. 5).

Over the years, however, general supervisory practice largely maintained a line-staff separation, with the former in control. Whatever engagement of staff has taken place was still done within administrative control, with instructional supervision as an administrative function (Eye & Netzer, 1971).

The growing incidence of teaming with cooperative planning by middle level school staff teams created a need to change that arrangement. Increasing staff interaction in more middle level schools is now approaching the hopes of Eisner (1978):

I would like one day to see a school in which teachers can function as professional colleagues, where a part of their professional role was to visit the classrooms of their colleagues, and to observe and share with them in a supportive, informed, and useful way what they have seen (p. 622).

Why has this been so slow to evolve? Venerable supervision literature long recommended increasing such staff involvement in improving instruction. Burton and Brueckner (1955) stated:

The aim of supervision is the improvement of the total teaching-learning process, the total setting for learning, rather than the narrow and limited aim of improving teachers in service (p. 13).

Gwynn (1961) added, "Supervision is an expert technical service primarily aimed at studying and improving *cooperatively* all factors which affect the quality of instruction" (p. 19).

Crosby (1957) believed it was critical that supervisors gain effective staff participation and involvement in curriculum and program improvement:

The supervisor knows that they who participate grow. She knows that voluntary participation is the only kind of participation that is real. Her efforts to help others recognize a mutual responsibility toward organized action to improve the curriculum is of much importance (p. 113).

From that perspective, supervision for instructional improvement has to become a shared staff function. The New York State Association for Supervision and Curriculum Development Report (Harnack et al, 1977) defined staff roles as part of a broad-based supervisory process.

Whether the supervisor/curriculum worker behaves as a coordinator, change agent, philosopher, curriculum theorist, researcher, or facilitator of in-service education, his task will be that of a supportive staff member in the school system. Realistically, his task will be to provide supportive services such as assistance in analyzing instructional problems, helping to remove barriers which might hinder orderly progress in terms of encouraging change or instilling confidence in the teaching staff (p. 6).

The report identified specific competencies needed to provide that support. The central issue was to gain staff participation to develop ownership in instructional improvement targets. In turn, staff also have to understand ways in which line supervisory efforts can support those efforts.

Alfonso, Firth, and Neville (1975) developed propositions that could lead to improved instructional supervisory behavior. A number of them defined essential conditions that have also emerged in evolving middle level instructional practice.

Proposition 10: A change effort will be more effective if it is perceived as building on existing practice rather than threatening it (p. 187).

The development of middle level practices such as cooperative learning, thematic instructional units, and more heterogeneous grouping required understanding of and support from building leadership personnel. Middle level line personnel have had to work closely with staff to understand the nature of those departures as they developed. Line personnel need to become knowledgeable of what those changes entail to seek the support of parents and community. That knowledge is also essential for effective evaluation of staff working in those programs.

This writer has observed that instructional leadership priorities are markedly higher among middle level administrators than among high school administrators. That priority may account for the growth of peer coaching, mentoring, and delegation of instructional improvement responsibilities in middle level instructional programs. Those innovations have not threatened staff members and have encouraged their involvement and participation.

Proposition 13: The effectiveness of change efforts will be improved when those restraining factors which inhibit an individual's normal desire for change have been recognized and dealt with deliberately (p. 188).

Middle level school staff ownership in instructional improvement has increased as line leadership has reduced and/or removed inhibiting factors and conditions.

Proposition 20: Change will be more readily accepted if it can be demonstrated to be practicable to the target system or a close approximation of it (p. 190).

Middle level instructional improvement has been most successful when proposed changes have been piloted among enclaves of staff that are interested in and ready to develop them. As the staff at large sees the advantage of those changes, they are more willing to expand upon them. Alfonso, Firth, and Neville noted that "supervisors should place more emphasis on local demonstration of change rather than importing the idea from outside" (p. 20). That makes it all the more important to establish conditions in which significant progress toward local instructional improvement can be successfully undertaken.

Proposition 21: Change will be effective when the conditions that exist within the target system are those which encourage change processes (p. 191).

As line personnel assume such a supportive posture, they encourage staff to consider ways of improving instructional practice in areas of concern to them. Middle level principals confirm that staff interactions help teachers identify and develop program and instructional improvement changes. Those interactions have created a climate for change that surpasses the identification of improvement targets by line personnel alone.

Middle level school line personnel have also moved from vertical to more horizontal interactions with staff. This leveled playing field has built staff understanding of the respective contributions line and staff each bring to identifying instructional improvement goals.

This facilitates suggestions for change from all members of the combined group and allows them to agree on how those suggestions should be processed and refined. It does not detract from line and staff prerogatives in other matters. It also established the following condition:

Proposition 29: A change effort will be more effective when it recognizes and utilizes the strength of group norms (p. 193).

As Wiles (1967) recommended, successful shared decision-making practices in middle level school programs have empowered both line and staff to interact cooperatively: "Teachers and administrators have the opportunity to tell each other frankly what they expect from each other and the help they would like to receive from each other" (p. 18).

Interaction to improve specific instructional and program practice has at times been developed. The development of models that successfully build that interaction across the range of program and instructional improvement needs remains an elusive challenge, however.

NEW APPROACHES FOR EVOLVING INSTRUCTIONAL NEEDS

As discussed earlier, elementary and high schools were the original units in the American school system. The developmental differences between children and adolescents created instructional practices appropriate at both levels. However, the subsequent emergence of middle level educational programs created its own unique supervisory support needs. First, it interfaced with the upper years of the former and lower years of the latter unit. Second, middle level schools have focused on the unique nature of young adolescents in developing instructional practices which differed from those appropriate for children and for maturing adolescent/young adult populations.

Middle level administrative and supervisory needs were often delivered through means developed in elementary and high schools or as adaptations of those procedures, however. Middle level program differences continue to require supervisory services developed to meet that uniqueness.

This writer does not agree that school restructuring can deliver those procedures. By definition, "restructuring" means rearranging existing elements in a new order or sequence. This is frequently the extent of restructuring supervisory services. Such approaches seldom result in more than new bottles for the old wine. Before restructuring, Toepfer et al (1993) recommended that middle level schools first "re-vision" or reconceptualize their current program goals. It is also important to identify and develop supervisory services necessary to monitor and improve them.

In most cases, *all* elements in existing supervisory programs are ineffective in terms of middle level program needs. If this is the case, it is necessary to identify which supervisory procedures are strong enough to be retained, which need to be improved, and which need to be discarded. Only as individual elements are strengthened and new ones developed to replace those identified as inadequate can restructuring be undertaken to develop an effective supervisory ends-means relationship.

Curriculum planning has both content and process dimensions. Supervisory procedures must likewise deal with needs in these dimensions. Unless those involved in changing curriculum are involved in defining new supervisory services, the results exemplify school restructuring at its worst. Traditional supervisory support solely developed upon elementary and high school program needs *have not* realistically improved middle level educational practice. The range of learning needs among young adolescents is wider than at elementary and high school.

Supervision in middle level schools needs to work at putting many old assumptions aside and replacing them with principles such as these:

1. Not all students need the same things to the same extent.
2. Not all students need the same things at the same time.
3. At any given time, some needs of students may be so urgent that they require immediate attention and experiences outside the curriculum prescribed at that point in time.

Middle level school supervisory needs vary further, depending on the grades involved in the local program and how that relates to local elementary and high school programs. There is no single, ideal middle level school/program grade pattern (Epstein, 1990; Epstein & MacIver, 1990). The issue of "which grades in the middle level school/program" depends on the local reasons for their inclusion.

Program effectiveness, not a grouping of grades, should be the primary concern. Supervisor needs will vary widely in terms of those conditions. The following three situations are illustrative of differing middle supervisory support needs in specific situations.

Multiple School Levels in a Single Building

Braddock, Wu, and McPartland (1987), and Coldiron, Braddock, and McPartland (1988) stated that there is no trend based upon pedagogic reasons or educational advantages to merge elementary and middle or middle level and high school programs into a single facility. Space and other logistical needs, however, do require that in some small districts.

Movement away from the self-contained classroom usually begins in the middle level program. Effects of middle level grade shifts on vertical program articulation must also be assessed. K–8 elementary schools should consider whether or not it is appropriate to continue self-contained instruction in the middle level grades housed in those schools. Shifts to different instructional organization in the latter grades of K–8 schools should be based upon the maturity and readiness of local students for something other than self-contained instruction.

Where self-contained classes continue through grade eight in such schools, supervision in the middle level grades is delivered from an elementary school perspective. Schools which shift to teaming in the latter grades of K–8 schools have found it necessary to supervise teachers in those grades differently.

In situations where middle level and high school programs are housed in a single facility, middle level program needs are often not supported as much as high school program needs. This is exacerbated if supervisory personnel do not understand the differences between instructional improvement needs at each level. Middle level–high schools need to pay attention to the following:

- Wherever possible, assign faculty exclusively to either middle level or high school programs.
- Provide a supervisor primarily concerned with the middle level program.
- Provide staff development that meets differing and/or separate needs of middle level and high school staff.
- Establish bell schedules that separate high school from middle grade students to the degrees desired (in fact, middle level schools may not have bells at all).

If concerns are not accommodated, the assignment of support systems, allocation of facilities, and staff development emphases usually favor high school program needs. Program needs in both middle level and high school programs in such facilities require specification so that both levels are adequately supported. Shared staffing issues also need to be identified and means developed that accommodate middle level and high school program needs within the building. Such arrangements should not curtail middle level instructional and curriculum articulation needs.

Staff with split middle level–high school teaching assignments find difficulty in putting high school teaching focus aside when they move to teach their first middle level class. If it can be done, teachers' middle level courses should be scheduled before their high school assignments. Some staff, however, will have to teach their high school courses before their middle level assignments.

Faculty who teach their high school courses before their middle level courses identify a common difficulty. Most teachers with such split loads agree they are less effective in their first middle level class if it immediately follows a high school class. They find it difficult to "shift down" to the lower cognitive and maturity at the middle level and feel they are much more effective in teaching their second middle level class.

That problem can be reduced. For example, if a science teacher has a high school class followed immediately by two middle level classes, the teacher can schedule a planning period or nonteaching duty between the first middle level one. Teachers find that this allows them to shift down and become more effective in the first middle level course they teach after their high school course assignments.

Teachers with split middle level–high school assignments agree they can more readily "shift up" to high school student and instructional focus after their middle level classes. Blocking teacher responsibilities at one level and then the other eliminates their having to go back and forth during their teaching day.

Effective supervision of staff with split loads requires attention from personnel at each level. High school supervisors seldom understand middle level pedagogy and instructional needs well enough to take on that responsibility. This chapter will later discuss ways that deal successfully with this situation.

Horizontal Articulation Issues

Cognitive and affective concerns should be interfaced, not separated. Cognitive achievement improves when program planning is based on their affective concerns (Beane, 1990). Collaborative instructional and learning arrangements assist students in articulating their educational experiences across the school day. This will help define the learning skills and processes students need to integrate, recall, and use those data more effectively.

Departmentalization is a vestige from the era when early secondary instructional procedures were modified high school practices. Departmentalization emphasizes in-depth study by organizing learning within separated subject areas. It neither seeks to correlate or integrate learning among different content areas nor facilitates the collaborative interaction teachers need to plan and integrate learning across content areas.

Since articulation of learning across content areas is a major middle level educational objective, middle level schools should carefully assess any advantages claimed for departmentalization. Feldlaufer, Midgley, and Eccles (1987) found departmentalization to be the least desirable pattern for organizing effective instruction in middle level grades. They wrote that in the fifth through the eighth grades, self-contained classrooms provide more correlation of learning and learning opportunities than departmentalization. In that regard, there are clear advantages of self-contained over departmentalized classrooms at the middle level. However, this writer is unaware of any studies that identify advantages for self-contained classrooms over teaming arrangements at the middle level.

Teaming helps reduce problems experienced in departmentalized subject isolation, if it's properly organized. Although it cannot eradicate separate subject curriculum organization, teaming can facilitate the articulation and even integration of learning across subject areas (Toepfer, 1988).

- make certain that concerns to integrate learning are identified in all areas of the school program
- identify opportunities to integrate learning within each subject area
- identify approaches especially appropriate for integrating learning among subject areas
- develop middle level teaching strategies particularly suited for integrating learning among subject areas (p. 4).

The initial concern of teaming should be the collaborative planning and development of programs for those students whom team members commonly teach. Such conjoint planning provides the essential keystone for true "team" teaching, rather than "turn" teaching. In itself, interdisciplinary teaming will not assure that curriculum integration will occur. Beane (1993) commented:

Interdisciplinary teaming does not necessarily lead to interdisciplinary curriculum organization (p. 33).

What interdisciplinary teaching does take place is simple correlation of subject areas (p. 34).

Interdisciplinary planning unfortunately has too frequently focused solely upon how to loosely connect information in separated subject areas. Beane (1992) pointed to the importance of focusing on planning integrated learnings in specific situations.

Curriculum planning in an integrative context begins with collaborative discussion about young people's questions and concerns and identification of the themes they suggest. Once a theme and the related questions they suggest are clear, curriculum planning turns to identifying activities the group might use to answer the questions. It is after these "what" and "how" concerns are addressed that questions of knowledge, skill, and resources are appropriate (p. 39).

This requires supervisory support of teacher teams that goes beyond traditional one-on-one approaches developed for self-contained and departmentalized instruction.

Two-Grade Middle Level Schools

Students spend considerable time adjusting to the instructional and organizational changes during their first middle level school year. Their familiarity with that environment enhances their success in school experiences in their remaining middle level experiences. This is reduced in two-grade settings. Two-grade middle level schools have a 50 percent turnover of students each year and require students to move through three different schools (elementary, middle level, and high school) within four years. Young adolescence is probably the most confusing time in one's school-aged years. Adjusting quickly to three such changes is particularly difficult and distracting during early adolescence.

Toepfer (1982) described a two-year team arrangement of middle level teachers and students. Even when local conditions require a two-grade middle level facility, internal articulation of the middle level program is improved when teams of students and teachers remain together for those two grades. Following their two-year cycle, students matriculate to the high school program and the teaching team moves back to begin another 80-week cycle with a new group of seventh grade students.

Two-year teams in two-grade middle schools reduce the fragmented experiences students have with different teachers in seventh and then eighth grade. In a two-year cycle, teachers gain extended, first-hand knowledge of the dramatic developmental changes experienced by some students, as well as the differing needs of others who progress more slowly. Student guidance and advisement can also be tied to teams. Study hall and other learning support programs can be focused within such arrangements across the two grades in the school. This provides the basis to plan and adjust curriculum and learning challenges accordingly beyond a single school year.

Teachers in 80-week programs confirm that knowing their students at the beginning of the second year provides several additional weeks of engaged teaching time beyond what occurs in a 40-week experience. Teachers develop an extended relationship with students and their families. Shifts of some individuals to different settings are made because of particularly severe personality clashes or other issues. Where necessary, that typically occurs in less than 3 percent of students and usually declines the longer the two-year team arrangement is continued.

Teachers in 80-week patterns do not have to learn the names and faces and needs of a new group of students each year. Teachers can readily see the changes—physical and otherwise—which some students make over the intervening summer, something teachers do not recognize when they get new students in eighth grade. This extended relationship also helps teachers to prepare students for the adjustments they will face when they enter high school.

No educational advantages have been identified in two-grade middle level school arrangements. Research by George, Spruel, and Moorefield (1987) confirmed that student learning achievement significantly increases when groups of middle level teachers and students remain together for longer than a single school year. Aside from the practice just described, multiple-year teacher-student teams are increasingly being used to extend relationships and improve student achievement in other middle level school configurations.

A more radical possibility is to have an 80-week experience in which teachers and students move together from one building level to the next. Such arrangements also require differing supervisory support specific to instructional needs at both school levels. Those needs must be understood by those who develop and implement those approaches. Two exemplary instances of this departure will be discussed latter.

EFFECTIVE MIDDLE LEVEL SUPERVISORY PRACTICE

The three situations considered in the last section each developed collaborative learning arrangements different from single-teacher regimen in either self-contained elementary or high school departmentalized patterns. However, supervisory services have largely been organized to deal with single-teacher settings. Supervisory needs in earlier cooperative programs (e.g., the Dalton, Massachusetts High School Plan and the Winnetka, Illinois Plan in the 1920s and the New York City Cooperative Group Plan in the Winnetka, Illinois Plan) never evolved (Shaplin, 1964). Shaplin noted that the New York Plan's radical departure from traditional practice, not its successful initiation of teaming, led to its rapid demise.

However, middle level school instructional departures like the three discussed in the previous section were increasing. Their benefits were more readily seen and they threatened no establishment. They did require reorganizing supervisory services and patterns to effectively monitor and facilitate instructional improvement in those circumstances. This also raised the question of the need for middle level supervisory personnel to develop expertise in new dimensions involved in those programs.

Berman and Usery (1966) pondered the need to deliver more personalized supervision. They believed that the supervisor should gain specific experience in the school environment in which he or she was to provide service.

Should the "supervisor-to-be" be required to matriculate in a residency experience? If so, what specific opportunities for experience should be included that are not now commonly found in programs for the preparation of supervisors? (p. 32)

The three middle level situations just discussed dealt with instructional middle level school environments. It is hard to imagine that supervisors who had not worked at the middle level could readily adapt supervisory procedures developed in either elementary or high schools to meet teacher needs in the situations sketched. The use of general supervisors at all school levels persists, however. When direct interventions are appropriate in middle level programs, the collaborative dimensions of teaming may require more than one-to-one supervisory-teacher interactions. Berman and Usery had a notion of what middle level supervisors now face: "How can supervisors evaluate the impact upon teaching of groups of teachers working without direct supervisory intervention on the improvement of the teaching process?" (p. 33)

Ideas for group interaction in supervision (Anderson & Snyder, 1993; Beck & Reinhartz, 1989; Doll, 1983; Glickman, Gordon, & Ross-Gordon, 1995; Joyce, Hersh, & McKibben, 1983) have developed over the years. The questions posed by Berman and Usery, however, framed the need to redefine and deliver effective instructional supervision in middle level team situations.

What techniques for small group interaction might be effective? What factors related to teaching could be handled more effectively in a group setting than in an individual conference? (p. 34)

What can be done in a group supervision situation which will enable supervisors to develop unique supervisory styles? (p. 35)

Teaming approaches in middle level schools were already under way when these questions were raised in the supervisory literature. Supervisory practices specific to team teaching needs have largely failed to emerge, however. In his interactive model applied to supervision, Boyd (1966) engaged teachers in dialogue, but only through supervisor led activities. In the introduction to Denemark's chapter, "Coordinating the Team," Lucio (1969) wrote the following:

We must abandon the concept of the "omnicapable" teacher working in lonely professional isolation. We must instead, according to George W. Denemark, view teaching as participation in an instructional team including a broad range of properly coordinated professional and paraprofessional workers. He notes how new developments affect the supervisor and his relationship to the teacher and his staff, and he analyzes the work of paraprofessionals and teacher aides as supporting staff for the classroom teacher (p. 83).

Citing schools in which teaming had been implemented, Denemark (1969) went on to discuss supervisory roles which could be shared with teachers. This involved delegating the responsibility for supervision of teachers and paraprofessionals on teaching teams to the designated team leader or coordinator. Denemark recommended empowered sharing of functions and noted:

What we need to do right now, in my opinion, is advance a different kind of hypothesis for change. I believe we ought to consider the possibility of becoming truly professional in education and in supervision (p. 89).

In describing "supervisory purpose" in such new relationships, Denemark concluded:

Supervisors cannot do anything and everything. . . .They must learn to use themselves in such a way that what they do makes a difference (p. 101).

However, Denemark's concept of team teaching was a hierarchical one. Although it delegated many supervisory functions to the team leader, it only decentralized traditional top-down supervisory procedures. Unruh and Turner (1970) noted that team teaching provided a hierarchical means for decentralizing linear supervisory approaches. "Sometimes the team teacher spends part of his time in the role of the subject supervisor" (p. 11). Hierarchical teams defined leadership skills that were given to the team member who was best prepared to deal with supervisory and administrative responsibilities in leading the team.

Earlier, Shaplin, and Olds (1964) had described a range of team arrangements, from egalitarian to hierarchical. The former provided settings in which team members could deal with staff concerns in need of support while working to improve instructional practices within specific team environments. Egalitarian team models even allowed team leadership to rotate among team members on a term basis.

Anderson (1966) described the supervisory needs of teaming approaches that were evolving in many middle level schools. His definition of team teaching described the collaborative environment in which a more decentralized, traditional supervisory paradigm was needed to monitor and facilitate instructional improvement within teaching teams.

Team teaching is a formal type of cooperative staff organization in which a group of teachers accepts the responsibility for planning, carrying out, and evaluating an educational program or some major portion of the program for an aggregate of pupils (p. 83).

Delegating program evaluation to teams, rather than just to the team leader, was a major departure. Anderson discussed informal and formal teaming approaches, including hierarchical models. In the ideal conception of team teaching he noted:

All team members participate periodically (weekly, if possible) in evaluation sessions of the overall as well as the current program. . . . And finally, each team member is the beneficiary of at least one weekly conference in which episodes of his own teaching (preferably those to which one or more colleagues were witnesses) are carefully and objectively analyzed and out of which specific suggestions and ideas for professional improvements emanate (pp. 91–92).

Anderson was the first to focus on the implications of team teaching for redefining supervisory services in schools that moved to team teaching.

Team teaching has built-in supervisory potentialities—if by supervision we mean influencing the professional performance of a teacher through discussion, observation, and related procedures. Team teaching permits supervision through group work and cooperative efforts. It therefore offers opportunities for leadership to those career teachers who have talents in the supervisory (or exemplary and inspirational) area and at the same time provides a nourishing and stimulating atmosphere in which beginners and other teachers can work (p. 105).

Middle level schools that successfully brought supervision into such collaborative settings have dealt more effectively with the "scope of involvement issues" that Wilhelms (1973) viewed as a major concern.

No other messages teachers receive are quite as powerful as those which tell them how much—or how little—their professional judgments are valued. Human beings create significance; they need to feel that they "count." Professional people have a special need for that freedom of decision and that participation in decision-making which are the very touchstone of a profession. If all the "big" decisions are made elsewhere, by other people, they soon get the message: that they are all right to "teach little things to children," but not quite part of the councils of the grown-ups. And if that is what they feel, their growth will be stunted, no matter how abundantly pater-nalistic kindness and courtesy may flow over them (pp. 41—42).

Bringing teachers into what Wilhelms called "the councils of grown-ups" was a central concern in middle level schools trying to redefine supervisory practice in the late 1960s and 1970s. Leadership and vision were common ingredients in those efforts. Daniel Weppner, principal of Mill Middle School in Williamsville, New York, introduced an innovative approach that has been refined over the quarter century since he left the district.

Weppner developed a leadership cabinet of team leaders that integrated supervisory responsibilities within teams. Team members became involved in defining general leader-ship and supervisory needs as well as variations of proce-dures to meet such needs within individual teams. Teachers took on the responsibility of monitoring, supervising, and evaluating each other's instructional performance according to collaboratively developed, agreed-upon standards.

Those standards have been reviewed and altered as needs changed, team members left, and new persons replaced them. Team members also evaluate their team leaders. They make suggestions for improving supervisory and other processes in individual teams and in the general team rubric. Clinical supervisory approaches have evolved and the peer coaching component developed in the district has also been utilized within teams.

Building administrators and district content area supervi-sors have found that teams involve them for specific and focused help as necessary. This collegiality developed over the years at the classroom level in Mill Middle School. This tradition and practice of empowerment substantially reduced most of the adversarial concerns Blumberg (1974) observed in so many situations. Not a panacea, this concept refined at Mill has established a remarkably successful supervisory para-digm. Professional growth activities are largely defined, implemented, and monitored within the teams themselves.

Clinical supervision has separated teacher evaluation from professional growth needs in many middle level team teach-ing settings. Cogan (1973) contended that supervision could become "clinical" only as it provided direct, trained observa-tion of manifest behaviors in the classroom. Snyder (1988) noted that clinical supervision has developed: "a useful man-agement and supervisory tool for observing teaching and as an observational system which supervisors and principals use in gathering data on teaching performance" (p. 261).

Clinical supervision allows individual teachers to develop instructional goals with the supervisor and establish an action plan for that teacher's evaluation. However, there is no direct interface of clinical supervision with team teaching arrange-ments. As a result, team teaching in middle schools has dealt with program improvement concerns as a staff-based func-tion. Line personnel have worked with staff where staff involved them and sought their expertise for suggestions and feedback. External review or validation of judgments made within the team can be requested as necessary. Tewell (1989) maintained that clinical supervision could "educate teachers to self-examine performance; counsel them on how to learn from analysis of failures" (p. 76).

Peer coaching has facilitated peer supervision in middle level school team teaching settings well beyond what clinical supervision has achieved. It has demonstrated the capacity to monitor instructional improvement at the locus of control of those concerned in specific instructional situations. Teachers in teaming arrangements have been able to identify and determine areas of need, ranging from instructional proce-dures to teacher behaviors in need of improvements. Active, ongoing involvement between the teacher and the person selected as the most appropriate person to do the coaching functions in that circumstance. Problem-solving, two-way communication among peers is developed by and for both the teacher and the coach (Garmston, 1990).

In coaching, teachers define the role of the observer and bestow the power to raise critical issues in that interaction (Garmston, 1990). Teachers do not worry that an area of weakness or need addressed through coaching will "creep" into their evaluation dossiers. This channels the evaluation of total performance of teachers into evaluative channels. It can eliminate anxieties as to whether communication between a supervisor and teacher remains confidential and privileged.

Costa and Kallick (1993) noted that: "Every student and educator too needs a trusted person who will ask provocative questions and offer helpful suggestions" (p. 49).

Like mentors, coaches should not have a line authority relationship with persons they are coaching. Costa and Kallik note that, free of line-staff concerns, a coach can more read-ily develop the trust needed to examine a particular circum-stance. The coach needs to:

- be clear about the nature of the relationship, and not use it for evaluation or judgment;
- listen well, clarifying ideas;
- offer value judgments only upon the request of the learner;
- respond to the learner's work with integrity; and,
- be an advocate for the success of the work (p. 40).

Coaching enhances teacher autonomy by defining the inter-dependence they need to identify professional growth experi-ences in areas the teacher has targeted. Garmston, Linder, and Whitaker (1993) stated:

The ultimate goal of Cognitive Coaching is teacher autonomy: the ability to self-monitor, self-analyze, and self-evaluate. In early cycles of Cognitive Coaching, the coach must draw these capacities from the teacher, but as the cycles continue, a teacher begins to call upon them internally and direct them toward an area of personal interest (p. 58).

In team teaching situations, coaches have to understand the team's program, individual teacher roles on the team, and the instructional procedures employed there. That knowledge helps the coach deal more effectively with the areas in which the teacher seeks clarification and assistance. Garmston, Linder, and Whitaker (1993) further noted:

"When faced with self-analysis, the teachers searched every corner of their minds, letting feelings and ideas surface that might have other-wise gone untapped" (p. 59).

Middle level schools have found coaching to be a powerful, nonthreatening way for teachers to identify personal pedagogical areas that need improvement. Team teachers have contributed to identifying areas with their colleagues, but often those selected to coach are colleagues from other teams who teach the same content areas. Costa and Garmston (1994) believe that teacher confidence in coaching may have the greatest current potential for staff and program improvement.

PUSHING THE ENVELOPE: TWO SITUATIONS

This section describes two situations that feature innovative and effective instructional improvement practices. These practices and supervisory services have developed as responses to the kinds of middle level instructional and supervisory issues and needs discussed earlier.

Manatee Middle School, Naples, Florida

The Manatee Education Center includes the Manatee Middle School, which comprises sixth through eighth grades, and its feeder elementary school. Organized in a house plan, the middle school accommodates the 2,000 students in sixth, seventh, and eighth grades who matriculate from the elementary school. Staff at the K–8 Manatee Education Center longitudinally planned this interfaced elementary–middle level program.

The students come from a population that speaks 47 different languages. A central concern was to provide extended student–teacher relationships. The goal was to maximally engage learning time to accommodate students' diverse cultural, ethnic, and racial backgrounds in helping all to achieve well.

After their preschool and kindergarten experience, students move to a teacher who remains with them through second grade. They then move to another teacher for their third and fourth grade. They then move to another teacher for fifth and sixth grade. Grade five is again self-contained.

The students and their teacher then move together across the campus to the middle school for grade six. There, the teachers engage with another colleague who has also moved with his or her class. They begin to do some two-teacher teaming for both classes. This deals effectively with concerns students and parents often have about moving to the middle school. The extended relationship with their teacher facilitates student adjustment to the new setting.

Gradual instructional changes from their elementary self-contained experiences to beginning teamed experiences provide a stable transition and matriculation for students. After sixth grade, students move to four teacher teams who will remain with them through eighth grade. The Manatee middle school is organized into four vertical houses to extend personal relationships. As students' individual needs allow, brothers and sisters of students go through the same houses to build family relationships and understandings.

There are facilitative support choices available for staff with the principal, dean, curriculum coordinator, and other staff

members at Manatee. These include peer coaching, mentoring, and personal–professional growth plans. Those options have facilitated staff planing to develop appropriately challenging and rigorous learning for students.

The middle school principal, the dean, and the curriculum coordinator at Manatee continue to facilitate a range of supportive activities for the staff. With that support, teachers have developed a series of benchmarks against which longitudinal student skill development can be identified. This has taken advantage of the 80-week span of student–teacher relationships. Teachers have developed inventories of growth and achievement, including both test benchmarks and authentic assessment, using portfolios of student work.

Evaluation of total teacher performance at Manatee is provided through clinical supervision in both the elementary and secondary buildings. Each beginning teacher works with a three-person team consisting of the building principal, a teacher, and another educator in the building whom the beginning teacher elects. Teachers remain the basic support team for 90 days. If progress is satisfactory the teacher may elect to continue that group and change the two members selected for the remainder of their period of probationary service.

Several options have been developed for situations in which clinical supervision identifies a teacher to be in difficulty. Staff are given the option of selecting the kind of team provided for beginning teachers to assess the difficulty and identify steps to correct those difficulties. The infrequency with which this option needs to be used confirms the effectiveness of the professional growth options available to staff and the high priority they have developed for continued professional growth.

Professional growth options separate out to choices made by the teacher. Available options include peer coaching, mentoring, and selection of a two- to four-person cohort professional support group. Once on continuing contract, teachers have the option of continuing a clinical rubric for their formal evaluation or electing a two- or three-year professional development plan. The latter involves identifying the area or areas in which the teacher intends to develop or extend skills and background, an outline of the experiences to be pursued in those areas, and definition of how the individual's progress will be identified and reported. This then becomes a contract which can be used for annual updating.

In combination with available peer coaching and mentoring options, this approach is elected by most teachers and has proven highly effective for professional development. An option for annual assessment by the administration is also available but is being elected less frequently. The two- to four-person professional cohort support group mentioned earlier has proven very effective with the middle level staff. They choose individuals particularly suited to the two-year sequence they teach. The middle school curriculum coordinator and dean are both widely chosen. The middle school principal and elementary school assistant principal are often chosen by fifth and sixth grade teachers to examine areas of program transition from one building to the next.

Working with teams as groups, the Manatee principal, dean, and curriculum coordinator have been able to facilitate a range of team instructional needs. Sergiovanni and Starratt

(1988) defined groups as "a collection of persons which is mutually reinforcing." Although they did not relate this to team teaching, a number of their points apply to team teaching. In considering whether or not groups make better decisions and are more efficient than individuals, they noted:

By and large, experts seem to suggest that group decisions are indeed better, although there are exceptions. Often the most informed person in the group can make a better decision if left alone. Indeed, group pressure can bring this person down to the group level. But it seems clear that for the most part, decision-making efficiency improves within the group context (p. 165).

Sergiovanni and Starratt concluded that supervision needs to take on more of a group character. The two opportunities they identified have also been used with middle level school teaching teams.

Opportunities for interaction and communication should be provided to enable groups to discuss intergroup problems with the aim that the groups will be better coordinated. Opportunities for rotation of members among groups should be provided to stimulate mutual understanding and empathy (p. 167).

Supervisory personnel at Manatee have worked to support the needs and demands of staff for continued professional development in extending this unique program.

Dallastown Area Middle School, Dallastown, Pennsylvania

The Dallastown Area Middle School spans the sixth to eighth grades and serves students from five feeder elementary schools. It currently houses 1,300 students, with further growth anticipated. Dallastown has developed an approach designed to restructure the middle school, its staff, and programs through a range of means for curriculum planning and staff development.

Clinical supervisory procedures separate evaluation of total teacher performance from program and instructional improvement. The principal and assistant principal devote a major portion of their time to a variation of the clinical model that encourages teachers to initiate multiple postobservational conferences to review procedures refined beyond the initial clinical observation.

Based on Glickman et al's notion (1995) that developmental supervision seeks to improve student learning, the purpose of the Dallastown Middle School's restructuring process is "to provide our teachers with the best professional practice skills necessary in order that our students receive the best education possible."

The staff development program incorporates a wide range of professional growth options, including peer coaching, mentoring, staff release time, bringing college courses related to specific staff development goals to the middle school, and "turn-key" programs and seminars offered by staff who have developed and successfully implemented new instructional practices.

Personal professional or group (team) staff development projects have the following support allocations: Each teacher has eight school days of professional release time every four school years. They can use release days to gather information, visit other sites, and pursue other professional development activities that achieve the goals of their approved improvement projects. Teachers are not limited to taking two days annually; they can petition for additional days if their needs in a particular staff development project require more than the eight-day total.

Each teacher is also allotted $2,100 to attend conferences over a four-year period. In addition to that amount, the administration has a pool of another 140 conference days to which teachers can be "assigned" if their allotted conference budget has been exhausted and their projects warrant such additional support.

The district retains the services of a nationally recognized consultant to work with middle level staff. Line and staff personnel have found the consultant's background in middle level education, supervision, and curriculum development to be a highly valuable asset to this program. The consultant provides 25 days per school year and conducts an annual summer workshop for staff. Additional consultant time is negotiable. This longitudinal involvement on an ongoing basis has provided benefits in several dimensions.

Service and support by the consultant include advisement and help in planning and developing specific activities, substantive information (references to information, sources, and sites where practices of interest are functioning), and suggestions for designing or carrying out activities. When requested, the consultant schedules time to meet with teaching teams during team planning time to discuss initiatives or concerns they wish to discuss. This assistance in professional growth initiatives has raised staff confidence and comfort in working with the consultant.

The consultant provides a unique function jointly defined by administration and staff. The consultant can be asked to deliver professional concerns and suggestions which staff want brought to the attention of line administrators. This has facilitated important professional concerns being forwarded with confidentiality and guarantees staff anonymity. Privileged confidentiality governs all of the consultant's interactions in the school.

Both line and staff have identified a "back door" kind of "serendipitous" evaluation that has emerged in that relationship. Since the consultant operates in a confidential relationship with them, staff have increasingly asked for evaluative feedback in particular circumstances. Teachers can ask administrators, counselors, staff colleagues, and the outside consultant to sit in on their classes and provide solicited feedback. Confidentiality is required between the teacher and observer in those situations.

This gives teachers access to expertise in a truly non-threatening setting. Their active participation overcomes Sergiovanni's and Starratt's concern (1983) regarding teacher participation in traditional supervisory conferences. They noted that "teachers generally assume passive roles and are exposed to logically structured programs or activities" (p. 331). This use of the consultant at Dallastown provides an independent opportunity for teachers to reflect and identify possibilities beyond the interactions teachers normally have with line supervisors.

A list of substitute teachers recommended and approved by teachers is used to release teachers for professional growth activities. Those substitutes are also used to cover classes when other particular duties, occur (e.g., the Teacher Steering Committee meets during the school day six times during the year).

The Teacher Steering Committee is an appointed group. Not a decision-making body, it receives issues from the staff for specific staff development initiatives. The final decision on initiating particular projects is made by the faculty as a whole along with the principal and assistant principal. The Teacher Steering Committee conducts regular building surveys to identify areas that are excelling, as well as staff concerns that might be developed into specific project proposals for the staff development program. For example, the successful use of portfolio assessment with students has raised the suggestion that portfolio evaluation for teachers be considered. A staff development proposal would require teacher union and school board approval.

A Building Council of staff volunteers represents every grade level and as many subject areas as possible. The principal, assistant principal, and a guidance counselor also meet with the council. The Building Council meets after the school day as needed.

The Middle Level Parent Advisory Group includes representatives from the Teacher Steering Committee and meets on a regular basis to obtain parents' input and provide answers to parents' questions. The principal and assistant principal attend as requested to give advice and answer questions.

Each year teams establish goals and evaluate results. Teams select an outside person (e.g., a teacher not on the team, a counselor, the principal or assistant principal, or the outside consultant) to participate in the evaluation.

A School Rumor Committee consists of three teachers who are recommended by the faculty. Trained in conflict-resolution skills, they track down erroneous information and deal with rumors to help assure that perception of conditions, occurrences, and incidents in the school are accurate. Wilson, Madison-Byar, Shapiro, and Schell (1969) pointed to the need to reconstruct supervisory services in ways that better facilitate teacher development needs.

What was needed was a conscious reconstruction of the supervisory role around the facilitation of inventiveness. By definition, inventiveness, since it breeds diversity, leads, first, to the teacher-role differentiation, and then to role inter-dependence of the type which must be reflected in institutional structures (p. 26).

Some may question the relationship of the Building, Council Middle Level Parent Advisory Group, and School Rumor Committee to the professional growth of staff. The availability of those elements at Dallastown provides effective means of separating and addressing specific concerns that affect teachers. Those channels substantially enhance the school environment for teachers and allow professional growth opportunities to focus more specifically on teachers' professional and pedagogical needs and concerns.

The Teacher Steering Committee coordinates those concerns and suggests possibilities for dealing with those needs. Conference participation support, mentoring, peer coaching, staff and college seminars, the outside consultant, and released time provide a range of opportunities to specifically address those needs at the staff level.

The Dallastown Middle School staff and administration agree that this program has opened up new and successful ways of stimulating teacher development. They concur that this program has established a culture that has effectively prmoted staff development. During its three years, this program has provided specific support service for instructional improvement. It has enabled staff to identify, meet, and address instructional improvement and program refinement needs.

Staff, administration, parents, and the Dallastown Board of Education have found that the continued results of this program justify the costs required to maintain it.

Both the Manatee and Dallastown programs illustrate ways in which middle level schools have sought to empower staff decision-making in improving instruction in their environments. There is a combined gain of staff ownership and esteem with acceptance of line leadership personnel. Those practices reflect another of Alfonso, Firth, and Neville's principles (1975):

Proposition 25: Change will be more effective when leadership and acceptance from within the group to be influenced come from an individual with group membership and esteem (p. 192).

That focus has also probably contributed to the development of successful practices such as cooperative learning, team teaching, heterogeneous grouping, and integrated curriculum in both schools.

Clinical supervision has improved evaluation of individual teacher performance. Models in which line evaluation of the total effectiveness of team and other collaborative teaching settings have not been developed, however. Lacking such approaches, middle level school practice is delegating greater instructional improvement responsibilities to the locus of staff decision-making. While gains from those approaches will be evaluated longitudinally, administration and staff at Manatee and Dallastown both concur that the staff-based activities described have led to noticeable faculty development and program improvement.

Improvements developed by individual teachers are communicated to other colleagues members through team planning. That frequently causes other team members to consider implementing them and to obtain the skills needed to do so. This emulates group learning and use of individual student progress in classroom cooperative learning arrangements.

Administrators in both schools have also found many teachers are bringing heightened awareness of their instructional strengths and needs to their clinical supervision activities. Teachers have carried over the results of their clinical supervisory post-conferences to staff interaction opportunities. These experiences have helped to increase their abilities to identify, develop, and refine those instructional skills.

Glickman, Gordon, and Ross-Gordon (1995) used the Johari window to visualize the needs for such programs. Its four panes indicate: (I) the public self; (II) the blind self; (III) the private self; and (IV) the unknown self.

In pane I (the public self) are the behaviors that both supervisor and teachers know the supervisor uses. In pane II (the blind self) are the behaviors unknown to the supervisor's self but known by teachers. In pane III (the private self) are behaviors about which the supervisor has knowledge that teachers do not. In pane IV (the unknown self) are actions taken by the teacher of which neither supervisor nor teacher is aware.

The confidential role of the consultant at Dallastown shows potential for moving supervisory practices from panes II through IV to Pane I. Until an interfaced line-staff supervisory model is developed to do that, it seems that an independent source is needed to emulate the consultant's contributions in the Dallastown program.

Delegation of staff and instructional improvement in the two situations described here has accommodated such needs in ways that line supervisory arrangements have not. Despite the accomplishments achieved by delegating program and instructional improvement to teachers, the need to interface line and staff operations in developing more broadly effective supervisory services persists at the middle and all school levels.

RETHINKING LEADERSHIP FOR INSTRUCTIONAL IMPROVEMENT

Innovations in middle level instructional improvement services present a threshold for rethinking educational supervisory leadership practices. Chaos theory (Wheatley, 1992) holds an interesting potential for that consideration. It maintains that order can emerge out of chaos. Fixed and rigid systems for running organizations now need to be replaced by new models that provide flexibility and the capacity to change. Wheatley notes that in natural systems, order is not imposed from without but emerges from within, reflecting on ways that organizations could similarly respond to events as they occur and improve their effectiveness. A greater dynamic is similarly needed to identify and access appropriate information that addresses needs for staff improvement.

Wheatley (1992) identifies "meaning" as one of the strongest forces that shapes an organization. That is driven by how our participation shapes efforts and develops more effective outcomes. She noted:

I believe in my bones that the movement towards participation is rooted, perhaps subconsciously for now, in our changing perceptions of the organizing principles of the universe. This may sound grandiose, but the quantum realm speaks emphatically to the role of participation, even to its impact on creating reality. As physicists describe the participatory universe, how can we fail to share in it and embrace it in our management practices? Will participation go away? Not until our science changes (p. 143).

Wheatley described how business organizations are finding that collaborative team planning dramatically improves upon results of isolated planning by individuals. Outside the middle level, however, schools have advocated such a concept more than they have embraced it. Mintzberg (1994) wrote that to improve their effectiveness in our society of increasing information, schools need to develop planning mechanisms that differ from isolated, linear procedures. Although middle level practice has moved in that direction, schools have traditionally attempted to avoid chaos and process operations through fixed procedures.

This chapter has maintained that line supervisory arrangements have had diminishing returns in assisting staff improvement. The ratio of supervisors to those whom they supervise has continued to increase. In most situations, opportunities for the focused, personalized interactions needed to help staff improve skills are either inadequate or nonexistent. There clearly is a critical need for new approaches to deal with those unmet and growing needs.

In any school, such needs will be serendipitous, even chaotic. According to Chaos theory, order can emerge out of such chaos. Educational supervisors might consider Wheatley's concerns about "'fractal organizations."

The potent force that shapes behavior in fractal organizations, as in all natural systems, is the combination of simply expressed expectations of acceptable behavior and the freedom available to individuals to assert themselves in non-deterministic ways. Fractal organizations, though they may never have heard the word fractal, have learned to trust in natural organizing phenomena. They trust in the power of guiding principles or values, knowing that they are strong enough influences on behavior to shape every employee into a desired representative of the organization. These organizations expect to see similar behaviors show up at every level in the organization because those behaviors were patterned into the organizing principles at the very start (p. 132).

Wheatley referred to this unaccountable force in shaping behavior as the behavior of "strange attractors." Strange attractors are defined as something at work within the organization which shapes the behavior of all within it. Longitudinally, strange attractors define limits in which patterns of activity and support evolve and function. Strange attractors are seen as a strong creative force that can guide members to shape an organization and make it flourish, even during chaotic times. Supervisory efforts to improve instruction can be defined by identifying the strange attractors within a school or school district's environment.

For example, three-dimensional computer models have found that while short-range weather forecasting is inconsistent, long-term plotting of those phenomena identify the "strange attractors" in the patterns and the limits around them.

Senge (1990) identified "circles of causality" which parallel Wheatley's notions about strange attractors. In causality circles, the tensions are growth against limits, establishing the dynamic of tension which Senge viewed as setting up a balancing phenomenon.

In each case of limits to growth, there is a reinforcing (amplifying) process of growth or improvement that operates on its own for a period of time. Then it runs up against a balancing (or stabilizing) process, which operates to limit the growth (p. 97).

Senge also spoke of developing "creative tensions" in systems thinking within organizations.

The key (to more effective creativity) is "creative tension," the tension between vision and reality. The most effective people are those who can "hold" their vision while remaining committed to seeing current reality clearly. This principle is no less true for organizations. The hallmark of a learning organization is not lonely visions floating in space, but a relentless willingness to examine "what is" in light of our vision (p. 226).

He viewed this as the potential for schools to organize dynamic planning that responds more effectively to instructional and learning needs. Senge's notion poses a challenge to traditional linear and "top-down" supervisory procedures. The "circle of causality" clearly requires parity of involvement for those seeking improvement. Their focus on self-improvement optimally should be the initiator of efforts for personal improvement.

Wheatley observed that information both informs and forms us. The success of clinical and coaching approaches to instructional improvement needs reflects her contention that relations are all that there is and that results are limited when individuals work separately or in isolation from one another.

Finally, Wheatley maintained that, within organizational operations, individuals can no longer function effectively by themselves. She believed it was essential that team members know how to talk to each other, how to listen, how to communicate with each other, how to support each other, and how to solve problems.

Middle level schools are high-energy places, but educational folklore contends that they are chaotic. Middle level school educational advances reflect chaos theory's contention that order can emerge out of chaos. Shared decision-making and delegated decision-making to staff have empowered them to bring professional resources to bear upon specific middle level school instructional improvement needs. Moving that farther ahead will require shifting traditional line-staff supervisory patterns to collegial, interdependent line-staff arrangements.

WAITING FOR GODOT

Supervision has had minimal success in improving the long-standing problem of teacher perception of the place and function of supervisory service. Neville (1968) noted:

Teachers continue to recognize a contradiction and express strong ambivalence about the place and function of supervisory services. Keep in mind—they may be wrong! Supervisors, in fact, may be human-relations oriented; they may have the skills to help teachers study the process of teaching—but if so, we have not measurably communicated these facts to those who stand to profit from our services (p. 416).

This writer maintains that the problem goes beyond perception alone. In this regard, there has been some lack of willingness and/or ability of supervisors to deal with the following (Toepfer, 1973):

The specific problem appears to be that supervision has not probed the expected potential of innovative efforts to improve the broad level of instruction on a systematic continuum. . . . The need for supervision to involve all factors in cooperative decision-making remains largely unfulfilled as most school districts consider possible innovations. Initial failure of these efforts centers about an unwillingness to delegate sufficient authority to involve a broad professional base in planning how innovative departures can be most effectively implemented (p. 740).

The linear, top-down, administrative–supervisory rubric has frustrated efforts to make supervision a shared or a staff function. Mark Twain mused about the reports of his death being premature. The decline of inspectorial, autocratic supervision envisioned by Douglas and Boardman (1961) was even more premature.

The influences which led to the decline of inspectorial, autocratic supervision are quite fundamental. One is the recognition of the falsity of the assumption that there are definite best methods of teaching in which the supervisor, because of his superior knowledge, can direct teachers. . . . Autocratic supervision suppresses teaching initiative and originality, producing pattern teaching and mediocrity (p. 2).

Those conditions persist and supervision has yet to deal with them as the authors thought. In what they saw as the "modern concept of supervision," Douglass and Boardman maintained that "good supervision is democratic."

Democracy in education includes the ideal of cooperation, of teachers and supervisors working together on common problems. The emphasis is placed on teacher growth, on teacher discussion, and determination of the various aims, plans, methods, and procedures for the improvement of education, and on development of the teachers' powers of self-direction (p. 3).

The success of supervisors in responding to changing instructional needs over the years has not been outstanding. The lock of linear approaches focused on administrative control remains a difficult one to open. Although the medical model has many faults, hospital administrators run the hospital as efficiently as possible, but they do not supervise physicians. The notion of educational supervision as an administrative function has some persisting flaws which require correction.

First, effective school administrative skill and instructional practice are not and should not be assumed as mutually inclusive. Second, criteria need to be established for those assigned instructional supervision responsibilities. Instructional supervisors should either have been or be very effective teachers and have an excellent understanding of effective teaching/learning practice. Third, supervisors need to keep abreast of developments in those areas and their own continuing growth in that area monitored. Fourth, line supervisory responsibilities need to be reconceptualized to extend staff authority, responsibility, and involvement in instructional evaluation. Developments in teaching and learning continue to bear out Burnham's (1962) concern:

Supervisors are challenged today as never before to continue their study on the job. The many demands for rapid change in the instructional program have brought about this challenge (p. 163).

The development of programs and procedures that "supervise supervisors" and identify ways to provide for their continuing needs for professional growth continues to elude us. The failure of supervision to move in those directions may have contributed to Starratt's (1992) suggestion to abolish supervision. He suggested that

teacher supervision by building level or system level administrators be abolished as a practice in all schools and school systems. To some that may sound outrageous, indefensible, even arbitrary. I am not using that suggestion for shock value. Rather, I am proposing the abolition of supervision for serious consideration. I want to make it clear at the outset what I mean by supervision. I am speaking of supervision as experienced by most teachers, as evaluation of classroom teaching. Whether that practice follows procedures under the rubric of clinical supervision, human resource supervision, developmental supervision, democratic supervision, classroom effectiveness supervision, or whatever, it does not matter. No matter how sophisticated the procedures, if it involves a supervisor observing a classroom teaching episode, a post observation conference with the teacher, and a written report that goes into the teacher's file, then that is supervision and I propose we abolish it (p. 14).

Evolving middle level instructional practice requires a supervisory model based upon the equatarian notion of Burton and Brueckner (1955).

The improvement of teachers is not so much a supervisory function in which teachers participate as it is a teacher function in which supervisors cooperate (p. 10).

Developmental supervision (Glickman et al, 1995), clinical supervision, coaching, and peer supervisory arrangements have provided windows to develop supportive arrangements based upon middle level instructional needs.

However, needs for staff involvement in teacher evaluation persist. Unless such practice evolves, there is a possibility that Starratt's suggestion to abolish supervision will become a serious consideration. Taken to the ultimate conclusion, teacher empowerment will bring about staff assimilation of functions previously "done" to them.

In response to Starratt, Waite (1992) discussed what a supervisory paradigm shift might look like. In dealing with the issue of power, Waite cited Dunlap and Goldman (1991), who viewed facilitative power as "an act of relationship between equals where acts of domination are the least desired alternatives" (p. 6).

Waite noted that in Dunlap's and Goldman's definition, "power with" replaces "power over" in "creating conditions to facilitate each other's success" (p. 26). Waite raised pivotal questions:

Do supervisors somehow block teachers' empowerment or their control over instruction and curriculum? If so, how? Do supervisors' unconscious interactional processes belie the ideas of equality? Is the supervisor's role simply the control of teachers through evaluation or other means, either overt or covert? (p. 26)

Waite's final question asks: "Why should co-equal relations between teacher and supervisors be readily accepted by teachers?" (p. 27). The collaborative middle level instructional improvement activities discussed in this chapter suggest that middle level staff are willing to accept and have accepted such opportunities. The "why" for that acceptance seems to be grounded in professional commitment to improve teaching and learning in middle level school programs.

This reflects Glickman's long-standing view of "supervisory glue as the metaphor for success" (Glickman, Gordon, & Ross-Gordon, 1995, p. 5) in which the ultimate goal of supervision is the improvement of student learning. In that sense, evolving middle level supervisory practice tests the rule of tradition. Middle level schools have not embraced Starratt's notion to abolish supervision but, in many respects, have simply done an "end run" around supervision. However, failure to develop new supervisory paradigms could make it the platform for gaining that empowerment.

Tinkering with linear supervisory models will not meet the needs for a reconceptualized middle level supervisory system. This is a reality that has to be faced. Waite (1992) concluded with this admonition:

The future is ever unfolding. Supervisors may contribute to the paradigm shift and help create schools and relationships reflective of democratic values. Or supervisors and their charges may be swept along by other people's agendas (p. 27).

Current needs provide an important opportunity to design new paradigms that will allow supervision to develop exciting possibilities for consideration at other school levels as well. The failure of supervision to embrace the opportunity at this watershed point in education could result in more disruptive solutions. Even if Kriegel and Patler's (1991) notion—"if it ain't broke . . . BREAK IT!"—comes to pass, it should not be by default.

CONCLUSION

From this writer's experience, middle level education has demonstrated interest and willingness to participate in identifying ways to improve supervisory practice. The kinds of middle level instructional practices discussed in this chapter have created needs for different supervisory support. The response of beginning collaborative and interactive line-staff supervisory practice in middle level schools warrants serious attention. It has established differences of kind and degree that have broken from traditional line-directed approaches to instructional improvement.

Middle level school staff have gained confidence in the empowerment they have realized in horizontal interaction with line personnel. This has, in turn, led to growing staff ownership and commitment to extend and push those efforts forward. Improvement in instruction and individual teacher practice attributed to those activities has reached a point in which careful analysis of claimed advantages can now be designed and undertaken. Elementary, high school and district-wide supervision would do well to study these middle level departures. They appear to offer valuable suggestions for developing paradigms that respond more effectively to demands for improved supervisory support.

REFERENCES

Acheson, K. & Gall, M. (1980). *Techniques of clinical supervision of teachers: Preservice and in-service applications* (3rd ed.). New York: Longman.

Adams, H. & Dickey, C. (1953). *Basic principles of supervision.* New York: American Book Company.

Alfonso, R. & Goldsberry, L. (1982). Colleagueship in supervision. In T. Sergiovanni (Ed.). *Supervision of teaching,* 1982 ASCD Yearbook. Arlington, VA: ASCD.

Alfonso, R., Firth, G., & Neville, R. (1975). *Instructional supervision: A behavioral system.* Boston: Allyn & Bacon.

Anderson, R. (1966). *Teaching in a world of change.* New York: Harcourt, Brace, & World.

Anderson, R. & Snyder, K. (1993). *Clinical supervision: Coaching for higher performance.* Lancaster, PA: Technomic.

Barr, A. (1937). *An introduction to the scientific study of classroom supervision.* New York: D. Appleton & Company. *Kappan, 76*(8), 616–622.

Beane, J. (1990). *Affect in the curriculum: Toward democracy, dignity and diversity.* New York: Teachers College Press.

Beane, J. (1992). Turning the floor over: Reflections on a middle school curriculum. *Middle School Journal, 12*(5), 1–5.

Beane, J. (1993). *A middle school curriculum: From rhetoric to reality* (2nd ed.). Columbus OH: National Middle School Association.

Beane, J., Toepfer, C. Jr., & Alessi, S., Jr. (1986). *Curriculum planning and development.* Boston: Allyn & Bacon.

Beck, D. & Reinhartz, J. (1989). *Supervision: Focus on instruction.* New York: Harper & Row.

Berman, L. & Usery, M. (1966). *Personalized supervision.* Washington, D.C.: ASCD, National Education Association.

Blumberg, A. (1974). *Supervisors and teachers: A private cold war* (2nd ed.). Berkeley, CA: McCutchan Publishing Company.

Boardman, C., Douglass, H., & Bent, R. (1953). *Democratic supervision in secondary schools.* Cambridge, MA: The Riverside Press.

Boyd, R. (1966). An interactive model applied to supervision. In J. Raths. & R. Leeper (Eds.). *The supervisor: Agent for change in teaching* (pp. 11–24). Washington, D.C.: ASCD, National Education Association.

Bovee, C. (1967, April). Is war too serious for the generals? *Impact on Instructional Improvement, 2*(2), 5–10.

Braddock, J., Wu, S., & McPartland, J. (1988, March. *Practices in the middle grades: National variations and effects.* Baltimore: The Center for Research on Elementary and Middle Schools, Johns Hopkins University.

Briggs, T. (1920). *The junior high school.* Boston: Houghton Mifflin.

Briggs, T. & Justman, J. (1952). *Improving instruction through supervision.* New York: Macmillan.

Bunker, F. (1909). Minutes of the November 30, 1909 meeting, *Board of Education Minutes.* Berkeley, CA.

Burnham, R. (1962, December). In-service education of supervisors. *Educational Leadership, 20*(3), 163–166.

Burton, W. & Brueckner, L. (1955). *Supervision: A social process* (3rd ed.). New York: Appleton-Century-Crofts.

Clark, D. & Clark, S. (1994). *Restructuring the middle level school: Implications for school leaders.* Albany: State University of New York Press.

Cogan, M. (1973). *Clinical supervision.* Boston: Houghton Mifflin.

Coldiron, R., Braddock, J., & McPartland, J. (1987, April). *Description of school structures and classroom practices in elementary, middle, and secondary schools.* Baltimore: The Center for Research on Elementary and Middle Schools, Johns Hopkins University.

Costa, A. & Garmston, R. (1994). *Cognitive coaching: A foundation for renaissance schools.* Norwood, MA: Christopher-Gordon Publishers.

Costa, A. & Kallick, B. (1993, October). Through the lens of a critical friend. *Educational Leadership, 51*(2), 49–51.

Crosby, M. (1957). *Supervision as cooperative action.* New York: Appleton-Century-Crofts.

Denemark, G. (1969). Coordinating the team. In W. Lucio (Ed.). *The supervisor: New demands—new dimensions* (pp. 83–101). Washington, D.C.: ASCD, National Education Association.

Doll, R. (1983). *Supervision for staff development: Ideas and approaches.* Boston: Allyn & Bacon.

Douglass, H., Bent, R., & Boardman, C. (1961). *Democratic supervision in secondary schools.* Cambridge, MA: The Riverside Press.

Dunlap, D. & Goldman, P. (1991). Rethinking power in schools. *Educational Administration Quarterly, 27*(1), 5–29.

Eichhorn, D. (1966). *The middle school.* New York: Center for Applied Research in Education (Jointly reprinted in 1986 by the National Association of Secondary School Principals, Reston, VA, and the National Middle School Association, Columbus, OH).

Eisner, E. (1978, May). The impoverished mind. *Educational Leadership, 35*(3), 622.

Eliot, C. (1898). *Shortening the elementary school and extending the high school. Educational reform: Essays and addresses.* New York: Century Company.

Epstein, J. (1990, February). What matters in the middle grades—grade span or practices? *Kappan, 71*(6), 438–444.

Epstein, J. & MacIver, D. (1990, Winter). The middle grades: Is grade span the most important issue? *Educational Horizons. 68*(2), 88–94.

Eye, G. & Netzer, L. (1971). *Supervision of instruction: A phase of administration.* New York: Harper & Row.

Feldlaufer, H., Midgley, C., & Eccles, J. (1987). *Student, teacher, and observer perceptions of the classroom environment before and after the transition to junior high school.* Ann Arbor, MI: University of Michigan.

Galloway, C. & Mulhern, E. (1973). Professional development and self renewal. In J. Frymier (Ed.). *A school for tomorrow* (p. 34). Berkeley, CA: McCutchan.

Garmston, R., Linder, C., & Whitaker, J. (1993, October). Reflections on cognitive coaching. *Educational Leadership, 51*(2), 57–79.

Garmston, R. (1990, Spring). Is peer coaching changing supervisory relationships? Some reflections. *California Journal of Curriculum and Supervision, 3*(2), 21–27.

George, P., Spruel, M., & Moorefield, J. (1987). *Long-term student-teacher relationships.* Columbus, OH: National Middle School Association.

Gittell, M. (1971). Supervisors and coordinators: Power in the system. In V. Haubrich (Ed.). *Freedom, bureaucracy, and schooling,* 1971 ASCD Yearbook (pp. 161–173). Washington, D.C.: ASCD, National Education Association.

Glickman, C., Gordon, S., & Ross-Gordon, J. (1995). *Supervision of instruction: A developmental approach* (3rd ed.). Boston: Allyn & Bacon.

Goldhammer, R., Anderson, R., & Krajewski, R. (1993). *Clinical supervision: Special methods for the supervision of teachers* (3rd ed.). New York: Harcourt Brace Jovanovich.

Grimmett, P., Rostad, O., & Ford, B, (1992). The transformation of supervision. In C. Glickman (Ed.). *Supervision in transition,* 1992 ASCD Yearbook (pp. 185–202). Alexandria, VA: ASCD.

Gruhn, W. & Douglass, H. (1947). *The modern junior high school.* New York: The Ronald Press.

Gwynn, J. M. (1961). *Theory and practice of supervision.* New York: Dodd, Mead, & Co.

Hall. G. S. (1905). *Adolescence, its psychology and its relations to physiology, anthropology, sociology, sex, crime, religion and education* (Vol. II). New York: D. Appleton & Company.

Hammock, R. & Owings, R. (1955). *Supervising instruction in secondary schools.* New York: McGraw-Hill.

Harnack, R. et al. (1977, March). The supervisor and curriculum worker: Commitment and competence. In C. Toepfer (Ed.). *Impact on Instructional Improvement, 13*(1), 1–36.

Harnack, R. (1967, April). Freedom to plan and teach. *Impact on Instructional Improvement, 2*(2), 31–36.

Johnston, J. H. et al. (1985). *An agenda for excellence at the middle level.* Reston, VA: National Association of Secondary School Principals.

Joyce. B., Hersh, R., & McKibben, R. (1983). *The structure of school improvement.* New York: Longman.

Kramer, R. (1985). Adolescence: Is it really necessary? *Transescence: The Journal on Emerging Adolescent Education, 18*(2), 44–50.

Kriegel, R. & Patler, L. (1991). *If it aint' broke . . . break it!* New York: Warner Books.

Leeper, R. (Ed.). (1969). *Changing supervision for changing times.* Washington, D.C.: ASCD, National Education Association.

Lucio, W. & McNeil, J. (1962). *Supervision: A synthesis of thought and action,* (3rd ed.). New York: McGraw-Hill.

Lucio, W. (Ed.). (1969). *The supervisor: New demands—new dimensions.* Washington, D.C.: ASCD, National Education Association.

Melton G. (1995, November 6). Personal conversation with C. F. Toepfer.

Mintzberg, H. (1994). *The rise and fall of strategic planning: Reconceiving roles for planning, plans, planners.* New York: The Free Press.

Myers, A., Kifer, L., Merry, R., & Foley, F. (1924). *Cooperative supervision in the public schools.* New York: Prentice-Hall.

National Education Association. (1907). The report of the committee on the equal division of the twelve years in the public schools between the district and the high school, *Journal of Proceedings and Addresses at the Forty-sixth Annual Meeting.* Chicago, IL: University of Chicago Press.

National Middle School Association. (1995). *This we believe.* Columbus, OH: Author.

Neville, R. (1968, February). The supervisor we need. *Educational Leadership, 25*(5), 414–417.

Pajak, E. (1993). *Approaches to clinical supervision: Alternatives for improving instruction.* Norwood, MA: Christopher-Gordon, Publishers.

Roderick, M. (1991, March). Unpublished paper reported in *Education Week,* p. 18.

Senge, P. (1990). *The fifth discipline: The art of practice of the learning organization.* New York: Doubleday & Company.

Sergiovanni, T. (1987). The theoretical basis for cultural leadership. In L. Shrieve & M. Schonheit (Eds.). *Leadership: Examining the elusive* (p. 121). Alexandria, VA: ASCD.

Sergiovanni, T. & Starratt, R. (1988). Supervision and group effectiveness *Supervision: Human perspectives* (4th ed.) pp. 149–171. New York: McGraw-Hill.

Shawan, J. (1910). *Annual report of the board of education of the city of Columbus for the year ending August 31, 1909.* Columbus, OH: Board of Education. Chicago: University of Chicago Press.

Shafer, H. (1967, October). Who becomes the voice of the turtle? *Impact on Instructional Improvement, 3*(1), 5–9.

Shaplin, J. (1964). Antecedents of team teaching. In J. Shaplin & H. Olds, Jr. (Eds.). *Team teaching* (pp. 24–56). New York: Harper & Row.

Shon, D. (1988). Coaching reflective teaching. In P. Grimmett & G. Erikson (Eds.). *Reflection in teacher education.* New York: Teachers College Press.

Sizer, T. (1992). *Horace's school: Redesigning the American high school.* Boston, MA: Houghton Mifflin.

Smith, S. (1990). *The collaborative school: A work environment for effective instruction.* Eugene, OR: ERIC Clearinghouse on Educational Management.

Snyder, K. (1988). Clinical supervision. In R. Gorton (Ed.). *Encyclopedia of school administration and supervision.* Phoenix, AZ: Oryx Press.

Starratt, R. (1992, July). A modest proposal: Abolish supervision (Paper presented at the Annual Meeting of the Council of Professors of Professional Supervision, Houston, TX, November 1991). *Wingspan, 8*(1), 14–19.

Tewell, K. (1989, April). Collaborative supervision theory into practice. *NASSP Bulletin, 76*(4), 34–38.

Toepfer, C., Jr. (1973, May). The supervisor's responsibility for innovation. *Educational Leadership, 30*(8), 740–744.

Toepfer, C., Jr. (1982). Organizational strategies for two-grade middle level schools. *Dissemination services on the middle grades.* Springfield, MA: Educational Leadership Institute.

Toepfer, C., Jr. (1986, November). Middle level transition and articulation issues. *Middle School Journal, 18*(1), 9–11.

Toepfer, C., Jr. (1990). Revisioning middle level education: A prelude to restructuring. *Educational Horizons, 68*(2), 95–99.

Toepfer, C., Jr. et al. (1993). *Achieving excellence through the middle level curriculum.* Reston, VA: National Association of Secondary School Principals.

Unruh, A. & H. Turner. (1970). *Supervision for change and innovation.* Boston: Houghton Mifflin.

Waite, D. (1992). What would a paradigm shift in supervision look like? (Paper presented at the Annual Meeting of the Council of Professors of Professional Supervision, Houston, TX, November 1991). *Wingspan, 8*(1), 25–28.

Wheatley, M. (1992). *Leadership and the new science: Learning about organizations from an orderly universe.* San Francisco: Berrett-Koehler.

Wiles, K. (1955). *Supervision for better schools* (rev. ed.). New York: Prentice-Hall.

Wiles, K. (1967). *Supervision for better schools* (3rd ed.). Englewood Cliffs, NJ: Prentice-Hall.

Wilhelms, F. (1973). *Supervision in a new key.* Washington, D.C.: ASCD, National Education Association.

Wilson, C., Madison-Byar, T., Shapiro, A., & Schell, S. (1969). Supervision: Heir to the planning function. *Sociology of supervision* (pp. 25–38). Boston: Allyn & Bacon.

26

SUPERVISION IN
SECONDARY SCHOOLS

Judith A. Aiken

UNIVERSITY OF VERMONT

Daniel Tanner

RUTGERS UNIVERSITY

INTRODUCTION: HISTORICAL BACKGROUND AND PERSPECTIVES

Teacher development has received increased attention in the educational literature and has become the focus of numerous efforts to solve educational problems and reform current educational practice (Courter & Ward, 1983; Fullan & Hargreaves, 1992; Heath, 1986; Hollingsworth & Sockett, 1994; Holmes Group, 1986; Holmes Report, 1986; Lieberman, 1992; Lieberman & Miller, 1984; Task Force on Teaching as a Profession, 1986; Zumwalt, 1986). There has been a resurgence amid this scene of interest in the theory and practice of school supervision and what the practice of supervision means in relationship to the reform of education (Garman, 1986). Although supervision has long been viewed as the means by which teachers and teaching can be improved, the understandings that lead to the improvement of teaching remain complicated (Baldwin, 1900; Barr & Burton, 1926; Blumberg, 1980; Briggs & Justman, 1952; Brim, 1930; Buckham, 1882; Burton, 1922; Calkins, 1882; Chancellor, 1904; Cogan, 1973; Crosby, 1957; Fullan & Hargreaves, 1992; Glickman, 1992; Gwynn, 1961; Harman, 1947; Harris, 1963; Hosic, 1928; Lewis & Miel, 1972; Melby, 1926; Melchoir, 1933; Mosher & Purpel, 1972; National Education Association [NEA] Department of Superintendence, 1930; Nutt, 1920; Rorer, 1942; Sergiovanni & Starratt, 1983; Spears, 1953; Taba, 1962; Tanner & Tanner, 1987, 1995; Zumwalt, 1986). The exact role of the educational supervisor

in relationship to educational improvement is not clearly understood within our schools (Bolin, 1983, 1988; Brim, 1930). It is, in the words of Alfonso and Firth (1990), the "lack of a clear definition and the inability to identify who supervisors are and what they do" (p. 181) that contributes to the problems of practice and research (Anderson, 1982; Blumberg, 1980; Bolin, 1988; Lucio & McNeil, 1969; Sergiovanni, 1982).

Improvement of Instruction

Much of the current research in the field of school supervision focuses on the idea that supervision is a domain needed to insure the improvement of instruction. As Grimmett, Rostad, and Ford (1992) point out, most of the literature on supervision converges around ideas that "help to bring about change in teachers' instructional practices" (p. 185). Alfonso and Firth (1990), agreed with this assessment in their criticism of the research on school supervision. They stated: "The paucity of serious research about supervision in education is disturbing, especially in light of the extraordinary claims made about its importance" (p. 188). According to Alfonso and Firth, the literature tends to fall into three categories: descriptive research that examines what supervisors do overtly; prescriptive research that identifies typical activities and objectives of supervision; and a third body of research that addresses the importance of supervision and its responsibility for the improvement of instruction (pp. 181–182). Alfonso and Firth call for a new research agenda that focuses on the critical issues being raised about the

The authors gratefully acknowledge the comments on this chapter by Dennis C. Buss and H. Jerome Freiberg.

field of supervision and encourages a move away from the singular focus on the improvement of instruction (p. 183).

Smyth (1989) also challenged the extant views that place supervision in the "mainstream of educational management" (p. 165). Smyth (1986) argued for a change from a service delivery model of supervision to one that empowers teachers and supervisors to begin to transform the conditions, organizational structures, instructional practices, and social relationships that have come to define school supervision (p. 338). As Smyth forcefully put it:

The major problem with traditional forms of supervision (and clinical supervision is by no means immune) is that they are conceptualized as a delivery of service to those who need it. No matter how benevolently it is done, efforts of this kind are largely self-defeating. Precisely because they are premised on managerial and undemocratic ways of working, these forms of supervision create dependence rather than independence. Issues and concerns that are being addressed are not the teachers' agenda, but rather those of someone within the administrative or bureaucratic hierarchy (Smyth, 1986, pp. 331–332).

An Untenable Dualism

The current controversy places the field of school supervision between two ideologies of supervision, a production efficiency model and a professional growth model (Tanner & Tanner, 1987). Finding roots in the inspectoral function of supervision, a function that is no longer tenable in the current educational scene, the production-efficiency approach continues to model the school along the lines of the "efficient industrial enterprise" (Tanner & Tanner, 1987, p. 122). This factory model of schooling treats supervisors as managers, teachers as workers, and students as products. Productivity and managerial efficiency are assessed by outputs such as minimum competency testing, standardized achievement test scores, national standards, international comparisons, and outcome-based education. These "outputs" are looked at in relation to "inputs," which include the time and financial resources available to the schools. There is a tendency to prescribe to teachers what they need to know in order to generate specific, previously decided student outcomes or behaviors. The teacher is perceived as a technician with limited freedom to participate in a high degree of autonomy and decision-making about important curricular issues. Zumwalt (1988) drew a similar conclusion:

Essentially what is emerging is a technical conception of teaching. Teachers are trained to exhibit a defined set of skills, knowledge, and attitudes which lead to predetermined learning outcomes (that is, test scores) for students. Teachers and students can easily be evaluated because the outcomes have been clearly and behaviorally described. Increasing the effectiveness and efficiency of teachers becomes the goal of curriculum makers and administrators. Professional autonomy and discretion are minimized in the name of maintaining high standards for all (p. 153).

Trapped within this managerial ideology, supervision continues to be treated as a scientifically based technology relegated to methodology, problem fixing, and inspectorial forms of teacher appraisal. The production model of schooling and supervision views the teacher more as a technician

than as a professional who is capable of displaying a high degree of autonomy. Under these circumstances, the teacher tends to regard the supervisor as an inspector whose principal functions are to see to it that the teacher is on task and to evaluate the teacher accordingly. By regarding the teacher as technician and by focusing singularly on the improvement of classroom instruction, responsibility for the determination and development of the curriculum is left largely to the educational policymakers and to various national commissions, committees, and panels outside of the schools, who greatly influence matters of curriculum design and policy (Tanner & Tanner, 1987). Thus, the responsibility of the secondary school teacher under this model of supervision is primarily the delivery of instruction within a subject-centered curriculum that is predetermined at a higher jurisdictional level.

A professional-growth model of supervision, however, is viewed as a developmental process involving a collaborative effort toward understanding, diagnosing, and solving substantive problems in the classroom and school (Tanner & Tanner, 1987). This model encourages the full participation of the classroom teacher and supervisor in curriculum development and in the process of democratic-participative problem solving for educational improvement. A professional growth model of supervision recognizes that, in order to meet the instructional needs of students, the professional needs of teachers, and the educational goals of the school, supervision must be organized to give attention to curricular problems across departmental lines and subject divisions. Supervision must in effect be seen in the context of curriculum development.

The Curriculum Paradigm and the Supervisor

The curriculum legacy has demonstrated that educational improvement does not result from the segmental adoption and implementation of new programs under the watchful eye of the supervisor (Cady, 1988). Curriculum development requires that the interdependence of knowledge, learners, teaching, and the philosophical aims of the educational program be recognized (Burton & Bruckner, 1955; Callahan & Button, 1964; Dewey, 1916; Schwartz, 1988; Taba, 1962; Tanner & Tanner, 1987; Tyler, 1949). It is the supervisor who works directly with classroom teachers and who conceives the curriculum according to this paradigm. The supervisor is in the unique position to help diagnose classroom and schoolwide problems and to bring a strong history of curriculum knowledge to bear on these problems (Schwartz, 1988). If the purpose of school supervision is to provide for the improvement of teaching and learning, then the functions of supervision need to be viewed in the perspective of this goal, which cannot be carried out independently of curriculum improvement. Teacher effectiveness needs to be based on the development of the capacity and the commitment of teachers to solve educational problems and to enhance the growth of learners through their continuous involvement in curriculum development.

Interdependence of Supervision and Curriculum

Current research bears out that a "planned, articulated curriculum-supervisory system can enhance student achievement, which is the ultimate goal of education" (Pohland & Cross, 1982, p. 150). All supervisory functions should be arranged in order to provide optimum educational opportunity for learners. The path to educational renewal requires that supervisors and curricularists work with teachers on the improvement of instruction by cooperatively planning and developing curricula (Barr, Burton, & Brueckner, 1938; Burton & Brueckner, 1955; Dewey, 1915; Glanz, 1992; Glickman, 1992; Joyce, 1971; Mintz, 1980; Oliva, 1989; Spears, 1953; Tanner & Tanner, 1987). Glanz (1992) wrote, "Curriculum efforts that eschew necessary supervisory strategies are an abysmal failure" (p. 226). Schwartz (1988) also supported the involvement of supervisors and teachers in curriculum. She wrote:

The supervision of in-service teachers has, in the main, been conducted mechanically and without regard for the teacher's role in solving curriculum problems. For the teacher has a role; if indeed these problems are to be solved, the "buck" ends at the teacher's door, no matter what policies are adopted at other levels (p. 44).

Other researchers lament the fact that the bureaucratic and technocratic functions of supervision have served to widen the gulf between teachers and supervisors and have diminished their opportunity to work collaboratively on solving significant educational problems across subjects and departmental lines (Aiken, 1992; Blumberg, 1980; Glickman, 1995; Joyce, 1971; Oliva, 1989; Tanner & Tanner, 1987). Glickman (1985) defined supervision as "the glue of a successful school" (p. 4) and believed that only by linking supervision with curriculum development and direct assistance to teachers are schools able to realize their goals. Oliva (1989) gave further support to the unity of supervision and curriculum and wrote that curriculum development is a "joint endeavor of all school personnel but primarily a cooperative activity of supervisors and teachers" (p. 263). What is evidenced by the research of these theorists is that supervision is destined to be an essential part of the curriculum development process, which includes decisions about the structure and content of the curriculum, the improvement of teaching, and the evaluation of the entire educational process—all of which are transformed to school development and improvement (Neagley & Evans, 1980).

Reform and Counterreform

School leaders are under constant pressure and influence from various bodies representing conflicting interests. They find themselves shifting their priorities in successive epochs in accordance with the dominant wave of a particular period. These reform shifts are often a succession of reactions and counterreactions to previous excessive and misguided reform measures. Schools continue to find themselves in a position of moving from one trendy fad to the next. As a result, "what is deemed appropriate one year, is deemed inappropriate the next" (Tanner, 1988, p. 45). According to Tanner, "this generates confusion and blurs sound educational principles such as the need to see the learner, learning processes, and content interrelatedly" (p. 45). Unless supervisors are consciously aware of the various sources, forces, and pressures for edu-

cational change, the schools will be vulnerable to whatever pressures or fashions are dominant at a particular time, and supervisors will continue to find themselves in authoritative postures with a tendency to impose measures for change from above. As school leaders attempt to respond to external pressures and forces upon the schools, they resort to segmental adoption of new practices, projects, packages, or policies, with little or no consideration of teachers, students, or consonance with the philosophical outlook of the school (Tanner & Tanner, 1987).

If secondary schools continue to believe that educational improvement and curriculum changes occur mainly in response to external mandates, rather than through a continuous, cooperative problem-solving process that engages the full participation of teachers, then changes will continue to be segmentally adopted and discarded, with no opportunity for systematic evaluation and comprehensive educational restructuring. When schools adopt innovations merely in response to external pressures or fashions, the innovations tend to be implemented superficially and often become little more than slogans or labels. The result is a succession of waves of reform by reaction and counterreaction. Such shifting and contradictory tides for change represent a great deal of movement but little progress (Tanner & Tanner, 1987).

Managerial Ideology Although the field of supervision has made advances toward curriculum leadership, supervision continues to be linked to a form of instructional improvement which too often comes down to methodological know-how and teacher appraisal (Eisner, 1982). Supervision in education appears to be trapped within a managerial ideology that supports the purpose of supervision as the means to assure compliance with one-way top-down edicts or external pressures rather then to provide the instructional leadership needed to insure educational improvement. Accountability issues, subject-specific educational outcomes as evidenced by standardized curricula and tests, teacher appraisal, and organizational efficiency continue to dominate the field. Supervision should be a collaborative relationship that encourages full participation of the classroom teacher and supervisor in curriculum development and democratic-participative problem solving for educational improvement. This, however, remains an elusive goal.

Supervision for Curriculum Development

The idea of the interrelationship between supervision and curriculum in educational improvement is not new. Glanz (1992) analyzed past efforts by supervisors and curriculum leaders to work collaboratively, describing the 1930s and 1940s as a time when coordinated efforts took on great importance. He stated:

By the 1930s, due largely to the perceived need by supervisors to alter their inspectatorial and production-oriented methods in favor of more democratic and collegial ones, it was apparent that supervisors and curriculum workers needed to unify their efforts. Supervisors could no longer involve themselves in instructional matters without attention to and knowledge about curriculum. Curriculum workers also realized that an affiliation with supervision would be necessary to effectively carry out curriculum revisions in the schools (p. 232).

Glanz was, no doubt, drawing from the works of two of the most prominent writers in the field of curriculum, H. L. Caswell and D. S. Campbell (1935). Caswell and Campbell recognized a critical link between supervision and curriculum and viewed the role of supervision in curriculum development as the means for teachers and supervisors to see problems of instruction in relationship to each other. According to Caswell and Campbell (1935):

A comprehensive curriculum program provides a complete related view of the problems of instruction. Each phase of work is seen in relationship to the other phases. With such a basis, supervision can relate the specific problems more adequately to other phases of instruction. Supervision can be most effective when it is based on a comprehensive curriculum program (pp. 75–80).

Further testimony to the concept of interrelatedness of supervision and curriculum can be found in the history of the field. In 1922, under the direction of Jesse Newlon, committees of teachers were relieved of their daily instructional responsibilities and were provided opportunities to work with curriculum specialists on instructional-curricular problems. This project came to be known as the Denver Plan and this process for curriculum revision became a prototype for curriculum development in the 1920s (Tanner & Tanner, 1980).

One of the greatest testimonies to the proper relationship between supervision and curriculum in the secondary school is found in the research of the Eight-Year Study (Aikin, 1942; Giles, McCutchen, & Zechiel, 1942). Funded by the General Education Board of the Rockefeller Foundation and sponsored by the Progressive Education Association, the experiment was spearheaded by such recognized educational leaders as Buros, Taba, Alberty, Mackenzie, and Tyler. Viewed as one of the greatest educational studies ever undertaken, the study was conducted over a period of eight years (1933 to 1941). Freed from their traditional college entrance requirements, which determined the secondary school curriculum to a great extent, 30 schools were allowed to experiment with new curricular arrangements and were given an opportunity to demonstrate the effectiveness of their own instructional programs. Each school decided its curriculum according to the unique needs of its students and community, rather than the usual subject and unit requirements. This new freedom, interestingly, generated further problems for practitioners. The schools were so accustomed to remaining within the boundaries defined by the subject matter curriculum that revising the instructional program according to the needs of adolescents and problems of living was difficult. To solve this problem, the experimental schools moved toward the development of integrated core-type programs that cut across subject matter lines and called for new relationships among staff based on collaborative planning and teaching. Teachers and supervisors moved away from a process of curriculum revision that was dependent on subject matter specialists or subject supervisors who wrote the segmental subject curriculum. They began to work together on curriculum articulation

according to a problem-solving process. The plan worked. Follow-up studies conducted by an independent research team and by the colleges revealed that the students who attended the experimental schools did at least as well as their college preparatory compeers. They actually earned a slightly higher total grade point average, earned higher grade averages in all areas except foreign languages, and received more academic honors. The outcomes were markedly more favorable for the graduates from the more experimental schools (Chamberlin, Chamberlin, Dought, & Scott, 1942). Teachers and supervisors recognized the value of working together on substantial problems of curriculum and instruction that grew out of the teaching-learning environment and transcended the subject curriculum and departmental domains.

Following the Eight-Year Study, Stratemeyer and her associates (1947) strengthened the relationship between supervision and curriculum in an important program she developed to link the curriculum with life. In *Developing a Curriculum for Modern Living*, they outlined a plan for curriculum improvement that recognized the significance and necessary role of the supervisor in the process. She wrote:

Perhaps no leadership role has been so strikingly redefined in the past three decades as that of the supervisor. From a responsibility which was limited to inspection, rating, and overseeing the use of courses of study, the supervisory role has evolved into one of assisting the professional staff to grow in ability to study and solve instructional problems . . . Supervision through individual and group work has become inextricably interwoven with curriculum development (p. 689).

John Dewey showed the earliest support for the involvement of teachers and supervisors in curriculum problems in 1901. In an article titled, "The Situation as Regards the Course of Study" which he wrote for the National Education Association, Dewey stated:

I have already alluded to the fact that at present the teacher is hardly enabled to get a glimpse of the educative process as a whole reduced to adding together the various external bits into which unity is broken. . . . As long as the teacher, who is after all the only real educator in the school system, has no definite and authoritative position in shaping the course of study, that is likely to remain an external thing to be externally applied to the child. . . . This unity and completeness must, however, be cared for somehow. Connections must somehow be made between the various fractional parts—the successive grades. The supervisor, the principal is the recourse (pp. 340– 341).

The fractionated subject curriculum of the secondary school makes it even more critical for curriculum workers, supervisors, and teachers to come together on issues and problems of curriculum and instruction. Despite successful past efforts, such as the Eight-Year Study, supervision in practice and theory is too often isolated from its role in curriculum improvement.

The Estrangement between Supervision and Curriculum

The body of literature that seeks to inform both the theoretical and practical understandings of school supervision has recently given attention to the alleged problem concerning the estrangement between curriculum and supervision (Aiken, 1992; Common & Grimmett, 1992; Consulting Editors, *Journal of Curriculum and Supervision*, 1992; Glanz, 1992; Pohland & Cross, 1982; Tanner & Tanner, 1987). Some writers question whether or not the "estrangement" is real, whereas others claim that the development of the fields of educational supervision and curriculum has followed disparate pathways (Grimmett & Common, 1992; Pohland & Cross, 1982). As stated by Pohland and Cross:

Our reading in the fields of curriculum and supervision suggests that each has developed largely independently of the other. However productive this strategy may have been for the maturing of separate disciplines, it has been equally limiting in its joint impact on the teacher's world (p. 150).

In an effort to bring understanding to the question of estrangement, several of the leading researchers in the field of school supervision sought to identify various practices that either contributed to the estrangement between supervision and curriculum or are simply manifestations of it. (See *Journal of Curriculum and Supervision*, Spring, 1992.) Their investigation led to a number of conclusions:

1. Responsibilities for supervision of teachers and for curriculum development in middle and secondary schools are often spread over several different offices or individuals, and are designated by the separate subject fields with little or no opportunity for coordination and collaboration. Supervision is viewed as a function of administration and is too often identified exclusively with teacher appraisal and evaluation.
2. Professional organizations rarely provide forums for curriculum leaders and supervisors of instruction to engage with each other in substantive dialogue and conversation.
3. Institutions of higher education that prepare individuals for positions in curriculum leadership and school supervision often do so in separate departments and programs, with supervision being placed in departments of administration and curriculum being merged with teacher education.
4. Professors tend to hold membership in separate professional societies, which discourages purposeful interaction and shared research.
5. Different orientations about the principles and assumptions that undergird supervision and curriculum, the technical and interpretive language that conveys meaning and understanding through different frameworks about the two fields, and the historical evolution of each contribute to the separation between supervision and curriculum. (Journal of Curriculum and Supervision, 1992)

School policies, professional role definition, divisions of labor, and working relationships in schools give evidence that there is indeed an estrangement between curriculum and supervision, both in theory and in practice (Common & Grimmett, 1992). Whether or not these segmented practices contribute to the estrangement or are results of the dualistic treatment of curriculum and supervision, this process is detrimental to the improvement of teaching and learning and the professional roles of the classroom teacher and supervisor (Tanner & Tanner, 1995).

Special Problems of Supervisors When curriculum and instruction are separated, and curriculum decisions are determined by those outside the realm of education and the classroom, supervisors and teachers are put in a vulnerable position of having to accept every dominant external mandate and reform that is thrust upon them. In this process, the determination of what students are to learn is conducted externally to the educational situation. When those outside the schools serve as the key participants in curriculum change, educational improvement is considered separate from the educational situation in which it is supposed to happen. The response from within the school is often overt compliance or covert resistance. This situation has contributed to special problems for school supervisors and instructional leaders. Issues such as restructuring, school climate, teacher evaluation, staff development, assessment, and curriculum coordination and articulation persist (Tanner & Tanner, 1987).

A Mission Unfulfilled

The estrangement of supervision and curriculum is reflected in the confusion over the function of supervision in professional literature, including the body of research on supervision. Indeed, the historical accounts of the field reveal the shifting and conflicting functions of the supervisor. This has had profound implications for school improvement to this day. Supervision has historically passed through many diverse transformations. Supervision began as inspection of teachers and has since been viewed variously as the means to achieve bureaucratic efficiency, to create democratic institutions, and to provide continuous support for teachers in class (Barr, Burton, & Brueckner, 1947; Bobbitt, 1913; Cogan, 1973). Too often, however, it has responded to the demand of managerial efficiency rather then the need for curriculum-instructional leadership.

A review of research leads to the claim that the field of supervision is buffeted by inherent difficulties that inhibit the development of effective supervision in the schools. The purpose of this chapter is to examine the historical antecedents that define the relationship between secondary school supervision and curriculum in an effort to understand why supervisors have yet to take their rightful place as curriculum leaders—a role that recognizes that instructional improvement and improved learning are inseparable from curriculum improvement. The first section of this chapter traces some of the turning points leading to the modern-day professionalization of school supervision. The second section presents an analysis of the literature from the evolving field of school supervision since 1900, particularly those aspects that concern the teacher–supervisor relationship in the curriculum development process. The final section discusses the resulting consequences for curriculum and supervision theory, research, and practice.

PROFESSIONALIZATION OF SUPERVISION

The mid-nineteenth century marks the beginning of school supervision as a profession and the growth of professional groups and associations concerned with the advancement of instructional leadership. It was becoming increasingly clear that although the superintendency was established to take over the work of supervision from lay committees, which had gotten out of hand, superintendents had virtually no professional preparation. Superintendents, however, devoted most of their time to school visitation and the supervision of teachers (Balliet, 1880; Barnard, 1856; Morrison, 1860; Parker, 1887, 1891; White, 1883, 1894). Nevertheless, by 1865, the Department of Superintendence of the National Education Association emerged to become a major force in the professionalization of school supervision. Through this organization, the early superintendents corresponded with each other, exchanged ideas, and began to meet on a regular basis (Griffiths, 1966). A number of education journals sprang up, and the new school supervisors became major contributors to these publications. Superintendents formed their own professional organization, the National Association of School Superintendents, which has organized annual meetings and conferences. Education had come to be recognized as a legitimate field of study with the establishment of courses on educational methods, child study, and the so-called science of teaching (Good, 1956). In 1875, William H. Payne published *Chapters on School Supervision*, which is credited as the first text written on school supervision (Button, 1961). Many others followed suit. Normal schools began to expand their program offerings to include four years of study, and departments of education began to appear in the universities.

School supervision was looked upon as a profession by the end of the nineteenth century. Supervisors had began to organize themselves into professional associations for mutual discussion of common problems. University study was expected for entrance into the field. Theories of supervision evolved as a growing number of articles and textbooks about teaching practices and school supervision were published (Ayer & Barr, 1928; Bush, 1930; Good, 1956; Tanner & Tanner, 1987). The scope of supervision was outlined in an 1870 resolution by the American Institute of Instruction and included such responsibilities as, "the arrangement of school buildings, appointment of teachers, classification of pupils, ordering of studies, methods of teaching, examination of results, and all the matters which pertain directly to the interest of public schools" (Showalter, 1924, p. 483). Ayer and Barr (1928) found it difficult to assess the full effects of these developments on supervisory practice, but felt they had great importance for modern supervisory practice. The theory and practice of school supervision was established with the professional treatment of subject matter, the introduction of supervised practice teaching, the organization of summer teacher institutes, and the development of new supervisory devices (Ayer & Barr, 1928, p. 8).

The supervisory legacy that grew out of the early national period and the common-school era brought changes to the purposes, arrangements, and functions of school supervision. First, the responsibility of the townspeople was transferred to the hands of a so-called expert, the school superintendent. Second, the responsibility of supervision in the improvement of teaching grew increasingly important, and the beginnings of a supervisor–teacher relationship formed through classroom contact. The organization of professional teacher training schools and opportunities for in-service development through teacher institutes became new and important supervisory devices. Third, school boards transferred the primary responsibility for curriculum development to the superintendents. Given the new graded arrangements and classification of pupils of the common schools and the push to expand the curriculum, the demand to adapt the curriculum to the new school organization became the responsibility of an educational expert—the school superintendent (Tuttle, 1942). The beginnings of a "science of teaching" (Good, 1956), was emerging as witnessed by the publication of professional teacher books and articles, the forming of teacher training schools, and the organization of teacher institutes. The seeds of an idea—that there are professionally agreed-upon principles of education from which teaching could be based—strengthened the earliest and most important function of supervision—the improvement of teaching. The most important outcome of that era, however, was the sweeping belief and profound faith that supervision of schools was necessary to contribute to the overall improvement of education and did not exist solely for the purposes of external control or regulation. Supervision had been established as an important professional function in American education.

An extensive description of the professionalization movement is provided by Firth. (See Chapter 36 of this volume devoted to "Governance of School Supervision.")

The Rise of State Authority

By the last quarter of the nineteenth century, schools were experiencing changes in authority and control. With the inevitable success of the common-school movement, education became more and more of a state responsibility. There was massive effort to strengthen state authority with the attempt to unify education, to elevate teaching standards, and to raise taxes in support of public education (Butts & Cremin, 1953; Tanner & Tanner, 1987). One of the most significant efforts was the establishment of state and county superintendents. The role and function of these new state-level officers initially was to ensure that school monies were properly spent and that schools were being maintained according to state law, in recognition of education as a state function. In time, however, these individuals assumed more authority and took over more responsibility from the local level. Cubberley (1923) claimed that new powers of state and county superintendents came from a gradual "gathering-up process" that eventually "deprived districts of their early powers and authority" (p. 38). Someone had to take responsibility for monitoring the state's demands, and this meant supervision (Tanner & Tanner, 1987).

One of the most significant developments during that era was the establishment of a state superintendent, often referred to in the literature as the state superintendent of common schools (Butts & Cremin, 1953). The first state superintendent's position was established in 1812 in New York. The requirements of the position were to develop a plan for the unification and improvement of the common school system, to create a report for the collection and expenditure of school monies, and to report these to the state legislature (Butts & Cremin, 1953). Cubberley (1923) described the duties of the state superintendent as almost entirely "clerical, statistical, and exhortatory" (p. 29). The greatest impact, however, was felt at the local level, especially in the cities. City school superintendents now had a new master to serve along with their boards: namely, the state. They were burdened with more and more responsibilities, which grew out of local conditions as well as mandates coming from the state level. As a result, their work took on a more distinctive administrative character and they assumed responsibility for more of the business and financial matters of the school. Responsibilities associated with the instructional program and teacher education were given over to the new cadre of school supervisors. The rising forms of state control served to influence the forms and functions of supervision that evolved at the local school level.

Tides of Change

The period from 1870 to the end of the nineteenth century was a time of dramatic growth and change in American society and the field of education. It was during that time that school supervision evolved into an organized practice and a professional field of study. By the beginning of the twentieth century, the system of free public education had taken form and spread over the country, especially at the elementary level. More and more students attended school each year, the school year had been lengthened, and compulsory school laws had been passed in most states (Cubberley, 1920). An intense effort was underway in the cities to create a unified system of education. Tyack (1974) noted that the blueprint for education, a system in which groups of students would proceed through grades and follow a uniform curriculum under the supervision of a superintendent, became the urban model of modern schooling. The ladder system of American education was becoming more articulated, especially with the establishment of the kindergarten and the public high school. Although the real battle for the public high school took place between 1880 and 1920, it was during the latter part of the nineteenth century that public high schools gained the "numerical lead" (Krug, 1964, p. 5) among different types of secondary institutions.

The changing social and economic conditions were adding to the growing complexity to American life and creating a demand for more formalized education. America was experiencing rapid growth in areas of manufacturing, transportation, and communication, as well as a growing interest in industrialism and the alleged value being given to business principles and practices. Many school superintendents were greatly influenced by the growth of industry and began to model their schools according to business and industrial-managerial practices (Callahan, 1962). Corporations were growing in size and cities were "exploding in population" (Butts & Cremin, 1953, p. 301). A second and larger wave of immigrants was entering the country and remaining in cities where low-paying and unskilled jobs were available. Farming, too, was experiencing

a revolution, as new knowledge and advanced machinery were altering the conditions of the family farm. With the passage of the Morrill Act in 1862, each state was granted 30,000 acres of public land in order to establish colleges of agriculture and mechanical arts (land-grant colleges) which were to evolve into the great state universities. As new knowledge was created, there was a greater demand for skilled labor both in the factories and on the farms.

The purposes and functions of public education were coming under scrutiny. The schools were looked upon as the institutions that could provide education to meet the demand for skilled labor in industrial America. The public schools also came to be viewed viewed as institutions that could help solve the problems of social living and the insufferable conditions that resulted from growing industrialism. The cities, particularly, were experiencing an increase in crime, poverty, and disease. What resulted was a series of reform efforts that eventually led to progressivism in education. Cremin (1961) stated:

Actually, progressive education began as part of a vast humanitarian effort to apply the promise of American life . . . to the puzzling new urban-industrial civilization that came into being during the latter half of the nineteenth century. In effect, progressive education began as progressivism in education: a many-sided effort to use the schools to improve the lives of individuals (p. viii).

The Struggle for Control of the Curriculum

During the last quarter of the nineteenth century, curriculum became a major concern. The forces that came to affect the American curriculum had grown in power and strength and, by 1890, the "struggle for control of the curriculum" (Kliebard, 1988, p. 1) was well underway. The conflict, according to Kliebard, resulted from the changing role of education in American society and from the different interest groups growing out of society, which placed altering values on what should be taught in American schools. Kliebard (1986) articulated it this way:

The route between the knowledge a society values and its incorporation into the curriculum becomes infinitely more tortuous, however, where we take into account the fact that different segments in society will emphasize different forms of knowledge as most valuable for that society . . . . Hence, we find different interest groups competing for dominance over the curriculum (p. 8).

For Cremin (1961), the struggle was "related to the broader currents of social and political progressivism" (p. 22). The battles involved the farmers, university people, urban settlement workers, city people, publicists, businessmen, labor unions, parents, and teachers (Cremin, 1961). The question about the purposes of schooling and what should be taught became especially important at the secondary level. Throughout most of the eighteenth and nineteenth centuries, and extending into the early years of the twentieth century, secondary education was looked upon as a preparation for college. With the addition of more practical coursework and the American philosophy that secondary education should be extended to all youth, the high school curriculum became a major concern. Callahan (1959) captured the conflict in these words:

What was to be the nature of the high school in a democracy? Would it be an extension of the common school which all children would attend? If so, what kind of a program would be offered? If the classical curriculum was not acceptable for all students, was it the best preparation for college? If so, how could such a program be set up alongside the noncollege preparatory curriculum? (p. 133)

Curriculum by Committee

Cremin's questions, coupled with the confusion over the lack of uniformity in college entrance requirements, became topics of discussion which eventually led to a study by two committees appointed by the National Education Association—the Committee of Ten on Secondary School Studies in 1893 and the Committee of Thirteen on College Entrance Requirements in 1899. The outcomes were critical and became the foundation upon which the American secondary curriculum was based. The Committee of Ten agreed on four parallel programs for the high school—Classical, Latin Scientific, Modern Language, and English—all of which served the college preparatory function. The report of the Committee on College Entrance Requirements followed with the proposal that a fixed number of units of study of the various subjects outlined in the Committee of Ten's report be required of all college entrants. Butts and Cremin (1953) summarized the outcomes as follows:

Of the two, the report of the Committee of Ten was probably the more discussed. By and large, it determined the course of American secondary education for a generation following its publication . . . The assumption throughout was that those courses which best prepare for college entrance also best prepare for the duties of practical life. Thus, most of the report was devoted to a proper organizing and harmonizing of traditional college-preparatory subjects. Moreover, the recommendation was that every subject be taught the same way (p. 390).

Needless to say, reports "perpetuated the traditional subjects and methods for the next quarter century" (Tanner & Tanner, 1990, p. 71). Although the ensuing arguments and battles challenged the findings of these two committees, the status quo won out, according to Krug (1964). Another American educational phenomenon was established—the idea of curriculum making by external committee and by those external to the daily realm of the teacher and student. Now that this uniform and predetermined subject curriculum was settled, at least temporarily, there was but one major task left for supervision—to focus on teaching or instruction. By the close of the nineteenth century, teacher improvement had become synonymous with instructional improvement, and instructional improvement focused on methodology in the classroom. This focus on method began the dualistic treatment of curriculum and instruction that had been fortified during the final decade of the nineteenth century by the recommendations put forth by NEA-sponsored committees. The committees had established the curriculum to be the traditional list of academic subjects. The chief function of school supervisors was instructional improvement in the separate academic subjects.

Nevertheless, as supervision moved into the new century, supervisory policies and practices signaled the beginnings of

a profession. Supervision had begun to cultivate its own philosophy, and had risen to a more prominent place in American schools, both at the local and state levels. The dilemma of just what the American curriculum should be in the growing industrialized nation raised new questions and challenged school leaders. Instrumental to these changes were the opportunities to elevate the competencies of the teaching force, and school supervision was defined by these purposes. At the close of the nineteenth century, curriculum as a force was just beginning to exert its influence on supervision.

Fueled by the torment of the last quarter of the nineteenth century, public education took on new momentum after 1900, greatly influenced by the social, political, scientific, and industrial forces that were changing American life. Amidst these myriad forces, special-interest groups emerged to compete for dominance over the curriculum. Proponents of the traditional subject curriculum, who advocated the training of the mind and development of the intellect, were challenged by the new thinking about education that recognized the biosocial development of the child and a curriculum that was more in harmony with the interests and needs of students (Kliebard, 1988). The battle for curriculum dominance was further complicated by the growing belief in some circles that education and its institutions were to be directed for the improvement of society. Even this group was divided philosophically, as "social efficiency" and "social progress" came to have different meanings in the curriculum (Callahan, 1962; Cremin, 1961). Some viewed the schools as agencies of social reform and social progress, whereas the others viewed the schools as instruments of social control (Kliebard, 1988). Another catalyst to the controversy was the fact that a truly American pedagogy was evolving which would further define and shape the system of free, public education (Meyer, 1957).

An American Philosophy

One of the strongest exponents for an American philosophy of education was John Dewey. Through his prolific writings and the inauguration of his famous laboratory school in 1896, Dewey sought to resolve the competing forces, or "dualisms" as he called them (Dewey, 1916). He viewed education as a fundamental means of social reform and progress. Dewey proposed a democratic purpose to education that called for new and more integrated studies, new learning experiences, a unitary structure for the school through twelfth grade, and the professionalization of teaching. Dewey's problem method, or method of intelligence, involved applying the scientific method (reflective thinking) to all kinds of real problems that students encounter in their studies and in life (Dewey, 1901, 1910, 1910b, 1916). Dewey's classroom would be modeled according to a miniature democracy, where students and teachers would form a social system in which they would apply the process of problem solving (Joyce, 1975). Dewey's organization was one of social interaction and cooperation among students; education was the means for building social power and insight through social problem solving (Tanner & Tanner, 1990).

Dewey's view and perception of education represented a massive challenge to the more traditional conceptions of knowledge and social progress. Dewey's philosophy was an orchestration of the leading progressive ideas that were growing during the early years of the twentieth century, ideas that were developing in harmony with the ideals of American democracy. His ideas, however, contrasted sharply with the values and practices embraced by many leaders in the business and industrial sectors of society.

Efficiency Experts and Scientific Management

Callahan (1962) cited 1910 as the year that the "efficiency expert made his grand entrance into American society" (p. 42). A newfound respect for business principles exerted strong pressures on the schools, especially the high school, to be organized and to operate in a "more business-like way" (p. 6). A call rang out for a more practical and useful curriculum. One idea was that vocational education should be offered through specialized vocational schools (Krug, 1964; Tanner, 1972). The strongest influence during these years, however, was the efficiency movement or what came to be known as scientific management (Callahan, 1962). Spearheaded by Frederick Taylor's time-and-motion studies, efficiency became synonymous with increased production at lower costs. "By the time Taylor published his classic *Principles of Scientific Management* (1911) he was already recognized as the prophet of a new order in industrial society," wrote Kliebard (1988, p. 95). The movement gained momentum and found support from many different circles, especially school people. School superintendents, having become victims of much negative press and muckraking journalists, embraced the new ideology (Callahan, 1962). Callahan (1962) described how, between 1911 and 1912, every popular journal and professional publication leveled attacks against the schools, charging that they were "inefficient and impractical" (p. 47).

Although all sectors of education were attacked, the most serious attacks were against school administrators. Struggling with enormous problems associated with their growing school systems, school superintendents were eager to latch onto something that appeared to be the grand panacea to their problems. Turning to their business counterparts, they saw the corporate model as their answer. According to Tyack (1974),

To many schoolmen the corporate model of school governance was not only modern and rational, but the answer to many of their problems. They wished to gain high status for the superintendent—and here he was compared with that prestigious figure, the business executive. . . . They wanted to make of school administration a science—and here was a ready-to-use body of literature on business efficiency to adapt to the school (p. 134).

Tyack devoted his entire work, *The One Best System,* (1974) to the business and industrial ideology that came to shape the system of American education and school leadership. He described an emerging system of public education that required new geographical locations; the sorting, grouping, and grading of students; increased student testing and evaluation; standardized and uniform curricula; increased teacher training and appraisal; standardized examinations; and "at the top of the system a superintendent who became the captain of education" (p. 134).

Principles taken from business and industry worked well with the ideas evolving from the work of mental-measurement proponents, who supported a quantitative approach to education (Bennett, 1917; Carr, 1901; Greenwood, 1888). These theorists believed that interpretation and explanation of human behavior and learning could be scientifically determined. Here, they seemed to be confusing quantification or scientism with science. Thorndike's invention of a scale unit to measure educational achievement ushered in a whole new field of standardized testing. Educators believed that Thorndike's scale concept could be developed to measure everything—intelligence, aptitude, achievement, methodology, and just about every aspect of educational practice found in the schools (Cremin, 1961).

Nevertheless, although much of the historic literature today is highly critical of the mental-measurement movement, aptitude testing was seen by many progressivists early in the twentieth century as a significant mechanism for uncovering and unleashing potentials that might otherwise remain unrecognized and undeveloped as the result of social and economic conditions. In this connection, it was seen as the means in which opportunity for education through high school and college would be transformed through measures of merit as opposed to social advantages or privilege. "As far as the tests assisted this goal," wrote Dewey in 1922, "they could serve the cause of progress; insofar as they tended in the name of science to sink individuals into numerical classes, they were essentially antithetical to democratic social policy" (p. 36).

Supervision for Efficient Teaching

The influence of business and industry and the so-called efficiency experts, along with the ideas put forth by mental measurement theorists, vastly affected school supervision during the early years of the twentieth century. With supervision being directed at the improvement of teaching, the surveys and rating scales that evolved from these early efforts of scientific management were to be the instruments through which supervisors were to determine the mechanisms of good teaching. An ever-increasing focus on educational method dominated the developing theory on school supervision (Brueckner, 1929; Button, 1961; Tuttle, 1942). Supervisors embraced the new scientism, and by 1929, the leading professional organization for school supervisors dedicated its yearbook to these developments. The contributors to the appropriately titled *Scientific Method in Supervision* (Hosic, ed. 1929) had great faith in the new techniques of supervision and how these activities would contribute to more efficient teaching (Brueckner, 1929). "The use of the scale technique by a large number of trained observers," claimed Brueckner, "makes it possible for the supervisor to conduct as comprehensive a survey of teaching as is desired and to secure a picture of the general status of teaching in the schools" (p. 25). Other writers identified the new standard measurements as a means for school supervisors to move away from subjective measures of evaluation of teaching to one that provided so-called objective data that were supposedly more reliable and effective in improving the daily work of the classroom teacher (Bliss, 1915).

Committee on the Economy of Time One of the strongest forces contributing to the changing direction of school supervision came from the Department of Superintendence of the National Education Association. As superintendents became more influenced by the ideas of business efficiency, they began to turn their attention to developing a more efficient curriculum and more efficient teachers. For years, they had been struggling with the growing number of subjects and curriculum crowding and congestion, especially in the secondary school. With scientific management and a new system of industrial management sweeping the country, the Department of Superintendence organized the Committee on Economy of Time in 1911 to study the problem of waste in education. Their approach was to hire nationally recognized educational leaders who would conduct a thorough review of curriculum and classroom activity in existing school districts (Kliebard, 1979). This pattern of electing those outside the schools to solve substantive problems of educators had found a place in the development of American education and was to plague school supervision with mounting regularity. Hundreds of surveys of schools were made on every aspect of the educational system. Surveys worked "hand-in-hand" with the educational testing movement, since both appeared to provide "tangible evidence of efficiency in the schools" (Callahan, 1962, p. 100).

The reports of the Committee on the Economy of Time appeared in several yearbooks of the National Society for the Study of Education between 1915 and 1919. The basic general findings of the Committee supported the idea that economy of time in education could be achieved by eliminating nonessential subjects or subject matter, by improving instructional methods, and by arranging the school system and the curriculum so that each part would be presented according to the development of the learner (Whipple, 1916; Wilson, 1917, 1919). The determination of the most efficient methods and assurance that these methods were being implemented in the classroom became the primary job of the school supervisor. In these endeavors, the teacher was further removed from the process of curriculum development which bolstered a further distinction between curriculum and instruction. The role of the school supervisor was simple. The supervisor needed only to assume the role of a kind of managing foreman in the new school organization (Tanner & Tanner, 1990).

Professional Support Many leading superintendents and college professors came out in support of the principles of scientific management that were applied to school supervision. One of the strongest proponents was Franklin Bobbitt, a professor of educational administration at the University of Chicago. In the Twelfth Yearbook of the National Society for the Study of Education, *The Supervision of City Schools* (1913), Bobbitt articulated his industrial model of school supervision. Bobbitt connected the operation of the schools with scientific management principles. The "workers" in the school were teachers. Supervisors were "managers" who were charged with the task of measuring the teaching methods being used in relationship to student outcomes, or "products." In the words of Bobbitt: "Directors and supervisors must keep the workers supplied with detailed instructions as to the work

to be done, the standards to be reached, the methods to be employed, and the materials and appliances to be used" (p. 8). It was the job of the supervisor to determine the most efficient method for attaining these standards and to make sure the teachers followed them exactly. Bobbitt and some of his followers went so far as to recommend the use of scorecards to measure teacher performance and efficiency in the classroom. Bobbitt and his followers believed that the method was scientific, because it eliminated the arbitrary and personal bias of supervisors and replaced it with principles that were allegedly deduced through empirical methods.

Under scientific management, supervisors had access to teacher rating scales, scorecards, standardized tests, surveys, and numerous other measures of efficiency (Boyce, 1915). Specific standards for teaching effectiveness were determined and supervisors measured teachers against these standards as listed on various rating forms. A method for controlling, classifying, and standardizing every aspect of education became available (Bagley, 1908, 1912; Spaulding, 1913). The primary function of supervision was to aid efficient school administration by creating efficient teachers (Anderson, 1916). Standards were set and there did not appear to be room for individual differences among teachers; uniformity and conformity were all-important (Ayres, 1913; Bagley, 1908; Cubberley, 1916; Spaulding, 1913). Teachers had little or no voice in the development of curriculum and were losing ground in the determination of method. This thinking is captured in the following excerpt, which appeared in a 1911 publication of the *NEA Proceedings* (Warriner, 1911):

The course of study for the most part is a fixed quantity, while the method of teaching should be optional. Supervision should say what is taught. . . . To hand over without reservation to a group of teachers the absolute and final decision as to the course of study or textbook is a dangerous policy for the welfare of the schools (p. 312).

The writing which appeared in prominent textbooks from the field and articles which appeared in leading professional journals for school administration between the years of 1910 and 1920 supported this approach to school supervision (Aiken, 1992; Button, 1961; Tuttle, 1942). A lot of literature referred to schools as factories in which children were looked upon as raw material to be shaped and fashioned to meet various demands of life (Cubberley, 1916). Supervisors were to adopt efficiency plans that would eliminate all waste from schools, so that classrooms could operate like well-run machines (Bagley, 1908). Provisions on how to provide an exact procedure for virtually every classroom activity were outlined in various supervision texts; procedures addressed how to line up for fire drills, how to pass lines, how to move to and from the blackboard, and how to hang up coats (Bagley, 1908). Exact measures of time were allocated for the school year, the school day, recess, and the teaching of each and every subject (Bagley, 1908). Little was left to the discretion of the teacher. Leading theorists from the field denied teachers a voice in developing curriculum, which was no longer considered an issue since it was assumed that curriculum was a matter of policy and that the new instruments of educational measurement provided the necessary scientific evidence as to how each and every subject should be taught. In the words of Bagley (1908):

The responsibility of determining the subjects of instruction seldom rests with the classroom teacher. In case the local or county authorities do not prescribe a definite course of study, that prescribed by the state department of public instruction should be used. The teacher frequently has some latitude, however, with certain "accessory" subjects, especially in schools that are not under the control of a principal or superintendent (p. 53).

Administrative Support Professional support for the new "scientific" approach to school supervision was also to be found in the voices of writers whose articles appeared between 1915 and 1916 in a new journal, *Educational Administration and Supervision.* This publication provided a forum for the discussion and the backing of the new "scientific" model of supervision. Supported by many individuals in school leadership and university positions, the debate concerning the proper role and function of school supervision persisted. The writers called for an application of so-called scientific methods to the study of all phases of education and applauded the use of standardized measurements (Bliss, 1915; Corson, 1906; Crabbs, 1925; Snedden, 1916). Educational leaders praised the arrival of the "efficiency expert who would help eliminate waste in school" (Anderson, 1916, p. 477), and embraced quantitative teacher-rating systems in order to evaluate teacher efficiency (Landsittel, 1916, p. 297). Even the superintendents and supervisors themselves were not immune to scrutiny. As stated by Anderson (1916):

Another misfortune which must be admitted even though lamentable is the presence of altogether too many inefficient teachers, supervisors, principals, and superintendents. . . . Teachers, supervisors, principals, and superintendents should be studied in a definite and thorough-going manner. Their functions, qualifications and methods should be scientifically determined (p. 479).

The Rebuttal In response to the rigid and autocratic practices that had contributed to the bureaucratization of supervision, teachers began to fight back. The NEA's Department of Classroom Teachers became a voice for protest in 1914 as they began to speak out against the practices of supervision in their schools. In his study of the first 100 years of the National Education Association, E. B. Wesley (1957) stated that "the members lost no time in airing their grievances and proclaiming their demands. . . . In fact, the first few meetings remind one of a broken dam releasing long-pent pressures" (p. 281). Teachers felt alienated and, compounded with their low status, poor salaries, and overloaded schedules, they raised numerous protests against business management methods being applied to their work (Elsbree, 1939). The Proceedings of the National Education Association during the years between 1913 and 1920 revealed that the method of industrial management—the analogy of the factory, efficiency ratings, and principles of scientific management—continually came under attack by the Department of Classroom Teachers (Bogan, 1919; Crabtree, 1914; Gardner, 1919; Parrott, 1914; Skinner, 1920). Teachers spoke out against efficiency measures and especially the mechanical rating schemes imposed

upon them (Crabtree, 1914). They called for the "abolishment of the teacher rating systems in place" (Parrott, 1914, p. 1170) and advocated a system that would be based on how well the teacher applied the recognized theory of teaching to the improvement of learning in their classrooms, which the so-called efficiency rating forms could not evaluate (Crabtree, 1914).

The problem became so controversial that the superintendents themselves criticized the kinds of supervision taking place in the schools (Clark, 1920; Hosic, 1920; Hunter, 1913; Weet, 1919). In 1908, the National Society for the Study of Education dedicated its Seventh Yearbook, Part I, *The Relation of Superintendents and Principals to the Training and Professional Improvement of Their Teachers,* to the relationship between supervision and teaching. School leaders recognized that teachers were gravely discontented over the matter of supervision as it was being applied in the schools. Clearly, from the discussion in the yearbook, the most important task of supervision remained the improvement of teaching (Lowry, 1908). Conversations, however, were not about principles of scientific management as being applied in the name of efficient teaching; instead, the writers of the yearbook turned to the importance of teachers and supervisors working together on matters of curriculum. Charles Lowry (1908), then superintendent of the Chicago schools, was clear regarding the role of teachers and supervisors in curriculum development and how a more democratic approach would result in better teaching. Lowry called for "a systematic consideration by committees of principals and teachers of the various topics in the course of study" and viewed this process as "continuous study into the values and methods used in schools" (p. 24).

Little by little, educational leaders recognized that efficiency in education did not lie in the authoritative imposition of so-called efficiency principles upon teachers; efficiency in education was to be realized by the cooperative participation of teachers and supervisors in the important task of curriculum making (Bogan, 1919; Dewey, 1915; Gardner, 1919; Hosic, 1920; Hunter, 1913). As a result, supervision moved in a new direction.

The Democratic Supervisor

No doubt, democratic ideals were popularized in the nation after 1915, as a result of World War I. The schools, like all institutions, were affected. In some ways, school supervision was probably forced to change as themes and causes for democracy took precedence. Publications on school supervision and curriculum were beginning to challenge scientific management principles based on Taylorism as more democratic approaches to school supervision began to evolve. Even before "educational efficiency" became the slogan of the day, many educational leaders and school superintendents clung to the belief that they were learned scholars, that their mission was to develop an understanding of principles of the art of teaching in the teachers, and that teacher participation in curriculum development was paramount (Arnold, 1898; Dewey, 1901; Lowry, 1908; McMurray 1903; Parker, 1883; Seeley, 1903). The language of Colonel Francis Parker (1883), who defined supervisors as "guides" (p. 173) and teachers as "leaders" (p. 171), reiterated these important roles. "The true method of teaching," claimed Parker, "is the exact adaptation of the subject taught, or means of growth, to the learning mind" (p. 170). For Parker, this adaptation was totally dependent on the "creative ability" (p. 166) of the teacher.

An article by Sarah L. Arnold, which appeared in the *NEA Proceedings* in 1898, recognized the teacher as one who knows the subject matter better than most supervisors and should be included in discussions and meetings about curriculum. Arnold's democratic thrust was most evident in her description of the qualifications needed by the school supervisor:

The unnameable quality which brings out the best in coworkers, this is his qualification. . . . The school system in his mind never sinks into a machine, method never becomes formal, directions are never dictatorial. He asks no blind following, no servile allegiance. He stands before his teachers to help them to the truth which shall make them free (p. 236).

Democratic ideals were advanced most powerfully, when John Dewey (1901) argued that the teacher "is the only real educator in the school system" (p. 341) and must be considered a critical participant in "shaping the course of study" (p. 341). Dewey wrote that an approach to curriculum development that granted exclusive power for determining the course of study to superintendents, supervisors, boards of education, or "a power outside the teacher in the classroom" (p. 341) could not succeed.

Teacher as Curriculum Maker The democratic model of school supervision viewed teachers as being continuously engaged in curriculum development work, in cooperation with supervisors. Even as procedures and policies for scientific management dominated supervisory theory, many educators supported more democratic models of school supervision and insisted on the essential role of teachers and supervisors in curriculum development. Dewey (1915) spoke out about how the principles of scientific management had invaded the public schools and contended that teaching had to remain an "intellectual enterprise" (p. 121) and not a "routine mechanical exercise." For this reason, Dewey supported teacher involvement at all levels of education, including the development of curriculum and instruction. In the words of Dewey (1915):

When teachers have as little to do, as they have at present, with intellectual responsibility for the conduct of the schools; when teachers who are doing most, if not all, of the teaching have nothing whatsoever to say directly about the formation of the course of study and very little indirectly; when they have nothing save ways of informal discussion and exchange of experience in teachers meetings or very little to say about methods of teaching or discipline; when they have no means for making their experience actually count in practice; the chief motive to the development of professional spirit is lacking. Now, either teaching is an intellectual enterprise or it is a routine mechanical exercise. And if it is an intellectual exercise . . . there is no better way calculated to retard and discourage the professional spirit than methods which so entirely relieve the teachers from intellectual responsibility as do the present methods (p. 121).

Experimentalists and Progressive Reform

At the same time that businessmen and industrialists were searching for more efficient ways to manage their factories and school leaders were busy adapting principles of industrial efficiency to their schools, a sharply different thrust in education came from another circle. Described as "an awakening of social conscience" (Cremin, 1961, p. 59), Americans were becoming more aware of the ills and abuses of industrial society. Cuban (1979) stated it this way:

The cold-water dousing of America by the consequences of immigration, unrestrained industrialism, and urban growth awakened lay and professional reformers to slums, poverty, and ignorance. They needed tools to attack problems. . . . Cadres of reformers imbued with a religious faith in science, knowledge, and civic morality saw the school as a splendid tool of reform (p. 147).

During this time, a variety of institutions and activities evolved with the purpose of promoting and implementing social reform and improvement in the living conditions of the poor and the lives of children (Cremin, 1988). Concerns about crowded, unhealthy living conditions, abuses of child labor, and other industrial casualties all give support to what was known as the Progressive Era. Education was the grand panacea. "Proponents of virtually every progressive cause from the 1890's through World War I had their own programs for the schools," wrote Cremin (1988, p. 85). Cremin went on to say, "Humanitarians of every stripe saw education at the heart of their effort toward social alleviation" (p. 85). Progressivists not only recognized the school as a force for social change, but extended efforts to make the school more progressive as well. The capstone following World War I was the extension of educational opportunity through the unitary, comprehensive, or cosmopolitan high school (Commission on the Reorganization of Secondary Education, 1918). Lunch programs, guidance services, special services, playgrounds, libraries, health services, shops, laboratories, and improved facilities made their way into public schools (Good, 1956).

Cremin (1988) identified several major themes that dominated progressive reform efforts and affected schools and the evolving forms of school supervision. First, the programs of study and functions of the curriculum were broadened to include health concerns, vocational needs, and the importance of family and community life. Second, more "humane, more active, and more rational pedagogical techniques" (p. 228) were applied in the classroom, along with new instructional approaches that addressed the diverse needs of different kinds of children and adolescents attending public school. A review of the literature reveals countless examples of progressive experiments in education and stories of the "pedagogical pioneers" who strained against the "one best system" (Aiken, 1992; Gross & Chandler, 1964; Tyack, 1974). A chief turning point was the extension of education upward, with universal secondary education emerging from vision to reality through the comprehensive high school (Commission on the Reorganization of Secondary Education, 1918). This created a vast and unprecedented need for secondary school supervision and led to the emergence of the field of adolescent study (Cremin, 1961).

New Organizational Patterns

Aside from having a monumental impact on advancing the cause and providing the framework for universal education by means of the uniquely American comprehensive high school, the report of the 1918 Commission on the Reorganization of Secondary Education held that "the democratic organization and administration of the school itself, as well as the cooperative relations of pupils and teacher, pupil and pupil, and teacher and teacher, are indispensable" (p. 14). The Commission held that the widest aims and functions of education should determine organization, rather than the other way around, pointing to the danger that departmentalization would create curricular segmentation, subject by subject, and teacher isolation. The Commission's report went on to discuss the problems of the high school principal with regard to supervision. Although the principal was theoretically seen as responsible for supervising the teaching and directing all activities of the school, the Commission's report pointed out that, from a practical standpoint, principals are under shifting pressures that divert them from these functions. The Commission then proposed that the principal form a council composed of teachers and that the council include directors of curriculum, guidance, health, and other areas, along with teacher committees all working cooperatively to develop a broad educational point of view. (This approach would engage a large number of teachers in cooperative schoolwork while, at the same time, it would not in any way diminish the ultimate responsibility of the principal).

The report of the Commission on the Reorganization advocated many other promising practices which were gaining credence in the professional literature. Progressive innovations included such ideas as unit plans, the project method, individualized instruction, the activity curriculum, and learning experiences organized around central themes that took into consideration the natural interests and experiences of the learner (Good, 1956; Gross & Chandler, 1964; Tanner & Tanner, 1990). All of these innovations helped to move the curriculum away from its strict adherence to separate subjects and graded organizational patterns. Many of these plans were eventually criticized for their overemphasis on child centeredness and disappeared. The philosophy that there are alternatives to the formal and rigid practices in the schools, however, remained a progressive legacy. The progressive reform movement provided an experimental departure from the traditional curriculum and the strict bureaucratic, uniform, and lockstep pattern that had become the standard in most school systems (Cremin, 1961, Cuban, 1984).

Supervision for Progressive Reform

The role of the teacher was vastly transformed as progressive innovations and curricular changes made their way into the public schools. School administration was also affected as more systematically organized and rational approaches to school management were implemented (Callahan, 1962; Cremin, 1961; Cuban, 1984). This transformation, in turn, forced a change in the purposes, functions, and organization of school supervision as new curricular approaches and purposes of public education challenged the roles of and relationships between teachers and supervisors. Instead of supervision influencing teaching, approaches to teaching and learning forced supervisors to become involved in curriculum development. As innovative ideas made their way into the practices and processes of American education and new thinking about how children learn affected teaching methodology, the need for someone who could help teachers apply the new pedagogy became an important force in school supervision.

Points of Conflict

The events brought about by the experimentalist progressives evolved into two major forces which vastly affected curriculum and school supervision during the early years of the twentieth century. Scientific management, based on principles of social efficiency and business and industry, and progressivism, based on a concern for social reform and child study, both directly affected curriculum and school supervision between 1900 and 1930. It was during this time frame that the untenable dualism that set supervision apart from its important relationship with curriculum development was cast. Research into major writings of the leading theorists, whose work appeared in official publications of professional organizations, defined the evolving supervision–curriculum relationship and the role of the classroom teacher in this process (Ayres, 1913; Bagley, 1908; Burton, 1922; Cubberley, 1916; Elliott, 1914; Hollister, 1914; Sears, 1918; Spaulding, 1913). School supervision tended to follow two oppositional paths: one that might be termed the "bureaucratization of supervision" and the other the "democratization of supervision."

Bureaucratization conceived of supervision as a top-down flow of communication, in which the school climate was "permeated by an air of authoritative managerial efficiency" (Tanner & Tanner, 1987, p. 170). Teachers were viewed as workers or technicians and were often excluded from participation in important curriculum decisions. Successful teaching was equated with efficiency, as measured by standardized rating instruments, checklists, scorecards, and tests (Bagley, 1908; Bobbitt, 1913; Reynolds, 1914; and Spaulding, 1913). Curriculum was determined by specified tasks for social utility and how well learning activities helped students attain predetermined specific objectives. Bobbitt, however, sought to conceive the curriculum in terms of specified life skills; these were defined behavioristically in terms of adult tasks. Furthermore, the goals of education were to be shaped according to how well the curriculum could accommodate young people under existing conditions, rather than helping them develop the knowledge and skills needed to improve conditions (Tanner & Tanner, 1980).

The democratic model of supervision viewed teachers as being continuously engaged in curriculum development and conceived of supervision as a problem-solving process that contributed to continuous professional growth and development. The supervisor provided the leadership that supported teachers in the process of curriculum development and instructional improvement. The curriculum was to grow out of the interests and needs of the learner and to be based on principles of human development and societal improvement. Education was to take on a democratic purpose of helping to prepare young people for participation in a democratic society, and supervisors were to assist teachers in the educational process.

Supervision as Democratic Instructional Leadership

After 1915, the literature on supervision showed a notable transition toward less autocratic models and functions. The professional writings of leading theorists from the field of school supervision confirmed that supervisors needed to improve themselves in their work and their relationships with teachers (Newlon, 1923; Nutt, 1920; Sears, 1918). Instead of supervision serving as the arm of administration, or supervisors serving as production managers or efficiency experts, supervisors were called upon to serve as instructional leaders who worked cooperatively with teachers and helped solve classroom problems, specifically as they related to subject matter (Barr & Burton, 1926; Burton, 1922). Supervisors began to establish themselves as instructional experts in the schools. It became evident that the so-called scientific methods of surveys, rating scales, and scorecards did not lead to the solutions of important educational problems. Nor did the hostility projected by teachers allow supervisors to do what they were traditionally intended to do (Button, 1961; McNeil, 1982; Tuttle, 1942).

Superintendents, supervisors, and scholars from higher education began to advocate more democratic approaches to school organization and administration (Barr and Burton, 1926; Bogan, 1919; Burton, 1922; Dewey, 1915; Gardner, 1919; Hosic, 1920; Hunter, 1913; Kilpatrick, 1925; Knapp, 1919; Kyte, 1923; Lull, 1923; Newlon, 1923; Nutt, 1920; Sears, 1918; Skinner, 1920; Thayer, 1925). Their writings embraced more democratic approaches to school supervision, which included greater collaborative involvement of the classroom teachers. Attempts were increasingly made to reduce the antagonistic feelings that had developed between teachers and supervisors (Foote, 1924; Hosic, 1920; Kilpatrick, 1925). New definitions of supervision viewed the field as democratic instructional leadership and favored greater involvement of teachers in all matters of education, especially in important curriculum matters (Burton, 1922; Foote, 1924; Knapp, 1919; Thayer, 1925; Tietrict, 1914; Wilson, 1920). Cooperative relationships were encouraged, and teachers were given more opportunity to participate as curriculum decision makers (Bacon, 1926; Hunter, 1924; Undegraff, 1921). In addition to important curriculum issues, teachers also had a greater voice in deciding school policy and certain matters of administration and supervision (Bogan, 1919; Gardner, 1919). In-service education, teacher councils, and teacher advisory committees became important new tools that fostered the active participation of the teacher in all matters of education (Clark, 1920; Skinner, 1920). One of the strongest advocates of democratic supervision came from the writings of James Fleming Hosic, President of the Chicago Normal School (1920). In his article titled, "The Democratization of Supervision," published in the *Proceedings of the National Education Association,* Hosic defined supervision as:

democratic leadership in a group of co-workers to the end that pupils of the schools may make the largest possible growth of desirable ideals, interests, knowledge, power and skills with the least waste of energy and the greatest amount of satisfaction to all concerned. . . . This is the real justification for supervision. This is why discipline must be supplanted by cooperation. This is why teachers should be consulted regularly by supervisors (pp. 414–415).

Supervision and Curriculum Although supervision was still viewed as that process that supports the improvement of teaching, it began to be recognized and accepted that the democratic participation of the teacher in important matters of curriculum development was the primary means of fostering teacher growth (Adair, 1926; Barr, 1929; Clements, 1927; Collings, 1924; Hunter, 1924). The new language of supervision focused on problems associated with "the organization of subject matter, testing, and the improvement of teachers in service" (Adair, 1926, p. 733), as writers began to recognize that teacher involvement in curriculum development provided one of the "best means for training teachers in service" (Adair, 1926, p. 733). In 1927, Clements went so far as to blame the then current dilemma of education on the fact that supervision had generally "ignored the curriculum and its relationship to curriculum making in its quest to improve teaching" (p. 174). Clements, a professor at the University of Illinois, offered his "preamble to the written constitution on the supervision of instruction":

Supervision of instruction and curriculum making represent two of the most important phases of secondary education. The interrelation existing between the theory of supervision and of curriculum making is evident. Certain aspects are so interrelated that it is difficult to separate them even for analytical purposes. In fact, in practice, they always are supplementary to one another. Theoretically considered, they represent fundamental but complementary aspects of a unified educative process (pp. 171–177).

Professional Organization The dramatic shift in theory was strengthened after 1920. Supervisors organized themselves into their own professional organization called the National Conference on Educational Method, and began to exercise responsibility for their new professional role. They turned away from issues of accountability and efficiency and focused on matters of curriculum and instruction. In 1921, they founded *The Journal of Educational Method* in an attempt to build a complementary, cooperative relationship between supervisors and teachers. In their opening pages, the editors stated that the journal would be entirely devoted to the improvement of teaching and would "provide means of unification of effort in the field of supervision and teaching" (1921, p. 1). The new journal seemed to represent those individuals in the schools who were practicing teachers, supervisors, and curriculum directors, rather then school superintendents and college professors. They wrote from their own viewpoints and from the realities of their classrooms. In one of the first issues of the journal, J. Cayce Morrison (1921) wrote about the changing role of the school supervisor and offered his "cardinal points" (p. 131) of school supervision:

To insure that all children have equivalent instructional opportunity, to coordinate properly all the instructional activities of the school, to provide every teacher with fullest opportunity to give her best in service and to organize conditions so that every teacher will continue to grow in service—they are the cardinal points of school supervision (p. 131).

It was through the *Journal of Educational Method* that the idea of supervision and curriculum as forming an important relationship was established. The supervisor was to take more responsibility for enlisting teachers as important participants in the curriculum development process (Barr, 1929; Collings, 1924; Cutright, 1929). Supervisors were prodded to "get into the advance guard rather than the rear guard of the curriculum-revision program" (Cutright, 1929, p. 407). An analysis of the many discussions in the *Journal of Educational Method* (eventually renamed *Educational Method*) provided evidence that concern for curricular aims, innovative and progressive curriculum changes, pupil achievement, and teacher involvement were fundamental concerns and responsibilities of school supervisors. Cooperative relationships between teachers and supervisors and supervisory leadership in the development of curriculum represented essential themes in school supervision literature.

By 1929, this group had become the Department of Supervisors and Directors of Instruction of the NEA. This organization published its own yearbook, in which greater support for democratic models of supervision and the link between supervision and curriculum could be forged (Brueckner, 1929; Burton, 1922; Hosic, 1928; Kilpatrick, 1925). The Department's first yearbook, appropriately titled *Educational Supervision* (1928), offered a review of current views, theories, and practices of prominent writers from the field, including A. S. Barr, W. H. Burton, J. Cayce Morrison, W. H. Kilpatrick, and J. R. Hosic. The yearbook served to further define the purpose of supervision as the process intended to help teachers with their work by enlisting their fullest possible active direction and to involve them in all phases of curriculum development (Kilpatrick, 1925).

Curriculum Redefined Professional journals, yearbooks, and textbooks confirmed the democratic purposes of supervision that had evolved during the first three decades of the twentieth century. The new theory of school supervision gave further testimony to the democratic purposes of the schools and the important relationship between supervision and curriculum. Backed by the tenets of social research, endorsed by universities and colleges, and sanctioned by the public schools, literature from the field was prolific. The meaning of curriculum and the relationship of supervision and teaching to curriculum underwent a radical transformation between 1900 and 1930. Curriculum came to mean something more than the "course of study" and list of subjects (Kliebard, 1988; Rugg & Counts, 1927; Tanner & Tanner, 1990, 1995). The scientific knowledge on child development and the social purposes of the schools continued to exert a force upon curriculum makers, which, in turn, forced greater attention toward the selection and organization of subject matter, the development of purposeful learning activities, and the evaluation of student learning. Curriculum writers began to define curriculum as all

the activities or experiences a learner has under the auspices of the school, which constituted an abrupt break from the traditional conceptions of curriculum (Cady, 1988; Caswell & Campbell, 1935; Rugg & Counts, 1927; Sears, 1918). Recognizing that what students learn is no longer limited to the formal course of study but is affected by the total school environment, a broader definition of curriculum was needed (Tanner & Tanner, 1980). With this change in definition and meaning of curriculum came changes in the application of school supervision and the role of the classroom teacher in the process. It was generally recognized after 1920 that curriculum was to mean "all activities through which a child learns" (Caswell & Campbell, 1937, p. 152) including the "organized program of study and the entire teaching process as carried on in the schools" (Caswell & Campbell, 1937, p. 153). The artificial dualism that had been growing between curriculum and instruction was challenged by this new thinking about curriculum. With these changes came an important focus for supervision—democratic instructional leadership and the engagement of teachers in the activities and important tasks of curriculum development. As the curriculum was looked upon more as experience shaped by the environmental conditions of the school and classroom, there was no question that the teacher was needed as a curriculum maker. Thus, the purposes of supervision, as well as the role of the teacher in the supervisory-curriculum relationship, were transformed.

Professional Support Jesse Sears (1918), a prominent writer in the field of supervision, supported this new definition of curriculum and the role of the supervisor and teacher in the process. Drawing from Dewey (1902), he stated:

The term curriculum usually brings to our minds a printed course of study or a collection of textbooks. We tend to think of the child and of the curriculum as two unrelated objects of concern for the teacher. . . . So it is that we are likely to set the one over against the other. If, however, we turn to our definition of education we are reminded that to learn is not merely to master the printed page, to get information, but that it is to develop, to grow, to experience, to live (pp. 144–145).

Following this lead, texts that appeared after 1920 fortified democratic principles and practices of school supervision (Barr & Burton, 1926; Burton, 1922; Dewey, 1929; Elliott, 1914; Gates, 1923; Hollister, 1914; Nutt, 1920; Sears, 1918; Wilson, Kyte, & Lull, 1924). Concern for cooperative relationships between teachers and supervisors, teacher participation in school policy development, increased attention to the curriculum, and selection and organization of subject matter by the teacher under the leadership of the supervisor represented the new tenets of supervisory theory. At a time when supervision was being severely criticized and challenged, democratic models depicted in popular texts on supervision and curriculum advocated increased involvement of teachers in educational planning and leadership.

The supervisor was there, as an educational expert, to guide, assist, direct, and help improve teaching. Supervisors were newly required to become "conversant with the literature" (Nutt, 1920, p. 25) and to have a great deal of curriculum expertise. Teacher appraisal was not aimed at the measurement of teacher efficiency based upon some external, predetermined standard of qualification, but was a tool to be used to help teachers improve themselves. In the words of Burton (1922):

Efficiency in supervision, in attaining the desired educative results, demands a unification and coordination of the efforts of every individual engaged in the different processes within the big complex (p. 396).

Experimental Attitudes The change from the alleged scientific approach as advocated by Bobbitt and his followers—which called for the supervisor to determine specific learning objectives and the teaching methods needed to attain them—to one where supervisors and teachers experimented together, "activated by a spirit of inquiry" (McNeil, 1982, p. 20), was another important change of this era. Supervisors were no longer doing "to" teachers but were working with teachers to develop applications of more scientific approaches in the classroom (Barr & Burton, 1926; McNeil, 1982). As stated by McNeil: "Supervisors and teachers together were to adopt an experimental attitude, testing new procedures and studying the effects of each newly introduced means of improvement until satisfactory results were attained" (p. 20).

Science Versus Scientism It was during this era that Dewey (1929) systematically addressed the problem of applying the scientific method in education and qualified the differences between science and scientism. Drawing from the field of measurement as an illustration, he cited the distinction between using measurement as a means to "guide the intelligence of teachers" (p. 36) and using it as the method to "dictate the rules of action" (p. 36) as the new meaning of science in education. Dewey was one of the earliest writers to recognize the important role of the teacher as an "investigator" (p. 46) of classroom problems and as a major contributor to the experimental process for educational improvement. The literature was advocating more experimental attitudes in the classroom for both teachers and students as the key to the improvement of teaching and learning, instead of authoritative, dogmatic supervision (Dewey, 1910a, b).

Supervision for Teacher Growth

Teacher improvement continued to be recognized as a fundamental purpose of supervision between 1920 and 1930. Teacher improvement, however, could not be separated from instructional improvement, which came about through the mutual and cooperative activities of the supervisor and teacher. Teacher growth was a prerequisite to teaching improvement and resulted from the involvement of teachers in curriculum development, research, professional development, and self-evaluation—all of which was to be directed and facilitated by the school supervisor.

Supervisors as Subject Specialists As supervisors became more recognized and valued as instructional leaders, they sometimes adopted a narrow view of their role. Curriculum

was just beginning to break from its subject-centered organization, even though it had come to be looked upon as all the activities provided for students under the auspices of the school. The newly found position of instructional leader was too often reduced to "subject specialist" (Stone, 1929; Uhl, 1929), often resembling the earlier role of the "special supervisors" who had provided teachers assistance with such special subjects as drawing, music, or manual arts when they first addressed the curriculum. Supervisors had not yet arrived at the point where time was given to providing for a study of the interrelationships of subjects and the applications of the curriculum to the life of the learner and to the wider world of social problem solving. This would come later. Supervisors most often worked in a leadership role in helping to establish course aims, standards for achievement, materials, and activities for each subject area in cooperation with teachers. They were, in many ways, subject specialists, too often required to work with teachers in one subject or subject field in isolation from other studies, and worked separately from other supervisors. Although the work of school supervisors continued to be directed at the classroom level, the ideas that curriculum was a primary concern of school supervisors and that teachers should play a vital role in its development were important supervisory legacies that grew out of the years between 1900 and 1930.

Democratic Instructional Leadership By 1930, supervisors had attained their own professional status as measured by their prominent place in the schools, their professional organizations, their professional publications, their advanced study in the university, and by the growing number of textbooks that had been written on the theory and practice of school supervision. In the space of 30 years, supervisors had been transformed from inspectors, to teachers of teachers, to efficiency experts, and eventually to instructional leaders. Teacher improvement was still seen as the primary function of supervision, but the means for improving teaching had changed. Supervisory techniques, formerly limited to reading circles, summer institutes, and observations and conferences, had expanded to include a full range of in-service education, graduate study, and curriculum development.

Autocratic, inspectorial models of supervision had been replaced with more cooperative and democratic approaches. In progressive school districts, teacher councils had evolved and teachers were more involved in the policy and planning of the educational program. In reaction to the rigid and bureaucratic supervisory models and the efficiency mania that swept the country between 1911 and 1920, supervisors saw the opportunity to affect teacher growth and development through instructional and curricular improvement. As curriculum had grown into a field of study, supervision seemed to take on greater importance, as it became recognized that all curriculum improvement programs required the expert leadership of an individual who understood the nature of the curriculum development process—the school supervisor.

By 1930, the leading professional organization for school supervision, the Department of Supervisors and Directors of Instruction, stated that the most important function for supervision was to learn how their profession would improve education by focusing on the course of study and the act of teaching. Writers for the 1929 Yearbook for the Department attempted to analyze classroom teaching by applying the newest methods of scientific research to supervisory procedures. The supervisors who lived and worked during the early years of the twentieth century embraced the challenge, but the struggle for democratic supervision and especially for recognition of the interdependence of curriculum and instruction was to continue to this day. It would not be until the 1930s that the democratic model of school supervision and the complementary relationship between supervision and curriculum were to emerge in full concert in the literature.

THE STRUGGLE FOR PROFESSIONALISM

The years between 1930 and 1965 represented an era shaped by philosophical debates over the purposes of public education, unprecedented progress in the sciences and technology, a sociological climate that raised new questions about the value of schooling to American society, and enormous expansion and growth. Student enrollment mushroomed during this era and the need for a population of professionally trained teachers was critical. In 1920, 2.5 million students were enrolled in public secondary schools in the United States; by 1960, the secondary school enrollment exceeded 9.5 million. In 1920, less than one-third of the age group was enrolled in secondary school; by 1960, almost 90 percent was enrolled (Tanner, 1972). The number of public school teachers needed to handle the influx of students at all levels increased from 20,000 in 1920 to over 2 million in 1965 (Lee, 1966). The dramatic increase in the high school enrollment demanded college-trained teachers. In 1930, only one out of every 20 teachers had been educated beyond high school; by 1960, 82 percent of all elementary school teachers and 98 percent of all secondary teachers were college graduates (Langworthy, 1990).

Teacher Education

The improvement of teaching continued to be an important focus of school supervision after 1930, for both preservice and in-service education. However, there were changes in the educational preparation of teachers and in the conditions under which they worked (Evenden, 1938). Teachers were better prepared and had to meet more rigorous certification requirements in order to qualify for employment. Qualifications, standards, and certification requirements for entry into the profession were totally transformed between the years 1930 and 1965. Education as a field of study had found a respected and valued place with the transformation of teachers' colleges into comprehensive colleges and universities. Teacher education programs were subjected to accreditation standards by newly formed organizations such as the National Council for Accreditation of Teacher Education (NCATE). Whereas preservice education curricula prior to 1900 had consisted mostly of "methods and devices of teaching and a review of the subjects to be taught" (Evenden, 1938, p. 33), preservice programs for teacher education after 1930

involved a professional field of study, principles and techniques of curriculum construction, and methods and procedures for measuring learning and teaching effectiveness (Evenden, 1938). Professional organizations for teachers became firmly established and teachers had a voice in the development of their professional status. By midcentury, responsibility for the preparation, licensure, and certification of teachers had moved out of the hands of local superintendents and to state departments of education (Wesley, 1957).

New Demands

Major groups during a time period marked by significant world events—the Great Depression, World War II, the Cold War, and the space race—looked upon schools as the means of addressing critical social and economic problems and reconstructing postwar society (Kliebard, 1988). Kliebard wrote that the "struggle for the American curriculum" (p. 181) transpired during the early years of the twentieth century, with the battles waging on well after 1930. Democratic, intellectual, and technocratic purposes for education came into conflict, and the school curriculum too often served as the battleground. Educators were faced with major challenges as various groups promoted their own special interests for the curriculum. Often, the school supervisor was put on the front line.

The Process of Curriculum Reform

During the years between 1930 and 1965, a new professional organization evolved. Its purpose was to deal directly with curriculum. A small "federation of curriculum specialists" became the Society for Curriculum Study. In 1936, they teamed up with members of the Department of Supervisors and Directors of Instruction of the NEA to form the Joint Committee on Curriculum. This committee studied current trends in the organization, evaluation, selection, and arrangement of learning materials and learning experiences. It explored the many progressive curriculum projects that had been taking place throughout American schools. They published their findings in *The Changing Curriculum* (Joint Committee on Curriculum, 1937), which became an important text, contributing to a greater understanding of the process of curriculum planning and development. What was significant, however, was that two organizations, one primarily concerned with curriculum and the other with supervision, came together to work on this project. For the Joint Committee on Curriculum, supervision and curriculum formed a natural unity.

Experimental Attitudes Curricular experimentalism during these years was encouraged and was related in large measure to the new social purposes of the school. Curriculum reorganization in the more progressive schools represented a radical departure from the traditional disciplines as experimentalists developed new curricula around important social issues, themes, and problems. Educators attempted to fuse social concerns and needs or interests of students into major areas of study (Caswell & Campbell, 1935; Collings, 1934; Cox & Langfitt, 1934; Kliebard, 1988; Rippa, 1980; Tanner, 1972). Struggling against the pressures of college dominance, schools experimented with new forms of curriculum that centered on problems common to adolescents, believing that there were many avenues of study and experience that would prepare youth for higher education (Aikin, 1942; Tyler, 1971). These developments placed new demands on secondary school supervision.

The focus for secondary school supervision was changing dramatically from merely enlisting the cooperative support of teachers in matters of curriculum and policy. Writers challenged these ideas as simply making autocratic practices more benevolent (Alberty & Thayer, 1931; Rorer, 1942). The new school supervisor had to serve as a dynamic leader who was able to create the conditions in the school that would make "all relationships more social so that the full and free interplay among all groups" (Alberty & Thayer, 1931, p. 236) could exist. The full participation of all members of the school community was needed for the democratic process. The NEA's Department of Supervisors and Directors of Instruction came out in strong support for this new thinking (Department of Supervisors and Directors of Instruction, 1933, 1938). The sixth Yearbook, *Effective Instructional Leadership* (1933), discussed the new role of educational leadership:

Those seeking freedom must first help create the conditions which make freedom possible; freedom must itself be an emergent quality in the personal and group life of all members. . . . Educational leadership must so organize the work of teachers, principals, and supervisors that interplay of mind is facilitated, initiative is rewarded, and cooperation is encouraged (pp. 131–133).

Professional Support

Given the social milieu of the 1930s and 1940s, concerns about democratic purposes and aims of the curriculum, coupled with increased attention to the supervisor as the instructional leader who could help schools meet these aims, were popular themes in the literature that appeared after 1930 (Alberty & Thayer, 1931; Barr, Burton, & Brueckner, 1938; Burton, 1940; Culbertson, 1964; Harman, 1947; Norton, 1931; Reschke, 1932; Rorer, 1942; Taba, 1945). As stated earlier, the strongest voices in support of democratic social philosophy came from the membership of the Department of Supervisors and Directors of Instruction. This professional group became a department of the National Education Association in 1928, due largely to the efforts of James Hosic, who wanted to establish an organization for educators who had a special interest in supervision. The department's earliest yearbooks, and the yearbooks that would follow throughout the century, reflected their interest and concern for the developing field of school supervision. Themes of cooperation, democratic leadership, scientific research to advance supervision and curriculum development, new relationships with staff, and democratic social purposes of schools reverberated through the many chapters of the yearbooks.

Initially, the writers for the Department's yearbooks attacked the industrial model of schooling that had been adopted by schools prior to 1920 in favor of more democratic organizations. They advocated an education that would contribute to the "growth and development of all the members of the orga-

nization, including administrators, supervisors, teachers, and pupils" (Department of Supervisors and Directors of Instruction, 1933, p. 19). From their writings, there emerged a new definition of instructional leadership and a vital role for the school supervisor. The Department's committee for the 1933 Yearbook, *Effective Instructional Leadership*, wrote:

Effective leadership will invite participation in the formation of instructional policies, will stimulate variation in educational thinking and planning, will encourage and allow freedom in experimentation. . . . and will provide for the maximum development of self-direction, self-appraisal and self-control of the teaching staff. Thus the instructional organization, which represents a desirable integration of supervisory organization and activities, should be dominated by a democratic philosophy (p. 2).

Democratic Classrooms Teachers, too, were expected to provide classroom environments that would meet the needs of students and democratic purposes. Contributors to the Eleventh Yearbook for the Department of Supervisors and Directors of Instruction entitled *Cooperation: Principles and Practices* (1939) expressed concern that the kinds of classrooms and school organizational patterns that had evolved in American schools did not promote important social relationships necessary for living in a democratic society. The department dedicated the entire yearbook to a study of the problem. "The school and home must function democratically," they wrote, "if children are to be expected to learn the full meaning of democracy as a way of desirable social interacting" (p. 80). This new responsibility to create democratic classroom environments became the obligation of the classroom teacher, and the supervisor played a critical role in the process.

Pupil Growth Through Teacher Growth Although the literature after 1930 continued to support the function of supervision as the improvement of teaching, "improvement" was conceived and measured in new ways (Barr, Burton, & Brueckner, 1938, 1947; Burton & Brueckner, 1955; Courtis, McSwain, & Morrison 1939; Heffernan, 1940; Lindquist, 1933; Rankin, 1934; Spears, 1953). The idea that teacher growth would contribute to pupil growth was more strongly recognized in the supervision literature after 1930 (Barr & Burton, 1926; Burton, 1922; Courtis et al, 1939; Rankin, 1934). In *Scientific Method in Supervision* (1934), the committee writing for the Seventh Yearbook of the Department of Supervisors and Directors of Instruction stated: "The foregoing generalization directs attention to the only justification for supervision, namely, providing for the growth and improvement of teachers as a means of insuring the growth and development of pupils" (p. 24). Equally important, leading writers from the field recognized that teacher growth was directly related to their participation in curriculum development. In the 1940 Yearbook, *Newer Instructional Practices of Promise*, the department made the following statement:

An era of continuous cooperative development of curriculum is taking place. This change in curriculum development puts the responsibility for leadership upon the supervisor and makes curriculum improvement a major function of supervision. Modern supervisors are inviting the participation and cooperation of teachers, specialists, administrators, and representatives of lay organizations. Such cooperative leadership not only results in improved curricula for children, but seems to be an excellent means of stimulating the professional growth of teachers (p. 345).

Their thesis was simple. Improved student learning was to come about through a process of supervision that was creative, cooperative, and involved teachers in self-directed approaches to substantive curriculum problem solving.

Teacher as Problem Solver Problem solving became an important aspect of the democratic and cooperative process that had come to define school supervision. Teachers were called upon to work on problems that were significant to them as practitioners (Gilchrist, Fielstra, & Davis, 1957; Richey, 1957). These problems, however, were no longer isolated to a single teacher or restricted to his or her classroom. Problems were viewed in relationship to the entire instructional program and the school's overall aims and purposes. The instructional-curriculum improvement process had moved out of the individual classroom and into the arena of the entire school (Spears, 1953). The group process and group attack upon instructional and curricular problems became vital and integral aspects of supervision. In *Supervision: Democratic Leadership in the Improvement of Learning*, Barr, Burton, and Brueckner (1938) stated that "one of the very best means of coming to some fairly substantial understanding of professional education is for teachers to study carefully and systematically the problems sensed by them in their everyday work as teachers" (p. 737). Almost two decades later, Burton and Brueckner (1955) still held the conviction that a "co-operatively determined attack upon significant local educational problems" (p. 9) was the best way to stimulate the entire staff toward continuous growth and development and sound educational improvement.

Supervision and Curriculum

The perspective of supervision as a democratic social purpose created a different role for the supervisor, especially in relationship to the curriculum development process. The supervisor now had to be much more than an instructional expert. In this evolving educational leadership position, the supervisor was required to bring about the necessary environmental conditions for an open and democratic exchange among faculty members to exist. It had come to be accepted in many quarters that curriculum was far more than a list of subjects. Aims and objectives that supported the "imperative needs of youth" and the goals of a democratic society became the focus of curriculum reconstruction, and school supervisors were newly challenged to think how the curriculum should be reconstructed to meet these goals.

Supervision Redefined Yearbooks, journals, and textbooks published in the field of supervision confirmed that democratic social purposes of supervision were reinforced after 1930. The purpose of supervision was to release all the cre-

ative abilities of the teacher so that he or she could be self-directive, solve classroom and school-wide problems, and contribute to improved learning of students (Melchoir, 1933; Norton, 1931; Reschke, 1932). The idea that supervision and curriculum form an inextricable relationship and the acknowledgment that supervision was to take the lead in the curriculum development process had been increasingly advanced (Harap, 1940; Zeller, 1940). Themes of teacher participation, freedom, group leadership, and new supervisory procedures were topics of discussion in innumerable articles and books (Alexander, 1947; Burton, 1940; Corey, 1949; Kelly, 1945; Mackenzie, 1945). Supervisors who supported the democratic social processes rejected the traditional, autocratic procedures that had been practiced in the schools by supervisors in earlier decades. New supervisory techniques included inservice workshops and programs, curriculum experimentation, action research, and group planning. These new organizational structures provided the democratic environments for teachers and supervisors to come together to attack and solve real problems.

The new definition of democratic leadership—the leader who encourages initiative and experimentation, who values individual contributions, and who supports group planning and problem solving—became an important issue for school supervision. Although some writers clung to earlier supervisory models and traditional views of curriculum, others challenged these methods, claiming that they had not enlisted the cooperative thinking and contributions of all members of the school but merely maintained the administrative hierarchy (Alberty & Thayer, 1931; Brown, 1933; Hunkins, 1931). Research into interpersonal relationships, working environments, organizational patterns, decision-making processes, and leadership style produced a different image of administration, which changed the role of the school supervisor (Culbertson, 1964).

The new democratic thrust in secondary school supervision appeared to emerge from the growing desire to make the curriculum more responsive to the needs of youth and changing social conditions. The experimentalists and progressivists had sought to renew the curriculum by promoting democratic social living. Alberty and Thayer (1931), two of the leading writers in the field, wrote that supervision in the secondary school had an important responsibility in this endeavor:

In view of this situation, our educational problem, particularly upon the secondary level, is to provide such training as will most likely equip individuals to become active participants, rather than mere spectators, in directing the changes in our social life. In this reconstruction, the curriculum must play a vital role. . . . Happily such a program may be made to serve as a vital instrument for improving the conditions for teacher and pupil growth, which is the heart of supervision (p. 219).

This vision marked a dramatic departure from earlier models of curriculum organization. Teachers, supervisors, and students were to create the curriculum as they moved along and in response to the needs of learners and the demands of a free society, which were dynamic rather than static (Barr, Burton, & Brueckner, 1938, 1947; Collings, 1934; Cox & Langfitt, 1934).

Democratic purposes of schooling, heterogeneous grouping, work-study, vocational education, curriculum integration, and common cores of learning were characteristic of the curriculum reform efforts during the post-Depression years, especially at the secondary school level of education. The "youth problem" became the catalyst for major reform of the secondary school curriculum. The vanguard educational reform efforts aimed to meet the "needs of youth" (National Society for the Study of Education, 1944), and the role of the school supervisor took on a new function. What evolved was a process in which supervisors were called upon to take a leadership role in the attempts to link the process of curriculum development to the critical needs of adolescents and the social purposes of the schools. Teachers were to play a greater role in this process. As the 1952 Yearbook of the National Society for the Study of Education (1953) stated:

Especially important to a continuing program of curriculum study is an emphasis by the administrative staff on teaching and learning situations which seem to have the promise of meeting the needs and interests of youth. Supervisory policies must anticipate developmental teaching programs by emphasizing teaching outcomes which will promote rather than obstruct curriculum revision (p. 90).

Unity in Theory There was consistent support for the relationship of supervision to curriculum and the involvement of the teacher in the curriculum-development process. The literature on school supervision, by midcentury, demonstrated a unity in theory (Adams & Dickey, 1953; Ayer, 1954; Briggs & Justman, 1952; Burton & Brueckner, 1955; Melchoir, 1950; Reeder, 1953; Spears, 1953; Wiles, 1950). Curriculum was defined as all the experiences and activities provided to the learner under the auspices of the school that would contribute to the agreed-upon goals and aims of the educational program; supervision was recognized as the means for developing this curriculum. The goals and means were viewed as interdependent. Teachers were encouraged to experiment in order to develop methods and materials that would foster student learning. They were given back their right to select educational materials, fashion methods, and determine curriculum objectives (Spears, 1953). A new technique known as "action research" (Corey, 1949) emerged to serve as an opportunity for practitioners to solve practical problems in their classrooms and schools.

The talents and expertise of teachers were needed to develop new curriculum materials and experiences, especially since traditional college preparatory texts were no longer appropriate for meeting the needs of youth. More emphasis was put on curriculum evaluation, as teachers and supervisors attempted to assess how their curriculum was preparing young people for their roles in a democratic society. A leading curriculum writer during this time who expressed this concern was Hilda Taba (1945). She wrote:

No one will doubt that curriculum revision for postwar education faces many serious problems, the solution of which may require a marked reorientation of time-honored procedures and principles. . . . In many areas fundamental changes have taken place in the basic orienting concepts, problems, and ideology. . . . The ideals of democracy, equality of opportunity, freedom, and the basic concepts permeating our teaching of civics, history, and literature are acquiring a new meaning (p. 80).

A Curriculum Paradigm The ability to use scientific tools to evaluate the teaching and learning processes created new responsibilities for supervisors. The expanding body of research on learning theory and the concern for democratic principles forced new elements into the development of supervision and curriculum. Drawing upon the curriculum of the Eight-Year Study of Ralph Tyler's *Basic Principles of Curriculum and Instruction* appeared in 1949. This concise handbook became the base upon which supervisors could build their work as they sought to find a balance among the needs of learners, the goals of a democratic society, and the proper place of subject matter in this process. Tyler's handbook put supervisors and teachers in the center of the curriculum development process, since they were directly involved in the development of curricular aims and objectives, the selection of materials and learning activities, the appraisal of student progress, and the evaluation of the instructional program (Tyler, 1949).

Professional Supervision The journal *Educational Method* emerged as the chief voice for supervisors. The journal's editors and contributors reflected the changing direction and philosophy of school supervision during the middle of the century. The writers moved closer to the realization that supervision and curriculum are inextricably linked in the important endeavor of educational improvement and that the teacher is a central participant in the process. The "marriage" of supervision and curriculum had taken place when the Department of Supervisors and Directors of Instruction merged with the Society for Curriculum Study, becoming the Department for Supervision and Curriculum Development in 1943. By 1947, they were known as the Association for Supervision and Curriculum Development. The Association renamed their journal *Educational Leadership*, and the relationship of supervision and curriculum in the improvement of instruction was established.

It was recognized by midcentury that the improvement of learning was contingent upon the full participation of the entire professional staff—teachers, supervisors, specialists, and administrators—and that the supervisor would create the democratic environments to support the process. To do this, the supervisor had to possess considerable knowledge in areas of democratic social planning, curriculum development, human relations, and evaluation. Teachers began to acquire the background preparation and experience that helped to establish them as expert resources to plan and administer the curriculum (Richey, 1957). New theorizing led to new and important meanings for in-service education. No longer valued as the means to correct some deficit of the teacher, in-service education was considered to be a way for the entire teaching staff to solve curricular and school-wide problems as a professional group (Richey, 1957). The supervisor was a critical participant in the new in-service structure, and the literature provided evidence that in some cases the term "supervisor" was replaced with other titles, such as "consultant," "coordinator," "advisor," or "resource person" (Spears, 1953). There was even room in these new democratic environments for "leadership to emerge from the teaching staff" itself (p. 66). The new definition of supervision reflected the type of leadership that promoted the growth of pupils, teachers and the supervisory staff (Melchoir, 1950). Most importantly, the purpose of schools at midcentury was tied strongly to democratic principles, and it was concluded that all work of supervision was directed toward achieving this goal. In the words of Spears (1953):

As supervisors, teachers, school administrators, and laymen continue to work with the problems of school operations, they must recall that all public schools have their foundation firmly rooted in the American heritage, the preservation of which in the final analysis is the principal motive of all supervisory effort (p. 454).

Culmination of Thought With the publication of the text, *Supervision: A Social Process*, by William Burton and Leo Brueckner (1955), the thought and research regarding the status of the field of supervision was aggregated. The text synthesized the ideas and ideals that the inter-connected fields of supervision and curriculum, and left its readers with few doubts about the interpretation of supervision as a democratic social process in the schools. In the words of these authors:

Supervision is recognized as a social process; in our country the co-operative democratic process. Group planning, group attack on problems, experimentation are central. Co-operation among all agencies of society which deal with childhood and youth . . . is inescapable. Supervision becomes co-extensive with, or at least intimately related to, the entire setting for learning (p. 9).

These authors charted a unified and democratic approach to school supervision and its relationship to curriculum (p. 366). They outlined how supervisors could contribute to the effective improvement of teaching and learning and to the betterment of society. Their book solidified the unity between supervision and curriculum, holding that teachers and supervisors must be cooperatively involved in the complex process of curriculum renewal (p. 83). For Burton and Brueckner, supervision had not only moved out of the classroom and into the wider arena of the entire school, but was to "reflect the aims and aspirations of the social order within which the school operates" (p. 3).

School Mobilization for National Security

The National Defense Education Act was passed in 1958, and millions of dollars were made available for the improvement of curriculum and instruction in science, mathematics, and foreign languages. The National Science Foundation became the primary agency to utilize funds for discipline-centered curriculum-reform projects in the sciences and mathematics. Within these reform efforts, teachers again became the primary target for change. The National Science Foundation sponsored year-long training institutes to instruct teachers in how to use the new curriculum packages, which came ready-made and invited little or no participation from the teacher or school supervisor in their development. There was also some sentiment that teachers generally lacked background in the subject fields. Measures were also enacted to improve teachers' undergraduate education in their subject specialties.

Another urgency was to induce more students to pursue careers in the sciences, mathematics, and engineering to meet the nation's technological needs. The personal and social needs of youth seemed to go into eclipse, and nationalistic priorities came to center stage (D. Tanner, 1972). As Daniel Tanner so succinctly put it:

A curriculum revolution was promised as university scholars developed new courses for the high school. Little attention was given to adolescent problems or interests in the new curriculum packages. . . . Also neglected were the interrelationships between and among the various subjects in the total school curriculum (p. 75).

Admiral Hyman Rickover (1963) argued that America's national security was threatened and that progressivism had jeopardized the safety of the nation. James Conant (1959), former president of Harvard and chairperson of the Educational Policies Commission Report, *Education for ALL American Youth* (Educational Policies Commission, 1944, 1952), seemed to succumb to the pressure of Sputnik I and the Cold War, when in 1959, he issued a new report, *The American High School Today*, in which he recommended a curriculum that followed more traditional subject matter and called for a greater focus on the academic disciplines. Nevertheless, Conant's data gave full support to the comprehensive high school.

Intellectual Leadership Following the conservative attack and claims of anti-intellectualism in American schools, the National Academy of Sciences held an educational summit known as the Woods Hole Conference (Bruner, 1960). Attended by a group of 35 respected scientists, mathematicians, and psychologists, the conference developed strong recommendations for restructuring of the school curriculum. Financed with funds from the federal government and private foundations, this group produced a report titled *The Process of Education* (1960) under the leadership of Jerome S. Bruner. Earlier reform proposals had centered on the needs of youth and how to make the curriculum responsive to *all* students, whereas members of the Woods Hole Conference were concerned with the "top quarter of public school students, from which we must draw intellectual leadership in the next generation" (Bruner, 1960, p. 10). The commission recommended that curriculum reform be based on the structure of the disciplines and that knowledge was to be viewed much the way a "scholar specialist" (Tanner & Tanner, 1980, p. 523) viewed his work. Major outcomes of the conference resulted in several curriculum recommendations: curriculum was to be organized according to the separate academic subject disciplines, students were to be grouped homogeneously, university scholar-specialists were to create the discipline-centered curriculum packages, and student achievement was to be based on the results of national testing programs.

The efforts that grew out of the Woods Hole Conference represented a dramatic departure from the kinds of curriculum projects, teacher involvement, and supervision that had been developed by experimental schools over the course of several decades (Cremin, 1961). The post-Sputnik reformers believed that each academic discipline is monolithic in structure and that the curriculum must be organized into discrete disciplines. The mission of the Woods Hole Conference was to respond to the alleged crisis in national security that had been spurred by the launching of Sputnik I by the Soviets. The new or neo-essentialist curriculum they proposed was designed to meet the scientific and technological needs of the nation. To ensure that their mission was fulfilled, the new curriculum packages were designed to be "teacher proof." It was, anachronistically, the student who was to become engaged in disciplinary inquiry, whereas the teacher was to "deliver" the curriculum. The interrelationships of knowledge and curriculum synthesis, which the core programs of the 1930s and 1940s had attempted to provide, were ignored. The interpretation that democratic aims are best served when the needs of youth and important social issues are confronted in the curriculum had no place in the new curriculum packages. The belief that important curricular decisions required the active involvement of the teacher had no place in the neo-essentialist reform efforts. The process of curriculum development was now placed in the hands of university scholar-specialists and tied to the national security needs of the nation.

Conflicting Imperatives

In the span of 30 years, curriculum development had passed between two major reforms—one precipitated by the youth problem and one motivated by academic specialism and national security. Several forces affected reform efforts, as educators vacillated among the needs of youth, social concerns, intellectual training, and nationalistic imperatives. Within these conflicts, the definition and purposes of school supervision, the supervisory-curriculum relationship, and the role of the supervisor and classroom teacher were, once again, reconstituted. Supervision tended to veer off in two directions—supervision as a democratic social process and supervision as a technological production process.

Supervision as a democratic social process embraces the democratic cooperative approach to problem solving, which involves group planning and a group attack on significant problems of youth and society. Supervision and curriculum development team together to provide the greatest level of instructional leadership and student achievement. Teacher effectiveness is based on how well teachers and supervisors continuously reconstruct the curriculum to meet the needs of youth in consonance with a democratic society. Curriculum improvement is viewed as a continuous process rather than segmental attempts to revise existing courses of study. This process, most importantly, can only take place within administrative arrangements and practices embracing democratic philosophy.

If supervision is conceived as a technological process, however, the supervisor serves more as a technician whose primary responsibility focuses on instructional methodology and student achievement as measured by standardized, quantifiable assessments. Curriculum is a policy matter and comes from a place external to the school. This model forces a separation of curriculum and instruction, and the curriculum is determined at a higher level of authority. Neither teachers nor supervisors are participants in the curriculum reform process and they have little or no involvement in matters of curriculum design, development, and evaluation. Teachers tend to regard the supervisor as the "inspector whose principal functions are to see to it that the teacher takes on the task of implementing preplanned curriculum packages in the classroom and to evaluate the teacher accordingly" (Tanner & Tanner, 1987, p. 180). The teacher simply needs to implement a curriculum that is determined by educational policy makers and designed by university scholar-specialists. The process of curriculum development and supervisory implementation takes on an orderly, hierarchical, authoritative structure.

New Urgencies

With the Supreme Court ruling outlawing segregated education in 1955 and the growing Civil Rights movement, much more was being expected of America's educational institutions (McClure, 1971). Although the Cold War priorities for curriculum improvement in the sciences, mathematics, and modern foreign languages continued to hold firm, there was also a growing concern for "disadvantaged" children and adolescents. Concern for these students and attention to individual differences forced a variety of curriculum reform efforts which would create new roles for supervisors. Other federal legislation was passed which supported such programs as Head Start and Upward Bound. These programs were designed to "compensate" for the social and economic inequalities in society. Billions of dollars were distributed to schools through federal legislation such as the Elementary and Secondary Education Act of 1965.

Private foundations and corporations also demonstrated increased support of public education. Schools and businesses entered into contracts in which innovative technology was introduced into the schools in the form of programmed learning and performance contracting (Nissman, 1976). These efforts led to many technological innovations in the schools: learning packages, audio-visual equipment, video recorders, and a staff-training model known as micro-teaching (Nissman, 1976). With increased spending on education, evaluation took on new importance, and schools were subjected to increased pressures and measures for accountability. Standardized testing provided the needed accountability data for leaders from government and industry, since they equated the success of the new curricular innovations and teaching with increased scores on standardized forms of measurement.

These events forced a change in the attitudes, intellectual dispositions, and professional participation of classroom teachers and supervisors.

Supervision as a Technological Process

As the theory and models of school supervision became more technical, a more mechanistic or behavioristic approach toward the improvement of teaching and learning emerged (Lovell, 1967). The underlying assumption was that the improvement of instruction was contingent upon some change in the teacher's classroom behavior (Harris, 1963, 1965). The supervisor was supposed to possess all the skills and knowledge associated with effective instruction, and had to have all the skills and techniques required to facilitate a change in the teacher's classroom (instructional) behavior (Anderson, 1967). This approach to supervision was typical of technological models and fit with the new accountability mandates. It was believed that student learning could actually be treated as a product resulting from some change in the teacher's performance or classroom behavior. Harris (1963) provided a supportive narrative for this idea. He wrote:

To view supervision in the context of the total school operation we must begin by focusing upon the central goal of the operation—learning—and the teaching activities involved. . . . Teaching implies behaviors related to instruction. Learning implies the learner. Another way of thinking about this is to regard pupils as the raw material and instruction as the central processes that are applied to produce the end product (p. 7).

The literature after 1960 often spoke of the "instructional behavior of teachers" (Curtin, 1964) and the "supervisory behavior" (Harris, 1963) of school supervisors. Supervisors were now referred to as "change agents," "facilitators," "engineers," or "strategic coordinators" (Harris, 1963; Lucio & McNeil, 1969; Swearingen, 1960). In books about supervision, school supervisors were perceived to be properly assigned to certain narrow, technical functions within the schools. Supervisors were no longer called upon to help create democratic environments in which teachers and supervisors worked on common curricular problems that would lead to the improvement of teaching and learning. They were enlisted to "design systems, engineer strategies, or create climates" (Heald, Romano, & Giorgiady, 1970, p. 197) for new teaching tactics or behaviors that would contribute to better student achievement as measured by standardized tests (Lawler, 1961).

Quantifiable measurements of teacher evaluation took on a greater importance and the improvement of instruction substituted for the improvement of teacher effectiveness. The preoccupation with teacher evaluation centered on attempts to establish three goals—characteristics of good teaching, good teaching as measured behavioristically, and conditions of good teaching (Harrison, 1968; Neagley & Evans, 1980). The search for acceptable "teacher competencies" was actively discussed in the literature (Joyce, 1975).

Back to the Classroom This focus on the "teaching act" forced supervisors to move back into the classrooms where these skills or techniques could be observed and assayed quantitatively. Supervisors and teachers became isolated from the wider purposes of schooling, and supervision was aimed at correcting alleged teaching deficiencies (Gwynn, 1961; Harris, 1963). Haan (1964) attacked democratic models, claiming that they distracted school leaders from the immediate task of assaying classroom instruction.

The conception of supervision by remote control—through working with teachers on curriculum committees and in workshops—although productive of other benefits, has not focused enough on the immensely complex and vital classroom situation. The withdrawal of school leadership from classroom study and participation followed the discrediting of a directive, inspectatorial type of supervision and curriculum consultation (p. 285).

Classroom observation was advanced as the primary means for improving teaching effectiveness in the classroom, so that the supervisor would be able to "focus on specific teacher behaviors" (Harris, 1963, p. 162) and "not be bothered by other elements involved in the classroom situation" (Harris, 1963, p. 162).

Curriculum and Instruction Once again, curriculum was severed from instruction. Terms such as "strategic planning for curriculum change" (Neagley & Evans, 1980, p. 284) came to be equated with the system that the supervisor was required to set up in order to help teachers shift to the new federally endorsed programs. This process involved a change in teaching behavior and, in many cases, a change in attitude as well. For these reasons, concern for human relations and positive school climates found their way back into the literature (Gwynn, 1961). "Good relations," however, meant the degree to which the teachers supported the new curriculum proposals. In some cases, teachers had to be reoriented toward the academic disciplines; in other situations, teachers had to develop competencies and behaviors that would allegedly lead to improved technical skills and more teaching effectiveness.

Concerns for effective leadership skills and the challenges of providing for individual differences contributed to these new conceptions of supervision. One of the most significant changes within these new "supervisory systems," however, was the lack of involvement of educators in the curriculum development process, especially at the local level. Whereas the progressives viewed curriculum as educative experience and supported the direct involvement of the teacher in the curriculum reform process, university scholar-specialists conceived of curriculum as discrete academic disciplines. The teacher's only role was that of a technician expected to "deliver" the curriculum. In *Supervision: Perspectives and Propositions* (1967), Lovell clearly articulated this view:

The function of instructional supervisory behavior in providing specialized assistance is . . . to provide a source of expert information, knowledge, theoretical formulations, and skills from organized disciplines to enrich the content in the instructional program, and to determine implications for teaching methodology (p. 23).

Out of this technological model came new supervisory instruments and devices that supervisors could use to observe teacher and student behavior. Joyce (1975) examined the work of researchers who developed an array of systems for analyzing the "transactions of teaching in specific behavioral terms" (p. 136). According to Joyce, these researchers intended to identify specific components of teacher behavior that were directly related to pupil growth (p. 137). One of the most popular was the Flander's system of interaction analysis that was supposed to supply the supervisor and teacher with objective and reliable information about teaching, specifically the verbal interactions that take place in the classroom (Beach & Reinhartz, 1989). These measures, however, did not observe the complex nature of classroom dynamics and the variety of interpretations, responses, values, and meanings that affect teacher-pupil relationships and student learning.

The Divorce In 1960, the Association for Supervision and Curriculum Development Yearbook, *Leadership for Improving Instruction*, stated: "In the mid-twentieth century, conditions surrounding those who carry responsibility for instructional leadership in American education are characterized by some degree of confusion and conflict" (p. 23). The writers for the yearbook recognized that education, especially school supervision, was caught in the "tensions and pressures of contemporary society" (p. 6). Pressures brought on by the Cold War, the space race, and the civil rights movement during the years after mid-century forced them to look at school leadership. The yearbook authors made an appeal to school leaders to respond with "conviction and action to present day challenges" (p. 23) and to reexamine our democratic values and purposes in this process. In the closing argument of the yearbook, they stated:

The goal and responsibility of democratic educational leadership is the improvement of instruction in America's schools. The heart of the instructional improvement program is the fostering of teacher effectiveness in the classroom. Democratic practices help teachers to see themselves positively, enable them to accept themselves and others, and to give them a high degree of identification with their associates. Sharing freedom and responsibility enables teachers to provide students with opportunities to think of themselves as responsible citizens and contributing members of society (p. 186).

Nevertheless, shortly after 1960, the literature supported a process and model of supervision that placed the supervisor as the expert technical assistant to the teaching staff, whose primary role was to help implement a curriculum that came from university scholar-specialists. The improvement of curriculum and instruction was replaced with the improvement of teaching effectiveness. From a responsibility that was originally limited to inspection, but had evolved into a professional role that enabled teachers to grow in ability to study and solve educational problems, supervision was again delimited by the political and national events at midcentury. In this process, supervision became divorced from the curriculum (Aiken, 1992).

PROGRESS, RETREAT, AND REFORM OF SECONDARY SCHOOL SUPERVISION

The period since the mid-1960s in American education has been characterized by increased federal involvement, a continued struggle for civil rights, accelerated criticism of public schools, demands for accountability through standardized testing, and a call for "excellence" and "restructured" schools. It has also been distinguished by a sense of enormity based on the resurgence in enrollments, the waves of new immigrants, the influence of technology, and the move toward consolidated or regionalized school districts.

In addition to these forces, the development of education over the second half of the twentieth century was shaped by enduring philosophical debates, forcing a continued examination of the purposes that the public schools were to serve. The basic arguments tend to fall between traditionalism, which advocates a curriculum limited to the traditional academic subjects and supports "back to basics," ability grouping, disciplinarity, and managerial efficiency in school supervision and administration, and progressivism, which envisions a curriculum that will meet the needs of a diverse student population and the extension of educational opportunity to all individuals within the framework of a democratic comprehensive secondary school. The progressives advocate interdisciplinary programs of general education along with several broad goals for our schools—academic, social/civic, vocational, and personal (Clark, 1988). School leadership is viewed by the progressives as a democratic social process that includes the involvement of teachers in all matters of curriculum and instruction. Although this argument has persisted since the 1800s, the progressive and traditionalist spirits are ingrained in the culture of American education and help to explain the conflicting paths that educational reform often takes.

Throughout the course of the twentieth century, American education has faced myriad problems brought about by shifting social trends, nationalistic needs, worldwide political and economic changes, increased numbers and diversity of students served, conflicting expectations for solutions to problems, and the requisite lack of agreement on how to settle and resolve new and recurring issues. These problems clearly will not be left behind as the new millennium begins. Whereas concern for discipline-centered knowledge production dominated throughout most of the Cold War and space race, expanded opportunity for minorities and the disadvantaged dominated the 1970s. The "structure-of-the-disciplines" doctrine (Bruner, 1960) came to be challenged by the calls for social "relevance" in the student protests of the late 1960s. By the 1980s, government and business leaders once again took the lead in the educational reform efforts by forming national panels, commissions, and committees to make recommendations concerning the alleged plight of American education (Carnegie Foundation for the Advancement of Teaching, Boyer, 1983; National Commission on Excellence in Education, 1983; National Science Board of the National Science Foundation, 1983; Task Force on Education for Economic Growth, 1983). Whereas in the era of the Cold War the schools were blamed for our alleged lag in military and space technology, during the 1980s critics condemned the schools for the nation's decline in the global industrial marketplace and the corresponding rise of Japan and Germany in this sphere (National Commission on Excellence, 1983).

A decade later, a "revolutionary transformation of the schools" was promised with the endorsement of *America 2000* by Congress—a "manifesto" for national goals (Goals 2000) to be attained by all schools by the year 2000 (U.S. Department of Education, 1991). Although concern for issues of literacy, violence, substance abuse, poverty, and preschool readiness are conditions that significantly affect the success of young people in school, major priority of *Goals 2000* was given to meeting high achievement standards in certain subjects, especially in science and mathematics. The new federal programs dictated that public education be held accountable for ensuring that students meet "world class standards" in core academic subjects, namely science, mathematics, history, and language arts (Boyer, 1983; Goodlad, 1966, 1984; Smith, Fuhrman, & O'Day, 1994;

Tanner & Tanner, 1995; U.S. Department of Education, 1991; D. Tanner, 1997).

Further Implications of Nationalizing Initiatives

Two major inferences can be drawn from the events since mid-twentieth century. First, most major initiatives on the secondary school curriculum originated at the national level and involved government influence—namely, from business leaders and various individuals or agencies outside of the schools (Adler, 1982; American Association for the Advancement of Science, 1989; Bennett, 1987; Boyer, 1983; Bruner, 1960; Coleman, 1974; Conant, 1959; Goodlad, 1984; Kohl, 1969; National Commission on Excellence in Education, 1983; National Commission on the Reform of Secondary Education, 1973; National Education Goals Panel, 1992; National Panel on High School and Adolescent Education, 1976; Rand Educational Policy Study, 1974; Silberman, 1970; Sizer, 1984; Task Force on Education for Economic Growth, 1983; Task Force on Teaching as a Profession, 1986; U.S. Department of Education, 1991). Educational leaders, teachers, supervisors, and community members assumed less and less responsibility for curriculum development and instructional improvement. Second, schools have become increasingly susceptible to all forms of social, political, and economic pressures (Fuhrman, 1994; Fuhrman & Elmore, 1994; Tanner, 1986). Given these developments, school blaming has become a surefire attraction for audiences in the mass media. The ensuing pressures have exerted considerable influence on schools and upon local autonomy in educational planning and curriculum development. The question "Who is the maker of the American curriculum?" has been debated increasingly in the literature (Clark, 1988; Fuhrman & Elmore, 1994; L. Tanner, 1988, Tanner & Tanner, 1995).

Clark (1988) assigns responsibility for curriculum decisions to ten different sources. Included in his list are the public, political leaders, textbook publishers, test publishers, the media, higher education, professional organizations, central administration, teacher groups, and individual teachers. In this process, the role and function of the secondary school supervisor has been subjected to increased confusion, crisis, and conflict (Anderson, 1982; Blumberg, 1980; Bolin, 1987; Gwynn, 1968; Lucio & McNeil, 1969; Mosher & Purpel, 1972; Smythe, 1989; Spears, 1953). Supervisors have too often been put in a position of having to change and respond to whatever crisis is perceived by the current political leadership or mass media at the time, which continues to challenge their critical role as leaders in the curriculum renewal process.

Restructured Schools In the later 1980s, another wave of reform efforts evolved, commonly referred to as the "restructuring movement" (Tanner & Tanner, 1995, p. 602; Jenkins & D. Tanner, 1992). Whereas in the previous movement the focus was on achieving excellence through increased course requirements, longer school years, more rigorous academics, better prepared teachers, new certification requirements, external testing, and centralized control from state capitals, the second wave was organized around the concept of restructured schools and shifted to issues surrounding teacher

education, curriculum and instruction, and "bottom-up participation from teachers and principals" (Lieberman, 1992). A report by the National Governors Association, which tracked restructuring efforts since 1987, presented a framework for school improvement identifying four major areas of restructuring—curriculum and instruction, authority and decision-making, staff roles, and accountability (O'Neil, 1992, p. 4). Fuhrman and Elmore (1990) and Joyce (1991) noted that the second wave of restructuring encompassed several major orientations—technical aspects that address curriculum and instruction, political and social changes that affect decision-making and roles and relationships of school staff, and occupational structures that address school governance and collegial workplaces. David (1991) identified several key features that distinguish restructuring from previous methods: it focuses on the idea that allegedly "all students can and must learn at higher levels; and it is a long-term commitment to fundamental, systemic change" (p. 11). Presumably, instead of trying to "change one piece at a time in a system of many interlocking pieces, restructuring . . . tackles all the pieces" (p. 11). Most significant about the "restructuring movement," however, was a return to the important dialogue about curriculum decisions and a renewed quest to concentrate on the problem of what students need to learn in order to be successful, to solve complex problems, and to exercise personal and social responsibility in their adult lives (Boyer, 1991).

Teacher Role

Throughout every reform period, the concern for more and better teachers has been reiterated. Since mid-twentieth century, it has become more common for professional groups to reexamine the qualifications, professional preparation, and professional improvement plans for teachers. Recurrently, it is seen that the key to educational change is the teaching force, with the idea that the quality of the educational program typically rests with the quality of its teachers (Langworthy, 1989). The roles and functions of secondary school supervisors and their rightful place in the processes of instructional improvement, curriculum development, and teacher improvement have been subjected to conflicting demands and shifts in priority.

Competency-Based Teacher Education Perhaps the most influential approach aimed at improving teacher education taking hold in the 1970s were the performance- or competency-based teacher development programs supported by some national reform groups (Cruickshank, 1985). This process-product approach sought to organize teacher preparation around specific teaching competencies that were stated in terms of observable teacher behavior. This approach worked hand in hand with the new curriculum designs and technological applications in the schools. Growing out of the research in behavioristic psychology, competency-based or performance-based teacher education equated teaching effectiveness with specific teaching behaviors that would allegedly promote student achievement (Gage, 1976; Gage & Winne, 1975). Because the curriculum was determined at a higher level, the implementation of curriculum in the classroom and the competencies that teachers would need to operationalize the curriculum became a major focus on teacher development. Specific teaching skills were determined and teacher "trainees" were trained in the specific skills or competencies to be learned.

Competency-based teacher education was based on microteaching. This method was promoted as a brief teaching encounter that provided initial training, followed by practice and corrective feedback, usually involving peers (Cruickshank, 1985). Additional cycles of instruction, practice, and feedback were available as needed. In addition to microteaching, minicourses and brief internships were organized (Allen & Ryan, 1969). In the words of Gage and Winne (1975):

Teaching strategies were analyzed into relatively discrete teaching skills. The trainee then practiced these skills individually with a small number of students for a brief period. Following the micro-teaching, the trainee received corrective feedback and usually did additional microteaching (p. 149).

Competency-based programs found support at both the state and local levels due to the new demands for accountability placed upon the schools by the federally sponsored programs. Microteaching and minicourses also represented quick and efficient means to train teachers in the use of the many new innovative technologies that were rapidly being introduced into the schools (Koran, 1969). The new teacher education strategies were easily injected into in-service education programs, to be utilized as the means to make practicing teachers more competent and accountable for implementation of the new curriculum packages and tools of technology. The role of the secondary school supervisor was critical to this process.

Humanistic Teacher Education As stated earlier, the 1960s and 1970s in America were periods of social and political ferment; and ways for meeting the needs of diverse student populations were addressed. Attempts to revise curriculum in order to make it more "relevant;" to recognize the contributions of all ethnic groups; and to eliminate bias, racism, and sexism from curriculum were important reform efforts. New federal mandates that supported educational opportunity addressed the need for teachers to become familiar with diverse learning styles and to develop appropriate teaching strategies for "at-risk" or disadvantaged learners. A concern for human relations, fostering positive self-concepts in minority children, and using community resources in teaching held new implications for teacher education and school supervision.

Differentiated Staffing The literature of the 1970s suggested another approach to teacher education reform that would allegedly produce more competent teachers (Allen, 1971; Allen & Ryan, 1969; Boutwell, 1972; Dempsey & Smith, 1972; Keefe, 1971; Long, 1977; Trump & Vars, 1976). Differentiated staffing was soon promoted as a process of reorganizing teaching staffs according to new roles—professional teacher, teacher assistant, and staff specialist. The idea began with J. Lloyd Trump in 1959 when he served as the chairperson for the Commission on Staff Utilization appointed by the National

Association of Secondary School Principals. The committee produced a report entitled *Focus on Change: Guide to Better Schools* (Trump, 1961). According to the plan, differentiation could be applied to all levels of workers according to function and role. Through the use of paraprofessionals and team teaching, students could be taught in small groups, large groups, or individually by incorporating learning carrels, audiovisual aids, teaching machines, and built-in listening or recording apparatuses (Trump, 1977). Teachers were supposed to have more opportunities for professional development and more time to work with other colleagues as master teachers, because responsibilities formerly assigned to teachers were allegedly subsumed by paraprofessionals and technology (Boutwell, 1972; Freiberg, 1984).

The Trump plan, and those that followed, had its critics who argued that these instructional approaches formed a hierarchical arrangement, with an emphasis on specialization of labor and a concern for the efficient utilization of staff (Edelfelt, 1972; Flanders, 1970; Skinner, 1968; Tanner, 1972). The goal of providing increased opportunities for teachers with different competencies and specialties to work together for curriculum and instructional improvement was replaced with the goals of managerial efficiency, as master teachers took over supervisory responsibility for those teachers who performed at a lower level, paraprofessionals assumed teaching responsibilities, and new technological teaching aids were added to the classroom (Edelfelt, 1972). There were other reasons for the lack of success of differentiated programs. Teacher resistance, low morale, scheduling rigidities, and reduced school funding were some of the problems identified (Lange, 1967; Nissman, 1976). The most serious mistake, however, was to confuse professional growth with remediation. This alienated teachers who viewed their input as essential in determining needs for in-service education and staff development. For these reasons, as well as shifts in education priorities, the Trump plan was never fully realized.

Conflicting and Contradictory Reform: Implications for Secondary School Supervisors

History documents that successive periods of political and social change are invariably accompanied by renewed demands upon the schools (Goodlad, 1966; Kliebard, 1988; D. Tanner, 1986; Tanner & Tanner, 1987, 1990, 1995). Within the context of the contemporary era, our schools have been subjected to reforms, counterreforms, and counter-counter-reforms aimed at improving schools, teaching, learning, and society. Instead of engaging a professional core of educators in a problem-solving approach to seek solutions to persistent and recurring problems, too often the initiatives have been "directed at undoing the excesses of the reform measures taken by schools . . . in the predecessor period" (Tanner & Tanner, 1987, p. 317).

Recommendations for change and assorted measures for curriculum improvement over the past 30 years, especially at the secondary level of schooling, tend to be imposed from outside the educational setting, emanating from federal and state agencies, radical critics, the media, colleges and universities, business organizations, professional associations, parents, and various private interests. In the words of Tanner and Tanner (1995):

In each instant of shifting demands and expectations the schools have been impelled to respond in a segmental way—whether in embarking on a return to the fundamentals, adopting disciplinary curriculum packages, employing specialized educational innovations, instituting ad hoc compensatory programs for the disadvantaged, or implementing accountability machinery through the use of narrow testing measures (p. 573).

With each succeeding reform movement, curriculum has come to be viewed more and more in the purview of policy-makers and higher levels of administration. Educators who are expected by society to help determine the curriculum are often left out of the process.

As school supervisors, especially those at the secondary level, have endeavored to meet the demands of instructional improvement and curriculum development, their roles and functions have been challenged and confounded by the conflicting and contradictory reports and initiatives for educational reform throughout the past 50 years. They have found themselves situated among contending demands and crosscurrents of purpose. Nationalistic priorities, evinced by the endless barrage of reports of various commissions, committees, and panels organized around the agenda of school reform, have brought about corresponding shifts in the role and function of school supervisors.

The Plight of the Supervisor

After 1960, the direction and function of the secondary school supervisor was seriously called into question as forces both inside and outside of education pushed their agendas upon the schools (Leeper, 1965, 1969; Lucio, 1969). Writers from the field were trying to make sense of the conflicting and confusing prescriptions for educational change and the role of supervision in leading the educational reform process (Eye & Netzer, 1965; Feyereisen, Fiorino, & Nowak, 1970; Franseth, 1961; Leeper, 1969; Lewis & Miel, 1972; Nowak, 1970; Sergiovanni & Starratt, 1971). Lewis and Miel (1972) fortified this tension:

The increasing distance between the standards of living of the affluent and the poor and the growing gap between level of aspiration and level of realization, both in material and human terms, has led to a growing uneasiness about the American society and distrust of one of its key institutions, the school. . . . A crucial area of improvement is the process of instruction—we must consider what is the most productive way to teach. Those with supervisory responsibility and their colleagues with whom they work closely on matters of instruction are in key positions to bring about such improvement (p. v).

Moreover, the reluctance of supervision to contribute to the process of educational improvement at a time when authority structures were being challenged in all aspects of society contributed to these tensions (Markowitz, 1976). Alfonso, Firth, and Neville (1984) addressed this issue:

In all too many cases, supervisors have spoken with little authority. Unsure of their own esteem and organizational status, they have too

often spoken timidly and behaved conservatively. They have been reactors, consultants, and instructional counselors, rather than intervention agents seeking to influence teachers directly (p. 342).

In 1960, the Association for Supervision and Curriculum Development issued *The Supervisor: New Demands and New Dimensions* (Lucio, ed.), based on the work of a special commission to look into the problems of supervisors and to take the "leadership in establishing the theory and identifying the context of supervision upon which changing roles and functions must be built" (p. ix). The writers recognized that the place of the supervisor was threatened by changing events and the "politics of curriculum change" (p. 13). The commission clearly came out in support of the supervisor's professional responsibility for determining curriculum change, and it valued the participation of the teacher in this process.

A second attempt to redefine the role and function of the school supervisor came from a collection of addresses from the Twenty-Fourth Annual Conference of the Association for Supervision and Curriculum Development. These addresses were reproduced in *Changing Supervision for Changing Times* (Leeper, 1969). As Lucio's committee was writing in response to the many changes thrust upon the schools, the Leeper collection of papers proposed to look at the "plight of the supervisor" (p. 43) within the context of accelerating change. The authors strongly urged supervisors to "take the initiative in professionalization of their own specialty" (p. 60). Crosby (1969) provided some contradictory rhetoric in casting the supervisor as a catalyst and leader who must bend with the wind in order to survive:

The supervisor is the keeper of the dream, the American dream of human dignity and brotherhood. The supervisor is catalyst of the American scene, perceiving change, weighing its implications for education, providing leadership in planning to meet it. The supervisor is realist, accepting the fact that . . . the ability to bend with the wind means survival (p. 63).

Given the mandates for change that came down from the federal and state government, the innovations propelled by the business-industrial complex, and the conflicting prescriptions for improvement of public education that appeared in the numerous commissioned reports and the media, secondary school supervisors were often called upon to serve "more as technicians ministering to the equilibrium of the organization" (Lucio, 1969, p. 212) or as "referees" (Wiles & Lovell, 1975, p. 134) than as educational leaders. Unfortunately, neither of these ASCD efforts generated a viable theory about the role of school supervision. What did evolve was the consultative approach to school supervision, which provided a temporary and only partial answer to the problem.

EMERGING PATHS FOR SECONDARY SCHOOL SUPERVISION

Clinical Supervision

Since midcentury, secondary school supervision can be described as having followed different paths. One of the strongest directions was a consultative approach to supervision, which appeared in the form of clinical supervision. Although consultative supervision found expression in other models, the clinical model and its various interpretations best represented this approach to school supervision (Cogin, 1973; Goldhammer, 1969).

First appearing in *Clinical Supervision*, by Robert Goldhammer (1969), the ideas that formed the clinical model grew out of the Harvard-Newton Summer Program where, in 1962, Morris Cogan and others were engaged in the task of developing new "training mechanisms for principals, supervisors, and teachers in leadership positions" (Goldhammer, 1969, p. iv). Goldhammer regarded clinical supervision as a process in which the supervisor's foci for analysis are the observational data on classroom teacher behavior, and such data are used as a basis for working with teachers on instructional improvement in a consultative relationship. This approach represented a change from earlier models of supervision, which were criticized as being conducted from a distance, and for engaging in curriculum development (Goldhammer, 1969). Clinical supervision is conducted in the normal setting of the classroom environment and school, and involves the gathering of data from direct observation of actual teaching-learning events and conditions, with the goal of improving classroom instruction. Teacher improvement was equated with changes in the teacher's method at the exact point where the teacher interacts with students.

The clinical model worked well with the reform initiatives of the 1960s and 1970s because the responsibility of the teacher was primarily the "delivery" of instruction in connection with a curriculum that was decided at a higher jurisdictional level. The supervisor was the technical expert who assisted teachers with the implementation of the discipline-centered high school curriculum and who made sure that teachers complied with the new curricular mandates. As a result, supervisors had to move into the classroom in order to focus more directly on instructional methodologies and specific acts of teaching (Amidon, Kies, & Palisi, 1970; Anderson, 1967; Bridges, 1970; Goldhammer, 1969; Harris, 1965; Lucio, 1962; Malone, 1970; Morley, 1970; White, 1970).

Secondary Supervision as Consultation

In 1964, Haan claimed that, in reaction to the inspectoral models of supervision, supervisors had moved their focus away from the individual classrooms and were attempting to work more with groups of teachers on problems of curriculum. Haan was writing, no doubt, in reference to the more democratic models of supervision that had evolved in earlier decades. In this process, he alleged that not enough focus had been on the "vital and complex" (p. 285) classroom situation. Since the curriculum reform efforts of the 1950s and 1960s had removed both the teacher and supervisor from their important roles as curriculum developers, Haan saw this as the time to refocus supervisory efforts on the classroom. Accepting curriculum and instruction as separate realms, he defined the function of supervision as the improvement of instruction and the need to assist teachers with the implementation of new innovations and the new national curriculum

packages developed by university scholar-specialists in response to the Cold War. Curriculum development was to be left to educational policymakers and others outside the schools. Haan was not alone in his thinking, because other writers from this era encouraged secondary supervisors to support and assist with the implementation of the national curriculum programs and other educational reforms in the classroom (Allen, 1971; Ayers, 1970; Berliner & Gage, 1976; Corey, 1967; Gleason, 1966; Hass, 1960, 1961; Klausmeir & Lambert, 1961; Lange, 1967; Lumsdaine, 1961; Meyer, 1966; Miller & Goldberg, 1963; Miller & Hudspreth, 1966; Schiller, 1971; Spaulding, 1958; Toepfer, 1973; Unruh, 1974, 1977; Witt, 1963).

Supervisor as Change Agent

Consultative models of school supervision helped advance the agenda for reform and reestablished a purpose and function for secondary school supervisor's. Much support appeared in the literature. In *Educational Leadership* (Miller and Hudspreth, 1961, p. 659) reinforced the supervisor's "catalytic position" in bringing about change in the school. Hence, it was the supervisor's responsibility to "bring to the teacher the pertinent ideas, in an atmosphere of inspiration, and help guide the change process that occurs" (p. 659). Wear (1966), also writing for *Educational Leadership*, referred to the supervisor as a "coordinator of multiple-consultation" (p. 653) and reassigned the supervisor to the role of "coordinator" or as one who would mediate among "college people, state departments of education, members of professional organizations, representatives of state and federal governments, textbook consultants" (p. 653) and others who had their agenda for curriculum reform. Van Til (1968) advocated the use of consultation as a means for implementing change in the school and advocated that supervisors serve more as "facilitators" (p. 45) of change than instructional leaders.

Consultative approaches of the late 1960s were equally concerned with the plight of disadvantaged or "at-risk" students, as well as the exploding "youth problem" (Broadhead, 1967; Brown, 1975; Coleman, 1966; Conlin & Haberman, 1967; Downing, 1964; Ether, 1969; Freedman, 1966; Galloway, 1967; Graham, 1975; Hittinger, 1969; Rollins, 1968; Schreiber, 1966; Skobjak & Pautler, 1979; Smith, 1966; Wattenberg, 1966). It was held that supervision and special training were especially important in addressing the problem of allegedly reluctant, fearful, and resentful teachers, so that they could better work with at-risk students. The focus, however, was mostly concerned with specific actions or personality traits of teachers, rather than on providing attention to important curricular and instructional problems that arose in response to the needs of diverse learners.

Clinical Supervision Triumphant

Even though consultative approaches to supervision evolved in response to the many changes affecting secondary school curricula and school supervisors after mid-twentieth century, it was the clinical conception of supervision that came to be recognized as the most popular model. With the publication of the works of Goldhammer (1969) and Cogan

(1973), it was assumed that, by changing teaching behavior, instruction would change, and a new basis for all supervisory work in the schools would evolve. Supervision was to be basically analytical, requiring a constant reexamination of teaching behavior within the classroom (Goldhammer, 1969, p. 368). The device or major method of clinical supervision rested almost entirely on the classroom observation, followed by consultative conferences between the teacher and supervisor. Cogan (1973) made the following statement:

Supervision may therefore be defined as the rationale and practice designed to improve the teacher's classroom performance. It takes its principal data from the events of the classroom. The analysis of this data and the relationship between teacher and supervisor form the basis of the program, procedures, and strategies designed to improve the student's learning by improving the teacher's classroom behavior (p. 9).

Collegiality and mutual respect were important aspects of clinical models, continued Cogan:

In colleagueship the teacher and clinical supervisor work together as associates and equals, and they are bound together by a common purpose. This purpose is the improvement of the teacher's instruction. . . .(p. 68).

It was from Cogan's writings that the more formalized programs for improving teaching behavior found their way into the schools. Behavioral systems of interaction analysis (Flanders, 1970), microteaching, observational systems, and technological simulations became important devices for supervisors to use in the analysis of classroom behavior. Moreover, it was held that clinical supervision would help elevate the diminished role of the school supervisor because he or she was now in a critical position of helping the teacher improve—this would come about through the assistance and "analysis" (Cogan, 1973, p. 66) provided by the supervisor.

Observation as Supervision Clinical supervision viewed supervisors as having all the skills and knowledge about effective teaching to facilitate a change in the teacher's behavior (Anderson, 1967; Bridges, 1970). Underlying the theory of clinical supervision is the belief that "technical improvement" (Goldhammer, 1969, p. 56) translates into improved teaching. Clinical supervisors were to assist teachers in understanding how specific teaching acts affect student learning (Amidon, Kies, & Palisi, 1970). Definite supervisory activities were advanced in support of this thesis (Harris, 1965; Malone, 1970; White, 1970). The literature that popularized clinical or consultative approaches to secondary school supervision emphasized the importance of certain activities, to be followed by supervisors largely centered on the classroom observation. Harris (1965) wrote: "Systematic classroom observation is essential to diagnosis of teaching. This is the only way to find out about the problems that exist at the classroom level" (p. 495). Malone (1970) also stressed the importance of classroom observational techniques as the means to collect "unbiased, non-judgmental data" (p. 130) that could be used to analyze and interpret classroom behavior in an effort to improve instruction. Theorists who supported clinical super-

vision believed that, that a process provided a medium for colleagueship. In mutually examining teaching behavior, through consultation with the teacher, its affect on student learning would be better understood.

The Separation of Curriculum and Instruction The focus given to the analysis of instruction in clinical supervision presupposes that matters pertaining to curriculum design, development, and evaluation are preordained at higher levels. The classroom teacher's main locus of responsibility is on instructional style and the specific student outcomes in connection with planning and conducting an individual lesson (Tanner & Tanner, 1987). Clinical supervision supported a separation of curriculum and instruction, and leading texts from the field provided little reference to the work of teachers and supervisors in the curriculum development process. Responsibility for the writing and revising of curriculum was outside the realm of the teacher and "outside of the classroom" (Cogan, 1973, p. 9). Goldhammer (1969) supported this separation under the seemingly arrogant allegation that:

Even when the teachers get hold of relatively good curriculums, they often ruin them. From what I observe in the schools, it would seem that "professional growth" resulting from in-service curriculum workshops is often represented by the substitution of new stupidities for old ones. Having done with curriculum, let's stay, for a time, with problems of teaching, remembering that our goal is to illustrate a context of scholastic bedlam in which a professional discipline of clinical supervision can be developed (p. 11).

From Classroom Change to Institutional Change

Although clinical supervision appeared to be the dominant form of supervision advocated in the literature between 1960 and 1970, other researchers were forming different ideas about the role and function of school supervision. A different model of consultation evolved, which attempted to move supervisors out of the safety of the classroom and to look at educational problems in the context of the entire situation. Writers believed that the real concerns of teachers had been discounted in the process of clinical supervision. Compounded with the conflicting and confusing prescriptions for improving the secondary school curriculum, supervision was seen as increasingly significant in helping lead the educational reform process (Feyereisen, Fiorino, & Nowak, 1970; Lewis & Miel, 1972; Sergiovanni & Starratt, 1972).

Janowitz (1969), a sociologist unsightfully criticized the school as built upon a segmental or specialized model of organization and function through "*ad hoc* adaption by introducing on a piecemeal basis, new techniques, new programs, new specialists, and even new administrative procedures" (p. 42). As the teaching process is broken up into increasingly specialized roles and techniques, continued Janowitz, the teacher's role in curriculum development is subordinated to specialists (pp. 24-25). Janowitz proceeded to call for an aggregate or holistic model of institution building for schooling, enhancing the teacher's role in curriculum development and school governance. He recommended that the pupil testing system be converted into a system for evaluating organizational effectiveness (p. 33).

Secondary School Supervision for Human Resources

Humanistic supervision, a term which often appeared in the literature, marked a turning point away from the clinical preoccupation with classroom teaching behavior (Abrell, 1974). The emerging fashion in the use of the term *human resources* in the social sciences found many proponents of humanistic supervision advocating supervision for human resources (Abrell, 1974; Association for Supervision and Curriculum Development, 1970; Blumberg, 1981; Combs, 1962, 1970; Lewis & Miel, 1972; Randolph, 1978; Sergiovanni, 1982; Sergiovanni & Starratt, 1971, 1979; Wiles & Lovell, 1975). Human resources supervision also provided a consultative approach but assumed that by encouraging human growth and development, the entire organization can improve. Human resources supervisors sought to understand and release the feelings, values, and potential creativities of the teachers within the context of the entire school organization. Improved teaching performance became synonymous with better self-concepts and enhanced teacher roles. Organizational theory and human development theory were integral to the development of this model (Bartky, 1953; Berman, 1966; Broudy, 1971; Chase, 1970; Combs, 1970; Eash, 1966, 1968; Graham & Scobey, 1970; Mackenzie, 1961; McKean & Mills, 1964; Ogletree, 1962, 1965, 1972).

Instead of focusing solely on specific teaching behavior as it evolves in the classroom, supervision for human resources included concern for motivation theory, leadership style, organizational climates, and the "self-actualization of individuals" (Sergiovanni & Starratt, 1971, p. 205). Supervision for human resources did not focus so much on the teaching act as on the teacher as a person. Whereas clinical models of supervision tended to focus on instructional behavior apart from matters of curriculum improvement, supervision for human resources related teacher improvement to the understanding of curriculum development, taking into account the individual needs, motives, and attitudes of the learners (Mosher & Purpel, 1972). Teachers and supervisors would explore themselves and others, their ideas, purposes, and personal decision-making as they related to problems of the classroom (Cruickshank, 1985). Human growth was the primary goal of the instructional program, and supervision provided the leadership in aligning the curriculum with this goal. Given the concerns for meeting the needs of disadvantaged and minority youth, the improvement of affective domains of classroom instruction gathered support, as issues of multiculturalism, race, gender equity, and "at-risk" youth took on greater importance (Conlin & Haberman, 1967; Cruickshank, 1975; Davis, 1975; Downing, 1964; Galloway, 1967; Havighurst & Gottlieb, 1975; Kelly, 1974; Macdonald, 1974; West & Millsom, 1975).

To change institutions, the people who worked in these institutions had to change. "A major effort of any supervisory act," wrote Sergiovanni and Starratt (1971), "is the changing of some aspect of a person's concept of self, way of behaving, attitude set, or relationship to the school and within the school as an organization" (p. 12). Humanistic supervision was to focus on concerns of people, their individual growth, and how they could contribute to the overall goals of the

organization. Issues of leadership, authority, organizational and human dynamics, and human motivation were critical in the process. Whereas clinical supervision was intended to change classroom behavior, supervision for human resources had additional goals—beyond teaching performance—to foster human growth and development and to improve the health and well-being of the entire organization (Abrell, 1974; Feyereisen, Fiorino, & Nowak, 1970; Randolph, 1978; Sergiovanni, 1982a; Sergiovanni & Starratt, 1971; Wiles & Lovell, 1975). Sergiovanni (1982) believed that supervision was responsible for helping teachers develop their full range of talents and creative abilities in order to accomplish the goals of the school.

Supervision for Human Growth

A major theme of supervision for human resources was to increase individual teachers' opportunities for "enrichment, challenge, and self-development" (Sergiovanni & Starratt, 1971, p. 127) and to create environments which encouraged human growth and fulfillment (Abrell, 1974; Combs, 1970; Maslow, 1962; McMaster, 1966; Wiles & Lovell, 1975). The link between the development of human potential and the health of the organization was an important aspect of supervision for human resources, and it helped move the process of supervision beyond the perimeters of the classroom (Abrell, 1974; Randolph, 1978; Sergiovanni & Starratt, 1971). Although the goal of changing behavior remained an issue, if any change was going to take place, it was to be based upon theories of human motivation and self-actualization (Maslow, 1970). Sergiovanni (1982) believed that supervisors had the important job of helping teachers develop their full range of talents, insights, experiences, and "creative abilities" (p. 110). Additional support came from Combs (1962), who wrote: "Administrators and supervisors may help to provide the quality of experience and the emotional climate for teachers which will help to free them to become their best selves" (p. 74). The supervisor was viewed as a helper or facilitator for growth, not as a technical assistant in clinical supervision. Wiles and Lovell (1975) stated: "They are, above all, concerned with helping people value each other. . . . The supervisor's role has become supporting, assisting, and sharing, rather than directing" (p. 20). The supervisor would effectively release the human potential and creative abilities of teachers through a series of consultative conferences, where an open, trusting, and collegial relationship would be formed. The supervisor would work with the teacher to identify problems and possible solutions. The fundamental tenet of supervision for human resources was the belief that each individual has the capacity to solve his or her own problems and that the primary role of the supervisor was to assist the teacher in this process (Abrell, 1974).

Curriculum Reconsidered In response to the civil rights movement of the 1960s, demands for curriculum relevance were placed upon the schools. These demands often evolved into a series of uncoordinated curriculum reform efforts that would allegedly better meet the needs of a diverse, multicultural society. Issues of civil rights, population changes, minorities, changing family structures, youth employment, and technology all had an impact on education (Ayres, 1970). Supervision for human resources evolved in part to these pressures. The solution was to support the kind of curriculum that nurtured the growth and development of individuals and supported all students as human resources. In the 1970 Yearbook of the Association for Supervision and Curriculum Development, the need for the school to "nurture humane capabilities" was emphasized. These words appeared in the introduction:

Much has happened during the past three years to confirm our belief that developing humane capabilities is an educational imperative. The nation has been racked with group tensions and domestic disorders. At the same time, not much has happened to convince us that American educators have made progress in nurturing humane capabilities (p. ix).

The response of the yearbook committee differed from those methods that had been advocated earlier. Instead of a proliferation of curriculum innovations and technological devices in the schools, humanistic writers spoke of the need to understand and use the curriculum and new technologies to solve some of these humanistic problems (Chase, 1970; Combs, 1970; Loughary, 1970). Writers discussed the "human curriculum" (Sergiovanni & Starratt, 1971, p. 281) and defined it almost romantically as a curriculum that emphasized the qualities of human beings—"feeling, thinking, valuing, and symbol creating" (Sergiovanni & Starratt, p. 281). Within this changing theory, the curriculum was to be returned to the realm of the school supervisor and teachers were, once again, to be given a role in curriculum planning and design in order to better respond to the needs of learners (Lewis & Miel, 1972; Mosher & Purpel, 1972; Sergiovanni & Starratt, 1971; Wiles & Lovell, 1975). In 1972, Fred T. Wilhelms addressed this concern in his introduction to Mosher and Purpel's book, *Supervision: The Reluctant Profession* (1972):

Most directly at stake is the ability of our teachers to teach effectively. . . . But even more fundamentally at issue is the curriculum itself, the program of the school and its very purposes. If, as a profession, we are unable to diagnose, plan and act at this level, we are done for (p. v).

Supporters of supervision for human resources wanted to restore school supervision to its rightful place in curriculum leadership. Mosher and Purpel (1972) were clear about the role of the supervisor when they stated: "The supervisor, in brief, is the principal curriculum and instructional leader in the school. . . . A sophisticated concept of curriculum is a sine qua non for supervisors. Without it, a supervisor would be like a conductor unable to read music" (p. 65).

Many supporters of humanistic supervision saw the return of secondary school supervision to the position of curriculum leadership as the proper response to the problems in education. They believed that this improvement had a direct relationship to the improvement of teaching, claiming that teacher improvement happens when teachers are required to apply "inquiry skills of scholarship to curriculum, instruction, and formal learning as it actually occurs in the lives of stu-

dents" (Mosher & Purpel, 1972, p. 192). Many of the national curriculum projects, the entrance of big business into the field of curriculum, educational technology, and new instructional patterns had put distance between the teacher and important curriculum decisions (Mosher & Purpel, 1972). For some, it had become a "private cold war" (Blumberg, 1980) between school supervisors and teachers. Supervision for human resources, however, required that supervisors and teachers work together again on important matters of curriculum and instruction. This shift in theory and thinking is captured realistically in the words of Mosher and Purpel (1972):

Specialized knowledge of curriculum theory and development is therefore a prerequisite to a comprehensive analysis of teaching. This requirement is explained by the argument that decisions about what knowledge is of most worth affects decisions about content which, in turn, affect and are mediated by teaching which, in part, determines what is learned. . . . These variables must be dealt with as interdependent elements in a logical whole (p. 84).

The Many Faces of Supervision

By 1982, the tensions and conflicts between supervision as a clinical process and supervision as a humanizing process were apparent. With the publication of the 1982 Yearbook for the Association for Supervision and Curriculum Development, *Supervision of Teaching*, the struggle was most evident. The yearbook offered a chapter-by-chapter description of the theoretical interpretations of supervision that had evolved over the past twenty years in an attempt to reconcile the "many competing faces of supervision" (Sergiovanni, 1982, p. vi). While Sergiovanni attempted to integrate the differing theoretical constructs, Karier (1982) believed that competing views and related practices simply had to "coexist" (p. 1). He stated:

In any given period, however, competing views of supervision exist among those within the scholarly and professional education communities. Teaching as a science, for example, and supervisory strategies based on technical rationality are dominant today. But these views and related practices coexist with more aesthetic and humanistic views and practices (p. 1).

Throughout the 1960s and 1970s, supervisors were asked to serve as change agents, facilitators, monitors, referees, colleagues, consultants, and counselors. They were rarely defined as curriculum leaders. The important task of leading teachers in the curriculum renewal process was removed from much of the supervisory literature. Classroom observation, teacher-supervisor conferences, and a focus on changing the behavior of teachers were the mainstays of supervision, as important curriculum questions were left to persons, groups, committees, and government and business leaders outside of the schools.

The 1980s opened with differing and vacillating models of school supervision. The emphasis ranged from narrow, segmental, technical requirements to the personal, therapeutic needs of the classroom teacher. Concern for substantive curriculum problems and issues were just beginning to work their way back into the literature on school supervision.

Compared to supervisory theory prior to 1950, however, the relationship of school supervision and curriculum leadership took on a much smaller role.

The New Emphasis on Excellence in Academic Standards

By the early 1980s, the curriculum retrenchment era and back-to-basics movement had been replaced with a call for "excellence" in education. Excellence was equated with the development of intellectual skills and rigorous academic achievement. Concerns for excellence called into question, once again, matters of curriculum and teaching.

Undergirding most of the educational reform reports that appeared during the 1980s and 1990s was a belief that education must aim at improving the intellect through the acquisition of organized knowledge, the development of intellectual skills, and mastery of academic subjects (Adler, 1982; Bennett, 1987; National Commission on Excellence, 1983; Task Force on Education for Economic Growth, 1983). The fundamental belief that education must provide the essential foundation for lifelong learning so that new skills can be acquired for new careers and citizenship participation was also stressed (National Commission on Excellence, 1983). Strong support for renewed emphasis in science and mathematics resounded in ways reminiscent of the Cold War (National Science Board Commission on Precollege Education in Mathematics, Science, and Technology, 1983). Other priorities advanced for the schools were concerned with helping students to think critically, preparing students for the world of work, assisting students to fulfill their social and civic obligations, and mastery of fundamental processes (Boyer, 1983; Goodlad, 1984).

America was considered a "nation at risk," unable to compete economically with Japan and Germany in global industrial markets because of the nation's allegedly poor schools. Whereas the schools were blamed for alleged Soviet military superiority during the Cold War and the space race, now the schools were blamed for the failure of the nation's industrial complex to meet the Japanese industrial threat. The demand for excellence was based on two postulates: the belief that success depends on high standards (test results) and the need for a profession of well-educated teachers (Task Force on Teaching as a Profession, 1986).

The Professionalization of Teaching

The commissions and committees organized during the excellence movement had their own prescriptions for teacher improvement. Like their earlier counterparts, the "excellence" wave of reformers recognized that successful outcomes of the new reform efforts—more academic courses, longer school days, more stringent graduation requirements, and so forth— all depended on the attitudes and abilities of teachers to implement these reforms (Lichtenstein, McLaughlin, & Knudsen, 1992; Zeichner, 1994). In the policymakers' quest for excellence, teacher preparation programs were to undergo more rigorous entrance standards and teacher licensing was to be based on the ability of the teacher to demonstrate competence according to a set of predetermined standards about what teachers needed to know and be able to do (Holmes Group, 1986; A Nation Prepared, 1986). Some reformers suggested the elimination of teacher education as part of the undergraduate experience, advocating a fifth-year apprenticeship that would meet the professional knowledge needs of teachers (Adler, 1982; Boyer, 1983). Most reforms, however, eventually centered on the improvement of teacher preparation programs and on the professional lives of practicing teachers by offering recommendations for entrance standards, selection processes, reward structures, relicensing criteria, and working relationships between schools and universities (Holmes Group, 1986).

Secondary School Supervision as Production

The production model of school supervision views teachers and supervisors as part of a production unit or as technicians segmentally focused on the improvement of instruction, while the determination and development of curriculum are left to the educational policymakers and subject-matter specialists. State departments of education and local school boards are influenced greatly on matters of curriculum by the national commissions and committees who determine educational outcomes and standards that students must allegedly meet. Teachers and supervisors are often bypassed in the design, development, and evaluation of curriculum. Their role and responsibility have been limited primarily to the "delivery" of instruction. Supervisors have struggled with the concerns of "how" to teach, based on the assumption that there are technical skills or instructional methods that can be applied or are transferable across all areas of the curriculum. These issues have too often remained separated from decisions about "what" to teach, and the separation of supervision and curriculum is perpetuated. While supervisors turned their attentions to classroom practices, important decisions about curriculum have been left to administrative levels outside of the school. As a result, the professional roles of the teacher and the supervisor were greatly diminished. The problem becomes one of insufficient attention to curriculum integration and the relationships between and among the various disciplines and grade levels. The direct involvement of teachers and supervisors on matters of curriculum coordination and articulation is critical to teacher development and educational improvement. Production models of supervision, however, limit the professional roles and responsibilities of teachers and supervisors in curriculum matters and continue to perpetuate an artificial separation between curriculum and instruction.

Although respect for the involvement of the classroom teacher in the curriculum development process is recognized by most leading writers in the field of school supervision, much of the literature that has appeared through the 1980s and 1990s gives increasing attention to issues of administrative organizational theory, with curriculum receiving relatively little attention (Glatthorn, 1987; Glickman, 1981; Hoy & Forsyth, 1986; Lovell & Wiles, 1983; Marks, Stoops, & King-Stoops, 1985; Morphet, Johns, & Reller, 1982; Sergiovanni & Starratt, 1983). This practice is reflected in the placement of secondary school supervision programs in departments of administration by colleges of education instead of in departments of curriculum and teaching. This has, in effect, only exacerbated the separation of curriculum from supervision. Educators preparing for supervisory positions in secondary schools take very few courses in curriculum theory and development. They focus more on administrative theory and the technomanagerial aspects of supervision, such as teacher observation, performance, and evaluation.

Texts on supervision have supported this technomanagerial thesis and the separation of curriculum and supervision over many years. Morphet, Johns, and Reller (1982) proffered that although school administrators must serve as instructional leaders, they are only required to "have some familiarity with the field of curriculum" (p. 311). Sergiovanni and Starratt (1983) advocated the decreased focus on curriculum:

One of the problems with many texts nominally devoted to supervision is that they neglect the functions of direct assistance and overplay curriculum development and related nonsupervisory matters. . . . The authors avoid that tendency by dealing much less with curriculum theory and a more general concern with educational programs, and much more with classrooms, instruction, and teaching (p. xiv).

In *Effective Supervision: Theory into Practice*, Hoy and Forsyth (1986, 1995) presented their theory of supervision within the framework of organizational theory and gave particular attention to activities designed to improve the teaching-learning process. These activities included a cycle of systematic planning between teachers and supervisors, classroom observation, and analysis of the teaching-learning process. Hoy and Forsyth are silent regarding matters of curriculum development and make little or no reference to curriculum.

Glatthorn (1987) believes educational leadership encompasses curriculum leadership, supervisory leadership, and organizational leadership. Although Glatthorn sees these processes as interrelated and interactive, they tend to be carried out by various individuals at different levels in the school district and according to different roles. Secondary school supervisory leadership, according to Glatthorn, is designed to focus on staff development, individual development, informal observations, and teacher evaluation, with the goal of providing those "supervisory services" (p. 86) needed to insure the successful implementation of curriculum that is developed by a team of "curriculum specialists and expert teachers" (p. 191). Harris (1985) wrote that the function of supervision involves those activities that are "highly instructional" (p. 6). He defined supervision of instruction as something that is "done with adults and things to maintain or change the school operation in ways that directly influence the teaching processes employed to promote pupil learning" (p. 10). Harris viewed learning as product, instruction as productive process, and the pupils as "raw materials" (p. 3). Although Harris listed curriculum development as a supervisory "task" (p. 10), he made no mention of teacher involvement in this process.

Professional Cultures and Curriculum Change Researchers have started to look at the relationship between teacher

development and educational reform through a different lens (Barth, 1990; Bickel & Artz, 1984; Buss, 1987; Courter & Ward, 1983; Fullan, 1990; Fullan & Hargreaves, 1992; Lieberman, 1992; Lieberman & Miller, 1984; Louis, 1992; Nelson, 1986; Nolan & Francis, 1992; Pfeiffer & Dunlap, 1982; Schubert, 1989; Smythe, 1989; Tanner & Tanner, 1995; Zeichner, 1994). Fullan and Hargreaves (1992) noted that since the late 1970s there has been a shift from the "innovative-focused" approach (p. 1), which equated teacher development with the successful implementation of innovations, to a realization that "teacher development is tantamount to transforming educational institutions" (p. 6). According to Fullan and Hargreaves, critical elements of effective implementation of innovations typically consisted of "alterations in curriculum materials, instructional practices and behavior, and beliefs and understandings on the part of the teachers involved in given innovations" (p. 1)—all of which fell to the responsibility of the supervisor. A more comprehensive program of teacher development that supports educational reform, however, involves a change in both the context and culture in which teachers work, an understanding of the various ages, career stages, gender, and experiences of teachers, a fostering of "interdependent collegiality" (Grimmett & Crehan, 1992, p. 81) and the involvement of teachers in curriculum planning and policy development (Fullan & Hargreaves, 1992; Stoll, 1992). The 1990s witnessed, in some quarters, the need to turn from reform to renewal by holistically addressing problems of teacher professionalism, curriculum development, student learning, curricular access, school climate, and the ways that organizations function most effectively.

Supervision as a Collaborative Problem-solving Process

The recognition of supervision as a collaborative problem-solving process, with supervision seen as the means for professional growth and educational improvement, has reappeared in the current literature (Eisner, 1982; Fullan & Hargreaves, 1992; Glickman, 1992; Grimmett, Rostad, & Ford, 1992; Leithwood, 1990; Lieberman & Miller, 1982; Oliva, 1989; Tanner & Tanner, 1987). The teacher and supervisor are, once again, viewed as critical players in the curriculum development process. This contrasts sharply with the underlying assumptions of consultative and clinical models of supervision, which hold that the most effective path to educational improvement is either by working with individual teachers on the improvement of classroom instruction through a focus on instructional behavior or by counseling teachers in order to assist them in developing new behaviors. Professional development models place high school teachers and supervisors at the center of the educational improvement process. Consultative models view teaching and instruction separately from the improvement of curriculum, whereas developmental school supervision regards the learning environment of the school, the learning process, and the continuous development of the curriculum as interdependent. It requires that teachers work collaboratively with supervisors, administrators, and students in the curriculum renewal process. Developmental approaches recognize the teacher as a problem solver and support the teacher as an inquirer of learning who makes critical decisions regarding curriculum and instruction. This model also challenges the idea that it is possible to link particular behaviors of teachers to the production of increased student achievement. The focus has been shifted to the contexts of teaching and how to develop productive or "collaborative, inquiring workplace environments for teachers and students" (Lieberman, 1992, p. 8). Teachers are no longer viewed as technicians but as "reflective practitioners" and "teacher researchers" (Hollingsworth & Sockett, 1994). In the words of Hollingsworth and Sockett (1994): "Both reflective practice and teacher research have emerged, each giving strong support to the ideology of educational improvement through professional autonomy" (p. 7).

Reflective practitioners and teacher researchers are those professionals who work at a high level of curriculum development or at what Tanner & Tanner (1995) defined as the "generative-creative level" (p. 628). Professional teachers think about what they are doing and try to find more effective ways of teaching. Supervisors and teachers at the generative-creative level are able to diagnose problems that emerge from the teaching-learning situation and formulate hypotheses for solutions. They experiment in their classrooms and communicate their learning to colleagues. They seek greater responsibility for curriculum decisions at the school and the classroom levels. Teachers at the generative-creative level exercise independent judgment in selecting curriculum materials and transforming them for local needs. They regard themselves as professionals and, as such, are continually involved in seeking solutions for the improvement of practice. Noffke, Mosher, and Maricle (1994) gave support to these ideas:

The picture painted of the curriculum in high school classrooms over the past decade is not a very cheery one. . . . Only recently has there been a rebirth of efforts to involve practitioners in the study of their own practice. While a whole range of collaborative efforts involving university-based researchers and educational practitioners is beginning to be noticeable . . . very little has been done to involve teachers in the critical and collaborative analysis of the knowledge they make available to students—the ways they select, organize, and treat that knowledge, and the factors which may influence their actions. . . . If attempts are to be made to expand the community of educational researchers beyond the academy to include teachers, then ways to involve teachers . . . in the production of knowledge about curriculum, must be more fully explored (p. 167).

The Legacy for Secondary School Supervision

Supervision as a field of study has always been linked to the improvement of teaching and learning. The professional growth needs of teachers and the instructional learning needs of students are met when supervision is organized so as to give attention to curricular problems that grow out of all the educational experiences within the school. In effect, educational improvement and teacher development must be seen in the context of curriculum development, with the supervisor serving as the individual within the school who is in the unique position to help identify classroom and schoolwide curricular problems. Supervisors are in the unique position to

help schools counter the "cycles of fashions" (Tanner, 1980, p. 13) and the pervasive penchant for educators and school administrators to "seek instant recipes and to follow the tides of fad, fashion, and external pressures" (Tanner & Tanner, 1987, p. 201) to perform and reform.

Teacher Development Versus Teacher Deficit Supervision has long been a part of the educational enterprise of schooling. The most important legacy of secondary school supervision is that educational improvement is dependent on the interrelatedness of supervision, curriculum, and teaching. From this legacy, school supervision has come to be looked upon as that human enterprise that seeks to help teachers improve in their work. Beginning with the clear need to elevate the professional knowledge and practices of teachers, generations of school supervisors have struggled with how to improve teaching. The idea that an "expert," possessing all the teachers' knowledge or skills, was needed has also become an important legacy of supervisory theory and has been played out in various models of supervision through contemporary times. Supervision has been looked upon as that agency that could repair or remedy omissions and weaknesses of teachers or could refine or enlarge the scope of existing teaching competencies. With each major curriculum reform or counterreform, secondary school supervisors have been called upon to rally to the cause and ensure that the teachers implement the new curriculum policies and practices mandated from outside the schools.

Deficit approaches to teacher improvement have ignored fundamental principles of democratic organizations as well as some very important aspects of adult learning and development. Teachers come to the classrooms with a wide range of experience, knowledge, skills, and interests. Their motive for continued learning is not to repair or remedy an inadequacy but to find greater satisfaction as practitioners. Teacher improvement necessitates the integration of instructional improvement with curriculum development, especially since teachers are important decision makers and the true interpreters and implementers of the curriculum.

The professional development model of supervision values teachers and supervisors as professionals capable of diagnosing problems, forming solutions, searching out best practices, using research to generate new knowledge, reflecting on current practices, and continuing to grow professionally. Within the professional model, teachers and supervisors find themselves in stronger positions to examine and critically evaluate proposals and propositions for reform. John Dewey (1938) contended: "Nothing has brought pedagogical theory into greater disrepute than the belief that it is identified with handing out to teachers recipes and models to be followed in teaching" (p. 393). For Dewey, means and ends must be contiguous. Teaching, learning, and curriculum are inseparable (Dewey, 1916). It is, in effect, counterproductive to divorce supervision from curriculum. The program of curriculum improvement must remain the primary concern for supervisory leadership. Supervisors need to understand that consideration of the needs of learners, the needs and ideals of a democratic society, and the design and organization of the curriculum must be treated interrelatedly. The legacy is to recognize supervision as a collaborative professional process for renewing schools through an aggregate approach to problem solving as opposed to segmental change.

The Compartmentalized Curriculum of the Departmentalized High School

The 1990s have witnessed the rediscovery of the need for an interdisciplinary or integrated core curriculum, coupled with higher-order thinking (Tanner & Tanner, 1995). This requires a concerted program to break down the compartmentalized curriculum of the departmentalized high school.

Supervision in the high school has traditionally been divided according to subject matter specializations. The consequence is that the subject fields are treated as independent domains. The structure of the high school derives from the departmentalized structure and knowledge specializations of higher academia. Acculturated by their education to regard themselves as subject specialists, secondary school teachers have lacked the interest, commitment, and knowledge base for correlating and integrating their subjects to other studies in the total school curriculum.

This situation presents enormous problems for curriculum directors and secondary school principals, who are expected to articulate the curriculum with broad districtwide goals in the face of the departmentalized mindset that has been so pervasive in the high school. Despite the rediscovery of the need for curriculum integration during the 1990s, and the notable efforts in this direction (Tanner & Tanner, 1995), there remains the persistent problem of faculty identification in the high school as subject specialists divided along departmental lines under department heads who may have supervisory functions. It may well be that the departments and subject specializations constitute boundaries that define faculty allegiances and subcultures in the high school. From their survey of teachers of academic subjects in 16 high schools, Grossman and Stodolsky (1995) reported that "high school teachers belong to distinctive subject subcultures" (p. 5). They commented: "We urge the research community to investigate the role of subject matter in secondary school teaching more systematically in analyses of teaching and to use a subject-matter lens in interpreting extant research" (p. 8). In

reaching this recommendation, Grossman and Stodolsky contended that school subjects are marked by inherent differences, concluding: "Those engaged in professional development will need to be responsive to the subject-specific concerns teachers may raise about proposed reforms or practices" (p. 10).

However, the inherent differences among the disciplines of knowledge are created by the knowledge specialism of the discipline-centered university. When designs for curriculum correlation and integration are implemented to the extent that the curriculum meets the criteria of generality and practicality, the so-called inherent differences soon disappear. This is what has occurred at schools and colleges engaged in systematic efforts for curriculum articulation for general education from the time of the Eight-Year Study (Aikin, 1942) to the present day (Tanner & Tanner, 1995). In the same vein, leading professional schools have found that interdisciplinary curricular designs are necessary for problem solving as related to professional practice (Williams, 1980). In effect, the lines of separation that mark the boundaries of the traditional disciplines become less and less distinct when the curriculum is connected to the real world of general living. The development of an interrelated or integrated curriculum obviously places enormous responsibility on the school supervisor, curriculum coordinator, and administrative leadership, given the subject-centered departmentalized culture of high school and college faculty.

The departments of a high school—taken together with their faculties, courses of study, and subject supervisors—do not add up to a curriculum. Unless concerted efforts are undertaken to make connections, the students cannot be expected to do what the professional staff will not do.

The recent rediscovery of the need for an integrated curriculum presents a great challenge and opportunity for supervision and teacher education, both preservice and in-service. In an age of knowledge specialization, the need for knowledge synthesis becomes increasingly paramount in a democratic society marked by common concerns in the midst of diversity and special interests. Supervisors and teachers need to renew their concerns and capabilities for strengthening the unifying as well as the diversifying functions of the high school.

REFERENCES

Abrell, R. L. (1974). The humanistic supervisor enhances growth and improves instruction. *Educational Leadership, 32,* 212–216.

Adair, C. S. (1926). What teachers want in supervisors. *Proceedings of the National Education Association, 66,* 729–733.

Adams, H. & Dickey, F. G. (1953). *Basic principles of supervision.* New York: American Book Company.

Adler, J. M. (1982). *The paideia proposal: An educational manifesto.* New York: Macmillan.

Aiken, J. A. (1992). *The divorce of supervision from curriculum: Implications for practice.* Doctoral dissertation, Rutgers University, New Brunswick, NJ.

Aikin, W. M. (1942). *The story of the eight-year study.* New York: Harper & Brothers.

Alberty, H. B. (1947). *Reorganization of the high school curriculum.* New York: Macmillan.

Alberty, H. B. & Thayer, V. T. (1931). *Supervision in the secondary school.* New York: D.C. Heath.

Alexander, W. M. (1947). Can we supervise through group planning? *Educational Leadership, 4,* 218–221.

Alfonso, R. J. & Firth, G. R. (1990). Supervision: Needed research. *Journal of Curriculum and Supervision, 5,* 181–188.

Alfonso, R. J., Firth, G. R., & Neville, R. (1984). The supervisory skill mix. *Educational Leadership, 4*(9), 16–19.

Alfonso, R. J. & Goldsberry, L. (1982). Colleagueship in supervision. In T. J. Sergiovanni (Ed.). *Supervision of teaching* (pp. 90–107). Alexandria, VA: ASCD.

Allen, D. (1971). In-service teacher training: A modest proposal. In L. J. Rubin (Ed.). *Improving in-service education* (pp. 109–120). Boston, MA: Allyn and Bacon.

Allen, D. & Ryan, K. (1969). *Micro-teaching.* Reading, MA: Addison-Wesley.

American Association for the Advancement of Science. (1989). *Science for all Americans.* Washington, D.C.: Author.

Amidon, E. J., Kies, K. M., & Palisi, A. T. (1970). Group supervision: A technique for improving teaching behavior. In J. E. Heald, L. G. Romano, & N. P. Georgiady (Eds.). *Selected readings on general supervision* (pp. 218–224). New York: Macmillan.

Anderson, D. A. (1916). The efficiency expert in education. *Educational Administration and Supervision, 2,* 477–482.

Anderson, R. H. (1967). Supervision as teaching: An analogue. In W. H. Lucio (Ed.). *Supervision: Perspectives & propositions.* Washington, D.C.: ASCD.

Anderson, R. H. (1982). Creating a future for supervision. In T. J. Sergiovanni (Ed.). *Supervision of teaching* (pp. 181–190). Alexandria, VA.

Arnold, F. (1910). *Textbook of school and class management.* New York: Macmillan.

Arnold, S. L. (1898). The duties and privileges of the supervisor. *Proceedings of the National Education Association, 37,* 228–236.

Ashby, L. W. (1958). Today's challenge to in-service education. *Educational Leadership, 15,* 270–273.

Association for Supervision and Curriculum Development. (1946). *Leadership through supervision* (1946 Yearbook). Washington, D.C.: Author.

Association for Supervision and Curriculum Development. (1960). *Leadership for improving instruction* (1960 Yearbook). Washington, D.C.: Author.

Association for Supervision and Curriculum Development. (1962). *Perceiving, behaving, becoming: A new focus for education* (1962 Yearbook). Washington, D.C.: Author.

Association for Supervision and Curriculum Development. (1965).

Role of supervisor and curriculum director in a climate of change (1965 Yearbook). Washington, D.C.: Author.

Association for Supervision and Curriculum Development. (1968). *Youth education* (1968 Yearbook). Washington, D.C.: Author.

Association for Supervision and Curriculum Development. (1970). *To nurture humaneness: Commitment for the 70's* (1970 Yearbook). Washington, D.C.: Author.

Association for Supervision and Curriculum Development. (1971). *Freedom, bureaucracy, and schooling* (1971 Yearbook). Washington, D.C.: Author.

Association for Supervision and Curriculum Development. (1982). *Supervision of teaching* (1982 Yearbook). Washington, D.C.: Author.

Association for Supervision and Curriculum Development. (1984). *Using what we know about teaching* (1984 Yearbook). Washington, D.C.: Author.

Association for Supervision and Curriculum Development. (1986). *Improving teaching* (1986 Yearbook). Washington, D.C.: Author.

Association for Supervision and Curriculum Development. (1992). *Supervision in transition* (1992 Yearbook). Alexandria, VA: Author.

Ayer, F. C. (1954). *Fundamentals of instructional supervision.* New York: Harper.

Ayer, F. C. & Barr, A. S. (1928). *The organization of supervision.* New York: D. Appleton.

Ayres, R. U. (1970). The technological revolution. In M. M. Scobey & G. Graham (Eds.). *To nurture humaneness* (pp. 63–74). Washington, D.C.: ASCD.

Ayres, L. P. (1913). The economy of time through testing the course of study. *Proceedings of the National Education Association, 51,* 131–149.

Bacon, F. L. (1926). Supervision in the secondary school. *Proceedings of the National Education Association, 66,* 713–729.

Bagley, W. C. (1908). *Classroom management: Its principles and technologies.* New York: Macmillan.

Bagley, W. C. (1912). The need of standards for measuring progress and results. *Proceedings of the National Education Association, 49,* 240–243.

Baldwin, J. (1900). *School management and school methods.* New York: D. Appleton.

Balliet, T. M. (1880). The work of the city superintendent. *Proceedings of the National Education Association, 28,* 183–184.

Barnard, H. (1856). School supervision. *The American Journal of Education, 2,* 534–535.

Barr, A. S. (1923). Making the course of study. *The Journal of Educational Method, 8,* 371–378.

Barr, A. S. (1929). *The supervision of elementary subjects.* New York: D. Appleton.

Barr, A. S. & Burton, W. H. (1926). *The supervision of instruction.* New York: D. Appleton.

Barr, A. S., Burton. W. H., & Brueckner, L. J. (1938, 1947). *Supervision: Democratic leadership in the improvement of learning.* New York: Appleton-Century-Crofts.

Barth, R. S. (1990). *Improving schools from within.* San Francisco: Jossey-Bass.

Bartky, J. A. (1953). *Supervision as human relations.* Boston, MA: D.C. Heath.

Beach, D. M. & Reinhatz, J. (1989). *Supervision: Focus on instruction.* New York: Harper.

Bennett, H. E. (1917). *School efficiency.* New York: Ginn.

Bennett, W. J. (1987). *James Madison High School.* Washington, D.C.: United States Department of Education.

Berliner, D. C. & Gage, N. L. (1976). The psychology of teaching methods. In N. L. Gage (Ed.). *The psychology of teaching methods* (75th Yearbook of The National Society for Study of Education, Part I; pp. 1–20). Chicago, IL: The University of Chicago Press.

Berman, L. M. (1966). What should be the crux of supervision? *Educational Leadership, 23,* 615–617.

Bestor, A. (1956). *The restoration of learning.* New York: Alfred A. Knopf.

Bickel, W. E. & Artz, N. J. (1984). Improving instruction through focused team supervision. *Educational Leadership, 41*(7), 22–24.

Bliss, D. C. (1915). School measurement and school administration. *Educational Administration and Supervision, 1,* 79–88.

Blumberg, A. (1980). *Supervisors & teachers: A private cold war* (2nd ed.). Berkeley, CA: McCutchan.

Bobbitt, F. (1913). Some general principles of management applied to the problems of city school systems. In *the supervision of city schools* (12th Yearbook of The National Society for the Study of Education, Part I; pp. 7–96). Bloomington, IL: Public School Publishing Company.

Bobbitt, F. (1924). *How to make a curriculum.* New York: Houghton Mifflin.

Bogan, W. J. (1919). The value of teachers. *Proceedings of the National Education Association, 57,* 387–389.

Bolin, F. S. (1988). Does a community of scholars exist? *Journal of Curriculum and Supervision, 3,* 297–298.

Bolin, F. S. (1983). *The language of instructional supervision: An historical study of the writings of six leaders in instructional supervision, 1922–1982.* Doctoral dissertation, Teachers College, 1983

Bolin, F. S. (1987). Perspective and imperatives on defining supervision. *Journal of Supervision and Curriculum, 2,* 368–380.

Bolin, F. S. & Panaritis, P. (1992). Searching for a common purpose: A perspective on the history of supervision. In C. D. Glickman (Ed.). *Supervision in transition* (pp. 30–43). Alexandria, VA: ASCD.

Boutwell, C. E. (1972, August). Differentiated staffing as a component in a systematic change process. *Educational Technology,* 20–24.

Borrowman, M. L. (ed.). (1965). *Teacher education in America.* New York: Teachers College Press.

Boyce, A. C. (1915). Methods for measuring teachers' efficiency. In A. C. Boyce (Ed.). *Methods for measuring teachers' efficiency* (14th Yearbook, Part II). Chicago, IL: The University of Chicago Press.

Boyer, E. L. (1983). *High school.* Carnegie Foundation for the Advancement of Teaching. New York: Harper.

Boyer, E. L. (1991). *Ready to learn: A mandate for the nation.* Princeton, NJ: Carnegie Foundation for the Advancement of Teaching.

Bridges, E. M. (1970). Instructional leadership: A concept re-examined. In J. E. Heald, L. G. Romano, & N. P. Georgiady (Eds.). *Selected readings on general supervision* (pp. 189–198). New York: Macmillan.

Briggs, T. H. & Justman, J. (1952). *Improving instruction through supervision.* New York: Macmillan.

Brim, O. G. (1930). Changing and conflicting concepts in supervision. *Educational Methods, 9,* 131–140.

Broadhead, C. A. (1967). Ghetto schools—an American tragedy. *Educational Leadership, 25,* 24–27.

Broudy, H. S. (1971). Democratic values and educational goals. In R. M. McClure & H. R. Richey (Eds.). *The curriculum: Retrospect and prospect* (70th Yearbook of the National Society for the Study of Education, Part I; pp. 113–152). Chicago, IL: The University of Chicago Press.

Brown, E. J. (1933). *Everyday problems in classroom management.* New York: Houghton Mifflin.

Brown, G. I. (1975). The training of teachers for affective roles. In K. Ryan (Ed.). *Teacher education* (74th Yearbook of the National

Society for the Study of Education, Part II; pp. 173–303). Chicago, IL: The University of Chicago Press.

Brueckner, L. J. (1929). Descriptions of instructional practices in the earlier school surveys. In J. F. Hosic (Ed.). *Scientific method in supervision* (2nd Yearbook of The National Conference on Educational Method). New York: Teachers College, Bureau of Publications.

Bruner, J. S. (1960). *The process of education.* Cambridge, MA: Harvard University Press

Buckham, H. B. (1882). *Handbook for young teachers.* Syracuse, NY: C. W. Bardeen.

Burton, W. H. (1922). *Supervision and the improvement of teaching.* New York: D. Appleton.

Burton, W. H. (1940). Supervision in the new school. *Educational Method, 14,* 210–215.

Burton, W. H. & Brueckner, L. J. (1955). *Supervision: A social process* (3rd ed.). New York: Appleton-Century-Crofts.

Bush, M. G. (1930). Elements common to all good supervision. *Educational Method, 9,* 462–466.

Buss, D. C. (1987). Relevant comments on New Jersey's plan for supervision of instruction: Recognizing the obstacles. *Focus on education, 31*(1), 45–53.

Button, H. W. (1961). *A history of supervision in public schools, 1870–1950.* Doctoral dissertation, Washington University, 1961.

Butts, R. F. & Cremin, L. A. (1953). *A history of education in American culture.* New York: Henry Holt.

Cady, J. M. (1988). *The curriculum-instruction dualism: Implications for practice.* Doctoral dissertation, Rutgers University, New Brunswick, NJ.

Calkins, N. A. (1882). School supervision. *Proceedings of the National Education Association, 22,* 497–500.

Callahan, R. E. (1962). *Education and the cult of efficiency.* Chicago, IL: The University of Chicago Press.

Callahan, R. E. (1959). *An introduction to education in American society* (rev. ed.). New York: Alfred A. Knopf.

Callahan, R. E. & Button, H. W. (1964). Historical change of the role of the man in the organization: 1865–1950. In D. E. Griffiths & H. G. Richey (Eds.). *Behavioral Science and Educational Administration* (63rd Yearbook of the National Society for the Study of Education, Part II; pp. 73–94). Chicago, IL: The University of Chicago Press.

Carr, J. W. (1901). Developing greater efficiency in the teaching force. *Proceedings of the National Education Association, 40,* 280–285.

Carter, J. G. (1866). Outline of an institution for the education of teachers. *American Journal of Education, 16,* 77–78.

Caswell, H. L. & Campbell, D. S. (1935). *Curriculum development.* New York: American Book.

Caswell, H. L. & Campbell, D. S. (1937). *Readings in curriculum development.* New York: American Book.

Chamberlin, D., Chamberlin, E., Dought, N. E., & Scott, W. E. (1942). *Did they succeed in college?* New York: Harper.

Chancellor, W. E. (1904). *Our schools: Their administration and supervision.* New York: D. C. Heath.

Chancellor, W. E. (1910). *Class teaching and management.* New York: Harper.

Chase, F. S. (1970). Educational implications of changing knowledge. In M. M. Scobey & G. Graham (Eds.). *To nurture humaneness* (pp. 93–108). Washington, D.C.: ASCD.

Clark, M. G. (1920). The part the teacher should play in the school administration. *Proceedings of the National Education Association, 58,* 93–95.

Clark, R. W. (1988). Who decides? The basic policy issue. In L. N. Tanner (Ed.). *Critical issues in curriculum* (87th Yearbook of the National Society for the Study of Education, Part I; pp. 175–204). Chicago, IL: The University of Chicago Press.

Clement, J. A. (1927). Supervision of instruction and curriculum making in secondary schools as complementary processes. *Educational Administration and Supervision, 13,* 170–177.

Cocking, W. D. (1928). *Administrative procedures in curriculum making for public schools.* New York: Teachers College.

Cogan, M. L. (1973). *Clinical supervision.* Boston, MA: Houghton Mifflin.

Coleman, J. S. (1966). *Equality of educational opportunity.* Washington, D.C.: Office of Education, U.S. Department of Health, Education, and Welfare.

Coleman, J. S., Ch. (1974). Panel on Youth of the President's Science Advisory Committee. *Youth: Transition to adulthood.* Chicago, IL: The University of Chicago Press.

Collings, E. (1924). The meaning and function of creative supervision. *Educational Method, 9,* 457–462.

Collings, E. (1934). *Supervisory guidance of teachers in secondary schools.* New York: Macmillan.

Combs, A. W. (Ed.). (1962). *Perceiving, behaving, becoming: A new focus* (1962 Yearbook). Washington, D.C.: ASCD.

Combs, A. W. (1970). An educational imperative: The human dimension. In M. M. Scobey & G. Graham (Eds.). *To nurture humaneness* (pp. 173–188). Washington, D.C.: ASCD.

Combs, A. W. (Ed.). (1971). *Freedom, bureaucracy, and schooling* (1986 Yearbook). Washington, D.C.: ASCD.

Commission on the Reorganization of Secondary Education. (1918). *Cardinal principles of secondary education* (Bulletin, No. 35). Washington, D.C.: United States Government Printing Office.

Common, D. L. & Grimmett, P. P. (1992). Beyond the war of the worlds: A consideration of the estrangement between curriculum and supervision. *Journal of Curriculum and Supervision, 7,* 209–225.

Conant, J. B. (1959). *The American high school today.* New York: McGraw-Hill.

Conant, J. B. (1963). *The education of American teachers.* New York: McGraw-Hill. Conference on Curriculum Reorganization and Revision. (1932).

Conlin, M. R. & Haberman, M. (1967). Supervising teachers of the disadvantaged. *Educational Leadership, 24,* 393–398.

Conlin, M. R. & Haberman, M. (1992). Estrangement between curriculum and supervision: Personal observations on the current scene. *Journal of Curriculum and Supervision, 7,* 245–249,

Corey, S. M. (1949). Curriculum development through action research. *Educational Leadership, 7,* 145–152.

Corey, S. M. (1967). The nature of instruction. In P. C. Lange, H. G. Richey, & M. M. Coulson (Eds.). *Programmed instruction* (66th Yearbook of the National Society for the Study of Education, Part II; pp. 5–27). Chicago, IL: University of Chicago Press.

Corson, O. T. (1906). The superintendent's authority and the teacher's freedom. *Proceedings of the National Education Association, 46,* 80–85.

Corwin, R. G. (1975). The new teaching profession. In K. Ryan (Ed.). *Teacher education* (74th Yearbook of the National Society for the Study of Education, Part II; pp. 230–264). Chicago, IL: The University of Chicago Press.

Counts, G. S. (1932). *Dare the school build a new social order?* New York: John Day Company.

Courter, R. L. & Ward, B. A. (1983). In staff development for school improvement. *Staff development* (82nd Yearbook of the National Society for the Study of Education, Part II; pp. 185–209). Chicago, IL: The University of Chicago Press.

Courtis, S. A., McSwain, E. T., & Morrison, N. C. (Eds.). (1939). *Cooperation: Principles and practice* (11th Yearbook of the Department of Supervisors and Directors of Instruction). Washington, D.C.: National Education Association.

Cox, P. W. L. & Langfitt, R. E. (1934). *High school administration and supervision.* New York: American Book Company.

Crabbs, L. M. (1925). *Measuring efficiency in supervision and teaching* (Contributions to Education, Teachers College, No. 175). New York: Teachers College.

Crabtree, J. W. (1914). Rating of teachers. *Proceedings of The National Education Association, 52,* 1165–1167.

Cremin, L. A. (1988). *American education: The metropolitan experience, 1876–1980.* New York: Harper.

Cremin, L. A. (1961). *The transformation of the school: Progressivism in American education, 1876–1957.* New York: Alfred A. Knopf.

Cremin, L. A. & Borrowman, M. L. (1956). *Public schools in our democracy.* New York: Macmillan.

Crosby, M. (1957). *Supervision as co-operative action.* New York: Appleton-Century-Crofts.

Crosby, M. (1969). The new supervisor: Caring, coping, becoming. In R. R. Leeper (Ed.). *Changing supervision for a changing time* (pp. 43–63). Washington, D.C.: ASCD.

Cruickshank, D. R. (1985). *Models for the preparation of American teachers.* Bloomington, IN: Phi Delta Kappa.

Cuban, L. (1979). Determinants of curriculum change and stability, 1870–1970. In J. Schaffarzick & G. Sykes (Eds.). *Value conflicts and curriculum issues* (pp. 139–195). Berkeley, CA: McCutchan.

Cuban, L. (1984). *How teachers taught: Constancy and change in American classrooms, 1899–1980.* New York: Longman.

Cubberley, E. P. (1915). *State and county educational reorganization.* New York: Macmillan.

Cubberley, E. P. (1916). *Public school administration.* Boston, MA: Houghton Mifflin.

Cubberley, E. P. (1920). *The history of education.* Boston, MA: Houghton Mifflin.

Cubberley, E. P. (1923). *The principal and his school.* Boston, MA: Houghton Mifflin.

Culbertson, J. (1964). The preparation of administrators. In D. E. Griffiths & H. G. Richey (Eds.). *Behavioral science in education* (63 Yearbook of the National Society for the Study of Education, Part II; pp. 303–330). Chicago, IL: The University of Chicago Press.

Curriculum making in current practice (Report of conference held at Northwestern University, October 30, 1931). Evanston, IL: Northwestern University.

Curtin, J. (1964). *Supervision in today's elementary schools.* New York: Macmillan.

Cushman, C. L. & Taulane, J. B. (1945). Curriculum planning is an in-service job. *Educational Leadership, 3,* 13–17.

Cutright, P. (1929). Teacher participation in curriculum construction. *Educational Method, 8,* 404–407.

David, J. I. (1991). What it takes to restructure education. *Educational Leadership, 48,* 11–15.

Davis, C. (1975). Learning disabilities: Need for a total effort. *Educational Leadership, 32,* 511–512.

Davis, O. L. (Ed.). (1976). *Perspectives on curriculum development* (1976 Yearbook). Washington, D.C.: ASCD.

Dempsey, R. A. & Smith, R. P. (1972). *Differentiated staffing.* Englewood Cliffs, NJ: Prentice-Hall.

Department of Supervisors and Directors of Instruction. (1933). In R. D. Lindquist (Ed.). *Effective instructional leadership* (6th Yearbook) Washington, D.C.: National Education Association.

Department of Supervisors and Directors of Instruction (1934). Scientific Method in Supervision (7th Yearbook). Washington, D.C.: National Education Association.

Department of Supervisors and Directors of Instruction. (1939). Cooperation: Principles and Practices (11th Yearbook). Washington, D.C.: National Education Association.

Department of Supervisors and Directors of Instruction. (1940). Newer Instructional Practices of Promise (12th Yearbook). Washington, D.C.: National Education Association.

Dewey, J. (1901). The situation as regards the course of study. *Proceedings of the National Education Association, 40*, 332–348.

Dewey, J. (1910a). Science as subject-matter and as method. In R. D. Archambault (Ed.). *John Dewey on education.* Chicago, IL: The University of Chicago Press.

Dewey, J (1910b). *How we think.* New York: D. C. Heath.

Dewey, J. (1915). Professional spirit among teachers. *American Teacher, 4*, 115–116.

Dewey, J. (1916). *Democracy and education: An introduction to the philosophy of education.* New York: Macmillan.

Dewey, J. (1922). Mediocrity and individuality. *The New Republic, 33*, 35–37.

Dewey, J. (1929). *The sources of a science of education.* New York: Liveright.

Dewey, J. (1938). *Experience and education.* London: Collier Books.

Dewey, J. (1956). *The child and the curriculum* (1902) *and the school and society* (1915). (Com. Ed.). Chicago, IL: The University of Chicago Press.

Douglass, H. R., Bent, R. K., & Boardman, C. W. (1961). *Democratic supervision in secondary schools* (2nd ed.). Boston, MA: Houghton Mifflin.

Downing, G. L. (1964). A supervision experiment with the disadvantaged. *Educational Leadership, 21*, 433–435.

Eash, M. J. (1966). Preparatory programs for supervisors. *Educational Leadership, 23*, 358–362.

Eash, M. J. (1968). Supervisors: A vanishing breed. *Educational Leadership, 26*, 73–80.

Edelfelt, R. A. (1972). Differentiated staffing: Where are we? *National Elementary Principal, 52*(4), 46–48.

Educational Policies Commission. (1944). *Education for ALL American youth.* Washington, D.C.: National Education Association (revised, 1952).

Eisner, E. W. (1982). An artistic approach to supervision. In T. J. Sergiovanni (Ed.). *Supervision of teaching* (pp. 53–58). Alexandria, VA: ASCD.

Eisner, E. W. & Vallance, E. (1974). *Conflicting conceptions of curriculum.* Berkeley, CA: McCutchan.

Elliott, E. C. (1914). *City school supervision* (School Efficiency Series). New York: World Book.

Elsbree, W. S. (1939). *The American teacher.* New York: American Book.

Engler, W. H. (1973). *Radical school reformers of the 1960's.* Unpublished doctoral dissertation, Rutgers University, New Brunswick, NJ.

Ether, J. A. (1969). Cultural pluralism and self-identity. *Educational Leadership, 27*, 232–234.

Evans, H. M. (1949). The adjustment problem in the senior high school. *Educational Method, 6*, 354–358.

Evenden, E. S. (1938). Contributions of research to the education of teachers. In G. M. Whipple (Ed.). *The scientific movement in education* (37th Yearbook of the National Society for the Study of Education, Part II; pp. 33–52). Bloomington, IL: Public School Publishing Company.

Eye, G. G. & Netzer, L. A. (1965). *Supervision of instruction: A phase of administration.* New York: Harper.

Feyereisen, K. V., Fiorino, A. J., & Nowak, A. T. (1970). *Supervision and curriculum renewal: A systems approach.* New York: Appleton-Century-Crofts.

Fitch, H. N. (1931). *An analysis of the supervisory activities and techniques of the elementary school training supervisor* (Contributions to Education, No. 476). New York: Teachers College.

Flanders, N. A. (1970). *Analyzing teacher behavior.* Reading, MA: Addison-Wesley.

Flexner, A. (1923). *A modern college and a modern school.* New York: Doubleday, Page.

Foote, I. P. (1924). How can a superintendent provide for teacher participation in the administration of a city school system? *Educational Administration and Supervision, 10*, 221–227.

Franseth, J. (1961). *Supervision as leadership.* Evanston, IL: Row, Peterson.

Freedman, M. K. (1966). Backgrounds and deviancy. In W. W. Wattenberg & H. G. Richey (Eds.). *Social deviancy among youth* (65th Yearbook of the National Society for the Study of Education, Part I; pp. 28–58). Chicago, IL: The University of Chicago Press.

Freiberg, J. H. (1984). Master teacher programs: Lessons from the past. *Educational Leadership, 42*(4), 16–21.

Fuhrman, S. H. (1994). Legislatures and educational policy. In R. F. Elmore and S. H. Fuhrman (Eds.). *The governance of curriculum.* Alexandria, VA: ASCD.

Fuhrman, S. H. & Elmore, R. F. (1994). Governors and education policy in the 1990's. In R. F. Elmore & S. H. Fuhrman (Eds.). *The governance of curriculum.* Alexandria, VA: ASCD.

Fullan, M., Bennett, B., & Rolheiser-Bennett, C. (1990). Linking classroom and school improvement. *Educational Leadership, 47*, 13–19.

Fullan, M. & Hargreaves, A. (1992). *Teacher development and educational change.* Washington, D.C.: The Falmer Press.

Gage, N. L. (Ed.). (1976). *The psychology of teaching methods* (75th Yearbook of the National Society for the Study of Education, Part I). Chicago, IL: The University of Chicago Press.

Gage, N. L. & Winne, P. H. (1975). Performance-based teacher education. In K. Ryan (Ed.). *Teacher education* (74th Yearbook for the National Society for the Study of Education, Part II; pp. 146–172). Chicago, IL: The University of Chicago Press.

Galloway, C. (1967). The plight of the inner-city. *Educational Leadership, 25*, 15–23.

Gardner, E. M. (1919). Constructive participation in organization and administration by teachers. *Proceedings of the National Education Association, 57*, 378–380.

Garman, N. B. (1986). Clinical supervision: Quackery or remedy for professional development. *Journal of Curriculum and Supervision, 2*, 148–157.

Gates, C. R. (1923). *The management of smaller schools.* Boston, MA: Houghton Mifflin.

Gilchrist, R. S., Fielstra, C., & Davis, A. L. (1957). Organization of programs of in-service education. In N. B. Henry (Ed.). *In-service education* (56th Yearbook of the National Society for the Study of Education, Part I; pp. 285–310). Chicago, IL: The University of Chicago Press.

Giles, H. H., McCutchen, S. P., & Zechiel, A. N. (1942). *Exploring the curriculum.* New York: Harper and Brothers.

Gist, A. S. (1925). The art of supervision. *The Journal of Educational Method, 5*, 192–196.

Glantz, J. (1991). *Bureaucracy and professionalism: The evolution of public school supervision.* New Jersey: Fairleigh Dickinson University Press.

Glantz, J. (1992). Curriculum development and supervision: Antecedents for collaboration and future possibilities. *Journal of Curriculum and Supervision, 3*, 226–244.

Glatthorn, A. A. (1984). *Differentiated supervision.* Alexandria, VA: ASCD.

Glatthorn, A. A. (1987). *Curriculum leadership.* Glenview, IL: Scott Foresman.

Gleason, G. (1966). Will programmed instruction serve people? *Educational Leadership, 23*, 471–482.

Glickman, C. D. (1981). *Developmental supervision: Alternative practices for helping teachers improve instruction.* Alexandria, VA: ASCD.

Glickman, C. D. (Ed.). (1992). *Supervision in transition* (1992 Yearbook). Alexandria, VA: ASCD.

Glickman, C. D. & Gordon, S. P. (1987). Clarifying developmental supervision. *Educational Leadership, 44,* 64–70.

Glickman, C. D., Gordon, S. P., & Ross-Gordon, J. M. (1995). *Supervision of instruction: A developmental approach.* Needham Heights, MA: Allyn & Bacon.

Goldhammer, R. (1969). *Clinical supervision: Special methods for the supervision of teachers.* New York: Holt, Rinehart and Winston.

Good, H. G. (1956). *A history of American education.* New York: Macmillan.

Goodlad, J. L. (1966). The curriculum. In J. L. Goodlad & H. R. Richey (Eds.). *The changing American school* (65th Yearbook of the National Society for the Study of Education, Part II; pp. 32–58). Chicago, IL: University of Chicago Press.

Goodlad, J. L. (1984). *A place called school: Prospects for the future.* New York: McGraw-Hill.

Graham, G. & Scobey, M. M. (Eds.). (1970). *To nurture humaneness: Commitment for the 70's.* Washington, D.C.: ASCD.

Graham, R. (1975). Youth and experiential learning. In R. J. Havighurst & P. H. Dreyer (Eds.). *Youth* (74th Yearbook of the National Society for the Study of Education, Part I; pp. 161–192). Chicago, IL: The University of Chicago Press.

Gramlich, E. M. & Koshel, P. P. (1975). *Educational performance contracting: An evaluation of an experiment.* Washington, D.C.: The Brookings Institute.

Green, J. (1987). *The next wave: A synopsis of recent educational reform reports* (Report No. TR-87-1). Denver: Education Commission of the States.

Greenwood, J. M. (1888). Efficient school supervision *Proceedings of the National Education Association, 36,* 519–528.

Griffiths, D. E. (1966). *The school superintendent.* New York: The Center for Applied Research in Education.

Griffiths, D. E. & Richey, H. G. (1964). In D. E. Griffiths & H. G. Richey (Eds.). *Behavioral science and educational administration* (63rd Yearbook of the National Society for the Study of Education, Part II). Chicago, IL: University of Chicago Press.

Grim, P. & Anderson, V. (1949). Is the American high school serving today's youth? *Educational Method, 6,* 338–348.

Grimmett, P. P. & Crehan, E. P. (1992). The nature of collegiality in teacher development: The case of clinical supervision. In M. Fullan & A. Hargreaves (Eds.). *Teacher development and educational change.* Washington, D.C.: The Falmer Press.

Grimmett, P. P., Rostad, O. P., & Ford, B. (1992). The transformation of supervision. In C. D. Glickman (Ed.). *Supervision in transition* (pp. 185–202). Alexandria, VA: ASCD.

Gross, B. M. (1964). The scientific approach to administration. In D. E. Griffiths & H. G. Richey (Eds.), *Behavioral science and educational administration* (63rd Yearbook of the National Society for the Study of Education, Part II; pp. 33–72). Chicago, IL: The University of Chicago Press.

Gross, C. H. & Chandler, C. C. (1964). *The history of American education.* Boston, MA: D. C. Heath.

Grossman, P. L. & Stodolsky, S. S. (1995). Content as context: The role of school subjects in secondary school teaching, *Educational Researcher, 24,* 5–11.

Gutherie, E. R. (1942). Conditioning: A theory of learning in terms of stimulus, response, and association. In N. B. Henry, (Ed.). *The psychology of learning* (41st Yearbook of the National Society for the Study of Education, Part II; pp. 17–60). Chicago, IL: The University of Chicago Press.

Gwynn, J. M. (1961). *Theory and practice of supervision.* New York: Dodd, Mead.

Haan, A. (1964). The teaching complex: Focus of in-service education. *Educational Leadership, 21,* 285–287.

Hammock, R. C. & Owings, R. S. (1955). *Supervising instruction in secondary school.* New York: McGraw-Hill.

Hanus, P. H. (1913). Improvement of the school system by scientific management. *Proceedings of the National Education Association, 51,* 247–258.

Harap, H. (1940). Curriculum materials suited to creative supervision. *Educational Method, 14,* 378–383.

Harman, A. C. (1947). *Supervision in selected secondary schools.* Doctoral dissertation, University of Pennsylvania, Philadelphia, PA.

Harris, B. M. (1963, 1985). *Supervisory behavior in education.* Englewood Cliffs, NJ: Prentice Hall.

Harris, B. M. (1965). Emergence of technical supervision. *Educational Leadership, 22,* 494–496.

Harrison, R. H. (1968). *Supervisory leadership in education.* New York: Van Nostrand Reinhold.

Hart, J. S. (1871). Schools for professional education of teachers. *The American Journal of Education, 22,* 401–409.

Hass, G. H. (Ed.). (1960). *Leadership for improving instruction.* Washington, D.C.: ASCD.

Hass, G. H. (1961). Who should plan the curriculum? *Educational Leadership, 19,* 2–4.

Havighurst, R. J. & Gottlieb, D. (1975). Youth and the meaning of work. In R. J. Havighurst, P. H. Dreyer, (Ed.). *Youth* (74th Yearbook of the National Society for the Study of Education, Part I; pp.145–160). Chicago, IL: The University of Chicago Press.

Hawley, W. D. (1985). Design and implementation of performance career ladders. *Educational Leadership, 43*(3), 57–61.

Heald, J. E., Romano, L. G., & Giorgiady, N. P. (1970). *Selected reading on general supervision.* New York: Macmillan.

Heath, D. H. (1986). *Improving teaching* (1986 Yearbook). Alexandria, VA: ASCD.

Heffernan, H. (Ed.). (1940). *Newer instructional practices of promise* (12th Yearbook of the Department of Supervisors and Directors of Instruction). Washington, D.C.: National Education Association.

Hillway, T. (Ed.). (1964). *American education: An introduction through readings.* Boston, MA: Houghton Mifflin.

Hittinger, M. S. (1969). Bilingualism and self-identity. *Educational Leadership, 27,* 247–249.

Hofstadter, R. (1962). *Anti-intellectualism in American life.* New York: Alfred A. Knopf.

Hollingsworth, S. & Sockett, H. (1994). Positioning teacher research in educational reform: An introduction. In S. Hollingsworth & H. Sockett. (Ed.). *Teacher research and educational reform* (93rd Yearbook of the National Society for the Study of Education, Part I; pp. 1–23). Chicago, IL: University of Chicago Press.

Hollister, H. A. (1914). *The administration of education in a democracy.* New York: Charles Scribner's Son's.

Holmes Group. (1986). *Tomorrow's teachers: A report of the Holmes Group.* East Lansing, MI: The Holmes Group.

Holt, J. (1976). *Instead of education.* New York: E. P. Dutton & Co.

Hosford, P. H. (Ed.). (1984). *Using what we know about teaching* (1984 Yearbook). Washington, D.C.: ASCD.

Hosic, J. F. (1920). The democratization of supervision. *Proceedings of the National Education Association, 58,* 414–420.

Hosic, J. F. (Ed.). (1928). *Educational supervision* (1st Yearbook of the National Conference on Educational Method). New York: Teachers College.

Hosic, J. F. (Ed.). (1929). *Scientific method in supervision* (2nd Yearbook of The National Conference of Supervisors and Directors of Instruction). New York: Teachers College.

Hoy, W. K. & Forsyth, P. B. (1995). *Effective supervision: Theory into practice.* New York: Random House.

Hunkins, R. V. (1931). *The superintendent at work on smaller schools.* Boston, MA: D. C. Heath and Company.

Hunter, F. M. (1913). How can supervisors and assistant superintendents render the most efficient service in their relationships to principals and teachers? *Proceedings of the National Education Association, 51*, 300–301.

Hunter, F. M. (1924). The relationship of supervision to the attainment of the major objectives of elementary education. *Proceedings of the National Education Association, 62*, 890–908.

Hunter, M. (1984). Knowing, teaching, and supervising. In P. H. Hosford (Ed.). *Using what we know about teaching* (pp. 169–192). Alexandria, VA: ASCD.

Illich, I. (1971). *Deschooling society*. New York: Harper.

Illich, I. (1972). The alternative to schooling. In J. L. Nelson, K. Carlson, & T. E. Linton (Eds.). *Radical ideas and the schools* (pp. 368–381). New York: Holt, Rinehart and Winston.

Jacobs, H. H. (1989). *Interdisciplinary curriculum: Design and implementation*. Alexandria, VA: ASCD.

Janowitz, M. (1969). *Institution building in urban education*. New York: Russell Sage Foundation.

Jenkins, J. M. & Tanner, D. (Eds.). (1992). *Restructuring for an interdisciplinary curriculum*. Reston, VA: National Association of Secondary School Principals.

Joint Committee on Curriculum. (1937). *The changing curriculum*. New York: D. Appleton-Century.

Joyce, B. R. (1971). The curriculum worker of the future. In R. M. McClure & H. G. Richey (Eds.). *The curriculum: Retrospect and prospect* (70th Yearbook of the National Society for the Study of Education, Part I; pp. 307–355). Chicago, IL: The University of Chicago Press.

Joyce, B. R. (1975). Conceptions of man and their implications for teacher education. In K. Ryan (Ed.). *Teacher education* (74th Yearbook of the National Society for the Study of Education, Part II; pp. 111–144). Chicago, IL: The University of Chicago Press.

Joyce, B. R. (1991). The door to school improvement. *Educational Leadership, 48*, 59–62.

Judd, C. (1925). The curriculum: A paramount issue. *Proceedings of the National Education Association, 55*, 173–180.

Kaestle, C. F. (1983). *Pillars of the republic: Common schools and American society*. New York: Hill and Wang.

Karier, C. (1982). The genesis of supervision. In T. J. Sergiovanni (Ed.). *Supervision of teaching*. Alexandria, VA: ASCD.

Karr, G. M. (1939). Utilizing community resources in an integrated program. *Education Method, 18*, 209–213.

Katz, M. B. (Ed.). (1971). *School reform: Past and present*. Boston, MA: Little, Brown.

Keefe, J. W. (1971). Differentiated staffing—its rewards and pitfalls. *NASSP Bulletin, 55*, 112–118.

Kelly, E. C. (1945). Why all this talk about workshops? *Educational Leadership, 22*, 200–204.

Kelly, F. (1974). A system approaches multicultural education. *Educational Leadership, 32*, 183–186.

Kilpatrick, W. H. (1925). *Foundations of method*. New York: Macmillan.

Klausmeier, H. J. & Lambert, P. (1961). Teaching machines and the learning process. *Educational Leadership, 18*, 273–283.

Kliebard, H. M. (1979). Systematic curriculum development. In. J. Schaffarzick & G. Sykes (Eds.). *Value conflicts and curriculum issues* (pp. 197–235). Berkeley: McCutchan.

Kliebard, H. M. (1988). The effort to reconstruct the modern American curriculum. In L. E. Beyer & M. W. Apple (Eds.). *The curriculum* (pp. 19–31). Albany: State University of New York Press.

Knapp, T. J. (1919). Practicing democracy in school administration. *Educational Administration and Supervision, 5*, 463–473.

Knight, E. W. & Hall, C. L. (1951). *Readings in American educational history*. New York: Appleton-Century-Crofts.

Knoll, J. W. & Kelly, S. P. (1970). *Foundations of education in America*. New York: Harper.

Knudsen, C. W. (1932). *Evaluation and improvement of teaching*. New York: Doubleday, Doran.

Kohl, H. R. (1969). *The open classroom*. New York: Random House.

Koran, J. J. (1969). Supervision: An attempt to modify behavior. *Educational Leadership, 26*, 754–764.

Krug, E. A. (1964). *The shaping of the American high school*. New York: Harper.

Kyte, G. C. (1923). The cooperative development of a course of study. *Educational Administration and Supervision, 9*, 517–536.

Landsittel, F. C. (1916). A score card method of teacher-rating. *Educational Administration and Supervision, 2*, 297–309.

Lange, P. C. (1967). Future developments. In P. C. Lange, H. G. Richey, & M. M. Koulson (Eds.). *Programmed instruction* (66th Yearbook of the National Society for the Study of Education, Part II; pp. 284–325). Chicago, IL: The University of Chicago Press.

Langworthy, S. B. (1990). *Schooling 1600–1990*. Glassboro, NJ: Rowan University.

Lawler, M. R. (1961). New frontiers for supervision. *Educational Supervision, 19*, 82–85.

Lee, G. C. (1966). The changing role of the teacher. In J. I. Goodlad (Ed.). *The changing American school* (65th Yearbook of the National Society for the Study of Education, Part II; pp. 9–31). Chicago, IL: The University of Chicago Press.

Leeper, R. R. (Ed.). (1965). *Role of the supervisor and curriculum director in a climate of change*. Washington, D.C.: ASCD.

Leeper, R. R. (Ed.). (1969). *Changing supervision for changing times* (Address presented for the 24th Conference, Chicago, IL). Washington, D.C.: ASCD.

Leeper, R. R. & Wilhelms, F. T. (Eds.). (1969). *Supervision: Emerging profession*. Washington, D.C.: ASCD.

Leithwood, K. (1992). The principal's role in teacher development. In M. Fullan & A. Hargreaves (Eds.). *Teacher development and educational change*. Washington, D.C.: The Falmer Press.

Lewin, K. (1942). Field theory of learning. In N. B. Henry (Ed.). *The psychology of learning* (41st Yearbook of the National Society for the Study of Education, Part II; pp. 215–242). Chicago, IL: The University of Chicago Press.

Lewis, A. J. & Miel, A. (1972). *Supervision for improved instruction*. Belmont, CA: Wadsworth.

Lichtenstein, G., McLaughlin, M. W., & Knudsen, J. (1992). Teacher empowerment and professional knowledge. In A. Lieberman (Ed.). *The changing contexts of teaching* (91st Yearbook of the National Society for the Study of Education, Part I; pp. 37–58). Chicago, IL: The University of Chicago Press.

Lieberman, A. (1992). Introduction: *The changing contexts of teaching* (91st Yearbook of the National Society for the Study of Education, Part I; pp. 1–10). Chicago, IL: The University of Chicago Press.

Lieberman, A. & Miller, L. (1984). *Teachers: Their world and their work*. Alexandria, VA: ASCD.

Lindquist, R. D. (Ed.). (1933). *Effective instructional leadership* (6th Yearbook of The Department of Supervisors and Directors of Instruction). New York: Teachers College, Columbia University.

Long, D. H. (1977). Competency-based staff development. In C. W. Beegle & R. A. Edelfetl (Eds.). *Staff development/staff liberation* (pp. 81–82). Washington, D.C.: ASCD.

Loughary, J. W. (1970). Educating for humaneness in the technological society. In M. M. Scobey & G. Graham (Eds.). *To nurture humaneness* (pp. 75–84). Washington, D.C.: ASCD.

Louis, K. S. (1992). Restructuring and the problem of teachers' work. In A. Lieberman (Ed.). *The changing contexts of teaching* (91st Yearbook of the National Society for the Study of Education, Part I; pp. 138–156). Chicago, IL: The University of Chicago Press.

Lovell, J. T. (1967). A perspective for viewing instructional supervisory behavior. In J. T. Lovell & W. H. Lucio (Eds.). *Supervision: Perspectives and propositions*. Washington, D.C.: ASCD.

Lovell, J. T. & Wiles, K. (1983). *Supervision for Better Schools,* 5th Ed. Englewood Cliffs, NJ: Prentice-Hall.

Lowry, C. D. (1908). (Ed.). The relation of principals and superintendents to the training and improvement of their teachers. (7th Yearbook of the National Society for the Scientific Study of Education, Part I; pp. 11–65). Chicago, IL: University of Chicago Press.

Lucio, W. H. (1962). Instructional improvement: Considerations for supervision. *Educational Leadership, 20,* 211–217.

Lucio, W. H. (Ed.). (1969). *The supervisor: New demands new dimensions.* Washington, D.C.: ASCD.

Lucio, W. H. & McNeil, J. D. (1969). *Supervision: A synthesis of thought and action.* (2nd ed.). New York: McGraw-Hill.

Lull, H. G. (1923). Teacher-training in curriculum making. *Educational Administration and Supervision, 9,* 290–303.

Lumsdaine, A. A. (1961). Teaching machines and auto instruction programs. *Educational Leadership, 18,* 266–270.

Macdonald, J. B. (1974). Cultural pluralism as ASCD's major thrust. *Educational Leadership, 32,* 167–169.

Mackenzie, G. N. (1945). The in-service job. *Educational Leadership, 1,* 2–6.

Mackenzie, G. N. (1961). Role of the supervisor. *Educational Leadership, 19,* 86–90.

Madden, M. (1921). Some problems of method in supervision. *The Journal of Educational Method, 1,* 10–12.

Malone, C. F. (1970). A design for productive classroom evaluation. In J. I. Heald, L. G. Romano, & N. P. Georgiady (Eds.). *Selected readings on general supervision* (pp. 251–258). New York: Macmillan.

Markowitz, S. (1976). The dilemma of authority in supervisory behavior. *Educational Leadership, 33,* 367–372.

Marks, J. R., Stoops, E., & King-Stoops, J. (1995). *Handbook of educational supervision: A guide for the practitioner* (2nd ed.). Boston, MA: Allyn and Bacon.

Maslow, A. H. (1970). *Motivation and personality* (2nd ed.). New York: Harper.

Maslow, A. H. (1962). Some basic propositions of a growth and self-actualization psychology. In A. W. Combs (Ed.). *Perceiving, behaving, becoming: A new focus for education* (pp. 34–39). Washington, D.C.: ASCD.

McClure, R. M. (1971). The reform of the fifties and sixties: A historical look at the near past. In R. M. McClure & H. G. Richey (Eds.). *The curriculum: Retrospect and prospect* (70th Yearbook of the National Society for the Study of Education, Part I; pp. 45–78). Chicago, IL: The University of Chicago Press.

McKean, R. C. & Mills, H. H. (1964). *The supervisor.* Washington, D.C.: The Center for Applied Research in Education.

McLain, J. (1971). Opening the system from inside *Educational Leadership, 28,* 472–475.

McMaster, A. L. (1966). Supervision: Loneliness and rewards *Educational Leadership, 23,* 339–342.

McMillan, M. L. (1958). Wings over our shoulders. *Educational Leadership, 15,* 339–342.

McMurray, C. A. (1903). *The elements of general method based on the principles of Herbart.* New York: Macmillan.

McNeil, J. D. (1982). A scientific approach to supervision. In T. J. Sergiovanni (Ed.). *Supervision of teaching.* Alexandria, VA: ASCD.

Melby, E. O. (1929). *Organization and administration of supervision* (Contributions to Education, School of Education Series, No. 1, Northwestern University). Bloomington, IL: Public School Publishing Co.

Melchoir, W. T. (1933). Preventative supervision for creative teaching. *Educational Method, 12,* 519–525.

Melchoir, W. T. (1950). *Instructional supervision.* Boston, MA: D. C. Heath.

Meyer, A. E. (1957). *An educational history of American people.* New York: McGraw-Hill.

Meyer, H. K. (1966). Televised learning. *Educational Leadership, 23,* 463–470.

Miller, C. W. & Goldberg, A. L. (1963). Technology and progress. *Educational Leadership, 20,* 431–433.

Miller, E. E. & Hudspreth, D. (1966). The supervisor and media. *Educational Leadership, 23,* 656–659.

Mintz, P. P. (1980). *A model and a rationale for supervision as the process of curriculum building.* Doctoral dissertation, Teachers College, Columbia University, 1980, New York.

Morley, F. P. (1970). The commercial package and the local supervisor. *Educational Leadership, 27,* 792–795.

Morphet, E. L., Johns, R. L., & Reller, T. L. (1982). *Educational organization and administration* (4th ed.). Englewood Cliffs, NJ: Prentice Hall.

Morrison, J. C. (1921). Supervision from the teacher's viewpoint. *The Journal of Educational Method, 1,* 131–138.

Morrison, T. (1860). Methods of instruction—general principles. *The American Journal of Education, 9,* 295–305.

Mosher, R. L. & Purpel, D. E. (1972). *Supervision: The reluctant profession.* New York: Houghton Mifflin.

National Commission on Excellence in Education. (1983). *A nation at risk: The imperative for educational reform.* Washington, D.C.: U.S. Department of Education.

National Commission on the Reform of Secondary Education. (1973). *The reforming of secondary education.* New York: McGraw-Hill.

National Conference on Educational Method. (1921). Introduction. *The Journal of Educational Method, 1,* 1–2.

National Education Association Department of Superintendence. (1930). *The superintendent surveys supervision* (8th Yearbook). Washington, D.C.: National Education Association.

National Education Association Department of Superintendence. (1938). *Youth education today* (16th Yearbook). Washington, D.C.: National Education Association.

National Information Center for Children. (1991). The education of children and youth with special needs: What does the law say? *NICHY News Digest, 1*(1), 1–15.

National Science Board Commission on Precollege Education in Mathematics, Science, and Technology. (1983). *Educating Americans for the 21st century.* Washington, D.C.: National Science Foundation.

National Society for the Scientific Study of Education. (1906). *The education and training of secondary teachers* (4th Yearbook, Part I). Chicago, IL: The University of Chicago Press.

National Society for the Study of Education. (1908). *The relation of superintendents and principals to the training and professional improvement of their teachers* (7thYearbook, Part I). Chicago, IL: The University of Chicago Press.

National Society for the Study of Education. (1915). *Methods for measuring teachers' efficiency* (14th Yearbook, Part II). Chicago, IL: The University of Chicago Press.

National Society for the Study of Education. (1915). *Minimum essentials in elementary-school subjects: Standards and current practice* (14th Yearbook, Part I). Chicago, IL: The University of Chicago Press.

National Society for the Study of Education. (1916). *Standards and tests for the measurement of the efficiency of schools and school systems* (15th Yearbook, Part I). Chicago, IL: The University of Chicago Press.

National Society for the Study of Education. (1917). *Second report of the committee on minimum essentials in elementary school subjects* (16th Yearbook, Part I). Bloomington, IL: Public School Publishing Company.

National Society for the Study of Education. (1919). *Third report of* the committee on economy of time in education (17th Yearbook, Part I). Bloomington, IL: Public School Publishing Company.

National Society for the Study of Education. (1938). *The scientific movement in education* (37th Yearbook, Part II). Bloomington, IL: Public School Publishing Company.

National Society for the Study of Education. (1942). *The psychology of learning* (41st Yearbook: Part II).. Chicago, IL: The University of Chicago Press.

National Society for the Study of Education. (1944). *Adolescence* (43rd Yearbook, Part I). Chicago, IL: The University of Chicago Press.

National Society for the Study of Education. (1945). *American education in the postwar period: Curriculum reconstruction* (44th Yearbook, Part I). Chicago, IL: The University of Chicago Press.

National Society for the Study of Education. (1946). *Changing conceptions in educational administration* (45th Yearbook, Part II). Chicago, IL: The University of Chicago Press.

National Society for the Study of Education. (1953). *Adapting the secondary-school program to the needs of youth* (52nd Yearbook, Part I). Chicago, IL: University of Chicago Press.

National Society for the Study of Education. (1957). *In-service education* (56th Yearbook Part I). Chicago, IL: The University of Chicago Press.

Neagley, R. L. & Evans, N. D. (1980). *Handbook for effective supervision of instruction*. (3rd ed.). Englewood Cliffs, NJ: Prentice-Hall.

Nelson, B. S. (1986). Collaboration for colleagueship. *Educational Leadership, 43*(5), 50–52.

Newlon, J. (1923). Reorganizing city school supervision. *Educational Method, 9*, 404–409.

Nissman, B. S. (1976). *A study of performance contracting and its application to education*. Doctoral dissertation, Rutgers University, New Brunswick, NJ.

Noffke, S., Mosher, L. & Maricle, G. (1994). Curriculum research together: Writing our work. In S. Hollingsworth & H. Sockett (Eds.). (93rd Yearbook of the National Society for the Study of Education, Part I; pp. 166–185). Chicago, IL: The University of Chicago Press.

Nolan, J. & Francis, P. (1992). Changing perspectives in curriculum and instruction. In C. D. Glickman (Ed.). *Supervision in transition* (pp. 44–60). Alexandria, VA: ASCD.

Noll, J. W. & Kelly, S. P. (1970). *Foundations of education in America*. New York: Harper.

Norton, M. A. (1931). How adequate supervision can bring about better articulation of the units of American education. *Educational Method, 10*, 387–389.

Nutt, H. W. (1920). *The supervision of instruction*. Boston, MA: Houghton Mifflin.

Ogletree, J. R. (1962). Preparing educational supervisors. *Educational Leadership, 20*, 163–165.

Ogletree, J. R. (1965). Professionalization of supervisors and curriculum workers. *Educational Leadership, 23*, 153–156.

Ogletree, J. R. (1972). Changing supervision in a changing era. *Educational Leadership, 29*, 507–510.

Oliva, P. F. (1989). *Supervision for today's schools*. (3rd ed.). New York: Longman.

O'Neil, J. (1992). Piecing together the restructuring puzzle. *Educational Leadership, 47*, 4–10.

Ooley, I. A. (1945). Growth through in-service action. *Educational Leadership, 3*, 126–128.

Parker, F. R. (1887). Discussion of Higbee's city and county supervision. *Proceedings of the National Education Association, 26*, 110–112.

Parker, F. R. (1891). The school of the future. *Proceedings of the National Education Association, 30*, 89–91.

Parker, F. W. (1883). *Notes of talks on teaching*. New York: E. L. Kellogg.

Parrott, A. L. (1914). Abolish the rating of teachers. *Proceedings of the National Education Association, 52*, 1168–1173.

Payne, B. (1908). How can the training of kindergarten and primary teachers contribute to economy in the education of children. In B. J. Gregory (Ed.). *The co-ordination of the kindergarten and the elementary school* (7th Yearbook of the National Society for the Scientific Study of Education, Part II; pp. 35–49). Chicago, IL: The The University of Chicago Press.

Payne, W. H. (1875). *Chapters on school supervision*. New York: American Book.

Pfeiffer, I. L. & Dunlap, J. B. (1982). *Supervision of teachers: A guide to improving instruction*. Phoenix: Oryx Press.

Pickard, J. L. (1898). *School supervision*. New York: D. Appleton.

Pohland, P. & Cross, J. (1982). Impact of the curriculum on supervision. In T. J. Sergiovanni (Ed.). *Supervision of teaching* (pp. 133–152). Alexandria, VA: ASCD.

Postman, N. & Weingartner, C. (1969). *Teaching as a subversive activity*. New York: Dell.

Rand Educational Policy Study. (1974). *How effective is schooling?* Englewood Cliffs, NJ: Educational Technology Publications.

Randolph, E. S. (1978). Maximizing human potential. *Educational Leadership, 35*, 601–608.

Rankin, P. T. (Ed.). (1934). *Scientific method in supervisory programs* (7th Yearbook of The Department of Supervisors and Directors of Instruction). New York: Teachers College.

Rankin, P. R. (Ed.). (1935). *Leadership in instruction*. Commission on Instruction Leadership, Department of Superintendence. Washington, D.C.: National Education Association.

Reeder, E. H. (1953). *Supervision in the elementary school*. Boston, MA: Houghton Mifflin.

Report of the Panel on the Preparation of Beginning Teachers. (1984). *The preparation of beginning teachers*. Princeton, NJ: The Henry Chauncey Center.

Reschke, L. K. (1932). The humanistic movement in supervision. *Educational Method, 12*, 41–44.

Reynolds, S. (1914). By what standard or tests shall the efficiency of a school or system of schools be measured? *Proceedings of the National Education Association, 52*, 261–265.

Rice, J. M. (1969). *Public school system of the United States*. New York: Arno Press and The New York Times.

Richey, H. G. (1957). Growth of the modern conception of in-service education. In N. B. Henry (Ed.). *In-service education* (56th Yearbook of the National Society for the Study of Education, Part I; pp. 35–56). Chicago, IL: The University of Chicago Press.

Rickover, H. (1963). *American education—a national failure*. New York: Dutton.

Rippa, S. A. (1980). *Education in a free society*. (4th ed.). New York: Longman.

Rollins, S. P. (1968). Youth education: Problems. In R. H. Muessig (Ed.). *Youth education: Problems, perspectives, promises* (pp. 2–19). Washington, D.C.: ASCD.

Rorer, J. A. (1942). *Principles of democratic supervision* (Contributions to Education, No. 858. New York: Teachers College.

Rugg, H. & Counts, G. (1927). A critical appraisal of current methods of curriculum-making. In G. M. Whipple (Ed.). *Curriculum-making: Past and present* (26th Yearbook of the National Society for the Study of Education, Part I; pp. 425–447). Chicago, IL: The University of Chicago Press.

Rugg, H. & Shumaker, A. (1928). *The child-centered school*. Chicago, IL: World Book.

Sarason, S. B. (1971). *The culture of the school and the problem of change*. Boston, MA: Allyn and Bacon.

Schiffer, J. (1980). *School renewal through staff development.* New York: Teachers College Press.

Schiller, J. (1971, May). Performance contracting: Some questions and answers. *American Education,* 3–5.

Schreiber, D. (1966). Work-experience programs. In W. W. Wattenberg & H. G. Richey (Eds.). *Social deviancy among youth* (65th Yearbook of the National Society for the Study of Education, Part I; pp. 280–314). Chicago, IL: The University of Chicago Press.

Schubert, W. H. (1989). Teacher lore: A neglected basis for understanding curriculum and supervision. *Journal of Curriculum and Supervision, 4,* 282–285.

Schwartz, H. (1988). Unapplied curriculum knowledge. In L. N. Tanner (Ed.). *Critical issues in curriculum* (87th Yearbook of the National Society for the Study of Education, Part I; pp. 35–59). Chicago, IL: The University of Chicago Press.

Sears, J. B. (1918). *Classroom organization and control.* Boston, MA: Houghton Mifflin.

Seeley, L. (1903). *A new school management.* New Yorky: Hinds, Noble, & Eldredge.

Sergiovanni, T. J. (1982a). The context for supervision. In T. J. Sergiovanni (Ed.). *Supervision of teaching* (pp. 108–118). Alexandria, VA: ASCD.

Sergiovanni, T. J. (1982b). Toward a theory of supervision practice: Integrating scientific, clinical, and artistic views. In T. J. Sergiovanni (Ed.). *Supervision of teaching* (pp. 67–78). Alexandria, VA: ASCD.

Sergiovanni, T. J. (1985). Landscapes, mindscapes, and reflective practice in supervision. *Journal of Supervision and Curriculum, 1,* 5–17.

Sergiovanni, T. J. & Starratt, R. J. (1971). *Emerging patterns of supervision: Human perspectives.* New York: McGraw-Hill.

Sergiovanni, T. J. & Starratt, R. J. (1983). *Supervision: Human perspectives.* New York: McGraw-Hill.

Showalter, B. R. (1924). The development of supervision of instruction. *Educational Administration and Supervision, 10,* 481–495.

Silberman, C. E. (1970). *Crisis in the classroom: The remaking of American education.* New York: Random House.

Sizer, T. (1984). *Horace's compromise.* Boston, MA: Houghton Mifflin.

Skinner, B. F. (1968). *The technology of teaching.* New York: Appleton-Century-Crofts.

Skinner, J. (1920). The place of the classroom teacher in administration of school affairs. *Proceedings of the National Education Association, 58,* 95–96.

Skobjak, B. L. & Pautler, A. J. (1979). Factors in youth unemployment. *Educational Leadership, 38,* 241–243.

Smith, M. S., Fuhrman, S. H., & O'Day, J. (1994). National curriculum standards: Are they desirable or feasible? In R. F. Elmore & S. H. Fuhrman (Eds.). *The governance of curriculum.* Alexandria, VA: ASCD.

Smith, R. (1966). Educating youth in a revolutionary society. *Educational Leadership, 23,* 331–340.

Smyth, J. (1986). Clinical supervision: Technocratic mindedness or emancipatory learning. *Journal of Curriculum and Supervision, 1,* 331–340.

Smyth, J. (1989). An alternative vision and an "educative" agenda for supervision. *Journal of Curriculum and Supervision, 4,* 162–186.

Smyth, J. (1991). Instructional supervision and the redefinition of who does it in schools. *Journal of Curriculum and Supervision, 7,* 90–99.

Snedden, D. (1916). Scientific methods in educational administration. *Educational Administration and Supervision, 2,* 279–283.

Solden, L. (1901). The organization of work of inspection and supervision. *Proceedings of the National Education Association, 40,* 276–279.

Spaulding, F. E. (1913). The application of the principles of scientific management. *Proceedings of the National Education Association, 51,* 259–280.

Spaulding, W. B. (1958). Satellites, rockets, missiles: Their meaning for education. *Educational Leadership, 16,* 4–7.

Spears, H. (Ed.). (1943). *Leadership at work* (15th Yearbook of the Department of Supervisors and Directors of Instruction). Washington, D.C.: National Education Association.

Spears, H. (1953). *Improving the supervision of instruction.* Englewood Cliffs, NJ: Prentice-Hall.

Spring, J. (1994). *The American school, 1642–1993* (3rd ed.). New York: McGraw-Hill.

Staples, I. E. (1971). The "open-space" plan in education. *Educational Leadership, 28,* 458–465.

Stoll, L. (1992). Teacher growth in the effective school. In M. Fullan & A. Hargreaves (Eds.). *Teacher development and educational change.* Washington, D.C.: The Falmer Press.

Stone, C. R. (1929). *Supervision of the elementary school.* Boston, MA: Houghton Mifflin.

Stratemeyer, F. B. (1947, 1957). H. L. Forkmer, M. Mckin, & A. H. Passow. *Developing a curriculum for modern living.* New York: Teachers College, Columbia University.

Study, H. P. (1940). Cooperative administration as a means to teachers' growth. *Educational Method, 20,* 23–28.

Suzzallo, H. (1906). *The rise of school supervision in Massachusetts* (Contributions to Education, No. 3). New York: Teachers College.

Swearinghen, M. E. (1960). Identifying needs for in-service growth. *Educational Leadership, 17,* 332–335.

Taba, H. (1945). General techniques of curriculum planning. In N. B. Henry (Ed.). *American education in the postwar period* (44th Yearbook of the National Society for the Study of Education, Part I; pp. 80–114). Chicago, IL: The University of Chicago Press.

Taba, H. (1962). *Curriculum development: Theory and practice.* New York: Harcourt, Brace & World.

Tanner, D. (1971). *Secondary curriculum: Theory and development.* New York: Macmillan.

Tanner, D. (1972). *Secondary education: Perspectives and prospects.* New York: Macmillan.

Tanner, D. (1973, March). Performance contracting: Contrivance of the industrial-government-education complex. *Intellect,* 361–365.

Tanner, D. (1982). Curriculum history. In J. E. Mitzel (Ed.). *Encyclopedia of educational research* (5th ed.). New York: The Free Press and Macmillan.

Tanner, D. (1986). Are reforms like swinging pendulums? In H. J. Walberg & J. W. Keefe (Eds.). *Rethinking reform: The principals dilemma.* Reston, VA: National Association of Secondary School Principals.

Tanner, D. (1989). A brief historical perspective of the struggle for an integrative curriculum. *Educational Horizons, 68*(1), 6–11.

Tanner, D. (1991). *Crusade for democracy: Progressive education at the crossroad* (A publication of the John Dewey Society for the Study of Education and Culture). Albany, New York: State University of New York Press.

Tanner, D. (1993). A nation truly at risk. *Phi Delta Kappan, 1,* 288–297.

Tanner, D. (1997). Standards, standards: High and low, 75, 115–120.

Tanner, D. & Tanner, L. N. (1980). *Curriculum development: Theory into practice* (2nd ed.) New York: Macmillan.

Tanner, D. & Tanner, L. N. (1987). *Supervision in education: Problems and practices.* New York: Macmillan.

Tanner, D. & Tanner, L. N. (1990). *History of the school curriculum.* New York: Macmillan.

Tanner, D. & Tanner, L. N. (1995). *Curriculum development: Theory into practice* (3rd ed.) Englewood Cliffs, NJ: Prentice Hall.

Tanner, L. (1988). Curriculum issues in historical perspective. In L. N. Tanner (Ed.). *Critical issues in curriculum* (87th Yearbook of the

National Society for the Study of Education, Part I; pp. 1–15). Chicago, IL: The University of Chicago Press.

Tanner, L. N. & Kridel, C. (1987). The uncompleted past: The society for the study of curriculum history celebrates its tenth anniversary. *Journal of Curriculum and Supervision, 3,* 71–74.

Task Force on Education for Economic Growth. (1983). *Action for excellence.* Denver: Education Commission of the States.

Task Force on Teaching as a Profession. (1986). *A nation prepared: Teachers for the 21st century.* New York: The Carnegie Forum on Education and the Economy.

Thayer, V. T. (1925). Democratic school administration. *Educational Administration and Supervision, 11,* 361–372.

Thut, I. N. (1957). *The story of education.* New York: McGraw-Hill.

Tietrict, R. B. (1914). How to secure more effective supervision. *Proceedings of the National Education Association, 52,* 286–289.

Toepfer, C. F. (1973). The supervisor's responsibility for innovation. *Educational Leadership, 30,* 740–743.

Trow, W. C. (1925). *Scientific method in education.* Boston, MA: Houghton Mifflin.

Trump, J. L. (1961). *Focus on change: Guide to better schools.* Reston, VA: National Association of Secondary School Principals.

Trump, J. L. (1977). *A school for everyone.* Reston, VA: National Association for Secondary School Principals.

Trump, J. L. & Vars, G. F. (1976). How should learning be organized? In William Van Til (Ed.). *Issues in secondary education* (75th Yearbook of the National Society for the Study of Education, Part II). Chicago, IL: The University of Chicago Press.

Turner, R. L. (1975). An overview of research in teacher education. In K. Ryan (Ed.). *Teacher education* (74th Yearbook of the National Society for the Study of Education, Part II; pp. 87–110). Chicago, IL: The University of Chicago Press.

Tuttle, F. B. (1942). *The theory of the supervision of instruction, 1875–1920.* Doctoral dissertation, Yale University, New Haven, CT.

Tyack, D. B. (Ed.). (1967). *Turning points in American educational history.* Waltham, MA: Blaisdell.

Tyack, D. B. (1974). *The one best system: A history of American urban education.* Cambridge, MA: Harvard University Press.

Tyler, R. W. (1949). *Basic principles of curriculum and instruction.* Chicago, IL: The University of Chicago Press.

Tyler, R. W. (1971). Curriculum development in the twenties and thirties. In R. M. McClure & H. G. Richey (Eds.). *The curriculum: Retrospect and prospect* (70th Yearbook of the National Society for the Study of Education, Part I; pp. 26–44). Chicago, IL: The University of Chicago Press.

Uhl, W. L. (1929). *The supervision of secondary subjects.* New York: D. Appleton.

Undegraff, H. (1921). Part of teachers in school management. *Proceedings of the National Education Association, 59,* 284–293.

United States Department of Education. (1991). *America 2000: An education strategy.* Washington, D.C.: U.S. Government Printing Office.

Unruh, G. G. (1977). Instructional supervision: Trends and issues. *Educational Leadership, 34,* 563–565.

Unruh, G. G. & Alexander, W. M. (1974). *Innovations in secondary education* (2nd ed.) New York: Holt, Rinehart, & Winston.

Van Geel, T. (1979). The new law of the curriculum. In J. Schaffarzick & G. Sykes (Eds.). *Value conflicts and curriculum issues* (pp. 25–75). Berkeley, CA: McCutchan.

Van Til, W. (1968). Supervising computerized instruction. *Educational Leadership, 26,* 41–48.

Van Til, W. (1975). Back to basics—with a difference. *Educational Leadership, 33,* 8–13.

Walker, D. F. (1977). The hard lot of the professional reform movement. *Educational Leadership, 35,* 83–85.

Warriner, E. C. (1911). Unity of ideals and purposes in teaching: As

gained from school supervision. *Proceedings of the National Education Association, 48,* 311–312.

Wattenberg, W. W. (1966). Review of trends. In W. W. Wattenberg & H. G. Richey (Eds.). *Social deviancy among youth* (65th Yearbook of the National Society for the Study of Education, Part I; pp. 4–27). Chicago, IL: The University of Chicago Press.

Wear, P. W. (1966). Supervisor: Coordinator of multiple consultations. *Educational Leadership, 23,* 652–655.

Webster, E. (1929). The curriculum in the making. *Educational Method, 5,* 159–165.

Weet, H. S. (1919). Necessity and difficulty of supervision in a city school. *Proceedings of the National Education Association, 57,* 504–505.

Wesley, E. B. (1957). *NEA: The first hundred years.* New York: Harper.

West, T. & Millsom, C. (1975). Learning disability funding. *Educational Leadership, 32,* 503–506.

Whipple, G. M. (Ed.). (1916). *Standards and tests for the measurement of the efficiency of schools and school systems* (15th Yearbook of the National Society for the Study of Education, Part I). Chicago, IL: The University of Chicago Press.

White, E. E. (1883). School supervision. *Proceedings of the National Education Association, 32,* 185–194.

White, E. E. (1894). *School management.* New York: American Book.

White, E. L. (1970). The package and the supervisor. *Educational Leadership, 27,* 788–791.

Wiles, K. (1950). *Supervision for better schools.* New York: Prentice Hall.

Wiles, K. (1963). *The changing curriculum of the American high school.* Englewood Cliffs, NJ: Prentice Hall.

Wiles, K. & Lovell, J. T. (1975). *Supervision for better schools.* Englewood Cliffs, NJ: Prentice Hall.

Wilhelms, F. T. (1946). *Leadership through supervision.* Washington, D.C.: ASCD.

Wilhelms, F. T. (1972). Foreward. In R. L. Musher & D. E. Purpel. *Supervision: The reluctant profession.* New York: Houghton Mifflin.

Williams, G. (1980). *Western Reserve's experiment in medical education and its outcome.* New York: Oxford University Press.

Williams, L. (1966). The consultant-teacher transaction. *Educational Leadership, 23,* 541–544.

Wilson, H. B. (1917). *Second report of the committee on minimum essentials in elementary school subjects* (16th Yearbook of the National Society for the Study of Education, Part I). Bloomington, IL: Public School Publishing Company.

Wilson, H. B. (1919). *Third report of the committee on the economy of time in education* (17th Yearbook of the National Society for the Study of Education, Part I). Bloomington, IL: Public School Publishing Company.

Wilson, H. B. (1920). The participation of the teaching staff in school administration. *Educational Administration and Supervision, 6,* 61–67.

Wilson, H. B., Kyte, G. C., & Lull, H. G. (1924). *Modern methods in teaching.* New York: Silver, Burdett, and Company.

Wirth, A. G. (1966). *John Dewey as educator.* New York: John Wiley & Sons.

Witt, P. W. F. (1963). Instructional technology: A challenge to curriculum workers. *Educational Leadership, 20,* 424–425.

Woodring, P. (1975). The development of teacher education. In K. Ryan (Ed.). *Teacher education* (74th Yearbook of the National Society for the Study of Education, Part II; pp. 1–24). Chicago, IL: The University of Chicago Press.

Zeichner, K. M. (1994). Personal renewal and social construction through teacher research. In S. Hollingsworth & H. Sockett (Eds.). (93rd Yearbook of the National Society for the Study of Education, Part I; pp. 66–85). Chicago, IL: The University of Chicago Press.

Zeller, D. (1940). The role of the teacher in supervision. *Educational Method, 14,* 383–393.

Zumwalt, K. K. (1986). *Improving teaching* (1986 Yearbook). Alexandria, VA: ASCD.

Zumwalt, K. K. (1988). Are we improving or undermining teaching? In L. N. Tanner (Ed.). *Critical issues in curriculum* (87th Yearbook of the National Society for the Study of Education, Part I; pp. 148–204). Chicago, IL: The University of Chicago Press.

27

SUPERVISION IN DISTRICT CENTRAL OFFICES

Edward F. Pajak
THE UNIVERSITY OF GEORGIA

Pamela G. Adamson
CLAYTON COUNTY (GEORGIA) SCHOOLS

Jean M. Rhoades
POLK COUNTY (GEORGIA) SCHOOLS

The supervisory role at the school district-central office level in curriculum and instruction has largely been ignored by researchers and theorists, and is often misunderstood and maligned by policy makers. It is poorly defined in practice and theory, and despite its explicit link to the fundamental task and purpose of schooling, the position of central office supervisor of curriculum and instruction remains tenuous and in constant jeopardy, especially during times of financial exigency (Anderson, 1988; Costa & Guditus, 1984; Rowan, 1982). The current restructuring movement in public education, which embraces school-based decision-making as a panacea, has brought new questions to the forefront of the national policy debate about the district-level supervisory role, its purpose, and its place in public education (Steller, 1994).

A DEMOCRATIC FOUNDATION

The supervisory role of the central office originated in the late nineteenth and early twentieth centuries, as urban school districts grew larger and became more centralized (Callahan, 1962; Tyack, 1974). The seminal source for both supervision and administration as areas of study and practice in education was a volume entitled *Chapters on School Supervision*, by William Payne (1875), a Michigan school superintendent (Culbertson, 1988; Glanz, 1977).

In the early twentieth century, however, the field of supervision began to produce a literature and philosophy distinct from that of educational administration. In a book entitled *City School Supervision*, Edward C. Elliott (1914) highlighted the importance of "the democratic motive of American education" to supervisory practice. He distinguished "administrative effi-

ciency," which required "centralization of administrative power" from "supervisory efficiency," characterized by "*decentralized, cooperative, expert* supervision" (p. 78, emphasis in original). Elliott argued that administrators stifled the individuality of teachers and children when administrative control was misapplied to the work of teachers and the achievements of students. In the decade that followed, other influential authors also expressed the view that democracy should be a guiding principle of supervisory practice in education (Ayer & Barr, 1928; Barr & Burton, 1926; Burton, 1927; Hosic, 1920; Stone, 1929).

While Frederick Taylor's industrial logic had a major impact on educational administration in the early twentieth century (Callahan, 1962; Tyack, 1974), its influence on instructional supervision was considerably less profound. In 1926, Barr and Burton noted, for example, that Franklin Bobbitt's (1913) adaptation of Taylor's principles of scientific management "has never been especially popular and seems to have had little influence" (p. 75) on the supervision of instruction. The reason that scientific management failed to significantly influence educational supervision has been attributed to the fact that "the problems of supervision and of teaching method were not readily amenable to investigation in the management frame of reference nor with the techniques available" (Callahan & Button, 1964, p. 90).

As a field of study and practice, supervision continued to distinguish itself from administration during the 1930s by aligning itself with the process of curriculum development and through the establishment of a new organization, the Association for Supervision and Curriculum Development (ASCD; Callahan & Button, 1964). In the early 1930s, publications of the Department of Supervisors and Directors of Instruction (one of ASCD's forebears in the National Education Association) advocated Dewey's (1929) consciously reasoned cooperative prob-

ACKNOWLEDGMENTS Special thanks to Patricia Reeves for her careful and diligent assistance in the final preparation of this chapter.

lem solving as a major guiding principle for supervisory practice and called for greater involvement of teachers in decisions related to instruction, as well as group deliberation and experimentation in solving problems (Department of Supervisors and Directors of Instruction [DSDI], 1932, 1933, 1934). In the most influential supervision textbook of the 1930s and 1940s, Barr, Burton, and Brueckner (1938) called for responsible leadership through democratic supervision that would rely on scientific reason and experimentation for direction.

Dewey's (1929) combination of democracy and scientific thinking thus had a much greater influence on the evolution of supervision than is generally recognized. His definition of scientific problem solving differed considerably from that of Bobbitt and other advocates of measurement, however, and should not be confused with scientific management (McKernan, 1987; McNeil, 1982). When Dewey called for the application of the scientific method to solve educational problems, he was referring to consciously deliberate *reflective inquiry* as a guide to practice in schools.

From the 1940s through the early 1960s, the ASCD published literature that for the most part refined and elaborated on the concept of supervision as an expression of democratic leadership (ASCD, 1948, 1951, 1960; DSDI, 1943; Van Til, 1946). The 1960 ASCD Yearbook may be the most cogent statement of democratic leadership in the supervision literature. Focusing on "the premise that democracy is ever in the state of becoming what people make it" (ASCD, 1960, p. 26), the book emphasized the importance of leadership that emerges from the group and the idea that all individuals in the school and community have leadership potential that should be cultivated and exercised (Pajak, 1993). Such progressive thinking clearly anticipated contemporary notions of participative governance and school-based decision-making. But public education, and supervision, in the United States followed a very different course for the next 30 years.

EARLY RESEARCH AND A SHIFT TOWARD MANAGEMENT

Authors have long recognized that the position of district-level supervisor is poorly defined in both theory and practice (Blumberg, 1984; Harris, 1967; Sergiovanni & Starratt, 1979). A variety of titles—associate or assistant superintendent for curriculum or instruction, supervisor of instruction, curriculum coordinator or director, and director of instruction, among others—are used in different school systems to describe positions that perform very similar functions (Costa & Guditus, 1984; Hall, Putman, & Hord, 1985; Speiker, 1976). At the same time, job descriptions for district-level curriculum and instructional leaders tend to be all-encompassing, so that specific task responsibilities can vary appreciably even when job titles are similar (Pajak, 1989).

Although quite general and context-free, the "classic description" (Hall, Putman, & Hord, 1985) of supervision as an organizational phenomenon was developed by Harris (1963, 1975), who identified "ten tasks" encompassing the range of supervisory responsibilities that can directly or indi-

rectly affect the quality of instruction. These tasks include: developing curriculum, organizing for instruction, staffing, providing facilities, providing materials, arranging for in-service education, orienting new staff members, relating special services, developing public relations, and evaluating.

Despite the obvious potential relevance of the district-level role to maintaining and improving the quality of instruction in schools, research on central office supervisors has been meager, especially compared to other professional roles in education (Bridges, 1982; Fullan, 1982; Hall, 1987). Wimpelberg (1987) has observed that "we have the largest research base on teachers and principals and a lengthy literature on the chief school superintendent. Unfortunately, we know considerably less about the instructional leadership behavior of central office supervisors . . ." (p. 103). At best, he observes, we have only "a sketchy sense . . . of the work of line administrators between the superintendent and the school" (p. 104).

The preponderance of research that does exist on the central office supervisor has been reported in doctoral dissertations. Most of these studies, especially those conducted prior to the 1980s, sought to define the district-level supervisory role by surveying supervisors or their role senders (i.e., teachers, principals, and superintendents) with questionnaires to determine their perceptions of effective, actual, and ideal supervisory duties and behaviors (Smith, 1983).

In a review and synthesis of 99 such studies conducted between 1955 and 1969, Carman (1970) reported greater unanimity between teachers and supervisors in their perceptions of the actual and ideal role of supervisors than either group had with administrators. The most frequently enacted supervisory duties, as perceived by local school personnel, included responsibility for in-service training, consultative instructional assistance, human relations, and coordination of instruction. The duties identified as most helpful included curriculum development, providing special materials and resources, and providing practical assistance to address specific problems. The most effective supervisor behaviors identified in Carman's review included sincerity, consideration, willingness to help, unobtrusiveness during classroom visits, ability to inspire teachers to improve, and supportiveness of teacher decisions. Activities related to curriculum and instruction received the highest priority, while the major obstacles to supervisory success were said to be budget restrictions, lack of time, and resistance to change.

During the 1970s and early 1980s, doctoral dissertations and other studies continued to focus mainly on perceptions of supervisory role incumbents and role senders, usually relying on surveys as the primary data source (Afifi, 1980; Beach, 1976; Boucree, 1981; Brown, 1975; Cantrell, 1979; Crews, 1979; Ferguson, 1976; Fidler, 1986; Gantt, 1977; Lovell & Phelps, 1976; Mayo, 1983; Melord, 1979; Perrine, 1978, 1984; Raske, 1979; Spears, 1980; Thomas, 1981; Walker & Hamm, 1981). The results of these studies tended to be consistent with earlier findings in terms of the kinds of tasks associated with district-level instructional leadership (Simonton, 1990). A review of research on the central office supervisor conducted by Floyd (1986) indicated that, among teachers, four categories of functions were associated with satisfaction or perceived effectiveness of supervisors' performance:

(a) interpersonal skills (Capper, 1981; Cawelti, 1980; Colbert, 1966; Cook, 1983; Cotton & Savard, 1980; Danley & Burch, 1978; Fraser, 1980; Hopkins, 1982; Kyle, 1984; Rentz, 1969; Young & Heichberger, 1975); (b) response and relevance to teacher need and teacher involvement (Colbert, 1966; Cotton & Savard, 1980; Franseth, 1972; Fraser, 1980; Humphries, 1981; Kyle, 1984; Loftus, 1980; Miller, 1959; Rentz, 1969; Young & Heichberger, 1975); (c) technical skills and professional competency (Cawelti, 1980; Danley & Burch, 1978; Hopkins, 1982; Kyle, 1984; Rentz, 1969); and (d) management skills (Danley & Burch, 1978; Loftus, 1980; Rentz, 1969).

According to Floyd's (1986) review, interpersonal skills and relevance to teacher needs were generally viewed by teachers as more important than any technical skills that supervisors might possess.

District office supervisors and members of their role set (teachers and administrators) continued to agree, according to most surveys conducted during the 1970s, that the primary purpose of supervision was improvement of classroom instruction. Less consensus between supervisors and their role senders was evident, however, regarding the actual and ideal behaviors or appropriate tasks for accomplishing this end (Cawelti & Reavis, 1980; Simonton, 1990). The literature seems to indicate that, particularly during the 1970s, teachers began to view district-level supervisors as more often performing administrative, coordinating, and managerial functions than helping to improve instruction (Carlton, 1970; Floyd, 1986; Fraser, 1980; Kyle, 1984; Smith, 1975; Young & Heichberger, 1975).

Esposito, Smith, and Burbach (1975), for example, drew up a list of supervisory activities from the literature to structure a survey of 86 percent of all district-level supervisors in Virginia. The researchers suggested that supervisory tasks fell into four categories. Two of the categories—direct assistance and indirect assistance to teachers—clearly fit the traditional view of supervision as an organizational function that supports and facilitates teaching. Two others—administration and evaluation—signaled a shift in the nature and emphasis of the district-level supervisory role.

Another study of supervisors in Virginia that same year (Evans, 1975) sought to replicate research conducted almost 10 years earlier in Texas (Cardenas, 1966). Both studies relied on eight vignettes, based on Harris' (1963) work, that described supervisory problems. Teachers, supervisors, and administrators were asked to rank responses that they considered most appropriate to each situation. In the Texas study, statistically significant differences in expectations about the role of instructional supervisor were not found, though some limited disagreement between teachers and supervisors was apparent (Cardenas, 1966). The 1975 Virginia study, however, revealed greater differences. Elementary supervisors were distinguished from teachers at a statistically significant level in placing greater importance on "organizing for instruction" and "evaluating instruction tasks." Teachers, in contrast, placed greater importance on the supervisory tasks of "curriculum development" and "providing materials" (Evans, 1975).

Holder (1977) also replicated an earlier survey (Gott, 1967) of system-level instructional leaders in Georgia. She found that supervisory tasks, such as program planning, in-service training, evaluation, demonstration teaching, and research remained fair-

ly constant over a 10-year period. However, tasks associated with "administration and personnel" increased in frequency of performance from 1967 to 1977.

Further evidence of a divergence from the task of supporting teachers to managerial functions among district-level supervisors during the 1970s is offered by Nasca (1976), who used job descriptions of elementary supervisors from 10 school districts and interviews with six supervisors to generate a list of 27 supervisory tasks. The tasks were classified into six areas: curriculum, instruction, classroom management, testing, professional duties, and administrative duties. A survey of teachers and supervisors showed that tasks related to providing instructional assistance at the classroom level were most valued by both groups. Supervisors, however, reported low frequency of involvement in a number of tasks that were highly valued by teachers, such as gathering instructional materials, suggesting curriculum ideas, demonstrating new instructional materials or strategies, providing opportunities for teachers to engage in professional meetings and in-service workshops, and participating in team or grade level meetings. Teachers conversely perceived little value in supervisors administering tests, but supervisors reported high frequency of involvement in this task.

Disagreement concerning the frequency with which supervisors actually and ideally performed tasks related to curriculum development, assistance, human relations, communication, and coordination of instruction was not limited to teachers. Douglass (1979) reported significant disagreement between superintendents and supervisors in Alabama about the actual and ideal tasks performed by supervisors. He concluded that such disagreement increased the likelihood of conflict between them.

Increasing pressure during the 1970s and early 1980s for supervisors to attend to managerial tasks at the expense of direct assistance to teachers was widely recognized in the supervision research literature (Burch & Danley, 1980; Sullivan, 1982). This trend, attributed at the time to increasing federal and state regulations, mandates, assessments, and testing requirements (Unruh, 1977), led Sturges (1979) to conclude that two distinct types of supervisors were needed in schools: *administrative* and *consultative*.

Sturges (1979) advocated separate academic preparation programs and different state certification requirements for these two functions. The administrative supervisors, he proposed, would be responsible for federal programs, teacher evaluation, and quality control. Consultative supervisors would concentrate exclusively on helping teachers improve learning opportunities for students. Sturges' recommendations, however, did not materialize. The gulf between managerial and consultative duties eventually resulted in a synthesis of sorts: the emergence of a conception of the supervisor of instruction as "change agent" within a burgeoning education bureaucracy.

EMERGENCE OF THE CHANGE AGENT

The apparent shift in behaviors among district-level supervisors during the 1970s, away from tasks that directly supported instruction and toward managerial duties, can be traced to at least three factors, all of which originated or accelerated during the 1960s and 1970s. These factors include: (1) the increased federal role in public education, (2) the appearance of collective bargaining by teachers in many states, and (3) the increasing size and complexity of schools and school districts (Pajak, 1993).

During the 1960s, federal funds appropriated for education increased from $5.4 billion to $12 billion, which subsidized programs such as Operation Head Start, the Vocational Education Act, and the Elementary and Secondary Education Act. Federal policies such as the War on Poverty and efforts to racially integrate schools also had an effect, as well as educational innovations that included the "new" mathematics, team teaching, bilingual education, audiovisual technology, and open classrooms (Morris, 1976). The result of all these changes was that schools became instruments of national policy and supervisors came to be viewed primarily as "change agents" (Pajak, 1993).

Shortly after World War II, Benne (1949) recommended that educational leaders should become agents of change as a means of contributing to a more democratic society. A clearly defined social engineering perspective did, in fact, emerge in the 1960s and 1970s, and this perspective shifted the initiative for change from classroom teachers to district-level supervisors. Supervisors were told in the education literature that it was less important to be concerned with whether their behavior was democratic than with whether it was effective in bringing about change (McCoy, 1961). This position directly contradicted Dewey's collaborative problem solving and the supervision literature of the 1920s, 1930s, and 1940s that drew heavily on his thinking.

Supervision literature during the 1960s touted the change-agent role as a means of empowering supervisors who felt "alienated from the educational scene" (Klohr, 1965) and as a solution to the "state of confusion in many schools" (Babcock, 1965) that arose from "accelerating change" in American culture (Holmes & Seawell, 1965). Calls for supervisors to become change agents continued into the 1970s (Bagby, 1972; Harris, 1975), resulting in the observation that the terms "change" and "innovation" had acquired the status of "God words" among educators (Hughes & Achilles, 1971).

Responses to "the needs of our rapidly changing society" seemed to predominate over the needs of students and the problems of teachers and administrators among some authors (Ogletree, 1972; Sommerville, 1971). Much of the supervision literature during the 1960s and 1970s, in fact, was heavily concerned with gaining teacher compliance in accepting innovations. Action research became a means to "shatter complacency which results from long experience" (Heffernan & Bishop, 1965), rather than a way in which supervisors could solve problems in collaboration with teachers. Instead of helping teachers to change the situations in which they worked, supervisors as change agents were advised to be more concerned with changing teachers and their behavior (Drummond, 1964; MacDonald, 1966).

During the 1960s and 1970s, supervision authors often portrayed teachers as a source of "resistance" to change, who had to be overcome, rather than as a source of creative ideas and solutions to problems (Mosher & Purpel, 1972; Toepfer, 1973). Broad involvement in the change process was urged because of its "functional" value in overcoming resistance to change and ensuring that "changes are carried out" (Harris, 1966, 1969). Supervisors were to keep teachers informed so that they understood the rationale for the innovation and how implementation should occur (Toepfer, 1973).

Though probably necessary and undeniably admirable in their intentions, the social programs and educational innovations of the 1960s and 1970s effectively removed the initiative for change from educators in local schools. The long-standing tradition of leadership in supervision, based on democratic principles derived largely from the educational philosophy of Dewey, was thereby gradually dislodged (Pajak, 1993). As a result, supervision in education faced a loss of meaning and purpose—a crisis from which, in many respects, it has yet to emerge.

Increased militancy among teachers' unions during the 1960s added to the turmoil in education and made supervisors' traditional appeals to a single profession seem irrelevant (Kinsella, Klopf, Shafer, & Young, 1969). Supervisors had been in the forefront of efforts to give teachers more power and to involve them in decisions during the 1940s and 1950s. But collective bargaining effectively usurped the supervisor's tools of cooperative planning and problem solving, and reinterpreted decisions affecting instruction and curriculum as conditions of employment. A specially appointed ASCD Commission on Problems of Supervisors and Curriculum Workers struggled with the fact that unionization and collective bargaining in education suddenly placed district supervisors and curriculum directors in an untenable no man's land between management and labor (Kinsella et al., 1969; Young, 1969).

Throughout the 1970s, the notion of democratic leadership lost ground in the supervision literature to the more managerial view that leadership is a function of position in the organization and should be adaptable to fit the requirements of different situations. The increasing size and complexity of schools and school districts in the United States required supervisors to devote more time and attention to organizational goals, long-range planning, and strategies for change (Alfonso, Firth, & Neville, 1975; Campbell, 1977; Ogletree, 1972).

Theories of leadership from business management and industrial psychology, such as McGregor's Theory X and Theory Y, Blake and Mouton's Managerial Grid, and Reddin's 3-D Theory, became prominent in supervision textbooks (e.g., Sergiovanni & Starratt, 1979) as more school districts became large, bureaucratized organizations. Writers urged supervisors to select a leadership style based on utilitarian "contingencies" instead of philosophical or educational conviction. Several texts defined supervision and leadership in terms of "behaviors" (Harris, 1975; Sergiovanni & Starratt, 1979; Wiles & Lovell, 1975). Others suggested that effectiveness was enhanced by organizationally conferred status and recommended that supervisors lead others in a direction determined by the supervisor (Alfonso, Firth, & Neville, 1975). Business management theories and the concept of the supervisor of instruction as an agent of change within the district organization continued to dominate the supervision field well into the 1990s.

CHANGE AND STABILITY

From 1973 to 1978, the Rand Corporation conducted a national study of four substantively different federally funded programs intended to introduce and support innovative practices in the public schools (McLaughlin, 1990). The so-called "Change Agent Study" greatly influenced perceptions of planned change in education, concluding that local expertise, organizational routines, and resources available to support planned change efforts generated fundamental differences in the ability of practitioners to plan, execute, or sustain an innovative effort.

Following publication of the Rand study, several authors identified the presence of change facilitators as a key factor contributing to a school's or district's ability and willingness to implement innovative programs (Berman, 1981; Fullan, 1982; Hall & Hord, 1987). Instructional supervisors had been urged since the 1960s to be at the forefront of the change process and to define their role as change agents within the structure of the district organization. Early in the 1980s, Fullan (1982) indicated that central office supervisory support was critical for successful change in districtwide practice, but observed that little was known about the specific contribution of district-level staff in introducing and responding to new ideas, following through with innovative programs, and supporting implementation and continuation.

Loucks and Cox (1982) confirmed that district-level supervisors were involved in every stage of an instructional change program they scrutinized. Effective district-level supervisors were described as getting their hands "dirty" working in the school with teachers and administrators to find out what they need, arrange or give training, assist with implementation, support follow-up training, and help to maintain innovative practice once it is put into place.

The next year, Cox (1983) reported that district-level supervisors played an important part in the institutionalization of change:

From the Study of Dissemination Efforts Supporting School Improvement we have learned that . . . central office personnel—curriculum coordinators, program directors, and specialists—have emerged as significant actors in the process of change. In fact, central office staff may well be the linchpins of school improvement efforts, linking together the external assisters and the building level administrators and teachers. They appear to be the most appropriate local sources of assistance in actually using new practices (p. 10).

As linchpins of school improvement efforts, district-level "local assistors" were familiarizing themselves with the needs of students in individual schools in their districts; locating and helping select new practices; knowing the content of the new practice, its purpose, and the benefits that were to result from its use; helping to arrange and conduct training in the new practice; working with external assisters; arranging funding and other support from the district or other sources; obtaining endorsements for the new practice from the superintendent, school board, principal, and teachers; working with teachers who were already using the practice in the classroom; working out "bugs" and overcoming obstacles; assist-

ing in evaluation; and helping plan the continuation and institutionalization of the new practice (Cox, 1983).

Drawing data from 12 case studies, Huberman and Miles (1984) observed that district-level supervisors were very closely involved in the adoption and implementation of innovations:

Much of the district-level dynamism for school improvement came from the central office administrators, often coordinators or assistant superintendents for curriculum and instruction, who kept their eyes open for promising practices outside the district or energetically promoted a local product. The central office administrator thus became the prime advocate of the new practice, often reaching directly into the schools to implement it and thereby leaving the building level principals to play a secondary role (p. 271).

Other researchers reported that innovation and impetus for change in high schools frequently originated with the district office (Hall & Guzman, 1984). Recognizing this fact, Hall, Putman, and Hord (1985) called for more research into the role of central office supervisor as change agent:

The stereotype of the roles of district office staff that are held by the public at large and by teachers in school do not appear to be congruent with their actual activities. There is much to be done by researchers that can inform us about the functions of persons in the district office and much that district office personnel can do to become clear about their roles and functions and how they can be more effective, especially as it relates to facilitating change in schools (pp. 156–157).

Wimpelberg (1987) similarly suggested that the central office is a potentially powerful source of instructional leadership, given too little notice in the discussion of school effectiveness and improvement. He supported this notion with five propositions:

(1) Instruction in most schools is not likely to improve unless district leadership acts to forge linkages between schools and central office, among schools, and among teachers. (2) The best linkages are forged, not through centralized instructional prescriptions but through an exchange process in which the central office and school administrators simultaneously challenge and support each other. (3) The central office personnel with the highest potential for exercising instructional leadership are intermediate administrators who have the organizational authority to supervise and evaluate principals and the expert and referent authority to support them. (4) The primary responsibility of the intermediate administrator is to see that every school principal develops both a technical and cultural consciousness of the school. (5) The instructional leadership role of the central office administrator requires a new kind of intimacy with schools (pp. 106–111).

Research on the district-level supervisor as an agent of change indicated that an innovation has a significantly better chance of succeeding when the central office is involved from the outset (Cox, French, & Loucks-Horsley, 1987) because district supervisors play such a significant part in support of teacher change (Hord, Rutherford, Huling-Austin, & Hall, 1987). The implementation of innovations calls for careful, systematic planning that is often led by district-level supervisors (Madrazo & Hounshell, 1987) who monitor the progress of implementation of the innovation (Butt, 1981). Such findings led Oliva (1989) to propose that instigating change is what supervision is all about. He suggests that the nature of supervisors' roles offers a unique opportunity to lead change efforts, especially when supervisors have established a sense of trust with other school personnel.

Some evidence in the literature, however, indicates that the role of change facilitator is not easily attained by district-level supervisors. Hall and Guzman (1984) hypothesized that central office coordinators are spread so thin and are involved in so many basic maintenance activities in relation to the curriculum that they are often unable to serve as a dynamic force for change.

A more recent case study of an urban school district's capacity for systemic structural change and support of school-based innovations similarly indicated that overextending duties for central office supervisors resulted in diminished expertise and a lack of accountability (Bogotch, Brooks, MacPhee, & Riedlinger, 1992). Because central office personnel operated within a closed system, innovative thinking was severely limited to a narrow group of individuals. The researchers found that, given the large number of responsibilities that central office supervisors face, not much time is available for researching or soliciting new, external ideas (Bogotch et al, 1995).

On the other hand, Pajak (1989) notes that much of the work done by district-level supervisors has an "invisible" quality to it. Many of the tasks that supervisors engage in "either have intangible outcomes or take place outside the direct view of others and so go unnoticed" (p. 179). Due largely to their diverse responsibilities and the fragmented nature of their jobs, district-level supervisors often initiate and support a process of change, but the tasks related to actual implementation are accomplished by others. Successful district-level supervisors make suggestions, provide materials, and introduce information and ideas continually, while allowing groups of teachers to develop their own identities and ultimately select their own direction. The invisible and intangible nature of supervisory tasks is further amplified by the successful supervisor's tendency to "give credit" for success to others (Pajak, 1989).

The importance of stability or continuity in the operation of schools balanced against the imperative for change in existing programs has long been recognized (Harris, 1985; McLaughlin, 1990; Tanner & Tanner, 1987), but it is usually ignored. Harris (1985) described the supervisory dilemma regarding stability versus change as a continuum ranging from total resistance to any form of change in an organization to redesigning or changing many if not all practices associated with a particular operation. He observed that a distinction between supervision for change and supervision that is concerned with maintaining stability was long overdue. Schools are all too often overwhelmed with calls for reform in various guises, so a critical feature of central office support may lie in simply providing a stable environment with respect to school organizational patterns (Louis, 1989). When schools are confronted with mandates, multiple innovative programs, and new requirements, priorities become unclear and efforts are diffused. Anderson (1988) noted that diverse and often contradictory political pressures can immobilize supervisory

effectiveness. The resulting inability to focus on a single reform strategy will actually inhibit school improvement (Louis, 1989; McLaughlin, 1990). A school or district thus can suffer from too much change going on at any one time as well as from too little change.

The central office supervisor's role thus can be understood, paradoxically, as advocating and facilitating change, growth, and improvement, while simultaneously providing stability, predictability, and continuity to the district organization. Much supervisory work contributes to reducing uncertainty in the ambiguous, unpredictable, and unstable reality of schools. When supervisors are successful in providing necessary clarity, predictability, and stability, teachers and administrators respond by investing confidence in them, and more willingly follow the supervisor's subsequent introduction of uncertainty in the form of innovations that improve effectiveness or promote equity (Pajak, 1989). Stability and change are not mutually exclusive if one thinks of change in schools as an interactive and evolutionary process instead of a revolutionary process. Supervisors may function most effectively as "patient realists" who facilitate the emergence and development of changes within schools, which serve to gradually modify and rejuvenate the existing organizational culture (Pajak, 1989).

APPLICATIONS OF MINTZBERG'S FRAMEWORK

Consistent with the growing influence of business management theory on the practice of supervision at the time, two studies conducted in the early 1980s sought to document the work performed by district-level supervisors of curriculum and instruction by applying Mintzberg's (1973, 1975) ten categories of managerial behavior. These categories included: figurehead, leader, liaison, monitor, disseminator, spokesperson, entrepreneur, disturbance handler, resource allocator, and negotiator.

In the first instance, Sullivan (1980, 1982) used Mintzberg's categories as a framework for structured observation to classify the work of six instructional supervisors in a large metropolitan school district. She reported that 98 percent of supervisors' activities were consistent with Mintzberg's classifications, with especially high concentrations in the categories of resource allocator (30 percent), monitor (19 percent), and disseminator (16 percent). In a similarly structured study, Donmoyer and Neff (1983) observed central office curriculum directors in three different school districts, but supplemented Mintzberg's descriptive behavioral categories with field notes to gain insight into how the exhibited behaviors might relate and contribute to supervisory effectiveness.

The findings of Sullivan (1980) and Donmoyer and Neff (1983) complement each other in a number of ways. In each instance, supervisors' work schedules were found typically to be comprised of a variety of brief and fragmented activities. Both studies suggested, however, that supervisors have somewhat more control over the pace of their work and personally initiated more of the tasks in which they engaged than was reported in similar studies of principals and superintendents (e.g., Martin & Willower, 1981; Pitner, 1978). Instead of frantically responding to immediate crises and external forces, district-level supervisors were depicted as being more proactive and having more opportunity for individual interpretation and self-determination of behavior than their line administrator colleagues.

Sullivan (1980, 1982) and Donmoyer and Neff (1983) reported that the largest portion of time spent by central office supervisors was in verbal interactions that were generally self-initiated and involved others within the school organization. In both cases, the researchers highlighted the "monitoring" function of management—the process of actively seeking and receiving a wide variety of information about the organization. The finding that supervisors also spent a great deal of time "disseminating information" and "allocating resources," led Sullivan (1980) to conclude:

The supervisor's primary position is that of information broker, or hub of communication, and the major task accomplished through the exchange and filtering of information is that of maintaining day-to-day operation of the school system as an organization (p. 37).

Sullivan (1980) speculated further that the number and variety of individuals and organizational units with which supervisors interact represent an informal communication network. This network, which is constructed by the supervisor, facilitates the flow of information within the school district. Sullivan suggested that because supervisors are central to this network, they are able to control processes such as decision-making by selectively regulating the flow and content of information that they transmit to others.

In contrast to Sullivan's (1980) content-neutral observational data, Donmoyer and Neff's (1983) field notes documented that central office supervisors actually spent a substantial amount of time with curriculum- and instruction-related matters. They found that many observed tasks that appeared to be purely managerial were revealed by the participants in interviews to be related directly to "the content and process of teaching" (p. 25). Donmoyer and Neff reported that, although considerable time and energy were frequently spent resolving immediate and concrete problems, supervisors actually viewed themselves as dealing mainly with abstract, long-range issues.

Instead of depicting supervisors as victims of uncertainty and ambiguity, Donmoyer and Neff (1983) portrayed the lack of clearly prescribed duties as a source of autonomy and flexibility that enabled supervisors to "choose to behave in a quite unmanagerial way and still meet the requirements of their role" (p. 44). They suggested that more research was needed into the way that supervisors negotiated between "an action oriented environment of generally concrete problems and a substantive field often characterized by abstraction" (p. 24). Donmoyer and Neff concluded that:

[T]he curriculum leader's role should be a focal point both for those interested in questions of knowledge utilization and for those who wish to conduct research which will examine more thoroughly linkages between the organizational aspects and the curricular and pedagogical functions of schools (p. 48).

Donmoyer and Neff (1983) further suggested that, in order to comprehend what supervisors do, the focus of inquiry should be broadened beyond simply identifying and describing behaviors and counting the frequency of their occurence. The subjective experience of being a district-level supervisor should also be considered in any adequate conceptualization of the role. Only by considering both objective and subjective realities, they noted, could the role of district-level supervisor be fully appreciated and an understanding of what constitutes effectiveness achieved. Although Donmoyer and Neff began their research with a theoretical framework derived from business management theory, their study resulted in decidedly unbusinesslike recommendations.

STUDIES OF MEANING AND SUCCESS

By the 1980s, it became apparent that the absence of a clear conception of the district-level supervisory role had serious practical as well as theoretical implications (Costa & Guditus, 1984; Hall, Putman, & Hord, 1985). The ambiguity of tasks associated with the role made central office supervisory positions vulnerable, especially when resources became scarce (Anderson, 1988). An analysis of data in California, for example, showed that, during the period from 1930 to 1970, the number of general instruction and curriculum-related positions increased along with other district-level positions (Rowan, 1982). The number of instruction and curriculum positions, however, lagged behind other staff positions related to business operations, personnel management, guidance, and psychological services. Most striking was the finding that of 17 district-level staff position titles, those related to curriculum and instruction were the two least stable and least likely to survive from one five-year period to the next. The three most stable district-level positions were those related to business affairs, cafeteria services, and health (Rowan, 1982).

In 1982, the ASCD established a Task Force on Research on Central Office Supervision in response to concerns of the Association's members that over the previous decade, "the number of district-wide instructional supervisors [had] slowly but steadily declined" (Costa & Guditus, 1984). The ASCD Task Force, comprised of a number of noted scholars in the field of supervision, was charged with documenting the effectiveness of supervisory personnel. The implicit expectation was that the work of district-level supervisors could be described in precise and measurable terms (Anderson, 1988).

In a final report, the Task Force concluded that it may be impossible to develop a general measure of central office supervisor productivity and effectiveness because "the role expectations of the positions . . . [are] simply idiosyncratic to each situation" (Blumberg, 1984, p. 3). The report added that variety of duties and expectations that comprise the supervisory role suggests that "questions of effectiveness must be answered in the specific situation and not through any sort of broad measuring instrument." The Task Force report further noted that district office supervisors typically relied on "personal measures" of effectiveness such as a "sense" of rapport with teachers and a "sense" of being welcome in a school, rather than any objectively definable standard of performance (Blumberg, 1984). These conclusions echoed Donmoyer and Neff's (1983) observation that the personal and subjective realities of supervision were essential to truly understanding the role.

Hall, Putman, and Hord (1985) found very little literature addressing the position of district office supervisory personnel. Their interview-based research, along with the findings of others (Cox, 1983; Huberman & Miles, 1984), indicated that support from district-level supervisors was essential to the success of innovation and school improvement. The authors cautioned policy makers, therefore, that the consequence of reducing the number of district-level positions "can be long term bankruptcy of the district's instructional program" (Hall, Putman, & Hord, 1985, p. 42). They also advised district office supervisors to take responsibility for defining, clarifying, and legitimizing work activities associated with their role. The researchers indicated a need for intensive and ongoing ethnographic field studies of central office functioning.

As an alternative to the many earlier, broad-based, quantitative surveys of tasks and studies based on a priori constructs, Floyd (1986) suggested that qualitative methodology might provide insights into effective district-level supervision by focusing on subjective role conceptions shared by outstanding supervisors. She conducted a descriptive study based on in-depth, open-ended interviews with four practicing central office supervisors in Georgia who had won at least one of two statewide awards for outstanding performance. Floyd identified themes from transcribed interviews, with the intention of developing a theoretical explanation of the influence exerted by these "outstanding" district level instructional leaders.

Floyd (1986) proposed three interactive conceptual constructs that contributed to the influence that outstanding district office supervisors exerted—influence, credibility, and flexibility. The construct of flexibility was further subdivided into three component themes, which included a fragmented focus, paradoxical visibility, and authority ambiguity. She concluded that outstanding central office supervisors possessed highly developed capacities for dealing with conceptual complexity and recommended that training in cognition be included in preparation and professional development programs for supervisors.

In a more comprehensive, interview-based study of 10 successful central office supervisors in New York State and Georgia, Pajak (1986, 1989) concluded that the very characteristics that pose a problem of definition and clarity for researchers and policy makers appear to allow incumbents in the supervisory role to be effective. Diversity, ambiguity, fragmentation, and multiplicity, he suggested, provide the "requisite variety" (Weick, 1978) for supervisors to act effectively as mediums of information and help others make sense of what goes on in schools.

Pajak (1989) agreed with Sullivan (1982) that district-level supervisors are at the hub of communication patterns, but he noted that they are in a position to do much more than simply control the flow of information. He suggested that effective central office supervisors help others construct meaning around a core value, which one district-level leader described as "a sincere concern for the well being of children and a commitment to quality instruction for their benefit" (p. 10). According to Pajak, this core value represents the focal point around which the experiences, events, processes, and goals of successful school districts are organized through a contin-

uous process of interpretation, reinterpretation, and counter-interpretation of norms, roles, and tasks that is orchestrated by the central office supervisor for curriculum and instruction.

Pajak (1989) suggests that districtwide instructional leadership consequently requires an ability to influence and even change established norms, roles, and tasks that govern teacher and administrator behavior in order to ensure consistency with the core value of benefiting students through instruction. Changes mandated from above, either by agencies outside the district or from the central office itself, however, are likely to have little effect at the classroom level unless the interpretation of social reality that exists among teachers changes as well. By arranging for active teacher participation in processes of curriculum planning and staff development, successful central office supervisors encourage teacher ownership of changes for instructional improvement, as the existing collective definition of the situation is also structured and reformulated. Norms and expectations that prevail among teachers and administrators gradually approximate the core value, as ongoing discussion of issues related to instruction leads to renewed consensus of meaning (Pajak, 1989).

Successful supervisors compared the process of interpretation, reinterpretation, and counterinterpretation of reality to solving a jigsaw puzzle: it involves fitting together fragments to construct a whole. This construction of reality, through ongoing discussion of instruction at all levels within the school district, incorporates past, present, and future realities (Pajak, 1989). Interpretations of materials, resources, ideas, policies, and events coalesce into images and anecdotes that contribute to the district's cultural narrative, which in turn guides the enactment of professional roles and tasks. The complexity, diversity, and ambiguity of the instructional supervisor's position can be understood, according to Pajak (1989), as serving to enhance the supervisor's capacity to facilitate a rich interpretation of social reality in ways that can benefit students.

Supervisors reported that they consciously model professional norms of integrity and a willingness to work hard as they interact with teachers and administrators. Organizational norms of teamwork and cooperation, fairness and equality, and reciprocity are also deliberately reinforced by effective district-level supervisors as they attempt to define and redefine social interactions. Managing conflict and encouraging the ritual exchange and sharing of "credit" for success are other important supervisory functions that seem to facilitate the development of positive and stable normative definitions of social reality in school districts. This resolution of normative uncertainty provides clarification of expectations surrounding professional roles and coordination of those roles to accomplish broad instructional purposes and tasks (Pajak, 1989).

Several processes facilitated by supervisors apparently contribute to both clarification and coordination of roles performed within the district by simplifying and supplementing information available to teachers and administrators. Pajak (1989) suggests that these include: standardizing curriculum, materials, and routines as a way of ensuring equity and simplifying procedures; planning and setting goals at the classroom, department, school, and district levels to establish a consistent and predictable direction of effort; and establishing a network of overlapping task forces, work groups, and standing committees that enrich communication as a means of improving coordination, commitment, and professional growth.

Supporting the task of instruction may be a routine and fairly unglamourous aspect of the central office supervisor's role. Pajak (1989), however, notes that it is absolutely essential for ensuring the stable functioning of the organization at its technical core: in the classroom. He observes that the identification, location, and provision of resources by supervisors contributes routinely to the maintenance and improvement of quality instruction in classrooms. Information, in the form of practical ideas, and praise for accomplishment help to reduce psychological uncertainty among teachers and principals, making them more secure about what they are already doing and more willing to risk doing things differently in the future. The following supportive functions performed by district-level supervisors appear to be especially important in reducing ambiguity, uncertainty, and instability related to instructional tasks: securing resources for instructional improvement, locating materials and information, providing in-service opportunities, validating worth, building confidence, and developing a mutually reinforcing network of collegial support (Pajak, 1989).

Much of the influence exerted by central office supervisors, according to Pajak (1989), is "earned" through frequent interactions with teachers and principals, which generate trust, mutual respect, and understanding. Successful central office supervisors constantly renew their credibility at the building level by facilitating the work of teachers and principals and demonstrating personal competence and dedication. This mutual or reciprocal influence, however, is not contrived or strategically planned. Supervisors seem to consider reciprocity of influence to be a part of the natural order of things (Pajak, 1989).

The exchange of resources and information for support and cooperation from teachers and principals may be understood at a purely functional level. Supervisors, however, emphasize that attending to "little things" that facilitate teachers' work has symbolic significance as well. Beyond the mundane functional level of exchange, a more abstract dimension of professional exchange exists, which relates to meaning, values, and professional growth. Successful district-level leaders view themselves as fostering higher degrees of achievement among other professionals in the service of children. Such supervisors strive to empower others, improve their competence, and increase their willingness to accept responsibility for the quality of instruction. Thus, rather than directly exercising personal or positional influence, successful supervisors view their work in terms of facilitating the expertise of others (Pajak, 1989).

As a transactional leader, the central office supervisor functions primarily as a resource for teachers and principals, helping to reduce uncertainty by performing and expediting routine tasks that promote feelings of security and trust among people working in the local schools. Pajak proposes that the supervisor receives support and cooperation in exchange for this reduction of uncertainty and is subsequently allowed by teachers and administrators to *introduce* uncertainty in attempting to improve general effectiveness or equity. Thus,

transactions at the practical level serve to define reality within the district as stable, yet capable of change, growth and development (Pajak, 1989).

Successful supervisors also function as transformational leaders who exercise moral influence by personally representing and advocating the core value of the education profession—benefiting students through instruction. Successful supervisors elevate routine processes into events that have a moral and symbolic meaning derived from the core value. By facilitating the interpretation and reinterpretation of norms, roles, and tasks around the core value, successful supervisors help principals and teachers renew their commitment and collectively engage in constructing a districtwide narrative of social reality that reflects this ideal (Pajak, 1989).

WORKING "BACKSTAGE"

Successful supervisors often use theatrical imagery while discussing their work. Pajak reports (1986, 1989) that they describe it as "invisible" and say that it occurs "backstage" or "behind the scenes." He proposed that a theatrical metaphor may be useful, therefore, to supplement the mechanistic metaphors that commonly dominate descriptions of how schools operate. Much of the work of district-level supervisors can, thus, be understood as happening "backstage" of the official "onstage" public performance enacted by teachers, principals, the superintendent, and the school board.

When viewed in terms of dramaturgical imagery, the district office role is seen to involve more than merely technical adjustments to the instructional program and efforts to control information. Supervisors among Pajak's (1989) participants noted that it is not sufficient for educators simply to do a good job; others must *perceive* them as doing a good job. Both functional and expressive dimensions of events and processes are considered by effective district supervisors, including an awareness and anticipation of reactions from multiple audiences, such as students, parents, teachers, administrators, and taxpayers (Pajak, 1986, 1989).

Frequent contact with teachers is necessary for district-level supervisors of curriculum and instruction to establish the trust required for teachers to allow them access to the "backstage" reality of the classroom. An obstacle to trust is the psychological and social distance that may develop due to the difference in status accorded supervisors and teachers by the organization. Successful central office supervisors deliberately seek to diminish this hierarchical gap between teachers and themselves by being open, approachable, and trustworthy in their behavior. This allows supervisors to work more as helpful backstage "directors" than as theater "critics" of the instructional performances exhibited "onstage" by teachers in classrooms and by principals in schools (Pajak, 1989).

Due to the inherent tension between local school and districtwide perspectives, working successfully with principals is one of the most imposing challenges that central office supervisors face. This struggle between local autonomy and the need for consistency, equity, and coordination of operations throughout the district has been heightened with the recent movement toward site-based management.

Principals ideally view the central office supervisor as a resource and service provider, someone who can be trusted to work "behind the scenes," rather than as a competitor or "spy" for the superintendent. Establishing and maintaining credibility with principals, therefore, is an important consideration for district-level supervisors. Those supervisors who have had personal experience as building-level administrators may find it easier to establish positive working relationships with principals because such prior experience provides a foundation for trust. First-hand knowledge of the principal's role may also make the expectations of novice supervisors more realistic (Pajak, 1989).

Although personal experience as a principal can ease the initial transition into the role of supervisor, it is no guarantee of long-term success. District supervisors must continuously prove themselves to principals by demonstrating a willingness to listen and consider their problems and ideas. District supervisors sometimes even assist "behind the scenes" by advocating a principal's position in the district office. On the other hand, successful supervisors carefully guard against becoming entirely subordinated to building administrators by insisting that principals take the process of instructional improvement seriously. Supervisors and principals ideally establish a reciprocal relationship of professional cooperation based on mutual respect, understanding, and consistency of expectations (Pajak, 1989).

Some central office supervisors, usually assistant or associate superintendents, exercise formal line authority over principals (Bogotch & Brooks, 1994). Even these administrators have to rely more often on indirect sources of influence, Pajak (1989) reports, because of the considerable autonomy that exists at the local school level. The principal is nominally the instructional leader of the school, and successful central office supervisors scrupulously avoid undermining this designation. Successful supervisors essentially view their responsibilities as encouraging, supporting, and complementing the principals' "onstage" efforts to improve the quality of instruction in the local schools (Pajak, 1989).

The theatrical imagery used by Pajak's (1989) participants acknowledges that teachers and principals are not passive or powerless objects. They are autonomous beings who think, evaluate, and communicate with each other and take action independent of supervisory control. Teachers and principals are active participants as well as audiences of each others' performances in the construction of social reality, particularly at the school and classroom levels.

The notion of supervisors working backstage or behind the scenes is also useful to understand how the supervisory role relates to that of the superintendent. Most superintendents deal primarily with issues originating in the district's environment, like finance and politics. Supervisors focus much more on matters internal to the district, especially those related to instruction and curriculum. One could say that the superintendent works with matters of external adaptation that affect and are dependent on the district's public "image." The supervisor, in contrast, concentrates on maintaining internal integration or the collective "vision" among professionals within the district that gives meaning and direction to their work. In keeping with their backstage perspective, successful supervisors emphasize that the superintendent should always "take the credit" for success and be "in the limelight" in dealings with the public and external agencies (Pajak, 1989).

The work of supervisors involves much more than simply tending to impression management, however. The collective agreement concerning goals and expectations that supervisors facilitate among the professional educators in a district is tangibly manifested in the curriculum, which is the medium through which instruction is transmitted and enacted. The curriculum can be viewed as a kind of "script" that guides behavior related to instruction, and provides concrete meaning and direction to the diverse and various tasks that district-level supervisors, administrators, and teachers all engage in. The social reality that adults create in schools, whether consciously or unconsciously, is another script that students live day after day. Ideally, these districtwide scripts represent consensual narrative understandings that "set the stage" for students' experiences in school. Such narratives are important because they teach students who they are and what they are capable of becoming. Instead of enacting tragedies or comedies, Pajak (1989) urges educators to "author scripts wherein students are prepared to experience their lives as heroic epics in which they determine their own destinies" (p. 235).

CONTENT SPECIALISTS

Supervision often conforms to the organizational context in which it operates (Firth & Eiken, 1982). Therefore, district supervisory structure or configuration is a salient factor when considering the role of district-level supervisors. An important decision in organizing leadership at the central office, for example, is whether supervisory functions are better performed by curriculum generalists or content specialists.

Little research exists on the relative merits of employing curriculum generalists or specialists to supervise instruction; however, arguments have been made for the importance of both (Oliva, 1989). The generalist ideally is expert at teaching, knows what constitutes good general instructional methods, has a broad view of curriculum which facilitates comparisons across grade levels and content areas, has an overall perspective of curriculum and instructional programs, and can serve as a unifying force. Specialists possess many of the same skills, but their expertise and attention are typically concentrated on a particular grade level or content area.

The importance of specialized content knowledge to successful supervision has been recognized by many writers. In their model of clinical supervision, Mosher and Purpel (1972) note significant implications of subject matter expertise for the analysis of what is to be taught in classrooms:

Clinical supervision is predicated on specialized, expert knowledge of content and curriculum. The supervisor is, first, a content specialist, because it is not feasible to analyze teaching effectiveness independently of the content of what is being taught (p. 83).

Oliva (1989) reasons that it is imperative to provide curriculum specialists to support instruction, especially at the secondary level, "because content and methods have changed—and continue changing—so rapidly that no generalist can possibly keep up with the changes in all fields" (p. 72). He further suggests that specialists can usefully provide technical help to teachers regarding assessment techniques, instructional support materials, instructional methodologies, and content knowledge in their areas of expertise.

Nolan and Francis (1992) have called for a shift in the focus of supervision, from exclusive emphasis on general instructional considerations to the inclusion of content-related issues and questions. They argue that the supervisory process is most effective when it addresses content-specific strategies and methods as well as general pedagogical matters.

Other authors, however, express concern about the limited view of curriculum and instruction that may be typical of subject specialists. They warn that it is crucially important for specialists to understand how their particular subject relates to other content areas in the curriculum. Many experts consequently support a role for both curriculum generalists and content specialists in school supervision (Firth & Eiken, 1982; Oliva, 1989; Tanner & Tanner, 1987).

Smith (1990) uncovered differences between generalists and specialists in the importance they attached to several dimensions of supervisory practice, as part of a larger study sponsored by the ASCD in 1989 (Pajak, 1990). Smith surveyed 324 central office supervisors in the United States and Canada who had been nominated as outstanding instructional leaders and assessed their perceptions of the importance of 12 dimensions of supervisory practice, both as their jobs currently existed and as they ideally should be. All 12 dimensions of practice were viewed by district-level supervisors as important. Ranked by mean score with respect to importance to the central office role "as it should be," the dimensions are as follows:

1. communication,
2. planning and change,
3. staff development,
4. instructional program,
5. motivating and organizing,
6. curriculum,
7. problem solving and decision-making,
8. personal development,
9. community relations,
10. service to teachers,
11. research and program evaluation, and
12. observation and conferencing.

In terms of perceived importance of their roles as they currently existed, statistically significant differences were found between district-level curriculum generalists and content specialists for four dimensions. District-level generalists viewed planning and change, problem solving and decision-making, and research and program evaluation as more important to their role than subject-matter specialists did. Content specialists, in contrast, considered service to teachers to be more important to their role as it currently existed than did curriculum generalists (Smith, 1990). Service to teachers and observation and conferencing were viewed as more important by content specialists with respect to how their job

should be enacted. Curriculum generalists, on the other hand, perceived research and program evaluation and personal development as ideally more important to their role.

Although the duties performed by curriculum generalists and specialists are often similar, the role incumbents that Smith (1990) surveyed viewed the relative importance of their various responsibilities differently. Specialists tended to be oriented toward working with individual teachers to provide quality instruction in schools. Generalists placed more importance on solving problems and planning changes to improve instructional programs districtwide. These findings led Smith to conclude that both generalist and specialist positions were necessary for a comprehensive supervisory program that would address both teacher and organizational issues.

Adoption of the National Education Goals in 1990 by President Bush and the nation's governors stimulated new interest in curriculum content, especially in the areas of mathematics and science, which were targeted specifically for improvement as "Goal 5." Partly in response, various national professional associations in both science and mathematics education have launched initiatives to improve curriculum and instruction in those content fields. Such efforts include: the Agenda for Action and the Curriculum and Evaluation Standards, both published by the National Council of Teachers of Mathematics (Adamson, 1994), as well as the National Science Education Standards, Project 2061 of the American Association for the Advancement of Science, and the National Science Teachers Assocation's Scope, Sequence, and Coordination Project (Anderson & Pratt, 1995).

A national survey by Madrazo and Motz (1983) asked teachers and school administrators to rank a range of duties for science supervisors in the order that best fit their needs. The results were as follows:

1. instruction,
2. curriculum,
3. staff development,
4. implementation,
5. management,
6. assessment, and
7. assignment, transfer, and equalization of teacher load.

Anderson and Pratt (1995) note that these findings are very consistent with those reported by Loucks and Cox (1982) concerning the contributions made by district-level supervisors to change and improve schools.

Beisenherz and Yager (1991) argue convincingly for the employment of subject-matter supervisors as a sound way to stimulate improvement of a school district's instructional program. These authors offer an extensive list of responsibilities for district-level science supervisors related to goals, curriculum, instructional policies, assistance to teachers, in-service training and other forms of professional development, and program funding that contribute to effective science instruction.

A study by Adamson (1994) lends credence to the practice of including content specialists on district office staffs. Examining the effects of several factors on school and district mathematics innovations, Adamson found that most variation among school and district mathematics programs was explained by the structural configuration of district mathematics leadership. Schools and districts that employed mathematics specialists at the central office level were significantly more mathematically innovative than districts that only had curriculum generalists at the district level. This pattern held true despite differences in district and school size, location, and per pupil expenditure.

Adamson (1994) used four categories associated with implementing innovations—developing supportive organizational arrangements, training, consultation and reinforcement, and monitoring (Hord, Rutherford, Huling-Austin, & Hall, 1987)—as a framework for studying perceptions of educational leaders regarding their roles as change agents in mathematics programs. After comparing responses of leadership personnel from innovative school districts, she found that district-level mathematics supervisors perceived a larger number of supportive functions as being important to the mathematics program than principals and department heads did. These supportive behaviors included: seeking and providing materials, seeking and acquiring funds, developing positive attitudes, increasing knowledge, reviewing information, holding workshops, modeling and demonstrating use of innovation, assisting individuals in solving problems, sharing tips informally, facilitating small groups in problem solving, providing practical assistance, administering end-of-workshop questionnaires, and conferencing with teachers about the progress of innovation use.

The assigned duties of curriculum generalists and specialists often overlap. Research on the merits of staffing with some combination of these roles is very sparse. Expert opinion and some evidence suggest, however, that generalists and specialists view the importance of their various responsibilities differently. Subject-matter specialists interpret their roles in terms of providing service and advice directly to individual teachers, whereas curriculum generalists are more oriented to districtwide concerns. Curriculum specialists can contribute to innovations in the instructional program of their particular content area and may place greater emphasis on a range of activities that support instruction than do school-based leadership personnel.

RESTRUCTURING

Greater teacher participation in administrative decisions, more parental choice and involvement, deregulation and decentralization of policy making, and site-based management are prominent changes that are being widely touted during the 1990s as solutions to a variety of problems facing public education. Such governance innovations, which collectively fall under the rubric "school restructuring," may drastically alter the roles and functions of teachers, building-level administrators, and central office supervisors.

Restructuring requires new forms of leadership to better initiate and sustain change efforts, as well as empower and support school staff (Bamberger, 1991; Evans, 1993). Supportive, facilitative, and democratic forms of leadership have long been part of the supervision tradition. But advocates of restructuring suggest a need to review the roles of

supervisors and established supervisory practice in terms of promoting the interests of teachers and students under alternative and emerging forms of school organization.

School restructuring does not necessarily mean that district office leadership is no longer relevant. In fact, restructured schools are changing the conditions of leadership (Murphy, 1991). Fullan (1993a) recently declared that neither top-down nor bottom-up strategies will work to improve schools and called for a systemic change process involving two-way relationships of pressure, support, and continuous negotiation. Calling for a fundamental shift of mind about the concept of educational change itself, he proposes that the new problem of change is centered on this question: What would be required to make the educational system a learning organization where change would be a normal part of work?

District-level support of schools involved with restructuring is recognized as extremely important (Bamberger, 1991; Hill & Bonan, 1991; Louis, 1989). Without the visible and active endorsement of the superintendent, efforts to restructure schools are very likely to end in failure (Bogotch & Brooks, 1994; Murphy & Hallinger, 1993; Rowley, 1992; Tewel, 1991). Superintendents are also in the strategic position to provide or withhold financial resources, political support, and protection to a school involved in the process of restructuring (Prestine, 1993). Superintendents can buffer a restructuring school from external interference, allow a school to bend the district's policies, and indirectly support restructuring efforts by working to eliminate barriers to change (Tewel, 1994).

Lack of district support has been documented as contributing to the failure of site-based governance councils in the Salt Lake City school system (Malen & Ogawa, 1988). A more recent case study of a junior high school involved with Theodore Sizer's Coalition of Essential Schools indicated that the restructuring process is inhibited when districtwide support of school-level efforts is withdrawn or inconsistent (Prestine, 1993). Another report on three case studies of Baltimore elementary schools indicated that support from the district office was essential to maintaining site-based innovation (Slavin, Madden, Shaw, Mainzer, & Donelly, 1993). Tension between district and local school policies was problematic, however, and continued district support became less evident with the departure of a reform-minded superintendent.

Louis (1989) argues that district-level support for school improvement efforts may be characterized by the adage "less is more" with respect to rules and regulations. She suggests that two especially salient dimensions affecting the quality of the relationship between school and district are the degree of engagement and the level of bureaucratization. Engagement requires shared goals and objectives and depends upon the consistency of clear communication and mutual coordination. The level of bureaucratization depends on whether control is enacted through rules and regulations or through personal relationships. Engagement appears to support school restructuring efforts, while a strong bureaucratic rule orientation serves as an inhibitor of such efforts. For restructuring to succeed, the bureaucratic rule orientation should attend to central policy setting and support for school-based improvement instead of centralized control over student learning outcomes (Louis, 1989).

Louis (1989) believes that, while district support of restructuring efforts is vital to sustaining innovation, such support does not necessarily mean that the district office directly participates in innovation at the school level. The primary function of district-level support is to help maintain the vision set by the school rather than become intimately involved in day-to-day operations. The quality of the innovation is best maintained by the school-level personnel (Louis, 1989).

Other writers indicate the need for district-level leaders to play a more active part in restructuring efforts. Supervisory practices that foster a trusting and supportive environment confirm district-level support and influence positively the ability of administrators and teachers to collaborate for school improvement (Chudek, 1989). District-level supervisors who voice and actively demonstrate their endorsement of collaboration, risk taking, and change efforts at the school level foster a culture that values restructuring. They can also support and assist restructuring by arranging release time for school staff members and by providing training in team building, renewal, and process skills (Elmore, 1990). According to this view, the district office must be transformed from a bureaucracy to a series of "service centers that advocate and facilitate innovation" (McWalter, 1992, p. 10). The major challenge of restructuring for the central office then becomes one of assisting schools and guaranteeing quality in a system that values variety rather than uniformity (Hill & Bonan, 1991).

Central office supervisors may also facilitate restructuring by helping to form networks among teachers and schools that share this common interest. Isolated outposts of innovation rarely survive, and access to a network of other schools involved in restructuring can provide needed support for teachers' professional development (Slavin et al, 1993). A summary of eight longitudinal case studies of restructuring schools suggested that staff development which encourages the "cross-fertilization of ideas" may be especially useful (Murphy & Hallinger, 1993). Cross-fertilization of ideas occurred when faculty from one restructuring school visited and worked with the faculty of another. Another study similarly reported that a key to success for an elementary school involved in a restructuring project was the teachers' ability to develop collegial relationships with other teachers, both inside and outside their schools (Short & Greer, 1993).

Some authors suggest that district-level supervisors can facilitate restructuring by introducing innovative approaches to accountability. Traditional, top-down, bureaucratic models of accountability generally appear to inhibit the restructuring process. Duignan (1990) suggests that Rizvi's (1990) idea of horizontal accountability complements the concept of schools as learning organizations because it emphasizes responsibility to peers and school communities. According to Cohen (1990), the local district should reorient "schools toward performance, rather than procedure . . . the district provides enabling tools and resources rather than restraints" (p. 265). The central office may also have to manage the district environment to ensure that schools are not subjected to premature demands from the public for information regarding student performance (Louis & King, 1993). Restructured schools need alternatives to address accountability, with the question of accountability being redefined collaboratively by the

school, the district office, and the school board (Bamberger, 1991; Hill & Bonan, 1991).

The distinction between district office supervisors as administrative officers with line authority and supervisors as staff members responsible for supporting principals and teachers seems to have gotten lost, or at least confused, among the numerous calls for decentralization and site-based governance. Both line and staff supervisors are typically and unfairly lumped together indiscriminately as members of the faceless bureaucracy that is portrayed as the source of organizational inadequacies.

A number of authors in educational supervision have argued for some time that central office supervisors operate more effectively as staff than in line positions (Dull, 1981; Harris, 1985; Lovell & Wiles, 1983; Oliva, 1984; Wiles, 1967). Indeed, line and staff central office supervisors view their duties quite differently (Smith, 1990). Supervisors in line positions place greater importance on supervisory tasks related to organizational issues, including community relations, planning and change, communication, classroom observation, problem solving and decision-making, research and program evaluation, and motivating and organizing. Supervisors in staff positions are more consciously dedicated to providing service to teachers in the classroom (Smith, 1990).

An important point to consider in light of school restructuring is that supervisors as support staff represent neither "top" nor "bottom" perspectives. Their position in the district structure defies dichotomous thinking of the sort that insists on locating mutually antagonistic positions at different levels of the organization. The very ambiguity of staff positions may make such supervisors uniquely suited for facilitating the simultaneous "top-down" *and* "bottom up" efforts that successful restructuring seems to require.

The potential effectiveness of staff supervisors to facilitate restructuring, however, is compromised both by their lack of formally sanctioned authority to influence principals and by a loss of credibility with teachers for having left the frontline of the classroom. Supervisors who specialize in supporting instruction traditionally lack the "cache" of change agents or program managers because the latter concepts are more consistent with the logic of a professional bureaucracy.

If the school restructuring movement continues, it is very likely that the role and function of the supervisor will undergo a metamorphosis along with the roles of teacher and principal. This would require a comprehensive and simultaneous change in both the culture of the school and the culture of supervision. While this seems a daunting challenge, organizational restructuring may never succeed without a parallel reculturing of this sort.

A QUESTION OF BALANCE

Fullan (1993b) asserts that a focus on the changing relationship between schools and districts is missing in the research on restructuring schools. He views research that places the district office in the position of simply waiving requirements and allocating resources as incomplete. Fullan suggests that a systematic, symbiotic relationship is required between restructuring schools and school districts. An emerging body of literature is contributing to our understanding of this reciprocally interdependent relationship.

Research on effective schools during the 1970s and 1980s that included the district office supervisor as an element of study confirmed the importance of the central office supervisory position (Wimpelberg, 1988). Most of the available evidence has indicated that instruction is not likely to improve in many schools without leadership from the central office that can forge links between schools and the district office, among schools, and among teachers within schools (Fullan, 1982; Pajak & Glickman, 1989; Wimpelberg, 1988).

As school districts move away from a hierarchical structure and toward a more decentralized and participative form of organization, however, tensions can increase between the press for local school autonomy and the need for a degree of system-level accountability and coordination of programs (Chapman, 1990; Elmore, 1990). Furthermore, as leadership is shared and becomes diffused, it is less likely to be confined to a single role or be prescribed by a set of tasks assigned exclusively to a particular individual (Elmore, 1990; Tye, 1992). The resulting conflicts and confusion can lead to inconsistencies and even failure of sincere attempts to restructure within a district.

Rowley's (1992) 12-year case study of the Sequoia Valley School District in California, for example, found that the district encouraged a strong philosophy of school-based management and site councils, but the board and superintendent also established a number of competing programs over a period of time which resulted in oppositional dynamics for change. The researcher concluded that a coordinated balance between centralization and decentralization in restructured school settings had not been achieved, and suggested that an optimal balance might result in a simultaneous codevelopment of schools and the district office.

Several other authors have suggested that educators and policy makers should sort out and determine in advance which decisions ought to be assigned to the school site and which to the district office in order to achieve better coordination (Cohen, 1990; Pajak & Payne, 1991; Tyack, 1990; Wimpelberg & Boyd, 1990). Paradoxically, an increase in both centralization and decentralization may be required because participative models for decision-making are "not equally appropriate for all tasks" (Tyack, 1990, p. 187).

An "integrated decentralization," involving simultaneously strong local diversity and centralized coordination, has been suggested by Murphy (1989) as a way to attain an effective balance between district-level control and local autonomy. He suggests that the central office can maximize the benefits of integrated decentralization by shifting away from monitoring and enforcing policy and moving toward providing services, facilitating, and coordinating. He proposes that the central office should attend most closely to those schools that have problems and unrealized potential, whereas schools that are already successful should have maximum freedom to pursue their own destinies.

Although favoring the idea of integrated decentralization, Pajak (1992) encourages central office supervisors to take a more proactive position toward restructuring. He suggests

that a new balance of supervisory functions is emerging between schools and district offices, which generally reflects a movement away from bureaucratic monitoring and standardization and toward greater tolerance and facilitation of diversity in schools and classrooms. He notes that the 12 traditional supervisory functions are likely to be enacted differently in school districts engaged in restructuring.

According to Pajak (1992), as school districts decentralize supervisory duties and rely on shared decision-making at the school level, information should flow more freely throughout the district and action can be initiated at any level. *Communication* becomes richer and more inclusive, and more opportunities are created for people to participate and commit themselves to an emerging vision. *Staff development* needs are identified by teachers themselves, who actively plan programs and make presentations to colleagues. The *instructional program* in a restructuring school district is more likely to be coordinated by groups of teachers who share the same students, subject, or grade level and who engage in frequent discussions about teaching. *Planning and change* are guided by a clear vision and sense of mission within the district instead of being directed by uniform policies. Innovation, experimentation, and risk taking are encouraged in order to rethink and redesign how things are done.

Motivating and organizing in restructuring districts are based on group participation and contribution to the achievement of collective aims as measured by multiple indicators of success. Classroom *observation and conferences* are tasks more often performed by teachers themselves in peer coaching arrangements. Less able teachers learn from observing their more competent colleagues, and beginning teachers are paired with more experienced mentors. *Curriculum* is developed and coordinated by teachers on grade-level or subject-matter teams who are familiar with student needs and interests. Curriculum is viewed as a relevant, vital, and never-ending process instead of a sterile document that sits on a shelf. *Problem solving and decision-making* are delegated to teachers and administrators who are closest to problems of practice in restructuring districts. They have the autonomy and flexibility to deal with problems immediately and are encouraged to experiment and learn while doing so (Pajak, 1992).

In restructuring school districts, *service to teachers* in the form of resources and materials is targeted toward helping groups achieve the agendas they have set for themselves. Teachers rely more often on their colleagues to both give and receive assistance and support. *Personal development* is determined by individuals and groups as they reflect on their values, beliefs, and practices, and redefine their roles, responsibilities, and relationships in the school to move beyond current practice. *Community relations* are focused on educating parents and taxpayers about what is happening in schools and involving them in decisions at the local school level to attain consensus from diverse perspectives and constituents. *Research and program evaluation* in restructuring districts are aimed toward making classrooms and schools centers of inquiry. New knowledge is generated through action research, which informs teachers' decisions about practices that work best for students in each school (Pajak, 1992).

A case study of a school district in Florida, which sought to transform its organization to reflect a collaborative ideology, reported consistency between supervisory behaviors and these same 12 dimensions of supervisory practice (Fitzgerald, 1991). Congruent with Pajak's (1992) viewpoint, supervision generally shifted from emphasizing control, enforcement, and monitoring to providing service, fostering site-based management and shared decision-making, and facilitating professional growth of the instructional staff (Fitzgerald, 1993).

Fitzgerald (1993) also reports that central office supervisors in the restructuring district he studied coordinated the strengths of different groups within the district to create a dynamic that gave individuals and groups ownership and responsibility for problems and situations. He found that district-level supervisors made a critical difference in the success of restructuring by facilitating the flow of information among the schools involved. They also facilitated the movement of needed resources and coordinated programs and staff development at the department, school, and district levels (Fitzgerald, 1993).

Another study examined the distribution of responsibility for the 12 dimensions of supervision in schools and districts involved with the national Coalition of Essential Schools and the Georgia–based Program for School Improvement (Rhoades, 1995). Central office supervisors viewed most supervisory functions as being shared equally between the school and the district, whereas principals perceived the school as having assumed most responsibility. District-level supervisors and principals agreed that community relations, staff development, and observation and conferencing functions should be situated at the school level. Supervisors believed more strongly than principals, however, that duties related to planning and change, communication, curriculum, instructional program, service to teachers, problem solving and decision-making, program evaluation, motivating and organizing, and personal development should be shared equally between schools and districts (Rhoades, 1995).

The size of a school district may be a mitigating factor in defining the appropriate balance between district and school-level control. Wills and Peterson (1995) reported a difference between larger and smaller districts in Maine, as superintendents sought to reduce uncertainty and chaos, which were apparently heightened by the attempt to restructure. In smaller districts, effective superintendents engaged directly in supervisory roles, including coordination of curriculum and staff development, while revising staff evaluation procedures to validate and assess change. In larger districts, effective superintendents more often delegated supervision of restructuring to assistant superintendents; however, they engaged in frequent communication with them. Superintendents in larger districts also exercised strong administrative control at meetings of steering committees, board committees, administrative teams, and various community groups.

Murphy (1995) studied Kentucky superintendents whose districts were engaged in "serious transformational reform efforts," to gain an understanding of the ways in which the roles of superintendents and other central office staff change in response to school restructuring. Superintendents perceived an abandonment of bureaucratic control by central office staffs and the emergence of a service orientation, which emphasized support and facilitation. The 35 participating superintendents viewed their own role as changing in terms of working more democratically, acting as enablers in the background rather than directing efforts from the apex of the organization.

Central office staff members are portrayed by Murphy (1995) as having experienced two types of "growing pains." The first resulted from a tremendous increase in work demands. The nascent service orientation required more meetings and more paperwork associated with new tasks and responsibilities. Superintendents believed that additional district office staff were needed to deal effectively with this increased workload. A second theme reflected "a sense of loss among central office staff." The definition of their jobs was challenged as schools became more autonomous and supervisors had less direct daily contact with schools. Murphy concludes that superintendents and their staffs are essential for promoting the successful evolution of new roles for principals, teachers, and students, and calls upon policy makers to carefully nurture this transformation of the central office and its functions.

Tewel (1995) cautions that restructuring can result in a psychological paralysis of central office staff at the very time that their services are most needed. A remedy is suggested by Bogotch and Brooks (1994), who examined relations between principals and central offices within a context of school restructuring in an urban district. The authors found that innovations seemed to be most successful when accompanied by "a clear district philosophy embodied in superintendency leadership" and "staff development for both central office and school level personnel." They conclude that staff development is especially crucial for overcoming traditional structural-functional relationships that hinder innovation and reorientation of values consistent with restructuring. Staff development may be the key to accomplishing a simultaneous transformation of central office and school-level roles.

SUMMARY AND CONCLUSIONS

The school district central office instructional supervisory position first emerged during the late nineteenth and early twentieth centuries as urban districts grew larger and more centralized. One of the earliest descriptions of the role, prior to the 1920s, represented district supervision as emphasizing democratic principles and decentralized, cooperative practice in education, and as offering a counterpoint to newly centralized administrative power.

Literature published during the 1930s and 1940s by the Department of Supervisors and Directors of Instruction and by the Association for Supervision and Curriculum Development during the 1940s and 1950s consciously advocated John Dewey's group deliberation, scientific reasoning, cooperative problem solving, and reflective practice. By the early 1960s, this body of professional literature was specifically defining supervision as the expression of democratic leadership. District supervision seemed to be conceived more in terms of democratic process than in terms of organizational structure.

Serious research on the district central office supervisory role is meager, especially in comparison to the number of studies of teachers, principals, and superintendents. Most studies of district supervisors of curriculum and instruction have been doctoral dissertations, usually focusing on supervisors in a single state and typically using survey methodology. With a few exceptions, the earliest available research was completed during the 1960s and concentrated primarily on identifying tasks performed by district supervisors. Many studies surveyed supervisors and others to compare perceptions of real and ideal supervisory behaviors. Both supervisors and members of their role set tended to favor supervisory practice that relied on interpersonal skills to support teachers and improve classroom instruction.

During the 1970s, however, these types of studies and replications of earlier work began uncovering comparatively lower perceived frequencies of supervisor involvement in the tasks most highly prized by teachers. Teachers increasingly viewed supervisors as performing more administrative, managerial, and evaluative functions. Growing pressure for supervisors to engage in administrative tasks was mentioned in the professional literature of the time, which attributed this trend to increasing federal and state mandates, regulations, assessments, and testing requirements.

The 1970s witnessed the emergence of the district supervisor as a "change agent" in a burgeoning educational bureaucracy. State and federal involvement in education, along with changing demographics, resulted in a rapid growth in the size and complexity of many school districts. Collective bargaining simultaneously redefined curricular and instructional issues as conditions of employment. Supervisors, most of whom held staff positions, became isolated in a no man's land between teachers and administrators.

Federal initiatives generally sought to institutionalize values consistent with schooling in a democratic society, but teachers were often portrayed as obstacles or resistance to be overcome. Some authors advocated the deliberate use of group process as a tool to shatter complacency and ensure teacher compliance. Although the goals of federal and state programs were usually commendable, their implementation effectively removed the initiative for change from the hands of educators in local schools. Dewey's philosophy of cooperative problem solving, which provided the roots for supervision during much of the twentieth century, became suddenly dislodged. In its place, perspectives derived from business management began to appear and eventually predominated in the most popular supervision textbooks.

The 1980s witnessed the most serious efforts to understand the central office supervisory role, although most research focused primarily on the concept of the supervisor as an agent of change. District supervision was related in several studies to school effectiveness and the successful adoption and implementation of innovations. Supervisors' responsibilities and overextension of duties, however, made the change agent's role very difficult. Several authors and researchers called attention to the supervisor's parallel responsibility to provide stability and predictability within the district organization. For the most part, however, inquiry into this stabilizing function continues to be neglected.

Studies based on observations and interviews with district-level supervisors began to appear in the early 1980s. Some of the studies applied categories of behavior derived from business-management literature. The supervisory role was fragmented and disjointed in its enactment, according to the studies, though it allowed more opportunity for personal control. Supervisors engaged primarily in large numbers of interpersonal interactions with others, while constantly seeking and receiving a variety of information about the organization. Supervisors' autonomy and flexibility allowed them to behave in unmanagerial ways to accomplish tasks that they viewed as closely related to improving curriculum and instruction.

Several authors called attention to the invisibility and lack of definition of the central office supervisory position, which resulted in vulnerability during times of financial constraint. An ASCD Task Force was formed to address this issue. It echoed the findings of other studies that emphasized the idiosyncratic and subjective realities of district-level supervision in its report and called for ethnographic approaches to understanding the district supervisor's role. During the mid-to-late 1980s, several qualitative studies portrayed the supervisor as a facilitator of "meaning-making" within the district organization. According to one such study, this function encourages the interpretation, reinterpretation, and counterinterpretation of organizational norms, roles, and tasks around a core value of commitment to providing high-quality instruction for the benefit of students. Related to this view is the theatrical notion of the district supervisor working backstage to enhance the performance of teachers, principals, and superintendents relative to instruction and curriculum.

The restructuring movement of the 1990s raises new questions about the relevance of district central office supervision of curriculum and instruction. Innovations like site-based management, participative governance, and calls for schools to become learning organizations, however, are actually remarkably consistent with early twentieth-century supervisory principles of democracy, decentralization, and cooperative problem solving. The evidence suggests that district-level commitment and active support of school restructuring are essential to the success of such efforts.

The central office supervisory position is once again being reconfigured to adapt to a new organizational reality. Key issues for the district appear to be: establishing an optimal balance between local autonomy and central control, reducing the conflict and confusion that often increase as leadership is diffused and roles become less clearly defined, and dealing with the explosion of information that occurs as teachers and principals are empowered.

With American education in the midst of a restructuring movement, it appears that district-level supervisors of curriculum and instruction can still play an important part in supporting the improvement efforts of schools. As districts adopt more decentralized forms of organization and the locus of decision-making shifts to the local schools, however, the prescriptive and inhibiting rule orientation that gained ascendancy during the 1960s and 1970s is being abandoned in favor of approaches that support school-based improvement efforts. At the same time that teachers are participating more in school governance and the principal's role is changing from instructional leader to leader of instructional leaders, the district-level supervisory role is returning to its original function of supporting the efforts of principals and teachers. District-level supervisors are again called upon to be supportive facilitators who are committed to sharing leadership while motivating teachers to pursue their school's mission in tandem with the district's vision.

SUGGESTIONS FOR FURTHER RESEARCH

The role of the central office supervisor of curriculum and instruction during any particular period during the twentieth century has been characterized by a constant state of evolution while addressing ever-changing educational realities. It is not surprising, therefore, that a clear, concise definition of the parameters of the role remains elusive, especially within the context of current restructuring in education. Although research efforts underscore the importance of the district supervisor's role in fostering the success of innovation and school improvement, more in-depth investigation of this role is needed.

Conceptual images of district-level supervisors have tended to emphasize the regulatory functions of the role. Only a handful of studies have examined the cognitive and normative structures and processes that provide meaning and stability to life in schools. Clearly, answers to the driving issues regarding the role of the central office supervisor in today's

environment call for greater attention to qualitative methods of inquiry. Survey methodology, though useful in framing the research agenda in earlier decades, does not provide the optimal venue for exploring "how," "what," and "why" questions—and it is to these more probing issues that the focus of inquiry should be drawn.

The literature is replete with indications that teachers need and value support and assistance at the classroom level. In this era of restructuring, how can supervisors of curriculum and instruction, who are ideally situated in a liaison capacity between the central office and the school, maximize this unique position to provide much needed support for teachers? How can the finely honed interpersonal skills of supervisors be employed to ensure meaning and purpose in education? Why do some district structures provide more fertile ground for the expression and enactment of democratic principles than others?

Here, at the threshold of the twenty-first century, lies an abundance of research opportunities for those interested in studying district-level supervision. Restructuring has given teachers, principals, parents, and the general public greater voice and choice in matters relating to education. Expectations for classrooms and schools change almost daily as competing agendas vie for influence at the local, state, and national levels. It will be incumbent upon researchers to answer this central question: What conditions of leadership must be in place to nurture the core value of the education profession—benefiting students through instruction?

REFERENCES

Adamson, P. (1994). The influence of structure and leader perceptions on mathematics innovativeness in selected schools and districts (doctoral dissertation, The University of Georgia). *Dissertation Abstracts International, 55,* 2649A.

Afifi, J. W. (1980). A study of the actual and ideal role perceptions of instructional supervisors in the public schools in the counties of Tennessee (doctoral dissertation, East Tennessee State University). *Dissertation Abstracts International, 41,* 1849A-1850A.

Alfonso, R. J., Firth, G. R., & Neville, R. F. (1975). *Instructional supervision: A behavior system.* Boston: Allyn and Bacon.

Anderson, R. D. & Pratt, H. (1995). *Local leadership for science education.* Dubuque, IA: Kendell/Hunt Publishing.

Anderson, R. H. (1988). Political pressures on supervisors. In L. N. Tanner (Ed.). *Critical Issues in Curriculum,* 87th Yearbook (pp. 60–82). Chicago, IL: National Society for the Study of Education.

Association for Supervision and Curriculum Development. (1948). *Group processes in supervision.* Washington, D.C.: Author.

Association for Supervision and Curriculum Development. (1951). *Instructional leadership in small schools.* Washington, D.C.: Author.

Association for Supervision and Curriculum Development. (1960). *Leadership for improving instruction,* 1960 Yearbook. Washington, D.C.: Author.

Ayer, F. C. & Barr, A. S. (1928). *The organization of supervision: An analysis of the organization and administration of supervision in city school systems.* New York: D. Appleton.

Babcock, C. D. (1965). The emerging role of the curriculum leader. In R. R. Leeper (Ed.). *Role of supervisor and curriculum director*

in a climate of change, 1965 Yearbook (pp. 50–64). Washington, D.C.: ASCD.

Bagby, G. (1972). Help wanted: Instructional leadership. *NAASP Bulletin, 57,* 40–46.

Bamberger, R. (1991). *Developing leaders for restructuring schools: New habits of mind and heart* (Report of the National LEADership Network Study Group on Restructuring Schools). Washington, D.C.: National LEADership Network.

Barr, A. S. & Burton, W. H. (1926). *The supervision of instruction.* New York: D. Appleton.

Barr, A. S., Burton, W. H., & Brueckner, L. J. (1938). *Supervision: Principles and practices in the improvement of instruction.* New York: D. Appleton-Century.

Beach, T. A. (1976). The perceptions of teachers, principals, and supervisor of the instructional supervisory support services in the public schools of Tennessee (unpublished doctoral dissertation, The University of Tennessee). *Dissertation Abstracts International, 37,* 5466A.

Beisenherz, P. C. & Yager, R. E. (1991). The school science supervisor: A necessity for a quality program. *School Science and Mathematics, 91*(4), 152–156.

Benne, K. D. (1949). Democratic ethics in social engineering. *Progressive Education, 26*(7), 201–207.

Berman, P. (1981). Educational change: An implementation paradigm. In R. Lehmig & M. Kane (Eds.). *Improving schools: Using what we know* (pp. 253–286). Beverly Hills: Sage.

Blumberg, A. (1984). *Report of the A.S.C.D. Committee on Central Office Supervisors.* Alexandria, VA: ASCD.

Bobbitt, F. (1913). *The supervision of city schools* (12th Yearbook, Part I, National Society for the Study of Education). Chicago: University of Chicago Press.

Bogotch, I. & Brooks, C. (1994). Linking school level innovations with an urban school district's central office. *Journal of School Leadership, 4*(1), 12–27.

Bogotch, I. E., Brooks, C., MacPhee, B., & Riedlinger, B. (1992). An urban district's knowledge of and attitudes towards school-based innovation. Paper presented at the annual meeting of the American Educational Research Association, San Francisco, CA.

Bogotch, I. E., Brooks, C., MacPhee, B., & Riedlinger, B. (1995). An urban district's knowledge of and attitudes towards school-based innovation. *Urban Education, 30*(1), 5–26.

Boucree, O. E. (1981). Role perceptions and expectations of central instructional supervisory personnel as held by principals and teachers (unpublished doctoral dissertation, George Peabody College for Teachers of Vanderbilt University, 1979). *Dissertation Abstracts International, 41*, 4221A.

Bridges, E. M. (1982). Research on the school administrator: The state of the art, 1967–1980. *Educational Administration Quarterly, 18*(3), 12–33.

Brown, K. R. (1975). The leadership role of the elementary school supervisor as perceived by elementary teachers and supervisors in selected school systems of Northeast Louisiana (unpublished doctoral dissertation, Northeast Louisiana University). *Dissertation Abstracts International, 36*, 1933A.

Burch, B. G. & Danley, W. E., Sr. (1980). The instructional leadership role of central office supervisors. *Educational Leadership, 37*, 636–637.

Burton, W. H. (1927). *Supervision and the improvement of teaching.* New York: D. Appleton.

Butt, R. L. (1981). The transitional curriculum. *Educational Leadership, 39*(2), 117–119.

Callahan, R. (1962). *Education and the cult of efficiency.* Chicago: University of Chicago Press.

Callahan, R. E. & Button, H. W. (1964). Historical change of the role of the man in the organization: 1865–1950. In D. E. Griffiths (Ed.). *Behavioral science and educational administration* (63rd yearbook of the National Society for the Study of Education) pp. 73–92. Chicago: University of Chicago Press.

Campbell, A. (1977). Are instructional leaders still needed? *Educational Leadership, 35*(1), 11–14.

Cantrell, R. T. (1979). Analysis of the function of the curriculum director in staff development programs of Georgia school systems with pupil enrollment between 2,500 and 10,000 (unpublished doctoral dissertation, Auburn University). *Dissertation Abstracts International, 40*, 1766A.

Capper, G. H. (1981). A study of supervisory procedures and behaviors in relation to teacher morale in selected Cook County schools. *Dissertation Abstracts International, 41*, 4223A.

Cardenas, J. A. (1966). Role expectations for instructional supervisors as expressed by selected supervisors, administrators, and teachers. *Dissertation Abstracts International, 27*, 2022A.

Carlton, C. G., Jr. (1970). Role of instructional supervisors as perceived by teachers and principals in selected Florida elementary schools. *Dissertation Abstracts International, 31*, 4406A.

Carman, B. D. (1970). Roles and responsibilities in general supervision of instruction: A synthesis of research findings, 1955–1969. *Dissertation Abstracts International, 31*, 4406A–4407A.

Cawelti, G. (1980). Effective instructional leadership produces greater learning. *Thrust for Educational Leadership, 9*(3), 8–9.

Cawelti, G. & Reavis, C. (1980). How well are we providing instructional improvement services? *Educational Leadership, 38*, 236–240.

Chapman, J. D. (1990). School-based decision-making and management implications for school personnel. In J. Chapman (Ed.). *School-based decision-making and management* (pp. 221–244). New York: Falmer Press.

Chudek, R. A. (1989). Administrative support of collaboration: A district school improvement experience (doctoral dissertation, University of Oregon). *Dissertation Abstracts International, 50*, 11A.

Cohen, M. (1990). Key issues confronting state policymakers. In R. F. Elmore (Ed.). *Restructuring schools: The next generation of educational reform* (pp. 250–287). San Francisco: Jossey-Bass.

Colbert, J. E. (1966). A study of effective and ineffective supervisory behavior. *Dissertation Abstracts International, 27*, 2306A.

Cook, K. E. (1983). The relationship between teacher perceptions of supervisory behavioral style and perceived teacher burnout. *Dissertation Abstracts International, 44*, 0925A.

Costa, A. & Guditus, C. (1984). Do district-wide supervisors make a difference? *Educational Leadership, 41*(6), 84–85.

Cotton, K. & Savard, W. G. (1980, December). *The principal as instructional leader. Research on school effectiveness project: Topic summary report.* Portland, OR: Northwest Educational Laboratory.

Cox, P. L. (1983). Complementary roles in successful change. *Educational Leadership, 41*(3), 10–13.

Cox, P. S., French, L. C., & Loucks-Horsley, S. (1987). *Getting the principal off the hotseat: Configuring leadership and support for school improvement.* Andover, MA: Regional Laboratory for Educational Improvement of the Northeast and Islands.

Crews, C. (1979). Instructional supervision: The winter and the warm. *Educational Leadership, 36*(7), 519–521.

Culbertson, J. A. (1988). A century's quest for a knowledge base. In N. J. Boyan (Ed.). *Handbook of research on educational administration* (pp. 3–26). New York: Longman.

Danley, W. E. & Burch, B. G. (1978). *Supervisory roles: A study of supervisor's commitments.* Memphis, TN: Tennessee Association for Supervision and Curriculum Development and the Bureau of Educational Research and Services, Memphis State University.

Department of Supervisors and Directors of Instruction. (1932). *Supervision and the creative teacher,* 5th Yearbook. New York: Teachers College, Columbia University.

Department of Supervisors and Directors of Instruction. (1933). *Effective instructional leadership,* 6th Yearbook. New York: Teachers College, Columbia University.

Department of Supervisors and Directors of Instruction. (1934). *Leadership at work.* Washington, D.C.: Author.

Department of Supervisors and Directors of Instruction. (1943). *Scientific method in supervisory programs,* 7th Yearbook. New York: Teachers College, Columbia University.

Dewey, J. (1929). *The sources of a science of education.* New York: Horace Liveright.

Donmoyer, R. & Neff, A. R. (1983). Work activities of central office curriculum leaders: An observational study. Unpublished manuscript.

Douglass, J. M., Jr. (1979). Role of instructional supervisors as perceived by instructional supervisors and superintendents in Alabama. *Dissertation Abstracts International, 40*, 5414A.

Drummond, H. D. (1964). Leadership for human change. *Educational Leadership, 22*(3), 147–148.

Dull, L. W. (1981). *Supervision: School leadership handbook.* Columbus, OH: Merrill.

Duignan, P. A. (1990). School-based decision-making and management: Retrospect and prospect. In J. Chapman (Ed.). *School-based decision-making and management* (pp. 327–346). New York: Falmer Press.

Elliott, E. C. (1914). *City school supervision.* New York: World Book.

Elmore, R. F. (1990). *Restructuring schools: The next generation of educational reform.* San Francisco: Jossey-Bass.

Esposito, J. P., Smith, G. E., & Burbach, H. J. (1975). A delineation of the supervisory role. *Education, 96*(1), 63–67.

Evans, R. (1993). The human face of reform. *Educational Leadership, 51*(1), 19–23.

Evans, R. L., Jr. (1975). Task expectations for the elementary supervisor role as expressed by elementary teachers and supervisors (unpublished doctoral dissertation, The Ohio State University). *Dissertation Abstracts International, 36,* 4901A–4902A.

Ferguson, F. M. (1976). A study of practices of elementary school supervisors (K–8) in the state of Louisiana as perceived by supervisors of instruction, principals, and teachers (unpublished doctoral dissertation, The Louisiana State University). *Dissertation Abstracts International, 36,* 3292A.

Fidler, D. A. (1986). Supervisory skills, knowledge, and values perceived as important by special education supervisors and their teachers. *Dissertation Abstracts International, 47,* 2541A.

Firth, G. R. & Eiken, K. P. (1982). Impact of the schools' bureaucratic structure on supervision. In T. J. Sergiovanni (Ed.). *Supervision of teaching* (pp. 153–169). Reston, VA: National Association of Secondary School Principals.

Fitzgerald, J. H. (1991). Management practices: A case study of district level supervisors and directors of curriculum and instruction in one school district (unpublished doctoral dissertation, University of South Florida). *Dissertation Abstracts International, 52,* 3781A.

Fitzgerald, J. H. (1993). Management practices: A profile of district-level supervisory activity in one school district. *Journal of Curriculum and Supervision, 8*(2), 128–139.

Floyd, M. K. (1986). Meanings that outstanding central office instructional supervisors associate with their role (unpublished doctoral dissertation, The University of Georgia). *Dissertation Abstracts International, 47,* 1946A.

Floyd, M. K. (1987). Flexibility and central office supervisors: The instrumental function of fragmentation, invisibility, and ambiguity. Washington, D.C. Paper presented at the annual meeting of the American Educational Research Association (ERIC Document Reproduction Service No. ED 282 311).

Franseth, J. (1972). *Supervision in rural schools: A report on beliefs and practices.* Washington, D.C.: U.S. Department of Health, Education, and Welfare (ERIC Document No. ED 054 873).

Fraser, K. P. (1980). Supervisory behavior and teacher satisfaction. *The Journal of Educational Administration, 18,* 224–231.

Fullan, M. (1982). *The meaning of educational change.* New York: Teachers College Press.

Fullan, M. (1993a). *Change forces: Probing the depths of educational reform.* Philadelphia: The Falmer Press.

Fullan, M. (1993b). Coordinating school and district development in restructuring. In J. Murphy & P. Hallinger (Eds.). *Restructuring schooling: Learning from ongoing efforts* (pp. 143–164). Newbury Park, CA: Corwin Press.

Gantt, G. A. (1977). Organizational and personal sources of role conflict involving principals and supervisors in select Georgia school systems (unpublished doctoral dissertation, The University of Georgia). *Dissertation Abstracts International, 38,* 6431A.

Glanz, J. (1977). A historicism and school supervision: Notes toward a history. *Educational Leadership, 35*(2), 149–154.

Gott, P. L. (1967). *The role of the curriculum worker in Georgia.* Carrollton, GA: Division of Education.

Hall, G. E. (1987). The role of district office personnel in facilitating school-based change: Hypotheses and research dilemmas. In R. Vandenberge & G. E. Hall (Eds.). *Research on internal change facilitation in schools* (pp. 163–180). Leuven, Belgium: Academic Publishing Company.

Hall, G. E. & Guzman, F. M. (1984). Sources of leadership for change in high schools. Paper presented at the annual meeting of the American Educational Research Association, New Orleans, LA (ERIC Document Reproduction Service No. ED 250 815).

Hall, G. E. & Hord, S. (1987). *Change in schools: Facilitating the process.* Albany, NY: State University of New York Press.

Hall, G. E., Putman, S., & Hord, S. (1985). District office personnel: Their roles and influence on school and classroom change: what we don't know. Paper presented at the annual meeting of the American Educational Research Association, Chicago, IL.

Harris, B. M. (1963). *Supervisory behavior in education.* Englewood Cliffs, NJ: Prentice Hall.

Harris, B. M. (1966). Strategies for instructional change: Promising ideas and perplexing problems. In J. Raths & R. R. Leeper (Eds.). *The supervisor: Agent for change in teaching* (pp. 85–95). Washington, D.C.: ASCD.

Harris, B. M. (1967). Roles of supervisors and curriculum workers. In R. P. Wahle (Ed.). *Toward professional maturity of supervisors and curriculum workers* (pp. 1–12). Washington, D.C.: ASCD.

Harris, B. M. (1969). New leadership and new responsibilities for human involvement. *Educational Leadership, 26*(8), 739–742.

Harris, B. M. (1975). *Supervisory behavior in education* (2nd ed.). Englewood Cliffs, NJ: Prentice Hall.

Harris, B. M. (1985). *Supervisory behavior in education* (3rd ed.). Englewood Cliffs, NJ: Prentice-Hall.

Heffernan, H. & Bishop, L. J. (1965). In R. R. Leeper (Ed.). *Role of supervisor and curriculum director in a climate of change,* 1965 Yearbook (pp. 87–143). Washington, D.C.: ASCD.

Hill, P. T. & Bonan, J. (1991). *Decentralization and accountability in public education.* Santa Monica, CA: RAND Publications.

Holder, C. W. (1977). Task analysis of selected leadership personnel responsible for instructional supervision and/or curriculum development in local school systems of Georgia (doctoral dissertation, The University of Georgia). *Dissertation Abstracts International, 38,* 4546A.

Holmes, G. W. & Seawall, W. H. (1965). Further studies for administrators and supervisors—purpose and scope. *High School Journal, 48,* 242–249.

Hopkins, D. W. (1982). The identification and validation of critical competencies for instructional supervisors in Georgia. *Dissertation Abstracts International, 43,* 218A.

Hord, S., Rutherford, W., Huling-Austin, L., & Hall, G. E. (1987). *Taking charge of change.* Alexandria, VA: ASCD.

Hosic, J. F. (1920). The democratization of supervision. *School and Society, 11,* 331–336.

Huberman, A. M. & Miles, M. (1984). *Innovation up close: How school improvement works.* New York: Plenum.

Hughes, L. W. & Achilles, C. H. (1971). The supervisor as a change agent. *Educational Leadership, 28*(3), 840–843.

Humphries, J. D. (1981). Factors affecting the impact of curriculum innovation on classroom practice: Project complexity, characteristics of local leadership (unpublished doctoral dissertation, The University of Georgia). *Dissertation Abstracts International, 42,* 2471A.

Kessler, R. (1992). Shared decision-making works! *Educational Leadership, 50*(1), 36–38.

Kinsella, B. W., Klopf, G. J., Shafer, H. T., & Young, W. T. (1969). *The supervisor's role in negotiation.* Washington, D.C.: ASCD.

Klohr, P. R. (1965). Looking ahead in a climate of change. In R. R. Leeper (Ed.). *Role of supervisor and curriculum director in a climate of change,* 1965 Yearbook (pp. 144–163). Washington, D.C.: ASCD.

Kyle, J. D. (1984). Teacher perception of the instructional specialist: Essential behavior expectations, role preference, and selected sources of effective instructional support. *Dissertation Abstracts International, 41,* 3268A.

Loftus, W. J. (1980). The role of the central office instructional leader in selected public elementary school districts. *Dissertation Abstracts International, 40,* 5675A.

Loucks, S. F. & Cox, P. L. (1982). *School district personnel: A crucial role in school improvement efforts.* Paper presented at the annual meeting of the American Educational Research Association, New York (ERIC Document Reproduction Service No. ED 250 779).

Louis, K. S. (1989). The role of the school district in school improvement. In M. Holmes, K. A. Leithwood, & D. F. Musella (Eds.). *Educational policy for effective schools* (pp. 145–167). New York: Teachers College Press.

Louis, K. S. & King, J. A. (1993). Professional cultures and reforming schools: Does the myth of Sisyphus apply? In J. Murphy & P. Hallinger (Eds.). *Restructuring schooling: Learning from ongoing efforts* (pp. 216–250). Newbury Park, CA: Corwin Press.

Lovell, J. T. & Phelps, M. S. (1976). *Supervision in Tennessee: A study of the perceptions of teachers, principals, and supervisors.* Murfreesboro, TN: Tennessee Association for Supervision and Curriculum Development and the Office of Continuing Education, Middle Tennessee State University.

Lovell, J. T. & Wiles, K. (1983). *Supervision for better schools* (5th ed.). Englewood Cliffs, NJ: Prentice Hall.

Lucio, W. H. & McNeil, J. D. (1979). *Supervision: A synthesis of thought and action.* New York: McGraw-Hill.

MacDonald, J. D. (1966). Helping teachers change. In J. Raths & R. R. Leeper (Eds.). *The supervisor: Agent for change in teaching* (pp. 1–10). Washington, D.C.: ASCD.

Madrazo, G. M. & Hounshell, P. B. (1987). The role expectancy of the science supervisor: Results of research in science supervision. *Science Education, 71*(1), 1–2.

Madrazo, G. M. & Motz, L. (1983). Do we link school science to science supervisors as a resource? In *Science teaching: A profession speaks,* NSTA Yearbook (pp. 76–78). Washington, D.C.: NSTA.

Malen, B. & Ogawa, R. T. (1988). Professional-patron influence on site-based governance councils: A confounding case study. *Educational Evaluation and Policy Analysis, 10*(4), 251–270.

Martin, W. J. & Willower, D. J. (1981). The managerial behavior of high school principals. *Educational Administration Quarterly, 17*(1), 69–90.

Mayo, B. R. (1983). The relationship between perceptions of organizational characteristics and role conflict among instructional supervisors in Virginia (unpublished doctoral dissertation, University of Virginia). *Dissertation Abstracts International, 43,* 3173A.

McCoy, R. F. (1961). *American school administration.* New York: McGraw-Hill.

McKernan, J. (1987). Action research and curriculum development. *Peabody Journal of Education, 64*(2), 6–19.

McLaughlin, M. W. (1990). The RAND change agent study revisited: Macro perspectives and micro realities. *Educational Researcher, 19,* 11–16.

McNeil, J. D. (1982). A scientific approach to supervision. In T. J. Sergiovanni (Ed.). *Supervision of teaching,* 1982 Yearbook (pp. 18–34). Alexandria, VA: ASCD.

McWalter, P. (1992). Handing accountability and authority to schools. *The School Administrator, 49*(1), 9–10.

Melord, M. S. (1979). A comparison of role and role expectations of supervisors in select public school districts in Kentucky. Unpublished doctoral dissertation, Western Kentucky University.

Miller, D. W. (1959). Teachers' appraisals of selected supervisory practices. *Dissertation Abstracts International, 20,* 3157A.

Mintzberg, H. (1973). *The nature of managerial work.* New York: Harper & Row.

Mintzberg, H. (1975). The manager's job: Folklore & fact. *Harvard Business Review, 53,* 49–61.

Morris, R. B. (1976). *Encyclopedia of American history.* New York: Harper & Row.

Mosher, R. L., & Purpel, D. E. (1972). *Supervision: The reluctant profession.* Boston: Houghton-Mifflin.

Murphy, J. T. (1989). The paradox of decentralizing schools: Lessons from business, government, and the Catholic Church. *Phi Delta Kappan, 70*(10), 808–812.

Murphy, J. (1991). *Restructuring schools: Capturing and assessing the phenomena.* New York: Teachers College Press.

Murphy, J. (1995). Restructuring in Kentucky: The changing role of the superintendent and the district office. In K. Leithwood (Ed.). *Effective school district leadership: Transforming politics into education* (pp. 117–133). Albany, NY: State University of New York Press.

Murphy, J. & Hallinger, P. (1993). Restructuring schooling: Learning from ongoing efforts. In J. Murphy & P. Hallinger (Eds.). *Restructuring schooling: Learning from ongoing efforts* (pp. 251–272). Newbury Park, CA: Corwin Press.

Nasca, D. (1976). How do teachers and supervisors value the role of the elementary supervisor? *Educational Leadership, 33,* 513–518.

Nolan, J. & Francis, P. (1992). Changing perspectives in curriculum and instruction. In C. D. Glickman (Ed.). *Supervision in transition* (pp. 30–43). Alexandria, VA: ACSD.

Ogletree, J. R. (1972). Changing supervision for a changing era. *Educational Leadership, 29,* 507–510.

Oliva, P. F. (1984). *Supervision for today's schools.* New York: Longman.

Oliva, P. F. (1989). *Supervision for today's schools.* New York: Longman.

Pajak, E. (1986, April). The backstage world of central office supervision. Paper presented at the annual meeting of the American Educational Research Association, San Francisco, CA.

Pajak, E. (1989). *The central office supervisor of curriculum and supervision: Setting the stage for success.* Boston: Allyn and Bacon.

Pajak, E. (1990). Dimensions of supervision. *Educational Leadership, 48*(1), 78–80.

Pajak, E. (1992). A view from the central office. In C. D. Glickman (Ed.). *Supervision in transition* (pp. 126–138). Alexandria, VA: ASCD.

Pajak, E. (1993). Change and continuity in supervision and leadership. In G. Cawelti (Ed.). *Challenges and achievement of American education,* 1993 Yearbook (pp. 158–186). Alexandria, VA: ASCD.

Pajak, E. & Glickman, C. (1989). Dimensions of school district improvement. *Educational Leadership, 46*(8), 61–64.

Pajak, E. & Payne, P. (1991, April). Principals' perceptions of district office roles and school reform. Paper presented at the annual meeting of the American Educational Research Association, Chicago, IL.

Perrine, W. G. (1978). Teacher and supervisor perceptions of leadership behaviors of elementary supervisors (unpublished doctoral dissertation, Rutgers University, The State University of New Jersey). *Dissertation Abstracts International, 39,* 590A–591A.

Perrine, W. G. (1984). Teacher and supervisor perceptions of elementary science supervision. *Science Education, 68*(1), 3–9.

Pitner, N. J. (1978). Descriptive study of the everyday activities of suburban school superintendents: The management of information (doctoral dissertation, The Ohio State University). *Dissertation Abstracts International, 39,* 6448A.

Prestine, N. (1993). Feeling the ripples, riding the waves: Making an essential school. In J. Murphy & P. Hallinger (Eds.). *Restructuring schooling: Learning from ongoing efforts* (pp. 32–62). Newbury Park, CA: Corwin Press.

Raske, D. E. (1979). The role of general school administrators responsible for special education programs. *Exceptional Children, 45*(8), 645–646.

Rhoades, J. M. (1995). A study of school and district responsibility for dimensions of supervisory practice in schools undergoing restructuring (doctoral dissertation, The University of Georgia). *Dissertation Abstracts International, 56,* 1613A.

Rizvi, F. (1990). Horizontal accountability. In J. Chapman (Ed.). *School-based decision-making and management* (pp. 299–324). New York: Falmer Press.

Rowan, B. (1982). Instructional management in historical perspective: Evidence on differentiation in school districts. *Educational Administration Quarterly, 18*(1), 43–59.

Rowley, S. (1992). School district restructuring and the search for coherence. Paper presented at the 1993 annual meeting of the American Educational Research Association, San Francisco, CA.

Sergiovanni, T. J. & Starratt, R. J. (1979). *Supervision: Human perspectives* (2nd ed.). New York: McGraw-Hill.

Short, P. M. & Greer, J. T. (1993). Restructuring schools through empowerment. In J. Murphy & P. Hallinger (Eds.). *Restructuring schooling: Learning from ongoing efforts* (pp. 165–187). Newbury Park, CA: Corwin Press.

Simonton, S. H. (1990). Tasks of the system-level instructional leader as perceived by superintendents, principals, and system-level instructional leaders in Georgia (doctoral dissertation, The University of Georgia). *Dissertation Abstracts International, 51,* 2975A.

Slavin, R. E., Madden, N. A., Shaw, A. H., Mainzer, K. L., & Donnelly, M. C. (1993). Success for all: Three case studies of comprehensive restructuring of urban elementary schools. In J. Murphy & P. Hallinger (Eds.). *Restructuring schools: Learning from ongoing efforts* (pp. 84–113). Newbury Park, CA: Corwin Press.

Smith, B. (1983). *A literature review on what makes central office supervisors effective.* Athens, GA: The University of Georgia, Effective Supervisors Project of the ASCD.

Smith, G. E. (1975). Teachers' perceptions of supervisors in Virginia (unpublished doctoral dissertation, University of Virginia, 1974). *Dissertation Abstracts International, 35,* 2512A.

Smith, R. (1990). The importance of the twelve dimensions of effective supervisory practice derived from educational literature as perceived by selected district-level supervisors (doctoral dissertation, The University of Georgia). *Dissertation Abstracts International, 51,* 2625A.

Sommerville, J. C. (1971). Leadership that "rocks the boat": A boat that needs rocking! *Educational Leadership, 29*(1), 45–49.

Spears, M. D. (1980). A comparison of the observed and ideal roles of the supervisor of instruction as perceived by supervisors, principals, and teachers in the state of Louisiana. *Dissertation Abstracts International, 41,* 2397A.

Speiker, C. A. (1976). *Curriculum leaders: Improving their influence.* Alexandria, VA: ASCD.

Steller, A. (1994). Taking stock on Central Street. *ASCD Update, 36*(8), 2.

Stone, C. R. (1929). *Supervision of the elementary school.* Boston: Houghton Mifflin.

Sturges, A. W. (1979). Instructional supervisors: A dichotomy. *Educational Leadership, 36,* 586–589.

Sullivan, C. G. (1980). The work of the instructional supervisor: A functional analysis (unpublished doctoral dissertation, Emory University). *Dissertation Abstracts International, 41,* 3068A.

Sullivan, C. G. (1982). Supervisory expectations and work realities: The great gulf. *Educational Leadership, 39*(6), 448–451.

Tanner, D. & Tanner, L. (1987). *Supervision in education: Problems and practices.* New York: Macmillan.

Tewell, K. J. (1991). A case study of reform. *The American School Board Journal, 178*(10), 30–33.

Tewell, K. J. (1994). Central office blues. *The Executive Educator, 16*(3), 31–35.

Tewell, K. J. (1995). Despair at the central office. *Educational Leadership, 52*(7), 65–68.

Thomas, K. O. (1981). The status and role perceptions of the supervisor of instruction in Louisiana public schools (unpublished doctoral dissertation, University of Southern Mississippi). *Dissertation Abstracts International, 42,* 2430A–2431A.

Toepfer, C. F. (1973). The supervisor's responsibility for innovation. *Educational Leadership, 30*(8), 740–743.

Tyack, D. (1974). *The one best system: A history of American urban education.* Cambridge, MA: Harvard University Press.

Tyack, D. B. (1990). "Restructuring" in historical perspective: Tinkering toward utopia. *Teachers College Record, 92*(2), 170–191.

Tye, K. A. (1992). Restructuring our schools: Beyond the rhetoric. *Phi Delta Kappan, 74*(1), 8–14.

Unruh, G. G. (1977). Instructional supervision: Issues and trends. *Educational Leadership, 34,* 563–566.

Van Til, W. (1946). Exploring educational frontiers. In *Leadership through supervision* (1946 Yearbook). Washington, D.C.: ASCD.

Walker, W. L. & Hamm, R. L. (1981). *Twelve-year follow-up study: Role and status of curriculum workers in Indiana* (ERIC Documentation Reproduction Service No. ED 211 455).

Weick, K. (1978). The spines of leaders. In M. W. McCall, Jr. & M. M. Lombardo (Eds.). *Leadership: Where else can we go?* (pp. 37–61). Durham, NC: Duke University Press.

Wiles, K. (1967). *Supervision for better schools* (3rd ed.). Englewood Cliffs, NJ: Prentice Hall.

Wiles, K. & Lovell, J. R. (1975). *Supervision for better schools* (4th ed.). Englewood Cliffs, NJ: Prentice Hall.

Wills, F. & Peterson, K. (1995). Superintendents' management of state-initiated reform: A matter of interpretation. In K. Leithwood (Ed.). *Effective school district leadership: Transforming politics into education* (pp. 85–116). Albany, NY: State University of New York Press.

Wimpelberg, R. K. (1987). The dilemma of instructional leadership and a central role for central office. In W. Greenfield (Ed.). *Instructional leadership: Concepts, issues, and controversies* (pp. 100–117). Boston: Allyn and Bacon.

Wimpelberg, R. K. (1988). Instructional leadership and ignorance: Guidelines for the new studies of district administrators. *Education and Urban Society, 20*(3), 302–310.

Wimpelberg, R. K. & Boyd, W. L. (1990). Restructured leadership: Directed autonomy in an age of educational reform. *Planning & Change, 21*(4), 239–253.

Young, J. M. & Heichberger, R. L. (1975). Teacher perceptions of supervision and evaluation. *Education, 96,* 10–19.

Young, W. F. (1969). Influencing professional negotiation. In W. H. Lucio (Ed.). *The supervisor: New demands, new dimensions* (pp. 29–45). Washington, D.C.: ASCD.

·28·

SUPERVISION IN INTERMEDIATE AGENCIES

Billie J. Sherrod

GEORGIA DEPARTMENT OF EDUCATION

Working together for improvement is a time-honored tradition in education. Teachers frequently enlist the assistance of fellow teachers, for example, to better meet the needs of their students. By sharing ideas and resources, teachers increase their repertoire of instructional strategies and broaden the spectrum of educational opportunities for students.

Cooperation among teachers became easier in the late 19th and early 20th centuries as one-room school houses were consolidated into multiple-graded elementary and secondary schools. Coinciding with the consolidation of schools was a move towards centralization of authority. In order to operate schools in an organized and efficient manner, the role of superintendent of schools emerged. A primary function of the superintendent during this time was supervision of instruction. Believing teachers to be subordinate in ability and relying primarily on authority, superintendents spent a considerable portion of their time sharing their knowledge, experience, and intuitions with teachers (Glanz, 1982). Although frequently an autocratic practice, this sharing of ideas was a means of improving classroom instruction.

With the population growth of the 20th century and the increase of public high schools' size and complexity, the superintendent was no longer able to single-handedly provide the needed instructional supervision. Therefore, central office instructional supervisory specialists were employed (Neagley & Evans, 1980). While maintaining the concept of centralization, the district level supervisors worked in concert with teachers, both individually and in groups, to share ideas, to increase skills, and to improve instruction.

As public schools continued to grow, society's expectations and demands on education increased. It became evident that many school systems, particularly smaller and rural ones, did not have the necessary resources to meet the challenge. Educators believed one way to alleviate such problems was for systems to draw on the concept of sharing, to join together, to pool their resources, and to provide the needed services for all systems so aligned. An outcome of systems cooperatively working together for educational improvement was the creation of educational service agencies (ESAs).

These intermediate agencies or ESAs exist as a structural layer between local school systems and the state education agency. Due to their unique position, ESAs have the potential for operating in a supervisory capacity and directly impacting instructional improvement in schools. It is necessary, therefore, to define the term supervision so that the role, function and impact of educational service agencies can be more clearly understood.

Several authors interpreted supervision in a broad view of services that support and promote instructional improvement in schools. Kimball Wiles viewed supervision as service activities designed to improve instruction. In 1967, he wrote "Supervision consists of all the activities leading to the improvement of instruction, activities related to morale, improving human relations, in-service education, and curriculum development" (Wiles, 1967). The idea of supervision as a mechanism for instructional improvement was also supported by Peter Oliva who wrote that "Supervision is a means of offering to teachers specialized help in improving instruction" (Oliva, 1976).

Other authors expanded their view of supervision to include the learner as the beneficiary of instructional improvement. Ben Harris, for example, defined supervision as "what school personnel do with adults and things for the purpose of maintaining or changing the operation of the school in order to directly influence the attainment of the major instructional goals of the school. Supervision has its impact on the learner, then, through other people and things" (Harris, 1963). William Burton and Leo Brueckner also emphasized the learner as a major component of instructional supervisory support. Included in their list of principles governing the operation and purpose of supervision are the following: (1) Supervision is ordinarily concerned with improving the setting for learning in particular; and (2) The ultimate purpose of supervision is the promotion of pupil growth, and hence eventually the improvement of society (Burton & Brueckner, 1955). Instructional supervision was defined by

Robert Alfonso, Gerald Firth, and Richard Neville as "Behavior officially designated by the organization that directly affects teacher behavior in such a way as to facilitate pupil learning and achieve the goals of the organization" (Alfonso, Firth, & Neville, 1981).

For the purposes of this chapter, supervision is defined as those services and practices that promote and support instructional improvement in schools and assist in achieving desired learner outcomes. In their role as cooperative agencies serving many school systems, ESAs provide numerous supervisory services supporting instructional improvement such as staff development, curriculum development and individual consultative assistance to teachers. Unfortunately, only a minor portion of the research on ESAs addressed their supervisory practices.

Originally, the purpose of this chapter was to only review the literature relative to instructional supervision in educational service agencies. A close examination of the research on ESAs revealed that interest focused not on the supervisory practices of these agencies but rather on other topics such as their inception, growth and development, cost effectiveness, governance, etc. Research on ESAs nationally is limited; studies of the services provided by ESAs that are supervisory in nature are extremely sparse. The result is that little is known about these intermediate agencies and their role in educational improvement. It seems important, therefore, to include in this chapter not only those studies conducted on ESAs relative to instructional supervision but also other research chronicling their inception and existence in the educational environment. This chapter explores the development of educational service agencies, their role, and the available research conducted on these agencies. Topics addressed include the origin, purpose, types, legislative mandates, mission, governance, funding sources, characteristics, services, evaluations, and need for additional research.

ORIGIN OF EDUCATIONAL SERVICE AGENCIES

Educational service agencies developed as a result of studies on efficiency in educational services. Geographic problems combined with political constraints prevented the consolidation of many small school systems into large districts serving greater student populations. ESAs were viewed as an alternative to consolidation by providing services to several school systems within a geographic area.

The best ways of providing educational services to students has historically been a frequent topic of educators. Often questions raised have resulted in research studies. During the 1950s and 1960s, several studies were conducted relating to the optimal number of students a school system should serve in order to operate services efficiently and economically. In each study, the conclusion was the same—a school system needed a minimum of 10,000 students to be self-sufficient in providing all needed services (Jacobson, Mrdjenovich, Solberg, & Wileman, 1975; Sherrod, 1991; Swanson, King, Nelson, & Good, 1978). The administration of education in the United States at the turn of the 20th century

consisted of a plethora of small districts. Throughout the 20th century, small school systems across the nation consolidated into slightly larger ones. Lavin and Sanders (1974) reported that although school consolidations reduced the number of school districts from 127,649 in 1932 to 17,000 by the early 1970s, sixty percent of all school districts in the nation still had a student enrollment of less than 1,200. Political and demographic problems frequently resulted in school district consolidations rarely extending beyond a county boundary. The result has been the continuation of many small local school systems.

The problems of demographics, geography, and politics can be exemplified by studies conducted in Wisconsin and in Georgia. Jacobson et al (1975) reported that the population sparsity over a large geographic area in Wisconsin resulted in 48 percent of the school systems enrolling fewer than 1,000 students each. A similar situation existed in Georgia. In 1965, Georgia had a total of 196 school systems, including 159 county and 37 city systems. Only 7 percent, or 13 school systems, had student populations of 10,000 or more; the majority of the systems served 3,000 or fewer students. The state superintendent of schools at the time envisioned consolidating the Georgia school districts into only 54 systems, thereby providing the student population and funding needed for comprehensive educational programs in grades 1–12 across the state. However, legislation delegated responsibility for public school administration to the county as the official basic unit. Consolidation required a constitutional amendment and faced heavy political opposition (Sherrod, 1991). Recognizing the improbabilities of overcoming physical and political roadblocks such as those in Wisconsin and Georgia prompted the studies on minimum student enrollment to recommend an alternative to the consolidation of small school districts that would allow for the retention of efficiency in providing educational programs for students. The recommendation was for the creation of intermediate units or educational service agencies. One of the studies underscored its belief in the potential benefits for small systems' membership in an educational service agency (ESA) by suggesting that systems with a student enrollment of less than 2,400 needed to participate in an educational service agency (Swanson et al, 1978).

The implication in the literature is that the development of ESAs would promote supervisory practices for instructional improvement in schools. The focus of the studies on minimum enrollment was on cost savings to school systems. However, it seems reasonable that school systems wanting to operate both efficiently and economically would also expect instructional improvement as an additional outcome. The ESAs were to be the source for providing instructional supervision resulting in improvement in the schools.

The ESA, sometimes referred to as the intermediate education agency or the intermediate unit (IU), generally bridges the gap of services between state and local levels. It serves as an intermediate agency to assist local school systems in providing services that they might not otherwise be able to efficiently provide. The National Education Association defined the ESA in 1963 as "an agency that operates at a regional level, giving coordination and supplementary services to local school districts and serving as a link between these basic administrative units and the state education authority" (Levis, 1983, p. 1).

The earliest recorded data on ESAs described those created in 1829 in Delaware (Levis, 1983). Of the relatively small number of ESAs developed in the 19th and early 20th centuries, most were created to perform regulatory functions for the state education agency (SEA). The philosophy supporting ESA development shifted during the 20th century from a base for state regulation to one of providing services for local school systems (Jones, 1975; Strain, 1984). The shift in philosophy combined with the increased educational demands on local school systems accentuated the need for ESAs and caused a rise in their development during the second half of the 20th century. ESAs grew rapidly in number during the 1960s as the federal government provided funding for the development of ESAs through the Elementary and Secondary Education Act and as states attempted to improve education by providing services and strengthening the connection between the state education agency and the local education agency (LEA) (Levis, 1983; Yin, Gwaltney, & Molitor, 1981). The number of ESAs has grown throughout the United States in the 20th century until, today, the majority of states have some type of intermediate service agency (Hopper, 1976).

Although most states have ESAs, limited research has been conducted to chronicle their inception in the various states and describe their development longitudinally. Only three studies were found which provided this information. Kachris (1987) used the political, economic, and demographic situation in New York to describe the origin and development of the Boards of Cooperative Educational Services (BOCES) in that state from 1948 to 1982. The types of ESAs and the services they provided in Georgia from 1966 to 1990 were described by Sherrod (1991). In both studies, the researchers used primary documents and interviews to provide a descriptive historical account of ESA development. While both studies were comprehensive in reporting influences impacting changes in ESAs, each was restricted to a single state. The third study was not written for the express purpose of describing ESA development. Instead, in addressing the issues of providing bilingual education, Buckel (1988) included a brief history of the ESAs in Texas.

The lack of longitudinal research on ESAs has resulted in educators not having a national perspective on how these agencies have operated and of effective supervisory models implemented by these agencies in providing services to local system personnel. Additionally, the lack of data has frequently resulted in noneducators, especially legislators and other policy makers, questioning their continued existence during periods of limited financial resources. With most states currently having a history of at least 30 years of ESA operation, the timing and need for additional longitudinal research on ESAs is optimal.

PURPOSE OF EDUCATIONAL SERVICE AGENCIES

The original purpose of the educational service agencies as they expanded rapidly during the 1960s was to assist small and rural school systems in providing services to their students. Most of the research related to the purpose of ESAs focused on the cost savings for ESA-member school systems as opposed to any instructional benefits received for school improvement. All of the studies cited on the purpose of ESAs are approximately 15–25 years old. No data were found to either support or refute whether the original purpose of ESAs remains intact.

A review of the literature nationally indicated agreement as to the purpose of the educational service agencies. The ESAs were created as an attempt to help alleviate the problems small, rural local school systems encountered in providing high cost, low incident services to students. The combining of resources allows for the production of programs and the delivery of services to be expanded at a reasonable cost for local school systems. Waller, Kemp, and Scanlon (1976) listed six purposes for ESAs. These are: (1) to improve the quality of existing services provided by the local system; (2) to improve the quality of existing services available to the residents of the area; (3) to combine local funds to provide a service too expensive for individual school systems; (4) to enable participating school systems to realize cost savings through economy of scale programs; (5) to enable local school systems to combine funds to provide programs directly to students when those programs could not be provided economically and efficiently by the individual school system; and (6) to increase the flow of federal and state resources into a region. It is interesting to note that only the first two items in this list of ESA purposes relate to instructional supervision. Instead, the emphasis was placed on the potential financial benefits of ESA membership.

The purposes of ESAs as identified have led educators to expect that participation in an ESA will lead to the provision of services at a reduced cost. However, the research provides conflicting information as to the accuracy of this perception. Several authors reported the benefits of ESA participation. Swanson et al (1978) cited a study conducted in Illinois in 1970 which concluded that school districts did in fact experience a greater economy of scale through ESA participation. Waller et al (1976) interviewed the system superintendents participating in ESAs in the Appalachian region and concluded that the ESA programs and services met all six of the identified purposes of ESAs. He further specified that the ESA-provided services of the development of policy manuals, psychological services, and in-service programs would not have been provided by the local systems acting alone. Waller did not expand on how the ESA programs improved the existing school services. However, a logical conclusion is that the ESA-provided in-service programs constituted an instructional supervision function, which led to the accomplishment of the first stated purpose of ESAs—that of improving the quality of existing school programs.

In another study, Popper (1982) interviewed the superintendents of systems participating in ESAs in Massachusetts and concluded cost effectiveness to be the major advantage of collaboratives. Because of this perceived advantage, the superintendents indicated that they expected declining student enrollment and reduced financial resources would result in an increased demand for ESA services by the membership.

The benefits of ESA membership were also supported by Strain (1984). This study, consisting of a questionnaire randomly sent to system superintendents in Ohio, found that a strong perception of need for the ESA services existed and that the ESAs provided services at a cost lower than the local systems working individually could have maintained. The superintendents agreed that sharing services is an important component in the education program of local school districts. Unfortunately, the types of supervisory services provided by the Ohio ESAs in this study are unknown. Similar studies have documented the financial benefits of ESA membership (Hopper, 1976; Notestone, 1982).

Other research has brought into question the notion of cooperative services saving local school systems money. Lane (1984) studied the financial relationships of the Boards of Cooperative Educational Services (BOCES) in Colorado. He concluded that the belief of ESAs assisting lower income school districts in stretching their limited budgets to make additional programs available to students is untrue. Concern with the equity of services prompted a study of the factors influencing participation in cooperative ventures in New York (Galvin, 1991). The findings concluded that a local system's level of participation depended not solely on the possibility of saving money while providing services but instead was affected by the structure of the cooperative in which the local system was organized. Moreover, the differences in participation were associated with variations in the cost of providing cooperative services relative to alternative means of production (Galvin, 1991).

A study to determine the cost effectiveness of ESA services relative to local system production was conducted in Wisconsin. Using selected services and programs, a cost analysis of ESA-provided services was compared to the cost of a local system providing these same services individually. The results found that some services were more cost effective if provided by the ESA whereas others were so if provided by the local system. More specifically, the ESA achieved the most financial benefit to the local system by employing personnel in the positions of business manager, curriculum coordinator, special education director, vocational education director, and food service director and by providing the necessary equipment for drivers' education. Although Brey did not specify the role and function of the personnel identified, the implication was that ESA-provided instructional supervisors were more cost effective in assisting systems in school improvement. Minimal savings for the local system were found in collaborative participation in audiovisual machine repair, substitute teacher service, and in-service programs. Additionally, the school system was determined to be better off financially by locally providing computer services and a Chapter I coordinator (Brey, 1981).

The research to substantiate the purpose of ESAs as cost effective collaboratives for small rural school systems appears inconclusive. The majority of the research supports the contention that ESA membership provides a financial savings for local school systems. However, the findings consist primarily of perceptions of superintendents and other educators as opposed to financial data. Additionally, much of the research dates back to the 1970s—a time when many of the ESAs were in their infancy and struggling to determine their role. Brey conducted the only research which included a cost effectiveness analysis. However, his study was limited to a single school system and as such, cannot be generalized to other school systems of varying student population and financial resources. Any research conducted today has the potential to evaluate the financial aspects of the sharing of services by local school systems of different sizes and economic situations over a 30 year period. More importantly, research conducted today could identify the current purposes of ESAs and the worth of ESA-provided instructional supervision services in assisting both ESAs and school systems in accomplishing their purposes.

Regardless of the absence of abundant data to confirm the worth of ESAs as cost savings cooperatives and as providers of instructional supervision services, they have continued to grow nationally. Local system personnel have supported the concept that cooperative arrangements for the provision of specific services is superior to schools working in isolation (Cox, 1981). Membership in ESAs in states with strong intermediate agencies continues to be high. For example, in Georgia in 1994, 176 out of a total of 182 local school systems belonged to the ESA in their area. Of the six nonmembers, four were large and two were mid-sized school systems. This high level of voluntary participation in ESAs suggests that the benefits include not only the belief in a cost savings but also the collegial sharing of ideas, the generating of solutions to problems, and the provision of supervisory assistance for instructional improvement to which a price tag cannot be attached.

TYPES OF EDUCATIONAL SERVICE AGENCIES

Three types of educational service agencies have emerged as dominant—the special district agency, the regionalized agency, and the cooperative agency. Two primary factors differentiate these agencies—the locus of control and the recipients of services. Over time, an agency's type and function frequently change. No data exist comparing the type of agency with the effectiveness of the instructional supervision services provided.

The literature suggests that several types of intermediate units exist for various purposes. Different authors have assigned different names to these agencies. Fletcher and Cole (1991) combined the definitions of Baugh (1987), Fletcher et al (1988, 1990), and McKibbon (1981) to describe ESAs in the following way as interdistrict cooperatives:

Interdistrict Cooperatives—Formal educational organizations, between the state-education-agency level and the local-education-agency level, enabled or mandated by the State for the purpose of sharing costs and services between or among autonomous districts and designed to provide participating districts with joint responsibility for administering and implementing programs.

Other authors have broken down this global description of intermediate agencies by identifying more specific types of ESAs. Lavin and Sanders (1974) suggested two main types of cooperatives—those where local systems voluntarily join together for the development of specific programs or services, and those consisting of multi-district agencies created by action of the state legislature. Reporting on the ESAs in the Appalachian Region, Waller et al (1978) listed three types of ESAs. They were:

(a) Individual—An independent legal entity recognizable by the state government and capable of receiving and expending public funds. The local board of control has the sole responsibility for organization and control of its policies.

(b) Sponsored—Legally sponsored by some existing institution such as a member local education agency that acts as the fiscal agent. The staff are employees of the fiscal agent. The ESA operates independent of the fiscal agent and follows the policies of its board of control.

(c) Institutionally linked—A component of an existing institution such as a local education agency or the state education agency. The local board of control makes most of its policy in cooperation with the parent organization.

Perhaps the best known types and the names of ESAs most frequently quoted are the ones identified by the American Association of School Administrators (AASA) in 1979 (Stephens Associates, 1979, p. 6). These were:

(a) Special district agency—This type of ESA is a legally constituted unit of school government between the state education agency (SEA) and a group of local education agencies (LEAs). It is created by the state or by the state and LEAs with the purpose of providing direct services to both the SEA and LEAs.

(b) Regionalized agency—An ESA of this type is established and functions as a branch of the SEA. Its primary purpose is to provide direct services to LEAs.

(c) Cooperative agency—In this configuration, two or more LEAs join together and support an ESA. The ESA provides common services exclusively to all LEAs in its membership.

The major difference among the three types of ESAs identified by the AASA focuses on the locus of control. The cooperative agency provides maximum autonomy for the local systems. They voluntarily join together and collectively determine the programs and services that best meet the needs of their area. Through formal collaboration, local school districts increase their power to act and achieve both their individual and collective goals. This type of cooperative provides the most flexibility to the LEA membership; frequently, the guidelines are so unrestrictive that each agency is able to develop as a reflection of local attitudes. In the special district agency, the decision-making authority is shared by both the local systems participating in the ESA and the state education agency. The local systems determine many of the programs and services to be provided to the membership but the ESA also performs tasks for the SEA by assisting local systems in implementing state-required programs. The third type, the regionalized agency, serves as a regional office of the SEA. It func-

tions simply to ensure that local systems in the area have the knowledge and skills needed to implement state-required programs.

The issue of locus of control or autonomy versus dependence was frequently cited in the literature. Some researchers stated emphatically that the philosophy supporting ESA development is service-oriented and, therefore, ESAs should not engage in enforcing the rules and regulations of the SEA. The authors expressed fear that performing such tasks would severely hamper the chances for developing effective, cooperative relationships with member local school systems (Jacobson et al, 1975; Stephens, 1974). Others were concerned that ESAs established as cooperative agencies in their states were moving away from that original intent to become arms of the state agency. One such study involved the educational service agencies or BOCES of New York. Morton (1988) maintained that the New York SEA had attempted to exert greater control over local school systems through different agencies and had turned its focus to the BOCES. He concluded that the BOCES were, in fact, annually wielding expanding control over participating LEAs.

The literature did not identify one type of agency as better than the others; instead, it simply suggested that each served a different purpose. The cooperative agency was portrayed as having more positive impact because this type of agency delivered those services identified by its members. The special district and the regional agencies, on the other hand, were viewed as delivering more mandated services. The desire to maintain local autonomy indicated that most local educators preferred the cooperative agency. However, when faced with the realities of increased programmatic demands and limited financial resources, many educators realized that autonomy and survival have to be carefully balanced. For example, Jacobson et al (1975) reported that due to the strong belief in local autonomy in Wisconsin, the local school systems both wanted and needed a type of educational service agency that would not challenge the "de facto" autonomy of the local school districts. One year later, Stefonek (1976) found that ESA directors in Wisconsin were ambivalent in their views of whether the legislature should mandate programs for the ESAs to deliver. They recognized that legislated programs lessened local autonomy but provided the financial security for the continuation of the agencies. A similar situation was found to exist in Georgia. In interviewing ESA directors, it was determined that those directors serving since the agencies' inception in 1966 resisted any movement away from local control whereas the more recently employed directors were more willing to forego total local autonomy in favor of expansion and continuation (Sherrod, 1991).

As is evident, the type of intermediate agency established varies among the states. Yin et al (1981) studied the ESAs of three states and reported that the agencies in Colorado were true cooperatives with total local autonomy whereas the ESAs of New Jersey operated as regional offices of the state education agency. Of the 36 states reporting on their interdistrict collaboratives in 1991, six states indicated having regionalized agencies while the other 30 reported various types of cooperative or special district agencies (Fletcher & Cole, 1991). In addition, the type of agency sometimes changes in function according to need, finance, and politics. The literature indicates at least three examples of ESAs changing their type and, therefore, their function. Morton (1988) suggested that the ESAs of New York were moving from cooperative agencies to regionalized agencies and the Pennsylvania Budget and Finance Committee (1976) expressed concern that a similar transition was occurring to the intermediate units in that state. The ESAs in Georgia were designated to be cooperative agencies when originally established but served as special district agencies in 1990. It is anticipated that the type of agencies serving educators in these three states as well as the ESAs in other states will change again as local situations change. This fluidity or the ability to change to meet local and state needs remains as one of the strengths of the intermediate agency.

Only one study was found which related the organizational structure of the ESA to the types of services provided. Galvin (1991) reported that a complicated set of relationships existed between the ESA structure in New York and the type of services offered. He further suggested that ESA structure strongly influenced a local school system's level of participation in ESA services. However, he did not specify whether the services were supervisory or administrative. Research is needed to determine if the type of ESA impacts the types of instructional supervision services offered. Furthermore, data are needed to evaluate the worth of instructional supervision services in assisting ESAs and local systems in accomplishing their goals of instructional improvement.

LEGISLATION CREATING EDUCATIONAL SERVICE AGENCIES

Frequently, educational service agencies were created across the nation as a result of state legislation. The legislation varied among the states from permissive to prescribed. Legislation in some states simply granted permission for ESA development if needed, while other legislative acts specified ESA membership and the services that ESAs would provide. There are no current studies comparing the effectiveness of ESA services with legislative mandates.

Educational service agencies came into existence across the nation either through local initiation or by state legislation. Todd (1980) studied the ESA network in 26 states and found that the ESAs in 19 of the states were mandated through legislation. The ESAs in some states originally began by local initiative but circumstances changed, which resulted in legislation providing for the creation of educational service agencies. This change can best be illustrated by describing the development of ESAs in Georgia.

In 1966, grant monies became available in Georgia for local systems to pool their resources and collaboratively provide educational services for students across county lines. These cooperatives prospered in Georgia and grew from only four agencies in 1966 to a total of 12 fully operational coalitions in 1972. Several issues arose during the six years that suggested the possibility of and posed a need for a legal sanction regarding the sharing of services. First, the projects were dependent on annual appropriations from the Georgia General Assembly. With no legal basis, the continuation of the ESAs remained

uncertain each year. Second, the absence of a legal sanction limited the state department of education to the disbursement of funds to only a single local school system in each coalition. A problem arose in that the system serving as the fiscal agent for the cooperative was required to pay benefits and retirement for personnel carried on its payroll who, in actuality, were not its employees. A third issue was also related to the location of the coalition within a school system. In more than one instance, the superintendent of the system providing the physical location and fiscal support felt the ESA director was "his" employee. The superintendent would frequently request more than his system's pro rata share of services from the agency.

Another issue centered on special education. Federal legislation required that local school systems meet the needs of all special education students by 1976. Although all school systems in the state had to comply, most did not have the necessary resources. Many systems began searching for an agency or other methods to assist in providing special education services.

A final issue, which may have had the greatest impact, was related to the location of governmental agencies providing services to Georgia citizens. Governor Jimmy Carter commissioned a reorganization study to explore possible ways that state government might better serve the population of the entire state. Governor Carter believed that governmental services were most effective if provided regionally and that geographic location and size were determiners of utmost importance in providing direct services to the people of Georgia.

The best way to resolve these issues in Georgia appeared to be through legislating ESAs. The Georgia General Assembly in 1972 passed Senate Bill 538, the Cooperative Educational Services Act. This legislation empowered the state board of education to create Cooperative Educational Service Agencies (CESAs) with the express purpose of sharing services designed to improve the effectiveness of the educational programs of member local school systems.

Situations similar to those described in Georgia resulted in the passage of legislation in the 1960s and 1970s in several states for the creation of ESAs. The laws varied from enabling legislation which permitted the voluntary formation of ESAs to mandatory legislation requiring ESAs. Permissive legislation passed in Colorado in 1965 allowed the development of ESAs "whenever feasible" whereas legislation passed in Michigan in 1962 mandated not only the establishment of ESAs but also required all local systems to become members of the intermediate agencies (Yin et al, 1981). Other states reporting ESA legislation included Oklahoma, Massachusetts, New Jersey, New York, North Carolina, Pennsylvania, and Wisconsin (Avants, 1975; Kemp, Waller, & Scanlon, 1976; Lavin & Sanders, 1974; Pennsylvania Legislative Budget and Finance Committee, 1976; Popper, 1982; Stefonek, 1976; Swanson et al, 1978; Yin et al, 1981).

Legislation in the states also varied in the prescribed requirements for ESAs. Frequently, the legislative acts included specific services that ESAs were to provide. It is ironic that a major purpose of ESAs was to improve the quality of school services to students but that legislation, for the most part, did not encompass instructional supervisory services. Some legislation, such as in the state of New Jersey, restricted the ESAs by stipulating that they were only to provide knowledge utilization services to LEAs while legislation in Pennsylvania and Wisconsin specified that ESAs were to provide special education services as well as other services. The Wisconsin legislation suggested additional services that the ESAs could provide including "such programs as research, special student classes, data collection, processing and dissemination, and in-services programs" (Jacobson et al, 1975). One interesting aspect of the Pennsylvania legislation was that it not only determined the services for ESAs to provide, but also specified the types of schools to be served. One of the requirements of the law was that ESAs provide the services of special education, testing, guidance and counseling, remedial education, and English as a second language to both public and nonpublic schools (Pennsylvania Legislative Budget and Finance Committee, 1976). The inclusion of nonpublic schools as potential ESA members was not found in any state other than Pennsylvania. Additionally, the Pennsylvania law required an annual report to the legislature detailing the services provided, an expenditures analysis, the sources of revenue and the number and types of personnel employed (Cober, 1978).

The studies on ESAs identified in this section included the legislative mandates governing the operation of the ESAs as part of their data. No attempt was made in any study which identified legislative mandates to determine the effectiveness of services provided by the ESAs created by permissive legislation with voluntary membership as opposed to those services provided by ESAs that were legally mandated with required LEA membership and prescribed services. Perhaps, this omission was due to the fact that most of the research which noted the legislative mandates was conducted during the 1970s, a few short years after ESA legislation was implemented in most states. The majority of the research on ESAs conducted in the 1980s and early 1990s did not indicate if the original legislation was still in effect or if amendments had changed the required services or service delivery programs. Kemp et al (1976) found that ESAs tended to look somewhat alike from state to state although they have diverse legislation and regulatory provisions. Research is needed to determine the validity of this conclusion twenty years later and to evaluate the impact of legislated services versus locally-determined needed services. This type of research will provide educators with the knowledge needed to make the best decisions about the ESA-provided instructional supervision services which support instructional improvement in the schools.

MISSION OF EDUCATIONAL SERVICE AGENCIES

A statement of mission provides direction for an organization or agency. Unfortunately, the ESAs nationally were not provided a clear mission. This omission has left ESAs without needed support and frequently resulted in confusion about the types of services they should provide. It seems evident that a clear mission which addresses services is needed. Such a mission statement would identify the instructional supervision services for ESAs to provide local systems and the func-

tion of such services in assisting school systems in improving curriculum and instruction.

One of the ways that research measures the effectiveness of a new program is to compare its accomplishments with the stated mission. Only limited data relating to ESAs and their mission was available. This lack of data was not localized to a single state or region but appeared nationally as well. The limited existing research on ESAs nationally suggested an absence of a mission and an unclear focus (Martisko, 1985; Pennsylvania Budget and Finance Committee, 1976; Snider, 1973). The ESAs were not provided a common foundation on which they could base their operations. The omission of a well-defined description of overall functions and limitations on activities has frequently caused confusion about the purpose of ESAs. Often, the only semblance of a mission for the ESAs was a charge to attempt to help alleviate the problems small, rural local school systems encountered in providing high cost, low incident services to students. The ESAs, therefore, were left on their own to either determine their own mission and act accordingly or to conduct daily activities without the advantage of a clear direction or a means to measure progress. The lack of a clear mission also resulted in the employment of some ESA directors who possessed limited knowledge of the concept of an ESA and of any external expectations for the agency. Left virtually unsupervised and functioning in isolation from each other allowed the ESAs initially established in some states, such as Georgia, to become distinct agencies providing diverse services to their constituencies.

Recognizing the problem of a lack of a stated mission, Martisko (1985) studied the ESAs in Minnesota in order to develop a planning process for developing a common mission statement to facilitate the statewide delivery of ESA services. Using ESA directors and governing board members to determine and cluster goals, Martisko concluded that the ESA mission should address the services that ESAs provide. The primary ESA services identified in Minnesota on which a mission could be developed included program development and in-service, research and development, liaison and communication activities, planning, and direct cooperative services that support district administration. It seems evident from Martisko's study that, due to the types of services the ESAs in Minnesota provided, they were operating in an instructional supervisory capacity. A mission statement focusing on services is clearly needed to provide support for ESAs in order to establish them as leaders in instructional supervision whose primary function is to assist schools in instructional improvement.

Although mission statements were rarely formalized, some states began providing direction and purpose for ESAs through legislation. However, the direction ranged from the very broad to the specific. For example, the 1965 permissive legislation passed in Colorado allowed the formation of ESAs "whenever feasible" while the 1977 New Jersey legislation established four ESAs with the express purpose of operating as regional arms of the state education agency (Yin et al, 1981). Sometimes as existing legislation was amended or new legislation was enacted, the mission became more clearly stated. The legislation in Georgia provides such an example. The 1972 Georgia legislation establishing ESAs stated in general terms that the purpose of the ESAs was for "sharing services which are designed to improve the effectiveness of the educational programs of member local school systems." When new legislation was passed in 1986, it still did not specify a mission. Instead, it partially determined a mission by assigning the state board of education responsibility for determining that ESA activities conform to state law. However, the 1987 legislative amendment specified five areas of service and required that all ESAs provide assistance to member school systems in each of the five areas. This program of mandated uniform statewide needs consisted of the following five service areas: (a) planning and research, (b) staff development, (c) instruction and curriculum, (d) assessment and evaluation, and (e) educational technology (Sherrod, 1991). Each of the five mandated services "illustrates" that ESAs in Georgia are to provide instructional supervisory assistance to school systems. Although a mission statement was not clearly delineated in the legislation, the identification of the five required service areas has been interpreted to mean that the provision of these services is, in part, the mission of the ESAs in Georgia. No research has been conducted to measure the effectiveness of these services in accomplishing the mission.

No other research exists related to the development of a common statement of mission. The lack of a clearly definitive mission statement has frequently limited the impact that ESAs could have on instructional supervision. Without a mission, ESAs in many states have often provided services that are administrative rather than focusing on those instructional supervision services which would lead to instructional improvement in schools. Additionally, the lack of a mission has fueled the flame between critics of ESAs who say they do not know what the ESAs do and why they do it and ESA educators who claim to provide needed services to member LEAs.

GOVERNANCE OF EDUCATIONAL SERVICE AGENCIES

The governing structure for ESAs across the nation is similar. ESAs are governed by boards composed of member system personnel. The responsibilities and authority of the boards varies based on the type of ESA agency. Studies of ESAs have reported the governing structure in existence but have not focused on relating the governance to ESA effectiveness.

The research on the governance structure of ESAs is limited; however, existing research suggests general consistency among the agencies. The most prevalent pattern of governance found was usually established by legislation and consisted of two boards: (1) a governing board, frequently referred to as a board of control, and (2) an advisory board (Kemp et al, 1976; Todd, 1980; Yin et al, 1981). The governing board functions as the decision-making authority while the advisory board makes recommendations to the governing board. The membership of the two boards varies among the ESAs nationwide. In some instances, the governing board consists of the superintendents of school systems participating in the ESA; in other agencies, the board members are elected by the local board of education to represent the school system. Generally, membership of the advisory board is determined in the reverse manner from the governing board. That is, an ESA whose governing board consists of local system superintendents has an advisory board of elected representatives from the local systems and vice versa.

The decision-making authority of the governing board is dependent on the type of ESA in existence. In the cooperative agencies, the governing board maintains sole responsibility for all decisions. This responsibility is shared with the state education agency in some special district agencies and in regional agencies. The governing board is charged with employing the agency director who handles the daily operations of the agency and approves the programs and services that the agency provides. The governing board, therefore, provides direction for the agency and directly influences the type and extent of instructional supervision services offered. Usually, the ESA governing boards do not require ESA members to participate in all available services; local systems are given the option of choosing those programs and services in which they want to participate. Member school systems wanting instructional improvement would use the supervisory services of the ESA; other systems might opt to only use administrative and other types of services offered by the ESA. The governing boards are also empowered to establish annual membership fees. Such fees partially cover the costs of ESA operational expenses since state legislation frequently specified that the agencies have no taxing power and no power to own property.

Only one research report was identified which addressed the governance structure and its impact on the provision of ESA services. Fletcher and Cole (1991) studied the level of satisfaction of the state education agencies with the implementation of required special education services provided by the ESAs. Fletcher and Cole concluded that no single governance pattern prevailed as more effective in the ESA delivery of services. Furthermore, they indicated that the governance structure did not make the cooperative work although they maintained that active participation by the governing board made a more effective ESA overall.

FUNDING SOURCES FOR EDUCATIONAL SERVICE AGENCIES

Typically, educational service agencies receive funds for maintenance and operations from three sources—the federal government, the state government and local member systems. The dependence on funding from various sources combined with the annual uncertainty of the continuation of funding has caused problems for ESAs and raised some criticism about the types of services offered.

The establishment of any new program or service usually requires funding to support its inception and continued maintenance. The creation of educational service agencies provides one example of the need for funding to support a new and innovative idea. Frequently, funding sufficient for the development and continuation of ESAs by a single source was unavailable. In such instances, state education agencies and local school systems interested in establishing collaboratives sought alternative funding sources. One source investigated was monies available through the federal government. Federal funding available through Title III of the Elementary and Secondary Education Act (ESEA) of 1965 provided for the initial establishment of many of the ESAs developed during the 1960s and 1970s. This piece of legislation did more to promote and expand the concept of local system cooperative ventures than any other (Jacobson et al, 1975; Jones, 1975). Although the ESEA legislation funded the establishment of many educational service agencies, the monies frequently were not sufficient to pay all expenses or fund all agencies. Alternative sources such as state funds and local system membership fees were frequently enlisted to establish ESAs.

The continuation of collaborative agencies in providing programs and services also required funding. The literature consistently indicated that continued funding ESAs was not by a single source of revenue but instead consisted of a combination of local, state and federal funding sources (Cober, 1978; Firestone, 1981; Lavin & Sanders, 1974; Pennsylvania Legislative Budget and Finance Committee, 1976; Yin et al, 1981). This combination of funding sources was necessary because no single source provided the amount necessary to maintain the agencies.

The financial dependence of ESAs on several sources has frequently resulted in criticism of the funding procedures and of the agencies. The federal funds were usually grant funds that were awarded on a competitive basis or were designated to "flow through" the state agency for specific programs. Supporters of the federal grants claim that ESAs have increased federal monies available to the local area. These monies expanded the number and type of programs available to students in the area because ESAs applied for and were awarded federal grants that local systems could not have received (Waller et al, 1976). Critics maintain that ESAs' need for funding for continued survival and growth results in their being less service oriented and less attuned to the needs of the local area. Instead of ESAs providing the instructional supervision services and other services deemed as needs by the local area, they are sometimes accused of providing only those services for which funding is available. The need for and acquisition of federal funds has been given as a reason that in several instances, programs identified as a local need were not implemented (Firestone, 1981; Kemp et al, 1976; Yin, 1981).

Concern over state funding of ESAs also exists. State funds have typically been appropriated annually by the state legislature. This annual allocation of funds has frequently resulted in uncertainty of the ESAs' continued existence each year and, therefore, in instability in staff and programs from year to year. Additionally, the dependence on state funds has raised questions over the extent of control the state education agency may exert over the local collaboratives.

An additional source of revenue for ESAs consists of member local system fees. The ESA governing board establishes the local system contribution at each agency. The fee configurations vary from state to state and among agencies within a state. Options include a set annual figure, an amount based on the number of students in the system, a charge for only those services utilized, or any combination of these methods for assessing fees. The requirement of a local system partially financing ESA services has sometimes resulted in a disproportionate delivery of services among member systems. Swanson et al (1978) found that wealthy systems in New York purchased more services than their poorer counterparts but the poor districts made a larger proportion of their expenditures through the ESA. A difference was found to exist in Colorado as well. Lane (1984) found that the higher income districts paid the most money to the ESAs but reported a large number of unmet needs. The large districts participated in many low priority programs which caused Lane to conclude that, by their participation, the large districts were subsidizing the smaller, poorer ones.

Calls for changing the method of funding for ESAs are prominent in the literature. Recommendations for a uniform state funding formula were consistently cited as far back as twenty years ago (Jones, 1975; Pennsylvania Legislative Budget and Finance Committee, 1976; Sherrod, 1991; Yin, 1981). A uniform funding formula is proposed as a way of ensuring the continuance of the ESAs while releasing them to focus on the instructional supervision needs of the member local systems. However, requests for continued state funding have resulted in legislators asking questions related to the current role and effectiveness of the ESAs' programs and services. Currently, hard answers to such questions posed by legislators and others do not exist. This absence of data has perpetuated the ESA reliance on funding from federal grants, state appropriations, and member local system fees.

CHARACTERISTICS OF EDUCATIONAL SERVICE AGENCIES

Characteristics are traits that distinguish and identify an organization or agency. Limited research has been conducted to determine if all ESAs nationally possess similar traits or characteristics. The majority of the studies that exist have focused on external demographic qualities of ESAs such as their geographic size, student population of member systems, and organizational structure. A few studies, however, examined the internal supervision of the agencies and of the services ESAs provide. Overall, few similarities deemed as characteristic of ESAs were found.

Perhaps the best way to view organizations such as the educational services agencies across the nation is by comparing their similarities and differences. However, little research has been conducted to determine the characteristics of these agencies except in broad terms and results of this limited research are not in agreement. Kemp et al (1976) studied the ESAs of the Appalachian region and concluded that the agencies looked basically very similar among the nine states although they had different legislative mandates and regulations. Five years later, Firestone (1981) disagreed, stating that ESAs within a state and between states differ substantially in organizational structure and patterns of governance. He maintained that ESAs share only two limited characteristics: (1) serving as an agency midway between the state education agency and local education agencies, and (2) facilitating communication among local systems and between the state education agency and local school districts. Firestone did not indicate what impact, if any, these characteristics have on the supervision of ESAs or on the instructional supervisory services they provide to local school systems.

Other studies examined the membership of ESAs. The literature suggests that the memberships of ESAs most frequently include small, rural school systems because the intended purpose of ESAs was for small rural local systems to collaboratively provide educational services for their students which each would have had difficulty providing alone. Swanson et al (1978) found that size of school system pupil enrollment did reflect on ESA membership. In studying the ESAs of New York, he found that, the smaller the local school district enrollment, the greater the reliance upon the ESA and its services. Swanson's study supports the belief that smaller systems are not financially able to provide instructional supervision services for their teachers and, therefore, rely on their ESA for assistance. Swanson did note, however, that legislation creating the ESAs did not allow the five big city districts in the New York City area with a large percentage of the state student enrollment to join the ESAs. In comparing ESAs in Michigan, New Jersey, and Colorado, Yin et al (1981) found a completely different situation. He maintained that pupil enrollment was not indicative of ESA membership because all of the local school districts in Michigan including the large metropolitan ones, participated as members in their local ESA. Yin et al did concede, however, that local school systems' membership in an ESA in Michigan was mandatory, not voluntary. ESA membership in this state was required for all systems regardless of size in an effort for ESAs to perform services for the state education agency consistently throughout Michigan.

Georgia provided another example of the diversity of school system size and its lack of relationship on ESA membership. Of the 16 ESAs in Georgia, the membership of one consisted entirely of large metropolitan Atlanta systems. In forming this cooperative, the LEA leadership indicated that, although each system provided its own instructional supervisors for the major content areas, the systems shared common problems that smaller systems did not have and that the ESA provided a collegial bond for solving them. The membership of the remaining 15 ESAs was comprised of smaller systems; only one of the five large school districts outside of the Atlanta area chose to join an ESA. The smaller systems indicated that they did not have the resources to provide instructional supervisors and relied on the ESA for this service.

Just as ESA membership by local school system size varies nationally, the geographic regions of ESAs appear inconsistent as well. Firestone (1981) reviewed the ESAs in Pennsylvania and reported that some had responsibility for providing services in very large geographic regions whereas others covered a very small area. The physical terrain and population density contributed in many instances to the variations in ESA geographic size. In other situations, the local systems determined the geographic service area of the ESA. For example, the Georgia legislature divided the state into 18 areas of comparable geographic size for the development of

ESAs. The local systems, however, in four of these areas voluntarily chose to combine into two ESAs, making a total of 16 coalitions for the state. The research on ESAs readily acknowledges the differences in ESA geographic size; however, no research has been conducted to determine the impact of size on the quality of the instructional supervision services provided or on the effectiveness of the ESAs.

Although the majority of the research on ESAs found diversity among the membership and size, Popper (1982) found positive attitudes for collaboration to be characteristic of ESA members. In studying the commonalities of local school systems who voluntarily joined an ESA, he concluded that each possessed the following three characteristics: (a) a positive view of the available ESA services, (b) a perceived need for additional collaborative services, and (c) an official school attitude that was positive toward interdistrict collaboration.

Perhaps the most interesting studies on the characteristics of ESAs relate not to the ESA itself but to the leadership style of the ESA director and the impact style has on the overall operation of an ESA. Two studies focused on the characteristics of the internal supervisory leadership exhibited at the ESA and the effects on the provisions of educational programs and services. Jacobson et al (1975) found a direct relationship between the provision of ESA services and the leadership style of the director. He contended that not only were different programs and services provided to local school systems based on the educational philosophy, personality and leadership ability of the ESA director but the style of the director also influenced the type of communication and interaction between the educational service agency and the member local school systems. The importance of internal supervision was supported by Fletcher and Cole (1991). Examining the four factors of governance, demographics, managerial style, and organizational style to determine which leads to successful interdistrict cooperatives, they concluded that managerial and organizational styles have the most direct impact on the operation of the ESA. Likewise, a study of the services provided by the ESAs in Georgia found as an unanticipated result that the personality and style of the director was specifically related to the type and number of services offered by the agency. None of these studies suggested which internal supervisory style was best in ensuring that ESAs provide effective instructional supervision services to member school systems. Additional research is needed to verify these studies and to make recommendations as to which supervision style is most effective for the operation of the ESA.

Nicholls (1983) examined the views of internal ESA supervisors to determine if differences exist between their viewpoints and those of system superintendents on issues facing education, educational philosophies, and job requirements. He surveyed ESA directors and compared their responses with the results of the National Study of the American School Superintendent. The results suggest that superintendents and ESA directors share similar perceptions of educational issues but, due to opposing organizational philosophies, differ in their job responsibilities and in the ways to address educational concerns. The consistency in the views of both ESA and local system leadership concerning education suggests that ESAs offer services needed by local systems and that local systems are receptive to these services. This shared vision of education is critical if ESAs are to be successful in providing instructional supervisory assistance to local systems and assist them in their efforts for instructional improvement.

The only additional study relating to the characteristics of ESAs concerned perceptions of needed components in developing a statewide ESA network. Aycock (1981) analyzed the ESAs in 12 states in the South to determine common characteristics. He used the results to survey system superintendents, department of education personnel, and legislators in several southern states to identify ESA components to be used as the basis for developing the intermediate agencies in Mississippi. He found that services ESAs should provide include direct instructional supervision, instructional-related supervision, and planning services. It seems apparent that instructional supervision is characteristic of the services provided by ESAs.

As is evident, the research on ESA characteristics is sparse at best. Existing data suggest that these agencies have more variables than consistent elements. More importantly, the research simply illustrates the differences among the agencies with no data to support or refute the effectiveness of one characteristic over another. The data most significant for students of supervision concerns the internal supervisory style and its effect on ESA programs and services and the supervisory services provided to local systems. More data are needed about ESA characteristics that support their role in providing instructional supervisory services for local school systems.

SERVICES PROVIDED BY EDUCATIONAL SERVICE AGENCIES

ESAs were developed nationally to assist local school systems in providing quality programs and services for students. ESAs provide services to local school systems who in turn use the skills and knowledge learned to improve the instructional program for their students. Many of the services, therefore, are various types of instructional supervision activities. Much of the literature refers to these as basic services of ESAs. Unfortunately, the studies completed on ESA services have not evaluated the worth of the instructional supervision services in assisting local systems in accomplishing their goals. Instead, studies of ESA services have focused on items such as the use of services, the most frequently provided service, changes in services, and future service needs.

The role of the ESA in assisting local educational agencies in providing educational programs to students has frequently centered on two issues—the type of agency established and the types of services provided by the agency. As previously indicated, most ESAs were developed to assist local systems in providing services that they would have been unable to provide efficiently if acting alone.

The literature suggests that ESA services vary among the agencies nationwide in both the number and type of services offered. This variation results from the local autonomy for identified needs, from federal and state legislation, and from requirements imposed by the state education agency. Todd

(1981) identified 26 ESA-provided programs and services to determine their inclusion in the ESAs of 27 states. The services consisted of both instructional supervision services as well as administrative tasks. Todd concluded that 12 of the 26 programs and services were provided by a majority of the ESAs and that the provision of the service was unrelated to the type of ESA (i.e. cooperative, special district, or regional). According to Todd's findings, the regional educational service agency which served as an arm of the state education agency was as likely to provide instructional supervision services as the cooperative agency. Of the states in Todd's study, the ESAs in Indiana were determined to provide the least number of services. A similar study conducted within a single state, Pennsylvania, revealed that the intermediate units of that state differed substantially in their provision of services. Some agencies provided as few as six services while other agencies offered as many as 20 services. The types of services varied from instructional supervision for teachers to ESA consultants working directly with students (Pennsylvania Budget and Finance Committee, 1976). Swanson et al (1978) also found ESA consultants providing services directly to students. He suggested that the ESAs of New York were originally created for that purpose—to only provide itinerant teaching services. It was only after the ESAs were perceived as successful in delivering this service that the legislature granted the authority for ESAs to provide instructional supervisory services.

Although services varied among agencies nationally, one ESA-provided service was consistently cited in the literature. The federal regulation which has impacted ESA services most strongly is the required provision of educational services for the handicapped. In fact, the passage of federal legislation, 94–142, created such a need for ESA services that, in many instances, it shaped the mission for ESAs. Most local school systems were not able to economically identify student needs and provide the legally required special education services, so they turned to their local ESAs for assistance. Cober (1978) found a substantial increase in ESA staff in Pennsylvania during the late 1970s and reported that most were employed to provide special education services. These services accounted for over 50 percent of the entire ESA budget. Waller et al (1976) concluded that the ESAs of the Appalachian region focused on special education as one of their major service delivery areas and Popper (1982) reported that the same condition existed in Massachusetts. A similar situation existed in Georgia in the 1970s; all ESAs provided special education services and two of these ESAs concentrated almost exclusively on the provision of these services (Sherrod, 1991). Additionally, Yin et al (1981) identified special education as one of the five service areas provided by the ESAs in Michigan and New Jersey. The special education services consisted of two types: (1) ESA consultants who served as itinerant teachers and worked directly with students, and (2) ESA consultants who served as instructional supervisors and worked with local system special education teachers.

Not only were special education services frequently provided, but they were also well received and valued by the ESA membership. Jacobson et al (1975) found that special education services were the most used of the services provided by the ESAs in Wisconsin. Stefonek (1976) interviewed the ESA directors and found that they perceived the special education services as the most successful ESA service. Litigation in Pennsylvania resulted in local system superintendents indicating that special education services were the most important ESA-provided service (Pennsylvania Budget and Finance Committee, 1976). The studies on special education services grouped itinerant teaching and instructional supervision together as a single special education service. No reference was made as to whether one aspect of special education was more frequently used or more highly valued than the other.

One of the positive attributes of ESAs has been their flexibility in the provision of services; they provide the service as long as local systems need them but move on to other areas when the need no longer exists. Local systems expressed a strong need for assistance in providing special education services in the 1970s. However, as the number of students to receive special education services increased during the 1980s at the local level, many LEAs began providing for disabled students locally and demand for ESA-provided special education services declined (Sherrod, 1991). This example of ESA-provided special education services illustrates how these intermediate agencies frequently assist local systems with start-up programs that may eventually be conducted by the local school system.

The research on ESAs in the 1970s frequently listed the services provided by the agencies under study or suggested services that should be provided. Often these lists overlapped; services suggested in one state were provided in another and vice versa. The services included a mix of both instructional supervison services and administrative functions. The most common types of supervision services indicated were (1) demonstration teaching in classrooms by supervisory content specialists, (2) in-service education, (3) curriculum development, and (4) grant writing. Frequently, ESAs were expected to provide both instructional supervison and administration services. For example, Waller et al (1976) suggested that ESAs should provide a mix of services such as grant-funded experimental or demonstration special projects, basic services including in-service education, cooperative purchasing and driver education; and liaison services to provide a forum to discuss issues. Other studies projected the services that ESAs needed to provide in the future. Commeret (1971) concluded that pupil personnel and management services needed to be provided by the Jefferson County BOCES; Erlund (1975) forecast that ESA consultants in Texas in the late 1970s would have to demonstrate skills in the areas of program planning, development, and evaluation; and Kirk (1980) questioned experts who influenced policy decisions in Pennsylvania to project that bulk purchasing and the standardization of data processing services among the state department of education and the ESA were the services most likely to be implemented before 1990. As evident, the lack of a mission caused ESAs nationally to proceed in various directions. Agencies with some states in the late 1970s were planning to expand the instructional supervisory services that would help schools in instructional improvement while other states were expanding the administrative role of the ESAs. Regardless of the direction the ESAs were taking, they frequently had staff in insufficient numbers to fulfill the expectations. Avants (1975) concluded that the 20 ESAs in Oklahoma were greatly understaffed to accomplish the instructional supervisory tasks for which they were created.

Little research was conducted on the ESAs during the 1980s and most of what exists did not directly address the services provided by the ESAs. McCoy (1981) studied the perceptions of the recipients of ESA services in Utah. He concluded that both teachers and principals believed that ESAs were important to the educational efforts in Utah and, therefore, the services provided by these agencies should be expanded. Martisko (1985) found that, although the ESAs in Minnesota were created primarily to provide local systems with the service of planning, the ESAs' dependency on their constituencies for annual membership resulted in their providing only short term or topical planning. Martisko maintained that annual appropriations of funding for ESAs generally had caused this service to be deficient for all ESAs across the nation. Sherrod (1991) concurred that the service of planning has been a frequent point of criticism of ESAs. Short term planning often has focused on program implementation without consideration of its advantages or disadvantages and eliminates program evaluation. The impact on instructional supervision is apparent. Supervisors in ESAs who practice only short term planning are severely limiting the impact that their services in staff development, curriculum development, and research and evaluation could have on local school systems.

The most comprehensive study on the provision of services was conducted in Georgia. This study described the services provided by the ESAs from their inception in Georgia in 1966 through 1990 and determined how and if the ESA services changed over the 24-year period indicated (Sherrod, 1991). Sherrod found that the ESAs were established in the 1960s as cooperative ventures among local school systems. Each ESA employed content specialists who functioned as instructional supervisors for schools in their area. These supervisors worked with teachers individually to improve the instruction in the classroom. Demonstration teaching was the most frequently cited service provided, although other services included curriculum development and grant writing. As ESA membership increased and demand for their services grew, it became evident that individual consultative assistance to teachers was no longer possible. The ESA supervisors in Georgia redirected their efforts and began providing large group staff development. Simultaneously with the change in the function of ESA supervisors, the ESAs' role in general changed to include administrative tasks.

Each of the types of services included in the Georgia study had been listed in the earlier studies of other states. The services, including both instructional supervison and administrative tasks, were described by the following categories: (a) planning and research, (b) staff development, (c) instruction and curriculum, (d) assessment and evaluation, (e) educational technology, (f) special education, (g) direct services to students, (h) business management including cooperative or bulk purchasing, audiovisual equipment repair, business machine and computer repair, and printing, (i) state department of education requirements, and (j) miscellaneous services specific to an individual ESA.

Sherrod concluded that all ESAs in Georgia provided services in each of the categories, although the extent of the service as well as the service delivery method differed among the agencies. Additionally, the data suggested the following changes had occurred during the 24 years considered in the study: (a) a shift in emphasis from classroom demonstration teaching and individual consultative assistance with teachers to group instruction on global programmatic issues; (b) a change in focus from simply reacting to system requests to a proactive mode of providing leadership and direction for local systems as well as responding to their needs; (c) an expansion of staff development programs to include all categories of certified and noncertified personnel; (d) a fluctuation in special education services depending on the needs of local school systems; (e) a shift from providing only those services requested by member school systems to providing services mandated by law, services requested by the state department of education, and services requested by school systems; (f) an expansion in technical services resulting from a broadened interpretation of the ESA mission and from technological advancements; and (g) a change in the development and implementation of programs based on the availability of grant funding. Although the research did not exist to validate the conclusions in Georgia as also occurring nationwide, it is anticipated that similar changes in the ESAs of all states have occurred. The significance of these findings for supervision is that instructional supervision has been an integral component of the ESAs' purpose since their inception and continues to be so. Supervisors have become proactive at ESAs and are providing educators the leadership and direction needed to improve the instructional program of schools. In many small systems, the ESA supervisors are the only instructional leaders; the teachers rely heavily on the skills and knowledge of the ESA supervisors for instructional assistance.

The only additional research available on the provision of ESA services listed a service function that was not specifically addressed in the Georgia study. Cappa (1988) conducted a nationwide study of the cooperative service agreements between local school systems, ESAs, and local governments. He concluded that ESAs most often provided services to local governments when they had entered into a service agreement relating to health services, vocational or career education, social services, adult education, purchasing, recreation programs, or library services.

The limited data available suggest positive reactions to the provision of ESA services. For example, when questioned about the value of the services of the intermediate agencies in Pennsylvania, 75 percent of local system superintendents rated them as "good" (Pennsylvania Legislative Budget and Finance Committee, 1976). These superintendents listed as the most important services that they received from the ESA as the instructional supervision functions of curriculum development, in-service education for all staff, special education and instructional media, and the administrative tasks of bulk purchasing and data processing. Kloster (1978) reviewed the functions of intermediate education agencies and concluded that they provide high cost, low incident services, and that a direct relationship exists between an ESA's size and type and

its levels of service. Urquhart (1971) concluded that the instructional supervision services provided by one ESA in Georgia in the areas of curriculum, instruction, and professional growth had a positive impact on member systems. He also noted, however, that many educators were uninformed of services provided by the ESA and stated that teachers frequently did not use the instructional supervision services because they were less knowledgeable than administrators about the types of services available through the ESA. The lack of awareness of available services was cited in other studies as well. Avants (1975) found that educators in Oklahoma did not use ESA services because they did not know of their availability. Stefonek (1976) found that the public was unaware of the services ESAs provided to local school systems in Wisconsin. He reported, however, that the majority of ESA directors were not concerned with this omission because local system superintendents and the boards of control were knowledgeable about the ESA services.

Several studies addressed issues relating to the use or lack of use of ESA services. In two of these studies, Waller, Kemp, and Scanlon (1976) and Stefonek (1976) concluded that ESA services were well used because of the economy of scale that they provided local school systems. Yin et al (1981) also found that ESA services were used by local systems in the states of Colorado, Michigan, and New Jersey. However, he maintained that the instructional supervision services of curriculum consultation and in-service programs were used most in Michigan. Yin et al identified four reasons for the use of these services: (1) the ESAs were responsive to the user needs; (2) the services were credible; (3) the services were based on strong interpersonal ties between the ESA staff and local system staff; and (4) the services involved mutual exchanges. Yin's conclusions suggest that the supervisors in Michigan were more successful than in other states because they were delivering needed instructional services of a high quality while maintaining collegial relationships with the educators in the schools.

In studying use of services, Popper (1982) found a relationship between the size of the school system and the superintendent's perceived need for additional services. He suggested that the smaller districts more frequently expressed a need for both instructional supervision and noninstructional administrative services than did larger systems. Tolson (1982) illustrated that the perception of use of services sometimes differed between groups. He compared superintendents' perceptions with those of ESA directors and found that the superintendents believed that the ESAs provided more services in public relations than the directors perceived. Additionally, the superintendents believed that the local systems used the services more frequently than did the directors. Keeley (1982) determined why ESA services were not utilized. He surveyed and interviewed system superintendents in one ESA district in South Dakota and found that the use of ESA services was not related to the need for or the quality of the service; instead, the use of services correlated to the lack of awareness of the potential of collaboration and to obstacles of tradition and continuity.

Users and nonusers of ESA services project differing degrees of optimism about future service needs. Michalski

(1987) studied school system personnel who actively participated in ESA services and those persons who participated in less than 25 percent of ESA services to determine if a difference existed in their perceptions of future ESA services. No indication was given as to why ESA services were used or not used by the participants. Overall, Michalski found that the users of ESA services projected more optimism about the future. However, he concluded that no difference existed between the two groups concerning desirable services ESAs should provide in the future. Instead, both groups maintained that the primary factor determining the ESAs' future would be the leadership.

The instructional supervision programs and services that ESAs provide are often critical to local school systems in their mission of providing students with the best education possible. However, data are not currently available to substantiate what existing supervisory services ESAs currently provide, to determine the worth of such services, or to project future needs. Much of the data on ESA services that does exist is from 15 to 20 years old, an eternity if measured by the advancements made within technology during that time period. During these twenty years, the role of the supervisor has been more clearly delineated. The available research, therefore, should not be used to assess the instructional supervision services ESAs currently provide. New research is needed on ESA services in general and instructional supervisory services specifically if these agencies are, in fact, going to effectively impact school improvement and bridge the gap between state and local levels as the educational system enters the 21st century.

EVALUATIONS

One way to measure the worth of a program, service, or agency is to evaluate it. Frequently, as new educational programs are implemented, an evaluation component is included. The results of such evaluations are often used to demonstrate the success of the program, or justify funding for the continuation of the program, or to call for the conclusion of the program.

During the rapid rise in the number of ESAs nationally in the 1960s and 1970s, these agencies were viewed as new entities. The United States was exploring new educational methods and emphasis was placed on demonstrating and verifying the value of new programs. However, limited research exists related to the evaluation of the ESA agencies or of the services that they provided. Although annual reports have been developed by ESAs in many states, questions have continually arisen throughout the years concerning the types of services provided by these agencies and their associated effectiveness. As previously stated, the ESAs in many states have been and continue to be dependent in part on annual appropriations from the state legislatures. Each year, many of these legislatures have questioned the continuation of funding for agencies about which so little is known. This situation has certainly been the case in Georgia. A common complaint among members of the Georgia legislature concerning the ESAs has been that they cannot understand exactly what the ESAs are

doing, and, therefore, cannot determine the educational benefits derived from their existence. The inability of ESAs to conclusively convey their value to legislators has jeopardized their future existence on more than one occasion.

The legislators' complaints have been substantiated by an absence of research data. The lack of information concerning the activities and effectiveness of ESAs was not confined to Georgia but appeared as a nationwide concern. Research to evaluate the effectiveness of ESA services was almost nonexistent, although the need for such data has been documented (Lavin & Sanders, 1974; Pennsylvania Legislative Budget and Finance Committee, 1976). The absence of research could be due, in part, to the attitude of the educators in decision-making positions in ESAs. Stefonek (1976) found that ESA directors in Wisconsin did not want any type of external evaluation of the effectiveness of their services. Instead, the directors maintained that answering to their local boards of control sufficiently evaluated their services. Waller et al (1976) and Kemp et al (1976) found similar attitudes with the ESA directors in Appalachia. These ESA directors acknowledged that they had no quantitative way of knowing if the ESAs were meeting their objectives but suggested that the continuation of support by their local system superintendents and boards of control indicated that objectives were in fact being met.

Of the limited research that exists, qualitative data or the perceptions of educators were often the measures to determine the effectiveness of a specific program or service. For example, Buckel (1988) compared the differences of opinions of ESA staff with local system personnel to determine the effectiveness of ESA-delivered bilingual educational programs in Texas. The results indicated that the programs were effective but weak in providing support material for bilingual education in the various content areas. Dickhudt (1987) examined the perceptions of principals and the characteristics of ESAs and local districts to assess the effectiveness of transferral of information from ESAs to local school districts in Minnesota. He concluded that the service was ineffective because principals had varying levels of understanding of the service and in general did not use the service. A third example of using educators' perceptions to evaluate effectiveness was a study conducted in Georgia. Urquhart (1971) surveyed administrators and teachers in one ESA area to measure the effectiveness of the ESA programs related to curriculum and instruction and to professional development. He concluded that the programs were effective because they provided a balance of services for both rural and nonrural school systems. He further suggested that an evaluation of the services of all ESAs was needed but that the diversity among the agencies required the development of individual evaluation instruments.

The use of educators' perceptions was also used in two studies to determine overall effectiveness of the ESA. Vice (1976) used the perceived impact of the implementation by the ESAs in Kentucky of the programs funded through Title III of the Elementary and Secondary Education Act, to conclude that the ESAs in that state were effective. Avants (1975) studied the ESAs in Oklahoma to access the extent to which they accomplished their objectives for the 1974–75 school year. The findings suggested that the ESAs were not measuring up to their potential, that school personnel were unaware of their services so they did not use them, and that the ESAs were greatly understaffed to accomplish the tasks for which they were established.

The most recent and potentially the most influential research related to factors promoting successful interdistrict cooperatives for special education. Fletcher and Cole (1991) studied the governance, demographics, managerial style, and organizational structure of ESAs providing special education services to determine the composition of the most effective ESAs. They concluded that (a) cooperatives providing multiple services are more effective than those with a single purpose such as providing special education services; (b) cooperatives are more effective when staff members have clearly defined roles and responsibilities that are communicated to member systems; (c) cooperatives are very effective if they provide more than fifty percent of the leadership in assessing needs, long range planning, public relationss and in-service training; (d) cooperatives are very effective when they communicate to members about the financial benefits of sharing services and of the resources needed to implement and maintain programs; and (e) cooperatives are very effective when they have a high level of involvement by the governing board. Although this research addressed the effectiveness of special education cooperatives, it has implications for all types of ESAs. Additional research is needed to verify or refute the findings of Fletcher and Cole. Such research has the potential of changing the structure of ESAs nationwide.

The only research available that evaluated the effectiveness of ESAs that was not based on educators' perceptions related to the financial benefits to school systems participating in ESAs. Hopper (1976) defined effectiveness in terms of financial costs to implement a program and compared the costs expended by ESA members with those of nonmembers. He found that ESAs expended substantially less money for group-oriented services than nonmembers paid for the same services. Hopper concluded that a major factor contributing to this situation was that ESAs had the ability to secure outside funding for some services while local systems often had restrictions on the number of grants that they could receive.

Most of the limited data that exists on ESAs did not address the effectiveness of either the educational service agency as a whole or of the component programs or services they deliver. Of the research on ESAs that exists, most was presented earlier in this chapter as it related to the topic under discussion. The remaining ESA data did not address ESA effectiveness or directly relate to previous topics. Rather, the remaining research explored issues such as attitudes towards ESAs (Nachatilo, 1977; Wain, 1977), the development of a self-evaluation instrument (Williams, 1979), the role of the director (McWhorter, 1977), frequency of services (Mueller, 1976), and types of services provided directly to students (Grund, 1976; Thero, 1979). As previously stated, an absence of evaluation research has apparently caused ESAs to be the target of considerable criticism. Legislators and policy makers have frequently suggested that data is needed to demonstrate the worth of entities such as ESAs in order to justify their continuation. The limited data that exists on the effectiveness of ESAs was generally positive. The two studies suggesting that

the ESA services were ineffective based their conclusions not on the worth of the program but on educators' lack of awareness of their existence. The small quantity combined with the lack of recency of most data perpetuates criticism and illustrates the continued need for research on these agencies. An abundance of research on ESAs is needed to end the controversy between critics and supporters and to assist educators in making the most appropriate educational decisions for students.

NEED FOR ADDITIONAL RESEARCH

This chapter has described the inception, role, and function of the educational service agencies in the United States by citing the available research. A careful reading of the literature reveals that the ESAs remain a virtually untapped source of information. Perhaps no other educational entity exists that has had such limited research about its purpose and worth. Studies have frequently focused on educational issues within an ESA service area; rarely was the ESA the topic of the research. Most of the available research on ESAs was conducted during the 1970s or very early 1980s; few studies have been conducted on these agencies within the last ten years. During the same time period, educational research on topics such as how children learn and effective instructional strategies for teachers has been abundant. Additionally, technological advancements within the last ten years have transformed the educational environment. Given the length of time that ESAs have been in existence and the potential impact the programs and services provided by these agencies have on instructional supervision for both local school systems and state education agencies, it seems incredible that so little research has been conducted on them.

The questions for researchers to investigate are plentiful. Possible questions include the following: (a) Is district geographic size a factor in the effectiveness of ESA services? (b) Are educational services provided by generalists more effective than similar services provided by specialists? (c) Is one service delivery method more effective than another? (d) Are ESA-provided technical services cost efficient for local school systems? (e) Is district student population a factor in the effectiveness of ESA services? (f) To what extent does system wealth influence the number and types of services that local systems receive? (g) What impact does the governance structure have on the effectiveness of ESA services? (h) Are ESAs that are proactive in their delivery of services more effective than those who operate solely in a reactive mode? (i) Is one type of ESA more effective than another in meeting the needs of local systems? (j) Does a requirement of annual membership affect the types and effectiveness of ESA-provided services? (k) What impact does the method for funding ESAs have on the provision and effectiveness of services? (l) Are ESAs in which membership is voluntary more effective than those that require membership? (m) Do ESA services result in a positive educational change in member school systems for the delivery of instruction to students? (n) Are ESAs that specialize in a few services more effective than those that provide a broader menu of services?

The list of possible questions to be researched is practically endless. The absence of available and, especially, current research on ESAs combined with the extensive number of these agencies nationwide provides an abundance of issues for researchers to address. Such research is needed for two primary reasons. First, the data could be used to answer the questions of legislators and other policy makers who are frequently asked to provide funding for agencies about which so little is known. Secondly, and most importantly, educators could make more informed decisions about collaborative efforts and the best ways of providing and improving educational opportunities for students.

REFERENCES

Avants, T. W. (1975). An assessment of regional education service centers in Oklahoma. *Dissertation Abstracts International, 36,* 5192.

Aycock, K. H. (1981). The degree of desirability of certain components of education service agencies for Mississippi. *Dissertation Abstracts International, 43,* 322.

Brey, W. J. Jr. (1981). A comparative study of differential cost between regional and local educational service delivery systems in the state of Wisconsin. *Dissertation Abstracts International, 42,* 1480.

Buckel, K. J. (1988). Perceptions of regional education service centers' effectiveness in supporting bilingual education in Texas. *Masters Abstracts, 27,* 20.

Cappa, T. P. (1988). Education and local government cooperation in metropolitan areas: Service cooperation agreements between local governments and school districts/ESAs of metropolitan areas. *Dissertation Abstracts International, 49,* 3213.

Cober, J. G. (1978). *An analysis of intermediate unit services 1975–1976—1976–1977. Addendum.* Harrisburg, PA: Pennsylvania State Department of Education (ERIC Reproduction Service No. ED 165 357).

Commeret, C. E., Sr. (1971). A study of the perceptions of local school teachers and administrators of Jefferson County as to the adequacy of the current school programs and the possible role that BOCES might play to improve these programs. *Dissertation Abstracts International, 32,* 2298.

Cox, B. B., III. (1981). Administrative criteria for the establishment of regional educational service agencies for special education. *Dissertation Abstracts International, 42,* 3821.

Dickhudt, T. M. (1987). Perceptions of elementary and secondary principals of information services offered by educational cooperative service units in Minnesota. *Dissertation Abstracts International, 48,* 15.

Erlund, O. J. (1975). A forecast of critical tasks for the role of planning and evaluation specialists in Texas regional education service centers. *Dissertation Abstracts International, 36,* 4901.

Firestone, W. A. (1981). *Regional educational service agencies supporting knowledge utilization: The intermediate unit of Pennsylvania.* Washington, DC: National Institute of Education (ERIC Document Reproduction Service No. ED 232 245).

Fletcher, R. & Cole, J. T. (1991). *Factors related to the successful operation of special education interdistrict cooperatives.* Las Cruces, NM: New Mexico State University (ERIC Document Reproduction Service No. ED 342 568).

Galvin, P. F. (1991). The structure of school district cooperatives: Factors that influence participation in cooperative ventures (educational finance). *Dissertation Abstracts International, 52,* 77.

Glanz, J. (1982). Ahistoricism and school supervision: Notes toward a history. In E. E. Grimsley & R. E. Bruce (Eds.). *Readings in educational supervision* (pp. 8–13). Alexandria, VA: ASCD.

Grund, W. E. (1976). A comparative case study of factors associated with programming practices for handicapped children in school districts using local versus cooperative service delivery. *Dissertation Abstracts International, 38,* 2703.

Hopper, D. L. (1976). A study of a regional education service agency in Mississippi. *Dissertation Abstracts International, 37,* 6872.

Jacobson, D., Mrdjenovich, D., Solberg, R., & Wileman, C. (1975). *The cooperative educational service agency.* Madison, WI: Wisconsin State Department of Public Instruction (ERIC Document Reproduction Service No. 120 979).

Jones, T. H. (1975). *Financing Connecticut's regional service centers.* State Advisory Committee to the Study of Educational Service Centers (ERIC Document Reproduction Services No. ED 133 851).

Kachris, P. T. (1987). A history of the district superintendency and BOCES, 1910–1982 (New York). *Dissertation Abstracts International, 51,* 699.

Keely, M. P. (1982). Education service units: A case study of the corn-belt cooperative. *Dissertation Abstracts International, 43,* 322.

Kemp, D. M., Waller, J. D., & Scanlon, J. W. (1976). *Report on regional education service agencies in Appalachia.* Washington, D.C.: Urban Institute (ERIC Document Reproduction Service No. 141 876).

Kirk, W. R. (1980). A forecast of postulated events in the provision of intermediate unit services in Pennsylvania. *Dissertation Abstracts International, 41,* 855.

Kloster, A. J. (1978). *A study of intermediate school district functions and organizational structure.* Research prepared for the Michigan Association of Intermediate School Administrators (ERIC Document Reproduction Service No. ED 166 820).

Lane, M. E. (1984). Colorado boards of cooperative educational services: factors influencing member districts' financial support (BOCES, school district). *Dissertation Abstracts International, 45,* 3068.

Lavin, R. J. & Sanders, J. E. (1974). *Organizing for improving delivery of educational services in Massachusetts. Volume 2: A review of educational cooperatives and their various forms.* Chelmsford, MA: Merrimack Education Center (ERIC Document Reproduction Service No. ED 098 692).

Levis, R. M. (1983). *The education service agency—Where next?* Arlington, VA: The American Association of School Principals.

Martisko, D. D. (1985). A study of educational cooperative service units in Minnesota: Mission as perceived by board members and directors (agencies, regional programs, planning). *Dissertation Abstracts International, 46,* 2151.

McCoy, J. W. (1981). A study of the current services offered by the Utah regional service centers as perceived by patron teachers and principals. *Dissertation Abstracts International, 42,* 485.

Michalski, J. A. (1987). Forecasting the future of education cooperative service units (ECSU's) in Minnesota: An exploratory study using the delphi methodology. *Dissertation Abstracts International, 48,* 2610.

McWhorter, D. G. (1977). Role and function of special education directors in a regional education service agency. *Dissertation Abstracts International, 39,* 2183.

Morton, C. (1988). Intermediate education units as control systems: The case of New York boards of cooperative educational services (BOCES). *Dissertation Abstracts International, 49,* 3225.

Mueller, R. C. (1976). A comparison of intermediate school districts in Michigan and intermediate units in Pennsylvania. *Dissertation Abstracts International, 38*, 6447.

Nachatilo, W. R. (1977). The educational cooperative service unit as perceived by school board presidents, administrators, and teachers in planning regions one and two of northwestern Minnesota. *Dissertation Abstracts International, 38*, 6447.

Neagley, R. L. & Evans, N. D. (1980). *Handbook for effective supervision of instruction* (3rd ed.). Englewood Cliffs, NJ: Prentice Hall.

Nichols, D. A. (1983). Comparative profiles of three types of intermediate district superintendents. *Dissertation Abstracts International, 45*, 369.

Notestone, L. L. (1982). Cooperative purchasing in the public school districts of the United States: Statutory authority and practices. *Dissertation Abstracts International, 43*, 1779.

Pennsylvania Legislative Budget and Finance Committee. (1976). *Report on the Pennsylvania intermediate unit system* (ERIC Document Reproduction Service No. ED 131 542).

Popper, W. J. (1982). Superintendents' perceptions of cooperative educational service agencies in Massachusetts. *Dissertation Abstracts International, 43*, 2524.

Sherrod, B. J. (1991). A description of the services provided by the educational service agencies in Georgia, 1966–1990. *Dissertation Abstracts International, 52*, 4176.

Snider, M. C. (1973). Guidelines for developing and implementing regional education service agencies. *Dissertation Abstracts International, 34*, 2282.

Stefonek, T. (1976). *Cooperative educational service agencies: the CESA coordinators' perspective* (Information Series Vol. 6, No. 2 Bulletin No. 7229). Madison, WI: Wisconsin State Department of Public Instruction (ERIC Document Reproduction Service No. ED 145 551).

Stephens Associates. (1979). *Planning for state systems of Education Service Agencies: Some conceptual and methodological considerations.* Arlington, VA: The American Association of School Administrators.

Strain, D. L. (1984). An analysis of need for county offices of education as perceived by randomly selected local school superintendents in Ohio. *Dissertation Abstracts International, 46*, 1779.

Swanson, A. D., King, R. A., Nelson, E. A., & Good, P. C. (1978). *A study of regional services and school district organization in New York state.* New York, N: New York State Department of Education (ERIC Document Reproduction Service No. 159 804).

Thero, J. J. (1979). A study of stated opinions held by internal school publics concerning programs of occupational education operated by boards of cooperative educational services in upstate New York. *Dissertation Abstracts International, 40*, 3991.

Todd, S. M. (1980). Comparison of Indiana RESA units with national RESA units as to programs and services and delivery of services and determination of satisfactory governance and finance patterns of national RESA units. *Dissertation Abstracts International, 46*, 1779.

Tolson, R. B. (1982). Utilization of regional services in the development of school-community relations programs in small school districts of Texas. *Dissertation Abstracts International, 43*, 1786.

Urquhart, D. C. (1971). The impact of the Heart of Georgia shared service project as viewed by participating administrators, teachers, and shared service consultants. *Dissertation Abstracts International, 32*, 4335.

Vice, W. C. (1976). Evaluating the perceived impact of the eastern Kentucky educational development corporation through its regional services. *Dissertation Abstracts International, 37*, 4836.

Wain, D. L. (1977). Attitudes of local educational policy-makers toward inter-district cooperation through regional service units and the relationship of these attitudes to selected personal and school district characteristics. *Dissertation Abstracts International, 38*, 1173.

Waller, J. D., Kemp, D. M., & Scanlon, J. W. (1976). *An assessment of the Appalachian regional commission's regional education service agencies program.* Washington, D.C.: Urban Institute (ERIC Document Reproduction Service No. ED 141 875).

Waller, J. D., Kemp, D. M., & Scanlon, J. W. (1976). *Supporting analyses for an assessment of the Appalachian regional commission's regional education service agencies program, and appendices.* Washington, D.C.: Urban Institute (ERIC Document Reproduction Service No. ED 141 874).

Williams, L. M. (1979). The design, development, and validation of a comprehensive self-evaluation study of a Texas regional education service center. *Dissertation Abstracts International, 40*, 6139.

Yin, R. K. & Gwaltney, M. K. (1981). *Organizations collaborating to improve educational practice.* Cambridge, MA: Abt Associates, Inc. (ERIC Document Reproduction Service No. ED 207 190).

Yin, R. K., Gwaltney, M. K., & Molitor, J. (1981). *Case studies of three interorganizational arrangements.* Cambridge, MA: ABT Associates, Inc. (ERIC Document Reproduction Service No. 207 189).

· 29 ·

SUPERVISION FROM STATE EDUCATION DEPARTMENTS

Dennis J. Nielsen

SOUTH CAROLINA STATE UNIVERSITY

Barbara S. Nielsen

SOUTH CAROLINA STATE SUPERINTENDENT OF EDUCATION

INTRODUCTION

Most all of us have general notions of what is and what is not research—what is and what is not supervision. Some of our notions are tightly bound to strict definitions while others include as much within their definitions as can reasonably be argued. We will differ. Whether we agree or disagree on what is or what is not, for the purpose of this chapter, we have determined the boundaries of understanding, of research and supervision that will be used throughout this analysis.

Within this chapter is a brief history of the changes in supervisory practices by state departments of education, a prototype with examples of primary initiatives in the State of South Carolina, the supervisory and research link, and future directions.

What Is And What Is Not

Research Directing rigorous experimental research has never been viewed as a primary mission of state departments of education. Thus, little research defined as a formal, systematic application of the scientific method to the study of problems has been conducted in state departments of education. However, if one extends the definition to include the analysis and transmission of the results of data collection on educational issues to the public, general assemblies, schools, students, and parents, state departments of education become one of the largest sources of research information in every state. For this chapter, the meaning of research will include the collection, analysis, and reporting of educational data.

Supervision According to Ben Harris (1975), "supervision of instruction is what school personnel do with *adults* and *things* to maintain or change the school operation in ways that *directly* influence the teaching processes employed to promote pupil learning" (pp. 10–11). Perhaps more than ever, state departments of education are working with adults and things to influence educational processes to enhance student learning. They are rejecting the historic approach of directing, prescribing and inspecting used for so many years and are well on their way to employing long advocated enlightened supervisory practices.

THE PAST ROLE OF RESEARCH IN STATE DEPARTMENTS OF EDUCATION

Research in the Organization

The organizational patterns of typical local school districts seem to be modeled on the organizational pattern of state departments of education. Generally, the positions that are defined in a state department are present in the local school district. Boards of education and superintendents have been appointed or elected to their office in both local and state organizations. Assistant and associate superintendents are customarily hired to be responsible for finance and curriculum and instruction. Directors with expertise in subject areas such as mathematics, language arts, performing and visual arts, physical education, and science are common positions in both traditional state departments and local districts. Other directors responsible for programs related to student service areas such as guidance and counseling, food service, evaluation, testing, and transportation; directors of programs that relate to specific student populations such as early childhood, gifted and talented, special needs, vocational, and adults; and directors of specially funded state and federal programs such as those noted in Chapter 1 legislation, are all specific job positions at the state and local levels. As positions formed at the state level (often due to new program areas funded by state legislatures or federal agencies), a new position was formed at the local level. The size of the bureaucracy continued to grow focusing on independent programs and disregarding research.

The scarcity of research in state departments of education is indirectly affected by federal funding agencies. Federal requirements for program funding emphasize the need for evaluative data but rarely include the need for research. The traditional evaluative data collected by federal funding agencies consist mainly of evidence used to support the meeting of specified objectives of the funded program. These data are not collected to support or reject research hypotheses but rather to justify continuation of a program. The type of data collected depends on the results specified in the program objectives. These data range from simply counting procedures (number of participants) to statistical analysis of outcomes. A major difference in these evaluation procedures and the strict definition of research is the lack of rigorously defined control groups. Most often, summary data are attributed to the effects of the program even though many other factors could account for much of the result.

A large amount of summative evaluation data is collected by state departments, federal agencies, and local districts. These data are reported and often aggregated in order to draw general conclusions of program effects.

From their early inception, state departments of education never viewed the conduct of rigorous research experiments as a primary mission and, thus, neither have local districts. Whether state leaders viewed the research function as the responsibility of colleges and universities or whether research was not viewed as a vital component in the educational process, rigorous research was not a substantial function of state departments of education nor, therefore, of local school districts.

State Regulation

Prior to the 1950s, state departments of education served primarily to provide teacher certification, goal setting, and general expertise. Their role focused on implementing the intents of individual state constitutions. In the late 1950s and early 1960s, a dramatic role change occurred. Perhaps influenced by the space race and the projected goals of the Soviet Union to destroy the United States, the call for renewed efforts in mathematics and science was made. The solution to being the first country to land on the moon was through a strong educational system. Because the need was so immediate, the quickest way to upgrade the schools was through the federal

government and state departments of education. New curricula were developed to expose students to advanced mathematics and science at earlier ages with an emphasis on the theoretical structures of mathematics and science.

During this time, research in universities on the teaching of mathematics and science was at a peak. Research findings were immediately transmitted to teachers and into classrooms through in-service, staff development and graduate education. Teachers were encouraged to return to college and many were paid by the federal government through the National Defense Education Act to obtain advanced degrees in mathematics and/or science education. Both graduate and undergraduate enrollments in those areas increased significantly. In 1900, 10 percent of the nation's population graduated from high school, school met for 140 days, and four percent of the population was registered to vote. By the year 1995, 42 percent of the nation's population were graduated from a four-year college and another 23 percent graduated from two-year institutions. The need for education was ever widening.

The landing on the moon in 1969 made the United States the obvious winner of the space race. Successful accomplishment of that mission provided strong evidence of the ability of the federal government and state agencies to produce results in education. Their oversight of the educational system to overcome large odds encouraged the federal government and state agencies to address other educational needs. Education had demonstrated its relevance to the future of the United States during the 1970s and in the early 1980s, under President Carter, education was elevated to a position on the Cabinet level. This new United States Department of Education was to serve as a central focus for the collection and dissemination of data relevant to education.

With no more moon races to win, attention was directed to the many social problems facing this nation. Out of the 1960s came new federal laws which placed the solution of full and complete integration on the public schools. Meeting the need for a larger segment of students to attend institutions of higher education was solely a responsibility of the educational system. The rebellious nature of students in the 1960s affected judgments about what should be taught in public schools. State legislatures, looking for help to solve these and other problems, gave their state departments increased responsibilities for the management of schools. And state departments responded to the challenge by becoming agencies of compliance and regulation. States began to "take control" of the entire system of education by establishing the number of hours students were required to be in class, the number of days a student must be in school to pass, the number of books a library must have, the specifications for new school buildings, and a set of required curriculum offerings. The traditional supervisory facilitating role of state departments was replaced with that of directing, controlling and regulating. Unlike the support for changes in mathematics and science, none of these changes in organizational power was supported by research.

In 1983, *A Nation at Risk,* a publication of the National Commission on Excellence in Education, warned the public about a failing educational system. Reforms in virtually every area of American education were judged by the authors to be necessary for the United States to reestablish its leadership in education. Since no specific solutions to the problems of fixing schools were offered by the report, state education departments were granted powers by their legislatures to correct the flaws in the system.

Due in part to the success of the mathematics and science efforts of the 1950s, state education departments began efforts to improve the system, program by program. As programs were identified for improvements, persons with special interest in one constituent group affected by a program reinforced the rising power of federal and state decision-making in education. Once state education departments received legal authority to regulate local schools, they began focusing on input variables they felt would have dramatic impact. They:

1. recommended significant increases in teacher salaries (In South Carolina, teacher salaries were raised by 60 percent over 7 years.);
2. advocated new sources of funding for targeted populations (In South Carolina, an additional penny sales tax was devoted solely to educational priorities.);
3. raised graduation requirements (In South Carolina the number of courses required to graduate from high school increased from 18 to 20, and recently to 24.);
4. defined the number of minutes a class must be offered (In South Carolina, a defined minimum program laid out the specific courses and classroom minutes which must be offered.);
5. defined minimum basic skills a high school graduate must possess upon graduation (In South Carolina, Basic Skills Assessment Program measures were developed in reading, writing and mathematics which students had to reach in order to graduate. The tests were administered at the tenth grade level and if failed could be taken again in the junior and/or senior years.);
6. established standards for teacher certification (In South Carolina, passing the Educational Entrance Examination competency assessment, meeting or surpassing a specified score on the National Teacher Examination, and submitting to a Federal Bureau of Investigation check were required for new teachers.);
7. offered incentives to schools (In South Carolina, based on test results comparing similarly situated school districts, a monetary reward was granted.); and
8. relied on a model for more effective schools (In South Carolina, the Educational Improvement Act (1983) included the requirement that six components of the Effective School Model be implemented in the schools. The degree of school success was determined by the achievement of the goals for each of these six components.).

From these input factors, a new set of rules for schools emerged. At an ever increasing rate, state department employees became auditors of rules and regulations. "Amid this blizzard of activity, it became easy to lose sight of the central aim: improving the teaching and learning process to support higher levels of student achievement" (ECS, 1995, p. 7). It became much easier to check and report to the state legislators the degree to which the new rules and regulations were being implemented.

Despite the lack of research evidence to support the emphasis on rules and regulations over this period, some gains were realized, but too slowly to meet present and future workforce demands (ECS, 1995). The changes have not translated into a significant number of graduates with world class skills (ECS, 1996). The demands by business, parents, and the public in general were not sufficiently met through the heavy emphasis on rule and regulation compliance. If public educational organizations were to survive, other changes seemed necessary.

RESEARCH: NEW BASIS FOR EDUCATIONAL CHANGE

Research Drives Systemic Change

Though little research has been conducted by state departments of education, the use of research results, both experimental and applied, have led state departments of education in their efforts to improve educational results through a reengineering of schools for the 21st century. At the heart of systemic change is a major reorientation in content and pedagogy to focus on learning. State education departments are relying on research to identify what is to be taught, to determine how best to teach and to measure what has been taught. The intent is to establish high standards and constantly raise the bar, aiming for continuous improvement by everyone who is part of the system.

Prompted by international comparisons, which have shown American educational results to be embarrassingly low, and by the widely perceived need for the United States to be the leader in the global economy, the search for new paradigms was in order. To be competitive in the new global marketplace, the American society recognized the need for a work force that is educated beyond the basics, that can work in group settings, whose members are on the cutting edge of technology and that can communicate at a high level, not only with English-speaking nations, but other nations as well.

To stay competitive in the international marketplace, major United States corporations realized the need for their own organizational change. Restructuring, downsizing, redistributing, retooling, and out-sourcing have been common words for change within the business community. If corporations are to deal with a new world, not only must the quality of their products improve, but the structure of the organization itself must change.

Following the swift movement of business to make use of enlightened supervisory practices, state departments have begun to alter their approaches. As with business, state departments realized that in order to produce a new product of quality, a new organizational paradigm must replace the old. With a renewed emphasis on meeting the needs of a variety of customers in the educational system, educators must deal with the shift in dynamics and the changes it brings. Whatever approach to change is used, the process should be comprehensive, practical, and effective. One such approach is the philosophy and attending concepts of Total Quality Management (TQM). W. Edwards Deming developed 14 principles most often associated with TQM. These principles reflect many of the same principles of enlightened supervision of the early 1970s. The principles are:

1. create constancy of purpose;
2. accept the new philosophy;
3. end dependence on mass inspection;
4. stop the practice of doing business on price tag alone;
5. improve the system of production and service;
6. establish programs of training;
7. initiate leadership;
8. drive out fear;
9. break down barriers between departments;
10. eliminate slogans, exhortations, and targets for the workforce;
11. eliminate numerical quotas and management by objectives;
12. remove barriers to pride and joy of workmanship;
13. institute a vigorous program of education and retraining; and
14. take action to accomplish the transformation (Aguayo, 1990).

A change in the organizational paradigm is necessary for the implementation of a total quality philosophy. Whether state departments of education follow the teachings of TQM or some other plan for facilitating and supporting organizational change, the need for structural change is clear. According to the Status Report of State Systemic Education Improvements (CCSSO, 1996), 43 states (no data on three-states) are under a reorganization plan while 40 states report a governance and management change. Reinforced by the principles underlying the new paradigm, state educational leaders are transforming the once fragmented educational system into a unified system with its parts interconnected for a common purpose. As state departments of education move away from a bureaucratic aim of sustaining the present to one where competitive barriers between departments are removed and collaboration is rewarded, state departments of education become more effective and efficient. When these fundamental structural changes in state departments of education become modeled within local education systems, dramatic change in the way education is delivered will result.

The Focus of Change

While program components are the heart of the change efforts in state departments, past experiences have shown that to change programs alone will not result in the significant reform necessary for significant improvement. Thus, the research for systemic change has been relied upon to help educational organizations set a new structural environment for improved results. A move to return to the importance of basic supervision practices of facilitating rather than directing, supporting rather than controlling and providing for participatory decision-making rather than managing the system are becoming the standard operating practices of state departments of education.

Figure 29.1 displays the basic elements of an educational program. Curriculum is defined simply as intended learning

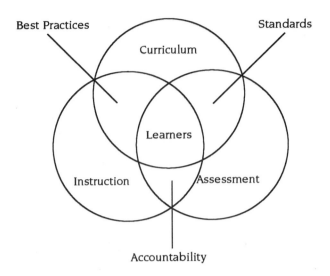

FIGURE 29.1. Program Components

goals, instruction as the means of delivering the curriculum to learners and assessment as the measure of learning results. All components are directed toward learners. Best practices are those researched instructional means which have been shown to provide learners with the best opportunities to reach the learning goals. Standards are the set of concrete achievement objectives that detail measurable skills and competencies that students should master in specific curricula at every step in the educational process. Accountability is the measure of the effectiveness of instructional efforts to assist learners in meeting educational standards.

Figure 29.2 displays specific program supports that require coordinated systemic change. Focusing on changing the basic system rather than changing each part separately was reflected in the philosophy shared by the nation's governors in their 1990 educational goals report, when they said, "We cannot continue to tinker with an educational machine whose fundamental design is defective. Instead, fundamental and dra-

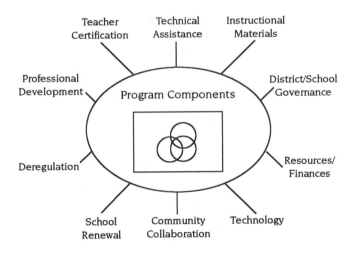

FIGURE 29.2. Program Supports

matic changes in the very design and structure of the educational system must be made." Because state departments have been given specific powers to affect directly local schools, they are in the best position to provide leadership for reform. Many state legislatures, well aware of the pressing national need, passed legislation resulting in a dramatic reformation in education.

The commitment to change seems firmly in place. The emphasis on inputs has been replaced by an emphasis on standards and the redesign of a controlling state system by reducing regulations and placing more and more decisions at the local level. Specifically, according to the Council of Chief State School Officers (CCSSO, 1996):

1. thirty-two states (one state did not report) have content standards under review or development in areas which include: Mathematics, Science, Health, English, Social Studies, Foreign Language, Arts, Health/PE, School To Work, Tech. Prep, Apprenticeships, Reading, Writing, History, Geography, Civics, Music, Visual Arts, Dance, Theater, Communication Skills, Computer Science, English As a Second Language, Languages Other than English, Language Arts, Language Usage, Technology, Vocational Technical Education, Biological and Physical Sciences, Citizenship, Integrated Learnings, Career Education, Multiculturalism, Communications, Technology, Environment/ Ecology, Home Economics, Health & Safety;

2. thirty-nine states (two states did not report) have content standards ready for implementation in Mathematics, Science, Health, English, Social Studies, Foreign Language, Arts, Health/PE, School To Work, Tech. Prep, Apprenticeships, Reading, Writing, History, Geography, Civics, Music, Visual Arts, Dance, Theater, Communication Skills, Computer Science, English As a Second Language, Languages Other than English, Language Arts, Language Usage, Technology, Vocational Technical Education, Biological and Physical Sciences, Citizenship, Integrated Learnings, Career Education, Multiculturalism, Communications, Technology, Environment/Ecology, Home Economics, Health & Safety;

3. forty-seven states (one state did not report) have student assessments consisting of one or more criterion referenced test, norm referenced test, portfolio assessment, performance test, of the following writing samples;

4. forty states (one state did not report) have student performance standards in place or under development;

5. fourteen states (three states did not report) have policies, programs, or strategies for opportunity to learn standards;

6. forty-seven states (one state did not report) have teacher policies on professional preparation;

7. forty-one states (one state did not report) have or are developing a state technology plan;

8. forty-three states (four states did not report) have policies, programs, or strategies for governance and management change;

9. forty-three states (four states did not report) have State Educational Agency reorganization underway;

10. forty-six states (two states did not report) reported a bottom-up community involvement policy, program, or strategy; and

11. forty-seven states (two states did not report) reported collaboration/integration of services.

A transfer of decisions from state educator departments to local school districts is a high priority in most states. When the CCSSO conducted a survey of the states during the months of October through December 1993 to determine the status of systemic reform planning and implementation, it found that state departments are changing the form and function of their organizational structures to lead, guide, and support state systemic reform initiatives at district and school levels. At that time, 42 states indicated that they either started or recently completed the reorganization (line and staff relationships by role, function, and responsibility) at their state departments of education. Of the other eight states, three reported that they have not reorganized, three did not respond to the survey section on state department of education reorganization, and two states did not respond to the survey. In 35 states, actions to reorganize departments to support state and local initiatives were driven by chief state school officers' recommendations to state boards of education. The primary rationale for changing the form and function of state departments of education from monitoring to service and technical assistance is support for educational reform. Eighteen states reported that their reorganization of state staff resources will provide direct services to local school district efforts through the formation of operational components such as cross-cutting field service teams; assignment of state staff to local district school improvement teams; use of local district staff in conjunction with state staff in the development of standards and assessments; and use of state-supported and state-staffed regional instructional services and support centers.

After years of working in a hierarchical organizational structure, many state department of education staff are not prepared to undertake the role and function changes required to operate in a new system. Few have ever experienced the structural requirements of working "across the system" or, more importantly, the changes this means in the behavior and attitude of state staff and their relationships with both internal and external clientele. State leaders recognize this as an organizational dilemma that must be worked at long and hard over an extended period. Changing structures and personal relationships to enable working across the organization to better align roles and functions requires significant behavioral and attitudinal changes among career personnel. To accomplish this, at least five states are using a quality management approach as the vehicle to make necessary changes in their respective state departments of education. Rather than create more monitoring strategies, state department staffs now need to support and sustain district site based initiatives that require shared decision-making, risk-taking, and further deregulation of the state bureaucracy. For South Carolina, as with other states, a process of strategic school/district renewal planning for meeting the educational goals of the state and nation has been established. The strategic school/district renewal plans are created locally by a collaborative effort of school personnel, local business leaders, parents, and members of the community. This strategy offers the public a vital opportunity to participate in determining what their school system is to do and why.

SOUTH CAROLINA: AN EXAMPLE

According to *Bridging the Gap: School Reform and Student Achievement* (Education Commission of the States, 1995) "research shows that certain reform policies and strategies can make a profound difference in student performance." Successful reforms have focused on improving the teaching and learning process, strengthening the interaction between teachers and students, and enhancing the curriculum (Wang, Haertel, & Walberg; April, 1995). Research-based systemic change involving a renewed supervisory effort seems well on its way to improve education.

South Carolina is one of many states where significant educational changes are taking place. Today, South Carolina has an educational system driven by high standards which are evident in every aspect of public schools. The focus is on lettering. A 1997 document entitled *"It's All About Learning"* details the effort. This document outlines the vision for educational reform in South Carolina and describes the inititatives that comprise the system-wide approach.

South Carolina is building its educational system from the ground up, replacing an outdated model with a high performance mode, geared to a more dynamic and more demanding century. High standards for student achievement are the heart of education in South Carolina, driving the goals set for learning and directing every other aspect of what is done to support teaching and learning in the classroom.

Like other states, South Carolina is responding to alarms first sounded more than a decade ago, when the nation began to recognize that times were changing and schools were failing to keep pace. On one hand, America's economy continues its move from the low-skill manufacturing jobs that once dominated the national marketplace to the high-skill, high-technology jobs of the present age. At the same time, our society is growing increasingly complex, with more poverty, less time for family interactions, and greater violence and crime.

Current challenges demand that schools teach more and teach it better to all students, at a time when there are more and greater obstacles in the path. History has demonstrated that these obstacles cannot be overcome using the same system designed for an earlier age.

In 1991, a vision was created with 57 Educational Excellence Teams consisting of thousands of South Carolinians. The charge to these Educational Excellence Teams was to evaluate the needs of the state's educational system and help chart the future course. Several central beliefs were accepted in order to create a new system of education for the 21st century in South Carolina. Among them are the following:

1. that all children can learn and do so at high levels;
2. that we can promote advanced achievement by replacing minimum expectations with rigorous academic standards all students are expected to meet, and by focusing all aspects of the educational system on achievement of those high standards;
3. that adequate resources must exist in every school to enable all students to achieve at higher levels;
4. that there is no single formula for excellence in education,

which is a function of local innovation and local commitment. The educational system must change from a top-down, state-managed system to one in which the state ensures strong system-wide support for effective schools but allows local schools and local communities the freedom to excel; and

5. that sustained and continuous improvement is promoted when all components of the educational system are accountable for efficiency and effectiveness in the use of learning resources.

Based on research and implemented with a strong emphasis on enlightened supervisory practices, South Carolina is one of the states leading the nation in development of standards that will enable students to compete with any in the nation or the world and in reorganizing and refocusing the entire system to help *all* students reach those standards.

Two Decades of Educational Reform Legislation in South Carolina

The question of what students should know and be able to do was first addressed in the Basic Skills Assessment Act (BSAA) of 1978. The answer proposed by the BSAA placed greater emphasis on basic skills, traditionally and minimally defined. Learning objectives were to be established in reading, writing, and mathematics at every grade level. The Education Improvement Act (EIA) of 1979 added science as a basic skill, required that Black history be included as a regular part of history and social studies courses, and mandated that students be provided with knowledge related to the intervention, prevention, and treatment of alcohol and drug abuse.

Target 2000—School Reform for the Next Decade Act of 1989 represented a radical shift in the response to what students should know and be able to do in two respects. First, the inclusion of the visual arts, music, dance, and drama moved the curriculum beyond a purely academic focus. Second, emphasis on higher order thinking and problem solving meant students were expected to do more than memorize and routinely apply it.

Passage of the Early Childhood Development and Academic Assistance Act (Act 135) in 1993 provided a more futuristic outlook. Specifically, Act 135 stated that students, by the end of third grade, should possess the skills that are required to succeed in the fourth grade. The School-to-Work Transition Act (STW), passed in 1994, continued the futuristic orientation by focusing on analysis of knowledge needed for adult living. In STW, the emphasis was on preparation for life after school. Therefore, high school students are expected to acquire competencies in five areas: resources, interpersonal, information, systems, and technology. They are also expected to attain marketable occupational skills and appropriate work-place behaviors.

Programmatically, several changes have occurred in the legislation over the past two decades. Through the EIA, diversity replaced sameness, through Target 2000, innovation replaced tradition; and through Act 135, was remediation replaced by prevention.

Legislators have increasingly recognized the need for qualified, well-educated teachers and administrators in South

Carolina schools. The view of "teachers-as-technicians" which was prevalent immediately after the Educator Improvement Act (Act 187) of 1979 has given way to "teachers-as-professionals." While technicians may be trained, professionals must be educated. Principals are now expected to be instructional leaders in their schools. The notion of "principals-as-leaders" represents a fundamental shift from the traditional view of "principals-as-managers."

Finally, one of the more obvious changes in the recent past has been the movement from state control of education to local control of education. As a consequence, local schools, school boards, and district authorities must now take on greater responsibility and authority for providing quality education to all students. With this shift has come the need for the state education agency to concentrate on three primary functions: (1) stretching the vision by constantly upgrading goals for the educational system; (2) monitoring educational effectiveness; and (3) either providing or arranging for the provision of technical assistance to those schools and districts in greatest need of it.

The State Department of Education has taken significant steps to systemically change itself and the local schools through priority initiatives found in the South Carolina Plan for Improvement of Public Education. Figure 29.3 displays the model. Each initiative is specifically described through the answers to the following two questions: *What is the initiative?* and *How does the initiative support achievement of high academic standards?*

SOUTH CAROLINA CURRICULUM FRAMEWORKS AND ACADEMIC ACHIEVEMENT STANDARDS

What Is the Initiative?

Since the early 1990s, teams of K–12 teachers, higher education faculty, business experts, and community members have been working to set broad guidelines for what students should know and be able to do in each of the subject areas taught in the schools. This has been done through development of academic blueprints known as curriculum frameworks. The process South Carolina adopted to develop the curriculum frameworks has won national attention for its emphasis on public input and consensus. All of South Carolina's frameworks have been subject to review and comment by thousands of interested citizens. All have been extensively revised to reflect those comments, making them truly consensus documents for what students should know and be able to do at each stage and at the conclusion of their public school academic careers.

How Does the Inititative Support Achievement of High Academic Standards?

The purpose of curriculum frameworks is to raise expectations for student achievement by defining high standards for

The Initiatives

Curriculum Frameworks
Statewide Systemic Initiative
Professional Development
Instructional Materials
Educational Technology Plan
Teacher & Administrator
 Certification & Licensure
Teacher Assistance, Development,
 and Evaluation
Tech Prep/School-to-Work Transition
Community Education
Service Learning
Young African-American Males
 Action Team
Character Education
Deregulation
District Strategic Planning/School
 Renewal Planning
School & District Profiles
School Districts in Greatest Need
 of Assistance
Instructional Improvement Initiative
School Incentive Reward
In$ite - Finance Analysis Model (FAM)
Fiscal Operations Improvements
Support Services
Continuous Needs Assessment & Research

The Model

FIGURE 29.3.

student learning. Recognizing that higher standards alone will not raise achievement for all students, the frameworks also provide a road map for changes in all other activities that affect teaching and learning to support achievement of these higher goals. Based on the research of best practices, recommendations presented in the frameworks guide the work of the department of education and schools in improving instruction, providing better professional development opportunities, identifying instructional materials that support advanced achievement, and improving statewide assessments.

The frameworks assist schools, districts, and the state to:

1. develop and revise curricula by providing guidelines and direction regarding knowledge, skills, and instructional strategies specific to each discipline;
2. develop, select, and adopt instructional materials;
3. develop more effective assessment of student learning;
4. provide effective professional development programs for teachers, administrators, and school board members;
5. develop more effective teacher and administrator preparation programs by establishing requirements for certification and licensure in specific areas and providing direction for preservice education; and
6. communicate expectations for student learning and classroom teaching to parents and the public at large.

Standards and Assessments The broad objectives for student achievement outlined in the curriculum frameworks are translated into more concrete achievement standards that detail the skills and competencies students should master in specific subjects at every grade. These achievement standards are benchmarked on national and international standards which provide the basis for a statewide assessment system. The statewide assessment system helps determine not only whether students are learning basic skills but how well they are meeting the higher standards defined through the frameworks.

In addition to gathering achievement data through state tests and a nationally standardized test, South Carolina also participates in the National Assessment of Educational Progress (NAEP), a national criterion-referenced assessment that measures achievement against high standards.

SOUTH CAROLINA STATEWIDE SYSTEMIC INITIATIVE

What Is the Initiative?

The South Carolina Statewide Systemic Initiative (SSI) is a key part of South Carolina's effort to improve and enhance the educational system. A permanent statewide collaborative K–12 and higher education network supporting teaching and learning in mathematics and science has been established through state funds and a grant from the National Science Foundation. This network not only supports and enriches local school district efforts to provide the best instruction in mathematics and science as outlined in the state's curriculum frameworks and the South Carolina Technology Plan but also

meets the Governor's Mathematics and Science Advisory Board's vision.

How Does the Initiative Support Achievement of High Academic Standards?

The SSI supports regional science and mathematics centers, a network of people and ideas dedicated to improving mathematics and science achievement for all students. The centers use successful teaching methods and materials from within the region, around the state, and across the nation to share with other teachers and schools. Each hub is represented by a regional advisory council consisting of every school district superintendent and college president in the region, business and industry representatives, teachers, and parent groups.

Each center offers a variety of opportunities, including curriculum leadership institutes for teachers, administrators, scientists, and mathematicians to teach and learn from each other. The centers collect, display, and share state-of-the-art instructional materials in mathematics and science.

The vision of the SSI is for every child to learn the habits of mind, analytical skills, and essential ideas of mathematics and science. The overarching goal is to provide quality and effective learning experiences in science and mathematics to all students by effecting strategic, systemic changes. To that end, the systemic change process goals of the SSI are threefold:

1. to strengthen and make permanent collaboration and communication among South Carolina's partners for improvement;
2. to communicate ideas for improvement and empower the agents of change—teachers and administrators—and to provide them with the skills and tools for translating these ideas into action; and
3. to enlist informed support from policymakers, parents, and local communities.

Collectively, these goals are articulated in the state's curriculum frameworks for mathematics and science; therefore, they are viewed as the vehicle for meaningful and long-lasting reform. These goals are tied to programs of teacher education and arts and sciences efforts at the college level in South Carolina so the benefits of research and dissemination of this information can be obtained.

PROFESSIONAL DEVELOPMENT

What Is the Initiative?

This initiative promotes excellence and equity in education by providing programs and services which extend opportunities to educators for assessing and developing their professional knowledge and skills in two ways: The first is through the South Carolina Leadership Academy, which is designed to help school districts select and train new personnel, to develop training to enhance the professional skills of current educators, and to provide up-to-date information on ideas and approaches to teaching and educational leadership. The second is by supporting individuals, schools, and districts in efforts to reshape teaching and school organizations.

How Does the Initiative Support Achievement of High Academic Standards?

This initiative has a dozen aspects as follows:

1. serves as a professional development resource;
2. compiles a database of staff development programs;
3. makes referrals regarding quality professional development consultants and activities;
4. reviews data and plans to determine professional development needs;
5. provides information to evaluate professional development;
6. helps administrators develop more effective oral communication skills;
7. engages participants in the Leadership Academy with a variety of writing activities;
8. provides comprehensive long-term skill development in six critical areas for practicing or potential school administrators who are assessment center graduates;
9. assists school districts by providing for an intensive, structured assessment of leadership and management skills prior to first-time principal appointments;
10. provides training in essential leadership and management skills for newly appointed principals;
11. assists school leaders in improving and enhancing instructional leadership skills; and
12. provides teacher, parent, and student needs assessment survey instruments, analyses, and technical assistance to schools and school districts.

INSTRUCTIONAL MATERIALS

What Is the Initiative?

The adoption of instructional materials and technology resources by the South Carolina State Board of Education which supports the content standards outlined in the South Carolina Curriculum Frameworks and occupational competencies.

How Does the Initiative Support Achievement of High Academic Standards?

Since 1992, adoption of instructional materials has been aligned with high, rigorous academic standards. Each review panel is required to use the curriculum frameworks as a basis for evaluating materials offered for bid.

The process has been made much more flexible for districts and schools to choose materials that meet the needs of the students in their communities. The menu of possible instructional material choices has increased from three to an unlimited number. The number of items which a school can adopt in each subject area has grown from five to an unlimited number. The regulations that guide the adoption process have been revised to include an option that encourages local districts to submit additional materials for review if materials on the state-adopted

list do not fully meet the needs identified for their students. A second major change is the inclusion of a public review process of the materials by parents and citizens in 27 sites throughout the state.

SOUTH CAROLINA EDUCATIONAL TECHNOLOGY PLAN

What Is the Initiative?

The goal of the South Carolina Educational Technology Plan is to provide all students access to the instructional materials and information resources made possible with the installation of the technology infrastructure.

How Does the Initiative Support Achievement of High Academic Standards?

The K–12 technology public/private partnership initiative provides access to a telecommunications infrastructure, a video and broadcast infrastructure, training for teachers, library media specialists, and all instructional staff in the effective use of technology throughout the curriculum. The plan ensures that students have at their fingertips the resources that provide the content information in an understandable format needed for them to achieve the high standards set in the curriculum frameworks. The plan includes:

1. a telecommunications infrastructure that provides Internet access to every school, district office, public library, and math/science center in the state (completed in 1997);
2. a video and broadcast infrastructure which has installed South Carolina Educational Television satellite dishes and two receivers at all schools in the state and enables districts to conduct short-distance learning and staff development broadcasts to meet local community needs;
3. training for teachers and instructional staff. The library media specialists in every school are identified as the leaders of this technology plan and have received training in how to use the technology provided, and in how to most effectively integrate the technology into the curriculum to have maximum impact on student learning. A major portion of resources is being provided for teacher professional development to enhance the quality of teaching/learning.
4. local video distribution system pilot projects to explore emerging technologies and their capacity to provide cost effective alternatives to integrated video, data, and audio access.

TEACHER AND ADMINISTRATOR CERTIFICATION AND LICENSURE

What Is the Initiative?

In 1995, a Teacher Certification/Licensure Steering Committee was appointed to review the current status of teacher preparation and certification in South Carolina with the objective of proposing recommendations to develop an improved system for licensing educators. By redefining what students should know and be able to do in the curriculum frameworks, a redefinition of what teachers and administrators should know and be able to do is an important element of the committee's work.

How Does the Initiative Support Achievement of High Academic Standards?

To strengthen the subject matter preparation of teachers and administrators and encourage higher academic achievement, the Licensure Steering Committee made the following recommendations:

1. to develop a performance-based system of certification;
2. to establish nationally accredited and highly accountable teacher and administrator preparation programs;
3. to reduce the number of certification/licensure areas;
4. to require professional development plans at the local level for certification/licensure renewal;
5. to continue interstate reciprocity of teaching licenses; and
6. to encourage teacher participation in the National Board Certification program.

TEACHER ASSISTANCE, DEVELOPMENT, AND EVALUATION

What Is the Initiative?

A collaboration among the state education department, educators from local school districts, and teacher education programs developed the South Carolina System for Assisting, Developing, and Evaluating Professional Teaching (ADEPT). ADEPT is an integrated system of state standards, guidelines, and strategies designed to promote excellence in the teaching profession. The ADEPT system replaces current statutes, regulations, instruments, and procedures which have been in place since 1977.

How Does the Initiative Support Achievement of High Academic Standards?

The likelihood of achieving high academic standards may be maximized by assuring that all students are taught by competent, professional teachers. ADEPT accomplishes this by:

1. establishing new state standards which redefine and upgrade the expectations for what all South Carolina teachers should know and be able to do as competent and effective professionals. The standards provide a common focus for all programs and strategies for assisting, developing, and evaluating preservice teachers, as well as teachers employed under provisional, annual, or continuing contracts. The standards view teaching as an integrated process as opposed to a recipe of isolated skills, and as done in context as opposed to generically;
2. establishing flexible guidelines and strategies for teacher education programs to use, in collaboration with school dis-

tricts, for designing and implementing innovative programs to evaluate and assist student teachers. Student teachers are provided with guidance and assistance throughout their student teaching assignment and formal written feedback on their performance with respect to state standards;
3. establishing flexible guidelines and strategies for school districts to use, in collaboration with teacher education programs, for providing provisional contract teachers with formalized induction programs during their first year of teaching. Induction programs provide teachers with comprehensive guidance and assistance throughout the school year and formal written feedback on their strengths and weaknesses relative to state standards;
4. establishing flexible guidelines and strategies for school districts to use for selecting and/or developing valid and reliable assessment processes for conducting formal evaluations of annual and continuing contract teachers, relative to state standards;
5. providing school districts with an optional assessment process that may be used to conduct formal evaluations of annual and continuing contract teachers, relative to state standards; and
6. establishing flexible guidelines and strategies for school districts to use for promoting the continuous professional growth of continuing contract teachers through individualized professional development plans and by encouraging pursuit of National Board Certification.

TECH PREP/SCHOOL-TO-WORK TRANSITION

What Is the Initiative?

Tech Prep is an educational reform initiative which combines a strong secondary and postsecondary education to prepare students for technology careers in the 21st century. The purpose of Tech Prep is to make the United States and South Carolina more competitive in the world economy by developing the academic and occupational skills of all segments of the student population.

After completing a strong academic and technical program, Tech Prep students are well prepared to enter full-time employment or pursue postsecondary education options. Tech Prep acts as a catalyst for reform that transcends barriers that have traditionally prevented the majority of high school students from reaching their full potential.

The South Carolina School-to-Work initiative establishes a structure that provides all students the opportunity to develop meaningful, high-level academic skills and to connect what they learn in school with the real world through educational experiences in participating businesses.

How Does the Initiative Support Achievement of High Academic Standards?

This initiative is intended to fulfill the following goals:

1. Tech Prep stresses the retooling of teachers and administrators through meaningful professional development

opportunities such as training in applied methodologies and learning styles;

2. Tech Prep raises standards by emphasizing high-level academics through courses based on the academic achievement standards but taught in an applied rather than in a theoretical approach;

3. Revised occupational and applied academic competencies stress the importance of interdisciplinary instruction and integration of the occupational and academic curricula; and

4. School-to-Work calls for work-based learning experiences for students to provide for real-world application of academic skills. Mentorships, internships, service learning, youth apprenticeships, registered apprenticeships, shadowing, and cooperative education are activities that allow students to apply what they are learning in the classroom to real-life situations.

COMMUNITY EDUCATION

What Is the Initiative?

This initiative is intended to implement a process that fosters extended or joint use of the school facilities, community involvement and participation, and interagency collaboration for children, families, and schools in the community.

How Does the Initiative Support Achievement of High Academic Standards?

Community education interagency activities are many and varied. Each in its own way is linked with the achievement of high academic standards. A brief explanation of a few of the activities are:

1. Linking Intergenerational Networks in Communities (LINC) partners youth with senior citizens in community service teams;

2. Healthy Schools is a collaborative program with the Department of Heath and Environmental Control to assist local school districts in developing healthy schools by providing training and technical assistance to schools and districts in parent/community involvement, health promotion, health education, school environment, counseling and social services, nutrition services, health services, and physical education;

3. Business/Education Partnerships is a program to foster and support an atmosphere of involvement and communication between business and education, to enlarge and enrich learning opportunities for all students, to challenge and support citizen-to-citizen understanding between schools and businesses in meeting academic standards and preparing for the economic future of communities;

4. Downtown As a Classroom is a program that joins downtown communities and education to stimulate supportive relationships;

5. World Class Partnerships is a program dedicated to providing the knowledge, skills, and cultural understanding essential for successful competition in the world. The initiative features international partnerships between schools in South Carolina and schools around the world;

6. Parenting Support Services is a program to enable parents to enhance their child's development in the critical years from birth to age five. The state education department provides training and technical assistance in parenting education, support for parents in their role, developmental screening for children who are enrolled in the program, and opportunities for parents to improve their own education; and

7. A partnership with businesses and other governmental agencies supports The Coach, which is a fully equipped, technologically state-of-the-art mobile literacy training facility that provides staff development in computer literacy, family literacy program development, and literacy skills.

SERVICE LEARNING

What Is the Initiative?

Service learning is a teaching methodology that integrates community service into the school curriculum. Service learning gives students the opportunity to make a difference in their communities by applying what they learn in the classroom to serving community needs.

How Does the Initiative Support Achievement of High Academic Standards?

Service learning links schools with their communities as students perform community service work that is integrated into and complements the standards outlined in the curriculum frameworks. Service learning helps students develop a sense of civic responsibility and community pride.

YOUNG AFRICAN-AMERICAN MALES ACTION TEAM

What Is the Initiative?

Grade failure rates, poor performance on standardized tests, and high participation in special and remedial programs indicate that African-American males have not fared as well as their counterparts in reaching their full potential. These educational statistics were the impetus to form a diverse group of more than 60 students and adults from across the state to examine the issues facing young African-American males and make recommendations for improvement.

How Does the Inititative Support Achievement of High Academic Standards?

The recommendations which are being implemented include:

1. the establishment of curricula that facilitates and inspires learning among African-American males in grades K–12;
2. designing, developing, planning, and implementing strategies for conflict resolution and conflict reduction;
3. the identification of educational programs, activities, and strategies that have potential for improving the ability of students to succeed in school.

CHARACTER EDUCATION

What Is the Initiative?

Character education is an effort to have a positive impact on student behavior and to help respond to problems of youth violence and school discipline by refocusing on traditional traits of good character.

How Does the Initiative Support Achievement of High Academic Standards?

Effective character education initiatives improve student achievement by encouraging the basic behaviors that contribute to learning. The approach to character education emphasizes community leadership in establishing character traits to be emphasized, with schools supporting and reinforcing character development in ways the local community identifies as appropriate. This program is not a course or a specific curriculum but is a central focus in the mission of schools.

DEREGULATION

What Is the Initiative?

A major effort to provide more local district control helped establish the deregulation initiative to eliminate, consolidate, and condense the number of regulations which set parameters for management of school curricula, programs, and practices.

How Does the Initiative Support Achievement of High Academic Standards?

Rollback of state regulations allows greater flexibility for grades K–12 and greater local control by providing flexibility in course offerings, weekly time requirements, textbook selection, administrator/teacher certification, pilot program approval, dual credit, course time requirements, attendance, class scheduling, and correspondence courses. Students are much more likely to achieve at high academic levels when their individual learning needs are specifically taken into account.

DISTRICT STRATEGIC PLANNING/SCHOOL RENEWAL PLANNING

What Is the Initiative?

The intent of this initiative is to challenge all districts and schools to raise their expectations for all students, to ensure that all students progress successfully through the educational system, and to ensure that all students are able to meet the high academic standards that are required to be productive citizens in the twenty-first century.

How Does the Initiative Support Achievement of High Academic Standards?

Plans in this initiative address:

1. how schools will provide appropriate education to preschool and primary students to ensure that they will be ready for fourth grade;
2. how schools will accelerate the learning of students who fall behind as an alternative to year-long, pull-out remediation;
3. how schools will provide for increased collaboration with parents and the community, particularly health and human services agencies; and
4. how schools will provide for voluntary parenting education and encourage parents to upgrade their literacy levels.

SCHOOL AND DISTRICT PROFILES

What Is the Initiative?

Each year South Carolina Education Profiles are published for the state, each district, and every school. Statistical profiles of each county provided information on features such as population, family characteristics, income levels, and the industrial base. These are followed by a detailed profile of the school district within that county that included information on students, school finance and staffing, and academic achievement for the past five years. The separate district and school profiles give grade-by-grade and indicator-by-indicator information that is further disaggregated by demographic data including gender, ethnicity, school lunch status, and other factors.

How Does the Initiative Support Achievement of High Academic Standards?

In order to make the best possible decisions about curriculum and program changes, districts and schools need access to the most accurate information possible about communities, students, and achievement. The five years of data related to each school and community provide a long-range view of student progress and enable each school to develop a plan of action to meet student learning needs. The profiles also provide the background for parents, community members, and local school boards to formulate questions about how each of those stakeholders can contribute to the long-term academic success of students in their area. Information on student achievement is essential for accountability at all levels.

SCHOOL DISTRICTS IN GREATEST NEED OF ASSISTANCE

What Is the Initiative?

An annual evaluation of schools is conducted to determine the quality of student performance based on test scores, standards reflecting accreditation deficiencies, dropout rates, and student and faculty attendance. School districts that fail to meet at least two-thirds of the minimum criteria are designated "highest priority for technical assistance." When a district is identified as "highest priority," a Review Committee is appointed to study educational programs in the district and identify factors affecting quality.

Since 1992, volunteer partnerships were formed with districts that were not designated as "highest priority" but were experiencing difficulty with student achievement. The partnerships are for a three-year period for the purpose of providing technical assistance to address deficiencies and improve the educational program in the districts.

How Does the Initiative Support Achievement of High Academic Standards?

By providing the following types of assistance to the school districts named as "highest priority for technical assistance," student achievement is expected to improve:

1. initiating and financially supporting the strategic planning and benchmarking processes with the South Carolina School Boards Association;
2. assessing the curriculum and providing strategies that can be included in the district strategic plan and school renewal plans to address areas where the curriculum is out of alignment with the academic achievement standards;
3. assisting in the development of a core curriculum implementation plan, which emphasizes standards, articulation between course and grade levels, instructional strategies, and evaluation techniques as defined by the curriculum frameworks;
4. providing on-site, long-term, in-class instructional support to teachers and administrators;
5. working with districts to implement collaborative partnership programs to encourage the involvement of business, parents, and other community groups and organizations;
6. reviewing with districts and interpreting test data for implications for curriculum changes and other district improvements; and
7. developing on-site, continuous staff development activities.

INSTRUCTIONAL IMPROVEMENT INITIATIVE

What Is the Initiative?

The Instructional Improvement Initiative, begun during the 1995–1996 school year, seeks to raise academic achievement of students in the schools—often in high poverty areas—that have traditionally been characterized by low test scores. On-site assistance is provided for teachers at participating schools with an emphasis on raising their expectations for students and improving their teaching skills, particularly in the areas of reading and mathematics. Master teachers on sabbatical provide direct assistance to teachers.

How Does the Initiative Support Achievement of High Academic Standards?

The Instructional Improvement Initiative helps teachers to:

1. raise expectations for student achievement;
2. develop more effective instructional skills, particularly with the lowest achieving students;
3. align curriculum and instruction to the frameworks and content standards; and
4. improve content knowledge as defined in the curriculum frameworks.

SCHOOL INCENTIVE REWARD

What Is the Initiative?

The School Incentive Reward is a program that recognizes schools with significant gains in student achievement. The primary criterion of the program is student achievement as evidenced by scores from statewide testing.

Schools meeting the achievement criteria receive a per-pupil monetary reward, a certificate, and a flag. The monetary reward may be enhanced by meeting additional criteria in student attendance, teacher attendance, and persistence rates.

How Does the Initiative Support Achievement of High Academic Standards?

The School Incentive Reward initiative supports improved achievement by:

1. emphasizing the gain in actual student achievement levels;
2. emphasizing the competition of each school against its own prior performance while seeking constant improvement;
3. allocating funds to recipient schools for the enhancement of the instructional program; and
4. focusing the school's attention on student achievement and other factors important for school success.

FINANCE ANALYSIS MODEL

What Is the Initiative?

South Carolina is the first state in the nation to introduce an innovative cost analysis system that fundamentally changes the way educational finance is analyzed and reported. The Finance Analysis Model, developed by the national accounting firm of Coopers and Lybrand L.L.P., complements the current financial accounting system by focusing on clear, complete, and useful management and public information. Its purposes are to serve as a management and planning tool for schools and districts and as an accountability tool for South Carolina's taxpayers.

The Finance Analysis Model analyzes cost data by function, location, and program. The five functions in the model are instruction, instructional support, operations, other commitments, and leadership. The model also allows separation of costs by location, such as school-site, central office, or nonallocated (which includes pass-through costs or payments to other agencies).

Further detailed breakdown of data is possible by reporting expenditures by program classifications such as special education, Title I, etc. Finally, the third level of reporting is by individual school. This allows costs to be separated by level or type of school such as elementary, middle, high, alternative, vocational, or special.

How Does the Initiative Support Achievement of High Academic Standards?

The Finance Analysis Model permits school personnel and the community to monitor the financial decisions of the local district. These data support that monies are spent directly in the classroom and greatly enhance decision makers to determine the cost of specific educational priorities.

FISCAL OPERATIONAL IMPROVEMENTS

What Is the Initiative?

Among the efforts of the Fiscal Operational Improvements initiative are: reducing the reporting requirements for federal and restricted grants funding; increasing, within allowed limits, funds advanced to school districts; automating the reporting of teacher/pupil data; formation of a statewide Financial Steering Committee comprised of school business officials from across the state to give input and advice on policy issues; conducting regional sharing meetings to gather information concerning problem areas, concerns, and suggestions on how to improve fund flows and accounting practices; and providing timely fiscal information for planning.

How Does the Initiative Support Achievement of High Academic Standards?

The goal of each of these efforts is to expedite the delivery of resources to the classroom. Allowing as much flexibility in the expenditure of funds as possible enables local officials to apply resources as needed to meet local conditions. Minimizing reporting and accounting requirements reduces administrative costs-freeing funds and personnel to support instructional initiatives.

SUPPORT SERVICES

The state department of education delivers many services in support of effective learning, including transportation, cafeterias, and facilities.

What Is the Initiative? How Does the Initiative Support Achievement of High Academic Standards?

These support services have a daily impact on the students' readiness to learn.

1. students need safe, dependable transportation to and from school and for transportation to special programs during the school day;
2. they need healthy, nutritious meals to ensure they are prepared to learn; and
3. instructional facilities must be designed to adequately support the curriculum, to insure student security and safety, and must be cost effective to operate.

CONTINUOUS NEEDS ASSESSMENT AND RESEARCH

What Is the Initiative?

To assist efforts for school reform and improvement in South Carolina, the SouthEastern Regional Vision for Education (SERVE) established a Policy Office at the State Department of Education. The role of SERVE's Policy Office is to assist in the identification and assessment of South Carolina's greatest reform needs and coordinate a variety of activities through SERVE to aid in such reform. The Policy Office facilitates the exchange of information on education topics and conducts policy studies and research. This is done on a local, regional, and national level by coordinating with other policy offices in the southeast and educational laboratories throughout the United States.

How Does the Initiative Support Achievement of High Academic Standards?

SERVE's purpose is to ensure that those involved in educational improvement in South Carolina have access to the best available research. SERVE's efforts are designed to help South Carolina educators, policy makers and communities improve schools and help all students reach their full potential.

All pieces of the system have been reengineered to focus on learning. Changes are being made in what personnel do with adults and things to improve the schools in ways that directly influence the teaching process to promote student learning. These changes rely on best practices as determined by research. Renewed supervisory behaviors and research have become primary tools for educational improvement. Throughout the initiatives of South Carolina and other states run the powerful threads of research and supervisory practices to produce best instructional results.

THE FUTURE OF RESEARCH IN STATE EDUCATION DEPARTMENTS

The public schools are functioning in an accountability environment where the level of performance of students must rise at the very time of declining social and political cohesion. Amid these constraints, schools must develop ways to attain better results with whatever resources presently exist. Changing the way education is delivered to an ever changing population is a challenge the public schools can no longer avoid with a rhetoric of excuses. The nation's need for a highly educated labor force in the 21st century is dependent upon educational institutions finding ways to increase productivity (Report From the Consortium on Productivity in the Schools, 1995).

The Report From the Consortium on Productivity in the Schools (1995) emphasizes the belief that increased productivity through research and development is the solution to bringing students up to national and international standards. "A major source of productivity gains is developing better practices and improving existing ones. . . . There is clear evidence that increased investments in R & D in the private sector result in productivity payoffs. In the global economy, countries supporting industrial R & D are moving ahead of those that are not. Much of modern society is a direct result of research" (p. 13).

Many of the basic tools for systemic change in education have come from the private sector. The paradigm shift in education has been led by the experiences of the private sector. Education has modeled the private sector through restructuring, downsizing, planning, staff development, use of technology, and new management principles to name but a few. The one area which has not seen the impact of the private sector experience is in research and development. As the private sector spends approximately three percent of its total costs on research, the federal government, as the primary funder of research and development in education, spends 0.08 percent of the sector's available funds. At the same time, total federal expenditures are 13.2 percent in research and development for national defense and 13.6 percent for research and development in health.

Traditionally, policymakers in education have believed in the notion of program dissemination as a means of making change in schools. If an educational program has evidence of success and can be demonstrated to others, these improved practices will spread throughout the educational arena and the necessary changes will be made. Indeed, the federal government's Joint Dissemination and Review Panel was one such effort. This endeavor funded the dissemination of programs to all that were interested if the program could support its success claims through evaluation or research evidence. A program developer would appear before a selected panel to present evidence of program success. If the panel accepted the information, this program would be presented to other schools and school districts with the opportunity to receive funded training and implementation strategies to replicate the approved program. Perhaps because the disseminated program was isolated and was not necessarily interconnected to systemic change, the effects of these programs did little to improve the educational standing of schools.

Where should the role of research in education lie? First, the federal government should follow the reformation of

state education departments and remove themselves from a reward and punishment system. The development of national goals and standards are appropriate for federal consideration because education sustains our form of democracy and insures our future as a nation to new citizens. The resources the federal government now uses to design, implement, and monitor programs should be redirected toward research that supports the improvement of educational organizations and of educational practices. The states and local districts should be the source of program innovation. A small portion of the new federal research funds should be used for the collection of large-scale databases for use by researchers. States should have a block portion of the funds, not to conduct research themselves, but to become the clearinghouse for determining the practical research needs of the schools. The remainder of the research funds should be competitively distributed among many disciplines that can relate their efforts to educational needs with a small portion for the dissemination of significant research findings. Psychological studies on learning, social psychological studies on educational organizations, science studies on neurological problems, on the use of drugs to monitor student behavior, and on the genetic connections with learning, should be encouraged.

Second, state education departments should consider taking an active role in research. The implementation and research of pilot programs prior to full program implementation could avoid large financial outlays that often prove to be ineffective. Monitoring (not controlling) research within the field of education is essential to support those studies which enhance the interconnectiveness of educational programs and that support student learning. Setting the tone for the importance of research, the state education department should provide professional development in action research at the classroom, school, and district levels; provide for the dissemination of research results; make available large informational databases on local schools, and insist upon research evidence when new programs are being promoted.

Third, since the private sector has a key interest in the employment of the products of the educational system, it should have the opportunity to be involved in the planning and oversight of research efforts in the various states.

SUMMARY

There is a new framework for educational systems in the states designed to permit continuous change; to interconnect its parts; and to replicate the process of renewal, community by community, district by district, school by school, and even classroom by classroom. The system should move decision-making from the state to local districts; focus its resources on the classroom; and adapt to future needs and changes. The system should have high expectations for student performance, actively involve the public in its plans and functions, and base decisions on best practices. This system should implement enlightened supervisory practices throughout, and provide for reconstruction, even of itself.

REFERENCES

Aguayo, R. (1990). *Dr. Deming: The American who taught the Japanese about quality*. New York: First Carol Publishing.

Augenblick, J., Van de Water, G., & Fulton, F. (1995). *How much are schools spending? A fifty state examination of expenditure patterns over the last decade*. Denver: Education Commission of the States.

Bauer, L. (1994) School-to-work transition. *In better education through informed legislation*. National Conference of State Legislatures.

Cawelti, G. (1994). *High school restructuring: A national study, ERS report*. Arlington, VA: Educational Research Service.

Chubb, J. E. & Moe, T. (1990). *Politics, markets and American schools*. Washington, D.C.: Brookings.

Cohen, D. K. (1990). The classroom impact of state and federal education policy. School of Education: Michigan State University.

The Council of Chief State School Officers. (1995). *The status report: State systemic education improvements*. Washington, D.C.: CCSSO.

The Council of Chief State School Officers. (1995). *State education accountability reports and indicator reports: Status of reports across the states*. Washington, D.C.: CCSSO.

The Council of Chief State School Officers. (1996). *The status report: State systemic education improvements*. Washington, D.C.: CCSSO.

Cuban, L. (1990). Reforming again, again, and again. *Educational Researcher, 19*. Washington, D.C.: American Educational Research Association, pp. 3–13.

David, J., Cohen, M., Honetschlager, D., & Traiman, S. (1990). *State actions to restructure schools: First steps*. Washington, D.C.: National Governors' Association.

Dianda, M. R. & Corwin, R. G. (1994, September). Start-up experiences: A survey. *Educational Leadership*. ASCD.

Duttweiler, P. C. (1988, October). The dysfunctions of bureaucratic structure. *Insights on Educational Policy and Practice*. Southwest Educational Development Laboratory.

Education Commission of the States (1995). *Bridging the gap: School reform and student achievement*. Denver, CO: Author.

Education Commission of the States (1996). *Standards & education: A roadmap for state policymakers*. Denver, CO: Author.

Elmore, R. F. et al. (1990). *Restructuring schools: The generation of educational reform*. San Francisco, CA: Jossey-Bass.

Elmore, R. F. & McLaughlin, M. W. (1988). *Steady work: Policy, practice and the reform of American education*. Santa Monica, CA: Rand Corporation.

Finn, C. E. & Ravitch, D. (1995, August). *Education reform 1994–1995*. Educational Excellence Network.

Firestone, W. A., Fuhrman, S. H., & Kirst, M. W. (1989). *The progress of reform: An appraisal of state education initiatives*. New Brunswick, NJ: Rutgers University, Center for Policy Research in Education.

Glanz, J. (1995, Winter). Exploring supervision history: An invitation and agenda. *Journal of Curriculum and Supervision 10*, 95–113.

Harris, B. M. (1975). *Supervisory behavior in education* (2nd ed.). Englewood Cliffs, NJ: Prentice-Hall.

MacDonald, J. T. (1994). An analysis of survey data on the transformation of state departments of education. *Transforming state education agencies to support wducation reform*. National Governors' Association.

McMullen, P. (1995). *Taking stock: The impact of reform*. Providence, RI: The Annenberg Institute for School Reform.

Medler, A. L. (1994). *Examples and summaries of state initiatives to develop goals, standards and outcomes*. Denver: Education Commission of the States.

The National Commission on Excellence in Education (1983). *A nation at risk: The imperative of educational reform*. Washington, D.C.: Author.

National Governors' Association. (1995). *State progress in school-to-work system development*. Washington, D.C.: Author.

Perez, A. (1995, June). *Legislative oversight of federal funds*. National Conference of State Legislatures. Legislative Finance Paper. Number 98.

A Report from the consortium on productivity in the schools. (1995). *Using what we have to get the schools we need*. COS.

South Carolina Department of Education (1997). *It's all about learning*. Columbia, SC: Author.

Tracy, S. J. (1995, May–June). How historical concepts of supervision relate to supervisory practices today. *Clearing House, 68*, 320–325.

Uchida, D., with Cetron, M. & McKenzie, F. (1966). *Preparing students for the 21st century*. American Association of School Administrators.

United States Department of Education. (1990). *National education goals*. Washington, D.C.

Wang, M. C., Haertel, G. D., & Walberg, H. J. (1995). *Effective practices and policies: Research and practitioner views*. National Center on Education in the Inner Cities. Paper presented at the annual meeting of the American Educational Research Association, San Francisco, CA.

·30·

INSTRUCTIONAL IMPROVEMENT
IN HIGHER EDUCATION

Karron G. Lewis
UNIVERSITY OF TEXAS AT AUSTIN

"Any service rendered to teachers that eventually results in the improvement of instruction, learning, and the curriculum, can be considered a form of supervision" (Neagley & Evans, 1980, p. 2). "Supervision" in this definition refers to what happens in grades K–12 to facilitate the improvement of teaching and learning. While the definition is consistent with what happens in higher education, the improvement of teaching and learning in higher education is not referred to as "supervision." It is usually referred to as "faculty development," "professional development," or "staff development." Faculty development is the preferred "umbrella" term encompassing systematic efforts to increase the effectiveness of faculty in all their professional roles and has evolved over time to include the following areas:

- Instructional improvement—a systematic effort to improve the teaching and learning process through individual and group consultation—common activities include classroom visits by professional staff, the use of video to analyze teaching styles and techniques, the development of teaching portfolios, and the use of peer review and mentoring as instructional improvement strategies;
- Organizational development—an attempt to bring about instructional improvement by changing the environment in which the faculty member operates by focusing on the relationships among the various units (e.g., departments, colleges—common activities include workshops, seminars, and individual consultation with administrators and faculty; and
- Personal development—takes a more holistic approach to the individual faculty member by attempting to enhance interpersonal skills, promote wellness, and assist with career planning—common activities include workshops, seminars and individual consultation, personal counseling, peer support group meetings, and retreats.

In this chapter, we will use the term "faculty development" to denote all of the activities and programs that are typically used in the improvement of teaching and learning in higher education. Today, faculty development programs are increasingly including all or most of the types of "development" listed above.

Francis (1975, p. 720) defines faculty development as ". . . an institutional process which seeks to modify the attitudes, skills, and behavior of faculty members toward greater competence and effectiveness in meeting student needs, their own needs, and the needs of the institution. Successful programs change the way faculty feel about their professional roles, increase their knowledge and skills in those roles, and alter the way they carry them out in practice."

In this chapter, we will look first at the history of faculty development in higher education and what changes in society and the economy have led to more emphasis on the improvement of teaching and learning at that level. We'll then provide an overview of the structures and functions of several models of faculty development programs. Finally, the research on teaching and learning in higher education will be reviewed and proposals given for future research and directions in faculty development.

BRIEF HISTORY OF FACULTY DEVELOPMENT IN HIGHER EDUCATION

Originally, faculty development in higher education meant developing expertise in one's discipline. It had been assumed, for many years, that if you knew the subject, you could teach it. So, to help faculty members keep up to date in their fields, most institutions of higher education offered support for sabbatical leaves, travel to professional meetings,

721

conducting research, and completing an advanced degree. The sabbatical leave, begun at Harvard University in 1810, is the oldest form of faculty support and was the model for this type of support for the next 150 years (Cochran, 1989). Usually, sabbaticals were competitive and given for research projects that could not be completed on the professor's home campus and required both travel and free time (Eble & McKeachie, 1985). Janet G. Donald (1977, p. 11) notes, "Because expertise and leadership in one's discipline are of paramount importance at this level of education, it has proved more difficult to examine the other important factors involved in the teaching process." So what has now caused a shift in emphasis?

Changes in Society and the Economy

In the late 1960s and early 1970s, student protests "attacked irrelevant courses and uninspired teaching" (Gaff & Simpson, 1994, p. 168). These protests took place primarily at large universities where the leading scholars were working, and they exposed the myth that all that was required to teach well was a thorough knowledge of the subject matter. In addition, "replacing homogeneous populations of the past [were] older students, part-time students and students from ever-increasing ethnic, cultural, and socioeconomic diversity" (Gaff & Simpson, 1994, p. 174). This diversity challenged the traditional ways of teaching and innovative methods had to be developed to keep the students interested in learning.

The OPEC-induced recession of the 1970s made it almost impossible for institutions of higher education to hire unlimited numbers of faculty or to "buy" a desired faculty member away from another institution. This forced administrators to deal with maintaining institutional vitality without staff turnover. For example, at "innovative" institutions created in the 1960s (e.g., Evergreen State), over 60 percent of the faculty would not be scheduled to retire until after the year 2000. Long-established universities found themselves "tenured in" with over 90 percent of the faculty holding tenure (Gaff, 1975, pp. 1–2). Concurrently, the population of college-age students was declining and few faculty were able to enjoy the mobility of the previous decade. In 1969, Nevitt Sanford and some associates at the Graduate Theological Union in Berkeley, California interviewed a random sample of faculty members at various colleges in the San Francisco area. "Most faculty in the study sample expressed a sense of vulnerability and threat apparently deriving from the [above] changes in the milieu of higher education" (Cochran, 1989, p. 6).

Beginnings of Faculty Development in Higher Education

Faculty members found they had to remain at one institution for longer periods of time and began to look to the institutions to provide opportunities and support for their professional and personal growth. The monograph developed by the Group for Human Development in Higher Education, *Faculty Development in a Time of Retrenchment* (Astin et al, 1974), provided some powerful suggestions for dealing with these problems. Some of these suggestions include:

1. making teaching a public activity, and open to collegial scrutiny;
2. developing self-reflectiveness about the activity of teaching and learning;
3. methods for training future professors to upgrade teaching effectiveness;
4. instituting campus-wide programs or institutes for assisting faculty in their quest for knowledge and skills concerning teaching and learning;
5. developing grants for enhancing pedagogical competence;
6. developing collegial groups based on shared interests in methodologies, pedagogical puzzlements, and so forth rather than just by discipline; and
7. providing ways to help faculty make mid-career transitions to other fields or even out of academia.

Unfortunately, the wheels of change move very slowly in higher education and many of the recommendations put forth in this monograph are only now becoming widespread actions in faculty development programs.

In the late 1970s and early 1980s, colleges and universities began responding to these changes by establishing faculty and instructional development programs (Clark & Lewis, 1985; Eble & McKeachie, 1985; McMillan, 1975; Toombs, 1983). The first programs emphasized instructional development. "The focus of their activities is the curriculum, or the class, not the faculty member. These centers are concerned with behavioral objectives, the design of learning experiences, and more efficient use of instructional devices and aids and orderly evaluation" (Freedman, 1979, p. viii). This emphasis on instructional development was in reaction to the criticism of the undergraduate student body of the 1960s. In 1975, McMillan surveyed 88 public and 27 private universities with advanced graduate programs and student enrollments greater than 5,000. He reported, "The primary purpose of the agencies I reviewed is to influence faculty to improve the quality of instruction. The location of the agency is usually within the central administration of the university, with typically two to four full-time faculty-administrators, support staff, and graduate assistants as personnel" (p. 19).

Many of these first faculty and instructional development programs were funded, either totally or in part, from grants from private foundations or public agencies. The Danforth Foundation, Exxon Education Foundation, Lilly Endowment, W.K. Kellogg Foundation, and Andrew W. Mellon Foundation were actively involved in supporting these early programs. Federally funded agencies such as the National Endowment for the Humanities, National Science Foundation, and the Fund for the Improvement of Postsecondary Education (FIPSE) were also strong supporters of this movement.

Because community college faculty have typically not emphasized research and other traditional scholarly activities, the need for instructional development programs was not seen as important at first. However, by the early 1970s, community colleges were also faced with changing conditions that led them to institute faculty development programs. Often faculty "renewal" programs were identified with "in-service training," a catch-all term for activities conducted by the college that were presumed to have an effect on an instructor's professional functioning (Cohen & Brawer, 1977). More often than not, these activities were required of all new and returning faculty members, much like the in-service training conducted by public school systems. A 1970 American Association of Junior Colleges survey disclosed that most faculty development programs included workshops and short course in-service programs focusing on education, curriculum development, and learning theories (O'Banion, 1972).

It seems rather ironic that in American education there is definitely a gap between the preparation experienced by elementary and secondary school teachers, on the one hand, and by college teachers, on the other. Osgood and York (1992) note that certification requirements for elementary and secondary school teachers demand that the future teachers take a series of courses dealing with pedagogical theory and practice. For college and university faculty, however, there is no credential required other than the possession of a graduate degree in an academic discipline. Yet, Osgood argues, the differences in teaching at the various levels of education are not so far removed from each other that one should require a year or more of deliberate training in how to teach while the other requires none. The Group for Human Development in Higher Education likened teaching in higher education to being a part of a "pedagogical amateurs' hour" (Astin et al, 1974).

The 1980s brought about a new paradigm for faculty development. This was triggered by the intensification of all the conditions that provoked the first surge of faculty development activities in the 1970s. "The most often cited deteriorating conditions of academic life include: reduced clerical support, reduced travel budgets, and massive amounts of deferred maintenance" (Cochran, 1989, p. 9). Faculty members also lost about 13 percent of their earning power (as measured in constant 1985–1986 dollars) from 1972 to 1986 (Stern, 1988). During the 1980s, the survey literature in educational research began to identify the widespread existence of "academic burnout" due to the continuing deterioration of the conditions of the academic workplace. In response to these conditions, the faculty development movement broadened its scope to include the personal dimensions of faculty life. With the inclusion of workshops and seminars focusing on "stage-of-the-life-cycle" events (e.g., mid-life crisis, career consulting, wellness programs, employee assistance programs, retirement planning programs), faculty development moved into more "holistic" development activities.

The Current Upsurge in Faculty Development

The 1990s have brought additional cries for "accountability" in higher education. Since parents and legislators are concerned that they are not getting what they are paying for, colleges and universities are instituting faculty development programs or centers for teaching and learning to help ensure that the undergraduates who attend are being exposed to the best possible teaching/learning conditions. At the end of the 1960s, only 40 to 50 faculty development programs existed (Sullivan, 1983). By 1975, 41 percent of all four-year institutions in the United States indicated they had organized faculty development programs (Centra, 1976). In a survey done by Erickson in 1986, it was found that 44 percent of all four-year institu-

tions had faculty development programs. During the winter of 1992–1993, Crawley (1995), in his study of faculty development programs at research universities, found that 67 or 64 percent of the 104 research universities as classified by the Carnegie Foundation for the Advancement of Teaching have an individual designated as the coordinator or director of a faculty or instructional development program or unit on their campus. Respondents to Crawley's survey indicated a high level of support for many of the 67 program initiatives typically used to support faculty and instructional development.

The number of new faculty development programs appears to be increasing steadily. In 1995 alone, the author received requests for information about starting a faculty development center from at least 20 institutions. Certainly, colleagues who are currently directors of faculty development centers also received such requests. In addition, the past five years have seen rapid increases in memberships in: (a) the Professional and Organizational Development (POD) Network in Higher Education (the professional home of many faculty and instructional developers at mostly four-year institutions); and (b) the National Council of Staff, Program, and Organizational Development (NCSPOD) and the National Institute for Staff and Organizational Development (NISOD) (the professional organizations of choice for "staff" developers at two-year institutions). Comparisons of their organizational membership lists show striking evidence of new centers and programs being started across all categories of postsecondary institutions.

Moreover, this renewed interest in faculty development programs has been given incentive by a growing body of research on the conditions under which these types of programs are effective and succeed in helping faculty members improve the quality of their teaching. Wright and O'Neil (1994) surveyed the teaching improvement practices in the United States and Canada. They found that improvements in the academic reward system to promote teaching, having deans and department chairs who recognize and foster the importance of teaching, and the existence of a teaching center were viewed by the survey respondents as the most promising avenues to improve instruction on their campuses. It is also due, in part, to the expanded commitment among college educators to provide "the highest quality education possible to an increasingly diverse student population" (Guskey, 1988, p. 124).

In the 1990s, many colleges and universities have expanded, or are expanding, the scope of activities included under the faculty development umbrella. They have discovered that faculty development is closely tied to institutional vitality and have begun to develop new priorities for these programs. Graf, Albright, and Wheeler (1992) cite some of these priorities as:

- *The Establishment and Retention of New Faculty.* Most institutions with faculty development centers provide intensive activities to orient new faculty to the campus and provide support for their teaching (Cresswell et al, 1990). Institution-wide seminars and orientations are frequently supplemented by formal and informal orientations offered at the college or departmental levels. A number of institutions provide mentoring programs for junior faculty members and peer visit programs are becoming more widespread. These programs can be especially helpful in retaining female and minority faculty members who are just entering college teaching, but they are beneficial for all incoming faculty members. Well-developed, exemplary programs in this area may be found at: Long Beach State University in California, the University of Georgia, and the University of Maryland.

- *Multicultural Sensitivity.* The ethnic and social diversity of colleges and universities is changing rapidly. Between 1976 and 1986, minority enrollment at U.S. colleges and universities increased 33 percent (Carter, 1990). Helping faculty members understand the characteristics, value systems, and learning styles of these populations has become an important function of faculty development programs. The University of Hawaii at Manoa and the University of Missouri at Columbia are examples of institutions with focused programs in this area.

- *Leadership and Support of Department Chairs.* It is becoming more and more obvious that department chairs are front-line faculty developers (Cresswell et al, 1990; Lucas, 1994; Seldin et al, 1990). Faculty development offices are increasingly conducting workshops, seminars, and individual consultations for chairs on how to facilitate faculty growth in all areas, including teaching. Exemplary department chair support programs exist at the University of Nebraska at Lincoln and Fairleigh Dickinson University.

- *Preparation of Teaching Assistants.* Teaching assistants (TAs) play a vital role in most universities and carry much of the lower-division teaching responsibility. Many institutions have developed courses or other types of programs to train TAs in such areas as course organization and management, teaching methods, availability of campus resources, and so forth. Special attention has also been given to the training in both language and pedagogy for international teaching assistants (ITAs). These programs contribute to the preparation of future faculty members and can make a noticeable difference in the quality of undergraduate education. Institutions with extensive TA/ITA training programs include the Universities of Washington, Texas at Austin, Nebraska at Lincoln, Michigan, Colorado at Boulder, Ohio State University, and Syracuse University. A national conference is held on this topic every other year.

- *Assessment.* Administrators in higher education are being held more accountable by the public, including legislatures and regents, for the quality of education being provided at their institutions. The skills and knowledge of the graduates at commencement and upon entrance into the workforce are used to determine the quality of education they received. Faculty developers are sometimes asked to help institutions develop assessment measures to meet these legislative requests. The University of Tennessee is a leader in the area of assessment.

- *Holistic or Enhanced Faculty Development.* More and more faculty development programs are incorporating personal development and organizational development to help faculty improve the personal and professional areas of their lives. The University of Georgia and Appalachian State University are leaders in this kind of programming.

- *Distance Education.* The delivery of courses via distance education technologies is quite different than teaching in a standard classroom. Faculty development programs are increasingly being called upon to provide comprehensive training programs to help faculty members operate effectively in this arena. The University of Wisconsin and Virginia Polytechnic Institute & State University have developed active training programs for faculty members involved in teaching at a distance.

- *Preparation of Part-Time Faculty.* Part-time faculty have been a part of higher education for a long time, but as economic pressures mount, the use of faculty members in this category is likely to increase. Especially in the Community College setting, these persons may have had limited experience in higher education and no training in course management or pedagogical methods. Faculty development programs are being asked to provide support services for these individuals. California State University at Fullerton has developed an excellent program for supporting the teaching and learning activities of part-time faculty.

- *Curriculum Development* (including the use of new technologies). Often faculty development is accomplished in the departments through curriculum development activities. Faculty developers, with expertise in course and curriculum design or redesign, can facilitate these changes through departmental consultations. Increasingly, faculty development centers are also providing training and assistance to faculty who want to use computer technology to enhance learning in their classes. Syracuse University Center for Instructional Development is a leader in the area of curriculum design and Southwest Texas State University has a "state of the art" program and facilities for helping faculty members use computer technologies effectively.

STAFFING FACULTY DEVELOPMENT PROGRAMS

The quality of the staff in a faculty development center is vital to its success. Faculty Development programs in higher education are typically staffed in one of three ways:

- a full-time staff member hired specifically for the position;
- experienced faculty members in academic departments serving part-time as faculty development specialists; and
- graduate students fulfilling assistantships in the center" (Graf, Albright, & Wheeler, 1992, p. 105).

Some larger centers may employ more than one full-time professional along with part-time faculty consultants and graduate assistants.

Sell and Chism (1991) looked at the advantages and disadvantages of each of these staffing alternatives and found that full-time professionals were preferred for those institutions able to afford that option. The advantages brought to faculty development programs by *full-time specialists* include more stability and continuity, full-time commitment to the functions of the center, professional training and experience as a faculty developer, and greater commitment to professional growth and activity in the faculty development field. *Experienced faculty members* serving as part-time developers are likely to have established respect and status in the institution and may be able to encourage others to engage in faculty development activities. Where *graduate students* serve as part of the faculty development staff, they receive excellent training for themselves and provide less costly personnel to the center. (Usually graduate students provide supplementary staff positions and experienced faculty or professional faculty developers direct the center.)

Some faculty development programs at smaller institutions are coordinated by faculty committees with members serving on a rotating basis. Lunde and Healy (1991) found that these committees are usually quite successful in providing workshops, publications, and grants for instructional improvement activities.

Appropriate academic preparation for professional faculty developers is something that is currently being studied closely. Sell and Chism (1991, pp. 23–24) have identified seven competencies that are of primary importance:

1. engage in needs assessment activities;
2. design and develop strategies that promote individual, pedagogical, curricular, and organizational growth ;
3. organize and implement specific programs, projects, and studies;
4. plan and deliver oral presentations;
5. conduct research about teaching and learning, and the evaluation of instruction;
6. produce print and non-print communications; and
7. establish and maintain consulting relationships.

Though many colleges and universities offer courses in college teaching, none have developed a graduate program specifically to prepare faculty developers for positions in higher education. Thus, "most practicing faculty developers today have attained their skills through self-study, attendance at conferences and workshops, networking, and on-the-job experience" (Graf, Albright, & Wheeler, 1992, p. 107). Fortunately, through the Professional and Organizational Development (POD) Network and other national and international conferences and workshops, there are many opportunities to gain skills and expertise in this area.

Of course, in order for a faculty development program to offer many or most of the activities previously discussed, there must be active support from the administration (i.e., money, personnel, and up-to-date equipment). Though this support is beginning to be offered, most faculty development programs are still operated on minimal budgets with one or two faculty developers for every 500-800 faculty members. Corporations are spending billions of dollars to train their employees (Eurich, 1985) and they maintain on-going research projects to discover how people learn. "In contrast to faculty in higher education, corporate trainers expect frequent ongoing evaluation, both in terms of achievement of course objectives and the methodology used, and frequent updating of training" (Lucas, 1991, p. 134).

Nevertheless, much progress has been made over the last 20 years. Moreover, the outcomes of these programs are showing that they *are* improving the quality of teaching and learning on many campuses (Ward, 1995). For example, in a study of individual teaching consultation conducted by Wilson (1986, pp. 209–210), it was found that "the consultation process was associated with statistically important change in overall teaching effectiveness ratings for 52 percent of the faculty clients." In addition, the comparison group "showed no significant change in the ratings of their teaching." The significance of existing research data indicates that teaching consultation services are indeed one of the driving forces for the improvement of teaching.

CHARACTERISTICS OF FACULTY DEVELOPMENT PROGRAMS IN HIGHER EDUCATION

If there is one thing that can be said about faculty development programs in higher education, it is that none of them are exactly alike. Each program's staffing, activities, governance structure, funding, and so forth, are determined by the type of institution in which it operates and the culture of that particular institution. Thus, a program that is very successful at one institution might not work at another institution, even though it is similar in size and mission. To provide some understanding of this, it is essential to consider those factors that influence these programs and several different models for faculty development programs.

Influences

A number of areas influence the specific elements contained in each faculty development program. These are:

Leadership The key people who support the program also influence what the program might contain. The individual areas of expertise of each of these leaders and what they see as the primary purpose or overall goals of the program greatly influence what activities are included, how the program is funded, and where the program is located in the overall structure of the institution.

Campus Community Elements like institutional mission, size, student traits, and faculty roles contribute to the unique needs and possibilities of the program. "If the prevailing organizational climate at a given institution is not favorable for improving teaching, then the change process may need to begin with reexamination of the institutional mission, reevaluation of administrative policies and procedures, and assessment of faculty motivation and educational values" (Ward, 1995, p. 39).

Local Faculty In order for a program to be successful, it must relate to the needs perceives by the faculty. If the program is to succeed in the long term, these needs must be addressed.

Age and Historical Evolution One must consider whether there has been some faculty/student development at the institution or whether a new program is being started "from scratch."

Availability of Resources Financial, human, and informational resources place constraints on the program. The number of desired goals and activities have to be prioritized to match what is perceived as the most valuable outcomes. In addition, in order for faculty development to be successful at a particular institution, the organization as a whole typically has to go through a developmental process. This process, says Francis (1975), consists of three stages:

1. Consciousness-raising stage—during this stage current attitudes are challenged in order to induce heightened awareness.
2. Focal-awareness stage—in this stage concentrated attention is directed to substituting new attitudes and behavior patterns for old.
3. Subsidiary-awareness stage—during this stage new attitudes or behaviors become firmly established and no longer acquire conscious attention.

The success of any given instructional development program in any institution depends upon its congruence with the level of awareness about instruction that has been attained. Conferences and workshops, student evaluations, instruction, and official institutional actions will be more or less effective depending upon how well they fit prevailing attitudes about instruction at that institution. Different kinds of workshops, different evaluation programs, and different policies will "take" at different awareness stages. By accurately assessing these stages, program planners will be able to make sounder judgments concerning which programs are likely to be effective, and they will be better able to understand why programs of comparable quality but different emphases are not equally effective (Francis, 1975, pp. 721–722).

Ward (1995, p. 30), in his "gleanings from research" article, indicates that there are three main factors that appear to be involved in the process of improving teaching:

1. driving forces—factors which tend to support improvement of teaching (e.g., faculty intrinsic motivation, consultation services related to improvement of teaching and a positive institutional climate for teaching;
2. neutral forces—factors which might be expected to have considerable influence on teaching improvement efforts, but which, according to research findings, actually have negligible impact (e.g., faculty career age, end-of-course student ratings that are not supplemented with consultation or other assistance, and the institutional reward system; and
3. restraining forces—factors which tend to oppose improvement of teaching (e.g., low perceived need to improve teaching among faculty, high sense of self-competence in teaching, and a negative institutional climate for teaching).

Ward concludes that

". . . any promising approach to improving teaching across an entire campus should begin with a thorough assessment of driving and restraining forces peculiar to the specific institution. After identifying the opposing forces that affect efforts to improve teaching, the strength of each force needs to be estimated. On campuses where restraining forces are dominant, the overall quality of teaching among the majority of instructors is not likely to change significantly in response to instructional improvement programs. Where driving forces slightly outweigh restraining forces, broad scale improvements may be possible if systematic intervention strategies are sustained over time, but the improvements are likely to be gradual and incremental in nature. Only when driving forces significantly outweigh restraining forces can extensive improvements be expected over a relatively short period of time" (p. 39).

Structural Variations and Program Models There are four major structural variations in current faculty development centers: the Campus-Wide Center, the Multi-Campus Cooperative Program, the University with Decentralized, Special Purpose Centers, and Development Components of other Academic Programs (Wright, 1988). Their typical organizational charts, a description of how they operate and what programs they may offer are discussed below.

CAMPUS-WIDE CENTER (Figure 30.1.)

Locus—Usually located under the chief academic officer.

Staffing—Often leadership person is selected from local faculty. There is, however, a growing pool of experienced faculty developers who may increase availability of external expertise. Staff typically includes:

Director*
Assistant/Associate Director*
Faculty Developers (1–2)*
Part Time Graduate Assistant
Secretary

Budget—Often supported by institution's teaching budget. Many are supplemented by grant funds for special aspects of

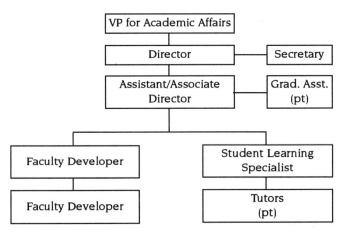

Figure 30.1. Campus-Wide Center

---

* May hold faculty rank or may be professional staff.

the program. Budgets vary greatly depending on program elements. Most have adequate funds to support a multi-activity program.

Audience—Usually serve faculty in all stages of their careers. Programs designed not only for troubled faculty but for all faculty at one time or another. Often also serve TAs and offer workshops and seminars to help them teach more effectively. Some centers also provide services for student learning such as study skills, tutoring, and so forth.

Programs—Each Campus-Wide Center may include all or some of these services, depending on funding, mission, etc.

—*For Faculty Development*—Most programs have gone beyond traditional grants, leaves, and travel for development. They typically include new information and skill-building workshops, seminars, conferences, retreats, and so forth.

- Written information—booklets, flyers, newsletters, library/reading resource room
- Individual consultation services
- Assistance in curricular review and revision
- Participation in teaching awards and grants
- Service on special teaching committees
- Some include associated programs such as:
  - TA training and development
  - student learning skill assistance
  - examination and evaluations services
  - media production services
  - career development
  - faculty exchange programs

—*For TA Training and Development*—If Campus-Wide Centers are also involved in TA training and development, they often offer services such as:

- Written information—booklets, flyers, newsletters, library/reading resource room
- Individual consultation services
- Workshops/seminars (sometimes leading to a "Certificate in Higher Education Teaching," e.g., University of Colorado, Boulder)

—*For Student Learning Skills*—If the Student Learning Skills Center is incorporated into the Campus-Wide Center, they often offer services such as:

- Tutors (often for specific courses)
- Resource room/library
- Workshops and seminars on learning and study skills, speed reading, etc.
- Audio-Visual and/or computer-assisted instructional modules
- Staff members who will work with faculty to help them design learning and study strategies for their courses

—*For Examination and Evaluation Services*—If the Campus-Wide Center is also charged with examination and evaluations services, they typically offer such services as:

- Scoring of op-scan exams
- Distribution and tabulating student evaluations of instructors
- Testing services for GRE, MCAT, etc.

—*For Media Assistance*—If Campus-Wide Centers have a media service, they often offer such services as:

- Equipment/personnel for showing films, slides and videos
- Graphic artists to help design overhead transparencies
- Video and/or computer graphics assistance
- Computer-assisted instruction specialists to help faculty develop programs for use in their classes

—*For Career Development Services*—The Campus-Wide Center might also offer assistance to faculty who are considering a career change or need career counseling. To facilitate this, centers might provide the following:

- Written materials on faculty careers and non-faculty careers
- Inventories and tests to help determine one's skills and aptitudes
- Career counselors

MULTI-CAMPUS COOPERATIVE PROGRAMS
(Figure 30.2.)

Locus—Usually have a central office which coordinates efforts and administers resources for a number of institutions. There are also usually individuals on each campus who are charged with local communication and coordination.

Staffing—Usually have a central coordinating council made up of academic administrators, faculty, and sometimes students from each campus. A central administrator is also a part of this council. (Central staffs vary from 1–3 people.) In addition, each campus may have a faculty committee and resource center with staff which complement the central multi-campus resources.

Budget—These tend to be large, but are divided among several institutions. A number of these budgets began with funds from grants.

Program—Unique opportunities for inter-institutional communication include:

- Grants for travel, leave, research, summer fellowships, etc. with competition from all campuses
- Weekend and summer conferences (frequently discipline-based)
- Inter-campus communication—newsletters, electronic bulletin boards
- Seldom has individual consultation unless campuses provide their own consultants

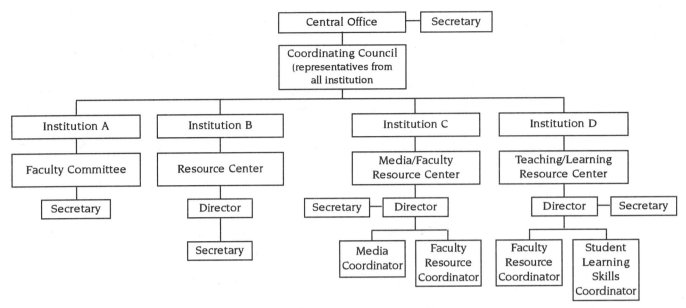

FIGURE 30.2. Multi-Campus Cooperative Programs

SPECIAL PURPOSE CENTERS (Figure 30.3)

Locus—Each of these special purpose centers may serve the whole campus, but each has a specific focus (e.g., student learning, media resources). Large campuses often have a number of special purpose centers to manage the various programs described under "Campus-Wide Center" above.

Staffing—Staffs have special expertise consistent with the goals of each center. Typically, there are one to three professionals plus support staff in each of the special purpose centers.

Budget—Some began with grant funds but most are part of the institution's budget or they generate income from services offered to outside clientele.

Program—Varies according to specific goals. Newsletters, workshops, publications, and resource materials are used to communicate with the clientele. Some examples of special purpose centers are:

- Career Development Program—Loyola University in Chicago
- Center for Faculty Evaluation & Development—Kansas State University Division of Continuing Education (serves other

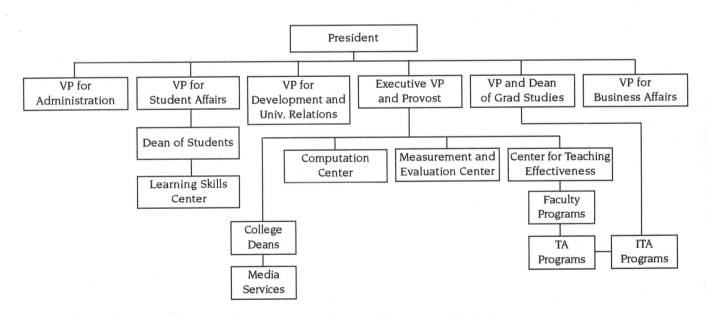

FIGURE 30.3. The University with Decentralized, Special Purpose Centers

colleges and universities—does workshops and publishes print material on a national scale)

- Graduate Teacher Program—University of Colorado, Boulder
- Thinking and Learning Center—Pace University
- External Studies Program—University of Pittsburgh
- Learning Skills Center—The University of Texas at Austin (serves the students in study skills, tutoring, etc.; serves the faculty by being a resource to design learning and study strategies for their courses)

DEVELOPMENT COMPONENTS OF OTHER ACADEMIC PROGRAMS (FIGURE 30.4.)

Locus—Organized under another unit such as a Dean's Office or a Faculty Development Committee.

Staffing—Faculty with released time or an administrator has this assignment as part of his or her workload.

Budget—Depends upon unit priorities and numbers being served.

Program—Program development usually the responsibility of a faculty committee, with some faculty release time. Scope may be limited by resources.

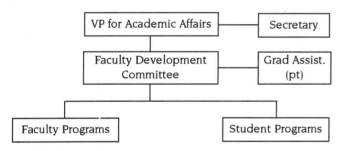

FIGURE 30.4. Development Components
of Other Academic Programs

The above descriptions offer a broad overview of typical faculty development program components. However, for a more detailed description of a wide variety of programs at various types of institutions, see Weimer (1991, pp. 174–199) and *Program Descriptions* published by the POD Network. This latter publication contains descriptions of over 75 faculty development programs in the United States and Canada.

JUNIOR AND COMMUNITY COLLEGES

In the 1960s, the community college emerged to take its place between the high school and the university. During the ten-year period between 1960 and 1970, the number of two-year colleges increased by 61 percent and the number of students increased by 271 percent. In that same time period, the

number of staff members increased by 327 percent (O'Banion, 1981) When the growth spurt slowed somewhat in the 1970s, the community colleges had a chance to look at where they were and how they had arrived at this point. As they reviewed programs, it became clear that

the quality of education in the community college did not depend primarily on numbers of students, or on the diversity of the programs, or on expanded facilities, or on new structures for decision-making, although these factors certainly contribute to the development of quality. The quality of education in the community college depended primarily on the quality of the staff. If the community college . . . is to realize even a modicum of its potential, then community college leaders must begin to pay as much attention to their staffs as to students, programs, buildings, and organizational structures (O'Banion, 1981, p. 1–2).

In their survey of community college chief academic officers, Smith and Hawthorne (1993, p. 11) found that "a center for teaching and learning on a university campus would most likely be a faculty development center, whereas on a community college campus it is likely to mean a learning resources center for students." Given that many entering community college students "lack the basic skills in reading, writing and/or mathematics to succeed in college-level studies" (Gratton & Walleri, 1993, p. 39), focusing on student development makes a great deal of sense. In addition, many centers at community colleges include non-academic staff development as well as faculty and student development. Thus, these centers might provide programs to improve clerical skills, management skills, and so forth (Lucas, 1981, pp. 83–100) through workshops usually conducted by an office of human resources at a four-year or graduate institution.

The Smith and Hawthorne (1993) study also found the following:

1. in general, responses (from the CAO's) confirmed limited support and commitment for instructional effectiveness;
2. the highest level of perceived commitment was in the area of campus environment and culture, including such ideas as faculty ownership of the curriculum, faculty confidence in administrative leadership, and a feeling of institutional pride;
3. the lowest level of reported commitment was in regard to instructional development activities, including faculty workshops, colleague support mechanisms, and organized campus units to promote effective teaching; and
4. compared to data from the study of four-year institutions, two-year college CAO's reported higher commitment for all the areas except for employment practices and policies (Cochran, 1989, p. ii).

RESEARCH ON TEACHING IN HIGHER EDUCATION

In his comprehensive review of the history of research on college teaching in the 20th century, McKeachie (1990) identifies five areas that have been the focus of study: class size, teaching/learning methods, evaluation of teaching, teaching and technology, and cognitive psychology. A majority of the research reviewed, and which has produced the most conclusive findings, has focused on teaching methods and student ratings of instruction. Findings tend to agree that different teaching methods may be effective for different purposes and that no individual method is superior for all situations (Costin, 1972; Dubin & Taveggia, 1968; McKeachie, 1970). There is also agreement that teaching effectiveness is dependent upon the particular subject matter being taught, the students enrolled in that particular class, and the setting (e.g., type of room, kind of institution) (Barnes & Barnes, 1993; McKeachie, Pintrich, Lin, & Smith, 1986). Finally, research indicates that student ratings of instruction are reasonably valid and reliable (Cohen, 1980; Feldman, 1989; Feldman, 1993; Marsh, 1984).

One thing that hinders conducting extensive research on teaching in higher education is that "teaching, unlike research and publishing, remains very much a private professional act, rarely open to collegial scrutiny" (Astin et al, 1974). This is slowly changing, with the advent of Angelo and Cross' *Classroom Assessment Techniques* (Angelo & Cross, 1993). The classroom research that is accomplished using these techniques is usually conducted by the faculty member rather than by a researcher specializing in higher education teaching research, though the faculty developer may facilitate the process and data analysis. According to Angelo (1991), "Classroom Assessment consists of *small-scale* assessments conducted *continuously* in college classrooms by discipline-based *teachers* to determine what students *are* learning in *that class*" (p. 9). Descriptions of how this technique has been used in a variety of disciplines and the teaching and learning changes that have occurred are detailed in *Classroom Research: Early Lessons from Success* (Angelo, 1991).

The new emphasis on effective teaching and learning in higher education has brought about the development of teaching techniques such as collaborative learning, active learning, team based learning, supplemental instruction, etc. (Bonwell & Eison, 1991; Bosworth & Hamilton, 1994; Martin & Arendale, 1994; Meyers & Jones, 1993; Michelson, 1992). By focusing more on the learner, faculty members are being encouraged to broaden their repertoire of teaching methods. Faculty development programs are assisting in this endeavor. The next step will be to develop ways in which faculty members and faculty developers can analyze these teaching strategies to determine when, where, and with what kinds of materials each strategy might contribute most to student learning. To make this information accessible, faculty members will have to be encouraged to publish their findings in teaching-oriented disciplinary journals—and colleges and universities will need to give appropriate recognition for this type of scholarship.

RESEARCH ON INTERVENTIONS TO IMPROVE COLLEGE TEACHING

Interventions with Faculty

For more than two decades, faculty development and instructional improvement programs in higher education have generated projects, research reports, and conferences. Many campuses support activities to benefit faculty and enrich the education of students. Most of the interventions to improve college teaching cluster in five categories: grants for faculty projects, workshops and seminars, feedback from student ratings, practice-based feedback (microteaching, individual consultation, and minicourses), and concept-based training (protocols). In 1981, Levinson-Rose and Menges conducted a critical review of the research in this area and concluded that "research on improving college teaching is not a well-defined field" (p. 418). Weimer and Lenze (1991) conclude their review of the literature with *"more research must be undertaken . . . instructional interventions are being used with virtually no empirical justification as to their effectiveness"* (p. 327). Nevertheless, an analysis and evaluation of Bush Foundation funded programs (Eble & McKeachie, 1985), in conjunction with the Levinson-Rose and Menges study, indicate that effective programs typically share the following four general characteristics:

1. There is a balance of faculty and administrator planning in the program, rather than domination by either group.
2. Change is seen as a gradual process that requires strong administrative support.
3. Faculty members receive feedback on the results of their efforts.
4. Faculty members receive continued support and follow-up activities.

Though these four characteristics seem quite "common sense" in nature, this combination of characteristics is not very common in college and university faculty development programs. Incorporating all of them requires a high level of commitment and cooperation among administrators and faculty members.

Problem of Focus Part of the problem, as stated by Smith (1995), is that most faculty members are still not convinced that teaching is really that important in the grand scheme of things. Robert Diamond (1993) in his work, *Recognizing Faculty Work: Reward Systems for the Year 2000,* summarized the problem well when he said, "the focus on research and publication and the mad dash for federal funds and external grants has diverted energies away from important faculty work and has had a direct and negative impact on the quality of classroom instruction" (p. 8). In addition, "most faculty-development efforts focus primarily on improving teaching—and only secondarily, if at all, on improving learning" (Angelo, 1994, p. 4). "The culture of the academy doesn't seem to include much discussion of differences in learning styles, or of adapting teaching to individual differences" (Smith, 1995, p. 17). In addition, Blackburn and his colleagues (1980) found that 92 percent of the faculty members they surveyed considered their teaching to be above average. Of these same faculty members, however, only 74 percent considered the teaching of their departmental colleagues to be above average. Thus, the rate of participation in faculty development programs aimed at improving teaching is typically rather low. It is reported that "no more than approximately 40 percent (and quite possibly fewer) of the teachers participate in workshops on specific teaching methods or audio-visual aids, and even fewer—less than 25 percent—participate in workshops on general educational issues (Blackburn et al, 1980; Centra, 1976; cf. Eble & McKeachie, 1985; Maxwell & Kazlauskas, 1992, p. 353).

Campus-Wide Workshops and Seminars Participation in campus-wide workshops and seminars can, however, help to create community. At the University of Texas at Austin, two campus-wide seminars are offered each year: *The Hitchhiker's Guide to the University: A Teaching/Orientation Seminar for New Faculty,* and the annual *Experienced Faculty Conference* (Lewis, Svinicki & Stice, 1985; Lewis, Svinicki, & Stice, 1989). A consistent comment on the final evaluation forms is that the faculty look forward to being able to meet and renew acquaintances with people from all across the campus. The *New Faculty Seminar's* three-day duration gives the participants time to make acquaintances with other new faculty members—many associations which continue for the duration of their time at the university. Then, the *Experienced Faculty Conference* ensures them of a time, at least once a year, to get together again.

Individual Consultation In most faculty development programs, where there is a center for teaching effectiveness or a teaching and learning center, individual consultation is one of the most documented and successful means of improving instruction. "Through this type of individual work with faculty members, we are able to focus on each person's strengths and concerns to facilitate discovery of alternative teaching methods, better testing methods, confidence in themselves as public speakers, or whatever will help each one do a more effective job as a faculty member in an institution of higher education" (Lewis, 1988, p. 19). In an individual consultation program, instructional consultants study and analyze the teaching materials (e.g., syllabi, handouts, exams), student feedback (e.g., end-of-semester evaluations, mid-semester evaluations, verbal feedback sessions), in-class observation data, faculty self-evaluation data, and anything else that may influence the way a course is taught. Through this analysis, the consultant and faculty member determine how well students are learning the material and what the faculty member is doing to facilitate or hinder this learning. In their monograph in the *New Directions for Teaching and Learning* series, Theall and Franklin (1991) have compiled the current thinking and day-to-day activities of those involved in teaching improvement efforts. This volume provides guidelines for effective practice to anyone involved in this endeavor. Brinko (1993) and Brinko and Menges (1996) have done extensive research to determine which individual consultation methods are most effective and the outcomes experienced by faculty members who take advantage of this service.

Programs in Community Colleges Most of the research on interventions done in community colleges has examined programs rather than outcomes (i.e., changes in the teachers or students). Additionally, the measures selected for study have usually consisted of general ratings of the programs rather than direct observation of them. One major factor that has been "studied" in both community colleges and four-year institutions/universities is the "rate of participation in workshops." Rather than look at the amount of participation in specific activities—for example, syllabus writing skills development—researchers have lumped all of the workshops and seminars together to get an overall participation level.

Shea (1990) and Schmidt (1987) found that the most important factor in a faculty development program's success was the instructional experts providing individualized services to the faculty. Surveys in community colleges indicate that expert consultation by colleagues on specific teaching matters and classroom visits with feedback sessions were among the less frequently used, but more effective, types of development. In addition, programs that provide small grants to faculty for the development of new methods in a course are rated as one of the most successful of all means of instructional development (Centra, 1976; Richardson & Moore, 1987).

Interventions with Graduate Teaching Assistants

In many, if not most, of the doctoral degree granting institutions in the United States, the graduate teaching assistantship is an important means for providing financial support to graduate students. In recent years, criticism has surfaced concerning the extensive use of TAs to instruct undergraduates in lower-division courses and labs. TAs are frequently criticized for their lack of communication and pedagogical skills even though in many fields it is assumed that if the person teaching has an undergraduate or graduate concentration in the subject being taught, he or she is qualified to teach.

In 1986, concern about the training and employment of graduate teaching assistants resulted in the first National TA Conference which was held in Columbus, Ohio. The conference was initiated in order to provide a forum to disseminate information on TA training program models and research and to share training materials and other resources. The participants represented 117 United States universities, located in 43 states and the District of Columbia, and two Canadian institutions. "Approximately one-third of the undergraduate students enrolled in private and public four-year colleges and universities in the United States (6.1 million total) and graduate students (1.34 million total) were represented by institutional members participating in the conference" (Chism, 1987, p. vi). Since 1986, this group has continued to convene every other year. In November 1995, the Fifth National Conference on the Training and Employment of Graduate Teaching Assistants was held in Denver, Colorado. This conference included over 600 participants, consisting of TAs, faculty, TA developers, administrators, and faculty members.

From each of the National TA Conferences has come a book of selected readings (Chism, 1987; Heenan & Jerich, 1995; Lewis, 1993; Nyquist, Abbott, Wulff, & Sprague, 1991). Many of the articles published in these books detail the research that is being undertaken in this area. An additional source for publication and dissemination of information on the training and development of TAs is *The Journal of Graduate Teaching Assistant Development,* edited by Karron G. Lewis and published by New Forums Press, Inc.

TA training has caught the attention of a number of funding agencies and foundations. One extensive program, *Preparing Future Faculty (PFF),* is jointly sponsored by the

Association of American Colleges and Universities and the Council of Graduate Schools and funded by a grant from The PEW Charitable Trusts. In this program, 17 large research universities are paired with three to five smaller four- or two-year institutions in their vicinity. The TAs from the research institution are given opportunities to visit the partner campuses, talk to faculty, administrators and students, and, in some cases, team teach courses. These experiences provide the TAs with a wider view of the faculty member's role in higher education. They learn there are more role models than the one they typically see at the research institution where they are pursuing their Ph.D. (Dennee, 1995).

In terms of preparing college and university faculty members to teach more effectively, this movement is unparalleled. Currently some type of TA training or development activities are in place at hundreds of institutions in the United States. and Canada. This area of training and development also provides a ripe source for conducting research on teaching and learning in higher education since it is usually possible to enlist greater participation from TAs than from their faculty counterparts.

Interventions Involving Department Chairs and Other Administrators

In her book, *Strengthening Departmental Leadership,* Ann Lucas (1994) indicates that Parker Palmer, a well-known scholar in the area of the improvement of teaching and learning in higher education, states that "little talk about teaching—good or otherwise—will take place if presidents and provosts, deans and department chairs do not expect and invite it into being on a regular basis" (Palmer, 1993, p. 9). "If effective teaching is to become more important in higher education, leadership of department chairs will be crucial in improving the overall quality of instruction in every department" (Lucas, 1994, p. 99). However, Lucas found that only one third of the chairs who attended at National Conference for Academic Chairpersons Kansas State University in 1991, indicated that they had had success in motivating poor teachers to improve the quality of their teaching. Before academic chairs will be able to do this effectively, *they* will have to become better informed about pedagogy, learning theory, and motivation.

In 1992, Boice completed a longitudinal study of 185 new faculty members at several comprehensive institutions. He found that the primary pedagogical approach of these new faculty members was a "facts and principles style of teaching" (p. 68). Being uncomfortable in the classroom was a major problem for new faculty, yet, they resisted change. When they received low student evaluations, they usually reacted defensively at first, and then focused on improving their lecture notes to make sure they had all their facts straight. The possibility of changing the *method* used for teaching never entered their minds.

Through the work of faculty developers such as Weimer (1990), we now know that most faculty can benefit from thinking and reflecting on how they teach as the first step to becoming a better teacher. Then, by combining observer feedback with an increased understanding of how students learn, faculty can focus on the teaching-learning process. Next, through readings and observing other teachers, an awareness of alternative pedagogical methods can be developed. The final step is to help chairs bring this awareness and openness to discussions in the department.

Lucas (1994, pp. 106–114) offers the following strategies for improving teaching effectiveness in a department:

1. *Make teaching effectiveness a high-priority goal of the department.* This means chairs must talk about teaching! They need to discuss their own teaching and what they are attempting to do, based on how things went the previous semester. Then, chairs can inquire about innovations or techniques faculty members are using in their own classes.

2. *Let faculty know that teaching effectiveness, like learning, is a life-long process.* Chairs must set the goal of ongoing professional development in teaching. They need to share with the faculty that teaching effectiveness must be continually monitored and thought about in order to improve.

3. *Create a climate of trust and support so that faculty's visits to each other's classrooms are acceptable and non-threatening.* Chairs can emphasize classroom observation as positive feedback and an opportunity to receive additional perspectives on teaching.

4. *Invite a few faculty members to observe one of the classes.* To emphasize the value of feedback, chairs can announce their own intention to solicit feedback. The chairs may suggest questions that will give them meaningful, affirming feedback and set the stage for encouraging others to try this.

5. *When advertising for new faculty, include the potential for effective teaching as one of the requirements for the position.* In *The Role of the Department Chair,* a document distributed by the American Sociological Association, the authors make a strong recommendation that considerable effort be devoted to assessing the candidate's teaching ability (Bowker, Mauksch, Keating, & McSeveney, 1992). Documentation of teaching ability should precede the campus interview and may include such things as a videotape of a lecture or discussion led by the candidate, sets of teaching evaluations, course syllabi, statements of teaching philosophy, and any other written evidence that relates to their teaching ability.

6. *Require all applicants for faculty positions to make a presentation to faculty and students before receiving a faculty appointment.* The document cited in item 5 also recommends that "candidates for teaching positions should be kept on campus for at least two full days, during which they should teach three or more regular classes in addition to the scholarly lecture often delivered to an audience of faculty members. Bring them in as guest lecturers to a regularly scheduled class" (p. 20). After the candidate's visit, faculty and students who were present for the guest lectures should sit down and discuss the positive and negative aspects of the pedagogical methods used.

7. *Reward good teaching.* A great deal of money is not the only reward one can give for excellence in teaching. Chairs should brainstorm with faculty to come up with a list of items the faculty would find reinforcing. Some possibilities might be: release time for course development, courses in using technology in the classroom, a little money to hire an undergraduate student assistant to help with clerical tasks or classroom research projects, etc.

8. *Sponsor departmental workshops on different aspects of teaching.* These workshops could be conducted by faculty members who have read several articles or a book on a particular topic or who have attended faculty development workshops. The staff members of the institution's faculty development center (or one at a nearby institution) could also present a workshop tailored to an individual department to answer a particular question raised by the faculty in that department.

9. *Share course syllabi with all department members.* Trask (1989) points out that nothing makes faculty members more thoughtful about preparing a syllabus than knowing that all of their colleagues will be reading it.

10. *Provide feedback to department members by circulating an anonymous list of grade distributions for all courses offered by the department.* This intervention may be used when there are several individuals whose grades are excessively high or low. Usually, when they see how different their grading is from the rest of the department, they will adjust to a more realistic distribution. If nothing else, this will provide an "opening" for discussing faculty's bases for grading and their individual expectations.

11. *Begin a teaching committee.* This group can work with new faculty and share relevant issues about teaching with the rest of the department. It might be divided into subcommittees for curriculum revision, classroom instruction and colleague observations.

12. *Build a departmental library on teaching.* The literature on pedagogy, learning, and motivation is becoming very extensive. Chairs might contact their faculty development center for a list of books and other materials that would be appropriate for such a library. Having something in the department will make it easier for faculty members to find the answers to their questions and make them aware of the vast number of resources that are available to them.

13. *Use student and colleague evaluations as feedback to celebrate good teaching.* Good teaching should not be taken for granted. Chairs need to recognize those teachers who have shown improvement and provide support for those who need assistance.

14. *Develop a mentoring system.* One form of mentoring suggested in the literature (Katz, 1985; Katz & Henry, 1988; Wunsch, 1994) pairs two faculty members who interview approximately three students from each other's classes once a week. The interviews focus on how the students read the assignments and prepared for class and the teacher-student interactions during the class. The faculty members meet once a week to discuss how these interviews can be used to improve the course.

15. *Introduce classroom research techniques for evaluating the effectiveness of teaching strategies and aiding understanding of what is going on in the classroom.* When discussing teaching in departmental meetings or individually with faculty, chairs can bring up the topic of classroom research and how faculty members can use these techniques to acquire feedback about their teaching. A copy of Angelo and Cross' (1993) book should be available in the departmental office library.

16. *Send interested faculty to workshops on teaching and have them run a workshop when they return.* This is an excellent way to get the most from travel money. Have the funded faculty member present a workshop so everyone can benefit from what that person learned.

17. *Invite faculty and students to brown-bag lunches, so that students can share what classroom experiences are meaningful to them.* If chairs prepare both the students and the faculty concerning the focus of the discussion (not using specific persons' names), then these types of interactions can give faculty a whole new perspective on how students view their academic experiences.

18. *Pass on the good news whenever you hear students commenting about exciting classes or interesting projects.* This not only reinforces good teaching, but also creates the norm that good teaching is a topic worthy of discussion.

19. *Create a tolerance for risk taking, so that individuals are willing to try new things in their classrooms.* Innovations are not failures if faculty learn something from them. By encouraging discussions of successes and "things that didn't quite go as planned," faculty will be more open to sharing their ideas and "bouncing" new ideas off colleagues.

20. *Experiment with the teaching portfolio.* Though teaching portfolios are especially useful for new faculty and for those preparing for promotion and tenure, the introspection and analysis involved in this process can benefit everyone, including the department as a whole.

21. *Use team teaching.* In order for team teaching to be a learning experience, both teachers must attend all classes. If each simply teaches half the course, there are no benefits gained from observing another faculty member teach, handle questions, and involve students.

22. *Encourage faculty to make videotapes of their teaching.* These videotapes may be viewed in private using a list of statements that relate to a variety of teaching skills. Or, the instructor can invite someone to act as a consultant, making recommendations about areas where improvements might be made. Having someone from the faculty development center do this the first time can relieve some of the anxiety about having a peer critique one's teaching.

23. *Recommend that faculty collect their own student evaluations early in the semester, while there is still time to make adjustments in the course.* This technique lets students know that the instructor cares about students' responses to the teaching approaches employed and can also initiate dialogue about what is and is not working. (Note: These early evaluations should not replace those normally used by the university in the last third of the semester.)

24. *Have faculty who teach related courses meet informally on a regular basis to talk about common problems and strategies.* These support groups might also offer mutual help to each other by offering to observe each other's classes.

Accompanying this list of strategies, Lucas includes some teaching topics that are worth talking about along with resources for outside reading. Some of the teaching topics she lists are the following (pp. 115–118):

- What constitutes effective teaching? What can faculty do to enhance their own teaching effectiveness?
- What are some of the better ways of handling students who come to class unprepared?
- Are there special approaches to teaching college freshmen?
- How can large sections be taught most effectively?

Department chairs may use this list in several ways:

- Distribute the list and ask faculty which topics they would like to discuss or which topics would provide interesting content for a workshop.
- Discuss the list with informal leaders of the department to get their ideas and suggestions about what activities might be the most appealing.
- Organize brown-bag lunches with the most effective teachers and anyone else who is interested. Then, have one person from this group report at subsequent faculty meetings on the new ideas about teaching this group has generated.
- Distribute short articles on some aspect of teaching at intervals during the semester.

Thus, with some creativity and a little work, department chairs could have a substantial impact upon the quality of teaching and learning in their departments. Without this, though, there will be little hope for permanent change in a majority of the faculty members.

FUTURE DIRECTIONS OF TEACHING AND LEARNING IN POSTSECONDARY EDUCATION

Though there have been some promising finishes in the research done on faculty development, the approach taken by many faculty development administrators is essentially intuitive. The research that has been done in instructional development and the resulting theories have "not often been used as a basis for these programs or as a means of evaluating the effectiveness of alternative faculty development methods" (Maxwell & Kazlauskas, 1992, p. 358). Instead of *opinions* about the improvement of teaching, there is a need for direct measures of change in faculty instruction, teaching and student learning in relation to faculty development programs.

Research is needed to determine which faculty development programs and activities are effective and the conditions under which colleges and universities should establish such programs. We also need to find out what would make professors eager to take advantage of these programs. What are their motivations, needs, and dreams for becoming effective (or great) teachers? Many signs point to a change in the reward system. That is, if the rewards (promotions, raises, etc.) were based on effective teaching rather than almost solely on research productivity, faculty members would look upon teaching differently. They would probably be more inclined to spend additional time improving their courses, considering learning theory, or honing teaching skills. The importance of this topic is shown in the Annual Conference on Faculty Roles and Rewards sponsored by the American Association for Higher Education (AAHE). The fourth such conference was held in January 1996.

This change in emphasis can be related to Boyer's report, *Scholarship Reconsidered: Priorities of the Professoriate* (1990). Boyer says,

We believe the time has come to move beyond the tired old "teaching versus research" debate and give the familiar and honorable term 'scholarship' a broader, more capacious meaning, one that brings legitimacy to the full scope of academic work. Surely, scholarship means engaging in original research. But the work of the scholar also means stepping back from one's investigation, looking for connections, building bridges between theory and practice, and communicating one's knowledge effectively to students. Specifically, we conclude that the work of the professoriate might be thought of as having four separate, yet overlapping, functions. These are: the scholarship of discovery; the scholarship of integration; the scholarship of application; and the scholarship of teaching (p. 16).

This report has prompted higher education to reconsider what constitutes faculty work and how that work should be rewarded. Teaching well is becoming a criteria for promotion and tenure and faculty development provides the means for helping faculty members do that.

AAHE is also holding conferences and conducting research on "School/College Collaboration," "Assessment & Quality," "Teaching, Learning and Technology," to name a few areas. Higher education is definitely beginning to focus on enhancing the quality of teaching and learning and some well-developed research studies will be forthcoming.

In the areas of teaching, learning, and technology, enormous advances are being made. "The frenetic pace of technological change in society at large is carrying over to our campuses. Exciting new instructional programs and services involving technology are being established all across the country, some of which have significant implications for the way that teaching and learning will be conducted in the future" (Albright & Graf, 1992, p. 2).

Although the technology experience may not be universal, the presence of technology in the learning environment is increasingly common: an e-mail address on a course syllabus; electronic mail as a supplement to office hours; class sessions held in computer labs; desktop computers in faculty offices; commercial software and simulations as part of the resources provided by textbook publishers; and course assignments that sent students to World Wide Web (WWW) sites in search of information resources (published articles, conference papers, digitized images, and just-released data files). These examples and others reflect the new significance of information technology in the instructional domain—across almost all disciplines (from art history to zoology) and in virtually all types of campus contexts, from elite research universities to community colleges to distance-education programs (Green, 1996, p. 24).

In response to this explosion in the use of technology, faculty developers are being called upon to "bring the faculty up to speed." Depending on their discipline and resourcefulness, some faculty members are more reluctant than others to start using these new tools for teaching. Sometimes, all they need is suggestions about how these tools can be incorporated into the teaching and learning in their courses. At other times, one-on-one instruction in computer usage is necessary.

The POD Network is also deliberating some of the research that is needed to help faculty developers do their job more effectively. Some of the questions being raised are:

- What is the correlation between faculty/organizational development and student learning?
- What is "scholarship" in faculty development?
- How can POD facilitate communication to the public/legislators about what faculty actually do?
- What skills or competencies do people need to do faculty development well and how can they get them?

POD is currently working in conjunction with The International Consortium for Educational Development (ICED), a new international consortium made up of persons in faculty development from around the world. The main thrust of this organization is to provide world-wide resources to facilitate the improvement of teaching and learning. Much research and work has been done in the areas of teaching and learning, but it is almost impossible for researchers from one part of the world to access this information if it has been compiled in another part of the world. Rather than "reinvent the wheel," the hope is to provide, in one location (e.g., a WWW site), a wide array of resources to assist in solving teaching and learning problems/puzzles.

CONCLUSIONS

In 1991, Derek Bok, President Emeritus of Harvard University, summed up why faculty development programs need to be a part of institutions of higher education:

The fact is that many faculty members need help, and efforts to give such help must play an important part in any comprehensive program to improve the quality of instruction. Furthermore, even if professors teach well at the moment they are tenured, there is no guarantee that they will continue to do so during their decades of service thereafter. Something more must be done to encourage and reward good instruction throughout the whole career cycle (p. 239).

Faculty development personnel and programs can facilitate the development of the "driving forces" in higher education referred to by Ward earlier in this chapter. Though much research still needs to be done in this field, it is a growing, developing, and exciting area with much potential to transform teaching and learning in higher education.

REFERENCES

Albright, M. J. & Graf, D. L. (Eds.). (1992). Teaching in the information age: The role of educational technology. New Directions for Teaching and Learning (Vol. 51). San Francisco, CA: Jossey-Bass.

Angelo, T. A. (Ed.). (1991). Classroom research: Early lessons from success. New Directions for Teaching and Learning (Vol. 46). San Francisco, CA: Jossey-Bass.

Angelo, T. A. (1994, June). From faculty development to academic development. AAHE Bulletin, 46(10), 3–7.

Angelo, T. A. & Cross, K. P. (1993). Classroom assessment techniques: A handbook for college teachers (2nd ed.). San Francisco, CA: Jossey-Bass.

Astin, A. W., et al. (1974). Group for human development in higher education. Faculty development in a time of retrenchment. New Rochelle, NY: Change Magazine.

Barnes, L. L. B. & Barnes, M. W. (1993). Academic discipline and generalizability of student evaluations of instruction. Research in Higher Education, 34(2), 135–149.

Blackburn, R.T., Boberg, A., O'Connell, C., & Pellino, G. (1980). Project for faculty development program evaluation: Final report. Ann Arbor, MI: Center for the Study of Higher Education, University of Michigan.

Boice, R. (1992). The new faculty member: Supporting and fostering professional development. San Francisco, CA: Jossey-Bass.

Bok, D. (1991). The improvement of teaching. Teachers College Record, 93(2), 236–251.

Bonwell, C. C. & Eison, J. A. (1991). Active learning: Creating excitement in the classroom. ASHE-ERIC Higher Education Report No. 1. Washington, D.C.: The George Washington University, School of Education and Human Development.

Bosworth, K. & Hamilton, S. J. (Eds.). (1994). Collaborative learning: Underlying processes and effective techniques. New Directions for Teaching and Learning (Vol. 59). San Francisco, CA: Jossey-Bass.

Bowker, L. H., Mauksch, H. O., Keating, B., & McSeveney, D. R. (1992). The role of the department chair. Distributed by the American Sociological Association Teaching Resources Center, 1722 N Street, N.W., Washington, D.C. 20036.

Boyer, E. L. (1990). Scholarship reconsidered: Priorities of the professoriate. Special report of the Carnegie Foundation for the Advancement of Teaching. Princeton, NJ: Princeton University Press.

Brinko, K. T. (1993). The practice of giving feedback to improve teaching. Journal of Higher Education, 64(5), 574–593.

Brinko, K. T. & Menges, R. J. (Eds.). (1996). Practically speaking: A sourcebook for instructional consultants in higher education. Stillwater, OK: New Forums Press.

Carter, D.J. (1990). Racial and ethnic trends in college participation:

1976 to 1988. Research Briefs, 1, 3. Washington, D.C.: Division of Policy Analysis and Research, American Council on Education.

Centra, J.A. (1976). *Faculty development practices in U.S. colleges and universities.* Princeton, NJ: Educational Testing Service.

Chism, N. (Ed.). (1987). *Institutional responsibilities and responses in the employment and education of teaching assistants.* Columbus, OH: Center for Teaching Excellence, The Ohio State University.

Clark, S.M. & Lewis, D.R. (Eds.). (1985). *Faculty vitality and institutional productivity: Critical perspectives for higher education.* New York: Teachers College Press.

Cochran, L. H. (1989). *Administrative commitment to teaching: Practical, research-based strategies to strengthen college teaching effectiveness* (ERIC Educational Document Reproduction Service No. ED 318 334).

Cohen, P. A. (1980). Effectiveness of student-rating feedback for improving college instruction: A meta-analysis of findings. *Research in Higher Education, 13,* 321–341.

Cohen, A. M. & Brawer, F. B. (1977). *The two-year college instructor today.* New York: Praeger Publishing.

Costin, F. (1972). Lecturing versus other methods of teaching. *British Journal of Teaching, 3,* 4–30.

Crawley, A. L. (1995). Faculty development programs at research universities: Implications for senior faculty renewal. *To Improve the Academy, 14,* 65–90.

Creswell, J. W., et al. (1990). *The academic chairperson's handbook.* Lincoln, NE: University of Nebraska Press.

Dennee, P. (Ed.). (1995, July). *In Progress: The newsletter of Preparing Future Faculty.* Washington, D.C.: Association of American Colleges and Universities.

Diamond, R. M. (1988). Faculty development, instructional development, and organizational development: Options and choices. In E. Wadsworth (Ed.). *A handbook for new practitioners* (pp. 9–11). Professional & Organizational Development Network in Higher Education (POD Network). Stillwater, OK: New Forums Press, Inc.

Diamond, R. M. (1993). Changing priorities and the faculty reward system. In R. M. Diamond & B. E. Adams (Eds.). *Recognizing faculty work: Reward systems for the year 2000. New Directions for Higher Education* (Vol. 81) pp. 5–12. San Francisco, CA: Jossey-Bass.

Donald, J. G. (1977). Research report: The search for teaching competencies in higher education. In A. B. Smith (Ed.). *Faculty Development and Evaluation Newspaper, 3*(2), 11–14.

Dubin, R. & Taveggia, T. C. (1968). *The teaching-learning paradox: A comparative analysis of college teaching methods.* Eugene, OR: Center for the Advanced Study of Educational Administration, University of Oregon.

Eble, K. E. & McKeachie, W. J. (1985). *Improving undergraduate education through faculty development.* San Francisco: Jossey-Bass.

Eurich, N. P. (1985). *Corporate classrooms.* Princeton, NJ: Carnegie Foundation for the Advancement of Teaching.

Feldman, K. A. (1989). Instructional effectiveness of college teachers as judged by teachers themselves, current and former students, colleagues, administrators, and external (neutral) observers. *Research in Higher Education, 30*(2), 137–194.

Feldman, K. A. (1993). College students' views of male and female college teachers: Part II—evidence from students' evaluations of their classroom teachers. *Research in Higher Education, 34*(2), 151–211.

Francis, J. B. (1975). How do we get there from here? Program design for faculty development. *Journal of Higher Education, 46*(6), Nov/Dec, 719–732.

Freedman, M. (1979). *Academic culture and faculty development.* Berkeley, CA: Montaigne, Inc.

Gaff, J.G. (1975). *Toward faculty renewal: Advances in faculty, instructional, and organizational development.* San Francisco: Jossey-Bass.

Gaff, J. G. & Simpson, R. D. (1994). Faculty development in the United States. *Innovative Higher Education, 18*(3), 167–176.

Graf, D. L., Albright, M. J., & Wheeler, D. W. (1992). Faculty development's role in improving undergraduate education. In M. J. Albright & D. L. Graf (Eds.). *Teaching in the information age: The role of educational technology. New directions for teaching and learning* (Vol. 51) pp. 101–109. San Francisco, CA: Jossey-Bass.

Gratton, M. & Walleri, R. D. (1993). An integrated systems approach in support of institutional effectiveness: The roles of staff and organization development and institutional research. *The Journal of Staff, Program & Organization Development, 11*(1), 35–47.

Green, K. C. (1996). The coming ubiquity of information technology. *Change, 28*(2), 24–31.

Guskey, T. R. (1988). *Improving student learning in college classrooms.* Springfield, IL: Charles C. Thomas.

Heenan, T. & Jerich, K. (Eds.) (1995). *Teaching graduate students to teach: Engaging the disciplines.* Urbana-Champaign, IL: Office of Conferences and Institutes, University of Illinois at Urbana-Champaign.

Katz, J. (Ed.). (1985). Teaching as though students mattered. *New Directions for Teaching and Learning* (Vol. 21). San Francisco, CA: Jossey-Bass.

Katz, J. & Henry, M. (1988). *Turning professors into teachers.* New York: Macmillan.

Levinson-Rose, J. & Menges, R. J. (1981). Improving college teaching: A critical review of research. *Review of Educational Research, 51*(3), 403–434.

Lewis, K. G. (Ed.). (1993). *The TA Experience: Preparing for multiple roles.* Stillwater, OK: New Forums Press, Inc.

Lewis, K. G. (1988). Individual consultation: Its importance to faculty development programs. In K. G. Lewis & J. Povlacs (Eds.). *Face to face: A sourcebook of individual consultation techniques for faculty/instructional developers* (pp. 19–32). Stillwater, OK: New Forums Press.

Lewis, K. G. & Povlacs, J. (Eds.). (1988). *Face to face: A sourcebook of individual consultation techniques for faculty/instructional developers.* Stillwater, OK: New Forums Press.

Lewis, K. G., Svinicki, M. D., & Stice, J. E. (1985). Filling the gap: Introducing new faculty to the basics of teaching. *Journal of Staff, Program, & Organization Development, 3*(1), 16–21.

Lewis, K. G., Svinicki, M. D., & Stice, J. E. (1985). A conference on teaching for experienced faculty. *Journal of Staff, Program, & Organization Development, 7*(3), 137–142.

Lindquist, J. (1978). Approaches to collegiate teaching improvement. In J. Lindquist (Ed.). *Designing teaching improvement programs* (pp. 7–19). Berkeley, CA: Pacific Soundings Press.

Lucas, A. F. (1991). Moving towards a shared vision or maintaining the status quo. *Proceedings of the Eighth Annual Conference, Academic Chairpersons: Improving effectiveness and efficiency* (pp. 23–35). Manhattan: Kansas State University.

Lucas, A. F. (1994). *Strengthening departmental leadership: A team-building guide for chairs in colleges and universities.* San Francisco, CA: Jossey-Bass.

Lucas, J. (1981). The De Anza College staff development program. In O'Banion, et al (Eds.). *Community college staff development programs for the 80's* (pp. 83–100). Frederick, MD: University Publications of America, Associated Faculty Press, Inc.

Lunde, J. P. & Healy, M. M. (1991). *Doing faculty development by committee.* Stillwater, OK: New Forums Press, Inc.

Marsh, H.W. (1984). Students' evaluations of university teaching: Dimensionality, reliability, validity, potential biases, and utility. *Journal of Educational Psychology, 76,* 707–754.

Martin, D. C. & Arendale, D. R. (Eds.). (1994). Supplemental instruction: increasing achievement and retention. *New Directions for Teaching and Learning* (Vol. 60). San Francisco, CA: Jossey-Bass.

Maxwell, W. E. & Kazlauskas, E. J. (1992). Which faculty development methods really work in community colleges? A review of research. *Community/Junior College Quarterly, 16,* 351–360.

McKeachie, W. J. (1970). Research on college teaching: A review. Washington, D.C.: ERIC Clearinghouse in Higher Education (ERIC Document Reproduction Service No. ED 043 789).

McKeachie, W. J. (1990). Research on college teaching: The historical background. *Journal of Educational Psychology, 82*(2), 189–200.

McKeachie, W. J., Pintrich, P. R., Lin, Y. G., & Smith, D. A. F. (1986). *Teaching and learning in the college classroom: A review of the research literature.* Ann Arbor: National Center for Research to Improve Postsecondary Teaching and Learning, The University of Michigan.

McMillan, J. H. (1975). The impact of instructional improvement agencies in higher education. *Journal of Higher Education, 46*(1), 17–23.

Meyers, C. & Jones, T. B. (1993). *Promoting active learning: Strategies for the college classroom.* San Francisco, CA: Jossey-Bass.

Michaelsen, L. K. (1992). Team learning: A comprehensive approach for harnessing the power of small groups in higher education. In D. H. Wulff & J. D. Nyquist (Eds.). *To improve the academy: Resources for faculty, instructional, and organizational development, 11,* 107–122. Professional and Organizational Development Network in Higher Education (POD Network). Stillwater, OK: New Forums Press, Inc.

Neagley, R. L. & Evans, N. D. (1980). *Handbook for effective supervision of instruction.* (3rd ed.). Englewood Cliffs, NJ: Prentice-Hall.

Nyquist, J. D., Abbott, R. D., Wulff, D. H., & Sprague, J. (Eds.). (1991). *Preparing the professoriate of tomorrow to teach.* Dubuque, IA: Kendall/Hunt Publishing Company.

O'Banion, T. (1972). *Teachers for tomorrow.* Tucson, AZ: University of Arizona Press.

O'Banion, T., et al. (1981). *Community college staff development programs for the 80's.* Frederick, MD: University Publications of America, Associated Faculty Press, Inc.

Osgood, A. F. & York, P. A. (1992). *Faculty teacher training at the post-secondary level* (ERIC Educational Document Reproduction Service No. ED 362 511).

Richardson, R. & Moore, W. (1987). Faculty development and evaluation in Texas community colleges. *Community/Junior College Quarterly, 11,* 19–32.

Schmidt, W. D. (1987). *Learning resources programs that make a difference: A source of ideas and models from exemplary programs in the field.* Washington, D.C.: Association for Educational Communications and Technology.

Seldin, P. et al. (1990). *How administrators can improve teaching: Moving from talk to action in higher education.* San Francisco, CA: Jossey-Bass.

Sell, G. R. & Chism, N. V. (1991). Finding the right match: Staffing faculty development centers. *To improve the academy: Resources for faculty, instructional, and organizational development, 10,* 19–29.

Professional and Organizational Development Network in Higher Education (POD Network). Stillwater, OK: New Forums Press, Inc.

Shea, M. A. (1990). Constructing a compendium of good ideas on teaching. *The Journal of Staff, Program, & Organization Development, 8*(1), 5–16.

Smith, A. B. & Hawthorne, E. M. (1993, April/May). *A national study of community college chief academic officers' perceived commitment to instructional effectiveness.* Paper presented at the Annual Meeting of the Council of Universities and Colleges at the Annual Convention of the American Association of Community Colleges, Portland, OR (ERIC Document Reproduction Service No. ED 355 991).

Smith, R. A. (1995). Reflecting critically on our efforts to improve teaching and learning. *To improve the academy: Resources for faculty, instructional, and organizational development, 14,* 5–25. Professional and Organizational Development Network in Higher Education (POD Network). Stillwater, OK: New Forums Press, Inc.

Stern, J. (Ed.). (1988). *The condition of education: Post-secondary education.* Washington, D.C.: National Center for Educational Statistics.

Sullivan, L. L. (1983). Faculty development: A movement on the brink. *College Board Review, 127,* 20–21, 29–31.

Toombs, W. (1983). Faculty development: The institutional side. In R. G. Baldwin & R. T. Blackburn (Eds.). *College faculty: Versatile human resources in a period of constraint. New Directions for Institutional Research* (Vol. 40) pp. 85–94. San Francisco: Jossey-Bass.

Trask, K. A. (1989). The chairperson and teaching. In A. F. Lucas (Ed.). *The department chairperson's role in enhancing college teaching. New directions for teaching and learning* (Vol. 37) pp. 99–107. San Francisco, CA: Jossey-Bass.

Ward, B. (1995). Improving teaching across the academy: Gleanings from research. In E. Neal & L. Richlin (Eds.). *To improve the academy: resources for faculty, instructional, and organizational development* (Vol. 14) pp. 27–42. The Professional and Organizational Development Network in Higher Education (POD Network). Stillwater, OK: New Forums Press.

Weimer, M. (1990). *Improving college teaching: Strategies for developing instructional effectiveness.* San Francisco: Jossey-Bass.

Weimer, M. & Lenze, L. F. (1991). Instructional interventions: A review of the literature on efforts to improve instruction. In J. Smart (Ed.). *Higher education: Handbook of theory and research* (Vol. 7) pp. 294–333. Bronx, NY: Agathon.

Wilson, R. C. (1986). Improving faculty teaching: Effective use of student evaluations and consultants. *Journal of Higher Education, 57,* 196–211.

Wright, Delivee L. (1988). Program types and prototypes. In E. Wadsworth, L. Hilsen, & M. A. Shea (Eds.). *A handbook for new practitioners* (pp. 13–17). The Professional & Organizational Development Network in Higher Education (POD Network). Stillwater, OK: New Forums Press.

Wunch, M. (Ed.). (1994). Mentoring revisited: Making an impact on individuals and institutions. *New directions for teaching and learning* (Vol. 57). San Francisco, CA: Jossey-Bass.

Part

·VI·

RELATIONSHIPS TO AFFILIATED FIELDS

INTRODUCTION

Ben M. Harris

UNIVERSITY OF TEXAS AT AUSTIN

The chapters in Section VI report on separate domains of educational research and professional practice which are each uniquely differentiated in the literature, yet each makes both direct and indirect contributions to the field of supervision of instruction. School administration, instructional development, curriculum development, staff development, and organization development each provide a unique perspective on strategies for maintaining and improving the character of educational programs. Interestingly, the persistent use of the word development in four of the five chapters is more than an accidental reminder of the essence of modern supervision as leadership for change and improvement in the quality of the educational enterprise.

SUPERVISION AND THE SUPERINTENDENCY

Chapter 31, written by Woodward primarily from the perspective of the superintendent of schools and central staff, focuses on instructional leadership as a unifying and linking concept between supervision and school administration. Five sections of this chapter focus on leadership theories underlying both administration and supervision, relationships of each to the other, instructional leadership as a function of the superintendency, and implications for practice and further research. The author gives special focus in the first portion of the chapter by posing several questions:

- What forces are affecting supervision and administration?
- Are lines between them blurring?
- Are they mutually exclusive or is one imbedded in the other?

In the latter half of the chapter, the focus shifts from relationship to ". . . the instructional leadership function of the school superintendent . . ." and that of the "superintendent's team."

In a wide ranging review of current leadership theory responding to "changing conditions in our world and new knowledge about leadership and organization," social systems theory concepts are cited with open-systems, interdependence, collaborative relationships, and transformational purposes depending heavily on interpersonal relationships for effectiveness. The changing view of leadership dictated by open systems theory is discussed using contingent and situational theory. Role concepts proposed by various scholars are identified, including such diverse tasks as coaching, consulting, inspiring, teaching, persuading, designing, and transforming, all relying upon relatively little coercion or power.

In summarizing this wide ranging review of current thought on leadership from an open-systems perspective, the author identifies six emerging concepts about leaders and draws inferences about the application of these concepts to leadership for both administration and supervision. The author suggests that the emphasis of supervision as related to promoting school effectiveness has been influential in linking administration to supervision with a common commitment to instructional leadership. Hence, the author concludes that a "new supervision" is emerging out of the same theoretical influences that are reshaping administration and management in schools.

The portion of this chapter addressing relationships between administration and supervision tackles the differentiation vs. integration issue using the literature describing tasks and dimensions of administrative and supervisory practice as well as studies of leader effectiveness. The findings produce mixed results at best. "There continues to be considerable dialogue about what supervision is and how it relates to administration." The author ventures forth with a conclusion that "the common ground between supervision and administration appears to be . . . instructional leadership." This, it is argued, "creates the need for an integrated systems approach with differentiation in focus and priority . . ."

The last half of this chapter focuses primarily on the superintendent of schools in relation to the "instructional leadership function." The author carefully reviews studies on "the superintendency," changing views of the position and the influence of the role. Attention is also given to "the superintendents team" and principal–superintendent interactions. Before turning to a section on implications for practice, the author summarizes what might be concluded even though hard evidence is limited. These conclusions about both the superintendent and "the district" in a wider sense relate to "influence on conditions of teaching and learning," the impact of both "direct and indirect" superintendent activities, and the "establishing and implementing vision, action, beliefs and collaboration." The author argues that effectiveness of entire systems, especially as related to changing instructional programs, is not an issue of either "decentralized or centralized" leadership but one of integrated and sustained efforts at all levels.

A part on implications for practice completes this chapter with specific proposals for practitioner actions and for further research. Proposals are given useful elaboration by raising critical questions and citing important considerations related to each. Closing remarks return to a major theme of this chapter, "that there is a needed integration of supervision and administration."

SUPERVISION AND INSTRUCTIONAL DEVELOPMENT

Acheson, Shamsher, and Smith join forces in authoring Chapter 32 which draws heavily upon case reports from both the U. S. and Canada. They purposely select a rather limited focus on five programs with similar features referred to as "peer consultation." They utilize both research and direct participation with these programs as the basis for systematically comparing and contrasting their features, strengths, and consequences as models for instructional development.

The introduction to this chapter is a discussion of the research-practice dilemma in education. The focus of many researchers is on isolated "variables" while practitioners need

complex models that improve instructional programs. "Most systematic, widespread change in educational practice involves implementation of models, not variables." The problem they cite associated with this dichotomy is that research on variables tends to be "quite good," while that on models is rare. The dilemma grows with the recognition that, in the absence of rigorous research and evaluation of instructional models, the overly positive view of developers about their new models is often misleading.

Using "peer consultation" as their selected innovation, the authors identify and analyze four alternative "types" in practice in both the U. S. and Canada. They suggest a continuum for analyzing operating examples of each type. The continuum from prescription to autonomy, from coaching to consultation, and from skills development to reflective practice is the framework used to describe, compare, and contrast programs of instructional development.

Peer coaching as implemented using the Hunter model is described and studies are reported. At higher levels of the continuum, peer observation programs in the U. S. and in Canada are described and rigorous evaluation efforts reported.

The authors, admitting a bias for the consultative types of peer consultation, report in some detail on an evaluation study of schools and districts implementing these models. Promising findings about these programs are their persistence in districts and their spread to other districts. The authors conclude that "All of the programs we have analyzed have merit. . . . Giving supportive feedback requires knowing how to observe systematically and communicate effectively in nonthreatening ways." This may be the greatest challenge of all for researchers and practitioners alike.

SUPERVISION AND CURRICULUM DEVELOPMENT

In Chapter 33, Oliva provides a wide-ranging review of conceptions about curriculum development as an integral part of a larger field closely related to instructional improvement and staff development. The author identifies various models of curriculum development, analyzes 12 "components," and details an array of recognized principles, issues, and trends.

Assuming that curriculum development is an integral part of supervision as practiced and widely recognized by scholars, the author introduces the review with attention to definitional questions relating to who are the curriculum developers, how are curriculum and instruction related, and even what is curriculum itself? Positing an essential close relationship between curriculum development and instructional improvement, an interesting array of eight models is briefly identified and schematically illustrated "as viewed by practitioners and theorists."

A major portion of this chapter provides a carefully detailed "suggested model for curriculum improvement." While this is a familiar linear model calling for a sequence of plan, implement, and evaluate, the author enumerates a 17-task sequence. This sequence is discussed and analyzed as "twelve components" in a way that ". . . integrate curriculum and instruction."

The concern for "defining a conception of curriculum" is given emphasis in a section that follows Oliva's suggested model. Here a century-long controversy is briefly reviewed, ranging from "essentialist philosophers" to progressive education. The place of testing programs in "explicitly mandating standardized testing" is cited as a critical influences on curriculum and instruction. This issue leads to a well-documented section on various forces and influences on curriculum and, hence, on curriculum development. Government mandates, reform movements, and pressure groups are discussed and controversial issues are examined.

Trends in curriculum development are identified by the author, including decentralization and shared responsibility. In a summarizing overview of "the more recent and futuristic aspects" of the curriculum, the author also suggests the need "to see what the past holds of value to the present." Needed research is also addressed here briefly with suggestions that virtually the entire field is open to scholarly inquiry.

SUPERVISION AND STAFF DEVELOPMENT

Chapter 34 by Gordon and Nicely represents an effort to synthesize a vast literature in a way that gives more in the way of structure and alternative perspective than is common in the few comprehensive source books in this field. These authors address definitional problems with a brief historical overview emphasizing terminological confusions. They move on to show the extent to which staff development is and has been deeply imbedded in the general literature of supervision of instruction for some 70 years.

The unique flavor of this chapter is found, however, in an extended section on alternative "frameworks" which gives careful attention to the emergence of scholarly reports and studies on many different practices that share common ground. These fragments are documented in terms of their relationships to supervision and staff development in a way that helps the reader make sense out of a fragmented literature. Yet other sections on levels of practice, orientations toward staff development, designing programs, and related processes provide insights and perspectives that are also truly rewarding.

In addressing 'levels," the authors deal succinctly with international, national, and regional, down to "the individual level," giving very brief but pointed reminders of the diversity and extensiveness of the field in practice even though not fully recognized by either scholars or practitioners.

One of the most provocative and original sections deals with "orientations." Here the authors identify different orientations reflected primarily in the literature on practices. The orientations identified and discussed in some detail are "transmission," "transaction," and "transformation." Each of these is defined and discussed in terms of a philosophical orientation. This section provides a very natural introduction to the section on purposes and offers a set of concepts for further research and theory building.

A brief section on characteristics of and barriers to effective staff development leads into designing programs with issues and various planning sequences reviewed. The alternative frameworks section provides the reader with brief overviews of actual designs utilizing training, peer coaching, induction and mentoring, action research, curriculum development, and others to clearly illustrate and document the extent to which staff development has evolved as a sophisticated area of supervisory practice. The literature sources cited in discussing the characteristics and supporting each of many alternative "frameworks" is a contribution in its own right. However, the extensive treatment of so many diverse program designs offers great challenges to researchers. The chapter makes clear that creative alternative program frameworks have been developed and are in practice. Determining their relative effectiveness, unique strengths, and limitations is the challenge for research and evaluation largely ignored to date.

SUPERVISION AND ORGANIZATIONAL DEVELOPMENT

As authors of Chapter 35, Hall and Shieh have produced a monumental re-analysis of organizational development as a field of inquiry and practice which has a long and relatively independent history. The authors trace the origins and evolving character of the field from World War II to the present, in an effort to deal adequately with ". . . the quantity of literature and the vagaries of the field during the last fifty years." They also update the reader with decade-by-decade descriptions of evolving perspectives with human relations and systems theory emerging as dominant in the 1960s while, in the 1970s, the dominant emphasis was on applications of behavioral science knowledge to improving organizations. In the 1980s, the field is described as moving to broader perspectives of changing whole organizations, ". . . as a systems approach to the total set of functional and interpersonal role relationships in organizations." The evolving character of OD as a field of inquiry and practice, both in and out of the world of the school, is described as having matured through the 1980s to the point of having a set of principles clearly applicable to the task of improving overall organizational functioning.

Criticisms of OD are clearly addressed and the future of theory and research is discussed in the context of needs for embracing various disciplines, responding to environmental changes, and increasing the emphasis on organizational culture.

The extended reporting on the historical and developmental perspectives guiding theory, research, and practice in this field leads the authors to address research needs, to review the limited number of rigorous studies, and to cite some of the efforts to apply OD principles and practices to school situations on a systematic rather than casual basis. The need to infuse OD practices into organizational life to be effective is the conclusion which leads these authors to begin to focus on the relationship of OD to school supervision. They suggest that supervisors at work in coaching, planning, training, and monitoring are already reflecting practice directly related to OD consultant efforts. They argue that both school supervisors as internal consultants and OD specialists as external consultants might be joined to produce a team to "guide the development of the whole system."

Using the term "Hybrid OD/Supervision role," the authors advance nine specific suggestions relating the two fields for sharing responsibilities and skills. As a final effort to challenge both fields, three questions are discussed relating to mutual interests in change, the needs to transform practitioners into active OD teams, and how ethical problems can be addressed.

Hall and Shieh offer a rich and well documented portrayal of Organizational Development as a field of inquiry and professional practice, now fully mature in the sense of being ready for more systemic application to the field of education. The critical concerns about limitations in theory and research bases are recognized, but not seen as barriers to creative applications to the function of instructional supervision. The authors only scratch the surface of documenting the realities of the world of supervision from an OD perspective, but their masterly treatment of organizational development as a field of practice leads the way for scholars in supervision to address the issues of new and better relationships between the two fields.

·31·

SUPERVISION AND THE SUPERINTENDENCY

Karen C. Woodward

ANDERSON (SOUTH CAROLINA) SCHOOL DISTRICT 5

THE CONTEXT

Superintendents, principals, and supervisors grapple on a daily basis with a complex set of issues, such as multiple goals, political agendas, social problems, diverse needs, special interests, conflicting demands, limited resources, and increasing accountability. The search for more effective schools and appropriate education for all children is complicated by:

- increasing fragmentation of public attitude toward government, taxes, and schools
- declining job security
- decline of home stability and community life
- growing media influence

Since the early 1980s, there has been increasing demand for educational accountability from many sources—politicians, press, parents, and business. Numerous proposals, varied solutions and legislative acts have been advanced for educational reform. Suggestions for restructuring come from many venues seeking to change the way schools operate (accountability, assessment procedures, school organization, leadership and management philosophy, instructional strategies, and roles and responsibilities of all stakeholders). With this attention to educational effectiveness has come increasing emphasis on instruction, instructional leadership, and the role of those involved in supervision of instruction. The changes in the way schools are being configured and operated have much to do with the way both supervision and administration have developed and are viewed, in light of this current context of social, economic, and political change. It is timely to review the changing role of supervision as it relates to school administration.

This chapter needs to be viewed in relation to the context described above and the other chapters. Previous sections of this book have focused on different aspects of supervision, including philosophies, practices, specialized areas, and levels of supervision. Subsequent chapters will deal with supervision as a profession, supervision theories, forces that affect supervision, and future implications. This section of the handbook is intended to connect the aspects of supervision of instruction to certain affiliated fields. Supervision by its very nature is carried out within the context of many relationships, and thus, complete treatment of the subject must include the relationship of supervision to the affiliated fields of school administration, instructional development, curriculum development, staff development, and organizational development.

Supervision is a responsibility of many, and improvement of instruction is a major function of administrators along with others in various positions. Techniques for improving instruction vary and are emerging rapidly under changing contexts indicated above (Harris, 1985). This chapter attempts to place administration in the discussion of supervision and instructional leadership, making appropriate connections that have implications for school effectiveness and instructional improvement.

The specific purpose of this particular chapter is to explore the relationship between supervision and school administration. Instructional supervision will be related to the field of school administration from both a research and practical perspective. The chapter is organized into five sections:

1. leadership and management theories underlying administration and supervision
2. relationships between supervision and administration
3. instructional leadership function and the superintendent
4. implications for practice
5. recommendations for future research

The fundamental focus of the chapter is *instructional leadership*. This focus suggests the need to begin with discussions of general leadership, supervision, and administrative theories; the effects of differing views on supervision and administration in action; and implications for their relationships. Thus, the first half of the chapter presents an overview of leadership, and of supervision, and administration as fields of study. This discussion includes definitions, dimensions, and similarities and differences between the two fields. Particular attention is devoted to the questions: *What forces are affecting supervision and administration? Are the lines between administration and supervision blurring? Are they mutually exclusive terms or is one embedded in the other?* The research on school administration referenced in this chapter relates primarily to instructional leadership and supervision. The section on the instructional leadership function in school systems moves the discussion from research to practice, raising the question of the need for instructional leadership, how roles and responsibilities are determined, and how instructional leadership is or can be carried out by administrators. In the second half of the chapter, major attention is given to the superintendent and the superintendent's team in instructional leadership. Focus is on the questions: *How important is the instructional leadership function for the school superintendent? How can this be provided by the superintendent and the superintendent's team? How can this discussion improve schools?* Implications for practical application of instructional leadership, including problems, priorities, strategies, interrelationships, and the potential synergy for school improvement are included. Finally recommendations for future research are offered.

LEADERSHIP AND MANAGEMENT THEORIES UNDERLYING ADMINISTRATION AND SUPERVISION

To understand supervision and administration, and their relationships, it is necessary to understand: (1) the underlying theories of leadership and management that have a bearing on how supervisors and administrators act; (2) the concept of administration; and (3) the concept of supervision. People act on what they believe or theorize to be true; thus, it is important to understand the current thinking regarding leadership, management, and the implications for administration and supervision theory.

Leadership and Management Theories

New models for educational leadership are emerging from changing conditions in our world and new knowledge about leadership and organizations. Technology and globalization are transforming work and the way work is done. New rules of operation are being created—flattened hierarchies, empowered workers, work teams. Hierarchial business cultures and rigid work rules are being replaced by flexible, self-directed workers who continuously acquire new skills to keep up with competition, new technologies, and new knowledge. Globalization and technology have "forced managers in the U.S. to rethink the autocratic, top-down approach developed by Frederick Taylor and others at the turn of the century. Now, more and more employers are forming problem-solving teams in factories and offices and are relying increasingly on collaborative efforts—both the employee-

manager kind and between the company and its suppliers and customers" (Business Week, October 1994).

These theories and practices of leadership and management are coming out of social systems theory, and systems theory (Demings' *New Economics*, Covey's *Principle-Centered Leadership*, Peters and Waterman's *In Search of Excellence*, Naisbett's book *Global Paradox*, and Senge's *The Fifth Discipline*). New definitions of leadership move away from emphasis on power and control (Taylor and Scientific Management), the personal authority of the leader or the position, and management by objectives. Attention is being given to the power of intrinsic motivation (Deming, 1995); empowerment versus control, emphasis on shared vision and values of the organization (Peters & Waterman, 1984); organizational culture, organizations as learning communities (Senge, 1990); and the moral responsibility of the leader. Long-term results and continual improvement in a less centralized organization replaces the quick fix for immediate results. Contingent and situational leadership replace rigid rules of action in a chain of command in this new work leadership environment.

Systems Thinking

One of the most powerful concepts influencing leadership is systems thinking (Downey, Frase, & Peters, 1994). A system is "a network of interdependent components that work together to try to accomplish the aim of the system" (Deming, 1993). Management of a system requires knowledge of the interrelationships between all the components within the system and of the people that work in it (Deming, 1993). Using school systems as an example, Deming described a system of schools not as merely pupils, teachers, school boards, and parents working separately to achieve their aims. A school district should be a system in which these groups work together to achieve the aims the community has set for the school (Deming, 1993).

Systems can be thought of as interdependent components, people and processes with a common purpose (Senge, 1990). In this way, a system is a whole whose elements "hang together because they continually affect each other over time and operate toward a common purpose" (Senge, 1990). By its very nature, systems thinking points out interdependence and the need for collaboration. The art of systems thinking includes learning to recognize the ramifications and tradeoffs of the action chosen. Thus, teamwork and team learning are important concepts in systems thinking. According to this view, team learning is vital because teams, not individuals, are the fundamental learning unit in modern organizations (Senge, 1990). Senge (1990) identifies systems thinking as the essential discipline to an effective organization because it is the conceptual cornerstone of a learning organization.

The concept of an organization being a learning organization or a community of learners comes out of systems theory in the search for more effective management of organizations and new leadership philosophy. Senge (1990) described a "learning organization as an organization that is continually expanding its capacity to create its future." Senge proposes that organizations that will excel in the future will be those that discover how to tap people's commitment and capacity to learn at all levels in an organization (Senge, 1990). Learning organizations are distinguished from traditional authoritarian "controlling organizations" by systems thinking and team learning. Such organizations exist where people are continually discovering and learning. Communities of learners engage in openness, local decisions connected by mission, values, and vision, and systems thinking. Learning organizations demand a new view of leadership (Senge, 1990). That centers on leaders as designers, stewards, and teachers. Leaders are responsible for building organizations where people continually expand their capabilities to understand complexity, clarify vision, and improve shared mental models.

In systems theory, components re-enforce each other to accomplish the aims of the system. To do this calls for a "transformation" of the current management style (Deming, 1993). Deming's management method is described in his well-known Fourteen Points. Essentially, leadership should be the job of management with his/her aim to assist people to do a good job. This new management style of the system leader is characterized by driving out fear, breaking down barriers, instituting self improvement, planning long-term improvement, and ceasing inspection. Eliminating the need for mass inspection can be accomplished by initially building quality into the process. The new philosophy of management is that quality does not come from mass supervision but from the improvement of the process. The old way of supervising bad quality out is replaced by building good quality in. New relationships between managers and staff are created. Collaboration, horizontal communication, cooperation, self-monitoring and inspection, and team responsibility are emphasized in the new management paradigm (Bradley, 1993).

One important way in which systems thinking influences organizations is to serve as a catalyst for changing the structure of organizations. System structure is the pattern of key interrelationships among components of the system (Senge, 1990). Senge suggests an integrated webbed organizational structure in which power is shared and structures are fluid as more in keeping with the concept of learning organizations. This is also in keeping with Demings admonition to break down barriers. In sum, systems thinking and quality focus are concepts that are causing a new way of thinking about management and leadership. Collaboration, integration of people and function, sharing power and accountability, and developing the capacity for all to lead, thereby creating learning organizations, are contributions of the systems approach.

Changing View Of Leadership

In shifting from the more traditional view of leadership to a "new" view, current thought tends to pull from a variety of theories of leadership and management, as well as systems thinking. Peter Nutty (1987) observed that in recent years there has been less support for the bureaucratic structure in modern organizations. New viewpoints are focusing on culture, schools as open systems not closed systems, contingent leadership, schools as learning communities, and linkages or shared responsibilities rather than pervasive bureaucratic structures. New structures are rising from these new theories

or schools of thought. Decentralization, school-based management, and participatory decision-making, empowerment, and systems thinking have emerged.

Considerations of culture and new knowledge about leadership are fundamental to the changing views of administrative thought and behavior. The work of Peters and Waterman, and others coming out of the corporate world, have directed attention to the role of organizational culture as a distinguishing feature in excellent companies. Effective leaders create effective companies by establishing an open organization with shared beliefs, mission, internal motivation, innovation, shared decision-making and, most importantly, trust, thus creating an organizational culture.

Of major influence on management recently has been the work of Deming and Ouchi. Out of their work came "Theory Z," concerned with the culture of the entire organization (Lunenberg & Ornestein, 1991) rather than leadership behavior as in "Theory X and Theory Y" (McGregor, 1960). Considerable attention is being given to the culture of the entire school organization, and to presenting schools as communities. Culture includes the values, mores, and ethos in which the institution is embedded (Lunenberg & Ornstein, 1991) as well as the personality and roles of those in the organization. Thus, the beliefs, feelings, attitudes, norms, and expectations determine the mission and standards for success. Effective organizational cultures are created by personalities, traditions, rituals, and communication networks, and have shared values and common beliefs (Peters & Waterman, 1984).

In addition to the corporate view of organizational culture, another consideration is the concept of cultural politics as discussed by Bates (1987). This concept recognizes the external factors that educational leaders must negotiate. Educational leaders must deal with "educational and social ideas as well as with pragmatic decisions about the formal organization of school practices" (p. 17). This, Bates suggested, is far from the "manipulative imposition of 'corporate culture.'" Additionally, there is increasing expectation of collaboration and integration of the school into the community culture.

Effective schools research has examined school culture and the role of the principal in establishing that culture as a primary factor in school effectiveness. The principal shapes the culture by creating a vision, developing shared purposes, demonstrating action and symbols, communicating ideas, and sharing decision-making (Firestone & Wilson, 1985). The principal develops norms of high expectations, academic emphasis, and climate conducive to instruction (Achilles, 1987).

In the ASCD publication, *Leadership for Tomorrow's Schools* (Patterson, 1993), described leadership as "the process of influencing others to achieve mutually agreed upon purposes for the organization" (p. 24), distinguishing managing (coordinating people and resources to produce a product) from leadership. Though a part of what a leader must do, managing is not the same as leading (Patterson, 1993). The new leader, according to Patterson, embraces values of participation, diversity, and reflection, replacing values based on personal power and control with core values based on the power of the organization. Others distinguish leading as doing the right thing and managing as doing things right, thus differentiating efficiency, control and rules (managing) from direction, purpose, and family feeling (leading) as described by Covey (1989).

Leadership is also being viewed as contextual with different situations requiring different approaches (Bolman & Deal, 1992). Bolman and Deal propose that an able leader as educational administrator must be able to operate in four leadership frames: (1) structural, (2) human resources, (3) political, and (4) symbolic. Because of our complex and ambiguous world, the ability to use more than one frame increases one's ability to make clear judgments and act effectively. The authors investigated their hypotheses by examining the relationship of these frames to effective principal behavior. The results suggest that "the ability to use multiple frames is critical to principal's effectiveness as both manager and leader" (Bolman & Deal, 1992, p. 328).

The idea that leader behavior must change based on certain conditions is proposed in contingent theory and in situational leadership. Task complexity and follower maturity, among other factors, determine the leadership approach to be taken. Although research on contingent and situational theory has been limited, there is evidence to support these theories (Lunenberg & Ornstein, 1991).

The literature since 1985 has focused heavily on vision, culture, reflection, and transformation (Pajak, 1993a; Pajak, 1993b). In transformational leadership, the purposes of the leader and group members are joined by mutual goals and mission of the organization (Pajak, 1993b) to create the restructuring emphasis of the 1980s and 1990s. The literature is replete with such concepts as: the leader as designer, steward, and teacher (Senge, 1992); intellectual leader (Schlechty, 1990); and cultural leader assigned such tasks as coaching, transforming, consulting, inspiring, teaching (Covey, 1989; Schlechty, 1990). The "new" leader relies less on position and authority and more on knowledge and persuasion (Deming, 1993; Schlechty, 1990). Research on sources of leader influence indicate that expert power (ability and knowledge) and referent power (personality and charisma) have been positively correlated to subordinate satisfaction and performance. Coercive power (control/punishment) has been negatively related. Expert power has also been found more effective in acceptance of change by subordinates than either coercive or legitimate (position) power (Lunenberg & Ornstein, 1991). Educational studies found that teacher satisfaction increased when principals were perceived as experts rather than as coercive administrators (Lunenberg & Ornestein, 1991).

Administration

There is a call for a new emphasis in leadership and management in educational administration (Chubb & Moe, 1990; Goodlad, 1978; Schlechty, 1990; Sergiovanni, 1993). Much of the thinking presented by those writers and others parallels that of general leadership in the private sector, including systems theory, adapted to the unique context of schools and schools districts. Educational administration has been defined as a social process that takes place within the context of a social system (Castetter, 1981; Getzels, Lephen, & Campbell, 1968) to be seen from three different points of view:

- structurally as a hierarchy of relationships;
- functionally as allocating and integrating roles and facilities to achieve system goals; and
- operationally as processes involving person-to person interaction.

An administrator, therefore, is a member of the professional staff who has been granted the authority to organize, direct, and control the work of subordinates or who renders assistance to other administrators (Castetter, 1981).

Sears (1950) observed that administration derives its nature from the essence of the service it directs as opposed to the general concept. Griffiths (1988) pointed out that administrative theory is in transition, especially in recognizing the effects of context in understanding administration. There is increasing recognition that educational administration is instrumental in accomplishing the organizational and societal purposes of schools and school districts. In that context, then, schools exist to educate students, and administration should serve that purpose (Willower, 1988).

Developments in educational administration parallel those in the broad field of administration theory. Indeed, educational administration for decades has followed movements in the social and behavioral sciences (Hoy, 1982). For example, closed systems theory has been replaced by open systems theory and contingent leadership theory has begun to replace universal leadership theory. Administrative theory, too, has evolved from the classical view—concern for efficiency—through a period of intense emphasis on human relations and psychology to the consideration of organizations as open social systems and the contingency theory of leadership (Hoy, 1982; Lunenburg & Ornstein, 1991). A closed system is insulated from outside forces or can accurately predict the affect of outside forces. The school meets neither of these characteristics of a closed system. The school is interdependent with its external environment and that environment has been unpredictable (Hoy, 1982). Primary concern with the internal relations of the school system (closed system view) is now commonly considered an inadequate approach to considering school organization and administration. It is now generally accepted that schools and school districts are open systems. Thus, closed systems theories, such as scientific management, are inadequate.

Another shift in leadership theory from emphasis on universal leadership to emphasis on contingent leadership, is based on the theory that the practice of leadership is too complex to rely on one set of behaviors or traits (Hoy, 1982; Lunenburg & Ornstein, 1991). It is generally accepted that effective leadership involves traits, leader behavior, and factors in a particular situation. Contingency factors, such as power, size, culture and environment, affect the behavior of leaders and, thus, the organization (Hoy, 1982). If schools are open systems affected by unpredictable external forces, then, contingent leadership theory takes on more meaning.

Administration has traditionally been seen as a technology of control (Bates, 1987). School reforms during the 1980s renewed interest in an administrative strategy that stressed control and scientific management though much different from the traditional form (Sergiovanni & Starratt, 1993). The *neo-scientific management* was a reaction to the human relations approach and the lack of accountability. In the new scientific management, emphasis was placed on measurement of end results (i.e., test scores, since in this view, what is measured gets done). Thus, the control factor became accountability of job performance.

Monitoring the achievement of the assigned task and accompanying objectives took precedence over personal supervision, unlike traditional scientific management which required heavy direct supervision of individuals. Employees under the neo-scientific management approach would be controlled by job accountability measures and would have minimal personal interaction with supervisors.

Critics have charged that this reliance on outside authority and emphasis on measurement leaves out the necessary human dimension (Sergiovanni & Starratt, 1993). They charge that this is a philosophy based on lack of trust in the employees' ability to be as concerned about the organization as that of the manager or administrator (Sergiovanni & Starratt, 1993).

These views of leadership are expressed in schools as site-based management, shared decision-making, participatory management, and team collaboration. The theory is that creating higher morale and job satisfaction through participation and increased autonomy results in increased productivity (Lunenberg & Ornstein, 1991). The results from studies of participatory management and site-based management in educational settings are as yet inconclusive regarding increases in student achievement. As systems theory would suggest, perhaps the notion should be interdependency rather than autonomy. More study is needed to explore the possibilities and options of various structures in this area.

Such approaches are required of leaders throughout the organization at all levels of the organization. Schlechty (1990) and Deming (1993) made the point that the authority figure must be involved for any substantial organizational change to be effective. Transformation of an organization can only take place under a leader. Effective schools research also found that leadership of the principal was present in such organizations.

Recent, though limited, research on the superintendency found that leadership of the superintendent is necessary for substantive change (Fullan, 1991).

Organizational theory and leadership theory influence how schools are organized and managed as well as the role and style of those managing and leading those organizations (i.e., administrators). Differences in leadership, organization, processes, locus of control, sources for authority, administrative reward, and structure are major distinguishing factors of the different approaches to administrative thought (Lunenberg & Ornstein, 1991). Each of these affects certain dimensions of organizational structure including job specialization, departmentalization, decision-making, authority and responsibility, delegation of authority, extent of centralization/decentralization, line/staff assignments, and span of control. Views on such matters result in varying organizational and decision-making approaches: (bureaucratic, participatory, or site-based) and in the roles, responsibilities, and relationships among those in the organization, including how supervision and administration are operationalized.

In sum, educational administration reflects the changing view of leadership and leaders, moving from a bureaucratic model to a democratic model. The emerging theories are most compelling in their effects on administration supervision, and, ultimately, educational effectiveness. Summarized below are the emerging concepts that depict a "new" emerging leadership and leader, thus, "new" educational administrative thought:

1. *Leadership is contextual and contingent.* Public school districts are open social systems affected by complex and multiple influences. Schools have an array of constituencies, goals, and external and internal forces. Leaders must use multiple approaches matched to the context, situation, task, and characteristics of followers.
2. *Leaders build organizational culture.* Values, vision, systems thinking, relationships, organizational norms, symbols, and rituals form a culture for organizational transformation.
3. *Leaders must expand traditional forms of control.* Authority of position and reward structures are being replaced by new forms of control including expertise; organizational culture, norms, and socialization processes; self control vs close supervision; empowerment with accountability and responsibility; data-driven decisions and results-driven leadership.
4. *Leaders are able to influence others through expert power or referent power.* The new leaders must be able to integrate ideas, knowledge, and methods and to create theories—use synergy—to transform an organization. New leaders must be informed, thus providing intellectual leadership and service as coach, mentor, and teacher integrating the vision, purpose, and values of the organization. Leaders must be reflective.
5. *Leaders are found at all levels.* Leadership must be neither bottom-up nor top-down but integrated. Those in authority must provide leadership for change to occur. Leaders and group members must be closely tied by mutual mission and goals.
6. *There is a necessary mix of bureaucratic and cultural leadership responsibilities.* Although there is a move away from bureaucratic, authoritarian models of leadership and administrative behavior, the range of responsibilities requires a mix of cultural and bureaucratic leadership. Ironically, much of the power and influence outside the profession has been directed toward increasing bureaucratic, controlling, nondemocratic modes of operation (Harris, 1985).

This changing view of leadership and leaders is reflected not only in general leadership and in administrative behavior but in the "new" supervision, and what appears to be influencing a change in the relationship between supervision and administration.

Supervision

While leadership is the process of influencing and facilitating others to achieve the purposes of the organization, general supervision is *"To provide the conditions and promote the behavior necessary for the achievement of organizational goals"* (Alfonso, Firth, & Neville, 1981, p. 6). In its classic sense, supervision is "to support and enhance an organization's work system, and to ensure productivity, quality, and achievement of organizational goals" (Bruce & Grimsley, 1987). By broad definition, supervision would encompass all aspects of the system and all staff of the system. Indeed the emerging concepts of administration, supervision, and leadership discussed thus far would apply across the system, including support services. A function found in all organizations, supervision is operationalized within each organization to reflect that management philosophy, leadership philosophy, and the nature of the goals to be achieved. More narrowly construed as supervision of instruction, supervision would be directed toward providing the conditions and promoting the behaviors that are necessary for students to learn that which is valued by the community served.

Two points are necessary to our current discussion. First, *there is new emphasis on supervision coming out of school effectiveness research.* According to Sergiovanni and Starratt (1993), supervision is at "a critical point in its evolution . . . supervision is emerging as a key role and function in the operation of schools." Sergiovanni and Starratt see supervision moving away from administrative matters to instructional matters aimed at increased school effectiveness.

Since the 1980s, supervision has been a major focus of policy makers, legislators, and school administrators. States have mandated systems of supervision, including staff development for teachers and administrators and evaluation systems primarily related to school effectiveness research. Supervision for more effective instruction and effective schools has become a more prominent part of administrators' job responsibilities. Strong school leadership has been linked to school effectiveness. Indeed, "instructional leadership" has been the predominant phrase of the 1980s and early 1990s.

Second, *there is emerging a "new supervision" coming out of the new theories of leadership, management, and administrative thought.* Reviewed earlier are the changing concepts of leadership and leaders: Viewing schools as open, complex social systems and learning communities; leadership as cultural, contextual, and contingent, using new forms of control; leaders found at all levels; less reliance on authority and position and more on expert, intellectual, and persuasive power; and a mix of bureaucratic and cultural leadership responsibilities. Recognizing the changes in leadership and administrative theory and the concomitant emerging changes in school structures, accountability, and views of teaching and learning, there is a call for change in the theory that underlies supervision. The question is, will supervision take the direction of increasing control and regulation of teachers and teaching or that of enhancing the professionalism of teachers and their decision-making (Sergiovanni & Starratt, 1993).

Review of books published in the last several years is indicative of the transition occuring in supervision. Sergiovanni and Starratt (1993) have redefined supervision as a process that is hierarchically independent and role free and based on a democratic, human resource model and on moral responsibility. Supervision is part of the system, not separate. It is a

process designed to help teachers and supervisors learn more about their practice and be better able to use their knowledge and skills to create for the school a more effective learning community. Sergiovanni and Starratt apply greater emphasis to professional development than quality control. Control, they suggested, is achieved through self-control of professionals, socialization to the norms of the organization, and building interdependence based on shared vision and values rather than standardized work outputs and direct supervision.

Similarly, Gordon (1992) proposed a new paradigm shifting from traditional supervision to a reconception of leadership, teaching, and change. Believing that "traditional supervision is becoming less effective at solving the problems in today's schools," his new supervision is characterized by empowerment, integrated functions, diversity, continuous collegial support, professional inquiry, and organic change. The goals of supervision remain the improvement of instruction but through empowerment rather than control. His new supervision integrates the functions of leadership development, improvement of the school environment, curriculum development, school-wide instructional improvement, staff development, classroom-based instructional assistance, and improvement of assessment.

In Gordon's paradigm, supervision is "identified more with a leadership process than with any single role." The new conceptions of supervision include both directive, collaborative, nondirective, and indirect approaches. In his developmental supervision model, Glickman (1985), suggests that supervisors match the approach to the developmental cognitive and maturity level of the teacher. He applies this approach to direct assistance to teachers as well as curriculum development, in-service education, and action research, all of which are considered dimensions of supervision. Costa and Garmston (1994) designed a supervision process called Cognitive Coaching, a nondirective approach in which the teacher and supervisor see reflective learning as the goal of supervision.

The "new" supervision closely parallels the concepts summarized previously in the discussion of the "new educational administration and leadership." Summarized below is a list of emerging concepts of the "new" supervision for school effectiveness, thus achieving the organizational goal of student learning:

1. There is increased interest in supervision for improved school effectiveness. The new supervision extends beyond the classroom to the school as a social system, thus recognizing that supervision as an integral and pervasive function.
2. Supervision is best viewed as contextual and culturally based. The new theories are based on the concept of teaching as a series of intellectual teacher decisions within varied teaching conditions. Thus, at times different models of supervision are effective dependent on the circumstances. The fundamental approach is best based on a democratic, human resource, moral and ethical theoretical base rather than on an approach based on scientific management and authority. Supervision should place greater emphasis on professionalism and less on quality control procedures. Supervision should include directive, collabo-

rative, and nondirective processes considering the culture and context of the situation. Supervisory models based on this point of view include developmental supervision, reflective supervision, clinical supervision, and peer supervision.

3. Supervision is hierarchically independent and role-free. The new supervision is characterized by empowerment, integrated functions, and diversity of processes carried out by anyone charged with school effectiveness. Supervision is part of, not separate from, the system.

4. There is increased focus on human resource development. Knowledge of practice and cognitive development of teachers, including developing decision-making capabilities and the capacity for abstract thinking, are being emphasized.

The emerging thoughts on supervision are based on a belief in teachers' ability and internal motivation to improve. The supervisory approach must be adjusted based on diversity of development and motivation.

In the 1992 ASCD Yearbook, entitled *Supervision in Transition*, Glickman writes, "Supervision is in such throes of change that not only is the historical understanding of the word becoming obsolete, but I've come to believe that if instructional leadership were substituted each time the word 'supervision' appears in the text and 'instructional leader' substituted for 'supervisor,' little meaning would be lost and much might be gained . . . as a field we may no longer need the old words and connotations. Instead, we might be seeing every talented educator (regardless of role) as an instructional leader and supervisor of instruction" (p. 3). If so, indeed the old order will have crumbled. The shifts or transitions described in that publication included school based collegial processes, reflection, coaching, professional development, critical inquiry, study, and research groups. Glickman's statement gives clues to the relationship between supervision and administration in any discussion of *instructional leadership*.

THE RELATIONSHIP BETWEEN SUPERVISION AND ADMINISTRATION

The relationship between supervision and administration has been a longstanding conversation. In Pajak's (1993) discussion of this, he points out that the field of supervision "distinguished itself from administration during the 1930s by aligning itself with the process of curriculum development" and during the 1940s with the newly formed Association of Supervision and Curriculum Development. In 1953, Spears observed that, with the addition of supervisors to school management, there was an effort to draw a line between administration and supervision. He wrote of three positions taken in the discussion: (1) setting-up vs. carrying-out, (2) authority vs. service, (3) whole vs. part. He surmised that administration reflects more authority than supervision and that supervision implies direction of the instructional program. In 1943, Rorer wrote that "In democratic education, administration and supervision are coordinate, correlative, and complementary functions having as their common purpose the provision of all

means and conditions favorable to teaching and learning. Thus, there is no sharp distinction between the two" (Rorer, 1943, p. 374).

Harris considers supervisory behavior as a special form of leadership, closely related to but distinct from administrative leadership. Although in practice it is difficult to determine where supervision ends and administration begins, there are distinctive endeavors for each (Harris, 1985). Harris defined supervision as a functional area of school operation that is highly related to instruction. He distinguished supervision from teaching in that teaching provides direct pupil-related services and supervisors provide teacher-support services in the area of instruction (Harris, 1985). He distinguished administration from both teaching and supervision as being noninstructional, including the tasks of coordinating, facilitating, and controlling that are characteristic of the work of principals, superintendents, and others related to the entire operation of the school system. Harris further described common tasks among management, administration, supervision, and teaching although contributed to in functionally different ways (Harris, 1985).

According to Harris, supervision is focused on instruction. Seen as a major function of the school operation, not a task, it is "what people do with adults and things to maintain or change the instructional operation of the school in order to facilitate the learning process" (Harris, 1985, p. 23). The tasks of supervision, in his view, are not exclusively supervisory but "are highly instructional related, thus appropriately labeled supervisory." The work of supervisors, coordinators, consultants curriculum specialists, principals, and classroom teachers are included as supervisors in Harris' (1985) description of supervision. According to this view, administrative endeavors exert power and influence on instructional endeavors and give "unity to the entire operation." Administrative endeavors are related to all areas of the system-teaching, pupil services, management, and supervision of instruction.

In a similar view, Oliva (1993) described supervision and administration as a continuum rather than a strict dichotomy with one pole strict supervision and the other pole strict administration. He contends that roles are blended by changing decision-making and expectations regarding school effectiveness.

Dimensions/Tasks of Supervision and Administration

A way to look at the relation between supervision and administration is to compare the dimensions and tasks assigned to each area. The 13 task dimensions of the principal's job identified by Sashkin and Huddle (1986) support the notion that there are some specifically administrative or bureaucratic tasks necessary for effective management of schools (finance, maintenance, support services, staffing, monitoring, relations with central office) as opposed to instructionally-related responsibilities imbedded in developing cultural linkages including responsibilities directly related to instructional leadership (working with groups and committees, observational methods for assessment, and coaching skills) and indirect influences (establishing an atmosphere conducive to learning, and organizational/interpersonal communication using symbols).

Although recognizing that there is no pure supervisory task, Harris (1985) identifies five core supervisory services: developing curriculum, providing staff, providing materials, arranging for in-service training, and evaluating instruction. Organizing for instruction, providing facilities, orienting staff, relating special pupil services, and developing public relations are considered five other supervisory tasks. Many of these tasks are shared between administration and supervision. For example instructional materials are budgeted for (administration), selected (supervision), purchased (management), used in the classroom (teaching), and employed in training (supervision).

Cawelti (1982) identified four major components of effective training for administrators: leadership behavior, management skills (planning, organizing, directing, and controlling), instructional leadership (curriculum development, clinical supervision, staff development, and teacher evaluation), and generic administrative topics (finance, law, personnel, theory, collective bargaining, public relations, and community relations). According to Cawelti (1982), the instructional leadership component is essential to increasing principal productivity in school improvement. His conclusion is based on the effective schools research of such researchers as Brookover, Edmonds, and Lezotte.

In a study commissioned by ASCD, Pajak (1990) identified 12 dimensions of supervision: community relations, staff development, planning and change, communication, curriculum, instructional program, service to teachers, observation and conferencing, problem solving, research and program evaluation, motivating and organizing, and personal development. The study found a high degree of consensus on what knowledge defines supervisory practice and agreement on effective practice. Although Pajak found that there exists a set of values, attitudes, and preferences that distinguish supervision from related functions in schools such as administration (Pajak, 1989), he also concluded that the proficiencies identified in each of these dimensions "represent duties of instructional leaders at all levels of the organization; they are not the sole responsibility of any single individual or position . . . any one position (e.g., superintendent, principal, lead teacher, department chairperson) requires close attention to the performance of certain supervisory functions and less attention to others" (p. 78). In Pajak's study, the traditionally administrative functions of facilities, student discipline, and personnel evaluation were excluded from consideration (Pajak, 1989).

Waite (1993) reported on his findings from a study of novice supervisors' understanding of supervision. When asked about the tasks, traits, relationships, and domains of supervision, these practitioners did not make major distinctions between administration and supervision. Indeed, they included administration as one of the domains of supervision. Waite's advice, given the strong sentiment in the literature that "bifurcation" of the two fields is "artificial and erroneous," was to desist from trying to establish the difference between administration and supervision and examine the implications of the relationship. For example, should there be more administrative training for supervisors and more supervision training for administrators? In doing so however, Waite did acknowledge some tasks to be exclusively administrative (e.g., budgets, monitoring, hiring, dismissal). More experienced supervisors of instruction gave strong and persistent priorities to staff development, curriculum planning and clinical interactions with individual teachers (Hord, 1990; Knezek, 1993; Pajak, 1990). Knezek's study of the involvement of assistant superintendents for instruction in instructional leadership provided new support for overlapping administrative and supervisory roles. Hord's (1990) analysis of superintendent perceptions of their roles in supervision of instruction gave support to strong involvement but selective emphasis on staffing and organizing. Ho's (1992) study of staffing effects of superintendent's active involvement in personnel selection had a significant relationship to the absentee rate of the classroom teacher and offers further support for overlapping and differentiated relationships among administrators and supervisors in the ways they provide leadership to instructional events.

The Changing Relationship

There continues to be considerable dialogue about what supervision is and how it relates to administration. The most distinguishing factor has been that supervision is focused upon improvement of instruction as opposed to more maintenance-related administrative responsibilities. The continuing dialogue has sought to distinguish between "supervision," "instructional supervision," "administration," "school leadership," "educational leadership," and, most recently, "instructional leadership."

As supervision for more effective instruction and effective schools has become a more prominent part of administrators' job responsibilities, the discussion has accelerated. Strong school leadership has been linked to school effectiveness. Indeed, instructional leadership has become the predominant phrase for school and district level administrators as a major job responsibility.

Increasing complexity of the school operation, the emphasis on school effectiveness, instructional leadership, systems theory, and changing views of leadership have called for an integration of supervision and administration, or, at the very least, increased overlap in the relationship of supervision and administration. In light of these issues, some educators propose that an embedded or integrated relationship between supervision and administration is required (Downey, Frase, & Peters, 1994). Further, new ways of viewing teaching and learning have also influenced the relationship between administration and supervision .

Although there may be some distinctions in the tasks of supervision and administration (accepting the notion that supervision applies to instruction) and there are some administrative tasks that are not instructionally related, what seems to be happening is that supervisors *and* administrators supervise instruction and provide instructional leadership. Because of the complexity of the public school mission, the few people available in supervisory positions, the new conceptions of leadership, and the focus on school effectiveness, all educators are expected to provide instructional leadership. *The common ground between supervision and administration appears to be the responsibility for instructional leadership.*

That responsibility creates the need for an *integrated systems approach* with differentiation in focus and priority by task and level of intervention. What do we know about instructional leadership? What are the implications for the chief school administrator of a school system, the superintendent? Discussion of instructional leadership and the superintendency offers further understanding of the relationship between supervision and administration.

THE INSTRUCTIONAL LEADERSHIP FUNCTION AND THE SUPERINTENDENT

Synthesis of educational and psychological research concerning schools shows that improving the amount and quality of instruction can result in vastly more effective and efficient academic learning (Walberg, 1984). Many factors affecting learning can be altered or influenced by educators. The two instructional factors identified by Walberg's synthesis of 3000 studies are: (1) the amount of time the student is engaged in learning and (2) the quality of the instructional experience, including psychological and curricular aspects. These instructional variables are complex and suggest the impact that superintendents and their team of professionals have on both administration and supervision (teacher quality, curriculum development, staff development, performance evaluation, and other such tasks).

The notion of instructional leadership, although not new, came into prominence with the school effectiveness research of the 1980s and was focused primarily on the principal. That research established that strong principal leadership affects student achievement and that successful schools are characterized by a clear sense of purpose supported by instructional leadership of the principal (Brookover & Lezotte, 1977; Cawelti, 1982; Edmonds, 1982). Other research has reported that student achievement is affected by what principals do (Chubb & Moe, 1990) and by teacher perception of the principal as instructional leader (Heck, 1992; Smith & Andrews, 1989).

The definition of instructional leadership as "those actions taken or delegated to promote growth of student learning" includes both direct and indirect actions (Kleine-Kracht, 1993). Typically, the direct functions or tasks involved in instructional leadership include communicating purposes, establishing vision and mission, clarifying goals, setting standards, monitoring student and teacher performance, recognizing and rewarding good work, providing staff development, offering technical assistance, implementing programs of known effectiveness, obtaining resources for learning, planning curriculum, and organizing for instruction. Indirect activities include establishing the physical and cultural context for instruction, developing leadership in others, acquiring resources, and maintaining the system (Kleine-Kracht, 1993). These tasks are responsibilities at both the district and school levels.

District administrators, especially the superintendent, are being held more accountable for student learning. Many states have set standards for school performance. For example, state departments of education, mayors, and governors

have actually taken control when school districts failed to meet standards. A new proposal of accountability recently under study by the South Carolina legislature would remove the superintendent and school board if certain basic standards in student achievement for the district are not met after two years of state assistance. In the case of an individual school not meeting standards, the principal could be removed. In Texas, poor patterns of student achievement result in loss of accreditation. The expectation is that strong instructional leadership is to be given by administrators at the district level. Superintendents are being held accountable for the school level performance. These requirements are based on the belief that district administrators are responsible for school effectiveness and that district leadership is an essential ingredient in improvement and change.

The Superintendency

An examination of the superintendency can demonstrate how supervision and administration come together and, indeed, are integrated. Empirical research has been primarily focused on the principal rather than other administrative positions (Pitner & Ogawa, 1981) and research on the superintendent, the superintendent's staff, and district organization is sparse. There is renewed interest in the superintendent and the influence of that role on school reform and improvement. Until recently, there had been little discussion of the superintendent's role in reform or restructuring. This lack of attention to the superintendent/CEO is unlike the reform of the 1960s and current corporate restructuring (Ouchi, 1981) where much attention is given to the system leadership. Wissler and Ortiz (1988) propose that schools are not understood "because in fact the schools have not been studied as total organizations. The research efforts have concentrated at the classroom level and school levels rather than the district level" (Weisler & Ortiz, 1988, p. 36). The influence and involvement of the superintendent and district level staff in instructional leadership have implications for the relationship between administration and supervision.

The position of superintendent has existed since the mid-1800s as city school districts appointed individuals to oversee the daily operations of a number of schoolhouses (Glass, 1992). The original role of the superintendent was that of "schoolmaster." The board of education made the major decisions and the superintendent was responsible for carrying out those decisions. By the end of the 19th century, superintendents had become managing administrators. Although early superintendents' efforts were on improvement of schools, they were also aware of the need to be knowledgeable in curriculum and instruction, teacher preparation, and staff development (Glass, 1992). When first established, the superintendency had five main responsibilities of supervision and management: business administration; supervision of the school plant; appointment of teachers and janitors; administration of curriculum; and supervision of teaching. Initially the board retained primary responsibility for the first three and the superintendent assumed responsibility for the other two functions (Spears, 1953). By the late 19th century, there was agreement that two administrative positions, that of business manager and that of superintendent, were needed. The superintendent at that time was directly responsible for the academic or instructional activities. Subsequently, the superintendent emerged as the chief executive officer (Glass, 1992). As the superintendency gained professional standing in the 20th century, the superintendent became directly responsible for the management of facilities, personnel, and finance and withdrew substantially from the responsibilities for teaching and learning. With that development, supervision was viewed as primarily administrative. The idea of a special instructional leader was yet to be envisioned (Spears, 1953).

Supervisory responsibilities were prominent among items discussed during informal meetings of superintendents who subsequently established the National Association of School Superintendents as their own professional organization. Evidence of continuing leadership by the Department of Superintendence within the National Education Association caused Aiken and Tanner to acknowledge its emergence by 1865 as "a major force in the professionalization of school supervision." (See Chapter 26 of this volume devoted to "Supervision in the Secondary School.") Similar credit to AASA for contributions along these lines is provided by Firth. (See Chapter 36 of this volume devoted to "Governance of School Supervision").

Among its most important contributions to supervision were the Department's publication on *Leadership in Instruction* (Rankin, 1935) and its 8th yearbook (NEA, 1938). The organization evolved into the American Association of School Administrators and separated from the NEA in 1971.

As the years passed, the recognition grew that the superintendent must assume responsibility for instructional leadership. Indeed, the 30th yearbook of the American Association of School Administrators, *The American School Superintendency* (1952), identified instruction as the most important function of the superintendent. The authors wrote:

All other responsibilities of the superintendent are secondary to the task of providing the facilities and conditions that make effective teaching and learning possible . . . the paramount function of the superintendency is instruction. The complexities of operating a modern school system today have made it increasingly necessary, however, for the superintendent to delegate the actual program of improving curriculum and instruction to other staff members (pp. 196–197).

At the time of that publication, the superintendent devoted an average of approximately one-fifth to one-fourth of his time directly to instruction. The conclusion drawn by the yearbook staff was that the superintendent who shares in planning for instruction and who brings the other elements of the system to bear on instruction is responding to his duty to that function. Included along with instruction as a responsibility of the superintendent were the functions of personnel, business, and auxiliary services. In sum, the superintendent was charged with seeing that all functions and processes made maximum contribution to instruction. The view was that "it is an unfortunate division when any one of the service functions—personnel, finance, school plant auxiliary service—is separated administratively from the superintendent and the instructional program. Planning and coordination should at every point mesh the decisions on the service functions into the educational processes in which learners are engaged."

The 35th yearbook of the American Association of School Administrators was entitled *The Superintendent as Instructional Leader* (1957). Once again, the administrators identified good instruction as the ultimate goal of a school system and improving instruction as the most important task of the superintendent. The book identified ways of "doing better the things superintendents are now doing to improve instruction—especially in the areas of personnel relations and cooperative undertakings" (p. 19). The yearbook called attention to the common problem of lack of attention to instruction by the superintendent because of the need to attend to business and administrative detail (AASA, 1957).

The view was that separation of the service function—personnel, finance and school plant—for the superintendent and the instructional process was not desirable. Accordingly, planning and coordination should mesh the service sector decisions into the educational process of learners.

The 1960s and 1970s were a time of extreme social tension and change in public education. The Civil Rights movement, desegregation, rise of unionism, problems in inner cities, and increasing numbers of disadvantaged students were subjects that absorbed the superintendent and school board and created tension between policy and management. Hierarchical bureaucracy and scientific management developed during this period (Glass, 1992). The pressures of the day increasingly pulled the attention of the superintendent from direct involvement with instruction, although instructional leadership was still considered an important function. In the 1971 and 1982 AASA studies of the superintendency, collective bargaining and finance ranked as the key concerns. The 1992 AASA survey of superintendents reported a return to an instructional focus, and listed student assessment/testing, general district accountability, and developing selected new programs as the most serious challenges along with finance and changing demographics.

The Changing View of the Superintendent

In the view of some scholars, the Superintendency is now emerging as executive level leadership rather than a position (Harris & Wilson, 1991). Current literature on the superintendency supports the view that the superintendent should be an executive leader focusing on the quality of the school's "product." The responsibility of the Chief Executive Office (CEO) is to improve productivity (e.g., improve student achievement, reduce dropouts, improve learning climate).

The superintendent is expected to facilitate the vision of the district and accomplish its mission, while managing the political, financial and social issues of a complex social system. The superintendent must lead in a world where products are being invented, organizations of unknown configuration are being designed, and whole new constellations of client needs are being addressed (Harris, 1985).

Schlechty writes that "the primary role of the superintendent is to educate the community about education, promote the articulation and persistent pursuit of a compelling vision, and ensure results, rather than programs, dominate the attention of all" (Schlechty, 1990, p. 131). Schlecty proposes that the "moral authority" of the school system resides in the office of the superintendent and that superintendents who do not use their office will "create a system incapable of leadership in the community" (Schlechty, 1990, p. 128)."In the long run" he writes "who the superintendent is, what the superintendent values, and the style of operation supported by the superintendent will manifest throughout the system" (Schlechty, 1990, p. 128).

The superintendent is the CEO but how much of his or her time is spent in instructional leadership? During the period when other pressures seemed to consume the superintendency, Goodlad (1978) lamented the lack of instructional leadership by school district administration. He described three eras of educational leadership. The pre-1950 era was characterized by strong interest in instructional management. Since then, the second era has seen administration focus on noninstructional matters. Goodlad called for a third era in which the focus would return to instructional leadership.

Research conducted before 1988 essentially confirmed that the superintendent gave scant attention to instructional matters. Cuban (1976) and Blumberg and Blumberg (1985) found that political and managerial roles dominated and that instructional and curriculum matters were dealt with infrequently by chief school officers.

Rowan (1982) found that superintendents spent approximately 20 percent of their time in instructional management. Wirt (1991) suggested that the missing link in instructional leadership was the attention of the superintendent. He argued that superintendents gave their attention, instead, to conflict management and maintenance activities, thus leaving little time for instructional leadership. The resolution of conflict was found to be the central problem for superintendents (Zeigler, Kehes, & Reisman, 1985). Few superintendents have been able to use politics and management to elevate instruction to the central focus.

Much of the discussion surrounding the effects of the superintendency focuses on the indirect controls or influence used. The position calls for "choreographing" district activities toward the district mission (Crowson 1987). Pitner and Ogawa (1981) found a choreographing role of superintendents in their 1977 and 1979 studies of the day-to-day behavior of the superintendents. Their analysis showed that "superintending is communicating" and that superintendents, though constrained by social and organizational structures, exert an important organizational influence. Pitner (1981) found that superintendents, rather than being single-minded about directing their organizations, responded to the diversity of the social system in which they worked. They exerted primarily symbolic leadership "at best indirect influence on organizational performance." Superintendents, in the Pitner study, attended primarily to structural aspects of the system such as programs, budgets, facilities, and schedules. Those activities were only loosely coupled with instructional activities. The absence of administrative control over instructional activity, Pitner and Ogawa suggested, is affected by two conditions: (1) uncertainties surrounding the technology of instruction; and (2) the lack of consensus regarding preferred outcomes. The Pitner framework suggested that the effect of administrator leadership on productivity depends on the characteristics of the faculty and staff, the conception of the teaching task, and the organization influencing whether a

leadership style enables the administrator to motivate, direct, and control teacher performance (Pitner, 1988). At the same time, superintendents saw instructional staffing competence (recruitment, selection, induction, and staff development) as significantly related to effective superintendents' tasks (Ho, 1992).

The fact that school organization is "loosely coupled" results in its structure being unconnected to the organization's work activity (Weick, 1976). Thus, the superintendent becomes disconnected from curriculum and instruction and school operations and assumes that others are taking responsibility and doing those jobs (Wirt, 1991). Being unconnected from the schools works against the productivity of the superintendent. The school district must be viewed as a total system; the superintendent is responsible for orchestrating the district as a system and must remain connected to the school operation. This requires knowledge of the interrelationships among all components of the district and the people in the district (Downey, Frase, & Peters, 1994).

Superintendent's Influence

There are some recent indications that superintendents have been entering Goodlad's third era (1978). In studying the superintendent's role, researchers have found that district-wide change is not possible without the support, encouragement, and involvement of the superintendent (Griffin, 1994). There is some evidence that superintendents do indeed affect instruction. Crowson (1987) found that superintendents in "instructionally effective" districts establish tight control over student achievement using indirect influence with schools, especially in the areas of curriculum and instruction. Larocque and Coleman (cited in Crowson, 1987, p. 60) reported a "strong district presence in higher-performing districts with superintendents setting achievement expectations, monitoring school performance data closely, and emphasizing school accountability." Studies have shown that superintendents' perceptions of their competence in instructional leadership tasks and the importance of their engaging in them are strong (Hord, 1990; Sulfani, 1987; Wan, 1991). In her study of six superintendents, Griffin (1994) found that each superintendent had an impact on the district's school effectiveness plans. "Each superintendent, as a leader and through his or her behavior, shaped the organization and created the setting for goal accomplishment within the school system" (p. 25). Griffin identified three areas of superintendent activity: (1) focus (vision, active involvement, alignment of curriculum—intended, taught, and tested—and accountability for results); (2) support (recognition of district staff as professionals, disaggregate analysis used as tool for improvement and staff development emphasis); and (3) beliefs (all children can learn) linked to action. These six superintendents were actively involved in and\or led program planning, curriculum alignment, and staff development (district-wide and site-based); interacted with teachers, principals and community; visited schools (all wished to visit more); and evaluated principals (focused on student achievement).

Murphy and Hallenger (1988) studied 12 instructionally effective school districts in California. They found "a higher than anticipated degree of coordination between district, school, and classroom in the areas of curriculum and instruction, and discovered the "superintendents were actively engaged in technical core operations" (p. 175). Districts in this study focused on improving student learning through systematic focus, long-term orientation, analysis of data, and application of results. They found support for the notion that districts can take active roles in setting goals, establishing district-wide curriculum and instructional focus with consistency, and coordinating of instructional activities. Strong instructional leadership was displayed by the superintendent by: providing direct leadership in the areas of curriculum and instruction, setting goals, promoting district-wide staff development, pressing for district and school goal coordination, and supervising and evaluating school principals. Superintendents monitored the instructional and curricular focus through the supervision and evaluation of principals and by checking on the implementation level of preferred teaching strategies and the achievement of curriculum objectives. Student test scores were taken seriously. Achievement scores and personnel evaluations were linked and other indicators of effectiveness were monitored. Progress on school-level goals was followed up at the district level, especially by the superintendent. District control was maintained while appropriate school autonomy was encouraged. There was balance or "dynamic tension" between school autonomy and district level direction and consistency among schools. Autonomy in the schools was found at the input and implementation stages. In the six districts studied, the system, perspective was evident and much attention was given to orientation of all persons involved. Strong leaders used collaborative methods of operation. The researchers concluded that these instructionally effective districts are different from the majority of the districts because "the attention to curriculum and instruction, the consistency of technical core factors, the strong instructional leadership of the superintendents, the emphasis on inspection of processes and outcomes, and the high degree of coordination between district, school and classroom set these districts apart from many of their counterparts" (Murphy & Hallenger, 1988, p. 180). Although excited and optimistic about these findings, the researchers cautioned against over-generalization from this small sample in which none of the districts possessed all characteristics. They believe, however, that this study is a good beginning for more complete studies on the role and effectiveness of districts in promoting educational effects and improvement (Murphy & Hallenger, 1988).

Joyce and Showers (1988) echo the finding of the importance of the superintendent and district organization in their work on staff development for improving student achievement. Properly focused and supported district staff development is needed for school improvement. They suggested that a district staff development council needs to work in cooperation with schools to select systemic initiatives that are coordinated with site-level initiatives. The point is not to overload schools with too many initiatives. In the view of Joyce and Showers (1988), active leadership from the superintendent is necessary for this approach to be successful.

The Superintendent's Team

Fullan (1991), in his review of the research and literature in the field of school effectiveness, suggested that, rather than considering superintendents separately, it would be best to exam-

ine the district administration as a whole because of the complex interrelationships involved in school improvement. District administrators are usually the critical source for initiating innovations (Huberman & Miles, 1984). As a force for change, two-way communication about specific innovations is necessary for success (Fullan, 1991). Fullan further found that the chief administrator, more than any other individual in the district, sets the tone and pace regarding the climate of communications. Fullan concluded that effective districts use "simultaneous top-down\bottom-up approaches" for sustained change and improvement. Whereas centralization is ineffective because it attempts to standardize curriculum and performance inappropriately, decentralization is ineffective because individual schools lack the capacity to manage sustained change and have difficulty in the effective assessment of changes. He cited the findings of Levin and Eubanks (1989), who reported that research to date had found neutral or disappointing results on empowerment and site-based management rather than encouraging or positive results. They cited problems of delegation, training, skill requirements, time, and others. Moreover, school councils rarely tackled instructional improvements or second-order changes (Levin & Eubanks, 1989). The evidence showed some positive changes in teacher satisfaction and professional practices within schools but very little evidence of schools addressing substantive instructional issues and agreeing on an instructional focus. This is not to say that site-based management should be abandoned. Some significant restructuring efforts are underway that may lead to better understanding of how site-based management within a total systems perspective can work. The school is the unit of change but how that is best operationalized has yet to be determined. Elmore (1988) raises the pertinent question, "how to change dominant modes of instruction that discourage engagement and how to change a bureaucratic structure that discourages people with a strong professional interest in teaching and learning" (p. 11).

Louis (1989) analyzed the relationship between five schools and their districts and found two dimensions that affected the quality of the relationship: (1) the degree of engagement (frequency of interaction and communication, mutual coordination and influence, some shared goals and objectives) and (2) the level of bureaucratization (presence of extensive rules and regulations governing the relationship). The "clearly positive district contexts" was one of high engagement and low bureaucracy. Louis concluded "Essentially the picture is one of co-management, with coordination and joint planning enhanced through the development of consensus between staff members at all levels about desired goals for education" (Louis, (1989, p.61). It was the schools with this district profile that had successful improvement projects.

LaRocque and Coleman (1989a, p.190) have hypothesized that the most effective "district ethos" was characterized by six sets of activity:

1. taking care of business (a learning focus)
2. monitoring accountability (an accountability focus)
3. changing policies/practices (a change focus)
4. consideration and caring for stakeholders (a caring focus)
5. creating shared values (a commitment focus)
6. creating community support (a community focus)

They concluded that effective districts have an active and evolving accountability ethos that combined interactive monitoring while respecting school autonomy.

Knezek's (1993) study of the improvement of student achievement test scores in 91 school districts and the contribution of assistant superintendents of instruction to those efforts showed strong relationships between those test scores and the responsibility of those central office staff leaders for technical support to principals. Those findings suggested the need for a model of collaboration involving the schools and a strong district presence by the superintendent and the superintendent's team to focus on instruction. Berry (1987) suggested that the work of central staff supervisory personnel acting under the leadership of the superintendent is important in providing to the schools technical skills often lacking in both principals and teachers.

Thus, it is no longer centralization vs. decentralization because it is clear that all levels of the system are involved—the classroom, the school, the school district, and beyond. Schools cannot redesign themselves. The role of the district is crucial for sustained, continuous, and long-term school improvement. Fullan proposed that the relationship which works is one of interactive pressure and support, initiative-taking, and empowerment through coordinated action. Moreover, he proposed that sustained improvement requires a change in the interrelationships of the school district toward this collaborative model. Fullan concludes that the matter of school and district balance has no final solution but that effective superintendents continually negotiate and monitor this relationship with school staff, "attempting to stay within an acceptable corridor of mutual influence" (Fullan, 1991, p. 211). In doing so, the paramount task of the district administrator is not to implement any specific innovation but to "build the capacity of the district and the schools to handle any and all innovations" (Fullan, 1991, p. 214).

Affecting Principal Instructional Leadership

The superintendent's supervision of principals is an important dimension of his/her instructional leadership in light of recent studies identifying activities principals can use to shape instruction and student learning. Bossert, Dwyer, Rowen, and Lee (1982) hypothesized that effective school-level management can affect instructional practice regarding instructional time, class size and composition, instructional grouping, curriculum pacing and articulation, student evaluation, and classroom task characteristics. Bossert et al.'s model of the principals' influence on students identified district characteristics that affect the instructional management behavior of principals (Bossert, Dwyer, Rowan, & Lee, 1982); those characteristics were rules and policy, community expectations, and teacher collective bargaining agreements. Duckworth (1983) asserted that the impact of district policy and management comes from the changes in the conditions of teaching and learning. The district factors affecting conditions of teaching and learning include staffing ratios, technical support, policies and regulations, employment contracts, fiscal resources, school size, and socioeconomic profile. Almanza (1980) and

Berry (1987) both studied elementary schools reported to be innovative and found principal and teacher active involvement directly linked to change; however, both also found central office staff involvement to be significant.

Rosenholtz (cited in Fullan, 1991) studied 78 elementary schools in eight districts and characterized some schools as "moving" and some as "stuck." In districts where "moving" schools were identified, the superintendents expected themselves, the principals, and the teachers to be continuous learners, they involved principals and teachers in goal setting and policy development. Districts with "moving" schools selected and cultivated principals whose foremost concern is student learning and who are skilled in instructional leadership. Superintendents in districts where "moving"schools were found respected the professionalism of teachers and actively sought to provide teachers with the necessary support to accomplish goals.

Peterson (1989) proposed that systems of control can affect principal instructional responsibilities such as observing teachers, monitoring student progress, building a coordinated instructional program, promoting staff development, and acting as an instructional resource. He identified six controls that can be used by the superintendent with principals to stimulate the principal to be an instructional leader: (1) supervision, (2) resource allocation, (3) input/output, (4) selection of the principal, (5) socialization to system norms and values, and (6) environmental controls. The financial input controls included per capita budgeting, contingency funds, and ability to transfer funds among budget categories. Instructional input controls included discretion in the initial hiring and transfer of teachers. Peterson found that there were more controls in administrative areas than in instructional areas. "Output controls" included standardized testing and public reaction. The patterns of control found were a subtle balance between control and autonomy. Principals were constrained by output controls but were granted autonomy in determining means to achieve ends, Fulfill tasks and select faculty. Peterson concluded that multiple controls influence principals' work, arguing the needed balance of control and autonomy that allows principals to be instructional leaders and still respond to the demands of a complex role can be attained (Peterson, 1987).

Hallinger and Murphy (1987) identified three influences of the district office on principal instructional leadership: (1) providing support resources, staff training, time, technical assistance, increased authority, and better information; (2) establishing a district culture of excellence in which teaching is a top priority by using symbolic leadership; and (3) implementing formal and informal controls including principal evaluation, clinical supervision, and accountability. Hallinger and Murphy concluded that there is "little doubt that the district shapes the leadership behavior of principals." Doing so, however, involves a complex set of actions that are affected by the context of individual districts and schools.

Smith and Andrews (1989) also concluded from their work that strong, supportive supervision of school principals is significant in promoting school reform and improvement practices. They suggested new supervisory practices such as role modeling and clinical supervision that is collegial and collaborative with the goal being improvement of instruction.

Superintendent's Instructional Leadership Role

The 1992 AASA *Study of the American School Superintendency* (Glass, 1992) resulted in several pertinent findings that urge a shift in the activities of the superintendency toward instructional leadership:

1. School boards are much more interested in the superintendent as an instructional leader than in past years.
2. Three of the five most serious challenges are instructionally related: student assessment/testing, general district accountability, and development of new programs. Finance and changing demographics were the other two serious challenges.
3. Preparation and training most important to the effectiveness of the superintendent included establishing a positive learning environment, developing effective instructional and curriculum programs, and managing district finances.

The emphasis on instruction is greater than in previous decades, reflecting an increasing importance of instructional leadership to superintendents. This increased emphasis on instructional leadership by the superintendent is reflected in the eight professional standards identified by AASA. Curriculum Planning and Development and Instructional Management are two of the eight standards. The other standards are Leadership and School Culture, Policy and Governance, Communications and Community Relations, Organizational Management, Human Resources Management, and Values and Ethics. Under these standards related to instruction, superintendents are expected to demonstrate knowledge in curriculum design, strategic planning for continuous improvement of teaching and learning, instructional taxonomies, cognitive development and learning theory, assessment, classroom and management techniques, technology, effective instructional strategies, and methods of monitoring student achievement and teacher performance.

The standards related to instruction can initiate needed dialogue about the role of the superintendent. They can further the discussion and investigation into the superintendent's effect on student achievement and training. Research should be designed around these standards to further knowledge about the superintendency and effective schooling in varying contexts such as different size districts and rural, suburban, or city settings.

Another study has identified the leadership domains and task areas of the school superintendent as groundwork to developing a diagnostic and professional development system for school system executives. Sponsored by AASA, the project developers have identified six leadership domains: General Education, Instructional Leadership, Administrative Leadership, Human Relations, Personal Capabilities, and Multicultural Perspectives. Forty two tasks of instructional leadership for executives were identified under the task areas of instructional planning, staffing for instruction, organizing for instruction, human resources development, and evaluating instruction (Harris, Nolan, Lovels, & Cartee, 1992; Harris & Wilson, 1991). The selection of these task areas grew out of the work of Hoyle, English, and Steffy (1985) which emphasized the impor-

tance of instructional program knowledge for the superintendent. Additionally, a study conducted by Scalfani and others in corporation with AASA compared perceptions of skills of superintendents identified as "exemplary" with those of a stratified random sample of superintendents. That study confirmed that practitioners view instructional leadership skills as important (cited in Harris & Wilson, 1991).

Because of the complexity of the superintendent's position, there has been little research. Thus, there is little evidence linking the activities of superintendents with a *direct* effect on the academic performance of students, improvement of teaching, or performance of principals (Cuban, 1994). The context of such research presents multiple problems of intervening variables. Some limited efforts in these directions have been made in the studies of Muller (1982) on the relationship of student achievement and superintendent leadership competence in which he found positive results. In another study, Ho (1992) reported that superintendents' involvement in staffing for instruction is a significant factor in teacher motivation.

Although there is much more to learn about instructional leadership generally and the role of the superintendent specifically, sufficient evidence is available to indicate the following:

1. *Instructional leadership influences the effectiveness of schools and school districts.* The amount and quality of instruction results in increased student learning. The superintendent has strong influence on conditions of teaching and learning which in turn affect learning. Of importance is the responsibility of the superintendent to create the conditions supportive of change, developing the capabilities of those at the district and school levels to initiate, facilitate and lead change. The ability to effectively lead instructional change should be found at the district and school levels.
2. *Superintendents exert instructional leadership through direct and indirect activities.* Direct activities include building vision, setting goals, monitoring results, assessing outcomes, promoting staff development, providing technical assistance, establishing standards, implementing effective programs, and providing resources for learning, curriculum planning, and organizing for instruction. Indirect activities include establishing a culture of excellence in learning, developing the capacity for leadership and knowledge in self and others, providing resources, ensuring maintenance, and overseeing budget development as well as directing central staff technical support personnel to assist principals and teachers in instructional improvements.
3. *A strong district presence is evident in high performing districts.* Instruction is influenced by the efforts of a district-level team to set achievement expectations, to monitor school performance, to emphasize accountability, to develop human resources, and to provide technical support related to instructional improvement, staffing, and program evaluation.
4. *District-wide change must have strong instructional leadership from the superintendent in establishing and implementing vision, action, beliefs, and collaboration.* Productivity focus, systemic improvement focus, long-term orientation, problem solving orientation, and people orientation are

part of this leadership by the superintendent. Human resource development is central to this responsibility.

5. *A model of collaboration and integration including the superintendent, the superintendent's team, and the school staff is needed.* A climate of trust, support and sense of efficacy for employees is basic to the interrelationship among the superintendent, district level team, and school staff. Research has suggested that a high degree of engagement and low degree of bureaucracy is the most effective model with balance between school-level autonomy and district-level direction. Simultaneous bottom-up/top-down collaboration demands collegial relationships. In the effective district, the system is neither decentralized nor centralized but integrated for sustained change and improvement.

6. *Effective superintendents are systematically involved in instructionally related activities.* Setting goals, selecting staff, supervising and evaluating principals, supervising and supporting professional development, focusing on curriculum and instruction, and monitoring district and school progress/productivity are important responsibilities of the superintendent.

7. *Superintendents can influence the principal as instructional leaders.* Through supervision, input and output control, selection, socialization, and environmental controls using various methods of supervision (role modeling, clinical supervision, and collaboration), the superintendent and his\her team can affect school productivity. Emphasis should be placed on supervision of processes rather than direct supervision of people.

IMPLICATIONS FOR PRACTICE

A changing relationship between administration and supervision is resulting as the two concepts move toward integration. There is a blurring of the lines separating the two fields even though there remains some differentiation based on the focus and priority by tasks and the level and type of intervention employed by each. This integration of the two fields is consistent with recently articulated theories of instructional leadership. Increased accountability of administrators for student outcomes, the current recognition of responsibilities for instructional leadership on the part of administrators, and emerging evidence that school effectiveness has been influenced by the instructional leadership of the superintendent and the district organization are factors that have affected and can furthur affect the practice of administrators.

Accepting this integrated view of supervision and administration through instructional leadership has important implications for practice and raises some very practical questions and considerations to be addressed in this new relationship:

1. *Superintendents and district staff should reexamine leadership, management, and decision-making practices along with governance structures in light of new knowledge about leadership and supervision.*

Questions. What is the district culture? How is it developed? Is there a climate of trust? openness? caring? cooperation? collaboration? and empowerment? Are staff treated with respect and professionalism? How is teamwork developed and nurtured? Is there a balance of top-down and bottom-up decision-making? Do integrated decision-making structures exist? Is there clear understanding of roles and responsibilities for decisions? Has adequate training for new leadership roles and structures been provided? Is there clear understanding of what site-based decision-making is and how participatory management works? How are schools developed as learning communities?

Considerations. If, as some suggest, the most difficult task is to obtain the appropriate balance between efficacy and control, how could a team approach integrating top-down and bottom-up, school-level and district-level decision-making work best? School systems need to explore governance structures that support the notion that the system is not a collection of individual schools but a complex system of interrelated and connected sites, processes, and structures connected by common vision, mission, and values; that the focus of change and improvement must be the school and classroom and the agents of change a team of district, school, and community stakeholders whose actions are based on cooperative planning

The discussion, however, should not rest on who makes the decision but what decision is in the best interest of children. The evidence thus far on site-based decision-making is a warning that overconcern with the structure of decision-making can interfere with primary focus on instructional and curricular matters such that real change may not occur. Structure, however, is necessary to facilitate action and communication and to prevent misunderstanding and confusion about the decision-making process. Different decision-making structures need to be tested along with tools to facilitate balanced decision-making. Murphy's and Hallenger's (1988) model for integrated decentralization has promise as does the integrated, webbed organizational structure suggested by Senge (1990) and Downey et al (1994). Deming's Fourteen Points also offer potential for developing new structures. Another approach to governance and decision making in keeping with the new leadership principles is the concept of adhocracy as proposed by Waterman (1990). Adhocracy uses temporary groups to accomplish a particular task rather that the static structures of bureaucracy (Downey et al, 1994), thereby increasing involvement and integration of stakeholders.

Shared decision-making and participatory management also offer potential for new management and governance structures. Well understood vision, mission, and values provide principles to guide shared decision-making, site-based management, and restructuring proposals. It might be argued that the most important guiding principle is the genuine belief that those affected by a decision should be part of the decision-making process.

All of these considerations for leadership, management, decision-making, and governance call for a primary focus to be on building capacity for leadership and personal responsibility at all levels. Such new structures call for commitment to excellence, a strong knowledge base, and high levels of professionalism. Training in decision-making and in new instructional practices would be essential and have important implications for the professional development of staff at all levels. A vital question might be asked: Are the norms and culture that create the conditions necessary for sharing decision-making, taking risks, and accepting accountability evident? If not, how can they best be developed?

2. *Superintendents should place instructional leadership as the major responsibility.*

Questions. How much time does the superintendent spend on instructional matters? What kinds of messages does the superintendent send about the importance of instruction? Does the superintendent spend time talking about and being actively involved in instructional matters? What strategies does the superintendent use to facilitate his or her instructional leadership role? Are noninstructional processes used by the superintendent to further instruction? Does the superintendent initiate, authorize, and support instructional initiatives? Is excellence in teaching and learning the driving force throughout the organization? Are there clear instructional expectations and accountability mechanisms? Is the necessary support to carry out instructional decisions provided for teachers, principals and district staff? Is there a well designed professional development program for teachers, principals, and district level supervisors/coordinators? How are new principals chosen and socialized into the system? What supports and controls do superintendents use that support principals as instructional leaders? What is the relationship between the superintendent and the principal regarding the linkages for instructional improvement? How are principals evaluated? Is there a philosophy of teaching and learning?

Considerations. The literature reveals the need for instructional leadership by the superintendent, but a minimal number of superintendents have responded. Admittedly, the challenge is great in the face of the daily requests from competing interests. The complexity of the position has increased. Ironically, it is these circumstances that make instructional leadership even more important. A major consideration is how the superintendent can organize his or her job responsibilities in order to put instructional leadership as priority. Of special consideration is the degree of engagement (Louis, 1989) that is needed for effective instructional leadership and what specific activities are important. Unfortunately, few models or approaches are well defined. District size and community context affect the approach that the superintendent and the superintendent's team might take. Additionally, staffing patterns will have implications. It may be that executing instructional leadership in differing contexts (Large/small; urban/rural; diverse/homogenous) is more different in degree than kind of direct or indirect activities. Or, perhaps more importantly, is how superintendents think about supervision. How they execute instructional leadership will be shaped by their beliefs about leadership, supervision, teaching, and learning. Research indicates that school districts should be clear that student learning is the priority, and the superintendent should be the major source of that message.

In light of this, the superintendent needs to examine the opportunities he or she has to further progress in noninstructional and instructional areas. For example, if the budget is viewed as the financial plan for implementing the instructional program (which is the focus of our mission), then budget-making takes on a unique tone. Instruction becomes the focus of recommendations from schools and departments. Under such a philosophy, instructional items take priority when considering all budget decisions other than safety and legal items. Making decisions about what to fund with limited resources can be agonizing, but becomes less so if instruction is the priority of the district.

Another example of using non-instructional tasks for instructional purposes is in the area of facilities. A top priority in the mission of a facilities department is to meet the needs for instructional support after safety and legal needs are met. When work orders are reviewed, those affecting the instructional areas should receive priority. When developing facilities plans the first step is for school personnel to define the educational specifications. Such principles help to establish a mind set toward instructional matters and have the effect of furthering instructional priorities. Yet another example is for the superintendent to use his or her office to cut through red tape, waive policy and procedure, and guide policy development in such a way as to support schools in innovation and change.

Another opportunity for influence occurs when the district or school is implementing a new program, teaching technique, or educational practice. The superintendent's ability to Marshall resources affects the level of implementation or change. Partial or half hearted provision of supplies, staff development, equipment, facilities, training, and technical assistance necessary for effective implementation sets the program up for failure, reduces the trust in the district leader, and cools enthusiasm for innovation and change. Proactive support results in more effective implementation, better chances for success, and more positive attitudes toward change. Great satisfaction results in implementing a program completely and well. The superintendent has the ability to control the conditions for improvement in the instructional program by the decisions he or she makes and the support he or she gives. Any number of opportunities for the superintendent are available to support instruction and send important messages that instruction is the district priority concern.

3. *School practitioners should examine strategies for achieving productivity and improvement.*

Questions. How should productivity be determined? What should be assessed? How should achievement and improvement be assessed? How can systems theory be used for improved productivity? Does the system operate on a theory of teaching, learning, supervision, and administration? Is there a systematic plan for systemwide improvement? Who should assume what responsibilities? What are effective teaching strategies? What are effective supervision strategies? Of principals? Of teachers? Are processes monitored rather than people? What staff development is most effective? How is curriculum aligned and monitored? What is the vision for schooling? What are the home, church, community, and mass media influences to be considered?

Considerations. The answers to these questions, if based on the discussions in this chapter, could dramatically change the way schools and school districts operate and could potentially increase their productivity and effectiveness. In answering these questions, school systems would need to explore changes in student assessment; implement alternative supervision models such as clinical/peer supervision for teachers and principals; develop system-wide strategic plans; establish techniques for accountability; and restructure district organizations, roles, and responsibilities. For example, in following the recommendations of systems theory and the quality movement, the focus of the district management team would be on continuous improvement and process management not simply bottomline thinking (Downey et al, 1994). Administrators' roles would ensure that everyone in the system is working for excellence in all processes. Data orientation to decision-making and a disciplined method of inquiry or problem solving would be used. Deming (1991) recommends the problem-solving method of Plan-Do-Study-Act (PDSA). Benchmarking or the practice of searching for best practices and processes not limited to the organization and standardization of those best practices would be included as possible strategies for achieving productivity and improvement. The district mission and vision would drive all activity under the systems concept.

4. *Preparation programs and on the job training programs for superintendents and supervisors must be redesigned.*

Questions. What theories of leadership, supervision, and administration are taught in preparation programs for administrators and supervisors? Do preparation programs prepare leaders or managers? What training is provided for superintendents in instructional leadership? What preparation is available in team building, mediation, participatory management and shared decision-making, and collaboration? What tools for data analysis and systems thinking are included? Is training reality based or field tested as well as theoretical? Is the program rigorous in expectations of knowledge, skills, and attitudes? What provision is made in school districts for continuous learning? Is the school district a learning organization? What is the infrastructure for organizational learning?

Considerations. The "new leader" will require new skills for new leadership processes and a systems perspective. College and university preparation programs for superintendents need to be examined to ensure that the content and practices include current views of leadership, supervision, and administration and increased attention to effective instructional leadership. Opportunities are needed for both acquiring knowledge and developing skills. Continuous learning will be essential. In-service education opportunities must be reexamined. Superintendents must initiate action to provide structured well-planned growth experiences for administrators, supervisors, and the superintendent. To lead, the superintendent must know, and be able to do. The proposed AASA standards will be helpful in redesigning preparation programs and planning for the continuing education of superintendents. Preparation programs for supervisors should also be reexamined to be certain that adequate attention is devoted to leadership, management, and instructional improvement.

5. *New supervisory and administrative structures, processes, and strategies for providing instructional leadership at the district level and school level are needed.*

Questions. How has the district office role been defined? How are schools developed as learning communities? How do schools and district office personnel support one another? What procedures are in place to monitor instruction? Is there strong district-level leadership for planning, implementation,

alignment, and assessment? What are the procedures for providing technical assistance to schools and teachers? What are the processes for collaboration?

Considerations. The relationship between the superintendent, the principal, and the district staff is important regarding the management linkages for instructional improvement. Integrated top-down/bottom-up decision-making appears most effective. Such district-level administrative/supervisory roles might include: providing technical assistance and facilitation, ensuring equity and excellence, assessing accountability, ensuring articulation across the curriculum and curriculum alignment, reviewing requests for waivers from district and state regulations, reallocating resources, and modeling and supporting shared decision-making and collaboration. District instructional personnel would work with school principals, lead teachers, department heads, instructional facilitators, and school or district teams, or on instructional matters. When needed, district staff could provide targeted direct assistance to schools through focus teams to collaborate on special projects as well as on instructional supervision. As facilitators, district staff provide technical assistance, advice, and support; initiate ideas; troubleshoot, and analyze research and information on effective practices. At the school level, participatory management structures such as leadership teams; grade level teams; and mentoring, coaching, and peer supervision are needed.

6. *The school district must have formal and informal, and direct and indirect ways of developing the capacity of teachers and principals to lead.*

Questions. How do teachers enhance their skills and knowledge in teaching and leadership? How do principals increase their knowledge and skills in leadership, supervision, and instructional improvement? Is there a well thought out plan for developing and enabling staff throughout the system at all levels to develop and utilize leadership skills? Is there balance between school-level and district-level staff development? What linkages exist between staff development and performance? What are the processes for providing technical assistance to the schools?

Considerations. Knowledge and reflection are foundations for the new leadership. Innovation and effectiveness require generating new knowledge from study, data analysis, conversation, and reflection on ideas. Teachers and principals must be seen as professionals intrinsically motivated to learn and grow. Thus, multiple growth opportunities are needed. Districts and schools must become learning communities of professionals who study together, cooperate in action research, participate in school-based and district-wide professional development, engage in peer observation, and serve as mentors. Of special importance is the ability of those in the system to effect change. The objective of the system desiring change and improvement is to develop experts in change at the district and school levels (Fullan, 1991).

Taken individually, these implications and examples of practice may accomplish little. Implemented together with other practices the impact can be powerful. These are suggestions for how superintendents should think about supervision of instruction. How superintendents use these guidelines depends on the context of individual schools and the total district. Essential to this entire process is the superintendents's role of increasing the capacity of the entire organization—teachers, principals, district staff—to learn more about their crafts and be better able to use their knowledge and skills to create an effective learning community. Capacity building produces commitment to continuous improvement rather than compliance.

Assuming this role, the superintendent demonstrates how administration and supervision are integrated–even embedded.

RECOMMENDATIONS FOR FUTURE RESEARCH

If schools are to accomplish the educational tasks set before them, better and more information is needed about what works in multiple situations for supervisors and administrators charged with improving instructional practices, processes, and organizations. Educational administration has been criticized for the lack of attention to the effects of leadership on student learning (Bossert, 1988). Bossert (1988) identified three reasons for the importance of administrative focus on instruction: (1) public demand for improved student achievement is increasing accountability of administrators for the "products" of schools; (2) the study of educational administration rests on an "assumed but indirect link" between the organization and student learning; and (3) organizational theory has consistently acknowledged the relationship between productive technology and administrative functioning. Thus, Bossert concludes that research must relate the productive technology of the school to the organization and its processes.

Throughout the review of research and literature, the dearth of data available has been emphasized. Not only is there scant research but some of the results are of questionable value. The lack of attention to the position of superintendent and the central office team leaves an incomplete picture of how to achieve educational productivity. School effectiveness research must now focus on the *total school system* and the influence of the superintendent and the superintendent's team.

Specific attention needs to be given to the roles and responsibilities of administrators, supervisors, and other school leaders and to the contributions of organizational structures, processes, and procedures for administration and supervision in providing instructional leadership. Below are some recommendations for future research:

1. More well defined research is needed on emerging practices and theories of leadership, supervision, and administration associated with new models of teaching and decision-making.
2. New models for roles and organizational structures in administration, supervision, and leadership within varying contexts need study (e.g., collegial supervision, clinical supervision of principals, empowerment, and superintendent controls). More information is needed about site-based management and the balance of top-down/bottom-up, centralization/decentralization organization and decision-making structures (for example, the flattened web). Additional models for an integrated organization are needed.

3. Added research is needed to define instructional leadership more precisely and how it can be best operationalized in a school system. The varying contexts of schools and districts should be addressed.
4. More research is needed on instructional improvement and school effectiveness within different contexts. If instructional leadership is to be achieved, more knowledge is needed about the results of instructional practices under varying conditions.
5. The study of school improvement and reform\restructuring should include the effects of district level activities as well as those in schools and classrooms. A systems view of the total organization is needed for district-wide improvement rather than focusing primarily on individual schools or on certain schools. A systems view prevents inequity and uneven improvement in schools.
6. More research is needed to determine the direct effect of actions by the superintendent on academic achievement of students and the improvement of teacher or principal performance. Specific attention is needed on the effects of indirect and direct influences and controls employed by the superintendent.
7. Additional research is needed on the superintendent's position in general in order to understand the constraints, challenges, and expectations of the job. A better understanding of how the superintendent spends his/her time (e.g., politics, risk management, administrative tasks) would be helpful in further understanding the superintendent's role and responsibility for instructional leadership. School district size and other contexts should be included in such studies.
8. Research needs to be more multi-dimensional. Studies are needed on well-developed models or theories of effective superintendents and school district organizations testing many variables rather than correlational or one dimensional. Longitudinal studies are needed. Moreover, studies should focus on leadership for fundamental change instead of narrow superficial change. More data are needed here about transformational leadership, macro leadership, and systemic change, embracing the total curriculum, the total school, the total community, and the total system.

In addition to such research, the need exists for improved processes for connecting research to practice. Interestingly, the public ranks research on educational productivity higher in priority than most other natural and social sciences (Gallup, 1983 cited in Walberg, 1984). The interchange between researchers and practitioners is currently too limited to provide the basis for improved research and practice.

CLOSING SUMMARY

The purpose of this chapter was to explore the relationship between supervision and administration. Certainly there is much unknown about supervision and administration individually as well as their relationship both as practiced and as should be practiced. There is still much to understand about instructional leadership in general and as the link integrating administrative and supervisory practices. Caution must be exercised about expectations until more is known. However, the complexity of the issue is indelibly clear. It is because of this complexity and emerging knowledge about leadership and organizations that a changed relationship is obvious. What seems to be at work here is greater consensus that there is a needed *integration* of supervision and administration. Instructional leadership is increasingly considered by superintendents and by researchers to be a major responsibility of administrators including superintendents. There are certain tasks that might be considered primarily, even exclusively, administrative (finance, student discipline, transportation, food service, maintenance, property control, personnel management). However, these are shared tasks in the context of new leadership approaches and new administrative and supervisory theories. These tasks provide indirect influence on instructional effectiveness. Finally, supervision of instruction as part of educational leadership is the responsibility of many in the school and district. Certainly superintendents are in a strategic position to ensure that instruction receives priority attention. Educational leaders at all levels must assume responsibility to initiate, support, encourage, and assess school effectiveness and instructional improvement. To do so in a school system, administration and supervision must be integrated.

REFERENCES

Achilles, C. M. (1987). A vision of better schools. In W. Greenfield (Ed.). *Instructional leadership: Concepts, issues and controversies* (pp. 17–37). Boston: Allyn and Bacon.

Alfonso, R. J., Firth, G., & Neville, R. (1981). *Instructional supervision: A behavior system* (2nd ed.). Boston: Allyn and Bacon.

Almanza, H. K. (1980). *Plummer: A study of in-service education programming associate with high innovative programs in selected elementary schools.* Unpublished doctoral dissertation, University of Texas at Austin, Austin, TX.

Bates, R. J. (1987). Corporate culture, schooling, and educational administration. *Educational Administration Quarterly, 23*(4), 79–115.

Berry, G. D. (1987). *A study of instructional leadership competencies and in-service education programs associated with selected successful elementary schools.* Unpublished doctoral dissertation, University of Texas at Austin.

Blumberg, A. & Blumberg, P. (1985). *The school superintendent.* New York: Teachers College Press.

Bolman, L. G. & Deal, T. E. (1992). Leading and managing: Effects of context, culture, and gender. *Educational Administration Quarterly, 28*(3), 314–329.

Bossert, S. (1988). School effects. In N. J. Boyan (Ed.). *Handbook of research in educational administration* (pp. 341–352). White Plains, NJ: Longman.

Bossert, S., Dwyer, D., Rowen, B., & Lee, G. (1982). The instructional management role of the principal. *Educational Administration Quarterly, 18*(3), 34–64.

Bradley, L. G. (1993). *Total quality management for schools.* Pennsylvania: Technamic Publishing Company, Inc.

Brookover, W. B. & Lezotte, L. W. (1977). *Change in school characteristics coincident with changes in student achievement.* Michigan: College of Urban Development, Michigan State University (ERIC Document Reproduction Service No. ED 181 005).

Bruce, R. E. & Grimsley, E. E. (1987). *Readings in educational supervision* (Vol. 2). Arlington, VA: ASCD.

Castetter, W. B. (1981). *The personnel function in educational administration* (3rd ed.). New York: Macmillan.

Cawelti, G. (1982). Tracing the effective school administrator. *Educational Leadership, 39*(5), 324–329.

Chubb, J. & Moe, T. (1990). *Politics, markets, and America's schools.* Washington, D.C.: Bruskings Insitute.

Costa, A. L. & Garmston, R. J. (1994). *Cognition coaching: A foundation for renaissance school.* Norwood, MA: Christopher-Gordon Publishing, Inc.

Covey, S. R. (1989). *The labels of highly effective people.* New York: Simon & Schuster.

Crowson, R. L. (1987). The local school district superintendency: A puzzling administrative role. *Educational Administration Quarterly, 23*(5), 49–69.

Cuban, L. (1994). Muddled reasoning will limit standard impact. *Educational Leadership, 9*(2), 8.

Deming, W. E. (1993). *The new economics for industry, government, and education.* Cambridge, MA: Massachusetts Institute of Technology.

Downey, C. J., Frase, L. E., & Peters, J. J. (1994). *The quality of education challenge.* Thousand Oaks, CA: Corwin Press, Inc.

Duckworth, K. (1983). Specifying determents of teacher and principal work: A descriptive study. *Journal of Educational Administration, 18*(1), 5–26.

Edmonds, R. R. (1982). Programs of school improvement: An overview. *Educational Leadership, 40*, 4–11.

Fireston, W. A. & Wilson, B. L. (1985). Using bureaucracy and culture linkages to improve instruction: The principal's contribution. *Educational Administration Quarterly, 21*(2), 7–30.

Fullan, M. G. (1991). *The new meaning of educational change.* New York: Teachers College Press.

Getzels, J. W., Lephen, J. M., & Campbell, R. F. (1968). *Educational administration as a social process.* New York: Harper & Row.

Glass, T. E. (1992). *The study of the American school superintendency.* Arlington, VA: American Association of School Administrators.

Glickman, C. D. (1985). *Supervision and instruction: A developmental approach.* Boston, MA: Allyn & Bacon.

Glickman, C. D. (Ed.). (1992). *Supervision in transaction.* Arlington, VA: ASCD.

Goodlad, J. I. (1978). Educational leadership: Toward the third era. *Educational Leadership, 35*, 322–331.

Gordon, S. P. (1992). Paradigms, transition, and the new supervision. *Journal of Curriculum and Supervision, 8*(1), 62–76.

Griffin, G. (1994). The superintendent's impact in school effectiveness: Profiles of six school districts. *Spectrum: Journal of School Research and Information, 12*(4), 20–27.

Griffiths, D. E. (1988). Administrative theory. In N. J. Boyan (Ed.). *Handbook of research on educational administration* (pp. 27–51). New York: Longman, Inc.

Hallinger, P. & Murphy, J. (1987). Instructional leadership in the school context. In W. Greenfield (Ed.). *Instructional leadership: Concepts, issues, and controversies* (pp. 179–203). Boston, MA: Allyn & Bacon.

Harris, B. M. (1985). *Supervisory behavior in education* (3rd ed.). New Jersey: Prentice-Hall.

Harris, B., Nolan, E., Lovels, J., & Cartee, D. (1992). Professionalizing the profession: Evolving a multi-site rational executive development center. *Educational Management and Administration, 29*(1), 58–64.

Harris, B. M. & Wilson, L. (1991). Instructional leadership specification for school executives: A preliminary validation study. *Journal of Personal Evaluation in Education, 5*(8), 21–30.

Heck, R. G. (1992). Principals' instructional leadership and school performance: Implication for policy development. *Educational Evaluation and Policy Analysis, 14*(1), 22–34.

Ho, W. R. (1992). *The study of relationships between institutional staffing competence, superintendent and selected personnel practices.* Unpublished doctoral dissertation, The University of Texas at Austin, Austin, TX.

Hord, S. E. (1990). *An investigation of institutional leadership perceptions among district level executives.* Unpublished doctoral dissertation, The University of Texas at Austin, Austin, TX.

Hoy, W. K. (1982). Recent developments in theory and research. *Educational Administration Quarterly, 18*(3), 1–11.

Hoyle, J., English, F., & Steffy, B. (1985). *Skills for successful school leaders.* Arlington, VA: American Association of School Administrators.

Huberman, M. & Miles, M. (1984). *Innovation up close.* New York: Plenum.

Joyce, B. & Showers, B. (1988). *Student achievement through staff development.* White Plains, NY: Longman, Inc.

Kleine-Kracht, P. (1993). Inherent instructional leadership: An administrator's choice. *Educational Administration Quarterly, 29*(2), 187–212.

Knezek, D. C. (1993). *A task analysis profiling the instructional leadership role of the assistant superintendent for instruction: White-layer school district in Texas.* Unpublished doctoral dissertation, The University of Texas at Austin, Austin, TX.

Levin, D. & Eubanks, E. (1989). *Site-based management: Engine for reform or pysidreen?* Unpublished manuscript.

Louis, K. (1989). The role of the school district in school improvement. In M. Holmes, K. Leithum, & D. Musella (Eds.). *Educational policy for effective schools* (pp. 145–167). Toronto: OISE Press.

Lunenberg, F. C. & Ornstein, A. C. (1991). *Educational administration: Concepts and practices.* California: Wadsworth, Inc.

McGregor, D. (1960). *The human side of enterprise.* New York: McGraw-Hill

Murphy, J. & Hallenger, P. (1988). Characteristics of instructionally effective school districts. *Journal of Educational Research, 8*(31), 175–181.

Naisbett, J. (1994). *Global paradox.* New York: Easton Press.

National Education Association Department of Superintendence. (1938). *The superintendent surveys supervision* (8th yearbook). Washington, D.C.: National Education Association.

Nulty, P. (1987). The economy of the 1990s: How managers will manage. *Fortune, 115*, 47–50.

Oliva, P. (1993). *Supervision for today's schools* (4th ed.). New York: Longman.

Ouchi, W. (1981). *Theory Z: How American business can meet the Japanese challenge.* Reading, MA: Addison-Wesley.

Pajak, E. (1989). *Identification of supervisiory proficiencies project.* Arlington, VA: ASCD.

Pajak, E. (1990). *Dimensions of supervision.* Arlington, VA: ASCD.

Pajak, E. (1993a). *Approaches to clinical supervision: Alternatives for empowering instruction.* Norwood, MA: Christopher-Gordon Publishers, Inc.

Pajak, E. (1993b). Changes and continuity in supervision and leadership. In G. Cawelti (Ed.). *Challenges and achievement of American education* (pp. 158–186). Arlington, VA: ASCD.

Patterson, J. L. (1993). *Leadership for tomorrow's schools.* Alexandria, VA: ASCD.

Peters, T. J. & Waterman, R. H. (1984). *In search of excellence: Lessons from America's best-run companies.* New York: Warner.

Peterson, K. D. (1987). Administrative control and instructional leadership. In W. Gwenfield (Ed.). *Instructional leadership: Concept, issues, and controversies* (pp. 139–152). Newton, MA: Allyn & Bacon.

Pitner, N. J. (1988). The study of administrator effects and effectiveness. In N. J. Boyan (Ed.). *Handbook of research on educational administration* (pp. 99–122). White Plains, NY: Longman.

Pitner, N. J. & Ogawa, R. T. (1981). Organizational leadership: The case of the superintendent. *Educational Administration Quarterly, 17*, 45–65.

Rakkin, P. R. (Ed.). (1935). Leadership in instruction. Commission on instructional leadership. Department of superintendence. Washington, D.C.: National Education Association.

Rethinking work. (1994). *Business Week*, October, 74–117.

Rorer, J. G. (1943). Principals of denveration supervision. *Teacher College Record, 44*(5), 374–375.

Rowan, B. (1982). Instructional management in historical perspectives: Evidence on differentiation in school districts. *Educational Administration Quarterly, 28*(1), 43–59.

Sashkin, M. & Huddle, G. (1986). *A synthesis of job analysis research on the job of the school principal.* Unpublished manuscript, Office of Educational Research and Improvement, Washington, D.C.

Schlechty, P. C. (1990). *Schools for the 21st century: Leadership imperatives for educational reform.* San Francisco, CA: Jossey-Bass.

Sears, J. B. (1950). *The nature of the administrative process.* New York: McGraw-Hill.

Senge, P. M., Kleener, A., Roberts, C., Ross, R., & Smith, B. (1994). *The fifth discipline handbook.* New York: Doubleday.

Senge, P. M. (1990). *The fifth discipline: The art and practice of the learning organization.* New York: Currency-Doubleday.

Sergiovanni, T. J. & Starratt, R. J. (1993). *Supervision: A redefinition* (5th ed.). New York: McGraw-Hill.

Smith, W. F. & Andrews, R. L. (1989). *Instructional leadership: How principals make a difference.* Arlington, VA: ASCD.

Spears, H. (1953). *Improving the supervision of instruction.* New York: Prentice Hall.

Sulfani, S. (1987). *AASA guidelines for the preparation of school administrators: Do they represent the important job behaviors of superintendents?* Unpublished doctoral dissertation, The University of Texas at Austin, Austin, TX.

The American School Superintendency 30th Yearbook. (1952). Washington, D.C.: Author.

The Superintendent as instructional leader. (1957). AASA 35th Yearbook. Washington, D.C.: American Association of School Superintendents.

Waite, D. (1993, April). *Novice supervisors' understanding of supervision.* Paper presented at the annual meeting of the American Educational Research Association, Atlanta, GA.

Walberg, H. J. (1984). Improving the productivity of America's schools. *Educational Leadership, 41*(8), 19–27.

Wan, Y. (1991). *Instructional leadership competencies: Self-estimated capabilities and importance as perceived by executive-level educators.* Unpublished doctoral dissertation, University of Texas at Austin.

Waterman, R. H., Jr. (1990). *Adhocracy: The power to change.* New York: W. W. Norton.

Weick, K. E. (1976). Educational organizations as loosely coupled systems. *Administrative Science Quarterly, 21*(1), 1–19.

Wissler, D. F. & Ortiz, F. I. (1988). *The superintendent's leadership in school reform.* New York: Falmer Press.

Willower, D. J. (1988). Synthesis and projections. In N. J. Boyan (Ed.). *Handbook of research on educational administration* (pp. 729–45). White Plains, NY: Longman, Inc.

Wilson, R. E. (1960). *The modern school superintendent: His prejudices and practices.* New York: Harper & Brothers Publishing.

Wirt, T. M. (1991). The missing link in instructional leadership. In P. W. Kurston, & P. P. Zodhiates (Eds.). *Advances in educational administration* (pp. 159–189). Greenwich, CT: JAI Press Inc.

Zeigler, H., Kehes, E., & Reisman, J. (1985). *City managers and school superintendents.* New York: Praeger.

SUPERVISION AND INSTRUCTIONAL DEVELOPMENT

Keith A. Acheson

UNIVERSITY OF OREGON

Mohammed Shamsher

BRITISH COLUMBIA TEACHERS ASSOCIATION

Neil Stephenson Smith

MALASPINA UNIVERSITY COLLEGE

This chapter is devoted to the consideration of Supervision and Instructional Development. The ERIC Thesaurus defines supervision as:

"the process or function of directing and evaluating activities in progress, and of providing leadership and guidance to the employees or staff involved."

The same source defines instructional development as:

"systematic approach to design, production, evaluation, and utilization of instructional systems and programs, including the management of these components."

To examine the research on directing and evaluating; providing leadership and guidance to staff; designing and producing, utilizing and implementing, managing, and evaluating instructional programs is more than can be captured in one chapter. Doing all these at once (in practice, as well as in research) comes close to what is being called "restructuring." Inclusion of the word "supervision" leads to staff development as one outcome for all of the above.

One might consider the use of supervision processes within instructional development, for example, frequent observation and feedback for teachers who are implementing a new curriculum. Another possibility is to look at instructional development within the field of supervision, that is, programs of instruction that prepare persons to be supervisors.

We decided to analyze several case studies in recent years that have combined elements from all or most of the above, with the expectation of finding patterns that can guide future research and development efforts in these areas. The instructional programs that we have chosen are not curricula for students in schools but programs for teachers that incorporate supervision, coaching, mentoring, or collegial observation and collaboration as essential elements in the mix.

A look at restructuring staff development for teachers in schools and colleges in North America can anticipate a number of desirable outcomes—teacher empowerment, collaboration, school-based management, cooperative learning (by teachers, not just students), shared leadership, and peer consultation. The programs we have chosen in each case have operated for several years, and, although there is inevitable diversity in their development and application, our concentration is on similarities that can be categorized and analyzed. There are increasing numbers of experiments and demonstrations that provide examples of the kinds of programs that might work. We shall describe only a few for which there is a base of research evidence.

RESEARCH AND PRACTICE

The tenuous relationship between educational research and educational practice has often been noted. One of the most important reasons why the impact of research on education seems so haphazard is that educational research is primarily engaged in a search for variables that *may* relate to improved outcomes, whereas educational innovations are primarily searching for models that *work*.

The search for relationships among conceptually distinct variables is, of course, the hallmark of quantitative research in education. We study, for example, the effects on student achievement of such variables as time on task, level of questioning, teacher enthusiasm, and use of advance organizers. Each of these variables can be described clearly in a few words, and each has its own research literature and conceptual basis. The information produced in such studies is often useful to practitioners, and can contribute substantially to the knowledge presented in educational psychology and other preservice and in-service courses.

Yet systematic, wide-scale change in educational practice usually comes about in a different way, through the adoption (and inevitable adaptation) of models. Models are instructional programs or school organizational schemes composed of many individual variables that may or may not be closely related to one another, and may or may not be derived from research. Slavin (1990) describes these as *complex models*. Programs such as Microteaching (Gage), DISTAR (Becker & Carnine, 1980), Assertive Discipline (Canter & Canter, 1976), Man, a Course of Study (Bruner, 1966), Another Set of Eyes (ASCD, 1987), and the Program for Quality Teaching (Smith & Acheson, 1991) would fit the category described by Slavin as complex models. These complex models are very different from one another, but they have several characteristics in common. One is that they all include quite different elements; none of them could be described in a few sentences. Another is that they all have well-developed training procedures for teachers and, in most cases, detailed training manuals and instructional materials. The provisions for supervision are less clear in some (perhaps most) models.

Most systematic, widespread change in educational practice involves implementation of models, not variables. For example, educational psychology texts for two decades recommended advance organizers, but their actual use in practice was probably rare until the widespread adoption of Hunter's Instructional Theory into Practice (ITIP) program. The effectiveness of the use of group contingencies was well established by the mid-1970s and they are often seen in practice as part of Canter and Canter's Assertive Discipline program.

This discussion is not intended to suggest that the adoption of models has uniformly positive results. Many models are ineffective or even counter-productive, and many more have never been adequately researched. Nor do we suggest that models tend to be faithfully implemented and maintained over time. What we do suggest is that when school districts are serious about innovation, they most often implement models, not variables. Even when they are convinced on the basis of variables, what they implement is models. When schools are concerned about teacher expectations, they may implement the Teacher Expectation and Student Achievement (TESA) model (Martin, 1973). When they are concerned about higher-order thinking skills, they may implement a thinking skills program (deBono, 1994) or other specific models (Adams, 1989). There is a problem in this state of affairs.

Although educational research on variables is, in the aggregate, quite good, educational research on models is seriously lacking in quantity as well as quality. There are many reasons for this. Perhaps the main reason is that the academic reward system clearly favors research on variables, because

research on variables builds theory and theory is the hallmark of serious scholarly inquiry. Most models are researched by their developers or other strong advocates. No matter how carefully and conservatively they actually do their research, this fact always places their findings under suspicion. At a minimum, anyone who has invested much time and money in development of a model, it is argued, can be expected to present evaluation results in the most positive light.

A characteristic of educational innovation is that each solution for a problem about instruction or a problem about school organization creates its own problems. Solving these new problems makes the difference between success or failure of the innovation. For example, individualized instruction was based on the well-supported observation that students learn best when taught at their own level and pace, but often failed because in operation the application of the principle reduced time for direct instruction by the teacher and introduced much procedural time and down time for students. Individualization, in solving the problem of adapting to individual differences, creates problems of time management, motivation, and lack of direct instruction which must be solved to make the program effective. When these problems are solved, individualized models can be successful (Slavin, Madden, & Leavy, 1984), but the solution may not have anything to do with individualized instruction per se.

Another problem of implementing variables without regard for the context is that the active ingredients are unclear. For example, increasing time on task is a sound principle, yet it apparently matters a great deal how time is increased. The most straightforward method of increasing time, adding to the school day, has been ineffective. More promising have been studies of complex models for improving classroom management skills (Everson, Weade, Green, & Crawford, 1985).

Whatever one believes about the relative utility of models versus variables as the basis for instructional or organizational innovation, it is clear that there is a demand for models among school districts, teachers, and other innovators. Therefore, it is a worthwhile goal of educational research to study and improve the quality of a model offered to potential users and policy makers.

Complex, coherent models provide one direct means of having research impact on practice. The programs we have selected for analysis can be subsumed under the label, "Peer Consultation." Ideally, research should identify the conditions under which a program such as Peer Consultation would work.

PEER CONSULTATION COMPARED TO RELATED SCHOOL PRACTICES

We define peer consultation as a school-based process in which teachers work with colleagues to provide one another with descriptive feedback and discourse about observed teaching for the purposes of enhancing their professional growth and organizational development. To clarify what this means, peer consultation can be related to educational processes that share similar characteristics.

This section compares peer consultation with three other educational processes: team teaching, clinical supervision, and mentoring. Each has similar characteristics but is designed to generate different outcomes.

Different peer consultation types can be found operating in school systems in North America today. In the next section, the types will be analyzed on a continuum that runs from those that are prescriptive and use "peer coaching" as a means of implementing prescribed instructional practices in the classroom to those whose outcomes are determined by teachers who use them collaboratively to achieve personally defined outcomes. The goals, content, and implementation patterns of the respective programs will be compared, as well as the ways in which they have been implemented.

Mentoring, team teaching, clinical supervision, peer supervision, and peer coaching all share certain attributes with peer consultation. The attitude that "there is nothing new under the sun" always holds some truth, especially in education. In this spirit, one might say that peer consultation simply represents a new combination of practices that have been a common part of the educational landscape for decades. This section and the next should illuminate similarities and differences among the various practices that involve teachers working with teachers.

Team Teaching

The first of these practices to be analyzed is team teaching. Reaching its peak in the late sixties, having teachers share classroom teaching responsibilities was tried as a way to enrich instruction, reduce isolation, and increase teacher autonomy. Meyers and Cohen (1971) studied the degree to which these expectations were met. They found that teachers experienced increased communication with colleagues on task-related issues and that professional satisfaction increased slightly, but teacher autonomy in the areas of decision-making remained fairly unchanged. Charters (1979) found that teachers in team teaching situations experienced a significant drop in teacher autonomy in making decisions, both at the level of classroom instruction and at the school level. He also found that there was no change in the level of professional satisfaction experienced by teachers. Simply put, team teaching reduced isolation but at the expense of autonomy.

Martin (1975) took a different approach by studying the interactive processes of partners. The skills used in problem-solving between successful team teachers were found to be very sophisticated. In partnerships that functioned well, a surprising number of complex strategies were used to solve day-to-day problems.

These studies of team teaching reveal the host of complications borne in attempts to bring teachers together in productive working relationships. Although challenging and rewarding for some, team teaching took its toll on others. It remains unclear whether different personality types, teaching styles, communication patterns, or organizational factors were the principal problems precipitating a reduction of teacher autonomy and gradual attrition among those who attempted team teaching.

What is the relationship between peer consultation and team teaching? First, peer consultation is a way to help teachers pursue common professional goals. It is also a problem-solving process colleagues can use in an environment of reduced isolation (as is team teaching). However, peer consultants are not responsible for ongoing functions of planning, implementing, and evaluating instruction, whereas team teachers are. Team teachers work together with students for up to six hours per day; peer consultants are only involved with colleagues in intermittent work focused specifically on the colleague's teaching.

This raises the question does peer consultation reduce or increase teachers' autonomy in making decisions that affect their work? Further, what kinds of interactions take place when the process does help teachers reach their goals?

Clinical Supervision

Another practice introduced in the 1960s and currently practiced in many North American schools (and other parts of the world) is clinical supervision. In clinical supervision, the aim is to help teachers solve their instructional problems. Although it is most often initiated by the supervisor, the teacher is invited to select specific areas of instruction in a pre-lesson conference. The supervisor observes the teaching, gathers specific data, then provides the teacher with objective information relating to the selected areas of interest. The supervisor's role is to facilitate the teacher's self-evaluation to promote instructional improvement.

The greatest obstacle blocking the potential success of a clinical supervisor is that the information emerging from a series of "observations" is usually tied to the teacher's evaluation report. It is not surprising that teachers' general sensitivity to the process of evaluation dampens the likelihood of risk-taking or instructional experimentation during such observations. It is only the brave, or naive, teacher who strays into the teacher evaluation process without a failsafe lesson to satisfy the evaluator. Experimenting with new techniques or strategies while being observed by a supervisor is treading heavily through a pedagogical minefield, given that the supervisor will soon be writing a summative evaluation.

Teacher-evaluation practices are also fraught with problems. One constraint is that they are designed primarily to serve the need for public accountability and administrative personnel decisions rather than to serve the needs of teacher development. Like a large net dragged through the ranks of teachers to snag only the lowest performers, clinical supervision, when tied to the summative teacher-evaluation processes, has caused resentment among teachers, particularly those whose unconventional styles have caused them to be caught up in the net.

Robinson (1979, 1983) and Barber (1985) in separate studies of teacher-evaluation concluded that, even in districts using merit pay ostensibly requiring highly refined teacher-evaluation systems, practices were subjective, poorly conceived, or poorly administered. Barber further suggested that the most significant reason for the failure of teacher-evaluation programs involves the perceived use of aversive control. Most teachers see any form of control initiated through evaluation systems, both reward and punishment, as aversive. Hence, they often respond with passive resistance or outright defiance to what they perceive as unfair control measures.

Administrators charged with the responsibility of evaluating teachers often resort to focusing on functions of teaching that are most easily evaluated. Such procedures are most often brief, superficial, and "pro forma" affairs (Stiggins & Duke, 1987). Attention to motivation, professional involvement, concern for children, and creativity is often forsaken in pursuit of simplicity and measurability. Teachers compelled to participate in such evaluation schemes become increasingly cynical with each new "pilot project" in teacher evaluation.

Although clinical supervision is a process intended to shift the focus of attention from the evaluator's subjective view to the teacher's perspective, the ubiquitous summative evaluation report forces the evaluator's judgment and bias, thus cancelling the possibilities for objective analysis by the teacher. The final written report inevitably represents the evaluator's judgments based upon personally defined criteria. At the root of the problem is the fact that the two goals, organizational accountability and teacher professional growth, are mutually incompatible:

Accountability systems strive to affect school quality by protecting students from incompetent teachers. However, because nearly all teachers are at least minimally competent, the accountability system directly affects only a very few teachers who are not competent (Stiggins & Duke, 1987).

In their study of 32 teacher-evaluation programs that were using clinical supervision, Stiggins and Duke (1987, p. 35) noted the frequency with which key characteristics of clinical supervision were employed. They found that pre-conferences (88%), observations (100%), post-conferences (100%), and action planning following the evaluation (88%) were taking place, which indicated that people were following the steps in the general model. However, there was little evidence that anyone in the process was promoting self-evaluation, which is one of the central aims of clinical supervision. Teachers reported that administrators controlled most of the evaluative functions. Moreover, the study revealed that the intended relationship between teacher evaluation and teacher growth was rarely achieved. Whereas most administrators believed that their practices of teacher evaluation promoted professional growth, most of the teachers who were surveyed believed the opposite. Clinical supervision was considered successful only in schools where the supervisor had exceptional skills and sensitivity in communication and classroom-observation skills and had cultivated healthy relationships with the teachers.

Many educators have suggested that teachers may be in a better situation to gain benefits from clinical supervision without the intervention of administrators. Teachers would be able then to use the process with one another (e.g., see Acheson & Gall 1987, p. 194; Stiggins & Duke 1987). Stark and Lowther (1984, p. 7), in a survey of approximately 100 teachers, reported that 89% of the teachers indicated that self-assessment was clearly the most appropriate method of evaluation.

What, then, is the relationship between peer consultation and clinical supervision? Is peer consultation merely a by-product of clinical supervision? Proponents disagree. They state that peer consultation begins with the technical analysis of teaching found in clinical supervision, but that peer consultation goes further by emphasizing the nurturing of peer relationships that support and foster the mutual analysis and understanding of teaching. In the Program for Quality Teaching implementation design, for example, any formal connection to teacher evaluation is shunned.

Is it conceivable that the two could be married in some safe union that would not threaten the inherent virtues of one or the other? Clinical supervision, in its classic form conceived by Cogan (1973) and Goldhammer (1969), aims at teacher self-criticism and self-evaluation. If at the first level teachers express the desire to become masters of their own professional fate, it behooves them to move to the next level of taking action and being willing to accept the feedback necessary to engage in meaningful reflection on their practice. For most, this kind of reflective process represents a giant step away from everyday teaching practice. The proponents of peer consultation believe that it offers a structure in which teacher self-evaluation can safely happen. Subsequent chapters will chronicle the attempts in the Program for Quality Teaching (PQT) to make peer consultation successful.

Mentoring

Next to be reviewed is the practice of mentoring. The word mentor originally meant trusted guide and counsellor, and a mentor-protege relationship implied a deep and meaningful association (Galvez-Hjornevick, 1986). One example of teacher-teacher mentoring is found in an extensive program in California (California Teacher-Mentor Program, 1987), which was spearheaded by the state superintendent and supported by a budget of 50–million dollars in 1986–1987. In the program, a teacher entering a new context of teaching (for example, a first-year teacher, or a teacher assuming a different assignment) is matched to the knowledge and wisdom of a more experienced person—the mentor. The mentor's professional knowledge and practice become the reference criteria against which the progress of the mentored teacher is judged. The program is typically centrally initiated, administered, and funded.

The main difference between mentoring and peer consultation is that the former tends to position one person as the expert and the other as the recipient of knowledge. Operating from an expert orientation, mentoring starkly contrasts with peer consultation's emphasis on reciprocity or mutuality.

To summarize the three processes just reviewed: team teaching, clinical supervision, and mentoring employ practices similar to those in peer consultation, but seek outcomes that are essentially different. Team teaching aims at a full-time process of collaborative decision-making between teaching partners. Clinical supervision is often associated with formal evaluation. Mentoring involves an expert working with a person less experienced. Peer consultation involves colleagues ("equals") working periodically and collaboratively to observe and give one another feedback on teaching.

Peer Consultation

There is confusion about peer consultation because of lack of understanding about several different collegial processes currently in use. These procedures employ peers (that is, fellow teachers) as observers, mentors, coaches, or collaborators. The processes are often lumped together as "peer coaching," an easy, catchy term. Unfortunately, such wholesale grouping precludes critical analysis by educators in regard to substantial differences in these various practices.

At its most basic level, peer consultation is a strategy for teachers to exchange knowledge, insights, or understandings, and study the practice of their own teaching. However, this description broadly includes radically different programs that vary according to the interpretation of the architects, implementers, and practitioners.

As educators, we need to discriminate intelligently among different peer consultation types. Such discrimination has not been prominent in the literature and there is little evidence that practitioners understand the not-so-subtle differences. Hence, what follows will offer a comparison of different types with the hope that this analysis will reduce the confusion and misunderstanding about the various options. After some fundamental distinctions are described among four major thrusts, each is considered in more detail.

Major Distinctions

The main differences among peer consultation practices can be addressed by four groups of questions:

1. Who initiated the program and who controls it? Was it mandated from district administration, or through decisions made by democratic vote at the building level, or was it a teacher-initiated process?
2. Are the program outcomes "prescribed"? Is there an explicit intention to adopt a specific model of instruction? Is the model of instruction imported from external sources, or is it influenced by the teachers' knowledge and research of their own teaching?
3. From what psychological theory of learning and human development does the program operate—from a behaviorist, cognitivist, or humanist foundation?
4. By what criteria does the program evaluate its success? Is it evaluated in terms of student achievement, the degree of teachers' behavioral (instructional) change, or by assessing what it has done to support teacher professionalism?

These questions separate programs that we call "peer coaching" from those that can be called "peer consultation" in the sense of colleagues working together on what someone herself or himself wants to change or improve, *not* what someone else wants.

To really decide what the architects had in mind one would have to know them as persons, and know their styles of operating, communicating, investigating, and coping. We don't know that about all of them, but we know some of them and are willing to hypothesize about others.

So, using the questions listed above, an investigation of the literature, and personal experience in the field as practitioners and researchers, here's what we see. The discussion begins with an examination of the purposes and goals as stated by the architects of each of the types, noting possible dis-

crepancies between these intents and those of trainers in the field and also the teachers who are actively engaged in classroom practice. Paradoxically, those who implement new ideas in the field often interpret them more narrowly and literally than the principal architects intended. The architects' theories are often more "liberal" and "broad-sighted" than are the practices one sees at the school level.

The last part of the analysis examines what the research says about the effectiveness of each of the peer consultation processes, that is, how well they actually achieve their purposes as stated.

Four Types of Peer Consultation There are several peer consultation processes operating in school systems today that roughly fit our generic definition. Within each of these types there are additional differences in purpose, theory, and intended outcomes. To assist in the analysis of the predominant types, we shall use the following categories:

1. Peer Coaching with focus on (a) Principles of Teaching or (b) Teacher Effectiveness.
2. Peer Coaching with focus on Models of Teaching
3. Peer Consultation with focus on (a) Instructional Finetuning and Reflection or (b) Reflective Practice and Innovation
4. Peer Consultation with focus on Organizational Development

The types considered in this analysis range from processes that concentrate on learning and developing specific instructional skills (type one) to processes that emphasize developing inter-colleague communications and problem-solving systems (type four). The first two types refer to their procedure as "coaching," which, as the name implies, engages teachers in helping colleagues to finetune specific skills or strategies of teaching. The last two, called peer "consultation" for our purposes, are less technically oriented in terms of their demand for a prescribed classroom outcome.

It is helpful to arrange the types on a continuum. At one end are the "peer coaching" types that prescribe scientific or technical approaches to instruction as means to school improvement. At the other end of the continuum are the "peer consultation" types that emphasize the development of social-interactive relationships and reflective processes designed to improve teachers' knowledge and understanding of their work. Another way of interpreting the continuum is to relate it to teachers' autonomy in instructional decision-making, moving from less autonomy on the right toward increased autonomy on the left (as shown in Figure 32.1). Two of the major types have been broken into subcategories in order to accommodate examples that illustrate variations within the main themes.

TYPE 1(A): PEER COACHING WITH A FOCUS ON PRINCIPLES OF TEACHING This category can be characterized by a program called Instructional Theory into Practice (ITIP), implemented in the Napa Valley in 1982. It was developed as a comprehensive system of instruction, based on a series of instructional principles drawn from a synthesis of teacher effectiveness literature by Madeline Hunter. The program promotes the practice of combinations of specific teaching behaviors to

Types of Peer Consultation

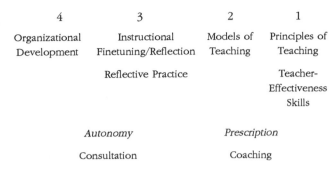

FIGURE 32.1.

be applied on the basis of established theoretical principles. Peer coaching, initially performed by external consultants, then by teachers, is employed as the central vehicle through which teachers learn to apply the system in their teaching.

TYPE 1(B): PEER COACHING WITH A FOCUS ON TEACHER EFFECTIVENESS SKILLS The main purpose of programs in this category is to build a bridge between teacher effectiveness research and the classroom. An example is Teacher Effectiveness Training (TET), led by Carol Cummings, designed to have teachers coach teachers to acquire specific instructional skills that have been identified through research as effective in promoting student learning. TET seems to pay less formal attention to theoretical principles which underpin the instructional skills than the Hunter-based program (ITIP). The implementation of TET also places stronger emphasis on the peer coaching system.

Peer *coaching* in the first two categories fosters relationships in which teachers are expected to be expert critics, guiding colleagues toward the adoption or refinement of specific teaching skills. The word "coaching" is aptly used in these programs, as it implies judging and assisting another's ability in specific skills, but does not pretend to advance the image of self-evaluation and critical reflection in teaching. Such programs are often grounded in behaviorist theory, implemented through a top-down (central office) style, and are evaluated by standards that are quantifiable, either through teacher performance behaviors or student achievement on standardized tests.

TYPE 2: PEER COACHING WITH A FOCUS ON MODELS OF TEACHING "Coaching to Models" differs from the two examples in Type 1 in that it begins by presenting an eclectic orientation to a broad spectrum of teaching possibilities. Once teachers have identified a specific model, however, the coaching function as conceived by Joyce and Showers takes on the characteristics of Type 1 programs. The coaching process becomes a fundamentally directive activity, with one teacher providing criticism of another's teaching in relation to their ability to apply the steps of a specific model of teaching. Abbreviated teacher in-service training sessions may shift the teaching partner's role to that of observing new teaching models in another's classroom without extensive interaction either prior to, or

after, the observation. Attaining fidelity with the model seems to be the central goal. With communication between colleagues reduced, this method becomes more of a peer *teaching* model than a model of consultation. In terms of supervision styles, it is didactic and direct as opposed to heuristic and indirect.

TYPE 3(A): PEER CONSULTATION (OR OBSERVATION) WITH A FOCUS ON FINETUNING AND REFLECTION Unlike the types mentioned thus far, peer observation of this type does not operate within strictly defined instructional models or skills. Rather, it focuses on professional development through the teacher's eyes, and is designed to promote opportunities for general reflection and refinement of teaching. Two archetypal programs are Jean Rudduck's British "Partnership Supervision" (Rudduck, 1987) and the Palatine "Teacher-2-Teacher" program in Illinois (Berlin & others, 1987). Rudduck states that this process is to be used exclusively for professional development among peers.

TYPE 3(B): PEER CONSULTATION WITH A FOCUS ON REFLECTIVE PRACTICE AND INNOVATION This type combines a number of the elements of the foregoing examples and is best exemplified by the Program for Quality Teaching (PQT) of the British Columbia Teachers' Federation. First, it employs the technical functions of analysis of teaching found in clinical supervision and peer observation types. It combines this with the perspective underlying the "models of teaching" type—that an eclectic approach to teaching is best. Finally, it relies upon the development of teachers' critical self-analysis of their personal understanding of curriculum and instruction and their roles as teachers. Collegiality and reciprocity are seen as important support systems. In direct contrast to the examples given thus far, this type places more emphasis on the processes of building collaborative working relationships among peers, and less on learning a system of specific instructional skills.

TYPE 4: PEER CONSULTATION WITH A FOCUS ON ORGANIZATIONAL DEVELOPMENT The final type to be considered is Organizational Development (OD). At first the inclusion of OD may appear somewhat incongruous, given that its primary focus is on group development and not on instructional development. It is included in our typology because it concentrates on what may be one of the most salient aspects of peer consulting—the development of productive interactions between teachers, problem-solving, and group decision-making for the purpose of promoting a healthy school climate for change. OD "teams" act either as peer consultants within their own schools or in the schools of other colleagues.

OD shares the basic principle espoused within all types of peer consultation, that the key source of school change and development rests in the strength of educators at the school level, and that teachers are in the best position to facilitate and negotiate the professional well-being and growth of fellow teachers. To achieve this aim, OD proponents such as Schmuck, Runkel, Fullan, and Miles suggest that healthy communications among teachers must be established before the success of specific instructional innovations can be anticipated. OD practice contrasts with all the other types reviewed in this analysis in that it emphasizes building inter-colleague and group processes and does not direct teachers toward pre-established standards or intended outcomes. It is included because of its proven track record in providing the foundational support for different school interventions and its effectiveness in improving professional relations in schools.

ANALYSIS OF PEER CONSULTATION TYPES

The first stage of examining the peer consultation types in detail involves the statement and clarification of the purposes of each. Discrepancies have arisen between the purposes as understood by those who have conceived the processes and those who are in the field acting as trainers and users of the processes. These are evident in the literature. Our investigation into the purposes of each type will disclose some of these discrepancies.

Second, a discussion of the theoretical perspectives of the principal architects will involve two levels of inquiry: (1) what are their theories about how *teachers* should learn? and (2) what are their theories about how *children* should learn? In cases where the theories are not made explicit, an attempt to interpret the theories will be made. The last part of the analysis will look at what the research says about the effectiveness of each of the peer consultation processes, that is, how well the stated purposes are achieved.

Type 1—Peer Coaching: Principles of Teaching or Teaching Effectiveness

The best known example of our first type is the Hunter-based, Instructional Theory Into Practice (ITIP) program which promotes specific teaching behaviors applied on the basis of established theoretical principles. Within this program, coaching is seen as the means for helping teachers apply the selected system of instructional skills in the context of their classrooms. Hunter does not call the Principles of Teaching a "model." However, if we accept Beaton's (1985) definition of a model as "a whole new repertoire of skills," then ITIP can be referred to as a model. Certainly it is much more than a random collection of "principles."

The Napa County implementation of the Hunter-based system has been selected as the archetype for this category because it was studied intensively by nationally recognized researchers over a four–year period using qualitative and quantitative research methods in two schools with control groups. The stated purposes or intended outcomes of the project were: (1) to develop specific teacher instructional skills based on the ITIP model, (2) to increase student engaged time in mathematics and reading, and (3) to increase student achievement scores in both math and reading (Stallings & Krassavage, 1986). The goal of the coaching process was to ensure that the instructional skills were successfully transferred to classroom practice.

The learning theory that underlies her model has been most clearly represented in Hunter's "Principles of Instruction" that derive from what she terms "the science of teaching" (1977). Based in behaviorist theory and developed from a synthesis of results from empirical studies on effective instruction, Hunter's work evolved from its foundation in the original ITIP program. The titles of some cornerstone books lend some insight into her theories of learning: *Motivation, Retention, Reinforcement,* and *Teaching for Transfer* (1979). Learning and teaching are presented as technical, rational activities that demand teachers to identify the key variables in a student's program, manipulate them to change student behaviors, and reinforce the behaviors that are desired.

The Hunter-based model for classroom instruction retains theoretical consistency when applied to the pursuit of "training" teachers in the instructional skills. The theory that guided the implementers' work in the Napa Valley project is characteristically behaviorist in its orientation. First, it follows a staff development model similar to that of Joyce and Showers (1980), the essential steps of which are: (1) introduction to theory, (2) modelling the new practice, (3) practice with feedback, and 4) on-site coaching (Stallings, 1986).

Second, and perhaps more interesting, is the fact that for the first four years the coaches in this implementation were "expert coaches" employed by the project. They were available to coach each teacher twice per month. In status, they were neither peers nor supervisors. They were entirely separate from line staff. It was thought that teachers would eventually assume the coaching roles. Joyce and Showers (1982) stressed that they believed coaching was an appropriate activity for administrators, coordinators, and supervisors. The theory of the "expert" reinforcing the correct teaching behavior, however, proved to be problematic in the fourth year of the program, when the classroom teachers were expected to assume gradually the coaching responsibilities.

During the implementation, the instructional skills training workshops were intensive, averaging 12 release days per year supported by the twice-monthly coaching sessions. Teachers were trained thoroughly in the instructional skills, but no training or preparation was provided for prospective peer coaches.

The program evaluators reported the results of the study on an annual basis. The outcomes revealed that the teachers experienced success in meeting the goals in the first three years, but in the fourth year student achievement scores in math and reading dropped to below those of the control groups (Stallings, 1986). The teachers' use of "appropriate instructional skills" (Robbins, 1987) also dropped significantly in the fourth year. Teachers reverted to former teaching processes, and the anticipated transfer of coaching responsibilities did not occur. Responses to the research reports varied.

Robbins and Wolfe (1987) defended the project by downplaying the significance of the research, noting a "stark contrast" between the quantitative and qualitative data, and stating that very positive changes had occurred in "collegiality, collaborative work, and shared responsibility for decisions in their schools." Stallings (1986) had reported that interviews and surveys indicated increased feelings of collegiality but dissatisfaction with perceived constraints of the Hunter model. Teacher "burnout" and disaffection were suggested as possible causes for the decline in student scores and teacher performance.

Hunter (1986) felt that her program had been misinterpreted and narrowly defined by the project; hence, teachers had received a distorted adaptation of her theories. Her major concern was that the Principles of Instruction, the basis of ITIP, had not been properly understood and adopted. This observation lost some impact, however, when compared with her lavish praise regarding the first three years of the project. An earlier paper (Hunter, 1976) had described teaching as a "series of decisions and the implementation of those decisions which increases the probability of intended learning." Perhaps the teachers had not been taught (or encouraged) to use the principles flexibly and were, therefore, unable to apply them within strategies of learning (other than direct, didactic ones), for example, discovery or inquiry methods. This phenomenon has not been limited to the Napa Valley, in our experience. The lack of flexibility is reinforced when evaluators use the principles as a checklist for classroom observations.

The role that coaching of teachers played in this project is difficult to separate from the model of instruction that was being advocated. Teachers were trained for the new system in a manner consistent with the way students were learning, through controlled practice, feedback, and refinement. However, this process was not used to train peer coaches. Perhaps it was assumed that coaching with a colleague would be a natural extension of the principles of instruction or a simple mimicking of the modelling of the expert coaches without need for guided practice, checking for understanding, or reinforcement.

Another example of a Type 1 program is Teacher Effectiveness Training (TET) led by Carol Cummings. It bases desired teaching outcomes on the teacher effectiveness research of recent years and places emphasis on a systematic process of peer coaching. One implementation of the program was intensively studied by university researchers in a district they called "Cragleaf" (a fictitious name). The staff development strategy can be viewed in the light of Fullan's "fidelity" model in which the instructional skills were not to be tinkered with or adapted by the practitioners at the school level.

The purpose of Cragleaf's TET program was to help teachers adopt specific instructional skills as defined in TET. The purposes of coaching were carefully conceived. Whereas the Napa Valley project initiated expert coaching to guide teachers' learning, the Cragleaf District intended to "establish a network for peer coaching both among principals in the district and teachers within schools" (Grimmett, 1986). The purposes of peer coaching were twofold. First, coaches were to help teachers learn and refine the instructional effectiveness skills. Second, coaching was seen as a process of empowering teachers by placing them in charge of their own workplace and working lives for the ultimate purpose of achieving "positive classroom and student self-concepts." Unlike the Napa Valley project, the Cragleaf designers did not assume the peer coaching process would be a self-starting, self-sustaining endeavor. It was systematically structured and peer coaches were trained in the techniques of providing feedback.

In TET, the theory underlying instructional skills and coaching skills is consistent with behaviorist principles. It concentrates on teacher-centered strategies of instruction with attention given to skill acquisition. The theory on coaching includes a unique "typology of conferencing" that includes different levels of colleague intervention. At the entry level, the observing colleague provides only descriptive or objective feedback to the partner. At what is described as the higher level, the colleague overtly judges the teacher's ability to implement the prescribed instructional patterns and skills correctly.

A program evaluation was completed three years after the project's inception (Grimmett, 1986). It concentrated more directly on the outcomes of the peer coaching process than on student outcomes. Much of the data came from structured interviews with teachers and principals. Many participants reported "improved professional competence, increased professional confidence, a growing sense of professionalism and collegiality, and a beneficial impact on students." On the other hand, many also stated that the process was "too time consuming" and required extreme effort and work at all stages, from initial planning conferences to feedback sessions. They remarked on the difficulty of establishing balanced relationships with colleagues, finding the process "threatening," and feeling "defensive." Others felt that the process was "formalized and contrived," and criticized the process of district supervisors training principals, and principals selecting teachers and engaging actively in the process as "peer" coaches.

Some teachers were concerned (as were some in Napa Valley) that the instructional skills program was constraining in its structure, with overemphasis on *direct* teaching processes. Their attitude about the coaching process, however, was different. Whereas the teachers in Napa Valley never expressed resentment about the project coaches, some teachers in the Cragleaf program felt betrayed by the fact that their principals used the same criteria as those in TET for evaluating teacher performance. When teachers had initially become involved in the program, they saw it as a different system of instructional skills that had been adopted for professional development purposes, separate from evaluation. Many resented the fact that they were having their formal evaluations based on their ability to implement the system, regardless of the situational context. Teachers were upset by the fact that some evaluators did not acknowledge the usefulness of different strategies of instruction. As one might suspect, having principals involved in "peer coaching" produced role conflicts. Some felt that it meant being both "player" and "umpire," simultaneously.

The coaching process, as in the Napa Valley project, seemed to fulfill the technical side of its stated purpose with some degree of success; teachers practiced and refined their instructional skills using the TET model. Teachers were nonetheless reluctant to commit themselves to the process, despite the fact that they had developed skills for teacher effectiveness and peer coaching. The project was impaired by problems in relationships within teams and with the administration. Teachers' statements reflected that they felt threatened by the process. A lack of trust seemed to exist between the various stakeholders. TET also suffered from the teachers' perception that it was "laid on." The initiation of the project was district dominated. No input was sought from teachers for whose benefit it was intended. It can be concluded that the program fell short of its second goal of empowering teachers through coaching.

In both ITIP and TET, teachers expressed resentment at being constrained by a model of instruction in which they felt little freedom to move. Although the theorists may suggest that Principles of Instruction (Hunter) or Teacher Effectiveness Training (Cummings) can be adapted to different methods of instruction, teachers seemed unaware of this adaptability and flexibility. This factor seems to have seriously impeded the successful implementation of instructional skills in both projects. It is difficult to sort out how much bearing the teachers' negative disposition toward the instructional program had on their acceptance of peer coaching. Coaching and instructional skills are as inseparable as "curriculum and instruction" and defy serious attempts to isolate one from the other for the purpose of analysis. The level of teacher commitment has emerged (in our view) as the primary problem which impeded successful implementation of the instructional program and peer coaching in both cases.

Type 2—Peer Coaching: Models of Teaching

The principal architects of our example for this type are Bruce Joyce and Beverly Showers, who incorporated peer coaching into their staff development model. It is based on research findings that revealed the difficulties teachers have transferring new models of teaching from in-service workshops to the classroom. It promotes a process of peer coaching that is associated not with just one model of teaching but with several.

The general theory of instruction is more eclectic than those of either Hunter or Cummings. Teachers are challenged to avoid the dogma of any one model and to develop an ever-expanding repertoire (as described in Joyce and Weil, *Models of Teaching*. This perspective, however, shares some theoretical ground with ITIP and TET in that, once the teacher chooses a model, it is adopted as an internally coherent system of instruction, to be implemented with a minimum of modification during the first several attempts at classroom application. The key difference is that teachers are encouraged to choose from a variety of models which cover a full range of learning psychologies. They also explore the theoretical underpinnings of the model. But, once a specific model is chosen, fidelity of implementation is expected. The goals of this approach to instructional development and peer coaching are:

- to study the theoretical base or the rationale of the method
- to observe persons who are relatively expert in the model
- to practice and obtain feedback in relatively protected conditions
- to coach one another as they work a new model into their repertoire, providing companionship by helping each other learn the appropriate responses to their students, and figuring out the optimal uses of the model in their courses by providing each other with ideas and feedback.

Following the observations, each teacher is encouraged to apply the model 10–30 times before a reasonable level of skill can be expected.

Additional goals of peer coaching are: (1) to build communities of teachers who continuously engage in the study of

their craft; (2) to develop a shared language and a set of common understandings necessary for the collegial study of new knowledge and skills; and (3) to provide follow-up training that is essential for acquiring new skills and strategies.

As in TET, peer coaching in this model is closely integrated with the content of the instructional program; similarly, peer "coaching" is the term employed. Some insight into the interpretation of coaching by the architects of this program comes from a quote by a university football coach: "We'll generally make you worse before we make you better . . .!" The emphasis is on "overlearning" skills until they become automatic, as in sports where there is not time to deliberate before deciding. This implies training and regimen, controlling, directing, and judging.

The research on applications of Type 2 programs, Coaching to Models, has produced mixed reviews. It indicates that peer coaching tends to facilitate transfer of training and helps to develop norms of collegiality and experimentation among teachers. Showers (1985) reported that teachers who are coached generally, but not always, practice new strategies more frequently and develop greater skill in the actual moves of a new strategy than uncoached teachers. Earlier reports also gave evidence that coached teachers used new strategies more appropriately in relation to their own instructional objectives.

Baker (1983), in a follow-up study, found that teachers who are coached by peers exhibit greater long-term retention of knowledge and skills with models and show a stronger understanding by demonstrating their abillity to apply the models in different situations with different instructional problems. However, only some of the teachers used the model when asked to do so.

Beaton (1985) looked for evidence of institutionalization of change connected with peer coaching. He found that the training programs were successful to the extent that teachers were able to perform the behaviors that they had been unable to do, yet there was little evidence that such behaviors became a part of the teachers' classroom routine. His study identified a pattern similar to that of ITIP and TET—significant short-term behavioral change, but little evidence that long-term goals have been attained.

Fullan (1987) suggests that three levels of change be considered when examining school innovations: (1) learning materials, (2) learning activities, skills, behaviors, and practices, and (3) beliefs or understandings. It appears that the examples of Type 1, ITIP and TET, met the first and second criteria on a short-term basis, but did not promote change in beliefs or understandings. Studies of Type 2 programs, Coaching to Models, have demonstrated that some shifts in teacher beliefs and understandings about teaching took place (for example, the teachers indicated they and the students liked using the models), but that long-term adoption of the models was not clearly demonstrated.

It appears that teachers experience difficulty making the transition from using the models in a rote-mechanical manner to a point where it becomes a smooth and natural part of their repertoire. The goal of "building communities of teachers who continuously engage in the study of their craft" seems not to have been corroborated by research. In the practice of peer coaching, where time is always limited, technical command of selected teaching strategies has taken priority over building group commitment and encouraging critical reflection.

Type 3—Peer Observation or Peer Consultation with Focus on Reflective Practice and Innovation

Type 3(a)- Peer Observation Peer Observation is different from previous types of coaching in that it is intended to provide teachers with skills of classroom observation to be used primarily as a source of professional reflection and refinement of teaching for self-selected kinds of professional growth. It has no formal affiliation with any specific regimen of instructional skills or models of teaching. In the types reviewed thus far, peer coaching has been closely linked to one or more specific instructional models.

One example of peer observation is Partnership Supervision (Rudduck, 1987). Although the word "supervision" usually implies evaluation, Rudduck points out that the process is designed exclusively for purposes of professional development "among peers." It borrows from the technical functions of clinical supervision; preobservation conferences, data collection, and post-observation conferences are used by the teachers to help them analyze their teaching.

Another program with almost identical purposes is the Palatine Teacher-2-Teacher (T-2-T) developed by the Palatine school district in Illinois (Berlin et al, 1987). The architects stress that there is also a political side to peer consultation, that teachers gain a sense of "empowerment" and control over their own situation. They also propose that staff development should be planned by teachers at the building level so that they will feel ownership and be more likely to participate enthusiastically. Moreover, only teachers should be involved and participation is voluntary. They do not *criticize*; they report, "this is what I saw," not "this is how it should be."

It seems clear that with these two examples passage has been achieved from what Thomas Sowell (1987) would call a "constrained" vision of what teachers are supposed to do into an "unconstrained" vision of their potential. He cites many examples—from politics, economics, law, and other domains of the social order—in which influential thinkers line up on one side or the other of this division of views about human nature. The constrained view would see teachers as limited in their capacity to be self-analytic and reflective whereas the unconstrained vision would picture them as burgeoning with potential and yearning to improve themselves as responsible professionals.

Research reports indicate that teachers welcome the process but still have fears that opening themselves to help from others may make them vulnerable to having classroom events shared indiscreetly in the faculty room. Reports of reduced feelings of isolation after a year of operation reveal the other side of that coin. To learn of the possibilities for building trust and commitment over a longer period of time, another example is helpful.

Another Type 3 example is the Program for Quality Teaching (PQT) of the British Columbia Teachers' Federation. It conducted its first training sessions in the summer of 1986

but the program had been under development within the federation for at least two years before that. We have called it *Peer Consultation: Reflective Practice and Innovation* in our typology. Because we participated in the development, implementation, and research activities of this project, we shall describe it from the perspective of participant observers rather than as dispassionate analysts.

The goals and purposes are closely related to the previous two Type 3 examples. PQT differs from the others in the emphasis that is given to the interactive process in the peer conferences. It stresses that teachers become adept in the use of non-judgmental and non-critical discourse in their work with colleagues. This is not easy for teachers who are used to evaluating, correcting, and controlling others in their work with students. The reciprocal relationship between consultants in this program, however, brings home the inherent defensiveness that teachers feel about their own efforts and, vicariously, those of colleagues.

PQT accepts the theory that any judgment of a colleague's work tends to diminish the likelihood of self-evaluation and undermines the confidence and trust necessary for a teacher to take risks in experimenting with new solutions. We have hypothesized that in other programs instructional strategies perceived as prescriptive by the participants may have inhibited their acceptance and diminished the zeal with which teachers applied them. Adding a bossy nurse to a bitter pill is unlikely to lead to continued use once the patient is released. Teachers who have been in this program for at least four years tell us that they have built a level of trust that allows them to be much more direct in giving feedback than could have been tolerated at the start.

The success or failure of a program that relies on peer coaching or peer consultation is probably more dependent on the inner workings of personal relationships than it is on the external, structural arrangements. These inner workings are difficult to tap. In our case, we visited a number of the schools during the first years of the program, met with teachers in groups and individually, in addition to surveying all participants via a questionnaire. Smith recorded, transcribed, coded, and analyzed many interviews and meetings as well as observing a number of preobservation and postobservation conferences, and making classroom observations along with the peer observer. Acheson revisited three of the original four districts at the end of the fourth year of operation and interviewed individuals who were still actively involved in the program. A questionnaire similar to the one used the first year was circulated during the fourth year and the returns were analyzed by Paul Goldman at the University of Oregon.

Ruth Wade (1982), summarizing an analysis of a large number of in-service teacher education studies, considered coaching to be one of the factors that could positively affect programs, but found that it was a much more sensitive process than it might appear to be at first glance. In a study of 225 organizations including schools and businesses, she found coaching to be "only moderately effective." She cited the importance of the psychology of coaching as an often neglected consideration that can lead to failure in the field of management. She suggested four reasons why coaching might fall short of its potential as a development technique:

- The coach and the trainee rarely have the psychological time to develop the kind of relationship based on mutual respect that is necessary for coaching.
- Because there usually is not much tolerance for giving people much time to grow, the coaching relationship is often impaired by pressure from superiors to get information from coaches that might be used against the trainee.
- Coaches often do not know how to foster independence; therefore, quick solutions are sometimes proposed that do not fit the complexity of the problem.
- The coaching situation is in danger of being blocked by the universal feeling of rivalry and its accompanying fears.

Wade's observations shed light on what we were able to learn from our analysis of the applications of peer coaching within ITIP and TET and Models of Teaching. There appeared to be little time devoted to helping teachers develop supportive channels of communication and problem-solving procedures. Instead, the processes that were employed fostered teachers' dependence on externally-driven theory and techniques, not the development of mutual respect and trust for each other. The personal and interactive practices necessary for an environment where critical reflection could be practiced seem incompatible with the design and intents of peer coaching.

Judith Warren Little (1985), writing on "the delicacy of collegial leadership," emphasizes the importance of developing reciprocity in collegial relationships:

Skillful pairs build trust by acknowledging and deferring to one another's knowledge and skill and by talking to each other in ways that preserve natural dignity, and by giving their work together a full measure of energy, thought and attention (1985).

Certainly to achieve this level of communication, healthy group dynamics and interpersonal communications are essential. Ironically, most people have a healthy (albeit at times, false) perception of their personal skills in communication. It is a common misunderstanding that good communication means simply the ability to articulate one's ideas clearly. Teachers, indeed, are paid to spend most of their time actively instructing, directing, and judging the work of others. They are in the role of expert-helper. Unfortunately, the range of interactions typically found in this kind of relationship with others does not lend itself positively to the peer consultative mode which requires respect for and understanding of another's ideas, beliefs, and teaching abilities. In our culture, a person's teaching is conceived to be both individual and personalized. Hence, it should follow that, if a teacher is working intensively with a colleague, the utmost in sensitivity is needed to foster a safe and productive climate for their work together.

This perspective lies in stark contrast to the analogy of the football coach who needs to have his players pretty well in line and following the prescribed behavioral patterns before the "skill players" break out into their individualized accomplishments. Teachers have never responded well to patronizing attitudes from anyone, especially peers. Advocates of peer coaching suggest that nearly any teacher who has been through a

training process can learn to provide feedback to another teacher. Perhaps true, but surely the success of the process relies on more than the technical act of giving feedback. Descriptive feedback provides only the starting point from which teachers can begin to create a dialectical process of inquiry, self-criticism, and consequent restructuring of teaching.

What are the implications for peer consultants? Beaton (1985) suggests they may need the same communication skills as trainers:

Although trainers, by their use of coaching, have closed the gap between solution-giving and process-helping consultancy, there is still a need for practitioners, either individually or more desirably as a team, to combine organization development and teacher professional development strategies and skills. This seems particularly necessary if peer coaching is to become established.

The program architects of PQT suspected that the most important function of the *inner game* of peer consultation may be found in a teacher's ability to engender trust, confidence, and respect while working with colleague partners. If teachers subscribe to the importance of this condition, then they must be given the time and ways of building strong and trusting relationships before being expected to excel in collegial development and critical analysis of teaching.

PQT has made use of a number of theoretical perspectives. The committee that initiated the program believed that teachers should be able to:

Use collegial support to acquire greater personal control over knowledge gained about their own teaching, ascribing meaning to that teaching and learning what is involved in genuinely autonomous growth as a professional (PQT, 1986).

The intent is much like Rudduck's or Berlin's: that teachers themselves have the power to understand, challenge, and ultimately transform their practices.

One theoretical perspective came from clinical supervision (Acheson & Gall, 1980, 1987, 1992). The particular version used has been described by the authors as "observing as if you were B. F. Skinner and giving feedback as if you were Carl Rogers." Most of the facilitators and some of the participants were familiar with this approach through the programs of their regional universities.

Another theoretical perspective came from Ted Aoki, who took part in the training sessions. This highly respected Canadian educator and senior statesman encourages teachers to think about their own teaching on three levels: technical, theoretical, and existential. In this light, peer consultation becomes legitimate for teachers who are seeking a more personal understanding of their own teaching and relationships with students, without feeling they have to strive for a prescribed set of specific teaching behaviors.

PQT, then, is the result of a blend of these theories. It is based on the belief that teachers can bring to their teaching a heightened sense of awareness and critical reflection without stringent control measures imposed from above.

Schon (1983) suggests that professionals are profoundly, but often unwittingly, aware of the decisions they make in their practice. His notions of "reflection-in-action" and "reflection-on-action" are attempts to bridge the gulf between theory and practice of professions:

As the professional moves toward new competencies, he gives up some familiar sources of satisfaction and opens himself up to new ones. He gives up the rewards of unquestioned authority, the freedom to practice without challenge to his competence, the comfort of relative invulnerability, the gratifications of deference. The new satisfactions open to him are largely those of discovery—about the meaning of his advice to his clients (his students), about his knowledge-in-practice, and about himself. When a practitioner becomes a researcher into his own practice, he engages in a continual process of self-education . . . the practice itself is a process of self-renewal. The recognition of error, with its resulting uncertainty, can become a source of discovery, rather than an occasion for self-defense.

The proponents of PQT, both the architects (planners, developers, presenters, facilitators) and the doers (participants: teachers and principals in practice), see it as a blend of systematic analysis of teaching and their own intuitive understandings of professional knowledge. Through its structure, they are able to practice critical appraisal of their teaching (principals as well as teachers), test new ideas, and restructure their teaching on the basis of what they discover in the reflective process

The intended outcomes are distinct from those of the peer *coaching* types since it is the teacher or teacher group that determines the goals and content of what is to be worked on using the peer consultation process. In the situations where it has worked best, this is exactly what has happened. Where it has not persisted, other priorities have intervened, sometimes in the guise of "administrative intrusions".

Research results, based on intensive efforts during the first two years of operation, the fourth–year interviews and survey, sixth–year interviews, and subsequent monitoring, can be summarized as follows:

1. Participants were almost unanimous in their positive reaction to the program. They expressed high satisfaction with the structure and content, with the support level from the teachers' federation, district, and building administrators, and with the impact on individual professional development and collegial relationships.
2. The numbers of districts, schools, and individuals have continued to increase and districts have tended to send new groups in successive years.
3. It should be noted that, as volunteers, program participants were presumably predisposed to respond favorably; positive responses may merely reflect a strong fit between these teachers and this program (Goldman & Smith, 1991).
4. The program is not for everyone; not everyone volunteers. Some have not continued the program beyond their initial commitment, usually because of time pressures or job movement by the participant or a partner.
5. The unusual collaboration among the federation, the districts, and the teachers—all as stakeholders—has had a positive effect on the way the program has been received.
6. Given the nature of the goals of the program, the research has had to rely on teachers' reports of how it has affected them, either through surveys or interviews rather than

through direct observation of behavior or quantitative measures such as tests. Goldman (1991) points out that "there is inevitable distortion whenever people report on what they used to believe." On the other hand, "some of the change figures are striking. These teachers clearly believe they are closer to their colleagues than they were a few years ago."

Type 4—Peer Consultation: Organization Development

The missing link in the implementation of the programs studied thus far may be found in the investigation of organizational development (OD). It is different from the others in important respects, but deserves inclusion because of some of its unique aspects.

OD differs because it is not employed as a safeguard for instructional performance, especially prescribed forms of instruction. Nor is it intented specifically to improve the technical or reflective capabilities of the classroom teacher. It does, however, specifically attend to the human relations skills that are critical to all types of peer consultation: exercising healthy interaction techniques, clarifying individual standards and group goals, and improving group problem-solving and decision-making.

What are the purposes, theories, and architects of OD? What elements does it share with other peer consultation types? Schmuck and Runkel (1987) call it a sustained effort at organizational change over time that focuses on the internal dynamics of the social system. Fullan, Miles, and Taylor (1980) described OD as:

a coherent, systematically planned, sustained effort at system self study and improvement, focusing explicitly on change in formal and informal procedures, processes, norms, or structures, and using the concepts of behavioral science. The goals of OD are to improve organizational functioning and performance. OD in schools has direct focus on educational issues.

It can also affect the system *indirectly* in ways that affect the structure. In a sense, the process amounts to overhauling the school's culture. Schmuck and Runkel (1985) note that:

The tenacity of a school's culture lies in the power of norms, how well they are adhered to, how resistant they are to change. Norms are shared expectations, usually implicit, that help guide the psychological processes and the behaviors of the group members.

How then does OD accomplish organizational introspection that strikes at the center of the school's culture and unveils the the school's norms and power relationships? Michael Fullan (1982) describes the general goals of OD: (1) To develop clear communication networks up and down and laterally; (2) To develop new ways of solving problems through the creative use of new roles; and (3) To involve more people at all levels in decision-making. Lubin and Lubin (1979) add another dimension to Fullan's goals: (4) To build trust among individuals and groups throughout the organization; (5) To supplement the authority associated with role or status with the authority of knowledge and competence; (6)

To increase sense of ownership of organizational objectives. The last goal is often thought of as seeking a balanced understanding of the relationship between organizational goals and individual goals.

Some basic assumptions about the ways individuals and groups function in schools underlie the goals of OD. One premise is that a group cannot be treated merely as a collection of individuals. Groups take on their own characteristics. Changing the norms and culture in a school requires understanding the dynamics and character of the groups affected. Changing the subsystems within a school may be easier than transforming the individuals. Within each group, members' feelings and goals are still seen as important, but they must be viewed in relation to the overarching organizational goals.

Kurt Lewin, whose theories underlie much of the OD movement, held that organizations are shaped by interactions, not by structure. Organizational behavior is not static habit or custom but a dynamic balance of forces working in various directions. Changing the social equilibrium in an organization, like changing the course of a river, requires attention to all the forces and influences that are at work. The leaders in OD experimentation and research, after 20 years of extensive experience, conclude that these forces are best attended to through groups.

How is OD related to peer consultation as we have defined it? OD teams have worked most effectively as peer consultants with school staffs and subgroups by helping develop a strong base of organizational support for change and innovation. Unlike the previous types, which attempt to institute processes for conferences and observations involving pairs of teachers, OD uses groups to provide the setting and support for descriptive feedback, problem-solving, and communication among several individuals rather than between just two.

How effective is OD, and under what conditions does it work best? Syntheses of the considerable research reveal that OD has been responsible for facilitating significant long-term success in the innovations with which it has been associated. The research shows that there has been success only in situations where all the basic conditions for change are present. Success is more likely when there is sustained support from top management, close partnership between inside and outside consultants, and participants who see OD as a continuing way of life. Where the emphasis is on personnel development focused on individual growth, the rate of success has been very low. The implication for peer consultation of the kinds we have described is that, in addition to the pairs who observe and confer, there needs to be group support for the enterprise. In PQT schools that have sustained enthusiasm for several years, there appears to be this sort of group spirit.

Research on Program for Quality Teaching

This section describes research on the Program for Quality Teaching (PQT) in which three principal questions were asked: First, what is peer consultation as practiced in the program? Second, why did teachers choose to become involved? Third, under what conditions does it appear to work best?

Initial data were obtained from feedback notes by participants at the end of each day of the five–day retreat and by interviewing participants and administrators of two pilot districts during the first two years of implementation. The information extracted from interviews must be seen in this context: the interviewers were also consultants in the design and implementation of the program and are among the authors of this chapter.

Three additional sources of research supplemented the interview procedure. First, a questionnaire was sent to 79 PQT participants at the end of the first year of the program's implementation . While the interviews concentrated on only two districts, the information drawn from the questionnaires represented four districts. The survey checked whether the general patterns described in the interviews were being experienced by other participants. The questions identified some basic behaviors and attitudes in regard to peer consultation. A similar survey was conducted at the end of the fourth year of implementation when the number of participants had passed 300. Additional interviews were conducted in three of the original four districts at the end of the fourth year.

Another source of information came from observation in the schools. Although this was not a primary source of data, on a limited number of occasions the authors were able to observe PQT participants in conferences, while teaching, in groups, or at faculty meetings.

Third, group interviews and informal written in-service evaluations helped to ensure that interviews were being adequately cross-referenced from different sources.

The Interview Process

Because the interviewers were known by the participants as being involved with PQT, to some degree their impressions may have been "managed." In contrast to this source of bias is the nature of those hardy individuals who volunteered to participate in the early days of this innovative program and whose candor surprised us. Nonetheless, participants could be expected to adjust their stories and shape their comments to what they expected we would want to hear. This was difficult to account for in the analysis of the data. Second, because we were program participants as well as researchers, there was inevitable distortion in the way the information was analyzed. Third, we chose to use semi-structured interviews. Rather than to aim at quantifying interview data, this choice concentrated on key themes and issues that arose naturally through questioning. Before the process is described, let us elaborate on the limitations.

Our dual role in the program as facilitators and researchers was the most obvious problem. All those interviewed, with the exception of 11 individuals who were non-PQT participants, knew us from the initial five-day professional-development sessions and subsequent meetings. Consequently, they were influenced by relationships previously established. The degree to which these relationships tainted the dialogue is difficult to assess. A review of transcripts made from tape-recorded interviews reveals that interviewees unabashedly related their problems, crises, and successes. It seemed that our association with the participants prior to the interviews, although causing an undetermined degree of distortion, created an environment in which the interviewees felt comfortable to speak in an open and honest manner.

Most of these interactions were reviewed by coding and analyzing transcripts taken from audiotape recordings of the interviews to monitor interviewer bias. Questions or responses that could be leading the interviewees and interactions that introduced our own biases appear to have been kept to a minimum. An independent reviewer with expertise in the area of qualitative research analyzed several transcripts and found that the interactions did not appear to be steering interviewee response. Beyond the verbal communication, however, it is important to acknowledge that tacit communications may distort interviewees' perceptions in unknown ways.

Another factor probably balanced the participants' understanding of our role. We were independent consultants and researchers, free of any formal institutional role with any of the stakeholding organizations (the school, the district, or the teachers' federation). They seemed to understand that we were not carrying any secret agendas.

Third, we were clear about the purpose of the interviews and emphasized that we were interested in finding out about their experiences in relation to their personal goals and expectations. We were not attempting to evaluate their experience in respect to some externally defined criteria. This was congruent with the message they received in the training sessions, where school groups and individuals were exhorted to develop their own goals and criteria for success. The principal message of PQT was that participants should adapt and implement the peer-consultation process in their schools as they saw fit. Diversity of interpretation was not only expected, it was encouraged. We explicitly stated that our central goal as researchers was to study the *process* of peer consultation, and any assessment of "success" would be in relation to criteria that had been established by the school group and individual teachers.

The open-ended structure of the program goals encouraged diversity, perhaps to a fault. Participants were urged to refer to their own internally developed standards and expectations and to entertain externally suggested standards only after healthy scrutiny. Consequently, interviewees openly related stories that in any other situation might have appeared to be highly unorthodox; but, because of the unprescribed nature of the program, all outcomes were seen as fair.

In three instances, school groups deviated in the extreme. These three schools stretched PQT to serve purposes that were antithetical to the basic principles of the program. The first example was a large secondary school in which PQT somehow became linked to teacher evaluation. In another school, PQT was mandated on a school-wide basis involving everyone on staff, not just volunteers. In a third school, PQT was introduced as a required activity for all first-year teachers.

The first example represented a clear breach of one of the fundamental premises upon which PQT was founded: that peer consultation was to be distinct from teacher evaluation. The second and third examples were schools that circumvented the basic program principle that participation should be voluntary. These three examples demonstrate the degree to which people deviated from the principles. In the follow-up, it was understood that the interviewees were not made to feel that they were being judged—even by these standards.

The interviewees, even in these extreme cases, were honest and matter-of-fact about their interpretation of their work. They were consistently candid in their accounts. While fully aware that they had diverged from the basic principles of the program, they were nonetheless comfortable with the understanding that their explanations and interpretations of the program were being respected.

In this way, the interview process was consistent with the philosophy of the program because it was carried out with positive regard for different interpretations of the program. Although the deviant schools contravened the principles, the PQT committee and the research group were nonetheless both supportive and curious about the possible outcomes that this might bring. Our role as participant observers and interviewers did not appear to constrain peoples' responses, most of which were forthright and almost disarming in their frankness.

A sharp contrast between the responses of people who were known personally and those who were not was evident in the interviews. Those few interviewees with whom we were not acquainted interacted in a more conservative and guarded manner. Their responses generally seemed sterile and carefully structured, perhaps filtered by a sentiment that we were there from the "outside" to judge their experience. Devoid of any interesting personal perspectives about teachers' experiences, discussions with these strangers gained only skeletal descriptions of what was happening in their schools.

We concluded that whatever was lost in not being impartial interviewers was balanced by the interviewees' trust of our role in the process. They seemed to be secure in the idea that we did not represent some hidden accountability on which they would have to tread lightly. Also, the conversational style and open-ended approach in the interviews seemed to be in tune with the way that people naturally communicate with others. When there is trust in a relationship, a less inhibited disclosure of personal truths can be anticipated.

Two additional factors probably worked in our favor. The five-day training sessions had been conducted in retreat settings and had included a number of informal social occasions. We were treated, therefore, as friends in our follow-up activities. In the training sessions, presenters and facilitators took part in the microteaching groups and also subjected themselves to feedback from demonstrations in the large-group sessions. We were probably regarded as regular people (which is how we saw ourselves).

This method of research is certainly open to many levels of criticism, not the least of which is the accusation that it is primarily concerned with feelings, wishes, and emotions of the individuals involved, rather than the outcomes established by studying an independent variable such as a definitive examination of the program "output." Critics of this form of research contend that too much emphasis is being placed upon people's perceptions, and not enough to what really happened in a particular social phenomenon.

Counter to this is the contention that in educational interventions the real picture emerges from the personal meaning that different players ascribe to social phenomena. People's interpretations and perceptions are critical to building a complete understanding of complex events. We chose a method that can be criticized by some as "soft" research but took steps to corroborate the accuracy of the interviewees' interpretation of events by comparing their personal stories with other independent sources of information—surveys, observations, and interviews with non-participants.

The interviews disclosed many doubts, concerns, problems and also many personal successes with peer consultation. From the analysis of this information, it appeared that people were not attempting to tailor their responses toward an external standard. While personal bias and the interviewees' propensity for managing impressions have certainly influenced our conclusions to some degree, the resulting richness of the interviews led us to believe that the participants' trust in our role probably helped them feel more comfortable with personal disclosures of their experiences than if we had been totally objective strangers following a structured interview pattern.

Participant Selection The purpose of the research was explained to the school groups in the fall of 1986 at the first follow-up in-service day. The participants were informed that the research would be qualitative in nature, using a descriptive approach relying primarily upon the information collected in interviews. They were informed that the general goal was to learn about their experience with peer consultation in their schools. All the participants seemed to understand and be agreeable to the general structure and purpose of the research. Participants for the individual interviews were selected by the school groups, usually on the grounds of their willingness to make themselves available on three or four occasions during the first year of implementation. The school groups also consented to attend two or three group interview sessions during the school year.

Interview Process Interviews were held with 75 individuals, 29 school groups, and 4 district groups. The interviews averaged 45 minutes to one hour. They were held in staff rooms, school libraries, or private spaces with minimal disturbances. The interview was introduced by describing its purpose; anonymity was promised and any information not to be quoted could be discussed with the tape recorder off. Each participant was invited to describe what he or she had been doing in PQT and to discuss personal perceptions of the process.

In the early interviews, it was useful to use standard questions to ensure that key topics had been addressed, but the formality of this practice gave way to a more conversational approach thereafter.

Managing and Analyzing Interview Data The greatest disadvantage of the open-ended interview is the unwieldy manner in which the information is gathered. As one might expect, interviewees tend to meander and weave through their experiences in haphazard fashion. On the positive side, their natural thought patterns were unimpaired by the constraints of a structured interview. On two occasions, dialogue digressed to the point where the interviews were rescheduled so that the discussion returned to the main topic at hand. Questions were avoided that would lead interviewees to assume that there were right or wrong viewpoints, or that the interviewer had an opinion.

There was another incidental outcome that influenced the experience of the interview participants. The interview process was satisfying for them in that it provided another opportunity to examine their work with peer consultation.

Only twice did people object to being taped. In one instance, a teacher was making confidential remarks about an administrator that it was felt should not be recorded. In another, a school group was embroiled in interpersonal controversy and felt that the tape inhibited the flow of discussion.

Individuals were interviewed at three-month intervals for the first year. Although the initial plan had assumed the interviews would end after the first year of implementation, all the original school interviewees were revisited in May of the second year to inquire about what had happened in the schools during that period. Moreover, some of these individuals and groups were revisited at the end of the fourth year of the program.

Taping, Transcribing, Coding, and Analyzing Most interviews were transcribed into word-processing documents. Over half of the tapes were transcribed in their entirety. With the other half, information that was irrelevant to the research was omitted.

A computer program enabled data from the interview transcripts to be coded and stored in a data base, analyzed using various organizers, and easily retrieved in later searches. This system made it possible to find occurrences and recurrences of different phenomena at all the various school sites.

Questionnaire/Survey

In May 1987, all the participants during the first year of PQT's implementation were surveyed for information about their experiences and professional outcomes to determine the degree to which the basic findings from interviews were consistent with the experience of a broader sampling of participants. The questionnaire contained 45 multiple-choice items and three open-ended questions. Of 78 forms sent, 63 were returned (80.7%). Although the questionnaire was not expected to generate in-depth information about the participants' experience, it provided a surface description of what the teachers and principals were doing in PQT. Second, it provided all participants with an opportunity to describe their experiences through a different medium than interviews or discussion groups.

In the spring of 1990, a version of the questionnaire similar to the first form was sent to more than 300 persons who had participated in the program up to that point. An analysis was reported at a national meeting (Smith & Goldman, 1991). The results corroborated the earlier findings.

Interviews were also conducted in the spring of 1990 with individuals and groups who had participated in the first four training sessions in 1986–1987. No effort was made to randomize the population. Instead, the interviewer chose individuals and groups who seemed likely to have experiences and insights that might illuminate our understanding of what had made this program successful and well received in general, but more so in some settings and situations than in others.

What the interviewer found was that forces outside the parameters of our original research were the prime influences on what was happening to the program. These forces can be classed as political. In one district, the training had been taken over by central office staff. The training time and location had been changed (reduced and weakened). The trainers had been replaced with others whose commitment we would question. In another district, the superintendent had substituted a training program with an emphasis on evaluation by administrators, even though it was based on the same tenets as PQT.

Perhaps the most convincing result is one that persists aside from interviews and surveys. Most of the districts that have sent participants to training sessions and have paid for substitute time and other costs continue to do so for additional groups.

Another convincing outcome is that additional school districts have opted to join the program over the years of its operation. During the initial phases, the districts which became involved were in the metropolitan areas of the province. Over time, rural (even remote) areas have joined. Peer consultation appeals to teachers, and administrators, in a variety of settings

and situations. It is also *not* appealing to a number of others teachers, administrators, settings, and situations. The program has been in operation for a decade and plans are underway for its expansion through several adaptations.

CONCLUSION

All of the programs we have analyzed have merit. There is merit in learning instructional strategies that are coherent and consistent with research on student achievement and teacher effectiveness. There is merit in understanding and being able to use a variety of strategies and techniques. There is merit in working closely with colleagues and getting supportive feedback from someone you respect and trust. Giving supportive feedback requires knowing how to observe systematically and communicate effectively in non-threatening ways. Receiving feedback from colleagues requires overcoming the natural defensiveness that teachers have about their teaching. An additional element appears to be necessary in many cases: group support beyond just one partner.

The implications for instructional supervision and staff development are not modest. The amounts of training, practice, follow-up, release time, and other forms of support are considerable. Our investigation of the literature, our own research, and first-hand experience tells us that the results are worth such efforts.

REFERENCES

An Analysis of the Proposed College of Teachers. (April, 1987). Vancouver: BCTF.

Analyzing determinations: Understanding and evaluating the production of social outcomes in schools. (1980). *Curriculum Inquiry, 10*(1), 55–76.

From civility to warfare—in just 16 years. (1984, January–February). *The BC Teacher, 63*(3), 105–106.

Acheson K. & Gall, M. (1980, 1987, 1992). *Techniques in the clinical supervision of teachers.* New York: Longman.

Adler, M. (1982). *The Paideia proposal.* New York: MacMillan.

Aitchison, K. M. *Individuals' reasons for dissatisfaction with B.C.T.F.* 106 Internal M Memorandum, BCTF Records, Membership file.

Anderson, J. G. (1968). *Bureaucracy in education.* Baltimore: Johns Hopkins.

Anderson, R. & Snyder, K. (1982). Why such an interest in clinical supervision? *Wingspan, The Pedamorphosis Communique, 1,* 1–10.

Aoki, T. & Shamsher, M. (Eds.). (1990). *Voices of teaching* (Vol. 1). Vancouver, B.C.: Teachers' Federation Publication Services.

Apple, M. W. (1979). *Ideology and curriculum.* London: Routledge & Kegan Paul.

Arendt, H. (1978). The life of the mind. New York: Harcourt, Brace Jovanovich.

Aronowitz, S. & Henry G. (1985). *Education under siege: The conservative, liberal, and radical school in South Hadley, MA: Bergin coaching strategy on teachers' transfer of training to classroom practice: A six month follow-up study.* Paper presented to AERA, 1984.

Association for Supervision and Curriculum Development (ASCD). (1987). *Another set of eyes: Techniques of classroom observation, techniques of conferencing.* Videotapes and manuals.

Baker, R. G. (1983). *The contribution of coaching to the transfer of training: An extension study.* Unpublished doctoral dissertation, Dept. of Teacher Education, U. of Oregon.

Ball, S. J. (1987). *The micro-politics of the school.* London: Methuen.

Ball, S. J. & Goodson, I. F. (1985). Understanding teachers: Concepts and contexts. In S. J. Gall & I. F. Goodson (Eds.). *Teachers' lives and careers* (pp. 1-26). Lewes, UK: Falmer Press.

Bateson, G. (1980). *Mind and nature, a necessary unity.* New York: Bantam Books.

Beaton, C. R. (1985). *Identifying change agent strategies, skills and outcomes.* Unpublished Doctoral Dissertation; University of Oregon.

Becker, W. & Carnine, D. (1980). Direct instruction: An effective approach for educational intervention with the disadvantaged and low performers. In B. Lahey and A. Kazdem (Eds.). *Advances in Child Clinical Psychology, 3.*

Bennett, W. (1982, February). *Transcript, excerpts from statement by Premier William Bennett."* BCTF, University of British Columbia, The Library. Special Collections Division, Larry Kuehn Papers, Box 1, file 12.

Bennis, W. (1969). *Organization development: Its nature, origins and prospects.* Reading, MA: Addison-Wesley.

Berlin, B. et al. (1987). Teacher–2–Teacher: The Palatine peer coaching program. *Journal of Staff Development, 8*(2), 21–23.

Berman, P. & McLaughlin, M.W. (1978). *Federal programs supporting educational change, Vol. VIII: Implementing and sustaining innovations*. Santa Monica, CA: The Rand Corporation.

Berman, P. et al. (1976). *Federal programs supporting educational change, Vol. X: Executive summary*. Santa Monica, CA: Rand.

Blake, D. E. (1985). *Two political worlds: Parties and voting in British Columbia*. Vancouver: The University of British Columbia Press.

Brandt, R. S. (1987). On teachers coaching teachers: A conversation with Bruce Joyce. *Educational Leadership, 44*, 12–17.

Brierly, M. & Berliner, D. (1982). The elemenary teacher as learner. *Journal of Teacher Education, 33*(6), 37–40.

British Columbia Teachers Federation. (1984). *Report on Teacher Evaluation*. An Unpublished Document. Vancouver, B.C.

Bruneau, W. A. (1977, May–June). What's so new about CORE and PLAP? *The B.C. Teacher, 56*(5) 156–158)

Bruner, J. (1966). *Toward a theory of instruction*. Cambridge, MA: Belknap Press of Harvard University.

Canter & Canter (1976). *Assertive disciplines: A take charge approach for today's educator*. Seal Beach, CA: Canter & Assoc.

Carr, W. & Kemmis. S. (1986). *Becoming critical: Education, knowledge and action research*. London: Falmer Press.

Carson, T. R. (1986). Closing the gap between research and practice: Conversation as a mode of doing research. *Phenomenology Pedagogy* (Vol 4, No. 2).

Carson, T. R. (1990). *Pedagogical reflections in reflective practice in teacher education*. Unpublished paper presented at the Bergamo Conference on Curriculum Theorizing and Practice, Ohio.

Charters, W. W. Jr. (1978). *The effects of team organization of elementary schools*. MITT Project CEPM. Eugene, University of Oregon.

Congratulations to All Concerned. (1970, December). *The BC Teacher, 50*(3), 116.

Conley, S. C. & Bachrach, S. B. (1990, March). From school-site management to school-site management. *Phi Delta Kappan*.

Connell, R. W. (1985). *Teachers' work*. Sydney: George Allen & Unwin.

Connelly, F. M. & Clandinin, D. J. (1987). On narrative method biography and narrative unities in the study of teaching. *Journal of Educational Thought, 21*(3), 130–139.

Cook, T. D. & Reichardt, C. S. (1979). *Qualitative and quantitative methods in evaluation research*. Beverly Hills, CA: Sage.

Dewey, J. (1933). *How we think*. Boston: Heath.

Dillon-Peterson, B. (1981). *Staff development/organization development*. Alexandria. VA: ASCD.

Doyle, W. & Ponder G. (1977). The practical ethic and teacher decision-making. *Interchange, 8*(3), 1–12.

Dunlop, D. & Goldman, P. (1991, February). Rethinking power in schools. *Educational Administration Quarterly, 27*(1), 5–29.

Fieman-Nemser, S. & Floden, R. E. (1986). The cultures of teaching. In M. C. Wittock (Ed.). *Handbook of research on teaching thinking* (3rd ed). New York: Macmillan.

Foucault, M. (1980). *Power/knowledge: Selected interviews and other writings*. New York: Pantheon.

Fullan, M. G. (1987). Implementing the implementation plan. In M. F. Wideen & I. Andrews (Eds.). *Staff development for school improvement* (pp. 213–222). London: Falmer Press.

Fullan, M., Matthew B. M., & Gib T. (1980). *Organization development in schools: The state of the art*. Final report to the National Institute of Education. Toronto; OISE press.

Fullan, M. (1982). *The meaning of educational change*. Toronto, Ontario M5S 1V6: OISE Press.

Gage, N. *Celebrating 100 years: Research and scholarship at Stanford.*

Gall, M. (1987, June). An evaluation response to a paper on staff development & peer coaching.

Garmston, R. J. (1987, February). How administrators support peer coaching. *Educational Leadership, 44*, 18–26.

Glatthorn, A. A. (1987, November). Cooperative professional development: Peer-centered options for teacher growth. *Educational Leadership, 45*, 31–35.

Goodman, J. (1984). Reflection and teacher education: A case study and theoretical analysis. *Interchange, 15*(3), 9–26.

Gosine, K. (1986). Bureaucracy, needs and teacher satisfaction. *Canadian Administrator, 10*(1) 1.

Greenfield, T. B. (1975). Theory about organization: A new perspective and its implication for schools. In M.G. Hughes (Ed.). *Administering education: International challenge* (pp. 71–99). London: Athlone Press.

Grimmett, P., Housego, I., & Moody, P.(1986). *A study of a district level initiative to establish a network for peer coaching among principals and teachers*. Center for the study of Teacher Education. Vancouver: University of British Columbia.

Guba, E. G. & Lincoln, Y. S. (1985). *Effective evaluation*. San Francisco: Jossey-Bass.

Guskey, T. R. (1985, April). Staff development and teacher change. *Educational Leadership, 42*, 57–60.

Hargreaves, A. (1984). The significance of classroom coping strategies. In A. Hargreaves & P. Woods, (Eds.). *Classrooms and staffrooms* (64–85). Milton Keynes, UK: Open University Press.

Hauwiller, J. G.(1986, November) Diversified staff development using models of teaching RIE.

Hodgkinson, C. (1978). *Towards a philosophy of administration*. Oxford: Basil Blackwell.

Hopkins, D. (1987). Teacher research as a basis for staff development. In M. F. Wideen & I. Andrews (Eds.). *Staff development for school improvement* (pp. 111–128). London: Falmer Press.

Howser, M. (1989) *Reluctant teachers: Why some people learn and grow and others do not*. Unpublished Dissertation, University of Oregon.

Hoyle, E. (1986). *The politics of school management*. London: Hodder and Stoughton.

Hunter, M. (1976, April) Teacher competency: Problem, theory, and practice. *Theory Into Practice, 15*, 2.

Hunter, M. (1986). Comments on the Napa county, California, follow-through project. *Elementary School Journal, 87*, 2.

Hunter, M. (1987, February) Beyond rereading Dewey, . . What's next? A response to Gibboney. *Educational Leadership*.

Hunter, M. (1977, April). Humanism vs. behaviorism. *Instructor, 86*.

Hunter, M. (1979). *Theory into practice*. El Segundo; ITIP Publications.

Ingvarson, L. & Greenway P. (1984). Portrayals of teacher development. *The Australian Journal of Education, 28*(1), 45–65.

International School Improvement Project. (1986). *Making school improvement work*. Leuven, Belgium: ACCO Publishing Co.

Johnson, S. M. (1989). *Schoolwork and its reform. Politics of education association yearbook*. Harvard.

Joyce, B. (1981). A memorandum for the future. In B. Dillon-Peterson (Ed.). *Staff development/organization developmentt* (ASCD 1981 Yearbook) pp. 113–127. Alexandria, VA: ASCD.

Joyce, B. (1987, February). On teachers coaching teachers: A conversation with Bruce Joyce. *Educational Leadership*.

Joyce, B. & McKibbon, M. (1982, November). Teacher growth states and school environments. *Educational Leadership* (pp. 36–41).

Joyce, B. & Showers, B. (1980, February). Improving in-service training: The messages of research. *Educational Leadership* (pp. 379–385).

Joyce, B. & Showers, B. (1982, October). The coaching of teaching. *Educational Leadership, 40*, 1.

Joyce, B. & Showers, B. (1983). *Power in staff development through research on training*. Washington: ASCD.

Joyce, B., Showers B., & Rolheiser-Bennett, C. (1987, October). Staff development and student learning: A synthesis of research on models of teaching. *Educational Leadership, 45*, 11–23.

Joyce, B. & Weil, M. (1980). *Models of teaching* (pp. 1–20). Englewood Cliffs, NJ: Prentice-Hall.

Kahn, R. (1976). Organizational development: Some problems and proposals, in readings in organizations: Behavior, structure, processes (p. 341). In J. Gibson, J. Ivancevich, & J. Donnelly Jr. (Eds.). Dallas: Business Publications.

Kanter, R. M. (1984). Women and power in organizations. In F. Fisher & C. Sirianni (Ed.). *Organization and bureaucracy* (pp. 241–269). Philadelphia: Temple University Press.

Katz, D. M. & Kahn, R. L. (1978). *The sdocial psychology of organizations.* New York: John Wiley.

Keddie, N. (1984). Classroom knowledge. In A. Hargreaves & P. Woods (Ed.). *Classrooms and Staffrooms* (pp.108–122). Milton Keyes, UK: Open University Press.

Kemmis, S. (1987). Critical reflection. In M. F. Wideen & I. Andrews (Ed.). *Staff development for school improvement* (pp. 73–90). London: Falmer Press.

Keutzer, S. (1971). Laboratory training in a new social system. Evaluation of a consulting relationship with high school faculty. *Journal of Applied Science, 7,* 493–501.

Keys, B. & R. L. Kreisman (1978). Organization development, classroom climate, and grade level. *Group and Organization Studies, 3,* 224–238.

Knowles, M. (1978). *The adult learner: A neglected species.* Houston: Gulf.

KottKamp, R., Provenzo, E., & Cohn, M. (1986, April). Stability and change in a profession: Two decades of teacher attitudes 1964–1984 (replication of Lortie's study). *Phi Delta Kappan,* 555–567.

Kundera, M. (1984). *The unbearable lightness of being.* New York: Harper and Row.

Kundera, M. (1988). *The art of the novel.* New York: Grove Press.

Lacy, C. (1977). *The socialization of teachers.* London: Methuen.

Lanier, J. E. & Little, J. W. (1986). Research on teacher education. In M. Wittrock (Ed.). *Handbook of research in teaching* (pp. 527–569). Washington, D.C.: American Educational Research Association.

Lawn, M. & Grace, G. (1987). *Teachers: The culture and politics of work.* London: Falmer Press.

[A] *Legacy for learners: The report of the royal commission of education.* (1988) Victoria, Province of British Columbia.

Lewin, K. (1951). *Frontiers in group dynamics. Field theory in social science.* New York: Harper and Row.

Lieberman, A. & Miller, L. (1979). *Staff development.* New York. Teachers College Press.

Lieberman, A. & Miller, L. (1983). *Teachers and their work.* New York: Teachers College Press.

Little, J. W. (1982). Norms of collegiality and experimentation: Workplace conditions of school success. *American Educational Research Journal, 19,* 325–340.

Lofland, J. & Lofland, L. H. (1984). *Analyzing social settings.* Belmont, CA: Wadsworth.

Lortie, D. (1975). *Schoolteacher: A sociological study.* Chicago: The University of Chicago Press.

Louden, W. (1988). *Knowledge and reflection: A case study and conceptual analysis of teaching.* Ph.D. thesis proposal. The Ontario Institute for Studies in Education.

Lubin, B., Goodstein, L., & Lubin, A. (1979). *Cases in organization development.* La Jolla University Associates.

Lyotard, J. (1987). *The postmodern condition. In after philosophy: end or transformation?* Cambridge: MIT Press.

Lyotard, J.-F. (1984). *The postmodern condition: A report on knowledge.* Minneapolis, University of Minnesota Press.

Martin, W. (1975). Negotiated order of teachers in team teaching situations. *Sociology of Education, 48,* 202–222.

McLaughlin & Marsh (1979). Staff development and school change—ASCD. In A. Lieberman & L. Miller (Eds.). *Staff development.* New York: Teachers College Press.

McNeil, L. M. (1986). *Contradictions of control.* London: Routledge & Kegan Paul.

Meyer J. & Cohen, E. (1971). *The impact of the open space school upon teacher influence and autonomy: The effects of an organizational innovation.* Technical Report No. 21. Stanford Center for R.& in Teaching.

Miles, M. & Huberman, M. (1984). *Qualitative methods: A sourcebook for methods.* Los Angeles, CA: Sage.

One hundred Years: Education in British Columbia. (1972, September) Victoria: Queen's Printer. 25. *School Act, Revised Statutes of British Columbia, chapter 375, consolidated. Behaviors of Effective Teachers as Rated by Elementary Teachers and Principals in British Columbia 1985–1986.* Unpublshed Doctoral Dissertation. Salt Lake City; Dept. of Ed. Admin. Brigham Young University.

Riseborough, G. F. (1985). Pupils, teachers' careers and schooling: An empirical study. In S. J. Ball & I. F. Goodson (Ed.).*Teachers' lives and careers* (pp. 202–265). Lewes, UK: Falmer Press.

Robbins, P. & Wolfe, P. (1987, February). Reflections on a Hunter-based staff development project. *Educational Leadership.*

Robert, M. (1974). *Loneliness in the schools.* Nile, IL: Argus Communications.

Rosennhotz, S. J. (1985, January). Political myths about education reform: Lessons from research on teaching. *Phi Delta Kappan.*

Rothberg, R. A. (1986, November). *Improving school climate and reducing teacher isolation.* RIE.

Rubin, L. (1987). Curriculum and staff development. In Wideen, Marvin, & I. Andrews (Eds.). *Staff development for school improvement.* Barcombe, East Sussex: Falmer Press.

Rudduck, J. (1987). Partnership supervision as a basis for professional development of new and experienced teachers. In Wideen, Marvin, & I. Andrews. (Eds.). *Staff development for school improvement.* Barcombe, East Sussex: Falmer Press.

Runkel, P. J. & Schmuck, R. (1987). *Research on organizational development in schools.* Eugene; UCEA Center on Organizational Development: University of Oregon.

Sahakian, W. (1976). *Introduction to the psychology of learning.* Chicago: Rand McNally.

Sarason, S. (1971). *The culture of the school and the problem of change.* New York: Allyn & Bacon.

Schlenker, B. R. (1980). *Impression management.* Monterey, CA: Brooks Cole Publishing.

Schmuck, R. A & Runkel, P. J. (1985). *The handbook of organizational development in schools.* Palo Alto: Mayfield.

Schon, D. (1983). *The reflective practitioner: How professionals think in action.* New York: Basic Books.

Servatius, J. D. & Young, S. E. (1985, April). Implementing the coaching of teaching. *Educational Leadership, 50.*

Shalaway, L. (1985, September). Peer coaching . . . does it work? R. & D. Notes. National Institute of Education (pp. 6–7).

Shamsher, M. (1988). *Program for quality teaching: Report.* Unpublished Document.Vancouver; British Columbia Teachers Federation Press.

Shamsher, M. (1986). *Program for quality teaching: Handbook.* Vancouver: British Columbia Teachers' Federation Press.

Shamsher, M. & Smith, N. (1988). *Program for quality teaching: Prospectus.* Unpublished Document.Vancouver: British Columbia Teachers Federation Press.

Showers, B. (1985, March). *Improvement through staff development: The coaching of teaching.* RIE.

Showers, B. (1985, April). Teachers coaching teachers. *Educational Leadership, 42,* 43–48.

Showers, B., Joyce, B., & Bennett, B. (1987, November). Synthesis of research on staff development: A framework for future study and a state-of-the-art analysis. *Educational Leadership, 45,* 77–87.

Sikes, P. J., Measor, L., & Woods, P. (1985). *Teachers' careers*. Lewes, UK: Falmer Press.

Sizer, T. R. (1984). *Horace's compromise*. Boston: Houghton Mifflin.

Smith, N. (1987). *Program for quality teaching: An interim report*. Unpublished Document. Vancouver; British Columbia Teachers Federation.

Smith, N. S. & Acheson, K. A. (1991). *Peer consultation: An analysis of several types of programs*. Eugene, Or. Oregon School Study Council.

Smyth, W. J. (1984, January). Teachers as collaborative learners in clinical supervision: A state of the art review. *Journal of Education for Teaching, 10*(1) 24–38.

Smyth, W. J. (1985). Developing a critical practice toward clinical supervision. *Journal of Curriculum Studies, 17*(1) 1–15.

Sowell, T. (1987). *A conflict of visions*. New York: William Morrow and Company.

Stallings, J. & Krasavage, E. M. (1986). Program implementation and student achievement in a four-year Madeline Hunter follow through project. *The Elementary School Journal, 87*(2) 117–138.

Stallings, J. & Krasavage, E. (1986, May). Effects of instruction based on the Madeline Hunter model on students' achievement: Findings from a follow-through project. *Elementary School Journal* (pp. 571–588).

Stallings, J. (1986). Allocated academic time revisited, or beyond time on task. *Educational Researcher 9*, 11–16.

Stallings, J. (1987, February). For whom and how long is the Hunter-based model appropriate?: A response to Robbins and Wolf. *Educational Leadership* (pp. 63).

Stark, J. S. & Lowther, M. A. (1984). Predictors of teachers' preferences concerning their evaluations. *Educational Administration Quarterly, 20*(4), 76–106.

Stiggins, R. J. & Duke, D. (1987). Research on teacher evaluation; Unpublished.

Stiggins, R. J. Teacher evaluation: Accountability and growth—different purposes. *NAASP Bulletin, 70*(490), 51–58.

Van Maanen, J. (Ed.). (1983). *Qualitative methodology*. Beverly Hills, CA: Sage.

Van Maanen, J. (1985). Cultural organization: Fragments of a theory. In Peter Frost et al. (Eds.). *Organizational culture*. Beverly Hills: Sage.

Wade, R. (1984, December). What makes a difference in in-service teacher education? A meta-analysis of research. *Educational Leadership*.

Waller, W. (1982). *The sociology of teaching*. New York: Wiley.

Waters, M. (1989, March). Collegiality, bureaucratization, and professionalization: A Weberian analysis. *American Journal of Sociology, 95*(5), 45–72.

Weick, K. (1976). Educational organizations as loosely–coupled systems. *Administrative Science Quarterly, 21*(3).

Wideen, M. F. (1987). Perspectives on staff development. In M. F. Wideen & I. Andrews (Eds.). *Staff development for school improvement* (pp. 1–15). London: Falmer Press.

Wildman, T. M. & Niles, J. A. (1987, July–August). Reflective teachers: Tensions between abstractions and realities. *Journal of Teacher Education, 38*, 25–31.

Withall, J. & Wood, F. (1979). Taking the threat out of classroom observation and feedback. *Journal of Teacher Education, 30*(1).

Wood, F. H., Thompson, S. R., & Russell, Sister Frances (1981). *Designing effective staff development programs*. In B. Dillion-Peterson (Ed.). (ASCD 1981 Yearbook) pp. 59–91. Alexandria, VA: ASCD.

Woods, P. (1979). *The divided school*. London: Routledge & Kegan Paul.

Yarger, S. et al. (1980). *In-service teacher education*. Palto Alto, CA: Booksend Lab.

Yin, R. K. (1984). *Case study research*. Beverly Hills, CA: Sage.

Zahorik, J. A. (1987). Teachers' collegial interaction: An exploratory study. *Elementary School Journal, 87*(4) 385–396.

·33·

SUPERVISION AND CURRICULUM DEVELOPMENT

Peter F. Oliva

GEORGIA SOUTHERN UNIVERSITY

Two decades ago, I attempted to construct a model of supervision which would answer this question: What is it that supervisors do? (Oliva, 1976; Oliva, 1993).* From an examination of the roles and tasks of supervisors—regardless of their titles—I conceptualized the tasks of these staffpeople as falling into three domains: instructional development, curriculum development, and staff development. It was my perception that these leaders—often referred to with the rather imprecise title of "instructional supervisors"—work at one time or another in all three domains. Some concentrate on one domain; others labor in two or all three domains. In fact, supervisors sometimes find themselves in all three domains simultaneously.

While working in one or more of the three domains, instructional supervisors fulfill at least four roles: coordinator, consultant, group leader, and evaluator. The domains and roles rest on a base of 13 foundations. Schematically, the model appears as shown in Figure 33.1. No barriers exist between the domains. Instructional supervisors, being versatile people, switch back and forth from one domain to the other, depending on the particular needs being served. The roles depicted indicate that supervisors sometimes coordinate, sometimes consult, sometimes lead groups, and, to the dismay of some of the experts in supervision, sometimes evaluate.

It is no secret that the job of instructional supervisor lacks precision and that conceptions of the domains, roles, functions, and tasks of supervisors differ among those people who have studied the field. We have continually asked ourselves such thorny questions as:

Is supervision administration?
Is supervision leadership in improving instruction?

Is supervision clinical assistance to individual teachers?
Is supervision staff development?
Is supervision curriculum development?

Perhaps the only way we can respond to questions like these is on the basis of prevailing practices and opinions of the researchers and experts. Let's see if curriculum development, i.e., the planning, implementation, and evaluation of the curriculum, falls within the responsibility of various supervisors. From the job descriptions of a sampling of supervisors, the following responsibilities are found among their many duties:

Provides leadership to schools in the area of curriculum (Assistant Superintendent of Curriculum).
Administers, plans, and analyzes the development of curriculum. (Director of Curriculum and Instruction).
Provides leadership in planning and conducting curriculum studies. (Elementary Education Director).
Evaluates, develops, and reviews curricular offerings. (Building Principal).
Assists teachers in interpreting curriculum . . . cooperates in constant evaluation of curriculum. (Assistant Principal).
Acts as a resource person for department teachers on curriculum questions. (Department Chairperson).

These statements from actual job descriptions reveal the difficulty of separating supervision from administration. In simplistic terms—with the full understanding that very little need in the education profession can be described in simplistic terms—administrators are *line* personnel who are legally charged with both management and supervisory responsibilities, including

---

*Excerpts from Oliva (1993) are from Peter F. Oliva, *Supervision for Today's Schools,* 4th ed. (White Plains, NY: Longman). © 1993. Reprinted by permission of Longman Publisher.

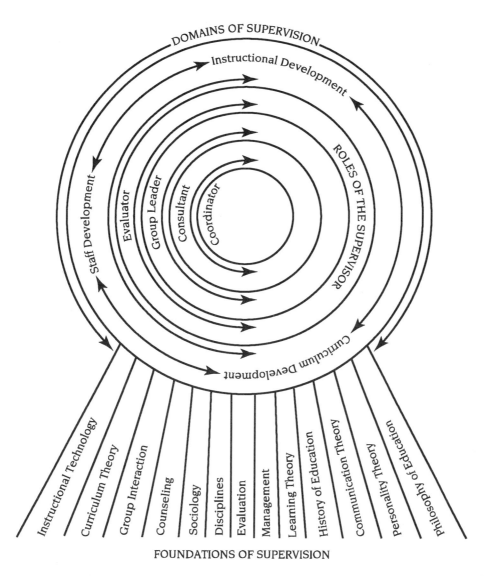

FIGURE 33.1. A conceptual model of supervision. Source: Peter F. Oliva,
Supervision for Today's Schools, 4th ed. (White Plains, NY: Longman, 1992), p. 22.
Reprinted by permission of the publisher.

instructional supervisory duties. Instructional supervisors, as *staff* persons without line responsibilities, are assigned duties by their superiors. These duties may be of both an administrative and instructional supervisory nature. The prevailing, though far from unanimous, sentiment among advocates of instructional supervision is that, because their primary mission is to help teachers, instructional supervisors should be as far removed from the practice of administration as possible. The Association for Supervision and Curriculum Development (ASCD) Working Group on the Roles and Responsibilities of Supervisors, chaired by A. W. Sturges, helped to clarify the administrative/supervisory dilemma by recommending two types of instructional supervisors: administrative and consultative (Sturges, 1978).

The issue of the relationship between supervision and administration is more properly the province of pages elsewhere in this handbook. Whether the instructional supervisor carries out administrative duties by law or by assignment, instructional supervisors do have responsibilities in the area of curriculum development.

When we speak of supervision and curriculum development as affiliated fields, we run the risk of fostering the impression that we are talking about two separate entities. Sometimes authorities talk of instructional development, curriculum development, and supervision, as if supervision were distinct from instructional development and curriculum development. Thus, they impart a conception of supervision limited to leadership in staff development/in-service education or to clinical assistance to individual teachers in their classrooms. The conception of supervision presented in this chapter departs from that view and holds that instructional development and curriculum development, along with staff development, are integral parts of instructional supervisory behavior.

Many authorities agree that leadership in curriculum development is a commonly expected part of the job of the supervisor. Lucio and McNeil (1969) said, "Verification of successful public school service of candidates for supervision often includes . . . participation in activities such as curriculum development" (p. 52). In a chapter entitled "Supervision is Curriculum Development," Lovell and Wiles (1983) commented, "Supervision has the responsibility for facilitating continuous curriculum improvement" (p. 145). In his book on supervision, Glickman (1985) included a chapter on curriculum development and described supervisory leadership responsibilities in these terms: "the supervisor should choose format, sources, and types of curriculum development that will increase teachers' choice and commitment to curriculum implementation" (p. 324). Wiles and Bondi (1986) included "Designing and Developing Curriculum" among the tasks of the supervisor (pp. 106–135). In both historic and current theory and practice, supervisors must exercise leadership in curriculum development.

WHO ARE THE CURRICULUM LEADERS?

Both popular and professional usage have made the term *instructional supervisor* a generic title that really encompasses all three domains: instruction, curriculum, and staff development. This term is shorthand for more awkward terms designed to encompass these domains. I am somewhat uncomfortable with the term, however, because it suggests a limited view of supervision: namely, clinical classroom supervision focusing on the improvement of instruction. I suppose if we must restrict our terminology, "instructional supervisor" is as good as any term since the ultimate goals of all three domains are the improvement of the teacher's instructional skills and the students' achievement. In this chapter, the terms "instructional supervisor," "curriculum supervisor," and "curriculum leader" are used interchangeably.

Where do we find these staff persons whom we can call "curriculum leaders"? Omitting those who work on a state level, we meet curriculum leaders at either the district, central-office, or the school-building levels. They may be generalists, who supervise several disciplines, or specialists, who have responsibilites for supervision in a specific field. Figures 33.2 and 33.3 show examples of generalist and specialist supervisors at the central-office and school-building levels. You will notice numerous titles. At the district level, some of the supervisors also carry administrative responsibilities and their instructional supervisory responsibilities are more limited. Specialists at the district level are consultants who help teachers in a particular discipline, such as language arts, or in a particular field, such as exceptionalities. At the school-building level, an assistant principal for curriculum and instruction may have primarily instructional supervisory responsibilities or more often shares some administrative duties. Lead teachers fulfill a generalist curriculum role at the school-building level, whereas team leaders and grade-level coordinators are specialists in elementary or middle schools, and department heads at middle schools and high schools are specialists in their own disciplines.

If you do not view elementary and middle school education as fields of specialization, I see no real problem in conceptualizing team leaders and grade-level coordinators as generalists, since they do assist teachers in several areas.

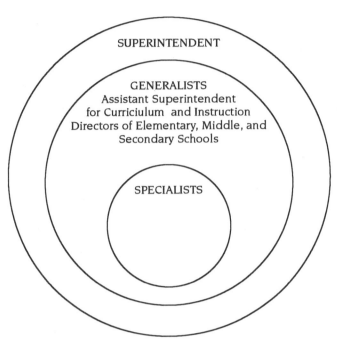

FIGURE 33.2. Generalist and specialist supervisors at the district level. Source: Peter F. Oliva, *Supervision for Today's Schools*, 4th ed. (White Plains, NY: Longman, 1993), p. 76. Reprinted by permission of the publisher.

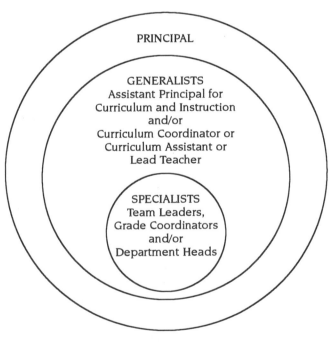

FIGURE 33.3. Generalist and specialist supervisors in an individual school. Source: Peter F. Oliva, *Supervision for Today's Schools*, 4th ed. (White Plains, NY: Longman, 1993), p. 76. Reprinted by permission of the publisher.

The issues in which methods of organizing for supervision are most effective—generalist versus specialist and central-office versus school-building—will be examined later in this chapter.

THE RELATIONSHIP OF CURRICULUM TO INSTRUCTION

Although supervisors may work in all three domains, they may perform duties in a single domain at a particular time or they may engage in tasks in two or three domains simultaneously. When supervisors write proposals for a new program for children at risk, they are working in the field of curriculum development. When supervisors propose techniques for instructing these children at risk, they are in the domain of instructional development. When supervisors conduct workshops on teacher burnout, they are leading a group in staff development. Supervisors frequently, however, work in two domains at the same time, such as when an instructional supervisor asks teachers to specify instructional objectives which will meet stated curriculum goals. The supervisor may also engage in all three domains at the same time, such as instructing teachers in the goals, objectives, and teaching strategies of a new program.

Distinguishing between domains is easier done in theory than in practice. Whether a practitioner's title is "director of curriculum and instruction," "director of instruction," or "director of curriculum," an instructional supervisor will demonstrate leadership responsibilities in curriculum development, instructional development and, to the extent he/she works with individual teachers and groups, staff development.

Curriculum Defined

Elsewhere I have listed more than a dozen definitions of the word "curriculum" (Oliva, 1992). I agree with Caswell and Campbell (1935), who perceived curriculum as "all the experiences children have under the guidance of teachers" (p. 66) and with Taba (1962), who wrote, "A curriculum is a plan for learning" (p. 11). I defined curriculum as:

a plan or program for all the experiences which the learner encounters under the direction of the school. In practice, the curriculum consists of a number of plans, in written form and of varying scope, that delineate the desired learning experiences. The curriculum, therefore, may be a unit, a course, a sequence of courses, the school's entire program of studies—and may take place outside of class or school when directed by the personnel of the school. (Oliva, 1992, p. 9).*

If curriculum signifies plans or programs, instruction refers to those techniques, strategies, or procedures which teachers use to translate the plans or programs into action. The simplest way for me to view the distinction between curriculum and instruction is to regard curriculum as the "what" and instruction as the "how."

Establishing Priorities

The relation between curriculum and instruction is comparable to the question "Which came first, the chicken or the egg?" We may substitute "curriculum" and "instruction" for "chicken" and "egg." Which *does* come first? I find myself in agreement with Macdonald (1965) who averred that curriculum planning precedes instruction.

Although it would seem logical that teachers would want to know what they wish to accomplish before they decide how to accomplish it, not all practitioners demonstrate that sequence. They jump into activities and decide what they wish to achieve afterward. In fact, some practitioners behave as if there were little or no correlation between what they wish to accomplish and how they will get there.

I have conceptualized the relationship between curriculum and instruction as viewed by practitioners and theorists in the form of eight models, four of which have appeared elsewhere (Oliva, 1992). I labeled these models:

Dualistic Separatist
Dualistic Cooperative
Reversible
Interlocking Horizontal
Interlocking Vertical
Concentric
Symbiotic
Cyclical

The Dualistic Separatist Model

The Dualistic Separatist Model, which appears in Figure 33.4, shows Curriculum and Instruction as two separate and independent entities. They go their own ways without concern for each other. Curriculum guides outlining the scope and sequence of the curriculum gather dust. Instructional goals and objectives may or may not have relevance to pronounced curriculum goals and objectives. The curriculum

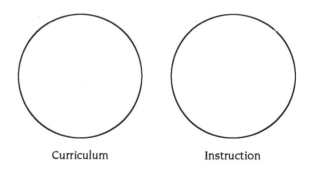

Curriculum   Instruction

FIGURE 33.4. The dualistic separatist model. Source: "The dualistic model," Peter F. Oliva, *Developing the Curriculum*, 3rd ed. (New York: HarperCollins, 1992), p. 10. Reprinted by permission of HarperCollins College Publishers.

---

*Excerpts from Oliva (1992) are from Peter F. Oliva, Developing the Curriculum, 3rd ed. (New York: HarperCollins). c 1992. Reprinted by permission of HarperCollins College Publishers.

planners and the instructional staff work independently and never the twain shall meet. I made this analogy: "Like siblings who have not seen each other in years, one may be sick without the other's ever knowing it " (Oliva, 1992, p. 14).

Dualistic Cooperative Models

Polarity is still present in the Dualistic Cooperative Models, but the three variants of this model, depicted in Figures 33.5, 33.6, and 33.7, show Curriculum and Instruction to be at least aware of each other's existence. In Dualistic Cooperative Model A, Curriculum and Instruction figuratively shake hands. The handshake holds out the promise of some working relationships between them. Like two great powers, each maintains its sovereignty, although an element of cooperation has crept in for the mutual benefit of both. The curriculum planners and the instructional designers have mutually agreed to enter into dialogue.

If the cooperative arrangement proves mutually satisfying, Curriculum and Instruction may walk hand in hand for some distance like a romantic couple, as seen in the diagram of Model B. The relationship depicted in this variation of the Dualistic Cooperative Model is somewhat more intimate. The curriculum planners and the instructors continually talk to each other and even appear to enjoy each other's company.

A third variant of the Dualistic Cooperative Model reflects an even closer relationship, as shown in the diagram of Model C. Curriculum and Instruction have become very chummy

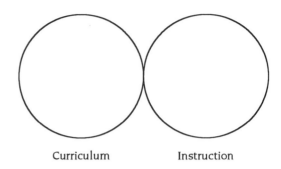

Curriculum   Instruction

FIGURE 33.7. Dualistic cooperative Model C.

and readily cooperate without a great deal of urging. It should not be forgotten, however, if we may use the analogy of these two entities as a heterosexual couple, that one remains very much an ERA proponent and the other continues as a chauvinist. While they may enjoy each other's company, each remains strongly independent.

Reversible Model

Instruction is the alter ego of Curriculum when a conceptual model depicts Curriculum as one side of a coin and Instruction as the other side. If we follow the metaphor of the two faces of the coin, the Curriculum-Instruction relationship is more like the Native American and the buffalo on the old U.S. nickel than Lincoln and his memorial on the penny, for the Native American and the buffalo are aware of each other's presence. What would the Native American have been without the buffalo or vice versa, the buffalo without its guardian and nemesis? When shown as the two faces of a single coin, Curriculum and Instruction are two different perspectives of the same substance. What is viewed programmatically may also be viewed in terms of implementation. The questions of which is the head of the coin and which is the tail or which the front and which is the back are of no significance. Curriculum and Instruction are viewed as integrated, etched into the same piece of metal. We might wish to view the coin itself, with Curriculum as one face and Instruction, as the other to signify the two faces that Schooling presents to the world. The schematics of the Reversible Model would look like Figure 33.8.

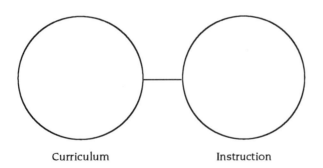

Curriculum   Instruction

FIGURE 33.5. Dualistic cooperative Model A.

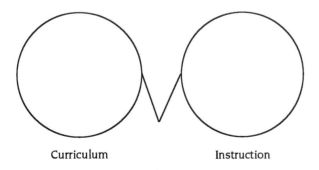

Curriculum   Instruction

FIGURE 33.6. Dualistic cooperative Model B.

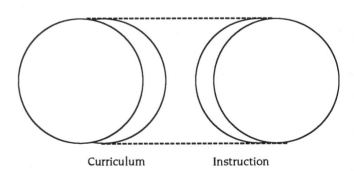

Curriculum   Instruction

FIGURE 33.8. The reversible Model.

Interlocking Models

Some people perceive Curriculum and Instruction as linked either horizontally (Figures 33.9 and 33.10) or vertically (Figures 33.11 and 33.12). Unlike dualistic models, in which Curriculum and Instruction are separate or barely touching, these two entities when interlocked do demonstrate a measure of interdependence.

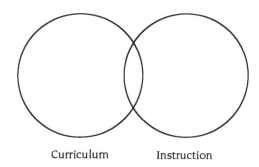

Curriculum   Instruction

FIGURE 33.9. Interlocking Model A. Source: Peter F. Oliva, *Developing the Curriculum*, 3rd ed. (New York: HarperCollins, 1992), p. 11. Reprinted by permission of HarperCollins College Publishers.

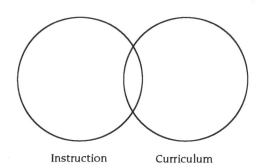

Instruction   Curriculum

FIGURE 33.10. Interlocking Model B. Source: Peter F. Oliva, *Developing the Curriculum*, 3rd ed. (New York: HarperCollins, 1992), p. 11. Reprinted by permission of HarperCollins College Publishers.

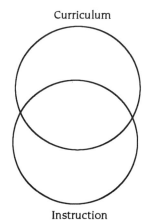

Curriculum

Instruction

FIGURE 33.11. Interlocking Model C.

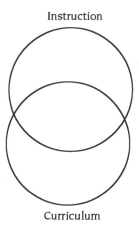

Instruction

Curriculum

FIGURE 33.12. Interlocking Model D.

Interlocking models force us to recognize that Curriculum and Instruction cannot exist whole without the other. Take one away from the other and you inflict damage. I would not attach a great deal of significance to the relative positions of Curriculum and Instruction when linked horizontally, although you might make a good case for priority of the entity to the left since in our culture we read from left to right. However, we can detect an element of supremacy of one over the other when we link Curriculum and Instruction vertically. In effect, the interlocking vertical models suggest subservience on the part of the entity on the bottom to the entity on top. I regard the proper place of Instruction as subservient to Curriculum rather than vice versa.

Concentric Models

Concentric models A and B, shown in Figure 33.13 and 33.14, picture one entity surrounding the other, making one the sub-system of the other. There is no question as to which entity is paramount. In Model A, Instruction is clearly dependent for its sustenance on Curriculum, whereas the latter is dependent on and secondary to Instruction.

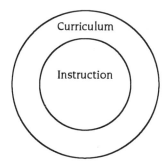

Curriculum

Instruction

FIGURE 33.13. Concentric Model A. Source: Peter F. Oliva, *Developing the Curriculum*, 3rd ed. (New York: HarperCollins, 1992), p. 12. Reprinted by permission of HarperCollins College Publishers.

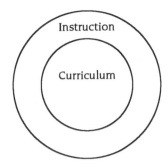

FIGURE 33.14. Concentric Model B. Source: Peter F. Oliva, *Developing the Curriculum*, 3rd ed. (New York: HarperCollins, 1992), p. 12. Reprinted by permission of HarperCollins College Publishers.

Symbiotic Model

When Curriculum is equated to Instruction, you have a Symbiotic Model, as seen in Figure 33.15. If you tell me that you see one circle, I would reply that you are looking at two circles—one superimposed over the other. You are looking at a model constructed of two congruent circles, which we might label Curriculum-Instruction. Most people would claim the existence of two entities, Curriculum and Instruction. They could point out that school systems employ Directors of Curriculum *and* Instruction and that universities often establish Departments of Curriculum *and* Instruction.

Some practitioners nevertheless act as if there was only one entity. When they equate curricular—i.e., programmatic—goals with instructionl goals, they are treating the two entities as one and the same. When they write instructional objectives and call them curriculum objectives, they are confusing or equating the two.

Cyclical Model

Figure 33.16 depicts Curriculum and Instruction as two independent and equally important entities engaging in continuous and mutual feedback. Instruction impacts on Curriculum and vice versa. It does not clarify the priority question—which comes first, Curriculum or Instruction—unless we agree that the entity to the left, as in the interlocking vertical models, indicates primacy. However, except in the cases of totally new programs where Curriculum should cer-

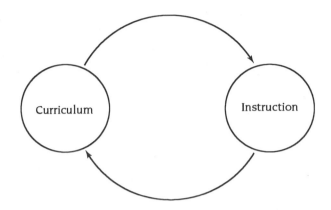

FIGURE 33.16. The Cyclical Model. Source: Peter F. Oliva, *Developing the Curriculum*, 3rd ed. (New York: HarperCollins, 1992), p. 12. Reprinted by permission of HarperCollins College Publishers.

tainly precede Instruction, the priority issue may be academic. Instructors are busy carrying out already established curricula. Feedback from Instruction modifies the Curriculum which in its turn modifies Instruction—a neverending cycle.

An Additional Model

Graduate students in curriculum courses sometimes create their own conceptual models of the relationship between Curriculum and Instruction. Westcot depicted this relationship in the form of a Möbius strip, which reveals a continuous, unbroken flow of one entity into the other, a very defensible conception (Westcot, cited in Oliva, 1992).

When we are considering models for any phase of the educational process, we cannot say that one model is "right" and another "wrong." Advocates express their preferences for one model over the other. We need to select models with which we feel most comfortable and which yield the best results. Of the models depicted in this chapter, my choice is the Cyclical Model, which provides continuous feedback or flow from one entity to the other, inseparability, and interdependence.

From the discussion of the intimate relationship between Curriculum and Instruction, we can deduce that supervisors charged with providing leadership in curriculum development will inevitably engage in both curriculum development and instructional development.

SKILLS AND TASKS OF CURRICULUM DEVELOPMENT

How then should we delineate the tasks of supervisors in curriculum development? They must demonstrate a broad repertoire of skills in order to carry out the various tasks of curriculum development. Curriculum leaders must exhibit skills which enable them to help teachers and others to (1) plan, (2) implement, and (3) evaluate the curriculum. We might

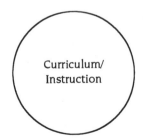

FIGURE 33.15. Symbiotic Model.

schematically cast the leaders' areas of responsibility in the form of a simple model of curriculum development as follows:

Each of these three areas of responsibility subsumes a body of knowledge and a set of skills and requires making a multitude of decisions. For example, planning requires describing the conception of curriculum on which plans will be based, uncovering unmet needs, designing plans for meeting those needs, and identifying human and material resources and costs. Implementing the curriculum calls for knowledge of both traditional and innovative responses to curriculum needs, putting resources to work, and translating plans into action. Evaluating the curriculum comprises analysis of the degree to which the plans which have been implemented have been successful. This chapter will provide a model that details steps in planning, implementing, and evaluating the curriculum and instruction.

Curriculum leaders must possess a companion body of knowledge and set of skills in working with groups when planning, implementing, and evaluating the curriculum. They must be experts in group dynamics, conflict resolution, and consensus building.

Most curriculum development involves (or should involve) working with groups. Curriculum leaders seek input from several constituencies both internal and external—to the school—teachers, administrators and supervisors, students, parents, and laypeople from the community. They provide leadership to a variety of schoolwide and districtwide curriculum committees, councils, and advisory groups. To help in deliberations, they often bring in consultants from inside or outside the system.

As they are working with groups, curriculum specialists must possess skills in keeping participants on task for curriculum development, which, if it is to be successful, must be a task-oriented process. Most participants, like the leaders, want to achieve results. They do not wish to be bogged down in endless processing of participants' beliefs, values, attitudes, likes, and dislikes. They must allow sufficient processing for people to express themselves and feel that their ideas are valued, but they must move the group forward to accomplish its main task: curriculum improvement.

One of the oldest—and, in my opinion, still one of the most useful—analyses of the dynamics of a group with implications for group process is offered by Benne and Sheats (1948). Somewhere along the line, most educators have encountered the Benne-Sheats identification of roles of individuals in groups.

Benne and Sheats broke roles played by individuals when working in groups into three categories: task, building/maintenance, and individual. Examples from 12 task roles are the *opinion seeker,* the *elaborator,* and the *energizer.* The seven roles played by those who wish to build and maintain the progress of the group include the *harmonizer,* the *gate keeper,* and the *standard setter.* Individuals attempt to satisfy their own needs through roles such as the *recognition seeker,* the *blocker,* and the 8 *dominators*

Using the Benne-Sheats classification system, curriculum leaders can identify roles played by individuals in a group setting, capitalizing on contributions made by those fulfilling roles which enhance the group's progress and channeling those who play negative roles into more constructive behavior.

Curriculum developers face a formidable task in resolving conflicts and achieving consensus on issues among and within constituencies. They must resolve differences and achieve agreement on a conception of curriculum. They must reach consensus on the school's philosophy and aims, on curriculum goals and objectives, and on establishing priorities of curricular needs. They must build consensus on plans for improving and evaluating the curriculum. These tasks can be accomplished only in a group setting.

A SUGGESTED MODEL FOR CURRICULUM IMPROVEMENT

A general utility model which fits many educational undertakings reinforces the understanding that, while instructional supervisors help teachers to (1) plan, (2) implement, and (3) evaluate the *curriculum,* they also assist teachers to (1) plan, (2) implement, and (3) evaluate *instruction.* Following this premise, we can enumerate tasks in a total process of curriculum development. The supervisor will help teachers to:

1. Specify the needs of students in general.
2. Specify the needs of society.
3. Write a statement of philosophy and aims of education.
4. Specify the needs of students in your school(s).
5. Specify the needs of the particular community.
6. Specify the needs of the subject matter.
7. Specify the curriculum goals of your school(s).
8. Specify the curriculum objectives of your school(s).
9. Organize and implement the curriculum.
10. Specify instructional goals.
11. Specify instructional objectives.
12. Select instructional strategies.
13. Begin selection of evaluation strategies.
14. Implement instructional strategies.
15. Make final selection of instructional strategies.
16. Evaluate instruction and modify instructional components.
17. Evaluate curriculum and modify curricular components (Oliva, 1992, pp. 174–175).

Identifying these tasks as components, I have placed them into a model for curriculum development that integrates Curriculum and Instruction. That model is shown in Figure 33.17.

The model portrays the tasks of the instructional supervisor in the domains of curriculum development and instructional development. The model consists of 12 components. Eight of these are "planning phases," which include specification of needs of students in general, needs of society, and aims and philosophy of education (I); needs of particular stu-

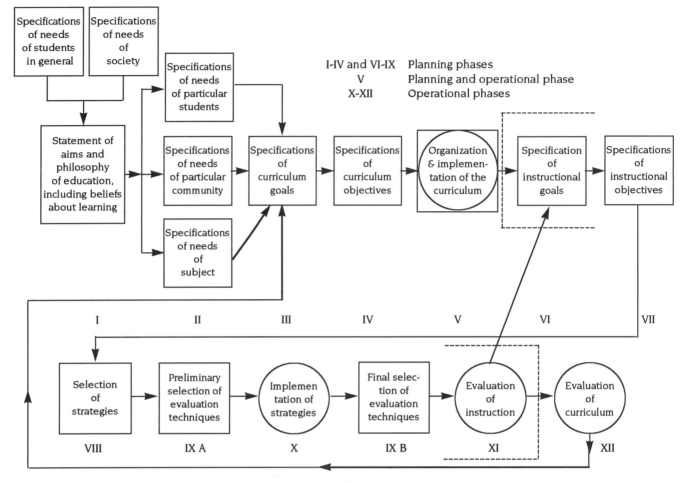

FIGURE 33.17. Model for curriculum development. Source: Peter F. Oliva,
Developing the Curriculum, 3rd ed. (New York: HarperCollins, 1992), p. 12.
Reprinted by permission of HarperCollins College Publishers.

dents, needs of particular community, and needs of the subject (II); curriculum goals (III); curriculum objectives (IV); instructional goals (VI); and instructional objectives (VII). You will also note selection of strategies (VIII), preliminary selection of evaluation techniques (IXA), and final selection of evaluation techniques (IXB) in the planning phases. Three components are operational phases, including implementation of strategies (X), evaluation of instruction (XI), and evaluation of curriculum (XII). Phase V, Organization and Implementation of the Curriculum, exhibits characteristics of both a planning and an operational phase.

Two Submodels

The total model for curriculum development integrates two submodels that could stand alone: a Curriculum Model (Components I–V and XII), which is actually a simplified curriculum development model, and an Instructional Model (Components VI–XI), which some experts might call a general model of instruction. By placing an instructional model

within the context of a curriculum development model, I mean to stress once again the interdependence of curriculum and instruction. You will note my indebtedness to theorists like Tyler whose (1949) "Rationale" has been widely accepted in the profession.

Feedback Lines

You should also observe the feedback line denoting a cyclical process from Component XII (Evaluation of the Curriculum) back to Component III (Specification of Curriculum Goals), and through the model until it once again reaches Component XII. The total model calls for modification of components as supervisors and teachers experience the need for modification. Even Components I and II need to be revisited periodically, since philosophies, needs of society, needs of particular communities, needs of students (both in general and in particular), and expanding knowledge in various disciplines require revision and restatement from time to time. You might well make an argument for bringing the feedback line to Component I rather than Component III. My rationale for cycling the feedback line to Component III instead of I was to imply that Components I and II call for review less frequently than the remaining components. A faculty hopefully will not flip-flop in its philosophy every year or err so far in identifying needs of students, society, or exigencies of the subject matter that they must constantly revise those components. Components III through XII call for continuous review and assessment.

When you are attempting to delineate the tasks of instructional supervision in any domain, it is useful to design a model which graphically depicts those tasks. In designing a model, you quickly come to realize that it is next to impossible to chart a single model on which all nuances appear. We are also unlikely to design a single model which meets all the preferences of curriculum workers. The instructional supervisor should design and follow a model with which he or she feels comfortable. He or she should test it in practice and revise as necessary.

THE TWELVE COMPONENTS

The foregoing model for curriculum development visualizes the supervisor's role in the domains of curriculum and instructional as leadership in carrying out 12 component tasks in sequence. Let's briefly examine each of these components when the model is followed during a periodic comprehensive study of the school's curriculum.

Component I: Specification of Needs of Students in General; Specification of Needs of Society; Specification of Aims and Philosophy of Education

The first component calls for broad general education of the participants in curriculum development, especially the instructional supervisor. Since the component calls for specification of needs of students in general, the supervisor directs curriculum planners to look at common needs of learners throughout our society. The planners must identify problems faced by young people as human beings, as Americans, and as inhabitants of an interdependent world.

The planners must also stay informed of ever-changing needs of American society. Often identification of general needs of students and needs of society will overlap. Basic skills are significant not only for the learners but also for society. A country cannot maintain its standard of living unless its citizens possess a reasonable mastery of the fundamental processes of reading, writing, and arithmetic. This chapter, however, is not the place to go into the much-publicized deficiencies in those areas.

Specification of students' needs and society's needs would certainly pinpoint cultural, linguistic, mathematical, and computer employment literacy, technology; health; cultural diversity; and environment as needs which must be recognized when shaping a curriculum for the late 1990s and beyond.

When needs of students in general and of society are identified, planners will cast those needs in the form of aims or purposes of education and express their philosophical beliefs. Stated in broad terms, an aim points the direction of the education system. An example of an aim is a simple statement: "The purpose of education is to teach students to think," or "The purpose of education is to develop literate citizens," or, "The purpose of education is the fostering of a democratic society."

A statement of philosophy expands on the planners' specification of aims of education and clarifies in narrative form the planners', and ultimately the school's, beliefs about the nature of schooling, learning, and the learners. "We hold these Truths to be self-evident, that all Men are created equal . . ." is an illustration of political philosophy. "We, the faculty, believe that every child should master in school the knowledge and skills necessary to live successful and productive lives in our industrialized society" is a statement of educational philosophy.

Component II: Specification of Needs of Particular Students, Specification of Needs of the Particular Community, and Specification of Needs of the Subject

Curriculum planners must identify needs of students and society generally, but they must at the same time specify the needs of students in their own schools and the needs of the local community. General needs of students and society would, of course, obtain throughout the nation. Students in one community, however, may demonstrate needs that differ from needs of students in other communities. The needs of students in Miami, Florida, for example, differ in some respects from those of Miami, Ohio. Curriculum planners must be aware of students in the demographic data of their communities, down to and including neighborhoods. Children from prosperous enclaves have needs which differ from children from low-income housing projects.

Requirements of the subject matter are usually the best-defined aspects of curriculum development. Textbooks and curriculum guides set forth the content to be taught. Dated textbooks, old curriculum guides, and outmoded courses of study, however, make periodic examination of content essential. We might say that there comes a time when we must stop teaching that the earth is flat.

Component III: Specification of Curriculum Goals

This model distinguishes goals from objectives and curriculum goals and objectives from instructional goals and objectives. Goals are ends that are neither observable nor measureable. Objectives, with the exception of those in the affective domain, are both observable and measureable.

Curriculum goals are statements of the curriculum's purpose. Curriculum goals may simply be reiteration of broad aims of education as applied to a particular school or statements created uniquely for a particular school. "Students of this school will demonstrate a command of the fundamental processes" is a typical, longstanding curriculum goal. It speaks to the purposes of basic skills curricula, although it does not tell us which fundamental processes or the level of mastery in each. "Students will develop an appreciation for the maxim 'healthy mind in a healthy body'" is another example of a curriculum goal.

The specification of curriculum goals is an excellent starting point at which to involve people other than teachers and administrators—namely, parents, representatives of business and industry in the community, and, depending on their maturity, students. Instructional supervisors will lead curriculum planners in stating curriculum goals that are selected from outside sources or created specifically for the particular school. The planners will need to set priorities from among the many curriculum goals that they may generate.

Component IV: Specification of Curriculum Objectives

Curriculum objectives turn curriculum goals into observable and measureable ends. When specifying curriculum objectives, curriculum planners must answer this question: "What do students have to do to make the goals observable and measureable?"

Let's take this aforementioned goal: "Students will demonstrate a command of the fundamental processes." We are thinking about achievement of all students, so we might design the curriculum objective: "By the end of the year, 75 percent of the students diagnosed with math deficiencies at each grade level of this school will have raised their scores on the national standardized test of achievement in mathematics by 10 percentile points." For the curriculum goal "Students will develop an appreciation of the maxim 'healthy mind in a healthy body,'" we might generate this curriculum objective: "The number of teenage pregnancies among girls of this school will be cut 10 percent each year for the next five years."

Curriculum objectives focus on students' accomplishments in the school as a whole. We can often spin out many curriculum objectives for a particular curriculum goal. One subtask of the instructional supervisor, when helping teachers to specify either curriculum objectives or instructional objectives, is to assist them in establishing priorities and deciding when enough is enough.

Component V: Organization and Implementation of the Curriculum

Once curriculum goals and objectives have been specified, curriculum planners must decide on ways to put the curriculum into operation, using what some people might call "delivery systems." In practice, of course, planners rarely have the opportunity to create all new delivery systems, except perhaps in new schools. Instead, they have the obligation of reviewing current delivery systems and revising them as necessary.

This is the one component of the model that is depicted as both a planning phase and an operational phase, for curriculum developers must first decide upon the delivery systems which best suit the curriculum goals and objectives and then establish them so that instruction can begin.

The planners must make numerous decisions, some of which are administrative, such as courses to be offered, extra class activities, scheduling, staffing patterns, provision for the handicapped, provision for the gifted, and extent of content integration.

Component VI: Specification of Instructional Goals

Component VI begins the process of bringing the curriculum alive by translating it into instruction in the classrooms.

Teachers breathe life into what at this point consists only of written plans.

At this stage in the instructional process, teachers are still in a planning mode. They now must select content and decide on methods to enable students to encounter the content.

Teachers now review the curriculum goals and objectives in order to identify instructional goals and objectives. Instructional goals are derived from the curriculum goals and objectives. They state in nonobservable and nonmeasureable terms what the teacher wishes each student in his or her classroom would achieve.

The math teacher, for example, might review the curriculum goal "Students will demonstrate command of the fundamental processes" and the curriculum objective "By the end of the year, 75 percent of the students designated with math deficiencies at each grade level of this school will have raised their scores on the national standardized test of achievement in mathematics by ten percentile points." The teacher can identify a large number of instructional goals and objectives which could accomplish the curriculum goal and objective. For example, the teacher might include in his or her lesson plans this instructional goal: "The student will develop an understanding of the process for dividing by fractions." The social studies or health teacher might consider how to accomplish the curriculum goal "Students will develop an appreciation for the maxim 'a healthy mind in a healthy body'" and the curriculum objective "The number of teenage pregnancies among girls of this school will be cut 10 percent each year for the next five years." He or she might choose the instructional goal "The student will become aware of the extent and consequences of teenage pregnancy."

Component VII: Specification of Instructional Objectives

At this point, teachers specify what are widely known as behavioral or performance objectives. Experts in instructional design (Mager, 1975; Popham, 1970; Tyler, 1949) have long advocated specification of instructional objectives. Like curriculum objectives, they must be both observable and measureable.

Countless teacher trainees have been encouraged over the past 40 years to write behavioral objectives into their lesson plans. The practice is so widespread and accepted now that we need not defend it as we once did. Teachers routinely write objectives which contain the behaviors to be performed by the student; some teachers strive for completeness by including the conditions under which the behavior takes place and the level of mastery sought.

The teacher, following the instructional goal "The student will develop an understanding of the process for dividing by fractions," can design instructional objectives that call for pupils to demonstrate their understanding. One such objective is: "The student will solve 20 problems on dividing by fractions with 90 percent accuracy." The social studies or health teacher, implementing the instructional goal "The student will become aware of the extent and consequences of teenage pregnancy," could specify this instructional objective: "Using library and other resources, the student will determine and summarize in a written report information that describes how widespread the problem of teenage pregnancy is in the nation, this state, and this community."

In practice, you will discover that experienced teachers often bypass the stage of writing instructional goals and proceed directly to specification of instructional objectives. Such practice is infinitely better than omitting both instructional goals and objectives entirely or in stating nonobservable and nonmeasureable instructional goals and labeling them instructional objectives. The end products in the sequence from curriculum goals to curriculum objectives to instructional goals to instructional objectives are the last-named instructional objectives.

You might infer that I agree with Gagné (1967) who observed that there is no activity called "Selection of Content." I would not be adverse to including a block called "Selection of Content" if the model designer wishes to call attention to the fact that the teacher sifts through textbooks, curriculum guides, and other aids when writing instructional goals and objectives. I have simply made the assumption that the teacher must examine material before writing instructional goals and objectives. In many cases, the instructional goals and objectives reveal the content. I point out also that curriculum planners take a first cut at selecting content, in somewhat broader terms than the classroom teacher, when they consider needs of the subject in Component II.

Component VIII: Selection of Strategies

When they select strategies of instruction, teachers must choose those that fit the discipline, the students, the community, the resources available, and the teacher's own beliefs and skills. The teacher who is a poor lecturer will select other techniques for presenting subject matter. The teacher who believes in the efficacy of cooperative learning will make use of small, collaborative groups. Independent study may be appropriate for more mature, self-directed learners. Teachers with outgoing, extroverted personalities will choose strategies more appropriate to their styles than to the styles of instructors with reserved, introverted personalities. Instruction on birth-control techniques may generate conflicts among patrons of the school unless it has been sanctioned by the community. Computer instruction requires the availability of both hardware and software.

The research on effective teaching over the past 20 years has revealed a wide variety of generic teaching competencies—skills, strategies, methods, and techniques which all teachers should master and include in their repertoires. Set induction, oral questioning, and variation of stimuli are three examples of these generic skills (Allen & Ryan, 1969; Berliner et al, 1976; Hunter & Russell, 1977; Rosenshine, 1979).

Component IXA—B: Preliminary and Final Selection of Evaluation Techniques

Component IX is split to convey the notion that evaluation is a continuous process. Teachers should be thinking about how to evaluate student achievement even before beginning presentation of instruction. Preliminary selection of evaluation techniques is shown prior to implementation of strategies and

final selection of evaluation techniques. To be more accurate, the model should show continuous selection of evaluation techniques during implementation of instruction.

Preassessment of entry knowledge and skills prior to implementation of strategies of instruction is also understood but not explicitly shown. Teachers design evaluation techniques not only for final assessment but also for preassessment.

Instructional supervisors help teachers to plan and carry out assessment techniques. Looming large is the generic skill of testing. In addition to employing written and objective tests, teachers should devise additional means for assessing student achievement, such as observation, written and oral reports, and actual skill performance.

Component X: Implementation of Strategies

We might have labeled Component X "Presentation of Instruction." This is the point in the model which the layperson generally recognizes as "teaching." Teachers display a variety of methods for motivating and managing students and confronting them with the subject matter.

It is at this point that both administrative and consultative supervisors evaluate teacher performance, albeit for different purposes. The administrator evaluates primarily for the purpose of making personnel decisions and secondarily for improving instruction; the instructional supervisor observes and provides feedback primarily for improving instruction and occasionally to assist in personnel decisions.

Component XI: Evaluation of Instruction

Evaluation of Instruction is the implementation of techniques whose purpose is assessment of student achievement at the conclusion of the presentation, which some people refer to as final or terminal assessment. In truth, no assessment is or should be terminal. Every assessment points the direction to continuing encounters with the subject matter. Assessments demonstrate the need for reteaching, remediation, review, and advancement.

While conducting a terminal assessment, teachers wish to know whether students have mastered the instructional objectives which were stated in Component VII. Curriculum experts point out the necessity for "curriculum alignment," that is, the correlation of learning activities and evaluation techniques with the instructional objectives and with each other.

Component XII: Evaluation of the Curriculum

We evaluate to determine not only if students achieve instructional objectives but also to discover whether the curriculum is working. If students demonstrate mastery of the *instructional* objectives, we have one important piece of evidence that the curriculum is providing desired experiences for the learners. Student success in meeting classroom objectives, however, is but one indicator of the effectiveness of the curriculum.

We also want to know whether the curriculum has met its stated *curriculum* objectives. Let's recall the examples of curriculum objectives stated earlier. We still will wish to know whether 75 percent of the targeted students have raised their scores 10 percentile points. We'll want to know whether the number of teenage pregnancies has dropped by 10 percent.

A curriculum needs assessment conducted as a part of Component II will uncover deficiencies in the curriculum. The curriculum planners will have placed the curriculum needs in priority and will have specified curriculum goals and objectives aimed at meeting those priorities. Curriculum evaluation discloses whether those curriculum objectives have been met and whether the deficiencies have been overcome.

The administrators will also want to know, even if the curriculum planners do not, whether the curricula established by the planners is cost-effective. A thorough curriculum evaluation will divulge those data.

SOME GUIDING PRINCIPLES

As they carry out their tasks as curriculum leaders, supervisors should demonstrate an understanding of several guiding principles. First, supervisors are change agents. They should constantly help teachers implement better ways to achieve goals. Supervisors must be proponents of change, not for the sake of change, but to improve curriculum and instruction. They must sense when to promote an innovation and when to hold for further research and examination. Alfonso, Firth, and Neville (1981) perceived grounding in change theory as an integral part of an instructional supervisor's behavior system.

Second, supervisors must involve others in curriculum development: teachers, administrators, consultants, parents, other laypeople, business and industry, and students. As Miel (1946) attested, "the nature of curriculum change should be seen for what it really is—a type of social change, change in people, not mere change on paper" (p. 10).

Third, curriculum improvement comes after an examination of the existing curriculum. The astute supervisor does not lead a group of teachers into a new program without assessing the nature, strengths, weaknesses, and needs of the present program. English and Kaufman (1975) explain the necessity for conducting curricular needs assessments and described a comprehensive process for doing so.

Fourth, curriculum development is a continuous process. The curriculum will never reach perfection. Without continuous examination, it is not possible to determine whether a curriculum needs refinement, expansion, or replacement.

In fulfilling his or her role as curriculum leader, the supervisor combines the skills of educator, teacher, planner, manager, communicator, evaluator, group leader, sociologist, philosopher, and psychologist. The multifaceted task of the curriculum leader is awesome, touching the lives of so many students, teachers, administrators, supervisors, parents, and other laypeople.

These guidelines have been incorporated into a more complete set of principles, which I have referred to as axioms:

- Curriculum change is inevitable and desirable.
- The curriculum is a product of its time.

- Curriculum changes of earlier periods often coexist with and overlap curriculum changes of later periods.
- Curriculum change results only as people are changed.
- Curriculum development is a cooperative group activity.
- Curriculum development is basically a process of making choices among alternatives.
- Curriculum development never ends.
- Curriculum development is more effective if it is comprehensive, not piecemeal.
- Curriculum development is more effective when it follows a systematic process.
- Curriculum development starts from where the curriculum is (Oliva, 1992, pp. 31–45).

PROBLEMS AND ISSUES IN CURRICULUM DEVELOPMENT

Defining a Conception of Curriculum

Defining a conception of curriculum is both a task and problem for the curriculum leader. Earlier in this chapter, I offered a definition of curriculum. However, I observed that many interpretations of curriculum can be found.

The search for a definition of curriculum is far from simple. Tanner and Tanner (1980) spoke of the changing conceptions of curriculum in the twentieth century. One's conception of curriculum is colored by his or her philosophies of education and philosophy of life. Thus, you may agree with essentialist philosophers like Bagley (1938) and the National Education Association Committee of Ten (1894) that the curriculum consists of academic subject matter designed to transmit the cultural heritage. You may subscribe to progressive philosophy espoused by its leading exponent, Dewey, who held that curriculum consists of those experiences designed to promote individual growth and socialization of the child (Dewey, 1929).

Essentialist thinking strongly affects current efforts at curriculum development. District and state assessment programs seek to measure students' achievements in the academic areas, mainly through both norm-referenced and criterion-referenced tests. On a national level, the National Assessment of Educational Progress periodically measures student performance in a number of curriculum areas. To translate national goals (U.S. Department of Education, 1990; *Goals 2000 Educate America Act*, 1994) into action, national standards in five core academic subjects (English, mathematics, science, history, and geography) and instruments for assessing achievement of those standards are currently under development and piloting (National Council on Education Standards and Testing, 1992).

To many people, curriculum consists of exposure to that content which will enable students to successfully pass the various standardized and nonstandardized tests. The content of the tests has become the curriculum in many instances. Madaus and Tan (1993) ascribed the growth in testing to four social forces, one of which is the "array of legislation, at both federal and state levels, promoting or explicitly mandating standardized testing programs." Madaus (1988) analyzed the effects of testing programs from both inside and outside the school system and cautioned:

What is needed at this juncture in American education is more discussion of creative counterstrategies that have curriculum and instruction driving testing rather than testing driving curriculum and instruction counterstrategies in which testing is the servant not the master of curriculum, instruction, and learning (p. 117).

Although there is no "right" or "wrong" conception of curriculum—since reasonable people can, do, and should formulate their own interpretations of curriculum—it is essential that those engaged in curriculum development analyze their beliefs and ultimately achieve consensus. The curriculum leader assumes the heavy responsibility of helping participating groups to reach agreement on a definition with which they can live.

Governmental Mandates and Reform Movements

Reform movements brought on by public dissatisfaction have periodically swept the schools. Thus, waves of reform efforts can be tracked from the nineteenth century to the present. Reform efforts can be attributed in part to the status of the economy (Firestone, Fuhrman, & West, 1991) and to public shifts in values (Cuban, 1990).

The 1980s saw a flurry of curriculum development as demand for school reform swept state after state. The electorate, dissatisfied with the products of the public schools, demanded improvement. Hence, state assessment of student achievement, increase in number of credits required for high school graduation, teacher certification tests, and state-prescribed teacher and administrator evaluation systems were established.

In their zeal to remedy supposed failings of the past, states jumped to specify instructional objectives in the various disciplines, learning activities, and means of evaluating students' mastery of content. Teachers began to feel that they could not exercise their own professional judgments about what students in their charge should learn and how they should be taught. Whether this attitude was accurate or not, local school personnel perceived the state was limiting—even usurping—their prerogatives.

Working with a state committee charged with development of an instrument for statewide evaluation, I suggested that building principals should demonstrate leadership in planning, implementing, and evaluating the curriculum. Several members of the group strongly opposed the concept of responsibility for planning the curriculum, maintaining that the curriculum was all planned for them by the state and that they had no freedom to plan.

It is true that state mandates, though well-intentioned, can restrict local schools' autonomy. However, even in those situations where the curriculum is detailed for the schools, state, prescriptions are usually meant to be minimal, allowing schools to proceed beyond the minimum. We all know from previous experience, unfortunately, that the minima often become the maxima.

The reform efforts of the 1980s centered largely on strengthening academic content and improving teacher effectiveness. The reform efforts of the 1990s have concentrated on restructuring school operations which will be discussed later in this chapter.

Whether the reforms of the 1980s will hold is problematical. Firestone et al (1992), reporting on a study by the Center for Policy Research in Education of educational reform in six states from 1986 to 1991, concluded that state efforts have met with only modest success and those reforms which were easier to implement have continued.

Perelman (1992) would go in a different direction. He is critical of current efforts at reform, such as *America 2000* and its state and local derivatives. He labeled reform a "hoax" and advocated abandonment of the traditional public education system in favor of privatization of learning which harnesses the latest in technology.

Since curriculum leaders, like all school personnel, must live within the context of state mandates, adapting state requirements to local needs poses a continuing problem. On the other hand, the problem of adaptation may not be as large as at first believed. Firestone et al (1991) reported that school districts offered little resistance to state requirements to increase academic subject matter. In some cases, the districts' curricula were already ahead of state mandates. State mandates in those cases affirmed district practices and priorities.

Pressure Groups

Whereas church and state were intimately entwined—even congruent in some cases—in early colonial days, a wall separated the school from society throughout the nineteenth and early twentieth centuries. By tradition, the public maintained its distance from the schools, allowing school officials to conduct schooling as they saw fit. School personnel saw no need for enlisting the assistance of the community beyond financial support. Both the public amd school faculties concurred that schooling was best left to the professionals.

Annual reports from the schools to the public, solicitation of volunteers, open houses, back-to-school nights, partnerships with business and industry, formation of advisory groups, and surveys of the public's attitudes toward the community's schools are creations of the latter half of the twentieth century. The movement toward empowerment of teachers and the local citizenry is one response to a widespread dissatisfaction with the accomplishments of the public schools. Public school personnel, in an age of intense competition from private and home schools, are keenly aware of the necessity for building strong community support.

The concomitant result of community support—in the American tradition—is the formation of groups of citizens with their own agendas for the schools. The curriculum is especially vulnerable to attack by pressure groups. Name almost any curricular issue and you will find camps on both sides and in between. One measure of successful school administrators today is their ability to deal with groups whose philosophies and agendas may be antithetical to their own.

Controversial Curriculum Issues

Ever since America's first schools were established in the seventeenth century, curriculum leaders have faced the task of making decisions many of which turn out to be controversial. Examples of the many, often weighty decisions curriculum leaders contended with in the distant and near past included: whether to add science and modern foreign languages to the curriculum, whether to offer tax-supported secondary education, whether to combine disciplines into broad fields, whether to establish vocational or comprehensive high schools, whether to offer a core curriculum in the junior high school, and whether to replace the junior high school with the middle school.

The current scene presents its share of controversial issues which call out for resolution: To what extent shall the curriculum be multicultural? Shall special education students be mainstreamed or promised special classes? What are the best means for developing computer competence? How do schools combat cultural illiteracy on the part of students? How do we eliminate gender discrimination? What kinds of alternative education should be provided for students with academic and behavioral problems? To what extent shall values education be incorporated into the curriculum? What kind of curriculum best promotes development of thinking skills? How shall schools respond to demands for censorship of materials, incorporation of special-interest programs, and abandonment of programs to which special interests object? Shall the whole-language approach replace other approaches to language instruction? To what degree should the practices of cooperative learning be incorporated into in the classrooms? Can high school students be required to perform community service as a condition for graduation?

Adding these somewhat newer issues to older, continuing issues, like general education versus vocational education; the place of religion in the public schools; how to best assess student achievement and on what criteria; and how to provide for the differing needs of slow, average, and rapid learners, and you have examples of the numerous controversial curricular problems facing curriculum leaders and the constituencies with which they work.

Type and Locale of the Curriculum Leader

The superintendent and school board must decide how to best organize for curriculum development. They must address two continuing questions to which school systems make differing responses. First, what types of curriculum leaders are needed? Shall they be generalists who can assist teachers across all levels and disciplines? Should they be specialists with fields of specialization who can assist teachers in their own areas of specialization? Second, where should the curriculum leaders be housed, in the central office or in the individual schools?

Generalist versus Specialist Educational philosophy and demographics certainly play important roles in deciding which personnel to employ and where to house them. If administrators believe that teaching has common elements regardless of the discipline or level, they can gravitate toward employing generalists who can supervise in many areas. They reason that generalists are knowledgeable and proficient in generic teaching skills, those competencies which should be in the repertoires of every teacher. Generalists will possess special competencies in one or more teaching fields in which they have been trained.

Specialists bring to curriculum consulting expertise in a particular field. The teaching of foreign languages, for example, calls for some methodologies which differ from those of social studies. Differing teaching fields certainly call for a different body of knowledge of the content of the discipline. A specialist would, of course, be expected to possess a knowledge of the content of his or her discipline that a generalist who has not been trained in that field would not possess. It is interesting to note that most of the help provided teachers through clinical supervision or other school system staff development activities focus on methods of teaching, rather than on remedying deficiencies in content.

Central Office versus Individual School Not only must school administrators resolve the issue of whether to employ generalists or specialists, they must decide where to house them. Shall they station them in the district office or shall they deploy them to the individual schools?

In making decisions regarding choice and location of personnel, school officials must take into consideration number of schools, number of students, geographical size of the school district, concentration and isolation of schools, and, of course, costs of providing for curriculum development. The bottom line remains what the school system can afford. While school officials may ardently desire to place, for example, a curriculum consultant in every school and offer specialist help from the central office for teachers in every discipline, ordinarily their budgets preclude them from doing so.

The traditional answer to provision for curriculum consultants typically has been the employment of generalists who are based in the central office. This is the most economical way to provide consultant help. School administrators can assign personnel more easily when they do not have to consider fields of specialization. A generalist working in a number of areas obviates the need for specialists in every area. A staffing pattern placing curriculum leaders in the central office means, of course, that a relatively few consultants will be spread among however many schools there are in the district. It means also, as Pajak (1989) pointed out, that central office supervisors must carry "extremely diverse and global" responsibilities (pp. 4–5).

A common complaint of instructional supervisors at the school district level is that they do not have sufficient time to visit all teachers and all schools with any degree of frequency. Under a centralized system, teachers often feel that consultants are never available when you need them. The role of curriculum consultants under a centralized system often devolves into troubleshooting, distributing information, and managing group staff development activities.

A variety of staffing patterns have been created to resolve the central office/individual school and generalist/specialist dilemmas. They may rely heavily on generalists or they may establish a judicious mixture of generalists and specialists. They will often employ a limited number of generalists at the district level, make more effective use of the generalists and specialists already on the individual school's faculty, and provide the services of specialists in a limited number of areas, such as mathematics, science, and special education. Whatever staffing pattern is in existence, there is a pronounced trend toward placing greater responsibility on the individual school for its development and management.

TRENDS IN CURRICULUM DEVELOPMENT

Decentralization

The decentralization movement of the 1980s and 1990s encompasses both states' delegation of responsibility for educational reform to the school districts and the districts' delegation of responsibility to the local schools. The decrease in state control requires a corresponding increase in local initiative and responsibility within relaxed state mandates.

Goodlad (1984) viewed the individual school as the appropriate locus for decision-making. Common buzzwords in school administration today are "site-based management" and "empowerment." These terms comprise a host of practices designed to decentralize the management and operation of the individual school. Administrators are granted some discretion not only in budgetary decisions but also in making curriculum decisions. Teachers, parents, and mature students are "empowered" to the extent that they are called on to participate in decision-making on a formalized rather than casual basis. Their ideas and suggestions are given serious consideration and often implemented. Schools are reaching out either voluntarily or through state or district directives to involve many citizens in making decisions about what the schools should teach in the light of needs of students and community.

Under decentralized plans for curriculum development, school-based personnel are designated to help teachers modify curriculum and improve instruction. Some regularly employed staff persons may function as curriculum consultants: assistant principals for curriculum and instruction, department heads, grade coordinators, and team leaders. Master teachers on the staff may serve as mentors to induct and assist beginning teachers. Those school systems that can afford them may hire lead teachers whose primary task is to work with faculty in the areas of curriculum and instruction.

While teachers, parents, and students are joining administrators and supervisors in site-based management, schools are enlisting the help of other laypeople, community leaders, and representatives of business and industry to examine offerings, propose solutions, and provide students with learning experiences both inside and outside the school.

Decentralization and site-based management are often referred to as "restructuring." Although decentralization is a prime feature of reform movements of the 1990s, Firestone et al (1991) noted that efforts at decentralization occur simultaneously with efforts at centralization. The CPRE study of educational reform in six states, referred to earlier, found evidence that moderation between the tendencies to decentralize and centralize entered the picture. States which had moved too far in centralizing responsibility extended more responsibility to the local districts; states which had customarily been strong advocates of decentralized responsibility moved toward more mandating.

Decentralization of responsibility and authority from district to school level is not without its problems. The placement of responsibility on the local school can diminish coordination efforts and can result in greater unevenness in quality among the schools of a district. Pajak affirmed the need for district-level leadership to maintain linkages within the school system (Pajak, 1992).

Fullan (1993) cited a number of studies that revealed local initiatives like school improvement programs have enhanced the decision-making process but have not necessarily resulted in improvements in curriculum and learning. Murphy (1989) advocated the blending of the forces of centralization and decentralization with "strong leadership at both the bottom and the top of school systems" (p. 809). In a like vein, Fullan (1993) observed that the key to the centralization/decentralization issue is restructuring so "the bottom-up and top-down initiatives can feed on each other" (p. 131). Fullan commented that "centralization errs on the side of overcontrol, decentralization errs toward chaos" (p. 128).

Shared Responsibility

A concomitant (though not absolute) consequence of decentralization is the sharing of responsibility. Curriculum development was historically perceived as the primary responsibility of the status person on the superintendent's staff, such as the director of curriculum and instruction. This person exercised leadership functions, enlisting help from other constituencies—teachers, parents, students—as he or she found desirable and necessary. Other constituencies remained to a great extent in a passive, reactive capacity.

Schools established curriculum committees composed of teachers on their faculties at those times when they were seeking accreditation by the regional associations. After fulfilling their mission—responding to accreditation procedures—the committees were dissolved. School principals here and there named standing curriculum committees to advise on curriculum matters and permitted such groups to make minor recommendations.

Schools also historically refrained from soliciting assistance of parents, projecting the attitude that the education is best left to professionals. Parents tended to accept that philosophy and were reluctant to offer advice on such esoteric matters as the curriculum. Parental involvement in school affairs most often took the form of passive participation in parent-teacher association meetings and back-to-school nights.

As years passed, the wall between schools and community began to crumble. School leaders perceived the aid of parents and other laypeople in the community as valuable extensions of curricula. Schools issued periodic reports to the community on their achievements and, sometimes, their deficiencies. They tapped residents of the community to serve as resource persons who could share their expertise with students. They began to build a cadre of volunteers who could provide assistance to the school in a variety of ways.

A wall originally separated not only schools from parents and other laypeople but also schools from business and industry. Each operated within its own sphere. Representatives of business and industry made an occasional appearance on career days and nights.

Perceptive curriculum leaders began to realize that business and industry offered great potential for enhancing the curriculum. Responding to this change in attitude and to the criticisms of business and industry concerning deficiencies in the schools, curriculum leaders began to reach out for financial and academic assistance.

Schools now invite experts in various fields to talk with students. They have entered into arrangements for fieldwork and training of students in business establishments and industrial plants.

The movement toward enlisting those resources outside of the schools—parents, other laypeople, business, and industry–in the programs has grown from isolation to casual participation on invitation to more formal relationships, including arrangements which implement the concept of empowerment.

Empowerment implies the planned involvement of persons inside and outside of the school system in the decision-making process. In one sense, it emulates the concept of quality-control circles—often attributed to the Japanese— found in the industrial world (Ouchi, 1981). Whereas industries seek advice and recommendations from their employees in order to maintain and improve the quality of their products, empowered constituencies make recommendations for improving operations of the school, including the curriculum.

Although *empowerment* is one of the watchwords of the day and is a pronounced trend, it is not without stresses and strains. Principals steeped in tradition do not relish erosion of their authority, which can happen when an empowered group takes its work seriously. Questions remain on how to constitute advisory groups, who should be represented, how to choose participants, how many participants the group should have, and what their responsibilities and powers should be.

That shared responsibility has problems that can be observed in Florida's experience with *Blueprint 2000* (Florida Department of Education, 1993) in which each school is required to develop a plan designed to meet state goals and to establish school advisory councils "to assist in the preparation and evaluation of the school improvement plan and . . . provide such assistance as the principal may request in preparing the school's annual budget and plan" (Florida Department of Education, 1993).

The thrust of the Florida legislation is to permit local schools to develop their own plans for improving their programs by inviting participation of the various constituencies. Schools have experienced difficulty in spelling out measures of progress toward achieving *Blueprint 2000* goals and in recruiting parents to serve on the advisory councils.

In spite of any problems that must be resolved, this genie will not be pushed back into the bottle. Today's school administrators must be willing to work with representatives of the various constituencies in the community. In fact, prevailing sentiment, both public and professional, encourages school leaders to seek out and welcome help from outside the confines of the school. Not only is the trend toward expanded participation of constituent groups sound academ-ically, but it is also expedient. Despite severe pressures, criticism, and attack, public schools can build their base of support by encouraging meaningful involvement of people from the community that they serve. If the trend toward empowerment continues, empowered groups may eventually become more than advisory in nature, since they already wield considerable power in the decision-making process.

As the role of the instructional supervisor has evolved over the years from inspector to colleague (Alfonso & Goldsberry, 1982; Bolin & Panaritis, 1992; Garman, 1982), a continuing redefinition of the role of curriculum leader can be expected. Educational, philosophical, economic, political, social, and cultural factors all exert influence on roles of school personnel.

For both strategic and economic reasons, central office supervisors may assume more coordination responsibilities and less direct contact with individual teachers. School based personnel will shoulder the responsibilities for working directly with teachers. In an era of emphasis on human relations and the development of human resources, authoritarian behavior of leaders is viewed as less acceptable and, consequently, less productive in achieving organizational goals. The rise of "empowerment" of not only teachers but also parents requires a style of leadership that seeks to bring out the talents of the empowered (Sergiovanni, 1987). Patience and tolerance for ambiguity are virtues to be cultivated by leaders, particularly in working with laypeople who come from many different backgrounds and are unfamiliar with educational programs and practices.

Curriculum leadership in an era of decentralization and shared responsibility may in some respects prove more challenging than under centralized and more authoritarian structures.

Looking Forward and Backward

Educational personnel and school boards can justifiably point with pride to many recent and futuristic aspects of curriculum and instruction. They can extol the emphasis that faculty places on computer literacy, computer-assisted instruction, business machines, interactive video, closed-circuit television, and radio and television production. They can point to their magnet schools with specialized curricula from science to drama to medical arts. They can indicate how teachers implement cooperative learning, whole language, early intervention, and programs for the gifted.

What is even more interesting, perhaps, is that the curriculum leaders should look over their shoulders to see what the past holds. In the heady days of the 1950s, schools were engaged in a ferment of experimentation, including team teaching, programmed instruction with teaching machines, instructional television, continuous progress plans, language laboratories, core curriculum, and flexible and modular scheduling. Some of these promising practices have survived. Team teaching remains strong at the middle school level. Programmed instruction has dropped by the wayside. The practice of herding large groups of students into an auditorium to watch televised programs on a number of monitors has died out, though television is widely used in other forms.

Once installed, high school language laboratories often gather dust.

Although they may not be called trends at this point, several innovations from the past are gathering strength. Schools are once more looking at nongraded or continuous progress schools as a viable alternative to the traditional practice of tailoring students to time which is held constant. Instead, they tailor time and free students to develop at their own speeds (Anderson & Pavan, 1993).

High schools are supplanting their single uniform period schedules with rotating schedules and double periods, using the same rationales as were used in the 1950s (Oliva, 1992). Reaching even farther back efforts at integrating the curriculum have breathed new life into the concept of the core curriculum, which correlated disciplines or fused subject matter following broad themes or topics (*Educational Leadership*, 1991; Vars, 1991).

The American zeal for newness often ignores contributions of the past. One of the competencies required of curriculum leaders is knowledge of research, experimentation, and past practices. Yesterday's innovation for that time may, indeed, be today's innovation for the present.

Cuban (1990) addressed the repetition of reforms, including the continuing issue of centralization versus decentralization of authority. Cuban observed that reforms return "again and again." Noting that recurring reforms have failed to solve problems for which they were designed, and he ventures that the problems were incorrectly diagnosed to begin with and, therefore, the solutions proposed were incorrect.

Curriculum developers may find solutions to some current curriculum problems in schools' experiences of the past.

Needed Research

Curriculum development remains, as it always has been, a fertile ground for research. We could still profitably explore, for example, the relative merits of nongraded schools versus graded schools. We need to determine the efficacy of year-round schools. We need to determine whether and under what conditions cooperative learning results in higher student achievement than through traditional, large-group, didactic methods. It would be fruitful to discover whether students have benefitted when teachers and parents participate in site-based management.

The curriculum researcher can study the uses of interactive video and the adaptation of the computer to instruction. This need exists for far more studies that reveal whether practices and programs make any difference in *student achievement*. In almost every aspect of the school curriculum, from identification of needs to organization to evaluation, curriculum workers can identify areas in need of inquiry.

This chapter concludes as it began by affirming that the domain of curriculum development is an integral, complex, and challenging part of the task of the instructional supervisor.

REFERENCES

Alfonso, R. J., Firth, G. R., & Neville, R. F. (1981). *Instructional supervision: a behavior system*. Boston, MA: Allyn and Bacon.

Alfonso, R. & Goldsberry. L. (1982). Colleagueship in Supervision. In T. J. Sergiovanni (Ed.). *Supervision in teaching* (1982 Yearbook). Alexandria, VA: ASCD.

Allen, D. & Ryan, K. (1969). *Microteaching*. Reading, MA: Addison-Wesley.

Anderson, R. H. & Pavan, B. N. (1993). *Nongradedness: Helping it to happen*. Lancaster, PA: Technomics Publishing Company.

Bagley, W. C. (1938) An Essentialist's Platform for the Advancement of American Education. *Educational Administration and Supervision, 24*(4), 251–252.

Beane, J. A., Toepfer, C. F., & Alessi, S. J., Jr. (1986). *Curriculum planning and development*. Boston, MA: Allyn and Bacon.

Benne, K. D. & Sheats, P. (1948). Functional Roles of Group Members. *Journal of Social Issues, 4*(2), 43–46.

Berliner, D. C. et al. (1976). *Phase III of the Beginning Teacher Effectiveness Study*. San Francisco: Far West Laboratory for Educational Research and Development.

Bolin, F. S. & Panaritis, P. (1992). Searching for common purpose: A perspective on the history of supervision. In C. D. Glickman (Ed.). *Supervision in Transition* (1992 Yearbook). Alexandria, VA: ASCD.

Caswell, H. L. & Campbell, D. (1935). *Curriculum development*. New York: American Book Company.

Cuban, L. (1990). Reforming again, again, and again. *Educational Researcher, 19*(1), 3–13.

Darling-Hammond, L. & Snyder, J. (1992). Curriculum studies and the traditions of inquiry: The scientific tradition. In P. W. Jackson (Ed.). *Handbook of research on curriculum*. New York: Macmillan.

Dewey, J. (1902). *The child and the curriculum*. Chicago, IL: The University of Chicago Press.

Dewey, J. (1929). *My pedagogic creed*. Washington, D.C.: Progressive Education Association.

Educational Leadership (1991). Integrating the curriculum, *49*(2), 3–75.

Eisner, E. W. & Vallance, E. (1974). *Conflicting conceptions of curriculum*. Berkeley, CA: McCutchan.

English, F. W. & Kaufman, R. A. (1975). *Needs assessment: A focus for curriculum development*. Alexandria, VA: ASCD.

Firestone, W. A., Fuhrman, S. H., & West, M. W. (1991). State educational reform since 1983: Appraisal and the future. *Educational Policy, 5*(3), 233–250.

Florida Department of Education (1993). *Blueprint 2000: A system of school improvement and accountability*. Tallahassee, FL: Author.

Fullan, M. (1993). Innovation, reform, and restructuring strategies. In G. Cawelti (Ed.). *Challenges and achievements of American education* (1993 Yearbook). Alexandria, VA: ASCD.

Gagné, R. M. (1967). Curriculum research and the promotion of learning. In *Perspectives of curriculum evaluation* (AERA Monograph Series on Evaluation, No. 1). Chicago: Rand McNally.

Garman, N. B. (1982). The clinical approach to supervision. In T. J. Sergiovanni (Ed.). *Supervision of teaching* (1982 Yearbook). Alexandria, VA: ASCD.

Glickman, C. D. (1985). *Supervision of instruction*. Boston, MA: Allyn and Bacon.

Goals 2000: Educate America Act (1994, March). Public Law 108–227, 103rd Congress. 108 STAT. 125–280.

Goodlad, J. I. (1984). *A place called school: Prospects for the future*. New York: McGraw-Hill.

Hunter, M. & Russell, D. (1977). How can I plan more effective lessons? *Instructor, 87,* 74-75, 88.

Jackson, P. W. (1992). Conceptions of curriculum and curriculum specialists. In P. W. Jackson (Ed.). *Handbook of research on curriculum.* New York: Macmillan.

Jackson, P. W. (Ed.). (1992). *Handbook of research on curriculum.* New York: Macmillan.

Lovell, J. T. & Wiles, K. (1983). *Supervision for better schools* (5th ed.). Englewood Cliffs, NJ: Prentice Hall.

Lucio, W. H. & McNeil, J. D. (1969). *Supervision: A synthesis of thought and action.* New York: McGraw-Hill.

Macdonald, J. B. & Leeper, R. R. (Eds.). (1965). *Theories of instruction.* Alexandria, VA: ASCD.

Madaus, G. F. (1988). The influence of testing on the curriculum. In L. N. Tanner (Ed.). *Critical issues in curriculum* (87th Yearbook of the National Society for the Study of Education, Part I). Chicago, IL: The University of Chicago Press.

Madaus, G. F. & Kellaghan, T. (1992). Curriculum evaluation and assessment. In P. W. Jackson (Ed.). *Handbook of research on curriculum.* New York: Macmillan.

Madaus, G. F. & Tan, A. G. A. (1993). The growth of assessment. In G. Cawelti (Ed) *Challenges and achievements of American education* (1993 Yearbook). Alexandria, VA: ASCD.

Mager, R. F. (1975). *Preparing instructional objectives* (2nd ed.). Belmont, CA: Pitman Learning.

Miel, A. (1946). *Changing the curriculum: A social process.* New York: D. Appleton-Century.

Murphy, J. T. (1989). The paradox of decentralizing schools: Lessons from business, government, and the Catholic church. *Phi Delta Kappan, 70*(10), 808–812.

National Council on Education Standards and Testing. (1992). *Raising standards for American education.* Washington, D.C.: U.S. Government Printing Office.

National Education Association Committee of Ten. (1894). *Report of the committee of ten on secondary school studies.* New York: American Book.

Oliva, P. F. (1976). *Supervision for today's schools.* New York: Crowell.

Oliva, P. F. (1992). *Developing the curriculum* (3rd ed.). New York: HarperCollins.

Oliva, P. F. (1993). *Supervision for today's schools* (4th ed.). White Plains, NY: Longman.

Ouchi, W. G. (1981). *Theory Z: How American business can meet the Japanese challenge.* Reading, MA: Addison-Wesley.

Pajak, E, (1989). *The central office supervisor of curriculum and instruction: Setting the stage for success.* Boston, MA: Allyn and Bacon.

Pajak, E. (1992). A view from the central office. In C. D. Glickman (Ed.). *Supervision in transition* (1992 Yearbook). Alexandria, VA: ASCD.

Perelman, L. J. (1992). *School's out: Hyperlearning, the new technology, and the end of education.* New York: William Morrow.

Popham, W. J. (1970). *Systematic instruction.* Englewood Cliffs, NJ: Prentice Hall.

Rosenshine, B. V. (1979). Content, time, and direct instruction. In P. J. Peterson & H. J. Walhberg (Eds.). *Research in teaching: Concepts, findings, and implications* (pp. 28–56). Berkeley, CA.

Schubert, W. H. (1986). *Curriculum: Perspective, paradigm, and possibility.* New York: Macmillan.

Sergiovanni, T. J. (Ed.). (1982). *Supervision of teaching* (1982 Yearbook). Alexandria, VA: ASCD.

Sergiovanni, T. J. (1987). The theoretical basis for cultural leadership. In L. T. Sheive & M. B. Schoenheit (Eds.). *Leadership: Examining the elusive* (1987 Yearbook). Alexandria, VA: ASCD.

Snyder, J., Bolin, F., & Zumwalt, K. (1992). Curriculum implementation. In P. W. Jackson (Ed.). *Handbook of research on curriculum.* New York: Macmillan.

Sturges, A. W. (1978). *The roles and responsibilities of instructional supervisors.* Alexandria, VA: ASCD.

Taba, H. (1962). *Curriculum development: Theory and practice.* New York: Harcourt Brace Jovanovich.

Tanner, D. & Tanner, L. N. (1980). *Curriculum development: Theory into practice* (2nd ed.). New York: Macmillan.

Tyler, R. W. (1949). *Basic principles of curriculum and instruction.* Chicago, IL: The University of Chicago Press.

U.S. Department of Education. (1990). *National goals for education.* Washington, D.C.: Author.

Vars, G. (1991). Integrating curriculum in historical perspective. *Educational Leadership, 49*(2), 14–15.

Wiles, J. & Bondi, J. (1986). *Supervision: A guide to practice* (2nd ed.). Columbus, OH: Merrill.

Wiles, J. & Bondi, J. (1993). *Curriculum development: A guide to practice* (4th ed.). New York: Merrill.

SUPERVISION AND STAFF DEVELOPMENT

Stephen P. Gordon
SOUTHWEST TEXAS STATE UNIVERSITY

Robert F. Nicely, Jr.
PENNSYLVANIA STATE UNIVERSITY

In this chapter, definitions of staff development and the relationship of supervision and staff development are examined by comparing the positions of scholars within the field. Three broad orientations to staff development are discussed; alternative purposes of staff development are reviewed; various levels of staff development are examined; characteristics of and barriers to effective staff development are outlined; alternative models for designing staff development programs are discussed; a variety of staff development frameworks are reviewed, with each review including a discussion of the relevant research; relationships of staff development and related processes are examined; staff development evaluation is discussed; and finally, trends and issues in staff development are presented.

DEFINING STAFF DEVELOPMENT

Definitions of staff development range from simple to complex. An example of the former is proposed by Sparks and Loucks-Horsley (1990): "Staff development is defined as those processes that improve the job-related knowledge, skills, or attitudes of school employees" (p. 5). An example of the latter is Heideman's (1990):

Staff development offers a process for growth to all professional educators. It is designed to influence their knowledge, attitudes, or skills, thus enabling them to create educational concepts and design instructional programs to improve student learning. These programs should be based on needs identified at the local, state, national or global level—often the result of societal changes. The concept of strategic planning, involving both a scan of the internal educational environment as well as the external one, is a part of successful staff development (pp. 5–6).

While there currently exists a wide range of definitions of staff development, Dillon-Peterson (1991) notes that the term was not generally used until the mid-1970s. Prior to that period, "in-service training" and "in-service education" were the prevalent terms. Since the 1970s, the terms "staff development" and "in-service education" have coexisted, with considerable disagreement within the field as to their relationship. One general view is that there is no distinction between the two terms. For example, Fullan (1990) and Tanner and Tanner (1987) treat in-service education and staff development synonymously.

A second general view is that in-service education is a subset of staff development, although there is considerable disagreement among those who share this view concerning definitions of the two terms. Daresh (1989) considers the common view to be that "*in-service education* covers those activities directed toward remediating a perceived lack of skill or understanding and *staff development* refers to an ongoing process that promotes professional growth, rather than remediation" (p. 252). He considers both in-service education and staff development to be important, suggests that artificial distinctions between them be minimized, and points out that in schools little difference is recognized between the two terms. Heideman (1990) differentiates in-service education and staff development as follows:

In-service education is only part of staff development, being almost exclusively informational in nature. In contrast, staff development goes beyond the informational stage; it involves adaptations to change with the purpose of modifying instructional activities, of changing teacher attitudes and improving student achievement. Staff development is concerned with personal as well as professional and organizational needs (p. 4).

Orlich (1989) also considers in-service education to be a subset of staff development, and describes in-service education as short-term training. He discusses the relationship of in-service education and staff development as follows:

Whereas in-service education is oriented toward immediate training objectives, staff development implies persistent and personally significant activities. In essence, staff development subsumes in-service education projects and also addresses the larger issue of developing organizational problem-solving capacities and leadership skills. The totality of building human and institutional resources in the organization becomes the goal of staff development (pp. 5–6).

Glickman's (1990) distinction between staff development and in-service education focuses on the scope of learning:

Staff development is the total of learning experiences available to a professional that are both directly and indirectly related to his or her work. In-service comprises the specific learning experiences, sanctioned and supported by the school and district, directly related to the instructional goals of the school and district (p. 310).

While agreeing that in-service education is a subset of staff development, Harris's (1989) explanation of staff development differs significantly from those discussed above. For Harris, staff development consists of staffing and training. Staffing involves selecting, assigning, evaluating, retiring, and dismissing. Training includes in-service education and advanced preparation. In-service education is training to improve an individual's performance in a current position. Advanced preparation is training for a new, advanced position.

A third general view of the relationship between in-service education and staff development (overlapping to some extent with the "in-service as subset" view) is that staff development has evolved from in-service education and is more teacher-centered, collaborative, systematic, and developmental (in short, more sophisticated) than in-service education (Hyde & Pink, 1992). Implicit in the evolutionary view is the notion that traditional in-service education will increasingly be viewed by scholars and practioners as archaic and inappropriate. This view is indirectly supported by the fact that in recent years the use of the term "staff development" has increased and "in-service education" has decreased both in literature and practice. Whether this trend reflects a mere change in terminology or a significant change in belief systems, content, and process remains to be seen, but historical reviews of practice lend support to the latter explanation (DeLuca, 1991; Dillon-Peterson, 1991).

Sergiovanni and Starratt's book *Supervision: A Redefinition* (1993) raises additional issues of terminology. In earlier editions (1979, 1983, 1988), one chapter was entitled "Supervision as Staff Development." In the 1993 edition, the chapter was retitled "Supervision as Teacher Development and Renewal." Building on the work of Bolin and Falk (1987), Sergiovanni and Starratt discuss "in-service programs," "staff development," and "renewal" as "alternative frameworks for creating a growth-oriented supervision" (p. 265), and place the three frameworks on a continuum from other- to self-directed, with in-service programs at the other-directed end of the continuum. The authors make the following proposal concerning the three frameworks: "All three have a role to play, but the full range of growth opportunities for teachers,

we suggest, is available only when renewal is emphasized and supported by staff development as needed. In contrast, in-service programming should play a very limited role" (pp. 265–266). Sergiovanni and Starratt have been trendsetters in the field of supervision, but the long-term impact of the three-framework classification and call for a primary emphasis on renewal remains to be seen.

Other authors have distinguished terms like "teacher development," "continuing education," "professional development," and "professional growth" from "in-service education," "staff development," and each other. In the mid-1990s, however, no proposed differentiation of these terms is commonly accepted. They are still used interchangeably by a large number of authors and practitioners. For the present, the tongue-in-cheek exercise developed by Nicholson, Joyce, Parker, and Waterman (1976, p. 92) still applies:

To form a suitable synonym for "in-service education"—(1) choose one word from Column A and/or one word from Column B; and then (2) choose one word from Column C:

A	B	C
"continuing"	"staff"	"development"
"continuous"	"professional"	"growth"
	"teacher"	"education"
	"personnel"	"preparation"
		"renewal"
		"improvement"

RELATIONSHIP OF SUPERVISION AND STAFF DEVELOPMENT

As early as 1922, Burton listed "the improvement of teachers in service" (p. 10) as a function of supervision and devoted a full chapter to that function. In the chapter, he discussed such topics as teachers' meetings, institutes, conferences, bibliographies, intervisitation, leaves of absence, coursework, lectures, participation in policy determination, and "curricula making." Discussions of "improvement" or "training" of teachers "in service" were present in the supervision literature throughout the 1920s and 1930s (Barr, 1931; Barr & Burton, 1926; Barr, Burton, & Brueckner, 1938). In the second edition of Barr, Burton and Bruecker's *Supervision: Democratic Leadership in the Improvement of Learning* (1947) the authors broke with the tradition, stating that "the expression 'training of teachers in service' is no longer in good repute" and titled the relevant chapter "Facilitating Teacher Growth."

In *Supervision for Better* Schools (1950, 1955), Wiles reflected the growth view, entitling one section "How Can Teacher Growth be Continued." In Melchior's (1950) *Instructional Supervision: A Guide to Modern Practice,* six chapters were devoted to "in-service education." Other mid-century authors, however, continued to refer to "in-service training." McNerney, for example, included a chapter entitled "The In-service Training Program" in his 1951 book *Educational Supervision.*

By the 1960s, the term "in-service education" had become prevalent in the supervision literature (Franseth, 1961; Harris, 1963; Wiles, 1967). Arranging for in-service education was one of Harris's (1963) often-cited ten tasks of supervision introduced in his book *Supervisory Behavior in Education*. In their *Handbook for Effective Supervision of Instruction*, Neagley and Evans (1964, 1970, 1980) devoted part of a chapter to working with groups in in-service education. Eye and Netzer (1965) stated that "the in-service development of teachers is one of the prime responsibilities of the supervisory staff" (p. 137). Not all supervision texts of the 1960s and early 1970s agreed. Popular texts by Blumberg (1974), Lucio and McNeil (1962, 1969), and Mosher and Purpel (1972), for example, did not focus on traditional in-service education as a component of supervision.

By the 1970s, the term *staff development* was being discussed within the supervision literature. Wilhelms (1973) encouraged the use of the term. In his booklet, *Supervision in a New Key*, Wilhelms entitled a section "The New Media of Staff Development," in which he highlighted a number of staff development offerings available from the Far West and Northwest regional laboratories. The fourth edition of Wiles and Lovell's *Supervision for Better Schools* (1975) discussed "continuing staff development" under the supervisory function of improving instruction and included a chapter titled "Staff Development in the Local School." In the first edition of *Supervision for Today's Schools*, Oliva (1976) proposed "teacher development" (a term he changed to "staff development" in later editions) along with "instructional development" and "curriculum development" as three "domains" of supervision. In each edition of his text, Oliva (1976, 1984, 1989, 1993) has written several chapters on teacher or staff development, including a chapter called "Helping Teachers Through In-service Programs." Sergiovanni and Starratt (1979) promoted staff development as a subset of supervision with a chapter entitled "Supervision as Staff Development" in the second edition of their book *Supervision: Human Perspectives*.

Alfonso, Firth, and Neville (1981) added a chapter on staff development to the second edition of *Instructional Supervision, a Behavior System*, but differentiated staff development from instructional supervision: "Staff development has the responsibility for systematic and continued learning in order to improve oneself professionally. Instructional supervision is responsible on a daily basis for monitoring and improving teaching and learning" (p. 400). The authors recognized the direct relationship between staff development and supervision and the importance of instructional supervisors' involvement in staff development planning. They maintained, however, that the supervisor should not be involved in the "actual conduct and operation" (p. 399) of staff development activities. They argued that doing so would cut into the supervisory role and cause the supervisory function to suffer.

Many other authors of the 1980s considered staff development or in-service education to be a subset of supervision. Wiles and Bondi (1980) considered supervision of in-service programs to be one of six "leadership roles." Dull (1981) considered staff development to be one of nine "functions" of supervision, stating that "supervision of staff development is the most important ingredient in school organization" (p. 110). In-service education continued to be one of Harris' (1985) ten tasks and became one of Glickman's (1985) five tasks of supervision. Tanner and Tanner (1987) included a chapter called

"Establishing and Administering the In-service Education Program." For Beach and Reinhartz (1989), staff development was one of seven "dimensions" of supervision. Daresh (1989) included a chapter entitled "Supervision as Effective Staff Development and In-service Education." He stated that "in many ways the responsibilities of supervisors are those of staff development" (p. 251). Pajak (1989) described staff development as an important supervisory responsibility.

Not all supervision texts from the 1980s treated staff development or in-service education as an important aspect of supervision. Blumberg's (1980) second edition, like his first, did not address traditional staff development in any significant manner. Although Krey and Burke (1989) described staff development as an "implementation target," and included a chapter entitled "Professional Status," they included little discussion of traditional staff development.

In the 1990s, staff development has become one of Wiles and Bondi's (1991) six "skill areas of supervision," remains one of Oliva's (1993) three "domains," and is one of Glickman, Gordon, and Ross-Gordon's (1995) five "tasks" of supervision. In the 1990s, authors considering staff development as a subset of supervision have placed increasing value on staff development as a supervisory task. Wiles and Bondi (1991) assert that "planning staff development activities is the major method of improving instruction for the supervisor" (p. 21). Starratt (1992) goes so far as to argue for the abolishment of traditional supervision, after which supervisors would assume only two roles: "teacher evaluator and facilitator of staff development" (p. 85).

Glatthorn (1990) discussed staff development as a "related process" rather than a subset of supervision. Glatthorn's definition of staff development differentiates it from both supervision and evaluation:

Staff development is the use of formal and informal programs, other than supervision and evaluation, designed to improve the performance of role incumbents; such programs are typically presented to groups of staff members and are typically designed in response to both organizational and individual needs (p. 224).

McQuarrie and Wood (1991) describe supervision and staff development as "discreet, yet connected" (p. 91). They identify similarities and differences between the two processes:

Both supervision and staff development focus on helping teachers become more effective in the classroom. Supervision accomplishes this by helping teachers refine skills they have already learned. Staff development stresses teaching and learning new skills. In addition, both processes are judgment-free; thus, they are designed to assist teachers as they improve their instructional practices in a non-threatening atmosphere (p. 94).

McQuarrie and Wood (1991) also discuss "connections" between supervision and staff development: supervisory data can be used for planning staff development; supervision can be used to refine and expand skills learned during in-service training; and staff development is used to prepare educators for supervision programs.

A significant body of literature on staff development exists separately from the supervision literature. This "independent" staff development literature includes a variety of books[1] and a rapidly expanding number of articles and research papers.

The relationship between the supervision literature and the separate staff-development literature takes the form primarily of common purposes and frameworks. For example, curriculum development, enhanced teacher decision-making, and instructional improvement are purposes which run through both the supervision and staff development literature. Frameworks like coaching and action research are found throughout both bodies of literature. Even clinical supervision is discussed as a format for staff development within the staff development literature (Caldwell, 1989; Harris, 1989; Loucks-Horsley et al, 1987) To summarize, while there is disagreement among supervision and staff development scholars about whether staff development can properly be called a subset of supervision or a related process, the two fields overlap considerably in the literature. This overlap is mirrored in practice, where supervisors often are assigned responsibility for coordinating staff development efforts.

ORIENTATIONS TOWARD STAFF DEVELOPMENT

Miller and Seller (1985) described three "metaorientations" to curriculum: transmission, transaction, and transformation. These three terms also can be used to describe the major orientations to staff development. In this section, origins and beliefs of the three orientations, as well as contemporary staff development models reflecting each orientation, will be discussed.

Transmission Orientation

The transmission orientation is related to the educational philosophies of perennialism and essentialism and has been influenced by behavioral psychology. Those who possess this orientation toward staff development believe that staff development should be a vehicle for conveying an externally validated body of knowledge, skills, and attitudes to teachers. Sources of the content to be transmitted have varied throughout the history of staff development. In the mid-eighteenth century teacher institutes, the first systematic forms of in-service training (Spring, 1994), were focused on transmitting subject-area knowledge and "moral character" (DeLuca, 1991; Spring, 1994). By the turn of the century, the focus of the institutes had shifted to training in methods of teaching (DeLuca, 1991). In the early 1900s, in-service training was based on the principles of scientific management derived from the industrial efficiency studies carried out by Frederick Taylor and others, and translated into educational terms by individuals like Franklin Bobbit and W. W. Charters. Curriculum was to be based on analysis of skills needed in adult life, and in-service training was concerned with instructing teachers in the most efficient methods of transmitting that curriculum.

During the 1960s, the behavioral science approach led to "teacher-proof" curricula and materials developed by outside researchers and publishers. In-service education was used to train teachers to use the packaged curricula. The neoscientif-

ic approach which emerged in the early 1970s relied on externally defined student performance objectives and standardized achievement tests to transmit student learning expectations to teachers. Under the neoscientific approach, in-service education is necessary to provide teachers with the instructional skills needed to meet those expectations.

Another form of transmission is based on the effective teaching studies that began in the early 1970s. These studies identify generic teaching behaviors which correlate positively with high scores on standardized achievement tests. Those who espouse the use of in-service training to transmit these behaviors to other teachers believe that teachers who use the same instructional *processes* observed in the effectiveness studies will attain the same positive student *outcomes* that were measured in the studies.

The transmission of instructional skills usually takes the form of training sessions followed by classroom inspection, reinforcement of desired instructional behaviors, and remediation when desired behaviors are not present. The effective teaching practices are often broken down into discreet "building blocks," "basic competencies," or "essential elements." This simplifies transmission as well as the measurement of skill acquisition. The most popular example of the transmission orientation in recent years is the Madeline Hunter Model (1984). The content of Hunter's training program is based partly on the effective teaching research, but also on her translations of research in psychology, sociology, neurology, and anthropology into principles for effective teaching. Hunter (1984) stated: "Translation of research-based theory into practice has now been accomplished" (p. 174). She believed that there now exists a "science of teaching which is generalizable to all goals in all content" (p. 170).

Hunter's (1984) discussion of the teacher's role reflects the transmission orientation:

Teaching involves factor-analyzing . . . goals into dependent and independent sequences of learning, diagnosing students to determine what each has achieved in that sequence, and employing psychological principles that contribute to the speed and effectiveness with which each student acquires new learning in those sequences (p. 170).

The instructional skills that Hunter (1984) transmits to teachers include the following:

1. setting the learning objective at the correct level of difficulty;
2. directing teacher and learner effort and energy toward the learning objective;
3. using principles of learning; and
4. monitoring student's learning and adjusting teacher and learner behaviors accordingly.

Hunter's seven elements of lesson design (anticipatory set, statement of the lesson's objective and purpose, input, modeling, checking for understanding, guided practice, and independent practice) are consistent with the effective teaching studies of the 1970s and 1980s (Rosenshine, 1983).

Hunter (1984) proposed that comprehensive training in the science of teaching be provided, "then implemented in classrooms with accountability for its infusion into the program being systematically monitored" (p. 191). The supervisor's role in the Hunter model includes classroom observations in which the supervisor prepares a "script tape" (verbatim transcript) of the lesson. The supervisor reviews the script tape to analyze the teacher's decisions about lesson content, learner behavior, teacher behavior, the lesson design, and the presence or absence of the four types of instructional skills previously listed. In a postobservation conference aimed at instructional improvement, the supervisor identifies productive behaviors, provides alternative behaviors, invites teacher analysis, identifies areas for improvement, or promotes continued teacher growth.

Hunter's model possesses all of the attributes of the transmission orientation: supervisor control of the learning process, transmission of scientific knowledge and skills, monitoring of instruction, reinforcement of desired teaching behaviors, and diagnosis and remediation of deficit behaviors.

Transaction Orientation

The transaction orientation[2] can be traced to Dewey's educational philosophy of experimentalism. Cognitive and cognitive-developmental psychology also have influenced the transaction position. Transactional staff development is primarily concerned with teacher problem solving and reflection aimed at fostering improved teacher decision-making. Dewey believed that the purpose of education is growth. He maintained that growth is fostered through interaction with one's social environment, especially through solving problems encountered within the environment. Dewey held that social interaction and problem solving make possible the continuous reconstruction of experience and knowledge, which enables personal and social improvement.

Transactional staff development also is rooted in the theories of social psychologists like Lewin (1946). Lewin's work focused on group dynamics and experiential learning. Johnson and Johnson (1982) summarized Lewin's concept of experiential learning:

When you generate an action theory from your own experiences and then continually modify it to improve its effectiveness, you are learning experientially. Experiential learning can be conceived of in a simplified way as a three-stage cycle: (1) the learner takes action by trying out the strategies and procedures in his action theory; (2) the learner experiences the consequences of his action, receives feedback on his behavior, and examines and reflects on his experiences, and (3) the learner organizes present information and experiences into a (new) action theory (pp. 17–18).

According to Lewin, experiential learning causes cognitive restructuring and attitudinal change and expands the learner's repertoire of skills, which can be utilized in similar situations that occur in the future (Johnson & Johnson, 1982).

For Schon (1988), as for Dewey and Lewin, the most important transaction is between experience and reflection. The reflective practitioner can engage either in reflection *in* action or *on* action. Reflection *in* action is defined as "reflection on phenomena, and on one's spontaneous ways of thinking and acting, undertaken in the midst of action to guide further action" (p. 22). Reflection *on* action is reflection on phenomena, thinking and acting within a particular situation carried out after the fact, also with the purpose of guiding future action.

Tanner and Tanner's (1987) view of problem solving within a democratic environment also reflects a transactional view:

The more effective schools are characterized as having a professional staff with a problem-solving orientation and a democratic-participative organizational climate—with structure, resources, and incentives for collaboration, cooperative decision-making, mutual support, and continuing commitment to the active search for problem solutions (p. 318).

A contemporary example of a staff development framework reflecting a transactional orientation was developed by Langer and Colton (1994). The purpose of the model is to develop teacher reflection. The framework includes (1) a *professional knowledge base* interacting with (2) a *cycle of inquiry* to construct knowledge and meaning, (3) *personal characteristics* which can promote reflective thinking within, (4) a *collegial environment*, and (5) a variety of specific *strategies* for developing reflective thinking.

The *professional knowledge base* consists of information "that needs to be accessed and considered in interpreting experiences and making decisions" (Langer & Colton, 1994, p. 2). The knowledge base includes content, students, pedagogy, context, prior experiences, personal values, feelings, and scripts. Langer and Colton (1994) explain these various aspects as follows:

A teacher planning a lesson on rocks and minerals might consider the essential concepts of the curriculum (CONTENT), the prior knowledge and interest of STUDENTS, how cooperative learning might be incorporated into the lesson (PEDAGOGY), the school's and community's current emphasis on scientific thinking skills (CONTEXT), and the results of the last time this was taught (PRIOR EXPERIENCES). The teacher's commitment to developing scientific reasoning (PERSONAL VALUES) and his or her own feelings of frustration or joy in the act of teaching on a particular day (FEELINGS) may also have an effect on the decisions made.

Another influence will be SCRIPTS—automatized routines in action or thinking. With experience, teachers acquire the ability to handle routines with little conscious thought. . . . Professionals also develop automatic self-questioning (metacognitive) routines that help them analyze their actions and decisions (pp. 2–3).

The *cycle of inquiry* consists of (1) observing and gathering information, (2) analyzing and interpreting, (3) hypothesizing, and (4) acting and experimenting. *Personal characteristics* desirable for reflective thinking include consciousness (metacognition), flexibility, social responsibility, caring, and efficacy. The authors maintain that teacher reflection develops in "*a collegial environment*—a place of trust where relationships are open and honest" (p. 3). Strategies recommended for developing reflective thinking include reflection on personal histories, video and audio self-assessment, journal writing, cognitive coaching, discussion and writing of cases, problem framing, action research, and role playing. All of these strategies are consistent with the transactional goal of growth through interaction with one's environment and reflection on that interaction.

Transformation Orientation

The transformation orientation includes two related approaches to staff development: the humanistic and the cultural-change approaches. The humanistic approach focuses on facilitating the individual teacher's self-directed growth. The cultural-change approach focuses on the transformation of the school culture through critical analysis of, and changes in, assumptions, values, norms, roles, and relationships.

Humanistic staff development is consistent with the broad educational philosophies of romantic naturalism and existentialism. Humanistic staff development has been directly influenced by humanistic psychology, including the work of Rogers, Maslow, and Combs. Rogers' (1961) "client-centered therapy" focuses on the notion of the individual's capacity for personal growth. According to Rogers, "the individual has within himself the capacity and the tendency, latent if not evident, to move forward toward maturity. In a suitable psychological climate this tendency is released, and becomes actual rather than potential" (p. 35). Rogers (1961) proposed that through genuineness, acceptance, empathy, and a nondiagnostic, nonevaluative approach, the facilitator can foster a client's growth toward autonomy.

Maslow (1970), another humanist, also proposed that individuals were capable of self-directed growth, but that hierarchy of four "deficiency needs" (physiological needs, safety needs, need for belonging and love, and need for esteem) must be met before addressing the need for self-actualization; the need "to become everything that one is capable of becoming" (Maslow, 1970, p. 46).

A third psychologist who has influenced humanistic staff development is Combs. For Combs, the helper's role is to create an atmosphere that will allow the client to improve his or her self-concept by confronting and reinterpreting past experiences or engaging in new experiences "calling for a different view of self" (Combs, Avila, & Purkey, 1978, p. 29). Creating such a "helping atmosphere" involves being authentic, genuine, and accepting; creating an environment that is both challenging and nonthreatening; and removing barriers to client involvement, including preoccupation with the past, evaluation, and fear of making mistakes. Change in the client's behavior is based on change in the client's self-concept (Combs et al, 1978).

A humanistic approach has been evident in a number of staff development models. Kelley (1951) described the use of humanistic principles to foster self-directed change by teachers attending a series of highly acclaimed workshops at Wayne State University. Berman's *Supervision, Staff Development, and Leadership* (1971) reflected a humanistic approach with such topics as "Perceiving," "Communicating," "Concerning," "Valuing," and "Facing Reality." Berman held that teachers' growth could be facilitated by establishing a climate of mutual trust and by freeing teachers from impediments. In their book, *Staff Development, A Humanistic Approach*, Dobson, Dobson, and Kessinger (1980) applied humanistic beliefs to staff development. They argued that a primary purpose of staff development should be to assist teacher decision-making by facilitating teachers' examination of the level of congruency among their educational beliefs,

their teaching practice, and the day-to-day operation of the school.

Clark (1992) presented a rationale for self-directed professional development:

First, we need to recognize that adult development is voluntary. No one can force a person to learn, change, or grow. When adults feel they are in control of a process of change that they have voluntarily chosen, they're much more likely to realize full value from it than when coerced into training situations in which they have little say about the timing, the process or the goals. Second, because each teacher is unique in important ways, it is impossible to create a simple, centrally administered, and planned program of professional development that will meet everyone's needs and desires. Why not let the individual be in charge of asking and answering the timeless questions: "Who am I? What do I need? How can I get help?" Third, I advocate self-directed professional development because I think it is the way that the best teachers already operate (p. 77).

The *cultural change approach* to transformational staff development is consistent with the broad educational philosophy of reconstructionism. It also is congruent with critical educational theorists like Apple (1982, 1984), Freire (1970, 1985), and Giroux (Giroux, 1983, 1985; Giroux & McLaren, 1986, 1989). Those who espouse the cultural change approach believe that the hierarchical organization of schools, the history of external inspection and control of teachers, teacher isolation, and traditional in-service training all restrict the teacher growth called for by humanists. They believe that growth can only take place if radical changes are made in the school's culture. The school culture is to be transformed through critical reflection on and changes in institutionalized assumptions, norms, values, roles, and relationships. The cultural change approach involves several interactive processes, including teacher empowerment, development of a collegial culture, and professional inquiry leading to "conscious development of teachers' own theories of practice," (Holland, Clift, Veal, Johnson, & McCarthy, 1992, p. 174).

Smyth's (1989a,b) "critical reflection" is an example of transformational staff development. Smyth argues that teachers have historically been oppressed by social and political forces of which they have little awareness, and that they often have been in unwitting collusion with those forces. He maintains that before teachers can begin to change the cultural conditions that frustrate and restrain them, they must first understand those conditions (Smyth, 1989b). Smyth (1989a) has put his critical perspective into practice while working with a group of teachers in an alternative approach to staff development. He engaged teachers in a process consisting of four phases: describing, informing, confronting, and reconstructing.

In the *describing phase*, participants recorded in a journal ordinary critical incidents they experienced while teaching. These descriptions of practice were the basis for group dialogue concerning the participants' practice. This dialogue included describing aspects of the teachers' worlds that alienated and confused them. In this phase, participants began to challenge the notion of a universal set of "good teaching" practices.

The *informing phase* of the project involved teachers in finding the meaning behind the teaching behaviors and dilemmas they had described in the earlier phase. Teachers in the project developed "local theories" about specific incidents which occurred in their teaching. This phase reinforced the teachers' belief that universal laws and "experts'" interpretations of effective teaching were not especially relevant to their efforts to make sense of the behaviors and dilemmas they were analyzing. According to Smyth (1989a) the teachers' "local theorizing" allowed them to go beyond the "habitualness and taken-for-grantedness" of teaching practice, and to "gain a measurement of control and ownership over what counts as knowledge" about teaching (p. 490).

In the *confronting phase,* the teachers focused on the causes of the teaching theories that were expressed in their practice. This phase involved reflection on how social and institutional forces influenced assumptions and values underlying classroom practices. When teachers in the project challenged their own local theories during this phase, they did so while examining the social causation of such theories, rather than ascribing inconsistent or problematic theories to personal deficiencies. By sharing journal entries and confronting local theories with colleagues, participants found that, rather than finding a simple problem to be solved, they identified a whole series of questions about classroom situations which needed to be addressed. As a result of dialogue with colleagues concerning these questions, teachers became conscious of the fact that many of their counterproductive and previously unarticulated and unquestioned theories about teaching were actually the result of social, cultural, and political structures beyond their classrooms.

The final phase of Smyth's project was the *reconstructing phase.* In this phase, teachers focused on what they might do differently in the future, including actions that teachers could take to overcome the institutional forces that influenced past practice. By this point in the project, dialogue had shifted from "how-to" questions typically associated with instructional assistance to questions about "what" gets taught to students and "why" it gets taught. While not all participants had restructured their teaching by the end of the project, all had been given the opportunity to critically reflect on their practice, an activity which Smyth holds to be a prerequisite to meaningful change.

PURPOSES OF STAFF DEVELOPMENT

A broad spectrum of staff development purposes is discussed in the literature. Part II of the 1983 Yearbook of the National Society of the Study of Education focused on staff development (Griffin, 1983). Chapters by prominent scholars addressed such staff development purposes as teachers' cognitive development, school improvement, improvement of teaching skills, and curricular and instructional change. Fielding and Schalock (1985) discussed three broad purposes of staff development: "(a) to foster the growth or increase the effectiveness of individual educators . . . (b) to foster the implementation or improvement of an instructional program, and (c) to improve the effectiveness of a school as an organization" (p. 6). Howey (1985) proposed six purposes: pedagogical development, understanding and discovery of self, cognitive development, theoretical development, professional development, and career development.

A work on staff development edited by Wideen and Andrews (1987) included emphases on developing critical reflection among teachers, improving instruction, teacher induction, school improvement, and curriculum development. In the same book, Bradley (1987) describes staff development as all those activities that lead to:

1. the teacher's improved performance in the present job;
2. the enhancement of the teacher's prospects of career development;
3. the teacher being able to help the school strengthen its present performance; and
4. the school being able to prepare itself to meet future demands on it (p. 192).

Orlich (1989) has proposed four general goals or foci of staff development: furthering the organization, promoting individual competence, changing roles, and developing a cadre of specialized trainers. Orlich matches several specific staff development models with each of his four purposes.

While most lists of staff development purposes focus on desired outcomes, some are process oriented. Lambert (1988) writes that facilitators of professional development should assist professionals in the following:

- inquiring into and reflecting on practice;
- bringing to the surface and sharing knowledge of the craft;
- identifying and creating options;
- leading and working collaboratively;
- learning about the state-of-the-art in the profession; and
- designing school and district systems that open opportunities and encourage participation (p. 668).

Lieberman and Miller (1991) recommend that professional development revolve around "(a) developing a culture of support for teacher inquiry in schools, (b) considering the professional growth opportunities appropriate to particular school cultures, and (c) working through the inevitable problems and tensions raised as part of the change process" (p. 5).

Some of the purposes of staff development clearly reflect one of the three orientations to staff development discussed previously. For example, the development of teacher competence can be related to a transmission orientation, cognitive development reflects a transaction orientation, and self-discovery relates to a transformation orientation. Most purposes of staff development, however, cannot be matched *a priori* with a single orientation. For example, a curriculum development or school improvement purpose could involve transmission, transaction, or transformation, depending on the specific goals of the staff development program.

LEVELS OF STAFF DEVELOPMENT

Staff development is discussed in the literature at the international, national, regional, state, intermediate, district, school, and individual levels. Each of these levels is discussed in this section. Depending on the level of staff development being addressed, policies, influences, dissemination of information and resources, and types of staff development will be considered.

International Level

Although they all are based in the United States, the American Educational Research Association (AERA), the Association for Supervision and Curriculum Development (ASCD), and the National Staff Development Council (NSDC), are, in effect, international organizations that significantly influence staff development throughout the world. AERA is the primary international forum for sharing formal research and scholarly papers on staff development. ASCD traditionally has taken a multifaceted view of educational leadership, including emphasis on curriculum development, instruction, supervision, and staff development. The rapidly growing NSDC has focused on staff development and organizational development. Both ASCD and NSDC place their primary focus on the practitioner and sponsor a variety of publications, audio and audiovisual productions, networks, affiliates, conferences, academies, institutes, and workshops on staff development. Both showcase effective staff-development programs at their annual conferences. There are also international staff development forums outside of the United States. The Commission of the European Communities (1988) has conducted international surveys and national case studies on staff development and identified priority staff development issues for the European community. International Seminars on Staff and Educational Development (ISSED) have been hosted by institutions in different nations (Documentation and Information Centre of the European Communities, 1991).

Examples of staff development in various nations can be found throughout the literature. George (1990) discusses staff development in Japan; Millin and Barta (1991) describe human resource development for the use of computers in Israeli schools; Pajak and Hooghoff (1992) discuss the Netherlands's national system for providing schools and teachers with professional support; and Bell and Day (1991) describe a range of professional development programs in Great Britain. Comparisons of different national approaches also are available in the literature. Takemura and Shimizu (1993) compare staff development for science teachers in Japan to staff development in the United States. Thompson and Cooley (1987) and Dahawy (1992) compare in-service education in the United Kingdom to in-service in the United States.

National and Regional Levels

Although most policies and programs of the federal government directed at PK–12 education influence staff development to some degree, several programs of the Office of Educational Research and Improvement in the U.S. Department of Education have had significant impact on PK–12 staff development. The National Diffusion Network (NDN) supports validation and dissemination of field-tested educational programs. These programs include some staff development programs but a far greater number of other types of educational programs with staff development components (Leuthheuser, 1994). The Educational Resources Information Center (ERIC) disseminates a wide educational knowledge base in print and microfiche form, including research and literature on staff development. Research and

Development Centers (RDC) have as their mission the development and dissemination of new knowledge in education. Individual centers have been established for separate content areas, for elementary, middle and secondary levels, and for teacher education. Much of the research generated by the centers has implications for staff development.

The Regional Educational Laboratories serve 10 federally designated regions, with the purpose of improving educational policy and practice by assisting in *application* of the available knowledge base. Despite the common purpose, particular laboratories have taken different approaches to improving educational practice in general and staff development in particular. For example, the Far West Laboratory for Educational Research and Development has made extensive use of the case study method in mentoring beginning teachers, teaching diverse students, and reforming middle grades. The North Central Regional Educational Laboratory (NCREL) has pioneered the use of audionetworks; audioseminars; and interactive, multimedia learning environments for supporting professional development. A primary focus of the Southwest Educational Development Laboratory has been the change process, including the dissemination of research reports, literature reviews, and resources; the training, assistance, and support of change agents; and case studies of change efforts. The Regional Laboratory for Educational Improvement of the Northeast and Islands, in affiliation with the nonprofit organization NETWORK, Inc., has been extremely active in staff development, making a variety of programs, publications, and other resources available. The popular publications *Building Systems for Professional Growth* (Arbuckle & Murray, 1990) and *Continuing to Learn* (Loucks-Horsley et al, 1987) were both co-published by the Regional Laboratory. The other regional laboratories, to varying degrees, have incorporated staff development efforts into their overall missions. A final example of a federal program that provides regional assistance is the National Program for Mathematics and Science Education, which sponsors regional consortia and a national clearinghouse. The regional consortia provide information, resources, and technical assistance to states and school districts.

Beyond national associations and federal programs, new national and regional networks that are part of the broader school reform movement clearly have implications for professional development. Such networks include the Accelerated Schools, the Coalition of Essential Schools, the Comer Schools, the League of Professional Schools, and Outcomes Based Education Schools. All of these networks promote reconceptualization of schools, teaching, and learning. Staff development would seem to be an essential component for any of the popular models for school reform.

State and Intermediate Levels

Statewide staff development efforts in recent years often have been tied to state initiated educational reforms. For example, state-level staff development efforts in Pennsylvania are tied to new curriculum guidelines calling for student learning outcomes, restructuring, and authentic assessment. Pennsylvania has required school districts to submit strategic plans for achieving student learning outcomes, including teacher induction and professional development plans. The state has placed a heavy emphasis on training of trainers programs to assist school districts in the educational reform efforts. Individual school districts are required to select a staff development committee to plan and be involved in the implementation and ongoing evaluation of the district's professional development program. The committee must include teachers who are chosen by teachers and administrators who are chosen by administrators.

Whether or not staff development is tied to larger educational improvement efforts as in Pennsylvania, policies and procedures put in place by state legislatures and state departments of education affect staff development at the local level to some extent. Many states require that a minimum number of days or hours per school year be devoted to staff development. Many also require staff development in particular areas. For instance, the majority of states now require induction programs for beginning teachers. In many states, mandated staff development programs are accompanied by state funding and other resources, leadership training, and technical support. State mandates not directly linked to staff development can nonetheless affect local staff development efforts. For example, statewide standardized achievement tests and teacher evaluation systems clearly set expectations for teacher performance and thus affect staff development needs and programs.

Major universities, especially land grant universities, often affect staff development throughout their home states. An example of this is Pennsylvania State University's Office of Staff Development and School Improvement, which for several years developed long-term staff development partnerships with school districts, schools, and intermediate agencies throughout Pennsylvania. Other universities and colleges tend to influence staff development within smaller geographic areas through the development of consortia, networks, and more recently, professional development schools. Many partnerships include business, industry, and other stakeholders. For example, Chalker (1992) reports on a consortium for improving teacher effectiveness in rural schools, which included Western Carolina University, seven rural school systems, two community colleges, parents, business leaders, government officials, and other institutions concerned with rural education. Consortium activities included collaborative staff development programs, grant projects, beginning teacher programs, and collaborative research.

State intermediate agencies and state supported consortia often provide staff development services. In Pennsylvania, 29 intermediate units (IUs) provide staff development among myriad other services. In the mid-1990s, a significant amount of that staff development is focused on preparing and assisting Pennsylvania educators to implement the aforementioned statewide reforms, including preparation programs on establishing student learning outcomes, strategic planning, authentic assessment, and inclusion. Most of the intermediate units, however, also have their own unique approaches and emphases. For example, Central IU 10 has moved from offering generic staff development programs toward helping individual school districts develop their own "customized" staff development plans. Northeastern IU 19 places a heavy emphasis on follow-up to a variety of initial staff development programs. Follow-up includes both peer coaching programs developed by IU 19 and on-site follow-up by IU 19 staff members. And Bucks County IU 22 has developed a variety of advisory councils, a middle school consortium, leadership cadres, and an extensive array of in-service courses and workshops. In addition to intermediate units, Pennsylvania's statewide system of lead-teacher training centers places a significant emphasis on staff development:

Teachers in these new leadership positions are to receive training regarding effective leadership strategies and instructional pedagogy. These lead teachers are to work cooperatively with their colleagues to provide assistance for the improvement of instruction, curriculum development, and the educational program of the school. The training for lead teachers is to be provided by a regional lead teacher center, managed by a director and shaped by a local governing board (Piscolish, 1993, pp. 2–3).

The activities of one of Pennsylvania's lead-teacher training centers are described in the discussion of teacher leadership as a staff development framework later in this chapter.

Another example of staff development at the intermediate level is Ohio's system of regional teacher training centers. The centers focus on five general goals:

- providing teacher-centered professional development experiences that build on the values of collegiality, collaboration, diversity, experimentation, and solving problems of teaching and learning;
- strengthening teacher leadership in educational improvement and change;
- providing opportunities for professional development of teachers in new instructional strategies and school organization;
- assisting curriculum development, integration, and revision, including improved assessment practices; and
- utilizing the integration of new technologies and telecommunications (Ohio Department of Education, 1991, pp. 4–5).

Planning committees for each center are made up of a majority of teachers and may include representatives from school districts, business, and higher education. The committees facilitate collaboration among stakeholders; develop needs assessments; and design, implement, and evaluate professional development activities for their respective state regions.

A final example of intermediate-level staff development is California's use of regional school networks to promote reform in the middle grades (Slater, 1993). Each network consists of one "foundation" school and 8 to 12 partner schools, receiving initial funding from private foundations, and assigned a California Department of Education (CDE) staff member as a resource person and liaison to CDE. The foundation school in each network was initially supposed to provide network leadership, but eventually formal network leadership structures evolved, include core steering committees. Network activities include regular regional meetings, interschool visitations by principals and teachers, annual regional conferences, and other networking and staff-development activities. The networks have led to the adoption and expansion of the interdisciplinary team concept, which in turn led to a variety of other reforms, including changes in instructional strategies, improved teacher-student relations, curriculum integration, heterogeneous grouping, the use of active learning strategies, and new advisory programs (Slater, 1993).

District Level

Along with decentralization and site-based management, the late 1980s and 1990s have seen a significant shift from district-based to school-based staff development. This shift has been based on the assumption that in most cases the school unit is the level at which significant educational change is most feasible. Despite this assumption, there is still a widespread agreement that some aspects of staff development need to be managed at the district level. Metzdorf (1989) maintains that "neither individual entrepreneurial efforts nor school-based improvement projects are likely to have lasting impact unless they are embedded within a supportive district-level program" (p. 14).

He goes on to propose several essential district-level functions:

- development of the district's philosophy, goals, and expectations;
- administration/coordination of staff development programs and resources within the district;
- coordination linkage with outside programs and resources;
- provision of quality control and evaluation of staff development;
- provision of district-level training and curriculum implementation;
- budgetary support; and
- "cheerleading" (providing vision and support) (p. 15).

Despite the general agreement that some staff development functions will remain at the district level, there is also consensus that in the 1990s the role of the central office in staff development is changing significantly. Asayesh (1994) points out that decentralization and site-based management mean that the central office role changes from dictating to supporting and enabling change. Wood (1989) concurs:

The central office no longer is totally responsible for deciding the who, what, how, and when of change. Decisions about which specific improvements are to be implemented in schools should be made by faculty members in each school. The central office management team facilitates rather than directs (p. 36).

An example of the changing central office role is provided by Middleton, Smith, and Williams (1994), who report on efforts by district personnel in Columbus, Ohio public schools to move from directing to supporting school initiatives.

Just as networks and partnerships have in recent years proliferated at the national, regional, state, and intermediate levels, individual districts have entered into partnerships with higher education, business and industry, and other stakeholders. For instance, Auger and Odell (1992) describe a partnership of 25 years between Albuquerque public schools and the University of New Mexico. The partnership has included a teacher/intern exchange program, a renewal program for career teachers, and a career development program. In another example, Zide and Colbert (1992) describe a collaborative project involving the Fitchburg, Massachusetts public schools and Fitchburg State College that allowed staff members to gain a certificate of graduate study in professional development. Participants developed skills in organization development, planned change, staff development, and action research, enabling collaborative efforts at restructuring the school system.

School Level

Decisions about staff development have traditionally been made at the district level, and the focus of staff development has been on the individual teacher. In the 1980s and 1990s, the emphasis has shifted to the school as the center for decision-making about staff development as well as the focus of staff development efforts. As noted earlier, the new emphasis on school-based decisions concerning staff development is related to the larger movement toward site-based management and decentralized decision-making. Wideen (1987) reflects on the relatively recent assumption that staff development should be focused on the school rather than the individual:

In some quarters this emphasis appears to be intended to counter the isolation experienced by teachers. Among others it appears to represent the recognition that a teacher's behavior is the product of a set of norms determined at the school level; any attempt that a teacher makes to change that behavior can occur only if the norms of the school change (p. 9).

Goodlad's (1984) notion of "the school as the unit of improvement" (with the district too large and the individual teacher too small a unit for meaningful educational change) has certainly given impetus to school-based staff development. Although Goodlad (1983, 1984) notes that school-based development is more of an item of faith than a researched-based concept, his ecological view of educational improvement supports the general concept of school-level development:

There is little point in concluding that our schools are in trouble and then focusing for improvement only on teachers, or principals, or the curriculum. All of these and more are involved. Consequently, efforts at improvement must encompass the school as a system of interacting parts, each affecting the others (Goodlad, 1984, p. 31).

A number of school-based staff development models are available in the literature (Douglas, 1991; Edelfelt, 1983; Hopkins, 1987; Meyers & Beall, 1992; Wood, 1989). Wood (1989) maintains that the following questions need to be asked during the initial stages of transferring primary responsibility for staff development to the school:

- What organization is required for successful school-based change?
- What should be the role and mission of staff development in this context?
- What staff development practices are most appropriate to school-based improvement?
- How should staff development be organized and managed to facilitate school-based improvement goals and plans?
- What training programs will be necessary for central office personnel, principals, and staff developers as the district enters school-based improvement goals and plans? (p. 35)

As is often the case with popular conceptions of staff development, empirical research has not kept abreast of the expanding theory on school-based development. Much of the existing research consists of case studies (Douglas, 1991) and reports on perceptions of those involved in school-based programs. A typical study reported by Lipman (1991), was based on focused interviews with representatives of eight elementary and four secondary schools participating in school-based staff development pilot projects. The schools reported a wide variety of staff development foci. The most often reported activities were conference attendance, in-service sessions led by staff members, cross-grade and cross-division planning, and staff retreats. Benefits included a more focused approach toward identifying goals and needs, increased conference participation, collaborative thinking and planning, staff cohesiveness, increased teacher participation and leadership, benefits to students (learning and self-esteem), and sharing of materials and ideas. One obstacle to the success of school-based staff development was insufficient time for meeting, planning, implementing, sharing, and following up. The most frequent suggestions to other schools beginning school-based development programs were to have regular lines of communication about the project, staff commitment, simplicity, shared decision-making, involvement of all staff, and needs assessment. The growing popularity of school-based staff development among both scholars and policymakers will in all probability lead to a significant increase in both the number and sophistication of research studies on school-based programs.

Individual Level

Staff development at the individual level can be formal or informal, based inside or outside of the school organization, and sanctioned or unsanctioned by the organization. It is curious that while staff development traditionally has focused on the individual—especially on improvement of individual instructional performance—there has been little effort to *individualize* staff development to meet the developmental levels, career stages, needs, and interests of particular teachers. Individualized staff development sponsored by the school organization is not necessarily self-directed staff development; it can be designed for the teacher by the supervisor (this usually occurs in remedial professional development linked to a teacher evaluation system), collaboratively planned by the supervisor and teacher, or self-directed with the organization's approval and support.

The assistance provided teachers who are engaged in individualized professional development can be quite varied. For example, Mathis and Gross (1989) reported that one district's support included tailored courses, minigrants, mentoring, skill training, peer coaching, visits to other schools, teacher exchanges, released time for special projects, videotaping, and videotape analysis. The offerings in individualized programs focused on coursework are by nature extensive, with the professional growth value of some courses questioned by critics. For instance, some of the less traditional courses in an individualized staff development program reported by Welch (1985) were aerobics, jazzercise, financial planning, auto repair, bridge, cooking, and dancing. Levine (1989) offers a counterargument to those who question the value of these types of courses within a staff-development program:

Since personal and professional growth are intertwined, ideas for individualized development might be broadened to include time for hobbies or attention to family matters. When adults are preoccupied

with concerns outside of school, overwhelmed with school work, or simply tired, such seemingly "unprofessional" activities can have a powerful impact on attitude and performance (p. 239).

Self-directed staff development is one of the staff development frameworks discussed in detail later in this chapter.

EFFECTIVE STAFF DEVELOPMENT: CHARACTERISTICS AND BARRIERS

This section will review a set of general characteristics of effective staff development as well as barriers to effective staff development. The following list of characteristics of effective programs is derived from reviews of research, program evaluations, and literature (Berman & McLaughlin, 1978; Griffin, 1983; Loucks-Horsley et al, 1987; Orlich, 1989; Wood, 1989; Wood & Thompson, 1993). The characteristics are:

1. involvement of participants in program planning and other program decisions;
2. integration of individual and organizational goals;
3. long-range planning and development;
4. collegiality and collaboration;
5. principal involvement in all aspects of the program;
6. incentives and rewards for participation;
7. differentiated learning experiences for participants with different needs;
8. adequate time for staff development;
9. follow-up to implement and sustain desired change;
10. ongoing staff development;
11. sustained administrative leadership and support; and
12. open and flexible staff development leadership.

Another way to better understand effective staff development is to examine the barriers to effective programs. After investigating four urban improvement projects, Pink (1989) identified 12 barriers. The barriers are summarized by Fullan (1991):

1. an inadequate theory of implementation, resulting in too little time for teachers and school leaders to plan for and learn new skills and practices;
2. district tendencies toward faddism and quick-fix solutions;
3. lack of sustained central office support and follow-through;
4. underfunding the project, or trying to do too much with too little support;
5. attempting to manage the projects from the central office instead of developing school leadership and capacity;
6. lack of technical assistance and other forms of intensive staff development;
7. lack of awareness of the limitations of teacher and school administrator knowledge about how to implement the project;
8. the turnover of teachers in each school;
9. too many competing demands or overload;
10. failure to address the incompatibility between project requirements and existing organizational policies and structure;

11. failure to understand and take into account site-specific differences among schools; and
12. failure to clarify and negotiate the role relationships and partnerships involving the district and the local university (pp. 316–317).

Fullan (1991) concluded that the presence of these barriers is the norm rather than the exception, but argued that with sufficient effort they can be overcome. Little's (1989) cross-site analysis of staff development in 30 California school districts revealed the presence of a number of Pink's barriers and the absence of many of the characteristics of effective staff development listed above.

DESIGNING STAFF DEVELOPMENT PROGRAMS

Hirsh (1993) discussed 11 issues to be considered prior to planning a staff development program. She warned that if the issues are ignored, they may create roadblocks to the planning process. The 11 issues follow:

1. *Personnel:* Who will participate?
2. *Schedule:* How long do we have?
3. *Incentives:* What can we offer (to individuals on the planning committee)?
4. *Measurement criteria:* How will success (of the planning process) be measured?
5. *Facilitation:* Who will lead the process?
6. *Budget:* Will there be funds to support the plan?
7. *The Retreat:* Are we willing to provide the time and money to take people to a retreat setting (for program planning)?
8. *Approval:* Who has the power to veto the plan?
9. *Commitment:* Who will ensure the success of the project?
10. *Trust:* Do we have an organizational context? (Are trust and support present within the system?)
11. *Knowledge:* Do the members of the planning team have the necessary knowledge base to support the development of a quality plan? (pp. 10, 11)

The Readiness, Planning, Training, Implementation, Maintenance (RPTM) model, proposed by Wood and colleagues (Wood, 1989; Wood, Thompson, & Russell, 1981) is a five-stage model for designing staff development programs:

- *Readiness.* Faculty members study, select, and make a commitment to new behaviors and programs that focus on improving professional practice and student achievement.
- *Planning.* Faculty members develop long-range plan(s) to achieve the changes identified in the first stage.
- *Training.* In-service training sessions are conducted based upon what is known about adult learners.
- *Implementation.* Participants integrate new professional behaviors and knowledge into daily work activities with follow-up assistance.
- *Maintenance.* Changes in practice are monitored to ensure continued high levels of performance (Wood, 1989, p. 28).

Parker (1990) has developed a "human resource model" with five elements: assessment, planning, implementation, evaluation, and participant empowerment.

- *Assessment:* Parker recommends multiple assessment methods, including personnel evaluation, interviews, questionnaires, the Nominal Group Process, the Delphi Technique, and official records.
- *Planning:* Two stages of planning are "Getting Ready" and "Developing the Plan." Getting Ready involves establishing a broad-based governance structure, developing a philosophy or mission statement, and stating program goals. Developing the Plan involves (1) writing objectives, (2) considering knowledge about adult learning, (3) considering the change process, (4) attending to teacher career stages, (5) designing activity formats, and (6) selecting delivery systems.
- *Implementation:* This element includes "Roles and Competency Modeling," and "Monitoring Tasks and Activities." The former involves (1) teachers, administrators, and board members assuming new roles, (2) the use of media for modeling, providing feedback, and self assessment, and (3) the use of networks to share ideas and resources. The monitoring stage, also referred to by Parker as the maintenance stage, includes support and supervision by administrators as well as incentives for participating in staff development.
- *Evaluation:* This phase consists of measuring the effects of the staff development program on participants, students, and the organization as well as the extent of program implementation. Parker recommends formative and summative as well as process and outcome evaluation.
- *Participant Empowerment:* This phase places teachers in leadership roles, increases their knowledge and skills, and involves them in decision-making concerning all aspects of the staff development program.

Although they are presented in linear form, staff development designs like the RPTIM model and Parker's human resource model can fairly easily be converted to continuous improvement models. Figure 34.1, for example, illustrates a continuous improvement cycle which includes most of the components found in both the RPTIM and Parker models. The initial needs assessment in this continuous improvement model would be a comprehensive one like that suggested by Parker. Subsequent needs assessments would be "reassessments," based primarily on findings from the program evaluation carried out in the last phase of the previous cycle.

In contrast to all of the models discussed above, Stake (1987) advocates "an evolutionary view of programming staff development":

Evolutionary change is gradual, internally "planned", in harmony with the organic system, and adaptive to the habitat . . . when changing any staff development milieu, new values and techniques need to be moderated and adapted to the previous ways of supporting teachers' efforts to improve (p. 55).

Under Stakes' evolutionary approach, formal "planning" would consist of designing naturalistic studies which would generate rich descriptions of efforts by teachers to improve their practice. These descriptions would provide other teachers with "vicarious experience," which in turn would stimulate teacher reflection, personal understanding, internal con-

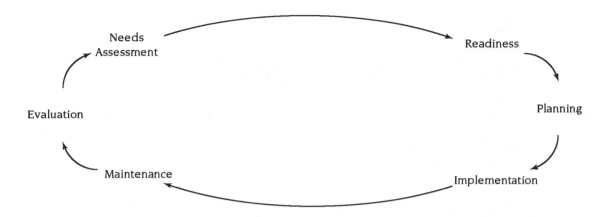

FIGURE 34.1. Continuous Improvement Cycle

viction, and self-directed change. Fullan (1987) critiqued Stakes' evolutionary programming:

> The main advantage of the evolutionary approach is that by definition it grafts onto people's natural experiences. Its disadvantage (some would say virtue) is that it does not set high expectations for change, and that its method (generating and presenting natural descriptions) remains to be tested in terms of how much development it would produce; this approach also appears to take the organizational and institutional conditions as given without recognizing their powerful inhibiting effects (p. 219).

ALTERNATIVE STAFF DEVELOPMENT FRAMEWORKS

The alternative frameworks for staff development reviewed in this section have all been widely discussed in the literature. They have sometimes been referred to as "approaches to teacher development" (Loucks-Horsley et al, 1987), "designs for learning" (Levine & Broude, 1984), or "promising practices" for promoting adult growth in schools (Levine, 1989). The frameworks discussed here are:

1. training;
2. peer coaching;
3. teacher induction and mentoring programs;
4. action research;
5. curriculum development;
6. teacher leadership;
7. teachers as writers;
8. collegial support groups and networks;
9. teacher and professional development centers; and
10. self-directed professional development.

These frameworks are not mutually exclusive. Within long-term staff development programs, one may evolve into or merge with another. Comprehensive staff development programs often are based on several frameworks that overlap and compliment each other. With these realities in mind, the selected frameworks are discussed below.

Training

Alternative training formats are listed here. General characteristics of effective training programs are reviewed. Research on three specific training designs that have gained considerable popularity—the Madeline Hunter, Reflective Use of Time (RUOT), and Joyce and Showers designs—are discussed.

Staff development has historically focused on the transmission of knowledge, skills, and attitudes through training. Training has traditionally been delivered through a variety of formats, including institutes, workshops, courses, minicourses, academies, clinics, programmed instruction modules, instructional television, videotapes, audiotapes, and computer-assisted instruction. Almost all of the 97 programs examined by Lawrence (1974) in his often cited review of research on in-service education involved some type of training. Lawrence defined an effective program as one which met its objectives. He found the following characteristics to be associated with effective programs:

1. differentiated training experiences for different teachers;
2. teacher in active role (constructing and generating materials, ideas, and behaviors);
3. demonstrations, supervised trials, and feedback;
4. teachers share and provide assistance to each other;
5. activities that are linked to a general effort of the school;
6. teachers . . . choose goals and activities for themselves; and
7. self-initiated and self-directed training activities (pp. 17-18).

Attempting to compare research on different training formats sheds little light on what constitutes more or less effective training, since program designers tend to identify such formats differently than staff development theoreticians. For example, despite clear differences in definitions found in the literature for terms like "institute," "workshop," and "clinic," in practice the same type of training might be called an institute in one program, a workshop in a different program, and a clinic in a third program. A comparison of specific training designs is hence more informative than comparison of practitioner-identified formats. The research on three popular training designs is reviewed here.

Hunter Training Design Considering the popularity of the Madeline Hunter training design over the last two decades, research on the Hunter model has been sparse, with mixed results. Stallings and Krassavage (1986) examined a four-year Hunter follow-through project that included a training program extending over three academic years. Training began with five one-day training sessions on the Hunter instructional model, followed by five to nine follow-up classroom visits and feedback from project staff. The following school year, additional training was provided on the topics of classroom management, directions, grouping, monitoring, test-taking strategies, motivation, retention, and a review of Hunter's lesson design. These sessions were again followed up by classroom visits and feedback by workshop presenters. During the next school year, the intent was to turn over primary program responsibility to principals and teachers, to "institutionalize" the program. During that year, teachers were provided four release days to attend additional in-service programs and a retreat, and project staff visited the participating schools weekly to observe and assist teachers. During the program, training and support were also provided for principals of participating schools.

Stallings and Krassavage reported on changes in instructional skills (for set, instruction, guided practice, and independent practice), student engaged rate, and student achievement in reading and mathematics. They found significant positive changes in teachers' skill scores from winter to spring of the second year and for the third year, but decreased scores for the fourth year of the program. They found a significant increase in student-engaged rate for the third year, but a reverse pattern for the fourth year. There was no significant gain in reading achievement from winter to spring of the second year, a significant gain in the third year, but a significant decrease in the fourth year. There was a significant gain in mathematics achievement from winter to spring of the second year, no gain in the third year, and a significant decrease the fourth year. The investigators reported significantly higher reading achievement for control schools compared to experimental schools, and no significant difference in mathematics achievement between experimental and control schools.

Manderville and Rivers (1988/1989) studied a Hunter-based program in South Carolina entitled the Program for Effective Teaching (PET). The investigators surveyed approximately 200 elementary teachers who had received the Hunter training. Respondents expressed positive perceptions of the training, and two-thirds of the program participants reported daily use of PET concepts in their lesson planning. Only 57 percent of the sample reported follow-up coaching at least once per year. The investigators found no significant difference in reading and mathematics achievement for the first to fourth grades between students of PET-trained teachers and students of teachers in control schools. In an expanded study, the investigators found no significant difference in achievement between students of over 900 PET-trained teachers and students of over 3,000 teachers not trained in PET. Sparks (1988/1989) has criticized the Mandeville and Rivers' study for not adequately addressing the question of whether PET-trained teachers were implementing the Hunter model, especially in light of the inadequate coaching provided.

Donovan, Sousa, and Walberg (1992) reported on a four-year study of a Hunter-based staff development program called the West Orange Project. Teacher preparation consisted of a training program and five types of follow-up: collegial groups, coaching by district trainers, peer coaching, instructional skills resource teachers in each building, and training of administrators and supervisors in Hunter's version of clinical supervision. The investigators collected data on 1,699 students, including 62 students who participated in all four years of the study, and 126 teachers. Surveys showed that most participating teachers, supervisors, and administrators perceived that (1) the Hunter model was implemented, (2) collegial groups and coaches had supported implementation, (3) teaching was more efficient and effective as a result of implementation, and (4) use of the Hunter model had increased feelings of professionalism and led to the use of common terminology among colleagues. Based on normal curve equivalent scores, elementary school students showed significant pre–post gains in reading but not in mathematics. Middle school students showed significant gains in both subjects. High school students showed no significant changes in mathematics achievement and a significant decrease in reading scores. The investigators reported that most of the variance in test scores was accounted for by pretest achievement (students with high pretest scores tended to finish with high scores). The study found little relationship between student achievement and coaching or collegial group meetings.

A two-year study by Pasch and Harberts (1992) of a staff development program using Hunter's approach led to more positive conclusions concerning links between Hunter training and student achievement. Teachers in two low achievement schools received 60 hours of training on the Hunter model, followed up by classroom coaching. Classroom observations revealed that teachers used instructional methods defined as effective by the Hunter model. Teacher interviews revealed a shift from a more technical to a more reflective view of teaching. Achievement gains of students in schools involved in the program were greater than both control schools and the average district gains. Teachers who had participated in the program for two years showed more improvement in instructional decision-making than teachers who had participated for one year. Pasch and Harberts (1992) concluded that an "unequivocal causal link" could not be made between the Hunter-based staff development program and gains in student achievement because of other initiatives taking place in both schools, including school–business partnerships and school improvement projects. For additional discussion of research on the Hunter model, see Orlich, Remaley, Facemyer, Logan, and Cao (1993).

RUOT Training Design The RUOT staff development program described by Stallings (1989) has resulted in changes in teachers' behaviors and significant gains in student reading scores compared to control groups. The content of the training program was based on earlier research by Stallings and associates, which identified over 30 instructional variables identified with reading gains. These variables were the basis for a series of six on-site workshops for small groups of secondary teachers. The training design calls for teachers to experience the following:

1. they become aware of a need for improvement through their analysis of their own observation profile;
2. they make a written commitment to try new ideas in their classroom the next day;
3. they modify the workshop ideas to work in their classroom and school;
4. they try the ideas and evaluate the effect;
5. they observe in each other's classrooms and analyze their own data;
6. they report their success or failure to their group;
7. they discuss problems and solutions regarding individual students and/or teaching subject matter;
8. they need a wide variety of approaches; modeling, simulations, observations, critiquing video tapes, presenting at professional meetings; and
9. they learn in their own way to set new goals for professional growth (Stallings, 1989, pp. 3–4).

Stallings goes on to list the following as cornerstones of the staff development program:

- learn by doing—try, evaluate, modify, try again;
- link prior knowledge to new information;
- learn by reflecting and solving problems; and
- learn in a supportive environment—share problems and successes (Stallings, 1989, p. 4).

In one study of the RUOT program, students of the 26 teachers in the treatment group showed a six month gain in reading scores compared to a control group. In another study, all teachers in two schools received RUOT training. The students in the treatment schools experienced an eight month gain in reading scores compared to the two control schools. In a third study, absent a control group, all teachers in a school district received the training. A group of students tracked from eighth through tenth grade showed steady increases in percentile rank on reading scores.

Joyce and Showers Training Design Based on a series of studies, Joyce and Showers (1988) developed a training design which has become increasingly popular over the last several years. Their design includes the following:

- an exploration of the theory underlying the skill;
- demonstration or modeling of the skill;
- practice of the skill under simulated conditions and feedback on skill performance; and
- classroom coaching.

Joyce and Showers (1988) reported the largest effect sizes for developing knowledge, demonstrating skill, and transfer of training when all four elements were included in a training program.

The Joyce and Showers model also has led to positive changes in student behavior and academic achievement. Joyce, Murphy, Showers, and Murphy (1989) used the basic training model, collegial study groups, faculty-generated school improvement goals, and assistance from a cadre of administrators and teachers to introduce a variety of teaching models to schools in Richmond County, Georgia. Initial models taught in the training program were cooperative learning, mnemonics, concept attainment, inductive reasoning, and synectics. After the new models were introduced, student disciplinary referrals decreased, and faculties showed an increasing willingness to address common problems. The investigators compared reading and social studies achievement of students taught by teachers who had reached "executive control" in their use of new models of teaching with achievement of students taught by teachers who were demonstrating only "mechanical use" of the models. At the elementary level the researchers found little difference between reading levels of the two groups. However, on the 5th grade social studies tests from the Iowa Test of Basic Skills, median scores and grade equivalents of the executive control group were considerably higher than the group that taught at the mechanical level. The investigators also found that achievement in social studies from the 6th to the 8th grade was six months higher in grade equivalents than the students' previous growth rate.

While studies like those conducted by Stallings (1989) and Joyce and Showers (1988) demonstrate that training can have positive effects on instruction and student achievement, they also point out the complexity, intensity, and time necessary for effective training programs.

Peer Coaching

Peer coaching is defined in this section. Different types of peer coaching are discussed. Research-based suggestions for effective peer coaching programs and results of studies on the effects of coaching are also reviewed.

Valencia and Killion (1988) define peer coaching as "the process where teams of teachers regularly observe one another and provide support, companionship, feedback, and assistance" (p. 170). Ackland (1991) has identified three characteristics of peer coaching: "Peer coaching programs are (a) nonevaluative, (b) based on the observation of classroom teaching followed by constructive feedback, and (c) aimed to improve instructional techniques." Glickman (1990) equates the peer coaching process with peer clinical supervision, involving a preconference; classroom observation, analysis and interpretation; postconference and critique of previous steps. Different types of peer coaching can be classified according to the *purpose* of the coaching as well as the *relationship* of participants.

Garmston (1987) describes three types of coaching based on purpose: technical coaching, collegial coaching, and challenge coaching.

- Technical coaching helps teachers transfer training to classroom practice, while deepening collegiality, increasing professional dialogue, and giving teachers a shared vocabulary to talk about their craft. . . . Technical coaching generally follows staff development workshops in specific teaching methods (p. 18).
- The major goals of collegial coaching are to refine teaching practices, deepen collegiality, increase professional dialogue, and to help teachers to think more deeply about their work. . . . The observed teacher's priority, rather than an instructional method presented in an in-service workshop, determines the coaching focus (p. 20).
- Challenge coaching helps teams of teachers resolve persistent problems in instructional design or delivery. The term challenge refers to resolving a problematic state (p. 21).

Ackland (1991) has proposed that actual peer coaching often involves a combination of technical, collegial, and challenge coaching. He classifies peer coaching into two categories: "(a) *coaching by experts* (specially trained teachers with an acknowledged expertise who observe other teachers to give them support, feedback, and suggestions, and (b) *reciprocal coaching* (teachers observe and coach each other to jointly improve instruction)" (p. 24).

A number of researchers and practioners have made recommendations for effective coaching programs. A representative set of suggestions, proposed by Munro and Elliott (1987), is summarized below:

- identify the purpose of peer coaching;
- do careful planning, with support of administrative staff;
- allow teachers themselves to decide on instructional improvement goals;
- train participants in observation and feedback skills;
- develop a system of accountability for observations and conferences;
- arrange periodic sharing sessions for coaches;
- provide opportunities to change partners and for interdisciplinary teams; and
- have a program facilitator responsible for coordination, accountability, scheduling, and substitute teachers.

Based on studies of technical coaching (coaching for transfer of workshop training to the classroom), Joyce and Showers (1988) found that, compared to uncoached teachers who had experienced identical training, coached teachers:

1. practiced new strategies more often and developed greater skill in the new strategies;
2. used new strategies more appropriately;
3. had greater long-term skill retention and increase in the appropriate use of the new strategies;
4. were more likely to teach new strategies to their students; and
5. better understood the purposes of the new strategies.

At the other end of the "coaching continuum" from the technical coaching described by Joyce and Showers is the purely collegial model. This model does not focus on the transfer of instructional skills from training sessions to teachers' classrooms. In fact, the only teacher training linked to the "pure" version of collegial coaching is that which develops coaching skills, such as observation and conferencing skills. The goals of collegial coaching typically include increased sharing of existing instructional methods and materials, teacher dialogue, reflection on teaching, collaborative experimentation, and improvement of the school's professional culture. The focus of the classroom observation is determined in a preobservation conference and may vary from one coaching cycle to the next. Rather than being predetermined, any instructional improvement goals emerge from analysis of observation data and reflective dialogue during coaching cycles.

Teachers in a collegial peer coaching program studied by Gordon (1990b) reported that they gained new perspectives on students and teaching, reflected more on their instruction, broke out of established patterns of teaching, and engaged in more professional dialogue as a result of their participation. Phillips and Glickman (1991) reported a significant increase in the conceptual levels of teachers participating in a collegial peer coaching program. Participants also reported that the peer coaching program was helping them to "(a) focus on the specifics of teaching, (b) gain new ideas and/or information, and (c) develop new insight or awareness about the teaching process" (p. 24).

More common than either purely technical or collegial coaching programs are those that include elements of both models. Such hybrid programs include workshops on effective teaching research, generic instructional skills, or models of teaching, as well as workshops on peer coaching skills. Peer coaching in such programs is loosely coupled to the workshops on instruction; participants are encouraged but not required to implement and coach each other on instructional skills addressed in workshops. Individualized instructional improvement goals linked to the content of the workshops on instruction often provide a general direction for the peer coaching, while allowing considerable choice concerning the specific focus of each coaching cycle.

A number of exploratory studies on programs combining technical and collegial coaching (hybrid programs) have been reported. A program described by Munro and Elliott (1987) included presentations on effective teaching research, self-assessment by teachers, an introduction to observation and feedback skills, teacher-designed action plans for instructional improvement, and peer coaching throughout the school year. Instructional processes to be observed by peer coaches were not predetermined. In the program evaluation, the majority of participants reported the following:

- they had achieved their instructional goals;
- peer coaching had made a significant difference in their instruction;
- peer coaching was more effective in helping them achieve instructional goals than direct classroom supervision; and
- peer coaching fostered more sharing of instructional methods among teachers.

Sparks and Bruder (1987) investigated programs at two schools that involved videotaping of participants' teaching for the purpose of self-assessment, training on observation and feedback, review of effective teaching practices, peer coaching, and follow-up videotaping and self-analysis. Through questionnaires and interviews, participating teachers reported that peer coaching improved collegiality, experimentation, and student learning. Gordon and colleagues (Gordon, 1993a,b; Gordon, Nolan, & Forlenza, 1995) carried out a series of studies on programs involving both technical and collegial coaching. In each of these programs, teachers attended a series of workshops on instructional models and skills, with peer coaching between workshops. In all three programs, teachers were given the choice during each coaching cycle between (1) technical coaching on skills learned during previous workshops, and (2) collegial coaching focused on concerns or goals identified by the individual teacher who was being coached. One of the programs that was studied used expert coaching (Gordon, 1993a), a second program used reciprocal coaching (Gordon, Nolan, & Forlenza, 1995), and a third program used a combination of expert and reciprocal coaching (Gordon, 1993b). Through questionnaires and interviews, participants in each program reported that their participation resulted in more open communication and dialogue among teachers, increased reflection on teaching, and changes in teaching behaviors.

Research on technical coaching is presently at a more advanced stage than research on collegial or "hybrid" models. Studies of technical coaching have documented skill transfer to classroom teaching. Most of the research on collegial and hybrid models, although promising, has been limited to the measurement of participant perceptions.

Teacher-Induction and Mentoring Programs

Here, environmental difficulties and specific needs of beginning teachers, as well as effects of having unmet needs, are discussed. The purpose and typical goals of teacher induction programs are presented. Several studies on mentoring, the chief component of most induction programs, are reviewed. Literature on selecting, training, assigning, and supporting mentors is discussed. Research on the types of support commonly provided to beginning teachers by mentors is summarized. Forms of beginning teacher assistance beyond mentoring are presented. Finally, the effects of teacher induction and mentoring are discussed.

Based on a review of the literature, Gordon (1991a) has identified six "environmental difficulties" within the traditional school organization awaiting beginning teachers: difficult work assignments, unclear expectations, inadequate resources, isolation, role conflict, and reality shock. The last of these is defined by Veenman (1984) as "the collapse of the missionary ideals formed during teacher training by the harsh and rude reality of classroom life" (p. 143). Gordon (1991a) also lists 12 specific research-based needs of beginning teachers, including needs for assistance with:

1. managing the classroom;
2. acquiring information about the school system;
3. obtaining instructional resources and materials;
4. planning, organizing, and managing instruction and other professional responsibilities;
5. assessing students and evaluating student progress;
6. motivating students;
7. using effective teaching methods;
8. dealing with individual students' needs, interests, abilities, and problems;
9. communicating with colleagues, including administrators, supervisors, and their teachers;
10. communicating with parents;
11. adjusting to the teaching environment and role; and
12. receiving emotional support (p. 5).

Formal assistance to address needs of novice teachers traditionally has not been provided. The results of having unmet needs have been devastating to many beginners, and include emotional, physical, attitudinal, and instructional problems. Without induction support, teachers tend to view themselves,

their teaching, their students, their teacher preparation, and their profession more negatively at the end than at the beginning of their first year of teaching (Gordon, 1991a). The attrition rate for each of the first two years of teaching has been reported at around 15 percent (Schlechty & Vance, 1983). Forty to 50 percent of teachers leave the profession within the first seven years (Estes, Stansbury, & Long, 1990; New Mexico State Department of Education, 1988; Wisconsin Department of Public Instruction, 1984).

In recent years teacher induction programs have been developed in a large number of school districts, to provide formal, ongoing assistance to beginning teachers. Huling-Austin (1988) has identified five common goals of induction programs:

1. to improve teaching performance;
2. to increase the retention of promising beginning teachers;
3. to promote the personal and professional well-being of beginning teachers;
4. to transmit the culture of the system to beginning teachers; and
5. to satisfy mandated requirements related to induction and certification (p. 9).

Although the assignment of a mentor to the beginning teacher is usually an important component of a teacher induction program, a comprehensive program includes a variety of support persons and structures. Gordon (1991a) recommends that a program development team be formed, including representatives of the central office, school administration, the local teachers' association, teachers at large, and, if possible, a university consultant. The development team designs, supports, monitors, and evaluates the induction program. Gordon (1991a) also suggests that a support team be assigned to each beginning teacher. The support team would include, among others, the principal, a mentor, and other experienced teachers with whom the beginner will be working closely.

Mentors The mentoring component of a teacher induction program includes selection, training, assignment, and support of mentors, as well as mentor responsibilities and activities. There is considerable discussion in the literature regarding criteria for selecting mentors. A representative set of criteria is provided by Odell (1990a):

1. demonstrated excellence in teaching;
2. demonstrated excellence in working with adults;
3. demonstrated sensitivity to the viewpoints of others;
4. demonstrated willingness to be an active and open learner; and
5. demonstrated competence in social and public relations (pp. 13–14).

Odell (1990a) also lists 10 topics as essential to mentor training, including:

- rationale for teacher induction programs;
- concerns of beginning teachers;
- fostering self-esteem in beginning teachers;
- stages of teacher development;
- fostering self-reliance in beginning teachers
- working with adult learners;
- teacher mentoring;

- classroom observation and conferencing skills;
- teacher reflection; and
- teacher coaching (p. 14).

The primary concern with mentor assignment is the match between mentor and beginner. It is commonly accepted that a good match includes a mentor on the same campus who teaches the same grade or subject matter as the beginner (Huffman & Leak, 1986). Matches of personality and educational philosophy are also critical. The importance of personal and philosophical matches supports the practice of informal interaction between beginners and potential mentors prior to mentor assignment and the consideration of the matching preferences of beginners and mentors (Gordon, 1991a). Although there is no research on teacher mentoring that supports age and gender matching, the general literature on mentoring suggests that the mentor should be 8 to 15 years older than the protege and that male-female mentoring relationships have more potential liabilities than same-gender matches (Odell, 1990b).

In case studies of mentor teachers, their proteges, and their principals, Ackley and Gall (1992) identified the top five sources of mentor support: the mentor-protege match, empathy with the protege, previous experience with adults, administrative support, and mentor training. Although intrinsic rewards for mentors like professional growth, personal relationships, personal growth, and the satisfaction of helping another teacher are considered to be more powerful than extrinsic rewards (Ackley & Gall, 1992), most experts recommend that external awards be provided to mentors. Such rewards can include public recognition, released time, stipends, tuition waivers at local colleges or universities, professional development credit for mentor training and service, and support for travel to professional development activities (Hirsh, 1990; Odell, 1990a).

Mentoring is the most important component of most teacher induction programs. Odell (1990b) discusses four phases of the mentoring process: developing the relationship, determining the mentoring content, applying effective mentoring styles and strategies, and disengaging the relationship when the beginning teacher reaches self-reliance. Based on her research on mentors' actual support activities, Odell (1990b) has described nine support categories: systems information, resources-materials, instructional, emotional, student management, scheduling-planning, environment, demonstration teaching, and parental. Specific mentoring activities reported throughout the literature include: information sharing, informal interaction, problem solving, demonstration teaching, coteaching, peer coaching, and collaborative action research (Ackley & Gall, 1992; Bernhardt & Flaherty, 1990; Bradley & Gordon, 1994; Gordon, 1991a; Huling-Austin, 1992; Wildman, Magliaro, Niles, & Niles, 1992).

Other Forms of Induction Support There is strong support in the literature for forms of beginning-teacher assistance beyond mentoring. A beginners' orientation day prior to the beginning of the school year is often recommended. Gordon (1991a) recommends that beginners receive an orientation to the community, district policies and procedures, the curriculum, the induction program, the school, and the beginner's specific responsibilities. Additional, ongoing forms of support for beginners are discussed in the literature, including beginning-teacher handbooks (Cole, 1990); skill training (Gordon, 1991a); cohort support groups (Huling-Austin, 1992; Thies-Sprinthall & Gerler, 1990); study groups (Odell, 1990a); monthly newsletters (Odell, 1990a); seminars (Bernhardt & Flaherty, 1990); interschool visitations by beginners (Cole, 1990); induction-team meetings consisting of the principal, mentor, and beginning teacher (Gordon, 1991a); team assistance with the development of professional improvement plans (Gordon, 1991a; Hirsh, 1990); and providing beginners with social opportunities (Hirsh, 1990).

Effects of Induction and Mentoring Programs Studies on induction programs have reported a variety of positive effects on beginning teachers, including improved instruction (Colbert & Wolff, 1992; Henry, 1988; Schaffer, Stringfield, & Wolfe, 1992), more positive attitudes about teaching (Henry, 1988; Parker, 1988), increased ability to motivate students (Parker, 1988), better classroom management (Colbert & Wolff, 1992; Parker, 1988), and more ability to develop positive relationships with students (Parker, 1988). Based on classroom observations of beginning teachers participating in a support program, Colbert and Wolff (1992) reported that participating beginners "used more effective instructional planning practices, provided more learning opportunities for students, and had higher student engagement rates than nonproject participants" (p. 197). Mager, Cianfarano, and Corwin (1990) concluded that beginners who participated in a mentor-internship more quickly developed views of themselves as possessing a set of teaching strengths and developed a stronger commitment to teaching than nonparticipating beginners.

Varah, Theune, and Parker (1986) found that administrators received fewer student referrals, parent calls, and student complaints involving beginning teachers who were provided induction support. Administrators in three induction programs studied by Hawk (1987) reported that being members of induction teams helped them to grow professionally, to better understand qualities of good teaching, made them more aware of teachers' needs, and improved their relationships with teachers. In a study reviewed by Odell (1990a), principals reported that the interaction and collaboration emphasized in an induction program improved the school atmosphere. Experienced teachers and principals in an induction program described by Colbert and Wolff (1992) reported increased collegiality among teachers as a result of the program.

Most studies on successful teacher-induction programs have concluded that mentoring is a vital program component (Colbet & Wolff, 1992; Huffman & Leak, 1986; Huling-Austin & Murphy, 1987; Mager, Cianfarano, & Corwin, 1990; Warring & Lindquist, 1989). The following conclusion by Huling-Austin and Murphy (1987) is typical of induction studies:

The assignment of a support teacher may well be the most cost effective induction practice available to program developers. First-year teachers who were assigned designated support teachers consistently reported that those persons were who they relied upon most heavily for assistance (pp. 35–36).

Studies of induction programs with mentoring components have identified benefits for mentors as well as proteges. Mentors have reported that program participation has helped them to refine their teaching (Warring & Lindquist, 1989), increase their confidence, broaden their perspectives, add to their knowledge of teaching and learning, and improve their communication skills (Odell, 1990a). Mentors have also reported that mentoring enhanced their professional experience, improved their collegial and process skills, brought them recognition for their professional expertise, and allowed them to make an important contribution (Godley, Wilson, & Klug, 1986–1987).

Follow-up studies of teacher induction programs indicate that they can increase the retention of teachers. Colbert and Wolff (1992) found that over 95 percent of teachers who participated in a beginning teacher support program were still teaching in urban classrooms after three years. Odell and Ferraro (1992) reported that 96 percent of teachers who were located were still teaching four years after their initial, mentored year. These percentages are far above typical teacher retention rates reported in the literature. Induction programs seem to have lasting effects beyond teacher retention. Mager et al (1990), found that many mentors and interns in a one-year mentor teacher-internship program continued informal relationships into a second and third year. In a number of follow-up studies, participants in teacher induction programs have continued to report positive effects in the years following their formal program participation (Manley, Siudzinski, & Varah, 1989; Odell, 1990a; Rossetto & Grosenick, 1987).

Action Research

In this section, action research is defined, the stages of action research are outlined, and teachers' reasons for doing action research are given; a summary of the history of action research is provided; different types of action research are described; supportive conditions for action research are discussed; and three studies of action research at multiple sites are reviewed. The literature abounds with definitions of action research. McKay (1992) captures the concept of action research particularly well:

Educators involved in action research think about a specific group in a particular setting with the main goal of finding better ways to do their job. Action research takes place when educators initiate and control the research in conjunction with the other day-to-day activities of leading a school or classroom. It is a search for answers to questions relevant to educators' immediate interests, with the primary goal of putting the findings immediately into practice (p. 18).

Holly (1991) lists six stages or steps in the action research cycle:

1. problem analysis—the initial formulation of the problem;
2. data collection—fact finding or, as Lewin (1946) referred to it, reconnaissance;
3. data analysis and conceptualization;
4. planning of an action program;
5. implementation of the action program; and

6. evaluation—monitoring the effects of the action program and judging the quality of the changes (p. 144).

Dowhower, Melvin, and Sizemore (1990) illustrate the value of action research as staff development in their discussion of the four reasons for teachers to do action research: empowerment, improved teaching and observing, more critical use of research, and becoming learners together.

Holly (1991) provides an excellent overview of the history of action research, dividing it into six time periods. In Period One, from 1900 to 1930, action research gained two of its primary characteristics: the scientific approach and teacher participation in solving educational problems. In Period Two, the 1930s, Kurt Lewin—credited by many to be the founding father of full-fledged action research—integrated his research cycle, an emphasis on research for social change, and group dynamics. In Period Three, the late 1940s and early 1950s, action research in education thrived in the United States largely through the efforts of Stephen Corey and Hilda Taba. After the early 1950s, however, action research in American education declined, due primarily to four factors: a retreat to scholarly research separated from practice, attacks on the action research methodology, questions about whether action research was meeting its promises, and the rise of a positivistic evaluation industry.

Period Four, the 1960s and 1970s, saw action research rise to popularity in Great Britain through the efforts of individuals like Lawrence Stenhouse, Robert Rapoport, and John Elliott, and projects like the Classroom Action Research Network (CARN). In Period Five, the late 1970s and early 1980s, the return of action research to the United States was fostered by projects involving a new breed of advocates, including Betty Ward, Ann Lieberman, and Sharon Oja. Holly calls Period Six, from the mid-1980s onward, the Era of Collaborative Inquiry. He asserts that the spirit of action research lives on, characterized by:

1. practitioner inquiry;
2. the belief in the centrality of teachers in research and change;
3. practical problem solving using self-evaluation;
4. the demystification of research;
5. team and whole-staff self-evaluation; and
6 increased awareness of the complexities of classroom learning.

Action research has been classified in a number of different ways. Calhoun (1993) uses three categories: *individual teacher research,* focused on changes in a single classroom; *collaborative action research,* involving classroom inquiry by a team consisting of practitioners and staff from a university or other external agency; and *schoolwide action research,* in which a school faculty focuses on a problem of collective concern. Houser (1990) differentiates educational research based on the teacher's role in the research. In *traditional research,* he views the role of university researcher and classroom teacher as completely separate, with teachers in the role of "minimally informed participants." In *action research,* Houser sees the roles of researchers and teachers as still separate but directly influencing each other. In what he refers to as *teachers as researchers,* praxis occurs as the roles of researcher and teacher are unified: "Within this framework teachers . . . initiate every aspect of a research project. They are responsible for formulating the questions, selecting the tools, and collecting, analyzing and interpreting the data" (p. 58).

A final way of classifying action research relates to the basic purpose of the research. Soltis (1984) has classified pedagogical research as *empirical, interpretive,* and *critical.* Holland et al (1992) have applied these three research perspectives to teachers' professional inquiry. Empirical inquiry can involve "a careful study of actual classroom events and particular teaching methods or practices" (p. 173). Interpretive inquiry may take the form of teachers examining their espoused educational platforms "and the influence those espoused platforms have on their practice and on their interpretations of the practice of others" (p. 174). Critical inquiry might involve "examining the relationships between instructional practices and larger economic and political contexts" (p. 174). Holland et al (1992) note that action research can incorporate all three types of professional inquiry.

Regardless of the type of action research being conducted, there is agreement across the literature that the presence of certain conditions will greatly enhance the likelihood of action research succeeding. Miller and Pine (1990) provide a representative list of supportive conditions:

- the provision of time for action research as part of teachers' regular work load;
- freedom of inquiry;
- technical and consultative assistance;
- material and financial support;
- university or staff development credit for carrying out research;
- opportunities for teachers to share their research; and
- administrative support of action research as a staff-development strategy.

Since the mid-1980s, there has been a rapid acceleration of studies on action research. Three studies, each examining a different model of action research, are discussed below.

The Action Research on Change in Schools (ARCS) Project This NIE-funded project (Oja & Pine, 1987) involved two collaborative action research teams, one in New Hampshire and the other in Michigan. The study focused on individual teachers at various stages of adult development on each team. Both teams consisted of teachers from the same school, a university researcher, and a research assistant. The common goals shared by all team members were to produce research on teacher morale and school scheduling practices, but teachers at different developmental stages proceeded in individual ways. Specific research problems were continuously redefined based on the emergence of new data and new context throughout the two-year project. Thus, the phases of action research were recursive rather than linear. Teachers involved in the action research reported the following outcomes:

(a) an increased understanding of the relationship between scheduling, curriculum, and school philosophy; (b) the creation of new patterns of communication, sharing, and collegiality; (c) the building of a common body of knowledge; and (d) an increased ability to identify, analyze, and solve classroom problems (Miller & Pine, 1990, p. 57).

Project Learn The League of Educational Action Researchers in the Northwest (Project Learn), a partnership consisting of Washington State University and area schools, facilitated school staffs wishing to bring about school improvement through action research (Sagor, 1991). Action-research teams began their participation with a two-day workshop regarding the basic steps of action research. At the end of the training program, each team wrote an action plan, including a problem statement, data-collection methods, and technical or logistical needs. As the teams conducted their action-research projects, assistance was available from "critical friends," a cadre of trained volunteers with research experience. A one-day follow-up workshop was held in mid-January. Project participants and other action researchers made presentations on their research at an international symposium held each spring. A continuing program providing networking and advanced training was available for teams that continued to conduct research after their first year of participation. Sagor (1991) reported sharp contrast between the school environments of action–research teams that succeeded and those that failed. Successful teams reported important projects; external support; and teams with drive, commitment, and "chemistry." Failed teams reported unimportant projects, lack of extrinsic support, and devisive and leaderless teams.

The League of Professional Schools The League of Professional Schools is a network of over 100 schools that is coordinated by an office within the College of Education, at the University of Georgia. Acceptance in the League is contingent on at least 80 percent of a school faculty voting by secret ballot to join the League. Schools joining the League agree to pursue "shared governance, instructional initiatives that promote student learning, and action research" (Calhoun & Allen, 1994, p. 4). School teams that join the League receive:

1. four days of meetings, including training on shared decision-making and action research, and sharing of school initiatives;
2. an informational retrieval system;
3. a network newsletter;
4. consultation; and
5. a one-day on-site visit by a facilitator.

Individual, collaborative, and schoolwide action research are encouraged within the league, but the primary emphasis is on action research for school improvement. Schools in the league have focused action research on such areas as student learning goals, instructional innovations, curriculum changes, inclusion, scheduling, student motivation, school communication, the school environment, and developing core values for a school philosophy (Calhoun & Allen, 1994).

Results of action research in the League have varied from school to school. Examples of *effects on students* include increases in student achievement, reductions in referrals and suspensions, improved attendance, improved self-esteem, improved attitudes toward mathematics, new learning experiences for students, and increased student participation in schoolwide decisions. Examples of effects on *school culture* include increases in shared decision-making; improvement in schoolwide communication; collection and sharing of schoolwide data about students; data-based changes; involvement of students and/or parents in decision-making; studying professional literature; and reflection on archival school data (Calhoun & Allen, 1994).

Calhoun and Allen (1994) identified impediments to action research within some league schools:

1. the lack of time;
2. the number of initiatives pursued (too many);
3. the manner in which goals and initiatives are selected (too much reliance on external information and resources);
4. the lack of awareness and provision of serious staff development;
5. the rare use of schoolwide data on a regular basis to modify action; and
6. the lack of involvement of students in the collective study process (p. 18).

Based on their study of action research within the league, Calhoun and Allen (1994) offered six recommendations for supporting schoolwide action research:

1. seek and work with policy-makers to ensure time for collaborative work;
2. use an inquiry mode for learning to conduct school-wide action research; one does not have to be "ready" or all-knowing to begin the journey;
3. develop and tend to a core group to lead the effort;
4. include students in the action research process;
5. keep the focus on student learning; and
6. seek technical assistance, if needed, and provide staff development for innovations (p. 22).

Curriculum Development

This subsection discusses curriculum development within a staff-development framework. Here, the interrelationship of staff development and curriculum development is discussed; principles that become critical when tying staff development to curriculum development are presented; and finally, examples from the literature of staff development within a curriculum development framework are provided.

Rubin (1987) argues that curriculum development is, in fact, a form of staff development:

It has become apparent that involvement in curricular issues, in itself, is a healthy form of staff development. When, for example, teachers reflect on which subject matter is critical, how content matter can be connected with previously acquired knowledge, ways of individualizing learning and instruction through which broad intellectual skills are developed, their professional knowledge base, sophistication, and technical skill are likely to increase (pp. 170–171).

Killion (1993) maintains that staff development and curriculum development are "two sides of the same coin." She points out that the two processes have common goals, characteristics, and rigor. In her discussion of common goals, she proposes the following:

Curriculum developers build knowledge of the subject area, curriculum organization and design, group processes, conflict resolution, content-specific pedagogy, budget, and resources management.

Not only are curriculum developers increasing their knowledge in these areas, but they are also called upon to demonstrate expertise. Frequently they conduct pilot or field tests and evaluate the results. In addition, curriculum developers may alter their attitudes about effective instruction and curriculum, collaboration with peers, and school and district improvement efforts. These goals of curriculum development are also significant staff development outcomes (p. 39).

Rubin (1987) argues that, in addition to the general characteristics of effective staff development identified in the research literature, there are additional principles that become critical when staff development is tied to curriculum development:

1. direct linkage between staff development programs and specific curricular targets;
2. collaborative policy-determination by teachers and administrators;
3. management procedures which treat continuous staff development as an essential aspect of curriculum evaluation;
4. mechanisms through which teachers and administrators jointly participate in curriculum evaluation;
5. use of the school faculty as a curriculum problem-solving unit;
6. communication devices which enable good instructional practices to be exchanged from teacher to teacher;
7. faculty commitment to the instructional program;
8. provisions for enhancing the staff's command of subject matter;
9. stress on reflective approaches to teaching;
10. emphasis on continuous self-training; and
11. efforts to incorporate cognitive skill development in the instruction (p. 176).

The literature provides numerous examples of staff development within a curriculum development format. Miller (1992) described three programs at "Mid City School District." One of the programs, "Project Primetime," involved nearly 100 teachers who redesigned the K–3 curriculum over a four-year period. Work groups of four to eight teachers assumed responsibility for particular teaching areas. Teachers developed their own group structure and work process, discussed their teaching, gathered and classified instructional materials and plans that had proven successful, researched issues, consulted experts, debated, compromised, and learned from one another. Teachers at each grade level developed a *Primetime Digest* that had practical advice on how to organize learning and instructional resources.

In a second curriculum development effort described by Miller (1992), middle and high school teachers reorganized the math curriculum for grades seven through twelve. In the first phase of the project, a small work group designed a five-year accelerated math sequence. Work-group inquiry included contacting other schools, the College Board, and college math departments; polling teachers; surveying students; researching student records; visiting outstanding math programs; and researching the literature on math education. The second phase of the project involved all math teachers. Several work groups were involved in different areas of investigations, with teachers assuming the roles of researchers and expert practitioners. Courses were added, dropped, and revised, and course sequences were changed. In the new curriculum, students were placed in higher-level math courses once they showed mastery of computational skills. Math teachers, rather than the guidance department assumed responsibility for student placemen. In short, the math curriculum for grades seven through twelve was totally restructured.

In a third project discussed by Miller (1992), "The Writing Project," teachers who were trained and designated as writing specialists formed teacher writing groups as structures for curriculum development. The writing groups consisted of 15 to 20 teachers and met biweekly to share, critique, revise, and edit their own writing. The teachers also began to share concerns about teaching writing and ideas for improving the teaching of writing. The group eventually evolved into a curriculum study group. During the second year of the project, the two specialists visited all of the district's schools, presenting demonstration lessons, meeting with study groups, starting new writing groups, distributing literature, answering questions, and observing classes. The writing project eventually involved more than half of the district's teachers.

According to Miller (1992), all three of the projects described "provided an opportunity for teachers to assume new roles, take control of their professional growth, and develop levels of expertise that heretofore they had associated with outside consultants" (p. 104). In all three projects, curriculum development and staff development became "indistinguishable."

A variety of other programs reported in the literature combine staff development and curriculum development. Branham (1990) described a three-year program developed by a consortium of an educational service agency and five school districts in the Hartford, Connecticut area to provide training and long-term technical support for district teams to evaluate and revise their K–12 math curricula. Hamner (1992) reported on a four-year program in the Eagle County, Colorado School District that combined curriculum and staff development in the planning, drafting, piloting, and implementing of a K–12 language arts curriculum. Miranda, Scott, Forsythe, Spratley, and Conrad (1992) described a comprehensive multicultural educational program in the Columbus, Ohio Public Schools that interrelated staff development and curriculum development components. Brown (1992) reviewed a decade of efforts in the Cambridge, Massachusetts Public Schools to design staff and curriculum development for multicultural education.

Teacher Leadership

Teacher leadership can be a vehicle for staff development both for teachers in leadership roles and for the teachers to whom they provide assistance. In this section, teacher leadership is discussed both in general terms and under the more specific term *lead teacher;* aspects of the lead teacher concept are reviewed; lead teacher selection criteria and preparation are addressed; results of research on skills of successful lead teachers are summarized; conditions influencing the success of lead teachers, as well as research on the effects of and constraints to the lead teacher role, are reviewed and, finally, research on the related concept of the *leadership cadre* is discussed.

At a general level, Fessler (1990) proposed a variety of teacher leadership options as strategies for teacher empowerment, including teacher leadership in preservice teacher education, mentoring of new teachers, research, professional organizations, peer staff development/in-service, peer coach-

ing/supervision, and curriculum development. In a study of K–12 grade teachers in Michigan, Hatfield, Blackman, and Claypool (1986) found that more than 10 percent of the teachers surveyed had one or more leadership roles. The investigators classified over 50 leadership activities into five categories: (1) staff development and consultation, (2) curriculum improvement, (3) administration, (4) policy and planning, and (5) evaluation.

The lead teacher (or teacher leader) role, while certainly under the teacher leadership umbrella, represents a more clearly defined concept than teacher leadership in general. Smylie and Denny (1990) describe three aspects of the lead teacher concept:

- The specific responsibilities of lead teachers should not be prescribed a priori but should be varied, flexible, and idiosyncratic to individual schools to meet specific and changing local leadership needs.
- Objectives include improving professional learning opportunities for other teachers, engendering collegiality and collective responsibility among school staff members, and promoting classroom and school improvement.
- The lead teacher concept suggests that teacher leadership roles be built around a classroom teaching assignment comparable to that of other teachers but on a reduced schedule (pp. 157–158).

While arguing for the "empty socket" approach to the responsibilities of lead teachers, Devaney (1987) proposed six potential responsibilities for lead teachers: their own teaching and instructional improvement, review of school practice, school-level decision-making, leadership of in-service education, assistance to individual teachers, and teacher evaluation.

Berry and Ginsberg (1990) proposed a number of lead teacher selection criteria: (1) proficient teaching; (2) knowledge of subject matter, child development, and learning theory; (3) organizational, interpersonal, and communication skills; (4) understanding of public education and their school; and (5) at least three years of experience in their school. Berry and Ginsberg (1990) also proposed a selection process involving a district-level committee of teachers; school-based selection teams made up of the principal and representative teachers; and lead teacher job descriptions, application procedures, and protocols for interviews with and observations of lead teacher candidates. Berry and Ginsberg's suggested selection criteria and process stand in sharp contrast to the research of Hatfield et al (1986), who found that the vast majority of teacher-leaders in their study were selected by "administrative appointment."

Zimpher (1988) proposed five "knowledge domains" necessary for the preparation of teachers for leadership roles. The domains are local district needs, interpersonal and adult development, classroom processes for school effectiveness, instructional supervision and observation, and a disposition toward inquiry. Lieberman, Saxl, and Miles (1988) studied 17 successful teacher-leaders to identify the skills, abilities, and approaches they used to build collegiality in schools. The investigators identified six skill clusters: building trust and rapport, organizational diagnosis, managing the change process, using resources (people, ideas, materials, and equipment), work management, and building skill and confidence in others (see Lieberman et al, 1988, pp. 152–159).

As with all staff development frameworks, the success of teacher leadership depends to some extent on the presence of certain conditions. Little (1988) discussed five such conditions: the perceived importance of the work that teacher leaders do, their symbolic role, the nature of ground rules made by stakeholders, incentives and rewards (or disincentives), and the level of district policy support. After examining a Colorado teacher leader program, Carter and Powell (1992) identified five "success factors" and concluded that the absence of any of the five factors will lessen a teacher leader's effectiveness. The factors—time and access, credibility, clear role descriptions, district support and training, and a collaborative environment—are essentially consistent with Little's five conditions. Gordon (1991b) suggests that schools design comprehensive lead teacher programs that address:

1. governance;
2. mission;
3. roles and functions of lead teachers;
4. lead teacher selection;
5. lead teacher preparation;
6. staff needs assessment;
7. data-based assistance activities;
8. dissemination of information about the program;
9. support and rewards for lead teachers; and
10. program evaluation and revision.

Empirical research on the *effects* of formally designated teacher leaders is still in the exploratory stage. In a study by Smylie and Denny (1990) of teacher leadership in a metropolitan school district, teacher-respondents were asked to discuss benefits of the activity of the teacher leaders. Sixty-five percent of the respondents identified benefits for the schools, 57 percent reported benefits for the district, and 48 percent identified benefits for themselves. The most frequently cited personal benefit was growth relative to classroom practice. The school benefit most often identified was an improvement in building-level staff development. The district-level benefits most often reported were professional recognition and rewards.

Smylie and Denny (1990) also identified a number of constraints to the teacher leaders' role development and performance. The teacher leaders were uncertain about whether other teachers understood their leadership roles and what principals and teachers expected of them as leaders. The teacher leaders also spent a great deal of time in program meetings, making building level decisions, designing curricula, and developing curriculum and instructional materials. These activities were inconsistent with their own definitions of their leadership roles, which focused on providing direct help and support to other teachers. The teachers experienced tensions over the allocation of time between classroom and leadership responsibilities, between their responsibilities to administrators and other teachers, and between their leadership roles and their principals' leadership roles. Smylie and Denny concluded that the development and performance of teacher leaders are mediated by their organizational context. They recommended that "teacher leadership development should be approached as an issue of organizational change and not merely as a task of enhancing individual opportunity and capacity" (p. 257).

Much of the research on teacher leaders has used the case study methodology. An excellent work by Wasley (1991) presents three case studies of teacher leaders, followed by a discussion of constraints, supports, and issues identified across the three studies. Wasley also discusses problems, paradoxes, and possibilities in teacher leadership and presents a process for creating or redesigning teacher-leadership positions.

An approach to teacher leadership that is related to the lead teacher concept is the teacher *leadership cadre,* a group of specially trained teachers who collaborate with each other and other staff members in change efforts at the school or district level. The change effort might focus on organizational, staff, curriculum, or instructional development; but it often takes the form of cadre members providing staff development workshops and follow-up support to other staff members.

After interviewing over 100 classroom teachers, Wu (1987) identified a number of reasons why teachers often prefer other teachers as staff developers. Teachers perceive that teacher-directed staff development creates a comfortable atmosphere for sharing ideas, places participants in a more active role, and includes practical ideas that can be applied immediately in the classroom. Teachers perceive that teachers who are staff developers better understand the resources and time available to other teachers, and using teachers as staff developers increases the number of staff developers and reduces expenses.

Teachers who are members of leadership cadres have reported numerous professional benefits for themselves. Gordon and colleagues (Gorden 1993a; Gordon, Badiali, & Nolan, 1992) studied a staff development leadership cadre throughout a year-long preparation program and its first year of operation as it provided instructional skills workshops and follow-up coaching to teachers. Teachers who were cadre members reported that they became more aware of teacher and student behaviors in their own classrooms, used a greater variety of instructional strategies, and engaged in more experimentation and reflection as a result of their participation. Cadre members also reported increased collegiality and a greater commitment to collective action among program participants. These teachers also reported some negative aspects of their membership in the leadership cadre, including logistical problems with and insufficient time to carry out their staff development responsibilities. Some nonparticipating teachers perceived the teachers in the cadre as unduly privileged and elitist.

Considerable research on teacher leadership still is needed, including research on different forms of teacher leadership like individual lead teachers and leadership cadres. Despite political and structural problems with this model that must be addressed, it seems to have considerable potential as a vehicle for professional development.

Teachers as Writers

Here, the relationship between effective writing, professional growth, and adult growth are discussed and, additionally, four forms of teacher writing described in the staff development literature are reviewed.

Levine (1989) discussed the relationship between effective writing, professional development, and adult growth. First, all three require *reflection:*

Writing, is by nature, a reflective activity. Professional development—such as reading and independent study or clinical supervision and peer coaching—necessitates observation and feedback. Adults gradually increase their ability to see and know themselves as they continue to develop (p. 223).

Effective writing, professional development, and adult growth also all require *collaboration:*

Contrary to popular belief, writing is not a solitary act. Instead writers refine their thinking and expression by sharing and receiving feedback. Most forms of professional development require internal as well as external supports. And (adult) development . . . takes place within the context of interpersonal relationships (p. 223).

All three, finally, require *ownership:*

When adults determine their own directions for change, changes are more likely to take place—and to stick. It is a lot easier to disown something we say than it is to divorce ourselves from what we write. Professional development activities are far more likely to be engaging and sustaining when teachers and administrators have a hand and a voice in their determination. Adult development is an active process, not a passive one (pp. 223–224).

With growing recognition of the links between writing, professional growth, and adult development, teacher writing has received increasing acceptance as a vehicle for staff development. Forms of teacher writing include journal writing, case writing, autobiography, and writing for professional publication. Each of these forms is discussed below.

Journal Writing Teachers can use journal writing to describe and reflect on events, beliefs, emotions, concerns, questions, problems, and future plans (Gordon, 1990a). When teachers share their journals with each other, collegial dialogue, mutual support, and collaborative problem solving can result. Killian (1991) described a project in which teacher-partners within a journal network wrote and shared journals as they implemented ideas from previously attended staff development workshops. Journal writing was supplemented by letters, phone conversations, and visits by the teachers to their respondents' classrooms. Based on journal review, interviews, surveys, and project summaries written by participants, the project evaluation indicated that the journal network fostered collegiality, voluntary perseverance with staff development, openness to experimentation, and opportunities for teacher leadership.

Teacher Cases A case contains three features. It is: (1) descriptive rather than analytical (although an analysis may accompany a case), (2) descriptive of teaching practice, and (3) intended to bring about specific teacher learning (Richert, 1991). Based on several years of research on the use of cases for teacher learning, Richert (1991) has concluded that having teachers themselves write cases and then discuss the cases with each other is an especially powerful form of staff development:

Preparing the case and then discussing it with colleagues brought their knowledge to a new level of consciousness and understanding. Other teachers reported that the process of creating a case, or discussing someone else's, helped them discover new knowledge or rediscover old knowledge in new ways. Writing the case was particularly powerful in this regard (p. 126).

Richert's research indicates that, through the writing-speaking-listening process, teachers who collaboratively create and analyze cases construct new knowledge beyond the understanding of particular teaching situations described in the cases.

Autobiography In addition to being a methodology for acquiring knowledge about teachers and teaching, teacher autobiography also has been used as a form of professional inquiry and staff development. Raymond, Butt, and Townsend (1992) described a four phase activity in which cooperative groups of teachers and their administrator focused on developing "collaborative biographies." The four phases include (1) a description of the context within which the teachers work, (2) a description of their current teaching practice, (3) reflections on their past personal and professional lives, and (4) their preferred professional futures based on a critical analysis of the accounts given during the first three phases. While the autobiographies are individual, they are developed through collaborative reflection. After each teacher has developed an individual professional development plan, the cooperative group identifies its collective concerns, then designs and carries out a common project which addresses both individual and collective agendas.

Writing for Professional Publication Greenwood (1991) proposed several reasons for educational practioners to write for publication, including thought clarification, information sharing, ego boosting, promotion of change, and financial rewards (when the school district offers incentives for writing). Lewis (1992) recounted personal benefits of writing for publication, including evaluating teaching experience, analyzing students' growth, gaining the respect of other professionals and increasing personal credibility, and ideas which lead to new student and teacher projects.

Lewis (1992) also discussed obstacles to teachers writing for publication, including insufficient time, writer's block, the absence of a professional reward system, difficulty accepting criticism, and an unwillingness to share creative ideas because of the fear of losing ownership. One historical problem with teachers writing for publication has been the sparsity of publications that feature practitioner writing. In recent years, national publications like the *Journal of Staff Development* and *Educational Leadership* have placed an increasing emphasis on giving voice to PK–12 teachers. More important to widespread teacher publication, a growing number of local and statewide publications have been created with the express purpose of disseminating teacher writing. An example is Pennsylvania's *Journal of Teacher Leadership*, a high quality publication consisting primarily of articles by teachers, published and edited "by teachers, for teachers."

Collegial Groups and Networks

In this section, functions and types of collegial groups are discussed; studies of successful collegial groups are summarized; differences and relationships of collegial groups and networks are described; benefits of networks are discussed; and, finally, examples of effective networks used as staff development frameworks are presented.

Collegial groups generally include study groups and support groups. The two types of groups theoretically have different functions. For example, Murphy (1992) proposes that the three functions of *study groups* are to help "implement curricular and instructional innovations, collaboratively plan school improvement, and study research on teaching and learning" (p. 71). Watson and Stevenson (1989) suggest six reasons for *support groups:* sharing successes, sharing frustrations, educating without indoctrinating, sharing best classroom practice, political action, and disseminating information. A review of the literature on these two types of collegial groups, however, reveals that in practice similar functions are found both in groups labeled as study groups and those identified as support groups.

There are myriad specific types of collegial groups. Boytim and Dickel (1988) list 28 different types of support groups for teachers. A sample of collegial group activities described in the literature include establishing a culture for change (Davis, McCarty, Shaw, & Sidani-Tabbaa, 1991); supporting the use of alternative models of teaching (Joyce et al, 1989; Murphy, 1992); studying educational research (Powell, Berliner, & Casanova, 1992); supporting a literature-based approach to reading instruction (Matlin & Short, 1991); reviewing professional books (Schmale, 1994); planning, presenting and analyzing action research (Keedy, 1992); applying whole language curricula (Salzer, 1991; Watson & Stevenson, 1989); improving communication skills across the curriculum (Schoenbach, 1994); and supporting special educators (Cook, 1992). Levine (1989) points out that groups develop and shift their purpose over time. An example of support-group development is described by Rich (1992):

As the group matured and grew from seven to 30 members over the course of 14 years, meetings gradually evolved from study sessions, during which members read and reacted to professional articles, to the critiquing and writing of new curriculum documents, to the presentation of workshops for other teachers, and finally to the review of classroom research (p. 33).

Examples of successful collegial groups were described by Gibboney and Gould (1987) in their review of "the dialogue approach to staff development." This process has the aims of empowering participants, improving learning-teaching and administrative practices, and increasing the capacity of participants to change organizational structures. The dialogue process is based on encouraging inquiry, reading books, and democratic dialogue. Its essential characteristics include:

1. dialogue involving participants from at least two levels in the school hierarchy (e.g., teachers and principals);
2. an initial focus on a general problem rather than a specific problem or solutions;
3. a body of ideas that inform and criticize the ideas and values learned over years of practice;
4. sufficient time;
5. dialogue that is both rigorous and flexible; and
6. a knowledgeable moderator.

Gibboney and Gould (1987) recommend that the democratic dialogue take place on the equivalent of five full days a year. They state that the preliminary results occur in six to 12 months and that changes in the structure of schooling occur in three to five years.

Gibboney and Gould (1987) reported positive outcomes in case studies of the dialogue process in two school districts. In one district, teachers were heavily involved in professional decisions, the staff improved the teaching-learning environment, and the K–12 curriculum was reorganized. Among the dialogue group at one high school in another school district, morale, job satisfaction, and appreciation of self and others increased. Ideas and values of teachers in the dialogue group changed; they valued a more intellectual, active student learning process. The dialogue group's teachers also changed their practice; they elicited more active student responses and used more small-group work, student talk, and less superficial content coverage. Several structural changes were made at the school level, including the creation of a discipline policy and a philosophy in learning and teaching, and three additional staff development days per year. District-level changes attributed to the high school dialogue group included a voluntary dialogue group of district administrators, and a change in the fine and practical arts grading system.

The distinction between collegial groups and *networks* is not precise, although collegial groups tend to function within individual schools, single districts, or local geographic areas, and networks tend to link educators with common interests across a relatively large geographic area, often at the state, national, or international level. A collegial group can be *part* of a network. For example, over 200 local support groups commonly known as Teachers Applying Whole Language (TAWLS) together form an international whole-language network (Salzer, 1991). Loucks-Horsley et al (1987) discuss a number of benefits of networks: expanding members' boundaries, sharing experiences and ideas, developing a common language, continuing growth, supporting norms of professionalism and collegiality, increasing participants' sense of efficacy, recognition of progress, and celebration of accomplishments.

The Foxfire Teacher Networks are examples of effective networks specifically intended to be frameworks for staff development. The networks are described by Smith and Wigginton (1991). The "Foxfire approach" is based on reflective thinking, problem solving, community involvement, and the democratic process (for the 11 "core practices" of the Foxfire approach, see Smith and Wigginton, 1991). Participation in the Foxfire program begins with teachers attending an intensive course on the Foxfire approach, which includes designing a project intended to teach a "chunk" of curriculum according to Foxfire principles.

The teacher networks form in regions where the Foxfire course has been taught, and eventually assume responsibility for teaching the course as well as providing support for teachers who are implementing the Foxfire approach. Networks vary from region to region but all are expected to be laboratories for field-testing the approach, arenas for classroom research, and centers for dialogue between Foxfire coordinators and teachers. All Foxfire networks have coordinators, courses, newsletters, small group meetings, retreats, and writing workshops. In some networks, teachers are linked by computers. Teachers who have completed the Foxfire course eventually assume responsibility for teaching it. An advanced course is offered for teachers who have completed the first course.

A teacher-outreach office coordinates the networks and meetings of coordinators, documents individual teacher's projects, publishes a newsletter with teacher case studies, dispenses grant funds, tracks relevant educational trends and research, and coordinates program evaluation. Systematic evaluations have been carried out to determine the effectiveness of the course and the extent of classroom implementation of the Foxfire approach by teachers who have completed the course. Smith and Wigginton (1991) reported network members' perceptions of benefits to them, which included continued growth in the instructional approach, opportunities to practice leadership, and teacher empowerment.

Teacher and Professional Development Centers

Here, the teacher center concept is defined, and a brief history of teacher centers is provided. Several teacher centers described in the literature are discussed. Loucks-Horsley et al (1987) describe teacher centers as follows:

Teachers' centers are professional development structures operating within a school or district, or between collaborating organizations such as schools, colleges, teachers' associations, and businesses. While no two teachers' centers look alike, they share certain purposes; they respond to teachers' continuing learning needs, as determined by the teacher; they provide an environment where teachers can work individually or in groups on developing classroom materials and projects; and they advise and assist teachers in their own improvement in a nonevaluative, supportive situation (pp. 94–95)

The height of the teacher-center movement in the United States came in the late 1970s and early 1980s as a result of federal legislation: Public Law 94–482. Ninety teacher centers were established with federal funding; they typically served single school districts and were housed on a district campus. Policy boards made up of a majority of teachers were responsible for developing, monitoring, and evaluating programs and activities. On average, teacher centers sponsored about 60 programs and activities per year, including courses, seminars, and workshops. Most programs and activities were short-term and focused on the improvement of instruction (Yarger, 1990).

Federal funding for teacher centers established under PL 94–482 lasted only three years, and the heyday of the teacher center had passed. A variety of centers have been established since the early 1980s, however. They have been funded by districts, universities, intermediate units, consortia, and state, federal, and private grants. Although the terms *teacher development center*, *professional development center*, and *staff development center* have different connotations, the functions of those centers that are discussed in the literature are for the most part indistinguishable. The three terms are thus viewed as interchangeable for the purpose of this review.

The Pittsburgh, Pennsylvania Public School District's Schenley High School Teacher Center is a well documented example of a successful center (Bickell, Denton, Johnston, LeMahieu, & Young, 1987; LeMahieu et al, 1989; Wallace, LeMahieu, & Bickel, 1990; Wallace et al, 1984). Schenley was reorganized and staffed with outstanding teachers from across the district. Many of these teachers became specially trained Clinical Resident Teachers (CRTs). Over a four-year period, groups of secondary educators from throughout the district participated in orientation and self-assessment at their own schools. They then completed eight-week mini-sabbaticals at Schenley "built around activities that addressed the refinement of instructional skills, sensitivity to adolescents as learners, knowledge within subject and content areas, individual professional enrichment, district wide initiatives, and follow-through of home schools for continued professional growth" (Wallace et al, 1990, p. 186). In addition, visiting professionals were teamed with CRTs, who helped the visitors plan lessons, watched them teach, and provided feedback.

Follow-through included individual follow-up plans, collaboratively designed by visiting professionals and CRTs, to be implemented by the visitors in their home schools. Follow-through was eventually expanded to include activities intended to renew the professional climates of home schools, including "Center of Excellence" projects to improve the home school environment and districtwide innovations like common departmental planning and the conversion of the role of department chairperson to that of "Instructional Team Leader." During the time the Schenley center was in operation, student achievement in reading and language increased dramatically across the districts' secondary schools, with even greater increases in reading and language achievement at Schenley itself. The teacher center concept later was extended to elementary and middle schools within the district.

Although the Schenley High School Teacher Center may be the most widely recognized center in recent years, a variety of regional centers funded by colleges, consortia, and state governments illustrate the fact that the teacher center concept did not die along with PL 94–482 funding. A regional professional development center located at Fitchburg State College, Massachusetts was described by Zide and Colbert (1992). The center includes a professional library; a variety of on-site courses, seminars, and networks; and long-term staff development consultation to area schools. The Regional Staff Development Center, created by the Southeastern Wisconsin Educators' Consortium, is described by Letven and Klobuchar (1990). The center has a threefold mission: teacher *support* (academic alliances, networks, study committees, and a beginning teacher/mentor program), *recognition* ("Educators Hall of Fame," "Educators Showcase," and mini-grants), and *training* (drug-free school programs, a science fellows program, and a regional in-service day). In Ohio, the Southwestern Regional Professional Development Center is one of eight such centers established by the Ohio Department of Education. The Center serves three subregions, each with its own subregional council and representation on the regional council. The center makes extensive use of subregional and regional needs assessments, collaborative planning, and the training of trainers to meet teachers' professional development needs (Southeastern Regional Professional Development Center, 1993).

A number of "specialized" centers have emerged across the nation. An example is the Southeastern Teacher Leadership Center, one of Pennsylvania's lead teacher training centers (Hynes & Summers, 1990). It is funded by a grant from the Pennsylvania Department of Education to the Philadelphia School District and is based at West Chester University. The primary activity of the center is the Leadership Seminar, offered to school instructional teams made up of teachers and at least one building administrator. The program begins with an assessment of participants' leadership skills and roles, continues with four days of seminars tailored to the assessment results, and concludes with follow-up seminars in the fall and spring of the following academic year. Other services provided by the center include technical assistance with school needs assessment, a variety of workshops, school consultation, and an annual conference on educational leadership (Hynes & Summers, 1990).

The North Carolina Center for the Advancement of Teaching (NCCAT) in Cullowhee, North Carolina is committed to rewarding, renewing, and retaining outstanding North Carolina teachers (Kirk, 1991). Its primary vehicle is an interdisciplinary seminar planned by specialists in the arts, humanities, and sciences and designed to foster creativity and problem solving skills. Kirk (1991) describes the seminar:

Because of their experiential or hands-on approach, seminars at NCCAT are sometimes referred to as "living seminars." They involve a varied range of activities. Examples include such things as repelling off mountain sides, gem mining, participating in anthropological digs, star gazing, scientific file studies, visits to a local Indian reservation, day trips to historical sites, story telling, folk dancing, and poetry writing. These highly participative activities are augmented by readings, media presentations, demonstrations, and addresses by visiting experts. The idea is to immerse participants in a more natural environment and rekindle the child-like curiosity and creativity that was once theirs. To help participants escape the myopia which sometimes prevents them from looking at everyday events in a holistic manner (p. 5).

All expenses for the week-long seminar are met by the state of North Carolina.

Teacher and resource centers focused on particular content areas are found throughout the United States. For example, Brinckerhoff (1989) described a variety of science resource centers across the nation. Perhaps the most comprehensive guidelines for establishing teacher centers have been prepared by Kahn (1991). Kahn's report includes sections on the philosophy, possible functions, and management of centers.

Self-Directed Professional Development

In this section, characteristics and dimensions of self-directed staff development are presented; reasons for and problems with self-directed growth are discussed; guides for and stages of self-directed development are summarized; and, finally, the career lattice model for structuring personalized staff development is described.

Self-directed professional development is characterized by individual teachers completing a self-assessment, identifying their own improvement goals, planning their own improvement strategies, and assessing their own growth. Loucks-Horsley et al (1987) explain that self-directed development

varies along four dimensions: it may be formal or informal, solitary or interactive, short term or long term, and micro (focused on one's own classroom) or macro (involving cooperation with other teachers in the school). Glatthorn (1990) reviews reasons for self-directed programs: the assumptions that self-directed development is consistent with the principles of adult learning, that it responds to changing developmental needs of the teacher, and that the current emphasis on the professionalization of teaching "connotes self-regulation and autonomous performance" (p. 201). Problems with self-directed development discussed by Glatthorn (1990) include the frequent failure of teachers to set challenging goals, teachers' insufficient use of feedback, and teachers' lack of constructive assessment of what they have accomplished. In addition to reviewing these difficulties, Glatthorn (1990) proposes a variety of methods for dealing with each.

Caffarella (1993) offers a six-step guide for developing a learning plan:

1. Develop the learning objective.
2. Identify learning strategies and resources.
3. Specify the evidence of accomplishments.
4. Describe the evaluative criteria and designate who will evaluate the evidence.
5. Develop a time-line.
6. Work with a peer consultation team and facilitator (pp. 31–32).

As suggested in Caffarella's step six, "being self-directed does not necessarily mean learning alone . . . the key is that the learner takes the *primary* lead for fostering his or her own growth and development" (p. 30). Caffarella (1993) suggests a number of tasks for staff developers to perform when facilitating individuals: assisting learners to identify learning objectives, strategies, resources, and evaluation criteria; providing resources; training process facilitators and matching them with learners; serving as the primary facilitator; and arranging for meetings of peer consultation teams.

Wilshire (1991) reported on a self-directed program with five stages:

1. *Invitation:* After an awareness session, teachers wishing to participate completed biographical data sheets, which were used to match participating teachers with facilitators from a nearby university.
2. *Assessment:* Facilitators taped structured interviews with teachers designed to determine teachers' staff development needs and preferences. Facilitators analyzed interview transcripts in order to generate staff development options to share with teachers.
3. *Validation-Negation:* Facilitators shared themes found in interview transcripts and staff development options with teachers. Teachers could select, reject, or elect to reflect further on staff development options. By the end of this phase, the teacher, with the assistance of his or her facilitator, developed professional development goals, objectives, activities, assessment plans, and lists of needed resources and materials.
4. *Disclosure:* The teachers shared their plans during a group meeting of teachers and facilitators. Collaboration among teachers with similar plans was encouraged.

5. *Implementation:* Teachers met with administrators for plan approval, then began implementation. Teachers were expected to complete their plans within two years and to share products with the district. District funds and facilitators were available to assist teachers as they implemented their plans. Individual projects included curriculum development, interdisciplinary team teaching, and gathering information on successful educational practice to share with other teachers.

McDonnell and Christenson (1990) propose the *career lattice* as a model for structuring personalized staff development. An alternative to career ladders, which have focused more on career development and performance incentives than on staff development, the career lattice integrates self-directed professional development, teacher empowerment, and teacher leadership. McDonnell and Christenson's model includes four components. The first component is *role options.* The options are arrayed across the horizontal axis of a matrix and include "learner," "knowledge producer," "peer coach," "teacher educator," "mentor," and "leader." The second component is *teaching responsibilities.* The responsibilities are listed along the vertical axis of the matrix and include "student evaluation," "planning," "curriculum," "instructional strategies," "materials," "classroom management," "discipline," "climate," "communication," "professionalism," and "co-curricular." The third component is the identification of *the initiator of an activity.* Initiators can be the teachers, peers, administrators, students, or parents. The fourth component includes *empowerment experiences.* Examples of empowerment experiences are education or training, experience, development activities, organizational work, research or reading, school or classroom visitation, and released time (McDonnell & Christenson, 1990). A format developed by McDonnell and Christenson integrates the career lattice components. It includes sections to enter professional development goals, role option, area of teaching responsibility, empowerment activities and resources, evaluation evidence, and the evaluator's comments and approval (McDonnell & Christenson, 1990). The career lattice seems to have significant potential for incorporating one or more of the previously discussed staff development frameworks within an individualized staff development program.

STAFF DEVELOPMENT AND RELATED PROCESSES

Adult development, the change process, organization development, and school restructuring are processes intimately related to staff development. They are discussed here to the extent that they directly affect or are directly affected by staff development.

Staff Development and Adult Development

Here, effects of adult stage development both on teachers' staff development needs and on teachers' responses to staff development are discussed; strategies for adapting staff development to teachers functioning at different stages of development are presented; studies on efforts to foster teachers'

stage development are reviewed; and, finally, life cycle theory and related developmental needs of adults are discussed.

At the most general level, adult development relates to staff development in two ways. First, teachers' developmental stages and life cycle phases affect their staff development needs and the way that they respond to staff development efforts. Second, staff development can be designed to stimulate the growth of teachers toward higher stages of adult development. *Stage development* includes such areas as cognitive, conceptual, moral, and ego development (Glickman, Gordon, & Ross-Gordon, 1995). Thies-Sprinthall (1984), in a course for supervising teachers, and Oja and Pine (1987), in a collaborative action research project, found that the developmental stages of participating teachers had a strong effect on how they responded to staff development programs. Oja and Pine (1987), for example, concluded that "teachers at different developmental levels reacted differently to collaborative action research; behaved differently in action teams; thought differently about authority and leadership, conceived of change differently; and understood the goals and outcomes of research differently" (p. 101).

Glickman, Gordon, and Ross-Gordon (1995) discuss three stages of staff development: orientation, integration, and refinement. They propose that as teachers move through these stages, staff development should be matched to teachers' developmental levels by tailoring the experience impact (Harris, 1989), degree of structure, sequence, and pace of staff development activities. Glickman, Gordon, and Ross-Gordon (1995) also suggest that as teachers who were initially functioning at lower developmental stages experience growth, the experience impact, structure, sequence, and pace of staff development activities be modified accordingly.

In a course for supervising teachers, Thies-Sprinthall (1984) provided more structure and guidance for teachers of low conceptual levels and less structure, more theory, and research projects for teachers of moderate and high conceptual levels. Built into the course were five conditions necessary to promote psychological and cognitive growth:

1. role-taking experiences;
2. careful and continuous guided reflection;
3. balance . . . between real experience and discussion/reflection;
4. both personal support and challenge; and
5. continuity (p. 54).

Teachers who completed the course experienced substantial gains on measures of conceptual level, principled judgment, and communication skills.

Phillips and Glickman (1991) reported on a peer coaching program (referred to earlier in this chapter) that incorporated Thies-Sprinthall's five conditions to promote psychological and cognitive growth. In staff development sessions, teachers learned observation, problem solving, and interpersonal skills through lectures, demonstrations, practice observations, conference role playing, outside readings, discussion, and reflection. The participating teachers observed and conferenced with each other during four peer coaching cycles, with each cycle followed by a group debriefing session. Phillips and Glickman reported significant increases in the conceptual levels of teachers who had participated in the program.

Life cycle development is a different dimension of adult development that also is relevant to staff development. Life cycle theory is focused on age-linked phases of adult development and the developmental tasks of each phase. Krupp (1989) discusses developmental needs over four decades:

Individuals in their 20s often determine their career direction and, therefore, seek information on careers and validation for their own competence. Individuals turning 30 come face-to-face with career and identity decisions. Those in their 40s often find themselves in positions of authority and express a desire to improve their leadership skills. Individuals in their 50s have generally settled into their careers and appreciate opportunities to give to others (p. 49).

Krupp (1981, 1989) describes adult life cycle phases in detail, relates them to the teaching career, and suggests staff development strategies appropriate for each phase.

Levine's *Promoting Adult Growth in Schools* (1989) provides extensive discussions of "stages of adult development" (stage theory), "phases of adult development" (life cycle theory), and professional development practices for promoting educators' growth. Glickman, Gordon, and Ross-Gordon (1995) discuss adult development theory and implications for both supervision and staff development.

Staff Development and the Change Process

In this section, the relationship between staff development and the change process is discussed; change factors that need to be analyzed by staff developers are reviewed; and sources of additional information on change relevant to staff development are provided.

Fullan (1990, 1991) has discussed the relationship between staff development and change on three different levels. First, the successful implementation of specific innovations requires staff development:

Effective implementation consists of alterations in curriculum materials, practices and behavior, and beliefs and understandings by teachers vis-a-vis potentially worthwhile innovations. . . . Put more simply, successful change involves learning how to do something new. As such, the process of implementation is essentially a learning process. Thus, when it is linked to specific innovations, staff development and implementation go hand in hand (Fullan, 1990, p. 4).

Second, new staff development programs are themselves innovations:

A second useful, but still limiting perspective, is to consider major new staff development projects as innovations in their own right. In particular, new policies and structures that establish new roles, such as mentors, coaches, and the like, are and can be considered as innovations in the sites and districts in which they are adopted (Fullan, 1990, p. 8).

On a third level, Fullan views staff development as a key ingredient in *institutional development,* "changes in schools as institutions that increase their capacity and performance for continuous improvement" (Fullan, 1990, p. 11). At this level, staff development is a long-term strategy for developing schools as collaborative workplaces (Fullan, 1991).

Shroyer (1990) maintains that staff development leaders need to analyze: (1) what change means to the organization and individuals within the organization, and (2) the innovation itself. Organizational factors to be analyzed include school characteristics, decision-making processes, and experiences with past change attempts. Additional organizational factors are the level of collaboration and support within the school, the school's purpose, and whether the proposed change is consistent with that purpose. Individual factors to be analyzed by staff developers include how individuals will react to change, as well as individuals' needs, concerns, backgrounds, and abilities. Other individual factors to be considered are leadership sources, identification of roles, how to encourage participation, and implementation assistance. Shroyer recommends that analysis of the change itself should focus on envisioning a program that is theoretically sound and technically manageable, provides clarity, and allows flexibility. Additional factors to be considered are whether the innovation's benefits outweigh its costs, its practicality, and whether it matches teacher, organizational, and community priorities.

Although a review of the change literature is beyond the scope of this chapter, a number of reports based on research and best practice are listed here for the reader's information. Reviews on educational change particularly relevant to staff development include Fullan's (1991) assumptions about change; Miles, Saxl, and Lieberman's (1988) key skills for educational change agents; and Miles' key success factors for change projects (Fullan, 1990). Additional relevant summaries include Tafel and Bertani's (1992) conclusions about systematic change; Glickman, Hayes, and Hensley's (1992) complexities of school change; and Hyde's (1992) essential elements for change among veteran teachers. Loucks-Horsley and Stiegelbauer (1991) review connections between staff development and the Concerns-Based Adoption Model (CBAM). Their review includes discussions of six principles of working with change, levels of concern about the innovation, and functions of interventions by change facilitators (also see Hall & Hord, 1987).

Staff Development and Organization Development

The relationship between organization development (OD) and staff development is discussed in this section. Goals and subgoals of OD are presented. Distinctions and relationships between staff development and OD are discussed; and programs integrating staff development and OD described in the staff development literature are reviewed.

Schmuck and Runkel (1985) propose that the chief goal of OD is "that the school achieve a sustained capacity for solving its own problems" (p. 10). They list subgoals: clarifying communication, establishing clear goals, identifying and resolving conflicts, decision-making that results in commitment, and assessment of development efforts.

In recent years, OD has received increasing emphasis in the staff development literature. The 1981 Yearbook of the Association for Supervision and Curriculum Development (ASCD) was entitled *Staff Development/Organization Development.* The National Staff Development Council

(NSDC) has placed considerable emphasis on OD. For example, the theme of the winter 1990 issue of NSDC's *Journal of Staff Development* was "Organization Development for Improving Schools." The differences between staff development and OD and their interrelationship are discussed in the literature. Vojtek (1992) defines staff development as "professional development for *individuals* to improve *student instruction*" and OD as "professional development for *groups* to improve *school climate*" (p. 4). Although Dillon-Peterson (1981) essentially agrees with Vojtek's distinction, she emphasizes the interrelationship of staff development and OD:

Seldom are individual development and institutional development or change discreet entities, even though they are often viewed that way. Rather, they are dependent correlates. Without one or the other—or if they operate in isolation—the potential for significant, positive change is materially decreased. Organizations are successful in fulfilling their missions only to the degree that the individuals within them understand and contribute to the achievement of mutually acceptable goals (p. 3).

While most authors agree that staff development and OD are complimentary and that there is considerable overlap between the two, there is also general agreement that the staff developer who becomes involved in OD efforts is assuming an expanded role requiring additional skills beyond those required for staff development leadership. Killion and Harrison (1990) propose that "to be successful in this new role, staff developers must develop skills in group process, facilitation, team building, decision-making strategies, and communication" (p. 25). In a nationwide survey of staff developers, Vojtek (1992) found that respondents were becoming more involved with OD, and generally rated their knowledge and use of individual OD skills (problem solving, decision-making, trust building, team building, leadership) higher than their knowledge and use of OD macrodesign elements (diagnosis, OD training, survey-data procedures, evaluating OD).

There is a consensus across the literature that the learning required of staff members for professional development is different from the learning required of staff for OD. For example Lipton and Greenblatt (1992) list 16 types of knowledge, skills, and attitudes required for OD, and 17 types of knowledge, skills, and attitudes for staff development.[3] While the lists are complimentary, only three types of learning appear in both lists: assessment alternatives, empathy, and risk taking.

A variety of descriptions of programs integrating staff development and OD are available within the staff development literature. Overviews of three representative reports are provided below. Killion and Harrison (1990) describe how a Colorado district used an OD approach to site-based management. Components of the program included the following:

- defining roles, including redefining central office personnel as support personnel, establishing a director of school improvement, monitoring of principals by the superintendent rather than central office personnel, and staff developers as facilitators of change;
- changing policies and procedures to support site-based management and participatory leadership;
- expanding training programs to include process skills;
- establishing flexible expectations for shared decision-making; and

- modeling of shared decision-making by the superintendent's cabinet and staff development department.

Walters and Henkelman (1990) describe two types of OD interventions based on programs funded by the Maryland State Department of Education (MSDE). In "Total School Intervention Projects" (intended primarily for secondary schools), OD consultants from the MSDE:

- provided leadership development workshops for school-based instructional leaders;
- facilitated school team meetings;
- assisted with data collection and analysis;
- facilitated a goal setting process;
- promoted collaborative decision-making and problem solving; and
- assisted in planning school-based staff development (p. 16).

In the "Teacher decision-making Project," (intended primarily for elementary schools) MSDE facilitators focused on the improvement of instruction and classroom management as well as training in facilitation skills, follow-up, and coaching of school-based leadership teams that facilitated school change projects. Based on several evaluation studies, Walters and Henkelman reported a variety of positive outcomes for staffs and students at schools involved in both types of projects.

Saltrick, Johnston, and Bickel (1991) described how Pittsburgh public schools established OD strategies for Phase II of the Schenley Teacher Center Staff Development Program discussed earlier. "Phase II Facilitators" in secondary schools taught half-time and were responsible for facilitating school-based staff development and shared decision-making. Facilitators were trained in group dynamics, team building, communication skills, conflict management, consensus building, and trust building. They were introduced to systems for observing individuals' behaviors in small groups. Logistical support and coaching were also provided for facilitators. The facilitators' tasks included the following:

- coordinating and facilitating activities related to the development, implementation, and dissemination of Centers of Excellence (school improvement projects aimed at meeting both district and school needs and focused on improving both student achievement and the school environment);
- serving as a liaison between the school and the Director of Centers for Excellence;
- providing feedback to the school's instructional cabinet and other related groups about group process;
- identifying school training and resource needs; and
- coordinating school-wide professional development activities with a special emphasis on peer observation, teaching clinics, and seminars (p. 53).

The facilitators also provided training to the instructional cabinet in conflict management, consensus building, and the feedback process.

The examples provided above not only show the relationship of staff development and OD, but also illustrate how OD can serve as one vehicle for school restructuring, a broader and more amorphous process.

Staff Development and School Restructuring

Here, the meaning of the term *school restructuring* is discussed; four relationships between staff development and restructuring are described; and the need to change the concept and role of staff development in order to better facilitate school restructuring is addressed.

According to Owen, Loucks-Horsley, and Horsley (1991), "The term *restructuring* has come to mean everything from changing one dimension of school life (for example, the governance structure, class schedule, or curriculum development process), to changing everything (that is, literally starting from scratch to design a new way of doing business" (p. 11). Joyce (1991) discusses five major emphases or "doors to school improvement," all intended to eventually change the school culture:

1. *collegiality:* developing cohesive and professional relations within school faculties and connecting them more closely to their surrounding neighborhoods;
2. *research:* helping school faculties study research findings about effective school practices or instructional alternatives;
3. *site-specific information:* helping faculties collect and analyze data about their schools and their students' progress;
4. *curriculum initiatives:* introducing changes within subject areas or, as in the case of the computer, across the curriculum area; and
5. *instructional initiatives:* organizing teachers to study teaching skills and strategies (p. 59).

As one reviews Joyce's list, staff development links to each emphasis are not difficult to draw. Rubin (1987) points out that "staff development is a major component in most school improvement efforts" (p. 174). Fullan (1991) argues that "staff development cannot be separated from school development" (p. 331). Owen, Loucks-Horsley, and Horsley (1991) discuss three roles of staff development in school restructuring, including staff development as (1) a vehicle for developing knowledge, skills and attitudes, (2) an unfreezing influence leading to consideration of restructuring, and (3) the heart of restructuring: promoting the school as a learning community. Based on a review of that body of literature which discusses the integration of staff development and school restructuring, the author has identified four categories of relationships between staff development and school restructuring: staff development as (1) precursor, (2) prerequisite, (3) ongoing dimension, and (4) central focus of school restructuring.

Staff development as precursor of school restructuring is equivalent to Owen, Loucks-Horsley, and Horsley's "unfreezing" role. Many schools initially not ready for comprehensive restructuring can gradually become aware of the need for it through participation in effective staff development programs. Such staff development programs contain many of the characteristics of successful restructuring programs, including collection and analysis of data, collaborative planning, participatory decision-making, and problem solving. Thus, staff development can be both a microcosm of and impetus for school restructuring. Initiating school restructuring through staff development has been described as "going in the back door" (Diegmueller, 1991). The well-known school restructuring programs in the Pittsburgh public schools and Richmond County, Georgia

schools, for example, both evolved from more limited staff development programs (Diegmueller, 1991).

Staff development as a prerequisite of school restructuring refers to the need to prepare school teams for restructuring by providing them with knowledge and skills necessary to participate in restructuring projects. For instance, Halcomb (1993) describes the content of training sessions in the School-Based Instructional Leadership program, designed to empower school leadership teams (including administrators, teachers, and other stakeholders) for school restructuring efforts. The sessions focus on:

* exploring the research and process;
* examining effective schools;
* defining district and school roles and responsibilities;
* improving schools through teamwork;
* affirming mission and beliefs;
* gathering, analyzing, and reporting data;
* developing and implementing the school improvement plan; and
* creating change in the school culture (p. 5-6).

Moller and Bohning (1992) and Maeroff (1993) describe other preparation programs for school improvement teams. The importance of this type of staff development to school restructuring is supported by the fact that districts that have not emphasized preliminary training have had to incorporate it into their projects after experiencing difficulty with initial attempts at restructuring (Diegmueller, 1991).

Staff development as an ongoing dimension of school restructuring is essential to any school restructuring effort (Levine, 1991; Parkay & Damico, 1989). For example, Johnson, Snyder, and Anderson (1992) describe staff development as one of four interdependent dimensions of the "work culture" that provide direction and energy for school restructuring. The other three dimensions are program planning, program development, and school assessment. Regardless of the direction that school restructuring takes, once restructuring goals have been identified and improvement plans made, effective implementation in any of Joyce's five emphasis areas (collegiality, research, site-specific information, curriculum initiatives and instructional strategies) invariably requires some type of staff development.

Staff development as the central focus of school restructuring, according to Owen, Loucks-Horsley, and Horsley (1991), means "promoting a vision of the school as a learning community" (p. 12). They go on to describe the vision:

In such a community there is much collaboration for learning. Risk taking is seen as necessary for learning, inquiry is encouraged, and failure is accepted as it feeds additional learning. Learners of all ages have input into what they will learn and make real choices. Depth of understanding is valued over superficial coverage, and opportunity is provided for focused study that takes place over time. The learning process pays attention to prior knowledge, construction of conceptual understanding, and repeated application to real life situations (p. 12).

Watson (1994) agrees that an important function of staff development for school restructuring is the development of a shared vision, and that the vision should include changing the role of the student "from passive to active, from dependent to independent" (p. 26). He argues that changing the role of the student requires new roles and skills for educators, as well as a new approach to staff development. Watson goes on to propose a number of implications for staff development, including new emphases on: (1) reflection; (2) inquiry and problem solving; (3) the exchange of ideas and creative thinking; (4) facilitating a needs-based, shared vision and corresponding plans, technical skills, and leadership skills; (5) teamwork and communication; and (6) professional development as a tool of discovery (for all of the implications, see Watson, 1994). Katzenmeyer and Reid (1991) also maintain that if staff development is to make a substantial contribution to school restructuring it must restructure its own rules, roles, and relationships and increase its emphasis on team building, capacity building, and organization development.

EVALUATION OF STAFF DEVELOPMENT

Marshall (1988) has identified five purposes of staff development evaluation, including the provision of information for program improvement, information for accountability, information for program planning, information for staff planning, and mentoring to staff developers. Most staff development evaluation models are adaptations of more generic program evaluation models. For instance, Marshall (1989) provides examples of case study, systems, goal-based, and quasi-legal models applied to staff development evaluation; Simmons (1982) and Todnem and Warner (1993) apply variations of cost-benefit analysis to staff development; and Loucks and Melle (1982) as well as Hoffman and Reed (1994) utilized aspects of the Concerns-Based Adoption Model (CBAM) to assess staff development programs.

Mullins (1994) has written one of the few recent publications entirely devoted to the evaluation of staff development programs. His work includes "Standards and Indicators of Quality" for program evaluation that encompass the following areas:

1. framework for staff development;
2. needs assessment policy and procedures;
3. advisory committee;
4. staff development objectives;
5. the instructional content;
6. instructional process;
7. staff development trainers;
8. meeting course/activity objectives;
9. follow-up and reinforcement; and
10. participant contribution (pp. 89–93).

In his book, Mullins applies the proposed standards and indicators to six vignettes, including:

1. the evaluation of needs assessment activities;
2. the use of staff development advisory committees;
3. how well staff developers use the principles of adult learning theory;
4. workshops for at-risk students;
5. a multicultural appreciation program; and
6. self-esteem workshops.

Staff development evaluation plans range from a narrow, goal-based focus to a wide, comprehensive focus. An example of the former is proposed by Ryan and Crowell (1982):

1. precise definition of program goals, in terms of measurable processes and outcomes;
2. identification of indicators that goals are being achieved;
3. identification of instrumentation for documenting presence and nature of indicators;
4. identification of instrumentation designers or of existing instruments;
5. identification of data collectors and/or monitors;
6. identification of appropriate dates for making formative evaluation decisions;
7. identification of procedures for analyzing data; and
8. identification of value judgments to be made and appropriate criteria for making those judgments (p. 167).

At the other end of the continuum, Glickman, Gordon, and Ross-Gordon (1995) take a broad view of what should be included in the evaluation plan. They suggest the following components:

1. evaluation of needs assessment;
2. evaluation of program design;
3. evaluation of readiness;
4. implementation evaluation;
5. evaluation of outcomes (intended and unintended); and
6. cost-benefit analysis.

Whether narrow or broad in focus, staff development evaluation typically includes the measurement of program outcomes. A number of writers have identified various categories of outcomes. Ryan and Crowell (1982) identify five types of outcomes and corresponding levels of assessment: teacher perceptions, teacher knowledge, teacher behavior, student classroom behavior, and student outcomes. Both Little (1982) and Loucks-Horsley et al (1987) propose similar classification schemes, with Little proposing "greater collegiality" and Loucks-Horsley et al suggesting "changes in organizational capacity" as additional possible outcomes.

There is a general consensus in the staff development literature that program evaluations should include multiple data sources (administrators, teachers, students, archival data) and multiple data collection methods (questionnaires, interviews, observations, document review, pre- and postmeasures, group discussions), with selected sources and methods based on the evaluation questions. There is growing agreement that program participants should be involved in all phases of staff development program evaluation. Crosby (1982) was an early proponent of this view, calling for participant involvement in each of the following:

• clarifying program goals and success indicators;
• designing the evaluation study;
• developing measurement methods;
• responding to interviews and other instruments;
• analyzing information; and
• reporting on the evaluation study.

Trends + Issues

...ral that different ...should be pre- ...various groups ...chnical or non- ...ff development ...ian (1982) has ...rd increasingly ...on

...ELOPMENT

...sea... in general and ...owing trends in

...d interaction of ...extent that it will ...h one from the

...transmission and ...d transformation; ...evelopment, with ...lopment so it can ...t, and increasing efforts to integrate individual development... with school-based development;

- increased efforts to include teachers in all aspects of staff development leadership, including planning, implementation, and evaluation of staff development programs;
- increasing incorporation of the research on adult development and the principles of adult learning into staff development efforts;
- increasing use of a variety of staff development frameworks rather than training frameworks alone, and increasing integration of multiple frameworks in comprehensive staff development programs;
- increasing integration of supervision and staff development with a variety of other improvement processes, including participatory school governance; leadership development; strategic planning; school restructuring; organization development; curriculum development; instructional program development; development of alternative forms of student, teacher, program, and school assessment; and career development;
- continued growth of staff development partnerships and consortia involving schools, business and industry, government agencies, and other stakeholders;
- an increasing variety of staff development networks at the intermediate, state, multistate, national and international levels, with increased opportunities for network members to share resources over distance and to engage in multimedia-based, interactive, distance education;
- an increased demand by stakeholders for more systematic, rigorous staff development evaluation, including the measurement of long-term effects on student and school performance; and

- inclusion of all adult members of the school community in staff development, with both differentiated and common staff development activities included within the total staff development program.

The current state of staff development, including the trends listed above, leads us to a number of issues that will have to be addressed by theoreticians, researchers, and practitioners in the coming years. Some of the more critical issues are:

- whether current cultural, economic, and political conditions within and outside PK–12 education will allow for the provision of adequate resources to support staff development that reflects research and best practice;
- whether district administrators will be willing and able to assume a facilitative rather than a directive role in staff development and whether campus administrators will develop the knowledge, skills, and attitudes to become effective staff development leaders, due to the increasing emphasis on school-based staff development;
- whether district and school administrators will be willing to allow teachers to participate fully in planning, implementing, and evaluating staff development programs, and whether significant numbers of teachers will be willing to assume such new reponsibilities;
- whether the trend toward school-based staff development and its implication of collective action can be successfully integrated with the need for staff development to address individual needs, concerns, interests, and abilities;
- whether PK–12 education will be able to overcome the current emphasis on piecemeal, short-term staff development efforts and move toward comprehensive, continuous, long-term staff development programs;
- whether it will be possible to determine empirically the most effective frameworks and combinations of frameworks for particular staff development goals, educational situations, groups, and individuals. Due to the idiosyncratic nature of "effective" staff development, this issue may well be best addressed through collaborative action research and case studies at the local level, shared with the profession through staff development networks and information banks;
- to what extent it will be possible to measure the interactions and effects of supervision and staff development integrated with other improvement efforts (organization development, curriculum development, improvement of assessment). As with alternative staff development frameworks, effects of mixing and matching the myriad ingredients of school improvement may be best studied at the local level, with networks and information retrieval services disseminating local program descriptions and research to interested parties;
- given the variety of intervening variables in the school environment, a more specific issue is how the effect of staff development on students can be measured validly. A parallel issue is concerned with how to develop better methodologies for measuring how multiple school

improvement efforts that include staff development affect students; and

- all of the above issues point to the general issue of what relationships should be developed among policy makers at the national and state level, local school boards; teacher associations; higher education; and other key stakeholders in planning future directions for staff development policy, practice, and research.

Despite the variety of conceptions of staff development, debate on whether staff development is part of supervision or is a related process, and issues concerning the current effectiveness and future direction of staff development, there are few educators who would dispute the tremendous potential of well conceived staff development for improving schools, teaching, and learning in the coming years.

REFERENCES

Ackland, R. (1991). A review of the peer coaching literature. *Journal of Staff Development, 12*(10), 22–27.

Ackley, B. & Gall, M. D. (1992, April). *Skills, strategies and outcomes of successful mentor teachers.* Paper presented at the Annual Meeting of the American Educational Research Association, San Francisco.

Alfonso, R. J., Firth, G. R., & Neville, R. F. (1981). *Instructional supervison: A behavior system.* Boston: Allyn & Bacon.

Apple, M. W. (1982). *Education and power.* Boston: Routledge & Kegan Paul.

Apple, M. W. (1984). The political economy of text publishing. *Educational Theory, 43*(4), 307–319.

Arbuckle, M. A. & Murray, L. B. (1990). *Building systems for professional growth.* Andover, MA: The Regional Laboratory for Educational Improvement of the Northeast and Islands.

Asayesh, G. (1994). The changing role of central office and its implications for staff development. *Journal of Staff Development, 15*(3), 2–5.

Auger, F. K. & Odell, S. J. (1992). The school-university partnerships for teacher development. *Journal of Teacher Education, 43*(4), 262–268.

Barr, A. S. (1931). *An introduction to the scientific study of classroom supervision.* New York: D. Appleton and Company.

Barr, A. S. & Burton, W. H. (1926). *The supervision of instruction.* New York: D. Appleton and Company.

Barr, A. S., Burton, W. H., & Brueckner, L. J. (1938). *Supervision: Principles and practices in the improvement of instruction.* New York: D. Appleton-Century.

Barr, A. S., Burton, W. H., & Brueckner, L. J. (1947). *Supervision: Democractic leadership in the improvement of learning* (2nd ed.). New York: Appleton-Century-Crofts.

Beach, D. M. & Reinhartz, J. (1989). *Supervision: Focus on instruction.* New York: Harper & Row.

Beegle, C. W. & Edelfelt, R. A. (Eds.). (1971). *Staff development: Staff liberation.* Washington D.C.: ASCD.

Bell, L. & Day, C. (Eds.). (1991). *Managing the professional development of teachers.* Milton Keynes: Open University Press.

Berman, L. E. (1971). *Supervision, staff development, and leadership.* Columbus, OH: Merrill.

Berman, P. & McLaughlin, M. W. (1978). *Federal programs supporting educational change, Volume 8: Implementing and sustaining innovations.* Santa Monica, CA: Rand Corporation (ERIC Document Reproduction Service No. ED 159 289).

Bernhardt, V. L. & Flaherty, G. M. (1990). Assisting new teachers in isolated, rural districts. *Journal of Staff Development, 11*(4), 38–42.

Berry, B. & Ginsberg, R. (1990). Creating lead teachers: From policy to implementation at. *Phi Delta Kappan, 71,* 616–620.

Bickel, W. E., Denton, S. E., Johnston, J., LeMahieu, P. G., & Young, J. R. (1987). Teacher professionalism and educational reform. *Journal of Staff Development, 8*(2), 9–14.

Bishop, L. J. (1976). *Staff development and instructional improvement.* Boston: Allyn & Bacon.

Blair, N. & Lange, R. (1990). A model for district level staff development. In P. Burke, R. Heideman, & C. Heideman (Eds.). *Programming for staff development: Fanning the flame* (pp. 138–167). London: Falmer Press.

Blumberg, A. (1974). *Supervisors and teachers: A private cold war.* Berkely, CA: McCutchan.

Blumberg, A. (1980). *Supervisors and teachers: A private cold war* (2nd ed.). Berkely, CA: McCutchan.

Bolan, R. (Ed). (1982). *School-focused in-service training.* London: Heinemann Education Books.

Bolin, F. S. & Falk, J. M. (Eds.). (1987). *Teacher renewal: Professional issues, personal choices.* New York: Teachers College Press.

Boytim, J. A. & Dickel, C. T. (1988). *Helping the helpers: Teacher support groups* (ERIC Document Reproduction Service No. ED 321 199).

Bradley, H. (1987). Policy issues concerning staff development. In M. Wideen & I. Andrews (Eds.). *Staff development for school improvement* (pp. 185–195). New York: The Falmer Press.

Bradley, L. & Gordon, S. P. (1994). Comparing the ideal to the real in state-mandated teacher induction programs. *Journal of Staff Development, 15*(3), 44–48.

Branham, L. A. (1990). Tying professional development to math curriculum development. *Journal of Staff Development, 11*(3), 2–6.

Brinckerhoff, R. E. (1989). Resource centers serve the needs of school science teachers. *School Science and Mathematics, 89*(1), 12–18.

Brown, B. B. (1992). Designing staff/curriculum development content for cultural diversity: The staff developer's role. *Journal of Staff Development, 13*(2), 16–21.

Burke, P., Heideman, R., & Heideman, C. (Eds.). (1990). *Programming for staff development: Fanning the flame.* London: The Falmer Press.

Burns, J. M. (1978). *Leadership.* New York: Harper & Row.

Burton, W. H. (1922). *Supervision and the improvement of teaching.* New York: D. Appleton and Company.

Caffarella, R. S. (1993). Facilitating self-directed learning as staff development. *Journal of Staff Development, 14*(2), 30–34.

Caldwell, S. D. (Ed.) (1989). *Staff development: A handbook of effective practices.* Oxford, OH: National Staff Development Council.

Calhoun, E. F. (1993). Action research: Three approaches. *Educational Leadership, 51*(2), 62–65.

Calhoun, E. F. & Allen, L. (1994, April). *Results of schoolwide action research in the league of professional schools.* Paper presented at the Annual Meeting of the American Educational Research Association, New Orleans.

Carter, M. & Powell, D. (1992). Teacher leaders as staff developers. *Journal of Staff Development, 13*(1), 8–12.

Chalker, D. M. (1992, October). *Project STEPE: A collaborative model for improving teacher effectiveness in rural schools.* Paper presented at the Annual Convention of the National Rural Education Association, Traverse City, MI.

Clark, C. M. (1992). Teachers as designers in self-directed professional development. In A. Hargreaves & M. G. Fullan (Eds.). *Understanding teacher development* (pp. 75–84). New York: Teachers College Press.

Colbert, J. A. & Wolff, D. E. (1992). Surviving in urban schools: A collaborative model for a beginning teacher support system. *Journal of Teacher Education, 43*(3), 193–199.

Cole, A. L. (1990). Helping teachers become "real": Opportunities in teacher induction. *Journal of Staff Development, 11*(4), 6–10.

Combs, A. W., Avila, D. L., & Purkey, W. W. (1978). *Helping relationships: Basic concepts for the helping professions* (2nd ed.). Boston: Allyn & Bacon.

Commission of the European Communities. (1988). *Commission work programme relating to the promotion of innovation in secondary education in the European Community* (COM[88] 545 final). Brussels: Author (ERIC Document Reporduction Service No. ED 326 748).

Cook, L. (1992). *Support groups for practicing special education professionals.* Reston, VA: National Clearinghouse for Professions in Special Education (ERIC Document Reproduction Service No. ED 347 745).

Crosby, J. (1982). Participation in evaluation as staff development. *Journal of Staff Development, 3*(1), 147–155.

Dahawy, B. M. (1992). *In-service education within schools: A comparative perspective* (ERIC Document Reproductin Service No. ED 362 431).

Daresh, J. C. (1989). *Supervision as a proactive process.* New York: Longman.

Davis, N. T., McCarty, B. J., Shaw, K. L., & Sidani-Tabbaa, A. (1991, April). *Communication for a shared understanding: The role of semiatics in establishing a culture for change.* Paper presented at the Annual Meeting of the American Educational Research Association, Chicago (ERIC Document Reproduction Service No. ED 332 238).

DeLuca, J. R. (1991). The evolution of staff development for teachers. *Journal of Staff Development, 12*(3), 42–46.

Devaney, K. (1987, March). *The lead teacher: Ways to begin.* Paper prepared for the Task Force on Teaching as a Profession, Carnegie Forum on Education and the Economy, New York.

Diegmueller, K. (1991). Staff development is essential in school restructuring. *Journal of Staff Development, 12*(3), 6–9.

Dillon-Peterson, B. (Ed.). (1981a). *Staff development/organization development.* Alexandria, VA: ASCD.

Dillon-Peterson, B. (1981b). Staff development/organization development—perspective 1981. In B. Dillon-Peterson (Ed.). *Staff development/organization development.* Alexandria, VA: ASCD.

Dillon-Peterson, B. (1991). Reflection on the past, present, and future of staff development. *Journal of Staff Development, 12*(1), 48–51.

Dobson, R., Dobson, J., & Kessinger, J. (1980). *Staff development: A humanistic approach.* Washington, D.C.: University Press of America.

Documentation and Information Centre of the European Communities, Charles University. (1991). *Tenth international seminar on staff and educational development: Final report.* Kaprova, Czechoslovakia: Author (ERIC Document Reproduction Service No. ED 347 915).

Donovan, J. F., Sousa, D. A., & Walberg, H. J. (1992). The Hunter

model: A four year longitudinal study of staff development effects. *Journal of Research and Development in Education, 25*(3), 165–172.

Douglas, B. (1991). Teachers as experts: A case study of school-based staff development. In L. Bell & C. Day (Eds.). *Managing the professional development of teachers* (pp. 88–109). Milton Keynes: Open University Press.

Dowhower, S. L., Melvin, M. P., & Sizemore, P. (1990). Improving writing instruction through teacher action research. *Journal of Staff Development, 11*(3), 22–27.

Dull, L. W. (1981). *Supervision: School leadership handbook.* (1981). Columbus, OH: Charles E. Merrill.

Edelfelt, R. A. (1983). *Staff development for school improvement: An illustration.* Ypsilanti, MI: Eastern Michigan University, National Center on Teaching and Learning.

Edelfelt, R. A. & Johnson, M. (Eds). (1975). *Rethinking in-service education.* Washington, D.C.: National Education Association.

Estes, G., Stansbury, K., & Long, C. (1990). *Assessment component of the California new teacher project: First year report.* San Francisco: Far West Laboratory for Educational Research and Development.

Eye, G. C. & Netzer, L. A. (1965). *Supervison of instruction: A phase of administration.* New York: Harper & Row.

Fessler, R. (1990). The teacher as leader. In P. Burke, R. Heideman, & C. Heideman (Eds.). *Programming for staff development: Fanning the flame* (pp. 57–67). London: The Falmer Press.

Fielding, G. D. & Schalock, H. D. (1985). *Promoting the professional development of teachers and administrators.* Eugene, OR: University of Oregon.

Franseth, J. (1961). *Supervision as leadership.* Evanston, IL: Row, Peterson, & Company.

Freire, P. F. (1970). *Pedagogy of the oppressed.* New York: Continuum Publishing Corporation.

Freire, P. F. (1985). *The politics of education.* South Hadley, MA: Bergin & Garvey.

Fullan, M. G. (1987). Implementing the implementation plan. In M. F. Wideen & I. Andrews (Eds.). *Staff development for school improvement* (pp. 213–222). New York: The Falmer Press.

Fullan, M. G. (1990). Staff development, innovation, and institutional development. In B. Joyce (Ed.). *Changing school culture through staff development* (1990 Yearbook of the Association for Supervision and Curriculum Development; pp. 3–25). Alexandria, VA: ASCD.

Fullan, M. G. (1991). *The new meaning of educational change* (2nd ed.). New York: Teachers College Press.

Garmston, R. J. (1987). How administrators support peer coaching. *Educational Leadership, 44*(5), 18–26.

George, P. S. (1990). Staff development: Japanese style. *Journal of Staff Development, 11*(3), 42–46.

Gibboney, R. A. & Gould, J. M. (1987). *Staff development and educational renewal through dialogue in two school systems: A conceptual and empirical assessment* (ERIC Document Reproduction Service No. ED 290 215).

Giroux, H. A. (1983). *Theory and resistance in education: A pedagogy for opposition.* South Hadley, MA: Bergin & Garvey.

Giroux, H. A. (1985). Teachers as transformative intellectuals. *Social Education, 49*(5), 376–379.

Giroux, H. A. & McLaren, P. (1986). Teacher education and the politics of engagement: The case for democratic schooling. *Harvard Educational Review, 56*(3), 213–238.

Giroux, H. A. & McLaren, P. (1989). *Critical pedagogy, the state and cultural struggle.* Albany, NY: State University of New York Press.

Glatthorn, A. A. (1990). *Supervisory leadership: Introduction to instructional supervision.* Glenview, IL: Scott Foresman.

Glickman, C. D. (1985). *Supervision of instruction: A developmental approach.* Boston: Allyn & Bacon.

Glickman, C. D. (1990). *Supervision of instruction: A developmental approach* (2nd ed.). Boston: Allyn & Bacon.

Glickman, C. D., Gordon, S. P., & Ross-Gordon, J. M. (1995). *Supervision of instruction: A developmental approach* (3rd ed.). Boston: Allyn & Bacon.

Glickman, C. D., Hayes, R., & Hensley, F. (1992). Site-based facilitation of empowered schools: Complexities and issues for staff developers. *Journal of Staff Development, 13*(2), 22–26.

Godley, L. B., Wilson, D. R., & Klug, B. J. (1986–1987). The teacher consultant role: Impact on the profession. *Action in Teacher Education, 8*(4), 65–73.

Goodlad, J. I. (1983). The school as a workplace. In G. Griffin (Ed.). *Staff development* (82nd Yearbook of the National Society for the Study of Education, Part II; pp. 36–61). Chicago: University of Chicago Press.

Goodlad, J. I. (1984). *A place called school: Prospects for the future.* New York: McGraw-Hill.

Gordon, S. P. (1990a). *Assisting the entry-year teacher: A leadership resource.* Columbus, OH: Department of Education.

Gordon (1990b, April). *Teacher-directed peer clinical supervision: Participants' reactions and suggestions.* Paper presented at the Annual Meeting of the American Educational Research Association, Boston.

Gordon, S. P. (1991a). *How to help beginning teachers succeed.* Alexandria, VA: ASCD.

Gordon, S. P. (1991b). Teacher leadership programs: The need for structure and flexibility. *Pennsylvania Educational Leadership, 11*(1), 36–40.

Gordon, S. P. (1993a, April). *Leadership cadre, phase II: Teachers as leaders and learners.* Paper presented at the Annual Meeting of the American Educational Research Association, Atlanta.

Gordon, S. P. (1993b, October). *The insrurctional leadership triad: University professors, school administrators, and teacher-leaders.* Paper presented at the Annual Convention of the University Council for Educational Administration.

Gordon, S. P., Badiali, B. J., & Nolan, J. (1992, April). *Teacher administrator leadership cadre, phase I: Preparing instructional leaders.* Paper presented at the Annual Meeting of the American Educational Research Association, San Francisco.

Gordon, S. P., Nolan, J. F., & Forlenza, V. A. (1995). Peer coaching: A cross-site comparison. *Journal of Personnel Evaluation in Education, 9*(1), 69–91.

Greenwood, S. C. (1991). Encouraging educational practitioners to write. *Journal of Staff Development, 12*(4), 16–19.

Griffin, G. A. (1983). *Staff development* (82nd Yearbook of the National Society for the Study of Education, Part II). Chicago: University of Chicago Press.

Halcomb, E. L. (1993, January). *School-based instructional leadership: A staff development program for school effectiveness and improvement.* Paper presented at the Annual Meeting of the International Congress for School Effectiveness and Improvement, Norrkoping, Sweden (ERIC Document Reproduction Service No. ED 358 561).

Hall, G. E. & Hord, S. M. (1987). *Change in schools: Facilitating the process.* Albany, NY: State University of New York Press.

Hamner, M. (1992). Toward successful curriculum implementation in Eagle County, Colorado. *Journal of Staff Development, 13*(1), 2–5.

Harris, B. M. (1963). *Supervisory behavior in education.* Englewood Cliffs, NJ: Prentice-Hall.

Harris, B. M. (1985). *Supervisory behavior in education* (3rd ed.). Englewood Cliffs, NJ: Prentice-Hall.

Harris, B. M. (1989). *In-service education for staff development.* Boston: Allyn & Bacon.

Hatfield, R. C., Blackman, C. A., & Claypool, C. (1986, February). *Exploring leadership roles performed by teaching faculty in K–12 schools.* Paper presented at the Annual Meeting of the American Association of Colleges for Teacher Education, Chicago (ERIC Document Reproduction Service No. ED 281 828).

Hawk, P. (1987). Beginning teacher programs: Benefits for the experienced educator. *Action in Teacher Education, 8*(4), 59–63.

Heideman, C. (1990). Introduction to staff development. In P. Burke, R. Heideman, & C. Heideman (Eds.). *Programming for staff development: Fanning the flame* (pp. 3–9). London: The Falmer Press.

Henry, M. A. (1988). *Project credit: Certification renewal experiences designed to improve teaching.* Terre Haute: Indiana State University, Department of Secondary Education (ERIC Document Reproduction Service No. ED 291 681).

Hirsh, S. A. (1990). Designing induction programs with the beginning teacher in mind. *Journal of Staff Development, 11*(4), 24–26.

Hirsh, S. (1993). Staff developers as planning facilitators. *Journal of Staff Development, 14*(2), 8–11.

Hockman, E. (1982). Staff development data banks: Taking evaluation beyond "happiness quotients." *Journal of Staff Development, 3*(1), 71–83.

Hoffman, N. E. & Reed, W. M. (1994, April). *The impact of studying, conducting, and reporting action research on teacher attitudes toward research.* Paper presented at the Annual Meeting of the American Educational Research Association, New Orleans.

Holland, P. E., Clift, R., Veal, M. L., with Johnson, M., & McCarthy, J. (1992). Linking preservice and in-service supervision through professional inquiry. In C. D. Glickman (Ed.). *Supervision in transition* (pp. 169–182). Alexandria, VA: ASCD.

Holly, P. (1991). Action research: The missing link in the creation of schools as centers of inquiry. In A. Lieberman & L. Miller (Eds.). *Staff development for education in the 90s* (2nd ed.) pp. 15–60. New York: Teachers College Press, Columbia University.

Hopkins, D. (1987). School-based review and staff development. In M. F. Wideen & I. Andrews (Eds.). *Staff development for school improvement* (pp. 55–69). New York: The Falmer Press.

Houser, N. O. (1990). Teacher-researcher: The synthesis of roles for teacher empowerment. *Action in Teacher Education, 12*(2), 55–60.

Howey, K. R. (1985). Six major functions of staff development: An expanded imperative. *Journal of Teacher Education, 36*(1), 58–64.

Howey, K. R., Bents, R., & Corrigan, D. (Eds.). (1981). *School-focused in-service: Descriptions and discussions.* Reston, VA: Association of Teacher Educators.

Huffman, G. & Leak, S. (1986). Beginning teachers' perceptions of mentors. *Journal of Teacher Education, 37*(1), 22–24.

Huling-Austin, L. & Murphy, S. C. (1987, April). *Assessing the impact of teacher induction programs: Implications for program development.* Paper presented at the Annual Meeting of the American Educational Research Association, Washington, D.C. (ERIC Document Reproduction Service No. ED 283 779).

Huling-Austin, L. (1988, April). *A synthesis of research on teacher induction programs and practices.* Paper presented at the Annual Meeting of the American Educational Research Association, New Orleans.

Huling-Austin, L. (1992). Research on learning to teach: Implications for teacher induction and mentoring programs. *Journal of Teacher Education, 43*(3), 173–180.

Hunter, M. (1984). Knowing, teaching, and supervising. In P. L. Hosford (Ed.). *Using what we know about teaching* (pp. 169–192). Alexandria, VA: ASCD.

Hyde, A. A. (1992). Developing a willingness to change. In W. T. Pink & A. A. Hyde (Eds.). *Effective staff development for school change* (pp. 171–190). Norwood, NJ: Ablex.

Hyde, A. A. & Pink, W. T. (1992). Thinking about effective staff development. In W. T. Pink & A. A. Hyde (Eds.). *Effective staff development for school change* (pp. 3–29). Norwood, NJ: Ablex Publishing.

Hynes, J. L. & Summers, P. F. (1990, November). *The Southeastern teacher leadership center: A program for the development of teacher leaders*. Paper presented at the Annual National Conference of the National Council of States of In-service Education, Orlando (ERIC Document Reproduction Service No. ED 326 535).

Joans, K., Clark, J., Figg, G., Howarth, S., & Ried, K. (1989). *Staff development in primary schools*. Oxford, UK: Basil Blackwell.

Johnson, D. W. & Johnson, F. P. (1982). *Joining together: Group theory and group skills* (2nd ed.). Englewood Cliffs, NJ: Prentice-Hall.

Johnson, W. L., Snyder, K. J., & Anderson, R. H. (1992). Organizational productivity and the school-based restructuring challenge. *Journal of Staff Development, 13*(4), 46–50.

Joyce, B. (Ed.). (1990). *Changing school culture through staff development*. Alexandria, VA: ASCD.

Joyce, B. (1991). The doors to school improvement. *Educational Leadership, 48*(8), 59–62.

Joyce, B., Murphy, C., Showers, B., & Murphy, J. (1989). School renewal as cultural change. *Educational Leadership, 47*(3), 70–77.

Joyce, B. & Showers, B. (1988). *Student achievement through staff development*. New York: Longman.

Kahn, H. (1991). *Teachers' resource centers*. London: Commonwealth Secretariat (ERIC Document Reproduction Service No. ED 341 384).

Katzenmeyer, M. H. & Reid, G. A. (1991). Compelling views of staff development for the 1990s. *Journal of Staff Development, 12*(3), 30–33.

Keedy, J. L. (1992, April). *Teacher facilitator leadership and school organization mediational effects: Implications on work redesign for instructional supervisors*. Paper presented at the Annual Meeting of the American Educational Research Association, San Francisco.

Kelley, E. C. (1951). *The workshop way of learning*. New York: Harper & Brothers.

Killian, J. E. (1991). Colleague journals as a staff development tool. *Journal of Staff Development, 12*(2), 44–46.

Killion, J. P. (1993). Staff development and curriculum development: Two sides of the same coin. *Journal of Staff Development, 14*(1), 38–41.

Killion, J. P. & Harrison, C. R. (1990). An organization development approach to change. *Journal of Staff Development, 11*(1), 22–25.

Kirk, J. J. (1991). *Cullowhee: A place of renewal and professional growth* (ERIC Document Reproduction Service No. ED 340 544).

Krey, R. D. & Burke, P. J. (1989). *A design for instructional supervision*. Springfield, IL: Charles C. Thomas.

Krupp, J. A. (1981). *Adult development: Implications for staff development*. Colchester, CT: Project Rise.

Krupp, J. A. (1989). Staff development and the individual. In S. D. Caldwell (Ed.). *Staff development: A handbook of effective practices* (pp. 44–57). Oxford, OH: National Staff Development Council.

Lambert, L. (1988). Staff development redesigned. *Phi Delta Kappan, 69*(9), 665–668.

Langer, G. M. & Colton, A. B. (1994). Reflective decision-making: The cornerstone of school reform. *Journal of Staff Development, 15*(1), 2–7.

Lawrence, G. (1974). *Patterns of effective in-service education: A state of the art summary of research on materials and procedures for changing teacher behaviors in in-service education*. Tallahassee FL: Florida State Department of Education (ERIC Document Reproduction Service No. 176 424).

LeMahieu, P. G., Piscolish, M., Johnston, J. R., Young, J. R., Saltrick, D., & Bickel, W. E. (1989, March). *An integrated model of program evaluation, administration and policy development*. Paper presented at the Annual Meeting of the American Educational Research Association, San Francisco.

Letven, E. & Klobuchar, J. (1990). A regional staff development center model. In P. Burke, R. Heideman, & C. Heideman (Eds.). *Programming for staff development: Fanning the flame* (pp. 168–179). London: The Falmer Press.

Leutheuser, J. (Ed.). (1994). *Educational programs that work: Catalogue of the National Diffusion Network* (20th ed.) Longmont, Colorado: Sapris West.

Levine, D. V. (1991). Creating effective schools: Findings and implications from research and practice. *Phi Delta Kappan, 72*(5), 389–393.

Levine, S. L. (1989). *Promoting adult growth in schools*. Boston: Allyn & Bacon.

Levine, S. L. & Broude, N. (1989). Designs for learning. In S. D. Caldwell (Ed.). *Staff development: A handbook of effective practices*. Oxford, OH: National Staff Development Council.

Lewis, B. A. (1992). From teacher to writer: How does it happen? *Social Education, 56*(1), 40–42.

Lewin, K. (1946). Action research and minority problems. *Journal of Social Issues, 2*, 34–46.

Lieberman, A. & Miller, L. (1991). Challenges and opportunities: Professional development in the year 2000. *Journal of Staff Development, 12*(1), 4–5.

Lieberman, A., Saxl, E. R., & Miles, M. B. (1988). Teacher leadership: Ideology and practice. In A. Lieberman (Ed.). *Building a professional culture in schools* (pp. 148–166). New York: Teachers College Press.

Lipman, P. (1991). *School-based staff development: Focused interviews in pilot schools*. Ontario, Canada: Scarborough Board of Education, Research Centre Program Department (ERIC Document Reproduction Service No. ED 359 149).

Lipton, L. & Greenblatt, R. (1992). Supporting the learning organization: A model for congruent system-wide renewal. *Journal of Staff Development, 13*(3), 20–25.

Little, J. W. (1982). Making sure: Contributions and requirements of good evaluation. *Journal of Staff Development, 3*(1), 25–47.

Little, J. W. (1988). Assessing the prospects for teacher leadership. In A. Lieberman (Ed.). *Building a professional culture in schools* (pp. 78–106). New York: Teachers College Press.

Little, J. W. (1989). District policy choices and teachers' professional development opportunities. *Educational Evaluation and Policy Analysis, 11*(2), 165–179.

Loucks, S. F. & Melle, M. (1982). Evaluation of staff development: How do you know that it took? *Journal of Staff Development, 3*(1), 102–117.

Loucks-Horsley, S., Harding, C. K., Arbuckle, M. A., Murray, L. B., Dubea, C., & Williams, M. K. (1987). *Continuing to learn: A guidebook for teacher development*. Andover, MA: The Regional Laboratory for Educational Improvement of the Northeast and Islands.

Loucks-Horsley, S. & Stiegelbauer, S. (1991). Using knowledge of change to guide staff development. In A. Lieberman & L. Miller (Eds.). *Staff development for education in the 90s* (2nd ed.) pp. 15–36. New York: Teachers College Press.

Lucio, W. H. & McNeil, J. D. (1962). *Supervision: A synthesis of thought and action*. New York: McGraw-Hill.

Lucio, W. H. & McNeil, J. D. (1969). *Supervision: A synthesis of thought and action* (2nd ed.). New York: McGraw-Hill.

Maeroff, G. I. (1993). Building teams to rebuild schools. *Phi Delta Kappan, 74*(7), 512–519.

Mager, G. M., Cianfarano, S., & Corwin, C. (1990). *A follow-up on the experiences of intern teachers: A report to the State Education Department of the New York State Mentor Teacher-Internship Program for 1986–1987 and 1987–1988*. Syracuse, NY: Syracuse University, School of Education (ERIC Document Reproduction Service No. ED 328 528).

Manderville, G. K. & Rivers, J. L. (1988/1989). Effects of South Carolina's Hunter-based PET program. *Educational Leadership, 46*(4), 63–66.

Manley, M. L., Siudzinski, L., & Varah, L. J. (1989). Easing the transition for first-year teachers. *NASSP Bulletin, 73*(515), 16–21.

Marshall, J. C. (1988). A general statement on staff development evaluation. *Journal of Staff Development, 9*(1), 2–8.

Marshall, J. C. (1989). Assessing program effects. In S. D. Caldwell (Ed.). *Staff development: A handbook of effective practices* (pp. 92–113). Oxford, OH: National Staff Development Council.

Maslow, A. H. (1970). *Motivation and personality* (2nd ed.). New York: Harper & Row.

Mathis, W. J. & Gross, S. J. (1989). Staff development fuels your teachers' drive to succeed. *The Executive Educator, 11*(2), 22–23.

Matlin, M. L. & Short, K. G. (1991). How our teacher study group sparks change. *Educational Leadership, 49*(3), 68.

McDonnell, J. H. & Christenson, J. C. (1990). The career lattice—a model for structuring personalized staff development. In P. Burke, R. Heideman, & C. Heideman (Eds.). *Programming for staff development: Fanning the flame* (pp. 117–137). London: The Falmer Press.

McKay, J. A. (1992). Professional development through action research. *Journal of Staff Development, 13*(1), 18–21.

McNerney, C. T. (1951). *Educational supervision.* New York: McGraw-Hill.

McQuarrie, F. O. & Wood, F. H. (1991). Supervision, staff devleopment, and evaluation connections. *Theory Into Practice, 30*(2), 91–96.

Melchior, W. T. (1950). *Instructional supervison: A guide to modern practice.* Boston: D.C. Heath & Company.

Metzdorf, J. (1989). District level staff development. In S. D. Caldwell (Ed.). *Staff development: A handbook of effective practices* (pp. 14–25). Oxford, OH: National Staff Development Council.

Meyers, K. & Beall, J. W. (1992). *The principal and school-based staff development.* Bloomington, IN: Phi Delta Kappa.

Middleton, J. A., Smith, A. M., & Williams, D. (1994). From directing to supporting school initiatives: One district's efforts. *Journal of Staff Development, 15*(3), 6–9.

Miles, M. B., Saxl, E. R., & Lieberman, A. (1988). What skills do educational "change agents" need? An empirical view. *Curriculum Inquiry, 18*(2), 157–193.

Miller, D. M. & Pine, G. J. (1990). Advancing professional inquiry for educational improvement through action research. *Journal of Staff Development, 11*(3), 56–61.

Miller, J. P. & Seller, W. (1985). *Curriculum: Perspectives and practice.* New York: Longman.

Miller, L. (1992). Curriculum work as staff development. In W. T. Pink & A. A. Hyde (Eds.). *Effective staff development for school change* (pp. 95–109). Norwood, NJ: Ablex.

Millin, D. & Barta, B. Z. (1991). Six years of computer penetration into primary education: The case of Israel. *Education and Computing, 7*(3–4), 171–178.

Miranda, A. H., Scott, J., Forsythe, J., Spratley, F., & Conrad, B. (1992). The implementation of a comprehensive multicultural program. *Journal of Staff Development, 13*(2), 2–6.

Moller, G. & Bohning, G. (1992). School improvement leadership training. *Journal of Staff Development, 13*(1), 36–39.

Mosher, R. L. & Purpel, D. E. (1972). *Supervision: The reluctant profession.* New York: Houghton Mifflin.

Mullins, T. W. (1994). *Staff development programs: A guide to evaluation.* Thousand Oaks, CA: Corwin Press.

Munro, P. & Elliott, J. (1987). Instructional growth through peer coaching. *Journal of Staff Development, 8*(1), 25–28.

Murphy, C. (1992). Study groups foster schoolwide learning. *Educational Leadership, 50*(3), 71–74.

Neagley, R. L. & Evans, N. D. (1964). *Handbook for effective supervision of instruction.* Englewood Cliffs, NJ: Prentice-Hall.

Neagley, R. L. & Evans, N. D. (1970). *Handbook for effective supervision of instruction* (2nd ed.). Englewood Cliffs, NJ: Prentice-Hall.

Neagley, R. L. & Evans, N. D. (1980). *Handbook for effective supervision of instruction* (3rd ed.). Englewood Cliffs, NJ: Prentice-Hall.

New Mexico State Department of Education. (1988). *Preliminary report: New Mexico enrollment and teacher needs projections.* Santa Fe: New Mexico State Department of Education.

Nicholson, A. M., Joyce, B. R., Parker, D. W., & Waterman, F. T. (1976). *The literature on in-service teacher eduction: An analytic review* (ISTE Report III). Washington D.C.: Office of Education, Teacher Corps (ERIC Document Reproduction Service No. Ed 129 734).

Noble, D. L. (1987). What are the effects of the training experience on staff development trainers? *Journal of Staff Development, 8*(1), 29–31.

Odell, S. J. (1990a). A collaborative approach to teacher induction that works. *Journal of Staff Development, 11*(4), 12–16.

Odell, S. J. (1990b). *Mentor teacher programs: What research says to the teacher.* Washington, D.C.: National Education Association.

Odell, S. J. & Ferraro, D. P. (1992). Teacher mentoring and teacher retention. *Journal of Teacher Education, 43*(3), 200–204.

Ohio Department of Education. (1991). *Ohio's plan for establishing regional teacher training centers.* Columbus, OH: Author.

Oja, S. N. & Pine, G. J. (1987). Collaborative action research: Teachers' stages of development and school contexts. *Peabody Journal of Education, 64*(2), 96–115.

Oliva, P. F. (1976). *Supervision for today's schools.* New York: Thomas Y. Cowell Company.

Oliva, P. F. (1984). *Supervision for today's schools* (2nd ed.). New York: Longman.

Oliva, P. F. (1989). *Supervision for today's schools* (3rd ed.). New York: Longman.

Oliva, P. F. (1993). *Supervision for today's schools* (4th ed.). New York: Longman.

Orlich, D. C. (1989). *Staff development: Enhancing human potential.* Boston: Allyn & Bacon.

Orlich, D. C., Remaley, A. L., Facemyer, K. C., Logan, J., & Cao, Q. (1993). Seeking the link between student achievement and staff development. *Journal of Staff Development, 14*(3), 2–8.

Owen, J. M., Loucks-Horsley, S., & Horsley, D. L. (1991). Three roles of staff development in restructuring schools. *Journal of Staff Development, 12*(3), 10–14.

Pajak, E. (1989). *The central office supervisor of curriculum and instruction: Setting the stage for success.* Boston: Allyn & Bacon.

Pajak, E. & Hooghoff, H. (1992). How the Netherlands supports curriculum and instruction. *Educational Leadership, 50*(3), 75–78.

Parkay, F. W. & Damico, S. B. (1989). Empowering teachers for change through faculty-driven school improvement. *Journal of Staff Development, 10*(2), 8–14.

Parker, L. S. (1988). A regional teacher induction program that works for rural schools. *Journal of Staff Development, 9*(4), 16–20.

Parker, L. S. (1990). A prototypic human resource model. In P. Burke, P. Heideman, & C. Heideman (Eds.). *Programming for staff development: Fanning the flame* (pp. 87–116). London: The Falmer Press.

Pasch, M. & Harberts, J. C. (1992). Does coaching enhance instructional thought? *Journal of Staff Development, 13*(3), 40–44.

Phillips, M. D. & Glickman, C. D. (1991). Peer coaching: Developmental approach to enhancing teacher thinking. *Journal of Staff Development, 12*(2), 20–25.

Pink, W. T. (1989, March). *Effective staff development for urban school improvement.* Paper presented at the Annual Meeting of the American Educational Research Association, San Francisco.

Pink, W. T. & Hyde, A. A. (Eds.). (1992). *Effective staff development for school change.* Norwood, NJ: Ablex.

Piscolish, M. A. (1993). *The Pennsylvania lead teacher program 1992–1993 evaluation: Final report.* Harrisburg, PA: Pennsylvania Department of Education.

Powell, J. H., Berliner, D. C., & Casanova, U. (1992). Empowerment through collegial study groups. *Contemporary Education, 63*(4), 281–284.

Raymond, D., Butt, R., & Townsend, D. (1992). Contexts for teacher development: Insights from teachers' stories. In A. Hargreaves & M. G. Fullan (Eds.). *Understanding teacher development* (pp. 143–161). New York: Teachers College Press.

Rich, S. J. (1992). Teacher support groups: Providing a forum for professional development. *Journal of Staff Development, 13*(3), 32–35.

Richert, A. E. (1991). Using teacher cases for reflection and enhanced understanding. In A. Lieberman & L. Miller (Eds.). *Staff development for education in the 90s* (pp. 113–132). New York: Teachers College Press.

Rogers, C. R. (1961). *On becoming a person.* Boston: Houghton Mifflin.

Rosenshine, B. (1983). Teaching functions in instructional programs. *The Elementary School Journal, 83,* 335–351.

Rosseto, C. & Grosenick, J. K. (1987). Effects of collaborative teacher education: Follow-up of graduates of a teacher induction program. *Journal of Teacher Education, 38*(3), 50–52.

Rubin, L. (Ed.). (1978). *The in-service education of teachers.* Boston: Allyn & Bacon.

Rubin, L. (1987). Curriculum and staff development. In M. F. Wideen & I. Andrews (Eds.). *Staff development for school improvement: A focus on the teacher* (pp. 170–181). New York: The Falmer Press.

Ryan, T. F. & Crowell, R. A. (1982). Evaluation for nonevaluators: Assessing staff development outcomes. *Journal of Staff Development, 3*(1), 156–169.

Sagor, R. (1991). What project LEARN reveals about collaborative action research. *Educational Leadership, 48*(6), 6–10.

Saltrick, D. S., Johnston, J. A., & Bickel, W. E. (1991). Establishing organization development strategies in secondary schools. *Journal of Staff Development, 12*(1), 52–55.

Salzer, R. T. (1991). TAWL teachers reach for self-help. *Educational Leadership, 49*(3), 66–67.

Schaffer, E., Stringfield, S., & Wolfe, D. (1992). An innovative beginning teacher induction program: A two-year analysis of classroom interactions. *Journal of Teacher Education, 43*(3), 181–192.

Schiffer, J. (1980). *School renewal through staff development.* New York: Teachers College Press.

Schlechty, P. C. & Vance, V. (1983). Recruitment, selection, and retention: The shape of the teaching force. *The Elementary School Journal, 83*(4), 469–487.

Schmale, R. L. (1994). Promoting teacher reflection through guided book reviews. *Journal of Staff Development, 15*(1), 30–33.

Schmuck, R. A. & Runkel, P. J. (1985). *The handbook of organization development in schools* (3rd ed.). Prospect Heights, IL: Waveland Press.

Schoenbach, R. (1994). Classroom renewal through teacher reflection. *Journal of Staff Development, 15*(1), 24–28.

Schon, D. A. (1988). Coaching reflective teaching. In P. P. Grimmett & G. L. Erickson (Eds.). *Reflection in teacher education* (pp. 19–29). New York: Teachers College, Columbia University.

Sergiovanni, T. J. & Starratt, R. J. (1979). *Supervision: Human perspectives* (2nd ed.). New York: McGraw-Hill.

Sergiovanni, T. J. & Starratt, R. J. (1983). *Supervision: Human perspectives* (3rd ed.). New York: McGraw-Hill.

Sergiovanni, T. J. & Starratt, R. J. (1988). *Supervision: Human perspectives* (4th ed.). New York: McGraw-Hill.

Sergiovanni, T. J. & Starratt, R. J. (1993). *Supervision: A redefinition* (5th ed.) New York: McGraw-Hill.

Shroyer, M. G. (1990). Effective staff development for effective organization development. *Journal of Staff Development, 11*(1), 2–6.

Simmons, J. M. (1982). Fighting the budget battle with evidence: Cost-effectiveness, data-based decision-making. *Journal of Staff Development, 3*(1), 118–146.

Slater, J. K. (1993). Using regional school networks to orchestrate reform in California middle grades. *The Elementary School Journal, 93*(5), 481–493.

Smith, H. & Wigginton, E. (1991). *Foxfire teacher networks.* In A. Lieberman & L. Miller (Eds.). *Staff development for education in the 90s* (pp. 193–220). New York: Teachers College Press.

Smylie, M. A. & Denny, J. W. (1990). Teacher leadership: Tensions and ambiguities in organizational perspective. *Educational Administration Quarterly, 26*(3), 235–259.

Smyth, J. (1989a). A critical pedagogy of classroom practice. *Journal of Curriculum Studies, 21*(6), 483–502.

Smyth, J. (1989b). A research agenda: An alternative vision and an "educative" agenda for supervision as a field of study. *Journal of Curriculum and Supervision, 4*(2), 162–177.

Soltis, J. F. (1984). On the nature of educational research. *Educational Researcher, 13*(10), 5–10.

Southeastern Regional Professional Development Center. (1993). *Regional plan II.* Unpublished document.

Sparks, G. M. (1988/1989). Caution! Research results ahead. *Educational Leadership, 464,* 64.

Sparks, D. & Loucks-Horsley, S. (1990). *Five models of staff development.* Oxford, OH: National Staff Development Council.

Sparks, G. M. & Bruder, S. (1987). Before and after peer coaching. *Educational Leadership, 45*(3), 54–57.

Spring, J. (1994). *The American school, 1642–1993* (3rd ed.). New York: McGraw-Hill.

Stake, R. (1987). An evolutionary view of programming staff development. In M. F. Wideen & I. Andrews (Eds.). *Staff development for school improvement* (pp. 55–69). New York: The Falmer Press.

Stallings, J. (1989, March). *School achievement effects and staff development: What are some critical factors?* Paper presented at the Annual Meeting of the American Educational Research Association, San Francisco.

Stallings, J. & Krassavage, E. M. (1986). Effects of instruction based on the Madeline Hunter Model on students' achievement: Findings from a follow-through project. *Elementary School Journal, 86*(5), 571–588.

Starratt, R. J. (1992). After supervision. *Journal of Curriculum and Supervision, 8*(1), 77–86.

Tafel, L. & Bertani, A. (1992). Reconceptualizing staff development for sytematic change. *Journal of Staff Development, 13*(4), 42–45.

Takemura, S. & Shimizu, K. (1993). Goals and strategies for science teaching as perceived by elementary school teachers in Japan and the United States. *Peabody Journal of Education, 68*(4), 23–33.

Tanner, D. & Tanner, L. (1987). *Supervision in education: Problems and practices.* New York: Macmillan.

Thies-Sprinthall, L. M. (1984). Promoting the developmental growth of supervising teachers: Theory, research programs, and implications. *Journal of Teacher Education, 35*(3), 53–60.

Thies-Sprinthall, L. M. & Gerler, E. R. (1990). Support groups for novice teachers. *Journal of Staff Development, 11*(4), 18–22.

Thompson, J. C. & Cooley, V. E. (1987, November). *An English perspective on in-service: A comparative analysis to practices and views in the United States.* Paper presented at the Annual Meeting of the National Council of States on In-service Education, San Diego.

Todnem, G. & Warner, M. P. (1993). Using ROI to assess staff development efforts. *Journal of Staff Development, 14*(3), 32–34.

Valencia, S. W. & Killion, J. P. (1988). Overcoming obstacles to teacher change: Direction from school-based efforts. *Journal of Staff Development, 9*(2), 2–8.

Varah, L. J., Theune, W. S., & Parker, L. (1986). Beginning teacher: Sink or swim? *Journal of Teacher Education, 37*(1), 30–34.

Veenman, S. (1984). Perceived problems of beginning teachers. *Review of Educational Research, 54*(2), 143–178.

Vojtek, R. O. (1992, April) *Integrating staff development and organization development: An empirical study of staff developers.* Paper presented at the Annual Meeting of the American Educational Research Association, San Francisco (ERIC Document Reproduction Service No. ED 348 746).

Wallace, R. C., LeMahieu, P. G., & Bickel, W. E. (1990). The Pittsburgh experience: Achieving commitment to comprehensive staff development. In B. Joyce (Ed.). *Changing school culture through staff development* (pp. 185–202). Alexandria, VA: ASCD.

Wallace, R. C., Young, J. R., Johnston, J., LeMahieu, P. G., & Bickell, W. E. (1984). Secondary education renewal in Pittsburgh. *Educational Leadership, 41*(6), 73–77.

Walters, P. S. & Henkelman, J. (1990). Organization development and the process of school improvement in Maryland. *Journal of Staff Development, 11*(1), 14–19.

Warring, D. F. & Lindquist, M. (1989, February). *A collaborative mentor-mentee program based on the Bloomington, Minnesota Public Schools.* Paper presented at the Annual Meeting of the Association of Teacher Educators, St. Louis (ERIC Document Reproduction Service No. ED 305 328).

Wasley, P. A. (1991). *Teachers who lead: The rhetoric of reform and the realities of practice.* New York: Teachers College Press.

Watson, D. J. & Stevenson, M. T. (1989). Teacher support groups: Why and how. In G. S. Pinnell & M. L. Martin (Eds.). *Teachers and research: Language learning in the classroom* (pp. 118–129). Newark, DE: International Reading Association.

Watson, R. S. (1994). The role of professional development in restructuring schools. *Journal of Staff Development, 15*(2), 24–27.

Welch, R. (1985). A district-wide approach to individualized staff development. *NASSP Bulletin, 69*(483), 119–122.

Wideen, M. F. (1987). Perspectives on staff development. In M. F. Wideen & I. Andrews (Eds.). *Staff development for school improvement* (pp. 1–15). New York: The Falmer Press.

Wideen, M. F. & Andrews, I. (1987). *Staff development for school improvement.* New York: The Falmer Press.

Wildman, T. M., Magliaro, S. G., Niles, R. A., & Niles, J. A. (1992). Teacher mentoring: An analysis of roles, activities, and conditions. *Journal of Teacher Education, 43*(3), 205–213.

Wiles, K. (1950). *Supervision for better schools.* New York: Prentice-Hall.

Wiles, K. (1955). *Supervision for better schools* (2nd ed.). New York: Prentice-Hall.

Wiles, K. (1967). *Supervision for better schools* (3rd ed.). Englewood Cliffs, NJ: Prentice-Hall.

Wiles, J. & Bondi, J. (1980). *Supervision: A guide to practice.* Columbus, OH: Charles E. Merrill.

Wiles, J. & Bondi, J. (1991). *Supervision: A guide to practice* (3rd ed.). New York: Macmillan.

Wiles, K. & Lovell, J. T. (1975). *Supervision for better schools* (4th ed.). Englewood Cliffs, NJ: Prentice-Hall.

Wilhelms, F. T. (1973). *Supervision in a new key.* Washington, D.C.: ASCD.

Wilshire, D. K. (1991). *Teachers in transition: An exploratory study of self-directed change and educational planning in professional development.* Unpublished doctoral dissertation, Penn State University, University Park, PA.

Wisconsin Department of Public Instruction. (1984). *Final report of the state superintendent's task force on teaching and teacher education.* Madison, WI: Author.

Wood, F. H. (1989). Organizing and managing school-based staff development. In S. D. Caldwell (Ed.). *Staff development: A handbook of effective practices* (pp. 26–43). Oxford, OH: National Staff Development Council.

Wood, F. W. & Thompson, S. R. (1993). Assumptions about staff development based on research and best practice. *Journal of Staff Development 14*(4), 52–57.

Wood, F. H., Thompson, S. R., & Russell, F. (1981). Designing effective staff development programs. In B. Dillon-Peterson (Ed.). *Staff development/organization development* (pp. 59–91). Alexandria, VA: ASCD.

Wu, P. C. (1987). Teachers as staff developers: Research, opinions, and cautions. *Journal of Staff Development, 8*(1), 4–6.

Yarger, S. J. (1990). The legacy of the teacher center. In B. Joyce (Ed.). *Changing school culture through staff development* (pp. 104–116). Alexandria, VA: ASCD.

Zide, M. M. & Colbert, R. (1992, February). *School community-college collaboration: A certificate of advanced graduate study in staff development and a professional development center.* Paper presented at the Annual Conference of the Association of Teacher Educators, Orlando (ERIC Document Reproduction Service No. ED 346 076).

Zimpher, N. L. (1988). A design for the professional development of teachers. *Journal of Teacher Education, 39*(1), 53–59.

NOTES

1 Examples include Beegle and Edelfelt, 1971; Bell and Day, 1991; Bishop, 1976; Bolan, 1982; Burke, Heideman, and Heideman, 1990; Caldwell, 1989; Dillon-Peterson, 1981; Griffin, 1983; Edelfelt and Johnson, 1975; Fielding and Schalock, 1985; Harris, 1989; Howey, Bents, and Corrigan, 1981; Jones, Clark, Figg, Howard, and Reid, 1989; Joyce, 1990; Joyce and Showers, 1988; Lieberman and Miller, 1991; Loucks-Horsley, Harding, Arbuckle, Murray, Dubea, and Williams, 1987; Orlich, 1989; Pink and Hyde, 1992; Rubin, 1978; Schiffer, 1980; Wideen and Andrews, 1987.

2 The use of the term "transaction" in this chapter should be distinguished from that of Burns's (1978). Burns considered transactional leadership to be that which takes place when "one person takes the initiative in making contact with others for the purpose of an exchange of valued things," which might be "economic or political or psychological in nature" (p. 19). In this chapter, the term "transaction" denotes teachers' interaction with their educational environment. Thus, "transactional staff development" is an extension of transaction as defined by Miller and Seller (1985) rather than by Burns.

3 For *organization development*, they list change process, varied examples of current practice, research design, assessment alternatives, characteristics of adult learning and development, team building, group dynamics, flexible, ongoing planning, articulation of core values, establishment of a shared vision, facilitation of individual and organizational growth, tolerance for ambiguity, empathy, risk taking as a value, norms of collegiality, and change as opportunity. For *professional development,* they list child development, student learning styles and culture, assessment alternatives, current information, content and curriculum, research on effective practice, instructional models, classroom management, classroom discourse, questioning/responding, decision-making, planning/implementation/reflection, curriculum development, coaching, reflective practice, empathy, flexibility, risk taking, efficacy, and lifelong learning (Lipton & Greenblatt, 1992).

·35·

SUPERVISION AND
ORGANIZATIONAL DEVELOPMENT

Gene E. Hall

UNIVERSITY OF NORTHERN COLORADO

Wen-Haur Shieh

HUALIEN TEACHER'S COLLEGE, TAIWAN

A chapter on organizational development in a handbook on school supervision may seem incongruous at first. Organizational development is generally seen as something that is done to improve the organization, while supervision centers on the development of the people. Organizational development has traditionally been the province of *external* consultants, while supervision has been seen as a key part of *internal* roles. Organizational development has been seen as a *temporary* effort of consultants, while supervision is expected to be a *continuing* function of supervisory personnel. Organizational development is supposed to be nonevaluative and address *all aspects* of organizational life, while supervision's predominant focus is on *one individual* at a time and is related to personnel evaluation. As simplistic as these comparisons may be, they still can serve as a useful starting place to introduce key features of organizational development and contrast these with features of school supervision.

As different as these two fields may seem at first glance, they can be presented in ways that illustrate how they relate to many of the same organizational processes and objectives. Both organizational development and school supervision are designed to address people aspects of organization life. Both use an array of process interventions and data collecting techniques, and both address aspects of change. A related commonality is that each has a very large body of literature about practices, models, and techniques and a relatively limited quantity of systematic studies of results and effectiveness.

An important decision made early in the preparation of this chapter was to restrict the scope and meaning of the term "organizational development." We could have taken a very broad view, one that encompassed a number of different theories and models about how, in a generic sense, organizations can be improved. A number of related models for bringing about change in organizations, such as the Concerns-Based Adoption Model (Hall & Hord, 1987) and the Diffusion perspective (Rogers, 1995), could have been included. In order to limit and contain the review, however, we chose to focus on the narrower use of the term. In the last 50 years, a genre of literature and professional practice has developed that is commonly referred to as "organizational development." The first purpose of this chapter is to review and critique the scope and characteristics of this view of organizational development. The second purpose is to explore applications and implications of this perspective for school supervision.

When we began to review the literature for this chapter, we expected to easily summarize the field of organizational development, and to quickly move into an analysis of the relationships and implications of organizational development for school supervision. The review and analysis of the organizational development literature turned out to be problematic, however. First of all, there is a very large quantity of written material. Second, the definition of the term "organizational development" varies widely. Third, there is a 50-year history of literature and practice that is loosely referred to as organizational development. To compound the search and review process further, there has been a continuing evolution of definitions and meanings for decades. Before we explore implications of the field of organizational development for school supervision, we must define and review the field of organizational development itself.

Due to the quantity of literature and the vagaries of the field during the last 50 years, this chapter begins with a short presentation of different definitions of the term "organizational development." This section is followed with a more extensive analysis and synthesis of how organizational development has evolved in meaning and processes. The last of these sections offers some discussion of the emerging and needed roles and functions of organizational development in the 1990s. The remainder of the chapter deals directly with the current and possible relationships between organizational development and school supervision. One of our most salient recommendations is that those who are engaged in more traditional forms of supervision need to increase their understanding and use of organizational development concepts and processes. There is a bigger mission for supervision that can only be accomplished by incorporating an organizational perspective.

One last point in this introduction: The term "OD" is often used in place of the words "organizational development." We will admit that, at the outset of this review, we thought we could easily interchange the two. As you will see, the way the field has evolved and the wide range of uses of both terms have made it nearly impossible to make bottom-line definitions. We will use the term "OD" throughout the chapter, but the reader needs to use caution in inferring all that may or may not be subsumed therewith.

EVOLVING DEFINITIONS OF ORGANIZATIONAL DEVELOPMENT

The years immediately following World War II were a period of development on many fronts. The economy, which had been exhausted during the war years, was in recovery. The Cold War was no longer simply a matter of having a strong military but increasingly involved a global political process. There was a need to convert manpower from warfare to peacetime endeavors. A new generation of children needed schools, with an increasingly more sophisticated curriculum and better prepared teachers. The returning GIs were entitled to higher education, and the war-torn countries of Europe and the Pacific needed to be redeveloped.

To accomplish all of these development goals at the needed pace required continuing advances in all aspects of education, training, supervision, administration, and leadership. Various training and development approaches that had been created during World War II were available, as were the wartime psychologists and trainers who had pioneered many of these tactics and strategies. The times, as reflected in the marketplace, demanded rapid increases in the functioning and effectiveness of all organizations. These pressures called for specialized development efforts aimed at public and private organizations. One result was the beginning of an effort to find and apply specialized processes to develop the skills of people working in organizational contexts (i.e., organizational development).

Beginning Models: Training and Planning

The beginning methods employed to improve organizational effectiveness can be grouped into two categories: (1) personnel training and (2) long-range organizational planning (French, 1971; McGill, 1977). Of the many personnel training methods which emerged in the postwar years, the one to have most profound impact on the development of OD was the *basic skill training group,* which was also known as the T-group, laboratory training, and sensitivity training (McGill, 1977). The basic assumptions of laboratory training are: (1) that the problems of organizational performance are problems of improper attitudes and improper behavior of organizational members; (2) changes of members' attitudes, values, and behavioral styles will lead to changes of organizational performance; and (3) training in laboratory conditions will help members examine their own attitudes and behavior in real settings and try new ones.

Laboratory training designs typically have participants engaging in group work with artificial (rather than job-specific) tasks. The training process emphasizes collecting data and receiving feedback about one's own behavior and the behavior of the group. The process also emphasizes using the feedback to better understand oneself and others. It was observed that feedback about participants' interactions in the laboratory settings provided rich personal learning experiences that were relevant and appropriate to organizational situations. Laboratory training was used to enrich individuals' learning experiences; and it was believed that the participants could take the experiential learning from the laboratory and relate it to organizational settings. Laboratory training placed its focus on increasing individuals' skills in the group process. Laboratory training programs did not address how to help individuals apply training outcomes to real settings. Instead, it was assumed that the participants could make the job-related transfer. The second thrust of OD training was to orient organizational improvement efforts toward a long-range planning perspective. To achieve this end, an array of systematic planning steps, processes, and techniques were employed, such as survey feedback.

Survey Feedback

Survey feedback was originally developed by Floyd Mann at the University of Michigan (Mann & Likert, 1952). The main functions of survey feedback were to collect information about member attitudes and opinions; to provide survey information to organizational units as feedback; and to design corrective actions based on the feedback information. The development of surveying devices and the corrective actions involved the use of an external consultant and an in-depth analysis of the organization. McGill describes a classic example of survey feedback used to improve organizational effectiveness, the establishment of the Action Service division of a national department store (McGill, 1977). Survey data about the operation of the Action Service division indicated how consumer complaints were related to organizational problems and how those problems were diagnosed through the survey of employees' opinions and then solved through group discussions. Survey feedback proved to be an efficient way to improve organizations based on data about members' opinions.

Organizational improvement efforts in the 1950s defined the emergence of what is commonly called organizational development. The efforts emphasized improving organizational effectiveness through behavioral changes of individual organization members. Two branches of academic thought contributed to the emphases. First, the human relations movement of the 1940s introduced the importance of linking human interaction skills and the crucial role of members' feelings toward their work environment with organizational performance. It was assumed that laboratory training in groups could provide members with the needed interpersonal skills, and that techniques such as survey feedback could provide information about members' feelings as inputs into organizational processes. A related movement was the emergence of systems theory in the 1950s. In systems theory, the organization is viewed as composed of different subparts, and organization members are regarded as only one part of the important elements or subsystems. For these reasons, training leading to individual improvement was seen as an efficient means of improving organizational performance. Individual improvement, in conjunction with long-range planning, were considered the primary targets for organizational improvement.

The resultant organizational improvement efforts in the 1950s paved the way for rapid growth of OD in the 1960s and its continued evolution in the 1970s, 1980s, and 1990s. An important and, in some ways, problematic characteristic of OD is that the field itself has evolved. As a result, supervisors and others who are interested in organizational development must keep in mind that the meaning of the term "OD" can be very different from decade to decade and author to author. Illustrations of how the definition and meaning of OD have varied along with a few implications are presented next.

Changing Definitions of OD

As consultants and practitioners gained experience with training and group processes and as more experts emerged, the definition of OD continued to evolve. This evolutionary process has continued to this day. The reason for addressing this pattern of continuing evolution of definition is not simply one of semantics. There are serious substantive implications that must be kept in mind when selecting a working definition of OD. For example, will a behaviorist or a constructivist set of assumptions serve as the basis for a developmental effort? Depending upon which decade and which authors are selected, very different assumptions can be in place, and, therefore, the resultant interventions can be quite different. Here, we quote several OD definitions to illustrate the diversity in and evolution of OD meanings.

Behavioral Perspectives In the 1960s, Beckhard (1969) defined OD in this way: "Organization development is an effort (1) planned, (2) organization-wide, and (3) managed from the top, to (4) increase organization effectiveness and health through (5) planned interventions in the organization's 'processes,' using behavioral-science knowledge (p. 9)." To

Beckhard, OD is a top-down change effort, and its purpose is to increase organizational effectiveness and health through improving organizational processes and using behavioral science knowledge.

Values Perspective Although OD is seen as an application of behavioral science to organizations, some researchers have placed their attention on the value issue of OD. For example, Derr (1974) regards OD as a value system. Kimberly and Nielsen (1975) include philosophy in their OD definition. Derr defined OD in this way: "OD is a theory, a method and a value system (often hidden) for improving the human side of organizational life and thereby improving the task-goal accomplishment of their complex organizations" (p. 11). All OD efforts entail valuing of some elements over others, as Derr pointed out in the early 1970s. Kimberly and Nielsen (1975) offer yet another definition:

Organization development (OD), a philosophy of and technology for producing organizational change, has been implemented in a variety of organizations. Growing out of the human relations tradition in the forties and fifties, it is actually a pastiche of techniques developed in the behavioral sciences which focus on problems of organizational learning, motivation, problem solving, communication, and interpersonal relations (p. 191).

McGill (1977) considered OD to be a normative process:

Organization development is a conscious, planned process of developing an organization's capabilities so that it can attain and sustain an optimum level of performance as measured by efficiency, effectiveness, and health. Operationally, OD is a normative process of addressing the questions: "What are we?" "Where do we want to be?" "How do we get from where we are to where we want to be?" This process is undertaken by members of the organization using a variety of techniques, often in collaboration with a behavioral science consultant (p. 3).

Individual Welfare Perspectives Turning to the 1980s, individual welfare is included in OD definitions. The following definitions reflect this trend:

Organization development in school districts is a coherent, systematically-planned, sustained effort at system self-study and improvement, focusing explicitly on change in formal and informal procedures, processes, norms or structures, using behavioral science concepts. The goals of OD include improving both the quality of life of individuals as well as organizational functioning and performance with a direct or indirect focus on educational issues (Fullan, Miles, & Taylor, 1980, p.135).

Organization development is the process undertaken by an organization, or part of an organization, to define and meet changing self-improvement objectives, while making it possible for individuals in the organization to meet their personal and professional objectives (Dillon-Peterson, 1981, p.3).

Organization development is an emergent discipline that provides concepts and skills for improving the climate and problem-solving ability of organizations. Applied to education, its goal is to help members of school organizations (faculties, administrators, community members) develop communities which effectively solve problems, initiate needed changes, and provide support for their members (Roark & Davis, 1981, p. 37).

OD is a planned and sustained effort at school self-study and improvement, focusing explicitly on change in both formal and informal norms, structures, and procedures, using behavioral science concepts, and experiential learning. It involves the school participants themselves in the active assessment, diagnosis, and transformation of their own organization (Schmuck, 1987, pp. 1-2).

The most basic value of organization development is that of joining and working together collaboratively with educators, students and parents to create democratic social structures, and humanized interpersonal relationships. Attendant values include expanding all participants' consciousness about how others think and feel, as well as finding more and more choices for new action (Schmuck, 1987, p. 2).

Shifts Toward a Constructivist Perspective The definitions presented in the early 1990s offer the first hints of a move away from behavioristic and structural frames and toward ones that may be more constructivist. For example Burke (1994) defines OD as: ". . . a planned process of change in an organization's culture through the utilization of behavioral science technologies, research, and theory" (p.12)."

A CLOSER LOOK AT OD BY DECADES

In its first 50 years, the meaning and emphasis of OD seemed inconsistent from decade to decade. The emphases of OD in the 60s were somewhat different than those in the 1970s, the 1980s, or the 1990s. In each decade, important emphases were added. In many ways, this evolution in definition and emphasis reflects a core value of OD—continuous learning. As OD practitioners and theorists learned more about their craft and as organizations became more sophisticated, the models and techniques of OD changed. This evolution in meaning of OD, by the decades, is highlighted in this section. Again, the reason for doing so is to illustrate to school supervisors that the many images and meanings of OD must be considered as context in exploring implications for supervisory practice. The philosophical orientation and role of supervision can be quite different depending on the perspective selected. Also, this review is important as a frame of reference for considering how the human processes of an organization can be viewed, understood, and developed. The ultimate application should be in constructing direct links between considerations of strategies for improving organizational life and developing the effectiveness of its members.

Organizational Development in the 1960s

The 1960s were a time of rapid development for OD. Many scholars invested in learning more about OD and introduced the importance and purpose of OD to practitioners in business, government, and education. Sanzgiri and Gottlieb (1992) attribute the growth of OD in the 1960s to several advantageous conditions: a period of relative economic stability and affluence, a culture that demonstrated a heightened willingness to engage in a dialogue about participation and democracy, inspiration of practitioners and university-based consultants to make organizations more flexible, a long-term commitment to organizational life, and an economically secure environment that encouraged experimentation with new organizational designs.

Focus on Human Relations and Systems Under these conditions, human relations thought and systems theory were the dominant perspectives of OD. Both the social movement of the 1960s and contemporary scholars' theories and research findings helped shape the beliefs that personnel factors were a significant contributor to organizational success and that organizations are subsystems of the larger system. This perspective interestingly is diametrically opposed to the widespread corporate philosophy of the 1990s that celebrates downsizing as a way to reward stockholders with short-term financial gains, while many employees lose their jobs.

The Civil Rights movement had a large impact on organizational improvement efforts. Workers' became more conscious of protecting their rights in work settings. Organization members became more involved in their organizations' decision-making processes. They saw involvement as a way to promote the quality of their working environment. Organization executives recognized the impact of this new consciousness and saw the importance of meeting workers' psychological needs as a strategy to promote organizational performance. Keep in mind that human relations thought, developed in the 1940s, and systems perspectives of organizations, developed in the 1950s, still influenced executives' thinking. The new perspective on the workers' place in the organization was added to these earlier frameworks.

Theories and empirical research findings provided evidence to support human relations thought and the systems perspective. Maslow's (1954) need theory, Herzberg's (1966) motivator-hygiene theory, and McGregor's (1960) Theory Y are among an array of theories that emphasize the importance of the relationship between individual personality and organizational dynamics. These theories maintain that, to improve job satisfaction, organizations must adjust their internal processes to help members develop more positive attitudes toward the organization. An important thrust of OD efforts during the period was how to create an environment that would foster trust, commitment, and willingness among members.

While theorists with a psychological perspective were concerned about the satisfaction of members' psychological needs in pursuing organizational outcomes, other theorists with a systems perspective argued that organizations could ensure their success by adjusting their internal structural processes to better match the external environment. Organizations are supposed to be systems continuously interacting with their external environments. These assumptions, too, were supported by empirical studies.

Based on their empirical studies, Burns and Stalker (1961) argued that organizations with organic and flexible structures perform better; Lawrence and Lorsch (1969) pointed out that integration and differentiation functions of organizations are contingent on the environment; and Likert (1967) contended that the extent of organizational performance could be predicted through systems analysis of organizations. These theories and study findings led OD efforts toward a focus on improving the internal structure of organizations.

Separate and Distinct Activities There have been many earnest attempts to apply behavioral science to various organizations. Past attempts have generally been oriented either toward personnel's psychological satisfaction or long-range organizational planning; they have rarely been concurrently combined. The many OD efforts in the 1960s reflected this dichotomy. Those efforts can be categorized as either human relations or systems changes. OD efforts in the early 1960s saw the development of individuals and the development of organizations as separate and distinct activities, and each was pursued as such. McGill (1977) describes the separation as "contemporaneous but not cooperative" (p. 17).

Organizations, however, are not only gatherings of people; people's efforts within organizations need to be coordinated and oriented toward organizational goals. Organizational improvement leaning only toward human relations perspectives or system perspectives are doomed to fail (Blake & Mouton, 1964). Blake and Mouton's Managerial Grid Program was one of the few cases of OD efforts at the time that systematically addressed elements of both individuals and organizations (Blake & Mouton, 1964). The Managerial Grid includes two major components: concern for people and concern for production. Six training phases are involved to help managers work toward the goals of OD:

1. laboratory-seminar training,
2. team development,
3. intergroup development,
4. organizational goal setting,
5. goal attainment, and
6. stabilization.

The Managerial Grid Program included a body of social science knowledge, and obviously represented a systematic attempt to transfer behavioral science concepts into organizational action.

To summarize the OD efforts in the 1960s, several characteristics can be observed:

1. They were a reflection of the social movement developing in the external environment.
2. They were based on scholars' perspectives of organizations.
3. External consultants were to be involved in dealing with the complexities of OD efforts.
4. They were initiated from the top.
5. They were seen by practitioners and researchers as experimental actions.
6. Both individuals and organizations were emphasized, but there was a lack of focus on skills to combine both.

Organization Development in the 1970s

The research and practice of OD in the 1970s was evolving into a period of adolescence (Burke, 1976; Friedlander, 1976). On the one hand, OD concepts were accepted by more and more organizational practitioners and were being put into practice in an ever expanding variety of organizations. On the other hand, researchers showed a stronger interest in studying OD, attempting to understand OD better, and to further establish models of OD for use in practice.

Economic Competitiveness Several factors combined to produce momentum for OD in the 1970s. The competitive world economy and the increase of behavioral science and technology knowledge were pushing OD to grow rapidly. After the continuous growth of the 1960s, the world economy had become more competitive. New market pressures made organizational practitioners alert to changes in the external environment and forced them accordingly to be more pragmatic in the operations of their organizations. In response, executives had to select strategies to improve organizational efficiency and effectiveness, or their organizations could no longer survive in the more competitive arena.

The oil embargo and recession of 1972-1973 made organizational adaptation more demanding. Organizations cut back, especially in the "soft" areas of training and human development. In a competitive era, observable benefits and direct impact on the bottom line were always companies' priorities. Benefits were indicated by measurable outcomes that could be compared. If techniques could not be viewed as cost-effective, they were not implemented. OD practitioners had to prove that their OD practices did work and brought tangible benefits to the organizations. Practitioners with less experience and less competency were weeded out. Those who survived had to quickly learn the concepts and skills required to practice effectively in a competitive environment (Burke, 1994).

The Search for Skills Practitioners were watching for whatever technologies became available as they improved their organizations. Any technological invention was soon tried in practice. With the input of new technologies, the personnel-technology relationship had to be adjusted and managerial styles needed to be changed so that the new technology could provide maximum benefits to organizations.

Other factors contributing to OD progress in the 1970s were advances in behavioral science. The continuing development of behavioral science since the 1940s provided testimony and some evidence relating OD factors and their applications to increases in organizational efficiency. Knowledge about organizations increased largely in the area of members' feelings and attitudes, job satisfaction, organizational climate, interpersonal relationships, communication problems, and group processes. As organizational practitioners became familiar with new concepts or skills in this area, they tried them in practice where OD programs provided them the opportunities.

In the academic arena, behavioral science was becoming more and more dominant. It seemed as if behavioral scientists were trying to reduce and simplify all behavioral phenomena to operational definitions and numerical explanations. Researchers in the behavioral sciences suggested that "OD need(s) to prove itself as science, one capable of producing quantitative data supporting the contention that humanistic processes did indeed lead to more productive organizations"

(Sanzgiri & Gottlieb, 1992, p. 61). Their suggestions were in accordance with organizational practitioners' appeals for measurable outcomes of OD. With the same emphasis on quantitative measures, cooperation between researchers and practitioners in promoting OD was a natural result.

OD in the 1970s was results-driven in order to meet the requirements of the economic environment. With the help of newly created behavioral science knowledge, the concepts and practice of OD in the 1970s evolved into a new period with a pragmatic orientation.

SYSTEMS THEORY CONTINUES IN IMPORTANCE. With the earlier establishment of systems theory, researchers used this perspective to view organizations as open systems. In an open system, there are ongoing interactions among internal elements of the system and continuous exchanges between the system and its external environment. Researchers attempted to explain and predict the interaction and exchange patterns. The systems perspective was used to explain OD concepts in the 1970s.

The systems perspective claimed that organizations are composed of various components or subsystems. The interactions among these components follow patterns which could be described and used to predict future actions. Since subsystems are part of the whole system, change in one component could lead to change in other components. One implication was that one should expect the effects of an OD intervention in one subsystem to interact with and affect behavioral patterns in other subsystems. With the systems perspective in mind, organizational practitioners in the 1970s believed that organizational performance could be promoted through planned efforts by causing changes in organizational processes. They believed that, with the help of existing knowledge of organizational and behavioral science, they could implement certain means to achieve organizational goals in an efficient way. OD was seen as a useful set of interventions to cause organizational change.

INFLUENCE OF BEHAVIORAL SCIENCE. OD was seen in the 1970s as the practical use of behavioral science knowledge to increase organizational performance. The emphasis of OD can be illustrated by how it was defined at that time. For example, French and Bell (1973) defined OD in this way:

Organization development is a long-range effort to improve an organization's problem-solving and renewal processes, particularly through a more effective and collaborative management of organization culture—with special emphasis on the culture of formal work teams—with the assistance of a change agent, or catalyst, and the use of the theory and technology of applied behavioral science, including action research (p. 15)

Heisler (1975) defined OD in a similar way:

Organizational development (OD) is the name generally applied to an emerging behavioral science discipline; this discipline seeks to improve organizational performance and effectiveness through planned, systematic, long-range efforts focused on the organization's culture and its human and social processes (p. 77).

McGill's (1977) definition was:

Organization development is a conscious, planned process of developing an organization's capabilities so that it can attain and sustain an optimum level of performance as measured by efficiency, effectiveness, and health . . . (p. 3).

There is much similarity among these three OD definitions. OD was seen as planned, with long-term effort, using behavioral science knowledge, with emphasis on developing appropriate team processes, and increasing organizational capacities to solve problems. The purpose of OD was to improve organizational performance which could be measured in terms of efficiency and effectiveness.

LIMITED RESEARCH AND THEORY TO SUPPORT PRACTICE. The goal of organizational practitioners had long been to improve organizational performance. It was not exclusively the domain of OD practitioners. The methods used by OD practitioners made OD different from the traditional management training approach. French and Bell (1973) pointed out seven characteristics that differentiated OD interventions from more traditional interventions: emphasis on group and organizational processes, emphasis on the work team as the key unit for learning more effective modes of organizational behavior, emphasis on the collaborative management of the work team culture, emphasis on the management of the culture of the total system, the use of an action research model, the use of a behavioral scientist change agent, and viewing the change effort as an ongoing process (French & Bell, 1973).

Early in the 1970s, researchers and practitioners tended to rely on existing organizational knowledge to orient their efforts. Yet, organizational knowledge systematically developed through research at that time was too limited to provide OD with a sound theoretical base for practical use. Researchers either offered their subjective prescriptions of OD practice or conducted survey research to increase understanding of efficient OD implementations. For example, French and Bell (1973) believed that there are three components in OD: the diagnostic component, the action component, and the process-maintenance component. McGill (1977) wrote that the OD process consisted of nine phases: convergence of interest, establishing the charter, legitimation and sponsorship, problem identification, general plan, action hypothesis, action step, formative evaluation, and problem reidentification. Lists of elements and components such as these do not form an overarching model or theory, however.

The relative absence of theoretical OD knowledge, along with the presence of extensive OD practice, suggested two important issues for OD researchers. The first was the need to identify and verify OD approaches used by practitioners that were generally more effective than others regardless of the situation in which they were applied. The second issue dealt with the need to identify factors that have a general influence on the success or lack of success of OD efforts as a change strategy or technique (Franklin, 1976). One identifiable strategy employed by several researchers was to propose categories of OD practice.

In a comparative study of successful and unsuccessful organizational development, Franklin (1976) proposed eight categories of OD practices:

1. characteristics of the organization's environment;
2. characteristics of the organization itself;
3. initial contact between development/research personnel;
4. formal entry procedures and commitment;
5. data-gathering activities and posture of organizational members toward them;
6. characteristics of the internal agents;
7. characteristics of the external agents; and
8. exit procedures.

In his survey of OD patterns in practice, Heisler (1975) selected six factors as variables used in his research: knowledge of OD, use of constants, level of program origination, impetus of OD program, focus of OD effort, OD techniques, and satisfaction and criticism of OD.

In their review article about empirical studies of school OD, Fullan, Miles, and Taylor (1980) identified several factors that contributed to school OD success at the stages of entry, transition or initial use, and institutionalization. Major factors included organizational readiness (such as time spent to warn people about the OD necessity and people's willingness to invest a certain amount of time and energy); active involvement, support, and understanding of the program by top management; sustained training and work over a period of two years; establishment and use of internal OD consultants combined with proactive use of external consultants; and viewing OD as a standard part of the district budget.

THE SEARCH FOR AN INTEGRATED MODEL. The factors used as variables in OD survey research and comparative studies of OD success reflected major concepts held by OD practitioners at the time. Researchers were attempting to capture OD in a more integrated model. According to Burke (1976), researchers' efforts could be accounted for as: (1) refinement in building models and tying methodology more directly to theory, (2) consolidation in terms of generating strategies of change for a total system, and (3) readjustment, especially with respect to values and questions of advocacy. Despite these efforts, no integrated OD model or theory was widely recognized in the 1970s.

Burke (1976) observed that the field of OD in the 1970s had moved into "adolescence". He wrote that OD was "searching for self-identity and self-concept, and sometimes overly autonomous if not rebellious, rather than more settled and adult" (p. 23). Friedlander (1976) compared OD to a strapping youth—"eager, energetic, confused, looking for an identity, looking to prove himself, wondering what he will be and do when he grows up, wondering if he ever will" (p. 17).

Organizational activities imply a set of complex behavioral phenomena. It is not an easy task to offer a comprehensive model that can indicate to OD practitioners in a certain way to improve organizations. One of the difficulties was that the concept of OD in the 1970s represented people's efforts to understand and improve organizations in various ways. As Kahn (1974) pointed out, OD was a convenient label for a variety of activities and did not represent a concrete concept or simple model of organizational activities.

Friedlander (1976) suggested that OD concepts in the 1970s included the interplay of three values—rationalism, pragmatism, and existentialism. Rationalism pushed OD to become more scientific, more theoretical, and more conceptual; pragmatism pushed OD to become more useful; existentialism pushed OD to become more humanistic, more aware, and more oriented toward people and growth. The interplay of these three values defeated efforts to develop a single integrated model, but they did help the field of OD to become more mature.

Experience with Whole Systems In the 1960s, OD practitioners devoted their efforts to enhancing participants' positive feelings toward organizations. Individuals were regarded as crucial elements of organizational effectiveness. In the 1970s, the efforts shifted toward promoting the process functions of whole systems. Although OD practitioners did not neglect individuals and their effectiveness, they did focus in the 1970s more directly on activities related to the operations of whole organizations. Building mutual trust, reducing barriers to communication, enhancing team process, establishing a positive organizational climate, participative methods of problem identification and problem solving, task forces, ad hoc groups, temporary organization structures, job design, and joint objective setting were the processes and techniques most frequently described by the OD practitioners as valuable (Patten, Skjerheim, & Shook, 1973; Rush, 1973).

The findings of one survey of OD practice in the 1970s can be used to illustrate aspects of OD at that time. In a survey of OD implementation, Heisler (1975) found that only 39 percent of the CEOs responding to the survey felt that they had substantial or good knowledge of the discipline. This lack of OD knowledge on the part of clients and OD practitioners could be accounted for, at least in part, by the absence of a widely accepted theoretical base for OD.

With insufficient theory and models to guide practice, the focus of OD efforts relied heavily on practitioners' experiences. If experience was the driver, naturally the more concrete difficulties faced by clients would be the major OD intervention targets. Organizational issues of the time, such as decision-making, problem solving, goal-setting processes, communication problems, interfacing relations, and planning methods became topics for training. Team building, management by objectives (MBO), systems analysis, and job enrichment/enlargement were the commonly used training techniques (Heisler, 1975). Heisler (1975) found that selection of the OD practices to be targeted originated mainly at the top management level, in response to internal forces or a combination of internal and external forces. He also found that the use of external and internal consultants was evenly divided.

A list of the major types of OD interventions summarized by French and Bell (1973) can also be used to show the prominent aspects of OD practice in the 1970s. French and Bell categorized OD interventions as diagnostic activities, team-building activities, intergroup activities, survey-feedback activities, education and training activities, techno-structural activities, process consultation activities, grid organization development activities, third-party peacemaking activities, coaching and counseling activities, life- and career-planning activities, and planning and goal-setting activities.

In analyzing French and Bell's categories of OD interventions, it is apparent that OD practice in the 1970s consists of five major areas:

1. the data gathering area, such as diagnostic and survey-feedback activities;
2. the group process area, such as team-building activities, intergroup activities, and third-party peacemaking activities;
3. the human resource area, such as education and training, process consultation, coaching and counseling, and life- and career-planning activities;
4. the organizational structural area, such as technostructural and grid organization development activities; and
5. planning and goal-setting area.

Again, these categories indicate that OD practice at that time was based on a systems perspective. OD was used to promote the functions of whole organizations. Organizational structural processes were the focus, not individuals. OD practitioners not only attempted to survey participants' collective feelings, but offered educational and training activities to enlarge their contributions to their organizations.

The 1970s was a period of continued evolution for OD. Researchers prescribed OD practice for practitioners, and practitioners were trying various OD procedures to improve their client organizations. Several aspects of the concepts and practices can be used to summarize the characteristics of OD during that period (Burke, 1976; French & Bell 1973; Friedlander, 1976; Sanzgiri & Gottlieb, 1992):

1. *Field:* OD expanded from a process for business/industrial organizations to a process applied to widely different organizational types.
2. *Pragmatism:* OD was adopted as a response to the requirements of external change and internal needs. Increasing efficiency and effectiveness were the major purposes of OD, while usefulness was the criteria for judging specific OD procedures.
3. *Top-down:* OD was initiated by managers at the top level to solve problems they faced in running organizations.
4. *System perspective:* Researchers advocated that OD practice center on generating change for a total system and that organizational change should be emphasized more than individual change. The role of the OD practitioner changed from working almost exclusively with management to working with both managers and persons at all organizational levels. Connection of people with technology was also considered.
5. *Long-term ongoing process:* OD was not presented as a one-shot event. Instead, it was seen as a long-term, planned, and systematic effort to change organizations.
6. *Experience-based:* No integrated OD theory could be applied. Practitioners relied heavily on their own experiences.

7. *Behavioral science base:* In addition to personal experience, practitioners in the 1970s applied behavioral science knowledge to developing OD intervention strategies and techniques.
8. *Context-bound:* Self-diagnosis and self-reflection exercises were commonly used to lead to strategies for change. OD practitioners shifted from advocating a specific managerial style to emphasizing the situation or contingency approach.
9. *Normative-reeducative strategy:* OD practitioners emphasized the importance of training and educating people across time in order to accomplish organizational change.
10. *Consultant's role:* OD practitioners no longer merely concentrated their effort on group processes. They also prescribed specific managerial styles. Their effort was not process-oriented, but content-oriented. This shift in the role of the consultant demanded that managers and administrators within the organizations become change agents, with the help of external consultants.

Another characteristic of the 1970s was rapid expansion in the types of organizations where OD was applied and the extent of its use. Without a sound theoretical base, however, practitioners relied heavily on available behavioral science knowledge. Continuous attempts to address existing organizational problems did occasionally produce effective solutions and did promote OD from a training status to a status of organizational legitimacy. Heavy reliance on behavioral science knowledge, however, made practitioners neglect the value domains in OD practice. Without addressing the value issues, OD could at most benefit organizations within the limitation of the organization's status quo. To cause a fundamental change, an integrated theory was needed; otherwise OD would continue to be seen mostly as a collection of various techniques used by organizational practitioners in trial-and-error ways to address topics of immediate client concern.

Organization Development in the 1980s

OD was previously used primarily as a response to an organization's technological orientation and its inflexible bureaucratic structure. Human values had been the major issue for OD. In the 1960s and 1970s, OD practice was concerned with members' psychological feelings, job satisfaction, cooperation, coordination, and personal growth. In the 1980s, environmental diversity became more prominent. Business was becoming more competitive internationally, and the composition of the work force was changing. Turbulence characterized the socioeconomic context (Sanzgiri & Gottlieb, 1992).

In the 1980s, the world economy was developing into a global system of which the United States was a part. In the global economy, business sectors had to struggle against competition from other countries. Various approaches had to be designed to enhance an organization's chances of survival. Lower production costs and higher product quality were the new priorities. Downsizing, mergers, acquisitions, leveraged buyouts, and the creation of multinational corporations were widely adopted strategies (Fagenson & Burke, 1990). One consequence of these changes was the concurrent layoff of a large number of individuals throughout organizations. A direct effect of these pressures and changes was the psychological impact on the feelings of employees who had to leave and those who remained. Another effect of these changes was the need for the remaining organization members to make adjustments, including their management styles, individual work and relationships, and the development of new corporate cultures (Fagenson & Burke, 1990).

The changing composition of the workforce was another factor. In the 1980s, an increasing number of women and minorities entered the workforce, bringing with them different values and career expectations. Faced with the high proportion of new workers, organization managers were forced to adopt new leadership styles.

The changing context of the 1980s oriented OD efforts toward enhancing organizations' capacities to adjust themselves to the new situation. The emergence of multinational corporations, the diversity of cultural values in organizations, and the changing workforce within organizations forced OD practitioners to address the challenge of helping management adjust to the new cultural diversity. Cultural and value differences and similarities were crucial factors that needed to be considered in formulating OD intervention strategies (Jaeger, 1986). The challenge for OD now was to develop organizational capabilities to cope with multidimensional and complex demands of international business (Woodman, 1989), to help organizations adjust to the changing work force, and to establish new organizational value clusters (Sanzgiri & Gottlieb, 1992).

External Environmental Factors The organizational development field had traditionally been more "micro" than "macro" in orientation; more focused on individual and group behaviors than on organization-wide processes, and more concerned with the tactics of intervention design and conduct than with strategies for changing whole systems (Woodman, 1989). The perspective of open systems used in the 1970s was still valued in the 1980s. However, the concept of OD was broadened. OD researchers no longer considered OD practice to be merely a change process following a fixed model or sequences. Instead, they thought more systemically and regarded OD as a complex activity involving various factors and processes (Greiner & Schein, 1988; Woodman, 1989).

This broader perspective brought with it an assumption that OD efforts had to be concerned not only with factors within an organization but with environmental factors outside the organization. Researchers viewed organizations as open systems whose effectiveness could be enhanced not only by modifying organizational structures and processes but by connecting them with environmental factors. For example, Beer and Walton (1987) stated: "Thus as a field, organization development will have to become concerned with the theory and practice of managing the continual adaptation of internal organizations to changes in the external environment" (p. 340). They believed that OD fostered organizational adaptation to environmental change. Nord (1989) expanded the OD paradigm by adding a political and economic framework. Lundberg (1989) viewed OD as organizational learning activ-

ities focusing on task adjustment, adapting to a changing environment, and preparing for new futures. Greiner and Schein (1988) suggested that OD practice needed to be combined with power utilization in organizations.

Norman and Keys (1992) summarized the definitions of OD implied in the literature of the 1980s as an educational strategy adopted to bring about planned change; as a systems approach to the total set of functional and interpersonal role relationships in organizations; as a long-range process directed at improving employee satisfaction, attitudes, and the effectiveness of organizations; as a planned program of change aimed at removing barriers to high performance and enhancing the system's capacity for adjustment to future demands; as a total, systemwide approach to planned change; and as a planned change effort involving a systematic diagnosis of the organization, the development of a strategic plan for improvement, and the mobilization of resources to carry out the effort. This summary of definitions indicates that OD requires long-term effort. It involves planning and mobilizing with the purpose of causing change in individuals and organizations.

SYSTEMIC CHANGE. With this broader perspective and agenda, the view of OD processes was modified. OD efforts were assumed to be linked to strategic management so that a system change could be made (Woodman, 1989). There was a growing understanding that fragmented efforts would not lead to OD success and that, instead, effective organizational change should be regarded as a long-term process. This strategic perspective assumed that OD should be oriented toward causing changes in the role of leadership and organizational culture over an extended period of time.

The role of leadership was required to shift from initiating routine improvement efforts to causing organizational transformation to ensure systemic changes. Organizational culture was seen as an important factor in promoting or hampering systemic change (Woodman, 1989). OD practitioners were asked to produce transformational leadership and favorable organizational cultures which would sustain organizational change.

Lippitt, Lippitt, and Lafferty (1984) suggested three broad trends that might affect the direction of OD professionals' consulting efforts: macrosystem trends, human resource system trends, and an emphasis on individuals in organizational systems. They suggested that these three broad system trends be taken into account when OD professionals provided consulting services. Based on their analysis of OD trends, Lippitt et al offered their prescriptions from a systems perspective.

Considering the macrosystem trend, Lippitt et al suggested that OD consultants have to understand the impact of organizational culture on overall organizational health and develop OD competency accordingly. OD consultants also have to employ a systems perspective to utilize organizational resources, to address issues of centralization vs. decentralization, to solve organizational conflict, and to promote interorganizational collaboration.

Based on recognition of human resource system trends, the OD professional would have to help organizations merge the line and staff functions, link the existing human resources, adjust to the increasing pluralism among members, and develop an efficient information system. Lippitt et al acknowledging the emphasis on individuals in the OD trends, urged OD professionals to promote individuals' self-recognition and intrinsic motivation and to help individuals change effectively. OD consultants should understand that healthy individuals make healthy organizations and thus increase the interdependence between individuals and their organizations. Self-selected excellence and intrinsic motivation factors would be seen as a key to greater productivity and a basic strategy in both human resource development and OD.

The Need for Theory Continues. With the advances in OD concepts, and the emphasis on systemic change, there was an even greater cry for a comprehensive theory on which OD practice could be based. Although behavioral science knowledge had been used in OD efforts for a long time, and a body of evidence on OD activities existed, no single theory encompassed most OD research and practice. In their review of OD research, Sashkin and Burke (1987) claimed that they did not find any real coherence among the various theoretical contributions or see any theoretical synthesis. Woodman (1989) offered a similar conclusion: "There is no shortage of theories and models of change and changing. What is needed is more comprehensive frameworks, categorization schemes, or models that will allow us to make sense of the theory and knowledge that already exists" (p. 211).

Although no comprehensive OD theory appeared in the 1980s, researchers' efforts did bring some contributions to the theory-building process. For example, Weisbord (1987) offered four guidelines for a general planning model: (1) assessing the potential for OD action; (2) getting the whole system in the room; (3) focusing on the future; and (4) structuring systems tasks so people can do for themselves. Porras (1987) suggested a comprehensive implementation theory called stream analysis, positing that the work setting consists of four dimensions or streams: organizing arrangements, social factors, technology, and physical setting.

Another advance in the OD theory-building arena in the 1980s was the refinement of key research variables. Several OD variables were reconceptualized and their meanings in practice were explored. For example, the meanings of participation, technology, and the role of expectations were examined in more detailed ways (Woodman, 1989). Researchers challenged the traditional assumption that participation is valued by all participants by positing that members' attitudes toward participation are mediated by a number of structural, relational, and societal factors. Researchers also expanded the traditional concept of technology to include information technology.

One of the contributions that became prominent during this time was the change concept offered by Golembiewski, Billingsley, and Yeager (1976). They proposed a conceptual clarification of the concept of "change" by identifying three types: alpha change, beta change, and gamma change. Alpha change involves a variation in the level of some existential state, given a constantly calibrated measuring instrument related to a constant conceptual domain. Beta change involves a variation in the level of some existential state, complicated by the fact that some intervals of the measurement

continuum associated with a constant conceptual domain have been recalibrated. Gamma change involves a redefinition or reconceptualization of some domain, a major change in the perspective or frame of reference within which phenomena are perceived and classified, in what is taken to be relevant in some slice of reality. Their clarification of the change concept offered a new way of OD thinking and OD research design.

In the 1980s, OD was viewed from a broader perspective, and some theory-building efforts were initiated. Remember that Friedlander (1976) used the metaphor of an adolescent to describe the development of OD theory in the 1970s. Despite a number of efforts, no "mature" OD theory emerged in the 1980s. Researchers did, however, contribute new direction for theoretical development of OD.

Integration of Structure and Behavior OD in the 1980s was a prevailing paradigm. Casual observers as well as practitioners found much less strangeness in the field and assumed a much greater sense of responsibility for organizational development. People felt that OD practice did cause substantial positive effects (Sashkin & Burke, 1987). Researchers and practitioners came to understand that OD needed to be integrated with other aspects of organizational activity.

Two predictions, offered by researchers and practitioners in the early 1980s, illustrate the increasing acceptance and understanding of OD. In 1981, Morrison (1981) predicted that the changing context would lead practitioners to use the following OD interventions: integrating high technology into the workplace; transforming technical experts into managers; managing rapid change; developing management styles to enhance productivity, efficiency, and the ability to compete with foreign industries; and accommodating the creativity and changing values of people in the workforce. OD was obviously no longer considered an add-on to existing practice; it was a systemic effort used to cause overall improvement. This understanding was not limited to researchers. OD practitioners thought of OD in a similar way.

In a study conducted at almost the same time as Morrison, OD practitioners were asked to predict what OD interventions would be used in the 1980s. Practitioners' responses included: power and influence training, stress management, career development, quality of work life, a systems approach to OD, greater use of OD to increase productivity and profitability, organizational diagnosis and design, long-term change, integration of women and minorities into the organization, and strategic planning and forecasting (Jones, Spier, Goodstein, & Sashkin, 1980). Both the researchers' and the practitioners' predictions indicated that OD was no longer considered as a one-shot effort, but an ongoing program that had to be integrated with organizational goals, leadership, technology, structural processes, strategic management, human values, and changes in the external environment.

OD practice in the 1980s verified the predictions described above. OD efforts in the 1980s involved and integrated more aspects of organizational life. There was an effective integration which resolved the long-standing conflict over whether structural concerns or behavioral process issues were the focus of OD activities, and the integration did cause improvements. Sashkin and Burke (1987) suggest that the increasing clarity of research findings of positive OD impacts owes much to the integration of task structure and behavioral process-based OD approaches and of people-centered with profit-centered OD values. Sashkin and Burke's observation places emphasis on the OD integration of organizations and individuals. People appeared to understand that organizational goals could not be achieved without attending to both individuals and organization needs.

Sanzgiri and Gottlieb (1992) offered a similar description of the integration function of OD effort. According to their description, the OD principles emphasized in the 1980s included: simultaneous long- and short-term involvement, interdisciplinary knowledge base, simultaneous internal and external focus, emphasis on quality management, emphasis on multiple research methods, and attention to both hierarchical and consensus-based modes of power. Their description indicates that OD practitioners had shifted their emphasis from singular functions to a greater focus on improving overall organizational functioning. OD practice was to be based on a systemic perspective.

EMERGENCE OF CULTURE AS AN OD CONCEPT. To integrate organizational activities, organizational culture became a crucial factor. The influence of organizational culture permeates all parts of organizational life. Collective norms within organizations, individuals' belief systems and behavior, members' commitment to organizations, and interpersonal relationship were all influenced largely by organizational culture. The persistent nature of organizational culture could be related to sustaining OD effects. To produce a lasting effect of an OD effort, organizational culture could not be ignored. This belief was supported by research on organizational culture, which began to appear in the 1980s.

OD practitioners, too, began to believe that organizational culture was an important vehicle for systemic change. Cultural change has to come before organizational change. One of the main OD tasks was to cause cultural change in organizations. This focus on culture was a move away from the earlier focus on climate and the conceptual and methodological problems that were associated with that approach (James & Jones, 1974). However, the culture focus was not from a pure process viewpoint but rather from the more structural perspective commonly used by organizational sociologists (Sashkin & Burke, 1987).

The emphasis on cultural change naturally led OD back to team building, which was helpful in addressing organizational culture and integrating organizational activities. Team building had previously been used to improve interpersonal relations. In the 1980s, OD practitioners used team building more to help teams accomplish their tasks. From the broader perspective of OD, team building was seen as the socio-technical systems approach that could serve as a means for integrating the task structure and behavioral process (Sashkin & Burke, 1987).

OD INTERVENTIONS There is little comprehensive research on the interventions used by OD practitioners in the 1980s. One survey of research on OD practitioners' activities and interventions during that period was conducted by Fagenson and Burke

(1990). These authors indicate that practitioners in the 1980s knew more about strategy, structure, reward systems, corporate culture, human resource development, technology, and the nature of the business of their organizations. Practitioners were actively involved in strategic planning and management, structural change, and forecasting and establishing long-range goals. Fagenson and Burke attribute these foci to the highly competitive environment of the time. Fagenson and Burke (1990) categorized OD interventions used by practitioners into five domains: employee development, strategy development, management-style enhancement, culture change, and technology integration. The OD activities practitioners engaged in most frequently were management style enhancement and strategy development. Data analysis indicates that practitioners in the 1980s were involved in a greater number and more varied set of interrelated activities. Human process interventions also appeared to have been less prevalent in the 1980s. Their use nonetheless appears to be linked to shaping the culture of the organization and developing employees, rather than merely being isolated interventions. This finding is consistent with Sashkin and Burke's (1987) observation that the two basic approaches to OD—the human processual and techno-structural—appear to have merged to some extent. The empirical data offered by Fagenson and Burke prove again that OD practice was based on a systemic perspective and was used to integrate organizational activities. This observation leads to a practical question: What competencies are required in the OD intervention process?

OD COMPETENCIES. In an investigation, Eubanks, O'Driscoll, Hayward, Daniels, and Connor (1990) identified six clusters of behavioral competencies that were considered to be effective intervention behavior by OD practitioners and clients: contracting, data utilization, implementing the intervention, interpersonal skills, managing group processes, and maintaining the client relationship. In another study of effective consulting, O'Driscoll and Eubanks (1993) identified the competency areas of effective OD consultants as knowledge, consulting skills, conceptual abilities, interpersonal skills, technical skills, integrative skills, communication skills, self-awareness and personal impact awareness, and change and influence skills.

O'Driscoll and Eubanks (1993) point out that the consultants' ability to use relevant information (data utilization) and establish specific goals for the intervention were the two most significant contributors to both consultant and client perceptions of the overall success of an intervention. The findings of the two studies cited indicate that OD was not a technical effort focused on a specific event, but an ongoing effort merged into organizational activities. One implication is that OD practitioners are now required to have all understanding of organization knowledge so that their efforts can be fully integrated and used to cause substantial effects.

CRITICAL ISSUES FOR OD IN 2000 AND BEYOND

OD has been developing and used in organizations for nearly 50 years. OD has evolved from a laboratory experience for developing human potential to a series of extensive strategies and multivariate models for improving the functioning of people in a wide variety of organizations. OD has been considered by many to be a useful approach to organizational improvement. An extensive body of descriptive literature about OD is available. However, there are continuing questions about what OD is and how valuable it can be.

Is OD really an effective way of improving organizations? If OD really works, shouldn't there be, after four decades of effort, a widely accepted theory or at least systematic descriptions of ideal practices that are derived from an articulated theory or model? Why isn't use of OD more widespread, especially in schools and higher education? Is OD merely a generic term for all kinds of organizational improvement efforts? Does OD have a unique thrust? And how will these questions be addressed in the year 2000 and beyond?

Sashkin and Burke (1987) predicted three possible scenarios for OD in the future. The first scenario showed OD to be stagnating, retrenching, and imploding. The second scenario showed OD to be healthy and stable, entering a period of slow but steady and productive growth in which the primary task would be refinement and consolidation. The third scenario showed OD moving in new, exciting directions—structure, culture, and leadership. Sashkin and Burke (1987) predicted that the second or the third scenario had the highest chance of unfolding. Earlier Friedlander and Brown (1974) had argued that the future of OD rested in part on its values and the degree to which its practice, theory, and research would be congruent with those values. Their argument was made in the 1970s, but it still holds true. Expectations for OD in the future need to be grounded in the past. A brief review of OD criticisms may offer hints about future trends.

Criticisms of OD

In their comprehensive review of OD in schools, Fullan, Miles, and Taylor (1980) summarized the factors suggested in OD literature that raised questions about its future:

1. The lack of a real theory of OD.
2. Unclear goals and the lack of a coherent and comprehensive conception of just what constitutes OD.
3. Fundamental dilemmas and discrepancies among the values and assumptions of OD, and between espoused values, actual practices, and their consequences.
4. Superficial and partial uses of OD.
5. Using OD without proper diagnosis, entry, start-up procedures, time frames, and other necessary operating characteristics.
6. Lack of attention to OD research and evaluation and failure to substantiate some claims.
7. Limited documented diffusion of OD programs and results. In general, the problem can be characterized as the predominance of diffuse OD practice with limited or unknown rigor and limited exchange of information about the experience of OD (pp. 171–172).

Fullan, Miles, and Taylor (1980) also summarized scholars' criticisms of OD. Those criticisms range from exasperation at the number of OD definitions to questions about its underlying values. Major criticisms include:

1. OD consultants typically represent the control needs of management;
2. OD consultants function as restabilizing agents or protectors of the status quo, rather than as change agents;
3. most OD assumptions blind theories to the differences and pluralism of organizations and the real, structural sources of conflict; and
4. superficiality, commercialism, and mistaken assumptions about the consultant's role.

Those summaries were offered in the early 1980s, but are still valid. The future of OD depends on how well those dubious factors and criticisms are dealt with. In reviewing the development of OD in the past, the potentials for its future are equally worthy of discussion. The following are some of the contributions that might be expected from OD in the future.

Future Theory Building

Any organizational improvement effort should have a theoretical basis. To sustain OD efforts, relevant and internally consistent OD theories need to be built. Until now, there has been no widely accepted comprehensive OD theory, but that does not mean there is no chance of one emerging.

Researchers have been attempting to identify interventions that most benefit organizations, yet the evidence is not conclusive. In some ways, the failure to produce conclusive findings of effects limits the establishment of OD theories. O'Driscoll and Eubanks (1993) suggest that this failure is due to the fact that most OD studies have restricted themselves to comparisons between techniques (such as survey feedback, process consultation, technostructural design change, and management development) instead of studying the actual behaviors exhibited by consultants during the intervention process. Their claim is that the inability of research to identify key behaviors that lead to improved effectiveness has been a major inhibitor of the advancement of OD as a science and as a profession.

Action research appears to be an appropriate method to promote OD knowledge which may lead to the establishment of OD theory. By involving practitioners in OD research, more knowledge about the occurrence and processes of OD may be generated. In fact, action research has been suggested as a methodology that can contribute to the advancement of social theory (Whyte, 1989; Whyte, Greenwood, & Lazes, 1989).

Methodological refinement is a requisite of any theory. To build a theory, however, it is more important to refine the nature, assumptions, and values of the issues. A primary step in establishing an OD theory is to refine OD definitions. What are the nature and goals of OD and what constitutes OD? In the past, OD was always regarded as on application of behavioral science. Its purpose was to improve organizational effectiveness, or it was presented as a change model. OD was viewed as a value-free tool. OD is far from value-free, however. OD approaches include many explicit and implicit values, such as the importance of using training activities that are not based on job content and that are context-free. As other ways of viewing, such as critical theory and constructivism, become more prevalent in OD, the underlying values may be questioned more directly. For example, OD has emphasized personal growth. Should personal growth itself be the goal, or is it a means to achieve higher organizational performance? If OD is supposed to increase organizational effectiveness, what are the criteria of organizational effectiveness? Different perspectives may involve different organizational components and may lead to different OD configurations. In the past, this ambiguity in OD values may have been a key reason for the absence of a commonly accepted OD model or theory.

It is natural that those attempting to offer theoretical contributions address issues of the nature of OD and its values. Discussions of OD values must be related to the nature of organizations and be combined with the other disciplines of organizational science. This combination could lead to a better understanding of what constitutes OD and how OD should be used.

With a better understanding of the values and components of OD, greater rigor in research methodology will be possible. As problematic as it is, OD researchers will have to make their research designs more elaborate and conduct studies in natural settings. They will have to explore the relationships among OD components, OD variables, and other organizational variables in ways that facilitate interorganizational and cross-study comparisons. They will need to tighten study designs in order to determine what effects are caused by OD interventions. As more and more research appears, there will be a greater opportunity for the emergence of a commonly accepted OD theory.

Integration with Other Disciplines and Approaches

In the past, OD was based on applied behavioral science, which was characterized as objective and possessing a "neutral-value" perspective. Knowledge used in OD need not be limited to behavioral science, however. More direct use of knowledge from other disciplines could provide added insights. For example, ontological knowledge in philosophy could help people understand human values; phenomenology may help explain organizational life; and critical theories in sociology may help practitioners justify equity in organizations. As organizational activities become more diversified, more knowledge from other disciplines needs to be applied not only to design interventions, but to ask basic questions about the effects, values, and directions of OD.

The use of OD in organizations should not lead to the rejection of other approaches to organizational improvement, such as staff development, leadership development, and other management or change strategies. OD should instead be combined with them, in theory, research, and practice.

Sensitivity to Environmental Changes

As environments change more rapidly and competition among organizations becomes more intense, OD practitioners in the 1990s have had to be more alert to challenges from environmental factors. External changes in the 1990s include the changing demographics of the work force, continuous downsizing, mergers and acquisitions, international competition, and the resulting changes in organizational culture and climate (Offerman & Gowing, 1990). There also are increasing demands for "corporate responsibility." The shortsighted interest in stockholder's financial gains are increasingly being weighed against worker and community losses. It is a challenge for OD practitioners to face these changes. For example, Offerman and Gowing (1990) suggest several strategies for addressing environmental changes, such as optimizing organizational structure, restructuring work, maximizing the use of technology, and creating an effective work environment. They claim that "the challenge to future management is to maintain organizational competitiveness and productivity through new models of structural design and creative approaches to work assignments that maximize human and machine resources. Future managers must simultaneously deal with a new, diversified work force characterized by changing attitudes and values" (p. 101).

In the 1980s, OD came to be one approach to systemic change. Another approach to change, the concerns-based adoption model (Hall & Hord, 1987), came into its own during this same time period. Now, as organization-environment interactions become more, environmental factors, both internal and external, are taken into account more by all agents who are designing organizational activities. All OD practitioners in the 1990s are being asked to help organizations become more capable of adapting to and surviving in changing environments. They will be involved internally in combining workers' human values with organizational goals and connecting individuals' performances with organizational efficiency. Their external efforts will be oriented toward integrating structural processes with the nature of the business to increase the organization's competitive strengths and to demonstrate that the organization is comprised of responsible citizens. As the rate of environmental change increases, OD practitioners will not only have to help organizations adapt to existing environmental conditions, but will have to foresee the patterns and trends that are foreshadowing future changes.

Increasing Emphasis on Organizational Culture

A major paradigm shift has occurred with the movements, away from the 1970s focus on climate to the 1990s focus on culture. Where climate descriptions focused more on participants' perceptions of their place in and satisfaction with the organization, culture involves the participants' understanding of the multifaced characterization of what the organization values. Culture regulates participants' behavior and orients collective efforts toward achieving organizational goals. The significance of organizational culture in OD is that organizational culture influences members' attitudes and values. For example, organizational socialization is the process through which new members are indoctrinated and learn what is important in an organization (Schein, 1968). Schein (1985) advocates that organizational culture, by providing consensus among members, can help organizations adapt to the external environment and seek solutions to internal integration issues.

The emerging focus on culture has been triggered in part by use of systems perspectives in OD work (Sashkin & Burke, 1987). In the 1970s, OD consultants would use various surveys and self-assessment measures to determine the individual's perceptions of their organization and derive a scaling of the organizational climate through aggregation of the individual data (James & Jones, 1974). In the 1990s, there has been paradigm shift toward considering the culture of an organization, which requires reliance on qualitative methods for assessment and constructivist paradigms for interpretation (Stassens, 1993; Stassens & Vandenberghe, 1994).

There is general acknowledgement that cultural factors affect organizational performance; but more knowledge is needed about organizational culture as a concept, techniques that influence it, and variables used in assessing it. Definition of salient components of organizational cultures are needed, and classification of the types of cultures that are most favorable to certain kinds of organization functions would be instructive. People need to know how to influence cultural changes in organizations. Thus, OD researchers need to continue the exploration of organizational culture, understanding the nature of organizational culture and the role it plays in bringing about and shaping organizational change. OD practitioners need to give greater consideration to cultural factors when formulating their strategic actions.

As one example of the increasing emphasis on organizational culture, Burke (1994) advocates the use of OD to bring about changes in its character. He explains that the direction of change should be toward an organizational culture with the following characteristics:

1. Growth and development of organization members is just as important as making a profit or meeting the budget.
2. Equal opportunity and fairness for people in the organization is commonplace; it is the rule rather than the exception.
3. Managers exercise their authority more participatively than unilaterally and arbitrarily, and authority is associated more with knowledge and competence than role or status.
4. Cooperative behavior is rewarded more frequently than competitive behavior.
5. Organization members are kept informed or at least have access to information, especially concerning matters that directly affect their jobs or them personally.
6. Members feel a sense of ownership of the organization's mission and objectives.
7. Conflict is dealt with openly and systematically, rather than ignored, avoided, or handled in a typical win-lose fashion.
8. Rewards are based on a system of both equality-fairness and equity-merit.
9. Organization members are given as much autonomy and freedom to do their respective jobs as possible, to ensure both a high degree of individual motivation and accomplishment of organizational objectives (Burke, 1994, pp. 196-197).

Burke's description offers practitioners a prescription for cultural changes, but it is about the achieved cultural status of organizations. OD practitioners need to understand how to orient the culture of an organization as well. Different organizations have different types of organizational culture issues. Determining an intervention game plan to develop a particular organization's culture will be contingent upon the specifics of that situation. In some settings, traditional types of OD interventions may work well. In other settings, leadership development or classic sensitivity training may be more effective. Since organizations are multivariate, plotting their development requires being able to assess a number of possible leverage points and having access to a broad portfolio of possible interventions.

There is a great need to understand more about how to customize OD interventions and achieve a better fit with the needs and goals of specific organizations. This is not just a local problem. Most current approaches to OD consultation have been built on models and techniques that were developed within the United States. The applicability of these models to other cultural contexts has not yet been determined. Since there are more and more multinational organizations, there is an increasing need for research on cultural similarities and differences and how to bring about change through OD interventions (O'Driscoll & Eubanks, 1993).

OD Evaluation and Research Methods

The future of OD will be largely determined by the availability, or absence, of convincing evidence of its effectiveness. With the continued emphasis on downsizing, global competitiveness, and budget cuts, the cost of OD functions will be scrutinized as never before. There will be continuing questions about whether OD is marginal fluff and what the return on investment is likely to be in the next quarter. Its continued viability will depend in large part on careful definition of aims, the use of economic means, and efficient measures of effects. In the OD literature, there is no lack of testimony about effectiveness, but more rigorous measures of direct effects are lacking. Studies need to document how OD efforts bring about benefits and in what ways. Studies should also be designed to document that the effects were not due to other factors. The measurement difficulties obviously increase as OD has become oriented more toward organization-wide processes, systemic changes, and long-term effects. System effects and the related benefits cannot be calculated easily or by simplistic indicators such as short-term profits. More advanced measures of OD effectiveness are needed, keeping in mind the need to be cost-effective. A critical key to accomplishing this goal will be to conceptualize OD assumptions, processes, and purposes more carefully; in other words, to be theory-based.

Needed Rigor in Research

Since there is such an extensive history of OD practice and applications in a wide array of settings, it would seem reasonable to expect that there is an equally extensive set of research and evaluation reports about its effects. This is not the case, unfortunately. We suspect that, as with many innovative efforts, most of the "innovation" experts (i.e., OD consultants) were so busy with their clients that there was little time left over to develop rigorous measures and conduct systematic studies. Whatever the reason, there are still far too few studies of OD, and most of the reported studies are of one particular intervention strategy and for one client setting, rather than multisite, multivariate samples. Controlled evaluation studies involving large samples and many sites to determine the effectiveness of particular interventions or to determine the ultimate consequences of OD projects are few in number.

Research Design Needs

One early synthesis of OD studies was reported by Porras and Berg (1978). They analyzed 35 studies that had assessed the impact of OD activities. These authors started by identifying five sets of activities which make up their definition of OD: (1) laboratory training with a process emphasis, (2) laboratory training with a task emphasis, (3) managerial grid or grid OD, (4) survey feedback, and (5) complementary techniques (techniques that are used in conjunction with one of the first four). Porras and Berg offer two well-thought out schema of research variables, one for process and one for outcomes. They concluded that there was little systematic evidence that showed overall effects of OD. For example: "One common assumption—that the most important effect of OD is to make people happier and more satisfied—was not supported by the data, which showed that several types of satisfaction measures changed relatively infrequently in OD programs" (p. 263). The effects on task and people-oriented variables were the same, and the effects of organizational processes and outcomes were the same.

These last two findings are particularly interesting in light of the expressed intent of OD to influence the people processes. The study analyses did show an impact primarily on the individual level of process variables, not on the overall organizational process. As with most OD studies, this one points out some of the definitional (What is change?), methodological (What kind of change is being measured?), and related design issues (What are the systematic biases in pre-measures?) that are embedded in OD research.

Miles, Fullan, and Taylor (1978) conducted a large sample analysis of the extent of implementation and sustained use of OD by school districts in Canada and the United States OD programs had been carried out. They first reviewed the OD literature about the assumptions, values, goals, and definitions of OD, its operating characteristics and effects, and the future of OD. They then conducted two empirical studies of OD practice in school districts. The first empirical study involved OD consultants from 76 school districts. Multiple regression analyses were carried out to determine the influence of district characteristics and various operating factors on the outcomes of OD efforts. The second empirical study contained three case studies, which were employed to analyze in more detail different types of OD programs and their uses. The systematic studies represented the first large-scale quantitative analysis of OD programs in school districts, and generated some significant findings. For example, OD programs were more frequently found in large districts; OD programs and more chance to continue after being carried out for a year and half; structured, system, and task-oriented approaches to organizational functioning were evidently more effective; and more individualistic (personnel development) or indeterminate approaches and accountability approaches were less effective.

Berg (1984) provided another meta-analysis of OD research based on Fullan, Miles, and Taylor's (1980) review article about school OD, articles critical of OD, empirical studies of OD, and interviews with OD researchers. Berg's meta-analysis was intended to "shed light on the question of OD's applicability to schools from as many angles as possible" (p. 1). It generated significant findings which might promote understandings of OD practice in schools. The major findings included:

1. OD has its roots in social psychology and is influenced by sociotechnical approaches,
2. an OD project is shaped by the interaction of the integral parts of a school and its environment,
3. OD is a process strategy rather than a product strategy for bringing about change,
4. an OD project has effects on school activities such as improved communication and more open relations,
5. there are no general, fundamental criteria by which OD's effects on schools can be measured, and
6. views on the future of OD in North American schools are at present in a state of confusion.

Miles, Fullan, and Taylor's (1978) and Berg's (1984) review articles provide a detailed description of the state of the art of school OD and the achievements of OD research through the early 1980s. Their analyses highlight the need for further OD research in school settings from a microperspective, i.e., the processes of OD and the interactions among the elements related to OD activities. In addition, research is needed that examines development and change from a systems perspective.

An early, well-designed study by Kimberly and Nielsen (1975) examined the impact of an OD effort on organizational performance. In this study, a model of causal linkages was applied to a planned change in an automotive division of a large, multiplant, multidivision corporation. The OD program entailed the standard steps of initial diagnosis, team-skills training, data collection, data confrontation, action planning, team building, and intergroup building. Significant positive changes were found in target group attitudes and perceptions, quality of output, and profit. No change in productivity was found, however. The inference was that productivity was "outside the direct control of plant management" (p. 191).

Kimberly and Nielsen's study is highlighted here since it addressed many of the necessary aspects of study design and was well-conceived to test the effects of an OD intervention effort. Although the authors studied only one plant, there were 2,600 hourly workers and 200 salaried employees. This was a sufficient sample size with which to have confidence in statistical findings. The researchers documented the OD change program. They developed a conceptual model using causal linkages to construct testable hypotheses. They related their study to the literature and had four years of data from the plant to use in the analyses. This study, unfortunately, is deficient in the same way as so many others. No information is provided about the quality of the questionnaires! No information about reliability, validity, or conceptual basis of the measures is presented.

The weakness in the Kimberly and Nielsen study seems to be symptomatic of OD research on intervention practices. There are a plethora of questionnaires and surveys for use in training and other OD interventions. At the same time, there is a dearth of basic statistical information about reliability and validity of these measures. One direct implication of this situation is that although OD, in one form or another, has been practiced for over 50 years, there is very limited empirical information to support or refute its impact and effectiveness.

The Positive-Findings Bias Debate

A consequence of the lack of rigorous studies is the risk of over generalizing from the findings of single studies. One indication of this is the increasing debate about the potential of a "positive-findings bias" in OD evaluations. Terpstra (1981) proposed that there is a negative relationship between the methodological rigor of an evaluation and the reported success of the intervention being evaluated. In other words, the higher the quality of the evaluation design, the less the relationship with participant positive reports of the intervention's results. Since that time, other studies have been designed to examine Terpstra's positive-finding bias hypothesis. Some researchers have reported inconsistent findings (Bullock & Svyantek, 1983; Neuman, Edwards, & Raju, 1989; Woodman & Wayne, 1985). Others have reported findings that are consistent with a positive-findings bias (Golembiewski & Sun, 1990; Guzzo, Jette, & Katzell, 1985).

Roberts and Robertson (1992) conducted a meta-analysis using 58 published studies. They reported that the approach used to determine the rigor of an evaluation is critical; and it may not be possible to develop rigorous measures that will meet everyone's expectations. Since such a measure becomes the independent variable in the positive-bias question, the findings that follow come under question as well. The bottom line on positive bias, then, is that OD practitioners and evaluators of OD initiatives need to be sensitive to the potential for positive bias creeping into their measures, study designs, and intervention practices. Close attention must be given to maintaining an objective perspective in weighing the potential and effects of OD efforts.

The Role of OD Consultants

OD is intended to cause long-term systemic changes; it is not a one-shot event. While OD can indeed make a positive difference, it still should be integrated with other organizational processes. In the past, external consultants provided OD interventions. Consultants typically withdrew after completion of a contract or termination of a project. As understanding of the potential importance of OD is recognized, OD needs to be seen less as a tool to manage crises and more as part of regular organizational activity.

If OD is to be a regular part of organizations, then institutionalization of the function is necessary. In other words, if we are to have "learning organizations" (Senge, 1990), OD resources and practices should be incorporated into the permanent structures and functions of organizations. To accomplish this goal, some of the traditional functions of external consultants should be handled by *internal* OD units. External OD consultants would still be needed to provide consultations to all levels of the organization, and to conduct some formal training sessions. Much of the necessary day-to-day coaching, planning, training and monitoring should be done internally, however. In other words, supervisors in more traditional assignments and roles should be taking on more of the internal OD functions. In addition, there is need for permanent roles for internal OD specialists.

This proposed approach is being tried in some U.S. school districts such as Gwinnett County, Georgia and Douglas County, Colorado. Two of the key challenges in this approach—successful in school districts as well as in businesses—have to do with the strategic perspectives of the people who become internal OD resources and their ability to be credible to most, if not all, levels of the organization. Too often, the selected internal consultants have many of the technical skills, but are unable to develop a strategic perspective of the organization. There also is a never-ending challenge to work in ways that develop and maintain credibility with employees at all levels. Internal consultants tend to be more effective with certain levels of employees and certain functions. These two potential gap areas then become the focal points for the external OD resource persons.

A priority task for all OD consultants will continue to be the attempt to infuse OD into organizational life. In other words, the culture needs to realize how and why OD is an integral strand of ongoing organizational activity along with manufacturing and sales, or teaching and learning. In these settings, the expertise required of consultants will not be limited to OD knowledge and services. OD consultants will have to be familiar with all aspects of the organization's business. It is possible that managers will take on some of the aspects of the traditional role of OD consultants. This may be more possible as the technology used in organizations becomes more advanced. It will require major rethinking of basic elements of the OD process and consultant role, however. New challenges can be envisioned, such as the needed ability to work across levels within an organization, issues of confidentiality, and accepting the manager as OD consultant. One way to begin integrating internal OD in school districts would be to restructure the traditional role of staff development. For example, in Douglas County, Colorado, the internal OD capacity is being developed by evolving the role of the director of staff development and placing a full-time, highly trained master teacher and OD specialist, called a building resource teachers (BRT), in each school. This internal OD team is linked with several external OD consultants. This set of internal roles partnering with an external set of consultant resources represents a strong, effective, and long-term viable model for schools to institutionalize an OD capacity.

THE RELATIONSHIPS OF OD AND SUPERVISION

The extensive review of the history and sampling of current issues of OD has been presented here for a number of important reasons. One major purpose is to point out that there is a larger organizational development context that needs to be acknowledged and understood by school supervisors. Also, the role and place of supervision, as currently defined in practice, is extremely narrow and limiting. Personnel in schools and school districts desperately need to develop a better understanding of their organization's functioning. They also need to be more skilled in using the processes and frameworks of OD. Although rarely mentioned, the current organizational health of most school districts and schools is problematic. The demand for change is constant. For example, the relentless pressure to downsize (Berg, Hall, & Difford, 1996) and the demands to respond to the never-ending cascade of new state and federal mandates require all school administrators to have higher levels of competencies in facilitating organization functioning and in developing more healthy organization cultures. No one internally is representing these capacities, however, and few school districts are investing in use of external OD resources. This situation is an opportunity! There is a clear need to redefine the function of supervision and the role of supervisors.

At the risk of being painted as heretics, we suggest that serious consideration be given to expanding the operational functions and roles of supervisors beyond the traditional contents of curriculum and instruction to facilitating schools and school districts in continuously developing as effectively functioning organizations. This change would not be easily accomplished nor would it be without risk. The current situation is not constructive either, however. There is a desperate need. This is a time when transforming changes are essential (Hall, 1994). The need, the opportunity, and the potential are inspiring.

In theory, a number of OD concepts and processes are similar to those of supervision. In practice, unfortunately, the intersection between the two fields seems to be minimal. In theory, supervisors in educational organizations should be concerned about the continuing development of not only individuals, but groups and the organization as a whole. In theory, OD consultants should be concerned about the effectiveness of curricular and instructional practices. In most education settings, there are factors that inhibit supervisors from viewing the whole organization and generic external OD consultants addressing teaching and learning. For example, the pressure to complete required annual evaluation cycles on individuals can leave supervisors with little or no time for thought or action targeted to groups or development of the whole organization. On the OD consultant side, the contract with the client may not include sorely needed work with individuals, or there may be a conflict of interest that prohibits the implementation of certain development efforts. There also is the likely possibility that the OD consultant contract will end at the diagnosis stage, perhaps before whole organization development efforts materialize. Depending on which definition or model of OD is being used and which definition or model of supervision is being used, the extent of overlap between supervision and OD can vary greatly

Aspects of an Expanded Role

To help in considering an expanded role for OD and supervision. We wish to examine some additional aspects of these different roles and the potential categories of OD/supervision targets. First of all, note that supervision has been considered to be an *internal* function, while the OD consultant has been seen as *external.* The stereotypical OD consultant traditionally focussed on *group process* and the related individual skills in a generic sense, while the stereotypical supervisor focuSed on *teaching* and *curriculum skills* for individuals. In the ideal setting, the internal supervisor and the external OD consultant would not only be aware of each other's work, they would act as a team in what they do. As an internal-external OD team, they should guide the development of the whole system.

There are some other factors that are worthy of consideration. For example, the concepts of "climate" and "culture" need to be addressed. In the past, climate was a key target of the work of OD consultants. As James and Jones (1974) stated, traditionally this aspect of the OD field was absent from careful concept definition and rigor in empirical studies. To bring order, James and Jones (1974) proposed that distinctions be made among three concepts: (1) *the situation:* actual descriptions of the setting; (2) *psychological climate:* the individual's perception of the climate; and (3) *organizational climate:* the sum of the individual perceptions. When offering training, developing measurement devices, or evaluating an organization, it is critical that there be clarity about which of these concepts is being measured, and which is thought to be the center of attention for training. In the past, the instruments too often did not measure what was espoused (i.e., validity was lacking), there was no evidence to indicate whether the measures were consistent in scores across repeated assessments (i.e., estimates of reliability were missing), and/or the instruments were used without an understanding that they were measuring something else (i.e., it measures very well something different from what it was reputed to).

Organizational culture has emerged as a focus in the 1990s. This approach is heavily based in the constructivist or interpretivist perspective. From this frame, the focus is not on the "facts" but the participants' interpretations of the actions and events that go on in organizational life. From this perspective, it is not what the supervisor/OD consultant does that counts as much as how the client interprets the actions. Each individual develops an interpretation. Through interactions, there is "social construction" of a group interpretation. Assessing aspects of culture requires the use of more qualitative techniques, which brings a new round of methodological issues such as trustworthiness and veracity (for a good example of assessing school culture, see the work of Stassens & Vandenberghe, 1994).

FEATURES OF A HYBRID OD/SUPERVISION ROLE

The descriptions above have highlighted key aspects of the relationship between OD and supervision, implying that it is possible to make supervision and OD complement each other. The following are some of the features and implications of having a hybrid OD/supervision role:

1. Focusing on promoting continuous organizational renewal and personal growth instead of focusing on either of them individually.

Supervision is traditionally used to promote individual members' growth. The relationship of the individual to organizational growth has been implicit. From a systems perspective, any organizational element influences and is influenced by others. Personal growth and organizational renewal are intertwined. This means that supervisors, in promoting personal growth, should take into account organizational renewal. Organizational renewal provides the necessity and favorable conditions for personal growth. Personal growth will similarly lead to organizational renewal. Organizational renewal and personal growth are matters of long-term processes, rather than occasional events.

2. Increasing problem-solving abilities of organizations and individuals instead of solving problems for them.

OD consultants have to withdraw when an OD contract terminates. OD consultants thus need to help organizations increase their problem-solving abilities so that organizations can solve their problems in spite of the consultants' absence (Schmuck and Runkel, 1994). Using the OD perspective in supervision, supervisors should focus their efforts on increasing members' problem-solving abilities, rather than offering prescriptions to them or continuing to remain central in their development of each new set of skills. Given the job complexity and the increasing professional specialization, as well as the time available, supervisors cannot offer prescriptions or be the primary resource for all emerging problems. Supervisors need to help members develop their skills at analyzing problems and finding solutions. Supervisors should also promote collaboration among members. In this way, supervisors are helping members to solve problems independently and in developing networks to others who can become resources in the future.

3. Integrating organizational goals with individuals' psychological needs instead of overly focusing on either of them.

In the early stages of OD evolution, satisfaction of workers' psychological needs was seen as a means to improve organizational effectiveness. As occupational dignity and job autonomy are emphasized more, job satisfaction is no longer seen merely as a means to organizational goals, but as something valuable in itself. Workers' psychological needs are seen as human values issues. In the OD field, consultants have been trying to integrate organizational goals with workers' psychological needs. Applying this perspective in supervision means that supervisors should deal with the achievement of organizational goals *and* workers' psychological needs—an integration of both. Supervisors have to address how workers feel about their jobs. They should also help members develop a sense of meaningfulness and ownership in the performance of the whole organization. Increasing the workers' sense of meaningfulness and ownership will help them integrate into the organization and derive a sense of satisfaction from the achievement of organizational goals.

4. Establishing a favorable culture instead of relying on close inspection.

Organizational culture is seen by OD consultants as a condition which can increase organization members' psychological welfare. It is also a tool used to stimulate organizational learning activities and to preserve OD intervention effects. Organizational culture enables members to understand what is valued by the organization and what behaviors are acceptable. It generates an invisible force to regulate members' behavior. A favorable organizational culture orients members' behavior toward the achievement of organizational goals. Cultural effects could be used by supervisors to improve organizational supervision. Supervisors could design and establish a favorable organizational culture which promotes members' learning activities and encourages mutual supervision and coaching among members. As a favorable culture develops, there will be "invisible supervisors" leading members' performance toward the achievement of organizational goals. Cultural effects can take the place of supervisors' close inspection.

5. Focusing on planned and long-term efforts instead of offering one-shot training.

OD is a planned, long-term effort to cause systemic change in organizations, and its greater effects do not appear immediately following an OD intervention. It is possible that the external OD consultant has withdrawn from the organization before the larger effects of the OD interventions are observed. Through careful design and implementation, OD effects can last a long time. This approach could be applied to supervision. Since supervisors are internal agents and will stay in their organizations longer, we can expect effective supervision to accumulate long-term macrosystem effects. Supervisors with an OD perspective would perform supervision as planned and with a long-term perspective. Effective supervisors would first formulate long-term goals and then design effective supervision procedures. As with OD, we would not expect effects at the macrosystem level from supervision to occur immediately, but over time we would see organizational improvements.

6. Enhancing efficiency through overall structural change instead of relying merely on personal growth.

Organizational structure can be thought of as the formalized interaction patterns among organization members. Organizational structure defines the division of labor, work relationships, and the roles members play. A well-designed structure specifies job descriptions for each member and thus increase coordination and integration among members' tasks. Structural change can be employed by OD consultants to generate systemic change and could be used by supervisors to promote organizational improvement. Applying the idea of structural change to the hybrid role of OD/supervision would mean that the structural placement of the OD/supervision role and function would need careful consideration. It would no longer be the responsibility of one person or one level in the organization. There would also need to be substantive input from the OD/supervision specialist about the design of any and all structural changes.

7. Provoking changes in participants' value systems and assumptions instead of merely modifying behavior.

Members' behavior in organizations is decided by their value systems and their assumption about the organization. To cause organizational change, OD consultants try to develop new value assumptions and process systems among members through involvement in organizational learning activities. Supervisors could provide assistance in this effort. They may help members reflect on organizational goals, organizational processes, and the meaning of their performance. Through this process, members may modify their value systems and assumptions and, over time, develop a consensus on organizational goals and the means to reach them.

8. Applying behavioral science knowledge to supervision instead of depending on subjective judgment.

A common criticism of supervision is that supervisors tend to evaluate members' performance or offer prescriptions based on their subjective judgments. Often, workers consider supervisors' judgments to be inadequate or irrelevant to the work environment. This criticism could be avoided through the application of behavioral science knowledge to supervision. Behavioral science knowledge has long been used by OD consultants to understand and improve organizational processes, and this approach has proved to be useful. In supervision, behavioral science knowledge may help workers understand and analyze organizational problems and formulate alternatives to solving the problems.

9. Playing supervisory roles as catalysts instead of as monitors.

OD consultants play their roles as catalysts in an OD effort. They withdraw from the organizations when contracts terminate. In the long run, organizations are expected to continue operating at a higher level without the consultants' presence. Supervisors are not expected to monitor members' performance all the time, but act as catalysts in promoting growth in job skills. The hybrid OD/supervisors would enable organizations to keep growing through organizational learning activities and to make individuals capable of self-improvement.

CAN OD BECOME A CHANGE MODEL FOR SUPERVISION, OR WILL OD CONTINUE TO BE ONLY A SOURCE OF INTERVENTIONS?

In summary, we raise three questions, each of which is in line with the themes that have been developed in this review. First of all, historically OD has been presented as a change model. For most of its practitioners and for most supervisors, however, OD has been used mainly as a source of interventions. In other words, instead of using the concepts and models of OD as a way to think about the development of schools and school districts *as organizations*, supervisors and staff developers have turned to OD as a source of training exercises and gimmicks for teacher workshops; only to a lesser extent has OD been the content for administrative in-service sessions and been used in long-term plans for developing schools and school districts as organizations.

The second theme is to consider how the practice of supervision and the role of supervisors would be transformed if OD became the basis for the job description and action. To what extent is it possible and desirable for school districts and schools to develop an internal OD capacity? If it was done, to what extent would OD become a responsibility of all professional personnel? What would be the role and capacity of the internal professional supervisor/OD consultant? How would a school district be organized to house an OD capacity? Would the OD role reside in a new central office position or be assumed as a new responsibility by existing role groups? Can a new conception of how to staff the OD function be conceived when the majority of personnel in the organization are education professionals? In business, this capacity typically resides in a separate quasi-independent office that reports directly to the CEO.

The third theme that needs to be addressed has to do with the ethics of supervision in an OD context. In most schools and school districts, supervision is currently seen as a nonjudgmental and "safe" process. What are the potential problems if serious attention is given to expanding the role and function of supervision to address development of the organization? Could supervision professionals, who tend to be former classroom teachers and not managers, assume an effective and credible role as internal OD professionals? How would confidentiality be defined and maintained? How would the leadership in a school district go about creating readiness to consider establishing an OD function? To what extent can school districts and schools consider, and be allowed by their many constituencies to consider transforming themselves, through a serious organizational development effort?

OD and the Change Literature

Throughout the history of OD, the proponents have presented it as a change model. They strongly believe that the organization whose members have mastered the many generic individual and group skills of OD will be more effective and successful at dealing with change. OD training and consultation are thus intended to bring about change through the acquisition of individual skills and group which will be helpful to the organization in accomplishing its many work-related changes. In this way of thinking, OD "interventions" are designed to develop generic skills which the members of an organization can then use to meet whatever substantive changes come their way.

As a change model, OD is one among many. There are various other theories and models of change that could be, and perhaps should be, considered (e.g. diffusion, Rogers,

1995; linkage, Havelock, 1971; concerns-based, Hall & Hord, 1987). These other models offer a number of additional factors and concepts that should be considered when engaged in a change effort. Based on a review of the citations in the OD literature, it appears that most OD proponents are not reading related change literature. With the notable exception of a few of the early OD experts, such as Miles (1971), there has been little cross linkage between the world of OD and change model experts in other fields such as education, business, communication, rural sociology, technology transfer, dissemination, and knowledge utilization.

Knowledge and understanding of the concepts from the general change literature would have been helpful in explaining some of the findings from OD consultation experience and research. For example, many do not recognize that OD in and of itself is not a change model; instead, it is an *innovation.* When the OD consultant arrives and the training sessions begin, the *consultant* may think of his or her training as *interventions. To the participants,* however, the consultant *and* the training are an *innovation.* The participants are being asked to learn and implement a new set of skills and tasks (i.e., to make a change). We hypothesize that one of the main reasons that OD efforts have resulted in so little long-term change (Miles, Fullan, & Taylor, 1978) is the failure of OD consultants to understand and appreciate that these efforts are an innovation and, as such, the prospective *users* of their innovation will experience the phenomenon of implementation.

Just as with any other innovation, the "adoption and implementation" of OD in each new organization will result in the participants going through the same stages of concern and levels of use (Hall & Hord, 1987) that occur with any other innovation. Thus, the change process for implementation of OD must be planned and developed in the same way as is necessary for any other change. An early study which linked the use of OD and change process was reported by Ruch and Hall (1982). In this case, the change was reorganization of a school of education. The change process was diagnosed and monitored using stages of concern and OD was used as the source of interventions.

Another implication for OD from the change literature, in this case using the diffusion perspective, has to do with the characteristics of "early adopters." It seems reasonable to hypothesize that many of the organizations in the past that "adopted" OD were led by what the rural sociologists would call "innovators" (Rogers, 1995). These individuals are the first to adopt new ideas, as well as the first to drop them for the next new idea. The innovators make it easy for developers of innovations (e.g., OD consultants) to make their first sales look easy. Unfortunately for the OD consultant, those that have studied the characteristics of adopters point out that only 2.5 percent of the potential users are innovators, and they are always on the look for the next new idea. Long-term institutionalization of change within an organization and widespread use across many organizations require that developers of innovations, including OD, must figure out how to work with other categories of adopters such as the "early adopters" and the "early majority." Without moving on to these more stable and careful categories of adopters, there will be little long-term sustained use of an innovation. The initial rate of adoption may be high (as was the case for OD in the 1970s), but in the long run—say, 50 years—sales will decline unless the innovation is customized to fit the perceived needs of the adopter categories in larger numbers.

Transforming Internal Roles and Structures to Incorporate OD

The proposal to incorporate OD as an internal function that is closely tied to supervision is not a new idea. For example, Pajak addressed some of the important implications for supervision and OD in 1982. He placed heavy emphasis on the importance of considering the systemic nature of organizations:

What may first come to mind is the direct application of the principles of group dynamics to the immediate task, such as in the formation and development of teams of teachers for the purpose of collaboratively improving instruction. But the issue is not simply one of applying technique, for a fundamental assumption of OD is the interdependence of elements and processes within a system. That is, a change in any single element or process within a system such as an organization cannot be easily confined and is believed likely to result in changes in other parts of the system as well (p. 245).

Pajak's point is an important one, and one that is missed by too many teachers and supervisors. Teachers do not exist in isolation in their classrooms; whether aware of it or not, they are part of a very large organizational system (Lowham, 1995). The decision to systematically add a new function to the operation of that system—for example, an internal OD capacity—will have systemwide implications.

Where ever the OD function is placed in the organization, the emphasis in our proposal is not to view OD as a simple additional element of instructional supervision as has been done in the past. Our emphasis is on establishing an internal capacity to enhance organizational processes and the organizational culture. Perhaps creating an OD office and placing it on the organizational chart would work; or there could be a reorganization of current district functions, especially the staff development and curriculum development roles. Another possibility would be to develop OD skills in all administrators. An important addition to this last option would be to draw in teachers and develop their understanding of and skill with OD concepts.

The strong and coherent systemwide OD emphasis that we envision would have a number of special characteristics. First of all, all members of the organization become knowledgeable about *organizational* processes and the skills and functions used to enhance development *of the organization.* Wallin and Berg (1983) defined this as the distinction between organizational development in schools and developing schools as organizations. A large portion of the past OD efforts in schools has been directed at developing teachers in classrooms, the design of in-service training, and enhancing school climate. There has not been a concerted effort to develop the capacity and functioning of schools and school districts as organizations.

In a number of ways, the typical past application of OD in schools is a mutation of the basic designs and intents of OD.

As frequently happens in education, an idea from business and industry was transferred to schools and applied to perceived problems. In the case of OD, skill exercises have been transferred to invigorate workshops for teachers and principals. What has been lost in the transfer is the emphasis on development of the organization. As noted previously, there is a tendency among educators to underestimate, if not downright ignore, the fact that they are members of an organization. Along with this denial is lack of interest in or understanding of the need to develop teachers and administrators as members of a large organizational system.

It will be important to establish a set of goals (and perhaps standards) for how educators and their organizations can best function and be developed. With these ideas explicated, it will then be possible to address how the supervision function can be realigned with the traditional OD function to create a hybrid set of roles and capabilities. The placement of these hybrid functions in the organizational structure will take some experimentation and will most certainly be based on the personalities and skills of individuals. But the overall goal should be to institutionalize an internal capacity in schools and school districts that combines the functions of instructional supervision with continuing development of the capabilities of the organization. In many ways, what we are talking about for school systems is what is done currently in some human resource offices of large corporations. In addition to the personnel and training functions, some human resource units also include OD consultants that offer development workshops and serve as internal consultants to all levels of the organization. Since this function does not currently exist in school systems, one way to introduce it would be to incorporate it into the transformation of the traditional supervision roles and functions.

Ethical Issues and OD in School Systems

We conclude this chapter with the topic of ethics. Little tends to be said about ethics, unfortunately. Another part of the legacy of the first 50 years of OD, however, are authors who have considered ethical issues in depth. In a 1979 article, Miles examined ethical issues in terms of OD interventions. He cautioned:

Though OD practitioners show few signs of wanting to clarify and promulgate ethical guidelines, more precision about ethics is needed. When we talk about OD, we are talking about people's work lives and how they live them; we are talking about the expenditure of a good deal of time and money; and we are talking about an emerging profession which is trying to deal with ancient and near-intractable issues in a competent way. The stakes are not small (p. 1).

Miles divided his analysis of ethical issues in OD interventions into five categories: (1) prior to the OD program, (2) goal setting, (3) the targets of change, (4) the means of intervention, and (5) the results of OD interventions. His questions and discussion in relation to each of these elements are still timely and relevant to the themes of this chapter. For example, whose interests are to be served in a goal setting: the total system or a particular subsystem? Will individual or organizational priorities take precedence? Will the OD program

bring about changes or serve the status quo? In examining ethical issues related to the targets of change, Miles (1979) observed, "Thus questions of how much 'say' the targets of change have in the very decision to designate them as targets and the character of the 'informed consent' involved in their decision to participate in intervention events are quite crucial" (p. 6). For example, do subordinates (e.g. teachers) really have a choice when a superior (e.g. principal) says that participation in an OD workshops is *voluntary*?

Another set of ethical issues is raised by the works of Victor and Cullen (1988) and others who have been studying what they call "ethical work climate." In these studies, the focus is not those aspects of typical organizational practices and procedures that have ethical content. These studies entail an analysis of how employees answer the metaphorical question "What *should* I do?" Their answers are based on their perceptions of what is prescribed, implied, and permitted by the organization in regard to moral obligations.

As part of the organizational development of schools and school districts—especially in this time of downsizing and restructuring, being "mean and lean," and responding to major policy changes, such as the release from court-ordered busing—answering the question "What should I do?" has special import. How can the organizational culture of schools be developed so that the traditional moral standards of the educator are not lost in the clash with the popular morality of corporate raiders and others who are focused solely on the here and now? What are the necessary ethical imperatives of managers and executives in education systems that need to be developed and preserved? How can the inevitable clash between the so-called idealism of educators be balanced with the urgencies of today's problems and the needs of clients and stakeholders?

One important part of answering these ethical questions is described by Murphy (1989), who suggested that "ethical business practices stem from ethical corporate cultures" (p. 81). There is no simple way to develop and nurture a corporate culture so that it emphasizes the importance of ethical considerations. A number of strategies can be implemented toward this end, however, including training workshops, ethics audits, corporate credos, and codes tailored to the specific needs of each functional area.

One of the important points to emphasize in any discussion of ethics is that we are not talking about absolutes. Instead, ethics deal with a *process* of examination and development of a value position relative to organizational behavior. Pruzan and Thyssen (1990) have addressed what they call "organizational ethics" with this frame in mind. They argue that ethics are "rationalistic." In these areas, there are no universal norms. Their second point is that the development of an ethical position is the result of interaction and open dialogue. They further advocate the use of "ethical accounting statements." These statements are developed through dialogue by the organization's stakeholders and are used in an annual audit which is conducted by the stakeholders.

Ethical accounting statements have been used in corporations in Denmark (Pruzan & Thyssen, 1990). If this process was applied to education organizations, the various stakeholders would engage in a process to develop the statements and to do the annual accounting. Pruzan and Thyssen point out important provisions in this approach: (1) management must itself live up to the statement; (2) the statements should be built into employment policy; and (3) management must support stakeholders in their ethical dilemmas.

In this brief discussion, our emphasis has been less on identifying specific ethical issues and more on highlighting some of the trends in the considerations of ethics in OD. Much less has been written about ethical issues, unfortunately. There are, however, some interesting and promising trends, as we have highlighted in the brief descriptions of ethical cultures and ethical accounting statements. Regardless of the amount of effort those engaged in traditional supervision practices wish to assign to OD, it is imperative that they find time to consider the ethical dimension of their practice. In this time of limited resources and short-term perspectives, the professionals must assert themselves and catalyze the necessary dialogue around the basic question "What should we do?"

CONCLUSION

For 50 years, the field of organizational development (OD) has offered much to supervision, especially in the form of concepts and skill exercises for individuals and groups. The field of OD interestingly has been unable to offer stability in terms of definition of itself. The operational definition of OD has varied from decade to decade. The field of OD has masterfully evolved and adapted to meet the shifting dynamics, needs, and characteristics of its customers. There has, unfortunately, been very limited empirical research on OD processes and effects, especially at the organization and system levels. Thus, at this time we know a great deal about philosophic assumptions, and there is a very large inventory of strategy and tactic OD-style interventions. We know much less about how to combine and evolve the resources of OD to develop the culture of organizations. Still, the frames offered by different OD models and

experts for considering basic aspects of organization functioning and the vital role of group and individual processes are crucial to improving the functioning of all organizations, including schools and school districts.

This chapter has two primary purposes: (1) to review the evolution of the definition of OD and highlight a few of the many conceptions, practices, and research findings that represent the 50 year legacy of OD; and (2) to propose that the field of supervision needs to be transformed from its singular focus on teacher's instructional development by incorporating a systematic emphasis on *organizational* development through training and coaching of all district employees. We would further suggest that this transformation should involve broad consideration of ways in which elements of OD could be of value to most if not all education stakeholders.

In many ways, a number of the current innovative efforts are skirting with OD issues. The coordinated and integrated service models certainly could benefit from OD. Many of the challenges of site-based councils are based in OD factors. The restructuring of central offices, charter schools, and release from court-ordered busing represent other major changes where OD skills and processes could be facilitative. The classroom is another venue where OD concepts and processes could be applied more consciously. After all, in many ways the class and the classroom incorporate features of an "organization." Perhaps introducing OD to teachers as an instructional approach would be one way to arouse their interest in and understanding of the school and school district as organizations.

In all of these ways, it is reasonable to advocate the introduction and incorporation of OD into schools and school districts. Education is a complex enterprise. There is a need to derive ways for the system and its members to work more effectively and efficiently. These are OD goals. What is needed is an OD capacity in schools and school districts to accomplished these goals. Are those engaged in the theory, research, and practice of supervision ready for the transformation?

REFERENCES

Beer, M. & Walton, A. E. (1987). Organization change and development. *Annual Review of Psychology, 38,* 339-367.

Berg, G. (1984). *OD in North American schools: A Scandinavian view, with comments by Matthew Miles and Michael Fullan.* Sweden: Uppsala University (ERIC Document Reproduction Service No. ED 249 607).

Berg, J., Hall, G., & Difford, G. (1996, June). Downsizing: The route to rightsizing or capsizing. *School Administrator, 53*(6), 23–26.

Beckhard, R. (1969). *Organization development: Strategies and models.* Reading, MA: Addison-Wesley.

Blake, R. R. & Mouton, J. S. (1964). Breakthrough in organization development. *Harvard Business Review, 42,* 133–153.

Bullock, R. J. & Svyantek, D. J. (1983). Positive-findings bias in positive-findings bias research. In K. H. Chung (Ed.). *Academy of Management best paper proceedings* (pp. 221–224). Wichita, KS: Academy of Management.

Burke, W. W. (1976). Organization development. *Journal of Applied Behavioral Science, 12*(1), 22–43.

Burke, W. W. (1994). *Organization development: A process of learning and changing.* Reading, MA: Addison-Wesley.

Burns, J. M. & Stalker, G. (1961). *The management of innovation.* London: Tavistock.

Derr, C. B. (Ed.). (1974). *Organization development in urban school systems.* Beverly Hills, CA.: Sage.

Dillon-Peterson, B. (1981). Staff development/organization development—Perspective 1981. In B. Dillon-Peterson (Ed.). *Staff development/organization development* (pp. 1–10). Washington: ASCD.

Eubanks, J., O'Driscoll, M., Hayward, G., Daniels, J., & Connor, S. (1990). Behavioral competency requirements for organization development practitioners. *Journal of Organizational Behavior Management, 11,* 77–97.

Fagenson, E. A. & Burke, W. W. (1990). Organization development practitioners' activities and interventions in organizations during the 1980s. *Journal of Applied Behavioral Science, 26,* 285–297.

Franklin, J. L. (1976). Characteristics of successful and unsuccessful organizational development. *Journal of Applied Behavioral Science, 12,* 471–492.

French, W. (1971, August). *A definition and history of organization development: Some comments.* Proceedings of the 31st Annual Meeting of the Academy of Management, Atlanta, GA.

French, W. L. & Bell, Jr. C. H. (1973). *Organization development: Behavioral science interventions for organization improvement*. Englewood Cliffs, NJ: Prentice-Hall.

Friedlander, F. (1976). OD reached adolescence: An exploration of its underlying values. *Journal of Applied Behavioral Science, 12,* 7–21.

Friedlander, F. & Brown, L. D. (1974). Organization development. *Annual Review of Psychology, 75,* 313–341.

Fullan, M., Miles, M. B., & Taylor, G. (1980). Organization development in schools: The state of the art. *Review of Educational Research, 50*(1), 121–183.

Golembiewski, R. T., Billingsley, K., & Yeager, S. (1976). Measuring change and persistence in human affairs: Types of change generated by OD designs. *Journal of Applied Behavioral Science, 12,* 133–157.

Golembiewski, R. T. & Sun, B. C. (1990). Positive-findings bias in QWL studies: Rigor and outcomes in a large sample. *Journal of Management, 16,* 665–674.

Greiner, L. E. & Schein, V. E. (1988). *Power and organization development*. Reading, MA: Addison-Wesley.

Guzzo, R. A., Jette, R. D., & Katzell, R. A. (1985). The effects of psychologically based intervention programs on worker productivity: A meta-analysis. *Personnel Psychology, 38,* 275–292.

Hall, G.E. (1994, April). *Examining the relative size of innovations: A scale and implications*. Paper presented at the Annual Meeting of the American Educational Research Association, Atlanta, GA.

Hall, G. E. & Hord, S. M. (1987). *Change in schools: Facilitating the process*. Albany, NY: State University of New York Press.

Havelock, (1971). *Planning for innovation through dissemination and utilization of knowledge*. Ann Arbor, MI: University of Michigan, Institute for Social Research.

Heisler, W. J. (1975). Patterns of OD in practice. *Business Horizons, 18*(1), 77–84.

Herzberg, F. (1966). *Work and the nature of man*. Cleveland, OH: World.

Jaeger, A. M. (1986). Organizational development and national culture: Where's the fit? *Academy of Management Review, 11,* 178–190.

James, L. R. & Jones, A. P. (1974). Organizational climate: A review of theory and research. *Psychological Bulletin, 81,* 1096–1112.

Jones, J. E., Spier, M. S., Goodstein, L., & Sashkin, M. (1980). OD in the eighties: Preliminary projections and comparisons. *Group and Organization Studies, 5,* 5–17.

Kahn, R. L. (1974). Organizational development: Some problems and proposals. *Journal of Applied Behavioral Science, 10,* 485–502.

Kimberly, J. R. & Nielsen, W. R. (1975). Organization development and change in organizational performance. *Administrative Science Quarterly, 20,* 191–206.

Lawrence, P. R. & Lorsch, J. W. (1967). *Organization and environment: Managing differentiation and integration*. Boston: Division of Research, Harvard Business School.

Likert, R. (1967). *The human organizations*. New York: McGraw-Hill.

Lippitt, G., Lippitt, R., & Lafferty, C. (1984). Cutting edge trends in organization development. *Training & Development Journal. 38*(7), 59–62.

Lowham, J. (1995). Evolution of intentions: From state policy development to teacher implementation. In D. S. G. Carter & M. H. O'Neill (Eds.). *Case studies in educational change: An international perspective*. Washington, D.C.: The Palmer Press.

Lundberg, C. C. (1989). On organizational learning: Implications and opportunities for expanding organizational development. In R. W. Woodman & W. A. Pasmore (Eds.). *Research in organizational change and development* (Vol. 3) pp. 61–82. Greenwich, CT: JAI Press.

Mann, F. C. & Likert, R. (1952, Winter). The need for research on the communication of research results. *Human Organization,* 15–19.

Maslow, A. H. (1954). *Motivation and personality*. New York: Harper & Brothers.

McGill, M. E. (1977). *Organization development for operating managers*. New York: AMACOM.

McGregor, D. (1960). *The human side of enterprise*. New York: McGraw-Hill.

Miles, M. B. (1971). *Innovation in education*. New York: Columbia University.

Miles, M. B. (1979). Should we care? Ethical issues in OD intervention. *A Publication of the OD Network, 11*(3), 1–10.

Miles, M. B., Fullan, M., & Taylor, G. (1978). *OD in schools: The state of the art*. Washington, D.C.: National Institute of Education.

Morrison, P. (1981). High technology, rapid change, and world competition in the eighties: The place for OD. *Group and Organization Studies, 6,* 395–411.

Murphy, P. E. (1989). Creating ethical corporate structures. *Sloan Management Review, 30*(2), 81–87.

Neuman, G. A., Edwards, J. E., & Raju, N. S. (1989). Organizational development interventions: A meta-analysis of the effects on satisfaction and other attitudes. *Personnel Psychology, 42,* 461–489.

Nord, W. R. (1989). OD's unfulfilled visions: Some lessons from economics. In R. W. Woodman & W. A. Pasmore (Eds.). *Research in organizational change and development* (Vol. 3) pp. 39-60. Greenwich, CT: JAI Press.

Norman, A. J. & Keys, P. R. (1992). Organization development. *Administration in Social Work, 16*(3–4), 147–165.

O'Driscoll, M. P. & Eubanks, J. L. (1993). Behavioral competencies, goal setting, and OD practitioner effectiveness. *Group and Organization Management, 18*(3) 308–327.

Offerman, L. R. & Gowing, M. K. (1990, February). Organizations of the future: Change and challenges. *American Psychologist,* 95–108.

Pajak, E. F. (1982). Organization development: Implication for supervision. *Planning and Changing, 12*(4), 245–254.

Patten, T. H., Skjerheim, T. F., & Shook, J. L. (1973). *Characteristics and professional concerns of organization development practitioners*. Madison, WI: American Society for Training and Development.

Porras (1987). *Stream analysis*. Reading, MA: Addison-Wesley.

Porras, J. I. & Berg, P. O. (1978). The impact of organization development. *Academy of Management Review, 3,* 249–263.

Pruzan, P. & Thyssen, O. (1990). Conflict and consensus: Ethics as a shared value horizon for strategic planning. *Human Systems Management, 9*(3), 135–151.

Roark, A. E. & Davis, Jr., W. E. (1981). Staff development and organization development. In B. Dillon-Peterson, (Ed.). *Staff development/organization development* (pp. 37-58). Washington: ASCD.

Roberts, D. R. & Robertson, P. J. (1992). Positive-findings bias, and measuring methodological rigor, in evaluations of organization development. *Journal of Applied Psychology, 77,* 918–925.

Rogers, E. M. (1995). *Diffusion of innovations* (4th ed.). New York: Free Press.

Ruch, C. P. & Hall, G. E. (1982, February). The effects of OD interventions on stages of concern (SoC). *Journal for Specialists in Group Work,* 39–47.

Rush, H. M. (1973). *Organization development: A reconnaissance*. New York: The Conference Board.

Sanzgiri, J. & Gottlieb, J. Z. (1992). Philosophic and pragmatic influences on the practice of organization development, 1950–2000. *Organizational Dynamics, 21*(2), 57–68.

Sashkin, M. & Burke, W. W. (1987). Organization development in the 1980's. *Journal of Management, 13,* 393–417.

Schein, E. H. (1968). Organizational socialization and the profession of management. *Industrial Management Review, 9,* 1–16.

Schein, E. H. (1985). *Organizational culture and leadership*. San Francisco: Jossey-Bass.

Schmuck, R. A. (1987). *Organization development in schools: Contemporary conceptual practices.* Eugene, OR: Center on Organizational Development in Schools, Oregon University (ERIC Document Reproduction Service No. ED 278 119).

Schmuck, R. A. & Runkel, P. J. (1994). *The Handbook of Organization Development in Schools and Colleges* (4th ed.). Prospect Heights, IL: Waveland Press.

Senge, P. M. (1990). *The fifth discipline: The art and practice of the learning organization.* New York: Doubleday.

Stassens, K. (1993). Identification and description of professional culture in innovating schools. *Qualitative Studies in Education, 6*(2), 111–128.

Staessens, K. & Vandenberghe, R. (1994). Vision as a core component in school culture. *Journal of Curriculum Studies, 26*(2), 187–200.

Terpstra, D. E. (1981). Relationship between methodological rigor and reported outcomes in organization development research. *Journal of Applied Psychology, 66,* 541–543.

Victor, B. & Cullen, J. B. (1988). The organizational bases of ethical work climates. *Administrative Science Quarterly, 33,* 101–125.

Wallin, E. & Berg, G. (1983). Research into the school as an organization, III: Organizational development in schools or developing the school as an organization? *Scandinavian Journal of Educational Research, 27,* 35–47.

Weisbord, M. R. (1987). Toward third-wave managing and consulting. *Organizational Dynamics, 15*(3), 5–24.

Whyte, W. F. (1989). Introduction. *American Behavioral Scientist, 32,* 502–512.

Whyte, W. F., Greenwood, D. J., & Lazes, P. (1989). Participatory action research: Through practice to science in social research. *American Behavioral Scientist, 32*(5), 513–551.

Woodman, R. W. (1989). Organizational change and development: New arenas for inquiry and action. *Journal of Management, 15,* 205–228.

Woodman, R. W. & Wayne, S. J. (1985). An investigation of positive-findings bias in evaluation of organization development interventions. *Academy of Management Journal, 28,* 889–913.

Part

• VII •

SUPERVISION AS AN ORGANIZED PROFESSION

INTRODUCTION

Robert F. Nicely, Jr.
PENNSYLVANIA STATE UNIVERSITY

Iris M. Striedieck
PENNSLYVANIA STATE UNIVERSITY

The six chapters in Section VII illuminate multiple issues related to the characterization of education, and hence, supervision as a profession. The issues that are presented and critiqued include the debated status of education/supervision as a profession in relation to how other established professions are characterized, the nature of supervisory preparation programs and their attendant values and beliefs, the central issues and necessary considerations for the prospect of "teaching supervision," policy and legal considerations that impact classroom visitation, curriculum work, staff development, the moral dimensions of instructional supervisory actions and intentions, and finally, an international perspective of "school supervision" as educational services.

The demarcation of these respective topics falsely connotes a sense of discreteness and unconnectedness. Indeed, those who actively engage in educational supervision and who reflectively consider the various ways in which school, community, and the broader social context influence all aspects of teaching and learning will recognize the shared dilemmas, triumphs, and implications embedded in each topic.

GOVERNANCE OF SCHOOL SUPERVISION

Chapter 36 is a collaborative and impressive effort by Firth and five graduate students to synthesize five complementary educational studies which sought "not only to analyze and anticipate research, but to participate in its creation as well." Seven sections provide character and substance to the subject of governance in instructional supervision. Each of the sections—professionalism/professionalization; image/identity; preparation/accreditation; licensure/certification; evaluation/enforcement; current status of research; and agenda for future research—starts with a historical perspective against which research findings are examined. While the demarcation of sections is presented for organizational purposes, the content of each is recursive in nature.

Firth and his students begin by noting the absence of a comprehensive and agreed-upon definition of a profession and its vital characteristics. They report numerous studies that sought to unearth characteristics, variables, and criteria depicting an ideal profession. Focus is upon the values identified by Strauss as providing a concept of professionalism/professionalization.

Consideration of education as bonified profession is still open to debate.

The second section examines the identity of practitioners of school supervision and the image of those who ply this craft. The authors assert that the field of education is doomed in forging a professional identity without having a shared and accepted understanding of the unified nature of curriculum and instruction, and related measures of effectiveness. Hall and Marshall's 1992 work provides the six aspects—perceptions, antecedents, titles, functions, theory, and research—on which the identity and image of school supervisors are critiqued in detail. In light of the multiple efforts to provide clarity and uniformity to the roles and functions of instructional supervisors and curriculum leaders, the authors note the appropriateness of considering the Association for Supervision and Curriculum Development (ASCD) as the guiding organization in such an endeavor.

Under the dimension of preparation/accreditation, Firth and his students examine the voluntary status of accrediting agencies and the obvious absence of governmental authority as a characteristic unique to the United States. An exceptional feature of this section is an explication of the six preparation/accreditation components identified by Firth: extent of surveillance, factors evaluated, type of standard, composition of agency, selection of agency membership, and level of agency jurisdiction. The authors report that the National Council for Accreditation of Teacher Education continues to clarify the vision of instructional supervision and to influence "educational preparation programs toward an increased standard of professionalization."

The fourth section details certification as a dimension of the professional virtue of licensure. Issues of malpractice by unqualified individuals coupled with retaining the rights of individual practitioners are the primary objectives for substantiating systems of professional certification. The authors utilize eight components identified by Firth as critical to the dimension of licensure/certification: extent of surveillance, factors evaluated, means of insuring standards, type of standard, designation of certificate, composition of agency, selection of agency membership, and level of agency jurisdiction. The persistent argument for nonattainment of consistent and meaningful certification requirements is the nebulous understanding of professional responsibilities in education. Firth and his co-workers note the efforts by the National Board for Professional Teaching Standards to enact an exemplary but voluntary national system for teacher certification designed to supersede the minimalistic approach taken by many state regulators.

In the final dimension of evaluation/enforcement, Firth and his co-authors reiterate the importance of establishing protocol for "enforcing high standards of ethical conduct to preserve public esteem and professional autonomy." Specific components of this dimension, identified by Firth, include extent of surveillance, factors evaluated, means of insuring standards, relationship between professional self-discipline and legal provisions, composition of agency, selection of agency membership, and level of agency jurisdiction. Because no unifying code of ethics prevails in education, state and local agencies have amalgamated statements of codes and

professional standards boards with adaptations from the National Education Association.

In Section VI of this chapter, each of the five dimensions of supervisory governance is revisited based on contemporary teaching. Some contemporary educational reformers contend that a fundamental flaw exists with the professional model, rather than with the actions of education professions. Furthermore, notions of hierarchy are perceived as flying in the face of democratic educational reforms which value collegiality and teachers as generators of knowledge.

Emerging from this extensive review and synthesis of supervisory governance are five major research questions, each associated with and profiling one of the dimensions. In essence, the authors seek to know: "What is the difference between the preferred and perceived profile(s) of the concept of professionalism/professionalization; identity/image; preparation/accreditation; licensure/certification; and evaluation/enforcement school supervision? For each, Firth and his students propose a model which incorporates the (1) four values of professionalism/professionalization, (2) six aspects of identity/image, (3) six components of preparation/accreditation, (4) eight components of licensure/certification, and (5) seven components of evaluation/enforcement in addition to reflecting contextual social forces (i.e., demographic, economy and finance, technology, etc.) and school factors (i.e., identity, structure, innovation, etc.). On a hopeful note, the authors surmise that it is possible—even probable—that education's status may be more in confluence, congruence, and/or communion with the postmodern dimensions of professionalism than those that have traditionally guided professionalization.

PREPARATION PROGRAMS IN SUPERVISION

Daresh begins Chapter 37 by speculating about how an individual is prepared to become an educational supervisor. A review of the historical trends in the field reveals certain images and metaphors to which professional development has ultimately conformed. In reviewing more contemporary visions of school supervision, Daresh points out that, while alternative models have emerged, many of the beliefs and values evident in the earlier traditional approaches still prevail.

This chapter considers the assumptions that school supervision is a process that provides educational leadership and that individuals are prepared to actualize related responsibilities. The author reports on opposing historical views of the supervisors' responsibilities, the trends affecting supervisory practice, and hence, the implications for supervisors' professional development. Supervision as inspection, as science, and as human relations, each entails different assumptions about teachers, practice, and inherent implications for preparing supervisors.

Several current perspectives of educational supervision still draw from former models. Those based on accountability and productivity value the inspection and scientific outlooks of supervision. The human relations perspective has led to the notion of human resource development in which productive organizations work to create satisfied and productive employees. Total Quality Management (TQM) and client-based supervision emphasize "the development of organizational plans and priorities directed toward increasing the sense of satisfaction felt by those who are the clients or customers of organizations—an air of teamwork and continuous improvement, to name a few."

Individuals interested in supervising in a human resource environment craft personalized visions of educational effectiveness while addressing the "people side" of schools. TQM supervisors would hone skills to determine "client needs" by working effectively with groups external to the school.

After a brief look at the research on beginning educational leaders, Daresh identifies ". . . limits on technical expertise, difficulties with socialization to the profession in general and individual school settings, and problems with role clarification and self awareness" as the three prime challenges of beginning school leaders. The omission of these key features in most educational and administrative preparation models provides credence for his Tri-Dimensional Model for Leadership Development which he describes.

Daresh claims that the regulations and policies of state education agencies and universities have largely influenced preparatory experiences of supervisors-to-be. He asserts that academic preparation, field-based learning, and personal formation enhance understanding of "how to supervise" or "to be a supervisor," which is more valuable than learning about supervision. For each, he elaborates on the assumptions, rationale, and limitations. In conclusion, Daresh points out that, by embracing a comprehensive perspective of leadership development, this model addresses and thwarts the common challenge that beginning educational leaders experience.

TEACHING OF SUPERVISION

In an attempt to holistically and critically conceive of the teaching of supervision, Badiali begins Chapter 38 by emphasizing how little the practice of supervision has changed over the past three decades. He notes in particular the multiple and sometimes conflicting interpretations of the purpose(s), definition, role, function, and preparation make problematic a vision of school supervision in which adult learning, critical reflection, and collaboration are central issues and necessary considerations. Badiali builds this argument in a way that juxtaposes historical and contemporary trends and perspectives, capturing how supervision has been taught and conjecturing about how it might be taught.

In the context of education, Badiali revisits the discussion of whether school supervision should be considered a subject or a field, a role or a function, or a combination of all of them. He explores whether school supervision should be taught as a discrete set of tasks or as a way of thinking. He also argues for the differentiation of instructional supervision from curriculum development.

The literature is rife with research about the practice of supervision; yet there is a scarcity of research indicating the value of supervision to enhance teaching and even less research providing insights into the "teaching" of supervision. Badiali claims that this situation exists because of the diffused nature of the discipline and the persistent and unresolved issues related to it, including differing conceptions of schools, purposes, teachers, teaching, and learning, as well as distinctions between

preservice and inservice settings. Following a comprehensive overview and chronology on the evolution of supervisory roles, Badiali advocates maintaining a broader definition of supervision, one which centers on democratic and professional virtues.

Badiali appeals for more explicit and more public rendering of the teaching of supervision to enhance understanding of the field and of practice. He suggests that teaching of and learning about school supervision are filtered through and influenced by the attendant assumptions and values derived from world views and life experiences.

Badiali draws implications from two models of teaching. The first model is predicated upon behavioristic attributes, in which teachers strive for characteristics of "effective teaching" while supervisors seek to translate related research for teachers and monitor its implementation in the classroom. An alternative model emphasizes reflective teaching and contextual considerations. The teacher tends to reflect on his or her own teaching as well as student learning, cultural differences, and a notion of multiplicity of problem posing and problem solving. Supervisors in this second context provide for teacher reflection and personal meaning-making while considering issues of power and unexamined assumptions which influence events of the classroom and school.

Badiali draws from research and practice in his examination of clinical supervision and problem-based learning as two metaphors for teaching supervision. He concludes that problem-based learning is a sound theoretical and practical construct from which to approach the teaching of supervision in which adult learning, critical reflection, collaboration, and a general process of constructing professional and democratic educational communities are valued.

POLICY AND LEGAL CONSIDERATIONS IN SUPERVISION

When school supervision is undertaken as a role, individuals too often are narrowly engrossed with the rituals and demands required by the immediacy of the situation. Without some prompting incident, the legal ramifications of educational supervision appear largely unknown. In Chapter 39, Hazi draws from school law, educational policy, teacher education, instructional improvement, curriculum development, and staff development to provide a comprehensive overview and national perspective regarding regulation of school supervision. Her focus is on the more recent developments of the past two decades. To establish common understanding of concepts and terms, she presents definitions of law and policy and represents school supervision as a practice dealing with classroom visitation, curriculum improvement, and staff development. Within each of these three aspects of school supervision, Hazi explicates the process and consequences of regulation, and directions for future research.

Classroom visitation is considered the most controlled aspect of school supervision because of teacher evaluation with the potential for dismissal. Moreover, evaluative procedures have become more inflexible because of federal, state, and district regulations, coupled with a desire to avoid litigation and financial straits. This has resulted in the establishment of guidelines and practices such as: evaluation must be job-related, uniformly administered, and nondiscriminatory; teachers must be assured of due process; and evidence must illustrate a pattern of events or actions. Hazi provides further insights into these and other regulations through actual case studies. She calls for additional case studies to assist in unfolding the complexity of law analysis and interpretation and to encourage contextual considerations of school law, instructional supervision, and educational practice. The National Board for Professional Teaching Standards, the Center for Research on Educational Accountability and Teacher Evaluation, and the Personnel Evaluation Standards represent just some of the national efforts to codify teacher practices.

A second aspect of school supervision involves development, implementation, and evaluation of curriculum. As defined in this writing, curriculum policy is the formal body of law and regulation that pertains to the content to be taught in schools and the methods for doing so. Regulations that inform such policy generally represent a progressive state role and at times an episodic nature. Publications such as *A Nation at Risk* (1983) prompted more rigorous regulation, resulting in numerous low cost, high visibility state reforms. Hazi reasons for more case studies on how supervisors and other curriculum workers negotiate curriculum policy, including how district curriculum guidelines are influenced by state policymakers, and examines the contributions and collective importance of participants in curriculum policy making.

Staff development is the least regulated of the three aspects of school supervision. Hazi broadly defines this component "as teacher development." Beginning with preservice education and spanning inservice education, she indicates a blurring of distinctions between the two. Regulations that inform staff development include: state control of entry through concurrent increase in requirements for initial certification and for inservice education; staff development policy influenced episodically at the national level as exemplified by the Teacher Center Initiative in response to the needs of teachers, Goals 2000 with staff development as a national goal, and the National Staff Development Council standards for effective professional development; and teacher participation in staff development policy through planning program and involvement in broader school decisions.

Due to limited case law related to staff development, Hazi calls for comprehensive examination at various levels of staff development, including aspects of continuing education, professional development, entry teachers, internships, mentor or lead teachers, and special initiatives.

SUPERVISION AS MORAL AGENCY

In Chapter 40, Starratt and Howells echo Badiali's observation that the past 30 years of research has yielded little new information about school supervision beyond technical and behavioristic emphases. The authors integrate key aspects from both traditional and contemporary approaches to build a vision of school supervision as moral agency. Their objective is to "go beyond the general structures often contained in lists of moral and ethical principles to explore the intrinsic moral content of the work of (school) supervision." Inherent in this discussion is a need to interrogate that which counts as legitimate learning and teaching and the conditions needed for learning. This objective is also emphasized in the six general subtopics: moral agency, moral agency in organizational life, school as moral action, school supervision as empowering, supervision in and for community, and restructuring agenda as moral action.

According to the authors, two levels of moral agency exist. The first level involves formal ethical frameworks, founded on qualities of autonomy (willingness to acknowledge one's own actions and to accept the consequences), connectedness (relationships with family and friends, environment, culture, history, and time and space), and transcendence (extension beyond self, ordinary, and expected on behalf of others to invest in a large collective cause) which are nurtured and actualized.

A second level of moral agency involves synthetic frameworks. A formal basis for ethical choice can occur at this level, given considerations of ethics of justice (fairness), ethics of care (respect for human dignity), and ethics of critique (concern for deeper structural issues of injustice and institutional transformation for the common good). Starratt and Howells poignantly assert that "when we place those questions against the backdrop of the moral landscape . . . we see more clearly that supervisor activity is concerned not only with effectiveness, not only with professional standards, but also with moral agency."

Moral agency may manifest itself in a transactional form within the normal constraints of organizational life by maintaining the agreed-upon rules, interacting fairly, and performing work with integrity and commitment. Starratt and Howells contend that a higher form of moral agency that is the transformation, which seeks to more incisively pursue organizational goals in light of larger human and social purposes. Implications for school supervisors entail not only the challenge to restructure practice, but to unearth the assumptions and beliefs that sanction practice.

In considering schooling as moral action, Starratt and Howells include learning, teaching, and supervising. For the supervisor, moral action is inherent in interactions as individuals who are ". . . concerned to promote the integrity of learning. . . . Any conversation supervisors have with teachers about their techniques and pedagogy needs to be nested in this larger inquiry."

When considered as empowerment, the traditional intent of supervision to control and evaluate teachers becomes problematic. Starratt and Howells emphasize that every relationship between individuals involves power. It, therefore, behooves supervisors to conceive of their practice as one that centers on leadership, rather than a specific role, and to recognize the dynamics of empowerment to foster respectful relationships between supervisors and teachers and among teachers.

The authors provide insights into the concept of supervision in and for the community. They cite the need for schools to purposefully create caring relations among administrators, supervisors, teachers, students, and parents. They contend that supervisors can be auspicious participants in shifting from the bureaucratic factory model to the democratic communitarian model. Moral commitment "actually requires the technical competence of consensus building, conflict resolution, and arbitration, but also involves concern with vision and purpose and human fulfillment and the building up of the civic community."

When considered as a restructuring agenda, moral action supersedes personal caring for the purpose of fashioning "a more humane workable learning community [and toward] the transformation of an institution." The authors call for qualitative research on actions of current supervisors engaging in moral leadership, attempting to empower teachers, and rising to the challenge of school restructuring. Such insights would be incorporated into the traditional forms of supervision and utilized to redefine those roles.

SUPERVISION SERVICES IN THE NETHERLANDS

In Chapter 41, Gorter presents, through an international and potentially comparative view, comprehensive conception of school supervision known as educational services. Responding to his own question, "Does 'school supervision' exist in the Netherlands and in other countries outside the USA?" Gorter answers both "yes" and "no." While general trends in practice, theory, and research are shared, Gorter observes that supervision as practiced in Europe prevails in social work, rather than in the school domain. He clarifies further the difficulty in writing about "supervision" from an international and comparative viewpoint. Foremost, for much of the European community, supervision connotes an element of control over work settings and people related to government bureaucracy. Secondly, supervision is deemed but one aspect of a more comprehensive educational system. Lastly, supervision which encompasses responsibility over an entire school staff or district (as evidenced in the United States) is not a practice of most educational systems in Europe.

Gorter contends that understanding particular educational systems and their internal developments comprise the prior and shared knowledge needed to comprehend the supervision services in other countries. The characteristics of educational systems are shaped by forces both within and outside schools. These forces have implications not only for the structure of the provider service, but the form of service implementation. Such influences include society (i.e., national events and market economies), decentralization (i.e., shared government and local control), freedom of choice (i.e., pri-

vate versus public education), school autonomy and quality (i.e. continuous negotiation between school and government for finances, regulations, and general school structure), and curriculum and student achievement (i.e. issues of national curriculum and educational outcomes).

Gorter notes the multiple and differing conceptions of supervision as espoused by American and European educators. Whereas no direct translation for supervision can be made in the Netherlands or any other European country, terms like *counsel, advise, guide,* and *consult* are readily heard in these countries. Similarly, peer and clinical supervision commonly discussed in the United States have no comparable counterparts in other countries. Rather, clinical supervision is considered "an intervention that is applied during the implementation of new practices." What is similar in nature between America and European countries are the topics of and approaches to supervision/educational services deemed "effective" and "ineffective." Overall, educational support in the Netherlands is only offered by request of the schools and this support is rendered in a nonhierarchical way.

The *Model for Description of Education Service and its Effectiveness* evolved from an intensive review and compilation of sources related to the educational support system in the Netherlands. This synthesis consists of five categorical sections—context for providers, input at provider's level, conditions for managing the primary process, through-put/performance/primary process, and output—each with subsequent subcategories. Gorter describes the literature search process for educational service providers in different countries and then presents a matrix summarizing the educational services found in the Netherlands, Belgium, Luxembourg, and Israel.

This chapter offers insights into the structure and values of education in representative countries which encourage comparative analysis among supervisory service providers. Gorter notes that particularly in the Netherlands, where a "well elaborated system of school support" is intact, the opportunity exists for ample and resolute monitoring and assessment. He extols the virtues of engaging in more comparative educational studies to further enhance the integrity of educational service providers, including supervision, as well as to reveal "issues that are relevant for the review of the effectiveness of the provided services in the various countries."

GOVERNANCE OF SCHOOL SUPERVISION

Gerald R. Firth

UNIVERSITY OF GEORGIA

"I hold every man a debtor to his profession . . . as men do of course seek to receive countenance and profit so ought they of duty to endeavor themselves by way of amends to be a help and an ornament thereunto."

Francis Bacon (1561–1626)
Preface, *Maxims of the Law*, 1596

"We have to create a new professionalism that has a civic character. . . . Civic professionals should align their practices with the processes that create a public."

David Mathews
President, Kettering Foundation

The public's disenchantment with professionalism:
Reasons for rethinking academe's service to the country.
Journal of Public Service and Outreach, Spring 1996

INTRODUCTION/PROLOGUE

Few educators would deny that instructional supervision is a noble calling. However, the field remains an enigma. Those who pursue supervision as a career—from university researcher to kindergarten coordinator—may display the trappings characteristic of other portrayals or masquerade in other guise. Not only do instructional supervisors readily accept duties acknowledged to be part of other specialties, but they also eschew opportunities to challenge those who invade their own province of expertise.

Members of any group, be it family, company, community, or party, automatically inherit the responsibility to improve its welfare, enhance its prestige, and extend its cause. Such obligations accrue to those engaged in instructional supervision, whether through formal joining of those ranks or by acceptance of the functions that operationally define the craft.

This chapter focuses on agenda, activities, and/or actions of organizations, agencies, and/or groups to identify, clarify, and

Contributions to this chapter by Ken A. Banter, Melinda R. Castleberry, Jan W. Otter, Janice S. Stowe, and Nancy G. Williams are acknowledged with pride, praise, and appreciation.

professionalize instructional supervision through establishing criteria for preparation, admission to membership, and/or enforcement of standards, as well as forums for related issues.

It would be tempting to dismiss, disregard, or denigrate the focus of this chapter on the premise that the functions of instructional supervision, and perhaps also the related but distinct companion, curriculum development, have lately been transformed from the activities of an individual at the district level to those of a multimember team at the school level. The merits of site-based management, shared governance, and/or participatory democracy are not debated here. The analysis presented in this chapter assumes the continued existence and relevance of instructional supervision in American public education, regardless of genre, form, or configuration. Furthermore, the presumption is made that persons who serve in such leadership capacities should be expected by noblesse oblige to be professional in every sense that term implies.

The respective statements regarding the nature of professions and/or professionalism by Bacon and Mathews cited at the beginning of the chapter from sources separated by four centuries highlight the interrelatedness of specialized service and public benefit. Variations in emphases on these fundamental considerations provide a rationale for comparing and/or contrasting views held on many occupations over the years by practitioners and clients.

The invitation to develop this chapter was recognized and embraced by this author as an opportunity not only to analyze and anticipate research, but to participate in its creation as well. A team of five graduate students majoring in instructional supervision in the Department of Educational Leadership, College of Education, University of Georgia, contributed companion pieces of research conducted during 1994. Their reports were drawn from an earlier research project that involved 24 University of Georgia graduate students in instructional supervision. The work of the five students spanned an entire year, drew upon three advanced courses in instructional supervision, and resulted in five distinct but coordinated studies.

The research design involved triangulation of three distinct, separate, related, and coordinated approaches using common constructs: literature search, document analysis, and companion studies.

In each section of this chapter, historical perspective derived from the literature is compared with the research findings. The five complementary research studies drew from a common data pool of 117 references that included research/technical papers, books, journal articles, dissertations, opinion/position papers, information analyses, descriptive reports, and legal/legislative/regulatory material. The five reports, which contributed invaluable data to portions of this chapter, are: *Professional Self-Discipline of Instructional Supervision: Vision, Identity, and Image* (Castleberry, 1994); *Professional Self-Discipline of Instructional Supervision: Standards, Preparation, and Accreditation* (Stowe, 1994); *Professional Self-Discipline of Instructional Supervision: Qualifications, Licensure, and Credentialing* (Otter, 1994); and *Professional Self-Discipline of Instructional Supervision: Criteria, Performance, and Enforcement* (Banter, 1994). The fifth and most comprehensive study, which constituted an applied project for the Specialist in Education degree, ana-

lyzed *Professional Self-Discipline of Instructional Supervision: Influences of National Leadership Organizations* (Williams, 1994). Williams (1994) examined a total of 128 textbooks on instructional supervision published during the 120-year period from 1875 to 1994.

A document analysis was executed by utilizing the data base assembled by the members of the research team and augmented by additional students in three graduate courses at the University of Georgia. The results of all five of the related investigations are drawn upon at appropriate places throughout the chapter.

The chapter begins with this Introduction/Prologue and ends with Predictions/Epilogue. The remainder of its content is presented in seven sections, each concerned with a different facet of the overall topic of governance in the field of instructional supervision. Section I is concerned with professionalism and professionalization; Section II deals with image and identity; Section III discusses preparation and accreditation; Section IV considers licensure and certification; Section V focuses on evaluation and enforcement; Section VI examines the current status of inquiry; and Section VII establishes an agenda for future research.

The demarcation between early efforts in the categories described in Sections I through V and those comprising the current status of inquiry described in Section VI was the publication in 1976 of *Educating a Profession* by the American Association of Colleges for Teacher Education. (Howsam, Corrigan, Denemark, and Nash, 1976). The goal of this report by the Bicentennial Commission on Education for the Profession of Teaching was "to stimulate recognition of teaching as a profession rather than an occupation" (p. 173). Regarded as a pivotal event, the report was republished in 1985 with a postscript.

Only material published since 1980 was regarded as appropriate for inclusion in Section VI, most of which focuses on education in general or teachers in particular rather than on leadership roles in instructional supervision and/or curriculum development.

Within each section of the chapter, comparison and contrast are provided among exemplars from established professions, situations in the field of education, and conditions in the craft of school supervision. Because the sections were developed independently, each has its own list of references.

The consideration of professional status for education in general and its leadership specializations, particularly instructional supervision, presents a long and continuing saga. This chapter describes relationships—actual or perceived—with other occupations accorded the designation of "profession". It traces the evolution of the concept of "profession" as applied to education from early inception through flagging efforts into renewed activity sparked by recent school reforms. For this author, who has been observer, participant, and supporter in many related ventures, it has been difficult to maintain the objective view that a research report requires. Several reviewers have conscientiously sought to hold the author to the standard of objectivity. It is hoped that any occasional departures from objectivity which suggest advocacy, criticism, and/or judgment will receive pardon if not acceptance from the reader.

REFERENCES

Bacon, F. (1596). Preface to *Maxims of the law.* In J. Spedding, R. L. Ellis, & D. D. Heath (Eds.). (1857–1874), *The works of Francis Bacon* (Vol. VII). London: Longmans and Company, Ltd. Reprinted 1968 New York: Garrett Press.

Banter, K. A. (1994). *Professional self-discipline of instructional supervision: Criteria, performance, and enforcement.* Unpublished research project in Educational Leadership, University of Georgia, Athens, GA.

Castleberry, M. R. (1994). *Professional self-discipline of instructional supervision: Vision, identity, and image.* Unpublished research project in Educational Leadership, University of Georgia, Athens, GA.

Howsam, R. B., Corrigan, D. C., Denemark, G. W., & Nash, R. J. (1976, 1985). *Educating a profession.* (Reprint with postscript). Report of the Bicentennial Commission on Education for the Profession of Teaching. Washington, D.C.: American Association of Colleges for Teacher Education.

Mathews, D. (1996, Spring). The public's disenchantment with professionalism: Reasons for rethinking academe's service to the country. *Journal of Public Service and Outreach, 1*(1), 21–28.

Otter, J. W. (1994). *Professional self-discipline of instructional supervision: Qualifications, licensure, and credentialing.* Unpublished research project in Educational Leadership, University of Georgia, Athens, GA.

Stowe, J. S. (1994). *Professional self-discipline of instructional supervision: Standards, preparation, and accreditation.* Unpublished research project in Educational Leadership, University of Georgia, Athens, GA.

Williams, N. G. (1994). *Professional self-discipline of instructional supervision: Influences of national leadership organizations.* Unpublished applied project for the Specialist in Education degree in Educational Leadership at the University of Georgia, Athens, GA.

SECTION I.
THE CONCEPT OF PROFESSIONALISM/PROFESSIONALIZATION

INTRODUCTION

This section considers the quest for the status and esteem of a profession (professionalization) within the context of the attainment of such a distinction by an occupation (professionalism).

Findings are presented in each of the following 10 categories: definitions of terms; general considerations; exemplars from established professions; situations in the field of education; conditions in the craft of school supervision; literature review; research reports; document analyses; values of professionalism /professionalization, including expertise, autonomy, responsibility, and commitment; and critique.

DEFINITIONS OF TERMS

For the purpose of this analysis, the term *professionalism* is defined as "an ideology and associated activities found in diverse occupational groups where members aspire to professional status" (Vollmer & Mills, 1966, p. viii); and the term *professionalization* is defined as "the process by which those engaged in an occupation alter circumstances in an attempt to turn it into a profession and themselves into professionals" (Hughes, 1958, p. 46).

GENERAL CONSIDERATIONS

The rise of professions and their professional organizations was heralded by Carr-Saunders (1928) to be of great importance to society:

All in all, the growth of professionalism is one of the hopeful features of the time. The approach to problems of social conduct and social policy under the guidance of a professional tradition raises the ethical standards and widens the social outlook. There is thus reason to welcome a development of which the result will be to increase the influence of professional associations upon character, outlook, and conduct (p. 31).

A craft labeled as a profession sets itself apart from typical employment (Counts, 1925). Wilkin (1938) explained the quest for professionalization in these words: "The professional spirit sets its seal against self-seeking and self-aggrandizement. It awakens a social consciousness and a conscience . . . . The professions are founded upon merit. They impose standards of admission and standards of practice. A position in a profession must be earned . . . but the professions are open to all who will submit to their discipline" (pp. 160–161).

As late as 1962, little had been written on the history of professions (Stinnett, 1962), even though Lieberman observed in 1956 that the idea of professions apparently grew out of the conviction that certain services were deemed so important that everyone should be guaranteed access to them (Lieberman, 1956). These important services eventually became the "classic" professions of law, medicine, and theology. Until the end of the sixteenth century, the professions were under the dominance of the church.

There is no single, recognized, authoritative definition of a profession or agreement about essential characteristics. Lieberman (1956) asserted that, "In order to be a profession, an occupational group must have unique, definite, and essential social functions to perform" (p. 19). He accorded this requirement primacy and majesty among the "complex of characteristics" which distinguish professions from occupations. The other characteristics identified by Lieberman (1956) included: an emphasis upon intellectual techniques in performing service, a long period of specialized training, a broad range of autonomy for both individual practitioners and for the group as a whole, practitioner acceptance of personal responsibility for judgments and actions, an emphasis upon service rather than gain, a comprehensive self-governing organization, and a code of ethics enforcing practitioner conduct (pp. 1–6).

In 1992, Hart and Marshall (1992) examined numerous sources in the literature regarding characteristics, variables, and criteria describing an ideal profession. The reports, which represented the period from 1930 to 1983, included those of Dreeben (1970), Edmonson (1930), Goode (1969), Greenwood (1957), Horton (1944), Lam (1983), Lieberman (1956), Ornstein (1979), Tyler (1964), and Weil and Weil (1971). From their analysis, Hart and Marshall (1992) identified five fundamental aspects of a profession: (1) possesses a specific body of knowledge; (2) is committed to an ideal of service; (3) adheres to agreed-upon ethical codes; (4) exercises autonomy; and (5) is identified by a distinctive culture (p. 2). Earlier works by Flexner (1915), Lippitt and This (1962), and Dull (1981) produced essentially the same results.

Professionalization is viewed in the literature as a process by which an organized occupation obtains the exclusive right to perform a particular kind of work, control training for and access to it, and control the right of determining and evaluating the way the work is performed (Vollmer & Mills, 1966).

"Professionalization is [also] a result of individual and group maturation," according to Krey and Burke (1989).

The group status is dependent not only upon the maturation of individual members but also upon the individual's capacity to be a productive member of the group. Many people, thoroughly competent in the skills of their own vocation, may be extremely slow in achieving those skills which make them productive group members (p. 353).

Dumont (1970) rejected the notion that credentialism is the sole determinant of professionalism. Rather, professionalization must develop in terms of characteristics such as uniqueness of preparation and exclusiveness of service which distinguish an occupational group from others.

EXEMPLARS FROM ESTABLISHED PROFESSIONS

Experience of established professions is a major resource for occupational groups that aspire to professional status or by groups that are regarded as professions but do not possess an altogether clear title to such a claim. The history of established professions clearly indicates that systematic attention to professionalization by its practitioners is always prerequisite to the attainment of professionalism by any occupation.

The National Manpower Council (1953) described the evolution from occupation to profession in these words:

The history of the professions also reflects changes in society's evaluation of certain occupations. . . . Acceptance as professions [is] . . . largely the result of the special efforts of an occupational group to set themselves apart from others, to establish standards of training and

practice, to regulate the conduct of their members, and to advance their knowledge (pp. 38–39).

Experience of other occupations, however, cannot serve as an automatic direction finder for education in its quest for professional status. One source of error lies is the tendency to overlook the weaknesses of other professions. "It is unwise to glorify education as a profession, but it is equally unwise to glorify medicine or law or any other occupation. All have shortcomings as professions" (Lieberman, 1956, p. 16).

SITUATIONS IN THE FIELD OF EDUCATION

The field of education is casually referred to as a profession. However, there are many, even among the ranks of educators, who contend that education has not yet attained acceptance as a true profession and may not be able to do so in the future. Among the reasons given is the assertion that educational practitioners generally are unable, unqualified, or unwilling to assume the responsibilities for self-discipline, a characteristic jealously guarded by other professionals. By intent, avoidance, and/or acquiescence, governance of education is remanded to others, typically laymen, whose judgment over educational practice and practitioners is substituted for that of educators.

Citizens in a typical community elect a board of education legally responsible for operating the schools. The school board employs a superintendent responsible for carrying out the policies of the school board. The superintendent or his or her authorized representative selects teachers whose job it is to follow the directives of the superintendent. Essentially, this theory makes the school board the ultimate source of moral authority for the superintendent and the superintendent the ultimate source of moral authority for teachers. This approach may be efficient, but it is not professional.

The very essence of a profession is a high degree of *personal* responsibility. Lieberman (1956) stated, "To the extent that teachers are subject to the orders of an administrator whom they have not chosen, who is not responsible to them, and over whom they have no control, the teachers have the status of hired hands rather than professional workers. . . . The responsibility of the professional worker to the client is *direct* and *personal*" (p. 57).

A genuine profession of education would not accept *any* lay determination—local, state, or federal—of what to teach and how to teach. Neither would it accept that teachers are free to teach whatever pleases them. Any limits on personal actions would be determined by the members of the profession.

Before 1969, a large proportion of educational practitioners were members of a single organization—the National Education Association (NEA). The predecessor National Teacher's Association was established in 1857 as the first national organization of teachers in the United States. Merger of the NTA with other organizations in 1870 to form the NEA brought together teachers, principals, supervisors, curriculum specialists, superintendents, higher education faculty, and agency personnel under a single aegis. The directions set by NEA were to dominate the organized profession for nearly a century (Howsam et al, 1979, p. 67). Major NEA efforts toward professionalization were conducted through the National Commission on Teacher Education and Professional Standards, later dissolved with its activities incorporated into a division of Instruction and Professional Development (Howsam et al, 1979, p. 69).

Competition for teacher allegiance arose from the American Federation of Teachers (AFT), which advocated that union tactics rather than a "unified profession" could more effectively advance salary and other benefits. A wedge was driven between teachers, the largest single constituency, and others. The National Association of Secondary School Principals (NASSP) and the Council of Chief State School Officers (CCSSO) separated from the NEA operationally in 1969, followed rapidly by the National Association of Elementary School Principals (NAESP), the American Association of School Administrators (AASA), and the Association for Supervision and Curriculum Development (ASCD) in 1971.

CONDITIONS IN THE CRAFT OF SCHOOL SUPERVISION

Earlier in this volume, the contributions of school superintendents informally and through the National Association of School Superintendents, the Department of Superintendence within the National Education Association, and, more recently, the American Association of School Administrators (AASA) to the professionalization of instructional supervision were described and acknowledged.

More specific efforts along these lines owe their beginning to the establishment in 1920 of their own professional organization by school supervisors. Called the National Conference on Educatonal Method, it founded a publication in 1921 which was eventually abbreviated from *The Journal of Educational Method* to simply *Educational Method*. The movement distinguished instructional supervisors, curriculum directors, and classroom teachers from publications dominated by school superintendents and college faculty. In 1928, this group became the Department of Supervisors and Directors of Instruction within the National Education Association. Direction was set for DSDI in its first two yearbooks: *Educational Supervision* (Hosic, 1928) and *Scientific Method in Supervision* (Hosic, 1929). Both were edited by James Hosic who had sought an organization within the NEA to focus specifically on school supervision.

Similar sentiments were echoed in significant DSDI yearbooks over the next 15 years (Lindquist, 1933; Rankin, 1934; Courtis, McSwain, and Morrison, 1939; Heffernan, 1940; Spears, 1943).

Merger of DSDI with the Society for Curriculum Study created the Department of Supervision and Curriculum Development in 1943 which became the Association for Supervision and Curriculum Development in 1947.

Many significant contributions of these organizations to the professionalization of school supervision are examined in detail by Aiken and Tanner. (See Chapter 16 of this volume devoted to "Supervision in Secondary Schools).

Frymier urged the professionalization of instructional supervision in his 1969 address to an ASCD symposium with these words:

"It is possible [for instructional supervisors] to attain truly professional status. . . . We must work to become truly professional, not because it will make us more money—although it will—and not because it will raise our prestige level in the eyes of others — although it will do that, too—but because we have to become truly professional in order to be effective. Being professional is the only way we can guarantee providing the highest quality service to those we seek to help" (p. 90).

Drawing upon Abrahamson (1967), Frymier asserted that any person or any group which is truly professional must be characterized not in some, not in most, but in each and every one of six different ways. The provision of an essential service for other people is the first, and probably the most important, characteristic of a profession. The others are a methodology unique and peculiar to that group; a practice built upon the best that is known from research; judgments and decisions that affect the lives and well being of those served; a code of ethics; and a national professional organization with the power to impose a discipline upon the membership that requires every member of the group to adhere to the professional way (Frymier, 1969, pp. 91–93).

Shafer (1965) examined the report of Abraham Flexner on deficiencies in medical preparation to determine its implications for educators in general and for instructional supervisors and curriculum leaders in particular. Based on his analysis, Shafer suggested that instructional supervisors and curriculum leaders should devote serious attention and united effort in the following areas:

1. Studying systematically conditions nationwide which hinder professionalization
2. Establishing standards for recruitment and selection of future instructional supervisors and curriculum leaders
3. Strengthening preservice preparation to insure programs which include theoretical studies, field work, and specialization
4. Establishing standards for appropriate certification by working with licensing agencies
5. Assuming responsibility through the ASCD for policing the membership and for acting upon violations of acceptable practice
6. Developing programs nationally, statewide, and locally to improve the public image of instructional supervision and curriculum development
7. Emphasizing the fact that professional preparation is an expensive venture in which the amount of financial support and investment is directly related to quality (p. 238).

In the final analysis, the professionalism of any group tends to be judged by the level of autonomy that the group as a whole exercises in defining the nature, conditions, and procedures of its work (Speiker, 1978). Instructional supervisors and curriculum leaders report that they often feel as though they have little control over their own positions and designated activities (Bartoo, Speiker, & Sturges, 1976).

Professionalism/professionalization is also determined by the manner in which a group self-regulates itself, serves the public, and ensures that each member contributes to society.

LITERATURE REVIEW

William H. Payne (1875) published chapters on school supervision in 1875, credited by Button (1961) to be the first textbook written on school supervision. Of the 128 books on instructional supervision published over the 120-year period from 1875 to 1994, 24 (19%) addressed the concept of professionalism. The greatest emphasis occurred during the 75-year period 1875–1949, when five of the 18 books (28%) mentioned professionalism. Since that period, emphasis was greatest during the decade 1960–1969, when five of the 23 books (22%) mentioned professionalism (Williams, 1994).

RESEARCH REPORTS

Professionalization of instructional supervision has been addressed in studies from several vantage points.

Organizations, Institutions, and Agencies

In 1958, the National Commission on Teacher Education and Professional Standards, established by the NEA in 1946, developed the New Horizons Project to reexamine its purposes, goals, and procedures (Lindsey, 1961). That project has been credited with helping to stimulate "professional groups [in education] to reexamine their own qualifications, their preparation, and their responsibility for professional improvement" (Mackenzie, 1961, p. 87).

Hart and Marshall (1992), synthesizing literature on professions in general and the teaching profession in particular, advocated that fundamental values be addressed in preparation programs, thereby providing future practitioners with a sense of collegial togetherness and support.

Lieberman (1956) provided a comprehensive academic examination of *Education as a Profession*. He considered the topics of professional function, professional autonomy, accreditation, certification, professional ethics, and professional associations in relation to established professions.

Doctoral Dissertations

Firth (1959) conducted an extensive pragmatic study of "Professional Self-Discipline of Public School Personnel" which focused on accreditation, certification, and enforcement in comparing and contrasting education with the five established professions of law, medicine, engineering, public accounting, and psychology. Firth surveyed 61 teacher preparation institutions, 48 state teachers associations affiliated with the NEA, and 19 state teachers associations affiliated with the AFT. In addition, he interviewed executive secretaries of the

five established professions at both the state and national levels. The study examined the efforts of professional organizations in establishing, implementing, and improving standards.

In an ASCD-endorsed study, Spier (1994) found that all 50 competencies categorized in the four domains of functional, programmatic, contextual, and personal/interpersonal were considered appropriate to be included in preparation programs for educational leaders. In addition to the membership of the Council of Professors of Instructional Supervision, respondents included 600 each of elementary principals and assistant principals, high school principals and assistant principals, superintendents and associate superintendents, curriculum directors and coordinators, and school-based and central-office based supervisors.

DOCUMENT ANALYSES

Williams (1994) distilled the treatment of professional self-discipline by authors of 128 textbooks on instructional supervision published over the 120-year period from 1875 to 1994 (Tables 36–1 and 36–2). She investigated references to the concept of professionalism/professionalization, and the respective dimensions of preparation/accreditation, licensure/certification, and evaluation/enforcement derived from Firth (1959). Her six time categories comprised the first 75 years from 1875 to 1949 (18 books), the 1950–1959 decade (15 books), the 1960–1969 decade (23 books), the 1970–1979 decade (21 books), the 1980–1989 decade (40 books), and the last half decade from 1990 to 1994 (11 books).

Books published on instructional supervision from the early 1900s to the mid-1960s contained more information on professionalism, preparation, and evaluation. The emphasis then shifted to evaluation and professionalism through the mid-1980s with modest attention to professionalism only through the early 1990s. Reference to certification was minimal throughout the 120 years. Expectations related to professionalism, preparation, certification, and evaluation have emerged from the discussions, descriptions, and debates regarding supervision. The literature of the 1990s has more to say about professionalism than the three dimensions of accreditation, certification, and enforcement. The characteristics of community and caring appear to have been added to the characteristics of the profession of supervision.

Williams (1994) hypothesized that authors who addressed professionalism and the three dimensions of self-discipline thought that professionalization of instructional supervision

TABLE 36–1. Occurrences of the Dimensions of Preparation, Licensure, and Evaluation Noted in Textbooks on Instructional Supervision Published During the 120-Year Period 1875 to 1994 Regarding the Concept of Professionalism Expressed by Number and Percentage

Time Period	No of Texts	Professionalism	Preparation	Licensure	Evaluation
1875–1949	18	5 (28%)	4 (22%)	1 (6%)	6 (33%)
1950–1959	15	1 (7%)	3 (20%)	1 (7%)	4 (27%)
1960–1969	23	5 (22%)	8 (35%)	4 (17%)	9 (39%)
1970–1979	21	4 (19%)	2 (9%)	2 (9%)	9 (43%)
1980–1989	40	7 (18%)	3 (8%)	2 (5%)	9 (23%)
1990–1994	11	2 (18%)	1 (9%)	0 (0%)	1 (9%)
Totals	128	24 (19%)	21 (16%)	10 (8%)	38 (30%)

Source: Williams, 1994, p. 23.

TABLE 36–2 Books on Instructional Supervision Published 1875–1994

Year	Author(s)	Title	Prof	Accr.	Cert	Cnf.	Label
1993	Anderson & Snyder	Clinical Supervision: Coaching Higher Performance					s
1993	Delano	Supervisor's Log: A Professional's Graffiti					s
1993	Goldhammer, Anderson, & Krajewski	Clinical Supervision, 3rd Edition					s
1993	Oliva	Supervision for Today's Schools, 4th Edition				550–57	s
1993	Pajak	Approaches to Clinical Supervision					s
1993	Sergiovanni & Starratt	Supervision: A Redefinition, 5th Edition	48–51				s
1993	Tracy, Saundra, & MacNaughton	Assisting and Assessing Educational Personnel					s
1992	Acheson & Gall	Techniques in the Clinical Supervision of Teachers, 3rd Edition					s
1991	Glanz	Bureaucracy and Professionalism	110–16	110–112			s
1990	Glatthorn	Supervisory Leadership: Introduction to Instructional Supervision					
1990	Glickman	Supervision of Instruction: A Developmental Approach					s
1989	George & Protherough	Supervision in Education					s
1989	Luehe	Principal and Supervision					pr, s
1989	Krey & Burke	Design for Instructional Supervision	349–355				s
1989	Daresh	Supervision as a Proactive Process	270–271				s
1989	Oliva	Supervision for Today's Schools, 3rd Edition				553–55	s
1989	Beach & Reinhartz	Supervision: Focus on Instruction					pr
1989	Pajak	The Central Office Supervisor of Curr. and Supervision					s
1988	Schain	Supervising Instruction					s
1988	Sergiovanni & Starratt	Supervision: Human Perspectives, 4th Edition					s
1988	Gorton, Richard, Schneider, & Fisher	Encyclopedia of School Admin. and Supervision					s
1987	Schon	Educating the Reflective Practitioner		3-17			prof
1987	Acheson & Gall	Techniques in Clinical Supervision of Teachers, 2nd Edition					s
1987	Champagne & Hogan	Consultant Supervision: Theory and Development					s
1987	DuFour	Fulfilling the Promise of Excellence					l
1987	Furman	Supervision: Evaluation of Teaching					s
1987	Knoll	Supervision for Better Instruction					s
1987	Tanner & Tanner	Supervision in Education: Problems and Practices	30–31				s, pr, supt
1986	Hoy & Forsyth	Effective Supervision: Theory into Practice					s
1986	Wiles & Bondi	Supervision: A Guide to Practice, 2nd Edition					s
1985	Glickman	Supervision of Instruction: A Developmental Approach					s
1985	Harris	Supervisory Behavior in Education, 3rd Edition				289–29	s
1985	Marks Stoops & King-Stoops	Handbook of Educational Supervision, 3rd Edition	614–628				s, s pr
1984	Oliva	Supervision for Today's Schools, 2nd Edition				563–56	s
1984	Cooper	Developing Skills for Instructional Supervision					s
1983	Doll	Supervision for Staff Development				355–38	s
1983	Lovell & Wiles	Supervision for Better Schools, 5th Edition				285–29	s
1983	Schon	The Reflective Practitioner	11–13				prof
1983	Sergiovanni & Starratt	Supervision: Human Perspectives, 3rd Edition					s
1982	Bellon & Bellon	Classroom Supervision and Instruct. Improvement, 2nd Edition					ad, l
1982	Goldstein	Supervision Made Simple					s
1982	Pfeiffer	Supervision of Teachers: A Guide				171–17	s
1981	Champagne & Hogan	Consultant Supervision: Theory and Development					s
1981	Dull	Supervision—School Leadership Handbook	89–90	103–10	91	276–29	s
1981	Alfonso, Firth, & Neville	Instructional Supervision: A Behavior System	335–33	336	337	337	s
1981	Gillespie	Creative Supervision					s
1980	Acheson & Gall	Techniques in the Clinical Supervision of Teachers					s
1980	Blumberg	Supervisors and Teachers : A Private Cold War, 2nd Edition					s
1980	Goldhammer, Anderson,& Krajewski	Clinical Supervision, 2nd Edition					s
1980	Neagley& Evans	Handbook for Effective Supervision of Instruction, 3rd Edition				330–33	s
1980	Wiles & Bondi	Supervision: A Guide to Practice					s
1979	Lucio & McNeil	Supervision in Thought and Action, 3rd Edition		51–62	50-51		s
1979	Eisner	The Educational Imagination					c, ed l
1979	Sergiovanni & Starratt	Supervision: Human Perspectives, 2nd Edition					s
1978	Marks, Stoops, & King-Stoops	Handbook of Educational Supervision, 2nd Edition	614–624			601–60	s
1978	Stoller	Supervision and Improvement of Instruction					s
1976	Bellon & Bellon	Classroom Supervision and Instructional Improvement					ad, l
1976	Oliva	Supervision for Today's Schools				416–41	s
1975	Alfonso, Firth, & Neville	Instructional Supervision: A Behavior System	335–33	297–31	305-30	317–32	s
1975	Harris	Supervisory Behavior in Education, 2nd Edition					s
1975	Wiles & Lovell	Supervision for Better Schools, 4th Edition				285–29	s, as-co
1974	Blumberg	Supervisors and Teachers: A Private Cold War					s
1973	Cogan	Clinical Supervision					s
1972	Lewis & Miel	Supervision for Improved Instruction				243–24	s
1972	Williams	New Dimensions in Supervision				243–25	s
1972	Mosher & Purpel	Supervision: The Reluctant Profession					s
1971	Berman	Supervision, Staff Development and Leadership					ibst, ed, l

TABLE 36–2 Books on Instructional Supervision Published 1875–1994 (*continued*)

Year Author(s)	Title	Prof	Accr.	Cert	Cnf.	Label
1971 Marks, Stoops & King-Stoops	Handbook of Educational Supervision	197–212			794–79	s
1971 Sergiovanni & Starratt	Emerging Patterns of Supervision	60				s
1970 Feyereisen & Fiorino	Supervision and Curriculum Renewal—Systems Approach					s
1970 Neagley & Evans	Handbook for Effective Supervision, 2nd Edition				278–28	s, pr, supt
1970 Unruh & Turner	Supervision for Change and Innovation				288–29	s
1969 Goldhammer	Clinical Supervision					s
1969 Lucio & McNeil	Supervision: A Synthesis of Thought and Action		53–65	52–53		s
1969 Wilson, Byar, & Shapiro	Sociology of Supervision					s
1968 Evans	First-line Supervision in Public Schools					
1968 Harrison	Supervisory Leadership in Education		102–10	14, 102		s
1967 Cox	History School-system Supervision-GA		119–120			s
1967 Elsbree, McNally,& Wynn	Elementary School Administration and Supervision, 3rd Edition					pr
1967 Hyman	School Administrator's Faculty Supervision Handbook					s
1967 Wiles	Supervision for Better Schools, 3rd Edition				291–30	s
1965 Eye & Netzer	Supervision of Instruction; Phase of Administration					sp. s
1965 Stoops	Elementary School Supervision	315–331			301–31	s pr
1964 Bradfield	Supervision Modern Elem. Schools				160–16	pr
1964 Curtin	Supervision in Today's Elem. Schools	6		6	277–29	s, pr, co, con
1964 Neagley & Evans	Handbook for Effective Supervision				216–22	s, pr, supt
1963 Harris	Supervisory Behavior in Supervision					s
1962 Lippitt & This	Issues in Human Relations Training	117–118				prof
1962 Lucio	Supervision: A Synthesis of Thought and Action	219	52–61	51		s
1962 Swearingen	Supervision of Inst.: Foundations and Dimensions		194–196		228–25	s
1961 Franseth	Supervision as Leadership				298–34	s
1961 Douglass, Bent, & Boardman, C.	Democratic Supervision in Secondary Schools		13–15			s, pr, d
1961 Gwynn	Theory and Practice of Supervision		443–444		385–39	s
1960 Cramer, & Domian	Administration and Supervision in the Elementary School					pr, s
1960 Hicks	Educational Supervision in Principle and Practice	202–20	422		410–42	s, pr, cons
1959 Elsbree, & McNally	Elementary School Administration and Supervision, 2nd Edition					pr
1957 Crosby	Supervision as Co-operative Action		14–16			s
1955 Burton, & Brueckner	Supervision, a Social Process				445–47	s
1955 Hammock	Supervising Instruction in Secondary Schools		296–302			s, supt, d
1955 Wiles	Supervision for Better Schools, 2nd Edition				315–32	s
1954 Ayer	Fundamentals of Instructional Supervision					s, supt, d
1953 Adams & Dickey	Basic Principles of Supervision		11, 12		258–27	s
1953 Bartky	Supervision as Human Relations					s
1953 Peckham	Principles and Techniques of Supervision					s
1953 Spears	Improving the Supervision of Instruction			169–171		s, co, d, con
1951 Elsbree	Elementary School Administration and Supervision					pr
1951 Flexner	Readings in the Social Aspects of Education	553–556				prof
1951 McNerney	Educational Supervision					s
1950 Melchior	Instructional Superv.-Guide to Modern Practice					s
1950 Wiles	Supervision for Better Schools				269–28	s
1947 Barr, Burton, & Brueckner,	Supervision: Democratic Leadership in Improv. of Instruction		912–930		930–94	s, e-i tech a
1939 Foster	High School Supervision		78–80			s, ap
1939 Myers	Problems in Public School Supervision					s
1938 Barr, Burton, & Brueckner,	Supervision				797–86	s
1938 Briggs	Improving Instruction: Superv. by Prins. of Sec. Schools				259–26	s
1938 Myers, Kifer	Cooperative Supervision in Public Schools					s
1932 Anderson, & Simpson	The Supervision of Rural Schools				403–43	s, a
1931 Alberty & Thayer	Supervision in Secondary School					s, pr
1931 Kyte	Problems in Supervision	39				s
1930 Kyte	How to Supervise					s
1927 Collings	School Supervision in Theory and Practice					s
1926 Barr & Burton	The Supervision of Instruction: A General Volume	547–54	540–546		494–52	s
1925 Anderson, Barr, & Bush	Visiting the Teacher at Work					s, pr, supt
1925 Pittman	The Value of School Supervision					ht, s
1921 Wagner	Common Sense in School Supervision	97–101				s
1920 Nutt.	The Supervision of Instruction	7–9			231–26	s
1890 Pickard	School Supervision	16–19	32	32		supt, o
1875 Payne	Chapters on School Supervision					supt

Label Key   a=administrator   c=critic   d=director curriculum/instruction   ed l=educational leader   ht=helping teacher
  i=instructor   l=leader   o=overseer   s=supervisor   pr=principal
  prof=professional   sp=specialis   sp r=supervising principal   supt=superintendent

Source: Williams, 1994

could be achieved through a more consistent and collaborative approach to preparation programs, certification requirements, and enforcement of standards to assure ethical and professional behavior. More emphasis on professionalism and the three dimensions of self-discipline occurred during the 1875–1949 and 1960–1969 periods.

VALUES OF PROFESSIONALISM/ PROFESSIONALIZATION

Strauss (1963) delineated four "values" associated with professionalism: expertise, autonomy, responsibility, and commitment. Each of these values is elaborated here.

Expertise

Established professions. The authority based on expertise derives from the fact that a professional occupation has clients, while a nonprofessional occupation has customers. Customers determine the services and/or commodities they want and shop around until they find them. Their freedom of decision rests upon the premise that they possess the capacity to determine their own needs and to judge the potential of the service or of the commodity to satisfy those needs. In a professional relationship, however, the professional determines what is best for the client (Greenwood, 1957, p. 49).

Every profession is identified by a codified, systematic body of knowledge which is neither possessed by any other professional group nor by the general public, and which is necessary to help solve specific problems. It is the possession of such expertise that sets the professional apart from lay people. To attain this knowledge, the professional must go through a lengthy period of specialized preparation. The nature and duration of this period of preparation will vary, but must be demanding enough to convince society to regard professionals as experts. Trust by society is critical to the acceptance of an occupation as a profession.

Education field. The existence and nature of a codified body of knowledge for teaching remains a hotly contested issue in education (Beyer et al, 1989; Carter, 1990; Feiman-Nemser & Floden, 1986; Grossman, Wilson, & Shulman, 1989; Lortie, 1975; Ornstein, 1981; Shulman, 1987; Spring, 1985; Sockett, 1989; Tom & Valli, 1990). One school of thought views teaching knowledge as scientifically based, objective, and lawlike. This conception has led to emphasis upon the technical skills needed to teach (Beyer et al, 1989; Lortie, 1975; Tom & Valli, 1990). A second school of thought views teaching knowledge as practical and site-specific. This conception has led to emphasis on understanding of self, students, and the contexts in which the teacher functions (Feiman-Nemser & Floden, 1986).

A survey of the literature by Hart and Marshall (1992) indicates that between these two views there is general agreement on at least two points. First, teaching is acknowledged to be a complex, multidimensional act which calls on many different types of knowledge, actions, behaviors, and decision-making abilities (Ayers, 1990; Barnes, 1989; Feiman-Nemser & Floden, 1986; Florio-Ruane, 1989; Spring, 1985). Second, in response to this complexity, teachers must have an understanding of both subject matter and pedagogy as well as the intricate relationships between them (Beyer et al, 1989;

Dreeben, 1970; Grossman et al, 1989; Howsam et al, 1976; Macklin, 1981; McDiarmid, Bell, & Anderson, 1989; Shulman, 1987; Tamir, 1988). These two areas constitute what is broadly thought of as the knowledge base of teaching (Hart & Marshall, 1992, p. 9).

Instructional supervision. Far less agreement exists regarding a distinct knowledge base for instructional supervision and curriculum development (Harris, 1963; Macdonald, 1965). Expertise in a profession also requires awareness of what it does not include. Frymier cautions that instructional supervisors cannot do anything and everything. The essence of a true professional lies in making judgments. "[Supervisors] must learn to use themselves in such a way that *what they do makes a difference.* . . . Unless the supervisory activity makes a direct contribution to improved teacher effectiveness, then it must be defined as beyond the professional sphere" (1969, p. 101).

Autonomy

Established professions. Professional autonomy refers to the scope of independent judgment reserved for practitioners of a profession because of the expertise that they possess (Macklin, 1981; McPeck & Sanders, 1974). Professionals are expected to use their own judgment since they know more about what should be done than the layman. "If there is no scope for independent judgment, there is no autonomy and no profession" (Lieberman, 1956, p. 89).

Education field. "The desire for autonomy," according to Bartoo (1978), "is the primary motivation for group actions, such as setting standards for preparation, licensing, populating licensure boards, promoting certain legislation, and `policing the ranks' of the group" (p. 1).

In education, however, it appears from the writing of Lieberman in 1956 that professional autonomy was not being *taken away* so much as it was being *given away.*

The reluctance of educators to assume responsibilities which are customary in other professions is a rather ironic commentary on some current controversies concerning public education. In recent years, a number of self-styled Paul Reveres, including a sizable number of college professors, have raised an alarm throughout the land concerning the efforts of "professional educators" [primarily public school administrators and employees of the state departments of education] to seize control of the schools from a supposedly complacent public. A sober look at the evidence indicates that . . . the professional educators are relinquishing whatever claims to professional status they might have by their acceptance—active encouragement even—of lay determination of professional matters (p. 106).

Lieberman (1956) listed nine aspects of education that can be categorized either as functions of group or national autonomy, or functions of individual or local autonomy. The five aspects identified as functions of group or national autonomy were: qualifications for admission to preparation programs; standards for entrance and expulsion; standards of professional conduct; power to judge if and when practitioners have violated those standards; and choice of individuals to lead the profession and speak on its behalf. The four aspects of education identified as functions of individual or local autonomy were: the subjects to be taught and the materials to be used in teaching them; the criteria to be used in determining students to be admitted, retained, and graduated at all levels; the forms to be used in reporting student progress; and school boundary lines and the criteria for permitting students to attend schools outside the boundary lines (p. 91).

Teachers exercise their collective professional autonomy by participation in self-governing and self-regulating professional organizations, particularly the NEA and the AFT. Although these organizations are designed to work on behalf of teachers, they have had little to do with the kinds of decisions noted earlier regarding the profession's standards. The need for strong professional organizations that would control the preparation and certification of teachers has been and continues to be discussed in the literature (Darling-Hammond & Goodwin, 1993; Darling-Hammond, Wise, & Klein, 1995; Howsam et al, 1976, 1985; Leeper,. 1965; Lieberman, 1956; Ornstein, 1981; Shanker, 1985; Spring, 1985; Stinnett, 1962).

As with group autonomy, teaching has not yet succeeded in gaining much local autonomy as a profession. Many teaching decisions are made by others (e.g., administrators, textbook publishers, and/or state policymakers) or heavily influenced by the decisions made by others (e.g., state legislators and/or school boards) (Hart & Marshall, 1992, p. 16). The opportunity for teachers to make decisions on matters which directly affect them has been improved by the emphasis on shared governance during the reform movement of the 1980s. However, in practice, the governance that was most freely shared often involved relatively trivial matters (Allan, 1993; Allan & Glickman, 1992; Glickman, 1993).

Responsibility

Established professions. Professions are too often viewed in terms of their superior prestige and income (Counts, 1925). Too often ignored is the fact that the full meaning of professionalization requires acceptance of greater responsibilities on the part of practitioners (Horton, 1944; Ornstein, 1981; Weil & Weil, 1971). There are grave dangers in permitting an occupation to assume the designation of profession while permitting the practitioners to evade professional responsibilities.

Self-regulation is a key responsibility of a profession. Monitoring the behavior of its members is critically important. The specific knowledge base required for the practice of the profession means that only those who share that knowledge base are qualified to pass judgment on the quality, conduct, and practice of the profession (Becker, 1962).

Education field. Professionalization of education would call for a transformation of practitioner responsibilities. Educators must, as do practitioners of the established professions, demonstrate as much concern for their professional obligations as for their professional prerogatives. Time must be devoted to such matters as accreditation, certification, and enforcement of professional ethics.

The notion of education as a profession appears utopian to many educators. Some teachers and educational leaders assert that they do not want to attend professional meetings, formulate professional policies, or discipline professional behavior. Such comments are often made by teachers who have not been encouraged or expected to accept nonclassroom duties and who work under conditions of employment which are not conducive to the acceptance of such responsibilities. The challenge is to change conditions of employment that developed when there was no thought of an autonomous, self-governing profession of teachers (Lieberman, 1956, p. 508).

Some professions have been able to expand services through effective utilization of semiprofessional or subprofessional assistants. The possibility of a similar pattern in education would allow delegation of lesser tasks and create the time needed for attention to nonclassroom professional obligations.

Establishing a profession of education would require changes that would affect everyone concerned with the educational enterprise (Lieberman, 1956, p. 509). It would require basic changes in the legal and administrative structure of public education. It would also require changes in preparation programs. Most importantly, relationships would have to be considered in a new perspective, as educators assumed responsibility for professional competence and professional discipline.

International Supervision All educational personnel, regardless of qualifications or power over others in a school system, are encouraged to believe that they are members of a single unified profession. Since control over teachers is inconsistent with the idea that a profession is a community of equals, disparate qualifications and differential power often are treated lightly (Lieberman, 1956, 1960).

This situation lends itself to hypocrisy of the worst sort. . . . The supervisor is presumably an expert; otherwise, there would be no point in the role. But the modern approach is that supervision must not be forced on the teacher . . . because it would be undemocratic and unprofessional for one member of the profession to control the behavior of other members. . . . Thus we are left with the problem of how to make sure that the superior technical competence of the supervisor is reflected in the work done by the teacher. This problem is a negligible one in other professions, where different levels of professional competence are recognized from the beginning (Lieberman, 1956, p. 503).

Commitment

Established professions. Every profession has its own norms, values, and symbols which are usually formed around professional organizations. Every profession also has its own purposes for existence which are accepted by each member of the profession. Through these shared purposes, a unity is formed among the individual practitioners which provides the structure of the profession as a whole (Greenwood, 1957; Hart & Marshall, 1992; Langford, 1978).

The rigorous and lengthy preparation required of most professions serves as an "ordeal of training" (Dreeben, 1970). Grueling internships for physicians and the demands of bar examinations for attorneys are examples of this ordeal of training. Surviving such rigors requires future professionals to work together and provides a unique, identity-forming bonding experience. "They have all survived to become `one of them'—a crucial self-perception" in the commitment of a neophyte to the profession (Hart & Marshall, 1992, p. 7). Another evidence of commitment is the acceptance of a profession as a life's work; professionals tend to stay in their chosen professions throughout their careers.

Education field. The preparation that teachers receive is usually seen as lacking the rigors needed to provide a true "ordeal of training" experience (Dreeben, 1970). The overall lack of ordeal in the training of teachers seems to encourage the development of an individual, rather than a group, identity (Dreeben, 1970; Hart & Marshall, 1992; Lortie, 1975).

Instructional supervision. Efforts have been made toward professionalization of school leaders, including supervisory personnel. An ASCD Commission on the Preparation of Instructional Leaders, established in 1959, described its charge during the initial year:

Other professional organizations and lay groups look to ASCD as an organization for leadership in the areas of instructional supervision and curriculum development. . . . Therefore, to offer [instructional] supervisors and curriculum workers an opportunity to develop plans for their own self-discipline and professional maturation and to allow them to speak out through the Association seems to be not only an important function for ASCD but, more significantly, a primary responsibility (ASCD, 1960).

Upon recommendation of the Commission on the Preparation of Instructional Leaders, the ASCD Executive Committee dedicated itself in 1961 to cooperating with the AASA, the NAESP, and the NASSP in establishing a Joint Committee on the Professionalization of Administrators and Supervisors.

In 1963, another significant step was taken by the ASCD when the Executive Committee designated the National Council for Accreditation of Teacher Education (NCATE) as the agency for approving preparatory institutions. A budget allotment was subsequently made to the NCATE for the development of standards to be used in accrediting programs.

Also in 1963, the final report of the Commission on the Preparation of Instructional Leaders recommended that the ASCD Executive Committee appoint a Standing Committee on Professionalization of Supervisors and Curriculum Workers. This committee and its successors have continued the work of the original commission.

The Standing Committee on Professionalization of Supervisors and Curriculum Workers spent its first year in 1964 researching the status of instructional supervisors and curriculum directors. It was soon apparent that any significant progress on the national level would require comparable action within each state. Consequently, state ASCD presidents were encouraged to create Committees on Professionalization of Supervisors and Curriculum Workers within each affiliate. With approximately 70 percent of the states responding, representative groups met in five regional areas during 1965–1966. From these regional meetings, 15 state affiliates sought to determine the current status of instructional supervisors and curriculum directors and design action programs to advance their quality and status (Ogletree, 1965). Seven ASCD affiliates currently are involved in pilot states with the NCATE and its 28 constituent members.

In 1973, the ASCD charged a working group with the task of addressing the professional responsibility of certificating curriculum leaders. During the deliberations, it became clear that the issues of certification were inextricably entwined with the concerns of preparation and accreditation. The result of that group's efforts was the publication entitled *Curriculum Leaders: Improving Their Influence* issued in 1976 (Bartoo, 1978).

CRITIQUE

The placement of education among the established professions is an issue of intense debate, both within the field and by society at large. General guidelines and standards have been proposed for programs of preparation, certification to practice, and enforcement of ethical standards. The integrity of a profession—indeed, its hallmark—rests upon control of these three factors (Firth, 1977).

Consensus of 24 of the 128 books examined by Williams (1994) was that the professionalism of instructional supervisors required organizing a distinct group with standards, traditions, body of knowledge and skills, policies enforced by a professional group, and discipline of members to guarantee effective, ethical, and professional behavior.

REFERENCES

Abrahamson, M. (1967). *The professional in the organization*. Chicago, IL: Rand McNally & Company.

Allan, L. R. & Glickman, C. D. (1992, March). School improvement: The elusive faces of shared governance. *NASSP Bulletin, 76*(542), 80–87.

Allan, L. R. (1993). *The role of voice in shared governance: A case study of a primary school*. Unpublished doctoral disseration in Educational Leadership at the University of Georgia, Athens, GA.

Anderson, A. W. (1962). The teaching profession: An example of diversity in training and function. In N. B. Henry (Ed.). *Education for the professions* (61st Yearbook of the National Society for the Study of Education, Part II; pp. 140-167). Chicago, IL: The University of Chicago Press.

American Association of School Administrators. (1993). *Professional standards for the superintendency*. Arlington, VA: Author.

Association for Supervision and Curriculum Development Commission on the Preparation of Instructional Leaders. (1960). Mimeographed working paper. Washington, D.C.: ASCD, NEA.

Ayers, W. (1990). Rethinking the profession of teaching: A progressive option. *Action in Teacher Education, 12*(1), 1–5.

Barnes, H. (1989). Structuring knowledge for beginning teachers. In M. C. Reynolds (Ed.). *Knowledge base for beginning teachers* (pp. 13–22). New York: Pergamon Press,

Bartoo, E., Speiker, C. A., & Sturges, A. W. (1976). Summary and recommendations. In C. A. Speiker, (Ed.). *Curriculum leaders: Improving their influence* (pp. 63–71). Washington, D.C.: ASCD.

Bartoo, E. (1978). Curriculum leaders: Improving their influence. In A. W. Sturges (Ed.). *Certificating the curriculum leader and the instructional supervisor* (pp. 1–11). Washington, D.C.: ASCD.

Becker, H. S. (1956, Winter). Some problems with professionalization. *Adult Education, 6*(2) 101–05.

Becker, H. S. (1962). The nature of a profession. In H. B. Henry. (Ed.). *Education for the professions* (61st Yearbook of the National Society for the Study of Education, Part II; pp. 27–46). Chicago, IL: The University of Chicago Press.

Beyer, L. E., Feinberg, W., Pagano, J. A., & Whitson, J. A. (1989). *Preparing teachers as professionals: The role of educational studies and other liberal disciplines*. New York: Teachers College Press.

Brubacher, J. S. (1962). The evolution of professional education. In N. B. Henry, (Ed.). *Education for the professions* (61st Yearbook of the National Society for the Study of Education, Part II; pp. 47–67). Chicago, IL: The University of Chicago Press.

Bucher, R. & Strauss, A. (1961, January). Professions in process. *The American Journal of Sociology, 66*(4), 325–334.

Button, H. W. (1961) *A history of supervision in public schools, 1870–1950*. Doctoral dissertation. Washington University.

Butts, F. & Cremin, L. (1953). *A history of education in American culture*. New York: Henry Holt & Company.

Caplow, T. (1954). *The sociology of work*. Minneapolis, MN: University of Minnesota Press.

Carr-Saunders, A. M. (1928, May). *Professions: Their organization and place in society.* Herbert Spencer Lecture at Oxford, Oxford: Clarendon Press.

Carr-Saunders, A. M. & Wilson, P. A. (1933). *The professions.* Oxford: Clarendon Press.

Carter, K. (1990). Teachers knowledge and learning to teach. In R. W. Houston, M. Haberman, & J. P. Sikula (Eds.). *Handbook of research on teacher education* (pp. 291–310). New York: Macmillan.

Cogan, M. L. (1953, Winter). Toward a definition of a profession. *Harvard Educational Review, 23*(1), 33–50.

Cogan, M. L. (1955, January). The problem of defining a profession. *Annals of the American Academy of Political and Social Science, 297*(1), 105–111.

Counts, G. S. (1925, January). The social status of occupations. *School Review, 33*(1), 16–27.

Courtis, S. A., McSwaim, E. T., & Morrison, N. C. (Eds.). (1939) *Cooperation: Principles and practice* (11th yearbook of the Department of Supervisors and Directors of Instruction). Washington, D.C.: National Education Association.

Darling-Hammond, L. & Goodwin, A. L. (1993). Progress toward professionalism in teaching. In G. Cawelti (Ed.). *Challenges and achievements of American education* (ASCD 1993 Yearbook; pp. 19–25). Alexandria, VA: ASCD.

Davies, A. F. (1952, June). Prestige of occupations. *British Journal of Sociology, 3*(2), 134–147.

Dreeben, R. (1970). *The nature of teaching.* Glenview, IL: Scott, Foresman.

Dull, L. W. (1981). *Supervision-school leadership handbook.* Columbus, OH: Charles W. Merrill Publishing Company.

Dumont, M. P. (1970). The changing face of professionalism. In L. A. Netzer, G. G. Eye, M. E. Dimock, M. P. Dumont, L. Homme, F. E. Kast, & S. J. Knezevich (Eds.). *Education, administration and change: The redeployment of resources.* New York: Harper and Row.

Edmonson, J. B. (1930). Professional standards as they relate to teaching. *The Nation's Schools, 6*(5), 21–25.

Edmonson, J. B. (1953). Some policies of states governing the granting of college charters and related problems. North Central Association Quarterly, 28(4), 215–217.

Elsbree, W. S. (1939). *The American Teacher.* New York: American Book Company.

Feiman-Nemser, S. & Floden, R. E. (1986). The cultures of teaching. In M. C. Wittrock (Ed.). *Handbook of research on teaching* (pp. 505–526). New York: Macmillan.

Firth, G. R. (1959). *Professional self-discipline of public school personnel.* Unpublished doctoral dissertation in Educational Administration, Teachers College, Columbia University, New York.

Firth, G. R. (1978). Preface. In A. W. Sturges (Ed.). *Certificating the curriculum leader and the instructional supervisor.* Washington, D.C.: ASCD.

Flexner, A. (1915). Is social work a profession? In *Proceedings of the national conference of charities and corrections.* Chicago, IL: Hildemann Printing Company, 576–590.

Florio-Ruane, S. (1989). Special organization of classes and schools. In M. C. Reynolds (Ed.). *Knowledge base for beginning teachers* (pp. 163–172). New York: Pergamon Press.

Frymier, J. R. (1969). The supervisor and his professional identity. In W. H. Lucio (Ed.). *The supervisor: New demands, new directions* (pp. 83–102). Washington, D.C.: ASCD, NEA.

Glickman, C. D. (1993). *Renewing America's schools: A guide for school-based action.* San Francisco, CA: Jossey-Bass Publications.

Goode, W. J. (1969). The theoretical limits of professionalization. In A. Etzioni (Ed.). *The semi-professions and their organization: Teachers, nurses, social workers* (pp. 263-313). New York: The Free Press.

Grambs, J. B. (1957). The roles of the teacher. In L. J. Stiles (Ed.). *The teacher's role in American society* (14th Yearbook of the John Dewey Society; pp.73–102). New York: Harper and Brothers.

Greenwood, E. (1957, July). Attributes of a profession. *Social Work 2*(3), 45–55.

Grossman, P. L., Wilson, S. M., & Shulman, L. S. (1989). Teachers of substance: Subject matter knowledge for teaching. In M. C. Reynolds (Ed.). *Knowledge base for beginning teachers* (pp. 23–36). New York: Pergamon Press.

Harris, B. M. (1963, November). Need for research on instructional supervision. *Educational Leadership, 21*(2), 129–136.

Hart, S. P. & Marshall, J. D. (1992). *The question of teacher professionalism* (ERIC Document and Reproduction Service No. ED 349 291, July 1992, 34p).

Hartman, G. A. (1934, October). Prestige of occupations. *Personnel Journal, 13*(5), 144–152.

Hatt, P. K. (1950, May). Occupation and social stratification. *American Journal of Sociology, 55*(6), 533–543.

Heffernan, H. (1940) Newer instructional practices of promise (12th yearbook of the department of supervisors and directors of instruction), Washington, D.C.: National Education Association.

Horton, B. J. (1944). The professor: Ten criteria of a genuine profession. *Science Monthly, 58*(2), 164.

Hosic, J. F. (1920). *The democratization of supervision.* Proceedings of the National Education Association, 58, 414–420

Hosic, J. F. (1928). *Educational supervision* (1st yearbook of the National Conferences on Educational Method). New York: Teacher's College, Columbia University.

Hosic, J. F. (1929). Scientific method is supervision (2nd yearbook of the National Conference of Supervisors and Directors of Instruction. New York: Teachers College.

Howsam, R. B., Corrigan, D. C., Denemark, G. W., & Nash, R. J. (1976). *Educating a profession.* Washington, D.C.: American Association of Colleges for Teacher Education.

Hughes, E. C. (1958). *Men and their work.* Glencoe, IL: The Free Press.

Hughes, E. C. (1969). Professions. In K. S. Lynn (Ed.). *The professions in America.* Boston, MA: Beacon, 1–14.

Krey, R. D. & Burke, P. J. (1989). *A design for instructional supervision.* Springfield, IL: C. C. Thomas Publishing Company.

Lam, J. Y. L. (1983). Determinants of teacher professionalism. *The Alberta Journal of Educational Research, 24*(3), 168–179.

Langford, G. (1978). *Teaching as a profession.* Manchester, England: Manchester University Press.

Leeper, R. R. (Ed.). (1965). *Role of supervisor and curriculum director in a climate of change* (ASCD 1965 Yearbook). Washington, D.C.: ASCD.

Lieberman, M. J. (1956). *Education as a profession.* Englewood Cliffs, NJ: Prentice-Hall.

Lieberman, M. J. (1960). *The future of public education.* (Chicago, IL: The University of Chicago Press.

Lindquist, R. D. (Ed.) (1933). *Effective instructional leadership* (6th yearbook of the department of supervisors and directions of instruction). New York: Teachers College, Columbia University.

Lindsey, M. (1961). (Ed.). *New Horizons for the teaching profession.* Washington, D.C.: National Education Association, National Commission on Teacher Education and Professional Standards.

Lippitt, G. & This, L. (1962). Is training a profession? In *Issues in human relations training* (pp. 117–118). Washington, D.C.: National Education Association.

Lortie, D. C. (1975). *Schoolteacher: A sociological study.* Chicago, IL: The University of Chicago Press.

Macdonald, J. B. (1965, November). Knowledge about supervision: Rationalization or rationale. *Educational Leadership, 23*(2), 161–163.

Mackenzie, G. N. (1961, November). Role of the supervisor. *Educational Leadership, 19*(2), 86–90.

Macklin, M. (1981). Teaching professionalism in the teaching profession. *The Australian Journal of Education, 25*(1), 24–36.

Markowitz, S. (1976, February). The dilemma of authority in supervisory behavior. *Educational Leadership, 33*(5), 367–372.

Marshall, T. H. (1939, August). The recent history of professionalism in relation to social structure and social policy. *Canadian Journal of Economics and Political Science, 5*, 325–340.

McDiarmid, W. G., Ball, D. L., & Anderson, C. W. (1989). Why staying one chapter ahead doesn't really work: Subject-specific pedagogy. In M. C. Reynolds (Ed.). *Knowledge base for beginning teachers* (pp. 193–206). New York: Pergamon Press.

McPeck, J. E. & Sanders, J. T. (1974, August). Some reflections on education as a profession. *Journal of Educational Thought, 8*(2), 55–66.

National Association of Elementary School Principals. (1991). *Proficiences for principals: Elementary and middle school* (revised). Alexandria, VA: Author.

National Association of Secondary School Principals. (1992). *Twelve skill dimensions.* Reston, VA: Author.

National Commission for the Principalship: National Association of Elementary School Principals and National Association of Secondary School Principals. (1990). *Principals for our changing schools: Preparation and certification.* Fairfax, VA: Balmar Printing.

National Manpower Council. (1953). *A policy for scientific and professional manpower.* New York: Columbia University Press, 38–39.

Ogletree, J. R. (1965, November). Professionalization of supervisors and curriculum workers. *Educational Leadership, 23*(2), 153–155.

Ornstein, A. C. (1979, Fall). Toward greater teacher professionalism. *Illinois Schools Journal, 59*(3), 3–14.

Ornstein, A. C. (1981, November). The trend toward increased professionalism for teachers. *Phi Delta Kappan, 63*(3), 196–198.

Parsons, T. (1939, May). The professions and social structure. *Social Forces, 17*(4), 457–467.

Payne, W. H. (1875) *Chapters on school supervision.* New York: American Book Company.

Rankin, P. T. (Ed.). (1934). *Scientific methods in supervisory programs* (7th yearbook of the department of supervsors and directors of the Department of Supervisors and Directors of Instruction). New York: Teachers College, Columbia University.

Sergiovanni, T. J., (1975). (Ed.). *Professional supervision for professional teachers.* Alexandria, VA: ASCD.

Shafer, H. T. (1965, December). What does the Flexner report say to ASCD? *Educational Leadership, 23*(3), 235–238.

Shanker, A. (1985). The making of a profession. *American Educator, 9*(3), 10–17, 46, 48.

Shulman, L. S. (1987). Knowledge and teaching: Foundations of the new reform. *Harvard Educational Review, 57*, 1–22.

Sockett, H. (1989). Research, practice and professional aspiration within teaching. *Journal of Curriculum Studies, 21*(2), 97–112.

Spears, H. (1943). *Leadership at work* (15th yearbook of the development of supervisors and directors of instruction). Washington, D.C.: National Education Association.

Speiker, C. A. (Ed.). (1976). *Curriculum leaders: Improving their influence.* Washington, D.C.: ASCD.

Speiker, C. A. (1978). Shaping policies for certification. In A. W. Sturges (Ed.). *Certificating the curriculum leader and the instructional supervisor* (pp. 35-43). Washington, D.C.: ASCD.

Spring, J. (1985). *American education: An introduction to social and political aspects.* White Plains, NY: Longman.

Stinnett, T. M. (1962). *The profession of teaching.* Washington, D.C.: Center for Applied Research in Education.

Strauss, G. (1963, May). Professionalism and occupational associations. *Industrial Relations, 2*(3), 7–31.

Tamir, P. (1988). Subject matter and related pedagogical knowledge in teacher education. *Teaching & Teacher Education, 4*(2), 99–110.

Tom, A. R. & Valli, L. (1990). Professional knowledge for teachers. In R. W. Houston, M. Haberman, & J. P. Sikula (Eds.). *Handbook of research on teacher education* (pp. 373–392). New York: Macmillan.

Tyler, L. L. (1964, May). Is teaching a profession? *Educational Forum, 28*(4), 413–421.

Vollmer, H. M. & Mills, D. L. (1966). *Professionalization.* Englewood Cliffs, NJ: Prentice-Hall.

Weil, P. E. & Weil, M. (1971). Professionalism: A study of attitudes and values. *The Journal of Teacher Education, 22*(3), 314–318.

Wilkin, R. N. (1938). *The spirit of the legal profession.* London: Oxford University Press.

Williams, H. G. (1994). *Professional self-discipline of instructional supervision: Influences of national leadership organizations.* Unpublished applied project for the Specialist in Education degree in Educational Leadership at the University of Georgia, Athens, GA.

Wilensky, H. J. (1964, September). The professionalization of everyone. *American Journal of Sociology, 70*(2), 137–158.

TEXTBOOKS ON INSTRUCTIONAL SUPERVISION LISTED BY THE SEVEN ERAS PUBLISHED DURING THE 120-YEAR PERIOD 1875–1994

The First 75 Years (1875–1949)

Alberty, H. & Thayer, V. (1931). *Supervision in the secondary school.* Boston: D. C. Heath.

Anderson, C., Barr, A., & Bush, M. (1925). *Visting the teacher at work.* New York: D. Appleton-Century.

Anderson, C. & Simpson, I. (1932). *The supervision of rural schools.* New York: D. Appleton-Century.

Barr, A. & Burton, W. (1926). *The supervision of instruction.* New York: D. Appleton-Century.

Barr, A., Burton, W., & Brueckner, L. (1938). *Supervision: Principles, and practices in the improvement of instruction.* New York: D. Appleton-Century.

Briggs, T. (1938). *Improving instruction.* New York: Macmillan.

Collings, E. (1927). *School supervision in theory and practice.* New York: Thomas Crowell.

Foster, H. (1939). *High school supervision.* New York: T. Nelson.

Kyte, G. (1930). *How to supervise.* Boston: Houghton Mifflin.

Kyte, G. (1931). *Problems in school supervision.* Boston: Houghton Mifflin.

Myers, A., Kifer, L., Merry, R., & Foley, F. (1938). *Cooperative supervision in the public schools.* New York: Prentice-Hall.

Myers, A. & Kifer, L. (1939). *Problems in public school supervision.* New York: Prentice-Hall.

Nutt, H. (1920). *The supervision of instruction.* Boston: Houghton Mifflin.

Payne, W. (1875). *Chapters on school supervison.* New York: American Book.

Pickard, J. (1890). *School supervision.* New York: D. Appleton-Century.

Pittman, M. (1925). *The value of school supervison.* Baltimore: Warwick and York.

Wagner, C. (1921). *Common sense in school supervision.* Milwaukee, WI: Bruce Publishing.

The Decade 1950–1955

Adams, H. & Dickey, F. (1953). *Basic principles of supervision.* New York: American Book.

Ayer, F. (1954). *Fundamentals of instructional supervision.* New York: Harper.

Bartky, J. (1953). *Supervision as human relations.* Boston: D. C. Heath.

Burton, W. & Brueckner, L. (1955). *Supervision, a social process.* New York: Appleton-Century-Crofts.

Crosby, M. (1957). *Supervision as co-operative action.* New York: Appleton-Century-Crofts.

Elsbree, W. (1951). *Elementary school adminstration and supervision.* New York: American Book.

Elsbree, W. & McNally, H. (1959). *Elementary school adminstration and supervision* (2nd. ed.). New York: American Book.

Flexner, A. (1951). What are the earmarks of a profession? In B. Smith (Ed.). *Readings in the social aspects of education* (pp. 553–556). Danville, IL: Interstate Printers and Publishers.

Hammock, R. (1955). *Supervising instruction in secondary schools.* New York: McGraw-Hill.

McNerney, C. (1951). *Educational supervision.* New York: McGraw-Hill.

Melchior, W. (1950). *Instructional supervision.* Boston: D. C. Heath.

Peckham, D. (1953). *Principles and techniques of supervision.* Dubuque: IO. W. C. Brown.

Spears, H. (1953). *Improving and supervision of instruction.* New York: Prentice-Hall.

Wiles, K. (1950). *Supervision for better schools* (2nd ed.). New York: Prentice-Hall.

The Decade 1960–1969

Bradfield, L. (1964). *Supervision for modern elementary schools.* Columbus, OH: C. E. Merrill Books.

Cox, J. (1967). *A history of school-system supervision in Georgia.* Ann Arbor, MI: University Microfilms.

Cramer, R. & Domian, O. (1960). *Administration and supervision in the elementary school.* New York: Harper.

Curtin, J. (1964). *Supervision in today's elementary schools.* New York: Macmillan.

Douglass, H., Bent, R., & Boardman, C. (1961). *Democratic supervision in secondary schools.* Boston: Houghton Mifflin.

Elsbree, W., McNally, H., & Wynn, R. (1967). *Elementary school administration and supervision.* New York: American Book.

Evans, G. (1968). *First-line supervision in the public schools.* Minneapolis, MN: Educational Research and Development.

Eye, G. & Netzer, L. (1965). *Supervision of instruction.* New York: Harper and Row.

Franseth, J. (1961). *Supervision as leadership.* Evanston, IL: Row, Peterson.

Goldhammer, R. (1969). *Clinical supervision.* New York: Holt, Rinehart, and Winston.

Gwynn, J. (1961). *Theory and practice of supervison.* New York: Dodd and Mead.

Harris, B. (1963). *Supervisory behavior in education.* Englewood Cliffs, NJ: Prentice-Hall.

Harrison, R. (1968). *Supervisory leadership in education.* New York: American Book.

Hicks, H. (1960). *Educational supervision in principle and practice.* New York: Ronald Press.

Hyman, R. (1967). *School administrator's faculty supervision handbook.* Englewood Cliffs, NJ: Prentice-Hall.

Lippitt, G. & This, L. (1962). Is training a profession? In I. Weschler & E. Schein (Eds.). *Issues in human relations training* (pp. 117–118). Washington, D.C.: National Training Laboratories.

Lucio, W. (1962). *Supervision: A synthesis of thought and action.* New York: McGraw-Hill.

Lucio, W. & McNeil, J. (1969). *Supervision: A synthesis of thought and action.* (2nd ed.). New York: McGraw-Hill.

Neagley, R. & Evans, N. (1964). *Handbook for effective supervision of instruction.* Englewood Cliffs, NJ: Prentice-Hall.

Stoops, E. & Marks, J. (1965). *Elementary school supervision.* Boston: Allyn and Bacon.

Swearingen, M. (1962). *Supervision of instruction: Foundations and dimensions.* Boston: Allyn and Bacon.

Wiles, K. (1967). *Supervision for better schools* (3rd ed.). Englewood Cliffs, NJ: Prentice-Hall.

Wilson, L. (1969). *Sociology of supervision.* Boston: Allyn and Bacon.

The Decade 1970–1979

Alfonso, R., Firth, G., & Neville, R. (1975). *Instructional supervision: A behavioral system.* Boston: Allyn and Bacon.

Bellon, J. & Bellon, E. (1976). *Classroom supervision and instructional improvement: A synergetic process.* Dubuque, IO: Kendall/Hunt Publishing.

Berman, L. (1971). *Supervision: Staff development and leadership.* Columbus, OH: C. E. Merrill.

Blumberg, A. (1974). *Supervisors and teachers: A private cold war.* Berkeley, CA: McCutchan Publishing.

Cogan, M. (1973). *Clinical supervision.* Boston: Houghton Mifflin.

Eisner, E. (1979). *The educational imagination.* New York: Macmillan.

Feyereisen, K. & Fiorino, A. (1970). *Supervision and curriculum renewal.* New York: Appleton-Century-Crofts.

Harris, B. (1975). *Supervisory behavior in education* (2nd ed.). Englewood Cliffs, NJ: Prentice-Hall.

Lewis, A. & Miel, A. (1972). *Supervision for improved instruction.* Belmont, CA: Wadsworth Publishing.

Lucio, W. & McNeil, J. (1979). *Supervision in thought and action* (3rd ed.). New York: McGraw-Hill.

Marks, J., Stoops, E., & King-Stoops, J. (1971). *Handbook of educational supervision.* Boston: Allyn and Bacon.

Marks, J., Stoops, E., & King-Stoops, J. (1978). *Handbook of educational supervision* (2nd ed.). Boston: Allyn and Bacon.

Mosher, R. & Purpel, D. (1972). *Supervision: The reluctant profession.* Boston: Houghton Mifflin.

Neagley, R. & Evans, N. (1970). *Handbook for effective supervision of instruction* (2nd ed.). Englewood Cliffs, NJ: Prentice-Hall.

Oliva, P. (1976). *Supervision for today's schools.* New York: Crowell.

Sergiovanni, T. & Starratt, R. (1971). *Emerging patterns of supervision: Human perspectives.* New York: McGraw-Hill.

Stoller, N. (1978). *Supervision and the improvement of instruction.* Englewood Cliffs, NJ: Educational Technology.

Unruh, A. & Turner, H. (1970). *Supervision for change and innovation.* Boston: Houghton Mifflin.

Wiles, K. & Lovell, J. (1975). *Supervision for better schools* (4th ed.). Englewood Cliffs, NJ: Prentice-Hall.

Williams, S. (1972). *New dimensions in supervision.* Scranton, PA: Intext Educational Publishers.

The Decade 1980–1989

Acheson, K. (1980). *Techniques in the clinical supervision of teachers: Preservice and inservice applications.* New York: Longman.

Acheson, K. (1987). *Techniques in the clinical supervision of teachers: Preservice and in-service applications.* New York: Longman.

Alfonso, R., Firth, G., & Neville, R. (1981). *Instructional supervision: A behavior system* (2nd ed.). Boston: Allyn and Bacon.

Beach, D. & Reinhartz, J. (1989). *Supervision: A focus on instruction.* New York: Harper and Row.

Bellon, J. & Bellon, E. (1982). *Classroon supervision and instructional improvement: A synergetic process* (2nd ed.). Dubuque, IA: Kendall/Hunt Publishing.

Blumberg, A. (1980). *Supervisors and teachers: A private cold war* (2nd ed.). Berkeley, CA: McCutchan Publishing.

Champagne, D. & Hogan, R. (1981). *Consultant supervision: Theory and skill development.* Bloomington, IL: CH Publications.

Champagne, D. & Hogan, R. (1981). *Consultant supervision: Theory and skill development* (2nd ed.). Bloomington, IL: CH Publications.

Cooper, J. (Ed.). (1984). *Developing skills for instructional supervision.* New York: Longman.

Daresh, J. (1989). *Supervision as a proactive process.* New York: Longman.

Doll, R. (1983). *Supervision for staff development.* Boston: Allyn and Bacon.

DuFour, R. (1987). *Fulfilling the promise of excellence.* Westbury, NY: J. L. Wilkerson.

Dull, L. (1981). *Supervision: School leadership handbook.* Columbus, OH: C. E. Merrill.

Furman, R. (1987). *Supervision: Evaluation of teaching.* New York: Vantage Press.

George, N. & Protherough, R. (Eds.). (1989). *Supervision in education.* Hull, Humberside, Quebec: University of Hull.

Gillespie, K. (1981). *Creative supervision.* New York: Harcourt, Brace Jovanovich.

Glickman, C. (1985). *Supervision of instruction: A developmental approach.* Boston: Allyn and Bacon.

Goldhammer, R., Anderson, R., & Krajewski, R. (1980). *Clinical supervision: Special methods for the supervision of teachers.* New York: Holt, Rinehart, and Winston.

Goldstein, W. (1982). *Supervision made simple.* Bloomington, IN: Phi Delta Kappa.

Gorton, R., Schneider, G., & Fisher, J. (Eds.). (1988). *Encyclopedia of school administration and supervision.* Phoenix, AZ: Oryx Press.

Harris, B. (1985). *Supervisory behavior in education* (3rd ed.). Englewood Cliffs, NJ: Prentice-Hall.

Hoy, W. & Forsyth, P. (1986). *Effective supervision: Theory into practice.* New York: Random House.

Knoll, M. (1987). *Supervision for better instruction: Practical techniques for improving staff performance.* Englewood Cliffs, NJ: Prentice-Hall.

Krey, R. & Burke, P. (1989). *Design for instructional supervision.* Springfield, IL: C. C. Thomas.

Lovell, J. & Wiles, K. (1983). *Supervision for better schools* (5th ed.). Englewood Cliffs, NJ: Prentice-Hall.

Luehe, B. (1989). *The principal and supervision.* Bloomington, IN: Phi Delta Kappa.

Marks, J., Stoops, E., & King-Stoops, J. (1985). *Handbook of educational supervision* (3rd ed.). Boston: Allyn and Bacon.

Neagley, R. & Evans, N. (1980). *Handbook for effective supervision of instruction* (3rd ed.). Englewood Cliffs, NJ: Prentice-Hall.

Oliva, P. (1984). *Supervision for today's schools* (2nd ed.). New York: Longman.

Oliva, P. (1989). *Supervision for today's schools* (3rd ed.). New York: Longman.

Pajak, E. (1989). *The central office supervisor of curriculum and supervision.* Boston: Allyn and Bacon.

Pfeiffer, I. & Dunlap, J. (1982). *Supervision of teachers: A guide to improving instruction.* Phoenix, AZ: Oryx Press.

Schain, R. (1988). *Supervising instruction.* New York: Educators Practical Press.

Schon, D. (1983). *The reflective practitioner.* New York: Basic Books Publishers.

Schon, D. (1987). *Educating the reflective practitioner.* San Francisco, CA: Jossey-Bass Publishers.

Sergiovanni, T. & Starratt, R. (1983). *Supervision: Human perspectives* (3rd ed.). New York: McGraw-Hill.

Sergiovanni, T. & Starratt, R. (1983). *Supervision: Human perspectives* (4th ed.). New York: McGraw-Hill.

Tanner, D. & Tanner. L. (1987). *Supervision in education: Problems and practices.* New York: Macmillan.

Wiles, J. & Bondi, J. (1980). *Supervision: A guide to practice.* Columbus, OH: C. E. Merrill.

Wiles, J. & Bondi, J. (1980). *Supervision: A guide to practice* (2nd ed.). Columbus, OH: C. E. Merrill.

The Last Half Decade 1990–1994

Acheson, K. (1992). *Techniques in the clinical supervision of teachers: Preservice and inservice applications.* New York: Longman.

Anderson, R. & Snyder, K. (Eds.). (1993). *Clinical supervision: Coaching for higher performance.* Lancaster, PA: Technomic.

Delano, J. (1993). *The supervisor's log: A professional's graffiti: A handbook for supervision.* New York: Teachers College Press.

Glanz, J. (1990). *Bureaucracy and professionalism: The evolution of public school supervision.* Madison, WI: Fairleigh Dickinson University Press.

Glatthorn, A. (1990). *Supervisory leadership.* Glenview, IL: Scott, Foresman/Little, Brown.

Glickman, C. (1990). *Supervision of instruction: A developmental approach.* Boston: Allyn and Bacon.

Goldhammer, R., Anderson, R., & Krajewski, R. (1993). *Clinical supervision* (3rd ed.). Fort Worth, TX: Harcourt Brace Jovanovich.

Oliva, P. (1993). *Supervision for today's schools* (4th ed.). New York: Longman.

Pajak, E. (1993). *Approaches to clinical supervision.* Norwood, MA: Christopher-Gordon.

Sergiovanni, T. & Starratt, R. (1993). *Supervision: A redefinition.* New York: McGraw-Hill.

Tracy, S. & MacNaughton, R. (1993). *Assisting and assessing educational personnel.* Boston: Allyn and Bacon.

SECTION II.
THE IDENTITY/IMAGE OF SCHOOL SUPERVISION

INTRODUCTION

This section considers the identity of practitioners of instructional supervision and the image of instructional supervisors to themselves and to others.

Findings are presented in each of the following 10 categories: definitions of terms; general considerations; exemplars from established professions; situations in the field of education; conditions in the craft of school supervision; literature review; research reports; document analyses; aspects of identity/image, including perceptions, antecedents, titles, functions, theory, and research; and critique.

DEFINITIONS OF TERMS

For the purpose of this analysis, the term *identity* is defined as the set of behavioral or personal characteristics by which an individual is recognizable as a member of a group; and the term *image* is defined as the impression of an individual or a group that is projected to and/or held by the public.

GENERAL CONSIDERATIONS

Occupations, to a considerable extent, serve to fix people to a position in society. Among the links between the larger social life and occupations, one of the more obvious involves social status and prestige. In all complex societies, characteristics of the way people earn their living confers status upon individuals. Those occupations which rank higher in socioeconomic status may facilitate the practitioner's upward mobility (Vollmer & Mills, 1966).

Persons who successfully learn the language and skills of an occupation emerge not only with an internalized commitment but also with an identification with the collectivity, the brotherhood (Moore, 1970). Every profession lives in a world of its own. The language which is spoken by its inhabitants, the landmarks so familiar to them, their customs and conventions can only be thoroughly learned by those who reside there" (Carr-Saunders & Wilson, 1933, p. i). In effect, each profession possesses a sort of subculture, composed of the manners, mores and folkways peculiar to the calling, the legends about it, and the symbols that it displays (Caplow, 1954).

Members of a highly familiar occupation are continuously aware of their role as decreed by tradition. They can predict with reasonable accuracy the manner in which they will be received in any company, and the status which will be accorded to them. Where the expectations are very definite, they will even be likely to assume the appropriate personality traits (Caplow, 1954).

The professional's conduct is assumed to reflect not only personal standards, or the lack of them, but professional standards as well. All professionals cringe at the conspicuous misconduct of a fellow; conscientious members even feel aggrieved at misconduct that does not become public (Moore, 1970).

Ideally, the position of the professional is balanced by a set of duties and restraints in dealings with clients, peers, administrators, and the general public. The rules of competence and honorable conduct are likely to be specific to particular professional fields; however, implicit or explicit obligations usually include admonitions to respect the public interest, the duty to perform, and the duty to learn, as well as to preserve and enhance the image (Znaniecki, 1960).

Within a dynamic model of professionalism, an important factor is the meaning which the professional identity has for the individual's self-image (Elliott, 1972).

EXEMPLARS FROM ESTABLISHED PROFESSIONS

Most professional roles, at least those of the traditional professions, are generally recognizable by others in society outside any particular work situation. The latent status attributes attached to professionals do not simply reflect lay ignorance; they arise out of the profession's need to guarantee itself before society. In the guarantee, status and character may be as significant as capability (Elliott, 1972).

In a real sense, professional roles can be said to be total when the practitioner is aware that certain standards of behavior or a particular life-style are expected because of his or her professional identity (Elliott, 1972). Adopting a professional identity has an impact on thought and behavior through the development of distinct professional ideologies.

Specialties and subspecialties develop when a few persons within an occupation take a particular position on some aspect of "professional identity." Through association activities, these persons organize their work in a manner which sets them apart from others in their occupations. Leadership evolves and specific procedures are developed for the conduct of work (Bucher & Strauss, 1961).

SITUATIONS IN THE FIELD OF EDUCATION

The education profession cannot claim elite status. With the spread of literacy, it has lost any esoteric knowledge base. With the growth of white-collar employment, teachers have also lost in relative income and become "the economic proletarians of the professions" (Mills, 1951, p. 129). Employed as they are in bureaucratic institutions, teachers lack both professional authority and independence: They do not control recruitment to the profession, nor preparation, nor certification; nor do they determine their own practice or conditions of service. They cannot turn away clients or fix fees. They swear no oath to a code of ethics and, if such a code existed, the teachers' loosely organized colleague group lacks the necessary disciplinary powers for its enforcement. Although an elite profession may maintain status in the context of bureaucratic employment, as do lawyers in the field of industry, no profession can win this standing for the first time in such an environment (Leggatt, 1970).

At the same time, it would be foolish to deny teachers the title of professionals. Etzioni's preference for "semiprofessional" (1969), though perhaps advancing analytic precision, seems unlikely to become a stable category. The group of occupations most easily distinguished are those with the highest prestige, and these are readily identifiable under the title, enshrined in popular usage, of the elite or established professions. Leggatt (1970) suggests that a more descriptive title for Etzioni's semiprofessions might be the "bureaucratic professions." The outstanding characteristics of teachers as an occupational group are the large number of practitioners, high proportion of female members, low social class composition, small measure of autonomy, and extensive internal segmentation (Leggatt, 1970).

The continuing challenge for improvement of instruction and the need for effective school organization both require specialization in educational leadership. Support for a corps of instructional leaders was articulated in 1963 by a joint committee of the American Association of School Administrators (AASA) and the Association for Supervision and Curriculum Development (ASCD). This committee's report, entitled *Organizing for Improved Instruction,* states:

The assumption that underlies this whole report is that classroom teachers and all staff members in a school system of whatever size need support and stimulation, their growth and competency and vision need nourishment, and their awareness of responsibility for change needs sharpening. To us this posits a necessary role for resource people not identified as administrators. These people are assistant superintendents for instruction or for curriculum, curriculum workers, supervisors, researchers, instructional material workers, and others who provide services designed to support and enrich the learning experiences of children (AASA/ASCD, 1963, p. 8).

Van Til (1965) described these support people as the "pivotal professional educators [who are] at the center of educational enterprises in thousands of American communities."

The good superintendent knows and works with the complex intermeshing of human and physical resources characteristic of the involved social institution called a school system. The good supervisor knows the ways of working with teachers to foster their professional growth. . . . The good curriculum director [provides for] learning opportunities which are based soundly upon philosophical, psychological, and sociological foundations and which draw upon many subjects and areas. So it is also with the good historian of education, the educational psychologist, the methods specialist, and so on through a long list of specialized competencies. . . . In short, the good professional educator is also a scholar in his own specialization (p. 26–7).

Any list of professional educators invariably includes supervisors of instruction, and yet, of all educational specialists, they are perhaps the most difficult to define. The curriculum field is in much the same quandary, also much maligned regarding identity and image. Surveys that have attempted to reconcile what curriculum people do or feel they should do, what curriculum textbooks say, and what curriculum courses teach, have revealed a level of disagreement which makes it very difficult indeed to reach an acceptable understanding of the identity or effectiveness of the curriculum field.

The identity of the field determines what knowledge (in the broadest sense) the potential curriculum leader obtains and the effectiveness of the field determines how that knowledge is enhanced. The curriculum field cannot create the need for the curriculum leader, but can only react to the need. It is suggested that the curriculum field become more agreeably defined from the perspective of the curriculum leader. [emphasis in the original] (Bartoo, Speiker, & Sturges, 1976, p. 64).

Sets of agreed-upon tasks do exist for curriculum leaders and instructional supervisors. Moreover, there are general distinctions between the tasks of the former and the tasks of the latter. Various reports differentiate between the "program-type" responsibilities of the curriculum director and the "people-type" responsibilities of the instructional supervisor. Speiker (1978) reported that, based on the findings of the working group and the correspondence that resulted in the development of *Standards and Guidelines for the Evaluation of Graduate Programs Preparing Curriculum Leaders* (1983), "the instructional supervisor is viewed as a person concerned with processes more than, but not at the exclusion of, products" (p. 37).

CONDITIONS IN THE CRAFT OF SCHOOL SUPERVISION

Because of the many variations on the theme of instructional supervision in theory and in practice, it is difficult to grasp a "vision" of the role. This vision may be created or at least approached through consideration of the identity of its practitioners and/or the image that they project.

Identity of School Supervisors

Discussion of governance requires identification of those subjects to be governed. Unfortunately, the problem of determining the collective characteristics by which an individual is recognized as a member of the group has posed serious difficulties for instructional supervision. Because it has not been possible to determine *who, what, where,* or *when* is a supervisor, the question of *why* is a supervisor is frequently raised.

The problem of lack of identity also has deleteriously affected the image of instructional supervision projected to others within education and to lay citizens. It is extremely difficult to "get a fix" on the parameters of instructional supervision. As a craft, it is simultaneously viewed as an extension of teaching, an adjunct of administration, a concommitment of curriculum, a representation of instruction—among others. Instructional supervision operates in shadow, as a gray area somewhere between teaching and administration. Its practitioners choose to remain obscure, giving credit to others and accepting responsibility without commensurate authority. Instructional supervisors consider their job done well when their effects have been so deft as to escape detection. Pajak (1989) likens them to stage managers whose job is to see that the performance of others goes as it should.

The downside of such altruism is that the efforts of instructional supervisors are often undervalued, particularly by those who call upon them most (McMaster, 1966). At best, their services are so unobtrusive and so intangible that their knowledge and skill are easily dismissed, as if anyone could do the work of supervisors. At worst, their services are presumed to be expendable, with the predictable result that supervisors are often the first to be redefined, reassigned, or eliminated completely during periods of financial exigencies.

It has been alleged that this invisibility of instructional supervision is both desired and deliberate, because it allows its incumbents to flow into and out of situations without the typecasting that accompanies other leadership positions (Pajak, 1989). Indeed, there is often a chameleon expectation that the instructional supervisor will be flexible from one situation to another and adaptable over time.

Numerous role studies (Bradshaw, 1970; Bartoo, Speiker, & Sturges, 1976; Christensen, 1976; Holder, 1977; Srisa-an, 1967; Sturges, 1978) have identified what instructional supervisors most frequently do. Seldom is the relative appropriateness of such tasks and functions considered. Research is less often focused on the matter of who instructional supervisors are or should be. Even more rare are investigations of when an individual becomes an instructional supervisor and by what authority such designation is conferred.

Harris (1967) stated that the confusion among educators and lay citizens about roles and responsibilities is "one of the serious obstacles to professionalization of [instructional] supervision." The confusion itself has serious consequences, according to Harris. It "prevents effective pre-service preparation, makes selection and placement practices haphazard, places supervisors under a cross-fire of conflicting perceptions and expectations from other educators, and frustrates efforts at in-service development of supervisory competencies" (p. 4).

Harris describes seven factors contributing to confusion regarding the roles and responsibilities of instructional supervisors:

1. Lack of product visibility, due to difficulty in identifying the supervisor's accomplishments
2. Unspecific clientele, due to efforts to serve teachers, the principal, the school board, and/or the public
3. Shared responsibilities with teachers, principals, and others, causing difficulties in assigning priorities
4. Change orientation of the supervisor, producing ambivalence—even resistance—from various sources
5. Indistinctive techniques that do not set the supervisor apart from other specialists

6. Itinerant operation, due to lack of a particular location or facility where the supervisor does his or her job
7. Hybrid image due to concentration on instructional improvement in collaboration with teachers and on organizational structure with administrators. (pp. 4–5)

No other position in educational leadership has received so much attention resulting in so little definition (Firth, 1986). The superintendency is not comparably indistinct because, in most states, the role is defined by law. Similarly, the principal's duties are clarified in state school codes. This is not true for instructional supervisors. Such individuals may have different responsibilities but the same title, or identical responsibilities but different titles (Firth, 1986). As a result, titles do not offer much help in clarifying responsibilities.

Leaders in the ASCD have reacted differently to the definitional problem. Greene (1967) explains the committee's rationale in their ASCD 1965 Yearbook, *Role of Supervisor and Curriculum Director in a Climate of Change* (Leeper, 1964).

In most school systems throughout the nation, various persons have assumed supervisory responsibility. The ASCD 1965 Yearbook, Role of Supervisor and Curriculum Director in a Climate of Change, makes no attempt to give titles to all the persons with supervisory responsibility. Instead, the yearbook committee used the term in the broadest sense to indicate . . . any person in an instructional leadership role who contributes to the improvement of teaching and/or the development of curriculum (Greene, 1967, pp. 44–45).

Considerable potential for professionalization of instructional supervisors may lie in establishing a leadership organization with restricted membership that enforces performance and provides specialty recognition through national certification. Such an organization could influence, in collaboration with other groups, accreditation of preparation, certification to practice, and perhaps even the types of positions in which instructional supervisors can serve.

Harris (1967) emphasized the need to establish role definition for professionals in instructional supervision with these words:

Leadership for instructional improvement must be clearly designated as the primary responsibility of a professionally competent group. Such professionals can effectively assume this complex leadership responsibility only when they focus on those tasks that are most relevant to instructional improvement, are provided with a unique set of working relationships, and have competencies necessarily for efficiently accomplishing the designated tasks (p. 12).

Difficulties regarding identity stem in part from differences in the three ways individuals are recognized as possessing qualifications to serve as instructional supervisors: by district appointment, by state certification, and by institutional endorsement. A brief review of these by Firth (1987) illustrates the need for an innovative mechanism that will set appropriate professional standards for these roles and recognize those who have met them.

District appointment. A familiar way that educators become instructional supervisors or curriculum directors is through appointment by the superintendent of a school district or intermediate agency, followed by board of education approval. The placement decision, which may ignore many potential candidates, is often based on perceptions of performance in another role, particularly that of effective teacher. It is assumed, perhaps rashly, that the transition from teacher of students to teacher of teachers is a simple one. Appointees, who may have little preparation for their duties, often then seek admission to higher education institutions offering appropriate formal studies focused on instructional supervision. In effect, then, superintendents determine both the prospective students for the relevant graduate programs and the individuals to be licensed by the state departments of education.

State certification. In most states, instructional supervisors and curriculum directors must meet some requirements, ranging from minimal teaching experience and a specified pattern of courses to completing a master's or even a specialist-level graduate program. Where state certificates are granted to instructional supervisors, individuals are expected to hold or be eligible for them prior to employment in the applicable role. In practice, people are often employed first and allowed a period of time in which to complete the requirements for the certificate.

Institutional endorsement. Where the only road to certification is through graduate programs, admission and completion standards at institutions of higher education often constitute actual licensure requirements. Some college and university programs require documentation that candidates are employed in relevant leadership positions or have been designated for appointment in the near future. Where certification depends primarily on academic preparation, professional standards may become particularly haphazard if the completion requirements of various institutions differ considerably. Course prerequisites, availability, and scheduling naturally influence access to the programs.

Organizational recognition. A clear model for a better mode of entry into professional roles has been established in other professions, notably in law, medicine, engineering, accounting, and psychology. That model is organizational recognition. The compelling reality is that the field of instructional supervision involves 50 separate state education agencies and more than 15,000 local and intermediate school districts. A logical couse to professional identity for instructional supervisors is for the ASCD to create a national specialty board that could certify individuals as having met appropriate professional criteria (Firth, 1987). Such an approach is described later in this chapter in reference to the dimension of licensure/certification.

In establishing the parameters of the theme developed in the ASCD publication describing *Professional Supervision for Professional Teachers* (1975), Sergiovanni declared that: "Identity, commitment, and motivation to work, then, are the ingredients needed in any approach to supervision" (p. 7).

Image of School Supervisors

According to psychological theory, behavior is determined largely by an individual's perception of self and role. Moreover, research indicates that the expectations of others create, at least in part, this self-image which directs behavior (Guss, 1961).

Guss (1961) coordinated a study by the Research Committee of the Indiana Association for Supervision and Curriculum Development for the purpose of ascertaining perceptions of instructional supervision held by a stratified random sample of 50 representatives of each of six groups: school administrators, principals, supervisors, teachers, parents, and faculty members in colleges of education. All groups except teachers viewed the contributions of school supervision to lie in the areas of instructional improvement, curriculum development, and teacher assistance. Teachers, however, thought of supervision as "a program dealing with materials, ideas, and schedules rather than with the teaching–learning situation as it affects personal relationships" (p. 100).

At all levels, supervisory roles require "a clear perspective of the school's goals, awareness of its resources and qualities, and the ability to help others contribute to this vision and to perceive and act in accordance with it" (Lucio & McNeil, 1969, p. 46).

Crosby (1961) noted that supervision can be a potent force when it is conceived as a service function that demands leaders who work "with the staff, not for the staff" (p. 111). This perception of supervision demands instructional supervisors who render service of leadership, spur teachers' self-direction, and share in the solution of problems in learning.

Perceptions of role held by instructional supervisors themselves, as well as by others, appear particularly relevant to image—and hence to behavior.

LITERATURE REVIEW

Although 89 (70%) of the 128 books on instructional supervision published over the 120-year period from 1875 to 1994 referred to supervisors strictly by that title, many different images and roles were described by the authors. The common thread was that the variety of situations in which supervisors work make every position unique. In the ever-changing field of education, supervisors have not clearly defined their roles as professionals, a condition which allows others to dictate their job functions (Castleberry, 1994). Of the five national leadership organizations, only the CCSSO has a restricted membership. The AASA, ASCD, NAESP, and NASSP all have open membership and include more than the specific group that they are assumed to represent (Williams, 1994).

RESEARCH REPORTS

Insights concerning the identity and/or image of instructional supervisors are often obtained from studies that were initiated to investigate other facets of instructional supervision.

Organizations, Institutions, and Agencies

Although designed for the purpose of investigating role, functions, tasks, and/or responsibilities of instructional supervisors and curriculum directors, a series of studies conducted in Georgia over the decade 1967–1977 also offers insights into the identity and image of such positions.

Gott and co-workers (1967) surveyed the entire 602 curriculum personnel employed in Georgia to investigate status, responsibilities, and perceptions of the role. Finding a definite lack of understanding that the curriculum worker's functions should deal only with instruction and curriculum (p. 53), Gott and colleagues (1967) recommended the curriculum worker be assigned minimum administrative responsibilities. Paradoxically, some replies to the survey expressed need for more administrative authority to be vested in the position of curriculum leader. The broad range of activities engaged in by curriculum leaders prompted recommendations that efforts be made to narrow their responsibilities and that the ASCD lead in the development of job descriptions for the role.

Doctoral Dissertations

Srisa-an (1967) surveyed educational leaders in Minnesota for the purpose of investigating perceptions and expectations of the role of curriculum director. Findings indicated that the position of curriculum director is characterized by substantial variation in title, incumbency, and role dimensions. Role expectations expressed by the three respondent groups all endorsed involvement of curriculum directors in activities that were program-centered, developmental, and directly or indirectly related to matters of curricular or instructional concern. However, discrepancies were found when comparing the curriculum directors' description of their actual roles with the principals' and superintendents' expectations of what the role ideally ought to be. Administrators expected curriculum directors to be less involved than they were in such matters as administration of personnel and management of supplies and equipment, and more involved than they were in research, public relations, and supervisory activities. Srisa-an concluded that the nature of responsibilities of curriculum directors is unique enough to require its own major preparation program. He also suggested that, since the overwhelming majority of persons serving as curriculum directors had not received preparation for such functions, inservice education should be provided by institutions of higher education to upgrade their effectiveness.

Bradshaw (1970) surveyed curriculum personnel in Georgia for the purpose of investigating role definition. He recommended that preparation programs focus on activities in which instructional supervisors actually engage, presumably even if such activities were not considered within the scope of that role.

Holder (1977) surveyed instructional supervisors from local school systems plus personnel from the cooperative educational service agencies (CESA) in Georgia for the purpose of task analysis. She found instructional supervisors and/or curriculum leaders in Georgia involved in tasks, particularly administrative, to the neglect of supervisory duties. She cautioned that "encouraging or directing instructional supervisors and/or curriculum leaders to perform duties outside of their primary role [is] dysfunctional and casts doubt about the worth of supervision among groups both internal and external to professional education" (p. 114).

In her survey of educational leaders in 50 states, Jensen (1977) explored the standards, credentials, and titles applied to individuals responsible for implementing staff development. She found a pervasive "lack of concern" for titles. "This inconsistent application of titles to individuals with similar responsibilities, or the use of the same title for individuals having very different duties [inevitably leads to] faulty communication with colleagues and the community" (p. 253). Jensen stressed the need for state education departments to issue certificates with titles descriptive of major responsibilities expected of individuals holding them.

Master's Theses and Specialist Projects

Turpin (1960) surveyed 96 instructional supervisors in Georgia for the purpose of obtaining perceptions and insights on problems in rendering services. Problems mentioned most often included insufficient time to render all supervisory services in a satisfactory manner; unfavorable attitudes of teachers and principals toward change; and inadequate funds for travel, study, and material. Instructional supervisors also reported that the scope of the job was extensive, responsibilities were numerous, and time was insufficient to accomplish all tasks involved.

Johnson (1966) analyzed selected educational literature, descriptive documents from universities in 24 states, and certification requirements in the 50 states to establish guiding principles to improve job descriptions, preparation programs, and certification standards for the curriculum supervisor. Johnson found no consensus concerning the tasks that curriculum supervisors performed in the schools. He recommended that studies be conducted of the positions occupied by supervisors in service to achieve greater commonality in title and role definition.

DOCUMENT ANALYSES

Castleberry (1994) examined 17 documents on instructional supervision published during the 33-year period 1957–1991 for references related to the six aspects of the vision of identity and/or image derived from the analysis by Hart and Marshall (1992) and others: perceptions, antecedents, titles, functions, theory, and research (Table 36–3). She noted the greatest occurrence of references to perceptions, which appeared in all 17 publications, followed by titles which appeared in 15 publications. Three of the other aspects—antecedents, theory, and research—were mentioned in more than half of the publications. Castleberry indicated that she was unable to distinguish between the aspects of title and of function.

ASPECTS OF IDENTITY/IMAGE

The six aspects of the vision of identity/image (Hart & Marshall, 1992) (perceptions, antecedents, titles, functions, theory, and research) are examined in detail.

Perceptions

Instructional supervisors are perceived as multitalented individuals, identified in the literature by their various roles or responsibilities: curriculum developers, teachers of teachers, improvers of instruction, administrators of personnel, coordinators of services, human relations experts, and organizational developers.

Curriculum developers. Instructional supervisors are expected to initiate opportunities or provide structure for curriculum change. However, existence of ill-defined relationships among teachers, administrators, and supervisors, as well as conflicting perceptions of respective roles may combine to inhibit consideration of change (Urick & Frymier, 1963).

Christensen (1976) surveyed 500 curriculum leaders in public schools to ascertain their perceptions of their competencies and their confidence to fill the role. Most curriculum leaders rated both their confidence and competency high.

TABLE 36–3. Occurrences of the Aspects of Perceptions, Antecedents, Titles, Theory, and Research Regarding the Vision of Identity and Image Noted in Documents on Instructional Supervision Published During the 33-Year Period 1959–1991

Author	Year	Perceptions	Antecedents	Titles	Theory	Research
Lucio & McNeil	1962	x	x	x	x	x
Harris	1967	x	x	x	x	
Wahle	1967	x	x	x		
Frymier	1969	x	x	x	x	
Leeper	1969	x	x	x		x
Lucio & McNeil	1969	x		x	x	
Mosher & Purpel	1972	x		x		
Blumberg	1974	x				x
Alfonso, Firth, & Neville	1975	x	x	x	x	x
Glanz	1978	x	x	x		
Struges	1978	x		x		
Alfonso, Firth, & Neville	1981	x	x	x	x	x
Krajewski	1985	x		x		
Bolin	1988	x			x	x
Oliva	1989	x			x	x
Pajak	1990	x	x	x	x	x

Source: Castleberry, 1994, p. 5.

They cited efforts in specific content areas (reading, mathematics, language arts) as major accomplishments. They also reported that educators generally understood the importance of curriculum planning, but that communities did not.

His findings indicated that the role of the curriculum leader and its organizational dimensions were unclear, no common title was applied to the position, and the certification classifications were "as numerous as the states and education agencies" (p. 62). The researcher recommended establishing uniform standards for preparation and certification of curriculum leaders.

Teachers of teachers. Anderson (1967) viewed supervision as an analogue, analyzing common elements and describing, in particular, the teaching aspects of supervision: "Supervision and teaching may be seen as roles with many of the same dimensions, and hence with similar problems and similar satisfactions. . . . For the zealous and professionally minded supervisor, the analogue of supervision as a teaching role seems to offer a wholesome and promising perspective" (p. 29).

The notion of the instructional supervisor as essentially a teacher of teachers is not new. Although this has not been generally viewed as the central concept around which the supervisor's preparation and activity should be organized, the argument can be made that it should be. "[Supervisors] major concern should be with the elements that directly relate to the instructional programs they develop for professional improvement of the teachers they supervise" (Turney, 1966, p. 665). Turney specifically stated that:

The supervisor's major objective should be to help the teacher master the substantive content he may not understand; attain competency in teaching techniques he may not know; and catalog, classify, and test the countless resources that may be brought to bear on the specific learning problems he may encounter. With skills such as these at his command, the teacher will be in a position to create that rare blend of professional competence and personal understanding which results in the fine and sensitive decisions vital to the development of superior programs of classroom instruction (p. 667).

Turney's "main objective" for the supervisor implies that particular competencies are needed by the supervisor. He recommends that preservice and inservice programs for instructional supervisors emphasize the analysis of teaching, individual and group counseling techniques, instructional media, and the structure of knowledge in the content areas. Mallan and Creason (1968) suggested that the fundamental aim of instructional supervisors should be reflective practice, that is, learning to assess such things as who he or she is, what he or she knows, and the types of evidence he or she accepts for knowing—for themselves and for assisting teachers to do so as well.

Improvers of instruction. The role of instructional supervisor has always been synonymous with efforts to improve instruction (Lucio, 1962). Acceptance of improvement of instruction as the raison d'etre of supervision mandates acceptance of an accompanying professional mandate: Those acting in a supervisory capacity must work in close relationship with personnel most directly concerned with instruction, the classroom teachers. Courses in preparation programs and ideal behavior in literature have emphasized interpersonal relations as the main route to instructional improvement. Consequently, the role of instructional supervisors is frequently equated to that of human relations expert with a strong commitment to humanistic values in the instructional program and in professional relationships (Eash, 1968).

Neville (1966) argued for an educational supervisor "who acts directly and effectively to improve the instructional program . . . an authority on teaching, a resource person, and an expert in group dynamics, and more recently [also] conceived of as a catalyst or an agent of change. This constitutes a general statement of the supervisor we need" (pp. 634–635).

If principals consider improvement of instruction as the first responsibility, it becomes imperative that the choice of supervisory personnel be carefully made. Prater (1961) warned that, "School staff itself must understand and accept the significant role of [instructional] supervisors in the constant struggle to attain the educational objectives of the school system" (p. 129).

Administrators of personnel. Instructional supervision shares with personnel administration the basic objectives of doing whatever is necessary to make sure that all who work within the school system have the competencies, will, and working conditions for providing the best educational program (Rutrough, 1967, pp. 54–55). Personnel administrators must be able to deal with complexities of human nature and implications for organizational behavior. The instructional supervisor has an important role to play in assisting the personnel division in coordinating the multiplicity of activities involved in its broad field of operation.

Rutrough (1967) stated that the instructional supervisor could effectively contribute to personnel activity in the areas of "orientation, inservice education, morale, and personal adjustment and motivation" (p. 225).

Coordinators of services. Coordinating contributions of the many and varied consultants now available to assist in improving school personnel and educational programs is often viewed as a responsibility of instructional supervisors. Such consultants may include teachers with special competencies, faculties at institutions of higher education, staff of state education departments, representatives of publishing companies, and lay citizens with particular expertise.

Utilization of multiple consultative services has become a necessity in a rapidly changing society, and coordination of such services is becoming recognized as a central function of instructional supervisors. The ability to act as coordinator of services requires that the supervisor possess broad comprehension of the total school program and of the role played by each staff member in the school's operation, development, and evaluation (Wear, 1966).

Human relations experts. Manley (1958) surveyed teachers, principals, superintendents, and instructional supervisors in Georgia regarding perceptions of supervisory services. The four responding groups were in agreement that the most beneficial services rendered by supervisors were in the area of human relations.

Cox and Lott (1961) examined perceptions of their role held by instructional supervisors in Georgia as well as by teachers and principals with whom they worked. Descriptions drawn from a Q-sort of 100 behaviors were ranked in terms of "most liked" and "least liked" in an ideal instructional supervisor. Each group of respondents ranked highest those behaviors which related to belief in people, acceptance of contributions of each child and teacher, and respect for individual differences of teachers.

Organizational developers. There have been those who doubt that instructional supervision will endure in any of its familiar roles. In addressing supervision as "the reluctant profession," Mosher and Purpel (1972) asserted that "the term 'supervisor' probably has too many negative connotations to survive" (p. 91). Instead, the authors advocated a new concept of leadership for curriculum and instruction in the person of a "clinical professor" who would develop alternative educational modes.

Glanz (1978) described a concerted effort by school supervisors to emphasize, at least in theory, a more democratic professional approach to decrease emphasis on the bureaucratic procedures characteristic of centralized management systems. However, because the process was not always well-defined, many instructional supervisors found that they were engaging in tasks previously the responsibility of other organizational agents. In effect, the supervisors ended up serving as technicians committed to maintaining the equilibrium of the organization rather than serving as educational leaders. Some hold that the main task of supervision is to answer the question of who will make decisions determining the kind of knowledge, skills, and attitudes to be fostered in schools.

Allan (1966) viewed the respective trends toward cooperative development of curriculum and team approach to supervision as reinforcing the need for educational leaders to direct and guide group efforts.

Antecedents

Two important antecedents of school supervision are the traditions from small, rural elementary schools which evolved into statewide programs and from the segregated "Negro" schools of the South.

Grimsley and co-workers (1974) chronicled a history of the development of instructional supervision in Georgia. Its rich legacies illustrate similar patterns in other states. Beginning in 1734 with assignment of responsibility for inspection of colonial church schools and early public schools, this model remained basically unchanged for 150 years. By the turn of the century, full-time supervisors appeared in both white and Negro school systems to assist principals who had earlier been released from their own classroom responsibilities to assist other teachers.

In 1934, Marvin S. Pittman, as president of South Georgia Teachers College (now Georgia Southern University), drew upon research in South Dakota and Michigan published in his book *The Value of School Supervision* (1925). Pittman's belief in the importance of professional preparation ultimately resulted in state certification which produced a separate professional identity for supervisors. In 1969, the state board of education approved criteria for common certificates to be issued to administrative and supervisory personnel in Georgia. Institutions of higher education developed preparation programs to ensure that students in administration and supervision both studied supervision, curriculum, administration, and the psychological

and sociological foundations of education, as well as other related fields. The new Administration/Supervision (A/S) certificate reflected the idea that leadership for instructional improvement was a shared responsibility. However, the certification of both supervisors and administrators with a single certificate implied a singularity which supervisors, at least, denied.

During the post-Civil War years when the races were educated separately in the South, a "Jeanes teacher" was a "member of the Negro race who work[ed] on a county-wide basis in the employ of county school officials to help improve the work of the schools and community life of the Negroes" (Georgia Association of Jeanes Curriculum Directors/Southern Education Foundation [GAJCD/SEF], 1975, p. 7).

The word *Jeanes* in the title was used because financial stimulation for this program was provided by Anna T. Jeanes, a Quaker of Philadelphia who supported Negro education through her philanthropy. In 1907, she donated 1 million dollars for the Negro Rural School Fund, commonly known as the Jeanes Fund, to encourage development of rural schools for black children. Introduced by the Henrico County Schools of Virginia in 1908, the "Jeanes teacher" became the Jeanes supervisor of Negro schools (GAJCD/SEF, 1979).

During the early years, salaries for the supervisors in the Negro schools were paid entirely by the Jeanes Fund. Three other funds—the Peabody Fund, the Virginia Randolph Fund, and the John F. Slater Fund—were combined with the Jeanes fund in 1937 to form the Southern Education Foundation (GAJCD/SEF, p. 13).

The Jeanes plan, a unique effort for improving education, spread throughout Alabama, Arkansas, Florida, Kentucky, South Carolina, Tennessee, Texas, Virginia, and the Virgin Islands. Because of its success in the United States, it was gradually introduced to the school systems of other countries, including Kenya, Liberia, Malawi, Zaire, Zambia, and Zimbabwe. Its influence reached Latin America and the Near East. Such extension of the Jeanes plan is impressive evidence of its value. Indeed, it has been said that "the Jeanes idea is considered one of the distinct contributions of America to the educational world" (Cousins, 1945).

Titles

As public school systems have been confronted with problems of accommodating new program opportunities or mandates from state or federal levels, many new job titles have appeared on the leadership roster. Personnel already employed have frequently been asked to assume revised or additional responsibilities. As a result, the titles of those in instructional leadership roles have lost precision in communicating job responsibilities.

"Supervisor" was used by Mackenzie (1961) as a generic term to include all whose unique or primary concern was instructional leadership. Supervisors were identified by such titles as helping teachers, department heads, curriculum consultants, curriculum directors, curriculum coordinators, general or special subject supervisors, or assistant superintendents in charge of instruction. The word *role* indicated what the holder of a position did. Local variations in skills and interests of holders of various positions, combined with differing patterns of organization, further obscured the exact roles of specific individuals and how improvement of curriculum and instruction was accomplished.

In 1965, Babcock stated that it was imperative to define the roles of specialists in curriculum and instruction, regardless of title, in the functional organization of the school system. He said, "This task must be faced squarely if the schools are to meet their responsibility of providing the best possible educational opportunities for all children and youth" (Babcock, 1965, p. 50). To date, that challenge still remains unanswered.

Functions

According to Bartoo (1976), instructional supervision and curriculum development were, prior to World War II, seen as separate functions. During the war years, the distinction became ambiguous and this ambiguity was encouraged for several years. The ASCD 1965 Yearbook on the *Role of Supervisor and Curriculum Director in a Climate of Change* (Leeper, 1965) represented the high-water mark for attempts to integrate instructional supervision and curriculum development. After that date, some scholars began actively to urge that the two functions again be recognized as distinct specialties.

Some conceptual basis for the separation was provided with the distinction of planning in curriculum as "preactive" and planning in instruction as "active" (Macdonald, 1965); and with establishing "intended learning outcomes" contrasted with "implementation" (Johnson, 1967). "The result [was the] conceiving of curriculum development as the adoption and management of a series, or set of projects, or programs, and by conceiving of the improvement of instruction as the twofold effort of matching types of teachers to program demands and the improvement of techniques" (Bartoo, 1976, p. 26).

Many variables complicate the definition of the separate roles of instructional supervisor and curriculum director: supervision takes place in settings that are complex and varied, the supervisor's place in the organizational structure of a school district is often ill-defined, and the existence of similar circumstances regarding curriculum development and the role of the curriculum director exacerbates the difficulties of role distinction.

It may not be possible, or even necessary, to define the role of instructional supervisor with precision. However, Babcock (1965) insisted that

It is essential that the channels for curriculum change be cleared . . . subject as the schools are to an increasing variety of curriculum pressures and to an evergrowing diffusion of the curriculum decision-making function. We must examine critically the roles and functions of the total administrative structure and the problems of interrelationships among the various parts. Finally, as specialists in the area of curriculum and instruction, we must make positive proposals for the establishment of organizational patterns which will release the full potential of all persons who are concerned with the educational processes (p. 64).

In describing preparation programs and certification standards, reference is routinely made to the nature of the craft of instructional supervisors and curriculum directors, and to the tasks they perform. Roles and functions of instructional supervisors and curriculum directors to a large extent determine, therefore, who enters preparation programs, the nature of such programs, and the licenses received. Study of roles and functions is an essential and imperative first step toward professionalization.

Although the duties of instructional supervisors and curriculum directors cannot be defined once and for all, neither can their roles be left undefined and unexamined. Rather, it is necessary that roles and functions be analyzed periodically in order to modify preparation programs, certification standards, and performance evaluations. This will ensure that instructional supervisors and curriculum directors can carry out the tasks assigned them and can function in new roles as these emerge (Hartsig, 1966).

Christensen and Turner (1978) surveyed a stratified random sample comprising 500 each of instructional supervisors, superintendents, and professors of supervision from the ASCD membership list for the purpose of identifying roles and preparation of instructional supervisors.

No definition of "instructional supervisor" or "curriculum director" was provided; respondents were expected to react on the basis of their own definitions. The sample of three populations was asked to indicate whether each of a set of 20 tasks was part of their expectations for instructional supervisor, curriculum director, or neither. Although such a list cannot be considered exhaustive, it included the major tasks typically assigned to either of these two roles.

Four tasks were agreed upon as most appropriate to the role of instructional supervisor: develop standards of teaching effectiveness; conduct staff meetings; conduct in-service programs; and observe teaching. Six tasks were agreed upon as most appropriate to the role of curriculum director: determine educational goals; conduct research; select curriculum content; work with community groups; prepare courses of study; and evaluate programs. Neither group viewed staff evaluation as being an appropriate activity for curriculum directors.

Theory

Problems of identifying and clarifying the roles of instructional supervisors and curriculum directors are compounded, according to Mackenzie (1963), by the underdeveloped state of the theory of the respective fields, and also by the low levels of preparation of some practitioners. Obviously, well-developed theories as to the nature of curriculum and of instruction would allow a better understanding of the functions which leaders in those areas could perform for the benefit of the educational program (p. 2).

Research

Although instructional supervision is one of the oldest subprofessions within the field of education, its attainment of maturity through research is, for the most part, yet to be realized. Effectiveness of various supervisory activities and programs employed for the purpose of influencing persons and situations toward more effective instruction demands to be thoroughly researched. Personal characteristics of instructional supervisors, and the relationship between those characteristics and educational change, merit extensive investigation. Harris (1963) specifically called for rigorous study of the forces that foster and resist educational change, both as action research by practitioners and as institutional studies of more elaborate design.

One of the most important steps toward improving supervisory practice and placing it on a truly professional level could come from a large-scale program of research on activity effectiveness. "The known supervisory activities need to be precisely tested for relative effectiveness in a series of situations, directed toward various problems, with diverse personalities involved" (Harris, 1963, p. 130). An ambitious research project on such a scale might be sponsored by the ASCD and/or financed by agencies or foundations interested in excellence for education.

Exacting studies of supervision programs as distinguished from specific activities or isolated supervisory endeavors are almost nonexistent. Lacking conceptual models, instructional supervisors rely more on experience and expectation than experimentation and evidence. Research is scant and, when it does exist, casts too little light for guidance. Cuban (1968), commenting on how little the frontiers of knowledge about the crafts of instructional supervisors and curriculum directors have advanced, contends that the professions are "at that primitive stage of relying on personal observation, intuition, or 'feeling'" (p. 363). As Harris (1963) points out, "Each subprofession borrows from others, relies on 'folk wisdom' where research is lacking, and extracts the relevant findings from research in related fields. Yet each profession which grows to maturity as an applied science does so partly because of the efforts of that group to promote and employ researches which are directly related to the unique problems and circumstances of that subprofession" (p. 129).

In 1965, the ASCD Research Institute focused upon Research and Development in Supervision. "As noble as this theme appears to a major organization with a commitment to [instructional] supervision . . . the institute planners were hard pressed to find research in supervision" (Macdonald, 1965, p. 161). The ASCD 1965 Yearbook, *Role of Supervisor and Curriculum Director in a Climate of Change*, gave almost no attention to research studies or research efforts in the field.

Although common sense indicates that teachers need and use assistance, perhaps even direction, research tells almost nothing about how to implement these aims. Macdonald (1965) observed that the basic question of whether instructional supervision has any value at all still remains unanswered (p. 161). Harris (1963) quotes one researcher as saying, "There is, in fact, little sound evidence that teachers change at all, to say nothing about change in relation to supervisory efforts" (p. 394).

Macdonald's impression that many central leadership personnel in general and instructional supervisors in particular were reluctant to research supervisory practices seems overly harsh. However, evidence, and the lack of it, suggest that instructional supervisors do not appear very eager to assess their own performance.

More effort must be devoted to visualizing varieties of supervisory patterns and to evaluating these patterns in operation. Macdonald (1965) adds, "It would facilitate matters a great deal if the values applied to the supervisory process were clearly identified and related to some kinds of operational criteria that could be evaluated" (p. 163). He goes on to suggest some specific "operational criteria":

If instructional supervision is to be "product" oriented, then changes in teacher behavior and/or teaching conditions that are possible and desirable must be clearly specified. If instructional supervision is to be essentially political in communicating and/or facilitating school ideology and goals, then these functions ought to be objectified for evaluation purposes. Or, if instructional supervision is to be essentially humanistic in providing help and support for humanizing the bureaucratic aspects of schooling, then this function should be specified clearly (p. 163).

The need to study itself as requisite to professionalization of instructional supervision has never been contested. Yet, for whatever reason, there have been essentially no pleas to engage in research on instructional supervision over the past three decades.

Alfonso and Firth (1990) call the paucity of serious research about supervision "disturbing, especially in light of extraordinary claims made about its importance" (p. 181). They concede that "the historical lack of clarity about who supervisors are and what they do persists. This problem at least partly explains the inadequate research base. Still, the educational profession should have confronted these issues by now" (p. 181).

CRITIQUE

Professional identity, status, and/or autonomy have long been denied both instructional supervisors and curriculum directors. Numerous attempts to clarify their roles and functions have been conducted by the ASCD since its formation in 1943 by the merger of the Society for Curriculum Study with the NEA Department of Supervisors and Directors of Instruction. Various officers as well as task forces, commissions, committees, councils, and working groups have considered the appropriateness of ASCD as the professional organization to represent both instructional supervisors and curriculum directors.

Respective summaries of numerous research studies regarding curriculum leaders and instructional supervisors by Bartoo, Speiker, and Sturges (1976) and Speiker (1978) can be categorized in terms of the concept of professionalism/professionalization, the visions of identity/image, and the respective dimensions of preparation/accreditation, licensure/certification, and evaluation/enforcement.

In 1969, Frymier made a passionate plea: "Somehow, someway, we have to devise a means of circumscribing our effort and circumscribing our group so we can give real power to the concept of [instructional] supervision in education. Adopting the professional model would be an exciting but complex and unsettling chore . . . [but] the rewards are worth whatever effort might be required to accomplish this" (Frymier, 1969, pp. 101–102).

REFERENCES

Alfonso, R. J. & Firth, G. R. (1990). Supervision: Needed research. *Journal of Curriculum and Supervision, 5*(2), 181–188.

Allen, R. S. (1966, January). Role and function of supervisors and curriculum workers. *Educational Leadership, 23*(4), 330–333.

American Association of School Administrators and Association for Supervision and Curriculum Development. (1963). *Organizing for improved instruction.* Washington, D.C.: The Associations.

Anderson, R. H. (1967). Supervision as teaching: An analogue. In W. H. Lucio (Ed.). *Supervision: Perspectives & propositions.* (pp. 29–41). Washington, D.C.: ASCD, NEA.

Association for Supervision and Curriculum Development. (1977). *Standards and guidelines for the evaluation of graduate programs preparing curriculum leaders.* Washington, D.C.: The Association.

Association for Supervision and Curriculum Development. (1983). *Evaluating graduate programs preparing curriculum leaders: Standards and guidelines* (p. 16). Alexandria, VA: The Association.

Babcock, C. D. (1965). The emerging role of the curriculum leader. In R. R. Leeper (Ed.). *Role of supervisor and curriculum director in a climate of change* (pp. 50–64). (ASCD 1965 Yearbook). Washington, D.C.: ASCD.

Bartoo, E. (1976). Who is the curriculum worker? In C. A. Speiker (Ed.). *Curriculum leaders: Improving their influence* (pp. 6–30). Washington, D.C.: ASCD.

Bartoo, E., Speiker, C. A., & Sturges, A. W. (1976). Summary and recommendations. In C. A. Speiker (Ed.). *Curriculum leaders: Improving their influence* (pp. 63–71). Washington, D.C.: ASCD.

Bradshaw, R. S. (1970). *A study of the local level supervisor of instruction in Georgia.* Unpublished doctoral dissertation in Instructional Supervision, University of Georgia, Athens, GA.

Bucher, R. & Strauss, A. (1961, January). Professions in process. *American Journal of Sociology, 66*(4), 325–334.

Caplow, T. (1954). *The sociology of work.* Minneapolis, MN: University of Minnesota Press.

Carr-Saunders, A. M. & Wilson, P. A. (1933). *The professions.* Oxford: The Clarendon Press.

Castleberry, M. R. (1994). *Professional self-discipline of instructional supervision: Vision, identity, and image.* Unpublished research project in Educational Leadership at the University of Georgia, Athens, GA.

Christensen, D. J. (1976). The curriculum worker today. In C. A. Speiker (Ed.). *Curriculum leaders: Improving their influence* (pp. 52–62). Washington, D.C.: ASCD.

Christensen, M. & Turner, H. (1978). The roles and preparation of instructional supervisors. In A. W. Sturges (Ed.). *Certificating the curriculum leader and the instructional supervisor* (pp. 20–34). Washington, D.C.: ASCD.

Cousins, R. L. (1945). Extent and influence of the Jeanes work. Atlanta University Summer School Release, mimeographed. In Georgia Association of Jeanes Curriculum Directors (1975) *Jeanes supervision in Georgia schools.* Atlanta: The Southern Education Foundation, Inc., 231–233.

Cox, J. V. (1961). The supervisor at work. *Educational Leadership, 19*(2), November, 131–138.

Cox, J. V. & Lott, J. G. (1961). *A study of the perceptions of the supervisor's role.* Unpublished study in Instructional Supervision at the University of Georgia, Athens, GA.

Crosby, M. (1961, November). Coordinating a supervisory program. *Educational Leadership, 19*(2), 111–114.

Cuban, L. (1968, February). The powerlessness of irrelevancy. *Educational Leadership, 25*(5), 393–396.

Eash, M. (1967). Guidelines for preparatory programs for supervisors and curriculum workers. In R. P. Wahle (Ed.). *Toward professional maturity of supervisors and curriculum workers* (pp. 19–24). Washington, D.C.: ASCD.

Eash, M. J. (1968, October). Supervision: A vanishing breed? *Educational Leadership, 26*(1), 73–79.

Elliott, P. (1972). *The sociology of the professions.* London: Macmillan Press, Ltd.

Esposito, J. P., Smith, G. E., & Burbach, H. J. (1975). A delineation of the supervisory role. *Education, 96*(1), 63–67.

Etzioni, A. (Ed.) (1969). *The semi-professions and their organization: Teachers, nurses, social workers.* New York: Free Press.

Firth, G. R. (1959). *Professional self-discipline of public school personnel.* Unpublished doctoral dissertation in Educational Administration, Teachers College, Columbia University, New York.

Firth, G. R. (1986, September). Message from the president—specialty recognition options available to school leaders. *ASCD Update, 28*(6), 2.

Firth, G. R. (1987, March). Message from the president—recognition by professional organizations: A better way to clear up role confusion. *ASCD Update, 29*(3), 2.

Frymier, J. R. (1969). The supervisor and his professional identity. In W. H. Lucio (Ed.). The supervision: New Demands, new directions (pp. 83–102). Washington, D.C.: ASCD, NEA.

Georgia Association of Jeanes Curriculum Directors. (1975). *Jeanes supervision in Georgia schools.* Atlanta, GA: The Southern Education Foundation, Inc.

Glanz, J. (1977). *Bureaucracy and professionalism: An historical interpretation of public school supervision in the United States, 1875–1937.* Unpublished doctoral dissertation, Teachers College, Columbia University, New York.

Glanz, J. (1977, November). Ahistoricism and school supervision: Notes toward a history. *Educational Leadership, 35*(2), 149–154.

Glanz, J. (1978). From bureaucracy to professionalism: An essay on democratization of school supervision in the early twentieth century (ERIC Document and Reproduction Service, No. ED168 169, November, p. 18).

Glanz, J. (1979). The bureaucratic-professional dilemma for supervisors and curriculum workers: An historical analysis of a persistent problem (ERIC Document and Reproduction Service, No. ED168 168, April, p. 19).

Gott, P. L., Johnson, C., Johnson, H., Threatt, R., & Bryant, H. (1967). Georgia association for supervision and curriculum development. *The role of the curriculum worker in Georgia.* Carrollton, GA: Division of Education, West Georgia College.

Grimsley, E. E., Burnham, R. M., Cox, J. V., Hussey, J. B., Singletary, H. T., Jr., & Woodard, A. (1974). Georgia association of curriculum and instructional supervision. *Instructional supervision in Georgia.* Athens, GA: Publishing Systems, Inc.

Greene, J. D. (1967). Implications for educational practice. In W. H. Lucio (Ed.). *Supervision: Perspectives and propositions* (pp. 42–53). Washington, D.C.: ASCD, NEA.

Guss, C. (1961, November). How is supervision perceived? *Educational Leadership, 19*(2), 99–102.

Harris, B. M. (1963, November). Need for research on instructional supervision. *Educational Leadership, 21*(2), 129–136.

Harris, B. M. (1967). Roles of supervisors and curriculum workers. In R. P. Wahle (Ed.). *Toward professional maturity of supervisors and curriculum workers* (pp. 1–12). Washington, D.C.: ASCD, NEA.

Hart, S. P. & Marshall, I. D. (1992) The question of teacher professionalism. ERIC Document and Republican Service. No. Ed 349 291, July 1992, p. 34).

Hartsig, B. A. (1966, December). Professionalization of supervisors and curriculum workers. *Educational Leadership, 24*(3), 268–271.

Holder, C. W. (1977). *Task analysis of selected leadership personnel responsible for instructional supervision and/or curriculum development in local school systems of Georgia.* Unpublished doctoral dissertation in Instructional Supervision, University of Georgia, Athens, GA.

Jensen, E. W. (1977). *Guidelines regarding individuals responsible for continued professional development programs for teachers in local education agencies.* Unpublished doctoral dissertation in Instructional Supervision, University of Georgia, Athens, GA.

Johnson, D. A. (1966). *An examination of current preparation and certification programs for school curriculum supervisors.* Unpublished master's thesis, University of Minnesota, Minneapolis, MN.

Leeper, R. R. (Ed.). (1965). *Role of instructional supervisor and curriculum director in a climate of change.* (ASCD 1965 Yearbook). Washington, D.C.: ASCD.

Leggatt, T. (1970). Teaching as a profession. In J. A. Jackson (Ed.). *Professions and professionalization* (pp. 153–177). London: Cambridge University Press.

Lucio, W. H. (1962, December). Instructional improvement: Considerations for supervision. *Educational Leadership, 20*(3), 211–217.

Lucio, W. H. (Ed.). (1967). *Supervision: Perspectives and propositions.* Washington, D.C.: ASCD, NEA.

Lucio, W. H. (1967). The supervisory function: Overview, analysis, propositions. In W. H. Lucio (Ed.). *Supervision: Perspectives and propositions* (pp. 1–11). Washington, D.C.: ASCD, NEA.

Lucio, W. H. & McNeil, J. D. (1962, 1969, 1979). *Supervision: A synthesis of thought and action.* New York: McGraw-Hill.

MacDonald, J. B. (1965, November). Knowledge about supervision: Rationalization or rationale. *Educational Leadership, 23*(2), 161–163.

Mackenzie, G. N. (1961, November). Role of the supervisor. *Educational Leadership, 19*(2), 86–90.

Mackenzie, G. N. (1963). *Roles of supervisors and curriculum workers.* Statement prepared for discussion by state affiliates. Washington, D.C.: ASCD.

Mallan, J. T. & Creason, F. (1968, February). A necessary frame of reference. *Educational Leadership, 25*(5), 414–417.

Manley, J. A. S. (1958). *A study of the services rendered by supervisors of instruction in Georgia.* Unpublished master's degree study at the University of Georgia, Athens, GA.

McMaster, A. L. (1966, May). Supervision: Loneliness and rewards. *Educational Leadership, 28*(8), 626–629.

Mills, C. W. (1951). *White collar: The American middle classes.* New York: Oxford University Press.

Moore, W. E. (1970). *The professions: Roles and rules.* New York: Russell Sage Foundation.

Mosher, R. & Purpel, D. (1972). *Supervision: The reluctant profession.* Boston: Houghton Mifflin.

National Association of Supervisors and Consultants. (1979). *The Jeanes story.* Atlanta, GA: The Southern Education Foundation, Inc.

Neville, R. F. (1966, May). The supervisor we need. *Educational Leadership, 23*(8), 634–640.

Pajak, E. F. (1989). *Identification of supervisory proficiencies project (final report).* University of Georgia (available from the Association for Supervision and Curriculum Development, 1250 N. Pitt Street, Alexandria, VA 22314-1403).

Petrie, T. A. (1969, May). To improve instruction, supervision, and evaluation. *Educational Leadership, 26*(8), 772–777.

Pittman, M. S. (1925). *The value of school supervision.* Baltimore, MD: Warwick and York.

Prater, J. (1961, November). Improving the skills of teaching. *Educational Supervision, 19*(2), 95–98.

Rutrough, J. E. (1967, December). The supervisor's role in personnel administration. *Educational Leadership, 25*(3), 249–255.

Sergiovanni, T. J. (1975). Introduction: Beyond human relations. In T. J. Sergiovanni (Ed.). *Professional supervision for professional teachers* (pp. 1–8). Alexandria, VA: ASCD.

Speiker, C. A. (Ed.). (1976). *Curriculum leaders: Improving their influence.* A report from the ASCD working group on the role, function, and preparation of the curriculum worker. Washington, D.C.: ASCD.

Srisa-an, W. (1967). *A macroscopic analysis of role dimensions of curriculum directors: Perceptions and expectations of superintendents, curriculum directors, and principals.* Unpublished doctoral dissertation, University of Minnesota, Minneapolis, MN.

Sturges, A. W. (Ed.). (1978). *The roles and responsibilities of instructional supervisors.* Unpublished report from the ASCD working group on the roles and responsibilities of supervisors. Washington, D.C.: ASCD.

Sturges, A. W. (1979, May). Instructional supervisors: A dichotomy. *Educational Leadership, 36*(8), 586–589.

Turney, D. T. (1966, May). Beyond the status quo: A reappraisal of instructional supervision. *Educational Leadership, 23*(8), 664–669.

Turpin, H. R. (1960). *Determining the causes of major problems encountered by instructional supervisors in Georgia.* Unpublished master's degree study at the University of Georgia, Athens, GA.

Urick, R. & Frymier, J. R. (1963, November). Personalities, teachers, and curriculum change. *Educational Leadership, 21*(2), 107–111.

Van Til, W. (1965). In a climate of change. In R. R. Leeper (Ed.). *Role of supervisor and curriculum director in a climate of change* (pp. 7–29). (ASCD 1965 Yearbook). Washington, D.C.: ASCD.

Vollmer, H. M. & Mills, D. L. (1966). *Professionalization.* Englewood Cliffs, NJ: Prentice-Hall.

Wear, P. W. (1966, May). Supervisor: Coordinator of multiple consultations. *Educational Leadership, 23*(8), 652–655.

Znaniecki, F. (1960). *The social role of the man of knowledge.* New York: Columbia University Press.

SECTION III.
THE DIMENSION OF PREPARATION/ACCREDITATION

INTRODUCTION

This section considers the specific components of accreditation of programs within the general dimension of professionalism regarded as preparation.

Findings are presented in each of the following 10 categories: definitions of terms; general considerations; exemplars from established professions; situations in the field of education; conditions in the craft of school supervision; literature review; research reports; document analyses; components of preparation/accreditation, including extent of surveillance, factors evaluated, type of standard, composition of agency, selection of agency membership, and level of agency jurisdiction; and critique.

DEFINITIONS OF TERMS

For the purpose of this analysis, the term *preparation* is defined as the graduate program of studies provided by an institution of higher education in which individuals obtain the competencies essential to practice a profession. The term *accreditation* is defined as the process by which an institution or program of study is "recognized by some agency or organization which establishes standards or requirements that must be met in order to secure approval" (Zook & Haggerty, 1936, p. 18).

GENERAL CONSIDERATIONS

A major intent of accreditation is to protect the public against deficient institutions, which would offer the cheapest possible programs with inferior teachers and facilities (Haberman & Stinnett, 1973). Accreditation provides "assurance of external evaluation of the institution or program, and a finding that there is conformity to general expectations in higher education or in the professional field" (COPA, 1982, p. 5).

There is widespread consensus that such higher education and professional programs ought to be held to published standards. Zook and Haggerty (1936) asserted without equivocation or exception that a college, like all other social institutions, must be constantly subject to "the scrutiny, criticism, and even regulation of the society in which it lives and which it serves" (p. 14).

Compliance with accreditation standards, however, is usually optional on the part of the college or university, at least in theory. Accrediting bodies in the United States are voluntary agencies; they lack any legal authority to compel institutions to comply. Be that as it may, the necessity for accreditation is usually acknowledged by institutions that are eligible to receive it; indeed, in many instances accreditation takes on a life-or-death significance (Mayor & Swartz, 1965).

This situation is unique to the United States. Most other nations maintain direct control over higher education through a central Ministry of Education or its equivalent. Under the American federal system, jurisdiction over education is reserved to the states which have, in practice, chosen to exercise little of their potential authority. The result of such a laissez-faire policy has been a great diversity among higher institutions in both the content and quality of their programs. Accreditation evolved from a need to bring a semblance of order to increasing variation among institutions (Mayor and Swartz, 1965). In addition, it serves as the primary means for assuring better programs of preparation and for protecting superior institutions against competition from inferior ones (Shafer & Mackenzie, 1965). The significance of preparation was addressed by Dewey: "I doubt whether we, as educators, keep in mind with sufficient constancy the fact that the prob-

lem of training teachers is one species of a more generic affair—that of training for professions. Our problem is akin to that of training architects, engineers, doctors, lawyers, etc. Moreover, since (shameful and incredible as it seems) the vocation of teaching is practically the last to recognize the need of specific professional preparation, there is all the more reason for teachers to try to find what they may learn from the more extensive and matured experience of other callings" (Dewey, 1904, p. 10).

EXEMPLARS FROM ESTABLISHED PROFESSIONS

Initiative for accreditation of programs of professional preparation has come chiefly from the professions themselves. The movement toward accreditation of professional schools or departments within colleges and universities in the United States was initiated with the publication in 1910 of Abraham Flexner's historic report entitled *Medical Education in the United States and Canada*. The Flexner report revealed that many medical schools were mere diploma mills, offering woefully inadequate programs, faculty, resources, and facilities. The conditions revealed by this report were so shocking that the American Medical Association immediately moved to professionalize medical education. The same effect was achieved for dentistry after publication of the Gies report (1926). During the years that followed, other professional associations took similar action: law in 1921, architecture in 1927, pharmacy in 1932, engineering in 1934, and so on. Professional schools for virtually every profession now are subject to accreditation by some agency.

It may be, as some suggest, that the internationally recognized excellence of professional preparation programs offered by American colleges and universities is due in some part to the uniquely American absence of governmental regulations on institutions of postsecondary education. "The American system of accreditation," according to the Council on Postsecondary Education (COPA), "[promotes] quality without inhibiting innovation" (1982, p. 1).

Detailed discussion of professional accreditation for preparation programs was provided long ago by Zook and Haggerty (1936) and by Pinkham (1954). The principles of accrediting institutions of higher education expressed by Zook and Haggerty (1936) were viewed as based on "the most comprehensive and constructive study of this particular problem which has ever been made" to that time (p. ix). The authors considered the issue of accreditation as exemplifying the eternal struggle between individual liberty and social responsibility (p. 142).

Pinkham (1954) presented tenets intended to bring accreditation under control, define its role, and provide direction to its impact on higher education so that institutions would be served rather than enslaved. He encouraged support by the American Association of Colleges for Teacher Education (AACTE) for the NCATE which has "emerged as a project of the Commission on Teacher Education and Professional Standards of the National Education Association" (p. 53).

SITUATIONS IN THE FIELD OF EDUCATION

Although schools have existed in the United States since Colonial days, the concept of teacher education as professional preparation is relatively recent. Departments of teacher education were not widely introduced into liberal arts colleges until 1915, when the North Central Association of Colleges and Schools required teachers in high schools approved for membership to have 11 semester hours of study in education (Lieberman, 1956).

The American Association of Teachers Colleges (AATC), established in 1917, began a formal accreditation process for teacher education programs in 1927, but no institutions other than teachers colleges were involved. Although the AATC was a national organization, it represented only a small fraction of the total number of institutions preparing teachers.

In 1948, the AATC merged with two other institutional-member organizations: the National Association of Colleges and Departments of Education, and the National Association of Teacher Education Institutions in Metropolitan Districts. The new, larger organization was the American Association of Colleges for Teacher Education.

The AACTE then expanded accreditation from the original base of teachers colleges to encompass all higher education institutions engaged in teacher preparation, if they applied for membership. The AACTE carried on accrediting functions from 1948 to 1954, when accrediting was transferred to the National Association for Accreditation of Teacher Education. NCATE. At that time, some 284 institutions were listed as AACTE members (Firth, 1959).

The NCATE is the only organization officially accepted by the Commission on Recognition of Professional Accreditation (CORPA) and the U.S. Department of Education as having the authority to accredit education programs. Thus, it is to the present operation of the NCATE that consideration is directed in this chapter.

The cancellation of financial contribution to the NCATE in 1972 enabled the NEA to achieve parity with higher education in regard to accreditation of teacher preparation programs (Howsam et al, 1976, p. 69). Since that time teachers participate fully and equally in all NCATE processes. However, in its negotiations with the NCATE, the NEA had to concede its position on mandatory accreditation and endorse the NCATE policy of voluntary accreditation. Annual delegate assemblies of the NEA evidence continuation of interest in certification requirements and ethical standards.

The NCATE is composed of 28 constituent members, including all six national leadership organizations. The CCSSO was a charter member in 1954, subsequently joined by the AASA in 1978, the NAESP in 1987, the National Middle School Association (NMSA) in 1988, the Association for Supervision and Curriculum Development (ASCD) in 1989, and the National Association of Secondary School Principals (NASSP) in 1993.

Only about 500 of more than 12,000 institutions engaged in teacher preparation are NCATE accredited. The NCATE has not overtly exerted pressure on institutions to become accredited. Nor is national accreditation for teacher education an explicit goal of the NCATE at this time, although it has received advocacy recently. Some of NCATE's most ardent supporters have stated that "NCATE accreditation should be a real mark of distinction which not all teacher preparing institutions can hope to achieve" (Lindsey, 1961).

Institutional participation in NCATE is voluntary. In an effort to develop a single system of accreditation, the NCATE promotes partnership arrangements with state agencies and regional accrediting organizations. At this time, 39 states maintain a collaborative relationship with the NCATE. State departments of education in all partnership states are working with this organization to conduct joint reviews of preparation programs in education. A few states (e.g., Arkansas, North Carolina, and Nevada) require national accreditation for some aspect of state approval. Some states (e.g., Florida and Kentucky) also include joint reviews with Board of Regents or State Higher Education Commissions.

Although the NCATE's authority is not universally acknowledged, effecting accreditation of preparation programs in the field of education is perhaps more necessary than accreditation of such programs in other professions. American citizens have considerable freedom of choice among privately employed professionals such as physicians or attorneys, but they have very little say in the matter of choosing teachers for the public schools in their communities. Consequently, greater protection is needed to safeguard the public from substandard institutions preparing teachers than from substandard institutions preparing practitioners in other professions. In theory, the school board or superintendent, acting on behalf of the community and the parents, can and should avoid employment of teachers and leadership personnel prepared in inadequate programs. However, this cannot be done without established standards.

It has been argued that educators themselves should have a keener interest in the accreditation of preparation programs than practitioners of other professions have in their own preparation programs. In education, certification is routinely granted to anyone who has completed an approved preparation program. In established professions, prospective practitioners usually face the additional hurdle of state board examinations formulated and evaluated by the professional group. These examinations provide assurance that institutions have prepared candidates who meet minimum standards set by the profession. Absence of official examinations for teacher certification would seem to call for a greater emphasis upon accreditation procedures to protect the public and the profession. This has not been the case.

Although the initial date that accreditation of teacher education programs began—1927—compares favorably with other, established professions, the field of education has presented a significant contrast to the united support for accrediting procedures displayed by other professions. There is little or no evaluation of professional competence after the completion of professional training, but there has also been little effective evaluation of preparation institutions by teachers themselves (Lieberman, 1956). Evaluation of the overall collegiate program is generally used as the quality index of professional preparation for education. In other fields, accrediting agencies place considerable weight on professional aspects of the preparation program (Firth, 1959).

CONDITIONS IN THE CRAFT OF SCHOOL SUPERVISION

Accreditation is a little understood yet potentially powerful factor in improving preparation for instructional supervisors and curriculum directors. Preparation programs for instructional supervisors exist to help individuals acquire knowledge, skills, and attitudes for their work as educational leaders.

Such programs are based on certain assumptions and subsequent operational decisions. These include goals or purposes held for the program, selection and admission of students, content deemed necessary for the desired educational outcomes, institutional arrangements for courses and/or experiences facilitating those desired outcomes, availability and utilization of materials and resources contributing to the learning of the necessary content, and behavior in the learning relationship with students. Improvements in preparation programs are assumed to be achieved through modification of one or all of these six aspects (Ogletree, Edmonds, & Wear, 1962). Preparation programs for instructional supervisors and curriculum directors have been described as combinations of idiosyncratic projections of faculty preferences and compromises generated by the exigencies of academic politics. The wide variation in programs is taken as evidence of a lack of systemic foundations (Eash, 1966). According to Eash (1966), the roots of many problems in preparation programs resided in the major issues involved in professionalization. "Since one of the dominant characteristics of a profession is the possession of a general and systematic knowledge not readily available to the public, preparation programs for the aspirants to the profession receive much attention." He goes on, "Seldom has so much faith been invested in so little empirical evidence . . . The formulation of programs of professional preparation [for supervisors] still resides in the realm of the occult" (Eash, 1966, p. 359).

If the knowledge base of the profession lacks definition, procedures for admission to the profession have been found in much the same condition. No specific requirements have been identified for admission to the specializations of instructional supervision or curriculum development. Rather, "there are only two kinds of selection procedures being carried on in most of the preparing institutions. One is self-selection . . . [The other is] to meet the general requirements for admission to graduate study" (Thurman, 1966, p. 589).

Such procedures are considered by many to be inadequate and inappropriate for a profession. Identification of prospective instructional supervisors and/or curriculum directors is viewed as the mutual responsibility of preparation institutions and school districts which, together, are encouraged to develop a plan for admission and retention of persons who demonstrate professional promise. Standards for selection are expected to include intellectual ability, academic and professional preparation, and commitment to professional ethics. Some advocate that only those individuals officially admitted by the preparation institution be permitted to study in the program (Hartsig, 1966).

Even though extensive research is needed to determine the nature of effective preparation programs for instructional supervisors and curriculum directors, some guidelines can be recommended based on evidence available from experience in education and studies in other professions.

Sufficient opportunities are needed to provide students a broad orientation to educational and social theory, learning theory, personality theory, and diverse learning styles based on ethnicity, gender, and/or culture. Preparation programs should also include knowledge from the related areas of educational administration, guidance, pupil personnel, and measurement and evaluation. In addition, students preparing for careers in instructional supervision or curriculum development are expected to obtain advanced study in an area of specialization. The professional sequence should demand a minimum of two years of study beyond the bachelor's degree and should combine formal academic classwork with supervised field experience. That combination bears a direct relationship to demands that all instructional supervisors and/or curriculum directors will face in actual practice. Finally, the number of preparation institutions should be limited in order to bring a balance between supply and demand, and to assure quality programs (Hartsig, 1966).

The detailing of preparation programs, insofar as selection of courses and their sequence is concerned, is addressed by Daresh in Chapter 37 of this handbook.

The confused state of preparation programs in instructional supervision and curriculum development is exacerbated by, and perhaps is at least in part a result of, variation in the perceptions of leadership roles in education. During the 1980s, the ASCD took a lead in attempting to codify those roles and the preparation they required. Supervision and instruction were included with curriculum as integral parts of professional studies in *Standards and Guidelines for Evaluation of Graduate Programs Preparing Curriculum Leaders*, published originally by the ASCD in 1977–1978 and revised by Firth and Sturges in 1982–1983. Somewhat later, the ASCD attempted to develop criteria for specialty areas in supervision (Clark, Glickman, & Knoll, 1988), curriculum (Oliva, Berman, & Gould, 1988), and instruction (Sparks, Della-Dora, & Hanes, 1988) to be applied through the NCATE. Respective committees composed of three recognized experts were appointed by the ASCD. Draft reports were prepared for each area during a year of effort. Workshops were held at several annual conferences. In spite of considerable interest and effort, however, the ASCD's direct involvement in the accreditation process was not fully implemented until its collaboration with other national leadership organizations through the National Policy Board for Educational Administration (NPBEA).

Eventually, the project was abandoned. Its demise was attributed largely to the difficulty of distinguishing among roles in instructional supervision, curriculum development, and instructional design. Significantly, the 1988 ASCD committee on instructional supervision submitted its proposed NCATE criteria under the heading of "instructional leadership." Another factor believed by ASCD officials to account for the situation was the changing perception of supervision as distributed among several leadership roles rather than vested in a particular specialist—the supervisor. The ascendancy of the principalship as the instructional leader in the late 1980s and early 1990s was part of this paradigm of shared supervisory responsibility, along with restructuring of schools and school districts. The ASCD joined other national leadership organizations to develop guidelines for preparation programs which were approved by NCATE in October 1995 (Carter, 1994).

LITERATURE REVIEW

Preparation programs for instructional supervisors have not, historically, received a great deal of attention from the profession. Of the 128 books on instructional supervision published over the 120-year period from 1875 to 1994, only 21 (16%) even addressed the dimension of preparation. During the 75-year period 1875–1949, four of the 18 books (22%) mentioned preparation. Emphasis was greatest during the decade 1960–1969 when eight of the 23 books (35%) mentioned preparation (Williams, 1994).

Collaboration to attain consistency of preparation programs for educational leadership is advocated by the NPBEA. Representing the five national leadership organizations, including the AASA, ASCD, NAESP, NASSP, and CCSSO, the NPBEA is helping to generate guidelines for preparation programs in the 39 states presently participating with the NCATE on joint approval. Williams (1994) recommended that the other states join NCATE's State Recognition Board to ensure that accreditation of preparation programs be consistent across all states. She also recommended that instructional supervision be identified as a specialty area, so it could have its own representative(s) on the accreditation, certification, and enforcement collaborative convened by the NPBEA.

RESEARCH REPORTS

Very few studies have looked at issues involved in the accreditation of preparation programs for instructional supervisors.

Organizations, Institutions, and Agencies

Mayor and Swartz (1965) conducted a study under the auspices of the National Commission on Accrediting to determine the influence of accreditation of teacher education on institutions of higher education. As of 1964, only 36 percent of teacher education institutions were accredited by the NCATE; however, these graduated some 70 percent of the new teachers. Many of those not accredited by the NCATE were either prestigious liberal arts colleges with no strong motivation for NCATE approval, or weak institutions that were fearful of not meeting NCATE requirements.

A finding of this study was that national accreditation of teacher education encouraged flexibility in state certification requirements: "[Despite] widespread and valid public concern about the rigidity of state requirements for teacher certification . . . national accreditation of teacher education . . . is in a position to contribute to the lessening of this rigidity. There is evidence that national accreditation has already contributed to increased flexibility in this area" (p. 220).

Mayor and Swartz concluded that the leadership that national accreditation would provide was sorely needed.

"Differences in the quality of education regionally are already much too obvious" (p. 228). They felt that national accreditation of teacher education, "soundly conceived and administered," would benefit the profession in two ways. First, it would stimulate educational improvement and innovation. Second, it would help teacher education gain respect in the eyes of the public and among its peers in higher education as well (p. 238).

The NCATE was seeking to explore the question of situating education among its professional peers when it commissioned a study (Yff, 1992) to compare the standards used by the specialized accrediting agencies from 10 professions: Architecture,. business administration, engineering, law, medicine, nursing, pharmacy, physical therapy, social work, and teacher education. The analysis encompassed five topics: objectives of accreditation, program levels reviewed, program versus unit review, input versus output variables, and multicultural and cultural diversity concerns. The standards of all accreditors were examined in the five categories of organization and administration, resources, students, curriculum, and outcomes. In practice, it can sometimes be difficult to draw a clear distinction between input and output criteria, especially in the category of curriculum. For example, whereas curriculum may be taken as a process dealing with sequences (and, therefore, an input), curriculum standards are often cast in a way that implies an outcome. Some national accrediting agencies describe elements of curriculum in terms of what graduates "will become" or "will be able to do." All accreditors speak to general outcomes, such as improving the profession and maintaining the public trust, but some also mention more individual outcomes.

The results of Yff's analysis suggest that the accreditation standards in education are more like than unlike those in other professions in terms of levels, topics, and objects of review.

There are, however, some areas in which accreditation in education is unique. One major difference between the NCATE and other accrediting agencies is its lack of autonomy. Except for designating its members, other professional groups exercise no authority over the NCATE. While it may thus be protected from detrimental political pressures, no other profession utilizes an accrediting agency that is not directly responsible to the professional group. Other professions do not generally require that preparation programs maintain approval by regional associations to be accredited by the national organization. Although this requirement serves as a practical measure, considering the number of institutions involved, lack of approval of the general program by regional associations may inappropriately tend to dilute NCATE accreditation.

The new NCATE standards refer to the qualifications necessary for a candidate to enter education. Most institutions, however, are pressured to admit any teacher within the state who is seeking a leadership position. This is a significant contrast to the requirements for advanced professional study applied by schools of law and medicine.

A third major difference between the NCATE and other accrediting agencies is that the NCATE distinguishes clearly between professional studies and specialty studies (the latter being the discipline that the student is preparing to teach).

This is a unique use of the idea of "specialization" among the accreditors, in that subject specialties and studies at particular levels are included as part of the basic-level program in teacher education. Specialization in other fields occurs after a first degree has been earned. The pattern is roughly analogous to advanced work in instructional supervision, curriculum development, or educational administration.

NCATE standards include content for initial teacher preparation as well as advanced studies. Some inquiry has sought to discover what should constitute the program of preparation for individuals who plan to work in instructional supervision. Sturges and Kollar (1976) surveyed state ASCD affiliates, universities, and school districts for the purpose of obtaining competency statements to guide preparation of curriculum leaders. There was general agreement regarding the necessary areas of competence, and the total list provided a detailed description of the necessary areas of competence and the level of learning expected of the student. The competencies were grouped into the following 10 categories: inservice, administration, evaluation, leadership, curriculum, research, instruction, communications, organization, and community relations.

Krajewski (1978) surveyed 48 universities in order to examine graduate programs to prepare instructional supervisors. Of the 45 institutions responding, 27 (60%) offered such programs through the department of educational administration. The four courses most frequently required were in administration, curriculum, supervision, and educational psychology.

Standards and Guidelines for Evaluation of Graduate Programs Preparing Curriculum Leaders (1977–1978, 1982–1983), developed by the ASCD, focused on professional studies, supporting fields, practicum/internship, resources and facilities, organization and governance, faculty, student services, evaluation, program review, and planning.

Doctoral Dissertations

Flintom (1962) described a project in North Carolina which produced "Criteria for Approved Programs for the Preparation of Supervisors." The seven guidelines for master's and specialist levels focused on the thorough understanding of the nature of the learner and psychology of learning, dynamics of human behavior, curriculum development, supervisory techniques, organization and administration, academic specialization, and research and statistics.

Evaluation of preparation programs for instructional supervisors and/or curriculum directors is complicated by the fact that they are often assigned to departments not specifically focused on them, that is, departments of educational administration, policy, or leadership rather than departments of curriculum and supervision or curriculum and instruction. Even when such is the case, distinctions between supervision and curriculum are typically ambiguous. A continuing lack of clarity in this regard is evidenced by doctoral dissertations and master's studies completed at the University of Minnesota (Johnson, 1966; Srisa-an, 1967) and the University of Georgia (Petersohn, 1974).

Firth's dissertation (1959) compared preparation programs and accreditation procedures of five established professions with those of education at that time. He predicted the evolution of the NCATE in recommending increased responsibility for

practitioners in the approval of preparation programs for educational personnel.

Master's Theses and Specialist Projects

Johnson (1966) proposed that preparation programs for curriculum supervisors and school administrators begin in a similar manner. He recommended that, beyond an initial core of experiences, each should develop distinctive emphases commensurate with the unique skills required of their respective roles. The curriculum supervisor should have fewer courses in administrative and managerial skills, and additional courses in the behavioral sciences, psychology and learning, and research design and techniques.

DOCUMENT ANALYSES

Stowe (1994) analyzed 18 documents, published during the 33 years between 1959 and 1991, which contained proposals for determining the influence on professional self-discipline of instructional supervision by standards, preparation, and/or accreditation. The documents were analyzed in terms of the six components of accreditation developed by Firth (1959): extent of surveillance, factors evaluated, type of standard, composition of agency, selection of agency membership, and level of agency jurisdiction.

Not all of the components were discussed in all of the documents. For example, all 18 of the documents dealt with the extent of surveillance and the factors to be evaluated. However, only nine of the 18 documents discussed the composition of the proposed accrediting agency; six considered level of jurisdiction; and only three mentioned membership of the agency they were supporting (Stowe, 1994). Stowe's findings on each of the six components are described later in this section as the "Instructional Supervision" aspect.

Stowe noted that different groups of individuals were considered appropriate for inclusion in many of the documents. She attributed this to the lack of a clear definition of an instructional supervisor. One publication included everyone who worked with teachers; others embraced combinations that drew "supervisors" from among administrators, superintendents, central office personnel, and college professors.

Although differing on specific recommendations, all 18 documents were in agreement that the accreditation process serves the profession well.

COMPONENTS OF PREPARATION/ ACCREDITATION

Six components of the dimension of preparation/accreditation (Firth, 1959)—extent of surveillance, factors evaluated, type of standard, composition of agency, selection of agency membership, and level of agency jurisdiction—are examined in regard to exemplars from established professions, situations in the field of education, and conditions in the craft of instructional supervision (Table 36–4).

TABLE 36–4. Occurrence of the Components of Extent of Surveillance,
Factors Evaluated, Type of Standard, Composition of Agency, Selection of Agency
Membership, and Level of Agency Jurisdiction Regarding the Dimension of
Preparation/Accreditation Noted in Documents on Instructional Supervision
Published During the 33-Year Period 1959–1991

Author	Year	Surveillance	Factors	Standards	Composition	Membership	Jurisdiction
Firth	1959	x	x	x	x	x	x
Lucio & McNeil	1962	x	x				
Leeper	1965	x	x	x	x		
Stemnock & NASSP	1968, 1969	x	x	x	x	x	x
Educational Leadership	1969	x	x	x	x		
UCEA	1973	x	x				
Sturges	1978	x	x	x	x		x
ASCD	1978	x	x		x		x
AASA	1979	x	x				
Hoyle, English, & Steffy	1985	x	x	x			
Pavan	1986	x	x				
Bolin	1986	x	x				
NAESP	1986	x	x	x			
Gousha	1986	x	x	x			
UCEA	1987	x	x	x	x	x	x
NAESP & NASSP	1989	x	x		x		
NAESP	1990	x	x	x			
Hill	1991	x	x	x	x		x

Source: Stowe, 1994, p. 47

Extent of Surveillance

Established professions. Law, medicine, engineering, and psychology have specific criteria which are utilized to evaluate institutions (law and medicine) or programs (engineering and psychology). Actual on-site visitations to participating institutions and re-inspections are made, either by teams from the accrediting agency or by representatives of the respective professional association. A list of approved programs is published and circulated widely. Since practitioners in most professions are adversely affected by allegations of program deficiencies in their preparatory institutions, they usually are willing to support high standards of professional preparation. However, higher standards require increased expenditures for faculty and resources.

Education field. The NCATE has established criteria for professional schools and developed procedures for evaluating preparation programs. It also publishes a list of approved institutions and programs that meet the guidelines of national professional associations.

Instructional supervision. As in medicine, engineering, and psychology, practitioners usually constitute at least half of the NCATE visitation teams. However, instructional supervisors tend to be underrepresented compared to other educational leadership categories.

Factors Evaluated

Established professions. The institution's plant, facilities, and finance; personnel policies; and curriculum and instruction are evaluated by accreditors in most professions. Schools of business administration also evaluate the student personnel program. Law, medicine, and engineering evaluate general organi-

zation and administration; the same three also evaluate professional laboratory experiences. Law and engineering include the future success of graduates in their assessments (Yff, 1992).

The commonalities among accreditors include concern for nondiscrimination and achieving diversity. Both architecture and social work make reference to multiculturalism as an element of curricular content during professional studies (Yff, 1992).

Education field. NCATE standards cover such aspects of preparation programs as general organization and administration; plant, facilities, and finance; staff personnel policies; curriculum and instruction; student personnel programs and services; and professional laboratory experiences. These are common to all professions (Yff, 1992).

A common set of 85 curriculum guidelines for NCATE accreditation of preparation programs in educational leadership was proposed in 1994 by the NPBEA. Presented in five areas, the number of guidelines devoted to each topic appears in parentheses: Strategic leadership, including professional and ethical leadership (8) and management and evaluation (4); Organizational leadership, including organizational management (5), interpersonal relationships (8), financial management and resource allocation (5), and technology and information systems (4); Instructional leadership, including curriculum, instruction, supervision, and the learning environment (13), professional development and human resources (8), and student personnel services (7); Political and community leadership, including community and media relations (7); and educational law, public policy, and political systems (12); and Internship (4) (NPBEA, 1994, pp. 15-29).

NPBEA standards approved by the NCATE in 1995 include information regarding the qualifications of candidates for admission to the preparation programs and reference to assessment of performance of candidates pursuing study at the institution. Multiculturalism as curriculum content also appears in the NCATE criteria as part of professional studies. Prior to the team visitation, the NPBEA will review curriculum folios to determine whether the institutional program generally complies with the guidelines of the national professional association.

Instructional supervision. Publications describing accreditation of preparation programs in instructional supervision focus on essential skills such as communicating, goal setting, planning, organizing, directing, evaluating, and working with people. Recommendations for improving preparation programs include greater emphasis on internships and/or inservice education. "Skills for successful leaders" appear as lists of proficiencies, performance domains, or building blocks. Discrepancies between preparation programs and certification requirements have been noted as an issue that the education profession needs to address.

Type of Standard

Established professions. No absolute preference for quantitative or qualitative criteria by accreditors can be identified. Whereas standards in law and psychology are essentially quantitative on some factors, qualitative aspects are sought on others. Engineering also uses both. Only medicine, which has achieved the enviable position of having no unapproved medical schools now operating in the United States, has standards that are primarily qualitative (Yff, 1992).

No accreditor appears to rely solely on dimensions of either program or unit capability; that is, the standards imply evaluation of program(s) in the context of institutional capability to carry out the program(s) effectively.

Education field. With respect to program versus unit evaluation, the NCATE is the only accrediting agency among those analyzed by Yff (1992) that refers to unit accreditation. Even so, NCATE standards do not support a clear distinction between program and unit characteristics.

Instructional supervision. Suggestions are beginning to surface that call for performance-based assessment. Some scholars advocated that full licensure be delayed until after there is evidence of a period of successful performance in a supervisory position (Stowe, 1994). Propositions such as these indicate a shift toward a more qualitative method of evaluating graduates of preparation programs in instructional supervision.

Composition of Agency

Established professions. In all professions employing an accreditation process, judgments are made by a special advisory board composed of a combination of practitioners and other members. The experience of the established professions indicates that practitioners should have at least as important a voice in the accreditation process as do representatives of preparatory institutions.

Education field. The preference for involving lay citizens who are noneducators to represent the public interest is at times viewed as more political than practical. Accreditation would seem to demand a professional judgment that such

persons cannot provide. CORPA and the U.S. Department of Education now require representatives of the public to participate on such bodies in other professions as well as education. The review teams formed by accrediting agencies should be composed primarily of practitioners and representatives of the institutions preparing educators.

Instructional supervision. There appears to be agreement that the NCATE is the appropriate agency for accrediting preparation programs in instructional supervision. There are also advocates for a more active role by the ASCD. The success of such ventures would only be as strong as the support of ASCD membership to accept such responsibility (Stowe, 1994).

Selection of Agency Membership

Established professions. Members of accrediting agencies in law, medicine, and psychology are chosen through representative delegates by election at an annual conference. However, final decision on the committees' recommendations rests with the representatives themselves in general assembly. In engineering, those who comprise the accrediting agency are named by representatives appointed by the executive committees of the constituent societies (COPA, 1982).

Education field. The experience of other professions as well as the clear preference of respondents to various questionnaire studies indicates that practitioners in education desire to exercise greater responsibility in the selection of members of the accrediting agency. The natural choice is democratic processes within the professional organizations. However, distribution of educators among memberships in many organizations with differing agenda, policies, and influence may make the use of indirect selection as now used in engineering more appropriate.

Instructional supervision. The membership of appropriate professional organizations is considered the logical pool from which to select individuals to serve on accrediting bodies in instructional supervision. Another suggestion proposed by the University Council for Educational Administration (UCEA, 1987) was that the NPBEA should form a national academy of professional school leaders to conduct accreditation activities. Under the UCEA proposal, the academy would be composed of individuals who have evidenced exemplary performance over an extended period of time.

Level of Agency Jurisdiction

Established professions. In all cases, professional accreditation is done at the national level. While many states also must approve institutions of higher education within their borders, they commonly use, either completely or with minor adaptation, the standards of the national group to evaluate those institutions.

Education field. In education as well as in other professions, the national level is considered to be the most advantageous for conducting the accreditation process. However, it is also essential that coordination be achieved, particularly with education agencies at the state level, to ensure that the professional standards receive legal recognition.

Instructional supervision. Widespread agreement exists that accreditation of preparation programs for instructional supervisors and curriculum leaders should to be conducted at the national level (Stowe, 1994).

CRITIQUE

In their review of the literature on professions in general and the teaching profession in particular, Hart and Marshall (1992) suggested that programs seeking to advance professionalism need to address such fundamental aspects as body of knowledge, ideal of service, distinctive culture, autonomy, and ethical codes.

The NCATE has successfully established criteria for professional schools and developed procedures for evaluating the programs of preparatory institutions. The NCATE has made an excellent beginning, and undoubtedly can do more. This organization is in a unique position for exerting influence upon educational preparation programs toward an increased standard of professionalization.

Preparation programs for instructional supervisors, however, reflect the general confusion caused by the lack of agreement of who instructional supervisors are and what they are supposed to do. Programs of study and specific standards have not been established, since there is no clear division of the roles of educational administrator, curriculum director, and instructional supervisor. Until these lines have been established, it may be difficult to convince an agency to assume responsibility for accreditation (Stowe, 1994).

Although technically the accreditation of programs is separate and distinct from certification to practice, a close relationship exists between the preparation of professionals and granting them a license. Elsbree and Reutter (1984) precisely state the inextricable association of the two processes in education: "Ultimately the standards of training sought by certification procedures cannot be divorced from the quality of training offered at preparing institutions" (p. 52).

REFERENCES

Association for Supervision and Curriculum Development. (1977). *Standards and guidelines for evaluation of graduate programs preparing curriculum leaders.* Alexandria, VA: Author.

Association for Supervision and Curriculum Development. (1983). *Evaluating graduate programs preparing curriculum leaders: Standards and guidelines.* Alexandria, VA: Author.

Carter, G. R. (1994, January). Message from the executive director—We need new standards for leadership programs. *ASCD Update, 36*(1), 2.

Clark, D., Glickman, C., & Knoll, M. (1988). *Guidelines for program standards in instructional supervision/leadership,* Preliminary Report of the ASCD Sub-committee to Prepare Program Standards for NCATE. Alexandria, VA: ASCD.

Council on Postsecondary Education. (1982). *Policy statement on the role and value of accreditation.* Washington, D.C.: The Council.

Dewey, J. (1904). The relationship of theory to practice. In C. A. McMurry (Ed.). *Principles of Pedagogy* (3rd Yearbook of the National Society for the Study of Education, Part 1). Chicago: The University of Chicago Press, 9–30.

Eash, M. J. (1966, February). Preparatory programs for supervisors. *Educational Leadership, 23*(5), 358–362.

Eash, M. J. (1967). Guidelines for preparatory programs for supervisors and curriculum workers. In R. P. Wahle (Ed.). *Toward professional maturity of supervisors and curriculum workers* (pp. 19–24). Washington, D.C.: ASCD.

Elsbree, W. S. & Reutter, E. E. (1954). *Staff personnel in the public schools.* New York: Prentice-Hall.

Flexner, A. (1910). *Medical education in the United States and Canada.* New York: The Carnegie Foundation for the Advancement of Teaching.

Flintom, M. (1962, December). Preparation and certification of supervisors. *Educational Leadership, 20*(3), 160–162, 209.

Firth, G. R. (1959). *Professional self-discipline of public school personnel.* Unpublished doctoral dissertation in Educational Administration, Teachers College, Columbia Universitym, New York.

Gies, W. J. (1926). *Dental education in the United States and Canada.* New York: The Carnegie Foundation for the Advancement of Teaching.

Haberman, M. & Stinnett, T. M. (1973). *Teacher education and the new profession of teaching.* Berkeley, CA: McCutchan Publishing Corp.

Hart, S. P. & Marshall, J. D. (1992). *The question of teacher professionalism.* (ERIC Document and Reproduction Service, No. ED349 291, July, p. 34.)

Hartsig, B. A. (1966, December). Professionalization of supervisors and curriculum workers. *Educational Leadership, 24*(3), 268–271.

Howsam, R. B., Corrigan, D. C., Denemark, G. W., & Nash, R. J. (1976, 1985). *Educating a profession.* (Reprint with postscript). Report of the bicentennial commission on education for the profession of teaching. Washington, D.C.: American Association of Colleges for Teacher Education.

Johnson, D. A. (1966). *An examination of current preparation and certification programs for school curriculum supervisors.* Unpublished master's thesis, University of Minnesota, Minneapolis, MN.

Krajewski, R. J. (1978, October). Existing programs for preparation of instructional supervisors. In A. W. Sturges (Ed.). *The roles and responsibilities of instructional supervisors* (pp. 60-66). Unpublished report of the ASCD working group on the roles and responsibilities of instructional supervisors. Washington, D.C.: ASCD.

Lieberman, M. (1956). *Education as a Profession.* Englewood Cliffs, NJ: Prentice-Hall.

Lindsey, M. (1961). *New horizons for the teaching profession.* Washington, D.C.: National Education Association, National Commission on Teacher Education and Professional Standards.

Mayor, J. R. & Swartz, W. G. (1965). *Accreditation in teacher education: It's influence on higher education.* Washington, D.C.: National Commission on Accrediting.

National Council for Accreditation of Teacher Education. (1992). *NCATE standards, procedures, and policies for the accreditation of professional education units.* Washington, D.C.: The Council.

National Policy Board for Educational Administration. (1994, November). *Proposed NCATE curriculum guidelines: Advanced programs in educational leadership for superintendents, principals, curriculum directors and supervisors.* (5th draft). Fairfax, VA: Author.

Ogletree, J. R., Edmonds, F., & Wear, P. W. (1962, December). Preparing educational supervisors. *Educational Leadership, 20*(3), 163–166.

Oliva, P. F., Berman, L., & Gould, J. (1988). *Guidelines for program standards in curriculum*, Preliminary report of the ASCD Sub-committee to Prepare Program Standards for NCATE. Alexandria, VA: ASCD.

Petersohn, R. L. (1974). *The development of a framework and an instrument for analysis of supervision of curriculum development.* Unpublished doctoral dissertation in Curriculum and Instruction, University of Georgia, Athens, GA.

Pinkham, F. O. (1954). Teacher education and the national commission on accrediting. In *Seventh Yearbook. The American Association of Colleges for Teacher Education* (pp. 43–56). Oneonta, NY: The Association.

Shafer, H. T. & Mackenzie, G. N. (1965). Securing competent instructional leaders. In R. R. Leeper (Ed.). *Role of supervisor and curriculum director in a climate of change* (pp. 65–86). (ASCD 1995 Yearbook). Washington, D.C.: ASCD.

Sparks, G., Della-Dora, D., & Hanes, R. (1988). *Guidelines for program standards in instruction*, Preliminary report of the ASCD Subcommittee to Prepare Program Standards for NCATE. Alexandria, VA: ASCD.

Srisa-an, W. (1967). *A microscopic analysis of role dimensions of curriculum directors: Perceptions and expectations of superintendents, curriculum, directors, and principals.* Unpublished doctoral disserration, University of Minnesota, Minneapolis, MN.

Stinnett, T. M. (1951). *The accreditation of institutions for teacher preparation.* Unpublished doctoral dissertation in Education, University of Texas at Austin, Austin, TX.

Stinnett, T. M. & Huggett, A. J. (1963). *Professional problems of teachers.* New York: Macmillan.

Stowe, J. S. (1994). *Professional self-discipline of instructional supervision: Standards, preparation, and accreditation.* Unpublished research project in Educational Leadership, University of Georgia, Athens, GA.

Sturges, A. W., & Kollar, V. (1976). Competencies for curriculum workers. In C. A. Speiker (Ed.). *Curriculum leaders: Improving their influence* (pp. 42–51). Washington, D.C.: ASCD.

Thurman, R. S. (1966, April). Identifying potential leaders for supervision and curriculum work. *Educational Leadership, 23*(7), 587–593.

Thurman, R. S. (1967). Identifying and selecting potential supervisors and curriculum workers. In R. P. Wahle (Ed.). *Toward professional maturity of supervisors and curriculum workers* (pp. 13–18). Washington, D.C.: ASCD.

University Council for Educational Administration. (1987). *Leaders for America's schools.* The report of the National Commission on Excellence in Educational Administration. Columbus, OH: The Council.

Williams, N. G. (1994). *Professional self-discipline of instructional supervision: Influences of national leadership organizations.* Unpublished applied project for the Specialist in Education degree in Educational Leadership at the University of Georgia, Athens, GA.

Yff, J. (1992). *Analysis of standards used by specialized accrediting bodies in ten professions* (pp. 18 plus addenda). Unpublished report prepared for the National Council for Accreditation of Teacher Education. Washington, D.C.: The Council,

Zook, G. F. & Haggerty, M. E. (1936). *Principles of accrediting higher institutions* (Vol I.). In a series of seven monographs on the Evaluation of Higher Institutions. Chicago, IL: The University of Chicago Press.

SECTION IV.
THE DIMENSION OF LICENSURE/CERTIFICATION

INTRODUCTION

This section considers the specific components of certification to practice within the general dimension of professionalism regarded as licensure.

Findings are presented in each of the following 10 categories: definitions of terms; general considerations; exemplars from established professions; situations in the field of education; conditions in the craft of school supervision; literature review; research reports; document analyses; components of licensure/certification, including extent of surveillance, factors evaluated, means of insuring standards, type of standard, designation of certificate, composition of agency, selection of agency membership, and level of agency jurisdiction; and critique.

DEFINITIONS OF TERMS

For the purpose of this analysis, the term *licensure* is defined as the generic regulatory device by which the state protects the public from malpractice of incompetent individuals by allowing professional groups to set up standards of admission to and internal control of their ranks (Black, 1951).

The term *certification* is defined as a process of legal sanction varying by state which authorizes an individual to perform prescribed services in public schools through maintaining standards of preparation and employment (Kinney, 1964).

GENERAL CONSIDERATIONS

A profession is "an occupation requiring expert knowledge that justifies a monopoly of services granted by government licensing" (Spring, 1985). A necessary criterion for a profession is the establishment of quasi-legal policies and regulations which establish minimum requirements for the certification of individuals to practice. These certification requirements affirm the individual's competency and serve to regulate the quantity as well as the quality of practitioners. A profession must also have the means to enforce the professional ethics and standards through provisions for revoking certification for cause (Hallberg, 1966).

Professional autonomy customarily includes control by the professional group itself over entry into and expulsion from the profession. Control over entry means that the profession sets the standards of professional preparation which must be satisfied for admission to practice. Educational institutions which prepare professionals may add requirements of their own but they have no authority to waive or modify requirements established by the profession.

Since the professions are regulated by the states, matters of licensure (admission to practice) and revocation of license (expulsion from practice) are vested in boards. Professional control over these vital issues is maintained by control of the respective boards, and also by securing legislation providing that membership of the boards be composed of practicing members of the professions involved. Virtually all professions except education regulate themselves in this manner (Stinnett, 1962).

Implicit in the very concept of a profession is the fellowship among its members. A profession is sometimes defined as a "horizontal community." The underlying idea is a powerful one: that a profession constitutes a *community of equals*. This is not to imply that every practitioner is equal in skill or ability to every other practitioner, nor does it rule out specialization within the profession. A horizontal community is one in which all members have equal responsibilities and rights in formulating policy. In the professions, this equality is based upon the assumption that the inevitable differences among practitioners are less important than the similarities, at least when it comes to formulating professional policy. Professions can be contrasted with "vertical communities," such as business organizations or the armed forces. Vertical communities exhibit several different occupational levels, each involving highly disparate functions, rights, responsibilities, and skills (Lieberman, 1956).

It is not always easy to decide whether two occupations should be regarded as specializations within a single profession or as two separate professions. If both groups have common service and vocational objectives, if one professional organization serves the purposes of both groups, and if their duties require a considerable amount of training in common, there is specialization within a single profession. Multiple certification may be desirable where the specializations involved should be regarded as separate professions, but in other cases it tends to divide groups which ought to be united in one profession.

EXEMPLARS FROM ESTABLISHED PROFESSIONS

For the most part, regulation of professions in the United States has been left to the states. As a result, professional control over entry and expulsion has usually taken the form of professional control of the state boards which license the practitioners of the various professions (Lieberman, 1956). Throughout the United States' 200-year history, state governments have continuously sought ways of reconciling the demands of special groups with the public interest. Licensure of the practitioner was one means by which states regulated and controlled special occupational groups, such as the professions. This function was ordinarily delegated to state boards created for this purpose. According to Fesler (1942), some state boards were controlled by the professions, while others were not. The degree of professional autonomy attained by particular professions bore a direct relationship to the extent those professions were able to control licensing.

As a result of political pressure from older professional societies during the period from the late eighteenth into the early twentieth century, state governments enacted legislation which assigned the responsibility for the licensing of practitioners to the professions (Council of State Governments, 1952). This function was ordinarily delegated to professional licensing boards which were empowered to grant licenses, either at their discretion or when a legal, prearranged set of standards was met (Fesler, 1942).

Transfer of responsibility for licensure from medical schools to state boards of medical examiners (1873–1895) and establishment of the National Board of Medical Examiners (1915) were viewed by a visiting German physician as necessary protection of the American public (Sigerist, 1934, pp. 135–137). By 1934, however, Sigerist contended that state examinations had outlived their usefulness, medical schools had matured to the point of again being entrusted to issue licenses, and state control could more appropriately be exerted through approval of preparation programs (pp. 163–164).

Requirements varied from profession to profession because of the historical settings in which they were developed and the unique factors that distinguished each group from the other. Nevertheless, most have followed similar steps in their evolutionary development (Stinnett, 1956). First, most professions require that the candidate for licensure take and pass a statewide test. In some cases, the professional association has developed an examination that is used in several states. For example, all states except one use an identical examination prepared by the American Institute of Accountants. In dentistry, medicine, and nursing, state boards typically use examinations which are prepared, administered, and graded by national professional associations. In the legal profession, sentiment is increasing for a uniform national bar examination for prospective attorneys. In most professions, the trend has been first, to introduce examinations in the few states that have not required one, and then to use examinations prepared by the national professional association.

SITUATIONS IN THE FIELD OF EDUCATION

Educators possessed of widely varying qualifications have served in the classrooms of the U.S. public school system since its beginning. Development of requirements for certification of educational personnel has been irregular both in terms of different types and among various states.

According to Elsbree (1939), the original purpose of teacher certification during the Colonial period was "not primarily, as one might suppose, to protect children against an illiterate or incompetent teacher, but rather to guard against the employment of religious dissenters" (p. 47). From churchmen, the authority was transferred by law and custom to town officers, but for half a century the granting of licenses to teach remained strictly a local function. From these lay school committees, the process gradually evolved through town and county superintendents or special examining boards to state authorities.

The two objectives generally approved for the establishment and maintenance of an efficient system of professional certification are to guard the state and its citizens from malpractice of unqualified persons, and to preserve the rights of the individual practitioner.

In most professions, authority to issue a license to practice is vested exclusively in a state board. Education has been moving in the same direction since 1900, when only a handful of states were characterized by statewide teacher certification. By 1955, 43 states had centralized the authority to certify teachers exclusively in a state agency (Armstrong & Stinnett, 1957). All states currently exercise legal authority over the certification of teachers and some specialists within the profession. The criteria generally include provisions regarding character and knowledge expressed as educational requirements. These historically have been developed by the state education departments and state boards of education without direct participation by practitioners.

During the 1980s, one major trend was an attempt to prescribe more closely the duties and functions of teachers, supervisors, and administrators. Regardless of the potential benefits and drawbacks of such plans, an alarming fact is that legislatures and courts in some states have taken the initiative in defining these duties and functions with little consultation from educators.

Educators should have a strong interest in certification issues because the fate of each individual is closely tied to the competence of other teachers. A certificate is essentially a license to teach—or be an instructional supervisor, curriculum director, or educational administrator—according to the terms and conditions of the certificate. The certificate itself does not guarantee a position, any more than a license to practice medicine or law guarantees employment. The certificate simply means that the holder is legally qualified to practice the profession. An individual or agency interested in employing a candidate is free to insist upon additional qualifications.

Requirements for certification vary considerably from state to state. There is also considerable variation in the requirements for different certificates within a state, including variations in the duration of a certificate and in the combination of subjects and grades that they authorize the holder to teach (Lieberman, 1956; Sturges, 1976).

Institutions of higher education typically configure their preparation programs to conform with state certification requirements. These institutions may, if they choose, exceed the minimum certification requirements set by the state. The extent to which they choose to exceed them depends in large part on the scope of certification requirements. Some states specify so much of the preparation program that institutions cannot add substantially to the basic requirements without extending the overall time needed to obtain a degree. An institution would hesitate to take such action alone, since it would risk losing a substantial number of students by adding requirements not shared by other institutions in the state. If certification requirements do not specify a very large part of the preparation program, institutions are freer to devise programs of their own. However, programs cannot be discussed realistically apart from an analysis of certification requirements as they operate in specific states (Lieberman, 1956).

Certificates in education are different in many ways from licenses in other occupations. Two kinds of differences are fundamental. The first difference is *functional certification*, which refers to the fact that certificates prescribe the specialization an educator may perform. Individuals are not certified simply as educators; they are certified as elementary teachers, high school teachers of a particular subject, elementary principals, secondary principals, guidance counselors, instructional supervisors, curriculum directors, superintendents, and so on. The extent of functional certification varies from state to state, but its use is so widespread that it is a general condition in education.

The second difference is *hierarchical certification*, which exists whenever there are substantial differences in the duration and quality of preparation needed to secure different certificates. Indeed, hierarchical certification is the norm; it takes more years to become an administrator than to become a teacher. Hierarchical certification is a serious obstacle to professionalization because of the vertical structure it creates (Lieberman, 1956).

State boards of education have a great deal of authority over policies, programs, and personnel of schools within their borders. Unlike established professions, state boards of education are typically composed of both practitioners and lay people. They control not only entry and expulsion, but many other matters which appear to be professional in character. It would seem desirable, therefore, to consider the reasons advanced by supporters of lay membership on state boards of education.

The most popular argument in support of lay state boards seems to be that education, as a "public profession," should be under public control. It is contended that the people as a whole must control the schools; otherwise, there is too great a probability that the schools will be used for partisan purposes. It is often said that, in the last analysis, everyone is affected by public school programs. Since it is desirable that those affected by a policy have a voice in the determination of the policy, boards which control education should be staffed by persons who represent the public instead of the profession.

While plausible, the phrase "public profession" may be misleading. Every profession, insofar as it deserves the title, is organized for the protection of the public. Indeed, professions arose because people deemed it essential that certain services be available to whoever needed them. Physicians and attorneys as well as other professionals regard themselves as members of a "public profession"—certainly not a private one. For example, according to an authoritative study of the legal profession in the United States, conducted under the auspices of many of the country's most distinguished lawyers and judges, "The legal profession is a public profession. Lawyers are public servants. They are the stewards of all the legal rights and obligations of all the citizens" (Blaustein & Porter, 1954). Lieberman (1956) makes the case even more strongly:

Indeed, if the phrase "public profession" means simply "affected with a public interest," it appears that many professions in which the practitioners are fee takers have a better claim to be regarded as a public profession than does education. Every doctor, dentist, and lawyer must meet standards for licensure, laid down by a public authority before he is qualified to practice. On the other hand, in many states teachers in private schools are not required to pass any publicly administered tests of professional competence at all, nor are they subject to public control in the performance of their private teaching duties. . . . The clear implication of this is that the public is not as much concerned with the competence of teachers as it is with the competence of doctors or lawyers (p. 107).

Nevertheless, lay control has always been the norm. The NEA itself passed a resolution in favor of lay control in 1921. That position was reaffirmed in 1927 and, insofar as it pertains to lay control of state boards of education, has never been modified since. A 1949 publication of the United States Office of Education (USOE) states that, "best practice indicates that requirements of occupational and area representation as well as certain educational attainment for board membership are undesirable" (USOE, 1949, pp. 4–6). Two years later, another publication of USOE strongly reiterated the same opinion: professional educators should not control state boards of education: "It is improbable that anyone would advocate that a board of education should be composed mostly of educators . . . or of persons from other one professional or vocational group (USOE, 1951, p. 22).

Lieberman (1956) stated that, ". . . the soundest procedure, and one generally followed in the established professions, is for a state board [to be] composed of practitioners of the profession itself" (p. 92). Except for education, most of the professions in the United States have steadily moved toward this criteria of professionalization for almost half a century.

In another way, state oversight of education is unique. State board examinations are the overwhelming rule in the established professions. The foundation of an adequate professional approach for entrance to practice has typically been the statewide examinations under the control of the professions. Proposals to reinstate them in education meet with spirited opposition, especially from institutions engaged in preparing educators. Statewide examinations conducted by a centralized authority with the power to insist on professional standards of achievement could be a powerful lever to force institutions of lesser quality to improve or cease preparation of educators. The fate of their graduates on certification examinations would soon produce either higher standards or a decreased enrollment in such institutions. In any case, changes in the manner that educators are licensed to practice, that is, certified, would have to be made at the state level.

Practitioners of medicine and law established standards of practice through their professional associations many years ago. Various educational organizations—including the NEA, NAESP, NASSP, AASA, and ASCD—have proposed standards to define and guide professional practice. Such standards, it is reasoned, could simultaneously improve practice, restore public confidence, and enhance the prestige of the education profession.

An ambitious effort to establish standards of practice for teachers has been undertaken by the National Board for Professional Teaching Standards, funded by the Carnegie Corporation. The NBPTS has identified standards of practice for teachers with the purpose of offering a voluntary national certification system. Unlike state certification, which is compulsory and documents only attainment of minimally acceptable entry-level preparation and performance, national board

certification is envisioned as a mark of distinction that would certify the attainment of an advanced level of proficiency (Pajak, 1989, p.2).

The concept of specialty recognition is well established in other professions. Specialty boards in medicine, for example, certify physicians in such fields as surgery, internal medicine, radiology, and dermatology, to name just a few. It is distinct from licensure by state education departments or additional categories of certification earned through graduate study.

Lieberman (1960, 1972) proposed establishment of a system of extra-legal teacher certification tentatively entitled "Educational Specialty Boards." National specialty boards in education would not demand any change in state licensure procedures; such recognition would not be required for a regular education certificate. Specialty board certification, however, would be accepted automatically in any state, since the holder would have been designated as possessing a "superior level of professional skill and competence" by an agency under the auspices of established national organizations in education. Faculty of institutions of higher education as well as public school personnel would be considered eligible to seek certification by national specialty boards.

As envisioned by Lieberman, specialty board certification would be advantageous to educational practitioners and to the institutions that employ them. Successful applicants would be able to obtain additional compensation wherever they served. It is expected that teachers would pay for specialty board examinations, inasmuch as the rewards for becoming board certified would make such cost worthwhile. The same practical logic underlies the willingness of accountants to become certified public accountants or of physicians to become board certified in the various medical fields. Board certification would be of value to institutions of higher education and to school districts as a reliable way of identifying superior individuals.

The basic issue is public and professional confidence that the designation "board certified" actually reflects a superior level of professional skill and competence.

Support for specialty recognition has come from the Carnegie Task Force on Teaching as a Profession. Its report, *A Nation Prepared: Teachers for the 21st Century* (1986), recommended specialty certification by a professional standards board as part of the restructuring of teachers' professional roles and the reorganization of schools.

CONDITIONS IN THE CRAFT OF SCHOOL SUPERVISION

Based on his research, Firth (1959) supported specialty certification of other public school personnel, particularly instructional supervisors and curriculum directors. Ideally, professors of instructional supervision and practitioners of supervision in schools would become "board certified."

The competencies that distinguish roles in supervision, curriculum, and instruction from each other and from other roles in education would first have to be agreed upon in order to be able to confer specialty recognition. Once professional standards are established, a training program would obviously need to be conducted, allowing those who can stand muster to acquire and demonstrate the defined competencies. This initiative suggests some interesting possible future functions for national leadership organizations in education.

The opportunity for doing so rests logically with the ASCD. In fact, the concept of specialty recognition was endorsed by the board of directors at the 1986 annual conference. Later that year, the Executive Council approved a proposal to "move forward with all deliberate speed" (Firth, 1987).

Precipitated by its decision to embark on a program of specialty recognition in supervision, curriculum, and instruction, the ASCD issued in 1987 a request for proposals to establish a research base for national certification. A proposal from the University of Georgia for "The Identification of Supervisory Proficiencies Project" was approved. Directed by Pajak (1989), the project involved a research team of nine doctoral students majoring in instructional supervision supplemented by an advisory committee of faculty members in the Department of Curriculum and Supervision at the University of Georgia.

The project identified 12 supervisory proficiencies, ranked in the following order: (1) communications, (2) staff development, (3) instructional program, (4) planning and change, (5) motivating and organizing, (6) observing and conferencing, (7) curriculum, (8) problem solving and decision-making, (9) service to teachers, (10) personal development, (11) community relations, and (12) research and program evaluation. It is interesting to note the low placement of "service to teachers," often heralded as the sine qua non of instructional supervision; "curriculum," which is often closely linked with instructional supervision; and "research and program evaluation," which indicates low priority for improving practice.

This research has been extended significantly through dissertation studies by seven of the nine members of the original research team. The 12 dimensions have since been utilized in several other doctoral studies in instructional supervision, including competencies for professional preparation programs (Spier, 1994), instructional supervision in mathematics (Adamson, 1994) and music (Porter, 1994), and school restructuring (Rhoades, 1995), as well as studies in other fields. Moreover, the original project report was translated into Dutch and Arabic for use by educational organizations in the Netherlands and Egypt.

During this same period, another development was proceeding. In May 1989, the National Policy Board for Educational Administration, consisting of representatives from 10 national organizations including the ASCD, recommended substantial changes in the preparation and certification of school administrators and supervisors, and called for the formation of a national professional standards board.

LITERATURE REVIEW

Of the 128 books on instructional supervision published over the 120-year period from 1875 to 1994, 10 (8%) addressed the dimension of licensure. It is noteworthy that during the 75-year period 1875–1949, only one of the 18 books (6%) mentioned licensure. Emphasis on this dimension was greatest dur-

ing the decade 1960–1969 when four of the 23 books (17%) mentioned licensure (Williams, 1994).

The NAESP and the NASSP have published materials which addressed certification. They cosponsored the National Commission for the Principalship which planned collaboratively, through the NPBEA, a national certification process based on documents entitled, *Principals for Our Changing Schools: Preparation and Certification* (1990) and *Principals for Our Changing Schools: Knowledge and Skills* (Thompson, 1993).

Because "strong certification requirements . . . increase the professional status, prestige, and image of a professional group," Williams (1994) recommends that standards for the certification of instructional supervisors be developed under the auspices of the NPBEA. The NPBEA/Commission for the Principalship provides a collaborative model for defining standards for the certification of principals.

RESEARCH REPORTS

Certification of educational leaders in general and of instructional supervisors and/or curriculum directors in particular has been the direct and indirect focus of numerous inquiries.

Organizations, Institutions, and/or Agencies

A number of studies have focused on state boards that regulate professions, education among them; others have specifically attempted to compare state boards of education with state boards of established professions.

A study of their historical development by Schrammel (1926) revealed an increase in the number of state boards of education from 29 to 41 during the 35-year period from 1890 to 1925. He also found that, with the exception of the governor and the chief state school officer, ex officio members had been virtually eliminated. Responsibility for appointments to the state board of education was vested in the governor in nearly all states.

Fesler (1942) conducted a study of state regulatory agencies to determine the effect of professional autonomy and regulation upon the professions being licensed, and the public interest. He concluded that some sort of liaison or channel of communication should be established between the professional specialists on the boards and the public; that the requirements for professional candidates should be raised no higher than necessary to keep out the inefficient; and that the government should impose more effective means of control over the professions.

In 1952, the Council of State Governments reported that legislation was enacted requiring education and/or experience as well as licensing as conditions for entrance into the practice of nearly 75 occupations. The licensing boards wielded considerable power bestowed by the state.

Will (1964) found a discernible trend in state government toward a central agency conferred with all powers and duties for administering the system of education. The state board of education, composed of representatives of the people, constituted the legislative component of the agency (p. 34). Depending upon the state, selection of board members was found to occur through election by the people or their representatives, appointment by the governor, appointment ex officio or by other office or position, and appointment by the chief state school officer (p. 15).

Molinari (1967) conducted a nationwide study for the purpose of comparing and contrasting the composition, characteristics, and current practices of state licensing boards for educational administration with the seven established professions of law, medicine, engineering, accountancy, dentistry, nursing, and architecture. He found that in the comparative professions, except for law, most members of state boards (75%) were appointed by the governor of that state. Ultimately, however, the professions controlled the membership because the state professional societies usually recommended a list of names from which the governor would select new board members. This list typically consisted of respected practitioners perceived as both knowledgeable and experienced in their field. Board members for the legal profession were selected either by the state supreme courts or the state bar commission.

State boards responsible for certification in educational administration, in contrast, were composed of lay citizens and professional practitioners from fields other than education. These boards were usually responsible for executing the legislative enactments dealing with education. In practice, they established the standards that determined whether or not a candidate was eligible for a license, and then delegated the licensing to the state superintendent of education or a section or a unit within the state department of education. The presence of lay members on state boards was viewed as preventing educational administration from exercising control over entry into and expulsion from its ranks as practitioners did in the seven comparative professions.

Molinari (1967) also noted that, in keeping with the professional independence of the boards for the seven comparative professions, operating expenses, such as office space, staff, and so on, were financed either by fees alone, or by a combination of fees and dues. In contrast, state boards responsible for certification in educational administration were supported by appropriations. The public, through lay representatives who served on state boards responsible for certification in educational administration, determined professional requirements, licensing practices, and fiscal policy.

Reviewing steps considered requisite for autonomy in education, Kinney (1964) asserted that establishment of the regulatory licensing board was essential. "This board would be responsible for . . . preparation and licensure of personnel. . . . Professional examinations might or might not be required . . ." (pp. 137–139). The board would also handle such issues as license reciprocity, out-of-state credentials, and appeals.

Other studies have sought to determine what might be appropriate standards for certification in educational specializations. Sturges (1976) found great differences among states in his survey of certification practices regarding the curriculum director. Questionnaires were sent to the department of education in each of the 50 states and to each of the 78 universities listed as offering a doctoral program for curriculum leaders approved by the NCATE. Responses were received from all 50 state departments of education and 50 universities

(65%). Although certification requirements for curriculum directors were reported for 32 states, footnotes by respondents indicated the inclusion of such titles as supervisor and coordinator. The majority of university professors responding to Sturges' questionnaire agreed that certification should remain the responsibility of the state department of education. However, approved preparation programs deserved consideration as a viable route to certification.

Sturges was involved in another study (Givens, McNeil, & Sturges, 1978) that surveyed 43 presidents of ASCD affiliates and a senior certification officer in each state to determine the existence of certificates for the curriculum leader or plans for the creation of such a certificate. In this survey, 42 percent of respondents indicated they held certificates as curriculum leaders in their states, and about 30 percent of those responding from states without such certification expressed support for it.

In a 1979 study, Sturges surveyed the executive director and a representative member of seven national professional associations for the purpose of determining perceptions of instructional supervisors and recommendations for their preparation. The NEA, AFT, AASA, ASCD, NAESP, Council of Professors of Instructional Supervision (COPIS), and Professors of Curriculum were all involved (Sturges, 1979, p. 586).

According to Sturges (1979), 22 states did not have a specific certificate for supervisors, but treated them as administrators for certification purposes. The 17 states that offered a supervisor's certificate specified the number of credit hours required in supervision and/or administration. The majority of states combined supervision hours with administration hours, or did not specify the number of hours. Two states required completion of an approved program (p. 588).

Although congruent with the administrative role that instructional supervisors often occupy, such linkage diminished the importance of the consultative role that many people, especially teachers, regard as the essential emphasis of instructional supervision. Other leaders, after all, can administer; they cannot always bring to bear the "people skills" of a consultative instructional supervisor.

Findings suggested that instructional supervisors may occupy two distinct roles: *Administrative* and *consultative*. Duties of administrative supervisors included responsibility for federal programs, evaluating teachers for tenure and salary increments, and quality control at the district level. Some positions of the type included department head, principal, and assistant superintendent. Consultative supervisors were more directly involved with helping teachers improve methodology. Evaluating teacher performance from a diagnostic point of view, their efforts focused on learning opportunities for children.

Sturges posited that, if school supervision can indeed be differentiated in these ways, it would seem appropriate to have different preparation programs and different certification requirements for each of the two types of instructional supervisors. In addition, he contended that clearer distinction between administrative supervision and consultative supervision at the district level might enhance the success potential of both role types.

Doctoral Dissertations

The results of the ASCD-sponsored research project on the identification of supervisory proficiencies directed by Pajak (1989) at the University of Georgia provided the basis for additional studies. Over the next two years, a series of seven doctoral dissertations was conducted at that institution to verify the importance of the 12 dimensions of effective supervisory practice derived from educational literature as perceived by selected individuals identified as outstanding instructional leaders. Respective studies focused on instructional supervisors (Smith, 1990); principals at the elementary, middle, and high school levels (McAfee, 1990); mentor teachers and peer coaches (Carr, 1990); department chairs (Duke, 1990); assistant principals at the elementary, middle, and high school levels (Heitmuller, 1991); lead teachers and team leaders (Guerke, 1991); and superintendents (Tostensen, 1991).

Each study verified the importance of all 12 dimensions of supervisory proficiency to the particular leadership role as it currently exists and as respondents considered it should be. The 335 associated statements regarding knowledge, skills, and attitudes established by the Pajak (1989) project also were verified as relevant to effective performance in each of the positions of instructional leadership studied.

The findings of these studies clearly have potential for development of preparation/accreditation standards and licensure/certification qualifications. They also provide the basis for specialty certification. The latter was a major stimulus for the project originally at the ASCD. However, the emphasis has shifted to the dimension of preparation/accreditation through collaboration with other national leadership organizations in the work of the NCATE. Collaboration with other organizations as members of the NPBEA also has encouraged the ASCD to continue interest in licensure/certification.

Certification requirements for instructional supervisors and/or curriculum directors must be strengthened if professionalization of these leadership roles is to be attained.

DOCUMENT ANALYSES

Certification requirements for school supervisors vary dramatically from state to state. A survey by Hallberg (1966) found 71 certificates for instructional supervisors and curriculum leaders in 36 of the 50 states. Some certificates entitled the holder to supervise at either the elementary or secondary level, or both, with a few certificates undesignated. In two states, as many as 27 institutions offered courses to meet requirements for supervision certification. In another state which had only eight such institutions, the number of students completing the requirements for supervision certification was still far in excess of demand. Hallberg enumerated seven principles to consider in establishing and revising certification requirements, including one urging that "the number of training institutions should be limited in order to bring a balance between supply and demand to assure an adequate program" (p. 625).

The UCEA has sought to identify, reassess, and reformulate the purposes served by certification of school leaders (1973) and to model preparation programs for school leaders after those in established professions (1987).

O'Reilly (1989) found agreement among educators that state-controlled systems of program approval provided appropriate mechanisms but strong legal control of certification evidenced by diversity of regulation was "at variance with the sentiment of educators."

Results of a survey on widely varied practices in state licensure of school administrators conducted by the AACTE (Ashbaugh & Kasten, 1992) urged collaboration among groups with vested interest in quality of educational leadership; cooperation of state certification agencies with the NCATE and NPBEA; coordination of staff development opportunities; consideration of national examination and/or certification; and creation of advisory groups to preparation programs.

Otter (1994) analyzed 13 documents published during the 33-year period from 1957 to 1991 to determine the influences on professional self-discipline of instructional supervision by qualifications, licensure, and/or credentialing. The documents were analyzed in terms of the eight components of certification developed by Firth (1958): extent of surveillance, factors evaluated, means of insuring standards, type of standard, designation of certificate, composition of agency, selection of agency membership, and level of agency jurisdiction (Talbe 36–5).

Not all components were discussed in each of the documents. However, reference to extent of surveillance and level of jurisdiction did appear in all 13 of them. Most documents (N-11) discussed types of standards; nine considered the factors to be evaluated; eight explored the composition of the certifying agency; and seven addressed means of insuring standards. Only two documents mentioned selection of membership of the certifying agencies (Otter, 1994).

Otter's findings on each of the eight components are described as the "instructional supervision" aspect later in this section.

COMPONENTS OF LICENSURE/CERTIFICATION

Each of eight components of the dimension of licensure/certification (Firth, 1958)—extent of surveillance, factors evaluated, means of insuring standards, type of standard, designation of certificate, composition of agency, selection of agency membership, and level of agency jurisdiction—is examined in regard to exemplars from established professions, situations in the field of education, and conditions in the craft of instructional supervision.

Extent of Surveillance

Established professions. All recognized professions have established criteria for general practice covering character and knowledge expressed as preparation requirements. Each operates evaluation procedures to determine qualifications and accepts successful candidates into professional standing. Most professions register candidates and approved practitioners on a periodic basis in at least some jurisdictions. Annual or biennial license renewals are typical. Rejected candidates usually appeal for a review of the decision of the licensing agency although

TABLE 36–5. Occurrence of the Components of Extent of Surveillance,
Factors Evaluated, Means of Insuring Standards, Type of Standard,
Designation of Certificate, Composition of Agency, Selection of
Agency Membership, and Level of Agency Jurisdiction Regarding the Dimension
of Licensure/Certification Noted in Documents on Instructional Supervision
Published During the 33-Year Period 1959–1991

Author	Year	Surveillance	Factors	Means	Standards	Designation	Composition	Membership	Jurisdiction
Molinari	1966	x					x	x	x
UCEA	1973	x	x		x	x	x		x
ASCD	1978	x	x	x	x				x
Schulgasser	1985	x			x		x		x
White	1986	x		x	x	x	x		x
Gousha	1986	x	x	x	x				x
Fullan	1987	x	x	x	x	x	x	x	x
UCEA	1987	x	x	x	x	x	x		x
O'Reilly	1989	x			x	x	x		x
Battist	1989	x	x	x	x	x			x
NCP	1989	x	x						x
Richardson	1990	x	x		x				x
Ashbaugh	1992	x	x	x	x	x	x		x

Source: Otter, 1994, p. 33.

appeals of bar examiners are placed directly before the courts in some states. Individuals may bring a suit before the courts for alleged discrimination by any of the licensing agencies.

The professions place no restrictions on the license other than a renewal fee to keep it in force throughout a lifetime. Most practitioners are engaged in a profession as a life's work. Specialization within a profession has remained primarily a matter of professional concern which may or may not also be given legal status in the states.

Education field: As in other professions, established criteria exist for the certification of educators to practice. However, because of the great emphasis upon education as a "public profession" and as a governmental function of the particular state, far less agreement has been achieved among the standards from state to state than in other professional fields. Although state advisory councils and commissions technically provide machinery by which educators may exert influence over practitioners, they do not have the control, as do other professions, in determining certification requirements. Opinions of textbook authors and respondents to various questionnaire studies advocate practitioner participation in regulating certification in education.

Instructional supervision: Many different groups are included among practitioners certified in supervision. In Otter's review of 13 publications on instructional supervision, superintendents were mentioned in six; principals were discussed in six; instructional supervisors were discussed in five; and curriculum directors were discussed in one (Otter, 1994).

Factors evaluated

Established professions: The knowledge possessed by each applicant is considered as part of the licensure process by all professions; character is considered by most; and determination of the actual ability to perform certain duties — by all except law and medicine—appears to be left to the preparing institutions.

Education field: Practitioners in education and those responsible for their credentialing agree that personality, character, and ability to perform professional service are important factors. Performance ability receives particular support from the replies to questionnaire studies. In effect, however, education assumes that preparing institutions have dealt with these factors and that a degree received indicates that the candidate is acceptable for certification. Additional consideration needs to be given to other factors in the certification process. Personality is viewed as vital in education but not in other professions.

Instructional supervision: The characteristics of instructional supervisors and educational administrators seeking certification generally concern skills necessary to work effectively with teachers to improve the instructional process. Characteristics commonly mentioned as being needed were effectiveness in communication, pedagogy, management, and leadership; skill in human relations; subject specialization in the area to be supervised; ability to plan and conduct research; competence in the improvement of instruction; ability to develop standards of effective teaching; and skills necessary to lead, manage, and succeed in a restructured school system (Otter, 1994).

Means of insuring standards

Established professions: Educational requirements and a written examination are the only techniques used in common by professions. An internship in an approved situation is required in medicine, in psychology, and to some extent in public accounting. An internship requirement for the legal profession exists in only a few states but is assumed to take place naturally. Character investigations are specified only in law, but the factor of character is considered part of the record of experience in engineering, public accounting, and psychology. An agency generally issues the license in each of the professions except law, where it is usually done by the courts. No oath is sworn in engineering, public accounting, or psychology. However, an oath before the court is required by attorneys in most jurisdictions, and an oath is traditionally part of the graduation ceremonies of medical schools.

Education field: The importance attached to character, personality, and performance ability of education candidates, coupled with the unaccredited nature of preparation programs demands the use of additional evaluation procedures. Other professions employ an examination to determine the ability to apply knowledge to professional problems. Textbook authors in education advocate consideration of a written test for those seeking certification, and the opinions of state education associations tend to support them. It is important that the education profession set a minimum quality measure for its members.

Instructional supervision: The importance attributed to character both in textbooks and on questionnaire studies indicates the need for careful scrutiny of supervisor candidates. Supervision requires a background of experience, which would be virtually impossible without professional coordination. The experience of medicine, psychology, and accounting indicates the wisdom of close monitoring of practitioners by the national organization in an internship-type experience.

Otter (1994) noted from her review of literature that the means of enforcing standards mentioned most often was the "approved program." Several studies suggested a two-level certification process. Under that plan, the instructional supervisor or educational administrator would become fully certified only after completing an internship or upon successful performance in a monitored full-time position for a period of time, perhaps three years.

Type of standard

Established professions: Graduation from an institution accredited by the appropriate professional agency is mandated for licensure in law, medicine, and engineering. A written examination is required by most professions. Law, medicine, and public accounting have licensure standards demanding that a minimum score must be reached. Criteria for licensure in engineering and psychology are essentially qualitative in nature. Graduation from an approved institution is required in all professions except psychology. The preparation necessary is usually specified in years of study, although accounting and seven of the specialty boards in medicine specify courses. Experience may be substituted for formal professional preparation completely in engineering and to some degree in public accounting and psychology.

Education field: Textbook authors in education and respondents to questionnaire studies generally agree with the requirement of a professional qualifying examination as a standard. Those sources also concur on the importance of graduation from a professionally accredited institution. Educational literature indicates that it is considered essential to protect the gains made in certification criteria during recent years, lest a state authority with a shortage of public school personnel fashion ways to issue regular certificates to unqualified individuals.

Instructional supervision: The most widely accepted certification standard is completion of an approved program of study. The requirement of teaching experience from two to five years is also common. Other requirements in some states include examinations, performance assessment, field experience, staff

development, and a master's degree (Otter, 1994). A more unified standard for certification of instructional supervisors appears desirable.

Designation of certificate

Established professions: In all professions, an individual is licensed as a general practitioner. Two levels of practitioners exist in legal terms for both public accountants and psychologists. The few specialties currently recognized in law are left to the designation of the professional group separate and apart from legal certification. Specializations in medicine are determined by the various national professional boards and in engineering by members of the national professional organizations devoted to particular aspects of the field.

Education field: Educators clearly favor the plan that recognizes a hierarchy of educational positions in the certification standards. They also desire that certification standards be so drawn as to clearly discriminate among those qualified to perform various functions. Many educators are concerned about the threat to standards posed by conversion programs which allow teachers prepared at the secondary level and liberal arts graduates to obtain certificates for teaching in the elementary grades.

Instructional supervision: Many of the publications examined by Otter (1994) mentioned two-tier licensing. Although specifics varied, the most common formula was a Level One certificate which was granted to the entering supervisor. A monitored period of internship was required for the Level Two certificate. About half the states offer a generic certificate for all leadership positions. The rest of the states offer specific certificates for separate leadership roles, such as superintendent, principal, curriculum director, or instructional supervisor. The most common period of validity for a certificate is five years.

Composition of agency

Established professions: In all the established professions, licensure is conducted by a special board with legal authority. All or a majority of the board members must be experienced practitioners in the profession. In most cases, the extent of professional composition of the board is defined by statute.

Education field: As the history of other professions clearly indicates, licensure is a professional function. The inclusion of representatives of preparation institutions and/or laymen on a licensing board is considered to have no justification other than political. Certification in education is advocated as the responsibility of a special board composed entirely or almost entirely of practitioners.

Instructional supervision: The certifying agency is typically composed mostly of lay citizens as opposed to educators. According to Schulgasser (1985), these agencies are influenced more by university regents and state education departments than by the professional practitioners or the preparatory institutions.

Selection of agency membership

Established professions: In medicine, engineering, public accounting, and psychology, the usual practice is for the licensing board to be appointed by the governor from a list submitted by the professional association. In law, it is common for the highest court in the state to make the selection from the approved list; however, in eight states, the governing body of the integrated bar chooses the board. The medical society also directly selects the board members in some states.

Education field: Those in the field of education assert that the practitioners themselves should have a much greater voice in the selection of the members of the certification agency.

Instructional supervision: Otter (1994) found little mention in the literature regarding selection of agency membership for certifying instructional supervisors.

Level of agency jurisdiction

Established professions: Certification of general practitioners is done at the state level in all of the established professions. Specializations are determined at the national level through professional organizations: in law by committee approval of qualifications; in medicine by specific examinations; in engineering on the basis of admission to particular societies; and in the recognized specialties of psychology by examination.

Education field: The state level is considered the most appropriate level for the certification of educational practitioners. Specialization seems more appropriately determined at the national level.

Instructional supervision: Bartoo, Speiker, and Sturges (1976) viewed the state as the appropriate level of jurisdiction for certification of instructional supervisors and curriculum directors.

Based on the recommendations of the responses from certification officers and professors, the formal certification of [instructional supervisors and] curriculum leaders should be administered through an appropriate state department of education office (p. 70).

All of the publications examined by Otter (1994) which referred to level of jurisdiction focused on certification at the state level. Ashbaugh and Kasten (1992) recommended that each state establish a licensing board for educational administrators.

O'Reilly (1989) and Ashbaugh and Kasten (1992) shared the opinion expressed in two reports by the University Council for Educational Administration (1973, 1987) that national credentialing should be utilized as evidence that

practitioners had exceeded minimum standards for professional proficiency.

CRITIQUE

Preparation in a profession, like training in a craft, anticipates licensure. Lack of agreement on professional responsibilities in education is reflected in certification requirements.

Instructional supervisors and curriculum directors represent the very few leadership positions in education that do not require completion of a program that concentrates on the area in which the practitioner will work or possession of a certificate indicating that minimal standards in the area of expertise have been met. Evidence suggests that most present incumbents of such leadership positions were prepared as educational administrators.

Certification for instructional supervisors ranges from no certificate in some states to certificates for four different types of supervisors in other states. Most commonly a special certificate awarded for instructional supervision or curriculum development represents completion of specific courses as part of or in addition to a defined program of graduate study in education. Preparation programs generally do not appear to be either specific to a function or specialized (Eash, 1966).

Bartoo, Speiker, and Sturges (1976) are among those who advocate specialty certification within educational leadership. They assert that certification should follow the completion of the recommended program of studies for an instructional supervisor or a curriculum leader at an accredited institution. Programs should be designed through involvement of practicing instructional supervisors or curriculum leaders in the state. Their influence should be exerted as members of advisory committees or evaluation teams and as co-workers in field activities. Moreover, there should be a systematic sequence of courses, workshops, and institutes for instructional supervisors and curriculum leaders to enable the continued upgrading of their preparation. In all these cases, efforts should be directed to incorporate certification requirements and role functions into statutes and regulations governing education in the states.

Hopefully, such analyses would eliminate conditions where institutional programs exist without appropriate certification, and certificates exist without appropriate supporting programs.

REFERENCES

Adamson, P. G. (1994). *The influence of leadership structure and leader perception on mathematics innovativeness in selected schools and districts.* Unpublished doctoral dissertation in Educational Leadership, University of Georgia, Athens, GA.

Armstrong, W. E. & Stinnett, T. M. (1957). *A manual on certification requirements for school personnel in the United States.* Washington, D.C.: National Education Association.

Ashbaugh, C. R. & Kasten, K. L. (1992). *The licensure of school administrators: Policy and practice.* Washington, D.C.: American Association of Colleges for Teacher Education.

Association for Supervision and Curriculum Development. (1966). *Certification, supervisors, and curriculum workers.* Unpublished

report. Washington, D.C.: The Association.

Association for Supervision and Curriculum Development. (1986). *Minutes of the fall meeting of the ASCD executive council,* October. Washington, D.C.: The Association.

Barton, E. Speiker, C. A. , & Sturgis, A. W. (1976) Summary and Recoomendations. In C. A. Speiker (Ed.). *Curriculum Leaders: Improving their influence.* Washington, D.C.: ASCD

Black, H. C. (1951). *Black's Law Dictionary (fourth edition).* St. Paul, MN: West Publishing Company.

Blaustein, A. P., & Porter, C. O. (1954). *The American lawyer.* Chicago, The University of Chicago Press.

Carnegie Forum on Education and the Economy. (1986). *A nation prepared: Teachers for the 21st century*. Washington, D.C.: Carnegie Forum on Education and the Economy, Task Force on Teaching as a Profession.

Carr, L. C. (1990). *The importance of twelve dimensions of effective supervisory practice derived from educational literature as perceived by selected mentor teachers and peer coaching*. Unpublished doctoral dissertation in Instructional Supervision, University of Georgia, Athens, GA.

Council of State Governments. (1952). *Occupational licensing legislation in the states*. Chicago: Author.

Duke, B. R. (1990). *The importance of twelve dimensions of effective supervisory practice derived from educational literature as perceived by selected department chairs*. Unpublished doctoral dissertation in Instructional Supervision, University of Georgia, Athens, GA.

Eash, M. J. (1966). Preparatory programs for supervisors. *Educational Leadership, 23*(5) February, 358–62.

Elsbree, W. S. (1939). *The American Teacher*. New York: American Book Company.

Fesler, J. W. (1942). *The independence of state regulatory agencies*. Chicago: R. R. Donnelly and Sons, Company.

Firth, G. R. (1959). *Professional self-discipline of public school personnel*. Unpublished doctoral dissertation in Educational Administration, Teachers College, Columbia University.

Firth, G. R. (1986, September, 2). Message from the president—Specialty recognition options available to school leaders. *ASCD Update, 28*(6).

Firth, G. R. (1987). Message from the president—Recognition by professional organizations: A better way to clear up role confusion. *ASCD Update, 29*(3), March, 2.

Gilley, J. W. & Galbraith, M. W. (1986). Examining professional certification. *Training and Development Journal, 40*(6), 60-61.

Givens, H., McNeil, E., & Sturges, A. W. (1978). Certificating the curriculum leaders. In A. W. Sturges, (Ed.), *Certificating the curriculum leader and the instructional supervisor*. Washington, D.C.: ASCD 12–19.

Guerke, M. L. (1991). *The importance of twelve dimensions of effective supervisory practice derived from educational literature as perceived by selected lead teachers and team leaders*. Unpublished doctoral dissertation in Instructional Supervision, University of Georgia, Athens, GA.

Hallberg, H. I. (1966, May 6). Certification requirements for general supervisors and/or curriculum workers today-tomorrow. *Educational Leadership, 23*(8), 62325.

Heitmuller, P. J. (1991). *The importance of twelve dimensions of effective supervisory practice derived from educational literature as perceived by selected assistant principals*. Unpublished doctoral disseration in Instructional Supervision, University of Georgia, Athens, GA.

Kinney, L. B. (1964). *Certification in education*. Englewood Cliffs, NJ: Prentice-Hall, Inc.

Lieberman, M. (1956). *Education as a profession*. Englewood Cliffs, NJ: Prentice-Hall, Inc.

Lieberman, M. (1960). *The future of public education*. Chicago: University of Chicago Press.

Lieberman, M. B. (1972). Educational specialty boards. In B. Rosner, (Ed.). *The power of competency-based teacher education: A report*. Appendix B. Boston, MA: Allyn and Bacon, Inc.

McAfee, A. L. (1990). *The importance of twelve dimensions of effective supervisory practice derived from educational literature as perceived by selected principals*. Unpublished doctoral dissertation in Instructional Supervision, University of Georgia, Athens, GA.

Molinari, R. G. (1967). *A comparative study of state licensing boards and licensing practices for school administration and seven other selected professions*. Published doctoral disseration for Doctor of Education degree at the University of Denver, CO.

National Commission for the Principalship. (1990). *Principals for our changing schools: Preparation and certification*. Fairfax, VA: National Policy Board for Educational Administration.

Ogletree, J. R. (1967). Certification of supervisors and curriculum workers. In R. P. Wahle, (Ed.). *Toward professional maturity of supervisors and curriculum workers*. Washington, D.C.: ASCD.

O'Reilly, R. C. (1989, August, 16). *The instability of certification for educational administration*. (ERIC Document and Reproduction Service, No. ED309 575,)

Otter, J. W. (1994). *Professional self-discipline of instructional supervision: Qualifications, licensure and credentialing*. Unpublished research project in Educational Leadership at the University of Georgia, Athens, GA.

Pajak, E. F. (1989). *Identification of supervisory proficiencies project (final report)*, University of Georgia (available from the ASCD, 1250 N. Pitt Street, Alexandria, VA 22314-1403).

Porter, B. A. (1994). *The role of the music supervisor in Georgia: Perceptions of practicing supervisors/coordinators*. Unpublished doctoral dissertation in Instructional Supervision, University of Georgia, Athens, GA.

Rhoades, J. M. (1995). *A study of school and district responsibility for dimensions of supervisory practice in schools undergoing restructuring*. Unpublished doctoral dissertation in Instructional Supervision, University of Georgia, Athens, GA.

Schulgasser, M. R. (1985). *The development of administrative and supervisory educational certification in New York State, 1629-1984*. Unpublished doctoral dissertation, Teachers College, Columbia University, New York.

Schrammel, H. E. (1926). *The organization of state departments of education*. Columbus, OH: The Ohio State University Press.

Sigerist, H. E. (1934). *American medicine*. New York: W. W. Norton and Company, Inc.

Smith, R. G. (1990). *The importance of twelve dimensions of effective supervisory practice derived from educational literature as perceived by selected district level supervisors*. Unpublished doctoral dissertation in Instructional Supervision, University of Georgia, Athens, GA.

Spier, S. C. (1994). *Selected educational leaders' perceptions of the competencies necessary for professional preparation programs*. Unpublished doctoral dissertation in Educational Leadership, University of Georgia, Athens, GA.

Spring, J. (1985). *American education: An introduction to social and political aspects*. White Plains, NY: Longman.

Stinnett, T. M. (1956). *The teacher and professional organizations* (3rd ed.). Washington, D.C.: National Education Association.

Stinnett, T. M. (1962). *The profession of teaching*. Washington, D.C.: Center for Applied Research in Education.

Sturges, A. W. (1976). Certification: State requirements and selected professors' attitudes. In C. A. Speiker, (Ed.). *Curriculum leaders: Improving their influence*. Washington, D.C.: ASCD, 31-41.

Sturges, A. W. (1979, May). Instructional supervisors: A dichotomy. *Educational Leadership, 36*(8), 586-89.

Thompson, S. D. (Ed.). (1993). *Principals for our changing schools: Knowledge and skills*. Fairfax, VA: National Policy Board for Educational Administration.

Tostensen, H. D. (1991). *The importance of twelve dimensions of effective supervisory practice derived from educational literature as perceived by selected superintendents*. Unpublished doctoral dissertation in Instructional Supervision, University of Georgia, Athens, GA.

University Council for Educational Administration. (1973). *Prepara-tion and certification of educational administrators: A UCEA commission report and summary*. Columbus, OH: Author.

University Council for Educational Administration. (1987). *Leaders for America's Schools: The report of the national commission on excellence in educational administration*. Tempe, AZ: Author.

U.S. Office of Education, Federal Security Agency. (1949). *The structure of state departments of education*. Washington, D.C.: Government Printing Office.

U.S. Office of Education, Federal Security Agency. (1951). *State boards of education and chief state school officers*. Washington, D.C.: Government Printing Office.

Will, R. F. (1964). *State education: Structure and organization*. U.S. Office of Education, Department of Health, Education, and Welfare, Miscellaneous No. 46. Washington, D.C.: Government Printing Office.

Williams, N. G. (1994). *Professional self-discipline of instructional supervision: Influences of national leadership organizations*. Unpublished applied project for the Specialist in Education degree in Educational Leadership at the University of Georgia, Athens, GA.

SECTION V.
THE DIMENSION OF EVALUATION/ENFORCEMENT

INTRODUCTION

This section considers the specific components of enforcement of ethical practice within the general dimension of professionalism regarded as evaluation.

Findings are presented in each of the following 10 categories: definitions of terms; general considerations; exemplars from established professions; situations in the field of education; conditions in the craft of school supervision; literature review; research reports; document analyses; components of evaluation/enforcement, including extent of surveillance, factors evaluated, means of insuring standards, relationship between professional self-enforcement and legal provisions, composition of agency, selection of agency membership, and level of agency jurisdiction; and critique.

DEFINITIONS OF TERMS

For the purpose of this analysis, the term *evaluation* is defined as the process for ascertaining the nature and quality of service performed by instructional supervisors. The term *enforcement* is defined as monitoring the performance of members by a professional organization to assure that standards established in its code of ethics are being met and imposing sanctions upon practitioners who violate those standards.

GENERAL CONSIDERATIONS

Provisions must be in place for a professional organization to enforce ethical standards by the revocation of the license to practice when standards are violated. Reasons for revocation typically include findings of inability to perform competently, personal behavior detrimental to the profession, or professional behavior in conflict with an established code of ethics. The professional organization provides the machinery by which the members of the group can do collectively what it would be impossible for them to do individually (Lieberman, 1956, p. 257).

The establishment of a professional organization follows a pattern. First, a number of persons exist who possess expertise in a specific occupation. They wish to provide a way for the public to discern the capable and scrupulous from the incapable and unscrupulous. A professional association is formed with membership limited to those with demonstrated competence.

At first, the professional association may lack public recognition. Many practitioners, qualified and unqualified, may be outside its ranks. In their early stages of development, such associations often exclude persons for reasons other than incompetence. However, over time criteria unrelated to competence tend to be erased. Membership expands to include an increasingly larger percentage of practitioners. The association achieves greater public awareness and gains respect among clients.

The association then establishes rules of conduct to define the proper relationship between practitioners and clients and among the practitioners themselves. At first, these rules may be no more than guidelines for proper conduct. Eventually the membership of the association sets up machinery for enforcing high standards of ethical conduct to preserve public esteem and professional autonomy.

The average layman must depend on the integrity of the practitioners to maintain the quality of professional service. By defining and enforcing ethical practice of its members, the profession takes the stance of acting in the interest of the public (Lieberman, 1956).

EXEMPLARS FROM ESTABLISHED PROFESSIONS

The formulation and enforcement of a code of ethics by a profession has a twofold purpose: first, to derive a set of rules that ensure ethical and effective service to society and protection for its members; and, second, to assume responsibility for assuring the competency of its members and to prohibit the type of conduct which will bring the profession into disrepute. Unlike legal statutes, which apply to everyone within a certain jurisdiction, the code of professional ethics applies only to members of an occupational group.

The evaluation/enforcement of the code of ethics is the raison d'etre for a professional organization, according to Frymier (1969): "The ultimate purpose of professional organizations [is] guarantee that every member of the group functions in the most ethical, the most effective, the most professional manner known. Professional organizations are instrumentalities to assure the provision of the highest quality of service, and those groups which are truly professional use the power of the organization to require compliance from their peers according to an ethical code" (p. 93).

Like legal statutes, enforcement of professional codes requires interpretation and application. Potential conflict among local, state, and national organizations requires a clear understanding as to which code should prevail in case of multiple interests. According to Lieberman (1956), a common code, perhaps supplemented by rules that are unique to particular professions, could be extremely valuable in "helping to define the scope of professional autonomy and responsibility in a democratic society" (p. 450).

SITUATIONS IN THE FIELD OF EDUCATION

Enforcement of ethical codes by educational associations is rare. The NEA took disciplinary action against only one person from 1929 to 1955. This occurred in 1947 when the superintendent of the Chicago school system was expelled from the NEA for using the influence of his position to obtain adoption of a textbook he had authored (Perry, 1955, p. 79).

Because there is no one central association to which all educators belong, no single code of ethics is applicable to all members of the education profession. The NEA is generally recognized as the leader, but many organizations compete for the affiliation of educational practitioners at all levels.

The Georgia Education Association developed the first ethical code for teachers in 1896, followed by the California Teachers Association in 1904, and the Alabama Education Association in 1908. After five years of study, the representative assembly of the NEA officially approved a code in 1929; it has since been revised several times. All state associations have either developed their own statements of ethics or adopted the NEA code.

In 1952, the NEA Committee on Professional Ethics initiated a series of interpretations of the code. A booklet containing its official opinions on unethical practice was issued in 1955. The NEA, practically all state associations, and some local associations established a process for investigating accusations of professional misconduct against practitioners and imposing specific disciplinary actions. Enforcement is typically delegated to a commission or committee. This group either conducts the investigation or appoints a special investigating team to do so. A formal hearing is held and appropriate action recommended to the executive board of the education association.

Education, in contrast to the established professions, has demonstrated little ability to police its own ranks. Lieberman (1956) states: "To become a leading profession, teachers must reverse the trends toward lay control of professional behavior. However, it is not enough merely to eliminate lay control. Teachers must formulate defensible professional standards and devise the machinery to see that they are enforced. Otherwise, there will be no legitimate moral basis for professional autonomy for teachers" (pp. 448–449).

One obstacle to professional self-discipline in education is tenure law. Tenure is generally perceived by the public as a means of protecting incompetents. Such laws have made attempts to dismiss incompetent practitioners difficult and time-consuming.

This protection [tenure] strains the credibility of consumers, whose own jobs may be less secure, and who may fail to believe that the political conditions that made tenure necessary are still operating. As long as the public sees tenure as protection of mediocrity and incompetence in education, it is unlikely to be sympathetic to demands that state regulatory boards be turned over to those within the profession (Killian, Wood, & Bell, 1980, p. 179).

Another obstacle to professional self-discipline has been the willingness of some administrators to ignore sound educational practice in favor of politically expedient measures.

As long as conflicts are recognized by the public but disregarded by the profession, education will remain "the hostile recipient of legislation drafted for those who cannot or will not clean up their own act" (Killian, Wood, & Bell, 1980, p. 180). If education is to attain the status of a true profession in the eyes of the public, educators themselves must upgrade their profession from the inside instead of just defending it against accusations from the outside (Research Division, 1938, p. 184).

CONDITIONS IN THE CRAFT OF SCHOOL SUPERVISION

Self-policing by a professional group presents complex problems, and there is little experience within the field of education to guide action in this area. An appropriate course of action would be for the ASCD to identify highly qualified members of the profession to form the nucleus of a corps of practitioners who would speak with authority on problems and solutions within the profession (Mackenzie, 1961).

During the 1960s, supervision and supervisors received particular attention within the ASCD. The zenith of such interest was probably reached in 1963, when the Commission on the Preparation of Instructional Leaders recommended that a requirement for ASCD membership be instituted by 1968, specifying two years of preparation beyond the bachelor's degree for instructional supervisors, curriculum directors, and professors of supervision and of curriculum. Subsequently, the Committee on the Professionalization of Supervisors and Curriculum Workers, chaired by Gordon Mackenzie (who had served as ASCD president, 1955–1956) urged that such action be taken.

Fearing "disenfranchisement" of some current members, the ASCD Executive Committee, reporting to the Board of Directors in 1965, called the requirement of two years of preparation beyond the baccalaureate for instructional supervisors "a real tragedy to be avoided at any cost" (Firth, 1986, p. 71). The Board of Directors chose not to adopt the recommendation of the Commission on the Preparation of Instructional Leaders.

Psychologist Arthur W. Coombs (president, 1966–1967) proposed the formation of a professional "home" for supervisors within the ASCD, where supervision as a profession could deal with the issues of preparation, certification, and ethical conduct. In March 1967, incoming president J. Harlan Shores included in his inaugural address the same phrase, as he pledged to make the association a "home for supervisors."

A year later in 1968 at Chicago, the annual conference planned to focus on supervision was disrupted and redirected by a confrontational group within the association whose members demanded focus on cultural diversity. Their actions dramatically influenced the structure, policy, and programs of the ASCD then and subsequently. One result of the 1968 controversy was the abrupt resignation at the annual conference of then president Muriel Crosby, one of the strongest allies of instructional supervision.

In 1986, Gerald R. Firth (president, 1986–1987) compared the ASCD's discussions of instructional supervision in its 1965 yearbook and its 1982 yearbook. The two publications, nearly 20 years apart, present a "striking contrast in focus, content, and audience":

The 1965 yearbook, Role of Supervisor and Curriculum Director in a Climate of Change, devoted attention to professionalization of the supervisor among educational leaders . . . and served as a rallying cry for those committed to this goal. The 1982 yearbook, Supervision of Teaching, provided broad perspective on the field of instructional supervision [including] various approaches, human factors, and external forces. The difference in content reflects an apparent change in the Association's conception of supervision from a function performed primarily by a small group of specialists to one performed by many leadership personnel, as well as by teachers themselves (Firth, 1986, pp. 70–71).

Alfonso, Firth, and Neville (1981) placed strong emphasis on the need for accountability, maintaining that instructional supervisors are accountable for technical competence to themselves, to the organization, and to the profession.

LITERATURE REVIEW

Of the 128 books on instructional supervision published over the 120-year period from 1875 to 1994, 38 (30%) addressed the dimension of evaluation. Emphasis was greatest during the decade 1970–1979 when nine of the 21 books (43%) mentioned evaluation. It is noteworthy that evaluation also was mentioned in nine books in each of the decades 1960–1969 and 1980–1989, but this number represented only 39% of the 23 books and 23% of the 40 books published in those respective decades (Williams, 1994).

RESEARCH REPORTS

Studies on evaluation/enforcement have focused on lay boards as well as professional practitioners in education.

Organizations, Institutions, and/or Agencies

Lieberman (1956) surveyed 52 state and territorial education associations to determine activities to establish and enforce professional ethics. A committee empowered to handle cases of alleged unethical conduct existed in each of 25 associations; however, these committees were much less aggressive than their counterparts in other professions.

The results of a 13-state pilot study (Firth, 1956) indicated that existing educational associations at that time had been unable to achieve the expectations of many educators in discharging their disciplinary function.

Doctoral Dissertations

In his study, Dull (1960) developed a comprehensive set of criteria for evaluation of supervisory programs. Obtaining confirmation from 120 national leaders in educational supervision, Dull was able to demonstrate that the criteria could be applied to determine effective programs of supervision.

According to Firth (1959), practitioners should play a larger role in the enforcement of ethical standards in education. He recommended that each state association have an Ethics Committee, empowered by statute to appoint teams to investigate charges of alleged incompetence or misconduct and to enforce disciplinary action.

Master's Theses and Specialist Projects

After his review of related literature, Johnson (1966) noted that the dimension of evaluation/enforcement in the education profession was typically absent. He found that the professional qualifications of the supervisor were commonly stated only in general terms. He concluded that, "Meaningful research on significant professional qualifications of the supervisor is almost nonexistent" (p. 61).

DOCUMENT ANALYSES

Banter (1994) analyzed 16 documents published during the 33-year period from 1957 to 1991 for the purpose of determining the influence on professional self-discipline of instructional supervision by criteria, performance, and/or enforcement (Table 36–6). The documents were analyzed in terms of the seven components of enforcement developed by Firth (1958): extent of surveillance, factors evaluated, means of insuring standards, relationship between professional self-discipline and legal provisions, composition of agency, selection of agency membership, and level of agency jurisdiction.

Banter (1994) analyzed documents from seven professional organizations and seven states with professional standards

TABLE 36–6. Occurrence of the Components of Extent of Surveillance,
Factors Evaluated, Means of Insuring Standards, Relationship Between Professional
Self-Discipline and Legal Provisions, Composition of Agency, Selection of Agency
Membership, and Level of Agency Jurisdiction Regarding the Dimension of
Evaluation/Enforcement Noted in Documents on Instructional Supervision
Published During the 33-Year Period 1959–1991

Author	Year	Surveillance	Factors	Means	Relationships	Composition	Membership	Jurisdiction
Frymier	1969	x	x	x	x			
Krajewski	1976				x			
Davis	1978				x			
AASA & NSBA	1980				x			
APA	1980		x	x				

Source: Banter, 1994, p. 10

boards regarding self-discipline of instructional supervision. He considered membership eligibility, code of ethics for the membership, and standards of performance for the membership required by seven national leadership organizations: AASA, ASCD, CCSSO, NAESP, NASSP, COPIS, and the Instructional Supervision Special Interest Group of the American Educational Research Association (ISSIG/AERA).

Of the seven national leadership organizations examined, five had an open membership (AASA, ASCD, ISSIG, NAESP, NASSP and ISSIG), while two limited their membership (CCSSO

and COPIS). The five professional organizations that have an "open membership" do not encourage the establishment of specialist subgroups within their ranks.

A formal, established code of ethics was not evident for any of the seven national leadership organizations (Banter, 1994). None of the seven professional organizations police their membership according to a code of ethical standards. These organizations have not promoted professionalism within their memberships in ways urged by Frymier (1969) and Marks (1985).

TABLE 36–7. Characteristics of Independent State Professional Standards Boards

	California	Oregon	Minnesota	Georgia	Florida	Kentucky	North Dakota
CHARACTERISTICS							
Name	Commission on Teacher Credentialing	Teacher Standards and Practices Commission	Board of Teaching	Professional Practices Commission	Education Practice Commission	Education Professional Standards Board	Education Standards and Practice Board
Effective date	1970	1973	1973	1973	1980	1990	1995
Basis for authority	State statute	State statute	State statute	State statute	State statute	State statute	State statute
Accountability to	State legislature	State legislature	State legislature	State legislature	State legislature	State legislature	State legislature
Professionals governed	All certified educators	All certified educators	All certified educators	All certified educators	All certified educators	All certified educators	All certified educators
Number of members	15	17	11	17	13	15	9
COMPOSITION							
Teachers	7	8	6	8	5	8	5
School administrators	1	4	1	4	5	2	2
State school superintendent	1	0	0	0	0	1	0
Teacher education institutions	4	2	1	0	0	2	1
Local school board members	1	1	0	0	0	1	1
General public	4	2	3	0	3	0	0
Business	0	0	0	0	0	0	0
Professional educators	0	0	0	4	0	0	0
Commissioner of higher education	0	0	0	0	0	1	0
State board of education	0	0	0	1	0	0	0

Source: Banter, 1994, p. 20

In most states, legislatures, boards of education, and/or boards of regents have assumed the responsibility for monitoring the behavior of professionals in education or have established specific boards or commissions to develop and enforce such codes and certification requirements for every educator within the state. It is estimated that approximately half of the states now have such functioning boards or commissions. Eleven states (California, Florida, Georgia, Indiana, Iowa, Kentucky, Minnesota, Nevada, North Dakota, Oregon, and Wyoming) have formed independent boards of professional standards through statutes for the purpose of issuing credentials to educators (ECS, 1994). Seven of these same states (California, Florida, Georgia, Kentucky, Minnesota, North Dakota, and Oregon) have enacted codes of ethics or professional practice for educators. Table 36.7 provides an analysis of the professional standards boards in these seven states.

An examination of the activities by the Georgia Professional Practices Commission (GPPC) serves as an example of the manner in which these seven independent boards function and their relationship to the professional self-disciplining of instructional supervisors. Created by the state legislature in 1967, the GPPC was given responsibility for developing the standards of conduct and a code of ethics for educators. In addition, one of the major goals of the GPPC remains to resolve professional conflicts and controversies before they escalate into formal adversary situations (GPPC, 1994a).

The GPPC sought the advice of educators throughout the state to establish nine standards of performance as minimal for the education profession in Georgia. The three parts of the code—"Canons," "Ethical Considerations," and "Standards of Conduct"—were designed to complement each other. The code's intent was to: protect the health, safety, and general welfare of students and educators; assure that the education profession is accountable for acts of unethical conduct by its members; and define and provide notice to educators of acts of unprofessional conduct for which they are accountable (GPPC, 1994b, p. 34).

COMPONENTS OF EVALUATION/ENFORCEMENT

Each of the seven components of the dimension of evaluation/enforcement (Firth, 1959)—extent of surveillance, factors evaluated, means of insuring standards, relationship between professional self-discipline and legal provisions, composition of agency, selection of agency membership, and level of agency jurisdiction—are examined here in regard to exemplars from established professions, situations in the field of education, and conditions in the craft of instructional supervision.

Extent of Surveillance

Established professions. All five of the established professions have developed codes of ethics. Except for the profession of engineering, those codes in force at the state level are based on the standards of the related national organizations. All five of the professional groups evaluate charges of alleged violations and determine the degree of discipline to be invoked against those found guilty.

Education field. Educators endorse the establishment of a common code to govern the actions of practitioners. While various state education organizations have codes of ethics, many do not include all the principles advocated by the NEA. In some cases, a provision in one state contradicts a similar statement in another.

Educators themselves should evaluate charges of alleged violations, determine the degree of discipline to be invoked, and reinstate individuals who have been disciplined. Respondents to various questionnaire studies report a willingness among educators to take responsibility for reporting violations committed by their peers. This requires that procedures be established for accusations to be processed and resolved.

Instructional supervision. In states where an agency exists to deal with violations of ethics, written complaints against any holder of or applicant for a certificate in education must be submitted to that agency by a local board of education, a local superintendent, the state board of education, the state superintendent, the state department of education, resident(s) of the state, or member(s) of the professional standards board. The agency investigates possible violations and furnishes findings of fact, conclusions of law, and recommendations for action to the state authority responsible for licensure (Banter, 1994).

Factors Evaluated

Established professions. All five of the established professions have included ethical behavior and defined some aspects of competent service in their codes.

Education field. In addition to emphasizing ethical behavior and competent service in the code of ethics, educators responding to questionnaire studies have endorsed the inclusion of personal conduct in a social situation as a requisite for professionals in education.

Elsbree and Reutter (1954) explained what was needed: "Basically a standard of conduct prescribed in a code of ethics for a profession should cover those features which distinguish the conduct of the member from that of the nonmember, either because the situation or relationship treated does not pertain to the nonmember or because acceptable conduct in the situation is different for the member than the nonmember" (p. 406).

Instructional supervision. In most states, a group authorized to monitor professional practices investigates charges against members of the education profession to determine if there has been a violation of any of the following: (1) the laws of the state pertaining to educators or to the profession of education; (2) the operative code of ethics for the group; or (3) the rules, regulations, or policies of the state board of education, the monitoring agency, or the local board of education. Findings and recommendation(s) for action are delivered to the state body responsible for certification of members of the profession (Banter, 1994).

Means of Insuring Standards

Established professions. All five of the established professions investigate situations; conduct hearings to determine the issue of guilt or innocence; and reprimand, suspend temporarily, or expel permanently members of the professional association. At the state level, the respective boards may suspend temporarily or expel permanently from actual practice by revoking the license to practice medicine, engineering, public accounting, and psychology. The formal investigative body for attorneys may recommend such measures but actual suspension or expulsion from the legal profession is carried out by the courts.

Education field. Educators generally endorse in principle the procedures described by the five established professions for the enforcement of standards. In such professions, it is expected that practitioners themselves impose penalties up to and including suspension or expulsion from the professional group. In the case of education, coordination would be required with the legal authority for license revocation.

Instructional supervision. The provisions applicable to individuals engaged in instructional supervision are the same as those for other practitioners in education. The plans differ greatly from one state to another (Banter, 1994).

Relationship Between Self-Discipline and Legal Provisions

Established professions. In law, a relatively close relationship exists between the courts and the professional association in the enforcement of the codes of ethics. Although they are two simultaneous, separate methods of discipline, the courts in integrated and some voluntary bar states have shown the tendency to vest this function by statement or implication in the professional organization. In the other four established professions, the pattern has been to develop self-enforcement as an integral part of legal regulations.

Education field. The preference of practitioners and scholars in education expressed in questionnaire studies is that the enforcement process in that profession should be made an integral part of tenure legislation.

Instructional supervision. Because those engaged in instructional supervision constitute a leadership subset within the profession of education, the practices that apply to other practitioners in the field are appropriate to them as well (Banter, 1994).

Composition of Agency

Established professions. In all five of the established professions except law, the enforcement agency is the same as the certifying agency—a special board with statutory authority of which all or a majority of members are actual practitioners. Those in the legal profession rely on an ethics committee, composed of practitioners separate from the licensing body, to work with the courts in monitoring the behavior of attorneys. Similar ethics committees in the other four established professions typically investigate and recommend disciplinary action to the legal authority.

Education field. The preference of educators reflected in textbooks and reported from questionnaire studies is for maintaining at the state level a board with legal authority to act as the enforcing agency. In most states, this is the certification agency which currently works in close cooperation with the ethics committee of the state professional organizations only in some states.

Instructional supervision. In the review of literature, nothing was found to indicate that there is a unique agency to oversee those in instructional supervision. Members of that group are currently subject only to those ethical demands that extend to all practitioners in education (Banter, 1994).

Selection of Agency Membership

Established professions. For the legal control of all five of the established professions except law, state boards are commonly appointed by the governor from a list of practitioners recommended by the state professional association. Some medical boards are directly selected by the medical society. Within the structure of the five established professions, ethics committees and related groups in law and public accounting are designated by the president of the professional organization, in engineering and psychology by the executive committee, and in medicine by election among the members.

Education field. Educators agree that the members of a professional organization should have a direct responsibility for the selection from the membership of those who are to operate the enforcing agency.

Instructional supervision. As members of the broader field of education, those engaged in instructional supervision favor an enforcing agency composed of practitioners of their leadership specialization.

Level of Agency Jurisdiction

Established professions: Among the five established professions, self-discipline is usually exercised at the local and state level in law and medicine and at the state and national level in engineering, public accounting, and psychology. At present, monitoring in medicine is most important at the local level (county); for law, public accounting, and psychology, monitoring is conducted at the state level; and in engineering, monitoring occurs at the national level.

Education field. An enforcing agency for education has been established in every state and operates at the state level.

Instructional supervision. Educators in all states have been given standards and a code of ethics that are enforceable by law. Unfortunately, the standards and codes were neither formed solely by instructional supervisors nor designed solely for them. These standards and codes apply to all educators within a state. The circle advocated by Frymier (1969) and Marks (1985) cannot be drawn around supervisors, because the imposed standards of performance are not unique for them (Banter, 1994).

However, Bartoo, Speiker, and Sturges (1976) advocate that the quality of conduct by instructional supervisors and curriculum directors should be audited at the national level by colleagues in the profession. They propose an ethics committee at the national level to address this concern (p. 68).

CRITIQUE

Every profession has the responsibility to monitor and discipline the conduct of its members. Seven states have established commissions or committees charged with the development of such standards and codes for all educators. Because these commissions or committees are also given the authority to enforce the standards and codes as well as to police themselves, they help to professionalize the educators in those states. Instructional supervisors are considered part of the group of educators from these states. The standards and codes are not unique for supervisors, however.

None of the seven national professional leadership organizations involving instructional supervisors—AASA, ASCD, CCSSO, COPIS, ISSIG/AERA, NAESP, and NASSP—has instituted standards of performance or a code of ethics for its members. Therefore, no association is able to enforce regulations upon its members except for lack of dues payment or absence from meeting attendance.

All seven national leadership organizations have been unsuccessful in creating an appropriate professional home for instructional supervisors. A coalition of these professional organizations working together to attain professional status for instructional supervisors might constitute a viable avenue to explore. Instructional supervisors representing the seven national leadership organizations should lobby for supervision's professional identity. A body similar to the professional standards commissions of the seven states could be charged with development and enforcement of performance standards and an ethical code for instructional supervisors. The guidelines should allow the supervisors to govern themselves directly or through the Professional Standards Commission. This board would serve as a policing arm for initial admission and continued service in the profession. Its membership would be appropriately drawn from the seven national leadership professional organizations.

REFERENCES

Association for Supervision and Curriculum Development. (1977). *Standards and guidelines for evaluation of graduate programs preparing curriculum leaders*. Washington, D.C.: Author.

Association for Supervision and Curriculum Development. (1983). *Evaluating graduate programs preparing curriculum leaders: Standards and guidelines*. Alexandria, VA: Author.

Alfonso, R. J., Firth, G. R., & Neville, R. F. (1981). *Instructional supervision: A behavior system* (2nd ed.). Boston, MA: Allyn and Bacon.

Banter, K. (1994). *Professional self-discipline of instructional supervision: Criteria, performance, and enforcement*. Unpublished research project in Educational Leadership, University of Georgia, Athens, GA.

Bartoo, E., Speiker, C. A., & Sturges, A. W. (1976). Summary and recommendations. In C. A. Speiker (Ed.). *Curriculum leaders: Improving their influence*. Washington, D.C.: ASCD.

Dull, L. (1960). *Criteria for evaluating the supervision program in school systems*. Unpublished doctoral dissertation at Ohio State University, Columbus, OH.

Education Commission of the States. (1994). *Characteristics of independent state professional standards boards*. Denver, CO: Author.

Elsbree, W. S. & Reutter, E. E. (1954). *Staff personnel in the public schools*. New York: Prentice-Hall.

Firth, G. R. (1959). *Professional self-discipline of public school personnel*. Unpublished doctoral dissertation in Educational Administration, Teachers College, Columbia University, New York.

Firth, G. R. (1986). ASCD and supervision: The later years. In W. Van Til (Ed.). *ASCD in retrospect* (pp. 69–81). Alexandria, VA: ASCD

Frymier, J. R. (1969). The supervisor and his professional identity. In W. H. Lucio (Ed.). *The supervisor: New demands, new dimensions*. (pp. 83–102). Washington, D.C.: ASCD, NEA.

Georgia Professional Practices Commission (1994a). Georgia professional practice commission: Structure and functions. Atlanta, GA.

Georgia Professional Practices Commission (1994b). Rules of the professional practices commission. Atlanta, GA.

Killian, J., Wood, F. H., & Bell, P. E. (1980, December). Last call for professional self-improvement. *Educational Leadership, 38*(3), 221–223.

Leake, C. (Ed.). (1927). *Percival's medical ethics*. Baltimore, MD: The Williams and Wilkins Co.

Lieberman, M. (1956). *Education as a profession*. Englewood Cliffs, NJ: Prentice-Hall.

Mackenzie, G. N. (1961, November). Role of the supervisor. *Educational Leadership, 19*(2), 86–90.

Marks, J., Stoops, E., & King-Stoops, J. (1985). *Handbook of educational supervision* (3rd ed.) p. 616. Boston, MA: Allyn & Bacon.

National Education Association. (1993). Code of ethics for the education profession. *National education handbook 1993–1994* (pp. 376–377). Washington, D.C.: Author.

National Education Association of the United States. (1921). *Addresses and proceedings, 59*. Washington, D.C.: NEA.

Perry, C. G. (1955, January). A code of ethics for public school teachers. *The Annals of the American Academy of Political and Social Science, 297*(1), 76–82.

Research Division. (1938, September). Statutory status of six professions. *Research Bulletin* (p. 16). Washington, D.C.: National Education Association.

Research Division. (1940, March). The status of the teaching profession. *Research Bulletin* (p. 18). Washington, D.C.: NEA.

Van Til, W. (Ed.). (1986). *ASCD in retrospect*. Alexandria, VA: ASCD.

Williams, N. G. (1994). *Professional self-discipline of instructional supervision: Influence of national leadership organizations*. Unpublished applied project for the Specialist in Education degree in Educational Leadership at the University of Georgia, Athens, GA.

Yeager, W. A. (1954). *Administration and the teacher*. New York: Harper and Brothers.

SECTION VI.
THE STATUS OF CURRENT RESEARCH

INTRODUCTION

The roles of instructional supervisor and teacher overlap, complement, and/or merge wherever peer coaching, mentoring, and collegial supervision exist. Therefore, the professionalization of school supervisors may be best discerned by examining research pertaining to their primary clientele, teachers.

The AACTE Bicentennial Report on *Educating a Profession* (Howsam et al, 1976) provided an analysis of a theoretical basis for the professionalization of teaching as well as a detailed set of recommendations for improving its professionalism.

Following publication of *A Nation at Risk* by the National Commission on Excellence in Education in 1983, the Bicentennial Commission added a 1985 postscript to its report that reaffirmed its original position and reaffirmed the connection between greater professionalization of teachers and an improved educational system: "The nation is at risk when any of its professions is severely weakened. Teaching is such a profession. . . . The basis for the genuine, sound practice of pedagogy is substantial and growing dramatically. If the nation wants to reduce its risk, it must upgrade the teaching profession and the conditions under which teachers practice. The achievement of one goal is inextricably linked to the other" (p. 177).

However, during the years since publication of *Educating a Profession*, not much change appears to have occurred (Surdyk, 1995, p. 28).

CONCEPT OF PROFESSIONALISM/ PROFESSIONALIZATION

Although many years have elapsed since education in general and supervision in particular embarked on the quest for professionalism/professionalization, more recent reports contain much the same language as earlier ones. The recent literature does provide a new attempt through sociological research to ascertain the significance of professions.

Sykes (1989) explores the motivation for professional identity, particularly in the field of education. She points out that there are no alternatives that can provide, as does professionalism, the coveted presumption of status, income, autonomy, and competence (p. 254).

The AACTE Bicentennial Report (Howsam et al, 1976) cautions that "opting to use the name [profession] does not insure that the status of profession will thereby be achieved" (p. 6).

Definitions of Terms

A wide variety of definitions from which to choose are available to anyone attempting to determine a meaning for the term *profession,* according to Surdyk (1995, p. 11). Among them the view that "professions are exclusive groups applying somewhat abstract knowledge to particular cases" (Abbott, 1988, p. 8) is instructive, insightful, and integrative.

General Considerations

Armstrong (1985) brought some method to the difficult task of defining *profession* by describing three distinct approaches: the attribute approach, the professional dominance approach, and the process/structural approach.

Attribute approach. The attribute approach is characterized by lists of traits claimed to represent the common core of those occupations that can be considered professions (Johnson, 1972). Those occupations that conform most closely to the attributes are ranked highest as professions. As a pioneer of this approach, Flexner (1915) developed a list of the six defining attributes common to all professions. However, this approach has fallen into relative disuse and, to some degree, disrespect (Abbott, 1988; Armstrong, 1985; Friedson, 1988; Houle, 1980).

Professional dominance approach. Friedson (1970) moved beyond identification of autonomy as one distinguishing trait among others, elevating it to the status of professional sine qua non. In his later work, he (1988) further developed the concept of autonomy by relating it to the exercise of control over specific domains of knowledge.

In a related analysis, Abbott (1988) argued that jurisdiction rather than dominance is the most important exclusive property of a profession. Such jurisdiction includes control of professional recruitment, training, and licensing; rights of self-discipline and of unconstrained employment; and absolute monopoly over practice and payment for practice (p. 59).

Critics of the professional dominance approach have contended that its advocates have failed to situate the development of professions within historical or social contexts (Armstrong, 1985; LaDuca & Engel, 1994), or to recognize that the body of knowledge exercised by specific professions may not be held in equal value by all segments of society (Johnson, 1972).

Process/structural approach. This approach, ushered in by Butcher and Strauss (1961) and Hughes (1963), regards professions as "contextual, relational, and situational" (Surdyk, 1995, p. 18). Thus, professions can be identified only within the "contemporaneous intellectual, political, economic and social context" (Kimball, 1992, p. 17) in which they exist. According to Armstrong (1985), this approach provides new insight into the emergence and development of professions because it synthesizes insights from various sociological methodologies.

Exemplars from Established Professions

"Professions," said Rueschemeyer (1983), "strike a bargain with society" in which competence and integrity are exchanged for the trust of client and community, relative freedom from lay supervision and interference, protection against competition, and "substantial remuneration and higher social status" (p. 41). This bargain may be becoming increasingly unacceptable to a public which sees itself as denied involvement in its own most important concerns.

Mathews (1996) suggested that professions may eventually be forced to rewrite the contract made with the public around the turn of the century. The high wall separating professions from the public needs to be torn down, he argued, to allow "two-way traffic" between citizens and professionals (p. 26).

Despite problems faced by established professions, particularly demonstrating the same rigidity as other types of institutions, the AACTE Bicentennial Report asserted that "there can be no acceptable social alternative to professional service and professional organization. To abandon the professions is to deny the quest for improvement in the lot of humanity" (Howsam et al, 1976, pp. 40–41).

Situations in the Field of Education

In analyzing teaching in terms of commonly accepted criteria for professions, the AACTE Bicentennial Commission (Howsam et al, 1976) found a wide discrepancy between the established, older professions and education as it exits in the United States. However, a close correspondence was found between education and what Etzioni (1969) described as the "semiprofessions." Etzioni's assessment poses a tantalizing question: Is education a profession in an emergent state, or is it destined to remain forever at the level of a semiprofession? Some scholars believe that education will eventually meet the challenge of achieving professional status (Howsam et al, 1976, p. 39), whereas others disagree (Goode, 1969).

The AACTE Commission Report does not accept the usual "high wall" between the public and the professions as justification for education's inferior status. "The Commission's hope is that educators will continue to enlarge the meaning of professionalism so that it becomes more democratic, client-nurturing, and political than that which presently characterizes the established professions" (Howsam et al, p. 133). The same spirit is expressed in Boyer's statement published in 1996 after his death in 1995 urging that the university must "affirm its historic commitment to. . . the scholarship of engagement" (p. 11), thus allowing both "academic and civic cultures [to] communicate continuously and creatively" (p. 20).

The AACTE Bicentennial Commission admits that achieving professional status will be difficult. "Somewhere within society, within the school as an institution, within the organized profession, within preparation institutions, within the governance system, within the nature of the teaching act, and elsewhere exist forces which interact to inhibit what seems to be the destined thrust of teaching to mature professionally. Clearly there will be no simple solution" (Howsam et al, p. 3).

Soder (1990) questioned whether the question of professionalism per se should remain a central and practical concern. Herbst (1989), author of an extensive history of teacher education in the United States, viewed teaching as a "not quite" profession. He calls for the improvement of teacher education within the framework of overall educational reform.

Surdyk (1995) also embedded professionalization within contemporary reform movements. However, she notes that although these movements contain educators dedicated to the concept of increased professionalization, they also contain those who adamantly contest any efforts whatsoever toward that goal. Many educators are concerned that the models of professionalization offered by medicine or law seem inappropriate or inadequate in the context of teachers or supervisors (Hoyle, 1980; Jackson, 1987; Soder, 1990; Sykes, 1989). Others protest that the professional model itself is flawed, as it applies or would apply to educators (Bull, 1990; Labaree, 1994). Duffy (1994) indicated that the establishment of professional development schools implies "a caste system in which the professors are the gurus and the teachers are followers" (p. 596). This hierarchy of expertise—which, indeed, professionalism implies—is at odds with the current reform movements working toward reconfiguring schools as democratic and collegial workplaces.

Democratic educational reforms call for the reinvention of the roles of teacher and supervisor, and the reinvention of their relationship to one another. In the tradition of the process-structural approach to defining a profession, these redefined roles may yet produce a conceptualization of professionalization unique to education.

Three national educational leadership organizations have defined methodologies and/or established mechanisms to strengthen professionalism among members.

Twelve Generic Skill Dimensions (1975, 1985) developed by the NASSP have been implemented through processes of assessment centers initiated in 1975 and validated through studies conducted in 1981 and 1989. *Proficiencies for Principals* (1991) developed by the NAESP serves a similar function in guiding the case simulations utilized in the Administrator Diagnostic Inventory. *Professional Standards for the Superintendency* have been developed by the AASA.

The NPBEA was established on January 19, 1988 in Washington, D.C. to coordinate the efforts to professionalize national educational leadership organizations, including the AASA, NAESP, NASSP, ASCD, and CCSSO.

Conditions in the Craft of School Supervision

One of the characteristics enumerated in the AACTE Commission Report is particularly significant for instructional supervisors: "There is relative freedom from direct on-the-job supervision. . . . The professional accepts responsibility in the name of his or her profession and is accountable through his or her profession to the society" (p. 7).

Therefore, the emerging role of the supervisor as a collegial resource person whose role is to support the work of teachers can be viewed as a move toward professionalization.

Values of Professionalism/Professionalization

The four "values" associated with professionalism/professionalization—expertise, autonomy, responsibility, and commitment—were addressed as important to the current status of the concept.

Expertise. The AACTE Bicentennial Report identified expertise as a basic aspect of professionalism/professionalization; however, that report also stated that teachers' authority is currently rooted more in the in loco parentis tradition than in expertise. "Little progress will be made until educators develop and use a body of recognized professional expertise" (Howsam et al, 1976, p. 13).

Sergiovanni (1992) suggested that educational expertise cannot be, nor should it be, codified in a finite list of "appropriate technical skills." "Like other professionals, teachers cannot become effective by following scripts. Instead they need to create *knowledge in use* as they practice" (Sergiovanni, 1987). "This ability requires a [high] level of reflection, understanding, and skill" (p. 35).The concept of *knowledge in use* applies to supervisors as much as to teachers.

Darling-Hammond, Wise, and Klein (1995) pointed out that accreditation, licensing, and advanced certification are the three major quality control mechanisms for any profession. In the field of education, however, these three mechanisms have historically been weak, in large part because of lay governance. Government bureaucracies—state legislatures along with state boards and departments of education—have set themselves to govern education. The result has been hundreds of individual state mandates.

In recent years, however, at least three changes have occurred. Autonomous professional standards boards for teaching have been established in 10 states. The National Board for Professional Teaching Standards (NBPTS), established in 1987, provided the first set of standards for the advanced certification of highly accomplished teachers. The NCATE has strengthened standards for teacher education programs. Initiatives such as these represent professional concern with defining, establishing, and enforcing an acceptable level of expertise for all educational practitioners.

Autonomy. Friedson (1970) asserted that the true mark of a profession is autonomy—its ability to control the content and terms of its work, and to organize, control, and dominate the work of others in the division of labor (p. 134). It is Surdyk's (1995) judgment that Friedson viewed autonomy and the political activity resulting from control wielded in society by professions as both a necessary and sufficient cause for an occupational group to claim professional status (p. 14).

Howsam et al (1976) explained that most teachers are employed in public service; their authority to teach comes from a contract and an assignment (pp. 12–13). The conditions under which teachers work strongly mitigate against autonomy.

Responsibility. One of the accepted hallmarks of a profession is its responsibility for the quality and competence of its members. This responsibility is twofold: responsibility to the members of the profession that the investment they have made in their preparation will not be devalued and responsibility to the public at large that the knowledge and skills of the profession are present in its members (Holmes Report, 1986, p. 65).

One aspect of a profession's responsibility to the public is its guarantee that members of the profession are not only knowledgeable and competent but also that they are persons of good character who are committed to exemplary practice and also to the general welfare. From ancient times, the traditions of education have been imbued with moral gravity and practitioners have been held to the highest moral standards. Generally, however, the responsibility for enforcing these moral and ethical standards is given not to the profession, but rather to paragovernmental boards and agencies. The public through its elected representative has declared it does not trust educators to police their own ranks.

Responsibility for competence and for moral and ethical conduct devolves, therefore, upon the individual more than upon the profession as a whole. This requires what Aristotle called practical wisdom regarding the purposes of one's practice: "For professionals, being virtuous in this sense means being conscious that one's activities always have a significance beyond the immediacy of particular situations" (Flores, 1988, p. 9).

Commitment. Flores (1988) emphasizes that the substantial difference between acting ethically and being ethical "is obscured by restricting professionalism to the adherence to the rules" (p. 2). Teachers tend to be committed "to teaching rather than to the professionalization of their teaching" (Howsam et al, 1976, p. 12). The existence of and subscription to codes of ethics in education are essential to professionalization; however, conformance to a code without commitment to its ideals and values means going through the motions of ethical behavior. A person may behave ethically for ignoble reasons; for example, to avoid trouble and gain tenure. To quote Sergiovanni (1992), "Only when code-specific behavior and underlying ideals and values are connected—only when it is accepted that what teachers do and why they do it are connected—will professional codes cease to be rules of professional etiquette and become powerful moral statements" (p. 55).

VISION OF IDENTITY/IMAGE

There are many images of teaching as well as conceptions of teacher effectiveness. It is also clear that supporters of increased professionalism/professionalization of teachers find some relationship between effective teaching and recognition of teaching as a profession. It remains to be seen how teachers will embrace that relationship (Surdyk, 1995, p. 42).

General Considerations

The view of teaching is well established both in statute and practice as "an occupationally related social institution established as a means of providing essential instructional services in the schools. Also, teaching is concerned with one area of societal need or function—professional intervention to enhance learning in a variety of instructional settings" (Howsam et al, 1976, p. 10).

Exemplars from Established Professions

Surdyk (1996) describes influences that shape the identity and image of members of professions. Some philosophers and ethicists believe that how individuals choose to act in any given situation is determined by who they perceive themselves to be. Who they are, in turn, is determined by the various communities to which they belong. As human beings—members of the community of humankind—people also are members of a particular race, culture, country, family, and perhaps religious group. All these communities help to define them. Moreover, behavior is determined by what particular communities accept and communicate about how to judge right, wrong, and the gray area "in between." To join a profession is to choose to belong to a community of professional colleagues. The sense of right, wrong, and "gray" about how professionals act is determined by who these professionals perceive themselves to be, both as part of the group but also as defined by responsibilities to perform certain services in a complex society that cannot be provided by just anyone. Professionals are expected to have a moral obligation to those within the society for whom they perform their service as well as to members of the profession itself (pp. 4–5).

Situations in the Field of Education

The particular image of teaching that a practitioner holds affects the manner in which it is practiced and assessed (Fenstermacher & Soltis, 1992; Shavelson, Webb, & Burstein, 1986; Tom, 1984). Teaching has been characterized as labor, as craft, as art, and as science (Darling-Hammond & Goodwin, 1993; Glatthorn, 1996; Mitchell & Kerchner, 1983).

To espouse an image of teaching as labor "suggests work that is preplanned, highly structured and routinized, and closely supervised. . . . In this role, the teacher is charged with implementing 'a defined set of skills, knowledge, and attitudes which lead to predetermined learning outcomes'" (Darling-Hammond & Goodwin, 1993, p. 23). Such an image of teaching is clearly antithetical to that of the education profession operating from a specific knowledge base and free to make autonomous judgments regarding practice.

Teaching as craft characterizes work that is "more likely to be licensed to ensure minimum standards and quality and to protect the public. Though craftsmen exhibit specialized knowledge, their decisions are based on the application of standardized modes of practice" (Darling-Hammond & Goodwin, 1993, p. 24; Glatthorn, 1996). The executive approach to teaching (Fenstermacher & Soltis, 1992) is an example of teaching as craft. "[It] views the teacher . . . as a person charged with bringing about certain learnings, using the best skills and techniques available" (p. 4). Recognition of teaching as a craft is not generally regarded as supportive of a professional image for teaching, specifically because "craft" does not imply a scientific knowledge base for practice (Tom, 1984).

Finally, teaching is also viewed as an art, emphasizing personal creativity and adaptability (Darling-Hammond & Goodwin, 1993, p. 24; Glatthorn, 1996, p. 14). Attempts to develop this image strictly along the lines of the aesthetic, however, are doomed to failure (Tom, 1984) since artists are typically indifferent to clients and idiosyncratic in the application of their skills. There is a particular problem concerning the image of teaching as art in that artists are generally assumed to be born, not made; that is, artistic talent is innate

rather than taught. This is incongruent with the image of teaching as a profession. The development of professions must be through acquisition of a specific knowledge base.

All of these images of teaching—as labor, as craft, as art, and as science—are common among teachers. This may explain why it has been so difficult for teachers to move toward the development of a professional culture. A professional culture builds from common values, beliefs, and goals, but professional education is often derided and downgraded within the profession itself.

In the interest of developing professional standards for educators as a united body, the Holmes Group (1990) advocated establishment of professional development schools in cooperation with universities. Professional development schools would organize themselves in accordance with their "strongest conceptions of teaching and learning" (p. 83) and, to that end, would cultivate collaboration in a variety of ways. The school and the university would share faculty and staff who would work together to plan, implement, and evaluate of programs..

Conditions in the Craft of School Supervision

Although instructional supervision has long been considered an important element of the school system, there is little evidence that it has made significant contributions to teacher performance or learning outcomes. Like administration, supervision has been viewed as "out of sync" with the nature of the school and the professional work force. Potentially critical elements in teacher performance, supervision, and administration largely determine what teachers do with the preparation and experience they possess. Howsam et al (1979) state that "administrators and supervisors must keep in mind always that schools are *modern* organizations staffed by professionals; learning and teaching are sensitive processes which insensitive relationships often violate; and since learning has personal development both as its process and its intended outcome, emphasis must always be on the formative, helping relationship, rather than on the summative, decision-making side of institutional life" (p. 67). Alfonso and Firth (1990) concede that "the historical lack of clarity about who supervisors are and what they do persists. This problem at least partly explains the inadequate research base. Still, the educational profession should have confronted these issues by now" (p. 181).

Aspects of Identity/Image

The six aspects of identity/image—perceptions, antecedents, titles, functions, theory, and research—were addressed as important to the current status of the vision.

Perceptions. Professional culture has been defined by Lortie (1975) as the collective knowledge, skills, behaviors, attitudes, and values that constitute the bases for professional expertise and decision-making.

Teachers must perceive themselves as learners engaged in reeducating themselves and each other to become experts in another mode of teaching (Putnam, 1990). According to

Nolan and Francis (1992), "before teachers can use a new model of teaching effectively, they must acquire a deep, personalized understanding of the model. . . . Teachers must be looked on as generators of knowledge on learning and teaching, not merely as consumers of research" (p. 51).

This is at great variance to the perception of the teacher reported by the AACTE Bicentennial Commission (1976): "Basic to the problem of developing a professional culture is the long-held view that there is not much to teaching. . . . Teaching has been based more upon conventional wisdom, folkways, and personal experience than upon solidly validated professional knowledge and skill" (Howsam et al, 1976, p. 11).

Antecedents. Though many teachers are recognized as individually competent and skilled, education in general is characterized by the lack of a common body of knowledge and repertoire of behaviors and skills needed in practice. Rather, each teacher individually develops personal strategies (Howsam et al, 1976, pp. 10–11).

Titles. The Holmes Group (1986) argued that a differential structure which recognizes increased levels of expertise is a prerequisite for the "construction" of an education profession (p. 64). They suggested a tier of three levels: the instructor, who would be prepared to deliver instruction under the direction of a career professional teacher; the professional teacher, who would be prepared to assume full responsibility at the classroom level; and career professional teacher, who would be capable of assuming responsibility not only within the classroom but also at the school level (p. 65).

Role. The AACTE Bicentennial Commission (Howsam et al, 1976) predicted that the teacher's role in the future will be as part of a collegial team, rather than the independent but isolated model which is now customary. The essence of collegiality is interpersonal relationships characterized by mutual respect. In the context of schooling, it includes common membership in a community, commitment to a common cause, shared professional heritage, and shared professional values (Sergiovanni, 1992, p. 91).

Theory. A profession demands the acceptance of a validated knowledge base. Indeed, without principles, concepts, and theories to validate practice, the occupation is restricted to the level of a craft (Howsam et al, 1976, p. 11).

The large body of research on teaching supports a conception of teaching that is: based on the integration of knowledge about learners and learning, curriculum and instruction, and society and contexts; characterized by the use of multiple skills, appropriately applied to particular situations; and context-dependent as knowledge and skills address the needs of particular students and classes. As a consequence, emerging approaches to teacher assessment are based on application of knowledge of learning, teaching, and the social context of education to the tasks of teaching, including planning, instruction, diagnosis of student needs and assessment of learning, and classroom management, within the contexts of subject matter and students (Darling-Hammond, Wise, & Klein, 1995, p. 30).

Research. Different philosophies of education give rise to multiple paradigms of research, which tend to vary according to their basic orientation to the question of what makes effective teaching. Shulman (1986) labels "classroom ecology" as his particular interest which represents a recent trend in studies of teaching. This body of research utilizes various approaches characteristic of qualitative research, particularly ethnographic studies. Sometimes criticized for ambivalence and overgeneralization, such studies also have been commended for bringing together content and pedagogy in the context of practical wisdom and in relationship to specific instances or cases. Research in this tradition goes directly to the primary source for firsthand knowledge of teaching, that is, to teachers themselves (Surdyk, 1995, p. 40).

As research on teacher effectiveness has become more conceptually and methodologically sophisticated, it has become acknowledged that, in a complex and variable educational environment, generalized rules for teacher behavior cannot replace the need for sophisticated knowledge and professional judgment. It seems clear that effective teaching must be responsive to a number of variables involving students, classrooms, and school environments in ways that preclude the application of predetermined approaches (Joyce & Weil, 1972). Moreover, many factors other than teaching behavior have profound effects on student learning (Anderson, 1982; Centra & Potter, 1980; Mckenna, 1981).

Researchers who have adopted an ecological perspective for investigating teaching have also pointed out that teaching and learning are characterized by reciprocal causality—what the teacher does depends on what students do, and vice versa, in a continuous set of interactions that cannot be predetermined given the variability of human behavior and experience. This reality also limits the applicability of process-product research findings. Research grounded in this perspective has found that what students do affects teachers' behaviors and that the complexity of classroom life calls for teaching strategies responsive to environmental demands (Darling-Hammond, Wise, & Klein, 1995, pp. 28–29).

Research on the stability and generalizability of measures of teaching behaviors lends support to a context-specific view of teaching. Stability refers to the extent that a teacher's behavior as measured at one point in time correlates with measures taken at another point in time. Generalizability refers to the extent that such measures are stable across different teaching situations (e.g., subject areas, grade levels, student ability levels). The more knowledgeable the teacher, the greater the expectation that his or her teaching will be responsive to the many considerations of subject, learners, goals, and purposes that combine to produce different judgments (Darling-Hammond, Wise, & Klein, 1995, p. 29).

DIMENSION OF PREPARATION/ACCREDITATION

In the renewed efforts toward professionalization of education, accreditation of preparation programs is viewed as a significant factor. According to Darling-Hammond, Wise and Klein (1995), the foundation of the new accreditation standards is the growing body of knowledge about teaching and learning obtained from research and "wisdom of practice" (p. 10).

General Considerations

Accreditation serves two fundamental purposes. First, the process ensures employers that applicants have met minimum standards. Second, accreditation requirements provide a continuous stimulus for institutional self-improvement. Typically, accreditation is bestowed upon a particular preparation program following an initial successful investigation by some branch of the profession's governing board. The process demands that for continued accreditation there then be periodic reevaluation visits by board-appointed teams. The process of accreditation has been so well received that what is called a voluntary process has become an obligation for most programs and institutions.

Exemplars from Established Professions

That a profession should have total control over entry into membership and delivery of service has always been a source of concern to the public. The basic question is whether the profession can be trusted to put the public welfare ahead of its own. The AACTE Bicentennial Report (Howsam et al, 1976) predicted that the future will see increasing interaction between the public and the professions. The public will oversee the professions through representation on the governing councils of professional associations, accrediting bodies, and licensing boards (p. 123).

Situations in the Field of Education

At the time of the AACTE Bicentennial Report (Howsam et al, 1976), only 40 percent of preparation programs for teachers at institutions across the nation had sought and received NCATE accreditation. This low proportion likely is due to an assumption that the existing alternatives already provide sufficient indications of quality.

Howsam et al (1976) were critical of the quality of teacher preparation programs in general: "Preparation for and induction into the profession are tragically inadequate. The time and resources devoted to the professional aspects of teacher education are markedly lower than for any other profession or semiprofession" (p. 12).

Rather than urging increased participation in NCATE accreditation, however, the AACTE Bicentennial Commission (1976) argued that teacher organizations should involve themselves in the accreditation process and establish collaborative relationships with colleges of education (p. 122).

Conditions in the Craft of School Supervision

Guidelines on approval of preparation programs for educational leaders, including instructional supervisors, have been developed by the NPBEA. This group's proposed Curriculum Guidelines were approved by the NCATE in October 1995. These guidelines, formulated from dimensions, standards, and domains published by the participating national organizations, defined advanced programs in educational leadership for superintendents, principals, instructional supervisors, and curriculum leaders.

As noted by Alfonso and Firth (1980), however, preparation programs for instructional supervisors are seldom unique. "Previous studies have indicated only minor differences between preparation programs and certification requirements for supervisors and administrators. . . . Until the knowledge base of instructional supervision has been established, preparation programs likely will continue to be weak and vulnerable to personal preference and historical antecedent, if not accident" (p. 187).

Components of Preparation/Accreditation

Current efforts in the dimension of preparation/accreditation are examined in regard to each of the six components.

Extent of surveillance. The Holmes Group (1995) rejects the philosophy of caveat emptor. In its view, nothing about the professional preparation of educators should be left to chance. Like the AACTE Bicentennial Commission, the Holmes Group urges national professional accreditation as a potentially important lever in strengthening the education profession overall and assuring quality preparation programs for those pursuing careers in the field of education. "If an education school contributes good research but poor professional development, it should become a laboratory or a center or a department in arts and sciences and cease to pose as a professional school—for education schools bear the unique expectation that their faculty will themselves be good educators, and their students will indeed learn important things" (p. 96).

Factors evaluated. Some argue that tests such as the National Teacher Examinations and Praxis meet the need for the equivalency of state licensing boards in other professions. In addition, the 92 standards prepared by the Interstate New Teacher Assessment and Support Consortium (INTASC), sponsored by the CCSSO, is considered an appropriate way to establish a quality index of professional preparation for education.

An important component of teacher preparation is study in the academic specialization areas. Academic faculty often assume that when the education majors learn the research procedure, logic, and content of an academic specialty, their ability to think analytically, act wisely, and excite others about the value of the discipline will follow. This is not necessarily the case.

The preparation of teachers, like that of nurses, social workers, doctors, and counselors, requires a mastery of subject matter combined with an understanding of how a subject matter can be useful to students in discovering personal levels of meaning (Howsam et al, p. 85).

Means of insuring standards. Of particular significance regarding the professionalization of teaching within a policy domain is the current movement toward development of nationally recognized professional standards for teachers (Wise, 1994). Various reports have made specific recommendations related to the accreditation of preparation programs and teacher certification.

New, more rigorous accreditation standards for teacher education programs are being implemented through the auspices of the NCATE, which strengthened its standards in 1988. The standards are demanding; many programs, of course, choose not to apply. Approximately 20 percent of the programs that seek NCATE accreditation fail to meet the standards the first time through the process. After appropriate changes, most of them are successful the second time (Darling-Hammond, Wise, & Klein, 1995, p. 10).

Composition of agency. The certification process also serves as a quality control mechanism. The certification of teacher education graduates is usually an instructional programmatic matter because it requires completion of an approved preparation program. Program approval departs from broad curriculum guidelines established by state departments of education. Institutions then submit their programs for review. When official approval has been given, graduates of that program become eligible for a license to teach (Howsam et al, 1976, p. 123).

Selection of agency membership. The fragmented nature of education as a field of study tends to be carried over into the accreditation process. Establishment of different standards for each subfield complicates representation on policy boards of accrediting agencies. The Joint Commission on Accrediting, a forerunner of the National Commission on Accrediting, listed the following major problems of the accreditation process in education: too many agencies, too much duplication, costly evaluation, overemphasis on quantitative and superficial standards, domination by outside groups, and procedures that interfere with institutional prerogatives (Howsam et al, 1976, p. 123).

In 1991, the CCSSO adopted a resolution to collaborate with the NCATE to evolve a common national system of accreditation for teacher preparation programs, emphasizing performance as well as knowledge. Since in their respective states "the chiefs" are the individuals who direct the system that is the state alternative to NCATE, the resolution is a major development.

The general movement in education, then, is toward more professionally grounded and performance-based standards for both accreditation and certification. These trends are analogous to those that have occurred in other professions.

Level of agency jurisdiction. Each individual state department of education develops, adopts, and promulgates a set of standards which institutions must meet before its teacher education program is approved. This process is mandatory, because graduates of unapproved programs are not eligible for teaching certificates. Program standards and the review process tend to be similar in all states.

Although they have the authority to insist on quality in all teacher education programs, state program approval processes often fall short of the ideal in practice. Very few programs are ever denied approval and, should this happen, they are soon reinstated. Loss of state accreditation would be a serious, possibly even mortal, blow to smaller institutions; the political consequences associated with denial of accreditation are significant.

Nevertheless, so long as the primary responsibility for overseeing the quality of teacher education programs rests with the state departments of education, the quality of our nation's teacher preparation programs clearly depends on how seriously the states regard the enforcement of their own standards.

DIMENSION OF LICENSURE/CERTIFICATION

Efforts to develop and field test a national licensure system for teachers (Bradley, 1993, 1994) have been stimulated by the perceived relationship between improved professional status for teachers and improved schooling. Development of national standards links directly to efforts making teaching a true profession (Watkins, 1993). It has become common to apply the terms *licensure* and *certification* in ways that differ from tradition. *Licensure* is often now used to refer to the credentialing of an individual practitioner while *certification* is often used in discussing programs of preparation.

General Considerations

Wise (1990) contended that the beginning of teacher professionalism depends on trust in those awarded the title *teacher* (p. 54). He asserted that for teachers to enjoy the kind of confidence generally accorded by the public to their members would require a licensing structure similar to those in established professions (p. 54).

Exemplars from Established Professions

Darling-Hammond, Wise, and Klein (1995) compared the qualifying-exam approach as a means of enabling the profession to determine whether a prospective practitioner has mastered a minimum standard of knowledge and skill. "In the established professions, the requirement that all applicants take a licensing exam after graduation from a professionally accredited program determines that candidates have acquired at least some of the knowledge and skill needed for practice. In teaching, this assurance is even more sorely needed given the vast differences in the quality of preparation programs" (p. 13).

Situations in the Field of Education

Present methods of certifying people as qualified to teach, based almost entirely on completion of state-approved preparation programs, has not succeeded in convincing the public that licensing standards can discriminate those who are competent to teach from those who are not. An obvious manifestation of this lack of credibility is the granting of "emergency certification" to untrained practitioners when shortages occur (Bacharach, 1985).

The Holmes Group (1986) argued that teacher education's professional status can be improved only by bestowing genuine credentials that reflect the highest standards and the most rigorous preparation possible (p. 43). The same report, however, cautioned against employing the strategies that other professions have allegedly used on occasions to limit access to preparation programs and create artificial scarcities.

Conditions in the Craft of School Supervision

Alfonso and Firth (1990) strongly caution that lack of specialty certification may eventually result in a loss of professional identity for the instructional supervisor. "Research may provide evidence that the unique needs and characteristics of instructional supervision are being washed away in a multitude of other certificates under which the field is subsumed. [Such a study] might also result in clearer professional expectations and certification requirements" (p. 187).

Components of Licensure/Certification

Current efforts in the dimension of licensure/certification are reviewed in regard to each of the eight components.

Extent of surveillance. The AACTE Bicentennial Report (Howsam et al, 1976) recommended a three-level plan for teacher certification that would provide initial certification for the beginning teacher; continuing certification for the experienced teacher; and professional certification for the teacher-scholar. Under the proposed plan, primary responsibility for initial certification should reside with the colleges and universities, assisted by field-based personnel. Responsibility for the second level of certification should rest heavily on field evaluations of the candidate by professional colleagues from the school system and the organized profession. The third level should document a candidate's capacity to coordinate the teaching and learning efforts of others, and to adapt instruction and curricula to the needs of students from different backgrounds.

Each level would continue to relate to a state education agency, but with full recognition that major responsibilities be assumed by professionals in organizations, school systems, colleges, and universities (pp. 125–126).

Factors evaluated. Darling-Hammond, Wise, and Klein (1995) emphasized that the specific knowledge, skills, and dispositions must be identified which will reliably and validly sort those candidates who are prepared to practice from those who are not. They suggest: (1) basic intellectual skills; (2) general liberal arts knowledge; (3) subject-matter knowledge; (4) pedagogical and professional knowledge; and (5) teaching skills and dispositions (pp. 95–96). In addition, these authors emphasized the importance of helping prospective teachers develop a reflective stance toward all aspects of teaching.

Shulman (1987) classified the elements of teaching knowledge somewhat differently: (1) content knowledge; (2) general pedagogical knowledge, including classroom organization and management; (3) curriculum knowledge; (4) pedagogical content knowledge, an amalgam of content and pedagogy that comprise teachers' professional understanding; (5) knowledge of learners and their characteristics; (6) knowledge of educational contexts, including the characteristics of classrooms, schools, communities, and cultures; and (7) knowledge of educational ends, purposes, and values, and their philosophical and historical foundations (p. 8).

Darling-Hammond, Wise and Klein (1995) compared several taxonomies of teacher knowledge, including Shulman's, and found that there is widespread agreement on a core of such knowledge. It was noted, however, that some professional knowledge and dispositions are noticeably absent. These include moral and ethical considerations in teaching, legal rights and responsibilities to students, and collegial obligations to fellow practitioners (p. 35).

Means of insuring standards. A number of methods that currently exist for assessing teacher competence include on-the-job evaluations, simulated teaching, interviews, portfolios, open-ended paper-and-pencil tests, and multiple-choice or other closed-ended paper-and-pencil tests (Darling-Hammond, Wise & Klein, 1995, p. 72).

Several states (e.g., Minnesota and Florida) require that prospective teachers spend their first year of employment working on a probationary certificate; full certification is not granted until the experienced, supervising teachers have observed and evaluated the novice's classroom performance several times. This serves two purposes. First, it mandates a procedure for feedback and support during the typically difficult first year of teaching. Second, it attempts to provide the public with a higher level of assurance that new teachers are competent to practice (Darling-Hammond, Wise, & Klein, 1995, p. 5).

There is also a widespread feeling that permanent certification is unwise. The AACTE Bicentennial Report (Howsam et al, 1976) cautions that the educational profession "must commit itself to the concept of continual recertification by using as many means as possible to insure that educators remain up-to-date, effective practitioners" (pp. 115–116).

Type of standard. In 1992, the INTASC published performance-based standards for licensing of teachers: "The task force emphasized that 'common core' standards are not analogous to generic or context-free teaching behaviors. The assessment of specific teaching decisions and actions must occur within varied contexts that will require varied responses. In some cases, these are grounded in the discipline being taught; thus, subject-specific pedagogical decisions need to be evaluated within the context of subject-specific standards" (Darling-Hammond, Wise & Klein, 1995, p. 42).

In reference to its recommended three-tier licensing system, the Holmes Group (1986) conceded that such a system would require "new standardized examinations in reading, writing, academic subjects, pedagogy, and the foundations of education. New forms of examination for professional competence also would have to be devised and tested, so that practitioners could be certified on the basis of proven professional competence rather than competence as a student of a subject. Both of these are large assignments . . ." (p. 14). This group stated, however, that such assessments can be devised to discriminate those who know how to teach from those who [do not] (p. 14).

Designation of certificate. The possibility—and hope—has been advanced that instructional supervisors eventually may be drawn from the group of master, board-certified teachers who have excelled as leaders of a team of teachers and others. The three-tier licensing plan offered in the Holmes Report (1986)—instructor, professional teacher, career professional—would make it possible for districts to offer financial and status incentives to master teachers who choose to remain in the classroom. Those teachers would be known as career professionals. It would also motivate those identified as professional teachers to pursue graduate study and/or other avenues of professional development. Career professionals, expected to constitute only 20 percent of the teacher force, would be given roles in improving the educational effectiveness of other school personnel.

Composition of agency. The AACTE Bicentennial Report (Howsam et al, 1976) contended that the granting of certification should be a shared process, rather than the exclusive province of state departments, professional teacher groups, higher education institutions, or local communities (p. 116).

Working in collaborative relationships, these groups can provide one another with feedback and mutual assistance in ensuring a professional teacher force for American public education.

Selection of agency membership. The Holmes Group (1986) advocated the establishment of professional development schools to provide teachers with "opportunities to contribute to the development of knowledge in their profession, to form collegial relationships beyond their immediate working environment, and to grow intellectually as they mature professionally." Analogous to teaching hospitals in the medical profession, these professional development schools would be expected to bring educational practitioners together with university faculty so that the benefits of both theory and practice can be combined (pp. 66–67).

Level of agency jurisdiction. The AACTE Bicentennial Report (Howsam et al, 1976) argued that the state must be the source for formal certification. However, the report indicated that the profession must develop, recommend, and monitor a professional educator's continuing education (p. 116).

DIMENSION OF EVALUATION/ENFORCEMENT

The legal responsibilities of professions to the public have been considerably extended, enlarged, and/or enhanced to embrace ethical (Sergiovanni, 1992), moral (Starratt, 1994, 1996), and/or caring (Noddings, 1992) relationships.

General Considerations

The privilege of self-governance by professions requires certain guarantees to the public, such as careful recruitment and demanding preparation, formal organization, informal relationships among colleagues, codes of ethics, and enforcement of the provisions through professional courts or committees (Rueschemeyer, 1983, p. 41).

Exemplars from Established Professions

In most professions, peer review of *practice* is considered at least as important as the involvement of peers in the formal evaluation of *practitioners*. Peer review of practice occurs when professionals regularly consult each other regarding both general and specific problems. "Peer review also routinely engages professionals in evaluating the ongoing activities of their organization, diagnosing what is working well and what needs rethinking, and proposing solutions that will promote more effective practices" (Darling-Hammond & Goodwin, 1993, p. 46).

Situations in the Field of Education

Darling-Hammond and Goodwin (1993) lament the absence from education of the kind of self-regulation required to legitimate professions. They point out that a high-ly developed professional accountability structure has not yet been developed in teaching. No single professional organization represents the views of all members of the occupation. State professional practice boards, such as those that establish licensing standards and provide oversight of practice in established professions, are still rare in teaching. Moreover, educators have not yet been able to establish the kinds of peer review and other accountability mechanisms to guarantee that only those who meet acceptable standards are admitted, prepared, licensed, hired, and retained in the teaching profession (Darling-Hammond & Goodwin, 1993, pp. 22–23).

Instructional supervisors are no closer to attaining self-governance than they were 30 years ago. They are still without true professional status, because they cannot claim their own unique professional organization, standards of performance, or code of ethics (Banter, 1994).

A professional organization solely for supervisors or a coalition of existing professional organizations working together may be possible avenues to attaining professional status. Until such an organization or coalition exists, supervisors continue to be governed by state agencies which impose broad standards on all educators.

Conditions in the Craft of School Supervision

Sergiovanni (1992) emphasizes that a significant feature of established professions is the preservation of an individual's professional identity "no matter how far one rises in the administrative ranks" (p. 55). It is common among educators to separate those in leadership roles from teachers working directly with student clients. This phenomenon is characteristic of principals, guidance counselors, curriculum directors, and instructional supervisors even though they interact daily with teachers in various school situations. According to Sergiovanni, "School administrators have a special responsibility to share in the professional ideal of teaching, for whatever else they are, they are teachers first" (p. 55).

The tendency to talk about teachers and sdministraors as separate parties was considered to be self-destructive by The Holmes Group (1990).

Components of Evaluation/Enforcement

Current efforts in the dimension of evaluation/enforcement are examined in regard to each of the seven components.

Extent of surveillance. Various groups are engaged in the preparation of performance-based standards for teacher licensing. The National Board for Professional Teacher Standards (NBPTS) is developing a performance-based system to recognize advanced competence among experienced teachers. Meanwhile, the INTASC, as part of the CCSSO, is working in collaboration with teachers and teacher educators, state licensing officials, and the NCATE, among others, to generate performance-based standards for initial licensing of teachers compatible with those of the NBPTS (Darling-Hammond, Wise & Klein, 1995, p. 42).

Factors evaluated. According to Darling-Hammond and co-workers (1995), careful and systematic review of on-the-job performance in a structured internship program, supplemented by evaluation of performance on realistic and appropriately complex teaching tasks, provides opportunity for more successful assessment of professional competencies, particularly among beginning teachers.

Means of insuring standards. According to Darling-Hammond and Goodwin (1993), teacher evaluation should be changed from a process that fosters only minimum standards to a process of fosters collegial discussion of professional issues. Teacher evaluation needs to include both a complex, context-dependent view of practice and appropriate peer-review mechanisms for providing expert advice on problems of practice. New forms of evaluation, coupled with mechanisms allowing regular review of practice are required to move from inspecting classrooms to inducing teachers to assume major responsibility for professional behavior (Darling-Hammond & Goodwin, 1993, p. 48).

Relationship between professional self-enforcement and legal provisions. Decisions regarding employment, continuation, tenure, and dismissal are made locally by administrators representing the school district rather than the profession. Wise and Darling-Hammond (1987) express concern that delegation by states of licensure responsibilities to school districts will determine the outcomes of the entire process.

Unlike established professions which assume responsibility for defining, transmitting, and enforcing standards of practice, teachers currently have little or no control over most of the mechanisms that determine performance standards. Instead, in most states, authority for teacher preparation, licensure, and practice rests with governmental bodies (legislatures and school boards) and with administrative agencies (state departments of education and central offices). Such authority relationships ultimately produce bureaucratic rather than professional controls over the content and structure of education. Regardless of whether standards for education are being ostensibly raised or lowered, the extent and kind of knowledge reflected in the standards remains beyond professional control.

Because tests "[transfer] control over the curriculum to the agency which sets or controls the exam" (Madaus, 1988, p. 97), and licensure exceptions are created by state legislators, both the content of teacher preparation and the provisions of teacher certification are removed from the profession.

Composition of agency. It is a generally accepted principle among educators that entry into and continuation of service in teaching "must be strictly controlled by members within the profession through internally structured mechanisms that regulate recruitment, training, licensure, and standards for appropriate and ethical practice" (Darling-Hammond and Goodwin, 1993, p. 21).

Selection of agency membership. Recent discussions about evaluation/enforcement are moot in regard to the actual procedures by which educators should participate in the selection, recommendation, and/or endorsement of members of professional practice boards in education. Most imply, however, that educators should seek to be influential in this regard and to exert such influence through professional organizations.

Level of agency jurisdiction. It appears clear from both direct statement and implication that evaluation/enforcement in education should continue to function at the state level whether the preferred mechanism be the state department of education, professional practices board, professional organization, or some coalition of these and/or other agencies, organizations, and/or institutions.

REFERENCES

Abbott, A. (1988). *The system of professions: An essay on the division of expert labor.* Chicago, IL: The University of Chicago Press.

Armstrong, R. V. (1985). *Strategies for staking out occupational turf: An analysis of clinical dietetics and nurse anesthesia in the health care marketplace.* Unpublished doctoral dissertation, University of Illinois at Chicago, Chicago, IL.

Bacharach, S. B. (1985). *Teacher shortages, professional standards, and hen house logic.* Ithaca, NY: Organizational Analysis and Practice.

Benveniste, G. (1987). *Professionalizing the organization: Reducing bureaucracy to enhance effectiveness.* San Francisco, CA: Jossey-Bass Publisher.

Boyer, E. L. (1996, Spring). The scholarship of engagement. *Journal of Public Service & Outreach, 1*(1), 11–20.

Bradley, A. (1994, April). Pioneers in professionalism. *Education Week,* 18–27.

Bucher, R. & Strauss, A. (1961, January). Professions in process. *The American Journal of Sociology, 66*(4), 325–334.

Bull, B. (1990). The limits of teacher professionalization. In J. Goodlad, R. Soder, & K. Sirotnik (Eds.). *The moral dimensions of teaching* (pp. 87–129). San Francisco, CA: Jossey-Bass Publishers.

Burbules, N. & Densmore, K. (1991a). The limits of making teaching a profession. *Educational Policy, 5*(1), 44–63.

Burbules, N. & Densmore, K. (1991b). The persistence of professionalism: Breakin' up is hard to do. *Educational Policy, 5*(2), 150–157.

Darling-Hammond, L. (1988). Policy and professionalism. In A. Lieberman (Ed.). *Building a professional culture in schools* (pp. 55–77). New York: Teachers College Press.

Darling-Hammond, L. & Goodwin, A. (1993). Progress toward professionalism in teaching. In G. Cawelti (Ed.). *Challenges and achievements of American education* (pp. 19-52). (ASCD 1993 Yearbook). Alexandria, VA: ASCD.

Darling-Hammond, L., Wise, A. E., & Klein, S. P. (1995). *A license to teach: Building a profession for 21st-century schools.* Boulder, CO: Westview Press.

Dempsey, V. O. (1991). *Inside looking around: Toward a grounded theory of teacher professionalism.* Unpublished doctoral dissertation, University of North Carolina at Chapel Hill, Chapel Hill, NC.

Duffy, G. (1994). Professional development schools and the disempowerment of teachers and professors. *Phi Delta Kappan, 75*(8), 596–601.

Etzioni, A. (Ed.). (1969). *The semi-professions and their organization: Teachers, nurses, social workers.* New York: Free Press.

Fenstermacher, G. & Soltis, J. (1992). *Approaches to teaching.* New York: Teachers College Press.

Flexner, A. (1915). Is social work a profession? *School and Society, 1*(1), 902–903. (From a paper presented at the 42nd Annual Meeting of the National Conference of Charities and Corrections, Baltimore, MD, 17 May 1915).

Flores, A. (1988). What kind of a person should a professional be? In A. Flores (Ed.). *Professional ideals.* Belmont, CA: Wadsworth Publishing Company.

Friedson, E. (1970). *Professional dominance: The social structure of medical care.* New York: Atherton Press.

Friedson, E. (1983). The theory of professions: State of the art. In R.

Dingwall & P. Lewis (Eds.). *The sociology of the professions: Lawyers, doctors and others* (pp. 19–37). New York: St. Martin's Press.

Friedson, E. (1988). *Professional powers: A study of the institutionalization of formal knowledge.* Chicago, IL: The University of Chicago Press.

Glatthorn, A. A. (1996). *The teacher's portfolio: Fostering and documenting professional development.* Rockport, MA: Pro>Active Publications.

Goode, W. J. (1969). The theoretical limits of professionalization. In A. Etzioni (Ed.). *The semi-professions and their organization: Teachers, nurses, social workers* (pp. 266–313). New York: Free Press.

Goodlad, J. (1990a). *Teachers for our nation's schools.* San Francisco, CA: Jossey-Bass Publishers.

Goodlad, J. (1990b). The occupation of teaching in schools. In J. I. Goodlad, R. Soder & K. A. Sirotnik (Eds.). *The moral dimensions of teaching* (pp. 3–34). San Francisco, CA: Jossey-Bass Publishers

Hansen, D. (1993). From role to person: The moral layeredness of classroom teaching. *American Educational Research Journal, 30*(4), 651–674.

Herbst, J. (1989). *And sadly teach.* Madison, WI: University of Wisconsin Press.

Holmes Report. (1986). *Tomorrow's teachers.* East Lansing, MI: The Holmes Group.

Holmes Report. (1990). *Tomorrow's schools: Principles for the design of professional development schools.* East Lansing, MI: The Holmes Group.

Holmes Report. (1995). *Tomorrow's schools of education.* East Lansing, MI: The Holmes Group.

Howsam, R. B., Corrigan, D. C., Denemark, G. W., & Nash, R. J. (1976, 1985). *Educating a profession.* (Reprint with postscript). Report of the Bicentennial Commission on Education for the Profession of Teaching. Washington, D.C.: American Association of Colleges for Teacher Education.

Houle, C. O. (1980). *Continuing learning in the professions.* San Francisco, CA: Jossey-Bass Publishers.

Hoyle, E. (1980). Professionalization and deprofessionalization in education. In E. Hoyle & J. Megarry (Eds.). *World yearbook of education: Professional development of teachers* (pp. 42–54). London, England: Kogan Page.

Hughes, E. C. (1963) Professions. Daedalus, 92, 655–688).

Interstate New Teacher Assessment and Support Consortium. (1992). *Model standards for beginning teacher licensing and development: A resource for state dialogue.* Washington, D.C.: Council of Chief State School Officers.

Interstate New Teacher Assessment and Support Consortium, (1995). *Next steps: Moving toward performance-based licensing in teaching.* Washington, D.C.: Council of Chief State School Officers.

Jackson, P. (1987). Facing our ignorance. *Teachers College Record, 88*(3), 384–389.

Johnson, T. (1972). *Professions and power.* London, England: Macmillan.

Kimball, B. (1992). *The "true professional ideal" in America: A history.* Cambridge, MA: Blackwell.

Labaree, D. (1992). Power, knowledge, and the rationalization of teaching: A geneology of the movement to professionalize teaching. *Harvard Educational Review, 62*(2), 123–154.

LaDuca, A. & Engel, J. (1994, June). On the neglect of professions theory in professions teaching. *Professions Education Researcher Quarterly, 15*(4), 8–11.

Lortie, D. C. (1975). *Schoolteacher: A sociological study.* Chicago, IL: The University of Chicago Press.

Mathews, D. (1996, Spring). The public's disenchantment with professionalism: Reasons for rethinking academe's service to the country. *Journal of Public Service & Outreach, 1*(1), 21–28.

Mitchell D. E. & Kerschner, C. T. (1983). Labor relations and teacher policy. In L. S. Shulman & G. Sykes (Eds.). *Handbook of teaching and policy.* New York: Longman, 214–238.

National Commission on Excellence in Education. (1983). *A national at risk: The imperative for educational reform.* Washington, D.C.: Author.

National Policy Board for Educational Administration. (1989, May). *Improving the preparation of school administrators: An agenda for reform.* Charlottsville, VA: Author.

National Policy Board for Educational Administration. (1994, November). *Proposed NCATE curriculum guidelines: Advanced programs in educational leadership for superintendents, principals, curriculum directors and supervisors.* Fairfax, VA: Author.

Noddings, N. (1992). *The challenge to care in schools: An alternative approach to education.* New York: Teachers College Press.

Noddings, N. (1995, January). A morally defensible mission for schools in the 21st century. *Phi Delta Kappan, 76*(5), 365–368.

Nolan, J. & Francis, P. (1992). Changing perspectives in curriculum and instruction. In C. D. Glickman (Ed.). *Supervision in transition* (pp. 41–60). (ASCD 1992 Yearbook). Alexandria, VA: ASCD.

Rueschemeyer, D. (1983). Professional autonomy and the social control of expertise. In R. Dingwall & P. Lewis (Eds.). *The sociology of the professions: Lawyers, doctors, and others* (pp. 38–58). New York: St. Martin's Press.

Sergiovanni, T. J. (1992). *Moral leadership: Getting to the heart of school improvement.* San Francisco, CA: Jossey-Bass Publishers.

Shanker, A. (1985). *The making of a profession.* Washington, D.C.: American Federation of Teachers, AFL-CIO.

Shaverson, R., Webb, N., & Burstein, L. (1986). Measurement of teaching. In M. Whitlock (Ed.). *Handbook of research on teaching* (3rd ed.) pp. 50–86. New York: Macmillan.

Shulman, L. (1986). Paradigms and research programs in the study of teaching: A contemporary perspective. In M. Whitlock (Ed.). *Handbook of research on teaching* (pp. 3–36). New York: Macmillan.

Soder, R. (1990). The rhetoric of teacher professionalization. In J. Goodlad, R. Soder, & K. Sirotnik (Eds.). *The moral dimensions of teaching.* San Francisco, CA: Jossey-Bass Publishers.

Starratt, R. J. (1994). *Building an ethical school: A practical response to the moral crisis in schools.* London, England: The Falmar Press.

Starratt, R. J. (1996). *Transforming educational administration.* New York: McGraw-Hill.

Surdyk, P. M. (1995). *Professionalism and effectiveness: A grounded theory study of teachers' perceptions.* Unpublished doctoral dissertation, Loyola University of Chicago, Chicago, IL.

Surdyk, P. M. (1996). *Turning "pro": Reflections on professionalism and teaching.* Unpublished paper. Chicago, IL: Loyola University.

Sykes, G. (1989). Teachers and professionalism: A cautionary perspective. In L. Weis, P. Altback, G. Kelly, H. Petrie, & S. Slaughter (Eds.). *Crisis in teaching: Perspectives on current reforms* (pp. 253–273). Albany, NY: State University of New York Press.

Sykes, G. (1991). In defense of teacher professionalism as a policy choice. *Educational Policy, 5*(2), 137–49.

Tom, A. (1984). *Teaching as a moral craft.* New York: Longman.

Wise, A. E. (1990, April). Six steps to teacher professionalism. *Educational Leadership, 47*(7), 57–60.

Wise, A. & Leibrand, J. (1993, October). Accreditation and the creation of a profession of teaching. *Phi Delta Kappan, 74*(2), 133–136, 154–157.

SECTION VII.
AGENDA FOR FUTURE RESEARCH

INTRODUCTION

The information examined in the previous six sections of this chapter provides the direction and foci for needed research regarding governance of school supervision. More appropriate, accurate, and applicable investigations require attention to at least five major research questions:

1. What is the difference between the preferred and perceived profile(s) of the concept of professionalism/professionalization of school supervision?
2. What is the difference between the preferred and perceived profile(s) of the vision of identity/image of school supervision?
3. What is the difference between the preferred and perceived profile(s) of the dimension of preparation/accreditation of school supervision?
4. What is the difference between the preferred and perceived profile(s) of the dimension of licensure/certification of school supervision?
5. What is the difference between the preferred and perceived profile(s) of the dimension of evaluation/enforcement of school supervision?

Investigations stimulated by these five questions should be framed by (a) the four values of professionalism/professionalization, (b) the six aspects of identity/image, (c) the six components of preparation/accreditation, (d) the eight components of licensure/certification, and (e) the seven components of evaluation/enforcement. Professionalism/professionalization involves the values of expertise, autonomy, responsibility, and commitment. Identity/image involves the aspects of perceptions, antecedents, titles, roles, theory, and research. Preparation/accreditation involves the components of surveillance, factors, standards, composition, membership, and jurisdiction. Licensure/certification involves the components of surveillance, factors, means, standards, designation, composition, membership, and jurisdiction. Evaluation/enforcement involves the components of surveillance, factors, means, relationships, composition, membership, and jurisdiction. These five major categories offer 22 fruitful, valuable, and challenging areas for further inquiry.

GENERAL CONSIDERATIONS

None of the five major categories or 22 subcategories exists in a vacuum. Each is influenced, impacted, and perhaps ultimately determined by forces in the external society and/or by operational factors within schooling. This is consistent with the process/structural approach to "contemporaneous context" (Kimball, 1992), studies of teaching ecology (Shulman, 1986), and qualitative methods, particularly ethnography. A model for research in any of the defined areas should establish frames of reference for both the contextual forces of society and the operational factors of schools.

Contextual Forces

"It is increasingly clear that societal forces are often either unrecognized or not understood by many important actors associated with the educational enterprise" (Yates, 1992, p. 1). Yates analyzed the implications of forces on American education in general and special education in particular, including demographics (age, ethnicity, language minorities, minority youth, family conditions, and dropouts), economy and finance (international competition, cost benefits, and welfare), professionalism (teacher shortages, women's opportunities, and minority access), technology (computers, interactive video, and genetic engineering), and social values (political ideologies, business partnerships, intrusive litigation, and parental involvement) (Yates, 1992, pp. 1–41).

Ideas originally generated by Burrello for a 1990 paper delivered at Trinity University were further developed with Gregory into analyses of contextual forces of society leading to a paradigm shift in education. Within an overall trend ranging from support of existing forces to support for emerging forces, four major changes were described: (1) from political/bureaucratic to political/economic/social, (2) from coercive to empowerment, (3) from technical to innovation, and (4) from symbolic to cultural (Burrello & Lashley, 1992, p. 87). The works of several other researchers drawn upon by Burrello and Gregory included Goodlad (1984), Gregory and Smith (1987), Kearns and Doyle (1988), Kantor (1989), Perleman (1987), Peters (1987), and Senge (1990).

In 1996, graduate students in a seminar on supervision theory at the University of Georgia identified 10 contextual forces currently at work in American society which significantly influence public education in general and school supervision in particular. These 10 forces, each with its characteristic manifestations, are presented in Table 36–8.

These contextual forces and/or others as pervasive constitute the milieu in which schools and instructional supervision exist. Therefore, they may be embraced within the research design.

School Factors

"Schools mirror the various forces operating within our society" (Yates, 1992, p. 1). Recent changes in schools and schooling are viewed as a function of the shifting educational paradigm, a concept elevated to scientific discourse by Kuhn (1970).

Evidence that the paradigm shift has, in effect, turned schools upside down can be found by observing 10 school factors and describing the previous state and the evolving

TABLE 36–8. Manifestations of Contextual Forces
Influencing American Education

Force	Manifestations
Technology	Computers, communication, virtual reality, networking, cyberspace
Reorganization	Downsizing, shared decision-making, multinational corporations, conglomerates, out sourcing
Financing	Taxes, investment, nonsalary wealth, trusts, commissions
Marketing	Services, products, advertising, agreements, "bartering"
Enterprise	Jobs, consultancies, part-time work, contract work, freelance assignments, shared positions
Multiculturalism	Neighborhoods, communities, organizations, churches, workplaces, cemeteries
Lifestyles	Family structures, living space, locations, dress, travel
Institutionalism	Foster homes, hospitals, penitentiaries, halfway houses, surrogate parents
Environmentalism	Habitat, pollutants, congestion, beauty, violence, conservation, preservation, protection
Valuing	Family, relatives, parents, siblings, children, country, religion, church, job, company, career

stage of each: identity, people, structure, leadership/control, innovation, organization (for institution), technology, financial management/control, marketing, and accountability (Burrello & Lashley, 1992, pp. 88–93, and Sage & Burrello, 1994, pp. 5–7).

In a traditional paradigm, such school factors might be identified by such labels as goals and objectives, students, programs, structures, personnel, resources, facilities, and/or evaluation.

Another set of factors focused on schooling is provided by the report of the Secretary's Commission on Achieving Necessary Skills (SCANS) for the U.S. Department of Labor entitled *What Work Requires of Schools* (1991). The SCANS report for America 2000 anticipates that change from existing traditional schools will demand a change in perspective as well as in the characteristics of strategy, learning environment, management, and outcome (p. 22). The study defined five clusters of competencies needed in the workplace which, "in conjunction with a three-part foundation," lie at the heart of job performance (p. vi). The five clusters of competencies were: (1) resources (time, money, materials, space, and staff); (2) interpersonal (teamwork, teaching, serving, leading, negotiating, and relating to cultural diversity); (3) information (acquiring and evaluating, organizing and maintaining, interpreting and communicating, and computer processing); (4) systems (understanding and operating, monitoring and correcting, and designing or improving); and (5) technology (selecting, applying, and maintaining and troubleshooting). The three-part foundation consisted of: (1) basic skills (reading, writing, calculating, listening, and speaking); (2) thinking skills (creativity, decision-making, problem solving, visualizing, acquiring, and reasoning); and (3) personal qualities (responsibility, self-esteem, sociability, self-management, and integrity).

Other competencies and expectations have been identified in recent studies by the Carnegie Corporation through its Task Force on Meeting the Needs of Our Young Children (1994) and its Council on Adolescent Development (1995).

MODELS FOR RESEARCH

Five models are presented that suggest specific targets for further research related to school supervision. In each of the five models, school supervision as represented by its values, aspects, or components is viewed as one dimension of a cubistic model in which the contextual forces of society and operational factors of schools are viewed as the other two dimensions.

Concept of Professionalism/Professionalization

In this proposed model (Figure 36.1), the four values of the concept of professionalism/professionalization (expertise, autonomy, responsibility, and commitment) are considered as one edge of a cube involving 10 contextual forces of society and eight operational factors of schools.

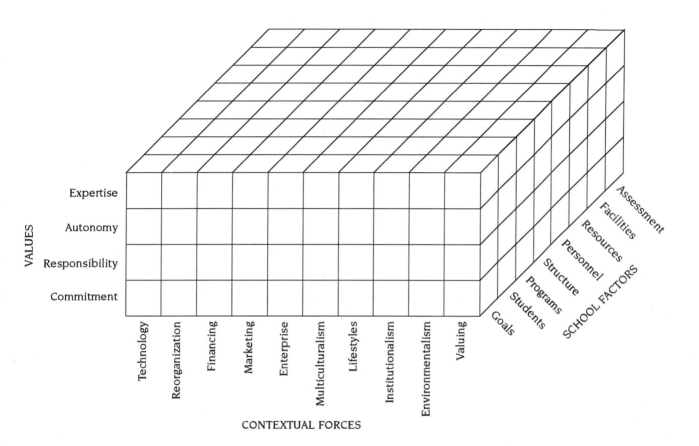

FIGURE 36.1. Proposed Model for Future Research Regarding Values
of the Concept of Professionalism/Professionalization of School Supervision

Vision of Identity/Image

In this proposed model (Figure 36.2), the six aspects of the vision of identity/image (perceptions, antecedents, titles, roles, theory, and research) are considered as one edge of a cube involving 10 contextual forces of society and eight operational factors of schools.

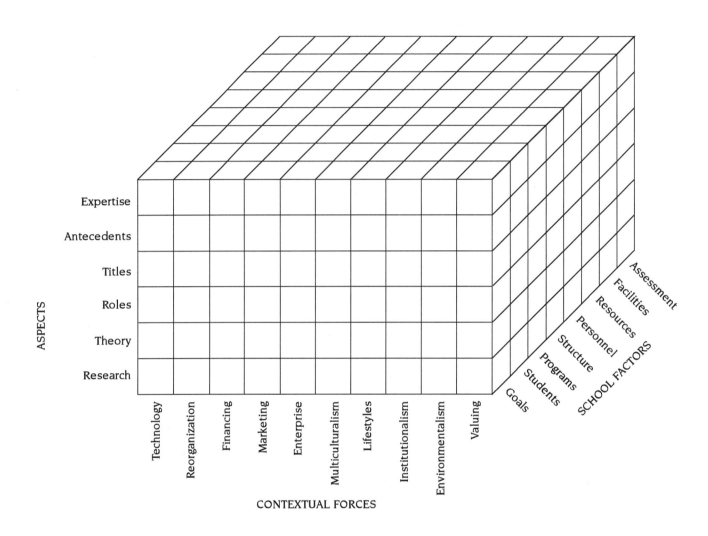

FIGURE 36.2. Proposed Model for Future Research Regarding Aspects
of the Vision of Indentity/Image of School Supervision

Dimension of Preparation/Accreditation

In this proposed model (Figure 36.3), the six components of the dimension of preparation/accreditation (surveillance, factors, standards, composition, membership, and jurisdiction) are considered as one edge of a cube involving 10 contextual forces of society and eight operational factors of schools.

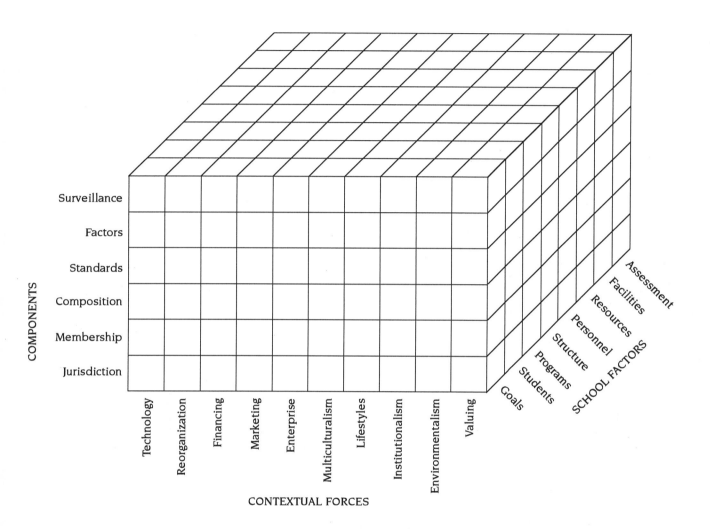

FIGURE 36.3. Proposed Model for Future Research Regarding Components of the Dimension of Preparation/Accreditation of School Supervision

Dimension of Licensure/Certification

In this proposed model (Figure 36.4), the eight components of the dimension of licensure/certification (surveillance, factors, means, standards, designation, composition, membership, and jurisdiction) are considered as one edge of a cube involving 10 contextual forces of society and eight operational factors of schools.

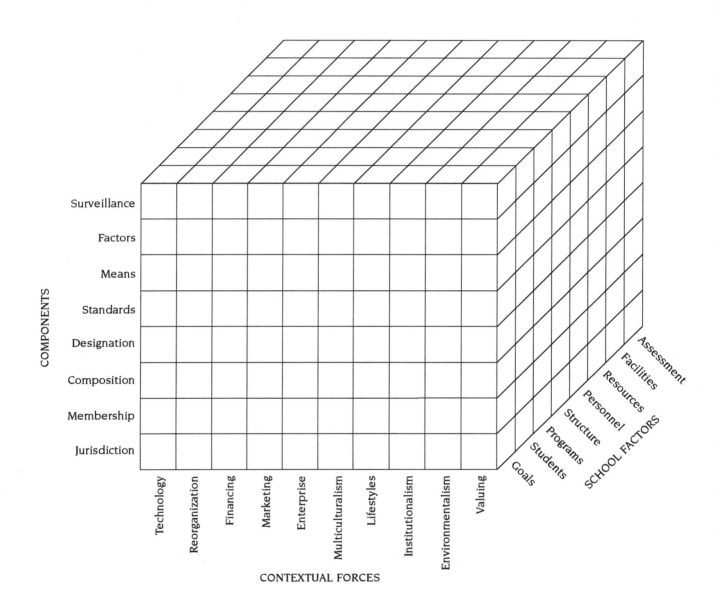

FIGURE 36.4. Proposed Model for Future Research Regarding Components
of the Dimension of Licensure/Certification of School Supervision

Dimension of Evaluation/Enforcement

In this proposed model (Figure 36.5), the seven components of the dimension of evaluation/enforcement (surveillance, factors, means, relationships, composition, membership, and jurisdiction) are considered as one edge of a cube involving 10 contextual forces of society and eight operational factors of schools.

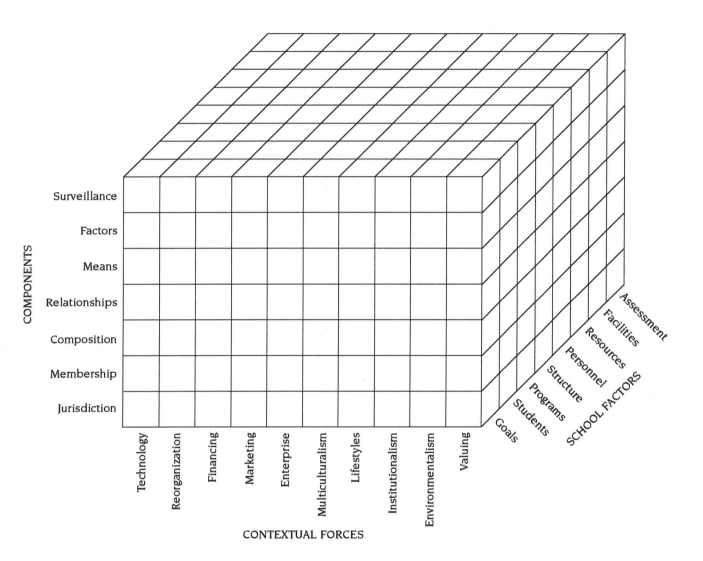

FIGURE 36.5. Proposed Model for Future Research Regarding Components
of the Dimension of Evaluation/Enforcement of School Supervision

SHIFTING PARADIGM OF PROFESSION

Rapid increases have recently occurred in the number of physicians, attorneys, engineers, and other acknowledged professionals employed by institutions, organizations, and agencies. Dynamic tension between professional integrity and bureaucratic expectations now effects many occupations in a manner historically characteristic of education. In this process, the paradigm of profession is being reshaped.

As education continues to move toward professional status, the nature of professionalism is taking new form. It is possible, even probable, that education's status may be more in confluence, congruence, and/or communion with the postmodern dimensions of professionalism than those that have traditionally guided professionalization.

REFERENCES

Boyer, E. L. (1995). *The basic school: A community for learning.* Princeton, NJ: Carnegie Foundation for the Advancement of Teaching.

Burrello, L. C. & Gregory, T. B. (1990). Paradigm shift: School turned upside down. In K. A. Waldron, A. E. Rieter, & J. H. Moore (Eds.). *Special education: The challenge of the future.* San Francisco, CA: Edwin Mellen Press.

Burrello, L. C. & Lashley, C. A. (1992). On organizing for the future: The destiny of special education. In K. A. Waldron, A. E. Riester, & J. H. Moore (Eds.). *Special education: The challenge of the future.* San Francisco, CA: Mellen Research University Press.

Carnegie Council on Adolescent Development. (1995). *Great transitions: Preparing adolescents for a new century.* New York: Carnegie Corporation.

Carnegie Task Force on Meeting the Needs of Young Children. (1994). *Starting points: Meeting the needs of our youngest children.* New York: Carnegie Corporation.

Goodlad, J. I. (1984). *A place called school.* New York: McGraw-Hill.

Gregory, T. B. & Smith, G. R. (1987). *High schools as communities: The small school reconsidered.* Bloomington, IN: Phi Delta Kappan Educational Foundation.

Kantor, R. M. (1989, November-December). The new managerial work. *Harvard Business Review, 67*(6), 85–92.

Kearns, D. & Doyle, D. (1988). *Winning the brain race: A bold plan to make our schools competitive.* San Francisco, CA: Jossey-Bass Publishers.

Kimball, B. (1992). "True professional ideas" is America: A history. Cambridge, MA: Blackwell.

Kuhn, T. S. (1970). *The structure of scientific resolutions.* Chicago, IL: The University of Chicago Press.

Perelman, L. J. (1987). *Technology and transformation of schools.* Washington, D.C.: National School Boards Association.

Peters, T. (1987). *Thriving on chaos: Handbook for a management revolution.* New York: Knopf.

Sage, D. D. & Burrello, L. C. (1994). *Leadership in educational reform.* Baltimore, MD: Paul H. Brookes Publishing Co.

Secretary's Commission on Achieving Necessary Skills. (1991). *What work requires of schools.* Washington, D.C.: U.S. Department of Labor.

Senge, P. (1990). *The fifth discipline.* New York: Doubleday.

Shulman, L. (1986). Paradigms and research programs in the study of teaching: A contemporary perspective. In M. Whitlock (Ed.). Handbook of Research on Teaching (pp. 3–36). New York: Macmillan.

Yates, J. R. (1992). Special education futures: Implications of national trends and forces. In K. A. Waldron, A. E. Riester, & J. H. Moore (Eds.). *Special education: the challenge of the future.* San Francisco, CA: Mellen Research University Press.

PREDICTIONS/EPILOGUE

In this report, the findings from theory and practice have been fused. The insights generated are enlightening, but the potential of the implications are frightening and should goad members of the field of instructional supervision into action.

These research efforts demand more than praise or endorsement. Roles and responsibilities of both instructional supervisors and curriculum directors must be defined to guide preparation/accreditation, licensure/certification, and evaluation/ enforcement.

Wilhelms (1973) called instructional supervision the "nervous system of the school."

It is not merely a system for updating methodology; it is not even merely a system for coordination of the many parts. It is, above all else, the mechanism for adaptation. It represents that ability to adapt to new conditions which an organism—or school—must have or die. This essential function cannot be shaken off. Teachers may dislike the traditional part of it that catches their eye; a few superintendents may acquire brief fame by "firing all the supervisors"; boards of education may pare their budgets first of all by cutting off everybody who doesn't work directly with children in the classroom. But the function still remains. It has to be performed, or the schools are doomed (p. 1).

The role [of instructional supervisor] will always be a very hard one to live up to: terribly demanding upon sheer physical and moral stamina, even more demanding upon insight and wisdom. They work in the midst of turbulence which may never subside. They deserve the best tools that can be had. Beyond that, they deserve, too, respect and the time and conditions needed for their way of life, to cultivate that inner strength and richness of resource which alone will enable them to surmount their problems. They deserve all this because they are the key to better education (p. 51).

Nothing less than the marshaling of unified professional statesmanship can ensure that those who bear the titles of instructional supervisors and curriculum directors possess those unique characteristics and skills that are essential for serving effectively in their respective roles the American educational enterprise in these times (Firth, 1978).

Evidence indicates that fulfillment of these high aspirations and expectations is not considered possible unless and until instructional supervision has attained the status of profession, accepted responsibility for self-governance, and assumed direction of its destiny.

The quest to accomplish such goals must be driven from deep within practitioners who claim ownership of their own identity. The image held of themselves is far more crucial than that held by others. The future of instructional supervision is more than a matter of mind and even of heart. Ultimately, it is a matter of soul.

REFERENCES

Firth, G. R. (1978). Preface. In A. W. Sturges (Ed.). *Certificating the curriculum leader and the instructional supervisor.* Washington, D.C.: ASCD.

Wilhelms, F. T. (1973). *Supervision in a new key.* Washington, D.C.: ASCD.

·37·

PREPARATION PROGRAMS IN SUPERVISION

John C. Daresh

UNIVERSITY OF TEXAS AT EL PASO

INTRODUCTION

How is one prepared to be an educational supervisor? Assuming that it is possible to prepare someone to step into this role, a number of conceptual problems first need to be addressed.

First, determining the particular role of a supervisor is a good starting point to try to ascertain the most appropriate strategies to prepare a future educational supervisor. Over the years, the nature of what supervision in schools should accomplish has changed, along with certain underlying assumptions about the nature of schooling, teachers, and educational leadership. As a result, the manner in which individuals are prepared to step into supervisory positions has naturally changed rather drastically over the years. This chapter will review several historical images of educational supervision, along with some consideration of the ways in which professional development of educational supervisors has had to conform to those images.

Second, and perhaps the most critical issue to be considered, is the perennial concern of whether supervision is a formal role or whether it is a process imbedded within a number of other, more established educational roles. Responding to this issue is a bit of an unending dilemma. There are people who are called "supervisors," but the current reality of school systems suggests that more attention is directed toward others—principals, directors of instruction, superintendents, subject department chairs, to name a few—who supervise. If that basic assumption is correct, the primary focus of this chapter must not be on how to prepare supervisors per se, but rather, how to prepare many— let us call them "educational leaders"—to engage in strong and proactive supervisory practice to make schools and school districts more effective in promoting student learning.

Another issue that always emerges in discussions of how to prepare educational leaders centers around the perennial debate regarding the probability that anyone can prepare others to be leaders. After all, many would claim that leaders are born, not made.

Regardless of these and other conceptual problems that might serve to block further discussion of how to prepare educational supervisors, in this chapter it is presupposed that supervision is a process of providing educational leadership, and that people can be prepared to carry out that critical responsibility. Having made that assumption, this chapter will examine how that preparation might be carried out, given what we know about the critical skills that must be shown by effective school leaders.

HISTORICAL TRENDS IN EDUCATIONAL SUPERVISION

Throughout the history of education in the United States, supervision in schools has had a variety of alternative definitions, each of which has been formed as a result of certain assumptions about what schools should be like, and what tasks teachers should perform. In turn, these definitions and assumptions have led to numerous competing visions of the exact responsibilities of supervisors. In this chapter, some of the different historical trends that have affected supervisory practice in the United States are reviewed, along with related implications for the preparation of supervisory personnel.

Supervision as Inspection

The issue of providing supervision for teachers in American schools is as old as the history of formal education in this country. In fact, the year 1642, when the first Massachusetts School Law was enacted, also marks the beginning of educational supervision in American schools. This first stage of supervisory development lasted until approximately the conclusion of the Civil War in 1865.

During these years, supervisors were primarily engaged in inspection—an approach based on the assumption that an educational supervisor's job was to find out what teachers were doing wrong in their classrooms. Although this description may seem rather harsh, it is important to recall some historical facts before judging seventeenth and eighteenth century supervisors as insensitive ogres who lacked compassion or basic respect for teachers. During the earliest days of American education, teachers often were not well educated and frequently stayed only a step or two ahead of their students in basic skills. Teachers often needed monitoring to make certain that minimally acceptable standards of performance were being maintained in classrooms and schools. Individual supervisors did not always agree with their assigned responsibilities. In fact, the judgmental nature of supervision during this time rested in job descriptions, not in personal interpretations.

The first stage of supervisory practice (ca. 1642–1865) could be further subdivided into two distinct eras: religious control and a more secular involvement. The first years of American public education were characterized, particularly in the New England colonies, by the assumption that local religious beliefs and values should be both preserved and transmitted from one generation to another. Supervision was defined largely in terms determined and accepted by religious leaders. The Massachusetts Bay Company of 1642 provides the earliest known description of educational supervision:

This Court, taking into consideration the great neglect of many parents and masters in training of their children in learning and labor, and other implyments which may be profitable to the common wealth, do hereupon order and decree, that in every town ye chosen men appointed for managing the prudential affairs of the same shall henceforth stand charged with the redress of this evil . . . and for this end, they, or the greatest number of them, shall have the power to take into account from time to time of all parents and masters, and of their children, especially of their ability to read and understand the principles of religion and the capital laws of this country.

These "chosen men" were either ordained ministers or elders in local congregations—an understandable phenomenon in light of the fact that the teaching and learning they reviewed was tied directly to matters of religion. If students were not learning how to read the Bible, their path to eternal salvation would be blocked because they would never be able to gain insight into the Scriptures or learn about God.

After the American Revolution, the duty of monitoring classroom procedures was increasingly entrusted to committees of laymen who were not associated with any specific religious group. This change no doubt occurred as part of the general secularization of American society taking place at this time. As the years went on, school officials placed less emphasis on the supervisor's responsibility to verify the quality of religious instruction and more emphasis on the supervisor's responsibility to oversee the quality of secular instruction. The assumption that teachers lacked basic competency, however, remained constant. Two popular definitions of supervision from the period reflect this shift in focus. Theodore Dwight and James Wickerman noted:

Visitation and careful examination are necessary to discover the teacher's merits in teaching and governing the attention, deserts, and improvement of the children. To render a teacher, in the first place, to convince him that he can, are the principal objects to be offered by a friend of education (Dwight, 1835, p. 21).

Such visitations [by supervisors] are necessary to secure the caretaking of the grounds, buildings, furniture, and apparatus; necessary to secure the most rapid progress on the part of the pupils; necessary to encourage competent teachers and to detect incompetent ones; in short, necessary to ensure the well-working of the whole school machinery (Wickerman, 1864, p. 9).

As these definitions show, the religious orientation in educational supervisory practice had given way to a more worldly and secular view by the mid-nineteenth century. On the other hand, these definitions continue to demonstrate some striking similarities in supervisory practice derived from a common set of assumptions held by educators throughout the first stage of supervisory development in American education.

Assumptions and Related Practices **Teachers were not to be trusted.** Perhaps the most basic premise of the earliest descriptions of supervision was simply that teachers, for the most part, were incompetents who could not be trusted to do their assigned jobs. At first, this assumption suggested a lack of trust in teachers' abilities to provide instruction in religion. The supervisor's responsibility, then, was to be present in classes as often as possible to safeguard against the spread of any religious heresy, either intentional or unintentional. Instruction was monitored closely, not so much to guarantee proper methods of teaching, but rather to make certain that proper interpretation of the Bible was maintained. Even when this religious focus became blurred and finally disappeared, teachers were still viewed as essentially incompetent employees who needed to be carefully watched.

Supervisors had the right to intervene directly in the classroom. During both stages of these early years, supervisors often engaged in activities that were descriptive in their own right; they deliberately tried to catch teachers in the act of making mistakes. Supervisors made frequent, usually unannounced, classroom visits, often intimidating even the most confident or competent of instructors. They frequently entered a classroom while a lesson was in progress and then openly and defiantly debated with a teacher about the accuracy of the information he or she was imparting.

Supervisors were meant to be inspectors. Supervisors were expected not only to monitor instructional processes and correct incompetent teachers in the midst of leading their classes, they were also expected to review the characteristics of the total school, not as consultants or facilitators, but solely as inspectors. They performed functions, such as overseeing the upkeep of the school building, instructional material, and equipment. Some of their tasks included, for example, verifying that the schoolhouse roof did not leak, that the fire in the stove was well stoked, and that there were sufficient slates and benches for all the pupils.

Implications for Preparing Supervisors Service as a supervisor during this earliest era in American education was clearly something that was not viewed as a career goal. Rather, those who supervised did so almost by default. They were individuals who were already educated, or had achieved a certain social (or religious) status that enabled them to make judgments about others' performance of teaching responsibilities. As a result, the idea of a specialized training or preparation programs for supervisors did not make sense. People became supervisors not because they knew about supervision, but because of what they knew about the subject matter being taught.

Interestingly enough, this impression that supervision of education is totally dependent on knowledge of subject content is, of course, still alive in current practice. Many continue to believe that all that is necessary to oversee instructional practice is knowledge of content, and that pedagogical technique is relatively unimportant. Thus, while there are few who would look fondly at "Supervision as Inspection" as a desirable era, many of the assumptions of that period in time remain with us today. In short, there are still many who do not believe that supervisors can be prepared.

Supervision as Science

From approximately the end of the Civil War until soon after World War I (ca. 1920), teaching procedures and educational practices in general were greatly influenced by experts whose primary interest was to improve organizational efficiency. William Payne set the stage for employing management principles with his 1875 proposal of precision and certainty of performance in schools: "The theory of school supervision . . . requires the superintendent to work upon the school through teachers. He is to prepare plans of instruction and discipline, which the teachers must carry into effect; but the successful working out of such a scheme requires constant oversight and constant readjustments. Hence arises the necessity for conference, instruction in methods, and correction of errors. The teachers of a graded school should be under continual normal instruction" (p. 4).

In 1914, E. C. Eliot offered this view: "Supervisory control is concerned with what should be taught, when it should be taught, to whom, how, and to what purpose" (p. 23).

Both of these views of supervision strongly imply that there is a single right way of doing things in education and that once this path is identified, it is the supervisor's responsibility to ensure that teachers know and follow it. The supervisor is also charged with the responsibility of planning, that is, of finding the most efficient and economical ways to attain organizational goals.

The views of various writers on corporate management, particularly Frederick W. Taylor (1916), whose scientific management principles were advocated as the way to ensure good practice in industrial organizations, also affected the beliefs of educators. A review of Taylor's major tenets provides a context for our discussion of this second period of supervisory thought and practice. Raymond Villers (1960, p. 78) outlined the essential points of Taylor's views below:

- Time study principle. All productive effort should be measured by accurate time study and a standard time established for all work performed in the shop.
- Piece rate principle. Wages should be proportional to output and their rates based on the standards determined by time study. As a corollary, a worker should be given the highest grade of work of which he is capable.
- Separation-of-planning-from-performance principle. Management should take over from employees the responsibility

for planning the work and making the performance physically possible. Planning should be based on time studies and other data related to production, which are scientifically determined and systematically classified; it should be facilitated by standardization of tools, implements and methods.

- Scientific-methods-of-work principle. Management should take over from workers the responsibility for their methods of work, determine scientifically the best methods, and train the workers accordingly.
- Management-control principle. Managers should be trained and taught to apply scientific principles of management and control (such as management by exception and comparison with validated production standards).
- Functional principle. The strict application of military principles should be reconsidered and the industrial organization should be so designed that it serves the purpose of improving the coordination of activities among the specialists.

These principles of scientific management imply that certain features of organizational life are so predictable that specific laws can be formulated to guide behavior in virtually every circumstance. Thus, in both educational and corporate views of supervision during this period, the belief reigned that behavioral formulas, when faithfully followed, would necessarily and automatically lead to predictable outcomes and products.

Scientific management principles clearly influenced the development of educational supervision during this period, but other facts also played a role. For example, many schools grew rapidly in both size and complexity, to the extent that larger organizational arrangements—districts and systems—were established across the nation, particularly in urban centers in the north and east. This increased organizational complexity was a major factor in the creation of a more segmented view of educational supervision. Larger school systems began hiring both— a business manager and a supervisor of instruction, who would function as equal partners in the hierarchical structure of the school district. Both were responsible to a third person in another newly created role, the superintendent of schools. This concept of dual administration (business and instruction) greatly influenced the development of modern administrative and supervisory practice. One product of this era in educational history, then, is what might be called the institutionalization and professionalization of the educational supervisor's role.

Assumptions and Related Practices Great faith was placed in educational laws. Organizations throughout society were awakening to the possibility that rules and principles derived from research could be established to guide practice. School administrators in particular were open to this line of thinking, because at this time a variety of problems were emerging from over two centuries of rather confused development. The notion that the educational practices of the past could be understood and even improved upon if some key facts and laws were learned was indeed tempting.

The outcome of this view, in terms of supervision, was that increasingly, the educational supervisor became a reviewer who verified that employees conformed to procedures which were determined and handed down by experts.

The supervisor's job was to make sure that the scientific rules of schooling were being followed. Thus, the emphasis in supervision was on the maintenance of acceptable teaching behaviors and particularly on ensuring that these were carried out efficiently.

The supervisory staff of a school system would determine the proper methods of instruction. This scientific approach to supervision emphasized a "top-down" orientation to defining and communicating information concerning instructional practices, and the supervisory personnel of a school or district became the legitimate experts in the field of instruction. Scientific management principles urging separation of management from employee control made unthinkable the possibility that teachers might work together to influence or define proper instructional techniques. Quite simply, teachers were viewed as the implementors of administrators' policies, and supervisors were around to make certain that the policies were being implemented faithfully.

To summarize, the overriding aim of educational supervision as it was practiced during this era was to develop teachers to be professionally efficient—that is, capable of self-analysis, self-criticism, and self-improvement—in order to conform to stated standards of performance. Those standards were determined at higher levels of the school district organization and then transmitted to the teachers. The educational supervisors' primary activity, then, was to provide either condemnations or commendations to teachers after classroom visits. Compromises between these two extremes were rarely possible.

Implications for Preparing Supervisors The prevailing motto of preservice preparation for educational supervisors during the scientific management era—if there had been such a practice in place at the time—would clearly have been something like, "There's a right way—and only one right way—to do everything." Supervision (and the preparation of future supervisors) consisted largely of teaching people how to do things in that one right way.

At the height of reliance on the precepts of scientific management as a guide for administrative performance, the role of the educational supervisor had not yet become so professionalized as to see formal preparation and certification programs in place across the United States. There can be little doubt, however, that those who were assigned supervisory responsibilities in schools were heavily influenced by the management trends and philosophies of the time. Thus, the practicing supervisor around the turn of the twentieth century would have been enamored with the use of scientific (or perhaps, "quasi-scientific") procedures as psychometric evaluation and statistical assessment of pupil performance and educational performance in general. No doubt, the writings of Thorndike heavily influenced how supervisors did their jobs by giving them the scientific, research-based findings on pupil learning and "correct" teaching practice that could be shared with classroom teachers. In short, the educational supervisor of this era was primarily viewed as a scholar and researcher who found the best ways to do things, and then shared those findings with the teachers.

This stage of development truly marked the beginning of the creation of supervision as a separate field of practice and study in education because of the transition of the supervisor as a lay authority figure, or simply a teacher who worked with colleagues in a more sophisticated and formalized role. Without that foundation in practice, supervisory preparation programs would not be part of university curricula today. As will be noted later in this chapter, however, the foundations of educational supervision derived from this scientific era have led to a conceptualization of supervisory preparation which is rooted almost exclusively in the acquisition of technical skills traditionally associated with the "science of supervision." Later, we will make the case that such traditional preparation may not be sufficient to assist educational supervisors in dealing with the complexities of their jobs.

Supervision as Human Relations

One consequence of the scientific era was the tendency to value the accomplishment of organizational goals more than the interests and needs of the people who worked in the organization. Scientific management often emphasized that all organizational components—employees included—were best understood as replacement parts. "One teacher is as good as another" could have been a motto of the time. Predictably, a vigorous reactive movement eventually emerged. A new philosophy of supervision took shape that focused on the needs of individuals who worked in schools and that emphasized satisfying their personal interests. Widespread support developed for cooperative group efforts as both an end and a means for change in schools. This was the human relations era (ca. 1920–1960).

Supervisors were encouraged to use every means possible to stimulate and encourage classroom teachers, with the assumed outcome being more effective instruction. Terms found in the literature describing supervision during this era included such words as coordinating, integrating, creativity, stimulating, and democratic relationships. Again, some definitions of supervision from the time provide a better understanding of the era. For example, the National Education Association (NEA) in 1930 stated: "[The following is a] fundamental philosophy of supervision: Supervision is a creative enterprise. It has for its objective the development of a group of professional workers who attack their problems scientifically, free from control of tradition and actuated by a spirit of inquiry. Supervision seeks to improve an environment in which men and women of high professional ideals may live a vigorous, intelligent, creative life" (p. 47).

What is truly remarkable about this definition, when compared to those in the earlier era of scientific supervision, is the sudden shift in emphasis from segmentation toward allowing employees to work together to define organizational goals and to create appropriate activities to meet those goals. The top-down emphasis on supervisory control had given way to a more democratic process. Two additional definitions support this view:

The supervisory function is described not much toward teachers and their methods as it is toward practices of advisement, student activities, pupil control of defensible subject matter, and personality adjustments of pupils and teachers (Cox, 1934, p. 33).

In general, to supervise means to coordinate, stimulate, and direct growth of teachers in the power to stimulate and direct the growth of every pupil through the exercise of his talents toward the richest and most intelligent participation in the society and world in which he lives (Briggs & Justman, 1952, p. 21).

A review would be incomplete if it did not include a description of the work of Kimball Wiles, often characterized as the chief advocate for the human relations approach to educational supervision. In 1967, he and a colleague provided the following definition of the role of supervisors:

The [supervisors] are expediters. They help establish communication. They help hear each other. They serve as liaisons to get people into contact with others who have similar problems or with resource people who can help. They stimulate staff members to look at the extent to which ideas and resources are being shared, and the degree to which persons are encouraged and supported as they try new things. They make it easier to carry out the agreements that emerge from evaluation sessions. They listen to individuals discuss their problems and recommend other resources that may help in the search for solutions. They bring to individual teachers, whose confidence they possess, appropriate suggestions and materials. They serve, as far as they are able, the feelings that teachers have about the system and its policies, and they recommend that the administration examine irritations among staff members (p. 11).

Clearly, there is a great difference between the perspectives of this human development era of supervision and those of the inspection and scientific eras. In the first two centuries of American education, there was very little concern for the individual needs of teachers and others in school systems. In Wiles's words, on the other hand, we find little or no concern for the priorities and needs of the organization. The focus had shifted dramatically from things to people.

Assumptions and Related Practices *If people are happy, they will be productive.* This is the fundamental premise of this era, and it is the key ingredient of any approach to managerial or supervisory practice that endorses the fulfillment of human needs. If happy employees are better, more effective employees, then supervisors must focus on the needs and interests of the workers. Thus, educational supervisors must spend a good deal of time seeking input from teachers and staff members concerning working conditions and other issues related to the quality of life in the organization. Supervisors must also emphasize discussion groups, shared decision-making, and group process skill development.

The improvement of the psychosocial climate of the school is a legitimate concern of supervisors. The human relations movement, which emerged quite forcefully during the 1920s and 1930s, was heavily influenced by the research and theory bases that were increasingly popular in the social sciences. During this period, the overall tenor of supervision was altered; it became acceptable for educational leaders to expend energy toward effecting positive feelings within the organization. Previously, only the measurable outcomes of organizations were considered to be the legitimate concerns of supervisors and administrators.

The supervisor is an in-between person in school systems. Whether it was a conscious modification or not is unclear and

probably unimportant, but during this period the formal role of the supervisor changed drastically from that of an authority figure to that of a process helper and consultant. In contrast with earlier periods when supervisors were either inspectors or efficiency experts, they became supporters, facilitators, and consultants to teachers. Two reasons might explain this shift. First, educational organizations and curricula were becoming more complex, and there was increasing specialization in many professional roles. The job of the supervisor probably reflected this change more than any other. Increasing demands for more varied curricula in school districts created the need for subject area specialists—one frequent conceptualization of the role of the supervisor—to work with teachers and provide them with expert assistance to help solve classroom instructional problems.

Second, a prevailing philosophical orientation of human relations management was that teachers and other workers needed supportive people to help them with their jobs. The supervisor's role was ideally suited to that function.

The nature of the supervisor's role continues to be debated, and as this debate continues, different views emerge of what should constitute effective preparation programs for supervisors.

Implications for Preparing Supervisors This period of human relations supervision and management actually ushered in two issues that have had an impact on the preparation of supervisors. At this time, states were adopting standards to certify those who would serve as educational supervisors (as contrasted with principals or superintendents), and these standards, of course, began to define the content of supervision preparation programs. By 1960, 21 states had established specific certificates or endorsements for professional education credentials that would allow people to be called "supervisors."

Two distinct perspectives about supervision began to emerge. One was based on the belief that supervisory personnel should be those who were prepared as subject area experts, and that their role was to work with teachers in refining curriculum. As a result, university-based supervision preparation programs (now a lucrative business because of emerging state certification standards) would often house supervision courses and programs in departments of curriculum and instruction, elementary education, or other similar graduate level section where the focus was truly on the refinement of teaching practice. In other cases, supervision continued to be associated with the management of schools, largely because of the view that supervisors were to evaluate teachers. In those institutions, the preparation of supervisors became an activity of the field of educational administration and management. In a relatively few cases, separate academic units were formed to focus strictly on the field of educational supervision as a separate entity. A prime example of this was the University of Georgia which for several decades retained separate departments of Educational Administration and of Curriculum and Supervision.

Also important during the human relations era was the determination of the subject matter included in programs—regardless of academic homes in universities—as essential knowledge and skills associated with supervision as a field of practice. In addition to such courses as advanced study of curriculum, instruction, and supervision as a separate field, aspiring supervisors were expected to take coursework designed to provide insights into the human side of their work. As a result, additional learning was now required in psychology, human relations, team development, and other similar areas that indicated the new vision of the supervisor as a human relations expert. Although such changes may have done much to change the "feel" of supervisory practice from a management role to a human development perspective, the structure of preparation programs still emphasized almost exclusively the acquisition of technical knowledge as a foundation for preservice preparation. One thing that did change, however, during this era of greater formal preparation of future educational supervisors was the recognition that people ought to gain some socialization to the "real world" of supervision by spending some time in the field. Internships, practica, and other forms of field experiences were added as requirements in virtually every state that had specific supervisory certification programs. Again, these experiences were added to increase aspiring supervisors' knowledge about their new future roles, but they may not have been sufficient to increase overall quality preparation, an issue to be addressed later in this chapter.

CURRENT PERSPECTIVES

Supervisory thought and practice today in some ways result from all three earlier perspectives, but in many ways bear no resemblance to any of them. Some educators now lean toward supervisory practices that stem from the earlier inspection and scientific philosophies of supervision; others have expanded the concept of human relations to develop an approach often referred to as human resource development. In recent years, there has been great interest in concepts associated with client-driven management behavior and a commitment to quality. In the next sections, some brief information will be provided about these alternative visions of supervision.

Return to Inspection

Few modern supervisors would openly admit to their belief that most teachers in their districts are incompetent and that supervisors are supposed to "catch" instructors teaching incorrectly or providing incorrect information to pupils. Yet this approach to supervision persists, frequently veiled in such jargon as "getting tough with those teachers who aren't performing." When school districts are faced with the unfortunate task of reducing the number of teachers or administrators because of budget cuts, declining enrollments, or other environmental pressures, there is often talk about laying off the incompetent teachers and administrators, not just those unlucky enough to be the most recently hired. This kind of rhetoric can lead to a climate where virtually all teachers feel threatened, and supervisors and administrators feel compelled to look for the worst rather than the best characteristics of their staffs.

The increasing acceptance of competency tests for teachers, which are required in a number of states and local school districts, is a very real manifestation of this approach. The unstated belief behind the calls for such testing is clearly that some teachers—an undetermined number—are doing a poor job and that these ineffective individuals must be weeded out from the ranks of public school teachers. The best way to do this, say proponents of competency testing, is to subject all teachers to an assumption of inadequate professional performance by requiring them either to take the tests or else lose their teaching credentials.

In some school systems, the percentage of widespread teacher incompetence has led supervisors and administrators to redefine their roles as those of inspectors. Such educators are likely to behave in such a way as to indicate a general lack of trust in their teaching staff. They may call for unannounced classroom visits to gather information about classroom activities. Discussions of procedures that require a collaborative relationship between teachers and supervisors become pointless. The use of clinical supervision, for example, a model that depends on open lines of communication, would be nearly impossible to implement.

Return to Scientific Supervision

A blind faith in the certainty that scientific laws can guide educational practice is by no means dead and buried. While the pontifications of the disciples of scientific management, such as Frederick Taylor, may seem to be foolish overstatements today, many educators continue to believe that educational practice can be understood according to predictable relationships among predictable variables. If we know how to mix chemicals to produce compounds in life-saving medicines, why can't we know exactly which ingredients should be mixed to form children who can read, write, and cipher?

The press for a return to scientific management in education comes from many sources. School boards, whose members often have strong ties to the world of private business, are still heavily influenced by the heritage of scientific management and often wonder why educators do things so inefficiently while those in the private sector effectively change raw materials into finished products. There is a strong desire to find predictability in educational practice. The number of products becomes an indicator of organizational effectiveness, and the assumption is often made that more is better.

Educational supervisors who agree with the assumptions of this approach would probably attempt to reduce more visible signs of productiveness in their schools, possibly in the form of higher scores on standardized achievement tests.

Human Resource Development

Rather than an outright return to human relations supervision equivalent to the revivals of inspection and scientific supervision, proponents of this approach have incorporated a basic ingredient of human relations (namely, the people in an organization hold the key to more effective supervision or management) into a variation known as human resource development. This method has dominated the literature of the past 20 years.

As its name implies, human resource development suggests that the most important activity of a supervisor is to help people within an organization (i.e., human resources) become as skillful and effective as possible. The organization will be improved because its most important features, employees, will be more effective.

There is a good deal of overlap between human relations and human resource development. Both approaches place tremendous emphasis on the needs of the people who work in the organization, and both views hold that organizational effectiveness is a desirable outcome of intervention by a supervisor. In addition, both views suggest that the key to organizational effectiveness is the extent to which workers can feel satisfied in their jobs.

Some important differences, however, keep human resource development from being a mere rehash of the earlier concept. Human relations advocates believed that emphasizing the happiness of an organization's employees would almost automatically guarantee that those employees would work harder, thereby increasing the overall effectiveness and productivity of the organization: "Happy people are productive people." The duty of the supervisor, then, would be to guarantee that workers were satisfied with the workplace and would therefore want to work harder. In school settings, the supervisor would ensure that teachers had what they wanted in terms of supplies and equipment and that they were reasonably satisfied with how they were treated. The human resource development approach, however, advocates that employees will be happier, more satisfied, and ultimately more productive only if they gain satisfaction through working in a productive organization: "Happy employees are productive employees if they work in a productive place." The supervisor thus becomes primarily interested in bringing about greater organizational effectiveness, thereby creating a setting where employees can gain satisfaction through their productivity. In many ways, then, human resource development supervision is an outcome of the human relations movement. The key distinction is the emphasis selected by the supervisor.

Proponents of human resource development criticize the earlier human relations perspective as highly manipulative because it assumed that a supervisor could be nice to employees and thereby make them buy into organizational goals without hesitation. Human relations believers, on the other hand, suggest that, because of its emphasis on organizational productivity, human resource development is but a thinly disguised return to scientific management. The real distinction seems to be more subtle, however. In human relations supervision, organizational effectiveness is a by-product of satisfying people's needs immediately. People tend to be comfortable in a human relations environment. The human resource development advocates, however, claim that people will eventually be satisfied if the organization is productive, even though the immediate impression may be that the supervisor is ignoring individual needs and that the results will be longer lasting. In fact, meeting the concerns of employees is a long-term goal for human resource development supervisors, who believe that immediate energy needs to be directed toward organizational effectiveness.

Client-Based Supervision and Total Quality Management

Total Quality Management (TQM) is probably the single movement that epitomizes management philosophy development in the past ten years. It is often described in the literature as emphasizing the development of organizational plans and priorities directed toward increasing the sense of satisfaction felt by those who are the clients or the customers of organizations. In other words, when the external environment perceives that it is satisfied with what takes place within an organization, then the organization is effective.

Focusing on the need to engage in absolute dedication to customer satisfaction is actually only one part of the philosophy of TQM. Ciampa (1992, p. 7) noted that TQM is directed toward producing results that fall into the following four qualities:

1. Customers are intensely loyal. They are more than satisfied because their needs are being met and their expectations are being exceeded.
2. The time to respond to problems, needs, and opportunities is minimized. Costs are also minimized by eliminating or minimizing tasks that do not add value. Moreover, they are minimized in such a way that the quality of goods or services given to the customer and the way the customer is treated is enhanced.
3. There is a climate that supports and encourages teamwork and leads to more satisfying, motivating, and meaningful work for employees.

There is a general ethic of continuous improvement. In addition, there is a methodology that employees understand for attaining a state of continuous improvement.

As one reflects on the vision of proper supervision suggested by an emphasis on TQM principles, it becomes clear that certain practices are exhibited by those who adhere to this approach. For example, top-down management is no longer valid, nor is any effort to use immediate and visible indicators of effectiveness. As a result, in school settings, it becomes increasingly difficult to imagine successful practice being identified solely in terms of increases in student achievement scores.

Implications for Preparing Supervisors

All of these recent perspectives on proper supervisory practice have implications for the preparation of educational supervisors. The return to inspection and scientific practice, for example, implies that those who would be effective supervisors would likely engage in training activities that place significantly more emphasis on learning proper, research-based information for the purpose of dictating effective practice. Human resource development would likely influence preservice preparation by emphasizing the need for future leaders to develop personalized visions of educational effectiveness. At the same time, future human resource supervisors would be expected to learn as much as possible about the "people side" of schools. TQM supervisors would increase their skills in working effectively with groups outside of the school as a way to determine "client" or "customer" needs.

Two general observations might be made about this last set of perspectives and their potential impact on preservice preparation. First, all who would practice any of these approaches would spend a considerable amount of time reviewing research and literature scrutinizing private sector applications. Human resource development, TQM, and most other recent approaches to effective management and supervision owe their histories to writers and observers of corporate management. School applications are extensive, but they tend to mirror those of the business world.

Second, whether these newer views of supervision are considered valid or not they all emphasize that preparation programs should involve learning more about effective practice. There is a strong research base that suggests that teaching about supervision, without equal attention being paid to learning how to supervise, or most importantly, what it means to an individual to become a supervisor is limited. Newer approaches to conceptualizing the ways in which individuals might become educational supervisors are long overdue and may represent yet another development of preparation programs for educational supervisors.

Research on Beginning Educational Leaders

To identify how leaders of schools might best be prepared, it is best to begin by examining what is known about the types of skills that are needed by those who are at the beginning of their careers. Research by Duke (1984), Daresh (1986), Weindling and Earley (1987), Daresh and Playko (1994), and van der Westhuizen and Legotlo (1996) has shown consistently that, regardless of such variables as level of school (i.e., elementary vs. middle vs. secondary), gender, or even the nation in which the study is carried out, beginning school leaders report that they face challenges in three specific areas: (1) limits on technical expertise (How do I do the things that "they" want me to do?), (2) difficulties with socialization to the profession in general and also individual school settings (What do "they" do around here?), and (3) problems with role clarification and self-awareness (Who am I, now that I'm a leader?). While studies have clearly shown that all three of these areas are critical for one to succeed in leadership roles in schools, some issues are more important than others. The area of role clarification and self-awareness is acknowledged by the majority of beginning administrators and supervisors, and also by their superordinates, as the most important area of development. Again, it must be noted that many also indicate that knowing how to do the job efficiently and effectively (technical skills), and how to adapt (socialization skills) are important. If one is to step into a new leadership role and "hit the ground running," however, one needs to possess a high degree of self-awareness, defined as: developing a personal response to matters calling for ethical concern, recognizing the moment of transfer from one professional self-identity to another new role or identity, and appreciating the fact that one's personal identity has been coded differently in the eyes of others.

The three areas of technical skills, socialization, and role clarification or self-awareness, then, are well-established as foci for preparing individuals to step into school leadership roles for the first time. It is evident, however, by looking at the ways in which most individuals have been actually prepared to serve as administrators or supervisors, that traditional training programs have not been complete.

PAST AND PRESENT PREPARATION

Preparation programs for educational supervisors have followed many different patterns over the years, depending largely on individual state certification requirements as well as local job descriptions and responsibilities. In some states, for example, specific certification has been created for supervisors. In most cases around the nation, however, individuals who serve in supervisory roles, as defined by the local employing school system, must meet statutory requirements for administrative certificates or licenses. In either case, the ways in which individuals have been prepared to serve as supervisors in schools have largely been a function of rules and policies of state education agencies and university practices.

For the most part, preparation of educational supervisors (and administrators) has been viewed primarily as a responsibility of the universities that have established approved preparation programs. In turn, most universities that have supervisor preparation programs rely on academic degree programs which is the stock and trade of institutions of higher education. Normally, people have been prepared (or certified or licensed) to serve as supervisors by completing a master's degree in education which includes a series of graduate level courses that focus on subjects prescribed by the certification or licensing agency. These courses, in turn, tend to focus on such issues as general supervisory skills, personnel management, curriculum design and evaluation, legal aspects of education, and other similar areas of content. Although specific requirements may vary from state to state, for the most part, required university course work centers on helping people to learn *about* supervision through the study of technical aspects of the field. Little background is provided on *how to supervise*, or *how to be a supervisor*.

In many states, university course work related to supervision is supplemented by requirements for aspiring leadership personnel to participate in some form of clinical learning experience as part of the credentialing process. These experiences are analogous to student teaching for future classroom teachers. For those who wish to qualify as supervisory personnel, there is typically a mandated period of time to observe practicing administrators or supervisors, and to actually participate in some of the work.

After completing the academic degree and any other requirements of the state, the graduate has, in essence, become a "supervisor," contingent, of course, upon a school system actually hiring him or her to serve in a formal supervisory role.

A PROPOSED PREPARATION MODEL

In the conventional preparation model described earlier, it is clearly assumed that, if a person is able to complete the academic requirements of a university (by learning about the technical side of supervision) and also do some field work, that will be sufficient preparation to form a practicing and, hopefully, competent educational supervisor.

This traditional approach to preparation has focused almost exclusively on only two of the dimensions of work identified as critical issues facing beginning educational leaders, namely technical skills and socialization to the role and profession. The development of skills and individual insights to assist new supervisors in the critical area of role clarification and self-awareness has not been addressed in most existing preparation programs.

If preparation programs for supervisors are to become more effective in assisting people to take on responsibility in an effective way, it may be possible to reconceptualize the ways in which preservice education is offered. Care must be taken not to ignore aspects of existing or past practice that have been successful. On the other hand, a new vision of supervisory preparation must include attention to elements of preservice training that have not been included in the past. The outcome of this effort to blend old and new practices is what will be described here as a "Tri-Dimensional Model for Leadership Development."

Dimension I: Academic Preparation

As noted earlier, traditional approaches to preparing educational supervisors have emphasized the acquisition of knowledge through the vehicle of graduate-level university courses. The content of these courses is viewed as critical to the skills associated with effective professional performance.

Assumptions and Rationale for Academic Preparation The reliance on university courses as a way to prepare future supervisors is rooted in a number of assumptions. These are related to the value of conventional courses as the "process by which a person learns and performs according to the norms, values, and behaviors held to be necessary for performing a particular professional role" (Blumberg & Greenfield, 1980, p. 221).

Academic preparation in the form of university-based courses is a practical way to assist future supervisors to develop a strong conceptual appreciation of a complex field of practice. The courses are useful in assisting people to acquire the basic "language" and knowledge base of their field. Learning the basic alternative models of curriculum evaluation, or the stages of clinical supervision, through a university lecture is more efficient than trying to learn these things from most other sources.

The assumptions for formal academic preparation originate from a view which holds that learning is essentially the product of a process of information assimilation (Little, 1981). The medium of learning is symbolic, wherein words are used to provide meaning to complex features of reality, and instructional techniques normally include lectures and seminar discussions. Learning takes place in classrooms and libraries.

Faculty members of the university have had the tradition-al role of overseeing academic preparation since they tend to focus attention on knowledge production rather than knowledge utilization. Those who live in the "ivory tower" can afford to engage in the type of inquiry that must take place in an environment not necessarily burdened by the daily "noise" and crises found in most schools. A group such as university faculty members must have time to examine issues that go beyond the solution of problems in the "here and now," and the best way for these perspectives to be shared with the practitioner community is through the traditional university course.

Limitations on Academic Preparation Academic preparation, particularly when defined as university course work, is far from a complete approach to preparing supervisors for their jobs. Perhaps the most basic problem is that the content of university courses is based on the choices of university faculty acting independently as self-defined "experts" in the teaching field of their choice. The self-interests of the academic community, therefore, are not only primarily served; they are virtually the only priorities that are addressed. Expertise, in the context of the university world, is defined through a professor's knowledge base, usually acquired through research findings. The learners are rarely consulted about the nature of what is to be taught. Dialogue between practitioners and academics might yield some important insights into the ideal content to be included as part of academic preparation.

Another traditional drawback to academic preparation concerns the issue of how the content of university courses is presented. A university course traditionally makes almost exclusive use of the information model of learning, as noted earlier. There is therefore great reliance on the lecture, with its emphasis on one-way communication from professor to students. Even if this large-group technique, which results in passive and reactive learners, is modified, other forms of instruction that are largely classroom-bound and oriented are likely used. Rarely do university faculty incorporate learning activities that enable students of supervision to experience the reality of leadership in schools. To be sure, some professors make an effort to expand their instruction by requiring students to interview practicing supervisors, engage in research projects out in schools, or by inviting practitioners to appear in classes. All of these activities create more relevant and lively classes; however, they are of lasting value only if they are tied to the instructional objectives of the classes, and if follow-up analysis and dialogue are also provided. If they are viewed as extra projects that are assigned to students because they might be "good experiences," they are then much more valuable as ornamentation than as a vital part of student learning.

No doubt other objectives and limitations might be voiced regarding the quality of the courses in many supervisory preparation programs, but there is value in these forms of learning as well. The critical issue is that if traditional university courses are viewed as addressing but one dimension of a comprehensive and conceptually oriented approach to preservice preparation of supervisors, limitations might be greatly reduced, and the value of academic preparation might be greatly enhanced.

Dimension II: Field-Based Learning

Many reformers of these preparation programs hold that to improve the training of future school leaders, field-based and experiential learning programs are necessary. More intense internships, planned field experiences, and other forms of practica have been suggested.

There is a strong progression toward preservice programs that are largely field-based in nature, and not necessarily tied to the traditional university structure. According to this view, universities should be places where people are educated, not "trained" or "prepared" in ways that practitioners are better able to do. This would also suggest that field agencies and practitioners would assume virtual control of the preparation of future generations of school supervisors.

As the movement toward greater field-based preparation has progressed, interest has heightened in the current status of university-based programs that attempt to increase opportunities for clinical learning. A review (Daresh & LaPlant, 1985) of these programs revealed the following characteristics:

1. Typical field-based learning experiences are not required of all students enrolled in administration or supervisor preparation programs but, rather, only of students seeking a formal certificate or license. When required, field-based activities are usually required toward the end of a student's program of studies.
2. Most programs operate in basically the same fashion: Students are expected to register for an academic credit-bearing course entitled "Internship," "Planned Field Experiences," or some similar title, and to spend anywhere from 10 to 40 hours per week during an academic term observing practitioners who, in turn, assign students tasks or projects to be carried out under their supervision.
3. Field-based programs normally provide academic credit, but student evaluation is of the pass/fail variety in most cases. Responsibility for evaluating student performance typically resides with the university faculty member who coordinates the practicum.
4. The university faculty coordinator is usually the only faculty member in an academic department who works with students enrolled in the practicum. Other than initial academic guidance for some students, the majority of the faculty is not active in supervising practica.
5. The duration of most field experiences is normally dictated by the length of the university's academic term and not by the time required to complete an assigned project or experience.
6. Students who participate in the majority of internships or field experiences are not paid for their work. As a result, most participate in field-based programs on a part-time basis while continuing to teach or perform other professional duties in the same schools where they are also engaged in their practica.

Assumptions and Rationale for Field-Based Learning Assumptions that field-based programs are a way to enhance the quality of traditional academic programs seem to be well-founded. Such programs enable future supervisors to apply theoretical learning and develop their skills through participation in a wide range of daily supervisory duties, apply knowledge learned in the classroom to a real-life setting, and adapt to the world of professional supervision. Field-based programs make it possible for the students to witness the practicalities associated with their intended roles, particularly if they are able to work with talented supervisory personnel who can serve as effective role models.

Limitations of Field-Based Learning Despite the relatively persistent emphasis on the need for field-based learning, some limitations derive from this form of learning, in large part when it is not combined with other models or dimensions of learning, most notably strong academic preparation. In the field of initial teacher education, many have questioned some fundamental assumptions about the value of the practicum as a learning device. From Dewey (1938) to Berliner (1984), Zeichner (1985), and Cruickshank and Armaline (1986), cautions have been offered that field-based learning experiences may actually be viewed as "miseducative," and that they create cognitive and behavioral traps which often close avenues to conceptual and social changes that may be warranted. In short, field-based learning programs too often may serve to prepare people only for what is at present and what was in the past—but not what might be in the future. The field experience for preparing future educational leaders cannot be viewed in the same vein as the apprenticeship used in the training of plumbers and electricians who are prepared for the future by learning the time-honored techniques that have worked in the past.

Field-based learning may be an extremely powerful tool for learning about a craft. Too great a reliance on the practicum, however, would be as unwise as attempting to prepare individuals for leadership roles "by the book," that is only through academic preparation or university courses.

Dimension III: Personal Formation

The most important dimension of supervisor preparation, one that is rarely addressed in a direct fashion, is referred to as "personal formation." It consists of those activities consciously directed toward assisting people to synthesize learnings acquired through other sources, and also to develop a personalized appreciation of what it means to be an educational leader. It is at this point that role clarification and self-awareness might be introduced in the preparation of future supervisory personnel. A major problem faced by the novice is the lack of understanding concerning what leadership, authority, power, and control mean on a very individual level. Personal formation may be a way to address this problem while also providing the means to construct a personalized moral and ethical stance that may be utilized in framing responses to a variety of future supervisory problems.

Structural Elements of Personal Formation Four specific elements comprise the personal formation: mentoring, reflection, platform development, and professional action planning.

Mentoring. Ashburn, Mann, and Purdue (1987) defined mentoring as the "establishment of a personal relationship for the purpose of professional instruction and guidance." Wasden (1987) noted, "The mentor is a master at providing opportunities for the growth of others, by identifying the situations and events which contribute knowledge and experience to the life of the [learner]. Opportunities are not happenstance; they must be thoughtfully designed and organized into a logical sequence. . . . The mentor takes great pains to help the [learner] recognize and negotiate dangerous situations . . ." (p. 1).

Mentors may work with aspiring supervisors to "show them how to do things" that are associated with the successful performance of a certain job. A role model may be consulted by a newcomer to the field to learn certain technical skills associated with the new job. A mentor, however, goes well beyond this function. He or she would be more inclined to prod novices to learn to perform a task according to their personal skills, talents, and limitations. In short, a mentor is more likely to raise questions than to provide answers to the novice.

The responsibilities and characteristics for mentors in a preservice program for educational supervisors include:

1. experience as an effective educational supervisor;
2. demonstration of generally accepted qualities of positive leadership;
3. ability to "ask the right questions" of protégés with whom they work, not simply give the "right answers";
4. acceptance of "other ways of doing things," and avoidance of the temptation to tell protégés that the only way to do something is "the way I've always done it";
5. expression of the sincere desire to see protégés go beyond their present levels of performance, even when that may mean going beyond the mentor's own abilities;
6. ability to model the values of continuous self-improvement, learning, and reflection;
7. comfort with the task of working with the developmental needs of adult learners; and
8. above all other qualities, the ability to listen to others, help others clarify their perceptions, and to "cause" others to reflect on their experiences.

Mentoring as part of the personal formation of supervisors is a critical responsibility, and most of the rest of professional development may be related to this element.

Reflection. A second element of personal formation is the development of skills related to personal reflection to guide supervisory performance. Reflection about one's professional performance in a role is simple to define. As Posner (1985) observed, concerning the use of reflectivity in preparing classroom teachers, individuals would benefit greatly from their experiences if they had the opportunity to prepare for and think about those experiences before and after they occur. This theme has been championed by Schon (1983) who advanced the concept of reflection as a guide to action in many professions. The simple idea is that an effective, reflective practitioner would be the person who realizes that, before he or she tries to solve problems, it is critical to think about the nature of the "right" problem to be solved.

Personal reflection would be realized by candidates for future supervisory positions keeping a diary, or reflective log, in which they would regularly record their personal descriptions of reality and their responses to some of the questions that are raised in daily practice. Writing observations down develops the skill of articulating important personal beliefs that may be of use in the future.

Educational platform development. Another important ingredient is the preparation of a formal statement of one's own educational philosophy, beliefs, and values. Sergiovanni and Starratt (1993) referred to this activity as the "development of a personalized educational platform." In their view, professional educators are encouraged periodically to review personal stances about important educational issues. In doing this, individuals would state the ideas that they espouse, in a similar way to the platform statements made by candidates running for a political office, with the major difference being that the educational platform should be designed to communicate a person's attitudes, values, and beliefs about education, even if these statements were contrary to the sentiments of the majority of people "out in the public."

Sergiovanni and Starratt suggested that an educational platform might include personalized responses to questions that come from the major issues such as (1) the aims of education, (2) major achievements of students, (3) the social significance of students' learning, (4) the image of the learner, (5) the value of the curriculum, (6) the image of the teacher, (7) preferred kind of pedagogy, (8) the primary language of discourse in learning situations, (9) preferred kinds of teacher–student relationships, and (10) preferred kind of school climate.

Preparing a platform helps in the process of personal formation by enabling persons to recognize their strongest beliefs (and perhaps unwanted biases as well) about significant issues in professional education. Some responses to these 10 areas will come about much more quickly than will others. These areas will serve as placeholders for concepts in which there is probably the strongest allegiance to certain values. The basis of these may be viewed as "core" or "non-negotiable" values for an individual. A second benefit is that it alerts individuals to probable conflicts that are likely to be ahead. When individuals have a good comprehension of their educational platforms, they may be able to foresee where sources of conflict will occur in relationships with organizations that also possess values. Understanding the exact sources or probable value disputes should assist most individuals in finding more effective ways of dealing with life in institutions.

Every educator should periodically articulate a personal educational platform. Further, there is considerable value in sharing this platform statement with mentors, colleagues, or others. This sharing process should take place with considerable regularity and frequency. This process is helpful in enabling others to gain insights into one's behavior and, perhaps even more importantly, to encourage an individual to be as clear as possible about the nature of personal values and beliefs. A platform is never really completed, but rather, it is a dynamic and ongoing activity carried out by every earnest school supervisor.

Professional action planning. The final element in personal formation is the articulation of a statement about one's overall personal professional development. This activity includes all of the insights gathered from academic preparation and field-based learning as well as those derived from mentoring, personal reflection, and platform development into a single, coherent action plan. Aspiring supervisors are encouraged at this point to indicate where they believe additional work may be needed. One of the greatest potential benefits of personal formation—the synthesis of learning—may occur through this activity. In addition, the most desirable objective of any learning activity, namely, control over learning by the learner, may take place.

Although personal professional action planning might be seen as the culminating activity of a preparation program, it should be incorporated as a part of a sequence of activities designed to address supervisory professional development needs. From the beginning of a future supervisor's first university course, there should be an explicit statement of the need to accept personal responsibility for translating course content into individual action. Each of the dimensions of the Tri-Dimensional Model presented here may be seen as occurring simultaneously with what goes on in the other features of the model. Personal formation must occur while academic preparation is going on, and field-based learning should be taking place to enhance academic preparation and clarify personal formation. The simultaneous nature of these three dimensions is depicted in the triangular diagram presented in Figure 37.1.

Assumptions and Rationale for Personal Formation An emphasis on personal formation is included as part of a preservice preparation program for school supervisors is based on two fundamental assumptions: (1) that beginning supervisors have the opportunity to do much more than respond to crises in a reactive fashion and have little time to engage in a review of their personal priorities, and (2) that adults need to learn in ways other than through the traditional information assimilation model used in university courses.

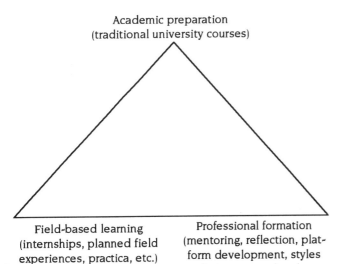

Academic preparation
(traditional university courses)

Field-based learning
(internships, planned field
experiences, practica, etc.)

Professional formation
(mentoring, reflection, platform development, styles
analysis, personal and professional development)

FIGURE 37.1. Diagram representing the tridimensional conceptualization of professional development for supervisors.

With regard to the first issue, the research conducted on beginning school leaders makes it clear that novices often have trouble with knowing exactly how to perform the functions of the job. Most beginners find ways to cope with a lack of technical skills rather quickly. They almost intuitively seek advice and counsel from others in the organization to "learn the ropes" when they are first hired. The aspect of "coming on board," which is rarely addressed in a structured fashion, is the appreciation for the personal demands that go along with having a new title of power and authority. Preparation programs rarely address the personal perceptions and sense of what it means to be "in charge." As a result, culture shock is experienced by many when they take their first positions. Many never recover from this initial shock. By adding the element of personal formation to a preservice preparation program, this initial trauma can be reduced and may also serve to determine whether the individual is really interested in supervision. Such self-selection can only be viewed as positive.

The second source of rationale for the concept of personal formation is that this dimension may add a different perspective to the predominant theory used in preparation programs. Existing programs tend to place considerable emphasis on the use of academic preparation as the primary preservice learning experience, with a pinch of field-based learning tossed in for good measure. These traditional approaches, then, tend to make almost exclusive use of the information assimilation mode of learning by students. The introduction of personal formation provides another approach, namely, experiential learning. The significant difference in this approach to learning, as contrasted with information assimilation, is that experiential learning places much emphasis on the ability of individual learners to control their own learning activities through a cycle of learning by doing, reflecting, formulating individual responses and understandings, followed by further experiences. This model is in accord with the prevailing assumptions found in current descriptions of adult learning (Bandura, 1977), and is an appropriate addition to programs designed to prepare adults to become school leaders.

Limitations on Personal Formation There are some limitations to this view as well. The most significant drawback to the concept of personal formation may be when this approach is used as a replacement for all other dimensions traditionally included in preparation programs. Some may suggest that the way to improve supervisory preparation is to remove universities from the business entirely, and to let practitioners handle all the training. The argument may be advanced that the only way to learn about supervision is to learn "at Nellie's elbow," or out in the field. Personal formation offers a tempting addition to this approach in that novices need mentors to assist in their experience-based learning. The problem with this perspective—a blend of personal formation with field-based learning alone—is that there is no room in this approach for beginners to learn basic concepts and principles of supervision. Furthermore, without a basis in strong academic preparation, there is likely to be little or no exposure to recent research on supervisory practice. Personal formation makes sense as an addition to existing preparation programs, but not as a complete replacement.

CONCLUSION

Many of the conceptual problems that have traditionally influenced the ways in which educational supervision is defined differently across the nation, and even in the ways supervisors are described in individual school systems, make it evident that more effective practice in the long run will be dependent on the creation of more efficient preparation programs. The object of this chapter has been to suggest not only modifications in existing practice, but also approaches that would change many fundamental assumptions and practices for the future.

REFERENCES

Ashburn, E. A., Mann, M., & Purdue, P. A. (1987). *Teacher mentoring: ERIC Clearinghouse on teacher education.* Paper presented at the Annual Meeting of the American Educational Research Association, Washington, D.C.

Bandura, A. (1977). *Social learning theory.* Englewood Cliffs, NJ: Prentice Hall.

Berliner, D. (1984). Making the right changes in preservice teacher education. *Phi Delta Kappan, 66*(2), 94–96.

Blumberg, A. & Greenfield, W. (1980). *The effective principal: Perspectives on school leadership.* Boston: Allyn and Bacon.

Briggs, T. H. & Justman, J. (1952). *Improving instruction through supervision.* New York: Macmillan.

Ciampa, D. (1992). *Total quality: A user's guide for implementation.* Reading, MA: Addison-Wesley.

Cruickshank, D. & Armaline, W. (1986, October). Field experiences in teacher education: Consideration and recommendations. *Journal of Teacher Education, 37,* 34–40.

Daresh, J. C. (1986). Support for beginning principals: First hurdles are highest. *Theory Into Practice, 3,* 168–173.

Daresh, J. C. & LaPlant, J. (1985). Developing a research agenda for administrator in-service. *Journal of Research and Development in Education, 18*(2), 39–43.

Daresh, J. C. & Pape, S. (1987). *Internships and other field experiences in the preparation of administrators and other professional educators: A status report.* Paper presented at the Annual Meeting of the Mid-Western Educational Research Association, Chicago.

Daresh, J. C. & Playko, M. A. (1994). Aspiring and practicing principals' perceptions of critical skills for beginning leaders. *Journal of Educational Administration, 32*(1), 35–45.

Dewey, J. (1938). *Education and experience.* New York: Macmillan.

Duke, D. R. (1984). *Transition to leadership: An investigation of the first year of the principalship.* Educational Administration Program. Portland, OR: Lewis and Clark University.

Dwight, T. (1935). *The school master's friend of the committee man's guide.* New York: Roe Lockwood.

Eliot, E. C. (1914). *City school supervision.* New York: World Book.

Galvez-Hjornevik, C. (1986). Mentoring among teachers: A review of the literature. *Journal of Teacher Education, 35*(1), 6–11.

Little, T. (1981). *History and rationale for experiential learning.* Washington, D.C.: National Society for Internships and Experiential Education.

Massachusetts Bay Company in New England. (1642). Records of the Governor and the Company (Vol. 3).

Payne, W. H. (1875). *Chapters on school administration.* New York: Wilson Hinkle and Company.

Posner, K. D. (1985). *Field experience: A guide to reflective teaching.* New York: Longman.

Schon, D. A. (1983). *The reflective practitioner: How professionals think in action.* New York: Basic Books.

Sergiovanni, T. J. & Starratt, R. J. (1993). *Supervision: Human perspectives* (5th ed.) New York: McGraw-Hill.

Taylor, F. W. (1916). The principles of scientific management. *Bulletin of the Taylor Society.*

van der Westhuizen, P. C. & Legotlo, M. W. (1996). *Perceptions of critical skills for beginning principals in multicultural settings.* Paper presented at the Annual Meeting of the Education of South Africa, Pochefstroom.

Villers, R. (1960). *Dynamic management in industry.* Englewood Cliffs, NJ: Prentice Hall.

Wasden, D. F. (1988). *A handbook for mentors.* Provo, UT: College of Education, Brigham Young University.

Weindling, D. & Earley, P. (1987). *Secondary headship: The first years.* Philadelphia: NFER Nelson.

Wickerman, J. P. (1864). *School economy: A treatise on the preparation, organization, employments, government, and authorities of schools.* New York: Perigree Press.

Wiles, K. & Lovell, J. T. (1967). *Supervision for better schools.* Englewood Cliffs, NJ: Prentice Hall.

Zeichner, K. (1985). *The ecology of field experiences: Toward an understanding of the role of field experiences in teacher development.* In L. Katz & J. Raths (Eds.). *Advances in Teacher Education* (Vol. 3). Norwood, NJ: Ablex Publishing.

·38·

TEACHING OF SUPERVISION

Bernard J. Badiali

MIAMI UNIVERSITY OF OHIO

"We teach to change the world."

Brookfield

INTRODUCTION

It has been almost 30 years since the publication of *Supervision: Emerging Profession* (Leeper, 1969), an anthology which compiled a decade of writing by educational scholars in the field of supervision. The 1960s was a time in which the continued existence of the supervisor as an instructional leader was at issue, and when the future existence of educational supervision as a field was in doubt. Leeper's anthology is an important work, a revealing collection of essays in which writers of that era address various aspects, motivation, techniques, and goals of supervision. The articles range widely in scope, revealing a period in which scholars were actively struggling to define, justify, promote, and professionalize a practice they referred to as supervision.

It is debatable as to whether substantial progress has been made during the last 30 years to come to terms with the problems and issues that faced supervision in the 1960s. An analysis of the 65 articles in Leeper's anthology suggests that many of the difficulties facing the field remain unmitigated. How supervision is defined, what functions it includes, what supervisors envision to be their role, what research informs the field, how supervisors are selected and prepared, and how supervision is actually taught are just a few of the unanswered questions still facing the field today. If it is fair to say that supervision has made little progress in emerging as a profession since 1960, then unresolved dilemmas about purpose, definition, role, function, and preparation are among the main reasons.

There has been less discussion in this decade regarding the professionalization of supervision than there was in 1969, and more discussion about the transformation of supervision as a field (Glickman, 1992; Gordon, 1992; Sergiovanni & Starratt,

1993). The role and functions of supervision may be less clear in the 1990s than they were in the 1960s. Shrinking resources, teacher empowerment, advances in technology, and new conceptualizations of how schools should be organized are factors that call into further question what supervision will mean in the future.

This chapter addresses the issue of how supervision is taught by providing some historical context and contemporary perspective. The way in which supervision has been taught is nested in the milieu of history, including a thicket of concepts, some complementary, some competing, with regard to how one views the practice. The chapter begins by problematizing supervision through discussing its traditions, definitions, undergirding philosophies, theories, practices, contexts, and world views. It concludes with some ideas about how supervision might be taught in the future to accommodate adult learning, critical reflection, and collaboration within the changing circumstances of schooling.

THE DILEMMA OF DEFINITION

To those outside the field, defining supervision is not difficult. Supervision is defined in the *American Heritage Dictionary* as "to oversee and direct." Indeed, 50 years ago the dominant function of supervision was oversight or inspection of schools and teachers. (In England educators continue to refer to supervision as "inspection.") Many teachers continue to have an emotional aversion to the term *supervision* because it conjures up notions of authoritarian directiveness. Mosher and Purpel (1972) used the term *snoopervision* to indicate teachers' discomfort and resistance to the practice. Today, however, only a small number of educators would accept this definition of supervision. During the last 30 years, defining supervision has been an exercise in variety and perspective. Supervision in education has come to mean something more and something different from supervision in the past and supervision in other fields. One issue that persists since before 1960 is that the term *supervision* is subject to many different interpretations. There seems to remain little consensus about its meaning.

Different definitions of supervision abound in the literature (Bolin & Panaritis, 1992; Oliva, 1993; Wiles & Bondi, 1980). To further complicate matters, a plethora of synonyms and modifiers have been used to describe supervision. Searching the literature since 1969, one finds terms like *administrative supervision, clinical supervision, consultative supervision, developmental supervision, differentiated supervision, instructional supervision, and peer supervision* (Oliva, 1993). Other terms such as *coordinator, coach, consultant, mentor, staff developer,* and *teacher-leader* have emerged as accepted synonyms for supervisor.

What makes defining supervision even more complex is that it is a subject to be taught at the university as well as a field in which practitioners work. While practitioners describe supervision in terms of "what is," professors often define supervision more in terms of what "should be." Supervisory functions vary widely from one school system to the next and one state certification program to the next. As a further complication, the functions performed by supervisors are distributed over a wide range of educational specialties that have been ascribed other identifications. When Harris (1963) described supervision decades ago as a "distributive function," he could have been describing the status of supervision in 1996.

The fact that there are many definitions of supervision make it difficult to describe how supervision is taught. (As an advanced certification or degree, one would assume that studies in supervision occur at the graduate level, where not much is known about how professors teach generally.) Is it taught as a role or a function or both? Is supervision taught as a discrete set of tasks or a way of thinking? Is supervision taught as both a field of study and a craft practice? As can be seen by the array of definitions presented in this handbook, individuals who write about it are hardly of one mind regarding the exact nature of supervision.

Scholars in supervision, however, are no different in this respect from scholars in curriculum, in that they find the field of supervision to be illusive and fragmentary (Ornstein & Hunkins, 1988). Ornstein (1995) suggests that supervision, curriculum, and instruction are so tightly interwoven that they interact in ways that are impossible to distinguish. He argues further that the relationship between supervision and administration has intensified in the 1990s because of the dramatic decline in supervisory personnel. As the numbers of supervisors have been reduced, their duties and responsibilities have been added to those of the principal.

PAUCITY OF RESEARCH

There is little empirical research on supervision either in the 1960s or the 1990s. According to MacDonald (1965), in the Association for Supervision and Curriculum Development

(ASCD) Yearbook, *Research and Development in Supervision*, little mention was made of any research studies in the field. Lamenting the lack of research evidence to be found regarding the impact of supervision, MacDonald wrote: "We are left with the still unanswered question of whether supervision has any value at all" (p. 161). Mosher and Purpel reiterate MacDonald's assertion: "But the inescapable conclusion to be drawn from any review of the literature is that there is virtually no research suggesting that supervision of teaching, however defined or undertaken, makes any difference" (1972, p. 50). With very few exceptions there is still little research in the field today (Nolan, Hawkes, & Francis, 1993).

If there has been a dearth of research on the general field of supervision, there is even less research on the "teaching" of supervision. Rarely is there mention in the literature as to how supervisors are taught and with what consequences. A persistent problem has been that there is very little reliable research done on who supervises and on what supervisors do to fulfill their responsibilities in schools. Research on the teaching of supervision is almost nonexistent.

There is no lack of writing on the practice of supervision, however. Dozens of articles have been published on supervisors and supervision during the last 30 years. According to Ornstein (1995), discussion about supervision has declined considerably in recent times. There are scores of textbooks on the topic, however, which suggests that there is a body of knowledge to which we can refer. We may even infer from these writings that there is a "curriculum of supervision" or more accurately, numerous curricula of supervision. Unfortunately, texts relate little about how a "curriculum" is taught or what approaches to instruction are popular or effective. Neither do we know the outcome of the work of students who, after experiencing the curriculum and instruction of supervision, become supervisors.

There appears to be little research on supervision in part because it is such a diffused discipline. Activities associated with it range from observing teachers and group dynamics to organizing curriculum and orchestrating systemic change. Research is associated with many of the activities related to supervision in schools, depending on how the practice is defined, but few studies focus solely on supervision. Studies in leadership, group dynamics, curriculum development, interpersonal relations, and so on, exist in the literature, but these areas are not the exclusive domain of supervisors. Supervision has not been defined in such a way as to distinguish it from other leadership positions such as administration and curriculum coordination. Specific characteristics have not been identified that set the supervisor apart from the principal, department chair, curriculum coordinator, mentor, or lead teacher.

PERSISTENT UNRESOLVED ISSUES

There are numerous issues that complicate any exploration of how supervision has been, or will be, taught. Specifying the role and function of the supervisor has been a conundrum (see Oliva, 1993, Chapter 2). Different conceptions of schools, teachers, teaching, and learning affect the manner in which supervisors are taught. Differing perceptions of the purpose schools serve influence the teaching of supervision. Whether supervisors are being prepared to work in preservice or in-service settings has also influenced the ways in which supervisors are taught.

The fact that supervision has had two different identities further complicates our understanding of how supervision is taught. Supervision may be thought of within the context of teacher preparation or school-based practice. It might be argued that supervisors serve two related but different purposes when the clients, expectations, power relationships, and responsibilities shift from working in preservice education to working with school-wide responsibilities. In teacher education, the emphasis is on providing a skilled service to aspiring teachers as they endeavor to enter the teaching profession. The focus is almost always on instructional issues. College supervisors, however, are instructors, performance evaluators, and part of a university community. Student teachers are in a highly dependent relationship with them. Because of the power differential, supervising student teachers is very different from supervising veteran teachers. Is it reasonable to believe that preparation of student teacher supervisors is, or should be, different from preparing in-service supervisors?

Supervisors in schools are also intensely concerned with instruction, but in addition to the organizational conditions that affect the school community. Their duties often include community relations, strategic planning, staff development, budgeting, and a variety of other responsibilities. Most certainly, in-service supervisors have a great deal in common with student teacher supervisors, but the term *supervision* takes on a somewhat different meaning depending on which reference point is used. In the past, the context for these two forms of supervision has been markedly different. With the advent of professional development schools and school/university partnerships, supervisors of student teachers may have more in common with in-service supervisors in the future.

SUPERVISION IN TRANSITION

A dilemma of supervision in education is not simply that many definitions exist, but also that its meaning has changed and evolved with the times. This section of the chapter will first briefly discuss the history of the nature of supervision and then examine teaching supervision in the future.

According to Wiles and Bondi (1980), the evolution of supervisory roles can be described as follows: 1750–1910: inspection and enforcement; 1910–1920: scientific supervision; 1920–1930: bureaucratic supervision; 1930–1955: cooperative supervision; 1955–1965: supervision as curriculum development; 1965–1970: clinical supervision; 1970–1980: supervision as management. Since 1980, approaches to supervision have included remnants of those in the past, but many new forms of supervision have been popularized during the last 20 years. From 1980 to the present, supervision has been characterized as human relations, human resources, democratic, collaborative/collegial, artistic, interpretive, and ecological (Oliva, 1993).

In a recent description of supervision, Tracy (1995) describes seven phases in the evolution of supervisory practice. She frames supervision as the act of assisting and assessing teachers and suggests that each historical phase of supervision has had a somewhat different emphasis and focus. Different skills were required to implement supervision at different times in history. As the purpose of supervision varied, so did its focus, assumptions, skills, and personnel.

Since 1980, rapid changes in supervision have made clear delineations very difficult. According to Pajak (1989), "the mid to late 1970s witnessed the culmination of one era and the beginning of another in the study of supervisory leadership in education" (p. 10). Pajak's assertion is supported by subsequent literature on supervision. The 1982 ASCD yearbook, *Supervision of Teaching* (Sergiovanni, 1982), for example, attempted to provide a current benchmark of the thinking of the times. The yearbook chapters defined "three faces of supervision: the artistic, the clinical, and the scientific" (p. v). In a very comprehensive study of supervision sponsored by the ASCD, Pajak (1989) identified and verified 12 dimensions of supervisory behavior. Collecting data from a national sample of university professors, school superintendents, principals, teachers, and other educational personnel, the following dimensions were identified: (1) community relations, (2) staff development, (3) planning and change, (4) communication, (5) curriculum, (6) instructional program, (7) service to teachers, (8) observing and conferring, (9) problem solving and decision-making, (10) research and program evaluation, (11) organizing and motivating, and (12) personal development (see Table 38–1).

As part of a comprehensive review of the literature from 1975 to 1989, Pajak and his colleagues linked these dimensions to the leading textbooks in the field (see Table 38–2). According to Pajak (1989), a high degree of consensus appears to exist among outstanding practitioners concerning the knowledge, attitudes, and skills that are most important to effective supervisory practice. Furthermore, the study suggests that there is strong agreement between practitioners and scholars. "No serious gap seems to exist, in other words, between those who study and write about supervision in education and those who actually practice it" (p. 149).

What Pajak and his colleagues seem to make clear about consensus is later called into question. In their chapter in *Supervision in Transition*, Bolin and Panaritis (1992) describe in detail the historical dilemma of defining supervision since before the turn of the nineteenth century. They argue that there has been only a loose consensus built over the years. Their conclusion is that the only points of consensus about supervision were; first, that the function of supervision is an important one whether it is carried out by a superintendent, supervisor, curriculum worker, or peer; and second, supervision is primarily concerned with the improvement of classroom practice for the benefit of students, regardless of what else may be entailed (p. 31). These authors go on to suggest that even this level of consensus is an illusion. Indeed, there are many definitions of supervision offered in the literature.

TABLE 38–1. The Importance of Twelve Dimensions of Supervisory Practice
as Rated by Outstanding Practitioners (n = 1075)

Dimension*	Strongly Agree	Agree	Disagree	Strongly Disagree	Mean
Communication	89.2%	10.4%	.4%	0%	3.89
Staff Development	88.2%	11.2%	.5%	.1%	3.88
Instructional Program	86.0%	13.6%	.4%	0%	3.86
Planning and Change	83.0%	16.2%	.8%	0%	3.82
Motivating and Organizing	80.1%	18.9%	.9%	.1%	3.79
Observation and Conferencing	77.2%	19.2%	3.1%	.6%	3.73
Curriculum	73.4%	25.5%	.9%	.2%	3.72
Problem Solving and decision-making	73.3%	25.3%	1.3%	.1%	3.72
Service to Teachers	72.6%	26.0%	1.3%	1%	3.71
Personal Development	70.8%	27.8%	1.2%	.2%	3.69
Community Relations	63.7%	33.6%	2.7%	.1%	3.61
Research and Program Evaluation	57.3%	39.3%	3.0%	.4%	3.54

*Rank is based on mean scores

Less conventional definitions of supervision began to appear later in this decade. Sergiovanni and Starratt (1989), for example, published the fifth edition of their popular supervision text and re-entitled it, *Supervision: a Redefinition*. Their definition disconnects supervision from traditional, hierarchical roles in the school organization and redefines supervision more in terms of democratic and professional processes. The new supervision they describe embraces peer clinical supervision, mentoring, action research, program evaluation, translations of school mission, and other processes that emphasize the idea of teachers as colleagues working together to increase comprehension of their practice. Further, they contend that staff development and supervision are now joined in such a way that they are often indistinguishable.

Teachers and supervisors are not viewed primarily as independent decision makers who calculate individually the costs and benefits of their actions, but rather as members of an educating community who respond to shared norms and values. Changing the metaphor of school as organization to school as community, Sergiovanni and Starratt assert that the context for supervision has changed. The supervisor emerges as an advocate, developer, and linch pin in relationship to the teachers' efforts to improve the process of teaching and learning (pp. xviii–xix).

Glickman (1992) has suggested that the term *instructional supervision* has outlived its usefulness. He seems to agree with Sergiovanni and Starratt that educators are thinking more democratically and dismantling long-standing hierarchies.

TABLE 38–2. Common Elements of Supervision

Historical phase	Method of improving teaching	Observation of classroom teaching	Face-to-face interaction
Community accountability	Direct-indirect intervention.	Visiting committees observed all aspects of school.	May have occurred. Not necessarily standard practice.
Professionalization	Group interventions such as teacher training and teacher institutes.	County superintendent observed classroom teaching. Late 1800s principals also assumed that role.	May have occurred. Not necessarily standard practice.
Scientific	Identify and solve instructional problems through scientific approach.	Supervisors or principals collected data to measure performance and student outcomes.	May have occurred. Not necessarily standard practice.
Human relations	Seeking to have socially and psychologically satisfied and motivated teachers.	Supervisors observed in order to assist, although in practice observation declined.	Interaction critical though not necessarily with a focus on instruction.
Second-wave scientific	Measurable outcomes and observation by systematic processes.	Supervisors systematically observed classroom events and measured student outcomes.	Face-to-face interaction decreased; the results of measurements indicated needs for change.
Second-wave human relations	Joint teacher/supervisor analysis of teaching patterns.	Supervisors collected data after discussion with teacher.	Face-to-face interaction in both a pre- and post-observation conference.
Human development	Selecting a style of supervision to best meet the teacher's needs.	Usually done, although process may vary with model selected.	Usually, but amount depends on model of supervision selected.

"When schools become decentralized, engage in shared governance, and see themselves as the center of action research, the term supervisor or supervision has little meaning to staff members" (p. 2). In this new paradigm, Glickman suggests, educators use terms such as *coaching, collegiality, reflective practitioners, professional development, critical inquiry,* and *study or research groups.*

WAYS OF TEACHING SUPERVISION

How supervision is actually learned depends heavily on the learners' as well as the teachers' orientation, perspective, and philosophy of education itself. Everyone's approach to supervision reflects his world view, how he perceives reality, what he values or deems important, and what amount of knowledge and experience he has about the field. Theoretical and practical principles of supervision are derived in part by having a perspective on the purpose for schools. How supervision is taught is "problematic," to use Dewey's (1938) term. According to Schon (1987), when practitioners (teacher of supervision) set a problem, they choose and name the items that they will notice; they select items for attention and organize them guided by their background, interests, and perspectives. Given the array of definitions, the wide possibilities in understanding supervisory tasks and functions, and the numerous perspectives on the purpose of school, teaching supervision can take many avenues.

Theory, Philosophy, and Approach

According to McCutchen (1995), theories in education are integrated clusters, bundles, or sets of interpretations, analyses, and comprehensions about educational phenomena. They are about the action we take when we teach as well as when we supervise. Theories have an empirical as well as an ethical dimension. Teaching, any teaching, has a moral basis from which decisions are made. Supervision scholars, like scholars in other fields, have a wide range of theoretical positions and opinions. Because those theories and opinions vary, we must speculate that approaches to teaching supervision in the past have varied as well.

A personal philosophy reflects life experiences, common sense, social and economic background, education, and general beliefs about people. Philosophy is a description, explanation, and evaluation of the world, or what social scientists call a "social lens" (Ornstein, 1995b). Philosophy determines principles for guiding action by serving as the foundation for educational decisions. Educators' values, attitudes, and beliefs spring from their philosophies—so do various approaches to supervision—and how to teach it.

McNeil (1982) argued that supervision should rely on a scientific approach, which holds to the theory that teaching is a science and, as such, can be examined and improved using the scientific method. An underlying assumption to this approach is that the efficiency of teachers would be increased through the guidance of a supervisor who would translate aims of the school into terms that the teachers understand. Tracing the progress of research on teaching effectiveness,

McNeil concluded that "There is little hope that (scientific) research will bring authoritativeness to supervision. Research does not cover the whole terrain of the classroom. Also, many of the scientific findings will be rejected on other grounds—political, economic. Further, teachers and supervisors will not agree that any finding is sufficiently established to serve as the final word of authority" (p. 32).

Eisner (1992) offers a competing theory that conceptualizes teaching as an art. According to Eisner, "One of the great ironies of contemporary education is that although teaching is often regarded as an art or a craft, it is most often studied as if it were, or aspired to be, a science. Almost any teacher will tell you that teaching is far from scientific. Yet the study of teaching and the conduct of supervision has, in general, been undertaken using scientific—some would say scientistic—assumptions and methods" (p. 53).

Sergiovanni and Starratt (1995) suggest that different theories of supervision and teaching compete with one another. Traditional scientific management, human relations, and neoscientific management represent three general theories of supervision. Each makes different assumptions about human nature, about authority, and about decision-making, which result in different expectations for the functions of supervision.

There are differences in theoretical and philosophical perspectives of supervision. Competing ideas are contextualized by beliefs about school curriculum and purpose. Ornstein and Hunkins (1988) identified five distinct approaches to curriculum that illustrate diverse positions on how individuals view schools: (1) behavioral-rational, (2) systems managerial, (3) intellectual-academic, (4) humanistic-ascetic, and (5) reconceptualist. Most supervisory orientations fall into one or more of these approaches as can be inferred when they are interpreted in light of the evolution of supervisory roles.

Given the dilemma of the definition of supervision, it seems appropriate to inquire about how individuals come to understand this concept. How one "knows" supervision, it stands to reason, will influence the way in which one "does" supervision; and more importantly, how one teaches supervision. How does one learn to supervise? Does how one "knows" and "does" supervision have anything to do with how one was taught supervision? How is supervision taught? Are there programs of study for supervision?

Looking back on the field and practice of supervision, it is apparent that there is a rich tradition filled with the best of intentions for bringing teachers and schools closer to their ideals. It seems that the tasks of supervision have been specified in each era to respond to the perceived needs of the time. The role of supervisor has evolved and transformed during the last century and with its evolution, the functions of supervision shifted to align with the roles. There is reason to believe that this evolution will continue.

One common thread running through the definition of supervision from age to age has been the idea that it is an "enabling activity." Supervisors aim to enable teachers to do a better job in helping students learn. They aim to enable schools to fulfill their purposes as organizations or as communities. While not much is written on this topic, supervisors have attempted to enable administrators to keep their very busy eyes on the quality and equity of education for all students.

If "enabling" is the common thread that carries through from age to age in supervision, is it also important to be more specific about enabling for what? Enabling is a means to an end—fulfilling the purpose(s) of schooling. According to Glickman, "All of our supervisory actions need to be taken in congruence with the higher principles of our American democracy" (p. 435). Answers to the following questions posed by Goodlad (1990) represent the ends.

What are public schools for in a democratic society? What should they be for, and for whom? Whose interests are served and whose should be served in a system of compulsory education? What is the nature and relationship between the interests of the individual, the family, the community, the state, and the society? Are there reasoned answers to these and like questions, or are there just an assortment of value positions, each as "good" as the other? Or, put another way, are there not fundamental normative positions derived from moral and ethical argument that serve to ground appropriate answers to crucial educational questions such as these? (p. ix)

According to Goodlad (1990), schools exist to prepare and enculturate future voting citizens so they may take part in a democracy. Glickman and co-workers (1995) elaborate on this idea:

"All students are created equal; that they are endowed by their Creator with certain inalienable Rights; that among these are an education that will accord them Life, Liberty, and the pursuit of Happiness; that whenever any public school becomes destructive of preparing students for these ends, it is the Right of the People to alter or abolish it" (p. 438).

In short, supervisors, because of their enabling focus, are vitally important school leaders and supervision should be thought of in terms of leadership. In Sirotnik's (1995) terms, leaders ". . . exercise significant and responsible influence." Supervision, like leadership itself, is a concept that requires a good deal of contextual interpretation and constructed meanings in particular settings, at particular times, for particular purposes, issues, and actions. It may not be sensible to define supervision in any more specific terms. Three key words in the brief definition are *influence*, the power to affect, sway, and persuade people; *exercise*, which conveys deliberate, decision-oriented, action taking; and *significant*, which means not without substance (pedagogical leadership). A fourth key word in the definition is *responsible*. According to Sirotnik (1995), embedded in this word is the moral code that derives from the tacit agreement entered into by educators by virtue of an occupation directed at significantly and profoundly influencing the lives of children.

To better understand supervision as a field and as a practice, it is necessary to explicate and promote the teaching of supervision. How can we understand the curriculum, the instruction of supervision, and the consequences of supervision if we have only a vague picture of how the practice is learned? For a field so long preoccupied with the instructional improvement of teachers, it is ironic that there is little explication of the instruction which goes on within the field itself. One reason that there is a lack of description of how supervision is taught may be the lingering concept that supervisors

must be master teachers, experts in the art and science of pedagogy. This concept suggests that "teachers of supervisors" need to be extraordinary teachers themselves, an intimidating thought. Yet if this is so, the curriculum and instruction of supervisors should stand as exemplars.

Little is known about how individuals learn to supervise. Since most formal experiences occur in graduate schools, it is necessary to explore not only the program of studies for supervision, but also the design and dynamics of the courses. Various textbook authors have staked out ideological territory to be sure, but understanding how those ideologies are conveyed in the classroom and in the field would be enlightening. There is obviously a limit as to what can be learned about supervision in a college classroom. Supervision, after all, is not a spectator sport. Any explication of teaching supervision would need to include a description of what field and practical experiences are used, what activities are performed, and with what consequences?

Clarifying how supervision is taught can do nothing but help the field. Research about teaching supervision should be conducted and reported regularly to the educational community so we can better define the teaching of supervision in the same way that we define other disciplines, for the purpose of enabling the teachers to examine and reflect upon the effects of their own teaching.

The balance of this chapter will be devoted to how supervisors might be taught to enable teachers, groups, and schools. It is impossible to discuss teaching supervision without discussing supervision itself. An effort has been made to separate "teaching supervision" from supervision, but at times this has been difficult.

Different Views of Teaching

Perhaps a key to a better understanding of how supervision is taught lies in the conception of teaching itself. The ideologies of instructors of supervision probably have implications for the content and processes used to prepare supervisors. Darling-Hammond and Sclan (1992) summarized two identifiably different views about teaching which influence supervision (and therefore the preparation of supervisors).

One view of teaching emphasizes the production of specific teacher behaviors thought to represent "effective teaching" (Hunter, 1984). Tracy and MacNaughten (1989) call this a "neo-traditionalist" approach and link its intellectual heritage to behavioral psychologists such as E. L. Thorndike. This view concerns specifying and producing teacher behaviors thought to increase those student behaviors believed to be associated with learning.

The neo-traditional view of teaching illustrates an epistemology derived from positivist philosophy. Technical rationality holds that practitioners are (at best) instrumental problem solvers (Schon, 1987). This view of teaching can be equated with the "effective schools" movement, proficiency testing, and other activities that attempt to reduce teaching to a set of controlled behaviors. In the struggle to define effective teaching using a technical rational approach, teaching has been reduced to a series of behaviors supported by "scientific" research. Such research has been almost always predicated on didactic methods used in elementary settings which seemed to produce high scores on tests of basic skills. One example of technical rationality in supervision is the Florida Performance Measurement System (FPMS) (Darling-Hammond & Sclan, 1992). The FPMS specifies an extensive list of teaching behaviors to be enacted by a classroom teacher and tallied by an evaluator, thus reducing teaching to a set of technical operations.

When the role of teacher is depicted in technical rational terms, supervision is concerned with translating research for teachers and monitoring its implementation in the classroom. Teaching supervision then becomes a matter of acquainting aspiring supervisors with the research on effective teaching, and making them proficient in the skills necessary to verify that research is being implemented in the classroom. The traditional view of teaching has been described by Nolan and Francis (1992) as follows:

1. Learning is a process of accumulating bits of information and isolated skills.
2. The teacher's primary responsibility is to transfer his (her) knowledge directly to students.
3. Changing student behavior is the teacher's primary goal.
4. The process of teaching and learning focuses primarily on the interactions between the teacher and individual students.
5. Thinking and learning skills are viewed as transferable across all content areas (p. 45).

Nolan and Francis have also described how technical rational supervisors and teachers conceptualize teaching and learning in basic education. Can this be extended? When supervisors conceptualize teaching and learning from a technical rational perspective, do they also expect that these principles apply to their own learning? If so, teaching supervision has much in common with teaching other subjects in elementary and secondary schools. These authors refer to these beliefs and related activities as "teacher-centered" (p. 46). In this approach, the supervisor and teacher come together to examine a teacher's observable behavior and to discuss it in light of generalizable teaching behaviors that have been identified by research as promoting student learning.

To be consistent with the technical rational orientation, the teacher of supervision would:

1. have clear and specific objectives for student learning that would relate to the perceived tasks and functions of supervision as described earlier,
2. organize and structure tasks and skills appropriate to supervision,
3. use examples and illustrations of this type of supervision,
4. model the appropriate application of the desired skills,
5. have students practice those skills so that they will be retained and eventually transferred to practice, and
6. assess students by requiring them to reproduce the desired knowledge and skill through some demonstration or test.

The format of numerous texts in the field of supervision suggests that the technical rational approach has been used to prepare supervisors (Boyan & Copeland, 1978; Oliva, 1993). Brookfield (1995) criticized teachers of adults with a reduc-

tionist cast of mind who believe that the dynamics and contradictions of teaching can be reduced to something linear and quantifiable as being "epistemologically challenged."

A second view of teaching is assumed when supervision focuses on the development of a reflective teaching orientation stimulated by the teachers' individual contexts and felt needs. Tracy and MacNaughton (1989) characterized this approach to supervision as "neo-progressive" because it can be traced to approaches advocated by Dewey, Piaget, and Bruner. According to Darling-Hammond (1992), "'neo-progressives' are concerned with developing deliberative classrooms that support both teachers and students in constructing meaning from their interactions with each other and with the world they study" (1992, p. 15).

In his book *Educating the Reflective Practitioner* (1987), Schon notes the contrast between a neo-progressive approach and a neo-traditional approach:

In the varied topography of professional practice, there is a high, hard ground overlooking a swamp. On the high ground, manageable problems lend themselves to solution through the application of research-based theory and technique. In the swampy lowland, messy, confusing problems defy technical solution. The irony of this situation is that the problems on the high ground tend to be relatively unimportant to individuals or society at large, however great their technical interest may be, while in the swamp lie the problems of greatest human concern. The practitioner must choose. Shall he remain on the high ground where he can solve relatively unimportant problems according to prevailing standards of rigor, or shall he descend into the swamp of important problems and non rigorous inquiry? (p. 3)

Schon refers to this second conceptualization of teaching and learning as springing from an "epistemology of practice." In contrast to the technical approach, which values conformity and reductionist thinking about teaching and learning, the neo-progressive view is that teachers are thoughtful, creative persons who use a set of principles and strategies derived from an informed personal philosophy of education and the multiple demands of learning contexts (Darling-Hammond, 1992). In this view, the dispositions, skills, and knowledge required for teaching include, but are not limited to, the disposition to reflect on one's own teaching and its effects on learners, to respect and value cultural differences, and to engage in critical and divergent thinking and problem solving with students (Darling-Hammond, 1992). Schon (1987) argues that the relationship between practice competence and professional knowledge needs to be turned upside down, that is, educators need to first focus on the artistry of practice competence, not professional knowledge.

Interestingly, such an approach requires educators to have an understanding of scientific inquiry and epistemology, as well as knowledge about behavior and cognition, cultures, human growth and development, social organizations, ethics, communication and language, learning contexts, and subject matter (Darling-Hammond referring to the Minnesota Internship Program [MBOT]). Schon (1987) describes this alternative epistemology as teacher artistry understood in terms of "reflection in action." He describes this form of professional artistry:

On this view, we would recognize as a limiting case situations in which it is possible to make a routine application of existing rules and procedures to the fact of particular problematic situations. Beyond these situations familiar rules, theories, and techniques are put to work in concrete instances through . . . a limited form of reflection in action. And beyond these, we would recognize cases of problematic diagnosis in which practitioners not only follow rules of inquiry but also sometimes respond to findings by inventing new rules, on the spot (p. 35).

Nolan and Francis (1992) offered principles of teaching and learning associated with this view:

1. All learning, except rote memorization, requires the learner to actively construct meaning.
2. Students' prior understandings of and thoughts about a topic or concept before instruction exert tremendous influence on what they learn during instruction.
3. The teachers' primary goal is to generate a change in the learner's cognitive structure or way of viewing and organizing the world.
4. Because learning is a process of active construction by the learner, the teacher cannot do the work of learning.
5. Learning in cooperation with others is an important source of motivation, support, modeling, and coaching.

There are at least two implications for teachers of supervision in this approach to teaching and learning. First they need to embrace an epistemology of practice and reflection; and second, the new epistemology would need to be manifest in their own teaching. For teachers of supervision who have been long immersed in the tradition of positivism, moving toward a different set of educational assumptions will not be easy. Changing one's world view never is.

Since Schon coined the term "reflective practitioner" in 1987, reflection has been co-opted to mean almost any retrospective thought about teaching. Smyth (1992) and Zeichner (1994) both pointed out that the term *reflective practice* becomes meaningless if it is used to describe any approach to teaching that is popular. Brookfield (1995) noted that everyone, regardless of his ideological orientation, has jumped on the bandwagon in using the term.

Artistry in teaching as described by Schon should not be confused with unexamined common sense. According to Brookfield, "unexamined common sense is a notoriously unreliable guide to action" (p. 4). This author argues that teachers need to exercise "critical reflection," a concept which has two distinctive purposes. The first purpose is for teachers to understand how considerations of power influence and distort educational processes and interactions. A common example that most teachers recognize occurs when a principal or supervisor comes to their classroom to observe a lesson. Suddenly, the teacher's behavior alters and students react to the change in predictable ways—those who want to help the teacher look good, become more active and attentive; those who want to embarrass the teacher become more unruly or lethargic. Because of the underlying influence of the observer's power, the climate of the classroom is distorted. Critical reflection requires the teacher to acknowledge and understand classrooms as places of some ideological conflict.

According to Brookfield (1995), teachers become aware of the pervasiveness of power and they begin to notice the oppressive dimensions of practices that they thought were neutral or even benevolent. They also begin to explore how power over learners can become power with learners (p. 9).

The second purpose of critical reflection is for teachers to uncover assumptions that they believe are in their own best interest, but that have actually been designed by more powerful others to work against them in the long term. Hegemony is the process by which ideas, structures and actions come to be seen by the majority of people as wholly natural, preordained, and working for their own good, when they are acutely constructed and transmitted by powerful minority interests to protect the status quo that serves those interests (Gramsci, 1978). Examples of hegemonic practices abound, but the most harmful may be commercialized products or programs that promise to solve all manner of instructional problems for teachers. Teacher proof curricula, canned discipline programs, and other commercially advertised techniques promoted to solve classroom dilemmas only serve to limit reflective practice and distort the manner in which teachers see their role.

To be consistent with an epistemology of practice, a teacher of supervision would: (1) honor the expansive reservoir of experiences of students and use it in any learning situation (Knowles, 1984); (2) help students inquire and problem solve and cope with their own emotional needs and tensions as well as the needs and tensions of those around them; (3) foster critical reflection; (4) facilitate self assessment with regard to the impact on the learning of others (5) rouse cognitive tensions and disequilibria in students without threatening their sense of self-worth and security; and (6) Model principles 1–5.

METAPHORS FOR TEACHING SUPERVISION

Good teaching is second only to good parenting in its complexity. It cannot be reduced to a formula. Teaching supervision carries with it a special responsibility since the potential impact of preparing educational leaders is profound. Although good teaching is complex and sometimes mysterious, it can and should be understood by those who do it.

Two models for teaching supervision combine various concepts of research and practice and should be applied metaphorically as well as literally. These models are not designed for mechanical application, but should be considered thought frames that have the potential to enhance the future supervisor's reflective practice. As Sergiovanni and Starratt (1993) explain, "Informed intuition and reflective practice are key concepts in understanding the link between knowledge and use. Neither is directly dependent upon models of teaching, but neither can evolve separately from such models" (p. 130).

Teachers of supervision are concerned with conceptual rather than instrumental knowledge. They strive to develop a reflective, professional knowledge that an accumulation of the referentially based decisions that supervisors make as they practice. The two approaches that follow are not the only approaches to teaching supervision by any stretch of the imagination, but they can be useful and powerful proposals for preparing supervisors in the future.

Clinical Supervision as a Metaphor

The term *clinical supervision,* like *reflection,* has unfortunately come to mean many different things to many different people. If one goal of teaching supervision is to enable the supervisor to work individually with teachers, then clinical supervision is an indispensable process. Developed in the 1970s by Morris Cogan and Robert Goldhammer (Garman, 1982), this approach to supervision has been interpreted, reinterpreted, and often misinterpreted by supervisors since its inception. The clinical supervision referred to here has been clearly described in the literature (Garman, 1982; Nolan, Hawkes, & Francis, 1993; and Pajak, 1993). Clinical supervision as a concept differs from the procedural orientation most often referred to in the literature. It is meant here as a metaphor for reflective practice very consistent with the notions of Schon (1987)and Brookfield (1995). It is not only a form of direct assistance to teachers (Glickman, Gordan, & Ross-Gordon, 1995), but also an approach to schooling that influences school culture.

Goldhammer, Anderson, and Krajewski (1980) describe the procedure of clinical supervision as follows: (1) preconference with teacher, (2) observation of classroom, (3) analyzing and interpreting observation, (4) postconference with teacher (5) critique of previous four steps.

This procedural approach was criticized by Garman (1982) after analyzing hundreds of conferences this way: supervisor officiates; teacher confesses his/her transgressions; supervisors suggest ways to repent; teacher agrees to recant; supervisor assists in penance; teacher makes "acts of contrition"; supervisor gives absolution; both go away feeling better.

Garman (1982) eschews the procedural approach. She argues that clinical supervision is more conceptual and reflective. She describes the process as a metaphor consistent with reflective practice:

A person becomes a clinical supervisor when he/she begins to think and act as if the "cycle of supervision" were a metaphor as well as a method; when observation and analysis are not only procedural phases for actions in classrooms, but also represent the empirical approach inherent in a skilled service; when the notion of conference not only means two people meeting before and after classroom visits, but also suggests dynamic forms of collaboration in educational alliances; when the image of "cycle" not only guarantees repeated performance, but also refers to high levels of involvement and commitment that press participants toward the "connectedness" of collegiality; when the teacher–supervisor relationship stands for ethical conduct as it is lived out in important choices. The specificity of the method can inform us about the unbounding qualities of the metaphor (p. 52).

Viewing clinical supervision as a metaphor, Garman describes the concepts of collegiality, collaboration, skilled service, and ethical conduct which must become the supervisors' habits of mind. These concepts represent principles by which supervision can be taught and learned. (For an explication of these concepts, see *The Clinical Approach to*

Supervision in Supervision of Teaching in the ASCD Yearbook, 1982).

Problem-Based Learning as a Metaphor

Problem based learning (PBL) has been described as a promising approach to professional development for educational leaders (Bridges and Hallinger, 1995); however, a growing number of professors of educational leadership have come to share the view that PBL may be more than simply a new teaching tool for preparing future educational leaders. They believe that PBL may also be a promising metaphor for supervision. This approach to professional preparation may undo the tradition and belief that knowledge is created at the university and passed down to practitioners. PBL, Murphy (1995) suggests, may help to solve one of the profession's most knotty problems—"that of the breach between the academic and practice arms of the profession" (in Bridges and Hallinger, 1995, p. x). PBL provides an approach to learning that recognizes and honors the array of beliefs, skills, and knowledge needed to be a successful school supervisor. For teachers of supervision, PBL provides students with an opportunity to work colleagially in groups on and with complex problems relevant to practice. PBL is an approach to leadership preparation based on principles of adult learning and strategies of integrated curriculum.

Programs that prepare and certify supervisors need to have an integrated approach to learning that deals with the problems of practice. Supervision cannot be learned as a series of discreet subjects to be studied and mastered. Problems and dilemmas are rarely separated into content areas in schools; rather, they are multidimensional and interrelated, that is "swampy." Fractionalization of subject matter does little to illustrate how supervision works in reality.

Whereas traditional preparation programs could be described as "content centered," PBL is an integrated approach that can be described as "problem centered." In contrast to a traditionally content-centered curriculum, PBL removes the emphasis on discreet subject areas and focuses on authentic educational problems, complex enough to draw a variety of content knowledge into play. Subject areas are drawn upon, but only insofar as they relate to a contextualized educational dilemma. Course work, then, is organized in seminars centered around themes that use problems found in the field.

PBLs come in as many varieties as there are problems of practice. They usually begin with a scenario and end with a charge to the group that is solving the problem. A good PBL is one in which learners can only succeed when they think, problem solve, and justify their solutions. PBL has the following characteristics:

- The starting point for learning is a (school-related, contextualized) problem for which an individual lacks a ready response.
- The problem is one that students are apt to encounter as future educational leaders.
- Knowledge that students are expected to acquire during their professional training is organized around problems rather than disciplines.

- Students, individually and collectively, assume a major responsibility for their own learning.
- Most of the learning occurs within the context of small group activity rather than in lectures (Bridges, 1992).

According to Bridges (1992), there are four propositions as a rationale for using PBL instead of a traditional curriculum: (1) Students retain little of what they learn when taught in a traditional lecture format. (2) Students often do not use the knowledge they have learned appropriately. (3) Since students forget much of what is learned or use knowledge inappropriately, instructors should create conditions that optimize retrieval and appropriate use of the knowledge in future professional practice. (4) PBL creates the three conditions that information theory links to subsequent retrieval and appropriate use of new information: activation of prior knowledge, similarity of context in which information is learned and later applied; and opportunity to elaborate on that information (p. 8).

Bridges (1992) discusses the cognitive, motivational, and functional grounds for using the PBL approach. This approach to curriculum is not new. In fact, it is similar to the problem-solving method John Dewey described as early as 1916 (Tanner and Tanner, 1995). Dewey argued that intellectual ability is the outcome of opportunity. He suggested that curriculum should link the individual with the environment—real world—and not depend on either memory or empty tradition. The underlying assumptions of PBL about knowledge are consistent with Dewian philosophy. PBL proponents assume that both knowing and doing are of equal value and importance.

Curriculum developers and program designers have been actively promoting integrated curricula and teaming (Jacobs, 1989; Drake, 1993; and Beane, 1995). They point to several reasons for taking an integrated approach to the preparation of supervisors. First, there has been unprecedented growth of knowledge in organizational development and leadership theory. (What is the basic information needed for supervisors in the twenty-first century?) Second, traditional preparation programs have been too fragmented. Students are often left on their own to make connections from one content course to another. Third, some students complain that course content is not relevant. Information seems too obscure to be helpful in practice. PBL has the potential to transcend these difficulties. It is relevant since the problems themselves come from practice. It is authentic because students must draw upon numerous areas of study to resolve a problem. Finally, the knowledge students use during PBL is more readily retained since it is introduced in context.

Dewey's problem-solving method rests on the principle that educational opportunity means shared knowledge and concerns:

the problem is one of learning together as well as what is learned. Learning together fosters the development of individual interests and talents as well as a sense of social responsibility. PBL requires that supervisors learn to work collaboratively with others in groups or teams. The hope is that students of supervision will extend the practice of collaboration in the workplace. A strong theme in problem-based teaching is that educational supervisors share a moral responsibility for creating a culture in school that contributes to the principles of democracy. In emphasizing teamwork and collaboration teachers of supervision model what must be done to create democratic schools.

Enough cannot be said about the benefits of dealing with real problems as a means of preparing supervisors. The act of finding and setting problems is important. Attention to the human and moral dimensions of schools is crucial. Working collaboratively in teams is more in step with the contemporary thinking which characterizes schools as communities.

CONCLUSION

This chapter has presented a profile of the troubled history of supervision. It has been demonstrated that teaching supervision depends on the contexts and referents that one uses as well as the ascription to a technical rational epistemology, or an epistemology of practice. Teaching supervision should include critical reflection through the use of two metaphors: clinical supervision and problem-based learning. Hopefully, the principles embedded in these two metaphors will assist those who teach supervision in the future.

PBL is a powerful approach to teaching supervisors, which has enabled professors to reexamine their own teaching. It is an approach that allows them to draw upon the wisdom and craft knowledge of practitioners. It provides opportunities to model collaborative problem-solving and democratic processes. PBL helps to address issues of power ethics on which a preparation program for supervision might rest. It enables students and professors alike to integrate subjects and disciplines within the fields of supervision, curriculum and leadership.

Beyond the classroom, PBL can provide a connection to practice as teachers of supervision work with schools. It has the potential to be a tool for mutual renewal between public school programs and university preparation programs. It contributes to co-reform which strengthens a growing network of educators in the field. PBL is more than a new or revisited instructional methodology, it can be the means by which educational community is constructed.

REFERENCES

Acheson, K. & Gall, M. (1987). *Techniques in the clinical supervision of teachers.* New York: Longman.

Alfonso, R., Firth, G., & Neville, R. (1981). *Instructional supervision: A behavior system.* Boston: Allyn and Bacon, Inc.

Beach, D. M. & Reinhartz, J. (1989). *Supervision: Focus on instruction.* New York: Harper & Row.

Beane, J. (1995). *Toward a coherent curriculum.* Alexandria, VA: ASCD.

Bolin, F. & Panaritis, P. (1992). Searching for a common purpose: A perspective on the history of supervision. In C. Glickman (Ed.). *Supervision in Transition* (pp. 30–43). Alexandria, VA: ASCD.

Boyan, N. A. & Copeland, W. (1978). *Instructional supervision training program.* Columbus, OH: Charles Merrill Publishing Company.

Bridges, E. A. & Hallinger, P. (1995). *Implementing problem-based learning in leadership development.* Eugene: ERIC Clearinghouse on Educational Management.

Brookfield, S. D. (1995). *Becoming a critically reflective Teacher.* San Francisco, CA: Jossey-Bass.

Corey, S. M. (1963, November). A more wholesome balance. *Educational Leadership, 21,* 67–68.

Darling-Hammond, L. & Sclan, E. (1992). Policy and supervision. In C. Glickman (Ed.). *Supervision in transition* (pp. 7–29). Alexandria, VA: ASCD.

Drake, S. (1993). *Planning integrated curriculum.* Alexandria, VA: ASCD.

Eash, M. J. (1969). Is systems analysis for supervisors? *Educational Leadership, 26*(5), 482–489.

Eisner, E. W. (1979). *The educational imagination of the design and evaluation of school programs* (2nd ed.). New York: Macmillan.

Eisner, E. W. (1982). An artistic approach to supervision. In T. J. Sergiovanni (Ed.). *Supervision of teaching* (pp. 53–66). Alexandria, VA: ASCD.

Garman, N. B. (1986). Reflection, the heart of clinical supervision: A modern rationale for professional practice. *Journal of Curriculum and Supervision, 2*(1), 1–24.

Garmen, N. (1982). The clinical approach to supervision. In T. Sergiovanni (Ed.). *Supervision of teaching* (pp. 35–52). Alexandria, VA: ASCD.

Glickman, C. D. (1993). *Renewing America's schools: A guide for school-based action.* San Francisco, CA: Jossey-Bass.

Glickman, C. D. (Ed.). (1992). *Supervision in transition.* Alexandria, VA: ASCD.

Glickman, C. D., et al. (1995). *Supervision of instruction: A developmental approach.* Boston: Allyn and Bacon.

Goodlad, J. I. (1990). *Teachers for our nation's schools.* San Francisco, CA: Jossey-Bass.

Goldhammer, R., Anderson, R., & Krajewski, R. (1980). *Clinical supervision* (2nd ed.). New York: Holt, Rinehart and Winston.

Gordon, S. (1992). Paradigms, transitions, and the new supervision. *Journal of Curriculum and Supervision, 8,* 62–76.

Gramsci, A. (1978). *Selection from the prison notebooks.* London: Lawrence and Wishhart.

Harris, B. M. (1985). *Supervisory behavior in education* (3rd ed.). Englewood Cliffs: Prentice-Hall.

Jacobs, H. (1989). *Interdisciplinary curriculum: Design and implementation.* Alexandria, VA: ASCD.

Leeper, R. R. (Ed.). (1969). *Supervision: Emerging Profession.* Washington, D.C.: ASCD, NEA.

MacDonald, J. B. (1965). Knowledge about supervision: Rationalization or rationale. *Educational Leadership, 23*(2), 161–163.

McCutchen, G. (1995). Curriculum theory and practice for the 1990s. In A. Ornstein & L. Behar (Ed.). *Contemporary issues in curriculum* (pp. 3–9). Boston: Allyn and Bacon.

McNeil, J. D. (1982). A scientific approach to supervision. In T. J.

Sergiovanni (Ed.). *Supervision of teaching,* (pp. 18–34). Alexandria, VA: ASCD.

McNeil, J. D. (1962). *Supervision: A synthesis of thought and action.* New York: McGraw Hill.

Mosher, R. & Purpel, D. (1972). *Supervision: The reluctant profession.* Boston: Houghton Mifflin.

Murphy, J. (1995). Foreward, *implementing problem-based learning in leadership development,* (pp. ix–xiii). Eugene: ERIC Clearinghouse on Educational management.

Nolan, J. & Francis, P. (1992). Changing perspectives in curriculum and instruction. In C. D. Glickman (Ed.). *Supervision in transition* (pp. 44–60). Alexandria, VA: ASCD.

Nolan, J., Hawkes, B., & Francis, P. (1993). Case studies: Windows into clinical supervision. *Educational Leadership, 51*(2), 52–56.

Oliva, P. (1993). *Supervision for today's schools* (4th ed.). New York: Longman.

Ornstein, A. & Behar, L. (1995). *Contemporary issues in curriculum.* (1st ed.). Boston: Allyn and Bacon.

Ornstein, A. & Hunkins, F. (1988). *Curriculum: Foundations, principles, and issues.* Englewood Cliffs: Prentice Hall.

Ornstein, A. C. (1995a). Curriculum, instruction, and supervision: Their relationship and the role of the principal. In A. C. Ornstein & L. S. Behar (Eds.). *Contemporary issues in curriculum* (pp. 281–287). Boston: Allyn and Bacon.

Ornstein, A. C. (1995b). Philosophy as a basis for curriculum decisions. In A. Ornstein & L. Behar (Eds.). *Contemporary issues in curriculum,* (pp. 10–17). Boston: Allyn and Bacon.

Pajak, E. F. (1989). *Identification of supervisory proficiencies project.* University of Georgia (available from the ASCD) Alexandria, VA: ASCD.

Pahak, E. F. (1993). *Approaches to clinical supervision: Alternatives for improving instruction.* Needham Heights, MA: Christopher-Gordon.

Schon, D. A. (1987). *Educating the reflective practitioner.* San Francisco, CA: Jossey-Bass.

Sergiovanni, T. J. (Ed.). (1982). *Supervision of teaching.* Alexandria, VA: ASCD.

Sirotnik, K. A. (1995). Curriculum: Overview and framework. In M. O'Hair & S. Odell (Ed.). *Educating teachers for leadership and change: Teacher education yearbook III,* (pp. 235–242). Thousand Oaks, CA: Corwin Press, Inc.

Smyth, W. J. (1992). Teachers' work and the politics of reflection. *American Educational Research Journal, 29*(2), 267–300.

Starratt, T. J. & Sergiovanni, R. J. (1993). *Supervision: A redefinition* (5th ed.). New York: McGraw-Hill.

Tanner, D. & Tanner, L. (1995). *Curriculum development.* Englewood Cliffs, NJ: Prentice Hall.

Tracy, S. J. (1995, May/June). How historical concepts of supervision relate to supervisory practices today. *The Clearing House, 68,* 320–325.

Wiles, J. & Bondi, J. (1980). *Supervision: A guide to practice* (1st ed.). Columbus, OH: Charles E. Merrill.

Zeichner, K. M. (1994). Research on teacher thinking and thinking and different views of reflective practice in teaching and teacher education. In G. H. I. Carlgren & S. Vaage (Eds.). *Teachers' minds and actions: Research on teachers' thinking and practice.* Bristol: Falmer Press.

POLICY AND LEGAL CONSIDERATIONS
IN SUPERVISION

Helen M. Hazi

WEST VIRGINIA UNIVERSITY

INTRODUCTION

Much has been written about instructional supervision (i.e., classroom visitation, curriculum work, and staff development) in general, but limited research from a legal perspective with a focus on supervision. It is hoped that this chapter fills this void and gives readers a framework for thinking about law and policy and research, with a focus on supervision in their own states.

In this chapter, information is synthesized from disparate disciplines and sources, making it accessible to practitioners and scholars who want to inquire into this dimension of supervision. The scope of this chapter is the regulation of supervision in the 50 states with a concentration in the past two decades. Citations span the 1940s through the present, range from the seminal to the illustrative, and include reviews of research and writings, legal research, and selected and relevant case law, statutes, and regulations.

This chapter is organized into five sections. The introduction includes definitions of law, policy, and supervision. The next three sections explicate the regulation of each of three aspects of supervision—classroom visitation, curriculum work, and staff development—and present directions for research. A final section has the conclusion.

Law, Policy, and Supervision Defined

In a society where individuals live in close proximity, law attempts to: protect individuals from violence and domination, prevent the destruction or seizure of property, and promote fairness and honesty in dealings with others. Thus, laws are "the minimum forms of protection for persons, property, and promises" (Hart, 1961, p. 195). Law promotes rules to govern these constantly recurring situations, appeals to individual conscience to maintain these rules, and enforces them when voluntary cooperation is not enough. Law is based on the principles of justice and impartiality. Justice maintains or restores a balance among individuals. Impartiality assures that law is applied without prejudice, interest, or caprice to all those situations that are alike (Hart, 1961).

Law comes from the legislative, judicial, and executive branches of government at the federal, state, and local levels. Law takes the form of legislation, case law, executive decree, and administrative regulation. School boards, state boards of education, legislators, judges, governors, attorney generals, and the President of the United States have legal authority and thus make law in their respective forms.

Those who have legal authority also have a persuasive power. They have the power to set policy or goals that serve as "guides to action" (which may or may not result in a form of law). For example, a governor, may issue a white paper for education in the year 2020. It contains a vision based on what is valued about education, but it has no force of law. The white paper may eventually result in regulations from a state board of education, but in this form it only has persuasive power. Thus, the policy milieu is the overarching, goal-oriented framework within which law (e.g., legislation) may be one tool for accomplishing goals. Allocating funds may be another policy tool used to regulate, control, promote services, or otherwise influence matters.

Complicating the policy arena is the existence of individuals or groups who have no legal authority, but are nonetheless influential. Individuals who have their own goals include lobbyists, business leaders, test and textbook publishers, state superintendents, teacher associations, taxpayer groups, and school critics. Their influence comes from their ability to persuade others to provide or deny funds or services, expand or limit choices or solutions to problems, or raise awkward questions that cannot easily be dismissed or addressed.

Thus, a policy is "a set of values expressed in words, issued with authority, and reinforced with power (often money or penalties) in order to induce a shift toward these values" (Marshall, Mitchell, & Wirt, 1989, p. 6). *Policy making* is a term used when referring to the political process by which different competing actors and groups influence the formulation of goals (and ultimately the formulation of law) at the local, state, or federal levels. The focus of this chapter is on those laws and policies in the states that concern supervision.

The authors of three dozen popular and representative supervision textbooks published in the past 60 years construe practice in terms of three functions (Holland, 1994). Supervision is a practice that deals with classroom visitation, curriculum work, and staff development. Regardless of job title, when individuals are engaged in any one of these three functions, they are engaged in supervision. Sometimes they are vested in one position called a supervisor; but this tends to be the exception, rather than the rule. For the purposes of this chapter, when the word *supervisor* is used, it means any individual who is engaged in any one of these three functions.

Classroom visitation is the most regulated aspect of supervisory practice nationwide. It is dominated by law from legislators, the courts, state boards of education, and local school boards. Curriculum work is less regulated nationwide by law than classroom visitation, but is dominated more by key actors in the policy arena. Staff development is the least regulated of the three, but is becoming an important tool in policy-making to improve teacher quality. The following three sections illustrate how each is regulated, what is the result of this regulation, and directions for research.

CLASSROOM VISITATION

Classroom visitation is the most regulated aspect of supervision. Classroom visitations may be done by administrators (or sometimes peers) and may be done for the purpose of offering assistance and/or for the purpose of conducting an annual performance rating for personnel decisions, which can ultimately result in teacher dismissal. Because there is so much regulation of teacher evaluation and teacher dismissal, classroom visitation, for any purpose, usually takes on a legal tone. As a result, supervisors may find themselves spending time and energy establishing legally defensible conduct.

Much has been written about teacher evaluation in general, but limited research exists from a legal perspective with a focus on supervision. Levin (1979), Millman (1981), and Soar, Medley, and Coker (1983) present useful summaries of practice and educational research prior to the 1980s. According to Levin (1979), much of the early literature presented theories, models, forms, and examples with limited research. Since the 1980s, authors such as Darling-Hammond, Wise, and Pease (1983), Wise, Darling-Hammond, McLaughlin, and Bernstein (1984), Millman and Darling-Hammond (1990) and Edward Iwanicki, founder of the *Journal of Personnel Evaluation in Education* have helped collect what has been typically fragmented writings and research of this emerging speciality.

Writings range from simple prescriptions based on wisdom of practice (e.g., Chirnside, 1984; Ellis, 1985; Jacobson, 1984)

to comprehensive analyses of law, policy, and practice based on research (e.g., Rebell, 1990; Wise et al. 1984). Research methods include: case study, legal analysis, policy analysis, interviews, and surveys of practice (e.g., Stiggins & Bridgeford, 1985). Some authors have proposed a research agenda (e.g., Strike & Millman, 1983). Still, writings more than research dominate the literature.

When those from the field of supervision write about teacher evaluation, they critique existing practice and its entanglements with supervision (e.g., Blumberg, 1974; Hazi, 1988; Smyth, 1986), its scientism (Hazi & Garman, 1988), and its pretense and quackery (Garman, 1986, 1987). Still others have attempted to explicate a theory of evaluation (e.g., Sergiovanni, 1984), promote models or effective practices (e.g., McGreal, 1983), and promote the integration of evaluation with other supervisory functions (e.g., McQuarrie & Wood, 1991). Few in supervision look at its legal dimensions (e.g., Hazi, 1994; Tracy & Smeaton, 1993).

The Regulation

When supervisors and others ask the question "What law regulates my classroom visits with teachers?" they have to look to three levels of legal activity, at the federal, state, and local levels. At the federal level, they must be aware of important legislation and cases ruled on by the federal courts. At the state level, they must look to school code, case law, and administrative regulation. At the local level, they must look to board policy, and, where they exist, to the collective bargaining agreement, and grievances. Further complicating this inquiry is the appearance of additional state law or policy which may not be titled *teacher evaluation* or *teacher dismissal,* but, nevertheless, is superimposed on existing law and complicates this aspect of practice. Supervisors may find rules governing classroom visitation in law regarding career ladders, internships, or mentor programs. Indeed, the act of observing teachers may be governed by a legal labyrinth, depending on the activity of boards of education, teacher associations, and legislators within a state.

This body of law has evolved over the past four decades. Prior to the 1960s, teacher evaluation was left to local discretion and educators were considered employees-at-will, where the school board could dismiss them for no good cause. When teachers began to challenge their dismissals in court, because they were denied their Fourteenth Amendment rights, their due process rights became established. As state and federal courts ruled on teacher dismissal cases, state legislatures and local school boards began to better define teacher evaluation in the 1970s and 1980s to avoid litigation (and its cost) and to make evaluation practices more rigorous and defensible.

State Stature Sets the Parameters for Evaluation, While District Policy Fills in the Details State statute or regulation typically specifies the purposes of evaluation, who evaluates and is evaluated, the frequency, what is evaluated, and that a post-evaluation conference will occur within some period of time. Evaluation procedures for beginning, probationary teachers are usually different from those who are tenured (Rebell, 1990; Tracy, 1992). Sometimes states mandate evaluator training, approved rating instruments, and local teacher input into the process; however, this is the exception, rather than the rule. States differ greatly on how prescriptive they are about evaluation practices (e.g., Darling-Hammond, 1992; Kuligowski, Holdzkom, & French, 1993; Tracy & Smeaton, 1993).

District policy may go beyond, but not violate, state statute. The teacher collective bargaining agreement, where one exists, may provide further details about evaluation. For example, it may require an orientation, association and/or committee involvement in formulating policy, when and how long observations occur, and how teachers are notified. It may also include details about information not to be used, evaluation report preparation and distribution, pre- and post-conferences, teacher response to the evaluation, how complaints are to be handled, and what happens if improvement is needed (Hazi, 1980).

Board policy may also include such details, but this usually depends on such factors as the number of problems that have occurred, activity of the teachers' association, and relationships between teachers and administrators. In either case, both policy and agreements become subject to court inspection, and, thus, what is written becomes the standard by which actual practice is judged.

Evaluation Must not be Arbitrary or Capricious According to guidelines of the Equal Employment Opportunity Commission, employee selection procedures, including supervisory evaluations, must be job-related, administered in a uniform manner, and must not discriminate against individuals (EEOC, 1978, 1993; Holley & Feild, 1975). If they do, the procedures may be found to be arbitrary and capricious and to violate an individual's civil rights.

This means that criteria must be explicit and made public to teachers. Reasons for dismissal "must be in simple language. . . to advise the employee of their nature so that he can properly prepare a defense . . ." (Rosenberger & Plimpton, 1975, p. 472). This need for well-defined criteria, in part, explains the popularity of teaching-evaluation models like explicit teaching (Rosenshine, 1986) and the Madeline Hunter model (Garman & Hazi, 1988). The Madeline Hunter model is a fairly detailed, seven-step lesson planning model that has been used by administrators as an evaluation template. In fact, at least one New Jersey teacher was successfully dismissed because she did not follow the Madeline Hunter model (*Moran v. Board of Education South Orange-Maplewood School District*, 1986; Hazi & Garman, 1988).

This also means that actual practice must comply with written policy. Supervisors have to be careful about introducing techniques that are not formally part of written policy. For example, if supervisors want to increase the number of observations, use different forms, or use a computer to script lessons, they must consider the consequences, if these actions are not the norm of local practice. The supervisor must consider whether these additives are justifiable and how they will be received. Such action might be considered arbitrary and capricious by teachers (e.g., Hazi, 1994) as well as the courts. Thus, actions and techniques recommended by experts in the field to improve classroom visitation may not always be defensible practice in the courts, if they are used on some, but not on others.

Teachers must be assured of due process Tenure or permanent contract creates an expectation of continued employment. When tenured teachers are dismissed, they are denied the opportunity to practice their livelihood. In the language of the Fourteenth Amendment, teachers cannot be deprived of such a property interest without due process. Tenured teachers also have a liberty interest. A dismissal can diminish the teacher's good name and reputation and limit future employment opportunities. Due process provides certain minimal procedures for protecting these interests.

Generally speaking, due process means that teachers are given "reasonable notification of the charges, an opportunity for a fair hearing before an impartial tribunal, representation by counsel at the hearing, an opportunity to examine adverse witnesses, and the right to appeal an adverse decision" (Rebell, 1990, pp. 343–344). In effect, teachers are given time and multiple contacts, slowing down what once was an all too hasty judgment process, when they were considered employees-at-will. *Board of Regents of State Colleges v. Roth* (1972) and its progeny established these due process procedures. [See Chapter 3 of Yudof, Kirp & Levin (1992) for the evolution of due process through case law.]

Evidence Must Be Substantial and Competent Generally, the courts assume that a certified, tenured teacher who teaches for a period of time without poor ratings is competent. Thus, the burden of proof is on the district to substantiate the dismissal.

The causes by which tenured teachers can be dismissed vary from state to state. The statutory causes include: incapacity, incompetency, inefficiency, insubordination, immorality, reduction in force, neglect of duty, and good cause (Rebell, 1990). Here the courts use no formula, but rather review the evidence and determine cause on a case-by-case basis. The burden of proof is on the person preparing the charge. For the purpose of this chapter, this discussion is limited to incompetency since it is the most problematic for supervisors.

For evidence to be substantial, it must show, especially in the case of incompetency, a pattern of events or reasons over time. Teachers tend not to be dismissed because of an isolated incident of incompetency, especially if they have received prior satisfactory ratings. The supervisor or designee must directly observe the teacher in the classroom over substantial ranges of time that are not too remote. These observations must also be documented. Documentation includes student grades, daily notes, lesson plans and tests, and anecdotal records (Rosenberger & Plimpton, 1975). This means that all supervisory records, even cursory notes or lesson transcripts, have the potential to appear in court one day.

Evidence is provided through testimony of individuals such as educators, students, and parents or community members. The expert opinion of educators is usually more persuasive. Expert opinion is more competent or credible if the expert has: (1) background, training, and certification in evaluation; (2) direct observation of the teacher and records of those observations gathered in a systematic way; and (3) another expert to corroborate the judgment (Rosenberger & Plimpton, 1975). The expertise of supervisors and others can be called into question, if they are not authorized to be in classrooms. In addition, peers can be called into court to provide testimony.

Incompetency is a Matter of Administrative Judgment Of all the grounds for teacher dismissal, incompetency is the most problematic for those who evaluate. Usually incompetency is not the sole cause for dismissal. When it is, incompetency includes: knowledge of subject matter, teaching methods, effect on pupils, and personal attitudes (or a combination of these). According to a review of case law related to teacher incompetency, teaching method (i.e., classroom control and organization) is used as a reason for dismissal more frequently, whereas knowledge of subject matter is used least frequently (Rosenberger & Plimpton, 1975).

The courts usually defer to the expert judgment of administrators. The courts do not decide on whether teachers are incompetent. Rather, they assure that procedures have been followed and that teachers have been provided their due process (Rebell, 1990).

It is worth noting, given the current climate of teacher accountability, that some teachers have been dismissed because of student learning rates. Reasons offered in cases prior to the 1950s include: poor results, the pupils did not learn very much, the pupils did not progress in accordance with their abilities, and the teacher did not teach pupils enough subject material called for in the course of study (Rebell, 1990; Rosenberger & Plimpton, 1975). In a noteworthy case, *Scheelhaase v. Woodbury* (1973), a nontenured Iowa teacher with 10 years of experience was not rehired solely because her students had low scores on the Iowa Test of Basic Skills (ITBS) and the Iowa Test of Educational Development. The district's program had been criticized by the North Central Examining Committee and was on the unapproved list of the Iowa Department of Public Instruction. The Superintendent insisted that "use of the ITBS scores as a measure of teacher competence stood as a reasonable and valid exercise of administrative discretion" (*Scheelhasse*, 1973, p. 239). Other experts for the teacher testified that it was improper to use these test scores as a basis for evaluating teacher performance. The court upheld the dismissal because the state had no tenure law creating an expectation of employment and because the teacher had been provided due process. The court was also reluctant to overturn the decision of the school board "because it believes the expert was wrong or the decision erroneous as long as it was made in good faith by the board" (Phillips, 1993, p. 725; Rebell, 1990).

More recent cases are found in Missouri and Delaware. In *St. Louis Teachers Union v. St. Louis Board of Education* (1987) the city schools initiated a policy to evaluate teachers based on the results of students' scores on the California Achievement Test (CAT). Teachers would receive a satisfactory evaluation if at least 50 percent of their students scored at or above the national norm on the CAT, achieved 10 months growth, or showed positive gain since the previous testing. If not, teachers would receive an unsatisfactory rating, have their salaries frozen, and could lose their jobs if they did not improve. After the second year of the policy, 22 teachers faced dismissal, until the teachers' association filed suit and successfully blocked the attempt. A district court judge denied the school district's motion to dismiss and called for a trial to determine whether the use of the CAT was arbitrary, capricious, and unconstitutional. The parties entered into negotiations and settled out of court (Hazi & Garman, 1988; Phillips, 1993).

In *Jones v. Indian River School District* (1994) a Delaware teacher with 9 years of experience was dismissed for incompetency and insubordination because she gave too many students D's and F's in her Algebra II class and did not use different instructional methods to improve student grades. Administrators claimed these negative grades gave students low self-esteem, turned them off to math, and proved that she was an incompetent teacher (Bradley, 1993). A state superior court judge found that the teacher was denied due process when the school board failed to review all exhibits in the case and when one board member who had children taught by the teacher was prejudiced. When the judge remanded the case back to the school board for a fair hearing, the teacher was reinstated (Jones, 1994).

Improvement Means Some Remediation Improvement of instruction is often a stated purpose of evaluation. It became an important purpose over the decades because one of the questions that courts asked administrators was whether the behavior of the dismissed teacher was remediable or irremediable. Thus, the legal meaning of improvement is remediation.

Irremediable behavior is when "irreparable damage has already been done to students, the faculty, or the school and the damage could not have been corrected if warnings had been given by the teacher's superiors when they learned of the cause" (Rosenberger & Plimpton, 1975, p. 472). Behavior that is remediable or correctable "will entitle a teacher to notice of the complaint against him and time within which to rectify his conduct" (Rosenberger & Plimpton, 1975, p. 472). As in the case of the Delaware teacher, the principal would have to determine whether the teacher's conduct was remediable or irremediable.

According to an analysis of statute and case law, Claxton (1986) warns us that there are no clear-cut definitions of what is irremediable. Although instances of immorality and the commission of crimes (e.g., rape, murder, and child abuse) may be clearer indicators, courts differ as to whether aspects of teaching such as student discipline and control problems are remediable.

Claxton (1986) provides guidance on both the general criteria to consider and the process for remediation. Conduct is irremediable if it: (1) has no positive educational aspect or legitimate professional purpose; (2) diminishes a teacher's effectiveness to teach or has done permanent damage to students, faculty or the school; (3) could not have been corrected had the teacher been warned by the administrators; or (4) has existed for such a long period of time so as to have become irremediable (p. 185). If the conduct is remediable, then Claxton (1986) recommends parameters for the process of remediation. Teachers receive due process for improvement as well: (1) the person or body so authorized should provide timely written notice to the teacher to dismiss, (2) the notice should state with specificity the reasons for finding a deficiency, (3) the teacher should be provided a reasonable amount of time to correct any deficiencies, and (4) an administrator or supervisor may be expected to assist the teacher in an effort to remediate the deficiencies. Improvement means time and assistance for both teacher and supervisor.

It should be noted that there is little guidance from case law on what is a "reasonable" amount of time to improve, unless specified in what Claxton calls a remediation statute. Eighteen states have remediation statutes. Although most do not define *reasonable,* several states define the time in terms of months (e.g., 1, 2, or 3 months) and 1 year (Claxton, 1986). There is also little guidance on what constitutes "assistance" from supervisors. Thus, determining what is remediable, time to improve, and assistance, are within the weighty judgment of those who conduct classroom visits that are associated with annual performance evaluations.

Directions for Research

Much law-based research can be done in this area. Since law constantly changes, updates on a topical, regional, or 50 state basis are periodically needed to track new developments. Topics especially relevant to supervisors include: new procedures for classroom visitation, whether supervisors are designated evaluators, the continuing definition of teacher incompetency, new details about the amount of time for improvement and the kinds of required assistance, and whether certain models of teaching or supervision are promoted.

A series of case studies, using multiple sources of data, can shed light on what regulates classroom visitation at state and local levels. The goal of such research would be to examine comprehensively the multiple sources of law that exist at various levels from the perspective of supervisory practice. Sources of data for analysis might include combinations of the following: relevant statutes, case law, state board regulation, selected collective bargaining agreements and grievances (where they exist), school board policy, and critical incidents of practice involving supervisors. Interviews with members of state departments of education and heads of state teacher associations might also be included.

One example that attempts to be comprehensive within a state is found in Utah. Sperry, Pounder, and Drew (1992) examined four separate pieces of legislation enacted over 19 years that contain elements of evaluation. Each was enacted independently to establish: grounds and procedures for employee termination, a professional practices commission, a career ladder, and evaluation. This analysis shows how additional state law, which may not be specifically titled "teacher evaluation," is superimposed on existing legislation and can result in new directions that influence this aspect of practice. Their contents examined in concert show vague, varied, and even contradictory language that results in multiple interpretations and potential sources of conflict in implementation. Although such analysis is useful for beginning to understand the interface of statutes within a state, it represents one step towards more comprehensively presenting how law impacts practice. Notably absent are findings of case law, grievances, and critical incidents of practice.

Two examples that portray the complexity and interface of law and practice are on the use of the Florida Performance Measurement System (Hazi, 1989a) and grievances filed against a New Jersey supervisor (Hazi, 1994). These case studies, combining legal analyses and critical incidents, make the issues and dilemmas come alive for practitioners as well as policymakers. Research that draws on multiple sources of data and reconstructs the incident into a story with its multiple contexts of law, supervision, and practice can provide new insights into this problematic aspect of the field.

Three recent national efforts related to teacher evaluation are important to track because of their potential to influence state law and policy makers. The first is the National Board for Professional Teaching Standards (NBPTS), which is developing teaching standards and performance assessments in 30 areas for voluntary, national teacher certification. Although NBPTS hopes to establish teaching as "both intellectual and technical work, as both art and science," standards will "show how a teacher's professional judgment is reflected in observable actions" (Barringer, 1993, p. 19). Although these standards can be characterized at this time as general, "they do privilege certain orientations and values about what constitutes effective teaching" (Stilley, personal communication, 8 June, 1994). NBPTS standards represent the profession's first attempt to codify teaching practices.

These standards could become part of state law and regulation. According to Lynn Cornett, director of the Southern Regional Education Board, a policy and research organization for southern states based in Atlanta, Georgia, the southern states await this board's work before attempting to revise their own statewide evaluations instruments (Cornett, personal communications, 20 November, 1992).

Another national effort is the establishment of a national evaluation center. Daniel Stufflebeam at Western Michigan University established the Center for Research on Educational Accountability and Teacher Evaluation (CREATE) in 1990 with a 5-year grant from the U.S. Department of Education. Its mission is to improve the theory and practice of educational evaluation in public and private schools in the 50 states. Three of its projects focus on improving teacher evaluation. This center has launched collaborative projects with researchers throughout the country. It also disseminates information to practitioners and local, state, and federal policymakers through annual conferences, publications, evaluation models, and kits (e.g., Wheeler, Haertel, & Scriven, 1993).

A third national effort is the development of *The Personnel Evaluation Standards.* The Joint Committee on Standards for Educational Evaluation (1988) produced this document to make evaluation "proper, useful, feasible, and accurate." It includes 21 standards to plan and assess systems for evaluating teachers and other educators. It represents an important attempt to codify this aspect of practice. CREATE uses these standards as a foundation for its evaluation models and projects (see also Stufflebeam & Sanders, 1990).

These three efforts have the potential to influence teacher evaluation law and policy (and therefore classroom visitation) in the future because of their national scope and the "sorry state" of existing personnel evaluation practice whose efforts have been described as "precipitous, simplistic, divisive, and hugely expensive" (Stufflebeam & Brethower, 1987, p. 127). Important, too, is the collaboration of practitioners and scholars from many disciplines, agencies, and professional associations throughout the states.

CURRICULUM WORK

Curriculum work is another regulated aspect of the practice of supervision. Curriculum work, i.e., curriculum development, evaluation, and implementation, is regulated differently than classroom visitation. It is regulated by key "actors" who have influence through various policy instruments (Walker, 1990). Curriculum work may be done by teachers or administrators, but curriculum policy is often regulated by key actors at the federal, state, and local levels. Sometimes teachers and administrators are among these key actors.

In the language of curriculum policy, curriculum workers audit, align, and guide the curriculum, assuring that it is in compliance with state and national law and policy (English, 1986–1987; Zirkel, 1990). Curriculum workers promote changes in curriculum and other supporting structures such as textbook adoption, testing, report cards, and staff development (Elmore & Fuhrman, 1994). Curriculum workers also translate and interpret curriculum for teachers and the public. Curriculum policy sets the parameters within which teaching and learning occur. Curriculum workers mediate this policy (Spillane, 1994).

For the purposes of this chapter, curriculum is broadly defined to include: goals, objectives, and purposes; content; materials and resources; activities; teaching strategies; evaluation; grouping; time; and space (Klein, 1991). Curriculum policy is the formal body of law and regulation that pertains to what should be taught in schools and how. Curriculum policy varies from state to state.

The seminal works of Walker (1990) and Elmore and Sykes (1992) have made important contributions to curriculum policy-making. Walker, a long-time writer on curriculum policy, presents useful concepts and frameworks for thinking about this topic, whereas Elmore and Sykes summarize and synthesize much of the writings and research. One of the keys to navigating this terrain, however, is deciding on point of view.

Educational policy can be viewed from the federal (e.g., Rabe & Peterson, 1988), state (e.g., Mitchell, 1988), or local levels (Burlingame, 1988). It can be examined from a politics of education approach or an educational policy research approach (Mitchell, 1988). The former approach, influenced more by political science, looks at policy and its actors from a power perspective, whereas the latter, influenced by the social sciences, looks at policy content and impact. Curriculum is but one corner of the educational policy arena.

Much of the curriculum policy research conducted has been "largely theoretical and largely lacking in empirical investigation," focusing instead on the development of reform strategies rather than on their implementation (Porter, Archbald, & Tyree, 1991, p. 21). Elmore and Sykes (1992) characterize curriculum policy research as an "artificially constructed field" that concerns government involvement with curriculum (p. 185). Further, they characterize it as "loosely organized, both topically and conceptually" (Elmore & Sykes, 1992, p. 185).

One can examine curriculum mandates (e.g., Henning, White, Sorgen, & Steizer, 1979), curriculum development (e.g., Short, 1983), curriculum politics (Unruh, 1983), case law related to the curriculum (e.g., McGhehey, 1978; van Geel, 1991), challenges to the curriculum (e.g., Adler & Tellez, 1992; McCarthy, 1993) and textbooks (Venezky, 1992). Curriculum policy can be considered by topic (e.g., censorship) or by special federal or state initiatives (e.g., vocational education, science and math, school desegregation, treatment of the handicapped, bilingual education, school effectiveness, and testing). Thus, how one defines "curriculum" also influences the research. And because of its multiple actors and complexity, one can also look at curriculum policy from the point of view of those curriculum workers who have to implement policy. Brooks (1991), for example, presents state policy messages learned as an assistant superintendent of instruction in a school district in New York.

The Regulation

To understand how curriculum work is regulated and the result of this regulation, one must start by examining the state's role. Regulation of the curriculum has accumulated incrementally dating back to when states first established their free system of schools. Regulation of the curriculum has also occurred episodically during crises (Walker, 1990).

Education (and thus Curriculum) is Primarily a State Responsibility, as implied in the Tenth Amendment of the U.S. Constitution. However, the states have had more authority over local schools than they have actually exercised, because of the long-standing belief in local control. Advocates of local control believe that most decisions, especially those regarding the curriculum, should be made by local elected officials, because local government is closest to the needs and interests of citizens (Elmore & Sykes, 1992). When such decisions are made by some remote centralized agency, they tend to be associated with negative images of "despotic government actions, high-handed officials, a petty bureaucracy replete with forms and documents, and probably, corruption" (Walker, 1990, p. 306).

Through their own constitutions, states have a duty to establish and maintain a "general," "thorough," "uniform," or "efficient" system of public schools (McGhehey, 1978). States have exercised this duty in various ways but have typically "left curriculum decisions to local school boards except for the barest directives" (Unruh, 1983, p. 106). Most states have required minimums concerning student attendance, the school calendar, the curriculum (requiring the teaching of some subjects and prohibiting others), graduation requirements, pupil records, program accreditation, personnel certification, and textbook adoption (Lawyers' Committee for Civil Rights Under Law, 1978; Walker, 1990). Such minimums appeared in legislation, but more so in department of education regulation. Sometimes when "newer" subjects needed to secure a place in the curriculum, special legislation was enacted to teach subjects such as vocational education, physical education, home economics, driver training, and more recently drug and AIDS education (Kirst & Walker, 1978). A minimalist approach characterizes state role toward curriculum policy through the 1970s (especially when states initiated student competency testing).

Since the 1980s and *A Nation at Risk* (The National Commission on Excellence in Education, 1983), the federal policy event that catalyzed state action, states have increasingly exercised more responsibility over education. They promoted programs for the disadvantaged, the limited-English-proficient, and the special education student. They increased graduation requirements (especially in science and math) and promoted new (and alternative) testing requirements. Some states enacted omnibus bills that completely overhauled education systems (e.g., Kentucky). The decade of the 1980s saw a 21 percent increase in state revenue for education (Fuhrman, 1994) and with this increased funding came more regulation.

Virtually every state was engaged in some form of low cost, high visibility reform activity. It has been estimated that there were 300 task forces, 700 statutes, and 39 reports generated by various groups in the states (Hazi, 1989b; Timar & Kirp, 1987). The school reform movement resulted in a whole new body of rules governing activities in local schools that had never before been regulated:

For students, there are rules about participation in sports and other extracurricular activities, about how much and what kind of homework must be done, and about how many times they may miss school before failing their courses. Students are also subject to rules about what kinds of courses they must take, how much time to devote to each subject each day, and what topics each class must cover. For teachers, there are rules regarding placement on career ladders and eligibility for merit pay. For local school trustees, there are rules requiring their participation in training programs. In some states, the law now prescribes how often daily announcements may be made over the school intercom system. There are even rules that permit state school officials to place schools deemed unsatisfactory into receivership and to fire school administrators and, presumably, trustees (Timar & Kirp, 1987, p. 309).

As a result, policy-making "has been fragmented and therefore, sometimes contradictory" (Fuhrman, 1994, p. 36). Curriculum policy-making during the 1980s appeared to be "complicated, irrational, disjointed, open, and unpredictable" (Walker, 1990, p. 326). In the 1990s, some call for "coherence" in curriculum policy (Beane, 1995).

Some states are more aggressive in their regulation than others. In states with centralized traditions, "educational policymakers are active agents for school improvement whatever the issue, and initiatives for school improvement frequently originate at the state level or, if they originate at local or national levels, rapidly find expression as state policies" (Walker, 1990, p. 315). States that hold to the tradition of local control give local districts "almost complete autonomy in curriculum matters that extend beyond the basics" and adopt a service orientation, seldom imposing their own policy agenda (Walker, 1990, p. 315). Southern and western states are more centralized in their curriculum decision-making than northern states (see Pipho, 1991, p. 77 for a listing).

While States are Responsible for Education, Curriculum Policy is also Influenced at the Federal Level The U.S. Supreme and federal courts, U.S. Congress, and the U.S. Department of Education are all influential (see, e.g., Kimbrough & Nunnery, 1988 and First, 1992 for a fuller and general account of federal and state involvements).

Commencing with *Brown v. Board of Education* (1954), the courts have become important forums for addressing educational issues ranging from school desegregation to educational malpractice (*Peter W. v. San Francisco Unified School District*, 1976; Brown & Cannon, 1993) to special education (e.g., *Board of Education v. Rowley*, 1982; Osborne, 1994;

Zirkel, 1993b) and to school finance reform (e.g., *San Antonio v. Rodriguez*, 1973; Dayton, 1992). The courts have a well established history on many topics concerning the curriculum. Some of them are:

- the flag salute (*West Virginia State Board of Education v. Barnette*, 1943);
- school prayer (e.g., Horner & Barlow, 1994; Kniker, 1989; *Lee v. Weisman*, 1992);
- the teaching of creationism (e.g., Daugherty, 1988; *Edwards v. Aguillard*, 1987; Nuger, 1988);
- teaching the non-English speaking (Irizarry, 1992; *Lau v. Nichols*, 1974; Levin, 1983);
- the removal of library books (*Board of Education v. Pico*, 1982; Hanna, 1993; McCarthy, 1993);
- sex education (*Cornwell v. State Board of Education*, 1969, 1970; Hazard & Einstein, 1983);
- student testing and promotion (e.g., *Debra P. v. Turlington*, 1984; Glaser & Silver, 1994); and
- tracking (*Hobson v. Hansen*, 1967, 1969; Gamoran, 1992; Oakes, 1985).

(Look for topical, as well as comprehensive, syntheses of case law and reviews of research such as van Geel, 1988 and those reviews listed.)

The federal government promotes certain educational goals when it is in the interest of the general welfare of the public. Federal goals are promoted through categorical aid legislation, conditional funding, numerous policy documents, special curriculum projects, research studies, and curriculum guides and materials. Federal programs have included those for the educationally disadvantaged, the handicapped, the bilingual, the gifted, the preschoolers, and those in desegregated settings. Programs have also promoted the arts, career education, consumer education, environmental studies, ethnic studies, foreign languages, Indian education, law-related education, libraries, math, reading, science, social sciences, and vocational education (Short, 1983; Unruh, 1983; van Geel, 1991).

A heightened time of federal involvement occurred during the 1950s and 1960s after Russia's launch of Sputnik when the public and its political leaders suspected the quality of education, teachers, textbooks, and graduates. Some of the major federal curriculum policy initiatives since the 1950s that Walker (1990) cites include: the National Defense Education Act of 1958, the Elementary and Secondary Education Act of 1965, the Vocational Education Act of 1968, the Career Education Act of 1972, and the Education for All Handicapped Children Act of 1975.

Most recently, as a result of *A Nation at Risk* and now Goals 2000, the federal government has become actively involved once again. Goals 2000: Educate America Act (1994) is an attempt to channel public and educator attention to accomplishing eight national goals. They concern: readiness to learn; increasing the graduation rate; adult literacy; becoming first in the world in mathematics and science; providing safe, disciplined, and drug-free schools; promoting parent participation; and promoting teacher training. An eighth and most important goal is national standards and voluntary national testing in the core subjects of English, mathematics, science, history, and geography (National Education Goals Panel, 1992, 1993). Many believe the latter goal will result in a national curriculum (Kellaghan & Madaus, 1991; Smith, O'Day & Cohen, 1991; Smith, Fuhrman, & O'Day, 1994; Viadero, 1994).

Education Issues Run in Cycles Downs (1972) believes that public attention cannot focus upon any one domestic issue for very long. He says that a problem "suddenly leaps into prominence, remains there for a short time, and then—still largely unresolved—gradually fades from the center of public attention" in an issue-attention cycle (p. 38). Problems particularly prone for such a cycle include those experienced by a minority (usually less than 15 percent) of the population. When the public-at-large realizes the complexity and cost of fixing an issue, largely through the news media, the issue fades from prominence, losing its initial excitement. Problems of social institutions such as education, that are tied to the economy, periodically get recycled.

Curriculum policy addresses issues (and values) most important to society. Democracy, quality, equity, efficiency, and more recently, choice are among those most fundamental and competing values of American society that shape education (and thus curriculum) policy (Marshall, Mitchell, & Wirt, 1989). The school is where these most pressing and recurring societal issues can be addressed. Education is everyone's business (especially since it is often the largest item in state budgets) in what Mitchell (1988) characterizes as America's "secular religion." What knowledge is worth knowing is a conversation in which diverse groups of people can easily participate.

"With each new generation there have been new curriculum controversies. Old issues, thought dead, have been revived as times and conditions have changed. So long as the schools are 'public' schools, the content of the curriculum will be subject to public pressure, which varies not only as to time, but also as to place" (McGhehey, 1978, pp. 140–141).

Citizens become episodically involved in education in various ways. Sometimes they use the courts. Those curriculum issues taken to state courts include: the establishment of kindergarten and the high school grades; the teaching of subjects such as bookkeeping, dance, evolution–religion, foreign language, and music (Fulbright & Bolmeier, 1964; McGhehey, 1978).

Citizens sometimes take their issues to their state elected officials. For example, leaders of the temperance movement in the late nineteenth century were the first to pass legislation impacting the classroom on the evils of alcohol. Then in the early twentieth century, various groups (e.g., religious as well as political fundamentalists) were effective in promoting the Bible and patriotism laws and banning Darwinism (Tyack & James, 1985). Starting in the late 1970s (and into the 1990s), state legislatures became influential once again. As mentioned, legislators dealt with many aspects of the schools that had never before been regulated.

Sometimes citizens take their issues directly to their local schools. They are mostly involved in negative actions such as the defeat of a bond issue, tax increase, or school board member; or the termination of controversial curriculum offer-

ings (Kirst & Walker, 1978). They may be influential individuals or well-organized groups with a specific agenda that may involve promoting or prohibiting certain topics or points of view in the curriculum. Pressure groups are those "which are concerned about language, procedures, and substance [in the curriculum] and which deliberately set out to promote their own agendas" (Marsh & Willis, 1995, p. 311). "Issues fanned by special interest groups change with time as they become resolved or obsolete, but new ones continually appear" (Unruh, 1983, p. 108). Issues include: censorship, religion, drug education, sex education, teaching values, and more recently, outcome-based education (e.g., McCarthy, 1993).

Curriculum Policy is Influenced by a Number of Key Actors in a State Knowing the actors helps to understand the process. The actors range from governors and other "insiders" at the state level to school boards, and special interest groups (see Kirst & Walker, 1978 and Schubert, 1986 for descriptions). All have their own values, preferences, and ideas about what they think should occur in the schools.

Chairs of House or Senate education committees and other lawmakers form the inner circle of influence within a state. Closest to these insiders are individuals such as the chief state school officer, members of the state board of education, heads of teacher organizations, and the governor. While the importance of policy elites may vary in individual states, educational researchers (and those in higher education) are usually among the least influential as policy "remotes" (Marshall, Mitchell, & Wirt, 1989).

Those actors who do influence curriculum policy are politically astute and sometimes charismatic. They seek advice from experts, digest information supplied by trained staffers, size up the political scene, align and disband other actors around issues, build long-term coalitions, then mobilize resources for action. Some believe that the massive school reform effort in Arkansas, for example, would not have occurred without the urging of Hillary Rodham Clinton, wife of then Governor Clinton. During her tenure, Arkansas dealt with issues such as higher graduation requirements, teacher testing, mandatory full-day kindergarten, class size, student competency testing, computer education, and policies on discipline, extracurricular activities, and homework (Nelson, 1993).

Actors are influenced by the history of their state political culture. Elected officials share implicit assumptions about what policy-making occurs in a state. Mitchell (1988) and Marshall, Mitchell, and Wirt (1989), following the work of Elazar (1972), assert that different regions of the country reflect the world view of their early settlers. In New England, for example, legislators embrace a moralist view of government, while those in the Mid-Atlantic region hold an individualistic view; southeasterners are traditionalists. Attitudes toward representation of their constituents, education, labor, and demography all shape their decisions; and, of course, state resources drive policy. The more that are available, the more experimentation can occur.

Actors operate in unified or conflicted policy contexts. "In a unified context like-minded individuals strive to develop policies that they prefer and that they hope to persuade the schools to adopt. In a conflicted context individuals with opposing views strive to develop a mutually acceptable policy" (Walker, 1990, p. 440). In a unified context consensus building and problem solving are easier because there exists some general consensus on problems and their solutions. In conflicted contexts, much negotiation and compromise take place and policies become "strange creatures of compromise" (Walker, 1990).

Actors in both contexts tend to view policy as simple assertions of fact. They believe that their policy is beneficial, feasible, and certain to solve the problem. If policy fails, they attribute it to the motives of those responsible for implementation, rather than to the complex situation or the lack of feasibility (Elmore & Sykes, 1992).

Actors are influenced by those in nearby states. Legislation in one state is frequently copied with little or no modification for use in a neighboring state. The phenomenon of regionalism has been so for collective bargaining issues, as well as general social issues (Saltzman, 1988). Mass media and formal educational policy networks (e.g., Education Commission of the States) help to promote the exchange of information (Mitchell, 1988; see Marshall, Mitchell, & Wirt [1989] for indepth insights into what influences key actors in the policy-making arena).

Policy Instruments Attempt to Influence Local Action States use a combination of policy instruments such as mandates, inducements, capacity building, and systemic change (Elmore & Sykes, 1992). Mandates are "rules governing the action of individuals and agencies that are intended to produce compliance" (p. 191). Inducements are transfers of money in return for certain immediate action. Capacity building is the investment of money in staff development to produce results over time. Systemic changes are the transfers of authority, such as the call for site-based management (Elmore & Sykes, 1992).

Porter, Archbald, and Tyree (1991) provide a useful perspective on policy instruments specific to curriculum:

Our understanding of curriculum control as a policy strategy has been developing at least since the early 1960s. Initially curriculum materials were the primary policy instrument of curriculum control. When materials alone failed to produce the desired results, policy instruments of student assessments (for accountability purposes) and curriculum frameworks were added. Most recently, policy researchers have distinguished control instruments along two dichotomous dimensions: (1) control of outcomes versus control of processes; and (2) requirements of teachers versus requirements of students (p. 19).

A curriculum control strategy is characterized by whether it is more or less prescriptive. "Generally the greater the number and type of outcomes and processes controlled, the more prescriptive the policy. Prescriptiveness is also enhanced through specificity" (Porter, Archbald, & Tyree, 1991, p. 19).

According to a six state policy study by Marshall, Mitchell, and Wirt (1989), changes in testing and program definition have been among the top targets to change the curriculum in a state. Policies specify the form or content of student tests. Program definition policies in these same states specify: "(1) setting higher program standards, (2) mandating the teaching of particular courses or subjects; (3) developing programs for special groups of students; and (4) changing program time requirements" (p. 81).

Curriculum alignment (also called instructional alignment) is another state policy control. While it emerged in the 1970s when states turned to minimum-competency testing (Elmore & Sykes, 1992), it dates back to the 1960s with Skinner and criterion-referenced instruction (Cohen, 1987). It is a process whereby curriculum goals, guides, textbooks, and tests are made consistent within a state (English, 1986–1987; Walker, 1990). Elmore and Sykes (1992) note that during the 1960s through the 1980s it was easier to assess basic skills and minimum competencies through paper and pencil tests; however, the new curriculum policy agenda that began to form in the mid-1980s—"advanced cognitive skills for all children, in-depth learning over superficial coverage, lively engagement with subject matter, and teaching for conceptual understanding"—required a different kind of assessment (Elmore & Sykes, 1992, p. 202). Thus was borne the alternative (sometimes called performance or authentic) testing movement (e.g., Glaser & Silver, 1994; Sheppard, 1992; Worthen, 1993) and portfolios for both students and teachers (e.g., Wolf, 1991).

Curriculum Policy has Varying Impact on Practice Some writers are of the opinion that policy has a major, negative impact on practice; others see a low, benign impact; still others believe that impact varies (Elmore & Sykes, 1992). Opinion seems to depend on the discipline out of which the research is conducted; assumptions made about teaching, learning, policy, and their interaction; state regulatory conditions; and who is asked about impact.

Writings about the negative impact on practice seem most persuasive. They include: the hyperrationalization of teaching (or legislated learning) (Wise, 1979), defensive teaching (McNeil, 1988a, 1988b, 1988c), the trivialization of the curriculum (Short, 1990), the de-skilling of teachers (Apple, 1986), teacher cynicism concerning the "come and go syndrome" of reform (Garman & Holland, 1997), and the effects of "teaching to the test" (which include the constriction and pruning of the curriculum and the elimination of innovative teaching methods, e.g., cooperative learning and team teaching) (e.g., Brooks, 1991; Smith, 1991).

Less is known about the impact of curriculum policy on curriculum workers. One case study is reported about a supervisor who resigned because of grievances filed against her as she attempted to observe teachers and align curriculum to the state test (Hazi, 1994). Other studies have been done by Spillane (1994) and Cantlon, Rushcamp, and Freeman (1991).

Curriculum Workers Mediate Policy "Policy statements usually lack sufficient detail to prescribe action fully…[and] usually require a high level of discretion and interpretation on the part of those who are supposed to carry them out" (Elmore & Sykes, 1992, p. 186). Curriculum workers act as "mediators" between state policy and teachers' practice (Spillane, 1994). They are "artists of policy adaption" whose hands are "both free and tied" (Schubert, 1986, p. 153).

Forewarned of a potential change before it becomes law, curriculum workers critically evaluate its potential impact on the many aspects of the system, given time requirements for implementation. Armed with data, they enter the policy arena, providing testimony to the key actors "to prevent the entrenchment of bad practice" (Elmore & Fuhrman, 1994, p. 215). Armed with knowledge about promising practices, instruction, research, staff development, and the complexities of teacher change, they serve to both stabilize and change the curriculum in their system. Once in place, they are also in the position of "fixing" policy (Walker, 1990). Curriculum workers are in a key position to recommend that policy be implemented as specified, or sometimes they can choose to limit or amplify its effects. They are more effective when they can creatively interpret policy so that it best serves the needs of students, teachers, and the school district.

Serving as a mediator requires the supervisor to think beyond the written rule represented by the policy. It requires the supervisor to: see problems as opportunities, not just inconveniences; develop expertise and cultivate professional policy networks; mobilize problem-solving skills and commitment to make them work; promote best practice, not professional self-interest; identify changes in curriculum guides, and other curriculum supporting structures such as textbook adoption, and report cards; provide teachers with incentives to adopt changes; provide staff development, and "push against the limits of policy" (Elmore & Fuhrman, 1994, p. 215; Spillane, 1994). Elmore and Fuhrman (1994) optimistically predict that

[a]utonomy will probably be increasingly defined as the capacity to push against state and national standards, to participate in the policy and professional networks that influence those standards and to develop innovative solutions to the basic problems posed by standardization, such as how to bring more challenging academic content to traditionally under-served students (p. 212).

Directions for Research

More studies about how supervisors and other curriculum workers mediate curriculum policy are necessary. For example, Spillane (1994) reports how one school district responded to a state-level reading policy through interviews with state and local personnel and through analyses of state and district documents. He found: changes in the district's reading curriculum guide to coincide with state policy; but, also "novel" instructional ideas that supported the reading philosophy of two of the district's administrators; alignment of textbooks and materials; and ambitious staff development with a state grant and national reading experts. This resulted in a refocusing of the district's reading curriculum and teaching practices whereby two key curriculum workers—the assistant superintendent and the director of elementary education—"interpreted the state policy to fit with their own personal instructional reform agenda" (p. 179). As "mediators," they "amplified" state policy.

Another example that focuses on curriculum specialists and uses multiple sources of data and methods is by Cantlon, Rushcamp, and Freeman (1991). The researchers interviewed curriculum specialists in three state departments of education and six local school district offices and analyzed curriculum-related documents to determine how district curriculum guidelines are shaped by state policymakers. They found a "dynamic and purposeful interplay" between the two levels

and identified two models. One they called the "autonomy/compromise model" wherein the district preserves the integrity of their local curriculum, while accommodating state directives. This usually occurs where there is local expertise, commitment, and resources to focus on local needs and priorities. The other is the "compliance/augmentation model," where districts adopt the state curricular frameworks and augment them by designing curriculum guidelines for subject areas not covered by state policy. Such research will contribute to our understanding of curriculum policy implementation from the curriculum worker's perspective.

Studies that represent the complexity of actors in curriculum policy-making situations are also needed. Adler and Tellez (1992), for example, examine challenges to the *Impressions* reading series in California by the religious right. Their study comprehensively illustrates the complex interaction of: fundamentalist ideology, state textbook adoption of the series, reasons for challenges, the media, influential church leaders, teacher and administrator reaction, and publisher response. Their qualitative case study shows the importance of looking at clusters of districts rather than single cases.

A dimension of such studies could include examining the roles that curriculum workers assume in curriculum controversies. For example, much has been written about Outcome-Based Education (OBE) (e.g, ASCD, 1993; Bradley, 1994a; Evans & King, 1994; Glatthorn, 1993; Harp, 1993; McCarthy, 1993; McKernan, 1993; O'Neill, 1994), but not on what effect such controversy has on the practice of curriculum workers. Curriculum workers are among those who explain the curriculum to the public. Do they become a "watch dog" for the critical consumer who can read and cite research (sometimes out of context)? As curriculum workers interpret and translate curricular and instructional practices, do they have to monitor the language of others to avoid jargon that may alienate or inflame special interest groups (e.g., Ledell & Arnsparger, 1993, pp. 16–17 for a list of "red flag terms")? How do they defend instructional practices, such as cooperative learning and mastery learning, when they are criticized by special interest groups ("What's Wrong with Outcome-Based Education?" 1993)? To what extent does academic freedom help teachers to justify their practice? (For a review of cases, see Zirkel, 1993b; see also Kemerer & Hirsh, 1981; Munnelly, 1970; Sacken, 1989; Smith, 1991).

Studies are needed to examine how the implementation of certain policies affects the practice of curriculum workers. For example, a number of school districts and states are beginning to issue warranties for their graduates (Goldman, 1992; Hazi, 1993; Kirkpatrick, 1992; Sommerfeld, 1992). The warranty is seen as a low-cost, risk-free, public relations attempt "to restore public and business confidence [to] education" that may cover basic or complex skills (Sommerfeld, 1992, p. 1). On its face, the warranty appeals to policymakers because this guarantee seems feasible and appears to require no cost. In reality, the idea may be fraught with problems of student and public notice, retest options, long-term costs, and remediation. The curriculum worker's role may also shift from improving instruction to guaranteeing warranties and the requisite readying and alignment of curriculum, teachers, and testing.

STAFF DEVELOPMENT

The staff development of teachers (also called in-service education, continuing education, professional development, and human resource development) is the least regulated of the three aspects of supervision. Depending on who one reads, staff development may be an aspect of supervision (e.g., Oliva, 1984); supervision may be a model of staff development (e.g., Sparks & Loucks-Horsley, 1990); or supervision and staff development may be discreet, yet connected, entities (e.g., McQuarrie & Wood, 1991). Its purpose may be the improvement or growth of individual teachers, the change of school cultures, or the professionalization of teaching. Staff development may take the form of workshops held on in-service days, university or college courses, programs for new teacher induction and mentoring, attendance at conferences, visitation of other teachers or schools, study groups, or educational travel. Supervisors and other staff developers are typically responsible for the design and delivery of in-service day workshops, but may also be involved in designing other training opportunities for teachers.

Narrow or expansive views of staff development exist in the writings, depending upon the adopted theory base. For example, writers have drawn on such work as, psychoanalytic psychology (e.g., Coffey & Golden, 1957), organizational development (e.g., Dillon-Peterson, 1981), change and innovation, (e.g, McLaughlin & Marsh, 1978), schooling (e.g., Goodlad, 1983), adult learning (e.g., Oja, 1991), action research (Holley, 1991), school improvement (Courter & Ward, 1983), and most recently, teacher reflection (e.g., Richert, 1991).

While Sparks and Loucks-Horsley (1990) and Huling-Austin (1990) present important syntheses of writing and research on the topics of staff development and induction, respectively, limited examples of law and policy research exist on the regulation of staff development in the states (see also earlier summaries by Gray & Gray, 1985; Lambert, 1989; Showers, Joyce, & Bennett, 1987). While the National Association of State Directors of Teacher Education and Certification (NASDTEC, 1994) annually records certification regulations in the states, Darling-Hammond and Berry (1988) were among the first to comprehensively examine teacher policy (that includes some items of staff development) between 1978 and 1986.

This chapter is best served by an expansive view of staff development that considers staff development as teacher development and begins with preservice and spans in-service (Griffin, 1991; Guskey, 1986; Sparks & Loucks-Horsley, 1990). A broad conceptualization is important because state policies are now blurring what were once separate spheres. Preservice has been used to refer to teacher training prior to initial certification; in-service has been used to refer to the continuing training of teachers once employed. Those laws and policies that are within its province include items of preservice certification, induction, and continuing training once teachers are in-service.

The Regulation

To understand how staff development is regulated—albeit to a limited degree—in the states and the result of this regulation, one must start by examining the state's role in preservice teacher education. This section draws on information from selected writings and research on staff development and selected law and policy in the states.

States Control Entry to the Profession Through Certification. Prior to the 1980s much of the substance of preservice teacher preparation was left to the discretion of higher education institutions and their national accrediting agency, the National Association for Accreditation of Teacher Education. Most states were concerned with only the barest minimum requirements for certification.

Starting in the late 1970s and into the 1980s, virtually every state enacted legislation (or passed state board regulation) to reform teacher education and certification in order to upgrade teacher quality. Reforms in many states included: increased admission requirements, the establishment of teacher testing and minimum grade point averages, more hours of field experience and supervision, and more courses in liberal arts and subject matter (sometimes at the expense of education course work). Some states even prescribed specific courses (e.g., child abuse and special education) and the proportion of hours in preservice programs. Ironically, as states moved to tighten certification requirements, many also waived such requirements (through alternative or emergency credentials) to counteract teacher shortages (Darling-Hammond & Berry, 1988). As requirements for initial certification advanced, so did requirements for in-service staff development.

While Much of Staff Development is Left to Local Discretion, it Is also Influenced by the State States have minimally regulated in-service staff development. Many states set the school calendar. They specify the minimum number of instructional days in a school year, but leave the number of in-service days to local discretion. School districts (and some states) also encourage staff development through the salary schedule. Salaries typically increase for years of experience and/or college credit and degrees received. In general, in-service staff development has been the responsibility of individual teachers and local school districts.

States also pass the occasional statute or regulation, calling attention to the general importance of staff development and/or the need for some special topic training. Topics mandated by some states in the 1970s included: accident prevention, career/vocational training, alcohol and drug education, and special education (especially writing individual educational plans) (Lawyers' Committee for Civil Rights Under Law, 1978). In the 1980s, some states added training on acquired immuno-deficiency syndrome (AIDS) and multiculturalism.

In the 1980s, however, the states began to blur the traditional boundaries between pre- and in-service education. Many states moved more into the in-service arena by eliminating life certificates. "Until recently, most states had few, if any requirements for teachers once they were initially certified. However, more states are disallowing the 'life' certificate—requiring teachers to continuously renew their credentials with additional formal college course work or in-service training" (Darling-Hammond & Berry, 1988, p. x). By 1994, all but seven states required course work, training, or some renewal activity to keep a certificate in force (NASDTEC, 1994, p. E-2).

States continued to blur the boundaries in the 1980s. Many adopted statutes or regulations for in-service teacher testing, mentor and internship programs, and performance-based compensation systems. By 1986, 46 states mandated tests in basic skills, subject matter, or professional knowledge for admission to teacher education, for certification, or for both. While basic skills tests were more prevalent, some states crossed over into what was traditionally in-service education by requiring assessment of on-the-job performance for first year teachers (Darling-Hammond & Berry, 1988).

While many states and districts required teachers to take the National Teacher Examinations (NTE) for certification, when they began requiring a certain cut score in the 1980s (especially in southern states), they set in motion legal challenges of discrimination by minorities. "Because . . . [such] exams have had a disproportionate adverse impact on minority candidates, teacher competency tests have triggered a number of large scale federal class suits" (Rebell, 1990, p. 346). The courts apply the EEOC Guidelines in their approach to these cases. A most notable example was *United States v. South Carolina* (1977) where use of the NTE, when validated, was upheld.

States, however, did not stay with competency testing for initial certification. Some, most notably Texas, sought to test practicing teachers for the purpose of job retention. This generated national controversy. In *Texas v. Project Principle* (1987), the testing of veteran teachers was upheld. Georgia and Florida developed beginning teacher programs with statewide performance assessment instruments. They began to use these same instruments with practicing teachers in performance compensation (also referred to as merit pay, career ladder, master teacher, or teacher incentive) systems (Darling-Hammond & Berry, 1988; see Cornett & Gaines, 1994 for status of initiatives).

When experienced teachers began to challenge the use of these preservice instruments, the lower courts gave conflicting signals. In *Kitchens v. State Department of Education* (1988), a Georgia superior court found the instrument and its procedures to be vague and arbitrary and reinstated the teacher. In *Sweeney v. Turlington* (1986) an administrative hearing judge found the instrument was reliable and ruled in favor of the state in denying a teacher a step on Florida's career ladder (Hazi, 1989a).

Staff Development Policy Is also Influenced Episodically at the National Level The U.S. Department of Education has influenced staff development in the states through funds that have accompanied federal curriculum initiatives. Examples of the 1960s and 1970s include projects of the National Science Foundation to promote science and math, and the effort to establish regional labs. Some projects rewarded teacher participation with stipends, tuition remission, graduate credit, and advanced degrees.

Of special note is the Teacher Center initiative. In the late 1970s, the federal government provided funds to support over 90 centers nationwide. "The teacher center movement spread gradually as an effort through which teachers could control their own continuing education, sharing craft knowledge on a peer-to-peer basis" (Elmore & Sykes, 1992, p. 201). Although funding lasted only a few years, it called attention to the belief that "staff development must be responsive to the needs of teachers" (DeLuca, 1991, p. 45; see also Zigarmi, 1978).

Staff development has recently caught the eye of national policymakers. It has been characterized as the "linchpin" of the national education standards movement and the "sleeping giant" of school reform (Richardson, 1994). It has also become one of the national education goals in the Goals 2000: Educate America Act. Goal 4 is: "By the year 2000, the Nation's teaching force will have access to programs for the continued improvement of their professional skills and the opportunity to acquire the knowledge and skills needed to instruct and prepare all American students for the next century" (Goals 2000: Educate America Act, Title 1, §102[4] [A] [1994]).

The National Staff Development Council (1994) also issued standards for effective professional development. These standards "reach far beyond one-shot workshops to call for training with intensive follow-up and support, study groups, research into promising classroom practices, and peer coaching. . . . The standards call for schools and districts to align staff development with their goals for improving education, to establish priorities based on data about students, to emphasize a challenging, developmentally appropriate core curriculum, and to address the need for quality education for all children through staff development (Bradley, 1994b, p. 5).

While the current standards address only educators at the middle school years, the council plans to set separate standards for elementary and secondary educators and to award implementation grants to schools. While these 55 standards have been issued to be used as a self-assessment and planning tool, they have the potential to be adopted by states that are in a standard setting mode.

Teacher Voice is Emerging in Staff Development Policy Starting in the 1960s, states—especially those with collective bargaining—have seen a movement for teacher control of their own professional development. Leiter and Cooper (1978) describe the sorry state of in-service training that prompted this movement. In-service training is "often reduced to a repetition of what has not worked offered by people doing the only thing they are comfortable doing for people who are disaffected and alienated and cynical about the process, all occurring on a budget either meager or nonexistent" (p. 109). Additional criticism includes: emphasis on correcting deficiencies, infrequent attention to classroom content and easily adaptable instructional strategies, little continuity and coordination, little relationship to student learning outcomes, and insufficient attention to other factors in the organization (Howey & Vaughan, 1983).

Cooper (1991), an activist with the American Federation of Teachers and founder and director of the New York City Teacher Centers Consortium, provides a perspective:

The condition of in-service education in the 1970s made it very clear that alternative approaches to in-service were necessary. The case for peer-driven (or teacher-centered) staff development under the sponsorship or with the collaboration of teacher organizations was an option whose time was at hand, and its coming to the fore paralleled the general growth of the union movement in the public sector. It was not difficult to make a convincing argument for channeling staff development through those in whom teachers placed their trust, particularly when the traditional top-down in-service models had been found to increase rather than decrease teachers' sense of alienation and powerlessness. Management-generated solutions imposed without regard to the need or will of those for whom they were fashioned lacked both justification and credibility. Thus a shift to more democratic in-service mechanisms gradually grew to fill the vacuum that we found (p. 83).

The seeds of this movement became visible first in the contents of collective bargaining agreements and then later in some state statutes. For example, Pennsylvania agreements in the late 1970s included far more provisions for in-service/staff development than teacher evaluation. They included details about: the number (and in some cases, the content of) in-service days; teacher and/or association involvement in arranging and conducting in-service training; orientation and supportive help for new teachers; access to sabbaticals, school visitations, and training outside of the district; and remuneration for college tuition (Hazi, 1980).

A more recent example also comes from Pennsylvania. Act 1986–178 (§1205) and subsequent state board regulation (§49.17) require school district administrators to develop continuing professional development plans in conjunction with teacher representatives. Activities can include: graduate course work, professionally related master's degree, state approved courses, curriculum development work, attendance at professional conferences, and supervised classroom observations of other professional employees. If superintendents fail to comply, their certificate or commission becomes inactive until the requirement is met.

Teacher voice (McDonald, 1988) was further legitimized nationally when directors of both the National Education Association and the American Federation of Teachers were included in the 1986 national policy document, *A Nation Prepared: Teachers for the 21st Century* (Carnegie Task Force on Teaching as a Profession, 1986). This policy document showed teachers as crucial to school reform and called for a fundamental redesign and restructuring of the educational system.

Some states not only called for teacher participation in their own continuing professional development, but also in broader school decisions. In 1988 and 1990, for example, West Virginia teachers actively lobbied and received greater involvement in site-based decision-making through the legislation of school improvement councils, and then curriculum teams, a mentor program, and faculty senates. Thus was born teacher empowerment (e.g., Ceroni & Garman, 1997) and the site-based management movement (e.g., Wohlstetter & Odden, 1992; Baldwin, 1993) in West Virginia, as well as other states.

Limited Case That Exists Relative to Staff Development Besides cases related to certification and testing, there is limited case law specific to staff development. One example, *Carnahan v. McWalters* (1988), concerns a mentor teacher program in New York. In 1986, the Rochester City School District established the Peer Assistant Review program, releasing teachers to work as mentors to train and assist first-year intern teachers and tenured teachers experiencing difficulty. Carnahan, president of the district's administrative and supervisory association, filed suit against superintendent McWalters, the board of education, and the teachers' association, claiming that the 22 mentor teachers were performing supervisory and administrative tasks—especially in observing and evaluating teachers—without proper credentials. Carnahan believed that this violated state regulations governing mentor programs and also felt that supervisory positions would be eliminated. This case occurred at the time when administrators were feeling threatened by the "growing responsibility that teachers [were] receiving as a result of educational reform" (Rodman, 1987a, p. 22).

A lower court dismissed the case, finding that the plaintiff lacked standing to file suit. The judge found that administrators experienced "no harmful effect" and that there was nothing in state regulations "which set forth the rights, privileges, or duties conferred by that certification, or that those rights, duties, or privileges are exclusively within the province of certified administrators" (Rodman, 1987b, p. 5). An appellate judge, however, ruled that Carnahan had standing to challenge the program, but ruled against her, finding that the program did not limit the duty of administrators to evaluate teachers (see also Hazi, 1988; Hazi, 1993a).

There is potential for more case law from the blurring of the lines between pre- and in-service teachers. The work of the NBPTS, mentioned in classroom visitation, further complicates this terrain. James Smith, NBPTS senior vice president, believes that these standards for certifying teachers should be an integral part of staff development as "criteria for creating staff development programs" (e.g., Sparks, 1994, p. 59). If they become criteria for evaluating teachers, a situation such as the following may occur: "If a school district enforces different standards for continued employment than for state licensure, it may be legally vulnerable to claims of unfair evaluation. If it enforces local standards for employment higher than the state's minimum standards, the district may deny a license to a candidate who could have been employed elsewhere" (Darling-Hammond & Berry, 1988, p. 35). Thus, while the policy lines between pre- and in-service have become less distinct, the legal implications have yet to be realized.

Directions for Research

Much law and policy research is needed to comprehensively identify mandates for staff development under its multiple labels on a 50 state or regional basis. This research should pay attention to special initiatives that may not be labeled as staff development per se but as continuing education, professional development, new teachers, internships, mentor, or lead teachers. Since the boundary between pre- and in-service training has become blurred in the states, some mandates may also be found within initiatives for preservice teacher education. These mandates may be found in statutes and state board regulations and may only be retrievable through interviews with department of education personnel. Comprehensive analyses are needed identify the number and content of in-service topics, as well as the form and substance of special initiatives.

Although the federal government has had limited and episodic influence on staff development, this level of law and policy cannot be neglected, especially if staff development remains as one of the eight national goals. The standards of the National Staff Development Council Standards (1994) should also be tracked to see if they begin appearing in federal initiatives or in the states as policy or law.

Although staff development case law is currently limited, future cases should be documented through case studies from the perspective of supervision. When court decisions occur in individual states they may seem to be anomalies. Nonetheless, they will accumulate over the next decades, as did teacher evaluation cases, and hold lessons for practice.

Little is known about how staff development is regulated at the local level. Since teacher voice is beginning to appear in selected state and national policy, an analysis of local policies or a case study of grievances (where they exist) could prove revealing. Where states have collective bargaining, the contents of selected agreements could be analyzed to determine what staff development issues are most important to teachers.

Research that examines the result of staff development initiatives is especially important with a focus on the new authority and leadership that may be granted to teachers. Ceroni and Garman (1997), for example, examine the lead teacher movement in Pennsylvania by interviewing teachers. They found teachers working in quasi-supervisory roles where they gave up valuable classroom and evening time to become "principal helpers" and "spies." Other teachers were resentful, resistant, and suspicious of their ambiguous roles. Lead teachers "receive[d] training in specific supervisory skills and [were] then charged with the duty of patrolling the classrooms of their colleagues to ensure the official teaching model [was] implemented." Where there were pockets of enthusiasm, the program was teacher-driven: roles and training "agendas [were] designed by teachers rather than those designed by administrators."

CONCLUSION

This chapter has drawn from the writings and research in school law, educational policy, teacher education, supervision, curriculum, and staff development to present a framework for the law and policy dimension of instructional supervision understanding. Sections have addressed how each of three aspects of supervision are regulated, the result of the regulation, and directions for future research.

Classroom visitation is the most regulated of the three aspects of supervision in the states. This regulation has occurred through statutes and case law that have accumulated at the federal and state levels over a period of four decades. The intent of these laws has been to protect teachers from arbitrary and capricious action and unjust dismissal, and to assure them their due process rights. When law is mixed with teacher evaluation policy at the local level (found in board policy and collective bargaining agreements, where they exist), the effect can seem like a labyrinth within which supervisors and others have to interpret and successfully chart a course for their day-to-day conduct as they work with teachers in classrooms.

As a consequence, evaluations (and classroom visitation for any purpose) have become more uniform, rigorous, and legally defensible. Legally defensible conduct requires that supervisors know about and comply with the letter of the law. This requires such assurances as explicit procedures, due process, documentation, time and assistance for remediation, and a uniform practice. While many procedures for classroom visitation have become regulated in some way, the criteria used to judge effective teaching still remain—for the time being—a matter of administrator discretion. Supervisors, however, should be cau-

tious about using student learning rates as a basis for evaluating and dismissing teachers.

Curriculum work, another aspect of supervision, is also regulated in the states. Its regulation has come primarily through state board of education regulation and the policy-making process. Curriculum is regulated both directly and indirectly in the states. It is regulated directly by mandates that prescribe curriculum time, content, and practices through legislation, regulation, and case law. It is also regulated indirectly through other policy instruments such as financial inducements, capacity building, and systemic changes. The degree of this regulation varies in a state, depending on the vigor of its law and policymakers, the political culture, the policy instruments used, and the amount of specificity and prescriptiveness. Regulation through statute and case law may also exist, but occurs episodically and directed to specific topics or practices. While the federal government has had limited and intermittent influence over the curriculum, it has been through highly particularistic policy when it has served the public's general welfare. Curriculum policy in a state sets the parameters within which teaching and learning occur and curriculum workers mediate that policy.

Staff development is the least regulated aspect of supervision. Its form and substance have been left largely to local discretion. When it has been regulated, it has been at the state level through state board regulation and/or statute. States primarily regulate the initial and continuing certification of teachers. If supervisors experienced any limitations, it was in the number of in-service days, their location within the school calendar, and/or an occasional statute or regulation specifying some special topic training. States depended on colleges of education to provide for the continuing development of teachers through course work. In the 1980s, however, states moved into the in-service sphere of staff development by eliminating life certification, and introducing special initiatives such as teacher testing, mentoring, and internship programs. These initiatives have tended to blur the lines between pre- and in-service teachers, making it important for supervisors to be in touch with developments in teacher education that may eventually have consequences for the practicing teachers with whom they work.

Prior to the 1980s, most states had practiced minimalism, leaving much to local discretion. During the 1980s and 1990s educators witnessed an unparalleled growth in the regulation of classroom visitation, curriculum work, and staff development. In the future we should see continued regulation with an increase, especially in the southern and western states, because these three aspects of supervision are interconnected and focus on teacher quality and student learning. The regulation will occur episodically or incrementally in a state vis-à-vis white papers, executive decree, statute, and/or case law and it may be layered upon existing (and perhaps contradictory) law, policy, and regulation. Its impact on practice will vary, depending on the scope of the law or policy event, the level at which it occurs, what is regulated, and the creative or stilted way in which it is interpreted, then mediated by supervisors.

Much has been written about supervision in general, but limited research exists from a legal perspective and with a focus on supervision. It is hoped that this chapter has given readers a framework to think about, and ideas, for research in this dimension of the field.

REFERENCES

Adler, L. & Tellez, K. (1992). Curriculum challenge from the religious right: The impressions reading series. *Urban Education, 27*(2), 152–173.

Apple, M. (1986). *Teachers and texts. A political economy of gender and class relations in education.* London: Routledge & Kegan Paul.

Association for Supervision and Curriculum Development. (1993, May). OBE in the news. *Program News* (p. 5).

Baldwin, G. (1993). *School site management and school restructuring.* Topeka, KS: National Organization on Legal Problems of Education.

Barringer, M. (1993). How the national board builds professionalism. *Educational Leadership, 50*(6), 18–22.

Beane, J. (1995). *Toward a coherent curriculum* (The 1995 ASCD yearbook). Alexandria, VA: ASCD.

Bird, T. (1990). The schoolteacher's portfolio: An essay on possibilities. In J. Millman & L. Darling-Hammond (Eds.). *The new handbook of teacher evaluation: Assessing elementary and secondary school teachers* (pp. 241–256). Newbury Park, CA: Sage.

Blumberg, A. (1974). *Supervisors and teachers: A private cold war.* Berkeley, CA: McCutchan Publishing.

Board of Education of the Hendrick Hudson Central School District v. Rowley, 458 U.S. 176 (1982).

Board of Education, Island Trees Union Free District #26 v. Pico, 457 U.S. 853 (1982).

Board of Regents of State Colleges v. Roth, 408 U.S. 564 (1972).

Bradley, A. (1993, September 15). Not making the grade: Teacher's firing spurs debate over standards, expectations for students. *Education Week* (pp. 1, 19–21).

Bradley, A. (1994a, June). Requiem for a reform: Shifting political winds uproot a Colorado districts' plans. *Education Week,* pp. 21–25.

Bradley, A. (1994b, April 27). Standards for professional development released. *Education Week 5.*

Brooks, M. (1991). Centralized curriculum: Effects on the local school level. In M. F. Klein (Ed.). *The politics of curriculum decision-making* (pp. 151–166). Albany: State University of New York Press.

Brown, S. & Cannon, K. (1993). Educational malpractice actions: A remedy for what ails our schools? *Education Law Reporter, 78,* 643–657.

Brown v. Board of Education, 347 U.S. 483 (1954).

Burlingame, M. (1988). The politics of education and educational policy: The local level. In N. Boyan (Ed.). *The handbook of research on educational administration* (pp. 439–451). New York: Longman.

Cantlon, D., Rushcamp, S., & Freeman, D. (1991). The interplay between state and district guidelines for curriculum reform in elementary schools. In S. Fuhrman & B. Malen (Eds.). *The politics of curriculum and testing.* (The 1990 yearbook of the politics of education association, pp. 63–80). London: The Falmer Press.

Carnahan v. McWalters, 536 N.Y.S.2d 345 (A.D.4 Dept. 1988).

Carnegie Task Force on Teaching as a Profession. (1986). *A nation prepared: Teachers for the 21st century.* New York: Carnegie Corporation, Carnegie Forum on Education and the Economy.

Ceroni, K. & Garman, N. (1997). The empowerment movement: Genuine collegiality or yet another hierarchy? In P. Grimmett & J. P. Neufeld (Eds.). *The struggle for authenticity: Teacher development in a context of educational change.* New York: Teachers College Press.

Chirnside, C. (1984). Ten commandments for successful teacher evaluation. *NASSP Bulletin, 68*(475), 42–43.

Claxton, W. (1986). Remediation: The evolving fairness in teacher dismissal. *Journal of Law & Education, 15*(2), 181–193.

Coffey, H. & Golden, W. (1957). Psychology of change within an institution. In N. Henry (Ed.). *In-service education for teachers, supervisors, and administrators.* (56th Yearbook of the National Society for the Study of Education, Part 1; pp.67–102). Chicago, IL: University of Chicago Press.

Cohen, S. A. (1987). Instructional alignment: Searching for a magic bullet. *Educational Researcher, 16*(8), 16–20.

Cooper, M. (1991). Stretching the limits of our vision: Staff development and the transformation of schools. In A. Lieberman & L. Miller (Eds.). *Staff development for education in the '90s: New demands, new realities, new perspectives* (2nd ed.) pp. 83–91. New York: Teachers College Press.

Cornett, L. & Gaines, G. (1994). *Reflecting on ten years of incentive programs: The 1993 SREB career ladder clearinghouse survey.* Atlanta, GA: Southern Regional Education Board.

Cornwell v. State Board of Education, 314 F.Supp. 340 (D.Md.1969), aff'd 428 F.2d 471 (4th Cir.1970), cert. denied 400 U.S. 942 (1970).

Courter, R. L. & Ward, B. (1983). Staff development for school improvement. In G. Griffin (Ed.). *Staff development.* (82nd Yearbook of the National Society for Study of Education, pp. 185–209). Chicago: University of Chicago Press.

Darling-Hammond, L. & Berry, B. (1988). *The evolution of teacher policy.* Santa Monica, CA: Rand Corporation.

Darling-Hammond, L. with Sclan, E. (1992). Policy and supervision. In C. Glickman (Ed.). *Supervision in transition.* (The 1992 ASCD Yearbook, pp. 7–29). Alexandria, VA: ASCD.

Darling-Hammond, L., Wise, A., & Pease, S. (1983). Teacher evaluation in the organization context: A review of the literature. *Review of Educational Research, 53*(3), 285–328.

Daugherty, R. F. (1988). *Creation/evolution in the public school: National policy as shaped through selected legal decisions.* Paper presented at the annual meeting of the National Organization on Legal Problems In Education, Washington, D.C.: (ERIC Document Reproduction Service No. ED 300896).

Dayton, J. (1992). An anatomy of school funding litigation. *Education Law Reporter, 77,* 627–648.

DeLuca, J. (1991). The evolution of staff development for teachers. *Journal of Staff Development, 12*(3), 42–46.

Debra P. v. Turlington, 730 F.2d 1405 (1984).

Dillon-Peterson, B. (Ed.). (1981). *Staff development/organization development* (The 1981 ASCD Yearbook). Alexandria, VA: ASCD.

Downs, A. (1972, Summer). Up and down with ecology—the "issue-attention cycle." *The Public Interest, 28,* 38–50.

Edwards v. Aguillard, 482 U.S. 578 (1987).

Elazar, D. (1972). *American federalism: A view from the state.* (2nd ed.). New York: Crowell.

Ellis, T. R. (1985). Teacher evaluation is hard work—and it should be. *Principal, 64*(4), 22–24.

Elmore, R. & Fuhrman, S. (1994). Education professionals and curriculum governance. In R. Elmore & S. Fuhrman (Eds.). *The governance of curriculum.* (The 1994 ASCD Yearbook, pp. 210–215). Alexandria, VA: ASCD.

Elmore, R. & Sykes, G. (1992). Curriculum policy. In P. Jackson (Ed.). *Handbook of research on curriculum* (pp. 185–215). New York: Macmillan.

English, F. (1986–1987). It's time to abolish conventional curriculum guides. *Educational Leadership, 44*(4), 50–52.

Equal Employment Opportunity Commission (EEOC). (1978/1993, July). Guidelines on employee selection procedures. *Code of Federal Regulations* §1607, 212–239.

Evans, K. & King, J. (1994). Research on OBE: What we know and don't know. *Educational Leadership, 51*(6), 12–17.

First, P. (Ed.). (1992). *Educational policy for school administrators.* Boston: Allyn & Bacon.

Fuhrman, S. (1994). Legislatures and education policy. In R. Elmore & S. Fuhrman (Eds.). *The governance of curriculum.* (The 1994 ASCD Yearbook, pp. 30–55). Alexandria, VA: ASCD.

Fulbright, E. & Bolmeier, E. (1964). *Courts and the curriculum.* Cincinnati: W.H. Anderson Company, American School Law Series.

Gamoran, A. (1992). Is ability grouping equitable. *Educational Leadership, 50*(2), 11–17.

Garman, N. (1986). Clinical supervision: Quackery or remedy for professional development. *Journal of Curriculum and Supervision, 1*(2), 148–157.

Garman, N. (1987). New Jersey's plan for the supervision of instruction and in-class supervision: Promise or pretense? *Focus On Education, 31*(1), 19–25.

Garman, N. & Hazi, H. (1988). Teachers ask, "Is there life after Madeline Hunter?" *Phi Delta Kappan, 69*(9), 669–672.

Garman, N. & Holland, P. (1997). The rhetoric of school reform reports: Sacred, skeptical and cynical interpretations. In R. Ginsberg & D. Plank (Eds.). *Commissions, reports, and reforms: Fashioning educational policy in the 1980s and beyond.* Praeger Publishers.

Glatthorn, A. (1993). Outcome-based education: Reform and the curriculum process. *Journal of Curriculum and Supervision, 8*(4), 354–363.

Glaser, R. & Silver, E. (1994). Assessment, testing, and instruction: Retrospect and prospect. In L. Darling-Hammond (Ed.). *Review of educational research, 20,* 393–419. Washington, D.C.: American Educational Research Association.

Goals 2000: Educate America Act, Pub. L. No. 103–227, 108 Stat. 125, 20 U.S.C. § 5801 *et seq.* (Mar. 31,1994)

Goldman, J. (1992). Satisfaction guaranteed or we'll take our graduates back! *The School Administrator, 49*(3), 22–24,41.

Goodlad, J. (1983). The school as workplace. In G. Griffin (Ed.). *Staff development.* (82nd Yearbook of the National Society for Study of Education, pp. 36–61). Chicago, IL: University of Chicago Press.

Gray, W. & Gray, M. (1985). Synthesis of research on mentoring beginning teachers. *Educational Leadership, 43*(3), 37–43.

Griffin, G. (1991). Interactive staff development: Using what we know. In A. Lieberman & L. Miller (Eds.). *Staff development for education in the '90s: New demands, new realities, new perspectives* (2nd ed.) pp. 243–258. New York: Teachers College Press.

Guskey, T. (1986). Staff development and the process of teacher change. *Educational Researcher, 15*(5), 5–12.

Hanna, R. (1993). *Censorship of written curricular materials in public schools: An historical investigation of legal parameters.* Paper presented at the Joint Conference of the Midwest History of Education Society and the History of Education Society, Chicago, IL. (ERIC Document Reproduction Service No. ED 362926).

Harp, L. (1993, September). Pa. parent becomes mother of 'outcomes' revolt. *Education Week,* 1, 19–21.

Hart, H. L. A. (1961). *The concept of law.* Oxford: Claredon Press.

Hazard, W. & Einsten, V. (1983). Legal aspects of sex education: Implications for school administrators. *Journal of Research and Development in Education, 16*(2), 34–40.

Hazi, H. (1980). *An analysis of selected teacher collective negotiation agreements in Pennsylvania to determine the legal control placed on supervisory practice.* Doctoral dissertation, University of Pittsburgh, *Dissertation Abstracts International,* 41:2423A.

Hazi, H. (1988, Spring). Instructional improvement in the courts: Lessons for supervisors. *Journal of the West Virginia ASCD.*

Hazi, H. (1989a). Measurement v. supervisory judgment: The case of Sweeney v. Turlington. *Journal of Curriculum and Supervision, 4*(3), 211–229.

Hazi, H. (1989b). *Teachers and the recht decision: A West Virginia case study of school reform.* Technical report published by Appalachia Educational Laboratory and made available through ERIC/CRESS, a clearing house on rural schools information (ED 318 597).

Hazi, H. (1993a). Legal limits on the practice of clinical supervision. In K. Snyder & R. H. Anderson (Eds.). *Clinical supervision landscapes: Coaching for higher levels of performance.* Lancaster, PA: Technomic

Hazi, H. (1993b). *Supervision in the next decade.* A presentation to the annual fall meeting of the Council of Professors of Instructional Supervision, Tampa, FL.

Hazi, H. (1994b). The teacher evaluation-supervision dilemma: A case of entanglements and irreconcilable differences. *Journal of Curriculum and Supervision, 9*(2), 195–216.

Hazi, H. & Garman, N. (1988). Legalizing scientism through teacher evaluation. *Journal of Personnel Evaluation in Education, 2*(1), 7–18.

Henning, J., White, C., Sorgen, M., & Steizer, L. (1979). *Mandate for change: The impact of law on educational innovation.* Chicago, IL: American Bar Association.

Hobson v. Hansen, 269 F. Supp. 401 (D.D.C. 1967), aff'd sub nom. Smuck v. Hobson, 408 F.2d 175 (D.C .Cir. 1969).

Holland, P. (1994, November). *What do we talk of when we talk of supervision?* Paper presented at the annual meeting of the Council of Professors of Instructional Supervision, New York.

Holley, P. (1991). Action research: The missing link in the creation of schools as centers of inquiry. In A. Lieberman & L. Miller (Eds.). *Staff development for education in the '90s: New demands, new realities, new perspectives* (2nd ed.) pp. 133–157. New York: Teachers College Press.

Holley, W. & Feild, H. (1975). Performance appraisal and the law. *Labor Law Journal, 26*(7), 423–430.

Horner, J. & Barlow, B. (1994). Prayer in public schools in light of Lee v. Weisman and its progeny. *Education Law Reporter, 87,* 323–328.

Howey, K. & Vaughan, J. (1983). Current patterns of staff development. In G. Griffin (Ed.). *Staff development* (82nd Yearbook of the National Society for Study of Education, pp. 92–117). Chicago, IL: University of Chicago Press.

Huling-Austin, L. (1990). Teacher induction programs and internships. In R. Houston (Ed.). *Handbook of research on teacher education* (pp. 535–547). New York: Macmillan.

Irizarry, M. (1992). Bilingual education and the law: Effectiveness of bilingual/bicultural program implementation in the Boston public schools (Massachusetts). *Dissertation Abstracts International, 53/02-A,* 360. (University Microfilms No. AAD92-19449).

Jacobson, W. (1984, February). We brought teachers up to snuff, and so can you. *The Executive Educator, 6*(2), 41, 46.

Joint Committee on Standards for Educational Evaluation. (1988). *The personnel evaluation standards: How to assess systems for evaluating educators.* Newbury Park, CA: Sage.

Jones, A. (1994, September). F is for fired. *NEA Today* (p. 23).

Jones v. Board of Education of the Indian River School District, 1994 WL 45428 (Del. Super. 1994).

Kellaghan, T. & Madaus, G. (1991). National testing: Lessons for America from Europe. *Educational Leadership, 49*(3), 87–93.

Kemerer, F. & Hirsh, S. (1981). The developing law involving the teacher's right to teach. *West Virginia Law Review, 84*(1), 31–90.

Kimbrough, R. & Nunnery, M. (1988). *Educational administration: An introduction.* New York: Macmillan.

Kirkpatrick, K. (1992, April). Education for life: Linking school to employment. Denver, CO: Education Commission of the States.

Kirst, M. & Walker, D. (1978). An analysis of curriculum policy-making. *Review of Educational Research 41*(5), 479–509.

Kitchens v. State Department of Education, Superior Court for the County of Fulton, Georgia, Civil Action File No. D-54773 (1988, July).

Klein, M. F. (1991a). A conceptual framework for curriculum decision-making. In M. F. Klein (Ed.). *The politics of curriculum decision-making: Issues in centralizing the curriculum* (pp. 24–41). Albany: State University of New York Press.

Kniker, C. (1989). A survey of state laws and regulations regarding religion and moral education. *Religion and Public Education, 16*(3), 433–457.

Kuliogowski, B., Holdzkom, D., & French, R. (1993). Teacher performance evaluation in the southeastern states: Forms and functions. *Journal of Personnel Evaluation in Education, 6*(4), 335–358.

Lambert, L. (1989). The end of an era of staff development. *Educational Leadership, 47*(1), 78–81.

Lau v. Nichols, 414 U.S. 563 (1974).

Lawyers' Committee for Civil Rights Under Law. (1978). *State legal standards for the provision of public education: An overview.* Washington, D.C.: National Institute of Education.

Ledell, M. & Arnsparger, A. (1993). *How to deal with community criticism of school change.* Alexandria, VA: ASCD.

Lee v. Weisman, 505 U.S. 577 (1992).

Levin, B. (1979). Teacher evaluation—a review of research. *Educational Leadership, 37*(3), 240–245.

Levin, B. (1983). An analysis of the federal attempt to regulate bilingual education: Protecting civil rights or controlling curriculum? *Journal of Law and Education, 12*(1): 29–60.

Leiter, M. & Cooper, M. (1978). How teacher unionists view in-service education. *Teachers College Record, 80*(1), 107–125.

Marsh, C. & Willis, G. (1995). *Curriculum: Alternative approaches, ongoing issues.* New York: Merrill.

Marshall, C., Mitchell, D., & Wirt, F. (1989). *Culture and education policy in the American states.* New York: The Falmer Press.

McCarthy, M. (1993). Challenges to the public school curriculum: New targets and strategies. *Phi Delta Kappan, 75*(1), 55–60.

McDonald, J. (1988). The emergence of the teacher's voice: Implications for the new reform. *Teachers College Record, 89*(4), 471–486.

McGhehey, M. A. (1978). Control of the curriculum. In C. Hooker (Ed.). *The courts and education* (77th Annual Yearbook of the National Society for the Study of Education, pp. 140–160). Chicago, IL: The University of Chicago Press.

McKernan, J. (1993). Some limitations of outcome-based education. *Journal of Curriculum and Supervision, 8*(4), 343–353.

McLaughlin, M. & Marsh, D. (1978). Staff development and school change. *Teachers College Record, 80*(1), 69–94.

McGreal, T. (1983). *Successful teacher evaluation.* Alexandria, VA: ASCD.

McNeil, L. (1988a). Contradictions of control, part 1: Administrators and teachers. *Phi Delta Kappan, 69*(5), 333–339

McNeil, L. (1988b). Contradictions of control, part 2: Teachers, students and curriculum. *Phi Delta Kappan, 69*(6), 432–438.

McNeil, L. (1988c). Contradictions of control, part 3: Contradictions of reform. *Phi Delta Kappan, 69*(7), 478–485.

McQuarrie, F. & Wood, F. (1991). Supervision, staff development, and evaluation connections. *Theory Into Practice, XXX*(2), 91–96.

Millman, J. (Ed.). (1981). *The handbook of teacher evaluation.* Beverly Hills, CA: Sage.

Millman, J. & Darling-Hammond, L. (Eds.). (1990). *The new handbook of teacher evaluation: Assessing elementary and secondary teachers.* Newbury Park, CA: Sage.

Mitchell, D. (1988). Educational politics and policy: The state level. In N. Boyan (Ed.). *The handbook of research on educational administration* (pp. 453–466). New York: Longman.

Moran v. South Orange-Maplewood School District Board of Education, (1986 November) NJ. School Law Decisions 2878.

Munnelly, R. J. (1970). Teacher-supervisor conflicts and the issue of academic freedom. *Educational Leadership, 27*(7), 673–677.

National Association of State Directors of Teacher Education & Certification (NASDTEC). (1994). *Manual on certification and preparation of educational personnel in the United States.* Dubuque, IO: Kendall/Hall.

The National Commission on Excellence in Education (1983). *A nation at risk: The imperative for education reform.* Washington, D.C.: Superintendent of Documents, U.S. Government Printing Office.

The National Educational Goals Panel. (1992). *Executive summary: The national education goals report.* Washington, D.C.: National Education Goals Panel.

The National Educational Goals Panel. (1993). *Handbook for local goals reports: Building a community of learners.* Washington, D.C.: National Education Goals Panel.

The National Staff Development Council. (1994). *National staff development council's standards for staff development, middle level edition.* Oxford, OH: National Staff Development Council.

Nelson, R. (1993). *The Hillary factor.* New York: Gallen Publishing Group.

Nuger, K. (1988). The U.S. Supreme Court applied the "Lemon" test to Louisiana's balanced treatment act. *Education Law Reporter, 46*(1), 1–15.

Oakes, J. (1985). *Keeping track: How schools structure inequality.* New Haven, CT: Yale University Press.

Oja, S. (1991). Adult development: Insights on staff development. In A. Lieberman & L. Miller (Eds.). *Staff development for education in the '90s: New demands, new realities, new perspectives* (2nd ed.) pp. 37–60. New York: Teachers College Press.

Oliva, P. (1984). *Supervision for today's schools* (2nd ed.). New York: Longman.

Olson, L. (1993, December 15). Who's afraid of OBE? *Education Week*, pp. 25–27.

O'Neil, J. (1994, March). Outcomes-based education comes under attack. *ASCD Update, 36*(3), 1, 4–5, 8.

Osborne, A. (1994). The idea's least restrictive environment mandate: A new era. *Education Law Reporter, 88*, 554–550.

Pennsylvania Act 178, 24 *Purdons* §12-1205.1, Regulations 22 *Pennsylvania Code* §49.17 (1986).

Peter W. v. San Francisco Unified School District, 60 Cal. App. 3d 814, 131 Cal. Rptr.854 (1976).

Phillips, S. E. (1993). Legal issues in performance assessment. *Education Law Reporter, 79*(3): 709–738.

Pipho, C. (1991). Centralizing curriculum at the state level. In M. F. Klein (Ed.) *The politics of curriculum decision-making: Issues in centralizing the curriculum* (pp. 67–97). Albany: State University of New York Press.

Porter, A., Archbald, D., & Tyree, A. (1991). Reforming the curriculum: Will empowerment policies replace control? In S. Fuhrman & B. Malen (Eds.). *The politics of curriculum and testing.* (The 1990 Yearbook of the Politics of Education Association, pp. 11–36). London: The Falmer Press.

Rabe, B. & Peterson, P. (1988). The evolution of a new cooperative federalism. *The handbook of research on educational administration* (pp. 467–485). New York: Longman.

Rebell, M. (1990). Legal issues concerning teacher evaluation. In J. Millman & L. Darling-Hammond (Eds.). *The new handbook of teacher evaluation: Assessing elementary and secondary school teachers.* Newbury Park, CA: Sage.

Richardson, J. (1994, May). Professional development advocated as a linchpin. *Education Week*, 8.

Rodman, B. (1987a, January). New York lawsuit highlights growing tension between principals, teachers over their roles. *Education Week*, 1, 22.

Rodman, B. (1987b, June 24). Court upholds 'mentor teacher' program in N.Y. *Education Week*, 5.

Rosenberger, D. & Plimpton, R. (1975). Teacher incompetence and the courts. *Journal of Law and Education, 4*(3), 469–486.

Rosenshine, B. (1986). Synthesis of research on explicit teaching. *Educational Leadership, 43*(7), 60–69.

St. Louis Teachers Union. v. Board of Education of St. Louis, 652 F. Supp. 425 (E.D. Mo. 1987).

Sacken, D. (1989). Rethinking academic freedom in the public schools: The matter of pedagogical methods. *Teachers College Record, 91*(2), 235–255.

Saltzman, G. (1988). Bargaining laws as a cause and consequence of the growth of teacher unionism. In D. Lewin, P. Feuille, T. Kochan, & J. Delaney (Eds.). *Public sector labor relations* (3rd ed.) pp. 53–129. Lexington, MA: Lexington Books.

San Antonio Independent School District v. Rodriguez, 411 U.S. 1 (1972).

Scheelhaase v. Woodbury Central Community School District, 488 F. 2d. 237 (8th Cir. 1973), cert. denied, 417 U.S. 969 (1974).

Schubert, W. (1986). *Curriculum: Perspective, paradigm, and possibility.* New York: Macmillan.

Sergiovanni, T. (1984). Expanding conceptions of inquiry and practice in supervision and evaluation. *Educational Evaluation and Policy Analysis 6*(4), 355–365

Sheppard, L. (1992). What policy makers who mandate tests should know about the new psychology of intellectual ability and learning. In B. Gifford & M. C. O'Connor (Eds.). *Changing assessments: Alternative views of aptitude, achievement and instruction* (pp. 301–328). Boston: Kluwer Academic Publishing.

Short, E. (1983). Authority and governance in curriculum development: A policy analysis in the United States context. *Educational Evaluation and Policy Analysis, 5*(2), 195–205.

Short, E. (1990). Challenging the trivialization of curriculum through research. In J. Sears & J. D. Marshall (Eds.). *Teaching and thinking about curriculum: Critical inquiries* (pp. 199–210). New York: Teachers College Press.

Showers, B., Joyce, B., & Bennett, B. (1987). Synthesis of research on staff development: A framework for future study and a state-of-the-art analysis. *Educational Leadership, 45*(3), 77–87.

Smith, M. (1991). Put to the test: The effects of external testing on teachers. *Educational Researcher, 20*(5), 8–11.

Smith, M., Fuhrman, S., & O'Day, J. (1994). National curriculum standards: Are they desirable and feasible? In R. Elmore & S. Fuhrman (Eds.). *The governance of curriculum.* (The 1994 ASCD Yearbook, pp. 12–29). Alexandria: ASCD.

Smith, M., O'Day, J., & Cohen, D. (1991). A national curriculum in the states? *Educational Leadership, 49*(1), 74–81.

Smyth, J. (1986). Clinical supervision: Technocratic mindedness, or emancipatory learning? *Journal of Curriculum and Supervision, 1*(4), 331–340.

Soar, R., Medley, D., & Coker, H. (1983, December). Teacher evaluation: A critique of currently used methods. *Phi Delta Kappan, 65*(4), 239–246.

Sommerfeld, M. (1992, January 15). Putting graduates under 'warranty' gains favor in districts and states. *Education Week*, 1, 16, 17.

Sparks, D. (1994). Staff development implications of national board certification: An interview with NBPTS's James Smith. *Journal of Staff Development, 15*(1), 58–59.

Sparks, D. & Loucks-Horsley, S. (1990). Models of staff development. In R. Houston (Ed.). *The handbook of research on teacher education* (pp. 234–250). New York: Macmillan.

Sperry, D., Pounder, D., & Drew, C. (1992). Educator evaluation and the law: A case study of common statutory problems. *Education Law Reporter, 75*(3), 965–979.

Spillane, J. (1994). How districts mediate between state policy and teachers' practice. In R. Elmore & S. Fuhrman (Eds.). *The gover-nance of curriculum.* (The 1994 ASCD Yearbook, pp. 167–185). Alexandria, VA: ASCD.

Stiggins, R. & Bridgeford, N. (1985). Performance assessment for teacher development. *Educational Evaluation and Policy Analysis, 7*(1), 85–97.

Strike, K. & Millman, J. (1983). Nontechnical questions about teacher evaluation systems in elementary and secondary schools: A research agenda. *Educational Evaluation and Policy Analysis, 5*(4), 389–397.

Stufflebeam, D. & Brethower, D. (1987). Improving personnel evaluations through professional standards. *Journal of Personnel Evaluation in Education, 1*(2), 125–155.

Sweeney v. Turlington and the State Board of Education, Final Order, Case No. 86-0023, Department of Education, Tallahassee, FL: (1986, September 22).

Texas v. Project Principle, 724 S.W. 2d 387 (Tex. 1987).

Timar, T. & Kirp, D. (1987). Educational reform and institutional competence. *Harvard Educational Review, 57*(3), 308–330.

Tracy, S. (1992). State mandated supervision of instruction: A status report. Bethlehem, PA: Unpublished report, Lehigh University.

Tracy, S. & Smeaton, P. (1993). State-mandated assisting and assessing teachers: Levels of state control. *Journal of Personnel Evaluation in Education, 6*(3), 219–234.

Tyack, D. & James, T. (1985). Moral majorities and the school curriculum: Historical perspectives on the legalization of virtue. *Teachers College Record, 86*(4), 513–537.

United States v. South Carolina, 445 F. Supp. 1094 (1977), aff'd 434 U.S. 1026 (1978).

Unruh, G. (1983). Curriculum politics. In F. English (Ed.). *Fundamental curriculum decisions.* (1983 ASCD Yearbook, pp. 99–111). Alexandria, VA: ASCD.

Van Geel, T. (1988). The law and the courts. In NJ. Boyan (Ed.). *Handbook of research on educational administration* (pp. 623–653). New York: Longman.

Van Geel, T. (1991). Two visions of federalism and the control of the curriculum. In M. F. Klein (Ed.). *The politics of curriculum decision-making* (pp. 42–66). Albany: State University of New York Press.

Venezky, R. (1992). Textbooks in school and society. In P. Jackson (Ed.). *Handbook of Research on Curriculum* (pp. 436–461). New York: Macmillan.

Viadero, D. (1994, January). Standards in collision: What will happen when all those ambitious plans reach the classroom? *Education Week*, 25–27.

Walker, D. (1990). *Fundamentals of curriculum.* New York: Harcourt Brace Jovanovich.

West Virginia State Board of Education v. Barnette, 319 U.S. 624 (1943).

What's wrong with outcome-based education? (1993, May). *The Phyllis Schafly Report, 26*(10).

Wheeler, P., Haertel, G., & Scriven, M. (1993, January). *Teacher evaluation glossary.* Kalamazoo: Western Michigan University.

Wise, A. (1979). *Legislated learning: The bureaucratization of the American classroom.* Berkeley, CA: University of California Press.

Wise, A., Darling-Hammond, L., McLaughlin, M., & Bernstein, H. (1984). *Teacher evaluation: A study of effective practices.* Santa Monica, CA: The Rand Corporation.

Wohlstetter, P. & Odden, A. (1992). Rethinking school-based management policy and research. *Education Administration Quarterly, 28*(4), 529–549.

Wolf, K. (1991). *Teaching portfolios: Synthesis of research and annotated bibliography.* San Francisco: Far West Laboratory for Education Research and Development.

Worthen, B. (1993). Critical issues that will determine the future of alternative assessment. *Phi Delta Kappan, 74*(6), 444–454.

Yudof, M., Kirp, D., & Levin, B. (1992). *Educational policy and the law.* (3rd ed.). St. Paul, MN: West Publishing Co.

Zigarmi, P. (1978). Teacher centers: A model for teacher-initiated staff development. *Teachers College Record, 80*(1), 172–187.

Zirkel, P. (1992). Will they sue? Will they win? The legal audit of curriculum. *International Journal of Educational Reform, 1*(1), 32–45.

Zirkel, P. (1993a). Special education law update III, *Education Law Reporter, 83*, 543–551.

Zirkel, P. (1993b). Academic freedom: Professional or legal right? *Educational Leadership, 50*(6), 42–43.

· 40 ·

SUPERVISION AS MORAL AGENCY

Robert J. Starratt

BOSTON COLLEGE

Marie L. Howells

MARTIN LUTHER KING, JR. HIGH SCHOOL, NEW YORK CITY

INTRODUCTION

Although there has been very little published and even less research conducted on the issue of the moral agency of supervision, nonetheless it seemed important to include an essay on the topic in this handbook. For the past 30 years, the emphasis of scholarship and research in supervision has tended to focus on the technical side of supervision, especially on clinical supervision (Cogan, 1973; Goldhammer, Anderson, & Krajewski, 1980). This emphasis reflected a predominantly behaviorist view of teaching and hence of supervision. That is, the focus was on the behavior of teachers, the objective recording of that behavior by the supervisor, the rational discussion of these observations by both teacher and supervisor (especially in light of research on effective, or exemplary teaching models), and the design of professional improvement plans based on these discussions. Although that view has been broadened to include differentiated supervision (Glatthorn, 1984), developmental supervision (Glickman, 1985), and cognitive coaching (Costa & Garmston, 1994), the field has tended to be dominated by a technical approach to supervision; that is, the field is focused on "effective" processes by which supervisors help teachers to improve their teaching skills.

More recently, however, new perspectives have been introduced which broaden (1) the concerns of supervision when schools are considered as learning communities or as communities with a foundational moral leadership (Sergiovanni, 1992, 1995), (2) supervision's role in the restructuring of schools (Sergiovanni & Starratt, 1993), and (3) supervision as "super-vision" (Sergiovanni & Starratt, 1993).

Supervision has come to be understood as a much more complex and multidimensional activity. This chapter attempts to build on the implications of both the traditional approaches as well as these more recent developments, in so far as they imply a moral agency in supervision.

This overview cannot ignore the more recent literature on moral issues in education in general as well as in educational administration. A recent annotated bibliography on ethical/moral issues in schooling can be found in Jackson, Boostrom and Hansen's *The Moral Life of Schools* (1993), and Starratt's "Building an Ethical School" (1994). This literature covers a broad spectrum of approaches, from an emphasis on "character development" (the best treatment is found in Lickona's [1989] *Educating for Character)* to an emphasis on growth in moral reasoning (Kohlberg, 1984), to a critique of the injustices and the moral vacuum in some schools (Apple, 1982; Giroux, 1988; Purpel, 1989) and to an emphasis on an ethic of caring in school (Beck, 1994; Noddings, 1984, 1992). An interesting study that does not espouse any particular view school of ethics, but simply points to the implicit moral agenda to be found in most classrooms is reported in Jackson, Boostrom, and Hansen (1993). They present extensive classroom scenarios that reveal either subtle attempts by the teacher to impart a moral lesson, or reveal morally ambiguous messages being sent by the teacher. The value of their work is to show how moral issues and concerns permeate even the most seemingly bland, neutral, and routine aspects of schooling.

This literature concerning the general moral agenda (or lack of it) in schools conveys our reflections on the moral agency (or lack of it) in supervision. Likewise, the literature dealing expressly with the moral agenda (or lack of it) of school administrators provides general insights for the more particular exploration of moral agency in supervision.

Bates (1984) and Foster (1986) reflect on the underlying moral challenges facing administrators, challenges that often go unnoticed in the press of bureaucratic demands that they encounter. These challenges concern the use of power and control in establishing what gets rewarded in the school and in defining and reinforcing the central meanings used to interpret what goes on in school. Beck (1994) introduces the ethic of caring to the work of administration. Although Beck does not emphasize that this is a feminine approach to administration, other women authors bring out the relational and interpersonal concerns that women tend to bring to administrative work (Ortiz & Marshall, 1988; Shakesaft, 1987). Strike, Haller, and Soltis (1988) employ a case study approach to explore ethical issues facing administrators. Supervisors would also be confronted with these ethical issues. Kimbrough (1985) attempts to provide a series of ethical principles implicit in the notion of educational administration as a profession.

This chapter, while clearly influenced by the authors just mentioned, will attempt to further expand the view of supervision as moral agency. At the outset, we acknowledge that the moral agency of supervision involves many "Thou Shalt Nots." We assume that supervisors follow the general rules prohibiting lying, cheating, violence, extortion, intimidation, racism, sexism, scapegoating, stereotyping, ridiculing, and all other misuses of the position's power, status, and authority. We acknowledge that, at a minimum, supervisory moral action should avoid all such misbehavior. Our objective, however, is to go beyond the general strictures often contained in lists of moral and ethical principles to explore the intrinsic moral content of the work of supervision. This work involves interactions with teachers and other administrators in an effort to improve learning and the pedagogies that lead to improved learning. Such work leads to a deep involvement with what is considered to be legitimate learning and teaching. This work also requires supervisors to explore the conditions for learning, that is, they must search for ways to make schools more user-friendly for learning, more flexible and responsive to a variety of student backgrounds and states of readiness, and more responsive to the concerns of parents as well as leaders in the civic community. These tasks necessarily involve supervisors in countless moral issues and concerns. This chapter, although not pretending to exhaust all the elements of supervisory moral agency, will attempt to explore how supervisors encounter moral issues and concerns deeply embedded in their work.

The chapter will also attempt to build an argument that supervision is indeed an act of moral agency, even in its more traditional forms of instructional supervision. Moreover, as we look at emerging perspectives on supervision in its relationship to empowerment, community building, and leadership in school restructuring, we can discover additional moral implications to the activity of supervision.

CONCEPT OF MORAL AGENCY

Initially, it may help to provide a foundation for thinking about supervision as moral agency by analyzing the notion of moral agency in itself. Moral agency has been studied and discussed by philosophers as ancient as Plato and Aristotle and as recent as MacIntyre (1984) Gewirth (1981), Heslep (1989, 1995), Taylor (1991), and many others. Our purpose is not to review the numerous theories of moral agency—an effort that would take use well beyond the scope of our topic—but to offer a general synthesis that may serve as a base to our discussion of supervision as moral agency. We believe this base encompasses enough points of view to satisfy a wide audience.

Moral agency can be discussed on two levels. On one level, there are formal ethical frameworks by which the moral content of actions and situations becomes ethically intelligible, and provides the moral agent with a reasonable basis for action. Beneath that level of analysis, one can find more foundational qualities of the moral agent that are predispositional to formal moral agency, that is, certain foundational human qualities are necessary for a fully human life, without which it would be impossible to engage in moral agency. On this deeper level, we will highlight three human qualities that appear to be foundational or preconditional to moral agency; namely, autonomy, connectedness, and transcendence (Starratt, 1994). On the next level, we will speak of a synthetic framework encompassing the ethics of justice, of care, and the ethics of critique (Starratt, 1991, 1994).

Foundational Qualities: Autonomy, Connectedness, Transcendence

For individuals to be moral agents, they must be autonomous. This suggests that individuals act according to their own understandings and desires and are willing to accept their actions and their consequences. Autonomy here is contrasted with unfreedom, the unfreedom of persons incapable of making an autonomous choice because of fear, ignorance, blind and unquestioning obedience to authority, or mental and emotional incapacity. Autonomous persons are those who, in the midst of social and cultural traditions and constraints, are nonetheless the conscious authors of their choices and actions. Autonomy, of course, is normally a mix of routine, of tacit knowing, and of self-reflective intentionality.

No one however, acts, completely independently. Every individual is a member of a community of language, memory, and culture, which influences and shapes the way members see the world and establish values. Moreover, we need others to reflect to us the significance of our actions, and indeed the sense of who we are as social beings. The second foundational quality of human beings, therefore, is that they are connected, namely to family and friends and enemies, to the natural environment, to a culture and a history. Individuals cannot act as human beings in total isolation from other human beings or from their immediate context. Those who appear to do so are classified as catatonic. Being connected, moreover, means being connected in time and space, here in this place with these people. Hence circumstances that define the particular context of our connectedness at any moment of the day call forth differentiated responses. What is permissible banter among old friends, for example, is inappropriate at a solemn occasion such as a funeral. Furthermore, the cultural traditions in which our lives are invested provide both opportunities for and limitations on human action.

Sometimes, however, ethical action requires moving beyond the narrow definitions of the culture. Such an attempt to transcend the culture, however, will itself be limited by power relationships and linguistic possibilities defined by the very culture we oppose. Here we encounter the third pre-conditional human quality for moral agency, the quality of transcendence. Transcendence is intended to refer to the movement beyond self, beyond the ordinary and mediocre. Transcendence is found in those human pursuits of excellence in the attempt to exceed the predictable and expected, in a struggle to stretch the limits placed on us by nature, in an effort to sing a purer note, to create a beautiful new design, to run a faster race, sometimes to reframe the ordinary way of looking at what is accepted as commonplace. In social relations, transcendence means going beyond the expected to extend ourselves on behalf of others. It means taking on the burdens of others, caring for them, helping them to finish a project. Transcendence also means investing energies in a large collective cause, such as protecting the environment, becoming politically active in an effort to influence public policy, joining a community service group. In general, then, transcendence involves going beyond self-interest for something larger than one's own life, one's group, one's interests.

These three foundational qualities complement and feed each other in everyday practice. Greene (1995) states: "Being autonomous only makes sense when one's autonomy can be (exercised) in relation to other autonomous persons, when the uniqueness of each person can be mutually appreciated and celebrated. Connectedness means that one is connected to someone or something different from oneself, hence, it requires an empathetic embrace of what is different for the autonomous actor to make and sustain the connection." Starratt (1994) writes: "Community enables the autonomous individual to belong to something larger; it gives the individual roots in both the past and the present. However, the community is not automatically self-sustaining, but it is sustained by autonomous individuals who transcend self-interest in order to promote the common good, who join with other individuals to recreate the community by offering satisfying and mutually fulfilling services for one another . . . (p. 40). While the three foundational qualities of autonomy, connectedness and transcendence provide the base for a mature and fulfilled human life, they also provide the foundational preconditions of mature moral agency."

A Formal, Multidimensional Framework for Ethical Choice: Justice, Care, Critique

Another framework seeks to provide a formal basis for ethical choice, based on traditions of ethical thought with long histories. This formal, multidimensional framework brings three schools of thought together as necessary components of a more comprehensive synthesis: justice, care, and critique. Individually, these three ethical choices are incomplete; when joined together, their unique strengths compensate for the deficiencies of the others. In some cases, applying the ethic of justice will reveal an unfairness in the appli-

cation of a rule (when some are held to the rule and some are not). In another case, an application of the ethic of care may reveal the lack of care and basic respect for the dignity of the human person reflected in bureaucratic processes. People may all receive the same treatment (thereby fulfilling the fairness principle), but this treatment may be humiliating and depersonalizing. In yet another instance, an institution might appear to afford people the same or equal treatment, and to do so with a certain caring attitude, but the institution itself might be fundamentally flawed in that it works to the benefit of some at the disadvantage of many, fixing whole classes and generations in subservient positions. The ethic of critique looks to deeper structural issues of injustice and seeks institutional transformation on behalf of a larger common good. The institution of slavery, for example, or the earlier feudal institution of land ownership and indentured servitude that governed the relationships between the aristocracy and the peasants, or the more recent institution of child labor in factories were seen to embody structural injustices that violated basic human rights, even though one could point to equal treatment and individual acts of kindness within those institutions. The joining of these three ethics into a multidimensional framework provides the moral agent with various interpretive views to understand the ethical content of situations and to make reasonable responses to these situations. "Each ethic needs the basic values embedded in the other two. The ethic of justice requires the profound commitment to the dignity of the individual person; the ethic of caring needs the larger attention to social order and fairness if it is to avoid the cynical and depressing ravings of the habitual malcontent; the ethic of justice requires the profound social analysis of the ethic of critique in order to move beyond the naivete found in a social system with inequities built into the very structures by which justice is supposed to be measured" (Starratt, 1994, p. 55).

Moral agency requires not only the exercise of the foundational human qualities of autonomy, connectedness, and transcendence, but also necessitates the application of the multidimensional ethical framework to provide greater intelligibility to the situations of everyday life. This is not to say that the moral agent will respond to every situation with the perfect mix of the foundational qualities and the ethical perspectives. This is an ideal type, a picture of human moral agency in the ideal.

In any given situation, individuals may respond under a distorted interpretation of the circumstances, seeing injustice where it is not present, or responding in a less than caring way to others involved in the case. Furthermore, a given situation may call for the application of an ethic of care, straight and simple, whereas another situation may call for the application of the ethic of critique. No one set of circumstances will exhaust the complex possibilities and requirements of moral agency.

Moral agency needs to be understood as something that endures over time. Over the course of many months, or many years, the quality of individuals' moral agency can be evaluated by their tendencies to act morally in a variety of circumstances. This does not mean that the person will never reveal moral flaws or lapses. We are concerned with moral agency as a general orientation to do the right thing autonomously, connectedly, transcendentally, with justice, care, and concern for structural respect of the common good. Moral agency in its fullest expression over a long period of time will therefore reflect the three qualities of autonomy, connectedness, and transcendence, as well as a happy blend of justice, care, and critique.

Application to Supervision

When thinking of supervision as implying moral agency, therefore, the following questions about supervisors can be applied–

Concerning foundational qualities:

- Do supervisors take ownership of their activities with teachers, or do they act as impersonal functionaries of the bureaucratic machinery? (autonomous)
- Do teachers encounter the authentic humanity of the supervisor, or do they encounter someone playing a one-dimensional authority role? (autonomous)
- Do supervisors tend to see problems in the school as everyone's responsibility, or do they isolate individuals for blame and judgment? (connected)
- Do supervisors work out a sense of partnership with teachers, or do they see themselves as evaluators who pass judgment on teachers? (connected)
- Do supervisors attend to their own professional development, so that they improve their own effectiveness every year? (transcendence)
- Do supervisors work in partnership with teachers and students to make the school more user-friendly and more productive? (connected, transcendence)

Concerning the multidimensional ethical framework:

- Do supervisors question how to make the whole institution of schooling work better for children? (justice, critique)
- Do supervisors encourage quality learning for all children, or promote a differentiated allocation of resources to some students at the expense of others? (justice)
- Do supervisors exhibit care for their teachers and for the students in the school on a regular basis? (care)
- Do supervisors seek to empower teachers and students or seek to control them? (care, critique)
- Do supervisors seek to eradicate all traces of racism and sexism in the school? (justice, care, critique)
- Do supervisors care about the quality of individual student performance, as well as school-wide increases in standardized test scores? (care, critique)
- Are supervisors as concerned about the social development and citizenship education of youngsters as about their academic achievement? (critique)
- Are supervisors concerned about the damaging labels schools attach to groups of youngsters ("disadvantaged," "at risk," "handicapped," etc.), and the subtle discrimination encouraged by the stereotypes these labels promote? (justice, critique)

Many of these questions could be asked of supervisors from a perspective of the "effective performance of their job" or from a perspective of "professional expectation." When the questions are placed against the backdrop of the moral landscape described earlier, however, it can clearly be seen that supervisor activity is concerned not only with effectiveness, not only with professional standards, but also with moral agency. As will be seen in the topics to follow, there are other questions to ask about the moral agency of supervisors. The questions presented here can lead to a beginning awareness of the genuine moral agency implied in the work of supervision.

MORAL AGENCY IN ORGANIZATIONAL LIFE

Moral agency becomes more complex when it is viewed in organizational life. Organizational life brings with it a host of responsibilities, rules, traditions, routinized cultural norms and expectations, as well as legal restraints. When becoming a member of an organization, especially an employee of an organization, there is an expectation of loyalty to the organization, as well as an expectation that the member agrees to and will seek to achieve the organization's goals. There are contractual obligations to observe the policies, rules, and standard operating procedures of the organization. There are, therefore, moral obligations to membership in organizations. There is an assumption, even if there are no explicit rules, that an employee is morally obliged by reason of one's contract to show up on time and stay to the end of the work day. Moreover, by reason of one's status as a professional educator, there is an assumption of moral obligation to one's students that flows from being a member of the teaching profession.

Organization Constraints

Organizational membership may place constraints on moral agency. Nevertheless, autonomy, connectedness, and transcendence can be exercised within the policies and procedures defined by the organization. Organizational policies, cultural definition, traditions, and standard operating procedures all channel the agency of members in certain directions and not in others. New members are socialized into the routines of the organization until they become second nature. The daily life of the organization nuances and shapes considerations of justice, care, and critique. If there are adversarial relationships between the management and the unions, for example, the way the employees care for their superior will be circumscribed by those adversarial relationships. In such circumstances, matters of justice are often defined by strict adherence to the contract.

Using language from structuration theory (Giddens, 1984), it may be said that the organization structures the moral agency of the members in such a way that the exercise of members' moral agency serves to reproduce the organization. The total context of the organization, the way it conducts its business in subtle and overt ways, therefore shapes the activities of organizational members. In its simplest expression, the organization produces the action of its members, and the action of the members reproduces the organization. Moreover, this tends to occur on the preconscious level, so that members are not aware of the organization's influence or control over their actions. Their actions seem perfectly normal, perfectly reasonable. Even the practice of the ethic of critique is often constrained by the organization's definitions of the way things are supposed to be.

Max Weber commented that modern organizations are, paradoxically, both the greatest threat to humanity's freedom and creativity, as well as the only places where humans can truly exercise freedom and creativity (Eisenstadt, 1968). The same might be said for moral agency. Organizations have a way of defining reality for their members in such a way as to preserve the legitimacy and functioning of the organization simply because it is a routine. It is not, however exempt from examination of its current applications. Ingrained organizational routines are hard to break, but they are possibly the precise sources of unfair or inhumane practices. The practice of tracking students in separate curricula, for example, is rationalized by school systems as beneficial to students with "lower abilities." Tracking has come to be accepted as one of the legitimate ways of running schools. Research studies (Oakes, 1985) have shown, however, that tracking simply places students in a situation where the possibility of school failure and alienation from the learning process is increased for those in the lower tracks. Nevertheless, teachers in the study maintained that they were working to improve the intellectual and personal development of students. This is an example of teachers working with good moral intentions in a situation structured by the school system that actually treated many students unfairly.

The practice of teacher evaluation is another example of an organizationally structured activity in school systems. This practice is rationalized as both a means to hold teachers to minimal standards of accountability, and as a way to help teachers improve their teaching. Yet this practice is fraught with uncertainties (Sergiovanni & Starratt, 1993; Starratt, 1983, 1992). Teachers report that supervisory episodes tend to be pro forma exercises that have little or no impact on their teaching (Juska, 1991; Starratt, 1983). Furthermore, there is no research that shows that any particular teaching protocol results in uniform student learnings at all levels in all circumstances. Yet supervisors evaluate teachers on their use or nonuse of protocols which are deemed "effective." Such forms of evaluation are not only unprofessional; Michael Scriven (1990) asserts that they verge on the unethical. Again, we find supervisors acting with good intentions in a situation, structured by the system as necessary and legitimate, that on closer reflection appears to routinely apply unjustifiable criteria to the evaluation of teachers.

Organization Opportunities

Having cited two close to home examples of how organizational routines tend to define the action of their members, thereby illustrating Weber's contention that organizations constrict human freedom and creativity (and moral agency), we now turn to the other part of his paradoxical statement. Modern organizations are the only arena for the genuine exercise of freedom and creativity. This can be taken to mean two things. First is the more accepted meaning that freedom and

creativity are always exercised in specific contexts. Those specific contexts place limitations on the freedom and creativity of the players. They are not free to do simply anything; rather, they are free to do what the contextual clues suggest is appropriate to that context. Every social context has cultural boundaries. Individuals socialized in that culture recognize what is culturally appropriate in various situations. One does not go to a funeral in a bathing suit. One does not go to the beach in white tie and tails. Those who do are usually thought to be crazy, unfree, and creative. Any setting, therefore, whether familial or in a formal organization, facilitates expressions of freedom and creativity (and moral agency) in culturally acceptable ways. It is possible, however, to be free and creative (and moral) in these circumstances, precisely because the culture accepts and promotes certain expressions of freedom and creativity. Athletes playing basketball are not free to do anything they want in the game, but they are free to improvise their shooting techniques on a fast break to the basket. The fans in the stands recognize that creativity. Concert piano players must master the rules of their music; once mastered, however, they are free to be creative in their interpretations of the music.

In this sense, then, Weber was saying that within the structures and procedures of organizational life, there is latitude for improvisation and personal creativity. The same can be said for moral agency. Within the constraints of organizational life, there are many possibilities for moral agency. Indeed, organizational life presupposes moral agency if it is to survive. Not only are the ordinary decencies to be expected; beyond them, people are expected to reach for morally high standards of interaction and work. The exercise of autonomy, connectedness, and transcendence is therefore possible in organizational life, and indeed to a high degree. The same is true for the practice of justice, care, and critique.

The second, and more profound meaning of Weber's paradox concerns the ongoing work of perfecting the organization itself. All organizations are, by definition, incomplete. They are less than perfect embodiments of the values the founders had in mind when the organization was started. Moreover, external circumstances and demands are always changing, requiring the organization to change in response. Inventive, intelligent, and courageous human beings change organizations. They are most free and creative when they recognize the limitations of the organization and work to transform those limitations into assets. More often than not, there is a moral challenge imbedded in the transformation of institutions. One of the greatest acts of moral agency, then, is the investment of one's moral energies in the continuing work of institutional transformation. This work does not issue in dramatic and instantaneous success. It usually requires years of ongoing reflection, self-criticism, as well as organizational criticism, sensitivity to the short-term needs of others in the organization, and a deep commitment to the values that will energize the transformation. According to Senge (1990), it is the work of creating a learning organization that is continually transforming itself.

Transactional and Transformational Moral Agency

Burns' (1978) distinction between transactional and transformational leadership can be used to distinguish moral agency in organizational life. The moral agency of individuals who act within the normal constraints of organizational life can be seen as transactional moral agency, that is, they transact their work and their relationships within the defined procedures and roles of the organization, but nonetheless perform these transactions in moral ways. This implies that they keep the rules that everyone has agreed to, that they treat each other fairly and with respect and care—again, within the standard operating procedures of the culture of the organization—that they perform their work with integrity and commitment to high quality standards, and that they critique behaviors that violate the rules of the organization, thus maintaining fairness and justice within the organization. Such transactional moral agency tends to assume that the organization is relatively healthy in its present form, or that it is the responsibility of someone else (usually the top administrators) to evaluate whether the organization is in need of correcting any basic flaws.

Transformational moral agency, on the other hand, seeks to bring the organization to a deeper pursuit of its goals, to bring the organization into harmony with larger human and social goals (e.g., to make the organization more environmentally sensitive, or more responsive to its clients, or to redesign the work of the organization to make it more humanly fulfilling even while improving productivity, or to encourage a more proactive policy of participating in the public life of the community in which it is housed). Usually the practice of the ethic of critique is called upon here to point out basic shortcomings of the organization, shortcomings that tend to be structural rather than incidental. The critique has to be blended with care, however, for these shortcomings are not usually due to bad will on the part of the leaders of the organization. Rather, basic flaws in organizations are usually due to oversight, drift, inattention to changing external environments, fixation on narrow goals, and so forth. The important work in transforming institutions is not to identify who is to blame, but to identify what needs to be changed, to bring to bear those value considerations that will motivate people to recreate a lost vision, to mobilize the stakeholders to invest in the needed changes. Leadership for institutional transformation acts to rekindle the foundational moral qualities in the members, to appeal to their autonomy, connectedness, and transcendence, and to nurture organizational arrangements that activate those qualities.

Transformational moral agency tends to be driven by altruistic ideals, by a passionate commitment to the heroic possibilities for human beings. This kind of moral agency is impatient with the enormous waste of human talent and energy to be found in organizational life. This waste is due to the tendency of organizations toward stability and predictability and hence to control as much as possible the discretion individuals in the organization can exercise. This leads to Weber's first part of the paradox: organizations are a threat to human freedom and creativity. Transformational moral agents want to release more of that freedom and creativity so that humans will be more fulfilled and more productive in their work. Hence, they will try to build in more flexibility to the organizational routines, more humanly

enriching teamwork, more customized work, more diversified ways to measure productivity, more responsiveness to the communities and clients the organization serves.

In making this distinction between the two forms of moral agency in organizational life, two points must be stressed. First, there is need for transactional moral agency. Much of the organizational day is spent in transactions. Bringing a moral sense to the demands of these transactions enables organizational life to run smoothly on human terms. Organizations are made up of human beings. The ordinary transactions of the organization therefore deserve the moral sensitivity that human beings require. The second point is that transformational moral agency is a higher form of moral agency, for it is involved in making the whole institution more morally reasonable. The effect of this kind of moral agency is much larger and longer lasting. Having said that, however, it is important to add that this kind of moral agency is more difficult and more demanding. In so far as transformational moral agents can invite their colleagues to also become transformational moral agents, then the work of transformation becomes possible, and indeed more fulfilling.

Implications for Supervision

Supervision is carried out within organizations called schools and school systems. Much of the work of supervisors is transactional in nature. Often, supervisory procedures are spelled out in teachers' contracts and in personnel policies. It is incumbent upon supervisors to see these transactions not simply as bureaucratic routines but more as actions of human beings who are serving moral as well as technical purposes, whose work is an arena for moral fulfillment as well as public service. Supervisors need to be aware of the foundational qualities needed to make those transactions humanly genuine, namely, that they respect the autonomy of the teachers, their mutual interdependence within the larger enterprise of promoting student learning, and the transcending value of their work together for both the students and their communities. Further, supervisors should recognize the need for caring relationships with their teachers. The ethic of care can become the cornerstone for the mutual work of teachers and supervisors to improve the learning of all students. That caring will incorporate and energize a concern for fairness in classrooms and a willingness to critique structural issues such as teaching arrangements, inappropriate curricular materials, grading schemes, and so forth.

The transactional moral work of supervision, however, will blend into transformational moral work, first as it uncovers the intrinsically moral nature of the act of learning and therefore of the acting of teaching; then as it begins to engage the agendas of teacher empowerment and of community building. Consideration of those moral agendas will be discussed later in this chapter. Before developing these agendas, a word is in order concerning the more structural–transforming moral agenda.

Seen from the pervasive public attention given to restructuring schools for the twenty-first century, the traditional practice of supervision in schools is coming to be seen as part of the problem, rather than part of the solution (Gordon, 1992). Those responsible for supervision are being challenged to restructure not only their practices, but also the assumptions and beliefs that legitimate their practice. That is to say, as elements of the restructuring agenda become clearer (site-based management, a focus on the core technology of the school as teaching and learning and on the student as the primary producer of knowledge in the school), a learning environment that is more responsive to diverse student talents, cultural interests, and language is called for. Such restructuring requires a greater understanding of the social nature of learning through group projects and peer reflection on learning, the structuring of teacher work in teams responsible for relatively self-contained groups for cross grades of students and interdisciplinary learning, and the promotion of teacher professional growth. The work of supervision necessarily must be rethought and reconstituted. Supervisory work must be redefined as restructuring work, as the work of transforming the school in an organically integrated process that recognizes the complexity and multidimensionality of the schooling agenda. That moral agenda will be taken up toward the end of this essay.

SCHOOLING AS MORAL ACTION

In this section, the intrinsically moral nature of learning will be explored. Focusing on learning as the student's work, the intrinsic connection between learning and the shaping of a moral person, between learning and moral performance, between learning and being grounded in a moral community, can be observed. The intrinsically moral nature of teaching, which derives its morality from the morality of learning, is also noted. The moral nature of teaching and learning is then used to illuminate the moral implications of supervisory work, which is deeply involved with teaching and learning.

Learning as Moral Action

When speaking of *learning,* we intend to encompass a vast range and variety of learning. In schools, for example, students learn about the world, their history, the biological functioning of various life forms, the structure of a symphony, the harmonies of the color wheel, international trade relationships, the engineering of bridges, the architecture of cities, the cultural forms of peoples, the geography of the planet, and the physics of the stars.

What does learning in this sense mean? It means coming to know something in some way, that is, coming into contact with a bite of reality and attempting to make sense of that reality: seeing that reality from a perspective such as an economic or political perspective, or a biological or religious perspective. It means grasping, understanding, seeing the usefulness of something (such as a wheel), the symbolic significance of something (such as a circle), the artistry of something (such as a poem), the comedy of something (the Emperor parading in his nonexistent clothing), the horror of something (The Holocaust), the symmetry of something (the Taj Mahal, a snow crystal, an isosceles triangle), the physics of something (the principle of gravity), the antiquity of some-

thing (the Grand Canyon). It means understanding relationships between mass and volume; democracy and freedom of speech; speed and resistance; fear and desire for control, church and state, poverty and wealth, fall and harvest, banks and loans, men and women, comedy and tragedy. It means knowing how to make things: apple pies, explosives, birdhouses, arguments, poems, bridges, peace settlements, dams, gardens, chemical compounds, profits, babies, and laws.

Learning involves the learner with the many complex understandings of the world that have already been achieved by those who preceded them. These understandings are explored in order to increase and expand the learner's knowledge of the human condition; of the way the social and natural world works. In the process of appropriating the knowledge produced by others, the learner has to produce that knowledge in her- or himself; it has to be personally appropriated and taken into a cognitive and affective interior landscape and integrated into the contour and colors and feelings of that landscape. Depending on the richness and depth of that prior interior landscape, the new knowledge will fill out empty spaces, or rearrange elements of the landscape into a new symmetry, or strike emotional chords already struck by earlier learnings, or enlarge and transform major interpretive maps in that landscape, or add depth and complexity to prior, simpler concepts. Often, the learning is very superficial and evanesces, leaving no discernible trace in that interior landscape. At other times, the prior views and understandings of how the world works may distort what is learned in order to fit it with other mental models of the interior landscape. Sometimes, the knowledge is communicated in unclear or confusing or nonsensical language and the student cannot make sense out of it.

The point of highlighting the diverse things youngsters are expected to learn is to suggest the range, the developmental sequencing, and the complexity of learning and to suggest some possible examples that will allow us to understand learning as an intrinsically moral action.

Let us use the analogy of interpersonal communications. There is an assumption that communications will be truthful. Telling the truth is a morally good action because it implies a respect for the other person, a desire not to deceive that person, an attempt to use the communication to carry the relationship with that person forward. We may not *like* the persons we are speaking with, but nonetheless we speak to those persons in a truthful way because that is what they deserve from us as human beings. Communication implies a moral quality such that deceptive or injurious communications are judged to be immoral, whereas truthful and caring communications are judged to be moral.

When persons come to know something, they may not distort or manipulate what they know to mean something other than as what they have come to know it. To engage intentionally in distorting what they know to make it appear to be something else, they are violating the integrity of that piece of reality and violating their own obligation to acknowledge it for what is is, to respect it for what it is they have come to know about it. Granted that psychotics distort reality to make it fit their fears or their fixations; that ignorance, inexperience, and cultural superstitions can lead to the misinterpretation of the meaning of something. In those cases, these people are not considered responsible for the distortion of what they have experienced and know. In other instances, when normal and healthy persons make mistakes about what they are learning, it is again acknowledged that there was no moral guilt there, because there was not a clear intent to distort or deceive. When people intentionally state that something is other than what they know it to be, that is called a lie. It is a lie, not only because it involves the attempt to deceive others, but because it does not reflect what they know about an element of reality. Knowing an element of reality carries with it an ineluctable responsibility to affirm that it is as we know it. Underneath the prohibition not to distort what we know is the tacit rule that we respect and acknowledge the realities that we are learning about. It does not mean that we have to like what we know. No one rejoices in the inescapable reality of death. No one likes the historical narratives of the Holocaust or the Rape of Nankin, the accounts of murder and violence in the world, of violations of public trust or cheating on taxes, but it cannot be denied that they have happened, that human beings actually do these things.

Underneath the widespread respect accorded to scholars is the acknowledgment of their dedication to uncover the truths of history, science, and society and to report their findings in as straightforward and unambiguous language as possible. There is a profound obligation on scholars to purify their knowledge of bias and distortion as much as possible, or at least to warn the public when the report moves from findings to speculation or interpretation—even after we admit that all knowledge is, in a sense, interpretation. Although the distracted 10-year-old does not bear the heavy moral obligation of the scholars, nonetheless, the roots of the moral quality of all learning and knowing are the same in both cases.

Beyond the natural obligation to respect the integrity of whatever element of reality one is studying, there is the further moral responsibility to act in accordance with what one knows. Knowledge puts us in a dynamic relationship with our world. When we learn that fire burns, we encounter the obligation to use fire cautiously so that we do not burn other children or burn down the family house, or the nearby forests. When we learn that certain chemicals pollute lakes and streams, we encounter the obligation to avoid putting those chemicals into water sources. When we learn about how automobiles work, how electricity works, how clothes are made and cleaned, how other children feel when they are insulted, how the postal system works, how money is used, these learnings and countless others place us in a complex web of relationships to other people, to our natural and social environment, and to the artifacts that clutter our lives. Knowledge of these realities brings knowledge of our relationship to these realities and therefore knowledge (albeit tacit and subliminal) of what those relationships require of us. In other words, our knowledge immerses us in the daily routines, expectations, rituals, and performances that carry obligations we have toward all of reality as a responsible human being. Knowledge equips us to engage the world—the world as both friendly and dangerous, the world as both beautiful and horrifying, the world as both mysterious and boring, the world as both an adventure and as a burdensome journey. We

can misuse our knowledge in an attempt to defy or bend those relational obligations, and therein we find the corruption not only of our knowledge, but the corruption of ourselves. Or we can use our knowledge to participate in the world in respect for those relational obligations.

We read exhortations that young people apply themselves to their studies so that they will be prepared for the competitive work place of the twenty-first century, so that they can return their country to economic dominance. There is a fervent moral undertone about these sweeping pronouncements concerning the failures and obligations of schools to prepare youngsters for the future work force. While educators resist the exclusive excessive focus on the schools' purpose to develop technological competencies, there *is* a legitimate claim on young people to prepare themselves well for their various adult roles in society. If the young refuse to learn those many lessons that will prepare them to vote intelligently, to be responsible parents and neighbors, as well as to be competent and inventive workers, then they are refusing to accept the burdens of citizenship, indeed, the burdens of their own humanity as social beings. To be sure, many students resist the lessons the school attempts to teach because the school is such a user-unfriendly place. Schools have to accept some of the blame for the enormous waste of the talent and the time of young people. That is the point. We acknowledge an obligation to learn so that we will be prepared to contribute. To refuse to learn is to refuse to be a moral person. We come to be more fully human, moral individuals by learning about all the complex relationships by which we are supported as *social* beings and by learning how to make those relationships work for our own and others' benefit.

This treatment of the morality intrinsic to learning has perhaps appeared overstated or unusual. This aspect of learning is seldom treated in the literature and research on learning, but that it is an aspect whose importance can be verified by further research. The moral aspect of learning, in fact, roots the whole moral enterprise of schooling. Turning now to the intrinsically moral nature of teaching and supervising, it can be noted that there are additional factors involved in determining the morality of that kind of action; the implication of teaching and supervising in the moral action of learning as described earlier, however, provides the essential moral grounding of their activity.

Teaching as Moral Action

Underneath the rhetoric about professionalism, among teachers, there is tacit awareness of their obligation to know the content of their curriculum thoroughly. This tends to be emphasized among high school teachers (Grossman & Stodolsky, 1995). This commitment arises not simply from their desire to provide the most complete curricular knowledge to their students, but also from an interest and caring about their subject matter field, from their earlier fascination with the world when seen from the window of American literature or classical ancient history or biology or geography.

Teachers were once students, and many continue to see themselves partially continuing in that role. As students, they experienced the tacit demand of reality to be respected in the action of learning, the engagement in knowing that led to appreciation and fascination. Theirs is an obligation that is partway between the school child and the scholar. While relying on the work of scholars, teachers experience the obligation to teach about the world with the particular integrity of someone instructing the young. We can find echoes, therefore, of the morality implied in the pursuit and expression of knowledge that was described in the section on learning when we analyze the moral quality of teachers' knowing and continuing learning.

Likewise, we can find echoes of the social responsibility which knowledge implies when we turn to the underlying purpose of teaching, namely, preparing youngsters to take their place in society through a gradual series of learnings that place them in the complex web of relationships to others, the natural and social ecology, and to the material artifacts and systems that facilitate and constrain adult life. As students have a moral obligation to themselves and to society to prepare themselves for mature participation in the communal life of society, teachers who serve as their guides and their coaches do so with an awareness that their task is weighted with moral consequences for youngsters *and* for society. To teach with an attitude of indifference toward those outcomes for the youngsters and for society is to neglect a moral responsibility of teaching. Hence, committed teachers will continue to remind students of the moral need to pursue a larger sense of social responsibility in applying themselves to their studies.

While these two moral aspects of teaching echo the moral aspects of learning, there are two additional moral aspects to teaching: caring for the individual student, and building a functional learning community. Children are often reluctant to go to school. It can be a humiliating experience for many children. Continuous academic failure and disciplinary sanctions can destroy self-confidence and breed alienation. Teachers sense an obligation to care for the youngsters in their charge. They recognize their vulnerability, inexperience, their awkwardness, and fragility in a competitive, bureaucratic environment. Teachers not only need a strong commitment to the subject matter; they need a strong commitment to nurture the young lives placed in their hands. To be sure, children have to learn to abide by rules, to overcome impulses, and learn social graces and common courtesy. These learnings often are acquired slowly through trial and error and through firm guidance from teachers. That firmness, however, must always be nested in a continuous and large-minded caring for children. Teachers who do not have time or energy to offer children a cheerful greeting, an understanding ear, a gentle reminder, and a pat of encouragement for a good job, are neglecting an essential component of their profession.

Beyond that moral aspect of their work, teachers also need to reach beyond their classrooms to involve themselves in the larger community of the school. One of the necessary moral learnings of children is how they are to live and work within communities. One way they learn this is to watch their teachers living and working in and for a community. Teachers who arrive as late and leave as early as their contract permits and rarely interact with and for other teachers are poor models of adults working to build up community in the school

(although some family and economic circumstances require some teachers to do this). Schools need adults who work together for school assemblies, special celebrations, family events, and other community-building activities, so that the students can experience their school as a friendly, cheerful, and caring place—a place where all the children feel welcomed and accepted. These kinds of school environments carry a strong message to children about the satisfaction of working together and sharing a common bond (Sergiovanni, 1994).

Supervision as Moral Action

Much of what will follow in succeeding sections of this chapter will elaborate on the moral quality of supervisory action. Here we simply want to root that elaboration in its relationship to the moral aspects of learning. From that vantage point, supervisors' actions are fundamentally moral because they are concerned with promoting the integrity of learning. Supervisors who do not attend to the integrity of learning, but simply concern themselves with technical aspects of teaching, such as a well-reasoned lesson plan, a good anticipatory set, evidence of checking of homework, and the sequencing of the learning tasks according to the sequences in the syllabus, may be missing the moral dimensions of supervision. Supervisors need to converse with teachers about how students are relating their classroom learning to everyday living and to the larger concerns about the community, to their own sense of history and the history of their families, and to the growing intelligibility of the network of relationships that their learning illuminates. In other words, supervisors need to attend to the multiple lessons youngsters are learning in the class, beyond their memorization of definitions, scaffolds, concepts, formulas for problem solving, to the larger sense and meaning youngsters are making from the classroom experiences. Any conversation supervisors have with teachers about their techniques needs to be nested in this larger inquiry: what are the youngsters really learning that makes a difference in their lives? As William James told his students, if what you are learning does not make a difference, then it is not worth learning. Supervisors need to ask concerning the lessons of the classroom: What can students do with this learning besides get the right answer on a test? By asking this question, supervisors will keep their conversations with teachers focused on the truly important things that should be going on in the classrooms, namely, the students' deep understanding of the subject matter. Conversations about pedagogy should concern seeking ways to enhance that kind of learning.

Additional aspects of supervision as moral agency, such as empowerment and community building, can now be considered. First, the more vexing issue of power will be discussed. In traditional schools, supervisors have power over teachers. That power relationship actually undermines the possibility of collegiality and shared moral responsibility for the students. By moving toward empowering relationships that are nested in a community that shares common norms and values, supervisors can free themselves from a dysfunctional, bureaucratic position vis à vis teachers and students for a more genuine moral activity in collaboration with teachers and students.

SUPERVISION AS EMPOWERMENT

The history of educational supervision is one of well-intentioned efforts to control teachers (Gordon, 1992). Supervisors have always been entitled to state and freely express their views on various situations and topics among their hierarchical colleagues and to others in the general school scene. Those surrounding the supervisor, however, have been limited in their capacity to express their responses to their supervisors. "While no one can give a person the power to be herself or himself, it is possible to limit or enlarge that power, especially when one is perceived to have 'power over' that person" (Sergiovanni & Starratt, 1993, p. 59).

Some educational leaders are less than enthusiastic about the word *empowerment*. Even some leaders committed to teacher enablement shy away from the word because it is so "value laden" and generates such strong emotion. The idea of teacher empowerment is inconsistent with the control view of supervision. There is intense debate and resistance generated by the concept of teacher empowerment. These reactions are typical in the flux between one model of behavior and a new emerging paradigm. Why should the control view of supervision be surrendered?

The answer lies in the current education crisis. American public education in general and curriculum and instructional leadership in particular have not successfully adapted to the rapid changing needs and problems of the nation and its young people. They are being called into question as never before. So far, the reaction to this crisis has been to expand rather than reduce control over teachers and instruction. This increasing control has lowered teacher morale and increased teacher stress and resentment, but has failed to solve any of the major problems facing our schools. Each new failure of the control view has resulted in an even more determined effort to increase control and an even more disappointing failure. For these reasons the control view underlying the old supervision is the subject of increasing criticism, and a shift toward the empowerment view seems to be gradually taking place (Gordon, 1992, pp. 65–66).

The notion of teacher empowerment is radically different from and inconsistent with the control view. It would be difficult, if not impossible, to merge these two different versions of what the supervisors' job description entails and the subsequent ability to perform the job.

Current well-meaning supervisors are ensnared in the difficulty of merging evaluation (judging for the purpose of personnel decisions) and supervision (helping for the purpose of teacher development) because they are two entirely different processes that cannot possess the same meaning in one word:

Attempts have been made to differentiate the two by purpose, by technique, by person, and by rhetoric. But . . . a seemingly well-intentioned supervisor tried to separate the two, and could not; because teachers did not perceive a difference, nor could they, given the nature of the law and the press for reform. The language that once helped us to skillfully differentiate the two, now only entangles us. This is the evaluation-supervision dilemma (Hazi, p. 37).

The time has come when supervisors will have to make a decision about how they intend to conduct their professional lives. From a moral standpoint, the empowerment choice is the most appealing as supervisors seek an alternative to the control model. Eventually there will be enough empirical evidence to warrant the mandating of new job descriptions. At present, supervisors can choose to become leaders into the new paradigm. "Educational supervision is nearing an either–or stage regarding the two views; authentic empowerment is currently being tested in a sufficient number of schools across the nation that comparisons with control supervision are inevitable" (Gordon, 1992, p. 66). Given the current crisis in education, if empowerment works where control has failed, the paradigm shift is most likely to accelerate emphatically. There are at least six transitions to be examined in beliefs about supervision, teachers, and change in the relationships found within schools.

Traditional Supervision	New Supervision
Control	Empowerment
Separate functions	Integrated functions
Sameness	Diversity
Occasional supervisor assistance	Continuous collegial support networks
Applied science	Professional inquiry
Mechanical change	Organic change

In traditional supervision, the first two items, control and separate functions, are about the purpose and function of supervision. The next two items, sameness and occasional supervisor assistance, are directed at beliefs about teachers and their needs. The last two items, applied science and mechanical change, look at the improvement process (Gordon, 1992). The first transition is the single most important one within the overall paradigm shift. It represents a change in beliefs about the very core of supervision.

The current educational renewal effort has generated a movement toward the empowerment of teachers, students, and those vital to the school's improved functioning. The term *empowerment* generally denotes the influence teachers can have on decisions and policy-making, especially when those decisions impinge upon students as well as teachers (Beck, 1993). Some teachers have felt, however, that empowerment is a ruse used by administrations to further exploit teachers. Whether this suspicion is justified, the empowerment literature has lacked a philosophical or moral base:

While the empowerment of teachers is supported by many arguments (professionalization of teaching, new career opportunities, organizational culture of schools, school improvement, etc.) . . . arguments for empowerment in the literature tend to concentrate on organizational functions and processes, guided by instrumental rationality or by theories of political participation and emancipation. While these have a legitimacy . . . they [do not] get close enough to the realities of the moral enterprise of teaching. Empowerment ought to have a philosophical base which illuminates its essentially moral qualities (Starratt, 1991, p. 1).

From a moral perspective, empowerment would enable individuals to become more than they were before, to transcend themselves, to become more capable of personal care even while expressing their critical opinion of others.

Terms Surrounding Empowerment

The terms *power, powerlessness, anxiety* and *alienation, choice, personal power* and *empowerment* mean different things to different people. An examination of these terms may be pertinent here.

To many, *power* certainly means experiencing a measure of "control" or "influence." Being in a position to control a situation or decide its outcome confers power (Kaufman & Raphael, 1983). There are many examples of power inherent in a situation. Employers have very real power over employees working in a business: employers can hire or fire employees as well as grant or withhold promotions or raises. That is power. It is exercised through granting freedoms, taking away privileges, and having the final say. Power..."is neither good nor bad; power just is. . . . Teachers have a very real power over their students, the power of a grade" (Kaufman & Raphael, 1983, p. 13). Many would hold that this perspective is essentially immoral because of the unjustified threat that is implied.

Work, school, and family are three crucial settings in which power is either explicit or inevitable. Every social group bears witness to the emergence of power through jockeying for positions of influence or control within the group. The former is the means by which dominance hierarchies begin to emerge within varied groups of people. Power is one motive propelling such social developments. It is a wellspring for many interpersonal negotiations, some of which are destructive.

Power rooted in a position of authority is an instance, but power stretches further into the human experience than is commonly understood. A closer look at the nature of power reveals that, "at another level of manifestation, power, becomes an inevitable undercurrent, if not entirely explicit, within each human relationship" (Kaufman & Raphael, 1983, p. 13). Every relationship between individuals, whether an adult or child, is a power relationship. This idea is pivotal to the view of power unfolding here: "Whenever we care about another's opinion of us, we give that person a measure of power to affect how we feel about ourselves. If someone's judgment counts with us, we are in a position of less power; we are likely to behave in ways to keep that judgment favorable" (Kaufman & Raphael, 1983, p. 13).

In these situations, power has been either freely given or relinquished inadvertently. The power given is no less real than power acquired directly through one's role or position. Either can be respected or abused. "Power has negative overtones to many when associated with coercion, force, threat, or violence. Power often is seen as delegated to the few, who then control the affairs of a community. From this perspective, empowerment implies the powerful impart some of their power to those they dominate" (Sergiovanni & Starratt, 1993, p. 56).

Everyone has experienced powerlessness; it is the earliest known experience. It is what sends the infant into a rage when a parent does not respond. It is the state everyone strives to remove himself from:

Powerlessness is the experiential ground from which emerges the earliest sense of self. It is powerlessness which gives birth to our need for power: to control our hands, to make our legs move as well, to control our bodies and all their functions, to speak our thoughts and have them listened to, to go where we will, to chart our own path according to our inner promptings, to control our own lives and destinies as best we can. It is the profound condition of helplessness in fancy, lasting over many months, which shapes our destiny to become in turn shapers of the social landscape in which we flourish (Kaufman & Raphael, 1983, p. 15).

The feeling of powerlessness that is rooted in our biological helplessness normally recedes through maturation. The feeling of powerlessness in adults, therefore, can be especially devastating especially when one of our primary security areas is threatened. "Either rage, subdued by present hostility, clinging behavior, depression, or hopelessness are prominent feeling states which can be activated by a perception of powerlessness" (Kaufman & Raphael, 1983, p. 16). The German term for this feeling is *angst* which denotes inordinate fear, fright, or anxiety.

The morally mature person is one who delicately balances both "me" and "I" amidst and through the exciting and mundane, the spontaneous and contrived experiences between individuals. That performance is worth not only applause, but, as with any fine art, worth viewing and reviewing. What is enacted is the moral integrity of the individual. This total performance reflects a quest for authenticity, an integration of need, perception of context and ideas. Because the balance is the handiwork of the morally mature individual, the persona created is an evolving response to the challenges that life presents. The quest for authenticity is particularly fulfilling when individuals are fortunate enough to find others honestly living out their own lives with similar authenticity. Mature moral persons can afford to remain loyal to their own dreams, yet also remain responsible to others they encounter in the larger communal landscape. The drama of social interaction must be seen, therefore, as the rich and complex performance of each individual in an encounter with others and with him or herself in experiences of social life.

There is a second dimension to powerlessness which is quite another matter. How is power given to another individual? Through offering a choice. When given a choice, persons feel a measure of power. Having a choice in a situation enables the self to feel a measure of control which then offsets feelings of helplessness. "Having a choice in a powerless situation is one vital route to restoring power. To see choices in a situation in which we feel powerless is a cornerstone in the foundation of competence" (Kaufman & Raphael, 1983, p. 16).

It is also the cornerstone of authenticity and autonomy necessary for moral behavior. This is the heart of the matter for the empowerment of teachers. The empowerment movement will make little difference if individuals do not choose to be empowered. The individual would necessarily have to be invited to make a choice to be authentic within him or herself, before any efforts to empower would make any difference.

The Most Basic Power: To Be Oneself

The power of self-determination has been a formative idea in American political life; it underlies the democratic ideal.

Self-determination is seen as the basis of living authentically. Modern consciousness has deeply ingrained the concept of authenticity, but it was not always so. Before the eighteenth century, no one thought that the differences between human beings had moral significance:

One way of describing its development is to see its starting point in the eighteenth century notion that human beings are endowed with a moral sense, an intuitive feeling for what is right and wrong. The original point of this doctrine was to combat a rival view, that knowing right and wrong was a matter of calculating consequences, in particular those concerned with divine reward and punishment. The notion was that understanding right and wrong was not a matter of dry calculation, but was anchored in our feelings. Morality has, in a sense, a voice within (Taylor, 1991, p. 26).

The most basic understanding of power is that which everyone possesses, namely, the power to be oneself.

The most unique power each person possesses is the power to be herself or himself. No one else has the power to be you. Only you can exercise that power. You may fail to use that power and instead try to to live up to an idea that others have of you, or to some fantasy image provided by popular culture. That power is the power to say yes and the power to say no to such images. The power may be heavily circumscribed by circumstances in your present context, but it is a power you never lose. You may turn it over to other people, but it always belongs to you. It is the power to be yourself, to sing your own song, dance your own dance, speak your own poetry. It is the power to be true to your best self, rather than the self that is fearful, jealous, or spiteful" (Sergiovanni & Starratt, 1993, p. 56).

This choice to be authentic requires living consciously on a daily basis. What is most important to learn about living life is given the least amount of attention: How can individuals feel an inner sense of competence as well as power in the world? Finding a direction and meaning for ourselves, coping with life's stresses, in addition to its uncertainties, are basic skills of living that are rarely addressed. Learning to feel secure in a rapidly changing environment while creating satisfying human relationships is a task largely ignored in school.

Dynamics of Empowerment

The "new" supervisor becomes a mentor of mentors and leader of leaders, an authentic colleague, and role model rather than control agent. In the new supervision, reciprocal, helping relationships develop between supervisors and teachers as well as among teachers. It acknowledges the teachers' right and obligation to make discretionary judgments about which teaching protocols are useful in their individual teaching contexts. Thus, while formally designated supervisors may be vital to teacher empowerment, the new supervision is identified more with a leadership process than with any single role, a process in which all teachers are invited to participate. In this process, the supervisor brings the school's unfinished agenda to the table for discussion. The supervisor may remind teachers of the school's values in order to encourage their own sense of purpose (Sergiovanni, 1995).

Supervisors as moral agents in the educational setting demonstrate a different attitude and character than in the traditional scheme of educational governance. Among the moral concerns of the supervisors is the issue of creating a " . . . mutual process of discovering what the power to be and the power to do means in a particular school, what positive qualities are attached to the exercise of that power, and what limitations are imposed by the circumstances of the communal effort at schooling" (Sergiovanni & Starratt, 1993, p. 59).

Supervisors' can to create an environment where masks can be removed by overcoming personal fear and mistrust. "Such a process of empowerment involves mutual respect, dialogue, and invitations; it implies recognition that each person enjoys talents, competencies, and potentials which are being exercised in responsible and creative ways for the benefit of the students" (Sergiovanni & Starratt, 1993, p. 59). It is a transition from viewing supervision as a means of controlling teachers' instructional behaviors to viewing supervision as a channel for teacher empowerment. Within this relationship, both teachers and supervisors exercise their power to be who they are with each other, to be their real selves, not someone simply filling a role in a system. "It implies that teachers legitimately and necessarily model what it means to be genuine in the way they conduct their relationships with their students and in the way they engage them in the learning material itself" (Sergiovanni & Starratt, 1993, p. 59). Supervisors would model authentic behavior in all their encounters. Within this atmosphere, empowerment may occur as part of a school's renewal efforts.

Empowerment in the Moral Heterarchal Structure

Moral empowerment certainly requires restructuring the hierarchy of the educational organization into a heterarchal and inclusive form of governance. It requires much more of a community structure composed of administrators, teachers, students, parents, and community members all taking part in their larger drama, than that which now exists, of a pyramid model stacked with groups and individuals disjointed from one another (Elmore, 1995). "Supervisors, by creating a trusting and supportive relationship with teachers, can enlarge the relational space teachers need to be more fully themselves: (Sergiovanni & Starrat, 1993, p. 59). In the heterarchal organization, education becomes the larger drama of the community and enjoins all participants to couple their own drama to it. The drama of empowered moral education invites all participants to allow their individual dramas to be honored, indeed, celebrated in the larger drama that includes intellectual activities of inquiry, debate, creative expression, authentic behavior, reflective thinking and play, conflict, struggle, and celebration. School and learning and growing can (even) be a joy.

School as a Theater for Action

If social life contains the drama of striving toward and creating the balance between the "me" and the "I" and others, then school is a natural setting for the social interactions that provide the culture for children to draw out the rough draft of their creations. This would be a school where children play and read, learn and decide, participate as individuals, and as teams. School must provide the space for the balance each person is seeking between personal integrity and mutuality with others. The school setting and the schooling process are conceived as large enough to provide this moral environment. School is a human construct comprised of individuals, of "administrators, teachers, students, parents, alumni and community members, active in their own struggle for moral beauty and their exchanges with each other" (Beck, 1994, p. 110). School then really can be recognized as drama, the natural setting, in which teachers become pivotal in "developing and implementing organization strategies." Supervisors in this paradigm are asked to support and dialogue with teachers. The dialogue between teachers and supervisors would focus and direct those strategies, but must go further conscientiously and circumspectly to "reassess personal and professional values. Resisting the equation of worth with academic achievement. They would treat students as instrinsically valuable and evaluate accomplishments as signs or indicators of growth and development" (Beck, 1994, p. 112). Supervisors and teachers' fundamental moral professional responsibility becomes the underscoring and enhancement of the basic dignity of all, rejecting the notion that achievement is the only goal in education (Beck, 1994).

Morally Empowering Teachers

Teachers spend the majority of their days in the classroom in direct contact with students. It is this aspect of their careers that they find most satisfying. Many consider this profession a "calling," not simply a job, and are deeply concerned about the welfare and progress of their students (Hansen, 1995). Many teachers refer to their students as "my kids." It is in this dimension that moral activity is manifested in schools. "Teachers are happy enough when their students score well on exams; however they are most fulfilled when their students delight in what they are learning. It is at this level that a supervisor engages the teacher in the moral dimensions of teaching. At this level supervisors engage in one of the fundamental aspects of empowerment" (Sergiovanni & Starratt, 1993, p. 56).

SUPERVISION IN AND FOR COMMUNITY

The wicked leader is he who the people despise. The good leader is he who the people revere. The great leader is he who the people say, "We did it ourselves."

Lao Tsu

Meaning of Community

The moral agent in an organizational setting such as the school needs to create an environment of caring that calls forth and bestows care among administrators, supervisors, teachers, students, and parents. The premise of this caring ethic is the inherent worth of the individual and the fundamentally com-

munal nature of education and schooling (Beck, 1994; Noddings, 1992). Educators adhering to this ethic believe that education is a human enterprise and that its finest purpose is promoting the fullest growth and development of persons (Buber, 1957; Gilligan, 1982; Noddings, 1992; Sergiovanni, 1994; Starratt, 1991). In addition, they are convinced "that the integrity of human relationships should be held sacred and that the school as an organization should hold the good of human beings within it as sacred" (Starratt, 1991, p. 195).

Perceptions

The standard psychology textbook picture of the old hag and young girl in a feathered hat may serve to illustrate a pertinent concept concerning perception. Some people see the old hag, others see the young girl, and still others can see both, although both cannot be seen simultaneously. Some cannot see either if not told that they are there to see. Perceptions about the world are that way—some are told to us and we never see the other one—sometimes we see both and have to make a choice between how we want to see the world. Our perceptions define our reality and some of us never see the possibilities for our own reality; hence, we only live our lives through the perceptions of others. The supervisors' perceptions create teachers' reality for better or for worse.

Gemeinschaft versus Gesellschaft

The terms *gemeinschaft* and *gesellschaft* are attributed to the German sociologist Ferdinand Tonnies. Gesellschaft describes a society based on an economic and instrumentalist model of society in which what individuals do and sell are more important than who people are in relationship to one another. According to Sergiovanni (1994), schools are learning the need to move toward gemenischaft. He describes three forms of gemeinschaft communities: by kinship, of place, and of mind. Kinship involves a unity of being, in the sense of "we," which families provide. Place is the sharing of common habitat or locale (e.g., my class, my school, my neighborhood, my town, my country). Gemeinschaft of mind forms by binding to a common goal, set of values, and *shared conception of being*. Gemeinschaft of mind represents the truly human and supreme form of *gemeinschaft* or community.

McWilliams describes gemeinschaft in Beck (1994) as "the dream of community which . . . has more than once helped support the effort to conquer nature in the hope that . . . it might lead humanity back to 'oneness'" (p. 21). The interrelatedness among people which community strives for is natural and desirable. The desire for relationships distinguishes humanity (Beck, 1993; Buber, 1957; Noddings, 1992). It compensates for "cosmic insecurity," in which life becomes reduced to mistrust and hostility, where there is nothing to support or sustain community (Buber, 1957).

Schools as Democratic Communities

Communities are made up of people who cluster together in a variety of groups. Groups function along two dimensions:

social and task. Successful groups are successful in interpersonal relationships and in working together on common tasks. Sometimes the social aspects predominate; sometimes they focus on a common task. The work on common tasks normally requires a minimal level of positive social relationships. Too great a concentration on social relationships sometimes gets in the way of the common tasks, as when students in a cooperative learning team fail to meet deadlines because they are having fun sharing stories.

In schools, the community is made up of groups of students and teachers and administrators. Students cluster in a variety of groups, depending on race, sex, interest (jocks, brains, nerds, druggies, drifters, etc.), common neighborhoods, ethnicity, and so on. They are often involved with several groups (an African-American female who plays on the girls' volleyball team and serves on the student government). Teachers cluster in groups such as subject matter departments, grade levels, cross-disciplinary teams, multiage class cohorts, as well as by race, sex, ethnicity, etc. Again, they are often involved with several groups such as the male art teacher who works with three grade level groups of teachers in a "writing across the curriculum" project, and serves on the school's grievance committee and the long-range planning committee. Generally, the more teachers and students participate in several groups, the greater likelihood there is of a stronger sense of community, for through these multiple involvements, they gain a larger view of the whole as it manages its institutional purposes.

Schools reorganize communities to provide landscapes of meaning for the participants in that community. In communities, people live in the shelter of each other. Sergiovanni (1995) defines community as "collections of people bonded together by mutual commitments and special relationships, who together are bound to a set of shared ideas and values that they believe in, and feel compelled to follow. This bonding and binding helps them to become members of a tightly knit web of meaningful relationships with moral overtones. In communities of this kind, people belong, people care, people help each other, people make and keep commitments, people feel responsible for themselves and responsible to others" (p. 100). Yet, these kinds of communities do not fall from the sky. They must be nurtured in a consistent environment of trust. They take time to develop.

Schools as communities have two purposes. One is the promotion of quality academic learning for all students. The second is the socialization of the group into the experience and practice of the community itself. Theoretically, the first purpose could be achieved through home instruction, or through the use of a tutor. Schools bring youngsters together, however, in sizable groups, not simply for reasons of efficiency (although in earlier factory models of schools that was a dominant theme), but primarily so that they will learn how to get along with others who are different from them, to learn the customs and rules of social intercourse, and to gain an initial experience of democratic community life.

While much has been written about the process of collaborative learning of academic subjects, the field is still exploring the many aspects of the second purpose of schooling, namely, the learning of the practice of democratic living. The recent

trend toward site-based management and participatory decision-making has been considered a major element in the school restructuring effort. Unfortunately, these reform strategies have been seen primarily as either technical challenges or political strategies, rather than as a move toward reconstituting schools away from the bureaucratic factory model to a democratic communitarian one.

Supervisors can play a significant part in the difficult process of moving away from the bureaucratic factory model to the democratic communitarian model. They can assist in this transition from a moral as well as a technical commitment. Moral commitment actually requires the technical competence of consensus building, conflict resolution, arbitration, building, but it also involves concern with vision and purpose and human fulfillment and the building up of the civic community.

Stages of Development in School Communities

As groups face their common tasks, they also face a range of decisions. The first decision is to decide what the common tasks are. Other decisions involve questions of who does what, who gets what to achieve the task, what kind of coordination mechanisms and processes are needed, how to monitor the quality achievement of the tasks, how to assess the final product, and more. As a group struggles with those decisions to reach consensus on issues, autonomous individuals have to give up their control of their own terrain for the solution of the problem on the table and be willing to act in behalf of the group's decision rather than their own. This is one essential of forming successful communities.

Each of us has a hand in this collective ideal, which makes for the integrity of the group, which in turn is the sacred thing, par excellence. Consequently, each of us shares the religious deference inspired by this ideal. The bond to the group thus implies, in an indirect but almost necessary way, the bond to other individuals; when the group ideal is only a particular manifestation of the human ideal—when the citizen-ideal merges in large measure with the generic ideal of mankind—then it is man qua man that we are bound, at the same time feeling more strongly linked with those in whom we find most clearly our society's particular conception of humanity [emphasis added]" (Durkheim, 1973, p. 82).

It behooves individuals to join in the community for at least two reasons: "It is better to plan for oneself, no matter how badly than to be planned for by others, no matter how well" (Caldwell & Spinks, 1988, p. 63). Second, groups effect change." In fact, the lone individual, reduced to his own resources, is unable to alter the social situation. One can act effectively upon society only by grouping individual efforts in such a way as to counter social forces with social forces" (Durkheim, 1973, p. 83).

As the group is forming, the individual is asked to come and participate with others. The individual moves from an atomized, passive existence to a potential of interaction with others. Morality can only occur in relation with others (Durkheim, 1973). Without the formation of a group, there is no opportunity for an individual to act morally. Schools in which isolation among administration, teachers, and students is the norm, cannot foster the emergence of moral behavior toward one another.

In the process of forming, all members of the group are moving from behind their masks and out of this shielded territory to give genuine views on the issue the group is discussing, all members are afforded the opportunity for their input. Within the formation process, the moral integrity of the group is forged. The individual is a moral agent by being able to remove his or her mask as an autonomous agent in a welcoming atmosphere. This gives the individual a chance to be moral. Each member adds to the collective group truth.

The authority of a decision, idea, or plan, then, is arrived at by group consensus, and derives its power not from one individual supported by several others. It derives its authority from the sacred authority vested in each individual who has contributed to the decision. The "sacred" authority in the arrived at norm of behavior, or decision, comes from each participant. However, it is the sum of all participants and thus is greater than any individual (Durkheim, 1973, p. 83). It represents a collective, developing community.

The collective conscience is an ideal formed by individual members of a group. Consensus is a decision all members of the group are willing to live with. As it is a representative group decision, it is infused with the ideal because it is collective. Underscoring this rationale, Zelenik and Moment (1964) clarify the nature of consensus as commitment: "Our meaning of consensus lies in the degree of personal commitment the members feel toward the group decision after it is reached. This means, for example, that even though some members might disagree with the decision on principle, they will accept it and personally carry out their part. Their emotional commitment to the group is measured by willingness to put the plan decided on into effect in their own personal behavior" (p. 142).

The essential ingredient of consensus is the extent of group loyalty shared by the members, so it is necessary to have all members feel that they belong and are needed regardless of their entire agreement with the decision at hand. "This is what explains the moral character ascribed to sentiments of interpersonal sympathy and acts prompted by such feelings. In themselves, they do not constitute intrinsic elements of the moral temperament; but they are closely linked to the most basic moral dispositions, while their absence may be taken to indicate—and not unreasonably—an inferior morality" (Durkheim, 1973, p. 83).

The former factory structure of schools therefore, displays an innate immorality in its structure of individuals using and being used to create workers rather than individuals working together, helping each other at a task or goal. The former structure does not allow space and time for people to interact in primarily human ways, and so does not permit the growth of morality among them.

Community Membership as Citizenship

These collective decisions are crucial to a community's learning to govern itself. Insofar as a group of people agree to treat each other in certain ways (e.g., with respect) and to avoid treating others in certain ways (e.g., with violence or contempt), they are agreeing to govern themselves in their everyday exchanges with one another. The community self-governance, in effect, creates a sense of citizenship among community members. They have certain rights as citizens of that community and they have concomitant responsibilities to respect the rights of fellow citizens.

In schools, there should be some form of covenant by which members of the school community bind themselves to one another (Sergiovanni, 1994). The terms of the covenant define, in a real sense, the terms of citizenship. These become the expectations and ideals that a school holds itself to. The large ideals of the covenant become the benchmarks for smaller agreements; for example, a teacher and class deciding the behavior that will be encouraged and the behavior that will be prohibited in the class. In these instances, it is easy to see the basic moral agenda: learning how to honor agreements, how to disagree nonviolently, how to forgive when the covenants are broken, how to celebrate in song and symbol the ideals of the covenant.

Sergiovanni (1994) spells out the details of the building of this community. After the initial covenant and its purposes have been established, community is built through the curriculum, through democratic processes in the classroom and the administration of the school, through the collaboration of teachers in service to the larger community, in all the co-curricular activities of the school, and through a strong partnership with adults in the home.

Because supervisors engage teachers and students both in classrooms and around the school, because they often sit on a large number of committees that link segments of the school together and segments of the school system together, they are in a very influential position to work for the building up of community in school. They can help first of all to build a covenant in the school, and then help to remind members of the school to bring the ideals of the covenant into their long- and short-term decisions.

THE RESTRUCTURING AGENDA AS MORAL ACTION

Supervisors, as an identifiable group of educators, have not been at the forefront of those calling for school restructuring or of those stepping forward with specific proposals for restructuring. This is due, in part, to the traditional role of supervisory oversight of teachers *as individuals* rather than oversight of what groups of teachers might be attempting. This traditional concern, moreover, has tended to focus exclusively on pedagogical skills rather than on the larger structural and policy environment of the school.

Supervisors, nevertheless, are in a unique position within the school to engage in the work of restructuring. They occupy that middle level in the schools between the teachers and higher administrators and policymakers. They can represent the concerns and aspirations of teachers to higher levels of administration as well as the concerns and aspirations of administrators to teachers. They can mediate and arbitrate apparent and real conflicts between the two levels. Furthermore, their work with teachers enables them to be spokespersons for their students as well, pointing out structural or policy hindrances to quality learning.

As several have pointed out, restructuring schooling requires a significant redesign of the work of the superintendent, principal, teachers, and schools (Sergiovanni, 1995; Starratt, 1996). It necessarily requires a redesign of supervisors' work (Sergiovanni & Starratt, 1993). If teachers are going to redesign their work to encourage the full involvement of students in the learning express, they are going to need to be involved in redesigning the whole school environment (use of space, time, school and community resources, etc.) to make it more user-friendly for an active student learning process (Elmore, 1995). Yet, teachers are unused to thinking about redesigning the whole school; their horizon has normally been restricted to their individual classrooms. The supervisor can move into the role of coordinating teachers' involvement in the work of school redesign, not as the "answer man" or as the control person for the superintendent, but as someone whose view of the school is more encompassing in that he or she is able to see the impact of one change on many elements in the system. During the planning and implementation phase of school restructuring, it makes no sense for the supervisor to carry on the traditional observation pattern, which assumes a process of teaching and learning that is the very object of many restructuring changes.

Supervisors as Change Facilitators

During this time of second-order change, there is a need for change facilitators. Donahue (1993) suggests that change agents for school improvement should: be a teacher and an administrator; be knowledgeable about teaching, curriculum, and assessment; know how to negotiate amidst political complexity; and be able to build consensus among groups. Most supervisors would fit that job description. Among other responsibilities, such change agents will need ". . . to prepare and organize the school for change, to identify the areas in which staff members are weak, such as leadership skills and group decision-making, and to provide the training they need; to help the principal adapt to a new management style . . . to keep the focus of activity on improved student achievement; and to recognize when schools are attempting too little or too much and then to help them establish the right pace of change." (Donohue, 1993, p. 30). Supervisors have the advantage over outside (and expensive) consultants, since they are already familiar with the individuals involved in the change. Rather than employing strangers who would require more time to familiarize themselves with who is who and what is what, the supervisors already have that information in hand. The cost of creating change need not be increased by the addition of a new position of change agent. Rather, supervisors are in the right position to take on many of these duties. These duties would require the transformation of the supervisors' work from overseer of individual teachers to enablers for the whole faculty.

Overcoming Resistance to Change

As the literature on second-order change makes abundantly clear, the process is messy, slow, and somewhat unpre-

dictable (Fullan, 1991). Many in the schools will resist, not out of some malicious conspiracy, but because the traditional routines of the school (eight class periods a day, grading, and labeling of children) and of the classroom (45-minute periods, discrete subject matter division, reliance on textbooks for curriculum context and sequence, teacher delivering instruction/curriculum to the children, etc.) have come to define the way things should be. The call for major changes often implies that everything that has been done up to now is wrong; hence, this implied accusation is resented and resisted. To let go of long accustomed routines is unsettling. There is concern that those involved would not be able to carry off the new protocol and that they may look incompetent under the new order of things; it is therefore better to stick with the "tried and true." Those leading change can end up being resented, ridiculed, and rejected. It is difficult to stay the course, holding to the dream or vision of what schooling might become.

Hence, it is legitimate to speak of the *discipline* involved in working at second-order change. That discipline assumes a deep moral commitment to school improvement by creating a user-friendly community that promotes high quality learning for all students. It is a moral commitment to those students who find school meaningless and alienating and for those in the middle who are not in the honors program, nor in the remedial programs. They are routinely processed as school statistics and predictable failures. This moral commitment is to help the school make a difference in every student's life and to offer a chance for personal success and recognition as someone who has something important to contribute.

Supervisors and teachers who embrace the risky business of redesigning their roles have an opportunity to engage in transforming leadership—the kind that raises people's sights toward higher moral goals of the community and for the community. It is an exhilarating reach to transcend narrow self-interest and to participate in an enabling endeavor for children; however, it will involve the endurance of conflict, misunderstanding, and the uneven, slow pace of change. That is moral action of a higher order. It goes beyond interpersonal caring to the building of a more humane workable learning community, to the transformation of an institution.

For the supervisor, moving into this new role will require initiative. It will involve building coalitions among teachers. It will mean teamwork with administrators who are struggling to redefine their roles. We like to think of this redefined role of supervisor as one who models reflective practice (Schon, 1983). Everyone in the school will be required to learn by a certain amount of trial and error. The change facilitator (the new supervisor) will help them reflect on what they are learning—bringing them to double-loop learning where they can recognize the structural or institutional constraints and possibilities (Argyris, 1977) that underlie a particularly problematic situation. The practice of reflection is something the new supervisor will attempt to institutionalize, for it is one of the chief marks of a learning organization (Senge, 1990). The new supervisor will also be a carrier of ideas—not the only carrier to be sure—one who, in moving from one working subgroup to another, will pollinate the groups with ideas he or she has picked up from another group. As the new supervisor moves from group to group, he or she will remind the groups to keep their priorities clear and to be guided by them. The new supervisor will pause to help teachers create a new conceptual framework that will enable them to reconceptualize their work or to see a problem from a fresh perspective.

The new supervisor will turn the definition of supervision on its head. The new work concerns "super vision," not looking over other's shoulders, but pointing to, creating, and discussing with the community of teachers a large vision of what the school needs to become. As a facilitator, the new supervisor keeps the groups working toward that Super Vision, helping them to interpret it for various elements in the school.

In suggesting this last role for the supervisor, we are clearly working in the optative mode. It is a form of thinking that is not based on any specific research. Rather, it is an attempt to project what seems to be a logical progression for supervisors to take. If the restructuring of schools continues on its course, the traditional role of the supervisor must of necessity change, if not entirely evanesce (Gordon, 1992). Moving toward the change agent/facilitator role enables the supervisor to function from the familiar middle-level position, but now with a much more ambitious and morally challenging agenda. Although the challenges are greater, the satisfaction should be deeper for this new kind of work.

FURTHER RESEARCH AGENDA

There remains a large research agenda for the future. Clearly one focus for research would be a series of in-depth interviews with supervisors to attempt to surface in their own words a vocabulary for identifying more adequately the moral leadership of supervision. Another series of studies needs to explore actual attempts of supervisors to empower teachers. This would require intense and sensitive supervisor–teacher interaction in order to build the level of trust needed to explore new dimensions of teaching. Building that collaborative relationship would be different with a veteran teacher than with a novice teacher. The personal and professional risks of collaborating with a supervisor and with other teachers must be met with a corresponding offer of support and acceptance. In other words, the moral integrity of the supervisor will be tested in a variety of ways. This more delicate and personalized supervisory approach would require a more qualitative type of research methodology in which the researcher's moral integrity would likewise need to be established.

The same sensitivity and integrity would be required of the researcher studying how supervisors build community around shared covenants. Levels of trust among teachers and supervisors might not initially be shared with the researcher who wants to "study them."

It would be interesting to discover whether there are any supervisors in the field who are engaged in the agenda of restructuring or involved in second-order change in the school. There must be, but they are probably supervisors who wear two or three other hats. Most likely, in the process of engaging in school restructuring, their supervisory activity has been gradually transformed, so that what supervising they do

is embedded in the collegial effort with teachers to enhance student learning, rather than a distinct formal exercise of a pre-announced and prescripted observation of a class. Careful studies of how supervision remains a legitimate responsibility of the supervisor, even though it is now more thoroughly integrated into collaborative efforts with teachers to create performative student work environments, could provide challenging contrasts to the previously more isolated and detached types of classroom observations and teacher evaluations. In-depth interviews with supervisors engaged in the larger challenge of restructuring should probe the possibility of increased moral satisfaction among supervisors in this kind of engagement with teachers. These studies could also reveal whether more traditional forms of supervision survive in this newer atmosphere of collaboration in restructuring the learning environment.

There is a need, finally, for studies that explore whether the called-for restructuring of the learning environment links three morally satisfying levels of work. If the restructured learning environment results in more authentic, personalized learning on the part of the student, then learning would come to be seen as a morally fulfilling activity, an activity that involves reverence for and appreciation of what is being learned, which simultaneously confers a sense of integrity to the learner. It is expected that as teachers listen to students talk about how and what they are learning, a more morally satisfying relationship with the learner develops. Now as mentor, coach, and guide, they would feel justifiable pride in the growth and achievements of the student. The teachers' commitments to their students, to nurture their growth would be rewarded by their students working hard to learn and to produce a quality piece of work. Teaching would become a growing source of moral, as well as professional, satisfaction. As teachers observe how learning gradually transforms and enriches the lives of their students, the "virtue" of teaching becomes more deeply apparent and appreciated.

Supervisors who see the results of their work with teachers bearing fruit from one learning setting to another would feel morally satisfied. The supervisor could see quality student performance and inventive teacher interventions in the learning process. The supervisors' own appreciation of the moral agency of the supervisor would grow through their understanding of the moral agency embedded in teaching and in learning. Few, if any, studies have yet to probe these limits.

Besides the research implications of this chapter, there are implications for the preparation of supervisors in professional development and university programs. It is suggested that prospective as well as practicing supervisors need to develop a much deeper appreciation of the many ways children and youths construct meaning out of what is presented in the curriculum. They have to appreciate the active nature of learning so as to understand a whole new way of teaching, a way that relies much more on the student mentally and imaginatively handling the material rather than on the teacher passing on information. They have to understand, moreover, what is morally at stake in the activity of learning, namely, the integrity of what is being learned and the self-construction of the learner in the process of learning. The change from viewing teaching as a series of protocols that the teacher performs to how the teacher structures learning activities and responds to the students in the process of their constructing meaning would develop from the supervisor's close attention to students as they learn; listening to and observing them as they are deciphering the learning activity, just the way teachers listen and observe. Only then can they begin to appreciate the many subtle ways the teacher responds to the student, leading the students to ask further questions of the material under study and to probe for additional information to what they already know. Practice in listening to and observing students and teachers engaged in learning needs to be built into course work and clinical experiences in the field.

Likewise, field-based clinics that develop teacher empowerment are called for. Beyond practicing this art, the supervisor-to-be should be immersed in community-building experiences. Besides the one-on-one trust-building exercises, they need to gain an experiential appreciation of how powerfully a community of educators can affect the quality of student learning and indeed the quality of life in the school. Supervisors must also learn to appreciate the many opportunities they have in the course of their work day to build up or tear down the sense of community among the staff.

Finally supervisors-to-be need to be confronted with their own moral responsibility to exercise leadership with the teachers in the arduous, complex, time-consuming work of making schools more responsive to diverse students with their diverse cultures, interests, and abilities so that all students become actively engaged in their own learning. Exercises in the design of classroom learnings, of whole programs, and of whole schools will help the supervisors-to-be

to participate on the job in the reconstruction of classrooms and schools.

All of this suggests that university programs for supervisors need to take stock of themselves. It is not unusual to find supervision professors lecturing to a class of 20 students on the importance of constructivist approaches to learning while students doze off. More supervision courses should be taught within courses for teachers on constructivist research in student learning. Supervisors need to attend classes and work on class projects with teachers so they will recognize and experience the collaboration between teachers and themselves. Working together will reinforce their moral commitments to their students and to the work of learning.

CONCLUSIONS

This chapter attempted to map the moral landscape of supervision. Since this aspect of supervision has rarely been researched, described, or even imagined, we felt relatively free to construct the map as it made sense to us. As such, it is a beginning to what we hope will be a developing conversation between theory, research, training, and practice. When supervision is viewed as a moral activity as well as a professional activity, it takes on a depth and importance and, indeed, a legitimacy that, in the minds of many, it lacks. We believe that by appreciating the moral dimensions of supervision, both teachers and administrators can view their own participation in the renewal of schools from a richer and more self-fulfilling perspective.

REFERENCES

Apple, M. (1982). *Education and power.* Boston, MA: Routledge & Kegan Paul.

Argyris, C. (1977). Double loop learning in organization. *Harvard Business Review, 55*(5), 115–125.

Bates, R. J. (1984). Toward a critical practice of educational administration. In T. J. Sergiovanni & J. E. Corbally (Eds.). *Leadership and organizational culture: New perspectives on administrative theory and practice* (pp. 260–274). Urbana & Chicago: University of Illinois Press.

Beck, L. (1994). *Reclaiming educational administration as a caring profession.* New York: Teachers College Press.

Buber, M. (1957). *I and thou.* Translated by Ronald Gregor Smith. New York: Scribner.

Burns, J. M. (1978). *Leadership.* New York: Harper & Row.

Cogan, M. (1973). *Clinical supervision.* New York: Houghton-Mifflin.

Costa, L. & Garmston, R. J. (1994). *Cognitive coaching: A foundation for renaissance schools.* Norwood, MA: Christopher-Gordon Publishers, Inc.

Donohoe, T. (1993). Finding the way: Structure, time, and culture in school improvement. *Phi Delta Kappan 75*(4), 298–305.

Eisenstadt, S. N. (Ed.) (1968). *Max Weber: On charisma and institution building.* Chicago, IL: University of Chicago Press.

Elmore, R. F. (1995). Teaching, learning, and school organization: Principles of practice and the regularities of school information. *Educational Administration Quarterly, 31*(3), 355–374.

Foster, W. (1986). *Paradigms and promises.* Buffalo, NY: Prometheus Books.

Fullan, M. G. (1991). *The new meaning of educational change.* New York: Teachers College Press.

Gewirth, A. (1982). *Human rights: Essays in justification and applications.* Chicago, IL: University of Chicago Press.

Giddens, A. (1984). *The constitution of society.* Berkeley, CA: University of California Press.

Gilligan, C. (1982). *In a different voice: Psychological theory and women's development.* Cambridge, MA: Harvard University Press.

Giroux, H. (1988). *Teachers as intellectual: Toward a critical pedagogy of learning.* Granby, MA: Bergin & Garvey.

Glatthorn, A. A. (1984). *Differentiated supervision.* Alexandria, VA: ASCD.

Glickman, C. D. (1985). *Supervision and instruction: A developmental approach.* Boston, MA: Allyn and Bacon.

Glickman, C. D. (1992). Introduction: Postmodernism and supervision. In C. D. Glickman (Ed.). *Supervision in transition* (pp. 1–3). Alexandria, VA: ASCD.

Goldhammer, R., Anderson, R. H., & Krajewski, R. J. (1980). *Clinical supervision: Special methods for the supervising of teachers* (2nd ed.). New York: Holt.

Gordon, S. P. (1992, Fall). Perspectives and imperatives: Paradigms, transitions, and the new supervisor. *Journal of Curriculum and Supervision, 8*(1), 62–76.

Greene, M. (1995). *Releasing the imagination.* San Francisco, CA: Jossey-Bass.

Grossman, P. & Stodolsky, S. (1995). Content as context: The role of school subjects in secondary school teaching. *Educational Researcher, 24*(8), 5–11, 23.

Hansen, D. T. (1995). *The call to teach.* New York: Teachers College Press.

Hazi, H. M. (in press). *The teacher evaluation-supervision dilemma: A case of entanglements and irreconcilable differences.* Morgantown, WV: West Virginia University.

Heslep, R. D. (1995). *Moral education for Americans.* Westport, CT: Praeger.

Jackson, P., Boonstrom, R. E., & Hansen, D. T. (1993). *The moral life of schools.* San Francisco, CA: Jossey-Bass.

Juska, J. (1991). Observations. *Phi Delta Kappa, 72*(6), 468.

Kaufman, G. & Raphael, L. (1983). *Dynamics of power: Fighting shame and building self-esteem.* Rochester, VT: Schenkman Books, Inc.

Kimbrough, R. B. (1985). *Ethics: A current study for educational leaders.* Arlington, VA: American Association of School Administrators.

Kohlberg, L. (1981a). *Essays on moral development: The philosophy of moral development* (Vol. 1). New York: Harper-Collins.

Kohlberg, L. (1981b). *The psychology of moral development. Essays on moral development* (Vol. 2). San Francisco, CA: Harper and Row.

Lickona, T. (1989). *Educating for character.* New York. Bantam.

Lightfoot, S. L. (1983). *The good high school: Portraits of character and culture.* New York: Basic Books.

MacIntyre, A. (1984). *After virtue.* Notre Dame, IN: University of Notre Dame Press.

Noddings, N. (1984). *Caring: A feminine approach to ethics and moral education.* Berkeley, CA: University of California Press.

Noddings, N. (1992). *The challenge to care in schools.* New York: Teachers College Press.

Oakes, J. (1985). *Keeping back: How schools structure inequality.*

Ortiz, F. I. & Marshall, C. (1988). *Women in educational administration.* In N. Boyan (Ed.). Handbook of research on educational administration (pp. 123–142). New York.

Purpel, D. E. (1989). *The moral and spiritual crisis in education: A curriculum for justice and compassion in education.* Branby, MA.: Bergen & Garvey.

Schon, D. (1983). *The reflective practitioner: How professionals think in action.* New York: Basic Books.

Scriven, M. (1990). Can research-based teacher evaluation be saved? *Journal of Personal Evaluation in Education, 4*(1), 19-32.

Senge, P. (1990). *The fifth discipline: The art & practice of the learning organization.* New York: Doubleday/Currency.

Sergiovanni, T. J. (1992). *Moral leadership: Getting to the heart of school improvement.* San Francisco, CA: Jossey-Bass.

Sergiovanni, T. J. (1994). *Building community in schools.* San Francisco, CA: Jossey-Bass.

Sergiovanni, T. J. (1995). *Leadership for the schoolhouse.* San Francisco, CA: Jossey-Bass.

Sergiovanni, T. J. & Starratt, R. J. (1993). *Supervision: A redefinition.* New York: McGraw-Hill.

Shakeshaft, C. (1987). *Women in educational administration.* Park, CA: Corwin Press.

Starratt, R. J. (1991, May). Building an ethical school: A theory for practice in educational leadership. *Educational Administration Quarterly, 30,* pp. 195–202.

Starratt, R. J. (1994). *Building an ethical school: A practical response to the moral crisis in schools.* London & Washington, D.C.: Falmer Press.

Starratt, R. J. (1996). *Transforming educational administration.* New York: McGraw Hill.

Taylor, C. (1989). *Sources of the self: The making of the modern identity.* Cambridge, MA: Harvard University Press.

Taylor, C. (1991). *The ethics of authenticity.* Cambridge, MA: Harvard University Press.

Zelenik, A. & Moment, D. (1964). *The dynamics of interpersonal behavior.* New York: Wiley.

·41·

SUPERVISION SERVICES
IN THE NETHERLANDS
AND OTHER COUNTRIES

Ruud J. Gorter

ASSOCIATION OF EDUCATIONAL ADVISORY CENTERS, THE HAGUE, THE NETHERLANDS

INTRODUCTION

The Netherlands may have one of the most elaborate systems of educational support in the world. There is a national center for curriculum development and another for testing services; there are three national innovation centers for secondary education and 63 local and regional educational service centers. All primary and special education schools have free, legal access to the service of their local center. Though other countries may organize educational support in other ways, similarities can be seen in the professional duties of the staff that execute "supervisory" work as external consultants. Even within and throughout the 50 states of the United States, different configurations can be observed through which support services are executed for schools. Can this work be seen as supervision, and what can research on educational support outside the United States add to the body of research on supervision?

Does "school supervision" exist in the Netherlands and in other countries outside the United States? Yes, and no. Yes, from what is known and observed about the practice of, theory of, and research on school supervision in the United States. The conclusion is that the same kind of work is done in the Netherlands and in other countries in Europe as well as in other parts of the world. The answer is "no" if we realize that in Europe, the term *supervision* is primarily used within the field of social work and has been used relatively little in the school sector (Dalin, 1993, p 151).

This term supervision has not been used for international communications either, for three reasons. The first is that *supervision* has a connotation in work settings of controlling

the work of others and that people in some countries, for example, in the former Eastern European bloc, associate the term with bureaucracy and authoritarian states and governments. The second reason is that, used in the educational field, supervision is seen only as one part of the professional repertoire of a comprehensive educational service (organization or system). The third reason is related to the second, that supervision in the United States is viewed as overseeing the whole range of educational practice of staff in a building or district, mostly in the public school system. These positions do not exist in many European countries.

One of the aims of this chapter, therefore, is to give a clearer description of educational services by providing a more comprehensive and internationally more useful terminology for *supervision*.

To describe the work and impact of educational services in a particular country we first need to look at its educational system and to the important developments within that country to understand the existence and foundation of educational service. This will include diverse factors and actors that are of great importance for the current legitimation of educational service (organizations and systems). The Netherlands will provide an example.

The next step will be to review descriptions of professional practices and theories, and relate these to literature on other countries. This will result in a clearer definition of educational service.

Another aim is to present research findings on educational service in the Netherlands, in some other countries in Europe, and, starting with Israel, in other regions of the world. To do so, we will present a model that merges our definition with several approaches that have been used by other authors who have reviewed educational service systems in the Netherlands and various other countries in Europe.

Although it is not our intention to present a comparative study, this chapter offers possibilities to compare the descriptions of educational service in the Netherlands and some other European countries with the United States. This is possible, because we will deal with significant and major factors that are described in other chapters of this handbook.

Our study is concentrated at the level of general compulsory education and includes levels of state kindergarten, infant, elementary, primary, and secondary sectors, which in most countries are the main subject of concern and are seen as a priority for educational support services. Because educational service in vocational and higher education differ substantially from that in general education, we will not deal with those sectors in this chapter.

THE EDUCATIONAL SYSTEM IN THE NETHERLANDS

The Dutch educational system will be described in this section. The system, as such, is more or less influential in defining the position, tasks, and operations of educational service providers.

Developments within the educational system will later be shown to have impact as well on the content of the work of the educational service system.

Primary Education

Primary education in the Netherlands is for all children between the ages of 4 and 12 years. Although it is only compulsory from 5 years of age in the Netherlands, 97 percent of all 4-years old students attend primary school. This is similar in Belgium, France, and Spain. The percentage of enrollment of 4-year-old children in the United States is 53 percent, comparable with Denmark, Ireland, Norway, Sweden, and Russia (Organization for Economic Cooperation [OECD], 1995). In the Netherlands it has recently been proposed to lower the age of compulsory education. The assumption is that within the 3 percent of children who do not attend kindergarten, there may be many latent talents.

In 1980 the total number of primary education schools in the Netherlands was 8,727. In 1994–1995 this was 7,860. At the same time the total number of students decreased from 1,743,000 in 1980 to 1,415,000 in 1992, but has been increasing since 1993. The total for the school year 1994–1995 was 1,451,000. This means that the total of students per school increased from 167 in 1991–1992 to 185 by 1994–1995 (Centraal Bureau voor de Statistiek [CBS], 1995a).

The effect of national policy to enlarge the size of all primary schools can be observed here. In the Netherlands, however, the total number of school boards and the average number of students per school will never grow so large in primary education that the external support services would be incorporated into the schools and school boards themselves. It is the official view of the Cabinet that this would lead to the fragmentation of expertise and to the inefficient use of money, time, and energy.

In 1985, kindergarten and elementary school merged into one school type, the primary school. Two years later almost one third of the schools had realized the content integration of both former types of schools; since then, however, the amalgamations have slowed down: in 1992 only two fifths of all schools had realized such amalgamations (Inspectorate of Education, 1994).

General Secondary Education: The Stage of Basic Education

Since 1993 the first stage of secondary education in the Netherlands has started with 2 or 3 years of basic education for all students between the ages of 12 and 15 years. Although the students attend different types of secondary schools–general secondary (pre-university education [VWO] like *gymnasium* and *athaeneum*), senior general secondary education (*havo*), junior general secondary education (*mavo*), and preparatory vocational education (VBO)–they have the same curriculum and examinations.

The total number of schools for general secondary education (VWO, havo, mavo) in 1980 was 1,511; by 1994–1995 this number decreased dramatically to 831. The total number of students decreased from 684,000 in 1990 to 666,000 in 1994–1995. In 1994–1995, 4 of 10 schools for secondary education had 1,000 or more students. Four years earlier this ratio was only 2 of 4 (CBS, 1995a.) This demonstrates once again the effect of the national government's policy to enlarge the size of schools, not only to offer a structure for the broad curriculum but also to provide more possibilities for their own financial and personnel management, which is an aspect of decentralization. The second phase of secondary education will be described in the various types of schools mentioned below. National policies are underway in current legislation.

Special Primary and Special Secondary Education

The total number of students in special education schools (about 950 schools in 1993) increased in the 1993–1994 school year by 3 percent. The policy of the national government, however, has been to limit the growth of special education in the last decade.

In Germany, Belgium, and the Netherlands more than 3.5 percent of all students attend schools devoted to special education. In contrast, other countries like Denmark, Sweden, and the United States have chosen to give these children special education in regular schools, which is known as inclusive education. This is also the case in the United Kingdom where every student with a special educational need has the legal right of access to the national curriculum. In these countries a maximum of only 2 percent of all students attend special schools.

The national government is now implementing its policy to provide general education with better facilities to educate as many children as possible within the regular schools, not only for reasons of equity and equality but also to avoid the high costs of the elaborate provisions for special education in the Netherlands. This policy includes providing schools with additional resources for personnel and materials, as well as introducing peripatetic counselors from special schools, networking between schools, and the installation of regional commissions that assess and judge the admittance of each child to special education schools. These commissions are additions to the educational service centers.

In summary, educational systems influence the educational services provided in two ways: First, they affect the position of the service providers, either opting in or opting out of the system. Second, they identify problems and challenges that must be met by the service providers.

CHARACTERISTICS OF EDUCATIONAL SYSTEMS

In this section, influences are described from inside and outside schools that have consequences for the structure and implementation of educational service providers.

Education and Society

After World War II, in most western European countries, there was the development of the welfare state, in which the national governments closely controlled public and private institutions. Visible aspects were an increasing number of regulations, a growing number of civil servants, and a substantial allocation for the social sector in the national budget. In the 1980s skepticism and disbelief in the positive influence of the welfare state grew. Liberalism, privatization, and businesslike and market-oriented concepts were favored. Input went out, output came in, as a reflection of free market forces.

Large-scale innovations in education took place in the years of the welfare state. Quality was centrally steered and mainly focused on new curricula, new organizational and didactical approaches, freely interpreting the mostly general and unspecified goals of education. Compatible with the welfare state were the arrangements for supporting schools and their innovations. The national governments appeared to assume responsibility for ensuring quality in schools rather than the schools themselves. Governments established inspectorates, superintendents, and examinations, and also created external support organizations that were fully funded by them, but operated quite independently, as is the case in the Netherlands since 1975.

In Belgium, powerful umbrella organizations founded agencies that were also financed by national governments. In England and Wales local education authorities (LEA) were responsible for educational services (in addition to the work of Her Majesty's Inspectorate which has existed since 1945). In Germany, individual states maintain support services for the school system. All these facilities emphasized control of inputs, just like schools.

This picture has changed rapidly in recent years for schools. They are gaining more autonomy and responsibility for quality in education, however, they must pay a price. The United Kingdom moved towards a national curriculum with tests of standards to evaluate the results of schools. The Netherlands implemented attainment targets and examinations together with a debate on the issue of introducing diagnostic tests at the entrance of kindergarten. More countries have set standards to direct school development. They are seen as a means to provide feedback to parents and agencies as well as diagnostic services for the schools. Providers of educational service have had to match their products and services to these new demands.

Decentralization

Although decentralization of schooling is considered an innovation in many countries, local control has a long tradition in the Netherlands: "A passion for education has characterized the Netherlands for centuries. The Netherlands common primary schools for all children were considered a responsibility of the State by the early part of the 19th century. In addition to their democratic character Dutch schools were noted by foreigners as having two unusual qualities, both of which continued to be valued: its governance was decentralized and its pedagogy was child centered. This tradition is richly continued today" (OECD, 1991).

Central governments generally have the option to decentralize their responsibility to lower levels, including those of the school boards and the local community authority. In the case of the school boards, the schools themselves can use internal expertise or can choose in-service training.

In the United Kingdom, centralization and functional decentralization coexist. At the level of the curriculum the United Kingdom remains massively centralized in terms of core and other defined subject areas. On the other hand, schools have the money to buy external support. It is very common for schools to look for outside expertise. This generally leads to the weakening of traditional ties between the schools and the LEA. The benefits of deciding on the long term are still to be demonstrated (Hopkins, Ainscow, & West, 1994, p. 16).

Decentralization is currently one of the main issues in the policy of the Dutch government as well. The national government recently implemented further territorial decentralization. Decentralization processes can be observed in all aspects of policy-making. In education the developments are substantial: the national government is relinquishing its responsibility to the 640 local authorities all over the country. Language education for migrants, educational priority areas, the ownership of school buildings, financing educational service centers, and permanent adult education are the main issues for a budget of about 1.7 billion U.S. dollars. (Rutten & Wijn, 1996, pp. 28–29.)

Freedom of Choice

Traditionally there is great freedom of education in the Netherlands (Dutch Constitution, Article 23) where parents have the right to found or to choose a school on the basis of their own religion, philosophy of life, or educational philosophy. These are classified as "private" schools and are often related to church affiliations. Local community authorities also have the right to found a school. The "public" schools comprise 31 percent of all schools. The national government has the duty to finance both "private" and "public" schools on an equal basis. The most recent minimum enrollment needed to found a school is 200 students. Historically the "private" system includes Protestant (27%), Roman Catholic (32%), and "neutral private" (8%) schools. According to recent demographic developments, the system includes also Islamic schools (2%). This comprehensive funding system and principles of choice can be found in many countries in Europe. The umbrella organizations for each of these different denominational schools negotiates with the national government to seek a balance of power between the central and school level. This negotiating system had been consolidated under the Christian Democrats who held a majority in government since 1917. In 1993 they lost their political majority in the national elections and it appears that the new government wants to further decentralize decision-making to the local level in the system. At the same time, parents are more often choosing alternative schools reflecting the philosophies of Montessori, Steiner, Freinet, Jenaplan within the denominational or public sector of the system.

It is very important to note here that the educational service in the Netherlands is not separated into these denominational pillars. All local and regional educational service centers work for all denominations in Dutch education.

School Autonomy and Quality

In countries with a federal government (e.g., Belgium, Germany, Switzerland) decisions on structures, educational planning, resources, and staff management are not made at the national but at the intermediate level (i.e., states and cantons). At the same time the schools are given little scope for local initiative (OECD, 1992).

In countries with a centralized educational system there are two levels: decision-making authority rests both with the schools and the intermediate levels as in Sweden or decision-making is shared between the central level and the schools as in France, Italy, Norway, Portugal, and Spain (OECD, 1991, 1992).

The Dutch education system is neither primarily centralized nor decentralized, but operates in a state of negotiated balance between national input (finances, regulations on personnel, school structure) and control (inspectorate) on the one hand, and decision-making by the individual school boards on the other (OECD, 1991). This situation of continuous negotiation between school and government is known as a *relative autonomy* of schools.

In many countries in Europe and other parts of the world, the educational system is in transition. In the Netherlands the national government has taken more responsibility for the curriculum. The format of attainment targets for each subject in the primary and secondary curriculum has been legislated. In secondary education, there are national examinations. This curricular power goes hand in hand with a policy of enlargement of the size of schools and the scope of power for school boards. At the same time, schools have been given more responsibility for spending their grant money and developing their own personnel policies. Schools, therefore, are held increasingly more accountable and, as a consequence, must report publicly on the quality and outcomes of the teaching program.

This increasing "relative" autonomy reveals the need for support to implement new financial systems, for the management of processes of cooperation between schools, merging of schools, teacher evaluation procedures, development of school management and information systems, developing total quality management (TQM) and TQM information systems. The growth of autonomy also generates the need to profile each school to better compete with other schools.

These recent changes are not the only reason for continued external support of schools. Leune (1992, 1994) mentions the risks of school autonomy that will doubtlessly require some form of external support. These risks are: decreasing coherence in the educational system, apathetic or contested use of competencies and public means, degradation of quality standards, increasing diversity among schools with a growing threat to equity and equality, and restraining innovations by defending the status quo of and by the individual school.

Curriculum and Student Achievement

In 1993, 8 years after the introduction of primary education in the Netherlands, consensus was reached about a common curriculum for all schools and attainment targets were legislated. This regulation in the law will be operational in 1998. After the attainment targets were released, however, the evaluation commission of the Inspectorate recommended a revision. Language and mathematics were specified as the core of the curriculum. The other disciplines in the curriculum will include both mandatory and optional objectives. The inspectorate warned that the attainment targets were too global and the curriculum was overloaded (Commisie Evaluatie Basisonderwijs [CEB], 1994). In fact, the governmental task force set up to revise the attainment targets did not operationalize them. It recommended that the National Institute for Curriculum Development (SLO) develop exemplary curricula. The revising commission neither wanted to restrict the curriculum to a core nor build in options (Commissie Heroverweging Kerndoeien Basisonderwijs, 1994). Schools, therefore, are preparing themselves in very different ways to meet the attainment targets in 1998. Here again, relative autonomy is visible.

The recommendation of the inspectorate to the government to pay more attention to teaching language and mathematics was based on research reports that 15 percent of all students that leave primary school have not mastered basic skills for reading and mathematics at a level appropriate to their chronological age. In the larger cities of the Netherlands, such as Amsterdam, Rotterdam, The Hague, and Utrecht, these percentages are higher because more students from lower socio-economic classes reside there (Leune, 1992).

The assumption that teaching language (Dutch) could be critical was also supported by international educational research. The OECD reported in 1995 that the Dutch public gave high priority to native language and that achievement of 9- and 14-year-old students in reading in Dutch schools was deficient compared with native language reading in other countries (OECD, 1995). Another problem is the relative underachievement of students from the immigrant population, especially from Morocco, Turkey, Netherlands Antilles, and Suriname, as well as students from lower socio-economic classes (Leune 1992). Given this evidence, the Ministry of Education, Culture and Sciences (ECS) founded a Language Expertise Center at the University of Nijmegen and declared teaching language as the number one priority in the innovation process for the future.

In secondary education, attainment targets came into operation in 1993. In the first 2 or 3 years, for all general secondary education schools, the teaching of the same 15 subjects and attainment targets became mandatory. These disciplines were: Dutch language, English, French, or German, history and civics, geography, economics, mathematics, science and chemistry, biology, day care and home economics, information technology, technique, physical education, and two disciplines from the arts. In contrast to primary education, national examinations have been introduced that are based on the attainment targets. In 1996, the first group of students who completed a 2-year program took those examinations. The National Institute for Testing Service (Cito) reported in 1996 that 10 percent of students of the lowest school level and 25 percent of students of the intermediate school level performed as well or sometimes even better than students in schools that were preparing for university. There is no analysis available as yet to explain these striking results.

In 1991, five percent of 16-year-old students left school without any diploma. This decreases the chances of young people in the labor market. In fact, 6.3 percent of all those between 15 and 24 years old were unemployed in the Netherlands in 1990. The international mean was 7.4 percent. Although the situation is better than a decade ago, it is still a challenge for the education system to improve the efficient attainment of one of the general education goals, namely, to allow every individual to actively participate in the economic society.

The mission of, and the market for, the current educational service providers will be influenced by the continued questioning of the assumptions underlying the welfare state together with an increasing demand for a free choice of schools, the growth of school autonomy, and the decentralization of power to local authorities. After a period of time in which a shift occurred from curriculum renewal to implementation and school development, a new interest in the curriculum is emerging. In place of intended learning outcomes the realization of learning outcomes is of greater concern in many countries. This broad public and political attention for educational outcomes affects the service providers' program of activities as they become driven by prescribed achievement factors associated with an educated work force.

THE SEARCH FOR A DEFINITION OF SUPERVISION AS EDUCATIONAL SERVICE

The reality of the welfare state, the relations between governments (federal and national, state, canton, provinces, districts, local) and schools, the changes in school systems and the curriculum and its outcomes are important factors that help determine the strategic position and working programs of educational service providers. These factors also influence, however, the way we talk and write about educational services in the different countries. In this section we will deal with the definition of supervision as educational service.

"The educational consultant comes (and goes) in many different shapes and sizes" (Fullan & Stiegelbaur, 1991, p. 215). Thus, the work done by educational consultants, both as indi-

viduals and as employees of an institution that provides educational consultancy, is defined in many different ways. In the Netherlands three major supportive consultancy labels are recognized: (1) educational and school counseling or guidance (onderwijs- en schoolbegeleiding), (2) educational and school advisory (onderwijs- en schooladvisering), and more recently (3) educational services (educatieve dienstverlening).

Translations of Supervision

The literal meaning of supervision as the overseeing of the work of others is widely used as an aspect of mentoring strategies; however, it is not particular to education. A translation of the word supervision (supervisie) is not used in the Netherlands, or in any other country in Europe, other than in an individual school where a faculty head might supervise colleagues. Sometimes the word is not known or is politically incorrect in former communist countries in Eastern Europe. Supervision there has the connotation of bureaucratic authority, including controlling mandates, rules, regulations, job descriptions, expectations and the related sanctions resulting from that control (compare with Sergiovanni in Glickman, 1992).

Translating the most common Dutch terms in English results in language such as "counseling," "advising," "guidance," or "consulting." Translations like "peer supervision" or "clinical supervision" are not used for the general definition of the work done in the Netherlands or other European countries. "Staff development" is mostly reserved as a synonym for "in-service training." This is not to say, however, that certain activities like peer supervision or clinical supervision are not recognized in the work of professionals in the various school systems, internal or external.

A Way of Defining "Educational Services"

The quotation by Fullan and Stiegelbaur, given earlier, is also relevant for definitions of educational services. Most definitions explain the term by reviewing phenomena that belong to it, by summing up elements or describing them, and/or giving examples as in denoted definitions. It is rare that definitions describe characteristics, either in an analytic or synthetic way, to create a whole set of characteristics ("Connotative definitions," Jozefzoon, 1985).

As far as we know there has only been one attempt to define in a connotative way the work of "supervision" in the Netherlands: "Planning, performing and evaluating of cyclic interventions, that are based on knowledge and skills and that are operated intentionally by a specific organized supporting system, which connects itself to an active participating client system in order to facilitate improvements in the structure, culture and performance of the client system, aiming that the client system can better realise its goals" (Timmer, 1985). This definition will be used here to describe the characteristics of supervision as an educational service for a broader audience and application.

Planning, Performing, and Evaluating Cyclic Interventions The planning, performing (executing), and evaluating of cyclic interventions are characteristic activities in interactive, direct situations—situations that can be seen as belonging to the professional settings of the daily work of educators. In these situations tests, curricula, and research may be used as aids to clarify problems or to offer possibilities for solutions. The development of these aids, however, cannot be seen as cyclic interventions. For this reason, research and development will be excluded from the definition and from this study.

What can be meant by "cyclic interventions" in the professional field of educational service? Recent research offers three models that describe the practice of educational services: (1) the *overall* model in which the consultant supports all the activities and interventions related to the three phases of an innovation process (initiation, implementation, and incorporation) and to all levels (administration, team, and classroom); (2) the *specific* model concentrates on all interventions for implementation at the classroom level only; and in (3) the guidance is *marginal:* only information and advice is given (Houtveen 1990). Slavenburg (1995) introduces the typology of "educational services." He distinguishes a number of interventions, categorized as: (1) guidance for school improvement and educational innovations (adoption, implementation, and incorporation); (2) support for organizational developments in schools; (3) counseling to help students with learning problems; (4) development of educational materials; (5) advising regional educational organizations; (6) information, and (7) cooperation with teacher training centers. This typology describes the services of most Dutch educational service centers.

After reviewing these models, the following remarks can be made: The model of Slavenburg is quite linear. Hopkins, Ainscow, and West (1994) proclaim a more cyclic approach of management in innovations: "The change process is not linear, but consists of a series of three stages, that merge into each other" (p. 37). Their first stage is not adoption but initiation. We would prefer this term, because this is more consistent to our philosophy that the client must be actively involved and can be the initiator of an innovation.

Clinical supervision can be seen as a intervention that is applied during the implementation of new practices. It is threefold: planning conference, classroom observation, and a reflective conference are brought together into a cyclic approach. This approach has evolved over time, being described by various groups and authors (Dingemans & Pajak, 1993; Pajak, 1993).

Recently, the developmental model has earned the most attention. Under the label of "cognitive coaching," Garmston (1994) defines the model as "an applied strategy to enhance another person's perceptions, decisions and intellectual functions" (p. 2). This type of intervention in educational settings is known in the Netherlands as "classroom consultation."

Hopkins, Ainscow, and West (1994) report on what does not work in educational services: one-shot workshops, when others besides the client system select topics, no follow-up support; too numerous activities for too many teachers from different schools; and settings without the necessary application to the individual situation. These authors also list what really works: namely, activities presented in combination, including the presentation of a theory or description of a skill or strategy, the modeling or demonstration of skills; practice in simulated and classroom settings; structured and open-ended feedback; and coaching for application using a hands-on approach in classroom situations. Reviewing implementation, Hopkins and his colleagues also report on crucial factors like clear orchestration of the process, and a mix of pressure and supports and rewards for teachers. Furthermore, evaluation is crucial in cyclic interventions. Research generally shows, however, that we know very little about the success of interventions related to project goals (Fullan & Stiegelbauer, 1991, pp. 216, 222).

Intentions The definition of social action is drawn from the official legislated intentions of the Dutch law on the support structure for schools: The support for schools aims to contribute to the maintenance and improvement of the quality of education. This aim may be seen as quite universal for all educational service providers in any country. Educational services are a mixture of directed tasks or missions and market for client-defined work. On the one hand, governments pay them to support schools for quality improvement in the long term; on the other hand, schools are asking for help, mostly related to short-term actions. In practice the needs of schools often reflect a mix of both school-specific and more general educational topics and indicate both short-term and medium-term strategies.

Knowledge and skills As a result of research on a broad review of literature on professional proficiences of supervision in the United States (Pajak, 1989) and of international cooperation, the Network of Local and Regional Support Services in the Netherlands (WPRO), recently re-named the Association of Educational Service Centers in the Netherlands, was able to develop a professional profile for supervisors that included not only knowledge and skills, but also professional attitudes. These knowledge, skills, and attitudes are related to nine professional fields, which can only be summarized here:

The provider system:

1. vision on supervision;
2. goal and objective oriented;
3. planned action;
4. strategical concept;
5. profile of the provider; and
6. using of and contributing to the expert system (theories and instruments; center of knowledge).

The client system

7. educational developments and needs; and
8. client organizations and human relations.

Contexts
9. education and society.

The attitude of the professional can be seen in the role of the consultant, which is usually called the process role. The main orientation of this role is not to use the expertise of the consultant to resolve the client's problem but instead, to help the client to understand the problem and to use organizational possibilities to solve it. The client decides what action to take. The many functions or roles include those of teacher (explaining), trainer, data gatherer, facilitator, model, third party, pusher, ombudsman, supporter, designer, researcher, and facilitator (Dalin, Rolff, & Kleekamp, 1993, 50–51).

Specific Organized Supporting System The definition of social change refers to the critical element of a specific organized system. This implies that, no matter how important this may be, interpersonal support that is not specifically organized to give educational support is excluded from the definition (and, as a consequence, from this study). These informal human interactions are very important processes for educational organizations (systems) and can be interpreted as supportive, without any bureaucratic, psychological, technical rational, professional, or moral authority other than from inside the person or an informal group (Sergiovanni, 1992). Educational service providers should also include these qualities in their work because they are essential for learning and healthy organizations.

The same sources of authority, therefore, can be recognizable from a micro to macro level, for example, (1) the person as a professional within a group of professionals; (2) the levels of authority within a school (building), a school board, district, state, province, or national department or ministry of education; (3) the level of umbrella organizations of school boards; (4) subsidized, dedicated educational support agencies; (5) organizations and institutions that have other core business but also can be seen as providers of educational services like universities, teacher-training colleges, research institutes; and (6) privatized or commercial organizations. Within each of these sources, there can be a specific organized system that provides educational service.

Connections Educational support in the Netherlands is only given on the request of schools. If the schools do not want to be served, then the agency will not get the money. There are no sanctions imposed upon the schools. If the schools want to be served, however, they have to sign a 4-year contract (WOV, Articles 26, 27). This law is very restrictive. Only schools within regions regulated by the national government can associate with the agency within that same region. This suggests a conflict with the autonomy of schools, but in practice it is not a problem. The Inspectorate reports that from 1987 until 1995, only 11 of 8,000 schools requested a transfer to another region. Every year schools and agencies together develop work plans for the next school year.

Another characteristic in the Netherlands is that the relationship between the service provider and the professional in the school is nonhierarchical (Dalin, Rolff, & Kleekamp, 1993, p. 151). In some other countries this differs in that the service provider is positioned within the hierarchical structure of the school system itself, and consultants also have a supervisory or inspecting role minimizing client-centered action.

Active Participating Client System The schools and educational organizations are given the support at their own request. This implies an active role. This support must contribute to the resolution of the problems of the school, therefore, it must be clear what the roles of the client, and the consultant are. The client for instance, is also supposed to be active in the final evaluation stage of the work.

Improvement in Structure, Culture, and Organization of the Client System The client and consultant should always be conscious that the work must have results throughout the client's organization. This means that the work must be detailed and incorporated.

Goals of the Client System Educational support systems must be aware of the goals the client has to realize. If the school is the client system, then consultants have to know the attainment targets of the school, which innovative policies and goals must be implemented, and how the school interpret this related to the school vision and policy statements.

Conclusion

Although this is a handbook on "supervision," it is not a term used to describe the work that is carried out in different settings in the Netherlands and other countries that serve schools to improve education.

Therefore, a term must be found that includes supervision in addition to essential activities in school improvement such as advising, consulting, and counseling. The terminology *educational services* will consequently be used, meaning a general activity to support schools to develop and to improve themselves. In that perspective, in this study we are seeking major, first-line support services for schools; thus, other support activities like long-term curriculum development, testing service, and educational research will be excluded. The terminology used here will include all professional activities performed in the first line of educational services, carried out by organizations and institutions, dedicated to providing educational services to schools and to other organizations committed to education. This service may incorporate the American term *supervision* in terms of professional aid and direction.

MODEL FOR THE DESCRIPTION OF EDUCATIONAL SERVICES AND THEIR EFFECTIVENESS

Before describing educational service in the Netherlands and in three other countries, it is necessary to develop a framework that can also be referred to for the development of comparative international overview of research on educational services. At present there is no comprehensive model to generate such an overview. Some Dutch contributions to international research findings will therefore be employed to review the status of the educational support system in the Netherlands.

To construct the framework, we will merge the description of the definition with five sources that show some comprehensive approach. The first is the work on standards of quality that have been developed by the Inspectorate of Education, which was used to review the quality of 45 school advisory centers (Inspectie van het Onderwijs, 1994). The second source is the work on criteria of the International Standards Organization (ISO), applied to educational organizations (Certiked) which are an experimental application for quality management of the educational service centers in the Netherlands (Certiked, 1995). The third source for the construction of the framework is the review of research on the work of educational service centers in the Netherlands by Van Gennip (1990). The fourth source is the review of Dutch research by Slavenburg (1996). Slavenburg's model was described earlier. The fifth source is the planned research on a systematic method of evaluation to measure the effects of educational support for schools by the Research Group for Applied Educational Technology (OCTO) at the University Twente in the Netherlands (Kramer, 1995). The content of these five sources will be outlined briefly.

(1) The Model of the Inspectorate (1994) The *model of the Inspectorate of Educational Support* includes 12 standards of quality that can be influenced more or less by the providers of educational support. The model excludes many of context factors outside the control of agencies; however these factors can be of great importance for the functioning of the delivery system. For that reason these context factors will be listed where the Inspectorate omits them in applying the standards in the areas of:

Context

- diversity of schools
- the willingness of schools to change
- capacity of schools to formulate their needs
- the policy capacity of school boards and administrators
- the awareness of local or regional educational problems and needs
- local policy for educational policy and improvement
- existence of a local educational priority area

Input

- financial resources (from national and local resources, also additional finances)
- expertise (professionals must be trained at the university level)
- policy, vision, mission
- cooperation with external actors (to enforce the quality of the work)

Throughput

- management (development and control of policy, vision, and mission)
- organization (adequate structure and procedures, efficiency)
- intensity of counseling (duration and frequency of interventions)

- level of interventions (work and effects must be visible at teacher level)
- use of facilities (accessible knowledge center for all professionals involved)
- quality control

Output

- client satisfaction
- use of materials and ideas

(2) The International Standards Organization Model (Certiked) (1995)
The primary process

- supply and demand (intake by provider and contract)
- execution of services (professional quality, time and financial management)
- evaluation and customer service (results at different levels; calculation)

Conditions

- mission, policy and organization
- research and development
- staffing (personnel management)
- external human and material resources
- training and experience
- center of knowledge/professional documentation

(3) The review of Van Gennip (1990)

- general scope of primary educational support for schools
- quantitative characteristics
- policy-making actors and general assignments
- results of school counseling: the measurement of the
  primary effects: the student level (achievement at all domains)
  secondary effects: instruction
  tertiary effects: school change, school organization
  quaternary effects: use of products and services of providers
    levels of use (no; additional/partial; fidelity; innovative)
    dimensions of use (scope; frequency; intensity; duration)
    conceptual use (effect on ideas)
- services assigned by the government
- services requested by the schools
- quality management and staff development
- cooperation and coordination (in the region)

(4) The Review of Slavenburg (1996)

- management of innovation or improvement
- adoption
- implementation
- incorporation
- organization development

- student counseling services
- developing educational materials
- information services
- advising regional organizations

(5) The OCTO Model (1995)

The model starts from the assumption that the main goals of the educational services provided to schools are:

- an increase of knowledge and skills of teachers or a changing attitude
- a change of behavior of teachers in teaching practice, improvement in behavior or achievement of students
- These goals should be measured at four interdependent levels:
- level 1: student level
- level 2: teacher behavior level in teaching practice
- level 3: teacher learning level (knowledge, skills, attitudes)
- level 4: service level, seen as: (a) satisfaction about the quality of product/service, (b) the service process

Model for Description

Context for Providers

THE NEEDS OF THE EDUCATIONAL SYSTEM. The situation in Dutch education and in various other countries has been presented in this chapter. Is this situation a legitimation for the work of the providers? Have reports of inspectorates, national assessment results, and public debate made an impact on the service program and raised the awareness about the results of the work of the provider? These questions concern national, regional, or local situations, and policies for improvement and innovation of education.

POSITION OF PROVIDERS.

Quantitative Characteristics Quantitative characteristics of support providers include the number and size of providers, budgets, and related resources. If available, comparable quantitative facts should be reported for comparative analysis.

Different Kinds of Providers Different kinds of providers were introduced earlier, ranging from micro to macro levels.

Monopoly or Competition Do providers carry out their services in a monopoly or competitive situation?

Image and Quality Are there reports or research on the image and quality of the service providers in society?

Political View Is there a major political view on the value of the support system or on the strategic position in the future?

Input at Providers' Level

FINANCIAL RESOURCES. Which financial resources such as national and local, or additional finances exist? Is there any research on the impact of levels of financing on the results of the services?

POLICY, VISION, AND MISSION. Does the organization have a policy, vision, and mission to direct the work of the organization?

EXTERNAL EXPERTISE. Does the provider organization buy external expertise and materials to support or stimulate the quality, effects, and results of its work? Does it cooperate and coordinate with other organizations, in or outside the pedagogical province?

STAFF. How is a sufficient level of expertise among staff ensured? At what levels are training centers available? What about the profile of the professional knowledge, skills, and attitudes in the nine fields? Is staff development for these professionals and supporting staff well planned and executed?

Conditions for Managing the Primary Process

CENTER OF KNOWLEDGE. Is a center of knowledge with professional documentation available, either at the level of each organization or at a macro level? Do providers share experiences (e.g., by networks, conferences, or a magazine)?

RESEARCH AND DEVELOPMENT. Research and development can be seen as an important condition for quality leading to actions and results of the providing system.

MONITORING AND STEERING QUALITY. The provision of the evaluation of interventions, feedback, and continuous improvement of crucial elements of the performance of the organization includes time, financial management, intensity, duration, and frequency of counseling interventions and subsequent verification procedures and efficiency.

Throughput/Performance/the Primary Process

INTAKE; SUPPLY AND DEMAND. The client (school) and the support agency agree on a *contract* (Hopkins, Ainscow, & West, 1994, p. 7). This term is used in the broad sense of the word *connections* which includes active participation by the client and a description of how providers will contribute to the improvement in structure, culture, goals, and the overall performance of the client system.

The organization that provides the support takes into account aspects such as the diversity of schools, the willingness of schools to change, the capacity of schools to formulate their needs, and the policy designed by school boards and administrators.

SERVICES PROVIDED.

Management of Innovation or Improvement These services are generally assigned by an authority outside the client system, such as the local or national government. Individual schools or groups of schools sometimes request these services. The activities of consultants are related to a cyclic series of interventions, passing through the stages of initiation, implementation, and incorporation.

Organization Development Services are normally requested by the schools and include activities like team building, management development, crisis intervention, merging of schools, and classroom organization.

Student Counseling Services Student counseling services may be requested by the schools, within the policy of inclusion, and may deal with diagnostic screenings, remedial support, and access to special education. Are these services delivered?

Developing Educational Materials Educational materials refers to the instruments that are used for interventions. Are these services delivered? Curriculum development and test development, as well as long-term research, are excluded from the analysis.

Information Services Information services can be offered in a wide range, from books and videos to electronic information. This service may make a difference in the client system.

Advising Organizations other than Schools Advice may be sought by departments of ministries of education, located in states, provinces, districts or local organizations. Organizations other than schools include parental organizations, teacher unions, and other groups, committed to education with a measurement of the impact for teaching and learning.

Output

Evaluation of results of educational service can take place on five different levels:

STUDENT LEVEL. Does educational service promote educational achievement at all domains?

TEACHER BEHAVIOR LEVEL IN TEACHING PRACTICE. Does educational service promote the desired changes in instructional behavior?

TEACHER LEARNING LEVEL. Do teachers gain knowledge, skills, and attitudes from educational service not only as an individual but also as a group (team)?

USE OF PRODUCTS AND SERVICES. Are levels of use, dimensions of use, and conceptual use observed?

SERVICE LEVEL. Are data available from the evaluation of satisfaction and quality of the products and services?

LITERATURE SEARCH ON EDUCATIONAL SERVICE PROVIDERS IN DIFFERENT COUNTRIES

The search for literature on the work of educational service providers in various countries began by selecting keywords and then applying these keywords to relevant sources. Reports from descriptive as well as from empirical research, if they are available, will be reported.

The Keywords

As described in the definitions of educational services, the following keywords should be used: *educational service, school support systems, teacher in-service training, staff development in school or education, education or school counseling services, education advice and advisory service or agency, education or educational consultant or consultancy, educational guidance, educational or clinical supervision.*

The Sources

DUTCH PUBLICATIONS. There are some Dutch publications in which educational services for schools in countries other than the Netherlands have been described very briefly: Voster (1982), Köllen (1990), an unpublished paper by Braaksma and Heinink (1990), and a series of booklets on education in Europe issued by the Open University in the Netherlands (Brodersen, Hooge, & Wielemans, 1994–1995). There are also some overviews of and references to international literature in Dutch research reports on the work of school support agencies. All Dutch literature on the subject has been reviewed by the author, thus, the underlying retrieval work has not been repeated.

THE ERIC INFORMATION SYSTEM. The basic retrieval system, accessed by Internet, was employed. The results of the queries via ERIC were: 64 publications on educational consultancy, 54 on staff development, 17 on teacher in-service training, 8 on regional educational service agencies (RESA), and 5 on educational advice. The abstracts on consultancy referred to a very broad variety of activities of consultants (from student counseling to implementation of innovations); staff development and teacher in-service training overlapped and referred mainly to courses for groups of teachers. *Guidance* and *Counseling* showed no results. The geographical identifications were mainly restricted to the United States, some to Canada, the United Kingdom, and one abstract referred to Germany. In that aspect, the search did not provide useful information for the description of systems in Europe.

THE INTERNATIONAL ENCYCLOPEDIA OF EDUCATION. The second edition of the encyclopedia, edited by Husén and Postlethwaite (1994) was chosen. This 12 volume source also offers entries by country name, but none of the country descriptions includes information on educational services.

EURYDICE. The European Commission for Education of the European Community maintains the information system Eurydice. Here, no relevant information for this study on educational services was retrieved.

Countries with Educational Service Providers

The Arlington-based American Association of Educational Service Agencies (AAESA) listed about 400 agencies in 35 states of the United States that provide educational services. Examples are the Educational Service District, Education Service Unit, regional Education Service Agency, Education Service Center, Board of Cooperative Educational Services,

Service Cooperatives, Intermediate School District, Area Education Agency, Intermediate Unit, and more. It is not known whether every province in Canada has such providers. No data are available for countries in South America, Africa, and Asia. In the Middle East the State of Israel offers support to its state schools through the Ministry of Education and by seven decentralized regions. Concerning Europe, it is not known whether all European countries offer an educational service to support schools. No information was found about educational services in Greece, Turkey, and most eastern European countries. There was some information about educational services in Austria, Italy, and Spain. It was reported that only the Inspectorate plays a role in the educational services for schools in those countries. In other countries, a variety of providers are responsible for the educational services at the same time and most of these organizations also have other core business, such as governmental, nongovernmental, as well as private organizations. These can be found in Denmark, France, Germany, Great Britain, Norway, and Sweden. The countries that have a more or less dedicated system for educational service are Belgium, Hungary, Luxembourg, the Netherlands, Portugal, and the Czech Republic. In this chapter, a description of the educational services will be given for four countries: the Benelux (Belgium, the Netherlands, and Luxembourg) and Israel.

BELGIUM

Context for Providers

THE NEEDS OF THE EDUCATIONAL SYSTEM. In Belgium, education is divided into three "nets": (1) the (official) education, governed and subsidized by each community in the federation, namely, Flanders, Walloon, and Brussels; (2) the subsidized official education governed by the provinces and local communities; and (3) the subsidized independent ("vrij") education. This education is mainly governed by Roman Catholic organizations.

The Belgian education system has to overcome the problems of the high average age of teachers and, as a result, the problems of replacement and ongoing training. It also needs to adapt the curriculum to scientific and technological changes and to economic objectives within an enlarged European context (Husén & Posthlethwaite, 1994, p. 503; Wielemans, 1994a, pp. 82–83).

Primary education in Flanders, the Dutch-speaking part of Belgium, is divided into two levels. The first is kindergarten and special kindergarten (2 1/2–5 year olds) and the second is elementary education (6–12 year olds) and elementary special education. Most levels are part of one school for primary education. About 10 percent of all kindergarten levels have an autonomous organization. In 1994–1995, 661,317 students attended primary education in Flanders. Although education is only compulsory from the age of 6 years, an average of 96 percent of all children between 2 1/2 and 5 years old were enrolled for first level. Minimal attainment targets (including developmental goals for kindergarten) have been issued from 1991.

The transition from kindergarten to elementary education has been a problem for years. This is demonstrated by the conflict of informal versus formal classroom organization (71 percent of all classrooms are nongrouped in comparison with 6 percent in the Netherlands and 31 percent in the United States; OECD, 1992, p. 172). Curriculum changes and strong variations in teacher preservice training are the main problems.

Special education is expanding yearly by about 2.4 percent. A total of 5.8 percent of all children aged between 2 1/2 and 12 years are in special education schools. The Belgian population includes 9 percent of migrants; therefore, intercultural education with Dutch as a second language, together with nondiscriminational behavior, are key issues in the curriculum.

There is (special) secondary education for 12–18-year-old students. Since 1994–1995, all the various traditional school types in Flanders merged into a unified school organization with four goals: extension of basic education for all, integration of all domains of development, inclusion of students with learning difficulties and social/emotional problems, and delay of vocational preparation. Achievement in the main subjects is higher in Flanders than in Walloon. In comparison with the 18 other industrial countries, Belgium scores under the mean of progress in reading comprehension achievement (OECD, 1995, p. 48). Explicit assignments to educational service agencies were not found.

POSITION OF PROVIDERS. The educational service agencies are operating on the basis of legislation, within the three "nets." Within these social structures there are two different kinds of providers: the Psycho Medical Social (PMS) Centers, which operate at the local and regional level, and the Pedagogical Guidance Agencies, which serve the schools throughout Flanders on a denominational basis.

There are no systematic cooperative efforts (Wulleman, p. 4). These providers are in a position to organize in-service training programs (Janssen-Vos & Laevers, 1996, p. 217). The formal position of these institutions has not changed in recent years (cfr. Voster, 1982, p. 25). Only the inspectorate reorganized its task: it rejected the task of aiding the service organizations and, instead, concentrated on inspecting schools, reporting to the service agencies, and setting their priorities (Köllen, 1990, p. 5).

Quantitative Characteristics There are 203 PMS Centers in Flanders and 163 in Walloon and the German communities. The PMS Centers' budget in Flanders is 90 million U.S. dollars, serving all students in primary and secondary education.

Different Kinds of Providers Service providers function at the state, province, and local community levels, and at the level of umbrella organizations of school boards. All service providers are subsidized and dedicated educational support agencies.

Monopoly or Competition The centralized establishment of these servicing agencies has minimized any form of competition for annual budgets.

No specific data are available for image and quality.

Political View In 1993 the Flemish Council for Education, established by the Ministry of Education in Flanders, published a policy paper in which the core business of the centers was reviewed and a more cooperative and efficient infrastructure was proposed (VLOR, 1993). Contacts with several PMS Centers made it clear that institutions are strongly encouraged to merge to improve their service quality.

Input at Providers Level

FINANCIAL RESOURCES.   In-service training programs will be facilitated by the national government in a lump sum for schools. For 1996–1997 the proposed budget for primary education in Flanders is 110 million francs (9.1 million U.S. dollars; or 137 U.S. dollars per student annually). This budget includes the budget for the educational service centers.

POLICY, VISION, AND MISSION.   No specific data are available on the way the providers have formulated their strategic issues and how effective those have been.

EXTERNAL EXPERTISE.   No specific data are available, however, informants from PMS centers confirm that the service providers do rely upon support from the universities in Flanders and from the Flemish Agency for the Development of Education (DVO), which executes curriculum development and research, the Dutch National Testing Service Institute and Dutch universities, innovation centers and educational service centers and their association, WPRO.

STAFF.   The staff of the Pedagogical Guidance Agencies consists of mainly former inspectors, former school administrators, consultants, teachers that have a current position in schools, and peripatetic teachers (Janssen-Vos & Laevers, 1996, p. 216).

Conditions for Managing the Primary Process

The inspectorate monitors the quality of the PM Social Centers and the pedagogical centers. No reports are available on the way this work has been executed or the results achieved.

Throughput/Performance/the Primary Process

INTAKE; SUPPLY AND DEMAND.   The basic assumption is that the needs of the school are the starting point for the services provided. The inspectorate of schools also has an important influence in programming the work of the PMS and the pedagogical centers. In the case of reported underachievement, the work of the service centers is more or less under continuous monitoring by the inspectorate of the Flemish Education Community in Brussels (Janssen-Vos & Laevers, 1996, p. 216).

SERVICES PROVIDED.

Management of Innovation or Improvement   The project Experience Based Kindergarten Education is a very complex innovation (Janssen-Vos & Laevers, 1996, p. 174). A national policy to influence and control the growth of special education is in operation. The education priority policy has been concentrated to provide more personnel in service agencies, and improve programs for in-service training in language and cultural diversity. This has been carried out throughout Flanders. The effect of these programs is not known (Fase, 1994, p. 96).

Organization Development   The Pedagogical Guidance Agencies offer process consultancy and advice for the improvement of the quality of schools.

Student Counseling Services   The PMS Centers offer counseling services mainly for students and their parents. These services include vocational orientation and choices as well as psychological and pedagogical advice and assistance.

Developing Educational Materials   No specific data are available on the results of the development of materials as an instrument for successful interventions in innovation or other principal services. The Kindergarten project does offer specific data concerning materials and planned interventions.

Information Services   The PMS Centers advise special schools on new methods for teaching. How this work is carried out and whether there are libraries for teachers in the service centers has not been reported. No specific data are available on advising regional organizations.

OTHER SERVICES.   The Pedagogical Guidance Agencies offer staff development programs (Janssen-Vos & Laevers, 1996, p. 215). Results have not been reported.

Output

STUDENT LEVEL.   Research on the project Experience Based Kindergarten Education is progressing. An early conclusion is that children demonstrate more initiative in their classrooms (Janssen-Vos & Laevers, 1996, p. 186).

TEACHER BEHAVIOR LEVEL IN TEACHING PRACTICE.   Teachers learn to observe from the project Experience Based Kindergarten Education, and vary their didactical behavior to help children with social/emotional problems (Janssen-Vos & Laevers, 1996, pp. 186–187). No specific data are available concerning the level of theory or attitudes teachers demonstrate after a specific intervention.

LEVELS, DIMENSIONS, CONCEPTIONS OF USE OF PRODUCTS AND SERVICES.   The dissemination of products of the project Experience Based Kindergarten Education is substantial. The ideas have been adopted on a wide scale in the teacher training centers. International recognition is growing (Janssen-Vos & Laevers, 1996, p. 174). No specific data are available on the level of service.

The educational service provided in Belgium is both functionally specialized and also fragmented within and between the different denominational and territorial sectors of the educational system. Within the different institutes, the PMS Centers are possibilities for interdisciplinary coordination and longitudinal approaches. Further document analyses are needed. It is expected that project documents of the service agencies, as well as their annual reports, will give more insight into the throughput aspects of the work in Flanders, but research on such evaluations is not yet available.

ISRAEL

Context for Providers

The education system in Israel includes kindergartens, primary schools, middle schools, secondary schools (including vocational and agricultural), teacher-training institutions, post-secondary schools for continued and vocational studies, colleges and universities. Pre-primary and kindergarten are attended by 320,000 children. Primary schools are attended by 697,200 students. In primary education there are 34,350 teaching positions.

The major needs of Israeli society are the social integration of all immigrants, absorption of immigrant students, and improvement of the level of achievement of the system and of every individual student.

According to Brickman in Husen and Postlewaithe's *International Encyclopedia of Education* (1994), the most important issues for the education system in Israel are quality preparation of teachers, better ethnic and linguistic absorption, and integration, adult education, and Bible teaching. His description, however, seems to be dated. Government reports show that the training of teachers has been addressed successfully.

Decentralization versus autonomy is one of the main issues in the education debate. As in most countries, the government is convinced that large-scale innovations will not be successful if these are adapted at the regional and local level. Although the State of Israel is under continuous existential pressure and demographic development—which mostly points to highly centralized systems—the balance of power in education between the three different governmental levels—national, the seven regions (Jerusalem, Northern, Haifa, Central, Tel Aviv, Southern, Recognized/Unofficial Education), and the local authorities—is still moving towards more decentralization and autonomy for decision-making at the local level.

The fields with the most power in Israel, in decreasing order, are: the curriculum, personnel policy, and the content of innovations.

THE CURRICULUM. The Curriculum Center of the Ministry of Education releases the national curriculum. These are syllabi for all compulsory disciplines, including guidelines for the division of teaching hours between compulsory and elective subjects. The core curriculum is the reference for new developments. An example of this is the syllabus for the discipline of English, issued in 1988, which serves the intermediate and upper schools (grades 5–12). It consists of 135 pages, which 133 contain based scope and sequences, one page with tips for situations and topics, and another dedicated to teaching English to "native speakers."

At the national level, chief inspectors have the opportunity to develop programs in addition to national priorities (see later) and to generate changes in the core curriculum. For teaching English, for example, a new project has been instated for improvement of education ("reading for pleasure"). This is due to concerns about the achievement of reading comprehension in Israel. Besides the mentioned syllabus, the chief Inspectorate

for English released an addendum in 1995, which is not a syllabus restricted to the content but rather a guide, including methodology, tips for the school library, and examples of book work for students. The English Inspectorate also publishes the magazine English Teachers Journal (started in 1971).

At the regional level, the curriculum can be adopted in various ways. There are electives that might be introduced or legislated by the regional authority.

At the school level, there is the freedom to adapt the guidelines to fit the teaching schedule. These must be approved by the national authority.

PERSONNEL POLICY. The regional heads continue to be responsible for the hiring and firing of teachers. Attempts to delegate that responsibility to the local authorities are debated. At the time of this research (June 1996) the teacher unions were opposed because the climate in the schools might deteriorate. Their standpoint was that giving the principals responsibility for firing and hiring would bring them into direct conflict with their staff.

The schools are financed by the national as well as by local authorities. This does not mean, however, that schools have the autonomy to decide how to spend their money for personnel matters. They must follow the national guidelines.

INNOVATIONS. A great deal of trust is extended to the schools to use their autonomy well, but there are many differences in how the schools wield this autonomy. Autonomy is most visible in projects for change. Schools write their own development plans for the following school year. They have the autonomy to set priorities, taking into account national and regional policies. It is not known at this time if priorities are set by the local authorities.

Innovations are indicators of the needs of a society to make changes in education. These innovations create new demands for change that influence agencies of educational support. The innovation priorities in Israel will be described in more detail.

Innovations from the Central Government The ministry of ECS in Israel issues yearly training programs for improving education with two main goals: greater economic growth and more equality. The following are the current official priorities for Israeli education:

1. Extension of the school day.
2. Promotion of science and technology studies. The implementation of the "Tomorrow 98" 5-year plan, begun in 1994, includes new curricula, revised teaching strategies, and the establishment and operation of science laboratories. Technological education in Israel has been strongly associated with vocational education. The Ministry of ECS has a separate science and technology division, which "supervises and guides, through centrally located supervisors, professional supervisors and other supervisory and guidance tools, arts and crafts instruction through the sixth grade, and technical and liberal arts instruction in junior high schools" (Technological Education in Israel, State of Israel, Ministry of ECS, January, 1996, p. 10).

3. Computerization of the education system, which includes training teachers to integrate computers in classroom activities, equipping schools with hard- and software, integrating information systems in teaching and learning, encouraging experiments, evaluation, and dissemination.

4. Promotion of programs for weaker/disadvantaged students. This policy includes (a) the implementation of the program "Together," which promotes students with special needs in regular schools, as well as mainstreaming or inclusion and (b) Improving weaker communities, which is a project that requires a holistic approach. The school system allows an external change agent to support the school.

5. Upgrading of the status of the teaching profession.

6. Expansion of higher education.

7. Improvement of education in the Arab and Druze sectors.

8. Classroom construction.

9. Immigrant absorption.

10. Broadening of humanistic education, Jewish education, education for international understanding, democracy coexistence, and peace.

Regional Innovations: Case of Central Region Schools are governed by local authorities that are organized into six regions or districts of Jerusalem, Manta, Northern, Haifa, Central, Tel Aviv, and Southern. We concentrated on one of them, the Central region, whose borders are drawn from Jerusalem to Tel Aviv, but do not include those two large cities. (While in Jerusalem, we heard that the local, regional, and national level of school governance have joined their efforts into one organization. This is related to the special status and problems of Jerusalem). All six regions develop yearly triannual plans for the improvement of education and report on an annual basis.

On their achievements, the Central region, where 23 percent of all Israeli students are taught, suggested various innovations from which schools at the local level can choose. This list demonstrates the "Special emphasis of the central region."

1. An increase in the number of "trailblazer" schools which demonstrate the following characteristics: (a) a high number of teacher in-service training hours, (b) development of unique initiatives, based on special needs of the school population, and (c) foreign language learning based on principles of Mcclosky's Global Village.

2. Development of autonomous student learning (in conjunction with Tel Aviv University).

3. Acquisition of computer skills for all students in grades 6–9.

4. Road safety for grades 1–2.

5. Improvement of the quality of decentralization project.

6. Special projects:
   (a) advancement of educational leadership.
   (b) improvement of mathematics education.
   (c) teaching strategies for heterogeneous classes.
   (d) holistic intervention (the 30 Settlement Project).
   (e) encouragement of Jewish studies in government schools.
   (f) creation of correct communication channels.
   (g) literacy skills: reading and writing.
   (h) to live in a better world: values, ethics, codes of behavior.

   (i) mainstreaming/inclusion of special education students.
   (j) Thursday forums of administrators in education.

The Innovations from Local Authorities The schools at the local level can choose not only from the list of the region but also can add a topic to the list that is group or site based. If this topic meets the requirements of both the national and regional authorities, the proposal of the school will be approved. This site-based priority setting might be seen as a kind of procedure to match supply and demand in the system. So far, at the national and regional level, the steering principle very strongly depends on the supply of the change agents (ministries, universities, and other agencies).

Local education authorities seem to have very little power over education, except in the larger cities, such as Jerusalem. Education is steered here by one authority, the Jerusalem LEA, which combines local as well as national responsibilities. The LEA was not included in this research, however.

POSITION OF PROVIDERS.

Quantitative Characteristics Data about education in Israel (1994) do not give the total number of schools, or personnel, involved with change agent institutions (supervisors from the ministry, regional, or local authorities). The publication "*There Is Another Way, Israel Believes in Education, Implementation of Major Policy Decisions*" of January 1996 does not give these numbers either; therefore the average ratio of external school change agents and the number of schools, teachers and students, for example, cannot be reported.

Expenditure for education in 1994 was 9 percent of the gross national product (GNP). The budget for primary education was 31 percent of 10.4 billion NIS or 3,224,000,000. There is no breakdown in internal and external expenditures of schools, so expenditures of the external support agencies like the ministry, regional, and local authorities cannot be reported.

DIFFERENT KINDS OF PROVIDERS OF EDUCATIONAL SUPPORT Policymaking, development, research, teacher training, and guidance and counseling in Israel are responsibilities of many organizations that operate at national, regional, and local levels. They are totally subsidized by the public government, either directly or through the schools, and in the free market.

The Ministry of Education, Culture and Sports. The Jerusalem Ministry of ECS based includes 10 departments. The Pedagogical Administration coordinates all preschool, primary and secondary education, examinations, The Science and Technology Center, curriculum development, special education and psychological counseling. The Pedagogical Secretariat is a steering platform within the Ministry, which is responsible for programming and financing major areas like: Arab and Druze education, Jewish studies, coexistence, Arab language and culture, education of the gifted, and the approval of textbooks, supervision, and guidance. It is not known if the Secretariat is also responsible for the Pedagogical Administration and who is responsible for coordination.

The ministry also houses the Curriculum Center, which is responsible for: developing and updating new curricula, elective developments, and school-based initiatives; developing educational materials; implementating and supervising the implementation; and evaluating the previously mentioned activities for all levels.

Excluding the movement towards decentralization and autonomy for schools, the national, central government plays an important role in supporting schools to implement the major policy in education. The Chief Inspectors and the Curriculum Center are the two principal bodies that are responsible for this role. The Chief Inspectors operating in the disciplinary fields have national counselors that can advise them on more general educational aspects of the curricula (e.g., using the computer, how to deal with weak learners, heterogeneous classes, etc.). The Chief Inspector for English includes 11 of these advisors that work with 18 district inspectors for English in conjunction with the counselors that visit the schools. These counselors present workshops and aid the teachers.

Networks, universities, and commercial providers. Networks operating at a national level, like the ORT movement network, the Amal network, and other networks of technological schools also provide educational services. These networks can be sponsored by the governmental levels. Schools can also pay for the support from their own budgets. Universities and colleges for teacher in-service training have alliances with the ministry and other governmental organizations. They have contracts for research, development, and consultation. Foreign institutions like Trenton State College (based in the United States but with international sites) also have access to the market of educational service, through their MED program, teaching English as a foreign and a second language.

Private institutions like the Branco Weiss Institute are also in powerful positions to develop programs and train teachers. Statistical data are not yet available, however. Further analysis of these institutes is needed to gain more insight into the work of those organizations.

The regional offices. All regions have support facilities for schools. In the case of Jerusalem, we visited a high school and spoke to a representative of the Jerusalem LEA. This LEA is responsible for all educational development in the Jerusalem area. Some examples were given in the field of science and technology. Here too, more facts are needed to complete the description.

Monopoly or Competition National innovations are implemented by support of central and regional organizations. In the case of the central region, time is allocated to schools that are most at risk. Criteria for this allocation are, for example, school achievement and social economic status.

Regional organizations might reserve budgets if schools have special demands or take their own initiative. The support can be given by any organization that has the desired expertise to help the schools. In the case of the central region, school-based innovations are financed and supported by the region if they fit into the innovation policy of the central government and of the regional authority. Regional innovations are supported by the regional authorities. School-based innovations are only subsidized if they fit into the current policy. In many cases, schools have to go to business and industry to sponsor their own innovations.

It can be concluded that the government provides much free support but there is no monopoly for any organization to provide schools with support. The experiences that were presented were not significant enough to conclude that there are regional protections. Most universities involved in providing educational support to schools are contracted because of their expertise, not for reasons of regional boundaries.

Input at Providers Level

FINANCIAL RESOURCES. Support services are free for schools. It is not clear, however, what the agreements or conditions are. Data are not available. Schools also collect money from local authorities, or from sponsors in business and industry, for additional, school-specific innovations.

POLICY, VISION AND MISSION. There do not appear to be any official statements about educational support services.

EXTERNAL EXPERTISE. Schools contract external expertise from a variety of organizations.

STAFF. Data were not located.

Conditions for Managing the Primary Process No research is available on the quality and effectiveness of educational service providers. It seems to be that judgments are made on the basis of common sense: "If our institute is still in existence for more than 5 years, it demonstrates that there is confidence among our clients and we have the right to exist."

Throughput/Performance/the Primary Process

INTAKE; SUPPLY AND DEMAND. THE Branco Weiss Institute publishes a newsletter with ideas and information on their products and services. Schools can sign up for orientation or contract for longer periods, including implementation activities. There is not yet a common culture in Israeli schools for long-term planning. Most schools, however, are very committed when they start an innovation process.

SERVICES PROVIDED. Referring to the section in which the innovation topics were described, it can be concluded that these topics can be seen as elements of management of innovation or improvement, organization development, and student counseling services.

Several institutes are developing educational materials as well; some also have information services. It is not known, however, if there has been any research or appraisal by the consumers and/or on the effectiveness of the services provided. Further investigation should provide insight in this field.

Management of Innovation or Improvement National innovation projects are supported by teacher-training programs, of which many are compulsory. The Ministry of Education reports on the number of teachers that participate. No qualitative results have been reported.

Developing Educational Materials The Ministry of Education may develop some materials, but in most cases, this is delegated to external institutions, like educational publishers. The Branco Weiss Institute, for instance, develops and implements materials, often of foreign origin (e.g., from the United States). This institute also translates Israeli publications into English.

No data was located concerning information services or advising (regional) organizations.

Output

STUDENT LEVEL. The results of education system improvement projects are reported in the yearly reports of the Ministry of ECS "Implementation of major policy decisions". Some examples of these results are: extension of the school day in elementary education from 37.4 weekly classroom and teaching hours in 1989–1990 to 47.2 hours in 1995–1996; an increase in the student:computer ratio: in 1989, the ratio was 1:30, in 1996, it was 1:10; the implementation grade of the science program in 1993–1994 was 55 percent, in 1995–1996, 90 percent.

The Branco Weiss Institute reported that they apply a model of evaluation at the student level and through clinical supervision they assess if programs for learning to think are successful. It is not clear and there is no evidence, however, that these results are related to the work of educational support agencies. Specifications to the following elements are not yet available: *teacher behavior level in teaching practice; teacher learning level; levels, dimensions, conceptions of use of products and services; and service level: quality of product and process of service.*

THE NETHERLANDS

Context for Providers

THE NEEDS OF THE EDUCATIONAL SYSTEM. In addition to locally defined needs the current national policy includes quality management, cultural diversity, and the implementation of attainment targets of the national curriculum. It is considered essential that educational service providers serve schools and the needs of the teaching profession.

POSITION OF PROVIDERS. "The Netherlands has a rich and elaborated educational support structure which is unique in all the world" (OECD, 1991). This support structure includes three specialized nationwide operating agencies, one for curriculum development, one for educational research, and one for testing service. There are three denominational (Public/Independent, Roman Catholic, and Protestant) innovation institutes operating for secondary education. Sixty three local and regional educational service centers serving all denominations, both public and private schools. We will concentrate on these 63 centers only, because they meet our definition of educational service.

This national funded system, legislated in the Educational Support Structure Act of December 1986, will expire in 1997 and be replaced by a decentralized system in which the national government will fund the local community authorities instead of the service centers. The local community authorities in their turn are obliged to fund the centers with this earmarked money provided by the national government during a 4-year transition period. The local community authorities, therefore, will have full control of the operations of the service centers. This may restrict the professional autonomy of the service centers and it will be monitored in the forthcoming years.

The decision to implement this decentralization to the local authorities has not been based on any research, but was the political initiative of the new government that came into power in 1994. If the Christian Democrat Party had stayed in power, they would have decentralized the responsibility for educational services directly to the school boards, according to the advice of the Scientific Council for Government Policy to the cabinet.

After the national government has transferred its responsibility for the support structure, schools for secondary education will get their own budgets to buy educational services. This should be financed with a part of the budget from the three national denominational innovation institutes, which serve secondary schools all over the country in the form of institutes and conferences but not by school-based interventions.

As the national and local governments pay for the full educational support service structure, all schools have the right to free educational service from the local and regional centers. This retains the service provided for primary schools in a protected, monopolized infrastructure. In contrast, the service for secondary schools will utilize the rules of the competitive market economy as these schools will have their own budgets to buy the educational support they need.

All local and regional educational service centers are affiliated with the Association of Educational Service Centers in the Netherlands (WPRO). The WPRO provides two yearly reports on the status of the ESCs in the Netherlands. From the most recent report (WPRO, 1995) we report some core quantitative characteristics of these centers:

	Total	Average per EAC
Number of educational service centers	63	
Number of schools	9,000	143
Number of students	1,600,000	25,000
Number of staff	2,600	41
Management	100	1.5
Professional staff	1,700	27
Support staff	800	12.5

Current evaluations show that clients are very satisfied with the services provided by the Dutch educational service centers. This is illustrated by the average score from relevant research (see Output, later), and on reports of the Dutch Inspectorate of Education (Inspectie van het Onderwijs 1992, 1994, 1995).

Again, in the eyes of the Association of Dutch Local Community Authorities (VNG), the educational service centers "are an important instrument" for local communities to implement local educational policies (Rutten & Wijn, 1996).

The political view on the future of educational services is that they have shifted from the national government to the local communities, which have to ensure the infrastructure for primary schools to get the support they need. School boards and authorities of local communities will negotiate in a standing local conference on the program of services from the educational service centers. After a period of 4 years, the national government will decide if the earmarked budget can be transferred to local authorities without designation. In that case, the local authorities will be responsible for guaranteeing the service infrastructure for schools.

The education policy of the national government is that local authorities and school boards have a better knowledge of the needs of the schools and local communities and that large-scale innovations steered centrally by the state are ineffective.

By bringing the focus of decision-making to a lower level, the possibility also arises to orchestrate educational policies like adult education, pre-school education, health and welfare for youth, migrant policy, and safety in and around schools with the programming of the Educational Service Centers.

The question has been raised as to the role of the national government will be to ensure the implementation of national innovation policies like attainment targets, inclusion, and early childhood education. Instead of the three national innovation institutes having the responsibility to coordinate such policies, the government introduced a so-called external process management for each innovation topic. It is suggested that this fragmented the coherence of educational innovations for teachers into an unmanageable situation. The government "repaired" this, however, by installing a National Innovation Process Management that has the task of stimulating schools to integrate national policies into their school-based policies and local priorities. At the same time, it will contact the educational service centers to support the implementation of the national issues by school boards that are responsible for integrating these policies when they request educational services.

Input at Providers Level

FINANCIAL RESOURCES. All 63 educational service centers are mostly co-subsidized by the national government and by the local community authorities. Every year the Dutch parliament decides on the budget for the service centers. The local communities follow that decision in determining their supportive funding. In 1995–1996 the national government allocated approximately 93 million Dutch guilders (60 million U.S. dollars). The local communities together contributed an additional 120 million Dutch guilders (80 million U.S. dollars). The budget per student in primary education was approximately 140 Dutch guilders (90 million US Dollars).

Funding by the national and local governments is also supplemented by third parties that buy services from the educational service centers, or sponsor them. These include schools for secondary education, which have their own budgets for external consultancy, organizations operating in the fields of environment, traffic safety, anti-discrimination policies, educational organizations, teacher-training centers for co-programming for in-service training, educational publishers, and international schools. The total part of earnings from third parties is between 4 and 20 percent of the regular total budget of the educational service centers (WPRO, 1995).

POLICY, VISION, AND MISSION. Counseling and advising schools, dissemination of information, development of educational materials, evaluation, and activities that promote an optimal school career for children (in primary education) are core activities, prescribed by the Dutch Educational Support Structure Act (WOV, 1986, Article 21). This law also prescribes that all support work primarily originates with requests made by schools.

The support for schools aims to contribute to both maintaining and improving the quality of education. It is directed both to re-enforcing the capability of schools to solve the problems they meet in realizing their goals and to encourage a systematic development and improvement of education. Support for schools includes services that are aimed at stimulating the functioning of the school as a whole (WOV, Article 2). The law also specifies the functions of the support agencies in general: they are to serve education, schools, and educational organizations, advise on national innovation policies; and cooperate to implement these policies (WOV, Article 3).

The Dutch Law on the Support Structure for Schools (WOV, 1986) prescribes that school advisory agencies must contribute to the maintenance and improvement of the quality of education by serving schools in the fields of pedagogy, methodology, disciplines, psychology, school organization, and educational change (WOV, 1986, Article 2). Most educational service centers have paraphrased these core tasks in their own strategic plans, which mostly have been developed under the influence of the recommendations to the government. which plans to decentralize the support system.

EXTERNAL EXPERTISE. Educational service centers do not hire significant external professionals to serve their clients. The numbers of professionals that are hired from similar institutes to work with schools as consultants are unknown. The exceptions are in the field of crisis management, the prevention of stress in the work environment, and in the case of highly specialized areas, such as education for children of political refugees. There is an open exchange of center staff expertise. National institutes also hire professionals from the local and regional centers to cooperate in more specialized projects.

STAFF. Approximately 2,000 consultants work in the educational service centers (WPRO, 1995). The Educational Support Structure Act requires minimum competencies. These imply that all consultants must have graduated from university or achieved a comparable level of education. The total staff number includes the heads of the educational information centers which are located at most educational service centers (see later).

The consultant profession is changing from a generalist to a specialized one because of a changing client attitude and by the increasingly broad spectrum of topics. At the same time, it is recognized that consultant work is separate more or less from "account management." Other staff members operate as "contact persons" who are responsible for the generation of contracts and subsequent evaluation.

On-the-job training for all the staff working in the educational service centers has been included in the state funded support infrastructure. The three denominational innovation centers have the task of professionalizing the staff of the local and regional centers. The yearly "Innovation Guide" offers a broad program that matches all the topics of the national innovation policy as well as the needs of the educational service centers. The latter also are served on a more commercialized basis.

Summer courses also have been offered by the national institutes and the Utrecht University. The University of Groningen offered a course for managers of the educational service centers. It is expected that the more commercialized approaches will replace the subsidized system because of the redundancy of the Educational Support Structure Act.

The most recent initiative has been to establish a professional organization for all consultants working in the field. In this organization the unions, other professional organizations, and the WPRO will cooperate to ensure opportunities for further professional development. The professional competencies profile (see definition section) is the unifying basis for this cooperation initiative.

Conditions for Managing the Primary Process The inspectorate that has the specific task of monitoring the quality of the work of the educational service centers reported positively on 60 of of the 63 centers (Inspectie Onderwijsverzorging, 1994).

Throughput/Performance/the Primary Process

The primary process of providing educational services to schools includes the intake, the service itself, and evaluation. The latter aspect will be described in detail later.

INTAKE; SUPPLY AND DEMAND.   How are the needs of schools and others handled by educational service centers and does the offer match the needs of the client system? There has been an assumption by some political parties in the Netherlands that the service offered by the Dutch support structure did not match the needs of the schools (Verhoeff, 1992), and that this matching would improve by giving schools the money to buy the educational services (Wetenschappelijke Raad voor het Regeringsbeleid [WRR], 1991). This specific purchasing power of schools has also been delegated in England and Wales.

Research, however, has demonstrated that the matching process in itself was of sufficient quality (Van Gennip, 1990), but that elements of the process could be improved (Koster, 1994). Koster referred to the need for improvement in defining actions, time, the involvement of schools themselves, and the definition of required outcomes and output.

THE SERVICE ITSELF.   Evaluation on the results and effectiveness of the work of educational service centers has been reviewed by Slavenburg (1995), director of the center in Rotterdam and professor at the University of Groningen. His conclusions follow.

Services in the Field of Innovation and School Improvement

Initiation. The influence of the work of the centers for the adoption of the educational ideas, crucial for the develop-

ment of primary education, has been of great importance (Slavenburg, 1995, p. 38).

Implementation. Most research has been concentrated on this stage of the innovation process. From 61 reports the general consensus is that only a combination of different interventions is effective: using training sessions related to clinical supervision and to teacher counseling seem to be the most productive combination of interventions (Slavenburg, 1995, p. 54).

Services in the Field of the Development of School Organization

Functioning of the school team. Although Slavenburg does not report research findings for this aspect, the development of "school work plans" is seen as a positive contribution to the establishment of teams in schools (Verhoeff, 1992).

School management. No substantial research has been reported on activities such as courses and seminars that have been offered by the centers in cooperation with teacher-training centers.

Diagnosis of the school organization. This activity claims to detect the strengths and weaknesses of organizations and then offers support for improving the school organization. No research on the results or effects for this organization is available.

Staff development. Educational service centers cooperate with teacher-training centers and colleges on different aspects of in-service training, such as in the field of computer technology, mathematics, and reading. Except for courses in reading, the satisfaction of schools and the reports of the inspectorate are very positive.

Services in the Field of Support for Schools to Teach Children with Learning Disabilities and Social/Emotional Problems

Approximately 50 percent of all the work of educational service centers is carried out in this field. Significant research has been reported and it is suggested that, by these interventions, a decrease of referral to special education schools of 2.1 percent of all students of primary education might be achieved (Slavenburg, 1995, p. 91).

Development and Dissemination

The larger educational service centers have the opportunity to develop and disseminate on a large scale textbooks and similar materials and then to evaluate the work. In addition, only the centers in the four large cities of Amsterdam, Rotterdam, The Hague, and Utrecht have the opportunity to use the research development and dissemination approach. Research did not refer to the effectiveness of educational service for schools. The other 60 educational service centers also develop and disseminate educational materials. Work is nationwide as in the example of education of the gifted and talented. There is little relevant research on the effectiveness of educational service.

Information Services

Almost every educational service center has an educational information center. The aim of this core activity is to stimulate the use of ideas that are promoted by the materials and demonstrate conceptual use. Almost 90 percent of all primary schools visit the centers and take information with them. Between 75 percent and 85 percent of the schools use the information for discussion and other conceptual activities in school (Slavenburg, 1995, p. 106).

Advising (Regional) Organizations

Most educational service centers not only give advice to schools, but also to other organizations such as networks of school boards, local community authorities, and cooperatives of local authorities. Parent organizations and teacher unions are target groups. Research indicates that educational services generally provide advice to these organizations as well (Slavenburg, 1995, p. 109).

Output

There has been significant research on the throughput of educational services in the Netherlands but only limited research on output. In the field of implementation of innovations it is known that some interventions are related very effectively to teacher behavior. The achievement of students, influenced by external educational services, have not been reported widely, with the exception of that by Houtveen, Booij, and Jong (1995) on the School Improvement Project, which was a cooperative effort of several educational service centers. Most research continues to evaluate the services performed and the conceptual use of them.

Conclusion

The Netherlands has a formal system of educational services so there has been significant research carried out on both the input and throughput of this system. More research is needed, however, at the output level of the system.

LUXEMBOURG

Context for Providers

THE NEEDS OF THE EDUCATIONAL SYSTEM. Schools have a limited influence in the Luxembourg elementary education system, comprised of 26,000 students. National and local authorities directly oversee teachers. Individual teachers have great freedom in interpreting the general features, but not specific formulated and centrally controlled curriculum. Principals of schools also have a limited influence.

According to the composition of the traditional population, three teaching languages, namely, French, German, and Luxembourg, are used in the schools. This multilingual situation is reinforced by the fact that 34 percent of all students in elementary education are from migrant foreign families. Students from elementary school take a central examination for admission to secondary education; 8.5 percent of all 12–15 year olds receive additional, complementary education, which is under critical review. Admittance to special classes is regulated by regional medical psychopedagogical commissions.

The secondary education system is in transition. After 3 years of orientation, students make a choice between 2 years of either classical or modern courses. They then must choose 2 years of various specializations. The multilingual situation, the high dropout rate, and the dysfunction of special classes suggests a need for the implementation of a nonselective school system (Husén & Posthlethwaite, 1994).

POSITION OF PROVIDERS. The Institute for Higher Pedagogical Training and Research (ISERP) organizes the training for future primary school teachers in Luxembourg. Those who are training to be secondary education teachers must get their in-service training in foreign countries. Practicing teachers get personal credits for in-service training. The Institute for Pedagogical Innovation and Research has been renamed as the Service of Coordination of Research and Innovation in Pedagogy and Technology (SCRIPT). This institution is working on innovation plans at a national level. At the local level, the inspectorate reports on the needs for support in the schools but there are no service teams. The Centers for Psychology and Study Guidance (CPOS), controlled by the national government, have the task of providing advice to students and parents on psycho/pedagogical issues and problems, and on vocational choices. These institutions do not work directly with teachers (Wielemans, 1994c). There are no data available about these educational services to schools, therefore, there is no evidence as to their effectiveness.

Conclusion

Further investigation using content analysis and codification of documents most likely will not add more information on throughput of this new service system.

EDUCATIONAL SERVICE IN SPECIFIC EDUCATIONAL FIELDS

The literature selected for generating data and describing educational service providers in different countries has also offered information on some specific areas of educational service. Two perspectives will be used to present an overview. One is the model for the description of educational services and their effectiveness, presented earlier; the other is on the use of an educational policy program. This includes topics referring to the curriculum, educational concepts, and to the general system of education.

Educational Services and Curriculum Implementation

National Curricula

The development and implementation of core curricula is executed in different ways in different countries. There has been little research concerning this (Gorter, 1986a,b).

In the United Kingdom, a national curriculum has been introduced under the Education Reform Act of 1983 and designated national tests in elementary and secondary education have been implemented. The British debate has been, and continues to be, intensive, as it is important to the major political parties. The former Thatcher administration privatized the agencies that would support schools and reduced the power of the local education authorities. This has led to the increased commercialization of the supply of educational services in the United Kingdom. These are evaluated as a part of the implementation process by the various commercial enterprises.

In the Netherlands, all primary schools must have implemented attainment targets by 1998. Previously there was no central orchestration of this nationwide implementation. In Dutch secondary education, the core curriculum for basic education was introduced in 1993. The national pedagogical centers had the responsibility to support schools as they implemented the curriculum. The results of this work at the different levels of teachers and students have not been reviewed systematically. The same situation is seen in Belgian Flanders, where a new national curriculum has been introduced to support the unification of secondary schools. In Israel the Ministry of Education, sometimes by its Inspectorate, is responsible for the development, implementation, and adaptation of the core curriculum. There is, nevertheless, some autonomy in using the core curriculum. Both at the level of the seven regions and of the individual schools, there are possibilities to adapt the curriculum to their specific situation.

Subjects and Disciplines

LANGUAGE ARTS, ESPECIALLY READING. At present, no research has been published on the results of educational service in the field of language arts and reading. In the Netherlands the teaching of reading has been given an extra impetus in primary education by nationwide in-service training. This training has focused more on theory than on practice in classrooms and 82 to 90 percent of all schools reacted positively to this provision (Slavenburg, 1995, p. 117).

Recently, a group of educational service centers in the Netherlands succeeded in producing a positive result in schools whereby specific interventions were integrated with language policy and improved facilities (Houtveen, Booij, & de Jong, 1995).

SECOND LANGUAGE FOR IMMIGRANTS. In the Netherlands, the United Kingdom, France, Germany, and Belgium, many publications refer to the issue of teaching the national language as a second language to immigrant children (Fase, 1994). Related to the immigrant policy of the State of Israel, bilingual education and teaching Hebrew as a second language have a very high priority. Many Israeli programs have been evaluated and adopted by other countries for the education of groups in education priority areas. Whether these implementation strategies are effective, however, is unknown. Research in this field generally shows slight achievement of these groups, but does not demonstrate that this is the effect of specific educational service.

FOREIGN LANGUAGE. One of the elements of implementing primary education in the Netherlands has been the introduction of English in grade 5 as a foreign language. In other European countries the policy of the European Community to introduce foreign languages has been carried out. No research has been undertaken yet to evaluate the effectiveness of educational support in implementing this policy of the Community.

In Israel English is compulsory. Interventions of the inspectorate include workshops, school visits, and information services, such as a journal. Here, too, no effects of these interventions have been demonstrated.

MATHEMATICS. The Netherlands has its unique success story on the introduction of realistic (context-related) mathematics education. It is evident that the network of the Freudenthal Institute at the Utrecht University, together with educational service centers, teacher-training colleges, inspectorate, the National Curriculum Development Institute, and educational publishers, has been of crucial significance to the nationwide acceptance of this innovation. Comparable situations in other European countries are not noted, defined, or reviewed in detail.

COMPUTER TECHNOLOGY. Dutch educational service centers have been quite successful in implementing computers and educational software in primary education. Other institutes have supported secondary schools in this field. This was achieved within the framework of national projects. The inspectorate of education has been very positive about the contribution of the local and regional educational service centers in this development (Inspectie van het Onderwijs, 1994).

In the State of Israel, computer technology is a high priority of the national government. The implementation of the 5-year plan "Tomorrow 98" is in full progress, steered and monitored by the Science and Technology Division of the Ministry of Education. The topic also has high priority at the regional level.

Educational Concepts

Learning by Experience for Early Childhood Education Most European countries see early childhood education as a priority, but the attention given to this area varies, including the enrollment of students as well as the introduction of new programs. In Belgium this field of educational service is dominated by the project "Learning by Experience," which has been described in earlier sections.

Gifted and Talented In a number of educational service centers in the Netherlands, special attention is given to teaching of gifted and talented children. This engagement has generated various publications from Bodegraven, Nijmegen, and Zoetermeer. The effects of specific interventions of external consultants, is not known, however. The education of the gifted in Israel, in contrast to the Netherlands, is a major official concern.

Educational System

Inclusion The continuing work of educational services is to make a difference by decreasing the number of students in special education and in integrating help for handicapped children into the mainstream of primary education. Educational service centers in the Netherlands provide early diagnosis together with special and remedial counseling and the provision of advice to teachers. For schools, this student counseling service is one of the most important needs for educational support. Fifty-one percent of all schools consider counsel meetings between consultants and teachers the most important activity. The next priority is attending training sessions (48%). The most effective intervention in theory, namely, clinical supervision, is not considered very important by schools.

The situations in the other countries described in this chapter differ substantially from the Netherlands. Only the Netherlands has such a rich variety of special education schools. This may be because only in the Netherlands are reviews available on the effectiveness of interventions that have been designed to decrease the growth of the special education school system.

Quality in Schools One of the priorities of educational policy in the Netherlands is that schools will be held more accountable for their quality of teaching than ever before. This implies that they should get more support from educational service centers. As this is a new issue in educational service, there are as yet no research results available.

Intercultural Education All four countries described here have policies on both education for immigrants and intercul-

tural education. Although results from research show that immigrant children achieve better in secondary education, there are major concerns about the little progress schools have made to implement intercultural education for all children. It is suggested that schools themselves do not request help in this field and, consequently, external consultants may have more power to facilitate schools to integrate this aspect in their organization and curriculum.

FURTHER RESEARCH

Educational service in the Netherlands is a well elaborated system of support for all schools. As this is a dedicated formalized system, the situation in this country is available for substantial monitoring and subsequent evaluation. In other countries the situation is less clear. It is important to gain more comparative information on educational services in these countries. The next step should be to concentrate on issues that are relevant to the review of the effectiveness of the provided services in these countries.

Discussion on the exemplary descriptions and communicating within a network of international correspondents, together with the linking of Europe with other countries, including Israel, the United States, Canada, and Australia, are essential to future progress.

REFERENCES

Beukering, J. T. E. van. (1991). *Interne begeleiding in de basisschool.* Amsterdam: GPI.

Braaksma, J. & Heinink, A. L. (1990). *Educational Support Agencies in some European Countries.* Not published.

Centraal Bureau voor de Statistiek. (1995a). *Kwartaalschrift Onderwijsstatistieken* (Vol. 2). Voorburg/Heerlen: CBS.

Centraal Bureau voor de Statistiek. (1995b). *Zakboek Onderwijsstatistieken 1994/1995. Onderwijs cijfergewijs.* The Hague: CBS.

Center for Educational Research and Innovation. (1992). *Education at a glance. OECD indicators.* Paris: OECD.

Commisie Evaluatie Basisonderwijs. (1994). *Zicht op kwaliteit.* The Hague: Inspectie van het Onderwijs.

Commissie Heroverweging Kerndoelen Basisonderwijs. (1994). *Doelbewust leren. Kerndoelen basisonderwijs in maatschappelijk perspectief.* Zoetermeer: Ministerie van Onderwijs, Cultuur en Wetenschappen.

Costa, A. & Garmston, R. J. (1994). *Cognitive coaching: A foundation for renaissance schools.* Norwood, CT: Christopher-Gordon.

Leune, J. M. G. (1994). *Onderwijskwaliteit en de autonomie van scholen.* In B. Creemers (Ed.). *Deregulering en de kwaliteit van onderwijs.* Groningen: RION.

Dalin, P., Rolff, H. G., & Kleekamp, B. (1993). *Changing the school culture.* London, England: Cassel.

Dingemans, M. & Pajak, E. (1993). *Approaches to clinical supervision.* In *School & Begeleiding, December 1993.* Hoevelaken: CPS.

Dingemans, M., Timmer, J., & Vermunt, H. (1995). *Een beroepsprofiel van onderwijsbegeleiders.* The Hague: WPRO.

Fase, W. (1994). *Ethnic divisions in western European education.* Münster, New York: Waxmann.

Fullan, M. G. & Stiegelbauer, S. (1991). *The new meaning of educational change.* London: Cassel.

Gennip, J. van. (1990). *Onderwijsbegeleiding onderzocht: Taken, werkwijzen en resultaten.* Nijmegen: ITS.

Glickman, C. D. (Ed.). (1992). *Supervision in transition.* Alexandria, VA: ASCD.

Gorter, R. J. (Ed.). (1986a). *Views on core curriculum. Contributions to an international seminar.* Enschede: SLO.

Gorter, R. J. (Ed.). (1986b). *Core curriculum in western societies. Conference report.* Enschede: SLO.

Gorter, R. J. (1993). *De toekomst van de onderwijsbegeleiding en WSNS.* In *Tijdschrift voor Orthopedagogiek.* Groningen: Wolters Noordhoff, *32,* 79–86.

Gorter, R. J. (1994). *Schoolbegeleiding in verandering.* In W. Tjerkstra (Ed.). *School voor kinderen.* Leeuwarden: GCO.

Groot, M. J. de. (1988). *The Dutch educational support system and its implications for Victoria.* Melbourne: Monash University.

Halter-Zeier, B. (Ed.). (1994). *Mittendrin. Informationen aus dem ZBS.* Luzern: ZBS.

Hooge, E. H. (1995). *Het onderwijs in Portugal.* Heerlen: Open Universiteit.

Hopkins, D., Ainscow, M., & West, M. (1994). *School improvement in an era of change.* London: Cassell.

Houtveen, A. A. M. (1990). *Begeleiden van vernieuwingen.* De Lier: Academisch Boeken Centrum.

Houtveen, A. A. M., Booij, N., & Jong, R. de. (1995). *Effectieve begeleiding en leerkrachtengedrag.* Utrecht: ISOR.

Husén, T. & Postletwaithe, T. N. (Eds.). (1994). *The international encyclopedia of education.* (2nd ed.). Oxford: Pergamon Press.

Inspectie Onderwijsverzorging. (1994). *Het functioneren van school-begeleidingsdiensten.Vijfenveertig instellingsevaluaties nader bekeken.* Breda: Inspectie van het Onderwijs.

Inspectie van het Onderwijs. (1992). *Verslag van de staat van het onderwijs in Nederland over het jaar 1991.* Zoetermeer: Ministerie van Onderwijs, Cultuur en Wetenschappen.

Inspectie van het Onderwijs. (1994). *Verslag van de staat van het onderwijs in Nederland over het jaar 1993.* Zoetermeer: Ministerie van Onderwijs, Cultuur en Wetenschappen.

Inspectie van het Onderwijs. (1995). *Verslag van de staat van het onderwijs in Nederland over het jaar 1994.* Zoetermeer: Ministerie van Onderwijs, Cultuur en Wetenschappen.

Janesick, V. J. & Hogan, M. (1982). *An annotated bibliography on recent research, development and practice in supervision.* Athens, GA: University of Georgia.

Janssen-Vos, F. & Laevers, F. (Eds.). (1996). *De opvang van en het onderwijs aan jonge kinderen. Een comparatieve studie betreffende de situatie in Vlaanderen en Nederland.* Zoetermeer: Ministerie van Onderwijs, Cultuur en Wetenschappen.

Joyce, B. & Showers, B. (1996). Staff development as a comprehensive service organization. *Journal of Staff Development, 17*(1).

Jozefzoon, E. O. I. (1985). Definities en definiëren. Enschede: SLO.

Jozefzoon, E. O. I. & Gorter, R. J. (1985). *Core curriculum. A comparitive analyses.* Enschede: SLO.

Köllen, E. (1990). *A review of education systems, teacher training courses and external educational support (in-service training and educational support organizations) in Belgium, Germany, England and Wales, Sweden, France, and the Netherlands.* Zoetermeer: Ministry of Education and Science.

Koster, A. J. (1994). Het aanbod van onderwijsverzorging. Groningen: RION.

Kramer, E. (1995). *Onderzoek naar een systematische evaluatiemethode voor het meten van effecten van schoolbegeleiding.* Enschede: OCTO.

Kuknyo, J. (1992). *Evolving county educational services. Change within the pedagogical institutes.* Nyíregyháza: The Hungarian Institute of Education. Rotterdam: CED/PI.

Leune, J. M. G. (1992). *Ontwikkelingen op het terrein van de onderwijsverzorging.* Rotterdam: RISBO.

Meijer, C. J. W., Pijl, S. J., & Hegarty, S. (Eds.). (1994). *New perspectives in special education. A six-country study of integration.* London: Routledge.

Organisation for Economic Co-operation. (1991). *Reviews of national policies for education: Netherlands.* Paris: OECD.

Organisation for Economic Co-operation/Unit for Education Statistics and Indicators. (1995). *Education at a glance 1995.* Paris: OECD.

Pajak, E. (1993). *Approaches to clinical supervision: Alternatives for improving instruction.* Norwood: Christopher-Gordon.

Pajak, E. & Hooghoff, H. (1992, November). *How the Netherlands supports curriculum and instruction.* In *educational leadership.* Alexandria, VA: ASCD.

Rutten, J. J. G. M. & Wijn, C. H. (1996). *Onderwijsbeleid op lokaal niveau.* The Hague: VNG.

Rubinstein, A. (1996). *There is another way. Israel believes in education. Implementation of major policy decisions.* Jerusalem: Ministry of Education, Culture and Sport.

Sergiovanni, T. J. (1992). *Moral Authoriy and the Regeneration of Supervision.* In C. D. Glickman (Ed.). *Supervision in Transition.* Alexandria, VA: ASCD.

Slavenburg, J. H. (1995). *Educatieve dienstverlening: Werkwijzen, effecten en waardering. Een overzicht van het Nederlands onderzoek naar educatieve diensten zoals die worden verleend door onderwijsbegeleidingsdiensten.* Rotterdam: Partners Training & Innovatie.

Slavenburg, J. H. (1996). *Dutch-Hungarian cooperation education support Institutes.* Rotterdam: CED/PI.

Sprinzak, D., Bar, E., & Levi-Mazioum, D. (1994). *Facts and figures about education and culture in Israel.* Jerusalem: Ministry of Education, Culture and Sport.

Stevens Brodersen, R. (1995). *Het onderwijs in Denemarken.* Heerlen: Open Universiteit.

Timmer, J. (1985). *Wat is onderwijsbegeleiding nu eigenlijk? Naar een definitie.* In E. Pelosi (Ed.). *Onderwijsbegeleiding, feiten en ideeën.* Groningen: Wolters-Noordhoff.

Verhoeff, C. C. (1992). *De toekomst van de onderwijsverzorging. Een analyse van meningen over de onderwijsverzorging.* The Hague: ABKO.

Vlaamse Onderwijsraad. (1993). *Naar een duidelijker profiel voor de PMS-centra Advies van de Vlaamse Onderwijsraad (Book 2).* Brussels: VLOR.

Voster, W. (1982). *De onderwijsverzorging internationaal vergeleken.* Zoetermeer: Ministerie van Onderwijs, Cultuur en Wetenschappen.

Wetenschappelijke Raad voor het Regeringsbeleid. (1991). *De Onderwijsverzorging in de toekomst.* The Hague: WRR.

Wielemans, W. (1994a). *Het onderwijs in Belgie.* Heerlen: Open Universiteit.

Wielemans, W. (1994b). *Het onderwijs in Italië.* Heerlen: Open Universiteit.

Wielemans, W. (1994c). *Het onderwijs in Luxemburg.* Heerlen: Open Universiteit.

WPRO. (1995). *Onderwijsbegeleiding in Cijfers VI.* The Hague: WPRO.

Wulleman, G. (Ed.). *De Nederlandse onderwijsbegeleidingsdiensten, verenigd in het WPRO en de Vlaamse PMS-centra en pedagogische begeleidingsdiensten.* Internal paper.

·VIII·

THEORIES OF SUPERVISION

INTRODUCTION

Allan A. Glatthorn

EAST CAROLINA UNIVERSITY

The chapters in this section examine the several dimensions or perspectives that might be used in understanding the nature and functions of supervision. In this sense, each individual chapter provides a lens for viewing supervision as a field of study and as an aspect of educational practice.

The availability of these multiple lenses through which to examine supervision theory and practice serves as a corrective to those who might otherwise be inclined to advocate and use a single perspective. Using only one lens, such as the scientific, provides a distorted view, excludes significant aspects of the field, and results in doctrinaire approaches to research and practice. Advocating the use of multiple perspectives, however, should not result in a mindless eclecticism: the scholar and the practitioner both need to bring to bear a critical understanding that enables them to identify potential limitations and strengths of each dimension.

SCIENTIFIC DIMENSIONS

Killian and Post begin the section with an analysis of the *scientific* dimension of supervision. As they use the term, *scientific* refers to structured application of specific principles under controlled conditions; *scientific supervision* is the process of systematically observing and analyzing instruction to determine the teacher's effectiveness in achieving predetermined outcomes. In their analysis of the history of scientific supervision, they identify its roots in the era of scientific management, grounded chiefly in Frederick Taylor's seminal work, *Principles of Scientific Management*. In this sense, sci-

entific supervision in its origins is closely allied with the industrial dimensions examined by Flinders in Chapter 46. As Killian and Post note, scientific management seemed to make a major impact on the administration of schools and in the development of curricula. Its advocates argued for ways to make the schools more efficient by using the principles of scientific management. Franklin Bobbitt, who was perhaps the earliest advocate of Outcomes Based Education, developed a curriculum model that used the principles of scientific management to develop curricula focusing on life roles. The supervisor practicing scientific supervision was expected to measure teacher performance, remediate in weak areas, and dismiss incompetent teachers. The authors argue convincingly that, although this early work in scientific management seemed to have an influence on educational thought, it had less impact on educational practice and declined in influence after 1930.

Scientific management is distinguished from *neoscientific management*, which more accurately describes several current elements of "scientific" practice; standardized testing; behavioral objectives; supervision through behavioral objectives; teacher rating scales; and merit pay systems. The pervasive and sustaining nature of scientific supervision is perhaps best evidenced, as the authors emphasize, in the widespread use by practitioners of the Hunter model of instruction and supervision: Hunter herself claimed a "20-year escalation of acceptance all over the world." Despite its ready acceptance by practitioners, the Hunter model attracted much criticism for its technological language, its rigidity, its insensitivity to subject-matter differences, and its weak research base. The authors conclude their chapter by deriving several enduring lessons from the past with respect to scientific supervision that they believe will be useful to both scholars and practitioners.

SOCIAL DIMENSIONS

Those using a social perspective to examine supervision are chiefly concerned with the way the culture of a particular society impacts upon the nature and functions of supervision. The core components of the culture are the internalized values of the people of that society that in turn influence the generally accepted norms of behavior and such behavioral manifestations as rituals, ceremonies, slogans, and stories. As the authors indicate, some theorists with a social perspective (e.g., Getzels, Guba, & Campbell) are chiefly concerned with the class as a social system, the type of leadership needed in such complex social systems, and the nature of conflict within the social system. Others (e.g., Shapiro, Benjamin, & Hunt) are more concerned with the school as a social enterprise, examining the larger issues of the school as an organization, the impact of the organization on supervisor and teacher behavior, and the processes by which such organizations change. Functioning in such organizations, the supervisor has a choice of roles: custodianship embracing a caretaking function, content innovation (i.e., emphasizing the adoption of alternative strategies, and role innovation, focusing on the development of alternative roles).

Other issues raised by those holding a social perspective include the influences of socioeconomic class stratification; the status of the supervisor's role; the impact of gender, race, and ethnicity; and the use of social systems theory in understanding supervisory function.

HUMAN DIMENSIONS

Wood examines the human dimensions of supervision, arguing for what she terms "transformative supervision" in a learning community. She points out that most teachers consider the principal (i.e., the chief supervisor of the teacher) as irrelevant and inaccessible. This has come about chiefly because the principal blurs the distinction between supervision and evaluation. Principals, she notes, are what they do and what they construe. Too many of them spend their time on the mundane and the routine. More important than what they do, however, is what they construe. Their beliefs about the purposes of those routine actions and their values about teaching and learning powerfully affect how they supervise. Their lack of conscious thought and reflection becomes a major impediment to their functioning as supervisors.

The solution to this dismal situation is transformative supervision, which Wood defines as a facilitator who works with the teacher in a collaborative relationship, creating and supporting a learning environment that reduces isolation and encourages teachers to reflect about their own teaching. Such a supervisory relationship can obviously flourish best in an organizational culture that views learning as a collaborative process, in an environment that is safe, failure-safe, and growth-oriented.

THE AESTHETIC DIMENSIONS

In the next chapter, Barone notes that the artistic lenses are now viewed as complementing the more familiar ones provided by the social sciences. As he indicates, artistic approaches to supervision are intended to help teachers become more talented at the practical art of teaching by employing the two fundamental processes: appreciation (i.e., interpreting and judging the quality of classroom events) and disclosure (i.e., publicizing the elements of artistry that have been appreciated). As Barone analyzes it, the appreciative dimension seems to include six components: the aesthetics of everyday life (chiefly as formulated by John Dewey); life in general as a story, embodied in personal narratives; the stories of teachers, as particular embodiments of the power of narrative; empathy as an artistic activity of supervisors; teaching as an art; and the act of appreciating teachers' artistry.

Artistic disclosure is marked by several characteristics: the use of expressive language; the use of contextualized language; the creation of virtual worlds; promotion of empathic understanding; the personal nature of composition; and the presence of a narrative format. In the act of disclosure, the supervisor functions as an educational critic, one who practices the art of educational connoisseurship and uses narrative storytelling as the chief form of disclosure. As an educational critic, the supervisor emphasizes three aspects (i.e., the descriptive, the interpretive, and the evaluative) and remains sensitive to the impact of the audience. Like other lenses, the aesthetic one has its own limitations: It is by nature subjective, it is labor-intensive, and it involves major issues of credibility and validity.

INDUSTRIAL DIMENSIONS

Flinders, in Chapter 46, is concerned chiefly with how the ideas of work in industrial settings apply to the theory and practice of school supervision. His retrospective analysis of industrial influences identifies three trends that have special relevance to the industrial dimensions of supervision: the bureaucratization of schooling (i.e., as schools became larger and their professionals more specialized); the spread of scientific management and social efficiency (i.e., the attempts to rationalize the profession); and social adaptation (i.e., chiefly as reflected in the "life adjustment" movement, which emphasized the role of the school in helping students adjust to the demands of the social order). As he notes, this emphasis on social adaptation is basically a conservative approach to the functions of schooling in a democratic society, which encourages supervisors to help teachers ensure that the school's products meet society's needs.

In Flinders' view, these same trends continue to have a major impact on schools today. He points to several contemporary examples: curricula shaped to accommodate the needs of industry; Total Quality Management (i.e., a set of beliefs and practices that sees schools as enlightened corporations, not as factories; and the use of the threat of world competition as an argument for school reform. Tying these three examples together is a common language and discourse that he sees as "pervasively anchored" in American industrial and business interests. In this common language, the school as a factory is the prevailing metaphor, teachers are the workers, and students the finished product. He delineates two significant implications of this analysis of language: Supervisors should be especially sensitive to the fluid and somewhat unpredictable nature of schools as nonrational organizations, and supervisors should realize that they are as much a part of the organization as are the teachers.

His analysis of teaching as work continues by identifying three major critics of industrial management as applied to schools. The work of Michael Apple is especially relevant in understanding two related trends. The deskilling of teaching results from the attempts of administrators to standardize and thus control the essential elements of teachers' work; the intensification of teachers' work is manifested in demands for increased teacher productivity. As he points out, supervisors may lose sight of these deleterious elements because their own work has become subject to the same influences.

The second critical analysis of industrial conceptions of teachers' work is Lipsky's theory of teachers as "street-level bureaucrats," whose collective actions add up to agency policy. As street-level bureaucrats, teachers tend to adopt a "processing mentality," which results in treating clients on the basis of standardized routines instead of being sensitive to their individual needs. The final critical element that Flinders examines is the emphasis of fidelity with respect to program implementation, in which implementation is viewed as a linear process governed through top–down management. The supervisor's role here is to check on how well the delivered curriculum matches the designed curriculum. On the contrary,

seeing implementation as program enactment emphasizes the teacher's role as an active shaper of the program, which is a key element in the co-creating of meaning.

INTERNATIONAL DIMENSIONS

While not topically consistent with the other chapters in this section, the chapter by Hough provides a very useful analytical system for categorizing studies in supervision—a system that goes beyond national boundaries. The categorization system proposed by Hough includes three frameworks: purpose, scope, and sociocultural context.

In the Hough system, the analysis of purpose yields a dichotomy: Studies are either action research, which focuses on localized understandings, or scientific research, which is concerned with producing generalized findings. The "scope" framework allocates studies in terms of the extent of the problem studied. Macrofocus research examines such large-scale issues as whole systems and their relationships, or whole cohorts of supervisors. Microfocus research is concerned with small-scale matters, such as the supervisor–supervisee relationship. The sociocultural context, as Hough sees it, is the most complex of the three frameworks. Societies are classified as members of one of three groups: agrarian economy, industrial/manufacturing economy, and service/information economy. Hough goes beyond simple classification, using the categories to make predictions. Thus, he believes that an agrarian context creates the need for small-scale action research.

These multiple perspectives provide several complementary lenses for scholars and practitioners through which both can view the nature of supervision.

· 42 ·

SCIENTIFIC DIMENSIONS OF SUPERVISION

Joyce E. Killian

SOUTHERN ILLINOIS UNIVERSITY AT CARBONDALE

Donna M. Post

SOUTHERN ILLINOIS UNIVERSITY AT CARBONDALE

INTRODUCTION

Educators and the public have recurrently looked to "scientific supervision" for an authoritative research base that will provide enduring formulas for teaching effectiveness and student achievement. Reconsideration of the contributions and limitations of science-based supervision lends perspective about why many efforts have fallen short of their promise and what forms of scientific supervision will continue to have an enduring influence on education.

The Art and Science of Teaching and a Definition of Terms

Educators have debated for many years whether teaching is an art, and therefore intuitive, creative, and expressive, or whether it is a science, and therefore a process to be studied, evaluated, and taught. Proponents of the "art" philosophy believe that the teacher is a performer who at times improvises in the practice of his or her craft, departing from certain rules, procedures, or teaching models to explore in detail unexpected twists and turns that may arise during the process of teaching and learning. As such, teaching is seen as performance to be critiqued on the basis of motivation and pacing, emotional reactions to other persons involved in the process, and the use of insight in achieving certain educational goals.

The artistic view of teaching is not incompatible with science if the latter is defined broadly enough to include question posing, experimentation, and discovery on the part of the teacher. Dewey (1929, pp. 13–15) argued that as long as this true scientific method is applied to teaching, the results can be both emancipatory and constructive. Opposition between art and science occurs, however, when the "experimentalist"

in any field begins to reduce findings to rules that are to be uniformly adopted or used simplistically in the identification of effective practices.

In contrast to Dewey are those "scientific" views of education that critique teaching on a narrower range of variables, using some rating of efficiency as a yardstick. In this latter view, teaching is a rational, technical, and predictive action that can be both taught and measured. This chapter will discuss in detail one such "scientific" philosophy of teaching and supervision that was shaped by the industrial model of scientific management early in this century. In order to examine this philosophy thoroughly and to understand its implications for teaching and learning, the chapter will explore scientific management theories in American business and industry and describe the nature of their expansion into education and schooling.

First, though, it is important to understand the meaning of three terms as they are used throughout this chapter. In this context, the term *scientific* in its narrowest sense refers to *structured application of specified principles under controlled conditions.* When it is conceived more broadly, it refers to the process of observing naturalistic phenomenon, asking questions, stating hypotheses, and drawing conclusions (at least tentatively). The term *scientific supervision* refers to the process of systematically observing and analyzing instruction to determine the teacher's effectiveness in achieving predetermined outcomes. *Scientific management* is a term used to describe the process of applying scientific processes in the administration of organizational behavior.

Scope of the Chapter

Like all approaches to supervision, the appeal of scientific management is recurrent. In describing and evaluating the effects of scientific management on supervision both past and present, the following questions will serve as organizers:

1. How have the theories and practice of scientific management influenced school supervision?
2. What is the nature of this influence, its strengths and limitations?
3. How has "scientific" supervision been studied and what are its lessons? What are the major gaps in this inquiry?
4. What lines of inquiry are most promising for future research? What should be the focus and implications of such research?

This chapter will begin by addressing the historical context of the scientific dimension of supervision. We will describe the context in which scientific management emerged, both in American business and industry, and in the broader American society. We will then trace the emergence of scientific management in the schools and examine documented examples of its implementation, including a discussion of the research that was conducted in those settings. We will next discuss the prevalence of scientific management practices in education, and conclude the historical section with a description of factors associated with its decline.

The second section of the chapter will deal with recurrent themes of scientific management in supervision. We will define *neoscientific* and identify its characteristics. We will then briefly describe several examples of neoscientific practices, including standardized testing, behavioral objectives, teacher rating scales, and merit pay. Examples will conclude with a detailed exploration of the Hunter model of supervision as a prevalent contemporary example of "scientific" supervisory practice. We will compare and contrast this modern example with earlier versions of scientific management practice and discuss issues related to the validity and generalizability of its research base.

We will conclude the chapter with a discussion of the present status of the influence of scientific management on supervision, the reasons for its enduring appeal, and its limitations. We will discuss the potential for a synthesis of scientific supervision with other forms of supervision and project the outlook for the future role of scientific supervision.

ROOTS IN THE PAST, 1900–1930

The Classical Period of Scientific Management

Any understanding of the scientific dimensions of supervision begins with a historical perspective on the scientific management movement. The initial impact of scientific management on schools and supervision was a by-product of the much broader movement that heavily influenced industry during the first quarter of this century. Taylor was the engineering consultant whose seminal work in setting standards for productivity made him the forefather of the efficiency movement in the United States. His 1911 *Principles of Scientific Management* described extensive field research in the steel industry, where he observed each task in the pro-

duction process and recommended changes in plant organization and worker assignments that would result in greatest efficiency. His meticulous observation and data collection were widely regarded as "scientific," a characterization that gave weight to his recommendations. His studies affected practice well beyond the original industrial sites, resulting in widespread application of such tactics as the piece-rate system and time standards for production. His "classical" scientific management model centered on an efficient organizational process, not on the workers' conditions or motivation, which had dominated in earlier supervision practices (Wiles & Bondi, 1991, p. 31).

Though many school leaders were skeptical about the application of "scientific" business practices to education, borrowing some of the aura of respectability from business was hard to resist. Scientific supervision got its foothold in education because it appeared to deliver a less personal and arbitrary authority for teacher supervision as it was promising greater gains in student achievement. Through empirical research, supervisors themselves were charged with discovering the most efficient procedures for performing teacher tasks and helping teachers acquire these methods in order to ensure maximum pupil achievement. By developing standards and performance checklists that reflected this "research," supervisors were able to monitor teaching effectiveness and evaluate teachers impartially (McNeil, 1982, p. 19).

Offshoots of scientific management in education were apparent in a variety of forms. Hallmarks were highly formalized, minutely specific written lists of goals, objectives, rules, regulations, and procedures. Like their business counterparts, scientifically managed schools had more stratified bureaucratic authority and a more specialized division of labor than had been present in school organization before this time. It is not coincidental that it was during this time that instruction, and then supervision, specialized by subject area (Wiles & Bondi, 1991, p. 6). Regimentation of classes and schedules was also a characteristic in many schools. As the expectation grew that teachers at each grade level would be doing roughly the same activities at the same time each day, part of the supervisor's role was that of an "efficiency monitor [who checked] to see that teachers were using time effectively and that the lessons were basically the same for all" (Beach & Reinhartz, 1989, p. 20). Thus, the *inspectional* concept of supervision became more entrenched. As the emphasis on scientific management and its stress on empirical research prompted supervisors to aspire to a science of teaching, the attempts of supervisors to control teacher behavior and its effect on student performance also accelerated (Alfonso, Firth, & Neville, 1981).

The Context in Which Scientific Management Emerged

National and International Roots of Scientific Management
Bureaucracy emerged in many aspects of American life around the turn of the century, concurrent with the growth of complex industrial organizations. As machine production and efficiency of operation became focal points in industry, "the relatively simple social and political structures of the preindustrial era seemed inherently inadequate" (Owens, 1991, p. 5).

Scientific management showed promise as a way of dealing impersonally with the conflicts that inevitably arose between people and organizations. The basic premise of the new model was that "if organizations followed established principles for efficiency, production would be high. Supervisors had but to assure the rigorous application of the principles" (Oliva, 1993, p. 8). The scientific management model surged in popularity early in the twentieth century, replacing the earlier inspection model of supervision at many work sites.

In the United States, particularly in the field of school supervision, the roots of scientific management are most frequently attributed to Frederick Taylor. In fact, Taylor's work was but a part of a larger national and international movement during the pre-World War I period, an era made uneasy by both worldwide occurrences of revolution and the rise of Communism, as well as by internal problems of labor unrest, waves of immigrants, and unplanned urban growth. During this period, practices associated with what became known as "Classical Organizational Theory" found outlet in the writings of Taylor as well as Max Weber, Henri Fayol, and Luther Gulick. Their writings encompass two different management perspectives: scientific management and administrative management. While Taylor and others of the scientific perspective focused on the management of work and workers, those of the administrative perspective focused on the management of the entire organization (Lunenburg & Ornstein, 1991, pp. 5–6).

Weber, a German sociologist, is credited with illuminating the character of bureaucratic authority in the modern Western world (Parsons, in Weber, 1947, p. 57). Weber described bureaucracy as by far the most efficient instrument of large-scale administration that had ever been developed and attributed its source of authority to its own impersonal order. In a bureaucratic structure, "each member of the staff occupies an office with a specific delimitation of powers and a sharp segregation of the sphere of office from his private affairs" (Parsons, in Weber, p. 58). Salaries are set according to rank, and a strict hierarchy determines control and supervision. Qualifications for a given position are determined by technical competence, which is often tested by examination and ensured by lengthy formal training as a condition of employment. Owens (1991, p. 6) observed that part of Weber's genius lay in the fact that he recognized both the potential and the dangers inherent in bureaucracy. Weber promoted bureaucracy's clear delegation of authority and responsibilities as a way of answering the era's concern with dealing fairly, impartially, and predictably with conflicts that inevitably arose in the workplace. Weber also warned that massive, uncontrollable bureaucracy could be one of the gravest threats to the modern world (p. 6).

Another theorist with the administrative perspective was a French mining engineer and industrialist named Henry Fayol. His years of experience as manager of a large coal-mining firm in France were the basis for his development of a set of five basic management functions and 14 management principles (Fayol, 1949). Urwick (1937) credited Fayol with directing minds to the need for studying administration scientifically. He pointed out similarities between Fayol and Taylor: While Fayol's industrial experience was less varied than

Taylor's, both men had been scientists before they were managers, and both approached practical problems with scientific enthusiasm. The men differed, however, in the starting point for their study: Whereas Taylor worked upward from the individual worker at his bench, Fayol worked downward from the managing director. Urwick (1937) summarized the unique contribution of Fayol's work:

For the first time a successful business leader of long experience submitted, not the work of others, but his own duties and responsibilities to close scientific analysis. He viewed what he had to do as an administrator with a detachment as rare as it is valuable. . . . Fayol showed beyond question . . . that better management is not merely a question of improving the output of labor and the planning of subordinate units of organization, it is above all a matter of closer study and more administrative training for the men at the top (p. 129).

Luther Gulick, who was another classical theorist with an administrative perspective, adapted Fayol's five basic management functions into "POSDCORB," his acronym for an outline of the functional elements of the work of a chief executive (i.e., planning, organizing, staffing, directing, coordinating, reporting, and budgeting). These seven major duties of the chief executive, he hypothesized, could be separately organized as subdivisions of the executive's office, with their number depending on the size and complexity of the organization of management (Gulick, 1937, p. 13).

Taylor, Weber, Fayol, and Gulick shared a pioneering influence in efforts to deal systematically with the organizational problems of a modern industrial society. They and others like them "approached administration and management as a scientist might, using the scientific tools of research, measurement, and analysis" (Wiles & Bondi, 1991, p. 31).

Frederick Taylor and the Scientific Management Movement in American Business and Industry

While Weber's, Fayol's, and Gulick's ideas about bureaucracy closely paralleled Taylor's and were written during roughly the same time period, those of Weber in particular were not translated and widely disseminated in the United States until after World War II (Campbell, Fleming, Newell, & Bennion, 1987, p. 63). In the United States prior to 1920, the management theories and practices of Frederick Taylor were most familiar to the public, and it was Taylor's theory and practice of scientific management in American steel industries that were later transferred into recommended school supervision practices.

Taylor, who began as an engineer in Pennsylvania at the Midvale and Bethlehem companies, was troubled by the inefficiencies that he observed in the production process. His interest in solving practical production problems led him to extensive field experimentation, and by 1915 he had become one of the nation's top engineering consultants. His techniques were labeled "scientific" because they were "scientifically validated" by painstaking observation and task analysis (Sergiovanni & Starratt, 1993, pp. 11–12).

Taylor's method can be summed up as, "Find the one best way and apply it consistently." In his 1911 *Principles of Scientific Management*, Taylor described the four managerial duties that are essential to implementing a scientific management approach in industry, contrasting them with earlier "initiative and incentive" practices that had prevailed in industry:

1. Develop a science for each element of a man's work, which replaces the old rule-of-thumb method.
2. Scientifically select and then train, teach, and develop the workman, whereas in the past he chose his own work and trained himself as best he could.
3. Heartily cooperate with the men so as to insure all of the work being done in accordance with the principles of the science which has been developed.
4. [Divide work and responsibility almost equally] between management and the workmen. The management take over all work for which they are better fitted than the workmen, while in the past almost all of the work and the greater part of the responsibility were thrown upon the men (pp. 36–37).

In summarizing how scientific management differed from systems that had gone before, Taylor (1911) stressed that his system shifted much responsibility from the worker to management. In his view, the single most prominent element was what he called "the task idea" (p. 39), (i.e., the notion that every worker's job is planned out at least a day in advance by management). At the start of the work day, the worker received detailed written instruction of what he was to accomplish, how it was to be done, and the exact time for doing it. Comparison of actual work with the task specified allowed for the application of the final critical element in Taylor's system: the bonus. When the worker accomplished the task correctly within the allotted time, he received a bonus the equivalent of 30–100 percent of his salary (1903, p. 60; 1911, p. 39).

Taylor explained the rationale for this bonus and how it should be allocated in his 1911 *Principles of Scientific Management*. He argued that workers had no capacity to produce well under conditions of deferred gratification:

A reward, if it is to be effective in stimulating men to do their best work, must come soon after the work has been done. . . . The average workman must be able to measure what he has accomplished and clearly see his reward at the end of each day if he is to do his best (p. 94).

He designated individual performance rather than group performance for the rewards based on his belief that personal initiative was a far more powerful incentive than was a desire for general welfare, noting that "the few misplaced drones, who do the loafing and share equally in the profits, with the rest, under cooperation are sure to drag the better men down to their level" (p. 95).

The Taylor System in Action The best known example of Taylor's principles in action was probably his description of how he streamlined the process of moving a surplus supply of pig iron onto railroad cars for transport. He described the steps that he took to define the "one best way" of doing this job in his 1911 *Principles of Scientific Management* (see pp. 40–48) and in several widely disseminated speeches he gave

during the period. The specific task was to lift a 92-pound pig of iron, carry it several feet, walk up an inclined plank into a railway car, and deposit the ore on the floor of the car. When Taylor began his work, the men were loading an average of 12.5 tons per day per worker. He undertook a time and motion study of the task, drawing on the series of earlier industrial experiments he had conducted to calculate the optimal time per day that a worker could operate "under load" and the time needed for rest. Taylor's calculations led him to determine that a first class worker could produce most efficiently if working under load only 43 percent of the day. With proper loading technique and strictly prescribed rest periods, he calculated that "a first-class man" could work at a steady pace all day without fatigue and produce almost four times the prevailing rate.

To ensure that the increased productivity was not implemented at the cost of conflict or a strike, Taylor counted on the bonus part of the plan to appeal to the workers. He "scientifically" calculated that the bonus rate for increased productivity on this task should be a 60 percent increase in pay, raising wages from $1.15 per day to $1.85. With the bonus and the scientific details of the task predetermined, Taylor turned his attention to finding the right man to do the job and inducing him to work according to specification at the desired speed.

The right one to handle pig iron was neither extraordinary nor difficult to find, Taylor (1911) observed, but "so stupid and so phlegmatic that he more nearly resembles in his mental make-up the ox than any other type" (p. 59). Taylor and his associate spent 3 or 4 days watching the gang of 75 pig-iron handlers. Four were selected who "appeared to be physically able to handle pig-iron at the rate of 47 tons per day." After a careful study was made of these four, including a study of their "character," "habits," and "ambition," one was selected (p. 43). Taylor went on to describe his conversation with Schmidt, "the little Pennsylvania Dutchman" he selected, and how he was handled in accordance with the principles of scientific management. After Schmidt had reached the desired level of productivity and had been rewarded his bonus, additional men were brought on and trained in the same manner until all of the pig-iron was handled at the 47 tons per day rate, and "the men were receiving 60 per cent. [sic] more wages than other workmen around them" (p. 47).

The Role of the Supervisor in the Taylor Model Supervisory responsibility at a given site took the form of several layers of highly specialized planners and supervisors. As Taylor described the hierarchy (see 1911, pp. 122–125), a management team in the planning department was responsible for the detailed daily written instructions that each worker received. While these planners did their work at desks free from interruption, other supervisors worked directly on the floor to ensure that workers both understood and carried out their written instructions.

This latter group of direct supervisors, whom Taylor alternately calls "teachers" and "functional foremen," acted as agents for the planning department and fell into seven categories: (1) the inspector, (2) the gang boss, (3) the speed boss, (4) the repair boss, (5) the time clerk, (6) the route clerk, and (7) the disciplinarian. These supervisors were in the shop at all times, helping and directing the workmen.

A final and less direct form of supervision was evident in Taylor's description of the product quality control, or what Taylor called "overinspection," to insure that no worker was slighting his work. He described the several layers of product sampling that comprised overinspection at a ball-bearing plant where a group of female employees had the job of sorting out defective bearings. The work of the workers was inspected and dummy samples were substituted for the regular work piles every two or three days. "Overinspectors" verified whether the first-level inspectors had found the proper number of defective bearings in the piles of each worker. In this way, Taylor concluded, all temptation to slight quality or cover up the shoddy work of others was removed (1911, pp. 90–91).

The Scientific Basis of the Taylor Model Because much of the appeal of Taylor's model rested on claims that its scientific basis made it superior to earlier forms of "initiative and incentive" management, it is important to examine the extent to which Taylor's model met scientific standards for validity, reliability, and generalizability.

There is abundant evidence that Taylor and his followers conducted painstaking time and motion studies, the reports of which often occupied thousands of pages. Most such analyses were simple and straightforward in their processes and could be conducted by a researcher with a stopwatch and a ruled notebook. Taylor described the steps of developing a simple law from such observations:

First. Find, say 10 or 15 different men (preferably in as many separate establishments and different parts of the country) who are especially skillful in doing the particular work to be analyzed.
Second. Study the exact series of elementary operations or motions which each of these men uses in doing the work which is being investigated, as well as the implements each man uses.
Third. Study with a stop-watch the time required to make each of these elementary movements and then select the quickest way of doing each element of the work.
Fourth. Eliminate all false movements, slow movements, and useless movements.
Fifth. After doing away with all unnecessary movements, collect into one series the quickest and best movements as well as the best implements (1911, pp. 117–118).

How such data were gathered and applied to simple tasks was documented in Taylor's published descriptions of such processes as handling iron ore, shoveling, and sorting ball bearings. Taylor was less thorough in describing how he conducted more complex time and motion studies. He characterized complicated industrial processes like cutting metals as the exception rather than the rule in industrial research and noted that they were extreme in their complication, and in the time required to develop the research base (1911, p. 115).

How Taylor measured the success of scientific management is also critical to its interpretation as research. The single indicator that Taylor reported consistently and precisely in numerous examples was the new system's comparative cost

benefit to the company over previous methods of management. Even though he often mentioned that the model benefited workers as well as owners and stockholders, Taylor was less clear in reporting how he measured the benefits of the model for workers. Rather, he stated these benefits in broad terms: "Out of the 140 workmen only two were said to be drinking men" (1911, p. 71); "Many, if not most of them, were saving money, and they all lived better than they had before" (p. 72).

In addition to his research on the work process itself, Taylor claimed a basis for his model in extensive investigations of human motivation. While conceding the variation among humans, Taylor said that broadly generalizable laws of human motivation guided his principles, laws based on the findings of a body of "accurate, carefully planned and executed experiments" which he had conducted over a period of years (1911, p. 119). What Taylor meant by "human motivation" was not clarified in his published writing of the period. Given the examples he used, it is likely that Taylor's view of human motivation was much narrower than were contemporary views. The term, as he used it, seemed to consider only the extent to which workers would produce more under a personal incentive plan. Because he did not amplify his reference to a research base with specific findings in either *Shop Management* (1903) or his subsequent book, *Principles of Scientific Management* (1911), it is impossible to assess the scientific merit of this aspect of his model.

While Taylor's findings in one industrial setting seem appropriately generalizable to other similar workplaces, generalization to more complex work processes and certainly to work sites outside the manufacturing industry have been criticized as an overextension. Taylor himself seemed somewhat ambivalent on the issue. He expressed confidence in wide application of the model early in *Principles of Scientific Management*, promising that his four elements could "be applied absolutely to all classes of work, from the most elementary to the most intricate" (1911, p. 40). Later in this same work, however, he cautioned against partial adoption or misapplication of the model, warning that if the method was applied without complete adherence to the principles behind it, then the results might be disastrous. He warned most emphatically against rushing implementation, noting that the process should take from 2 to 5 years and should not be undertaken without the full commitment of all concerned:

Even when men who are thoroughly in sympathy with the principles of scientific management undertake to change too rapidly from the old type to the new, without heeding the warnings of those who have had years of experience in making this change, they frequently meet with serious troubles, and sometimes with strikes, followed by failure (1911, p. 130).

Taylor's admonition did not deter hasty efforts to implement the model in settings ill-suited and ill-prepared for its use. As the evidence of the principles of scientific management began to appear in other social and family institutions of the period, it had clearly been extended beyond its roots in simple industrial processes. Callahan (1962, Chap. 10) noted that it was common to generalize the model beyond its scientific base, an overextension he blamed on both Taylor and those of his followers, who claimed that his principles were a panacea that could be applied to all institutions.

Popularity of the Model in Industry and Society The immense popularity attained by the scientific management movement became at its peak is evident in the writings of some of the period's historians. Taylor was referred to as the "Apostle of the American Gospel of Efficiency" and credited as the first man to proclaim the "truths" about mass production (Boorstin, 1973, p. 363). The model achieved its prominence as the result of a combination of historical events and good timing. The model received national attention when Louis Brandeis, "'the people's lawyer' and champion of labor" (p. 367), made reference to Taylor's work in the highly publicized public hearings on the Eastern railroad's requests for a rate hike. Brandeis praised Taylor's work repeatedly and used it (viz., *Shop Management*, 1903) to support his case against the railroad, arguing that the railroads did not deserve a rate hike when they had failed to take advantage of an existing management model that would have allowed them to be more efficient and profitable (Boorstin, 1973, p. 368).

Kliebard (1971) pointed out an ethical dimension to the attraction of the Taylor model for the period. Once pay rates could be scientifically connected to worker performance, hard work could be rewarded and laziness punished, which was a solution much in keeping with the tried and true virtues of the nineteenth century (pp. 77–78).

Callahan (1962) provided a thorough discussion of the impact of the scientific management movement on the broader American society. He noted that, while the Taylor system was well known only within engineering circles before 1910, it became almost an obsession in the press and throughout society after the railroad hearings of 1911. He cited several forms of evidence of the model's prevalence, including: (1) the hundreds of articles and scores of books that were published on various aspects of scientific management in the years between 1910 and 1916; (2) the discussion of the model in writings of the period about a wide range of professions and organizations, "including the army and navy, the legal profession, the home, the family, the household, the church, and . . . education (p. 23); (3) the spread of the model to other countries as evidenced in the translation of Taylor's *Principles of Scientific Management* into 10 languages; and, finally (4) the formation of Taylor societies and efficiency societies as special interest groups for those interested in promoting the principles of the model.

The Decline of the Taylor Model in Industry Despite its rapid rise and its widespread popularity, some inherent problems in the Taylor model exposed it to criticism from the start. Gross (1964) noted that there was widespread resentment among both management and workers about Taylor's insistence that they needed the assistance of his highly trained "scientific" experts. Workers complained of being reduced to mere automatons in the production process and expressed resentment toward what they perceived to be the model's lack of respect for their craftsman's knowledge. They also resisted the replacement of earlier cooperative work relationships

with Taylor's individual incentive system. Workers sought remedy through organized labor, and by 1912 their unions had obtained authorization of a formal investigation into Taylor's methods. The report of the special committee of the House of Representatives, which conducted this investigation, resulted in the 1915 adoption of an amendment that strictly prohibited the use of stop watches or the payment of bonuses in army arsenals. Another major blow was struck by the report of the United States Commission on Industrial Relations, which concluded that Taylor's method was more arbitrary than scientific and that it ignored important human factors in the workplace.

Other ammunition for criticism emerged in a growing body of research that called into question the assumptions underlying scientific management practice. By the late 1920s, Elton Mayo and his colleagues, F. J. Roethlisberger and William J. Dickson, were conducting a series of experiments at the Hawthorne plant of the Western Electric Company to investigate the effects of a variety of work conditions on productivity. Research was initially conducted much as it would have been in a Taylor time-and-motion study (i.e., based on the assumptions of industrial administration that wages and physical working conditions were the chief factors in employee motivation and productivity) (Getzels, Lipham, & Campbell, 1968, p. 33). In one study, the researchers sought to determine the lighting conditions that would produce optimal productivity on a telephone relay assembly line. They assigned two groups of workers to the same task in separate rooms. In the experimental room, illumination was incrementally altered, while it was held constant in the control. Findings indicated that whatever the change to the experimental condition, production improved for *both* experimental and control groups. The findings of no "sufficiently significant differences" in worker output in enhanced or diminished light confounded the researchers: "Somehow or other that complex of mutually dependent factors, the human organism, shifted its equilibrium and unintentionally defeated the purpose of the experiment" (Mayo, 1933, p. 56).

In an effort to understand what factors were confounding the findings, the researchers departed from the usual experimental approaches of the period and conducted a series of interviews with workers. Roethlisberger and Dickson (1949) described their central finding:

It became clear to the investigators that the limits of human collaboration are determined far more by the informal than the formal organization of the plant. Collaboration is not wholly a matter of logical organization. It presupposes social codes, conventions, traditions, and routine or customary ways of responding to situations. Without such basic codes or conventions, effective work relations are not possible (p. 568).

In his discussion of the findings, Mayo (1933, p. 73) suggested that an experimentally unintended modification of mental attitude had in fact overshadowed the effects of the intended variable. By consulting workers about their views on the upcoming changes and giving them veto power over managerial suggestions, the researchers had inadvertently introduced a new working milieu in which self-determination and social well-being ranked ahead of the work itself.

Scott (1981) described the impact of the Hawthorne project and subsequent studies of human motivation:

Additional studies carried out by the Harvard group . . . all served to call into question the simple motivational assumptions on which the prevailing rational models rested. Individual workers did not behave as "rational" economic actors but as complex beings with multiple motives and values; they were driven as much by feelings and sentiments as by facts and interests; and they did not behave as individual, isolated actors but as members of social groups exhibiting commitments and loyalties stronger than their individualistic self-interests. . . . At the social psychological level, the Hawthorne studies pointed to a more complex model of worker motivation based on a social–psychological rather than an economic conception of man; and at the structural level, the Hawthorne studies discovered and demonstrated the importance of informal organization (pp. 86-87).

What had begun as verification of the effect of workplace factors had taken an unexpected turn. Mayo and his colleagues increasingly directed attention to the social relations of the the workers. In time, they documented that the human relations approach was at least as important as the technical view of administration. Getzels, Lipham, and Campbell (1968, pp. 33–40) noted that these studies paved the way for the work of Mary Parker Follett, the first great exponent of the human relations point of view, and Chester Barnard, who sought to embed a theory of administrative relationships in the context of a social science framework.

Thus, the findings of the Hawthorne research suggested that a formula far more complex than Taylor's was essential for investigating workplace productivity. Researchers and management alike began to pay more attention to such factors as employees' motivation and satisfaction. This legacy has endured in a variety of empirically based human relations approaches to supervision through to the present.

Enduring Contributions Of Taylor's Model To Industry And Organizational Theory

The Taylor system was a boon to the industry of its time in terms of lowering costs of production while raising the level of productivity. The model waned, however, with shifting postwar political currents, and as researchers like Elton Mayo provided evidence of the complexity of human motivation in the workplace. Certain aspects of the Taylor model, however, have proved enduring, as Boorstin (1973) pointed out in his description of the effects of Taylor's scientific management system on bargaining well into mid-century:

Taylor's concept of time study and his notion of the elementary task were soon incorporated in the calculations both of manufacturers and of labor unions. By mid-century, General Motors, in its contracts with its workers, had divided the hour into six-minute periods, had fragmented the work to fit the periods, and the worker was being paid by the number of tenths of an hour that he worked. The United States Steel Corporation contract with the C. I. O. on May 8, 1946, defined a "fair day's work" as "that amount of work that can be produced by a qualified employee when working at a normal pace. . . . A normal pace is equivalent to a man walking, without load, on smooth, level ground at a rate of three miles per hour." In their wage-rationaliza-

tion program the next year, they described 1,150 jobs within 152 classifications. The Aluminum Company of America spent three and a half years and a half-million dollars developing a formula to rationalize and classify 56,000 jobs (p. 368).

The system had both lasting effects on bargaining and daily life in industry as well as a long-term influence on organizational research and theory. While Wiles and Bondi (1991) noted that Taylor and his followers ignored the human factors related to productivity, they credited Taylor with initiating and advocating the "meticulous observation and study of the work process." They also attributed to him "launching the serious study of organizational structure" and "reordering organizations along functional lines." Specific management strategies that they credited to him include such modern concepts as "specialization and standardization of work, use of mathematical models for production, the piece-rate system, and time standards for production" (p. 31). Owens (1970) also discussed Taylor's contributions in terms of their lasting impact on organizational theory. The present form of the scientific management model, which is now often referred to as"classical theory," or "formal organization," retains certain characteristics of organizations emphasized in Taylor's model: specialization, control, hierarchy, and division of labor.

SCIENTIFIC MANAGEMENT IN THE SCHOOLS

The Appeal of Scientific Management to Schools

Callahan (1962, Chap. 10) traced the events and circumstances that led to the wide adoption of forms of scientific management in schools. He noted that timing was critical; the period of 1910 to 1920 was ripe for what he characterized as the "tragic" impact of the efficiency movement on schools. The first contributing factor was the general public mood of suspiciousness toward all public institutions, fueled by the muckraking journalism of the period. A second factor was the transfer of the taint of railroad mismanagement to other public institutions, including schools, and the sense that Taylor's timely and attractive "scientific management" solution could also transfer. A third factor was the ascendance in the prestige of all aspects of business, including its leaders and its methods. This enamorment with business promoted scientific management methods in government in general and in the election of businessmen to school boards specifically. Finally, and of greatest importance, Callahan noted that educational administration was still immature and vulnerable as a profession in 1910. Lacking a genuinely educational, intellectual, and scholarly tradition of graduate training in administration, it could not defend itself against the overtures of those promoting the scientific model.

Button (1961) attributed some of the responsibility for the scientific direction that education took to decisions made by educators themselves. He speculated that the decision of the Committee of Fifteen in 1895 to reject the nascent qualitative area of child study in favor of more traditional subject-centered approaches had an enduring effect on the direction that supervision took. He noted that the committee's report and the kind of thinking it embodied precluded much influence from educational psychology for at least the next two decades, thus ensuring a clearer path for innovations inspired by developments in industrial and business management (p. 132).

Thus, for a variety of reasons, the popularity of scientific management soon spilled over into the schools. Whether because school people wanted to be attached to the "respectability" or "scientific detachment" of the movement, they adapted many of the strategies to supervision in schools. Owens (1991, p. 7) noted that attractiveness of the movement overwhelmed any doubts that administrators had about it: "There was a rush among school superintendents to get aboard the bandwagon of the day by adopting the jargon and practices of those with high status in society—business executives." J. Franklin Bobbitt, a professor of educational administration at the University of Chicago, had been involved in the implementation of a scientific management system in the Gary, Indiana, schools. In a 1912 article in *The Elementary School Journal,* he described a plan that could transform the Gary schools to run at 100 percent efficiency when legally unencumbered. Bobbitt was selected as editor of the National Society for the Study of Education's Twelfth Yearbook, and his high national profile both in the yearbook and in related speaking engagements helped to proliferate his view of the application of industry to education. The attitude and language of scientific management in education were common by mid-decade, as reflected in Ellwood Cubberley's (1916) characterization of schools as "factories in which the raw products . . . are to be shaped and fashioned into products to meet the various demands of life" (p. 338). The "products," of course, were children.

The Form of Scientific Management in Schools

In this conducive social and political climate, the procedure for implementing a more businesslike organization and operation in schools became well standardized in the first quarter of the century. After weighing school performance against the business criteria of economy and efficiency, critics pronounced schools below acceptable standards and suggested the substitution of a business or industrial practice (Callahan, 1962). With businessmen in charge of the solutions, school leaders were relegated to a secondary role. All they needed to do was determine how the change could be produced and "produce it without question" (Tanner & Tanner, 1975, p. 282). As Callahan (1962) observed of this shift, "Doubtless many educators who had devoted years of study and thought to the aims and purposes of education were surprised to learn that they had misunderstood their function. They were to be mechanics, not philosophers" (p. 84).

In addition, the educators who embraced scientific management were not discouraged by the limitations that the business model might have for direct application to education. Bobbitt (1913) ruled out constraints of the model, arguing that education was "a shaping process as much as the manufacture of steel rails; the personality is to be shaped and fashioned into desirable forms" (p. 12). Although he did grant that the many aspects of personality made schools an enor-

mously more complex process, he saw this only as a challenge, not a barrier. Thus, Bobbitt and others formulated the following educational equivalent of the four steps of the industrial model:

1. Draw up in detail for each social or vocational class of students in our charge a list of all of the abilities and aspects of personality for the training of which the school is responsible.
2. Determine scales of measurement in terms of which these many different aspects of the personality can be measured.
3. Determine the amount of training that is socially desirable for each of these different abilities and state these amounts in terms of the scales of measurement.
4. [Establish] progressive standards of attainment for each stage of advance in the normal development of each ability in question. (p. 49).

Proponents of scientific management planned to start with investigating simple, easily quantifiable processes such as mathematics computation and spelling, but they were optimistic that even more complex processes like composition could eventually be broken into steps to allow for their analysis and measurement. Before long, data collection exceeded researchers' time to measure the relative efficacy of the method used, and Bobbitt discouraged the undertaking of any new experiments until statistical analysis could catch up with data collection. The fact that the research base was incomplete, however, did not delay implementation of "scientific methods" in the schools. While the research base was being developed, Bobbitt advised, the supervisory staff should make decisions based on "the rough determination" that had resulted from comparative studies (1913, p. 55) or, lacking even that base, upon "the fixed stars" (p. 57) of certain general principles of education that the well-informed supervisor had in his command.

As to what life was like in a scientifically managed school, histories of school supervision suggest that it bore resemblance to life in the factories of the period. In preparation for the disciplined life of the workplace, students in such schools marched from place to place under a system of regimentation and rigidity, following a set of rules strictly overseen and enforced by a supervisor (Alfonso, Firth, & Neville, 1981). Administrative emphasis was on cost-per-pupil efficiency and rigid application of highly specific work and accounting procedures. Like their counterparts in industry, teachers were often given detailed written instructions; the expectation was that teachers at each grade level would follow "minute-by-minute, standard operating procedures" across the district (Owens, 1991, p. 7).

The Role of the Supervisor in the Scientifically Managed School

As in industry, scientific school supervision was touted as the replacement for earlier "personal" and "arbitrary" forms of supervision. Supervisors sought to create a science of teaching from which to derive their authority over teacher behavior and its effect on student performance (Alfonso, Firth, &

Neville, 1981, pp. 29–30). The way research was conducted and translated into supervisory practice is illustrated in one of the more thoroughly investigated areas of achievement, mathematics. Using an equation that included the factors of both speed and accuracy, researchers calculated children's average performance and derived tables of standard scores by grade level. Bobbitt translated these scores into grade level objectives that became the standard for student achievement: "At the end of a year's work, an eighth grade child should be able to . . . read simple one-step problems of approximately 30 words in length and decide upon the operation to be used in their solution at the rate of 8 examples a minute with an accuracy of 90 percent." Such equations had their equivalent in teacher performance as well: "In simple addition operations, the third grade teacher should bring her pupils up to an average of 26 correct combinations per minute" (1913, p. 21).

Having arrived at such scientific objectives for students and teachers, the role of the supervisor was to measure teacher performance, remediate in weak areas of performance, and dismiss teachers where necessary. Bobbitt asserted that scientific approaches to measuring teacher performance could provide supervisors with "incontestable" evidence (1913, p. 28). Though Bobbitt made no allowance for existing differences "in class ability, background, or previous performance" (Button, 1961, p. 157), he claimed that supervisors could compare the work done by students of a given teacher against the standard set for that grade level, and on that basis sort the weak teachers from the good teachers. Bobbitt asserted that, by such comparisons, the supervisor could know "absolutely" which teachers needed his help, in what particular area their strengths and deficiencies lay, and how to go about giving advice and assistance. In the case of the weak teachers who could not or would not cooperate with their remediation, the evidence of inefficiency would "instantly" overcome all earlier obstacles to removing, transferring, or retiring them (1913, pp. 27–28).

Scientific supervision took many forms, both direct and indirect, in the schools of the first quarter of this century. However, a few strategies were so prevalent in scientifically managed schools as to be considered hallmarks of the period's supervision. The first of these (i.e., the use of teacher rating scales) was reminiscent of the old inspection model of supervision in that at least some of the items on the scale required the supervisor to rate actual teacher performance. "Scientific" ratings differed from earlier versions, however, in that the ratings were quantifiable and presumed to be precise and objective. As editor of the *1915 National Society for the Study of Education Yearbook—Part II*, Arthur Boyce solicited evidence about the prevalence of rating forms. Responses from 242 superintendents of large districts nationwide suggested that their use was widespread; some contained only two categories of evaluation, whereas others rated 75 or 80 teaching factors. One of the forms distributed "1,000 points over 42 separate qualities of merit" (p. 18). After receiving more than 100 hundred rating forms during this survey, Boyce concluded:

Any attempt to summarize the qualities found in the many schemes proposed can be only partly successful, owing to the diversity of meaning for the same terms and difference in expression. An exami-

nation of 50 rating schemes revealed 150 factors which, however, were not all different. Thus we find six different ways of expressing Instructional Skill and ten different statements for Discipline. There is much overlapping among the qualities (p. 18).

Most ratings were of the "general impression" type, however, and were thus subject to rater bias. Boyce set out to remedy this situation by developing a more scientific rating scale of his own. That scale appears in Figure 42.1.

Button (1961) described the assumption of Boyce's scale: "The obvious virtues produced good teaching, although these attributes were and are vague and unobservable; they may be deduced from observation" (p. 171). Although Boyce's rating scale showed some reliability problems when implemented in a variety of schools, it was warmly received and widely adopted. The positive response probably resulted from both its ease of use and its backing from the prestigious *American School Board Journal* and the National Society for the Study of Education. Callahan (1962) noted that even when districts did not adopt the original Boyce scale, they tended to use it as a model. Thus, the numerous rating scales that appeared in subsequent education literature bore a striking resemblance to his (p. 105).

A superintendent's discussion of "Tests and Scales as Aids to the Supervisor" (Nietz, 1921) illustrates the problems that supervisors sought to remedy with rating scales and provides insight into their relationships with teachers. Nietz began with a discussion of the weaknesses of supervision of the past (i.e., what he termed "visitation type only"), noting that criticism of teachers resulting from such visits was nearly always personal opinion. He advocated a new approach (i.e., the "impersonal analysis" of the teacher and his or her work by means of standardized tests, scales, and other similar means for testing efficiency) (p. 47). He asserted that such means had many advantages:

They would lead many a lost teacher out of our educational wilderness. They help the supervisor to control and assist his teachers more effectively and scientifically. This is done in several ways. They help and assist in belittling the self-satisfaction and conceit of some egoistic but unsuccessful teachers. Many such teachers have good hidden ability but need to be humiliated by some other means than the personal criticism of a supervisor. The use of standardized tests will often reveal that she is not as good a teacher as she thought herself to be, so she may forget to see the "mote" in the other's eye and realize the "beam" in her own, and begin to remove it. Many a teacher who has reached the stage of self-sufficiency has seen it necessary to step off her self-exalted pedestal. Such one still has a future if self-improvement is sought (p. 47).

Less direct but equally prevalent supervision strategies were school research bureaus and school surveys. In the former case, district staff were assigned to independent units as researchers, much like the inspection department in the Taylor industrial model. From this "expert" perspective, the staff monitored testing of students and reported the extent to which teachers and students were meeting district standards. On the other hand, school surveys were conducted by personnel from outside the district, usually a panel of professors of educational administration. The size of the team, the duration of the study, and the content and quality of data gathered, varied greatly from site to site. What all school surveys had in common, however, was that they were economically motivated (Callahan, 1962), having been urged upon administrators as an excellent defense against critics as well as an invaluable instrument "for obtaining more money for the schools" (p. 115).

Issues of Reliability and Validity Related to Research Conducted in Schools

Any discussion of the prevalence and endurance of scientific management's effect on schools must be prefaced with a critique of the quality of the research base on which it was presumed to be grounded. This issue of quality has been discussed in the works of many leading writers in both curriculum and supervision, and consensus on that quality ranges from "weak" to "tragic." The present discussion will address general issues of quality and then discuss some of the most prevalent practices in scientific supervision in terms of their instrument and content validity and their generalizability.

The most persistent and substantive criticism of the movement is probably that it sacrificed accuracy for precision, which is a flaw that Sergiovanni and Starratt (1993, p. 211) described as analogous to looking for lost keys under the light at the corner even though they were lost in the darkness in the middle of the block. Much of the research of the period has been dismissed as *rationalistic* (i.e., as research that focused on what was easy to observe and measure) rather than on that which was really important in teaching and learning.

There is evidence that much of the period's research was fundamentally flawed. There seem to have been problems, both with *what* the educational researchers measured, and with *how* they measured it. In the first place, these researchers were trying to accomplish a task for which both they and the state of educational research as a field were ill-prepared. Unlike Taylor, who approached problems in industry as a skilled scientist, Callahan (1962) noted that educational administrators had neither the interest nor the ability to carry out his level of painstaking research. While these educational leaders rushed to claim the "scientific" label because of the status and authority it implied, there was in fact no *science* of education, only a rudimentary start in material that could be drawn upon from related fields, most notably the work of researchers in the areas of psychology and sociology like Thorndike, Bagley, Judd, and Counts. Educational administrators were not trained in the attitudes or skills of the researcher. More like craft apprentices, they learned to "do" research from the early leaders and then "taught their students as they had been taught" (Callahan, 1962, p. 247).

This superintendent's dismissal of the problems with variation in scales and testing was typical of the period:

Someone may assert that these variations with the use of the scale may in some cases be even greater than the teachers would have if they did not try to use the scale. This, however, is really exaggerated . . . But even if there is variation, it does not mean that the scale is useless. No two people read off precisely the same measurement of an article on a yardstick or a temperature on a thermometer. . . . The

variation now complained of in the use of the standard scales in school work will certainly grow less and less as these scales are perfected (Alexander, 1917, p. 66).

The superintendent likewise dismissed concerns with validity:

The most prominent objection is that these scales do not measure the really big things in school work. "These scales," say their enemies, "deal with the mechanical and formal elements. Education is too spiritual and intangible to be judged by such standards." . . . Of course, these scales do not measure the big things in life. No person ever really does that, not even with a thermometer or a yardstick. But there are times when the big issues of life are temporarily subordinated to smaller but more pressing things. When the baby is sick, we need the thermometer, not palaver about spiritual values. . . . And if these minor matters are promptly and efficiently attended to, there will be all the more time and energy left for the really big things (Alexander, 1917, pp. 66–67).

It is not surprising that such practical educational leaders of the period focused more on the driving daily issues of public school life than on the issues of scientific validity. The enduring problem that this created, however, was that their findings were accepted as scientific when in fact they were not. Callahan described this "tragedy" as fourfold:

Educational questions were subordinated to business considerations; administrators were produced who were not, in any true sense, educators; a scientific label was put on some very unscientific and dubious methods and practices; and an anti-intellectual climate, already prevalent, was strengthened . . . countless educational decisions were made on economic or on noneducational grounds (1962, pp. 246–247).

What these educational leaders researched in their school surveys and internal data collection, therefore, almost invariably boiled down to cost. Broader issues of quality in education were ignored in most school evaluations. The development of standardized scales and measurements was grounded in the preoccupation with providing the kind of comparative cost data that would allow administrators to identify the most economical schools that produced the best "units of product" at the lowest price. Such standardization would ultimately keep down costs by allowing "comparative cost calculations" between different schools and different cities (Bobbitt, 1913, p. 49). In his discussion of Frank Spaulding's widely published approach to school evaluation, Callahan (1962) translated some of the terms that Spaulding used into their real financial meaning. When Spaulding used the term *local considerations*, he really used per pupil costs and pupil recitation costs in his calculations. When he used the term *educational value*, he had actually computed the dollar value (p. 73).

How these leaders measured educational quality was similarly problematic. Their efforts for the most part focused on determining prevailing or median practice rather than conducting the experimental research that would have allowed them to attribute causality. In their discussion of one of the most ambitious efforts of the scientific management movement, the report of The Committee on Economy of Time, Tanner and Tanner (1975) noted that the quality of the research suffered from the fact that members of the commit-

Teacher _____ City_____ Grade Taught_____
        (indicate sex)   (or building)   (or subject)

        Experience _____ years.   Salary_____ per month.

Highest academic training_____

Extent of professional training _____

Detailed Rating		V.P.	Poor	Medium			Good	Ex.
I. Personal Equipment—	1. General appearance							
	2. Health							
	3. Voice							
	4. Intellectual capacity							
	5. Initiative and self-reliance							
	6. Adaptability and resourcefulness							
	7. Accuracy							
	8. Industry							
	9. Enthusiasm and Optimism							
	10. Integrity and sincerity							
	11. Self-control							
	12. Promptness							
	13. Tact							
	14. Sense of justice							
II. Social and Professional Equipment—	15. Academic preparation							
	16. Professional preparation							
	17. Grasp of subject-matter							
	18. Understanding of children							
	19. Interest in the life of the school							
	20. Interest in the life of the community							
	21. Ability to meet and interest patrons							
	22. Interest in lives of pupils							
	23. Co-operation and loyalty							
	24. Professional interest and growth							
III. School Management—	25. Daily preparation							
	26. Use of English							
	27. Care of light, heat, and ventilation							
	28. Neatness of room							
	29. Care of routine							
	30. Discipline (governing skill)							
IV. Technique of Teaching—	31. Definiteness and clearness of aim							
	32. Skill in habit formation							
	33. Skill in stimulating thought							
	34. Skill in teaching how to study							
	35. Skill in questioning							
	36. Choice in questioning							
	36. Choice of subject-matter							
	37. Organization of subject-matter							
	38. Skill and care in assignment							
	39. Skill in motivating work							
	40. Attention to individual needs							
V. Results—	41. Attention and response of the class							
	42. Growth of pupils in subject matter							
	43. General development of pupils							
	44. Stimulation of community							
	45. Moral influence							
General Rating								

Recorded by _____ Position_____ Date_____

FIGURE 42.1. Efficiency Record

Controlling the Rating of Teachers
(explanation of terms used in score card shown on opposite page)

I. Personal Equipment includes physical, mental, and moral qualities.
  1. General appearance—physique, carriage, dress, and personal neatness.
  3. Voice—pitch, quality, clearness of schoolroom voice.
  4. Intellectual capacity—native mental ability.
  5. Initiative and self-reliance—independence in originating and carrying out ideas.
  7. Accuracy—in statements, records, reports, and school work.
  10. Integrity and sincerity—soundness of moral principles and genuineness of character.
  13. Tact—adroitness, address, quick appreciation of the proper thing to do or say.
  14. Sense of justice—fairmindedness, ability to give all a "square deal."

II. Social and Professional Equipment includes qualities making the teacher better able to deal with social situations and particularly the school situation.
  15. Academic preparation—school work other than professional. Adequacy for present work.
  16. Professional preparation—specific training for teaching. Adequacy for present work.
  17. Grasp of subject-matter—command of the information to be taught or the skill to be developed.
  18. Understanding of children—insight into child nature; sympathetic, scientific, and practical.
  22. Interest in lives of pupils—desire to know and help pupils personally, outside of school subjects.
  23. Cooperation and loyalty—attitude toward colleagues and superior officers.
  24. Professional interest and growth—effort to keep up to date and improve.
  26. Use of English—vocabulary, grammar, ease of expression.

III. School Management includes mechanical and routine factors.
  29. Care of routine—saving time and energy by reducing frequently recurring details to mechanical organization.
  30. Discipline (governing skill)—character of order maintained and skill shown in maintaining it.

IV. Technique of Teaching includes skill in actual teaching and in the conduct of the recitation.
  31. Definiteness and clearness of aim—of each lesson and of the work as a whole.
  32. Skill in habit formation—skill in establishing specific, automatic responses quickly and permanently; drill.
  33. Skill in stimulating thought—giving opportunity for and direction in reflective thinking.
  34. Skill in teaching how to study—establishing economical and efficient habits of study.
  35. Skill in questioning—character and distribution of questions; replies elicited.
  36. Choice of subject matter—skill with which the teacher selects the material of instruction to suit the interests, abilities, and needs of the class.
  37. Organization of subject matter—the lesson plan and the system in which the subject-matter is presented.
  39. Skill in motivating work—arousing interest and giving pupils proper incentives for work.
  40. Attention to individual needs—teacher's care for individual differences, peculiarities, and difficulties.

V. Results include evidence of the success of the preceding conditions and skill.
  41. Attention and response of the class—extent to which all of the class are interested in the essential part of the lesson and respond to the demands made on them.
  42. Growth of the pupils in subject-matter—shown by pupils' ability to do work of advanced class and to meet more successfully whatever tests are made of their school work.
  43. General development of pupils—increase in pupils' ability and power along lines other than those of subject matter.
  44. Stimulation of community—effect on life of the community tending to improve or stimulate its various activities.
  45. Moral influence—extent to which the teacher raises the moral tone of the pupils or of the school.

FIGURE 42.1. (continued)

tee did not start their task with definitions of *best*, *satisfactory*, and *adequate* (p. 286). The rules that they attempted to generate from the "experimental" evidence they collected were likewise flawed by practices like sample size too small to permit generalization (p. 288).

Research specific to supervision was affected by many of the same problems. Like the school evaluation research of the period, schemes that attempted to assess teachers on the basis of test data about their students were no stronger than the tests and measurement skills of the employees in the inspection department. The rating scales widely used during the period allowed supervisors to record data in a quantified and standardized format, but there is no evidence that the data collected in such a manner was valid. Boyce and others attempted to upgrade the "overall impression" scales by adding sections that required raters to check items about teaching techniques and classroom management. Many items on the scales, however, elicited nothing more than the arbitrary personal opinions that Boyce was trying to eliminate, with items requiring raters to assess such areas as *integrity and sincerity*, *moral influence*, and *sense of justice*.

It is not surprising that studies of the use of rating forms showed great variance in multiple raters' rankings of the same teacher as well as in raters' ability to discriminate between the listed qualities. In concluding her critical study of the validity and reliability of the teacher efficiency scales of the period, Crabbs (1925) cautioned, "Teaching efficiency cannot be judged by supervisors accurately enough to be of any practical value" (p. 97). Such criticism did not curtail use, however, and scales continued to be widely adopted and used to evaluate, remediate, and even dismiss teachers.

The underlying validity problem of the research undertaken during the era seems to have been a mismatch of models. While the Taylor model may well have been appropriate in industrial situations where jobs consisted of discrete, predictable tasks, it was not a complex enough model to investigate the quality of life in schools or the effect of educational practices on a range of human variables. The appeal of scientific management to educators of the period spoke more of their need to align themselves with scientific respectability than with appropriateness of fit of the model to education or the accuracy of findings that it inspired.

Prevalence of the Scientific Management Model in the Schools of the Period

Historical discussions, of American schools of the period are consistent in attributing "a profound and long-lasting impact upon the ways in which schools were organized and administered" to scientific management (Owens, 1991, p. 7; Wiles & Bondi, 1991). While there is substantial evidence, of the prevalence of scientific management on *thought* within professional organizations and publications of the period, there is less convincing evidence of the movement's influence on practice. Scientific management permeated some functions of school organizations more than others. Button (1961) noted that general administration, rather than supervision, was the focus of interest during the period from 1905 to 1920. Whereas school finance, school surveys, school buildings,

and curriculum all received great attention, the older notion of a supervisor as a "teacher of teachers" was abandoned. Interest in supervision was secondary to shop management, and the function of supervision was "for the sake of businesslike administration, to produce efficient schools and efficient teaching" (pp. 183–184).

Curriculum seems to have been affected to a wide extent, at least in public high schools. Krug (1964) described a merger between scientific management and social efficiency:

Curricular implications . . . included socialized objectives (scientifically established); the judging of subjects by their proved contributions to these objectives; a strong feeling against foreign languages and traditional mathematics; an equally strong feeling for vocational or practical subjects; the substitution for history of what were coming to be known as the social studies; an acceptance of English, but in "socialized" or "functional" forms; and differentiation aimed at groups (pp. 322–323).

The impact of scientific management on the preparation of administrators is well documented. Callahan (1962, Chap. 8) described the predominance of the scientific management model in the graduate programs of major universities preparing educational administrators. He noted its influence on thousands of administrators who took master's level coursework between 1915 and 1929 and, even more significantly, on the hundreds of superintendents who received doctorates in educational administration. The latter group obtained a variety of powerful positions in education, as superintendents in major cites, officials in state departments of education, and, most important of all, as professors of education in colleges and universities, where they taught teachers and administrators and directed research studies for masters' and doctoral degrees.

From such influential positions, these educational leaders had a major impact on the way schools were organized, operated, and evaluated. The scientific management philosophy of such leaders was particularly apparent in the preoccupation with quantitative measurement that characterized the period's approach to evaluation. Callahan (1962) concluded that by 1920, rating scales were being used extensively and that surveys, investigations, and comparisons were being made in almost every school (pp. 110–111).

In their discussion of which scientific management practices actually predominated in public schools of the period, Callahan and Button (1964) distinguished between practices associated with two of the movement's foremost proponents. On the one hand, Bobbitt advocated adoption of a model close to the original Taylor principles, with administration guided by the interpretation of a body of scientific findings. By contrast, Spaulding's "cost accounting" version had a more superficial resemblance to the original Taylor model. Using graphs, charts, and a reference to "scientific" in the title, his presentations had many of the trappings of the movement. His recommendations, however, were generalized, from the cost accounting procedures that he had used successfully as superintendent of the Newton, Massachusetts, schools, not from scientific research. His essential message was how administrators could lower costs; recommendations from his Newton experience included the elimination of small classes and reduction in overall course offerings, moves that resulted in larger class size, fewer electives, and reductions in the teaching staff.

It was this Spaulding "cost accounting" model that predominated in the educational administration journal articles of the period and presumably in the practices of those administrators who sought to align themselves with the movement. Callahan and Button (1964) noted several reasons why Spaulding's model had more influence on practice than did Bobbitt's. First and foremost, the Spaulding model was an easy way to answer school critics. It achieved some measures of economy and created the appearance that schools were being run efficiently. By contrast, the Bobbitt model "required an elaborate and expensive research and planning division" (p. 84). This was an unaffordable luxury for most small districts, particularly in view of the fact that the general public made no clear distinction between cost efficiency and real efficiency. Furthermore, Callahan and Button noted, while Bobbitt's ideas received little public resistance within the profession, his notion of children as "products" and teachers as "workers" was well outside the mainstream view of administrators. Thus, his work contributed only in a more general way to administrative acceptance of business–industrial organizational patterns in education and to the increasingly authoritarian concept of school administration. Barr and Burton (1926, p. 75) also noted that the discussion provoked by Bobbitt's ideas far exceeded their actual influence and popularity. They attributed this lack of influence both to the distastefulness of the industrial model to many administrators and teachers as well as to the model's emphasis on compliance at the cost of true cooperation.

Other commentators on the history of school leadership question whether in fact scientific management's influence on the schools of the period may not have been overestimated, particularly in the area of supervision. Button (1961, p. 340) described a discrepancy between advocated practice and actual practice, noting that during the period when scientific practice was advocated, survey results showed that supervisors were neither being trained to practice scientific supervision, nor were they actually practicing it. They instead resorted to widespread use of rating procedures similar to those advocated as a part of scientific supervision.

Other authors have pointed out that scientific supervision was only one of many influences on supervision in the first quarter of the century. Glanz (1991, p. 184) noted that historical trends in supervision are not well confined to periods and that it is unrealistic to view scientific supervision as a trend that began at a given point in time and was immediately followed by a period of democratic supervision. Rather, the era was a time when many notions of supervision existed concurrently. Pajak (1993, p. 2) likewise noted that, whereas Taylor's work certainly influenced the early years of educational supervision, it was only one competing theme in its literature. To support this contention, Pajak traced the emergence of the theme of democracy as a guiding principle for education in the work of Edward C. Elliott and others.

Other writers suggest that the influence of scientific management may have been less extensive in supervision than in administration. Callahan and Button (1964) gave two reasons

for this difference. First, they noted that the problems of supervision and teaching method were particularly incompatible with the model's research methods. A second major difference in the supervision area was the growing professional alliance of those with supervisory interests with the newly formed Association for Supervision and Curriculum Development (ASCD).

Whereas the impact of scientific management on supervisory practice was neither modest nor pervasive, its hallmarks were quite apparent in certain areas of supervision, especially in evaluation. The leading text on supervision late in the period reflects the ambivalence of supervision leaders about the model. Barr and Burton (1926) used the Detroit Public School's statement of principles to exemplify their theory of supervision. This circular included six principles, the first of which is, "Supervision must be democratic" (p. 83). Principle number four, however, "supervision must be scientific" (p. 84), reflects the influence of Taylor and his educational allies in setting the following requirements for supervisors:

1. A common scientific background for principals, teachers, and supervisors
2. The development of definite, well-understood objective standards for judging and improving the quality of instruction
3. An experimental and laboratory study of instructional problems
4. Interpretive measurements of results (p. 84)

Thus, even by the end of the first quarter of the century, certain aspects of the scientific model were still well entrenched in the supervisory texts widely used in graduate programs and in the school supervision plans of major cities.

The Decline of Scientific Management in Education

Whereas vestiges of scientific management are recurrent throughout the twentieth century, the major first wave of the movement had peaked before 1920 and was in decline by 1930. Challenges to the practices had been present from the start, from forces both inside and outside the educational system. Rugg (1920, p. 670) noted that while nearly all school systems were using rating scales, there was substantial evidence that the scales were unreliable and that neither they nor teacher testing could measure the complex dynamic qualities that are essential to quality teaching. By 1920, the dissatisfaction with rating scales for teachers was just as extensive as their use, and resistance was taking the place of docile resentment.

Some of the strongest attacks came from organized teachers who protested the hierarchical and undemocratic nature of the reforms and the separation of educational management from classroom practice. Many of these protests had an element of gender conflict because the women who were predominant in the teaching force sought more equal representation in administrative ranks and decision-making (Tyack & Hansot, 1982, p. 114). Poetry on the cover of the March 1916 *American Teacher* expressed the teachers' "case against efficiency."

If Efficiency Means the Demoralization of the School System;

If Efficiency Means Dollars Saved
and Human Material Squandered;
If Efficiency Means Discontent, Drudgery,
and Disillusion—
We'll Have None of It! (p. 1)

Such protests were at least partly attributable to teachers' dissatisfaction with the application of industrial supervision practices to the schools. As Button noted (1961, p. 218), they were an indicator that the relationship between teachers and supervisors could not endure in their present form: "It was not adequate that the supervisor's role be acceptable [sic] in the eyes of the administrator or of his public or his board. It was also necessary that he perform some function which would justify him in the eyes of the teacher." The "insurgence" launched by the National Education Association and the American Federation of Teachers between 1914 and 1919 made public the teachers' dissatisfaction with scientific management practices. Whereas these protests did not have immediate success, they were a factor in the change in supervision after 1920 (Button, 1961, pp. 194–198). Supervision after 1920 began a shift toward more collaboration between teachers and supervisors:

The supervisor acknowledged the importance of securing the cooperation of the teacher; instead of seeing himself in the role of an efficiency expert he took the part of the scientist in education, and worked with a science which bore the hallmarks of child study, of science in general in the nineteenth century, and of the earlier industrial management studies (Button, 1961, p. 350).

The movement also lost its momentum as it became apparent that some of the techniques of scientific supervision were not compatible with the emergent world view. In the business world, the start of the Great Depression seriously tarnished the credibility of the notion that what was good management practice for business and industry would be good practice in all other institutions as well. In education, the pendulum was also swinging. As Dewey and others espoused the view that schools should be places to nurture democratic ideals, critics began to speak out against "scientifically managed" schools where cost accounting rather than the nurturing of individuality and creativity were the bottom line. Callahan (1962, p. 248) noted that forceful opposition of educators Jesse Newlon and George Counts after 1930 helped to reduce business influences on educational administration in major institutions. Under Newlon, the graduate program in educational administration at Teachers College, Columbia University shifted its focus to social policy, while Harvard University revised its catalog description to omit its reference to the superintendent as a "manager of the school plant" during the same period (p. 249).

There was also a growing awareness of the mismatch between the research methods of Taylor and his associates with the important questions that needed to be asked about educational effectiveness. Scientific management in education had been neither a philosophical nor a practical success. Callahan and Button (1964, p. 90) offered some explanations

about why administrators began to lose interest in using "scientific" approaches to the supervision of teachers. They pointed out that empirical investigations of the period in the field of teacher effectiveness had failed to generate replicable, generalizable findings. Just as the Hawthorne studies suggested that Taylor's research had failed to account for many of the important variables in productivity, educators began to suspect that the scientific management model was not complex enough to explain many of the factors that motivate and satisfy children and teachers. The conclusion among many leaders in educational administration was that Taylor's techniques and perspectives were not compatible with the problems of supervision and teaching methods. Glanz (1991, p. 103) summed up the decline of a period that had begun with high hopes among supervisors for legitimizing their existence: "This was a period of time in which cautious optimism slowly turned into confirmed despair for supervisors. As a result, supervisors in the 1920s began to search for new methods and conceptions in supervision."

Describing the end of the "Period of Efficiency Orientation, 1876–1936," Eye and Netzer (1965, pp. 6–7) noted some positive trends from that concept. The period's increased employment of full-time supervisors resulted in a shift back to face-to-face contact between supervisors and teachers and a focus on instructional improvement. The appearance in the supervisory literature during the period of such terms as *conference, advice, improvement, constructive,* and *growth* suggests a warming trend in the relationships between supervisors and teachers. Thus, Eye and Netzer concluded that, even though supervisors of the period had no deep understanding about how to improve "environmental conditions," they understood their importance and made some corrective efforts.

Enduring Effects of Scientific Management on Schools

While the effect of the scientific management movement waned after the first quarter of the century, the social movement that spawned it was so powerful that the decline was neither fast nor total. One of the enduring legacies in school organization was a change in the power and responsibilities of school supervisors. Wiles and Bondi (1991, pp. 5–6) traced the origin of the split between administration and supervision to the practices of the scientific management era. They noted that, as the responsibilities of the superintendent burgeoned, it was no longer feasible for the superintendent to conduct classroom visitations. These responsibilities were delegated to a supervisor who served as the superintendent's representative. This diminished authority relegated supervisors to an increasingly ineffective role. Wiles and Bondi noted that in the period that followed, school supervisors were increasingly perceived as "snoopervisors" whose focus in school visits was confined to mechanical observations and reports.

Many of scientific management's "mindsets" about education endure into the present as well. Tanner and Tanner (1975, pp. 282–283) described two of the policies that emerged from Bobbitt's model of a business-led educational system to become entrenched in America's approach to education: using economic grounds rather than educational grounds as the basis for educational decision-making and looking to business and industry for solutions to educational problems. Alfonso, Firth, and Neville (1981) noted the staying power of the period's disciplined mentality in an enduring legacy of regimentation and the expectation of unquestioned adherence to procedure and codes in public schools. Oliva (1993, p. 9) likened the present to the period in which Taylor's model was so attractive to educators, noting that "teaching is at a point in time when many, perhaps most, educators perceive it as a science whose component skills, i.e., generic competencies, can be identified, learned, and mastered." In this modern management climate, "scientific" supervisors base their evaluations on the match between the teacher's performance and a prescribed set of fixed principles drawn from research.

How have the ideas of the original model had such holding power? Callahan (1962) described the influence of administrators prepared in graduate programs of the era in perpetuating the practices. Their influence on certification requirements, texts, and curricula of preparation programs ensured that the emphasis on business and mechanical aspects of education would supersede instructional concerns well into the middle of the century. Even into the 1960s, their legacy endured in such prevalent practices as assigning clerical tasks and lunchroom monitoring to teachers and having teachers check in and out of their buildings in a clock-punching manner. Callahan concluded that it was no wonder "in 1959 when students just entering the teaching profession were asked what knowledge they thought they would need to be a teacher, a doctor, a typist, or a machinist that their responses for the job of teacher, typist and machinist were quite similar" (p. 255).

Evaluation practices of the period have also been perpetuated into the present in the form of standardized tests and teacher-rating scales. Callahan (1962, p. 118) linked the endurance of such practices to the public's perception of their origins: If this was how the "experts" and "authorities" chose to assess education and their work was scientific, then these must be the important elements of education.

RECURRING SCIENTIFIC PHILOSOPHY AND PRACTICE IN SUPERVISION

The turn-of-the-century brand of scientific management declined amid persistent questions about the limited validity of what its research measured and a rising interest in a more democratic and progressive view of life in schools. In the decades since, however, the influence of scientific management has been recurrent and its practices widely adopted. When classical scientific management from industry was applied to school supervision, it took the form of close monitoring of classroom practices regarding curriculum and instruction in order to ensure that teachers were in compliance with district guidelines and standards. While this face-to-face, manager-worker style of supervision is rare in American schools, some supervision historians and theorists speculate that the premises and precepts of scientific management have not changed, only the way the ideas are implemented has changed.

McNeil (1982) traced the course of scientific supervision through the decades after Taylor. Scientific approaches in the 1930s were characterized by a shift away from positivism to more of an emphasis on problem solving and active participation of the teacher in the research process. In this period, the attitude about research in schools shifted from regarding findings as "fixed" to thinking of data more as a way to sharpen the focus of observation and direct further thinking about the problem being investigated. While research in the 1940s continued to focus on instructional problems of significance to teachers, the wartime climate led researchers to apply only the scientific findings that were "consistent with the social values . . . and political ideologies of the time" (p. 20).

By the 1960s, scientific research in the schools was no longer the domain of teachers and supervisors; rather, it had been relegated to the "experts" in the behavioral sciences, who were well versed in complex psychological concepts as well as technically proficient in the methodology and statistics of quantitative research. Although concerted efforts were made to compile existing research and to conduct new research that would lead to causal explanations for student achievement, the era did not provide a definitive research basis for supervision. Research of the period, however, did reveal the complexity of classroom interactions and difficulty of solving the central problem of evaluating teaching (i.e., clarifying the criterion of teaching effectiveness) (McNeil, 1982), a quest that has remained with us.

One of the more enduring themes of scientific management can be seen in the continuing attempt, both at the state and district levels, to identify observable teacher behaviors that are clearly linked to measures of student achievement, and then to work with teachers to devise strategies for achieving and evaluating them (Oliva, 1993). The varied applications of scientific supervision have far more in common than they have differences: They have science-based teaching as their ideal that can be implemented with some certainty of effectiveness and assessed without contamination of supervisory bias.

Characteristics of Neoscientific Management

Sergiovanni and Starratt (1993, p. 13) described similarities and differences between protogenic forms of scientific management in schools and their more modern counterparts, which the authors termed *neoscientific*. Both focus on control, accountability, and efficiency, but neoscientific forms use more impersonal ways of achieving management objectives than did earlier forms. Both are concerned with production and outcomes, but modern forms emphasize teacher responsibility for the quality and pace of instruction, while expecting supervisors to monitor teaching and learning outcomes for evidence of "instructional excellence" (i.e., a contemporary version of "efficiency and effectiveness"). Described in this section are several examples of educational initiatives manifesting neoscientific characteristics.

Standardized Testing Sergiovanni and Starratt (1983, pp. 5–6) suggested standardized testing as a prime example of the way external control mechanisms have been substituted for the earlier inspection models of supervision. Because scores from these tests are often distributed publicly for comparisons by class and by school, the tests exert an "impersonal" control on what content teachers will emphasize. Like their scientific management counterparts, contemporary standardized tests can subordinate the human dimension and personal job satisfaction in pursuit of student performance goals. They can also result in oversimplified assessment: Comparing classrooms and schools on the basis of test results alone disregards important socioeconomic and cultural differences that significantly affect educational quality. The result in too many schools, modern critics argue, is that standardized testing promotes sterile and regimented instruction in schools, places undue stress on students and teachers to achieve narrowly specified objectives, and results in low student morale and low teacher acceptance (Brophy & Good, 1986; Eisner, 1967a, b; 1985; Rockler, 1987).

Behavioral Objectives Another example of neoscientific management is the behavioral objective—now more commonly called a performance objective or outcome—which requires that teachers specify the learning intent of any instructional sequence in behavioral and observable terms (Mager, 1962; Popham, 1969, 1970, 1971). While originally intended to assist teachers with instructional clarity and to focus students on critical learning outcomes, performance objectives were quickly adopted by instructional supervisors as benchmarks against which to measure teacher effectiveness. Like "the task idea" utilized by their counterparts in Taylorism, school supervisors seek to specify the intended outcome for a particular segment of the teacher's work and then determine the teacher's effectiveness or efficiency through documented evidence of goal achievement. In *Teacher Supervision Through Behavioral Objectives*, Piper and Elgart (1979) advocated joint development of instructional objectives by teachers and their supervisors with subsequent classroom observation by the supervisor for documentation purposes. This was a time-consuming and expensive task. In an effort to simplify the process, whole sequences of performance objectives were developed externally for many content areas and imposed upon teachers (Beyer & Apple, 1988, p. 195; Popham, 1970). The low implementation levels that resulted indicated that teachers either did not understand the objectives as written or failed to see their relevance. In a manner reminiscent of organized labor's response to Taylor's methods, many teachers perceived "supervision by objectives" to be another form of inspection and refused to relinquish their autonomy in the selection of instructional aims, goals, and objectives (Beyer & Apple, 1988, p. 195).

Teacher Rating Scales Process-product researchers of the 1970s, such as Rosenshine, Gage, and Medley, studied teacher behaviors and characteristics that predict or cause student achievement. The first three editions of *The Handbook of Research on Teaching* provided an extensive summary of this research base, the findings of which supported the efficacy of strategies like increased time on task and direct instruction (see Brophy & Good, 1986; Medley & Mitzel, 1963; Rosenshine & Furst, 1973). In many school districts, these findings became the basis for in-service and staff development initiatives intended to disseminate the research and to improve instruction and learning. At first, teachers were encouraged by the findings and the potential they offered for increased student achievement and decreased criticism of the public schools; however, as districts began to develop rating scales and supervision instruments to gather evidence that classroom teachers were, in fact, practicing "effective" or "efficient" teacher behaviors, dissatisfaction with the research and its intrusion into classroom practice began to grow. Teachers questioned whether the behaviors sought in their performance could truly be linked to student achievement. At the same time, critics suggested that the behaviors were not broadly generalizable across grade levels and content areas and to students in all socioeconomic and cultural contexts. Thus, in their haste to implement process–product research, school boards and administrators apparently repeated the mistakes of their counterparts in the Taylor era: They failed to recognize both controlled conditions under which the research had been conducted and prolonged commitment that was necessary among school authorities if implementation was to prove successful.

Merit Pay Systems Though interest in merit pay systems has waxed and waned over the last 90 years (cf., Greenwood, 1905, p. 467), their reemergence in the last decade as a form of teacher evaluation and control warrants placement among neoscientific forms of supervision. The intent of merit pay plans, from Taylor's time to the present, has been to provide incentives and rewards for personal achievement above normally anticipated levels. In education, this often translates to monetary rewards for teachers whose students outperform their peers on standardized tests or other common achievement measures. There are essentially two types of merit evaluation: "Old style" determines teacher merit on the basis of classroom performance and is characterized by rating scales and other instruments designed to measure agreed upon teacher traits and behaviors; "new style" uses student scores on standardized tests, "output factors," and other teaching indicators as the critical variables in determining the "degree" of merit to be awarded (Bacharach, Lipsky, & Shedd, 1984, pp. 26–28; Bhaerman, 1973, pp. 63–65). As with the other forms of neoscientific supervision, standardized test scores and rating scales have been criticized by teachers and their representatives who assert they are not valid indicators of teaching effectiveness. While merit pay systems, therefore, have appealed to certain teachers because of the financial rewards involved, widespread acceptance has not been manifest. On average, merit systems have lasted between two and six years in school districts where they were implemented (Guernsey, 1986, p. 9).

If we accept the label of "neoscientific," then, for any reform effort that focuses on efficiency, production, effectiveness, and accountability, the past two decades have provided an abundance of examples like those described here. No form of supervision, however, has been subjected to more criticism for its "neoscientific" conception and implementation than the Madeline Hunter model of instruction and supervision. Because the model has had such a profound effect on how supervision is currently conducted in schools across this country, the model merits detailed examination. The background, impact, and prevalence of the Hunter model is discussed first. This is followed by a description of criticism leveled against the model, particularly in terms of its research base, and then by an examination of its enduring legacy.

The Hunter Model of Instruction and Supervision

BACKGROUND. In the late 1960s, Madeline Hunter and associates of the University Elementary School at UCLA launched a 5-year program of research about teacher decision-making. Their quest was for a research based body of knowledge about learning that applied to students of "all ages, races, creeds, and socioeconomic or ethnic groups, regardless of the content being learned or the delivery system or organizational plan being used" (1975, p. 35). The result of this research was an identification of "eleven discrete but interrelated decisions" used by teachers in planning, implementing, and assessing instruction (Hunter, 1973, pp. 61–62).

Because Hunter and her colleagues sought an explicit model that teachers and their supervisors could learn and apply efficiently, they systematized the 11 decisions into a model. This model came to be known by a variety of names, including a Clinical Theory of Instruction, Instructional Theory Into Practice (ITIP), Mastery Teaching, Program for Effective Teaching (PET), Clinical Teaching, Target Teaching, the UCLA Model, and The Hunter Model (Hunter, 1985). The underlying premise of the model was that research-based theory about teaching effectiveness had been translated into guidelines for practice (Hunter, 1984). Based on this claim, Hunter urged educators to pursue the professionalization of teaching through systematic adoption and implementation of her instructional model.

The Hunter model specifies steps to be used in all stages of the supervisory process. In the preliminary planning stage, teachers make decisions about content and desirable learner and teacher behaviors. In the implementation stage, they consider and use elements of lesson design that include *anticipatory set*, a statement of the *objective and purpose*, input, *modeling*, *checking for understanding*, *guided practice*, and *independent practice*. In the assessment stage, a supervisor observes teaching directly and employs two of the hallmarks of the Hunter model: script-taping and the Teaching Appraisal for Instructional Improvement Instrument (TA III). The supervisor then conducts a postconference with the teacher to examine and discuss congruence of the teacher's performance with Hunter's model and its principles of learning.

IMPACT ON INSTRUCTIONAL SUPERVISION. Though widely referred to as a "clinical model" of supervision, several aspects of the Hunter model were at variance with the classical model of clinical supervision Goldhammer (1969) had conceived. First, there was no preobservation conference. Hunter explained that there was no need for such a meeting because the assessment instrument itself could give "concrete evidence of what the teacher has learned, or needs to learn, and what he is able

to apply in the classroom" (1973, p. 62). Second, there were prescribed principles of learning and corresponding classroom indicators that were to guide the supervisor's observation and data collection. Finally, there was an equally prescribed, semi-scripted approach to the postobservation conference. The supervisor was to follow procedures for one of six different types of supervisory conferences Hunter had developed and described (1980, 1983, 1984). The task was essentially to determine the teacher's skill in using all components of the Hunter model.

PREVALENCE OF THE MODEL IN PUBLIC SCHOOLS. Evidence of the prevalence of Hunter's Model is apparent in Slavin's (1987) description: "Scores of states and local districts have virtually institutionalized Hunter's model, even establishing teacher evaluation procedures based upon her theories. Supervisors visit classrooms, expecting to see 'Madeline Hunter' in every lesson" (p. 56). Wolfe similarly described the "Seven-Step Lesson Plan" as a familiar phrase "in schools all over the United States" (1987, p. 70). In October 1988, Hunter herself acknowledged the "20-year escalation of acceptance all over the world" (p. 29). A report from Garman and Hazi (1988, p. 670) looked at the impact on one state. They documented that "the Madeline Hunter/Clinical Supervision . . . movement . . . has swept—in the name of school reform—at least 61 percent of all Pennsylvania school districts." They also reported that "more than 1,700 principals, supervisors, and other central office administrators—representing 75 percent of Pennsylvania school districts"—had attended Hunter workshops.

CRITICISM. Despite the model's popularity and Hunter's claim of its base in defensible research (e.g., 1985, 1986a, b; 1987a, b), it attracted much criticism. Costa lamented the "language of *technology*" and scientific reductionism expressed in Hunter's work and the model's "categorizing the acts of teaching, learning, and supervising into precisely three decisions, seven steps, and six types" (1984, p. 196; italics in original). The model was subject to other charges, including the allegations that it impeded innovation and creativity, deprofessionalized teaching, reduced teacher autonomy, assumed a "best way" to teach, and created ethical dilemmas for supervisors (Gibboney, 1987a, b; Pavan, 1986; Slavin, 1987, 1989; Wolfe, 1987). Content area teachers in science and social studies criticized the model as inappropriate for certain instructional purposes (Berg & Clough, 1991, 1990–1991a, b; Wolfe, 1987). Practices of supervisors who used the Hunter model were likewise criticized: looking for all seven "steps" as they observed in classrooms; faulting teachers if a step was missing; and developing teacher evaluation forms that listed Hunter's Seven Essential Elements of Teaching to be checked off as *excellent*, *good*, or *needs improvement* (Garman & Hazi, 1988; Pavan, 1986; Wolfe, 1987).

RELATED RESEARCH. Although much of the early criticism of the Hunter model was philosophically rather than empirically based, pressure on Hunter for research studies to support her claims of better student achievement and teacher performance had intensified by 1985. At first, she referred her critics to 20 years of research in "psychology, neurology, sociology, and anthropology" (1984, p. 171) and to existing "teacher effectiveness research" in education journals. Critics argued, however, that the research to which she referred had limited generalizability because it had been conducted in the primary grades of inner-city schools with effectiveness measures limited to reading and math achievement test scores (Pavan, 1986, p. 67). Research on human learning systems and neuroprocesses, they said, yielded nothing to support widespread adoption of the Hunter model. Slavin (1987, p. 57) pointed out that requiring teachers to use Hunter-type lessons could not be justified given emerging research on the model. He made reference to a study in progress at several elementary schools in Napa County, California, and noted that results were not lending support to Hunter's claims. Hunter countered that perhaps Slavin had ignored "original validation of the model (Project Linkage) conducted by an independent investigator, Rodney Skagar, which substantiated impressive gains by students in an inner-city Los Angeles school" (Hunter, 1988, p. 29). Slavin persisted: "I wrote to Skagar to obtain his report. He responded that the study was unpublished, unavailable (even *he* had lost his copy), and deeply flawed" (1989, p. 78; italics and parentheses in original).

Slavin's criticism was borne out in the Napa Valley findings and in other research on the Hunter model. Four major studies about the model were reported in professional journals between 1982 and 1989, and though they represented initiatives in separate states, none was able to report that implementation of the Hunter model demonstrated significant and consistent gains in student achievement (Dildy, 1982; Donovan, Sousa, & Walberg, 1992; Mandeville & Rivers, 1988–1989; Stallings & Krasavage, 1986). In all cases, while early achievement data supported the model's use, longitudinal results suggested other factors (e.g., collegiality that developed between teachers and researchers, possible Hawthorne and halo effects, more frequent classroom observations, and improved teacher morale) as causes of temporary achievement gains.

Findings from the most exhaustive of these studies provide, insight about problems inherent in the model that emerged under rigorous scrutiny. Stallings and Krasavage (1986) reported longitudinal data from the Napa County and Vacaville, California, studies conducted over 4 years to investigate implementation of Madeline Hunter's "Follow-Through Project" and its impact on student achievement. The sample consisted of 102 students. Those in the experimental group were largely Chapter I eligible and of low socioeconomic status (SES); many were also of limited English-speaking (LES) ability. They were from schools where standardized test scores were low and where Chapter 1 assistants had been removed for the duration of the study. Students in control schools were from a much higher SES level, had fewer LES and public aid student percentages, and had retained previously assigned Chapter 1 assistants. Results demonstrated that student time-on-task in the experimental groups increased significantly in reading and math during years 1 and 2, but decreased significantly during years 3 and 4. In terms of student achievement, there were significant gains in years 1 through 3, but a significant drop in reading and a nonsignificant drop in math scores during year 4. Two unexpected

results were disclosed: *Over the duration of the study*, students in the control groups made greater gains in reading than did those in the experimental group, and LES students outperformed those whose native language was English in both reading and mathematics. Regression toward the mean was a factor. The authors concluded that inconsistent results could be attributed to ineffectiveness of the model or to decreased program maintenance during the fourth year of the study. Achievement gains during years 1 and 2 were explained as a possible Hawthorne effect.

Thus, despite extensive training of the teachers, supervisors, and researchers involved, the "scientific approach" of Hunter's model had failed to yield the significant increases in student achievement it had promised.

CURRENT STATUS. Though prior to 1990 the Hunter Model was implemented at all levels in schools and even extended into adult learning programs in the United States and abroad, the lack of research support for its claims seems to have limited further expansion into schools. No new research on the model has surfaced since 1992, nor have any additional states adopted it as a general supervisory plan. While some school districts have abandoned the model in favor of new initiatives, however, statewide and districtwide supervisory plans have institutionalized the model in many areas. Several factors seem likely to perpetuate the model's use for some time to come: Hunter's charismatic and contagious advocacy of the model until her death in 1994, the widespread existence of administrators and teachers trained in the model's use, and the belief among many administrators that the model allows them to evaluate teacher performance objectively.

The popularity and problems of the Hunter model provide an appropriate foundation for discussing the present and future of scientific supervision. Although the model was embraced with enthusiasm by many teachers and administrators, problems emerged much as they had with earlier scientific management plans: implementation preceded validated research; results were overgeneralized, overzealous proponents used the model in ways for which it was never intended, and "bandwagon effects" among administrators superseded debate about validity. Thus, most of the lessons to be learned were lessons from the past.

CONCLUSION

This section examined the present and projected status of the influence of scientific management on supervision. It concludes with suggestions about how lessons from past experience can guide future research and implementation of scientific supervisory practices.

Present and Future Status of the Influence of Scientific Management on Supervision

Looking back over a half century, Callahan (1962; Chap. 10) described the conditions that made this nation ripe for the rapid spread of scientific management: a general public mood of suspiciousness, a taint of mismanagement associated with major public institutions, a prevalent high regard for the views of business leaders, and, finally, a sense that education in general, and the field of educational administration in particular, suffer from a lack of maturity and respect as scholarly fields. The prevalence of Callahan's "conditions" today and in future generations may be a rough gauge as to how receptive the national climate is to scientific reform efforts. If such conditions set the stage, then it would seem likely that we will continue to see vestiges of scientific management in education.

Writers who have traced the impact of scientific management on supervisory practice predict its endurance with attitudes ranging from chagrin to enthusiasm. Most believe, however, that scientific approaches to supervision will remain the mainstream. Sergiovanni and Starratt noted that as long as we live "in a technical-rational society where that which is considered scientific is prized, scientific conceptions of supervision will continue to be readily accepted." They asserted that in such a society, claiming that supervision and teaching are applied sciences lends respect to those fields, and that trying to use research to identify the "one best practice" is attractive. The authors also noted, however, that "teaching and learning are too complex to be captured so simply. In the real world of teaching, none of the assumptions hold up very well and the related practices portray an unrealistic view of teaching and supervision" (1993, pp. 29–30).

A more optimistic view of the impact of the scientific model on supervision is that the concept of what is "scientific" will be broadened and synthesized with other approaches, most often human relations. Over the years, thinking about what is "scientific" has changed from the narrow observation and identification of Taylor's principles approach to one that pays more attention to conceptualizations that help us to understand complex processes that guide us through appropriate action (Fessler, personal communication, December 19, 1994). Attempts at such broadening and synthesis go back almost as far as Taylor's original work. The most enduring models of synthesis are social systems approaches. Getzels, Lipham, and Campbell, (1968, pp. 47–48) noted that one such model, Parson's *Theory of Social Action,* was having an influence on educational thought as early as 1938. This and subsequent social systems models stress the interdependence of the parts of any social system, the organization of these parts into a whole, and the intrinsic presence of both individuals and institutions within the system (Getzels, Lipham, & Campbell, 1968, p. 54). Later writers, including Getzels and Guba, have applied these ideas to school management and supervision.

In this tradition of synthesis, other modern writers in supervision continue to develop models or theories that present the best working explanations of existing observations and data. Fessler (1992, pp. 31–34) provided a model for such efforts and described the complex process by which it was used to develop a model of the Teacher Career Cycle:

The first step in the process is to gather data that present a view of the "real world." . . . Data sources used to develop this view included observing common practice, interviewing teachers, conducting case studies, and reviewing the literature. . . . Based on a synthesis of data collected, an explanation of the real world of teacher careers was hypothesized into a working model.

This model-building phase of theory development requires the synthesis and expansion of prior knowledge into a framework that adds new insights and structures for analysis. The working model developed at this stage should not be viewed as fixed, but rather as a tentative paradigm that offers the current best explanation of existing data. Subsequent data gathered should be cycled back into the model to make modifications and refinements (p. 31).

Other writers in the field of supervision also provide insight about how synthesis may affect supervisory practice. Oliva noted that even though supervision will continue "in a clinical mode" for the immediate future, a future synthesis of the best features of scientific and other approaches is possible, particularly when it becomes clear that there is no "single best approach" to supervision that guarantees success. The distinction between supervisory approaches will be more a matter of degree

between the supervisor who follows a scientific approach with some added dimensions of artistic, interpretive, ecological, and qualitative approaches and the supervisor who follows artistic, interpretive, ecological, and/or qualitative approaches with some added dimensions of scientific, and quantitative approaches (1993, pp. 578–579).

Krey and Burke (1989, pp. 15–16) also described evidence of synthesis, noting that they view the last 20 years as a "Period of Unification" for supervision. While supervisors have drawn from many seemingly contradictory approaches to supervision, ranging from "scientific" to collaborative, the diversity of these efforts does not reflect an absence of direction or creativity in supervision. Rather, it shows an evolution toward more unity in the perspectives of the historically important constituent groups in supervision: teachers, supervisors, and administrators. This new unity will ultimately assist in defining purposes for supervision.

Some Lessons from the Past

In our discussion of the problems and limitations of the various forms of scientific supervision that have come to prominence and decline over the past 80 years, several themes have emerged. These themes have been apparent from Taylor's day through present-day implementation of the Hunter model. Problems that plague applications of scientific management to supervisory practice typically include several of the following: overgeneralization of the model or its research base; rushed implementation; substitution of "bandwagon" claims for a research base; inattention to the importance of the variables of human motivation and creativity; failure to generate replicable, generalizable findings; and, finally, the problem of failing to clarify at the start what is meant by "teacher effectiveness." The following lessons from the past are derived from these themes and could be useful in guiding the efforts of future reform efforts that are scientific in their approach.

First, the model has to match the complexity of the context in which it will be implemented. Problems of overgeneralization have undermined efforts at scientific reform from the start. Although Taylor himself admitted that it was a relatively simple process to do a task analysis for handling pig iron, but a much more complex one to describe the interactions of a person and a machine in a tool-grinding factory, he still claimed that his model could apply in all work places. Bobbitt and his colleagues did painstaking research on simple mathematical processes, but got bogged down by reams of data and resorted to generalizing the "rough determination" of existing comparative studies to complex processes like composition. Hunter's model was likewise applied in contexts quite different from the elementary classrooms where the original research was conducted. When they tried to use the model in lessons with high-level cognitive or affective objectives, many teachers perceived the model to be a poor fit.

Second, adequate research and preparation need to precede implementation. Educational literature is replete with examples of well-intentioned innovations that failed to survive. Popularity and widespread acceptance of most scientific management models have been intense but short-lived, lasting only about a decade. Taylor himself warned that undertaking change too rapidly, without full support of administration and workers, would result in worker resistance and the downfall of his model (1911, p. 130). Failure to establish an adequate research base in advance of implementation results in an equally catastrophic course. When statistical analysis was unable to keep up with data collection, Bobbitt encouraged supervisors to be guided by using prevailing or median practice as a substitute for comparative data, or by the "fixed stars" of supervisory principles that every supervisor was presumed to have at his disposal (1913, pp. 55–57). Thus, intuition became the real basis for practice, while proponents continued to justify their decisions with the authority of a research base.

Third, human factors cannot be ignored or subordinated to productivity goals. Taylor's substitution of personal incentive bonuses for earlier cooperative worker relationships paid off in lowering production costs, but it drew such resistance from organized labor that components of his model were banned on many worksites. Bobbitt's analogies of children to "products" and of education to the steel manufacturing process were probably related to the fact that administrators were more likely to discuss than use his theories (Callahan & Button, 1964). Hunter's model was widely perceived as limiting teacher's professional autonomy: Many teachers resented the prescriptive and inspectional aspects of the model. Their attitudes may have led to low levels of implementation and even interfered with research on the model's effectiveness. What Mayo and Roethlisberger demonstrated in their research at the Hawthorne site has not changed: Underestimating the powerful needs for camaraderie in the workplace, as well as the value of intrinsic job satisfaction and professional autonomy, continues to undermine many scientific reform efforts.

Scientific management has had wide appeal across institutions and generations. Despite modest research support for the model's effectiveness in supervisory practice, it continues to be a major competing force in supervision. Scientific supervision promises to provide a defensible basis for making tough decisions that no one wants to make arbitrarily: Its hallmarks are hard data and definitive answers. As Sergiovanni and Starratt pointed out (1993, p. 211), we seem to prefer an exact answer to a wrong question rather than an approximate answer to the right question. The important issue thus becomes, not so much whether the legacy of scientific management will *endure*, but whether our predilection for the most simplistic of its forms can be tempered by some lessons learned about its failures.

REFERENCES

Alexander, C. (1917). Standard tests as an aid in supervision. *The American School Board Journal, 54* (1), 17–18, 66–67, 69.

Alfonso, R. J., Firth, G. R., & Neville, R. F. (1981). *Instructional supervision: A behavior system* (2nd ed.). Boston: Allyn & Bacon.

American Teacher, The. (1916, March). The case against efficiency [a poem]. *5* (3), 1.

Bacharach, S. B., Lipsky, D. B., & Shedd, J. B. (1984). *Paying for better teaching: Merit pay and its alternatives.* Ithaca, NY: Organizational Analysis & Practice.

Barr, A. S. & Burton, W. H. (1926). *The supervision of instruction.* New York: D. Appleton.

Beach, D. M. & Reinhartz, J. (1989). *Supervision: Focus on instruction.* New York: Harper & Row.

Berg, C. A. & Clough, M. (1990–1991a). Hunter lesson design: The wrong one for science teaching. *Educational Leadership, 48*(4), 73–78.

Berg, C. A. & Clough, M. (1990–1991b). Only an expensive horoscope. *Educational Leadership, 48*(4), 84.

Berg, C. A. & Clough, M. (1991). Forum: Generic lesson design—the case against. *The Science Teacher, 58*(7), 26–27, 29–31.

Beyer, L. E. & Apple, M. W. (Eds.). (1988). *The curriculum: Problems, politics, and possibilities.* Albany, NY: State University of New York.

Bhaerman, R. D. (1973). Merit pay? No! *The National Elementary Principal, 52*(5), 63–69.

Bobbitt, J. F. (1912). Elimination of waste in education. *The Elementary School Teacher, 12*(6), 259–271.

Bobbitt, J. F. (1913). Some general principles of management applied to the problems of city-school systems. In J. F. Bobbitt (Ed.). (12th Yearbook of the National Society for the Study of Education, Part I: The supervision of city schools (pp. 7–96). Chicago, IL: The University of Chicago Press.

Boorstin, D. J. (1973). *The Americans: The democratic experience.* New York: Random House.

Boyce, A. C. (1915). *Methods for measuring teachers' efficiency.* (14th Yearbook of the National Society for the Study of Education, Part II; pp. 9–81). Bloomington, IL: Public School Publishing.

Brophy, J. E., & Good, T. L. (1986). Teacher behavior and student achievement. In M. C. Wittrock (Ed.). *Handbook of research on teaching* (3rd ed.) pp. 328–375. New York: Macmillan.

Button, H. W. (1961). *A history of supervision in the public schools, 1870–1950*. Doctoral dissertation, Washington University.

Callahan, R. E. (1962). *Education and the cult of efficiency*. Chicago: University of Chicago.

Callahan, R. E. & Button, H. W. (1964). Historical change of the role of the man in the organization: 1865–1950. In D. E. Griffiths (Ed.). *Behavioral science and educational administration*. (63rd Yearbook of the National Society for the Study of Education, Part II; pp. 73–92). Chicago, IL: The University of Chicago Press.

Campbell, R. F., Fleming, T., Newell, L. J., & Bennion, J. W. (1987). *A history of thought and practice in educational administration*. New York: Teachers College Press.

Costa, A. L. (1984). A reaction to Hunter's knowing, teaching, and supervising. In P. L. Hosford (Ed.). *Using what we know about teaching* (ASCD 1984, Yearbook) pp. 196–2030.

Crabbs, L. M. (1925). *Measuring efficiency in supervision and teaching* [Number 175 in Contributions to Education series]. New York: Teachers College, Columbia University.

Cubberley, E. P. (1916). *Public school administration: A statement of the fundamental principles underlying the organization and administration of public education*. Boston: Houghton Mifflin.

Dewey, J. (1929). *The sources of a science of education*. [The Kappa Delta Pi Lecture Series]. New York: Liveright.

Dildy, P. (1982). Improving student achievement by appropriate teacher in-service training: Utilizing program for effective teaching (PET). *Education, 103*(2), 132–138.

Donovan, J. F., Sousa, D. A., & Walberg, H. J. (1992). The Hunter model: A four year longitudinal study of staff development effects. *The Journal of Research and Development in Education, 25*(3), 165–172.

Eisner, E. W. (1967a). Educational objectives: Help or hindrance? *School Review, 75*(3), 251–260.

Eisner, E. W. (1967b). A response to my critics. *School Review, 75*(3), 277–282.

Eisner, E. W. (1985). *The educational imagination: On the design and evaluation of school programs* (2nd. ed.). New York: Macmillan.

Elliott, E. C. (1914). *City school supervision*. Yonkers-on-Hudson, New York: World Book.

Eye, G. G. & Netzer, L. A. (1965). *Supervision of instruction: A phase of administration*. New York: Harper & Row.

Fayol, H. (1949). *General and industrial management*. (C. Storrs, Trans.). London: Sir Isaac Pitman & Sons.

Fessler, R. (1992). In R. Fessler & J. C. Christensen (Eds.). *Teacher career cycle: Understanding and guiding the professional development of teachers*. Needham Heights, MA: Allyn & Bacon

Garman, N. B. & Hazi, H. M. (1988). Teachers ask: Is there life after Madeline Hunter? *Phi Delta Kappan, 69*(9), 669–672.

Getzels, J. W., Lipham, J. M., & Campbell, R. F. (1968). *Educational administration as a social process: Theory, research, practice*. New York: Harper & Row.

Gibboney, R. A. (1987a). A critique of Madeline Hunter's teaching model from Dewey's perspective. *Educational Leadership, 44*(5), 46–50.

Gibboney, R. A. (1987b). The vagaries of turtle research: Gibboney replies. *Educational Leadership, 44*(5), 54.

Glanz, J. (1991). *Bureaucracy and professionalism: The evolution of public school supervision*. Cranbury, NJ: Associated University Presses.

Goldhammer, R. (1969). *Clinical supervision: Special methods for the supervision of teachers*. New York: Holt, Rinehart, & Winston.

Greenwood, J. M. (1905). An experience in helping teachers professionally. *Educational Review, 30*, 464–473.

Gross, B. M. (1964). The scientific approach to administration. In D. E. Griffiths (Ed.). *Behavioral science and educational administration* (63rd Yearbook of the National Society for the Study of Education, Part II; pp. 33–72). Chicago, CA: The University of Chicago Press.

Gulick, L. H. (1937). Notes on the theory of organization. In L. F. Gulick & L. F. Urwick (Eds.). *Papers on the science of administration* (pp. 115–142). New York: Institute of Public Administration.

Gulick, L. H. & Urwick, L. F. (Eds.). (1937). *Papers on the science of administration*. New York: Institute of Public Administration.

Guernsey, M. A. (1986). *Review of related literature and research: History of merit pay, differentiated staffing, and incentive programs* (ERIC Document Reproduction Service No. ED 267 513).

Hunter, M. (1973). Appraising teaching performance: One approach. *The National Elementary Principal, 52*(5), 60–62.

Hunter, M. (1975). The limits of accountability. *The National Elementary Principal, 55*(2), 34–37.

Hunter, M. (1980). Six types of supervisory conferences. *Educational Leadership, 37*(5), 408–410, 412.

Hunter, M. (1983). Script-taping: An essential supervisory tool. *Educational Leadership, 41*(3), 43.

Hunter, M. (1984). Knowing, teaching, and supervising. In P. L. Hosford (Ed.). *Using what we know about teaching*. Alexandria, VA: (ASCD 1984 yearbook). pp. 169–192.

Hunter, M. (1985). What's wrong with Madeline Hunter? *Educational Leadership, 42*(5), 57–60.

Hunter, M. (1986a). Madeline Hunter replies: Develop collaboration; build trust. *Educational Leadership, 43*(6), 68.

Hunter, M. (1986b). Let's eliminate the preobservation conference. *Educational Leadership, 43*(6), 69–70.

Hunter, M. (1987a). Hunterization (Response to Slavin). *Instructor, 96*(8), 60.

Hunter, M. (1987b). Beyond rereading Dewey . . . what's next? A response to Gibboney. *Educational Leadership, 44*(5), 51–53.

Hunter, M. (1988). Response to Slavin: Improving teacher decisions. *Educational Leadership, 46*(2), 29.

Kliebard, H. M. (1971). Bureaucracy and curriculum theory. In V. F. Haubrich (Ed.). *Freedom, bureaucracy, & schooling*. (ASCD 1971 yearbook). pp. 74–93, Washington, D.C.: ASCD.

Krey, R. D. & Burke, P. J. (1989). *A design for instructional supervision*. Springfield, IL: Charles C. Thomas.

Krug, E. A. (1964). *The shaping of the American High School*. New York: Harper and Row.

Lunenburg, F. C., & Ornstein, A. C. (1991). *Educational administration: Concepts and practices*. Belmont, CA: Wadsworth.

Mager, R. F. (1962). *Preparing instructional objectives*. Belmont, CA: Fearon.

Mandeville, G. K. & Rivers, J. (1988–1989). Effects of South Carolina's Hunter-based PET program. *Educational Leadership, 46*(4), 63–66.

Mayo, E. (1933). *The human problems of an industrial civilization*. New York: Macmillan.

McNeil, J. D. (1982). A scientific approach to supervision. In T. J. Sergiovanni (Ed.). *Supervision of teaching*. (ASCD 1982 yearbook) pp. 18–34. Alexandria VA: ASCD.

Medley, D. M. & Mitzel, H. E. (1963). Measuring classroom behavior by systematic observation. In N. L. Gage (Ed.). *Handbook of research on teaching: A project of the American Educational Research Association* (pp. 247–328). Chicago: Rand McNally.

Nietz, J. A. (1921). Tests and scales as aids to the supervisor. *The American School Board Journal, 62*(2), 47–48,

Oliva, P. F. (1993). *Supervision for today's schools* (4th ed.). White Plains, NY: Longman.

Owens, R. G. (1970). *Organizational behavior in education*. Englewood Cliffs, NJ: Prentice-Hall.

Owens, R. G. (1991). *Organizational behavior in education* (4th ed.). Englewood Cliffs, NJ: Prentice-Hall.

Pajak, E. (1993). *Approaches to clinical supervision: Alternatives for improving instruction*. Norwood, MA: Christopher-Gordon.

Pavan, B. N. (1986). A thank you and some questions for Madeline Hunter. *Educational Leadership, 43*(6), 67–68.

Piper, T. J. & Elgart, D. B. (1979). *Teacher supervision through behavioral objectives*. Baltimore, MD: Paul H. Brookes.

Popham, W. J. (1969). Probing the validity of arguments against behavioral goals. In R. C. Anderson, G. W. Faust, M. C. Roderick, D. J. Cunningham, & T. Andre (Eds.). *Current research on instruction* (pp. 66–72). Englewood Cliffs, NJ: Prentice-Hall.

Popham, W. J. (1970). The Instructional Objectives Exchange: New support for criterion-referenced instruction. *Phi Delta Kappan, 52*(3), 171173.

Popham, W. J. (1971). Performance tests of teaching proficiency: Rationale, development, and validation. *American Educational Research Journal, 8*(1), 105–117.

Rockler, M. J. (1987). *Improving the knowledge base in teacher education* (ERIC Document Reproduction Service No. ED 290 742).

Roethlisberger, F. J. & Dickson, W. J. (1949). *Management and the worker*. Cambridge MA: Harvard University Press.

Rosenshine, B. & Furst, N. (1973). The use of direct observation to study teaching. In R. M. W. Travers (Ed.). *Second handbook of research on teaching: A project of the American Educational Research Association* (pp. 122–183). Chicago: Rand McNally.

Rugg, H. O. (1920). Self-improvement of teachers through self-rating: A new scale for rating teachers' efficiency. *The Elementary School Journal, 20*(9), 670–684.

Scott, W. R. (1981). *Organizations: Rational, natural, and open systems*. Englewood Cliffs, NJ: Prentice-Hall.

Sergiovanni, T. J. & Starratt, R. J. (1983). *Supervision: Human perspectives* (3rd ed.). New York: McGraw-Hill.

Sergiovanni, T. J. & Starratt, R. J. (1993). *Supervision: A redefinition* (5th ed.). New York: McGraw-Hill.

Slavin, R. E. (1987). The Hunterization of America's schools. *Instructor, 96*(8), 56–58.

Slavin, R. E. (1989). On mastery learning and mastery teaching. *Educational Leadership, 46*(7), 77–79.

Stallings, J. & Krasavage, E. M. (1986). Program implementation and student achievement in a four-year Madeline Hunter follow-through project. *The Elementary School Journal, 87*(2), 117–138.

Tanner, D. & Tanner, L. N. (1975). *Curriculum development: Theory into practice*. New York: Macmillan.

Taylor, F. W. [1903] (1919). *Shop management*. Reprint. New York: Harper & Row.

Taylor, F. W. [1911] (1967). *The principles of scientific management*. Reprint. New York: W. W. Norton (Published by arrangement with Harper & Row).

Tyack, D. B. & Hansot, E. (1982). *Managers of virtue*. New York: Basic Books.

Urwick, L. F. (1937). The function of administration: With special reference to the work of Henri Fayol. In L. F. Gulick & L. F. Urwick (Eds.). *Papers on the science of administration* (pp. 115–142). New York: Institute of Public Administration.

Weber, M. (1947). *Max Weber: The theory of social and economic organization*. (A. M. Henderson & T. Parsons, Trans.). New York: Oxford University Press.

Wiles, J. & Bondi, J. (1991). *Supervision: A guide to practice* (3rd ed.). New York: Macmillan. [Previous editions copyrighted 1986 and 1980 by Merrill].

Wolfe, P. (1987). What the "seven-step lesson plan" isn't! *Educational Leadership, 44*(5), 70–71.

·43·

SOCIAL DIMENSIONS OF SUPERVISION

Arthur S. Shapiro

UNIVERSITY OF SOUTH FLORIDA

Arthur Blumberg

SYRACUSE UNIVERSITY

Supervision is primarily a sociological and cultural anthropological territory of knowledge.

L. Craig Wilson

We are what we know.

James Burke
The Day the Universe Changed

INTRODUCTION

Analyzing the field of supervision from the perspective of the social dimensions within which it functions is similar to moving the Earth with a lever. All one needs for the feat is a platform and a relatively lengthy and robust lever. Contemplating supervision from the perspective of the social context within which supervision and schooling take place similarly seems to be a gargantuan enterprise. It is hoped that the results may provide us with some notions of future directions toward which both practice and research may move. Either or both outcomes may legitimize the inquiry.

In order to provide a macroscopic overview of the field, this analysis commences with an overview of the social dimensions of a society and the nature of the often hidden and unconscious cultural constraints within which human behavior and thinking are focused. An overview of Craig Wilson's (1969) formulations of the phases of supervisory thought and practice is provided in order to generate a "big picture" perspective. The critical lack of theory in the field is the next focus, together with the crippling implications such a state of affairs produces in the field of practice and for prac-

titioners. A brief view of perceptions of the effectiveness of supervision and supervisors is treated. The construct of efficacy is introduced and briefly applied, as is Blumberg's concept of supervision as a craft.

Major facets of supervision promulgated by Kimball Wiles are briefly reviewed next, with John Lovell's additions of supervision as an instructional behavior system, and as coordinating and facilitating human development. Additional formulations of the field are presented, such as supervision as social process, as decision-making, and as the planning function. Supervision as a social function of education and schooling (e.g., as a social enterprise), and as a holistic behavior system are the next foci, after which the impact of the social functions of education on supervisors and supervision are explored.

A sampling of social dimensions of supervision is then delineated, such as culture and cultural trends, socioeconomic class stratification, and some social psychological perspectives, including positions, roles, role expectations, and role functions. Following that, such factors as race, gender, ethnicity, organizational theory/issues/factors including social systems theory and practice, and cyclical organizational phenomena are presented, succeeded by exploration of a number of the social functions of schools and schooling and their implications for educational supervision.

The impact of many facets of culture on supervision is next, including organizational culture, cycles, and climate, after which the American predilection for fads and bandwagoning is scrutinized. This is followed by an overview of the influence of the social dimensions upon the acceptance and use of a number of different supervisory models. Authority, power, influence, empowerment, and control and the role of the supervisor regarding these interrelated phenomena constitute the next arena of inquiry.

Implications for supervision by centralization and nationalization trends in education are analyzed, as is a broad brush treatment of reform efforts with their usual and expected limited success. An individualized organizational diagnostic, planning, and implementation construct is presented. School and district size research is explored for impact upon student achievement and other goals and for supervisory implications, as is the treatment of schools as professional bureaucracies. The value of a clear philosophy of education, of administration, and of supervision as well as of critical-analytical and problem-solving skills on evaluating such phenomena as fads, current trends, and varied educational practices is stated.

The chapter closes with a summary, conclusions, implications, and recommendations for practice and research.

CONSTRUCTING SOCIAL REALITIES

The social context in any society provides the structure and focuses the nature of the thinking and discussion of any issue in that society. Indeed, the social context in any society identifies the issues that will be considered, determines the interaction and discussion, and often determines which issues or concerns will and will not even become conscious matters for consideration. A society's most highly esteemed values point irrevocably toward certain key phenomena. In Japan, the core value of cooperation flows throughout society to mold behavior in industry, education, and family. America's individualism leads to great value being placed on competition, with its attendant results in schools, marketplace, churches, and family.

The extraordinary power of a culture's subtle, unperceived values and messages becomes evident in the work of two educational psychologists, Harold Stevenson and James Stigler (1992). These two men, who were puzzled why Asian students routinely did better at elementary mathematics than Americans, hypothesized that persistence might be a contributing factor. They experimented with a group each of American and Japanese students, giving them an unsolvable problem. Most American youngsters attacked the problem briefly and gave up, whereas Japanese students worked on and on endlessly. The researchers concluded that Americans believe that success in school depends upon one's ability; in contrast, Japanese students believe that persistence and, therefore, hard work determine success. A culture's subtle and not-so-subtle messages become deeply embedded and are rarely draw to the surface, let alone questioned.

The inhabitants of a society engage in activities the society prizes (e.g., play a good game of tennis, engage in social banter, worship one deity). They skulk with shame from the taboo (e.g., incest, child abuse, arson, animal sacrifice) and other stigmatizing behaviors (Goffman, 1963). Indeed, key significant objects for one society may be weeds in another's garden (Mead, 1934). American Indians prospered and fattened on the largesse they perceived abounding over the land, whereas early settlers starved, unable to redefine and rebuild their useless knowledge of perceived European-based significant objects and symbols in their new world.

American individualism and competition, supported by a social Darwinistic philosophy, for instance, has narrowly focused supervisory behavior into models of individually directed supervision (i.e., clinical supervision is obviously grounded in psychology, which is itself heavily aimed at individual behavior).

Berger and Luckman's (1966) *The Social Construction of Reality* made the point via its title. Each society, each culture and each subculture constructs its own social realities, (i.e., its own norms), practices, customs, and taboos over the forests of time. Each president has attempted to construct new social realities in his administration. For example, President Clinton pressed hard to pass the North American Free Trade Agreement (NAFTA) legislation, a new direction for the country. Some educators and spokespersons have been trying to redefine the nature of schooling in America by making school choice and vouchers a national reality.

On the local scene, it is rare that any group builds its social reality as a conscious, well-thought out, and articulated process, with people fully aware that they are attempting to redesign the norms of their culture or subculture. Developing such an awareness, plus knowledge of workable change strategies and of the building blocks of a society and its culture (e.g., norms, positions, roles, role expectations, social systems) may provide one with a considerably enhanced armamentarium of tools to accomplish such an intriguing goal. The creation of a social reality also serves as a formidable empowerment process and strategy.

On the organizational level, one assumption held by some ". . . is that organizations exist apart from people, thus making it possible to modify organizations or to design new ones without changing people. The second (assumption) is that the goals of an organization are independent of those held by the individuals in it. An alternative view conceives of the organization as a socially constructed reality within which individuals perceive rules, pressures, demands, powers, and dependencies [Greenfield, 1973, p. 555, Silverman, 1970]" (Levin & Simon, 1974).

This alternative view is a basis for this chapter.

PERSPECTIVES IN SUPERVISION

While the Roman god, Janus, only had two faces, each facing in opposite directions, supervision seems blessed (or cursed?) by a greater variety of facets and perspectives. The prevailing focus of the field has been the function of facilitating improvement of the individual teacher's professional practice. This seems to occupy the premier focus of literature for virtually all the decades of the twentieth century, and fits the American fixation on the individual as the basic unit of society.

Wilson's Three Phases of Supervisory Thought

Craig Wilson (1969) postulated three phases to supervisory thought, all taking place for the most part during this century (see Figure 43.1).

The purpose of the first phase—institutional control—obviously focused on controlling the organization and its teachers, which to this day is a dominant component of a considerable range of supervisory beliefs and practices. The second stage—program definition—"was to define the substance and the processes most appropriate for the newly-created [institutional] structure (of public education)" (p. 28). Wilson noted that content was easier to write than to transmit; therefore, the phase culminated in the testing and evaluation movement/stage, again, in order to ensure that the teacher was controlled. This stage obviously drives much of the curriculum and instruction today as exemplified by numerous state testing programs and calls for a national assessment program "to certify individual performance and thereby motivate students and their teachers to meet these standards." (SCANS Report, 1982). A form of centralized national control was clearly operative in this initiative, enacted into legislation in 1994.

The third and last phase of supervisory practices—growth processes—includes group processes, subject area development, and comprehensive planning (and, by implication, clinical supervision and human resources supervision [Miles, 1965; Sergiovanni & Starratt, 1979]), reaches to today. Wilson noted that subject area development often aimed at a "search for the common denominators of content (i.e., the structures of knowledge)" (p. 29), which led to "rebuilding of total curriculum designs around larger concepts and processes" (p. 29) (i.e., comprehensive planning).

Wilson summarized the first of these three phases (i.e., institutional control), as static because change in both process and product were minimal. The second phase (i.e., program definition), focused on producing "predictable products" (p. 29). The third, phrase (i.e., Growth Processes) "perceives of uncontrollable products but predictable processes" (p. 29). The behavior of the supervisor and the nature of supervision will obviously vary, "depending upon which phase is dominant." In addition, Wilson insightfully noted that all three phases may co-exist in an organization, with one dominant at a particular time.

Wilson stated emphatically, "I continue to believe that 'supervision' either results in *teacher empowerment* or it is worse than useless" (personal communication, Feb. 6, 1994).

The Role of Theory in Educational Supervision

Regardless of the enormous power and the indispensable contribution of theory to the natural sciences and the professions, theory is often viewed with contempt and derision in education and in school supervision. New teachers, administrators, and supervisors are urged to throw theory out the schoolroom window and to learn to be practical, an obvious impossibility because practice and action are based on theory. Educators insist that they do not wish to use tested and reputable scientifically based theories; instead preferring to employ their own untested and unarticulated theories, while simultaneously denying their existence.

A strange cultural contradiction immediately emerges when the medical profession is contrasted with education. Most people would not consider choosing a physician who ignores scientific findings. They would lead the exodus from the office or a physician who did not know and utilize the

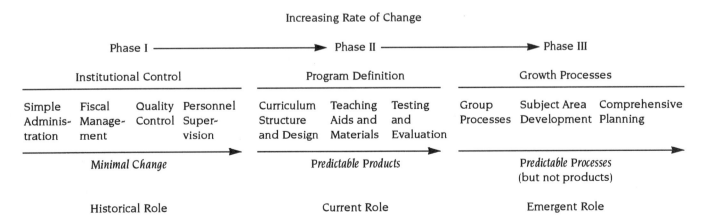

FIGURE 43.1. Stages in the Evolution of Supervisory Concepts and Practices

germ theory of disease, likely recommending removal of the person's license to practice.

The contribution of theory to every professional field is immense, essentially providing a lodestone to guide thinking and practice. Because theory describes, analyzes, and predicts phenomena, a great host of behaviors can be explained succinctly with one theoretical formulation. Theory assists attempts to become more objective and guides to new knowledge and action (i.e., if I do this, then this may result). Such astute thinkers as Dewey (1938), Coldadarci and Getzels (1955), and others firmly asserted that theory and practice are one, with each flowing from the other.

Other advantages result from theory development (in both education and social work); however, the field of supervision has not been blessed by a plethora of theories. In 1969, Shapiro, (Wilson et al, 1969) noted, "It is obvious, then, that this brief review of relevant literature (in both educational and social work supervision) has hardly turned up a theory of supervision" (p. 43). Not much has occurred since then. Most attempts to apply theories and models from administration and psychology to supervision have met with indifference.

One major problem referred to earlier rests on the fact that the placesetting of theory on the table of American culture lies well below the salt. Our culture is both antitheoretical and antiintellectual, particularly in the social sciences and in education. Modest efforts are largely ignored even by those in the fields.

THE EFFECTIVENESS OF SUPERVISORS AND SUPERVISION

Blumberg (1993), long a critic of supervisory practice, structured some assumptions in grasping the nature of supervision in order to consider its effectiveness.

1. The efficacy of supervision has never been demonstrated in any generalized way.
2. For the most part, the practice of supervision takes place in dyadic settings, but it does sometimes occur in a group setting, where there is more than one teacher present.
3. For the most part, as far as the teacher is concerned, meetings with supervisors are involuntary.
4. The extent to which a supervisor can be helpful to a teacher depends on her or his ability to engage a teacher in conversation about the teacher's work. This ability is related to the supervisor's credibility in the teacher's eyes as someone who has something valuable to offer, at minimal cost, as well as the supervisor's interpersonal skills.
5. It is the teacher who has control over the nature of the supervisor–teacher interaction [similar to Barnard's revolutionary thinking concerning the nature of the sources of power].
6. The supervisor is in the position, most of the time, of "selling" something the teacher does not want to "buy".

A summary of these assumptions would go: Supervision is a practice that has never proved to be systematically valuable. The practice itself takes place within an organizational and interpersonal environment that on the surface, seems not to be conducive to productive work relationships between the parties involved . . . (pp. 2–3).

Blumberg then referred to a number of studies (Blumberg & Amidon, 1965; Blumberg & Tallerico, 1988; Wiles, 1953) indicating that teachers do not consider supervisors to be valuable professional aides, or the supervisory process as presently practiced to be helpful. For instance, Blumberg (1993) cited a Wiles study where "only 4 percent of the teachers felt that the quality of supervision was good" (p. 4). regarding another Wiles study, Blumberg (1993) noted that "only 35 of 2500 teachers indicated that they considered their supervisor as the source of new ideas or changes in teaching practice" (p. 4).

The Blumberg and Amidon (1965) study pointed to "a sizeable percentage of teachers considered the time they spent with their supervisor as utterly wasteful, while a small percentage thought of it as time well spent" (p. 4). Based on the Blumberg and Tallerico (1988) study, Blumberg (1993) observed respondents "reported that only three out of 43 teachers studied reported that they had, in their recent memory, a productive conference with their supervisor" (p. 4).

Furthermore, Blumberg's and Tallerico's (1988) title, Supervision and the Schools: A Symphony in Discord, denoted an interesting conclusion. The authors perceived that the two systems were constructed upon differing premises. The school system is built on the concepts of order and control, whereas the philosophical base of supervision comprises a human relations perspective.

People writing in professional journals rarely make categorical, unqualified generalizations. After defining supervision as "experienced by most teachers as evaluation of classroom teaching" (p. 14), Starratt developed A Modest Proposal: Abolish Supervision (1992); in which he stated categorically, "To my knowledge there is no research that shows that supervision, as it is generally practiced, results in substantial, and sustained changes in teachers' teaching" (p. 15).

Starratt pointed to the "underside of supervision" (p. 15), referring to the "bureaucratic procedures that become administrative means, sometimes thoughtlessly used, to control teachers" (p. 14). Starratt addressed the impact of supervision on student learning, indicating that it "is at best inconclusive" (p. 15). "Other research efforts to trace relationships between discrete teacher behaviors and increased student performance have again and again resulted in inconsistent and contradictory findings" (p. 15).

Starratt returned to the idea that supervision can improve teaching, noting that the teaching act is extremely complicated, and producing his categorical statement quoted earlier. In addition, he declared,

"Given the picture of present classroom teaching—its craft nature; the multiple meanings associated with competence; the unpredictability of everyday life in classrooms; with the collectivity of students in the classroom; the layer upon layer of meanings, feeling, symbolic connecting and disconnecting; as well as the strong affective bond between teacher and class—how could a supervisor come into a classroom and presume to offer advice on how to teach the class better, based on one visit? Yet supervisors do this every day without the slightest hesitation" (p. 17).

In response to Starratt, Robert Alfonso (1992) noted: "We seem to be unable to evaluate supervision, judging when it is effective and when it is not" (p. 21). He added: "We have, however, largely ignored the issue of evaluating supervisory performance" (p. 21).

In his *A Response to Starratt's A Modest Proposal: Abolish Supervision*, Blumberg (1992) agreed with Starratt's indictment of supervision, but then foreshadowed a thesis of this paper in stating:

Whatever we call supervision, its focus has been, for the most part, on individuals without regard for (1) the organizational context in which those individuals work, and (2) the needs that teachers have and the rewards they seek (albeit not consciously) as adults from other adults in their work setting (p. 24).

Blumberg presaged a later section of this paper, which focused on supervision as social process and as a *system* of human behavior, not merely as individuals acting out social roles (which in itself implies a coherent, organized social system).

Pavan (1983) related clinical supervision to student achievement, concluding that due to numerous conditions affecting achievement, the territory proved difficult to assess. Nottingham and Dawson (1987) noted that in most schools teacher evaluation and supervision are seldom mutually exclusive. They asserted that whereas supervision is built on trust and a helping atmosphere, evaluation is judgmental and founded on law or policy statements. They cited a Rand Corporation study (1985) that reported five major problems with teacher evaluation processes: (1) principals' incompetence, (2) teachers' resistance or apathy, (3) lack of uniformity and consistency, (4) inadequate training for evaluators, and (5) shortcomings concerning secondary school staff evaluation.

Efficacy and Instructional Supervision

The emerging construct of efficacy (Bandura, 1992; Dusek, 1985) contributes some value to instructional supervision. Efficacy appears to be characterized by two benchmarks. In the first, the instructional supervisor asserts, "I *can* make a difference." The second says, "I know *how* to make a difference," which ensues from the supervisor having developed an armamentarium of realistic, workable, and viable options, techniques, and approaches that he or she uses effectively to achieve professional goals.

Bandura's Efficacy Theory (1986, 1992) seems useful to supervision. In addition, Bandura implied that *how* people conceptualized their ability determined whether their levels of perceived efficacy are increased or reduced. If people

perceived their abilities and talents to be changing, evolving, and growing, then they developed a higher sense of efficacy than did those who perceived their abilities and talents as rigid, fixed, static, and, therefore, limited, even if the latter began with higher levels of ability. The former self-conception, which led administrators, supervisors, and teachers to take responsibility for the performance of "their" students and teachers, was termed "ego-enhancing" (i.e., developed in work on attribution theory [Cooper & Burger, 1980]). Those who perceived their's and others' talents as static and fixed tended to take little responsibility for the performance of "their" students and teachers, and were termed "ego-defensive." Taking little responsibility, these individuals tended to blame other factors, such as poor socioeconomic conditions and poor family settings, pointing the finger of blame anywhere but at themselves.

A study by Hoy and Woolfolk (1990) determined that a most significant influence on teacher efficacy is the way the principal treated the teachers. A supportive role that helped "teachers maintain classroom order and solve instructional problems" (p. 367) increased teachers' sense of efficacy substantially.

The job of the instructional supervisor, with these insights as lodestones, manifestly metamorphoses first into facilitating people to shift conceptualization of their abilities and talents to see growth and potential in themselves and others. This has enormous implication for the beliefs and assumptions underlying many persistent retentions of young children, a practice for more than a century despite overwhelming research evidence of severe negative consequences. Teachers assume that such children will remain consistently behind in their growth and maturation and not mature and overtake their peers.

A second major function of instructional supervisors clearly becomes one of vastly increasing both their own and their supervisees' inventory of frames of reference, theories, strategies, processes, "tricks of the trade," and other alternatives that will increase confidence in knowing *how* to make a difference.

These concepts might be utilized as benchmarks in order to evaluate studies relating efficacy of supervisory behavior; however, studies of instructional supervision and supervision dealing with efficacy are relatively limited and scattered widely over special education, regular education, preservice education, counseling and social work, international education, higher education, effective leadership, organizational, and curriculum that such a process would be unwarranted. The most frequent focus was on preservice supervision and efficacy, followed by counselor and social work supervision, with less than a handful of studies applicable to supervision of regular classroom teachers. Such a scattered approach and the paucity of studies indicated that application of the concept of efficacy to explicate supervisory behavior was in a relatively early phase of development, and that related fields might be mined more appropriately.

Efficacy is typically one element, and often minor in importance, compared with other aspects of most studies in supervision. Notwithstanding, Licklider and Niska (1993) reported that a sense of efficacy appeared to be enhanced for 26 principals who participated in a 20-week in-service program. Their sense of effectiveness and of self-confidence similarly improved. Another study (Coladarci & Bretton, 1991) indicated that teachers' perceptions of the utility of supervision, not its frequency, significantly predicted teacher efficacy. In this study, the researchers conducted a factor analysis and found a personal efficacy factor, defined as "when any of my students show improvement, it is because I found better ways of teaching them." They were unable, however, to find a clearly defined general efficacy factor, stating that "the meaning of general efficacy needs to be clarified." They were similarly unable to compare the results of efficacy in their sample with those of other samples, stating that they could find no "standard by which to judge the level of teacher efficacy in any one sample" against that of another.

In his handbook on clinical supervision, Smyth (1984) delineated the four stages of the process. He performed a postobservation analysis of the process and concluded that the efficacy of the process may be considered a fifth stage.

Patterson (1986) applied nonrational theory to schools. Nonrational theory grew from instability caused by changing student demographics, legislation improving standards and access, and increasing community expectations. Nonrationality in the schools is further defined in terms of decentralized goals, power, decision-making, external environment, and teaching process. Patterson constructed two fictitious school districts (i.e., one a rational and the other a nonrational model) and found the nonrational model to be "a more accurate and logical interpretation of reality." Applying nonrational theory to schools demonstrated how efficacy and integrity could be enhanced.

Tinning (1983) found that university supervisors exercised a low impact on student teachers for a number of reasons, among which are that the advice given by the supervisor tends to be generalized, and that feedback is often delayed and infrequent.

Blumberg's (1974) *Supervisors and Teachers: A Private Cold War* essentially raised the question of efficacy in teacher peer supervision. He literally reprinted two articles—the first, "Group Supervision" (Amidon, Kies, & Palisi, 1966) and the second, "When Teachers Evaluate Each Other" (Abramson, 1972)—in his chapter dealing with the issue. The two articles reported peer supervisory models. The first involves a group of teachers providing nonevaluative feedback only on request to colleagues who audio taped segments of their teaching. The group used a Flanders matrix as the touchstone against which to analyze teaching behavior. The second article by Abramson (1972) reported on the Templeton School of Tigard, Oregon's program of team-based peer evaluation, and on Livonia, Michigan's individual-focused peer evaluation system. The authors saw intriguing possibilities with the processes. These pioneer projects predated efficacy construct development. Notwithstanding, the efficacy construct applies to them inasmuch as those projects reported positive findings, although all recommended further development of their models and more time to analyze results.

Utilizing the construct of efficacy to analyze supervisory behavior obviously, makes sense. In recommendations for further research, developing instruments to study supervisors' and administrators' efficacy will be proposed. Efficacy is a powerful tool in the armamentarium of constructs, theories, models, frames of reference, and concepts by which make better sense can be made of the swirling complexities of our increasingly complicated culture.

Supervision as a Craft

Blumberg (1989) initiated consideration of supervision as a craft. He cautioned, however, that "as we use the idea administration-as-craft, we are thinking metaphorically" (p. 26), as is the case with consideration of administration as a science or an art. Blumberg reflected on his dissatisfaction with formulations of administration as a science, citing Bridges' (1982) statement reviewing research on the school administrator from 1967 to 1980,

[T]he research seemed to have little or no practical utility. In short, there is no compelling evidence to suggest that a major theoretical issue or practical problem relating to school administrators has been resolved by those toiling in the intellectual vineyards since 1967" (p. 25).

In contemplating the nature of art, and then evaluating administrative behavior by those criteria, Blumberg followed Croce (1976). Croce considered art as "the expression of something called 'lyrical intuition'" (p. 557) (i.e., "a sort of pureness of expression of the imagination that reflects the apprehension of 'the pure throb of life in its ideality'" [p. 557]).

Blumberg then examined aspects of the craft metaphor, using Collingwood's (1938) formulations. Collingwood defined a *craft* as "the power to produce a preconceived result by means of consciously controlled and *direct* action" (p. 15). Blumberg asserted:

First, to be an administrator involves, above all, dealing with and relating to people in a variety of problem-oriented contexts. Second, our learning to deal with and relating to people is a function of our long and quite personal social history—a history which, for the most part, is buried beyond recall (p. 49).

Blumberg concluded that while the metaphorical analogy does not fit completely, it is the best approximation describing and analyzing what administrators actually do. He noted that teaching is a craft, and that by implication, so is supervisory behavior.

SUPERVISION: A PLETHORA OF FACETS

In considering the numerous viewpoints regarding instructional supervision, one major focus and function stands out:— to improve professional function to enhance teaching and learning.

Kimball Wiles' Perspectives

In his landmark, *Supervision for Better Schools*, Wiles (1950), ushered the field into a more behaviorally focused era, and delineated perspectives to analyze supervision. He denoted the major function of supervision as releasing human potential, as leadership, as communicating, as curriculum development, and as improving instruction. Lovell (1983), who completed a fifth edition of this textbook after Wiles' untimely death, viewed supervision as an instructional behavior system with a deliberate focus on the school's teaching behavior system. Lovell added sections on clinical supervision, coordinating and facilitating change, and facilitating human development, of which the latter two previously were implied by Wiles.

In the chapter on leadership, Wiles and, later, Lovell pointed briefly to research on the role of the supervisor in the group as an official leader in the organization. Both authors noted that the supervisory role has prescribed authority, prestige, and position and that it should be utilized constructively, or the supervisor and the position may suffer.

Perspectives on Supervision as Social Process

Two works provide insights into supervision as social process. One was by Getzels, Guba, and Campbell (1968), and the other was by Shapiro, et al (1993), who saw supervision as the social enterprise of decision-making.

Much as educational administration profited from Getzels, Guba, and Campbell (1968) on administration as social process, instructional supervision could benefit from the same perspective. Guba's and Getzels' first model (1957), augmented considerably by Thelen (1960) (see Figure 43.2) and expanded into a book and coauthored by the first two with Campbell (1968), provided intriguing insights into instructional supervision. The social process model was used to describe three styles of leadership, and then to explicate a number of sources of conflict for individuals, organizations, culture, and conflicts among all three.

Models of Leadership Styles The expanded social process model described three styles of leadership as nomothetic, idiographic, and transactional. The first, nomothetic, focuses

on requirements of the organization, its roles, and role expectations. A nomothetically-styled administration generates a relatively structured, control-oriented, universalistic approach to administration and supervision. With this model, all people are treated alike; rules and regulations are promulgated and followed relatively rigidly. The organization operates and feels more impersonal and bureaucratic.

The second style, idiographic or personal leadership, primarily attempts to meet individual needs in contrast to the organization's requirements, and could be described as particularistic. Rules and regulations are downplayed and policy is bent or designed to meet individual, human needs. The organization is flexible, focusing on individual or group needs. Hierarchies and regulations pale when confronted by people's needs.

The third style, transactional leadership, attempts to meld the first two styles by balancing elements of both. Thus, in this transactional style roles and role expectations of the organization are balanced with meeting personalities and need dispositions of individuals.

Potential Sources of Conflict The possibly greatest contribution of the expanded model to the administrator and supervisor lies in its pointing to varying potential and hidden sources of conflict for supervisors.

CONFLICT AMONG DIFFERING CULTURAL VALUES. American schools obviously teach students from a considerable variety of cultures. Norms of those varying cultures may conflict. For example, a supervisor may be agnostic, which may be acceptable to one culture or subculture, but definitely not to a fundamentalist, religious subculture within the areas served by the schools.

Another illustration of cultural conflict occurs when a female supervisor supervises men from ethnic cultures where women are considered distinctly inferior (e.g., in the Far East and Latin America). Where teachers of one gender resent being supervised by the other, difficult conflicts not easily resolvable may result.

Similar difficulties may occur when supervisor and supervisee represent differences in race, religion, nationality, and/or ethnicity.

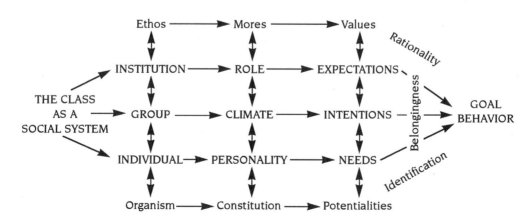

FIGURE 43.2.

CONFLICTS WITHIN AND BETWEEN ROLES. Conflicts within roles and role expectations may develop in a number of ways. Disagreement may arise within a reference group itself (e.g., where some English teachers emphasize form and style in students' writing, and others focus on content and meaning), presenting the supervisor with divergences of option that are not reconcilable. Mathematics teachers are presently in conflict over whether the priority teaching students to solve problems versus teaching computational skills. Research indicates that many mathematics teachers face considerable difficulty even comprehending teaching mathematics as a problem-solving format because they have been so socialized that mathematics is computation (Battista, 1994).

Conflicts between roles and role expectations are illustrated in the case of supervisors expected to trust staff and treat them as professionals in the face of many districts and states that mandate detailed supervisory procedures and expectations emphasizing high control. Both reference groups become caught in a mesh of conflicts that can seriously erode a trusting and cooperative relationship. Another illustration of this conflict is evidenced by role expectations that a principal, supervisor, and staff will work cooperatively, which is threatened by a highly controlling principal who views the school as his or her own turf.

The varied role expectations that individuals act out may conflict, with supervisors wanting to establish and maintain warm interpersonal relationships with their colleagues (i.e., the teachers). The superintendent may perceive supervisors to be members of an administrative team and, select them to represent the school district in a collective bargaining conference. This can become a clear role conflict in terms of teachers' perceptions.

SOCIAL SYSTEMS–CULTURE CONFLICT. An illustration of the culture conflicting with that of a social system occurs when a supervisor utilizes informal contacts in lounges, facilitating interactions with teachers in an easy, relaxed atmosphere. The culture of the school as a social system may have established separate lounges for men and women, automatically canceling some of the supervisor's opportunities for informal interactions. Another illustration of a social system–culture conflict occurs when the school establishes a smoking lounge and the supervisor is sensitive to smoke.

CONFLICT AMONG AND WITHIN SOCIAL SYSTEMS. Different reference groups/social systems may disagree on various issues. Principals feeling hard-pressed for time often want supervisors to evaluate teachers. Supervisors have historically been loath to do so, knowing that their relationships with teachers will be impaired.

Junior high school and high school coaches often feel separate from the faculty, particularly if they are hired as coaches and not as teachers. They are often reluctant to participate in meetings and in-service program. In contrast, principals, supervisors, and teachers favoring change generally want this social system to participate. This feeling is particularly exacerbated when junior high schools consider restructuring into middle schools, causing many coaches to fear losing their position as coaches (e.g., middle schools often move to intramural sports formats) and, therefore, of losing status.

PERSONALITY CONFLICTS. A series of difficulties predicted by the Guba–Getzels model involve personality conflicts (i.e., opposing need dispositions within the individual's personality). Some supervisors and administrators with a need to control find that they want to get the job done, assigning duties quickly to often reluctant staff, which is a process that elicits resentment. Still another aspect of the supervisors' and administrators' personality may press them to be caring, facilitative, and supportive, resulting in internal conflict within the individual.

Intrapersonality conflict can occur when new supervisors want to maintain and/or develop close, personal relationships between themselves and their teachers, and yet, also want to keep some social distance in the belief that familiarity reduces authority. Another example of this conflict can develop when stress is placed on an introverted supervisor to plan in-service workshops with teachers to prepare them for a new program; or to conduct meetings with parents to garner support for an innovation.

ROLE–PERSONALITY CONFLICTS. The last conflict anticipated by the model consists of conflicts between an individual's organizational roles and his or her personality needs. In such a conflict situation, the supervisor may want to be "one of the team", but his or her principal may want to initiate proceedings against a teacher with the supervisor's active and public participation as his role responsibility. A supervisor may have high needs for controlling his or her environment, yet the role expectations for his or her job may require a nonjudgmental Rogerian, or a democratic approach, a conflict that may cause considerable stress.

Summary of the Contribution of the Guba–Getzels Model The Guba–Getzels model, borrowed from educational administration, appears to provide considerable insight to a variety of supervisory areas. A theory or model specifically designed for instructional supervision as social process might produce insights and impact practice in similar or different ways.

Organizational Decision-making as Social Process

The second work to be cited for insights into supervision as social process consists of a construct of a theory/practice of organizational decision-making by Shapiro, et al (1993). It appears to bear considerable relevance to instructional supervision. Contending that decision-making in organizations is necessarily a *social enterprise*, the authors delineate a four-phase process of decision-making with the acronym, PINC. The PINC theory describes, analyzes, and predicts the essentially social processes involved in making decisions in both formal and informal organizations (see Figure 43.3).

The process follows:
"*Step #1: Sensing an issue, concern, need, situation, or problem—and developing a Plan.*" (Shapiro, et al, 1993, p. 453).

"The process of decision-making in organizations starts when one or more people [either in the organization or hovering about it] perceive or sense, [however vaguely], a discontinuity, or a problem, or a need, or a concern," (p. 453) or an issue or situation. This generally leads someone or several people into formulating some sort of a *plan*, however loosely perceived, to deal with whatever the person senses.

"*Step #2: Generating Interactions among people involved*" (p. 454).

The next step in making organizational decisions consists of this person or persons beginning to talk, to *interact* with others, getting key people together in the organization to deal with the concerns. The process of making organizational decisions occurs within an organization and is, therefore, a *social enterprise*. People and social systems begin to *interact* regarding the issue or concern. These interactions commence as people begin communicating their purposes and goals to define and solve a problem. Hidden issues often may arise at this time, such as power relations, gender equity, cynicism toward reform, and distrust of administrators.

"*Step #3: The process of Negotiating*" (p. 454).

"In the preceding second process, people interact to define their intentions, their purposes, their viewpoints, their interests, their hidden agendas, their institutional situations and limitations, and much more. As their interactions continue and ideas emerge, . . . a series of *negotiations* begin to emerge and develop" (p. 454). As potential lines of action or initiatives start to unfold, people *negotiate* various possibilities, various lines of action that they may prefer at the time.

"*Step #4: Consequences/outcomes*" (p. 455).

Some decisions are eventually made. In short, some *consequences* or outcomes develop from the *negotiations*.

As the agreed-upon consequences or lines of action are implemented, a new series of concerns develop from the consequences chosen. Thus, the PINC process recommences. The process is obviously cyclical, recurring again and again as the organizational decision-making process continues. In addition, the four processes may overlap, with people who are negotiating finding that they need more information about an issue, and then devising new plans to cope with the issue(s).

A case study may exemplify the process. Curriculum development may occur (Step 1) if individual teachers, supervisors, and/or administrators begin to sense a need and then to share, converting individual discontent into shared unrest (Blumer, 1951). The individual(s) who begin to share their dissatisfaction with this area of curriculum then develop a *plan* to do something about it. On the other hand, because many districts operate on a five-year curriculum revision cycle, that time may be nigh.

Proposals are floated to look at that area of curriculum, typically with a committee formed whose members *interact* (Step 2). Different interests begin to surface as divergent value sys-

tems emerge, leading people to *negotiate* their viewpoints (Step 3). For example, if the revision is in world history, some people may wish to include Asian history because about 50 percent of the world's population lives on that continent. This is discussed in various interactions, with negotiations taking place both within and outside the committee.

In the end, some *consequences* (Step 4) have to be reported to the administration which, in turn, may report to the board of education on the *outcomes* of the process. Asian history is perhaps included—or perhaps it is not. The organizational decision-making process is the focus.

Tripartite Theory of Organizational Change\

The third work on school supervision as social process to be examined in this section is a theory that focuses on supervision as the planning process. Wilson et al (1969) developed this third theory of supervision to be, sociologically based in nature. The theory essentially addresses four questions that relate to supervision in organizations.

1. Do organizations, like individuals, create a career, a pattern of phases through which they cycle in their life spans?
2. Why do organizations start with such great hope and at the end lose their sense of purpose and strength of vitality? Why do they run downhill, becoming entropic? Why do they decay?
3. What are the dynamics of these phases and process of organizational entropy?
4. How can organizations be sustained as viable, effective, and internally vigorous for more than a brief duration of months or years?

Stanton Leggett's Foreword expresses the case dramatically;

Two facts about the American way of life are apparent to even casual observers. First, Americans live their lives in a sea of formal organizations. Second, Americans truly believe themselves to be free men—they do not consider themselves slaves. Yet, if the authors of this work are correct, we are all enslaved by an apparently invariable cycle though which our organizations must pass.

This oppressive institutional cycle will prevail unless positive action is taken to alter its course. Sociology of Supervision presents an in-depth study of the basic theory that institutional change is predictable. It further states that such change can be consciously managed and directed (p. ix).

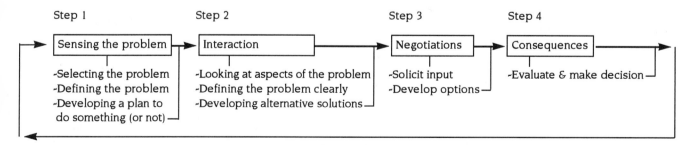

Step 1	Step 2	Step 3	Step 4
Sensing the problem	Interaction	Negotiations	Consequences
-Selecting the problem -Defining the problem -Developing a plan to do something (or not)	-Looking at aspects of the problem -Defining the problem clearly -Developing alternative solutions	-Solicit input -Develop options	-Evaluate & make decision

FIGURE 43.3. Steps in the decision-making process (generic)

In developing the first social theory of supervision, Wilson et al discovered empirically that organizations career uncontrollably through a life cycle of three phases. The theory attacks the question head-on as to why organizations, after productive and successful starts, inexorably slow down, become ossified, backward-looking, and cease being effective. At first glance, the Tripartite Theory of Organizational Power, Change, and Succession is basically a theory of organizational entropy (i.e., organizations, like physical systems in the universe, similarly are energy systems that slowly run downhill).

The book states that all organizations (e.g., individual schools, departments, school systems, colleges, businesses, hospitals, military units), like individuals, generate a career of phases though which they invariably move. The authors categorically predict the exact series of three phases with three accompanying leadership styles (plus a fourth synthesized style) through which organizations cycle in their careers.

Figure 43.4 diagrams the Tripartite Power Theory.

The succession of phases occurs in fixed rotational order as a result of internal struggles and progressive loss of purpose. Analysis of this three-phased process reveals that selecting the top executive in any organization unquestionably constitutes the most crucial decision any organization makes in its life cycle. Indeed, that decision creates the phase into which the organization remains or moves.

The theory noted that organizations typically languish, often for excruciatingly lengthy periods, in an unproductive phase during which red tape, rules and regulations, bureaucratic rituals and routines, and other restrictive phenomena are generated by people within the organization. The organization, in this position-oriented phase, is headed by a bureaucrat (e.g., Millard Fillmore, Calvin Coolidge, Neville Chamberlain). Because the bureaucrat focuses on order and efficiency rather than on effectiveness, he or she generally generates negative loyalty. Rather, loyalty is directed to the position (e.g., "Well, he's not much of a president, but we're loyal to the office of the presidency.") With little or no purpose in mind except survival, the organization lurches from crisis to crisis, with ceremonialism as a mainstay of function. The bureaucrat is more of a tinkerer (not even a mechanic). He or she stays *inside* the box and *builds* the box that encapsulates him or her. Most big-city school systems provide examples of the Position-Orientation Phase.

The organization can obviously neither prosper nor even survive for long with this defensive and purposeless strategy, particularly if the surrounding culture and/or environment is changing and dynamic. The superior administrator, or the board of directors, eventually perceive that the organization is plummeting toward disaster (i.e., that most institutional indicators are heading downhill). They remove the bureaucrat, and select a charismatic leader (e.g., John F. Kennedy, Lee Iacocca, Moses, Joan of Arc, Winston Churchill, John Dewey) to rejuvenate the organization, to develop a sense of purpose, and to galvanize it into action. The organization becomes oriented or attracted toward the charismatic leader (i.e., becomes Person-Oriented).

During this phase, vision is wide, action is often bold, and the organization is often caught up in a feeling of collective

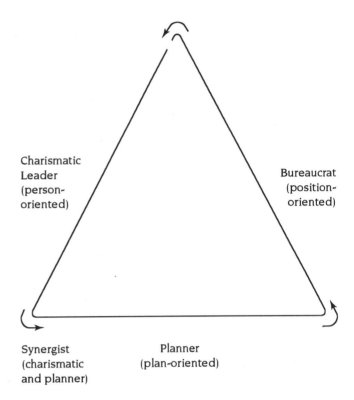

FIGURE 43.4. Phases of organizational change: Tripartite theory

excitement (Blumer, 1951). After a time, several possibilities unfold. Many members may begin to tire of the quick pace, the charismatic leader maybe recruited by a neighboring organization that perceives that it, too, is foundering and wants to rejuvenate into viability, or, the leader may be dismissed. The organization, anxious to maintain the leader's last ideas, recruits a planner to stabilize itself. People develop loyalty to the plan, hence Plan-Orientation, with all resources focusing on achieving the goals of the plan, as developed by the planner (e.g., Omar Bradley, Lee Iacocca, A. S. Neill), and, perhaps his or her team.

Several years later, however, the plan is becoming hazy, new personnel have entered who are not loyal to the plan because they did not participate in its development and job descriptions are generated defining (and limiting) expectations in order to achieve the plan. In short, red tape is generated to achieve the goals:routines develop, rules and regulations proliferate, purpose fades, and, slowly, the organization slides down the slippery slope into the Position-Oriented phase without the inhabitants being aware of their slow evolution into Position-Orientation.

A different leadership type characterizes each of the respective phases in the organization's career: charismatic, planner, and bureaucrat. Rarely, a fourth type of leader emerges who is both charismatic *and* a planner. This unique individual is called a synergist, a person who combines *both* the charismatic and the planning functions. Among synergists are Mao Tse Tung George Washington, Douglas MacArthur,

Golda Meier, B. Frank Brown, Robert Maynard Hutchins, and Lee Iacocca, and Ho Chi Minh.

A major contention of the Tripartite Theory of Organizational change for educational administration and for instructional supervision is that, in addition to other responsibilities, both constitute the planning function in organizations. Supervisors are expected to become involved in planning, a harbinger of functions and responsibilities delegated increasingly to the district by state authorities during the last decade.

Indeed, the planning function becomes a key responsibility of the position, inasmuch as the conceptual tools (together with change and planning strategies) are now available to move the organization into a more productive phase of its career (Person- or Plan-Orientation), rather than to languish for long periods of time in the unproductive, senescent, static Position-Oriented phase.

The overwhelming question raised by this theory is: How can internally-based structures and strategies be developed that keep an organization in a continual planning phase in its career, thus defeating the forces of entropy?

Supervision as a Social Function

Western societies generate several sociological institutions: the family, political, economic, educational, religious/spiritual, and health care and medicine. Some sociologists might add recreational institutions to this list. The educational institution generates a variety of functions, among which the instructional, administrative, and supervisory functions predominate. As Wilson et al (1969) indicated, the educational institution generated a supervisory function as early as the nineteenth century. Thus, the function of supervision appears to be deeply embedded into the woof and warp of education. Its purpose appears to shift depending upon the philosophy dominating the institution at the time Wilson (1969).

The Impact of Education's Social Functions on Supervisors

Institutions, and therefore organizations, mirror society's values. Because society's values become deeply ensconced in educational organizations, the social functions of education virtually and automatically carry out society's purposes and values in the educational process.

For some years, analysts have delved into the manifold social functions of education (i.e., socialization of students, social sorting, filling time, failing students). It is interesting that virtually all of these efforts have focused on the impact of the social functions on students. Education's social functions, however, also have enormous impact on instructional supervisors and school administrators as well as and on parents, the community, and the nation. Shapiro described the process in a paper titled, "Looking at the 'Oil Can' from the Outside: The Supervisor as Greek Chorus" (1994).

Supervisors, like all human beings, want to be accepted. To achieve this end in most organizations, the individual tends to go along to get along. He or she may endure persistent institutional practices about which educational research has raised serious question (retention, ability grouping, tracking) in order to become accepted.

VanMaanen and Schein (1979) point to three choices for people entering an organization and assuming a defined position and role (such as teacher, supervisor, or administrator in education). The first choice is that of custodianship, where the new role incumbent learns the substantive expectations of a position in a social system, and the strategies customarily utilized to achieve those expectations. This response comprises essentially a caretaker assumption toward role expectations. In this strategy, the new supervisor would not question the beliefs and practices of the people in the organization. Maslow's (1970) second and third levels of motivations, safety and meeting social needs, (focused on achieving acceptance within the school as an organization), operate strongly.

VanMaanen and Schein note a second option to socializing pressures for newcomers entering organizations content innovation, in which alternative strategies are selected instead of continuing present practices. In this option, changes or improvements are made in the knowledge base or strategic practices of the role. The newcomer does not accept unthinkingly all the norms, customs, practices, expectations, beliefs, and myths of those in the school's social systems.

The third option for new comers consists of role innovation, in which the incumbent of the position redefines the role by changing its purpose and focus. Van Maanen and Schein point out ". . . a genuine attempt is made by the role holder to redefine the ends to which the role functions" (pp. 3–4).

The preceding provides a theoretical framework whereby new and veteran supervisors (as well as administrators and teachers) may make rational choices regarding strategies in defining their roles and functions. With these insights, they may examine which strategy will produce optimal outcomes for the organization, teachers, students, and/or themselves.

Cooptation comprises a powerful force/process to socialize role incumbents into behavior desired by power holders in key social systems, which is behavior that usually supports the status quo. Many supervisors simply buy into the "box" of the system that defines their function. Shapiro pointed to an alternative role for supervisors: organizational trouble shooter instead of ratifier of the status quo to gain acceptance and belong.

Supervision as a Behavior System

Analyzing supervision as a behavior system can provide valuable and divergent insights. Hazi raised the question of the knowledge that would be generated if supervision was viewed from a mental health perspective (personal communication, November 7, 1993). Treating supervision as a social enterprise rather than as the behavior of individual supervisors facilitating individual teachers provides one key.

Barnard (1938) provided another, asserting that, to survive and prosper, any organization (or social enterprise) must develop a common purpose, a system of communication to ensure support of the purpose, and, a system of cooperation to achieve the purpose. All constitute indispensable elements of an organization. To achieve the purpose, supervisors need to develop a master plan that the great majority of participants support, and then supervisors need to implement the plan.

While this constitutes a tall order, the problem is both survival as well as growth in effectiveness and efficacy for instructional supervision. School supervisors, in concert with our culture's premier value (i.e., individualism) perceive themselves as lone individuals struggling uphill against great odds to improve instruction. Becoming members of a social enterprise changes such views greatly.

As a social function of education, supervision obviously has a core of behaviors that most practitioners utilize in their professional practice. Duncan Waite's "Instructional Supervisor as Cultural Guide" (1990) speaks to this issue by acknowledging the existence of a "supervisory culture." Approaching this from the perspective of an ethnographic or anthropological viewpoint, Waite conducted an in-depth analysis of a number of articles on supervision, concentrating on the relationship between novice teachers and supervisors. He perceived the interaction as a socialization process. Supervision from this standpoint therefore constitutes an enculturation.

Lipton and Starratt (1989) focused on the moral climate of schools, which is obviously an aspect of the culture of supervision. Their studies pointed to the contribution supervisors made to the culture of the school when they did not manipulate teachers, when they took responsibility for their mistakes, and when they were authentic and candid. These behaviors generated trust among staff members and helped them grow.

Every culture, and within it every profession, generates its own language. Blumberg (1986) studied the language of supervision from the mid-1800s to the present and found that whereas the basic problems appear to have remained the same, the language changed to mirror the society's larger social trends. Other facets of supervision as a behavior system appear in later sections of this chapter on culture, organizational culture, and organizational climate.

One phenomenon clouding ease of decision-making consists of the multiplicity of purposes involved in education. Indeed, Phi Delta Kappan's Commission on Educational Planning published a list of 18 different goals some years ago. Benjamin (personal communication, March 1, 1992) termed this "goal ambiguity," which obviously provides both intriguing difficulties and advantages for those attracted by challenge.

SOCIAL DIMENSIONS

Culture and Cultural Trends

The culture concept (that "all the learned customs, beliefs, values, knowledge, artifacts, and symbols that are constantly communicated among a set of people who share a common way of life (Light, Keller, & Calhoun, 1989) constitutes a fundamental construct in sociology and the social sciences. Every individual lives and swims in the all-enveloping cultural ocean of customs, norms, practices, beliefs, symbols, and artifacts that guide virtually all actions (except reflex responses), and about which the individual tends to be unaware. Individuals live, feel, believe, taste, and think as the culture

focuses us, and like the water we drink, neither taste it nor are aware of it. Culture consequently has an enormous impact upon instructional supervision and upon supervisors. It totally determines whether they exist and how they function. In a simpler culture, where teaching consists of informal processes within the family, formal educational institutions do not exist. The establishment of such positions and roles as teacher or supervisor is available. Parents and authority figures *are* the teachers and supervisors. Culture, therefore, literally determines *whether* positions and roles will be generated, and *how* they will be played.

In short, supervision is the child of the culture. Thus, in the nineteenth and early part of the twentieth century, supervision was authoritarian, as the culture dictated. With the rise of Scientific Management, a rationale for authoritarianism was promulgated, in which supervision became associated with high control and with time and motion studies.

Reflecting a change in thinking about organizational culture, the next administrative and supervisory philosophy to appear was that of Human Relations. This school of thought, starting in the late 1940s, influenced some organizations to reconstruct their supervisory practices. As the Human Relations movement played out, the next major approach was based on the behavioral sciences. The *behavior* of role incumbents and of others was analyzed, as illustrated in the Leader Behavior Description Questionnaire (LBDQ) developed by Halpin and others at The Ohio State University.

Every fad and fashion (e.g., MBO, Zero-Based Budgeting, OBE, and TQM) convinces, some supervisors to practice the new school of thought, although some of the basic approaches, such as Scientific Management (a la Theory X), persist in the majority of schools and organizations in the American culture. As noted earlier, supervisory practices tend to follow the dominant philosophy of the organization, and/or of the profession, and certainly of the culture.

A later section addresses organizational culture, climate, and other relevant phenomena that directly impinge upon supervision and supervisors.

Socioeconomic Class Stratification

Like culture, socioeconomic classes (thereby implying stratification) seem to abound in Western and many other societies. Depending upon the researcher, various formulations of classes have been constructed since Marx; their commonality consists of people perceiving that social classes acquire differential amounts of social status or prestige, economic status or wealth, and political status or power (Light et al, 1989). The implication of this for education and for supervisors is self-evident. Various social classes are treated differently in schools, and often attend different schools because they live in different communities. A great deal of literature has explored the disparate phenomena involved in differential treatment of students from varying socioeconomic classes, including Kozol's *Savage Inequalities* (1991), The Annie E. Casey Foundation's *Kids Count Data Book* (1994), Oakes' work on tracking (1986), Gray's *Why We Will Lose: Taylorism in America's High Schools* (1993), and Howard's *There May Be No Fair Play in American Rigged Schools*, (1989).

The "Oil Can" article previously cited refers to the dilemma faced by supervisors, teachers, administrators, and school board members because, they tend to support discriminatory practices (e.g., tracking, ability grouping, retention, and others) that exploit the lower socioeconomic classes. The "Oil Can" calls for supervisors to "do no harm," a challenge that many may not like or accept because it questions the comfortable status quo, and urges them to move into new territories.

Social Psychological Perspectives

The supervisor, sociologically speaking, is a position or status in the social structure. Other positions generated by educational institutions are principal, student, teacher, superintendent, school board member, and the like. Roles consist of the way the position is carried out (i.e., how a set of expected behaviors, attitudes, obligations, and privileges are acted out). As Linton (1936) observed, we occupy a status, but play a role. Each role has a series of expectations attached to it, which individuals learn though interaction, and which sociologists consider the socialization process.

As Katz and Kahn (1978) noted: "The idea of role as a set of expected activities associated with the occupancy of a given position assumes substantial agreement among the relevant people as to what those activities are" (p. 200). Sociologists further point out that communications are sent and received from role-incuments, leading Katz and Kahn to state:"In an organizational society, people acquire a kind of general expertise in the taking of organizational roles" (p. 202).

Role conflict was discussed in the earlier section dealing with the contributions of the Guba–Getzels model in predicting sources of conflict in organizations. Culture-role conflict was discussed, as were conflicts within and between roles, role-personality conflict, and others. Katz and Kahn "define role conflict as the simultaneous occurrence of two or more role expectations such that compliance with one would make compliance with the other more difficult" (p. 204), and then identify different sources of role conflict.

Benne and Sheats (1948) further analyzed roles into three sets of role functions, a construct that proved extremely useful in working with groups. The three include group task roles (i.e., initiator-contributor, information seeker, and recorder), group building and maintenance roles (i.e., encourager, gate-keeper, and harmonizer), and the idiosyncratic need-meeting roles of individuals (i.e., blocker, dominator, and self-confessor). Cook (1982) utilized the role concept in a program to improve supervisory behavior by clarifying the roles of teachers and of supervisors.

Individuals obviously have the latitude to act out each role differently. One can be a dominating supervisor, or a compassionate supervisor. A principal can welcome a supervisor as a major resource (i.e., provided the role incumbent has the skills and insights to be such an asset), or he or she can feel threatened by the supervisor. The principal can treat the supervisor as a colleague or as an intruder, as a ally to be involved in decision-making or as a enemy to be excluded from "school" territory. The "Oil Can" statement pointed to a supervisory role as a change agent. Wilson et al (1969) proposed that supervisors become organizational or institutional planners. However, the

supervisor, decides to play his or her role, the consequences become enormous.

Gender, Race, Ethnicity

A comparison of gender, racial, composition, and, to a lesser extent, ethnicity in regard to role expectations and participation from 1900 to the present in American society reveals enormous changes that will continue well into the next century. The impact on education and on the role of the school supervisor can hardly be exaggerated. Changes in attitudes concerning fair and equitable treatment both in the culture and in legal codes have made transformations in educational beliefs and practices. Previously, separate school systems have merged. African-Americans have moved into supervisory and other leadership posts in substantial numbers.

Gender and ethnic walls have been penetrated to some extent. For example, an increasing number of women have become high school principals (e.g., the author met the only female high school principal in Indiana in the late 1970s). Formerly excluded ethnic groups have increasingly attained supervisory and administrative roles.

However, the egalitarian ideal of the Declaration of Independence, which is the centerpiece of the three-and-one-half century Human Rights Movement remains to be achieved. Blumer (1951), a developer of elementary collective behavior, noted that general social movements proceed by fits and starts. At times a movement sometimes lurches forward, and at other times stumbles backward a step. "Progress" never occurs in a straight line. This is obviously the American experience with race, gender, and ethnicity.

At the present time, some retrogression with ethnicity is occurring illustrated an actual call for excluding an ethnic minority (i.e., Hispanics) from public schools in California. Indeed, Americans, a xenophobic nation of immigrants, tend to discriminate against immigrants, believing that they absorb too much social and financial capital. This contrasts with the reception immigrants receive in Israel, where the national population increased more than 30 percent in the first third of the 1990s. Americans express concern about a 0.4 percent annual increase. Indeed, careful studies (Shapiro, 1993) point out that immigrants are an advantage to the nation because schooling occurs in the immigrants' native country, and as adults they generally do not use social welfare and retirement benefits to which they contribute and become entitled.

Organizational Factors/Phenomena

Organizational theory, social systems (or group) theory, and cyclical organizational phenomena and personality factors are examined in this section.

Organizational Theory, Issues, and Processes As is self-evident, the milieu in which the school supervisor functions is an organization. It becomes essential, therefore, that supervisors study organizations, and become able to describe, analyze, and predict how people behave and social systems operate in organizations so that they can be more effective and efficient. Thus, the vast literature on organizations provides a cornucopian bonanza for the supervisor interested in self- and organizational improvement.

Organizational theory includes work on bureaucracy, varying theories of administration (e.g., X and Y, Z), decision-making, systems theory, role theory, social systems theory, leadership theory, motivational theory, theories of organizational change, culture, climate, and other areas. Organizational processes include acceptance, rejection, competition, hostility, cooperation, trust and distrust, and a number of other processes. Mintzburg (1979) viewed organizations as energy systems characterized by five flows. These include a system of formal authority, regulated (work) flows, informal communication, work constellations, and ad hoc decision processes (p. 35). Open systems (1) allow energy to flow, (2) become self-organizing to some extent, (3) generate quality circles, (4) are more dynamic and flexible, and (5) can evolve to meet individual and organizational needs. Fabun (1967) developed the concept of *The Corporation as a Creative Environment*, stating that organizations are energy systems. This offers an intriguing approach to working creatively with organizations. Weick's (1982) notion of the loosely-coupled organization is important for effective supervisory function. These constructs support organizational diversity within purpose, rather than the normal organizational thrust to weed out divergence by forcing everyone and every suborganization to look alike.

In addition, people and social systems in organizations create positions, roles, and subcultures. The supervisor who is aware of these and can utilize the preceding information effectively in his or her professional practice has a considerable advantage over one who is oblivious to this immense field of knowledge.

Earlier, a major role proposal called for supervisors to become change agents. It is difficult to imagine how anyone could move effectively into such a role without developing a clear grasp of effective change strategies (Bennis, Benne, & Chin, 1969; Lewin, 1952; Van Meter, 1980) and learning to employ them selectively in professional practice.

Deming (1982) generated considerable insight (and controversy) into administration and supervision by his approach. Changing the usual American practice of blaming problems on the lowest levels of the hierarchy (e.g., workers or teachers) he asserted that inasmuch as management is responsible for 85 percent of all quality problems, management has to take the lead in changing the systems and processes that created those problems. In short, the *system* created the problem, not the worker.

Social Systems Theory Any worthwhile supervisor must be aware of key social systems or groups (i.e., any two or more people in meaningful relationship) in any organization. Many case studies have been written witnessing the implosion of unwary or unwitting supervisors and administrators who failed to grasp key components of their organizations (Kowalski, 1991; Sergiovanni et al, 1992). To impact and influence, supervisors must become intimately cognizant of key social systems, core beliefs of the organization's culture, patterns of influence, and prestige.

The importance of recognizing the vital influence social systems/groups play in human affairs, human development, and organizations cannot be overstated. Ross (1993) cites Turner (1988, p. 66) for the following: "In group identification is an adaptive social-cognitive process that makes such prosocial relations as social cohesion, cooperation, and influence possible." He further asserted:

Groups are the central mechanism for providing individuals with their identity; rather than holding that individuals "sacrifice" part of their identity when they are part of a group, the perspective adopted here sees positive individual identity as possible only in the context of secure group attachments. . . . expulsion or exclusion from the group and its activities is terrifying, not only because of the physical threat to individual security but because the emotional separation is intolerable. The notion of the individual apart from the group is a product of western thought, not of the general human experience (p. 19).

Hamilton (1983) utilized social systems theory in research on school and classroom ecology. He noted that "marked differences in student behavior and school climate can be attributed to the beliefs and practices of teachers and administrators and the ways in which they interact to form a social system."

Anyone interested in organizational impact has to become aware of major external systems impinging on the organizations and social systems in which he or she is functioning, or else that individual is operating blindly.

Cyclical Organizational Phenomena In an earlier section, supervision was portrayed through the lens of the planning function. As such, the Tripartite Theory was briefly presented (Wilson et al, 1969). Two other theories of cyclical organizational change provide differing perspectives and insights for use in professional practice. Levin and Simon (1974) of the Ontario Institute for the Study of Education (OISE) proposed a cycle of seven phases that they induced from analyzing the development of new educational settings in elementary schools. The seven phases, in order, comprise (1) getting together to define the mission, (2) defining and obtaining support for the setting, (3) planning and assembling the setting, (4) getting started, (5) looking back and ahead: post-launching assessment, (6) starting again: stabilizing the setting, (7) looking ahead to the next year. Levin and Simon's time cycle consisted of one school year in contrast with the decade(s)-long focus of the Tripartite Theory.

Bernstein (1965) and his colleagues developed a model from a social group work perspective. Its five stages of development were based upon observations of formed clubs of youngsters, aged 9 to 16. The steps, which provide implications for supervisors, consist of (1) preaffiliation, (2) power and control, (3) intimacy, (4) differentiation, and (5) separation.

Organizational cycles provide considerable data to improve supervisory functioning because knowledge of literature can enable the astute supervisor to analyze the phase in which the school or district currently resides and to shape his or her behavior to meet the norms and assumptions operating. The supervisor may be able to predict the next phase down a cycle's road, to decide whether to support that phase, or to work to maintain the present phase. Such knowledge enables supervisors to function more effectively and efficiently. More effort to develop alternative models and theories might prove useful.

Personality Factors Personality factors seem to relate to supervisory and administrative behavior in organizations. The Myers–Briggs Type Indicator (MBTI) identifies many administrators and supervisors in a wide variety of fields who tend to cluster in several personality "types." For example, the ISTJ (introvert, sensor, thinking, judger) style and ESTJ (extravert, sensor, thinking, judger) style together comprised 25.68 percent of elementary and secondary school administrators (Myers & McCaulley, 1985, p. 139).

Does one kind of personality tend to become a Theory *X* supervisor, while another leans more toward Theory *Y*, and still another toward Ouchi's (1981) Theory *Z*? These present fruitful areas to explore. One dissertation (Kurtin, 1993) employed the MBTI to determine the relationship with the State of Florida Council on Educational Management administrator competencies (Crogan, Lake, & Schroder, 1983). Kurtin discovered:

educational administrators with Extraverted personality types scored significantly higher than administrators with Introverted types on Group ratings of Concept Formation, Self Confidence, Organizational Ability, Management Control, and Delegation. Educational administrators with Feeling personality types scored significantly higher than administrators with Thinking types on the Overall rating of Interpersonal Search, Presentation, and Achievement Orientation (pp. xi–xii).

Gregorc's (1982) Personality Style Delineator provides a quicker approach to diagnosing personality styles. His four styles (i.e., Concrete Sequential, Abstract Sequential, Abstract Random, and Concrete Random) can be utilized to diagnose personality, and then to develop appropriate lines of action to interact positively with each style, this provides a useful tool for the supervisor.

This area of research proffers a fertile field to cultivate, particularly in exploring the relationships of organizational factors, leadership style, and personality among supervisors and administrators. With such knowledge, supervisors may be able to work more effectively and efficiently by recognizing the research-based relationship between personality and leader style and the impact on organizational culture and climate. In addition, those who take such instruments generally begin to accept and respect personality styles that differ from their own, enabling them to work more successfully with a greater variety of people.

Social Functions of Schooling and Supervision

Social functions of schooling and supervision, as well as at their primary and secondary functions, merit consideration.

Schools exist in society to do more than teach concepts, skills, and attitudes to eager recipients, and to "transfer from one generation to the next of society's beliefs, values, sentiments, knowledge, and patterns of behavior" (Parelius & Parelius, 1978, p. 23). In addition to cultural reproduction, schools have other functions, some manifest and some murky, some magnificent and some mean, some constructive and some destructive. Parelius and Parelius pointed to the following social functions: social control through socialization, assimilating minority groups, developing patriotic citizens,

training competent workers, "selection and allocation of individuals for various positions in society" (p. 27), and supporting selected social change.

The rest of this section, based on work by Shapiro et al (1995), briefly explores the social functions of supervision to alert educational personnel to their existence and purposes, suggesting to supervisors and others that their professional responsibility is to question these practices.

Socialization Schools socialize students. They teach students how to behave, and to think the way the culture directs. Students learn many of the keys of their culture in schools, such as how to work together, how to share, how to take responsibility, how to eat lunch very fast, and when to raise a hand to ask a question or to go to the lavatory. They learn appropriate sophisticated behavior for a preteen and for a teen, such as what style of shoes to wear at various occasions or what girls are expected to do and what boys are expected to do. In short, students learn in schools the expectations of their and others' roles.

Schools also socialize teachers, supervisors, administrators, custodians, board members, parents, and legislators, to name a few. Parents rapidly learn that their teen-age-youngsters do not welcome their presence in high school. Supervisors quickly learn that they are perceived as having power when they know that they do not. New teachers quickly learn that secretaries and custodians are key players in getting things done. Principals eventually learn that secretaries know everything going on and can make or break them.

Schools socialize all of the children and huge segments of society simultaneously. *How* they socialize students and the rest of us constitutes the focus in analyzing the social functions of schooling and supervision.

Social Sorting An egalitarian society in which socioeconomic classes did not exist would not develop institutions and schools which would sort people, including children, by their place in the social structure. Ours, of course, has developed such a structure. Consequently, the schools typically provide social sorting mechanisms—unless they take major corrective action to eliminate this practice (Shapiro et al, 1994, pp. 72–73).

The vehicles carrying out this social function are ability grouping and tracking (Esposito, 1971; Goldberg, 1963; Oakes, 1986).

If anyone wanted to design a process to separate the socioeconomic classes, then that person could hardly generate better mechanisms than ability grouping and tracking. Upper middle class children enter school with considerable advantages over their lower socioeconomic classmates, and proceed to accelerate further through the grades. Howard (1989) observed that schools are rigged nine ways to produce winners and losers, including graded schools where unsuccessful pupils are retained, standardized testing programs, special courses for "less worthy" pupils, and others. According to Howard (1989), it is:

the letter grading system which forces teachers to communicate messages of unworthiness and failure to pupils on a regular basis, grouping and ranking practices which continuously remind our least successful pupils that the school thinks some pupils are better than they are, (p. 3),

Gray (1993) pointed to the elitism basic and endemic to our schools in his article, "Why We Will Lose: Taylorism in America's High Schools." The "Oil Can" concept earlier in this chapter deals with the responsibility of supervisors in this matter, recommending forcefully that they not buy into prevailing practices.

Failure Benjamin (Shapiro et al, 1994) analyzed education's use of the law of supply and demand to amplify the prestige of the high school diploma. Because scarcity produces greater value, he zeroed in on the widespread use of failure that enhances the diploma's value. If everyone who entered high school received a diploma, it would have virtually no worth. Use of failure consequently raises its prestige. New York State developed a Regent's Diploma for the more academically able, and one of considerably lesser prestige for other students unable to pass Regent's examination' standards.

Supervisors who support retention might wish to examine the human wreckage in its selective wake (Smith & Shepard, 1994). Two thirds of those retained once drop out of school. Over 95 percent of those failed twice never walk across the stage to receive a diploma. Citing the Annie E. Casey Foundation's *Kids Count Data Book* (1994), Raspberry (1994), asserted:

A recent study compared two groups of Americans: those who finished high school, got married, and reached age 20 before having their first child, and those who did none of these three things. Of the children in the first group, only 8 percent were living in poverty in 1992. In the second, the poverty rate was 79 percent (Sarasota Herald-Tribune, March 3, 1994).

Many caring, concerned teachers consign their children to this life of poverty under the mistaken assumption that retention will help them do better. Indeed, for almost a century research has clearly indicated the exact opposite, still the practice continues, and the human destruction continues.

Warehousing/Storing Students The author served as assistant superintendent in a district that developed an open high school. A major concern expressed at the daily morning coffee klatches held for small groups of parents was anxiety over where their adolescents were when they had no assigned classes. The school, which was a modified version of the model developed by J. Lloyd Trump eliminated study halls. Parents were relieved when they visited the huge instructional learning center and the large number of laboratories where students could work, study, and be gainfully occupied. They greeted the dawn-to-dusk availability of the cafeteria where their youngsters could socialize and work with each other and with teachers and counselors with considerably less joy because parents were uncomfortable with unstructured time.

Filling Time When the British extended the years of compulsory schooling after World War II, many secondary school teachers panicked over how they could fill students' time (based on the assumption that time must be filled or the ruffians could get out of hand). Schools obviously fill time for students, and for teachers. Indeed, when viewed objectively, teachers are as much prisoners of their schedules as students. Secondary school teachers teach five or six periods daily, and they must meet their classes.

Acquire Knowledge, Skills, and Attitudes/Values Parents and society expect students to learn a large number of ideas or concepts in their journey through school. Arithmetic concepts scientific ideas, historical facts, literary classics, geographic, data, and a host of other knowledge are perceived as required outcomes (Hirsch, 1988).

Students are similarly expected to learn a large number of skills. They are expected to be able to perform the four arithmetic processes proficiently. Controversy has developed in teaching mathematics, with many preferring students to solve mathematical problems, rather than to memorize computational skills. The research unfortunately indicates that many mathematics teachers have difficulty solving such problems themselves and that, as a consequence, cannot teach problem solving (Battista, 1994). The schools are also, expected to teach scientific techniques, map reading, and many others skills. Schools have been attempting to teach critical thinking skills for several decades, with questionable results.

The controversy over teaching values has obfuscated the self-evident nature of schooling and the learning process. Teachers serve as role models for many students who basically introject their instructor's value systems. Teachers and schools stand for honesty, integrity, responsibility, and concern. The most zealous protester against teaching values would hardly argue that schools should abandon teaching children not to cheat, not to plagiarize, not to do homework, not to forge parents' names, and not to disrespect authority.

Schools inculcate large numbers of attitudes and values in youngsters through experience. Indeed, the Commission on the Reorganization of Secondary Education (1918) established "civic participation" as one of "the seven cardinal principles of secondary education." The aim was to create adults who embraced citizenship values, such as voting and participating in the democratic process, certainly an intention to develop values and attitudes in the population, which still occurs without controversy in ninth grade Civics courses. Although the purpose and the course were created in 1918, its widespread use in one form or another endures.

Primary and Secondary Functions Primary and secondary functions of education can be attacked in a number of ways. In one view, Orlosky (personal communication, June 22, 1994) noted that the transmission of knowledge could be considered primary. Most other functions discussed earlier (i.e., social control, socializing, social sorting, warehousing, filling time) would be secondary. They hardly comprise goals toward which superintendents point with pride in their commencement addresses. In the tertiary function would be development of character, values, and the modeling impact of teachers upon students.

Other secondary functions appear to include developing constructive interpersonal relationships, interacting with the community, learning cooperative behavior, learning to share, and developing appropriate attitudes to become employable.

In summary, the preceding social functions, some manifest and some hidden, provide opportunity and challenge for school supervisors to alter their own roles and functions.

Cultural Factors of Schooling and Supervision

The next area for consideration as a social dimensions of supervision consists of the key factors of culture and their impact on school supervisors, including general cultural factors, organizational culture and climate, anti-intellectualism, faddism and bandwagoning, cooperation versus competition, and divergent models of supervision.

General Cultural Factors Culture has been defined as "all the learned customs, beliefs, values, knowledge, artifact, and symbols that are constantly communicated among a set of people who share a common way of life" (Light, Keller, & Calhoun, 1989). The general culture within which individuals live has generated a considerable number of factors impacting schools and making demands upon education. For example, all children are required to attend school, although states may vary the starting age. The distances people live from schools caused by American land usage patterns leads to establishing school boundaries. Most boards of education provide transportation to students living more than a specified distance from the school. Indeed, few other nations have developed a structure featuring district school boards as the ultimate governing body, most of which are locally elected.

The American culture's main thrust focuses on the individual, not on the group, the organization, the culture, or the system. The price paid for *malfunctioning systems* includes problems with *individuals*; therefore, blame is directed to those at the lowest levels (e.g., workers or teachers). The emphasis of supervision in America is to work with the particular worker or teacher, usually the new, the marginal, and the inadequate. (The subtlety and power of cultural messages was discussed earlier in the experiments of Stevenson and Stigler [1993] in terms of a culture's emphasis on persistence or talent). A subsequent section on reform efforts cites more from Deming (1982) on this matter.

Organizational Culture in American Education In the early 1980s, literature dealing with organizational culture (Deal & Kennedy, 1982; Ouchi, 1981; Peters & Waterman, 1982) sprang into prominence. Robert Owens (1991) quoted Edgar Schein (1985, pp. 19–20), who defined organizational culture as "the body of solutions to external and internal problems that has worked consistently for a group and that is therefore taught to new members as the correct way to perceive, think about, and feel in relation to those problems" (Owens, p. 171). Each organization generates its subculture over time (i.e., its norms and assumptions guiding each person's behavior). Proof of this is glaringly evident when comparing different organizations. The United States Marine Corps generates its own organizational culture, distinct from that of the Coast Guard, and certainly vastly dissimilar from that of a nursery school. The latter is considerably divergent from the subculture of a high school (e.g., no football games, no cheerleaders, no pep assemblies, no National Honor Society, no dances, no clubs, no lectures; instead, daily naps, snacks, play on the floors).

CBS's subculture diverges from that of NBC and both from CNN, and they all differ from that of a professional football team. The Catholic Church has generated its own overall culture, yet every nation's church is dissimilar from that of other countries. In addition, a place of worship differs in its culture, whether Quaker Meeting, Jewish synagogue, or a Muslim mosque.

The organizational culture comprises what members believe the organization is all about. It is essentially an agreed-upon cluster of norms, practices, beliefs, myths, and assumptions of the group, system, or organization. In short, it is a constructed reality (Berger, 1966). Some might consider it a group fantasy.

Practitioners effectively shear new teachers, supervisors, and administrators from their school-derived knowledge as they indoctrinate (i.e., socialize) them into the organizational culture (e.g., "Forget the theory you learned in school; this is the real, the practical world").

It is interesting that the culture of the organization shapes the organization, and the organization shapes its own organizational culture. In addition, the culture changes, sometimes slowly, and at other times rapidly. The Catholic Church of 1994 certainly differs from its predecessor in the 1950s, before Pope John XXIII altered the culture.

Zamanou and Glaser (1989) utilized an Organizational Culture Scale (OCS) to provide quantitative data in teamwork/conflict, supervision, involvement, climate/morale, and meetings over a two-year period with a governmental organization. Researchers found that communications skills training for the entire organization, involvement in decision-making, and establishing task force teams exerted the greatest impact on the organizational culture.

Organizational Cycles As organizations move through the phases of their cycles, the organizational culture changes. If one uses the Tripartite Theory (Wilson et al, 1969), an organization in its more senescent phase (Position-Orientation) is vastly different in energy levels and in enterprising efforts than one in Person-Orientation with a charismatic leader. The former organization would be characterized by caution, limited vision, little planning, conservatism, and generally high control from the top. Punishment is often meted out to those having the temerity to develop independent initiatives and to those perceived as disloyal to top levels. The external environment is often viewed suspiciously, development of turfs is rampant, and considerable energy is spent protecting territories from insiders perceived as competitors.

The organization in the Person-Orientation phase with its attraction to the charismatic leader supports initiative, even entrepreneurship, and generates many enterprises or actions, which are often uncoordinated, that may occur simultaneously. High support and reward for enterprise usually become a norm embedded in the organizational culture, which is generally not punitive and controlling. Its vision and sense of mission usually become expansive. The organization often abounds with excitement and ferment. Interaction among people within and outside the organization is supported and rewarded, ideas are tried out, and the leader is visible and dynamic. The contrast between the two leaders and the organizational subcultures is typically obvious.

The Position-Oriented leader (i.e., termed the *bureaucrat*) obviously lacks dynamism and charisma, does not facilitate, and is usually low on trust. The cultures develop in radically different directions. These differences provide enormous implications for the supervisor in his or her functioning within each organization.

Organizational Climate Using a term developed by Argyris (1958), Halpin and Croft (1963) generated the Organizational Climate Description Questionnaire (OCDQ). They constructed the OCDQ because it

permits us to portray the "Organizational Climate" of an elementary school. The Organizational Climate can be construed as the organizational "personality" of a school; figuratively, "personality" is to the individual what "climate" is to the organization (Halpin & Croft, p. 1).

The authors discovered six organizational climates using their procedures (i.e., Open, Autonomous, Controlled, Familiar, Paternal, and Closed) with four teacher and four principal behaviors characterizing each climate. The behaviors contrasted most between the Closed and Open climates, leading the authors to favor the Open over the Closed.

Other researchers approached climate somewhat differently, generating dissimilar results. Stern and Steinhoff (1958) developed the Organizational Climate Index (OCI), which produced divergent dimensions from those of Halpin and Croft (e.g., development press and control/task effectiveness press).

Owens (1991, p. 175) defined organizational climate as "the study of *perceptions* that individuals have of the environment in the organization." By this definition, Owens perceived the climate as the *individual's* perception of the organizational culture surrounding and embracing him or her.

Kennebrew and Sistrunk (1989) utilized an instrument modeled on the Ohio State Leader Behavior Description Questionnaire (LBDQ). Called the Supervisory Behavior Description Questionnaire (SBDQ) and the School Climate Survey (SCS), these questionnaires zeroed in on the principal's supervisory behavior with relationship to climate. When principals behaved collaboratively, positive results were obtained in contrast with directive supervisory behavior in such areas as curriculum and staff development, instructional organization, and program evaluation.

To summarize, the constructs of organizational climate and culture have considerable power for diagnosing crucial components of organizations. Inquiring into the nature of the norms and assumptions of any organization and the varied constructs used in different climate instruments provides supervisors and others remarkable insights into the way people in organizations behave, and how to work effectively with them.

Examples/Applications for Instructional Supervision Attitudes toward in-service programs in schools are heavily influenced by prevailing cultural norms and organizational assumptions, as well as the organizational climates generated. Faculties, including administrators, typically view in-service programs as boring, trivial, and inconsequential to them and to their professional practice. In-service is too often delivered in a lecture/telling format, despite widespread knowledge that involvement produces more impact. Those feeling the most social distance from the main body of the faculty, often coaches and administrators, therefore literally tend to distance themselves at in-service programs, usually sitting as far back in the room as possible. Principals most frequently do not attend, with excuses that they are too busy or that they do not need this particular in-service assistance, thereby devaluing both the in program and themselves.

Antiintellectualism and Antitheoreticalism

American antiintellectualism and antitheoretical biases (Parrington, 1927) strongly infect the schools and, therefore, supervisors and supervision. New teachers are invariably told by their veteran colleagues, to disregard theory and they often do. The result is that the profession takes relatively clear research findings either with a grain of salt, or ignores results completely. Thus, most teachers and administrators persevere with such practices as ability grouping, tracking, retaining children, graded schools, and so on.

These twin currents in American thought play out interestingly with administrators. Most people typically enter graduate programs for administration and supervision without the slightest idea that a theoretical base is enormously useful for educators, although recognizing that it is indispensable for physicians. As a consequence, they tend to go through a ritual dance (e.g., Bradshaw [1988] called it "a hypnotic trance" p. 36) in their courses, dutifully memorizing, but unaware of, the usefulness of theories to professional practice. When they become administrators, therefore, "they often do not have a clue about what they are doing and how they affect teachers and kids" (Armstrong, personal communication, 1993).

Armstrong, after researching administrator behavior, commented on large numbers of principals who simply have no idea that they have embraced Theory X in their behavior, with control and power as major motivations. As a result, they are unable to see the consequences of their behavior on teachers, students, parents, and on the education process itself.

The twin themes of antiintellectualism and antitheoreticalism play out in schools into suspicion or rejection of universities and colleges and thus of their potential contribution of resources, services, and ideas. As noted earlier, in-service programs are is similarly disdained.

Fads, Fashions, and Bandwagoning Cursed with a weak or nonexistent theoretical basis, educators (and key educational decision makers locally and nationally) become gullible victims to fads, with their attendant phenomenon, bandwagoning. Without a theoretical keel as underpinning, educators and the public fall prey to any notion that wanders into discourse and many tend to embrace it as an advocate. Hunter's approach, management by objectives (MBO), differentiated staffing, programmed budgeting, merit pay, ungraded schools (now making a comeback), zero-based budgeting, Skinner's behaviorism, Bruner's structure of the disciplines, the spiral curriculum, and so on all are examples of this tendency.

In the short term, the question emerges, Where will TQM, whole language teaching, site-based management, and other current vogues allow supervision to go?

Competency-based education seems to be in the process of decline, certainly for teachers and perhaps for administrators as well. The State of Florida focused its administrative credentialing process around supposed competencies (e.g., basic for average principals and high for highly effective principals, as determined by their superintendents). The state is reviewing the theoretical underpinning of this approach which has totally dominated the master's degree programs for both administrative and supervisory credentialing for more than a decade.

Competition vs. Cooperation

A major theme of American life is the high value placed on competition, as opposed to cooperation, which obviously extends throughout schools and society. There is only one winner and only the biggest and the best count. As noted, Barnard (1938) proposed three indispensable elements to any organization: a common goal, a system of communication, and a system of cooperation to achieve the goal. The American obsession with competition presents difficulties for our organizations, including schools and, therefore, supervisors. When control, domination, and monopolizing the limelight are acted out as organizational themes, cultures, and/or climates, complexities emerge that can distort a goal achievement. Chances for effective cooperation to become diminished.

Competition can be finessed with Taylor's (1968) Table of Human Talents, which is similar to the Table of Periodic Elements. Hypothesizing approximately 120 actual and potential human talents, which are clustered into families (e.g., academic, artistic, physical, organizing, decision-making, human relationships), Taylor noted that regarding any one talent, half the population is above average and half is below. Using six talents, 95 percent will be above average in at least one of them. Thus, most people are talented.

An interesting game, known as The Prisoner's Dilemma, illustrates problems generated by our culture's worship of competition. The hypothetical game has the following scenario. Two individuals are caught in a robbery and are interrogated separately. Thus, they cannot communicate. If both cooperate with each other, neither implicating the other, the judge will give them each one year in prison. If one defects and implicates the other, that person will get zero years and the other will get 12 years in jail. If both defect and implicate each other, each will get 10 years. Each faces The Prisoner's Dilemma. Therefore, the principles of the game are that everyone is better off if players cooperate and both are much worse off if they both defect.

The actions of the OPEC oil cartel nations provide intriguing insights into the principles of the game. The best interest of each nation is to cooperate by limiting oil production to levels set by OPEC to maintain high prices. Some nations defect, however, and exceed their publicly agreed-upon quotas to generate more income, causing prices to fall and deriving less income.

In education, a number of scenarios, although more complicated, look startlingly similar to The Prisoner's Dilemma. The concept of schools of choice certainly fits the game. The way the OPEC nations play their parts, everyone in the cartel loses. In schools of choice, it becomes difficult to avoid the same conclusion because schools will inevitably try to convince their clientele that they are superior to "competing" schools.

The practice of individual schools competing for rewards, honors, "incentive" grants, and other competitive goals is another illustration of the principles of the game. One teacher described her new principal's heavy focus on getting an award from the state as an exercise in which concern for the students, which was a major value of the organizational culture, was displaced in the pursuit of the empty, but symbolic paper honor. In essence, she was creating the Casino School (i.e., glitzy on the outside, hollow on the inside).

Divergent Supervisory Models

Supervisory visits by administrators have traditionally been rare. Large numbers of teachers have taught a decade or more without a visit from their principal. A number of authorities were cited earlier that pointed to the nonexistence, inadequacy, or destructiveness of supervision as presently practiced (Blumberg, 1993; Starratt, 1992, Wiles, 1953). New models have surfaced that could have the capacity to provide different results when and if carried out. As an example, the Florida Performance Measurement System (FPMS) used first in 1982 mandated that a first-year teacher in that state would have two summative observations to diagnose the assistance needed; in essence, a professional development plan. Two formative observations followed the assistance provided by a peer teacher and/or a supervisor or administrator.

While this could be considered a step in the right direction, it is insufficient to facilitate the growth new and veteran teachers require for professional and personal development. In 1993, unfortunately, the state of Florida ceased supporting the system, which required regular training to ensure that observations would be reliable. The task was delegated to each of the 67 school districts, but the state no longer mandated use of FPMS. Most districts used the plan for annual evaluation of all teachers, although the instruments were designed only for beginning teachers.

Some states have adopted or adapted Florida's model, while others have produced programs of their own. The structure of the Florida system of supervision was based on the teacher delivering direct instruction, which the state believed was easiest to manage and to measure. With the advent of the constructivist classroom (Brooks & Brooks, 1993), such an approach loses much of its value, and it may even augment a control purpose of the system.

Various clinical supervision models present interesting and divergent practices from the "typical" supervisory approaches so prevalent through the years. Pajak's (1993) book on clinical supervision listed three original models (i.e., two humanistic and one artistic), three technical and didactic models, and three developmental and reflective models. The field of alternatives has expanded considerably from the early days of Goldhammer, Cogan, and Mosher and Purpel. Implications for the professional practice of instructional supervisors become challenging. Which model can be utilized with which personality at what stage of an organization's career in what organizational culture and climate? Complex professional matters and decisions await the instructional supervisor (and administrator, as well).

Another set of models consist of peer supervision, such as that utilized in DeKalb, Illinois, some years ago in a study reported by Keedy (1991), and two earlier programs mentioned by Blumberg (1974) (Abramson, 1972; Amidon, Kies, & Palisi, 1966). In these approaches, a small number of teachers volunteer to meet to review their teaching practices. In some models the teacher makes a videotape of a small segment of his or her work, which can be analyzed nonjudgmentally against a matrix selected by the group. In one model, a university facilitator or a supervisor works with the group, but administrators are noticeably absent. Teachers generally report considerable satisfaction inasmuch as the focus is on their growth and development; evaluation is conspicuously absent.

The author spent several years as a social group worker, meeting with nine groups of children per week. Workers made summary recordings of all their meetings with the various groups, except for one in which a group process recording was done. This material was utilized in weekly meetings between the supervisor and the social worker in which the focus was on what goals he or she and the group had developed, what dynamics occurred, how did the worker function, what additional options were possible, how could the worker have improved his or her professional practice, and the like. In mental health counseling, a number of similar models have been developed in which the worker and supervisor meet weekly for an hour to an hour and a half, reviewing cases, and proceeding as discussed earlier. Such intensive approaches appear difficult for education with its staffing of one administrator to 20 or more teachers, and one supervisor to many more personnel.

Levine (1967) developed a group treatment model for social case workers, which could be utilized as a supervision model. In it, a group of social workers learned to work with groups with a supervisor as the instructor. As can be readily seen, this process could easily be adapted into a supervisory model for groups of teachers, many of whom lack the skills of working effectively with groups, and fear working with them.

The last two models suggested consist, first, of an approach in which the role of supervisor takes on the challenging task of facilitating fundamental organizational change. The second model consists of expanding the planning function as a major area for supervision, as delineated in the *Sociology of Supervision* (Wilson et al, 1969).

Authority, Power, Influence, Empowerment, and Control

The last major area regarding social dimensions of school supervision examines the impact on supervisory practice of authority, power, influence, empowerment, and control; the increase in national and state control of education; an indi-

vidualized diagnostic, planning, and implementation construct for reform efforts; some divergent generalizations on school size and student achievement; a view of schools as professional bureaucracies; and the need for developing a philosophy of education and sharpening problem-solving skills.

The definitive analysis of social power was by Bierstedt (1950). He related power, force, authority, and influence as follows: "(1) power is latent force; (2) force is manifest power; and (3) authority is institutionalized power" (p. 733). He further explicated:

Power itself is the predisposition or prior capacity which makes the application of force possible. Only groups which have power can threaten to use force and the threat itself is power. Power is the ability to employ force, not its actual employment, the ability to apply sanctions, not their actual application (p.733). Thus, power is stored force.

Bierstedt perceived that, once an organization or institution was established, positions are created which have more or less authority. A priest can absolve a sinner, and a principal can assign a teacher a subject to teach. Authority and power therefore become attached to a position, not to the person who fills it.

"Influence is persuasive, while power is coercive," asserted Bierstedt (p. 731). Max Weber's formulation of influence concurred because he perceived people influenced through persuasion, which occurs through force of personality, cogency of arguments, and/or prestige held by the individual (Blau & Scott, 1962).

This analysis enables us to discern the supervisor's role vis-à-vis power. He or she has none. The supervisor usually occupies a staff, not a line, position. The supervisor also do not have authority, as defined by Bierstedt. He or she has *influence*. Thus, the supervisor's access to teachers essentially rests on the good graces of the principal, or on other line officers.

In order to improve education, those in positions of power and influence, working under Theory X assumptions, have developed an excessive fixation with control and the use of power. The Excellence Movement, which is rising as a counter to the Egalitarian Movement, spawned increased testing in the name of objectivity and accountability. Thus, American education was to be controlled through relentless quantification, all in the pursuit of objectivity and accountability. By 1994, national legislation was passed and signed by President Clinton to establish national standards of education.

Benjamin (1989) denoted the power of tests to drive curriculum: As teachers attempt to meet requirements, competencies, and demands, one is struck by the notion that teachers have become serfs, attached to their jobs, driven by anxiety and, often, fear. Wilson (personal communication, July 10, 1994) asserted:

[T]he classroom teacher has been downgraded to such a low level that it appears to be subprofessional. The question is who will want the job? If the principal is the on-site manager, does his job become "indoctrination" (military style)? If so, who would want his job either? (p. 11).

In part, this explains the adversarial relationships that have developed between administrators and teachers, and between teachers and students. All three are driven to meet increasing expectations. The result produces increased alienation and decreased creativity, and, even, productivity. Indeed, in the pursuit of productivity, pressure exerted by administrators and teachers themselves tends to decrease the very end so energetically sought (Harrison, 1990).

Gougeon (1989) studied principals through the Principal Leadership as Social Control (PLASC) theory. The theory explains the social control of teachers though power- and authority-based interactions with their principals that bring expectations of teachers into agreement with expectations of their schools.

Smyth (1989) performed a historical analysis on clinical supervision from its beginning to the present. He noted that it began as a collaborative process. He found, however, that it had been coopted into a mechanism of teacher control with its progressive affiliation with forces of the conservative educational reform movement.

This is perhaps a hidden reason behind widespread and intensive efforts to empower teachers with such devices as site-based management and other restructuring constructs developed in such projects as The Coalition of Essential Schools (Sizer, 1984).

State Control and Nationalization of Education

Since publication of Campbell's and Bunnell's *Nationalizing Influences on Secondary Education* (1963), the forces promulgating those trends have increased considerably (Wilson, 1994). State control has become a major factor in district and school decision-making in certification, structural reform such as site-based management, administrator selection, desegregation, training and in-service education of teachers, and other areas. Indeed, a handful of states, have actually either restructured local schools, taken over districts, or threatened to do so.

In 1994, legislation passed both houses of Congress and was signed by the president establishing national goals for education. Indeed, national standards for education appears to be a euphemism for national testing, a development with enormous portent for supervision and education. In addition, other nationalizing influences, both public and private, such as the National Merit Scholarship Program, the National Science Foundation, the College Entrance Examination Board, the Scholastic Aptitude Test, and others have accelerated national forces influencing education. The impact on supervisors has been profound, with many specialties inundated in carrying out mandates, losing their mission and focus in the process. This situation undoubtedly will continue to plague the profession for some time to come.

Top–Down–Reform One Size Fits All

Reform initiatives mandated or promulgated by the nation or the state (e.g., Goals 2000, Florida's Blueprint 2000, which heavily pressed for site-based management), including those by voluntary organizations (e.g., The Annie E. Casey Foundation's New Futures Initiative and Theodore Sizer's

Coalition of Essential Schools), generally do not achieve the results they envision (Gordon, 1984; Muncey & McQuillan, 1993; Sarason, 1980; Sarason, 1990; Wehlage, Smith, & Lipman, 1992).

Many factors obviously enter into the extremely complex processes of "reforming" one school, let alone a total system. A major limitation lies in the processes utilized in many reform initiatives—they often tend to be a "'micro-management syndrome' in which rapid change is forced from the top down" (Wilson, 1994), and, as a consequence, generate copious quantities of cynicism, distrust, and resistance. In Florida's state-mandated Blueprint 2000, a fundamental thrust is site-based management. Its premise of school autonomy, however, becomes an oxymoron when delivered by a state-directed, top–down mandate narrowly defined by state and local district guidelines, and vigorously opposed by most superintendents and secondary school principals.

A major obstructing factor consists of superintendents' and principals' resistance to proposals they consider will reduce their power. This is particularly true of high schools, which generally do not move into reform arenas as rapidly as elementary and middle schools. Conversations with secondary principals indicate that they are extremely loath to reduce their power, which they strongly feel will occur in site-based management or any decentralizing or restructuring attempt. In addition, Cuban's (1982) studies indicated that the classroom has remained virtually the same in secondary schools since the turn of the century.

"One Size Fits All" (Shapiro, 1993) referred to the incredibly naïve notion that a state's or a foundation's large-scale reform effort (i.e., restructuring, site-based management, middle schools) can be implemented successfully with a single uniform change strategy applicable to every school and to every district. In contrast, with great care, thought, and involvement of all parties, an Individualized Educational Plan (IEP) is developed for *each student* involved with special education. It is incredible, however, that to reform schools fundamentally, to change an entire system, to institute massive system-wide alterations, a wholesale strategy is mandated which at best produces mediocre or poor outcomes.

A construct incorporating a diagnostic instrument, change process, and strategy is needed that can account for the major forces, dynamics, structures, systems, functions (and dysfunctions), cultures, and climates operating in *each* institution. It is interesting that just such a construct has been developed and utilized to *individualize* the analysis, planning, implementation, and evaluation of change and change strategies (Shapiro, 1993). Entitled organizational mapping, "Analysis of Dynamics of Change," the construct emerged from intensive work to construct major reform changes and change strategies in numbers of schools and other organizations (see Table 43–1).

Analysts utilizing this construct tease out major *issues, concerns, problems, and conditions* in the organization with a representative planning group. They then develop *conclusions and implications*, which are all done publicly. The next step is to discern *themes* underlying *conclusions and implications*. Once that is done, the group designs *potential initiatives and lines of action*. Care is taken to construct a *rationale* to support each *potential initiative*. Lastly, *outcomes*, or *consequences* are followed and evaluated.

This is obviously a highly individualized approach, certainly not wholesale, and manifestly not one that can be performed readily; however, not everyone can reconstruct such a complex organization as a school, or a district, or an entire state—and yet that is precisely what is expected in wholesale restructuring, reform efforts, and change strategies.

The danger is that legislators, institutions, and major players will realize that all their efforts, good will, energy, and money have not approached expectations. They will point fingers of blame at the schools, particularly at teachers as education's perpetual "fall guys", as Hunt observed (Shapiro et al, 1994). The reform effort will then be abandoned.

Wilson (1994), recognized the "sea of troubles" afflicting our society and education and the faulty assumptions upon which much reform effort is based: control of education by the testing movement, introduction of business approaches in school management, "pervasive infusion of confrontational relations . . . [with] children, teachers vs. students; administrators vs. teachers; and test makers and evaluation experts vs. everybody else" (p. 1). As a consequence, Wilson introduced the idea of "Peaceful Education." He noted: "At the present, schools are not peaceful places; they are test sites for power and demonstration centers for intergenerational conflict. 'Peaceful Education' thus becomes the educational issue of the century" (p. 2.). Designing a curriculum to introduce such a revolutionary construct into the schools presents a challenge.

Size: Small Schools and Small Systems

Although virtually ignored by key decision makers, the size of the school (Barker & Gump, 1964; Oxley, 1989, 1994) and the district (Fowler & Walberg, 1990) produces a major impact on student achievement and sense of self-worth. "The big school [for a high school over 700, 500 or fewer for elementary schools] has a negative impact on virtually all factors and indicators" (Shapiro et al, 1994, p. 138). The following is adapted from a table by Shapiro et al (1993, pp. 113–124) listing advantages and disadvantages of small and large schools. The list focuses on disadvantages of large schools:

Student achievement and test scores are lower.
Attendance is worse.
Dropouts are greater—a high school of 2000 generates twice the percent of dropouts as does a school of 600.
Costs are higher ("empirical evidence for cost savings only applies to very small schools" (Walberg & Fowler, 1987) "and if achievement and other positive schooling outcomes are not considered" (Fowler & Walberg, 1990).
Communication is top–down.
Climate is poor—greater social distance in part causing "destructive student subcultures [to] emerge" (Oxley, 1989, p. 28).
Little sense of community—little participation except for a small elite, little involvement.
Student involvement in school activities is decreased.
Relationships are impaired—anonymity, depersonalized, alienation.

Authority is externally imposed—social controls external.
Rates of vandalism and violence are higher (Lindsay, 1982; Pittman, & Haughwout, 1987).

The implications for education and supervision cannot be more clear; supervisors must stand for smaller and decentralized units to avoid the negatives of the large school.

Schools as Professional Bureaucracies

Schools and hospitals differ from the normal bureaucracy in a number of ways. First, both employ personnel with greater technical and professional expertise. Second, their norms differ from business because their purpose is to provide specialized service to clients. Professions are also characterized by colleague-oriented reference groups. Professionals are expected to evaluate situations and problems and then to make autonomous decisions within their sphere of expertise. Thus, autonomy plays a crucial role in developing a profession. It usually develops a special language that outsiders do not understand. In addition, professions have self-imposed control structures based on expertise and professional standards.

The seeds for organizational conflict are sown by the very nature of the expertise teachers and supervisors develop, and their expectations that they should be respected and listened to by administrators empowered to make decisions. One major problem is that administrators cannot possibly keep pace with the growth of knowledge and expertise of their teachers and supervisors.

Thus, by their nature, professional bureaucracies generate conflict between authority of position and authority of expertise. Respect for expertise of administrators consequently declines in a reciprocal manner: as teachers' expertise increases, their respect for administrators decreases. A number of models have been developed that may prove useful to supervisors in addressing this source of conflict. The ombudsman is one; decentralization is another. Japanese management philosophy constitutes another, as do organization development theories and processes. Conflicts can erode relationships and effectiveness if allowed to fester and grow. The concept of supervisor as trouble-shooter addresses this circumstances.

Hills (1975), a professor of educational administration at the University of British Columbia in Vancouver for a long time, became an elementary principal for 1 year. His subsequent reflective thinking provided further insight into our own enterprise. He recommended that "preparation programs for principals [and by implication, supervisors] should lead students to develop a relatively articulate, consistent, administrative philosophy" (p. 1). He also recommended that "preparation programs for principals should place heavy emphasis on the development of critical-analytical and problem-solving skills" (p. 2) because often "...administrators spent a great deal of time searching for solutions to un- or ill-defined problems" (p. 2). Possession of a coherent philosophy and perceptive analytical and problem-solving skills obviously enables a professional to operate with insight and consistency, and not to be swayed by fads and fashions that swoop by and onto which others latch eagerly.

SUMMARY AND CONCLUSIONS

This extensive overview of the social dimensions of supervision dealt first with the social dimensions of a society and of supervision, pointing toward the enormous impact of cultural phenomena on human thinking, and therefore, behavior. It was noted that each society and each organization constructs its own realities. To provide a context, the analysis commenced with Wilson's three phases of supervisory thought and practice. The inquiry next noted the lack of theory in supervision and its crippling impact on developing supervisory concepts. Several severe criticisms of the effectiveness of supervision were noted, application of the construct of efficacy to supervision was discussed, as was Blumberg's view of supervision as a craft.

Next, Wiles' major facets of supervision were mentioned, with Lovell's additions. Supervision was overviewed from varying perspectives, including Guba–Getzels' social process, a theory/practice of organizational decision-making as social process, as the planning function with supervisors as planners, as a social function of education and schooling, and as a holistic behavior system, with an example of supervision as a social enterprise. The major influence of social functions of education on supervisors was discussed using Dewey's "Oil Can" metaphor.

A number of social dimensions of supervision were delineated, including culture, socioeconomic class, and social psychological perspectives such as positions, roles, expectations, and functions. In addition, race, gender, ethnicity, and a number of organizational theories/issues/factors were analyzed. Discussions of social systems theory and practice, organizational cycles, and a range of social functions of schools followed, together with their implications for supervision.

Consistent with a major theme of this chapter that supervision constitutes a social enterprise, the wide-ranging and often subtle impact of culture on supervision and supervisory behavior was discussed, including organizational culture and climate, the relationship among organizational phenomena, leadership, and personality factors, and the American predilection for bandwagoning into quick-fix fads. Applications of the Prisoner's Dilemma to education and supervision were proposed, followed by an overview of the influence of social dimensions of schooling upon various supervisory models, some drawn from other fields. The related phenomena of authority, power, influence, empowerment, control, and their influence on the supervisory role were analyzed. The impact upon supervision by trends toward centralization and nationalization of education were reviewed, as was an overview of reform efforts, usually top–down and relatively limited in success. Research on school and district size was explored for its ramifications on supervision and schooling, as was the nature of the school as a professional bureaucracy. Hills' message to administrators and supervisors regarding the need to develop and use a coherent philosophy of education, administration, and supervision consistently, along with critical-analytical and problem-solving skills in defining and analyzing problems ended the discussion.

IMPLICATIONS FOR PRACTICE AND RESEARCH

At the beginning of this chapter, one of the goals established was to generate future directions toward which both practice and research might move. In a wide-ranging analysis such as this, numbers of conclusions and implications may be drawn and inferred. Several major conclusions, implications, and recommendations for practice and research will be stated.

The fundamental challenge to our field emerged from Hazi's question of Shapiro, a mental health therapist, (personal communication, November 7, 1993) at the annual conference of COPIS in Tampa. How would we treat supervision if we looked at it from a mental health perspective?

The question unlocked the following line of thought. If we change from perceiving supervision as an affair of individuals, and treat the field as a social enterprise (i.e., the thesis of this chapter), then we must follow the major lines of action social enterprises must generate to survive, as Barnard specified (1938). The first indispensable element must be to develop a common purpose, without which no enterprise can become or remain viable. The second indispensable element must be to establish a system of communication for members to understand and to buy into the common purpose, and to generate the third element. This third indispensable element consists of developing a system of cooperation so that the purpose held commonly becomes the focus of concerted action leading to its achievement.

Instructional supervision must therefore develop a common purpose to which its proponents subscribe, and then organize a master plan to implement those purposes collectively. Supervision has functioned for too long without a clearly articulated, common purpose and a master plan to achieve that purpose. To go this requires reconstructing our social realities. To do otherwise invites continuing ineffectiveness and inefficiency.

A second major conclusion is that supervisors tend to be coopted by the organization into supporting existent practices developed by their schools and districts, which are conventions that are manifestly harmful to students, staff, schools, and education. To counter this coopting process, alternative roles were recommended for supervisors and the supervisory profession to generate greater impact upon schools and districts. One recommended role consists of the supervisor as organizational trouble-shooter who is able to analyze an organization using various theoretical frameworks in order to deal with its basic issues and problems, and then to develop strategies to take effective action, and to be heavily involved in the action; in short, to be a change agent.

Another recommended role involves functioning as a comprehensive planner, a role rare in education and essential to avoid the stasis of residing in an unproductive phase of an organization's career. In addition, a major skill to hone is expertise in organizational decision-making. Being able to predict the phases of the decision-making process provides a powerful tool to the supervisor and an equally potent contribution to an organization.

The rationale behind these suggested roles and skills is that supervisors must create powerful roles as key players in

TABLE 43–1. Analysis of Dynamics of Change

Issues/Questions	Summary/Conclusions	Potential Lines of Action/Initiatives
Socioeconomic changes in community: From single home to duplexes. From parents to single parent. Reduced intramural participation. Reduced parents participation.	Changing students' values, attitudes: Value of education. Not doing homework. Impact on teachers: Reduced standards.	Major intramural program. Major recognition program. Major involvement of parents: Volunteers in school. Fund raisers. Administration, faculty involved. In-service programs to understand students.
Impact on Teachers: Feeling of high stress. High frustration. Morale collapsing. "Family" feeling collapsing. Considering leaving school.	Social organization holding school together, but fraying. Key teacher social systems upset, publicly considering leaving.	Develop grade level administrative teams. Develop teacher teams.
Hopelessness.	Need sense of hope.	Develop plan with purpose: Form three committees to reorganize. Planning. Guidance. Classroom management support team.
Passive, laissez faire administration not functioning: One of two deans not functioning. Guidance dysfunctional Administrative clock-watching spreading to teachers, students.	Administration, deans, guidance dysfunctional: Not cooperating. Not proactive. Limited work ethic affecting teachers, students. Teachers angry at students for this.	Proactive leadership to form and support: form and support: Planning and guidance committees.
Junior high school departmental organization dysfunctional.	Formal organization blocks effective action: isolates teachers. Teachers with same students do not see each other. Teachers disorganized.	Formal organization must change to facilitate cooperation: Form teacher teams, work in small decentralized units with same students. Form grade level administrative teams.
Department organization.	Little accountability.	Grade-level teams for administrators, teachers.
Norms (attitudes, practices, behavior).	Culture dysfunctional: Norms must change.	Establish new norms with above changes

schools and systems which are perceived as invaluable. These roles will enable supervisors to contribute significantly to schools, districts, and to education; in turn, this will enhance supervisors' worth. Research must of course, follow to point the way toward greater efficacy. The critical lack of both theory and a consistent philosophy by supervisors creates an absence of a fulcrum or centerpiece around which to organize thinking, and, therefore, professional practice. Thus, supervisors (and others) tend to fall prey to the endless quick-fix fads caroming across the American educational landscape. Putting the child first and believing in people's worth does not constitute a fad, nor does looking for talent and creativi-

ty in every individual. While creating theory tends to be serendipitous, considerably more theory needs to be produced to widen the existent base and to improve practice. Along with sharpened problem-solving skills, this would enhance the value of supervisors to the organization and to education.

Scholars' comments on the effectiveness of supervision indicated serious problems. The roles suggested earlier, along with others to be developed in the future, might impact this vacuum significantly. In addition, the construct of efficacy has considerable potential for improving supervisory practice. It is important to change the supervisors own as well as teachers' sense of effi-

TABLE 43–1. Analysis of Dynamics of Change (continued)

Rationale for Actions	Underlying Themes	Major Outcomes
Develop sense of belonging for all: Sense that teachers care, that parents care. Sense of pride. Teach parenting skills. Faculty, administration understand, accept students. Involve community.	Changing community changes students' attitudes: Decreasing respect for teachers, education. Teachers increasingly alienated from parents, students, each other, administration, guidance, central office.	Major intramural programs. Major recognition program for all. Major parent involvement program, with staff development. In-service program on nature of students.
Decentralize: Work/cooperate in small units. Make all visible/accountable. Personalize. Increase ownership, morale. Increase sense of belonging.	Teachers' control over professional life decreased: Feel powerless. School sliding downhill.	Grade-level administrative teams in place. Teacher teams in operation.
Teachers involved in reorganization: Increased ownership. Empowerment. Support groups.	Loss of morale, hope, positive attitude towards work, purpose.	Long-range plan developed. Reorganization support team functioning: Sense of hope. Strong teacher ownership of plan and support of reorganization support team.
Develop support by all reference (administration, deans, guidance, faculty, students, community, central office).	Passive, laissez faire administration functioning poorly No accountability.	Administration strongly supports plan, reorganization support team, process. Accountability clear, visible.
Decentralizing facilitates: Personalizing. Empowerment. Greater responsibility. Accountability-all visible. Cooperation. Interdependent operation.	Relationship between form and function: Organization dysfunctional-prohibits teachers with same students from working together. Centralized/decentralized. Central office indifferent.	Formal organization changed from a junior high school to a middle school: Grade-level administrative teams. Teacher teams with block of students. Implementing teacher as advisor program.
All organizational components become visible-thus, accountable.	Administrators, deans, guidance not accountable.	Accountability.
Decentralization increases students', teachers' cooperation, responsibility.	Norms need to support changes, work ethic, cooperation, responsible professional behavior, self-esteem, recognition for all, repersonalizing to a family.	Cultural norms, beliefs, practices changed.

cacy. More research on factors that affect supervisory and administrative efficacy have promise. Development of efficacy instruments specifically focused on functions and tasks of both administration and supervision could provide vital insights. The several role shifts recommended, including those of change agent/trouble shooter and comprehensive planner might serve as intriguing foci for research on effectiveness and efficacy. More work on Blumberg's concept of supervision (and, by implication, teaching and administration) as a craft might also provide interesting findings.

A number of varied facets by which supervision can be perceived merit attention. The Guba–Getzels model, designed for educational administration, provides intriguing insights into instructional supervision as a social process. It suggests that leadership styles can be utilized to predict sources and nature of conflict in organizations, augmenting the practicing supervisor's effectiveness. A construct designed specifically for supervision might shed more light.

A four-phase practice/theory of organizational decision-making as social process (PINC) might enable supervisors to predict the process of organizational decision-making, a tool of considerable potential to enhance function. The Tripartite Theory of organizational change and succession, has implications for predicting phases in an organization's career and attendant leadership styles characterized by each phase. The theory addresses a number of issues, one of which consists of predicting the virtually inevitable process of entropy in organizations. It also offers clues for avoiding this entropic process by creating internally based planning structures and strategies to maintain an organization in a perpetual planning phase. It provides the supervisor with insights into performing the planning function, a course of action designed to increase the value of the supervisor and supervision to the organization and to the profession. Research on the impact of using these theories seems advisable.

While virtually all literature on the social functions of education focused on their impact on students, this analysis of the influence of these functions on *supervisors* found major impact. In the process of trying to become accepted, most supervisors buy into the social functions institutionalized into education, including the current practices of retention, ability grouping, and tracking. This analysis recommended other options, such as creating alternative strategies and role innovation, in which incumbents change their roles and function in new ways. Supervisors should metamorphose into organizational trouble shooters and comprehensive planners, which are options to enrich their function significantly and to contribute to schools. Just as the Leader Behavior Description Questionnaire (LBDQ) contributed profoundly to the study of leadership and generated theory, additional theory and instruments need to be generated to study supervisory *behavior* and the behavior system of supervision.

The analysis of the American culture and cultural trends, concluded that supervision exists only if the culture decides that it is needed, and that its form is determined by the prevailing philosophies and views of the culture. Schools perform a social sorting function, which sends lower socioeconomic and minority children into lower ability and tracking levels. The implication for supervisors is "to do no harm" and to work to end these practices. Longitudinal research would be useful to capture long-term trends and drifts.

The review of social psychological factors, such as positions, roles, role expectations, and role functions, within organization, served as the basis for constructing divergent roles and role functions by which to improve supervisory effectiveness and efficiency within organizations. Once the supervisor recognizes that roles can be defined and interpreted differently (i.e., that options exist), he or she can avoid being a captive of the role designated by the organization or subculture. A range of these options might be studied for greater insight.

Organizations constitute the environment for the supervisor and for the supervisory function. Therefore, understanding organizational structure and processes becomes a key to effectiveness. A number of areas of organizational theory offer research potential.

Organizational diversity and openness were perceived as rich fields for supervisors to develop alternative roles to increase their effectiveness and efficiency. Because of the American focus on the individual, emphases on social systems, organizational theory and processes, and the organization as a system become crucial in improving supervisory

effectiveness and efficacy. Indeed, supervision viewed as social enterprise and as a social system itself constitutes areas for development and investigation.

The cycles of organizational behavior and supervisory behavior have been virtually ignored in literature and research. This area might be productive to explore for additional models. Further work on relationships among organizational factors, personality style, and leadership behavior appears to be a rich area of inquiry. Supervisors would certainly increase their repertoire of approaches in working with different people, leadership styles, and organizations in varying career stages. Further research could prove beneficial. By exploring the interrelations of various models of supervision, personality styles, and phases of an organization's career in relationship to organizational climate and efficacy.

Main social functions of schooling, including the socializing influence of schools (i.e., on students and on others, including supervisors), social sorting, failure, warehousing/storing children, filling time, and acquiring knowledge, skills, and attitudes/values promise acute insights into the ways these operations develops. Supervisors and others may be able to free themselves from constraints of accepting social functions uncritically. Supervisors must become more objective and work to change practices deleterious to students. In-depth, longitudinal research might prove productive.

Studies of organizational culture and organizational climate both are critical to diagnosing components of all organizations, are essential areas in which supervisors must develop insights.

Several additional areas for supervision, including the consequence of antiintellectualism and antitheoreticalism in the culture upon people entering the profession as well as on those presently practicing, invite investigation. Because many professionals tend to regard theory as valueless, research is necessary to find appropriate change strategies. A solid theoretical background could help supervision practitioners deal with the prevalent fads and bandwagoning in American education, which often create the Casino School (i.e., all glitzy but no substance).

A variation of the Prisoner's Dilemma applied to American education provides food for thought in terms of the value placed upon competition over cooperation. Several alternative models of supervision in education and various fields need to be developed and be better researched to provide alternatives.

In a chapter devoted to the social dimensions of supervision, the issues of authority, power, influence, empowerment, and control must be considered. With the American predilection for power, the supervisor, who functions with none and with only limited influence at best, must be a student of these issues. Because administrative style taps into people's power needs, the movement to empower those on the lowest rungs of the educational hierarchies makes sense. Empowerment strategies should be a component of every supervisor's armamentarium of strategies, concepts, and thinking as should research to assess practice and to point to new vistas.

The increasing nationalizing of education and the top–down, generally failure-prone nature of reform efforts provide areas for intensive research. As waves of reform efforts fail to impact the classroom (as Cuban noted) and the schools, key power holders may abandon public education either as unfixable or as not worth the effort.

Although some excellent work has been done on the relationship of size of school and districts to student achievement, this research has been all but totally ignored, except in some rural regions. The research clearly demonstrates the value of small school size on student achievement, self-worth, values, and a host of other factors. The time is perhaps now to mount a national campaign to publicize such findings and to influence those who are deciding to build large schools and to increase existing schools in the name of economy.

Because schools are professional bureaucracies, alternative strategies are needed for dealing with the inevitable internal conflicts emerging from this type of organization. A mediating and trouble-shooting role for supervisors appears appropriate. In addition, research could play a valuable part both in developing alternative roles as well as in determining their effectiveness.

Finally, the current indifferences regarding social dimensions of school supervision projected by scholars of and practitioners in the field must end. It is imperative for supervisors to design and implement a common purpose with an accompanying comprehensive plan and research strategy to confidently stride into the coming millennium with courage and conviction.

REFERENCES

Abramson, P. (1972, September). When teachers evaluate each other. *Scholastic Magazine*, 26–28.

Alfonso, R. H. (1992). A response by Dr. Robert H. Alfonso to Jerry Starratt's paper entitled a modest proposal: Abolish supervision. *Wingspan*, *8*(1), 20–22.

Amidon, E. J., Kies, K. M., & Palisi, A.T. (1966). Group supervision: A technique for improving teacher behavior. *National Elementary School Principal*, *45*(5); 54–58.

The Annie E. Casey Foundation. (1994). *Kids Count Data Book*. Baltimore, MD: Annie E. Casey Foundation.

Argyris, C. (1958, March). Some problems in conceptualizing organizational climate: A case study of a bank. *Administrative Science Quarterly*, *II*, 501–520.

Bandura, A. (1986). *Social foundations of thought and action: Asocial-cognitive theory*. Englewood Cliffs, NJ: Prentice-Hall.

Bandura, A. (1992). *Self-efficacy mechanisms in socio-cognitive functioning*. Paper presented at the American Educational Research Association, San Francisco.

Barker, R. G. & Gump, P. V. (1964). *Big school, small school*. Stanford, CA: Stanford University Press.

Barnard, C. I. (1938). *The functions of the executive*. Cambridge, MA: Harvard University Press.

Battista, M. T. (1994). Teacher beliefs and the reform movement in mathematics education. *Phi Delta Kappan*, *75*(8), 462–463, 466–468, 470.

Benjamin, W. F. (1989, Spring). From the curriculum editor. *Florida Association for Supervision and Curriculum Development (FASCD) Journal*, *5*, 2–4.

Bennis, W. G., Benne, K. D., & Chin, R. (1969). *The planning of change*. New York: Holt, Rinehart and Winston.

Benne, K. D. & Sheats, P. (1948). Functional roles of group members. *Journal of Social Issues*, *4*(2), 242–247.

Berger, P. L. & Luckmann, T. (1966). *The social construction of reality*. Garden City, NY: Doubleday

Bernstein, S. (1965). *Explorations in group work*. Boston, MA: Boston University School of Social Work.

Bierstedt, R. (1950). An analysis of social power. *American Sociological Review*, *15*(6), 730–738.

Blumberg, A. (1986). The language of supervision: Perspectives over time. San Francisco, CA: *American Educational Research Association* (ERIC Document Reproduction Service No. ED 277 110).

Blumberg, A. (1989). *School administration as a craft*. Boston, MA: Allyn & Bacon.

Blumberg, A. (1992). A response to Starratt's a modest proposal: Abolish supervision, *Wingspan*, *8*(1), 22–24.

Blumberg, A. (1993). *The human side of supervision*. Unpublished manuscript.

Blumberg, A. & Amidon, E. (1965). Teacher perceptions of supervisor-teacher interaction. *Administrator's Notebook*, Chicago, IL: Midwest Administration Center, University of Chicago, *14*(1), 1–4.

Blumberg, A. & Tallerico, M. (1988). *Supervision and the schools: A symphony in discord*. Unpublished manuscript.

Blumer, H. (1951). Collective behavior. In A. M. Lee (Ed.). *Principles of sociology* (pp. 167–222). New York: Barnes & Noble

Bradshaw, J. (1988). *Bradshaw on: The family*. Deerfield Beach, FL: Heath Communications

Brooks, J G. & Brooks, M. G. (1993). *The case for constructivist classrooms*. Alexandria, VA: ASCD.

Campbell, R. F. & Bunnell, R. A. (1963). *Nationalizing influences on secondary education*. Chicago, IL: University of Chicago, Midwest Administration Center.

Coladarci, T. & Breton, W. A. (1991). Teacher efficacy, supervision, and the special education resource-room teacher. Chicago, IL: *American Educational Research Association* (ERIC Document Reproduction Service No. ED330 684).

Coladarci, A. P. & Getzels, J. W. (1955). *The use of theory in educational administration*. Stanford, CA: Stanford University Press.

Collingwood, R. G.(1938). *The principles of art.* Oxford: The Clarendon Press.

Commission on the Reorganization of Secondary Education (1918). *Cardinal principles of secondary education.* Bureau of Education Bulletin 1918, No. 35. Washington, D.C.: U.S. Government Printing Office.

Cook, P. F. (1982). Improving supervision in teaching using behavior modeling techniques. Houston, TX: *American Association of Colleges for Teacher Education* (ERIC Document Reproduction Service No. ED213676).

Cooper, H. M. & Burger, J. M. (1980). How teachers explain students' academic performance: A categorization of free response academic attributions. *American Educational Research Journal, 17*(2), 95–109.

Croce, B. (1976). In A. Hofstatter & R. Kuhns (Eds.). *Philosophies of art and beauty.* Chicago, IL: University of Chicago Press.

Croghan, J. H., Lake, D. G., & Schroder, H. M. (1983). *Identification of the competencies of high-performing principals in Florida.* Tallahassee, FL: Florida Department of Education, Florida Council on Educational Management.

Cuban, L. (1982). Persistent instruction: The high school classroom. *Phi Delta Kappan, 64*(2), 113–118.

Deal, T. E. & Kennedy, A. A. (1982). *Corporate cultures: The rites and rituals of corporate life.* Reading, MA: Addison-Wesley.

Deming, W. E. (1982). *Quality, productivity, and competitive position.* Cambridge, MA: Massachusetts Institute of Technology, Center for Advanced Engineering Study.

Dewey, J (1938). *Experience and education.* New York: Macmillan.

Dusek, J. (1985). *Teacher expectations.* Hillsdale, NJ: Erlbaum

Esposito, D. (1971). Ability grouping: Good for children or not? *ERIC/IRCD Urban Disadvantaged Series.* NY: Teachers College, 1–6.

Fabun, D. (1967). The corporation as a creative environment. Oakland, CA: *Kaiser News*, Kaiser Companies.

Fowler, W. J. & Walberg, H. J. (1990). *School size characteristics and outcomes.* Unpublished manuscript.

Getzels, J. W., & Guba, E. G. (1957). Social behavior and the administrative process. *School Review, 65*(4), 423–441.

Getzels, J. W., Lipham, J. M., & Campbell, R. F. (1968). *Administration as social process.* New York: Harper and Row.

Getzels, J. W. & Thelen, H. A. (1960). The classroom as a social system. In N. B. Henry (Ed.). *The dynamics of instructional groups* (59th Yearbook of the National Society for the Study of Education, Part II; pp. 53–83). Chicago, IL: University of Chicago Press.

Goffman, E. (1963). *Stigma: Notes on the management of spoiled identity.* Englewood Cliffs, NJ: Prentice-Hall.

Goldberg, M. (1966). *The effects of ability grouping.* New York: Teachers College Press.

Gordon, D. (1984). *The myths of school self-renewal.* New York: Teachers College Press.

Gougheon, T. D. (1989). Leadership as social control: The high school principalship. Bellevue, WA: *Washington Educational Research Association* (ERIC Document Reproduction Service No. ED304 785).

Gray, K. (1993). Why we will lose: Taylorism in America's high schools. *Phi Delta Kappan 74*(5), 370–374.

Greenfield, T. B. (1973). Organizations as social inventions: Rethinking assumptions about change. *Journal of Applied Behavioral Science 9*(5), 551–554.

Gregorc, A. (1982). *Gregorc Style Delineator.* Columbia, CT: Gregorc Associates, Inc.

Halpin, A. W. & Croft, D. B. (1963). *The organizational climate of schools.* Chicago, IL: Midwest Administration Center, University of Chicago.

Hamilton, S. F. (1983). Highlights from research on school and classroom ecology. *Educational Leadership, 40*(5), 69.

Harrison, E. A. (1990). An investigation of the relationship between perceived teacher burnout and organizational climate in elementary schools. *Dissertation Abstracts, International, 51*, 11A.

Hills, J. (1975). Preparation for the principalship: Some recommendations from the field. *Administrator's Notebook, XXIII*(9), 1–4.

Hirsch, E. D. (1988). *Cultural literacy: What every American needs to know.* New York: Vintage Books.

Hoy, W. K. & Woolfolk, A. E. (1990). Socialization of student teachers. *American Educational Research Journal, 27*, 279–300.

Howard, E. (1989). There may be no fair play in American rigged schools. *Changing Schools, 17*(1), 2–3, 8.

Katz, D & Kahn, R. L. (1978). *The social psychology of organizations.* New York: John Wiley & Sons.

Keedy, J. L. (1991). Teacher collegial groups as a teacher self improvement strategy: Implications for instructional supervisors. Chicago, IL: *American Educational Research Association* (ERIC Document Reproduction Service No. ED334 675).

Kennebrew, J. L. & Sistrunk, W. E. (1989). Principal's supervisory behavior and school climate. Little Rock, AR: *Mid-South Educational Research Association* (ERIC Document Reproduction Service No. ED 312 764).

Kowalski, T. J. (1991). *Case studies in educational administration.* New York: Longman.

Kozol, J. (1991). *Savage inequalities: Children in America's schools.* New York: Crown Publishing.

Kurtin, K (1993). *Relationships between personality types and competencies of school administrators.* Unpublished doctoral dissertation, University of South Florida, Tampa, FL.

Leggett, S. (1969). Foreword. In L. C. Wilson, T. M. Byar, A. S. Shapiro, & S. H. Schell. *Sociology of supervision.* Boston, MA: Allyn & Bacon.

Leggett, S., Brubaker, C. W., Cohodes, A., & Shapiro, A. S. (1977). *Planning flexible learning places.* New York: McGraw-Hill

Levin, M. A. & Simon, R. I. (1974). From ideal to real: Understanding the development of new educational settings. *Interchange 5*(3), 45–54.

Levine, B. (1967). *Fundamentals of group treatment.* Northbrook, IL: Whitehall Company.

Lewin, K. (1952). Group decision and social change. In G. E. Swanson, T. M. Newcomb, & E. L Hartley (Eds.). *Readings in social psychology.* New York: Henry Holt.

Licklider, B. L. & Niska, J. M. (1993). Improving supervision of cooperative learning: A new approach to staff development for principals. *Journal of Personnel Evaluation in Education, 6*(4), 367–378.

Light, D., Keller, S., & Calhoun, C. (1989). *Sociology* (5th ed.). New York: Alfred P. Knopf.

Lindsay, P. (1982). The effect of high school size on student participation, satisfaction, and attendance, *Educational Evaluation and Policy Analysis, 4*, 57–65.

Linton, R. (1947). *The study of man.* New York: Appleton-Century-Crofts.

Lipton, L. & Starratt, R. J. (1989). The moral side of supervision. San

Francisco, CA: *American Educational Research Association* (ERIC Document Reproduction Service No. ED307 718).

Lovell, J. T. & Wiles, K. (1983). *Supervision for better schools* (5th ed.). Engelwood Cliffs, NJ: Prentice-Hall.

Mead, G. H. (1934). *Mind, self, and society.* Chicago, IL: University of Chicago Press.

Miles, R. (1965). Human Relations or Human Resources? *Harvard Business Review. 43*(4), 148–163.

Mintzberg, H. (1979). *The structuring of organizations.* Engelwood Cliffs, NJ: Prentice-Hall.

Muncey D. & Mcquillan, P. (1993). Preliminary findings from a five-year study of the Coalition for Essential Schools. *Phi Delta Kappan, 74*(6), 446–489.

Myers, I. B. & McCaulley, M. H. (1985). *Manual: A guide to the development and use of the Myers-Briggs type indicator* (p. 139). Palo Alto, CA: Consulting Psychologists Press, Inc.

Nottingham, M. & Dawson, J. (1987). Factors for consideration in supervision and evaluation (ERIC Document Reproduction Service No. ED284 343).

Oakes, J. (1986, September). Keeping track, part 1: The policy and practice of curriculum inequality. *Phi Delta Kappan,* 12–17.

Oakes, J. (1994). Organizing schools into small units: Alternatives to homogeneous grouping. *Phi Delta Kappan, 75*(7), 521–526.

Ouchi, W. G. (1981). *Theory Z: How American business can meet the Japanese challenge.* Reading, MA: Addison-Wesley.

Owens, R. G. (1991). *Organizational behavior in education* (4th ed.). Boston, MA: Allyn and Bacon.

Oxley, D. (1989). Smaller is better. *American Educator, 13*(1), 28–31, 41–52.

Oxley, D. (1994). Organizing schools into small units: Alternatives to homogeneous grouping. *Phi Delta Kappan, 75*(7), 521–526.

Pajak, E. (1993). *Approaches to clinical supervision: Alternatives for improving instruction.* Norwood, MA: Christopher-Gordon Publishers.

Parelius, A. P. & Parelius, R. J. (1978). *The sociology of education* (p. 23). Englewood Cliffs, NJ: Prentice-Hall.

Parrington, V. L. (1927). *Main currents in American thought.* New York: Harcourt, Brace, and Company.

Patterson, J. L. (1986). *Productive school systems for a nonrational world* (ERIC Document Reproduction Service No. ED274 028)

Pavan, B. N. (1983). Clinical supervision: Does it make a difference? DeKalb, IL: *Council of Professors of Instructional Supervision* (ERIC Document Reproduction Service, No. ED242 094).

Peters T. J. & Waterman, R. H. (1982). *In search of excellence: Lessons from America's best-run companies.* New York: Harper & Row.

Pittman, R. & Haughwout, P. (1987). Influence of high school size on dropout rate. *Educational Evaluation and Policy Analysis, 9,* 337–343.

Raspberry, W. (1994, March). How to predict a life of poverty. *Sarasota Herald-Tribune.*

Ross, M. H. (1993). *The culture of conflict.* New Haven, CT: Yale University Press.

Sarason, S. B. (1980). *The culture of the school and the problem of change.* Boston, MA: Allyn & Bacon.

Sarason, S. B. (1990). *The predictable failure of educational reform: Can we change course before it's too late?* San Francisco, CA: Jossey-Bass.

Schein, E. H. (1985). *Organizational culture and leadership.* San Francisco, CA: Jossey-Bass.

Secretary's Commission on Achieving Necessary Skills (1982, April). (SCANS Report), *Learning a living: A blueprint for high performance* (p. xiv). Washington, D.C.: Department of Labor.

Sergiovanni, T. J., Burlingame, M., Coombs, F. S., & Thurston, P. W. (1992). *Educational governance and administration* (3rd ed.). Boston, MA: Allyn & Bacon.

Sergiovanni, T. J. & Starratt, R. J. (1979). *Supervision: Human perspectives.* New York: McGraw-Hill.

Shapiro, A. S. (1993, November). *Organizational mapping: One size fits all: A construct and process facilitating diagnosing, planning, and implementing school improvement initiatives.* Paper presented at the meeting of the Southern Regional Council on Educational Administration. Orlando, FL.

Shapiro, A. S. (1995). Looking at the "oil can" from the outside: The supervisor as Greek chorus. *Wingspan, 11*(1), 23–25.

Shapiro, A. S., Benjamin, W. F., Hunt. J. J., & Shapiro, S. (1993). Enhancing teacher effectiveness, empowerment, and the restructuring process via an organizational decision-making process. In E. W. Chance (Ed.). *Creating the quality school: Selected readings.* Norman, OK.: University of Oklahoma.

Shapiro, A. S., Benjamin, W. F., Hunt. J. J., & Shapiro, S. (1994). *Organizational decision-making: What employees need to know to survive.* Unpublished manuscript.

Shapiro, A. S., Benjamin, W. F., Hunt, J. J. & Shapiro, S. (1995). *Curriculum and schooling: A practitioner's guide.* Palm Springs, CA: ETC Publications.

Shapiro, M. D. (1993) *The relevance of classical/libertarian principles in society today.* Unpublished paper presented for the Claude R. Lambe Fellowship, San Franscisco.

Smith, M. L. & Shepard, L. A. (1987). What doesn't work: Explaining policies of retention in the early grades. *Phi Delta Kappan, 69*(2), 129–134.

Silverman, D. (1970). *The theory of organizations.* London: Heinemann.

Sizer, T. (1984). *Horace's compromise: The dilemma of the American high school.* Boston, MA: Houghton Mifflin.

Smyth, W. J. (1984). Clinical supervision—collaborative learning about teaching. a handbook (ERIC Document Reproduction Service No. ED278 151).

Smyth, W. J. (1989). Problematizing teaching through a "critical" perspective on clinical supervision. San Francisco, CA: *American Educational Research Association* (ERIC Document Reproduction Service No. ED 307 256).

Starratt, R. J. (1992). A modest proposal: Abolish supervision. *Wingspan, 8*(1), 14–19.

Stern, G. G. & Steinhoff, C. R. (1958). *Organizational climate index.* Syracuse, NY: Evaluation Research Associates.

Stevenson, H. W. & Stigler, J. W. (1992). *The learning gap: Why our schools are failing and what we can learn from Japanese and Chinese education.* New York: Simon & Schuster.

Taylor, C. (1968, December). As well as knowledge dispensers. *NEA Journal,* 67–70.

Tinning, R. I. (1983). Supervision of student teaching: A behavioral critique (ERIC, 1983, Abstract No. ED227 082).

Turner, J. C. (1988). *Rediscovering the social group: A self-categorization theory.* Oxford: Basil Blackwood.

VanMaanen, J. & Schein, E. H. (1972). *Organizational careers: Some new perspectives.* London, England: Wiley and Sons.

Van Meter, E. (1980). Planned change in education. *Administrator's*

Notebook XXVIII(7), 1–4. Midwest Administration Center, University of Chicago.

Waite, D. (1990). Instructional supervisor as cultural guide. Boston, MA: *American Educational Research Association* (ERIC Document Reproduction Service No. ED 320 296).

Walberg, H. J. & Fowler, W. J. (1987). Expenditure and size efficiencies of public school, districts. *Educational Researcher, 16*(7), 5–13.

Weber, M. (1962). In Blau P. M. & Scott, W. R. (Eds). *Formal organizations* (pp. 27–32). San Francisco, CA: Chandler Publishing Company.

Wehlage, G., Smith, G., & Lipman, P. (1992). *Restructuring urban schools: The new futures experience.*

Weick, K. E. (1982). Administering education in loosely coupled schools. *Phi Delta Kappan, 63*(10), 673–676.

Wiles, K. (1950). *Supervision for better schools.* Englewood Cliffs, NJ: Prentice-Hall.

Wilson, L. C., Byar, T. M., Shapiro, A. S. & Schell, S. H. (1969). *Sociology of supervision.* Boston, MA: Allyn & Bacon.

Wilson, L. C. & Wilson, C. R. (1994). *The power of peaceful education: Programmable dimensions of high quality self-sustaining learning.* Unpublished manuscript.

Zamanou, S. & Glaser, S. R. (1989). Communication intervention in an organization: Measuring the results through a triangulation approach. San Francisco, CA: *Speech Communication Association* (ERIC Document Reproduction Service No. ED 314 808).

HUMAN DIMENSIONS OF SUPERVISION

Carolyn J. Wood
UNIVERSITY OF NEW MEXICO

INTRODUCTION

How is supervision practiced in schools? How is it perceived by teachers? What should be the purpose of supervision? How can supervision be changed from a one-on-one hierarchical interaction between a principal and teacher to a collaborative experience that facilitates possibilities and potential? What supervisory behaviors will facilitate transformative experiences for teachers? What is the supervisor's role in building communities of learners and learning communities? Answers to these and other questions regarding supervision are particularly important during an age of school reform.[1]

In addressing the preceding questions, this chapter begins by presenting several teacher perceptions of supervisors that appear to be as prevalent today as they were almost two decades ago. The problem with these images, however, is that teachers tend to perceive supervisors who emulate these identified approaches to supervision as irrelevant. With all of the emphasis on developing new and improved models of supervision, it is somewhat puzzling that this perceived irrelevance has continued. To shed light on reasons for this lack of progress, the focus shifts to a discussion of why supervisors behave in ways perceived by teachers as unhelpful. Two fundamental reasons are posited. First, socialization processes and other organizational factors are described to demonstrate how forces, many of which are perceived to be beyond principals' control, shape the manner in which principals practice their role. In other words, principals have tended to become what they have spent their time doing. Second, it is often difficult for principals to visualize and, thus, to act on the basis of alternative supervisory models because of the way in which they habitually have thought about their role. In other words, principals have tended to become what they have construed. In assisting principals to hold different conceptions of supervision, traditional and transformative supervision are contrasted in this section. The final portions of this chapter provide illustrations of two alternative models, which

resemble a more transformative approach to supervision. The first focuses on the attitudes and behaviors exhibited by a school principal as he attempted to practice transformative supervision. This is followed by a relatively extensive review of the actions and interactions of a group of individuals who worked in a transformative way with teachers in schools and the reactions of the teachers to these efforts.

TEACHER PERCEPTIONS OF SUPERVISORS

During the late 1970s, Pohland and Wood (1978) asked graduate students in courses on supervision of instruction to engage in an exercise that had very telling results. In an attempt to better understand perceptions of the supervisors with whom they had worked, teacher-students were asked to organize themselves into small groups and fantasize the characteristics of the "current" and "future" houses in which supervisors lived. They were then to reflect on and write about the meanings they attached to these descriptions. A wide variety of images resulted, ranging from the 1984-like malevolent images of "Big Brother" and "Gothic Horror" to their impressions of "Black and White" and the positive images projected in "On Call." The following brief excerpts from four of these images provide some of the flavor of those descriptions:

Big Brother: The supervisor lives in a penthouse atop the National Bank Building. The exterior of the penthouse is covered with eyes—blue, black, brown, green. The interior of the house is eyeless, but is traditionally conservative by way of furnishings and is immaculately sterile, everything in its place. . . . Of particular interest is the "eye control" room. It is furnished futuristically, containing many electronic devices. The room is designed to enable the supervisor to view the activities of any member of the staff whenever he/she chooses.

Gothic Horror: The house is situated high upon a steep rocky hill. It is not easily reached except by those sure-footed creatures experienced in climbing, for there are no well-defined paths to follow. . . .

From inside the house the view to the outside is obscured by the towering oak trees. The entrance to the house is a narrow, heavy oak door, always closed due to the lack of any screen door. . . . The windows are hung with heavy dark drapes which are usually drawn. The furnishings are very formal throughout the house. In the living room there are large over-stuffed chairs with high backs and an uncomfortable over-stuffed couch, not built for sitting. . . . There is a formal dining room in which the usual main course of baked baloney is served to dinner guests. . . . The entire appearance is one of immaculate rigidity.

Black and White: The supervisor lives in either a circular house or one that revolves on a turntable. Either way, the house will feature a "public side" and a "private side." The "public side" of the house has wide expanses of glass and projects an image of openness. The interior decor is formal; the color scheme neutral; and the place is immaculate (no kids or dogs allowed). A bar is well stocked to serve scotch, martinis, etc. In contrast to the "public side," the "private side" is casual and comfortable. The exterior walls are stucco or brick; the interior decor is informal; and there is easy access to a busy kitchen. Signs of children and animals abound, and the bar serves beer.

On Call: The supervisor of the future lives in a sturdy, mobile, weather controlled and solar heated houseboat having many gangplanks. An older car is parked on deck. The cabin has many windows and entry to the cabin is through squeaky revolving doors. The interior of the cabin is furnished with comfortable and many styled furniture. A wide variety of unique communication systems are present.

One of the most intriguing findings from the analysis of these data was that most of the images and explanations conveyed that supervisors were irrelevant in terms of attending to the needs and concerns of teachers. None of the "current" supervisor protocols addressed teacher needs and concerns, and only some of the "On Calls" of the "future" did so. The "current" houses described were uniformly bland, highlighting no features that might indicate that the supervisor was viewed as a resource provider or an instructional resource.

The total absence of any positive affect in the "present" protocols was a second more expected finding. Affect was either neutral or negative, generally depicting supervisors as inaccessible physically and psychologically and as indecisive, ambivalent, and unauthentic. Inaccessibility was suggested by such descriptors as "castle on a hill," "barbed wire," and "narrow doors [that are] always locked." Lack of concern for teachers was signified by references to teachers as "puppets," the "unlisted phone," and by the statement that teacher messages were "immediately gobbled up by a paper shredder." Signaling hope in the years to come (i.e., perhaps when they themselves became supervisors), positive affect was evident in some of the supervisor houses of the future. Accessibility, openness, warmth, authenticity, and professionalism were conveyed in those descriptions that indicated that the supervisor lived in a "tent," a "travel home," or a "houseboat with many gang planks," or else lived "nearer to the school than the central office," had "no fences," "many windows," "wide doors," and "unique communication systems." Positive images of the "future" were also conveyed through descriptions of houses containing a "sitting and listening room," a "pot-bellied stove," "a coffee pot with many cups," and "no clocks."

An interesting feature of the preceding findings is that they

are based on data provided by students in the late 1970s. Many of these former teachers are now the supervisors, principals, and central office administrators about whom current students write. Even though methods of acquiring data about supervision and supervisory practices in current courses have changed, the findings continue to indicate that supervisors are often perceived as irrelevant to the teaching and learning enterprise in schools. The following description, provided by Teacher-Graduate Student Arlene Kane,[2] demonstrates that things have not changed much over the years. Having secured the permission of both the science teacher (Jane Roberts) and assistant principal (Roy McCoy), Teacher-Student Kane was allowed to observe the evaluation/supervisory process in action at Parkview High School. Her account of the process follows:

A preconference was scheduled during Jane Roberts' prep period. Time allotted (but not used) by Mr. McCoy for this conference was thirty minutes. The conference began with an exchange of pleasantries about the weather and personal comments. Also, included were questions and comments directed to Ms. Roberts such as: "How are you enjoying this year?" "Are you able to get all the materials and books needed?" "Here are a few descriptors of your job. I'm sure you are meeting all areas." "This should be no problem for you. Probably just an interruption." "I will let you know when I am coming to observe."

The conference was controlled by Mr. McCoy in a very matter-of-fact way, while Ms. Roberts smiled or agreed. Her involvement was minimal, and she had no questions. Basically, the conference gave the administrator a chance to show his warm regard for the teacher, but it did not really direct or encourage any (what I would consider) meaningful exchanges between them. At no time did they discuss specific goals for the observation.

During the scheduled observation, which was held two days later, Mr. McCoy arrived after the bell rang and sat at the side of the room with a clipboard on his lap. I sensed massive tension not only from the teacher, but even the students appeared to be behaving strangely. Students sat erect and appeared to have been coached on proper classroom behavior. Throughout the entire lesson Mr. McCoy took very few notes and seemed preoccupied. He glanced at his wristwatch several times.

After class was over, Mr. McCoy smiled at Ms. Roberts and commented that she had done a "good job" and asked when she was available to come in for the postobservation conference. The date was set for the following day during Ms. Roberts' prep period.

During the postobservation conference, Ms. Roberts was handed a copy of the evaluation with a small paragraph which generally complimented her overall performance as being "good." The evaluation also included the rating portion which was marked with 100 percent outstanding performance ratings. After she read the evaluation, Mr. McCoy asked if she had any questions; and if not, to please sign the evaluation, and he would give her a copy. This exchange was seconds long and his parting comment was "Thanks for coming by. That's it for this year."

We both walked out together and briefly discussed her feelings about the evaluation. She commented that she was very glad it was over and that the entire process made her very nervous. She also stated that she thought the process was a bad joke (pp. 3–5).

McCoy had taken a graduate level course in supervision; he had participated in the district's mandatory training in clinical supervision. At Parkview High School, however, the supervisory process has been reduced to evaluation: one or two classroom observations per year and 10–20-minute pre- and postobservation interactions during which pleasantries are exchanged. There are no meaningful dialogues about the teacher's objectives or about what the teacher would like the supervisor to observe, nor is there any mention of collaboration among teachers or between the teacher and the supervisor, or any evidence of working to create a learning community or a community of learners.

The most troubling part of the preceding scenario is that the practices followed are not unique to this school or to this assistant principal. Rather, they currently are repeated in many schools throughout the country. This very well could be why a National Education Association (NEA) survey indicated that, while most teachers (i.e., more than 90 percent) tend not to fear principals' criticism of their plans or their competence, they do not perceive their supervisors as helpful. In fact, the survey indicated that "of 14 possible 'sources of knowledge and skills,' teachers rated consultation with building administrators among the *least* effective, ahead of only undergraduate education courses and in-service training provided by districts" (Shedd & Bacharach, 1991, p. 85).

With regularity, graduate students question me, "Did you teach Principal *X* or Administrator *Y* as a student in your courses?" When I answer in the affirmative, they ask, "Why didn't people seem to learn anything back then?" My response has typically been, "You become what you do and you are the way you construe." This is admittedly a simplistic answer to a very complex set of actions and understandings. This response, however, provides the foundation for discussing why many principals behave in ways that are not perceived by teachers as helpful.

SUPERVISORS BECOME WHAT THEY DO

University preparation programs attempt to assist students to become more reflective. Professors provide prospective administrators myriad alternative supervisory models, discuss how to facilitate the growth of teachers and other staff members, and create situations that give opportunities for prospective administrators to practice, to reflect, and to improve their interpersonal interactions and problem-solving skills. Graduate students voice their commitment to use these methods when they become practicing administrators. When they become principals, however, they tend to behave as their principals behaved. I always challenge students, as I did their predecessors, to "prove me wrong." They, in turn, remark, "This won't happen to me; I will do things differently when I become an administrator." It is sad, however, that this is precisely what their principals and supervisors said to me when they were graduate students, and many (but, thankfully, not all) became like their predecessors. Thus, in many schools, supervisory practices are reminiscent of the inspection/production model established during the early decades of the twentieth century (Tanner & Tanner, 1987) rather than representative of the growth-oriented models like cognitive coaching and reflective practice, the clinical and developmental approaches to supervision (Costa & Garmston, 1985; Garman,

1986; Glickman, 1985, 1992; Pajak, 1993; Zeichner & Liston, 1987), the school development practices recommended by Fullan (1991), or the more transformative approaches discussed by Darling-Hammond and McLaughlin (1995), Leithwood (1992), Lieberman (1995), and Poplin (1992).

One of the reasons supervisory practices have not changed appreciably over the years is because of the incongruence between the rhetoric espoused by principals and the posited reality of their situations. For example, based on the techniques used by Mintzberg (1973; 1976) in his classic studies of managers in corporations, Morris et al. (1982) and Kmetz and Willower (1982) examined high school and elementary school principals' work behaviors. Through their research they found that even though the professional literature and principals themselves indicate the importance of exercising various types of leadership, principals devote substantially more time to activities depicted as organizational maintenance than to those related to leadership. Both studies demonstrated that instead of devoting long stretches of time to curriculum, instruction, and concentrated interaction with teachers, principals tend to engage in a high volume of work at an unrelenting pace with tasks (e.g., including those related to curriculum and instruction) characterized in terms of variety, discontinuity, and brevity. In other words, principals' attention is constantly drawn away from working with teachers in a learning mode and is typically focused on such organizational requirements as teacher evaluation, maintaining order, and managing day-to-day disciplinary matters. The image portrayed is that of principals as managers who follow district policies and procedures and respond to state and federal mandates rather than as transformational leaders focusing primarily on teacher growth. Teachers consequently tend to view principals as compliance officers rather than as providers of resources and assistance, as umpires rather than coaches, and as wardens rather than leaders. To put it very simply, principals have tended to become what they have spent so much time doing. They have become managers instead of transformational leaders because they spend their time managing the organization rather than helping teachers to develop their talents and skills.

The role requirements and socialization processes that operate in organizations also tend to perpetuate the tendency of principals to become what they do. Even though the following section does not focus on the socialization processes that occur in K-12–institutions, it does demonstrate the manner in which attitudes and behaviors subtly are influenced by normative expectations and the activities in which people engage.

Socialization Processes and Role Requirements

Three illustrations provide convincing evidence that socialization processes, role requirements, and organizational routines literally shape people's attitudes and behaviors, often in ways contrary to their intentions. The first example, which is provided in Lieberman's (1956) classic study on the shaping power of organizational roles, supplies a clear illustration of how one's position affects his or her attitudes and perceptions. Lieberman measured the attitudes of employees in two appliance plants three times during a three-year period: first when employees were assembly-line workers, one year later when 23 had become foremen and 30 had been elected union stewards, and the third year when half of those promoted had returned to nonsupervisory jobs. During the first year, no significant differences existed between the attitudes of those who later became foremen and those who became union stewards. After their promotions, however, the foremen reported more favorable attitudes toward the company, top management, and toward the principle of incentive pay; those who assumed positions as union stewards evidenced more positive attitudes toward unions, top officials in their own union, and toward the principle of seniority rather than ability as the basis for wages. When they subsequently returned to the role of worker, the perceptions and attitudes of foremen and stewards alike tended to revert to those of workers. Their roles in the organization literally shaped their attitudes.

There is probably not a more poignant illustration of the shaping power of organizational roles than an experiment conducted by Zimbardo (1973). Middle class, Caucasian, college-age males were recruited to create a simulated prison. Half of the subjects were randomly selected to play the role of guards while the others were assigned the role of prisoners. To create the psychological conditions of imprisonment, the experimenters used a variety of techniques: The prisoners were confined, dressed in prisoners' clothes, and made almost totally dependent on the guards. Within a very brief span of time, the prisoners began to exhibit passive behaviors while the guards behaved in an extremely aggressive manner:

Typically the guards insulted the prisoners, threatened them, were physically aggressive, used instruments (night sticks, fire extinguishers, etc.) to keep the prisoners in line and referred to them in impersonal, anonymous, deprecating ways. . . . From the first to the last day there was significant increase in the guards' use of most of these domineering abuse tactics (pp. 48–49).

Because of the intense aggression exhibited by the guards, the experiment, which had been scheduled to last for two weeks, was terminated after six days. Whereas Lieberman's research demonstrated the manner in which one's position shapes his or her *attitudes and opinions*, Zimbardo's findings illustrated the impact of one's organizational position on *behavior*. The findings from the latter study are even more poignant when one learns that five days into the experiment one of the guards, who entered the experiment as a pacifist, tried to force-feed a prisoner who would not eat.

The third example of the shaping potential of organizations derives from an interview with a university professor who reflected on the socialization process she experienced during her doctoral program:

In my cohort doctoral program, we met with the faculty in January of our first year to discuss the program. Most of us were very vocal regarding our likes and dislikes. Although we were given an opportunity to air our feelings, nothing actually changed over the next year . . . at least I didn't think so until the following January when two cohorts of students met with the faculty. I can remember being fascinated as I watched the first year students describe the problems they were experiencing with the program. They were very forthright, and the passion of their beliefs was undeniable.

After the meeting the second year group voiced several comments: "Wasn't that an interesting experience?" "Did you see how angry Student X was?" It was then that I came to what I perceived at that time to be a rather startling realization: although the program hadn't changed, WE, the second year students, had changed! We had adapted to and perhaps even adopted the norms and values we had so forthrightly argued against the previous year.

These three examples suggest that, regardless of education, commitment, or previous experiences, people are subject to an intense socialization process from the day they assume their roles in organizations; however, they are usually only minimally aware of the ways in which their attitudes and behaviors are being transformed.

Organizational Forces Shape Supervisory Practices

How do socialization processes and organizational routines shape supervisory practices in schools? Better understanding of the answer to this question requires review of the manner in which supervisory and evaluation processes have been developed and implemented in school districts across the country. Since the mid-1980s, most districts have made a concerted effort to improve their evaluation/supervisory processes by having administrators and teachers join together to develop new policies and procedures. Intense discussions regarding the differences between supervision and evaluation have often resulted in the creation of parallel committees, one focused on supervision (i.e., focusing on teacher development and performance) and the other on evaluation (i.e., assessing and judging teacher performance for the purpose of personnel decision-making). The group concentrating on supervision may devise a training program to assist administrators in becoming supportive of teacher growth and to provide professional development activities that help principals engage in clinical supervision and/or coaching practices.

Desirous of ensuring that the evaluation instrument is valid and reliable, members of the evaluation committee conscientiously review the research on effective teaching as a basis for deriving the categories and descriptors on a rating scale instrument. In addition, they make certain that the instrument will assess observable teacher behaviors and develop the procedures that will guide the process. Extensive training for administrators also becomes part of the evaluation plan. The district may adopt the recommendations of the committees, but in many instances the supervisory/evaluation processes continue to be enacted as an annual ritual that resembles the scenario described earlier of Teacher Robert's experience with Administrator McCoy.

Even though the distinction between supervision and evaluation may exist in district policies and procedures, and in the minds of both teachers and administrators, other factors mitigate against the separation of these processes, making both irrelevant in terms of the professional growth of teachers. Four of these factors merit consideration: (1) embodiment of both processes in the role of the principal, (2) time factors, (3) the absence of a legal separation of evaluation and supervision, and (4) use of data obtained under the guise of supervision in an evaluative way.

First, regardless of the restructuring and reform initiatives that have taken place (or perhaps because of them), many districts across the country have abolished the positions of subject matter specialists and curriculum coordinators. Thus, in most school districts, both supervision and evaluation have become the responsibility of the principal.

Second, rather than relieve principals of some of their other responsibilities, supervision has simply been added to their already overloaded schedules. With a limited amount of time available, supervision has become a relatively mechanical and mindless process (Wood 1992b). Thus, even though an administrator may be committed to the principle of teacher development, instructional improvement has been reduced to the evaluation process in many districts. Because of the perceived lack of time available, the evaluation process is again short-circuited and becomes equated with completing the evaluation instrument. Figure 44.1 illustrates the scenario played out in many schools when supervision and improving instruction are viewed as synonymous with filling out evaluation forms for a specified number of teachers each year.

Third, in most states no *legal* differentiation has been made between supervision and evaluation (Hazi, 1994). This has perpetuated the ambiguity between the two processes that is often resolved in favor of evaluation when the Public School Code is silent regarding supervisory responsibilities in relation to teacher growth and development. In districts where principals' evaluations are based on whether staff appraisals are completed and turned in on time instead of on the basis of either the information contained in the appraisals or the learning opportunities available to teachers, it is reasonable that principals will be more inclined to attend to those responsibilities upon which their own assessment is based.

A fourth factor blurs the distinction between evaluation and supervision. The very processes that were implemented to help teachers grow have become what Grimmett, Rostad and Blake (1992) have labeled "sophisticated mechanisms of teaching inspection and instructional surveillance" (p. 187). Hazi (1994) commented on the way in which some districts use information generated through clinical supervision sessions as documentation for cases of teacher dismissal:

As teacher evaluation became the object of court scrutiny . . . administrators desperately needed techniques to legalize their impressions. . . . [W]hen clinical supervision came to mean the in-classroom supervision of teachers, the lessons from law were unmistakably clear: documentation of a consistent pattern of poor performance over time, notification with due process, and opportunities for improvement if remediable. . . . Data collection systems from the field of supervision allowed administrators to better document their impressions in ways that could pass arbitrator and court scrutiny. For those adept at scripting, verbal interaction could be captured to balance the inadequacy of frequency data. . . . The postobservation conference then provided administrators with the vehicle to deliver legally defensible data, yet assure teachers their due process (pp. 213–214).

This practice, of course, both succeeds in making clinical supervision irrelevant, and it increases teachers' distrust of any supervisory attempts on the part of the principal.

Regardless of administrators' good intentions, supervision in many schools has not changed substantially over the past few decades. Supervisory practices have instead continued to respond largely to environmental forces and the demands of the formal organization (Wood, 1992a; b). Such factors as school size, program complexity, state and district policies, and the multiplying requirements of the principal's role impede the ability of school administrators to focus on empowering teachers and actually assisting them to grow. Principals may want to create learning environments in their schools and to work in classrooms with teachers. The more they engage in evaluative and management-type activities, however, the less likely they are to engage in meaningful supervisory activities that promote teacher growth. This pattern of activity is what prompted one principal to state in an interview: "Supervision happens not because of the organization but in spite of it." In brief, many principals have become evaluators rather than supervisors because that is what they have spent their time doing.

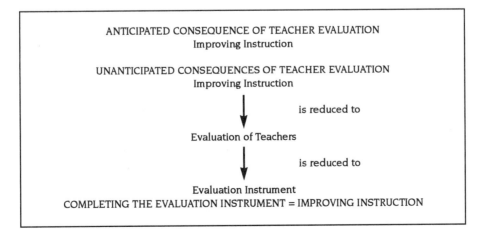

FIGURE 44.1. Anticipated and unanticipated consequences of improving instruction through teacher evaluation

SUPERVISORS ARE WHAT THEY CONSTRUE

Despite the fact that organizational norms, policies, and socialization processes exert a strong influence on administrators' attitudes and behaviors, evidence exists that some principals have overcome those forces that, in many instances, prevent them from becoming what we might call "transformational leaders." In this section, several studies are reviewed that have found a difference between average supervisors and those identified as leaders. In addition, by contrasting traditional and transformative supervision, attention is focused on how supervisors can become more effective.

An article that appeared in the newsletter of the National Center for School Leadership (Ames, 1989) described a study of how 81 elementary, middle, and high school principals' interpreted the activities surrounding their role. MetriTech, which is the firm that conducted the research, provided principals with electronic pagers. Each time the pager beeped, principals answered a series of questions regarding the activity in which they were engaged. Teachers and students in each school were also asked to complete surveys regarding their perceptions of both the leadership provided by the principal and the climate of the school. The findings indicated that principals spent a major portion of their days in a similar manner: They walked the hallways and playground, visited classrooms, and met with teachers; however, they tended to view these activities in two very different ways. Those principals who were perceived by students and teachers to be *less effective* interpreted these activities as routine, focused on keeping order, coordinating schedules, and maintaining the status quo. On the other hand, those principals who were viewed as *more effective* interpreted those same activities as opportunities to define school goals, supervise teaching, promote an instructional climate, affect student achievement, and praise the work of others.

The MetriTech study demonstrated that effective school supervision does not consist merely of acquiring a set of skills or engaging in particular activities. Rather, the *beliefs* principals hold about the activities in which they engage make an important difference. Bolman and Deal (1993) also found that the frameworks administrators use to think about their work are related to how well they perform: "Without our giving it a second thought, the frame we choose determines the reality we experience and the script that guides our actions" (p. 23).

Everyone interprets his or her activities through a set of beliefs and assumptions, even if they exist only at a subconscious level. As the studies by MetriTech and Bolman and Deal indicated, these beliefs and assumptions exert a profound influence over supervisors' actions and the manner in which they are perceived by others; therefore, although earlier sections of this chapter posited that *principals tend to become what they do,* this section will assert that *principals are what they construe.* In other words, their actions and behaviors are not necessarily determined by state and district policies, structured routines, or the socialization processes surrounding organizational roles. It is not so much the situation, the rules, or the procedures that have implications for principals' behaviors; rather, it is their *interpretation* that has consequences for how they behave (Csikszentmihalyi, 1990; Peterson, Maier, & Seligman, 1993;

Seligman, 1991, 1994; Senge, 1990; Wood, 1991) and subsequently for how they are perceived.[3] Those supervisors who view their engagements with staff members as routine interactions rather than as opportunities to create learning environments will, in all likelihood, continue to be perceived by teachers as irrelevant.

Because many principals habitually tend to think about supervision in terms of traditional practices, it is often difficult for them to visualize alternative models. They tend to perceive supervision as a one-on-one interaction based on classroom observations and tend to view their own role as that of providing expert knowledge and insights to assist teachers to improve their instructional skills. Review of the definition of *supervise* and its synonyms that appear in *Webster's New Twentieth Century Dictionary*, provides reinforcement for the preceding beliefs about the essence of supervision:

supervise, n.inspection

supervise, v.t.to oversee or direct (work, workers, a project); to superintend.

supervisor, n.a person who supervises; a superintendent; a manager; a director. In certain school systems, an official in charge of the courses of study for a particular subject and of all teachers of that subject.

superintend, v.t.to have or exercise the charge and oversight of; to oversee with the power of direction; to take care of or direct with authority; to control, to regulate, to supervise.

These dictionary definitions and traditional practice clearly indicate a management orientation to supervision, suggesting images of authority, dominance, control, compliance, and managing both a system and people. These definitions also characterize the supervisor as the expert and purveyor of knowledge.

If principals continue to view supervision in this manner, then the reality of their situations and the experiences of teachers are not likely to change. Thus, helping principals to think about supervision with a more "transformative" orientation is an important first step to changing the way they work with teachers. Transformational supervision[4] focuses on creating a learning environment rather than on managing a system and remediating posited teacher deficiencies. In addition, rather than a one-on-one hierarchical interaction between the principal and the teacher, the transformational supervisor works collaboratively with individuals and groups of teachers to facilitate possibilities and potential. Although the following provides Thayer's (1988) characterization of leadership, it also describes the transformational supervisor:

[O]ne who gives others a different sense of meaning of that which they do by recreating it in a different form, a different "face," in the same way that a pivotal painter or sculptor or poet gives those who follow him (or her) a different way of "seeing"—and therefore saying and doing and knowing in the world. . . . The leader is a sense-giver. The leader always embodies the possibilities of escape from what might otherwise appear to us to be incomprehensible, or from what might otherwise appear to us to be a chaotic, indifferent, or incorrigible world—one over which we have no ultimate control (pp. 250, 254).

Transformational supervision also inspires teachers "to transcend their own needs and interests for superordinate goals" (Quantz, Rogers, & Dantley, 1991, p. 97). Table 44–1 provides

TABLE 44–1. Differences Between Traditional
and Transformative Supervision

	Traditional Supervision	Transformative Supervision
Teaching Defined	Relatively mechanical process (e.g., following the "five-step" lesson plan) that can be observed and judged by the principal, even one untrained in the teacher's subject matter discipline.	Highly complex and uncertain process requiring continuous judgment and decision-making on the part of the teacher.
Supervision Defined	A one-on-one interaction between the teacher and the principal in which the teacher tends to assume a passive and reactive role while the principal dispenses information and judgments.	Interaction in which the supervisor and teacher(s) are active in creating and supporting a collaborative learning environment focused on reducing isolation and encouraging teachers to examine and reflect upon their teaching.
Who is the Supervisor?	The school principal, subject matter specialists, central office personnel	The person him- or herself, other teachers, subject matter specialists, the principal.
Role of the Supervisor	Critic who monitors and documents teacher behavior through classroom observation and evaluation.	Facilitator who assists in creating a learning environment by: (1) helping teachers obtain a sense of meaning and encouraging risk-taking; (2) rethinking schedules and staffing patterns in order to create blocks of time for team planning, sharing, learning, and evaluating; and (3) identifying resources (e.g., materials and opportunities) to facilitate teacher growth.
Supervisor–Teacher Relationship	Accountability and improving teaching performance and competence are the foci of the interaction. Thus, the relationship tends to be viewed as *hierarchical,* wherein the principal is viewed as the expert, passing along judgments and advice.	Interactions encourage risk-taking because: (1) teachers feel safe to disclose a variety of aspects of their teaching and to make and admit mistakes and (2) the focus of supervision is on building professional interdependence and creating teacher growth opportunities. Thus, the relationship is viewed as *interdependent,* wherein the teacher and supervisor collaborate and co-create, each contributing to the teaching and learning process through his or her expertise and experience.
Type of Evaluation Stressed	*Summative evaluation:* An annual or semi-annual event consisting of brief classroom visits by the principal followed by a judgment of the teacher's performance and competence based on a set of criteria identified as characteristics of effective teaching.	*Formative evaluation:* An ongoing process in which teachers engage in self- and peer evaluation by inquiring into the usefulness of their plans and actions and by exploring alternative strategies. It also includes the nonjudgmental, developmental, collegial examination of teaching and learning in which teachers and administrators struggle together to clarify their thinking though reflective questioning and inquiry.
Assumptions	A principal's insights and knowledge are more important than those of the teacher and his or her teaching colleagues.	Teachers generally learn more readily from interactions with collaborators than they do from interactions with evaluators.
	Teacher effectiveness research has identified criteria/teacher behaviors that should be modeled by teachers to increase student learning.	Student learning will increase if teachers teach in a manner they deem appropriate, considering their own talents and strengths and the characteristics of students.
	External accountability motivates teachers to improve their performance.	Teachers are professionals and have an internal commitment to learn and to improve their teaching.
Professional Development	A series of in-service workshops, attending a conference, or the assistance of a long-term consultant.	A wide array of opportunities in which to be involved; and creating, experiencing, and learning with and from other teachers in the school.
Policies Regarding Supervision	Quality control policies that focus on controlling or directing the work of teachers.	Capacity-building policies intended to develop teachers' capacity to respond to and be responsible for facilitating learning among students and themselves.

a listing of several differences between transformational and traditional supervision (Darling-Hammond & McLaughlin, 1995; Darling-Hammond & Sclan, 1992; Garmston & Wellman, 1995; Gitlin & Price, 1992; Lieberman, 1995; Nolan & Francis, 1992; Poole, 1994; Reitzug & Burrello, 1995).

In addition to thinking about supervision in traditional ways, many principals assume that the bureaucracy prevents them from adopting alternative supervisory practices. For example, they believe that state and district mandates for teacher evaluation, ubiquitous reports, and myriad other management responsibilities prevent them from arranging their time in a way that will help teachers to grow. Many are also convinced that they will be punished for not following district policies to the letter. Some principals fear reprisals for stepping out and using strategies that differ from those prescribed through policy and traditional practice, however, Sarason (1971) provides evidence that *conceptions of the system*, rather than the reality of the situation, tend to govern how principals perform their roles:

[T]he range in practices among principals within the same system is sufficiently great so as to suggest that the system permits and tolerates passivity and activity, conformity and boldness, dullness and excitement, incompetency and competency. . . . [T]here are principals who act as if they are primarily in control of their destiny, and there are those who act as if what they have been, are, and will be are largely a function of external conditions and forces over which they have had or will have little control (pp. 142–143).

In many ways, then, principals' thoughts create their own reality. As physicist David Bohm (1992) argued:

[T]hought doesn't know it is doing something and then it struggles against what it is doing. It doesn't want to know that it is doing it. And it struggles against the results, trying to avoid those unpleasant results while keeping on with that way of thinking (pp. 10–11).

In brief, Bohm states that "'thought creates the world and then says, I didn't do it'" (Kofman & Senge, 1993, p. 13). In like manner, Hawkins (1991) describes the power of thoughts and mental models in the following: "[I]t is with our thinking that we create the prisons in which we fall asleep" (p. 172). Changing supervision from what is perceived by teachers as an irrelevant activity to a meaningful engagement therefore entails altering the mental models principals carry in their heads. Although a principal may blame the bureaucracy for the school's problems, it is not necessarily the bureaucratic structure that is at fault. Instead, the internalization of norms, attitudes, beliefs, and values may perpetuate established organizational images and censor new ways of seeing. Rather than continue to perceive the district as an impenetrable bureaucracy that prevents people from learning and growing, principals need to envision the organization as a pliable, responsive entity capable of being molded and shaped into an environment that they (and other school personnel) desire.

How do principals and other supervisors change their mental models? How do they work with their staffs in nonbureaucratic, nonevaluative ways? How do they create communities of learners and learning communities? How can they facilitate learning for other educators? Two illustrations will prove instructive in this regard. The first focuses on Ed Stoddard, an

innovative principal, who replaced the district evaluation process at Westside Elementary School with a supervisory and learning system focused on teacher growth. The second example centers on the leaders involved in New Mexico-Fellows for the Advancement of Mathematics Education (NM-FAME), a project whose purpose was to change the way mathematics was taught in three school districts. The focus of the project was curricular and pedagogical reform; however, instead of in-service workshops, participants experienced a learning community and were subsequently able to create environments in their schools that made learning and teaching in new ways safe for classroom teachers. Neither Stoddard nor those associated with NM-FAME focused on organization rule following. Rather, they evidenced attitudes and behaviors suggesting that what counted was building a community of learners.

Emphasis on Teacher Growth: Westside School

Ed Stoddard, the principal of Westside Elementary School, is perceived by teachers and community members to be an instructional leader. He has stated that teacher development is more important than teacher evaluation, and he has found a way to focus his efforts on helping teachers to grow. Believing that teacher evaluation is a waste of everyone's time and that only 1–3 percent of the teaching staff in any district has serious performance problems that should result in being placed on formal evaluation and eventual termination, Stoddard does not "let the threat of legal action drive our whole system." His beliefs are obvious in the following scenario that was reconstructed from an interaction:

I believe that goal setting, not criticism, should be used to improve performance and that the most effective remedy for poor performance is to focus on the future rather than on the past. Focusing on the past is generally unproductive due to the fact that there is no way that the past can be undone. At the beginning of the year, I don't provide the staff with teacher evaluation packets, because I am afraid they will read them and begin to believe that they matter. They don't!

My role is to maximize the potential of each teacher and that is a very different orientation than "How do I get rid of teachers?" Each teacher already has in his or her head what is needed to become a better teacher. Some want to work on classroom management; some want to learn more about how to use the computer in their classroom; some want to concentrate on how to become better organized. Others want to understand how to assess student learning without using tests; or they want to spend time upgrading the content in their courses.

Teachers need to spend some time thinking about, "What do I want to learn this year?" When they get that sorted out, I ask them to schedule an appointment with me. I help them brainstorm how to get assistance and resources so they can accomplish what they want to accomplish. We outline the steps the teacher will take, list the people who need to be contacted and the things the teacher needs to do in order to learn what she or he wants to learn.

We then take the teacher evaluation instrument and substitute the teacher's goal and proposed action steps for the teacher competencies and items written on the district form. For example, item number one on the evaluation form might be: "The teacher communicates accurately and effectively . . . ." On a copy of the form, we cross that out and substitute one of the steps of the process through which the teacher plans to learn to use a computer (see Figure 44.2). Then, the teacher and I meet in the spring to determine the degree to which

---

TEACHER EVALUATION REPORT

Teacher Name _____   School _____

Evaluator Name _____   Year_____

Definition of Degree of Performance Ratings:

5   Outstanding Performance: Performance consistently exceeds acceptable standards. Direction is
           not necessary

4   Good Performance: Performance exceeds acceptable standards. Little direction and supervision are
           necessary

3   Satisfactory Performance: Performance meets acceptable standards. Some direction and
           supervision may be necessary

2   Performance Needs Improvement: Performance does not fully meet minimum acceptable standards.
           The employee has the potential to meet job requirements, but direction and periodic progress checks
           are necessary.

1   Unsatisfactory Performance: Performance does not meet minimum acceptable standards. Detailed
           direction and frequent progress checks are required.

                                                                  Goal
TEACHER ~~COMPETENCIES~~

To achieve level 1 proficiency in the use of computers [to use word processing programs with printing capabilities,
to use software to maintain and quickly access student records (i.e., attendance, grade books, etc.), to develop banners,
posters, fliers, newsletters, etc]

                                                                  Degrees of Performance

    1. To attend 5 in-service sessions at the Technology Support Center

    ~~1.   The teacher communicates accurately and effectively in the~~   1   2   3   4   5
         ~~content area and maintains a professional rapport with~~
         ~~students~~

    2. To have the necessary software installed on the computer in my classroom by
        the technology resource teacher in my building

    ~~2.   The teacher obtains feedback form and communicates with~~   1   2   3   4   5
         ~~students in a manner which enhances student learning~~
         ~~and understanding.~~

    3. To practice using the computer programs at least 5 hours per week

    ~~3   The teacher appropriately utilizes a variety of teaching~~   1   2   3   4   5
         ~~methods and resources for each area taught~~

    4. To request assistance from the technology resource teacher when I need help

    ~~4.   The teacher encourages the development of student involvement,~~   1   2   3   4   6
         ~~responsibility and critical skills~~

FIGURE 44.2. Example of a teacher evaluation report
used at Westside School

the goal and the steps have been met. If the teacher has completed all the steps and has reached the goal, we circle a 5 (the highest possible rating). If not, then we circle a 4 or 3. If the teacher does not get to an item, we cross it off the sheet. Of course, we don't send our substitute evaluation report to Central Office. The one we send looks like the report used by every other school in the district so no one ever questions what we are doing.

By following this course of action, we are not working for the form; rather the form is working for us. I definitely think there are advantages to this way of working: (1) it gives the teacher and principal control over the system and, thus, relieves a sense of helplessness that we can't do anything; (2) it encourages teachers to create their own meaning; (3) it gives the principal the opportunity to model the supervisory process by working with the teacher; (4) it is nonthreatening for both the principal and teacher; (5) it satisfies the bureaucracy because an evaluation report is on file for the teacher; and (6) it is certainly more energizing and fun.

Stoddard's images of supervision and evaluation and his view of what the system will tolerate differ from the conceptions held by many of his colleagues. His concern is not about what the district will and will not allow; he has created a supervisory system focused on developing teachers' abilities and strengthening their assets rather than one focused on teacher needs and the remediation of deficiencies.[5] As a consequence, continuous improvement, effort, and action steps have become the bywords for teachers at Westside Elementary School. Stoddard's philosophy and actions are based on two assumptions: (1) teachers want to improve their performance and (2) the best way to facilitate performance improvement is to encourage teachers to pursue their own leads. Instead of focusing on why things go wrong, Stoddard concentrates on how to assist teachers to accomplish what they wanted to accomplish.

In essence, then, Stoddard assumes the stance of a teacher developer rather than that of a problem solver. The important differences between these stances have been emphasized in the literature. In the following statements, Akin and Schultheiss (1990) and Kofman and Senge (1993) contrast the mindset and behaviors that represent the developer and creator with those of the problem solver:

[T]here is increasing recognition in a variety of fields that high performance or health is more than a lack of problems. In medicine, positive physical health is much more than a lack of disease. Athletes now train more with images of positive performance, developing strengths rather than merely working on overcoming deficits. Problem solving is a fundamentally conservative approach to organizational improvement. It is conservative in that it takes some prior, rational design as defining what is good, and constructs managing the system as minimizing the deviation from the standard. Problems are often defined as deviations from a standard. Managers as problem solvers tend to know more about how things go wrong than they know about how things go right. But if the capacity of an organization . . . is to grow, it will have to do more than solve problems (Akin & Schultheiss, 1990, p. 13).

Problem solving is fundamentally different from creating. The problem solver tries to make something go away. A creator tries to bring something new into being. The impetus for change in problem solving lies outside ourselves—in some undesired external condition we seek to eliminate. The impetus for change in the creating mode comes from within. Only the creating mode leads to a genuine sense of individual and collective power, because only in the creating mode do people orient themselves to their intrinsic desires (Kofman & Senge, 1993, p. 10).

Stoddard facilitated teacher growth by redirecting teachers' energies away from "responding to" external influences to "initiating" their own learning pursuits. Even though he worked in the same district as Assistant Principal McCoy, the mental model Stoddard carried in his head and his subsequent actions were very different from those of McCoy. There was also a corresponding difference in the way these administrators worked with and were perceived by teachers. Based on the findings of studies by Leithwood and Jantzi (1990) and Smith and Andrews (1989), Fullan (1991) described principals, like Stoddard, who direct their energies toward building a community of learners: "The role of the principal is not in implementing innovations or even in instructional leadership for specific classrooms. There is a limit to how much time principals can spend in individual classrooms. The larger goal is in transforming the culture of the school" (p. 161). McCoy spent time observing in classrooms and writing reports while Stoddard helped teachers to grow by assisting them to achieve their own goals. By placing an emphasis on the growth of all staff, Stoddard seemed to concur with a statement that appeared in the July 1991 edition of the *Queensland Association of State School Principals Newsletter*: "No restructured profession can be built on unrestructured individuals." His emphasis was on people and their development rather than on organizational structures and their maintenance.

Like Stoddard Karen Williams, director of the NM-FAME project and the FAME Fellows, concentrated on teacher growth by providing opportunities for teachers to learn and to garner new ideas and ways of working. Whereas Stoddard operated in an atypical fashion within a traditional school district, however, Williams and the Fellows were relatively unencumbered by the trappings that tend to surround the role of a principal, such as teacher evaluations, organizational maintenance responsibilities, and tradition. Being involved in an innovative program to change the way mathematics was taught, Williams and the Fellows felt free to design their own ways of working with teachers. Whereas Stoddard may have been successful in building a community of learners (i.e., teachers focused on improving their knowledge and skills so that their instructional capabilities would improve), Williams and the Fellows focused on creating a learning environment, where they, in the context of a group, collaborated in a number of ways to help each other become what they were capable of becoming.[6] In meetings, interviews, and focus groups, teachers associated with this project spoke of the way that the environment in which they operated had transformed their thinking both in terms of mathematics as well as in terms of a myriad of other areas. The NM-FAME program possessed many of the attributes of a learning environment, and Williams and the Fellows personified a more transformational approach to helping teachers grow than did most supervisors. What then are the characteristics of supervisors who facilitate learning in others? What operating values and environmental properties characterize a learning environment? The following scenario will help to answer these questions by reviewing the role of Williams and the FAME Fellows as transformational supervisors or leaders and the manner in which they worked to create environments that facilitated learning. One of the problems that plagues the adoption of a more transformative approach to supervision is the lack of models and successes to point the way. The following description will therefore include a liberal use of quotes from program participants in order to help provide the flavor of their experiences and to give the reader a better "feeling for" the nature of supervision in terms of creating a learning environment.

Emphasis on Teacher Growth: The NM-FAME Project[7]

The purpose of NM-FAME was to develop a cadre of K–5 teachers (called *Fellows*) who would change mathematics instruction in three school districts. The Fellows were classroom-based in 15 schools. In addition to full-time teaching responsibilities, their activities included: (1) completing seven higher level mathematics courses over a three-year period; (2) promulgating and implementing the *Curriculum and Evaluation Standards for School Mathematics* issued by the National Council of Teachers of Mathematics (NCTM, 1989); and (3) serving as teacher-leaders, working individually and in groups with teachers, providing continual support, developing teacher networks, and giving workshops in their schools and districts. The project director, Karen Williams, and two Fellows, called Resource Teachers, were released from their classroom responsibilities in order to engage in on-site collaboration for two to four days per month with each Fellow. The project director and resource teachers typically worked in the Fellows' classrooms, demonstrated new teaching techniques, collaborated with teachers in the building, or assumed classroom responsibilities so that a Fellow could work with other teachers or present district workshops. Each Fellow also selected and worked with three individuals called FAME-Teachers (i.e., one each year of this three-year project) who received mathematics training in the form of in-service workshops and who also served as team members and support persons in the schools. In essence, then, this intensive staff development effort provided support and training for 17 classroom teachers, who in turn collaborated with FAME-Teachers and non-FAME teachers in their schools to promote a better understanding and appreciation of mathematics.

The project director, resource teachers, and the Fellows can be thought of as supervisors (i.e., educators, who while engaged in learning themselves, helped to create environments that would facilitate learning in those with whom they collaborated). The project director and resource teachers facilitated the learning activities of the Fellows while the Fellows, in turn, assisted teachers in their schools. Three leadership/supervisory characteristics, along with four operating values that permeated NM-FAME, tended to be responsible for the growth of the individuals associated with the Project. The synopsis that follows highlights those characteristics and operating values that have important implications for principals and other supervisors as they work to transform their school environments into learning communities.

Leadership\Supervisory Characteristics

Participants frequently referred to three leadership or supervisory characteristics that facilitated learning through NM-FAME: (1) clear vision coupled with a belief in diverse methods of implementation; (2) unconditional valuing of others; and (3) enticing or inviting (rather than pushing) people into new attitudes and actions. Even though they are listed here as separate characteristics, the participants almost always referred to them in the same breath. They were, metaphorically speaking, more like threads of a whole cloth rather than different pieces of fabric sewn together.

Clear Vision The Fellows attributed much of the group's success to the power of Project Director Williams' vision, and they frequently mentioned its importance:

Karen has a vision. She knew right from the beginning what she was looking for. We didn't. She would talk to us and nurture us; and we came to make decisions. But I think they were decisions basically that Karen had already in mind. She kind of led us. You know in your classroom how you want kids to learn something, and you ask the right questions and make them feel good about themselves and pretty soon they come around to doing what you wanted them to do in the beginning. I think Karen does that (Fellow H, 1994 Interview, pp. 5–6).

She [Williams] sees a goal and goes straight toward it. She knows what to do to move it along and to move the people along with it. She has confidence. She gives you the feeling that she has a lot of confidence in you. She has confidence that you see the vision. It was never, "This is my vision, do you want to be part of it." It is more like, "I see something; can you see it too? Would you like me to help you, and we'll go towards it?" She is a wonderful flag bearer, and she just goes for it; but she'll help you keep up (Fellow L , 1994 Interview, pp. 36–37).

This overarching vision served as a constant guide for their activities; however, rather than standardize their procedures, the Fellows used implementation strategies that were suitable to them, depending on their personalities and their school situations. Williams described this approach by saying, "We did not say, 'A teacher-leader does 1, 2, 3, 4 ,5.' We said, 'You know your school; you know the problems. We want to support you in impacting your school'" (1994 Interview, p. 9). Fellow V referred to the uniting of the vision with multiple methods in the following way: "Our mission is there, and we are all aiming toward the same thing; but how you do it depends on how you fit at your school" (1994 Interview, p. 30).

Unconditional Valuing A clear vision of the change effort coexisted with absolute flexibility about the details of implementation, but the driving energy emanated from the fact that a focused vision was coupled with an unconditional respect for and belief in those who participated in the Project. For example, as she talked about the strength of Williams' vision, Fellow H emphasized the importance the director placed on people: "Nothing is more important than getting her dream fulfilled *except for the people*. She's willing to be flexible with the people because the people are the most important thing" (Fellow H, 1994 Interview, p. 6). The goal of the

Project was to create teacher-learners who would generate their own initiatives and develop their own strengths. Even though the project director and Fellows modeled teaching strategies and provided demonstration lessons, they did not intend for teachers to replicate these behaviors in their own classrooms:

I don't want them to clone me because if they clone me, they're not learning and they're not developing as themselves. . . . What I want them to do is to take in information, process through it, pick up the stuff that's applicable to them, throw the rest of the stuff away, and to grow. All they need is someone to ask questions, to expose them, and to give them confidence so they know they can go and do it (Karen Williams, 1992 Interview, p. 4).

Unconditional valuing was manifest in the many ways in which Williams helped the Fellows feel good about themselves: "She really wants everyone to be the best they can possibly be. . . . She worked very hard through listening and guidance to make us realize how knowledgeable and capable *we are*" (Fellow O Interview, Spring 1994, pp. 12–13). And Fellow C remarked, "She always gives *us* all the credit. She always sees good things *in us*" (1993 Interview, p. 19).

The Resource Teachers and Fellows followed Williams' lead and continually projected a belief in others. The ways in which they worked with other teachers is reminiscent of the story in Greek mythology of the sculptor named Pygmalion who carefully disengaged an image of a woman who was asleep in a block of marble. Pygmalion did not actually create the statue of the woman and bring her to life. She existed before he began to carve; Pygmalion *merely* delivered her from a marble prison. Rather than view their endeavors as shaping or controlling those with whom they worked, NM-FAME participants similarly described their efforts in terms of encouraging, releasing, and supporting others. That teachers reaped the benefits of this way of working can be seen in the following: "Fellow M urges you and gives you opportunities. She's so open and accepting. When I go to the math meeting and say, 'I really feel like a dummy,' she says, 'Everybody starts from a different place.' She values you so much for who you are and where you're coming from" (Non-FAME Teacher O, 1994 Interview, p. 4).

Inviting Rather Than Pushing NM-FAME participants created an interest both in the subject matter and in teaching the content in new ways. Like helpful supervisors, they provided opportunities for groups of teachers to meet, to see videotapes, and to talk about what they were doing in their classrooms. They also shared ideas, books, articles, materials, and problem-solving activities. Furthermore, they created professional libraries, gave demonstration lessons in their classrooms and in the classrooms of other teachers, and provided workshops on particular methods. In other words, the FAME *Fellows* created environments that fostered learning and provided ongoing support while teachers learned and tried out new teaching methods. Their strategies were relatively subtle and could be characterized as a soft-sell approach. For example, Fellow T helped to raise the consciousness of teachers in her building during the math adoption process by preparing

and giving each person a folder that described resource alternatives to textbooks. In another example, non-FAME Teacher G portrayed her interactions with Fellow K: "She will approach me and say, 'Hey, I got this book I thought you might like to look at. Can we go eat lunch in your room today? Tell your teammates to come too'" (1994 Interview, p. 12). And FAME Teacher P indicated the importance of the relationships promoted by the Fellows: "The thing that's important about FAME is the personal relationship between the Fellows, FAME Teachers, and other teachers. It's not pushy. It's like, 'Paula, do you want to come and see me do this lesson this afternoon?' And Paula might say, 'no;' but next time she might say, 'yes'" (1994 Interview, p. 19). Although inviting teachers to try new content and methods may have been a fundamental reason for their interactions, the NM-FAME participants did not perceive themselves as purveyors of subject matter and instructional strategies. Instead, they saw themselves as nurturers of people. Fellow K expressed a feeling shared by several others: "I certainly don't see myself as a leader; I'm more of a nurturer" (1992 Interview, p. 15).

The actions of the director, resource teachers, and fellows seemed quiet and unheroic when compared with supervisory behaviors of others that are portrayed as "taking a stand," "making things happen," or "creating a new order". The relatively routine, but constant, availability of the FAME participants appeared to provide precisely the type of assistance that encouraged teachers to develop and grow. Teachers thrived because they were enticed or invited into new ways of teaching rather than pushed. FAME participants then essentially created environments that invited teachers to join them.[8] FAME Teacher V said it clearly when she exclaimed, "Fellow M keeps sucking me into these things!" (1994 Interview, p. 16). In the two statements that follow, Williams illustrated how she drew in people by helping them to accomplish what it was *they* wanted to accomplish: "I take other people's ideas and support them and help them so that they perceive that they are in control of everything that is going on. I work *for them*. They are not working for me to accomplish my needs" (1992 Meeting 1, p. 5). "I saw my role as taking obstacles out of the Fellows' way so they could accomplish the things they were capable of accomplishing" (1994 Interview 2, p. 75).

In many ways, the three characteristics described earlier portray a "servant leader," who, according to Greenleaf (1991), is a person who has a goal, a dream, or vision: "A leader ventures to say: 'I will go; come with me!'" (p. 15). In his discussion of the servant leader, Greenleaf also characterizes the pygmalion features previously described when he commented that acceptance and empathy help people to develop: "People grow taller when those who lead them empathize and when they are accepted for what they are. . . ." (p. 21). To Greenleaf, the leader is a servant to the other person's needs first. Before one can lead, he or she must gain trust by making certain "that other people's highest priority needs are being served" (p. 13). As Sergiovanni (1992) indicated in the following statement, the notion of servant leadership helps supervisors literally to reframe their conceptions of supervision and leadership:

[I]nstead of worrying constantly about setting the direction and then engaging teachers and others in a successful march (often known as planning, organizing, leading, motivating, and controlling), the "leader" [or supervisor] can focus more on removing obstacles, providing material and emotional support, taking care of the management details that make any journey easier, sharing in the comradeship of the march and in the celebration when the journey is completed (pp. 43–44).

The three characteristics described earlier were important in setting the stage for teacher growth. Of equal significance, four operating values permeated both the Project as well as many of the school sites at which the Fellows taught. In most of the NM-FAME school settings, these operating values assumed the strength of norms that were constantly reinforced through attitudes, actions, and interactions. These operating values played a significant role in creating the learning environments associated with NM-FAME; thus, they are important to supervisors elsewhere who attempt to foster teacher growth.

Environmental Characteristics and Underlying Operating Values

Just as teachers try to provide classroom environments that support student learning, NM-FAME attempted to create learning environments for teachers that fostered growth and change. Four characteristics of these environments, and their underlying operating values, were mentioned repeatedly by teachers as having helped them to assume the role of teacher-learners: (1) a fluid environment where learning is viewed as a process, not an outcome; (2) a supportive environment where learning is collaborative, not competitive; (3) a safe environment where no one fails; and (4) a resource/full environment where growth opportunities are available, and facilitators are learners. The reader is again cautioned that, even though these environmental characteristics and operating values will be treated as discrete, it was in their coming together that they affected teachers in empowering ways.

A Fluid Environment Where Learning is Viewed as a Process, Not an Outcome The Fellows and FAME Teachers did not simply pay lip-service to becoming learners; they practiced being teacher-learners by enrolling in courses. As important as learning the content and higher level mathematics was to their growth, however, they indicated that having the courses taught in ways that modeled the NCTM Standards, which they were attempting to implement in their own classrooms, made this experience even more relevant to them. As Fellow T indicated: "The method of instruction is the key—it is forever holding my hand, questioning, suggesting, demonstrating, guiding—truly facilitating my understanding" (Journal Entry, Spring 1992, p. 4). Rather than merely talk about constructing their own learning, collaborating with others, and sharing noncompetitively, their courses gave them an opportunity to practice these strategies as learners. In addition, because of the manner in which their courses were taught, participants came to view their own and other people's learning in terms of a process that occurs over time. As Fellow M exclaimed: "We worry less about answers and more about process" (Meeting Fall 1992, p. 18). They also learned that, if they did not understand something when it was first introduced, then the material would be presented again at

a later date (i.e., there was a flow or fluidity to the instruction and they would revisit concepts and ideas in different contexts until they did understand). Fellow B talked about this as she described how she began to believe in her own ability in mathematics: "The trust that Ms. McGuire [the instructor of the Fellows' first three courses] helped us build in her was what did it. If we don't get it now, we knew she was going to come back around and hit it from another direction. And sooner or later we would get it" (Interview, Spring 1993, p. 33). Fellow C echoed Fellow B's experiences: "Ms. McGuire had so much faith in us, and she kept telling us that we could do it. And then I could see by working this way that I really did know it. She showed us that we understood stuff" (Interview, Spring 1993, pp. 22–23).

By assuming the role of teacher-learners in courses that emphasized process over product and experiencing the importance of "learning how" rather than knowing THE answer, the Fellows were encouraged to better engage with the task, by asking, "*how* do I do this problem?" rather than "*can* I do it?" Their experiences taught them to focus on alternative strategies rather than to struggle with the implications that a wrong answer had for their self esteem. They also better understood how to reshape the lessons in their elementary school classrooms because they had first-hand experience with instructional strategies that they could adopt as they worked with their pupils to enhance understanding.

Supportive Environment for Collaborating During the higher level mathematics courses, the Fellows and FAME teachers worked together in groups, sharing their thinking and devising alternative strategies to solve problems. Through McGuire's encouragement and example, they became coaches who worked to assist their peers. Rather than experience jealousy or self-depreciation because a colleague exhibited more skill, they came to value each other's expertise and learned to request assistance from each other. Fellow G made the following comment in this regard:

In the group there are people that have a much stronger mathematical base than I have. Yet, instead of feeling intimidated by it, I know there is somebody I can go to when I need their expertise. . . . Instead of feeling competitive, we use each other as resources (Interview, Spring 1994, pp. 5–6).

Several participants commented that, unlike other teaching situations, the environment created through the efforts of FAME was a supportive one in which learning was viewed as a collaborative venture rather than as one that fostered competition between and among colleagues.

Myriad comments from NM-FAME participants underlined their belief that various types of support were essential to their growth and development. FAME Teacher B commented on the importance of having "people who are there say, 'here's some ideas that you might use,' or 'why don't you come watch me do this?'" Fellow C talked about collaborative support in the form of having someone to share with and show things to:

Resource Teacher F is one of those fabulous supports . . . real interested in what I do and what I think, and interested in learning along with me in terms of what are the kids thinking, what are they doing, and what's gonna help these teachers? . . . She does things like wondering about "Why did this kid say that and did he really understand this?" (Interview, Spring 1993, pp. 27–28).

Non-FAME Teacher N focused on support in terms of sharing: "When I have an activity that has turned out great, I almost literally run down the hall or go find Fellow L . . . . I just know she will appreciate it, and she does. . . . It makes it more fun when you can share and say, 'Look how wonderful this thinking is'" (Interview, Spring 1993, pp. 32–33). Teachers who had no previous experience with the innovative methods discussed their need for a more direct type of ongoing support, helping in translating what they had learned during workshops and institutes into lessons that could be implemented in their classrooms. Assistant Principal H, for example, talked about needing this type of support when she was a classroom teacher :

[Fellow F would say] "It's okay, try this lesson, I'll be right next door. If it bombs, come talk to me." I remember my first math menu. It bombed dreadfully, and I wanted to chuck the whole thing. Luckily Fellow F was there to help debrief me and talk me through it and say, "What didn't work? What do you need to do differently? Try this; let's do this" (Interview, Spring 1994, pp. 48–49).

Non-FAME Teacher B also shared a poignant story about her inability to implement strategies "learned" at a workshop without ongoing support:

[After the workshop] I was really fired up, and I kept thinking, "Oh, I'm gonna do this, and I'm gonna do that!" And then when I got in my own classroom, it was scary. . . . I didn't know how to actually get started. I probably never would have if Fellow H hadn't been at our school. I had talked to her on several occasions and told her "I'd really like to do this, but I'm having a hard time getting started." The first thing that happened is she said, "Okay, I'll come in and demonstrate a lesson." . . . Even after she had given me some ideas, I still needed to go to her and say, "Well, what do they mean by this? What exactly do I need to do here?" I just needed her there to know that I was doing okay. And she would come in and check on me to see how things had gone (Interview, Spring 1994, pp. 5–6).

When participants talked about the significance of having a support person from whom they were able to learn and with whom they could share ideas and practices, they invariably indicated that it was vital to have that person located in the school instead of being a "visitor." They also spoke of the importance of working with people who possessed the following characteristics: "nonthreatening," "available," people who can "remove some of the isolation teachers experience," and someone who can help "to alleviate the fear." The supervisory support offered through FAME was very different from the support many of the participants had received from principals with whom they had worked—support came in response to questions the teachers asked and learnings they desired rather than in response to someone else's agenda. Unlike previous teacher evaluation experiences, access to genuine collaboration and mutual support led NM-FAME participants to feel safe: safe to admit they did not know an answer and safe to request assistance.

A Safe Environment Where No One Fails An attitude that permeated NM-FAME was that "no one will fail." This encouraged Fellows and teachers alike to take risks and to feel secure even when they experienced a "nonsuccess." That this attitude became a natural part of the Project can be seen in Fellow T's response to a question about the no failure rule: "I guess I don't even see it anymore as making mistakes. I think of them as opportunities for me to learn. . . . We are learners and mistakes will happen. This is the way kids and adults learn. It is just part of the learning process" (Interview, Spring 1994, p. 34). As Fellow K worked with children and teachers, she tried to create a safe environment by focusing on their strengths:

I try to approach children through their strengths. When you do this, it just makes them move up and feel so strong. I need to make a concerted effort to do that with all of the teachers I work with. They don't have to do it perfectly; what's important is for them to see themselves as succeeding and moving on. . . . That's what's important: valuing people and looking at ways of approaching them through their strengths. I wouldn't be here if it weren't for Karen Williams' earlier contacts and her valuing of me—seeing her believe in me when I wasn't confident enough to believe in myself (Interview, Spring 1992, p. 13).

Mistakes and occasional failures were viewed as providing information; they were seen as indicating that the person should do something in a different way rather than to indicate that he or she had failed. As the Fellows worked with others, they tended not to focus on weaknesses. Instead, they concentrated on creating a learning context by raising such questions as: "What are your strengths?" "Where are you in the learning process?" "What do you need?" "How can I help?"

A Resource/full Environment Where Growth Opportunities Are Available and Facilitators Are Learners While the Fellows attributed much of their growth to having been provided with a safe and supportive environment in which learning was viewed as a process rather than an outcome, they also indicated the importance of having what might be referred to as a "resource/full" environment. Funds were available (1) to purchase materials like manipulatives and mathematics kits; (2) to pay for substitutes, which allowed Fellows and other classroom teachers time to plan together; (3) to pay travel and registration fees for conference attendance; (4) to buy books and other materials for professional libraries; and so on. While regarding the funds available for these purposes as extremely beneficial, they expressed the belief that even more important in terms of their own growth was the availability of human resources: practitioners who behaved as learners rather than experts. For example, Fellow G talked about how others had served as role models and had enhanced her growth by sharing their insights about why lessons they had taught did not work well: "Well, for Pete's sake; if she can talk about it, so can we" (Interview, Spring 1994, p. 28). Such collaborative experiences propelled the Fellows to continue to learn and to share both their successes and nonsuccesses with others. A journal entry by Resource Teacher B portrays the reciprocity that characterized her work with classroom teachers. After describing how she and a FAME Teacher had worked together one morning, Resource Teacher B wrote, " Some days this resource teacher job is so exciting!!! I *always* learn so much *from* FAME Teacher X!"

(Spring 1992, p. 3). As described by FAME Teacher P, the two-way sharing was energizing: "It's really important that they're [the Fellows] on-site 'cause I can run over there and say, `Fellow F read this log.' And she'd do the same thing and run into my classroom. And that felt good 'cause I thought she had all this experience and knowledge, but she'd still come to me and ask me a question" (Interview, Spring 1993, p. 25).

Funds from external sources were invaluable in providing the Fellows and other teachers with myriad opportunities for professional development. Would they have achieved as much growth, however, if they had not experienced collaboration and support from others? Non-FAME Teacher K offered the following comments: "If someone gave me a blank check and said, 'Here, order whatever you wish,' I don't know that I would grow. You need access to other people that you respect and who have some answers for you. So support is that other person, that connection" (Interview, Spring 1993, p. 24). For some teachers, support in the form of assistance was important; however, for others, interacting with people who perceived themselves as collaborators in the learning adventure was what encouraged growth.

The environments created by and for teachers associated with NM-FAME shared at least the four operating values described earlier. The difference between the teachers associated with NM-FAME and many other classroom teachers appeared to be similar to the dichotomy between people who have "learning goals" and those who exhibit "performance goals."[9]

According to Dweck (1986), individuals who pursue learning goals choose "challenging tasks regardless of whether they believe themselves to have high or low ability. . . . Instead of calculating their exact ability level and how it will be judged, they can think more about the value of the skill to be developed or their interest in the task to be undertaken" (p. 1042). On the other hand, teachers whose behaviors are guided more by performance goals tend to focus more on making certain that they look good and less on mastering a skill. As Dweck stated; "Even individuals with high assessments of their ability may sacrifice learning opportunities (that involve the risk of errors) for opportunities to look smart" (p. 1042). The environments created in NM-FAME and in the Fellows' schools were structured to ensure positive attitudes regarding the content and methods. High involvement and engagement were encouraged while external controls like evaluation and curriculum audits were diminished or nonexistent. This led participants to invest their energies in learning rather than in performing for their supervisors.

In sum, the three supervisory attributes of the project director, resource teachers, and Fellows, and the four operating values that permeated NM-FAME led to the creation of learning environments in the schools. In turn, these learning environments, seemed to facilitate enthusiasm, as well as the growth and development of faculty. Because they appear to represent cornerstones in the development of a learning community, both the supervisory and environmental characteristics are illustrated in Figure 44.3.

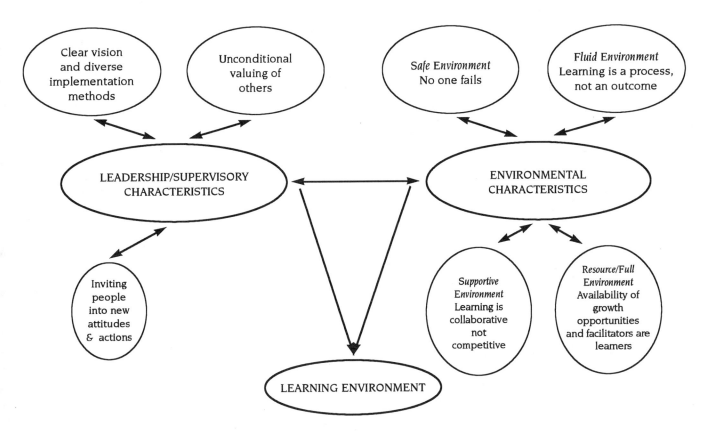

FIGURE 44.3. Leadership/supervisory and environmental characteristics that assist in creating a learning environment

SUMMARY OF THE CURRENT SITUATION

This chapter has addressed two fundamental questions regarding supervision. First, why have teachers tended to experience supervision as irrelevant? Second, how can supervisors facilitate growth and learning in classroom teachers?

Supervisory Practices: Why do They Lack Relevance for Teachers?

Although supervision at a future time may be perceived as relevant in school settings, most teachers do not view current practices as particularly useful for a variety of reasons. First, in most districts, the principal has been designated as the supervisor. From a teacher's point of view this creates a conflict in as much as the typical principal also assumes evaluation responsibilities. Most teachers would not choose to confide deficiencies and admit needing assistance to an individual who has the responsibility to determine their assignments, recommendations, promotions, and so on. Second, principals have been known to use data obtained under the guise of supervision for evaluation purposes, thus violating the trust necessary in a supervisory relationship. Third, the principal may not have training in the teacher's subject matter area, thus, in the teacher's mind, diminishing the principal's ability to offer useful assistance. Fourth, even if the principal were trained in the teacher's area of expertise, then he or she may be relatively unavailable to provide assistance because of a perceived lack of time.

All of the preceding have been mentioned by teachers as reasons why they do not view supervision as particularly relevant. These reasons, however, may merely be symptoms of two much larger problems: (1) how principals actually spend their time and (2) how they define and act on their interpretation of the supervisory role. First, the principalship tends to be characterized as a fast-paced, multiinteraction, varied-demand position where events and district mandates often-times seem to control the principal's agenda. This style of working is constantly reinforced by more crises, problems, meetings, and daily tasks that consume the principal's time and energy. Rather than assume primary importance, supervision has frequently become just one more responsibility to which the principal must attend, just one task among many to be checked off the daily "to do" list.

While the patterns of activity and ways in which principals spend their time provide important considerations in determining why supervision is perceived by teachers as irrelevant, principals' patterns of thought and reflection are equally important. Just as checking off the accomplishment of tasks represents a behavior, it also represents a pattern of thought, particularly if a principal characterizes a supervisory activity as "just one more task." Principals often stress that they do not have time to think, reflect, or plan. When they are governed by normative expectations that reports will be completed in a timely fashion, however, or that order in the building will be maintained, and that district policies and procedures will be followed, it is sometimes the subconscious rather than the conscious mind that rules. Wood (1992b) suggested that due to a lack of conscious thought and reflection, important activities such as supervision often are relegated to mindless tasks:

Because the principal's role has become marked by increasing complexity, diversity, and responsibility, most principals have developed the ability to operate on "automatic pilot" for self-preservation. This state leaves the conscious mind free for important problems and allows a principal to move with relative ease from discussing a problem with an angry parent, to finding someone to fix a broken water pipe, to completing a report. Through continued practice, the automatic pilot becomes very efficient in handling problems so that almost before the principal knows what the problem is, it is being solved by habit before new problems arise. However, in many instances, the mechanism becomes too efficient, and too automatic and, literally, may take over instructional leadership functions. . . . Without conscious realization, these functions can become mechanical, mindless tasks (p. 56).

Out of habit, rather than as a consequence of thought and reflection, many principals focus their attention on solving problems rather than on creating opportunities, on completing urgent tasks rather than on planning for the accomplishment of vital priorities and goals, and on evaluation forms rather than on teacher growth and development. When principals view teacher development as a problem to be solved or a task to be accomplished, they often sacrifice effectiveness for efficiency. In essence, then, when evaluation and supervisory tasks rather than people and their professional development become principals' primary focus, teachers perceive supervision as irrelevant; and it is.

Supervisory Practices: How To Facilitate Teacher Growth and Development By Building a Learning Community

Organizational requirements and expectations surrounding principals' positions may teach principals that they lack the time necessary to engage in effective practices and that they do not control their professional lives. As much of the literature (Ames, 1989; Bolman, & Deal, 1993; Csikszentmihalyi, 1990; Peterson, Maier & Seligman, 1993; Seligman, 1994; Senge, 1990; Wood, 1991) has indicated, however, it is not so much organizational rules, the formal expectations surrounding their jobs, or even time, or the lack thereof, that determine how supervisors will behave. Rather, it is their interpretation (i.e., their attitude), regarding the situation that has important consequences for their behavior and, subsequently, for how they are perceived by other educators.

The attitudes projected by Principal Stoddard and NM-FAME participants provided poignant illustrations of the ways in which perspective and interpretation can make a difference. Neither Stoddard nor the FAME participants believed in exerting control over the teachers with whom they worked. Rather, they put their energies into creating learning opportunities that invited, rather than mandated, teachers to change. For example, Stoddard eschewed the formal teacher evaluation processes of the district. Guided by an underlying belief that teachers themselves know what to do to improve their instructional practices, Principal Stoddard helped faculty members focus on building their capacity rather than on remediating their deficiencies. He facilitated their efforts to access the assistance and resources they would need in order to accomplish their goals. In essence, he redefined supervision by adopting the mindset of a teacher developer or a creator of learning opportunities rather than of an evaluator or problem solver focused on crisis management.

Although Williams, as director of NM-FAME, and the resource teachers and Fellows were different from Stoddard in that they did not serve as school principals, they were similar to him in that they viewed their role as assisting teachers to grow (i.e., as helping to create environments that would facilitate collaboration and learning). Their attitudes and the activities in which they engaged therefore have implications for principals and other supervisors of teachers. In addition to helping create learning environments for others, each was actively engaged in understanding new methods and content—they too were learners. Additional attributes that both made their attitudes and behaviors different from those typically adopted by more traditional supervisors and helped to facilitate learning in teachers are summarized in the following lists. They include leadership or supervisory characteristics that set the stage for teacher growth and the operating values that permeated the Project and subsequently the school settings:

- Leadership/Supervisory Characteristics
  - Clear vision coupled with a belief in diverse methods of implementation
  - Unconditional valuing of others
  - Enticing or inviting (rather than pushing) people into new attitudes and actions

- Operating Values
  - A fluid environment where learning is viewed as a process, not an outcome
  - A supportive environment where learning is collaborative, not competitive
  - A safe environment where no one fails
  - A resource/full environment where growth opportunities are available, and facilitators are learners

In conclusion, a more "can-do" attitude characteristic of learning communities is facilitated by supervisors who adopt the leadership/supervisory characteristics listed previously. Teachers, however, do not feel empowered simply because they perceive a direction and receive support. Is it also not sufficient that teachers interact in learning environments that

are characterized by certain operating values. Rather, these features in combination are what make the difference. Transformational supervision is much more than facilitating curricular and methods reform. It is literally assisting in the transformation of people and school cultures by redesigning ways in which educators work together; by emphasizing strengths rather than weaknesses; and by providing assistance such as training, support, and materials. Most important of all, however, transformative supervision is not a set of skills one learns. It is an attitude one adopts.

AGENDA FOR FURTHER RESEARCH

An examination of the supervision literature indicates that, in line with school reform efforts, new models of supervision continually are being proposed. In addition, teachers and principals alike have voiced their opinions over the years that traditional supervisory practices do not work. Old habits and public demands for accountability, however, die hard. The traditional model of supervision is alive and well in schools and districts across the country. Thus, the field is ripe for further research in at least three areas.

First, researchers need to identify those persistent factors that prevent schools and districts, and more particularly administrators and teachers, from moving away from more traditional forms of supervision and toward transformational supervision and the creation of learning environments. Can a lack of movement be attributed to fear, habit, lack of motivation, actual constraints imposed by state and district policies, or other forces?

Second, investigating the impact of the traditional and more transformative approaches on teachers, their motivation, teaching practices, and the like, is necessary to understand the effect, or lack thereof, of supervision. How do principals spend their time? How do they interpret the activities in which they engage? Do supervisory practices promote resourcefulness or do they produce feelings of helplessness in teachers? Does supervision encourage "playing it safe" or innovation? What types of assistance would teachers perceive as helpful?

Third, shadowing and providing case histories of exemplary supervisors and teacher growth situations has the potential to bridge the gap between theory and practice. Observations of the field that serve to document how supervisors have transformed their roles to make teacher development central has the potential to link practitioners and researchers in ways that will be helpful to both.

REFERENCES

Akin, G. & Schultheiss, E. (1990). Jazz bands and missionaries: OD through stories and metaphor. *Journal of Managerial Psychology, 5*(4), 12–18.

Ames, R. (1989). Quality, not quantity. *Leadership and Learning Newsletter, 2*(1), 1–3.

Bohm, D. (1992). *Thought as a system*. London, England: Routledge.

Bolman, L. G. & Deal, T. E. (1993). Everyday epistemology in school leadership: Patterns and prospects. In P. Hallinger, K. Leithwood & J. Murphy (Eds.). *Cognitive perspectives on educational leadership*. New York: Teachers College Press.

Costa, A. L. & Garmston, R. (1985). Supervision for intelligent teaching. *Educational Leadership, 42*(5), 70–80.

Csikszentmihalyi, M. (1990). *Flow: The psychology of optimal experience*. New York: Harper & Row.

Darling-Hammond, L. & McLaughlin, M.W. (1995). Policies that support professional development in an era of reform. *Phi Delta Kappan*, 76(8), 597–604.

Darling-Hammond, L. & Sclan, E. (1992). Policy and supervision. In C. D. Glickman (Ed.). *Supervision in transition* (pp. 7–29). Alexandria, VA: ASCD.

Dweck, C. S. (1986). Motivational processes affecting learning. *American Psychologist*, 41(10), 1040–1048.

Fullan, M. G. (1991). *The new meaning of educational change* (2nd ed.). New York: Teachers College Press.

Garman, N. B. (1986). Reflection, the heart of clinical supervision: A modern rationale for practice. *Journal of Curriculum and Supervision*, 2(1), 1–24.

Garmston, R. & Wellman, B. (1995). Adaptive schools in a quantum universe. *Educational Leadership*, 52(7), 6–12.

Gitlin, A. & Price, K. (1992). Teacher empowerment and the development of voice. In C. D. Glickman (Ed.) *Supervision in transition* (pp. 61–74). Alexandria, VA: ASCD.

Glickman, C. D. (1985). *Supervision of instruction: A developmental approach*. Boston, MA: Allyn & Bacon.

Glickman, C. D. (1992). Introduction: Postmodernism and supervision. In C. D. Glickman (Ed.) *Supervision in transition* (pp. 1–3). Alexandria, VA: ASCD.

Greenleaf, R. K. (1991). *Servant leadership: A journey into the nature of legitimate power and greatness*. New York: Paulist.

Grimmett, P. P., Rostad, O. P., & Ford, B. (1992). The transformation of supervision. In C. D. Glickman (Ed.). *Supervision in transition* (pp. 185–202). Alexandria, VA: ASCD.

Hawkins, P. (1991). The spiritual dimension of the learning organization. *Management Education and Development*, 22(3), 172–187.

Hazi, H. M. (1994). The teacher evaluation-supervision dilemma: A case of entanglements and irreconcilable differences. *Journal of Curriculum and Supervision*, 9(2), 195–216.

Kmetz, J. T. & Willower, D. J. (1982). Elementary school principals' work behavior. *Educational Administration Quarterly*, 18(4), 62–78.

Kofman, F. & Senge, P. M. (1993). The heart of learning organizations. *Organizational Dynamics*, 22(2), 5–23.

Leithwood, K. (1992). The move toward transformational leadership. *Educational Leadership*, 49(5), 8–12.

Leithwood, K. & Jantzi, D. (1990). *Transformational leadership: How principals can help reform school culture*. Paper presented at the American Educational Research Association Annual Meeting.

Lieberman, A. (1995). Practices that support teacher development: Transforming conceptions of professional learning. *Phi Delta Kappan*, 76(8), 591–596.

Lieberman, S. (1956). The effects of changes in roles on the attitudes of role occupants. *Human Relations*, 9, 385–402.

Mintzberg, H. (1973). *The nature of managerial work*. New York: Harper & Row, 1973.

Mintzberg, H. (1976). The manager's job: Folklore and fact. In W. R. Lassey & R. R. Fernandez (Eds.). *Leadership and social change* (2nd ed.) pp. 213–237. La Jolla, CA: University Associates.

Morris, V. C., Crowson, R. L., Herwitz, E., & Porter-Gehrie, C. (1982). The urban principal: Middle manager in the educational bureaucracy. *Phi Delta Kappan*, 63(10), 689–692.

National Council of Teachers of Mathematics. (1989). *Curriculum and evaluation standards for school mathematics*. Reston, VA: National Council of Teachers of Mathematics (NCTM).

Nolan, J. & Francis, P. (1992). Changing perspectives in curriculum and instruction. In C. D. Glickman (Ed.). *Supervision in transition* (pp. 44–60). Alexandria, VA: ASCD.

Pajak, E. (1993). *Approaches to clinical supervision: Alternatives for improving instruction*. Norwood, MA: Christopher-Gordon.

Peterson, C, Maier, S. F., & Seligman, M. E. P. (1993). *Learned helplessness: A theory for the age of personal control*. New York: Oxford University Press.

Pohland, P. A. & Wood, C. J. (1978). *Teachers' images of supervision*. Unpublished paper, University of New Mexico, Albuquerque, NM.

Poole, W. (1994). Removing the "super" from supervision. *Journal of Curriculum and Supervision*, 9(3), 284–309.

Poplin, M. (1992). The leader's new role: Looking to the growth of teachers. *Educational Leadership*, 49(5), 10–11.

Quantz, R., Rogers, J., & Dantley, M. (1991). Rethinking transformative leadership: Toward democratic reform of schools. *Journal of Education*, 173(3), 96–118.

Reitzug, U. C. & Burrello, L. C. (1995). How principals can build self-renewing schools. *Educational Leadership*, 52(7), 48–50.

Sarason, S. B. (1971). *The culture of the school and the problem of change*. Boston, MA: Allyn & Bacon.

Seligman, M. E. P. (1991). *Learned optimism*. New York: Alfred A. Knopf.

Seligman, M. E. P. (1994). *What you can change & what you can't*. New York: Alfred A. Knopf.

Senge, P. M. (1990). *The fifth discipline: The art & practice of the learning organization*. New York: Doubleday.

Sergiovanni, T. J. (1992). *Moral leadership: Getting to the heart of school improvement*. San Francisco, CA: Jossey-Bass.

Shedd, J. B. & Bacharach, S. B. (1991). *Tangled hierarchies: Teachers as professionals and the management of schools*. San Francisco: Jossey-Bass.

Smith, W. F. & Andrews, R. L. (1989). *Instructional leadership: How principals make a difference*. Alexandria, VA: ASCD.

Tanner, D. & Tanner, L. (1987). *Supervision in education: Problems and practices*. New York: Macmillan.

Thayer, L. (1988). Leadership/communication: A critical review and a modest proposal. In G. M. Goldhaber & G. A. Barnett (Eds.). *Handbook of organizational communication* (pp. 231–263). Norwood, NJ: Ablex.

Wood, C. J. (1991). Are students and school personnel learning to be helpless-oriented or resourceful-oriented? Part 1: Focus on students. *Journal of Educational and Psychological Consultation*, 2(1), 15–48.

Wood, C. J. (1992a). Are students and school personnel taught to be helpless-oriented or resourceful-oriented? Part 2: Focus on school personnel. *Journal of Educational and Psychological Consultation*, 3(4), 317–355.

Wood, C. J. (1992b). Toward more effective teacher evaluation: Lessons from naturalistic inquiry. *NASSP Bulletin*, 76(542), 52–59.

Wood, C. J. (1995). *You can't teach what you don't know: NM-FAME 1991–1994*. A longitudinal evaluation for the National Science Foundation and the Exxon Education Foundation.

Zeichner, K. M. & Liston, D. P. (1987). Teaching student teachers to reflect. *Harvard Educational Review*, 57(1), 23–48.

Zimbardo, P. E. (1973, April). A pirandellian prison (pp. 38–60). *New York Times Magazine*.

NOTES

1. This chapter has benefited from the review and critique of colleagues interested in and concerned about schools supervision: Franny Dever, Gerald R. Firth, Lois Folsom, Shirley M. Hord, John T. Macrostie, and Michael M. Morris.
2. Pseudonyms have been used throughout this manuscript.
3. The relationship between Person *A*'s actions and Person *B*'s perception of Person *A*'s behaviors is not necessarily a direct one. Rather, Person *B*'s perceptions are mediated by his or her *interpretation* of Person *A*'s behaviors.
4. Given the definitions posited earlier, one might be tempted to suggest that transformational supervision is actually an oxymoron. We should, perhaps, follow the lead of Glickman (1992) who, in the introduction to *Supervision in Transition*, stated that instead of supervision, we should use terms such as *"coaching, collegiality, reflective practitioners, professional development, critical inquiry and study or research groups"* (p. 2).
5. When principals focus on teacher assets, they assist teachers to think in terms of possibilities. In like manner, when teachers adopt a developmental rather than a remedial model, both teachers and students begin to think in terms of capacities and abilities rather than in terms of needs and deficiencies (Wood, 1991; 1992a).
6. In this chapter, the phrase *community of learners* is used to describe a collection of individuals who are desirous of continuous learning and who pursue opportunities to improve their knowledge and skills so that their instructional capabilities will improve. The phrases *learning environment* and *learning community* are used to signal that people, in the context of a group, are collaborating in a number of ways: learning together, building on each other's strengths, sharing, and helping each other to become what they are capable of becoming.
7. Information for this scenario is based on Wood (1995), which reports the activities and experiences of participants in NM-FAME, a 3-year project funded by the National Science Foundation and the Exxon Educational Foundation. While NM-FAME is the name of the program, pseudonyms have been used in place of the names of program participants.
8. As we discussed this phenomenon in a doctoral seminar, Tom Root posed the following to explain the difference between the exertion of force and effective leadership or supervision: The effective supervisor creates a context or an environment that spawns the will within someone to action. One cannot make the person take off his coat by the exercise of power or the exertion of direct force, but rather by creating a climate (i.e., warmth from the sun) in which the person arrives in his own mind at the need for a particular action and so does it willingly. (Seminar in Organizational Change, Fall 1995).
9. A cause–effect relationship actually cannot be posited without further research specifically designed to test the nature of the relationship that occurred. The qualitative data presented in Wood (1995) do, however, suggest the possibility of a relationship between the values that permeated NM-FAME and both the attitudes expressed and behaviors observed in those associated with the Project.

·45·

AESTHETIC DIMENSIONS OF SUPERVISION

Thomas E. Barone

INTRODUCTION

Over the decades of the 1980's and 1990's, educationists have increasingly attended to the aesthetic dimensions of education. Indeed, it has only recently been demonstrated that the arts offer valuable sets of lenses through which educational phenomena can be observed and appreciated. These artistic lenses are now viewed in many quarters as complementing the more familiar ones provided by the social sciences. They enable us to apprehend aesthetic qualities within daily schooling experiences that previously went unnoticed. Indeed, some educationists insist that focusing on these aesthetic facets can provide important new insights about the value of educational experiences within schools and classrooms that can lead to the improvement of educational practice.

The kinds of educational phenomena that can be observed through these artistic lenses are various. For example, some researchers have focused on aesthetic qualities in curriculum materials (Vallance, 1977). Others have considered the kinds of experiences that students have within a school setting or school program (Barone, 1983; Huenecke, 1992). Still others have attempted to apply aesthetic notions to the evaluation of activities of students and teachers (Donmoyer, 1980; Flinders, 1989; Hawthorne, 1992). Indeed, one can safely say that aesthetic qualities lurk within every conceivable facet of the processes of education and schooling, from school architecture to the life stories of school administrators; therefore, they can be attended to by conceptual tools that are forged within the crucible of the arts. This is not to say that a surfeit of literature that does so, presently exists. As noted, aesthetic lenses for viewing educational phenomena are recent inventions. While they remain underutilized, these lenses have nevertheless gained favor within some educational circles.

The dimension of schooling that is of most direct concern in this chapter is the supervision of school personnel, espe-

cially teachers at various stages of their careers, and more specifically, the aesthetic elements of supervision which will serve as the primary focus. Even more than the aesthetic side of other educational activities, however, the aesthetic side of supervision has remained underaddressed. Artistic approaches to educational supervision are still in their formative stages of development. The available literature, both theoretical and empirical, that attends directly to these kinds of approaches is relatively scant. This chapter attempts to distill some of the important pieces of that literature, and to synthesize it with the writings of various theorists (especially aestheticians) from within and outside the field of education.

Some of these theoretical writings by educationist authors serve as sources of legitimation for the application of aesthetic concepts to the realm of education generally and of supervision specifically. The notions of other theorists from outside the field of education are presented here as additional material, yet to be mined, but with the potential for serving the same legitimatory purposes. Finally, the chapter includes observations about what theoretical and applied work still needs to be undertaken so that the aesthetic dimensions of school supervision can be more fully addressed.

In exploring the aesthetics of school supervision, the focus is most intensely on the clinical activities of the supervisor. Cogan (1973) distinguished between *general supervision* and *clinical supervision*. The activities of general supervision include curriculum writing, reporting to parents, and evaluating the total educational program. The activities of general supervision take place primarily outside the classroom. On the other hand, clinical supervision has as its primary aim the improvement of teachers' classroom performance. For that purpose, data are secured primarily from the events that occur within the classroom. In artistic approaches to clinical supervision, however, information about teacher's lives outside of the classroom is sometimes also seen as relevant for understanding and improving their teaching; therefore, it may be attended to in the supervisory process. The main goal of the supervisory activity is still focused on helping teachers to become more talented at the practical art of teaching.

The phases or stages in various models of clinical supervision differ in kind and number (see Oliva, 1993, for a discussion of the phases of five models of clinical supervision.) In an artistic approach, there are two basic phases of the clinical supervisory process. These phases correspond to two fundamental activities of the supervisor as he or she attempts to achieve the primary goal of clinical supervision, the enhancement of teaching quality. The first is the phase of *appreciation*. In this part of the process, the supervisor observes, interprets, and makes judgments about the qualities within the educational events at hand. The artistic qualities in an act of teaching are often appreciated. Consideration, therefore, of the appreciation phase of arts-based supervision entails discussion of teaching as an artistic endeavor. The second phase is that of *disclosure* in which the supervisor publicizes the elements of artistry that he or she has come to appreciate, and invites reaction to and discussion about the content of the observations disclosed.

These two phases of the process of educational supervision (i.e., appreciation and disclosure) serve to structure the content of this chapter. First, the aesthetic elements within the act of observing educational events are discussed. This is followed by consideration of various arts-based approaches to disclosing which have been observed and appreciated. The primary purpose of this disclosure is enhancing the quality of educational experiences within the school setting. When taken together, these components comprise the two hemispheres of an artistic metaphor for the supervisory process. This is because the same two components (i.e., an appreciation of various qualities of lived experience and an imaginative recasting and revelation of those qualities) constitute the work of an *artist*.

AESTHETIC APPRECIATION AND THE SUPERVISORY PROCESS

Education and the Aesthetics of Everyday Life

It may seem unusual to some readers, and perhaps even pretentious, to equate the work of an educational practitioner such as a school supervisor with that of an artist. Indeed, within Western culture the process of making art has been held apart from and above the mundane affairs of everyday life. For example, classical and formalist aestheticians have insisted that works of art are ethereal things, lofty, spiritual objects that must be admired from a respectful distance in a museum or on a stage. Such works of art have been considered to be high achievements, and are never to be confused with the profane things of everyday commerce. Doing art is seen as the opposite of doing business: Our culture is suffused with Platonic dichotomies between (among other things) acts of imagination and practical acts. The former are seen as sublime, inspired, noble, engagements whose primary purpose is a moral uplift; the other kind of activity is crass, concerned only with the baser needs of the human animal.

Given this cultural milieu, it may indeed seem odd to suggest that an activity such as the supervision of teachers can be rife with aesthetic qualities, and that certain facets of it might be analogous to the activity of an artist. That some of us are able to entertain such a notion at all is due partly to the work of certain aestheticians who have challenged traditional ideas of art as an object bracketed off from daily life experiences. Among the first aestheticians to do so was John Dewey.

Throughout his writings, Dewey, following the German philosopher Hegel, sought to synthesize various dualisms that have pervaded Western culture, dualisms such as mind and body, spirit and matter, intellect and emotion, thought and action, society and individual, theory and practice, and so on. Dewey similarly aimed to challenge the rupture of the aesthetic from everyday life. "Why," he asked,

is there repulsion when the high achievements of fine art are brought into connection with common life, the life that we share with all living creatures? Why is life thought of as an affair of low appetite, or at its best a thing of gross sensation, and ready to sink from its best to the level of lust and harsh cruelty? (Dewey, 1934/1958, p. 20).

Dewey demanded an end to the segregation of the aesthetic from the everyday, asking his readers to see art as coterminous with being in the world, to see it as "prefigured within the very process of living" (Dewey, 1934/1958, p. 24). For Dewey, aesthetic experiences arise from within the interaction of human beings with their surroundings. Aesthetic qualities such as balance, harmony, rhythm, tension, and form are viewed as biological commonplaces, to be found in the most elemental activities of the human organism.

Dewey's connections between the artistic and the everyday meant that aesthetic qualities could now be sought out and observed in the practical affairs of daily living (e.g., in the realms of religion, morals, politics, business, and, yes, education, including teaching and clinical supervision of teaching). Before we can address the artistic nature of supervision, however, we must understand the nature of the artistry within that which is being supervised. We must review the literature on teaching as an artform.

Teaching as an Art

The teacher-as-artist metaphor is a familiar one in discourse about education. While technical parallels between teaching and art have been explored formally in print (Barone, 1983, 1993; Eisner, 1983; Greene, 1971, 1985; Grumet, 1988, 1993; May, 1993; Smith, 1971), it is not uncommon to hear comments about the "art of teaching" in informal discussions. At least two questions, however, about the supposed parallels between the work of teachers and of artists deserve responses: What characteristics of teaching resemble those of making art? Are there some aspects of teaching that do not fit the artistic metaphor? The following discussion concerning the artistic nature of teaching is not intended to be exhaustive. It will instead summarize portions of the work of five commentators on aesthetic theory and teaching who attempt to address these two questions. These theorists are Madeleine Grumet, Elliot Eisner, Thomas Barone, Maxine Greene, and Ralph A. Smith.

Grumet (1993) identified three key elements common to art and teaching. The first is the element of *naming*. Artists of all sorts help those who experience their art perceive and name features of the world they would otherwise have ignored. Teachers as artists can enable students to understand and name themselves, rather than only letting others define who they are. "Name-giving" is promoted by teachers who invite conscious reflection within students about their identities, thereby facilitating the making and discovery of those identities.

The second element is *curriculum*. Grumet (1993) insisted that the first curriculum is that which the student learns at home. All other curricula, including curriculum content mandated from outside the classroom, are improvisations on the order discovered in this first curriculum. The school is a "middle place" where the teacher as artist mediates the content, values, and relationships of the home (i.e., the private) with those of the world (i.e., the public) (Grumet 1993). This mediative process is analogous to the struggle of the artistic imagination with resistant materials: "We pull the furniture of the course into a web of relations that makes sense to the [students] who live it, and working with the given, we show children how to make it up all over again and make it their own" (Grumet, 1993, p. 207.)

The final key element in the art of teaching is *relation* (Grumet, 1993). This element emphasizes the communal, as well as the private, nature of the art of teaching. The art of teaching is more than dyadic, as Grumet argued (1993, p. 207): It does not "enclos[e] student and teacher in a private romance of learning." Artists work in both studio and gallery. The private studio of the classroom provides teachers with shelter against the bureaucratic press of the school and outside world, but the gallery offers teachers opportunities for reflection, space, and the critique of colleagues [and, Grumet might have added, the critiques of supervisors—more on this point later.]

Eisner's work has also helped to articulate the parallels between teaching and art. Eisner (1985) has discussed four such parallels. First, teachers, like other artists, make judgments that are qualitative in nature as events unfold in order to achieve a qualitative end result. Examples of qualities that exist within classroom events include tempo, tone, pace, and climate. The teacher, using qualitative judgment, will interpret the qualities that emerge and then respond appropriately in order to achieve the direction which he or she wishes the activities to take. For example, a teacher will listen for messages within the tone and pace of student's conversations in order to determine a desirable kind of orchestration of those conversations.

Second, the activity of teaching is influenced in unpredictable ways by classroom contingencies. It is an adventitious activity. When done well, it is not completely dominated by routines or recipes. This is not to say that the teacher will be devoid of a repertoire. Responses by the teacher, however, cannot be too rote or automatic lest the opportunity for ingenuity be lost.

Third, teaching can be an art insofar as the teacher seeks ends that are emergent rather than preformulated or known precisely in advance of the act of teaching. In art, ends are discovered through action, and they are not preconceived and efficiently attained. Eisner (1969) is famous for his cautions against the use of instructional objectives meant to describe precise educational outcomes of activities that have not yet occurred. Instead, Eisner argued, the ends of teaching must emerge from within the teaching act, not prior to it, lest teaching be reduced to a set of algorithmic functions that do not allow for artistry.

Fourth, Eisner (1985) suggested that teaching can be considered art when it is performed with "such skill and grace that for the student as well as for the teacher, the experience can justifiably be called aesthetic." Teaching experiences that are aesthetic contain both formal and substantive elements. They constitute acts of artistic expression that provide heightened awareness and deepened understanding.

Borrowing heavily from Dewey, Barone (1983) elaborated upon this connection between aesthetic experiences and educational ones. He emphasized that Dewey's approach to the quality of life experiences (like Dewey's approach to art in general) was not one of relativism. Some experiences are seen as more worthwhile than others. Dewey was similarly discriminatory about the affairs of education, holding that some schooling experiences are educational, while others are miseducational. An *educational* experience is a growth-inducing experience that grants the capacity for having even richer experiences in the future; a *miseducational* one, has "the effect of arresting or distorting the growth of further experiences" (Dewey, 1938/1963, p. 25). A miseducational experience can be one that turns off the student to the subject of study, or one that is lively and vivid but disconnected from other experiences, or one that increases the skills of a student but tends "to land him [sic] in a groove or rut" (Dewey, 1938/1963, p. 26).

Barone (1983) argued that educational experiences are more likely to possess the fundamental attributes of aesthetic experiences than the characteristics of anesthetic experiences. Educational experiences contain both aesthetic substance and aesthetic form. The content of an educational experience is material that will be useful to students as they create more profound future experiences. And like the aesthetic experience of responding to a novel, concerto, or drama, educational experiences proceed through Aristotle's identifiable phases of a story. Each phase has a distinct emotional quality, from a sense of expectancy and suspense, toward a growing elan, to a climax, and finally to a tired satisfaction as closure is reached. Deweyan-style aesthetic experiences, therefore, should be valued and fostered by teachers in an educational setting. Promoting aesthetic/educational experiences, Barone (1983) argued, requires artistry. Indeed, educational experiences are the fruits of good teaching, much as good art evokes an aesthetic response in the perceiver.

For Barone (1983), a good teacher selects and arranges the environment, including the curriculum content, into "activities with a catalytic potential for engaging students in an educational experience" (Barone, 1983, p. 25). This conscious arrangement implies a form of guidance by the teacher. This is so even though it is the student rather than the teacher (like the experiencer of a work of art rather than the artist) who ultimately constructs the experience for herself or himself. It is the student who interacts with the learning "material," (i.e., the content of the curriculum), wrestles with it, subdues it, shapes it, and incorporates it into her or his being. It is the teacher, however, who artfully selects appropriate, potentially engaging, material, and places it tantalizingly within proximity of the student. It is also the teacher who is present at the rendezvous between student and curriculum, offering support as the educational interactions ensue.

For Barone (1983), however, the parallel between teaching and art is not a perfect one. He emphasized one important way in which teaching is unlike art. The artist expresses an inner vision, transforming it to an outward aesthetic object. He or she does this without concern about whether a particular audience possess the capacity to respond to that vision. The art object embodies a personal "statement" in which the potential for an aesthetic experience may remain nascent. Indeed, some artwork may be appreciated only years after the demise of the artist and some may never be appreciated at all. Teachers, however, cannot be afforded the luxury of not communicating with their "audience" of students. Indeed, the fundamental purpose of acquiring empathic understanding with students is to determine the experiential and developmental readiness of students for encountering particular content. Thus, *Macbeth* may be great art, but to make it required reading for, say, seventh graders, is not necessarily artful pedagogy. Indeed, the result of such a pedagogical move may be a miseducational experience because it cannot be assumed that the grandeur of Shakespeare will speak for itself to those who are not prepared to hear it.

Other educational scholars have noted additional incongruities between teaching and making art. Smith (1971) suggested that the analogy between art and teaching is not a good one. For example, teaching is expected, in Smith's view, to have measurable results; the same does not hold for acting or performing. Moreover, teachers and artists make different kinds of judgments. In teaching, cognitive rather than aesthetic judgments are central; however, art, at least for Smith (1971), is not primarily cognitive.

Another theorist with reservations about the teacher-as-artist metaphor is Maxine Greene. Greene (1971) stressed the fact that poets and other artists require long periods of reflective "brooding." This contrasts starkly with the spontaneity demanded in teaching. Moreover, Greene (1971) expressed concern that the tight control of materials required by artists may translate into the molding of students by teachers toward their own preferred visions.

Concerning the last observation, Barone (1983) recognized a paradox. In education, the ends-in-view of the students must prevail; indeed, education means learning to exercise control in carving out meaningful experiences. The artistry of the teacher is found in artfully arranging the learning environment, thereby designing situations that promote the acquisition of control by the student. For Barone (1983),

this is a true act of expression on the part of the teacher because he or she transforms his or her own behavior into a conscious means to an end, thereby imbuing it with meaning. Barone was here following Dewey (1934), who spoke of this kind of action as a medium, because it is "employed in view of its place and role, and its relations, an inclusive situation—as tones become music when ordered in a melody" (p. 35). The end, of course, is this: The teacher aims to shape the situations that, like the products of the masters of the other arts, can result in recipient/student aesthetic experiences. In that sense, argued Barone (1983), teaching is "incipient art," if not "art" in the full-fledged sense of the term.

Appreciating the Artistry of Teachers: Supervisors as Educational Connoisseurs

The artistry of teaching, whether incipient or full-fledged, that is described by educational theorists is like other kinds of artistic activity: highly subtle and complex. Eisner (1985), perhaps more than any other author in the field of education, has emphasized this point. Teachers will make untold numbers of complex moves during the course of a teaching episode, and each action will be nested in a complex web of relationships that are often not immediately obvious. For a supervisor to make sense out of this rich and dense activity, he or she must know how to observe and to appreciate the many and varied nuances of meaning within it. That is, the supervisor must practice, in Eisner's [1985] term, *educational connoisseurship*).

As defined by Eisner (1985), connoisseurship is the art of appreciation. Eisner, however, did not limit the focus of connoisseurship to the arena of the fine arts. Instead, Eisner followed the lead of aestheticians such as John Dewey and Susanne Langer in connecting aesthetics to everyday life. Eisner argued that one can appreciate phenomena in nearly every kind of human activity and in the natural world as well. One may appreciate the subtle nuances in the moves of a baseball pitcher, have an appreciation of the qualities within Persian rugs, or may attend more fully to the tastes and flavors within wine or food. There is nothing, in principle, that cannot be the object of connoisseurship (Eisner, 1985, 218).

Educational connoisseurship occurs when the phenomena of interest are educational in nature. Eisner (1985) identified five subject matters of schooling that can serve as data sources for connoisseurship. First, the *intentional* dimension deals with the goals or aims that are formulated for the school or a classroom. Second, the *structural* dimension involves the ways in which schools are organized. Third, the *curricular* dimension focuses on the quality of the curriculum content and the activities employed to engage students in it. Fourth, there is the dimension that is of chief concern in clinical supervision—the *pedagogical* dimension. For Eisner, the pedagogical dimension includes the manner in which the curriculum is mediated by a teacher. Finally, there is the *evaluative* dimension. This subject matter includes evaluative practices and instruments, especially tests.

Connoisseurship, whether educational or otherwise, is acquired through noticing, and noticing requires *perceptivi-*

ty. Eisner (1991) suggested that perceptivity is the ability to differentiate the relationships between qualities in various phenomena. In this regard–perceptivity differs from, and goes beyond, *recognition*. When observing involves only recognition, it is truncated. That is, one who re-cognizes merely looks at an object in order to classify it, or to recall it as a member of a larger set of objects. One may recognize an object as a tree, and classify it as such, perhaps even sub-classify it as an oak tree. When the perception of the tree goes beyond mere recognition, however, the perceiver explores the ways in which a particular object is different from other members of its class. One perceives the distinctive qualities of this particular oak tree (e.g., the graceful curve in one of its two main branches, the peculiar odor being emitted from its rotting trunk, the mottled color of the leaves).

The observation of a teaching episode can likewise end with recognition of certain types of teaching moves, or it can go beyond to the kind of perception in which idiosyncratic qualities in the teaching are discerned and appreciated. Eisner (1985) expressed concern that, when observation schedules are used as mechanical tools, the result is a blinding of the supervisor to what may be significant in the observed teaching. By requiring the categorization of teaching moves, this kind of observation tool may prevent the supervisor from going beyond recognition to perception. Such devices may tend to retard the development of connoisseurship in the supervisor.

For example, an aspect of teaching performance such as the degree of enthusiasm, may be observed. A certain teacher may be ranked high on this particular competency. Simply recognizing and counting the number of enthusiastic gestures by that teacher, however, will tell little about the quality of enthusiasm, or about the contexts in which it is evidenced. One may counter with the observation that, generally speaking, an enthusiastic teacher is better than a dispassionate one, and for certain purposes that may be all the information needed; however, various styles of enthusiasm exist, some of which may be inappropriate in certain circumstances. For example, there is feigned enthusiasm about subject matter that a teacher finds boring. Many students may regard this as signifying a phony and overbearing demeanor. This perceived phoniness may even resonate with other elements of disingenuousness in the teacher's demeanor. One result may be alienation of students from the teacher, rather than the love for subject matter that the teacher was feigning.

These subtle distinctions in qualities may be overlooked as a result of using a rating scale or performance checklist. The supervisor who employs such a checklist may be discouraged from looking beneath the surface of phenomena at hand. The supervisor may recognize general qualities such as enthusiasm, but not move beyond recognition to the perception of important idiosyncratic facets within those qualities.

One necessary requisite for connoisseurship within any field of endeavor is wide experience within that field. For example, in order to appreciate the subtle distinctions in the performances of *Othello* by various actors, one must have had broad experience in the theatre. A connoisseur must carefully attend to the various elements of a performance in order to acquire a second important attribute of a connoisseur—a good memory. Among other things a connoisseur of Shakespeare possesses vivid recollections of the subleties in various Shakespearian performances that he or she has experienced. The memories of these experiences can serve as a backdrop against which the qualities within present and future performances can be contrasted.

Connoisseurship, therefore, implies a certain level of expertise, a degree of sophistication that is garnered through careful attention, and wide exposure to the area of interest. Acquiring this expertise takes much effort on the part of the observer. In other words, connoisseurship is earned. For that reason, lengthy exposure to a particular set of phenomena alone will not necessarily make one a connoisseur. The number of years spent observing in a classroom will not necessarily contribute to the development of educational connoisseurship in a supervisor if he or she is there primarily to recognize rather than to see. "To develop connoisseurship one must have a desire to perceive subtleties, to become a student of human behavior, to focus one's perception. Looking is a necessary condition, but looking is essentially a task one undertakes; it is seeing that is an achievement" (Eisner, 1985, p. 220)."

Pedagogical connoisseurship is therefore influenced by an ability to perceive and differentiate subtle and complex qualities within a teaching performance and to compare those qualities in one's sensory memory with other performances observed. Eisner (1991) insisted, however, that there is another important factor in connoisseurship—*antecedent knowledge*. Antecedent knowledge is the knowledge one has about factors that have a bearing on the qualities within the teaching episode that is experienced. Eisner (1991) provided an example of antecedent knowledge in relation to the appreciation of teaching:

In classrooms knowing something about the history of the situation, something about the teacher and the school, and the values that are regarded as important in the community can help us to notice and to interpret what we have noticed. What we might see and say about a first-year teacher would probably differ considerably from what we would say if we knew the teacher was a fifteen-year veteran. If we knew the students had a measured mean IQ of 140, our knowledge would influence what we would look for and how we would regard what we had seen. The point here . . . is that our perception and interpretation of events are influenced by a wide range of knowledge we believe to be germane to that classroom or situation. Our ideas about something make a difference in how we regard it (p. 66).

Antecedent knowledge will have a bearing on what we notice and interpret. Moreover, antecedent knowledge can be as much a hindrance as a help in the development of connoisseurship. How is this so? Whereas antecedent knowledge can provide new windows through which to see a situation, it can also limit perception. This is because antecedent knowledge can shape our expectations, influencing what we choose to attend to as well as the value we place upon that which we observe. For example, the Pygmalion effect is a well-known phenomenon among educationists. Teachers privy to certain information about a student's academic past may allow that history to lower their aspirations for those students. The teacher may then treat them in accordance with those lowered aspirations. It does not stretch the imagination to suggest that, just as easily as a positive outcome, a damaging "self-fulfilling prophecy" might also result from prior knowledge about a teacher held by a supervisor.

Antecedent knowledge about teaching, therefore, can include (among other things) theories of teaching and learning, and personal images of what constitutes acceptable teacher–pupil relationships (Eisner, 1991). One of the most crucial kinds of antecedent knowledge, however, involves the personal and professional life story of the teacher being supervised. That form of antecedent knowledge is acquired within a process called *empathic understanding*. We now turn to a discussion of life stories and empathy as part of the artistic activity of clinical supervisors by which they can become educational connoisseurs.

Supervision and the Life Stories of Teachers

In order to survive and flourish, human beings continuously attempt to make sense of the phenomena around us. In so doing, we construct an idea of who we are in relation to the world; that is, we create a personal identity. As the pragmatist philosopher George Herbert Mead (1934) put it, we construct a *self*. The idea that is one's self is developed and modified over the course of a lifetime as the person interacts further with the various elements in the physical and social environment. This self-identity is thus an achievement that is gained and altered through a process of moving upon and reacting to a world in which others are simultaneously achieving their own identities.

As phenomena and events are experienced over time, we tend to gather them together into a meaningful whole that reveals their relationship to each other and to us (i.e., we compose stories or narratives about our selves that describes and explains our growing or shifting identities). For the postmodern philosopher Ricoeur (1981), this growth and shift in the relationships between ourselves and the rest of the world constitutes the *plot* in the story of our lives. As with most stories, the plots of the ones we tell about ourselves possess the kind of structural unity found in Dewey's "aesthetic experiences." Indeed, it was Aristotle (1961) who first identified the three stages of a story (i.e., the beginning, the middle, and the end). Human lives contain those same phases. As Polkinghorne (1988) put it: "The self is that temporal order of human existence whose story begins with birth, has as its middle the episodes of a lifespan, and ends with death" (p. 152).

The stories or narratives that we weave about our relationships with the world are useful as we attempt to make meaning of newly encountered phenomena and act upon them. These phenomena are not perceived in isolation, with each one disconnected from the others. Rather, we bestow meaning upon these phenomena only upon interpreting them against the backdrop of our "funded biography," (Dewey 1938), which is the integral mass of our accumulated life experiences. Making sense of these phenomena also enables us to act upon them intelligently and coherently. These actions are in turn the source of adjustments in our life narrative. In other words, they advance its plot.

Indeed, literary critics and other aestheticians have noted that these processes of interpreting and acting upon perceived phenomena are *hermeneutical* activities that are not unlike the acts of writing and reading a work of literature. In literary texts, each new passage is crafted in light of what has already been written in previous acts of writing; each is interpreted by a reader in light of what has already been encountered inside and outside of the text. Polkinghorne (1988) explained the parallels between human actions and life stories as follows:

Narrative is the form of hermeneutic expression in which human action is understood and made meaningful. Action itself is the living and narrative expression of a personal and social life . . . and its organization manifests the narrative organization of human experience. Acting is like writing a story, and the understanding of action is like arriving at the interpretation of the story (pp. 142–143.).

Schoolteachers are among the kinds of people who, through their personal and professional activities, write the stories of their lives. This statement embodies a notion that has received increasing attention by some educational researchers over the last several years. Fictional and nonfictional stories of schoolpeople have, of course, been around for ages, crafted primarily by noneducationist authors (see Barone, 1992). Interest in linguistics and literary theory, however, as well as the work by prominent humanist scholars such as Bruner (1986, 1994) and Sarbin (1986), has promoted the notion of narrative storytelling as a legitimate form of human inquiry. This interest has spread to the community of educational researchers, many of whom are located in the fields of curriculum and teacher education, who have become intrigued with adapting the tools of the narrative research tradition to plumb their own domains of interest.

The most prominent researchers in the endeavor to explore the storied lives of educational practitioners, and to define and advance a methodology for doing so, have included Elbaz (1983, 1991), Connelly and Clandinin (1985, 1990), and Witherell and Noddings (1991). As as a result of these researchers and others, noted Carter (1993), "Story has become . . . more than simply a rhetorical device for expressing sentiments about teachers or candidates for the teaching profession. It is now, rather, a central focus for conducting research in the field" (p. 5).

The notion of story has rarely been related to the field of supervision within empirical research. It is so related, however, in the work of Holland (1989), even if this researcher did not focus on the lives of teachers outside of the supervisory experience. Instead, Holland (1989) collected stories of "critical incidents in supervision" as told by teachers. Of 72 such stories, 51 were accounts of negative experiences with supervisors, 19 were positive. The study departs from the many quantitatively oriented studies on perceptions of supervision in its attempt to "reveal participants weighting and giving meaning to events, and interpreting contexts and the actions of others according to their own unique blends" (p. 63). The researcher noted that the stories contained four recurring themes. Three of these involved the role of the supervisor (i.e., as authority, as critic, as resource), and the fourth concerned the teachers reaction to supervision. Holland (1989) related the essence of the teachers' stories using these three themes.

In research on stories of teachers, supervision by school building administrators plays a tangential role (Bullough, Knowles, & Crow, 1992; Bullough, 1989; Ryan 1992; Kane 1991; Wood, 1992) or a central role (Bullough 1990). Bullough (1990) identified and analyzed a first-year teachers' view of her self and her work. Using a methodology of narrative case study, the researcher identified three problems related to supervision that may generalize from this beginning teacher's experiences. First, beginning teachers who are technically competent may find that supervisors tend to withdraw, leaving the vulnerable and insecure beginner to ask for help. Second, the beginning teacher is tentative and cautious in establishing relationships with supervisors who are seen as summative evaluators. The importance placed by the beginner on a high rating works against the possibility of rapport. The third problem is this:

The emphasis on developing skills and rating performances results in a serious oversimplification of the process of becoming a teacher, who must be viewed in relationship to biography and conceptions of self-as-teacher and to the teachers' entire life situation (p. 357).

Bullough (1990) further stated that

each generalization points toward a constrained and destructively partial view of teacher development and the process beginning teachers go through as they try to negotiate a satisfying place in schools and to establish their professional identities (p. 357).

The supervision described in a book by Knowles, Cole, and Presswood (1994) is that of preservice teachers by university faculty members and school-based cooperating teachers. It, too, employs narrative forms of inquiry. The focus is on negotiating roles and developing professional relationships with cooperating teachers and university supervisors.

Empathy as an Artistic Activity of Supervisors

Advocates and practitioners of research on teacher narrative such as Holland (1989), Bullough (1990), and Carter (1993) argue that, in order for members of an outside audience to fully comprehend the meaning of a teacher's professional activity, they must first understand that activity in the context of the teacher's storied life. Such a position holds consequences for the field of supervision. It suggests that a supervisor will attain deeper antecedent knowledge and, therefore, connoisseurship, but only to the extent that he or she is able to interpret those phenomena in light of the full text of the teacher's (i.e., the actor's) biography. In order for this to occur, the supervisor must be able to participate vicariously within the form of life manifested in the pattern of actions exhibited and expressed by the teacher. They must engage in empathic understanding.

The practice of empathy rests on certain ordinary if implicit assumptions: (1) the "object" of attention is a fellow human being, (2) there is a shared reality in which all of us partici-

pate because we are persons, (3) each of us acts from within a unique *horizon* (Gadamer, 1975), a particular outlook on the world resulting from a fund of life experiences within a sociocultural milieu, and (4) that we can and do in fact imagine ourselves as acting from within the horizon of others.

Empathic understanding is more than mere intuition or feeling because what is striven for is an *idea* of a piece of subjective life, not purely emotional identification. Insofar as it involves interpreting meaning of actions, the process of acquiring this idea is analogous to the processes of writing and understanding the text of one's own life. The same hermeneutics of writing and understanding one's own life text, and the same interpretive activity involved in creating and interpreting a work of art, is evident in the process of a supervisor reconstructing the life story of the teacher. A particular action gains sensibility through its participation in a larger pattern, and the supervisor's awareness of the teacher's life story is enriched as this new piece of evidence is accommodated. Empathy grows as each new component contributes to and derives meaning from an emerging "whole."

In other words, as a teacher acts, he or she is also writing the story of a personal/professional life. When a supervisor interprets those actions in light of what it is that he or she knows about the text-of-that-life-so-far, he or she can arrive at a closer understanding of the meanings that those actions hold for the teacher/actor. We have seen that such empathic activity in which a supervisor goes about re-creating the lives of teachers in her or his imagination possesses certain artistic qualities, but is it enough for a supervisor to adopt the perspective of the teacher being observed? Is it sufficient for the supervisor to appreciate educational phenomena exclusively from the teacher's point of view? Is empathy enough? Should the teaching act be understood and judged through criteria that are external to the intentions of the teacher? Responses to these questions by educational theorists have generally depended on the critical stance taken in relation to the art of teaching. This stance has in turn usually reflected the author's theoretical positions on the nature of art and the appropriate role of the art critic.

Educational Connoisseurship and Judgment

Some educationists are aligned with theorists in the fields of literary and art criticism who hold that one may come to appreciate fully the nature of the art object by focusing solely on the psyche of the writer/artist, by ferreting out his or her intended meanings for the work. Other theorists disagree. They join with aestheticians who have held that a work of art always means more than, or at least can mean something different from, what the artist had in mind at the time of its creation. For some of these theorists, studying the inner and outer lives of the artist or teacher, and the cultural milieu in which he or she worked, can be interesting and enlightening. They would not diminish the importance of empathic understanding. These theorists argue, however, that the "effect" of the work is at least as important as the intentions of the artist. The completed work (i.e., the cultural artifact or text) ultimately belongs to those who come to experience the work, or read the text, from their own vantage point.

For example, consider the distinction made by the hermeneuticist scholar E. D. Hirch (1976) between *meaning* and *significance* in textual interpretation. For Hirsch, the term *meaning* refers to the whole, internal set of related understandings within a text, and *significance* to textual meaning in relation to a larger context (i.e., the "mind" of another reader, another era, a wider subject matter, an alien system of values, or any context beyond the text itself). This distinction is germane to the discussion on supervisor empathy of teachers if the structural relations in the personal and professional life of an individual teacher as perceived by that teacher is meant by *meaning*, and those relations as interpreted from within another perspective, such as that of a supervisor, is meant by *significance*. Barone (1979) noted that a shift from meaning to significance within the process of interpreting a teacher's performance occurs whenever the supervisor does any of the following:

1. Understands motives or "reasons" for the teacher's actions of which the teacher is not aware. Many levels of awareness of the sources of our actions exist. Some social theorists (e.g., Harland, 1975) have argued that an observer is in a better position to ascertain what was intended than the actor herself or himself at least in the case of unconscious intentions.
2. Discerns otherwise unrecognized "rulelike" patterns in the actions of the teacher. For example, a speaker cannot always reflect on the rules of grammar as he or she uses them, nor must he or she be able to formulate the rules of language in order to communicate through speech, even though those rules are explicit in what he or she says and how he or she says it. Other "hidden" cultural patterns of behavior may also be implicit in the actions of teachers.
3. Interprets a set of actions in terms of a particular social science theory of which the teacher is not aware. When a particular set of actions of a teacher is interpreted (e.g., in terms of reinforcement theory), there may be more learned about the "significance" of those actions than their experienced meaning for the teacher, depending upon the conscious awareness of the teacher in regard to the theory.

Whereas empathic understanding is therefore an important element in coming to interpret what a teaching event means, pedagogical or educational connossieurship, in Eisner's (1985) formulation of the term, is broader than empathy. It also includes the *valuing* of educational phenomena by the supervisor. Connoisseurship implies the judgment of the supervisor is assessing the *significance* of teacher performances. It involves judging their impact upon the educational lives of students.

As with the fine arts, there are degrees of goodness involved in the activities of teaching. Appreciation of a teaching act is not necessarily the same as liking it (Eisner 1991, pp. 68–69). One may appreciate the flaws in a work of art as well as the excellence. In observing a teaching performance, a supervisor may appreciate the weaknesses as well as the strengths. Educational connoisseurship implies being able to distinguish between the flaws and the strengths of teaching.

Judgments about the quality in any field of endeavor will be made on the basis of images that are construed from the observer's past experiences. These images are of the qualities perceived within the various phenomena. These images may be garnered through any of the senses; for example, there are auditory images of rap music, gustatory images of ahi tuna, olfactory images of Bluegrass perfume. These images allow us to discriminate between the various kinds of phenomena. An educational connoisseur will possess a storehouse of images of teaching.

Multiple modes or genres exist in any artistic medium. For example, in Western painting, there is cubism, abstract expressionism, pop art, and op art. Formal qualities will vary according to genre. Other complex human endeavors may also possess various modes and genres, each of which is characterized by its own morphology, or set of formal qualities. Teaching is one such complex endeavor. Different modes or genres of teaching include lecture, discussion, inquiry, and so on. Eisner (1991) argued that the images of qualities within each of these forms of teaching will differ, as will the criteria used to determine what constitutes excellence in terms of those qualities. In order to make an appropriate assessment, the educational connoisseur will apply different criteria to, for example, a teacher-centered classroom activity than to one that is child-centered.

If, however, judgments about quality are inherent in the act of appreciating pedagogical performances, then those judgments are not necessarily made public. Connoisseurship is a private endeavor. It does not *require* sharing of judgments with others, including the personnel observed. A clinical supervisor, of course, is indeed required or compelled to disclose his or her judgments in one form or another. When that form possesses certain aesthetic characteristics, then the educational supervisor-as-connoisseur becomes an *educational critic*. The next section of this chapter will address this and other issues related to the aesthetic dimensions of disclosure in the supervisory process.

ARTISTIC DISCLOSURE AND THE CLINICAL SUPERVISOR

Feminist scholar Madeleine Grumet (1988, 1993) has noted that not all of the work of a teacher is performed in a sealed-off studio, behind closed classroom doors, with only her students as an audience. A room of one's own, she wrote, can quickly become a bunker. Better that a teacher, despite the

terrible vulnerability [that] accompanies aesthetic practice, . . . express her understanding to the child and to the world of the children, to her sisters who are her colleagues, and to her sisters who are the mothers of the children. . . . The challenge for women who would be artists in their classrooms is to create the community that will encourage and receive their expression (1988, pp. 92–93).

A teacher (regardless of gender, other observers might claim) must move back and forth between the studio of the classroom and the gallery of the world outside. For Grumet, the outward movement is not solely for the purpose of defending and justifying the expressions of female teacher-artists to others with claims on the education of the child. Display can also lead to improvement of one's art when it is accompanied by an invitation for collegial critique and commentary (Grumet, 1993, p. 207).

In this view, the connoisseurship of a collegial observer (i.e., the private appreciations of teaching strengths and weaknesses by supervisor, peer, parent, or even student, that remain undisclosed) cannot foster the kind of critical self-reflection that can lead to an enhancement of teaching talent. For that, and for other important ends, to be achieved, the observer must move beyond silent appreciation to some form of disclosure of his or her impressions of the teaching performance. For some aesthetic educational theorists who write about the nature of school supervision, the disclosure by a supervisor of what he or she has come to appreciate within classroom teaching should itself be rife with aesthetic qualities such as sensitivity and expressiveness. In other words, these theorists would recommend *artistic* approaches to disclosure by clinical supervisors who spend time in the gallery.

Characteristics of Artistic Disclosure

A variety of different artistic genres exist through which a supervisor may choose to publicize that which has come to be appreciated in a school setting. These genres correspond to the various forms of arts-based qualitative research and evaluation in education that have been developed over the decades of the 1980s and 1990s. They include forms of literary (or "new") journalism, literary ethnography, teacher lore and student lore, literary case studies, life history, and even fictionalized storytelling and educational novels. The most prominent, widely discussed forms of arts-based disclosure are narrative storytelling and educational criticism. Those two genres serve as focal points of discussion later in this chapter. First, however, the focus is on similarities shared by all forms of arts-based disclosure and the distinctions between arts-based and science-based forms of expression.

Barone and Eisner (1997) have identified several elements common to arts-based (i.e., especially literature-based) forms of disclosure about educational phenomena. They include: (1) the use of expressive languages; (2) the use of contextualized and vernacular languages; (3) the capacity to create a virtual reality; (4) the capacity to promote empathic understanding; (5) the personal nature of the composition; and (6) the presence of an aesthetic format. Each will be described and discussed briefly. Depending upon the audience to whom the school supervisor is disclosing information, however, some of these elements will take on greater importance than others.

The Use of Expressive Language The kind of language employed in scientific and philosophical writing) aims at technical precision and avoids metaphorical playfulness. Writers of literature, on the other hand, use a language that can be described as evocative, connotative, and expressive. Rather than making propositional statements about phenom-

ena, poets and other literary authors call forth the reader's imaginative faculties, attempting to create meaning in a roundabout way. The aesthetician Langer (1942) distinguished between *representational symbols* and *presentational symbols*. The former, found in propositional discourse, are words that point directly to real-world referents. The latter are metaphors that do not signify a literal meaning, but enable the reader to experience that which they express through their form.

Artists are bound to "work within the limits of the material to create a form that expresses what has no name" (Eisner, 1975, p. 226). To capture the essence of particular qualities in phenomena one cannot rely upon direct statement, but must instead create a form that indirectly implies their nature. For the supervisor-as-artist to reveal the qualitative aspects of life in a classroom, he or she must connote, suggest, and intimate rather than denote, state, or assert. "Metaphor breaks the bonds of conventional usage to exploit the power of connotation and analogy. It capitalizes on surprise by putting meanings into new combinations and through such combinations awakens our senses" (Eisner, 1975, p. 226).

This characteristic of expressive, metaphorical, artistic language is helpful in avoiding what Eisner (1982) labeled the *fallacy of concreteness*, which is a fallacy indigenous to scientific forms of disclosure in supervision. These approaches focus on disclosing the manifest behavior of the teacher or student, rather than the expressed meaning and the quality of experiences. Artistic disclosures by supervisors do not have to be sublime poetry, but they often do employ evocative language that creates a semblance of what has been observed so that readers may imagine what the experience was like for the inhabitants of the classroom.

The Use of Contextualized and Vernacular Language A second characteristic of artistic language is its contextualized nature. Anthropologist-storyteller Clifford Geertz (1974) has used the term *thick description* to signify the closely observed, literary style of writing that honors the complexities found in cultural events. Thick description grounds phenomena observed in a particular context, adequately attending to rich complexities. Artistic language does not rely primarily on theoretical or technical grammar and vocabulary, which is language that tends to be abstract, one step removed from the primary qualities of cultural events. In contextualizing events, artistic language instead employs the rich vocabularies of everyday discourse. Such language is more likely to be useful in expressing the essence of schooling experiences than is the language of scientific research and theory, with its specialized terms (e.g., "advanced organizer" or "seatwork management") whose meanings are not necessarily self-evident. Many standardized forms for evaluating teachers also employ ordinary language that easily communicates to nonspecialists. It is only when the vernacular is used for contextualization purposes (e.g., as a tool for thick description) that it begins to perform a decidedly literary function.

One last point concerns use of the vernacular in artistic portraits of teaching performances. It may seem that composing a literary-style rendering is beyond the talents of most school supervisors, requiring a "virtuoso performance" from them (Oliva, 1993, p. 489.) It is true that thick descriptions of teaching episodes demand abilities not used in other forms of disclosure. For example, one cannot rely on a checklist of indicators to be marked, and must describe activities in one's own words. Beyond that, it is certain that some people are better writers than others. The task is rendered less formidable, however, when one considers that the ordinary language of daily conversation is the verbal medium to be used.

The Creation of Virtual Worlds Phenomenologist aesthetician Langer (1957) described art objects as *virtual entities.* In this kind of object, specific physical details are given over to the composition of an apparition (i.e., a semblance of a real object). Langer's notion resonates with Iser's (1974) ideas about the creation of a virtual world within a piece of literature. The virtual world of a story may be either fictional (i.e., honoring a specific set of characters and events that occurred in the order in which they are portrayed) or nonfictional (i.e., exhibiting a higher order of the imagination, and employing poetic devices such as composite characters and invented dialogue).

The virtual world of a story, whether fictional or nonfictional, is composed through the vivid rendering of particular empirical details of human activity. For this rendering, the author best uses the kind of expressive, contextualized, and vernacular language described earlier. Through the use of this language, the author locates these details within a sociohistorical context that is recognizable to the reader, thereby bestowing credibility upon the story. This attribute of narrative credibility was termed *verisimilitude* by Bruner (1987). In a story with verisimilitude, the reader is able to recognize qualities portrayed in the story from the realm of his or her own life experiences. Still, as with Langer's (1957) notion of virtual entities in the realm of the nonliterary arts, the primary focus in apprehending a literary work is more on the composed apparition (i.e., the virtual whole), than on the particulars.

The reader of a good story (i.e., fictional or nonfictional) may temporarily leave behind the world that is near at hand, and move into the virtual realm of the text. The apparition of the storied world, however, may become a kind of heuristic device that comments upon and raises questions about the more familiar "real" world. This activity may enable and persuade the reader to reflect upon the values and meanings that adhere to objects and practices previously taken-for-granted. Such critical reflection can be helpful in the field of education (Schon, 1991). For example, a supervisor, who has already become familiar with a teacher's professional life and approach to teaching, may cast his or her observations in the form of a vivid story, which could promote such distanced reflection.

The Promotion of Empathic Understanding Expressive language that is also contextual and vernacular can contribute another important element to artistic disclosure. This is its capacity for promoting empathy. As defined earlier in this chapter, empathic understanding is the ability to participate vicariously in a form of life as manifested in a particular pattern of actions. For example, Rorty (1989) has described the capacity of literature for promoting empathy in readers. Powerful descriptions enable a reader to recreate, in the act of reading, the mental atmosphere, the thoughts, the feelings, and the motivations of characters in a story, drama, or essay. The reader is allowed to imaginatively experience events from a different perspective or value nexus.

The importance of empathic understanding of teachers by supervisors as one element in appreciating classroom events has already been discussed. Artistic disclosure can, in turn, enable other readers of an arts-based report to dwell within the world of the supervised teacher. On the other hand, supervisors who use artistic forms of disclosure of classroom activities may choose to focus on the activities of students, vividly portraying events from their vantage points. It can often be difficult for teachers to distance themselves from their own perspectives of their classrooms. Disclosure that is focused on students may be extremely helpful to teachers, enabling them to empathize with students, and allowing them to perceive classroom events from another viewpoint. Supervisors may even choose to tell a story in which the main characters are administrators. Sharing vivid depictions of various ways of viewing school events may help to reduce the alienation that is often cited as inhabiting the technocratic superstructure of the school (Flinders, 1989; Miller, 1990).

The Personal Nature of the Composition The perspectives of its various characters are not all that is advanced within a piece of literature. The reality of an artistic disclosure is ultimately shaped by the author of the text. A literary-style text will often be crafted in accordance with the controlling insight (or insights) that it advances. This insight is the thesis of the text, and it serves a dual purpose of giving form to the text and of mediating the content to be included or excluded. For example, a supervisor who composes an artistic text of disclosure will need to determine the most significant idea(s) or point(s) he or she wishes to convey. This thesis (or theses) will in turn serve as a criterion (criteria) for selecting from among the qualitative phenomena that are candidates for inclusion in the composition, while simultaneously operating as a kind of patterning principle for revealing relationships between these phenomena.

The process of selecting one or more theses for a portrait of schooling phenomena requires that the author focus on educationally consequential qualities rather than on the ephemeral. This process can often prompt the supervisor/ author to think deeply about educational concerns as they relate to matters-at-hand. As mentioned, it will be important for the supervisor to consider the meaning of events from the vantage points of several players within a classroom setting, including teacher(s) and students. It is the supervisor/author, however, who will ultimately make judgments about educational significance; he or she will select the thesis and craft the disclosure. As with every arts-based form of inquiry, these texts embody the unique vision of the author. In that sense, each will display the signature of the supervisor/ author.

Still, the judgments embodied in the text are not meant as a declaration of a single, "correct" version of reality. One important characteristic of art is its perspectival nature (i.e., it is not positivistic in the sense of insisting upon itself as the embodiment of ultimate, impersonal truth). The text of an artistic publication is instead meant to serve as a starting point for deliberations with those who are being supervised. This fact has important consequences for the role and status of the supervisor vis-à-vis the supervised. As one who chooses to disclose artistically that which he or she has observed, a supervisor adopts the stance of an open-minded co-investigator rather than that of a closed-minded figure of authority.

The Presence of an Artistic or Narrative Format The last characteristic of artistic kinds of disclosure concerns format (Barone & Eisner, in press). Disclosure of observations by school supervisors can occur though any of several media. The disclosures can be oral, written, or even (i.e., in the minds of visionary educational aestheticians) comprised of nonliterary art products (i.e., paintings, sculpture, photographs, videos, multimedia presentations, and so on) that artistically convey their "findings" (Uhrmacher, 1983; Donmoyer, 1994). The focus of this article is on formats of disclosures within written and oral media.

First, let us consider what the format of any arts-based disclosure would *not* look like. The format found in scientific supervisory evaluation reports is often the format of a preselected observation instrument, such as a checklist or rating scale, that is used to collect and organize data about teaching performance. Such instruments often identify specific teaching competencies, skills, and behaviors to be observed by the supervisor. The number of times each behavior is performed will sometimes be tallied, and a numerical score will be calculated. These scores may be augmented by (usually) short commentary that embellishes upon the raw numerical data.

As a rule, artistic forms of disclosure appear otherwise. Narrative forms of disclosure do not employ standardized checklists, with their "advance organizers" that predetermine which qualities of a teaching performance or educational event are salient. The format is instead a less-restrictive one of narrative discussion. This narrative is usually more prolonged and extensive than that which accompanies standardized forms of disclosure. Any of several kinds of written artistic formats may be employed. These include the narrative formats of the art critic, literary essayist, and various sorts of storytellers. Each of these formats will be described more fully later in this chapter.

Eisner (1982) has identified two fallacies associated with scientific formats that are likely to be avoided by whatever the artistic kind of format employed. (Recall that, according to Eisner, the fallacy of concreteness is eliminated with the use of artistic language rather than format). These two fallacies are the *fallacy of additivity* and the *fallacy of method*.

The fallacy of additivity is committed when the supervisor uses an instrument that "assumes that the incidence of particular teaching behaviors—structuring, giving examples, positive and negative reinforcement, and so forth—all have equal pedagogical weight and can be added together to secure an index of the quality of teaching" (1982, p. 55). An artistic or narrative format implies a composition with a theme that serves to select information for inclusion in accordance with a general criterion of educational significance. Thus, the author of the disclosure is unfettered in the ability to make judgments about the degree of salience of particular elements of a teaching performance. Such a format promotes, but of course cannot guarantee, a more *accurate* portrayal of the quality of teaching observed.

Avoidance of a second fallacy (i.e., the fallacy of method) means that within an artistic disclosure format a *fuller* portrayal of the quality of teaching is more likely. For Eisner (1982), the fallacy of method occurs when aspects of teaching are neglected "that are immune to the criteria and instruments that the researcher employs (p. 56)." In the preceding discussion of educational connoisseurship, it was noted that observational checklists provide supervisors with categories of behaviors to be *recognized*, but do not promote the *perception* of nuances of meaning that may be salient to interpreting and judging the quality of a teaching performance. In that discussion, an example was provided of a teacher whose enthusiasm is recognized but whose phoniness is not perceived. An additional example of the fallacy of method in which a significant aspect of teaching is not perceived, and, therefore, not reported, follows.

Consider a supervisor who is using the observation instrument Flanders Interaction Analysis Categories (FIAC) (Flanders, 1972). The supervisor tallies the number of times a teacher who is responding to students "accepts or uses" their ideas. FIAC notes that a teacher is engaged in such behavior when he or she "acknowledges student talk [and] clarifies, builds on, or asks questions based on student ideas." However, this general description of a kind of communication event does not speak to subtle qualities within the event. For example, no mention is made about the appropriateness of the student talk to which the response is made. Are all student ideas worth a response? What if the student ideas are consistently expressed with the intent of diverting attention from course content? In addition, the analytical categories do not promote the reporting of different qualities in the kinds of questions asked by the teacher in response to student comments. What if the questions based on student ideas are often tinged with sarcasm? What if the teacher has a tendency to clarify questions that are already understood by all or most of the students in the class? These are a few examples of aspects of teaching that are immune to this checklist. Will making the checklist lengthier and more cumbersome mean avoidance of the fallacy of method? Probably not. For Eisner (1982), an artistic approach to disclosure is required that has a format offering the supervisor the flexibility needed to address the educationally significant but idiosyncratic subtleties that adhere to particular teaching performances.

As mentioned earlier, the media employed for disclosing findings may be (among other possibilities) written, oral, or a combination of both. A written composition will be more likely to provide sufficient space for a full exposition of the supervisor's findings than will an exclusively oral report. Moreover, a literary composition is more likely to "exploit the expressive, poetic, and often metaphorical potential of language to convey to teachers or to others whose decisions affect what goes on in schools, what has been observed" (Eisner, 1982, p. 55). Such a report may stand on its own or may be augmented with oral commentary and dialogue. For example, it may be presented to an observed teacher prior to a postobservation conference as a springboard for reflection and discussion.

Two Genres of Arts-Based Disclosure: Stories and Critiques

A variety of genres of disclosure that exhibit many or all of these six aesthetic characteristics have already been imagined, discussed, and utilized, albeit usually in conjunction with educational activities (e.g., research, program evaluation, teacher education, etc.) other than clinical supervision. Still other literary and artistic genres are waiting, available for transport into the educational arena from the fields of the arts and humanities, as soon as their potentials are noticed. The two arts-based genres of educational research and evaluation that have already been granted the most prominence are *narrative storytelling* and *educational criticism*. Each will now be discussed in turn.

In the earlier discussion of the appreciation dimension of arts-based forms of supervision, the notion of story was related to the affairs of everyday life in schools. The brief history of the work done to promote storytelling as a legitimate form of educational research and as a teaching tool was traced. It was suggested that a supervisor who is capable of empathy (i.e., performance able to comprehend the performance of a teacher in light of his or her life-story-thus-far), is more likely to understand deeply the meaning of that performance. In this section, narrative storytelling is discussed both in terms of appreciation and as a means of disclosure of information to the school personnel being supervised and to others who are charged with decision-making about the affairs of the school.

Narrative storytelling is indeed a second important arts-based genre through which information about teaching and teachers can be disclosed. What, then, is narrative storytelling? Narrative has been defined in various ways, but its root is in the Latin *narrare*, to relate. Narrators relate accounts of incidents and events. Many kinds of narrative accounts have been identified, including oral anecdotes and folklore, diaries, historical treatises, and so on (Connelly & Clandinin, 1990). Although some writers conflate the terms *narrative* and *story* (e.g., Nespor & Barylske, 1991), others suggest that the story (i.e., at least in the Aristotelian tradition) possesses certain aesthetic qualities that other forms of narrative may not.

Prominent among these qualities is *aesthetic form*. The dynamic aesthetic form, with its beginning, middle, and end, is an important element in a written, storied disclosure of a supervisor. Stories also contain portraits of people acting within vividly rendered psychological and social settings or *landscapes*. The incidents within the story are bound together by a *plot* that serves to bring order to the descriptions of events, personalities, and incidents in the story. *Voice* is an additional features of the narrative story to which the supervisor should attend. This last feature is discussed more fully later in the context of the nature of the supervisory confer-

ences in which arts-based forms of written disclosure serve as heuristics for productive dialogue.

A second genre of arts-based disclosure is called *educational criticism*. John Mann (1969) first mentioned the possibility of employing the tools of the art critic as a way to publicize insights into the affairs of education. Mann was focused primarily on the field of curriculum. The notion of arts-based criticism of educational phenomena, however, has been most deeply explored and widely disseminated by Elliot Eisner (1976, 1977, 1981, 1991, 1994). Eisner coined the term *educational criticism* and elaborated conceptually on the legitimacy of drawing from the arts for tools to use when inquiring into educational matters. Several of his students have followed in his path, contributing theoretically on educational criticism and providing examples of critiques of educational phenomena of various sorts (Barone, 1987; Donmoyer, 1980; McCutcheon; 1979; Vallance, 1978).

If educational criticism can be characterized as primarily Eisner's brainchild, then it is the Siamese twin to his notion of educational connoisseurship. Both concepts (i.e., connoisseurship and criticism) originated within the arts, but they have been linked by Eisner to the aesthetics of everyday life. For Eisner (1982) as for Dewey (see earlier discussion), educational affairs are part of everyday life, and this includes the affairs of the educational supervisor. Recall that educational connoisseurship is the art of appreciating educational phenomena. Educational criticism, then, is the art of disclosing what it is that has come to be appreciated. Connoisseurship, therefore, is a prerequisite to criticism. The powers of perception must be exercised by a critic if he or she is to make public subtle, complex, and important qualities within phenomena. As with connoisseurship, criticism involves judgment; indeed, as Dewey (1934/1958) stated in *Art as Experience*, "criticism *is* judgment." The judgment entailed in appreciation, however, is a private act. Only when the connoisseur reveals the fruits of judgment to an audience does he or she become a critic: criticism is the public side of connoisseurship. In other words, "criticism is the art of disclosing the qualities of events and objects that connoisseurship perceives" (Eisner, 1975, p. 223). As Dewey (1934/1958, p. 324) put it: "The aim of criticism is the reeducation of the perception of the work of art."

How does the critic practice her or his art of reeducation? There are three aspects to what critics do: they describe, they interpret, and they evaluate. McCutcheon (1977) and Eisner (1991) emphasized that these three elements appear intermingled in most texts of educational criticism. For analytical purposes, however, each may be examined separately to determine what they contribute to a critique.

The Descriptive Aspect of Educational Criticism What does the descriptive aspect of educational criticism entail? It demands particular attention to several of the six dimensions of artistic disclosure mentioned earlier. Educational critics use expressive, vernacular, contextualized language to create virtual worlds that enable the reader to gain a sense of what it is like to be in a particular culture, or a particular classroom. The critic uses descriptive prose in an artistic way, including shaping the text, feeling its rhythms, carefully choosing the right word or phrase, employing metaphors that are apt, and so on. In this manner, an accomplished writer can externalize the internal and produce a public text that is structurally isomorphic with his or her private experience.

The excerpt from an educational criticism by Donmoyer (1980) is the work of an educational critic who accomplishes this feat. It is a description of the interactions between a student-teacher and seventh grade students:

Tom Messinger [the student-teacher] . . . is in the front of the room leading the class in solving the problem. His gruff, somewhat ponderous and professional tone does not appear to command the same sort of natural respect and rapport engendered by [the regular teachers]. Hints of an us-against-them tug-of-war tension so commonplace between teacher and students in middle school classrooms and so remarkably absent from this classroom yesterday now begin to emerge. Students begin talking to each other, seemingly about extraneous matters; individual students begin making audible, joking aside. When these things occur, [the regular teacher] either raises his hand like a cheerleader trying to quiet booing fans at a football game, or he verbalizes what appears to be this classroom's normally unspoken commandment, "be serious above all." These unobtrusive interventions settle the offenders and Mr. Messinger and the class can proceed to solve the problem (p. 15).

The Interpretive Aspect of Educational Criticism Educational critics do not merely give an account of perceived educational phenomena; they also attempt to explain the meaning of that phenomena. This is accomplished within the second aspect of educational criticism—the interpretive aspect. *Interpretation* means contextualizing the actions that have been observed, including offering possible reasons for, and potential consequences of, those actions (Eisner, 1991, p. 95). The supervisor who has extensive experience in educational matters, and therefore a keener understanding of them, must use his or her interpretive powers in providing a critique that will reeducate the perception of the teaching performance by the supervisee.

In the following excerpt from an educational criticism of a fine arts program in a predominantly black elementary school, Barone (1987) attempted to place certain programmatic elements into historical and theoretical context:

In [one] art history . . . approach the classics represented the crowning glory of Western Civilization and were to be studied for the aesthetic and moral lessons they held . . . [t]races of this approach appear throughout the recorded history of Concordia School. . . . For example, just as in the heyday of this approach great works of a more recent vintage were ignored . . . likewise there were [in this school] . . . no prints representing paintings since the 1950's.

The emphasis on the study of art works and . . . ideas that have withstood the test of time is itself traditional to many educational philosophers who value a kind of "liberal education." This criterion of endurance is used as a guiding principle for judging what knowledge is of most worth and thus recommended for inclusion in the school curriculum. This content is, furthermore, often seen as constituting an essential core of common knowledge that should be the basis of a universal agenda. Eisner and Vallance (1974) have named these curriculum theorists academic rationalists . . . one of these [was] Robert Hutchins . . . [who] gathered together the most profound writings of humanity into a set of tomes called The Great Books of the Western World. Likewise, the history of art history/art

appreciation programs in American schools exhibits a nearly exclusive emphasis on European art (taught, of course, almost invariably to Americans of European ancestry) (p. 432).

To accomplish the task of interpretation, the educational critic, unlike that of authors of most other forms of arts-based educational disclosure, may borrow theory from the social sciences (i.e., at least as envisioned by Eisner, 1991). This borrowing is not for the traditional scientific purposes of prediction and control of future events, but rather to guide the perception of the critic/observer. The theory of the educational critic may not be already established; rather, it may be emergent, similar to that which the advocates of "grounded theory" in other forms of qualitative inquiry have described. Whether established or emergent, the theory may serve as a heuristic device in raising questions about educational phenomena, or it may serve to provide a more penetrating explanation of events observed.

Of course, theory has its limits in the interpretive enterprise. Theories are necessarily incomplete, and they compete with each other for shedding light on particular aspects of the subjects of inquiry. For that reason, Eisner (1991, p. 97) argued the phenomena observed must not be shaped to fit the theory, but the theory must be shaped to fit the phenomena. In other words, theory must be used flexibly in interpreting educational practices and events.

The Evaluative Aspect of Educational Criticism Finally, all educational critics necessarily make judgments. This is because education is a value-saturated enterprise (i.e., a normative undertaking). Indeed, the critic makes public the private judgments of the connoisseur. Eisner (1991) is clearly not a relativist when it comes to schooling experiences. Indeed, he cited Dewey's (1938) point that some schooling experiences are educational while others are miseducational—some foster intellectual and emotional growth in students, but some inhibit growth. Who is to make the judgments about how educational certain experiences are? That is the role of supervisor/critic, not the supervisee. As mentioned earlier, connoisseurship moves beyond empathic understanding of the supervisee to an assessment of quality using criteria that arise at least partially from within a different perspective (i.e., the perspective of the supervisor). The fact that a teacher can articulate the reasons for a particular set of actions does not free the supervisor from the responsibility to make his or her own assessments of their appropriateness and quality.

An excerpt from an educational criticism that provides a clear example of overt conclusions drawn by the evaluator comes from McCutcheon (1976):

On the whole, Mr. William's classroom appears to be a good place for children to be if they are bright, conversational, independent, and inquisitive, or if they need to learn and practice skills in conversation, problem-solving, creative use of language, dealing with complex information, writing reports, and interpreting stories and poems. In this classroom, children may learn grammar, reading, and language skills in context rather than in isolated drill. It is an intellectually intense, stimulating, and supportive environment. . . .

This case is an example of a situation in which parental involvement in schools met with unfortunate results. I do not mean to imply that parents should not be involved in schools or that all their involvement is deleterious. However, parental involvement is not always beneficial, either. Clearly, Mr. Williams is leaving teaching because he feels their pressure. Yet many features of his classroom were worthwhile for these children (p. 260).

Arts-Based Disclosure Texts and Supervisory Conferences

The focus thus far has been on the character of literary-style disclosures in clinical supervision. Attention is now turned to the character of the postobservational meetings between teacher and supervisor in which written disclosures are used as springboards for discussion.

It should be noted that fine artists (e.g., dancers, actors, sculptors, and the like) are rarely able to confer with the critics who analyze their work. One important aspect of clinical supervision of teachers, however, is the opportunity for the teacher/artist and supervisor/critic to confer about the meaning and significance of what has been observed and noted. The purpose of such postobservational conferences should be a formative one; namely, the enhancement of the quality of future teaching. What, then, are the characteristics of such meetings that will ensure that they are positive and productive?

One characteristic relates to the roles adopted by the conferees. Do the supervisor and supervised meet essentially as equals, or is one subordinate to the other? Addressing this issue, Tanner and Tanner (1989) distinguished between clinical and developmental supervision. The relationship between teacher and supervisor in the former is described as consultative. One shortcoming of the clinical approach, according to these authors, is the narrow focus on instructional matters rather than the curriculum, which tends to be predetermined at higher levels. Developmental supervision, on the other hand, is seen as democratic and participative in character: The curriculum is emergent, and the learning environment is mutually constructed rather than mandated from outside.

Some advocates of clinical supervision, however, do indeed see their approach as democratic, although in varying degrees. Some see a relationship between clinical supervisor and teacher that is mutually empowering and based upon collegiality and trust. They suggest that the role of supervisor as friend, confidante, and colleague be emphasized. For example, Garman (1982) proposed diminishing the psychological distance between supervisor and supervised. Others, however, find that a degree of detachment is both inevitable and potentially useful in an organizational entity such as the school.

The trick, it seems, is for the clinical supervisor to strike an appropriate balance between the two seemingly contradictory roles. In this view, the clinical supervisor is not acting undemocratically while playing dual roles of evaluator and helpmate (Oliva, 1993). This kind of balancing act requires a degree of tact and finesse. Relevant questions for the clinical supervisor who prepares an arts-based disclosure for a teacher include: How can critiques of, or stories about, the personal and/or professional characteristics and performances of teachers be crafted so that they will achieve the intended aim of enhancing the educational process? How can an appropriate balance be struck between empathic understanding and distanced, reflective evaluation, which is needed for a critique to be viewed as an invitation to genuine dialogue, an encouragement toward mutual problem solving, rather than a closed, summative, judgmental set of pronouncements that produce only fear and withdrawal? To ensure the necessary balance, there are at least two factors to consider: the nature and sources of the critiques, and the context in which they are read and discussed.

Issues in Composing the Written Disclosure One important question concerning written disclosures concerns who gets to write them and about whom. This brings us to the issue of voice, of whose version of events is indeed disclosed in criticism and storytelling, the "meaningful" version of the teacher/actor, or the "significance" that is presumably located by the observer/evaluator/supervisor. Voice is an important element in all forms of storytelling and has been a central concern in research on story and narrative in education. Holland (1991) has suggested that supervisors have failed "to learn an essential lesson about supervision: [they] afford [practitioners] no opportunity to express their own views in their own voices" (p. 76).

The notion of voice has been especially prominent in feminist writings (e.g., Britzman 1986; Miller, 1990) and in writings calling attention to oppressed or "silenced" groups (McLaughlin & Tierney, 1993). As Elbaz (1991) noted, however, the concept has also been prominent in research on teacher's knowledge and thinking; indeed, this research has played a prominent political role in legitimating the notion of "teacher's perspective" (Janesick, 1982; Tabachnick & Zeichner, 1986) or "frame of reference" (Clark & Peterson, 1986) in educational inquiry.

For Elbaz (1991, p. 10), the basic question about voice is this:

What kind of discourse is being used and to what extent does it allow the authentic expression of teacher's experiences and concerns? If it has been difficult for teachers to voice their own concerns, this is because the academic and professional discourse of teaching . . . does not allow for the formulation of those concerns (p. 10).

One issue, then, is who writes the story to be told. In "top–down" inspection and production models of supervision, the voice of the teacher is squelched, and he or she remains silent in the face of a powerful, authoritative, supervisor (Tanner & Tanner 1989). The more democratic clinical (and developmental) forms of supervision encourage a more vocal role for the teacher. Would it be wise, therefore, for educational supervisors, to invite disclosure from the teacher who is supervised before rushing to write a version of a teaching performance? Indeed, might there not be the possibility of multiple disclosures of teacher performance from many sources? A portfolio of stories may be gathered from colleagues, and even students, to stand beside (or perhaps be woven into) the critique by the supervisor. Reading about the teacher's version of events, seeing them embedded within the context of the teacher's personal/professional history, may greatly enhance the empathic awareness of the supervisor, thereby reducing those imbalances between significance and meaning, and between distance and intimacy that currently plague so much disclosure in the field of clinical supervision.

As Elbaz (1991) noted, however, the issue of voice does not pertain only to who gets to write. A more fundamental question is whose perspective is ultimately honored when decisions are made. Authentic expressions of teacher concerns can be provided by a sensitive onlooker who tells a story that conveys the tacit aspect of teacher's knowledge. Much craft knowledge of teachers is unarticulated and not logically sequenced and only partially patterned and organized; but it is imbued nevertheless with personal meaning. Moreover, that personal knowledge is always contextual, embedded within the culture of a particular school, and society as a whole. The voice of the teacher always speaks from within that realm of personal/professional context. Whoever ultimately tells the story, it is incumbent upon him or her to insure that voice is heard.

Related to the issue of voice in arts-based disclosure is the issue of *characterization*. Who are the characters in the classroom whose lives are portrayed in an educational story or critique? These characters are never reduced to an external, "objective" set of traits or behavioral patterns (Barone, 1980). Indeed, in no sense are these characters ever neutral entities whose "true" identities are revealed or expressed in the story text (Nespor & Barylske, 1992). Instead, the "selves" of teachers portrayed in a story or critique are always crafted and constructed, whether the story is autobiographical or composed by an onlooker. Context once again emerges as a crucial element in this construction. Nespor and Barylske (1992) elaborated on this point by quoting Kondo (1990):

Rather than bounded, essential entities, replete with a unitary substance and consciousness, identities become nodal points repositioned in different contexts. Selves, in this view, can be seen as rhetorical figures and performative assertions enacted in specific situations within fields of power, history, and culture (p. 304).

The notion that the selves of storied characters are never "unified" in substance or consciousness has been advanced by Bakhtin (cited in Holquist, 1990). For Bakhtin, as for other so-called postmodernist thinkers, there are no stable identities, and so boundaries between selves are illusory. Because this is so, it is no longer possible to think in terms of an author as sole proprietor of his or her story, or in terms of one characterization of a self as inherently privileged over another. One important consequence of this view for supervisors harkens back to the notion of voice: Single, univocal portraits of teachers should give way to a multiplicity of scenarios written from many different viewpoints because different voices create different versions of the same characters.

One last, more radically democratic, suggestion about characterization.: We have assumed thus far that the sole focal point of arts-based disclosures is the character of the teacher. What if stories and critiques written by teachers about the professional lives of supervisors were also shared in a supervisory conference? Might not such an egalitarian gesture promote a less-threatening atmosphere, a more candid and fruitful dialogue, and a more collegial problem-solving process?

A third concern involves the intended *audience* for the critique or story. In clinical supervision, the traditional audience for feedback has been the teacher who is supervised rather than, say, policymakers or members of other educational constituencies. Given that audience, how can a written disclosure be crafted to achieve that conduciveness to professional growth that Eisner (1991) called the "first ideal of an educational critique?"

Criticism and storytelling should be constructive rather than destructive. Negative feedback in any form, whether artistic or scientific has the potential for leaving psychological bruises and arousing defensive behaviors. Insofar as its style and content are personalized, an arts-based form of disclosure may appear to be potentially more damaging and less defensible than a traditional systematic, standardized evaluation form. It is relatively easy for an evaluator to hide behind the pretense that "low inference" standardized competency lists are not also subjective and value-based (i.e., the illusion that they are fairer because they are universally applied). For this and other reasons, the author of an arts-based disclosure must be especially careful to consider its potential effects on the audience to whom it is written, and to compose it accordingly.

Eisner (1991) therefore cautioned against total candor in an educational criticism. He also suggested, however, that shaping a critique or story with care and tact does not mean avoiding all negative criticism. He would simply have the author carefully consider factors such as (1) the relationship of the supervisor/author to teacher/reader, (2) the purpose that the feedback is intended to serve, and (3) who else will be privy to the text. It is most important that the storyteller or critic emphatically understand the intentions of the teacher, even as he or she suggests alternative viewpoints and perspectives (including, perhaps, those of students and parents).

Issues in Sharing the Written Disclosure The positive effects of an arts-based disclosure are equally dependent upon the quality of the text and upon the quality of the discussion that the text provokes. This discussion (partly) occurs in supervisory conferences between the author(s) and reader(s) of the critiques and stories. Meetings between clinical supervisors and teachers to discuss evaluation reports have traditionally been known as postobservational conferences. Many of the exemplary characteristics of traditional supervisory conferences are also desirable for those in which supervisors and teachers convene to discuss arts-based reports. Certain technical and interpersonal skills of the supervisor are helpful. For example, Glickman (1981) suggested the importance of an ability to detect whether a directive or nondirective approach will be most effective with a particular teacher and a flexibility in adjusting one's behavioral style accordingly.

Oliva (1993) noted that the entire supervisory process must take place against the backdrop of a long-standing rapport between the protagonists. Moreover, the conference itself must not be perceived as a summative assessment of teaching performance; rather, it is "an opportunity for the supervisor to provide valuable feedback for the teacher's consideration" (p. 497). Indeed, as Gitlin and Smith (1989) have argued, the act of supervisory criticism must be based in dialogue. For conferences in which arts-based reports are preferred, the text must be seen as one that is open and suggestive, not as a final, closed version of events. This approach to the reading of a written text is in accord with a school of literary criticism known as *poststructuralism*, or, as it is sometimes labeled, *postmodernism*.

Poststructuralism is most easily understood as a reaction to certain central notions of structuralism. Structuralists viewed written texts (i.e., especially texts of science or social science) as authoritative, as a true representation of reality garnered by the author. Within modernist Western culture, authors of texts have traditionally assumed a position of privilege, with special access to supposedly objective, and therefore politically neutral, truth, reason, and virtue. Their agenda has been to enlighten, educate, and perhaps even instill moral values in their readers. The persuasive power of the modernist text indeed resided in the assumption that a single, literal reading of the textual object existed—the one intended by the author. As Rosenau (1991) put it:

The modern author in society is a "legislator," defined as a specialist, a manager, a professional, an intellectual, or an educator. . . . they "know" and "decide things" by weighing the positive and negative and determining what is "true." [They] arbitrate in the sense of choosing between opposing points of view in controversy. What they select becomes "correct and binding" (Bauman 1987, p. 27).

Part of the post-structuralist intellectual attitude, however, is a repudiation of the modernist notion of textual authorship. An author may no longer claim to provide universal truth (i.e., a morally or politically neutral translation of reality). Her or his act of authoring is now exposed as arising from within a peculiar perspective that is bound up in issues of personal meaning, history, and power. For example, a supervisor can no longer claim that a list of teaching skills and competencies are value-free, that they do not arise from within a particular educational ideology, or that the question of whose interests are served by legitimating those particular talents over others is an irrelevant one. Poststructuralists would demand that agency and responsibility be acknowledged. For example, the standardized evaluation form must be challenged, "deconstructed," "interrogated," and examined for its hidden agenda of maintaining the political status quo.

What would such a post-structuralist spirit mean with regard to the manner in which educational texts of criticism and storytelling are shared? The supervisor would remind the teacher that he or she (i.e., the supervisor) is merely an interpreter of phenomena that have been perceived, that the disclosure preferred is not meant to contain claims of ultimate truth, and that it offers no nonnegotiable prescriptions. The critique or story is valid only insofar as it is personally meaningful to the teacher. It is valuable only to the extent that it enables the teacher to dwell within (an) alternative perspec-

tive(s), to perceive qualities in his or her teaching that may have previously gone unnoticed, and to reflect upon those in relation to the whole of his or her personal and professional life. The teacher is invited to pull only what is helpful to him or her from the text, and to disregard the rest.

The tone and demeanor of the supervisor would support this kind of open textual reading. He or she elicits a "deconstruction" of the text: Supervisor–writer and teacher–reader tear it apart together to be questioned and analyzed in order to ensure that its contents support the interests of students rather than those of other constituencies (e/.g., administrators). The supervisor encourages the brainstorming of a variety of alternative interpretations of the phenomena described and evaluated in the text. The conversation may also move outward from the text to important issues only implied within the story or critique. For example, discussion of forces that operate to constrain alternative possibilities in the classroom (i.e., external curriculum mandates, parental narrowmindedness, administrative fiats, etc.) may occur.

As with Tanner and Tanner's (1989) developmental supervision, this kind of clinical discussion gives recognition to the teacher as an inquirer and problem solver:

A fundamental premise of developmental supervision is that education is a process of growth rather than a process of end products. In a free society, education must be regarded as a process through which the learner grows in capacity to add meaning to experience and thereby to direct the course of ensuing experience with intelligence. In this sense, the individual gains in power and insight in controlling his or her own destiny. This applies not only to the student, but to the teacher as learner (p. 200).

The role of a clinical (or developmental) supervisor in writing and discussing an arts-based text with a teacher is to suggest additional meaning to professional and personal experience so that he or she might better direct aspects of teaching. The writing and discussion must therefore proceed with the premise that the arts-based text itself is an ongoing process, to be continuously reconsidered and rewritten, and never a closed, finalized "end product."

FUTURE RESEARCH ON AESTHETIC DIMENSIONS OF SUPERVISION

The area of arts-based approaches to supervision remains a fertile ground for both conceptual and empirical forms of research. As mentioned at the outset of this chapter, the dearth of empirical research in this field is a partial consequence of its newness. The notion of education and teaching as artistic (i.e., as opposed to scientifically based) activities has only (relatively) recently gained attention, and the possibility that what supervisors do may be regarded as artistic has likewise not been fully explored. This possibility is gaining increasing attention. It therefore behooves supervisionists to re-search their field in the new light cast on it by these possibilities. This final section of this chapter contains a list, which is by no means exhaustive, of questions that may need to be more fully explored in that new light.

First, there is the conceptual matter of whether supervision is indeed best viewed as an artlike activity. There is still no consensus on the wisdom of identifying teaching as an art. This is even more true for supervision. What are the advantages and disadvantages for doing so? The question could be rephrased: What facets of the supervisory process are, and which are not, aesthetic in nature? On the other hand, is the question: In what ways can the activity of supervisors be enhanced if pursued with more artistry, and with an eye to its aesthetic character? Conceptual clarification of these matters needs further attention.

The notions of educational connoisseurship and criticism are dependent upon the usefulness of the supervisor-as-artist metaphor. What are the strengths and weaknesses of thinking of supervisors as educational connoisseurs and critics? Do some supervisors already view themselves in this light? To what extent do they hear an objectionable elitist tone in the terminology? Does this metaphor tend to reinforce the antidemocratic relationship between authoritative, vocal supervisor and subservient, silent supervisee? Can the metaphor be maintained and the power of voices equalized?

Specific questions related to educational connosseurship include: Should supervisors be persuaded (educated?) to start thinking of themselves as educational connoisseurs? What level of educational connoisseurship do supervisors already possess? To what extent has their ability to *see* subtle and important nuances in teaching episodes been blunted by a habit of merely *recognizing* that which is pointed to by standardized evaluation checklists? Naturalistic case studies of supervisors acting as educational connoisseurs should enable us to answer such questions.

Similar questions relate to the notion of educational criticism: Do supervisors possess the skills and talents necessary to write educational criticisms that exhibit the qualities of good arts-based disclosure outlined earlier? Are they willing to acquire those skills? How would the training of supervisors need to be altered so that they might do so? Is the writing of educational criticism by clinical supervisors feasible? Is it too time-consuming, too labor-intensive? Published examples of educational criticisms (and other sorts of arts-based disclosures) written by supervisors for teachers (and teachers for their peers, and teachers for supervisors) would be enormously helpful. Studies of supervisors who have tried to move beyond standardized forms toward more descriptive, artistic texts of disclosure would also be an important contribution to our understanding.

The other major genre of artistic disclosure is narrative storytelling. Is it indeed a good idea for supervisors to encourage and attend to teacher narratives? To what extent is the teacher's storied life outside the classroom relevant to the supervisory act? To what degree do supervisors already empathize with teacher-supervisees? Can increased empathic understanding lead to more sensitive forms of disclosure and to enlightened guidance toward improvement of teaching? If so, how? Finally, with what other forms of artistically grounded disclosure (in addition to criticism and storytelling) might it be helpful for supervisors to experiment?

REFERENCES

Aristotle. (1961). *Poetics.* (S. H. Butcher, trans.) New York: Hill & Wang.

Barone, T. (1978). *Inquiry into classroom experiences: A qualitative holistic approach.* Doctoral dissertation, Stanford University, Stanford, CA.

Barone, T. (1983). Things of use and things of beauty: The story of the Swain County High School arts program. *Daedalus, 112*(3), 1–28.

Barone, T. (1987). On equality, visibility, and the fine arts program in a black elementary school. *Curriculum Inquiry, 17*(4), 421–446.

Barone, T. (1989). Ways of being at risk: The case of Billy Charles Barnett. *Phi Delta Kappan, 71*(2), 147–151.

Barone. T. (1992). A narrative of enhanced professionalism: Educational researchers and popular storybooks about schoolpeople. *Educational Researcher, 21*(9), 15–24.

Barone, T. (1993). Breaking the mold: The new American student as strong poet. *Theory into Practice, 32*(4), 236–243.

Barone, T. & Eisner, E. (1997). Arts-based educational research. In R. M. Jaeger (Ed.). *Complementary Methods for Research in Education* (2nd ed.). Washington, D.C.: American Educational Research Association.

Bauman, Z. (1987). *Legislators and interpreters: Modernity, postmodernity and intellectuals.* Ithaca, NY: Cornell University Press.

Bruner, J. (1986). *Actual minds, possible worlds.* Cambridge, MA: Harvard University Press.

Bruner, J. (1994). *Four ways to make a meaning.* Invited address at the Annual meeting of the American Educational Research Association, New Orleans, LA.

Bullough, R. V., Jr. (1989). *First year teacher: A case study.* New York: Teachers College Press.

Bullough, R. V., Jr. (1990). Supervision, mentoring, and self-discovery: A case study of a first-year teacher. *Journal of Supervision and Curriculum Development, 5*(4), 338–360.

Bullough, R. V., Jr., Knowles, G., & Crow, N. (1991). *Emerging as a teacher.* New York: Routledge.

Carter, K. (1993). The place of story in the study of teaching and teacher education. *Educational Researcher, 22*(1), 5–12, 18.

Clark, C. M. & Peterson, L. (1986). Teachers' thought processes. In M. Wittrock (Ed.). *Handbook of research on teaching* (3rd ed.) pp. 255–295. New York: Macmillan.

Cogan, M. (1973). *Clinical supervision.* Boston, MA: Houghton Mifflin.

Connelly, F. M. & Clandinin, D. J. (1990). Stories of experience and narrative inquiry. *Educational Researcher, 19*(5), 2–14.

Dewey, J. (1934/1958). *Art as experience.* New York: Capricorn Books.

Dewey, J. (1938/1963). *Experience and education*. New York: Collier Books.

Donmoyer, R. (1980). The evaluator as artist: A discussion of premises and problems with examples from two aesthetically based evaluations. *The Journal of Curriculum Theorizing, 2*(2), 12–26.

Donmoyer, R. (1994). *In their own words: A readers theater presentation of students' writing about writing and a discussion of the pros and cons of artistic modes of data display*. Annual meeting of the American Educational Research Association, New Orleans, LA.

Eisner, E. (1969). Instructional and expressive objectives: Their formulation and use in curriculum. In W. J. Popham (Ed.). *Instructional objectives* (pp.1–31). American Educational Research Association, Monograph on Curriculum Evaluation. Chicago, IL: Rand McNally.

Eisner, E. (1975). Educational connoisseurship and educational criticism: Their forms and functions in educational evaluation. *Journal of Aesthetic Education*, Bicentennial Issue.

Eisner, E. (1977). On the use of educational connoisseurship and educational criticism for the evaluation of classroom life. *Teachers College Record, 78*(3), 325–388.

Eisner, E. (1981). On the differences between scientific and artistic approaches to qualitative research. *Educational Researcher, 10*(4), 5–9.

Eisner, E. (1982). An artistic approach to supervision. In T. J. Sergiovanni (Ed.). *Supervision of teaching* (1982 Yearbook) pp. 35–52. Alexandria, VA: ASCD.

Eisner, E. (1983). The art and craft of teaching. *Educational Leadership, 40*(4).

Eisner, E. (1985). *The educational imagination: On the design and evaluation of school programs* (2nd ed.). New York: Macmillan.

Eisner, E. (1991). *The enlightened eye: Qualitative inquiry and the enhancement of educational practice*. New York: Macmillan.

Eisner, E. (1994). *The educational imagination: On the design and evaluation of school programs* (3rd ed.). New York: Macmillan.

Eisner, E. & Vallance, E. (Eds.). (1974). *Conflicting conceptions of curriculum*. Berkeley, CA: McCutchan.

Elbaz, F. (1983). *Teacher thinking: A study of practical knowledge*. London, England: Croon Helm.

Elbaz, F. (1991). Research on teacher's knowledge: The evolution of a discourse. *Journal of Curriculum Studies, 23*(1), 1–19.

Flanders, N. (1972). *Interaction analysis: Teacher handbook*. San Francisco, CA: Far West Laboratory for Educational Research and Development.

Flinders, D. J. (1989). *Voices from the classroom: Educational policy can inform policy*. Eugene, OR: ERIC Clearinghouse on Educational Management, University of Oregon.

Gadamer, H. (1975). *Truth and method*. (G. Barden and J. Cumming, trans. and ed.). New York; Seabury Press.

Garman, N. (1990). Theories embedded in the events of clinical supervision: A hermeneutic approach. *Journal of Curriculum and Supervision, 5*(3), 201–213.

Geertz, C. (1974). *The interpretation of cultures*. New York: Basic Books.

Gitlin, A. & Smith, J. (1989). *Teacher evaluation: Educational alternatives*. Philadelphia, PA: Falmer Press.

Glickman, C. (1981). *Developmental supervision: Alternative practices for helping teachers improve instruction*. Alexandria, VA: ASCD.

Goodson, I. (1992). *Studying teachers' lives*. London, England: Routledge.

Greene, M. (1971). Art, technique, and the indifferent gods. In R. Smith (Ed.). *Aesthetics and problems of education*. Urbana, IL: University of Illinois Press.

Grumet, M. (1988). *Bitter milk: Women and teaching*. Amherst, MA: University of Massachusetts Press.

Grumet, M. R. (1993). The play of meanings in the art of teaching. *Theory into Practice, 32*(4), 204–209.

Habermas, J. (1972). *Knowledge and human interest*. Boston, MA: Beacon Press.

Harland, R. (1975). Intention and critical judgment. *Essays in Criticism, 14*, 215–225.

Hawthorn, R. (1992). *Curriculum in the making: Teacher choice and the classroom experience*. New York: Teachers College Press.

Hirsch, E. D. , Jr. (1976). *The aims of interpretation*. Chicago: University of Chicago Press.

Holland, P. (1989). Stories of supervision: Tutorials in a transformative practice of supervision. *Peabody Journal of Education, 66*(3), 61–77.

Holquist, M. (1990). *Dialogism: Bakhtin and his world*. London, England: Routledge.

Huenecke, D. (1992). An artistic criticism of Writing to Read, a computer-based program for beginning readers. *Journal of Curriculum and Supervision, 7*(2), 170–179.

Iser, W. (1974). *The implied reader*. Baltimore, MD: Johns Hopkins University Press.

Janesick, V. (1982). Of snakes and circles: Making sense of classroom group processes through a case study. *Curriculum Inquiry, 12*(2), 161–189.

Kane, P. R. (ed.) *The first year of teaching: Real world stories from America's teachers*. New York: Teachers College Press.

Kondo, D. (1990). *Crafting selves*. Chicago, IL: University of Chicago Press.

Knowles, G., Cole, A., & Presswood, C. (1994). *Through preservice teachers' eyes: Exploring field experiences through narrative and inquiry*. New York: Merrill.

Langer, S. (1942). *Philosophy in a new key*. Cambridge, England: Harvard University Press.

Langer, S. (1957). *Problems of art*. New York: Charles Scribner's Sons.

McCutcheon, G. (1976). *The disclosure of classroom life*. Doctoral dissertation, Stanford University, Stanford, CA.

McLaughlin, D. & Tierney, W.G. (Eds.). *Naming silenced lives: Personal narratives and the process of educational change*. New York: Routledge.

Mann, J. (1969). Curriculum criticism. *Teachers College Record, 71*, 27–40.

May, W. T. (1993). Teaching as a work of art in the medium of curriculum. *Theory into Practice, 32*(4), 210–218.

Mead, G. H. (1934). *Mind, self, and society*. Chicago, IL: University of Chicago Press.

Miller, J. (1990). *Creating spaces and finding voices: Teachers collaborating for empowerment*. Albany: State University of New York Press.

Nespor, J. & Barylske, J. (1991). Narrative discourse and teacher knowledge. *American Educational Research Journal, 28*(4), 805–823.

Oliva, P. F. (1993). *Supervision for today's schools* (4th ed.). New York: Longman.

Polkinghorne, D. E. (1988). *Narrative knowing and the human sciences*. Albany, NY: State University of New York Press.

Ricoeur, P. (1981). *Hermeneutics and the human sciences*. (J. Thompson, ed. and trans.). Cambridge, England: Cambridge University Press.

Rorty, R. (1989). *Contingency, irony, and solidarity*. Cambridge, England: Cambridge University Press.

Rosenau, P. (1992). *Post-modernism and the social sciences: Insights, inroads, and intrusions*. Princeton, NJ: Princeton University Press.

Ryan, K. (Ed.). (1992). *The roller coaster year: Essays by and for beginning teachers*. Boston, MA: HarperCollins.

Schon, D. (Ed.). (1991). *The reflective turn: Case studies in and on educational practice.* New York: Teachers College Press.

Smith, R. (1971). Is teaching an art? In R. Smith (Ed.). *Aesthetics and problems of education.* Urbana, IL: University of Illinois Press.

Tabachnick, B. & Zeichner, F. (1986). Teacher beliefs and classroom behaviors: Some teacher responses to inconsistency. In M. Ben-Peretz, R. Bromme, & R. Halkes (Eds.). *Advances of research on teacher thinking,* (pp. 84–96). Lisse: Swets and Zeitlinger,.

Tanner, D. & Tanner, L. (1987). *Supervision in education: Problems and practices.* New York: Macmillan.

Witherell, C. & Noddings, N. (Eds.). (1991). *Stories lives tell: Narrative and dialogue in education.* New York: Teachers College Press.

Wood, D. R. (1992). Teaching narratives: A source for faculty development and evaluation. *Harvard Educational Review 62*(4), 535–550.

·46·

INDUSTRIAL DIMENSIONS OF SUPERVISION

David J. Flinders

INDIANA UNIVERSITY

INTRODUCTION

The purpose of this chapter is to examine how the impact, influences, and implications of work in industrial settings have shaped the theory and practice of school supervision. The linkages today between school and work are so pervasive that we often take them for granted. Moreover, it is common to think and talk as if education itself were a type of business or industry. Thus, schools both serve to prepare students for a future in which the world of work looms large, and they provide this service in ways and under conditions that are analogous to the domains of business and corporate management. As this largely implicit way of thinking circulates through the field of supervision, it deserves special scrutiny. At the very least, the school-as-business metaphor raises many unanswered questions. What and how much do we know about the cultural ties between work and education? What is the nature of this relationship, and what is its history? Do aspects of industrial management continue to shape the interactions of supervisors with their superiors, peers, and subordinates? How is this influence felt, and what are its consequences? When is research on work in other settings relevant to school supervision? What lessons are worth learning from this research?

The point is that this topic represents a thicket of questions and tentative assumptions rather than a well-defined or disciplined field of inquiry. It is necessary to clear away some of the underbrush that might otherwise derail a chapter of this kind. First, no coherent body of research obtained from industrial management or its parent disciplines stands ready to inform the practices of school supervision by means of any direct or systematic application of findings from one domain to another. To put this another way, the diffusion of supervision theory and practice is typically a less rational process than common sense would lead us to believe. Individual studies of business and industrial innovations do occasionally surface in the literature on school supervision, but these

studies tend to be isolated and relatively narrow in scope. Furthermore, their impact on the day-to-day work of instructional supervision is largely unknown. The broader (and probably stronger) influences on supervision practice, whether from the fields of management or elsewhere, are likely to take an indirect route that is mediated through other social institutions and fields of educational interest than supervision per se.

This is not just a matter of dealing with circuitous pathways. Rather, the nature of such diffusion is itself diffuse. That is, management and related theories are not likely to inform school supervision in quite the same way that scientific theories inform the fields of engineering and medicine. For example, economic theories that are based on notions of human motivation tend to get mixed up with all sorts of other cultural folkways before ever reaching the practices of education. The processes involved are ones of transformation rather than transmission. For this reason, a comprehensive review of management theories in isolation is beyond the scope of this chapter, and it would be of more interest to those outside the field of supervision than is called for here. Points of interest and opportunities for cross-fertilization are certainly worth our close attention, but my aim is to keep the following discussion well focused on issues specifically relevant to the practices of school supervision. I will be using this focus and the term itself (i.e., school *supervision*), to mean the activities engaged in by educational administrators and university liaisons when their intent is to describe, interpret, analyze, or appraise the work of teachers, student teachers, or teacher interns.

Again, it would seem foolish or at best naive to ignore the influences of management theories on school supervision for the very reason that these two domains of professional activity seem to share a good deal of terminology, language, and conceptual frames of reference. As I have just noted, specific points of common interest do offer opportunities for cross-fertilization. Furthermore, when I engage in the supervision of student teachers, which has long occupied a good deal of my time, or when I write about supervision as a field of study, I bring a set of questions to this work that I hope make it a more reflective process than would otherwise be the case. For example, these questions include: How is this activity framed? What do others expect of a supervisor, and why? How do I go about describing supervision, either as what I do or as a field, especially to those outside of education? In other words, how do I account for myself as a supervisor, and what does that account say about my underlying theories of practice?

Other supervisors in education perhaps struggle with similar questions, and this would be the context in which the industrial dimensions of supervision tacitly shape our thinking about a wide range of issues. Just below the surface of the field's practicality flows an intellectual history to which industrial metaphors have made a significant contribution. Thus, the rationale for attending to this contribution has more to do with understanding who we are and how the field has developed than it does with the potential transfer of management technologies.

Before pursuing this theme, however, I want to briefly mention the broader outlines of what is to follow. Chapters such as this one, which review theory and research, tend to be retrospective in their approach. As it is, the organization of this chapter does begin with an overview of historical studies. This is one area in which the beginnings of a well-developed literature will help situate the field as it has changed during the past century relative to the influence of industrial management theories and research. My overview of this research gives particular attention to three themes: (1) school bureaucratization, (2) the efficiency movement, and (3) social adaptation. This summary of historical studies is followed by a look at how industrial and management ideas play out in more contemporary settings. I will discuss several examples, including relatively well-defined "transplants" such as Total Quality Management. Nevertheless, my aim in this part of the chapter is to follow up on my thesis that the most significant influences of industrial management on school supervision are indirect, diffuse, and exercised through the language and discourse of supervision rather than through explicit efforts to inform (or reform) the field.

In the second half of the chapter, I will emphasize a more forward-looking approach. My aim is to suggest the range of issues that could be considered under the rubric of my title, the "industrial dimensions of supervision." First, I want to illustrate how metaphorical analysis brings into focus parallel trends in both school supervision and theories of organizational life. Second, I will selectively review research on teaching as work, giving special attention to scholarship that builds on the commonalities between teaching and similar occupations. In particular, this review examines the implications for school supervision obtained from analyses of work in three areas: (1) critical theory, (2) urban studies, and (3) program implementation.

Having covered this broad terrain, it also seems worthwhile to venture some recommendations for the next generation of research on school supervision. My final concern, therefore, will be to suggest related directions and lines of future research that promise to enhance our understanding and practices of school supervision.

WHERE WE HAVE BEEN

My primary interest is with the twentieth century, the age in which supervision in the United States has developed from an "inspector of schools" model, narrow in its official presence, to some semblance of the field we recognize today. The history of supervision is of course much older, as are the influences of an economic and even industrial framework for thinking about the formal education of youth. Karier's (1982) discussion of the common school era (1830–1850), which is a starting point that corresponds with the early waves of American industrialism, illustrates that the inclination to view education in economic terms was already well afoot. Karier cites Horace Mann's comment that "education has market value. . . . It may be minted and will yield a larger amount of statutable coin than common bullion" (p. 6). Mann did not use this metaphor simply as a rhetorical device; rather, he used it as an underlying basis for the justification of public education. In another place, Mann (1848) wrote:

Beyond the power of diffusing old wealth, it [education] has the prerogative of creating new. It is a thousand times more lucrative than fraud; and adds a thousand fold more to a nation's resources than the most successful conquests. Knaves and robbers can obtain only what was before possessed by others. But education creates or develops new treasures, treasures not before possessed or dreamed of by anyone (p. 88).

Karier (1982) refers to this notion of human capital as "the rationale for public schooling that would sustain the American nation for the next century" (p. 6). In many circles, this early economic rationale has yet to ebb or wane.

The common school era and the second half of the nineteenth century set the stage on which supervision was to develop as a field of professional interest. The field's early discourse and identity, as Bolin and Panaritis (1992) argued, "cannot be understood apart from the broader social trends that changed both the role of the school and that of the teacher during the twentieth century" (p. 30). Educational historians repeatedly cite three such trends that have special relevance to the industrial dimensions of supervision. The first is the bureaucratization of schooling that has steadily increased over the long course of American state-supported education. As public schooling grew in the number of students and expectations for what schools were to accomplish, so did the specialization of school people and the differentiation of school organization into patterns that resembled those of modern industry. The second is the spread of a technicist orientation, or what is alternately called social efficiency or scientific management. These terms refer to the notion that a wide variety of occupations, particularly nonprofessional work and the minor professions (e.g., teaching), can be made rational through the analysis and standardization of worker performance. The third trend, social adaptation, is exemplified in the aims of education to prepare students for life adjustment. Although broadly conceived in education, the life adjustment movement served specifically to reinforce some of the most direct ties between schooling and the world of work.

School Bureaucratization

A confluence of demographic and social factors (including broad trends such as urbanization, immigration, and industrialization) led to significant growth in elementary education in the second half of the nineteenth century, and was subsequently followed by significant growth in secondary education. More young people found themselves in school and were retained longer, state expenditures increased, and the scope of curricula began to expand. Students, particularly these in urban schools, became classed and graded, as did teachers and subjects of study. As expenditures rose and state authority broadened over the school's operation, formal accountability also became an issue. Moreover, school organization became increasingly complex and differentiated. The role of head teacher developed into that of school principal, and superintendents were hired to address administrative needs. American education had found what Tyack (1974) called "The One Best System."

Business and industry influenced the development of this system on a wide range of fronts: through the growing popular press, through ties between business and local government, through professional associations on both sides of the business/education fence, and later through the interests of vocational education. After all, some of the same demographic trends that led to growth in public education also spurred growth in business. By 1925, when Calvin Coolidge proclaimed that "the business of America is business", he was referring to an institution that had gained a leading influence over the nation's cultural identity (Callahan, 1962, p. 2). We may also surmise that education then was no less responsive to perceived social trends than it is today. Two developments can be used to illustrate the porous nature of school organization: the rise of school board governance and the role of higher education in the training of school administrators.

In the first decades of this century, educational reformers strove to remove schools from the turmoil of partisan politics by creating small local schoolboards that were, as Tyack (1974) wrote, "to emulate the process of decision-making used by men on the board of directors of a modern business corporation" (p. 126). Like education itself, these boards were to represent the best elements of the local community, and "best" increasingly meant the business sector. As Karier (1982) noted, "School boards in the progressive era [1890–1920] moved more under the control of business and professional leaders, and the disproportionate representation of these classes on school boards remains to the present day" (p. 9).

Local boards were created to delegate that power to superintendents and their administrative staff, not to operate schools. Nevertheless, business leaders had a relatively direct means of influence through the school boards on which they served. Those responsible for school supervision were not just accountable to the board; rather, they also ensured that this relationship shaped the organization of schools along hierarchical lines of authority. Regardless of informal networks, a corporate–industrial model was one that the board would likely understand. School leaders were thus encouraged to create at least a facade of businesslike routines and relationships. The reality of that facade as a symbol of ratio-

nal thinking is what gave school bureaucratization its particular flavor.

A second illustration of a business presence in the bureaucratic development of schools and the emergence of supervision as a field is reflected in the response of higher education to these developments. As supervisory and administrative roles in education became increasingly specialized, they came to be seen as justification for expert training, which is a special province of the university. Schools of education began offering courses in school administration soon after the turn of the century (Karier, 1982, p. 9). The idea of preparing the new middle management for education must have been appealing to many university people. Rather than struggle with the overwhelming task of training the growing ranks of classroom teachers, the university could concentrate on the preparation of a smaller yet potentially influential group—administrative specialists. These specialists could then tell teachers what to do and supervise their performance. This achieved the economy of training those who could then train others.

At the same time, some education schools sought to emulate successful schools of business, doing so in order to gain status on their home turf; that is, within the universities where education was relatively new and often perceived with some suspicion. Efforts to gain academic respectability, however, immediately raised conflicting demands between what the university valued and the practical needs of educational administrators. For example, Clifford and Guthrie (1988) wrote that:

[E]ducation pursued some of the same interconnected strategies employed by business schools. These included a broad curriculum that emphasized academic approaches or "applied social science" over functional specialization, the diversion of resources to graduate programs preparing for research careers at the expense of undergraduate "vocational" training, creating personal networks that enabled their advanced-degree holders to step into executive positions in the field, and curtailing the numbers of women in their programs (p. 163).

The impact of higher education on the practice of supervision and administration may thus have been somewhat blunted for the very reason that education emulated professional schools of business in tactics that were perceived as necessary to secure its academic standing. The extent to which practitioners simply ignored those in higher education, however, is open to question. If nothing else, the response of higher education recognized an emerging organizational structure based on school management roles. In the eyes of such historians as Cuban (1979), this structure was to have a stable and lasting influence on American schools. Moreover, an applied social science approach could be reshaped by administrators to help answer growing demands for educational efficiency.

The Efficiency Movement

Frederick W. Taylor is one of the few names that give students of industrial management and those of educational history something specific to talk with each other about without going outside their respective fields. Taylor's approach is often referred to as "scientific management," a term that pervades historical accounts of school administration, educational reform, and curriculum development. It represents one of the most explicit examples of a transplant from business and industry that has taken root in education. Taylor's most famous (and later most criticized) work was a time and motion study for Bethlehem Steel Corporation. The study focused specifically on manual labor, but Taylor's approach soon spread to all sorts of managerial concerns, from running railroads to reforming municipal government (Callahan, 1962, pp. 19–25).

Scientific management was conceived on the premise that there is an efficient method for performing any given task, and that this method could be discovered through systematic observation and analysis of that task. The manager's responsibility was for conducting this analysis and for teaching workers the most efficient method once it was known in detail. The techniques of the approach turned out to be less influential than its spirit of rationality because it was that spirit that historians describe as invading the ranks of educational management. For example, Beck and Murphy's (1993) historical examination of the principalship noted a shift during the 1920s and 1930s with respect to the image of the principal's role. Prior to that time, the image that had steadfastly served principals was one of moral leadership. Principals were responsible for being exemplary members of the community. When they were revered, it was on the basis of their moral (and often spiritual) good standing. This image was displaced first by the more practical image of manager, someone who could get things done, and then by the more polished image of school executive.

Beneath these changed images rested the allure of "social efficiency," an enticing ideology because it promised a utility that was almost too good to believe. In the industrial context, efficiency gained through scientific management promised the possibility of raising profits or wages, or both, without also having to raise prices. Moreover, the numbers were not insignificant. Taylor's analysis of one job at Bethlehem Steel claimed the potential to increase productivity by almost 400 percent. In education, scientific management promised a better product (more learning per student) for less expenditure. As Cuban (1988) put it: "Managerial efficiency, translated into dollars and cents, became the silver bullet that would improve schooling" (p. 56).

The magic of getting "more for less" must have been a strong inducement to a particular way of thinking about education for anyone connected with school politics. Callahan's work, however, suggested that still other factors help explain why expertise replaced moral standing as a basis for school management. Callahan is widely recognized for his book, *Education and the Cult of Efficiency* (1962), which is a study that began as an examination of the origins and influences of business on educational administration. In this book, he advanced what is known as the "vulnerability thesis." Briefly stated, this thesis proposes that the appeal of scientific management was enhanced by the relatively weak positions and susceptibility of educational administrators. As a symbol of rational thought and sound logic, scientific management would seem tailor-made (no pun intended) as a defense against growing public criticisms of educational waste. Callahan argued that opinion leaders increasingly portrayed the tradition-bound practices of education as being carried out by means of an antiquated and decrepit system. Administrators, who for various reasons already occupied a precarious role, found themselves in the position of needing to respond, and did so by cloaking their work in the guise of managerial efficiency.

Callahan's thesis has been criticized by Karier (1982, p. 8) for portraying school administration as victimized, a weak profession that too easily capitulated to the influences of business. Any validity the thesis has, however, would apply to supervision with special relevance because supervision has developed as a relatively low-status concern, at least in institutions of higher education (Clifford & Guthrie 1988, p. 115). Its association with the daily practice of teaching has unfairly, though perhaps unavoidably, led many supervisors to be anxious about justifying their work in terms perceived as respectable outside of the teaching profession. One might also argue that such anxiety need not automatically be viewed as a weakness, especially if it helps keep supervisors more open to a range of ideas than they might otherwise be.

We have come full circle today, given that some scholars in educational administration have begun a discussion of moral leadership based on a renewed interest in communitarian values (Sergiovanni, 1992). It is unlikely, however, that images of school administration can (or should) ever return to the earlier conception of educational leadership based on community recognition of an individual's moral character. This is what makes the turn-of-the-century's departure from that image significant. The ensuing advent of scientific management signaled a fundamental change. The issue since then has not been whether supervision would be based on expert knowledge; rather, it is on whose expert knowledge. Bolin (1987) makes this point in discussing the historical tensions revealed in how supervision has been defined within the field. For example, she noted the tensions between scientific management and developmental psychology in the writings of people such as Barr, Burton, and Brueckner. Kliebard (1985) also argued that scientific management and the broader currents of social efficiency did not go unchallenged. The significant challenges, however, were to be from other growing domains of expertise, imported as scientific management had been in the field's early years of its emergence as a specialized role.

Social Adaptation

Scientific management and the efficiency movement were oriented toward the *means* of producing a particular product. This orientation served in turn as the basis for applying managerial efficiency to school supervision aimed at ensuring effective job performance. The third trend to be considered—that of social adaptation—is closely related, but it gives greater emphasis to the ends, outcomes, and purposes of education. In doing so, it illustrates another type of industrial influence on supervision. This influence is again indirect, but it is significant nonetheless because of its relevance to fundamental conceptions of the teacher's role. Social adaptation specifically holds that the aims of teaching in particular and of education in general should be to prepare students for their future responsibilities as adults. For example, in his 1918 book on curriculum, Franklin Bobbit argued that education was not for the 10 or 15 years of childhood, but rather for the 50 years of adulthood. Bobbitt (1918) wrote: "Human life, however varied, consists in its performance of specific activities. Education that prepares for life is one that prepares definitely and adequately for these specific activities" (p. 42).

Education viewed as a form of preparation, especially as preparation for a person's vocation or means of livelihood, is a tradition that dates back well before the turn of the century. Bobbitt and his contemporaries simply brought this tradition up-to-date by recasting it into the language of modern efficiency and by asserting that the goals of education could be "discovered" through surveys and systematic studies of contemporary life. Their legacy turned out to be anything but trivial. The notion that schooling could be based on a dispassionate analysis of what people do, the problems they face, and so forth was one that would influence successive generations of educational writers, from Bobbitt through such prominent works as Ralph Tyler's *Basic Principles of Curriculum and Instruction* to examples of what is now called "needs assessment."

At the turn of the century, however, preparation for adult life had a special urgency because that tradition dovetailed remarkably well with the broad perception that schools could help "Americanize" an increasingly diverse population. Migration patterns and waves of immigration filled the nation's classrooms, and combined with poverty to raise serious concerns about class conflict and what a growing popular press characterized as the widespread disintegration of social order. "Policy makers in these years," wrote Tyack (1974), "saw pluralism as a peril" (p. 181). Textbook images of the nation as a melting pot gained credibility as an ideal, and the schools themselves took on an integrative purpose (i.e., helping more and more young people learn how to fit into their accorded social niche). In 1909, Ellwood P. Cubberley wrote that the task of education was "to assimilate and amalgamate" immigrants "as part of our American race" (p. 15).

Educators throughout the century have tended to view both Americanization and preparation for adult life in broad terms. In fact, the interpretations were often so broad as to be almost comical in efforts to categorize every conceivable facet of what it means to be a conscious being (Kliebard 1975). Nevertheless, the world of work has always commanded a central role in such schemes of adult life, partly because of its cultural status symbolized in the Protestant work ethic, and partly because work activities are relatively easy to specify in ways that do not make them sound trivial. The responses to what educators perceived as the necessities of real life were vocational education and a more practically oriented curriculum Schools came to grapple with renewed concerns for life adjustment during the depression era and the war years that followed. The proponents of this movement debated the over exact meaning of the term *life adjustment,* but its emphasis in the classroom often served to reinforce a common set of virtues: Punctuality, obedience, honesty, thrift, cooperation, and other habits were viewed as sound preparation for an economically productive existence (Kliebard, 1987, pp. 243–247).

The life adjustment movement in particular and the doctrine of social adaptation in general have tended to reflect a largely conservative point of view. Karier noted that "while a few educational leaders sought to change the social order through the schools, many more thought in terms of social harmony and life adjustment" (p. 11). For Bobbitt also, the central problem was not one of social reform, but the supposedly more technical issues of how to clearly identify the skills necessary to leading a productive life, how to analyze these complex skills into their component parts, and then how to organize the component parts into a curriculum. Referring to career education, a more contemporary example of life adjustment concerns. Eisner (1985) concluded: "Career education programs are not intended to encourage children or youth to consider alternatives to work as it is now generally defined or to question seriously the premises and values that give work such a central place in our lives" (p. 75). This conservative stance, albeit a variable feature of social adaptation, lends further support to conceptions of education as an economic resource or tool.

To put this another way, schools function on behalf of other segments of society. In this respect, social adaptation poses an interesting scenario. Business and industry require skilled and reliable workers who can be produced or supplied through vocational and career education or other life adjustment programs. Such programs carry the influence of industry directly to the schools, but they also tacitly reinforce a supply-and-demand logic that situates the schools as a supplier to industry. Control is principally located on the demand side of this relationship. It is the customer (i.e., industry) that specifies needs, removing that decision from the schools. Like Bobbitt, if one's orientation to education is largely technical to begin with, then this arrangement is exactly what might be wanted. The goals of schooling can be assumed as given, and educators can get on with the task of filling whatever order society has placed.

The implications for supervision are indirect but compelling in their own way. Business, industry, or some other societal interest is the customer on whose behalf the supervisor assumes the function of quality control. In this role, supervisors are expected to help others assure that the school's product meets specifications deemed appropriate to customer needs. It is unlikely that supervisors of this century have ever viewed themselves merely as functionaries of industry. The doctrine of social adaptation, however, did encourage school supervisors to view their work as serving broader social purposes, and that opened the door to the influence of industrial and business concerns. Combined with the increasing bureaucratization of American schools and the rise of managerial efficiency, the historical context in which supervision emerged as a field is one that favored cultural diffusion from business and industry to the field's growing sense of professional identity.

WHERE WE ARE NOW

The historical themes considered earlier (i.e., school bureaucratization, managerial efficiency, and social adaptation) are as much with us today as they have been in the past. Their persistence in shaping how contemporary scholars and researchers think about school organization, educational administration, and instructional supervision is so resilient that it raises the question of whether the educational trends of this century played out as historical studies suggest or whether we simply see in the past the familiar present. Whatever the case, it is not difficult to find a continuing influence of business and industry both in their impact on school practices and in their more diffuse contributions to present-day understandings of education. Three examples, chosen somewhat arbitrarily, serve to briefly illustrate this point.

Contemporary Examples

Three Cs Curriculum In the early 1980s, the California State Department of Education decreed that it was necessary for public schools to augment the traditional three Rs of basic education with the new three Cs: computer literacy, calculation, and communication. The three Cs suggest more a rearticulation, of the back-to-basics movement in a language that appeals to our information age, than they do an innovation. In the 1970s and early 1980s, California's economy had become increasingly dependent on the industries of high technology, and these industries were perceived as future growth areas. The three Cs curriculum was intended to assure that growth. The decree was at most symbolic (i.e., an exhortation for schools to better align their curriculum with the needs of a changing economy). Without discounting public relations, however, the department's aim was explicitly stated as to put educators on notice that California schools must take responsibility in preparing their students for employability.

Little research has been done on how such symbolic concerns have impacted school supervision or changed curriculum at the level of classroom practice. It is possible that statewide efforts shape the climate of school reform and conceptions of education more generally, and that this influence in turn impinges on how teachers and supervisors interact, how they set priorities, what they look for in the classroom, and what they see as good teaching. It is also possible that teachers and supervisors simply ignore state "leadership." Even if this were the case, however, curricular issues cannot be dismissed out of hand because curriculum has other and perhaps more direct connections with private enterprise. For example, Apple (1989) underscored that textbooks and materials represent an economic commodity. They are produced by business people whose decisions about the nature of their product are influenced by regulations, market considerations, competition, and the need to make a profit. Apple's work is relevant to supervision in other ways, addressed later in this chapter. The issue here is one of recognizing that, while supervisors and teachers typically approach curriculum as a part of classroom planning or as a field of educational studies, from a publisher's point of view, curriculum is the result of product development.

Total Quality Management A contemporary second example is Total Quality Management, widely enough recognized by the early 1990s to be known simply as TQM. This approach is one of the more recent programs in a long line of management techniques that have worked their way into the discourse of school supervision and educational administration. The roots of TQM go back to the 1940s and Shewhart's work at Bell Laboratories.

In an effort to improve the reliability of telephones, Shewhart's method was to infuse quality control (i.e., primarily new statistical procedures to reduce product variance) throughout the entire process of design and production (Bonstingl, 1992). In the 1970s and 1980s, the approach became more widely applied in business, partly through its loose connections with Deming and his work in postwar Japanese industry.

TQM did not have a powerful influence on education until 1990, but the number of books, journal articles, workshops, and conference presentations on TQM has burgeoned since that time. Almost every major educational journal has published articles on this topic, the overwhelming majority of which have focused on the applications of TQM, how-to explanations of its use, or case examples of what the approach looks like in practice. TQM has also been thoroughly analyzed in the literature from perspectives that include, for example, critical theory, structuralism, and the postmodern (Capper & Jamison, 1993). Reports of research on the effects of TQM are much less common, but what few studies have been reported suggest that TQM's influence was far more modest than its advocates typically imply (Brandt, 1992).

The high-profile/low-impact pattern that has emerged for TQM is not unfamiliar. For example, consider, Cuban's (1979) analogy between educational change and a hurricane sweeping across an ocean. Cuban compares the hurricane's turbulent winds and ocean surface with any recently heralded school reform. The winds of change are reflected in our professional journals and conference programs, but school practices lie protected well below the ocean's surface. At this depth, the ocean-floor at which teachers and school administrators go about their day-to-day work, the currents of reform are slow to shift in one direction or another, and practice remains largely undisturbed by even the most pronounced turbulences of educational innovation.

Cuban's hurricane metaphor may overstate the point. TQM has and will continue to have some influence over educational management concerns. However, nothing exists in research, equivalent to a Richter scale for gauging the impact of TQM at any level. One reason for this limitation is that, as TQM has made its way into education, definitions of the approach have also broadened from what was initially viewed as a management technique to a more encompassing orientation, now sometimes referred to as "quality philosophy." Philosophy in this expression is used not in its formal academic sense, but to signify a general set of principles. Some of these principles, such as the elimination of product variance and TQM's emphasis on the "customer's voice" in defining product quality, are easily traced back to the influence of business and industrial concerns. These same principles, however, have become increasingly *less* central to what educators and school administrators mean when they use the term *quality philosophy*. Emphasis now seems to be on a qualitative (even artistic) sense of quality rather than the quantitative sense of quality in which TQM has its origins.

Another general trend is also worth noting. Signs are already on the horizon that the TQM hurricane has begun to abate (or are we in the eye of the storm?). Perhaps one reason for this at least temporary abatement is that, as TQM or quality philosophy principles are more broadly defined, they seem less and less "new" to education (Brant, 1992). An innovation's tendency to undermine itself is one of the ironies of diffusion. To state it briefly, the more alike or congruent an innovation is to familiar practices, the greater its likelihood of adoption. At the same time, an innovation's similarity to existing ideas also reduces its impact. In other words, what seems to appeal to adopters are the noninnovative characteristics of an innovation. According to this view, TQM is perhaps not so much being *adopted* as it is being *coopted* by education.

What one finds is the continuous blending of ideas (i.e., old wine in new bottles, so to speak) that makes the influence of both TQM and the industrial dimensions of supervision extremely difficult to track. With these caveats noted, however, there is no reason to dismiss TQM as little more than sound and fury. At least for purposes of illustration, TQM represents fresh imprints of business and industrial thinking on the fields of school supervision and educational management. These imprints are born of contemporary needs, but they do not signal a radical departure from past ideas. As Sztajn (1992) noted, TQM urges educators to think of schools as enlightened corporations, not as factories, which is an updating of an old business metaphor.

Competitive Global Market A third example also is a contemporary development only in its particular form, and it is again one that is closely related to business concerns. This example is the increasingly common use of world competition as an argument for school reform. While the Cold War engendered beliefs that education was necessary to national security, threats from abroad dramatically shifted during the early 1990s. National security is still a pressing issue, but at stake today is economic not military security, and our chief adversaries are no longer Russia and the former Soviet Bloc, but Japan, Germany, and other exporting nations that have cut deeply into American consumer markets.

Many in education have drawn the parallels between economic and educational rivalry in explicit terms. Legislation that sets national goals for American schools (e.g., Goals 2000: Educate America Act) has taken up the language of economic security. These national goals speak of "productive employment" and "the skills necessary to compete in a global economy." For example, one goal states that "U.S. students will be first in the world in science and mathematics achievement" (Riley, 1995). Another cornerstone of the national educational reform strategy is the School-to-Work Opportunities Act, which is legislation that emphasizes occupational standards as criteria for student success.

Moreover, our leading journals are now filled with references both to standards and to "world-class" standards. Cuban (1993) wrote that in the 1980s and 1990s,

hundreds of formal reports from corporate leaders, foundations, professional associations, and federal agencies have consistently underscored how schools have failed in achieving their purposes and how important schools are to the nation's economic success (p. 108).

Kirst (1993), an astute observer of American politics and education, spelled out a now prevalent line of reasoning:

[A]rguments about whether the performance of our students has declined over time miss the point. The 1990 Oldsmobile was better

than any Olds made before. But was it good enough to meet worldwide competition in 1990? A similar question faces U.S. education: Are we good enough to stand up to world wide competition? (p. 613).

This argument, in part, serves important political functions in the interest of education. It is an argument that politicians readily understand, and one that holds public credibility in the contemporary context of national and state politics. As suggested earlier, however, the global competition argument is often directed toward neither politicians nor the public. Rather, it is preached to teachers and school administrators by those who seek to motivate change. Just as American business must adapt its products to a global market or risk failure, schools must also adapt.

Education is again framed in terms of economic metaphors: competition, employability, standards, and managerial efficiency. Supervisors in particular find themselves back in the role of quality control. Their work, however, is now overlaid with a new sense of obligation. Failure to assure that others meet market standards fails the system, and it also fails the nation's ability to compete and thrive in economic terms. Widely publicized comparisons of average test performance between American students and those of other countries further reinforce this point of view. When American schools do not fare well on the basis of such comparisons, education (like American business) is cast in terms of a growing crisis.

These three examples (i.e., California's three Cs Curriculum, TQM, and education in a global marketplace) illustrate that the historical connections between industrial concerns and American schooling are very much alive and well today. Other examples might have served just as appropriately: the increasing popularity of school-business partnerships (e.g., Howard 1995) or the accountability movement. Apple (1993), citing the Ryerson Plan of summer internships for teachers in businesses and corporations as yet another example, wrote: "Chairs of Free Enterprise devoted to economic education are springing up at universities throughout the country. Teaching the message of industry has become a real force" (p. 143). A common language and discourse pervasively anchored in American industrial and business interests ties these present-day examples together. Because this language is influential yet largely taken for granted, it will be addressed later as a topic in its own right.

The Factory Metaphor

However specialized, the professional socialization of school supervisors is inextricably linked to the historical themes noted above and to the broader field of contemporary education. Among the industrial metaphors that contribute to these fields of practice and study, the school as factory is often cited as a prominent framework (e.g., Schlechty, 1990, p. 22). Although more often implicit than explicit, this analogy plays out in the following way. Factories, like schools, are organized around a production sequence that is designed to transform raw materials into a standard product. Students represent the raw materials who are to be processed and from which schools produce an educated population. The early grades are devoted to forming a basic frame or chassis (consisting of the three Rs) on which curriculum components (i.e., subjects) can later be installed. Differences in the quality of the original material is called scholastic aptitude.

Teachers represent both the workers and the machinery used in transforming raw materials into a finished product. They do so through a division of labor whereby certain teachers take responsibility for adding different curriculum components (e.g., units of math, history, science, English, and so forth) as the students move from one step in the process to the next. The teachers work by a timeclock, and they negotiate the conditions of their work through collective bargaining. If one of these teachers malfunctions, then he or she has "burned out." School administrators represent middle management whose job it is to control the overall process of production and assure that product specifications are being adequately met. Finally, the school board sets company policy and decides on governing principles. The school's consumer market is society or some segment of society.

As suggested earlier, leading educators in the first half of this century did not hesitate to make this metaphor explicit. As Cubberley wrote in 1916:

Our schools are, in a sense, factories in which the raw products (children) are to be shaped and fashioned into products to meet the various demands of life. The specifications for manufacturing come from the demands of twentieth-century civilization, and it is the business of the school to build its pupils according to the specifications laid down (quoted in Lincoln, 1992, p. 81).

The factory metaphor is made explicit today almost solely in order to critique its emphasis on standardization, the implied passivity of the students, the resulting fragmentation of curriculum, and the overall reliance on formal lines of top–down authority. These contemporary critiques are anything but dispassionate, and their appraisals of the factory metaphor are overwhelmingly negative. For example, Hyman (1986) concludes in the *School Administrator's Faculty Supervision Handbook* that:

The factory metaphor is a deadly one. . . . It is deadly because it subverts humane interaction between the people involved in school life. Behavior according to the school as factory leads the teacher to treat the students as inanimate objects, as things (not people) to be processed, stamped out, and finished on the conveyor belt assembly line instead of as developing, emerging, evolving human beings. Unfortunately, there are adult citizens today who still demand that we "build" this year's model of students to the streamline specifications they have laid down (p. 4).

Condemned on the one hand but recognized as still influential on the other, the factory metaphor is a relatively easy target for criticism. Broad themes related to this metaphor do not fare any better. Tyack (1974), for example, criticizes "the one best system," (which is his term for the corporate-style bureaucratization of urban schooling) as having "ill-served the pluralistic character of American society" (p. 11). Karier (1982), another educational historian, has harsh comments for the influence of profit and efficiency:

Unexamined, unchecked, and uncontrolled, the criteria of efficiency cut deeply into our traditional views of the dignity of life, knowledge, the meaning of words, and the overall political process by which we govern ourselves. In such a world, words like democracy and freedom lose their traditional meanings as they take on a propaganda function (p. 15).

In a similar vein, Hold (1993) advised: "Attempts to link business with schooling should be treated with suspicion, since they often presage a shift away from the purposes of education —the development of the mind—toward the tasks of training—the inculcation of skills" (p. 22).

In short, the factory metaphor, together with other values associated with industrialism per se, have fallen out of favor among many leading segments of educational analysis. A parallel trend has developed in business education as well as in business scholarship. Management theorists in particular are questioning some of the same industrial implications that trouble educational writers. It is important to avoid the impression that even widespread criticism of the factory metaphor has effectively minimized or cut off its influence on considerations of educational processes. It would be naive to assume that analytic critiques of the factory model allow individuals to readily step outside its tacit power to shape perceptions. Changes in thinking are under way, but metaphors like the one at hand have a tenacious life of their own.

Lakoff and Johnson (1980) indicate one of the reasons for the die-hard nature of metaphorical thinking. Their point is that groups or families of related metaphors are linked together to form a coherent understanding that often stretches across several domains of experience. In this sense, many metaphors represent a stable network of meaning; not simply a single point of comparison, but an entire vocabulary and discourse for making sense of what people do (see also Reddy, 1979; Schon, 1979). Poet Robert Frost put this matter another way:

All metaphor breaks down somewhere. That is the beauty of it. It is touch and go with the metaphor, and until you have lived with it long enough you don't know where it is going. You don't know how much you can get out of it and when it will cease to yield. It is a very living thing (quoted in Cox & Lathem 1968, 33).

The network of educational metaphors that have a connection with industrial thinking and business values extends well into the structures and processes of schooling. These metaphors are often taken for granted, but a list would include such terms as:

school board
classroom management
portfolios
homework
instructional delivery
outcomes-based education
the child-care industry
central office
accountability
competition
curriculum packages
school–university partnerships

The power of such a vocabulary in shaping thinking about education would not be so impressive if it were limited to a handful of analogic metaphors of the type listed earlier. A more general metaphoric process is at work, however, where meanings are carried over from one domain to another through imagery rather than through analogic comparisons alone. These image words are sometimes called "iconic metaphors" (Bowers & Flinders, 1990). A relevant example of an iconic metaphor is the term *organization* used as a noun to refer to a business, corporation, or school. The conventional image of an organization typically includes a hierarchical structure, a common purpose shared by the organization's members, lines of formal authority through which the organization's governance is maintained, and a division of labor.

This iconic metaphor is one that organizational theorists have begun to question over the past two decades. For example, Hartman (1988) argued that classical images of an organization place far too much reliance on top management and their ability to plan or control even the organization's goals. As he stated:

An organization's actual as opposed to its claimed objectives are not necessarily what top management decides. In order for objectives to be genuine rather than mere inscriptions in a slick binder, they must have the requisite support within the organization. In most large organizations implementation of planning is an elaborate process of building political support, rather than just telling everybody exactly what to do. . . . Having a clear understanding of coherent ultimate objectives is enough for saints only, and does sinners less good (p. 107).

Hartman is not questioning the effectiveness of managers nor the virtues of workers; rather, he is commenting on the underlying image of organizations as highly rational entities.

A similar trend, which is more a redefinition of rationality than it is a shift away from it, is represented in writers such as Simon, March, or Schon. Whereas classical images of an organization suggested the activities of goal-setting, planning, management, and control, the work of these writers emphasizes a notably different vocabulary. Simon (1957) introduced the term *satisficing,* which is decision-making within the constraints of limited information and limited predictability. March (1984) wrote of ambiguous preferences, loose coupling, organized anarchy, and the process of muddling through ambiguous commitments. Schon's (1983) view of professional life is one that stresses uncertainty, complexity, trial and error, and the nontechnical processes of "reflection-in-action."

The shift in vocabulary represented by these authors signals a deeper shift in perceived reality. Their working theories (i.e., metaphors) bring several facets of organizational life into focus that might otherwise go unnoticed. The first of these is that decisions are rarely made outside the context of their implementation. For example, goal-setting is often an emergent process that illustrates a mutual influence between intentions and actions. Second, decisions are rarely made on a unilateral basis. Even top–down management requires some degree of negotiation between members of the organization. Third, the authority of official reports is limited. Hartman (1988) makes this point by noting that organizations "can be

neurotic, in the sense that management habitually can have poor control over what actually happens after policy or strategy is made" (p. 107). Examples of such weak ties between an official agenda and practice are not difficult to find in education. Thornton's (1988) research, for instance, reports a significant level of what he called "dissonance" among the intended curriculum, what happens in classrooms, and what students learn.

The point, however, is more than just the potential slippage between policy objectives and actual practice. Organizational theorists are attempting to explicate general phenomena, with one being the tendency for parts of the organization to tacitly subvert formal lines of authority. Emic or "insider" perspectives on organizational life consistently reveal a shadow culture behind the clean organizational charts of top–down decision-making. This is a central theme in much of Goffman's (1961, 1974) research: Whenever you create a system, you also create an underlife.

The lessons of theory and research have urged those interested in organizational life to re-think images of what counts as rational behavior within an organization. These efforts hold at least two direct implications for school supervision. The first is to recognize that intentions (e.g., professional development aims, lesson plans, and instructional objectives) are best understood within their organizational context. Moreover, that context is likely to follow its own logic reflected in the micropolitics and culture of a particular school. Like other members of the organization, teachers face uncertainties and inconsistent choices, compromise to fit the given constraints of their work, cope with ambiguities, and generally learn to muddle through on their own terms. Mistakes in practice may be frequent as demands are juggled, reprioritized to match the situation at hand, or simply ignored. Maintaining a facade of predictability and control may be part of the job, but so is learning to deal with unintended consequences. All of these concerns speak to the fluidity of organizational life, which in turn places special emphasis on the supervisor's ability to read the intricate context in which instructional activities unfold (Flinders, 1991).

The second implication involves recognizing that supervisors themselves are usually as much a part of the organization as those they seek to assist. The supervisor's intentions and decisions are shaped as much as anyone else's by the settings in which they work. They, too, face uncertainties, unpredictable outcomes, and conflicting demands. They, too, engage in a certain amount of trial and error. They, too, are unable to make unilateral decisions. Even the use of "objective" techniques such as low-inference checklists or observation schedules cannot free supervisors from the contexts of their work or from their subjective understandings of those contexts.

As Peshkin (1985) argued, subjectivity does not necessarily undermine the validity of a person's knowledge or observations. Under the right circumstances, subjective understandings can enhance the power of observations to inform others about experiences they themselves might otherwise take for granted. Whether subjectivity is a vice or virtue, however, depends on the observer's awareness of how his or her subjective beliefs and commitments enter into the process.

Peshkin (1988) suggested a number of heuristic strategies for increasing this awareness by helping observers keep track of their emotional responses to observed events, and by making explicit the normative basis on which those events are judged to be significant. As a general expectation, many supervisors believe that they should try to be conscious of their particular biases and do what they can to prevent those biases from leading to prejudicial assessments, but the notion of turning subjectivity to one's advantage has yet to be worked out in the context of supervision practices.

The organization as an iconic metaphor for patterns of supposedly rational behavior has been treated only briefly. Some organizational theorists tell us that such patterns are far more context-dependent and less subject to formal authority than was once assumed, which in itself holds important implications for supervision. Another iconic metaphor is "teaching as work." This is again a metaphor largely taken for granted, but it is useful as a basis for identifying some additional lines of research that are relevant to the relationship between business and school supervision.

TEACHING AS WORK

The perspective of teaching as work encompasses several broad categories of research and scholarship that are loosely connected by their shared interest in teaching as a means of livelihood, career, or occupation. Within this perspective, three representative, but still relatively narrow lines of scholarship are examined. The first is from critical theory and is focused particularly on Apple's writings. The second is from the field of urban affairs and is illustrated by Lipsky's theory of street-level bureaucracy. The third is from program implementation research and is devoted to models examined by Synder, Bolin, and Zumwalt.

Critical Theory Perspective

Critical theorists have been among the most strident critics of business' influence on education. They do not see that influence as being conspiratorial, but as sinister nonetheless. In their view, schools have long been subject to a business offensive, the effects of which have been to regulate class mobility, manage class conflict, and maintain the exploitative relations found in the larger society by producing a semi-skilled yet ideologically docile workforce. Although vehemently opposed to the involvement of mainstream business interests, the critical theorists have done more than other groups to promote an economic analysis of American education. Moreover, their scholarship often makes use of labor and work-related metaphors that are directly relevant to the industrial dimensions of supervision.

Within a critical theory perspective, Apple's work is prominent in its scope of considerations related to the political economy of schooling. One of the central themes of his research was to pursue a nonreductionist examination of managerial and business trends as they impact past and present school practices (Apple, 1986). Two concepts are illustrated by these trends, and both are problematic to a genuinely democratic education. The concepts are deskilling and work intensification. Each concept is considered in turn and then addressed the implications for school supervision.

Deskilling Apple (1986, pp. 39–40) argued that the efficiency movement in education influenced schools in much the same way that Taylor's scientific management strategies influenced American industry. In short, efficiency failed as a technique, but it succeeded on a more symbolic level. One of its most significant effects was to legitimize interventions that were intended to rationalize an individual's work. This rationalization was primarily analytic. Its approach involved breaking down a worker's performance into a sequence of discrete tasks, the aim being to simplify an otherwise complex job. As simplification becomes built into a production sequence, workers become more responsible for executing routine tasks and less responsible for how their work is conceived. This is the process of deskilling. Control over a given job (e.g., teaching or learning) is shifted from the worker to those with closer ties to management.

In education, deskilling has the potential to play out in ways that influence teachers and students alike. The student's work (i.e., learning skills or content) can be highly rationalized through instructional design systems, as in the case of programmed learning. When this approach becomes a dominant form of classroom practice, students may readily find themselves engaged in a type of goal displacement. Their aims are no longer to master certain skills or learn a given body of content; rather, they are to complete so many worksheets per day.

Similar types of displacement also threaten the work of teachers. The "teacher-proof" curriculum packages developed in the 1960s, especially scripted curricula such as the DISTAR reading program, are often cited in this context (McCutcheon, 1988). In the eyes of those who designed such programs, the teacher's job was narrowly defined so as not to go beyond an accurate delivery of the materials. When teachers remained true to this role, they often found the demands of covering a certain amount of material each day displaced the goal of helping students. Scripted programs again were not very successful as a curriculum design technique; however, they often signaled further erosion of the teacher's formal control over curricular and instructional decision-making.

Work Intensification The second concept relevant to labor's perspective is work intensification. Fiscal retrenchment and intense competition for resources have once again been used to support demands for increased productivity. In education, these demands take the form of higher standards, increased graduation requirements, and extending the school year. Because additional resources often do not accompany these demands, teachers and students find themselves expected to do more with less. The result is an intensification of one's work, which by Apple's (1986) description, "has many symptoms, from the trivial to the more complex—ranging from being allowed no time at all even to go to the bathroom, have a cup of coffee or relax, to having a total absence of time to keep up with one's field" (p. 41).

Whether intended or unintended, intensification functions to control the teacher's work. Part of this control is exercised through isolation. As the demands of work increase, individuals find less opportunity to socialize and interact with one another. My own analysis of teacher isolation supports this thesis. In a qualitative study of six high school teachers, I found that the patterns of their work indicated a form of self-imposed isolation. From the teachers' point of view, isolation was more than just a psychological state or physical separation from other adults; it was also a strategy for coping with their need to focus on the increasing demands of their work (Flinders, 1988).

Work intensification has other consequences as well, some of which are more immediately detrimental to instruction. Because the quantity of service provided to students is far more easily assessed than its quality, the need to cut corners is most likely to compromise instruction on the side of quality. At the same time, good teaching is often considered to be its own reward. Intensification undermines this intrinsic motivation for students as well as teachers when opportunity for the traditional interest in work well done is no longer available.

Deskilling and work intensification are important control mechanisms for the very reason that they often go unrecognized in the context of supervision. If unaware of how such tendencies arise or where they lead, a supervisor can unwittingly contribute to reducing the quality of instruction rather than improving it. Moreover, the issues at hand are not just ideological. Supervisors can guard against the specific concerns of deskilling and work intensification without embracing the premise of some critical theorists that schools are oppressive institutions. Supervisors must also not assume a radical stance in order to recognize that supervision has its own political basis and implications. It is only because supervision is rarely recognized in political terms that this perspective takes on special significance.

Many teachers, of course, actively resist the mechanisms of deskilling and work intensification through various forms of "creative insubordination" (Flinders, 1989). If this resistance can be recognized as a constructive attempt by teachers to maintain the integrity of their teaching or to improve the quality of their instruction, then it should be supported by whatever authority the supervisor has to offer. Learning to read a teacher's best efforts and challenges to official policy is part of the nontechnical (if not political) side of supervision. It requires a level of understanding that must be established through open dialogue between teachers and supervisors, and a willingness on the part of supervisors to support a negotiated agenda.

These issues are particularly easy to lose sight of in the day-to-day practice of supervision because a supervisor's work may be subject to similar mechanisms of deskilling and work intensification. The prerequisite conditions of work rationalization (particularly in the form of state-mandated observation instruments) and fiscal retrenchment would seem evident if not widespread within the field. Research, however, has yet to tell us much about whether or how such conditions have impinged on the practices of school supervision. Considerable resistance to deskilling and work intensification

might be found here too, as in teaching, with supervisors actively seeking ways to maintain control over their own work by subverting official policies.

Street-Level Bureaucracy

A second line of scholarship relevant to teaching as work is represented by Lipsky's (1980) theory of "street-level bureaucracy." Lipsky developed this theory based on studies of police, public service workers, teachers, and employees in various other human resource agencies. In this respect, the theory does not flow directly from the context of business or industry, nor is it as closely linked to socioeconomic factors as is, for example, critical theory. Lipsky's theory instead offers a framework that bridges industrial and business perspectives on the one hand with human service concerns on the other. It is useful in the context of school supervision because it brings into focus some of the same problems that concern critical theorists, but does so by taking a different approach.

Lipsky's theory is an attempt to describe the work practices of individuals who deal directly with clients in a public service setting. By Lipsky's definition street-level bureaucracies "are the schools, police and welfare departments, lower courts, legal services offices, and other agencies whose workers interact with and have wide discretion over the dispensation of benefits or the allocation of public sanctions" (1980, p. xi). Lipsky argued that street-level bureaucrats play a critical role because their collective actions add up to agency policy as it is experienced by those whose lives the policy is intended to change. In other words, the focus of this theory is on what services are like at their point of delivery.

Lipsky identified five conditions that both influence service and define the nature of work within street-level bureaucracies. The first condition is that the resources available to agency workers are typically inadequate to meet expected (or at least hoped for) outcomes. For example, teachers have limited time and information, but they also work with large numbers of students and a wide range of curricula. Still more to the point, the public defines the school's role in broad terms. The hope is that teachers will be able to get across some curriculum content and perhaps impart some basic skills, but while they are at it, teachers also are expected to build character, foster critical thinking, encourage creativity, promote self-esteem, help eliminate racist and sexist attitudes, give practical advice, and support family values, all of which could be just the beginning of a much longer list. Teachers would probably be the last to abandon such worthy goals, but these aspirations do begin to seem unrealistic when set against the limited resources available to education.

The second condition of work within street-level bureaucracies is that the demands for services increase to meet the availability of services. If availability goes up, then new demands will immediately fill in any discrepancy. In schools, there are always more students who can be identified as "at risk" or in need of services not previously available to them. Moreover, attending to individual differences, which is often viewed as one of the cornerstones of good teaching, is the type of practice that can induce an almost inexhaustible demand, whatever a teacher's time and energy.

A third condition of work is closely related to the first two. Goal expectations for human service agencies tend to be vague, ambiguous, or conflicting. In education, local politics usually demand that consensus over the aims of schooling can only be reached at considerable expense to specificity. It is easier to agree on broad principles than it is on the particulars of what or how a curriculum should be taught. In addition, schools do not have a single mission; rather, they serve multiple purposes. Some of these purposes, such as academic learning and vocational preparation, may compete with one another and lead to inconsistent practices.

The fourth condition of work in street-level bureaucracies is that worker performance oriented toward goal achievement is typically difficult to measure. The vagueness of educational goals and the potential for conflicting objectives do not help in this respect, but the nature of learning and its relationship to teaching is also at issue. A teacher can never be quite certain just what students have learned, or how much of that learning can be directly attributed to his or her instruction. No one has found a way to get inside another person's head to know what that person has learned. Thus, a teacher's performance can only offer approximations of his or her success.

The final condition of work is that clients are usually nonvoluntary. Compulsory education laws do not make this true in any absolute sense. Nevertheless, for people who cannot afford private schooling, the public schools have what amounts to a monopoly on education. More to the point, individual "clients" typically have quite limited choices about who, how, and what services a school provides.

Overall, these five conditions of work present a number of constraints, particularly with respect to the time and resources available to those who provide public service. In order to cope with the constraints of their work, street-level bureaucrats develop a variety of strategies. These strategies include rationing services, controlling clients, modifying goals, and routinizing procedures. Classroom teaching illustrates all of these strategies in one form or another. For example, the routine use of textbooks and worksheets, even though they are intended to promote learning, also allows teachers to standardize important aspects of their work. Classroom management techniques serve to control clients, and methods such as the use of reading groups in the primary grades permit teachers to ration their time and attention.

Such strategies again are highly adaptive to the conditions of a street-level bureaucracy. They allow workers to conserve scarce resources either by limiting service or by standardizing its delivery. The strategies make an otherwise impossible job manageable. Their secondary effects, however, are troublesome, particularly in the long run. As the work becomes increasingly routinized and as pressures persist to deal with large caseloads, street-level bureaucrats begin to take on what Lipsky calls a "processing mentality." This orientation may take different forms, one of which involves "processing" the work itself. In particular, workers come to view tasks as no longer means to an end, but as ends in themselves. For example, a teacher may set short-range objectives such as covering the first three chapters of the textbook by a certain date, grading so many papers each day, having the students learn so many vocabulary words per week, take so many quizzes, and so forth.

It is easy to become preoccupied with such tasks, losing sight of the context in which they are significant. Here again a subtle form of goal displacement takes place between helping students learn and the need to complete an arbitrary number of tasks within a specified amount of time. This type of displacement is not restricted to public service work alone. Businesses and industries have long been aware that workers can become cut off from their sense of purpose and involvement, which is a process similar to that of deskilling. Motivation and job satisfaction suffer as a result, as does the quality of the worker's performance.

A "processing mentality" can take another form that is more specific to public service work, and more invidious, than the task-oriented routines also common to business and industry. Lipsky refers to this alternate form as "client processing." The adaptive work strategies so important to street-level bureaucrats (e.g., rationing services, routinizing procedures, etc.) involve a built-in contradiction between being responsive to clients as individual cases and the need to treat them on the basis of standardized routines. Routines are effective for the very reason that they ignore individual differences. What they are effective *at*, however, is the goal of moving people through the system (i.e., getting them from one step in the process to the next).

The dangers of "client processing" are the same dangers of bureaucratic organization more broadly conceived. To be specific, the very clients the organization was created to serve become viewed in largely impersonal ways, either as case types (e.g., a behavior disordered child or a reading deficit problem) or as a number (e.g., percentage of students meeting graduation requirements or number of students receiving a particular service). If teachers respond too rigidly to the press of needing to deal with large numbers of students, they sacrifice opportunities for exercising discretion in their day-to-day work. This is the source of a bureaucracy's impersonal basis for dealing with its clients, and by which clients come to be recognized only in the terms that qualify them for a particular service.

How, then, does Lipsky's theory of street-level bureaucracy promise to inform either the practices or understandings of school supervision? Like destilling and work intensification, the concepts of work processing and client processing suggest specific tendencies for supervisors to be aware of and guard against. On this point, the criteria a supervisor uses to assess a teacher's performance are at issue. Criteria prespecified in terms of task completion or the amount of work accomplished without regard for its quality or how work routines impact relationships in the classroom are appealing because such criteria reduce ambiguity and can be measured with the type of precision that has at least the appearance of objectivity. Such criteria, however, may unintentionally reinforce the same coping strategies that lead to a processing mentality. On the other hand, criteria that recognize quality, the teacher's discretion in dealing with individual cases, and the involvement of students in instruction may be highly appropriate, although such criteria can only be assessed on a subjective basis. In this situation, supervisors face the dilemma of having to choose between relevance or rigor.

More specific to the classroom, work processing calls attention to the relationship between a teacher and his or her curriculum. In the context of supervision as deliberation and inquiry, the quality of that relationship can be addressed in ways that resist the early closure on possibilities, which is all too common in the routinization of practice. Where appropriate, supervision could take on the aim of helping teachers find new opportunities for engaging with their curriculum at an intellectual level. Because many individuals enter teaching with a special interest in their subject areas, helping them maintain this interest adds to job satisfaction as well as models continued learning, thus enhancing the quality of instruction.

Client processing calls attention to a quite different type of relationship (i.e., the one between a teacher and his or her students). Rapport, solidarity, or interpersonal competence are not easy concepts to pin down in terms of specific behaviors. Furthermore, most teachers do not have time within their daily schedules that is officially designated for interacting with students on a one-to-one basis. An imaginative approach to work routines, however, that does not foreclose early on a range of options can lead to work structures that promote one's professional discretion in this area. For example, many teachers have found routines that build in pockets of time each day or each week for allowing at least brief interactions with individual students. Supervision could not only recognize but encourage such routines.

Models of Program Implementation

Critical theory and street-level bureaucracy are contemporary lines of inquiry that hold specific implications for understanding some of the contextual and structural dimensions of teaching as work. This section of the chapter is fulfilled by considering a third area of research—that of program implementation. At first glance, program implementation research may seem unrelated to the industrial dimensions of school supervision. I want to make explicit, however, that this research is based on distinct conceptions of teaching as work. These conceptions of teaching can be linked with the industrial themes previously introduced, and they illustrate a growing sophistication with respect to understanding the nature of professional life in schools.

In order to emphasize both the development of this research and its relevance to teaching as work, I will draw on a review by Synder, Bolin, and Zumwalt (1992). These authors identify three models of implementation research, and these models have a bearing on supervision because each one brings into focus different aspects of teaching, including: (1) fidelity, (2) mutual adaptation, and (3) program enactment.

Fidelity The fidelity perspective best illustrates the historical assumptions of efficiency, school bureaucratization, and social utility. Implementation is viewed from this perspective as a linear process, governed through top–down management. The aim of fidelity research is to assess the degree to which a particular innovation or procedure is implemented as planned. The teachers' role is to execute a program's content and design as faithfully as their abilities permit. The supervisor's role is to check on how well a course of study matches the intent of its design, and to identify ways to facilitate the process of carrying out the program as intended. This usually involves developing a checklist of practices that correspond with desired program plans. That checklist is then used to gauge the degree of implementation.

The simplicity of this logic is appealing. As long as program goals can be clearly defined, worker responsibilities are relatively straightforward. Teachers are the conduit by which the program is delivered; their actions are thus goal-oriented and can be rationalized on that basis. This rationalization is one that stresses the application of techniques or methods, and, in doing so, echoes the parallels between the industrial uses of scientific management and its legacy in education. The legacy reproduced in the fidelity model, however, includes more than an emphasis on technique. It also reinforces the view of schooling itself as a means to social ends, and a significant subset of these social ends have traditionally represented business and economic interests.

Mutual Adaptation Although most program implementation research and many program evaluation efforts have employed the fidelity model, this approach leaves significant aspects of a teacher's work unrecognized and unexamined. The limitations of the fidelity model are illustrated particularly well by the Rand Change Agent Study. This four-year project focused on various school change efforts, concluding that successful change efforts are characterized by a more complex process of mutual adaptation, not by a simple act of adoption (McLaughlin, 1976). A mutual adaptation model is distinct in its emphasis on the processes of implementation. As Synder, Bolin, and Zumwalt defined the term:

Mutual adaptation is seen as that process whereby adjustments in a curriculum are made by curriculum developers and those who actually use it in the school or classroom context. This implies a certain amount of negotiation and flexibility on the part of both designers and practitioners (1992, p. 410).

Like fidelity, mutual adaptation still views implementation as a linear process, but the influence between plans and practice is regarded as a two-way street. Mutual adaptation also acknowledges that practitioners (e.g., teachers) modify plans as they put them into practice. Thus, the teacher is viewed as an active rather than passive agent, which corresponds with Lipsky's argument that street-level bureaucrats play a critical role in shaping organizational policy as that policy is experienced by clients. To put this another way, the focus of mutual adaptation is on how policies are played out within the context of their delivery.

This emphasis on the "in-process" modifications of work also undercuts the clean lines that are often assumed to be the hallmark of top–down management. Conditions of work are viewed as complex, thus demanding some degree of latitude in how the work is carried out. On this point, mutual adaptation is closer to the "enlightened corporation" metaphor than it is to the conventionally understood school-as-factory metaphor. In addition, mutual adaptation better accommodates the shift in organizational theory that has stressed ambiguous preferences, the processes of "satisficing," loose coupling as an organizational norm, and, more recently, what Charles Handy (1989) has called "upside–down thinking," which is an approach to looking at familiar business relationships in innovative ways.

Program Enactment A third implementation model—program enactment—takes mutual adaptation a step further in the direction of viewing the teacher's work as highly context-bound and teachers themselves as fully active agents in shaping the purposes of their work. From this point of view, teaching is neither thought of as the process of delivering a product (e.g., knowledge) nor as the process of building a model student on the basis of a prespecified set of plans. Teaching instead involves the cocreation of meaning whereby teachers and students act together in the construction of an educational experience. The goals of this process are largely emergent, and flexibility as well as individual distinctiveness are valued. In a sense, the students are hand-made rather than mass produced.

Synder, Bolin, and Zumwalt point out that implementation research focusing on enactment is relatively rare. Some research, including Hawthorne's (1992) study, "Curriculum in the Making," or Clandinin and Connelly's work (1992), conceive of the teacher as a curriculum developer. There are also studies reviewed by Synder, Bolin, and Zumwalt (1992, p. 427) that seek to examine what an enacted program looks like and what it means specifically to those most directly involved with its implementation. The results of such research have not yielded prescriptive recommendations, but they do suggest at least three broad themes.

The first theme is that the emergent nature of an enacted program makes it difficult to define the program prior to its implementation or outside the context of its enactment. Being in the classroom to interpret enactment strategies firsthand counts for supervisors. The second theme is that teacher and student investment in a program is positively related to its successful implementation. This theme raises the question of what recognizable features of a classroom are indicative of ownership. The third theme is that attempts to control or standardize the program have a negative effect on its implementation. By implication, the supervisor's role would need to be recast in more collaborative terms than is typically the case.

Although industrial metaphors are less evident in enactment-oriented implementation research, enactment may well accommodate and be informed by theories of organizational life. For example, Schon's (1983) concepts of "reflection-in-action" and "reflection-in-practice" speak to the emergence of purposes and the flexible applications of technique. Connections can also be drawn between enactment and critical theory. Because enactment views teaching as the joint construction of meaning, the authenticity of learning is determined at the level of classroom practice, not by an outside source. Thus, implementation depends on the empowerment of teachers and students, and this empowerment then becomes the implicit or explicit goal of support services (i.e., supervision).

One of the obvious conclusions one might draw from this section is that work in general (and teaching-as-work in particular) has been conceptualized from a wide variety of perspectives. Even within education, lines of scholarship such as those from critical theory, street-level bureaucracy, and program implementation represent a quite diverse family of theoretical orientations and research traditions. Some (e.g., critical theory) point to the broad similarities between teaching and other types of work. Others (e.g., implementation research) are more focused on the distinctive characteristics of work in schools per

se. Nevertheless, even an enactment model holds lessons for understanding the nature of work in general. Where enactment brings aspects of teaching into focus that traditional industrial metaphors neglect, it thereby sophisticates our understanding of those metaphors. Moreover, the diversity of perspectives that can be brought under the umbrella of teaching as work indicates the potential for extending these perspectives into the field of supervision research. The final comments address some of the possibilities in this area.

FUTURE RESEARCH

Contemporary concerns such as global competition and employability, organizational theories, and the studies of teaching as work cited in this chapter suggest that research on the industrial dimensions of supervision could well assume a forward-looking agenda. Whereas the technologies and values of industry have changed over the past century, how people make their livelihood through service, production, and so forth remains central to the social context of education. School supervision is responsive to that context, and it is also proactive to the degree that supervision shapes our conceptions of good teaching and professional practice.

On the specific question of how business and industrial concerns have influenced school supervision, historical studies remain the strong suit of current educational research. Even in this category, however, holes in the literature leave unanswered questions. On the one hand, studies that follow in the tradition of Callahan's research have examined the origins and adaptation of industrial values and practices in education and educational administration at large. On the other hand, writers such as Karier and Bolin focused on the intellectual history of supervision as a distinct enterprise, picking up strands of industrial influence as part of their analyses. The gap between these two approaches is the impact of industry specifically on school supervision. Moreover, direct efforts to address this impact in its historical context would likely reveal far more avenues of influence than I have considered in the themes of bureaucratization, scientific management, and social adaptation. Indeed, these themes serve only as points of departure for further research.

The contemporary influence of business and industry raises its own unresolved questions. The life cycle and trajectory of particular innovations (e.g., TQM) are not well understood. Have such innovations impacted supervision practices or ways of thinking as much as they have impacted the professional literature? Are such innovations "coopted" rather than adopted by education, as I have suggested? Have arguments for global competition shaped the political climate of school supervision? Is the nation's ability to compete economically at all related to how supervisors envision their work or to what instructional practices they view as credible? Have school–business partnerships had an influence on the parameters of teaching and supervision? How do today's closer ties between schools and business play out in terms of day-to-day instructional activities?

Any one of these business-related trends can be examined further by cross-referencing its intended or unintended influence on schools with the various concepts suggested in theories of teaching as work. For example, do school–business partnerships influence the rationalization of practice or the resource issues that may lead to deskilling and work intensification? How do such innovations play into or shape the conditions of work that characterize a street-level bureaucracy? Can innovations be carried out in ways that undermine what Lipsky calls a processing mentality? Is this mentality part of an innovation's cost? What influence will an innovation have on the enacted program? How does the innovation fit within the personal constructs of teachers and students? How is the innovation shaped through processes of mutual adaptation? Such questions, which are central to a wide range of educational reform efforts, suggest that researchers with any curiosity will not run short of significant opportunities to pursue their interests.

Furthermore, studies that contribute to understandings of teaching as work, whatever their particular theoretical approach, are important both for their implications with respect to supervision and for clarifying theory at more explicit levels of understanding. Supervisors tend to take their theories of teaching for granted, treating them as assumptions rather than as conceptual tools. The potential for future research is to help delineate these assumptions as a set of options that supervisors may use in their interpretations and appraisals of teaching. To put this another way, research and theories of teaching as work promise to contribute to the knowledge base on which the reflective nature of supervision depends.

Still another area of potential contribution suggested in this chapter is the knowledge that has been gained in understanding the complexities of organizational life. Some of the implications of this understanding have been discussed with respect to the supervisor's subjectivity as well as his or her ability to read the subtle qualities of organizational behavior. The trend in business has been to rethink the nature of organizations in ways that stress the limits of conventional rationality. In light of this reconceptualization and its emphasis on the vicissitudes of organizational life, two additional areas of research that deserve mention focus on supervision as a form of professional practice.

The first area concerns understanding the social context of supervision. In particular, researchers may find it useful to draw a parallel between what Becker (1982) has called "art worlds" in his research and the "supervision worlds" in which supervisors operate on a daily basis. An art world includes all of the people, materials, and conventional ways of acting that go into or are necessary in the production of an artistic work. By analogy, a supervision world would include all the people, materials, and conventional ways of acting that are necessary to supervision. This encompasses teachers, their students, the classroom, curriculum materials, those who wrote and produced the materials, and so forth. A supervision world would also include

the necessary and conventional norms on the basis of which supervision gets done. Such norms focus on the expectations people hold with respect to what supervision is and how supervisors should act. In this sense, supervision is viewed as a form of social organization.

This view of supervision raises several questions. What are the distinctive characteristics of supervision worlds that make them alike or different than, say, business worlds? With whom and how must supervisors cooperate in order to accomplish their work? What conditions will elicit uncertainty or arguments over how to proceed? When do conventional routines break down, and why? What are the practical concerns that motivate supervisors, and how do they describe the micropolitics of their day-to-day lives? The challenge for supervision research, especially research interested in supervision as a professional activity, will be to capture the particulars of practice in ways that contribute to broader thematic understandings of that practice.

A second area of research suggested by the complexity of organizational life, be it in business or in educational settings, involves the use of subjective appraisal. Schon's work in particular has emphasized the central role of subjective understandings in ordinary professional practice. Moreover, subjective appraisals are common to all sorts of practical activities, from cooking a meal or negotiating interpersonal relationships to closing a business deal or writing an academic paper. It might also be surmised that supervisors draw on a wide range of insights based on their own subjective appraisals. Very little, however, is known about the processes involved or how to go about characterizing the various types of subjectivity that come into play. Relatively little also is known about how appraisals are related to what teachers or others credit as good supervision.

Current efforts to reconceptualize the professional practice of school supervision lead outward to a fascinating spectrum of researchable questions, which suggests one final point. The industrial dimensions of supervision (i.e., those dimensions of practice informed by business or corporate interests) have their greatest influence through the type of complexities of organizational life that can only be revealed through studies of actual practice. Because the influence in question is indirect (i.e., it is filtered through the intellectual history and social discourse of educational traditions), researchers will find it difficult to disentangle the industrial dimensions of supervision from the structure of supervisory work or from the context in which that work is carried out. Be that as it may, the promise of future research on the industrial dimensions of supervision is not to disentangle or isolate discrete facets of practice; rather, it is to help us better understand how supervision, like other professional fields, is defined by its particular blend of social meanings.

REFERENCES

Apple, M. W. (1983). Curricular form and the logic of technical control. In L. Weis & M. Apple (Eds). *Ideology and Practice in Schooling,* (143–165). Philadelphia, PA: Temple University Press.

Apple, M. W. (1986). *Teachers and texts.* New York: Routledge & Kegan Paul.

Apple, M. W. (1989). Regulating the text: The sociohistorical roots of state control. *Educational Policy, 3,* 107–123.

Beck, L. G. & Murphy, J. (1993). *Understanding the principalship.* New York: Teachers College Press.

Becker, H. S. (1982). *Art worlds.* Berkeley, CA: University of California Press.

Bobbitt, F. (1918). *The Curriculum.* Boston, MA: Houghton Mifflin.

Bolin, F. S. & Panaritis, P. (1992). Searching for a common purpose: A perspective on the history of supervision. In C. D.

Glickman (Ed.). *Supervision in Transition*. Alexandria, VA: ASCD.

Bolin, F. S. (1987). On defining supervision. *Journal of Curriculum and Supervision, 2*, 368–380.

Bonstingl, J. J. (1992, November). The quality revolution in education. *Educational Leadership, 50*, 4–9.

Bowers, C. A. & Flinders, D. J. (1990). *Responsive Teaching*. New York: Teachers College Press.

Brandt, R. (1992). Are we committed to quality? *Educational Leadership, 50*, 3.

Callahan, R. E. (1962). *Education and the cult of efficiency*. Chicago, IL: University of Chicago Press.

Capper, C. A. & Jamison, M. T. (1993). Let the buyer beware: Total quality management and educational research and practice. *Educational Researcher, 22*, 25–30.

Clandinin, D. J. & Connelly, F. M. (1992). Teacher as curriculum maker. In P. W. Jackson (Ed.). *Handbook of Research on Curriculum*, (pp. 363–401). New York: Macmillan.

Clifford, G. J. & Guthrie, J. W. (1988). *Ed school*. Chicago, IL: University of Chicago Press.

Cobberly, E. P. (1909). *Changing conceptions of education*. Boston, MA: Houghton Mifflin.

Cox, M. & Lathem, E. C. (1968). *Selected prose of Robert Frost*. New York: Collier.

Cuban, L. (1979). Determinants of Curriculum Change and Stability, 1870–1970. In J. Schaffarzick & G. Sykes (Eds.). *Value Conflicts and Curriculum Issues*, (pp. 139–196). Berkeley, CA: McCutchan.

Cuban, L. (1993). Computers meet classroom: Classroom wins. *Teacher College Record, 95*(2), 105–114.

Cuban, L. (1988). *The managerial imperative and the practice of leadership in schools*. Albany, NY: State University of New York Press.

Eisner, E. W. *The Educational Imagination*, (2nd ed.). New York: Macmillan.

Flinders, D. J. (1988). Teacher isolation and the new reform. *Journal of Curriculum and Supervision, 4*.

Flinders, D. J. (1991). Supervision as cultural inquiry. *Journal of Curriculum and Supervision, 6*, 87–106.

Goffman, E. (1961). *Asylums*. New York: Anchor Books.

Goffman, E. (1974). *Frame analysis*. New York: Harper Colophon.

Handy, C. (1989). *The age of unreason*. Boston, MA: Harvard Business School Press.

Hartman, E. M. (1988). *Conceptual foundations of organizational theory*. Cambridge, MA: Ballinger.

Hawthorne, R. K. (1992). *Curriculum in the making*. New York: Teachers College Press.

Holt, M. (1993). Dr. Deming and the improvement of schooling: No instant pudding. *Journal of Curriculum and Supervision, 9*(1), 6–23.

Howard, C. (1995). Education and business go hand-in-hand into the future: Delco and IST form a partnership. *Chalkboard, Indiana School of Education Alumni Association, 42*(2), 8.

Hyman, R. T. (1986). *School administrator's faculty supervision handbook*. Englewood Cliffs, NJ: Prentice-Hall.

Karier, C. (1982). Supervision in historic perspective. In T. J. Sergiovanni (Eds.). *Supervision of Teaching*. Alexandria, VA: ASCD.

Kirst, M. W. (1993). Strengths and weaknesses of American education. *Phi Delta Kappan, 74*(8), 613–618.

Kliebard, H. (1975). The rise of scientific curriculum making and its aftermath. *Curriculum Theory Network, 5*, 27–38.

Kliebard, H. M. (1985). Three currents of American curriculum thought. In A. Molnar (Ed.). *Current Thought on Curriculum: 1985 ASCD Yearbook*. Alexandria, VA: ASCD.

Kliebard, H. M. (1987). *The struggle for the American curriculum, 1893–1958*. New York: Routledge and Kegan Paul.

Lakoff, G. & Johnson, M. (1980). *Metaphors we live by*. Chicago, IL: University of Chicago Press.

Lincoln, Y. S. (1992). Curriculum studies and the traditions of inquiry: The humanistic tradition. In P. W. Jackson (Ed.). *Handbook of Research on Curriculum*, (pp. 79–97). New York: Macmillan.

Lipsky, M. (1980). *Street-level bureaucracy*. New York: Russell Sage Foundation.

Mann, H. (1948/1957). Twelfth Annual Report (1848). In L. A. Cremin (Ed.). *The republic and the school*. New York: Teachers College Press.

March, J. G. (1984). How we talk and how we act: Administrative theory and administrative life. In T. J. Sergiovanni & J. E. Corbally (Eds.). *Leadership and Organizational Culture*. Urbana, IL: University of Illinois Press.

McCutcheon, G. (1986). Curriculum and the work, of teachers. In L. E. Beyer & M. W. Apple (Eds.). *The Curriculum* (pp. 191–203). Albany, NY: State University of New York Press.

McLaughlin, M. W. (1976). Implementation as mutual adaptation: Change in classroom organization. *Teachers College Record, 77*, 339–351.

Peshkin, A. (1985). Virtous subjectivity: In the participant observer's I's. In D. Berg & K. Smith (Eds.). *Exploring Clinical Methods for Social Research* (pp. 267–282). Newsbury Park, CA: Sage.

Peshkin, A. (1988). In search of subjectivity—one's own. *Educational Researcher, 17*, 17–22.

Reddy, M. J. (1980). The conduit metaphor—a case of frame conflict in our language about language. In A. Ortony (Ed.). *Metaphor and Thought* (pp. 284–324). Cambridge, England: Cambridge University Press.

Riley, R. W. (1995). The Goals 2000: Educate America act, providing a world-class education for every child. In J. F. Jennings (Ed.). *National issues in education: Goals 2000 and school-to-work*. Bloomington, IN: Phi Delta Kappa.

Schlechty, P. (1990). *Schools for the 21st century*. San Francisco: Jossey-Bass.

Schon, D. A. (1980). Generative metaphor: A perspective on problem-setting in social policy. In A. Ortony (Ed.). *Metaphor and Thought*, (pp. 254–283). Cambridge, England: Cambridge University Press.

Schon, D. A. (1983). *The Reflective Practitioner*. New York: Basic.

Sergiovanni, T. J. (1992). *Moral Leadership*. San Francisco, CA: Jossey-Bass.

Simon, H. A. (1957). *Models of Man*. New York: John Wiley and Sons.

Synder, J., Bolin, F., & Zumwalt, K. (1992). Curriculum implementation. In P. W. Jackson (Ed.). *Handbook of Research on Curriculum*, (pp. 402–435). New York: Macmillian.

Sztajn, P. (1992). A matter of metaphors: Education as a handmade process. *Educational Leadership, 50*, 36.

Thornton, S. J. (1988). Curriculum consonance in United States history classroom. *Journal of Curriculum and Supervision, 3*, 308–320.

Tyack, D. B. (1974). *The one best system, a history of American urban education*. Cambridge, MA: Harvard University Press.

COMPARATIVE INTERNATIONAL
STUDY OF SUPERVISION

Michael J. Hough

UNIVERSITY OF WOLLONGONG, NEW SOUTH WALES, AUSTRALIA

INTRODUCTION

In conceptualizing this chapter, the aim was to develop a usable categorization framework so that reported studies of research in supervision, whether historical, current, or future, can be analyzed on a more thoughtful and rigorous basis than a simple date/location/apparent purpose basis.

The chapter is organized into two sections: the development of the categorization frameworks and the application of the categorization frameworks. The major intellectual purpose of this chapter, therefore, is to and provide three conceptual frameworks by which comparisons can be made among international research studies in supervision. To achieve that purpose, the chapter avoids the approach of exhaustively listing the details of published research studies. Rather, it attempts instead to provide three decision frameworks against which the rapidly increasing body of research studies can be organized and explained. In addition, the nature of the frameworks themselves also provides a socioeconomic context for the research approaches used within supervision.

This categorization approach is also required by the rapid increase in electronic accessibility and the accompanying ease of accessing the literature on international (or any other) forms of supervision. The emergence of databases such as the Educational Resources Information Clearinghouse (ERIC) and the growing availability of compact disks with read-only memory (CD-ROM) and other forms of information technology-based access to literature has led to a devaluing, in relative terms, of the traditional requirement to "find" the studies, books, and reports. There is no doubt that if this chapter was written 20 years ago, it would have to meet the requirement of undertaking the hard work of finding the "glittering prizes" of the real-ly useful and significant references, obtained from *nondeveloped, nonintegrated* information systems.

A deliberate choice has therefore been made to focus this chapter on the task of developing the intellectual usage tools by which the increasingly more readily available *data* (i.e., references on international research in supervision) can be converted into higher order, usable *information*. In that sense, two obvious criticisms are anticipated and acknowledged:

- This chapter is deliberately biased toward analytic frameworks and systems of analysis, rather than toward providing an exhaustive listing of all the comparative international research studies in supervision.
- Readers in developing countries with limited or no access to technology-based information retrieval systems will find this a relatively sterile, nonuseful classification approach.

It is considered, however, that this last-mentioned user group will steadily diminish. As the cost of information technology (I.T.) decreases, its availability increases, as will the corresponding access of "developing country" users to integrated I.T. databases.

As a partial compensation, the chapter concludes with some illustrative approaches, including case studies of how the categorization framework could be useful for practitioners, as well as theorists, of educational supervision.

The remainder of this chapter, therefore, provides a matrix-style intellectual framework for *reviewing* and *organizing* the references obtainable through the electronic searches of databases containing research literature on supervision. It also illustrates how the framework can be used as an analytic tool to *predict* appropriate or required research approaches in international contexts for educational supervision.

DEVELOPING THE CATEGORIZATION FRAMEWORKS

The categorization matrix is based on three allocation frameworks (F):

F: The Purpose of the Study
F: The Scope of the Study
F: The Sociocultural Context of the Study

The three frameworks were selected by using the observational logic basis that researchers (and their research outcomes) are affected by three fundamental aspects when they carry out research, namely:

- The "breadth of impact" they intend for the outcomes from the research activity, which became the Purpose Framework.
- The "target group" that they have in mind for any meaning derived from the research activity, which became the Scope Framework.
- The "social and economic" situation prevailing in the country in which the research is being undertaken, which became the Sociocultural Context Framework.

The details of the overall matrix, and each allocation framework will now be provided to illustrate how different international, cross-cultural contexts for research in supervision can be developed or used.

Analyzing International Research in Supervision

The classification approach is based on a matrix that consists of three allocation decision frameworks, with each providing an analysis logic system that is sufficiently developed to enable the classification and subsequent location of a reference on research in supervision, in an international context.

The basic axes of the matrix are three analysis frameworks shown in Figures 47.1 and 47.2 using standard three-dimensional logic systems.

Each of these frameworks will now be expanded.

Initial Expansion: Basic Framework Choices The intent of this initial expansion is to show the basic intellectual decisions and choices to be made for each framework. In categorizing a reference on the matrix, a reader needs to make three broad classification decisions:

- Framework: The Purpose of the Research

This framework essentially requires a decision as to the main *purpose* of the research (i.e., the reference is categorized as either a context-specific study with *limited generalizability*, or as a study that explores or probes *general rules and relationships* that transcend the specific data and/or context of the study.

Comment: Limited generalizability research includes but is not necessarily restricted to a "Case Study" approach.

- Framework: The Scope of the Research

This framework essentially requires a decision as to the main *focus* of the research. The reference is essentially categorized either as a *macro* focus of studying the "organizational system or aggregated large group" context of supervision, or as a study that illustrates the *micro* focus of studying the "specific skills and knowledge of the individual/small group" context of supervision.

It should be noted that it is acknowledged that most research has "spillover" effects in outcomes where results are obtained in the "other" category to the one selected as the major category. This framework, however, attempts to classify research by identifying the main outcome group(s) *intended as recipients* for the research findings.

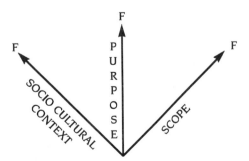

F = Framework for categorization decision

FIGURE 47.1. The basic analysis matrix

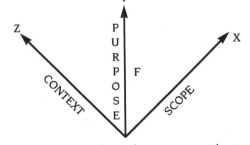

The matrix from a traditional perspective. The (x, y, z) logic will be used later in this categorization system

FIGURE 47.2. The basic analysis notation system

• Framework: The Sociocultural/Economic Context of the Research

This framework requires a decision as to the *closest economic/societal development phase* of the society within which the supervision is embedded. The basic analysis decision is to determine the location of each research study in the *developmental* continuum, as follows:

(e.g., See, Toffler, 1985, 1991, 1995).

In this type of analytic approach, the continuum represents a summary of the major societal development changes that occur across cultures. It essentially describes the emerging sociocultural characteristics that are the major emphases of that phase of societal development. It must be stressed that earlier emphases do not disappear; rather, the newer emphases layer over the earlier one(s) and reduce their relative importance.

As will be discussed later, it must be acknowledged that there are other cultural transition perspectives than the Toffler-type conceptualization that could be used as the basis of a sociocultural categorization. For example, a conceptualization that attempts to describe the transition from an elitist toward a mass (i.e., egalitarian?) society, might well provide useful categorization insights. The "sociocultural wave" conceptualization has been used in this initial analysis because it

is widely used in Western societies to analyze and explain societal change. It has the value of relative simplicity to illustrate the basic approach being argued and developed.

Another limitation is that the "Wave" conceptualization tends to treat countries and their societies as homogeneous within each country. This is not necessarily true, and it represents an initial oversimplification of most "real" societies. The initial analysis again suggests "whole country" analysis to illustrate the approach, but the conceptualization is perfectly capable of being used to illustrate or analyze subgroupings within a particular country, if that is required.

The development of the full matrix now begins, and it can be represented by the more sophisticated diagram following (Figure 47.3).

Detailed Expansion of Frameworks This final expansion section provides the full detail by which sophisticated choice(s) and decision(s) can be made on each framework, in order to allocate specific research studies to their appropriate location within the three-dimensional analysis matrix. In addition, this identifiable location can provide both insights into the situational characteristics of the particular research, and to locate it into a wider policy context of its sociocultural purpose.

• Framework: The Purpose of the Research (the Y Axis)

As illustrated by Figure 47.3 this framework provides a relatively clear allocation choice between the *intellectual purposes* underlying the research; essentially, it is a guide to the underlying *intent* of the researcher toward the degree to which any research findings can be generalized.

Researchers basically make the fundamental choice of *low generalizability "action research"* or *high generalizability tra-*

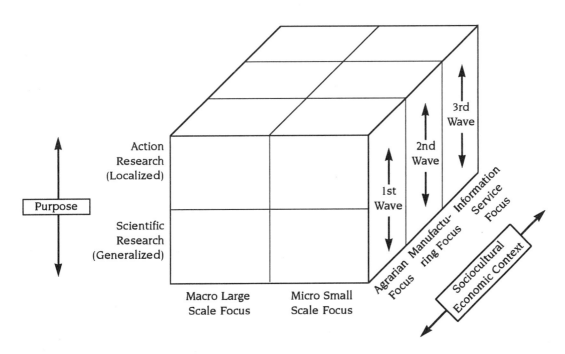

FIGURE 47.3. The decision matrix—first expansion

TABLE 47–1. The Decision Profiles For The
"Intellectual Purpose" Framework

Research/Researcher As "Technical Expert"	Research/Researcher As "Process Facilitation"
• Problem is stated in outcome/relationship terms (e.g., to improve the outcome x by manipulating y).	• Problem is stated in process improvement terms (e.g., to evaluate the change process used to facilitate z).
• Little or no involvement with subjects. The researcher is neutral and independent/uninvolved.	• Researcher–client involvement is accepted, and this relationship is developed as part of the research process.
• The solution/hypotheses are usually developed by the researcher.	• The solution is developed as part of the action research process.
• The researcher brings 'hard' research skills/techniques, usually based on inferential statistics.	• The research uses "grounded theory" or "soft" research techniques, often based on correlational, descriptive statistics or no usage of statistics.
• The researcher is seeking observable change that is quantifiable and testable, including replication and validation.	• The researcher is seeking explanations for dynamic change, which may be situation-specific and unlikely to be replicable.
• The researcher is seeking cause–effect, generalizable findings that are wider than and greater than the specific experimental/test setting.	• The researcher is seeking "site-specific" relationships that may not generalize or are generalizable only in terms of process characteristics, rather than in cause–effect relationships.
• Large-scale (system) accountability issues tested or explored.	• Specific (situational) issues are clarified and identified.

ditional or "empirical rational" research. This allocation choice involves identifying the quite different roles of the researcher. For example:

- Action research requires the role: "researcher as a process facilitator."
- Traditional research requires the role: "researcher as an uninvolved technical expert."

The following "indicators" are offered as the profile (i.e., guide) for the allocation decision to be made on this particular framework.

ALLOCATION DECISION GUIDELINE. If the purpose of the reference is localized "action research," then it is a different *purpose* to an article/reference focusing on traditional (i.e., generalizable) research. Table 47–1 provides the allocation decision details for this choice.

- Framework: The Intelligence Scope of the Research (The "X" Axis).

As illustrated by Figure 47.3, this framework essentially requires a decision as to the breadth of relationships probed by the research (i.e., *scope*). The underlying choice is where the research focus lies in the realm of '*macro*' (i.e., organizational system level issues) or on '*micro*' (i.e., individual relationship level issues). This framework requires a decision

choice as to the scope of the research, essentially by judging whether the focus level is on *large-scale organizational/system relationships*, or on *small-scale individual relationships within specific organizational settings*. The basic analysis is to determine the scope of each research study by using the profiles in Table 47–2 as a guide for the allocation decision to be made on this particular framework.

ALLOCATION DECISION GUIDELINE. If the purpose of the research is to categorize large-scale organizational relationships, then it has a different *scope* to a reference focusing on specific individual or specific group relationships. Table 47–2 provides the allocation decision details for this choice.

- Framework: The Sociocultural/Economic Context (The Z Axis).

Framework: The Sociocultural/Economic Context (The Z axis)
As first illustrated by Figure 47.3 this is the most complex of the three frameworks, and requires a sophisticated analysis of the *situational* location of a research study on supervision, within the detailed sociocultural framework.

Figures 47.4 and 47.5 present visual summaries of the key analysis factors. The analysis is based on the conceptual arguments presented by theorists such as Toffler (1985, 1991) that society has evolved through a series of socioeconomically related "waves," which represent the major job creation focus (i.e., "drivers") of that type of culture and society. This

TABLE 47–2. The Decision Profiles For The
"Intellectual Scope" Framework

Macro Focus Research (large scale)	Micro Focus Research (small scale)
This category of research approach deals with supervision relationships such as:	This category of research approach deals with supervision relationships such as:
• "whole organization" system relationships; • "whole cohort(s) of supervisors" relationships; • INTER (between) organizational relationships.	• "small group" context research; • specific "supervisor–supervisee" research; • INTRA (inside) organizational relationships.
Typical examples: Research on system-wide changes in training of supervisors.	Typical examples: Research on a specific training program to produce specific learning/skill outcomes in an identifiable cohort of supervisors.

"situational" type of analysis is developed from two underlying assumptions: new forms of (identifiable) societal change overlay, as distinct from replace, earlier practices, and specific societal practices (including supervision) also change to reflect these newer societal requirements.

The Toffler concept of "societal waves" underlying Figures 47.4 and 47.5 enables a whole range of culturally embedded practices, including supervision, to be related to one of the three sociocultural/economic frameworks that are represented by "*verticals*" on the main diagram (see Figure 47.5). The allocation decision is based on detecting sufficient profiling data from the categorizing choices offered by this diagram for the reference to be allocated to the closest one of the three basic sociocultural "waves" or "eras" as represented by each "vertical" shown in Figure 47.5. The three basic frameworks are initially shown by Figure 47.4.

In general, societies have transitioned from agrarian (V_1) to manufacturing/industrial (V_2) toward service economies (V_3) in periods of up to 150 years (e.g., United Kingdom, United States) to as little as 40 years (e.g., Hong Kong).

The "horizontals" on diagram Figure 47.5 represent a series of socialcultural–economic decision factors that essentially describe conditions or practices that change or evolve as the sociocultural/economic context changes. The "decision factors" selected to describe or reflect this sociocultural change are identified as either "key" or "background."

A "key" indicator provides a *direct* guide as to the likely categorization that should be allocated, whereas a background indicator provides contributing *support* for an allocation decision.

Based on the layout of Figure 47.5, each of the profiling factors will now be described. It is important to stress that *not all profile factors need to be present for an allocating decision to be made,* and a range of profiling factors is provided to anticipate the reality that each reference found will present varying types and levels of detail about the sociocultural context within which the research was conducted. The Figure 47.5 framework essentially enables supervision practice to be related to its broad sociocultural context by determining a pattern across at least some of the profiling factors, and allocating the reference to the appropriate closest "vertical" within the diagram.

It must be (re)acknowledged that this approach makes some fundamental assumptions; (1) The Toffler conceptualization of societal "Waves" is a preferred sociocultural explanation for the ways in which societies change and evolve, and (2) the same sociocultural analysis can be used to explain an entire nation. These assumptions will be maintained to illustrate the basic

value of the analytic approach, whereas acknowledging that alternate sociocultural theories could be substituted and subgroups analyzed for subsequent uses of the basic approach. Each "profiling" factor for Figure 47.5 is now described in sufficient detail to enable an allocation decision to be made, if a reference provides detail on that particular allocation factor. It must be restated and re-emphasized that an allocation decision can be made on the basis of evidence from only some of the suggested profiling factors. It is neither expected nor required that all profiling factors will be described within a specific reference to be categorized.

The descriptions commence from the top left of Figure 47.5. Whereas allocation details are summarized within the figure, the following are provided as expansion commentaries to assist with the allocation decision:

• Status of the Workforce

This is a key indicator, this attempts to describe the way that "people characteristics" change and evolve within a society as the workforce moves from simple, locally focused tasks connected with agriculture and subsistence through the demands of a regional- or nation-based manufacturing/industrial economy focusing on skills of production, toward the intellectual- and knowledge-based skills of a global, service-based economy. This indicator has direct bearing on identifying the approaches to supervision that are appropriate for different status workforce groups. For example, nondirective and collegial approaches to supervision evolve with the emergence of highly educated workforces.

• Status of Capital

A background indicator, this illustrates the emergence of capital as an important factor in supporting sophisticated sociocultural/economic structures such as a service focused economy. This factor provides only a "setting" within which supervisory approaches can be more clearly perceived.

• Attitude of Government

A background indicator, which illustrates how government attitudes and practices need to evolve and change as sociocultural needs evolve. This "setting" factor also provides a contribution to the understanding of supervisory approaches rather than a direct perspective.

• Probable Basis of Power

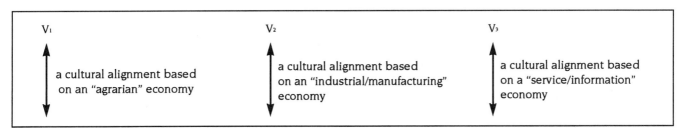

FIGURE 47.4. The major sociocultural relationships
underlying the detail of Figure 47.5.

Key Factor(s) and Spectrum of Change/Choice

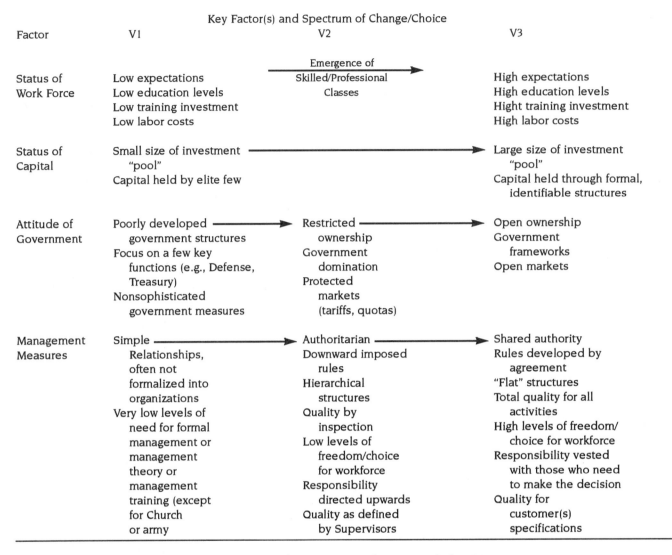

Factor	V1	V2	V3
Status of Work Force	Low expectations Low education levels Low training investment Low labor costs	Emergence of Skilled/Professional Classes →	High expectations High education levels Hight training investment High labor costs
Status of Capital	Small size of investment "pool" ————————————————→ Capital held by elite few		Large size of investment "pool" Capital held through formal, identifiable structures
Attitude of Government	Poorly developed ——→ government structures Focus on a few key functions (e.g., Defense, Treasury) Nonsophisticated government measures	Restricted ——————→ ownership Government domination Protected markets (tariffs, quotas)	Open ownership Government frameworks Open markets
Management Measures	Simple ————————→ Relationships, often not formalized into organizations Very low levels of need for formal management or management theory or management training (except for Church or army	Authoritarian ——→ Downward imposed rules Hierarchical structures Quality by inspection Low levels of freedom/choice for workforce Responsibility directed upwards Quality as defined by Supervisors	Shared authority Rules developed by agreement "Flat" structures Total quality for all activities High levels of freedom/choice for workforce Responsibility vested with those who need to make the decision Quality for customer(s) specifications

FIGURE 47.5. Labor (V1) / Capital (V2 / Knowledge (V3)
intensive societies and organizations

This is a key indicator that illustrates the changing power relationships and requirements of supervision. For example, the power relationship in agrarian economies is ultimately based on physical or religious coercion/force, which creates nonquestioning or acceptive social relationships that require little in the way of sophisticated supervisory knowledge or practice. At the "other end" of the continuum, sophisticated information/service economies require complex and supportive relationships between highly skilled individuals, increasingly within the context of nonhierarchical organizations emphasizing quality of customer service, (i.e., this is described as "Total Quality" organizations in the Figure 47.5 summaries.)

• Probable Economic Focus

This phrase covers an interrelated set of background indicators:

• phase of economy;
• emphases of production; and
• locus of main markets.

These three background indicators allow *patterns* of relationships to be described that trace the probable historical development of phases of economies, and also enable the location of a "specific" economy in comparative terms. For example, Western economies, such as the United States or Germany, are locatable as Third Wave; countries such as Australia or Canada are transitioning from Second Wave toward Third Wave; many Asian (e.g., Vietnam) and African countries are First Wave, whereas rapidly evolving economies such as the "Asian Tigers" of Singapore and Hong Kong, have probably effectively made the transitions from First- through to Third-Wave economies in periods of 50 years or less.

Key Factor(s) and Spectrum of Change/Choice

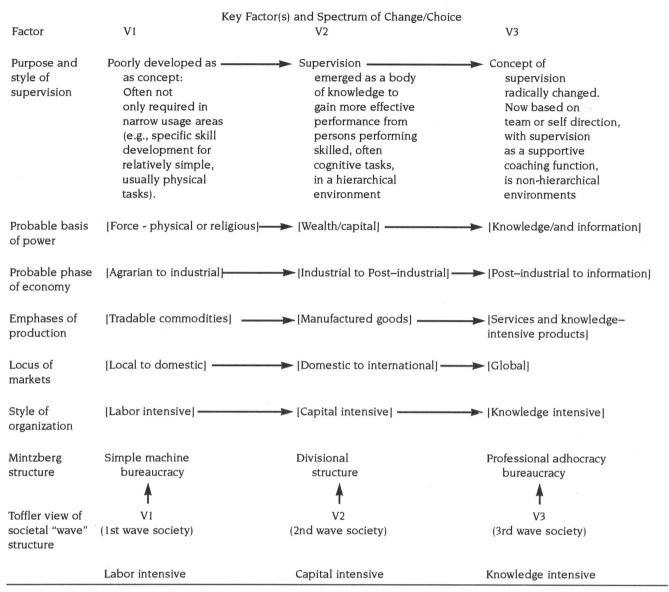

Factor	V1	V2	V3
Purpose and style of supervision	Poorly developed as as concept: Often not only required in narrow usage areas (e.g., specific skill development for relatively simple, usually physical tasks). ⟶	Supervision emerged as a body of knowledge to gain more effective performance from persons performing skilled, often cognitive tasks, in a hierarchical environment ⟶	Concept of supervision radically changed. Now based on team or self direction, with supervision as a supportive coaching function, is non-hierarchical environments
Probable basis of power	[Force - physical or religious] ⟶	[Wealth/capital] ⟶	[Knowledge/and information]
Probable phase of economy	[Agrarian to industrial] ⟶	[Industrial to Post–industrial] ⟶	[Post–industrial to information]
Emphases of production	[Tradable commodities] ⟶	[Manufactured goods] ⟶	[Services and knowledge– intensive products]
Locus of markets	[Local to domestic] ⟶	[Domestic to international] ⟶	[Global]
Style of organization	[Labor intensive] ⟶	[Capital intensive] ⟶	[Knowledge intensive]
Mintzberg structure	Simple machine bureaucracy ↑	Divisional structure ↑	Professional adhocracy bureaucracy ↑
Toffler view of societal "wave" structure	V1 (1st wave society)	V2 (2nd wave society)	V3 (3rd wave society)
	Labor intensive	Capital intensive	Knowledge intensive

FIGURE 47.5. Labor (V1) / Capital (V2 / Knowledge (V3)
intensive societies and organizations (continued)

It must be restated and stressed that *all* known economies contain elements of agriculture, manufacturing and service. The categorization or label as First-, Second- or Third-Wave economy refers to the major *drivers of job creation* for that economy (i.e., job creation sources may *NOT* be the major revenue source for the gross domestic product of a country however, leading to the fact that in some economies, such as Australia, much of the revenue still comes from "First Wave" industries, but job creation does not). In turn, more specific "microeconomic" practices, such as supervision, need to be related to this "macroeconomic" focus for a full understanding of their practices and intended outcomes. In simpler terms, the supervisory approaches that are required or appro-

priate in a highly educated Third-Wave (service) economy are strikingly different from those appropriate in a less-educated First Wave (agrarian) economy.

The assumption has therefore been made in developing this framework that the research issues in different countries reflect both this different context and different purpose, and that these differences lead to different categorizations under this framework approach. It is again acknowledged that more sophisticated developments of this basic approach may require the analysis to discriminate out sociocultural subgroupings within a single economy, and if that were to occur, then the analysis would be required to describe subgroup behaviors and patterns for specific subsets of an economy.

• Style of Organization

This phase covers the key indicators that represent the type of managerial approach and supervisory requirement that have evolved or are needed for a particular organizational context. It must be acknowledged that an assumption made in this initial conceptualization approach is that the contexts and practices of educational supervision are broadly similar to other organizational contexts and forms of supervision.

It should be noted that this assumption is probably strongest for First- and Third-Wave societies and weakest for Second-Wave ones. This claim is supported by the likelihood that in noncomplex, agrarian (i.e., First Wave) communities, all forms of work and education were largely undifferentiated; in complex, industrial societies (i.e., Second Wave) schools were separate structures from other forms of work, and although this is often described as a "factory model" of schooling, there is pervasive and repeated comment from this era that commercial, "for profit" organizations are so different from school and "not-for-profit" ones that completely different approaches to management are required. The "Total Quality" and "Learning Organization" type arguments of the information/service era (i.e., Third Wave), however, emphasize the need to focus on the human and human learning feature of organizational behavior.

In deciding categorizations from these factors, the specific allocation criteria are:

• the main "means of achieving organizational purpose":
  – labor-intensive organization (First-Wave Agrarian)
  – capital intensive organization (Second-Wave Manufacturing)
  – knowledge intensive organization (Third-Wave Information)

• the organizational "shape."

In making a profiling decision on this factor, the Mintzberg (1981) classifications describing forms of organizational structure are used:

Mintzberg "Organizational Type"	Most likely "Wave" for that "Type"
Simple structure	First-Wave Economies (Agrarian)
"Machine Bureaucracy" structure	Second-Wave Economies (Manufacturing)
"Divisional" Structure "Professional Bureaucracy" structure	Third-Wave Economies (Information)
"Adhocracy" structure	

This last profiling indicator (i.e., "organizational structure") provides a strong "clue" as to likely supervising behaviors and relationships required or used by organizations in particular sociocultural "waves." This is because the organizational concept has evolved, both in its structure and processes, to meet the needs of people interacting in working relationships who are within the societal context of acceptable practices for that era.

• Purposes of Management/Supervision

The following three descriptors are key indicators for allocating a research reference to the sociocultural context. The management/supervision changes described in the following, illustrate how the need for and purposes of management change as societies grow and evolve:

Era	Management/Supervisory Practices
"First-Wave" Societies (Agrarian)	• Management and supervision focused on simple technical skill tasks, with little concern for, or awareness of, sophisticated organizations. Education and training of managers/supervisors is very limited, and it is restricted to simple mechanisms such as "apprenticeship" or direct skill transfer techniques. Direct, simple instructional methods used for small numbers of recipients.
"Second-Wave" Societies (Manufacturing)	• Management and supervision reflect the needs of hierarchical, authoritarian organizations focusing on manufacturing, mass production era. Education and training of managers/supervisors growing and acknowledging the emergence of educated elites/professions. Sophisticated and symbolic training mechanisms evolved (e.g., widespread University/College/Technical Institutes) qualifications emerging. Mass education/training methods evolving to train large numbers of students. Then: The later *transition* phase: Management and supervision focus more on producing flexible workforces *within* hierarchical structures. Technology is used to educate managers/supervisors in new ways of working, including new ways of working within organizations to achieve required processes and outcomes. Collegial approaches to supervision (e.g., clinical supervision) were developed in this transition phase.
"Third-Wave" Societies (Information/ Service)	• Management and supervision change to meet the needs of flexible work teams in nonhierarchical organizations emphasizing total quality service for customers. Management/supervision training focus on new roles for managers, such as the skills of creating a "learning organization" with supportive/coaching functions, and the skills of strategic planning to create flexible new forms of organizations, including the "virtual organization" of rapidly changing (e.g., contract) relationships. Education and training are becoming more central to success, using learning technologies to assist both self-directed/self-initiated learning *and* to develop group skills and outcomes.

It should be noted that there is constant discussion and debate as to whether educational supervision/management is broadly similar to business management. Moreover, it is true that this sociocultural classification approach assumes similarity rather than difference. It is interesting to speculate on whether the difference/similarity issue is more a continuum than a clear choice, and that location on the continuum is also affected by societal "era." It is a tentative prediction that similarity would be a characteristic of First-Wave practice, difference is a characteristic of Second-Wave, and the development of Third-Wave business thinking and practice is strongly characterized by terms such as the "*Learning Organization,*" and is moving toward the "similarity" end of the continuum.

Usage of the Decision Matrix

Any international research article on supervision can now be classified by using a series of three allocation decisions based on selecting answers to questions derived from the three frameworks, with the resulting categorization summarized by the use of a traditional (-, -, -) style logic system, for example:

z: Is the sociocultural context (SC) that of an agrarian (A)-, manufacturing (M)-, or information (I)-based economy?

Notation: SC_A, SC_M, SC_I

y: Is the purpose (P) of the research that of localized action research (AR) or generalized traditional research (TR) ?

Notation: P_{AR}, P_{TR}

x: Is the *scope* (S) of the research that of macro (large system, L) or micro (small group/individual, S) research?

Notation: S_L, S_S

The answers to these three decisions are then representable by a notation (i.e., SC, P,S) selected from the following categorization choices:

Sociocultural Context	Purpose	Scope
SC_A	P_{AR}	S_L
SC_M	P_{TR}	S_S
SC_I		

Note: For ease of writing, the categories are allocated full upper case notation.

Each notation, therefore, and the analysis frameworks it represents, can be used to *classify* existing research references. In addition, by using this framework, it is possible to *predict* logical patterns of interest and relationship in supervision studies as sociocultural needs evolve with subsequent increased complexity and need representing the different purpose relationships within supervision. For example, some suggested major patterns are discussed next.

Agrarian Societies (First-Wave) In meeting the needs of localized and noncomplex organizations and the small-scale education systems that support them, supervision research studies are predicted as occasional, situation specific, and directed at micro (i.e., individual/small group context) supervision (i.e., SC_A, P_{AR}, S_S would be a dominant categorization).

Manufacturing/Industrial Societies (Second-Wave) In meeting the needs of large-scale, standardized hierarchical organizations, and the education/training institutions that support them, supervision studies are predicted as planned, generalized and directed at macro (i.e., large group context supervision). This is the era of the "general" theory of management/supervision, aimed at deriving generalized rules for supervisory relationships (i.e., SC_M, P_{TR}, S_L).

Within this general "era," a further trend is predictable as the industrial/manufacturing era enters the *transition* stage toward information/service economies in that the focus of supervision will also expand to include research on flexible, situation specific, small group focused supervision (i.e., SC_M, P_{AR}, S_S). It is important to stress that this pattern is still within hierarchical organizational structures as indicated by the SC_M notation.

Information/Service Economies (Third-Wave) In meeting the emerging needs of Third-Wave economies with their de-emphasis on structures and hierarchies, two probable patterns are predictable in nonhierarchical, flexible, customer-oriented service organizations emphasizing the "learning capacity" of individuals and workgroups as competitive advantage. The predicted supervisory patterns will be either:

- situation specific, localized action research emphasizing the specific supervisory needs of particular service organizations (i.e., SC_I, P_{AR}, S_S);

in parallel with

- supervisory research studies looking at the general process characteristics common across learning organizations emphasizing their intellectual capital as competitive advantage (i.e., SC_I, P_{TR}, S_S).

It could be noted that the common focus on small-scale scope research in the "Third-Wave" categories results from a predominant emphasis on the self-directed work team in the "total quality" or "learning" organization that typifies the early thinking of this era. This approach was initially detectable in the "situational leadership" type theories that emerged in the "late" Second-Wave era in response to the perceived inadequacies of "large-scale" leadership theories.

It is therefore predicted that "action research" type studies will be a growing phenomenon in societies transitioning from "late" Second-Wave manufacturing eras to Third-Wave information and service eras.

Matrix Prediction of Supervision Patterns

The most probable (i.e., numerous) research categorizations predicted by the logic systems can now be described.

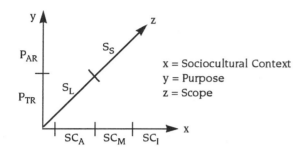

First-Wave (Agrarian)

SC_A, P_{AR}, S_S = the Agrarian society context creates a low level of need for predominantly small-scale, action research approaches to issues and problems of supervision.

Second-Wave (Manufacturing/Industrial)

SC_M, P_{TR}, S_L = the Manufacturing/Industrial society context creates the need for predominantly large-scale, traditional research into issues and problems of supervision (i.e., generalized rules and theories for standardized, hierarchical organizations).

Plus an observable trend toward:

SC_M, P_{AR}, S_S = the transitioning phase from manufacturing toward a service economy, which creates the need for research on the issues and problems of supervision focusing on effective ways of obtaining flexible outcomes with skilled staff working within hierarchical organizational structures.

Third-Wave (Information/Service)

- In this still-emerging societal context, two parallel trends are predicted as identifying the need for research on the new issues and problems of supervision:

SC_I, P_{AR}, S_S = Focusing on supervision for quality outcomes in specific work group situations.

and

SC_I, P_{TR}, S_S = Focusing on supervision for quality *processes* for all situations.

It should be noted that both patterns occur within non-hierarchical, flexible organizational structures.

The final section of this chapter describe the application of the frameworks to actual situations or examples of research in supervision.

USE OF THE FRAMEWORK TO CATEGORIZE A RESEARCH STUDY

The most common usage predicted for the framework will be to categorize single research reports by locating them on the three decision matrix. In many cases, however, the ease of categorization will be strongly influenced by the type of published detail provided. It is very probable that the range and type of data reported will be deliberately selected by the author(s) to suit the needs of the reporting vehicle (e.g., a particular journal).

It is therefore likely that the data provided by a reference will not enable a full, direct classification on all three aspects: sociocultural context, scope, and purpose. Of the three frameworks, the most difficult to categorize will undoubtedly be sociocultural context because articles often focus on the close detail of the research itself on the assumption that the reader is from the same sociocultural setting. Scope and purpose, therefore, are more likely to be clear (or at least directly commented upon), whereas sociocultural context is more often assumed, rather than explained, in many research reports.

A frequent categorization *challenge*, therefore, will probably be to decide the sociocultural context of the reported research. Figure 47.5 accordingly provide a wide range of criteria on which an allocation decision could be made. This decision framework is deliberately constructed so that it is *not* necessary that data on all criteria be available within this framework in order to make an allocation decision within the matrix.

A further acknowledged difficulty will be that many articles on supervision are essentially descriptive in that they "tell a story" or "summarize the details of a supervision situation." In essence, they are "fringe" articles that address or report the basis elements of a *research* situation.

As stated in the beginning of the chapter, the purpose has been to provide a more rigorous categorization system for supervisory research, than a simple geographic/time-based description. The frameworks suggested enable focus to move away from low-level detail toward an intellectually driven allocation decision based on sociocultural context, purpose, and scope. Some representative research reports are now categorized accordingly to illustrate the usage(s) of the framework.

Data Searches

By using a database search through ERIC, for example, and by the use of the ERIC thesaurus selected search terms of school supervision, supervisory methods, institutional leadership, teacher/supervisor, and research, it was a straightforward task to obtain a list of citations over specific years. Three simple examples of a typical database literature search (e.g., on ERIC or ABI) will now be provided to illustrate the use of the matrix.

Terms Selected for Search(s)	Era Selected	No. of Citations
S: School supervision x teacher supervision x supervisory methods x institutional leadership x models in developing (ERIC c.b.doc)	1987 onward	62 refs
S: School supervision x teacher supervision x supervisory methods x institutional leadership x models in developing (ERIC.a.doc)	1987 onward	49 refs
S: Supervision x leadership x study x studies (ABI.a.doc)	1980 onward	174 refs

These are typical search categorizations, carried out quite routinely with any modern library access to information systems, they illustrate the increasingly occurring fact that *data* (i.e., specific references) are now available readily and in ever-increasing volume(s) by using different databases through such systems as ERIC or the Abstracted Business Information (ABI).

From a personal review of the preceding references prior to classification by the matrix as comparative international research references, several obvious trends emerged:

- the absence of clear data for a comparative, sociocultural context allocation in most of the references obtained;
- there was very little explicit, cross-cultural comparison provided by the text, and the sociocultural context of each study was strongly assumed, rather than explained, by the author(s);
- the emphasis on situation-specific research was numerically strong; and
- there was much focus on the impact of situation specific research aspects on principal (or school) effectiveness.

These realities illustrate some important trends worth commenting on as follows:

1. most research is not explicitly about cross cultural or international context issues of supervision; and
2. most research is focused within specific cultures or cultural contexts for supervision.

Despite these limitations, the major frameworks of the matrix have been successfully used to provide categorization of sample references. This illustrates the manner in which the matrix approach enables higher-order analysis and categorization of the preceding data on issues of international, comparative supervision.

Illustrative Categorizations

The full details of the selected references are provided at the end of the chapter, and represent an illustrative selection of applying the allocation matrix to the above literature searches.

SC_A, P_{AR}, S_S - The Stereotypic Agrarian Society

The following represent action research, small-scale research reports in an agrarian sociocultural context:

Archibald, B. (1986), Australia; Brown, G. (1984), Thailand; Ekpunobi E. and D. (1984), Nigeria; Karagozoglu, G. (1986), Turkey; Smart, J. (1980), The Philippines.

SC_M, P_{TR}, S_L—The Manufacturing Society

The following represent traditional large-scale, large organizational relationship research studies in a traditional, hierarchical manufacturing environment

Bell, R. (1985), Australia; Gaziel, H. (1979), Israel; Hardy, C. and Zarrimuto, R. (1989), Brazil; Jones, A. (1986), Australia; Murphy, J. and Hallinger, P. (1986), United States; Retallick, J., Australia

SC_M, P_{AR}, S_S—The Later/Transitioning Manufacturing Society

The following represent small scale, intraorganizational research studies:

Cheung, Y. (1991), Hong Kong; Corfield, T. (1982), United Kingdom; Macpherson, R. (1990), Australia; Savey, L. et al (1992), Australia; Shannon, R. (1990), United States; Sternberg, J. (1992), U.S. Afro-Americanism.

SC_I, P_{AR}, S_S—The Information/Service Society

The following represent small-scale action research studies on supervision in new style work relationships:

Doyle, K. (1992), United States; Galor, C. and Meurice, G. (1993), United States; Ibe, M. and Sato, N. (1993) Japan; Poplin, M. (1992) United States.

These illustrative classifications show that the overall decision matrix provides frameworks that are useful for allocating context and meaning to some, *but not all* studies of research in supervision. It must be acknowledged that this framework was *not* appropriate for a number of references obtained by the searches, and it was specifically not appropriate when the reference was:

- not describing a research situation;
- not attempting to provide any international, cross-cultural comparison or perspective to the research; or
- not providing sufficient information to enable the categorization logic to be applied with any confidence or validity (e.g., the reference is too brief or not explicit enough).

In that sense, the ability to categorize a reference on the matrix represents a screening (or culling) for adequacy as a research document that is capable of providing international perspectives on research into supervision. On reflection, however, it is self-evident that many references do *not* set out to provide such a commentary.

Nevertheless, the preceding categorizations show that the framework can bring higher order meaning to research data, which is considered an improvement beyond the "location–date–outline" categorization approaches that have been the historically prevalent, previously available categorization systems. These previously available systems partly reflected the earlier, simpler demands of *non* I.T. (Information

Technology)-based retrieval systems. Moreover, *any* type of classification system suffers the deficiency that it cannot allocate a research reference to an international or cross-cultural categorization if international perspectives are just not addressed by the study. It should be noted that one of the additional, value-added perspectives provided by the proposed matrix is that it gives a wide range of sociocultural issues by which a research study could be allocated a categorization, provided that it gives *some* background or peripheral sociocultural indications for its research purpose and context.

Categorization Implications

There are a number of other perceived implications from the matrix categorization, for the general fields of research and policy development in supervision, as follows:

1. One application is the use of the decision matrix framework to develop more focused research activities probing into the relationships of the matrix itself (i.e., it identifies the need for "meta" research focused on the relationships between sociocultural context, purpose, and scope in research situations).
2. Another application would be to trace the change in research emphases across a time scale that could detect cultural changes (e.g., a decade-based time framework for detecting different patterns of emphasis in supervisory research).
3. There are policy development implications from the matrix decision framework for educational authorities. The issues and ideas of the categorization systems could be used as an analytic tool to explain or predict broader societal processes and their relationships to supervision and supervisory practices.

Some generic questions that this social policy approach should explore include, but are not limited, to:

- "in what ways do different sociocultural settings encourage or prevent supervisory efficacy?"
- "what supervisory approaches are optimized in their effectiveness by specific sociocultural contexts or settings?"
- "what style of supervision/supervisory approaches should a society develop or invest in to optimize socioeconomic development/school development/staff development?"

4. Finally, one application for the decision matrix approach is that it could become the intellectual organizing framework for an ongoing compendium or edited series on intranational *or* international studies in supervision. For example, previous "review" approaches, such as:

- the categorization and literature review work of Johnson (1987) between Canadian and Australian approaches to supervision; or
- the 1989 A.C.E.R. (Australian) publication, edited by Lokan and McKenzie, entitled *Teacher Appraisal: Issues and Approaches*; in particular, the chapter within that publication by Beare, which attempts to generate explanatory

models of international supervision, could be reanalyzed or restructured using the decision matrix categorization approach as could the categorizations used by Pajak (1990) in identifying the 12 dimensions of supervisory practice.

Prediction and Verification Profiles

The following represent three examples of different sociocultural approaches to education, with the categorizations of the decision matrix being used to analyze the types of supervisory practices predicted as appropriate for these differing societal contexts, thus enabling both predictive research to be generated and existing research to be verified and tested against predictions.

Case Study 1: SC_M to SC_A—This societal scenario is provided by the educational policy decisions taken by a prominent Middle East country in the 1980s. Because a large proportion of its population was still living in essentially "First-Wave" agrarian-type social conditions, the decision was made to abandon its Western society derived "Second-Wave" assumptions about the "categorizing and sorting for manufacturing employment" functions of its formal public school system. These "Second-Wave" educational purposes were essentially transplanted from the philosophies and practices of Western nations. In the latter, a major task of the education system was to prepare students for the appropriate level of employment in a manufacturing, technological economy. These transplanted assumptions and practices were consciously rejected by the Middle East country, which directed public education to focus upon living conditions and coping skills for a rural population in an economy based predominantly on agriculture and tourism.

In matrix categorization terms, this Middle East country adopted educational policies which altered (reverted) its school practices from an SC_M (Manufacturing) to a SC_A (Agrarian) context. Supervisory practices that may have been appropriate under the previous policy would accordingly become rapidly dysfunctional and inappropriate for this new set of expectations. Thus, the matrix categorization would be altered from an SC_M basis to an SC_A basis. The categorization assists in illustrating the need for changes in the purpose and scope of supervisory practices, including their accompanying research, to meet these new policy contexts.

This case study outline illustrates that supervisory purpose(s) and behavior(s), like other societally imbedded practices, depend for their appropriateness on their context–purpose relationship, as well as on their more specific details. The categorization matrix is capable of detecting and describing this context change and predicting the more specific practice aspects connected with scope and purpose.

The classification notations that reflect this situation would then be:

From an $SC_M > SC_A$ context, with policy preferred/required practices of SC_A, P_{TR}, S_L.

It should be noted that this is a dysfunctional classification by the "traditional" expectations of a Western society moving in continual transition toward a Third-Wave society. However, it represents an appropriate classification for a society deliberately selecting policies and practices that change this "traditional" pattern or expectation to suit its specific cultural needs.

Case Study 2: SC_A to SC_M—This case study describes the educational policies of a Far Eastern country, designed to distinguish between the practices (and outcomes) provided for three distinct racial/religious groups. This intent was to provide the highest quality educational experiences to its indigenous racial group, and lesser quality educational experiences to the other two racial groups. The latter were offered only limited opportunities for official positions and opportunities directly controlled by government. In essence, the government policies were aimed at creating different outcomes within the same country for three different social groups by encouraging different educational practices for each. Accordingly, supervisory and related educational practices are expected to attain different but controlled educational outcomes. The matrix analysis needs to be capable of discriminating between specific subpractices in the single overarching societal context.

In practice, the Asian country is in transition from an agricultural to a manufacturing economy (i.e., $SC_A > SC_M$). It appears to be encouraging its preferred elite to be educated for the "new" society being created. The educational practices for the preferred group need to be consistent with those that promote the SC_M outcome, *but* must operate parallel with other components of the educational system intended to produce SC_A related outcomes. Thus, appropriate educational approaches should create segmented supervisory practices aimed at different outcomes within the one broad system.

The matrix analysis is capable of producing such discrimination in its classifications (i.e., it can detect or predict practice difference(s) within this type of societal context).

Thus, a probable matrix analysis representing this situation is:

SC_A $\boxed{+=+=>}$ SC_M >SC_I for Group A in the population; $SC_A > SC_A$ for Group B; and $SC_A > SC_M$ for Group C, within the one country's cultural settings.

Thus, there should exist a deliberate range of supervisory practices that target each separate group for different outcomes, such as:

$$SC_A > SC_M \text{ using } SC_M, P_{TR}, S_L$$

followed by

$$SC_M > SC_I \text{ using } SC_I, P_{AR}, S_S, \text{ for that selected societal group only}$$

The other social subgroups would be handled by different, targeted educational practices, including supervisory approaches, that are consistent with the different outcomes required by social policy. For example:

$$SC_A > SC_A \text{ requires } SC_A, P_{TR}, S_S \text{ approaches}$$
$$SC_A > SC_M \text{ requires } SC_M, P_{TR}, S_L$$

It should be noted again that this outline case study illustrates the need for different subpractices, including supervision, predicted by the matrix logic for this complex educational policy situation. It illustrates the predictive, testable logic and behaviors required to support this nontraditional societal situation.

Case Study 3: SC_M to SC_I—This situation describes the educational practice requirements of a Far Eastern country with a strongly homogeneous racial grouping and an advanced economy in transition from manufacturing to an information focus. It has a well-educated population that has enjoyed the benefits of a properly funded 12-year public school system modeled on those of Western nations. The government wishes to promote growth and the transition to a post-manufacturing economy, while retaining the high standard of living currently supported by its initial successes in flexible, low-cost manufacturing. The dilemma is that the homogeneous Asian culture does not value or seek the strong individualism that underlies many Western cultures. The government also wishes to pursue education and social policies that promote the continued rise in standard of living, but not at the expense of societal homogeneity. In essence, it wishes to promote the $SC_M > SC_I$ transition without promoting the strong individualism that characterizes this transition in other Western economies.

The matrix can reflect this profile requirement but will essentially diagnose it, by Western standards as an apparently dysfunctional mix of an advanced societal context embedding the practices of a traditional earlier era.

Thus, the required sociocultural transition is $SC_M > SC_I$ but the accompanying educational practices are likely to be:

SC_I accompanied by SC_I, P_{TR}, S_S. (i.e., implementation techniques that do not usually accompany this sociocultural context in other economies).

It again should be noted that this outline case study outline illustrates the ability of the matrix classification to explain and/or predict appropriate supervisory behavior for a specific, nontraditional sociocultural situation. Such predictions then can be tested against actual practice for verification, and also used as a guide to policy implementation.

FUTURE DIRECTIONS

This chapter has assumed that improvements in information technology will continue to open up rapid access to larger number of articles and references on research in supervision. The challenge is to design intellectual frameworks capable of enhancing synthesizing data into higher order information and understanding.

The matrix methodology developed in this chapter represents the type of categorization that will need to be developed and applied in order to cope with the ever-increasing volume of specific reference detail offered by I.T.-based retrieval systems. This detail will need to be absorbed and analyzed, partly through the use of higher order classification systems that focus on organizing by themes and issues, rather than by simple time or geographically source-based systems.

The specific profiling and allocation frameworks suggested for this initial version of the matrix will themselves need constant revision and improvement, as the intellectual needs of information societies become clearer and better understood. The frameworks are offered as an example of logic for comparative international research studies in the context of a learning culture, in which the intellectual and analytical tools will themselves be the subject of continuous change and improvement.

REFERENCES

Archibald, B. (1986). *The Work of National Board Inspectors on the Victorian Goldfields.* Unpublished MBA Thesis. University of Melbourne, Australia (No. 33813).

Beare, H. (1989). The Australian policy context. In J. Lokan & P. McKenzie (Eds.). *Teacher appraisal: Issues and approaches.* Melbourne. A.C.E.R.

Beare, H. (1989). *Educational administration to efficient management: The new metaphor in Australian education.* Paper to A.E.R.A. San Francisco, CA.(ED308598).

Bell, R. (1985). *The changing role of the headmaster—1915–1974.* Unpublished MEd Thesis. University of Melbourne, Australia (30668).

Browne, G. (1984). *A study of the leader behavior of department heads in Thai teachers colleges.* Unpublished PhD Thesis. University of New England, Armidale, Australia, (26830).

Burkhardt, G. (1991). *Performance appraisal and assessment of educators.* Paper to 1991 Australian Council for Educational Administration Conference, Sea World.

Cheung, Y. (1991). Leadership style of principals and organizational process in secondary schools. *Journal of Educational Administration, 29*(2), 25–37.

Corfield, T. (1982). *The supervisor and the organized worker: Supervisor's self-development, Series 4. Institute of Supervisory Management,* Litchfield, England.

Doyle, D. (1992). Mastering motivation. *Incentive (IMK), 166*(3), 20–23.

Drucker, P. (1993). *Post capitalist society.* New York, Harper Business.

Early, J. (1991). Strategies for measurement of service quality. *Quality Forum, 17,* 10–14.

Ekpunobi, E. & D. (1984). *Supervisory procedures and methods of improvement in Nigeria.* E.D.R.S. ED261007.

Evans, B. (1987). *Reflecting on leadership practices through a cultural analysis of schools.* Paper to AARI, Christchurch, NZ (No. 39947).

Galor, C. & Meurice, G. (1993). Putting the power into empowerment. *Journal For Quality and Participation, 16*(1), 98–101.

Gaziel, H. (1979). Role set conflict and role behavior: An empirical study of the Israeli general inspector of schools. *Journal of Educational Administration, 17*(1), 58–67.

Hardy, C. & Zarrimuto, R. (1989). *Strategy, structure and style in Brazilian universities.* Paper to Annual Meeting ASHE, Atlanta, GA (ED 313971).

Ibe, M. & Sato, N. (1989). Educating Japanese leaders for a global age: The role of the international education centre. *Journal of Management Development, 8*(4), 41–47.

Johnson, N. (1989). Criteria for assessing the effectiveness of schools and principals. *Education Canada, 29*(2), 14–19 (EJ395663).

Johnson, N. & Holdaway, E. (1990). School effectiveness, principals effectiveness and job satisfaction: A comparison of three school levels. *Alberta Journal of Educational Research, 36*(3), 265–295 (EJ418923).

Jones, A. (1986). *The development of the role of inspectors of schools in South Australia.* Unpublished PhD Thesis. University of New England, Armidale, Australia (No. 34019).

Karagozoglu, G. (1986). Educational supervision in a developing country. Turkey (ED275079).

Kennedy, P. (1993). *Preparing for the 21st century.* New York, Random House.

Lokan, J. & McKenzie, P. (1989). *Teacher appraisal: Issues and approaches.* Melbourne: A.C.E.R., Education Review No. 28.

Mintzberg, H. (1981). Organizational design: Fashion or fit? *Harvard Business Review,*103–116.

Macpherson, R. (1990). *The radical reform of administrative policies in N.S.W. school education: Practical and theoretical implications.* Paper to AERA Association, Boston, MA.

Murphy, J. & Hallinger, P. (1987). The administrative control of principals in effective school districts. *Journal of Educational Administration, 25*(2), 161–192.

Naisbett, J. & Aburdane, P. (1986). *Reinventing the Corporation.* Futura Books.

National Industry Extension Service (NIES) (1990). *Quality: The strategic advantages.* AGPS, DEET.

Paine, J., et al (1992). *Total quality and education.* Sydney, Australia: Ashton Scholastic.

Pajak, E. (1990). *Identification of dimensions of supervisory practice in education: Reviewing the literature.* Paper to AERA Conference, Boston (ED320285).

Poplin, M. (1992). The leaders new role: Looking to the growth of teachers. *Educational Leadership, 49*(5), 10–11.

Porter, M. (1990). *The competitive advantage of nations.* London, England: Macmillan.

Retallick, J. (1989). *Clinical supervision and symmetrical communication: Towards a critical practice of supervision.* Unpublished Ph.D. Thesis. Deakin University, Geelong, Australia (PhD No. 56182).

Savery, L., Soutar, G., & Dyson, J. (1992). Ideal/Decision marking styles reported by deputy principals. *Journal of Educational Administration, 30*(2), 18–25.

Seaton, A. (1994). Creating a literate culture: A role for school administrators. *Practising Administrator, 16*(2), 38–40.

Shannon, R. (1990). The educational administration: Professor, expectations. *Vital Speeches, 57*(1), 26–30.

Smart, J. (1980). Teacher as community leader: A Philippine example. *Australian Journal of Education, 24*(1), 82–91.

Sternberg, J. (1992). Helping peacocks show their feathers: Portrait of an educational leader. *Journal of Applied Behavioural Science, 28*(2), 252–262.

Toffler, A. (1991). *Powershift.* Bantam Books.

Toffler, A. (1985). *The Third Wave.* Bantam.

Toffler, A. & Toffler, H. (1995). *Creating a new civilisation: The politics of the 3rd Wave.* Futura.

Part

◆ IX ◆

FORCES AND FACTORS

INTRODUCTION

Barbara Nelson Pavan

TEMPLE UNIVERSITY

During the early discussions with the editors, consultants, advisory board members, prospective chapter authors, and publishers regarding the content for this *Handbook of Research on School Supervision,* many chapters and sections took shape quite quickly. These were mostly the material that precedes this particular section; however, a number of aspects not solely related to school supervision, but vital to an understanding of supervision within an organizational context, kept surfacing as issues that needed to be addressed by those responsible for supervision within the schools. As such, these chapters provide background knowledge for all educators on issues—organizational; economic; cultural, ethnic, and gender; and technology as they relate to schooling in general and to supervision in particular.

I had expected to find the discrepancies between schools with limited resources and those of more fortunate circumstances to receive more emphasis, possibly because I had just come from school visits, including one to an inner-city school with low academic achievement and only a dozen very old computers. The other visit was to a highly rated suburban district where one classroom contained more than $25,000 worth of up-to-date computer equipment. The latter classroom had parents who work for Hewlett Packard and a teacher who is an experienced grant writer. No degree of understanding of ethnic, gender, or social class differences can make up for the very limited resources generally available in both rural and urban schools.

ORGANIZATIONAL FORCES

Valverde takes us on a journey in Chapter 48 through the past and to the future with respect to the models on paradigms commonly assumed for instructional supervision utilizing external and internal forces as his organizers. Administration and supervision in the schools moved uneventfully toward a bureaucratic model until the 1960s protest and Civil Rights movements. Innovation flourished and clinical supervision was developed. External forces continue to impact the schools in the 1980s and 1990s. Immigration has continued, with the demographics of schools, especially in urban areas, becoming increasingly more diverse, and technology has rapidly changed the workplace. Current national dynamics include increased mobility, which means that teachers often do not have students for the full school year, the re-engineering of the workplace, which leads to jobs requiring either low or high skills, and accountability or reform in both government and schools.

A new topology of five institutional forces is proposed by Valverde for consideration by supervisors. Boundary forces are the broad limits or parameters of action, consisting of national and state legislation, and rulings by federal and state courts. Controlling forces further limit actions in the form of state mandates, school board policies, and school administration rules and regulations. Environmental forces are the organizational structure, facilities, and professional climate. Liberating forces consist of the teaching talent within the school, multiple teaching ideologies, learning constructs, curricular choice, and the expertise in the community. Among the variable forces under control of policy makers are finances, instructional staff, and role definition.

The function of supervision may be assigned to line administrator who also evaluates teachers, to the staff consultant who functions as an expert to assist teachers, or it may evolve in more teacher-controlled ways as it does in site-based management or professional development schools. Both of the latter organizations have as basic premises that those in the school should collect data, develop a school improvement plan, and decide which people will do what to effect improved academic achievement. In the case of the professional development school, a school or college of education becomes a full partner with teachers, such that certain university faculty are assigned to the school. In these collaborative models, decisions about supervision are made by the school staff.

Other shaping forces on supervision include the competing dynamics of centralization versus decentralization, standardization versus creativity, specialization versus generalization, and conflicting interests.

ECONOMIC FORCES

Smyth begins Chapter 49 with a book excerpt describing a prisoner overwhelmed by the constant brightness and supervision in his powerless situation. He unapologetically indicates to the reader that he has written a polemic that may strike some readers negatively, but which will stimulate their thinking about his basic premise that school supervision is changing radically due to economic, political, and social forces external to education.

In the first part, the process of economic globalization, Smyth acknowledges the changing arena of business from national corporate identities to a world focus with increasing use of technology to improve productivity, a greater need to respond to market forces, restructured labor markets, improved accountability, international governmental regulations, and restructured work places utilizing more worker participation such as in total quality management. These business trends and the belief that education will solve national economic problems have forced teachers to become "pedagogical technicians" accountable for vocational training rather than a liberal education of their students.

"The consequences for teachers' work" lists many of the ways that teachers are being controlled, such as increasing accountability for student learning, and even suggests that school-based councils or teacher empowerment are really not attempts to broaden teachers' decision making, but to control them. One reference to school-based councils cited is an actual description of events in a school district where the superintendent kept close control over both teachers and administrators and inappropiately managed the process of participatory decision making. It is easy to cite examples of poor implementation in order to destroy the idea of teacher involvement/control in decision making, yet that is just what

Smyth is advocating. His detailed lists of the things that teachers need to do besides actual classroom teaching should be made clearer to the general public, including parents, community members, tax payers, and industrial managers. Because his lists are based largely on non-American schools, however, many of these activities would be extracurricular and bring extra pay to teachers in the United States. Of course, if schools here were truly site-based, then teachers would decide which activities would be available and which teachers would be responsible for them.

Smyth cautions that the role of supervisor is one of implied power due to its inspection aspect and to the control exerted over the dialogue even in the clinical supervision process, described in an earlier chapter, the latter was designed as a collaborative process with supervisor and teacher together in charge of the interaction. Numerous citations could have been given of teacher peer supervision, which is beginning to become a more common process. Smyth notes that the standards movement and competitive charter schools are ways to control teachers and supervisors, as well as administrators, rather than to allow teachers to decide what and how students should learn.

He considers that supervisors, not "politicians or their minders," are to seek answers to crucial questions like:

- What's worth teaching?
- Who says?
- Why are some ways of teaching superior to others?
- Whose interests are served (and whose denied) through particular representations?
- How can schools be made better places of learning, while being more socially just?

Smyth wants government to regulaterprivate business, but not public education. Excellence, quality, and accountability are considered code words for the regulation of teachers rather than an opportunity for teachers to determine what is best for their students. Business is now considered the customer of education as teachers are being supervised into making students become compliant workers. Smyth wants the voices of teachers to be heard, but appears to disenfranchise the parents, the community, and even the students themselves.

CULTURAL, ETHNIC, AND GENDER ISSUES

In Chapter 50, Gay reviews research on how culture, ethnicity, and gender affect academic achievement as these findings should inform the practices of teaching and supervision. She indicates that achievement is related to resource allocations, both material and human; to the quality of the learning opportunities; and the relationships between teachers and students in the classroom. Important aspects of schooling are both socialization to the "national mainstream culture" (i.e., acculturation) and the transmission to students of "their own cultural heritages and legacies" (i.e., enculturation). As such the practice of teaching and supervision should be "gender sensitive and culturally responsive."

Achievement data is discussed that indicates that students of color, with the possible exception of Asian Americans in technical subjects, have lower test scores than do European American students. Girls score higher in the "feminine" subjects such as reading, writing, and literature, whereas boys' scores are higher in the "masculine" subjects of math, science, history, and geography. Teachers are aware of these discrepancies, try to do what they think is best for their students, and are generally not malicious racists; therefore, Gay suggests "that inequitable educational practices are committed unknowingly and unintentionally because educators do not understand the interactive relationship between culture, teaching, and learning."

The steering of girls and people of color away from demanding courses and the insidious practice of assigning more students of color to lower tracks is probably even more damaging to their academic achievement and self-esteem than are gender and ethnically biased textbooks. Low-track classes focus on conformity, obedience, and rote memory activities, whereas high-track classes emphasize self-direction, higher order thinking, creativity, and active participation. Teacher expectations for students are affected by the students' assignment to tracks. This is further reinforced when teachers do not feel competent to teach these students so there is a need to increase teachers' repertory of multicultural pedagogical strategies.

Boys are called on more frequently by teachers to answer academic questions, and they are given more positive and negative feedback than girls. Teachers' comments to girls and students of color generally relate to social conformity rather than academics.

A fascinating section documenting numerous research studies entitled "Cultural Characteristics and Discontinuities," is divided into four sections (i.e., participatory structures, communication styles, learning styles, and ethnic identification and affiliation) and provides much food for thought. Cultural orientations of some Asian American groups emphasize self-discipline, control, and conformity, which may suggest why these students often do well in school. American Indian children would probably fare better in a John Dewey participatory classrooms as their tradition is one of collaboration and community. African American children might perform best within a classroom where there was high involvement of emotional, cognitive, and physical energy with participation not controlled, but where students "speak out" and comment on what they hear, as is often done in black churches (i.e., call-response). Novelty, variety, action in learning, presentation of visual images, groupness rather than individual competition, and story telling are also noted as cultural responsive learning strategies for African Americans and others.

Supervisors can raise the gender and cultural consciousness of teachers by using observational instruments to document how frequently and for what purpose different students are called on, to analyze classroom displays and materials for ethnic- and gender-equal status, and for videotaping teacher–student interactions. In addition, supervisors should obtain information and materials, many of which are suggested by Gay, train teachers to assess instructional materials for bias; and provide training on useful instructional strategies for gender and culturally responsive teaching.

TECHNOLOGY

Chapter 51 on instructional technology provides both the sophisticated and novice user a very complete understanding and history of educational media from Montessori's programmed instructional devices to the vivid vision in the open pages of a school using presently available technology. King, Wilkerson, and Okey stress that technology is a process, not just the materials and devices of educational media. Radio, films, television, and video are all described here as well as programmed instruction, which has moved from text, to Skinner's teaching machine, to computers with their branching capability to respond to individual needs.

Most of the media research has compared a particular aspect of technology with "conventional" education with inconsistent results or findings of no significant differences. Few studies have used acceptable research designs and many were conducted over brief time spans. It would be more useful to teachers to know specifically under what conditions which type of learners will achieve a given objective rather than generalized admonitions as to technology usage. In addition, costs associated with media need to be analyzed in relation to learning achievement. Adding media as a supplement or enrichment to the regular program is not cost effective. Integration of media into the regular program requires extensive teacher planning, but it might increase student achievement. Independent student usage of instructional materials without teacher mediation has the greatest potential for savings once materials are purchased. Design and utilization of instructional strategies are more closely related to the improvement of student achievement than to the particular media selected.

The current state of computer technology, information access through telephone lines with modems, the Internet, cable and satellite dish access to television, e-mail, and distance education are presented, including technical details such as the type of broad-band connections needed for speedy access to the Internet and the high cost of equipment necessary for two-way interactive distance learning. Because rapid evolution of technology will continue to change information sources, it is necessary for supervisors to work closely with school media specialists.

Instructional supervisors should keep in mind that no media form is superior to another, but should be selected to fit the instructional strategies and intended outcomes of a particular learning unit. Instructional materials should be evaluated for their fit with the students and learning objectives. The most cost efficient method should be selected for presenting the necessary stimulus to the learner.

The use of technology in the function of supervision was not discussed. Readers are certainly aware of audio- or videotaping classroom sequences for analysis. Some supervisors actually bring laptop computers into the classroom to record dialogue, and a small hand-held calculator has been programmed for recording Interaction Analysis. Teachers report being very distracted by the tapping sound from the laptops. If stationery video cameras are used frequently in the classroom, then both teachers and students forget their presence.

·48·

ORGANIZATIONAL FORCES AND SCHOOLING

Leonard A. Valverde

ARIZONA STATE UNIVERSITY

INTRODUCTION

Education, like other professions, does not occur in a vacuum, immune to societal events and dynamics. The practice of instructional supervision is also not isolated from the forces at work within school districts and schools. Because of these two realities, our discussion will cover both spectrums; to a limited extent, the external forces at work, and to a greater degree, the internal forces that shape the nature of school supervision. By external forces, my reference is to global, national, and other major environs outside of public schools. By internal forces, I am targeting influences that are found within organizations called *schools*. Beyond identifying and discussing external and internal forces, this examination will also cover how these dual forces help to formulate educational paradigms and determine the practice of supervision that commonly has taken place in schools.

The primary intent of this chapter is to provide a different perspective about how supervision has been defined in practice by societal and organizational forces rather than to recount research. The examples of these two major, categorical forces that shall be presented and discussed will therefore not reemphasize the typical scenarios found in the literature.

The chapter will conclude with a brief discussion of how the current forces in place are causing supervision to be in a continuous state of transition and redefinition.

SOCIETAL FORCES

Societal forces are numerous and exponential in influence when viewed through multiple cultural paradigms and the unique histories of various regions within the United States. Societal dynamics shape the context within which schooling takes place. The following discussion of specific societal forces does not attempt to be all inclusive; rather, the intent is to high-light, in broad strokes, some of the heretofore ignored major forces at work and to establish a framework tracing the historical development of supervision in public schools in the United States. It is hoped that this framework approach within a sociological perspective will stimulate others to identify additional, previously neglected, societal dimensions of the past and present that will help to provide a fuller understanding and a different view of the continuous development and the evolving nature of instructional supervision in public schools across the United States.

The Evolution of Supervision

The practice of supervision is not solely performed in public schools. In fact, the origins of supervision are found outside the field of education (Glickman, 1992). Business and industry are more likely to be the progenitors of supervision. Though there are relatively few historical studies about education, and even fewer students who trace the origins of supervision in education, it appears that the task of supervision came into practice in public schools about the late nineteenth century (Tyack, 1974). From approximately 1800 to 1875, public citizens who acted as trustees informally supervised teachers. America at this time was mostly rural with an agrarian economy; however, a few large cities (e.g., New York, Boston, Chicago, San Francisco, Los Angeles) were then becoming major commerce centers. In the last quarter of the 1800s, supervision became the responsibility of the school superintendent in such developing cities. Big business and major city governments were adopting bureaucracy as a form of organization and way of doing things. Prior to bureaucracy, businesses were small in size and physically located in one building. Their units were organizationally loosely arranged, their actions were uncoordinated, and their decision-making was local. As the population of the United States grew, however, particularly within cities, business and industry also expanded in size to accommodate the demands of potential markets. Because the greatest population growth occurred in cities, more schools were created. With the increased number of city schools, school districts were formed. In turn, districts adopted the bureaucratic characteristics then common in big business and major industry.

By the early 1900s, schools in cities could be described as having all the markings of a bureaucratic organization: hierarchical structure, clearly defined roles and responsibilities, division of labor, clear reporting lines, centralized decision-making, and multiple policies and rules to regulate actions. The creation of more schools now meant that public education was geographically located across the cities in many different buildings. Thus, the district superintendent could no longer directly supervise teachers as in the past. The task of supervision, therefore, was passed on to the school building principal and almost exclusively focused on monitoring and rating teachers. Supervision was not concerned with how well teachers were providing instruction; rather, it focused on how closely teachers were following the rules and regulations of the district. Supervision was a controlling mechanism at heart. Teachers were expected to conform and so supervision became an inspection process. Rigidity ruled within schools.

From 1900 until the 1920s, America was aggressively transforming itself into an industrial nation. Henry Ford created the United States automobile industry and, by inventing the assembly line, revolutionized America and its way of doing business. Other large industries that served the entire country, such as the telephone industry, followed the automobile model. Workers on the assembly line had a specific, repetitive task; telephone operators had a well-defined set of duties. These workers were watched regularly to make sure they were completing their task in the correct amount of time and in the way they were told to do their work. On occasion, telephone operators and other assembly-line like workers came upon a situation that they had to ask their superior to guide them through or to do for them because they did not have the proper author-

ity or permission to go beyond or to improvise in completing their prescribed duties. Supervisors in business and industry were physically stationed behind the line worker. Picture for yourself the telephone supervisor standing immediately behind the bank of seated switchboard operators.

During this 20-year time frame, supervision in schools rarely occurred (i.e., principals performed administrative and teaching duties). When principals wore their supervisory hats, their caps with the small letters were no different than their administrative caps. When they did supervise, they acted like business and industry supervisors (i.e., as overseers)!

In large school districts, during the 1930s, the position of supervisor (i.e., a person helping to improve instruction) began to emerge. With the creation of a position devoted full time to supervision, supervision was elevated from a task performed by superintendents and/or principals along with their many other administrative tasks to a full-fledged function. Supervisors were originally, generalists, working primarily with teachers; however, because they now had an entire day to supervise, their scope of involvement broadened to include curriculum. As comprehensive high schools took hold, the ranks of supervisors expanded to include specialists. It was the high school specialists who strengthened the task of curriculum development in the supervisor's role (see Table 48–1).

Most domestic enterprises were put on hold in the early 1940s during World War II. Many manufacturing facilities converted their efforts to produce military supplies (e.g., weapons, tanks, airplanes, ships, uniforms, food processing, etc.). Much of what the military created to win the war was infused, after the war, into the world of work, in the United States and in the conquered countries, (i.e., Japan and Germany). Some of the dominant features of the military were a clear chain-of-command, fixed organizational charts, the importance of accomplishing the objective no matter the cost, and so on. The human factor was a low priority and human relations were unimportant.

TABLE 48–1. The Emergence of Modern Instructional Supervision

Role Player	Leading Citizen	Superintentent	Principals	Supervisors: Generalist	Supervisors: Specialist	Principals: Supervisors	All: Admin. Supervisors Teachers	All:
Percentage of Time	Very Limited	Very Limited	Small Fraction	Full-Time	Full-Time		Some Percentage of Week	Some Percentage of Day
Definition	Checking	Task: Rating of Teachers	Task: Rating of Teachers	Function: Many Tasks	Function: Many Tasks		Process	Process
Frequency	Once in A While	Rarely	Occasionally	Regularly	Constantly		Constantly	Routinely
Number of Supervisors	One	One	One/School	Central Office Cadre	Central Office and Some Schools		School Based	School Based
Supervisory Approach	Laissez-Faire	Autocratic	Directive	Bureaucratic	Professional	Developmental Clinical	Reflective	Inventive
Time Line	1800	1875	1900–1920	1930–1950	1950–1960	1970–1980	1990	2000

With the end of World War II, and particularly due to the passage of Public Law 346, which is better known as the GI Bill, men leaving the military were able to enter college in large numbers. After finishing their higher education, many former military men entered the education profession. The GI Bill produced 238,000 teachers (*The Arizona Republic*, 1995). These men then moved quickly out of teaching and into school administration. The avenue of advancement for women in education was slower and channeled into supervision. From the late 1940s to the late 1950s, supervision was influenced by two countercurrents. The source that caused the countercurrents was gender. The men in administration were greatly affected by the military model of efficiency, with an emphasis on chain-of-command; the women were more prone to developing a teacher's capabilities and weighing the human side heavily. Male administrators wanted group uniformity and obedience in their teachers and students; women supervisors wanted individual growth and independence for teachers and students.

In the 1960s, schools, like all American institutions, faced an unprecedented challenge. During the Vietnam War, protest against authority at home was the order of the day. Political parties and government agencies were under frequent attack. The Civil Rights movement concurrently brought about civil and social unrest. Universities and schools were centers of attention due to desegregation orders. While change was being forced upon schools, in the main, educators resisted altering their way of operating to fit the circumstances. The resistance had many facets to it. For example, there was conflict within the teaching ranks between the new, young teachers and the old, experienced teachers. The older teachers were tied to conventional practice. They took the call for change as an indictment of their way of doing things. Conflict also materialized between teachers and administrators. Most school administrators during the 1960s were World War II veterans, tied to doing things one way—their way. Because the newly recruited teachers were of the "don't trust anyone over thirty" generation, it almost guaranteed a clash of ideals.

Despite the internal opposing camps, pockets of innovation were emerging across the country, particularly in big city school districts. They were fueled by the infusion of federal funds for the Elementary and Secondary Education Act, Title I Disadvantaged Youth, desegregation funds, and ESEA, Title VII Bilingual Children. All were funded during President Johnson's Great Society Program, circa 1965. In desegregation orders and in federal regulations, student/teacher ratios were lowered and set. Resource personnel such as teacher aides and reading and math specialists were required, and curriculum development and alternative methods were mandated.

Thus, beginning in the late 1960s and continuing on into the decade of the 1970s, instructional supervision came into full bloom. Supervision was studied, researched, discussed, and written about more than ever before (Glanz, 1991). More expansive definitions of supervision were drafted, new models of supervisory practice were formulated, multiple tasks were carefully delineated, techniques were enumerated, and approaches were critiqued. The force of protest, however, was the engine driving this accelerated supervision advancement, and protest also shaped the nature of supervision.

Whereas the new look to supervision was viewed by educators under the garment of professionalism (Sergiovanni, 1975), the real fabric was the protest movement. It was the era of protest and conflict. These two social forces created a liberating environment: Uniformity was out, variety was in, and lock step was out, flexibility was in. In addition, grouping was out and individuality was in. The melting pot theory of acculturation was challenged and multiculturalism was courted. In education, this became a time of projects, exploration, and model building. Standardized tests that concentrated on identifying norm reference scores were challenged; student assessment for diagnostic purposes was in vogue. Within supervision, this period was the dawn of the age of clinical supervision (Cogan, 1973). Supervisors were no longer interested in rating teachers, evaluating teachers, or making judgments about teachers' characteristics. Supervision was now clinically a formal and systematic way of observing the actions of teachers and helping the teachers to "see" and understand the consequences of their classroom behavior. Clinical supervision fit the time of assessment and diagnosis. Clinical supervision was a one-on-one affair, again fitting into the societal norms of the time: individualization, and science.

Through the 1970s and until the late 1980s, the immigration of Asians from the Far East and refugees from the Caribbean islands and the continued influx of Latin Americans from Mexico, Central America and South America began to accelerate the changing face of America, in particular the changing face of our school population. Because of the mismatch between poor, inner-city, first-generation, limited or non-English speaking, ethnic/racial minority students and middle class, suburban, fourth-generation, white teachers, supervisors were pressed to develop curriculum that related to these new students (i.e., multiculturalism) and to conduct staff development sessions for teachers to learn about the various cultures and the use of English as a second language approach (ASCD Journal, 1980–1984). Because of the heavy cultural-instructional demand, school districts began to promote and hire ethnic/racial minorities in supervisory positions.

A parallel shift of philosophy was taking place in public school administration. Administrative preparation programs in colleges of education were seeking out change-agent types for enrollment. College curricula was altered to emphasize strategies that facilitated organizational changes. For the first time in the history of public education, African Americans were being appointed to these leadership positions in greater numbers. As a result, the ethnic and racial composition of superintendents and principals of inner-city schools radically changed. A different philosophy and attitude about administration, instruction, and student learning came with these new appointments.

Global Societal Forces: Then and Now

With the brief historical narrative describing societal forces that shaped instructional supervision as background (i.e., big business, assembly-line industry, bureaucracy, urbanization, population growth, World War II veterans entering teaching/ administration, science emphasis, and protest era) the discussion will now turn to more current and direct forces that help to determine the contemporary concept and practice of supervision in schools. There are many external societal forces (i.e., too many in fact to include), so only three dominant, far-reaching and long-standing forces will be elaborated upon. The first force (i.e., immigration) has a long history and deep-rooted influence on society and schools. The second force (i.e., demographics) is derived from the immigration force. The third force (i.e., technology) has recently been accelerating, but it promises to have a lengthy future in society and a significant impact on education.

Immigration

From a European historical perspective, civilization began in the old world and, therefore, North America was discovered and colonized by European explorers, the Vikings, and Christopher Columbus. As is well known, however, there were many American Indian tribes populating North, Central, and South America. The earlier view of world population has prehistoric humans migrating from Asia over the Bering Straits into currently known Alaska and moving into Canada and down through North America. Other historians theorize that "natives" sailed the Pacific Ocean to South America and traveled up into Central and North America as well. While the question of how the Americas were first populated is still arguable, it is well accepted that the United States is a country created by immigration, through persons drawn to the "land of opportunity," or through *forced* migration (e.g., Africans as slaves and Chinese as coolies). The origins of other nonwhite ethnic and racial groups in the United States have created a two-class system that favors White America and exploits nonwhites.

The immigration has continued for more than 200 years and will most probably continue into the future. Since the beginning, the institution that has Americanized foreigners has been the school system. The Congressional Record is replete with negative attitudes expressed by elected representatives about Hispanics, Chinese, other Asians, and Eastern and Southern Europeans, as well as Catholics and Jews (Stewart, 1994). Public schools have reflected a bifurcated view about immigrants, as has Congress. For the previously named groups, the school philosophy has mirrored a negative viewpoint, therefore, schools have devoted their attention to transforming immigrants before providing instruction (i.e., devaluing the native culture so they can adopt new values and norms). This type of socialization policy has resulted in many detrimental outcomes. Through the school curriculum, the values, language, history, and customs of immigrant groups have until recently usually been denied and distorted.

The practice of supervision in schools predominant with these types of student bodies has been prescriptive, bureaucratic, and controlling. The majority of immigrant children have attended urban schools, both in the past and in the present. Supervisory positions emerged and profited first in metropolitan school districts. These three factors therefore reveal that the practice of supervision was partly shaped by society's view regarding immigrants.

Demographics

As the world and the United States mature, a second force (i.e., demographics) is substantially molding institutional prac-

tice. The U.S. Census, founded in 1790, is almost as old as the United States (Carson & Weisberger, 1989). The Census does more than just count the nation's population. It monitors familial status, tracks our movements, classifies our occupations, and assesses our wealth, to list just a few of the many statistical counts. Based on the results, our government redefines its political representation, and the Congressional count is the basis for the many important decisions (e.g., federal dollar allocation to such social responsibilities as education).

Educational attainment is among the many counts. Along with educational attainment are other subcounts relevant to education, such as the number of school-age children in a household, race or ethnicity, age of persons, length of time residing in current location, family income, and so on. For the past three decades, the findings show that school student bodies are growing in number and becoming highly diverse by race and/or ethnicity, language ability, different languages spoken other than English, and socioeconomic status. Furthermore, data collected by other educational agencies, such as the *Condition of Education*, U.S. Department of Education, shows that educational achievement is disproportional and inverse for nonwhite student populations (Hodgkinson, 1992). One proposed reason for the high drop-out rate is the mismatch between the low-income, urban, and culturally and linguistically diverse student body and a homogeneous teaching staff (i.e., white, middle class, suburban, English speaking only).

The consequence of recent demographic trends in schools has been to move away from the melting pot theory, which was ethnocentric in nature and rooted in an imperialistic national policy, and to move toward a multicultural educational approach, grounded in a cultural pluralism philosophy where cultures are seen as having equal value. Due to these two shifts, school demographics and the cultural paradigm in schools, supervision concomitantly altered its focus. For more than two decades (i.e., 1970–1990), staff development of teachers was heavily centered on multicultural education. Curriculum was inclusive instead of exclusive (e.g., the contributions of various ethnic and racial groups were included in textbooks). It is more important to note however, that supervision began to drift away from the bureaucratic, autocratic, and tractive approach to multiple approaches, such as the democratic, collaborative and dynamic approaches (Harris, 1985).

Technology

The third force of change (i.e., technology) exploded onto the American societal landscape in the mid-1970s via the introduction of personal computers. Technology promises to be another major determinant in education at all levels and far into the future. Personal computers have spread widely into the workplace, homes, and schools, and evolved equally rapidly in capability as they have infused themselves into daily life. Telecommunications have kept pace with the development of personal computers. This compound advancement has changed the ways people work and play.

Computers and telecommunication have fostered connectivity worldwide to an unprecedented degree. Information and people are now readily accessible. The storage and manipulation of facts and information is now unbounded. In addition to the array of hardware (i.e., multiple channel television, video and audio tape recorders, computer discs, and satellite transmissions), there are multiple advancements in the variety of computer software and programs, both for educational and recreational uses. All of these developments have caused the role of the classroom teacher to change drastically. Teachers are no longer the primary sources of information and the sole dispensers of knowledge; rather, they are now the managers of information and engineers in the use of technology in the classroom.

Armed with all these electronic instructional tools, students can learn through various mediums, based on an interactive mode. These technological mediums now potentially free the teacher to truly individualize instruction. To be specific, there are computer-developed software programs that permit computer-managed instruction. This means that the learner's knowledge base can be assessed by means of the computer, then the software can be adjusted to the level of program instruction that is compatible with the student's level of knowledge. As the student increases his or her knowledge base, the level of difficulty by testing and branching will also increase. This type of computer assisted instruction was pioneered by the military.

The use of the computer in schools, on its own, or in conjunction with other media, includes diagnostic use and remediation as described earlier, simple drill and practice, simulation and model building, research facilitation, and communication building (i.e., oral, written and interactive). These are all means to foster the underlying principles of teaching (i.e., active learning), promote problem solving, and stimulate creative thinking. Technology has the potential to change the school as an institution to a true learning environment (Rowe, 1985).

If classroom instruction is to be transformed by technology, then supervision must be at the helm that steers the new course. Teachers should be trained in the use of these new tools and guided during their practice with such tools. Supervisors will also have to incorporate such tools in their own practice. Clinical supervision is an excellent vehicle for the use of technology. The same principles apply to clinical supervision as to computer management instruction. The supervisor can observe the teacher, record behavior, and diagnose interactions. The supervisor then assesses consequences of actions with the teacher. The supervisor next suggests improvement either in training or in changed classroom behavior (Boyan, 1978). These three steps parallel the computer process of determining student knowledge level, offering up exercises equal to the level of difficulty, and then branching the student's achievement after testing.

Current National Societal Dynamics

In a compact period of time (e.g., 25 years), six significant societal dynamics emerged. The national dynamic of mobility and the re-emphasis of science/technology began in the late 1970s. Two other dynamics emerged in the late 1980s. Business initiated the re-engineering movement and, also within the business sector, new work skills as well as new jobs began to develop. In the 1990s, two additional dynamics surfaced: government reinvention and school reform. The umbrella for all these trends was *accountability*.

With the dawning of an information society and service-dominated employment industry, coupled with a changed family structure (i.e., two working parents or single-parent households), high divorce rates, and unstable marital status due to divorce and remarriage, the two social constructs of longevity and stability gave way to *short-term relationships* and *mobility*. People and families moved a number of times within cities, out of town, and across states. They also did not move just once or twice as they had in the past during certain traditional rites of passage (i.e., leaving the family home after finishing public school to go off to college or finding a home after getting married).

Persons and companies no longer felt a loyalty to each other. Companies would relocate without regard to employee continuity. Promotion and opportunity within corporations was no longer dominated by inward experience and length of term, commonly referred to as seniority. Persons changed companies as well as jobs (i.e., from working in sales in corporate America to working in advertising in small business). Even more drastic than changing jobs, people began to change careers, and, even more, they changed careers more than once (e.g., from being an engineer to becoming a high school teacher of mathematics to becoming a hotel manager).

The dynamic of mobility meant that public school teachers could no longer depend on having students for the entire year. Student enrollment become fluid; students leaving before the semester ends and new students entering at any time during the semester have become common (Seo, 1994). As a consequence, teachers now have a much shorter time to establish relationships with their students, students have to adjust to teaching styles more rapidly, and the class no longer has a common curriculum as a starting base.

Mobility is targeted to teachers as well as to students. Teachers are leaving the profession after a few years of service. Like other professionals, they are also leaving schools for better-paying school districts. Large school districts, such as New York and Los Angeles, offer the opportunity for teachers to move from school to school within the district at the end of the school year. Because many teachers are spouses to other professionals, they typically leave when their spouse is transferred out of town, and/or out of state.

With teachers and students in a state of transience, community building in schools is a problematic process. When you add teacher isolation to this phenomenon the implications for supervision becomes clear. Supervision should concentrate on building the capacity within teachers to diagnose student learning styles and construct a student knowledge base. Curriculum will have to be packaged into microunits that can be used independent from previous units. Computer-assisted instruction will have to be utilized. Above all, however, supervisors will want to build collaborative endeavors among teachers, encouraging them to work in teams of two or more. Teacher time will have to be changed so that part of their day is spent away from students and in conjunction with other teachers, planning cooperative lessons and interactive instruction, discussing students they have in common, and so on. By stressing this teacher interactive association concept, a bonding will occur and a team identity can be forged. Lasting friendships and relationships will bloom. These attitudinal underpinnings will reinstate the feeling of belonging and stability.

The paradigm shift from a postindustrial, manufacturing workforce to an information-based, service employment market caused corporate America and the business communities to institute a major *reengineering* process. With the changed business landscape, two basic types of employment were created: low-paying low-skill (e.g., McDonald's fast food jobs) and high paying high-skill (e.g., computer technicians). The new business culture, which included total quality management, greater employee responsibility, higher benchmarks, greater customer satisfaction, and less product error, was equally important. The assembly-line mentality wavered and gave way to group work, cooperative tasks, and multiple responsibilities.

This business movement produced pressure on public schools to provide a better educated workforce. A worker as a problem solver and as a team player, in addition to possessing basic reading, writing, and computing skills, has become the goal. Businesses of national stature (e.g., Motorola) were spending significant amounts of their operating budgets to instruct their employees in basic educational skills. These businesses were compensating for what schools had failed to do by providing remedial education on company time. This pressure was adding fuel to the accountability movement, which has been in force within schools since the early 1960s.

Elementary schools are being asked to instill fundamental skills among their students, while secondary schools are asked to generate a motivated individual who will be able to think clearly. School teachers are being asked to prepare students to enter the world of work 12 years into the future for still noninvented positions. For teachers to respond, supervision will need to develop a new facet to its approach: reflective leadership (Sergiovanni, 1991). Teachers will need assistance in contemplating the long view and the overall significance of their actions, goal setting, and understanding of the big picture.

With the start of the last decade in the twentieth century, the mounting wave for governmental *reform* crested with the 1992 presidential election and was sustained with the 1994 Congressional elections. The Clinton administration joined the business movement of re-invention by asking the vice president of the United States to lead the federal government's task in this effort. A wave of public dissatisfaction with the government surfaced after 35 years of requiring accountability for its public officials in the form of programs.

Although the social force of *accountability* gained a major foothold in education in the 1960s under President Kennedy's and President Johnson's administrations, its history goes back to the start of the twentieth century and the flowering of large urban cities (Martin, Overholt, & Urban, 1976). During the 1960s, when federal dollars were available to support school desegregation, the Elementary and Secondary Education Act, Title I funds for disadvantaged minority students and ESEA Title VII Bilingual Education, funds began to flow in sizeable amounts; accountability advocates required evaluation components. In the 1970s, accountability was manifested in school effectiveness studies (Edmonds, 1977, 1979, 1980). In the 1980s, accountability was evident in student assessment. In the 1990s, accountability was seen in the form of school reform.

With the emphasis of accountability on school personnel, particularly classroom teachers, the practice of supervision was directly shaped by the accountability movement. Supervisors were assigned to help teachers write behavioral objectives and to identify evidence to measure the objectives. Supervisors were also trained in program evaluation and were used to collect data on teachers and programs. The primary concept behind accountability and measurement permeated the thinking of educators; therefore, the concept and practice of classroom observation that emerged in the 1970s was based on the parallel and intersecting basis of observation and recorded data. Clinical supervision was to ground the discussion by the supervisor with the teacher on items that were tangible, concrete, counted, and recorded (Hunter, 1983).

In addition to being rooted in public unrest, accountability is closely tied to the principles of *science*. During the early 1960s, the United States was totally engulfed in space travel, and landed a man on the moon before the decade ended. The "hard" sciences (e.g., physics and chemistry) were emphasized, and the "soft" sciences (e.g., social sciences) were discounted to a lower level. The perspective changed from phenomemlogical understanding of things to quantitative analysis. Interpretation and speculation were eschewed and precision and verification were valued.

Today, after 35 years of accountability in schools, the unanticipated consequences are obvious. Teachers, instructional supervisors, and administrators were restricted in their thinking about their roles, constricted in their actions, and, as a result, have hindered the progress of the education profession. The 1990s is the school reform era, calling for new and creative schools and educational programs that will prepare children and youth to successfully cope with the unknown. School personnel are now being urged to be creative, original, and expansive in their thinking.

If school personnel are going to respond to the current public demand, then supervision will have to foster and promote insight, introspection, and spontaneity. Teachers, supervisors and administrators will have to return to principles of discovery and understanding. Qualitative research and examination will have to be practiced to a larger degree than in the past. Evaluation of teaching and instructional programs will need to be based on connoisseurship, which is an approach first advocated by Elliot Eisner in the earlier 1980s (Eisner, 1993).

The preceding treatment of both historical and societal forces should enable the reader to have a fuller understanding about how and why supervision has manifested itself in schools over time. The discussion now turns to forces that directly shaped the philosophy and conceptual constructs of instructional supervision in public schools.

INSTITUTIONAL FORCES

The second part of this chapter provides a new topology of institutional forces at work in public education. The five institutional forces are categorical; therefore, they are broad in scope and permit traditional organizational dynamics to be subsumed. The third part of the chapter will incorporate the typical organizational forces (e.g., school district arrangement, school site governance, etc.) and discuss how the practice of supervision manifests itself.

Under this new category of institutionally based forces, the concept of supervision is defined. The topology of institutional forces helps us to understand the boundaries within which schools operate, as well as to know what type of supervision comes into play, and to assess the *quality* of supervision (i.e., the effectiveness and efficiency). Five institutional forces will be presented for consideration. The five types of forces are termed *boundary, control, environmental, liberating,* and *variable.* (For an overall pictorial scheme, refer to Figure 48.1.)

Boundary Forces

Boundary forces form broad limits as to what should be done and how much can be done (see Figure 48.1, Slide 1). They set the parameters as to what is officially permissible or required. Boundary forces are consequently created by the passage of national and state legislation, or by federal and state court rulings. Most legislation and court rulings are either enabling, which causes certain actions to come into play, or protectionistic, which results in the prevention of certain kinds of behavior or treatment. Legislation or court rulings are typically initiated due to a combination of both stopping some pre-existing circumstance (i.e., considered detrimental) and creating a different (believed to be better) circumstance. Some examples of this include: the Federal legislation passed in 1965 that established the Elementary and Secondary Education Act, which focused our nation's public schools on developing compensatory education programs, and the 1975 passage of *Public Law 94-142,* which turned the attention of public schools to main-

streaming as many special education–designated children as possible.

Two court rulings demonstrate how court decisions can impact comprehensive educational matters. The 1954 *Brown v. Topeka Kansas School Board* ruling forced educators to stop desegregation practices and to develop instructional programs effective for African American students. The 1974 U.S. Supreme Court *Lau v. Nicholes* decision prevented school districts from placing non-English-speaking youngsters in "speaking English only" classes. It also required school districts to have either bilingual instruction or English as a Second Language programs.

Official policies spring from federal or state legislation as well as court decisions. Whereas laws and court decisions are enabling or expansive in nature, policies are typically prescriptive, which consequently narrows the options or interpretation of the meaning of the law. Policies translate general laws into more definite guidelines. For example, in 1974 after the U.S. Supreme Court ruled in the San Francisco *Lau* case, it ordered the Department of Education to come forth with a set of guidelines that school districts could adopt in order to be in compliance with the court's ruling. The U.S. Department of Education produced what was commonly referred to as the "Lau Guidelines" (Cardenas, 1976).

Controlling Forces

Controlling forces are restrictive by nature (see Figure 48.1, Slide 2). They limit the actions persons can take to comply with laws and policies. For example, they may grow out of the state mandates. The three types of controlling forces to be

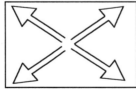  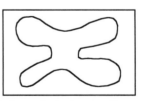

(1) Boundary forces delineate between society and schools. They are the outer limits. Everything within the square is considered schooling.

(2) Controlling forces reduce what is permissible within schooling, typically by prescriptive policies. Thus these forces narrow activity within the diamond.

(3) Envirnomental forces are further constricting in nature. Therefore they restrict behavior within the circle.

 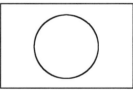

(4) Liberating forces expand the possibilities. They push out the pre-set boundaries. Thus the arrows are pointed outward.

(5) Variable forces fluctuate, sometimes permitting expansion sometimes causing restrictive movement. Thus the shape is irregular and wavering.

FIGURE 48.1. Institutional forces: five types

presented here for consideration are school district governing board regulations, administrative rules, and school procedures. Controlling forces narrow the margin of flexibility provided by laws, policies, and guidelines. They are specific in that they indicate who is responsible, timelines are specified, frequency is made clear, and typically documentation is required (i.e., forms are provided).

The most prolific of controlling forces probably emanates from state legislation and state departments of education. This proliferation is due to the fact that public education is primarily a state responsibility. Some states, like California, have a massive number of laws regulating all aspects of education, ranging from teacher certification, curriculum, and student enrollment, to administrative reporting. With so many state requirements passed since statehood (i.e., more than 100 years), some laws contradict one another. State Departments of Education are the administrative arm of the state legislature and have therefore become monitoring agencies.

Coinciding with the civil rights movement and as part of the protest decade of the 1960s, grass root and special interest groups have used the judicial system to right wrongs and to establish new treatment (Spring, 1993). When the accountability thrust discussed early in the chapter was added to this movement it becomes obvious why state departments and local school districts have been under an avalanche of compliance and bureaucracy. Discretion or flexibility of operation, at every level (i.e., classroom teacher, building principal, or district office personnel), was reduced greatly. Autonomy is a characteristic of any profession. As autonomy was substantially reduced in education, the profession was held back from advancing as far as it might have.

When one considers the progress of any major element in public education (e.g., curriculum development, instructional supervision, or teaching methods) during this time frame (i.e., 1965–1990), it is a credit to the profession that forward movement was accomplished under such a confining circumstance and debilitating era.

Environmental Forces

Environmental forces are human engineered (see Fig. 48.1, Slide 3). These forces, like the previous ones discussed, are still parameter setters, even though they are more contextual than confining. Environmental forces can be seen as capacity centered (i.e., what is physically or tangibly possible to accomplish). The three environmental forces are the facilities, professional climate, and organizational structure.

First, it is well understood that people adapt to their physical surroundings. How school buildings are constructed creates a pattern of how teachers and others act individually and collectively. School design also determines other school functions. Depending upon the number and age of the school buildings, the district can enroll only so many students. Because of space shortage, students may have to be bused to nonneighborhood schools or to another neighboring school district. Due to classroom types, only a certain number of science courses can be taught in the middle and/or high schools. Availability and size of school libraries, gymnasiums, auditoriums, cafeterias, and so on, will also influence the type of educational programs offered. School facilities help to determine schedules of activities. The configuration of buildings and rooms can determine team teaching and cooperative learning, whether it will occur and to what degree.

By reflecting on how school classrooms have been organized, one can ascertain major shifts in teaching philosophies. In pre-industrial time, one room school houses were arranged where the teacher's area (i.e., in the front of the room) was raised on a platform and students looked up to see the teacher. During the Industrial Age, multiple-room school buildings were designed to have regular and uniform space. All of the classrooms were organized such that the teacher's desk and area were still in the front of the room (minus the raised platform), and individual students' desks were screwed to the floor in straight rows. This classroom arrangement exemplified a teacher-centered orientation where students were empty vessels to be filled by and with the teacher's knowledge. In the Postindustrial Age, schools were designed with open and irregular spaces. Classrooms were arranged with moveable tables and chairs. Centers were set-up within a single classroom and the teacher's area was reduced to a desk, usually placed in the back or the side of the room. This arrangement represented a student-centered orientation where students learned through active, group activities. Learning was dynamic and affective as well as cognitive (Eisner, 1990).

Second, based on the professional climate established by the school board and the superintendent, district personnel mirror its actions to be in concert with the umbrella climate. Through their pronouncements and written statements the school board and the superintendent define and disseminate the district mission. Through their communication, such as the district newsletter or in-house television transmission, goals and expectations are made clear to school teachers and instructional support personnel. At the various unit levels, therefore, priorities are identified that fit into the general district goals and expectations. For example, if raising standards is a goal, then classroom teachers will establish priorities to increase student achievement levels. Instructional supervisors will help to determine what a reasonable increase of standards in the various disciplines at different grade levels might be.

Third, the way the district and schools are organized administratively depends upon both physical and philosophical considerations. Size in number of employees and schools are the physical aspect. Philosophical considerations, such as flat versus multiple layers of administration, centralized versus decentralized, change orientation versus status quo, bottom–up versus top-down communication, and so on, will mold the type of organizational arrangement. In turn, the daily district operations will be influenced by such organizational configurations. The district's organization will either promote productivity among its employees, cooperation with support groups such as parent and community volunteers, and collaboration with businesses, or it will cause separation and potential conflict with local teacher associations and other special interest groups.

Liberating Forces

As the name suggests, liberating forces are expansive in scope (see Fig. 48.1, Slide 4). They expand the boundaries put in place by the all too common controlling forces and help to overcome the environmental forces that are more restrictive than neutral. Liberating forces are conceptual in nature. They are philosophies grounded in beliefs that are then translated into human behavior and actions. Liberating forces are found in all schools at all times. The only difference is the degree to which they exist. Liberating forces are found in the following: (1) the human talent of the instructional staff, (2) pedagogic ideologies, (3) learning constructs, (4) curriculum, and (5) community participants. Brief discussion of each of these liberating areas will follow.

(1) Every school has an enormous potential of intellectual capacity that is typically expected from its teaching staff and instructional support staff. It is the responsibility of the principal and the instructional supervisory staff to unlock and harness this brain power and then use it to move the school goals and priorities forward. The unlocking process may be as simple as motivating persons through conversation to explore and experiment. It could be as elaborate as structuring regular staff development sessions, with scheduled state or national experts making presentations on selected topics. Channeling and sustaining the human talent on district goals and school priorities is more time consuming and requires more organization and planning. It need not cost much. For example, the principal could act as the instructional leader by convening focus groups on a weekly basis to generate ideas by teachers sharing what they are doing in their classrooms instead of holding the traditional staff meetings to make district or school announcements.

(2) Within any school, there are potentially as many teaching ideologies as there are teachers. Even though colleges of education are accused of having a lot of irrelevant curriculum in their teacher preparation programs, there is much variety across the country. Most teachers acquire their learning ideologies in college. Teachers will also alter what they learned in their college preparation program to suit their own strengths and weaknesses as well as adjust to the school children for whom they are responsible. Throughout a teacher's career, his or her teaching styles will change as he or she matures as an individual and develops as a teacher. Furthermore, teachers will use multiple approaches during the same semester as well as during a single day, based in part upon the subject matter for which they are responsible and the purpose of the lessons. In opposition to the public stereotype that teachers typically use a uniform teaching approach, all one has to do is to visit classrooms to see the multiplicity of pedagogy in use.

(3) The learning constructs that teachers harbor mentally and manifest in their classroom behavior with students are conceptually separated from the pedagogy, but closely tied in practice. In fact, for most practitioners, beliefs about their students' characteristics will determine the learning constructs they put into practice. Teachers who believe students learn the best by "doing" will structure lessons to have hands-on activities as the approach. Teachers who assume students learn

mostly by problem solving will ask questions and present situations where students are required to collect information and come to a conclusion. Teachers who feel students learn more by utilizing as many senses as possible will employ multimedia in their instruction. Teachers who think skill development is acquired by practice will offer repetitive exercises. Teachers who conclude that students learn easily from each other will organize students into teams to produce projects.

(4) Curricula is also an expanding force by way of opening the mind to heretofore unexplored options. Curricula come from many sources: textbooks, state departments, universities, professional associations, federal agencies, private consultants, businesses, foundations, think tanks, and so on. Two other sources, and possibly the most energetic producers, are classroom teachers and district curriculum writers or instructional supervisors. While every school district and school are required to utilize state-adopted textbooks and district-purchased supplemental curricula, teachers and instructional support staff are constantly modifying, supplementing, or complimenting the official curricula by way of securing or developing accompanying instructional materials and aides. In fact, curriculum development is the second-most time-consuming activity teachers and support staff involve themselves in beside teaching students. The more curricula choice available to teachers, the wider and richer the experience for teachers and students.

(5) Communities, whether they are in a poor-income rural town, an economically depressed urban ghetto, or a rich suburb, are support systems for public schools. In fact, as more communities become pluralistic in nature, their capacity to provide support increases. The schools have typically seen the increase in diversity as a problem (i.e., the district not having adequate cultural or linguistic resources to match the student demand). By reaching out to the surrounding community, parents and other adults could offset the school district's deficiency with their expertise. Any lack in the community to meet school needs could be compensated by and through community leadership efforts (i.e., business or civic leaders providing school access to resource agencies external to the local community). By schools forming partnerships with various constituents, the capacity of schools to meet the societal challenges placed upon them through the growing accountability factor and through the education profession's own increase of standards can be met.

Variable Forces

As implied in the name, variable forces can be either positive or negative factors (see Fig. 48.1, Slide 5). Depending on how these variables are manipulated, they can improve the circumstances or prevent progress. Unto themselves they are neutral. When put into play, however, they become freeing agents or restrictive components. It is the policy makers and administrative office holders who, for the most part, control the variable's direction toward a positive or negative status. The variable forces to be discussed here are finances, instructional staff, and role definition.

School budgets are the best variables to illustrate the accuracy of the preceding statements. Money by itself, whether in short or ample supply, is neither helpful nor harmful. While having more funds available to a school district increases the options of how to spend funds, it does not mean that better education will result. How the total amount is allocated for expenditure is more important than the amount of funds in school budgets. To illustrate this last point, let us take a simple example. School district Alfa has more dollars per pupil than school district Beta. Alfa school district board members decided to expend a substantial portion of its budget to the first-time purchase of computers for half of its schools and a minimal fraction on staff development. As a result computers being placed in schools for the first time are used infrequently and superficially by teachers without training or experience with computers and, in turn, by students. Beta school district decides to invest its limited funds in staff development and no funds to computers. By investing in increasing the teaching staffs' ability, it enables the district to maintain a satisfactory morale level. The two self-selected courses of action by each school district produce a different response.

Similar to school budgets, the number of instructional staff employed by a school district can also be a positive or negative factor. To have a low teacher–student ratio does not guarantee that better instruction will take place. How teachers are organized, how their time is distributed daily and over the academic year, how they are trained, what kind of assistance they are provided, how teachers are motivated as compared with rewarded monetarily, or, in short, how teachers are utilized are factors more important than numbers. To make this point, consider the following scenario. School District One annually employs a sufficient number of teachers to have a districtwide student–teacher ratio of 25:1. Because schools cannot control such factors as numbers of students by age and, therefore, by grade level or children living in certain parts of town, student enrollments per school will vary. Thus, in some grade levels in some schools the student teacher ratio will be higher or lower than 25:1. In reality, the true classroom ratio could vary as much as 19:1 to 31:1. Some teachers, therefore, will feel cheated or to some degree become disillusioned.

School District Two decides to have differentiated staffing and flexible use of instructional time. This means that some teachers are assigned to teach large numbers of students (e.g., 65–85) Monday, Wednesday, and Friday for half a day each. The remaining half day is spent on planning. On Tuesday and Thursday, these teachers act as school supervisors for the other teachers. Teachers who are not assigned large classes use their half of pupil-free time on Monday, Wednesday, and Friday to plan their lessons that compliment and supplement the large class instruction. Because there is time to plan together, collaborative teaching takes place. This planning time allows for social interaction to take place among teachers and builds up group association. Discussion about students also takes place so the sharing of information is facilitated. Many more benefits are derived by this differentiated approach, and a great majority of the district teachers feel good about their work load, even though it is varied.

The way persons will perform in a certain role, in this case the instructional supervisor's role, is usually determined by how the role is defined. Role definition does not mean the listing of duties to be performed. We refer instead to a general expectation (e.g., a change agent or a facilitator, an empowered position versus support status, an independent versus a dependent operator, product-driven or process-centered, an evaluative monitor or a technical assistant, curriculum-based or grounded in pedagogy, instructional leader versus middle management, and so on). These either/or descriptors should allow educators to think-up contrasting scenarios, thus illustrating the variety of role definition. Just to underscore the point, two of the preceding descriptors will be fleshed out.

An instructional supervisor whose role is defined primarily to *produce* results will direct energy and time to generate various outcomes. For example, in the area of curriculum, the supervisor would likely spend much time in putting together instructional packets. The more individual packets designed (i.e., number) or the fuller each packet (i.e., volume of materials), the better. In the area of working with teachers, the supervisor would probably choose to structure his or her interaction with the teacher to end with a tangible record. This could be the number of lesson plans written by teachers or a request for teachers to keep a written log of problems discussed, and then report how recommended actions appear to work out. In contrast, a supervisor, whose role is defined as *process* centered, would focus his or her effort and workday differently from the product-driven definition. In the curriculum domain, the supervisor would consequently concern him- or herself with designing a plan regarding how various persons (i.e., teachers, discipline specialists, principals, university faculty, private consultants, and others) could be tapped to play a role, the timeline involved, how generated materials will be evaluated, and so on.

The second example illustrates the evaluative monitor versus the technical assistant descriptor. An instructional supervisor who perceives his or her overall function to be one of an evaluator of teacher behavior to ascertain their compliance with a prescriptive teaching approach will be cast in the role of monitoring teachers for compliance purposes or making judgements. The supervisor who is in the role of technical assistant will observe teachers to collect data that can be used to diagnose teacher actions and pupil reactions, offer suggestions as to what a teacher can do to change behavior or reinforce certain behavior, and so on.

The preceding role descriptors are offered to demonstrate that role definition does make a difference in the action of supervisors. The intent is not to cast one definition in a negative light and the opposite definition in a positive light.

TRADITIONAL ORGANIZATIONAL FORCES

The previous section of the chapter ended with discussion about how a general interpretation of role definition influenced the type of supervisory approach played out in schools. This part of the chapter will move from the topology of general institutional forces to a discussion of how the practice of supervision is directly influenced by traditional organizational forces. This section will specifically show how supervision in schools has been shaped and determined by organizational forces.

Bureaucratic Structures

It was noted earlier in the chapter under the discussion of the evolution of supervision. that modern schools have come to adopt the Industrial Age business structure of bureaucracy. Even though society is transforming into an information age, most school districts and schools still cling tightly to bureaucratic characteristics. Present day supervision of instruction has therefore been directly formed to comply with the bureaucratic characteristics. This basically means that supervision of instruction is based on two bureaucratic characteristics: authority and levels of structure. By using these two characteristics as vertical and horizontal continuums, a two-by-four matrix can be constructed (see Table 48–2). The primary bureaucratic characteristic that has determined the practice of supervision in schools has been authority. Based on authority, two types of supervision have manifested: line and staff.

Supervision is predominately understood to be a support function to teaching specifically and instruction generally. In a bureaucratic organization, therefore, supervision is assigned to *staff* who are to be advisory and who, through their recommendations and suggestions, are to assist in the accomplishment of instruction. These staff persons therefore have no direct authority vested in their position. Because their purpose is to be helpful, their source of "authority" comes primarily from their competencies, skills, and knowledge acquired through formal training or practical experience. Supervisors in staff roles have to rely on a combination of human and technical skills in order to get teachers and others to respond to their recommendations.

Supervisors in a staff role, however, are compromised by the informal characteristics of a bureaucracy, which means that while the primary purpose of a supervisor is to help improve the quality of instruction that takes place in schools by assisting classroom teaching, administrators want access to the information collected by supervisors about teachers. Teachers will therefore comply with supervisor suggestions because they know that supervisors will be sharing informa-

TABLE 48–2. Supervision in Bureaucratic Type Schools

	Authority	
Level	Staff	Line
District	A core of supervisors who report to an associate superintendent or a director. The number will vary depending on the size of the district. Size will determine how supervisors are organized (i.e., by specialization or grade level; e.g., elementary, secondary, etc.). Core of supervisors is assigned to schools. Principals direct supervisors' actions. Supervisors report to principals about teachers. They can advise, recommend, and model to influence teacher behavior. They work on curriculum and staff development.	While there is a core of staff supervisors, the individual in charge of the staff is the line supervisor. Title is at the associate superintendent level or district director level. Core of supervisors report to this person. School principals also report to this person when matters concern instruction or curriculum. Person at one time (early in career) was recognized for outstanding classroom performance.
School	Usually one person, a teacher released of classroom duties. Typically identified because of expertise as teacher. Reports to principal. Does classroom observations. Models teaching methods. Organizes and conducts workshops for teachers. Title varies: lead teacher, resource teacher. Attends district wide state and national conferences to collect latest information. Classroom observation data and views are found in principal's annual evaluation of teachers.	Either the principal (if a small school) or the assistant principal (if a large school) is the supervisor. These persons probably are not experts in teaching of curriculum. Because of other responsibilities, supervisory function is minimal in practice and quality is questionable. Supervision is reduced to classroom observations for the purpose of annual teacher evaluations. Curriculum and staff development sessions are rare.
State Department	A cadre of supervisors whose title will vary, although "coordinator" is typically used. Viewed as experts in an academic specialization, like special education, math, science, and so on. Primary work load is curriculum development and information sharing through workshops. Field visits are typically at the district level and by way of invitation. Focus is usually on interpreting state requirements and/or new initiatives.	Dependent upon the size of the staff, there could be two to three persons as line supervisors (i.e., deputy superintendent) and two executive directors with areas divided (e.g., elementary and secondary). They are removed from any main line supervisory tasks. They communicate via newsletters and official information-centered memorandums about curriculum and instructional requirements.
Regional Centers	A small number of supervisors may be called consultants. Because of small numbers, they are generalists and experts in teaching methods. They typically share their knowledge by way of conducting in-service sessions for groups of teachers. These staff development sessions are sponsored by their center periodically and teachers travel to them. The consultants also develop curriculum and materials for use by teachers. These materials may be free or for purchase.	Commonly, only one person, two in large service centers. The title of director is generally applied. Person is very much an expert who stays current on general instructional and curriculum matters. Shares knowledge with staff and school people by way of a regular printed message of a substantive nature. Influential by expertness and invitation to help in problem solving.

tion about their performance and cooperation with their administrator, who in turn will evaluate them partly on the information that the supervisor provides. Teachers will comply under this practice but they will not be open to sharing their weaknesses or concerns with instructional supervisors because of the negative consequences that may occur after evaluation. The extreme polarization of teachers and supervisors is best elaborated by Blumberg (1980) in his book, *Supervisors and Teachers: A Private Cold War*.

This distortion of relationship caused by a bureaucratic organization is enhanced by another informal consequence. Teachers will respond to supervisory suggestions because they are working with a supervisor who has the approval of the teacher's administrator. In short, the instructional supervisor is speaking for and on behalf of the school principal. It is understood that the supervisor is acting in the principal's stead when it comes to providing assistance in teaching techniques. Furthermore, supervisors also have informal influence on administrators as well as on teachers. Supervisors, therefore, provide administrators with information about teachers and, based on the amount and quality of information, administrators formulate judgments and conclusions that result in their actions. Administrators are indirectly guided by the information provided by supervisors.

Finally, supervisors in staff roles also have responsibility in curriculum matters. Supervisors can and do recommend an adoption of textbooks, modify commercial curriculum materials for district/school use, and develop districtwide curriculum. Another major responsibility of supervisors is organizing and conducting staff in-service sessions for groups of teachers.

Distribution of Assignments

The amount of time supervisors in staff roles give to teacher assistance, curriculum development, and staff development will be dependent upon the number of supervisors and where they are located. For example, if the school district is small and has a few supervisors at the central office, then the time devoted to each of these functions will vary, but will typically be very limited. In metropolitan school districts, supervisory staff usually exists at all levels (i.e., central office), at school buildings, and even by discipline (e.g., music and art, science and math, etc.).

The practice of supervision in schools from a *line* position is different in some respect and the same in others. Line-type supervision is practiced to a much lesser extent in schools than staff/consultative supervision. Recall from the first part of the chapter that supervision first emerged as a task that was part of the administrator's responsibilities; however, as public schools grew in number, and as education expanded and society evolved, supervision became a function and the role of supervisor was created and proliferated. Even though supervision based on line authority exists to a lesser and probably minor extent, it is still in place.

At the school-district level where supervision is vested in an administrative position, the typical position is associate or assistant superintendent for curriculum and/or instruction. At the school-building level either the principal or the assistant principal has the responsibility of performing the supervisory

function. At the regional service center or state department of education, the administrative title is probably an executive director or director of elementary or secondary education.

Whereas the administrator assigned with the responsibility of helping teachers has the same purpose as a staff person, the relationship is based on superior–subordinate status. Because of multiple factors, such as lack of time, too many other administrative tasks to perform, and lack of expertise, line supervision performed with teachers is minimal in time, of low quality, and focused on evaluation of teacher performance. Classroom observations of teachers, therefore, turn out to be the minimum required by the district for teacher performance assessment. The information collected by the administrator is recorded more for measurement use than it is for diagnostic purposes. The focus is more on identification of weaknesses than on providing a balanced recording of strengths and weaknesses. Observation data are rarely used to problem solve. Such an approach clearly interferes with promoting effective supervision.

Persons in administrative roles are required and called upon to develop and hone their managerial skills and organizational knowledge. Technical expertise, which serves supervisors in staff roles, is consequently, often underdeveloped with line administrators. The line supervisor is much more concerned with making sure teachers are in compliance with school district and state requirements. Line supervisors are preoccupied with teacher accountability to parents (i.e., meeting grade level standards). Thus, instructional improvement is secondary to organizational policies.

Because line supervisors have to split their time between two functions (i.e., administrative and supervision), the function of supervision is reduced to a task. Line supervision translates into teacher observation and sharing district policy information, whereas other supervisory tasks go unattended such as curriculum matters, staff in-service sessions, instructional program development, and so on.

Because the number of staff supervisory positions is limited in a line supervisory organized school district, the quality of instructional assistance is also limited. Furthermore, because the emphasis by line supervisors is on compliance and accountability, the organization will be focused on maintaining an acceptable status quo; therefore, one purpose of supervision, instructional improvement, or organizational change is unlikely.

Other writers have presented more detailed descriptions as to how bureaucracy has determined the type of supervision practiced in schools. An excellent reference is by Firth and Eiken (1982). They have identified and discussed seven common bureaucratic models for supervision of instruction (see Table 48–3).

SUPERVISION PARADIGMS

The discussion up to this point has demonstrated fully how both external and internal forces had profoundly influenced what takes place in schools and how these forces can shape the type of teaching, supervision, and administration that occurs. By now it should also be apparent that societal and educational forces at play are not separate from one

TABLE 48–3. Summary of Advantages and Disadvantages Regarding Seven Common Bureaucratic Models for Supervision of Instruction

	Supervisory Pattern						
Areas of Impact	Staff Consultant	Line Authority	Multiple Central Office Support	Decentralized Area Support	Performance Assessment	Local School Support	Intermediate Service Agency Support
Leadership	Determines resource allocation but dependent on administrative priorities	Combines supervision with management but creates superior–subordinate relationship	Distributes responsibility for specific programs but encourages formation of competing coalitions	Accommodates to needs of different areas but dependent on style and tone set in each	Provides focus to assistance but limited by factors included in assessment	Designates responsibility for supervision but delegates most important functions	Provides additional options but requires appropriate selection
Technical Skills	Enhances opportunities for influence but dependent on requests from teachers or principals	Emphasizes managerial skills but requires on-the-job development of technical skills for supervision	Utilizes specialized skills but reduces opportunities for collaboration	Diffuses potential assistance but reduces resources available to a particular area	Utilizes those related to standards but neglects others needed by teachers	Provides on-the-job training but diminishes other types of skills	Supplements available services but duplicates some existing local skills
Communication	Encourages linkages as information broker but dependent upon administration for access to official channels	Establishes authenticity of messages but restrict information considered detrimental	Encourages interaction among peers but decreases interaction between members of different units	Increases knowledge of local situation but reduces contact with central office	Emphasizes assessment results but ignores other topics of importance to teachers	Increases interaction with teachers but reduces contact between teacher and principal	Offers additional information but provides contradictory views
Decision Making	Minimizes rash solutions with alternatives but dependent on persuasion of administrators	Clarifies prerogatives for supervision but compromises by management responsibilities	Permits consideration of varied alternatives but encourages protection of parochial interests	Encourages broad basis of involvement but risks loss of district policy integrity	Contributes to improved performance but limits attention to items in assessment	Encourages initiative by subordinates but removes decision from principal	Retains local prerogatives but questions loyalty of agency staff
Morale Functions	Provides sympathetic ally but dependent on others to alter circumstances	Possesses ability to resolve teacher problems but considered reluctant to do so	Promotes teamwork within unit but fosters suspicion between members of different units	Increases opportunities for assistance but dependent on resource availability	Establishes standard for assessment but distrusted due to general application	Enhances opportunities for assistance but confuses teacher allegiance	Enhances importance of supervision but requires request for assistance
Curriculum Responsibilities	Contributor to program development but limits opportunities to assist teachers	Accepts assignments readily but lacks appropriate qualifications	Encourages attention to each subject area but restricts consideration of total program	Increases responsiveness to local program needs but threatens total district direction	Promotes change for similarity but produces unstructured diversity	Increases potential for change but restricts marshaling of resources	Addresses particular concerns but may compromise district goals
Organizational Roles	Potential related to resource control but limited to relationships with principals	Possesses power to modify situation but holds allegiance to existing structure	Distinguishes particular characteristic but threatens collaborative efforts	Provides team for particular area but increases tendency for supervisors to become part of management.	Shapes organization to assessment but shifts responsibility for supervision	Frees principal for other duties but intrudes additional level of structure	Promises mutually supporting structure but requires clear distribution of responsibility
Value Assumption	Advise and counsel should be separate from power and direction	Power and responsibility for related operations should be combined	Specialization should be fully utilized	Responsibility should be assigned close to the operational level	Responsibility for evaluation and support functions should be separated	Sources of support should be immediately available and familiar with local situation	Resources should be shared rather than duplicated

another; rather they overlap and intertwine with each other. In the remaining section, attention will be directed toward discussion of the type of supervision paradigm that may likely appear on the education scene due to the forces presently at work. The closing discussion will address dynamics that are competing and likely to be continual for some time to come.

Emerging Forces and Supervision Approaches

Because society and many of its formal institutions are changing substantially and with greater rapidity than in the past, it is not surprising to find a change of view regarding the conceptualization and practice of supervision in the literature about supervision (i.e., in the 1990s). As the editor of the 1992 ASCD yearbook, Glickman stated:

It is perhaps time for those of us who have toiled, practiced, and written about supervision to "pretend to not know" that events in education are shaking our deep-rooted conceptions of instructional supervision. Might I even suggest that the term instructional supervision itself may be outliving its usefulness? The reordering and redefining of societies, governments, and economies have been in "the very air" (emphasis added). People are rethinking old ways of doing business, dismantling hierarchies, and formulating new expressions of "life, liberty and the pursuit of happiness." It is no historical accident that the democratization and decentralization of government across the world are happening at the same time similar activities are being asked of public schools (p. 1).

Just as business has experienced the creation of a new corporate culture through the promotion of the entrepreneurial spirit, downsizing, and the learning organization, schools are also attempting to bring about a new culture. Little (1991) and Weicks (1982) studied schools and found new school characteristics or cultures emerging. Little identified shared beliefs and values that constituted professional interdependence as a normative basis for action. Through interaction of teachers, a common language and shared referents were developed. These new elements fostered new behavior among teachers, such as openness to observe one another and a willingness to discuss classroom teaching. (Grimmett, Rostad, & Ford, 1992) Weicks found that in some schools where teachers held themselves accountable by tightly structured beliefs and values, a culture of collegial conditions developed. The administrative hierarchy of a bureaucratic organization gave way (Grimmett, Rostad, & Ford, 1992).

Schools, therefore, are beginning to move from the bureaucratic culture where such traits exist (i.e., isolationism, teachers working individualistically, communication is minimal among adults; labor is divided, physical space [e.g., classrooms] is separated from one other) to a collaborative culture of interaction where the following traits are substituted: teachers work together; communication is face to face and frequent, labor is shared through teaming, and teachers are together by way of meetings and common observations while in their classrooms. With schools in a state of transition, supervision will also follow suit and modify itself.

Since 1984 Glatthorn rationalized that supervision should be differentiated in practice. He provided three reasons, one of which is that:

teachers have different growth needs and learning styles. They differ, first, in the type of interaction they prefer. Copeland's (Boyan & Copeland, 1980) study is one of several that conclude that some teachers prefer a directive supervisory style, while others prefer nondirective interactions. Teachers differ also about the supervisory relationships they prefer. Young and Heichberge report that 62 percent of the teachers they surveyed preferred a "helping" relationship, while 36 percent wanted a "colleague-ship" relationship. And they differ in the kinds of environments in which they work and in their ability to learn in that environment. After studying several thousand teachers, Joyce and McKibbin (1982) concluded, "Enormous differences exist in the extent to which teachers pull growth-producing experiences from their environment and exploit personal and professional activities" (Glatthorn, 1984, p. 36).

Glatthorn proposes four types of supervisory approaches, (1) clinical, (2) cooperative, (3) self-directive, and (4) administrative monitoring. He defines each briefly as:

Clinical supervision is an intensive process designed to improve instruction by conferring with a teacher on lesson planning, observing the lesson, analyzing the observational data, and giving the teacher feedback.
Cooperative professional development is a collegial process in which a small group of teachers agree to work together for their own professional growth.
Self-directive development enables the individual teacher to work independently on professional growth concerns.
Administrative monitoring is a process by which an administrator monitors the work of the staff, making brief and unannounced visits simply to ensure that the staff are carrying out assignments and responsibilities in a professional manner (Glatthorn, 1984).

Since the start of the 1990s, the national dialogue and discussion has called for public schools to reform. The term reform has been used with the interpretation that schools have failed, and just as students who were found in the past to be incorrigible were sent to a reform school where discipline and punishment ruled, schools that have been found to be "bad" must reform. Educators have fortunately, gone beyond the criticism and are interpreting reform to mean they are being prompted to transform schools in creative and new ways. If this movement to reinvent schools is going to be successful, then another progressive supervision model will likely be needed.

Sergiovanni posits that "supervision can hardly be counted among educational successes. Most teachers consider supervision to be a nonevent—a ritual they participate in according to well-established scripts without much consequence" (Sergiovanni, 1992).

The societal talk of school reform has produced the practice of site-based management and has promoted professional development schools in colleges of education. These two developments have in turn caused educators to call for a changing role of supervision to accommodate the new situation (Burke & Fessler, 1994).

Site-Based Management

Site-based management is a state legislative response to a perceived lack of effective schooling. It is a move to foster greater participation by more stakeholders in the operation of public schools. It is a means by which parents, teachers, principals, and others have shared decision-making powers. Site-based management should help to promote community in schools, a concept Sergiovanni declared to be necessary to change teaching and in turn to cause a new kind of supervision to be practiced (Sergiovanni, 1992). The role of most school positions will change as site-based management spreads throughout the country. In the case of the supervisor, the new behaviors and foci may result.

Because site-based management is a vehicle to transform schools, it requires three basic tasks to be performed: (1) the entire school to be assessed, (2) a new vision statement to be created, and (3) a school improvement plan to be crafted. The role of the supervisor will need to become one of shared leadership (Glickman, 1992). The supervisor should facilitate the three tasks of site-based management. To be specific, supervisors will want to apply their skill in data design, collection, and interpretation. More important than the technical expertise, however, supervisors will have to be reflective and help others (i.e., teachers) to think seriously and deeply about the meaning of the school assessment. A new meaningful vision statement will only come forth with introspection and a comprehensive view. In fact, the most difficult task of school reform is to conceptualize a school that will mold a student for the twenty-first century. To craft a vision statement the supervisor will have to elevate his or her thinking as well as that of others to a higher plane. By so doing the supervisor will become an instructional leader, a curriculum visionary, an architect of school environment, a designer of space, and a creator of human interactions. The supervisor as a leader will not do these things alone; rather, he or she will stimulate others to join in the work and build consensus among the many thoughts so that a common and shared vision is the end product. The last characteristic of this new role the supervisor should play involves planning expertise. A school improvement plan will transform the vision into reality. Any school improvement plan calls for identifying necessary resources (both human and financial), activities to be performed, a time line, an evaluation component, and so on. The supervisor should be a major contributor to this process.

Professional Development Schools

The school reform movement has expanded beyond public schools into colleges of education. Colleges of education have the primary, but not exclusive, responsibility for training classroom teachers, principals, supervisors, superintendents, and other school personnel. Since the time when colleges of education shed their "normal school" title and characteristics, there has been a constant tension between public school people and college faculty as to how best to prepare teachers and what the curriculum should be. Practitioners accused college faculty of developing a curriculum that is overly theoretical and irrelevant to the real world of teachers. College faculty posit that teachers cannot be given "cookie cutter recipes" that will help the prospective teacher to cope successfully with each and every situation. The prospective teachers should be armed with theories that they can apply to different situations in the hopes that they will be able to be

effective. This tension is kept taut by college faculty and school teachers working apart from each other in the training of future teachers and in the continual upgrading of teachers. The only brief moment during which they may come together in the teacher training process is at the student teaching stage.

In the late 1960s when teacher preparation programs were under sharp attack from various sectors (e.g., state legislatures, teacher unions, school districts, federal government, professional organizations, and others) the threat to close colleges of education became serious. Colleges of education in Research I Universities were particularly hard pressed to demonstrate their viable contribution in the teacher preparation process because many of them had relegated this function as low priority. Adjunct faculty consequently taught teacher preparation courses, and student enrollment in these programs was reduced to a small number. Tenure track faculty concentrated their efforts in research and taught a few graduate-level courses per year. The threat of closure did not materialize, but a good number of colleges of education deans resigned or were replaced. The Holmes Group was organized in 1986 in response to the mounting criticism.

The Holmes Group was originally a collection of Research I University college of education deans meeting together with the expressed intent to improve the teacher preparation experience. After about 3 years, the Holmes Group was enlarged to include other colleges of education that were not in Research I universities. One of the strategies to improve the teacher education programs was the creation of professional development schools. Colleges of education were to work with local school districts to identify a school that would be designated a professional development school. Unlike the old university lab schools, where student enrollment was controlled and teacher selection was determined by the university, the professional development school represented a typical and natural school setting. Professional Development Schools would be places where university faculty, veteran teachers, and potential teachers would work together in learning about pedagogy and the effectiveness of curriculum through practice, implementation and research. Professional Development Schools were to simulate what the teaching hospital was for the medical profession. The major attraction of the Professional Development School was that it would bring all parties together in a real-world setting.

If professional development schools catch on and become a mainstay of teacher education programs, and present indications make this projection likely, then the role of the supervisor will need to change accordingly (Ishler et al, 1994). Professional Development Schools will be places where all players will have a shared reality, and an abundant set of opportunities will come into existence whereby college faculty, school personnel, and prospective teachers can work cooperatively both to improve teaching and to improve schools. A new reality will necessitate a new set of interactions. The college faculty member, the veteran teacher, the principal, and the instructional supervisor will all be performing a supervisory role at some point in their daily activity. The new role will be multifaceted (i.e., supervision will mean the person will have to be a mentor, coach, model, and researcher), and each of these roles will require skill in interaction and ability to reflect on occurrences. These new roles are one step beyond the clinical supervisor model. While observation and feedback through conferencing will be necessary, professional development school operations will now demand that the supervisor go beyond the more limited traditional role.

Future and Continuous Shaping Forces

Because of the multiplicity of the societal and school forces at play during any time period, no two schools are alike, even adjoining neighborhood schools. Supervisory models are also not practiced the same way, even though conceptualized and described in one way for all to understand. The practice of supervision (i.e., the approach formally adopted by the school district), whether as a behavior, a task, or a function, is never activating in the same way. The forces at work alter the concept to fit the circumstances. There will consequently always be variance between the abstract concept and the implementation.

As long as schools are formal institutions, regardless of the configuration they take, certain school dynamics are likely to be in existence. Supervision will continue to be pulled and stretched by competing dynamics. These push and pull struggles will modify and shape supervision in many ways. One of these competing dynamics is *central office versus school-based operations.* This is the perpetual pendulum swinging from centralization to decentralization and back. Another opposing set of dynamics is the pressure of *group activities versus individual behavior* (Pajak, 1989). This psychological stress is created by the person struggling between a proper balance of group norms and nonconformity. A corollary struggle is between *standardization and creativity.* These two outcomes are expected by the school. Schools need benchmarks to measure progress. This is the organizational dimension of schools. Because schools are also learning institutions, however, they also demand creativity. The creation of knowledge is ingrained in the professional cloth.

Specialization versus generalization will continue to shape the substance of supervision. The exponential development of knowledge in academic disciplines will fuel the debate over the question of how much a person should and can come to know. How the question is answered will decide what role teachers and supervisors will perform. Finally, another enduring force that should bring about a yin and yang effect on supervision will be *conflicting interest.* These various interests will be formed by different interpretations of worldly events.

They will represent the differing perspectives formed and held in the minds of individuals. Whenever a large number of people collectively attend to a common enterprise, there are bound to be conflicting interests. It is highly unlikely that given the preceding dynamics one way of doing things will be satisfactory or even possible.

CONCLUSION

In closing, because this coverage has addressed the forces that have created supervisory models in concept, as well as shaped the practice of these supervisory paradigms, it is appropriate to end the chapter with proposing a new purpose for supervision. It appears that supervision has outgrown its noble goal of being a process striving to reach and maintain instructional excellence (Pajak, 1990).

The turn of the century is upon us. When one examines the socioeconomic and scientific landscape of the United States, the dominant force seems to be expansion through discovery and invention or reinvention. This dimension of newness is nowhere better observed than in space exploration and technology. The human race has a sufficient amount of nomadic quality in its gene pool to cause generations to continue to expand the living experience to places where the human race has not inhabited before. In addition to space, there will be exploration into oceanic living, and, probably more importantly, individual expansion of personal frontiers on a psychological plane is more of a driving force than expansion of the physical dimension. Just as space exploration accelerated and advanced new technological inventions, however, so will the continued expansive attitude cause greater variety and options to be created and craved. Think of the vast variety of automobiles a person can choose from.

Change is and will continue to be a constant. As we enter the third millennium, we enter a new civilization based on information. Knowledge will be power. The educational enterprise will be at the core of the next century. Educational leaders will have to be inventors, creating options, providing variety, stimulating pluralism, and embracing diversity. They will also have to be explorers in the human arena of interaction. They will have to blaze new paths to build consensus within subunits and harness divergent options to coexist with each other in parallel environments. Hence, the next purpose for supervision to adopt is to become and foster an *inventive process* and for the supervisor to be self-evolving (Valverde, 1982).

REFERENCES

The Arizona Republic, Phoenix, AZ: June 4, 1995, p. A1.

ASCD Journal *Educational Leadership.* Series between the years 1980–1984.

Blumberg, A. (1980). *Supervisors and teachers: A private cold war.* Berkeley, CA: McCutchan Publication Corporation.

Boyan, N. & Copeland, W. D. (1978). *Instructional supervision training program.* Columbus, OH: Charles E. Merrill Publishing Co.

Brown v. Board of Education, Topeka, Kansas. 347 U. S. 483, 1954.

Burke, P. J. & Fessler, R. (1994, Spring). The Changing role of supervision in site-based management. In R. J. Krajewski (Ed.). *Supervision: New roles for all.* Madison, WI: ASCD publication.

Cardenas, J. A. (1976, January). Lau remedies outlined. *ERIC,* ED125148.

Carson, G. & Weisberger, B. A. (1989, November). The Great countdown. *Mass Mutual.*

Cogan, M. (1973). *Clinical supervision*. Boston, MA: Houghton Mifflin Company.

Edmonds, R. R. (1977, December). Search for effective schools: The identification and analysis of city schools that are instructionally effective for poor children. *ERIC*, ED 142610, p. 10.

Edmonds, R. R. (1979, September). Search for effective schools. *ERIC*, ED 170396, p. 66.

Edmonds, R. R. (1982, June). Search for effective schools. *ERIC*, ED 212689, p. 21.

Eisner, E. (1993). *The enlightened eye: Qualitative inquiry and the enhancement of educational practice*. New York: Macmillian International.

Firth, G. R. & Eiken, K. P. (1982). Impact of the schools' bureaucratic structure on supervision. In T. J. Sergiovanni (Ed.). *Supervision of teaching*. Alexandria, VA: ASCD.

Glanz, J. (1991). *Bureaucracy and professionalism: The evolution of public school supervision*. London, England: Associated University Press.

Glatthorn, A. A. (1984). *Differentiated supervision*. Alexandria, VA: ASCD.

Glickman, C. D. (1992). *Supervision in transition*. Alexandria, VA: ASCD.

Grimmett, P. P., Rostad, O., & Ford, B. (1992). The Transformation of supervision. In C. D. Glickman, (Ed.). *Supervision in transition*. Alexandria, VA: ASCD.

Harris, B.M. (1985). *Supervisory behavior in education*. (3rd ed.).

Hodgkinson, H. L. (1992, June). *A demographic look at tomorrow*. Washington, D.C.: Institute for Educational Leadership.

Hunter, M. (1983). Script taping: An essential supervisory tool. In *Educational Leadership*, ASCD Journal.

Ishler, R., Winecoff, S., Edens, K., Wieland, S., & Toner, T. (1994, Spring). Professional development schools call for new roles in supervision. In R. J. Krajewski (Ed.). *Supervision: New roles for all*. Madison: WI: ASCD.

Little, J. W. (1981) *The power of organizational setting: School norms and staff development*. Paper presented at the annual meeting of the American Educational Research Association. Los Angeles, CA.

Martin, D. T., Overholt, G. E., & Urban, W. J. (1976). *Accountability in american education: A critique*. Princeton, NJ: Princeton Book Company.

Pajak, E. (1989). *Central office supervision of curriculum and instruction: setting the stage for success*. Boston, MA: Allyn & Bacon.

Pajak, E. (1990). *Identification of dimensions of supervisory practice in education: Reviewing the literature*. Paper presented at the annual meeting of the American Educational Research Association. Boston, MA.

Rowe, M. (1985). *From a school system to a learning system: Educational innovations in Israel*. New York: Center for Cultural Resources.

Seo, D. (1994, November). A lesson in musical chairs. *Los Angeles Times*.

Sergiovanni, T. J. (Ed.). (1975, March). *Professional supervisors for professional teachers*. Alexandria, VA: ASCD.

Sergiovanni, T. J. (1991). *The Principalship: A reflective practice perspective*. Boston, MA: Allyn and Bacon.

Sergiovanni, T. J. (1992). Moral authority and regeneration of supervision. In C. D. Glickman (Ed.). *Supervision in transition*. Alexandria, VA: ASCD.

Spring, J. (1993). *Conflict of interest: The politics of American Education*. New York: Longman.

Stewart, D. W. (1994). *Immigration and education: The crisis and the opportunities*. New York: Lexington Books.

Tyack, D.B. (1974) *The One best system: A history of American urban education*. Cambridge, MA: Harvard University Press.

U.S. Department of Education (1975). *Condition of education*, Washington, D.C.: United States Government.

United States Government. (1974). *Lau v. Nichols*. 414 U. S. 563.

Valverde, L. A. (1982). The Self-evolving supervisor. In T. S. Sergiovanni (Ed.). *Supervision of Teaching*, Alexandria, VA: ASCD.

Weiick, K. E. (1982). Administering schools in loosely coupled schools. *Phi Delta Kappan*, 27, 2:673–676.

· 49 ·

ECONOMIC FORCES
AFFECTING SUPERVISION

John Smyth

FLINDERS UNIVERSITY OF SOUTH AUSTRALIA

INTRODUCTION

From a cylindrical core capped by a great glass dome four cell-blocks and two work-blocks radiated away at sixty degree intervals like spokes from the hub of a giant wheel. Beneath the dome was a central watch-tower from which a spectator could enjoy a clear view down the central walkway of all four cellblocks. The block roofs were mounted on smooth granite walls that overhung the top tiers by twenty feet. The kingposts, tie beams and rafters of the roof were constructed of wrought iron and covered with extravagant sheets of thick green glass. Through the glass streamed the all-seeing light of God: a permanent surveillance that induced in the cowering inmate a state of conscious and permanent visibility, and ensured the automatic functioning of power. Looking outside from the window of his cell the convict could see the encircling walls with their resident riflemen; from the bars of his door he saw the central observation tower with its cameras and guards. At night his cell was illuminated by a dim green bulb and the walls and walkways by spotlights. A man entering Green River said goodbye to darkness for the duration of his stay. Darkness permitted at least the illusion of privacy and invisibility, places where a man might try to reconstruct some sense of his own individual existence. Because the inmate was constantly visible he could never be sure whether he was being spied upon or not and thus became his own warder, perpetually watching himself on his jailor's behalf. Green River was an architecture of power built upon the paranoid fantasies of the guilty.

Tim Willocks, Green River Rising (1994)

In reexamining the changing nature of supervision in schools we are dealing with something that bears a strong resemblance to the changing architecture of power portrayed in the novel, *Green River Rising*. It is not that classrooms are coming to be constructed like prisons, for that is clearly not the case, rather, the way power is becoming sedimented into the structures and the processes of the way we lead our lives leads to the kind of metaphorical self-policing that is becoming increas-

ingly self-evident in the enactment of supervisory processes in schools. The similarity lies in the pervasive way in which supervision, thought about in terms of its language and its discourses, exerts an all-pervading force in shaping the nature of the way teaching is, and is thought about.

What constitutes supervision in schools is undergoing rapid change (see Smyth, 1991a), as is our understanding of what constitutes schooling and its role in contemporary society. It is impossible to understand something as complex as the changes currently being visited upon supervision in schools without also understanding something of the wider forces making things the way they are (Sultana, 1993, makes this point compellingly in respect of Europe). School supervision is undergoing some dramatic changes at the moment, but there is also implicit within supervision some extraordinarily strong tendencies towards continuity (Smyth, 1987). In other words, the more things change the more they stay the same.

It would be too simplistic an explanation to say that there is a deterministic set of relationships at work for something as complex and controversial as supervision. As George Herbert Mead (1934) put it, we are simultaneously the products as well as the creators of our history. In the field of supervision this means that wider forces both shape what is happening to supervision as a process and a practice, but what transpires under the rubric of supervision in schools also exerts a reciprocal shaping influence on the kind of society in which we live and work, and what we regard as valuable and important. This notion of the "praxis" of supervision is by no means new: As policy makers, researchers, and practitioners of supervision we have always had a strong sense of the way in which educational action impinges on, and is in turn influenced by, our theories of supervision and how theoretical predispositions are informed through the process of living out supervision in actual educational contexts. It is the mutual reciprocity of that lived relationship and how school people contextualize it, continually

1173

modifying what is feasible, practicable, and just, that makes supervision such a fascinating subject of study.

This chapter is intended as an excavation of the broader forces that are currently having a bearing on shaping the work of supervision (see Smyth, 1995, for a more detailed discussion of this), and to comment on what might be the likely effects of this on supervision as a practice and as a field.

As such my approach will be wide-ranging, and to some readers it may appear somewhat polemical, and for that I make no apology, but it is well to know that from the start. The issues I am trying to struggle with are diffuse and certainly not easy to come to grips with; consequently they require a different kind of treatment. At least in the early part of the chapter, I shall stylistically summarize large tracts of literature with which the reader may be unfamiliar, by a series of points. I do this rather than engage in detailed and complex discussion of ideas; after all, it is the tenor and direction I wish to point to in this chapter and the way in which I see this as a different way of framing what is happening in school supervision.

There will be four parts to the chapter: (1) the process of economic globalization; (2) the effect of global restructuring on the redefinition of education; (3) the consequences for teachers' work; and (4) the role of supervision in the changes to teachers' work. The essence of the argument is that supervision is changing radically and we need to be apprised of the wider genesis of these changes if we are to properly understand what is happening to the field.

THE PROCESS OF ECONOMIC GLOBALIZATION

The opening argument to this chapter is that we are currently experiencing some worldwide forces that are dramatically changing fundamentally the way we think and conceive of schooling, not to mention supervision. The economic epicenter of the world is rapidly shifting to the Pacific Rim and the Americas, in a context of massive international repositioning and restructuring. Spurred on by vastly improved means of information technology, instantaneous communication, and a capacity of international capital to move around the world at short notice to take advantage of local circumstances (i.e., cheap labor), this has meant that corporations as well as governments are faced with unprecedented levels of volatility, uncertainty, and unpredictability demanding quite different kinds of responses in terms of work organization and workplace skills. Among other things, these new circumstances are characterized by:

- flexible post-Fordist forms of production and restructured workplace organization;
- a greater reliance on market forces as a mode of regulation, rather than rules, regulations, and centralized bureaucratic modes of organization;
- more emphasis on image and impression management as a way of shaping consumers;
- a recentralization of control in contexts where responsibility for meeting production targets is devolved;

- resorting to increasingly technicist ways of responding to uncertainty; and
- a greater reliance on technology as the preferred means for resolving complex and intractable social, moral, and political problems.

Without going into it in any detail at this point, suffice to say that in schools as in industrial enterprises generally, these changes constitute quite a different regulative framework for the exercise of social control. We are now witnessing a worldwide dramatic shift of the boundaries of control from direct, overt, and bureaucratic forms of surveillance, to much more covert forms that take expression in the nature of the way in which work itself is being restructured. The "just-in-time" and "total quality management" processes touted in the management literature are particular cases in point. The very success of processes like these rely on somewhat more self-regulative procedures that are predicated on an intensification of work practices brought about by the harnessing of peer pressure through "teamwork" and "partnerships" aimed at responding to "customer needs," eliminating waste, and generally promoting a culture of continuous improvement (Delbridge, Turnbull, & Wilkinson, 1992). We are experiencing the emergence of these trends in schools through so-called processes of "empowerment" and the creation of schemes like "lead teachers" (Ceroni, 1995; Ceroni & Garman, 1991).

Decisions and steerage in contemporary capitalism, therefore, is increasingly being removed from the control of national (and democratically elected) governments, and placed into the hands of transnational economic forces that operate largely outside of the scope of government and which are accountable only to their head offices in London, New York, or Tokyo. This process of global economic rearrangement is producing a new international economic order as well as generating new international divisions of labor, and new and unstable settlements and sets of social forces that are time specific.

Castells (1989) argued that there are really three identifiable aspects to this wider economic restructuring: (1) a fundamental realignment of the relationship between capital and labor, such that capital obtains a significantly higher share in the benefits of the fruits of production; (2) a new role for the state in the public sector, which is more about changing of the style of government intervention in the economy, rather than a reduction of its role; and (3) a new international division of labor in which low-cost labor is profoundly shaping what is happening in the "developed" world.

There are a number of outcomes occurring regarding the first of these contemporary trends that might best be summarized as follows:

- higher productivity through technological innovation;
- lower wages, reduced social benefits, and less-protective working conditions;
- decentralization of production to regions of the world with more relaxed labor and environmental restrictions;
- greater reliance on the informal economy (i.e., unregulated labor);

- restructuring labor markets (to take growing proportions of women, ethnic minorities and immigrants); and
- weakening trade unions, which is the single most important factor in restoring the level of profits (Castells, 1989, pp. 23–25).

As to the second, Castells (1989) argued that we are not witnessing the withdrawal of the state from the economic scene; rather, we are seeing the emergence of a new form of intervention whereby new means and new areas are penetrated by the state, while others are deregulated and transferred to the market (p. 25). He saw this emerging redefinition of the role of the state as embracing:

- deregulation of many activities, including relaxation of environmental controls in the workplace;
- shrinkage of and privatization of productive activities, in the public sector;
- regressive tax reform favoring corporations and high income groups;
- state support for high-technology research and development and leading industrial sectors;
- priority and status for defense and defense-related industries;
- shrinkage of the welfare state; and
- fiscal austerity with the goal of a balanced budget.

These changes do have implications for the way in which schools are organized and administered, and these, along with their implications for supervision, will be addressed in later sections of this chapter.

Third, the opening-up of new markets through global expansion (or "internationalization") has been possible as a consequence of several noticeable developments:

- industry taking advantage of the most favorable conditions anywhere in the world;
- capital taking advantage of "around-the-clock capital investment" opportunities; and
- homogenizing markets, and making up market loss in one area through increases in another (pp. 26–28).

All of these have quite pronounced implications for schools, how they are organized, and what transpires within them.

THE EFFECT OF GLOBAL RESTRUCTURING ON THE REDEFINITION OF EDUCATION

The role and function of education is undergoing dramatic change in response to these economic imperatives. The notion of a broad liberal education is struggling for its very survival in a context of instrumentalism and technocratic rationality where the catchwords are *vocationalism, skills formation, privatization, commodification,* and *managerialism.* In circumstances like these, education "comes under the gun" because it is simultaneously blamed for the economic crisis

while it is being held out as the means to economic salvation—if only a narrow, mechanistic view of education is embraced.

The changes that are afoot are not ones that emerge either out of the heartland of education or from strictly pedagogical and curriculum matters. Rather, they are about how best to control education by making it do its economic work by changing the ideology as well as the discourse of schooling through reinvigorating notions like human capital. Coupled with this is a worldwide move towards recentralizing control over education through national curricula, testing, appraisal policy formulation, profiling, auditing, and the like, while giving the impression of decentralization and handing control down locally. The image of education is also revamped by reconfiguring the work of teaching so that teachers appear more as delivers of knowledge, testers of learning, and pedagogical technicians. The reality is that the work of teaching is increasingly routinized and proletarianized as teachers are subject to the discourses as well as the practices of managerialism: tighter control by outsiders, better forms of accountability, more sophisticated surveillance of outcomes, and greater reliance on measures of competence and performance.

THE CONSEQUENCES FOR TEACHERS' WORK

In all of this there are a number of quite contradictory tendencies shaping the work of teachers. At precisely the same time external forces are seeking to take a larger role in determining what counts as teaching, teachers are also being exhorted to exercise more control at the local level over what it is they do (Goodman, 1994). This recentralization within a rhetoric of devolution is difficult to reconcile, at least on the surface.

For example, in Australia, as well as in their equivalents in other parts of the world, there are:

- National Curricula, in the form of National Subject Profiles and Statements;
- Key Competencies, Standards, and Skills Formation;
- Performance Appraisal, Performance Management, and Performance Indicators;
- daily exposure to educational aerosol words like excellence and quality, which are the latest bouquet words to be sprayed around over our ever-so-slightly decaying educational institutions;
- a formidable armory of the latest surveillance and control gadgetry being foisted onto schools, teachers, and the work of teaching, like:
  - curriculum audits;
  - educational review units;
  - school charters;
  - mission statements;
  - strategic reviews;
  - profiles;

- benchmarks;
- line management;
- leaner organizations;
- quality assurance;
- advanced skills assessment;
- measurement of outcomes;
- total quality management;
- corporate managerialism; and
- international best practice.

Without going into matters in any detail, it is becoming clear that teachers' work is increasingly being subjected to a range of forces:

- It is being constrained by the intrusion of external agencies who require that schools operate in the "national interest," a claim that is invariably couched in the economic imperative of increased international competitiveness.
- The fiscal crisis of the state is reducing funding to schools, in contexts in which schools are exhorted to "do more with less."
- The breakdown of other social institutions is occurring at the same time schools are expected to take on a wider and more complex range of functions.
- Control is being recentralized, which has the effect of conveying the message to teachers that they cannot be trusted and that their work is devalued; this happens in contexts in which it is made to look as if teachers are being given more autonomy, self-control, and decision-making power at the school level.
- Schools are expected to operate more like private enterprises (i.e., to market themselves) to compete against one another for students and resources, which are functions that take them increasingly away from the reason for which they exist (e.g., teaching and learning).

All of the matters just alluded to are ones that are obviously ripe with implications for both teachers' and supervisors' work and their working relationships. As a consequence, we have a number of policy initiatives that:

- require teachers to work within more rigidly defined policy frameworks and guidelines, of one kind or another;
- place greater emphasis on determining the worth of teaching in terms of measurable outcomes;
- supposedly make teachers more accountable by linking outcomes to the actions and activities of individual teachers, classrooms, and schools;
- move teachers and schools in the direction of processes that are more appropriate to those of the corporate and industrial sector (e.g., performance appraisal, curriculum audits, or quality assurance); and
- preach that the virtues of education and schooling are no different from any other commodity (i.e., they are to be measured and calibrated according to quality standards; packaged and delivered to targeted audiences; and haggled

over in the artificially constructed user-pays marketplace of education).

On the other hand, there is another set of tendencies and trends appearing to point in the opposite direction. These all have the sounds of pseudoparticipation and quasi-democracy about them:

- devolution;
- competition;
- choice;
- autonomy;
- collegiality;
- collaboration;
- self-management;
- liberation management;
- teamwork and partnerships;
- networking and collegiality;
- flexibility; and
- responsiveness.

While the tendencies just listed might look and sound as if they are about giving teachers more control over their work, and it is true in some cases that they do, it is more a matter of appearances in most instances. There is a substantial contradiction. The work of teaching is increasingly brought under the influence of politicians, policy makers, and the captains of industry at the same time that claims are made that teachers and schools should take greater control of their own destiny:

- deciding on local priorities;
- exercising greater self-management;
- breaking away from expensive and inefficient bureaucratic forms of organization; and
- making schools into leaner organizations able to be more responsive.

Hargreaves and Dawe (1990) said that teachers are being urged "to collaborate more, just at the moment when there is less to collaborate about" (p. 228). Their words have a remarkable ring of authenticity about them. As one cynic put it, it feels like "school-based management emerged just when schools [around the world] were about to go broke." Processes of self-management, which was introduced in this kind of economic climate, can be about what Stephen Ball (1993) from the University of London has described as "the self-management of decline," rather than about enhancing the work of teaching. In the United States, where similar processes are afoot,

school-based resources and decision-making have been narrowed, not expanded. School-based councils feel "empowered" only to determine who or what will be cut. So fights fall along predictable lines of teachers versus parents . . . administrators versus teachers (Fine, 1993, p. 696).

This is all shrouded in confusion and contestation as teachers struggle hard with the ascendancy of management principles that would redefine and control the nature of their work.

How are we supposed to make sense of such contradictions, and what do they mean? How come schools, and the work of teaching, are being pulled in these opposing directions?

To summarize the argument so far, it is clear that economic restructuring worldwide has produced a remarkably similar set of circumstances that are characterized by uncertainty, unpredictability, volatility, and shrinking tax bases as multinationals move off-shore, loss of national sovereignty, and situations of virtual ungovernability in which democratically elected governments no longer have any real control over transnational economic agencies such as multinational corporations (Taylor-Gooby, 1994, p. 398).

Faced with circumstances that can only be described, at best, as that of "overload," governments have had to retreat, mostly from areas in which they have traditionally been providers (e.g., education, and a range of other public services). They have had to off-load these responsibilities onto the private sector. Where that has not been possible, they have had to convince the private sector (in order to have it continue to pay the bills), that public enterprises will be organized along the lines of those in the private sector. That is to say, governments have engaged in trade-offs with private enterprise in deals that have been struck to deliver skilled (and compliant) labor, in return for a further reduction in already shrinking tax bases. Part of the deal has been the government hardening its regulatory functions (directions, guidelines, and frameworks), while at the same time appearing to be fair and just by allowing for autonomy, flexibility, creativity, self-management, and responsiveness, and with all of this at a distance, while maintaining overall steering and setting of directions, as Kickert (1993) has noted!!

In schools, this means:

- giving schools and teachers responsibility to implement local decisions, but within firmly prescribed guidelines;
- allowing schools discretion over expenditures, but in an overall context in which real resources are shrinking, and where centrally provided services are being wound down through the dismantling of educational bureaucracies;
- fostering the notion that it is fair (and indeed "good") for schools to compete against one another (i.e., that the efficient will survive, and that competition will cause the rest to lift their game or go out of business) regardless of whether they are all operating on a level playing field or not;
- devolving responsibility for achieving learning outcomes, but within a context of accountability, where resources are tied to demonstrating the achievement of guaranteed targets; and
- redefining, at a policy level, who are the "consumers" of education so that there is a much closer connection between education and industry (i.e., industry is now the customer, and in the logic of the marketplace, the customer is always right, and we have to keep the customer happy).

The very nature of the work itself complicates whether (and in what ways) teachers are losing control of their work. Connell (1989) summarized this nicely when he said, regarding the task and circumstances of teaching:

[It] is a labor process without object. At best, it has an object so intangible—the minds of kids, or their capacity to learn—that it cannot be specified in any but vague and metaphorical ways. A great deal of work is done in schools, day in and day out, but this work does not produce any things. Nor does it, like other white collar work, produce visible and quantifiable effects—so many pensions paid, so many dollars turned over, so many patients cured. The "outcomes of teaching," to use the jargon . . . are notoriously difficult to measure (pp. 123–124).

Connell argued that the popular image of teaching as "talk-and-chalk in front of a class" (p. 124) is extremely misleading. Connell said that views like this fail to understand that teachers' work is like an "ever-receding horizon"—it is just never complete. That is to say, there is "no logical limit to the expansion of an individual teacher's work" (Connell, 1989, p. 125). He took a concrete example and examined it: a teacher talking at the blackboard, which is far from the standard approach to teaching. Although not apparent to the naked eye, as Connell (1989) suggested, it contained a complex interdependency of tasks:

- time spent preparing the lesson;
- time spent getting the class settled and willing to listen;
- time spent supervising exercises and correcting them;
- keeping order;
- dealing with conflicts between children;
- having a joke with them from time to time and building up some personal contact;
- discussing work with them individually;
- planning lesson sequences;
- preparing handouts and physical materials;
- collecting, using, and storing books and audiovisual aids;
- organizing and marking tests and exams;
- keeping records; and
- liaising with other teachers.

Most of this has to be done separately for each class—and that's for a conventional form of teaching !!! What about outside of the classroom?

- supervising kids in playgrounds, at the canteen, during sporting events, onto transport, on excursions;
- planning and arranging swimming carnivals, athletics days, football and netball matches, geography excursions, biology excursions, and so on;
- drama workshops, concerts, gymnastic displays, fetes, speech days, bingo nights;
- going to parent/teacher nights, parents and citizens association meetings, union meetings, staff meetings, department meetings;
- organizing and getting facilities for, and supervising, the school magazine, the chess club, the camera club, the debating team, the students' council, the end of class disco, the farewell to year 12;
- making school rules, policing them, administering punishments;

- being class patron (year teacher, form mistress, house master, team or grade leader) and coordinating information about members of the class, doing pastoral work, checking rolls, answering queries;
- counseling pupils in trouble, and dealing with personal crises, sexual and ethnic antagonisms, and bullying;
- sometimes dealing with agitated parents, welfare officers, police;
- modifying curricula, bringing programs up to date, integrating new materials;
- getting familiar with new techniques, new machines, new textbooks;
- attending in-service conferences and courses on new curricula;
- planning and taking kids on camps, bushwalking, canoeing, swimming; and
- writing end-of-term and end-of-year reports, final references, and other official documents.

This, Connell (1989) said, is far from a full tally!!

Little wonder that teachers are working as taxidrivers, insurance sales people, computer consultants, and the like. I am not surprised by Ashenden's (1989) quip that "army recruiters going into schools fishing for students report catching teachers instead" (p. 11).

An article in an Australian newspaper described what a teachers' working week looked like, from the inside:

- classroom teaching, 18 hours;
- in-school preparation and supervision, 8–10 hours;
- meetings, 3 hours;
- take-home preparation and marking, about 25 hours; and
- co-curricular activities and sport, 4–6 hours.

total: between 50 and 60 hours a week (Muller, 1993)

SUPERVISION AND CHANGES IN TEACHERS' WORK

Supervision has long been touted as being for "the improvement of instruction," as if that somehow made it immune from critical scrutiny. St. Maurice (1987) showed how even widely invoked and supposedly enlightened forms like clinical supervision (Cogan, 1973; Goldhammer, 1969) fail to adequately take account of (or be cognizant of) their own discourses of power, and how they operate to regulate teaching. The missing element, he claimed, is discussion of matters relating to power. Questions like the following are completely ignored or glossed over:

What is made into data, for whose purposes?
Whose power and truth are implicit in the analyses?
What do the notions of improvement mean to the teacher, the supervisor, and the regimes under which they live? (p. 244).

Because processes like clinical supervision fail to question their own power relations (Smyth, 1985; Smyth, 1986), St.

Maurice (1987) argued, what is reproduced is a methodology for "improving instruction" that emulates and is replete with the hierarchy and power relations of clinical medicine:

The teacher is asked to interact, but as a reclining patient in submission to the power of words, symbols, and tools that examine and claim to cure what may or may not be simply seen and felt. By first dissecting instruction into behaviors, then diagnosing the causes and treatments for events lived by the teacher and students, the clinical supervisor exercises an exclusive authority to name what goes on in classrooms. A face-to-face encounter with these clinicians is stacked in favor of the face that claims expert knowledge, its own language and systems of symbols, and tools that convey the power of truth (p. 246).

This is not to suggest, however, that teachers are completely helpless or powerless because there is scope for opposition and resistance even in such situations:

The gaze is assymetrical: the subject-as-object may seem powerless to gaze back and question its majesty and authority: to do so would be called inappropriate, unrealistic, and against improvement. Such resistance, and the invasive responses reserved for it by the eye of power, must be investigated elsewhere. At this point, it is enough to say that recognizing the gaze of power, and calling it by name, is the vital first step towards opposition (pp. 246–247).

Waite (1993) showed how supervisory encounters no longer need be viewed as "a one way phenomenon, an imposition of supervisory control on the docile teacher. . . . Although supervisors enjoy a privileged position in conferences . . . teachers' resources are not to be underestimated" (p. 697). Waite suggested that supervision that recognizes its own implications of power works in ways in which supervisors "quit blaming teachers . . . [and] simultaneously examine the micro and macro contexts and processes influencing teaching and learning" (p. 698). He said that they need to focus on supervising "contexts" rather than "teaching behaviors" (p. 698).

Yet, at the same time, however, history cannot be completely denied. Indeed, the history of teaching in America has long been one of supervision being the managerial tool for controlling the work of teaching so as to ultimately harness schools to industry. Whereas in England, as Eisner (1991) has noted, there had been a history of "inspectors" being involved in describing and understanding what transpires in classrooms so as to report on their strengths and weaknesses, the mode in the United States had been very different at least until the 1960s:

American models of supervision have been rooted in the industrial world. The cult of efficiency, as Callahan (1962) reminds us, was America's early effort to reduce teaching to a practical routine. The task of the supervisor, like that of a boss on the assembly line, was to see to it that the job was done right, and this meant according to specifications. Time and motion study became the method through which school productivity could be increased, since it was believed to optimize the workers' (teachers') efficiency by eliminating wasted motion (p. 12).

St. Maurice (1987) put the same point in even harsher terms:

the history of the American teaching "profession" is a story of laborers whose skills were defined entirely by management, struggling for power in classrooms under the eye of supervisors empowered to describe and judge every aspect of their work (p. 252).

Against this backdrop the role, purpose and definition of supervision become quite different from what they have been in the past. We can no longer regard supervision as being benign and apolitical, rather, it is riddled through and through with all manner of complex social, political, moral, and ethical questions (Smyth & Garman, 1989). Those of us involved in supervision, therefore, have an awesome responsibility to be reflexive of our own agenda. Supervision is not a branch of management. As such, it ought not to be concerned with the simple reproduction of other people's agenda. Those of us who research and practice in this area have a duty to pose and to seek answers to certain crucial questions:

- what's worth teaching ?
- who says ?
- in what ways ?
- why are some ways of teaching superior to others ?
- how is knowledge to be represented ?
- whose interests are served (and whose denied) through particular representations ?
- how can schools be made better places of learning, while being more socially just ?
- what kind of educational structures are most appropriate?

These, and questions like them, are fundamental questions that go right to the heart of the educational enterprise. They are not questions that can or should be left on the periphery to politicians or their minders, nor are they questions that are central to teaching and classrooms. As such, they lie squarely in the domain of supervisors and those who research the supervisory process in schools. They are questions that are at one and the same time contestable, provocative, perplexing, and uncomfortable. Above all, they are also generative and offer hope and possibility about how schools might be different, when not construed solely in econometric terms.

If schools are to be more than factories engaged in the mindless production of compliant labor, then we need teachers imbued with a strong sense of what it means to be a teacher in a genuinely self-determining school: That means leadership of a supervisory kind that is rapidly being extinguished at the moment. Teachers need passionate advocates who have a profound understanding of what kind of places schools are. They need allies prepared to take a stance against the economic moguls who say schools are primarily cost centers concerned with budgets, forms of testing, and conduits through which to redress unfavorable balance of payments.

We need supervisors prepared to:

- resist the conversion of fundamental moral and political questions into technical and administrative problems (Mac an Ghaill, 1991, p. 310);
- listen to teachers' voices more and publicly defend them against the shrill cries from the captains of industry;
- work in ways that both acknowledge and loudly celebrate teachers' theories of what works, and why;

- get the word out that teaching is a form of "intellectual struggle" (Reece, 1991), and put to rest forever the notion that teaching is mere technical work;
- demand that teachers be treated in more trusting ways, which means showing that teachers are indeed in control of what they do, and that they have workable ways of being accountable to one another;
- convince a skeptical public and a hostile media that when students do not learn as well as might be expected, we should be less hasty in pointing the finger at teachers, and look more closely at the context within which teachers work, and ask if they are being properly supported;
- make the point that curriculum should be constructed around the "lived experiences" of children and teachers, rather than crafted around national profiles that are allegedly aimed at making us more internationally competitive, or that aim to reduce the balance of payments;
- promote the circumstances in our schools in which teachers feel comfortable with and compelled to call into question the basic assumptions about teaching and learning, and to radically change those assumptions if experience tells them otherwise; and
- make the point resoundingly that teaching and schooling ought to be about engaging with the big questions that fire the imagination, the spirit, the feelings, and the intellect (adapted from Clifford & Friesen, 1993).

As we work these issues through as supervisors in our schools, the bottom line has to be:

- less measurement against standards of performance, and more concern with ways of enabling teachers to connect with the lives of their students;
- counteracting mindless administrative and managerial incursions into teachers' classrooms that have no educational foundation to them;
- seeing the ways in which teachers' voices are being progressively silenced in the debates about school reform, and how the media hype about accountability is being used as a way of legitimating managerialism; and
- forms of engagement with teachers that provide them with an active, informed commentary on one another's teaching, while helping them to appreciate the complexity, the contradiction and the confusion accompanying change (Smyth, 1991b, p. 75).

POST-FORDIST MODE OF SUPERVISION

One of the major consequences of this post-Fordist turn in the way we regard and organize our work relationships is that what had previously been overt forms of control have now become much more covert. Another way of putting it is that processes like supervision, which have historically been held in place by notions of bureaucratic and hierarchical authority, are rapidly coming to be replaced by forms of control that are embedded in the structure of work itself. I can make this point more directly by an illustration from Halberstam's (1986) *The Reckoning*, which is the story of the transformation of the U.S. automobile industry:

In the early eighties, American executives, because of joint production deals, were often visiting Japanese [automobile] factories, and they were finding out how good the Japanese were, especially at the basics. One executive who had made the trip and reached that conclusion a decade earlier was Hal Sperlich, then of Ford. Touring a Japanese auto factory in the early seventies, he had noticed that there were no repair bays alongside the [production] line, areas into which defective cars in the process of assembly were pulled for fixing.

"Where do you repair your cars?" Sperlich asked the engineer with him.

"We don't have to repair our cars," the engineer answered.

"Well, then," Sperlich asked, "where are your inspectors?"

"The workers are the inspectors," his guide answered (p. 716).

This example illustrates that post-Fordist production and forms of flexible specialization (and most schools are coming to be increasingly swept up in image and impression management in the attempt to capture so-called niche markets) are heavily implicated in the processes of shifting responsibility and blame (but not real power) closer to the workface or point of production. We can see this most graphically in the worldwide move to devolve educational administration to schools, while stoically ensuring that control is maintained or even intensified at the center through processes, guidelines, policy frameworks or the like. Supervision has not disappeared—it has merely undergone a profound transformation.

Waite (1995) has grappled with this in terms of "dialogic supervision" through an attempt to re–embed "supervision within the contexts of change." Drawing on Giddens (1990), Waite contended that schools exist within contexts of "radicalized modernity" and that as a consequence the "practices of conventional supervision are coming to be seen as increasingly inappropriate ways to deal with teachers, instruction, etc." (p. 2), largely because supervision as a process suffers from the dual crises of "scientific certainty and objectivity" and of "representation." As to the first, Waite said that "even as we gain some measure of understanding of social phenomenon, we change the phenomenon because of our understanding" (p. 4). As to "representation," Waite claimed that what gets portrayed or represented through the lens of conventional supervisory practices of "observing a lesson," "analyzing the data," and what is talked about as data in the "postconference," goes through a series of highly selective processes of partialling out of certain things, including others, while all the time giving the outward appearances of not doing so. He said that:

These reductionist practices, whether intended or not, serve particular aims and ignore or exclude others. . . . This is so because . . . classrooms are busy places, cognitively and perceptually dense. No one can see all that goes on in the classroom, and some of what goes on is invisible. . . . What finally gets discussed in a supervision conference is reduced still further. . . . Further reductionism is occasioned by the interactional face-to-face processes of the conference itself. Usually, the supervisor shares or reports the data from the observation to the teacher. . . . The teacher may respond. . . . Seldom is the teacher allowed to speak his or her mind. . . . Even in the most col-

laborative of conferences, it is the supervisor's data that frames the interaction (pp. 8–9).

The contrast is between supervision based on "authoritative discourse" (i.e., for monitoring, surveillance and control) that is monologic, and dialogic approaches to supervision (i.e., for growth and reflection) that are based on "internally persuasive discourse" that embody the language and perceptions of others. The latter is embedded in "reflections on one's practices and beliefs" (p. 22) that approximate "a moral conversation" (p. 29) in that "everything is held open to scrutiny and question" (p. 31).

Kell (1994) presented a portrayal of the way in which the "schools-as-factories" metaphor has been framed and held in place for nearly 180 years through notions of surveillance and supervision, even though the exact mode may have changed. Like Hartley (1992) and Miller (1988), he attributed modern notions of surveillance to Bentham's nineteenth-century notion of the panopticon: "an observation point which was a series of radial segments housing prisoners with a central observation point where a lone guard could supervise large numbers of prisoners" (p. 6). Hartley (1992) noted that the most significant feature of the panopticon was that "those being observed would not know if they were being observed at a given time" (p. 33). Bentham also believed that schools should be run along similar lines with a heavy emphasis on what he termed the "constant and universal inspection principle" and the "constant superintendency principle" (Kell, 1994, p. 6). Bentham's contributions were not limited either to prisons, poor houses, or asylums—his major contribution to education was through his book *Chrestomathia*, published in 1816, with its focus on "quality," "functions," and "performance," making it remarkably contemporary in flavor. Rather, he focused on "saving money," "saving time," "information-gathering," "record keeping," and having the teacher teach the student to an "agreed standard," which are all notions that were remarkably ahead of their time, if current trends are any indications. Bentham's ideas as they relate to education can best be summed up in his three principles of "hierarchical observation," "normalizing judgment," and "the examination" (Miller, 1988).

As Kell indicated, whereas school administration and supervision has since passed through the Tayloristic process of scientific management in which the tasks of schools are broken down into smaller and smaller fragments (i.e., through segmentation, measurement and quantification) in the illusory pursuit of efficiency and standardization, the current reform and restructuring, with its emphasis on "performance" and "indicators," has become the new embodiment of panopticism and surveillance. According to Hartley (1992), current preoccupations with a technocratic view of education, including "competence," "performance," "standards," and "appraisal," can all be directly traced back to Bentham and the disciplinary devices that came to govern the way prisons operated (and still do).

For current purposes, the most important legacy of Bentham's ideas is that "more and more, the 'observer' resides within ourselves. No longer are we ordered to comply; rather our consent is managed. No longer are we disciplined in the coercive sense; rather we discipline ourselves" (Hartley, 1992, pp. 34–35). The new technology of control and supervision is much less person-oriented. It is more of a kind that works through "slogan systems" (Apple, 1986) such as those in vogue at the moment (i.e., competencies, standards, learning outcomes, skills testing, curriculum audits, and performance indicators). Dow (1994) argued that:

Educational outcomes have entered our language at about the same rate as the notion that educational and economic objectives are linked. Whether there is any evidence to link the economic performance of a nation with the achievement of educational outcomes is a moot point, but there is little doubt that there is a powerful mythology about the link between an effective school system and a competitive economy (p. 1).

He claimed that outcomes, as a form of supervision, operates in two ways: The first is through the metaphorical equivalent of the central office military flyover:

These outcomes are a bit like the full size wood and canvas mockups of armored tanks used in warfare. If [head office] flies over the school in his or her spotter plane, he or she will see rows and rows of fierce looking outcomes nested in action plans and teachers' classroom plans, all pointing pugnaciously at the "targeted groups" cowering on the margins of the educational landscape (p. 2).

The second way in which the ideology of outcomes and performances works is through the language and discourse of schooling. According to Dow (1994) if you want to have a job, or to advance up the promotion ladder, then you have to mouth the rhetoric:

If you want a job in a promotion position these days you need to have an "outcomes orientation," and the achievement of outcomes has joined the ranks of the really important organizational mantras to be chanted in job interviews (p. 2).

Dow noted that we have become "entranced" and "mesmerized" by these ideas because of their seeming common sense and rationality, as well as what looks like their capacity to help educational administration escape from its history of "vagueness and untidiness" (p. 2). Setting targets, standards, and indicators in advance, and then checking later to see whether or not they have been achieved, sounds compellingly simple, which is precisely what we need in contexts of enormous uncertainty, confusion and complexity. Whether or not it actually works, is irrelevant; it is important that it gives the impression of being capable of doing so.

The suggestion here is that the personage of the supervisor, while important, may become less so as technologies of control have an increasing influence on shaping what occurs in schools and classrooms (Smyth, 1990). Whereas the kind of semantic mapping undertaken by Waite (1994) of "what supervision is?" and "what supervisors do" are useful, they are by no means the full story because of the risk they run of portraying even supervisors as having more real power then they in fact have. It is encouraging to hear of the possibilities of a "paradigm shift" in the direction of a more democratic style of supervision (Waite, 1992), but I suspect that such shifts might

be more illusory then real when the wider view is taken. We are increasingly experiencing processes, procedures, and technologies of control that are embedded in the work of teaching in ways that make face-to-face forms of supervision something less consequential.

An illustration of what this looks like in terms of how supervision works via technocratic/standardized curriculum is presented by Shanks (1994) in an ethnographic account of a primary school that was required by its new superintendent to move from teachers being in control of the curriculum (e.g., constructing it around the needs and interests of the students) to one in which supervisory processes were used to implement a "standardized" curriculum "structured for individual engagement." The teachers had previously operated in ways in which "curriculum guidelines" were used as "resources for planning," to a situation in which all teachers had to have a common set of objectives, textbooks were purchased for each subject, and "tests provided by the textbook companies . . . based on the textbooks" (p. 48). Shanks (1994) summed up the manner in which supervision-by-curriculum standardization impacted on the students, in the following ways:

The pattern was part of the "keep busy" ethic that helped the classrooms run smoothly. As long as the students looked occupied and did not cause any disturbances, they did not cause problems for their teachers. . . . As a result, they were subjected to a de-skilling process. "De-skilling is part of a long process in which labor is divided and then redivided to increase productivity, to reduce 'inefficiency,' and to control both the cost and impact of labor" (Apple & Weiss, 1983). The standardized curriculum effectively placed technical controls on students and their actions in order to increase "productivity"—as measured by test scores—and hopefully, to reduce inefficiency. The technical controls simplified the students' labor by dividing learning concepts into discrete elements. . . .

Students went step by step through the learning process in assembly-line fashion. Their progression through the steps lacked interaction with other students and teachers. They worked alone to complete the required assignments but had little incentive to do any additional work since they lacked control over it. The requirement for minimum achievement did not foster in-depth work in any curricular area.

Students . . . acted like factory workers who did only what they were told to do . . . they perceived learning and school simply as work to be done . . . work did not relate to their individual needs and interests, and it required neither their attention nor their involvement (pp. 56–57).

CONCLUSION

The focus on this chapter, unlike most of the others in this handbook, has been on the broader economic, political, and social forces working to shape supervision, and how what is meant by supervision is becoming redefined through what is happening to teachers' work through forms of wider global restructuring underway. The claim is made here that social control of teaching is being exercised less and less through face-to-face forms of supervision, although that has by no means disappeared (see Roberts, 1994), but rather through technologies of control (Smyth, 1990) that are becoming, at one and the same time, more distant and yet embedded in the work of teaching. While there are some productive sides to this in terms of teachers being urged to be more "reflective" and to operate with one another in more "collegial" ways (and even these have considerable downsides, see Smyth 1989a; Smyth, 1991c), in the final analysis many of these differ little in their final effect from "indirect" forms of control (Lawn & Ozga, 1986), which are increasingly being exercised through centralized curricula, outcomes-based education, forms of performance-based mea-sures, and testing. As I have argued elsewhere (Smyth, 1989b), if teachers are to be involved in genuinely liberating forms of teaching, then we need "an alternative vision and an 'educative agenda' for supervision as a field of study" one that is less con-cerned with grading, inspection, and quality control, and that is more inclusive of teachers and students as major actors in describing, becoming informed about, confronting, and recon-structing (Smyth, 1992) both the *practices* and the *surrounding wider context* within which teaching and learning occur.

REFERENCES

Apple, M. (1986). *Teachers and texts: Political economy of class and gender relations in education*. Boston, MA: Routledge & Kegan Paul.

Apple, M. & Weis, L. (Eds.). (1983). *Ideology and practice in school-ing*. Philadelphia, PA: Temple University Press.

Ashenden, D. (1989). Chucking the chooks: Restructuring the educa-tion industry. *Education Australia, 7*, 9–10.

Ball, S. (1993). Culture, cost and control: Self-management and entre-preneurial schooling in England and Wales. In J. Smyth (Ed.). *A socially critical view of the self-managing school* (pp. 63-82). London, England: Falmer Press.

Callahan, R. (1962). *Education and the cult of efficiency*. Chicago, IL: University of Chicago Press.

Castells, M. (1989). *The information city: Information technology, and the urban-regional-process*. Oxford: Blackwell.

Ceroni, K. (1995). Promises made, promises broken: A literary criti-cism of the Pennsylvania lead teacher programme). Unpublished doctoral dissertation, University of Pittsburgh.

Ceroni, K. & Garman, N. (1991, February). *The empowerment move-ment: Genuine collegiality or yet another hierarchy?* Paper to the International Teacher Development conference, Vancouver, pp. 14–16.

Clifford, P. & Friesen, S. (1993). A curious plan: Managing on the twelfth. *Harvard Educational Review, 63*(3), 339–354

Cogan, M. (1973). *Clinical supervision*. Boston, MA: Houghton Mifflin.

Connell, R. (1989). The labor process and the division of labor. In B. Cosin, M. Flude, & M. Hales (Eds.). *School, work and equality* (pp. 123–134). London, England: Hodder and Stoughton.

Delbridge, R., Turnbull, P., & Wilkinson. (1992). Pushing back the frontiers: Management control and work intensification under JIT/TQM. *New Technology, Work and Employment, 7*(2), 97–106.

Dow, A. (1994, November). *What's wrong with outcomes? A discus-sion of the impact of the focus on second order consequences in education*. Address to the Northern Adelaide Principals' Network, Adelaide.

Eisner, E. (1991). *The enlightened eye: Qualitative inquiry and the enhancement of educational practice*. New York: Macmillan.

Fine, M. (1993) [Ap]parent involvement: Reflections on parents, power and urban public schools. *Teachers College Record, 94*(4), 682–710.

Giddens, A. (1990). *The consequences of modernity*. Stanford, CA: Stanford University Press.

Goldhammer, R. (1969). *Clinical supervision: Special methods for the supervision of teachers*. New York: Holt, Rinehart, and Winston.

Goodman, J. (1994). External change agents and grassroots school reform: Reflections from the field. *Journal of Curriculum and Supervision, 9*(2), 113–135.

Halberstam, D. (1986). *The reckoning*. New York: Avon.

Hargreaves, A. & Dawe, R. (1990). Paths of professional develop-ment: Contrived collegiality, collaborative culture, and the case of peer coaching. *Teaching and Teacher Education, 6*(3), 227–241.

Hartley, D. (1992). *Teacher appraisal: A policy analysis*. Edinburgh: Scottish Academic Press.

Kell, P. (1994). Educational administration: Taking care of business. *Education Australia, 28*, 5–7

Kickert, W. (1993). *Steering at a distance: A new paradigm of public governance in Dutch higher education*. Department of Public Administration: Erasmus University, Rotterdam. Unpublished man-uscript.

Lawn, M. & Ozga, J. (1986). Unequal partners: Teachers under indi-rect rule. *British Journal of Sociology of Education, 7*(2), 225–238

Mac an Ghaill, M. (1991). State-school policy: Contradictions, confu-sions and contestation. *Journal of Education Policy, 6*(3), 299–313.

Mead, G. (1934). *Mind, self and society*. Chicago, IL: University of Chicago Press.

Miller, P. (1988). Factories, monitorial schools and Jeremy Bentham: The origins of the "management syndrome" in popular education. In A. Westoby (Ed.). *Culture and power in educational organiza-tions* (pp. 43–55). Milton Keynes: Open University Press.

Muller, D. (1993, November). Schools' turbulent year ends but new angst looms. *The Age*, 20.

Reece, P. (1991). Teachers' work as intellectual struggle. *Critical Pedagogy Networker, 4*(1), 1–5.

Roberts, J. (1994). Discourse analysis of supervisory conferences: An exploration. *Journal of Curriculum and Supervision, 9*(2), 136–154.

Rumberger, R., & Levin, H. (1984e). *Forecasting the Impact of New Technologies on the Future Job Market*. Stanford, CA: Institute for Research on Educational Finance and Governance, School of Education, Stanford University.

Shanks, J. (1994). Student reactions to a standardized curriculum: A case study. *Journal of Curriculum and Supervision, 10*(1), 43–59.

Smyth, J. (1985). Developing a critical practice of clinical supervision. *Journal of Curriculum Studies, 17*(1), 1–15.

Smyth, J. (1986). Clinical supervision: Technocratic mindedness, or emancipatory learning. *Journal of Curriculum and Supervision, 9*(4), 331–340.

Smyth, J. (1987). Cinderella syndrome: A philosophical view of super-vision as a field of study. *Teachers College Record, 88*(4), 567–588.

Smyth, J. (1989a). A critical pedagogy of classroom practice. *Journal of Curriculum Studies, 21*(6), 483–502.

Smyth, J. (1989b). An alternative vision and an 'educative' agenda for supervision as a field of study. *Journal of Curriculum and Supervision, 4*(2), 162–177.

Smyth, J. (1990). Teacher evaluation as the technology of increased centralism in education. In C. Bell (Ed.) *World yearbook of edu-*

cation: *Assessment and evaluation* (pp. 237–257). London, England: Kogan Page.

Smyth, J. (1991a). Instructional supervision and the redefinition of who does it in schools. *Journal of Curriculum and Supervision, 7*(1), 90–99.

Smyth, J. (1991b). *Teachers as collaborative learners: Challenging dominant forms of supervision.* Milton Keynes: Open University Press.

Smyth, J. (1991c). International perspective on teacher collegiality: A labor process discussion based on teachers' work. *British Journal of Sociology of Education, 12*(4), 323–346.

Smyth, J. (1992). Teachers' work and the politics of reflection. *American Educational Research Journal, 29*(2), 267–300.

Smyth, J. (Ed.). (1995). *Critical discourses on teacher development.* London, England: Cassell.

Smyth, J. & Garman M. (1989). Supervision-as-school reform: A 'critical' perspective. *Journal of Education Policy, 4*(4), 343–361.

St. Maurice, H. (1987). Clinical supervision and power: Regimes of instructional management. In T. Popkewitz (Ed.). *Critical studies in teacher education: Its folklore, theory and practice* (pp. 242–264). New York: Falmer Press.

Sultana, R. (1993, November). *Conceptualizing teachers' work in a uniting Europe.* Paper to the Third International Teacher Development Conference on "Teachers Reclaiming Teaching," Adelaide.

Taylor-Gooby, P. (1994). Postmodernism and social policy: A great leap backwards? *Journal of Social Policy, 23*(3), 385–404.

Waite, D. (1992). Supervisors' talk: Making sense of conferences from an anthropological linguistic perspective. *Journal of Curriculum and Supervision, 7*(4), 349–371.

Waite, D. (1993). Teachers in conference: A qualitative study of teacher-supervisor face-to-face interaction. *American Educational Research Journal, 30*(4), 675–702.

Waite, D. (1994). Understanding supervision: An exploration of aspiring supervisors' definitions. *Journal of Curriculum and Supervision, 10*(1), 60–76.

Waite, D. (in press). Understanding supervision: Re-embedding supervision within the contexts of change. In *Re-thinking instructional supervision: Notes on its language and culture.* London: Falmer Press.

Willocks, T. (1994). *Green River Rising.* London, England: BCA.

·50·

CULTURAL, ETHNIC,
AND GENDER ISSUES

Geneva Gay

UNIVERSITY OF WASHINGTON

INTRODUCTION

The ultimate purpose of teaching and supervision is to improve the academic performance of students. This task is becoming more problematic and pressing as disparities in the academic performance of students of color and European Americans, and between males and females continue largely unaffected from one generation to another. The increasing ethnic, racial, cultural, linguistic, and social diversity of the U. S. student population further complicates the issue. It is far less appropriate now than ever before to think of school achievement problems only in terms of European and African Americans, and the three Rs. Students from no ethnic group are doing as well in school as they could, and all are negatively affected in some way by the total complex of educational disparities. A case in point is the proficiency test scores in the academic core subjects. No ethnic groups at any age tested reached the level designated by the National Assessment of Educational Progress (NAEP) as "advanced level proficiency" in reading, writing, math, science, history, geography, or literature.

Supervisors need to have a thorough understanding of all of these issues if they are to succeed in helping teachers work better with diverse students toward improving their school achievement. This knowledge may be facilitated by analyzing the research and scholarship on how gender and ethnicity affect the educational opportunities, experiences, and outcomes of students. These findings can then be used to make teaching and supervision more gender sensitive and culturally responsive.

These purposes and assumptions give focus and direction to the discussion in this chapter, which begins with a brief presentation of the conceptual framework and philosophical assumptions that contour all subsequent analyses. This is fol-

lowed by an explanation of the current achievement status of students by gender and ethnic groups. It is offered as evidence of the need for radical changes in the educational services available to students who are marginalized in mainstream society and schools because of being female or persons of color.

The greater portion of the chapter is devoted to reviews of research and scholarship that provide some reasons for why discrepant ethnic and gender achievement patterns persist. The discussion is organized around three types of explanations. The first deals with curriculum differentiations by ethnicity and gender. The second examines research and theory about interactions between students and teachers in classrooms. The third discusses cultural traits of different ethnic and gender groups that may influence their educational opportunities and outcomes. These three issues (i.e., curriculum differentiations, classroom interactions, and cultural diversity) are assumed to be both pivotal obstacles and opportunities to improve the achievement of students of color and females.

In the last part of the chapter some implications for supervisory practice, extrapolated from the research on ethnicity and gender, are discussed. The suggestions made comprise the major anchor points of the general proposal for culturally responsive and gender sensitive supervision. A belief that teachers and supervisors should establish collaborative and reciprocal partnerships to design and implement educational reform for cultural diversity permeates all other ideas.

FRAMING THE ISSUES

Disparities in educational opportunities and outcomes correlate highly with the ethnicity and gender of students, which is a fact that is both persistent and paradoxical. Its persistence

1184

is apparent in academic patterns that prevail across time, place, level of schooling, subjects and skills, and types of assessment measures. This fact is paradoxical because achievement disparities continue largely unabated despite years of attempts at remediation in the midst of a culture that claims commitment to educational equity and excellence for *all* students.

Reasons abound for these achievement patterns and paradoxes. They cover the spectrum from genetics on one extreme, to the suspect validity of the measures used to assess academic achievement for culturally diverse students, to a deliberate conspiracy of educational institutions not to educate certain students, to discontinuity between the cultures of schools and some ethnic groups. Three streams of argument reoccur. First, achievement outcomes are related directly to resource allocations. Of these, "human resources" may be even more important than material and fiscal ones for directly impacting student performance. Second, there is a high correlation between kinds of learning opportunities students receive and the levels of their achievement outcomes. Third, the processes of teaching and learning that go on in classrooms are crucial, if not the ultimate, places where achievement quality is determined. In other words, the appropriateness and effectiveness of instructional strategies for culturally diverse students, as well as the quality of the personal relationships that exist between students and teachers, have significant effects on academic achievement.

On the other hand, educational programs and practices that are not *culturally embedded* in that they do not incorporate the experiences, contributions, and perspectives of females and ethnic groups of color are morally suspect, cognitively invalid, and pedagogically questionable. After all, one of the most basic functions of schools is socialization, of which an essential element is to transmit to students their cultural heritages and legacies. Pai (1990) described this as the *enculturative* function of education. It should operate in conjunction with the other key component of socialization, which is *acculturation*. This is achieved in schools by teaching all children the national mainstream culture. Cultural knowledge and self-affirmation also facilitate achievement in the academic subjects and skills for females and students of color. They are filters through which abstract concepts and ideas are made personally meaningful, and they provide the courage that is often required to pursue learning (AAUP Report, 1995; Banks & Banks, 1995; Grossman & Grossman, 1994; Hollins, King, & Hayman, 1995).

These observations have led to proposals that educational equity and excellence for female and ethnically diverse students are contingent upon curriculum, instruction, and performance assessment being *gender sensitive and culturally responsive*. These aspects of schooling must incorporate the wide range of diversifying factors that characterize the U. S. student population at the levels of policy, content, and process. Gay (1993) borrowed the concept of *segmented marketing* from business and industry to further explain this idea. It means using specifically designed strategies for targeted segments of consumers to enter into their circles of trust, and thus better market products and services to them, as well as increased sales. In the educational arena, culturally respon-

sive teaching is analogous to segmented marketing; learning is the "product" or "services"; females and students of color are "targeted and segmented consumers of learning." As a result, accepting the legitimacy of cultural pluralism, and modifying teaching styles to synchronize them with different ethnic learning styles are as important as including the contributions of ethnic groups and females in the content of different subjects. Others (Bennett, 1995; Banks & Banks, 1995; Shade, 1989) code these proposals as the *need for multicultural education* to permeate teaching and learning for all students in all subjects and school settings. Issues of diversity based in ethnicity, gender, social class, and language are of particular significance in culturally responsive or multicultural education.

A similar explanation applies to supervision. It, too, must be gender sensitive and culturally responsive if it is to be appropriate and relevant to the culturally pluralistic issues, challenges, and populations in today's and tomorrow's schools. At the heart of culturally responsive supervision is understanding why and how teaching, learning, and supervising are not culturally neutral, objectifiable, or transcendent processes. As Bowers and Flinders (1991) explained, however, everything that goes on in the classroom is pervasively influenced by the cultural backgrounds, experiences, and orientations of the participants. The responsibilities of supervisors, and the degree to which they are successful in meeting them, are determined in large part by their understanding of how cultural values, language, and behaviors influence the classroom activities of students and teachers, as well as their own. This seems to be a reasonable expectation because the supervisory function, according to Sergiovanni and Starratt (1993), encompasses moral, ethical, and technical dimensions. The role of supervisors is to help teachers do the right things better in order to best serve the needs of the students whom they teach. To do this well, supervisors must guide, teach, monitor, model, and mentor the teachers with whom they work.

This is the position taken and developed in the remainder of this chapter. It assumes that familiarity with the findings of research and scholarship about the cultural effects of ethnicity and gender on the educational process is a prerequisite for developing culturally responsive and gender-sensitive supervision and instruction strategies. These effects are discussed first in relation to how academic achievement is distributed among ethnic groups and by gender, second by how access to knowledge is differentiated by gender and ethnicity, and third by how classroom interactions between students and teachers are similarly affected.

ACHIEVEMENT PATTERNS

National trends in academic achievement are documented by annual and longitudinal reports published regularly by educational and governmental agencies. Among them are the NAEP "report cards" on proficiency in reading, writing, math, science, U. S. history, literature, and geography; *The Condition of Education* and the *Digest of Education Statistics* by the National Center of Education Statistics; and the

Statistical Abstract of the United States by the Bureau of the Census. Research projects conducted by scholars in local school sites and scholarly publications further substantiate the general trends presented by these national documents. A case in point is the *Handbook of Research in Multicultural Education* (Banks & Banks, 1995). The most prominently used data base for determining levels of academic achievement is scores on a variety of standardized tests.

These data sources indicate that European-American males tend to perform higher than do their female counterparts, and all other ethnic groups, male or female, on most measures of educational achievement. The most recent reports, based on data collected in 1992, show how general patterns of academic achievement commonly associated with gender are manifested across specific indicators. One of these is the higher proficiency levels of females in reading and writing for grades 4, 8, and 12. The same was true for the 1986 report card in literature. Twelfth-grade males performed better than females in math, but the achievement of fourth and eighth graders was comparable. The science achievement of males in all three age groups was greater than it was for females, and the gap increased as students advanced through school. Males had higher scores in U.S. history and geography, which were last tested in 1988 (*The Condition of Education*, 1994). Whereas these data are important and revealing, they are also limiting because they are not completely disaggregated by ethnic groups. Achievement information specific to American Indians and Asian Americans is frequently not included in data analyses. These "categorical data" also make it impossible to discern how males and females within different ethnic groups are performing in the various academic areas. Gender differences within ethnic groups are almost never reported in the NAEP report cards.

The achievement of ethnic groups in 1992 continued a long-established pattern. European-American students consistently perform much better than do students of color. The possible exception to this pattern is Asian Americans on some achievement measures. For example, Asian Americans scored better on the 1993 Scholastic Aptitude Test (SAT) than did European Americans in math by 41 points (535, compared with 494); however, they scored lower on the verbal portion of the test by 29 points (415 to 444) (*The Condition of Education*, 1994). It is difficult to determine, with much certainty, if these patterns persist in the academic skills because separate data for Asian-American performance in reading, writing, math, science, history, and literature are not provided in the latest statistical summaries reported in documents from the National Center for Education Statistics. This is also the case with Native Americans. These voids are attributed to the numbers of students from these groups in national education studies being too small to permit reliable and valid generalizations (*Characteristics of American Indian and Alaska Native Education*, 1995).

For the other two major ethnic groups of color on which data are routinely available, African Americans consistently have the lowest levels of achievement across time and in all academic skills areas. The performance of Latinos is slighter better, but not significantly so. The gaps between the achievement levels of these two groups of color and their European

American counterparts continue to be alarmingly large, and they tend to increase the longer students stay in school. In 1992, the differences in the science scores of African and European American 9-, 13-, 17-year olds were 39, 43, and 48 points, respectively. The gap for Latinos was 34, 29, and 34. Similar patterns existed in math, reading, and writing, but the range of the differences across ethnic groups was somewhat smaller, and there was some variance by age level as well. In math the Black-White gaps for 9-, 13-, and 17-year olds were 27, 25, and 26 points, compared to Latino-White gaps of 23, 20, and 20 points. (*The Condition of Education*, 1994; *NAEP 1992 Trends in Academic Progress*, 1994). In these areas 13-year-old Latinos and African Americans seemed to be making more progress toward closing the achievement gaps between themselves and European Americans than were their older and younger counterparts.

In reading, which is considered a prerequisite skill to successful performance in all other academic and intellectual tasks, only 25, 28, and 37 percent, respectively, of fourth, eighth, and twelfth graders reached the proficiency level on the 1992 assessments. The National Assessment Governing Board (NAGB) described "proficiency" in reading as the ability to understand literal and inferential information included in narrative text, and declared it the achievement level that all students should reach. In general, European and Asian Americans, students in advantaged urban areas, and females had higher reading proficiency levels than did Latinos, African Americans, American Indians, residents of disadvantaged urban and rural areas, and males. A summary of these achievement distributions for reading by grade, ethnicity, and gender is presented in Table 50–1.

As these data show, no ethnic group in any age category achieved a score of 300, which NAEP has established as the beginning cutoff point for a proficiency level in reading. Females performed higher than males by 8, 13, and 10 points in grades 4, 8, and 12. This pattern of gender advantage also prevailed at the other two achievement levels (i.e., by 10, 12, and 10 percent for grades 4, 8, and 12 for the basic levels, and 2 percent at each grade for the advanced proficiency levels). Differences in the reading performance of ethnic groups

TABLE 50–1. 1992 Reading Achievement Levels*
by Gender and Ethnicity

	Grade 4	Grade 8	Grade 12
ETHNICITY			
European Americans	226	268	297
African Americans	193	238	272
Latinos	202	242	277
Asian Americans	216	270	291
Native Americans (Indians)	208	251	272
GENDER			
Females	222	267	296
Males	214	254	286

*Average score on a scale of 0 to 500.

Source: Mullins, I. V. S., Campbell, J. R., & Farstrup. A. E. (1993). NAEP 1993 reading report card for the nation and the states. Washington, D.C.: U. S. Department of Education, National Center of Education Statistics.

ranged from 36 points (i.e., lowest African Americans; highest European Americans) for fourth graders to 30 points for eighth graders and 25 points for twelfth graders. In almost all grades the achievement of African Americans was lower than other groups of color, and that of Asian Americans was the highest. The one exception occurred in grade 12, where the scores of Native and African Americans were identical (Mullins, Campbell, & Farstrup, 1993; *NAEP 1992 Trends in Academic Progress*, 1994).

Four other disturbing trends are evident in these achievement profiles of females and students of color. First, no notable improvement has occurred in reading achievement since 1984 for any grade level, gender, or ethnic group. Second, in 1992 the level of reading proficiency was the lowest of all subjects for all groups, at almost every age level tested. The only exceptions were 17-year old African Americans and Latinos whose reading scores were slightly higher than their science scores. Their math scores were much higher than were their reading scores, by 25 and 21 points, respectively. Third, the overwhelming majority of students at all ages and from all ethnic groups are not performing at the advanced intellectual levels in any of the subjects tested. In 1992 only European-American twelfth graders achieved a score above 300, and only in math and science (*The Condition of Education*, 1994; *NAEP 1992 Trends in Academic Progress*, 1994). This is the score (on a range of 0 to 500) that the NAEP has established as indicative of the ability to demonstrate higher-order critical thinking and problem-solving skills, understand complex reading information, and write detailed, reasoned explanations to support claims and assertions. Fourth, the achievement levels of twelfth-grade African Americans are often lower than those of eighth-grade European Americans. This is true in science, reading, and writing. Their scores in math and history are higher, but not significantly so.

When available, data on gender patterns of educational attainment within ethnic groups show that these are not as consistent as those by ethnicity across groups. They vary by age, ethnicity, socioeconomic status, type of achievement indicator, and levels of schooling. The AAUP Report (1995) on *How Schools Shortchange Girls* provided several substantiations of these patterns. Among them are: (1) lower class girls have better test scores than their male counterparts in the elementary grades, but this advantage disappears by high school; (2) high socioeconomic boys from all racial and ethnic groups have better overall test scores than girls; (3) girls receive better subject grades than boys, regardless of ethnicity or economic status; (4) on NAEP reading assessments boys perform as well as girls on the expository passages, but lower on the literary ones; (5) boys read more nonfiction, while girls read more fiction; (6) gender disparities in math and science achievement tend to increase with the age of students and the complexity of skills; and (7) females who reject traditional gender roles have higher achievement in math than those who do not.

National reports usually do not disaggregate achievement data by gender within ethnic groups; however, several individual researchers have provided some analyses for various groups of color. In their summary of these, Grossman and Grossman (1994) report that:

- African-American, Latino, Asian-American, and European-American females develop verbal and visual–spatial skills earlier than do males, and they achieve higher test scores on them in both elementary and secondary schools.
- The gender gaps in elementary mathematics favor European, African, and Latino American females, but not American Indians. In high school no consistent gender gaps exist within ethnic groups on complex mathematical skills and word problems. There are, however, some indications that African- and Asian American females score better than do their male counterparts, while the reverse is true for European Americans.
- African American females perform better than males in science.

Paradoxes also exist across and within patterns of educational attainment for gender and ethnic groups. Schools are often criticized for their feminine ethos and ambiance, especially at the elementary levels, which would logically seem to facilitate higher achievement levels for females, yet this is not the case for all subjects. Females generally perform better in reading, writing, and literature, which are subjects traditionally thought to be "feminine." Males do better in the "masculine" subjects of math, science, history, and geography (*Digest of Educational Statistics*, 1994; Grossman & Grossman, 1994; Klein, 1982; Maccoby & Jacklin, 1974).

Some students of color, notably African-American males, are awarded and graded in classroom performance more for their social than academic competencies. One would expect, then, that they would have fewer problems with the social adjustments demanded by schools; instead, the reverse is true. African-American males have some of the highest dropout rates (exceeded only by Latinos) and disciplinary referrals of all ethnic groups (*The Condition of Education*, 1994). Asian Americans are often believed to be so successful in school that they are a "model" to be emulated by others. This is more myth than reality. In fact, their performance profiles are more bipolar than being consistently high for all subgroups within this ethnic category, vary by achievement measures, and are affected by socioeconomic status similar to other ethnic groups. Disproportionate numbers of Japanese, Chinese, and Korean Americans perform highly in math and science, but their achievement is very low in reading, writing, verbal, and social relations skills. Their persistence rates in school are very high, and their disciplinary problems are low. Low socioeconomic Asian-American students do not perform significantly better in reading and math than do other poor ethnic groups. Many Vietnamese, Thai, Cambodian, and other immigrants are experiencing major adjustment, achievement, and attendance problems in schools (Osajami, 1991; Yu, Doi, & Chang, 1986).

Educational critics and advocates alike point out that the achievement gaps between European Americans and students of color are declining, largely because of improvements made by the latter. The overall gains made are too small to have any noticeable effects on the patterns themselves. Furthermore, the achievement levels of all students continue to cluster in lower-level academic skills. None demonstrate higher-order thinking and problem-solving abilities in any of the subjects and skills routinely tested.

These achievement patterns and problems identify areas that should be targeted for change in educational reform. The AAUP Report (1995, pp. 4–5) explains how imperative these needs are with respect to gender equity:

Serious consideration of girls is not merely a matter of justice; it is an issue of economic survival and basic common sense. . . . To leave girls on the sidelines in discussion of educational reform is to deprive ourselves of the full potential of half of our work force, half of our citizenry, and half of the parents of the next generation. . . . By studying what happens to girls in school, we can gain valuable insights about what has to change in order for every student–every girl and every boy—to do as well as she or he can. Our children–and our nation deserve nothing less.

A similar case can be made for ethnicity. As West (1993) poignantly, yet so simply declared "race matters" in adequately assessing the perils and potentials of groups in U. S. society and institutions.

The question remains: How does one achieve more educational equity for females and students of color? The answer is dependent upon the reasons behind the achievement patterns—what is or is not happening in the processes of teaching and learning to cause the academic performance of ethnic and gender groups to be as it is. Until these explanations are revealed and understood, how to proceed with carefully planned and target-focused reform agendas that will improve the school achievement of females and students of color will continue to mystify educational leaders.

GENERAL EXPLANATIONS FOR ACHIEVEMENT DISPARITIES

Knowledge of the differential achievement patterns and trends of students of color and females is essential to making education more equitable for them; however, it is not sufficient. Genuine reforms address the *reasons* why these occur. Their quality and effectiveness are linked directly to the adequacy of the explanations provided for why the problems exist. Several general ideas have emerged from the massive, and continually growing, body of research, and theoretical scholarship on educational inequity based on gender, race, and ethnicity.

One explanation suggested is that teachers are driven by malicious racist and sexist intentions. This was a prominent theme in the early phases of the ethnic studies, multicultural education, and gender equity movements. It is less so now. Arguments have shifted more and more toward acknowledging that teachers are often as victimized as their marginalized students by the institutional ethos of schools that are strongly race, gender, and culturally biased in favor of Eurocentric, middle class, male experiences and perspectives.

Another explanation is that students of color and their parents are responsible for their failure problems. They lack the kind of motivation, initiative, aspirations, perseverance, and skills it takes for high-academic achievement in schools. This kind of reasoning underlies the National Center for Education Statistics explanations for why American Indians, Latinos, and African Americans exhibit lower levels of achievement on test scores in science and mathematics. It attributes causality to the large percentage of students of color with poverty backgrounds; the low-educational and high-unemployment levels of their parents; high discipline and safety problems in the schools they attend; the lack of persistent efforts and active involvement in school on the part of students; and the absence of rigorous academic curricula (*Understanding Racial-Ethnic Differences in Secondary School Science and Mathematics,* 1995).

This type of reasoning continues a tradition of what Ryan (1971) called "blaming the victims." He described this as "an ideological process, which is to say a set of ideas and concepts deriving from systematically motivated, but *unintended* distortions of reality" (p. 10). It places the onus of social inequalities on the individuals who are most negatively affected by them rather than on the institutional structures in which they live. Ryan (p. 60) explained applying this idea to the inequities that exist in schools for culturally different students:

We are dealing, it would seem, not so much with culturally deprived children as with cultural depriving schools. And, the task to be accomplished is not to revise, and amend, and repair deficient children but to alter and transform the atmosphere and operations of the schools to which we commit these children. Only by changing the nature of the educational experience can we change its product. To continue to define the difficulty as inherent in the raw material—the children—is plainly to blame the victim and to acquiesce in the continuation of educational inequality in America.

More current variations of Ryan's reference to "culturally deprived" children and "cultural depriving schools" are "at-risk children" and "risk-creating schools." With the exception of this minor adjustment in language, however, his poignant message is as applicable now as it was when he wrote it 25 years ago, and the constituents in whose interest he so argued are the same: children of color and poverty.

A third proposed explanation for disparities in academic achievement by ethnicity and gender is that academic success, like other resources in a competitive, capitalist society, is not limitless. Knowledge is a form of "cultural capital" (Giroux, 1992) and, like other resources, products, and services in the economic marketplace, it is distributed on the basis of merit and ability. In other words, in schools as in the rest of society, "to the victor belongs the spoils," and "the fittest survives the best." In such a society where other opportunities are unequal, schools merely reproduce these inequities in ways that give advantages to middle class, European-American males. Educational programs and practices are distributed in such a way as to perpetuate the hierarchical economic, political, and social systems that exist in society, and the positions of various groups in them (Bowles & Gintis, 1976; Grubb, 1995). This is a strong theme in current feminist, postmodernist, and critical pedagogy critiques (e.g., Giroux, 1992; Hlebowitsh, 1993; Sleeter & McLaren, 1995).

A fourth reason often given for the academic achievement of students of color and females is the nature of their socialization outside of school. This explanation was particularly prevalent in the early phases of the gender equity movement. It contends that the way boys and girls are initiated into sex-role attributions and expectations affects their own academic choices, as well as how curriculum programs are planned and delivered. If girls grow up thinking math is a "masculine" subject, then they avoid it because they do not want to appear "unfeminine." This is most evident in the developmental stages in the life cycle when being "masculine" and "feminine" becomes of major importance for the first time (which coincides with the middle school years). Many researchers (Hoyenga & Hoyenga, 1979; Maccoby & Jacklin, 1974; Wittig & Petersen, 1979) feel this explains why distinct gender differences in preferences and performance by skill areas and subjects (e.g., mathematical, spatial, and verbal abilities) do not appear much before age 11 or 12.

The ethnicity parallel to sex-role socialization is cultural conditioning. Two aspects of this explanation are possible. One is within the tradition of schools replicating society. The other is more transformative and will be discussed later. Within the context of the replication theory is the idea that negative images, evaluations, and expectations of people of color are promoted in society. Students come to school very much aware of how their ethnic groups are viewed. The internalization of these views creates self-fulfilling prophecies. Their ethnic groups are not seen as worthy members who make significant contributions to society, so they continue the tradition by not doing well in school. Students feel they are not expected to and are incapable of high achievement in school because they are American Indian, Latino, or African American, and, therefore, they do not do well academically. Persuasive support for these assertions are presented in *Looking in Classrooms* (Good & Brophy, 1978), *School Achievement of Minority Children* (Niesser, 1986), and the *Handbook of Research in Multicultural Education* (Banks & Banks, 1995). If these claims are true, then the current "at-risk" movement is troublesome and doomed to failure. Despite being cushioned in the ritual of reform, its efforts are framed within an ideology that emphasizes what students do not have and cannot do. "At-riskness," then, can be a form of subtle but powerful socialization that directs students toward school failure rather than success.

Viewpoints that attribute achievement patterns to malicious intentions of educators, lack of parent and student interest in education, and societal replication through traditional sex-role socialization and ethnic biases are nested in negativistic and predeterministic attitudes that are not conducive to positive reform efforts. They indict and blame, and it is most frequently the victims of educational inequities who are the objects of these indictments. Deficit, pathological, and accusatory orientations like these have initiated many compensatory education programs, such as Head Start, Upward Bound, Horizons, and BRIDGE. For the most part, these have been unsuccessful in improving or sustaining the educational attainment of significant numbers of students of color. A case in point is Chapter–1 funded initiatives to provide supplementary instruction in basic skills for students who are economically poor and academically "at-risk." They also often are members of ethnic groups of color. Even after more than 25 years of existence and billions of dollars spent, the academic achievement of the students Chapter 1 serves continue to lag behind that of their middle class counterparts.

Despite major limitations in the power of these kind of explanations to impact academic achievement positively, they do serve a useful "awareness" purpose for some. Lengermann and Wallace (1985) point this out in relation to feminist research and scholarship. They suggest that:

Feminism's critique of gender inequality has made whole sectors of our population 'see' what they had not previously recognized: that masculinity and femininity are associated with a complex system of social relationships, legitimated by distinctive beliefs, and shot through with what some claim is an oppressively unequal treatment of women. However people respond to these facts and claims, they are at least now aware of them (p. 134).

A parallel argument can be made for the ethnicity critique and its success in bringing the inequities groups of color suffer to the consciousness of schools and other social institutions. Awareness alone is not enough for educational leaders to reform schooling to make it more gender sensitive, and ethnically and culturally responsive; therefore, reasons for why long-standing patterns of gender and ethnic achievement persist that offer fresh insights and more positive directions for change are needed.

A more promising explanation (i.e., an alternative paradigm) is that inequitable educational practices are committed unknowingly and unintentionally because educators do not understand the interactive relationship between culture, teaching, and learning. Many teachers are not aware of the pervasive impact of culture on their own and their students' classroom behaviors. Good and Brophy (1978) suggested that teachers are not consciously aware of most of what goes on in the classroom. This unconsciousness may result from the fact that (1) teachers are too busy managing the many things that routinely occur in typical classrooms to think much about what they are doing (Goodlad, 1984); (2) cultural rules and values are normally embedded in behaviors at a level below conscious awareness and control (Spindler, 1987; Au, 1980); and (3) insufficient attention is given to cultural diversity in the professional preparation of educators (Dilworth, 1992; Phelan & Davidson, 1993).

Even teachers who are consciously aware of their classroom behaviors think they are doing what is best for all students. They do not realize that what they consider to be "normal and standard" ways of relating are culturally embedded, and not universally shared by all students (Bowers & Flinders, 1991). Pai (1990) contended that even those teachers who agree in principle that educational practices are shaped by particular sociocultural contexts "are not always clear and precise about the myriad ways in which cultural factors influence the processes of schooling, teaching, and learning" (p. v). When educators use only their own cultural criteria for regulating and interpreting the learning behaviors of culturally different students, they may be systematically creating guarantees of educational inequality. This lack of knowledge about and appreciation for how culture affects teaching and learning leads to unsound educational policies, ineffective school practices, and unfair assessment of learners (Banks & Banks, 1993; Pai, 1990). Shinn (1972) added that cultural insensitivity can negatively affect self-concepts, augment alienation, heighten social maladjustment, and encourage rebellion among culturally different students. Education that is not multicultural consequently has *comprehensive, destructive* consequences for students, and not just academic ones.

The existence of discontinuities and mismatches between the home cultures of diverse students and the culture of schools offer a sixth explanation for why ethnic disparities in school achievement persist. How individuals are socialized in their various ethnic groups and cultural communities does not match well with school attitudes, values, and behaviors that lead to high academic performance. The contentious issues are often more procedural and structural than substantive (Cazden, John, & Hymes, 1985; Alexander, Entwisle, & Thompson, 1987; Spindler, 1987). That is, *how* individuals from different cultures go about mastering and demonstrating learning is more variant than *what* they deem is worthy of learning. *Cultural ignorance, insensitivity, and incompatibilities* are therefore critical reasons why discrepancies exist in the educational opportunities and outcomes of females and students of color. This is the position taken by most multiculturalists and advocates of gender equity. Ladson-Billings (1994, 1995a, 1995b), Hollins, King, and Hayman (1994), Gay (1993), Shade (1989), and Spindler (1987) suggested that if cultural discontinuity is the militating force that stands in the way of diverse students achieving high levels of learning, then it is incumbent upon educators to understand the cultural traits of different groups, and to use them as leverages for change toward improving instruction and achievement.

Each of these possible explanations for discrepancies in the academic achievement of different ethnic and gender groups need to be examined thoroughly. This task is beyond the scope of this chapter. Instead, only three of them are explored in depth. They are curriculum differentiations, teacher expectations and interactions, and cultural characteristics and discontinuities.

CURRICULUM DIFFERENTIATIONS

The kinds of courses taken by females and students of color, and the substantive content about ethnicity and gender included in courses taught, have profound effects on achievement. If students are not exposed to equal status, high quality, socially desirable subjects and content, then this will have negative effects on their academic performance, social adjustment, personal perceptions of self, and other long-range consequences, such as postsecondary education and employment opportunities. Access to courses also pose significant challenges and invitations to reforming education to achieve academic equity and excellence for females and members of different ethnic groups. These general issues are examined further by looking at course-taking patterns, tracking, textbooks, and effects of equity curriculum reforms.

Course-Taking Patterns

According to data reported by *The Condition of Education* (1994) females in 1992 earned more high school course units in academic subjects than males (18.0 compared with 16.9), and fewer in vocational subjects (3.6 compared with 4.0). The

distributions of academic units earned by ethnic groups favored Asian (18.5) and European (17.6) Americans. By comparison American Indians compiled the least academic credits (16.0), followed in sequence by African Americans (16.7) and Latinos (16.9).

Ethnic and gender course-taking patterns within curriculum categories are another source of documentation for discrepancies in access to equal status knowledge. The *types* of courses differ significantly. A study of achievement status of African Americans conducted by the College Entrance Examination Board (*Equity and Excellence*, 1985) reported that they take less course work in mathematics, physical sciences, and social studies than do European Americans, and that the content of the courses taken is less intellectually challenging. While African Americans take courses like general, business, and remedial math, their European American peers take algebra, geometry trigonometry, and calculus. Similar patterns are evident for American Indian, Latino, and European American females from low socioeconomic backgrounds for math as well as for science. Their enrollments tend to be highly clustered in general science and biology, and much lower in chemistry and physics. Differences also exist among groups in foreign language courses taken. For instance, in 1992 at least 75 percent of college-bound European American graduates had taken two or more years of a foreign language in high school compared with 60 percent of their African American peers (Education Testing Service, 1989; Grossman & Grossman, 1994; *The Condition of Education*, 1994).

Content differentations also surface in vocational and computer science courses. The types and numbers of curricular offerings available in both of these areas favor economically advantaged communities and European Americans. Data from the AAUP Report (1995) indicate that schools with large concentrations of poor students teach 40 percent fewer vocational courses than do middle- and upper-class schools. European-American females and students of color (female and male) tend to enroll in vocational courses that train for low-status, low-paying jobs, such as cosmetology, clerical and secretarial, cabinet making, retail sales, building maintenance, and television repair. By comparison, European-American males enroll in vocational courses that offer managerial training, business finance, and industrial arts skills. These patterns seem to cut across ability levels. Even though the enrollments of gifted and talented students from all ethnic and gender groups are disproportionly underrepresented in vocational courses, they conform to other established trends.

Some researchers such as Archer (1984) and Canale and Dunlap (1987) feel that these vocational course-taking patterns reflect gender socialization, ethnic career aspirations, socioeconomic status, and the age of students. Grossman and Grossman (1994) offered additional support for these assertions. Their comprehensive review of gender issues in education shows:

Beginning in preschool, males and females tend to aspire to gender-stereotyped occupations and careers. Females are less likely to aspire to mathematics, science, or engineering careers. In comparison to African American, Hispanic American, Southeast Asian Americans, and working-class European American males, females, including those who are gifted and talented, aspire to less prestigious and lower paying occupations that typically do not require a college degree. This is especially true of females who have more traditional views of gender roles . . . [and] younger children because females' career aspirations become less gender stereotypical as they advance from kindergarten through high school (Grossman & Grossman 1994, pp. 26–27).

Students from low socioeconomic backgrounds, especially those of color who attend schools where their ethnic groups predominate, also have less access to microcomputers. Their computer teachers are less qualified, and their use of the computer as an instructional tool is restricted largely to drill and practice on basic literacy skills. European-American students, particularly males, take more computer courses and are encouraged to develop skills that relate to programming (*Equity and excellence*, 1985; Farmer & Sidney, 1985; Grossman & Grossman, 1994; *The Condition of Education*, 1994; Winkler et al, 1984; Oakes, 1985).

A study conducted by Linn (1985) in California illustrated these trends. Of the high school students surveyed, females represented 86 percent of all students enrolled in word-processing classes, but only 37 percent of those were in computer programming. Students' choices of computer courses may be influenced by what Burstyn (1993) called the "masculine model of hierarchy and scientific objectivity" (p. 118) with its emphasis on "structured programming" and "rule-driven systems" (p. 119) that pervades the field of educational technology. Female and male students enrolled in the same computer-programming classes engaged differently with assigned tasks. Turkle and Papert (1990) found that whereas males were concerned most with technical mastery of computer programs in rule-driven ways, females preferred to play with the elements of programs, move them around, and try different arrangements as if they were "words in a sentence, the notes in a musical composition, the elements in a collage" (p. 136). Linn (1985) hypothesized that differences in female and male students' access to computer knowledge and how they engage with the technology reflect gender patterns of leisure use of computers. Females tend not to participate as often as males in computer recreational games. As a result, they may require more explicit rule guidance, and be more reluctant to use the computer in academic tasks. Regardless of the reasons for their behaviors, females tend to take computer courses that are "less likely to foster higher cognitive skills" (Linn 1985, p. 22).

Tracking

Another revealing perspective on the ethnic and gender disparities embedded in curriculum differentiations is offered by research on tracking. In its 1994 report on curriculum differentiation in high schools, the National Center for Education Statistics reported that only 15 percent of the schools it surveyed indicated that they had "traditional tracking policies." Eighty one percent, however, offered core curriculum courses (e.g., math, science, English, social studies) that are differentiated by content, quantity and intensity of work, and expectations for individual tasks (*Curricular Differentiation in Public High Schools*, 1994).

The disproportionate representation of students of color in low-level, low-status curricular tracks and special education is a widespread practice. According to the AAUP Report (1995) two- thirds of all students in special education programs are male. The more "subjective" the criteria for diagnosis and the category of referral (e.g., learning disability, behavioral disorders, social maladaption), the higher the representation of males. Harry's (1992) research showed that students of color, except Asian Americans, are overrepresented in all mildly handicapped categories of special education. In the mentally retarded categories their representation is 35 percent, more than double their overall population (16) percentage. In gifted and talented programs they comprise only 8 percent. Because of these disparities, the AAUP Report concluded: "Rather than identifying learning problems school personnel may be mislabeling behavioral problems" (p. 30). Girls and ethnic students who sit quietly in classrooms are ignored; boys and students of color who act out are placed in special education programs that do no meet their needs.

The works of Oakes (1985, 1986a; 1986b) and Goodlad (1984) are indicative of the specific ways in which curriculum tracking impedes educational equity for students of color and females are manifested. Their findings reveal that a hierarchical class order of courses exists in both academic and vocational curricula, with European Americans at the top, and African Americans and Latinos at the bottom. These students "experience school in very different ways" (Oakes 1986a, p.14) because the kind of knowledge and quality of teaching accessible to them are fundamentally different.

To substantiate these conclusions Oakes described differences in academic activities she observed in the 300 high-track and low-track English classes selected from 38 schools throughout the United States. Students in the high-track classes were exposed to "high status knowledge," such as topics and skills required for college, classic and modern fiction, characteristics of literary genres, how to analyze narrative texts, writing thematic essays and research papers, critical thinking and problem solving about challenging and interesting issues, and vocabulary that would increase scores on college entrance exams. Instruction in the low-track classes emphasized basic reading skills and grammar, the use of drill through workbooks and prepackaged learning kits, writing simple paragraphs, filling out application forms, and memorizing facts. Similar discrepancies existed in the mathematics curricula. High-track classes focused on mathematical concepts, whereas low-track ones prioritized basic facts and computational skills (Oakes, 1985).

Anyon (1981) found the same patterns in social studies curricula across different socioeconomic level schools. In working- and middle-class schools, students were taught blind patriotism, and no conceptual tools for analyzing or criticizing U. S. society. Textbooks, assignments, and class discussions emphasized honoring country, upholding laws, and supporting the decisions of leaders. In upper-middle-class and wealthy schools, students were taught critical skills for analyzing society and generating solutions to social and political problems

Discrepancies in the academic skills emphasized led Goodlad (1984) to conclude that high-track courses cultivate a more independent, higher-order thinking type of education. In it self-direction, creativity, critical thinking, active involvement in the learning process, high expectations for achievement, and positive self-esteem for students are prioritized. By comparison, the focus of low-track classes is developing social conforming, rule obedience, and nonacademic types of behaviors that include working quietly, punctuality, cooperation, study skills, and getting along with others. These lead to low self-esteem, low teacher expectations for achievement, and the allocation of more classroom time to behavioral and disciplinary issues. The placement of students in low-track classes "predicts for them diminished access to what increasingly are being recognized as the most satisfactory conditions for learning" (Goodlad, 1984, p. 156). Oakes (1986b) cautioned that these differences should not be treated simply as cases of race and class discrimination. Of greater importance is the fact that

lower-track and vocational programs are often detrimental to the students in them. Ample evidence suggests that placement in these programs begins a cycle of restricted opportunities, diminished outcomes, and growing achievement differences between low-track students and their counterparts in higher tracks. These placements do not appear either to overcome students' academic deficiencies or to provide them with future access to high-quality learning opportunities (p. 150).

Rist's (1970) studies of African Americans from kindergarten through third grade revealed that the castelike grouping of students for instruction begins very early in the educational process and prevails largely unchanged thereafter. Students remained in the same level of reading group to which they were assigned on the eighth day of kindergarten throughout the third grade. This lack of movement across tracks also is documented by Rosenbaum (1976), Persell (1977), and Oakes (1985).

The academic emphases evident in high- and low-curriculum tracks can also be attributed to entire schools. In her own research and others she reviewed, Anyon (1981) observed that elementary schools in different social class neighborhoods taught and rewarded different kinds of work habits and personal attributes. Lower-class schools in both European- and African-American communities discouraged personal assertiveness and intellectual inquiry in favor of rote memory and conformist social behaviors. In middle- and upper-class schools students received more independent assignments, were rewarded for intellectual assertiveness, and engaged in activities demanded by professional and managerial careers (e.g., initiating and setting work priorities, negotiating and solving problems, and making procedural decisions for accomplishing tasks). Oakes (1986b) found that curricula vary among schools according to student populations. Schools with predominately students of color and high poverty levels tend to offer fewer advanced-level classes, more remedial courses, smaller academic track enrollments, and larger general and vocational tracks. By comparison, middle-class schools with largely European-American students offer more college-preparatory courses, science-related classes, and business-focused vocational programs.

In her review of the current educational status of Asian Americans, Pang (1995) pointed out that students are caught up into whatever is the prevailing institutional ethos toward achievement of the schools they attend. Schools plagued with social problems are driven by the need for control, order, and conformity, while those devoted to academics have an ambiance of intellectualism. Both institutional "sets" are shaped by European-American–based notions about how to best meet the needs of different social class, ethnic, and gender groups of students. The commitment to poor and visible ethnic minorities seems to be preparation for being followers, whereas it is directed toward developing leaders, for middle and upper class European Americans. The potential differential effects of these "cultural, academic, and social class "typecasted schools" on student achievement is underscored further by a publication of the National Center for Education Statistics. *Understanding Racial-Ethnic Differences in Secondary School Science and Mathematics Achievement* (1995) reported that in urban communities 50.2 percent of African Americans, 42.4 of Latinos, and 53.1 of American Indians attend disadvantaged schools, compared with 10.9 of European Americans and 20.2 of Asian Americans. The representational patterns are similar for rural areas as well, with 47.2 percent of Latinos, 47.6 of American Indians, and 33.0 percent of African Americans attending disadvantaged schools. The report concluded that "the quality of education in disadvantaged schools is known to be generally less than in other schools. . . . This difference is reflected not only in student achievement but also in teacher attitudes, school practices, and school climate" (p. 19). For example, in disadvantaged schools teachers' morale is lower, and their attitudes, expectations, and actions toward students are less positive, there are fewer teachers from ethnic groups similar to the student populations, and fewer numbers of students enroll in advanced level courses.

Because the practice of tracking by curricular options and schools is so often assumed to be based in rational arguments for accommodating differences in intellectual ability, it is not scrutinized as carefully as it should be for inherent ethnic and gender biases. As a consequence, it can lead schools to "unwittingly subvert their well-meaning efforts to promote academic excellence and to provide conditions that will enable all students to achieve it" (Oakes, 1986a, p. 17). Tracking can exaggerate initial differences among students rather than accommodate and build upon them to improve achievement. It can have long-range and even permanent negative effects for students of color and females.

Several researchers argue that tracking replicates in educational institutions the same kind of class, gender, and ethnic inequities in rights and privileges that exist in society at large. In these, middle-class European Americans, males, and some Asian-American groups receive preferential academic treatment because of differences in the status and quality of the curriculum they encounter compared with other ethnic groups of color and females. Alexander and McDill (1976) found that high school seniors who had comparable achievement levels became increasingly dissimilar in their academic performance and future aspirations after being placed in different curriculum tracks. Adelman (1991), Pollard (1993), and Yu, Doi, and Chang (1986) reported that even females and students of color who take high-status courses and are high achievers in school do not have aspirations for and actual achievement levels of career success equal to those of European American males.

The limited career opportunities and lifetime effects for students who spend their school years in low-track, low status curricula, and who are low achievers, are so persistent, pervasive, and profound that they have become conventional wisdom. Verdugo (1986) and Persell (1977) presented further documentation. They proposed that the curriculum options schools provide are agents of "legitimization" because they reproduce the social, political, and economic power, privilege, and prestige arrangements of society at large. Anyon (1988, p. 184) stated that the work habits and dispositions taught to students in different social classes "lends a circular causality and social legitimacy to a stratified society." The assumption is that the kind of education provided to lower- and upper-class students is justifiable because it is consistent with what they deserve and are capable of doing. Grant (1984) spoke directly to the negative consequences of tracking for African-American females. As a result of the tendency of the first grade teachers she observed to emphasize social skills over academic ones, Grant concluded:

Black girls' everyday schooling experiences seem more likely to nudge them toward stereotypical roles of black women than toward alternatives. These include serving others and maintaining peaceable ties among diverse persons rather than developing one's own skills (1984, p. 109).

Textbooks

How issues of gender and ethnicity are dealt with in instructional content, textbooks, trade books, and other resources is another important indicator of curriculum differentiation. It is also a powerful obstacle as well as an opportunity for improving educational quality, equity, and excellence for students. This is particularly so because of the dominance of textbooks as instructional materials. Woodward, Elliott, and Nagel (1986), Davis et al (1986), and Scott and Schau (1982) reported that as much as 90 percent of classroom instruction is regularly organized around textbooks.

Research on ethnic and gender biases in textbooks date back to the beginning of the twentieth century. It was most prolific during the 1960s, 1970s, and early 1980s. It first began with correcting the blatant stereotypical portrayals of African Americans in social studies textbooks, and gradually extended to include Native Americans, Latinos, Asian Americans, and women, as well as other content materials, such as literature, children's story books, math, science, geography, and basal readers. Factual information, visual images, illustrations, narrative prose, and "overall tone and impressions" have been scrutinized. Ethnic and gender criteria used to analyze instructional materials have moved from being primarily quantitative analyses about numerical inclusions to more qualitative assessments about cultural accuracy, authenticity, and inclusivity. An illustration of the latter are the six indicators Sadker and Sadker (1982) developed to evaluate materials for gender equity: linguistic bias, stereotyping, imbalance, unreality, fragmentation, and invisibility.

For the most part this history of research shows that blatant ethnic and gender stereotypes have been eliminated from textbooks and other instructional materials. The greatest progress appears to have occurred in young children's instructional materials, and in social studies and literature textbooks. While the issue of inclusion for groups of color and females across subjects seem to be largely resolved, the *quality* of their treatment needs further improvement.

These results are not unequivocal. The analyses of illustrations in seven popular elementary science series textbooks conducted by Powell and Garcia (1985) illustrate this point. Both males and females were depicted in a wide variety of science- and nonscience-related careers, but the number of males almost doubled the number of females. Less than 25 percent of the human illustrations represented ethnic groups of color, and they usually appeared in nonscience-occupational roles. This casts a shadow of doubt on the accuracy and authenticity of these portrayals. Higher percentages of males and females were depicted in traditional gender stereotypical roles (e.g., male doctors and managers; female nurses and homemakers). When adult males and females assumed occupational roles in the same illustrations, males were usually given the most prestigious position.

Images of children in science textbooks continue to perpetuate gender-typed roles. Boys are shown in assertive activities such as moving heavy objects, playing physical sports, and generally "doing" actions. The girls are depicted in passive, "decorative," and "observing" activities such as cheerleading, playing dress-up, and self-grooming. These findings led Garcia and Powell (1985) to reiterate the importance of role modeling (i.e., females and students of color seeing representatives of their own gender and ethnic groups in instructional materials). As a result they recommended that in science textbooks,

adult females and minorities should be depicted with greater frequency in a variety of occupational and nonoccupational roles. Such recommended changes would help to reduce stereotypic perceptions of women, minorities, and other societal groups in science and do much to help representatives of these groups perceive science as a field of endeavor (p. 531).

Similar findings and conclusions have emerged from analyses of social studies textbooks. Ellington's (1986) analysis of 12 secondary school economics textbooks revealed that controversial issues were avoided, overly optimistic images of prosperity were presented, and the illustrations of African Americans and Latinos included were largely decontextualized. These messages were conveyed specifically by using a descriptive mode of discourse when topics related to African Americans and Latinos were discussed, ignoring groups that are not prospering economically, including narrative text without any analytical passages, and making few linkages between the photographs of ethnic groups included and related topics discussed. These findings underscore the importance of Ellington's conclusion that "economics texts would be greatly improved . . . [by] the inclusion of even such rudimentary information as race-specific employment data" (1986, p. 66).

A study commissioned by People for the American Way to evaluate 31 eighth- and tenth-grade U.S. history textbooks generated both encouraging and disturbing results (Kretman & Parker, 1986; Davis et al, 1986). A set of eight qualitative criteria were used to conduct these analyses. They were authority, interpretation, significance, context, representativeness, perspective, engagement, and appropriateness. The "representativeness" criterion is particularly relevant to looking at issues of gender and ethnicity. The review panel characterized it as:

Pluralism, equity, and a full sense of identity are apparent in the textbooks; stereotypes and simplism are avoided. The history presented to students acknowledges the experiences and contributions of representative individuals and groups. It offers a positive but not a romanticized sense of Americans' personal and collective roots. Both famous and ordinary people are represented (Davis et al, 1986, p. 15).

For the most part the reviewers concluded that textbooks no longer ignore or obscure the contributions of diverse ethnic groups and women in the history, life, and culture of the United States; however, these books continue to have some major problems, the greatest of which is unevenness in the treatment of various groups and challenging issues. To support these conclusions, Davis et al (1986) pointed out that the coverage given to Latinos, Asian Americans, and American Indians is superficial and fragmentary. Textbooks "perpetuate their invisible roles in building this nation" (Davis et al, 1986, p. 10). The books were also overly concerned with minimizing the violence, conflict, and complexity in the U. S. story. Their narratives unduly stressed civility and compromise, and largely ignored conflicts that existed among the diverse peoples of the United States.

Results from Anyon's (1988) analyses of elementary and secondary social studies textbooks further substantiate these conclusions. These books provided tacit approval of U.S. existing social arrangements, privileges, and power distributions. This was achieved by "omitting social conflicts, misrepresenting realities of economic participation, delegitimating potential economic alternatives, and constraining approved methods of dissent and social change" (p. 185). To the extent that the achievement of equity for marginalized ethnic groups and females requires that the prevailing economic and political order is challenged and transformed, current textbooks continue to be more obstacles to, rather than catalysts for, reform.

McCarthy (1990) provided another telling illustration of how textbooks avoid dealing genuinely with social conflict. He described the perfunctory manner in which many textbooks treat slavery, noting that; they rarely deal substantially with the symbolic and physical violence in the daily lives of slaves, or the cultural genocide and immorality of the institution of slavery. In dealing with more contemporary African-American individuals and issues, textbooks show a clear preference for those who are most in line with mainstream priorities and values. Thus, individuals who challenge society in nontraditional ways (e.g., "militants" who use social change tactics other than voting and nonviolent protest) are ignored or treated disparagingly. In relating these tendencies to women, Tetreault (1985) suggested that the changes are more cosmetic than substantive, and that they inflate the real

progress history textbooks have made in incorporating authentic women's stories.

In her assessment of educational efforts to "integrate" curriculum and instructional materials since the 1954 *Brown v. Board of Education* Supreme court decision, Gay (1979) arrived at conclusions virtually identical to those of Ellington, Davis et al and associates, and Powell and Garcia. Her reasons for being cautiously positive about the status of ethnicity in texts are somewhat different. Troublesome features for her are the type of information about ethnicity presented and the extent of its integration into the mainstream or central cores of textbook content. Gay (1979) declared that just as considerable improvement in how textbooks treat groups of color is an indisputable fact, so is the need for further changes because:

subtle forms of racism and ethnic stereotyping persist. . . . The tendency prevails . . . for ethnic minorities having to be "super" in order to be acceptable, and for individual personalities to be emphasized over the masses. There also appears to be an inverse relationship between grade level and the integration of information about blacks and other minorities in textbook content. As the grade level increases . . . there appears to be a regression to a "desegregated format" in that ethnic content is set apart for separate topics, chapters, paragraphs, and sections (p. 243).

Studies of curriculum materials that focus primarily on gender issues have produced the same kind of mixed results as those on ethnicity. The reviews conducted by Grossman and Grossman (1994) reveal that textbooks, basal readers, and biographies are less sexist now, but they continue to overrely on stereotypical gender typing of males and females presented in the visuals and the narrative text. Blatant sexism had been reduced by decreasing the disparity between the number of females and males included, and showing females working in a variety of occupations. Yet male pronouns are overused, stories about males tend to outnumber those about females in readers for the higher grades and in biographies, and strong residues of traditional family roles remain. Males and fathers work in action-oriented, decision-making, and leadership careers (e.g., executives, scientists, firefighters, and builders), whereas females work in care-giving careers (e.g., teachers, nurses, doctors, social workers, and various "aides" or "assistants" positions). Men's leisure activities are many and varied, but those of females are narrower in range and more gender stereotypical. As with individuals of color, when women's contributions are discussed, those that fulfill more acceptable traditional female roles and images are included to the virtual exclusion of those who represent and speak from feminist perspectives.

Several common and recurrent ways textbooks and other instructional materials perpetuate biases toward women and ethnic groups of color emerge from these specific analyses. The AAUP Report (1995) identified six of these: *exclusion* of any references to perspectives and experiences different from the Eurocentric mainstream; *stereotypic portrayals* of the roles, identities, and cultures of non-European ethnic groups and females; *subordination* or *degradation* to European Americans and males; *superficiality* of discussions about contemporary ethnic and gender issues; and *cultural inaccuracy or isolation*, achieved by detaching individuals from their sociocultural communities and contexts. After reviewing 100 gender and ethnic equity programs, the National Association of Education developed a checklist of 11 common biases found in textbooks. In addition to some of those already discussed, it included double standards for females and males, and for European Americans and ethnics of color; condescension, tokenism, and denial of achieved status and authority; backlash; and divide-and-conquer strategies that praise individuals as better than or "exceptions" to others in their ethnic and gender groups (AAUP Report, 1995).

These analyses leave the impression that textbooks are far from being ideal in their treatment of women's and groups'-of-color issues, experiences, contributions, and perspectives. They continue to be driven by a Eurocentric "center" of reality. Their primary effort in dealing with diversity is to incorporate it along the peripheries of this center rather than to use women and ethnic contributions to challenge, deconstruct, and transform the central core of the fund of knowledge taught to students. These practices make it difficult, if not impossible, to give equal status treatment to "everybody's story," and to ensure that they are told with accuracy, integrity, and authenticity. McCarthy (1990) calls equal status treatment of diverse cultural experiences in instructional materials "emancipatory multiculturalism." He described it as "the critical redefinition of school knowledge" that "goes beyond the language of 'inclusivity' by emphasizing relationality and multivocality as the central intellectual forces in the production of knowledge" (p. 119).

Making this "paradigmatic shift" requires teachers to be knowledgeable about cultural and gender diversity. They also need to know how to "deconstruct" and "transform" existing textbook profiles of diversity. Supervisors can help to facilitate the development of these skills by demonstrating how to analyze instructional materials for ethnic and gender biases, distortions, inaccuracies, and oversights. How well they model and teach these skills depends upon their own personal competencies, convictions, and commitments to ethnic and gender equity in education.

Effects of Equity Curriculum

Understanding the effects that curriculum about gender and ethnicity has on students is important to continuing efforts to make the educational process more culturally responsive to diverse students and females. Most of the thinking on these thus far is based on theoretical assertions, logical deductions, and anecdotal evidence from localized projects and experiences. Only a few research studies exist on the effects of ethnic curricula. Most of them occurred in the 1970s, most deal with African Americans, most involved elementary students, and most focus on students' attitudes. Furthermore, "the studies tend to be short term, have measurement problems, and were rarely examinations of the relationships between expressed attitudes and behaviors" (Banks, 1991, p. 464).

Lee and Slaughter-Defoe (1995) included several more recent initiatives in their review of the impact of developments in ethnomathematics on teaching math to African Americans. Specific curricula that they examined included the

Algebra Project for middle school students in the Cambridge, Massachusetts, Public Schools, the Math Workshop Program for teaching calculus to college students, which was created by Uri Treisman at the University of California at Berkeley, and the historic work of Abdulalim Shabazz in training mathematicians at Atlanta-Clark University. All of these projects incorporated the culturally specific norms, experiences, frames of reference, and social knowledge of African Americans to improve their achievement in high-level mathematics, such as algebra and calculus. According to Lee and Slaughter-Defoe (1995, p. 360) Shabazz is explicit in explaining that his approach "links a sense of social activism, social responsibility, and cultural awareness, and includes a history of African and African American contributions to the history of mathematics." All of these projects have achieved impressive results.

Similar positive effects of culturally responsive curricula have been reported for Latinos, American Indians, and Native Hawaiians. Jamie Escalante's success in teaching advanced placement calculus to "at risk" high school Latino students in East Los Angeles (Escalante & Dirmann, 1990) was popularized in the film, *Stand and Deliver*. The Kamehameha Elementary Education Program (KEEP) has a history of more than 20 years of success with improving the reading and language arts achievement of Native Hawaiian young children by incorporating their cultural styles into the teaching processes (Gallimore, Boggs, & Jordan, 1974; Boggs, Watson-Gegeo, & Mcmillen, 1985; Au, 1993). Lomawaima (1995) described cultural projects in the Rough Rock Demonstration School on the Navajo Reservation, the Kickapoo Nation School, and the inclusion of Inupiat and Western Alaskan cultures into the curricula of the North Sloop Borough School District. These projects indicate that when their cultural values and experiences were included in curricula, American-Indian students "blossomed from silent, 'concrete' learners into talkative analytical students" (Lomawaima, 1995, p. 341), and their declining test scores were reversed. A recurrent theme relative to culturally responsive curriculum emerged from Nieto's (1995) and Garcia's (1991) reviews of policies and programs on educating Puerto Ricans, Mexican Americans, and other Latino groups: "the explicit and positive acknowledgment of Latinos' cultural base is valuable in the classroom experience" (Nieto 1995, p. 407). As school populations become even more ethnically, culturally, and linguistically pluralistic so do these needs. They are so important that Nieto believes linguistic and cultural maintenance and promotion, along with multicultural and bilingual education, must be the cornerstones of *all* educational reform efforts.

A large and growing body of research exists on gender and sex equity in school curricula. With the exception that virtually all of it focuses on European Americans, the other general traits of ethnic curriculum studies apply to gender equity curriculum as well. In these research traditions, either gender or ethnicity is examined; rarely are both explored in the same study. Lewis' (1982, p. 386) reminder that "the multidimensional nature of minority women's oppression dictates multidimensional approaches to obtaining equity" points to another major limitation of current research on gender equity curriculum. It does not examine how gender issues are contextualized in different ethnic groups' experiences; nor how equity instructional materials differentially affect the achievement of male and female students from various ethnic groups. This may be changing due to the research and scholarship of contemporary feminists of color such as Bell Hooks (1989), Cherrie Moraga and Gloria Anzaldua (1981), Patricia Hill Collins (1991), and Audre Lorde (1988).

Banks (1991), Klein (1982), and Scott and Achau (1982) provided helpful summaries of research on gender- and ethnically responsive curriculum. They reveal several common effects across these two types of reform. Among them are:

- The use of gender- and ethnic-equity materials in conjunction with instructional actions, such as class discussions, values analysis, and self-reflections, produce more positive race and sex attitudes than materials alone.
- Gender- and ethnic-equity materials have caused students from preschool through college to become less sex and race stereotypical in their attitudes and knowledge about roles, traits, activities, and occupational capabilities of women and groups of color.
- The longer the intervention treatments, the stronger the positive results.
- Younger children are more traditional and inflexible in their gender attitudes than are older ones. The reverse appears to be true for ethnicity. Glock, Wuthnow, Piliavin, and Spencer (1975) also found a reverse (but desirable) correlation between level of cognitive sophistication and racial and religious prejudices among adolescents. As cognitive ability increased, the prejudicial attitudes declined.
- Improved gender and ethnic attitudes do not necessarily lead to corollary changes in behaviors.
- The more comprehensive equity curricular and instructional approaches are, the greater the positive effects. Dealing with perceptions, attitudes, knowledge, and actions are more effective than knowledge alone.
- Improved ethnic and gender attitudes in one curricular area do not generalize to other areas not specifically addressed in the materials.
- For the most part, directions of change are similar for males and females, but the degree of change tends to favor females.

These findings led Scott and Schau (1982, pp. 225-226) to conclude:

[P]resenting just a few token females and males engaged in nontraditional activities will not influence pupils' sex role attitudes, knowledge, or behavior beyond the examples presented. Pupils need exposure to a sufficient quality of sex-equitable materials to allow them to incorporate nontraditional role behaviors and attitudes into their cognitive schemas and abstract principles about sex roles.

Parallel ideas apply to ethnicity. They undoubtedly inform the suggestions of multiculturalists that information about diverse ethnic groups, their cultures and experiences should be integrated into the curriculum and instruction of all school subjects for all students at all grade levels.

Additional support for sustained and substantive efforts to implement equity curriculum and instruction derives from research conducted by Gougis (1986). He examined the effects of racial prejudice and related stress on the academic performance of college-age African Americans. Although the study was a relatively small one, involving 90 students who were exposed to a contrived experimental treatment, the results are very revealing and instructive. The experimental group was asked to memorize a play embedded with expressions of racial prejudices. The control group memorized the same play devoid of the racial statements. A Differential Emotional Scale was used to assess the effects of these materials on the participants' emotional state, study time, note-taking skills, and recall of learned materials. The students exposed to the prejudiced materials had significantly higher levels of anger, disgust, and distress, and they had lower levels of joy. In addition, they spent less time studying and recalled less quantity and quality of content.

These results confirmed the hypotheses and were consistent with previous research findings. They indicated that (1) racial prejudices in curriculum materials and classroom instruction are stress-provoking for students whose ethnic groups are targeted; (2) stress and anxiety can reduce students' motivation to learn, time on academic tasks, and memory, comprehension, and other cognitive processes; and (3) the negative effects of prejudice-related stress on academic performance are cumulative. Gougis (1986, p. 149) argued that "as the process continues over the years . . . blacks will have spent less time trying to learn academic material and . . . made less efficient use of their cognitive skills." A learning deficit is created that worsens with each successive year of schooling: "Whites learn a little more each year, blacks learn less." If these assertions are generalizable across educational levels, contexts, and other groups of color, then they help to explain why the achievement gaps between some of these groups and European Americans are generally greater for twelfth graders than they are for fourth and eighth graders.

The evidence is clear from research to date that ethnic and gender equity in textbooks and other instructional materials is better now than it was in the past, but it still needs improvements, and that these kinds of curriculum resources have positive effects on students' attitudes. These findings have specific and significant implications for culturally responsive teaching and supervision. The facts that most of the studies reported are small-scale and short-term, none occur after the mid-1980s, and they deal either with gender or ethnicity but not both, are troubling. A nagging question is, Why has there been no noticeable research activity on these critical issues in the last 10 years? One answer may be that textbooks do not monopolize classroom instruction to the extent now that they once did. This logically, seems unlikely because their extreme dominance was so profoundly evident as recently as the mid-1980s.

Another possibility may be found in the cyclical nature of educational theory, research, and practice. Priorities in theories of equity pedagogy have changed over the duration of its existence. Since the beginning of the demands for ethnic and gender equity in education in the 1960s and 1970s, ideological and methodological proposals for how this can be accomplished have shifted from primary emphasis on curriculum content per se to instructional processes (i.e., from inclusion to transformation). A major indication of this shift is how multiculturalists define their field of specialization. It is now considered more as an ideology, a process, a perspective, a pedagogy, and a reform movement that permeates all other aspects of the educational enterprise, than a *separate, freestanding* instructional program on ethnic, cultural, racial, or gender diversity. It is a way of thinking, believing, and behaving that places cultural pluralism at the center of all educational policies, programs, procedures, and practices (Banks & Banks, 1993; Bennett, 1995; Gay, 1994a,b; Gollnick & Chinn, 1994; Sleeter & Grant, 1994). Research trends may simply parallel these philosophical orientations. Whatever the explanations are to these apparent gaps in equity curriculum research, they should be examined carefully and thoroughly, and corrected. Greater quantities and varieties of research are needed on effects of all kinds of equity education initiatives. The results will have a significant impact on how gender sensitive and culturally responsive teaching and supervision are operationalized in practice.

CLASSROOM INTERACTIONS

The importance of improving instructional materials and ensuring more equality in access to curriculum options and course content for females and students of color is unquestionable. These alone, however, are not sufficient to achieve full gender and ethnic equity in educational opportunities, experiences, and outcomes. Of equal, if not more significance is reforming the *process of instruction*, a centerpiece of which is the interactions that occur between students and teachers in classrooms. Both social and instructional interactions are crucial. Holliday (1985), Philips (1983), Cazden, John, and Hymes (1985), and Spindler (1987) asserted that in many instances the opportunity to participate in academic dialogue is contingent upon the social, interpersonal, and procedural competence of students (Holliday, 1985; Philips, 1983). As part of a five-part study of the educational experiences of Mexican American students in the Southwest, the U. S. Civil Rights Commission (1973, p. 6) declared:

The heart of the educational process is in the interaction between teacher and student. It is through this interaction that the school system makes its major impact upon the child. The way the teacher interacts with the student is a major determinant of the quality of education the child receives. Information on what actually happens in the classroom is thus important in assessing the quality of educational opportunity.

Holliday (1981; 1985) used a "transactional, theoretical perspective" (p. 117) to relate these general ideas to the educational opportunities and experiences African Americans have in schools. She explained that (1) these are determined by students' social competence and their academic abilities; (2) teachers' attitudes and perceptions affect and mediate children's academic achievement; (3) although both children's and teacher's interactional processes affect classroom interac-

tions, the effect of teachers on academic achievement are significant, while those of students are minimal; and (4) teachers' attitudes can transform African-American student achievement efforts into "learned helplessness" (p. 128). She further explained that demands for interpersonal excellence imposed by the institution are more directly linked to students' survival in school than their academic ability. Coupled with teacher attitudes and other transactional processes in the classroom, these encourage academic incompetence. Research on gender equity (Biklen & Pollard, 1993; Klein, 1985; AAUW Report, 1995) also points to student–teacher interactions as a crucial site where educational quality and equality are determined or denied for female and male students.

Whether the data sources are empirical, ethnographic, qualitative, anecdotal, or personal narratives, two persistent messages emerge from research on classroom interactions. One is that teachers control what happens in the classroom. By virtue of being unilaterally in charge of the classroom discourse, they decide who will have what kinds of opportunities to learn when, where, and how (Goodlad, 1984). The other is that both quantitative and qualitative discrepancies exist in the chances students have to participate in instructional interactions. These opportunities are differentiated according to many variables. Most of them have nothing to do with intellectual ability, yet, they make the difference between who learns and who fails. Race, gender, ethnicity, social class, and home language are of utmost importance among these variables.

The general patterns of these discrepancies were established by Rosenthal and Jacobson (1968) 30 years ago in the landmark study, *Pygmalion in the Classroom*. Their finding that teacher expectations of students' achievement affects how they behave toward students has continued largely unchanged ever since. Although more recent research has generated additional explanations for why differences in expectations exist, it has not produced any fundamental changes in the overall patterns of them. These indicate that students of color (especially African Americans, Latinos, and American Indians) are consistently disadvantaged in classroom interactions with teachers; in most cases, so are females.

Educational reformers need to understand the specific features of these interactional patterns if gender and ethnic inequities in educational opportunities and outcomes are to be eliminated. Two manifestations of these will be discussed here. They are *teacher expectations* and *discrepant classroom behaviors*. Both are major determinants of the quality of learning opportunities students receive. Each offers a powerful entree into culturally responsive and gender-sensitive teaching and supervision.

Teacher Expectations

One of the most thorough summaries of research on teacher expectations and related classroom behaviors is presented by Good and Brophy (1978) in *Looking In Classrooms*. They contend that "many students in most classrooms are not reaching their potential because their teachers do not expect much from them and are satisfied with poor or mediocre performance when they could obtain something better" (p. 70).

The research they review confirms this assertion. It also reveals several other significant points about teachers expectations and their effects on student learning. Although individual exceptions have been noted in the research, these patterns persist across teachers as a group.

First, expectations are powerful determinants of the quality of teachers' interactions with students, and the subsequent performance of students. Beliefs do not necessarily correlate with behavior, but expectations do. Teachers may believe that gender and ethnic diversity should be understood and appreciated, yet they do nothing about it in their classroom instruction. They may believe textbooks are not the best sources of information on women's contributions, but they continue to use them without making any modifications. If teachers *expect* students to be high or low achievers, then they will act in ways that cause this to happen. Good and Brophy (1978) referred to this as the "self-fulfilling prophecy effect," which is a concept first introduced by Rosenthal and Jacobson (1968). It means that "teachers' expectations affect the way they treat their students, and, over time, the way they treat their students affect the amount that students learn" (p. 67). The mere existence of an expectation does not lead to the self-fulfilling prophecy; rather, it is the behavior it produces. It is also not something that happens incidentally or instantaneously; it requires coherent and deliberate action over time. According to Good and Brophy (1978) the process includes five steps: (1) the teacher expects specific achievement from specific students; (2) the teacher behaves toward students according to these expectations; (3) the teacher's behaviors convey to the students what is expected of them, and are consistent over time; (4) students internalize teachers' expectations, and these affect their self-concepts, achievement motivations, and levels of aspiration; and (5) over time students' achievement and behavior become more and more attuned to what the teacher expects, unless they engage in deliberate resistance and change strategies.

Second, teacher expectations about student achievement are affected by assumptions that have no factual basis, and may persist even in the face of facts to the contrary. For example, research has shown that teachers who believe certain children had high IQs expected them to do well in reading. The students achieved at high levels even though their IQs were no better than those thought to be lower. This phenomenon may partially explain the "model minority" syndrome ascribed to Asian Americans. The high expectations teachers have for them generate high academic performance. Gender is a strong nonacademic factor that affects teacher expectations. In situations where teachers expect boys and girls to perform equally as well, they do. Palardy (1969) found this to be the case with reading achievement. Grossman and Grossman(1994), Bowie and Bond (1994), and Good and Brophy (1978) reported that teachers frequently associate substantive quality of academic performance with the language or dialect students speak. The work of students who speak African American and working-class versions of English is expected to be poorer, and is judged accordingly, than is that of students who speak mainstream Standard English.

Third, teacher expectations affect motivation, self-concept, and aspirations as well as achievement. Students who believe

that their teachers do not have any confidence in their ability to perform well internalize this, and their own self-confidence diminishes accordingly. They do not persist in efforts and learning tasks, and their performance declines. The achievement effects are exponential. As teachers' expectations for higher achievers increase, so does their performance, while that of low achievers becomes even less. The result is a further widening of the achievement gap between students. This cycle is particularly dangerous for low achievers. It can "confirm or deepen the students' sense of hopelessness and cause them to fail even where they could have succeeded under different circumstances" (Good & Brophy, 1978, p. 100). This process may be behind what Holliday (1985) meant by "learned helplessness." It certainly attests to the influence of "significant others" (Combs, 1962) in shaping students' academic lives, and helps to explain the cumulative school failure of some students

Fourth, teacher expectations and their corollary behaviors are not limited to students' academic achievement; they involve social adjustment skills as well. For example, teachers tend to expect students of color and males to create more disciplinary problems than European Americans and females. Males and students of color consequently receive more disciplinary referrals and harsher penalties. They also often expect correlations to exist between discipline and achievement (McFadden et al, 1992; Mickelson, 1990). Low achievers are expected to create more disciplinary problems in the classroom than are high achievers. Teachers help to make these expectations come true by punishing students of color for behaviors that are overlooked when committed by European Americans. Research conducted by Sheets (1995) shows teachers also can aggravate classroom conflicts by being inflexible, unapproachable, and unreceptive to students' attempts to explain their perspectives or extenuating circumstances surrounding disciplinary issues.

Fifth, teachers tend to have higher *universal* academic achievement expectations for European Americans than for students of color, with the exception of some Asian Americans. They are expected to do better in *all* subjects, tasks, and skills. These patterns of expectations are apparent as early as preschool and continue through college. In a study of teachers in 144 elementary and secondary schools in San Francisco, Wong (1980) found that teachers expected Asian-American students to be more academically capable, emotionally stable, and cheerful compared to European American students. These expectations transcended grade levels for they were the same for the third-, sixth-, eighth-, and eleventh-grade teachers who participated in the study. Studies reviewed by Grossman and Grossman (1994) indicated that female students of color are expected to perform better than their male counterparts across subjects, grades, and ability levels. When individuals do not conform to these expectations they are acknowledged as "exceptions to the rule," but no modifications are made in the rule. Gender-associated expectations for European Americans tend to vary by academic task, with females being expected to perform better than males in reading and writing, but males expected to do better in math, science, and computer technology (Biklen & Pollard, 1993; Hoyenga & Hoyenga, 1979; Klien, 1982; Maccoby & Jacklin, 1974).

Sixth, teachers' expectations and sense of professional efficacy are interrelated. Based on their review of research on this phenomenon, Pang and Sablan (1995) defined teaching efficacy as the beliefs teachers hold about their abilities to affect the academic achievement of students. Teachers who do not have high-performance expectations for students, also do not feel very efficacious about their own competencies with those students. On the other hand, those who have high levels of confidence in their abilities tend to have high achievement expectations for students, and their teaching behaviors reflect these. A significant number of the 175 preservice and in-service teachers in the Pang and Sablan study felt they could not effectively teach or influence African-American students in their classrooms. These attitudes were supported by other beliefs that lack of discipline from the home and a lack of interest in academic success are the main reasons for the achievement gaps that exist between African- and European-American students. These troubling results led Pang and Sablan (1995, p. 16) to posit that "teacher efficacy is an important construct in student achievement, and teacher educators need to seriously examine what teachers believe about their ability to teach children from various underrepresented groups." Thus, changing teachers' attitudes, expectations, and feelings of efficacy are imperative to achieving gender- and ethnic-equity in educational opportunities and outcomes. These reforms should occur in concert with developing more ethnic and gender sensitive interpersonal behaviors, and implementing pedagogical strategies that are more multiculturally inclusive.

Discrepant Behaviors

An implicit assumption of classroom interaction research is that there is sufficient communicative exchanges between students and teachers to generate a vital data base. Findings reported by Goodlad (1984) in his massive study of 1,000 classrooms in 38 schools cast shadows of doubt upon the validity of this assumption. He found that teachers spend 70–78 percent of classroom time on instructional tasks, with the amount increasing from elementary to high school. He admonished, however, that "time to teach and learn only provides the initial opportunity. There is then great variation in how this time is used by teachers and students" (p. 100). One of the most pervasive and persistent traits of classrooms in Goodlad's study is how infrequently students engage actively in learning with each other, and how rarely teachers initiate interactive dialogues with individual students. Teachers instead show a preference for unilateral control of instruction, frontal, total group teaching, giving of information, monitoring seat-work, and conducting quizzes. These observations are consistent with earlier studies (Good & Brophy, 1978) that show that classroom dialogues are monopolized overwhelmingly by teachers.

Other features that Goodlad observed about how classroom instruction is routinely conducted included little praise or correction of students' work; little guidance for how to improve performance; a very narrow range of learning activities available to students, most of which involved listening to teachers, writing answers to questions, and doing workbook assignments; and the lack of sufficient time for students to complete tasks. These traits tended to increase in frequency and magnitude with grade levels. Their preponderance led Goodlad (1984) to conclude that the general picture of classroom dynamics is one of "neutrality in human relations . . . considerable passivity among students and emotional flatness" (p. 113). Whether in elementary, middle, or high schools, the classrooms he observed were not characterized by "exuberance, joy, laughter, abrasiveness, praise and corrective support of individual student performance, punitive teacher behavior, or high interpersonal tension" (Goodlad 1984, p. 112). It is important to keep this overall scarcity of classrooms interactions in mind as teachers' relations with females and students of color are examined.

Both quantitative and qualitative variables are used to examine classroom interactions. Common among them are the frequency of teacher initiated contacts with students; the kinds of questions asked and to whom; the amount of wait time allocated for student responses; the kinds of feedback, criticism, and praise given to students; turn-taking procedures; the cues, prompts, and extensions teachers use in relation to student responses to instructional stimuli; and types of contacts students initiate with teachers. Results of research reported by Good and Brophy (1978), Philips (1982, 1985), Cazden, John, and Hymes (1982), and Greenbaum (1986) on these variables indicate (1) the differences evident in teachers' achievement expectations for females and students of color produce parallel kinds of variance in their classroom behaviors toward them, and (2) the directionality of the differences is the same across variables. That is, students for whom teachers have low-achievement expectations receive fewer academic and intellectually challenging contacts, and shorter wait time to formulate responses to questions. The results of these analyses show that significant inequities exist in the quantity and quality of teachers' interactions with females and students of color, and by gender within ethnic groups.

As might be expected from the other ethnic trends in educational opportunities discussed thus far, students of color, whether male or female, receive fewer and less-quality chances to participate in academic interactions than do European Americans (Damico & Scott, 1988; Good & Brophy, 1978; Sadker & Sadker, 1982; U. S. Civil Rights Commission, 1973). The reverse is true in some other types of interactions, such as disciplinary actions. For the most part, African American and Latino males fair even worse than do females. They receive the least and the worst kinds of academic interactions with teachers. Overall, students of color get less total attention, are called on less frequently, are encouraged to continue to develop intellectual thinking less often, are criticized more and praised less, receive fewer direct responses to their questions and comments, and are reprimanded more often and disciplined more severely. Grossman and Grossman (1994) noted that even when praise is given it tends to be qualified and general rather than specific and elaborated to academic tasks. Furthermore, African-American females are praised more often for good social behavior than their academic work. Routine, qualified, generalized, and social praise are less effective than sincere, unqualified praise for particular academic activities and accomplishments.

African Americans also do not receive encouragement to pursue learning comparable to that of European Americans. The same applies to Mexican Americans in the Southwest and to American Indians. Jackson and Cosca (1974, p. 227) suggested that these groups "receive substantially less of those types of teacher behavior presently known to be most strongly related to gains in student achievement."

In a study of Navajo and European-American preschoolers, Guilmet (1979) mentioned virtually identical effects. He witnessed situations in which "Navajo children, who are more in need of the teachers' and aides' help, receive less attention than the Caucasian children who are more prepared for learning in the public school environment" (p. 262). These disparities in the quantity of teachers' time and attention ethnic students of color receive create inequities in learning opportunities that may never be remediated throughout the duration of schooling unless deliberately targeted for change.

When more qualitative analyses are added to these quantitative ones the situation becomes even more disturbing. Students of color are also asked lower-order cognitive questions, given answers more frequently instead of being encouraged to find solutions to problems, receive fewer prompts and probes on their academic contributions, fewer of their comments are included and built upon in teacher explanations, and have disproportionately more procedural and managerial than substantive interactions with teachers. For example, they are asked, "Did you get the answer?," "What are the legal qualifications to be president of the United States," and "Did you include three reflections in your portfolio?" These are procedural and managerial exchanges. More substantive ones would be: "Explain how you arrived at that answer," "Why do you think she does not have a good chance of becoming president?," and "What distinguishes the main themes of your reflections from each other?" Anecdotal reports add another technique teachers frequently use in interacting with African-American, Latino, American-Indian, and some Southeast-Asian students. They simply ignore them, and function as if these students were not even present. No kind of contact is made with them as long as they do not disrupt the class. When contact is made it is invariably of a disciplinary nature. Relative to learning opportunities, this "silent treatment and invisibility" is the worst form of instructional discrimination and academic inequity.

Teachers interact with European-American females in similar, but somewhat more varied, ways than they do to students of color. On the whole, European-American boys have more interactions with teachers, both positive and negative, and verbal and nonverbal. These differences are particularly evident and consequential in more precise and task-specific praise, acceptance, criticism, and corrective feedback on both academic and social conduct (AAUP Report, 1995). Streitmatter (1994, p, 128) explained that, "males dominate the classrooms both in the positive sense as learners, as well as in a negative sense as behavioral problems." On the other hand, "the magnitude of this ratio varies with the nature of the communication, being greatest for disciplinary exchanges and smallest for instructional messages" (Good & Brophy 1978, p. 24). European-American males initiate more contacts with teachers, receive more encouragement, feedback, and praise, are cued,

prompted, and probed more, are rewarded more for academic accomplishments, are asked more complex, abstract, and open-ended questions, and are taught how to become independent thinkers and problem solvers. European-American females initiate less, receive less academic encouragement, praise, prompts, and rewards, are taught dependency in problem solving by being given answers more frequently, have less total interactional time with teachers, are asked more simple questions that require descriptive and concrete answers, are disciplined less frequently and less severely, and are rewarded more for social than for academic accomplishments (Brophy & Good, 1978; Grossman & Grossman, 1994; Sadker & Sadker, 1982; Scott & McCollum, 1993).

These patterns of treatment are similar for African-American females, but they are more extreme when compared with their European-American counterparts. Even when their actual achievement is equal to European-American females and males and greater than African-American males, and their attempts to initiate interactions with teachers are more frequent, African-American girls still receive less and lower-quality opportunities to engage in instructional interactions (Damico & Scott, 1988; AAUP Report, 1995). In the assignment of classroom managerial tasks, European-American females are given "trusted lieutenant duties and special high prestige assignments," (Grossman & Grossman, 1994, p. 90), while the duties given to African Americans involve social responsibilities. Damico and Scott (1988) found this to be the case in peer-assisted classroom instruction. Teachers asked African-American females to help other students with nonacademic tasks, whereas European-American females were directed to give academic assistance. These actions undoubtedly reflect the differences apparent in the vested interests of teachers in students. They typically demonstrate considerable concern and interest in the academic work of European-American females, but they pay more attention to the social behavior of African Americans (Grossman & Grossman, 1994).

Differential teacher behaviors like these toward females in general and African Americans in particular have long-term negative consequences. They discourage all females from acquiring the more active and assertive learning styles and skills that lead in the long run to greater academic achievement and leadership success within and beyond school. An additional negative effect accrues to African-American females. They have lower academic self-esteems and higher feelings of powerlessness and hopelessness about their ability to direct or control their academic destinies (Damico & Scott, 1987; Scott & McCollum, 1993). These, in turn, diminish learning efforts and time on task, which subsequently leads to lower levels of academic performance. For those students who engage in resistance strategies in opposition to this treatment, higher disciplinary actions also result.

Good and Brophy (1978), Oakes (1985; 1986a,b), and Goodlad (1984) report that teachers' interactions with low-achieving students parallels those with students of color and females. This is not surprising, given the kind of expectations associated with students in low-track classes, and the fact that membership in these groups is often overlapping, especially for American Indians, Latinos, and African Americans. High-achieving students are advantaged in both the quantity and quality of interactions they have with teachers. According to Good and Brophy (1978) they receive more questions and praise, more response opportunities, more wait time to formulate responses, more prompts, cues, and probes to extend thinking, and more complex questions that require higher order thinking skills. Thus, some students are triple disadvantaged relative to inequities in the opportunities they receive to participate in instructional interactions because of their ethnicity, gender, and intellectual ability, real or assumed.

Research on teachers' instructional interactions with low- and high-achieving students in reading substantiate these trends. The reviews conducted by Brown, Palincsar, and Purcell (1986) revealed several important and inequitable trends. Teachers interrupt poor readers more often than good readers, and give mostly graphemic/phonemic helping cues to poor readers, and semantic/syntactical ones to good readers. Instruction with good readers emphasize comprehension skills, such as inferring meaning from, thinking about, criticizing, and evaluating text. Much of the teaching time with poor readers is devoted to drills on pronunciation and decoding, and establishing procedural rituals such as turn-taking and hand-raising. Given this differentiated quality of instruction, and the high correlation between ethnicity, gender, and teachers' assessment of students' reading ability, the discrepancies that exist in national reading achievement scores are not surprising. If reading is indeed the most crucial anchor skill for achievement in all other areas, then high correlations between students' reading abilities and their performance in math, science, social studies, writing, and literature should be expected.

CULTURAL CHARACTERISTICS AND DISCONTINUITIES

In examining cultural characteristics for reasons why inequities exist in educational opportunities it is important to remember that cultural traits operate in interaction with other factors. As Sue and Okazaki (1990) suggested, in their attempt to explain the educational achievement of Asian-Americans, school success or failure results from a combination of factors. Among them are cultural traits, the functional value of education for mobility, accessibility to other social, economic, and political opportunities; and how different ethnic groups are perceived by society at large. Because cultural factors are often left out of these analyses, they are of major significance here. In assessing cultural traits that may provide some insights into the academic achievement of different ethnic students, the challenge is to determine those that are most germane because all aspects of culture are not pertinent. Sue and Okazaki (1990) proposed that this search be directed toward locating cultural values and socialization patterns that affect mediating variables, such as effort, motivation, and feelings of efficacy, which correlate strongly with achievement.

Ethnographers, anthropologists, multiculturalists, feminists, educationalists, and sociolinguists have identified four aspects of culture that are particularly pertinent to understanding and improving the educational experiences of students of color and females. They are *participation structures, communication styles, learning modalities and styles,* and *ethnic identification and affiliation.* These are closely interrelated, and separating them is artificial and arbitrary; however, research on them is discussed separately here in an attempt to identify discrete contributions each may offer to making teaching and supervision more gender sensitive and culturally responsive.

Participation Structures

Cultures have different rules and protocols for appropriate communication exchanges and interpersonal relations. They specify who can say what, when, to whom, and under what conditions, as well as who is to be in control. Sociolinguists and ethnographers refer to these as "participation structures" (Cazden, 1986; Cazden, John, & Hymes, 1985; Philips, 1983, 1985). They always reflect cultural values and socialization processes. Within the context of schooling these are commonly used ways of soliciting and allocating student involvement in classroom activities. The criteria of acceptability for these stem from middle class, European-American–based cultural values, norms, standards, and rules of order, etiquette, power relationships, thinking, communication, and interpersonal interactions (Shinn, 1972; Spindler, 1987; Samovar & Porter, 1991). Whereas discernible patterns of participation structures exist for ethnic and cultural groups, individual variations within groups do occur. These group trends may be mediated by such variables as gender, social class, education, assimilation, and ethnic affiliation.

Several elements of discourse and rules about interactional behaviors are typically studied to determine the participation structures of teachers and various ethnic groups in classrooms. They have both verbal and nonverbal dimensions. They include the tempo, pace, and directiveness of the speaker, techniques for gaining, managing, and maintaining attention, vocabulary, the amount of time allocated for responses, turn-taking rules, questioning strategies, the length of verbal reframes, and reactions to responses of the individuals participating in the discourse. These variables have been studied most often through research in international contexts (Samovar & Porter, 1991), with African Americans (Abrahams, 1970; Kochman, 1972, 1981; Smitherman, 1977), with different American-Indian groups (Dumont, 1985; Greenbaum 1985; Mohatt & Erickson, 1981; Philips, 1983, 1985), with European-American females (Belensky, Clinchy, Goldberger, & Tarule, 1986; Grossman & Grossman, 1994; Hoyenga & Hoyenga, 1979; Klein, 1982; Maccoby & Jacklin, 1974), and with Native Hawaiians (Au, 1980a,b, 1993; Au & Kawakami, 1994; Au & Mason, 1983; Boggs, Watson-Gegeo, & McMillen, 1985).

The results of these studies indicate that structures designed to regulate human interactions in various institutional, social, and interpersonal settings are reflections of cultural values (Hall, 1981; Cazden, John, & Hymes, 1985; Pai, 1990; Au, 1993). When values are not shared among ethnic and cultural groups their regulatory participation structures collide, which in turn makes quality interactions difficult if not impossible. This is often the case for culturally different students in classrooms. These "collisions" jeopardize effective teaching and learning.

Philips (1983) has identified four frequently used classroom participation or "participant" structures. The first is teachers talking to the whole class, and students participating in either choral responses, or individually on a "first-come, first-serve" basis. Both of these participation styles require teacher permission before initiation. The second is organizing students in small groups, and teachers interacting with each group in turn. Within-group interactions are arranged in "rounds of turns." Interactions across groups are duplicated in place and time so that teachers can monitor several groups at once, or groups participate one after another. The third participation structure is a one-to-one interaction between teachers and students. It usually occurs when students are doing deskwork, and individuals initiate requests for assistance from the teacher. The fourth participation structure is the lack of any interaction between students and teachers.

In all of these participation structures students are rather passive, and they work individually and are relatively isolated from each other. They are rewarded more for being assertive than affiliative, for solo instead of collaborative performance, and for speaking more than for listening (AAUP Report, 1995). Irrespective of which participation structure is used, the sequence of interactions is the same: teacher initiates, student responds, teacher evaluates student's response. Au (1993, p. 108) called this pattern "conventional classroom recitation." It is a facsimile of the linearity associated with rational thinking, and the predominant organizational schemata of middle class, European-American culture. The structures and conditions it imposes upon who participates, and how, in instructional interactions are not always appropriate for students from diverse ethnic, racial, social, and cultural backgrounds.

Goodlad's (1984) national study of elementary, middle, and high school classrooms, reported in *A Place Called School,* provides convincing evidence of the magnitude and pervasiveness of the use of these participation structures to organize and regulate instructional interactions. Teachers are the centrifugal force across these interactions. They dominate and direct everything that goes on in the classroom, all decisions stem from them, and they determine the pattern of flow of classroom activities, from what is discussed, to how, where, by whom, and in what sequential order. The prevailing tendency is for both the content and process of discussions to be directed toward the entire class, and with individual students taking sequential turns at participation after being granted permission by the teacher. Philips (1985) called this pattern of interactions a "switchboard participation structure." She named it this because of the monopolistic control teachers have over classroom discourse, the similarity of the roles students play, and the use of serialized and individualized turn-taking in which one student talks at a time, and only to the teacher.

Switchboard participation styles are preeminent in classrooms at all three levels of schooling (elementary, middle, and high). Teachers control, lead, and direct, while students submit, follow, and comply. Students spend most of their classroom time engaged in the same kinds of teacher-directed, passive, and linearly arranged activities. The most prolific of these are listening to explanations or lectures, completing worksheets, writing answers to chapter questions, and preparing for assignments or practicing work under teacher supervision. Their magnitude increases steadily from the primary grades through college. The patterns are so persistent across grades that Goodlad (1984, p. 105) predicted: "The chances are better than 50–50 that if you were to walk into any of the classrooms in our sample [a total of 1,000], you would see one of these three activities underway." His data also indicated that teachers rarely make any provisions for individual students' rates and styles of learning. While students were observed working independently in all levels of schooling, they were doing "identical tasks, rather than a variety of activities designed to accommodate their differences" (p. 105).

According to Sampson (1977) these kinds of participation structures are based upon and perpetuate the value of "self-contained individualism" (p. 769). It is pivotal in the cultural ethos of mainstream U.S. society. Embedded within this value are assumptions that appropriate school behaviors include self-sufficiency, rational thinking, controlled impulses and emotions, compressed motions and movement, inherent desires and aspirations for achievement, and separating importance of tasks from personal interest or needs (Gay, 1975; Boykin, 1994). Thus, teachers are often inclined to give priority to procedural routines and task mastery over the interest appeal and personal relevance of instruction for students. A case in point is how problem solving has come to be considered a set of sequential steps to be applied emphatically. They proceed from the identification of a problem to collecting information and judging its merits, identifying possible solutions, choosing the most valid solution, and assessing its appropriateness. There is some risk that conforming too rigidly to this procedure can supersede the significance of the problem itself.

The routinization, regimentation, and similarity of participation structures in the classrooms Goodlad (1984) observed caused him to liken them to "painting-by-numbers." By this he meant that teachers make all decisions about the focus, purpose, and parameters of assignments, and students merely follow directions within these established boundaries. Most learning tasks assigned and questions asked require simple "information production, and single-correct answers." Provocative, open-ended questions and thinking invitations are rarely extended to students. In Goodlad's opinion, this lack of instructional diversity, routines imposed upon students, the increasing rigidity of these as grade levels advance, and the corresponding decline of teachers' involvement with students as persons, "limit the school's role in the humanization of knowledge" (Goodlad, 1984, p. 126). As school grades increase teachers become more "distanced" from and dispassionate toward students, and the switchboard participation structure, in all its manifestations, is further entrenched. This is especially apparent in the middle school years, which is a time when students need personal involvement with and support from teachers in order to maintain their interest in school, and some psychosocial and emotional equilibrium as they traverse one of the most radical periods of change in the entire life cycle.

The rituals and routines of conventional school participation structures are compatible with the cultural orientations of some Asian-American groups (notably Japanese, Chinese, and Koreans), even though they may not share the underlying value of individualism. Kitano and Daniels (1988), Montero (1980), and Thu (1983) suggested that emphasis given to self-discipline, control, conformity, harmonious relations, and a formal hierarchical social structure in traditional Asian cultures show why students from these backgrounds do well in school. They may be able to adjust easier to the procedural protocols of schooling because of this socialization than can African Americans and Latinos, whose cultural priorities are different. If Holliday's (1985) theory is correct that social competence is often a prerequisite for academic opportunity, then this social adjustment aids their academic achievement.

Tong (1978) developed these ideas in greater detail for Chinese Americans. He explained that in traditional Chinese culture approaches to learning paralleled those of warrior training. They stressed obedience, form, precision, and control over one's actions and emotions. Mastery was achieved through a process of observation, imitation, memorization, and repetition. This socialization causes individuals to be very cautious, deliberate, meticulous, and methodological in thought and behavior. On the surface, these emphases are reminiscent of the ambiance in the classrooms Goodlad (1984) observed, and Au's (1993) description of the "conventional classroom recitation" process. They give the appearance of passivity and lack of engaging interpersonal interactions between students and teachers.

Chu (1995) contended that Korean-American students are likely to be nonexpressive, passionless, passive, and nonparticipatory in classrooms unless their involvement is solicited directly by teachers. He identified several cultural values that account for this demeanor. Korean youth are taught not to initiate conversations with elders, to be deferential to superiors, and to remain silent rather than display faulty understanding or poor command of a skill. They will nod politely while not understanding, attribute learning difficulty to their own lack of diligence, and resist expressing opinions for fear they may sound presumptuous. For Korean students "to be contentious is a sign of conceit" (Chu 1995, p. 152). This kind of persona fits well with the teacher domination, student passivity, and limited activity that characterize most U.S. classrooms.

Similar kinds of participation styles have been observed among Mexican Americans and American Indians. Cortes (1978) found Chicano students to be reserved and reluctant to speak out in ethnically mixed groups. This was not a function of language ability because students with excellent and limited English skills behaved the same way. Murillo (1976) attributed the classroom quietness of Mexican Americans to the value their culture attaches to showing courtesy to others, and deference to authority figures, such as family elders, priests, and teachers. He explained that while European Americans are taught to value openness, frankness, and directness, Mexican Americans give priority to diplomacy and tactfulness. Direct argument or contradiction are considered rude and disrespectful. Rather, "concern and respect for another's feelings dictate that a screen always be provided behind which a man may preserve his dignity" (Murillo 1976, p. 16). This cultural condition leads to rather nonaggressive, nonparticipatory styles in the classroom, especially in oral conversations with teachers.

A long history of research on different American-Indian groups dating back to the 1940s indicates that children from these ethnic backgrounds are culturally socialized to perform in ways that are often at odds with school norms and rules. In studying Hopi children, Dennis (1940) found that their communities placed little emphasis on power and prestige. As a result the children displayed less rivalry and desire to be important, superior, or distinguished. They seemed more concerned with working for the betterment of the group than achieving individual recognition. Similar results were revealed by research conducted by Havighurst and Neugarten (1955) with 1,000 children from six different tribal communities, Philips (1983, 1985) on the Warm Springs Reservation, Mohatt and Erickson (1981) with the Odawa, John (1985) with Navajo, and Dumont (1985) with the Sioux and Cherokee. In school contexts this socialization led to the perception that American Indians are "silent children" (Cazden, John, & Hymes, 1985) because they tend not to be very talkative, assertive, and individually competitive. Their outward appearance conforms to the pattern of relative inactivity that has been attributed to most classroom instruction, but the underlying motivation is different. While European-American students may not be active because the instruction is not provocative enough to stimulate their drive for individual competitiveness, American-Indian children may be reticent because the classroom does not accommodate their communal and collaborative styles of participation. Traditional American Indian cultures believe children acquire and retain knowledge better through imitation, experience, touching, and active participation in holistic learning contexts where physical, psychological, social, emotional, spiritual, intellectual, and environmental factors are considered simultaneously (Pewewardy, 1994). This participant style is reminiscent of Dewey's ideas of teaching the whole child and learning by doing, and McCaleb's (1994) conception of learning as a collaborative, communal effort.

There is considerable disjuncture between the passive, dispassionate, routinization of conventional classroom interactional structures and the participation styles of African Americans. These have been described by researchers such as Boykin (1982, 1986), Hale-Benson (1986), Kochman (1972, 1981), Pasteur and Toldson (1982), Baber (1987), and Smitherman (1977) as being active, spontaneous, intuitive, and interactive, with strong inclinations toward emotional, creative, and dramatic presentation. Individuals perform best within the context of and in interaction with a group. They invest their involvement with emotional, cognitive, and physical energy. They gain the right to participate in discourse by the strength of the personal need or impulse to be involved, and the persuasive power of the point they wish to make, rather than waiting for permission to be granted by a designated facilitator. In the classroom teachers consider these behaviors "speaking out of turn," and they penalize students for exhibiting them.

Pasteur and Toldson referred to these tendencies as "stylistic renditions" and "expressive movement" (p. 10), while Boykin (1986) identified them as "verve" and "affect." Salient attributes of them are "a propensity for relatively high levels of stimulation, to action that is energetic and lively," and "an emphasis on emotions and feelings, together with a special sensitivity to emotional cues and a tendency to be emotionally expressive" (Boykin, 1986, p. 61). Pasteur and Toldson employed an "insider's voice and perspective" to explain further that African Americans:

use motor behaviors in all areas of our lives. Our experiences are enriched by movements, and we learn innovative movements through our experiences. Where we black people are, there is action. We carry it with us and mold challenging conditions through the use of it (1982, p. 255).

The research of Guttentag (1972) and Guttentag and Ross (1972) validated the assertions about the proclivity of African Americans for motion and movement in learning. Both studies were conducted with preschool children. Guttentag observed African Americans and European Americans, without their knowledge, to determined if there would be any difference in their kinetic styles in play situations. The play opportunities provided were varied or not, with or without toys, music, and a playmate. The European-American children used less of the physical play space, and they engaged in passive, low-intensity, and individualized activities, such as lying down, sitting, and squatting. By comparison, the African-American children used all of the play space, engaged in more active, high-intensity, and varied actions such as walking, running, jumping, and dancing. They were more likely to include another child in their play activities.

In a related study, Guttentag and Ross (1972) used motion and movement as structured teaching tools to see if they had any effects on achievement. They had students act out concepts like over–under, above–below, loud–soft, high–low, and big–small. The theoretical assertions were again affirmed. Physical movement helped the African-Americans students learn the concepts quicker and with a higher degree of accuracy. Classroom observations conducted by this author revealed similar results. In one instance, a middle school math teacher was struggling, failing, and becoming increasingly frustrated with trying to teach students proportions such as half, quarter, and three quarters. Finally, in desperation he asked eight students to come to the front of the room and form a circle. By shifting numbers of individuals in and out of the circle the teacher was able to visualize and demonstrate what an eighth, fourth, and a half looked like when taken away from the whole, and what was left. The students were able to "experience and perform" the concepts, and see them in double image (e.g., see one-fourth and three-fourths simultaneously, as well as their relationship to each other). Within a matter of moments the same student who was totally baffled before the "performance" began grasped the concepts, as she moved in and out of the shifting shapes of the circle. With just a little additional prompting, she was able to explain the concepts fluently and with accuracy.

These cultural inclinations toward movement and emotion are the reasons why Kochman (1981) found, in his comparative study of African- and European-American communication styles, that interactions between these two ethnic groups are often very contentious. One specific point of contention that he described is the resentment African Americans felt when their attempts to interject emotional energy into debates were rejected by European Americans. While Blacks considered communicative structures that were inhospitable to feelings too constraining for genuine involvement and quality performance, Whites felt it was an infringement of procedural mandates to impose feeling upon them. Kochman also developed a profile of these groups' general participation and presentation types. He described the African-American mode of self-presentation as being high-keyed, animated, interpersonal, and confrontational. It is involving, engaging, heated, and affective. By comparison, middle class European Americans use a presentation style that is low-keyed, dispassionate, impersonal, and nonchallenging. The overall tone is cool, quiet, detached, rational, and unemotional.

Two other key dimensions of the participation structures of African Americans are identified by Marshall (1969) and Boykin (1979, 1982). These are novelty and variety in the formats of teaching and learning. Marshall studied the effects of novelty and changing sensory stimulation on the task performance of low- and middle-class kindergartners. The performance of the lower-class students was comparable to their middle class counterparts when the learning tasks had high interest appeal. The gamelike techniques that were used in the teaching stimulated the interest, motivation, involvement, and task-attending behaviors of the lower-class students, but they were distracters for the middle-class students that interfered with their task-attendance. Boykin examined the effects of varied formats for learning and practice on task mastery for third- and fourth-grade African and European Americans. Each group was presented the same tasks in unvaried and varied formats. The formats were varied by sequence, with no more than two of the same kind of activities juxtaposed to each other, and by differences in sensory stimulation (i.e., seeing, feeling, hearing, moving). The African-American students performed better with the varied formats. The European Americans performed equally as well with either varied or unvaried formats. Academic ability was not a significant factor in determining these preferences because high- and low-achieving students in both ethnic groups responded similarly. Their coping devices, however, varied by format and ethnic group. While the European-American students tried to make the unvaried tasks more interesting and persisted with them, the African-American students were easily distracted in unvaried formats, and they coped by engaging in off-task behaviors.

Boykin's and Guttentag's findings about the preferences of African Americans for variety and action in learning were further validated by Morgan (1990) and Shade (1994). Morgan's observational study of eighth graders in five classes showed that African-American students were five times more active than European Americans. Males engaged in even more activity than females. In two separate studies Shade surveyed African-American students in grades seven through nine to determine their perceptual and presentation preferences. They expressed a clear preference for visual images as sensory stimulation and physically active teaching–learning processes. From these findings Shade (1994) extrapolated some advice for teachers. She suggested that the pace, tempo, and types of experiences designed to facilitate learning should be more varied, actively engaging, and changed frequently. These will generate positive effects for African Americans without interfering with the educational quality of other students. The research of Lipsitz (1984) supports this contention. It revealed that even students and teachers who were not inclined to be very active in learning situations were not unduly distracted by high energy, movement, and activity classrooms.

These findings led Boykin to propose that European American students have a higher tolerance level for monotony, routine, and repetition in teaching than do African Americans. The potential negative consequences of their response patterns increase in magnitude when they are juxtaposed to Goodlad's compelling portrayals of classrooms as dull, uninspiring, repetitious, and homogeneous places where all students do the same things in the same ways. African-American students will disengage from these tasks earlier and more completely. This disengagement leads to lower academic achievement and can create discipline problems.

Analyses of gender issues in education have produced a participation profile of females that shares certain similarities with ethnic groups who have a rather passive, conforming, and deferential demeanor in the classroom. According to the reviews conducted by Maccoby and Jacklin (1974), Hoyenga and Hoyenga (1979), Wittig and Petersen (1979), and Grossman and Grossman (1994), analyses of gender have focused more on personality traits, motivation, and achievement by specific subject areas than on participation structures per se. The latter can be inferred from the former. The evidence shows that females in all ethnic groups, except African Americans, show more stress and anxiety in math and science classes than do males, but that males are more anxious in English. Females tend to be more willing to verbalize fears, anxieties, and other emotions related to academics than males. When males do express emotions they are more intense and they manifest as anger rather than as the sadness and depression that are more typical of females (Grossman & Grossman, 1994). These emotional dispositions have differential effects on achievement. Other research (Gougis, 1986; Speilberger & Sarason, 1978) has shown that there is a direct and inverse correlation between stress and academic efforts and outcomes: As the stress level increases, task focus, time, persistence, and mastery decrease.

Additional research findings (Belensky, Clinchy, Goldberger, & Tarule, 1986; Hoyenga & Hoyenga, 1979; Klein, 1982) reveal differences in how females and males negotiate relationships that affect their participation and presentation styles in instructional interactions. Although the results are not always definitive and unequivocal, several general directional tendencies emerge from them. They are: (1) males are assertive, aggressive, and domineering, while females are more altruistic, helpful, sensitive toward others, and egalitarian; (2) females are more cooperative and affiliative, and learn better through "connected knowing" (Belensky, et al, 1986), whereas males are competitive, individualistic, and challenging; (3) females are more inclined to avoid conflicts, but males confront and even instigate them; (4) females are less self-confident and more dependent on adult assistance and approval than males; (5) males dominate mixed-sex groups by being more initiating, talkative, and influential in decision-making, while females are more acquiescent and submissive; (6) females are more concerned with social aspects of situations, while males are interested in power relationships; and (7) females are externally motivated and males are intrinsically motivated.

Hoyenga and Hoyenga (1979) explain why reliance on external motivation places females in a tenuous and vulnerable position. Achievement for females is more fragile than it is for males because it is "dependent upon the whims of the environment supplying the motives, and because the extrinsic motivation interferes with the operation of the independent, intrinsic motive for accomplishing the same task" (p. 360). This dependency makes female students less willing to take major risks in learning environments for fear of failing, or of displeasing teachers or not receiving their approval. As a result, they may self-select out of the more challenging academic courses and experiences.

The degree to which these kinds of traditional gender-specific social dispositions and participation structures persist is influenced by culture, social class, age, and ethnicity. Individuals from traditional cultures and lower socioeconomic backgrounds exhibit these sex-type tendencies to a greater extent than do those from more modern societies and middle classes. Senour (1977) found support for this generalization in her reviews of research on Mexican-American women. She reported that throughout the larger Latino ethnic group, women are traditionally "expected to be gentle, mild, sentimental, emotional, intuitive, impulsive, fragile, submissive, docile, dependent, and timid." By comparison, men are expected to be "hard, rough, cold, intelligent, rational, farsighted, profound, strong, authoritarian, independent, and brave" (p. 330).

Gender differences in dispositions and their expression in classroom performance are less distinct before puberty than at and afterward (Hoyenga & Hoyenga, 1979; Maccoby & Jacklin, 1974). The gender and sex-role expectations of most ethnic groups parallel those described by Senour. They differ more in degree than kind. These similarities help to explain why the Women's Liberation Movement often anchors its advocacy agenda in common bonds of gender oppression that transcends ethnic-group identities and boundaries.

African Americans deviate significantly from many typical sex- and gender-typed behaviors, while Latinos and Asian/Pacific Islanders conform to them the most. Virtually no information is available on American Indians. Grossman and Grossman (1994) and Lewis (1975) attributed this difference to the historical subjugation and oppression of African Americans, which required females to be self-sufficient, aggressive, and assertive for sheer survival. This led to androgynous gender socialization, which continues even today. For the most part, individuals who grow up with androgynous socialization do not exhibit typical sex-typed attributes, and will be as successful in school as males. Wittig and Petersen (1979, p. 292) further explained that:

[I]n predicting individual differences in the potency of sex role as a mediator of intellectual functioning, . . . [and] controlling for intelligence one might predict:

1. Individuals who . . . [are] high in masculinity and high in femininity. . . will do well on most cognitive tasks regardless of the sex typing of the achievement domain.
2. High-masculine–low-feminine types will seek out and do best on masculine-typed intellectual tasks . . .
3. [H]igh-feminine–low-masculine people will . . . achieve in the fewer feminine areas and avoid or do poorly in the numerous masculine domains. . . .

As suggested earlier, ethnicity is a major mediating factor in these predictions about gender associated behaviors for students of color, especially African American females.

The individualistic competitiveness that features so prominently in the participation structures typically employed in classrooms also may be problematic for some students of color and females. Asian Americans, Latinos, Native Hawaiian, American Indians, and African Americans have been described as having communal or group-oriented cultures (Boykin, 1985; Cazden, John, & Hymes, 1985; Kagan & Madsen, 1971; Kibria, 1993; Kitano & Daniels, 1988 ; Marin, 1993; Martinez, 1977; Morris, Sather, & Scull, 1978; Ramirez & Castaneda, 1974; Shade, 1989). They are reluctant and find it difficult to participate easily in the highly individualistic and competitive modes expected in most classrooms. Instead of isolation, independence, self-sufficiency, and "dispassionate distance" from each other, teachers, and the content of their subjects, these students prefer learning environments that facilitate personal involvement, connectedness, collaboration, emotional investment, and a sense of community. Speaking on behalf of American Indians, Burgess (1978) explained that parents and children desire to be successful in school, "but in a manner that is consistent with the cooperative and non-competitive tribal, community, and family values and aspirations" (p. 46).

Foster (1994), Ladson-Billings (1994), and Cazden (1988) found that successful teachers with African-American and Latino students build upon their cultural affinities for groupness. These teachers establish bonds of personal caring and connectedness, build community, and develop cooperative, collaborative working relationships among students, and between students and teachers. They establish classroom rituals and routines to "reinforce this sense of collectivity and there are negative sanctions for belittling, humiliating, and embarrassing others" (Foster, 1994, p. 235). In describing the operations and effects of community, collaboration, connectedness, and reciprocity in the classrooms she studied, Ladson-Billings (1994, p. 73) noted that, "psychological safety is a hallmark of each of these classrooms. The students feel comfortable and supported. They realize that the biggest infraction they can commit is to work against the unity and cohesiveness of the group." This did not mean mindless submission to the group. Students also confronted group thinking and developed their own individual skills, all within the context of maintaining high intellectual, cultural, and ethical standards.

These findings suggest that individualism and communalism in the classroom do not have to be mutually exclusive. For some students, such as Latinos, Asian/Pacific Islanders, African Americans, and American Indians, the latter is a fundamental participation structure which facilitates the former. Culturally responsive supervisors understand that synchronizing classroom interactions with students' preferred participa-

tion structures can improve their level of involvement in academic tasks, which, in turn, may increase achievement levels. Both ethnic and gender variations in participation structures must be considered and accommodated.

Communication Styles

Many researchers agree on two major points about the interaction between communication, teaching, learning, and culture that have significant implications for achieving ethnic and gender equity in educational opportunities and outcomes. The first is that effective communication is imperative for successful teaching and learning. It becomes even more so in educational situations where students and teachers are from different cultural, ethnic, social, and gender backgrounds. Boggs (1985) lends additional support to these claims in explaining:

The attitudes and behavior patterns that have the most important effect upon children . . . [are] those involved in communication. The form of exchange between child and adult and the conditions in which it occurs will affect not only what is said, but how involved the child will become (p. 301).

The second point is that communication both reflects and transmits culture. As Byers and Byers (1985, p. 28) explained, "the organization of the processes of human communication in any culture is the template for the organization of knowledge or information in that culture." Goodenough (1981) adds that the proper unit of analysis for the study of culture is the local activities within which cultural structures are situated. The absence of commonly shared communicative frames of reference, procedural protocols, and rules of social etiquette makes it extremely difficult for culturally diverse people to understand and appreciate each other. Communication styles, or what Goodwin (1990) might call "communicative activities situated in specific social organizational frameworks," are therefore of equal importance as participation structures in understanding how culture influences teaching and learning, and using this knowledge to improve the educational experiences of diverse students.

In fact, participation structures are often characterized by analyzing communication and interaction styles. This practice is particularly notable in studies of American Indians, Native Hawaiians, and African Americans. The negative effects of "communication discontinuity" on the quality of task performance and interpersonal relations are described poignantly by Kochman (1972, 1981) in his comparative analyses of African- and European American communicative styles; by Philips (1983, 1985), Dumont (1985), John, (1985), Mohatt and Erickson (1981) and Greenbaum (1985) in their studies of the speech behaviors of American Indian children in classrooms; and in research on the home and school behaviors of Native Hawaiians by Au and Mason (1983), Boggs, Watson-Gegeo, and McMillen (1985), Au and Kawakami (1985, 1991, 1994), and Gallimore, Boggs and Jordan (1974). Little research is available on the sociocultural communication styles of Asian Americans and Latinos. It instead tends to focus more on linguistic structures and issues of bilingualism.

Research on gender communication styles in educational settings is also rather sparse. Most of the little that does exist involves comparative analyses of European-American males and females within the context of gender inequities, and sex-role expectations (Belensky, Clinchy, Goldberger, & Tarule, 1986; Grossman & Grossman, 1994; Maccoby & Jacklin, 1974). The resulting data identify gender-related communication roles without providing any details on the dynamics of actual communicative acts in the classroom.

The most valuable studies of ethnic communication styles for understanding and eliminating educational inequities emphasize sociolinguistic and sociocultural discourse rather than linguistic analyses, and employs ethnographic methodologies. Instead of examining structural elements of language systems, they explore a combination of verbal and nonverbal aspects of communicative behaviors as applied in various social contexts and interpersonal interactions. These studies focus on what Cazden (1985) calls "the communicative act" or "social interactional styles" (Au, 1993). The researchers concentrate on capturing the meaning of communication performances *as intended by the performers*, and the cultural norms, values, operating principles, and strategies that govern their production and interpretation within particular contextual or situational boundaries (Kochman, 1981).

In analyses of cultural communication styles within classroom settings, the primary concerns have to do with stylistic and social, rather than referential and structural features. As Hymes (1985) explained:

It is not that a child does not know a word, but that he pronounces it in one social dialect, rather than another. Not that a child cannot express himself or that a thought cannot be required of him, but that he expresses it in one style of expression rather than another. Not that a child cannot answer questions, but that questions and answers are defined for him in terms of one set of community norms rather than another, as to what counts as questions and answers, and as to what it means to be asked or to answer. . . . In these and many other cases the concern is not with something that is cognitively necessary to the child's intellectual growth, but with something that is considered socially necessary.

This position is consistent with that expressed by Spindler et al (1987) in *Education and Cultural Process*. They argued that the most contentious issues in intercultural relations are more procedural than substantive. Five of these components of communication have been identified by research as highly susceptible to cultural conditioning and insightful to understanding classroom dynamic: (1) relationship between speakers and listeners; (2) how thought processes and the content of discourse is sequenced; (3) how turn-taking opportunities are obtained; (4) response patterns; and (5) the range of communicative devices used. Each of these is a potential entree for culturally responsive teaching and supervision interventions.

In many classrooms, students, as participants in communicative acts, are expected to assume a *passive-receptive* posture (Kochman, 1981)—they are to listen quietly while the teacher talks. Once the teacher finishes, the student is then allowed to respond in some prearranged, rather stylized form, by asking or answering questions; validating and approving what was said, or taking a turn at talking. This verbal persona is accompanied by certain corollary nonverbal attending behaviors and speech-delivery mechanisms. These include little or no physical movement and maintaining eye contact with the speaker. Students are expected to be silent and look at teachers when they are talking, and to wait to be acknowledged before they take a turn at talking. Because of the central role teachers play in the classroom, they expect to control the flow of classroom communication by determining who talks when through regulating the turn-taking process (Philips, 1983). The speech behaviors are low-keyed, dispassionate, impersonal, nonchallenging, and employ what Bernstein (1964) identified as an "elaborated" delivery style. It is analogous to the "formal" and "frozen" styles described by Joos (1969). These performance styles emphasize always speaking in complete sentences that reflect logical development of thoughts, giving background details, word appropriateness, rules of usage, and careful attention to stylistic features. The structural forms of speaking are as important as the substantive content.

These communication protocols are not normative for all ethnic and cultural groups. Research (Smitherman, 1977; Kochman, 1981, 1985; Baber, 1987) has shown that *active, participatory,* and *reciprocal* relationship exists among African Americans, and between speakers and listeners. This style of interacting is often referred to as *call-response*. It involves listeners giving encouragement, commentary, compliments, and even criticism to speakers as they are talking. If a speaker says something that triggers a response (whether positive or negative; affective or cognitive) in them, then African-American listeners are likely to "talk back." This may involve a vocal or motion response, or both, sent directly to the speaker, or shared with neighbors in the audience. The speech performance style associated with it is restricted and context-specific (Bernstein, 1964); intimate, casual, and consultative (Joos, 1969); and has an aestheticism that is affective, animated, interpersonal, energetic, dramatic, and engaging (Baber, 1987; Boykin, 1986; Kochman, 1981; Pasteur & Toldson, 1982). It is characterized by a free-flowing interplay between speakers and listeners, an economy of words, and a high incidence of nonverbal features, such as facial expressions, gestures, and body movement. Delivery effectiveness is as important in conveying meaning as is the substantive content of the message. Verbal ability is perceived both as effect in conveying meaning, and as a tool for exercising power over people and situations through the artful use of persuasion, manipulation, innuendo, an astute sensitivity to what motivates others, and entertainment devices.

African Americans are consequently often described as verbal performers whose speech behaviors are fueled by personal investments, advocacy, emotionalism, fluidity, and creative variety (Abrahams, 1970; Baber, 1987; Leacock, 1985). These speech facilities and communication styles have been attributed to the oral–aural nature of African-American cultural and communal value orientations (Boykin, 1986; Hale-Benson 1986; Kochman, 1972, 1981). By comparison, European-American teachers and students tend to consider discourse that is characterized by high energy, affect, and personal investment of the speakers as irrational, tension-provoking, and potentially volatile.

A related practice was observed by Longstreet (1978) and described by Shade (1994) as "breaking in and talking over." It is a mechanism African Americans use to signal speakers that their purposes have been accomplished and there is no need to pursue the dialogue further. For individuals who do not understand and share these behaviors, they are considered rude, insulting, and inattentive. In classrooms teachers deem them "talking out of turn," and judge them disruptive and inappropriate.

Native Hawaiians use a discourse style that has some similarities to the call–response practice of African Americans. It is called "talk-story" or "conarration." Talk story involves several students working collaboratively and talking together to create an idea, form a thought, tell a story, or complete a learning task. Au (1993, p. 114) described this communication style:

During talk story children present rambling narratives about their personal experiences, usually enhanced with humor, jokes, and teasing. . . . Seldom in talk story does one child monopolize the right to speak as children are asked to do during conventional classroom recitation. What seems important to Hawaiian children in talk story is not individual performance in speaking . . . but group performance in speaking. Children who are leaders, those who are well liked by others, usually are those who know how to involve others in the conversation, not those who hold the floor for themselves. The value Hawaiian children attach to group versus individual performance seems consistent with the importance in Hawaiian culture of contributing to the well-being of one's family and friends, rather than working only for one's own well-being.

This communicative practice has been extensively documented by Au (1980a, 1993), Au and Kawakami (1985, 1991, 1994), Boggs, Watson-Gegeo, and Mcmillen (1985), and Gallimore, Boggs, and Jordan (1974), who have been studying the KEEP for the last 25 years. KEEP is a reading and language arts program designed to improve the literacy achievement of Native Hawaiian children in the early grades. Gender differences have not been a unit of analysis in this research.

Other observed ethnic communication behaviors that seem to stem from and conform to cultural values that give high status to group needs are students' response patterns to teacher-initiated questions in the classroom. Many African American, American Indians, Asian Americans, and Hawaiian Americans are reluctant to participate in classroom discourse that singles out individuals and demands that they perform without the accompaniment of the group. In his study of fourth- and fifth-grade European Americans and Choctaw Indians Greenbaum (1985) focused on nonverbal communication behaviors such as length of utterances, listening-gaze, turn-taking, and chorus versus individual speaking patterns. The Indian students consistently interrupted the teacher more, spoke in shorter reframes, responded more frequently in chorus, and spent more time gazing at their peers as the teachers talked. Durmont (1985), Mohatt and Erickson (1981), and Philips (1983, 1985) found that Sioux, Cherokee, Odawa, and Warm Springs Reservation Indian children were very hesitant about speaking out in individually competitive situations; gave few volunteer responses to teacher-initiated requests; spoke out without getting permission from the teacher; and talked more to each other than the teacher. In peer group learning arrangements, they were more verbally fluent, more task-focused and task-persistent for longer periods of time, and more well-behaved. Justin (1975) and Grossman (1984) observed similar classroom communication patterns among Latinos, as did Boykin (1979; 1983), Kochman (1981), and Shade (1989) with African Americans.

Studies conducted by Marin (1993) and Sabogal et al. (1987) validated the assertion that high value is attached to group affiliations by Latino Americans. This also affects how children relate and communicate in settings outside their cultural communities, including schools. They coded this preference "familialism," and defined it as "that cultural value which includes a strong identification and attachment of individuals with their nuclear and extended families, and strong feelings of loyalty, reciprocity, and solidarity among members of the same family" (Marin, 1993, p. 185). Marin used family obligations, support from family, and family as referent as variables to determine if familialism exists among different national origin Latino groups, and levels of assimilation. He found (1) that familialism is a central value shared by Mexican Americans, Puerto Ricans, Cuban Americans, and South Americans, and (2) as acculturation increases Latinos from all subgroups become less familistic in "family obligations" and "family as referent," but not in "support from family." This deeply ingrained socialization may be at play in classrooms when Latino students show preferences for working in groups, collaborating on tasks, and avoiding individualistic attention. They may, indeed, be responding to cultural prompts to solicit and provide "familial support." In this instance, "family" is more figurative than literal, cultural and ethnic than biological, or what anthropologist refer to as "fictive kinship."

This value of communalism may be the motivation for why Asian Americans routinely form study groups to deal with academic tasks; why Hawaiians "talk together" in constructing meaning; why African Americans persistently appeal to the "call–response dynamic" in verbal and nonverbal forms, and in both stylized (e.g., singing, dancing, sermoning) and regular daily interactions; and why American Indians systematically seek to include other members of their ethnic groups (and children generally when no other Indians are available) in their listening-gaze behaviors. All of these communicative behaviors represent various culturally determined ways of evoking group affiliation and participation.

Another salient characteristic of African American verbal communication styles is the frequent use of symbolism and metaphorical language. Their facility in these areas is diametrically opposed to claims by some teachers that African-American children are not very skilled in abstract thought and elaborated speech. Leacock (1985) suggested that metaphorical thought involves high levels of cognitive ability and abstraction. Combined with other performance traits, these present a picture of African-American speakers that is in marked contrast to the muted, inarticulate, adversarial behaviors, and need for simplistic discourse that many teachers ascribe to them. Cazden, John, and Hymes (1985) and Kochman (1981) attributed these differences in speech competence to the cultural congruency or incongruency of the contexts in which the actions take place.

In many ways, gender verbal communication patterns closely approximate those of European and African Americans. When ethnicity is not a factor, the tonal, but not the textual, elements of the communication styles of females are similar to those of European Americans, and those of males are more like African Americans. From the little that is known, gender communication styles parallel, and derive from, their participation and relational patterns (Sheldon, 1990; Tannen, 1990). Girls tend to use more affiliative, supportive, and accommodating verbal and nonverbal language mechanisms, while those of boys are more assertive, directive, managing, and controlling. Girls speak more politely and tentatively, use less forceful words, suggest and request rather than direct and command, are less confrontational, and are less intrusive when they enter into conversations. By comparison, boys interrupt more; use more commands, threats, and boast of authority, and give information more often (Grossman & Grossman, 1994; Hoyenga & Hoyenga, 1979; Maccoby, 1988). Maccoby (1988, p. 758) concluded, "speech serves more egoistic functions among boys and more socially binding functions among girls."

Furthermore, Hoyenga and Hoyenga (1979) found in their reviews of related research that "feminine communication styles" are associated with less intelligence, passivity, and submissiveness, irrespective of the actual gender of the speaker. They feel that these attitudes and behaviors reflect the influences of gender socialization in other aspects of human behavior and interpersonal relations. These portrayals, and their related effects on interpersonal relations and educational experiences, are strikingly similar to those that Kochman (1981) found in his comparative study of *Black and White Styles in Conflict*.

Some caution should be exercised in interpreting gender communication styles. Several reasons account for this: (1) the database is rather small, and much of it was generated 15–20 years ago; (2) social changes in the intervening years, such as the gender liberation and feminist movements, may have significantly affected gender styles of presentation, participation, and communication; (3) results across studies are not consensual and conclusive; and (4) gender communication patterns may vary significantly, depending upon setting, activity, age, ethnicity, and whether the interactions occur in sex-same or sex-mixed groups. For example, some research suggests that African American females are more demure and deferential when communicating with African American males, and follow their lead in cross-gender settings such as classrooms. In other words, they behave similarly to European-American females when interacting with male members of their own ethnic group (Sheldon, 1990; Tannen, 1990).

Goodwin (1993) found contrary results. In her study of community-based peer group interactions the communication of girls did emphasize equality, solidarity, and social relationships among the participants, but their moral concerns focused on "justice and rights," not the care, responsibility, harmonious, and supportive collaborations reported elsewhere for females in general (Abrahams, 1976; Belensky, Clinchy, Goldberger, & Tarule, 1986; Gilligan, 1982; Maltz & Borker, 1983). The "gender asymmetry" that often characterizes social structures and communications in other settings

was not present in the interactions of the children she studied. Rather, a strong ethic of egalitarianism in rights, roles, and speech behaviors prevailed. Kochman (1972), Smitherman (1977), and Baber (1987) described the same kinds of gender distributions in the various stylized communication techniques commonly used among African Americans, such as woofing, signifying, playing the dozens, braggadicio, and rapping. Some of these techniques are used more frequently by males or females, but none are the exclusive dominion of either gender, relative to the prerogative of use and performance ability. African American girls rap, roll, and cap as well as boys!

Different eye contact behaviors, as a form of nonverbal communication, have been observed among different ethnic groups, and found to be rather problematic in classrooms. African Americans, Mexican Americans, Puerto Ricans, some American Indian groups, and many Asian Americans practice eye aversion (Byers & Byers, 1985). They avoid establishing direct eye contact with adults in positions of authority, especially when they are being chastised. These behaviors signal respect and appropriate demeanors within some cultural communities. Teachers often associate eye aversion with inattention, dishonesty, distrust, disrespect, and confirmation of guilt on rule infractions. These disparate reactions illustrate the point made by Byers and Byers (1985, p. 21) that even if deliberate prejudice is not a motivating factor, "differing cultural practices that are quite out of the awareness of the people involved may act as the seeds of misunderstanding or conflict." The consequences are frequently punitive for students, and heightened restrictions on the possibility of them receiving equitable academic opportunities.

Hoyenga and Hoyenga (1979) reported that females use more and different types of eye contact than do males, and that they attach more significance to its role in communications. Females have been observed to be less talkative and more disconcerted when they cannot see the individuals to whom they are talking, while males are more talkative. The authors account for these differences by explaining that "if women are more sensitive to interpersonal cues than men are, and if affiliation is more salient for them than for men, then the greater importance of eye contact to women seems understandable" (Hoyenga & Hoyenga, 1979, p. 311). Because of the lower status ascribed to them, it may be more important for females to have access to eye contact and other nonverbal aspects of communication to help them better "read" the intentions and integrity of males. The same explanations have been made for why African Americans have such a keen sense and finely developed repertoire of nonverbal communication skills (Abrahams, 1976; Gay & Baber, 1987; Kochman, 1972, Smitherman, 1977). The impact of a long history of racism on their social, personal, educational, and political options makes being thoroughly informed about messages conveyed verbally and nonverbally imperative for their own self-protection and presentation.

Another feature of communication styles that can be contentious in culturally pluralistic classrooms and negatively affect educational opportunities for some students of color is how thoughts are organized and expressed. Two techniques are commonly identified: *topic-centered* and *topic-associative or topic-chaining.* European Americans seem to prefer the first, Latinos, African Americans, American Indians, and Native Hawaiians (Au, 1993; Goodwin, 1990; Heath, 1982; Michaels, 1981) are inclined toward the latter. To date no research is available on Asian American preferences.

In *topic-centered* discourse speakers focus on one topic at a time, arrange facts and ideas linearly, and make explicit relationships between facts and ideas: Their delivery moves inductively from discrete parts to a cumulative whole with a discernible closure. The structure, content, and delivery of its narrative style (i.e., its logical order) closely parallel the expository writing style commonly used in schools. A *topic-associative style* of talking is episodic, anecdotal, thematic, and deductive. Relationships among segments of the discourse are assumed or inferred rather than established explicitly (Cazden, 1988; Lee & Slaughter-Defoe, 1995). The thinking and speaking appear to be circular, not linear.

In actual performance topic-associative discourse sounds like storytelling. The elaborate verbal genres that African Americans have cultivated over time (e.g., Abrahams, 1976; Baber, 1987; Kochman, 1972; Smitherman, 1977) probably grew out of and helped to further validate the utility of this type of talking for a culture that places high value on verbal repartee, fluidity, creativity, and dramatic effect in delivery. Goodwin (1990) observed these communication features at work among the mixed-aged (4–14) African-American peer groups in a Philadelphia neighborhood as they told stories, shared gossip, resolved arguments, and negotiated relationships. She noted the ease and finesse with which a child could switch from a contested verbal exchange to an engaging story, and dramatically reshape dyadic interactions into multiparty conversations. By using a single utterance the children could evoke a broad history of events, a complex web of operative identities and relationships that all participants understood without elaborate details on any of the separate segments. The "talk-story" discourse style among Native Hawaiian operates in a similar fashion. Au (1993, p. 113) characterized it as a "joint performance, or the cooperative production of responses by two or more speakers." Hall (1981) contended that these interactional and communicative styles are possible because the speakers are members of "high context" cultures. This means that they live in close contact with each other, relative to shared residential space, experiential frames of reference, and historical and cultural experiences, perspectives, and worldviews.

Topic-associative talking is often problematic in conventional classrooms. Teachers generally consider it to be unfocused, illogical, rambling, and inappropriate for schools. Research by Michaels and Cazden (1986) indicate that European-American teachers find this talking style difficult to understand, and place less value on it. African American teachers give equal positive value to topic-centered and topic-associative styles of discourse. These teacher response patterns are troubling given present and future predicted school demographics. Teachers will more and more be European Americans, and more students will be ethnics of color. If teachers do not understand and value students' communication styles, then current achievement problems may intensify. This prospect could be counterbalanced if teachers were to

endorse Gee's (1989) contentions that topic-associative talking is more complex, creative, and literary than is topic-centered. Thus, cultivating it in classrooms may improve the achievement of students of color.

Discourse style preferences by ethnic groups are not limited to children. They are observable among adults as well. Lightfoot (1994) found a strong proclivity for topic associating in the conversations of the highly successful African-American adults she interviewed for *I've Known Rivers.* She identified the participants as "storytellers" rather than interviewees, and her research as a story, not a study. Her description of the relationship between herself and the six individuals whom she interviewed captured the essence of the communicative style and ambiance that undergird a topic-chaining or associative style of discourse, and lead to the creation of a "talk-story." As Lightfoot (1994, p. 640) explained:

These storytellers do not travel alone. I am with them; we are on the journey together. Their life stories emerge out of our constantly evolving relationship. The subtext here is the narrative of a relationship that is the vehicle through which the life story is remembered and expressed. Rather than being 'interviewed," these six people are 'collaborators' or 'cocreators' of their own life stories. The message and meaning of the stories come from the interaction, our duet, the convergence of our experience. I am both audience and mirror, witness and provocateur, inquirer and scribe. Sometimes I am also the storyteller.

For teachers working with students who use a topic-associating style of thinking and talking, their instructional processes may improve significantly by them being storytellers, too.

Learning Styles

The learning styles of students of color and females are reciprocally related to participation structures, communication patterns, and cultural identity and socialization. Many scholars and researchers (Banks & Banks, 1995; Hale-Benson, 1986; Morris, Sather, & Scull, 1978; Shade, 1989) suggested that the achievement problems of diverse students can be diminished by closer aligning teaching styles with their learning styles. These proposals are met with both hope and hostility, and problems and potentials. Some people think the notion of ethnic learning styles fosters stereotypes, and can be used as an excuse for teachers to justify their lack of instructional persistence with certain students. It is promising, however, "to the degree it illuminates cultural variables that influence the way children learn and helps teachers discover ways of strengthening academic achievement among learners of diverse cultural backgrounds" (Bennett, 1995, p. 164). The hopeful also see ethnic and gender learning styles as means to reducing the level of cultural discontinuity between how some students learn to learn in their cultural communities, and how they are expected to function in classrooms. Matching instruction to the learning styles of different ethnic groups and genders, therefore, can improve their focus on academic tasks, access to knowledge, and subsequent achievement. The skeptics point out that children are individuals, and they learn in their own unique ways; that learning style traits are stereotypes; and that discussions of ethnic learning styles imply that some groups cannot learn certain things.

These are common misconceptions associated with learning styles. They fail to acknowledge three important points: (1) learning styles deal with how individuals learn, not their intellectual ability; (2) children are members of cultures, and their individuality can never be totally separated from their socializing experiences; and (3) learning style characteristics are intended to be group profiles, not descriptions of specific individuals. To acknowledge that ethnic group learning styles exist is not to deny the importance of individual differences, rather, "it is to say that cultural differences are one important component of individual differences" (More 1987, p. 152). An essential component of culturally responsive supervision, therefore, is helping teachers analyze and monitor the extent to which they employ cultural factors and styles of learning in attending to the needs of individual ethnic students.

"Relevance," "connectedness," and "continuity" (e. g., "starting the instructional process where students are") are commonly accepted principles of good pedagogy. If these are applied to students of color and to females, then it is imperative for ethnic and gender learning styles, as well as "shared cognitive frameworks," to be central features in teaching culturally different students. Research support for these assertions are provided by Pandolfo (1985), Smith and Lewis (1985), and Hall, Reder, and Cole (1979). Pandolfo's research shows that reading comprehension increases when the schema linguistically different students use to interpret narrative text match closely with the content schema of the author. Smith and Lewis found that African-American students remember more details of stories about African-American characters than about European Americans. The bidialectic students in the Hall, Reder, and Cole study (1979) recalled more information and scored higher when they were tested in their cultural dialects than in standard English. Implicit in these findings is support for the notions that matching teaching and learning styles, including culturally relevant content in teaching (i.e., establishing cultural relevance and connectedness) improve the academic achievement of students of color. Belensky et al (1986) found this to be true for females as well. Learning for girls and women was more successful when it allowed them to emphatically engage and personally identify with the subject and situation being taught. The authors called this "connected knowing."

By the time students begin school as kindergartners, they already have acquired deeply entrenched cultural systems of rules and preferred methods for acquiring knowledge (Shade & New, 1993). These learning styles are instrumental in determining what information receives attention, the intellectual mediating processes used in solving cognitive problems, and the appropriate responses to display in learning situations (Shade, 1989). Culturally responsive and gender-sensitive teaching, therefore, should use the learning styles students bring from home to try to improve achievement before asking them to employ other systems of learning. It is for this reason that a review of research on gender and ethnic learning styles is important here.

Most scholars make a distinction between learning style and learning ability. More (1989) described learning style as the characteristic or usual manner in which individuals acquire, code, organize, and process information, whereas learning ability refers to one's intellectual capabilities. Guild and Garger (1985) declared that learning style is about process, not product. It can be understood by keeping in mind the basic functions people perform when they interact with situations, ideas, information, and each other. They identify the issue or challenge, think about it, react to it, and finally act upon it. Thus, the essential and differentiating features of learning styles can be described as cognition (i.e., ways of knowing), conceptualization (i.e., forming ideas and thinking), affect (i.e., feeling and valuing), and behavior (i.e., acting) (Guild & Garger, 1985).

Some relationships may exist between learning style and intellectual ability; they are not identical. Any correlations that have been observed may be more a factor of limitations of the measurement devices, the degree of cultural congruency in the diagnostic procedures, or successful adaptation to school protocols than intelligence per se. Guild and Garger (1985, p. 80) concluded that "it pays off in school to have certain stylistic characteristics that are more consistently successful with school tasks." It is not surprising, then, that students with high indices of field-independence in styles of learning will appear to be more intelligent than those who are field-dependent because most school measures of intelligence and achievement reflect field-independent structures, processes, and content. The fact that intellectual ability is conspicuously absent in the extensive work of Shade (1982, 1989, 1994; Shade & New, 1993) reveals its unimportance in identifying the essential nature and profiles of learning styles.

According to Shade and New (1993), a learning style is a *macrostructure* comprised of two fundamental components: a *perceptual style*, or preference for a certain sensory modality (e.g., sight, sound, touch, motion) for receiving and sending information, and a *thinking style*, or how information is processed, such as reasoning, planning, associating, classifying, inferring, appraising, and transforming. Individuals learn the basic structure and process of these within the framework of their cultures. Bennett (1995) offers a similar characterization of learning style as the cognitive, affective, and physiological behaviors students habitually employ in perceiving, interacting with, and responding to learning stimuli and environments. From these descriptions, it is clear that *a learning style is a preferred system of intellectual processing.*

Theoretical conceptions usually plot learning styles at polar position on a continuum ranging from gestaltism on one end to atomism on the other. For example, "whole" versus "parts" with all of their attendant dispositional and behavioral characteristics. The language used to name these learning style "types" is rich and varied. It suggests the disciplinary base in which the analyses are grounded, as well as their directional focus and emphasis. Shade (1989) added that the bipolar placement of learning styles is based on perceptual processing orientations, typical ways of organizing and representing information, and behavioral and intellectual strategies used to adapt to environmental forces. She provided a useful summary of these bipolar identities in relation to which of these three features they emphasize.

Identifiers for learning styles that focus on perceptual processing orientations include *field-independence versus field-*

dependence, *verbalizer versus visualizer, analytic versus synthetic, diffusive versus fixative,* and *levelling versus sharpening.* Across these labels are varying degrees of idea selection and representation, perceptions of images, details and specificity, and attention deployment. Descriptions of learning styles based on the organizational techniques used in information processing include *descriptive and relational versus inferential, abstractness versus concreteness, reflectivity versus impulsivity, convergent versus divergent,* and *serialistic versus holistic.* The polar positions they symbolize are distinguished by conceptual differentiation, how information is represented, and the sequencing and speed of thinking. Learning styles that emphasize adaptational strategies are identified as *extraversion versus introversion, closed-minded versus open-minded, constricted versus flexible control, internality versus externality, complex versus simple, integration versus dissociation,* and *field-independency versus field-dependency.* They deal with differences in attending behaviors, feelings of empowerment and responsibility for one's own actions, and the extent to which individuals feel obligated to their own cultural ideas, values, beliefs, and experiences (Shade, 1989).

Research and scholarship on learning styles (Bennett, 1995; Grossman, 1984; Morris, Sather, & Scull, 1978; Ramirez & Castaneda, 1974; Shade, 1989) have generated a consensual set of descriptive traits for each of the polar positions on the continuum. They emerge from analyses of different style variables and conceptualizations, a wide variety of measurement devices, and the participation of many ethnic groups. A descriptive profile of learning styles can be constructed from this composite body of research. Staying within the framework of polarities, Bennett (1995, p. 163) begins this construction as follows:

Some [students] work well in groups; others prefer to work alone. Some need absolute quiet in order to concentrate; others do well with noise and movement. Some need a great deal of structure and support; others are more independent and self-motivated. Some students grasp oral instructions quickly; others need to see instructions in writing. Some require a warm personal rapport with the teacher, while others do not. Some are intuitive; others prefer inductive or deductive reasoning. Some learn best in a formal environment, while others prefer a more relaxed atmosphere.

In most instances, in the organization of these ideas, the first ones stated are characteristic of the gestaltist pole, while the second ones mentioned fit better at the atomistic end of the learning style continuum. The exceptions are the quiet/sedentary/formality and the noise/movement/informality continua.

Several other learning style traits can be extrapolated from research and theory, and added to Bennett's sketch to create a more thorough and complete profile. These are presented in Table 50–2.

Four conclusions derive from research on learning styles that have major implications for designing ethnic- and gender-responsive educational reforms. First, there is a strong interactive relationship between culture, language, ethnicity, gender, and learning styles. Students from cultural backgrounds that are more communal, group-centered, and tradi-

TABLE 50–2. Characteristics of Bipolar Learning Styles

Atomistic	Gestalistic
Distracted by Enviromental/ Contextual Elements	Responsive to Environmental/ Contextual Elements
Perceive Discrete Parts	Perceive Holistic Patterns
Individual Oriented and Competitive	Group Oriented and Cooperative
Cognitive and Rational	Affective, Emotional, Moral, and Spiritual
Passive and Receptive	Active and Participatory
Intrinsically Motivated	Extrinsically Motivated
Object and Task Mastery Centered	Person and Relationships Centered
Inattentive to Social Environment	Social Environment is a Necessity to Learning
Learning Through Trial and Error	Learning Through Modeling and Imitation
Inductive Reasoning	Deductive Reasoning
"Objective" Impersonal References	"Subjective" Personal References
Expert/Authority-Based Knowledge Certification	Personal/Experienced-Based Knowledge Certification
Transmissive Relation to Knowledge	Transactive Relation to Knowledge
Spokesperson Ownership	Advocacy Ownership
Methodical, Purposeful, and Self-Constrained	Self-Assertive, Expressive and Spontaneous
Compartmentalized Response Patterns	Holistic Response Patterns
Individualism	Communalism
Reason and Emotion are Contradictory	Reason and Emotion are Complementary
Descriptive and Literal Speech	Symbolic and Metaphorical Speech
Prefer Verbal and Auditory Sensory Stimulation	Prefer Visual, Auditory, and Tactile Sensory Stimulation
Sequential Information Processing	Simultaneous Information Processing
Physical and Psychological Distance	Physical and Psychological Closeness

tional (on a scale of traditionality–modernity), groups of color, and females tend to cluster along the gestaltist end of the learning style continuum. The evidence in support of this tendency for African Americans, Latinos, American Indians, and Native Hawaiians is consistent and conclusive (Bennett, 1995; Boggs, Watson-Gegeo, & McMillen, 1985; Cazden, John, & Hymes, 1985; Hale-Benson, 1986; Hollins, King, & Hayman, 1994; Ramirez & Castaneda, 1974; Shade, 1989, 1994). One example of how these preferences operate in practice is combining social interactions with task performance. Establishing social relations, or engaging in "social stage setting," is often a *precondition* for task performance for Latinos, African Americans, Native Hawaiians, and Filipinos. Another variation of this preference is to "talk through tasks" as they are being performed. Teachers interpret these tendencies as unnecessary socializing and unfocused, off-task behaviors that interfere with quality task performance.

The situation is less clear and definitive for Asian Americans, especially Japanese, Chinese, and Koreans. They seem to be bistylistic. Tong (1978) offered a possible explanation for this in his analysis of traditional Chinese cultural values and the impact they have on learning styles. He says:

There are features of both field independence and field sensitivity in our styles of learning, particularly in the heterodox/warrior style. One is always sensitive to the field and one also operates in ways independent of what forces in the field would have one do. The emphasis throughout is on total control of one's actions (independence), with that control based on a keen ability to assess or understand whatever situation one finds himself in (sensitivity) (p. 93).

Bennett (1995) reported on some research that indicated that Hmong children have classic traits of field-dependent (or gestaltist) learning styles. Chan (1981) suggested that their traditional socialization has taught Indochinese students "to learn by listening, watching (observing) and imitating" (p. 42). They show a strong proclivity, however, toward group effort in preparation for task performance like other Asian groups.

There is not much research on the learning styles of females. The little that does exist deals with European and African Americans, and the results are often inconclusive on specific learning style aspects. The research generally suggests that ethnicity is a stronger indicator of learning styles among females than is gender. The way females in different ethnic groups approach learning tends to be more like male members of the same group than females in other groups. This tendency is not as strong for European Americans as it is for African Americans. European-American females exhibit some of the learning style traits typically associated with their ethnic group (atomistic/field-independence) to a lesser degree of intensity and magnitude than males. They also have more of the traits usually attributed to groups of color (gestaltist/field-dependence) than do their male counterparts. Among these are external locus of control, sociality, people and relationship orientations, preference for cooperative and collaborative learning, sensitivity to nonverbal cues, and dependency upon adult directions and feedback (Belensky, Clinchy, Goldberger, & Tarule, 1986; Grossman & Grossman, 1994; Klein, 1982).

Other characteristic features of females' ways of knowing include learning through empathy, trust in knowledge derived from personal experience and involvement, focus on understanding, not judging other people's thinking, and establishing bonds of kindredness with other learners and learning resources, or "passionate connected knowing" (Belensky et al, 1986). A composite summary of females, learning style attributes compiled from different research on gender issues in education is presented in Table 50-3. These attributes were symbolized in the preferred metaphors of the women studied by Belensky et al. They used speaking and listening metaphors to convey their preferences for dialogue, interaction, connection, conversation, and community in learning processes. These were at odds with the visual metaphors prolific in conventional schooling, which "equate knowledge with illumination, knowledge with seeing, and truth with light" (Belensky et al, 1986, p. 19).

A major insight derived from research on gender and ethnic approaches to learning is that *learning style is a holistic construct with multiple dimensions.* They include:

TABLE 50-3. Gender Learning Style Attributes*

Female	Issue	Male
Process Oriented Discovery/ Constructed	Education Aim How Knowledge Acquired	Goal Oriented Revealed/ Received
Intuition	Method of Analysis	Rationality
Synthesis	Learning/Life Relationship	Compartmental
Communal	Learning Structure	Solitary
Generalist	Learning Focus	Specialist
Support	Learning Condition	Challenge
Personal	Self/Content Connection	Impersonal
External Factors	Validation	Internal Factors
Listening	Experiencing Voice	Speaking

*Categories based on variables studied by Belensky et al (1986) in *Women's Ways of Knowing.*

- *Substantive*—Preferred content, such as math, science, literature, social studies; tasks such as mechanical or interpretative; and intellectual skills, such as memorizing, describing, analyzing, synthesizing, or criticizing.

- *Procedural*—Preferred ways of approaching learning tasks, including pacing, allocation of time, variety or monotony, novelty or predictability, passivity or activity, isolation or sociality, structure or freedom from constraints, types of task persistence, and choice of lecturing, didactic, or inquiry teaching.

- *Environmental*—Preferred physical and interpersonal settings for learning, including sounds, silence, lighting, temperature, space decorations, and the presence or absence of other individuals.

- *Organizational*—Preferred structural arrangements of work place, and study space, including proxemics or amount of personal space, relative empty or full learning spaces, clutter or carefully ordered space, individually owned or group-shared space, and rigidity or flexibility and mobility of the space inhabited.

- *Perceptual*—Preferred sensory modalities for receiving, processing, and sending information, including visual, tactile, kinetic, auditory, oral, or multiple modalities (Barbe & Swassing, 1979).

- *Relational*—Preferred interpersonal and social interactions in learning situations, including formality or informality, individual or group contexts, independence or kindredness, peer–peer or child–adult, authoritarian or egalitarian.

- *Motivational*—Preferred reasons for learning including self-desires and aspirations, self-esteem and self-concept needs, praise and accolades, internal versus external prompts, and conforming to expectations, norms, and pressures of various groups.

All of these have to be understood independently and in conjunction with each other to be most effective in guiding instructional reform. The more that is known about the many dimensions of learning styles, the more powerful the diagnoses and educational treatments of individual ones will be (Guild & Garger, 1985). Skewed, distorted, and incomplete conceptions, and inappropriate educational interventions are otherwise likely to result. When treated as gestalts the learning styles of ethnically and gender-diverse students may produce diagnoses very different from when assessments are based on only one or two components. Lomawaima (1995) makes this point in his explanation that American Indian children are field-dependent, yet they are private and silent learners. These attributes are not consistent with the sociality usually associated with field-dependent learners, yet they do not invalidate the overall diagnosis; rather, they are reminders that no learning style is ever a pure and totally discrete category.

The third lesson discerned from research is that learning styles are not exclusive, absolute, or intractable. Despite the fact that style, culture, ethnicity, and gender do correlate strongly, the full range of the continua of learning styles exist in all racial, ethnic, and social groups (Cooper, 1985). Only points of emphasis differ. As *preferred* and *usual* ways of engaging with intellectual challenges, they are the "centers," the "baselines," the "central tendencies" of learning processes. When faced with a learning task individuals invariably begin the process, focus on, and return to their own base of operations. There is some preliminary research evidence that suggests that as some individuals grow older shifts in learning styles occur, especially from field-dependence toward independence. It is also probable that no individuals remain in the same learning style format for all tasks, times, and circumstances. Inherent within each learning style is its own continuum. The dynamic nature of learning styles implies that teaching and supervision must engage them in multiple and varied ways, from diagnosing students' academic needs to practicing learning tasks to appraising performance mastery.

A final significant insight gleaned from research on learning styles is that evidence of the effects of matching teaching and learning styles is inconclusive. Few systematic, large-scale, and longitudinal studies have been conducted on this phenomenon, with the exception of with Native Hawaiians. Most research concentrates on diagnosing and describing learning styles, and involves small, isolated projects about the effects of educational programs designed to accommodate or reflect them. The emphasis has also been more on selected components rather than on the total construct of learning style attributes.

Although not always validating of and conclusive about theoretical assertions, preliminary findings on teaching to the learning styles of different ethnic groups are encouraging. Saracho's (1989) review of research on Mexican Americans indicates that students from both polar positions of the learning style continuum do better in school with teachers who use an atomistic/field-independent teaching style, or that no effects occur at all. This finding may be influenced by the fact that the measurements of achievement are traditional, and that the teaching and learning style features analyzed are not specific to any particular dimension, such as substantive, pro-

cedural, or motivational. Thus, analyzing learning and teaching styles as general gestalts may not be powerful enough to capture more discrete effects.

Several studies have demonstrated that responding educationally to selective aspects of learning styles does produce positive results. Greenbaum (1985), Phillips (1983), and other studies involving American Indians reported in Cazden, John, and Hymes' *Functions of Language in the Classroom* (1985) prove that adjusting instructional communications to synchronize better with American Indian children's interactional styles produce positive results. Participation in instructional discourse, verbal fluency, time on task, and academic achievement increase in quantity and quality. Lomawaima (1995) reports studies in which the use of nonverbal cues that communicate warmth in teaching and interactional styles with Athabascan and Eskimo college student increased their overall learning. Lee (1995), Piestrup (1973), and Foster (1989) have demonstrated that the use of verbal and nonverbal elements of African-American discourse styles improves students' comprehension of academic content and concepts. Other learning style features that have been shown to facilitate learning for African Americans when used in teaching are establishing feelings of community and solidarity, active and participatory learning, shared identity, interpersonal caring, warmth, informality, common struggle, linking the content of learning with lived experiences, and variability in learning formats (Boykin, 1979, 1982; Foster, 1989, 1991, 1994, 1995; Guttentag, 1972; King, 1991, 1994; Ladson-Billings, 1991,1994, 1995a,b; Piestrup,1973). In the Piestrup (1973) study the changes led to increased scores on standardized reading achievement tests for first graders. The others were observational studies that did not use standardized achievement test scores as a measure of the effects of matching learning and teaching styles. Reviews of research on cooperative learning conducted by Slavin (1995) give convincing evidence that this approach to teaching has positive academic, social, interpersonal, and personal effects for European Americans, Latinos, and African Americans.

The extensive research on Native Hawaiian children in the KEEP presents convincing and conclusive evidence about the positive effects of matching teaching–learning styles. This intervention has led to a phenomenal improvement of the students' performance on standardized measures of reading achievement. By using "a cultural synthesis of familiar and novel routines and participation structures which enable Hawaiian children to use their sociolinguistic skills in learning to read" (Boggs, Watson-Gegeo, & Mcmillen, 1985, p. 140) KEEP raised the students' reading scores from the thirteenth to the sixty-seventh percentile in 4 years.

KEEP is probably the best, the longest, and most comprehensive practical example of culturally responsiveness and matching teaching–learning styles that currently exists. The small database on other ethnic groups allows for only tentative interpretations. Much more reform and research of the type that exist in KEEP are needed to determine what happens when different dimensions of learning and teaching styles are matched for various ethnic, social, and cultural groups, and when multiple indicators of achievement are used.

Ethnic Affiliation and Identification

"Developmental appropriateness" and "readiness," along with "relevance" and "beginning with where the students are" are commonly evoked principles of teaching . Their definitions are frequently limited to prerequisite knowledge and intellectual maturation. Successful learning and teaching require much more than this. Readiness can be perceived as the psychoemotional and intellectual disposition of individuals to receive and engage with learning stimuli. A major factor embedded in this definition is the idea that how students feel about themselves has a significant impact, along with teacher expectations and learning styles, upon how they function in learning situations. These self-concepts, like other individual and cultural characteristics, are multidimensional. Thus, psychologists and educators are increasingly identifying physical/appearance, and personal, school, intellectual, social, and gender self-concepts (Clark, 1992; Pang, Mizokawa, & Olstad, 1985). Another concept of particular significant to the discussion is *ethnic identity development*.

Ethnic identity has been defined as the personal ownership of membership in a particular ethnic group, and the knowledge, understandings, values, attitudes, beliefs, and behaviors associated with this membership (Bernal et al, 1993; Phinney & Rotheram, 1987). It includes dimensions of identification and affiliation, cognition and affect, psychology and sociology, individual and group orientations. It is a dynamic, developmental, and sociopsychological process that develops gradually, and tends to increase in clarity, intensity, and significance with age (Phinney & Rotheram, 1987). It is an aspect of, and may even be a complement to, one's more global self-concept, but it is neither analogous nor predictive of it. According to Bernal et al (1993), ethnic identity has five major components: self-identification, constancy, role behaviors, knowledge, and feelings and preferences that reflect the cultural values of a given group.

Cross (1987, 1991) offers a comparable argument in distinguishing between personal identity and referent group orientation factors. He argued that both are important, but that they are not predictive of each other in constructing ethnic identities. He further explained that:

Black identity is not predictive of personal happiness, but it is predictive of a particular cultural-political propensity or worldview. PI [Personal Identity], though not predictive of a person's RGO [Referent Group Orientation], is predictive of ego strength, mental health, and interpersonal competence. PI tells us something about the mental health of a person, independent of his or her group identity. RGO data tells us a great deal about the person's worldview, independent of personality. Thus, each sector is capable of predicting extremely important factors, but each is a very poor predictor of each other (Cross 1987, p. 126).

It is not enough for teachers and supervisors merely to know the ethnic groups to which students belong. More important needs are understanding how individuals feel about and relate to their ethnic identity; how these perceptions affect learning, social, and personal behaviors; and how and why ethnic perceptions, attitudes and behaviors change over time. This knowledge helps to move the dialogue about

the interaction between culture and ethnicity beyond categorical levels of African, Asian, Latino, and European Americans. While ethnic group distinctions are imperative, they do not illuminate individual difference *within* these categories. Analyzing the processes of ethnic identity formation and transmission among individuals can facilitate this understanding (Bernal & Knight, 1993).

The body of available research on ethnic identity development from a positive perspective is relatively small but growing. Like other aspects of cultural studies, it is not evenly distributed across ethnic or gender groups, and the theoretical conceptualizations far exceed research analyses. Most of this research has been conducted with African Americans. A few studies do exist on the ethnic affiliation of Asian Americans, Latinos, and, more recently, European Americans. Prior to the mid-1970s most studies on ethnic identity dealt with establishing racial or ethnic preference among young children, and examining the "self-hatred" thesis with African Americans as epitomized by the Clarks doll preference research of the 1940s and the Horowitz' Show Me Test studies in the 1950s (Bernal & Knight, 1993; Cross, 1991; Helms, 1990; Phinney & Rotheram, 1987). Studies conducted by Gopaul-McNicol (1992) and Powell-Hopson and Hopson (1992) produced results similar to the ones the Clarks reported in the 1940s. Neither ethnicity, social class, nor national origin was a significant mediating factor. Although the intensity was somewhat different, both African- and European-American preschool children, lower and middle class, and African-American children in New York and Trinidad showed a preference for playing with white dolls while describing black dolls as "looking bad." Interventions that emphasized and modeled positive attributes of African Americans caused the children to reverse their opinions and preferences. These findings led Powell-Hopson and Hopson (1992) to recommend that programs to promote positive images of African Americans and combat racism be implemented for all children. These are imperative because "racial prejudice not only threatens the integrity and development of blacks but also impairs the ability of whites to understand and learn to accept cultural differences of other racial groups" (p. 188).

Cross (1987) advised that the results of studies like these should not be taken too seriously as conclusive proof that self-hatred is a strong presence among African Americans. Most of the children who participated in these "self-hatred" studies were quite young. Their youth means that they could not have developed very sophisticated concepts of race. The analytical focus of the research was on the consistency of their racially ascribed identities with their worldviews, but whether with children like themselves. The results on the former, however, have frequently been interpreted to be indications of the latter. Cross offered this explanation in further clarifying his proposal:

When black children show preference for white, it does not follow that they "hate" black or that they want to be "White," unless being White is taken in the following way. In young (normal) children the liquidity of their ego allows for some very interesting transformational fantasies which, if found operative in adults, might define psychosis. When children like something, they often play at being it. Thus in their own minds they can "become" a lion, a tiger, or an airplane. Why should we become alarmed when a black child express-es an attraction to the white world by playing white? (p. 130).

Four assertions related to ethnic identity development have major implications for creating culturally responsive educational programs for diverse students: (1) positive ethnic identity correlates with improved academic achievement; (2) positive ethnic identity is not automatically or easily achieved; often, it has to be deliberately constructed; (3) individuals of color with high levels of ethnic identification and affiliation are often seen as problematic in traditional school environments; and (4) ethnic identity and affiliation are key features of "readiness" to learn for students' of color. The extent to which classroom teachers, supervisors, and other educational leaders understand these processes, they can make better decisions about the scope, sequence, pacing, appropriateness, and effectiveness of instruction for diverse students.

One unit of analysis in research on ethnic identification and affiliation is level of acculturation. It was used by Chow (1981), Kitano and Daniels (1988), and Montero (1980) in their studies of Asian Americans, and by Marin's (1993) research on Mexican Americans. They found an inverse relationship between level of acculturation and ethnic identity/affiliation. As acculturation increased, compliance to indigenous cultural values, and association with members of the same ethnic group declined. Factors affecting the degree to which this occurs include generation, residential proximity to and frequency of contact with members of one's own ethnic group, and kinds of interactions with mainstream culture. With specific reference to Latinos, Martin (1993, p. 192) explained that "as length of exposure or stay in a new culture increases . . . the level of acculturation of the individual increases and the self-identification of the individuals changes toward a more 'biethnic identification."

Chow (1981) contended that the way Chinese-American females interact with their own ethnic group and mainstream European Americans is a reflection more of where they fall on a continuum of four personality types than generation or length of residence in the United States. *Traditionalists* comply with traditional cultural values and social codes; *assimilationists* disaffiliate from their own ethnic group, reject their ethnic identity, and often experience intense self-hate, and identify totally with mainstream culture; *pluralists* integrate elements of both Chinese and mainstream American culture into their values and behaviors; and *ambivalents* operate on the periphery of ethnic groups, are socially alienated, and are essentially culturally marginalized beings. Chow seems to imply that these are permanent psychological positions that individuals assume in relation to their own and other's ethnicity, rather than transitional stations in a developmental and progressional process.

These patterns of ethnic identification associated with degrees of assimilation for Asian Americans and Latinos do not apply as well to African Americans. For example, the very mature, privileged, and highly successful African Americans who participated in Lightfoot's (1994) study expressed very strong and deeply entrenched feelings of ethnic identity and affiliation. On this point, Lightfoot commented that

their own racial identity has . . . undergone transformation, reflecting personal developmental changes, changing political and cultural con-

texts and affiliations, and emerging reconnections with family origins. I would say that each of these storytellers has grown "blacker" as they have matured, stronger and less ambivalent in their identity as African-Americans (p. 604).

In the same vein, and with similar participants (e.g., upper-middle-class professionals), Edwards and Polite (1992) identified cultural consciousness and strong ethnic identity as salient and persistent traits of successful African Americans.

More recent research has concentrated on examining the sociopsychological developmental nature of ethnic identity formation. Notable contributors to this line of inquiry are Cross (1971, 1991), Atkinson, Morten, and Sue (1983), Phinney (1989, 1992, 1993), Banks (1979), Kim (1981), Phinney and Alipura (1990), Phinney and Tarver (1988), Phinney and Rotheram (1987), Helms (1990), Aries and Moorehead (1989), and Streitmatter (1989). None of these studies examined how or if gender interacts with ethnic identity development.

Cross (1990) synthesized previous research findings and theoretical conceptualizations in developing a model of stages of ethnic identity development among African Americans that was more thorough than any of its predecessors at the time. First introduced as the "Negro-to-Black Conversion Model" (Cross, 1971), it is based on what Cross called "the psychology of *nigrescence*, " or the process of becoming black. In this context "Black" is a philosophical orientation, a worldview, a cultural notation, and symbol of ethnic affirmation on a physiological descriptor. Cross' model asserts that (1) "blackness [or other ethnic identification] is a state of mind, not an inherited trait, and its acquisition often requires considerable effort" (Cross, 1991, p. 149); (2) achieving positive ethnic identity is a socio-psychological transformative process; (3) achieving positive ethnic identity does not necessarily lead to corollary changes in other aspects of self-concept development; and (4) ethnic identity development is personally liberating and empowering. Gay (1985, 1987, 1994c) built upon Cross' model and translated it from its original domain of social psychology to the arena of education. She suggested some curriculum designs and instructional strategies appropriate for the different stages of ethnic identity. Phinney used the general concepts of identity and ego formation introduced by Erikson (1968) and Marcia (1980) to create a model of ethnic identity development. She has tested it out with African-, European-, Latino-, and Asian-American students in middle schools, high schools, and colleges. The results indicate that the general model applies across ages and ethnic groups of color, although there are some variations in magnitude, intensity, and rate of growth. African Americans and Latinos are more consciously aware and clear about their ethnicity at all age levels than Asian Americans. European Americans have the most diffused or unclarified sense of ethnic identity, to the extent that Phinney (1993, p. 65) concluded "ethnicity was not a meaningful concept for these students."

Alba (1990), Helms (1990), and Tatum (1992) have conducted research on racial and ethnic identity development among European Americans. Alba proposed that a new sense of ethnicity is emerging among individuals and groups of European ancestry. Because it is associated with being from anywhere on the European continent rather than specific countries, he called it "symbolic ethnic identity." It is an outcome of cultural assimilation in a societal context where specific white ethnic affiliations (e.g., Irish, French, English, etc.) which were once important in the texture of U. S. social life, have receded into the background. They are being replaced with the categorical identification of being "European American."

While Alba's research deals with the construction of group ethnic identity, that of Helms and Tatum deals with individuals' ethnic identity development. They contend that White identity is closely intertwined with racism. The greater the extent of racism and the more it is denied, the more difficult it is for European Americans to develop a positive ethnic identity. As racism is confronted directly and deliberately, the process becomes easier. The other major and corollary feature of constructing a positive sense of White ethnic identity is becoming nonracist.

The psychological model of White Racial Identity Development created by Helms (1990) is a six-stage process, with each involving attitudes, emotions, and behaviors in which both African Americans and European Americans are significant referent groups. The stages are *contact, disintegration, reintegration, pseudoindependence, immersion/emersion,* and *autonomy.* The progression is from (1) a naive curiosity, timidity, or trepidation about African Americans, and a superficial awareness of being European American; (2) to conscious but conflicted and questioning conceptions of Whiteness; (3) to regressing back to believing in the inherent superiority of European Americans and the inferiority of African Americans; (4) or, beginning to genuinely question and deconstruct existing theories of raciality; (5) to searching for new and more accurate information to replace racial myths and stereotypes; (6) to finally, internalizing, nurturing, and applying new definitions of Whiteness, as well as becoming more racially and culturally pluralistic in one's total outlook and behaviors.

Several findings derive from studies of ethnic identity development as a sociopsychological progression of self-validation, self-acceptance, and self-creation that are important foundations for culturally responsive teaching and supervision. First, the process goes through discernible stages of development. These progress from nonconscious cognition, or self-denigration about one's ethnicity, to a conscious rejection of negative ethnic identity attributions, to a search for the reacclimation of authentic ethnic roots, to a clarification and internalization of positive conceptions of self-defined ethnicity. Second, individuals become psychologically healthier as they progress from self-negation to self-definition and self-acceptance. This improved state of personal well-being has positive effects on academic effort and achievement, interpersonal relations, receptivity toward the ethnicity of others, and overall pychosocial adjustment. Third, stage-specific psychological dispositions are transmitted through symbolic attitudes and expressive behaviors. Individuals in the self-denigration stages are very diligent about not exhibiting behaviors they think others consider typical of their ethnic group. Those who are rejecting out-group definitions of their ethnicity and are searching for their own ethnic roots may engage in exag-

gerated, highly stylized displays of ethnic ensignia, dress, and language. The ones who have accepted and internalized their ethnicity use no regularized symbols or conspicuous behavioral displays; rather, their ethnic self-acceptance permeates their total persona and style of being (Gay, 1987, 1994c). Fourth, some stages of ethnic identity development are more susceptible to internal and intergroup tensions than are others. For instance, the "awakening" and "search for roots" stages can lead to a lot of friction between individuals both within and among ethnic groups. Africans Americans in these stages can be as intolerant of other African Americans who have not yet begun the transformation process as they are of everyone who is not African American. These stages, separately and collectively, are "part of the development that oppressed people experience as they struggle to understand themselves in terms of their own culture, the dominant culture, and the oppressive relationship between the two" (Sue 1995, p. 651).

Some important lessons for educational reform can be extracted from research on ethnic identity development. Because positive ethnic identity is learned, it is teachable. If positive ethnic identity correlates with higher academic performance, then its facilitation should play a major role in educational programs designed to improve the achievement of students of color. Individuals in different stages of ethnic identity development have different needs. Educational interventions in this growth process should be developmentally appropriate to match the needs of the different stages. Like other traits that affect how students and teachers act and react toward each other, ethnic identity development occurs within particular cultural, ethnic, and socioecological contexts. As a result, the process can neither be fully understood nor responded to most effectively without *situated* or *contextualized analyses.* This means understanding the dialectical interaction that exists among ethnic identity, culture, communication, gender, individuality, environment, time, place, and referent group.

IMPLICATIONS FOR SUPERVISORY PRACTICE

A major premise of the research reviewed in this chapter is that sensitivity to gender and cultural diversity in classroom instruction can improve the academic achievement of females and students of color. This potential is currently not being sufficiently tapped. Too many educators are unaware, unknowing, and unappreciative of how culture, ethnicity, and gender affect instructional and learning behaviors, or unskilled in how to apply cultural diversity in teaching. Correcting these limitations is the major goal of gender sensitive and culturally responsive supervision. It should include developing *conscious awareness* about the dynamics of cultural diversity in the classroom; *knowledge* about specific components of cultural diversity; *appreciation* for the importance and vitality of cultural diversity for improving educational equity; and *technical or pedagogical skills* for making the educational enterprise culturally pluralistic.

The role of supervisors in this process is three-dimensional: assessing instructional activities in classrooms; helping teachers become more skillful in gender sensitivity and cultural responsiveness; and applying standards of gender and ethnic equity in the performance of their own roles and functions. It is consistent with Sergiovanni and Starratt's (1993) vision of supervision as a function intrinsic to the "reinvention" of schools that is currently being proposed by various reform movements. Because schools need "super-visions" of possibilities and hope, "those exercising supervisory responsibilities are in a unique position to nurture, develop, and articulate . . . [visions of] what a learning community can and should be" (p. xix). Supervisors should help classroom teachers design programs where students from all kinds of ethnic, racial, gender, cultural, and social backgrounds are enfranchised, empowered, and enabled for maximal intellectual, personal, social, and emotional development. Their leadership in these areas is based on the assumption that they are competent in ethnic, cultural, and gender diversity. This competence is contingent upon their own knowledge, values, skills and commitments. If supervisors are not personally and professionally committed to promoting gender and ethnic equity within the domain of supervision, getting teachers to do so in the classroom will be impossible because supervisors, like teachers with students, cannot lead, direct, guide, or facilitate in terrains they, themselves, do not know, value, or do.

Sergiovanni and Starratt (1993) view supervisors as advocates, developers, negotiators, arbitrators, and aides in improving teaching and learning. Both their roles and the results they expect to achieve are moral endeavors (i.e., doing what is good, right, and just for students, teachers, programs, and schools). Sergiovanni and Starratt (p. xviii) further explained that:

Supervision takes its moral character from its close involvement with the intrinsic moral qualities of teaching and learning. That is to say, teaching of its very nature assumes a caring for the one taught and a respect for the integrity of what is being taught and its connection to the past, present, and future life of the community. Not to care for the person being taught, or to distort the meaning of what is being taught, violates the very idea of teaching. Supervision is an activity that involves another in supporting and furthering that caring for the learner and respect for the significance of what is taught. The moral authority of the supervisor is joined with the moral authority of the teacher.

Because supervision is inextricably linked to teaching, it, too, must be culturally responsive and gender sensitive in order to fulfill the moral edict of making the educational process more equitable for females and students of color. Just as teachers who are moral in their instructional behaviors establish trusting, open, respectful, caring, and liberating relationships with students, supervisors must do likewise with teachers. Their engagements with teachers should exhibit human and professional respect, acceptance, integrity, honesty, and facilitation. Together, "these comprise the moral activity of empowerment" (Sergiovanni & Starratt, 1993, p. 61). Culturally responsive supervisors therefore help teachers to empower themselves to teach diverse students with competence and confidence; to acquire knowledge, attitudes, values, and skills about cultural diversity; and to apply these in instructional situations.

Creating culturally responsive and gender-sensitive education in the classroom requires a *reciprocal partnership of learning and doing* between teachers and supervisors. They must work closely together to understand and demonstrate what approach to education means in theory and practice. Banks (1992) explained that educational reform dealing with cultural diversity requires *transformative leaders* who are connected through shared values and goals, are motivated by the same vision of building a new order for their operational contexts, and who model the way for and enable each other in arriving at these new destinations. This reciprocity allows teachers and supervisors to capitalize on each others' strengths, and to facilitate the overall professional development of both (Guild & Garger, 1985) toward achieving greater gender and ethnic equity in education. Thus, teachers and supervisors who are culturally responsive in their respective educational functions are, by definition, transformative leaders.

Modeling is a critical feature of culturally responsive supervision. In good modeling *being and doing* are of equal importance. It is not enough for models to tell and to teach others what to do. They must be living embodiments of their own messages. In the context of classroom instruction and supervision, this means that supervisors must do in their own domains of functioning that which they expect teachers to do in working with students. Their supervisory attitudes and behaviors must *image* cultural responsiveness and gender sensitivity. In addition to lending credibility and integrity to their leadership, culturally responsive supervision establishes important points of reference for illustrating conceptual ideas and practical possibilities about similar needs in classroom instruction.

The research reviewed in this chapter indicates that gender sensitive and culturally responsive education requires *corrective and transformative action*. Educational programs, teaching practices, and instructional materials that deal adequately with ethnic, cultural, and gender diversity are currently the exception rather than the rule. In order to make these regular and routine features of the educational process, many existing practices need to be revised or replaced. Many teachers do not have the skills these reforms demand; they will have to be developed. Facilitating this kind of staff development falls within the purview of supervisory responsibilities.

Developing Self Awareness and Cultural Appreciation

Culturally responsive and gender-sensitive supervision helps teachers to develop *conscious awareness* about how culture affects individuals, processes, policies, and programs in schools and classrooms. In this respect, Good and Brophy's (1978) contention that most teachers are unaware of what they do in the classroom is important. One cannot start to solve a problem until after it is identified and recognized. If teachers do not know what they are doing in classrooms to minimize the educational opportunities of students of color and females, they cannot change their behaviors. Therefore, a critical element of culturally responsive supervision is *consciousness-raising* for both teachers and supervisors. This includes becoming aware of the cultural values embedded in and conveyed through their own and students' behaviors, and the existence of gender and ethnic disparities in teaching attitudes, expectations, assignments, and activities.

There are several simple but powerful ways in which this consciousness can be developed. First, using observation instruments to record how frequently students from different ethnic and gender groups are called on to answer what kinds of questions in instructional dialogues; praised; provided with intellectual probes, prompts, and cues; criticized and disciplined; and how often and in what ways the cultural experiences, contributions, and perspectives of women and ethnic groups of color are incorporated into curriculum content. Working together, teachers and supervisors can tabulate these results, analyze them for patterns and trends, and locate behaviors that need to be corrected. They can devise "Ethnic and Gender Equity Report Cards" for themselves as a means for continually monitoring and assessing their progress toward providing classroom instruction that is truly egalitarian for culturally diverse students. A second strategy for developing self-awareness is helping teachers to learn how to analyze their classroom decorations, images, and symbols for ethnic- and gender-equal status inclusion, accuracy, and authenticity. These are powerful conduits of tacit teaching about what and who are valued in the classroom. They can either alienate or affiliate, connect or isolate, praise or insult, or affirm or reject women and ethnic groups of color, thereby extending or obstructing learning opportunities provided in the more formal aspects of teaching.

A third means that can be used to bring teachers' interactional styles with students from different gender and ethnic group to a heightened level of awareness is video recordings. Videotapes can be made of teachers engaged in routine tasks and interactions. These provide mirror images of behaviors teachers may be unaware they are doing, Examining these analytically and critically can isolate attitudes and behaviors (both verbal and nonverbal) that facilitate learning for some students and impede it for others. Once they are identified strategies for change can be devised.

Spindler and Spindler (1993) and Bennett (1995b) offer more systematic models that can be used to facilitate teacher awareness about gender and ethnic disparities in classroom interactions. Both of these models are within the traditions of participatory action and participant–observation research. Heath (1983) used a similar technique in her ethnographic studies of young European and African American children's communication styles. The Spindler and Spindler model is called "Cultural Therapy." It is a process for bringing individuals' own culture to a level of cognitive consciousness, analyzing why the cultural behaviors of others are objectionable, irritating, or shocking, and making explicit unequal power relationships in the classroom. Essential features of cultural therapy include explicating culturally patterned assumptions that drive expectations, communications, and behaviors, culturally determined mechanisms for the expression, defense, and protection of "the self," cultural conflicts in the classroom between diverse students and teachers, and the various kinds of *instrumental competencies* and *situational self-efficacy* required for success in school, such as social etiquette, study skills, and interactional and bureaucratic protocols. It provides a way to respond to research findings that indicate that teacher

expectations and differences in cultural procedural and presentation styles are often more of an interference to academic success for students of color than intellectual ability.

Bennett's (1995) self-awareness model comes out of the theoretical framework of teachers as decision makers and reflective practitioners. Referred to as the "Teacher Perspective Framework," it facilitates self-reflection by having teachers diagnose their own perspectives of teaching prior to entering the classroom, and then studying their instructional actions to determine congruency between predicted and actual teaching behaviors. The participants' self-recorded observations are accompanied by periodic self-reflections and interviews to further heighten self-awareness and self-understanding of teaching modes. The users select perspectives that best describe themselves from among seven options (e.g., Nurturers, Friendly Pedagogues, Inculcators, Empowerers, Facilitators of Thinking, Friendly Scholars, Scholar Psychologists). Although this model was not designed specifically for analyzing teaching perspectives on cultural diversity, it can be easily adapted for this purpose. Some of the perspectives are more compatible for relating to diverse students and doing culturally responsive teaching than others. For example, Empowerers, who emphasize teaching for social change, and Nurturers,who give priority to establishing quality relationships with students, are more consistent with culturally responsive pedagogy than are Inculcators, who stress the transmission of academic knowledge.

Acquiring Cultural Knowledge and Appreciation

Responsiveness implies knowing, accepting, and acting. Therefore, for teachers to respond appropriately to ethnic and gender diversity in classrooms, they must have a clear understanding of facts about how these various traits are expressed in human behavior generally, and in educational contexts specifically. The position of supervisors in the organizational power structure of schools is strategically significant for helping teachers to acquire the knowledge and skills they need to be culturally responsive and gender sensitive in their instruction. They are responsible for identifying professional needs of teachers, and designing staff development programs to address them, or advising others to do so. Either way, supervisors possess real power for determining the kinds of in-service education teachers will receive.

Supervisors should be mindful of several key principles in designing these professional development experiences. First, the knowledge provided about ethnic and gender diversity should be *comprehensive*. It should deal with many different aspects of culture, especially those that are directly associated with teaching and learning. The four components discussed earlier—participation structures, communication styles, learning styles, and ethnic identity development—are imperative. Second, cultural knowledge needs to be *contextualized*— (i.e., interpreted and understood within specific groups, social settings, and the particular frameworks of the various job functions different educators perform). Thus, teachers need to understand specific cultural characteristics of African Americans, Latinos, Native Americans, Asian Americans, and European Americans. They need to understand how characteristic traits associated with females and males may be mediated by ethnicity and social class. They also need to know how using multicultural perspectives affect teaching math, reading, or science, and how to teach different ethnic and gender groups within particular subjects and school settings (predominately single group of color, European American, or racially mixed schools). Third, cultural knowledge should be both *cognitive* and *affective*. Factual information about different ethnic groups' values, customs, traditions, institutions, artifacts, major events, and heroes is essential, but it is not sufficient. It needs to be complemented with explorations of feelings, beliefs, and values related to ethnicity and gender, the interrogation of prejudices, stereotypes, racism, and sexism, and the examination of ethics and morality of cultural diversity, and equity of opportunities.

Many different techniques can be used to help teachers acquire the knowledge they need about ethnic and gender diversity in order to become more culturally responsive in their teaching. Their supervisors should negotiate the inclusion of multicultural competence in the accountability requirements for teachers. This could take two forms, including the study of ethnic and gender diversity in the contracted professional development experiences during a school year, and incorporating indicators of ethnic and gender sensitivity into the techniques routinely used for the performance appraisal of classroom teachers.

Available information and materials on gender issues and the cultures of ethnic groups are voluminous. There is no way that teachers can manage all of it; they must select those which are most relevant to their needs. Supervisors can provide invaluable assistance with this task, by developing a "premier" of "essential resources" on cultural attributes of women and ethnic groups of color. It should include books and articles produced by academic scholars, literary products (e.g., novels, autobiographies, poems, short stories) written by women and ethnic group members, and popular culture documents (e.g., films, recordings, documentaries). Many of the writings referenced earlier in this discussion can be included on this list, such as *Women's Ways of Knowing* (Belensky, Clinchy, Goldberger, & Tarule, 1986), *Expressively Black* (Gay & Baber, 1987), *Ethnic Identity: The Transformation of White America* (Alba, 1990), the *Handbook of Research on Multicultural Education* (Banks & Banks, 1995), and *Culture, Style and the Educative Process* (Shade, 1989). These readings should be accompanied by interpretative and reflective discussions. This is necessary because individuals may not clearly understand what they read if they have limited personal experiences with ethnic and cultural diversity. Supervisors should facilitate these discussions, assuming they are competent in the areas being studied.

Readings and discussions about cultural characteristics still may not be sufficient for some teachers to fully grasp the essence and image of how these traits function behaviorally. Including films and video recordings that portray these in the professional development experiences can be helpful. There are several high-quality feature length films, television programs, and educational media which can serve this purpose. Among them are "Racism 101," "Still Killing Us Softly," "Valuing Diversity," "Ethnic Notions," "Stand and Deliver," and "I am Joaquin."

Developing Culturally Responsive Pedagogical Skills

The success of culturally responsive education ultimately depends upon action. Teachers must understand, appreciate, and value it, and they must do it. They frequently need assistance in developing the technical skills gender sensitive and culturally responsive teaching requires. Supervisors should provide this assistance. Teachers need to develop application skills related to all of the areas discussed earlier which affect the academic achievement of students who are female and members of various ethnic groups of color.

Teachers and other school leaders are often admonished to decide if instructional materials are free of gender and ethnic biases, but rarely are they taught *how* to make this decision. Even most of the criteria for evaluating materials for these practices are more categorical than operational (i.e., they specify *what* to look for, but do not adequately explain *how* to "recognize" it). For example, a common criterion used in textbook analyses is, "Do the narrative text and visual illustrations present nonstereotypical portrayals of women and individuals and groups of color?" Another frequent proposal is for instructional materials and programs to include heroes and role models for females and ethnically diverse students to emulate. The validity of both proposals is endorsed by research findings on "connected knowing," but teachers uninformed about cultural characteristics do not know what a "nonstereotypical ethnic portrayal" is, or who are culturally appropriate heroes and heroines for different ethnic groups. Making these determinations becomes even more challenging as textbooks move away from presenting obvious and crass gender and racial stereotypes, yet continue to perpetuate more subtle ones. Teachers must be taught how to assess instructional materials for gender and cultural equity, and how to identify ethnic cultural heroes.

Supervisors can plan and facilitate training sessions to develop these skills. The sessions should include introductions to existing evaluation criteria, how to modify general criteria to serve specific purposes, demonstrations of how to apply the criteria to the narrative and visual texts of instructional materials, and guided practice in doing these analyses. These approaches can also be applied to media materials, such as magazine advertisements, television programs, and popular films. In some cases media analyses will be less threatening and easier to accomplish because the images are more graphic. They are somewhat removed also from the educators' professional arena. This distance can be beneficial in sharpening perspective and focus. Most commercial publishers and professional organizations have criteria for identifying gender, race, and ethnic biases in educational materials that can be used for these purposes. One example of these is the *Multicultural Curriculum Guidelines,* published by the National Council for the Social Studies. These can be modified and simplified for different settings and subjects.

Four other specific skill areas imperative to the implementation of culturally responsive and gender-sensitive education emerged from the research and scholarship reviewed earlier. Each falls within the role of supervisors as diagnosing needs, envisioning possibilities, and facilitating change in the professional development of teachers that will ultimately improve the school achievement of students who are female and members of various groups of color.

First, demonstrating and training teachers how to diagnose their teaching styles and the learning styles of students. This might begin by observing different students' preferences for certain learning stimuli, activities, and content in a variety of settings (e.g., formal instruction, play time, self-selected peer interactions). The observations can be conducted in person or through videotapes, and independently or with teachers and supervisors working collaboratively. One of the many instruments available (see Bennett, 1995; Guild & Garger, 1985; Ramirez & Castaneda, 1974, for samples) for diagnosing learning styles can be used to guide these observations, or be administered directly to teachers and students. After these learning-style characteristics are identified, the logical next step is to develop instructional techniques to accommodate them. The model created by Barbe and Swassing (1979) for teaching to modality strengths also may be helpful in developing instructional strategies to match different learning styles.

Techniques similar to identifying learning/teaching styles should be employed to help teachers clarify their own ethnic and gender identity development, and their attitudes toward this in students. Individuals in varying stages of these developmental processes can be very problematic to effective classroom instruction. Teachers who are vested in traditional gender roles may find students who are feminists and committed to gender liberation intolerable. The reverse is also true when the teachers are more gender liberated than are the students. Interacting with students in the midst of their ethnic identity transformations can be extremely stressful for teachers. Supervisors observing these dynamics may declare these classrooms "out of control" and recommend interventions that are inappropriate. The development of nontraditional ethnic and gender identities, however, is central to personal liberation and empowerment, which in turn, enhance academic achievement. To facilitate this growth teachers need to be able to recognize different stages of gender and ethnic identity development, and to create instructional strategies appropriate for each one. The identity development models suggested by Cross (1991), Helms (1990), Tatum (1992), and Phinney (1993), along with the instructional intervention strategies proposed by Gay (1985), can be helpful in these undertakings.

Third, teachers need to learn how to identify the language behaviors (both verbal and nonverbal) they use in the instructional process that are facilitative or obstructive to the participation of females and students of color. Students and teachers send out all kinds of signals as to whether they understand and value what each is saying. These are conveyed through a host of vocabulary, gestures, body postures, attitudes, and response mechanisms. Making lists of words and habits routinely used that are gender exclusive (e.g., using "he" as the universal pronoun) and inconsistent with ethnic preferences (e.g., referring to Asian Americans as "Orientals"; calling African American male students, "boys"; identifying groups of color as "you people"), and working diligently to avoid them can improve teachers' trust and credibility levels with students, and increase students' participation in instructional dialogues.

Fourth, supervisors should conduct training sessions for teachers on how to design curriculum and use instructional strategies that reflect the experiences, perspectives, orientations, and contributions of females and ethnic groups of color. This training should include three phases: (1) understanding the key generic components of curriculum and instructional development; (2) identifying the components of these design processes that are most amenable to incorporating gender and ethnic content; and (3) modifying the designs and strategies so that cultural diversity is placed appropriately in their respective components. Acquiring these skills can be expedited through *supervised practice*, and creating *demonstration prototypes* to illustrate how gender sensitive and culturally responsive curriculum and instruction are created. Supervisors can collaborate with curriculum, instruction, research, and development divisions of school districts, and expert consultants in gender and ethnic equity in education to produce a series of training videos. The videos should demonstrate the curriculum development process and show how culturally responsive teaching is enacted in actual classrooms.

SOME FINAL COMMENTS

Too many teachers continue to enter the profession without having received sufficient preparation in cultural diversity during their preservice education. The quick demise of so many other educational innovations that did not include a strong professional skills development component for teachers is too painful to be easily forgotten. What is at stake in promoting ethnic and gender equity in education is too important to risk yet another failure by not ensuring that teachers are prepared for the challenge. This need underscores everything that has been said about the leadership role supervisors must perform in helping schools and teachers implement culturally responsive and gender sensitive education.

Every educator in every aspect of the educational enterprise must join the struggle to make schooling more equitable and effective for students of color and females. They must work aggressively and uncompromisingly toward this end. The clarion call has been sounded and we cannot be timid about responding to its summon. Our children's and our own futures are too much in peril for anything less than a full-scale attack on educational injustices and inequities.

Garcia (1995) echoed the depth and immediacy of these needs. In speaking about the increasing numbers, and the academic status of ethnically, racially, socially, and linguistically diverse students in today's schools, he said:

[T]heir success is our success and their failure is our failure. They must succeed. We have no other alternative short of disbanding the "game." To think of disbanding education in this country is analogous in impossibility to thinking of disbanding the economy. Can education rise to this challenge and accommodate students it has historically underserved? There is no doubt that we have the resourcefulness to meet this challenge (pp. 377–378).

If resourcefulness is not the issue in making educational success a reality for females and ethnic students of color, then what is? This question brings back to mind Sergiovanni and

Starratt's point that teaching and supervision—in fact, the entire educational enterprise—are moral endeavors. Given this, then the question about the educational future of the United States is: Do we have the moral valor and the ethical will to do what is right by all of our children? If we do, and Garcia is correct in his assessment that the resources already exist, then we can make high level academic success a reality for all children, and a healthy, vital future for society will be ensured.

While research and theory on the complex interplay of ethnicity, culture, gender, and education do not always speak with a consensual and unequivocal voice on all specific details, general patterns and trends are firmly established. There is more than enough evidence about the incipient nature and persistent negative consequences of ethnic and gender disparities in education to justify a full-bloom transformative reform agenda. Supervisors are in a strategic position to lead the way in defining, championing, and even directing these initiatives. They hold positions of unheralded potential in this struggle. Their power and participation in the vanguard of equity reforms has heretofore not been capitalized. This oversight must be corrected in the future.

Supervisors are routinely expected to help schools, as institutions, envision and re-vision their missions and directions, to assist in assessing how their various dimensions are proceeding toward achieving desired goals, and to help educators in different institutional positions improve their effectiveness. No realistic future for schools can be envisioned or constructed without dealing directly with cultural diversity. Thus, meeting the needs of diverse students and fulfilling the mandate of providing *relevant, responsible,* and *ethical* supervisory leadership are closely interrelated.

At the heart of these goals, visions, and challenges is the implementation of educational programs and practices that incorporate the contributions, perspectives, experiences, and styles of the culturally diverse peoples who comprise the United States and its schools. To the extent that this happens, all students will receive an education that is self-validating, personally liberating, intellectually enabling, and socially empowering. Supervisors can contribute significantly to this achievement by being culturally responsive and gender sensitive in their own professional functions, and holding those with whom they work accountable for the same. Partnerships of vision, purpose, commitment, and action such as these make the possibility of students of color and females receiving just, equitable, and qualitative educational opportunities a more promising prospect.

REFERENCES

Abrahams, R. D. (1970). *Positively black.* Englewood Cliffs, NJ: Prentice-Hall.

Abrahams, R. D. (1976). *Talking Black.* Rowley, MA: Newbury House.

Adelman, C. (1991). *Women at thirty something: Paradoxes of attainment.* Washington, D.C.: U. S. Department of Education, Office of Educational Research and Improvement.

Alba, R. D. (1990). *Ethnic identity: The transformation of white America.* New Haven, CT: Yale University Press.

Alexander, K. A. & McDill, E. L. (1976). Selection and allocation within schools: Some causes and consequences of curriculum placement. *American Sociological Review, 41,* 969–980.

Alexander, K. L., Entwisle, D. R., & Thompson, M. S. (1987). School performance, status relations, and the structure of sentiment: Bringing the teacher back in. *American Sociological Review, 52,* 665–682.

Anyon, J. (1981). Social class and school knowledge. *Curriculum Inquiry, 11*(1), 3–42.

Anyon, J. (1988). Schools as agents of social legitimation. In W. F. Pinar (Ed.). *Contemporary curriculum discourses* (pp. 175–200). Scottsdale, AZ: Gorsuch Scarisbrick.

Archer, C. J. (1984). Children's attitudes toward sex-role division in adult occupational roles. *Sex Roles: A Journal of Research, 10*(1–2), 1–10.

Aries, E. & Moorehead, K. (1989). The importance of ethnicity in the development of identity of black adolescents. *Psychological Reports, 65* 75–82.

Atkinson, D. R., Morten, G., & Sue, D. W. (1983). Proposed minority identity development model. In D. R. Atkinson, G. Morten, & D. W. Sue (Eds.). *Counseling American minorities: A cross-cultural perspective* (pp. 191–200). Dubuque, IA: Willam C. Brown.

Au, K. H. (1980a). Participation structures in a reading lesson with Hawaiian children: Analysis of a culturally appropriate instructional event. *Anthropology and Education Quarterly, 11*(2), 91–115.

Au, K. H. (1980b). *Theory and method in establishing the cultural congruence of classroom speech events.* ERIC Document, ED 204 465.

Au, K. H. (1993). *Literacy instruction in multicultural settings.* New York: Harcourt Brace.

Au, K. H. & Kawakami, A. J. (1985). Research currents: Talk story and learning to read. *Language Arts, 62*(4), 406–411.

Au, K. H. & Kawakami, A. J. (1991). Culture and ownership: Schooling of minority students. *Childhood Education, 67*(5), 280–284.

Au, K. H. & Kawakami, A. J. (1994). Cultural congruence in instruction. In E. R. Hollins, J. E. King, & W. C. Hayman (Eds.). *Teaching diverse populations: Formulating a knowledge base* (pp. 5–23). Albany, NY: State University of New York Press.

Au, K. P. & Mason, J. M. (1983). Cultural congruence in classroom participation structures: Achieving a balance of rights. *Discourse Processes, 6*(2), 145–167.

Baber, C. R. (1987). The artistry and artifice of black communication. In G. Gay & W. L. Baber (Eds.). *Expressively black: The cultural basis of ethnic identity* (pp. 75–108). New York: Praeger.

Banks, C. A. M. (1992). The leadership challenge in multicultural education. In C. Diaz (Ed.). *Multicultural education for the 21st century* (pp. 204–213). Washington, D.C.: National Education Association.

Banks, J. A. (1988). *Multiethnic education: Theory and practice* (2nd ed.). Boston, MA: Allyn & Bacon.

Banks, J. A. (1991). Multicultural education: Its effects on students' racial and gender role attitudes. In J. P. Shaver (Ed.). *Handbook of research on social studies teaching and learning* (pp. 459–469). New York: Macmillan.

Banks, J. A. & Banks, C. A. M. (Eds.). (1993). *Multicultural education: Issues and perspectives* (2nd ed.). Boston, MA: Allyn & Bacon.

Banks, J. A. & Banks, C. A. M. (Eds.). (1995). *Handbook of research in multicultural education.* New York: Macmillan.

Barbe, W. B. & Swassing, R. H. (1979). *Teaching through modality strengths: Concepts and practice.* Columbus, OH: Zaner-Bloser.

Belensky, M. F., Clinchy, B. M., Goldberger, N. R., & Tarule, J. M. (1986). *Women's ways of knowing: The development of self, voice, and mind.* New York: Basic Books.

Bennett, C. I. (1995a). *Comprehensive multicultural education: Theory and practice* (3rd ed.). Boston, MA: Allyn & Bacon.

Bennett, C. I. (1995b). *Teacher perspectives as a tool for reflection, partnerships, and professional growth.* Paper presented at the Annual Meeting of the American Educational Research Association, San Francisco, CA.

Bernal, M. E. & Knight, G. P. (Eds.). (1993). *Ethnic identity: Formation and transmission among Hispanics and other minorities.* Albany, NY: State University of New York Press.

Bernal, M. E., Knight, G. P., Ocampo, K. A., Garza, C. A., & Cota, M. K. (1993). Development of Mexican American identity. In M. E. Bernal & G. P. Knight (Eds.). *Ethnic identity: Formation and transmission among Hispanics and other minorities* (pp. 31–46). Albany, NY: State University of New York Press.

Bernstein, B. (1964). Elaborated and restricted codes: Their social origins and some consequences. *American Anthropologist, 66*(6), 55–69.

Biklen, S. K. & Pollard, D. (Eds.). (1993). *Gender and education.* (92nd yearbook of the National Society for the Study of Education, Part I). Chicago, IL: University of Chicago Press.

Boggs, S. T. (1985). The meaning of questions and narratives to Hawaiian children. In C. B. Cazden, V. H. John, & D. Hymes (Eds.). *Functions of language in the classroom* (pp. 299–327). Prospect Heights, IL: Waveland Press.

Boggs, S. T., Watson-Gegeo, K., & McMillen, G. (1985). *Speaking, relating, and learning: A study of Hawaiian children at home and at school.* Norwood, NJ: Ablex.

Bowers, C. A. & Flinders, D. J. (1991). *Culturally responsive teaching and supervision: A handbook for staff development.* New York: Teachers College Press, Columbia University.

Bowles, S. & Gintis, H. (1976). *Schooling in capitalist America.* New York: Basic Books.

Bowie, R. & Bond, C. (1994). Influencing future teachers' attitudes toward black English: Are we making a difference? *Journal of Teacher Education, 45*(2), 122–118.

Boykin, A. W. (1979). Psychological/behavioral verve in academic task performance: Pretheoretical considerations. *Journal of Negro Education, 47,* 343–354.

Boykin. A. W. (1982). Task variability and the performance of black and white schoolchildren: Vervistic explorations. *Journal of Black Studies, 12,* 469–482.

Boykin, A. W. (1986). The triple quandary and the schooling of Afro-American children. In U. Neisser (Ed.). *The school achievement of minority children: New perspectives* (pp. 57–92). Hillsdale, NJ: Lawrence Erlbaum.

Boykin, A. W. (1994). Afrocultural expression and its implications for schooling. In E. R. Hollins, J. E. King, & W. C. Hayman (Eds.). *Teaching diverse populations: Formulating a knowledge base* (pp. 243–256). Albany, NY: State University of New York Press.

Brown, A. L., Palincsar, A. S., & Purcell, L. (1986). Poor readers: Teach, don't label. In U. Neisser (Ed.). *The school achievement of minority children: New perspectives* (pp. 105–143). Hillsdale, NJ: Lawrence Erlbaum.

Burgess, B. J. (1978). Native American learning styles. In L. Morris, G. Sather, & S. Scull (Eds.). *Extracting learning styles from social/cultural diversity: A study of five American minorities* (pp. 41–53). Normal, OK: Southwest Teacher Corps Network.

Burstyn, J. N. (1993). Who benefits and who suffers: Gender and education in the dawn of the age of information technology. In S. K. Biklen & D. Pollard (Eds.). *Gender and education.* (92nd year-

book of the National Society for the Study of Education, Part 1: pp. 107–125). Chicago, IL: University of Chicago Press.

Byers, P. & Byers, H. (1985). Nonverbal communication and the education of children. In C. B. Cazden, V. P. John, & D. Hymes (Eds.). *Functions of language in the classroom* (pp. 3–31). Prospect Heights, IL: Waveland Press.

Canale, J. R. & Dunlap, L. L. (1987). Factors influencing career aspirations of primary and secondary grade students. ERIC Document ED 288 164.

Cazden, C. B. (1986). Classroom discourse. In M. C. Wittrock (Ed.). *Handbook of research on teaching* (3rd ed.) pp. 432–463. New York: Macmillan.

Cazden, C. B. (1988). *Classroom discourse: The language of teaching and learning.* Portsmouth, NH: Heinemann.

Cazden, C. B., John, V. P., & Hymes, D. (Eds.). (1985). *Functions of language in the classroom.* Prospect Heights, IL: Waveland Press.

Chan, K-N. (1981). Education for Chinese and Indochinese. *Theory Into Practice, 20*(1), 35–44.

Characteristics of American Indian and Alaska Native education: Results from the 1990–91 school and staffing survey. (1995). Washington, D.C.: U. S. Department of Education, National Center for Education Statistics, Office of Educational Research and Improvement.

Chow, E. N. L. (1981). *Acculturation and self-concept of the Asian American woman.* ERIC Document, ED 224 848.

Chu, H. (1995). The Korean Americans. In C. A. Grant (Ed.). *Educating for diversity: An anthology of multicultural voices* (pp. 139–157). Boston, MA: Allyn & Bacon.

Clark, M. L. (1992). Racial group concept and self-esteem in black children. In A. K. H. Burlew, A. C. Banks, H. P. McAdoo, & D. A. ya Azibo (Eds.). *African American psychology: Theory, research, and practice* (pp. 159–172). Newbury Park, CA: Sage.

Collins, P. H. (1991). *Black feminist thought: Knowledge consciousness, and the politics of empowerment.* New York: Routledge.

Cortes, C. E. (1978). Chicano culture, experience, and learning. In L. Morris, G. Sather, & S. Scull (Eds.). *Extracting learning styles from social/cultural diversity: A study of five American minorities* (pp. 29–39). Normal, OK: Southwest Teacher Corps Network.

Cross, W. E., Jr. (1971). Negro-to-black conversion experience. *Black World, 20,* 13–27.

Cross, W. E., Jr. (1987). A two-factor theory of black identity: Implications for the study of identity development in minority children. In J. S. Phinney & M. J. Rotheram (Eds.). *Children's ethnic socialization: Pluralism and development* (pp. 107–113). Newbury Park, CA: Sage.

Cross, W. E., Jr. (1991). *Shades of black: Diversity in African-American identity.* Philadelphia, PA: Temple University Press.

Curricular differentiation in public high schools. (1994). Washington, D.C.: U. S. Department of Education, National Center for Education Statistics, Office of Educational Research and Improvement.

Damico, S. B. & Scott, E. (1987). Behavior differences between black and white females in desegregated schools. *Equity and Excellence, 23,* 63–66.

Davis, O. L., Jr., Ponder, G., Burlbaw, L. M., Garza-Lubeck, M., & Moss, A. (1986). *Looking at history: A review of major U. S. history textbooks.* Washington, D.C.: People for the American Way.

Dennis, W. (1940). *The Hopi child.* New York: Appleton Century.

Digest of education statistics. (1994). Washington, D.C.: U. S. Department of Education, National Center of Education Statistics.

Dilworth, M. E. (Ed.). (1992). *Diversity in teacher education: New expectations.* San Francisco, CA: Jossey-Bass.

Dumont, R. V., Jr. (1985). Learning English and how to be silent: Studies in Sioux and Cherokee classrooms. In C. B. Cazden, V. P. John, & D. Hymes (Eds.). *Functions of language in the classroom* (pp. 344–369). Prospect Heights, IL: Waveland Press.

Educational Testing Service. (1989). *What Americans study*. Princeton, NJ: Educational Testing Service.

Edwards, A. & Polite, C. K. (1992). *Children of the dream: The psychology of Black success*. New York: Doubleday.

Ellington, L. (1986). Blacks and Hispanics in high school economics textbooks. *Social Education, 50*, 64–67.

Equality and excellence: The educational status of African Americans. (1985). New York: College Entrance Examination Board.

Erikson, E. (1968). *Identity: Youth and crisis*. New York: Norton.

Escalante, J. & Dirmann, (1990). The Jaime Escalante math program. *Journal of Negro Education, 59*(3), 407–423.

Farmer, H. S. & Sidney, J. S. (1985). Sex equity in career and vocational education. In S. Klein (Ed.). *Handbook for achieving sex equity through education* (pp. 338–359). Baltimore, MD: Johns Hopkins University Press.

Foster, M. (1989). It's cooking now: A performance analysis of the speech events of a Black teacher in an urban community college. *Language in Society, 18*, 1–29.

Foster, M. (1991). "Just got to find a way": Case studies of the lives and practice of exemplary black high school teachers. M. Foster (Ed.). *Readings on equal education. Volume 11: Qualitative investigations into schools and schooling* (pp. 273–309). New York: AMS Press.

Foster, M. (1994). Effective black teachers: A literature review. In E. R. Hollins, J. E. King, & W. C. Hayman (Eds.). *Teaching diverse populations: Formulating a knowledge base* (pp. 225–241). Albany, NY: State University of New York Press.

Foster, M. (1995). African American teachers and culturally relevant pedagogy. In J. A. Banks & C. A. M. Banks (Eds.). *Handbook of research on multicultural education* (pp. 570–581). New York: Macmillan.

Gallimore, R., Boggs, J. W., & Jordan, C. (1974). *Culture, behavior, and education: A study of Hawaiian-Americans*. Beverly Hills, CA: Sage.

Garcia, E. (1991). *Education of linguistically and culturally diverse students: Effective instructional practices*. Washington, D.C.: Center for Applied Linguistics.

Garcia, E. E. (1995). Educating Mexican American students: Past treatment and recent developments in theory, research, policy, and practice. In J. A. Banks & C. A. M. Banks (Eds.). *Handbook of research on multicultural education* (pp. 372–387). New York: Macmillan.

Gay, G. (1975). Cultural differences important in the education of Black children. *Momentum, 2*, 30–33.

Gay, G. (1979). Impact of *Brown* on textbooks. *Crisis, 86*(6), 240–243.

Gay, G. (1985). Implications of selected models of ethnic identity development for educators. *Journal of Negro Education, 54*, 43–55.

Gay, G. (1987). Ethnic identity development and black expressiveness. In G. Gay & W. L. Baber (Eds.). *Expressively black: The cultural basis of ethnic identity* (pp. 35–74). New York: Praeger.

Gay, G. (1993). Building cultural bridges: A bold proposal for teacher education. *Education and Urban Society, 25*(3), 285–299.

Gay, G. (1994a). *A synthesis of scholarship in multicultural education*. Urban Monograph Series. Oak Brook, IL: North Central Regional Educational Laboratory.

Gay, G. (1994b). *At the essence of learning: Multicultural education*. West Lafayette, IN: Kappa Delta Pi.

Gay, G. (1994c). Coming of age ethnically: Teaching young adolescents of color. *Theory Into Practice, 33*(3), 149–155.

Gay, G. & Baber, W. L. (Eds.). (1987). *Expressively black: The cultural basis of ethnic identity*. New York: Praeger.

Gee, J. P. (1989). What is literacy? *Journal of Education, 171*(1), 18–25.

Gilligan, C. (1982). *In a different voice: Psychological theory and women's development*. Cambridge, MA: Harvard University Press.

Giroux, H. A. (1992). *Border crossings: Cultural workers and the politics of education*. New York: Routledge.

Glock, C. Y., Wuthnow, R., Piliavin, J. A., & Spencer, M. (1975). *Adolescent prejudice*. New York: Harper & Row.

Gollnick, D. M. & Chinn, P. C. (Eds.). (1994). *Multicultural education in a pluralistic society* (4th ed.). Columbus, OH: Merrill.

Good, T. L. & Brophy, J. E. (1978). *Looking in classrooms* (2nd ed.). New York: Harper & Row.

Goodenough, W. H. (1981). *Culture, language, and society* (2nd ed.). Menlo Park, CA: Benjamin Cummings.

Goodlad, J. I. (1984). *A place called school: Prospects for the future*. New York: McGraw-Hill.

Goodwin, M. H. (1990). *He-said she-said: Talk as social organization among Black children*. Bloomington, IN: Indiana University Press.

Gopaul-McNicol, S. A. (1992). Racial identification and racial preference of Black preschool children in New York and Trinidad. In A. K. H. Burlew, W. C. Banks, H. P. McAdoo, & D. A. ya Azibo (Eds.). *African American psychology: Theory, research, and practice* (pp. 190–193). Newbury Park, CA: Sage.

Gougis, R. A. (1986). The effects of prejudice and stress on the academic performance of Black-Americans. In U. Neisser (Ed.). *The school achievement of minority children: New perspectives* (pp. 145–158). Hillsdale, NJ: Lawrence Erlbaum.

Grant, L. (1984). Black females' "place" in desegregated classrooms. *Sociology of Education, 57*(2), 98–111.

Greenbaum, P. E. (1985). Nonverbal differences in communication style between American Indian and Anglo elementary classrooms. *American Educational Research Journal, 22*, 101–115.

Grossman, H. (1984). *Educating Hispanic students: Cultural implications for instruction, classroom management, counseling and assessment*. Springfield, IL: Charles C. Thomas.

Grossman, H. & Grossman, S. H. (1994). *Gender issues in education*. Boston, MA: Allyn & Bacon.

Grubb, W. N. (1995). The old problem of "new students": Purpose, content, and pedagogy. In E. Flaxman & A. H. Passow (Eds.). *Changing populations, changing schools* (94th Yearbook of the National Society for the Study of Education. Part II; pp. 4–29). Chicago, IL: University of Chicago Press.

Guild, P. K. & Garger, S. (1985). *Marching to different drummers*. Alexandria, VA: ASCD.

Guilmet, G. M. (1979). Instructor reaction to verbal and nonverbal-visual styles: An example of Navajo and Caucasian children. *Anthropology & Education Quarterly, 10*, 254–266.

Guttentag, M. (1972). Negro-White differences in children's movement. *Perceptual and Motor Skills, 35*, 435–436.

Guttentag, M. & Ross, S. (1972). Movement responses in simple concept learning. *American Journal of Orthopsychiatry, 42*, 657–665.

Hale-Benson, J. E. (1986). *Black children: Their roots, culture, and learning styles*. Baltimore, MA: Johns Hopkins University Press.

Hall, E. T. (1981). *Beyond culture*. (2nd ed.). Garden City, NY: Anchor Press/Doubleday.

Hall, W. S., Reder, S., & Cole, M. (1979). Story recall in young black and white children: Effects of racial group membership, race of experimenter, and dialect. In A. W. Boykin, A. J. Franklin, & J. F. Yates (Eds.). *Research directions of Black psychologists* (pp. 253–265). New York: Sage.

Harry, B. (1992). *Cultural diversity, families, and the special education system: Communication and empowerment*. New York: Teachers College Press, Columbia University.

Havighurst, R. J. & Neugarten, B. L. (1955). *American Indian and white children: A sociopsychological investigation*. Chicago, IL: University of Chicago Press.

Heath, S. B. (1983). *Ways with words: Language, life, and work in communities and classrooms*. Cambridge, England: Cambridge University Press.

Helms, J. (1990). *Black and white racial identity: Theory, research, and practice.* New York: Greenwood.

Hlebowitsh, P. S. (1993). *Radical curriculum theory reconsidered: A historical approach.* New York: Teachers College Press, Columbia University.

Holliday, B. G. (1981). The imperatives of development and ecology: Lessons learned from black children. In J. McAdoo, H. McAdoo, & W. E. Cross, Jr. (Eds.). *Fifth conference on empirical research in Black psychology* (pp. 50–64). Washington, D.C.: National Institute of Mental Health.

Holliday, B. G. (1985). Towards a model of teacher-child transactional processes affecting black children's academic achievement. In M. B. Spencer, G. K. Brookins, & W. R. Allen (Eds.). *Beginnings: The social and affective development of Black children* (pp. 117–130). Hillsdale, NJ: Lawrence Erlbaum.

Hollins, E. R., King, J. E., & Hayman, W. C. (Eds.). (1994). *Teaching diverse populations: Formulating a knowledge base.* Albany, NY: State University of New York Press.

Hooks, B. (1989). *Talking back: Thinking feminist, thinking black.* Boston, MA: South End Press.

How schools shortchange girls: AAUP report (1995). New York: Marlowe and Company.

Hoyenga, K. B. & Hoyenga, K. T. (1979). *The question of sex differences: Psychological, cultural, and biological issues.* Boston, MA: Little, Brown and Company.

Jackson, G. & Cosca, C. (1974). The inequality of educational opportunity in the southwest: An observational study of ethnically mixed classrooms. *American Educational Research Journal, 11*(3), 219–229.

John, V. P. (1985). Styles of learning—styles of teaching: Reflections on the education of Navajo children, In C. B. Cazden, V. P. John, & D. Hymes (Eds.). *Functions of language in the classroom* (pp. 331–343). Prospect Heights, IL: Waveland Press.

Joos, M. (1967). *The five clocks.* New York: Harcourt, Brace and World.

Kagan, S. & Madsen, M. C. (1971). Cooperation and competition of Mexican, Mexican-American, and Anglo-American children of two ages under four instructional sets. *Developmental Psychology, 6*(1), 49–59.

Kibria, N. (1993). *Family tightrope: The changing lives of Vietnamese Americans.* Princeton, NJ: Princeton University Press.

Kim, J. (1981). *The process of Asian-American identity development: A study of Japanese American women's perceptions of their struggle to achieve positive identities.* Unpublished Doctoral Dissertation, University of Massachusetts.

King, J. E. (1991). Unfinished business: Black student alienation and black teachers' emancipatory pedagogy. In M. Foster (Ed.). *Readings on equal education. Volume 11: Qualitative investigations into schools and schooling* (pp. 245–271). New York: AMS Press.

King, J. E. (1994). The purpose of schooling for African American children: Including cultural knowledge. In E. R. Hollins, J. E. King, & W. C. Hayman (Eds.). *Teaching diverse populations: Formulating a knowledge base* (pp. 25–56). Albany, NY: State University of New York Press.

Kitano, H. H. L. & Daniels, R. (1988). *Asian Americans: Emerging minorities.* Englewood Cliffs, NJ: Prentice Hall.

Klein, S. S. (Ed.). (1982). *Handbook for achieving sex equity through education.* Baltimore, MD: Johns Hopkins University Press.

Kochman, T. (Ed.). (1972). *Rappin' and stylin' out: Communication in urban Black America.* Urbana, IL: University of Illinois Press.

Kochman, T. (1981). *Black and white styles in conflict.* Chicago, IL: University of Chicago Press.

Kretman, K. P. & Parker, B. (1986). New U.S. history textbooks: Good news and bad. *Social Education, 50,* 61–63.

Ladson-Billings, G. (1991). Returning to the source: Implications for educating teachers of black students. In M. Foster (Ed.). *Readings on equal education. Volume 11: Qualitative investigations into schools and schooling* (pp. 227–244). New York: AMS Press.

Ladson-Billings, G. (1994). *The dreamkeepers: Successful teachers for African-American children.* San Francisco, CA: Jossey-Bass.

Ladson-Billings, G. (1995a). Multicultural teacher education: Research, practice, and policy. In J. A. Banks & C. A. M. Banks (Eds.). *Handbook of research on multicultural education* (pp. 747–759). New York: Macmillan.

Ladson-Billings, G. (1995b). Toward a theory of culturally relevant pedagogy. *American Educational Research Journal, 32*(3), 465–491.

Lawrence-Lightfoot, S. (1994). *I've known rivers: Lives of loss and liberation.* Reading, MA: Addison-Wesley.

Leacock, E. B. (1985). Abstract versus concrete speech: A false dichotomy. In C. B. Cazden, V. H. John, & D. Hymes (Eds.). *Functions of language in the classroom* (pp. 111–134). Prospect Heights, IL: Waveland Press.

Lee, C. D. & Slaughter-Defoe, D. T. (1995). Historical and sociocultural influences on African American education. In J. A. Banks & C. A. M. Banks (Eds.). *Handbook of research on multicultural education* (pp. 348–371). New York: Macmillan.

Lengermann, P. M. & Wallace, R. A. (1985). *Gender in America: Social control and social change.* Englewood Cliffs, NJ: Prentice-Hall.

Lewis, D. (1975). The black family: Socialization and sex roles. *Phylon, 36*(3), 221–237.

Lewis, S. (1982). Achieving sex equity for minority women. In S. S. Klein (Ed.). *Handbook for achieving sex equity through education* (pp. 365–390). Baltimore, MD: Johns Hopkins University.

Linn, M. C. (1985). Gender equity in computer learning environments. *Computers and the Social Sciences, 1,* 19–27.

Lipsitz, J. (1984). *Successful schools for young adolescents.* New Brunswick, NJ: Transaction Books.

Lomawaima, K. T. (1995). Educating Native Americans. In J. A. Banks & C. A. M. Banks (Eds.). *Handbook of research on multicultural education* (pp. 331–347). New York: Macmillan.

Longstreet, W. (1978). *Aspects of ethnicity: Understanding differences in pluralistic classrooms.* New York: Teachers College Press, Columbia University.

Lorde, A. (1988). *A burst of light.* Ithaca, NY: Firebrand Books.

Maccoby, E. E. (1988). Gender as a social category. *Developmental Psychology, 24*(6), 755–765.

Maccoby, E. E. & Jacklin, C. N. (1974). *The psychology of sex differences.* Stanford, CA: Stanford University Press.

Maltz, D. N. & Borker, R. A. (1983). A cultural approach to male-female miscommunication. In J. J. Gumperz (Ed.). *Communication, language, and social identity* (pp. 196–216). Cambridge, England: Cambridge University Press.

Marcia, J. (1980). Identity in adolescence. In J. Adelson (Ed.). *Handbook of adolescent psychology* (pp. 159–187). New York: Wiley.

Marin, G. (1993). Influence of acculturation on familialism and self-identification among Hispanics. In M. E. Bernal & G. P. Knight (Eds.). *Ethnic identity: Formation and transmission among Hispanics and other minorities* (pp. 181–196). Albany, NY: State University of New York Press.

Marshall, H. H. (1969). Learning as a function of task interest, reinforcement, and social class variables. *Journal of Educational Psychology, 60,* 133–137.

Martinez, J. L., Jr. (Ed.). (1977). *Chicano psychology.* New York: Academic Press.

McCarthy, C. (1990). Multicultural education, minority identities, textbooks, and the challenge of curriculum reform. *Journal of Education, 172*(2), 118–129.

McCaleb, S. P. (1994). *Building communities of learning: A collaboration among teachers, students, families, and community.* New York: St. Martin's.

McFadden, A. C., Marsh, G. E., Price, B. J., & Hwang, Y. (1992). A study of race and gender in the punishment of school children. *Education and Treatment of Children, 15*(2), 140–146.

Michaels, S. (1980). "Sharing Time": Narrative styles and differential access to literacy. *Language in Society, 10,* 423–442.

Michaels, S. & Cazden, C. B. (1986). Teacher/child collaboration as oral preparation for literacy. In B. B. Schieffelin & P. Gilmore (Eds.). *The acquisition of literacy: Ethnographic perspectives* (pp. 132–154). Norwood, NJ: Ablex.

Mickelson, R. A. (1990). The attitude-achievement paradox among black adolescents. *Sociology of Education, 63,* 44–61.

Mohatt, G. & Erickson, F. (1981). Cultural differences in teaching styles in an Odawa school: A sociolinguistic approach. In H. T. Trueba, P. Guthrie, & K. H. P. Au (Eds.). *Culture and the bilingual classroom* (pp. 105–119). Rowley, MA: Newbury House.

Montero, D. (1980). *Japanese Americans: Changing patterns of ethnic affiliation over three generations.* Boulder, CO: Westview Press.

Moraga, C. & Anzaldua, G. (Eds.). (1981). *The bridge called my back: Writings of radical women of color.* Watertown, MA: Persephone Press.

More, A. J. (1989). Native Indian students and their learning styles: Research results and classroom applications. In B. J. Shade (Ed.). *Culture, style, and the educative process* (pp. 150–166). Springfield, IL: Charles C. Thomas.

Morgan, H. (1990). Assessment of student's behavioral interactions during on-task activities. *Perceptual and Motor Skills, 70,* 563–569.

Morris, L., Sather, G, & Scull, S. (Eds.). (1978). *Extracting learning styles from social/cultural diversity: Studies of five American minorities.* Normal, OK: Southwest Teacher Corps Network.

Mullins, I. V. S., Campbell, J. R., & Farstrup, A. E. (1993). *NAEP 1992 reading report card for the nation and the states.* Washington, D.C.: U. S. Department of Education, National Center of Education Statistics, Office of Educational Research and Improvement.

Murillo, N. (1976). The Mexican American family. In C. A. Hernandez, M. J. Haug, & N. N. Wagner (Eds.). *Chicanos: Social and psychological perspectives* (pp. 15–25). St Louis, MO: C.V. Mosby.

NAEP 1992 trends in academic progress. (1994). Washington, D.C.: U. S. Department of Education, National Center for Education Statistics, Office of Educational Research and Improvement.

Neisser, U. (Ed.). (1986). *The school achievement of minority children: New perspectives.* Hillsdale, NJ: Lawrence Erlbaum.

Nieto, S. (1995). A history of the education of Puerto Rican students in U. S. mainland schools: "Losers," "outsiders," or "leaders"? In J. A. Banks & C. A. M. Banks (Eds.). *Handbook of research on multicultural education* (pp. 388–411). New York: Macmillan.

Oakes, J. (1985). *Keeping tracks: How schools structure inequality.* New Haven, CT: Yale University Press.

Oakes, J. (1986a,). Keeping track, part 1: The policy and practice of curriculum inequality. *Phi Delta Kappan, 68,* 12–17.

Oakes, J. (1986b). Keeping track, part 2: Curriculum inequality and school reform. *Phi Delta Kappan, 68,* 148–153.

Osajama, K. H. (1990). Breaking the silence: Race and the educational experiences of Asian-American college students. In M. Foster (Ed.). *Readings on equal education. Volume 11: Qualitative investigations into schools and schooling* (pp. 115–134). New York: AMS Press.

Pai, Y. (1990). *Cultural foundations of education.* New York: Merrill/Macmillan.

Palardy, J. (1969). What teachers believe—what students achieve. *Elementary School Journal, 69,* 370–374.

Pang, V. O. (1995). Asian Pacific American students: A diverse and complex population. In J. A. Banks & C. A. M. Banks (Eds.). *Handbook of research on multicultural education* (pp. 412–424). New York: Macmillan.

Pang, V. O., Mizakawa, D. T., & Olstad, R. G. (1985). Self-concept of Japanese American children. *Journal of Cross-Cultural Psychology, 16,* 99–108.

Pang, V. O. & Sablan, V. (1995). *Teacher efficacy: Do teachers believe they can be effective with African American students.* Paper presented at the Annual Meeting of the American Educational Research Association, San Francisco, CA.

Pandolfo, J. M. (1985). Prior knowledge and the reading comprehension of linguistically/culturally diverse students. ERIC Document, ED 255 863.

Pasteur, A. B. & Toldson, I. L. (1982). *Roots of soul: The psychology of black expressiveness.* Garden City, NY: Anchor Press/Doubleday.

Persell, C. H. (1977). *Education and inequality: A theoretical and empirical synthesis.* New York: Free Press.

Pewewardy, C. D. (1994). Culturally responsive pedagogy in action: An American Indian magnet school. In E. R. Hollins, J. E. King, & W. C. Hayman (Eds.). *Teaching diverse populations: Formulating a knowledge base* (pp. 77–92). Albany, NY: State University of New York Press.

Phelan, P. & Davidson, A. L. (Eds.). (1993). *Renegotiating cultural diversity in American schools.* New York: Teachers College, Columbia University.

Philips, S. U. (1983). *The invisible culture: Communication in classroom and community on the Warm Springs Indian Reservation.* Prospect Heights, IL: Waveland Press.

Philips, S. U. (1985). Participant structures and communicative competence: Warm Springs children in community and classroom. In C. B. Cazden, V. P. John, & D. Hymes (Eds.). *Functions of language in the classroom* (pp. 370–394). Prospect Heights, IL: Waveland Press.

Phinney, J. (1989). Stages of ethnic identity development in minority group adolescents. *Journal of Early Adolescence, 9,* 34–49.

Phinney, J. (1992). The Multigroup Ethnic Identity Measure: A new scale for use with adolescents and young adults from diverse groups. *Journal of Adolescent Research, 7,* 156–176.

Phinney, J. S. (1993). A three-stage model of ethnic identity development in adolescence. In M. E. Bernal & G. P. Knight (Eds.). *Ethnic identity: Formation and transmission among Hispanics and other minorities* (pp. 61–79). Albany, NY: State University of New York Press.

Phinney, J. & Alipuria, L. (1990). Ethnic identity in college students from four ethnic groups. *Journal of Adolescence, 13,* 171–183.

Phinney, J. S. & Rotheram, M. J. (Eds.). (1987). *Children's ethnic socialization: Pluralism and development.* Newbury Park, CA: Sage.

Phinney, J. & Tarver, S. (1988). Ethnic identity search and commitment in black and white eighth graders. *Journal of Early Adolescence, 8,* 265–277.

Piestrup, A. M. (1973). *Black dialect interference and accommodation of reading instruction in first grade.* Monograph of the Language Behavior Research Laboratory. Berkeley, CA: University of California.

Pollard, D. S. (1993). Gender and achievement. In S. K. Biklen & D. Pollard (Eds.). *Gender and education* (92nd Yearbook of the National Society for the Study of Education. Part 1; pp. 90–106). Chicago, IL: University of Chicago Press.

Powell, R. R. & Garcia, J. (1985). The portrayal of minorities and women in selected elementary science series. *Journal of Research in Science Teaching, 22*(6), 519–533.

Powell-Hopson, D. & Hopson, D. S. (1992). Implications of doll color preferences among Black preschool children and White preschool children. In A. K. H. Burlew, A. C. Banks, H. P. McAdoo, & D. A. ya Azibo (Eds.). *African American psychology: Theory, research, and practice* (pp. 183–189). Newbury Park, CA: Sage

Ramirez, M., III, & Castaneda, A. (1974). *Cultural democracy, bicognitive development and education.* New York: Academic Press.

Rist, R. C. (1970). Student social class and teacher expectations: The self-fulfilling prophecy in ghetto education. *Harvard Educational Review, 40,* 411–450.

Rosenbaum, J. E. (1976). *Making inequality: The hidden curriculum of high school tracking.* New York: Wiley.

Rosenthal, R. & Jacobson, L. (1968). *Pygmalion in the classroom: Teacher expectations and pupils' intellectual development.* New York: Holt, Rinehart & Winston.

Ryan, W. (1971). *Blaming the victim.* New York: Vintage Books.

Sadker, M. & Sadker, D. (1982). *Sex equity handbook for schools.* New York: Longman.

Samovar, L. A. & Porter, R. E. (Eds.). (1991). *Intercultural communication: A reader* (6th ed.). Belmont, CA: Wadsworth.

Sampson, E. (1977). Psychology and the American ideal. *Journal of Personality and Social Psychology, 35,* 767–782.

Scott, E. &. McCollum, H. (1993). Making it happen: Gender equitable classrooms. In S. K. Biklen & D. Pollard (Eds.). *Gender and education* (92nd Yearbook of the National Society for the Study of Education. Part I; pp. 174–190). Chicago, IL: University of Chicago Press.

Scott, K. P. & Schau, (1982). Sex equity and sex bias in instructional materials. In S. S. Klein (Ed.). *Handbook for achieving sex equity through education* (pp. 218–232). Baltimore, MD: Johns Hopkins University Press.

Senour, M. N. (1977). Psychology of the Chicana. In J. L. Martinez, Jr. (Ed.). *Chicano psychology* (pp. 329–342). New York: Academic Press.

Sergiovanni, T. J. & Starratt, R, J. (1993). *Supervision: A redefinition.* (5th ed.). New York: McGraw-Hill.

Shade, B. J. (1982). Afro-American cognitive style: A variable in school success? *Review of Educational Research, 52,* 219–244.

Shade, B. J. (Ed.). (1989). *Culture, style, and the educative process.* Springfield, IL: Charles C. Thomas.

Shade, B. J. (1994). Understanding the African American learner. In E. R. Hollins, J. E. King, & W. C. Hayman (Eds.). *Teaching diverse populations: Formulating a knowledge base* (pp. 175–189). Albany, NY: State University of New York Press.

Shade, B. J. & New, C. A. (1993). Cultural influences on learning: Teaching implications. In J. A. Banks & C. A. M. Banks (Eds.). *Multicultural education: Issues and perspectives* (2nd ed.). pp. 317–329. Boston, MA: Allyn & Bacon.

Sheets, R. (1995). *Student and teacher perceptions of disciplinary conflicts in culturally pluralistic classrooms.* Unpublished Dissertation, University of Washington, Seattle, WA.

Sheldon, A. (1990). Pickle fights: Gendered talk in preschool disputes. *Discourse Processes, 13,* 5–31.

Shinn, R. (1972). *Culture and school: Socio-cultural significances.* San Francisco, CA: Intext Educational Publishers.

Slavin, R. E. (1995). Cooperative learning and intergroup relations. In J. A. Banks & C. A. M. Banks (Eds.). *Handbook of research on multicultural education* (pp. 628–634). New York: Macmillan.

Sleeter, C. E. & Grant, C. A. (1994). *Making choices for multicultural education: Five approaches to race, class, and gender* (2nd ed.). Columbus, OH: Merrill.

Sleeter, C. E. & McLaren, P. L. (Eds.). (1995). *Multicultural education, critical pedagogy, and the politics of difference.* Albany, NY: State University of New York Press.

Smith, R. R. & Lewis, R. (1985). Race as a self-schema affecting recall in Black children. *The Journal of Black Psychology, 12.* 15–29.

Smitherman, G. (1977). *Talkin' and testifyin': The language of Black America.* Boston, MA: Houghton Mifflin.

Speilberger, C. & Sarason, I. (1978). *Stress and anxiety; vol. 5.* New York: Wiley.

Spindler, G. D. (Ed.). (1987). *Education and cultural process: Anthropological approaches* (2nd ed.). Prospect Heights, IL: Waveland Press.

Spindler, G. & Spindler, L. (1993). The process of culture and person: Cultural therapy and culturally diverse schools. In P. Phelan & A. L. Davidson (Eds.). *Renegotiating cultural diversity in American schools* (pp. 21–51). New York: Teachers College, Columbia University.

Streitmatter, J. L. (1989). Identity development and academic achievement in early adolescence. *Journal of Early Adolescence, 9,* 99–116.

Streitmatter, J. (1994). *Toward gender equity in the classroom: Everyday teachers' beliefs and practices.* Albany, NY: State University of New York Press.

Sue, D. W. (1995). Toward a theory of multicultural counseling and therapy. In J. A. Banks, & C. A. M. Banks (Eds.). *Handbook of research on multicultural education* (pp. 647–659). New York: Macmillan.

Sue, S. & Okazaki, S. (1990). Asian-American educational achievements: A phenomenon in search of an explanation. *American Psychologist, 45*(8), 913–920.

Tannen, D. (1990). *You just don't understand.* New York: William Morrow.

Tatum, B. D. (1992). Talking about race, learning about racism: The application of racial identity development theory in the classroom. *Harvard Educational Review, 62,* 1–24.

Tetreault, M. K. T. (1985). Phases of thinking about women in history: A report card on the textbook. *Women's Studies Quarterly, 13*(2/3), 35–47.

The condition of education. (1994). Washington, D.C.: U. S. Department of Education, National Center for Education Statistics, Office of Educational Research and Improvement.

Teachers and students. Report V. Differences in teacher interaction with Mexican American and Anglo students. (1973). Washington, D.C.: U. S. Civil Rights Commission, Mexican American Education Study.

Thu, H. B. (1983). Meeting the needs of Indochinese students. *Momentum, 14,* 20–22.

Tong, B. R. (1978). Warriors and victims: Chinese American sensibility and learning styles. In L. Morris, G. Sather, & S. Scull (Eds.). *Extracting learning styles from social/cultural diversity: Studies of five American minorities* (pp. 70–93). Normal, OK: Southwest Teacher Corps Network.

Turkle, S. & Papert, S. (1990). Epistemological pluralism: Styles and voices within the computer culture. *Signs: Journal of Women in Culture and Society, 16*(1), 128–157.

Understanding racial-ethnic differences in secondary school science and mathematics achievement. (1995). Washington, D.C.: U. S. Department of Education, National Center for Education Statistics, Office of Educational Research and Improvement.

Verdugo, R. R. (1986). Educational stratification and Hispanics. In M. A. Olivas (Ed.). *Latino college students* (pp. 325–347). New York: Teachers College Press, Columbia University.

West, C. (1993). *Race matters.* Boston, MA: Beacon Press.

Winkler, J. D., Stravelson, R. J., Stasz, C., Robyn, A., & Fiebel, W. (1984). *How effective teachers use micro-computers in instruction.* Santa Monica, CA: The Rand Corporation.

Wittig, M. A. & Petersen, A. C. (Eds.). (1979). *Sex-related differences in cognitive functioning: Developmental issues.* New York: Academic Press.

Wong, M. G. (1980). Model students?: Teachers' perceptions and expectations of their Asian and White students. *Sociology of Education, 53*(4), 236–247.

Woodward, A., Elliott, D. L., & Nagel, K. C. (1986). Beyond textbooks in elementary social studies. *Social Education, 50,* 50–53.

Yu, E. S. H., Doi, M., & Chang, C-F. (1986). *Asian American Education in Illinois: A review of the data.* Springfield, IL: Illinois State Board of Education.

·51·

TECHNOLOGY, COMPUTERS, AND TELECOMMUNICATIONS

James M. King, Gene L. Wilkinson, and James R. Okey

UNIVERSITY OF GEORGIA

INTRODUCTION

There is a long history of prophets who have predicted the vast impact that technology will have on education. As early as 1913, Thomas A. Edison was quoted as saying, "Books will soon be obsolete in the schools. Scholars will soon be instructed through the eyes. It is possible to teach every branch of human knowledge with the motion picture. Our school system will be completely changed in 10 years" (Saettler, 1968, p. 98).

Anyone who has been sitting back anticipating Edison's predicted change in the school system has had a long wait. Research on the diffusion and adoption of innovations indicates that a new development in education typically takes 50 years to reach widespread adoption (Rogers, 1983). However, with the rapid spread of microcomputers and VHS videorecorders in the schools, the development of interactive satellite communications, and the exponential growth of the Internet, this pattern may be changing. Consider a school, not of tomorrow, but one that incorporates a combination of things that are happening in schools across the country today:

- Both students and teachers begin their school day early by using their Personal Digital Assistants (PDAs) to log into the central school computer system before they leave home to check and make sure all assignments have been delivered and to see if special items need to be brought to school today. The PDA also collects a news clipping file for each student on the topics they have been assigned to research for the next week (e.g., Fadel, 1995).

- When students arrive at school and filter into classes they begin working on various activities. Many students work on individualized projects as teachers monitor progress and assist where needed. In a vocational class, a student touches an oxyacetylene torch to an object being welded and draws it across the surface. With too slow a movement, the surface metal melts and the object is ruined. This scene is all too often the case for beginning welding students, but the student is not disturbed and tries again to master the proper touch to complete a successful weld. The student is not working at a traditional welding station, but is interacting with a computer and multimedia welding lesson. "The input device looks and acts exactly like an oxyacetylene torch. The video monitor is laid flat in the position of a piece of metal to be welded. As the 'torch' is moved across the screen, the visual of the welding puddle responds to such factors as the speed of the movement and the height of the torch, just as would happen in an actual weld" (Nugent, 1987, p. 14). Students receive feedback from the computer and are allowed to practice until they consistently weld with acceptable levels of quality.

- In another classroom, 16 students work at computers interconnected to a Compact Disc-Read Only Memory (CD-ROM) Drive. At the touch of a key each student has instant access to the Compton's Encyclopedia, the American Heritage Dictionary, Roget's Thesaurus, a ZIP code directory, spelling checker, style book, and a book of quotations. In addition, hundreds of other CD-ROMs, including full-text journal databases, are on-line for instant access by students in any classroom. PDAs using infrared network connections collect and compile data for students as they prepare multimedia reports. Students can check their compositions for spelling and style errors with Microsoft's CD-ROM Reference Disc or check the Compton's CD-ROM Encyclopedia for a passage on early manufacturing processes and "paste" it into their research paper without having to retype the material (e.g., Marchionini, 1989; Large, 1994).

1228

- Down the hall, music students load "sampled" audio sounds from a CD-ROM library of thousands of realistic sounds into their synthesizer keyboards to create an entire orchestra of sound. They will later record the finished compositions onto a Compact Disc Record (CD-R) along with video images to accompany the music (e.g., Lalande, 1995).

- Students in a social studies class will work cooperatively today with a class in St. Petersburg, Russia, interactively discussing the conversion of the socialist state into a democratic republic. This interaction takes place over the Internet using high-speed lines capable of carrying both data and video signals simultaneously. These two classes will also poll other schools in both the United States and Russia to determine perceptions of the shift from a socialist system to a democracy (e.g., Wilson & Marsh, 1995).

- Today in this particular school 10 other classes will be conducted over the distance education network, providing advanced math, science, and language courses. Classes in 200 schools will benefit from the expertise of master teachers in subjects where there is a shortage of qualified teachers locally. These distance education classes are two-way interactive, using satellite transmissions and land lines for multisite connectivity (e.g., Dimock & Cornillon, 1994; Martin, 1993).

- Students in almost every class within the school will process data on-line through the Internet and search databases worldwide for the latest information on the topics they are studying. Teacher workstations in each classroom are connected to the central administrative computer, where student information is updated on a continuous basis. When teachers have any concerns about student progress, they can contact parents immediately through the interactive cable network regarding performance data. Testing is done on-line with each student's PDAs so that each student's records are available for both parent and teacher to discuss problems and possible solutions (e.g., Ridenour, 1987).

- At the end of the school day, students filter out to other activities including sports, recreation, and clues in which predecessors have participated for decades. When these students arrive at home, however, they plug back into the Internet and continue exploring the world of information, collecting data to prepare materials for the next day's classroom activities. They work in small study groups over the Internet, connecting with other study groups throughout the world and deciphering the data they need to prepare for another challenging school day (e.g., Wilson, 1995).

All of the activities just described sound like science fiction or those predictions from the 1950s that everyone's life would be totally automated. However, the technology currently is in place to implement each of these scenarios and many more—of which we can only dream. Today's technology has provided some wondrous tools to automate many of the repetitive tasks that are required in today's work places and school settings.

As instructional supervisors, it is important to understand how technology has evolved in schools, where it is heading, and how new technologies can best be used to increase effectiveness. School supervisors, as well as other educators, can better utilize new technologies in three broad areas: communication, research, and management. As a communication tool, technology can be used to send electronic mail, prepare presentations and build better communication links with those who are supervised. In the area of research, technology tools can be used for data collection, access to periodicals and electronic databases, and use of the Internet where widely dispersed information can be aggregated. Finally, new technologies can improve existing management practices by improving record keeping, speeding clerical functions while improving accuracy, and assisting with skill tracking of students and staff, while providing effective evaluation.

A look back at the history of the use of technology in schools will provide perspective for understanding where schools are headed. In conjunction with this historical base, a review of what is known about the effectiveness of technology and an examination of some of the newer developments in technology, computers, and telecommunications will help provide a foundation for educational leaders who must cope with innovations that are just beginning to have an impact on the workplace and in the schools.

HISTORICAL DEVELOPMENT OF EDUCATIONAL TECHNOLOGY

Educational technology first emerged as a distinct field within education during the 1960s through the merger of the older audiovisual education tradition with the developing programmed learning movement (Eraut, 1989). The field of educational technology is eclectic, reflecting the diversity of background and interests of the individuals who work in the field, and the various conceptual frameworks which have contributed to its growth. Coming from such areas as mass communications, education, library science, military and business training, psychology and learning theory, engineering, sociology, information science and cybernetics, and the fine arts, professionals in the field of educational technology share a common interest in the tools of teaching and learning, and a common concern with the role and function of technology in education. With such diversity, the problem of defining the field is both vital and complex.

Definition of Educational Technology

The definition of the field of educational technology has shown a continuing growth and development over the years. During the early 1960s, the field was called audiovisual communications and was defined by its major professional organization as:

[T]hat branch of educational theory and practice primarily concerned with the design and use of messages which control the learning process. It undertakes: (a) the study of the unique and relative strengths and weaknesses of both pictorial and nonrepresentational messages which may be employed in the learning process for any purpose; and (b) the structuring and systematizing of messages by men and instruments in an educational environment. These undertakings include the planning, production, selecting, management, and utilization of both components and entire instructional systems. Its practical goal is the efficient utilization of every method and medium of communication which can contribute to the development of the learner's full potential (Ely, 1963, pp. 18–19).

This definition was a culmination of the educational media movement in American education and established a number of themes which were to be elaborated as consensus was being developed on new terminology for the field.

In its monumental report to the U.S. Congress, the Commission on Instructional Technology (Tickton, 1970) noted two different ways of defining instructional technology. One of these definitions, "the media born of the communication revolution which can be used for instructional purposes alongside the teacher, textbook, and blackboard" (p. 21), is the traditional definition of educational media. Such a definition implies a consideration of machines and materials—the things (e.g., television, films, overhead projectors, computers) that are considered part of educational media. Because such an approach is expected by those outside of the field, it will be followed, to a degree, in this chapter. Such a definition, however, is too narrow. It excludes a number of issues that are, or should be, of concern to individuals looking at the quality of education.

The Commission's second definition goes beyond specific devices or media. Under this definition, instructional technology is defined as "a systematic way of designing, carrying out, and evaluating the total process of learning and teaching in terms of specific objectives, based on research in human learning and communication, and employing a combination of human and nonhuman resources to bring about more effective instruction" (Tickton, 1970, p. 21).

The growing acceptance of this second definition was one of the factors that led the major professional organization in the media field to change its name from the Department of Audiovisual Instruction to the Association for Educational Communications and Technology (AECT), and led to the initiation of the work of the AECT Task Force on Definition and Terminology (AECT, 1977). The definition, as proposed by the Task Force and accepted by AECT, stated:

Educational Technology is a complex, integrated process involving people, procedures, ideas, devices, and organization, for analyzing problems, and devising, implementing, evaluating and managing solutions to those problems, involved in all aspects of human learning. In educational technology, the solutions to problems take the form of all the *Learning Resources* that are designed and/or selected as Messages, People, Materials, Devices, Techniques, and Settings. The processes for analyzing problems, and devising, implementing and evaluating solutions are identified by the *Educational Development Functions* of Research-Theory, Design, Production, Evaluation-Selection, Logistics, and Utilization. The processes of directing or coordinating one or more of these functions are identified by the *Educational Management Functions* of Organization Management and Personnel Management (p. 59).

A simplification of this official definition states that "instructional technology is the theory and practice of design, development, utilization, management and evaluation of processes and resources for learning" (Seels & Richey, 1994, p. 9).

The more narrowly defined terms, *educational media* or *audiovisual communications,* are concerned primarily with two elements of the total domain model: materials and devices. The concern in schools is with the materials and the devices as well as with people who provide and operate them; the design, production, logistics and utilization: their organization and management; and their interaction with learners.

This broad concern with technology as process rather than as things is reflected by Acheson, Shamser, and Smith in Chapter 32 of the *Handbook* on instructional development, and by Oliva in Chapter 33, on curriculum development. Most individuals outside of the field of instructional technology, however, think of mechanical devices, such as computers or television, when the term is used in the context of education. This use of technology has a long history in American education and provides a context for a discussion of current trends.

Audiovisual Education Movement

Although the roots of instructional technology can be traced back to the middle ages, the field got its start early in the twentieth century with the school museum movement (Saettler, 1968, 1990). The period between 1918 and 1924 saw the first formal courses dealing with the use of educational media offered by colleges and universities, the publication of the first professional journals dealing with aspects of visual education, the initiation of research focused on visual instruction, and the beginnings of America's principal professional organization on instructional technology, now named the Association for Educational Communications and Technology, as the Department of Visual Instruction, to be changed to the Department of Audiovisual Instruction in 1947, within the National Education Association (Seibert & Ullmer, 1982).

The audiovisual education movement received its early emphasis from the development and application of educational motion pictures. Early studies of the effectiveness of motion pictures were conducted by Freeman (1924) at the University of Chicago, the Eastman Kodak Company (Wood & Freeman, 1929), and Knowlton and Tilton (1929) at Yale University. After a slight setback during the Great Depression, there was an expansive use of films, along with other forms of instructional media, in industrial and military training during World War II. During and after the war, more than 80 individual studies on film use were conducted for the armed forces at Pennsylvania State University (Carpenter & Greenhill, 1956; Hoban & Van Ormer, 1950). Research on films conducted by Lumsdaine for the Air Force looked at methods of eliciting and/or guiding overt student responses during instruction (Lumsdaine, 1963). The war experience firmly established motion pictures as the most significant form of instructional media, until the position of films was supplanted by television, videocassette recordings, and microcomputers.

The theoretical basis, to the extent that one existed, for the visual education movement was the conviction (1) that stimulus richness and variety would enhance student attention and motivation and (2) that the degree of abstraction or concreteness within the learning stimulus was a critical variable in learning (Erant, 1989). Early books on visualization of the curriculum by Hoban, Hoban, and Zisman (1937) and on audiovisual methods in teaching by Dale (1969) provided early direction and rationale for the field (Seels & Richey, 1994). These "rules of thumb" served as an ever-increasingly shaky foundation until the rapid development of television, without the involvement of audiovisual specialists and the emergence of teaching machines and programmed instruction led Finn (1960) to challenge both the name and focus of the field (Erant, 1989).

Radio, Television, and Mass Communications

The second major movement that merged into the field of instructional technology was the development of electronic communications and educational broadcasting. The oldest electronic medium is educational radio, which can trace its beginnings to the start of the first educational station at the University of Wisconsin in 1919 (Sandler, 1967). School radio programming began with the Ohio School of the Air in 1929 and expanded nationally with the Radio Corporation of America's Educational Hour on the National Broadcasting Company (NBC) network and the American School of the Air on the Columbia Broadcasting System (CBS) (Saettler, 1968, 1990). The use of educational radio in the schools continued to grow rapidly until the 1930s and 1940s, when it was the most common form of audio instruction (Jamison & McAnany, 1978). The use of educational radio declined during the 1960s with the growth of instructional television but it is still one of the most widely available educational media. In a national survey conducted for the Corporation for Public Broadcasting, Riccobono (1985) found that 88 percent of the nation's teachers had audio/radio programming available and that, of these teachers, 16 percent indicated weekly use of radio materials in the classroom.

Because of the pressures of World War II, television had a slow initial development following its public debut during the 1939 New York World's Fair. After the War, however, the pace of development was rapid. The first nonprofit television station was started at Iowa State College in 1945 (Walker, 1962). The initial programming of nonprofit television stations was primarily public affairs and cultural material rather than classroom related. Instructional broadcasting started during the mid-1950s. National educational broadcasting had its beginnings in 1952 with the founding of the Educational Television and Radio Center which later developed into National Educational Television and ultimately into today's Public Broadcasting System and the Corporation for Public Broadcasting (Saettler, 1990). One of the first school systems to integrate television into the total instructional program was Hagerstown, Maryland (Wade, 1967). The impressive gains reported for Hagerstown students from this innovation were likely due to the systematic curriculum design and instructional development that the integration of televised instruction required (Wilkinson, 1980). *Sesame Street* is another impressive example of the effects of systematic design and development of instruction (Ball & Bogatz, 1970; Children's Television Workshop, 1990; Milkie, 1990). Today, as a result of

cable and satellite transmission and the development of simple-to-use videotape recorders, instructional television (ITV) is one of the most commonly available and used educational media. Riccobono (1985) reported that 70 percent of the teachers in the United States had access to ITV and that, at the elementary level, 56 percent of teachers made use of it weekly.

The growth of broadcasting in the United States led to a concern with the process of communication. Building on earlier work by Shannon and Weaver (1949), Berlo (1960) developed a popular model of the communication process that described the circular relationship between senders, messages, channels, and receivers. Schramm (1954) also applied Shannon and Weaver's work to mass communications, emphasizing human behavior in the process of communication. Mass communications concepts and theories have provided one of the theoretical foundations of instructional technology (Seels & Richey, 1994). The instructional use of television has been one of the most thoroughly evaluated and studied aspects of education (Saettler, 1990). Many extensive reviews of this research have been developed (Reid & MacLennan, 1967; Chu & Schramm, 1967; Dorr, 1992).

Programmed Instruction and Computer-Assisted Instruction

Most of the early developments in media and technology began with a device and attempted to develop a theoretical rationale to justify existing practice. Programmed instruction (PI) was an exception. Tracing its roots back to early work in stimulus-response learning by Pavlov and Hull, PI grew from a strong theoretical foundation and experienced a long period of development that paralleled, but did not initially merge with, the audiovisual education movement. Montessori began developing programmed instructional devices during the first decade of this century. Pressy and others began experimenting shortly thereafter with programmed instruction (Saettler, 1968, 1990). The appearance of Skinner's (1954) work on teaching machines and programmed learning, popularized by Mager (1962), provided a rationale for the field in the area of behavioral psychology (Seels & Richey, 1994). The relationship of behavioral psychology to the audiovisual field was illustrated in major publications by Lumsdaine and Glaser (1960) and Lumsdaine (1964).

The early research and theory of teaching machines and text-based programmed learning provided the foundations for the development of the initial computer-based education applications. The development of computer-based education during the 1950s and 1960s was slow because of the reliance upon large, mainframe computer installations with terminals physically connected to the operating computer by cable (Heinich, Molenda, & Russell, 1993). Early applications were primarily confined to university settings, such as the PLATO project at the University of Illinois. Research on early computer applications at Stanford University has been reported on by Suppes and Morningstar (1972). The pattern of slow development of computer-based educational systems was not broken until the development of small, relatively inexpensive, personal computers by such companies as Apple Computer, Inc., in the early 1980s. The development of computer hardware, instructional software, and teacher support programs since then has been exponential.

Despite its long history, the place of media and technology in education is misunderstood by educators. In 1986, Donald Ely, then head of the ERIC Clearinghouse on Information Resources, identified five common misconceptions regarding media and technology: (1) media and educational technology are the same thing, (2) using media in the classroom will automatically bring about student learning, (3) one form of media is superior to another form of media, (4) a newly developed medium will solve problems that have not been solved already by existing media, and (5) research findings provide a justification for the use of media and technology in the classroom. That these are, in fact, misconceptions will be clear after an examination of the research on media and technology in education.

RESEARCH ON MEDIA AND TECHNOLOGY

Anyone seeking to do a comprehensive survey of the research dealing with educational media is faced with a frustrating task. From one point of view, the field of educational media is one of the newest and most comprehensively documented aspects of education, reaching maturity along with the methodology of educational research and evaluation during the forced growth of World War II and the expansion of graduate education programs during the 1950s and 1960s. From another point of view, the field is as old as the first primitive that scratched a crude drawing in the dust, and is an area rich in advocacy but poor in evidence. Many of the studies in the field were set up to demonstrate prior convictions rather than to examine carefully drawn hypotheses. The results of several decades of research can be summed up as "no significant difference."

A number of reviewers have attempted to give cohesion and direction to an understanding of the research on educational media and technology. In his book, *The Evolution of American Educational Technology*, Saettler (1990) traces developments from 1918 through the 1980s. Ely (1986) has identified five phases of media research during the same period. Comprehensive reviews have been developed by Wilkinson (1980b) and by Thompson, Simonson, and Hargrave (1992). Other authors have focused on research dealing with specific types of media, such as films (Hoban & Van Ormer, 1950; May & Lumsdaine, 1958), programmed instruction (Lumsdaine & Glaser, 1960), television (Chu & Schramm, 1967; Reid & MacLennan, 1967), and computers (Kulik, Bangert, & Williams, 1983; Kulik, Kulik, & Bangert-Downs, 1984; Kulik & Kulik, 1986; Roblyer, Castine, & King, 1988), or on specific aspects of media, such as Briggs' (1968) review of media and learner variables, Travers' (1967) publication on information transmission, and the work of Fleming and Levie (1978, 1993) on principles of instructional message design. The *Review of Educational Research* (e.g., Clark, 1983, Kozma, 1991; Jamison, Suppes, & Wells, 1974) and the *Encyclopedia of Educational Research* (e.g., Clark, 1992; Dorr, 1992, Feasley, 1992; Salomon, 1992) have published major reviews of media research on a regular basis. One of the most

important research reviews, in terms of giving direction to the field, was that by Lumsdaine (1963) in the *Handbook of Research in Teaching* and subsequent reviews by Levie and Dickie (1973) in the *Second Handbook,* and by Clark and Salomon (1986) in the third edition.

Historical Development of Media Research

Experiments dealing with the instructional use of media began near the end of World War I and grew with the development of commercial films and radio. One of the first major studies to look at the use of motion pictures in a public school setting was conducted at the University of Chicago (Freeman, 1924). This series of experiments, which ran during a period of three years in eight different school systems, produced a number of conclusions related to the relative effectiveness of motion, still visuals, and verbal instruction.

The Chicago film studies identified a number of conditions under which different media attributes interacted with program content, teaching strategies, and learner characteristics, and it could have provided a solid foundation for media research; however, they were neglected in favor of a more limited experimental design that still persists today: the comparative media study. Following the lead of early studies conducted by Eastman Kodak Company (Wood & Freeman, 1929) and Yale University (Knowlton & Tilton 1929), investigators compared the effectiveness of this medium with that medium, or with "conventional" instruction. Weber pointed out as early as 1930 that no further experiments on the comparative value of media were needed and that other questions should be examined. Weber's advice was ignored, however, and there was no major shift in the type of media research being conducted until the end of World War II.

Major military studies on the use of film in training during and after World War II (Hovland, Lumsdaine, & Sheffield, 1949; Carpenter & Greenhill, 1956), the exploration of television as a training tool by the Navy and by Pennsylvania State University, and the stimulation for research and innovation caused by the National Defense Education Act of 1958, led to both an expansion and an intensification of media research during the 1950s and 1960s. At the same time, there was great dissatisfaction with both the common designs being employed in media research and the questions being examined. Knowlton (1964), among others, pointed out that much of the research on media was based on false assumptions—that assuming the key variable to be the means of information transmission rather than some aspect of the message, content, or the learner would lead to false or contradictory conclusions. The realization that motion is motion whether presented in film, over television, or in a live demonstration, and that a unit of instruction that requires perception of motion will be more effectively taught if motion is employed, goes a long way toward clearing up some of the confusion and conflicting results of the comparative media studies. For example, Chu and Schramm (1967), concluded that there is no difference between learning from film and learning from television if they are used in the same manner.

Reacting to the problems inherit in the comparative media studies, a new direction for media research was suggested by

Lumsdaine (1963) and others. This approach, which dominated media research during the 1970s and 1980s, focused primarily on the "attributes" of media rather than on the media themselves. As stated by Levie and Dickie (1973), media attributes are.

properties of stimulus materials which are manifest in the physical parameters of media. The attributes of a medium, then, are the capabilities of that medium—to show objects in motion, objects in color, objects in three dimensions; to provide printed words, spoken words, simultaneous visual and auditory stimuli; to allow for overt learner responses or random access to information. Some attributes, such as the capacity to show objects in three dimensions, are properties of relatively few media (p. 860).

Research on media attributes, as summarized by Lumsdaine (1963), Briggs (1968), and Levie and Dickie (1973), continued to show the same conflicting results characteristic of comparative media studies. Levie and Dickie suggested that there was a need to turn "to the more complex problem of discovering the conditions under which different levels of attributes are differentially effective. What media attributes will facilitate learning for what kinds of learners in what kinds of tasks?" (p.877). A number of individuals suggested designs for generating and testing hypotheses about the interaction of media attributes and learner aptitudes (Clark, 1975; Snow, 1970; Snow & Salomon, 1968) and much work has been conducted in the area (Cronbach & Snow, 1977; Winn, 1978), but problems still persist. As this research improved in quality and reached a deeper understanding of media, however, it became necessarily unrepresentative of the real world and; therefore, it fell short of accomplishing the objective of improving educational practice (Salomon & Clark, 1977).

There has been a reaction within the last 10 years against quantitative, controlled research designs and a movement toward more qualitative research strategies. In 1986, Ely pointed out that the major research question presently seemed to be "Under X conditions (which includes the use of media), does Y type of learner achieve Z objectives?" (p. 6). Much of the current research on media and technology in education has more of a flavor of evaluation and in-depth case studies than of controlled experimental research. Before the past 70 years of research on media is rejected out of hand, however, some of the generalizations that have been established, deserve examination.

Comparative Effectiveness Studies

As each new medium (e.g., film, radio, television, programmed instruction, computers) has been introduced into the classroom, the natural question is, "Can students learn from this medium?" and if so, "Can they learn *better* from it than from some other medium?" As a result, the most common type of media research has been a study that compares a specific medium of instruction against one or more other media—most often "conventional" instruction.

The typical problem with research that purports to examine the effectiveness of one instructional media in comparison with another media or with conventional instruction is that the results are not consistent from one study to the next. At one point there is significant evidence for the use of media, then for conventional instruction, but the result has most often been no significant difference. For example, Hartley (1966) examined 112 studies that compared programmed instruction with conventional instruction and found that on measures of achievement 41 studies showed programmed instruction significantly superior, 6 showed programmed instruction significantly worse, and 37 showed no significant difference between the two treatments.

Part of the situation can be explained by problems in research design (Lumsdaine, 1963; Greenhill, 1967). For example, when Hartley applied minimal acceptance criteria to the studies that he was considering, he was left with only eight acceptable studies. In a similar way, Stickell (1963) examined 250 experiments that compared television with conventional instruction. When criteria were applied to determine if the research could be interpreted—(1) experimental and control groups of at least 25 subjects, (2) randomly assigned from the same population, (3) taught by the same instructor, (4) measured by a testing instrument judged to be reliable and valid, and (5) evaluated by acceptable statistical procedures—he was left with only 10 studies that met the full standards and 23 studies that were acceptable with minor problems. All 10 of the interpretable studies showed no significant difference. Among the acceptable studies, three favored television and none favored conventional instruction.

Despite the recurring indictment of the comparative media research design (Clark, 1983; Lumsdaine, 1963; Weber, 1930; Wilkinson, 1980b), such studies continue to be conducted with results that appear to astound the researcher. For example, Wesley, Krockover, and Hicks (1985) compared the effectiveness of programmed instruction delivered by means of printed text versus computer delivery. The researchers found no differences between the groups. This result, which was contrary to their expectations and hypothesis, was attributed to the short treatments or to the small sample size. "The authors evidently did not even consider the possibility that this nondifference is exactly what should be expected in a well-controlled study of this type" (Hagler & Knowlton, 1987).

In 1973, Schramm reviewed the media research literature in order to examine Gagné's (1965) contention that "most instructional tasks can be performed by most media" (p. 364). Schramm concluded that "how a medium is used may be more important than the choice of medium. Learning seems to be affected more by what is delivered than by the delivery system" (p. 273). It can safely be concluded, however, that "when they are carefully selected and/or produced—taking into account both media attributes and student characteristics—and systematically integrated into the instructional program, educational media have a significant impact on student achievement" (Wilkinson, 1980b, p. 39).

Kozma (1991, 1994) has attempted to reopen the debate of media effects on learning by presenting the argument that some media, through unique combinations of attributes such as the ability to represent motion, allow student manipulation, present complex contexts, and the like, do have the potential for affecting learning. As Morrison (1994), Clark (1994), and others pointed out in rebuttal to Kozma's arguments, however, the examples he provided do not present evidence of the effectiveness of media; rather, they show the effectiveness of the instructional strategies employed could be obtained by means of a number of different media or combinations of media.

The studies of comparative media effectiveness have been justifiably criticized. The research methodology has often been faulty, or the researcher mistakes the effects of novelty, systematic instructional design efforts, or instructional methods for the effects of the media. Clark (1983), who is one of the most consistent and scathing critics of comparative media studies, has made the observation that, when all variables are held constant except the delivery system, there is no reason to believe that there should be any difference between the experimental and control conditions. Clark suggested that "media are mere vehicles that deliver instruction but do not influence student achievement any more than the truck that delivers our groceries causes changes in our nutrition" (p. 445). Clark's analogy is both vivid and, on the surface, valid; however, the analogy can be taken a few steps further. Granted that, although the truck adds nothing to the nutritional value of the produce, the selection of the wrong truck can subtract from its value. For example, a flatbed semi-trailer is a poor choice for hauling sides of beef in July. The way in which the produce is packaged for transportation can also subtract value. Shoveling eggs loosely into a dump truck will definitely reduce their appeal, if not their nutritional value. The way in which the truck is driven also affects nutritional value. In more formal language, the expanded analogy suggests that there are questions that can be asked regarding media selection (e.g., the match of learning tasks with media stimulus characteristics), aspects of instructional packaging (e.g., degree of active student response or the application of perceptual principles to screen design), and different utilization strategies and patterns of classroom integration.

Media Selection

A number of different classification systems for media and procedures for the selection of appropriate media in specific instructional situations have been produced. In the 1940s ,Dale (1969) developed his "Cone of Experience," which placed different learning experiences, including types of media, on a continuum ranging from direct, purposeful experiences to visual and verbal symbols. Dale's contention was that students needed to develop a base of concrete experiences in order to benefit from more symbolic learning experiences. Media selection became a process of matching the student's level of experience with the level of teaching activities on the cone. More recent media classification systems include Bretz's (1971) taxonomy of communication media and Heidt's (1976) system of relating media attributes to learner traits.

Different systematic procedures have been developed to aid instructional planners in the selection of media. Most of these strategies take the form of branching decision trees. Kemp and Smellie (1994) present a series of branching questions that move from a consideration of group size (i.e., individualized, small group, or large group) through media attrib-

utes to specific media. Anderson (1983) presented a series of questions leading designers to different classifications of media or instructional aids that meet the needs of different instructional tasks. Reiser and Gagné (1983) identified a number of candidate media and questions to be considered for each of six basic instructional patterns (e.g., self-instruction for nonreading students). In contrast to these procedures, Braby et al (1975) developed a series of matrices that rate different instructional delivery systems in relation to the stimulus, instructional setting, and administrative criteria required for 12 different learning tasks ranging from recalling bodies of knowledge through attitude learning.

One of the problems with systematic media selection procedures is that they are often based on intuitive rather than empirical evidence. Schramm (1973) stated that "there is almost a complete lack of studies intended to ascertain *under what conditions* and *for what purposes* one medium may be superior to another" (p. 62). One approach to this problem was proposed by Allen (1967) when he attempted to define the appropriateness of various instructional media to different types of learning tasks. More recent approaches include the Mayer and Gallini (1990) study, which outlines four conditions necessary for effective use of illustrations in science instruction.

Some authors (Jamison, Klees, & Wells, 1978; Scanlon & Weinberger, 1973) have made use of the no significant-difference findings in comparative media studies to suggest that technology might be a means of improving the productivity of education. A number of cost studies dealing with the use of media in public schools have been conducted. These fall into three main categories: descriptive, predictive, and comparative (Wilkinson, 1973). Comparative studies are often referred to as cost-effectiveness or cost-benefit studies. The central purpose of a cost-effectiveness study is the evaluation of, and choice between, alternative means to achieve a given objective. The analysis can proceed from either of two orientations: the achievement of the most output for a set dollar cost or the achievement of the least dollar cost for a set level of output. No matter which of these approaches is employed, there are certain fundamental operations that need to be carried out in the study: (1) determination of objectives, (2) determination of feasible alternatives, (3) determination of relevant costs, and (4) presentation and interpretation of results.

Examples of media cost studies include a study by Carter and Walker (1969), which predicted and compared the cost of the widespread adoption of ITV and CAI by public schools; a General Learning Corporation (1968) study for the Department of Health, Education, and Welfare, which sought to compare a number of different media strategies under different conditions; and Kiesling's (1979) study of the University of Mid-America. More recent studies include examinations of the cost-effectiveness of distance education by Jones and Simonson (1993) and Caffarella et al (1992). Clark (1992) pointed out that there is a need for additional studies on the economics of media, suggesting that although media do not affect learning, "there is equally dramatic evidence that *media do influence the economic elements of learning.* That is, under certain conditions media can dramatically influence the *cost* of learning" (p. 812).

In order to achieve the benefits of economic savings, a number of authors have suggested that the media selection decision needs to be moved away from the classroom teacher and related more closely to instructional design or curriculum planning (Heinich, 1970). Wilkinson (1980a, 1992) pointed out that there are three basic patterns of media use in the schools, each of which has different potential effects of program cost and learning effectiveness.

Additive Approach Materials are added to regular instruction as supplementary or enrichment activities. As such, they are not necessary for the achievement of basic instructional outcomes. Media use is dependent on the classroom teacher, does not usually have a significant impact on student achievement, and represents and added expense for the educational system. This approach is not cost effective.

Integrated Approach Carefully selected or produced materials are integrated into regular instruction and become essential to the achievement of basic instructional outcomes. This approach represents an additional cost for the school/district and requires extensive teacher planning and preparation, but it has the potential for increasing student achievement.

Independent Approach Instruction is redesigned so that at least some basic instructional outcomes can be achieved through the interaction of students and instructional materials without the direct intervention of the classroom teacher. This approach represents a major initial cost to the school system, but it has the greatest potential for increasing the cost effectiveness of the instructional program.

Message Design

With the realization that media did not affect learning, efforts have turned to an examination of the attributes embedded in media, the characteristics of the messages conveyed by media that might affect student performance, and a concern with how such messages might be more effectively designed (Dijkstra, van Hout Wolters, & van der Sijde, 1990; Fleming & Levie, 1978, 1993; Jonassen, 1982). Grabowski (1991) outlined three thrusts of message design within the field of instructional technology: design for instruction (e.g., external to the learner—organization and sequencing of information, provision for practice and feedback, etc.), design for learning (e.g., internal to the learner—coding, integration, translation, etc.), and general principles (e.g., visual perception, legibility standards, etc.) that support both instruction and learning.

Much of the initial research on message design grew out of the early research on programmed instruction. For example, Lumsdaine (1963) and Levie and Dickie (1973) reviewed a number of research studies that dealt with such design issues as step size and position or negative reinforcement. Concern over the mixed results of earlier media research led to interest in the interaction of media attributes and learner characteristics (Clark, 1975; Cronbach & Snow, 1977; Snow, 1970; Snow & Salomon, 1968). Levie and Dickie (1973) suggested that "understanding media may be furthered by (a) specifying media in terms of attributes, (b) defining these attributes in

terms which relate to the ways in which information is processed internally, and (c) discovering relationships between these attributes and other important instructional variables" (p. 877).

A number of researchers have looked at different aspects of visuals in instruction (Gropper, 1966; Levie & Lentz, 1982; Mayer & Gallini, 1990; Willows & Houghton, 1987). Some of the studies focus on levels of abstraction or reality within the visuals (e.g., Dwyer, 1970). Others have looked at the strategies by which students employ pictures in learning (Levin, 1983) or the use of visuals in multiple-channel communications (Hartman, 1961; Severin, 1967). Brown, Lewis, and Harcleroad (1977) have drawn a number of general conclusions regarding visuals in instruction. Visuals are stimulating and aid student understanding and recall of information. Simple line drawings are often more effective than are realistic illustrations. Color does not necessarily add to the instructional effectiveness of pictures.

Other researchers have focused on such aspects of messages as the application of perceptual psychology (Winn, 1993), the use of color (van Hout Wolters, Kerstjens, & Verhagen, 1990; Lamberski, 1980: Snowberg, 1973), and print legibility (Adams, Rosemier, & Sleeman, 1965; Hooper & Hannafin, 1986). In a comprehensive review of research on illustrations and typography in the design of printed instructional materials, Wilson, Pfister, and Fleury (1981) determined that "illustrations can improve learning and retention if they are properly designed for the intended population" (p. 35) and suggested possible guidelines for the designers and evaluators of instructional texts.

Schramm (1973) examined the literature dealing with the effects of adding different channels to an instructional message and found that "such research as there is on this question almost invariably indicates that the addition of one or more supplementary or complementary channels of instruction makes a difference" (p. 67). This conclusion contradicts Travers (1966), who found that there is little or no advantage of two channels (audio and visual) over a single-channel presentation. Severin (1967) suggested that this conflict relates to the interaction of redundancy and/or relevancy of the information in the two channels. If the information in both channels is related or relevant, then there will be greater gain with two channels. If the information is totally redundant, then there will be no gain over a single channel. If the information is unrelated, then there will be interference and less information gain.

For all of the concern over other aspects of message design, the key element in student learning appears to be the instructional strategy that is built into the material. As Clark (1983) has suggested, "If learning occurs as a result of exposure to media, the learning is caused by the instructional method embedded in the media presentation" (p. 26). The foundations of instructional technology in learning research has been explored by Gagnè and Glaser (1987), and the research on the application of learning principles within the design of instructional messages has been summarized by Hannafin and Hooper (1993). The application of this research to instructional design has been elaborated as a series of principles and design guidelines by Yelon (1996). The tasks of designing specific types of instruction, such as computer-based instruction (Morrison, Ross, & O'Dell, 1991) and interactive instruction (Schwier, 1991), have been explored by other authors.

Utilization Strategies

Although they did not establish the superiority of one media over another, many of the comparative media studies did determine that specific classroom strategies can enhance the effectiveness of media use. For example, a study by Craig (1956) can be used as evidence in support of adapting materials to local school needs. The sample consisted of 124 students, aged 9 through 15, compared with 136 students that were matched on a common entrance examination. The first group had sound films on a variety of informational subjects. The second group saw the visual track of the films, but heard commentary by their own classroom teachers. The group that saw the silent film with the local commentary performed significantly better than the sound film group on a posttest.

Carpenter and Greenhill (1956) summarized the results of film research for the navy during World War II. In addition to concluding that well-produced films, used either singly or in a series, can be employed as the sole means of teaching some types of performance skills and conveying some kinds of factual data, they identified a number of utilization practices that can improve the effectiveness of film use. Postviewing tests increase learning when students are told what to look for in the film and that a test on the film content will be given. Students learn more if study guides are provided for each film. Note taking by students during the showing of a film should be discouraged because it distracts from the film itself. Successive showings of a given film can increase learning. Students can watch motion pictures for one hour without reduction in training effectiveness. The effectiveness of film learning should be evaluated by tests. After a film has been shown, major points should be summarized and discussed, lest students form misconceptions. Follow-up activities should be encouraged to provide carryover of generalizations.

In a summary of utilization guidelines that have been established by over 50 research studies or reviews of media research, Bowie (1985) identified 10 major guidelines for the effective use of media in instruction. All media materials should be previewed before being shown. Students should be formally prepared to view the materials through such activities as giving advanced assignments related to the content, posing questions that the material will answer, briefly outlining the content, or discussing the relationship of the material to previous learning. Students should be allowed the time and opportunity to discuss the material. Reinforcement of the material should be provided through follow-up activities and feedback to questions and student discussion of the material. As time allows, the entire presentation or at least the parts needing clarification as determined through discussion, should be repeated. Note taking during viewing of media presentations should be discouraged. Media materials should not be viewed in a completely darkened room. Noise levels in the room should be kept at a minimum.

Most of the research on media utilization has been focused on additive or integrated approaches to the use of instructional materials—on questions dealing with, "How do we ensure max-

imum learning from this ITV program, or this filmstrip?" The same factors, however, are operational in the independent approach to media utilization that is inherent in such newer technological developments as computer hypertext materials and interactive satellite distance education. The instructional strategy in such an independent approach is internal to the instructional materials and under the control of the instructional designer rather than external and under the control of the classroom teacher. The implications of this can be seen through an examination of some of the developments in educational computing and telecommunications.

DEVELOPMENTS IN EDUCATIONAL COMPUTER APPLICATIONS

By any measure, the history of computer applications in education is a short story. Computers first made their presence in instructional settings in the 1960s. This was almost exclusively in university environments with efforts conducted by computer scientists. PLATO and TICCIT, two mainframe, time-shared systems, first brought interactive computer-based instruction to colleges and high schools (Merrill et al, 1995).

Some initial high school–based sites set up in the late 1960s and early 1970s were networked to mainframe computer systems. Most efforts were directed at providing high school students vocational training in data processing skills. Computer applications were limited in scope and geography, and had little impact in terms of numbers of learners affected. These trials with large computers, however, set the stage for applications of computer technology in learning a decade-and-a-half later when microcomputers first appeared in the mid-1970s. The relative low cost and portability of the Apple II in 1978 made use of computers a possibility in schools.

"The early days of instructional computing saw much excitement for its potential and many prophecies of great educational improvement through computer-based instruction" (Allessi & Trollip, 1991, p. 2). Studies of computer-based learning have shown modest gains in what is learned by students using computers, as well as some efficiencies in time (Bangert-Drowns, Kulik, & Kulik, 1985). These studies have most often shown "no significant" difference between traditional instructional methods and computer assisted or augmented instruction. Even though there has been limited research support for computers as an aid to learning, however, the movement over the last decade has been moving relentlessly toward more and more computers (and related technological equipment) at all levels of education and in all subject areas.

Instructional Applications

In the sections that follow, different aspects of instructional computing are considered in relation to how teachers and students interact with computers on a daily basis. The intention in these descriptions is to focus on how teachers and learners are using computers and technology as aids to teaching and learning, rather than to focus on the effectiveness of this use. A focus on effectiveness research over the years in studies that compared computer use with traditional means of learning has generally been a fruitless pursuit. A reevaluation of this research using metaanalysis techniques (Kulik et al, 1983, 1984; Roblyer et al, 1988) has shown a general tendency in favor of computer-assisted instruction. Clark (1994), however, argues cogently that such media comparison studies invariably confuse the medium of instruction with the instructional strategies used and are thus not tests of the importance or value of using any particular medium (in this case computers) as an aid to learning.

Computer-Aided Learning Computer applications in learning have become so pervasive (in a content, not in a geographic, sense) that there is virtually no aspect of learning in any subject area to which computers have not been matched. Consider this statement from Bruce (1990) about computing in language arts:

Computers are now being used in classrooms for instruction in composition, literature, decoding, reading comprehension, spelling, vocabulary, grammar, usage, punctuation, capitalization, brainstorming, planning, reasoning, outlining, reference use, study skills, rhetoric, handwriting, drama, and virtually every other area of language arts. There are also programs specifically designed for learners in preschool, primary, upper elementary, middle school, high school, and college grades, as well as those in adult education, English as a second language, foreign language, bilingual, and special needs classes (p. 536).

A similar statement could be made about nearly every subject in school study ranging from the traditional academic areas to vocational and occupational fields, and the arts. Of course, the declaration that these widespread applications of computing are possible or that they occur somewhere does not mean that they are common in terms of actual use in schools. There have been enough computers available in schools during the 1990s for them to impact the learning of a significant number of students. While schools are adopting computers at a faster pace than any other technology in the history of education, the computer-to-student ratio is still relatively high. Peterson's Guides (1995) lists information on their World Wide Web Site indicating that 4,278,958 computers are used for instruction in the nation's schools, with the Macintosh being the most frequently purchased model. The number of students sharing a computer has declined to 12 students/computer from 125 students/computer 10 years ago and 20 students/computer in 1990–1991. This is a significant increase in accessibility, but the numbers are still not optimal for the full integration of computers into the curriculum.

While the growth in computing resources has been exponential for almost a decade, Becker (1994) stated: "If all computers in school inventories were used all day long, each student (working individually) would be able to use computers for about 30 minutes per day, or nearly 100 hours per school year." The goal in most school systems is to lower the computer-to-student ratio to below 5 students/computer in the next several years.

A conception of the role of the computer in schools put forth by Bitter and Camuse (1984) still describes accurately the use of computers in classrooms. The computer was described by Bitter and Camuse as being useful for tutoring students in a subject or topic by a computer program (e.g., in learning about life cycles of insects). They also described the comput-

er as a productive tool for word processing, data analysis, drawing, and record keeping. Finally, they described student authorship of programs directing computer to carry out some actions (e.g., doing some calculations or making projections in a problem situation). When microcomputers were first introduced into classrooms, much of the instruction dealt with becoming "computer literate" and learning to program the computer. Current emphasis in the classroom has shifted away from programming to the more important aspect of using the computer as a tool to assist students in acquisition of analytical and research skills. The three application areas outlined by Bitter and Camuse are still appropriate descriptors of what computers can do in school learning environments. New developments in both the capabilities of the computers and the vision of the developers, however, have enlarged the scope to include elaborate and sophisticated applications in the tutor, tool, and programming environments. Present computer applications allow elaborate simulations of phenomena that require higher order thinking, problem solving, and logical reasoning or explorations in elaborate learning environments, construction of tools for art, graphics, or animation, and multimedia authoring that puts control of the simulated environment in the hands of novice learners.

Information Access Computer applications that provide access to information have an even shorter history than do those for computer-aided learning. In information access, the focus is on using computer programs to locate information that is available either locally in a library or more remotely in another library or information source. Libraries in schools have automated their catalogs by providing a computer link to the holdings. Search procedures by topic, author, title, and source provide powerful and efficient means of identifying sources of information. Dictionaries, atlases, and encyclopedias that are available on CD-ROM can be readily accessed (King, Murwin, & Matt, 1990). While these sources provide the same materials that their print counterparts have always provided, they also include such features as word pronunciation, multiple language capabilities, and video and sound images in the encyclopedias.

Beyond these local links to sources of information are computers hooked by networking to remote sources of data and information. Through telephone lines (via modems hooked to computers) or through direct wire connections to worldwide computer networks, a learner with no more than a modest home or school computer can connect in moments to sites scattered throughout the world. Through these connections, mail messages can be sent and received, discussions held, and information accessed. Students may collaborate on research data gathering, teachers may locate lesson materials, or either may communicate directly with peers in a different culture. Through the linking of the computer to the rest of the world, the boundaries of the classroom change and the means of learning are altered. Students are able to conduct library searches of card catalogs of books, periodicals, and other sources to find abstracts and perhaps full text documents.

Presentation An increasingly common application of computers for classrooms is their use in presentations. The display from a single computer is made available to a group of learners by sending it to a video projector, a display device on an overhead projector, or a large-screen monitor. In this way, demonstrations of phenomena are available to all learners in a group setting. The computer displays may provide visuals, words, or sounds that serve as discussion points. A variety of software programs make the development of computer presentations a readily available and adaptable means of providing common images to a group. Students are being encouraged to prepare computer-based presentations incorporating, text, graphics, music and motion video in place of traditional print-based reports and term papers. Even children in the early elementary grades are working with multimedia production tools to prepare exciting visual reports of their work.

Assessment, Evaluation, and Records Applications

Consider some of the common tasks associated with teachers, learners, and schools: keeping rosters and records of students and their accomplishments, giving and grading tests of achievement, and reporting progress to students and parents. These are all examples of tasks important to teachers and schools to which computers can be applied, and they have been. From the earliest days of computers in schools, it was no stretch of imagination to see where computers could provide some labor saving and efficiency to tasks such as these. With the exception of word processing, the use of a grading/reporting program may be the single most common application of computer programs used by teachers in a school.

Computer capabilities have also allowed different kinds of record keeping. Portfolios of student work have been used with students for many years, but the capability of computers to maintain and access records has elaborated the idea of a paper portfolio (e.g., of writing samples) to include samples of work that incorporate text, speech, sound, video, and still images.

The use of classroom computers is steadily growing; and as new teachers are trained with the technology even more activity will occur. We do not yet know best how to use the power of these new computing devices in our classrooms, but many teachers and students are daily discovering exciting new activities that seem to reinforce the principle of a pathway of life-long learning. The new computing devices seem to place sufficient power in the hands of students that they may be the first generation to fully understand the implication of learning for life.

DEVELOPMENTS IN EDUCATIONAL TELECOMMUNICATIONS

The term *telecommunications* has had and continues to have various meanings to different people. If you talk to a television engineer or producer, they do "telecommunications." The *tele* in telecommunications refers to television. If you talk to the president of a phone or satellite transmission company, they also claim to be doing telecommunications. The *tele* in this case refers to telephone. The person carrying on distance education programs will also claim to be involved in telecommunications as will the coordinator of a computer or data processing facility. Telecommunications today is hard to tag with a single nar-

row definition. *Tele* in Greek means "far off," and Heinich, Molenda, and Russell (1993) defined a *telecommunication system* as a means for communicating over a distance; specifically, any arrangement for transmitting voice and data in the form of coded signals through an electronic medium. Because television was not included specifically, a broader more acceptable definition might be "the transmission of information over a distance by various electronic means for the purpose of communication." If you need to know the specifics of how this information is being transmitted and in what precise form, then you should be prepared to ask; "Just what do you mean by 'telecommunications'?" The following section will discuss four telecommunication areas that are impacting daily on schools and the management of school systems. These four technologies, including television, networking, electronic communications, and distance education, are where some of the most radical changes are taking place in our schools today, but, as Dempsey (1990) noted, the majority of classrooms remain locked in time.

Most classroom instruction, school buildings, and school managerial systems haven't changed since the creation of public education. A school teacher from 1890 could step out of a Winslow Homer painting and feel right at home teaching the same curriculum in a 1990 classroom. What business or other enterprise could exist exactly the same way for 100 years? (p. 8).

If the new technologies that are available to us are going to impact schools in far-reaching, positive ways and modify and update curricula, widespread, methodical adoption will be necessary.

Television

Television debuted to the public at the 1939 New York World's Fair and had a societal impact that has yet to be fully understood. Early studies on the effects of television on young children by Himmelweit, Oppenheim, and Vince (1958) and Schramm, Lyle, and Parker (1961) indicated that generally television does not have detrimental effects on the majority of children. However, Schramm et al noted:

For some children under some conditions, some television is harmful. For other children under the same conditions, or for the same children under other conditions, it may be beneficial. For most children under most conditions, most television is probably neither harmful nor particularly beneficial (p. 13).

Television infuses our daily lives and yet as an instructional tool television has had mixed reviews.

Instructional Programming Effectiveness Studies began in the late 1940s and continued into the 1970s to determine if television was an effective instructional tool. The majority of these comparison studies often lacked sufficient controls and are today viewed with a jaundiced eye by most contemporary researchers (Reeves, 1986). The general findings for many of these studies indicated that there were no significant differences between instruction by television and "traditional" methods. While not demonstrating significance, these studies did show that television, used properly, was effective and, in fact, was a cost-effective alternative to traditional instruction when used with large populations that lacked trained instructors.

Instructional television usage surged in the early 1950s and 1960s as school systems and state boards of education financed experiments in the use of classroom television. The Mid-West Program on Airborne Television (MPATI) was one of the more ambitious projects that used an airborne transmitter to reach 17,000 schools serving nearly 7 million students (Brown & Norberg, 1965). Classroom television usage dropped off in the 1960s and early 1970s because real-time viewing was necessary, and, as the novelty of the media decreased, fewer teachers made efforts to fit programming into their schools. While celluloid film was the prominent media format in schools prior to 1980, the 1980s and 1990s have seen a dramatic shift to videotape media for instruction and enrichment. Early use of television in classrooms required "real-time" viewing because the first instructional television programming was broadcast live at a time before video recorders were available to schools. The infusion of videorecording devices into schools, the fair use copyright laws, and the convenience of time shifting have allowed teachers to more easily incorporate video into instruction.

With the advent of inexpensive video recording devices, particularly the 1/2 inch VHS format available in the 1970s, classroom television use made a resurgence. Television in conjunction with the use of videocassette recorders continues to be one of the most-used media formats in schools today (Heinich et al, 1993). Teachers began to actively integrate video lessons into their curriculum, and schools were able to provide almost instantaneous access to a large collection of video footage that was available in the past only on film stored away at the system level or only available with advanced planning from rental sources.

Used as an integral part of a unit or lesson, video has proven to be an effective instructional technology format. Heinich et al (1993) stated that both videotape and videodisc are pedagogically more flexible than film. Both video formats have fast forward and reverse search capabilities, while film does not. Many publishers now coordinate text, video, and even computer data materials to provide an integrated instructional package for instruction. Most current video use relies on time shifting or time molding to allow the teacher to bring video into a lesson exactly at the point it is needed, not when someone else decides to broadcast it.

One form of "real-time" video is viable in many schools. Schools, particularly high schools, have been installing satellite reception dishes in the C and KU band range for the past 10–12 years. These one-way video systems provide foreign language, math, and science broadcasts that have proven to be both instructionally sound and cost effective for small school systems that cannot afford specialized teachers in, say, Russian, Japanese, chemistry, or advanced placement physics.

Commercial Programming Impact Commercial television programming raised a storm of controversy almost from its inception. Television has been accused of causing almost every ill that befalls our society, including the breakup of the nuclear family, increased violence (Baker & Ball, 1969), disrespect for authority, decline in reading and reading comprehension skills

(Himmelweit et al, 1958), low SAT and GRE scores, and even sexual perversion. While there is no doubt that television has changed our society, it should be noted that some aspects of television actually enhance or modify society for the good. Television has brought a nation closer together by sharing common experiences on a daily basis. While regionalism still exists, people realize that the nation as a whole is moving with common goals and interests. Television, particularly worldwide satellite transmissions, have also provided more of a sense of one-world and common goals of humanity. At the same time, television has brought the daily horrors and common gossip of the world into our living rooms, causing us to be more apprehensive of our future. Newscasts of current events, both violent and positive, give us a window on the world as never before.

Television is a shifting medium. In the 1950s, three major networks—American Broadcasting Company (ABC), National Broadcasting Company (NBC), and Columbia Broadcast System (CBS)—captured almost 100% of the television audience, with local affiliate stations re-broadcasting evening programming from the "Big Three." The networks share of the total audience recently has dropped significantly with cable television systems and direct satellite broadcasting expanding into many homes.

Cable Television: A Shifting Paradigm Cable television systems in the 1960s were first developed to provide clear, strong signals in outlying suburban or urban areas with poor reception. These cable systems simply rebroadcast programming being provided by the major networks. With the advent of geosynchronous communication satellites, cable systems began reaching out further for additional programming. Independent stations such as WLS Chicago and WTBS Atlanta suddenly became "Superstations." Ted Turner, recognizing the potential for satellite transmission and reception, started Cable News Network (CNN) as the first 24-hour all-news station. That was just the beginning. There are now hundreds of "world" channels from which to select.

AT&T, TCI Communications, and several other media companies, including Microsoft Corporation and Apple Computer, Inc., would have us believe that a 500-channel interactive two-way system will be in everyone's home by the turn of the century, although what we will do with 500 channels is not quite clear. The quality of programming that most of us currently have on 30 or 50 channel cable systems is questionable, with the exception of The Learning Channel, The Discovery Channel, Arts and Entertainment, and the local PBS affiliate. Cable operators are hurriedly converting their systems over to two-way interactive capabilities by installing fiberoptic cabling and high-speed routers. Cable operators and telephone systems seem to be on a collision course at the front door to provide interactive two-way services that include movies on demand, interactive video games, home shopping, computer data services, and phone services. In 1994, the FCC cleared the way for local phone companies to compete with cable TV firms. The new regulations will allow phone companies to offer "video dial" tones, which will let phone companies offer video over their networks.

Direct Broadcast Television Cable television companies are competing with local phone carriers, and new technologies may displace the current cable television system at a time when they are upgrading cabling to provide two-way interactive services. The Digital Satellite System (DSS) was introduced by RCA (Radio Corporation of America) in 1994, and it has expanded beyond all expectation. The 1994 Christmas shopping season found DSS with a shortage of systems for the consumer demand. The 18-inch digital satellite dish mounts unobtrusively almost anywhere and can bring over 150 channels of crisp video and digital audio signals into a home or school.

Sesame Street, Channel One, and Beyond High-quality educational and instructional television programming has been in existence since the mid-1960s when the Children's Television Workshop developed Sesame Street and, later, Electric Company. These innovative efforts set the standard for all future instructional and educational, or, more properly defined, "Edutainment" programming. Numerous research studies covering all aspects of Sesame Street have shown significant developmental gains in the targeted population (Children's Television Workshop, 1976, 1990; Mielke, 1990).

While Sesame Street, Electric Company, and other Public Television–funded operations have set new standards for children's programming, commercial interests also have set sights on the schools. Chris Whittle of Whittle Communications launched Channel One with much fanfare and a great deal of controversy. Whittle proposed to donate a satellite dish, televisions, VCRs, and cabling to schools in exchange for access to students for 12 minutes per day. His news and current events show was to be geared for middle and high school students. The catch and the controversy revolved around the two minutes of the 12 in which would carry advertising. Administrators and some teachers saw Channel One as a way to obtain much needed technology for their schools. Many parents and teachers, on the other hand, felt that students were already being bombarded with too much commercialism at home. Channel One has opened our schools to commercial advertisers in exchange for much needed technological support. Good or bad, this crack in the schoolhouse door has opened a path for future commercial ventures.

As Schneider and Wallis (1988) stated, "allied with home computers, satellites, and conventional communications systems, television introduces more than just new signs and representations; it also establishes an important new political formation: a class structure based not on wealth, but on access to information" (p. 85). We will see how these merging technologies may change the face of the world and, most surely, the way instruction is delivered in that world.

Networking

Wiring our schools for electronic communication could very well be one of the top priorities for our nation in the coming decade. Exponential growth in activity has occurred on the Internet, with almost all institutions of higher education adding thousands of users monthly. Vice-President, then senator, Al Gore's proposal for a National Research and Education Network (NREN) is still stirring much debate in both houses of Congress and in boardrooms of major corporations across the country as many consider the format of a national or international infor-

mation network. In May 1995, the Internet, which was begun more than 25 years ago with funding from the National Science Foundation, became a commercial venture, no longer receiving Federal funding. The Internet network, which was originally designed to assist researchers with transporting data and analyzing it using high-level computer systems not available on their local campuses, has turned into the "hot must have" for almost anyone with a computer.

The system has turned into a "free-form" eclectic collection of almost any information that can be imagined. More than 3 million people per day currently access different resources connected to the continually expanding Internet. Elementary and secondary schools are just now gearing up for a jump into the "Internet galaxy." Many elementary and secondary teachers, and a small percentage of students, have had access to the Internet in the past through special projects with colleges and universities. Independent service agencies and states are now making plans for all schools to be wired into the network by the year 2000. If Bill Gates, chairman and chief executive officer of Microsoft Corporation and the richest man in the world, has his way, the "information highway" will be the next "great commercial venture" (Gates, Myhrvold, & Rinearson, 1995).

Phone Based Networking Currently the majority of elementary and school access projects connecting to the Internet are using dial-in phone services. These are generally direct connection projects in which only a few computers have access to Internet services. Phone based connections are restricted to 56,300 bits per second transfer rate which is too slow for efficient graphic based data transfer. Special Integrated Services Digital Networks (ISDN) phone lines can provide higher transmission rates and cable television systems are now beginning to offer cable modems that can transmit data at several millions bits of information per second.

Local Area Networks Within Schools Many schools have networked their computers within labs to provide cost-effective ways to share software and monitor student usage, and even classroom management of testing and grading (Kurshan, 1994). Efforts are increasing to connect all computers within schools to Local Area Networks (LANs) so that every classroom will have access to electronic library catalogs and reference sources. Studies done on electronic card catalogs and electronic research show that students do more in-depth searches, find better information, and do it in a shorter time than do students using traditional research methods (Hindes, 1990).

Computers as management tools are beginning to be used more readily. While large school systems have used forms of data processing for record keeping for more than 30 years, teachers have usually not had direct access or input into these systems. Within the past ten years, programs such as MacSchool and Curriculum Management System (CMS) have begun to allow teachers to directly enter data on student progress, monitor student progress and attendance, and even streamline parent teacher conferences. Mann and Kitchens (1990) state that the CMS system encourages high expectations for student achievement and makes such expectations reasonable because each student is working on mastering content that is at the appropriate level. Parents receive highly detailed computer-generated reports every two weeks informing them of the student's progress. Teachers are enabled to identify objectives that have or have not been mastered at an acceptable level for each student. The LANs within school facilities make systems such as MacSchool and CMS possible.

Districtwide Networking For many years larger school districts have also maintained computer systems for moving statistical data and student records in electronic form. Most of these systems have relied on one-way access, with schools shipping data to the central office either over phone lines or through data tapes or computer diskettes. Information returning to the schools generally came in the form of printed reports or student grade reports. New network architectures are connecting schools within a district or systems to Wide Area Networks (WANs), which can provide continuous feedback with a steady flow of current data that can assist school-based administrators and teachers in making decisions that help effect change more quickly. The new structure of system-wide networks is also providing a cost effective architecture for directly wiring schools into the Internet.

Broad-band Internet Connections System-wide broad-band WANs can be connected by T1, T3, or ISDN phone lines directly to an Internet service provider. Tying all schools together into a WAN before making connections to the Internet is more cost effective than having individual schools each being connected directly to the Internet. With high-speed broad-band connection to the Internet, schools can begin accessing large graphic, audio, and video resources located anywhere in the world. Resources such as NetScape or Windows 95 are providing "user friendly" interfaces so students and teachers can begin to "surf" the worldwide network of information databases.

Future Directions for Networking It is not inconceivable that students from around the globe will interact on a minute-by-minute basis with other students from far reaching points in the near future. They will share common goals and interests and discover the delicious variety of culture and customs that abound in "our" world. Students will interact with students in Europe as easily as they interact with students across their community. In fact, WANs can bring schools within a community closer together because for the first time students will be able to "travel" across town and work on a project with students that have similar interests.

Electronic Communications

The electronic communications that can take place once networks are in place are boundless. E-mail currently appears to interest everyone on the Internet network, whereas just five years ago it was unusual for anyone but computer "geeks" to have an e-mail address on their business card. Anyone employed by a college or university today that does not have an e-mail address, is looked upon with suspicion about academic productivity. Commercial businesses are also "getting wired." Large and small companies alike access the Internet systems for communicating information, finding data,

transporting data to various sites needed, and achieving greater profits by working "smart" over the network.

Information Research and Retrieval Information access is a key aspect of being linked to the Internet. Schools are just beginning to explore the multiple resources available and ways that information can improve the local curriculum. Traditional on-line database services have been available for more than 20 years, but "for-profit" services such as Nexus/Lexus have generally been out of the price range for schools. Schools do have access to databases contained on CD-ROMs housed within schools, but with direct access through the Internet to government and university databases, many schools can now afford to provide up-to-the-minute resources that will assist their students. Johnson once said that "knowledge is of two kinds; we know a subject ourselves, or we know where we can find information about it." (Kaplan, 1992, p. 316). Being able to find information on the Internet will be an ever more important skill for our students and teachers. They will incorporate data gleaned for widespread sources into reports and projects on a daily basis.

Linking Classrooms As stated earlier, linking classrooms around the world will strengthen our understanding of other cultures, and broaden science and geography skills whether the connection might be in our own community or at the far corners of the globe. Projects such as the Voyage of the Mimi (Gibbon & Hooper, 1987) have already proven the feasibility of carrying students out of classrooms into the real world through communication networks and live television. With high-speed communication networks, students without experienced teachers can now collaborate with master teachers around the world. The eventual structure and form that these communication networks will take is still open to much speculation. On the one hand, many feel that schools should have unlimited access to resources on the Internet, or on whatever it is eventually named. On the other hand, forces in the business world want to privatize the Internet because they realize the potential for great profits. Whatever the eventual structure of the communications network, available evidence suggest that its form will be quite different than at present, but is insufficient to guide our imagination toward what shape it may take. Optomists envision that this worldwide communications network will lead to the next Renaissance. As Sculley (1987a) stated in a videotape of his keynote address to EDUCOM 1987:

The technologies we have seen today are only platforms. They are opportunities. They are possibilities. They are however, the tallest of platforms, the richest of opportunities and the broadest of possibilities that I know of. They will allow us to set loose an avalanche of personal creativity. And once we have thousands and thousands of ideas to harvest, we may have the chance once again to create a second Renaissance, perhaps every bit as important as the first.

Distance Education

As Heinich et al (1993) stated, distance education is a rapidly developing approach to instruction throughout the world.

The approach is being widely used by business, industry, and medical organizations. For many years, colleges and universities have experimented with distance education programs. States where populations are broadly dispersed over long distances, such as Utah and Alaska, have had some of the greatest successes with distance education programs.

For more than 40 years, distance education has attempted to take instruction out of isolated classrooms and move it into the communities where the information is needed. While current efforts to wire everyone into a communications network may eventually nullify many of the efforts of distance education advocates, replacing correspondence, radio, and television transmissions with integral data networks, distance education will only get stronger with these new and faster technologies.

Correspondence Courses Correspondence courses consisting of printed materials and, in later years, of audio and video cassettes and videodiscs have proven to be effective for many kinds of instruction. Findings (Billings, 1988) generally show that high student motivation is necessary for satisfactory completion of course work, but successful students learn and retain information on a par with traditional classroom instruction. While correspondence courses appear "low tech" compared with many of the electronic data and communication systems currently in development, they can still provide a cost-effective method for disseminating instructional materials to students located at great distances from the instructor.

One and Two-way Audio Communications Distance education initially began using land-based telephone lines for instruction in the 1950s. First, one-way audio over phone lines or radio transmissions proved the feasibility of distance instruction. Two-way systems later allowed instructors to confer with students at distant sites, which provided a form of interactivity. While audio-only systems work when students are motivated, the lack of visual feedback to the instructor sometimes causes real consternation when instructors realize, after long periods of silence, that no students were at a remote site listening to a lecture.

One-way Video Communications One-way video, with and without audio feedback, were some of the next distance education systems tried. While one-way video did not eliminate the problem of visual feedback for the instructor, students were at least now able to get more of a sense of presence of the instructor in a distant classroom. One-way video systems over land-based lines have again proved to be effective. Today's current crop of digital slow-scan systems even make it possible for distance education to transmit instruction over standard phone lines, thus reducing the per student hour contact costs.

Two-way Interactive Video Communications Two-way digital classrooms, where audio, video, and digital data can be transmitted over a series of phone lines capable of utilizing the high bandwidth necessary to carry video signals, have also been developed. Many of these two-way interactive systems still rely on slow-scan digital video, so the instructor may often look a little lethargic when moving about the classroom. The two-way video system allows an instructor to view the classroom or

classrooms where students are located. This visual feedback for the instructor seems to enhance the quality of learning (Massoumian, 1989) and allow students to be more interactive with the instruction. A 1991 survey in *Training Magazine* (Lee, 1991) showed that only 10% of training organizations in business and industry are using videoconferencing. While this percentage is increasing as technologies improve and costs decrease, it is fairly evident that elementary and secondary schools are not yet using two-way distance education systems for instruction to any great extent. Schools generally lag behind business and industry in adopting new technologies. Some state initiatives, such as the Georgia Statewide Academic and Medical System (GSAMS), are attempting to wire more sites for both instruction and medical diagnosis. Indiana has also entered into an agreement with Mid-West Bell to provide distance education access for all schools within the state.

Satellite The first geosynchronous communications satellite was launched by the National Aeronautics and Space Administration (NASA) in 1958. Since that time, hundreds of communications satellites have radically modified how people communicate over long distances. Teleconferences using satellites have been steadily growing as more transponders have become available on satellites. Expansion of satellites and a change from C to KU bands have allowed development of lower power, less expensive transmission systems.

One-way Satellite Transmission The most prevalent form of satellite conferencing is still one-way linkups where the instructor or presenter broadcasts a signal from a ground station to a satellite transponder, which is then beamed back to earth. Any satellite dish pointed at the correct satellite and tuned to the correct frequency can receive the televised signal. Students can query the instructor for feedback using a land-based phone line. Many schools have installed satellite reception dishes for bringing in programming from the distance education providers like the Texas Interactive Instructional Network (TI-IN) and Satellite Telecommunications Educational Programming (STEP). For example, Georgia has equipped every school in the state with dishes for the reception of instructional programming and in-service courses broadcast over the Peach Star satellite. Many of these programs are for courses which cannot be taught in the local school system for lack of qualified personnel. Courses such as Japanese, Russian, advanced math, chemistry, physics, and calculus have all proven popular.

Two-way Interactive Satellite Transmission Two-way interactive satellite programming is still restricted to organizations with large budgets. Ground transmission satellite systems are very expensive to install and require full-time engineers to keep them operational. While some states have tested two-way satellite based distance education programming, widespread adoption is not expected unless or until more satellites and transponders are made available. The cost of an uplink station and transponder time are currently beyond the means of all but state or regional agencies or private industry.

Future Directions for Distance Education It appears that distance education will continue to grow, with colleges and universities and public school agencies investigating its possibilities. While the technology is still in an embryonic state, the commitment from certain educational agencies is there to move ahead with widespread distance education initiatives. Georgia is currently spending more than $50 million to connect 200 classrooms throughout the state. A medical component of this same project is linking physicians and clinics with hospitals so that specialists can diagnose symptoms without requiring patients to drive long distances to regional medical centers. These two-way interactive land-based systems are attempting to provide instruction to rural and suburban areas where universities are not readily available.

The future of distance education systems and telecommunications will continue to evolve, but all school sites may eventually have an integral broad-band connection to the Internet of the future. Through fiber-optic cabling, this network will be capable of carrying high-definition video, digital audio, and data for true interactive instruction on demand into any classroom in the United States and eventually the world. As Sculley (1987b) suggested, these are the most exciting of times to be alive.

IMPLICATIONS OF CHANGING TECHNOLOGY FOR SCHOOL SUPERVISION

One of the inescapable aspects of modern life is change. New developments in computers, satellite communications, and electronic networks are constantly occurring, and these changes are creating pressure on schools to adapt and modify programs in order to prepare students and teachers to make effective use of new resources (Dwyer, 1994; Riel, 1994). Although some critics decry the effects of television on schools (Marc, 1995) and feel that the reality of networked telecommunications falls far short of the claims of its advocates (Stoll, 1995), technology is the driving force behind many current efforts to restructure American public education (Means, 1994; Reigeluth & Garfinkle, 1994).

Just as it was not possible to predict the impact that the microcomputer would have on the schools 10 years ago, it is not possible today to predict what the most significant technologies in education will be five or ten years from now. It is possible, however, to draw some general principles from the research literature that can provide guidance to instructional

supervisors as they attempt to cope with a changing technological environment:

- Although specific developments are hard to predict, the technology available to assist in the achievement of educational goals will continue to change and evolve at a rapid pace, increasing the media options for educators to use in instruction and learning.
- No single form of media or combination of media is (or can be) inherently superior to any other form or combination of media—if the media being compared have similar operational characteristics and are capable of presenting the necessary stimulus information to the learner.
- Instructional strategies and learning principles that are embedded into the materials or that are used to integrate the materials into the classroom are the significant factors that influence student learning from media rather than any specific characteristics of the media themselves.
- The selection of one form of media or combination of media over another form of media or combination of media, if both are capable of presenting the same instructional stimulus, should be influenced more by economic factors than by any inherent characteristics of the media.
- Instructional materials should be evaluated carefully to ensure that they are appropriate to the teaching strategy being employed, meet the needs and abilities of the students, and embody established design principles that facilitate communication and student learning.
- Technology is changing the way in which information is located and processed. It is expanding the sources that are consulted from beyond the textbook, school library, or local community to a worldwide network that students must be trained to access and use effectively.
- Keeping up with changing technology will require that instructional supervisors work closely with school media specialists (AECT, 1988), technology coordinators, and experienced school personnel to ensure that newer media are effectively integrated into the curriculum.

Media and technology are the tools of teaching and learning. These tools must be available when and where they are needed to meet the needs of the teachers and students who must use them. As the old adage states, "If the workman is not provided the tools necessary to do his job, he cannot be held accountable if the job is not completed properly."

REFERENCES

Adams, S., Rosemier, R., & Sleeman, P. (1965). Readable letter size and visibility for overhead projection transparencies. *AV Communication Review, 13*(4), 412–417.

Allen, W. H. (1967). Media stimulus and types of learning. *Audiovisual Instruction, 12*(1), 27–31.

Allessi, S. & Trollip, S. (1991). *Computer-based instruction.* Englewood Cliffs, NJ: Prentice-Hall.

Anderson, R. H. (1983). *Selecting and developing media for instruction* (2nd ed.). New York: Van Nostrand Reinhold Company.

Anglin, G. J. (Ed.). (1991). *Instructional technology: Past, present, and future.* Englewood, CO: Libraries Unlimited.

Association for Educational Communications and Technology & American Association of School Librarians. (1988). *Information power: Guidelines for school library media programs.* Chicago: American Library Association. Washington, D.C.: The association.

Association for Educational Communications and Technology. (1977). *The definition of educational technology.* Washington, D.C.: The association.

Baker, R. K. & Ball, S. (1969). *Mass media and violence*. Washington, D.C.: U.S. Government Printing Office.

Ball, S. & Bogatz, G. A. (1971). *The first year of Sesame Street: An evaluation*. Princeton, NJ: Educational Testing Service.

Bangert-Drowns, R., Kulik, J., & Kulik, C. (1985). Effectiveness of computer-based education in secondary schools. *Journal of Computer-Based Instruction, 12*(3), 59–68.

Becker, H. J. (1994). *Analysis and trends of school use of new information technologies* [Internet document]. (World-Wide-Web address: http://www.ota.gov/pubs.html). Washington, D.C.: U.S. Congress, Office of Technology Assessment.

Berlo, D. K. (1960). *The process of communication*. New York: Holt, Rinehart & Winston.

Billings, D. M. (1988). A conceptual model of correspondence course completion. *American Journal of Distance Education, 2*(2), 23–35.

Bitter, G. G. & Camuse, R. A. (1984). *Using a microcomputer in the classroom*. Reston, VA: Reston Publishing

Bowie, M. M. (1985). Media utilization in the classroom. *Drexel Library Quarterly, 21*(2), 105–125.

Braby, R., Henry, J. M., Parrish, W. F., & Swope, W. M. (1975). *A technique for choosing cost-effective instructional delivery systems* (TAEG Report No. 16). Orlando, FL: U.S. Navy, Training Analysis and Evaluation Group.

Bretz. R. (1971). *A taxonomy of communication media*. Englewood Cliffs, NJ: Educational Technology Publications.

Briggs, L. J. (1968). Learner variables and educational media. *Review of Educational Research, 38*(2), 160–176.

Brown, J. W., Lewis, R. B., & Harcleroad, F. F. (1977). *AV instruction: Technology, media and methods* (5th ed.). New York: McGraw Hill.

Brown, J. W. & Norberg, K. (1965). *Administering educational media*. New York: McGraw-Hill.

Bruce, B. (1990). *Roles for computers in teaching the English language arts* (Technical Report No. 522. Urbana, IL: Center for the Study of Reading, University of Illinois. (ERIC Document Reproduction Service No. ED 326 866).

Caffarella, E., et al. (1992). *An analysis of the cost-effectiveness of various electronic alternatives for delivering distance education compared to the travel costs for live instruction*. Greeley, CO: Western Institute for Distance Education (ERIC Document Reproduction Service No. ED 380 127).

Carpenter, C. R. & Greenhill, L. P. (1956). *Instructional film reports, vol. 2* (Technical Report 269–7–61). Port Washington, NY: Special Devices Center, U.S. Navy.

Carter, C. N. & Walker, M. J. (1969). Costs of instructional TV and computer-assisted instruction in public schools. In Committee for Economic Development, *The schools and the challenge of innovation* (pp. 320–341). New York: McGraw Hill.

Children's Television Workshop. (1976). *CTW research bibliography*. New York: Author.

Children's Television Workshop. (1990). *Sesame Street research bibliography: Selected citations related to Sesame Street, 1969–1989*. New York: Author.

Clark, R. E. (1975). Adapting aptitude-treatment interaction methodology to instructional media research. *AV Communication Review, 23*, 133–137.

Clark, R. E. (1983). Reconsidering the research on learning from media. *Review of Educational Research, 53*(4), 445–460.

Clark, R. E. (1992). Media use in education. In M. C. Alkin (Ed.). *Encyclopedia of educational research* (6th ed.) (pp. 805–814). New York: Macmillan.

Clark, R. E. (1994). Media will never influence learning. *Educational Technology Research & Development, 42*(2), 21–29.

Clark, R. E. & Salomon, G. (1986). Media in teaching. In M. Wittrock (Ed.). *Handbook of research on teaching* (3rd ed.) pp. 464–478. New York: Macmillan.

Chu, G. C. & Schramm, W. (1967). *Learning from television: What the research says*. Stanford, CA: Institute for Communications Research.

Craig, G. O. (1956). A comparison between sound and silent films in teaching. *British Journal of Educational Psychology, 26*, 202–206.

Cronbach, L. J., & Snow, R. E. (1977). *Aptitudes and instructional methods*. New York: Irvinton.

Dale, E. (1969). *Audio-visual methods in teaching* (3rd ed). New York: Holt, Rinehart and Winston.

Dempsey, E. (1990). First word. *Omni, 12*(7), 8.

Dijkstra, S., van Hout Wolters, B. H. A. M., & van der Sijde, P. C. (Eds.). (1990). *Research on instruction: Design and effects*. Englewood Cliffs, NJ: Educational Technology Publications.

Dimock, C. W. & Cornillon, P. (1994). Teaching high school physics using satellite imagery. *Physics Teacher, 32*(3), 156–158.

Dorr, A. (1992). Television. In M. C. Alkin (Ed.). *Encyclopedia of educational research* (6th ed.) pp. 1397–1400. New York: Macmillan.

Dwyer, D. (1994). Apple Classrooms of Tomorrow: What we've learned. *Educational Leadership, 51*(7), 4–10.

Dwyer, F. M., Jr. (1970). Exploratory studies in the effectiveness of visual illustrations. *AV Communication Review, 18*(3), 235–249.

Ely, D. P. (Ed.). (1963). The changing role of the audiovisual process in education: A definition and glossary of related terms. *AV Communication Review, 11*(1), Supplement No 6.

Ely, D. P. (1986). *Educational technology research: A status report on classroom applications*. Paper presented at EDUTEC '86, Tokyo, Japan (ERIC Document Reproduction Service No. ED 279 301).

Eraut, M. R. (1989). Conceptual frameworks and historical development. In M. Eraut (Ed.). *The international encyclopedia of educational technology* (pp. 11–21). New York: Pergamon Press.

Fadel, C. (1995). PDA's will come of age in the nineties. *Electronic Design, 43*(1), 104.

Feasley, C. E. (1992). Distance education. In M. C. Alkin (Ed.). *Encyclopedia of educational research* (6th ed.) pp. 334–342. New York: Macmillan.

Finn, J. D. (1960). Technology and the instructional process. In A. A. Lumsdaine & R. Glaser (Eds.). *Teaching machines and programmed learning: A source book* (pp. 382–394). Washington, D.C.: Department of Audiovisual Instruction, National Education Association.

Fleming, M. & Levie, W. H. (Eds.). (1993). *Instructional message design: Principles from the behavioral sciences*. (2nd ed.). Englewood Cliffs, NJ: Educational Technology Publications.

Freeman, F. N. (1924). *Visual education*. Chicago, IL: University of Chicago Press.

Gagné, R. (1965). *The conditions of learning*. New York: Holt, Rinehart & Winston.

Gagné, R. M. & Glaser, R. (1987). Foundations in learning research. In Gagné, R. M. (Ed.). *Instructional technology: Foundations*. Hillsdale, NJ: Lawrence Erlbaum Associates.

Gates, B., Myhrvold, N., & Rinearson, P. (1995). *The road ahead*. New York: Penguin Books.

General Learning Corporation. (1968). *Cost study of educational media systems and their equipment components*. Washington, D.C.: Department of Health, Education, and Welfare.

Gibbon, S. & Hooper, K. (1987, Spring). The voyage of the MIMI. *Learning Tomorrow: Journal of the Apple Education Advisory Council*, 195–207.

Grabowski, B. L. (1991). Message design: Issues and trends. In G. J. Anglin (Ed.). *Instructional technology: Past, present, and future* (pp. 202–212). Englewood, CO: Libraries Unlimited.

Greenhill, L. P. (1967). Review of trends in research on instructional television and film. In J. C. Reid & D. W. MacLennan (Eds). *Research in instructional television and film* (pp. 1–17). Washington, D.C.: U.S. Office of Education.

Gropper, G. L. (1966). Learning from visuals: Some behavioral considerations. *AV Communication Review, 14*(1), 37–70.

Hagler, P. & Knowlton, J. (1987). Invalid implicit assumption in CBI comparison research. *Journal of Computer-Based Instruction, 14*(3), 84–88.

Hannafin, M. J. & Hooper, S. R. (1993). Learning principles. In M. Fleming & W. H. Levie (Eds.). *Instructional message design: Principles from the behavioral and cognitive sciences* (2nd ed.) pp. 191–231. Englewood Cliffs, NJ: Educational Technology Publications.

Hartley, J. (1966). Research report. *NEW Education, 2*(1), 4 page reprint of article.

Hartman, F. R. (1961). Single and multiple channel communication: A review of research and a proposed model. *AV Communication Review, 9*(4), 235–262.

Heidt, E. U. (1976). *Instructional media and the individual learner: A classification and systems appraisal.* New York: Nichols Publishing Co.

Heinich, R. (1970). *Technology and the management of instruction* (Monograph No. 4). Washington, D.C.: Association for Educational Communications and Technology.

Heinich, R., Molenda, M., & Russell, J. (1993). *Instructional media and new technologies of instruction* (4th ed.). New York: Macmillan.

Himmelweit, H. T., Oppenheim, A. N., & Vince, P. (1958). *Television and the children.* London, England: Oxford University Press.

Hindes, M. A. (1990). *The search for processes and attitudes of students accessing CD-ROM resources: The study of two high school media centers.* Unpublished doctoral dissertation, University of Georgia, Athens, GA.

Hoban, C. F., Hoban, F. H., & Zisman, S. B. (1937). *Visualizing the curriculum.* New York: The Cordon Company.

Hoban, C. F. & Van Ormer, E. B. (1950). *Instructional film research, 1918–1950* (Technical Report No. SDC 269-7-19). Port Washington, NY: U. S. Naval Training Device Center.

Hooper, S. & Hannafin, M. J. (1986). Variables affecting the legibility of computer generated text. *Journal of Instructional Development, 9*(4), 22–28.

Hovland, C. I., Lumsdaine, A. A., & Sheffield, F. D. (1949). *Experiments on mass communication.* Princeton, NJ: Princeton University Press.

Jamison, D. T. & McAnany, E. G. (1978). *Radio for education and development.* Beverly Hills, CA: Sage Publications.

Jamison, D., Suppes, P., & Wells, S. (1974). The effectiveness of alternative instructional media: A survey. *Review of educational Research, 44*(1), 1–68.

Jamison, D. T., Klees, S. J., & Wells, S. J. (1978). *The costs of educational media: Guidelines for planning and evaluation.* Beverly Hills, CA: Sage Publications.

Jonassen, D. (Ed.). (1982). *The technology of text.* Englewood Cliffs, NJ: Educational Technology Publications.

Jones, J. I. & Simonson, M. (1993). Distance education: A cost analysis. In *Proceedings of Selected Presentations at the Convention of the Association for Educational Communications and Technology, New Orleans, LA* (ERIC Document Reproduction Service No. ED 362 171).

Kaplan, J. (1992). *Bartlett's familiar quotations* (16th ed.). Boston, MA: Little Brown.

Kemp, J. E. & Smellie, D. C. (1994). *Planning, producing, and using instructional technologies* (7th ed). New York: Harper Collins College Publishers.

Kiesling, H. (1979). Economic cost analysis in higher education: The University of Mid-America and traditional institutions compared. *Educational Communications and Technology Journal, 27*(1), 9–24.

King, J. M., Murwin, S. W., & Matt, S. R. (1990). Optical disc technology: Education trend of the future? *The Technology Teacher, 49*(8), 25–29.

Knowlton, D. C. & Tilton, J. W. (1929). *Motion pictures in history teaching.* New Haven, CT: Yale University Press.

Knowlton, J. Q. (1964). A conceptual scheme for the audiovisual field. *Viewpoints, Bulletin of the School of Education, Indiana University, 40*(3), 1–44.

Kozma, R. B. (1991). Learning with media. *Review of Educational Research, 61*(2), 179–211.

Kozma, R. B. (1994). Will media influence learning? Reframing the debate. *Educational Technology and Development, 42*(2), 7–19.

Kulik, C. C. & Kulik, J. A. (1986). Effectiveness of computer-based education in colleges. *AEDS Journal, 19*(2–3), 81–108.

Kulik, J., Bangert, R., & Williams, G. (1983). Effects of computer-based teaching on secondary students. *Journal of Educational Psychology, 75*(1), 19–26.

Kulik, J., Kulik, C., & Bangert-Downs, R. (1984). Effectiveness of computer-based education in elementary schools. *Computers in Human Behavior, 1*(1), 59–74.

Kurshan, B. L., et al. (1994). *An educator's guide to electronic networking: Creating virtual communities.* Syracuse, NY: ERIC Clearinghouse on Information Resources (ERIC Document Reproduction Service No. ED 372 772).

Lalande, R. (1995). LIM intelligent music workstations CD-ROM for Macintosh. *Computer Music Journal, 19*(2), 105–107.

Lamberski, R. J. (1980). *A comprehensive and critical review of the methodology and findings in color investigations.* Syracuse, NY: ERIC Clearinghouse on Information Resources (ERIC Document Reproduction Service No. ED 194 063)

Large, A., et al. (1994). A comparison of information retrieval from print and CD-ROM versions of an encyclopedia by elementary school students. *Information Processing and Management, 30*(4), 499–513.

Lee, C. (1991, October). Who gets trained in what? *Training,* 47–59.

Levie, H. W. & Dickie, K. E. (1973). The analysis and application of media. In R. M. W. Travers (Ed.). *Second handbook of research on teaching* (pp. 858–882). Chicago, IL: Rand McNally.

Levie, W. H. & Lentz, R. (1982). Effects of text illustrations: A review of research. *Educational Communications and Technology Journal, 30*(4), 195–232.

Levin, J. R. (1983). Pictorial strategies for school learning. In M. Pressley & J. R. Levin (Eds.). *Cognitive strategy research: Educational applications* (pp. 203–237). New York: Springer-Verlag.

Lumsdaine, A. A. (1963). Instruments and media of instruction. In N. L. Gage (Ed.). *Handbook of research in teaching* (pp. 583–682). Chicago, IL: Rand McNally.

Lumsdaine, A. A. (1964). Educational technology, programmed learning, and instructional science. In E. R. Hilgard (Ed.). *Theories of learning and instruction* (63rd yearbook of the National Society for the Study of Education, Part I). Chicago, IL: The University of Chicago Press.

Lumsdaine, A. A. & Glaser, R. (Eds.). (1960). *Teaching machines and programmed instruction: A source book.* Washington, D.C.: National Education Association.

Mann, G. & Kitchens, J. (1990, February). *Curriculum management system: A computer managed curriculum.* Paper presented at the Annual Meeting of the Association of Teacher Educators, Las Vegas, NV (ERIC Document Reproduction Service No. ED 319 679).

Marc, D. (1995). *Bonfire of the humanities: Television, subliteracy, and long-term memory loss.* Syracuse, NY: Syracuse University Press.

Marchionini, G. (1989). Information-seeking strategies of novices using a full-text electronic encyclopedia. *Journal of the American Society for Information Science, 40*(1), 54–56.

Martin, E. D. (1993). Student achievement and attitude in a satellite-delivered high school science course. *American Journal of Distance Education, 7*(1), 54–61.

Massoumian, B. (1989). Successful teaching via two-way interactive video. *Tech Trends*, *34*(2), 16–19.

May, M. A. & Lumsdaine, A. A. (1958). *Learning from films.* New Haven, CT: Yale University Press.

Mayer, R. E. & Gallini, J. K. (1990). When is an illustration worth ten thousand words? *Journal of Educational Psychology*, *82*(4), 715–726.

Means, B. (Ed.). (1994). *Technology and education reform: The reality behind the promise.* San Francisco: Jossey-Bass Publishers.

Merrill, P. F., Hammons, K., Vincent, B. R., Reynolds, R. L., Christensen, L., & Tolman, M. N. (1995). *Computers in education* (3rd ed.). Boston, MA: Allyn and Bacon.

Mielke, K. W. (1990). Research and development at the Children's Television Workshop. *Educational Technology Research and Development*, *38*(4), 7–16.

Morrison, G. R. (1994). The media effects question: "Unresolvable" or asking the right question. *Educational Technology Research and Development*, *42*(2), 41–44.

Morrison, G. R., Ross, S. M., & O'Dell, J. K. (1991). Applications of research to the design of computer-based instruction. In G. J. Anglin (Ed.). *Instructional technology: Past, present, and future* (pp. 188–194). Englewood, CO: Libraries Unlimited.

Nugent, R. (1987, January). *The language of interactivity.* Paper presented at the meeting of the Institute for Graphic Communications, Key Biscayne, FL.

Peterson's Guide. (1995). *The U.S. public school system* [Internet document]. (World-Wide-Web address: http://www.petersons.com/preview/k12.html). Princeton, NJ: Peterson's Education Center.

Reeves, T. C. (1986). Research and evaluation models for the study of interactive video. *Journal of Computer-Based Instruction.* *13*(4), 102–106.

Reid, J. C. & MacLennan, D. W. (1967). *Research in instructional television and film.* Washington, D.C.: Department of Health Education and Welfare.

Reigeluth, C. M. & Garfinkle, R. J. (Eds.). (1994). *Systemic change in education.* Englewood Cliffs, NJ: Educational Technology Publications.

Reiser, R. A. & Gagné, R. M. (1983). *Selecting media for instruction.* Englewood Cliffs, NJ: Educational Technology Publications.

Riccobono, J. A. (1985). *School utilization study: Availability, use, and support of instructional media. 1982–83 final report.* Washington, D.C.: Corporation for Public Broadcasting (ERIC Document Reproduction Service No. ED 256 292).

Ridenour, D. (1987). Allowing students read-access to their own computer records. *CAUSE/EFFECT*, *11*(2), 12–16.

Riel, M. (1994). Educational change in a technology-rich environment. *Journal of Research on Computing in Education*, *26*(4), 452–474.

Roblyer, M. D., Castine, W. H., & King, F. J. (1988). Assessing the impact of computer-based instruction: A review of recent research. *Computers in the Schools.* 5(3/4), 11–149.

Rogers, E. M. (1983). *Diffusion of innovations* (3rd ed.). New York: The Free Press.

Saettler, P. (1968). *A history of instructional technology.* New York: McGraw Hill.

Saettler, P. (1990). *The evolution of American educational technology.* Englewood, CO: Libraries Unlimited.

Salomon, G. (1992). New information technologies in education. In M. C. Alkin (Ed.). *Encyclopedia of educational research* (6th ed.) pp. 892–903. New York: Macmillan.

Salomon, G. & Clark, R. E. (1977). Reexamining the methodology of research on media and technology in education. *Review of Educational Research*, *47*(1), 99–120.

Sandler, J. (1967). *The hidden medium: A status report on educational radio in the United States.* New York: Herman W. Land Associates.

Scanlon, R. G. & Weinberger, J. A. (Eds.). (1973). *Improving productivity of school systems through educational technology: Final report of symposium.* Philadelphia, PA: Research for Better Schools.

Schneider, C. & Wallis, B. (Eds.). (1988). *Global television.* New York: Wedge Press.

Schramm, W. (1954). How communication works. In W. Schramm & D. F. Roberts (Eds.). *The process and effects of mass communication* (pp. 3–26). Urbana, IL: University of Illinois Press.

Schramm, W. (1973). *Big media, little media: A report to the Agency for International Development.* Stanford, CA: Institute for Communication Research, Stanford University.

Schramm, W., Lyle, J., & Parker, E. B. (1961). *Television in the lives of our children.* Stanford, CA: University Press.

Schwier, R. A. (1991). Current issues in interactive design. In G. J. Anglin (Ed.). *Instructional technology: Past, present, and future* (pp. 195–201). Englewood, CO: Libraries Unlimited.

Sculley, J. (1987a). *Keynote Address EDUCOM '87* [videotape]. Cupertino, CA: Apple Computer, Inc.

Sculley, J. (1987b). *Odyssey: Pepsi to Apple, a journey of adventure, ideas, and the future.* New York: Harper & Row.

Seels, B. B. & Richey, R. C. (1994). *Instructional technology: The definition and domains of the field.* Washington, D.C.: Association for Educational Communications and Technology.

Seibert, W. F. & Ullmer, E. J. (1982). Media use in education. In H. E. Mitzel (Ed.). *Encyclopedia of educational research* (5th ed.) pp. 1190–1202. New York: The Free Press.

Severin, W. (1967). The effectiveness of relevant pictures in multiple-channel communications. *AV Communication Review*, *15*(4), 386–401.

Shannon, C. & Weaver, W. (1949). *The mathematical theory of communication.* Urbana, IL: University of Illinois Press.

Snow, R. E. (1970). Research on media and attributes. *Viewpoints, Bulletin of the School of Education, Indiana University*, *46*, 63–89.

Snow, R. E. & Salomon, G. (1968). Aptitudes and instructional media. *AV Communication Review*, *16*, 341–357.

Snowberg, R. L. (1973). Basis for the selection of background colors for transparencies. *AV Communication Review*, *21*(2), 191–207.

Stoll, C. (1995). *Silicon snake oil: Second thoughts on the information highway.* New York: Doubleday.

Strickell, D. W. (1963). *A critical review of the methodology and results of research comparing televised and face-to-face instruction.* Unpublished doctoral dissertation, The Pennsylvania State University.

Suppes, P. & Morningstar, M. (1972). *Computer-assisted instruction at Stanford, 1966–1969: Data, models, and evaluation of the arithmetic program.* New York: Academic Press.

Taylor, R. (1980). *The computer in the school: Tutor, tool, tutee.* New York: Teachers College Press.

Tickton, S. G. (Ed.). (1970–1971). *To improve learning: An evaluation of instructional technology* (2 volumes). New York: Bowker.

Thompson, A. D., Simonson, M. R., & Hargrave, C. P. (1992). *Educational technology: A review of the research.* Washington, D.C.: Association for Educational Communications and Technology.

Travers, R. M. W. (1967). *Research and theory related to audiovisual information transmission.* Washington, D.C.: U.S. Office of Education.

van Hout Wolters, B. H. A. M., Kerstjens, W. M. J., & Verhagen, P. W. (1990). The use of color to structure instructional texts. In S. Dijkstra, B. H. A. M. van Hout Wolters, & P. C. van der Sijde (Eds.). *Research on instruction: Design and effects* (pp. 79–91). Englewood Cliffs, NJ: Educational Technology Publications.

Wade, S. (1967). *Hagerstown: A pioneer in closed-circuit televised instruction. New educational media in action: Case studies for planners.* Paris, France: UNESCO and the International Institute for Educational Planning.

Walker, J. (1962). *Channels of learning.* Washington, D.C.: Public Affairs Press.

Weber, J. J. (1930). *Visual aids in education.* Valparaiso, IN: Valparaiso University.

Wesley, B., Krockover, G., & Hicks, C. (1985). Locus of control and acquisition of computer literacy. *Journal of Computer-Based Instruction, 12*, 12–16.

Wilkinson, G. L. (1973). Cost evaluation of instructional strategies. *AV Communication Review, 21*(1), 11–30.

Wilkinson, G. L. (1980a). *Educational media, technology and instructional productivity: A consideration of cost and effectiveness* (Occasional Paper No. 2). Syracuse, NY: ERIC Clearinghouse on Information Resources (ERIC Document Reproduction Service No. ED 216 680).

Wilkinson, G. L. (1980b). *Media in instruction: 60 years of research.* Washington, D.C.: Association for Educational Communications and Technology.

Wilkinson, G. L. (1992). Instructional media/materials. In J. W. Keefe & J. M. Jenkins (Eds.). *Instructional leadership handbook* (2nd ed.) pp. 183–184. Restin, VA: The National Association of Secondary School Principles.

Willows, D. M. & Houghton, H. A. (Eds.). (1987). *The psychology of illustration.* New York: Springer-Verlag.

Wilson, D. L. (1995). Internet@home. *Chronicle of Higher Education, 41*(40), 20–22.

Wilson, E. K. & Marsh, G. E. (1995). Social studies and the Internet revolution. *Social Education, 59*(4), 198–202.

Wilson, T. C., Pfister, F. C., & Fleury, B. E. (1981). *The design of printed instructional materials: Research on illustrations and typography.* Syracuse, NY: ERIC Clearinghouse on Information Resources.

Winn, W. E. (Ed.). (1968). Aptitude treatment interaction. *AECT Research and Theory Division Newsletter, 8*(4), 2–38.

Winn, W. E. (1993). Perception principles. In M. Fleming & W. H. Levie (Eds.). *Instructional message design: Principles from the behavioral and cognitive sciences* (pp. 55–126). Englewood Cliffs, NJ: Educational Technology Publications.

Wood, B. D. & Freeman, F. N. (1929). *Motion pictures in the classroom.* Boston, MA: Houghton Mifflin.

Yelon, S. L. (1996). *Powerful principles of instruction.* White Plains, NY: Longman Publishers.

·52·

FUTURE DIRECTIONS FOR SCHOOL SUPERVISION

Carl D. Glickman and Dianne G. Kanawati

UNIVERSITY OF GEORGIA

This volume, the *Handbook of Research on School Supervision*, brought together the unique perspectives of more than 70 different authors looking at 50 different aspects of supervision in more than 50 different chapters. Although these authors are concerned with supervision as it is currently defined and practiced in a particular context, many of them have looked toward the future of the profession as well. It is interesting that there are wide areas of agreement as well as areas of disagreement about the future of school supervision. New models are proposed, familiar issues are brought forward for reconsideration, and various research emphases are suggested. This chapter first considers those models, issues, and research proposals and then speculates about the future of schooling and its implications for the future of supervision.

FOUR TRENDS

Throughout this book, the most striking commonality is the pervasive influence of organization and management theories from the field of business. Flinders pointed out that "education has always drawn from business and will continue to do so," citing examples from 1920's social efficiency to 1990's Total Quality Management. Although enthusiasm for this development is not universal (e.g., Smyth), there is a general consensus that organizational and managerial theories have much to offer the field of supervision either directly or indirectly.

The supervisory role is indeed common to all organizations, and schools are organizations that operate within most, if not all, of the same organizational dynamics and constraints as business and political organizations. However, the new models of supervision, which draw upon organizational development and/or quality management theories, represent a dramatic alteration in the ways that supervision is conceptualized and what its priorities ought to be.

The following is a list of four trends in supervision that were repeatedly cited by the authors of this *Handbook*. It is not coincidental that they are all congruent with organizational and managerial theories such as Organizational Development (OD) and Total Quality Management (TQM), which have had a significant impact on the field of business.

Shift From Individual to Group Focus

Clinical supervision, which has dominated supervisory theory and shaped practice in various configurations since the 1960s, has come under attack as limited, inadequate, and ineffective (Anderson & Snyder; Garmston, Lipton, & Kaiser; Hall & Shieh; Tracy; Shapiro & Blumberg).

One problem with the clinical model is its premise that, if an individual teacher's instruction can be improved, then student learning will improve. Research has been unable to confirm that clinical supervision has any significant impact upon student achievement. Another problem with the clinical model is its assumption that, if an individual teacher's instruction can be improved, then the organization as a whole will thereby be improved. Organizational theories indicate that this assumption is precisely inverted: The organization must first be changed, or meaningful individual change is probably not possible.

According to Garmston et al, "the culture of the workplace may itself be a more powerful influence upon practice than the acquisition of a pedagogical knowledge base." Wood noted that "socialization processes, role requirements, and organizational routines literally shape people's attitudes and behaviors, often in ways contrary to their intentions." Work, including teacher work, is a part of, and is therefore in large part determined by, the school's social and organizational system.

By shifting from an individual to a group focus, the supervisor's role becomes more likely to be welcomed as a resource provider than as a critic. Working with teams of teachers, the supervisor functions as "a visionary leader, a facilitator, a developer of talent, and one who empowers the team to produce results for students" (Anderson & Snyder).

Teachers and supervisors work together with mutual respect, which is motivating in itself (Tracy). Moreover, widening the supervisor's scope and sphere of activity beyond the classroom makes the school or district's "culture" a legitimate focus of supervisory interest and, it is hoped, influence.

Shift From a Preoccupation with Inspection and Evaluation Toward a Function of Facilitating Growth

According to Francis Duffy, supervision as inspection and evaluation has been the dominant model in practice, if not in theory, for the entire 300 years of American education. This approach typically ends by being prescriptive: the supervisor functions as the "expert" sent in to "fix" a problem. Using the terminology of Miller and Seller (1985), several authors called this the "transmission" model of supervision because the supervisor "transmits" skills and knowledge to the supervisee. The supervisee is presumed to be in a deficit position; otherwise, he or she would not warrant the supervisor's attention. This approach can create problems as well as solve them.

It is also not necessarily more effective to require teachers to generate their own professional development programs. Acheson, Shamsher, and Smith maintained that "mandating a program of self-improvement is counter-productive, contradictory, and dysfunctional." In the alternative vision, the supervisor invites teacher growth by "setting the stage," providing a "fluid environment where learning is viewed as a process, not as outcome" (Wood). This model assumes that "persons are capable of taking responsibility for their own growth, of being self-directed and self-supervising when the proper resources and support mechanisms are available" (Tracy).

The supervisor's job centers on providing resources and support mechanisms. The modeling and encouragement of reflective practice is one way in which this can be done (Gordon & Nicely; Starratt). Teachers and students need to become "major actors in describing, knowing, confronting, and reconstructing the practices and the context in which education occurs" (Smyth). The importance of context will be discussed more fully in the next section.

As a result of the reflective process, the supervisor in effect becomes a catalyst, a change agent, who "[provokes] change in participants' value systems and assumptions rather than merely seeking to modify behavior" (Hall & Shieh). Several authors used Miller and Seller's (1985) terminology and called this "transformative" supervision or "supervision for professional growth."

Shift From a Micro- to a Macroconceptualization of Supervisory Context.

A systems approach to supervision, one which considers the "total organizational environment," is strongly recommended by several authors (Garmston, Lipton, & Kaiser; Woodward; Waite; Valverde; Flinders). In this view, the school or district is considered as a social system, as a culture, and/or as an organization in which the people who fill a particular role form one subsystem from among many.

The importance of educational context is being highlighted in much of current supervisory thinking. Rather than con-

ceptualizing supervision as "an affair of individuals," according to Shapiro and Blumberg, it must be treated as a "social enterprise." Tracy said: "To improve the performance of any one individual, we must consider the total organizational environment in which that person works." Flinders pointed out that supervisors are as much a part of the organization as those they seek to assist, while their success simultaneously depends upon their ability "to read the intricate context in which instructional activities unfold."

This approach to supervision is compatible with the "facilitating growth" function discussed in the previous section; however, it is presumed that during the process of facilitating growth, organizational goals can be served at the same time and, indeed, should be given equal priority. If the system and its members are to work together effectively and efficiently, then personal growth and organizational renewal must be linked, instead of focusing on either one to the exclusion of the other (Hall & Shieh).

This approach obviously expands the supervisor's sphere beyond the classroom level. Waite asked:

What are the political, economic, structural, and historical sociological influences, patterns, and forces impinging upon supervision and its domain? Can these be connected, and if so how?

Valverde discussed the "dynamics" exerted by the particular internal and external forces that affect schools and which make each school unique, distinct from any other. Smyth "excavated" the broader forces that bear on the work of supervision, especially those that result from worldwide economic restructuring.

Those authors whose terminology is drawn directly from organizational/managerial theory call this approach to supervision "supervision for human resources" (Aiken & Tanner; Anderson & Snyder; Hall & Shieh). This model assumes that the entire organization will improve by encouraging human growth and development. There is an additional element involved in the managerial/organizational paradigm, however: The premise that identifying and working toward the goals of the organization (i.e., school or district) is a corollary supervisory responsibility.

Starratt described the process as:

[The supervisor is] a carrier of ideas (not the only carrier to be sure) who, moving from one subgroup to another, pollinates the groups with ideas from other groups . . . helping others to find a larger vision of what the school needs to become, and helping people work toward that vision.

Determining the shape of that larger vision, according to Anderson and Snyder, is done through an understanding of "client needs" (i.e., the needs of the students, parents, and community). "When it becomes clear what are the client needs, then school goals and strategic plans follow." They add:

Strategic thinking and planning, driven by client needs and systems thinking, can offset the traditional reliance on static laws, programs, and practices, and can alter the outcomes of schooling for all populations.

Emphasis on Creating Community, Both Within the School and with the Larger Community Which the School Serves

In effect, teams of teachers will supervise themselves. As they do so, they will work together, supporting and assisting one another in such endeavors as collecting data on student and teacher learning, and assessing overall team performance. The supervisor functions as a resource provider and facilitator, rather than being solely responsible as the initiator of the process. Fostering collegiality among teachers becomes a major supervisory goal.

In effect, the school becomes a community of life-long learners (Tracy), united in a common project: making the vision of what the school can become come to pass. Schoolwide acceptance of a common project based upon a common vision would require a dramatic change from the fragmented manner in which schools have typically operated. Starratt speaks of the supervisor's role as "building coalitions among teachers" and Swan expresses much the same sentiment when he advises "building bridges over the walls which allow the division of one group of educators . . . and one group of students, from another."

As there must be a shared vision of the school within the school itself, there must also be a shared vision of the school as a part of the larger community. Just as the school or district constitutes a social system, so does the community as well. In the managerial/organizational model, the school accepts its role in the larger community because identifying "client needs" requires it to do so. Rust et al envision the supervisor "reaching out to the community to promote involvement in and support for the arts program as well as to voice the rationale for it." The same could and should be done for other programs as well.

Securing community involvement through an effective public relations program ought to be regarded as an important aspect of a school's function. Local involvement has always been an important part of the American educational system, but the support of the community for its school cannot be taken for granted in times of diversity and conflict. "Promoting involvement and support" and "voicing the rationale" are crucial roles which supervisors should embrace.

Although these four trends in supervision are unabashedly drawn from managerial/organizational theories, not everyone welcomes the application of business theories to education. Smyth, in particular, cautioned that although supervision is allegedly becoming more participatory and collegial, he suspects that "such shifts might be more illusory than real [because] processes, procedures, and technologies of control are embedded in the work of teaching." Changes in the vocabulary of supervision may mask the fact that very little change of substance has actually taken place.

[While] teachers [are] being urged to be more "reflective" and to operate with one another in more "collegial" ways . . . in the final analysis many of these differ little in their final effect from "indirect" forms of control increasingly being exercised through centralized curricula, outcomes-based education, forms of performance-based measures, and testing.

FIVE ISSUES

The following is a list of five issues in supervision that were repeatedly cited by the authors of this handbook. It is essential that each be acknowledged, addressed, and hopefully, allayed.

Supervision Needs to Eschew Simplistic Solutions to Its Dilemmas Several authors make this same point, in almost the same words. There must be "respect for the complexity of human endeavor," according to Killian and Post; we must "take instructional supervision seriously as a complex human endeavor," said Hawthorne and Hoffman. There is a dangerous tendency to address the "grand complexity" of supervision with simplistic paradigms (Harris). Cook cautioned that "there is a vast difference between simple elegance and simplistic solutions. . . . elegant solutions emerge from risk-taking, from patience and persistence."

Goldsberry is even more direct:

The pretense that supervisory interventions can have predictable and reproducible consequences across contexts and teachers is puzzling to me. . . . Supervision is a form of human, interpersonal interaction. As such it is as variable as friendship, parenthood, sales, or any other form of people engaging other people.

Simplistic solutions are undeniably attractive. Killian and Post conclude that this is probably the basis for scientific management's wide appeal across institutions and generations. They quote Sergiovanni and Starratt's (1993) wry observation that people would rather have an exact answer to a wrong question than an approximate answer to the right question.

The predilection for simplistic solutions has brought education in general, and supervision with it, under fire for too readily adopting every passing fad and fancy. Shapiro and Blumberg lay the blame on a "weak or non-existent theoretical basis" that makes educators "fall prey to any notion wandering into discourse." Harris pointed out that the roads upon which the notions were wandering are always paved with good intentions: The changes were always sincerely intended to contribute to the improvement of teaching and learning.

Changes and reforms, however, are played out in the schools. Whatever becomes of them, it is the supervisors who are held responsible.

In all cases, supervisors were involved in virtually all of the change efforts—and thus to blame for the demise of sound programs, as well as the collapse of the ill-conceived [ones] (Harris).

Dealing with the forces of change when they arise, Harris said, is one of the roles of the supervisor. The supervisors' intervention can ideally turn positive forces to advantage, and blunt the impact of the negative ones. In practice, however, distinguishing the positive from the negative, especially when enthusiasm for the innovation is running high, is more easily recommended than accomplished.

The Relationship of Supervision and Curriculum Needs to be Reexamined

The separation of curriculum from supervision is a historical study in itself, but Oliva, Aiken, and Tanner, as well as Glatthorn, all argued that the two roles need to be reunited. Glatthorn defined educational leadership as encompassing curriculum leadership, supervisory leadership, and organizational leadership. Aiken and Tanner, however, pointed out that these processes, though "seen as interrelated and interactive by Glatthorn," tend to be carried out in practice by various individuals at various levels in the school district.

According to Aiken and Tanner, the long ascendancy of clinical supervision has favored the separation of curriculum from supervision. With its emphasis on classroom analysis of instruction, the clinical supervision model presupposes that curriculum matters are dealt with at higher levels.

Not everyone, however, is inclined to reunite—or undifferentiate—the two. Firth spoke of "instructional supervision, and . . . the related but distinct companion, curriculum development." He argued that sets of distinct, agreed-upon tasks do exist for curriculum leaders and for instructional supervisors, and that various reports differentiate between the "program-type" responsibilities of the curriculum director and the "people-type" responsibilities of the instructional supervisor.

This issue forms part of the larger issue of how supervision as a profession defines itself, or even whether it is important that it try to do so.

Supervision Needs to Strive for Recognition as a Profession

Firth identified four fundamental aspects of professions: expertise, autonomy, responsibility, and commitment.

Using these as a framework, he analyzed the reasons why the placement of educational specialties such as supervision among the established professions has been an issue of debate, both within the field and by society at large.

According to Firth, the integrity of a profession—indeed, its hallmark—rests upon control of three factors: programs of preparation, certification to practice, and enforcement of ethical standards. At the present, supervision as a profession controls none of the three.

Research in Supervision Needs to Demonstrate More Methodological Rigor

Several authors addressed this problem. Cook complained about research that is "haphazard" and "atheoretical." Killian and Post lamented the substitution of "bandwagon" claims for a research base, failure to generate replicable, generalizable findings, and the problem of "failing to clarify at the start" exactly what is meant by "teacher effectiveness." Goldsberry pointed out that too many supervision studies have been done during the first year of a program, which is too soon for productive teacher involvement to have developed.

Nolan listed several specific concerns, including a need for larger sample sizes, more longitudinal and sequential designs, more information about the raters when rating scales are employed, more information about participants as well as

contexts, more precise operational definitions of terms and constructs that are important to the study, more rigorous instruments designed specifically for the context of interest, and the need to limit overreliance on "self-reported satisfaction" as a measure of supervisory effectiveness.

Like Nolan, Shapiro and Blumberg specifically mentioned the need for the development of instruments generated specifically to study supervisory behavior and the behavior system of supervision.

Firth noted:

Unlike other professional fields, education generally and instructional supervision particularly do not possess respective bodies of scientific knowledge documenting by careful experimentation and experience the results of various methods and procedures. This has led to much difficulty in determining the adequacy of an individual supervisor, the supervisory program in a local school system, and/or contributions of instructional supervision in American education.

Supervision Needs a Moral Foundation

This question is central to Starratt's chapter 40, "Supervision as Moral Agency," but it was also a concern—stated or implied—in several others. Hall and Shieh note that "little tends to be said about ethics." Hawthorne and Hoffman complain of "the lack of a moral centering on matters of consequence in relation to . . . instructional supervision." Shapiro and Blumberg lament a "critical lack of theory and a consistent philosophy," which means that supervision has no "fulcrum or centerpiece around which to organize thinking and, therefore, professional practice." In their metaphoric prose, Shapiro and Blumberg described the challenge to:

design and implement a common purpose . . . to confidently stride into the coming millennium with courage and conviction.

Moral issues are raised in several chapters without being developed or resolved. Gay, who wrote Chapter 50, on "Cultural, Ethnic, and Gender Issues," invoked moral imperatives when she asked, "Do we [Americans] have the moral valor and the ethical will to do what is right by all of our children?" In Chapter 8, "The Psychology of Supervision," Garmston, Lipton, and Kaiser described supervision as "a fractal representation of similar values, assumptions, and beliefs that permeate the organization." The language of those urging organizational or managerial strategies upon the profession often seems to be couched in the lofty rhetoric of liberty and equality, presumably as an appeal to moral/ethical obligations to which supervisors must respond; however, what if the values, assumptions, and beliefs of the organization are antithetical to those of the supervisor—what then? This question is discussed by Hall and Shieh, who asked, "How can the inevitable clashes between the so-called idealism of educators become balanced with the urgencies of need of clients and customers?"

Shapiro and Blumberg made the point that ethical questions will inevitably arise. In order to deal with them when they do, "It is imperative that [supervisors] find time to consider the ethical dimension of their practice." Indeed, one of the fundamental aspects of a profession, according to Firth, is a professional code of ethics.

It is somewhat disconcerting to look over the many chapters in this volume and find so few that addressed a moral/ethical dimension of supervision. In general, the moral issue has been marginalized or ignored completely. This, itself, should be viewed as an issue of concern.

IMPLICATIONS FOR FUTURE RESEARCH: TRADITIONAL, INNOVATIVE, GAPING HOLES

Most of the chapters in the *Handbook* conclude with specific needs for research. This may well be the most valuable contribution of the *Handbook* to the future of the profession: the compilation of research on supervision extant at the date of publication may reveal holes in the informational fabric that had previously gone unnoticed. Some of the research needs are perennial, although that makes them more important, not less. Other research needs have been perceived, especially those derived from the qualitative research paradigm. Certain other areas seem to have never been researched at all. Each of these research questions may fruitfully serve as a guide for future directions in supervision research.

Traditional Research Questions

"Despite nearly a century of inquiry," Schoonmaker et al observed that "there remain pressing questions about supervision which continue to invite systematic inquiry. These questions beg a larger question, 'Why do the same questions keep coming up?'"

We seem to have encountered a set of problems without solutions, problems which persist despite the many ways in which we have made inquiry into them. The questions around persistent problems have contradictory answers.

Three "persistent problems" that are of concern to the authors of the *Handbook* will now be discussed.

How Does Supervision Affect Student Achievement? This is foremost among the "persistent problems." Schoonmaker et al noted that

a survey of the literature across time makes it quite clear that the topic of most interest to supervisors has been understanding the relationship between supervisory intervention, teaching practice, and student outcomes.

Oliva urged more studies of the impact by programs and practices on student achievement. Swan asked, "Under what conditions does the provision of effective supervision positively impact student achievement?" According to Cook, research in the field of supervision too often focuses on minor variables and ignores the central purpose of supervision: the enhancement of student learning.

This may be understandable in an era where we have difficulties in understanding student learning and how to assess it. However, this is

all the more reason why research in supervision should examine student learning in a broad perspective.

Gordon and Nicely agree with Cook that student learning is difficult to assess; they see a need for better methodologies to explore the interactions and effects of supervisory interventions on students. Tracy suggested that alternative methods of inquiry, such as action research, may yield such methodologies.

What Are the Factors in Supervisory Efficacy? This question is being asked in every supervisory context. Writing in the context of higher education, Lewis asked, "What skills or competencies do people need to do faculty development well, and how can they be taught?" Exploring supervision in the context of special education, Swan asked, "Which [supervisory] practices work most effectively in specific situations with given resources and constraints?"

Holland deplored supervision's lack of clear standards of practice or, for that matter, a clear rationale for existing practice.

As a practice with no standards of practice, supervision is characterized by processes and techniques reflecting both practical expediency and intellectual anarchy.

Shapiro and Blumberg expect research to point the way toward greater supervisory efficacy by identifying the roles and skills that enable supervisors to make significant contributions to their schools, their districts, and education. The authors would like to see the development of efficacy instruments "specifically focused on functions and tasks of both administration and supervision" in order to develop a "general efficacy construct."

How do Different Models of Supervision Compare? Although speaking in the context of school counselors, Nolan provides a list of research questions likely to yield valuable information in any context.

1. Of the supervisory models that have been advocated in the literature, which are most effective and under what conditions and constraints?
2. What models of supervision are currently being used in the schools?
3. Are there schools or districts that currently employ models of supervision that could be used as exemplars for others?

Such questions need to be addressed before widespread implementation of new supervisory models, as well as after. Killian and Post cautioned that adequate research and preparation need to precede implementation of new supervisory models or techniques. Although their chapter is focused on scientific management models of supervision, Killian and Post listed common difficulties encountered during applications of theory to practice which apply just as well to supervisory models in general. These difficulties include "overgeneralization of the model or its research base; inattention to the importance of human variables of motivation and creativity; [and] failure to generate replicable, generalizable findings."

Gordon and Nicely questioned "whether it will be possible to determine empirically the most effective frameworks and combinations of frameworks" for particular supervisory goals.

Innovative Research Questions

Although it may be difficult to do, the comparison of competing supervisory models is too crucial to leave unresolved simply because it is difficult. This is a serious weakness in the profession, if it cannot document what effect it has on students or decide what it does that works well and what works less well. Research using alternative methods of inquiry could yield more satisfactory answers.

How Can New Methods of Inquiry Inform Practice? "Those who wish to understand supervision and its effects need multiple forms of inquiry for exploration of myriad issues and practices of teachers and schools" (Schoonmaker et al); that is, for exploration of "the complex human activities encompassed by instructional supervision" (Hawthorne & Hoffman).

Cook noted that ethnographic research is "no longer in its infancy in education," but added that there has been relatively little done in supervision using this approach.

As we discover more about how people think, inquire, dream, create, and communicate, supervision itself takes on new dimensions and moves from the tradition linear model to a complexity full of life, wonder, and unexpected beauty. Research must accept and incorporate that complexity

Cook explained that "rich, textured descriptions" would enable the reader to grasp the ways in which teachers and learners conduct inquiry in science or in music, and how supervision can enhance such thinking and learning.

Barone conceptualized supervision itself aesthetically. He suggested narrative storytelling as another avenue toward understanding the art—as opposed to the science—of supervision.

Is supervision, like teaching, an art or a science? Is the supervisor's answer to this question reflected in his or her practice? Does attention to teacher narratives make supervision more effective? Are there other artistically grounded formats—in addition to criticism and narrative—which might be helpful for supervisors to explore?

Ethnographic or qualitative research can take various forms, of which description is only one. Glanz pointed out the potential value of historical research through such avenues as document analysis and biographical narrative. Flinders noted a need for historical research that would explore the impact of industry on school supervision. Wood posited that case histories of exemplary supervision could help to bridge the gap between theory and practice.

Waite mentioned what must be a valid concern: will research studies done with alternative methods of inquiry carry weight with decision makers such as boards of education, and what might to done to ensure that they do?

Most research in supervision to date has been done using the empiricist, quantitative approach to inquiry. Truth, however, may be more than a sum of the facts; perhaps, some of supervision's "persistent problems" will yet yield to examination through innovative means.

How Can a Historical Examination of Issues of Diversity (i.e., Issues of Race, Class, and Gender, Marginalization of Women, Poor, and Minorities) Inform Practice? Schoonmaker et al noted that when the literature on supervision is searched for the voices of diversity, "certain silences become apparent." The voices themselves have not been silent; rather, they were not reported in the literature at the time. Schoonmaker et al mentioned particularly the immigrants of the early years of the twentieth century, the migrant workers of the Depression years, African Americans during the years of segregated schooling, Native Americans in their still-segregated schooling on reservations, and women. It is particularly arresting that women should have been silenced because most teachers were women, and most supervisors were men.

Schoonmaker et al claimed that, maddeningly, "there is little in mainstream literature to suggest that there were any issues or challenges of cultural diversity that affected supervisory practice"; however, there are sources of valuable data. Schoonmaker et al mentioned *The Journal of Negro Education*; Firth cited publications about the Jeanes supervisors, the first supervisors in the "colored" schools of the South.

These considerations (i.e., race, class, gender) operate in ways that have largely gone unexamined. For example, Hawthorne and Hoffman found that male-dominated fields of practice do not have any equivalent to supervision of professional practice beyond initial preparation and licensure.

The assumption is that the professional practitioner has mastered the knowledge and skills that define the essence of the practice, will conduct themselves ethically, will actively seek and use new insights/skills, and will use standardized procedures and judgments to guide their practice.

In contrast, those professions that have historically been female dominated always have direct supervision of practice.

How do Issues of Diversity Manifest Themselves in the Profession Today? Nolan asks, "What roles do gender and culture play in producing the intended and unintended outcomes which result from school psychologist supervision?" The same question can be asked for supervision in any context.

In Chapter 50, on "Cultural, Ethnic, and Gender Issues in Supervision," Gay explored this issue in depth. Gay urged "culturally responsive and gender sensitive" supervision, and strongly recommended staff development specifically designed to help teachers reflect upon and recognize their own stereotypes and biases.

Waite speculated at length about the "culture" of supervision, wondering about the "deep personal meaning" attached to being a supervisor, what it means to be a supervisor of another race, class, or gender, whether or not more women are aspiring to supervisory positions, and what effect this will have on the profession.

The Same Questions Also Need to be Explored Concerning Issues of Authority, Power, Influence, Empowerment, and Control Hawthorne and Hoffman found little evidence that critical theory has become an active frame of reference in supervision research. They noted that

the dominance of positivist and practical (does it work?) perspectives about research and understanding appears to keep the research questions descriptive and utilitarian rather than interpretive and critical.

Nevertheless, concerns of power distribution are being discussed more often. According to Shapiro and Blumberg, empowerment strategies should be a component of every supervisor's strategies, concepts, and thinking.

What Knowledge, Skills, and Attitudes of the Supervisee Promote Effective Supervision? Although the factors that make a supervisor effective have always been a topic of research, several authors mentioned that the factors that make supervisees receptive to supervision ought to be investigated as well. Nolan pointed out that supervision is clearly a two-way street and suggested that more attention is needed to the knowledge, skills, and attitudes of the supervisee. Lewis would like research to identify the motivational factors of supervisees and investigate how such factors might be tapped.

Oja and Reiman asked to what degree teachers' characteristics, attitudes, career phases, conceptions of self, and intellectual, interpersonal, and moral dispositions determine the explicit and implicit interactions between the teacher and students or colleagues. Furthermore, they wonder to what degree psychological development (i.e., maturity) can be deliberately promoted by supervision?

How Can Managerial/Organizational Theories From the Field of Business be Used to Make Schools More Effective?

Organizational culture and climate are both critical to diagnosing crucial components of all organizations and are essential areas in which supervisors must develop insights and skills. Organizations constitute the environment for the supervisor and for the supervisory function. Therefore, understanding the structure and processes becomes a key to effectiveness (Shapiro and Blumberg).

Flinders suggests that business-related theories may help us understand "the complexities of organizational life." Gordon and Nicely would like to see clarification of the role that supervision can or should play within organizational reform efforts.

Hall and Shieh are confident that supervision and organizational development (OD) can be made complementary with one another. They caution, however, that OD has too often been presented as a set of techniques, with the crucial emphasis on the transformation of the organization ignored.

Gaping Holes

Although there were few areas in supervision that the authors who contributed to the *Handbook* identified as well or sufficiently researched, certain areas were found to have been investigated almost not at all.

Educational Service Agencies In Chapter 28 on educational service agencies (ESAs) Sherrod found no research at all that investigated the supervisory methods or effects of these intermediate agencies.

An absence of evaluation research has apparently caused ESAs to be the targets of considerable criticism. Legislators and policy makers have frequently suggested that data is needed to demonstrate [their worth]. . . . It is almost inconceivable that the agencies which provide the most supervisory services to countless schools in small districts across the nation have been virtually eliminated from evaluation (Sherrod).

"The list of possible questions to be examined," she concluded, "is practically endless."

School Counselors and School Psychologists Nolan, author of Chapter 21 on "Supervision in Service Areas," was also dismayed to find almost no literature that addressed either how the supervision of school guidance counselors and school psychologists is conducted or how it ought to be conducted. He closed by saying, "Given the scarcity of research in the field, almost any study would make a contribution."

Specific Areas of Specialization "There has been virtually no attention paid in recent years to supervision that is designed to address the specific characteristics of separate academic areas," according to Cook. In particular, she noted a surprising paucity of research pertinent to the use of generalist versus specialist supervisors. Which is more effective? Which do teachers prefer? Does effectiveness or teacher preference vary according to grade level or subject area?

Sheerer found a similar situation in early childhood education.

DEMOCRACY AND SUPERVISION

In speculating about the future of schools and of supervision, it is important not to gloss over some riveting problems. There has been a steady voice from practitioners in schools who simply do not see the word or connotation of supervision as currently practiced relevant to the changes and improvements of education in their own situations (see Glickman, 1992). Virtually no major research study about school improvement and increased student achievement contains any mention of the terms *supervision* or *supervisors* in the findings. Instead, focus is upon such factors as collegiality, the nature of authentic pedagogy and assessments, and the collective vision and educational practices of faculty, parents, students, and school leaders. If supervision as a field is to have meaning in the next decade, then its moral and ethical purpose clearly need to be examined and revitalized according to the fundamental purposes of education and society.

The issues of supervision defined in this book—simplistic solutions to dilemmas, reintegration with curriculum, recognition as a profession, and methodological rigor—can only be addressed if supervision as a profession is clear on its moral foundation. Shapiro and Blumberg characterized such a foundation as an essential "centerpiece to organize thinking and, therefore, professional practice." If a moral foundation of education can be established by school supervisors, clarification would be obtained for the future research needed on all the various issues that trouble them: student achievement; supervisory efficacy; different models and new methods of inquiry; historical and current examinations of diversity; explorations of authority, power, influence, empowerment, and control; necessary knowledge, skills, and attitudes; and appropriate use of managerial/organizational theories from other fields.

In other words, it is essential to first understand supervision as part of an overarching vision (a "super-vision") of education, and from that vision determine how the various discrete subfunctions are to be practiced. To avoid this foundational question is to leave the field, the research, and the practice racing madly upstairs and downstairs in a Tower of Babel. Our publications, conferences, workshops and materials are filled with whatever educational theories, models, innovations, or enterprises have lately caught the fickle interest of the educational marketplace. When today's promises prove false, we are ready to try tomorrow's.

If democracy as educative hope is a moral foundation for education upon which to stand and from which to work, is to be found, it must begin with the original view of democracy as an educative hope among people.

The foundation of public education is not a new vision of education; rather, it is an old, conservative idea about the relation between education and democracy. What appear in this book to be new challenges about working with people as individuals or as groups—trying to forge a purposeful community while respecting human growth and development; "reforming" a school into a center of inquiry; facilitating criticism, dissension, and creative problem solving while advocating common goals of a larger community—are not new at all. These are instead all the issues of trying to make a democracy live in practice rather than simply in rhetorical abstractions.

Public education's fundamental purpose has therefore always been, or should have always been, educating students to make wise individual and collective choices about present and future pursuits of "life, liberty, and the pursuit of happiness." For this "super-vision" of education to occur requires its practice as a way of learning and living among adults as well as with students in classrooms, schools, and communities.

The relationship between democracy and education has been implicit from the earliest days of the American Republic and, indeed, may have been more fully realized in America before the Republic. Thomas Jefferson, author of the Declaration of Independence, believed that free universal education was an essential condition for a democratic society. Jefferson wrote: "If a civilized nation expects to be ignorant and free . . .it expects what never was and never will be." Jefferson's argument was that the fundamental remedy for the abuse of power is education, giving the people free access to ideas and encouraging open discussion of those ideas.

The belief that citizens can educate themselves well, when ensured general diffusion of knowledge, freedom of expression, free press, open marketplace of ideas and tolerance for the pursuit of truth with a lower-case *t* so that each generation may uncover new and different truths, is central to Jeffersonian

democracy. These guarantees are more than constitutional rights; they are educative imperatives. They ensure access and participation in knowledge to safeguard the freedom of people so that *free* people define the public *domain* (free-dom) rather than the kings (king-dom).

Such an education would guarantee that all students experience and come to value the underlying principles of democratic life: liberty, equality, and fraternity (Rolheiser & Glickman, 1995). Liberty refers to personal rights and responsibilities. Equality encompasses fairness and impartiality and the acceptance of all citizens as equal. Fraternity deals with the importance of cooperative responsibilities and working with others (i.e., a social contract).

When the goal of democracy is practiced seriously in public schools, students succeed across specific educational subgoals, academic, vocational, aesthetic, and social pursuits. In effect, public schools must ensure a democratic threshold of learning experiences that gives all students the knowledge, skills, compassion, and understanding to participate in human affairs.

What does this mean for the work of supervision and school improvement. It must be acknowledged that most schools are profoundly undemocratic. Democratic beliefs—that the participation of all as equals through the general dissemination of knowledge, contrary perspectives, and equal participation constitutes the best means for deciding the common good—do not form the fabric of most schools. Democratic beliefs also do not typically form the fabric of staff development, curriculum development, or models and techniques of supervision. Most schools are composed, instead, of advisory groups or site-based councils or positional authority who have the control and influence to make decisions for the rest of the people. Thus, schools use non-democratic practices in trying to achieve democratic purposes for students.

Democratic Pedagogy: The Empirical Base

The word *democracy* has many different meanings to different people, so it is crucial to be quite precise about what is meant when stating that democracy is the most powerful pedagogy of learning (see Glickman, 1998; Dewey, 1916).

The four supervision trends in this book—(1) shift from individual to group focus, (2) shift from preoccupation with inspection and evaluation toward a function of facilitating growth, (3) shift from a micro- to a macroconceptualization of supervisory content, and (4) emphasis on creating community both within the school and with the larger community that the school serves—can be analyzed in terms of whether or not their outcome is conducive to greater democratic engagement, participation, and learning for all students and adults.

There is an accumulated base of research on learning practices that can be shown consistently to increase student achievement, learning satisfaction, and success in later life. These results are equally consistent across socioeconomic classes and race, ethnic, and gender compositions of students. For example, a study followed students who graduated from 30 high schools that used democracy as the central tenet of curriculum content and instructional practices, matched with students who graduated from traditional high schools. This study found that of 1,475 matched pairs of students, studied through four years of high school and for four years afterward, those who graduated from democratic schools had higher grades, received more academic and nonacademic honors, had a higher degree of intellectual curiosity, participated more in groups, and demonstrated a more active concern with national and international issues. Entitled the Eight-Year Study (Aiken, 1942), these results were published in 1942.

Fifty-four years later, 1996, study of 820 high schools and 11,000 students found that where academic programs were reorganized around "active learning and where this type of instruction is widespread throughout the school," students have significantly higher gains on all measured achievement domains of mathematics, reading, social studies, and science, as measured by the National Assessment of Educational Progress (Newman, Marks, & Gamoran, 1995; Lee, Smith, & Croninger, 1995).

The same results hold true for longitudinal studies of elementary and middle schools (Newman & Wehlage, 1995). Newman et al refer to this type of active learning as "authentic pedagogy." It consists of students constructing knowledge, using disciplined inquiry, and finding applications of learning outside of classroom and school settings.

Research referred to initially as "developmental" and more recently as "constructivist" has been built from the work of such cognitive scholars as Piaget (1974), Vygotsky (1978), Bruner (1960), Leinhardt (1993), and Gardner et al (1994). This work has repeatedly demonstrated that effective teaching that (1) is tailored to the natural curiosity and physical activity of the student; (2) creates disequilibrium with what a student knows by providing new information; and then, (3) carefully "scaffolds" with appropriate information, materials, activities, and questions to increase students' competence and desire to pursue further learning.

Furthermore, teaching and learning methods that use cooperative settings and group investigations and where "students learn to develop generalizations, hypotheses, and inferences" show higher achievement and attitudinal gains among students (Joyce & Weil, 1992; Rolheiser & Glickman, 1995). As Wood (1990) observed of such classrooms and schools, "[students] are doing things, not just watching someone else. Learning is not a spectator sport in these schools."

Democracy, when viewed and practiced as a method of participation, is therefore the most effective way of learning for all children, adults, supervisees, and supervisors, whatever the disciplines, subject, skills, or understandings.

Democratic Supervision and Pedagogy

How democracy can become revitalized to support and encourage individual liberty *and* community freedom *as a way of learning* is the issue for supervision or supervisors. Any supervisor or supervision program would need to bear the burden of proof for the justification of any techniques, models, or programs that is not prodemocratic. Research would have to show how methods of authoritarianism, obedience, and passivity can create educated, informed, and wise democratic citizens.

To realize the power of education for students, democratic pedagogy must be used and modeled by those formally responsible for the teaching and learning improvements of teachers. What are the standards of a democratic pedagogy that result in high achievement? Let us suggest the following:

1. Students actively working with problems, ideas, materials, and other people as they learn skills and content.
2. Students having escalating degrees of choices, both as individuals and as groups, within the parameters provided by the teacher.
3. Students being responsible to their peers, teachers, parents, and school community that educational time is being used purposefully and productively.
4. Students sharing their learning with each other, with teachers, and with parents and other community members.
5. Students deciding how to make their learning a contribution to their community.
6. Students assuming escalating responsibilities for securing resources (e.g., of people and materials outside of the school) and finding places where they can apply and further their learning.
7. Students demonstrating what they know and can do in public settings and receiving public feedback.
8. Students working and learning from each other, individually and in groups, at a pace that challenges all.

In effect, students learn physics best by using their knowledge and applying it to such an activity as designing a suspension bridge. They learn English best by writing, reading, performing, and, in general, participating in literate forms of communication with others. They learn history best by becoming historians, using archival materials to develop accounts of events. (See Meier, 1995, for amplifications on concrete activities and assessments of democratic pedagogy resulting in extraordinary accomplishments for all students.)

The concept of democratic pedagogy remains unchanged for supervisors working with adults. In other words, supervisors learn how to improve teaching and learning when they employ the techniques of reflective practice and take the time to think, deeply and critically, about goals for students and our current practice. This means informing themselves about other possibilities by talking, reading, visiting, and listening to colleagues, as well as by studying and observing successful practices. In order for all of this to work at a reflective and purposeful school level means activities, participation, and connections need to be made on the part of all adults.

The job of formal supervisors and supervision programs, therefore, is to utilize democratic pedagogy in schools in ways that build toward increasing faculty choice, participation, connection, and contribution around the core issues of teaching and learning within and across classrooms. The goal is for teachers to take on greater responsibility, individually and collectively, for their own learning about their own practice. If teachers do not readily initiate such discussions, studies, and observations, then it is not the job of the supervisor to give up and abandon them, but rather to remember Jefferson's words:

I know of no safe depository of the ultimate power of the society but the people themselves, and if we think them not enlightened enough to exercise their control with a wholesome discretion, the remedy is not to take it from them, but to inform their decision.

Democracy is predicated on psychological assumptions about humans; specifically, every individual is an active, curious learner who—given information, materials, and directions—will be able to utilize learning in meaningful ways to see connections, discover applications, and participate with others.

High performance on the part of both students and teachers is found in schools that use their organizational structures of shared governance, site-based decision-making, and action research to infuse democracy throughout normal, routine activities, including staffing; scheduling; student placement, assessment, discipline, and staff development; curriculum improvement; instructional strategy, and involvement with parents and community. The eternal concern of supervision, in research and practice, should be the unrelenting insistence that democracy and education live in day-to-day practice so that every adult and child acknowledges that he or she is a full, valued, and responsible member of a democratic public, and also understands and accepts the rights and duties required by such membership.

THE FUTURE OF SUPERVISION

The *Handbook of Research on School Supervision* provides the most comprehensive examination of the field of supervision ever undertaken. It explores previous developments, current trends, and research needed in the future. In the aggregate, it emphasizes the constant need for a moral and ethical center as a foundation for assessing roles, responsibilities, programs, and achievements. Without a moral foundation of education, little guidance exists for determining what supervisors and supervision programs should be doing or accomplishing.

The immediate future of supervision will be embedded in current conflicts about standards, productivity, and core learnings, as well as the concepts of professionalism, authority, autonomy, and local control. To resolve these conflicts and to forge better research, practice, and theory, the field of supervision must rededicate itself to the incessant struggle of making schools the center of democratic inquiry. Determining a better individual and collective future of, for, and with students, faculty, and communities can only be realized through the mastery of human judgment over the complex dilemmas and paradoxes inherent in the human condition itself. A daunting challenge, indeed—but is that not what education is all about?

REFERENCES

Aiken, W. F. (1942). *The story of the eight-year study.* New York: Harper and Brothers.

Bruner, J. (1960). *The process of education.* New York: Vintage Books.

Dewey, J. (1916). *Democracy and education: An introduction to the philosophy of education.* New York: Macmillan.

Gardner, H., Krechevsky, M., Sternberg, R. J. & Okagaki, L. (1994). Intelligence in context: Enhancing students' practical intelligence for school. In K. McGilly (Ed.). *Classroom lessons: Integrating cognitive theory and classroom practice* (pp. 105–127). Cambridge, MA: Bradford Books.

Glickman, C. D. (1998). *Revolutionizing America's Schools..* San Francisco, CA: Jossey-Bass.

Joyce, B. & Weil, M. (1992). *Models of teaching* (4th ed.). Boston, MA: Allyn & Bacon.

Lee, V. E., Smith, J. B., & Croninger, R. C. (1995, Fall). Another look at high school restructuring: More evidence that it improves student achievement and more insight into why. *Issues in restructuring schools.* Center on organization and restructuring of schools, University of Wisconsin (Madison). Report No. 9, pp. 1–10.

Leinhardt, G. (1993). On teaching. In R. Glaser (Ed.). *Advances in Instructional Psychology,* 4, 1–54.

Meier, D. (1995). *The power of their ideas: Lessons for America from a small school in Harlem.* Boston, MA: Beacon Press.

Miller, J. P. & Seller, W. (1985). *Curriculum: Perspective and Practice.* New York: Longman.

Newman, F. M. & Wehlage, G. G. (1995). *Successful school restructuring: A report to the public and educators by the Center on Organization and Restructuring of Schools.* Madison, WI: Wisconsin Center for Education Research.

Paget, J. (1974). *To understand is to invent: The future of education.* New York: Viking Press.

Rolheiser, C. & Glickman, C. D. (1995). Teaching for democratic life. *The Educational Forum,* 59(2), 196–206.

Sergiovanni, T.J., & Starratt, R.J. (1993). *Supervision: A redefinition.* New York: McGraw-Hill.

Vygotsky, L. L. (1978). *Mind in society.* Cambridge, MA: Harvard University Press.

Wood, G. H. (1990). Teaching for democracy. *Educational Leadership,* 48(2), 32–37.

NAME INDEX

Shafer, H., 605, 876
Shalit, S., 279
Shamsher, M., 740, 1249
Shanks, J., 1181
Shannon, C., 1231
Shapiro, 1249, 1251–1252, 1254
Shapiro, A., 615
Shapiro, D. A., 538–539
Shapiro, M. D., 1058, 1062, 1065, 1069
Shapiro, S. R., 513
Shaplin, J., 344, 611
Sharpton, L. F. H., 522
Shea, M. A., 731
Sheats, P., 789, 1067
Shedd, J. B., 164
Sheerer, M. A., 577, 584–586, 1254
Sheets, R., 1198
Sherrod, B. J., 579, 699–700
Sherwood, J. J., 194–195
Shewhart, 1128
Shieh, W., 741–742, 1251, 1254
Shiliff, K. A., 362–363
Shilling, C., 297, 302
Shimizu, K., 808
Shinn, R., 1189–1190
Shoemaker, F. F., 501
Shores, J. H., 62
Shor, I., 296
Short, K. G., 512
Showers, B., 85–86, 93, 253, 347–348, 356,
    545, 754, 769, 771, 813, 815–816
Shrigley, R. L., 493, 495
Shroyer, M. G., 829
Shulman, L., 84, 206, 459, 464, 928,
    931
Sigerist, H. E., 907
Sillane, J. P., 376
Silvern, S. B., 413
Simmel, G., 294–295
Simmons, J. M., 832
Simon, H. A., 1131
Simon, R. I., 1068
Simonson, M., 1232, 1234
Simpson, D. E., 565
Singleton, H. W., 44
Sireno, P. J., 522
Sirotnik, K., 409, 962
Sistrunk, W. E., 390, 499–501, 1072
Sizemore, P., 819
Sizer, T., 188–189, 605
Skau, K. G., 122, 210
Skinner, B. F., 247, 976, 1231
Slaughter-Defoe, D. T., 1195
Slavenburg, J. H., 1011, 1013–1014
Slavin, R. E., 8, 24, 764, 1049–1050, 1214
Smellie, D. C., 1234
Smith, 935, 1249
Smith, A., 181
Smith, A. B., 729
Smith, A. M., 810
Smith, C., 526
Smith, E. V., 170
Smith, G. E., 669
Smith, H., 825–826
Smith, J., 980, 1118

Smith, J. A., 391
Smith, M. S., 160
Smith, N. S., 740
Smith, R., 677
Smith, R. A., 730, 1105–1107
Smith, R. R., 1211
Smith, W., 592–593
Smith, W. F., 389, 755, 1094
Smitheram, V., 472
Smitherman, G., 1203, 1209
Smithson, J., 376–377
Smulyan, L., 478
Smylie, M. A., 822–823
Smyth, J., 207, 210–211, 220–221, 226, 230,
    234, 259, 301, 405–406, 622, 806–807,
    1154
Smyth, J. W., 125–126, 129
Smyth, W. J., 95, 493, 498, 501, 964, 1060,
    1075
Snarey, J., 467
Snedden, D., 57
Snippe, J., 498
Snook, I., 80–81, 83–84
Snow, C. A., 44
Snow, R. E., 473
Snyder, C. J., 331–332
Snyder, J., 129
Snyder, K. J., 356, 364, 370, 384–385
Soar, R., 969
Sobel, E., 563
Sockett, H., 654
Soder, R., 409, 925
Soltis, J. F., 101, 230
Sousa, D. A., 814
Sowell, T., 772
Sowers-Hoag, K., 546
Spafford, C., 428, 434, 481
Sparks, D., 978
Sparks, G. M., 451, 814, 816
Sparks-Langer, G., 414, 416
Spaulding, F., 1041, 1045
Spears, H., 5, 47, 155, 343, 640–641, 749
Spector, B., 194
Speiker, C. A., 888, 895, 915, 922–923
Spencer, H., 294
Spencer, M., 1196
Sperry, D., 972
Spier, S. C., 877
Spillane, J., 976–977
Spindler, G. D., 289–290, 292–293, 301,
    1190, 1197, 1207, 1219
Spindler, L., 289–290, 1219
Spira, L., 559
Spivey, D. A., 415
Spodek, B., 581
Spratley, F., 822
Sprinthall, N., 12–13, 475
Spruel, M., 610
Spruill, A. W., 132
Srisa-an, W., 890
Stake, R., 511–513, 812
Stalker, G., 845
Stallings, J., 404, 420, 439–440, 769,
    813–815, 1050
Stark, J. S., 766

Starratt, R. J., 66, 82–83, 85, 95–96,
    100–101, 157, 209, 220, 232–234, 260,
    298–299, 311, 314, 318, 347, 399–400,
    403, 431, 498, 501, 613–614, 618, 650,
    652, 748, 802–803, 870–871, 954,
    960–961, 964, 987, 989, 1041,
    1047–1048, 1052, 1058–1059, 1066,
    1185, 1218, 1249–1250
Staudt, J., 465
Steeples, M. M., 362
Stefonek, T., 692, 697–698, 700–701
Steinback, R., 24
Steinhoff, C. R., 1072
Stein, R. D., 481
Stenhouse, L., 819
Stephens, E. R., 378
Stephens, J. F., 522
Stern, A., 546
Sternberg, R. J., 465, 480
Stern, G. G., 1072
Stevenson, H., 1056
Stevenson, M. T., 825
Stice, C. F., 472
Stiegelbauer, S., 24, 172, 829, 1010
Stiggins, R. J., 153, 766
Stigler, J., 1056
Stocking, G., 291
Stoddard, E., 1092–1095
Stodolsky, S. S., 655
Stogdill, R. M., 231
Stokrocki, M., 511
Stoltenberg, C., 546, 561
Stone, R. K., 565
Stowe, J. S., 902
Strain, D. L., 691
Stratemeyer, F., 624
Strauss, G., 880, 924
Streitmatter, J., 1200
Strike, K., 406
Stringfield, 440
Stronck, D., 499
Stroufe, G. E., 319, 376
Stuart, M. R., 566
Stufflebeam, D., 972
Sturges, A. W., 669, 783, 895, 900, 902,
    911, 915, 922–923
Sue, S., 1201
Suhor, C., 494
Sullivan, C. G., 383–384, 672–674
Sullivan, D. G., 110–112
Summerfield, H. L., 327–328
Suppes, P., 1231
Surdyk, P. M., 926–927
Sutton, J. M., Jr., 549–550
Swanson, A. D., 318, 690, 696–698
Swanson, M., 422
Swan, W. W., 489, 539
Swartz, W. G., 901
Swassing, R. H., 1221
Swee, D. E., 565
Swetnam, L. A., 413
Sykes, G., 924, 973, 976
Synder, J., 1135–1136
Synder, K. J., 831
Sztajn, P., 1129

SUBJECT INDEX